D0745561

HARRAP'S
MINI
German
DICTIONARY

HARRAP'S

MINI

German

DICTIONARY

HARRAP
London

Distributed in the United States by
PRENTICE HALL
New York

First published in Great Britain 1988 by HARRAP BOOKS Ltd
Chelsea House, 26 Market Square, Bromley, Kent BR1 1NA

This dictionary is a shortened version of *Harrap's Concise German
and English Dictionary*, edited by Robin Sawers. The project was
carried out for Harrap by Lexus Ltd

Dieses Wörterbuch ist eine gekürzte Fassung des *Harrap's Concise
German and English Dictionary*, hrsg. von Robin Sawers. Diese
Kürzung erfolgte unter der Projektleitung von Lexus Ltd.

Editors/Mitarbeiter:
Horst Kopleck   Jimmy Burnett   Colin Arthur

Trademarks
Words considered to be trademarks have been designated in this
dictionary by *R.t.m.* However, no judgement is implied concerning
the legal status of any trademarks by virtue of the presence or
absence of such a designation.

Eingetragene Warenzeichen
Wörter, die unseres Erachtens eingetragene Warenzeichen
darstellen, sind in diesem Wörterbuch durch *R.t.m.*
gekennzeichnet. Weder das Vorhandensein noch das Fehlen dieses
Zeichens ist jedoch als Wertung bezuglich der Rechtslage
eingetragener Warenzeichen zu verstehen.

Reprinted 1989 (*twice*); 1990; 1991

ISBN 0-245-54579-4

In the United States, ISBN 0-13-383019-5

Library of Congress Cataloguing-in-Publication Data

Harraps mini German dictionary.
p.   cm.
A shortened version of Harrap's concise German and English
dictionary.
"First published in Great Britain, 1988 by Harrap Books Ltd. ...
London" — T.p. verso.
ISBN 0-13-383019-5 (Prentice Hall : $3.95 (est.)
1. German Language — Dictionaries — English.
2. English Language — Dictionaries — German.
1. Harrap's concise German and English dictionary
PF3640.H295   1990   89-48982
443'.21—dc20   CIP

Printed in England by Clays Ltd, St Ives plc

Preface

Treatment of entries

As in all other Harrap dictionaries, wide-ranging use is made of a system of 'labels'. These are abbreviations, printed in italics, and positioned before the translation, for example *Sp:* for sport, *Ch:* for chemistry or *Z:* for zoology. As far as possible we have used only easily recognizable short forms. To make the dictionary entries easy to work with we have used Roman numerals (**I.**, **II.** etc.) to subdivide grammatical categories (noun, verb etc.) and Arabic numerals (**1.**, **2.** etc.) and letters ((*a*), (*b*) etc.) to mark differences in meaning.

Compound nouns

One of the main difficulties in a German-English dictionary lies in the treatment of German compounds. In this dictionary we have, where appropriate, used a system of 'combining form' entries (*comb. fm.*). This shows – with examples – how to translate nouns that form the first part of a compound word. In this way it is possible to include more compounds in the dictionary than would be the case if each compound were given a separate entry. However, if a compound does not fit the pattern shown by the combining form then it is treated as a separate entry.

Structure of entries

Headwords are given in **bold** type. Main headwords are followed by a phonetic transcription in square brackets. Sub-headwords are only given stress marks unless their pronunciation differs substantially from that of the main headword. There then follows an abbreviation describing the part of speech. Then, if the word is a German noun, come the genitive and the plural ending (with the exception of compounds of which the second element is independently listed as a separate headword). For English nouns we give irregular plurals only. Irregular verbs are given in a separate list and marked up in the text with *irr.* The numbers given with certain irregular German verbs refer to the list of verbs which shows the pattern according to which the parts of these verbs are formed.

Attention should be paid to the use of brackets and obliques. Brackets are used for additional parts of a usage and the bracketed part will also appear in the translation, unless it is superfluous. Obliques are used to indicate alternative elements, for example in a set expression, and corresponding translations are given. Brackets are also used around typical objects of verbs and around nouns that are typically used with adjectives.

Abbreviation of headwords

In the German-English part of the dictionary a large number of the entries are compounds. Frequently a main headword is split by a vertical stroke (|). This is to show that the first element of the word is not repeated in the following compounds. These compounds consist of the initial letter of the word (big or small), a tilde (~) and the rest of the word, for example: **Förder|band, F~er, f~n** etc. Within the entry the word is abbreviated to its initial letter followed by a full-stop, as long as it is in exactly the same form as given at the beginning of the entry. If the word has a different ending, then the tilde replaces that part of the word at the beginning of the entry up to the vertical stroke. For example, in the entry with the main headword **Durchschlag** we have the verb **d~en** as well as the expression **d~ender Erfolg**. In the English-German part of the dictionary the tilde is not used. Instead all entries are written in full except when they are abbreviated to the initial letter as in example sentences.

Order of headwords

The headwords are alphabetically ordered with the exception of compounds which are listed under the first element of the compound. Entries like these are not interrupted just to maintain alphabetical order. So, for example, **Bau** is followed by **b~fällig, B~stein, B~werk** etc. and then by **Bauch**. German prefixes such as aus-, bei-, vor-, zu- etc. form an exception to this rule with compounds starting with these prefixes being given separate entries. New headwords run on within an entry are preceded by ◆.

Vorwort

Behandlung der Einträge

Wie in allen anderen Harrap-Wörterbüchern finden Sachbereichsangaben weitgehend Verwendung. Hierbei handelt es sich um kursiv gedruckte Abkürzungen, die der Übersetzung vorangestellt sind, wie z.B. *Sp:* für Sport, *Ch:* für Chemie oder *Z:* für Zoologie. Soweit dies möglich war, haben wir uns auf leicht erkennbare Kürzel beschränkt. Um die Einträge übersichtlicher zu gestalten, verwenden wir römische Zahlen (**I., II.** usw.) zur Unterteilung von grammatischen Kategorien (Substantiv, Verb usw.). Bedeutungsunterschiede werden durch arabische Ziffern (**1., 2.** usw.) sowie durch Buchstaben ((*a*), (*b*) usw.) gekennzeichnet.

Zusammengesetzte Substantive

Eine Hauptschwierigkeit in einem deutsch-englischen Wörterbuch besteht in der Behandlung der deutschen zusammengesetzten Substantive. Wir verwenden in diesem Wörterbuch, wo angemessen, sogenannte 'combining form'-Einträge (*comb. fm.*). Diese zeigen anhand von Beispielen, wie Substantive, die das erste Element einer Zusammensetzung bilden, zu übersetzen sind. Auf diese Weise können mehr Zusammensetzungen aufgenommen werden, als dies bei separaten Einträgen der Fall wäre. Wenn ein zusammengesetztes Wort nicht in das Muster der 'combining form' paßt, wird es als eigener Eintrag angeführt.

Struktur der Einträge

Stichwörter sind **fett** gedruckt. Einem Hauptstichwort folgt die phonetische Umschrift in eckigen Klammern. Untergeordnete Einträge erhalten lediglich Betonungszeichen, außer wenn ihre Aussprache abweicht. Hierauf folgt eine Abkürzung, die die grammatische Kategorie bezeichnet. Bei deutschen Substantiven folgen der Genitiv und der Plural (außer bei Zusammensetzungen, bei denen das zweite Wortelement als eigener Eintrag erscheint); bei englischen Substantiven wird der Plural nur angegeben, wenn er unregelmäßig ist. Unregelmäßige Verben sind in einer gesonderten Liste aufgeführt und im Text selbst durch *irr.* gekennzeichnet. Die Zahlenangaben bei einigen unregelmäßigen deutschen Verben verweisen auf Verben in der Liste, deren Formen nach dem gleichen Muster gebildet werden.

Weiterhin ist die Verwendung von Klammern und Schrägstrichen zu beachten. Klammern werden bei zusätzlichen Elementen einer Wendung benutzt, entsprechend erscheint dann auch der Klammerausdruck in der

Übersetzung, es sei denn, er ist überflüssig. Ähnlich bezeichnen auch Schrägstriche Alternativen, etwa bei einer Redewendung, mit Entsprechungen in der Übersetzung. Ebenfalls eingeklammert erscheinen bei Verben typische Objekte sowie bei Adjektiven häufig in Zusammenhang mit diesen verwendete Substantive.

Abkürzung von Stichwörtern

Im deutsch-englischen Teil besteht ein Großteil der Einträge aus Zusammensetzungen. Häufig wird ein Hauptstichwort durch einen vertikalen Trennstrich (|) unterteilt. Dies zeigt an, daß das Anfangselement des Wortes bei den darauffolgenden Zusammensetzungen nicht wiederholt wird. Diese Zusammensetzungen bestehen aus dem Anfangsbuchstaben des Wortes (groß oder klein), einer Tilde (~) und dem Rest des Wortes, also z.B.: **Förder|band, F~er, f~n** usw. Innerhalb des Eintrags wird das Wort mit seinem Anfangsbuchstaben abgekürzt, dem ein Punkt folgt, solange das Wort die gleiche Form wie das betreffende Stichwort hat. Hat das Wort eine abweichende Endung, ersetzt die Tilde jeweils das Hauptstichwort am Anfang eines Eintrags bis zum Trennstrich, z.B auf den Eintrag mit dem Hauptstichwort **Durchschlag** folgt das Verb **d~en** sowie der Ausdruck **d~ender Erfolg.** Im englisch-deutschen Teil des Wörterbuchs wird die Tilde nicht verwendet; alle Einträge, außer wenn sie in Beispielsätzen durch den Anfangsbuchstaben abgekürzt werden, erscheinen voll ausgeschrieben.

Folge der Stichwörter

Die Folge der Stichwörter ist alphabetisch, außer bei Zusammensetzungen, die jeweils unter dem ersten Element der Zusammensetzung erscheinen. Ein solcher Eintrag wird nicht durch andere Wörter unterbrochen, nur um die alphabetische Reihenfolge zu wahren: auf **Bau** folgen also **b~fällig, B~stein, B~werk** usw. und erst dann **Bauch.** Eine Ausnahme bilden deutsche Stichwörter mit Präfixen wie aus-, bei-, vor-, zu- usw., die jeweils eigene Einträge haben. Neue Stichwörter innerhalb eines Eintrages sind durch ◆ hervorgehoben. *

Abbreviations and Labels used in the Dictionary
Im Wörterbuch benutzte Abkürzungen und Bereichsangaben

A:	archaic	veraltet	*E:*	engineering	Ingenieurwesen
abbr.	abbreviation	Abkürzung	*East G:*	East German	ostdeutsch, DDR
abs.	absolute use	ohne Akkusativobjekt	*Ecc:*	ecclesiastical	kirchlich
			e.g.	for example	zum Beispiel
acc	accusative	Akkusativ	*El:*	electricity	Elektrizität
adj.	adjective; adjectival	Adjektiv; adjektivisch	*esp.*	especially	besonders
			etc.	et cetera, and so on	und so weiter
Adm:	administration; 'officialese'	Verwaltung; Beamtensprache			
			f	feminine	weiblich
adv.	adverb	Adverb	*F:*	colloquial(ism)	umgangssprachlich
Agr:	agriculture	Landwirtschaft			
Anat:	anatomy	Anatomie	*Fb:*	football	Fußball
approx.	approximately	ungefähr	*Fig:*	figurative	figurativ, übertragen
Arch:	architecture	Architektur			
art.	article	Artikel	*Fin:*	finance	Finanzwesen
Art:	art	Kunst	*fut.*	future	Futur, Zukunft
Astr:	astronomy	Astronomie			
Atom.Ph:	atomic physics	Atomphysik	*G:*	German	deutsch
			gen	genitive	Genitiv
attrib.	attributive	attributiv	*Geog:*	geography	Geographie
Aus:	Austrian	österreichisch	*Gram:*	grammar	Grammatik
Austral:	Australia; Australian	Australien; australisch	*H:*	household	Haushalt
Aut:	automobiles, motoring	Automobile	*Hist:*	history	Geschichte
			Hum:	humorous	scherzhaft
aux.	auxiliary	Hilfs-			
Av:	aviation; aircraft	Luftfahrt	*i.*	intransitive	intransitiv
			i.e.	id est, that is	das heißt
Biol:	biology	Biologie	*imp.*	imperative	Imperativ
Bot:	botany	Botanik	*imperf.*	imperfect	Imperfekt
Brit:	British	britisch	*impers.*	impersonal	unpersönlich
			Ind:	industry	Industrie
Ch:	chemistry	Chemie	*indef.*	indefinite	unbestimmt
Cin:	cinema	Kino	*inf.*	infinitive	Infinitiv
Civ.E:	civil engineering	Tiefbau	*insep.*	inseparable	nicht trennbar
Cl:	clothing	Kleidung	*int.*	interjection	Ausruf
coll.	collective	kollektiv	*interrog.*	interrogative	interrogativ
Com:	commerce, business	Handel, Geschäftswelt	*inv.*	invariable	unveränderlich
			irr.	irregular	unregelmäßig
comb.fm.	combining form	Zusammensetzungselement			
			j-d		jemand
comp.	comparative	Komparativ	*j-m*		jemandem
conj.	conjunction	Konjunktion	*j-n*		jemanden
Cu:	culinary; cooking	Kochkunst	*j-s*		jemand(e)s
			Jur:	jurisprudence, law	Rechtswesen
dat	dative	Dativ			
Data-pr:	data-processing	Datenverarbeitung	*Lit:*	literary usage; literature	gehobener Sprachgebrauch; literarisch
decl.	declined	dekliniert			
dem.	demonstrative	Demonstrativ-, hinweisend			

part 1

GRAMMAR NOTES

Articles

The form of the definite article (the) in German depends on whether the noun is masculine, feminine or neuter and on whether it is singular or plural. The forms are:

	sing.	pl.
m	*der*	*die*
f	*die*	*die*
n	*das*	*die*

For example:

sing.	pl.
der Hund	*die Hunde*
die Stange	*die Stangen*
das Heft	*die Hefte*

The definite article also changes according to the case it has in the sentence. There are four cases: nominative, accusative, genitive and dative:

	m	f	n	pl.
nom.	*der*	*die*	*das*	*die*
acc.	*den*	*die*	*das*	*die*
gen.	*des*	*der*	*des*	*der*
dat.	*dem*	*der*	*dem*	*den*

For example:

> der Lehrer trat herein
> ich sehe den Lehrer
> die Stimme des Lehrers
> ich habe mit dem Lehrer gesprochen

The indefinite article also varies according to the case and gender of the noun.

	m	f	n
nom	*ein*	*eine*	*ein*
acc	*einen*	*eine*	*ein*
gen	*eines*	*einer*	*eines*
dat	*einem*	*einer*	*einem*

Examples:

> ein Hund kam gelaufen
> ich sehe einen Hund
> der Kopf eines Hundes
> von einem Hund gebissen werden

Adjectives

If an adjective is used in front of a noun it is declined. The endings that the adjective will take depends on whether the noun is used with the definite article (der/die/das) or with the indefinite article (ein/eine/ein).

Endings with the definite article:

	m	f	n	pl.
nom.	*-e*	*-e*	*-e*	*-en*
acc.	*-en*	*-e*	*-e*	*-en*
gen.	*-en*	*-en*	*-en*	*-en*
dat.	*-en*	*-en*	*-en*	*-en*

Examples:

> der gute Freund
> den guten Freund
> des guten Freundes
> dem guten Freund
> die guten Freunde

Endings with the indefinite article:

	m	f	n
nom.	-er	-e	-es
acc.	-en	-e	-es
gen.	-en	-en	-en
dat.	-en	-en	-en

Examples:

> ein braves Kind
> ein braves Kind
> eines braven Kindes
> einem braven Kind

Endings when no article is used:

	m	f	n	pl.
nom.	-er	-e	-es	-e
acc.	-en	-e	-es	-e
gen.	-en	-er	-en	-er
dat.	-em	-er	-em	-en

Examples:

> feiner Wein
> feinen Wein
> feinen Wein(e)s
> feinem Wein
> feine Weine

If an adjective is used after a noun, it does not change its ending at all, for example:

> der Kaffee ist kalt
> die Frau war schön
> das Haus ist hoch
> die Mäuse waren tot

Verbs

There are two main groups of verbs: weak and strong. Present and imperfect tense endings for weak verbs are:

spielen

present	imperfect
ich spiel-*e*	ich spiel-*te*
du spiel-*st*	du spiel-*test*
er/sie/es spiel-*t*	er/sie/es spiel-*te*
wir spiel-*en*	wir spiel-*ten*
ihr spiel-*t*	ihr spiel-*tet*
Sie spiel-*en*	Sie spiel-*ten*
sie spiel-*en*	sie spiel-*ten*

Strong verbs are characterized by a vowel change in the verb stem. See the list of irregular German verbs on pages xv–xvi.

Here are two important German verbs: sein (to be) and haben (to have):

sein

present	imperfect
ich bin	ich war
du bist	du warst
er/sie/es ist	er/sie/es war
wir sind	wir waren
ihr seid	ihr wart
Sie sind	Sie waren
sie sind	sie waren

haben

present	imperfect
ich habe	ich hatte
du hast	du hattest
er/sie/es hat	er/sie/es hatte
wir haben	wir hatten
ihr habt	ihr hattet
Sie haben	Sie hatten
sie haben	sie hatten

List of German Irregular Verbs
Liste der deutschen unregelmäßigen Verben

	Infinitive	*Present Indicative*	*Past Indicative*	*Past Participle*
1	backen	bäckt	backte	gebacken
2	befehlen	befiehlt	befahl	befohlen
3	beginnen	beginnt	begann	begonnen
4	beißen	beißt	biß	gebissen
5	bergen	birgt	barg	geborgen
6	bewegen	bewegt	bewegte (bewog)	bewegt (bewogen)
7	biegen	biegt	bog	gebogen
8	bieten	bietet	bot	geboten
9	binden	bindet	band	gebunden
10	bitten	bittet	bat	gebeten
11	blasen	bläst	blies	geblasen
12	bleiben	bleibt	blieb	geblieben
13	braten	brät	briet	gebraten
14	brechen	bricht	brach	gebrochen
15	brennen	brennt	brannte	gebrannt
16	bringen	bringt	brachte	gebracht
17	denken	denkt	dachte	gedacht
18	dreschen	drischt	drosch	gedroschen
19	dringen	dringt	drang	gedrungen
20	dürfen	darf	durfte	gedurft
21	erkiesen	erkiest	erkor	erkoren
22	erlöschen	erlischt	erlosch	erloschen
23	erschrecken	erschrickt (erschreckt)	erschrak (erschreckte)	erschrocken (erschreckt)
24	erwägen	erwägt	erwog	erwogen
25	essen	ißt	aß	gegessen
26	fahren	fährt	fuhr	gefahren
27	fallen	fällt	fiel	gefallen
28	fangen	fängt	fing	gefangen
29	fechten	ficht	focht	gefochten
30	fliehen	flieht	floh	geflohen
31	fließen	fließt	floß	geflossen
32	frieren	friert	fror	gefroren
33	gären	gärt	gor	gegoren
34	gebären	gebiert	gebar	geboren
35	geben	gibt	gab	gegeben
36	gehen	geht	ging	gegangen
37	gelten	gilt	galt	gegolten
38	genesen	genest	genas	genesen
39	geschehen	geschieht	geschah	geschehen
40	gleichen	gleicht	glich	geglichen
41	gleiten	gleitet	glitt	geglitten
42	graben	gräbt	grub	gegraben
43	greifen	greift	griff	gegriffen
44	haben	hat	hatte	gehabt
45	halten	hält	hielt	gehalten
46	hängen	hängt	hing	gehangen
47	hauen	haut	haute (hieb)	gehauen
48	heben	hebt	hob	gehoben
49	heißen	heißt	hieß	geheißen
50	helfen	hilft	half	geholfen
51	kennen	kennt	kannte	gekannt
52	klimmen	klimmt	klomm	geklommen
53	kommen	kommt	kam	gekommen
54	können	kann	konnte	gekonnt

(xv)

55 kriechen	kriecht	kroch	gekrochen
56 laden	lädt	lud	geladen
57 lassen	läßt	ließ	gelassen
58 laufen	läuft	lief	gelaufen
59 leiden	leidet	litt	gelitten
60 leihen	leiht	lieh	geliehen
61 lesen	liest	las	gelesen
62 liegen	liegt	lag	gelegen
63 lügen	lügt	log	gelogen
64 mahlen	mahlt	mahlte	gemahlen
65 meiden	meidet	mied	gemieden
66 melken	melkt	melkte (molk)	gemolken
67 mögen	mag	mochte	gemocht
68 müssen	muß	mußte	gemußt
69 nehmen	nimmt	nahm	genommen
70 preisen	preist	pries	gepriesen
71 quellen	quillt	quoll	gequollen
72 riechen	riecht	roch	gerochen
73 rinnen	rinnt	rann	geronnen
74 rufen	ruft	rief	gerufen
75 saufen	säuft	soff	gesoffen
76 saugen	saugt	sog (saugte)	gesogen (gesaugt)
77 schaffen	schafft	schuf	geschaffen
78 schallen	schallt	schallte (scholl)	geschallt
79 scheinen	scheint	schien	geschienen
80 schelten	schilt	schalt	gescholten
81 scheren	schert	schor	geschoren
82 schieben	schiebt	schob	geschoben
83 schinden	schindet	schund	geschunden
84 schlafen	schläft	schlief	geschlafen
85 schlagen	schlägt	schlug	geschlagen
86 schleichen	schleicht	schlich	geschlichen
87 schmelzen	schmilzt	schmolz (schmelzte)	geschmolzen (geschmelzt)
88 schreien	schreit	schrie	geschrie(e)n
89 schweigen	schweigt	schwieg	geschwiegen
90 schwimmen	schwimmt	schwamm	geschwommen
91 schwören	schwört	schwor	geschworen
92 sehen	sieht	sah	gesehen
93 sein	ist	war	gewesen
94 senden	sendet	sandte (*Rad:* sendete)	gesandt (*Rad:* gesendet)
95 sieden	siedet	siedete (sott)	gesiedet (gesotten)
96 sinken	sinkt	sank	gesunken
97 sitzen	sitzt	saß	gesessen
98 sollen	soll	sollte	gesollt
99 stecken	steckt	steckte (stak)	gesteckt
100 stehen	steht	stand	gestanden
101 sterben	stirbt	starb	gestorben
102 stinken	stinkt	stank	gestunken
103 stoßen	stößt	stieß	gestoßen
104 treffen	trifft	traf	getroffen
105 treten	tritt	trat	getreten
106 tun	tut	tat	getan
107 wachsen	wächst	wuchs	gewachsen
108 waschen	wäscht	wusch	gewaschen
109 werden	wird	wurde	geworden
110 werfen	wirft	warf	geworfen
111 wissen	weiß	wußte	gewußt
112 wollen	will	wollte	gewollt
113 ziehen	zieht	zog	gezogen

German Pronunciation

The stress is shown by means of a stress mark ['] before the accentuated syllable, e.g. **Zucker** ['tsukər], **unmöglich** [un'mø:kliç]. Symbols in brackets show an optional sound which is sometimes included and sometimes omitted. We have also used the ˀ to indicate the glottal stop (a slight pause) in transcribing German words.

Vowels

Symbol	Examples	Symbol	Examples
[a]	h*a*t, h*a*rt	[ɔ]	P*o*st, *O*rt
[ɑ:]	B*a*d, B*a*hn, W*aa*ge	[ɔ̃, ɔ̃:]	Feuille*ton*
[ɑ̃, ɑ̃:]	Abonnement	[o]	M*o*ral, Adv*o*kat
[ai]	w*ei*ß	[o:]	B*oo*t, l*o*s
[au]	H*au*s	[ɔy]	h*eu*te, H*äu*ser
[e]	*e*gal, M*e*than	[œ]	g*ö*ttlich, *ö*ffnen
[e:]	B*ee*t, W*e*h	[œ̃]	Parf*um*
[ɛ]	B*e*tt, h*ä*tte	[ø]	*Ö*konom
[ɛ:]	w*äh*len, sp*ä*t	[ø:]	*Ö*l, sch*ö*n
[ɛ̃, ɛ̃:]	Terr*ain*	[u]	B*u*tter, Sch*u*ß
[ə]	B*e*hang, halt*e*	[u:]	*U*hr, Gr*u*ß
[i]	W*i*nd, m*i*t	[y]	Gl*ü*ck, Ph*y*sik
[i:]	v*ie*l, Br*i*se	[y:]	R*ü*be, f*üh*ren

Consonants

Symbol	Examples	Symbol	Examples
[b]	*b*esser	[n]	*n*ein
[ç]	i*ch*, trauri*g*	[ŋ]	la*ng*, de*n*ken
[x]	Ba*ch*, Lo*ch*	[p]	*P*akt, her*b*, ob*w*ohl
[d]	*d*a		
[dʒ]	*G*in	[r]	*r*ot, ze*rr*en, Vate*r*
[f]	Fa*ß*, *V*ieh, *Ph*on	[s]	Gra*s*, Ha*s*t, Gru*ß*
[g]	*G*eld	[z]	*S*orge, Ro*s*e
[h]	*H*aus	[ʃ]	*Sch*ein, *s*pät, sti*ll*
[j]	*j*a	[t]	*T*ag, *Th*ron, Ba*d*, Han*d*, Sta*d*t
[ʒ]	*G*enie, *J*ournal		
[k]	*k*alt, Sar*g*, Café, *Ch*or	[ts]	*Z*ar, Hin*z*, Hi*tz*e, Funk*t*ion, *C*äsar
[ks]	E*x*zellenz		
[l]	*L*ast, Nabe*l*	[tʃ]	Ma*tsch*
[m]	*M*ohn, *m*ein	[v]	*V*ase, *w*eit, et*w*as

A

A, a [aː], n -/- (the letter) A, a.

à la [aː], prep. Com: at.

Aal [aːl], m -(e)s/-e eel. ◆'**a∼en,** v.refl. F: sich a., to lounge about.

Aas [aːs], n -es/Äser 1. no pl carrion. 2. V: (Pers.) sod; **kein A.,** not a soul. ◆'**A∼geier,** m vulture.

ab [ap]. I. prep. + dat from (... onwards); **ab 3 Mark,** from 3 marks upwards. II. adv. 1. **ab und zu,** now and then; **von nun ab,** from now on. 2. off; **ab ins Bett!** off to bed with you! F: **der Knopf ist ab,** the button has come off.

'abändern, v.tr.sep. to alter (sth.). ◆**A∼ung,** f alteration.

'Abart, f variety. ◆'**a∼ig,** adj. abnormal.

'Abbau, m 1. dismantling. 2. (Senkung) reduction. 3. Min: mining. ◆'**a∼en,** v.tr.sep. (a) to take down (a stall, tent etc.); to dismantle (a machine, building); (b) to reduce (expenditure, staff); (c) to work (a mine); to mine (coal etc.).

'abbeißen, v.tr.sep.irr.4 to bite (sth.) off.

'abbekommen, v.tr.sep.irr.53 (a) to get; (b) **etwas/nichts a.,** to be damaged/undamaged; (Pers.) to be hurt/unhurt.

'abberufen, v.tr.sep.irr.74 to recall.

'abbestellen, v.tr.sep. to cancel.

'abbiegen, v.i.sep.irr.7 (sein) (Straße) to branch off; (Pers., Auto) to turn off; **nach rechts/links a.,** to turn right/left.

'Abbild, n image, likeness (of s.o.); portrayal (of sth.). ◆'**a∼en,** v.tr. to depict (sth.). ◆'**A∼ung,** f illustration.

'abbinden, v.tr.sep.9 (a) to untie; (b) Med: to ligature.

'abblasen, v.tr.sep.irr.11 F: to call off (a strike etc.).

'abblättern, v.i.sep. (sein) to peel (off).

'abblenden, v.sep. 1. v.tr. die Scheinwerfer a., to dip /N.Am: dim one's headlights. 2. v.i. (haben) Aut: to dip. ◆'**A∼licht,** m dipped headlights.

'abbrechen, v.sep.irr.14 1. v.tr. (a) to break off (a piece, relations etc.); (beenden) to stop; (b) to demolish (a house); **das Lager a.,** to strike camp. 2. v.i. (haben) to break off.

'abbremsen, v.tr.sep. to reduce (speed).

'abbrennen, v.i.sep.irr.15 (sein) to burn down; F: **abgebrannt sein,** to be broke.

'abbringen, v.tr.sep.irr.16 **j-n von etwas a.,** to dissuade s.o. from doing sth.

'Abbruch, m -(e)s/-e 1. demolition (of a building). 2. breaking off (of negotiations etc.). ◆'**a∼reif,** adj. (Haus) condemned.

'abdanken, v.i.sep. (haben) to resign; (Herrscher) to abdicate.

'abdecken, v.tr.sep. (a) to clear (a table); (b) (zudecken) to cover.

'abdichten, v.tr.sep. to seal; Nau: to caulk.

'abdrehen, v.sep. 1. v.tr. to turn off. 2.

---

v.i. (haben) to turn away.

'Abdruck, m 1. -(e)s/-e copy. 2. -(e)s/=e imprint. ◆'**a∼en,** v.tr.sep. to print.

'abdrücken, v.tr.sep. to fire (a gun); abs. to pull the trigger.

Abend ['aːbənt]. I. m -s/-e evening; **heute a.,** this evening, tonight; **am A.,** in the evening; **es wird A.,** it is getting dark, **zu A. essen,** to have supper. II. A∼-, comb.fm. evening (suit, sun, star etc.); ◆'**A∼brot,** n -(e)s/no pl supper. ◆'**A∼essen,** n dinner. ◆'**a∼füllend,** adj. full-length (film, programme). ◆'**A∼kasse,** f evening box office. ◆'**A∼kurs,** m evening class. ◆'**A∼land,** n -(e)s/no pl **das A.,** the West. ◆'**a∼lich,** adj. (of) evening. ◆'**A∼mahl,** n (Holy) Communion. ◆'**A∼rot,** n -s/no pl sunset. ◆'**a∼s,** adv. in the evening(s); **6 Uhr a.,** 6 p.m.

Abenteuer ['aːbəntɔyər], n -s/- adventure. ◆'**a∼lich,** adj. adventurous. ◆'**Abenteurer,** m -s/- adventurer.

aber ['aːbər], conj. but; oder a., or else; **das ist a. hübsch,** that's really pretty. ◆'**A∼glaube,** m superstition. ◆'**a∼gläubisch,** adj. superstitious. ◆'**a∼mals,** adv. again.

'aberkennen, v.tr.sep.irr.51 **j-m seine Rechte usw. a.,** to deprive s.o. of his rights etc.

abfahren, v.sep.irr.26 1. v.i. (sein) to leave. 2. v.tr. (a) (Polizei usw.) to patrol (a road etc.); (b) to wear out (tyres). ◆'**A∼t,** f 1. (Fahrtbeginn) departure; Sp: start (of a rally etc.). 2. (Talfahrt) downward trip. ◆'**A∼ts-,** comb.fm. departure (time etc.); starting (signal etc.).

'Abfall. I. m 1. (Abnahme) drop; 2. (Lossagung) defection (from a party etc.). 3. (Müll) usu.pl A∼e, rubbish, N.Am: garbage. II. A∼-, comb.fm. rubbish (heap etc.); Ind: waste (product etc.). ◆'**A∼eimer,** m rubbish bin; N.Am: trash can. ◆'**a∼en,** v.i.sep.irr.27 (sein) (a) (herunterfallen) to fall, drop (off); (b) (übrigbleiben) to be left over; (c) (sich neigen) to slope (down); (d) (sich lossagen) to break away; (e) (nachlassen) to decline, (schlechter werden) deteriorate; (Druck, Spannung usw.) to drop.

'abfällig, adj. adverse (judgement, criticism); disparaging (remark).

'abfangen, v.tr.sep.irr.28 (a) to intercept (a letter etc.); to catch (s.o.); (b) to bring (a car etc.) under control.

'abfärben, v.i.sep. (haben) (Farbstoff) to run; Fig: to rub off.

'abfertigen, v.tr.sep. (a) to attend to; F: **j-n kurz a.,** to snub s.o.; (b) to turn round (goods, an aircraft etc.); (Zoll) to clear (goods). ◆'**A∼ung,** f -/-en turn-round; (Zoll) clearance.

'abfeuern, v.tr.sep. to fire.

'abfind|en, v.tr.sep.irr.9 (a) to pay off (a

creditor); *Jur:* to compensate (s.o.); (*b*) **sich mit etwas** *dat* **a.,** to resign oneself to sth. ◆'**A~ung,** *f* -/-en settlement.

'**abflauen,** *v.i.sep.* (*sein*) (*Wind*) to drop; (*Interesse usw.*) to flag.

'**abfliegen,** *v.i.sep.irr.*7 1. *v.i.* (*sein*) to fly away; *Av:* to take off. 2. *v.tr.* to patrol.

'**abfließen,** *v.i.sep.irr.*31 (*sein*) to flow away.

'**Abflug,** *m* take-off.

'**Abfluß,** *m* -sses/¨sse (*Rohr*) waste pipe; (*Offnung*) outlet. ◆'**A~rinne,** *f* gully. ◆'**A~rohr,** *n* drainpipe.

'**abfragen,** *v.tr.sep.* to question; *Sch:* test (s.o.).

'**Abfuhr,** *f* -/no pl 1. collection of rubbish etc.). 2. (*Abweisung*) rebuff; **j-m eine A. erteilen,** to snub s.o..

'**abführen,** *v.sep.* 1. *v.tr.* (*a*) to take (s.o.) away; (*b*) to pay (off) (taxes, debts etc.). 2. *v.i.* (*haben*) to act as a laxative. ◆'**A~mittel,** *n* laxative.

'**Abgabe,** *f* -/-n 1. (*a*) (*Aushändigung*) handing over; (*Einreichen*) handing in; *Sp:* passing; (*b*) casting (of vote). 2. (*Geldleistung*) tax; **soziale A.,** social security contribution. ◆'**a~(n)pflichtig,** *adj.* taxable.

'**Abgang,** *m* (*a*) departure; leaving (*von Schule*); (*b*) *Th:* exit.

'**Abgas,** *n* exhaust fumes; *Ind:* waste gas.

'**abgearbeitet,** *adj.* worn out (person); worn (hands).

'**abgeben,** *v.tr.sep.irr.*36 (*a*) (*übergeben*) to hand in/over, deliver (a letter, parcel etc.) *Sp:* to pass (the ball) (an **j-n,** to s.o.); (*b*) (*verkaufen*) to sell (sth.); (*c*) to cast (one's vote); (*d*) to generate (heat etc.); (*e*) *v.refl.* **sich mit j-m/etwas a.,** to go round with sb/in for sth.

'**abgedroschen,** *adj. F:* hackneyed.

'**abgegriffen,** *adj.* worn (coins); well-thumbed (book).

'**abgehen,** *v.sep.irr.*36 1. *v.i.* (*sein*) (*a*) to go away; **von der Schule a.,** to leave school; (*b*) (*ablaufen*) to go off; (*c*) (*Knopf*) to come off; (*d*) (*fehlen*) F: **ihm geht jedes Gefühl für Humor ab,** he has absolutely no sense of humour. 2. *v.tr.* to walk along (sth.).

'**abgekartet,** *adj. F:* **a~es Spiel,** put-up job.

'**abgelegen,** *adj.* remote.

'**abgemacht,** *adj.* agreed, understood; **a.!** done! it's a deal!

'**abgeneigt,** *adj.* **a. sein,** to be averse to sth.

Abgeordnete(r) [ˈapgəˈʔɔrdnətə(r)], *m & f decl. as adj.* Member of Parliament, *U.S:* representative.

'**abgerissen,** *adj.* ragged.

'**Abgesandte(r),** *m & f decl. as adj.* envoy.

'**abgeschieden,** *adj. Lit:* secluded (position); remote (spot).

'**abgeschmackt,** *adj.* trite.

'**abgesehen,** *adj.* **a. von,** apart from.

'**abgespannt,** *adj.* tired (out).

'**abgestanden,** *adj.* flat (beer); stale (air).

'**abgestorben,** *adj.* numb (limb); dead (tree, tissue etc.).

'**abgewetzt,** *adj. F:* threadbare.

'**abgewinnen,** *v.tr.sep.irr.*3 **j-m etwas a.,** to win sth. from s.o.; **etwas** *dat* **Geschmack a.,** to get a taste for sth.

'**abgewöhnen,** *v.tr.sep.* **j-m etwas a.,** to break s.o. (of the habit) of sth.; **ich habe mir das Rauchen abgewöhnt,** I have given up smoking.

'**abgießen,** *v.tr.sep.irr.*31 to strain off (water etc.); to drain off (potatoes etc.).

'**Abglanz,** *m* reflection.

'**abgleiten,** *v.i.sep.irr.*41 (*sein*) to slip/slide off.

'**Abgott,** *m* idol.

'**abgöttisch,** *adv.* **j-n a. lieben,** to idolize s.o.

'**abgrenzen,** *v.tr.sep.* (*a*) to mark off; (*b*) to define (s.o.'s powers, field of action etc.). ◆'**A~ung,** *f* -/-en demarcation; (*b*) definition.

'**Abgrund,** *m* (*a*) abyss; (*b*) *Fig:* (*Verderben*) ruin.

'**abgucken,** *v.tr.sep.* (*a*) F: **j-m etwas a.,** to learn sth. by watching s.o.; (*b*) *abs. Sch:* to crib.

'**abhaken,** *v.tr.sep.* to tick off.

'**abhalten,** *v.tr.sep.irr.*45 (*a*) to keep (sth.) away; to keep (the rain etc.) off; **j-n von etwas a.,** to prevent s.o. from doing sth.; (*b*) **eine Sitzung a.,** to hold a meeting.

'**abhandeln,** *v.tr.sep.* (*a*) **j-m etwas** *acc* **a.,** to do a deal with s.o. for sth.; (*b*) (*behandeln*) to deal with (a subject). ◆'**A~lung,** *f* treatise (**über** + *acc,* on).

ab'handen, *adv.* **a. kommen,** to get lost.

'**Abhang,** *m* (downward) slope.

'**abhängen,** *v.* 1. *v.i.sep.irr.*46 (*haben*) (*a*) **von j-m, etwas a.,** to depend on s.o., sth.; (*b*) *Cu:* to hang (until tender). 2. *v.tr.* (*a*) *Rail:* to uncouple; (*b*) F: to get rid of (s.o.). ◆'**a~ig,** *adj.* dependent (**von** + *dat,* on); **von einer Bedingung a.,** subject to one condition. ◆'**A~igkeit,** *f* -/-en dependence (**von** + *dat,* on).

'**abhärten,** *v.tr.sep.* to harden (s.o.) (**gegen** + *acc,* to). ◆'**A~ung,** *f* hardening (**gegen** + *acc,* to).

'**abhauen,** *v.sep.irr.*47 1. *v.tr.* to chop off. 2. *v.i.* (*sein*) P: to clear off.

'**abheben,** *v.sep.irr.*48 1. *v.tr.* (*a*) to take off; *Tel:* to lift (the receiver); **Geld a.,** to draw money; (*b*) **sich a.,** to stand out. 2. *v.i.* (*haben*) (*a*) *Av:* to take off; (*rocket*) to lift off; (*b*) to cut (the cards). ◆'**A~ung,** *f* withdrawal.

'**abhelfen,** *v.tr.sep.irr.*50 (*haben*) **etwas** *dat* **a.,** to remedy sth.

'**abhetzen,** *v.tr.sep.* **sich a.,** to wear oneself out.

'**Abhilfe,** *f* -/no pl remedy; **A. schaffen,** to take remedial action.

abholen, *v.tr.sep.* (*a*) to fetch (sth.); to

collect (letters etc.); (b) to pick (s.o.) up.
'**abholzen**, v.tr.sep. to cut down.
abhören v.tr.sep. to tap (a telephone conversation etc.); Mil: to intercept (a message).
Abitur [abi'tuːr], n -s/-e school-leaving examination. ◆**A~ient(in)** [-turi'ɛnt(in)], m -en/-en (f -/-nen) school-leaving examination candidate.
'**abkaufen**, v.tr.sep. j-m etwas a., to buy sth. from s.o.; F: **das kaufe ich dir nicht ab**, I don't believe your story for a moment.
Abkehr ['apkeːr], f -/no pl estrangement; departure (**von einer Politik usw.**, from a policy etc.). ◆**a~en**, v.tr. **sich von j-m, etwas a.**, turn one's back on s.o., sth.
'**abklingen**, v.i.sep.irr.19 (sein) to die down.
'**abknicken**, v.tr.&i.sep. (haben) to snap (off).
'**abknöpfen**, v.tr.sep. F: **j-m Geld a.**, to sting s.o. for money.
'**abkochen**, v.tr.sep. to boil.
'**abkommen**. I. v.i.sep.irr.53 (sein) **vom Wege a.**, to lose one's way; **vom Thema a.**, to get off the subject. II. A., n -s/- agreement.
'**abkömmlich**, adj. dispensable. ◆**A~ling**, m -s/-e descendant.
'**abkoppeln**, v.tr.sep. to uncouple (a coach etc.), unhitch (a trailer etc.).
'**abkratzen**, v.sep. 1. v.tr. to scrape off. 2. v.i. (sein) P: to kick the bucket.
'**abkühlen**, v.sep. 1. v.tr. to cool. 2. v.refl.&i. (**sich a.**) (a) to cool down; (Wetter) to turn cool. ◆**A~ung**, f cooling.
'**abkürzen**, v.tr.sep. (abbrechen) to cut short; **den Weg a.**, to take a short cut. ◆**A~ung**, f -/-en (a) (Weg) short cut; (b) abbreviation (of a word etc.).
'**abladen**, v.tr.sep.irr.56 to unload.
Ablage, f place to put sth.; (Regal) shelf; **A. machen**, to do the filing.
ablagern, v.sep. v.tr. to deposit; **sich a.**, to settle, form a deposit. ◆**A~ung**, f -/-en deposit.
'**ablassen**, v.sep.irr.57 1. v.tr. to let out (water, air etc.); **Dampf a.**, to let off steam. 2. v.i. (haben) **von etwas a.**, to stop doing sth.
Ablauf, m 1. (Rohr usw.) drain. 2. (Ende) expiry, N.Am: expiration. 3. (Verlauf) **A. der Ereignisse**, course of events. ◆'**a~en**, v.sep.irr.58 1. v.i. (sein) (a) (abfließen) to run away; **an etwas dat a.**, to run down sth.; (b) (Ereignisse usw.) **gut/schlecht a.**, to go well/badly; (c) (Frist usw.) to expire. 2. v.tr. (a) **die Geschäfte a.**, to scour the shops (**nach etwas dat**, for sth.); (b) (abnutzen) **die Sohlen a.**, to wear out one's soles.
'**ablegen**, v.sep. 1. v.tr. (a) (ausziehen) to take off; (b) (aufgeben) to discard (old clothes, cards etc.); to drop (a name etc.); to give up (a habit etc.); (c) to put

down (a burden, the receiver etc.); (d) to file (documents etc.). 2. v.i. (haben) Nau: to cast off. ◆'**A~er**, m -s/- (a) shoot, cutting; (b) Com: offshoot (of a firm).
'**ablehnen**, v.tr.sep. to refuse (an invitation etc.); to reject (an offer, argument, organ etc.). ◆**A~ung**, f -/-en refusal, rejection.
'**ableiten**, v.tr.sep. (a) to divert (a river, traffic etc.); (b) (herleiten) to derive (a word, a formula etc.) (**aus/von + dat**, from). ◆**A~ung**, f -/-en 1. no pl (a) diversion; drainage (of water etc.); (b) derivation. 2. (Wort) derivative.
'**ablenken**, v.tr.sep. (a) to turn away, deflect (sth.); (b) to distract (s.o., s.o.'s attention, thoughts etc.); to divert (suspicion etc.). ◆'**A~ung**, f -/-en (a) deflection; (b) distraction, diversion. ◆**A~ungsmanöver**, n -s/- diversion.
'**ablesen**, v.tr.sep.irr.61 to read.
'**ableugnen**, v.tr.sep. to deny.
'**abliefern**, v.tr.sep. to deliver (goods, F: s.o.); (überreichen) to hand over (sth.). ◆'**A~ung**, f -/-en delivery.
'**ablösen**, v.tr.sep. (a) to remove (sth.) (b) to relieve (s.o.); (c) Fin: to redeem (a mortgage etc.). ◆'**A~ung**, f -/-en (a) removal; (b) Mil: relief; (c) Fin: redemption.
'**abmachen**, v.tr.sep. (a) (entfernen) to remove (sth.); (b) (vereinbaren) to arrange (sth.); to agree on (a date, price etc.). ◆'**A~ung**, f -/-en agreement.
'**abmagern**, v.i.sep. (sein) to lose weight. ◆'**A~ungskur**, f slimming diet.
'**Abmarsch**, m departure. ◆'**a~ieren**, v.i.sep. (sein) to march off.
'**abmelden**, v.tr.sep. to cancel; **sich a.**, to give notice of one's departure; (**vom Hotel**) to check out. ◆**A~ung**, f -/-en notification of departure.
'**abmessen**, v.tr.sep.irr.25 to measure. ◆'**A~ung**, f dimensions, measurements.
'**abmontieren**, v.tr. sep. to take off (a part); to dismantle (a machine etc.).
'**abmühen**, v.refl.sep. **sich a.**, to slave away.
'**Abnäher**, m -s/- dart.
Abnahme ['apnaːmə], f -/no pl 1. removal. 2. Com: taking delivery (of goods etc.). 3. (official) inspection (of a machine etc.). 4. (Nachlassen) decline, decrease.
'**abnehmen**, v.sep.irr.69 1. v.tr. (a) to take down (decorations etc.); to take off (a hat, lid etc.); to lift (the receiver); (b) **j-m etwas a.**, to take sth. from s.o.; F: **das nehme ich dir nicht ab!** I don't believe it! (c) Com: to purchase (goods); (d) (prüfen) to inspect (a machine etc.). 2. v.i. (haben) to decrease; (Fieber) to go down; (Kräfte usw.) to decline; (Pers.) to lose weight; (Mond, Interesse usw.) to wane. ◆'**A~er**, m -s/- buyer, purchaser.
'**Abneigung**, f aversion, dislike.

abnorm [ap'nɔrm], *adj.* abnormal.

'**abnutz**|**en**, *v.tr.sep.* to wear down, (*völlig*) wear out (a part, tyres etc.). ◆'**A~ung**, *f -/-en* wear.

Abonn|**ement** [abɔnə'mãː], *n -s/-s* subscription. ◆**A~ent(in)** [-'nɛnt(in)], *m -en/-en* (*f -/-nen*) subscriber. ◆**a~ieren** [-'niːrən], *v.tr.* to take out a subscription to (a periodical etc.).

Abort [a'bɔrt], *m -(e)s/-e* lavatory, toilet.

'**abpassen**, *v.tr.sep.* to wait for.

'**abpfeifen**, *v.tr.sep.irr.43* (*Schiedsrichter*) to blow his whistle. ◆'**Abpfiff**, *m* final whistle.

'**abprallen**, *v.i.sep.* (*sein*) (*Ball usw.*) to bounce; (*Geschoß usw.*) to ricochet.

'**abputzen**, *v.tr.sep.* to wipe off.

abquälen, *v.refl.sep.* sich mit etwas *dat* a., to struggle with sth.

'**abraten**, *v.tr.&i.sep.irr.13* (*haben*) j-m a., to dissuade s.o.

'**abräumen**, *v.tr.sep.* to clear away.

'**abreagieren**, *v.tr.sep.* to work off.

'**abrechn**|**en**, *v.sep.* **1**. *v.tr.* (*abziehen*) to deduct (expenses, VAT etc.); … abgerechnet, not counting … 2. *v.i.* (*haben*) to square accounts; *F:* mit j-m a., to get even with s.o. ◆'**A~ung**, *f* (*Rechnung*) account; (*Schluß*a.) settlement (of accounts).

'**Abreise**, *f* departure. ◆'**a~n**, *v.i.sep.* (*sein*) to set out.

'**abreiß**|**en**, *v.sep.* **1**. *v.tr.* (*a*) to tear (sth.) off; (*b*) to demolish (a building, bridge etc.). **2**. *v.i.* (*sein*) to stop abruptly.

'**abrichten**, *v.tr.sep.* to train.

'**abriegeln**, *v.tr.sep.* to block (a road); eine Gegend a., to cordon off an area.

'**Abriß**, *m* **1**. (*Übersicht*) outline. **2**. (*Abbruch*) demolition.

'**Abruf**, *m* auf A. on call; Waren auf A., goods for delivery as required. ◆'**a~en**, *v.tr.sep.irr.74* (*a*) to request delivery of (goods ordered); (*b*) *Data-pr:* to recall (information).

'**abrunden**, *v.tr.sep.* to round off.

abrupt [ap'rupt], *adj.* abrupt.

'**abrüst**|**en**, *v.i.sep.* (*haben*) to disarm. ◆'**A~ung**, *f* disarmament.

'**abrutschen**, *v.i.sep.* (*sein*) to slip (off/down).

'**Absage**, *f -/-e* cancellation; refusal (of an invitation etc.). ◆'**a~n**, *v.sep.* **1**. *v.tr.* to cancel (sth.). **2**. *v.i.* (*haben*) to cry off.

'**Absatz**, *m* **1**. paragraph. **2**. heel (of a shoe). **3**. *no pl Com:* sales. ◆'**A~gebiet**, *n* market.

'**abschaffen**, *v.tr.sep.irr.77* to abolish.

'**abschalten**, *v.tr.&i.sep.* (*haben*) to switch off.

'**abschätz**|**en**, *v.tr.sep.* to assess (s.o., property etc.); to estimate (value, weight etc.). ◆'**a~ig**, *adj.* adverse (judgment etc.), derogatory (remarks).

'**Abschaum**, *m* pej: scum.

'**Abscheu**, *m -(e)s/no pl* repugnance, loathing; j-s A. erregen, to repel/disgust

s.o. ◆**a~lich** [-'ʃɔylɪç], *adj.* revolting (sight, smell etc.); atrocious (deed).

'**abschicken**, *v.tr.sep.* to send off, (*per Post*) post, *N.Am:* mail (a letter etc.).

'**abschieben**, *v.tr.sep.irr.82* (*a*) to push (sth.) away; (*b*) *Jur:* to deport (s.o.).

Abschied ['apʃiːt], *m -(e)s/-e* farewell, parting. ◆'**A~s-**, *comb.fm.* farewell (visit, kiss, scene etc.); parting (gift, kiss, tear etc.).

'**abschieß**|**en**, *v.tr.sep.irr.31* (*a*) to launch (a rocket etc.); (*b*) to shoot down (an aircraft); to shoot (a bird).

'**abschirmen**, *v.tr.sep.* to shield (s.o., sth.) (gegen + *acc*, from).

'**abschlag**|**en**, *v.tr.sep.irr.85* (*a*) to knock (sth.) off; (*b*) to refuse (a request etc.). ◆'**A~szahlung**, *f* first instalment.

abschlägig ['apʃlɛːgɪç], *adj.* unfavourable.

'**abschleifen**, *v.tr.sep.irr.43* to sand (down).

Abschlepp- ['apʃlɛp-], *comb.fm.* breakdown (service etc.). ◆'**a~en**, *v.tr.sep.* to tow away.

'**abschließen**, *v.sep. irr.31* (*a*) to lock; (*b*) to conclude (an agreement etc.), complete (a book, deal etc.).

'**Abschluß**, *m* (*a*) extremity; (*Rand*) unterer/oberer A., bottom/top edge; (*b*) (*Ende*) end, conclusion (of a speech etc.); completion (of a deal etc.). **II**. '**A~-**, *comb. fm.* final (examination etc.). ◆'**A~bilanz**, *f* final (annual) balance-sheet. ◆'**A~feier**, *f* speech day.

'**abschmecken**, *v.tr.sep.* to season.

'**abschneiden**, *v.sep.irr.41* **1**. *v.tr.* to cut off (sth.). **2**. *v.i.* (*haben*) gut/schlecht a., to make a good/poor showing.

'**Abschnitt**, *m* **1**. (*a*) section; *Mil:* sector (of a front); (*b*) (*Stadium*) phase; stage (of a journey). **2**. (*abtrennbarer Teil*) stub (of a ticket etc.); (*Bon*) coupon.

'**abschnüren**, *v.tr.sep.* to cut off.

'**abschöpfen**, *v.tr.sep.* to skim off.

'**abschrauben**, *v.tr.sep.* to unscrew.

'**abschreck**|**en**, *v.tr.sep.* (*a*) to deter (s.o.); (*b*) *Cu:* to rinse (spaghetti etc.). ◆'**a~end**, *adj.* deterrent; a~endes Beispiel, warning example. ◆'**A~ung**, *f -/-en* deterrent.

'**abschreib**|**en**, *v.sep.irr.12* **1**. *v.tr.* (*a*) (*Abschrift machen*) to copy; (*b*) *Fin:* to write off (a loss, debt, *F:* a lost friend etc.). **2**. *v.i.* (*haben*) *Sch:* to crib (bei j-m, from s.o.). ◆'**A~ung**, *f Fin:* writing off (of debts, losses); (*Wertminderung*) depreciation.

'**Abschrift**, *f* copy, transcript.

'**abschürf**|**en**, *v.tr.sep.* to graze. ◆'**A~ung**, *f -/-en* graze.

'**Abschuß**, *m* **1**. firing (of a gun); launch (of a rocket). **2**. shooting down (of a bird, aircraft).

abschüssig ['apʃysɪç], *adj.* sloping.

'**abschwächen**, *v.tr.sep.* to lessen (an effect etc.); to tone down (one's remarks).

'**abschweifen**, *v.i.sep.* (sein) vom Thema a., to digress.

abseh|bar [apze:ba:r], *adj.* foreseeable. ◆'**a~en**, *v.sep.irr.92* 1. *v.tr.* (a) to foresee (sth.); es ist (noch) kein Ende abzusehen, there is no end in sight; (b) es auf j-n, etwas *acc* abgesehen haben, to be after s.o., sth. 2. *v.i.* (haben) (a) von etwas *dat* a., to ignore/disregard sth.; abgesehen von apart from; (b) von einem Plan/Besuch a., to abandon a plan/visit.

abseits, I. *adv.* a. vom Wege, off the road; *Fig:* sich a. halten, to keep in the background. II. A~, *n* offside.

'**absend|en**, *v.tr.sep.94* to send off, (per Post) post, *N.Am:* mail (a letter etc.). ◆'**A~er**, *m* sender.

absetz|bar ['apzɛtsba:r], *adj. Fin:* (von der Steuer) a., (tax) deductible. ◆'**a~en**, *v.sep.* 1. *v.tr.* (a) (abnehmen) to take off (a hat etc.); (hinstellen) to put down (sth. heavy, one's glass etc.); to drop (passengers); (b) (entfernen) to remove (an official etc.) from office; to depose (a monarch); (c) (ablagern) sich a. to settle; (d) *Com:* (verkaufen) to sell (goods); (e) (abziehen) Spesen usw. (von der Steuer) a., to deduct expenses etc (from tax). 2. *v.i.* (haben) to stop. ◆'**A~ung**, *f -/-en* (Entlassung) dismissal.

absicher|n, *v.tr.sep.* to make safe; sich gegen etwas a., to guard against sth. ◆'**A~ung**, *f -/-en* safeguard.

'**Absicht**, *f -/-en* intention; mit A., intentionally. ◆**a~lich**, 'ap~], *adj.* intentional.

absitzen, *v.sep.irr.97* 1. *v.i.* (sein) to dismount. 2. *v.tr. F:* eine Strafe a., to serve a sentence.

absolut [apzo'lu:t], *adj.* absolute.

absolvieren [apzɔl'vi:rən] *v.tr.* to complete (a course etc.); to pass (an examination).

'**absonder|n**, *v.tr.sep.* (a) to isolate (s.o., oneself), cut (s.o., oneself) off; (b) to secrete (bile, sweat etc.). ◆'**A~ung**, *f -/-en* (a) isolation; (b) *Biol:* secretion.

absorbieren [apzɔr'bi:rən], *v.tr.sep.* to absorb.

'**abspalten**, *v.tr.sep.* to split off (sth.).

'**abspeisen**, *v.tr.sep. F:* j-n mit Ausreden usw. a., to fob s.o. off with excuses etc.

absperr|en, *v.tr.sep.* (a) to lock (a door etc.); (b) to cordon off (an area). ◆'**A~ung**, *f -/-en* (road) block; barrier.

'**Abspiel**, *n Sp:* (a) pass; (b) *no pl* passing. ◆'**a~en**, *v.tr.sep.* (a) to play (a record); (b) *Sp:* to pass (the ball); (c) sich a., to take place; (Buch usw.) to be set (somewhere).

'**absplittern**, *v.tr.&i.sep.*(sein) to splinter (sth.); to chip (off) (paint).

'**Absprache**, *f* arrangement.

'**absprechen**, *v.tr.sep.irr.14* (a) man kann ihm das Talent nicht a., one cannot deny his talent; (b) sich (mit

j-m) a., to come to an arrangement (with s.o.).

'**abspringen**, *v.i.sep.irr.19* (sein) (a) to jump, *Sp:* take off; (b) (Farbe, Lack usw.) to chip off.

'**Absprung**, *m* jump; *Sp:* take-off.

'**abspülen**, *v.tr.sep.* to rinse (plates etc.); to rinse (sth.) off.

'**abstamm|en**, *v.i.sep.* (sein) (Pers.) to be descended (Wort) to be derived. ◆'**A~ung**, *f -/-en* descent, ancestry; derivation.

'**Abstand**, *m* distance, gap; in gleichen A~en, at equal intervals; er ist mit A. der Beste, he is far and away the best; von etwas *dat* A. nehmen, to abandon sth.

'**abstatten**, *v.tr.sep.* j-m einen Besuch a., to pay s.o. a visit.

'**abstauben**, *v.tr.sep.* (a) to dust (furniture etc.); (b) *F:* (entwenden) to swipe, pinch (sth.).

'**Abstecher**, *m -s/-* einen A. machen, to make a detour.

'**abstehen**, *v.i.sep.irr.100* (haben) to stick out.

'**absteigen**, *v.i.sep.irr.89* (sein) (a) to descend; in einem Hotel a., to put up at a hotel; (b) *Sp:* to be relegated.

'**abstell|en**, *v.tr.sep.* (a) to put away, store (furniture etc.); to park (a car, cycle etc.); (b) (abschalten) to stop (a clock, machine etc.), to turn off (gas, water, heating etc.); to switch off (a radio, an engine etc.); (c) (niedersetzen) to put/set down (a burden). ◆'**A~gleis**, *n* siding. ◆'**A~raum**, *m* store room.

'**abstempeln**, *v.tr.sep.* to stamp.

'**absterben**, *v.i.sep.irr.101* (sein) (Pflanze) to die (off), wither.

Abstieg ['apʃti:k], *m -(e)s/-e* descent; *Fig:* decline; *Sp:* relegation.

'**abstimm|en**, *v.sep.* 1. *v.tr.* (a) to tune (in) (the radio, a circuit etc.) (auf + *acc*, to); (b) to adjust (sth.) (auf *acc*, to suit sth.); Pläne usw. aufeinander a., to co-ordinate/bring into line plans etc. 2. *v.i.* (haben) to vote. ◆'**A~ung**, *f* 1. *Rad: TV:* tuning. 2. vote, voting.

abstinen|t [apsti'nɛnt], *adj.* abstemious; (vom Alkohol) teetotal. ◆**A~z**, *f -/no pl* teetotalism. ◆**A~zler**, *m -s/-* teetotal(l)er.

'**Abstoß**, *m* push (off); *Sp:* goal kick. ◆'**a~en**, *v.tr.sep.irr.103* (a) (mit Stoß bewegen) to push (s.o., sth.) away/off; *Fig:* seine Art stößt mich ab, I find his manner repellent; (b) *Com:* Waren a., to sell off goods. ◆'**a~end**, *adj.* repellent.

abstrakt [ap'strakt], *adj.* abstract. ◆**A~ion** [-tsi'o:n], *f -/-en* abstraction.

'**abstreiten**, *v.tr.sep.irr.* to deny.

'**Abstrich**, *m -(e)s/-e* 1. *Med:* smear. 2. (Abzug) deduction, cut.

'**abstufen**, *v.tr.sep.* (a) to terrace (land); (b) to grade (colours, salaries etc.).

'**Absturz**, *m* plunge; *Av:* crash.

'**abstürzen**, v.i.sep. (sein) to plunge (down); (Flugzeug) to crash.

absuchen, v.tr.sep. to search, scour (a district etc.), scan (the horizon).

absurd [aps'zurt], adj. absurd.

Abszeß [aps'tsɛs], m -sses/-sse abscess.

Abt [apt], m. -(e)s/-e abbot.

'**abtasten**, v.tr.sep. (a) to feel (s.o., sth.) all over; (Polizei) to frisk (s.o.); (b) TV: to scan (an image etc.).

'**abtauen**, v.tr.sep. to melt (ice); to defrost (the refrigerator).

Abtei [ap'tai], f -/-en abbey.

Ab'teil, n compartment. ◆'**a~en**, v.tr.sep. to divide up (a room); to partition off (part of a room). ◆**A~ung**, f [ap'tailuŋ] department; Mil: detachment. ◆**A~ungsleiter**, m head of department/division.

abtragen, v.tr.sep.irr.42 (a) to pull down (a building etc.); (b) **eine Schuld a.**, to pay a debt; (c) to wear out (clothes etc.).

abträglich [ɑptrɛːkliç], adj. harmful.

abtransportieren, v.tr.sep. to remove.

'**abtreiben**, v.sep.irr.12 1. v.tr. (a) to drive (a ship etc.) off course; (b) **ein Kind a.**, to procure an abortion. 2. v.i. (sein) (Schiff) to drift. ◆**A~ung**, f -/-en abortion.

'**abtrennen**, v.tr.sep. (a) to detach (a counterfoil etc.); to cut off (a button etc.); to divide off (part of a room).

'**abtreten**, v.sep.irr.105 1. v.tr. (a) (abnutzen) to wear out (a step, carpet etc.), wear down (heels); (b) (überlassen) to relinquish (a right). 2. v.i. (sein) (a) (Pers.) to withdraw; Mil: **a.!** dismiss! (b) (Regierung usw.) to resign.

Abtritt, m withdrawal.

'**abtrocknen**, v.tr.&i.sep. (haben) to dry.

abtrünnig [ɑptrʏniç], adj. renegade.

'**abtun**, v.tr.sep.irr.106 (übergehen) to dismiss (s.o., s.o.'s objections etc.).

'**abverlangen**, v.tr.sep. **j-m etwas a.**, to demand sth. from s.o.

'**abwandeln**, v.tr.sep. to modify.

'**abwandern**, v.i.sep. (sein) to migrate. ◆'**A~ung**, f migration.

'**abwarten**, v.tr.sep. (haben) to await, wait for (sth.); **warte ab**, wait and see.

abwärts ['apvɛrts], adv. down, downwards.

Abwasch ['apvaʃ], m -es/no pl F: washing up. ◆'**a~en**, v.tr.&i.sep.irr.108 (Pers. Geschirr) a.), to wash up.

'**Abwasser**, n -s/- sewage; Ind: effluent.

'**abwechseln**, v.tr.&i. (haben) sep. to alternate (two things); (Pers.) to take turns (**mit j-m**, with s.o.). ◆'**a~elnd**, adj. alternate, alternating. ◆**A~lung**, f -/-en (a) alternation; (b) variety; **zur A.**, for a change.

'**Abweg**, m auf **A~e geraten**, to go astray. ◆'**a~ig**, adj. out of the way; obscure (idea etc.); (verfehlt) off the point.

'**Abwehr**. I. f -/no pl (a) F: (Widerstand) A. **gegen etwas** acc, resistance to sth.; (b)

Mil: Sp: defence. II. '**A~-**, comb.fm. defensive (measure etc.). ◆'**a~en**, v.tr.sep. to ward off (danger, an attack etc.). ◆'**A~spieler**, m defender.

'**abweichen**, v.i.sep.irr.40 (sein) (verschieden sein) to differ (**von + dat**, from); (abgehen) **vom Kurs a.**, to go off course. ◆'**a~end**, adj. deviating; divergent (opinion etc.). ◆'**A~ung**, f -/-en deviation.

'**abweisen**, v.tr.sep.irr.70 (a) (fortschicken) to turn (s.o.) away; (b) (ablehnen) to reject, turn down (a candidate, request etc.). ◆'**a~end**, adj. **a~ende Geste**, dismissive gesture.

'**abwenden**, v.tr.sep.irr.94 (a) to turn away (one's eyes, face etc.); **sich a.**, to turn away/aside; (b) to ward off (danger); to avert (a disaster etc.).

'**abwerfen**, v.tr.sep.irr.110 to throw off; to shed (leaves, skin); to drop (bombs, pamphlets etc.).

'**abwert|en**, v.tr.sep. to devalue. ◆'**a~end**, adj. pejorative.

'**abwesen|d**, adj. 1. absent. 2. (zerstreut) absent-minded. ◆'**A~de(r)**, m&f decl. as adj. absentee. ◆'**A~heit**, f -/no pl absence.

'**abwickeln**, v.tr.sep. (a) (abrollen) to unwind; (b) (erledigen) to settle (a matter); to organize (an event).

'**abwiegen**, v.tr.sep.irr.7 to weigh out.

'**Abwurf**, m throwing; dropping (of bombs etc.).

'**abzahl|en**, v.tr.sep. to pay off. ◆'**A~ung**, f instalment.

'**abzählen**, v.tr.sep. to count (sth.).

'**Abzeichen**, n badge; Mil: etc: insignia.

'**abzeichnen**, v.tr.sep. (a) to draw, sketch (sth.); to copy (a picture etc.); (b) **sich gegen etwas** acc **a.**, to stand out against sth.

Abzieh|bild ['aptsi:bilt], n transfer. ◆'**a~en**, v.sep.irr.113 1. v.tr. (a) to take off (a ring); (b) to skin (an animal, a tomato etc.); to strip (a bed, paint etc.); (c) to print (a film, negative); (d) to deduct (an amount), subtract (a number); (e) to withdraw (troops). 2. v.i. (sein) (Nebel, Rauch usw.) to clear; (Gewitter) to pass; (Truppen) to withdraw; F: (Pers.) to go away.

'**abzielen**, v.i.sep. (haben) **auf etwas** acc **a.**, to aim at sth.

'**Abzug**, m 1. deduction; Com: (Rabatt) discount. 2. Phot: print. 3. (Raucha-) flue. 4. Mil: withdrawal. 5. trigger (of a gun).

abzüglich [ɑptsy:kliç], prep. + gen less.

'**abzweig|en**, v.tr.&i.sep. (sein) (a) (Straße usw.) to branch off; (Auto) turn off; (b) Com: etc: to divert (capital). ◆'**A~ung**, f -/-en turning (in road); (Gabelung) fork.

ach [ax], int. oh! ah! F: **mit A. und Krach**, by the skin of one's teeth.

Achse ['aksə], f -/-n 1. Aut: etc: axle. 2.

(Mittellinie) axis.

Achsel ['aksəl], f -/-n shoulder. ◆'A~höhle, f armpit. ◆'A~zucken, n -s/no pl shrug.

acht¹ [axt], num. adj. eight; (heute) in a Tagen, a week today. ◆a~e(r,s), num. adj. eighth. ◆'a~el, inv.adj. eighth (part) of … ◆'A~erbahn, f roller coaster. ◆a~zehn num. adj. eighteen. ◆'a~zig, num. adj. eighty. ◆a~ziger. I. inv. adj. die a. Jahre, the eighties. II. A., m -s/- octogenarian. ◆'a~zigste(r,s), num. adj. eightieth.

'acht2, in the vbl. phr. sich in a. nehmen, to be careful; etwas außer a. lassen, to disregard sth. ◆'a~en, v. 1. v.tr. (a) (respektieren) to respect (s.o., s.o.'s rights, age); to observe (the law). 2. v.i. (haben) auf etwas acc a., to pay attention to sth. ◆'a~geben, v.i.sep.irr.35 (haben) (aufpassen) to pay attention (auf etwas acc, to sth.); (sorgen für) auf j-n, etwas acc a., to keep an eye on s.o., sth.; gib acht! take care! ◆'a~los, adj. careless, heedless. ◆'a~sam, adj. heedful (auf + acc, of); careful. ◆'A~ung, f -/no pl 1. (Aufmerksamkeit) attention; A.! look out! 2. (Wertschätzung) respect.

ächten ['ɛçtən], v.tr. to ostracize (s.o.).

ächzen ['ɛçtsən], v.i. (haben) (Pers.) to moan, groan; (Dielen usw.) to creak.

Acker ['akər], m -s/= field. ◆'A~bau, m arable farming. ◆'a~n, v. 1. v.tr. to farm (land). 2. v.i. (haben) F: to slave away.

Adamsapfel ['aːdamsʔapfəl], Adam's apple.

add|ieren [a'diːrən], v.tr. to add up. ◆A~ition [-itsi'oːn], f -/-en addition.

Ad|el ['aːdəl], m -s/no pl (Klasse) nobility. ◆'a~(e)lig, adj. noble (family, descent); titled (person).

Ader ['aːdər], f -/-n vein; j-n zur A. lassen, A: Med: to bleed s.o.; F: to get money out of s.o.

Adjektiv ['atjɛktiːf], n -s/-e adjective.

Adler ['aːdlər], m -s/- eagle.

Admiral [atmi'raːl], m -s/-e admiral.

adopt|ieren [adɔp'tiːrən], v.tr. to adopt. ◆A~ion [-tsi'oːn], f -/-en adoption. ◆A~iv- [-'tiːf], comb.fm. adopted (child); adoptive (parents).

Adreßbuch [a'drɛsbuːx], n directory.

Adresse [a'drɛsə], f -/-n address; F: an die falsche A. geraten, to get the wrong person. ◆a~ieren [-'siːrən], v.tr. to address (an + acc, to).

adrett [a'drɛt], adj. smart.

Adria ['aːdria], Pr.n.f -. die A., the Adriatic.

Advent [at'vɛnt], m -(e)s/no pl Advent. ◆A~skranz, m advent wreath.

Adverb [at'vɛrp], n -s/-ien adverb.

Affäre [a'fɛːrə], f -/-n affair; F: sich aus der A. ziehen, to get out of it.

Aff|e ['afə], m -n/-n 1. Z: monkey; (Menschena.) ape. ◆'A~enhitze, f -/no

pl F: scorching heat. ◆'a~ig, adj. F: stuck-up.

Affekt [a'fɛkt], m -(e)s/-e strong emotion; im A. begangen, done in the heat of the moment. ◆a~iert [-'tiːrt], adj. affected.

Afrika ['afrika]. Pr.n.n -s. Africa. ◆A~ner(in), m -s/- (f -/-nen) African. ◆a~nisch, adj. African.

After ['aftər], m -s/- anus.

Ägäis [ɛ'gɛːis]. Pr.n.f -. die Ä., the Aegean.

Agent|(in) [a'gɛnt(in)], m -en/-en (f -/-nen) agent. ◆A~ur [-'tuːr], f -/-en agency.

Aggregat [agre'gaːt], n -(e)s/-e 1. aggregate. 2. El: system.

Aggression [agrɛsi'oːn], f -/-en aggression. ◆a~iv [-'siːf], adj. aggressive.

agil [a'giːl], adj. agile.

Agitation [agitatsi'oːn], f -/-en agitation. ◆A~ator [-'taːtor], m -s/-en agitator.

Agrar- [a'graːr-], comb.fm. agricultural (product, imports, policy etc.). ◆A~reform, f land reform. ◆A~wirtschaft, f farming industry.

Ägypt|en [ɛ'gyptən]. Pr.n.n -s. Egypt. ◆A~er(in), m -s/- (f -/-nen) Egyptian. ◆a~isch, adj. Egyptian.

aha [a'haː], int. (oh) I see!

Ahn [aːn], m -en/-en Lit: ancestor.

ähneln ['ɛːnəln], v.i. (haben) j-m, etwas dat ä., to resemble s.o.

ahnen ['aːnən], v.tr. (Vorgefühl haben) to have a foreboding of (sth.); to suspect (the truth etc.); ich habe es geahnt, I saw it coming. ◆'A~ung, f -/-en 1. foreboding; ich habe so eine A., als ob …, I have a feeling that … 2. (Vermutung) idea; hast du eine A.! fat lot you know about it! ◆a~ungslos, adj. unsuspecting.

ähnlich ['ɛːnlɪç], adj. similar; F: das sieht dir ä.! that's just like you! ◆'A~keit, f -/-en similarity; (im Aussehen) resemblance.

Ahorn ['aːhorn], m -s/-e maple.

Ähre ['ɛːrə], f -/-n ear.

Akadem|ie [akade'miː], f -/-n academy. ◆A~iker(in) [-'deːmikər], m -s/- (f -/-nen) university graduate. ◆a~isch [-'deːmɪʃ], adj. academic (career etc.); university (education etc.).

akklimatisieren [aklimati'ziːrən], v.refl. sich a., to become acclimatized.

Akkord [a'kɔrt], m -(e)s/-e 1. Mus: chord. 2. Ind: im A. arbeiten, to do piecework.

Akkordeon [a'kɔrdeɔn], n -s/-s accordion.

Akkusativ ['akuzatiːf], m -s/-e accusative (case).

Akne ['aknə], f -/-n acne.

Akrobat|(in) [akro'baːt(in)], m -en/-en (f -/-nen) acrobat. ◆a~isch, adj. acrobatic.

Akt [akt]. *m* -(e)s/-e 1. 2. *Art:* nude.
Akte ['aktə], *f* -/-n file; *pl* A~n, records, files; etwas zu den A~n legen, (i) to file sth.; (ii) *F:* to shelve sth. ◆**A~nschrank,** *m* filing cabinet. ◆**A~ntasche,** *f* briefcase. ◆**A~n- zeichen,** *n* reference.
Aktie ['aktsiə], *f* -/-n share. ◆**A~n-, comb.fm.** share, *N.Am:* stock (index, capital, price etc.); stock (market etc.). ◆**A~ngesellschaft,** *f* joint-stock com- pany.
Aktion [aktsi'o:n], *f* -/-en 1. action; in A~ treten, to come into action. 2. campaign; *Com:* (sales) drive. ◆**A~är(in)** [-'nɛ:r(in)], *m* -s/-e (f -/-nen) shareholder, *N.Am:* stock- holder.
aktiv [ak'ti:f]. I. *adj.* active; a~er Soldat, regular (soldier). II. A~, *n* -s/-e active voice. ◆**a~ieren** [-ti'vi:rən], *v.tr.* to get (business etc.) going; to get (people) moving; *Med:* to stimulate (activity). ◆**A~ierung,** *f* -/-en activation, stimula- tion. ◆**A~ität** [-vi'tɛ:t], *f* -/-en activity. ◆**A~saldo,** *m* credit balance.
Aktualität [aktuali'tɛ:t], *f* -/-en topical- ity. ◆**a~ell** [-'ɛl], *adj.* topical; current (fashion, style etc.); a~eller Bericht, up-to-date report.
Akupunktur [akupuŋk'tu:r], *f* -/-en acu- puncture.
Akustik [a'kustik], *f* -/no *pl* acoustics. ◆**a~isch,** *adj.* acoustic.
akut [a'ku:t] *adj.* acute.
Akzent [ak'tsɛnt], *m* -(e)s/-e accent; *Fig:* stress.
akzept|abel [aktsɛp'ta:bəl], *adj.* accept- able. ◆**a~ieren** [-'ti:rən], *v.tr.* to ac- cept (sth.).
Alarm [a'larm]. I. *m* -(e)s/-e alarm; *Mil:* alert. II. A~, *comb.fm.* warning (sys- tem, device etc.). ◆**a~bereit,** *adj.* on the alert. ◆**A~bereitschaft,** *f* standby. ◆**a~ieren** [-'mi:rən], *v.tr.* (a) (*Alarm geben*) to alert (troops, police etc.); (b) (*aufschrecken*) to alarm (s.o.).
Albanien [al'ba:niən], *Pr.n.n* -s. Alba- nia. ◆**A~ier(in),** *m* -s/- (f -/-nen) Alba- nian. ◆**a~isch,** *adj.* Albanian.
albern ['albərn], *adj.* silly (behaviour, person etc.); fatuous (remark). ◆**A~heit,** *f* -/-en silliness.
Album ['album], *n* -s/-ben album.
Algen ['algən], *fpl* seaweed.
Algebra ['algebra], *f* -/no *pl* algebra.
Algerien [al'ge:riən], *Pr.n.n* -s. Algeria. ◆**A~ier(in),** *m* -s/- (f -/-nen) Algerian. ◆**a~isch,** *adj.* Algerian.
Alibi ['a:libi], *n* -s/-s alibi.
Alimente [ali'mɛntə], *npl* alimony.
Alkohol ['alkoho:l], *m* -s/-e alcohol. ◆**a~frei,** *adj.* non-alcoholic, soft (drinks). ◆**A~iker(in)** [-'ho:likər(in)], *m* -s/- (f -/-nen) alcoholic. ◆**a~isch** [-'ho:liʃ], *adj.* alcoholic.
all [al]. I. *indef. pron.* 1. *sing.* a~es,

everything; das ist a~es, that is all; a~es in allem, all in all; vor a~em, above all; bei/trotz a~em, in spite of everything; sie war sein ein und a~es, she was everything to him. 2. *pl* a~e, all; (*Pers.*) everybody; a~e beide, both (of them). II. *adj.* all; in a~er Frühe, bright and early; a~e Menschen, all men; a~e zwei Tage, every other day. III. *adv. or pred. adj. F:* der Zucker ist a~e, there is no sugar left. IV. A., *n* -s/ no *pl* das A., the universe. ◆**a~e'dem,** *indef. pron.* trotz a~, in spite of all (that). ◆**a~e'mal,** *adv.* (a) ein für a., once and for all; (b) *F:* what- ever happens. ◆**a~en'falls,** *adv.* if the worst comes to the worst. ◆**a~er-, comb.fm.** + *superl.* (best, highest, most, most beautiful etc.) of all; very (best, highest etc.). ◆**a~er'dings,** *adv.* (a) (*bejahend*) certainly; (b) (*einschränkend*) sie ist a. keine Schönheit, admittedly she is no beauty. ◆**a~er'hand,** *inv. adj.* of all sorts/kinds; *F:* das ist ja a.! that's the limit! ◆**A~er'heiligen,** *n -/ no pl* All Saints' Day. ◆**a~er'lei,** *inv. adj.* all sorts/kinds of. ◆**a~er'letze(r,s),** *adj.* last. ◆**a~er'seits,** *adv.* (a) on all sides; (b) *F:* guten Mor- gen a.! good morning everybody! ◆**a~'jährlich,** *adj.* annual; *adv.* an- nually, every year. ◆**A~'tag,** *m* work- ing day; der A., everyday life. ◆**a~'täglich,** *adj.* (*täglich*) every- day (event etc.); daily (walk etc.); (*durchschnittlich*) ordinary (person, face etc.); mundane (occupation). ◆**a~- tags,** *adv.* on working days/weekdays. ◆**A~tags-, comb.fm.** everyday (life, language etc.). ◆**a~'wissend,** *adj.* omniscient. ◆**a~'zu,** *adv. comb.fm.* all too, only too (quickly etc.); far too (long, much etc.); nicht a~zuviel, not all that much. ◆**A~zweck-, comb.fm.** all- purpose (tool etc.).
Allee [a'le:], *f* -/-n avenue.
allein [a'lain]. I. *adj.& adv.* alone; sich von a~e schließen, to shut automati- cally; Gedanke ist schrecklich, the mere thought is terrible. II. A~-, *comb.fm.* (*einzig*) sole (proprietor, heir, agency etc.); (*ausschließlich*) exclusive (right, possession etc.). ◆**a~gang,** *m* single- handed effort; im A., on one's own. ◆**A~herrscher,** *m* autocrat. ◆**a~stehend,** *adj.* (a) (*Pers.*) single.
aller- *see* **all.**
Allergie [alɛr'gi:], *f* -/-n allergy. ◆**a~isch** [a'lɛrgiʃ], *adj.* allergic.
alles *see* **all.**
allgemein [algə'main], *adj.* general; im a~en, in general, generally. ◆**A~bildung,** *f* general education; (*A~wissen*) general knowledge. ◆**a~gültig,** *adj.* universal. ◆**A~heit,** *f/no pl* 1. die A., the general public. 2. generality. ◆**a~verständlich,** *adj.*

popular.

Alli|anz [ali'ants], f -/-en alliance. ◆**a∼iert**, adj. allied; **die A∼ierten**, the allies.

allmählich [al'mɛːliç], adj. gradual.

Alm [alm], f -/-en alpine meadow.

Almosen ['almoːzən], n -s/- alms; F: & N.Am: hand-out.

Alpen ['alpən]. I. Pr.n.pl **die A.**, the Alps. II. '**A∼**, comb.fm. alpine (pass, plant etc.); ◆**A∼enveilchen**, n cyclamen.

Alphabet [alfa'beːt], n -(e)s/-e alphabet. ◆**a∼isch**, adj. alphabetical.

Alptraum ['alptraum], m nightmare.

als [als], conj. 1. (a) (zeitlich) when; (b) (nach Komparativ) than; **ich bin älter a. er**, I am older than he is; (c) (außer) but, except; **nichts a.**, nothing but; (d) (in der Eigenschaft) as; **er kam a. letzter/erster**, he was the last/first to come. **a. ob, as if**.

also ['alzo], conj. & adv. therefore, so; **da bist du a.!** so there you are! **a. doch!** so I was right (after all)! **na a.!** what did I tell you! **a., ich glaube ...**, well, I think ...

alt¹ [alt], adj. old; **er ist immer noch der a∼e**, he hasn't changed at all; **wir lassen alles beim a∼en**, we are leaving things just as they are. ◆'**A∼bau**, m old building. ◆**a∼be'kannt**, adj. (old and) familiar ◆'**a∼be'währt**, adj. proven (remedy, methods); long-standing (friendship etc.). ◆'**A∼eisen**, n scrap iron. ◆'**a∼hergebracht**, adj. traditional. ◆'**a∼klug**, adj. precocious (child). ◆'**a∼modisch**, adj. oldfashioned. ◆'**A∼papier**, n waste paper. ◆'**a∼sprachlich**, adj. classical (studies). ◆'**A∼stadt**, f old (part of a) town. ◆'**A∼weibersommer**, m Indian summer.

'**Alt²**, m -s/-e Mus: alto; (weibliche) contralto; ◆'**A∼stimme**, f alto/(weibliche) contralto voice.

Altar [al'taːr], m -(e)s/-e altar.

Alter [al'tər], n -s/- age; (a) **im A. von 20**, at the age of 20; (b) (hohes) **A.**, old age. ◆'**a∼n**, v/i. (sein/haben) to age. ◆**A∼s-**, comb.fm. (a) age (group etc.); (b) (of) old age; (care etc.) of old people/the aged; Med: geriatric (complaints, medicine etc.). ◆'**A∼sgrenze**, f age limit. ◆'**A∼sheim**, n old people's home. ◆'**A∼sunterschied**, m difference in age. ◆'**A∼tum**, n -s/-er antiquity. ◆'**a∼tümlich**, adj. ancient; (altmodisch) antiquated (dress etc.); old-world (town etc.).

ält|er ['ɛltər], adj. (a) older; elder (son, brother etc.); **ä. werden**, to grow old; (b) (ältlich) **ein ä∼er Herr**, an elderly gentleman. ◆'**ä∼este(r,s)**, adj. oldest; eldest (son, brother etc.).

altern|ativ [altɛrna'tiːf], adj. alternative. ◆**a∼ative** [-'tiːvə], f -/-n alternative.

Alu|folie ['ɑːluːfoːliə], f baking foil. ◆**A∼minium** [alu'miːnium], n -s/no pl aluminium. N.Am: aluminum.

am [am], prep. 1. = **an dem**. 2. **am deutlichsten**, most clearly.

Amateur [ama'tøːr], m -s/- amateur.

Amazonas [ama'tsoːnas]. Pr.n.m -. the (river) Amazon.

Amboß ['ambos], m -sses/-sse anvil.

ambulan|t [ambu'lant], adj. j-n a. behandeln, to treat s.o. as an outpatient. ◆**A∼z**, f -/-en Med: outpatients' department; (b) Aut: ambulance.

Ameise ['aːmaizə], f -/-n ant. ◆'**A∼nsäure**, f formic acid.

amen ['aːmən], int. & A., n -s/- amen.

Amerika [a'meːrika]. Pr.n.n -s. America. ◆**A∼ner** [-'kaːnər], m -s/- American. ◆**A∼nerin**, f -/-nen American girl/woman. ◆**a∼nisch**, adj. American.

Amnestie [amnɛs'tiː], f -/-n amnesty.

Ampel ['ampəl], f -/-n traffic light(s).

Amput|ation [amputatsi'oːn], f -/-en amputation. ◆**a∼ieren** ['tiːrən], v.tr. to amputate.

Amsel ['amzəl], f -/-n blackbird.

Amt [amt], n -(e)s/-er 1. office; **ein A. bekleiden**, to hold an office/a position; 2. (a) (Behörde) (government) office/department; section (of a ministry); (b) (Gebäude, Raum) (post/tax etc.) office; Tel: exchange, N.Am: central ◆**a∼ieren** ['tiːrən], v.i. (haben) to be in/hold office. ◆**a∼lich**, adj. official. ◆'**A∼s-**, comb.fm. official (language, secret etc.); (holder, term, robes, oath etc.) of office. ◆'**A∼sgericht**, n district court. ◆'**A∼srichter**, m district court judge ◆'**A∼sweg**, m auf dem A., through official channels.

Amulett [amu'lɛt], n -(e)s/-e charm.

amüs|ant [amy'zant], adj. amusing. ◆**a∼ieren** [-'ziːrən], v.tr. to amuse (s.o., oneself); **sich über j-n, etwas acc a.**, to be amused at s.o., sth.

an [an]. I. prep. 1. + dat (a) (räumlich) at, on; (neben) by; **an sich**, in itself; as such; **an und für sich**, strictly speaking; (c) (zeitlich) on; **am Montag**, on Monday; **am Tage**, in the daytime. 2. + acc (a) (Bemerkung usw.) (directed) to (s.o.): (intended) for (s.o.); (b) **etwas an etwas acc binden/heften/nageln**, to tie/pin/nail sth. (on)to sth.; (c) (Richtung) at; (gegen) (up) against. II. adv. 1. **von Köln an**, from Cologne (on)wards; **von heute an**, (as) from today. 2. F: (a) **das Licht/Gas/Radio ist an**, the light/gas/radio is on; (b) **mit dem Mantel an**, with his/her coat on.

analog [ana'loːk], adj. analogous (zu + dat, to). ◆**A∼ie** [-lo'giː], f -/-n analogy.

Analphabet [analfa'beːt], m -en/-en illiterate.

Analy|se [ana'lyːzə], f -/-n analysis. ◆**a∼'sieren**, v.tr. to analyse.

Ananas ['ananas], f -/- & -se pineapple.
Anarch|ie [anar'çi:], f -/-n anarchy.
◆**A~ist(in)** [-'çist(in)], m -en/-en (f -/-nen) anarchist. ◆**a~istisch**, adj. anarchic.
Anatom|ie [anato'mi:], f -/-n anatomy.
◆**a~isch** [-'to:miʃ], adj. anatomical.
'anbahnen v.tr.sep. to pave the way for (negotiations etc.); (Sache) sich a., to be in the offing.
'Anbau, m 1. no pl Agr: cultivation (of wheat etc.). 2. (Bau) extension, annexe.
◆**'a~en,** v.tr.sep. (a) to grow (plants); (b) to build on (further rooms etc.).
an'bei, adv. herewith.
'anbeißen, v.tr.sep. 4 1. v.tr. to take a bite out of (an apple etc.); F: **zum A. aussehen,** to look adorable. 2. v.i. (haben) take the bait.
'anbelangen, v.tr. impers. sep. **was ihn anbelangt,** as far as he is concerned.
'anbeten, v.tr.sep. to worship.
'Anbetracht, f in A. + gen, in consideration of.
'anbetreffen, v.tr.impers.irr.104. **was mich anbetrifft,** as far as I am concerned.
'anbiedern, v.tr.sep. Pej: **sich bei j-m a.,** to curry favour with s.o.
'anbieten, v.tr.sep.irr.8 to offer (sth.) (j-m, to s.o.); **sich a.,** to offer one's services.
'anbinden, v.tr.sep.irr.9 to tie up (a boat, an animal etc.) (an + acc, to).
'Anblick, m sight. ◆**'a~en,** v.tr.sep. to look at (s.o., sth.).
'anbrechen, v.sep.irr.14 1. v.tr. to break into (provisions, stocks etc.); to start (a loaf), open (a bottle). 2. v.i. (sein) (Tag) to dawn; (Nacht) to fall.
'anbrennen, v.i.sep.irr.15 (sein) (a) to catch fire; (b) (Essen) to burn.
'anbringen, v.tr.sep. (a) (befestigen) to fix, fit (sth.); to put up (curtains, a sign etc.); (b) (vorbringen) to put forward (a request, a suggestion); (c) F: (herbeibringen) to turn up with (sth.).
Anbruch, m Lit: dawn (of a day, era).
Andacht ['andaxt], f -/-en 1. devotion. 2. (Gottesdienst) (short) service. ◆**'andächtig,** adj. devout.
'andauern, v.i.sep. (haben) to last. ◆**'a~d,** adj. persistent, continuous (rain etc.); constant (questions).
Anden ['andən]. Pr.n.pl **die A.,** the Andes.
Andenken ['andɛŋkən], n -s/- (Erinnerung) memory; (Sache) souvenir.
and(e)re(r,s) ['andərə(r,s)], adj. & pron. 1. other; **unter a~m,** among other things; **am a~n Tag/Morgen,** (on) the next day/morning. 2. (verschieden) other, different; **jemand/niemand a~r,** somebody/nobody else; **das ist etwas ganz a~s,** that's a different matter; **kein a~r als X,** nobody but X. ◆**'a~nfalls,** adv. otherwise.

◆**'a~rseits,** adv. on the other hand.
andermal ['andərma:l], adv. **ein a.,** another/some other time.
änder|n ['endərn], v.tr. (a) to change (one's attitude, direction etc.); to alter (plans, a dress, Nau: course etc.); **ich kann es nicht ä.,** I cannot help it; **sich ä.,** to change. ◆**A~ung,** f -/-en change.
anders ['andərs], adv. (a) differently, in different ways (als, from); (b) (sonst) jemand/niemand a., somebody/nobody else; **wer a. als er?** who (else) but he? ◆**'a~artig,** adj. different. ◆**'a~wo,** adv. elsewhere.
anderthalb ['andərt'halp], inv. adj. one and a half.
anderweitig ['andərvaitiç], adj. a. beschäftigt, otherwise engaged.
andeut|en, v.tr.sep. to indicate (sth.); to outline (a plan). ◆**A~ung,** f -/-en (a) indication; (b) implication.
'Andrang, m -(e)s/no pl rush (nach Karten usw., for tickets etc.); (Gedränge) crush.
androhen, v.tr.sep. **j-m etwas a.,** to threaten s.o. with sth.
aneign|en, v.tr.sep. (a) **sich dat etwas a.,** to appropriate sth.; (b) (lernen) **sich dat Kenntnisse usw. a.,** to acquire knowledge etc.
aneinander [anai'nandər]. I. pron. & adv. by/to one another; a. vorbei, past one another; a. denken, to think of one another. II. a~, comb.fm. (to join, tie etc.) to one another; (to grow, bind etc.) together. ◆**a~geraten,** v.i.sep.irr.13 (sein) (Parteien, Streitkräfte usw.) to clash (with one another).
anekeln, v.tr.sep. to sicken (s.o.).
anerkannt, adj. acknowledged, recognized (expert, authority etc.); established (right, author etc.).
anerkenn|en, v.tr.sep.&insep.irr.51 (a) (bestätigen) to recognize (s.o., a state, s.o.'s merits etc.) (als, as); to acknowledge (s.o.'s right, authority etc.), accept (s.o.'s right, authority etc.); Com: to accept (a bill etc.); (b) (würdigen) to respect (rules, other people etc.); appreciate (s.o.'s efforts etc.). ◆**'a~end,** adj. approving. ◆**'a~ennswert,** adj. ◆**'A~ung,** f -/-en recognition, acknowledgment; acceptance; (Würdigung) appreciation.
anfachen, v.tr.sep. Lit: to fan (flames etc.), stir up (passions etc.).
anfahr|en, v.sep.irr.26 1. v.tr. (a) (liefern) to deliver (coal etc.); (b) Aut: to run into (s.o., sth.); (c) F: (Pers.) to go for (s.o.). 2. v.i. (sein) (Auto usw.) to start (off).
Anfall, m attack. ◆**'a~en,** v.sep.irr.27 1. v.tr. to attack (s.o.). 2. v.i. (sein) (Kosten) to accrue; (Arbeit) accumulate.
anfällig ['anfɛliç], adj. prone, Fig: vulnerable (für etwas acc, to sth.).
'Anfang, m -(e)s/-̈e (a) (Beginn) beginning, start; **von A. an,** from the

beginning/the start; (b) pl (*Ursprünge*) the origins. ◆'**a~en**, *v.tr.&i.sep.irr.28* (*haben*) to begin, start; **was soll ich damit a.?** what am I to do with it?

Anfänger|er(in) ['anfeŋər(in)], *m -s/- (f -/ -nen)* beginner, learner. ◆'**a~lich**, *adj.* initial (hesitation etc.); early (symptoms etc.).

'**anfangs**, *adv.* at first, to start with. ◆'**A~buchstabe**, *m* initial (letter). ◆'**A~stadium**, *n* initial stage.

'**anfassen**, *v.sep.* **1.** *v.tr.* (a) (*berühren*) to touch (s.o., sth.); (b) *Fig:* to handle, tackle (a problem etc.); **etwas richtig a.**, to set about sth. the right way. **2.** *v.i.* (*haben*) **mit a.**, to lend a hand (**bei** + *dat*, with).

'**anfechten**, *v.tr.sep.29* to contest (an opinion, a statement etc.); to challenge (s.o.'s right etc.).

'**anfertigen**, *v.tr.sep.* (a) to produce, make (sth.); *Ind:* to manufacture (goods etc.); (b) to draft (a document etc.).

'**anfeuern**, *v.tr.sep.* to spur (s.o.) on.

'**anfliegen**, *v.sep.irr.17* **1.** *v.tr. Av:* (a) (*Flugzeug*) to approach (an airport etc.); (b) (*Fluglinie*) to serve (an airport, a city). **2.** *v.i.* (*sein*) (*Vogel*) to come flying up.

'**Anflug**, *m* **1.** *Av:* approach. **2.** *Fig:* (*Spur*) touch.

'**anfordern**, *v.tr.sep.* (a) to demand (sth.); (b) (*bestellen*) to order (an article). ◆'**A~ung**, *f* (a) demand; (b) *Com:* order (**von** + *dat*, for).

'**Anfrage**, *f* inquiry. ◆'**a~n**, *v.i.sep.* (*haben*) to enquire (**wegen** + *gen*, about).

'**anfreunden**, *v.refl.sep.* **sich a.**, to make friends.

'**anfühlen**, *v.tr.sep.* to feel (sth.); **sich hart/weich a.**, to feel hard/soft.

'**anführen**, *v.tr.sep.* (a) (*leiten*) to lead; (b) (*zitieren*) to quote (an author, passage); to state (one's reasons etc.); (c) *Fig:* to trick, fool (s.o.). ◆'**A~er**, *m* leader, *esp.* ringleader (of a revolt etc.). ◆'**A~ungszeichen**, *npl* quotation marks, inverted commas.

'**Angabe**, *f* **1.** (a) information; *Tchn:* data; (**nähere**) **A~n**, details, particulars; (b) (*Erklärung*) statement, declaration. **2.** (*Tennis*) service.

'**angeb|en**, *v.tr.sep.35* **1.** *v.tr.* (a) to give, state (one's name, reasons etc.); (*verzollen*) to declare (goods); (b) (*bestimmen*) to set (the pace etc.). **2.** *v.i.* (*haben*) *a* (*Tennis*) to serve; (b) *F:* to show off. ◆'**A~er**, *m -s/- F:* show-off. ◆'**A~erei**, *f -/-en F:* showing off. ◆'**a~lich**, *adj.* alleged (reason, thief etc.); ostensible (purpose etc.).

'**angeboren**, *adj.* innate, inborn (qualities etc.).

'**Angebot**, *n* (a) offer; *Com:* quotation; (b) (*Auswahl*) range; (*lieferbare Ware*) stock, supply; **A. und Nachfrage**, supply and demand.

'**angebracht**, *adj.* appropriate; apt (remark).

'**angebunden**, *adj.* **kurz a.**, curt, offhand.

'**angeheitert**, *adj. F:* tipsy.

'**angehen**, *v.sep.irr.36* **1.** *v.i.* (*sein*) (*Pflanze*) to take (root); (*Licht usw.*) to go on; (*Maschine, Motor usw.*) to start (up); (*Feuer*) to catch. **2.** *v.tr.* (a) (*angreifen*) to attack (s.o.); *Fig:* to tackle (a problem etc.); (b) **j-n um Geld, Hilfe usw. a.**, to turn to s.o. for money, help etc.; (c) (*betreffen*) to concern, affect (s.o.). ◆**a~d**, *adj.* future (teacher, pilot etc.); budding (artist etc.).

'**angehör|en**, *v.i.sep.* (*haben*) to belong (*dat*, to). ◆'**A~ige(r)**, *m & f* decl. as *adj.* member.

'**Angeklagte(r)**, *m & f* decl. as *adj. Jur:* accused; (*im Zivilrecht*) defendant.

'**angemessen**, *adj.* appropriate, suitable (moment etc.); (+ *dat*, for); apt (remark); **a~er Preis**, reasonable price.

'**angenehm**, *adj.* pleasant; **a.1** pleased to meet you!

'**angenommen**, *see* annehmen.

'**angeregt**, *adj.* lively, spirited.

'**angesehen**, *p.p. as adj.* respected (person); reputable (firm).

'**Angesicht**, *n* face. ◆'**a~s**, *prep.* + *gen*, in view of.

'**angespannt**, *adj.* intense (concentration etc.); tense (nerves, situation).

'**angestammt**, *adj.* hereditary.

'**Angestellte(r)**, *m & f* decl. as *adj.* (salaried) employee; (bank etc.) clerk; (shop) assistant.

'**angetan**, *adj.* **von j-m, etwas** *dat* **a. sein**, to be keen on s.o., sth.

'**angetrunken**, *adj.* tipsy.

'**angewiesen**, *adj.* **auf j-n, etwas** *acc* **a. sein**, to be dependent on s.o., sth.

'**angewöhnen**, *v.tr.sep.* **j-m etwas a.**, to get s.o. used to sth.; **sich** *dat* **etwas a.**, to get into the habit of (doing) sth. ◆'**A~wohnheit**, *f -/-en* habit.

'**angleichen**, *v.tr.sep.irr.40* to adjust, adapt (sth.).

'**angreif|en**, *v.tr.sep.irr.43* (a) (*überfallen*) to attack; (b) (*anbrechen*) to draw on (reserves etc.); (c) (*schädigen*) (*Krankheit usw.*) to affect (s.o.); (*Säure usw.*) to corrode (metal etc.). ◆'**A~er**, *m -s/-* attacker; (*Staat*) aggressor.

'**Angriff**, *m* **1.** attack; *Jur:* assault. **2.** **etwas in A. nehmen**, to set about (doing) sth. ◆'**A~s-**, *comb.fm.* offensive (weapon etc.); aggressive (spirit etc.).

Angst [aŋst], *f -/-e* (a) fear; (*Sorge*) anxiety; **A. (vor j-m, etwas) haben**, to be afraid/frightened (of s.o., sth.); **A. um**

j-n, etwas haben, to be anxious/worried about s.o., sth.; (b) mir ist/wird a. (und bange), I am scared stiff; j-m a. machen, to scare/frighten s.o. ◆'A~hase, m F: scaredy cat.

'ängst|igen ['ɛŋstigən] v.tr. to frighten, scare (s.o.); sich ä., to be frightened (vor + dat, of); (Sorgen haben) to be anxious (um + acc, about). ◆'ä~lich, adj. nervous, (scheu) timid (person, disposition etc.); frightened, scared (look etc.). ◆'ä~lichkeit, f -/no pl nervousness; anxiety.

'angucken, v.tr.sep. F: to look at (s.o., sth.).

'anhaben, v.tr.sep.irr.44 (a) to have (sth.) on; (b) F: das Licht a., to have the light on; (c) j-m etwas/nichts a. können, to be able/unable to harm s.o., sth.

'anhalt|en, v.sep.irr.45 1. v.tr. (a) (zum Stehen bringen) to stop (s.o., sth.); to bring (traffic, a train etc.) to a standstill; (b) (ermahnen) j-n zur Arbeit usw. a., to urge s.o. to work etc. 2. v.i. (haben) (a) (Fahrzeug usw.) to stop; (b) (andauern) (Wetter) to continue; (Zustand usw.) to persist. ◆'a~end, adj. lasting (effect); persistent (rain); sustained (interest). ◆'A~er, m -s/- F: hitch-hiker; per A. fahren, to hitch-hike. ◆'A~spunkt, m clue; pl evidence.

an'hand, prep. a. von Beispielen, with the help of examples.

'Anhang, m 1. (in einem Buch usw.) appendix. 2. coll. F: (Gefolge) hangers-on; (Angehörige) relatives; family.

'anhäng|en, v.tr.sep. (a) to hang (sth.) on; (befestigen) to fix, fasten (a label, tag etc.) (an + acc, to); (b) (ankuppeln) to hitch up (a coach, trailer etc.); (c) (hinzufügen) to add on (a paragraph etc.). ◆'A~er, m -s/- 1. trailer. 2. (Schmuck) pendant. 3. (Etikett) tag. 4. (Pers.: adherent (of a belief etc.); supporter (of a party, Sp: club etc.). ◆'A~erschaft, f -/no pl followers, adherents. ◆'a~lich, adj. affectionate; devoted (friend etc.). ◆'A~lichkeit, f -/-en affection. ◆'A~sel, n -s/- appendage.

'anhäuf|en, v.tr.sep. to accumulate (money etc.); (Arbeit usw.) sich a., to pile up. ◆'A~ung, f -/-en accumulation; pile (of work).

'anheben, v.tr.sep.irr.48 to lift, raise (sth.); to jack up (a car).

'anheimelnd ['anhaiməlnt], adj. homely.

'Anhieb, m F: etwas auf A. tun, to do sth. first go.

'Anhöhe, f rise; hillock.

'anhör|en, v.tr.sep. (a) (zuhören) to listen to (s.o., sth.); (b) das hört sich gut an, that sounds good; (c) man hört (es) ihm an, daß ..., one can tell from the way he speaks that ...

animieren [ani'mi:rən], v.tr. (anregen) j-n zum Trinken usw. a., to persuade s.o. to have a drink etc.

Anis [a'ni:s], m -es/-e aniseed.

'Ankauf, m purchase. ◆'a~en, v.tr.sep. to purchase (sth.).

Anker ['aŋkər], m -s/- anchor; vor A. gehen, to drop anchor. ◆'a~n, v.i. (haben) to anchor. ◆'A~platz, m anchorage.

'anketten, v.tr.sep. to chain.

'Anklage, f (a) accusation; Jur: charge; (b) Jur: (auch A~vertretung f) prosecution. ◆'A~bank, dock. ◆'a~n, v.tr.sep. j-n wegen etwas gen a., to accuse s.o. of sth.; Jur: charge s.o. with sth. ◆'Ankläger, m Jur: plaintiff.

'Anklang, m 1. (Ähnlichkeit) echo. 2. (bei j-m) A. finden, to meet with (s.o.'s) approval.

'ankleide|n, v.tr.sep. to dress (s.o.); sich a., to dress (oneself). ◆'A~raum, m dressing room, changing room.

'anklopfen, v.i.sep. (haben) bei j-m a., to knock at s.o.'s door.

'anknüpfen, v.sep. 1. v.tr. (a) etwas an etwas acc a., to tie sth. to sth.; (b) to start (a conversation etc.). 2. v.i. (haben) to carry on (where one left off).

'ankommen, v.i.sep.irr.53 (sein) (a) (eintreffen) to arrive. (b) (Erfolg haben) bei j-m (gut) a., to be a success with s.o., (Witz usw.) go down well with s.o.; gegen j-n, etwas acc nicht a. können, to be no match for s.o., sth.; (c) auf j-n, etwas a., to depend on s.o., sth.; F: ich lasse es drauf a.! I'll chance it!

'ankreuzen, v.tr.sep. to mark (sth.) with a cross.

'ankündig|en, v.tr.sep. to announce (sth.); to publicize (an event); Fig: to herald (a new era etc.). ◆'A~ung, f -/-en announcement.

'Ankunft ['ankunft], f -/=e arrival.

'Anlage, f 1. (a) (installation of apparatus etc.; (Bau) construction; (b) Fin: investment. 2. (Anordnung) layout; Tchn: system. 3. pl (a) öffentliche A~n, public gardens; (b) Sp: etc: facilities; Ind: plant; sanitäre A~n, lavatories and washrooms. 4. (Beilage) enclosure. 5. (Veranlagung) tendency (zu Allergien usw., to allergies etc.).

'Anlaß ['anlas], m -sses/=sse (a) (Grund) reason (zu + dat, for); (b) (Gelegenheit) occasion.

'anlass|en, v.tr.sep.irr.57 (a) to start (up) (an engine, machine); (b) F: to leave (the light, radio etc.) on. ◆'A~er, m -s/- starter.

anläßlich ['anleslic], prep. + gen on the occasion of.

'Anlauf, m 1. Sp: run-up; Fig: im/beim ersten A., at the first attempt. ◆'a~en, v.sep.irr.58 1. v.i. (sein) (a) to run up; (b) (Maschine, Motor usw.) to start (up); (Fahndung usw.) to get under way; (Film) to open; (c) (Scheibe, Brille usw.) to mist up; (Metall) to tarnish; (Pers.) vor Kälte blau a., to go blue with cold. 2. *v.tr.* **einen Hafen a.**, to call at a port.

anlege|n, *v.sep.* 1. *v.tr.* (*a*) **etwas an etwas** *acc* **a.**, to put/lay sth. on sth.; (*Pferd usw.*) **die Ohren a.**, to lay back its ears; (*b*) (*anziehen*) to put on; (*c*) (*zielen*) **auf j-n a.**, to aim at s.o.; (*d*) *Fin:* **Geld a.**, to invest/(*ausgeben*) spend money; (*e*) (*einrichten*) to lay out (a garden etc.); to design, plan (a bridge, road etc.); to draw up (a list, statistics etc.); to install (cables, pipes etc.). 2. *v.i.* (*haben*) to moor. ◆'**A~platz**, *m* ◆'**A~stelle**,*f* mooring.

anlehnen, *v.tr.sep.* (*a*) to lean (sth.) (**an etwas** *acc*, against sth.); (*Pers.*) **sich an j-n, etwas a.**, to lean on s.o., sth.; (*b*) **die Tür/das Fenster a.**, to leave the door/window ajar.

'Anleihe,*f* -/-n loan.

anleit|en, *v.tr.sep.* **j-n zu etwas** *dat* **a.**, to train s.o. in sth. ◆'**A~ung**,*f* instruction.

anlernen, *v.tr.sep.* to train.

anlieg|en. **I.** *v.i.sep.irr.62* (*haben*) (*a*) (eng) a., to fit closely; (*b*) (*Arbeit usw.*) to be pending. **II. A.**, *n* -s/- (*a*) request; **ein A. an j-n haben**, to have a favour to ask of s.o.; (*b*) (*Sorge*) concern. ◆'**a~end**, *adj.* (*a*) adjoining (property etc.); (*b*) (eng) a., close-fitting. ◆'**A~er**, *m* -s/- **A. frei**, access for residents (only).

'anmachen, *v.tr.sep.* (*a*) *Cu:* to dress (the salad); (*b*) *F:* to switch/turn on (the light, radio etc.).

anmaß|en, *v.tr.sep.* **sich** *dat* **ein Recht usw. a.**, to usurp a right etc. ◆'**a~end**, *adj.* presumptuous; (*hochmütig*) arrogant.

Anmeld|e- ['anmɛldə-], *comb.fm.* registration (form, fee etc.). ◆'**a~en**, *v.tr.sep.* (*a*) to register (a car, birth, death, business etc.); (*b*) **sich a.**, to register (*polizeilich*, with the police); (*beim Arzt*) to make an appointment (with the doctor); (*c*) (*ankündigen*) to announce (s.o.). ◆'**A~ung**,*f* (*a*) registration; announcement; (*b*) (*Büro*) registration office; (*im Hotel*) reception.

anmerk|en, *v.tr.sep.* **j-m etwas a.**, to notice sth. in s.o.; **laß dir nichts a.!** don't give yourself away! ◆'**A~ung**,*f* -/-en note.

Anmut,*f* -/no *pl* grace. ◆'**a~en**, *v.tr.sep.* **es mutet mich seltsam an**, it strikes me as odd. ◆'**a~ig**, *adj.* graceful; charming (manner etc.).

'annähen, *v.tr.sep.* to sew on (sth.).

annäher|n, *v.tr.sep.* **sich** (**etwas** *dat*) **a.**, to come closer to (sth.). ◆'**a~nd**, *adj.* approximate; *adv.* **nicht a.**, not nearly. ◆'**A~ungsversuch**, *m F:* **bei j-m A~ungsversuche machen**, to make advances/overtures to s.o.

Annahme ['annɑːmə],*f* -/-n 1. (*Annehmen*) acceptance. 2. (*Aneignung*) adoption (of a name etc.). 3. (*Vermutung*) assump-

tion.

annehm|bar ['anneːmbɑːr], *adj.* acceptable. ◆'**a~en**, *v.tr.sep.irr.69* (*a*) to accept (a gift, an invitation, a bill etc.); to take on (a job); to adopt (a resolution, name, attitude etc.); (*b*) (*vermuten*) to assume, presume (sth.); **angenommen, daß ...**, suppose/supposing that ...; (*c*) (*kümmern*) **sich j-s/etwas** *gen* **a.**, to take care of s.o./sth. ◆'**A~lichkeiten**, *fpl* amenities.

Annonc|e [a'nõːsə],*f* -/-n advertisement. ◆**a~ieren** [-'siːrən], *v.tr.&i.* (*haben*) to advertise.

annullier|en [anu'liːrən], *v.tr.* to annul (a marriage), cancel (a contract etc.).

anonym [ano'nyːm], *adj.* anonymous.

Anorak ['anorak], *m* -s/-s anorak.

anordn|en, *v.tr.sep.* (*a*) to arrange (objects); (*b*) (*befehlen*) to order. ◆'**A~ung**,*f* -/-en (*a*) arrangement; (*b*) order; (*Vorschrift*) regulation.

'anorganisch, *adj.* inorganic.

anormal ['anɔrmɑːl], *adj.* abnormal.

anpacken, *v.tr.sep.* (*a*) to seize (s.o., sth.); **ein Problem a.**, to tackle a problem.

anpass|en, *v.tr.sep.* to adapt (sth.). ◆'**A~ung**,*f* -/-en adaptation, (**an** *+ acc*, to). ◆'**a~ungsfähig**, *adj.* adaptable.

Anpfiff, *m Sp:* kick-off.

'anpflanzen, *v.tr.sep.* to plant.

'anpöbeln, *v.tr.sep. F:* to shout abuse at (s.o.).

'anprangern, *v.tr.sep.* to pillory (s.o.).

'anpreisen, *v.tr.sep.irr.70* to extol.

Anprob|e,*f* -/-n fitting. ◆**a~ieren**, *v.tr.sep.* to try on.

anrechn|en, *v.tr.sep.* (*a*) (*berechnen*) **j-m etwas a.**, to charge s.o. for sth.; (*b*) **j-m etwas als Fehler a.**, to consider sth. as a mistake on s.o.'s part; *Fig:* **wir rechnen ihm seine Hilfe hoch an**, we greatly appreciate his help.

'Anrecht, *n* right.

'Anrede,*f* address; opening (of a letter). ◆'**a~n**, *v.tr.sep.* to address (s.o.).

anreg|en, *v.tr.sep.* (*a*) (*vorschlagen*) to suggest (sth.); (*b*) (*beleben*) to stimulate (s.o., the circulation etc.). ◆'**a~end**, *adj.* stimulating. ◆'**A~ung**,*f* (*a*) encouragement; (*b*) (*Vorschlag*) suggestion.

'anreichern, *v.tr.sep.* to enrich.

Anreise,*f* (*a*) journey (there); (*b*) (*Ankunft*) arrival. ◆'**a~n**, *v.i.sep.* (*sein*) (*a*) to travel (there); (*b*) to arrive.

'Anreiz, *m* incentive, inducement.

Anrichte,*f* -/-n sideboard. ◆'**a~n**, *v.tr.sep.* (*a*) to prepare (a meal, dish); to dress (a salad); (*b*) to cause (confusion, disaster etc.).

'anrüchig, *adj.* disreputable (person etc.); sleazy (night spot etc.).

Anruf, *m* -(e)s/-e call. ◆'**A~beantworter**, *m* answering machine. ◆'**a~en**, *v.tr.sep.irr.74* (*a*) to call to (s.o.); (*b*) **j-n um Hilfe a.**, to appeal to s.o. for help; (c) *Tel:* to ring (s.o.) up, *N.Am:* call (s.o.). ◆'A~er, *m* -s/- caller.

'anrühren, *v.tr.sep.* (a) to mix (a sauce, mortar etc.); (b) (*berühren*) to touch.

ans [ans], *prep.* = an das.

'Ansage, *f* -/-n announcement. ◆'a~n, *v.tr.sep.* to announce; (b) er hat sich zum Mittagessen angesagt, he has told us he is coming to lunch. ◆'A~r(in), *m* -s/- (f -/-nen) announcer.

'ansammeln, *v.tr.sep.* to collect (objects etc.); to accumulate (goods, wealth); sich a., (*Staub usw.*) to collect; (*Menschen*) to gather; (*Vermögen usw.*) to accumulate.

ansässig ['anzɛsɪç], *adj.* resident.

'Ansatz, *m* first sign (of buds etc.); beginning; base (of the neck etc.); A. des Haars, hairline. ◆'A~punkt, *m* starting point.

'anschaffen, *v.tr.sep.* sich *dat* etwas a., to acquire sth. ◆'A~ung, *f* acquisition; (*Kauf*) purchase. ◆'A~ungskosten, *pl* prime cost.

'anschalten, *v.tr.sep.* to turn on.

'anschauen, *v.tr.sep.* to look at. ◆'a~lich, *adj.* clear (picture); vivid (description). ◆'A~ung, *f* -/-en opinion, view (über etwas *acc*, on sth.). ◆'A~ungsmaterial, *n* illustrative material; *Sch:* visual aids.

'Anschein, *m* appearance, look; (*täuschend*) semblance; allem A. nach, to all appearances. ◆'a~end, *adv.* apparently.

'Anschlag, *m* 1. (*Bekanntmachung*) (public) notice. 2. (*Überfall*) attack. 3. touch (of a pianist, piano etc.); 240 A~e in der Minute schreiben, to hit 240 keys per minute. 4. das Gewehr im A. halten, to hold the rifle in the aiming position. ◆'a~en, *v.sep.irr.85* 1. *v.tr.* (a) to put up (a notice, poster etc.); (b) to strike, hit (a note, a key etc.); (c) (*beschädigen*) to chip (a plate, glass etc.). 2. *v.i.* (*haben*) (a) to knock (an etwas *acc*, on/against sth.); (b) (*Hund*) to start barking. ◆'A~zettel, *m* bill.

'anschließen, *v.tr.sep.irr.31* (a) to join, attach (sth.); to connect (up) (an appliance); (b) to affiliate (a group); sich j-m a., to join up with s.o.; sich j-s Meinung a., to endorse s.o.'s ideas; (c) (*folgen*) sich an etwas *acc* a., to follow (immediately) after sth. ◆'a~d, *adv.* (immediately) afterwards.

'Anschluß, *m* 1. (*Verbindung*) connection. 2. (*Kontakt*) contact; sie sucht A., she wants to make friends. 3. im A. an + *acc*, following.

'anschmieren, *v.tr.sep. F:* to diddle, con (s.o.).

'anschnallen, *v.tr.sep.* to fasten the strap(s) of (a rucksack etc.); to put on (skates, skis); sich a., to put on one's seat belt.

'anschneiden, *v.tr.sep.irr.59* (a) to cut

into (a loaf); (b) ein Thema a., to broach a subject.

'anschreiben, *v.tr.sep.irr.12* (a) to write (sth.); (b) etwas a. lassen, to buy sth. on credit; *Fig:* bei j-m gut angeschrieben sein, to be in s.o.'s good books; (c) to write to (s.o., an authority etc.).

'anschreien, *v.tr.sep.irr.88* to shout at (s.o.).

'Anschrift, *f* address.

'Anschuldigung, *f* -/-en accusation; allegation.

'anschwellen, *v.i.sep.irr.71* (*sein*) to swell; (*Fluß*) to rise; (*Lärm usw.*) to grow louder.

'anschwemmen, *v.tr.sep.* to wash (sth.) ashore.

'ansehen. I. *v.tr.sep.irr.92.* (a) to look at (s.o., sth.); to watch (a programme); etwas mit a., to stand by and watch sth.; j-m etwas a., to see sth. from s.o.'s appearance; (b) ich sehe es als meine Pflicht an, zu ..., I regard it as my duty to ... II. A, *n* -s/*no pl* (a) respect. (b) ohne A. der Person, regardless of status. ◆'a~nlich, *adj.* considerable. ◆'a~nlich, *adj.* considerable.

'ansetzen, *v.sep.* 1. *v.tr.* (a) to place (a tool etc.) in position; to put (a glass) to one's lips; (b) (*festlegen*) to arrange (a meeting etc.); (c) to allow (an amount, a period); (d) (*Eisen*) Rost a., to get rusty, to rust; *F:* Fett a., to put on weight. 2. *v.i.* (*haben*) to start.

'Ansicht, *f* -/-en 1. (a) (*Meinung*) opinion; meiner A. nach, in my opinion; (b) (*Blick*) view; eine A. der Stadt Köln, a view of Cologne. 2. *Com:* zur A., on approval. ◆'A~skarte, *f* picture postcard. ◆'A~ssache, *f* matter of opinion.

an'sonsten, *adv.* otherwise.

'anspannen, *v.tr.sep.* (a) to harness (a horse) (an + *acc*, to); (b) to tighten (a rope); to tense (the muscles), strain (one's nerves).

'anspielen, *v.i.sep.* (a) *v.i.* (*haben*) (a) to start playing; (b) (*hinweisen*) auf j-n, etwas a., to allude to s.o., sth.; (*versteckt*) to hint at sth. ◆'A~ung, *f* -/-en allusion (auf + *acc*, to); (*versteckte*) A., hidden reference.

'Ansporn, *m* incentive (zu etwas *dat*, to do sth.) ◆'a~en, *v.tr.sep.* to spur (on) (one's horse); *Fig:* to spur, urge (s.o.) on.

'Ansprache, *f* speech, address.

ansprech|bar ['anʃprɛçbɑːr], *adj.* (*Pers.*) approachable. ◆'a~en, *v.sep.irr.14* 1. *v.tr.* to speak to (s.o.) (auf etwas *acc*, about sth.); to address (s.o., a crowd etc.). 2. *v.i.* (*haben*) (a) (*reagieren*) to respond; (b) (*gefallen*) to appeal. ◆'a~end, *adj.* appealing.

'anspringen, *v.i.sep.irr.19* (*sein*) (*Motor*) to start.

'Anspruch, *m* claim; (hohe) A~e stellen, to make (heavy) demands; j-n, etwas in

A. nehmen, to make demands upon s.o., sth. ◆'a~slos, adj. (bescheiden) modest; unassuming (person). ◆'a~svoll, adj. demanding.

anstacheln, v.tr.sep. to egg (s.o.) on.

Anstalt ['anʃtalt], f -/-en 1. institution. 2. pl A~en machen, etwas zu tun, to prepare to do sth.

'Anstand, m decency. ◆'a~slos, adv. unhesitatingly.

'anständig, adj. 1. proper (conduct etc.); respectable (person, dress etc.). 2. F: (ziemlich gutgroß) decent (meal, portion, hotel etc.); (richtig) real, proper.

anstarren, v.tr.sep. to stare at (s.o., sth.).

an'statt, conj. & prep. + gen instead of.

'anstecken, v.tr.sep.ir.14 to puncture (sth.); ein Faß a., to tap a barrel.

'ansteck|en, v.tr.sep. (a) (mit Nadel) to pin (sth.) on; (b) (anzünden) to set fire to (sth.); to light (a fire, cigarette etc.); (c) Med: to infect (s.o.). ◆'a~end, adj. infectious.

anstehen, v.i.sep.irr.100 (haben) to stand in a queue/N.Am: line, queue (up).

'ansteigen, v.i.sep.irr.89 to rise.

an'stelle, prep. + gen instead of.

'anstell|en, v.tr.sep. (a) (Pers.) sich a., to stand in a queue/N.Am: line; to queue (up); (einstellen) to take (s.o.) on; (c) (in Gang setzen) to start (machinery); ich weiß nicht, wie ich es a. soll, I've no idea how to set about it; (d) F: sich geschickt/dumm a., to show skill/act stupidly. ◆'A~ung, f -/-en employment.

Anstieg ['anʃtiːk], m -(e)s/-e (a) ascent, climb; (b) rise (der Preise usw., in prices etc.).

'anstift|en, v.tr.sep. to cause (confusion etc.); to instigate (a crime, revolt etc.); j-n zu etwas dat a., to incite s.o. to (doing) sth. ◆'A~er, m instigator.

'anstimmen, v.tr.sep. to strike up (a song); ein Gelächter a., to start laughing.

Anstoß, m 1. (Anlaß) impetus; A. zu etwas geben, to initiate sth. 2. (Ärgernis) offence. 3. Sp: kick-off. ◆'a~en, v.sep.irr.103 1. v.tr. (a) to give (s.o., sth.) a push/knock; (mit dem Ellbogen) to nudge s.o.; (b) abs. Sp: to kick off. 2. v.i. (a) (sein) an etwas acc a., to knock against sth.; (b) (haben) (mit den Gläsern) a., to clink glasses (with s.o.); (c) (haben) (ungrenzen) an etwas acc a., to be adjacent to sth.

anstößig ['anʃtøːsiç], adj. offensive.

'anstreich|en, v.tr.sep.irr.40 to paint (sth.); (b) to mark (a passage, mistake etc.). ◆'A~er, m (house) painter.

anstrengen ['anʃtrɛŋən], v.tr.sep. (a) to strain (one's eyes, voice); (b) sich a., to make an effort (to do sth.); (körperlich) to exert oneself. ◆'a~end, adj. strenuous. ◆'A~ung, f -/-en effort, exertion; strain (for the eyes etc.).

Ansturm ['anʃturm], m Mil: assault; (Andrang) rush.

Antark|is [ant'?arktis]. Pr.n.f -. die A., the Antarctic. ◆a~isch, adj. antarctic.

'antasten, v.tr.sep. to touch (an object, money etc.), Fig: touch on (a subject).

'Anteil, m 1. share, portion; (im Gemisch) proportion. 2. no pl A. an etwas dat nehmen, to take an interest in sth.; (besorgt) be concerned about sth. ◆'a~mäßig, adj. proportional. ◆'A~nahme, f -/no pl sympathy.

Antenne [an'tɛnə], f -/-n 1. aerial. 2. pl Z: antennae; F: feelers (of insect).

Anti-, anti- ['anti-], prefix anti-. ◆'A~alko'holiker(in), m, f teetotaller. ◆'a~autori'tär, adj. permissive. ◆'A~'babypille, f F: the pill. ◆A~biotikum [-bi'oːtikum], n -s/-ka antibiotic. ◆A~pathie [-pa'tiː], f -/-n antipathy ◆(gegen + acc, to).

antik [an'tiːk], adj. (a) classical (art, literature); ancient (Greece, Rome); (b) antique (furniture etc.). ◆A~e, f -/-n die A., the ancient world.

Antilope [anti'loːpa], f -/-n antelope.

Antiquar|iat [antikvari'oːt], n (e)-s/-e secondhand bookshop. ◆a~isch, adj. secondhand (book, bookshop).

antiquiert [anti'kviːrt], adj. antiquated.

Antiquität [antikvi'tɛːt], f -/-en usu. pl antique. ◆A~en-, comb.fm. antique (dealer, shop etc.).

Antrag ['antraːk], m -(e)s/-e (a) (Vorschlag) proposal; motion; (b) Adm: application; Jur: petition. ◆A~steller, m -s/- applicant.

'antreffen, v.tr.sep.irr.104 to find (s.o.).

'antreiben, v.tr.sep.irr.12 to drive.

'antreten, v.tr.sep.irr.105 1. v.tr. to set out on (a journey); to start (a job); to enter upon (a career); ein Erbe a., to come into an inheritance; sein Amt a., to take up office. 2. v.i. (sein) Mil: to fall in; Sp: gegen X a., to compete against X.

'Antrieb, m 1. drive. 2. Fig: motive; aus eigenem A., of one's own accord. ◆'A~s-, comb.fm. driving (axle, belt, motor etc.).

'antrinken, v.tr.sep.irr.96 F: sich dat Mut a., to take a drop of Dutch courage.

'Antritt, m start (of a journey etc.); taking up (an office). ◆'A~s-, comb.fm. inaugural (lecture, address etc.).

'antun, v.tr.sep.irr.106 j-m etwas a., to do sth. to s.o.; sich dat Zwang a., to restrain oneself.

Antwort ['antvort], f -/-en answer, reply; um A. wird gebeten, RSVP. ◆'a~en, v.i. (haben) to answer, reply.

'anvertrauen, v.tr.sep. (a) j-m etwas a., to entrust s.o. with sth.; (b) sich j-m a., to confide in s.o.

'anwachsen, v.i.sep.irr.107 (sein) (a) to grow; (b) (Pflanze) to take root.

Anwalt ['anvalt], m -(e)s/-e (a) lawyer; (b) Fig: (Verfechter) advocate.

'Anwandlung, f fit; in einer A. von Schwäche, in a weak moment.

'Anwärter(in), m (f -/-nen) candidate, Sp: contender.

'anweis|en, v.tr.sep.irr.70 (a) (zuteilen) to assign; j-m einen Platz a., to show s.o. to a seat; (b) (anleiten) to give (s.o.) instructions; to instruct (s.o.) (to do sth.); (c) (überweisen) to transfer (a sum). ◆'A~ung, f -/-en (a) assignment; (b) instruction; (c) (von Geld) transfer; (Schein) (money) order.

'anwend|en, v.tr.sep.irr.94 to apply (a method, rule, law etc.); (gebrauchen) to use (an object, energy, force etc.). ◆'A~ung, f -/-en application; use.

'anwesen|d ['anve:zənt], adj. present; die A~den, those present. ◆'A~heit, f -/no pl presence. ◆'A~heitsliste, f attendance list.

anwidern ['anvi:dərn], v.tr.sep. to disgust (s.o.).

'Anzahl, f number. ◆'a~en, v.tr.sep. to pay (a sum) as a deposit; to pay a deposit on (a TV etc.). ◆'A~ung, f deposit.

'Anzeichen, n indication, sign.

Anzeige ['antsaigə], f -/-n 1. announcement (of a death etc.); (Inserat) advertisement; A. gegen j-n erstatten, to report s.o. to the authorities. 2. Tchn: reading (on a gauge etc.); Data-pr: display. ◆'a~n, v.tr.sep. (a) (bekanntgeben) to announce (melden) to report (s.o., sth.) to the police. ◆'A~nteil, m advertisements. ◆'A~r, m indicator.

anzetteln, v.tr.sep. to instigate.

'anzieh|en, v.tr.sep.irr.113 (a) die Knie a., to draw up one's knees; (b) to put on (clothes, shoes etc.); sich a., to put on one's clothes; (c) (Magnet & Fig:) to attract (s.o., sth.); (d) (festschrauben) to tighten (a screw etc.). ◆'a~end, adj. attractive. ◆'A~ungskraft, f -/no pl attraction; A. der Erde, (force of) gravity.

'Anzug, m 1. suit. 2. no pl; im A. sein, (Sturm) to be gathering; (Gefahr usw.) to be imminent.

an'züglich ['antsy:kliç], adj. suggestive.

'anzünden, v.tr.sep. to light (a cigarette, fire etc.); to set fire to (sth.).

'anzweifeln, v.tr.sep. to question.

Apfel ['apfəl], m -s/= apple. ◆A~sine [-'zi:nə], f -/-n orange.

Apostel [a'pɔstəl], m -s/- apostle.

Apostroph [apɔ'stro:f], m -s/-e apostrophe.

Apotheke [apo'te:kə], f -/-n (dispensing) chemist's (shop); pharmacy. ◆A~r, m -s/- (dispensing) chemist; pharmacist; N.Am: druggist.

Apparat [apa'ra:t], m -(e)s/-e (a) coll. apparatus; (Gerät) device; (small) machine; (b) Rad: TV: set; Phot: camera; (c) telephone; am A., speaking. ◆A~ur [apara'tu:r], f -/-en equipment.

Appartement [apartə'mɑ̃:], n -s/-s luxury apartment.

Appell [a'pɛl], m -s/-e (a) appeal (b) Mil: roll-call. ◆a~ieren [apɛ'li:rən], v.i.

(haben) to appeal (an j-n, to s.o.).

Appetit [ape'ti:t], m -(e)s/-e appetite; guten A.! enjoy your food! ◆a~lich, adj. appetizing.

applau|dieren [aplau'di:rən], v.i. (haben) to applaud (j-m, s.o.). ◆A~s [a'plaus], m -es/-e applause.

Aprikose [apri'ko:zə], f -/-n apricot.

April [a'prıl], m -(s)/-e April. ◆A~scherz, m April fool joke.

Aquaplaning [akva'pla:nıŋ], n -(s)/no pl aquaplaning.

Aquarell [akva'rɛl], n -s/-e water-colour (painting).

Aquarium [a'kva:rium], n -s/-rien aquarium.

Äquator [ɛ'kva:tor], m -s/no pl equator.

Ära ['ɛ:ra], f -/no pl era.

Arab|er ['arabər], m -s/- Arab. ◆A~erin [a'ra:bərin], f -/-nen Arab woman. ◆A~ien [a'ra:biən], Pr.n.n -s. Arabia. ◆a~isch [a'ra:bɪʃ]. I. adj. Arabian; Arabic (language, numerals etc.). II. A., n -/no pl Arabic.

Arbeit ['arbait], f -/-en (a) work; sich an die A. machen, to set to work; bei der A., at work; (b) (Aufgabe) job. ◆'a~en, v. 1. v.i. (haben) (a) to work (an etwas dat, on sth.); (b) (Maschine usw.) to operate. 2. v.tr. to work (metal, wood etc.); Fig: sich nach oben a., to work one's way up. ◆'A~er(in), m (f) -s/- (f -/-nen) worker; Agr: labourer. ◆'A~er-, comb.fm. labour (movement, shortage etc.); working-class (family etc.). ◆'A~erschaft, f -/no pl (a) workforce (of a firm); (b) coll. workers. ◆'A~geber(in), m -s/- (f -/-nen) employer. ◆'A~nehmer(in), m -s/- (f -/-nen) employee. ◆'A~s-, comb.fm. (a) working (clothes, wage, method, day, week, title etc.); (b) labour (service, costs, camp, market, minister etc.); work (therapy, process etc.); (c) (certificate, contract etc.) of employment; (d) industrial (psychology, law, accident etc.). ◆'A~samt, n employment exchange. ◆'a~sfähig, adj. (Pers.) fit to work. ◆'A~sfläche, f work top. ◆'A~sgang, m operation (of a worker); working cycle (of a machine). ◆'A~sgemeinschaft, f study group. ◆'A~skraft f (a) worker; pl A~skräfte, manpower; (b) s.o.'s capacity for work. ◆'a~slos, adj. unemployed; die A~slosen, the unemployed. ◆'A~slosenunterstützung, f unemployment benefit. ◆'A~slosigkeit, f no pl unemployment. ◆'A~splatz, m (a) place of work; (b) (Stelle) job. ◆'A~steilung, f division of labour. ◆'a~sunfähig, adj. unemployable. ◆'A~szeit, f working hours. ◆'A~szimmer, n study.

Archäologie [arçeolo'gi:] f -/no pl archeology.

Architekt|(in) [arçi'tɛkt(in)], m -en/-en (f

-/-nen) architect. **◆A~ur** [-tɛk'tuːr], *f* /-en architecture.

Archiv [ar'çiːf], *n* -s/-e archive.

arg [ark], *adj.* bad (mistake etc.); *(unangenehm)* nasty (disappointment etc.); a~e **Schmerzen**, terrible pains.

Argentin|ien [argɛn'tiːniən], *Pr.n.n* -s. Argentina. **◆A~ier(in)**, *m* -s/- *(f* /-nen) Argentinian. **◆a~isch**, *adj.* Argentinian (meat etc.); Argentine (Republic).

Ärger ['ɛrgər], *m* -s/*no pl* (a) *(Unmut usw.)* annoyance, (Zorn) anger; (b) *(Scherei)* trouble. **◆'ä~lich**, *adj.* **1.** *(Sache)* annoying. **2.** *(Pers.)* annoyed. **◆'ä~nis**, *n* -ses/-se, *v.tr.* to annoy; **sich über j-n/etwas schwarz ä.**, to be hopping mad about s.o., sth.; **ärgere dich nicht!** don't let it upset you. **◆'A~nis**, *n* -ses/-se *(a)* *usu.pl* annoyance; *(b)* öffentliches **Ä.**, public nuisance.

arglos ['arkloːs], *adj.* unsuspecting; a~e **Bemerkung**, innocent remark.

Argument [argu'mɛnt], *n* -(e)s/-e argument. **◆a~ieren** [-'tiːrən], *v.i.* *(haben)* to argue.

Arg|wohn ['arkvoːn], *m* -(e)s/*no pl* suspicion. **◆a~wöhnisch**, *adj.* mistrustful, suspicious.

Arie ['aːriə], *f* /-n aria.

Aristokrat [aristo'kraːt], *m* -en/-en aristocrat. **◆A~ie** [kra'tiː], *f* / n aristocracy. **◆a~isch** [-'kraːtiʃ], *adj.* aristocratic.

Arkt|is ['arktis], *Pr.n.f* -. **die A.**, the Arctic. **◆'a~isch**, *adj.* arctic.

arm¹ [arm] *adj.*)

Arm² [arm], *m* -(e)s/-e arm; branch (of a river); **j-n auf den A. nehmen**, to pull s.o.'s leg. **◆'A~band**, *n* bracelet; *(Uhra.)* watchstrap. **◆A~banduhr**, *f* wristwatch.

Armatur [arma'tuːr], *f* /-en *usu. pl* fittings. **◆A~enbrett**, *n* *Aut:* dashboard; *Av: etc:* instrument panel.

Armee [ar'meː], *f* /-n army.

Ärmel ['ɛrməl], *m* -s/- sleeve; *F:* **etwas aus dem Ä. schütteln**, to produce sth. out of a hat. **◆'A~kanal**. *Pr.n.* **der Ä.**, the (English) Channel.

ärmlich ['ɛrmliç], *adj.* poor (family, area etc.); shabby (house etc.).

armselig ['armzeːliç], *adj.* *(mittellos)* destitute, impoverished; *(elend)* miserable (person, state, attempt etc.).

Armut ['armuːt], *f* -/*no pl* poverty; poorness (of soil etc.).

Aroma [a'roːma], *n* -s/-men (Geruch) aroma; *(Geschmack)* flavour, taste. **◆a~tisch** [aro'maːtiʃ], *adj.* aromatic.

Arrangement [arãʒə'mãː], *n* -s/-s arrangement. **◆a~ieren** [-'ʒiːrən], *v.tr.* to arrange; **sich a.** to come to an arrangement.

Arrest [a'rɛst], *m* -(e)s/-e detention.

arrogan|t [aro'gant], *adj.* arrogant. **◆A~z**, *f* -/*no pl* arrogance.

Arsch [arʃ], *m* -(e)s/⸚e *V:* arse, *N.Am:* ass.

Art [aːrt], *f* /-en *(a)* kind, sort; *Z:* species; *Bot:* variety; *(b)* *(Weise)* way, manner; *(c)* *(Wesen)* nature. **◆A~nverkalkung**, *f* arteriosclerosis.

artig [aːrtiç], *adj.* well-behaved, good (child etc.).

Artikel [ar'tiːkəl], *m* -s/- article.

Artillerie [artilə'riː], *f* /-n artillery.

Artischocke [arti'ʃɔkə], *f* /-u (globe) artichoke.

Artist(in) [ar'tist(in)], *m* -en/-en *(f* /-nen) (circus) artiste, performer.

Arznei [aːrts'nai], *f* /-en medicine. **◆A~mittel**, *n* -s/- medicine.

Arzt [aːrtst], *m* -es/⸚e doctor. **◆Ärzt|in** ['ɛːrtstin], *f* /-nen woman doctor. **◆'ä~lich**, *adj.* medical.

As [as], *n* -ses/-se ace.

Asbest [as'bɛst], *m* -(e)s/-e asbestos.

Asche ['aʃə], *f* /-n ash; ashes (of a fire); *(Schlacke)* cinders. **◆A~nbahn**, *f* cinder track. **◆'A~nbecher**, *m* ashtray. **◆'A~nbrödel/'A~nputtel**, *n* -s/- Cinderella. **◆A~r'mittwoch**, *m* Ash Wednesday.

Asi|at(in) [azi'aːt(in)], *m* -en/-en *(f* /-nen) Asian. **◆a~atisch**, *adj.* Asiatic. **◆A~en** [a'ʔziːən]. *Pr.n.n* -s. Asia.

asozial ['azotsioːl], *adj.* antisocial.

Aspekt [as'pɛkt], *m* -(e)s/-e aspect.

Asphalt [as'falt], *m* -s/-e asphalt. **◆a~ieren** [-'tiːrən], *v.tr.* to surface (a road) (with asphalt).

Assistent(in) [asis'tɛnt(in)], *m* -en/-en *(f* /-nen) assistant.

Assozi|ation [asotsiatsi'oːn], *f* /-en association. **◆a~ieren** [-tsi'iːrən], *v.tr.* to associate.

Ast ['ast], *m* -(e)s/⸚e branch.

Aster ['astər], *f* /-n aster.

Ästhet|ik [ɛs'teːtik], *f* -/*no pl* aesthetics. **◆'ä~isch**, *adj.* aesthetic.

Asthma ['astma], *n* -s/*no pl* asthma. **◆A~tiker** [-'maːtikər], *m* -s/- asthmatic. **◆a~tisch** [-'maːtiʃ], *adj.* asthmatic.

Astro|loge(-login) [astro'loːgə(-'loːgin)], *m* -n/-n *(f* /-nen) astrologer. **◆A~logie** [-loˈgiː], *f* -/*no pl* astrology. **◆A~naut** [-'naut] *m* -en/-en astronaut. **◆A~nomie** [-noˈmiː] *f* -/*no pl* astronomy. **◆a~nomisch** [-'noːmiʃ] *adj.* astronomical.

Asyl [a'zyːl], *n* -s/-e *(a)* **(politisches) A.**, (political) asylum; *(b)* *(Ort)* refuge; *(für Obdachlose)* home; *Fig:* sanctuary.

Atelier [atəli'eː], *n* -s/-s studio.

Atem ['aːtəm], *m* -s/*no pl* breath; **außer A.**, out of breath; *Fig:* **A. holen**, to pause for breath. **◆'a~beraubend**, *adj.* breathtaking. **◆'a~los**, *adj.* breathless. **◆'A~not**, *f* shortage of breath. **◆'A~pause**, *f* breathing space. **◆'A~zug**, *m* breath.

Atheis|mus [ate'ismus], *m* -/*no pl* atheism. ◆**A~t**, *m* -en/-en atheist. ◆**a~tisch**, *adj.* atheistic.

Athen ['aːtɛn]. *Pr.n.n* -s. Athens.

Äther ['ɛːtər], *m* -s/- ether.

Äthiop|ien [ɛti'oːpiən]. *Pr.n.n* -s. Ethiopia. ◆**ä~isch**, *adj.* Ethiopian.

Athlet|(in) [at'leːt(in)], *m* -en/-en (*f* /-nen) athlete. ◆**A~ik**, *f* -/no *pl* athletics. ◆**a~isch**, *adj.* athletic.

Atlantik [at'lantik]. *Pr.n.m* -s. der A., the Atlantic (Ocean). ◆**a~isch**, *adj.* Atlantic.

Atlas ['atlas], *m* -ses/At'lanten atlas.

atm|en ['aːtmən], *v.tr. & i.* (*haben*) to breathe. ◆**A~ung**, *f* -/no *pl* respiration.

Atmosphäre [atmos'fɛːrə], *f* -/-n atmosphere.

Atom [a'toːm]. **I.** *n* -s/-e atom. **II.** **A~-**, *comb.fm.* atomic (bomb, weight etc.), nuclear (power station, war etc.). ◆**a~ar** [ato'maːr], *adj.* atomic. ◆**A~energie**, *f* atomic/nuclear energy. ◆**A~meiler**, *m* atomic pile. ◆**A~müll**, *m* nuclear waste. ◆**A~sprengkopf**, *m* nuclear warhead. ◆**A~waffen**, *fpl* nuclear weapons.

Attacke [a'takə], *f* -/-n attack.

Attent|at ['atəntaːt], *n* -(e)s/-e assassination (attempt); **ein A. auf j-n verüben**, to make an attempt on s.o.'s life. ◆**A~äter(in)**, *m* -s/- (*f* /-nen) (would-be) assassin.

Attest [a'tɛst], *n* -(e)s/-e certificate.

Attraktion [atraktsi'oːn], *f* -/-en attraction. ◆**a~iv** [-'tiːf], *adj.* attractive.

Attrappe [a'trapə], *f* -/-n dummy.

Attribut [atri'buːt], *n* -(e)s/-e attribute. ◆**a~iv** [-bu'tiːf], *adj.* attributive.

ätz|en ['ɛtsən], *v.tr.* to corrode (metal). ◆**ä~end**, *adj.* corrosive; *Ch: & Fig:* caustic.

auch [aux], *adv. & conj.* **1.** (*zusätzlich*) (*a*) too, also; **ich bin müde—ich a.!** I am tired—so am I! (*b*) (*mit Negativ*) either; **ich a. nicht**, nor/neither do I; (*c*) (*außerdem*) what's more; **a. das noch!** that's the last straw! **2.** (*a*) (*sogar*) even; **a. wenn du nicht kommst**, even if you don't come; (*b*) (*wirklich*) **was hätte es a. für einen Sinn?** what would be the point anyway? (*c*) **wer/was a. (immer)**, whoever/whatever.

auf [auf]. **I.** *prep.* **1.** (*räumlich* + *dat/acc*) on; **a. dem Bild/der Welt**, in the picture/the world; **a. der Post**, at the post office; **es hat nichts a. sich**, there's nothing to it; **a. etwas** *acc* **zugehen**, to go towards sth. **2.** (*zeitlich*) + *acc* **a. einige Tage** for a longer period; **a. die Minute genau**, punctual to the minute; **a. einmal war es finster**, suddenly it was dark; **etwas a. morgen verschieben**, to put sth. off until tomorrow; **a. meine Bitte (hin)**, at my request. **3.** **a. dem kürzesten Wege**, by the shortest route; **a. diese Art/Weise**, in this way; **sich a.**

deutsch unterhalten, to converse in German. **II.** *adv.* up, upwards; **sich a. und davon machen**, to make off.

'aufatmen, *v.i.sep.* (*haben*) to draw a deep breath; (*erleichtert*) to breathe a sigh of relief.

'aufbahren ['aufbaːrən], *v.tr.sep.* to lay out.

'Aufbau, *m* **1.** no *pl* (*Aufbauen*) construction; erection of a tent, scaffolding etc.); assembly of a machine etc.). **2.** (*Zusammenstellung*) composition (of society, a picture etc.); structure (of a building, compound, organization, play etc.). ◆**'a~en**, *v.tr.sep.* (*a*) to construct (a building etc.); to assemble (a machine etc.); to erect (a tent, structure etc.); (*b*) to build up (reserves, a team etc.); **sich** *dat* **eine neue Existenz a.**, to build a new life for oneself; (*c*) (*Theorie usw.*) (**sich**) **auf etwas** *dat* **a.**, to be based on sth.

'aufbäumen, *v.tr.sep.* (*Pferd*) **sich a.**, to rear; (*Pers.*) **sich gegen j-n, etwas** *acc* **a.**, to rebel against s.o., sth.

'aufbauschen, *v.tr.sep.* to exaggerate.

'aufbereiten, *v.tr.sep.* to process.

'aufbessern, *v.tr.sep.* to improve (sth.); to raise (a salary etc.).

'aufbewahr|en, *v.tr.sep.* to keep (sth.) (safely), (*lagern*) store (luggage, furniture etc.). ◆**'A~ung**, *f* -/no *pl* **1.** safekeeping; (*Lagern*) storage. **2.** *Rail: etc:* (*Stelle*) left-luggage office.

'aufbiet|en, *v.tr.sep.irr.8* to muster, summon up (all one's tact, strength etc.).

'aufblasen, *v.tr.sep.irr.11* to inflate, blow up (a balloon, tyre etc.).

'aufbleiben, *v.i.sep.irr.12* (*sein*) (*Pers.*) to stay up; (*Geschäft usw.*) to stay open.

'aufblicken, *v.i.sep.* (*haben*) to look up.

'aufblühen, *v.i.sep.* (*sein*) (*a*) to blossom; (*b*) *Fig:* (*Handel usw.*) to prosper.

'aufbrauchen, *v.tr.sep.* to use up, exhaust.

'aufbrausen, *v.i.sep.* (*sein*) (*Pers.*) to flare up. ◆**'a~d**, *adj.* irascible (person), fiery (temperament).

'aufbrechen, *v.sep.irr.14* **1.** *v.tr.* to break open (a door etc.), force (a lock etc.). **2.** *v.i.* (*sein*) (*a*) to crack; (*Wunde*) to open, (*Knospe usw.*) burst; (*b*) (*Pers.*) to leave, set out (**nach** + *dat*, for).

'aufbringen, *v.tr.sep.irr.16* (*haben*) (*a*) to raise (money); to muster (courage, strength); (*b*) (*reizen*) to anger (s.o.).

'Aufbruch, *m* departure, start.

aufbürden ['aufbyrdən], *v.tr.sep.* **j-m etwas a.**, to saddle s.o. with sth.

'aufdeck|en, *v.tr.sep.* (*a*) to uncover (a bed etc.); (*b*) *Fig:* to expose (a plot, crime etc.), reveal (motives etc.).

'aufdrängen, *v.tr.sep.* **j-m etwas a.**, to force sth. on s.o.; **sich j-m a.**, to inflict oneself on s.o.

'aufdrehen, *v.tr.sep.* to turn on (a tap, the gas etc.).

'aufdringlich, *adj.* persistent, pushy (person); obtrusive (advertisement, object); loud (clothes, colours etc.).

aufein'ander, *adv. & comb.fm.* (a) *(über-einander)* on top of one another; (b) **a. losgehen,** to fly at one another. **♦a~folgen,** *v.i.sep.* (sein) to follow one another. **♦a~folgend,** *adj.* successive, consecutive. **♦a~prallen,** *v.i.sep.* (sein) *(Autos usw.)* to crash into one another; *Fig: (Ansichten)* to clash.

Aufenthalt ['aufɛnthalt], *m* -(e)s/-e (a) stay; (b) *Rail: etc:* stop. **♦A~serlaubnis,** *f* residence permit. **♦A~sraum,** *m* recreation room.

'auferlegen, *v.tr.sep.* to impose (taxes, a fine etc.), inflict (a punishment) (j-m, on s.o.).

'Auferstehung, *f -/no pl* resurrection.

'aufessen, *v.tr.sep.irr.25* to eat (sth.) up.

'auffahr|en, *v.sep.irr.26* **1.** *v.i.* (sein) (a) **auf ein anderes Fahrzeug a.,** to run into (the back of) another vehicle; (b) *(Pers.)* **verärgert a.,** to jump up angrily. **2.** *v.tr.sep.* to bring up (the guns). **♦A~t,** *f* -/-en drive; *(zur Autobahn)* access road. **♦A~unfall,** *m* collision.

'auffallen, *v.i.sep.irr.27* (sein) to attract attention; **ist Ihnen nichts aufgefallen?** didn't you notice anything? **♦a~d,** *adj.* striking (similarity, beauty etc.); marked (difference).

'auffällig, *adj.* flashy (dress etc.); showy (person); loud (colours etc.); **a~es Benehmen,** ostentatious behaviour.

'auffang|en, *v.tr.sep.irr.28* to catch (s.o., sth. falling); to pick up (words, *Rad:* signals etc.). **♦A~lager,** *n* transit camp (for refugees).

'auffass|en, *v.tr.sep.* (a) to understand, grasp (sth.); (b) *(deuten)* to interpret (sth.). **♦A~ung,** *f* (a) understanding; (b) view, opinion.

'auffindbar, *adj.* traceable; **nirgends a.,** not to be found anywhere.

'aufforder|n, *v.tr.sep.* **j-n a.,** etwas **zu tun,** to call on/*(dringlich)* urge/*(bitten)* ask s.o. to do sth. **♦A~ung,** *f* request; **A. zum Tanz,** invitation to dance.

'auffrisch|en, *v.sep.* **1.** *v.tr.* to refresh (one's memory); to brush up (one's knowledge). **2.** *v.i.* (sein/haben) *(Wind)* to freshen.

'aufführ|en, *v.tr.sep.* (a) *Th: Mus:* to perform (a play, a piece); to show, put on (a film); (b) **sich gut/schlecht a.,** to behave well/badly; (c) to list (names, items etc.). **♦A~ung,** *f* -/-en (a) performance; (b) listing.

'Aufgabe, *f* -/-n **1.** *no pl* (a) posting, *N.Am:* mailing; insertion of an advertisement); *Rail:* registering (luggage); (b) *(Verzicht)* giving up; relinquishment (of a right); *Sp:* retirement (from a race etc.). **2.** *(Auftrag)* task, job; *Mil: etc:* mission, assignment; *Sp: (Zweck)* function; (c) *Sch:* exercise; *Mth:* problem; **A~n** *pl (Hausaufgaben)* homework.

'Aufgang, *m* (a) rising (of the sun); ascent (of a star); (b) *(Treppe)* stairway.

'aufgeben, *v.tr.sep.irr.35* (haben) (a) to post, *N.Am:* mail (a letter); to send (a telegram); **seine Bestellung a.,** to place one's order; **eine Annonce a.,** to put an advertisement in the paper; **sein Gepäck a.,** to register one's luggage; (b) **j-m eine Arbeit a.,** to set s.o. a task; (c) to give up (a struggle, business etc.); to abandon (an attempt, a plan).

'Aufgebot, *n* **1.** array; contingent (of police etc.); *Sp: (Mannschaft)* team, squad. **2. unter A. aller Kräfte,** using all one's strength. **3.** *Ecc:* banns.

'aufgebracht, *adj.* angry.

'aufgedreht, *adj. F:* in high spirits.

'aufgedunsen, *adj.* puffy (face); bloated (stomach etc.).

'aufgehen, *v.i.sep.irr.36* (sein) (a) *(Sonne, Teig, Vorhang usw.)* to rise; (b) *(Tür, Augen usw.)* to open; (c) *(Pers.)* **in etwas** *dat* **a.,** to live for sth.

'aufgeklärt, *adj.* broad-minded; **(sexuell) a. sein,** to know the facts of life.

'aufgelegt, *adj.* **gut/schlecht a.,** in a good/bad mood; **zu etwas** *dat* **a. sein,** to be in the mood for sth.

'aufgeregt, *adj.* upset; agitated.

'aufgeschlossen, *adj. (Pers.)* open-minded; liberal (views).

'aufgeschmissen, *adj. F:* **a. sein,** to be in a fix.

'aufgeweckt, *adj.* quick-witted; *(klug)* bright (child).

'aufgießen, *v.tr.sep.irr.31* to make (tea, coffee).

'aufgreifen, *v.tr.sep.irr.43* (a) to pick up, catch (a criminal etc.); (b) to take up (an idea, a case etc.).

'aufhaben, *v.tr.sep.irr.44 F:* (a) *(tragen)* to be wearing (a hat, spectacles etc.); (b) *Sch:* to have (sth.) to do as homework.

'aufhalten, *v.tr.sep.irr.45* (a) to stop (s.o., sth.); to halt (progress etc., *Mil:* an advance); (b) *(vorübergehend)* to hold up, delay (s.o., traffic etc.); to obstruct (a development etc.); (c) to dwell on sth.; (d) **j-m die Tür a.,** to hold the door open for s.o.; *F:* **die Hand a.,** to hold out one's hand (for money); (e) **sich an einem Ort a.,** stay in a place.

'aufhäng|en, *v.tr.sep.* (a) to hang (sth.) up; to put up (curtains, a poster etc.); to hang (a picture etc.); **j-n/sich a.,** to hang s.o./oneself. **♦A~er,** *m -s/-* hanger.

'aufheben. **I.** *v.tr.sep.irr.48* (a) to lift (s.o., sth.) up; *(vom Boden)* to pick (sth.) up; (b) *(aufbewahren)* to keep (sth.); **gut aufgehoben sein,** to be well looked after; (c) *(abschaffen)* to lift (a ban, restrictions etc.); to cancel (an order etc.), abolish (a tax etc.); to cancel (out) (an effect). **II. A.,** *n -s/no pl* **viel A~s um j-n, etwas** *acc* **machen,** to make a great fuss about s.o., sth.

'aufheitern, *v.tr.sep.* to cheer (s.o.) up;

(*Himmel, Wetter*) **sich a.**, to clear up.

'**aufhellen**, *v.tr.sep.* to lighten (colours etc.); **sich a.**, (*Gesicht*) to light up; (*Wetter*) to clear up.

'**aufhetzen**, *v.tr.sep.* to stir up (people).

'**aufholen**, *v.tr.sep.* (den *Vorsprung*) **a.**, to catch up; **die Verspätung a.**, to make up for lost time.

'**aufhorchen**, *v.i.sep.*(*haben*) to prick up one's ears.

'**aufhören**, *v.i.sep.*(*haben*) to stop; (*Freundschaft usw.*) to come to an end.

'**aufklappen**, *v.tr.sep.* to open (a knife, book etc.), raise (a lid).

'**aufklär|en**, *v.tr.sep.* (a) to clear up (a misunderstanding, crime etc.); (b) **j-n über etwas** *acc* **a.**, to enlighten s.o. about sth.; (*sexuell*) **a.**, to explain the facts of life; (c) (*Wetter*) **sich a.**, to clear (up). ◆'**A~ung,** *f -/-en* clarification; enlightenment; *Mil:* reconnaissance; (*sexuell*) sex education.

'**Aufkleber**, *m -s/-* sticker.

'**aufkochen**, *v.tr.sep.* **etwas** (*kurz*) **a. lassen,** to bring sth. to the boil.

'**aufkommen**, *v.i.sep.irr.53* (*sein*) (a) (*Nebel*) to rise; (*Wind*) to spring up; *Fig:* (*Zweifel usw.*) to arise; (*Stil, Mode*) to come in; (b) **für j-n, etwas** *acc* **a.**, to be liable for s.o., sth.

'**aufladen**, *v.tr.sep.irr.56* (*haben*) (a) to load (baggage etc.); *El:* to charge (a battery).

'**Auflage**, *f -/-n* 1. (a) impression; **überarbeitete A.**, revised edition; (b) (*von Zeitung*) circulation. 2. (*Beschränkung*) condition, restriction.

'**auflassen**, *v.tr.sep.irr.57* (a) to leave (the door etc.) open; (b) to keep (a hat) on; *F:* to let (children) stay up.

'**auflauern**, *v.i.sep.* (*haben*) **j-m a.**, to waylay s.o.

'**Auflauf**, *m -(e)s/-e* (a) crowd; (b) *Cu:* approx. = soufflé. ◆'**a~en**, *v.i.sep. irr.58* (*sein*) (a) to run aground; (b) (*sich anhäufen*) to accumulate.

'**aufleben**, *v.i.sep.* (*sein*) (*wieder*) **a.**, to take on a new lease of/*N.Am:* on life; (*Pflanze usw.*) to revive.

'**auflegen**, *v.tr.sep.* (a) to put on; *Tel:* (**den Hörer**) **a.**, to hang up; (b) **ein Buch neu a.**, to reprint a book.

'**auflehn|en**, *v.refl.sep.* **sich a.**, to rebel (**gegen** + *acc*, against). ◆'**A~ung,** *f -/no pl* rebellion.

'**auflesen**, *v.tr.sep.irr.61* to pick up.

'**aufleuchten**, *v.i.sep.* (*haben*) (*Licht*) to flash; (*Augen*) to light up.

'**auflockern**, *v.tr.sep.* (a) to break up (the soil etc.); (b) (*entspannen*) to make (the atmosphere etc.) more relaxed.

'**auflös|en**, *v.tr.sep.* (a) to dissolve; to untie (knots, one's hair); to close (an account etc.); (b) to solve (a riddle etc.); (c) **sich a.**, to break up; (*Salz usw.*) to dissolve; (*Menge*) to disperse; (*Nebel, Wolke*) to clear (away). ◆'**A~ung,** *f -/-en* (a)

disintegration; dissolution; (b) *Com:* closing (of an account).

'**aufmach|en**, *v.sep.* 1. *v.tr.* (a) to open; to undo (buttons, string etc.); to unfasten (a dress); **ein Geschäft a.**, to set up a business; (b) **sich a.**, to set off. 2. *v.i.* (*haben*) to open. ◆'**A~ung,** *f -/-en* appearance (of s.o., sth.); layout (of a page).

'**aufmerksam**, *adj.* (a) attentive; (*beobachtend*) observant; (b) **auf j-n, etwas** *acc* **a. werden,** to notice s.o., sth.; (*höflich*) thoughtful. ◆'**A~keit,** *f -/-en* (a) attention; (b) (*Höflichkeit*) thoughtfulness.

'**aufmöbeln**, *v.tr.sep. F:* to do (sth.) up; to buck (s.o.) up.

'**aufmuntern**, *v.tr.sep.* to cheer (s.o.) up; (*Kaffee, Alkohol*) to buck (s.o.) up.

Aufnahme ['aufnaːmə]. *f -/-n* 1. opening (of negotiations etc.); establishment (of relations etc.). 2. (*Empfang*) reception; admission; **A. beim Publikum,** public reaction. 3. intake (of food, refugees etc.); 4. *Phot:* photograph; *Cin: TV:* shot; (*Banda.*) recording. ◆'**a~fähig,** *adj.* receptive. ◆'**A~prüfung,** *f* entrance examination.

'**aufnehmen**, *v.tr.sep.irr.69* (a) to pick (sth.) up; (*aufsaugen*) to absorb (water etc.); (b) to take up (an idea, the fight etc.); to start (work etc.); (c) (*annehmen*) to accept (s.o.) (as a member etc.), include (s.o.) (in a team etc.); (d) (*niederschreiben*) to take down (dictation, notes etc.); (e) *Phot:* to photograph, take a photograph of (s.o., sth.); (*auf Band*) to record (s.o., sth.).

'**aufopfer|n**, *v.tr.sep.* to sacrifice. ◆'**a~nd,** *adj.* self-sacrificial.

'**aufpassen**, *v.i.sep.* (*haben*) (a) (*achtgeben*) to pay attention; (b) **auf j-n, etwas a.**, to keep an eye on s.o., sth.

'**Aufprall**, *m* impact. ◆'**a~en,** *v.i.sep.* (*sein*) **auf etwas** *acc* **a.**, to strike sth.

'**Aufpreis**, *m -es/-e* supplement.

'**aufraffen**, *v.refl.sep.* **sich a.**, to pull oneself together; **ich konnte mich nicht dazu a.**, I could not bring myself to do it.

'**aufräumen**, *v.tr.&i.sep.* (*haben*) to clear up/away (toys etc.); to tidy (a room etc.).

'**aufrecht**, *adj. & adv.* upright. ◆'**a~erhalten,** *v.tr.sep.irr.45* to maintain (order, contact etc.); to uphold (a tradition etc.).

'**aufreg|en**, *v.tr.sep.* to excite (s.o.), (*beunruhigen*) upset (s.o.); **sich a.**, to get excited/*F:* worked up. ◆'**a~end,** *adj.* exciting. ◆'**A~ung,** *f* agitation; (*Spannung*) excitement.

'**aufreiben**, *v.tr.sep.irr.12* (a) to chafe (the skin); (b) (*zermürben*) to wear (s.o.) down, fray (s.o.'s nerves). ◆'**a~d,** *adj.* gruelling.

'**aufreißen**, *v.tr.sep.irr.49* 1. *v.tr.* to tear/rip (sth.) open; to fling (the door, window) (wide) open; to tear up (the road); **die Augen** (**weit**) **a.**, to stare wide-eyed.

'**aufreizen**, *v.tr.sep.* to provoke. ◆'**a~d**, *adj.* provocative.

'**aufrichten**, *v.tr.sep.* (*a*) to raise, erect (a mast, pillar etc.); to help (s.o.) up; (*im Bett*) to sit (s.o.) up; (*b*) *Fig:* to console (s.o.). ◆'**a~ig**, *adj.* sincere; upright (conduct); (*offen*) frank (opinion etc.). ◆'**A~igkeit**, *f -/no pl* sincerity; frankness.

'**aufrücken**, *v.i.sep.* (*sein*) (*a*) to move up; (*b*) (*befördert werden*) to be promoted.

'**Aufruf**, *m* (*a*) summons, appeal. ◆'**a~en**, *v.tr.sep.irr.74* to summon; to call out (a name) (s.o., a witness etc.).

'**Aufruhr**, *m -/no pl* (*a*) (*Tumult*) upheaval, commotion; (*b*) (*Aufstand*) rebellion; (*einer Meute*) riot.

'**Aufrührer**, *m -s/-* rioter; (*Aufständischer*) rebel. ◆**a~isch**, *adj.* rioting (crowd), rebellious (people).

'**aufrunden**, *v.tr.sep.* to round up, *N. Am:* round off.

'**aufrüsten**, *v.tr.&i.sep.* (*haben*) to (re)arm. ◆'**A~ung**, *f* (re)armament.

'**aufrütteln**, *v.tr.sep.* to shake (s.o.) up.

'**aufsagen**, *v.tr.sep.* to recite.

'**aufsammeln**, *v.tr.sep.* to pick up, collect.

'**aufsässig** ['aufzɛsiç], *adj.* refractory (child); rebellious (people).

'**Aufsatz**, *m -es/-e* 1. essay. 2. top (of a dresser etc.).

'**aufsaugen**, *v.tr.sep.irr.76* to absorb (*Schwamm*) soak up.

'**aufschauen**, *v.i.sep.* (*haben*) to look up.

'**aufschieben**, *v.tr.sep.irr.82* (*a*) to slide open (a window etc.); (*b*) (*verschieben*) to postpone (sth.).

'**Aufschlag**, *m* 1 (*Aufprall*) impact (of a bomb etc.). 2. *Sp:* service. 3. *Com:* surcharge. 4. (*Hosena.*) turn-up; (*Ärmela.*) cuff; (*Mantela.*) lapel. ◆'**a~en**, *v.sep.irr.85* I. *v.i.* (*a*) (*sein*) **auf den Boden (hart) a.**, to hit the ground (hard); (*b*) (*haben*) *Sp:* to serve; (*c*) (*sein*) (*Tür usw.*) to burst open; (*d*) (*haben*) (*Waren*) to go up (in price). 2. *v.tr.* (*a*) to break (sth.) open; to crack (an egg); to open (a book, paper, one's eyes etc.); (*b*) to put up (a tent etc.).

'**aufschließen**, *v.sep.irr.31* 1. *v.tr.* to unlock. 2. *v.i.* (*haben*) (*aufrücken*) to close up.

'**Aufschluß**, *m* **A. über etwas** *acc* **geben**, to provide information about sth. ◆'**a~reich**, *adj.* revealing (facts); (*lehrreich*) informative (talk etc.).

'**aufschnappen**, *v.sep.* 1. *v.tr. F:* (*Pers.*) to catch (s.o.'s words etc.). 2. *v.i.* (*sein*) to spring open.

'**aufschneiden**, *v.sep.irr.59* 1. *v.tr.* (*a*) to cut (sth.) open; (*b*) to slice (bread etc.). 2. *v.i.* (*haben*) *F:* to brag. ◆'**A~er**, *m -s/- F:* show-off.

'**Aufschnitt**, *m* (selection of) sliced cold meat; *N.Am:* cold cuts.

'**aufschrecken**, *v.sep.* 1. *v.tr.* to startle

(s.o.). 2. *v.i.irr.23* (*sein*) to start (up).

'**Aufschrei**, *m* cry, yell. ◆'**a~en**, *v.i.sep.irr.88* (*haben*) to cry out.

'**aufschreiben**, *v.tr.sep.irr.12* to write (sth.) down.

'**Aufschrift**, *f* writing; (*Etikett*) label.

'**Aufschub**, *m* delay.

'**aufschwatzen**, *v.tr.sep.* **j-m etwas a.**, to talk s.o. into buying sth.

'**Aufschwung**, *m* 1. upward swing. 2. *Fig:* upturn.

'**aufsehen**, I. *v.i.sep.irr.92* (*haben*) to look up. II. **A.**, *n -s/no pl* **A. erregen/verursachen**, to cause a stir; **ohne A.**, unnoticed. ◆'**a~enerregend**, *adj.* sensational. ◆'**A~er(in)**, *m -s/- (f -/-nen)* supervisor (*im Museum, am Marktplatz*) attendant; (*im Gefängnis*) warder.

'**aufsein**, *v.i.sep.irr.93* (*sein*) (*a*) to be open; (*b*) (*Pers.*) to be up.

'**aufsetzen**, *v.sep.* 1. *v.tr.* (*a*) to put on (a hat, the kettle); (*b*) to draft (a letter, contract etc.); (*c*) (*Pers.*) **sich a.**, to sit up. 2. *v.i.* (*Flugzeug*) to touch down.

'**Aufsicht**, *f no pl* supervision; **A. haben/führen**, to be in charge (of sth.). ◆**A~srat**, *m* board of directors.

'**aufsitzen**, *v.i.sep.irr.97* (*a*) (*sein*) to sit up; (*b*) (*sein*) (*Reiter, Fahrer*) to get on; (*c*) (*sein*) **j-m, etwas** *dat* **a.**, to be taken in by s.o., sth.

'**aufspannen**, *v.tr.sep.* to put up.

'**aufsparen**, *v.tr.sep.* to save up, keep (sth.).

'**aufsperren**, *v.tr.sep.* (*a*) (*Vogel/Tier*) to open (its beak/mouth) wide; (*b*) to unlock (a door).

'**aufspießen**, *v.tr.sep.* to spear (sth.).

'**aufspringen**, *v.i.sep.irr.19* (*sein*) (*a*) to jump up; **auf etwas** *acc* **a.**, to jump onto sth.; (*b*) (*Deckel usw.*) to spring open; (*Knospen*) to burst; (*Haut*) to crack.

'**aufspüren**, *v.tr.sep.* to trace (s.o., sth.), track down (a criminal).

'**aufstacheln**, *v.tr.sep.* to incite.

'**Aufstand**, *m* revolt, rebellion.

'**aufständisch**, *adj.* rebellious.

'**aufstecken**, *v.tr.sep.* (*a*) to put up (one's hair etc.); (*b*) *F:* to give up (a plan etc.).

'**aufstehen**, *v.i.sep.irr.100* (*a*) (*sein*) to stand up; (*vom Bett*) to get up; (*b*) (*haben*) (*Tür usw.*) to stand open.

'**aufsteigen**, *v.i.sep.irr.89* (*sein*) (*a*) to get on; (*b*) (*Ballon usw.*) to ascend; (*Rauch, Sonne etc.*) to rise; (*Nebel*) to lift.

'**aufstellen**, *v.tr.sep.* (*a*) to put up (a tent, statue etc.); to set up (a machine); (*b*) to place (chairs, a ladder etc.) in position; (*Pers.*) **sich a.**, to station oneself; (*in Reihen*) to line up; (*c*) to put up (a candidate); (*d*) to form (a team etc.); to set (a record); to draw up (a list, table); to draft (a plan); to lay down (rules, norms); **eine Behauptung a.**, to make a statement. ◆'**A~ung**, *f* 1. (*a*) erection; assembly (of a machine); (*b*) positioning; (*c*) *Parl:* nomination; (*d*) formation (of a team). 2. (*Liste*) list.

Aufstieg ['aufʃtiːk], *m* -(e)s/-e 1. climb; ascent (*esp.* of a rocket, balloon). 2. rise (**zur Macht usw.,** to power etc.); (*im Rang*) promotion.

'**aufstoßen**, *v.sep.irr.103* 1. *v.tr.* to push/ (*mit dem Fuß*) kick open (a door etc.). 2. *v.i.* (*sein*) (*Baby*) to burp; (*Betrunkener usw.*) to belch.

Aufstrich, *m* spread.

'**aufsuchen**, *v.tr.sep.* to look (s.o.) up; to go to see (a doctor).

'**auftakeln**, *v.tr.sep.* (*a*) *Nau:* to rig (a ship); (*b*) *F:* **sich a.,** to doll oneself up.

Auftakt, *m Fig:* opening.

'**auftanken**, *v.tr.&i.sep.* (*haben*) to fill up (a car); to refuel (an aircraft).

'**auftauchen**, *v.i.sep.* (*sein*) (*a*) to emerge; (*U-Boot, Taucher*) to surface; (*b*) (*Pers., Verlorenes*) to turn up.

'**auftauen**, *v.tr.&i.sep.* to thaw (sth.); *Fig:* (*Pers.*) to get going.

'**aufteilen**, *v.tr.sep.* to divide (sth.) up. ◆'**A~ung,** *f* division.

'**auftischen**, *v.tr.sep.* to serve up (food), dish up (a meal, *F:* lies etc.).

Auftrag ['auftraːk], *m* -(e)s/-e (*Aufgabe*) task; (*Bestellung*) order; **im A. der Firma X,** on behalf of Messrs X. ◆**a~en,** *v.tr.sep.irr.85* (*a*) to serve up (a meal); (*b*) to apply, put on (paint, make-up etc.); (*c*) **j-m etwas a.,** to instruct s.o. to do sth. ◆'**A~geber(in),** *m* (*f*) client.

'**auftreiben**, *v.tr.sep.irr.12* *F:* to get hold of (s.o., sth.); to raise (money).

'**auftreten**. I. *v.i.sep.irr.105* (*sein*) (*a*) (*Pers.*) **leise usw. a.,** to tread softly etc.; (*b*) (*Pers.*) to appear; **selbstbewußt a.,** to behave/act confidently. II. **A.,** *n* -s/*no pl* (*a*) appearance; (*b*) (*Benehmen*) bearing.

'**Auftrieb**, *m* (*im Wasser*) buoyancy; *Av:* lift; *Fig:* impetus.

'**Auftritt**, *m* (*a*) appearance; (*b*) *Th:* scene (of a play).

'**aufwachen**, *v.i.sep.*(*sein*) to wake up.

'**aufwachsen**, *v.i.sep.irr.107* (*sein*) to grow up.

Aufwand ['aufvant], *m* -(e)s/*no pl* expenditure.

'**aufwärmen**, *v.tr.sep.* (*a*) to warm up (food); *F:* to rehash (a story), rake up (s.o.'s past etc.); (*b*) **sich a.,** to warm oneself up; *Sp:* to warm up.

'**aufwarten**, *v.i.sep.* (*haben*) **mit etwas** *dat* **a.,** to come up with sth.

aufwärts ['aufvɛrts]. I. *adv.* upwards. II. '**A~,** *comb.fm.* upward (movement, trend etc.). ◆'**a~gehen,** *v.i.sep.irr.36* (*sein*) to get better; **mit ihm geht es aufwärts,** things are looking up for him.

'**aufwecken**, *v.tr.sep.* to wake (s.o.) up.

'**aufweichen**, *v.tr.* to soften (sth.); (*im Wasser*) to leave (sth.) to soak.

'**aufweisen**, *v.tr.sep.irr.70* **etwas a. können,** to have sth. to show for oneself.

'**aufwenden**, *v.tr.sep.* to spend (money, time), use up (material, energy); to de-

vote (effort, time). ◆'**a~ig,** *adj.* lavish; (*kostspielig*) costly.

'**aufwerten**, *v.tr.sep.* to revalue. ◆'**A~ung,** *f* revaluation.

'**aufwiegeln**, *v.tr.sep.* to incite.

'**aufwiegen**, *v.tr.sep.irr.7* to offset (sth.).

'**aufwirbeln**, *v.tr.sep.* to whirl (leaves etc.) into the air; *Fig:* **Staub a.,** to cause a stir.

'**aufwischen**, *v.tr.sep.* to wipe/mop up.

'**aufzählen**, *v.tr.sep.* to list. ◆'**A~ung,** *f* list.

'**aufzeichnen**, *v.tr.sep.* (*a*) to sketch (sth.); (*b*) (*festhalten*) to record. ◆'**A~ung,** *f* (*a*) sketch; (*b*) record; recording.

'**aufziehen**, *v.sep.irr.113* 1. *v.tr.* (*a*) to hoist (a sail, flag); (*b*) (*öffnen*) to open (a zip, drawer etc.); to draw back (the curtains); (*c*) to wind up (a clock etc.); (*d*) to bring up (a child), rear (an animal); (*e*) *F:* **j-n a.,** to tease s.o. 2. *v.i.* (*sein*) (*Sturm, Wolken*) to come up.

'**Aufzug,** *m* 1. procession. 2. (*Fahrstuhl*) lift, *N.Am:* elevator. 3. *Pej:* *F:* get-up. 4. *Th:* act (of a play).

'**aufzwingen**, *v.tr.sep.irr.19* **j-m etwas a.,** to force sth. on s.o.

Augapfel ['auk'apfəl], *m* eyeball; *Fig:* **er hütet es wie seinen A.,** he keeps it in cotton wool.

Auge ['augə], *n* -s/-n eye; **kein A. zutun,** not to sleep a wink; **vor aller A~n,** in public; **unter vier A~n,** in private; **j-n, etwas aus den A~n verlieren,** to lose sight of s.o., sth.; **etwas mit anderen A~n ansehen,** to view sth. differently; **ein A. zudrücken,** to turn a blind eye to sth. ◆'**A~n-,** *comb.fm.* eye (shade, trouble, drops, lotion etc.); optic (nerve etc.). ◆'**A~nblick,** *m* moment; **im A.,** at the moment. ◆'**a~nblicklich,** *adj.* (*a*) immediate; (*b*) (*derzeitig*) present (situation etc.). ◆'**A~nbraue,** *f* eyebrow. ◆'**A~nfällig,** *adj.* conspicuous; obvious. ◆'**A~nmaß,** *n* visual judgment (of distance). ◆'**A~nschein,** *m* *Lit:* **dem A. nach,** to all appearances. ◆'**A~nweide,** *f* sight for sore eyes. ◆'**A~nzeuge,** *m* eyewitness.

August [au'gust], *m* -s/-e August.

Auktion [auktsi'oːn], *f* -/-en auction. ◆**A~ator** [auktsio'naːtɔr], *m* -s/-en auctioneer.

Aula ['aula], *f* -/-len assembly hall.

aus [aus]. I. *prep.* + *dat* 1. (*Richtung*) (*a*) out of; **a. dem Haus,** out of the house; (*b*) from; **der Zug kommt a. Hamburg,** the train comes from Hamburg. 2. (*Material*) made of. 3. (*Grund*) from, out of (fear, habit etc.). II. *adv.* (*a*) (*Licht, Feuer*) out; (*Schalter*) off; (*b*) (*vorbei*) over; **es ist a. mit ihm,** it's all up with him; (*c*) **er geht bei ihm ein und a.,** he comes and goes in her house; *Fig:* **er weiß weder a. noch ein,** he is at his wits' end; **auf etwas** *acc* **a. sein,** to be set/bent on sth. **III. A.,** *n -lno pl Sp:* **im/ ins A.,** out of play.

'ausarbeiten, *v.tr.sep.* to think out (a plan etc.); draw up (a contract etc.).

'ausarten, *v.i.sep.* (sein) to degenerate.

'ausatmen, *v.tr.&i.sep.* (haben) to breathe out, exhale (air).

'ausbaden, *v.tr.sep. F:* to carry the can for (s.o.'s mistakes etc.).

'Ausbau, *m* 1. *Tchn:* removal (of a part). 2. (*Erweiterung*) widening; extension; (*Umbau*) conversion (of an attic etc.). ◆**'a~en,** *v.tr.sep.* (a) *Tchn:* to remove (a part, an engine); (b) to widen (a road); to extend (a house, network etc.).

'ausbessern, *v.tr.sep.* to repair, fix, (*behelfsmäßig*) patch up (sth., damage etc.); to mend (clothes).

'ausbeulen, *v.tr.sep.* (a) to knock out the dent(s) in (a hat, etc.); (b) to make (trousers etc.) baggy.

'Ausbeut|e, *f* yield; *Fig:* (Gewinn) gain. ◆**'a~en,** *v.tr.sep.* (a) to exploit (resources etc.), work (a mine etc.); (b) (*ausnutzen*) to exploit (s.o.). ◆**'A~er(in),** *m -s/- (f -/-nen)* exploiter; *F:* slave-driver. ◆**'A~ung,** *f -lno pl* exploitation; *Min:* working.

'ausbild|en, *v.tr.sep.* to train. ◆**'A~er(in),** *m* (f) instructor. ◆**'A~ung,** *f* training; (further/ university) education. ◆**'A~ungs-comb.fm.** training (camp, film, method etc.).

'ausbitten, *v.tr.sep.irr.10* **sich** *dat* **etwas a.,** to ask for sth.

'ausbleiben, *v.i.sep.irr.12* (sein) (Pers.) to fail to appear/(Wirkung, Erwartetes) materialize; **es konnte nicht a., daß ...,** it was inevitable that ...

'Ausblick, *m* (a) view; (b) *Fig:* prospect.

'ausbrechen, *v.i.sep.irr.14* (sein) (a) (Feuer, Krieg usw.) to break out; (Vulkan) to erupt; *Fig:* **in Tränen/Gelächter a.,** to burst into tears/laughter; (**aus dem Gefängnis**) a., to break out (of prison). ◆**'a~er,** *m -s/-* escaped prisoner.

'ausbreiten, *v.tr.sep.* (a) to spread out (wares, a map, wings etc.); to open out (a newspaper etc.); (b) **sich a.,** to spread.

'ausbrennen, *v.sep.irr.15* 1. *v.tr.* to burn out; *Med:* to cauterize. 2. *v.i.* (sein) to burn out.

'Ausbruch, *m* (a) (Beginn) outbreak; eruption (of a volcano); (b) escape (from prison, etc.); (c) outburst (of rage etc.).

'ausbrüten, *v.tr.sep.* to hatch out (eggs); *Fig:* to think up (a plan).

'Ausbuchtung, *f -/-e* bulge.

'Ausdauer, *f* staying power; (Durchhalten) perseverance. ◆**'a~nd,** *adj.* tenacious.

'ausdehn|en, *v.tr.sep.* (a) to stretch, expand (sth.); to extend (frontiers, contacts etc.); (b) **sich a.,** to stretch, extend; (Stadt, Handel, Ch: Gas) to expand. ◆**'A~ung,** *f -/-en* (a) expansion (b) (Fläche) expanse, extent.

'ausdenken, *v.tr.sep.irr.17* (a) **sich** *dat* **einen Plan usw. a.,** to devise a plan; (b) **es ist nicht auszudenken,** it doesn't bear thinking about!

'ausdrehen, *v.tr.sep. F:* to turn off.

'Ausdruck¹, *m -(e)s/-e* expression; **zum A. kommen,** to be expressed. ◆**'A~sweise,** *f* mode of expression.

'Ausdruck², *m -(e)s/-e Data-pr:* print-out.

'ausdrück|en, *v.sep.* 1. *v.tr.* (a) to squeeze out (water, juice etc.); to stub out (a cigarette); (b) to express (an opinion etc.); **anders ausgedrückt,** in other words. ◆**'a~lich,** *adj.* explicit; express (wish, command etc.).

ausein'ander, *adv. & comb.fm.* (a) apart; (b) (kaputt) in pieces. ◆**a~bringen,** *v.tr.sep.irr.16* to separate. ◆**a~fallen,** *v.i.sep.irr.27* (sein) to fall/come to pieces. ◆**a~gehen,** *v.i.sep.irr.36* (sein) (a) (Wege usw.) to diverge; *Fig:* (Meinungen usw.) to differ; (b) (Paar) to split up. ◆**a~halten,** *v.tr.sep.irr.45* (unterscheiden) to tell (people) apart. ◆**a~nehmen,** *v.tr.sep.irr.69* to take to pieces. ◆**a~setzen,** *v.tr.sep.* (a) (erklären) to explain (ideas etc.); (b) **sich mit einem Problem a.,** to come to terms with a problem; **sich mit j-m a.,** to have it out with s.o. ◆**A~setzung,** *f -/-en* (a) discussion; (Streit) argument.

'auserlesen, *adj.* select (people); choice (food, wine); exquisite (taste etc.).

'ausfahr|en, *v.sep.irr.26* 1. *v.tr.* (a) to take (s.o.) out for a drive; *Tchn:* to lower (Av: landing gear etc.); to raise (an aerial, periscope etc.). 2. *v.i.* (sein) to drive out; (Schiff) to leave harbour. ◆**A~t,** *f* 1. (Abfahrt) departure. 2. exit (from a garage, motorway etc.).

'Ausfall, *m* 1. (a) (Verlust) loss (of hair, earnings etc.); (b) (Absagen) cancellation; (c) (Versagen) failure; stoppage (in a factory). 2. *Mil:* sortie. ◆**'a~en,** *v.i.sep.irr.27* (sein) (a) (Zähne, Haare usw.) to fall out; (b) to turn out (well, badly etc.); (c) (Vorstellung, Zug usw.) to be cancelled; (Maschine usw.) to break down. ◆**'a~end,** *adj.* impertinent. ◆**'A~straße,** *f* arterial road (out of a town).

'ausfeilen, *v.tr.sep.* to file (sth.) to shape; *Fig:* to polish (a speech etc.).

'ausfertig|en, *v.tr.sep.* to draw up (a contract etc.), make out (a bill etc.); to issue (a passport etc.). ◆**'A~ung,** *f -/-en* (a) drawing up, making out; issuing; (b) (Exemplar) copy.

'ausfindig, *adj:* j-n, etwas a. machen, to locate s.o., sth.

'Ausflucht, *f -/-e* excuse, pretext.

'Ausflug, *m* excursion.

'Ausflügler(in), *f* ['ausfly:glər(in)], *m -s/- (f -/-nen)* day-tripper.

'Ausfluß, *m* (a) outflow (of water etc.); discharge (of sewage, *Med:* of pus etc.); (b) (Abfluß) drain, outlet.

'**ausfragen**, *v.tr.sep.* to interrogate, quiz (s.o.).

'**ausfransen**, *v.i.sep.* (*sein*) to fray (at the edges).

'**ausfressen**, *v.tr.sep.irr.25 F:* **was hat er ausgefressen?** what has he been up to?

'**Ausfuhr**, *f /-en* export.

'**ausführ|bar**, *adj.* **1.** exportable (goods etc.). **2.** (*durchführbar*) feasible. ◆**'a~en**, *v.tr.sep.* (*a*) to export (goods); (*b*) to carry out (an order, a plan, repair etc.); (*c*) to take out (a dog, a girl etc.); (*d*) to elaborate on (a question etc.). ◆**'a~lich**, *adj.* detailed; *adv.* in detail. ◆**'A~ung**, *f* **1.** (*Vollzug*) execution; (*Bau*) construction; (*Qualität*) workmanship. **2.** (*Bemerkung*) remark, comment. **3.** *esp. Com:* version; *Aut:* model; (*Lack, Appretur usw.*) finish.

'**ausfüllen**, *v.tr.sep.* (*a*) to fill up (a space); to fill in/*N.Am:* fill out (a form); (*b*) to occupy (time, s.o. etc.).

'**Ausgabe**, *f* **1.** (*a*) handing out, (*Verkauf*) sale (of stamps etc.); issue (of shares); (*b*) (*Schalter*) counter. **2.** edition (of a book, news broadcast etc.); issue (of a periodical). **3.** *usu. pl* **A~n**, expenditure.

'**Ausgang**, *m* **1.** way out, exit. **2.** (*a*) **A. haben**, to have time off; (*b*) (*Anfang*) beginning. **3.** (*Ende*) end; (*Ergebnis*) result. ◆**'A~s-**, *comb.fm.* (*a*) starting, initial (position etc.); original (condition, question etc.); (*b*) *El:* output (voltage, stage). ◆**'A~spunkt**, *m* starting point, point of departure.

'**ausgeben**, *v.tr.sep.irr.35* (*a*) to hand out, distribute (food etc.); to issue (tickets, *Fin:* shares, notes); (*b*) to spend (money); (*c*) **er gibt sich als Engländer aus**, he pretends to be English.

'**ausgebucht**, *adj.* fully booked.

'**ausgedehnt**, *adj.* extensive; (*riesig*) vast.

'**ausgefallen**, *adj.* off-beat (style etc.); eccentric (taste).

'**ausgeglichen**, *adj.* stable (person, etc.); even (temperament). ◆**'A~heit**, *f /no pl* (good) balance; stability.

'**ausgeh|en**, *v.i.sep.irr.36* (*sein*) (*a*) to go out; (*b*) *Fig:* **der Vorschlag von ihm aus**, the suggestion came from him; **gehen wir einmal davon aus, daß** ..., let us assume that ...; (*c*) (*Zähne, Haare usw.*) to fall out; (*Geld usw.*) to run out; (*d*) **die Sache ging gut/schlecht aus**, the affair ended well/badly; (*e*) (*Licht, Feuer*) to go out; (*f*) **auf etwas** *acc* **a.**, to set out to do sth.; **leer a.**, to come away empty-handed. ◆**'A~verbot**, *n* curfew.

'**ausgelassen**, *adj.* exuberant; (*wild*) unruly (child etc.); wild (party).

'**ausgemacht**, *adj.* (*a*) agreed, settled (terms etc.); (*b*) *F:* downright (stupidity etc.).

'**ausgenommen**. **1.** *prep.* + *gen/dat* except (for). **2.** *conj.* **a.** (*wenn*) **es regnet**, unless it rains.

'**ausgeprägt**, *adj.* marked.

'**ausgerechnet**, *adv.* **a. ihm mußte das passieren!** it had to happen to him of all people!

'**ausgeschlossen**, *pred. adj.* out of the question.

'**ausgesprochen**, *adj.* decided (preference etc.); pronounced (talent).

'**ausgestorben**, *adj.* extinct (animal); *Fig:* **wie a.**, (*Stadt usw.*) dead, deserted.

'**Ausgestoßene(r)**, *m & f decl. as adj.* outcast.

'**ausgezeichnet**, *adj.* excellent.

'**ausgiebig** ['ausgi:biç], *adj.* extensive (discussion etc.); **a. frühstücken/schlafen**, to have a really good breakfast/sleep.

'**Ausgleich**, *m* -(*e*)s/*no pl* **1.** (*Gleichgewicht*) equilibrium, balance. **2.** (*Entschädigung*) compensation. **3.** *Fb:* (*Tor*) equalizer. ◆**'a~en**, *v.tr.sep.irr.40* (*a*) to balance (weights, *Fig:* an account etc.); to reconcile (differences, opposites); to compensate/make up for (a loss, lack etc.); **sich a.**, (*zwei Sachen*) to cancel one another out; (*b*) *Fb:* **a.**, to equalize. ◆**'A~ssport** *m* keep-fit (exercises). ◆**'A~streffer**, *m Fb:* equalizer.

'**ausgrab|en**, *v.tr.sep.irr.42* also *Fig:* to dig (sth.) up; to excavate (ruins). ◆**'A~ung**, *f /-en* excavation, dig.

'**Ausguß**, *m* (*Becken*) sink; (*Abfluß*) plughole.

'**aushaben**, *v.tr.sep.irr.44 F:* **ich habe das Buch aus**, I have finished the book.

'**aushalten**, *v.tr.sep.irr.45* (*a*) to bear, stand (s.o., sth.); to endure (pain etc.); (*b*) *F:* to keep (s.o.); **er läßt sich von ihr a.**, he lives off her earnings.

'**aushandeln**, *v.tr.sep.* to negotiate.

'**aushändigen** ['aushɛndigən], *v.tr.sep.* to hand (sth.) over, hand out (prizes etc.).

'**Aushang**, *m* notice.

'**aushänge|n**, *v.sep.* **1.** *v.tr.* (*a*) to put up, post (a sign, notice etc.); (*b*) to take (a door) off its hinges. **2.** *v.i.irr.46* (*haben*) to be displayed. ◆**'A~schild**, *n* sign.

'**ausharren**, *v.i.sep.* (*haben*) to persevere.

'**aushelfen**, *v.i.sep.irr.50* (*haben*) (j-m) **a.**, to help (s.o.) out.

'**Aushilf|e**, *f /-n* (*a*) assistance; (*b*) (*Pers.*) temporary worker. ◆**'A~skraft**, *f* temporary worker, *F:* temp.

'**aushöhlen**, *v.tr.sep.* to hollow out (sth.), scrape out (a melon etc.); to undermine (a river bank etc.).

'**ausholen**, *v.i.sep.* (*haben*) **mit dem Arm a.**, to raise one's arm; *Fig:* **weit a.**, to go back a long way.

'**aushorchen**, *v.tr.sep.* to sound (s.o.) out.

'**auskennen**, *v.refl.sep.irr.51* **sich a.**, to know what's what/*F:* the ropes; (*in einem Ort*) to know one's way about.

'**auskippen**, *v.tr.sep. F:* to tip out/*N.Am:* dump (a plant etc.).

'**ausklammern**, *v.tr.sep.* to leave on one side, exclude (a topic etc.).

'**auskleiden**, *v.tr.sep.* (*a*) *Lit:* to undress (s.o., oneself); (*b*) to line (a wall etc.).

'**ausklingen**, *v.i.sep.irr.19* (*sein*) to come to an end.

'**ausklopfen**, *v.tr.sep.* to beat (a carpet etc.); to knock out (a pipe etc.).

'**auskommen. I.** *v.i.sep.irr.53* (*sein*) (*a*) **mit etwas** *dat* a., to make do/manage with sth.; (*b*) **mit j-m** a., to get on with s.o. **II. A.**, *n -s/no pl* **er hat ein gutes A.**, he is quite well off.

'**auskundschaften**, *v.tr.sep.* to reconnoitre (an area), spy out (a secret etc.).

Auskunft ['auskunft], *f -/-e* (*a*) (item of information); (*b*) (*Stelle*) information (desk/bureau); *Tel:* Enquiries.

'**auskuppeln**, *v.i.sep.* (*haben*) *Aut:* to let out the clutch.

'**auslachen**, *v.tr.sep.* to laugh at, (*verspotten*) make fun of (s.o.).

'**ausladen**, *v.sep.irr.56* **I.** *v.tr.* (*a*) to unload; (*b*) *F:* **einen Gast** a., to put off a guest. **2.** *v.i.* (*haben*) to jut out.

'**Auslage**, *f* 1. *pl.* A~**n**, outlay. 2. (*Schaufenster*) shop window; (*Ausgestelltes*) display.

'**Ausland**, *n* **das A.**, foreign countries; **im/ins A.**, abroad. ◆'**A~s-**, *comb.fm.* (*a*) foreign (business, department etc.); (*b*) international (relations, *Tel:* call etc.). ◆'**A~korrespondent(in)**, *m* (*f*) (*j*) (*Journalist*) foreign correspondent; (*b*) (*Sekretär*) bilingual secretary. ◆'**A~sreise**, *f* trip abroad.

Ausländ|er(in) ['auslɛndər(in)], *m -s/- (f /-nen)* foreigner. ◆'**a~isch**, *adj.* foreign.

'**auslass|en**, *v.tr.sep.irr.57* (*a*) to let out (steam, water, a dress etc.); (*b*) to leave out, omit (sth.); *F:* to leave off (a piece of clothing); (*c*) *Cu:* to melt (butter); (*d*) **seine schlechte Laune an j-m** a. to take it out on s.o.; **sich über etwas** *acc* a., go on about sth. ◆'**A~ung**, *f /-en* omission. ◆'**A~ungszeichen**, *n* apostrophe.

'**auslasten**, *v.tr.sep.* to use (a machine, etc.) to capacity; **voll ausgelastet**, fully occupied.

'**Auslauf**, *m* 1. outlet, outflow (for water etc.). 2. **der Hund hat hier keinen A.**, there's no space for the dog to run free here. ◆'**a~en**, *v.sep.irr.58 v.i.* (*sein*) (*a*) (*Flüssigkeit*) to run out, (*durch Leck*) leak; (*Farben*) to run; (*b*) (*Schiff*) to leave harbour; (*c*) (*enden*) to come to an end.

'**Ausläufer**, *m* 1. (*Rand*) fringe; spur (of a mountain). 2. *Bot:* runner. 3. *Meteor:* ridge (of high pressure); trough (of low pressure).

'**ausleeren**, *v.tr.sep.* to empty.

'**ausleg|en**, *v.tr.sep.* (*a*) to display (goods etc.); (*b*) to cover (a surface); (*c*) **für j-n Geld** a., to lend s.o. money; (*d*) (*deuten*) to interpret (a text, s.o.'s behaviour etc.). ◆'**A~ung**, *f /-en* interpretation.

'**ausleiern**, *v.tr.sep.* *F:* to wear out (a mechanism etc.); to stretch (elastic).

'**Ausleihe**, *f /-n* issue desk (in a library).

◆'**a~en**, *v.tr.sep.irr.60* (*a*) to borrow (money); to take out (a book); (*b*) to lend (sth.) (**an j-n**, to s.o.).

'**Auslese**, *f* 1. *no pl* selection. 2. elite of society etc.); (*Wein*) wine from specially selected grapes. ◆'**a~n**, *v.tr.sep.irr.61* (*a*) to select (flowers etc.); (*b*) to finish reading (a book etc.).

'**ausliefer|n**, *v.tr.sep.* (*a*) *Com:* to distribute (goods); (*b*) to hand over (s.o.); (*an einen Staat*) to extradite (s.o.). ◆'**A~ung**, *f* 1. *Com:* distribution. 2. handing over; extradition.

'**auslöschen**, *v.tr.sep.* (*a*) to extinguish, put out (a fire, candle etc.); (*b*) to efface (memories); (*c*) to annihilate (a people, lives).

'**auslös|en**, *v.tr.sep.* (*a*) to trigger off (an event etc.); to cause (surprise, joy etc.); to set off (an alarm etc.); (*b*) to redeem (pawned goods); to bail out (a prisoner). ◆'**A~er**, *m -s/-* trigger; *Phot:* (shutter) release.

'**auslosen**, *v.tr.sep.* to draw lots for (sth.).

'**ausmachen**, *v.tr.sep.* (*a*) (*Summe, Zahl*) to amount to (sth.); (*Sachen*) to constitute (a whole, part); (*b*) (*erkennen*) to make out (a ship etc.); (*c*) *F:* (*vereinbaren*) to agree (a time, meeting point etc.); (*d*) *F:* to turn off (the light, radio etc.); to put out (a cigarette etc.); (*e*) *F:* (*bedeuten*) to matter; **macht es Ihnen etwas aus, wenn ich rauche?** do you mind if I smoke?

'**ausmalen**, *v.tr.sep.* (*a*) to paint; (*b*) *Fig:* **sich** *dat* **etwas anders** a., to imagine sth. differently.

'**Ausmaß**, *n* (*Größe*) size; *Fig:* (*Umfang*) extent (of destruction etc.).

'**ausmerzen** ['ausmɛrtsən], *v.tr.sep.* to eliminate.

'**ausmessen**, *v.tr.sep.irr.25* to measure.

Ausnahme ['ausnaːmə], *f /-n* exception. ◆'**A~efall**, *m* exception, exceptional case. ◆'**A~ezustand**, *m* state of emergency. ◆'**a~slos**, *adv.* without exception. ◆'**a~sweise**, *adv.* as an exception; for once.

'**ausnehmen**, *v.tr.sep.irr.69* (*a*) to take (sth.) out; to gut (a fish etc.); (*b*) (*ausschließen*) to exclude, exempt (s.o.); (*c*) *P:* (*Geld abnehmen*) to fleece (s.o.); (*d*) *v.refl.* **sich gut/schlecht** a., (*Pers.*) make a good/bad impression. ◆'**a~d**, *adv.* exceptionally.

'**ausnutz|en**, *v.tr.sep.* (*a*) to exploit (a source of energy etc.); to utilize (time etc.); (*b*) *Pej:* to take advantage of (s.o.). ◆'**A~ung**, *f /no pl* exploitation.

'**auspacken**, *v.tr.sep.* to unpack (goods, clothes), unwrap (presents).

'**auspfeifen**, *v.tr.sep.irr.43* to boo.

'**ausplaudern**, *v.tr.sep.* to let out.

'**auspressen**, *v.tr.sep.* to squeeze (a lemon etc.), squeeze out (juice etc.).

'**ausprobieren**, *v.tr.sep.* to try (sth.) out.

'**Auspuff. I.** *m -(e)s/-e* exhaust (system).

II. **'A~-**, *comb.fm.* exhaust (pipe etc.).
◆**'A~topf**, *m* silencer, *N.Am:* muffler.
'ausradieren, *v.tr.sep.* to rub out.
'ausrangieren, *v.tr.sep. F:* to chuck out.
'ausrauben, *v.tr.sep.* to rob (s.o.); to loot (a shop); to empty (the till).
'ausräumen, *v.tr.sep.* to turn out (a drawer etc.); to clear (a room).
'ausrechnen, *v.tr.sep.* to work out.
'Ausrede, *f* excuse. ◆**a~n**, *v.sep.* 1. *v.i.* (*haben*) to finish speaking; **laß mich a.!** let me finish! 2. *v.tr.* **j-m etwas a.** a., to talk s.o. out of sth.
'ausreichen, *v.i.sep.* (*sein*) to suffice, be enough. ◆**'a~d**, *adj.* sufficient.
'Ausreise, *f* departure. ◆**'A~genehmigung**, *f/'A~visum*, *m* exit visa. ◆**a~n**, *v.i.sep.* (*sein*) to leave the country.
'ausreiß|en, *v.sep.irr.4* 1. *v.tr.* to pull/tear (sth.) out; to uproot (a plant etc.). 2. *v.i.* (*sein*) *F:* to run away (from home etc.), escape (from prison). ◆**'A~r**, *m -s/-* runaway.
'ausrenk|en, *v.tr.sep.* **sich** *dat* **die Schulter usw. a.,** to dislocate one's shoulder etc.
'ausrichten, *v.tr.sep.* (*a*) to align (sth.); (*b*) (*mitteilen*) **j-m etwas a.,** to tell s.o. sth.; **kann ich etwas a.?** can I take a message? (*c*) (*erreichen*) to achieve (sth.).
'ausrotten, *v.tr.sep.* to wipe out (a race etc.); *Fig:* to eradicate (abuses etc.). ◆**'A~ung**, *f -/no pl* extermination.
'ausrücken, *v.i.sep.* (*sein*) *Mil:* to march off; (*Feuerwehr*) to be called out; *F:* (*Pers.*) to run away.
'Ausruf, *m* exclamation. ◆**'a~en**, *v.sep.irr.74* 1. *v.i.* (*haben*) to exclaim. 2. *v.tr.* (*a*) to call out (names etc.); (*im Hotel usw.*) **j-n a. lassen**, to page s.o.; (*b*) to proclaim (a state of emergency etc.), call (a strike). ◆**'A~ezeichen**, *n* exclamation mark.
'ausruhen, *v. refl.* **sich a.,** to rest.
'ausrüst|en, *v.tr.sep.* to equip. ◆**'A~ung**, *f* equipment.
'ausrutschen, *v.i.sep.* to slide, slip.
'Aussage ['auszaːgə], *f -/-n* statement. ◆**'a~n**, *v.sep.* 1. *v.tr.* to state (sth.). 2. *v.i.* (*haben*) to make a statement; **vor Gericht a.**, to give evidence in court.
'Aussätzige(r) ['auszɛtsigə(r)], *m & f decl. as adj.* leper.
'ausschacht|en, *v.tr.sep.* to dig. ◆**'A~ung**, *f -/-en* excavation.
'ausschalten, *v.tr.sep.* (*a*) to switch/turn off (the light, radio etc.); (*b*) *Fig:* to eliminate (a competitor, mistakes etc.).
'Ausschank, *m -(e)s/-̈e* (*a*) sale of alcoholic drinks; (*b*) (*Theke*) bar.
'Ausschau, *f* **nach j-m, etwas A. halten,** to keep a lookout for s.o., sth. ◆**'a~en**, *v.i.sep.* (*haben*) **nach j-m a.**, to look out for s.o.
'ausscheid|en, *v.sep.irr.56* 1. *v.tr.* to

eliminate (sth. unsatisfactory); to excrete (waste matter). 2. *v.i.* (*sein*) to retire; *Fig:* **diese Alternative scheidet aus**, this alternative can be eliminated. ◆**'A~ung**, *f -/-en* 1. (*Körpera~ung*) excretion. 2. *Ch:* precipitation. 3. *Sp:* (*a*) elimination; (*b*) (*A~ungsrunde*) qualifying round. ◆**'A~ungsspiel**, *n* qualifying match/tie.
'ausschenken, *v.tr.sep.* to pour out, (*verkaufen*) sell (drinks).
'ausscheren, *v.i.sep.* (*sein*) to pull out.
'ausschlachten, *v.tr.sep.* (*a*) *F:* to cannibalize (a car, machine etc.); (*b*) *Pej: F:* exploit (a situation).
'ausschlafen, *v.sep.irr.84* 1. *v.i.* **sich a.**, to have a lie-in; (*b*) **seinen Rausch usw. a.**, to sleep off the effects of alcohol etc. 2. *v.i.* (*haben*) **ich habe noch nicht ausgeschlafen**, I have not slept enough.
'Ausschlag, *m* 1. *Med:* rash. 2. *Ph:* deflection (of a compass needle etc.). 3. **den A. geben**, to tip the balance. ◆**'a~en**, *v.sep.irr.85* 1. *v.tr.* (*a*) (*haben*) (*Pferd usw.*) to kick out; (*Pflanzen*) to sprout; (*Kompaßnadel usw.*) to show a deflection. 2. *v.tr.* (*a*) to knock out (s.o.'s teeth etc.); (*b*) to line (a box etc.); (*c*) (*ablehnen*) to reject, decline (an offer etc.). ◆**'a~gebend**, *adj.* decisive.
'ausschließ|en, *v.sep.irr.31* 1. *v.tr.* (*a*) to lock/shut (s.o.) out; (*b*) **j-n von/aus etwas** *dat* **a.**, to exclude/(*aus Partei*) expel s.o. from sth.; (*c*) to rule out (a possibility etc.). ◆**'a~lich**. **I.** *adj.* exclusive (right etc.). **II.** *prep. + gen.* exclusive of. ◆**'A~lichkeit**, *f -/no pl* exclusivity.
'Ausschluß, *m* exclusion; *Pol: Sch:* expulsion; *Sp:* suspension.
'ausschmück|en, *v.tr.sep.* to decorate (a room etc.); *Fig:* to embellish (sth.).
'ausschneiden, *v.tr.sep.irr.59* to cut (sth.) out.
'Ausschnitt, *m* 1. extract (*Zeitungsa.*) cutting. 2. neckline.
'ausschreiben, *v.tr.sep.irr.12* (*a*) to write out (a word); to make out (a cheque, prescription etc.); (*b*) to advertise (a post, competition etc.).
'Ausschreitung, *f -/-en esp. pl* **A~en**, excesses.
'Ausschuß, *m* 1. *Pol: etc:* committee. 2. *no pl Com:* (*also* **A~ware** *f*) rejects.
'ausschütten, *v.tr.sep.* (*a*) to pour out; to empty (a bucket etc.); (*b*) *Com:* to pay out (dividends etc.); (*c*) **sich vor Lachen a.**, to fall about laughing.
'ausschweif|en, *v.i.sep.* (*sein*) to indulge in excesses. ◆**a~end**, *adj.* dissolute, debauched (life); licentious (thoughts); *Fig:* extravagant (imagination). ◆**'A~ung**, *f -/-en* excess.
'ausschweigen, *v.refl.sep.irr.89* (*haben*) to maintain silence.
'aussehen. **I.** *v.i.sep.irr.92* (*haben*) to look; **nach etwas** *dat* **a.**, to look like sth.; **es sieht aus, als ob ...**, it looks as

though ...; F: **das Kleid sieht nach nichts aus**, the dress doesn't look anything special; **so siehst du aus!** you can think again! II. **A.**, *n* -*s*/*no pl* appearance; *F:* looks.

außen ['ausən]. I. *adv.* (on the) outside; **nach a. aufgehen**, to open outwards. II. **'A~-**, *comb.fm.* (*a*) (*äußere von zwei*) outer (wall, surface etc.); (*b*) exterior (lighting, angle etc.); outside (pocket, staircase, *Sp:* lane etc.); (*c*) foreign (trade, policy etc.). ◆**'A~bezirk**, *m* (outer) suburb. ◆**'A~bordmotor**, *m* outboard motor. ◆**'A~dienst**, *m* field work. ◆**'A~handel**, *m* foreign trade. ◆**'A~minister**, *m* foreign minister. ◆**'A~ministerium**, *n* foreign ministry. ◆**'A~politik**, *f* foreign policy. ◆**'a~politisch**, *adj.* with regard to foreign policy. ◆**'A~seite**, *f* outside. ◆**'A~seiter**, *m* outsider; *Fig:* (*Pers.*) misfit. ◆**'A~stehende(r)**, *m & f decl. as adj.* bystander. ◆**'A~welt**, *f* outside world.

'aussenden, *v.tr.sep.irr.94* (*a*) to send out (s.o., a patrol etc.); (*b*) to emit (rays, heat).

außer ['ausər]. I. *prep.* + *dat* 1. out of; **a. Hause essen**, to have a meal out; **a. Betrieb**, not working; *Fig:* (**vor Wut usw.**) **a. sich**, beside oneself (with rage etc.); **a. sich geraten**, to lose one's self-control. 2. (*a*) except (for); **alle a. einem**, all except one. II. *conj.* except; **a. wenn es regnet**, unless it rains. ◆**a~dem**, I. *adv.* (*noch dazu*) in addition, as well. II. *conj.* moreover. ◆**'a~ehelich**, *adj.* extra-marital. ◆**'a~gewöhnlich**, *adj.* exceptional. ◆**'a~halb**, *prep.* + *gen & adv.* outside. ◆**'a~ordentlich**, *adj.* extraordinary (situation, session etc.); exceptional (person, actor etc.); unscheduled. ◆**a~'stand(e)**, *adv.* **a. sein**, **etwas zu tun**, to be unable/in no position to do sth.

äußere(r,s) ['ɔysərə], *adj.* outer (layer, margin etc.); external (circumstances, appearance etc.).

äußerlich ['ɔysərliç], *adj.* (*a*) outward (appearance etc.); external (feature, use etc.); (*b*) *Fig:* (*oberflächlich*) superficial. ◆**'A~keit**, *f* -/-en outward characteristic; *pl* **A~en**, minor matters.

äußer|n ['ɔysərn], *v.tr.* (*a*) to express (an opinion, wish etc.); (*b*) **sich über etwas** *acc* **ä.**, to comment on sth.; (*c*) (*Merkmale*) **sich in etwas** *dat* **ä.**, to be apparent in sth. ◆**'A~ung**, *f* -/-en (*a*) (*Behauptung*) statement; comment; (*b*) (*Ausdruck*) expression (of sth.).

äußerst ['ɔysərst]. 1. *adv.* extremely. 2. *adj.* **ä~e(r,s)** (*a*) (*Ort*) furthest (end, limits etc.); (*b*) (*höchste*) (absolute) maximum (price, load etc.); extreme (danger, poverty etc.); supreme (effort, concentration); utmost (importance, caution etc.); **zum Ä~en entschlossen**, determined to

try anything; (*c*) (*schlimmste*) worst; **im ä~en Fall**, if the worst comes to the worst. ◆**'ä~en|falls**, *adv.* at the most/ worst.

'aussetz|en, *v.sep.* 1. *v.tr.* (*a*) to abandon (a child, dog etc.); (*b*) **j-n/sich einer Gefahr usw. a.**, to expose s.o./oneself to a danger etc.; (*c*) (*kritisieren*) **etwas an j-m auszusetzen haben**, to find fault with s.o.; (*d*) *Jur:* to suspend (proceedings etc.). 2. *v.i.* (*haben*) (*a*) to stop (suddenly); (*Motor*) to cut out; (*b*) to make a pause. ◆**'A~ung**, *f* -/-en (*a*) abandoning; (*b*) *Jur:* suspension.

'Aussicht, *f* (*a*) view; (*b*) *Fig:* prospect; *usu. pl* outlook; **j-m etwas in A. stellen**, to promise s.o. sth. ◆**'a~slos**, *adj.* hopeless (situation etc.); doomed (venture etc.). ◆**'A~spunkt**, *m* vantage point. ◆**'a~sreich**, *adj.* promising.

'aussiedeln, *v.tr.sep.* to evacuate, resettle.

'aussöhnen, *v.tr.sep.* to reconcile; **sich a.**, to become reconciled.

'aussortieren, *v.tr.sep.* to sort out (washing etc.), eliminate (unwanted items).

'ausspann|en, *v.sep.* 1. *v.tr.* to unhitch (a horse etc.); (*b*) to spread out (a net, wings etc.); to stretch (a rope etc.); (*c*) *F:* **j-m den Freund a.**, to steal s.o.'s boyfriend. 2. *v.i.* (*haben*) to relax.

'ausspar|en, *v.tr.sep.* to leave (sth.) empty/(a space) blank; to leave out.

'aussperr|en, *v.tr.sep.* to shut/lock (s.o.) out. ◆**'A~ung**, *f* -/-en Ind: lock-out.

'ausspiel|en, *v.tr. & i.sep.* (*haben*) (*a*) (*Kartenspiel*) to lead; (*b*) *Fig:* **j-n gegen j-n a.**, to play s.o. off against s.o. ◆**'A~ung**, *f* -/-en draw (of a lottery).

'Aussprache, *f* -/-en 1. pronunciation; (*Akzent*) accent. 2. discussion; **eine offene A.**, a frank exchange of views.

'aussprech|en, *v.sep.irr.14* 1. *v.tr.* (*a*) to pronounce (a word etc.); (*b*) to express (a wish, one's gratitude etc.); to deliver (a judgement); (*c*) **sich mit j-m a.**, to have a heart-to-heart (talk) with s.o.; **sich für/ gegen etwas** *acc* **a.**, to come out in favour of/against sth. 2. *v.i.* (*haben*) to finish speaking.

ausstaffieren [ausʃtaˈfiːrən], *v.tr.sep.* to rig (s.o, sth.) out.

'ausstatt|en, *v.tr.sep.* to provide (s.o., sth.) (**mit etwas** *dat*, with sth.); to equip (an office etc.). ◆**'A~ung**, *f* -/-en (*a*) (*Ausrüstung*) equipment; (*Kleider usw.*) outfit; (*b*) *Th:* scenery and costumes.

'ausstechen, *v.tr.sep.irr.14* (*a*) to cut (turf etc.); (*b*) (*übertreffen*) to outdo (s.o.).

'ausstehen, *v.sep.irr.100* 1. *v.tr.* to endure (pains, anxiety etc.); **ich kann ihn nicht a.**, I can't stand him. 2. *v.i.* (*haben*) (*Rechnungen usw.*) to be outstanding; (*Entscheidung*) to be pending.

'aussteigen, *v.i.sep.irr.89* (*sein*) (*a*) to get out (of a car), get off (a bus, plane etc.); (*b*) *F:* to drop out.

'ausstell|en, *v.tr.sep.* (*a*) to display (goods

etc.); to exhibit (pictures, products etc.); (b) to issue (a passport etc.); to make out (a cheque, bill etc.). ◆'**A~ung,** f 1. display; (Schau) show; Art: etc: exhibition. 2. Adm: issue.

'**aussterben,** v.i.sep.irr.101 (sein) to die out; Z: (Gattungen) to become extinct.

'**Aussteuer,** f dowry.

'**Ausstieg,** m -(e)s/-e exit.

'**ausstopfen,** v.tr.sep. to pad out (a cushion etc.); to stuff (an animal).

'**Ausstoß,** m (a) discharge; (b) Ind: output. ◆'**a~en,** v.tr. sep.irr.103 (a) (Schlot usw.) to emit (smoke, fumes etc.); (b) to expel, (aus der Gesellschaft) ostracize (s.o.).

'**ausstrahl|en,** v.sep. 1. v.tr. (a) to give out; (b) Rad: TV: to broadcast (a programme). 2. v.i. (sein) von/aus etwas dat a., to radiate from sth. ◆'**A~ung,** f (a) radiation; (b) Rad: TV: broadcast; (c) Fig: effect of an event etc.); charisma (of a person).

'**ausstrecken,** v.tr.sep. to stretch out.

'**ausstreichen,** v.tr.sep.irr.40 to cross out, delete.

'**ausströmen,** v.sep. 1. v.tr. to give off; Fig: to radiate (love etc.). 2. v.i. (sein) (Wasser, Gase usw.) to escape.

'**aussuchen,** v.tr.sep. to pick out, select (sth.).

'**Austausch,** m (a) exchange; (b) Tchn: replacement (of machine parts etc.). ◆'**a~bar,** adj. exchangeable (goods etc.); Tchn: interchangeable (parts etc.). ◆'**a~en,** v.tr.sep. (a) to exchange; (b) (ersetzen) to replace (Tchn: a part, Sp: player etc.). ◆'**A~motor,** m replacement engine.

'**austeilen,** v.tr.sep. to deal out (cards etc.), to distribute (clothes etc.); to dish out (soup, Fig: praise etc.).

'**Auster,** f 'austər, f -/-n oyster.

'**austoben,** v.refl.sep. sich a., to let off steam.

'**austragen,** v.tr. sep.irr.85 (a) to hold (a race, contest etc.); (b) to settle (a quarrel etc.); (c) to deliver (newspapers etc.). ◆'**A~ung,** f -/-en 1. delivery. 2. Sp: staging of a game etc.).

Austral|ia ◆'A~ier(in), m -s/- (f -/-nen) Australian. ◆'a~isch, adj. Australian.

'**austreiben,** v.tr.sep.irr.12 (a) to drive (people etc.) out; (b) Fig: j-m eine Unart usw. a., to cure s.o. of a bad habit etc.; böse Geister a., to exorcize evil spirits.

'**austreten,** v.sep.irr.105 1. v.tr. to stamp out (a fire etc.); to wear down (a path, steps etc.). 2. v.i. (sein) (a) (Gas) to escape; (b) F: a. (gehen), to go for a pee; (c) aus der Kirche a., to leave the church.

'**austrinken,** v.tr.sep.irr.96 to drink up; to finish (a drink), drain (a glass etc.).

'**Austritt,** m (a) escape (of gas); (b) resignation, withdrawal (aus + dat, from).

'**austrocknen,** v.sep. 1. v.tr. to dry (sth.) thoroughly. 2. v.i. (sein) to dry out.

'**ausüb|en,** v.tr.sep. (a) to practise (a profession etc.); to carry on (an activity); (b) to exercise, exert (pressure, an influence etc.). ◆'**A~ung,** f performance; exercise.

'**Ausverkauf,** m (clearance) sale. ◆'**a~en,** v.tr.sep. to clear (goods). ◆'**a~t,** adj. sold out.

'**Auswahl,** f (a) choice, selection; (b) range, assortment (of goods etc.); (c) Sp: picked team.

'**auswählen,** v.tr.sep. to choose, select.

'**Auswander|er,** m emigrant. ◆'**a~n,** v.i.sep. (sein) to emigrate. ◆'**A~ung,** f -/-en emigration.

'**auswärt|ig** ['ausvɛrtiç], adj. (a) non-local; a~ige Besucher, visitors from another town; (b) (ausländisch) foreign; das A~ige Amt, the (West German) foreign ministry. ◆'**a~s,** adv. (a) away from home; a. essen, to eat out; Sp: a. spielen, to play away; (b) er wohnt a., he lives out of town. ◆'**A~sspiel,** n away match.

'**auswechseln** v.tr.sep. to replace (a part etc.); Fb: to substitute (a player).

'**Ausweg,** m -(e)s/-e solution; als letzter A., as a last resort. ◆'**a~los,** adj. hopeless.

'**ausweichen,** v.i.sep.irr.40 (sein) j-m, der Versuchung usw. a., to avoid s.o., temptation etc.; einem Auto usw. a., to get out of the way of a car etc.; Fig: einem Thema usw. a., to evade an issue etc. ◆'**a~end,** adj. evasive.

'**ausweinen,** v.refl.sep. sich a., to have a good cry.

Ausweis ['ausvais], m -es/-e identification; (Personala) identity card. ◆'**A~papiere,** npl identification papers. ◆'**a~en,** v.tr.sep.irr.70 (a) j-n, sich a., to prove s.o.'s, one's identity; (b) (aus dem Land) to deport (s.o.). ◆'**A~ung,** f -/-en deportation.

'**ausweiten,** v.tr.sep. (a) to widen (a gap), enlarge (a hole etc.); to stretch (a glove, shoes etc.); (b) Fig: to expand.

'**auswendig,** adv. by heart.

'**auswert|en,** v.tr.sep. to evaluate (statistics etc.); to utilize (experiences etc.). ◆'**A~ung,** f -/-en evaluation; utilization.

'**auswirk|en,** v.refl.sep. sich auf etwas acc a., to have an effect/impact on sth. ◆'**A~ung,** f effect, impact.

'**auswischen,** v.tr.sep. (a) to wipe off (words on a blackboard etc.); (b) F: j-m eins a., to put one over on s.o.

'**Auswuchs,** m Fig: esp. pl A~e, excesses; das ist ein A. Ihrer Phantasie, that is a figment of your imagination.

'**auswuchten,** v.tr.sep. to balance.

'**auszahlen,** v.tr.sep. (a) to pay out (money), to pay off (creditors, workmen); to buy out (a business partner); (b)

Fig: sich a., to be worth it.

'**auszeichn|en**, *v.tr.sep.* (a) *Com:* to price (goods); (b) to honour (s.o.); (c) (*unterscheiden*) to distinguish (s.o., oneself, sth.). ◆'**A~ung**, *f* -/-en 1. *Com:* pricing. 2. (a) (*Ehrung*) distinction; award of a prize etc.; (b) (*Preis, Orden*) award.

'**ausziehen**, *v.sep.irr.113* 1. *v.tr.* (a) to pull out (a nail etc.); to extend (a table etc.); (b) to take off (clothes); j-n/sich a., to undress s.o./oneself. 2. *v.i.* (*sein*) to move out (of a house). ◆'**A~tisch**, *m* draw-leaf table.

'**Auszubildende(r)**, *m & f decl. as adj.* trainee.

'**Auszug**, *m* 1. move, removal (from a house etc.). 2. (*Ausschnitt*) excerpt, extract. 3. (*Kontoa.*) statement.

Auto ['auto]. I. *n* -s/-s car; **A. fahren**, to drive (a car). II. '**A~**, *comb.fm.* (a) car (ferry, dealer, tyre, key, insurance etc.); motor (industry, traffic etc.); (b) road (at-

las etc.). ◆'**A~bahn**, *f* motorway, *N.Am:* freeway. ◆'**A~bus**, *m* bus; (*für lange Strecken*) coach. ◆'**A~fahrer(in)**, *m* (f) driver (of a car); motorist. ◆**A~gramm** ['gram], *n* autograph. ◆**A~mat** ['moːt], *m* -en/-en vending machine. ◆**A~'matik**, *f* -/-en automatic mechanism; *Aut:* automatic transmission. ◆**a~matisch** ['-maːtiʃ], *adj.* automatic. ◆**A~nom** ['noːm], *adj.* autonomous. ◆'**A~nummer**, *f* registration number. ◆'**A~radio**, *n* car radio. ◆'**A~rennen**, *n* motor race. ◆'**A~unfall**, *m* car accident. ◆'**A~verleih**, *m* car hire. ◆'**A~werkstatt**, *f* garage.

Autopsie [autɔp'siː], *f* -/-n autopsy.

Autor ['autɔr], *m* -s/-en ['toːrən] author. ◆**A~in** ['toːrin], *f* -/-nen authoress. ◆**a~i'sieren**, *v.tr.* to authorize. ◆**a~itär** [-'iˈtɛːr], *adj.* authoritarian. ◆**A~ität** [-iˈtɛːt], *f* -/-en authority.

Axt [akst], *f* -/**Äxte** axe.

B

B, b [beː], *n* -/- (the letter) B, b.

Baby ['beːbi], *n* -s/-s baby.

Bach [bax], *m* -(e)s/⁻e stream. ◆**B~stelze**, *f* wagtail.

Back- [bak-], *comb.fm.* baking (powder etc.). ◆'**B~blech**, *n* baking sheet. ◆'**B~bord**, *n Nau:* port (side). ◆**b~en**, *v.tr.irr.* to bake (bread etc.), make (a cake, biscuits etc.). ◆'**B~fisch**, *m Cu:* fried fish. ◆'**B~obst**, *n* dried fruit. ◆'**B~ofen**, *m* (baker's/ kitchen) oven. ◆'**B~pflaume**, *f* prune. ◆'**B~röhr**, *n*/◆'**B~röhre**, *f* oven. ◆'**B~stein**, *m* (red) brick. ◆'**B~waren**, *fpl* bakery products.

Back|e ['bakə], *f* -/-n 1. cheek. 2. *Tchn:* (a) jaw (of a vice etc.); (b) (*Bremsb.*) brake shoe. ◆'**B~enbart**, *m* side-whiskers. ◆'**B~enzahn**, *m* molar.

Bäcker ['bɛkər], *m* -s/- baker. ◆**B~ei** [-'rai], *f* -/-en bakery; baker's shop.

Bad [baːt], *n* -(e)s/⁻er 1. (a) bath; (b) (*im Meer usw.*) swim, dip. 2. (a) (*B~ezimmer*) bathroom; (b) (*Schwimmb.*) (swimming) pool. 3. (*Kurort*) spa. ◆**B~e-** ['baːdə-], *comb.fm.* (a) bathing (cap, things, beach etc.); (b) (*fürs Bad*) bath (mat etc.). ◆'**B~eanstalt**, *f* swimming-baths. ◆'**B~eanzug**, *m* bathing suit. ◆'**B~ehose**, *f* bathing/ swimming trunks. ◆'**B~emantel**, *m* bathrobe. ◆'**B~emeister**, *m* swimming-pool attendant. ◆'**B~en**, *v.* 1. *v.i.* (*haben*) (a) (kalt/warm) b., to have a (cold/warm) bath; (b) (*schwimmen*) to bathe; *F:* (bei/mit etwas *dat*) b. gehen, to come a cropper (with sth.). 2. *v.tr.* to bath (a baby etc.); to bathe (a wound, eyes etc.). ◆'**B~eort**, *m* 1. seaside re-

sort. 2. (*Kurort*) spa. ◆'**B~etuch**, *n* bath towel. ◆'**B~ewanne**, *f* bath tub. ◆'**B~ezimmer**, *n* bathroom.

baff [baf], *adj. F:* flabbergasted.

Bagatelle [baga'tɛlə], *f* -/-n trifle; trifling matter/(*Geld*) sum.

Bagger ['bagər], *m* -s/- (*für das Flußbett*) dredger; (*für Erde*) excavator. ◆'**b~n**, *v.tr. & i.* (*haben*) to excavate. ◆'**B~see**, *m* (water-filled) gravel pit.

Bahn [baːn]. I. *f* -/-en 1. way, path; **auf die schiefe B. geraten**, to fall into bad ways. 2. *Astr:* course (of a star); orbit (of a planet); path (of a comet). 3. (a) *Sp:* (*Rennb.*) (race/running) track; (b) (*Fahrb.*) carriageway (of a road). 4. width (of material, wallpaper etc.). 5. (a) *Rail:* **mit der B. fahren**, to travel by train/rail; (b) (*Straßenb.*) tram. II. '**B~**, *comb.fm.* railway, *N.Am:* railroad (worker, official, line etc.); rail (connection). ◆'**b~brechend**, *adj.* revolutionary (idea, discovery etc.). ◆'**B~damm**, *m* railway embankment. ◆'**b~en**, *v.tr.* **sich** *dat* **einen Weg b.**, to clear a way/ path. ◆'**B~hof**, *m* (railway) station. ◆'**B~hofshalle**, *f* station concourse. ◆'**B~hofsvorsteher**, *m* station master. ◆'**B~schranke**, *f* level crossing barrier. ◆'**B~steig**, *m* platform. ◆'**B~übergang**, *m* level crossing. ◆'**B~wärter**, *m* crossing keeper.

Bahre ['baːrə], *f* -/-n stretcher; (*für Tote*) bier.

Bajonett [bajo'nɛt], *n* -(e)s/-e bayonet.

Bake ['baːkə], *f* -/-n beacon.

Bakterien [bak'teːriən], *fpl* bacteria, *F:* germs.

Balance [ba'lãːsə], *f* -/-n balance. ◆**B~akt**, *m* balancing act.

◆**b~ieren** [-'si:rən], v.tr. & i. (haben) to balance.

bald [balt], adv. **1.** soon; **b. darauf,** shortly afterwards; F: **bis b.!** see you soon! **2.** F: (beinahe) almost. **3. b. ..., b. ...,** now ... now ... ◆**b~ig** ['baldiç], adj. speedy.

Baldrian ['baldria:n], m -s/-e valerian.

balgen ['balgən], v.refl. **sich b.,** to tussle, scuffle.

Balkan ['balka:n]. Pr.n.m. **-s der B.,** the Balkans.

Balken ['balkən], m -s/- beam; (Stahl) girder.

Balkon [bal'kɔŋ], m -s/-s & -e **1.** balcony. **2.** Th: dress circle.

Ball¹ [bal]. I. m -(e)s/æ ball. II. **B~,** comb.fm. ball (game, boy etc.). ◆**b~en,** v.tr. (a) to form, press (snow, paper etc.) into a ball; **die (Hand zur) Faust b.,** to clench one's fist; (b) sich b., to gather (into a ball); (Wolken) to gather, mass. ◆**B~ung,** f -/-en compression; concentration; massing (of clouds etc.). ◆**B~ungsgebiet,** n densely populated (industrial) region.

Ball², m -(e)s/æ dance, ball. ◆**B~saal,** m ballroom.

Ballade [ba'la:də], f -/-n ballad.

Ballast [ba'last, balast], m -(e)s/no pl ballast; Fig: dead wood, lumber. ◆**B~stoffe,** mpl roughage.

Ballen ['balən], m -s/- **1.** Com: etc: bale (of straw, paper etc.). **2.** Anat: ball (of the hand/foot).

Ballett [ba'lɛt], n -(e)s/-e ballet. ◆**Ba'llettänzer,** m (male) ballet dancer. ◆**Ba'llettänzerin,** f ballerina.

Ballistik [ba'listik], f -/no pl ballistics.

Ballon [ba'lɔŋ], m -s/-s & -e balloon.

Balsam ['balza:m], m -s/-e balsam; Fig: balm.

Bambus ['bambus], m -ses/-se bamboo.

banal [ba'na:l], adj. commonplace, trite (remark etc.); trivial, banal (story etc.). ◆**B~i'tät,** f -/-en (a) no pl triteness; triviality; (b) trite remark.

Banane [ba'na:nə], f -/-n banana. ◆**B~nschale,** f banana skin.

Banause [ba'nauzə], m -n/-n philistine.

Band¹ [bant]. I. n -(e)s/æer **1.** (a) tape; (als Zierde) ribbon; (b) (metal) strip (for packing etc.); (c) hoop (of a barrel); (c) Rec: (magnetic) tape; (Fließb.) conveyor belt; F: **Fehler am laufenden B.,** one mistake after the other; (e) Anat: ligament; (f) Rad: waveband. **2.** m -(e)s/æe (Buch) volume. **3.** n -(e)s/-e (usu. pl) Lit: bond, tie (of friendship, love etc.). II. **B~,** comb.fm. tape (recording etc.). ◆**B~gerät,** n tape recorder. ◆**B~maß,** n tape measure. ◆**B~säge,** f band-saw. ◆**B~scheibe,** f intervertebral disc.

Band² [bɛnt, bænd], f -/-s band.

Bandage [ban'da:ʒə], f -/-n bandage. ◆**b~ieren** [-da'ʒi:rən], v.tr. to bandage

(a sprained wrist etc.).

Bande ['bandə], f -/-n (a) gang (of thieves, thugs etc.); (b) F: bunch (of people).

bändigen ['bɛndigən], v.tr. (a) to tame (a wild animal); (b) to control (a child, scared animal); Fig: to curb (one's anger etc.).

Bandit [ban'di:t], m -en/-en bandit, gangster.

bang(e) ['baŋ(ə)], adj. (a) anxious; **mir wurde angst und b.,** I got scared. ◆**b~en,** v.i. (haben) Lit: **um j-n, etwas acc b.,** to be anxious about s.o., sth.

Bank¹ [baŋk], f -/æe **1.** bench. **2.** (im Meer) (sand/mud)bank; (oyster)bed.

Bank². I. f -/-en Fin: bank. II. **B~,** comb.fm. bank (account etc.). ◆**B~direktor,** m bank manager. ◆**B~ier** [-ki'e:], m -s/-s banker. ◆**B~note,** f banknote; N.Am: bill. ◆**B~rott** [-'krɔt]. I. m -s/-e Jur: & Fig: bankruptcy; **B. machen,** to go bankrupt. II. b., adj. Jur: bankrupt; F: (Pers.) broke. ◆**B~überfall,** m bank robbery.

Bankett¹ [baŋ'kɛt], n -(e)s/-e banquet.

Bankett², n -(e)s/-e verge (of road).

Bann [ban], m -(e)s/-e **1.** spell; Fig: **j-n in seinen B. ziehen/schlagen,** to cast one's spell over s.o. **2.** Ecc: (decree of) excommunication. ◆**b~en,** v.tr. (a) to exorcize (ghosts); Fig: to hold (s.o.) spellbound.

Banner ['banər], n -s/- banner; standard.

Bar¹ [ba:r], f -/-s bar. ◆**B~dame,** f barmaid. ◆**B~hocker,** m bar stool. ◆**B~keeper,** m -s/- barman.

bar². I. adj. **1. b~es Geld,** cash; (etwas) (in) b. bezahlen, to pay cash (for sth.). **2.** Lit: bare (head etc.). II. **B~,** comb.fm. cash (payment, sale, transaction, purchase etc.). ◆**b~fuß,** adv. /'b~füßig, adj. barefoot. ◆**B~geld,** n cash. ◆**b~geldlos,** adj. **b~geldloser Zahlungsverkehr,** credit transactions. ◆**B~schaft,** f -/-en ready money. ◆**B~scheck,** m uncrossed cheque/N.Am: check.

Bär [bɛ:r], m -en/-en bear. ◆**b~beißig,** adj. surly, grumpy.

Baracke [ba'rakə], f -/-n hut; hutment; Pej: shanty.

barbarisch [bar'ba:riʃ], adj. (a) barbaric, barbarous; (b) F: dreadful (cold, hunger etc.).

Bariton ['ba:ritɔn], m -s/-e baritone.

Barkasse [bar'kasə], f -/-n launch.

barmherzig [barm'hɛrtsiç], adj. merciful; (mitfühlend) compassionate. ◆**B~keit,** f -/no pl mercy, compassion.

Barometer [baro'me:tər], n -s/- barometer.

Baron [ba'ro:n], m -s/-e baron. ◆**B~in,** f -/-nen baroness.

Barren ['barən], m -s/- **1.** (Gold usw.) bar, ingot. **2.** Sp: parallel bars.

Barriere [bari'ɛ:rə], f -/-n barrier.

Barrikade [bari'ka:də], f -/-n barricade.

barsch[1] [barʃ], adj. gruff; (kurz angebunden) curt.

Barsch[2], m -(e)s/-e perch.

Bart [ba:rt], m -(e)s/-e 1. beard. 2. web (of a key).

bärtig ['bɛ:rtɪç], adj. bearded.

Basar [ba'za:r], m -s/-e bazaar.

basieren [ba'zi:rən], v.i. (haben) auf etwas dat b., to be based on sth.

Basis ['ba:zɪs], f -/Basen base; (Grundlage) basis.

Baskenmütze ['baskənmytsə], f beret.

Basketball ['ba:(:)skətbal], m & n basketball.

Baß [bas], m -sses/-sse 1. bass. 2. (Instrument) double bass.

Bassin [ba'sɛ̃, ba'sɛ], n -s/-s pool.

Bast [bast], m -(e)s/-e raffia.

basta ['basta], int. F: b.! enough!

bastel|n ['bastəln], v. 1. v.i. (haben) (a) to do (home) handicrafts; (b) an etwas dat b., to tinker (around) with sth. 2. v.tr. to make, F: knock up (sth.). ◆'B~ler, m -s/- handicraft enthusiast; (Heimwerker) do-it-yourselfer.

Batterie [batə'ri:], f -/-n battery.

Bau [bau]. I. m -(e)s/no pl (a) construction (of roads, houses etc.); im B., under construction; (b) (Baustelle) building site; (c) Fig: (Aufbau) structure (of a play etc.); (d) (Körperbau) build. 2. -(e)s/-ten building, edifice. 3. -(e)s/-e (a) burrow (of a rabbit); earth (of a fox); (b) Min: pit. II. 'B~-, comb.fm. (a) building (firm, costs, material etc.); (b) structural (engineer, steel, drawing etc.). ◆'B~arbeiter, m building worker. ◆'B~art, f (a) architectural style; (b) = Bauweise; (c) Ind: design (of machine etc.). ◆'b~en, v. 1. v.tr. (a) to build (houses, a nest etc.); to construct (a machine, model etc.); to make (violins etc.); (Pers.) kräftig/schmal gebaut sein, to be of sturdy/slim build; (b) F: einen Unfall b., to have an accident. 2. v.i. (haben) (a) to build; (b) Fig: auf j-n b., to rely on/put one's faith in s.o. ◆'b~fällig, adj. dilapidated, tumbledown. ◆'B~gelände, n building site. ◆'B~genehmigung, f planning permission. ◆'B~gerüst, n scaffolding. ◆'B~herr, m initiator of a building project. ◆'B~jahr, n year of construction/manufacture; Aut: B. 1987, 1987 model. ◆'B~kasten, m (a) (child's) box of bricks; (Lego usw.) constructional toy; (b) (model) kit. ◆'B~leiter, m architect in charge. ◆'b~lich, adj. structural. ◆'B~satz, m kit (of parts). ◆'B~sparkasse, f building society. ◆'B~stein, m 1. building brick/stone. 2. Tchn: (Bestandteil) component; (Einheit) unit. ◆'B~stelle, f building site; (auf der Straße) roadworks. ◆'B~unternehmer, m building contractor.

◆'B~weise, f (method of) construction. ◆'B~werk, n building, edifice.

Bauch [baux]. I. m -(e)s/-e 1. abdomen; Pej: (dicker B.) paunch; F: (Magen) tummy. 2. (a) belly (of a vase etc.). II. 'B~-, comb.fm. belly (dancer, Av: landing etc.); Anat: abdominal (cavity, region etc.). ◆'b~ig, adj. bulbous (vase etc.). ◆'B~redner, m ventriloquist. ◆'B~schmerzen, mpl stomach ache. ◆'B~speicheldrüse, f pancreas.

Bauer ['bauər], m -n/-n 1. (a) farmer; (b) Pej: peasant. 2. (Schachspiel) pawn. ◆'B~nbrot, n coarse rye bread. ◆'B~nhaus, n farmhouse. ◆'B~nhof, m farm.

Bäuer|in ['bɔyərin], f -/-nen farmer's wife. ◆'b~lich, adj. rural; rustic (art etc.).

Baum [baum]. I. m -(e)s/-e tree. II. 'B~-, comb.fm. tree (roots etc.); (group) of trees. ◆'B~schule, f (tree) nursery. ◆'B~stamm, m tree trunk. ◆'B~stumpf, m tree stump. ◆'B~wolle, f cotton.

baumeln ['baumeln], v.i. (haben) to dangle.

Bausch ['bauʃ], m -(e)s/-e ball, wad (of cotton wool etc.); Fig: in B. und Bogen, wholesale, indiscriminately. ◆'b~en, v.tr. to puff (sth.) out; to fill (a sail); sich b., (Segel, Gardine usw.) to billow (out); (Kleider) to be baggy.

Bayer|(in) ['baiər(in)], m -n/-n (f -/-nen) Bavarian. ◆'b~(e)risch, adj. Bavarian. ◆'B~ern. Pr.n.n -s. Bavaria.

Bazille [ba'tsilə], f -/-n/B~us, m -/-illen bacillus.

beabsichtigen [bə'apzɪçtigən], v.tr. to intend (sth.).

be'acht|en, v.tr. (a) to observe (rules, regulations); (b) to heed (a warning etc.); j-n, etwas nicht b., to ignore s.o., sth. ◆b~lich, adj. considerable (sum, achievement etc.); important (position). ◆B~ung, f -/no pl 1. observation. 2. attention; B. verdienen, to be worthy of note.

Beamt|e(r) [bə'amtə(r)], m decl. as adj., B~in, f -/-nen official; (Funktionär) civil servant.

beanspruchen [bə'anʃpruxən], v.tr. (a) to claim (one's share, damages etc.); to take advantage of (s.o.'s help, hospitality etc.); to take up (space, time etc.); (b) to tax, strain (s.o.); Tchn: to stress (a machine etc.); stark beansprucht, (Stoff, Teppich usw.) subject to hard wear/Tchn: (Teil) heavy strain.

beanstand|en [bə'anʃtandən], v.tr. (a) to object to (sth.); (b) Com: to query (an invoice); to make a complaint about (goods). ◆B~ung, f -/-en objection (+to); complaint (+ gen, about).

beantragen [bə'antra:gən], v.tr. (a) to apply for (a permit etc.); (b) (bei einer

Sitzung) to propose (an adjournment etc.); b., daß ..., to move that ...; (c) *esp. Jur:* to call for, demand (a sentence etc.).

be'antwort|en, *v.tr.* to answer (a question, letter). ◆B~ung, f /-en answer.

be'arbeit|en, *v.tr.* (a) to work on, (*behandeln*) treat (sth.); *Ind:* to process (raw materials); (b) *Adm: Jur: etc:* to deal with, process (an application, a case etc.); (c) to edit (a book, text etc.); to adapt (a play etc.); *Mus:* to arrange (a piece). ◆B~ung, f /-en 1. *no pl* treatment; *Ind: Adm:* processing; *Lit:* adapting, revising; *Mus:* arranging; in B., (*Buch usw.*) in preparation; (*Fall*) being dealt with. 2. (*Ergebnis*) adaptation; (*Neub.*) revision; *Mus:* arrangement.

Beatmung [ba'?a:tmʊŋ], f /-no pl künstliche B., artificial respiration.

beaufsichtig|en [ba'?aʊfzɪçtɪgən], *v.tr.* to supervise. ◆B~ung, f /-en supervision.

beauftrag|en [ba'?aʊftra:gən], *v.tr.* to give (s.o.) the job (etwas zu tun, of doing sth.); to commission (an artist etc.); *Jur:* to brief (a lawyer); j-n mit einer Arbeit b., to assign a task to s.o. ◆B~te(r), m & f decl. as adj. representative; *Com:* agent.

be'bauen, *v.tr.* (a) to build on (a plot, piece of land); bebautes Gebiet, built-up area; (b) *Agr:* to farm (the land); to cultivate (a garden, field).

beben ['be:bən], *v.i.* (haben) to shake.

bebild|ern [ba'bɪldərt], *adj.* illustrated.

Becher ['bɛçər], m -s/- (a) (*Trinkb.*) beaker; (aus Glas) tumbler; (b) carton (of cream etc.); tub (of ice cream).

Becken ['bɛkən], n -s/- 1. (a) (wash)basin; (kitchen) sink; (WC) (lavatory) pan; (b) (*Bassin*) (swimming, paddling) pool. 2. *Mus:* cymbals. 3. *Anat:* pelvis.

bedacht [ba'daxt], adj. (a) careful, circumspect; (b) (*besorgt*) concerned (auf + acc, about); darauf b., etwas zu tun, intent on doing sth.

bedächtig [ba'dɛçtɪç], adj. deliberate, slow; (*Pers.*) thoughtful.

be'danken, *v.refl.* sich b., to express one's gratitude; sich bei j-m (für etwas acc) b., to thank s.o. for sth.

Bedarf [ba'darf], m -(e)s/no pl (a) need, *Com:* demand (an + dat, for); B. an etwas dat haben, to need sth.; bei B., if required; in case of need. ◆B~sfall m, im B., if necessary. ◆B~shaltestelle, f request stop.

bedauer|lich [ba'daʊərlɪç], adj. regrettable, unfortunate. ◆b~n. I. *v.tr.* (a) to feel sorry for (s.o.); er ist zu b., he is to be pitied; (b) to regret (sth.). II. B., n -s/no pl regret; mit B., regretfully. ◆b~nswert, adj. pitiable (person, condition); deplorable (situation etc.).

be'deck|en, *v.tr.* to cover (sth.); (*Himmel*)

sich b. to become overcast. ◆b~t, adj. covered; overcast (sky).

be'denk|en. I. *v.tr.irr.17* (a) (*überlegen*) to think (sth.) over; (b) (*berücksichtigen*) to bear (sth.) in mind. II. B., n -s/- thought, reflection; ohne B., without hesitation; B. haben (, etwas zu tun), to have doubts/reservations (about doing sth.); moralische B., scruples. ◆b~lich, adj. 1. (*Pers.*) thoughtful; doubtful (expression). 2. (a) (*verdächtig*) dubious (transaction etc.); (b) (*besorgniserregend*) worrying. ◆b~zeit, f /no pl time to think it over.

be'deut|en, *v.tr.* to mean (sth.); das hat nichts zu b., it is of no significance. ◆b~end, adj. important; distinguished (person); considerable (amount, sum). ◆b~sam, adj. (*bedeutend*) momentous. ◆B~ung, f /-en 1. (*Sinn*) meaning. 2. (*Wichtigkeit*) importance. ◆b~ungslos, adj. (a) meaningless; (b) unimportant. ◆b~ungsvoll, adj. significant.

be'dien|en, *v.tr.* (a) to serve, attend to (a customer, guest); bitte b. Sie sich! (do) help yourself! (b) to operate (a machine etc.); (c) sich j-s, etwas gen b., to make use of s.o., sth. ◆B~stete(r), m & f decl. as adj. employee. ◆B~ung, f -no pl 1. (a) service; (b) (*Kellnerin*) waitress. 2. operation (of a machine). ◆B~ungsanleitung, f operating instructions.

beding|en [ba'dɪŋən], *v.tr.* to cause (sth.); to bring (sth.) about. ◆b~t, p.p. & adj. (a) conditional (permission); qualified (praise, agreement etc.); (b) psychologisch b. sein, to have psychological causes. ◆B~ung, f /-en (a) condition, stipulation; unter der B., daß ..., on condition that ...; unter keiner B., on no account; (b) pl (*Verhältnisse*) conditions; (c) pl *Com:* terms. ◆b~ungslos, adj. unconditional (surrender, approval etc.); unquestioning (devotion, faith etc.).

be'drängen, *v.tr.* to press (s.o.) (hard); (*plagen*) to pester (s.o.).

be'droh|en, *v.tr.* to threaten (s.o., sth.). ◆b~lich, adj. threatening, menacing. ◆B~ung, f threat (des Friedens usw., to peace etc.).

be'drucken, *v.tr.* to print on (sth.); bedruckt, printed (notepaper, cotton).

be'drück|en, *v.tr.* to depress (s.o.); (*Sorgen usw.*) to weigh (heavily) on s.o. ◆b~end, adj. oppressive. ◆b~t, adj. depressed; downcast, subdued.

be'dürf|en, *v.tr.irr.20 Lit:* j-s, etwas b., to be in need of s.o., sth. ◆B~nis, n -ses/-se need, requirement. ◆B~nisanstalt, f public convenience. ◆b~nislos, adj. modest in one's requirements; frugal. ◆b~tig, adj. needy, poor. ◆B~tigkeit, f /no pl neediness, want.

beeiden [ba'?aɪdən], *v.tr.* to declare (sth.) on oath.

beeilen [bə'ʔailən], *v.refl.* **sich b.**, to hurry; **sich b., etwas zu tun**, to hasten to do sth.

beeindrucken [bə'ʔaindrukən], *v.tr.* to impress (s.o.).

beeinfluss|en [bə'ʔainflusən], *v.tr.* to influence. ◆**B~ung,** *f -/no pl* (use of) influence.

beeinträchtig|en [bə'ʔaintrɛçtigən], *v.tr.* to affect (s.o., sth.) (adversely); (*schädigen*) to damage (health etc.), encroach on (rights); (*mindern*) to lessen (effect, value); to impair (judgement etc.). ◆**B~ung,** *f -/-en* adverse effect (+*gen*, on); damage; encroachment.

beend|igen [bə'ʔɛnd(ig)ən], *v.tr.* to finish (sth.); to put an end to (a quarrel, s.o.'s career etc.).

beengen [bə'ʔɛŋən], *v.tr.* to restrict, hamper (s.o.'s movements, freedom etc.).

beerdig|en [bə'ʔerdigən], *v.tr.* to bury (a dead person). ◆**B~ung,** *f -/-en* burial; funeral. ◆**B~ungsunternehmen,** *n* (firm of) undertakers; *N.Am:* funeral parlor.

Beere ['be:rə], *f -/-n* berry.

Beet ['be:t], *n -(e)s/-e* (flower etc.) bed.

befähig|en [bə'fɛ:igən], *v.tr.* (*Eigenschaft usw.*) to qualify (s.o.); (*Umstände usw.*) to enable (s.o.) (to do sth.). ◆**B~ung,** *f -/no pl* **1.** ability, competence. **2.** qualification(s) (*zu + dat*, for).

befahr|bar [bə'fa:rbar], *adj.* (*Straße usw.*) passable (for vehicles); **nicht b.**, unfit for traffic. ◆**b~en,** *v.tr.irr.26* to drive along (a road etc.); **eine stark/wenig b~e Strecke**, a busy/little-used stretch of road.

befallen [bə'falən], *v.tr.irr.27* (a) (*Krankheit*) to attack (s.o., a plant etc.); (b) (*Angst usw.*) to seize, overcome (s.o.).

be'fangen *adj.* **1.** (*schüchtern*) shy; (*gehemmt*) self-conscious; (*verlegen*) embarrassed. **2.** *esp. Jur:* (*parteiisch*) biased. ◆**B~heit,** *f -/no pl* **1.** shyness; self-consciousness; embarrassment. **2.** *esp. Jur:* bias (of a witness).

be'fassen *v.refl.* **sich mit etwas dat b.**, to concern oneself with sth.; (*untersuchen*) to deal with sth.

Befehl [bə'fe:l], *m -(e)s/-e* (a) order; *Data-pr:* instruction; **zu B.!** yes sir! (b) *Mil:* command. ◆**b~en,** *v.tr.irr.* **j-m etwas b./j-m b., etwas zu tun**, to order/ command s.o. to do sth. ◆**b~igen,** *v.tr. Mil:* to command (an army etc.). ◆**B~shaber,** *m* commander. ◆**B~sverweigerung,** *f* insubordination.

be'festig|en *v.tr.* (a) to fix, attach (sth.); (b) to reinforce (a bridge, dam etc.); (c) *Mil:* to fortify (a town etc.). ◆**B~ung,** *f -/-en* **1.** *no pl* fixing, attaching. **2.** reinforcement. **3.** *Mil:* fortification.

be'feuchten *v.tr.* to moisten (sth.), humidify (the air).

be'find|en. I. *v.* **1.** (a) *v.tr.* **etwas für gut/richtig usw. b.**, to judge sth. to be

good/right etc.; *Jur:* **j-n (als/für) schuldig b.**, to find s.o. guilty; (b) *refl.* **sich b.**, (*Pers., Sache*) to be; (*Ort, Gebäude usw.*) to be situated. **2.** *v.i.* (*haben*) **über etwas** *acc* **b.**, to give a judgement on sth. **II. B.,** *n -s/no pl* **1.** (*Meinung*) opinion; judgement. **2.** (*Zustand*) state of health.

be'folgen, *v.tr.* to follow (advice), comply with (rules etc.).

be'förder|n, *v.tr.* (a) to transport (s.o., sth.); to convey, (*schicken*) send (letters, goods), *Com:* ship (goods); (b) to promote (s.o.) (**zum Direktor,** to the position of director). ◆**B~ung,** *f -/-en* **1.** *no pl* transport(ation), conveyance; *Com:* shipping. **2.** promotion.

be'fragen, *v.tr.* to ask, question (s.o.); to interrogate (a witness); to consult (a doctor, dictionary etc.).

be'frei|en, *v.tr.* (a) to release (a prisoner etc.), to free, liberate (s.o., a country etc.); to rescue (s.o.); (b) to clear (sth.), rid (s.o.) (**von etwas,** of sth.); (c) to exempt (s.o.) (**von Steuern usw.,** from taxes etc.). ◆**B~er(in),** *m -s/- (f -/-nen)* liberator; rescuer. ◆**B~ung,** *f -/no pl* **1.** liberation, release (**von** + *dat,* from); emancipation (of women). **2.** exemption. ◆**B~ungs-,** *comb. fm.* freedom (movement etc.).

befremden [bə'frɛmdən], **I.** *v.tr.* to take (s.o.) aback, shock (s.o.). **II. B.,** *n -s/no pl* amazement; shock; (*Entrüstung*) indignation.

befreunden [bə'frɔyndən], *v.refl.* **sich mit etwas dat b.**, to come to like sth.; **mit j-m (eng) befreundet sein**, to be (great) friends with s.o.

befriedig|en [bə'fri:digən], *v.tr.* to satisfy (s.o., a need etc.); to fulfil (a desire, demand etc.); **sich (selbst) b.**, to masturbate. ◆**b~end,** *adj.* satisfactory. ◆**B~ung,** *f -/no pl* satisfaction; fulfilment.

befristen [bə'fristən], *v.tr.* to limit.

befrucht|en [bə'fruxtən], *v.tr.* to fertilize (an egg, flower). ◆**B~ung,** *f -/-en* fertilization; **künstliche B.,** artificial insemination.

befug|t [bə'fu:gt], *adj.* **b. sein, etwas zu tun**, to be authorized to do sth. ◆**B~nis,** *f -/-se* authority; *pl* **B~se,** powers.

Befund [bə'funt], *m* result (of a test etc.); findings (of an inquiry etc.).

be'fürcht|en, *v.tr.* to fear. ◆**B~ung,** *f -/-en esp.* (*Bedenken*) misgiving.

befürworten [bə'fy:rvɔrtən], *v.tr.* to support (sth.), advocate (a policy etc.). ◆**B~er,** *m -s/-* advocate.

begab|t [bə'ga:pt], *adj.* gifted, talented. ◆**B~ung,** *f -/-en* gift, talent.

begatten [bə'gatən], *v.tr.* (*Tiere*) to mate with; **sich b.**, to mate.

be'geben, *v.refl.irr.35* (a) **sich an einen anderen Ort b.**, to proceed to another place; (b) *impers. Lit:* **es begab sich, daß**

..., it so happened that ... ◆B~heit, f
-/-en incident, occurrence.

begegn|en [bəˈgeːgnən], v.i. (sein) (a)
j-m, etwas dat b., to meet s.o., sth.; (b)
j-m freundlich/höflich b., to treat s.o.
kindly/politely. ◆B~ung, f -/-en meeting, encounter.

begeh|bar [bəˈgeːbaːr], adj. passable
(road etc.). ◆b~en, v.tr.irr.36 (a) to
walk along (a path etc.); (b) (feiern) to
celebrate (a birthday etc.); (c) (verüben)
to commit (a crime, blunder etc.);
einen Fehler b., to make a mistake.

begehr|en [bəˈgeːrən], v.tr. to want, cov-
et (sth.); to desire (a woman etc.); (heftig) to crave for (sth.). ◆b~enswert,
adj. desirable. ◆b~t, adj. sought after;
popular (dancing partner etc.).

begeister|n [bəˈgaistərn], v.tr. to arouse
enthusiasm in (s.o.); (Theaterstück usw.)
to delight, thrill (s.o., the audience etc.);
sich (für etwas acc) b., to get
enthusiastic/F: excited (about sth.).
◆b~t, adj. enthusiastic, thrilled.
◆B~ung, f -/no pl enthusiasm.

Begier|de [bəˈgiːrdə], f -/-n desire, (Ge-
lüste) craving, (Sehnsucht usw.) longing.
◆b~ig, adj. avid, eager.

Beginn [bəˈgin], m -(e)s/no pl beginning.
◆b~en, v.irr. 1. v.tr. to start (a conversation, work etc.); to set about (sth.).
2. v.i. (haben) to begin, start.

beglaubig|en [bəˈglaubigən], v.tr. to
authenticate (a document, etc.).
◆B~ung, f -/-en authentication.

be'gleichen, v.tr.irr.40 to settle, pay.

Begleit- [bəˈglait-], comb.fm. accompany-
ing (text etc.); attendant (symptom, circumstances etc.); Mil: etc: escort (aircraft, vessel etc.). ◆B~brief, m
accompanying/covering letter; Com: advice note. ◆b~en, v.tr. to accompany
(s.o., sth.). ◆B~er(in), m -s/- (f -/-nen)
1. companion. 2. Mus: accompanist.
◆B~erscheinung, f side effect.
◆B~musik, f Cin: TV: etc: background music. ◆B~ung, f -/-en 1. company. 2. Mus: accompaniment.

beglück|en [bəˈglykən], v.tr. to make
(s.o.) happy. ◆b~wünschen, v.tr. to
congratulate.

begnad|et [bəˈgnaːdət], adj. gifted.
◆b~igen, v.tr. to pardon (s.o.).
◆B~igung, f -/-en (free) pardon.

begnügen [bəˈgnyːgən], v.refl. sich mit
etwas dat b., to content oneself with sth.

Begonie [bəˈgoːniə], f -/-n begonia.

be'graben, v.tr.irr.42 to bury (s.o., sth.).

Begräbnis [bəˈgrɛːpnis], n -ses/-se
burial; (Feier) funeral.

begreif|en [bəˈgraifən], v.tr.irr.43 to un-
derstand (s.o., sth.), grasp (sth.).
◆b~lich, adj. understandable.

begrenz|en [bəˈgrɛntsən], v.tr. to limit,
restrict (sth.).

Begriff [bəˈgrif], m 1. concept; (Ausdruck)
term, expression. 2. conception, idea; für

heutige B~e, by present day standards.
3. im B. sein, etwas zu tun, to be on the
point of doing sth. ◆b~sstutzig, adj.
slow on the uptake; F: gormless (person,
expression).

be'gründ|en, v.tr. to justify (an action,
opinion etc.). ◆b~et, adj. well-
founded (hope, suspicion etc.); reasoned
(argument etc.). ◆B~ung, f seine B.
war ..., the reasons he gave were ...

be'grüß|en, v.tr. to greet (s.o.); to wel-
come (a guest, a suggestion etc.).
◆B~ung, f -/-en greeting; welcome.

begünstig|en [bəˈgynstigən], v.tr. (a) to
favour (s.o., sth.); (Umstände usw.) to
further (plans etc.); (b) (bevorzugen) to
give (s.o.) preferential treatment.
◆B~ung, f -/-en (a) favouring; further-
ance; (b) preferential treatment; (c) Jur:
aiding and abetting.

be'gutachten, v.tr. to give a professional
opinion on (sth.).

begütert [bəˈgyːtərt], adj. well-to-do.

behaart [bəˈhaːrt], adj. hairy.

behäbig [bəˈhɛːbiç], adj. (Pers.) portly
(and slow-moving); leisurely (pace etc.).

behagen [bəˈhaːgən], v.i. (haben) j-m
b., to suit s.o. ◆b~lich, adj. comfortable (armchair etc.); cosy (room, restaurant etc.).

be'halten, v.tr.irr.45 to keep; etwas (im
Gedächtnis) b., to remember sth.

Behälter [bəˈhɛltər], m -s/- container, receptacle; (für Flüssigkeiten) tank.

be'hand|eln, v.tr. (a) to treat; (b) (Buch,
Pers. usw.) to deal with (a subject).
◆B~lung, f -/-en handling (of an
affair); (Patient) in B., undergoing treatment.

beharr|en [bəˈharən], I. v.i. (haben) to
persist; auf/bei seinem Entschluß b., to
stick to one's decision. II. B., n -s/no pl
persistence. ◆b~lich, adj. persistent;
obstinate (silence, refusal etc.); dogged
(determination). ◆B~lichkeit, f -/no pl
persistence; perseverance.

behaupt|en [bəˈhauptən], v.tr. (a) to
maintain (sth.); sich (in einer Position)
b., to hold one's own; (b) to say (sth.,
the opposite etc.). ◆B~ung, f -/-en
statement; assertion.

be'heben, v.tr.irr.48 to rectify (an abuse,
defect); to repair (damage).

be'heizen, v.tr. to heat.

Behelf [bəˈhɛlf], m -(e)s/-e stopgap,
makeshift. ◆b~en, v.refl.irr.50 sich
b., to manage, make do. ◆b~smäßig,
adj. makeshift.

behelligen [bəˈhɛligən], v.tr. to bother
(s.o.).

behende [bəˈhɛndə], adj. Lit: nimble;
(geschickt) deft.

beherbergen [bəˈhɛrbɛrgən], v.tr. to put
(s.o.) up.

be'herrsch|en, v.tr. (a) to rule (over) (a
country etc.); (b) (Pers., Gefühl usw.) to
dominate (s.o., s.o.'s mind/life etc.); (c)

to be in control of (the situation etc.); to control (oneself, one's feelings etc.); (d) to master (an instrument, a language etc.). ◆B~ung, f -/no pl 1. hold, sway; domination. 2. control. 3. mastery; command (of a language); grasp (of a subject).

beher'zigen [bə'hɛrtsigən], v.tr. to heed (a warning etc.); to take (s.o.'s advice) to heart.

beherzt [bə'hɛrtst], adj. courageous.

behilflich [bə'hilfliç], adj. j-m b. sein, to help s.o. (with sth./to do sth.).

be'hinder|n, v.tr. to hinder, hamper (s.o.); to obstruct (traffic, Sp: an opponent etc.), impede (visibility etc.). ◆b~t, adj. (mentally/physically) handicapped. ◆B~ung, f -/-en (a) hindrance, impeding; Aut: Sp: obstruction; (b) (Hindernis) obstacle (+ gen, to); (c) Med: handicap.

Behörde [bə'hø:rdə], f -/-n authority; public body. ◆b~lich ['-hø:rtliç], adj. official.

be'hüten, v.tr. to protect (s.o., sth.) (vor + dat, from).

behutsam [bə'hu:tza:m], adj. cautious (person, words); gentle (treatment etc.).

bei [bai], prep. + dat 1. (Ort) (a) near; (nahe/dicht) bei der Schule, (right/just) by the school; (b) among (a number of people, things); (c) at; bei Tisch, at table; bei uns (zu Hause), (i) at our house; (ii) in our country; bei j-m wohnen, to live with s.o. in s.o.'s house; bei einer Firma arbeiten, to work for a firm; wie es bei Shakespeare heißt, as Shakespeare says; sie hatte kein Geld bei sich, she didn't have any money with/on her. 2. (Zeit) bei seiner Ankunft, on his arrival; when he arrived; er war (gerade) beim Abwaschen, he was (just) washing up (at that moment); bei Tag(e)/Nacht, by day/night. 3. by; j-n bei der Hand nehmen/beim Namen rufen, to take s.o. by the hand/call s.o. by name. 4. (im Falle von) with, in the case of (s.o., sth.). bei Regen, if it rains.

'beibehalten, v.tr.sep.irr.45 to retain (sth.); to keep up (a custom, habit).

'beibringen, v.tr.sep.irr.16 j-m etwas b., to teach s.o. sth.; F: wie soll ich es ihr b.? how shall I break it to her?

Beicht|e ['baiçtə], f -/-n confession. ◆b~en, v. 1. v.tr. to confess (one's sins etc.). 2. v.i. (haben) to confess; b. gehen, to go to confession.

beide ['baidə], adj. & pron. both; die b~n Schwestern, the two sisters; (betont) both (of) the sisters; die b~n, the two of them; (alle) b., both; b~s, both; eins von b~n, one or the other; keins von b~n, neither. ◆b~rlei, inv. adj. of both kinds. ◆b~rseitig, adj. on both sides; mutual (agreement etc.). ◆b~rseits. I. prep. + gen on both sides of (the road etc.). II. adv. on

beiein'ander, adv. (close) together.

'Beifahrer, m (front-seat) passenger. ◆'B~sitz, m front seat.

'Beifall, m 1. applause. 2. (Billigung) approval.

'beifügen, v.tr.sep. (a) to enclose (sth.); (b) (hinzufügen) to add (sth.).

beige [bɛ:ʒ], inv. adj. beige.

'beigeben, v.tr.sep.irr.36 1. v.tr. (a) to add (sth.) (etwas dat, to sth.); (b) to assign (a helper etc.) (j-m, to s.o.). 2. v.i. (haben) klein b., to give in, F: climb down.

'Beigeschmack, m (slight) taste, flavour (of sth. else); (scharf) tang.

'Beihilfe, f 1. Adm: financial aid; (einmalig) grant. 2. Jur: aiding and abetting.

Beil [bail], n -(e)s/-e hatchet; (butcher's) cleaver.

'Beilage, f -/-n 1. supplement. 2. Cu: accompaniment(s); Fleisch mit Nudeln als B., meat served with noodles.

'beiläufig, adj. passing (remark etc.); casual (inquiry, behaviour etc.).

'beilegen, v.tr.sep. (a) to enclose (sth.); (b) to settle (a quarrel, difference etc.). ◆B~ung, f -/-en settlement.

bei'leibe, adv. b. nicht, certainly not.

'Beileid, n -s/no pl condolences; sein B. aussprechen, to offer one's condolences. ◆B~s-, comb.fm. (visit, letter etc.) of condolence.

'beiliegen, v.i.sep.irr.62 (haben) einem Brief usw. b., to be enclosed with a letter etc. ◆b~d, adj. enclosed.

beim [baim] = bei dem.

'beimessen, v.tr.sep.irr.25 etwas dat Wichtigkeit/Bedeutung b., to attach importance to sth.

Bein [bain], n -(e)s/-e leg; auf den B~en, on one's feet; (nach einer Krankheit) up and about. ◆'B~bruch, m fracture of the leg.

beinah(e) ['baina:(ə)], adv. nearly.

beinhalten [bə'ʔinhaltən], v.tr. to contain (sth.); (Begriff usw.) to cover (sth.); (Brief usw.) to state (that ...).

beipflichten ['baipfliçtən], v.i.sep. (haben) j-m b., to agree with s.o.

'Beirat, m advisory committee.

beirren [bə'ʔirən], v.tr. to disconcert (s.o.); laß dich nicht b., don't let yourself be put off.

beisammen [bai'zamən], adv. & comb.fm. together. ◆B~sein, n -s/no pl (social) gathering.

'Beischlaf, m sexual intercourse.

'Beisein, n im B. von j-m/in j-s B., in the presence of s.o.

bei'seite, adv. (a) (auf der Seite) apart, on one side; Th: aside; (b) (an die Seite) aside, to one side; j-n, etwas b. schaffen, to get rid of s.o., sth.

'beisetz|en, v.tr.sep. to bury (a corpse). ◆B~ung, f -/-en burial; (Feier) funeral.

'Beispiel, n example (für etwas acc, of

sth.); **zum B.,** for example; **sich** *dat* **ein B.** an j-m, etwas nehmen, to take s.o., sth. as one's model. ◆**'b~haft,** *adj.* exemplary. ◆**'b~los,** *adj.* unprecedented. ◆**'b~sweise,** *adv.* for example.

beiß|en ['baisən], *v.tr. & i.irr.* (*haben*) (*a*) to bite; (*b*) (*Rauch, Wind usw.*) to burn; *F:* **die Farben b. sich,** the colours clash. ◆**'b~d,** *adj.* biting (cold, wind); acrid (taste, smell, smoke); *Fig:* caustic (wit, remark).

'Beistand, *m* assistance; (*Unterstützung*) support.

'beistehen, *v.i.sep.irr.100* (*haben*) **j-m b.,** to help/(*in Schwierigkeiten*) stand by s.o.

'beisteuern, *v.tr.sep.* to contribute.

'beistimmen, *v.i.sep.* (*haben*) **j-m, einem Vorschlag b.,** to agree with s.o., a proposal.

Beitrag ['baitra:k], *m -(e)s/=e* contribution; (*Mitgliedsb.*) subscription; (*Versicherungsb.*) premium; (*Zeitungsb.*) article. ◆**b~en** ['-gən], *v.tr. & i.sep.irr.85* (*haben*) to contribute (sth.).

'beitreten, *v.i.sep.irr.105* (*sein*) **einem Verein, einer Partei usw. b.,** to join a club, party etc.

'Beitritt, *m* joining (**zu einem Verein usw.,** of a club etc.).

'Beiwagen, *m -s/-* sidecar.

'beiwohnen, *v.i.sep.* (*haben*) **etwas** *dat* **b.,** to be present at sth.

Beize ['baitsə], *f -/-n* **1.** (*a*) corrosive; (*b*) *Cu:* pickle, marinade. **2.** (*für Holz*) stain.

bei'zeiten, *adv.* in good time.

bejahen [bə'ja:ən], *v.tr.&i.* (*haben*) to say yes (to a question); (*billigen*) to approve of (s.o., sth.). ◆**b~d,** *adj.* positive (attitude); affirmative (answer).

bejahrt [bə'ja:rt], *adj.* aged.

be'jammern, *v.tr.* to bewail (sth.).

be'kämpf|en, *v.tr.* to fight (an opponent, a pest, plan etc.); to combat (an epidemic, evil etc.). ◆**B~ung,** *f -/no pl* fight, battle (+ *gen.,* against).

bekannt [bə'kant], *adj.* **1.** well-known; (*berühmt*) famous. **2.** (*Tatsache, Person*) known (**j-m,** to s.o.); (*seit langem/von früher*) familiar; **mir ist das schon b.,** I know that already; **sie kam mir b. vor,** she seemed familiar; **darf ich Sie mit meinem Mann b. machen?** may I introduce you to my husband? ◆**B~e(r),** *m & f decl. as adj.* acquaintance; friend. ◆**B~enkreis,** *m* circle of acquaintances. ◆**B~gabe,** *f* announcement; disclosure. ◆**b~geben,** *v.tr.sep.irr.35* to announce (sth.). ◆**b~lich,** *adv.* as is well known; **er hat b. keine Geduld,** everybody knows he has no patience. ◆**b~machen,** *v.tr.sep.* to publish (findings, a discovery etc.). ◆**B~machung,** *f -/-n* (*a*) publication; (*b*) (*Anschlag*) notice. ◆**B~schaft,** *f no pl* acquaintance.

be'kehr|en, *v.tr.* to convert (s.o.). ◆**B~ung,** *f -/-en* conversion.

be'kenn|en, *v.tr.irr.51* to admit (one's mistake, guilt); to confess (the truth, one's sins, that …); **sich zu j-m b.,** to stand by s.o. ◆**B~tnis,** *n* (*Konfession*) denomination.

be'klag|en, *v.tr.* (*a*) *Lit:* to grieve over, lament (a loss, death etc.); (*bedauern*) to deplore (sth.); (*b*) **sich b.,** to complain. ◆**B~te(r),** *m & f decl. as adj.* defendant.

be'kleid|en, *v.tr.* (*a*) to dress (s.o.); (*b*) *Lit:* to hold (an office). ◆**B~ung,** *f* **1.** clothing. **2.** tenure (of an office).

be'klemm|en, *v.tr.* to oppress. ◆**b~end,** *adj.* oppressive; stifling (atmosphere). ◆**B~ung,** *f -/-en* feeling of oppression/(*Angst*) apprehension.

beklommen [bə'kləmən], *adj.* uneasy.

be'kommen, *v.irr.53* **1.** *v.tr.* (*a*) to get (sth.); to receive (a letter, permission, money, etc.); **ein Kind b.,** to have a baby; (*b*) (*sich verschaffen*) to obtain (sth.); **den Zug/Bus noch b.,** to catch the train/bus. **2.** *v.i.* (*sein*) **j-m b.,** (*Nahrung, Klima usw.*) to agree with s.o.

bekömmlich [bə'kœmliç], *adj.* wholesome; **leicht/schwer b.,** easily digestible/indigestible.

be'kräftig|en, *v.tr.* to confirm (an opinion, suspicion etc.), strengthen (s.o.). ◆**B~ung,** *f* confirmation.

be'kümmer|n, *v.tr.* to trouble, worry (s.o.). ◆**b~t,** *adj.* sorrowful; troubled.

be'kund|en, *v.tr.* (*a*) *Lit:* to manifest (one's feelings, intentions etc.); (*b*) *Jur:* to testify (that …).

be'lächeln, *v.tr.* to smile (condescendingly/pityingly) at (s.o., sth.).

be'laden, *v.tr.irr.56* to load (s.o., a lorry etc.); **schwer b.,** heavily laden.

Belag [bə'la:k], *m -(e)s/=e* **1.** (*Schicht*) coating; (*sehr dünn*) film; *Med:* fur (on the tongue); (*Zahnb.*) plaque. **2.** (road) surface; (floor-)covering; *Tchn:* lining (of brakes etc.). **3.** *Cu:* filling (for sandwiches etc.).

be'lager|n, *v.tr.* to besiege (a town etc.). ◆**B~ung,** *f -/-en* siege.

Belang [bə'laŋ], *m -(e)s/-e* **1.** *no pl* **von/ohne B.,** of consequence/no consequence; important/unimportant. **2.** *pl* **B~e,** interests. ◆**b~en,** *v.tr.* to sue, prosecute (s.o.). ◆**b~los,** *adj.* unimportant. ◆**B~losigkeit,** *f -/-en* **1.** *no pl* insignificance. **2.** trifling matter.

be'lassen, *v.tr.irr.57* to leave (s.o., sth.).

belast|en [bə'lastən], *v.tr.* (*a*) to place a load/strain on (sth.); *Fig:* to burden (oneself, one's memory etc.); (*b*) *Fin:* to debit (an account); (*c*) *Jur:* to incriminate (s.o.). ◆**B~ung,** *f -/-en* (*a*) load, (*Beanspruchung*) stress; **zulässige B.,** safe (working) load; (*b*) *Fig:* strain. **2.** *Fin:* debiting (of an account). **3.** *Jur:* incrimination. ◆**B~ungsprobe,** *f* load test; *Fig:* gruelling test (of s.o.). ◆**B~ungszeuge,** *m* witness for the prosecution.

be'lästig|en, *v.tr.* to bother (s.o.), (*Mann*) molest (a girl); to pester (s.o.) (with questions etc.). ◆**B~ung,** *f* -/-en (*a*) *no pl* bothering; molestation; (*b*) (*Besuch usw.*) intrusion; **etwas als B. empfinden,** to find sth. annoying.

be'laufen, *v.refl.irr.58* **sich auf 100 DM** *acc* **b.,** to amount to 100 marks.

be'lauschen, *v.tr.* to eavesdrop on.

be'leb|en, *v.tr.* (*a*) to give life to (s.o., sth.); (*b*) (*lebhafter machen*) to enliven (s.o., sth.); to stimulate (the economy etc.); to brighten (up) (a room etc.); **j-n neu b.,** to revive (s.o.). ◆**b~t,** *adj.* busy (road etc.); animated (conversation).

Beleg [bə'le:k], *m* -(e)s/-e (documentary) proof; (*Scheck*) voucher, receipt. ◆**b~en,** *v.tr.* (*a*) (*bedecken*) to cover (sth.); **Brote mit Käse b.,** to put cheese on pieces of bread; **b~te Zunge/Stimme,** coated tongue/husky voice; (*b*) (*reservieren*) to reserve (a seat, table, room); **Vorlesungen b.,** to enrol for lectures; (*c*) (*beweisen*) to substantiate. ◆**B~schaft,** *f* -/-en employees, personnel (of a firm).

be'lehren, *v.tr.* to inform, instruct (s.o.).

beleidig|en [bə'laidigən], *v.tr.* to offend (s.o., *Fig:* the eye, ear); (*abschtlich*) to insult (s.o.). ◆**B~ung,** *f* -/-en insult; *Jur:* slander, (*schriftlich*) libel.

be'leucht|en, *v.tr.* to light (a street, room etc.); *Fig:* to shed light on. ◆**B~ung,** *f* -/-en lighting; (*Licht*) light.

Belg|ien ['belgiən], *Pr.n.n* -s. Belgium. ◆**B~ier(in),** *m* -s/- (*f* -/-nen) & ◆**b~isch,** *adj.* Belgian.

be'licht|en, *v.tr.* to expose (a photograph etc.). ◆**B~ung,** *f* -/-en exposure. ◆**B~ungsmesser,** *m* light meter.

be'lieb|ig, *adj.* 1. *attrib.* any (at all/you like). 2. *adv.* **b. lange/viel,** as long/much as one likes; **etwas b. verändern,** to alter sth. at will. ◆**b~t,** *adj.* popular; **sich bei j-m b. machen,** to get into s.o.'s good books. ◆**B~theit,** *f* -/no *pl* popularity.

be'liefern, *v.tr.* to supply (s.o.).

bellen ['belən], *v.i.* (*haben*) to bark.

be'lohn|en, *v.tr.* to reward (s.o., patience etc.). ◆**B~ung,** *f* -/-en reward.

be'lüften, *v.tr.* to ventilate (a room etc.).

be'lügen, *v.tr.irr.63* to lie to (s.o.).

be'lustig|en, *v.tr.* to amuse, entertain (s.o.). ◆**B~ung,** *f* -/-en amusement.

be'mächtigen, *v.refl.* **sich j-s, etwas** *gen* **b.,** to seize s.o., sth.

bemängeln [bə'meŋəln], *v.tr.* to find fault with (s.o., sth.).

be'mannen, *v.tr.* to man (a ship etc.).

bemerk|bar [bə'merkba:r], *adj.* noticeable; **sich b. machen,** to draw attention to oneself/itself. ◆**b~en,** *v.tr.* (*a*) to notice (s.o., sth.); (*b*) (*sagen*) to remark (that ...). ◆**b~enswert,** *adj.* remarkable. ◆**B~ung,** *f* -/-en remark.

be'messen, *v.tr.irr.25* to calculate (a price

etc.); **meine Zeit ist knapp b.,** my time is limited.

be'mitleiden, *v.tr.* to pity, feel sorry for (s.o.).

be'müh|en. I. *v.tr.* (*a*) *Lit:* to trouble (s.o.); to call on the services of (a doctor, lawyer etc.); (*b*) **sich b.,** to try (hard); (*c*) (*sich kümmern*) **sich um einen Patienten usw. b.,** to attend to a patient etc. II. **B.,** *n* -s/no *pl* endeavour; **vergebliches B.,** wasted effort. ◆**B~ung,** *f* -/-en *esp. pl* efforts.

be'nachbart, *adj.* neighbouring (town etc.).

be'nachrichtig|en, *v.tr.* to inform. ◆**B~ung,** *f* -/-en notification.

be'nachteilig|en, *v.tr.* to treat (s.o.) unfairly. ◆**b~t,** *adj.* deprived. ◆**B~ung,** *f* -/-en (*a*) unfair treatment; (*b*) disadvantage.

be'nehmen. I. *v.refl.irr.69* **sich b.,** to behave. II. **B.,** *n* -s/no *pl* behaviour; **er hat kein B.,** he has no manners.

be'neiden, *v.tr.* to envy (s.o.); **j-n um etwas b.,** to envy s.o. sth. ◆**b~swert,** *adj.* enviable (success etc.); **nicht b.,** not to be envied.

be'nennen, *v.tr.irr.51* to name.

Bengel ['beŋəl], *m* -s/- rascal.

benommen [bə'nɔmən], *adj.* dazed, stunned. ◆**B~heit,** *f* -/no *pl* dazed state.

be'nötigen, *v.tr.* to require (sth.).

be'nutz|en, *v.tr.* to use. ◆**B~er,** *m* -s/- user. ◆**B~ung,** *f* -/no *pl* use.

Benzin [ben'tsi:n], *n* -s/-e petrol; *N.Am:* gas(oline). ◆**B~kanister,** *m* jerry can.

beobacht|en [bə'ʔo:baxtən], *v.tr.* (*a*) to watch, (*kontrollieren*) observe; (*b*) (*bemerken*) to notice (sth.). ◆**B~er,** *m* -s/- observer. ◆**B~ung,** *f* -/-en observation.

be'pflanzen, *v.tr.* to plant (a border etc.).

bequem [bə'kve:m], *adj.* (*a*) comfortable (chair, shoes etc.); (*b*) easy (route, life, way etc.); **b~e Ausrede,** convenient excuse. ◆**b~en,** *v.refl. esp. F:* **sich (dazu) b., etwas zu tun,** to deign to do sth. ◆**B~lichkeit,** *f* -/-en 1. comfort. 2. *no pl* (*Faulheit*) laziness.

be'rat|en, *v.tr.irr.13* 1. *v.tr.* (*a*) to advise (s.o.); **sich b. lassen,** to take advice; **gut b. sein, etwas zu tun,** to be well advised to do sth.; (*b*) (*besprechen*) to debate (sth.). 2. *v.i.* (*haben*) & *refl.* (*sich*) **mit j-m b.,** to confer with s.o.; **sie berieten (miteinander), was zu tun sei,** they discussed what was to be done. ◆**B~er(in),** *m* -s/- (*f* -/-nen) adviser. ◆**b~schlagen,** *v.i.* (*haben*) to confer. ◆**B~ung,** *f* -/-en 1. advice; *Med: Jur:* consultation. 2. (*Besprechung*) discussion.

be'rauben, *v.tr.* to rob (s.o.).

berech|enbar [bə'rɛçənba:r], *adj.* calculable. ◆**b~nen,** *v.tr.* (*a*) to calculate (sth.); (*schätzen*) to estimate (the price etc.); (*b*) **j-m etwas b.,** to charge s.o. for sth.; **j-m zu viel/wenig b.,** to overcharge/undercharge s.o. ◆b~**nend**, *adj.* calculating. ◆B~**nung**, *f* 1. calculation. 2. *no pl* mit B., deliberately.

berechtig|en [bə'rɛçtigən], *v.tr.* to entitle (s.o.); (*Pers.*) to authorize (s.o.) (to do sth.). ◆b~**t**, *adj.* justified (hope, complaint etc.); legitimate (reason, pride etc.). ◆B~**ung**, *f* -/-en entitlement; right; (*Befugnis*) authorization.

be'red|en, *v.tr.* (*a*) to talk (sth.) over; to discuss (sth.); (*b*) (*überreden*) to persuade (s.o.). ◆b~**t** [bə'reːt], *adj.* eloquent.

Be'reich, *m* (*a*) region, area; (*b*) field (of science, art, politics etc.).

be'reichern [bə'raiçərn], *v.tr.* (*a*) to enrich (oneself, a language etc.); to enlarge (a collection); (*b*) **sich b.**, to grow rich (**an** + *dat*, on).

be'reinigen, *v.tr.* to settle (an argument etc.); to clear up (a problem etc.).

be'reisen, *v.tr.* to tour (a country).

bereit [bə'rait], *adj.* ready; **sich b. halten**, to hold oneself in readiness; *Mil: etc:* (*einsatzb.*) to stand by; **sich zu etwas** *dat* **b. zeigen**, to show one's willingness to do sth. ◆b~**en**, *v.tr.* **j-m Sorgen/Kummer b.**, to cause s.o. worry/trouble; **j-m Freude/eine Überraschung b.**, to give s.o. pleasure/a surprise. ◆b~**halten**, *v.tr.sep.irr.45* to have (sth.) ready; (*für Notfälle*) to keep (sth.) handy. ◆b~**legen**, *v.tr.sep.* to put (clothes, a meal etc.) out (ready) (**j-m**, for s.o.). ◆b~**liegen**, *v.i.sep.irr.62* (*haben*) to be/lie ready. ◆b~**machen**, *v.tr.sep.* to get (s.o., sth.) ready. ◆b~**s**, *adv.* already. ◆B~**schaft**, *f* -/-en 1. (*a*) readiness; **in B. sein/stehen**, to be ready/*Mil:* on standby; (*b*) willingness (**zur Hilfe/zu helfen**, to help). 2. (*Polizeieinheit*) riot squad. ◆B~**schaftsdienst**, *m* emergency service. ◆b~**stehen**, *v.i. sep. irr.100* (*haben*) to be ready waiting. ◆b~**stellen**, *v.tr.sep.* to provide (machines, troops etc.); to make (funds etc.) available. ◆b~**willig**, *adj.* willing (etwas **zu tun**, to do sth.); *adv.* willingly, readily.

be'reuen, *v.tr.* to regret (sth., having done sth.).

Berg ['bɛrk]. I. *m* -(e)s/-e (*a*) mountain, (high) hill; (*b*) *Fig:* **jetzt sind wir über den B.**, the worst is behind us; (*c*) *F:* pile (of work etc.). II. *B~*-, *comb.fm.* 1. mountain (guide, hut etc.); climbing (boot etc.). 2. mining (engineer etc.). ◆b~**'ab**, *adv.* downhill. ◆B~**arbeiter**, *m* miner. ◆B~**auf**, *adv.* uphill. ◆B~**bau**, *m* mining. ◆b~**ig**, *adj.* mountainous. ◆B~**kamm**, *m* mountain ridge. ◆B~**kette**, *f* mountain range. ◆B~**mann**, *m* (*pl* -leute) miner. ◆B~**steigen**. I. *v.i.sep.irr.89* (*sein*) to go climbing/mountaineering. II. **B.**, *n* -s/*no pl* mountaineering. ◆B~**steiger(in)**, *m* -s/- (*f* -/-nen) mountaineer, climber.

◆'B~**werk**, *n* mine.

berg|en ['bɛrgən], *v.tr.irr.* (*a*) to salvage (cargo, a vessel); to recover (cargo, a dead body etc.); to rescue (accident victims etc.); (*b*) *Fig:* **Gefahren in sich b.**, to have hidden dangers. ◆'B~**ung**, *f* -/-en salvage; recovery; rescue.

Bericht [bə'riçt], *m* -(e)s/-e report; account (of an event, journey etc.); **B. erstatten**, to report. ◆b~**en**, *v.tr. & i.* (*haben*) to report (sth.); **über etwas** *acc* **b.**, to (give a) report on sth. ◆B~**erstatter**, *m* reporter, correspondent.

berichtig|en [bə'riçtigən], *v.tr.* to correct. ◆B~**ung**, *f* -/-en correction.

beritten [bə'ritən], *adj.* mounted (policeman etc.).

Berliner [bɛr'liːnər], *m* -s/- *Cu:* doughnut.

Bernstein ['bɛrnʃtain], *m* amber.

bersten ['bɛrstən], *v.i. irr.5* (*sein*) to burst; (*Boden usw.*) to develop cracks.

berüchtigt [bə'rʏçtiçt], *adj.* notorious; disreputable (area, house etc.).

berücksichtig|en [bə'rʏksiçtigən], *v.tr.* to take (sth.) into account; to consider (feelings, experience, an application etc.). ◆B~**ung**, *f* -*no pl* consideration.

Beruf [bə'ruːf], *m* -(e)s/-e occupation; (*freier B.*) profession; (*handwerklich*) trade. ◆b~**en**. I. *v.tr.irr.74* (*a*) **j-n zum Nachfolger b.**, to appoint s.o. as one's successor; (*b*) **sich b. auf** + *acc*, to refer to (s.o., the law etc.). II. *adj.* (*a*) (*fähig*) competent; (*b*) **er fühlt sich dazu b.**, he feels he has a vocation for it. ◆b~**lich**, *adj.* vocational (training etc.); professional (duties, advancement etc.); work (problems, prospects etc.). ◆B~**s**-, *comb.fm.* (*a*) professional (footballer, boxer, criminal, secret etc.); *Mil:* regular (soldier, officer, army); (*b*) vocational (training, school); (*c*) occupational (disease etc.); working (clothes etc.). ◆B~**berater(in)**, *m(f)* careers officer/ *Sch:* teacher. ◆B~**beratung**, *f* vocational/careers guidance. ◆b~**s-tätig**, *adj.* working (person). ◆b~**s-verbot**, *n* ban prohibiting a teacher, doctor etc. from practising his profession. ◆B~**ung**, *f* -/-en 1. appointment. 2. *no pl* vocation (**zum Arzt**, to become a doctor). 3. *no pl* reference (**auf** + *acc*, to); **unter B. auf j-n, etwas** *acc*, with reference to s.o., sth. 4. *Jur:* appeal.

be'ruhen, *v.i.* (*haben*) **auf etwas** *dat* **b.**, to be based on sth.; **eine Sache auf sich b. lassen**, to let a matter rest.

beruhig|en [bə'ruːigən], *v.tr.* to calm (s.o., the nerves etc.); to reassure (s.o.); to ease (one's conscience, pain etc.); **sich b.**, to calm down. ◆B~**ung**, *f* -/-en (*a*) *no pl* calming; reassuring; **zur B. der Nerven**, to calm the nerves; (*b*) reassurance, comfort. ◆B~**ungsmittel**, *n* sedative; (*gegen Depressionen*) tranquillizer.

be·rühmt [bə'ry:mt], *adj.* famous. ◆**B~heit,** *f -/-en* **1.** *no pl* fame. **2.** famous person, celebrity.

be·rühr|en, *v.tr.* (*a*) to touch (s.o., sth.); **sich b.,** to come into contact; *Fig:* (*Ideen usw.*) to have something in common; (*b*) to mention (a subject, point etc.); (*c*) to affect (s.o.). ◆**B~ung,** *f -/-en* contact; touch (of s.o.'s hand etc.).

be·sag|en, *v.tr.* (*Sache*) to say, mean (sth., nothing). ◆**b~t,** *adj.* aforesaid.

be·sänftig|en [bə'zɛnftigən], *v.tr.* to pacify (s.o.), calm (s.o.'s anger etc.). ◆**B~ung,** *f -/no pl* calming.

Be·satzung [bə'zatsuŋ], *f* (*a*) *Nau: Av:* crew; (*b*) *Mil:* occupying force, (*Garnison*) garrison. ◆**B~s-,** *comb.fm.* occupying (troops etc.); occupied (area etc.).

be·schädig|en [bə'ʃɛ:digən], *v.tr.* to damage (sth.). ◆**B~ung,** *f -/-en* **1.** *no pl* damaging. **2.** damage.

be·schaffen[1], *v.tr.* to obtain, *F:* get (sth.). ◆**B~ung,** *f -/no pl* obtaining.

be·schaffen[2], *adj.* **es ist so b., daß ...,** it is so constituted that ... ◆**B~heit,** *f -/no pl* consistency; texture (of skin, material etc.); (*Zustand*) condition; (*Struktur*) composition; (*Art*) nature.

be·schäftig|en [bə'ʃɛftigən], *v.tr.* to occupy (s.o., oneself); **j-n b.,** to keep (s.o.) busy; (*Problem usw.*) to exercise s.o.'s mind; **die Firma beschäftigt 200 Leute,** the firm employs 200 people. ◆**b~t,** *adj.* (*a*) busy; (*b*) **bei einer Firma b. sein,** to work for a firm. ◆**B~ung,** *f -/-en* (*Tätigkeit*) occupation; job.

be·schäm|en, *v.tr.* to make (s.o.) feel ashamed; to shame (s.o.). ◆**b~end,** *adj.* humiliating; shameful.

be·schatt|en, *v.tr.* to tail (s.o.).

be·schau|en, *v.tr.* to have a look at (sth.). ◆**b~lich,** *adj.* tranquil (life etc.).

Be·scheid [bə'ʃait], *m -(e)s/-e* **1.** (*a*) information; (*b*) *Adm:* (official) decision. **2.** *F:* **über etwas** *acc* **B. wissen,** to know about sth.; **ich werde Ihnen B. sagen,** I'll let you know.

be·scheiden, *adj.* modest. ◆**B~heit,** *f -/no pl* modesty.

be·scheinen, *v.tr.irr.79* to shine on (s.o., sth.).

be·scheinig|en [bə'ʃainigən], *v.tr.* to certify (sth.) (in writing); to acknowledge (receipt). ◆**B~ung,** *f -/-en* (*Schein*) certificate; (*Quittung*) receipt.

be·schenken, *v.tr.* to give (s.o.) presents.

Be·scherung [bə'ʃe:ruŋ], *f -/-en* giving out of (Christmas) presents; *F:* **eine schöne B.!** a nice mess!

be·scheuert [bə'ʃɔyərt], *adj. F:* (*Pers.*) dotty.

be·schießen, *v.tr.irr.31* to shoot at (sth.); to bombard (a town, *Ph:* nucleus).

be·schildern, *v.tr.* to signpost (a road).

be·schimpf|en, *v.tr.* to call (s.o.) names. ◆**B~ung,** *f -/-en* abuse.

Be·schlag [bə'ʃla:k], *m* (*a*) (metal) fittings

(of a door, chest etc.); (*b*) film, mist (on metal, window etc.); (*c*) j-n, etwas in B. **nehmen,** to take s.o., sth. over completely. ◆**b~en. I.** *v.tr.irr.85* **1.** *v.tr.* to put metal fittings on(to) (a door, etc.); to stud (boots etc.); to tip (a stick etc.) with metal; to shoe (a horse). **2.** *v.i.* (*sein*) (*Glas*) to steam/mist up. **II.** *adj.* well-informed; well up. ◆**B~nahme,** *f -/-n* confiscation; *Mil:* requisition. ◆**b~nahmen,** *v.tr.* to confiscate (sth.); *Mil:* to requisition (land, property etc.).

be·schleunig|en [bə'ʃlɔynigən], *v.* **1.** *v.tr.* to quicken (one's steps etc.); to speed up (work, a process etc.); to hasten (s.o.'s recovery, collapse). **2.** *v.i.* (*haben*) *Aut:* to accelerate. ◆**B~ung,** *f -/-en* **1.** quickening; speeding up. **2.** *Ph: Aut:* acceleration.

be·schließen, *v.tr.irr.31* (*a*) to decide (that ...); (*b*) to pass (a bill etc.); (*c*) (*beenden*) to end (a letter, speech etc.).

Be·schluß, *m* decision.

be·schmutzen [bə'ʃmutsən], *v.tr.* to get (sth.) dirty, soil (sth.).

be·schneiden, *v.tr.irr.59* (*a*) to trim (a hedge); to prune (a tree, *Fig:* expenditure etc.); (*b*) *Ecc:* to circumcise (s.o.).

be·schönigen [bə'ʃø:nigən], *v.tr.* to gloss over (a fault etc.).

be·schränk|en [bə'ʃrɛŋkən], *v.tr.* to limit, restrict (sth.); **sich auf etwas** *acc* **b.,** (i) (*Sache*) to be limited to sth.; (ii) (*Pers.*) to confine oneself to sth. ◆**b~t,** *adj.* (*a*) limited (means, time etc.); (*b*) (*Pers.*) (*geistig*) b., of limited intelligence; (*c*) (*engstirnig*) narrow-minded. ◆**B~theit,** *f -/no pl* **1.** (*a*) limited intelligence; (*b*) narrow-mindedness. **2.** limited nature. ◆**B~ung,** *f -/-en* limitation.

be·schrankt [bə'ʃraŋkt], *adj.* **b~er Bahn-übergang,** level crossing with barriers.

be·schreib|en, *v.tr.irr.12* (*a*) to describe (sth.); (*b*) to write on (a piece of paper etc.). ◆**B~ung,** *f -/-en* description.

be·schrift|en [bə'ʃriftən], *v.tr.* to write (on) (a label etc.); to label (a jar etc.). ◆**B~ung,** *f -/-en* **1.** *no pl* writing; labelling. **2.** (*Aufschrift*) inscription; label.

be·schuldig|en [bə'ʃuldigən], *v.tr.* **j-n b.,** to charge s.o., accuse s.o. ◆**B~ung,** *f -/-en* accusation.

be·schütz|en, *v.tr.* to protect (s.o., sth.). ◆**B~er,** *m -s/-* protector.

Be·schwerde [bə'ʃve:rdə], *f -/-n* (*a*) complaint; (*b*) *pl* pain, trouble.

be·schwer|en, *v.tr.* (*a*) to weight (down) (a roof, net etc.); (*b*) **sich b.,** to complain. ◆**b~lich,** *adj.* tiring, arduous.

be·schwichtig|en [bə'ʃviçtigən], *v.tr.* to pacify (s.o.); to placate (s.o., s.o.'s anger etc.); to ease (one's conscience). ◆**B~ung,** *f -/no pl* soothing; *esp. Pol:* appeasement; conciliation.

be·schwindeln, *v.tr. F:* to swindle (*belü-*

gen) to tell (s.o.) fibs.
beschwingt [bə'ʃvɪŋt], *adj.* gay, lively.
beschwipst [bə'ʃvɪpst], *adj. F:* tipsy.
be'schwören, *v.tr.irr.91* (*a*) to swear to (a statement etc.); (*b*) (*anflehen*) to implore (s.o.); (*c*) (*heraufb.*) to invoke (spirits etc.); *Fig:* to evoke (the past, memories etc.).
beseitig|en [bə'zaitigən], *v.tr.* to eliminate (mistakes etc.); to dispose-of (rubbish etc.). ◆**B~ung**, *f -/no pl* elimination; disposal.
Besen ['bezən], *m -s/-* broom. ◆**B~stiel**, *m* broomstick.
besessen [bə'zɛsən], *adj.* fanatical; **von einer Idee b.**, obsessed with an idea.
be'setz|en, *v.tr.* to occupy (a seat, post, *Mil:* a country); to fill (a space, vacancy, *Th:* part etc.). ◆**b~t**, *adj.* (*Sitz usw.*) taken; (*Toilette, Tel: Leitung*) engaged. ◆**B~tzeichen**, *n* engaged tone. ◆**B~ung**, *f -/-en* **1.** (*a* esp. *Mil:* occupation; (*b*) filling (of a vacancy); *Th:* casting (of a play). **2.** *Th:* cast.
besichtig|en [bə'zɪçtigən], *v.tr.* to look round (a school etc.); to view (a house); to see the sights of (a town). ◆**B~ung**, *f -/-en* look round; viewing; visit.
besied|eln [bə'ziːdəln], *v.tr.* to settle (in) (an area); **dünn/dicht besiedelt**, sparsely/densely populated. ◆**B~(e)lung**, *f -/no pl* settlement.
besiegeln [bə'ziːgəln], *v.tr.* to seal.
be'sieg|en, *v.tr.* (*a*) to defeat; (*b*) *Fig:* to overcome (doubts etc.). ◆**B~te(r)**, *m & f decl. as adj.* loser.
besinn|en [bə'zɪnən], *v.refl.irr.3* (*a*) **sich b.**, to think, reflect; **sich anders b.**, to change one's mind; (*b*) **sich auf j-n, etwas *acc* b.**, to remember s.o., sth. ◆**b~lich**, *adj.* contemplative. ◆**B~ung**, *f -/no pl* consciousness; (*wieder*) **zur B. kommen**, to regain consciousness; *Fig:* to come to one's senses. ◆**b~ungslos**, *adj.* unconscious.
Be'sitz, *m -es/no pl* **1.** property. **2.** (*das B~en*) ownership. ◆**B~er.irr.97** (*a*) to possess, own (property etc.); (*b*) to have (talent, courage etc.). ◆**B~er(in)**, *m -s/- (f -/-nen*) owner. ◆**B~ergreifung**, *f -/-en pl* taking possession; (*mit Gewalt*) seizure.
besohlen [bə'zoːlən], *v.tr.* to sole (a shoe etc.).
Besoldung [bə'zɔldʊŋ], *f -/-en* salary; *Mil:* pay.
besonder|e(r, s) [bə'zɔndərə(r,s)], *adj.* special; particular (reason, wish, care etc.). ◆**B~heit**, *f -/-en* peculiarity; special feature. ◆**b~s**, *adv.* particularly; (*e*)specially.
besonnen [bə'zɔnən], *adj.* prudent; (*umsichtig*) cautious; (*überlegt*) considered (opinion, judgement). ◆**B~heit**, *f -/no pl* prudence; caution.
be'sorg|en, *v.tr.* (*a*) to get (hold of), (*kaufen*) buy (sth.); (*b*) to see to (sth.);

◆**B~nis**, *f -/-se* anxiety. ◆**b~niserregend**, *adj.* worrying. ◆**b~t**, *adj.* worried, concerned. ◆**B~ung**, *f -/-en* (*Kauf*) purchase.
be'sprech|en, *v.tr.irr.14* (*a*) to discuss, review (a book, film etc.); **sich mit j-m b.**, to confer with s.o.; (*b*) **ein Tonband b.**, to record (one's voice) on a tape. ◆**B~ung**, *f -/-en* discussion; conference; (*Rezension*) review.
besser ['bɛsər], *adj.* better; **b. ist b.**, better safe than sorry; **du hättest b. geschwiegen**, you would have done better to keep quiet; (*oder*) **b. gesagt ...**, or rather ... ◆**b~n**, *v.tr.* to improve (sth.); to reform (a criminal etc.); **sich b.**, to get better; (*Pers.*) to mend one's ways. ◆**B~ung**, *f -/-en* improvement (+ *gen*, in); reformation; **gute B.!** get well soon! ◆**B~'wisser**, *m -s/-* know-all.
best- ['bɛst-], *comb.fm.* (*a*) best (paid, dressed etc.); (*b*) *F:* most (hated etc.). ◆**b~e(r, s)**, *adj.* best; **im b~n Fall(e)**, at best; **b~n Dank!** many thanks; **das B. wäre abzureisen**, it would be best to leave; **der/die/das B.**, the best; **es geschieht zu deinem B~n**, it is in your best interests; **er weiß es am b~n**, he knows best; **einen Witz zum b~n geben**, to tell a joke; **j-n zum b~n halten**, to pull s.o.'s leg. ◆**b~enfalls**, *adv.* at (the) best. ◆**b~ens**, *adv.* very well, excellently. ◆**B~leistung**, *f* best performance. ◆**b~möglich**, *adj.* best possible. ◆**B~zeit**, *f* fastest time.
Be'stand, *m* **1.** *no pl* continued existence; survival (of a nation, firm etc.); **B. haben/von B. sein**, to be enduring. **2.** stock (*an etwas dat*, of sth.). ◆**B~saufnahme**, *f* stock-taking. ◆**B~teil**, *m* component (part); *Fig:* element.
be'ständig, *adj.* (*a*) constant; (*b*) enduring (peace, friendship etc.); steadfast (friend etc.); reliable (worker etc.); settled (weather).
be'stärk|en, *v.tr.* to confirm (s.o.'s suspicions, doubts etc.).
bestätig|en [bə'ʃtɛːtigən], *v.tr.* to confirm (sth.); to verify (a statement etc.), endorse (an opinion etc.); (*bescheinigen*) to certify (sth., that ...). ◆**B~ung**, *f -/-en* confirmation; verification.
bestatt|en [bə'ʃtatən], *v.tr. Lit:* to inter (a corpse); to lay (s.o.) to rest. ◆**B~ung**, *f -/-en* funeral.
bestäuben [bə'ʃtɔybən], *v.tr.* (*a*) to dust (sth.); (*b*) *Bot:* to pollinate (a plant).
be'staunen, *v.tr.* to gaze at (s.o., sth.) in amazement/admiration.
be'stech|en, *v.tr.irr.14* (*a*) to bribe (s.o.); (*b*) *Fig:* to captivate (s.o.). ◆**b~end**, *adj.* fascinating (person, appearance etc.). ◆**b~lich**, *adj.* open to bribery; corruptible. ◆**B~ung**, *f -/-en* bribery, cor-

ruption.

Besteck [bə'ʃtɛk], n -(e)s/-e 1. cutlery. 2. *Med:* (set of) instruments.

be'stehen. I. v.tr.irr.100 1. v.i. (*haben*) (*a*) to exist; **es besteht ...**, there is ...; (*b*) **b. aus** + dat, (i) to be made of (rubber, metal etc.); (ii) to consist of (several parts, two members etc.); **der Unter-schied bestand darin, daß ...**, the difference was that ...; (*c*) **auf etwas** dat **b.**, to insist (up)on sth.; (*d*) *Sch:* **b.**, to pass the examination. **II.** v.tr. (*a*) to pass (*Sch:* an examination; *Tchn: Fig: etc:* a test). **II. B.**, n -s/no pl 1. existence. 2. insistence (**auf** + dat, on).

be'stehlen, v.tr.irr.2 to rob (s.o.).

be'steigen, v.tr.irr.89 to climb (a moun-tain etc.); to mount, get on(to) (a horse, bicycle etc.); to board (a train etc.); to ascend (the throne).

Be'stell-, comb.fm. Com: order (book, number etc.). ◆**b~en**, v.tr. (*a*) to order (goods, a meal etc.); (*b*) to book (a table, *Th:* seats etc.); (*c*) **j-n zu sich b.**, to sum-mon s.o.; (*d*) (*ausrichten*) **bestell deinem Bruder schöne Grüße von mir**, give my regards to your brother; **kann ich etwas b.?** can I take a message? (*e*) (*ernennen*) to appoint (a representative etc.), (*f*) to cul-tivate (the land, a garden etc.). ◆**B~schein**, m order form. ◆**B~ung**, f -/-en Com: order.

be'steuern, v.tr. to tax (s.o., sth.); to rate (a building).

besti'alisch [besti'ɑːlif], adj. bestial, bru-tal. ◆**B~ie**, f -/-n beast; *Fig:* (Pers.) brute.

be'stimm|en, v. 1. v.tr. (*a*) to fix, decide (on) (a price, time etc.); (*b*) to lay down (conditions, rules etc.); (*b*) to mean, in-tend (sth.); (*c*) **j-n/jmdn als Nachfolger b.**, to mark out(*ernennen*) appoint s.o. (as) one's successor; (*ermitteln*) to deter-mine the age, position of sth. etc.); to define (the meaning of a word etc.); *Bot:* to classify (plants); (*d*) to have a decisive influence on (s.o., sth.); (*regeln*) to gov-ern (the amount, size etc.). 2. v.i. (*ha-ben*) (*a*) **über etwas** acc (frei) **b.**, to be able to do what one likes with sth.; (*b*) (*anordnen*) to give orders. ◆**b~t**, adj. 1. definite (purpose, *Gram:* article); distinct (impression); **eine b~te Summe**, a cer-tain sum; (*b*) adv. certainly, definitely; **er wird es b. wissen**, he is sure to know. 2. particular, special; **hast du etwas B~es vor?** are you doing anything special? 3. firm, decisive (tone, manner etc.). ◆**b~theit**, f -/no pl 1. firmness, deci-siveness. 2. **etwas mit B. wissen/sagen**, to know/say sth. for certain. ◆**B~ung**, f -/-en 1. no pl fixing. 2. no pl (*Zweck*) ap-pointment; (*b*) (*Schicksal*) fate, destiny. 3. (*Ermittlung*) determination (of sth.); definition (of a word etc.). 4. (*Anordnung*) regulation; clause (of a contract). 5. no pl (*Zweck*) intended purpose.

◆**B~ungs-**, comb.fm. (port, country etc.) of destination.

be'straf|en, v.tr. to punish (s.o., sth.). ◆**B~ung**, f -/-en punishment.

be'strahl|en, v.tr. Med: to give (s.o.) ray(*mit Höhensonne*) sunlamp treatment. ◆**B~ung**, f ray/sunlamp treatment.

Be'streb|en, n -s/no pl endeavour; (*Ziel*) aim. ◆**b~t**, adj. at pains (to do sth.). ◆**B~ung**, f -/-en effort; (*Versuch*) at-tempt.

be'streichen, v.tr.irr.40 to spread (bread etc.).

be'streiten, v.tr.irr.41 (*a*) to dispute (a statement etc.); to challenge (s.o.'s right etc.); (*leugnen*) to deny (a fact, one's guilt etc.); (*b*) to pay for (sth.); to meet (costs); to provide (entertainment etc.).

be'streuen, v.tr. to sprinkle (sth.); *Cu:* to powder, dust (a cake etc.).

be'stürm|en, v.tr. (*a*) *Mil: etc:* to storm (the enemy, a town etc.); (*b*) to pester (s.o.) (**mit Fragen usw.**, with questions etc.).

be'stürz|en, v.tr. to dismay, alarm (s.o.), (*erschüttern*) stun (s.o.). ◆**B~ung**, f -/no pl dismay, alarm.

Besuch [bə'zuːx], m -(e)s/-e 1. visit; (*kurz*) call (**bei** j-m, on s.o.); **bei** j-m **ei-nen B. machen**, to pay s.o. a visit. 2. **der B. der Schule, Kirche usw.**, attend-ance at/going to school, church etc. 3. **B. bekommen**, to have visitors/a visitor. ◆**b~en**, v.tr. (*a*) to visit (s.o., a country etc.); (*kurz*) to call on (s.o.); (*b*) to attend (a meeting etc.); to go to (school, a museum, concert etc.). ◆**B~er(in)**, m -s/- (f -/-nen) visitor; *Th: etc:* patron. ◆**B~szeit**, f -/-en visiting time.

betätig|en [bə'tɛːtɪgən], v.tr. (*a*) to oper-ate (a machine etc.); (*b*) **sich b.**, to work, be active (**als, as**). ◆**B~ung**, f -/-en 1. no pl operation. 2. activity.

betäub|en [bə'tɔybən], v.tr. (*a*) (*Schlag usw.*) to stun, (*Lärm*) deafen (s.o.); (*b*) *Med:* to anaesthetize (s.o.); (*c*) to deaden (pain, a nerve etc.). ◆**b~end**, adj. 1. *Med:* anaesthetic (effect etc.); narcotic (drug). 2. (*berauschend*) intoxicating, heady (perfume etc.). ◆**B~ung**, f -/no pl 1. daze; dazed/stunned state. *Med:* anaesthetization; (*Narkose*) anaesthetic. ◆**B~ungsmittel**, n anaesthetic.

Bete ['beːtə], f -/-n **rote B.**, beetroot.

beteilig|en [bə'taɪlɪgən], v.tr. **sich b./ beteiligt sein an** + dat, to take part/ participate in (a game, competition etc.); to contribute to (a project, present etc.); **j-n an etwas** dat **b.**, to give s.o. a share in sth. ◆**B~te(r)**, m & f decl. as adj. person involved; participant; *Jur:* inter-ested party. ◆**B~ung**, f -/-en participa-tion; attendance (**an einem Kurs**, at a course).

beten ['beːtən], v.tr. & i. (*haben*) to pray.

beteuer|n [bə'tɔyərn], v.tr. to declare

(sth.) solemnly; to protest (one's innocence etc.). ◆B~ung, f -/-en declaration; protestation.

Beton [be'tɔŋ], m -s/-s & -e concrete. ◆b~ieren [-to'niːrən], v.tr. to concrete (a road etc.). ◆b~iert, adj. concrete.

beton|en [bəˈtoːnən], v.tr. to stress. ◆b~t, adj. 1. stressed (syllable etc.). 2. emphatic; studied (indifference, simplicity etc.). ◆B~ung, f -/-en emphasis, stress.

betören [bəˈtøːrən], v.tr. to bewitch, dazzle (s.o.).

Betracht [bəˈtraxt], m j-n, etwas in B. ziehen, (i) (erwägen) to consider (s.o., sth.); (ii) (berücksichtigen) to take s.o., sth. into account; j-n, etwas außer B. lassen, to disregard s.o., sth.; in B. kommen, to be possible. ◆b~en, v.tr. (a) to look at (s.o., sth., Fig: a problem etc.); (b) j-n als seinen Freund usw. b., to regard/look upon s.o. as one's friend etc. ◆B~er, m -s/- onlooker. ◆B~ung, f -/-en 1. no pl observation; bei genauerer B., on closer examination. 2. (Überlegung) reflection, meditation. ◆b~lich, adj. contemplative.

beträchtlich [bəˈtrɛçtlɪç], adj. considerable.

Betrag [bəˈtraːk], m -(e)s/-e amount, sum (of money). ◆b~en, I. v.tr.irr.85 (a) (Rechnung usw.) to amount to (1000 marks etc.); (b) sich b., to behave. II. B., n -s/no pl behaviour.

be'treff|en, v.tr.irr.100 to affect, concern (s.o., sth.); (sich beziehen auf) to refer to (s.o., sth.), Betrifft: …, re: …. ◆b~end, pres. & adj. relevant (person etc.). ◆b~s, prep. + gen concerning, with regard to s.o.

be'treiben, v.tr.irr.12 (a) to pursue (a hobby, policy, studies etc.); (b) to run (a business, a machine etc.).

be'treten. I. v.tr.irr.105 to enter, go into (a room, house etc.); to walk on (a lawn etc.); to step onto (a bridge etc.); B. verboten! keep out! II. adj. embarrassed; sheepish (smile).

betreu|en [bəˈtrɔʏən], v.tr. to take care of (s.o., sth.). ◆B~er(in), m -s/- (f -/-nen) (a) nurse; (im Hause) home help; (bei Unfällen usw.) relief worker; (b) Sp: coach. ◆B~ung, f -/no pl care.

Betrieb [bəˈtriːp], m -(e)s/-e 1. (Firma) concern, business; (Fabrik) factory, works. 2. no pl running, operation; in B., in use; (nicht defekt) working; außer B. (defekt) out of order. 3. no pl F: bustle; activity; (auf den Straßen) heavy traffic. ◆B~s-, comb.fm. 1. operating (costs, El: voltage etc.); working (capital, climate etc.); (b) staff, (Fabriks-) works (canteen, holidays etc.); company (doctor etc.). ◆B~sausflug, m staff outing/ N.Am: trip. ◆b~sfähig, adj. operational; in working order. ◆B~sgeheimnis, n trade secret. ◆b~sleitung, f management.

◆B~srat, m 1. works council. 2. (Pers.) works council member, approx. shop steward. ◆b~ssicher, adj. reliable (in operation). ◆B~sunfall, m accident at work. ◆B~swirt, m business administration graduate. ◆B~swirtschaft, f business administration; management (studies).

be'trinken, v.refl.irr.96 sich b., to get drunk.

betroffen [bəˈtrɔfən]. adj. upset; (bestürzt) taken aback; (gekränkt) hurt.

betrüb|en [bəˈtryːbən], v.tr. to sadden (s.o.). ◆b~lich, adj. sad; distressing (news etc.). ◆b~t, adj. sad; gloomy, (face etc.).

Betrug [bəˈtruːk], m -(e)s/no pl deception; (Betrügerei) cheating; trickery; Jur: fraud.

betrüg|en [bəˈtryːgən], v.tr.irr.63 1. v.tr. to deceive (s.o., oneself); to cheat (s.o.); Jur: to defraud (s.o.). 2. v.i. (haben) to cheat. ◆B~er(in), m -s/- (f -/-nen) deceiver; trickster; (beim Spiel usw.) cheat. ◆b~erisch, adj. deceitful (person); fraudulent (act etc.); in b~erischer Absicht, with intent to deceive.

betrunken [bəˈtrʊŋkən], adj.pred. drunk; attrib. drunken (man, driver etc.).

Bett [bɛt]. I. n -(e)s/-en bed; ins/zu B. gehen, to go to bed. II. B~-, comb.fm. bed (jacket, rest etc.); bedtime (reading etc.); bedding (box etc.). ◆B~bezug, m duvet/quilt cover. ◆B~decke, f (a) (aus Wolle) blanket; (gesteppt) quilt; (b) (Tagesdecke) bed spread. ◆b~en, v.tr. to lay, settle (s.o., sth.); sich b., to settle/lie down. ◆b~lägerig, adj. bed-ridden. ◆B~nässen, n bed-wetting. ◆B~tuch, n sheet. ◆B~vorleger, m bedside rug. ◆B~wäsche, f bed linen. ◆B~zeug, n F: bedding.

bettel|arm [ˈbɛtlʔarm], adj. desperately poor, destitute. ◆B~ei [-ˈlai], f -/-en 1. no pl begging. 2. (Flehen) pleading. ◆b~n, v.i. (haben) to beg.

Bettler(in) [ˈbɛtlər(in)], m -s/- (f -/-nen) beggar.

betulich [bəˈtuːlɪç], adj. fussy

Beug|e [ˈbɔʏgə], f -/-n bend. ◆b~en, v.tr. (a) to bend (one's arm, leg); to incline (one's head); (b) Lit: to break (s.o.'s will etc.); sich j-m, etwas dat b., to submit to s.o., sth.; (c) Gram: to inflect (a word). ◆B~ung, f -/-en 1. bending. 2. Gram: inflection.

Beule [ˈbɔʏlə], f -/-n 1. swelling. 2. (Vertiefung) dent.

beunruhig|en [bəˈʔʊnruːigən], v.tr. to worry (s.o., oneself). ◆B~ung, f -/no pl worry, anxiety.

beurkund|en [bəˈʔuːrkʊndən], v.tr. to register (births etc.); (beglaubigen) to certify (a statement etc.).

beurlaub|en [bəˈʔuːrlaubən], v.tr. (a) to grant (s.o.) time off/esp. Mil: leave; (b) Mil:Adm: to suspend (an official etc.).

beurteil|en [bə'ʔuːrtaɪlən], *v.tr.* to judge (s.o., sth.); to assess (value, s.o.'s work etc.). ◆**B~ung,** *f* -/-en **1.** judgement; (*Meinung*) opinion. **2.** (*schriftlich*) assessment.

Beute ['bɔytə], *f -/no pl* (*a*) booty; *Mil:* spoils; (*b*) (*Opfer*) prey.

Beutel ['bɔytəl], *m -s/-* bag; pouch (for tobacco, *Z:* of a kangaroo etc.).

bevölker|n [bə'fœlkərn], *v.tr.* (*Pers., Tier*) to inhabit (an area etc.); **eln dicht/dünn bevölkertes Land,** a densely/sparsely populated country. ◆**B~ung,** *f -/-en* population.

bevollmächtig|en [bə'fɔlmɛçtɪgən], *v.tr.* to authorize (s.o.); *Jur:* to give (s.o.) power of attorney. ◆**B~te(r),** *m & f decl. as adj.* authorized representative/*esp. Com:* agent; (*Beauftragter*) delegate. ◆**B~ung,** *f -/-en* (*a*) *no pl* authorization; (*b*) authority; *Jur:* power of attorney.

bevor [bə'foːr], *conj.* before.

bevormunden [bə'foːrmundən], *v.tr.* not to allow (s.o.) to make decisions.

bevorstehen [bə'foːrʃteːən], *v.i.sep.irr.100* (*haben*) (**unmittelbar/nahe**) **b.,** to be imminent; **ihm steht eine große Enttäuschung bevor,** he is in for a big disappointment. ◆**b~d,** *adj.* forthcoming. (**unmittelbar**) **b.,** imminent.

bevorzug|en [bə'foːrtsuːgən], *v.tr.* (*a*) to prefer (s.o., sth.); (*b*) (*begünstigen*) to give (s.o.) preferential treatment. ◆**b~t,** *adj.* privileged (person, position etc.). ◆**B~ung,** *f -/-en* preferential treatment; priority; (*ungerechte B.*) favouritism.

bewach|en [bə'vaxən], *v.tr.* to guard (a house, prisoners etc.). ◆**B~ung,** *f -/no pl* guarding; **unter B.,** under surveillance.

bewaffn|en [bə'vafnən], *v.tr.* to arm. ◆**B~ung,** *f -/-en* armament; (*Waffen*) arms, weapons.

bewahren [bə'vaːrən], *v.tr.* (*a*) to keep, preserve (sth.); (*b*) **j-n, etwas vor Schaden/einer Gefahr b.,** to preserve/protect s.o., sth. from harm/danger.

bewähr|en [bə'vɛːrən], *v.refl. sich b.,** to prove one's/its worth (*Einrichtungen usw.*) to prove a success. ◆**b~t,** *adj.* reliable, trustworthy (friend etc.); proven (remedy etc.); established (principle etc.). ◆**B~ung,** *f -/-en Jur:* probation. ◆**B~ungsfrist,** *f Jur:* (period of) probation.

bewahrheiten [bə'vaːrhaɪtən], *v.refl. sich b.,** to prove (to be) true (**an j-m,** in s.o.'s case).

bewältigen [bə'vɛltɪgən], *v.tr.* to cope with (problems, a pile of work etc.); to overcome (difficulties etc.); to get through (a task, *F:* food etc.).

bewandert [bə'vandərt], *adj.* well-versed.

bewässer|n [bə'vɛsərn], *v.tr.* to irrigate. ◆**B~ung,** *f -/no pl* irrigation.

beweg|en¹ [bə'veːgən], *v.tr.* (*a*) (*von der*

Stelle) to move (sth.); to shift (sth. large/heavy); **sich b.,** to move; (sich rühren) to stir; (*b*) (*rühren*) to move (s.o.); **Probleme, die uns alle b.,** problems which exercise all our minds. ◆**b~en²,** *v.tr.irr.* **j-n (dazu) b., etwas zu tun,** to make s.o. do sth. ◆**B~grund,** *m* motive. ◆**b~lich,** *adj.* **1.** movable (parts, feasts etc.); *Mil:* mobile (units, troops). **2.** (*rege*) active, agile (mind, person). ◆**D~lichkeit,** *f -/no pl* **1.** mobility. **2.** (*mental/physical*) agility. ◆**b~t,** *adj.* (*a*) (*Pers.*) moved, emotional (words etc.); (*b*) eventful (times, life etc.). ◆**B~ung,** *f -/-en* **1.** (*a*) movement; motion; (*b*) **körperliche B.,** physical exercise; (*c*) **eine religiöse/politische B.,** a religious/political movement. **2.** (*Erregung*) emotion. ◆**B~ungsfreiheit,** *f -/no pl* freedom of movement/*Fig:* action; *F:* elbowroom. ◆**b~ungslos,** *adj.* motionless.

be'weinen, *v.tr.* to weep for, mourn (s.o., sth.).

Beweis [bə'vaɪs], *m -es/-e* (*a*) proof, *pl.* **B~e,** evidence; (*b*) (*Zeichen*) sign, token. ◆**B~aufnahme,** *f Jur:* (hearing of) evidence. ◆**b~bar,** *adj.* provable. ◆**b~en** [-zən], *v.tr.irr.70* to prove (a fact, guilt, that ... etc.); to establish (innocence, the truth of sth. etc.). ◆**B~führung,** *f -/no pl* argumentation; (line of) argument. ◆**B~kraft,** *f* conclusiveness, cogency. ◆**b~kräftig,** *adj.* cogent, forceful. ◆**B~mittel,** *n* (piece of) evidence.

be'wenden, *v.tr.* **es dabei b. lassen,** to leave it at that.

be'werb|en, *v.refl.irr.101* **sich** (**um eine Stellung**) **b.,** to apply (for a job). ◆**B~er(in),** *m -s/- (f -/-nen)* applicant, candidate; *Sp:* contender (for a title etc.). ◆**B~ung,** *f -/-en* application.

bewerkstelligen [bə'vɛrk∫tɛlɪgən], *v.tr.* to manage, arrange (sth.).

be'werten, *v.tr.* to assess; to rate, evaluate (s.o.'s work etc.); *Fin:* to value (sth.).

bewillig|en [bə'vɪlɪgən], *v.tr.* to grant (credit etc.); (*genehmigen*) to approve (a new tax, payment etc.). ◆**B~ung,** *f -/-en* grant(ing); approval.

be'wirken, *v.tr.* to cause (sth.); to effect (a change, cure).

bewirten [bə'vɪrtən], *v.tr.* to entertain (guests etc.).

bewirtschaften [bə'vɪrt∫aftən], *v.tr.* to run (a farm etc.); to farm (land).

bewohn|bar [bə'voːnbaːr], *adj.* habitable; fit to live in. ◆**B~en,** *v.tr.* to occupy, live in (a house etc.); to inhabit (a region, country etc.). ◆**B~er,** *m -s/-* occupier, occupant; inhabitant.

bewölk|t [bə'vœlkt], *adj.* cloudy, overcast. ◆**B~ung,** *f -/no pl* (*Wolken*) clouds.

Bewunder|er [bə'vundərər], *m -s/-* admirer. ◆**b~n,** *v.tr.* to admire (s.o., sth.). ◆**b~nswert,** *adj.* admirable.

◆B~ung, f -/no pl admiration.

bewußt [bə'vust], adj. conscious; (a) **sich dat etwas gen b. werden**, to become aware/conscious of sth.; to realize sth.; (b) (absichtlich) deliberate (deception etc.); (c) (erwähnt) aforementioned.
◆b~los, adj. unconscious.
◆B~losigkeit, f -/no pl (state of) unconsciousness. ◆B~sein, n -s/no pl consciousness, awareness; bei (vollem) B., (fully) conscious.

be'zahl|en, v.tr.&i. (haben) to pay (s.o., an amount, price, bill etc.); to pay for (goods, Fig: a mistake etc.). ◆B~ung, f -/no pl payment.

be'zaubern, v.tr. to captivate, enchant (s.o.). ◆b~d, adj. enchanting.

be'zeichn|en, v.tr. (a) to mark (a spot, path etc.); (b) (nennen) to call (s.o., oneself, sth.) (als etwas acc, sth.).
◆b~end, adj. characteristic, typical (für j-n, etwas acc, of s.o., sth.).
◆B~ung, f -/-en 1. marking; indication; genaue/nähere B., specification 2. (Ausdruck) expression.

be'zeugen, v.tr. to bear witness to, testify (to) (sth.).

bezichtigen [bə'tsiçtigən], v.tr. j-n eines Verbrechens b., to accuse s.o. of a crime. ◆B~ung, f -/-en accusation.

bezieh|bar [bə'tsi:ba:r], adj. (Wohnung usw.) ready to be moved into, vacant. ◆b~en, v.tr.irr.113 (a) to cover, (neu b.) recover (an armchair etc.); die Betten frisch b., to change the bedclothes; (b) to move into (a house, flat etc.); Mil: to take up (a position etc.); Fig: adopt a standpoint; (c) to obtain (goods etc.); to take (a newspaper etc.); to receive (a salary, pension etc.); (d) etwas auf etwas acc b., to relate sth. to sth.; (Pers., Bemerkung usw.) sich auf j-n, etwas b., to refer to s.o., sth. ◆B~ung, f -/-en 1. (a) pl freundschaftliche/diplomatische B~en, friendly/diplomatic relations; gute B~en zu j-m haben, to be on good terms with s.o.; (b) pl contacts; (c) (Zusammenhang) connection; zwei Dinge zueinander in B. setzen, to connect/link two things. 2. (Verhältnis) relationship. 3. (Hinsicht) in dieser/jeder B., in this/every respect. ◆b~ungslos, adj. unrelated, unconnected. ◆B~ungsweise, adv. or.

Bezirk [bə'tsirk], m -(e)s/-e district.

Bezug [bə'tsu:k], m -(e)s/-e 1. cover (of a cushion etc.); loose cover, N.Am: slipcover (of a chair etc.); (pillow-)case. 2. no pl (Erwerb) obtaining; drawing (of a salary etc.). 3. pl B~e, salary, income. 4. (Zusammenhang) reference; mit B./in b. auf j-n, etwas acc, concerning/regarding s.o., sth. ◆b~sfertig, adj. vacant (house etc.); pred. ready to move into. ◆B~sperson, f person to whom one relates. ◆B~spreis, m purchase/subscription price. ◆B~squelle, f

source of supply; supplier.

bezüglich [bə'tsy:kliç], prep. + gen concerning, regarding.

bezwecken [bə'tsvɛkən], v.tr. to aim at (sth.).

be'zweifeln, v.tr. to doubt.

be'zwing|en, v.tr.irr.19 to conquer (an enemy, Fig: fear, mountain etc.); to vanquish (an opponent); Fig: to keep (one's curiosity, anger etc.) under control.

BH [be'ha:], m -(s)/-(s) F: bra.

Bibel ['bi:bəl], f -/-n Bible.

Biber ['bi:bər], m -s/- beaver.

Biblio|graphie [bibliogra'fi:], f -/-n bibliography. ◆B~thek [-'te:k], f -/-en library. ◆B~thekar(in), [-te'ka:r(in)], m -s/-e (f -/-nen) librarian.

biblisch ['bi:bliʃ], adj. biblical.

bieder ['bi:dər], adj. (a) honest, upright; (b) Pej: (spießig) bourgeois.

bieg|en ['bi:gən]. I. v.irr. 1. v.tr. to bend (wire, a branch etc.). 2. v.i. (sein) um die Ecke/in eine Straße usw. b., to turn the corner/into a street etc. II. B., n -s/no pl bending, curving; es geht auf B. oder Brechen, it's all or nothing. ◆b~sam, adj. flexible; pliable (material); supple (body, limbs). ◆B~ung, f -/-en bend.

Biene ['bi:nə], f -/-n 1. bee. 2. F: (Mädchen) bird. ◆B~n-, comb.fm. bee's, bee (sting etc.); (swarm etc.) of bees; B~n (honey). ◆B~nkönigin, f queen bee. ◆B~nkorb, m (basket-work) beehive. ◆B~nstich, m beesting; Cu: plain cake covered in grated almonds and sugar. ◆B~nstock, m beehive. ◆B~nwachs, m beeswax.

Bier [bi:r]. I. n -(e)s/-e beer; drei B., three beers/glasses of beer. II. 'B~-, comb.fm. beer (barrel, garden etc.). ◆B~brauer, m -s/- brewer. ◆B~deckel, m beer mat. ◆B~dose, f beer can. ◆B~krug, m beer mug.

Biest [bi:st], n -(e)s/-er (also Fig) beast.

biet|en ['bi:tən], v.tr.irr.8 to offer (sth.); to provide (shelter, an opportunity etc.); (tausend Mark) auf etwas acc b., to bid (a thousand marks) for sth.; das lasse ich mir nicht b.! I won't stand for that.

Bigamie [biga'mi:], f -/-n bigamy.

Bikini [bi'ki:ni], m -s/-s bikini.

Bilanz [bi'lants], f -/-en 1. balance; (schriftlich) balance sheet. 2. Fig: (net) result; die B. ziehen, to draw conclusions; (rückblickend) to take stock.

Bild [bilt]. I. n -(e)s/-er picture; das äußere B. der Stadt, the (outward) appearance of the town; in B~ern sprechen, to speak figuratively; bist du im B~e? are you in the picture? II. 'B~-, comb.fm. picture (editor etc.); pictorial (document, book etc.). ◆B~bericht, m photo-reportage. ◆B~erbuch, n picture book. ◆B~fläche, f screen; F: von der B. verschwinden, disappear from the scene. ◆B~hauer, m sculptor. ◆b~lich, adj. 1. pictorial (representation etc.). 2. figurative (expression etc.). ◆'B~nis, n -sses/-sse portrait. ◆'B~platte, f video disc. ◆'B~schärfe, f definition (of the image). ◆'B~schirm, m screen. ◆'b~schön, adj. gorgeous. ◆'B~text, m/'B~unterschrift, f caption.

bilden ['bildən], v.tr. (a) to form, (gestalten) shape (sth.); **die b~enden Künste,** the fine arts; *j-g:* **j-s Charakter b.,** to mould s.o.'s character; (b) (darstellen) to be (sth.); **die Regel/eine Ausnahme b.,** to be the rule/an exception; (c) (erziehen) to educate (s.o., oneself etc.). ◆'B~ung, f -/no pl 1. (Bilden) formation; (Formen) shaping. 2. (Erziehung) education; (general) knowledge, culture. ◆'B~ungs-, comb.fm. educational (policy, reform etc.). ◆'B~ungslücke, f gap in one's education. ◆'B~ungsweg, m type of education; **der zweite B.,** further education.

Billard ['biljart]. I. n -s/-e billiards. II. 'B~-, comb.fm. billiard (room etc.). ◆'B~kugel, f billiard ball. ◆'B~queue, n billiard cue.

billig ['bilıç]. I. adj. 1. (a) cheap; low (price); F: **b. davonkommen,** to get off lightly; (b) (dürftig) poor (goods); **b~e Ausrede,** feeble excuse. 2. **recht und b.,** right and proper. II. 'B~-, comb.fm. cheap (flight, goods); low (price). ◆'b~en [-gən], v.tr. to give (sth.) one's approval; (amtlich) to sanction (sth.). ◆'B~ung, f -/no pl approval.

Billion [bili'oːn], f -/-en billion; *N.Am:* trillion.

bimmeln ['bıməln], v.i. (haben) F: to ring.

Binde ['bındə], f -/-n (a) bandage; (b) (Armb.) armband; (c) F: (Damenb.) sanitary towel. ◆'B~glied, n (connecting) link. ◆'b~en, v.tr.irr.9 (a) to tie (a knot, shoelaces, s.o.'s hands etc.); (fesseln) to bind (s.o.), tie (s.o.) up; (zusammenb.) to tie/bind (sth.); to bind (a book, *Ch:* gases etc.); (b) **ich bin durch/an mein Versprechen gebunden,** I am bound by my promise; **ich will mich nicht nicht b.,** I do not want to commit myself/esp. get married yet. ◆'b~end, adj. binding; hard-and-fast (rule). ◆'B~estrich, m hyphen. ◆'B~faden, m string; **ein B.,** a piece of string. ◆'B~ung, f -/-en 1. tie, bond; (gefühlsmäßig) attachment; (Verpflichtung) commitment. 2. (Skib.) binding.

binnen ['bınən]. I. prep. + dat/occ. gen within; **b. kurzem,** shortly. II. 'B~-, comb.fm. inland (harbour, sea etc.); internal, home (trade etc.). ◆'B~land, n the interior of a country).

Binse ['bınzə], f -/-n Bot: rush; F: **in die B~n gehen,** to go west. ◆'B~nweisheit, f truism.

Bio|graph [bio'graːf], m -en/-en biographer. ◆'B~graphie [-a'fiː], f -/-en biography. ◆'B~loge [-'loːgə], m -n/-n biologist. ◆'B~logie [-lo'giː], f -/no pl biology. ◆'b~logisch, adj. 1. biological. 2. Agr: organic (cultivation).

Birke ['bırkə], f -/-n birch (tree).

Birn|baum ['bırnbaum], m 1. pear tree. 2. (Holz) pearwood. ◆'B~e, f -/-n 1. (a) (Frucht) pear; (b) (Baum) pear tree. 2. El: (light) bulb.

bis [bıs]. I. prep. + acc 1. until; **b. jetzt,** up to now; so far; **b. heute,** until today; (nachdrücklich) to this day; **von 9 b. 5 Uhr,** from nine to/till five; **von Montag b. Freitag,** from Monday to Friday, *N.Am:* Monday through Friday; **bald/später/morgen usw.,** see you soon/later/tomorrow etc.; **b. in die Nacht (hinein),** (far) into the night; **b. zum nächsten Mal/zum 1. Mai,** until the next time/May 1st. 2. (nicht später als) by; **b. dahin/Montag,** by then/Monday. 3. (räumlich) as far as; **b. wohin?** how far? **von oben b. unten,** from top to bottom. 4. (+etc.) **b. aufs höchste,** to the utmost; **b. ins kleinste/letzte,** down to the last detail. 5. **b. auf** (a) (inklusive) including; (b) (mit Ausnahme von) **b. auf dich sind alle fertig,** everyone is ready except (for) you. 6. (mit Zahlen) **b. zu,** up to. II. conj. until. ◆'b~'her, adv. so far, up to now ◆'b~'herig, adj existing (up to now). ◆'b~'lang, adv. so far, up to now.

Bischof ['bıʃɔf], m -s/-e bishop.

bischöflich ['bıʃøːflıç], adj. episcopal.

Biskuit [bıs'kviːt], n & m -(e)s/-s & -e *Cu:* sponge.

Biß [bıs], m -sses/-sse bite. ◆'b~chen, inv.s. **ein b.,** a bit.

Biss|en ['bısən], m -s/- bite, mouthful (of food). ◆'b~ig, adj. 1. vicious (dog etc.). 2. biting, caustic (remark etc.).

Bistum ['bıstuːm], n -s/-er bishopric, diocese.

bisweilen [bıs'vailən], adv. *Lit:* sometimes, from time to time.

bitte ['bıtə]. I. adv. please; **ja, b.?** yes? **b. schön!** (etwas anbietend) do have/take one! **vielen Dank!**—**b. sehr/schön!** thank you very much!—don't mention it/*N.Am:* you're welcome; (wie) **b.?** pardon? **na b.!** there you are, you see! what did I tell you? II. B~, f -/-n request; (dringend) plea. ◆'b~n, v.tr.&ri.irr. (haben) (j-n) **um etwas acc b.,** to ask (s.o.) for sth.; **j-n zu sich dat b.,** to ask s.o. to come to see one.

bitter ['bıtər], adj. bitter; **etwas b. nötig haben,** to need sth. desperately. ◆'b~böse, adj. (wütend) furious, livid; (übel) villainous. ◆'B~keit, f -/no pl bitterness; (Verbitterung) rancour; acrimony (of a remark etc.). ◆'b~lich, adv. bitterly.

Bizeps ['biːtsɛps], m -es/-e biceps.

bläh|en ['blɛːən], v.tr. (a) (Wind) to swell (sails); **sich b.**, (Segel) to swell, (Gardine) billow; (Nüstern) to flare; (b) Appr. (Speisen) to cause flatulence. ◆**B~ungen**, fpl flatulence, F: wind.

blam|abel [bla'maːbəl], adj. humiliating; ignominious (defeat). ◆**B~age** [-'maːʒə], f -/-n humiliation [-'maːʒə]. ◆**b~ieren** [-'miːrən], v.tr. to make (s.o.) look foolish/small; **sich b.**, to make a fool of oneself.

blank [blaŋk], adj. 1. shiny (metal, boots etc.). 2. (nackt) bare (skin, boards etc.). 3. (rein) pure, sheer (nonsense, envy etc.). 4. F: (pleite) (stony) broke.

blanko ['blaŋko], inv.adj. ◆**B~scheck**, m blank cheque.

Blas|e ['blaːzə], f -/-n 1. (a) bubble; Tchn: flaw (in glass etc.); (b) Med: blister. 2. Anat: bladder. ◆**B~ebalg**, m bellows. ◆**b~en**, v.irr. 1. v.tr. (a) to blow; (b) Mus: to play (a flute, oboe, a tune etc.). 2. v.i. (haben) to blow. ◆**B~instrument**, n wind instrument. ◆**B~kapelle**, f Mus: brass band.

blasiert [bla'ziːrt], adj. blasé.

blaß [blas], adj. (a) pale (face, person, colour etc.); Fig: colourless (style, description etc.); (b) (schwach) faint (hope); vague (memory, idea etc.).

Blässe ['blɛsə], f -/no pl paleness, pallor; Fig: colourlessness.

bläßlich ['blɛslɪç], adj. pallid, rather pale.

Blatt [blat], n -(e)s/¨er 1. leaf (of tree), leaf (of paper); Mus: **vom B. singen/spielen**, to sight-read; Fig: **das steht auf einem anderen B.**, that is another matter. 3. (Zeitung) (news)paper. 4. (Spielkarte) (playing) card; **ein gutes B. haben**, to have a good hand. 5. blade (of an oar, axe, a saw).

blätter|n ['blɛtərn], v.i. (a) (haben) in einem Buch b., to leaf/glance through a book; (b) (sich) (Farbe usw.) to flake (off). ◆**B~teig**, m puff pastry.

blau [blau], adj. 1. blue; **ein b~es Auge**, a black eye; **ein b~er Fleck**, a bruise; Aal/Forelle **b.**, boiled eel/trout; **eine Fahrt ins B~e**, a mystery tour. 2. F: (betrunken) tight. ◆**b~äugig**, adj. blue-eyed. ◆**B~beere**, f bilberry, N.Am: blueberry. ◆**B~licht**, n blue light. ◆**b~machen**, v.i.sep. (haben) F: to malinger, stay away from work. ◆**B~pause**, f blueprint. ◆**B~säure**, f prussic acid.

Blech [blɛç], n -(e)s/-e 1. sheet metal; (für Dosen usw. & Pej:) tin. 2. no pl Mus: brass. 3. no pl F: (Unsinn) rubbish, rot. II. **'B~-**, comb.fm. (a) tin (drum etc.); metal (shears etc.); (b) Mus: brass (instrument etc.). ◆**B~dose**, f tin, can. ◆**b~en**, v.i. (haben) F: to fork out. ◆**B~schaden**, m superficial damage (to the bodywork).

Blei [blai], n -(e)s/-e 1. lead. 2. (B~lot) plumb, lead. ◆**'b~ern**, adj. lead.

◆**'b~haltig**, adj. containing lead. ◆**'B~stift**, m pencil. ◆**B~stiftspitzer**, m pencil sharpener.

Bleibe ['blaibə], f -/-n F: place to stay. ◆**b~en**, v.i.irr. (sein) 1. to stay, remain; (a) **das bleibt unter uns**, (that's) strictly between ourselves; **bei der Sache b.**, to keep to the point; b. **Sie bitte am Apparat!** hold the line please! (b) F: **wo bleibst du denn?** what's keeping you? what's happened to you? (c) to remain, be left; **es bleibt keine andere Wahl**, there is no other choice [left]; (d) **bei seiner Meinung b.**, to stick to one's opinion; **es bleibt dabei**, that's settled/final. ◆**b~nd**, adj. permanent (damage etc.); lasting (effect etc.). ◆**b~nlassen**, v.tr.sep.irr.57 to leave/let (sth.) alone; **an deiner Stelle würde ich es b.**, I wouldn't do it if I were you.

bleich [blaiç], adj. pale, white (face etc.). ◆**b~en**, v.tr. to bleach.

Blend|e ['blɛndə], f -/-n 1. shield, shade (for the eyes). 2. Phot: diaphragm; (Öffnung) aperture, stop. ◆**b~en**, v.tr.&i. (haben) (also Fig:) to dazzle (s.o.); (blind machen) to blind (s.o.). ◆**b~end**, adj. dazzling (beauty etc.); magnificent (sight, spectacle etc.); brilliant (speech, achievements etc.); adv. marvellously, wonderfully; **es geht ihm b.**, he's in great form.

Blick [blik], m -(e)s/-e 1. (kurz) glance; **finsterer B.**, scowl; **die B~e auf sich acc ziehen**, to attract attention; **Liebe auf den ersten B.**, love at first sight. 2. (Aussicht) view. 3. **einen/keinen B. für etwas acc haben**, to have an/no eye for sth. ◆**b~en**, v. 1. v.i. (haben) (a) to look; (b) F: **sich b. lassen**, to show one's face. ◆**B~fang**, m eye-catcher. ◆**B~feld**, n field of vision. ◆**B~winkel**, m point of view.

blind ['blint], adj. 1. blind (für + acc, to); **ein B~er/eine B~e**, a blind man/woman. 2. cloudy (mirror etc.); dull, tarnished (metal); b~er **Alarm**, false alarm; b~er **Passagier**, stowaway. ◆**B~darm**, m appendix. ◆**B~darmentzündung**, f appendicitis. ◆**B~en-**, comb.fm. (home, school, Rad: programme etc.) for the blind. ◆**B~enhund**, m guide dog (for the blind). ◆**B~enschrift**, f braille. ◆**B~flug**, m instrument/blind flight. ◆**B~gänger**, m dud (shell); P: (Pers.) dud. ◆**B~heit**, f -/no pl blindness. ◆**b~lings**, adv. blindly; b. **rennen/stürzen**, to rush headlong. ◆**B~schleiche**, f -/-n slow-worm. ◆**b~schreiben**, v.i.sep.irr.12 (haben) to touch-type.

Blink- [bliŋk-], comb.fm. flashing (light etc.); ◆**B~anlage**, f Aut: hazard warning lights. ◆**b~en**, v.i. (haben) (Stern, Licht usw.) to twinkle; (regelmäßig/als Signal) to flash; Aut: etc: to signal. ◆**B~er**, m -s/- Aut: (flashing) indicator. ◆'B~**licht**, n indicator.

blinzeln ['blintsəln], v.i. (haben) to blink; (mit einem Auge) to wink.

Blitz [blits]. **I.** m -es/-e 1. lightning; ein B., a flash of lightning. 2. Phot:/ F: flash. **II.** 'B~-, comb.fm. (a) lightning (attack, war etc.); (b) Phot: flash (cube etc.). ◆'b~**ableiter**, m lightning conductor. ◆'b~**en**, v.i. (haben) v.i. impers. es blitzte, there was a flash of lightning; (b) to flash, sparkle. ◆'B~**licht**, n flash unit. ◆'B~**licht**, n flash(light). ◆'b~**schnell**, adj. lightning (movement, reaction etc.); split-second (decision); adv. with lightning speed.

Block [blɔk], m -(e)s/-e & -s 1. (pl -e) block (of stone etc.). 2. (a) ein B. Briefpapier, a writing pad; (b) Pol: bloc; (c) block (of houses). ◆'B~**ade** [-'ka:də], f -/-n blockade. ◆'B~**flöte**, f recorder. ◆'b~**frei**, adj. Pol: non-aligned (state). ◆'B~**hütte**, f log cabin. ◆'b~**ieren** [-'ki:rən], v. 1. v.tr. to block, obstruct (a road, Rail: line, Fig: decision etc.); to stop (traffic, supplies etc.); to jam (a machine, Tel: lines etc.); Aut: to lock (the wheels); Mil: to blockade (a port). 2. v.i. (haben) (Räder) to lock; (Motor usw.) to seize. ◆'B~**schrift**, f block capitals.

blöd(e) [blø:t, -də], adj. F: (a) silly, daft (person, remark etc.); (b) (ärgerlich) b~e Situation, stupid situation. ◆'B~**heit**, f -/-n stupidity; (Äußerung) stupid remark. ◆'B~**sinn**, m F: rubbish; P: crap. ◆'b~**sinnig**, adj. F: nonsensical (chatter); idiotic (behaviour, idea).

blöken ['blø:kən], v.i. (haben) (Schafe) to bleat; (Rinder) low.

blond [blɔnt], adj. blonde, fair (hair, beard); fair-haired (person). ◆B~**ine** [-'di:nə], f -/-n blonde (woman).

bloß [blo:s], adj. & adv. 1. bare; mit b~en Füßen, barefoot; mit b~em Auge, with the naked eye. 2. (a) mere (supposition, trifle etc.); (b) adv. F: only, just; (verstärkend) **mach das b. nicht wieder!** don't you dare do that again! **was soll ich ihm b. sagen?** what on earth am I going to tell him? ◆'b~**legen**, v.tr.sep. to expose (sth.). ◆'b~**liegen**, v.i.sep. 62 (sein) to be exposed. ◆'b~**stellen**, v.tr.sep. to compromise (s.o., oneself).

Blöße ['blø:sə], f -/-n 1. Lit: nakedness. 2. sich dat eine B. geben, to show one's weak spot.

blühen ['bly:ən], v.i. (haben) (a) to flower, be in bloom/(Bäume) in blossom; (b) Fig: (Pers., Geschäft usw.) to flourish, thrive; F: das kann dir auch noch b., that could happen to you too. ◆'b~**d**, adj. 1. (a) Bot: flowering; in flower/bloom; (b) thriving (person, business). 2. eine b~e Phantasie, a very fertile imagination.

Blum|e ['blu:mə], f -/-n 1. flower. 2. (a)

bouquet (of wine); (b) froth, head (on beer). ◆'B~**en**-, comb.fm. flower (bed, arrangement, garden, shop etc.); floral (design etc.). ◆'B~**enkohl**, m cauliflower. ◆'B~**enstrauß**, m bunch of flowers, bouquet; (klein) posy. ◆'B~**entopf**, m flowerpot. ◆'B~**enzwiebel**, f bulb. ◆'b~**ig**, adj. flowery.

Bluse ['blu:zə], f -/-n blouse.

Blut [blu:t], n -(e)s/no pl blood; mit B. befleckt, bloodstained; F: (nur) ruhig B.! keep calm! keep your hair on! **II.** 'B~-, comb.fm. blood (-bath, group, orange, sausage, transfusion etc.). ◆'B~**alkohol**, m blood alcohol level. ◆'b~**arm**, adj. anaemic. ◆'b~**befleckt**, adj. bloodstained. ◆'B~**bild**, n blood count. ◆'B~**buche**, f copper beech. ◆'B~**druck**, m blood pressure. ◆'B~**egel**, m leech. ◆'b~**en**, v.i. (haben) to bleed. ◆'B~**erguß** m effusion of blood; haematoma. ◆'b~**ig**, adj. 1. bloody, gory. 2. (verstärkend) complete (beginner, layman etc.). ◆'b~**jung**, adj. very young. ◆'B~**probe**, f blood test. ◆'B~**schande**, f incest. ◆'B~**spender**, m blood donor. ◆'B~**ung**, f -/-en bleeding; Med: haemorrhage. ◆'B~**vergiftung**, f blood poisoning.

Blüte ['bly:tə], f -/-n 1. flower, bloom; (von Obstbäumen) blossom. 2. (Blühen) flowering, blooming; blossoming. 3. Fig: in der B. seiner Jahre, in the prime of life. 4. F: dud (bank) note. ◆'B~**nstaub**, m pollen. ◆'b~**n-weiß**, adj. snow-white. ◆'B~**zeit**, f 1. flowering period; blossom-time (of a tree). 2. Fig: great period (of a culture etc.); (a) prosperity; (b) heyday; great period of a culture.

Bö [bø:], f -/-en gust; (Regenbö) squall.

Bock [bɔk], m -(e)s/-e 1. (a) Z: (Roh, Kaninchen) buck; (Ziegenb.) he-/F: billygoat; (Schafb.) ram; (b) F: der ist ein sturer B., he's as stubborn as a mule. 2. (Gestell) stand (for tools etc.); trestle (for a table); (Schemel) stool; Sp: (vaulting-) horse. ◆'b~**en**, v.i. (haben) (Pferd usw.) to dig in its heels; (sich aufbäumen) to rear; F: (Pers.) to be badtempered; Aut: (Motor) to fire unevenly. ◆'b~**ig**, adj. pigheaded. ◆'B~**shorn**, n F: j-n ins B. jagen, to put the wind up s.o. ◆'B~**wurst**, f large sausage for boiling.

Boden ['bo:dən]. **I.** m -s/- 1. ground; (Erde) soil; (Fußb.) floor; den B. unter den Füßen verlieren, to lose one's footing; (im Wasser) get out of one's depth; F: ich war am B. zerstört, I was absolutely shattered. 2. (Grundlage) basis; auf dem B. der Tatsachen stehen, to be firmly based on fact. 3. bottom (of a box etc.); B. des Meeres, sea bed. 4. (*Dachb.*) attic, loft. **II. B~**, *comb.fm.* ground (frost, *Av:* staff etc.); floor (area etc.); *Agr:* land (reform etc.). **◆'b~heizung,** *f* under-floor heating. **◆'b~los,** *adj.* abysmal (ignorance etc.); boundless (stupidity etc.). **◆'B~satz,** *m* -es/*no pl* sediment, *F:* dregs. **◆'B~schätze,** *mpl* mineral resources. **◆'B~see.** *Pr.n.m.* der B., Lake Constance. **◆'B~turnen,** *n* floor exercises.

Bogen ['bo:gən], *m* -s/- & [1]. 1. arch (of a bridge etc.); **die Straße macht einen B. nach links,** the road curves round to the left. 2. (*Waffe* & *Mus:* bow. 3. sheet (of paper). **◆'B~gang,** *m* arcade. **◆'B~schießen,** *n* archery. **◆'B~schütze,** *m* archer.

Bohle ['bo:lə], *f* -/-n (thick) plank.

Böhm|en ['bø:mən]. *Pr.n.n* -s. Bohemia. **◆'b~isch,** *adj.* Bohemian.

Bohne ['bo:nə], *f* -/-n bean. **◆'B~nkaffee,** *m* pure/*F:* real coffee. **◆'B~nstange,** *f* (a) beanstick; (b) *F:* (*Pers.*) beanpole.

bohner|n ['bo:nərn], *v.tr.* to polish (a floor). **◆'B~wachs,** *n* floor polish.

bohr|en ['bo:rən], *v.tr.* 1. *v.tr.* to bore. 2. *v.i.* (*haben*) (a) to drill (**nach** + *dat*, for); **in der Nase b.,** to pick one's nose; *Fig:* **b~ender Schmerz,** gnawing pain; (b) *F:* (*drängen*) to keep on; **b~ende Fragen,** probing/persistent questions. **◆'B~er,** *m* -s/- drill. **◆'B~insel,** *f* drilling platform/rig. **◆'B~loch,** *n* bore-hole. **◆'B~maschine,** *f* power-drill; *Ind:* drilling machine. **◆'B~turm,** *m* (drilling) derrick.

böig ['bø:iç], *adj.* gusty; squally.

Boje ['bo:jə], *f* -/-n buoy.

Bollwerk ['bɔlvɛrk], *n* (*also Fig:*) bulwark.

Bolzen ['bɔltsən], *m* -s/- bolt.

bomb|ardieren [bɔmbar'di:rən], *v.tr.* to bombard (a town etc.; *F:* s.o. with questions etc.). **◆'B~e** ['bɔmbə], *f* -/-n bomb. **◆'B~en-,** *comb.fm.* 1. bomb (attack, crater, damage etc.). 2. *F:* terrific, fantastic (success etc.).

Bon [bɔŋ], *m* -s/-s 1. (*Gutschein*) voucher. 2. (*Kassenzettel*) receipt.

Bonbon ['bɔŋbɔŋ, bõ'bõ], *m* & *n* -s/-s sweet; *N.Am:* (*sing.* & *pl.*) candy.

Bonus ['bo:nus], *m* -/-ses)/-(se) bonus; extra dividend.

Bonze ['bɔntsə], *m* -n/-n *F:* big shot/*N.Am:* wheel.

Boot [bo:t], *n* -(e)s/-e boat. **◆'B~s-,** *comb.fm.* boat (builder, hook, race, hire etc.). **◆'B~ssteg,** *m* landing-stage.

Bord[1] [bɔrt], *n* -(e)s/-e shelf.

Bord[2], *n* -(e)s/-e an B. (**eines Schiffes**), aboard/on board (a ship); **von B. gehen,** to go ashore. **◆'B~buch,** *n* log (book). **◆'B~funk,** *m* ship's radio. **◆'B~karte,** *f* boarding ticket. **◆'B~stein,** *n* kerb(stone).

Bordell [bɔr'dɛl], *n* -s/-e brothel.

borgen ['bɔrgən], *v.tr.* (a) **j-m etwas b.,** to lend sth. to s.o./lend s.o. sth.; (b) **sich** *dat* **etwas** (**bei/von j-m**) **b.,** to borrow sth. (from s.o.).

borniert [bɔr'ni:rt], *adj.* narrow-minded.

Börse ['bœrzə], *f* -/-n 1. *Fin:* stock exchange; (*Warenb.*) commodity market. 2. (*Geldbeutel*) purse. **◆'B~nmakler,** *m* stockbroker (on the Exchange).

Borst|e ['bɔrstə], *f* -/-n bristle. **◆'b~ig,** *adj.* 1. bristly. 2. (*grob*) surly.

Borte ['bɔrtə], *f* -/-n braid.

bös [bø:s], *adj.* = **b~e**. **◆'b~artig,** *adj.* 1. vicious (animal); malicious (person, remark etc.). 2. *Med:* malignant (disease etc.). **◆b~e** ['bø:zə], *adj.* 1. (a) evil, wicked (person, act etc.); **das B~e,** evil; (b) bad, nasty (illness); terrible (shock, mistake); **es war nicht b~e gemeint,** no harm was intended. 2. *F:* (*zornig*) angry, cross. **◆'B~ewicht,** *m* villain; scoundrel. **◆'b~willig,** *adj.* (a) ill-willed, malicious; (b) *Jur:* wilful (damage etc.).

Böschung ['bœʃuŋ], *f* -/-en slope; (*steil*) escarpment; (*Damm*) embankment.

bos|haft ['bo:shaft], *adj.* wicked, evil; (*böswillig*) spiteful, malicious. **◆'B~heit,** *f* -/-en 1. *no pl* malice, spite. 2. (*Bemerkung*) malicious remark.

Boß [bɔs], *m* -sses/-sse *F:* boss.

Botan|ik [bo'ta:nik], *f* -/*no pl* botany. **◆b~isch,** *adj.* botanical.

Bot|e ['bo:tə], *m* -n/-n messenger. **◆'b~engang,** *m* errand. **◆'B~schaft,** *f* -/-en 1. message. 2. (*Vertretung*) embassy. **◆'B~schafter(in),** *m* -s/- (*f* -/-nen) ambassador.

Bottich ['bɔtiç], *m* -s/-e tub; (*für Wein usw.*) vat.

Bouillon [bul'jõ, -jɔŋ], *f* -/-s broth; clear soup.

Bowle ['bo:lə], *f* -/-n punch.

box|en ['bɔksən]. **I.** *v.* 1. *v.i.* (*haben*) to box; **gegen j-n b.,** to fight s.o. 2. *v.tr.* to punch (s.o., *F:* sth.). **II. B.,** *n* -s/*no pl* boxing. **◆'B~er,** *m* -s/- boxer. **◆'B~kampf,** *m* boxing match; fight. **◆'B~sport,** *m* boxing.

Boykott [bɔy'kɔt], *m* -(e)s/-s & -e boycott. **◆b~ieren** [-'ti:rən], *v.tr.* to boycott (s.o., sth.).

brachliegen ['bra:xli:gən], *v.i.sep.irr.62* (*haben*) to lie fallow.

Branche ['brã:ʃə], *f* -/-n branch (of industry etc.); (*Gewerbe*) trade; (line of) business. **◆'B~nverzeichnis,** *n Tel:* classified directory; *Brit:* yellow pages.

Brand [brant]. **I. B~-,** *m* -(e)s/-e 1. fire, blaze; **in B. geraten,** to catch fire. 2. *no pl Med:* gangrene. **II. 'B~-,** *comb.fm.* (a) fire (-wall etc.); incendiary (bomb etc.); (b) burning (smell etc.). **◆'B~mal,** *n* burning (mark); *Agr:* (*Zeichen*) brand; *Fig:* stigma. **◆'B~marken,** *v.tr. insep.* to condemn (s.o., sth.) (publicly); to brand

(s.o.). ◆'B~**stifter**, m fire-raiser.
◆'B~**stiftung**, f arson. ◆'B~**wunde**,
f burn.

brand|en ['brandən], v.i. (haben) (Wellen
usw.) to break. ◆'B~**ung**, f -/no pl
surf.

Branntwein ['brantvain], m spirit; coll.
spirits.

Brasil|ianer(in) [brazili'ɑːnər(in)], m -s/-
(f -/nen) Brazilian. ◆**b~i'anisch**, adj.
Brazilian. ◆**B~ien** [bra'ziːljən]. Pr.n.n
-s. Brazil.

Brat- ['braːt], comb.fm. fried (fish etc.),
roast (meat); baked (apple). ◆**b~en. I.**
v.tr. & i.irr. (haben) to roast (meat, potatoes etc.); to bake (apples); (in der
Pfanne) to fry (meat, potatoes etc.); Fig:
(Pers.) in der Sonne b., to roast in the
sun. **II. B~en**, m -s/- (gebraten) roast;
(auch roh) joint; er hat den B~en ge-
rochen, he got wind of it/(Unangenehmes)
smelt a rat. ◆'B~**ensoße**, f
gravy. ◆'B~**hähnchen**, n roast
chicken. ◆'B~**kartoffeln**, fpl fried
potatoes. ◆'B~**pfanne**, f frying
pan. ◆'B~**rost**, m grill; (im Freien) barbecue. ◆'B~**wurst**, f fried sausage.

Bratsche ['braːtʃə], f -/-n viola.

Brauch [braux], m -(e)s/-e custom; (im
Geschäft usw.) practice. ◆'b~**bar**, adj.
usable (material, tool etc.); practicable
(idea etc.). ◆'B~**barkeit**, f -/no pl usa-
bility; practicality. ◆'b~**en**, v.tr. (a) to
need (sth.); du brauchst nicht hinzugehen, you don't have to/need to go there;
(b) (benutzen) to use (sth.).

Braue ['brauə], f -/-n (eye)brow.

brau|en ['brauən], v.tr. to brew.
◆'B~**er**, m -s/- brewer. ◆'B~e'**rei**, f
-/-en brewery.

braun [braun], adj. brown; bay (horse).
◆'b~**gebrannt**, adj. sun-tanned.

Bräun|e ['brɔynə], f -/no pl tan.
◆'b~**en**, v.tr. & i. (haben) (a) to turn
(sth.) brown; (in der Sonne) to tan (s.o.,
skin etc.); (b) Cu: to brown (meat, onions etc.). ◆'B~**lich**, adj. brownish.
◆'B~**ung**, f -/no pl 1. (Bräunen) brown-
ing; tanning. 2. brownness; (sun)tan.

Brause ['brauzə], f -/-n 1. (a) (für Blumen
usw.) (watering) rose, sprinkler; (b)
(Dusche) shower. 2. F: (Limonade) (fizzy)
lemonade. ◆'b~**n**, v.i. (haben) (a) to
roar; (b) (duschen) to have/take a shower.
◆'B~**pulver**, n fizzy lemonade powder;
Brit: sherbet.

Braut [braut], f -/-e bride; (Verlobte)
fiancée. **II. 'B~-**, comb.fm. bridal (bouquet, veil etc.). ◆'B~**jungfer**, f bridesmaid. ◆'B~**paar**, n bridal pair.

Bräutigam ['brɔytigam], m -s/-e (a)
fiancé; (am Hochzeitstag) bridegroom.

brav [braːf], adj. 1. good, well-behaved
(child etc.). 2. (bieder) worthy, honest
(man, citizen etc.).

Brech|bohne ['brɛçboːnə], f French
bean. ◆'B~**eisen**, n crowbar.

◆'b~**en**, v.irr. 1. v.tr. (a) to break
(sth., Fig: a record, contract, etc.); to
violate (a truce, an oath etc.); Med: to
fracture (a bone); die Ehe b., to commit
adultery; (b) Opt: to refract, bend (light
rays). 2. v.i. (a) (sein) to break; (b) (sein)
to burst, break out; (c) (haben) mit j-m/
einer Partei usw. b., to break with s.o./
break away from a party etc.; (d) (haben)
F: (sich übergeben) to vomit, be sick.
◆'D~**reiz**, m (feeling of) nausea.
◆'B~**stange**, f crowbar.

Brei [brai], m -(e)s/-e pulp; Cu: mash;
(Haferb.) porridge.

breit [brait], adj. wide (street, mouth
etc.); broad (shoulders, grin, base etc.);
die b~e Masse, the vast majority; die
b~e Öffentlichkeit, the general public.
◆'B~**e**, f -/-n 1. width, breadth of
shoulders etc.). 2. Geog: latitude.
◆'B~**engrad**, m (degree of) latitude.
◆'B~**gefächert**, adj. wide-ranging (interests etc.). ◆'b~**machen**, v.refl.sep.
F: sich b., to take up a lot of room.
◆'b~**schult(e)rig**, adj broad-
shouldered. ◆'b~**treten**, v.tr.sep.irr.
105 F: to flog (a subject), go on about
(sth.); to spread (a story etc.).
◆'B~**wand**, f wide screen.

Brems- [brɛms-], comb.fm. brake (light,
drum etc.). ◆'B~**belag**, m brake lining. ◆'B~e [brɛmzə], f -/-n brake.
◆'b~**en**, v. 1. v.tr. to slow down (a vehicle, Fig: development etc.); to hold
(s.o.) back. 2. v.i. (haben) to brake.
◆'B~**spur**, f braking/tyre marks.
◆'B~**weg**, m braking distance.

brenn|bar ['brɛnbaːr], adj. combustible;
(leicht) b., inflammable. ◆'b~**en**, v.irr.
1. v.i. (haben) (a) to burn; (Haus usw.) to
be on fire; es brennt! fire! F: wo
brennt's denn? what's (all) the rush? (b)
Fig: darauf b., etwas zu tun, to be dying
to do sth.; (c) (Licht, Lampe) to be alight;
das Licht b. lassen, to leave the light
on; (d) (Wunde, Augen usw.) to smart,
sting. 2. v.tr. to burn (sth., a hole etc.);
to fire (pottery, tiles etc.); to distil
(spirits). ◆'B~**holz**, n firewood.
◆'B~**material**, n -s/no pl fuel.
◆'B~**nessel**, f stinging nettle.
◆'B~**punkt**, m 1. Opt: etc: focal point.
2. Fig: centre, focus (of interest etc.).
◆'B~**spiritus**, m methylated spirits.
◆'B~**stoff**, m fuel.

brenzlig ['brɛntsliç], adj. F: risky,
dodgy.

Bretagne [bre'tanjə]. Pr.n. f Brittany.

Brett [brɛt], n -(e)s/-er 1. board; (dicker)
plank. 2. F: pl: (a) skis; (b) Th: die
B~er, the boards. ◆'B~**erzaun**, m
wooden fence. ◆'B~**spiel**, n board
game.

Brezel ['breːtsəl], f -/-n pretzel.

Brief [briːf], m -(e)s/-e letter.
◆'B~**beschwerer**, m -s/- paperweight.
◆'B~**freund(in)**, m (f) penfriend,

N.Am: penpal. ◆'B~**kasten**, *m* letter box, *N.Am:* mailbox. ◆'B~**kopf**, *m* letterhead. ◆'b~**lich**, *adv.* by letter. ◆'B~**marke**, *f* (postage) stamp. ◆'B~**marken**, *comb.fm.* stamp (collector, album etc.). ◆'B~**papier**, *n* writing paper, notepaper. ◆'B~**porto**, *n* letter rate. ◆'B~**tasche**, *f* wallet, *N.Am:* billfold. ◆'B~**taube**, *f* carrier pigeon. ◆'B~**träger**, *m* postman, *N.Am:* mailman. ◆'B~**trägerin**, *f* postwoman. ◆'B~**umschlag**, *m* envelope. ◆'B~**wahl**, *f* postal vote. ◆'B~**wechsel**, *m* correspondence.

Brigade [bri'gɑːdə], *f* -/-n brigade.

Brikett [bri'kɛt], *n* -s/-s (coal) briquette.

brillant [bril'jant]. I. *adj.* brilliant. II. B., *m* -en/-en brilliant, diamond.

Brille ['brilə], *f* -/-n 1. (pair of) spectacles, glasses; **eine B. tragen**, to wear spectacles/glasses. 2. toilet seat. ◆'B~**n-**, *comb.fm.* spectacle (wearer etc.).

bringen ['briŋən], *v.tr.irr.* (a) to bring, (*wegb.*) take (s.o., sth.); (b) to yield (profit, interest etc.); **die Möbel brachten viel Geld**, the furniture fetched a lot of money; *F:* **das bringt nichts**, it doesn't get you anywhere; (c) *F:* (*veröffentlichen*) to publish (an article etc.); *TV:* to screen (a programme etc.); *Rad:Th:* to put on (a play etc.); (d) **es zu etwas dat b.**, to achieve sth.; **es weit b.**, to go far; (+ *prep.*) **j-n auf die Idee b.**, to give s.o. the idea; **etwas hinter sich b.**, to get sth. over and done with; **j-n in Gefahr/Verlegenheit b.**, to endanger/embarrass s.o.; **j-n um etwas acc b.**, to deprive s.o. of sth.; **j-n zum Lachen/zur Verzweiflung b.**, to reduce s.o. to laughter/despair; **j-n dazu b., daß er etwas tut**, to get s.o. to do sth.

brisant [bri'zant], *adj. Fig:* explosive (question etc.); controversial (book etc.).

Brise ['briːzə], *f* -/-n breeze.

Brit|e ['briː(ː)tə], *m* -n/-n Briton; *N.Am:* Britisher. ◆**b~isch** ['briːtiʃ], *adj.* British.

bröck|e|lig ['brœk(ə)liç], *adj.* crumbly, crumbling. ◆'**b~eln**, *v.tr.* & *i.* (*haben*) to crumble.

Brocken ['brɔkən], *m* -s/- bit of (bread, meat etc.); lump (of coal etc.); snatch; *F:* snippet (of a conversation etc.); **ein harter B.**, a tough nut (to crack).

brodeln ['broːdəln], *v.i.* (*haben*) to bubble.

Brokat [bro'kɑːt], *m* -(e)s/-e brocade.

Brokkoli ['brɔkoli], *pl.* broccoli.

Brombeere ['brɔmbeːrə], *f* -/-n blackberry.

bronch|ial [brɔnçi'ɑːl], *adj.* bronchial. ◆**B~ien**, *fpl* bronchial tubes. ◆**B~itis** [-'çitis], *f* -/no *pl* bronchitis.

Bronze ['brõːsə], *f* -/-n bronze.

Brosche ['brɔʃə], *f* -/-n brooch.

Broschüre [brɔ'ʃyːrə], *f* -/-n (*Heft*) booklet; (*Flugschrift*) pamphlet.

Brot [broːt], *n* -(e)s/-e bread; **ein B. mit Käse**, a piece of bread and cheese; **belegte B~e**, open sandwiches. ◆'B~**erwerb**, *m* livelihood. ◆'B~**krume**, *f*/'B~**krümel**, *m* breadcrumb. ◆'b~**los**, *adj.* **das ist eine b~e Kunst**, there is no money in that.

Brötchen ['brøːtçən], *n* -s/- (bread) roll.

Bruch [brux], *m* -(e)s/-e 1. (a) breaking; bursting of a dike etc.); (b) (*B~stelle*) break; fracture (of metal part, *Med:* bone); *Med:* (*Riß*) rupture; (*Eingeweide*) hernia; (c) breach (of a contract etc.); break (**mit der Tradition**, with tradition); breaking-up (of a friendship etc.); (*Ehe usw.*) **in die B~e gehen**, to break up. 2. *Mth:* fraction. 3. *Com:* (a) (*B~schaden*) breakage; (b) damaged goods; *F:* junk. ◆'B~**bude**, *f* hovel. ◆'B~**landung**, *f* crash-landing. ◆'B~**stelle**, *f* break; (*im Glas usw.*) crack; *Med:* (point of) fracture. ◆'B~**stück**, *n* fragment; snatch (of a song, conversation etc.). ◆'B~**teil**, *m* fraction.

brüchig ['bryçiç], *adj.* brittle, (*bröckelig*) crumbly; cracked (leather, *Fig:* voice).

Brücke ['brykə], *f* -/-n 1. bridge. 2. (*Teppich*) rug.

Bruder ['bruːdər], *m* -s/- brother.

brüder|lich ['bryːdərliç], *adj.* brotherly, fraternal. ◆'B~**lichkeit**, *f* -/no *pl* brotherliness. ◆'B~**schaft**, *f* -/-en 1. **sie tranken B.**, they drank to their friendship (and to calling each other 'du'). 2. brotherhood.

Brüh|e ['bryːə], *f* -/-n 1. *Cu:* broth; clear soup; (*Grundlage für Suppe*) stock. 2. *Pej: F:* (*Wasser*) **schmutzige B.**, murky water. ◆'b~**en**, *v.tr. Cu:* to pour boiling water over, scald (meat, vegetables etc.). ◆'B~**würfel**, *m* stock cube.

brüllen ['brylən], *v.i.* (*haben*) (a) (*Vieh*) to low, (*Stier*) bellow; (*Raubtier, Fig: Kanonen*) to roar; (b) (*schreien*) to yell, bawl; *F:* (*Baby*) to scream, howl; *F:* **es war zum B.**, it was a scream.

Brumm|bär ['brumbɛːr], *m* -en/-en *F:* grouser, *Hum:* grumbleguts. ◆'b~**en**, *v.* -*i.* *v.i.* (*haben*) (*Insekten*) to buzz, drone; (*Bären*) to growl; (*Fig: Motor, Orgel usw.*) (*laut*) to boom; (*leise*) to drone; (*summen*) to hum; **mir brummt der Kopf/Schädel**, my head's throbbing. 2. *v.tr.&i.* (*haben*) (a) to sing (sth.) out of tune; (b) to grumble, grouse; (*etwas*) **b.**, to mumble (sth.). ◆'b~**ig**, *adj. F:* grumpy, surly.

brünett [bry'nɛt], *adj.* brunette (girl); brown (hair).

Brunnen ['brunən], *m* -s/- 1. well; (*Quelle*) spring. 2. (*Heilquelle*) spa water(s).

brüsk ['brysk], *adj.* brusque, curt. ◆**b~ieren** [-'kiːrən], *v.tr.* to snub (s.o.). ◆**B~ierung**, *f* -/-en snub.

Brüssel ['brysəl]. *Pr.n.n* -s. Brussels.
Brust [brust], *f* -*/e* 1. *no pl* chest; *Cu: Fig: & Lit:* breast. 2. (*der Frau*) breast; **einem Kind die B. geben**, to breastfeed a child. ◆'**B~bein**, *n* breastbone. ◆'**B~korb**, *m* thorax. ◆'**B~schwimmen**, *n* breaststroke. ◆'**B~umfang**, *m* chest measurement. ◆'**B~warze**, *f* nipple.
brüst|en ['brystən], *v.refl.* **sich b.**, to boast (**mit** etwas *dat*, about sth.). ◆**B~ung**, *f* -*/-en* parapet.
Brut [bru:t], *f* -*/-en* 1. incubation (of eggs). 2. brood (of birds, bees). ◆'**B~kasten**, *m* incubator. ◆'**B~reaktor**, *m* breeder (reactor). ◆'**B~stätte**, *f* (*also Fig:*) breeding-ground.
brutal [bru'ta:l], *adj.* brutal, (*grausam*) cruel. ◆**B~ität** [-ali'tɛ:t], *f* -*/-en* 1. *no pl* brutality, cruelty. 2. act of brutality.
brüt|en ['bry:tən], *v.* 1. *v.i.* (*haben*) (*a*) (*Vogel*) to brood, (*Henne*) sit (on her eggs); (*b*) (*Pers.*) **über** etwas *acc* **b.**, to ponder/brood over sth. 2. *v.tr.* to plot (revenge etc.). ◆**B~er**, *m* -s/- breeder (reactor).
brutto ['bruto], *adv. Com:* gross.
brutzeln ['brutsəln], *v.* 1. *v.i.* (*haben*) to sizzle. 2. *v.tr. F:* to fry (sausages etc.).
Bub [bu:p], *m* -en/-en boy. ◆**B~e** ['-bə], *m* -n/-n (*Spielkarte*) jack, knave.
Buch [bu:x], *n* -(e)s/*er* (*a*) book; (*b*) *Cin:* script; (*c*) *Com:* **die B~er führen**, to keep the books/accounts. ◆'**B~binder**, *m* -s/- bookbinder. ◆'**B~drucker**, *m* printer. ◆'**B~führung**, *f* book-keeping, accounts. ◆'**B~halter(in)**, *m* (*f*) bookkeeper. ◆'**B~haltung**, *f* 1. *no pl* book-keeping. 2. accounts department. ◆'**B~handel**, *m* book trade. ◆'**B~händler(in)**, *m* (*f*) bookseller. ◆'**B~handlung**, *f* bookshop, *N.Am:* bookstore. ◆'**B~macher**, *m* bookmaker. ◆'**B~prüfer**, *m* auditor.
Buch|e ['bu:xə], *f* -/-n beech (tree). ◆'**B~ecker**, *f* -/-n beechnut. ◆'**B~fink**, *m* chaffinch.
buchen ['bu:xən], *v.tr.* (*a*) to enter (a sum etc.); (*b*) to book (a seat etc.).
Bücher|bord ['by:çərbort], *n/* ◆'**B~brett**, *n* bookshelf. ◆'**B~ei** [-'rai], *f* library. ◆'**B~regal**, *n* bookshelves.
Buchse ['buksə], *f* -/-n (*a*) *Tchn:* bush; (*b*) *El:* socket.
Büchse ['byksə], *f* -/-n 1. (*a*) (*rund*) tin, *esp. N.Am:* can; (*aus Porzellan usw.*) jar; (*b*) (*verschließ.*) small box. 2. (*Jagdgewehr*) sporting rifle. ◆'**B~n-**, *comb.fm.* tinned, *esp. N.Am:* canned (fruit etc.). ◆'**B~nöffner**, *m* tin/*esp. N.Am:* can opener.
Buchstab|e ['bu:xʃta:bə], *m* -ns/-n letter (of the alphabet). ◆**b~ieren** [-ʃta'bi:rən], *v.tr.* to spell (out) (a word).
buchstäblich ['bu:xʃtɛ:pliç], *usu. adv.* literally.

Bucht [buxt], *f* -/-en bay.
Buchung ['bu:xuŋ], *f* -/-en 1. entry. 2. (*Reservierung*) booking, reservation.
Buck|el ['bukəl], *m* -s/- (*a*) *F:* back; (*b*) (*krummer B.*) hunchback; **die Katze machte einen B.**, the cat arched its back. ◆'**b~(e)lig**, *adj.* 1. hunchbacked (person). 2. *F:* bumpy (road etc.).
bücken ['bykən], *v.refl.* **sich b.**, to bend (down), stoop (**nach** etwas *dat*, to pick sth. up).
Bückling ['byklɪŋ], *m* -s/-e 1. *F: Hum:* (low) bow. 2. (*Fisch*) buckling.
Buddh|ismus [bu'dɪsmus], *m* -/*no pl* Buddhism. ◆**B~ist**, *m* -en/-en Buddhist.
Bude ['bu:də], *f* -/-n 1. (*a*) (*auf dem Markt usw.*) stall, booth; (*b*) (*Baub.*) site hut. 2. *F:* (*Bruchb.*) hovel, dump. 3. *F:* (*Mietszimmer*) digs; (*Wohnung*) place, pad.
Budget [by'dʒe:], *n* -s/-s budget.
Büfett [by'fɛt], *n* -(e)s/-s & -e 1. sideboard. 2. (*Theke*) (buffet) counter. 3. **kaltes B.**, cold buffet.
Büffel ['byfəl], *m* -s/- buffalo.
büffeln ['byfəln], *v. F:* 1. *v.i.* (*haben*) to cram, *Brit:* swot. 2. *v.tr.* to swot/*N.Am:* bone up (a subject).
Bug [bu:k], *m* -(e)s/-e *Nau:* bow(s); *Av:* nose.
Bügel ['by:gəl], *m* -s/- 1. (*Kleiderb.*) clothes-/coat-hanger. 2. (*a*) (*Steigb.*) stirrup; (*b*) (*hacksaw etc.*) frame; handle (of a bag etc.). 3. side-piece (of spectacles). ◆'**B~brett**, *n* ironing board. ◆'**B~eisen**, *n* (electric) iron. ◆'**B~falte**, *f* crease (in trousers). ◆'**b~frei**, *adj.* non-iron (material); drip-dry (shirt etc.). ◆'**b~n**, *v.* 1. *v.tr.* to iron (clothes etc.). 2. *v.i.* (*haben*) to do the/some ironing.
bugsieren [bu'ksi:rən], *v.tr. F:* to steer (s.o.), manoeuvre (sth.).
Buh|ruf ['bu:ru:f], *m* boo. ◆'**b~en**, *v.i.* (*haben*) *F:* to boo.
Bühne ['by:nə], *f* -/-n 1. *Th:* stage; *F:* **alles ging glatt über die B.**, everything went off smoothly. 2. platform; (*Hebeb.*) hydraulic lift. ◆'**B~n-**, *comb.fm.* (*a*) stage (lighting, version, words etc.); (*b*) dramatic (art etc.). ◆'**B~nbild**, *n* scenery, set. ◆'**B~ntechnik**, *f* production technique(s).
Bukett [bu'kɛt], *n* -s/-s & -e bouquet (of flowers/wine).
Bulgar|e [bul'gɑːrən], *m* -n/-n *Pr.n.n* -s. Bulgaria. ◆**b~isch**, *adj.* Bulgarian.
Bull|auge [bul'augə], *n Nau:* porthole. ◆'**B~dogge**, *f* bulldog. ◆'**B~e**, *m* -n/-n 1. bull. 2. *Pej: P:* (*Polizist*) rozzer; **die B~en**, the fuzz. ◆'**b~ig**, *adj. F:* 1. stocky, beefy. 2. scorching (heat).
Bumerang ['bu:məraŋ], *m* -s/-s & -e boomerang.
Bummel ['buməl], *m* -s/- *F:* stroll. ◆'**B~ant**, *m* -en/-en *F:* slowcoach; time-waster; (*Nichtstuer*) loafer. ◆'**B~elei**, *f* -/*no pl* dawdling; idleness.

◆'b~**eln**, *v.i. F:* (*a*) (*sein*) to stroll, saunter; (*b*) (*haben*) to dawdle, loiter; (*bei der Arbeit*) to waste time; (*faulenzen*) to loaf about. 2. *Pej:* = ◆**elant.**

◆'B~**elzug**, *m F:* stopping train.
◆'B~**ler(in)**, *m -s/- (f -/-nen) F:* 1. stroller. 2. *Pej:* = ◆**elant.**

Bund¹ [bunt], *n -(e)s/-e* bundle; bunch (of radishes etc.).

Bund², *m -(e)s/-e* 1. (*a*) bond (of friendship etc.); (*Verband*) association; *esp. Pol:* confederation; (*Bündnis*) alliance; **mit j-m im B~e sein,** to be associated/*Pej:* in league with s.o.; **der B.,** the Federation; (*Regierung*) the Federal Government. 2. *Cl:* waistband. ◆'B~**es-,** *comb.fm.* federal (capital, government, state etc.). ◆'B~**esbahn,** *f* Federal Railways. ◆'b~**esdeutsch,** *adj.* West German. ◆'B~**esgebiet,** *n -(e)s/no pl* federal territory; *West G:* (territory of the) Federal Republic. ◆'B~**eskanzler,** *m* Federal Chancellor. ◆'B~**esland,** *n West G:* Federal State; *Aus:* Province. ◆'B~**espost,** *f* (Federal) Post Office. ◆'B~**espräsident,** *m* President of the Federal Republic. ◆'B~**esrat,** *m* Upper House of the Federal Republic. ◆'B~**esrepublik,** *f* Federal (German) Republic. 1. *West G:* confederation. 2. (*Gliedstaat*) federal state. ◆'B~**esstraße,** *f* Federal Highway, main road. ◆'B~**estag,** *m* the Lower House (of the Federal Republic). ◆'B~**eswehr,** *f* Federal Armed Forces.

Bünd|**chen** ['byntçən], *n -s/-* neckband; (*an Ärmeln*) cuff. ◆'B~**el,** *n -s/-* bundle; wad (of banknotes). ◆'b~**eln,** *v.tr.* to tie (wood, banknotes etc.) into a bundle/bundles; to truss (hay, straw). ◆'b~**ig,** *adj.* 1. valid, convincing (argument etc.); conclusive (proof etc.). 2. (*kurz*) succinct, terse (answer etc.); precise (style). 3. *Tchn:* on a level, flush. ◆'B~**nis,** *n -ses/-se* alliance.

Bungalow ['buŋgalo], *m -s/-s* bungalow; *N.Am:* ranch house.

Bunker ['buŋkər], *m -s/-* bunker.

bunt [bunt]. **I.** *adj.* (*a*) coloured; (*vielfarbig*) colourful, multi-coloured; (*grell*) gaudy (colours, clothes etc.); (*b*) (*gemischt*) mixed, varied (programme etc.); (*wirr*) in a jumble; (*c*) *F:* **jetzt wird's mir zu b.!** I've had enough! that's going too far! **II.** *B~-,* *comb.fm.* coloured (glass, paper etc.). ◆'B~**stift,** *m* coloured pencil; crayon. ◆'B~**wäsche,** *f* coloureds.

Bürde ['byrdə], *f -/-n* burden.

Burg [burk], *f -/-en* castle. ◆'B~**friede(n),** *m* truce. ◆'B~**graben,** *m* moat. ◆'B~**ruine,** *f* ruined castle.

Bürg|**e** ['byrgə], *m -n/-n* guarantee; (*Pers.*)

guarantor. ◆'b~**en,** *v.i.* (*haben*) **für j-n, etwas** *acc* **b.,** to vouch/*Fin:* stand surety for s.o., sth. ◆'B~**schaft,** *f -/-en* guarantee, surety.

Bürger(in) ['byrgər(in)], *m -s/- (f -/-nen)* citizen. ◆'B~**initiative,** *f* (community) pressure group; (*Aktion*) public campaign. ◆'B~**krieg,** *m* civil war. ◆'b~**lich,** *adj.* 1. civil (rights, marriage etc.). 2. (*a*) middle-class (family etc.); *esp. Pej:* bourgeois (attitude etc.); (*b*) (*einfach*) plain, homely (cooking etc.). ◆'B~**meister,** *m* mayor. ◆'B~**pflicht,** *f* duty as a citizen. ◆'B~**recht,** *n* citizenship; *esp. pl* **B~rechte,** civil rights. ◆'B~**schaft,** *f -/-en* 1. citizens, townspeople. 2. (*in Hamburg/Bremen*) City Parliament. ◆'B~**steig,** *m* pavement, *N.Am:* sidewalk. ◆'B~**tum,** *n -s/no pl* middle class(es), bourgeoisie.

Büro [by'ro:], *n -s/-s* office. ◆'B~**angestellte(r),** *m & f decl. as adj.* office worker. ◆'B~**klammer,** *f* paper clip. ◆'b~**krat** [-o'kra:t], *m -en/-en* bureaucrat. ◆'B~**kratie** [-a'ti:], *f -/-n* bureaucracy. ◆'b~**kratisch** [-'kra:tiʃ], *adj.* bureaucratic. ◆'B~**schluß,** *m* (office) closing time.

Bursche ['burʃə], *m -n/-n* 1. lad, youth. 2. *F:* (*Kerl*) chap, bloke; *esp. N.Am:* guy. ◆'b~**ikos** [-i'ko:s], *adj.* 1. (*Mädchen*) (tom)boyish; (*Frau*) mannish. 2. (*salopp*) sloppy.

Bürste ['byrstə], *f -/-n* brush. ◆'b~**n,** *v.tr.* to brush (sth.).

Bus [bus], *m -ses/-se* bus; *Brit:* (*für Ausflüge/längere Strecken*) coach.

Busch [buʃ], *m -(e)s/-e* bush. ◆'b~**ig,** *adj.* 1. bushy (eyebrows etc.). 2. (*Gelände*) bush-covered. ◆'B~**werk,** *n* bushes; (*Sträucher*) shrubbery.

Büschel ['byʃəl], *n -s/-* tuft (of grass, hair); bunch, clump (of flowers etc.); cluster (of blossoms).

Busen ['bu:zən], *m -s/-* bosom. ◆'B~**freund(in),** *m (f)* bosom friend.

Buß|**e** ['bu:s-], *comb.fm.* (sacrament etc.) of penance/repentance. ◆'B~**e,** *f -/-n* 1. *Ecc: no pl* penance. 2. *Jur:* fine. ◆'B~**geld,** *n* fine.

Bussard ['busart], *m -s/-e* buzzard.

büß|**en** ['by:sən], *v.tr.&i.* (*haben*) (**für**) **etwas b.,** to pay the penalty for (sth.); **für seine Sünden b.,** to atone for one's sins. ◆'B~**er,** *m -s/-* penitent.

Büste ['bystə], *f -/-n* bust. ◆'B~**nhalter,** *m* brassière, *F:* bra.

Butter ['butər], *f -/no pl* butter; *F:* **es ist alles in —** everything's just fine. ◆'B~**blume,** *f* buttercup. ◆'B~**brot,** *n* slice of bread and butter. ◆'B~**brotpapier,** *n* greaseproof paper. ◆'B~**dose,** *f* butter dish.

C

C, c [tse:], n -/- (the letter) C, c.

Café [ka'fe:], n -s/-s café.

Camp [kɛmp], n -s/-s camp. ◆'**c~en**, v.i. (haben) to camp. ◆'**C~er**, m -s/- (Pers.) camper. ◆'**C~ing**, n camping. ◆'**C~ingplatz**, m camp site/N.Am: ground.

Caravan ['karavan], m -s/-s (a) (motor) caravan, N.Am: camper; (b) (Kombi) estate car, N.Am: station wagon.

Cell|ist(in) [tʃe'list(in)], m -en/-en (f -/-nen) cellist. ◆'**C~o**, n -s/-lli & -s cello.

Chamäleon [ka'mɛːleɔn], n -s/-s chameleon.

Champagner [ʃam'panjər], m -s/- champagne.

Champignon ['ʃampinjɔ], m -s/-s mushroom.

Chance ['ʃãːsə], f -/-n (a) chance; die C~n stehen gleich/zwei zu eins, the odds are even/two to one; (b) (Gelegenheit) opportunity.

Chaos ['kaːɔs], n -/no pl chaos. ◆**cha'otisch**, adj. chaotic.

Charakter [ka'raktər], m -s/-e [-'teːrə] character. ◆**c~i'sieren**, v.tr. to characterize (s.o., sth.); (schildern) to portray, depict (s.o., sth.); (kennzeichnen) to typify (s.o., sth.). ◆**C~istik** [-'ristik], f -/-en characterization; (C~bild) character sketch. ◆**c~istisch** [-'ristiʃ], adj. typical, characteristic. ◆**c~lich**, adj. (qualities etc.) of character; adv. in character. ◆**c~los**, adj. insipid (colour, taste); characterless (person, building). ◆**C~losigkeit**, f -/no pl insipidness. ◆**c~schwach**, adj. spineless, weak-kneed. ◆**c~stark/c~voll**, adj. full of character; (person) of strong personality. ◆**C~zug**, m trait.

charmant [ʃar'mant], adj. charming; delightful. ◆**Charme** [ʃarm], m -s/no pl charm.

Charter- [(t)ʃartər-], comb.fm. charter (flight etc.). ◆**c~n**, v.tr. to charter (a plane etc.).

Chauffeur [ʃɔ'føːr], m -s/-e chauffeur; (taxi) driver.

Chaussee [ʃɔ'seː], f -/-n [-'seːən] high road.

Chauvin|ismus [ʃovi'nismus], m -/no pl chauvinism. ◆**C~ist**, m -en/-en chauvinist. ◆**c~istisch**, adj. chauvinistic.

checken ['tʃɛkən], v.tr.&i. (haben) to check (s.o., sth.).

Chef(in) ['ʃɛf(in)]. I. m -s/-s (f -/-nen) head of a firm, school etc.); F: boss. II. C~-, comb.fm. chief (engineer, editor etc.). ◆**C~arzt**, m chief consultant, superintendent (of a hospital).

Chem|ie [çe'miː], f -/no pl chemistry. ◆**C~iefaser**, f man-made fibre. ◆**c~ikalien** [-i'kaːliən], fpl chemicals.

◆'**C~iker(in)**, m -s/- (f -/-nen) chemist. ◆'**c~isch**, adj. chemical; **c~ische Reinigung**, (i) dry cleaning; (ii) (Geschäft) dry cleaner's.

Chicoree ['ʃikore:], f -/no pl chicory.

Chiffre ['ʃifrə], f -/-n 1. number. 2. (code) symbol, cipher. 3. (Anzeigenc.) box number. ◆**c~ieren** [ʃi'friːrən], v.tr. to encode (a text), put (a message etc.) into code.

Chile ['ʃiːle]. Pr.n.n -s. Chile. ◆**C~ne** [tʃi'leːnə], m -n/-n Chilean. ◆**C~nin**, f -/-nen Chilean (woman). ◆**c~nisch**, adj. Chilean.

Chin|a ['çiːna]. Pr.n.n -s. China. ◆**C~ese** [çi'neːzə], m -n/-n Chinese. ◆**C~esin**, f -/-nen Chinese (woman). ◆**c~esisch. I.** adj. Chinese. **II.** C., -s/no pl Chinese.

Chinin [çi'niːn], n -s/no pl quinine.

Chip [tʃip], m -s/-s 1. usu. pl C~s, (potato) crisps/N.Am: chips. 2. (Spielc.) chip. 3. Data-pr: chip.

Chirurg [çi'rurk], m -en/-en surgeon. ◆**C~ie** [-'giː], f -/-n 1. no pl surgery. 2. (Abteilung) surgical unit. ◆**c~isch**, adj. surgical.

Chlor [kloːr], n -s/no pl chlorine. ◆**C~oform** [kloro'fɔrm], n -s/no pl chloroform.

Choke [tʃouk], m -s/-s choke.

Cholera ['koːlɔra], f -/no pl cholera.

Choleriker [ko'leːrikər], m -s/- irascible person.

Chor [koːr]. **I.** m -(e)s/-e choir; (also Th:) chorus; im C. sprechen, to speak in unison. **II.** 'C~-, comb.fm. Mus: choral (concert, music, work etc.); (Chor) (practice etc.). ◆'**C~gestühl**, n choir stalls. ◆'**C~knabe**, m choirboy.

Choral [ko'raːl], m -s/-e chorale.

Choreograph [koreo'graːf], m -en/-en choreographer. ◆**C~ie** [-a'fiː], f -/-n choreography. ◆**c~isch** [-'graːfiʃ], adj. choreographic.

Christ(in) ['krist(in)], m -en/-en (f -/-nen) Christian. ◆'**C~baum**, m Christmas tree. ◆'**C~enheit**, f -/no pl Christendom. ◆'**C~entum**, n -s/no pl Christianity. ◆'**C~kind**, n das C., the infant Jesus. ◆'**c~lich**, adj. Christian. ◆'**C~us**. Pr.n.m gen. Christi. Christ.

Chrom [kroːm], n -s/no pl Ch: chromium; Aut: etc: F: chrome.

Chromosom [kromo'zoːm], n -s/-en chromosome.

Chron|ik ['kroːnik], f -/-en chronicle. ◆'**c~isch**, adj. chronic. ◆**c~ologie** [-olo'giː], f -/-n chronology. ◆**c~ologisch** [-o'loːgiʃ], adj. chronological.

Chrysantheme [kryzan'teːmə], f -/-n chrysanthemum.

circa ['tsirka], *adv.* (*abbr.* **ca.**) about, approximately.

City ['siti], *f* *-/-s & Cities* city centre.

Clique ['klikə], *f* *-/-n* clique; gang.

Clou [klu:], *m* *-s/-s F:* (*a*) main attraction, highlight; (*b*) **der C. (an) der Sache ist ...**, the whole point about it is ...

Clown [klaun], *m* *-s/-s* clown.

Computer [kɔm'pju:tər], *m* *-s/-* computer.

Conferencier [kõferãsi'e:], *m* *-s/-s* compère.

Container [kɔn'te:nər]. I. *m* *-s/-* container. II. **C~-**, *comb.fm.* container (ship, traffic etc.).

Couch [kautʃ], *f* *-/-(e)s* couch, sofa.

Coupé [ku'pe:], *n* *-s/-s* Aut: coupé.

Coupon [ku'põ:], *m* *-s/-s Com:* voucher, coupon; (*zum Abreißen*) counterfoil.

Courage [ku'ra:ʒə], *f* *-/no pl* courage.
◆**c~iert** [-a'ʒi:rt], *adj.* courageous; *F:* plucky.

Cousin [ku'zɛ̃], *m* *-s/-s* (male) cousin.
◆**c~e** [ku'zi:nə], *f* *-/-n* (female) cousin.

Creme ['kre:m], *f* *-/-s* cream.
◆**c~farben**, *adj.* cream(-coloured).
◆**c~ig**, *adj.* creamy.

Curry ['kœri], *n* *-s/-s* curry.

D

D, d [de:], *n* *-/-* **1.** (the letter) D, d.

da [da:]. I. *adv.* **1.** (*räumlich*) there; **da sind wir**, here we are; **ich bin gleich wieder da**, I'll be back in a minute; **ist noch etwas Brot da?** is there any bread left? **2.** (*zeitlich*) then; **von da an**, from then on; II. *conj.* (*Ursache*) as, since.

dabehalten ['da:bəhaltən], *v.tr.sep.irr.45* to keep (s.o.) there.

dabei [da'bai], *adv.* **1.** (*a*) (*räumlich*) **dicht d.**, close by; (*b*) **with it**; (*im Paket usw.*) enclosed; (*c*) *F:* **ich habe kein Geld d.**, I have no money on me. **2.** **d. bleiben**, to stick to one's point; **es bleibt d.**, it's settled; **es ist doch nichts d.!** (i) there's no harm in it! (ii) (*leicht*) there's nothing to it! **was ist schon d.?** what does it matter? **3.** (*a*) (*im Begriff*) **j-n d. erwischen**, to catch s.o. in the act; **d. sein, etwas zu tun**, to be (in the process of) doing sth.; (*b*) (*gleichzeitig*) while doing so; **er hat sich nichts d. gedacht**, he didn't mean anything by it; **d. kam es heraus, daß ...**, in the process it came out that ...; (*c*) (*auch noch*) what is more; (*d*) (*dagegen*) yet; **d. darf man nicht vergessen, daß ...**, at the same time one must not forget that ... ◆**d~bleiben**, *v.i.sep.irr.12* (*sein*) to stay there; (*bei einer Tätigkeit*) to stick to/at it. ◆**d~haben**, *v.tr.sep.irr.44* to have (s.o., sth.) with one. ◆**d~sein**, *v.i.sep.irr.93* (*sein*) to be present (**bei +** *dat*, at).

'dableiben, *v.i.sep.irr.12* (*sein*) to stay (here/there).

Dach [dax]. I. *n* *-(e)s/-er* **1.** roof; **er wohnt unter dem D.**, he lives in the attic; **unter D. und Fach**, under cover; (*sicher*) in safety; (*erledigt*) settled; (*fertig*) finished. II. **'D~-**, *comb.fm.* (*a*) roof (*beam, gable etc.*); (*b*) (*im Dach*) attic (*room, flat etc.*). ◆**D~boden**, *m* loft, attic. ◆**D~decker**, *m* roofer. ◆**'D~first**, *m* ridge (of the roof). ◆**'D~fenster**, *n* dormer window; (*Luke*) skylight. ◆**'D~luke**, *f* skylight. ◆**'D~pappe**, *f* roofing felt. ◆**'D~pfanne**, *f* pantile. ◆**'D~rinne**,

f gutter. ◆**'D~schaden**, *m* **1.** roof damage. **2.** *F: Hum:* **er hat einen leichten D.**, he's not quite right in the head. ◆**'D~ziegel**, *m* roof tile.

Dachs [daks], *m* *-es/-e* badger.

Dackel ['dakəl], *m* *-s/-* dachshund.

dadurch [da'durç, *emphatic* 'da:durç], *adv.* **1.** (*a*) (*hindurch*) through it/them; (*b*) by it; **was hat er d. gewonnen?** what has he gained by it? **2.** [da'durç] because of this/that.

dafür [da'fy:r, *emphatic* 'da:fy:r], *adv.* **1.** (*a*) for it/them; (*statt dessen*) instead; **ein Beweis d., daß ...**, proof (of the fact) that ...; (*b*) **d. sein**, to be for/in favour of it; **d. spricht, daß ...**, (i) a point in its favour is that ...; (ii) (*Bestätigung*) this is confirmed by the fact that ... **2.** ['da:fy:r] (*a*) **er arbeitet langsam, d. aber gründlich**, he works slowly, but makes up for it in thoroughness; (*b*) **d., daß er nicht lange hier ist, beherrscht er die Sprache sehr gut**, considering that he hasn't been here long, he is very good at the language. ◆**d~halten**, *v.i. sep.irr.45* (*haben*) **d., daß ...**, to think/be of the opinion that ... ◆**d~können**, *v.i.sep.irr.54* (*haben*) **er kann nichts dafür**, he can't help it; it's not his fault.

dagegen [da'ge:gən, *emphatic* 'da:ge:gən], *adv.* **1.** (*a*) against it/them; **d. hilft nichts**, there's nothing you can do about that; (*b*) opposed to it; **haben Sie etwas d., wenn ich rauche?** do you mind if I smoke? **2.** **was kann ich d. eintauschen?** what can I exchange for it? **3.** (*im Vergleich*) **dieser ist nichts d.!** this is nothing in comparison. **4.** (*andererseits*) but, on the other hand; ◆**d~halten**, *v.tr.sep.irr.45* to argue, object.

da'heim, *adv.* at home; **bei uns d.**, back home.

daher [da'he:r, *emphatic* 'da:he:r], *adv. & conj.* (*a*) from there; (*b*) (*deshalb*) **d. dieser Brauch**, hence this custom; **d.!** that's why!

dahin [da'hin, *emphatic* 'da:hin], *adv.* **1.** (*a*) there, to that place; (*b*) **bis d.**, (i) that far; (*im Buch usw.*) up to that point; (ii) (*zeitlich*) until then; up to that time; (*Zukunft*) by then; (*c*) (*soweit*) to that point; **j-n d. bringen, daß er etwas tut,** to persuade s.o. to do sth. **2.** [da'hin] (*vorbei*) over; (*verloren*) gone; **die Ernte ist d.,** the crops are ruined. ◆**d~gehen,** *v.i.sep.irr.36 (sein)* to go (along); (*Zeit*) to pass. ◆**d~gehend,** *adv.* to this/that effect. ◆**d~gestellt,** *adv.* **es bleibt d. ob ...,** it remains to be seen whether ...; **es d. sein lassen(, ob ...),** to leave it open (whether ...).

da'hinten, *adv.* back there; over there.

dahinter [da'hintər, *emphatic* 'da:hintər], *adv.* behind it/them; ◆**d~kommen,** *v.i.sep.irr.53 (sein)* F: to get to the bottom of it; **endlich kam ich dahinter, was los war,** I finally got wise to what was going on. ◆**d~stecken,** *v.i.sep.* (*haben*) F: to be behind it/(*Pers.*) at the bottom of it. ◆**d~stehen,** *v.i.sep.irr.100 (haben)* to be behind it, (*unterstützen*) back it.

Dahlie ['da:liə], *f -/-n* dahlia.

'dalassen, *v.tr.sep.irr.57* F: to leave (s.o., sth.) (here/there); (*vergessen*) to leave (sth.) behind.

damalige(r,s) ['da:ma:ligə(r, s)], *attrib. adj.* of that time; (fashion etc.) of the day; **der d. Präsident,** the then president.

damals ['da:ma:ls], *adv.* then, at that time; **d., als ...,** (in the days) when ...

Damast [da'mast], *m -(e)s/-e* damask.

Dame ['da:mə], *f -/-n* **1.** lady; *Sp:* **400 Meter der D~n,** women's 400 metres. **2.** (*Spiel*) draughts, *N.Am:* checkers. **3.** (*Schach, Kartenspiel*) queen. ◆**'D~brett,** *n* draughtboard. ◆**'D~n-, comb.fm.** (*a*) lady's (glove, shoe, bicycle etc.); ladies' (hairdresser, tailor, toilet etc.); (*b*) *Sp:* women's (team etc.). ◆**'D~nbinde,** *f* sanitary towel, *N.Am:* napkin. ◆**'d~nhaft,** *adj.* ladylike. ◆**'D~nwahl,** *f* ladies' choice. ◆**'D~nspiel,** *n* draughts, *N.Am:* checkers.

Damhirsch ['damhirʃ], *m* fallow deer.

da'mit [*emphatic also* 'da:mit]. **I.** *adv.* (*a*) with it; **sie war d. einverstanden,** she agreed to it; *F:* **her d.!** hand it over! **hör auf d.!** stop it! (*b*) **was willst du d. sagen?** what do you mean by that? **d. bewies er seine Unschuld,** he thereby proved his innocence. **II.** *conj.* so that.

dämlich [de:mlɪç], *adj.* F: silly, stupid.

Damm [dam], *m -(e)s/⁻e* embankment of a road, railway etc.); (*Deich*) dike, *N.Am:* levee; (*im Fluß usw.*) dam; (*Hafend.*) mole; F: **nicht (recht) auf dem D.,** under the weather.

dämmen ['deman], *v.tr.* to dam (a river).

dämm(e)rig ['dem(ə)rɪç], *adj.* dim (light); gloomy (day etc.).

Dämmerlicht ['demərlɪçt], *n* twilight; (*am Abend*) dusk. ◆**'d~n,** *v.i.* (*haben*)

to grow light/dark; **es dämmert,** (i) day/dawn is breaking; (ii) dusk is falling; *F:* **jetzt dämmert's bei mir!** now I see! now I'm beginning to get it! ◆**'D~ung,** *f -/-en* twilight; (*abends*) dusk; (*morgens*) dawn.

Dämon [dɛːmɔn], *m -s/-en* [dɛˈmoːnən], demon. ◆**d~isch** [-ˈmoːnɪʃ], *adj.* demonic.

Dampf [dampf]. **I.** *m -(e)s/⁻e* steam; (*chemische*) *Z~e,* vapours; (*giftige Z~e,* toxic fumes. **II.** **'D~-, comb.fm.** steam (power, pressure, pipe, turbine, *H:* iron etc.). ◆**'D~en,** *v.i.* (*a*) (*haben*) (*Suppe, Kessel usw.*) to steam; (*b*) (*sein*) (*Schiff, Zug*) to steam (along). ◆**'D~er,** *m -s/-* steamer. ◆**'D~kochtopf,** *m Cu:* pressure-cooker. ◆**'D~maschine,** *f* steam engine. ◆**'D~schiff,** *n* steamship, steamer. ◆**'D~walze,** *f* steamroller.

dämpfen ['dempfən], *v.tr.* (*a*) to deaden, muffle (sound); to soften (light); cushion (a blow etc.); *Fig:* to curb (anger etc.); to dampen (s.o.'s enthusiasm etc.); (*b*) *Cu:* to steam (fish, potatoes); (*c*) *H:* to steam-iron (sth.).

danach [da'na:x, *emphatic* 'da:na:x], *adv.* (*a*) (*räumlich*) after it/them; (*dahinter*) behind it/them; (*b*) (*zeitlich*) afterwards; (*c*) (*demgemäß*) in accordance with it/them; (*d*) **ich habe d. gefragt/mich d. erkundigt,** I asked/enquired about it; (*e*) **es sieht (ganz) d. aus,** it looks (very) like it.

Däne ['dɛːnə], *m -n/-n* Dane. ◆**'D~emark.** *Pr.n.n -s.* Denmark. ◆**D~in,** *f -/-nen* Danish girl/woman. ◆**d~isch,** *adj.* Danish.

daneben [da'ne:bən, *emphatic* 'da:ne:bən], *adv.* (*a*) beside it/them; **dicht/gleich d.,** right next to it/them; (*b*) (*außerdem*) in addition; (*gleichzeitig*) at the same time; (*c*) (*im Vergleich*) by comparison. ◆**d~gehen,** *v.i.sep.irr.36 (sein)* (*a*) (*Schuß*) to miss (the target); (*b*) F: to go wrong; (*Plan*) to misfire.

Dank [daŋk]. **I.** *m -(e)s/no pl* thanks, gratitude; **vielen/besten/schönen/herzlichen D.,** thank you very much; many thanks. **II.** *a., prep. + gen/occ. + dat* thanks to. ◆**'d~bar,** *adj.* **1.** grateful; **sich (j-m) d. zeigen/erweisen,** to show one's gratitude. **2.** rewarding, worthwhile (task etc.). ◆**'D~barkeit,** *f -/no pl* gratitude; thankfulness. ◆**'d~e,** *see d~en* **1.** (*b*). ◆**'d~en,** *v.* **1.** *v.i.* (*haben*) (*a*) to say thank you; **j-m für etwas d.,** to thank s.o. for sth.; **nichts zu d.,** don't mention it; (*b*) **danke (schön/sehr)!** thank you (very much)! **wie geht es Ihnen?—danke gut,** how are you?—very well, thank you. **2.** *v.tr.* **ich habe es ihr zu d.,** I have her to thank for it; **niemand wird es dir d.,** no one will thank you for it. ◆**'d~enswert,** *adj.* deserving (of thanks); **d~e Bemühungen,** commendable efforts. ◆'D~**sagung**, f -/-en (expression of) thanks.

dann [dan], adv. (a) then; **d. und wann**, now and then; **bis d.!** see you (then)! (b) (in dem Fall) then; **selbst/nur d., wenn ...**, even/only if ...

daran [da'ran, emphatic 'da:ran], adv. 1. (a) on it/them; onto it/them; (b) at it/ them; **er arbeitete lange d.**, he worked at/on it for a long time; (c) **wir gingen d. vorbei**, we went past it; **nahe d.**, close to it/them; **im Anschluß d.**/d. **anschließend**, immediately after that. 2. **es ist nichts Wahres d.**, there is no truth in it; **es liegt d., daß ...**, the reason for it is that ...; **mir liegt viel d.**, it is very important to me. ◆**d~gehen**, v.i.sep.irr.36 (sein) d., etwas zu tun, to set to work to do sth. ◆**d~setzen**, v.tr.sep. **alles/sein letztes d., um etwas zu erreichen**, to do one's utmost to attain sth.; **sich d.**, to get down to it.

darauf [da'rauf, emphatic 'da:rauf], adv. 1. (a) on it/them; **oben d.**, on top of the pile); (b) **d. zugehen/losgehen**, to go towards it/them; **d. zielen/schießen**, to aim/shoot at it/them. 2. after that; 3. (a) **wie kommst du d.?** what gave you that idea? **ich komme jetzt nicht d.**, I can't think of it at the moment; (b) **d. steht Todesstrafe**, the penalty for that is death; (c) **es kommt d. an**, it all depends. ◆**d~folgend**, adj. next, following. ◆**d~'hin**, adv. 1. (im folgenden) as a result. 2. (mit Blick darauf) with this in view.

daraus [da'raus, emphatic 'da:raus], adv. 1. (räumlich) from it/them. 2. **d. wird nichts**, (i) nothing will come of that; (ii) that's out of the question; **ich mache mir nichts d.**, I'm not keen on it.

Darbietung ['da:rbi:tuŋ], f -/-en Th: performance; item (in a programme).

darin [da'rin, emphatic 'da:rin], adv. (a) in it/them; inside; (b) (emphatic) there; **d. unterscheiden wir uns**, that's where we differ.

darleg|en, v.tr.sep. to set forth (a plan, reasons); to expound (a theory etc.). ◆'D~**ung**, f -/-en exposition; demonstration (of a theory).

Darlehen ['da:rle:ən], n -s/- loan.

Darm [darm]. I. m -(e)s/⁻e 1. Anat: intestine; pl D~e, bowels. 2. (a) (für Saiten usw.) gut; (b) (sausage) skin. II. 'D~-, comb.fm. Med: intestinal (ulcer, disease, haemorrhage etc.); **d.** (cancer etc.) of the bowels. ◆'D~**saite**, f catgut string.

darstell|en ['da:rʃtɛlən], v.tr. (a) (bildlich) to portray, (oft symbolisch) represent (s.o., sth.); (b) (in Worten) to portray (s.o., sth.); (c) Th: to present (arguments, facts, etc.); (c) Th: to play the part of (the hero etc.); **sich (als etwas) d.**, to show oneself/itself (to be sth.). ◆'D~**er(in)**, m -s/- (f -/-nen) Th: actor,

actress; interpreter (of a part). ◆'D~**ung**, f -/-en 1. representation; portrayal; Th: interpretation (of a part); **bildliche D.**, pictorial representation; **schematische D.**, diagram. 2. (Schilderung) description; account (of the facts etc.); **für: falsche D. (des Sachverhalts)**, misrepresentation (of the facts).

darüber [da'ry:bər, emphatic 'da:rybər], adv. 1. (a) over it/them; **laufe nicht d.!** don't walk over/across it; (b) above, beyond (it); (zusätzlich) in addition; **es geht nichts d.**, nothing can touch it; (c) (Zahlen usw.) more; (Preis) higher; **Männer von sechzig Jahren und d.**, men of sixty and over. 2. (dabei) in the process; **d. vergaß ich meine eigenen Sorgen**, that made me forget my own troubles. 3. **sich d. freuen/ärgern**, to be pleased/ angry about it.

darum [da'rum, emphatic 'da:rum], adv. 1. (a) round it/them; (b) **d. geht es nicht**, that's not the point; **es geht ihm d., zu ...** his aim is to ... 2. (mit Verben) (to ask, fight etc.) for it; **d. wetten**, to bet on it. 3. (Folge) so; (Grund) that's (the reason) why; F: **warum denn?—d.!** but why?—because!

darunter [da'runtər, emphatic 'da:runtər], adv. 1. (a) (räumlich) beneath it/them; (b) (Zahl, Preis) less; (c) (unter mehreren) among(st) them. 2. (mit Verben) from/by it; **d. kann ich mir nichts vorstellen**, that doesn't mean anything to me.

das [das], see **der**.

dasein ['da:zain]. I. v.i.sep.irr.93 (sein) (a) to be there/(anwesend) present; (b) to exist; **es ist alles schon mal dagewesen**, there is nothing new under the sun; **noch nie dagewesen**, unheard of. II. D., n -s/ no pl existence, life.

'dasitzen, v.i.sep.irr.97 (haben) to sit (there).

das'jenige, see **derjenige**.

daß [das], conj. that; **es ist zwei Jahre her, d. wir das Haus gekauft haben**, it is two years since we bought the house; **d. du ja nicht zu spät kommst!** don't you dare be late!

das'selbe [das'zɛlbə], see **derselbe**.

'dastehen, v.i.sep.irr.100 (haben) (a) to stand (there); (b) **gut/schlecht d.**, to be in a good/bad position; **jetzt steht er ganz allein da**, now he is all alone in the world.

Datei ['da:tən], npl data; (persönliche) **D.**, particulars. ◆'D~**bank**, f data bank. ◆'D~**verarbeitung**, f -/no pl data processing.

datieren [da'ti:rən], v.tr. & i. (haben) to date (aus + dat, from).

Dativ [da:ti:f], m -s/-e dative (case).

Dattel ['datəl], f -/-n date.

Datum ['da:tum], n -s/Daten date; **welches D. haben wir heute?** what's the date today? **ohne D.**, undated. ◆'D~**s-**, comb.fm. date (stamp etc.).

Dauer ['dauər]. **I.** f -/no pl (a) length, duration; Jur: term (of contract etc.); es war von kurzer D., it did not last long/ (Begeisterung usw.) was short-lived; für die D. eines Jahres, for (a period of) a year; (b) von D., lasting; auf die D. gewöhnt man sich daran, you get used to it in the long run. **II.** 'D~-, comb.fm. (a) permanent (condition, symptom etc.); lasting (success, solution etc.); continuous (rain, Mil: fire etc.); constant (speed etc.); (b) Sp: etc: endurance (run etc.). ◆'D~auftrag, m standing order. ◆'d~haft, adj. enduring (peace etc.); durable (material etc.). ◆'D~haftigkeit, f -/no pl permanence. ◆'D~karte, f season ticket. ◆'D~lauf, m (a) long-distance run; (b) im D., at a jogtrot. ◆'D~lutscher, m F: lollipop; ◆'d~n, v.i. (haben) last (an hour etc.); das dauert (mir) zu lange, that takes too long (for me). ◆'d~nd, adj. (a) lasting (peace, effect etc.); (b) continual; d. etwas tun, to keep doing sth.; ◆'D~ton, m continuous tone. ◆'D~welle, f permanent wave. ◆'D~wurst, f hard smoked sausage (e.g. salami).

Daumen ['daumən], m -s/- thumb; j-m den D. drücken/halten, to keep one's fingers crossed for s.o

Daune ['daunə], f -/-n downy feather; pl down. ◆'D~ndecke, f eiderdown (quilt).

davon [da'fon, emphatic 'dɑːfon], adv. 1. (Entfernung) (away) from it/them; wir sind noch weit d. entfernt, we still have a long way to go. 2. was habe ich denn d.? what do I get out of it? das kommt d.! that's what you get! er ist nicht d. betroffen, he is not affected by it; 3. (a) (Menge) of it/them; das Gegenteil d., the opposite of this); (b) (to hear, talk etc.) about it; d. kann gar keine Rede sein! that's out of the question! ◆d~gehen, v.i.sep.irr. (sein) to walk/go away; ◆d~kommen, v.i.sep.irr.53 (sein) to get away/off; mit dem Leben/dem Schrecken d., to escape with one's life/a fright. ◆d~laufen, v.i.sep.irr. (sein) to run away. ◆d~machen, v.refl.sep: sich d., to make off. ◆d~tragen, v.tr.sep.irr.85 to carry (s.o., sth.) away); to receive (injuries etc.); den Sieg/den ersten Preis d., to win a victory/first prize.

davor [da'foːr, emphatic 'dɑːfoːr], adv. 1. (a) (Ort) in front of it/them; (b) (Zeit) before it/that; (zunächst) first; (c) Angst d. haben, to be afraid of it/them; j-n d. schützen, to protect s.o. from it/them.

dazu [da'tsuː, emphatic 'dɑːtsuː], adv. (a) to it/them; er sah die Menge und stellte sich d., he saw the crowd and joined them; (b) with it/them; es wurde Salat d. gereicht, salad was served with it; (c) as well, in addition; d. kommt, daß ich

kein Geld habe, what's more I haven't any money; (d) for it; sie hat keine Lust d., she does not feel like (doing) it; d. bereit/fähig, ready to do/capable of it; ◆d~gehören, v.i.sep. (haben) (a) to belong to it/them; es gehört schon einiges dazu, that takes quite some doing. ◆d~gehörig, adj. belonging to it/ them. ◆d~kommen, v.i.sep.irr.53 (sein) (a) to come (along), appear (on the scene); (b) (hinzugefügt werden) to be added. ◆'d~mal, adv. A: & Hum: in those days. ◆d~tun, v.tr. sep.irr.106 to add (sth.).

dazwischen, adv. between them; in between. ◆d~fahren, v.i.sep.irr.26 (sein) to intervene in a quarrel, fight etc.); (unterbrechen) to interrupt. ◆d~kommen, v.i.sep.irr.53 (sein) (a) wenn nichts dazwischenkommt, if nothing goes wrong; (b) er ist den Fingern dazwischengekommen, his fingers got caught in it. ◆d~reden, v.i.sep. (haben) to interrupt. ◆d~treten, v.i.sep.irr.105 (sein) to intervene.

Debatte [de'batə], f -/-n debate; das steht nicht zur D., that's beside the point. ◆d~ieren [-'tiːrən], v.tr.&i. (haben) to debate (sth.).

dechiffrieren [deʃi'friːrən], v.tr. to decipher (a code etc.).

Deck [dɛk], n -s/-s Nau: deck; unter D. gehen, to go below; alle Mann an D.! all hands on deck! ◆'D~adresse, f cover address. ◆'D~bett, n duvet, continental quilt, N.Am: comforter. ◆'D~e, f -/-n 1. cover; (Bettd.) blanket; (Bettüberwurf) bedspread; (Reised.) rug; mit j-m unter einer D. stecken, to be hand in glove with s.o. 2. (Tischtuch) tablecloth. 3. (Zimmerd.) ceiling; an die D. gehen, to hit the roof. ◆'D~el, m -s/- lid; (zum Aufschrauben) screw-top cap; (Buchd.) (back/front) cover. ◆'d~en, v.tr. to cover (sth.); a) den Tisch d., to lay/set the table; das Dach d., (mit Ziegeln) to tile/(mit Stroh) thatch the roof; (b) (schützen) to shield (s.o., sth.); Fig: to cover up for (s.o., s.o.'s misdemeanours); Fb: etc: einen Spieler d., to mark a player; (c) Kosten, seinen Bedarf usw. d., to cover expenses, one's needs etc.; (d) sich d., (Berichte, Aussagen) to tally; (Ansichten usw.) to coincide. ◆'D~en-, comb.fm. ceiling (plaster etc.). ◆'D~farbe, f opaque paint; body colour. ◆'D~mantel, m Fig: pretence; cover (für etwas acc, for sth.); unter dem D. der Religion, disguised as religion. ◆'D~name, m assumed name; Lit: pseudonym; Mil: code name. ◆'D~ung, f -/no pl 1. covering. 2. (a) Mil: etc: cover; (b) Sp: defence; Fb: marking; (c) covering up (of a crime etc.). 3. meeting of a demand, need). 4. Fin: cover; security (for a sum); guarantee (for a loan etc.). ◆'d~ungsgleich, _adj._ congruent.

Defekt [de'fɛkt]. **I.** _m_ -(e)s/-e defect; fault (in a machine etc.). **II.** _a.,_ _adj._ defective (part etc.); (_Maschine_) out of order.

defensiv [defɛn'ziːf], _adj./D~,_ _comb.fm._ defensive (warfare, measures etc.). ◆**D~e** ['-ziːvə], _f_ /-n defence.

defin|ieren [defi'niːrən], _v.tr._ ◆**D~ition** [-ni'tsioːn], _f_ /-en definition. ◆**d~itiv** ['-tiːf], _adj._ definitive (edition etc.); final (offer, decision etc.).

Defizit ['deːfitsit], _n_ -s/-e deficit.

deftig [deftiç], _adj._ F: **1.** filling (food); **d~e Mahlzeit**, solid/hearty meal. **2.** coarse (jokes).

Degen [de'gɔn], _m_ -s/- sword.

degenerieren [degene'riːrən], _v.i._ (_sein_) to degenerate.

degradieren [degra'diːrən], _v.tr._ to downgrade (s.o.).

dehn|bar [deːnbaːr], _adj._ (material etc.) that stretches; tensile (metal etc.); expansive (solid etc.); elastic (material, _Fig:_ concept, rules etc.); expanding (bracelet etc.). ◆**D~barkeit**, _f_ /_no pl_ elasticity. ◆**d~en**, _v.tr._ to stretch (sth.); to lengthen (a vowel etc.); **sich d.**, to stretch. ◆**D~ung**, _f_ /-en stretching.

Deich [daiç], _m_ -(e)s/-e dike, seawall.

Deichsel ['daiksəl], _f_ /-n (a) (_einfach_) pole; (b) (_Gabeld._) shafts of a cart etc.). ◆**d~n**, _v.tr._ F: to wangle (sth.).

dein [dain], _poss. adj._ your. ◆**d~e(r,s)**, _poss. pron._ yours; **sind das d.?** are those yours? **das D.**, (i) your property; (ii) (_Anteil_) your share. ◆**d~er**, _pers. pron._ (_gen_ of **du**) of you. ◆**d~erseits**, _adv._ on your part. ◆**d~esgleichen**, _pron._ (of) your (own) kind. ◆**d~etwegen/um 'd~etwillen**, _adv._ for your sake; because of you. ◆**d~ige**, _poss. pron._ _decl._ _as adj._ _Lit:_ **der/die/das d.**, yours.

dekaden|t [deka'dɛnt], _adj._ decadent. ◆**D~z**, _f_ /_no pl_ decadence.

Dekan [de'kaːn], _m_ -s/-e dean.

Dekolleté [dekɔl'teː], _n_ -s/-s (low) neck-line, décolleté.

Dekor [de'koːr], _m_ -s/-s decoration (on glass etc.); _Th: etc:_ décor. ◆**D~ateur(in)** [-a'tøːr(in)], _m_ -s/- (_f_ /-nen) (a) (_house_) decorator; (b) _Com:_ window-dresser. ◆**D~ation** [-atsi'oːn], _f_ /-en (a) _no pl_ decoration; _Com:_ (window) dressing; (b) (_Auslage_) display; _Th: Cin: etc:_ set. ◆**d~a'tiv**, _adj._ decorative. ◆**d~ieren** [-'riːrən], _v.tr._ to decorate (sth., s.o. with a medal); _Com:_ to dress (a shop window).

Delegation [delegatsi'oːn], _f_ /-en delegation.

delikat [deli'kaːt], _adj._ **1.** delicious (dish, fruit etc.). **2.** (_heikel_) delicate (matter, situation). ◆**D~esse** [-'tɛsə], _f_ /-n delicacy. ◆**D~essengeschäft**, _n_ delicatessen.

Delikt [de'likt], _n_ -(e)s/-e _Jur:_ (indictable) offence.

Delle ['dɛlə], _f_ /-n dent.

Delphin [del'fiːn], _m_ -s/-e dolphin.

Delta ['dɛlta], _n_ -s/-s & -ten delta.

dem [deːm], _dat. sing._ of **der, das** _see_ **der**.

Dementi [de'mɛnti], _n_ -s/-s (official) denial. ◆**d~eren** [-'tiːrən], _v.tr._ to deny (rumours etc.).

dem|ent'sprechend, _adj._ corresponding; (_passend_) suitable; _adv._ accordingly. ◆**'d~ge'mäß**, _adv._ accordingly. ◆**'d~nach**, _adv._ according to that/this; (_also_) so, consequently. ◆**'d~'nächst**, _adv._ shortly.

Demo|krat [demo'kraːt], _m_ -en/-en democrat. ◆**D~kratie** [-a'tiː], _f_ /-n democracy. ◆**d~kratisch**, _adj._ democratic.

demolieren [demo'liːrən], _v.tr._ to wreck (sth.); F: to smash up (a car etc.).

Demonstr|ant(in) [demɔn'strant(in)], _m_ -en (_f_ /-nen) _Pol:_ demonstrator. ◆**D~ation** [-atsi'oːn], _f_ /-en demonstration. ◆**d~ativ** [-a'tiːf], _adj._ **1.** illuminating (example etc.). **2.** ostentatious (action). **3.** _Gram:_ demonstrative. ◆**d~ieren** [-'striːrən], _v.tr. & i._ (_haben_) to demonstrate.

Demoskopie [demosko'piː], _f_ /_no pl_ opinion polling/research.

Demut ['deːmuːt], _f_ /_no pl_ humility.

demütig ['deːmyːtiç], _adj._ humble. ◆**d~en** ['-igən], _v.tr._ to humble (s.o., oneself); (_erniedrigen_) to humiliate (s.o.). ◆**D~ung**, _f_ /-en humiliation.

'demzu'folge, _adv._ consequently, therefore.

den [deːn], _acc._ of **der**, _q.v._

denen ['deːnən], _dat.pl_ of **der, die, das** _see_ **der**.

Denk|art ['dɛŋk?art], _f_ /-en (a) way of thinking; (b) (_Gesinnung_) mentality. ◆**d~bar**, _adj._ conceivable. ◆**d~en. I.** _v.irr._ **1.** _v.tr._ to think (sth., a thought etc.); **das läßt sich d.**, that's understandable; **das kann ich mir d.**, I can well believe it; **er dachte sich nichts Böses dabei**, he meant no harm by it; **das ist für dich gedacht**, this is meant for you. **2.** _v.i._ (_haben_) to think (an + _acc._, of; über + _acc_, about); F: **wo denkst du hin!** what can you be thinking of? **denk mal an!** you don't say! **denkste!** that's what you think! **großzügig/kleinlich d.**, to be of a liberal/petty turn of mind; **ich denke nicht daran, das zu tun**, I wouldn't dream of doing it; **solange ich d. kann**, for as long as I can remember. **II. D.**, _n_ -s/_no pl_ (way of) thinking; thought. ◆**'D~er**, _m_ -s/- thinker. ◆**d~fähig**, _adj._ capable of thought; rational (being); thinking (person). ◆**'d~faul**, _adj._ mentally lazy. ◆**'d~fehler**, _m_ error of logic. ◆**'D~mal**, _n_ memorial; (_Plastik usw._) monument. ◆**'d~würdig**, _adj._ memorable. ◆**'D~zettel**, _m_ F: (unpleasant) reminder; awful warning.

denn [dɛn]. **I.** _conj._ **1.** (_weil_) because; _Lit:_ for. **2. mehr/besser d. je**, more/better than ever. **II.** *adv.* **1.** was ist d. eigentlich passiert? what really did happen? warum d. nicht? why not? **2.** es sei d. (, daß) ..., unless ...

dennoch ['dɛnɔx], *adv.* nevertheless; however.

Denunziant(in) [denuntsi'ant(in)], *m* -en/-en (*f* -/-nen) informer.

Deodorant [de'odo'rant], *n* -s/-s deodorant.

deponieren [depo'niːrən], *v.tr.* to deposit (valuables).

Depot [de'poː], *n* -s/-s depot; (*für Möbel, Waren*) warehouse; (*Lager*) store.

Depress|**ion** [depresi'oːn], *f* -/-en depression. ◆**d~iv** [-'siːf], *adj.* depressed.

deprimieren [depri'miːrən], *v.tr.* to depress (s.o.); deprimiert, depressed.

der [deːr], *m* (*acc* den, *gen* des, *dat* dem), **die** [diː], *f* (*acc* die, *gen/dat* der), **das** [das], *n* (*acc* das, *gen* des, *dat* dem), **die**, *pl* (*acc* die, *gen* der, *dat* den). I. *art.* the; der **Mensch**, man; die kleine Gabi, little Gabi; den **Kopf schütteln**, to shake one's head; zieh dir die **Schuhe an**, put your shoes on. II. *dem. pron.* (*gen m & n* **dessen**; *gen f & pl* **deren**; *dat pl* **denen**) (*a*) (*Pers.*) he, she; the one; they; those; the ones (*Sache*) that; the one; that those; the ones; (*b*) (*betont*) **der ist es getan**, 'he/'she did it; der war es, it was him; der/die mit dem grünen Hut, the one with the green hat; ach der! oh him! der, den ich kenne, the one (that) I know; (*c*) that; das ist mein **Vater**, that is my father; das waren **Zeiten**, those were the days; wie dem **auch sei**, however that may be; um die und die **Zeit**, at such and such time. III. *rel. pron.* (*gen m & n* **dessen**, *f & pl* **deren**; *dat pl* **denen**) (*Pers.*) who; *acc* whom; *gen* whose; *dat* to whom; (*Sachen*) which, that; of which.

derart [deːr'aɾt], *adv.* (+ *adj.*) so; (*in solchem Maße*) so much, to such an extent. ◆**d~ig**, *adj.* such, like this/that.

derb [dɛrp], *adj.* (*grob*) uncouth (person, manners etc.); crude (person, features, expression, joke etc.); (*unsanft*) rough (treatment etc.). ◆**D~heit**, *f* -/no *pl* (*Grobheit*) uncouthness, crudeness.

deren ['deːrən], *see* der, II, III.

dergleichen [deːr'glaiçən], *inv.* I. *dem. adj.* such; of this/that kind. II. *dem. pron.* things like that; nichts d., nothing of the kind.

derjenige ['deːrjeːnigə], *m*/**diejenige** *f*/ **dasjenige** *n dem. pron.* (*Pers.*) he, she; the one; (*Sachen*) that; the one; *pl* those, the ones.

dermaßen ['deːrmaːsən], *adv.* so; to such an extent.

derselbe [deːr'zɛlbə], *m*/**dieselbe** *fl* **dasselbe** *n dem. adj.* the same.

derzeit ['deːrtsait], *adv.* at present, at the moment. ◆**d~ig**, *adj.* present.

des [dɛs], *see* der I.

Desert|**eur** [dezɛr'tøːr], *m* -s/-e deserter. ◆**d~ieren** [-'tiːrən], *v.i.* (*sein/haben*) to desert.

desgleichen [dɛs'glaiçən], *adv.* likewise.

deshalb ['dɛshalp, *emphatic* dɛs'halp], *adv.* because of this/that; (*also*) therefore.

Desin|**fektion** [dɛzin-, dɛs'infɛktsi'oːn], *f* -/no *pl* disinfection. ◆**D~fektions-mittel**, *n* disinfectant. ◆**d~fi'zieren**, *v.tr.* to disinfect.

Desinteresse [dɛs'intəresə], *n* -s/no *pl* lack of interest; indifference. ◆**d~iert** [-'siːrt], *adj.* uninterested.

dessen ['dɛsən], *see* der II, III. ◆**d~ungeachtet**, *adv.* nevertheless.

Dessert [dɛ'seːr], *n* -s/-s dessert, *Brit:* sweet.

Destill|**ation** [dɛstilatsi'oːn], *f* -/-en (*a*) no *pl* distilling; (*b*) *Ch:* distillation. ◆**d~ieren** [-'liːrən], *v.tr.* to distil.

desto ['dɛsto], *adv.* (*before comp.*) je eher, d. lieber, the sooner, the better.

destruktiv [dɛstruk'tiːf], *adj.* destructive.

deswegen ['dɛs-, dɛs'veːgən], *adv.* = deshalb.

Detail [de'tai], *n* -s/-s detail. ◆**d~liert** [detai'jiːrt], *adj.* detailed.

Detekt|**ei** [detɛk'tai], *f* -/-en detective agency. ◆**D~iv** [-'tiːf], *m* -s/-e detective.

deut|**en** ['dɔytən], *v.* **1.** *v.tr.* to interpret (a text, dream etc.) (**als**, as); to read (the stars, s.o.'s hand etc.); to foretell (the future). **2.** *v.i.* (*haben*) to point (**auf j-n**, **etwas**, at s.o., sth.); *Fig:* (*Zeichen usw.*) **auf eine Änderung usw. d.**, to point to a change etc. ◆**d~lich**, *adj.* (*a*) clear; distinct (improvement etc.); (*b*) (*eindeutig*) explicit; (*grob*) blunt (answer etc.). ◆**D~lichkeit**, *f* -/no *pl* (*a*) clarity; (*b*) bluntness. ◆**D~ung**, *f* -/-en interpretation.

deutsch [dɔytʃ]. **I.** *adj.* **1.** German; die **D~e Demokratische Republik** (*abbr.* **DDR**), the German Democratic Republic (*abbr.* GDR), East Germany. **2.** (*a*) d. sprechen, to speak German; (*b*) geschrieben, written in German; (*b*) das D~e, the German language; ins **D~e übersetzen**, to translate into German. **3.** ein **D~er/eine D~e**, a German (man/woman); die **D~en**, the Germans; sie ist **D~e**, she is (a) German. **II.** D., *n* -(s)/no *pl* German. ◆**D~land**. *Pr.n.n* -s Germany.

Devise [de'viːzə], *f* -/-n. **1.** motto. **2.** *pl* **D~n** foreign exchange/currency. ◆**D~nkurs**, *m* rate of exchange.

Dezember [de'tsɛmbər], *m* -(s)/- December.

dezent [de'tsɛnt], *adj.* discreet; (*gedämpft*) subdued (lighting, music); (*geschmackvoll*) tasteful (pattern, furnishings etc.).

dezimal [detsi'maːl], *adj.* decimal (system etc.). ◆**D~bruch**, *m* decimal (fraction). ◆**D~zahl**, *f* decimal.

dezimieren [detsi'mi:rən], v.tr. to decimate (a population etc.).

Dia ['di:a], n -s/-s slide.

Diabet|iker(in) [dia'be:tikər(in)], m -s/- (f -nen) *Med:* diabetic. ◆d~**isch**, adj. diabetic.

Diagnose [dia'gno:zə], f -/-n diagnosis.

diagonal [diago'na:l], adj. diagonal. ◆**D~e**, f -/-n diagonal.

Diagramm [dia'gram], n -s/-e diagram; (statistical) chart.

Dialekt [dia'lɛkt], m -(e)s/-e dialect. ◆d~**frei**, adj. standard (language).

Dialog [dia'lo:k], m -(e)s/-e dialogue.

Diamant [dia'mant], m -en/-en diamond. ◆d~**en**, adj. diamond (bracelet, *Fig:* wedding etc.).

Diapositiv [diapozi'ti:f], n -s/-e transparency; (*gerahmt*) slide.

Diät [di'ɛ:t]. I. f -/-en 1. diet. 2. *pl Pol:* allowance. II. d., adv. d. leben/essen, to be on a diet.

dich [diç], 1. pron. acc of *du, q.v.* you. 2. refl. pron. yourself; **wasch(e) d.**, wash (yourself).

dicht [diçt], adj. 1. dense (fog, forest, traffic, population etc.); thick (hedge, hair, crowd etc.); close (weave etc.); d. **tight**, packed (programme etc.); d. **bevölkert/bewohnt**, densely populated. 2. adv. (*Lage*) close (**an/bei** + dat, to); d. **hintereinander folgen**, to follow in quick succession. 3. leakproof; (*wasserdicht*) waterproof (shoes etc.); watertight (container); *F:* **er ist nicht ganz d.**, he isn't all there. ◆**D~e**, f -/-n 1. thickness; density (of population etc.); *Cl:* closeness (of weave). 2. *Ph:* density. ◆**d~en¹**, v.tr. to make (a roof, tap etc.) watertight; to seal (a joint). ◆**d~halten**, v.i.sep.irr.45 (*haben*) *F:* to keep one's mouth shut. ◆**D~ung|**, f -/-en seal; (*Material*) packing; gasket. ◆**D~ungsring**, m -(e)s/-e washer.

dicht|en², v. 1. v.tr. to write a poem, novel). 2. v.i. (*haben*) to write poetry. ◆**D~er(in)**, m -s/- (f -/-nen) poet(ess); (*Verfasser*) author(ess); (*Schriftsteller*) writer. ◆**d~erisch**, adj. poetic. ◆**D~kunst**, f -/no pl (art of) poetry. ◆**D~ung²**, f -/-en (a) (*Lyrik*) poetry; (b) fiction.

dick [dik], adj. thick; fat (person, *F:* book, cigar, *Hum:* salary etc.); d~e **Bohnen**, broad beans; d. **machen**, (*Kleid*) to make one look fat; (*Essen*) to be fattening; d~e **Luft**, stuffy/*Fig:* tense atmosphere; *Fig:* **mit j-m durch d. und dünn gehen**, to go through thick and thin with s.o. ◆**D~darm**, m colon, large intestine. ◆**D~e**, f -/-n thickness; (*Pers.*) fatness. ◆**d~fellig**, adj. *F:* thick-skinned. ◆**d~flüssig**, adj. viscous. ◆**D~icht**, n -(e)s/-e thicket. ◆**D~kopf**, m *F:* pig-headed person. ◆**d~köpfig**, adj. *F:* pig-headed. ◆**d~lich**, adj. stoutish (person); chub-

by (baby); thickish (liquid). ◆**D~milch**, f curd; (*saure Milch*) curdled/sour milk.

die [di:], see der.

Dieb(in) ['di:p ('di:bin)], m -(e)s/-e (f -nen) thief; (*Einbrecher*) burglar. ◆**D~esbande**, f pack of thieves. ◆**D~esgut**, n stolen goods; *F:* loot. ◆**d~isch**, adj. impish (delight etc.); **sich d.** (*über etwas acc*) **freuen**, to be full of glee (over sth.). ◆**D~stahl**, m -(e)s/-e theft; *Jur:* larceny; **geistiger D.**, plagiarism.

diejenige ['di:je:nigə], pron. f see **derjenige**.

Diele ['di:lə], f -/-n 1. (floor)board. 2. (*Vorraum*) hall.

dien|en ['di:nən], v.i. (*haben*) to serve (j-m s.o.); *Mil:* to serve (one's time); (*Sache*) **damit ist mir nicht gedient**, that is no help to me; **es dient dem Fortschritt**, it is an aid to progress. ◆**D~er(in)**, m -s/- (f -/-nen) 1. servant; (*Dienerin*) maid. 2. (*Verbeugung*) bow. ◆**D~erschaft**, f -/no pl domestic staff. ◆**d~lich**, adj. useful; **j-m, einer Sache d. sein**, to be of help to s.o., a cause.

Dienst [di:nst]. I. m -(e)s/-e service; **j-m einen guten/schlechten D. leisten**, to do s.o. a good/bad turn. 2. (a) (*Arbeit*) work; (*Stellung*) job; **j-n in D. nehmen**, to engage s.o.; **außer D.**, retired; (b) **öffentlicher D.**, Civil Service; ◆ *Mil: etc:* duty; **D. tun/haben**, to be on duty; **Offizier vom D.**, Officer of the Day. II. **'D~,** comb.fm. official (secret, matter etc.); esp. *Com:* business (trip etc.). ◆**D~abteil**, n guard's compartment. ◆**d~bereit**, adj. (*Apotheke usw.*) on duty. ◆**D~bote**, m (domestic) servant. ◆**d~eifrig**, adj. zealous; (*übertrieben*) officious. ◆**D~grad**, m grade; *Mil:* rank. ◆**d~habend**, adj. (doctor, officer etc.); on duty. ◆**D~leistung**, f service (rendered). ◆**D~leistungsgewerbe**, n service industry. ◆**d~lich**, adj. official (communication, matter); d. **verreist**, away on business. ◆**d~pflichtig**, adj. liable for compulsory service. ◆**D~plan**, m duty roster. ◆**D~schluß**, m end of office hours; **nach D.**, after work. ◆**D~stelle**, f (administrative) office; **zuständige D.**, competent authority. ◆**D~stunden**, fpl office hours. ◆**d~tauglich**, adj. (person) fit for (*Mil:* active) service; able-bodied. ◆**D~weg**, m **auf dem D.**, through official channels. ◆**D~zeit**, f 1. working hours. 2. *Mil: etc:* term of service.

Dienstag ['di:nsta:k], m Tuesday. ◆**d~s**, adv. on Tuesdays.

dies [di:s]. I. dem. pron. this. II. adj. = **dieses**. ◆**d~bezüglich**, adj. relevant (documents etc.); (statement etc.) in this connection. ◆**d~jährig**, adj. of this

year; this year's (programme etc.).
◆'d~mal, adv. this time.
◆'d~seitig, adj. 1. on this side. 2. Lit:
earthly. ◆'d~seits. I. prep.+ gen &
adv. on this side (of). II. D., n -/no pl
Lit: das D., this earthly life; this world.

Diesel ['diːzəl], m -(s)/- diesel (engine/oil).
dieselbe [diː'zɛlbə], dem. pron. f. see derselbe.

diesig ['diːziç], adj. hazy, misty.
Dietrich ['diːtriç], m -s/-e skeleton key.
diffamier|en [difa'miːrən], v.tr. to slander
(s.o.). ◆D~ung, f -en defamation;
Pol: etc: smear.

Differen|tial [diferɛntsi'aːl], n -s/-e Mth:
differential. ◆D~tialgetriebe, n differential (gear). ◆D~tialrechnung, f differential calculus. ◆D~z ['rɛnts], f /
-en 1. Mth: etc: difference; (Rest) balance; (Überschuß) surplus. 2. pl disagree-
ments. ◆d~zieren, v.tr. & i. (haben)
to differentiate. ◆d~ziert, adj. varied;
discriminating (taste, judgement); sophisticated (method).

digital [digi'taːl], adj. digital.
Dikt|at [dik'taːt], n -(e)s/-e dictation.
◆D~ator, m -s/-en dictator.
◆d~atorisch [-a'toːriʃ], adj. dictator-
ial. ◆D~a'tur, f -/-en dictatorship.
◆d~ieren [-'tiːrən], v.tr. to dictate
(letters etc.). ◆D~iergerät, n dictating
machine.

Dilemma [di'lɛma], n -s/-s dilemma.
Dilett|ant(in) [dilɛ'tant(in)], m -en/-en (f
/-nen) dilettante. ◆d~antisch, adj.
amateurish.

Dill [dil], m -(e)s/-e dill.
Dimension [dimɛnzi'oːn], f -/-en dimension.

Ding [diŋ], n -(e)s/-e thing; pl -e nach
Lage der D~e, according to circumstances; es ist ein D. der Unmöglichkeit, it's a physical impossibility; das
geht nicht mit rechten D~en zu, there
is something odd about it; F: das ist so
ein D.! well, honestly! what next! (Verbrecher) ein D. drehen, to do a job.
◆'d~fest, adj: j-n d. machen, to arrest
s.o.

Diphtherie [difte'riː], f -/-n diphtheria.
Diplom [di'ploːm]. I. n -s/-e diploma;
(akademischer Grad) degree. II. D~,
comb.fm: holding a diploma, qualified (librarian etc.). ◆D~ingenieur, m (academically) qualified engineer.
Diplomat(in) [diplo'maːt(in)], m -en/-en
(f /-nen) diplomat. ◆D~ie [-a'tiː], f /
no pl diplomacy. ◆d~isch, adj. diplomatic.

dir [diːr], pers. pron. dat of du (a) to/
from/for you; (b) refl. tun d. die Füße
weh? do your feet hurt? nimm d. ein

Stück, help yourself to a piece; wünsch
d. was! have a wish! (c) (with prep.) nach
d.! after you! bei d., at your home.

direkt [di'rɛkt], adj. 1. direct.
◆D~heit, f -/no pl directness; (Offenheit) frankness. ◆D~ion [-tsi'oːn], f /
-en 1. (Vorstand) (board of) directors. 2.
(Büro) director's office. ◆D~or(in)
[-'rɛktor, -(r)k'toːrin)], m -s/-en (f /
-nen) director; (von Bank, Theater) manager; Sch: head teacher; esp. N.Am: principal. ◆D~übertragung, f live transmission.

Dirig|ent [diri'gɛnt], m -en/-en conductor
◆d~ieren [-'giːrən], v.tr. (a) (also
abs.) Mus: to conduct (an orchestra); (b)
(lenken) to direct (the traffic etc.).

Dirne ['dirnə], f -/-n F: tart; N.Am:
tramp.

Diskont [dis'kont], m -s/-e discount.
◆D~satz, m discount rate.

Diskothek [disko'teːk], f -/-en dis-
co(theque).

Diskrepanz [diskre'pants], f -/-en discrepancy.

diskret [dis'kreːt], adj. discreet.
◆D~ion [-etsi'oːn], f -/no pl discretion.

diskriminieren [diskrimi'niːrən], v.tr. to
discriminate against (s.o.).

Diskus ['diskus], m - & -ses/-se & -ken
discus.

Diskussion [diskusi'oːn], f -/-en discussion (über + acc, about, of); (Debatte) debate; zur D. stehen, to be on the agenda. ◆D~sbasis, f/D~sgrundlage, f
basis for discussion. ◆D~steilneh-
mer(in), m -s/- (f /-nen) panellist.

diskut|abel [disku'taːbəl], adj. worth dis-
cussing; nicht d., out of the question.
◆d~ieren [-'tiːrən], v.tr. & i. (haben)
(über) etwas acc d., to discuss sth.

disponieren [dispo'niːrən], v.i. (haben)
(a) to plan (ahead), make arrangements;
(b) über j-n, etwas acc d., to have s.o.,
sth. at one's disposal.

Disput [dis'puːt], m -(e)s/-e dispute

Disqualifi|kation [diskvalifikatsi'oːn], f -/
-en disqualification. ◆d~zieren
[-'tsiːrən], v.tr. to disqualify (s.o.).

Dissertation [disertatsi'oːn], f -/-en dissertation, (doctoral) thesis.

Dissident(in) [disi'dɛnt(in)], m -en/-en (f
/-nen) dissident.

Distanz [dis'tants], f -/-en distance; Fig:
(Abstand) detachment. ◆d~ieren
[-'tiːrən], v.tr. sich d., to keep one's
distance; Fig: sich von j-m, etwas dat
d., to dissociate oneself from s.o., sth.
◆d~iert, adj. detached.

Distel ['distəl], f -/-n thistle.

Disziplin [distsi'pliːn], f -/-en discipline.
◆d~arisch [-i'naːriʃ], adj. discipli-
nary. ◆d~ieren [-i'niːrən], v.tr. to discipline (s.o., oneself). ◆d~los, adj. un-
disciplined.

divers [di'vɛrs], adj. various; (einzelne)
miscellaneous; (unterschiedlich) diverse

(opinions etc.).

Divid|ende [divi'dɛndə], *f* **-/-n** dividend. ◆**d~ieren** [-'diːrən], *v.tr.* to divide (a number etc.) (**durch** + *acc*, by).

Division [divizi'oːn], *f* **-/-en** division.

doch [dɔx], *conj. & adv.* but; (*dennoch*) yet, however; (*trotzdem*) after all; **es geht d. nicht,** it just won't work/do; **wenn er d. käme!** if only he would come! **du kommst d. (oder)?** you are coming, aren't you? **sei d. ruhig!** do be quiet! **siehst du es nicht?—D.!** can't you see it?—Oh yes, I can; **d.,** yes, yes O.K.

Docht [dɔxt], *m* **-(e)s/-e** wick.

Dock [dɔk], *n* **-s/-s** dock.

Dogge ['dɔgə], *f* **-/-n** (**englische** D., mastiff; **dänische/deutsche** D., Great Dane.

Dogma ['dɔgma], *n* **-s/-men** dogma. ◆**d~tisch** [-'maːtiʃ], *adj.* dogmatic.

Dohle ['doːlə], *f* **-/-n** jackdaw.

Doktor ['dɔktɔr], *m* **-s/-en** doctor. ◆**D~and(in)** [-'rant (-'randin)], *m* **-en/-en** (*f* **-/-nen**) doctoral candidate. ◆**D~arbeit,** *f* doctoral thesis. ◆**D~titel, m/D~würde,** *f* doctorate.

Doktrin [dɔk'triːn], *f* **-/-en** doctrine. ◆**d~är** [-'nɛːr], *adj.* doctrinaire.

Dokument [doku'mɛnt], *n* **-(e)s/-e** document. ◆**D~ar-** [-'taːr-], *comb.fm.* documentary (film, programme). ◆**D~arbericht,** *m* documentary/on the spot report. ◆**D~ation** [-tatsi'oːn], *f* **-/-en** documentation. ◆**d~ieren** [-'tiːrən], *v.tr.* to document (sth.); (*belegen*) to prove (sth.) by documents.

Dolch [dɔlç], *m* **-(e)s/-e** dagger.

Dollar ['dɔlar], *m* **-s/-s** dollar; **5** D., five dollars.

dolmetsch|en ['dɔlmɛtʃən], *v.tr.&i.* (*haben*) to interpret (a speech etc.). ◆**'D~er(in),** *m* **-s/-** (*f* **-/-nen**) interpreter.

Dom [doːm], *m* **-(e)s/-e** cathedral. ◆**'D~pfaff,** *m* **-en/-en** bullfinch.

domin|ant [domi'nant], *adj.* dominant. ◆**D~anz,** *f* **-/-en** dominance. ◆**d~ieren,** *v.tr. & i.* (*haben*) to dominate (s.o., sth.).

Domizil [domi'tsiːl], *n* **-s/-e** abode.

Dompteur [dɔmp'tøːr], *m* **-s/-e** /**Dompteuse** [-'tøːzə], *f* **-/-n** (animal) tamer.

Donau ['doːnau], *Pr.n.f.* **die D.,** the (River) Danube.

Donner ['dɔnər], *m* **-s/-** thunder. ◆**'d~n,** *v.i.* (*haben*) (*a*) (*also Fig:*) to thunder; **f~an die Tür d.,** to hammer at the door; *Fig:* **d~nder Beifall,** thunderous applause; (*b*) *F:* (*schimpfen*) to raise hell, fume. ◆**D~wetter,** *n* **1.** *F:* (*Rüge*) telling off. **2.** *int.* (**zum** D.**!**) (*nochmal*)**!** good heavens!

Donnerstag ['dɔnərstaːk], *m* Thursday.

doof [doːf], *adj.* (*a*) silly, daft; (*b*) (*langweilig*) deadly boring.

Doppel ['dɔpəl]. **I.** *n* **-s/-. 1.** (*Zweitschrift*) duplicate. **2.** (*Tennis*) doubles. **II. 'D~-,** *comb.fm.* (*a*) double (bed, room, knot, line, window, chin, murder etc.); (*b*) dual (meaning, *Th:* role etc.). ◆**'D~decker,** *m* **-s/-. 1.** *Av:* biplane. **2.** double-decker (bus). ◆**'D~deutig,** *adj.* ambiguous. ◆**'D~gänger,** *m* (*Pers.*) double. ◆**'D~haus,** *n* semi-detached/ *N.Am:* duplex house. ◆**'D~punkt,** *m* colon. ◆**'d~seitig,** *adj.* (*a*) double-sided; (*b*) (*in Zeitung*) two-page (advertisement etc.). ◆**'d~sinnig,** *adj.* ambiguous. ◆**'D~stecker,** *m El:* two-way adapter. ◆**'d~t,** *adj.* **1.** double; **in d~ter Ausführung,** in duplicate; *adj.* verglast, double-glazed. **2.** twice the (length, size etc.); **das Buch habe ich d.,** I've got two copies of that book. ◆**'D~verdiener,** *m* **1.** person with two sources of income. **2.** (*Ehepaar*) **sie sind** D., they are both earning. ◆**'d~züngig,** *adj.* two-faced.

Dorf [dɔrf], *n* **-(e)s/-er** village. ◆**'D~bewohner(in),** *m* **-s/-** (*f/-nen*) villager.

Dorn [dɔrn], *m* **1.** **-(e)s/-en** thorn. **2.** **-(e)s/-e** (*a*) punch, awl; (*b*) spike (of a running shoe etc.). ◆**'D~busch,** *m* briar, thornbush. ◆**'d~ig,** *adj.* thorny (plant etc.). ◆**D~röschen** *Pr.n.n* **-s.** Sleeping Beauty.

Dörr- ['dœr-], *comb.fm.* dried (meat, vegetables, fruit).

Dorsch [dɔrʃ], *m* **-(e)s/-e** cod(fish).

dort [dɔrt], *adv.* there; **d. oben,** up there; **d. drüben,** over there; **d. herum,** thereabouts. ◆**'d~'her,** *adv.* (**von**) **d.,** from there. ◆**'d~'hin,** *adv.* there; to that place. ◆**'d~ig,** *adj.* in/of that place.

Dose ['doːzə], *f* **-/-n 1.** box; (*für Tabak usw.*) jar; (*für Zucker*) bowl. **2.** (*aus Blech*) tin; *esp. N.Am:* can. **3.** *El:* socket. ◆**D~n-,** *comb.fm.* tinned, *esp. N.Am:* canned (meat etc.). ◆**D~nmilch,** *f pl* evaporated/ condensed milk. ◆**D~nöffner,** *m* tin/ *N.Am:* can opener.

dös|en ['døːzən], *v.i.* (*haben*) *F:* to doze. ◆**'d~ig,** *adj. F:* drowsy; (*stumpfsinnig*) dopey.

dos|ieren [do'ziːrən], *v.tr.* to measure out (medicine etc.). ◆**D~is** ['doːzis], *f* **-/ Dosen** dose.

Dotter ['dɔtər], *m & n* **-s/-** yolk.

Dozent(in) [do'tsɛnt(in)], *m* **-en/-en** (*f* **-/-nen**) lecturer; *N.Am:* assistant professor.

Drache ['draxə], *m* **-n/-n** dragon.

Drachen ['draxən], *m* **1.** kite. **2.** *P:* (*Frau*) shrew. ◆**'D~flieger,** *m* hang-glider.

Dragée [dra'ʒeː], *n* **-s/-s** sugar-coated sweet/*N.Am:* candy/*Med:* pill.

Draht [draːt]. **I.** *m* **-(e)s/-e** wire; *Pol:* **heißer** D., hot line; *F:* **auf** D. **sein,** to know one's stuff. **II. 'D~-,** *comb.fm.* wire (brush, basket, fence etc.). ◆**'D~haar,** *n* wire hair. ◆**'D~haar-,** *comb.fm.* wire-haired (terrier etc.).

◆'d~ig, *adj.* wiry (hair, person). ◆'d~los, *adj.* wireless (telegraphy etc.). ◆'D~seil, *n* (*a*) wire rope; cable; (*b*) (*für Seiltänzer*) tightrope. ◆'D~seilbahn, *f* cable railway; (*Kabine*) cable car. ◆'D~zange, *f* wire pliers. ◆'D~zieher, *m Fig:* string puller.

drall¹ [dral], *adj.* plump, buxom (girl, woman).

Drall², *m* -(e)s/*occ* -e spin (of a ball, bullet).

Dram|a ['drɑːma], *n* -s/-men drama. ◆D~atiker [-'mɑːtikər], *m* -s/- dramatist, playwright. ◆d~atisch [-'mɑːtiʃ], *adj.* dramatic.

dran [dran], *F:* = daran; **du bist d.,** it's your turn; **gut d. sein,** to be well off. ◆'d~bleiben, *v.i.sep.irr.12* (*sein*) *F:* (**an etwas** *dat*) **d.,** to hold on (to sth.); *Tel:* **bleiben Sie (bitte) dran!** hold the line please! ◆'d~kommen, *v.i.sep.irr.53* (*sein*) *F:* to have one's turn.

Drang [draŋ], *m* -(e)s/=e 1. (*Druck*) pressure. 2. (*innerer Trieb*) urge; (*plötzlich*) impulse; **D. nach Freiheit,** yearning for freedom.

drängeln ['drɛŋəln], *v.tr.&i.* (*haben*) to jostle (s.o.).

drängen ['drɛŋən], *v.* 1. *v.tr.* (*a*) to push, shove (s.o.); (*b*) **j-n zu etwas** *dat* **d./j-n d., etwas zu tun,** urge s.o. to do sth.; **er wollte sie nicht d.,** he didn't want to rush her. 2. *v.i.* (*haben*) (*a*) (*Menschenmenge usw.*) to push, shove; (*b*) **auf Zahlung usw. d.,** to press for payment etc.; *Fig:* **die Zeit drängt,** time is running short.

drastisch ['drastiʃ], *adj.* 1. drastic (measures etc.). 2. (*derb, direkt*) uncompromising.

drauf [drauf], *F:* = darauf; **d. und dran sein, etwas zu tun,** to be on the point of doing sth. ◆'D~gänger, *m* -s/- go-getter; (*waghalsig*) daredevil. ◆'d~gehen, *v.i.sep.irr.36* (*sein*) *F:* (*a*) to kick the bucket; (*b*) (*Zeit, Geld*) to be spent. ◆'d~zahlen, *v.tr.sep. F:* to pay (sth.) on top.

draußen ['drausən], *adv.* outside; (*im Freien*) out of doors; **da d.,** out there.

Dreck [drɛk]. I. *m* -(e)s/*no pl* 1. *F:* muck; (*Schlamm*) mud; **j-n, etwas in den D. ziehen,** to run s.o. sth. down. 2. *P:* (*Sache*) business; (*Kleinigkeit*) trifle. 3. *P:* **ein D./der letzte D. sein,** to be utterly worthless(*Pers.*); the lowest of the low. II. **'D~,** *comb.fm. F:* dirty, (*stärker*) filthy (work, thing, *Fig:* hole, paw etc.); (*mies*) lousy (weather etc.). ◆'d~ig, *adj. F:* dirty (hands, *Fig:* joke etc.); muddy (path etc.); filthy (weather, *Fig:* book etc.); **ihm geht es d.,** he's in a bad way(*finanziell*) hard up.

Dreh [dreː]. I. *m* -(e)s *F:* 1. (*Einfall*) idea; (*Trick*) knack. 2. (*Drehung*) turn; *Fig:* **einer Geschichte einen D. geben,** to give a story a twist. II. **'D~,** *comb.fm.* (*a*) revolving (door etc.); (*b*) rotary (motion etc.); (*c*) swivel (chair, *Tchn:* joint etc.). ◆'D~arbeiten, *fpl* shooting (of a film). ◆'D~bank, *f* (turning) lathe. ◆'d~bar, *adj.* rotatable; revolving (chair, *Tchn:* stage etc.); (*schwenkbar*) swivelling. ◆'D~buch, *n* (film) script; screenplay. ◆'d~en, *v.* 1.*v.tr.* (*a*) to turn (a key, handle, one's head etc.); (*im Kreis*) to rotate, (*schnell*) spin (a wheel etc.); (*b*) sich d., to turn; (*im Kreis*) to rotate, (*schnell*) spin; **sich um etwas** *acc* **d.,** to revolve around sth., (*Gespräch usw.*) be concerned with sth.; *Fig:* **alles dreht sich um ihn,** he is the centre of everything; (*b*) to roll (a cigarette); *Cin:* to shoot (a film), film (a scene). 2. *v.i.* (*haben*) (*a*) (*Schiff usw.*) to turn; (*b*) (*Wind*) to change; (*c*) **an etwas** *dat* **d.,** to turn, *Fig:* twist sth. ◆'D~er, *m* -s/- turner; lathe operator. ◆'D~kreuz, *n* turnstile. ◆'D~orgel, *f* barrel organ. ◆'D~scheibe, *f* (*a*) turntable; (*b*) (*Töpferei*) potter's wheel. ◆'D~stuhl, *m* swivel chair. ◆'D~ung, *f* -/-en turn; (*um die Achse*) rotation; (*im Kreis*) gyration. ◆'D~zahl, *f* (number of) revolutions; speed. ◆'D~zahlmesser, *m* revolution counter.

drei [drai]. I. *num. adj.* three. II. **D.,** *f* -/-en (number) three. ◆'D~eck, *n* triangle. ◆'d~eckig, *adj.* triangular. ◆'D~eck(s)tuch, *n* 1. shawl. 2. *Med:* triangular bandage. ◆'D~ecksverhältnis, *n* ménage à trois. ◆'D~einigkeit, *f* -/*no pl* trinity. ◆'d~er'lei, *adj.* of three kinds. ◆'d~fach, *adj.* threefold, triple; **in d~facher Ausfertigung,** in triplicate; **das D~fache,** three times as much. ◆'D~faltigkeit, *f* -/*no pl* trinity. ◆'d~jährig, *adj.* three-year-old (child etc.); three-year (appointment etc.). ◆'d~könige, *pl/*D~königsfest *m* Epiphany. ◆'d~mal, *adv.* three times. ◆'D~rad, *n* tricycle; *Aut:* three-wheeler. ◆'d~ßig. I. *adj.* die d. Jahre, the thirties. II. **D.,** *m* -s/- person in his/her thirties. ◆'d~ßig**jährig,** *adj.* thirty-year old (person); thirty years' (war etc.). ◆'d~ßigste(r,s), *num. adj.* thirtieth. ◆'d~stellig, *adj.* three-figure (number). ◆'d~teilig, *adj.* in three parts; *Cl:* three-piece (suit). ◆'d~'viertel, *adj.* three quarters; **d. voll,** three quarters full. ◆D~viertel'stunde, *f* three quarters of an hour. ◆D~'vierteltakt, *m* three-four time.

dreinreden ['drainreːdən], *v.i.sep.* (*haben*) (*unterbrechen*) to interrupt; (*sich einmischen*) to interfere.

dreist [draist], *adj.* (*kühn*) audacious; (*frech*) impudent. ◆'D~igkeit, *f* -/-en audacity; impudence.

Dresch|e ['drɛʃə], f -/no pl F: thrashing, hiding. ◆'d~**en**, v.tr.irr. (a) to thresh (corn etc.); Fig: **Phrasen d.,** to talk in platitudes; (b) to thrash (s.o.).

Dress|eur [drɛ'søːr], m -s/-e (animal) trainer. ◆d~**ieren** ['siːrən], v.tr. to train (an animal); ◆**D~ur** ['suːr], f -/-en training.

Drill [dril], m -(e)s/no pl drill. ◆'D~**bohrer,** m -s/- (spiral) drill. ◆'d~**en,** v.tr. to drill.

Drilling ['driliŋ], m -s/-e triplet.

drin [drin], F: = **darin; mehr ist nicht d.,** you can't expect any more.

dring|en ['driŋən], v.i.irr. (a) (sein) **durch etwas** acc **d.,** to penetrate sth.; **aus etwas d.,** to break/(Flüssigkeit) leak out of sth.; (Geräusch) to come from sth.; **bis zu j-m d.,** to get as far as s.o.; (b) (haben) **auf etwas** acc **d.,** to press for sth. ◆**d~end,** adj. urgent (matter, Tel: call etc.); imminent (danger). **d. verdächtig,** strongly suspected. ◆d~**lich,** adj. urgent. ◆**D~lichkeit,** f -/no pl urgency.

Drink [driŋk], m -s/-s (alcoholic) drink.

drinnen ['drinən], adv. inside.

dritt [drit]. I. adv. phr. **zu d.,** in a group of three; **wir waren zu d.,** there were three of us. II. **'d~,** comb.fm. third (largest, smallest etc.). ◆**d~e(r,s),** adj. third; **aus d~er Hand,** at third hand; indirectly; also Jur: **D~e(r),** third party; **im Beisein D~er,** in the presence of others. ◆**D~el,** n -s/- third. ◆**d~eln,** v.tr. to divide (sth.) into three. ◆**d~ens,** adv. thirdly.

Drog|e ['droːgə], f -/-n drug. ◆**D~enabhängige(r),** m & f drug addict. ◆**D~erie** [drogə'riː], f -/-n (non-dispensing) chemist's shop, N.Am: drugstore. ◆**D~ist(in)** [dro'gist(in)], m -en/-en (f -/-nen) (non-dispensing) chemist, N.Am: druggist.

Droh|brief ['droːbriːf], m threatening letter. ◆**d~en,** v.i. (haben) to threaten. ◆**d~end,** adj. threatening (attitude etc.); menacing (tone, gesture etc.); imminent (danger). ◆**D~ung,** f -/-en threat.

dröhnen ['drøːnən], v.i. (haben) to boom, (hallen) resound; (sehr laut) to roar; (Maschinen usw.) to throb, (in der Ferne) usw.) to throb, (in der Ferne) usw.

drollig ['drɔliç], adj. funny; (niedlich) sweet; (seltsam) quaint.

Drops ['drɔps], m & n -/- (fruit) drop, boiled sweet; N.Am: hard candy.

Droschke ['drɔʃkə], f -/-n cab.

Drossel ['drɔsəl], f -/-n thrush. ◆'d~**n,** v.tr. (a) to throttle (an engine); (b) to cut down (speed, imports etc.).

drüben ['dryːbən], adv. over there.

drüber ['dryːbər], adv.F: = **darüber.**

Druck¹ [druk], m -(e)s/-e pressure; squeeze (of s.o.'s hand); Fig: **j-n unter D. setzen,** to put pressure on s.o.; F:

in/im D. sein, to be pressed for time. ◆**'D~knopf,** m (Verschluß) press-stud; (klein) snap fastener. ◆'D~**luft,** f -/no pl compressed air.

Druck² [-]. I. m -(e)s/-e 1. no pl (a) printing; **in D. gehen,** to go to press. 2. (Kunstd.) print, engraving. II. '**D~,** comb.fm. (a) printing (costs, process etc.); (b) (gedruckt) printed (pattern, page, Cl: material etc.). ◆'D~**buchstabe,** m block letter. ◆**d~en,** v.tr. to print (a book etc.). ◆'**D~er,** m -s/- printer. ◆'**D~erei,** f -/-en printing works, F: printer's. ◆'**D~erschwärze,** f -/-n printer's ink. ◆'**D~fehler,** m misprint. ◆'**D~sache,** f printed matter. ◆'**D~schrift,** f block capitals/letters.

Drück|eberger ['drykəbɛrgər], m -s/- shirker; Mil: malingerer. ◆'**d~en,** v. 1. v.tr. (a) to press (s.o., sth.); **j-n an sich/ an die Brust d.,** to embrace/hug s.o.; **der Schuh drückt (mich),** this shoe is too tight; (b) F: **sich vor etwas** dat/**um etwas** acc **d.,** to dodge/evade sth. 2. v.i. (haben) to press; **auf den Knopf d.,** to press the button. ◆'**d~end,** adj. heavy (burden, debt etc.); oppressive (heat etc.). ◆'**D~er,** m -s/- (a) door handle; (b) push-button; F: **am D. sein/sitzen,** to be in control.

drum [drum], adv. F: = **darum; mit allem D. und Dran,** with all the trimmings.

drunter ['druntər], adv. F: = **darunter; d. und drüber,** upside down.

Drüse ['dryːzə], f -/-n gland. ◆'**D~n-,** comb.fm. glandular (fever etc.).

Dschungel ['dʒuŋəl], m -s/- jungle.

Dschunke ['dʒuŋkə], f -/-n junk.

du [duː]. I. pers. pron. you; **mit j-m auf du und du stehen/per du sein,** to be on familiar terms with s.o. II. **Du,** n -(s)/-(s) you; **j-m das Du anbieten,** to suggest to s.o. that he/she use the familiar form of address.

Dübel ['dyːbəl], m -s/- wallplug.

duck|en ['dukən], v.tr. (a) to humble (s.o.); F: to do (s.o.) down; **sich d.,** to duck. ◆'**D~mäuser,** m -s/- cringer; F: yes-man.

dudel|n ['duːdəln], v. 1. v.i. (haben) to tootle; (Radio usw.) drone (on). 2. v.tr. to drone out (a song, tune). ◆'**D~sack,** m -(e)s/-e bagpipes.

Duett [du'ɛt], n -(e)s/-e duet.

Duft [duft], m -(e)s/-e scent, fragrance (of flowers etc.); aroma (of coffee, a cigar etc.). ◆'**d~en,** v.i. (haben) to smell, be fragrant. ◆'**d~ig,** adj. fine, gauzy (material); light, dainty (dress etc.).

duld|en ['duldən], v.tr. to bear (pain etc.); to tolerate (injustice etc.); **etwas stillschweigend d.,** to shut one's eyes to sth. ◆'**d~sam,** adj. tolerant. ◆'**D~ung,** f -/-en toleration.

dumm [dum], adj. 1. (a) stupid (person, action); N.Am: dumb (person); (töricht) foolish, silly; **d~es Zeug reden**, to talk nonsense; (b) **er ist immer der D~e dabei**, he always comes off worst. 2. *F:* (*unangenehm*) stupid, awkward (business, time etc.); **zu/wie d.!** what a nuisance! **die Sache wird mir zu d.**, that's too much. ◆'**d~dreist**, *adj.* impudent. ◆'**D~heit**, *f -/-en* l. *no pl* stupidity; (*Leichtsinn*) silliness, foolishness. 2. stupid thing, folly. ◆'**D~kopf**, *m F:* fool; ass

dumpf [dumpf], *adj.* dull (sound, *Fig:* pain etc.); (*gedämpft*) muffled (sound).

Düne ['dy:nǝ], *f -/-n* dune.

Dung [duŋ], *m -(e)s/no pl* dung.

Düng|emittel ['dyŋǝmitǝl], *n* fertilizer. ◆**d'~en**, *v.tr.* to fertilize, manure (a field etc.). ◆'**D~er**, *m -s/-* fertilizer, (*Mist*) manure.

dunkel ['duŋkǝl]. I. *adj. a* dark; **es wird den.**, to get dark; (*also Fig:*) **im d~n**, in the dark; (b) *Fig:* (*unbestimmt*) vague (idea, memory, suspicion etc.); (*unklar*) obscure (passage etc.); (c) (*zweifelhaft*) **dunkle Geschäfte**, shady deals. II. **D.**, *n -s/no pl Lit:* darkness. ◆'**D~heit**, *f -/no pl* darkness. ◆'**D~kammer**, *f* darkroom. ◆'**d~n**, *v.* 1. *v.i.* (*haben*) to grow dark. 2. *v.tr.* to darken (colours etc.). ◆'**D~ziffer**, *f* unpublished but suspected figure/statistic.

Dünkel ['dyŋkǝl], *m -s/no pl Lit:* conceit. ◆**d~haft**, *adj. Lit:* conceited

dünn [dyn], *adj.* thin; (a) slim (figure, volume); spindly (legs); (b) (*schwach*) weak (coffee etc.); *Fig:* **d. gesät**, few and far between. ◆'**D~darm**, *m* small intestine. ◆'**d~flüssig**, *adj.* thin, watery (liquid).

Dunst [dunst], *m -es/=e* mist; (*in der Ferne, aus Abgase usw.*) haze; (*Dampf*) vapour. ◆'**d~ig**, *adj.* misty, hazy; (*verräuchert*) smoky.

dünsten ['dynstǝn], *v.tr. Cu:* to steam (fish, vegetables); (*schmoren*) to braise (meat etc.).

Dünung ['dy:nuŋ], *f -/-en* swell.

Duo ['du:o], *n -s/-s* duo.

Duplikat [dupli'ka:t], *n -(e)s/-e* duplicate; (*Abschrift*) copy.

Dur [du:r], *n -/-* major (key); **A-D**, A major.

durch [durç]. I. **prep.** + *acc* (a) through; (*mittels*) **d. die Post**, by post; **d. Zufall**, by chance; **etwas d. Lautsprecher bekanntgeben**, to announce sth. over loudspeakers; (b) (*von*) **d. ein Erdbeben zerstört**, destroyed by an earthquake. II. **adv.** 1. (*zeitlich*) (a) **den Sommer d.**, throughout the summer; (b) *F:* (*vorbei*) **es ist schon elf Uhr d.**, it's already gone eleven. 2. **d. und d.**, thoroughly.

'durcharbeiten *v.tr.sep.* 1. *v.tr.* to study (sth.) thoroughly. 2. *v.i.* (*haben*) to work without a break; **die ganze Nacht d.**, to work right through the night.

'durchatmen *v.i.sep.*(*haben*) to breathe

deeply.

durchaus ['durç(')²aus], *adv.* 1. (*unbedingt*) absolutely, at all costs. 2. **es ist d. möglich/richtig**, it is perfectly possible/correct; **d. nicht**, not at all.

'durchbeißen *v.tr.sep.irr.4* (a) to bite through (sth.); (b) *F:* **sich d.**, to struggle through.

'durchblättern *v.tr.sep.* to glance/thumb through (a book etc.).

'Durchblick *m* 1. view. 2. *F:* overall view; **den D. verlieren**, to lose track (of things). ◆'**d~en**, *v.i.sep.* (*haben*) (a) to look through (**durch etwas** *acc*, sth.); (b) **etwas d. lassen**, to make sth. clear; **blickst du hier durch?** can you make anything of this?

Durch|blutung, *f -/no pl* circulation.

durch'bohren *v.tr. insep.* (*Messer usw.*) to pierce (sth.); *Fig:* **j-n mit seinem Blick d.**, to transfix s.o. with a glance.

durchbrechen *v.irr.14* 1. ['durçbrɛçǝn] *v.tr.sep.* to break (sth.) in two; to break through (a wall etc.). 2. ['durçbrɛçǝn] *v.i.sep.* (*sein*) (a) (*Stock usw.*) to break in two; (b) (*Sonne, Mil: Truppen*) to break through. 3. [durç'brɛçǝn] *v.tr.insep.* to break/burst (through) (sth., a dam etc.).

'durchbrennen, *v.i.sep.irr.15* (a) (*huben*) (*Ofen usw.*) to keep burning; (b) (*sein*) **die Sicherung ist durchgebrannt**, the fuse has blown; (c) (*sein*) *F:* to run away.

'durchbringen *v.tr.sep.irr.16* (a) to get (s.o., sth.) through, pull (a patient) through; (b) (*vergeuden*) to squander (money).

'Durchbruch, *m* breakthrough; cutting (of teeth).

durch'denken, *v.tr.insep.irr.17* to think (sth.) over; **gut durchdacht**, well thought out.

'durchdrehen, *v.sep.* 1. *v.tr.* to put (meat etc.) through the mincer. 2. *v.i.* (*haben*) (a) (*Räder*) to spin; (b) *F:* (*Pers.*) to panic, go round the bend.

durchdringen, *v.irr.19* 1. ['durçdriŋǝn], *v.i.sep.* (*sein*) (**durch etwas** *acc*) **d.**, to penetrate (sth.). 2. [durç'driŋǝn] *v.tr.insep.* to penetrate (sth.); **j-n d.**, (*Gefühl usw.*) to fill s.o.; (*Idee*) to seize s.o.'s imagination.

'durchdrücken, *v.tr.sep.* (a) to press, force (sth.); *F:* to push through (a plan etc.); (b) to straighten (one's knees, back).

durchein'ander. I. *adv.* (*Sachen usw.*) jumbled (up); *Pej:* in a mess; **ich bin ganz d.**, I'm all mixed up. II. **D.**, *n -s/no pl* disorder; mess; (*Verwechslung usw.*) mix-up. ◆**d~bringen**, *v.tr.sep.irr.16* to confuse (s.o.); to muddle up (papers, words etc.). ◆**d~reden**, *v.i. sep.* (*haben*) **alle redeten durcheinander**, everyone was talking at once.

durchfahren, *v. irr.26* 1. ['durçfa:rǝn] (*sein*) *v.i.* to drive/travel through (sth.); **der Zug fährt bis X durch**, the train doesn't stop until X. 2. [durç'fa:rən] *v.tr.insep.* to travel/*Aut:* drive through (an area, country etc.); *Fig:* (*Schreck, Gedanken usw.*) to pass through (s.o., s.o.'s mind).

'Durchfahrt, *f* -/-en **sie sind nur auf der D.,** they are just passing through; **D. verboten,** no thoroughfare.

'Durchfall, *m* diarrhoea. ◆**d∼en,** *v.i.sep.irr.*27 (*sein*) (*a*) (**durch etwas** *acc*) **d.,** to fall through (sth.); (*b*) *Th:* (*Stück*) to be a flop; (**bei der Prüfung**) **d.,** to fail (the examination); **j-n d. lassen,** to fail s.o.

'durchfinden, *v.i. & refl.sep.irr.*9 (*haben*) (**sich**) **d.,** to find one's way through.

durch'forschen, *v.tr.insep.* to explore.

durch'froren, *adj.* frozen stiff.

'durchführ|bar, *adj.* practicable. ◆**d∼en,** *v.sep.* 1. *v.i.* (*haben*) **durch etwas d.,** to go through sth. 2. *v.tr.* (*a*) **j-n** (**durch etwas** *acc*) **d.,** to take s.o. through, show s.o. round (sth.); (*b*) (*verwirklichen*) to carry out (a plan, task, an order etc.); to complete (work etc.); to hold (a meeting); to make (a count). ◆**D∼ung,** *f* -/-en carrying out; (*Vollendung*) completion.

'Durchgang, *m* -(e)s/=e 1. passage (through), way through; **D. verboten,** no thoroughfare. 2. (*Stadium*) phase; *Sp:* round. ◆**D∼s-** *comb.fm.* through (road, station etc.); *esp.Com:* transit (visa, trade etc.). ◆**D∼slager,** *n* transit camp. ◆**D∼sstadium,** *n* transitional stage. ◆**D∼sverkehr,** *m* through traffic.

durchgängig ['-gєniç], *adj.* general; universal (opinion etc.).

'durchgehen, *v.irr.sep.*36 1. *v.i.* (*sein*) (*a*) (**durch etwas** *acc*) **d.,** to go of(*Pers.*) walk through (sth.); (*b*) (*Antrag, Gesetz usw.*) to go through; **etwas d. lassen,** to let sth. pass; **j-m etwas d. lassen,** to let s.o. get away with sth.; (*c*) (*Pferd*) to bolt; *F:* (*durchbrennen*) to run away. 2. *v.tr.* (*sein*) to go/look through (a list, book etc.). ◆**d∼d,** *adj.* 1. through (train, ticket, carriage etc.). 2. continuous; **d. geöffnet,** open day and night; (*Geschäft*) no lunchtime closing.

'durchgreifen, *v.i.sep.irr.*43 (*haben*) (*a*) (**durch etwas** *acc*) **d.,** to reach through (sth.); (*b*) to take (decisive) action.

'durchhalten, *v.sep.irr.*45 1. *v.i.* (*haben*) to hold out. 2. *v.tr.* to see (sth.) through; **er kann das Tempo nicht d.,** he cannot stand the pace.

'durchkämpfen, *v.tr.sep.* (*a*) to fight (sth.) out; *Fig:* to achieve (sth.) (after a struggle); (*b*) **sich** (**durch etwas** *acc*) **d.,** to fight one's way through (sth.).

'durchkommen, *v.i.sep.irr.*53 (*sein*) (*a*) to come through, (*Regen usw.*) come in; *Tel: etc:* to get through; (*b*) (*Patient*) to pull through; (*c*) to manage/get by (with sth.); *F:* **damit wirst du (bei ihm) nicht**

d., that won't get you anywhere (with him).

durch'kreuzen, *v.tr. insep.* to thwart (s.o.'s plans etc.).

'durchlassen, *v.tr.sep.irr.*57 to let (s.o., sth.) (pass) through; **Wasser d.,** to leak.

'durchlässig, *adj.* (*a*) (*wasserd.*) porous (material, soil etc.); leaky (shoes, roof etc.); (*b*) (*lichtd.*) transparent.

durchlauf|en, *v.irr.*58 1. ['durçlaufən], *v.i.sep.* (*sein*) (**durch etwas** *acc*) **d.,** to run through (sth.). 2. [durç'laufən] *v.tr.insep.* (*a*) to pass through (stages etc.); (*b*) *Sp:* to cover (a distance). ◆**D∼erhitzer,** *m* constant flow water heater.

durch'leben, *v.tr.sep.* to live through (a period), experience (sth.).

'durchlesen, *v.tr.sep.irr.*61 to read (sth.) through.

durch'leuchten, *v.tr.insep.* to X-ray (s.o., sth.); *Fig:* to examine (a case, s.o.'s past etc.); *F:* to screen (s.o.).

durch'löchern, *v.tr.insep.* to punch holes in (sth.); **von Kugeln durchlöchert,** riddled with bullets.

'durchmachen, *v.tr.sep.* to go through (school, hard times etc.); to undergo (training, a process, an operation etc.).

Durchmesser, *m* -s/- diameter.

durch'nässen, *v.tr.insep.* to drench (s.o., sth.), soak (clothes etc.) (through).

'durchnehmen, *v.tr.sep.irr.*69 *Sch:* to go through, *F:* do (a text, etc.).

durchnumerieren, *v.tr.sep.* to number (pages etc.) consecutively.

'durchpausen, *v.tr.sep.* to trace (a picture etc.).

'durchpeitschen, *v.tr.sep.* (*a*) to whip (s.o.) soundly; (*b*) to rush (a law etc.) through.

durchqueren [durç'kve:rən], *v.tr.insep.* to cross.

'Durchreiche, *f* -/-n service hatch. ◆**d∼n,** *v.tr.sep.* to hand (sth.) through.

'Durchreise, *f* -/-n journey through (**durch ein Land usw.,** a country etc.); **auf der D. sein,** to be passing through. ◆**D∼visum,** *n* transit visa.

'durchringen, *v.refl.sep.irr.*19 **sich zu etwas** *dat* **d.,** to make up one's mind finally to (do) sth.

'durchrosten, *v.i.sep.* (*sein*) to rust through.

durchs [durçs], *prep.* = **durch das.**

'Durchsage, *f* -/-n announcement; *F:* (news)flash.

'durchsagen, *v.tr.sep.* to announce (information etc.).

durch'schau|bar, *adj.* obvious, transparent (motives etc.); **schwer d.,** puzzling. ◆**d∼en,** *v.tr.insep.* to see through (s.o., a trick, motives etc.).

'durchscheinen, *v.i.sep.irr.*79 (*haben*) (*Licht*) to shine through; (*Muster usw.*) to show through. ◆**d∼d,** *adj.* translucent (material).

'**Durchschlag**, *m* -(e)s/-e **1.** carbon copy.
2. *Cu:* colander; strainer. ◆**d~en**,
v.sep.irr.85 **1.** *v.tr.* (*a*) to break (sth.)
through/in half; (*b*) **sich d.** to struggle
through; **sich alleine d.,** to fend for oneself. **2.** *v.i.* (*haben*) (*Tinte, Farbe usw.*) to
come/show through. ◆'**d~end**, *adj.* effective (measures etc.); powerful (effect
etc.); convincing (argument, evidence);
d~ender Erfolg, sensational success.
◆'**D~skraft,** *f -/no pl* (*a*) penetrating
power; penetration (of a shell etc.); (*b*)
Fig: force (of an idea, argument); effec-
tiveness (of proof etc.).

durchschneiden, *v.tr.irr.59* **1.** ['durʃ-
ʃnaidən] *v.sep.* to cut (sth.) through/(*in
zwei Teile*) in half. **2.** [dʊrç'ʃnaidən]
v.insep. to cut through (sth.).

'**Durchschnitt**, *m* **1.** average; **über/unter
dem D.,** above/below average. **2.**
(*Schnitt*) section (through sth.). ◆'**d~-
lich,** (*a*) *adj.* average; (*b*) *adv.* on
(an) average. ◆'**D~s-**, *comb.fm.* (*a*)
average (age, price, speed, temperature
etc.); (*b*) ordinary (education etc.).
◆'**D~smensch,** *m* man in the street.

'**Durchschrift**, *f* carbon copy.

'**durchsehen**, *v.sep.irr.92* **1.** *v.i.* (*haben*)
(*durch etwas acc*) **d.,** to see through
(sth.). **2.** *v.tr.* (*a*) to look/go/(*flüchtig*)
glance through; (*prüfend*) check (a book,
papers etc.).

durchsetzen *v.tr.* **1.** ['dʊrçzɛtsən] *v.sep.*
(*a*) to get (*mit Gewalt*) force (a reform,
etc.) through; **seinen Willen d.,** to get
one's own way; (*b*) **sich d.,** to assert oneself, (*seinen Willen d.*) get one's way;
(*Produkt*) to catch on; **er kann sich nicht
d.,** he has no authority. **2.** [dʊrç'zɛtsən]
v.insep. to intersperse (sth.) (with sth.).

'**Durchsicht**, *f -/no pl* inspection; **zur D.,**
for information. ◆'**d~ig,** *adj.* transparent (material); *Fig:* obvious (plan, deception etc.). ◆'**D~igkeit,** *f -/no pl* transparency.

'**durchsickern**, *v.i.sep.* (*haben*) (*Blut usw.*)
to seep/trickle through; *Fig:* (*Geheimnis*)
to leak out.

'**durchsieben**, *v.tr.sep.* to sieve, sift (flour
etc.); *Fig:* to sift through.

'**durchsprechen**, *v.tr.sep.irr.14* to discuss
(sth.) (thoroughly).

'**durchstehen**, *v.tr.sep.irr.100* to come
through (difficulties, a test etc.); to withstand (pressure); **das Tempo d.,** to stand
the pace.

durch'stöbern, *v.tr.insep.* to rummage
through (drawers, clothes etc.); to ransack (a house, room etc.).

'**durchstreichen**, *v.tr.sep.irr.40* to cross
out, delete (a word etc.).

durch'such|**en**, *v.tr.insep.* to search (s.o.,
a house etc.); (*Polizei*) to frisk (s.o.).
◆**D~ung,** *f -/-en* search.
◆**D~ungsbefehl,** *m* search warrant.

'**durchtrainiert**, *adj. Sp:* in top condition.

durch'tränken, *v.tr.insep.* to soak (sth.).

durch'trieben, *adj.* cunning, sly.

'**durch'wachsen**, *adj.* streaky (bacon).

'**durchwählen**, *v.i.sep.* (*haben*) *Tel:* to
dial direct.

durchweg ['dʊrçvɛk], *adv.* without exception.

'**durchzählen**, *v.tr.sep.* to count (all the
people/things).

durchziehen, *v.irr.113* **1.** ['dʊrçtsi:ən]
v.tr.sep. (*a*) **etwas (durch etwas acc) d.,**
to pull sth. through (sth.); (*b*) *F:* to see
(sth.) through; to complete (sth.); (*c*)
(*Idee, Motiv usw.*) **sich durch ein Werk
d.,** to run through a work. **2.**
[dʊrç'tsi:ən] *v.i.sep.* (*sein*) to pass/go
through; to march through. **3.**
[dʊrç'tsi:ən] *v.tr.insep.* to pass/go through
(an area, *Fig:* s.o.); (*Motiv usw.*) to run
through (a work etc.).

'**Durchzug**, *m* **1.** passage through. **2.**
(*Zugluft*) through draught/*N.Am:* draft.

dürfen ['dʏrfən], *modal aux. vb.* (*a*) **etwas
tun d.,** to be allowed to do sth.; **darf ich
mitkommen?—ja, du darfst,** may I come
too?—yes, you may; **hier darf nicht ge-
raucht werden,** smoking is not permitted
here; **darfst du das?** are you allowed to
do this? (*b*) (*Höflichkeitsformeln*) **darf ich
Sie bitten, mir zu folgen?** would you follow me please? **wenn ich bitten darf,** if
you don't mind; please; (*im Geschäft*)
was darf es sein? can I help you? (*c*) **du
darfst dich nicht darüber aufregen,** you
mustn't worry about it; **sie darf nichts
davon wissen,** she must not know anything about it; **das hätte er nicht tun d.,**
he ought not to have done that; (*d*) **das
darf doch nicht wahr sein!** it can't be
(true)! **er dürfte bald kommen,** he will
probably come soon.

dürftig ['dʏrftiç], *adj.* **1.** poor (dwelling,
garment etc.); meagre (wages etc.); (*b*)
(*unzulänglich*) inadequate; poor (piece of
work, excuse, substitute etc.).
◆**D~keit,** *f -/no pl* (*a*) poverty; mea-
greness; (*b*) inadequacy; poor quality.

dürr [dʏr], *adj.* **1.** dry (branches etc.);
arid (desert); barren (soil, *Fig:* years). **2.**
(*hager*) gaunt (person); scraggy (limb,
neck). ◆**D~e,** *f -/-n* **1.** (*Regenmangel*)
drought. **2.** *no pl* aridity; dryness.

Durst [dʊrst], *m* -(e)s/*no pl* thirst
(**nach +** *dat*/**auf +** *acc,* for); **D. haben,** to
be thirsty. ◆'**d~ig,** *adj.* thirsty
(**auf +** *acc,* for).

Dusche ['du:ʃə], *f -/-n* shower. ◆**d~n,**
v.i. (*haben*) & *refl.* **(sich) (kalt/warm) d.,**
to have a (cold/warm) shower.

Düse ['dy:zə], *f -/-n* nozzle; jet (of a carburettor). ◆'**D~n-**, *comb.fm. esp. Av:*
jet (bomber etc.).

Dussel ['dʊsəl], *m* -s/- *F:* sucker.

düster ['dy:stər], *adj.* gloomy (room,
light, *Fig:* mood etc.); sombre (colours,
landscape etc.). ◆'**D~keit,** *f -/no pl*
darkness; (*also Fig:*) gloom.

Dutzend [dʊtsənt], *n* -s/-e dozen.

◆'d~ **mal**, adv. a dozen times; F: dozens of times. ◆'D~**mensch**, m run-of-the-mill type. ◆'d~**weise**, adv. by the dozen.

duz|en ['du:tsən], v.tr. j-n d., to call s.o. 'du', be on familiar terms with s.o. ◆'D~**freund(in)**, m (f) close friend (whom one calls 'du').

Dynam|ik [dy'na:mik], f -/no pl 1. dynamics. 2. Fig: vitality. ◆d~**isch**, adj. dynamic.

Dynamit [dyna'mi:t], n -s/no pl dynamite.

Dynamo ['dy:namo], m -s/-s dynamo, generator.

Dynastie [dynas'ti:], f -/-n dynasty.

D-Zug ['de:tsu:k], m express train.

E

E, e [e:], n -/- (the letter) E, e.

Ebbe ['ɛbə], f -/-n low tide.

eben ['e:bən]. **I.** adj. flat (surface, country etc.); level (ground); (glatt) smooth. **II.** adv. 1. (verstärkend) just; (a) (genau) precisely, exactly; (b) simply; **dann muß er e. hier bleiben**, then he'll just have to stay here. 2. (gerade) e. noch, only just; **ich komme, wenn ich e. kann**, I'll come if I possibly can; **ich wollte e. gehen**, I was just about to leave. ◆'E~**bild**, n Lit: image. ◆e~**bürtig**, adj. of equal birth/rank; worthy (opponent). ◆'e~**'da**, adv. in that very place; (bei Zitaten) ibidem (usu. abbr. ibid.). ◆'E~**e**, f -/-n 1. Geog: plain. 2. Mth: (Fläche) plane. 3. Fig: (Stufe) level. ◆'e~**erdig**, adj. on the ground/N.Am: first floor. ◆'e~**falls**, adv. also. ◆'E~**heit**, f -/no pl evenness; smoothness. ◆'E~**maß**, n -es/no pl harmony; regularity (of features). ◆'e~**so**, adv. just as (wie, as). ◆'e~**sogut**, adv. er hätte e. hier bleiben können, he might just as well have stayed here. ◆'e~**soviel**, adv. just as much/(pl) many. ◆'e~**sowenig**, adv. just as little/as few.

Eber ['e:bər], m -s/- boar.

ebnen ['e:bnən], v.tr. to level, smooth (ground, a surface etc.).

Echo ['ɛço], n -s/-s echo.

echt [ɛçt], adj. (a) genuine; real (pearls, silk, leather, Fig: problem etc.); true (feelings, friendship etc.); (b) adv. F: (verstärkend) really; **das ist e. Peter!** that's typical of Peter! ◆'E~**heit**, f -/no pl sincerity (of feelings etc.); authenticity (of a painting etc.).

Eck [ɛk]. **I.** n -s/-e(n) = **Ecke**; übers E., diagonally. **II.** 'E~, comb.fm. corner (house, cupboard, stone, table, room, Sp: throw, hit etc.). ◆'E~**ball**, m corner (kick). ◆'E~**e**, f -/-n (a) corner; es fehlt an allen E~n und Enden, there is a shortage of everything; (b) Sp: corner (kick, throw). ◆e~**ig** ['ɛkiç], adj. angular; square (brackets etc.); Fig: awkward (movements). ◆'E~**zahn**, m canine tooth.

edel ['e:dəl], adj. noble; fine (food, wine); precious (metal, stones). ◆'e~**mütig**, adj. noble-minded. ◆'e~**stahl**, m high-grade steel. ◆'E~**stein**, m pre-

cious stone.

Efeu ['e:fɔy], m -s/no pl ivy.

Effekt [ɛ'fɛkt]. **1.** m -(e)s/-e effect. 2. E~en pl Fin: securities; stock. ◆E~**hascherei**, f -/no pl straining after effect; Th: etc: showmanship. ◆e~**iv** [-'ti:f], adj. 1. (wirksam) effective (method, steps etc.). 2. actual (price, weight, value etc.). ◆e~**voll**, adj. striking.

egal [e'ga:l], adj. 1. uniform. 2. F: **das ist mir ganz e.**, it's all the same to me; **er muß es machen, e. wie**, he must do it, it doesn't matter how.

Ego|ismus [ego'ismus], m -/no pl selfishness. ◆e~**ist**, m -en/-en egoist. ◆e~**istisch**, adj. selfish. ◆e~**zentrisch**, adj. self-centred.

eh [e:], adv. (a) F: (sowieso) anyway; (b) **wie eh und je**, as always; **seit eh und je**, since time immemorial.

ehe[1] ['e:ə], conj. before. ◆e~**dem**, adv. Lit: formerly. ◆e~**malig**, adj. former (king, officer, champion etc.). ◆e~**mals**, adv. Lit: formerly. ◆'e~**r**, adv. 1. (früher) sooner. 2. (wahrscheinlicher) more likely. 3. rather; (a) (lieber) **er würde sich e. umbringen**, he would sooner kill himself; (b) (mehr) **ich würde das e. als Nachteil ansehen**, I would regard that rather as a disadvantage; (c) F: (ziemlich) somewhat; e. häßlich, pretty ugly.

Ehe[2] ['e:ə], f -/-n marriage; Ecc: matrimony; **die E. schließen**, to get married (**mit** + dat, to); **in der E.**, ◆'E~, comb.fm. (a) marriage (partner etc.); (b) married (life etc.). ◆'E~**brecher(in)**, m (f) adulterer; f adulteress. ◆'e~**brecherisch**, adj. adulterous. ◆'E~**bruch**, m adultery. ◆'E~**frau**, f wife. ◆'E~**gatte**, m spouse. ◆'e~**lich**, adj. 1. legitimate (child, descent etc.); e. geboren, born in wedlock. 2. marital (harmony, duties etc.); conjugal (rights). ◆'E~**mann**, m husband. ◆'E~**paar**, n married couple. ◆'E~**ring**, m wedding ring. ◆'E~**scheidung**, f divorce. ◆'E~**schließung**, f marriage.

Ehr|e ['e:rə], f -/-n honour; zu seiner E. muß ich sagen, daß..., to give him his due, I must say that...; j-m E. machen/ Lit: zur E. gereichen, to be a credit to s.o.; etwas in E~n halten, to treasure sth.; **was verschafft mir die E.?** to what do I owe the honour of your visit? ◆'**e**~**en,** v.tr. to honour (s.o., sth.). ◆'**E**~**en,** comb.fm. (a) honorary (member, title etc.); (b) (guest, man etc.) of honour. ◆'**e**~**enamtlich,** adj. honorary (chairman, post etc.). ◆'**E**~**enbürger,** m freeman. ◆'**E**~**enhaft,** adj. honourable. ◆'**e**~**enrührig,** adj. defamatory. ◆'**E**~**enrunde,** f lap of honour. ◆'**E**~**ensache,** f point of honour; **das ist doch E.!** that goes without saying! ◆'**E**~**entag,** m red-letter day. ◆'**e**~**envoll,** adj. honourable. ◆'**E**~**enwort,** n word of honour; F: **E.!** honest(ly)! ◆'**e**~**erbietig,** adj. deferential. ◆'**E**~**furcht,** f (Verehrung) reverence; (Scheu) awe. ◆'**e**~**fürchtig,** adj. reverent. ◆'**E**~**gefühl,** n sense of honour. ◆'**E**~**geiz,** m ambition. ◆'**e**~**geizig,** adj. ambitious. ◆'**e**~**lich,** adj. (a) honest (person, feelings, opinion etc.); fair (dealings etc.); genuine (concern); sincere (wish etc.); **e. gesagt,** quite honestly, to be honest. ◆'**E**~**lichkeit,** f -/no pl honesty; sincerity (of feelings etc.). ◆'**e**~**los,** adj. dishonourable. ◆'**E**~**ung,** f -/-en 1. honour. 2. no pl honouring. ◆'**e**~**würdig,** adj. venerable (old man etc.).

ei[1] [ai], int. oh! **ei, ei, was seh ich?** aha, what's this?

Ei[2] n -(e)s/-er 1. egg. 2. Biol: ovum. ◆'**Eier-,** comb.fm. egg (spoon etc.). ◆'**Eierbecher,** m egg cup. ◆'**Eierkuchen,** m pancake. ◆'**Eierlikör,** m & m egg flip. ◆'**Eierschale,** f eggshell. ◆'**Eierstock,** m ovary.

Eich|**e** [ˈaiçə], f -/-n oak (tree). ◆'**E**~**el,** f -/-n Bot: acorn. ◆'**E**~**en-,** comb.fm. oak (leaf, table etc.). ◆'**E**~**hörnchen,** n -s/- squirrel.

eich|**en** [ˈaiçən], v.tr. to calibrate (measuring instruments). ◆'**E**~**maß,** n standard measure. ◆'**E**~**ung,** f -/-en standardization; calibration.

Eid [ait], m -(e)s/-e oath. ◆'**e**~**esstattlich,** adj. **eidesstattliche Erklärung,** statutory declaration.

Eidechse [ˈaidɛksə], f -/-n lizard.

Eidotter, n & m (egg) yolk.

Eier, comb.fm. see Ei.

eiern [ˈaiərn], v.i. (haben) F: (Rad) to wobble.

Eifer [ˈaifər], m -s/no pl zeal; (Begeisterung) eagerness; F: **im E. des Gefechts,** in the heat of the moment. ◆'**E**~**erer,** m -s/- zealot. ◆'**E**~**ersucht,** f jealousy. ◆'**e**~**ersüchtig,** adj. jealous (auf j-n, etwas of s.o., sth.). ◆'**e**~**rig,** adj. keen; eager (pupil etc.).

Eigelb, n egg yolk(s).

eigen [ˈaigən], I. adj. 1. own; **etwas sein e. nennen,** to call sth. one's own; **sich dat eine Meinung/Theorie zu e. machen,** to adopt an opinion/a theory; **eine Wohnung mit e**~**em Eingang,** a flat

with its own entrance; **mit dem ihr e**~**en Charme,** with her characteristic charm. 2. (seltsam) odd (ideas etc.); difficult (person). II. '**E**~**-,** comb.fm. (a) own (property, capital, make etc.); intrinsic (value etc.); (b) self-(financing etc.). ◆'**E**~**art,** f peculiarity; persönliche E., (personal) idiosyncrasy. ◆'**e**~**artig,** adj. (a) von e~artiger Schönheit, of singular beauty; (b) (seltsam) odd, strange. ◆'**E**~**bedarf,** m own personal requirements. ◆'**E**~**gewicht,** n Ph: specific gravity; Com: net weight. ◆'**e**~**händig,** adj. own (signature); personal (letter etc.). ◆'**E**~**heim,** n own home; owner-occupied house. ◆'**E**~**heit,** f -/-en peculiarity (esp. of a person). ◆'**E**~**liebe,** f -/no pl vanity. ◆'**E**~**lob,** n self-praise. ◆'**e**~**mächtig,** adj. high-handed (person, action etc.); arbitrary (decision); (unbefugt) unauthorized (action). ◆'**E**~**name,** m proper name. ◆'**e**~**nützig,** adj. self-interested. ◆'**e**~**s,** adv. expressly. ◆'**E**~**schaft,** f -/-en 1. quality, (Merkmal) characteristic (of a person, material); property (of a substance). 2. (Funktion) **in seiner E. als Vormund,** in his capacity as guardian. ◆'**E**~**schaftswort,** n adjective. ◆'**E**~**sinn,** m obstinacy. ◆'**e**~**sinnig,** adj. obstinate. ◆'**e**~**tlich,** adj. real; true (value, meaning etc.); **ich sollte ich jetzt arbeiten,** strictly speaking I should be working now; **wie gern es ihm e.?** how is he, I wonder? ◆'**E**~**tum,** n -s/no pl property. ◆'**E**~**tümer,** m -s/- owner; proprietor (of a hotel, business etc.). ◆'**e**~**tümlich,** adj. peculiar; **ein e~tümlicher Geruch,** a strange smell. ◆'**E**~**tumswohnung,** f freehold flat; N.Am: condominium. ◆'**e**~**willig,** adj. 1. (e~sinnig) wilful (child etc.). 2. (Pers.) of independent mind; highly individual (interpretation etc.).

eign|**en** [ˈaignən], v.refl. to be suitable. ◆'**E**~**ung,** f -/-en suitability.

Eil- [ˈail-], comb.fm. express (messenger, letter etc.). ◆'**E**~**bote,** m -n/-n. ◆'**E**~**brief,** m express letter. ◆'**E**~**e,** f -/no pl hurry, haste; **das hat keine E.,** there's no hurry about that; **◆'e**~**en,** v.i. (a) (sein) to hurry; **j-m zu Hilfe e.,** to rush to s.o.'s aid; (b) (Sache) to be urgent. ◆'**e**~**ig,** adj. hurried; **es e. haben,** to be in a hurry; (b) (dringend) urgent (business, letter etc.). ◆'**e**~**igst,** adv. posthaste. ◆'**E**~**zug,** m semi-fast train.

Eileiter, m -s/- Fallopian tube.

Eimer [ˈaimər], m -s/- bucket; F: **im E.,** (Sachen) up the spout; (Pers.) done for.

ein[1] [ain]. I. num.adj. one; **e. für allemal,** once and for all; **er ist ihr e. und alles,** he is everything to her; **e**~**es Tages/Morgens,** one day/morning. II. num.pron. (a) (Pers.) one; someone; **e**~**er nach dem anderen,** one after another;

wenn man das sieht, wird e~em schlecht, it makes you feel ill when you see that; (b) (Sache) one; **ich habe kein Glas, hast du e~(e)s?** I haven't got a glass, have you got one? **III.** indef.art. a, an; **e. jeder,** each one; **IV.** ein-, adj.comb.fm. one-(armed, eyed, legged, dimensional etc.). ◆**'e~gleisig,** adj. single-track.

ein², adv. **e. und aus,** in and out; **er weiß weder e. noch aus,** he is at his wit's end.

einander [ain'andər], pron.inv. one another; **e. im Wege,** in each other's way.

einarbeiten, v.tr.sep. (a) to break (s.o.) in (to a new job); (b) to show (s.o.) the ropes; (b) v.refl. **sich e.,** to settle in (to the work).

einatmen, v.tr.&i.sep. (haben) to breathe in, inhale (sth.).

Einbahn-, comb.fm. one-way (traffic etc.). ◆**'E~straße,** f one-way street.

Einband, m binding.

Einbau. **I.** m 1. no pl building in; fitting (of a cupboard, engine etc.); installation (of central heating, plumbing etc.); 2. built-in unit. **II.** **'E~-,** comb.fm. built-in (shelves etc.). ◆**'e~en,** v.tr.sep. to install (central heating etc.); Fig: incorporate (an episode etc.); to fit (a part, an engine). ◆**'E~küche,** f fitted kitchen. ◆**'E~möbel,** npl built-in furniture.

einbegriffen, adj. included; **alles e.,** altogether.

einberuf|en, v.tr.sep.irr. 74 (a) to summon (a meeting etc.); (b) Mil: **j-n (zum Heer) e.,** to call s.o. up/N.Am: draft s.o. (into the army). ◆**'E~ung,** f -/-en (a) no pl summoning; (b) Mil: conscription; N.Am: draft.

einbetten, v.tr.sep. to embed (sth.).

Einbettzimmer, n single room.

einbezieh|en, v.tr.sep.irr. 113 to include (s.o., sth.), (berücksichtigen) take (sth.) into account. ◆**'E~ung,** f /no pl inclusion; **unter E. von + dat,** including.

einbiegen, v.i.sep.irr.7 (sein) to turn.

einbild|en, v.refl.sep. (a) **sich dat etwas e.,** to imagine sth.; (b) **was bildest du dir eigentlich ein?** who do you think you are? **darauf brauchst du dir nichts einzubilden!** that's nothing to be proud of! ◆**'E~ung,** f /-en 1. (Phantasie) imagination; **es ist reine E.,** it is purely imaginary. 2. (Hochmut) conceit. ◆**'E~ungskraft,** f /no pl imagination.

einblenden, v.tr.sep. to fade in (a scene, music etc.).

Einblick, m insight.

einbrech|en, v.tr.sep.irr.14 **1.** v.tr. to break in/down (a door etc.), to smash in (a window). 2. v.i. (a) (sein) (Dach usw.) to cave in; (b) (sein/haben) (Einbrecher usw.) to break in; (c) (sein) (Nacht) to fall; (Dämmerung) to set in. ◆**'E~er,** m -s/- burglar; (am Tag) housebreaker.

einbringen, v.tr.sep.irr.16 to bring in (money, the harvest etc.); to earn (money, profit, Fig: a reputation etc.); **es bringt nichts ein,** it doesn't yield any profit.

Einbruch, m 1. (Sturz) collapse (of structure, support etc.); Com: Fig: slump. 2. burglary; **E. in eine Bank,** break-in at a bank. 3. **bei E. der Kälte,** when the cold weather sets in; **bei E. der Dunkelheit,** at nightfall.

einbürgern, v.tr.sep. (a) to naturalize (a foreigner); (b) **sich e.,** (Pers.) to settle down; (Brauch) to become accepted; **es hat sich eingebürgert, daß ...,** it has become the custom that ...

Einbuße, f -/-n loss, Jur: forfeiture (**an Geld usw.,** of money etc.).

einbüßen, v.tr.sep. to lose (money, influence, one's life etc.); to forfeit (one's rights etc.).

eindecken, v.tr.sep. (a) to cover (sth.) up/over; (b) **sich mit etwas e.,** to lay in a supply of sth., stock up with sth.

eindeutig, adj. clear (instructions, lead etc.); unambiguous (reply, meaning etc.). ◆**'E~keit,** f /-en clearness; unambiguity.

eindring|en, v.i.sep.irr.19 (sein) (a) **e. in + acc,** (also Fig:) to penetrate (sth.); to force one's way into (a room etc.); (Truppen usw.) to invade (a country, town etc.); to infiltrate (enemy lines etc.); Fig: to get to the bottom of (a mystery etc.); (b) **auf j-n e.,** to close in on s.o.; Fig: to urge s.o. **II. E.,** n -s/no pl intrusion; penetration; Mil: invasion. ◆**'e~lich,** adj. urgent (warning etc.); pressing (request etc.); forceful (speech, language etc.). ◆**'E~ling,** m -(e)s/-e intruder.

Eindruck, m impression; **er machte einen unglücklichen E.,** he seemed unhappy. ◆**'e~svoll,** adj. impressive.

eindrücken, v.tr.sep. to press/push in (a knob etc.); (zerdrücken) to crush (a tin, s.o.'s chest etc.).

eineinhalb, num.adj. one and a half.

einengen, v.tr.sep. (a) **j-n e.,** to restrict s.o.'s movements; **eingeengt,** cramped; restricted (space etc.); (b) to restrict (s.o.'s freedom, rights etc.).

einer ['ainər], see **ein.** ◆**'e~lei.** **I.** inv.adj. & adv. (egal) immaterial; **das ist mir ganz e.,** that's all the same to me. **II. E.,** n -s/no pl sameness. ◆**'e~seits,** adv. **e. ... andererseits ...,** on the one hand ... on the other hand ...

einfach ['ainfax], adj. 1. single (thread, width etc.); Med: simple (fracture); **e. gefaltet,** folded once. 2. (a) (leicht) simple; (b) adv. simply, just. 3. (schlicht) ordinary (people); plain (food); simple (life). ◆**'E~heit,** f /no pl simplicity.

einfädeln, v.tr.sep. (a) to thread (cotton, film, tape etc.); (b) F: to arrange (sth.).

einfahr|en, v.sep.irr.26 1. v.i. (sein) (ankommen) to arrive. 2. v.tr. to run/N.Am: break in (a car, etc.). ◆**'E~t,** f 1. entry; *(Ankunft)* arrival. 2. *(a)* entrance; E. freihalten, keep (entrance) clear; keine E.! no entry; *(b)* (motorway/N.Am: freeway) access road.

'Einfall, m 1. idea; einem plötzlichen E. folgend, on a sudden impulse. 2. Ph: incidence (of light/rays). 3. Mil: invasion; *(kurz)* raid. ◆'e~en, v.i.sep.irr.27 *(sein)* *(a)* *(einstürzen)* (Gebäude) to collapse; *(b)* (Licht) to fall/shine in; *(c)* *(mitmachen)* to join in; *(d)* Mil: in ein Land usw. e., to invade a country etc.; *(e)* dabei fällt mir ein ..., that reminds me ...; ihm fiel keine bessere Ausrede ein, he couldn't think of a better excuse. ◆'e~slos, adj. unimaginative. ◆'e~sreich, adj. imaginative; *(klug)* ingenious. ◆'E~sreichtum, m imaginativeness; ingenuity.

'einfältig ['ainfɛltiç], adj. simple; *(naiv)* naive.

'Einfamilienhaus, n (undivided) family house; N.Am: one-family house.

'einfangen, v.tr.sep.28 to capture.

'einfarbig, adj. in one colour; plain (material).

'einfass|en, v.tr.sep. *(a)* to surround a lawn, plot of land etc.); to edge (a garment, tablecloth etc.); *(b)* to set (a jewel). ◆'E~ung, f edge; setting.

'einfinden, v.refl.sep.irr.9 sich e., to turn up; *(Menge)* to gather.

'einfließen, v.i.sep.irr.31 *(sein)* in etwas acc e., to flow into sth.

'einflößen, v.tr.sep. *(a)* j-m Arznei/ Wasser e., to give s.o. sips of medicine/ water; *(b)* Fig: to inspire (respect, admiration etc.).

'Einfluß, m influence. ◆'E~bereich, m sphere of influence. ◆'e~reich, adj. influential.

'einförmig, adj. uniform. ◆'E~keit, f -/no pl uniformity.

'einfrieren, v.sep.irr.32 1. v.i. *(sein)* to freeze (up) *(Schiff)* to become icebound. 2. v.tr. to freeze.

'einfüg|en, v.tr.sep. *(a)* e. in + acc, to fit (an object) into (sth.), insert (a word etc.) into (a text etc.); to add (a remark); *(b)* (Pers.) sich e., to fit in. ◆'E~ung, f insertion.

'Einfühlungsvermögen, n (power of) empathy.

'Einfuhr. I. f -/-en no pl importation (of goods etc.); *(b)* imports of (a country). II. 'E~, comb.fm. import (regulations, restrictions, licence etc.).

'einführ|en, v.tr.sep. *(a)* to introduce (s.o.); to bring in (sth. new, a law, a reform etc.); *(b)* *(einfügen)* e. Med: to insert (sth.); *(c)* Com: to import (goods). ◆'E~ung, f introduction; insertion. ◆'E~ungs-, comb.fm. introductory (course, price etc.).

'Eingabe, f 1. *(Gesuch)* petition; application (an acc, to s.o.). 2. Data-pr: input.

'Eingang, m 1. entrance; kein E., no en-

try. 2. *(Ankunft)* arrival (of mail etc.); nach E. Ihres Briefes, on receipt of your letter. 3. *(Anfang)* beginning. ◆'e~s. I. adv. at the beginning. II. prep. + gen at the beginning of. ◆'E~s-, comb.fm. *(a)* entrance (hall etc.); *(b)* opening (words, speech etc.); *(c)* Com: (date etc.) of receipt; *(d)* El: input (voltage etc.).

'eingeb|en, v.tr.sep.irr.35 *(a)* j-m eine Medizin usw. e., to administer a medicine etc. to s.o.; *(b)* Data-pr: to feed (data). ◆'E~ung, f -/-en inspiration.

'eingebildet, adj. *(a)* (Pers.) conceited; *(b)* imaginary (illness etc.).

'Eingeborene(r), m & f decl. as adj. native.

'eingedenk, adv. + gen bearing in mind.

'eingefleischt, adj. confirmed (bachelor, pessimist etc.); inveterate (opponent etc.).

'eingehen, v.sep.irr.36 1. v.i. *(sein)* *(a)* esp. Com: (Briefe, Geld) to come in, be received; *(b)* in die Geschichte e., to go down in history; *(c)* e. auf + acc, to agree to (a demand, request etc.); *(d)* auf eine Frage usw. (näher) e., to go into a question (more closely); auf j-n e., to take an interest in s.o. *(e)* (Tier) to die; (Firma, Zeitung usw.) to fold. 2. v.tr. *(haben)* to enter into (an alliance, obligation); to take on (a bet); to take (a risk). ◆'e~d, adj. *(gründlich)* thorough.

'eingelegt, adj. 1. inlaid (work etc.). 2. Cu: marinaded.

'Eingemachtes, n decl. as adj. preserved/ bottled fruit, vegetables etc.

'eingemeinden, v.tr.sep. to incorporate.

'eingenommen, adj. von etwas e., taken with sth.; gegen j-n, etwas acc e., prejudiced against s.o., sth.

'eingeschrieben, adj. registered.

'eingesessen, adj. (old-)established; *(ansässig)* resident.

'Eingeständnis, n confession; admission.

'eingestehen, v.tr.sep.irr.100 to admit (sth.).

'Eingeweide ['aingəvaidə], npl viscera, F: guts; Z: entrails; Cu: offal.

'eingewöhnen, v.tr.sep. sich e., to settle down.

'eingießen, v.tr.sep.irr.31 to pour (a drink).

'eingliedern, v.tr.sep. to incorporate (sth., a place), insert (details, facts etc.), integrate (s.o.).

'eingraben, v.tr.sep.irr.42 *(a)* to bury (valuables etc.); sich e., to dig in; (Tier) to burrow.

'eingreifen, v.i.sep.irr.43 *(haben)* *(a)* to intervene; *(sich einmischen)* to interfere; *(b)* (Zahnräder usw.) (in etwas acc) e., to mesh (with sth.)/engage (sth.).

'eingrenzen, v.tr.sep. to narrow down (a subject etc.).

'Eingriff, m 1. intervention. 2. Med: operation.

'einhaken, v.tr.sep. sich bei j-m e., to

link arms with s.o.

'Einhalt, *m etwas dat* E. **gebieten,** to call a halt to sth. ◆**e~en,** *v.tr.sep.irr.45* 1. *v.tr.* (*a*) to keep (a promise, an appointment, one's distance); to keep to (a plan, diet etc.); to follow (a course); to observe (a contract, rule, holiday etc.). 2. *v.i.* (*haben*) to stop; to pause.

'einhändig, *adj.* one-handed; *adv.* with one hand. ◆**'e~en,** *v.tr.sep.* to hand (sth.) over, (*einreichen*) hand (sth.) in.

'einhängen, *v.tr.sep.* (*a*) *den (Hörer)* e., to hang up; (*b*) *sich bei j-m* e., to link arms with s.o.

'einheimisch, *adj.* (*eines Landes*) native (population, plants etc.); domestic (product, market); (*einer Stadt usw.*) local (residents, industry etc.); **die E~en,** the locals.

'Einheit ['ainhait], *f -/-en* 1. (*a*) unity (of a nation, party, *Th:* the drama etc.); (*b*) (*Ganzes*) **eine E. bilden,** to form a (homogeneous) whole. 2. *Meas: Mil: etc:* unit. ◆**'e~lich,** *adj.* uniform; (*a*) homogeneous (whole, work of art etc.); coherent (argument etc.); (*b*) *Com:* standard (price, tariff etc.). ◆**'E~s-,** *comb.fm.* standard (value etc.); uniform (clothing etc.).

einhellig ['ainheliç], *adj.* unanimous.

'einholen, *v.tr.sep.* (*a*) e. **gehen,** to go shopping; (*b*) **Auskunft** e., to make inquiries; **j-s Rat/Erlaubnis** e., to get s.o.'s advice/consent; (*c*) to take in (a sail), draw in (a fishing net); to strike (a flag); (*d*) *j-n/ein Auto* e., to catch up with s.o./a car; **verlorene Zeit** e., to make up for lost time.

'Einhorn, *n* unicorn.

'einhüllen, *v.tr.sep.* to wrap (s.o., sth.) up.

einig ['ainiç], *adj.* 1. (*geeint*) united (nation, people etc.). 2. (*in Übereinstimmung*) **mit j-m** e. **sein,** to agree with s.o. ◆**'e~en** [-gən], *v.tr.* (*a*) to unify (a country etc.); (*b*) **sich** (**mit j-m**) e., to come to an agreement with s.o. ◆**'E~keit,** *f -/no pl* unity; (*Übereinstimmung*) agreement. ◆**'E~ung,** *f -/-en* unification (of agreement.

einige(r,s) [ainigə(r,s)], *indef.pron. & adj.* 1. *sing.* (*etwas*) some; (*ein bißchen*) a little, a bit of. 2. *pl* (*a*) (*ein paar*) a few; (*mehrere*) several; (*b*) *pron.* some, a few; **e. wenige,** a few. 3. (*ziemlich viel*) **e~s kosten,** to cost quite a bit. ◆**'e~'mal,** *adv.* a few/several times. ◆**'e~r'maßen,** *adv.* to some extent; *F:* **wie geht es dir?—so e.,** how are you?—not too bad/so-so.

'einjagen, *v.tr.sep.* **j-m Angst/Schrecken** e., to give s.o. a real fright/scare.

'einjährig, *adj.* (*a*) one-year-old (child, animal etc.); (*b*) *Bot:* **e~e Pflanzen,** annuals.

'einkalkulieren, *v.tr.sep.* to take (sth.)

into account, allow for (a possibility, *Fin:* an expense).

'Einkauf, *m* (*a*) *no pl* buying; (*b*) purchase; **E~e machen,** to do some shopping. ◆**'e~en,** *v.tr.sep.* to purchase (sth.); **e. gehen,** to go shopping. ◆**'E~s-,** *comb.fm.* shopping (street, basket, bag etc.).

'einklammern, *v.tr.sep.* to bracket.

'Einklang, *m* harmony (of ideas etc.); **etwas (mit etwas** *dat*) **in** E. **bringen,** to reconcile sth. (with sth.).

'einkleiden, *v.tr.sep.* to clothe (s.o.).

'einklemmen, *v.tr.sep.* **etwas (in etwas** *acc*) e., to wedge, jam sth. in(to sth.).

'einknicken, *v.tr.&i.sep.* (*haben*) to bend (wire etc.) (at an angle); **seine Knie knickten ein,** his knees gave way.

'einkochen, *v.tr.sep.* to preserve, bottle (fruit, vegetables etc.).

'Einkommen, *n -s/-* income, earnings; revenue (from estates). ◆**'E~(s)steuer,** *f -/no pl* income tax.

'einkreisen, *v.tr.sep.* to surround.

'Einkünfte ['ainkynftə], *pl* earnings; (*Gewinn*) proceeds.

'einladen, *v.tr.sep.irr.56* 1.to load (goods) (**in einen Lastwagen usw.,** onto a lorry etc.). 2. to invite (s.o.); **komm, ich lade dich ein,** come on, I'll treat you. ◆**'e~end,** *adj.* inviting; tempting. ◆**'E~ung,** *f -/-en* invitation.

'Einlage, *f.* 1. *Fin:* investment; deposit. 2. *Cu:* **Suppe mit E.,** soup with added ingredients (noodles, dumplings etc.). 3. (*in Schuhen*) arch support. 4. (*Zahne.*) temporary filling. 5. *Th: etc:* interlude.

'Einlaß ['ainlas], *m -sses/=sse* 1. admittance. 2. *Tchn:* inlet, intake.

'einlassen, *v.tr.sep.irr.57* (*a*) to admit (s.o.), let (s.o., sth.) in; (*b*) **e. in** + *acc,* to let (sth.) into (concrete, a wall etc.); (*c*) **sich** e. **auf** + *acc,* to get involved in (sth.).

'Einlauf, *m* 1. *Sp:* finish. 2. *Med:* enema. ◆**'e~en,** *v.sep.irr.58* 1. *v.i.* (*sein*) (*a*) (*Läufer, Pferde usw.*) to come in; (*b*) (*ankommen*) to arrive; (*c*) (*Wasser usw.*) to run/flow in; **das Badewasser** e. **lassen,** to run the bathwater; (*d*) (*Stoff, Kleidung*) to shrink. 2. *v.tr.* (*a*) **j-m das Haus** e., to pester s.o. with requests/troublesome visits; (*b*) to break/wear in (shoes); (*c*) **sich** e., *Sp:* (*Läufer usw.*) to warm up.

'einleben, *v.refl.sep.* **sich** e., to get used to one's new surroundings.

'Einlegearbeit, *f -/-en* inlaid work. ◆**'e~en,** *v.tr.sep.* (*a*) **etwas in etwas** *acc* e., to insert sth. in sth.; (*b*) *Cu:* to pickle (cucumbers etc.), marinate (fish etc.); (*c*) **eine Pause** e., to have a break; (*d*) **Protest** e., to lodge a protest; *Jur:* **Berufung** e., to appeal; (*e*) **für j-n ein gutes Wort** (**bei j-m**) e., to put in a good word for s.o. (with s.o.). ◆**'E~sohle,** *f* inner sole; (*loose*) insole.

'einleit|en, *v.tr.sep.* to begin, start (sth.); to write an introduction to (a book etc.); to initiate (measures); **eine Geburt (künstlich) e.**, to induce a birth. **◆'e~end**, *adj.* introductory (words); preliminary (measures). **◆'E~ung**, *f* introduction; initiation; (*Vorspiel*) prelude.

'einleuchten, *v.i.sep.* (*haben*) **das leuchtet mir ein**, I can see that. **◆'e~d**, *adj.* convincing.

'einliefer|n, *v.tr.sep.* j-n ins Gefängnis/ Krankenhaus e., to take s.o. to prison/ (the) hospital.

'einlösen, *v.tr.sep.* to cash (a cheque); to redeem (securities, sth. from pawn etc.); *Lit:* to make good (one's promise).

'einmachen, *v.tr.sep.* to preserve.

'einmal, *adv.* 1. (*a*) once; noch e., once again; noch e. so lang, twice as long; (*b*) e. hier, e. da, now here, now there; (*c*) (*in Zukunft*) e. wird die Zeit kommen, wo ..., one/some day the time will come when ...; (*d*) (*zuvor*) (once) before; at one time; es war e. ..., once upon a time there was ...; (*e*) auf e., at the same time; (*plötzlich*) suddenly, all at once. 2. (*verstärkend*) nicht e., not even; das ist nun e. so, that's the way it is. **◆E~'eins**, *n* -*/no pl* 1. das (kleine/große) E., multiplication tables (up to 10/from 10 to 20). 2. rudiments, basics. **◆'e~ig**, *adj.* 1. (*a*) single (reading etc.); non-recurring (payment etc.); (*b*) (*einzig in seiner Art*) unique (opportunity etc.); unrepeatable (offer); das war e. schön, that was absolutely beautiful. **◆'E~igkeit**, *f* -*/no pl* uniqueness.

'Ein'mannbetrieb, *m* one-man operation (of buses etc.); *Com:* one-man business.

'Einmarsch, *m* marching in; entry. **◆'e~ieren**, *v.i.sep.* (*sein*) to march in.

'einmischen, *v.refl.sep.* sich e., to interfere (in etwas acc, in/with sth.). **◆'E~ung**, *f* interference.

'einmünd|en, *v.i.sep.* (*sein*) e. in + acc, (*Fluß*) to flow into (the sea); (*Straße*) to lead into, join (another road/river).

'einmütig ['ainmy:tiç], *adj.* unanimous.

'Einnahme ['ainna:mə], *f* -*/-n* 1. taking (of a medicine etc.). 2. *Mil:* capture. 3. *usu.pl* E~n, earnings; (*Ertrag*) takings. **◆'E~quelle**, *f* source of income.

'einnehmen, *v.tr.sep.irr.69* (*a*) to take (medicine etc.); (*b*) *Com: etc:* to take/ (*verdienen*) make (money); (*c*) *Mil:* to take (a town, fortress etc.); (*d*) to take (one's seat); to take up (a position, *Fig:* standpoint); (*e*) to occupy (space, a position etc.); (*f*) j-n für sich acc e., to win s.o. over; j-n gegen sich e., to prejudice s.o. against one. **◆'e~d**, *adj.* captivating, charming.

'einnicken, *v.i.sep.* (*sein*) *F:* to nod off.

'einnisten, *v.refl.sep.* *F:* sich bei j-m e., to instal oneself in s.o.'s home.

Einöde ['ain'ø:də], *f* desert, wilderness.

'einordnen, *v.tr.sep.* to arrange (objects)

in proper order; sich e., (i) (*Pers.*) to fit in; (ii) *Aut:* to get into (the right) lane.

'einpacken, *v.sep.* 1. *v.tr.* to pack (sth.); to wrap up (a present etc.). 2. *v.i.* (*haben*) to pack (up), (*also Fig:*) pack one's bags.

'einpendeln, *v.refl.sep.* sich e., to level off.

'einperchen, *v.tr.sep.* to pen (sheep); to pack (people) into a small space).

'einpflanzen, *v.tr.sep.* to implant (an idea, *Med:* an organ etc.) (j-m, in s o.).

'einplanen, *v.tr.sep.* to include (sth.) in one's plans; (*berücksichtigen*) to allow for (sth.).

'einpräg|en, *v.tr.sep.* (*a*) to imprint (a mark, design etc.); (*b*) *Fig:* j-m etwas e., to imprint (sth.) on s.o.'s mind; sich dat ein Gedicht usw. e., to memorize a poem etc. **◆'e~sam**, *adj.* memorable; catchy (tune).

'einrahmen, *v.tr.sep.* to frame (a picture etc.).

'einrasten, *v.i.sep.* (*sein*) to snap into position.

'einräum|en I. *v.tr.sep.* (*a*) das Geschirr e., to put away the crockery; (*b*) (*gewähren*) j-m ein Recht, *Fin:* einen Kredit usw. e., to grant s.o. a right, credit etc.; (*c*) (*zugeben*) to admit.

'einrechnen, *v.tr.sep.* to include (sth.).

'einreden, *v.tr.sep.* j-m, sich etwas e., to persuade s.o., oneself of sth.

'einreiben, *v.tr.sep.irr.12* sich dat das Gesicht mit Creme e., to rub one's face with cream; j-m den Rücken e., to rub oil etc. on s.o.'s back.

'einreichen, *v.tr.sep.* to submit (a petition, an application etc.).

'einreihen, *v.tr.sep.* sich e., to take one's place (in a queue etc.); *Fig:* to fall into line.

'Einreise, *f* entry (into a country). **◆'e~n**, *v.i.sep.* (*sein*) (in ein Land) e., to enter a country.

'einreißen, *v.sep.irr.4* 1. *v.tr.* (*a*) to tear (sth.); to split (one's fingernail etc.); (*b*) (*niederreißen*) to pull down (a house, wall etc.). 2. *v.i.* (*sein*) (*a*) to tear; (*b*) *Fig:* (*Gewohnheit usw.*) to gain a hold.

'einricht|en, *v.tr.sep.* (*a*) to furnish (a house, room etc.); to fit out (a kitchen, shop etc.); *F:* sich häuslich e., to make oneself at home; (*b*) (*anordnen*) to arrange (sth.); sich auf etwas acc e., to make arrangements for sth. **◆'E~ung**, *f* 1. (*a*) *no pl* furnishing; fitting out; (*b*) equipment; (*Möbel*) furniture. 2. (*Anordnung*) arrangement; set-up of a workshop etc. 3. (*a*) (*Anstalt*) institution; (*b*) (*Brauch*) practice. 4. *Tchn:* (*Gerät*) device; (*Anlage*) installation.

'einrosten, *v.i.sep.* (*sein*) to rust (up); *F:* (*Glieder*) to get stiff; (*Kenntnisse*) to get rusty.

'einrücken, *v.sep.* 1. *v.i.* (*sein*) (*a*) (*Truppen*) in ein Land e., to enter a country;

(b) (einberufen werden) to be called up (for military service). **2.** *v.tr.* (a) to indent (a line etc.); (b) to insert (an advertisement).

eins¹ [ains]. **I.** *num.adj.* one; **um e.,** at one o'clock; **es kommt auf e. heraus,** it comes to the same thing. **II. E.,** *f* -/-*en* (figure) one.

eins², *indef.pron. see* **ein.**

'einsalzen, *v.tr.sep.* to salt, cure.

einsam ['ainzaːm], *adj.* (a) lonely, solitary (person, existence); isolated, lonely (place); (b) *F:* **e~e Spitze,** the tops. ◆**'E~keit,** *f -/no pl* loneliness, solitude.

'einsammeln, *v.tr.sep.* to gather (fruit etc.); to collect (money, tickets etc.).

'Einsatz *m* **1.** *(Teil)* insert, *Tchn:* element (of a filter etc.). **2.** *(Spiele.)* stake; *Fig:* **unter E. des Lebens,** at the risk of one's life. **3.** *(a) (Gebrauch)* use of labour, machines, police etc.); (b) *Mil:* mission. **4.** *Mus:* entry. ◆**'e~bereit,** *adj. Mil: (Truppen)* ready for action; **sich e. halten,** to be on standby. ◆**'E~kommando,** *n* task force.

'einschalten, *v.tr.sep.* (a) to switch on (a light, radio etc.); to connect (up) (a circuit, battery); *Aut:* to engage (a gear); **sich e.,** to switch itself on/*(Heizung usw.)* come on; (b) *(einfügen)* to insert (a word, sentence etc.); to interpolate (a phrase, remark etc.); (c) to bring in (the police, experts etc.); **sich e.,** to intervene; **sich in ein Gespräch e.,** to join in a conversation.

'einschärfen, *v.tr.sep.* **j-m etwas e.,** to impress sth. on s.o.

'einschätzen, *v.tr.sep.* to assess (s.o., sth.); *(bewerten)* to estimate the value of (sth.); **j-n, etwas hoch e.,** to value s.o., sth. highly. ◆**E~ung,** *f* assessment; *(Meinung)* opinion; appraisal (of a situation etc.).

'einschenken, *v.tr.sep.* to pour out (wine, water etc.) (j-m, for s.o.); to fill (a glass, cup etc.).

'einschicken, *v.tr.sep.* to send in (sth.).

'einschieben, *v.tr.sep.irr.82* (a) to push/*F:* shove sth. into sth.; (b) to insert (a quotation etc.); to add (an extra item etc.).

'einschiffen, *v.tr. & refl.sep.* **(sich) e.,** to embark.

'einschlafen, *v.i.sep.irr.84* *(sein)* to go to sleep.

'einschläfern, *v.tr.sep.* to send (s.o.) to sleep; *(töten)* to put (an animal) to sleep. ◆**'e~d,** *adj.* soporific.

'Einschlag *m* **1.** impact (of bomb etc.). **2.** *Fig:* **orientalischer E.,** oriental touch. ◆**'e~en,** *v.sep.irr.85* **1.** *v.tr.* (a) to hammer in (a nail, post etc.); (b) to break (a window), knock down (a door); **j-m den Schädel e.,** to smash s.o.'s head in; (c) *(einpacken)* to wrap up (a present etc.) (in paper, cloth etc.); (d) **eine andere Richtung e.,** to change direction; **eine Lauf-**

bahn e., to enter upon a career; (e) *(beim Nähen)* to turn (sth.) over/down. **2.** *v.i.* *(haben)* (a) **der Blitz/die Bombe hat hier eingeschlagen,** the lightning/bomb struck here; *F:* **der Film schlug (gut) ein,** the film was a hit; (b) to shake hands **(auf etwas** *acc,* on sth.); (c) **auf j-n/ein Tier e.,** to shower s.o./an animal with blows.

einschlägig ['ainʃleːgiç], *adj.* relevant (literature, authority etc.).

'einschleichen, *v.refl.sep.irr.86* **sich** *(in* **etwas** *acc)* **e.,** to creep in(to sth.); **sich in j-s Vertrauen e.,** to insinuate oneself into s.o.'s confidence.

'einschließ|en, *v.tr.sep.irr.31* (a) to lock (s.o., sth.) up; (b) *(umgeben)* to encircle (sth., troops); (c) *(aufnehmen)* to include (s.o., sth.); **X eingeschlossen,** including **X.** ◆**'e~lich. 1.** *adv.* inclusive. **2.** *prep. + gen* including.

'einschmeicheln, *v.refl.sep.* **sich bei j-m e.,** to ingratiate oneself with s.o. ◆**'e~d,** *adj.* ingratiating (manners, ways); silky (voice).

'einschnappen, *v.i.sep. (sein)* (a) to click shut/home; (b) *F: (Pers.)* to take offence.

'einschneiden, *v.tr. & i.sep.irr.59 (haben)* **(in) etwas** *acc* **e.,** to cut into sth. ◆**'e~d,** *adj.* radical (change); decisive (event).

'Einschnitt *m* **1.** (a) cut, *esp. Med:* incision; *(Kerbe)* notch; (b) gap (in hills etc.). **2.** *Fig:* turning point.

'einschränk|en, ['ainʃrɛŋkən], *v.tr.sep.* (a) to restrict (sth.); **sich e.,** to economize; (b) to qualify (a statement, condition etc.). ◆**'E~ung,** *f -/-en* (a) restriction; (b) qualification; **ohne E.,** without reservation.

'Einschreib|ebrief, *m* registered letter. ◆**'e~en.** **I.** *v.tr.sep.irr.12* (a) to write (sth.) down; to enter (sth.) (**in eine Liste,** on a list); (b) to register (s.o.); **sich e.,** to enrol; (c) to register (a letter, parcel). **II. E.,** *n* **per E.,** by registered post/*N.Am:* mail. ◆**'E~ung,** *f* enrolment, registration.

'einschreiten, *v.i.sep.irr.41 (sein)* to intervene.

'Einschub, *m* insertion.

'einschüchtern, *v.tr.sep.* to intimidate.

'einschulen, *v.tr.sep.* to send (a child) to school (for the first time).

'einschweißen, *v.tr.sep.* to shrink-wrap (a book, record).

'einsehen. I. *v.tr.sep.irr.92* (a) to inspect, examine (documents, books etc.); (b) to see, realize (one's mistake etc., that ...). **II. E.,** *n* **ein E. haben,** (i) *(Verständnis haben)* to show understanding; (ii) *(vernünftig sein)* to listen to reason.

'einseifen, *v.tr.sep.* to soap.

einseitig ['ainzaitiç], *adj.* (a) unilateral (treaty, decision); *Fig:* one-sided (person, training etc.). ◆**'E~keit,** *f -/no pl* one-sidedness.

'einsend|en, *v.tr.sep.irr.94* to send (sth.) in, submit (an article etc.). ◆**'E~er**, *m* sender. ◆**'E~eschluß**, *m* closing date (for entries). ◆**'E~ung**, *f* entry (for a competition); (*Beitrag*) contribution.

'einsetzen, *v.sep.* 1. *v.tr.* (*a*) to put (sth.) in; to insert (*Cl:* a patch etc.), fill in (the date etc.); (*b*) (*ernennen*) to appoint (s.o., a committee etc.); (*r*) to call in (troops, police etc.); (*anwenden*) to use (a weapon, tactics, all one's strength etc.); *Sp:* bring on (a player); (*d*) to bet (an amount); *Fig:* to risk (one's life); (*e*) **sich für eine Sache e.,** to champion a cause; **sich für j-n e.,** to stand up for s.o. 2. *v.i.* (*haben*) to start; (*Regen usw.*) to set in; *Mus:* to come in.

'Einsicht, *f* 1. examination. 2. (*a*) (*Verständnis*) insight; (*Erkenntnis*) realization; (*b*) (*Vernunft*) **E. zeigen,** to show sense. ◆**e~ig**, *adj.* (*vernünftig*) sensible; (*verständnisvoll*) understanding. ◆**'E~nahme**, *f /-n* examination; *Jur:* search.

Einsiedler ['ainzi:tlər], *m* hermit; recluse.

einsilbig ['ainzilbiç], *adj.* monosyllabic (word, person, reply); (*Mensch*) taciturn.

'einsinken, *v.i.sep.irr.96* (*sein*) **in etwas** *acc* **e.,** to sink in(to sth.); (*Boden usw.*) to subside.

Einsitzer, *m* **-s/-** single-seater.

'einspannen, *v.tr.sep.* (*a*) to clamp (sth.) into position; **ein Blatt Papier e.,** to insert a sheet of paper (into the type-writer); (*b*) to harness (a horse); (*c*) *F:* to rope (s.o.) in (for a job).

'einsparen, *v.tr.sep.* to economize on (materials, expenses etc.); to cut down (expenditure etc.).

'einsperren, *v.tr.sep.* to lock up, *F:* jail (s.o.).

'einspielen, *v.tr.sep.* **sich e.,** (*Musiker*) to practise; (*Sportler*) to warm up; (*Unternehmen*) to get under way; **sie sind gut aufeinander eingespielt, they work together as a good team.

'einspringen, *v.i.sep.irr.19* (*sein*) **für j-n e.,** to stand in for s.o.

'einspritzen, *v.tr.sep.* to inject.

'Einspruch, *m* objection.

'einspurig ['ainʃpu:riç], *adj.* single-track (line, road).

einst [ainst], *adv. Lit:* 1. (*früher*) once, in the past. 2. (*in Zukunft*) one day.

'einstampfen, *v.tr.sep.* to pulp (books).

'Einstand, *m* (*beim Tennis*) deuce.

'einstecken, *v.tr.sep.* (*a*) to put/stick (sth.) in; to plug in (the radio etc.); to post (a letter); (*b*) to pocket (money, profits etc.); (*c*) (*hinnehmen*) *F:* to suffer (an insult, defeat, criticism etc.), take (blows etc.).

'einstehen, *v.i.sep.irr.100* (*sein*) **für j-n, etwas** *acc* **e.,** to vouch for s.o., sth.; **für die Folgen e.,** to answer for the consequences.

'einsteigen, *v.i.sep.irr.89* (*sein*) to get on (the train, bus etc.); (**in ein Auto**) **e.,** to

get in(to a car).

'einstell|bar, *adj.* adjustable. ◆**'e~en**, *v.tr.sep.* (*a*) to put (away) (a vehicle); (*b*) (*beschäftigen*) to take on (s.o.); (*c*) (*aufhören*) to stop (work, smoking etc.); to suspend (payments); (*d*) *Tchn:* to adjust (a machine, screws, volume etc.); **einen Sender e.,** to tune in to a station; *Fig:* (*Pers.*) **sich auf j-n, etwas** *acc* **e.,** to adapt oneself to s.o., sth.; (*e*) **sich e.,** (*Pers., Jahreszeit*) to arrive; (*Schmerzen usw.*) to start; (*Zweifel, Schwierigkeiten*) to arise. ◆**'E~ung**, *f* 1. cessation (of hostilities, production etc.); stoppage of work; suspension of payments etc.). 2. *Tchn:* adjustment. 3. *Cin:* *TV:* (*Aufnahme*) take. 4. (*Haltung*) attitude. 5. engagement (of staff, workers).

'Einstieg, *m* **-(e)s/-e** entrance (of a bus etc.).

einstig ['ainstiç], *adj.* former.

'einstimm|en, *v.i.sep.* (*haben*) (*Instrument, Stimme*) to come in; **in den Jubel usw. e.,** to join in the cheering etc. ◆**'e~ig**, *adj.* 1. *Mus:* unison (singing etc.). 2. unanimous (decision etc.). ◆**'E~igkeit**, *f /no pl* unanimity.

'einstöckig ['ainstœkiç], *adj.* one-storey.

'einstreichen, *v.tr.sep.irr.86* *F:* to rake in (money, profits etc.).

'einstudieren, *v.tr.sep.* to study (a piece of music, *Th:* part etc.); to rehearse (a play).

'einstürmen, *v.i.sep.* (*sein*) **auf j-n e.,** to rush at/*Mil:* attack s.o.; *Fig:* (*mit Fragen usw.*) to bombard s.o. (with questions etc.).

'Einsturz, *m* collapse; caving in (of ground etc.). ◆**'E~gefahr**, *f* (*Schild*) danger falling masonry.

'einstürzen, *v.i.sep.* (*sein*) (*Gebäude usw.*) to collapse; (*Dach*) to cave in.

einstweil|en [ainst'vailən], *adv.* (*vorläufig*) for the time being; (*inzwischen*) meanwhile. ◆**e~ig**, *adj.* temporary.

eintägig ['ainte:giç], *adj.* one-day (visit etc.).

'eintauchen, *v.sep.* 1. *v.tr.* to dip; (*auf längere Zeit*) immerse (sth.). 2. *v.i.* (*sein*) (**ins Wasser**) **e.,** to dive in(to the water).

'eintauschen, *v.tr.sep.* to exchange, *F:* swap (sth.).

'einteil|en, *v.tr.sep.* (*a*) to divide (sth.); to classify (animals, plants etc.); (*b*) to map out (one's time, day etc.); (*verteilen*) to distribute (workload, expenditure etc.); (*c*) **j-n zu einer Arbeit e.,** to allot s.o. a task. ◆**'e~ig**, *adj.* one-piece (swimsuit etc.).

eintönig ['aintø:niç], *adj.* monotonous. ◆**'E~keit**, *f /no pl* monotony.

'Eintopf, *m* hot-pot; stew.

'Eintracht, *f /no pl* harmony; (*Frieden*) peace.

einträchtig, *adj.* harmonious; peaceful.

'Eintrag, *m* **-(e)s/-e** entry (in a diary, list etc.). ◆**'e~en**, *v.tr.sep.irr.85* (*a*) to put/write (sth.) down; to enter (sth.); (b) to enrol (s.o.) (**als Mitglied**, as a member); to register (a birth, trade mark etc.); **eingetragener Verein**, incorporated society; (*Pers.*) **sich e.**, to enter one's name; (*im Hotel*) to check in. ◆**'E~ung**, *f* -/-en 1. (*Eintrag*) entry. 2. registration.

einträglich ['aintrɛːklɪç], *adj.* lucrative.

'eintreffen, *v.i.sep.irr.104* (*sein*) (a) (*ankommen*) to arrive; (b) (*Prophezeiung usw.*) to come true; (*Ereignis*) to happen.

'eintreiben, *v.tr.sep.irr.12* to recover, collect (outstanding debts, money etc.).

'eintreten, *v.sep.irr.105* 1. *v.i.* (*sein*) (a) (*Pers.*) to enter, come in; **e. in** + *acc*, to enter (the room, a convent, the war etc.); **in einen Verein usw. e.**, to join a club etc.; (b) (*Ereignis*) to occur, take place; (*Zustand*) to set in; (c) **für eine Sache e.**, to support a cause. 2. *v.tr.* to kick (sth.) in.

'Eintritt, *m* 1. (*Eintreten*) entering; entrance; **E. verboten!** no admittance. 2. (a) (joining (**in einen Verein usw.**, of an association etc.); (b) entry (**in Verhandlungen**, into negotiations); (c) **bei E. der Dunkelheit**, when darkness sets in. ◆**'E~s-**, *comb.fm.* admission (ticket etc.).

'eintrocknen, *v.i.sep.* (*sein*) to dry up.

'einüben, *v.tr.sep.* to practise (a piece of music, dance step etc.).

einverleib|en ['ainfɛrlaibən], *v.tr.sep. & insep.* (a) to incorporate (sth.); (b) *Hum:* (*Pers.*) **sich dat einen Kuchen usw. e.**, to consume a cake etc.

'Einvernehmen, *n -s/-* understanding; **im E. mit dem Chef**, with the agreement of the boss.

'einverstanden, *pred.adj.* **e. sein**, to be in agreement; **e.!** OK!

'Einverständnis, *n* (a) agreement; (*Billigung*) consent; (b) (*Einigkeit*) understanding.

'Einwand, *m* -(e)s/¨e objection (**gegen etwas** *acc*, to sth.). ◆**e~'frei**, *adj.* satisfactory; (*tadellos*) perfect.

'Einwander|er, *m* immigrant. ◆**'e~n**, *v.i.sep.* (*sein*) to immigrate. ◆**'E~ung**, *f* immigration.

einwärts ['ainvɛrts], *adv.* inward(s).

'Einweg-, *comb.fm.* non-returnable (bottle etc.).

'einweichen, *v.tr.sep.* to soak (washing etc.).

einweih|en, *v.tr.sep.* (a) to open (a building, road etc.), consecrate (a church etc.); (b) to initiate (s.o.); **j-n in ein Geheimnis usw. e.**, to let s.o. in on a secret etc. ◆**'E~ung**, *f* -/-en 1. official opening; *Ecc:* consecration. 2. initiation.

einweis|en, *v.tr.sep.irr.70* (a) **j-n ins Krankenhaus usw. e.**, to send s.o. to (the) hospital etc.; (b) **j-n in eine Tätigkeit e.**, to introduce s.o. to a job. ◆**'E~ung**, *f* -/-en (a) assignment; E.

ins Krankenhaus, hospitalization; (b) introduction (**in** + *acc*, to).

'einwenden, *v.tr.sep.94* to object; **dagegen läßt sich nichts e.**, there is no objection to that.

'einwerfen, *v.tr.sep.irr.110* (a) to throw in (the ball, *Fig:* a remark etc.); to post (a letter); to put in (a coin, money); (b) to smash (a window etc.).

'einwickeln, *v.tr.sep.* to wrap up.

einwillig|en, *v.i.sep.* (*haben*) (**in etwas**) *acc* **e.**, to agree/(*erlauben*) consent (to sth.). ◆**'E~ung**, *f* -/-en agreement; consent.

'einwirken, *v.i.sep.* (*haben*) **auf j-n, etwas** *acc* **e.**, to have an effect on s.o., sth.; (*beeinflussen*) to influence s.o., sth. ◆**'E~ung**, *f* effect; (*Einfluß*) influence.

'Einwohner|in, *m -s/- (f -/-nen*) inhabitant; resident (of a village, estate). ◆**'E~meldeamt**, *n* registration office. ◆**'E~schaft**, *f -/no pl* resident population.

'Einwurf, *m* 1. *Sp:* throw-in; **E. DM 2.**, put 2 marks in the slot. 2. (*Öffnung*) slot. 3. (*Bemerkung*) interjection; (*kritisch*) objection.

'Einzahl, *f Gram:* singular.

'einzahl|en, *v.tr.sep.* to pay in (money) (**auf j-s Konto**, into s.o.'s account). ◆**'E~ung**, *f* -/-en payment (into the bank).

'einzäunen, *v.tr.sep.* to fence (in) (a plot etc.).

'einzeichnen, *v.tr.sep.* to draw in (details).

Einzel ['aintsəl]. I. *n -s/-* (*Tennis*) singles. II. **'E~-**, *comb.fm.* (a) separate (question, element, state, edition etc.); (b) single (volume, bed, garage etc.); individual (packaging, *Sp:* contest etc.); (c) (*einzig*) sole; only (child etc.). ◆**'E~gänger(in)**, *m (f)* (*Pers.*) outsider; *F:* lone wolf. ◆**'E~haft**, *f* solitary confinement. ◆**'E~handel**, *m* retail trade. ◆**'E~händler**, *m* retailer. ◆**'E~teil**, *f* -/-en detail. ◆**'e~n**, *adj.* 1. (a) (*alleinstehend*) individual, (*gesondert*) separate (parts etc.); **jeder e~ne**, every single one; **e. verpackt**, individually wrapped. 2. (*einige*) some, a few. 3. **das e~ne**, the details; **im e~nen**, in detail. ◆**'E~teil**, *n* component (part). ◆**'E~zimmer**, *n* single room.

einzieh|en, *v.sep.irr.113* 1. *v.tr.* (a) to pull/draw in (nets, a rope etc.); to take in (sails, claws etc.); to strike (the flag); to duck (one's head); to retract (the undercarriage); (b) to withdraw (a passport, licence etc.); *Jur:* to seize (s.o.'s property etc.); (c) to collect (debts, taxes etc.); **Erkundigungen über j-n e.**, to make inquiries about s.o.; (d) *Mil:* to call s.o. up, *N.Am:* draft (s.o.). 2. *v.i.* (*sein*) (a) (*Pers.*) (**in eine Wohnung, ein Haus usw. e.**), to move in(to a flat, house etc.); (b) (*Feuchtigkeit usw.*) to be soaked up.

einzig ['aintsiç], *adj.* (a) only (possibility, child etc.); **nur ein e~es Mal!** just once! **er konnte keine e~e Frage beantworten,** he couldn't answer a single question; (b) **e. (in seiner Art),** unique. ◆**'e~artig,** *adj.* unique; (*unvergleichlich*) incomparable.

'Einzug, *m* (a) entrance (of s.o., an army, band); (b) moving in; move (**in die neue Wohnung,** into the new flat).

Eis [ais]. I. *n* -es/*no pl* 1. ice. 2. *Cu:* ice (cream). II. **E~-,** *comb.fm.* (a) ice (-hockey, dancing, *Nau:* -breaker etc.); (b) ice cream (seller, wafer etc.). ◆**'E~bahn,** *f* ice/skating rink. ◆**'E~bär,** *m* polar bear. ◆**'E~becher,** *m* sundae. ◆**'E~bein,** *n Cu:* cured knuckle of pork. ◆**'E~berg,** *m* iceberg. ◆**'E~blume,** *f* frost-flower (on a window). ◆**'E~decke,** *f* frozen surface; (*Schicht*) (layer of) ice. ◆**'E~diele,** *f* ice cream parlour. ◆**'e~ig** ['aiziç], *adj.* icy (wind, *Fig:* manner etc.). ◆**'E~kaffee,** *m* iced coffee. ◆**'e~kalt,** *adj.* icy, freezing (room, weather etc.); ice-cold (drink). ◆**'E~kunstlauf,** *m* figure skating. ◆**'E~lauf,** *m* skating. ◆**'e~laufen,** *v.i.sep.irr.58 (sein)* to skate. ◆**'E~pickel,** *m* ice-axe. ◆**'E~schießen,** *n approx.* = curling. ◆**'E~schrank,** *m* refrigerator. ◆**'E~zapfen,** *m* icicle. ◆**'E~zeit,** *f* Ice Age.

Eisen ['aizən], *n* -s/- iron. ◆**'E~bahn,** *f* railway, *N.Am:* railroad. ◆**'E~bahn-,** *comb.fm.* railway, *N.Am:* railroad (line, station etc.); rail (journey, network etc.). ◆**'E~bahner,** *m* -s/- *F:* railwayman; *N.Am:* railroader. ◆**'E~erz,** *n* iron ore. ◆**'e~haltig,** *adj.* containing iron; ferrous (compound).

eisern ['aizərn], *adj.* (a) iron; (b) relentless (energy etc.); *F:* **darin bin ich e.,** I won't budge on that.

eitel ['aitəl], *adj.* vain. ◆**'E~keit,** *f* -/-en vanity.

Eiter ['aitər], *m* -s/*no pl* pus. ◆**'e~n,** *v.i. (haben)* to suppurate. ◆**'e~ig** ['aitriç], *adj.* suppurating.

'Eiweiß, *n* (a) egg-white; (b) *Biol:* protein.

'Eizelle, *f* ovum.

Ekel ['e:kəl]. 1. *m* -s/*no pl* (a) repulsion (**vor** + *dat,* to); **E. über etwas acc empfinden,** to be sickened by sth. 2. *n* -s/- *F:* (*Pers.*) beast; (*Mann*) bastard, (*Frau*) bitch. ◆**'e~erregend,** *adj.* nauseating. ◆**'e~haft/'ek(e)lig,** *adj.* (a) nauseating (smell etc.); (b) (*unangenehm*) beastly (person, job, weather etc.); horrible (sight etc.). ◆**'e~n,** *v.tr. v.impers.* **es ekelt mich/mir vor ihm,** I am disgusted by him; I loathe him; (b) *v.refl.* **sich vor j-m, etwas dat e.,** to loathe s.o., sth.

Ekstase [ɛk'staːzə], *f* -/-n ecstasy.

Ekzem [ɛk'tseːm], *n* -s/-e eczema.

Elan [e'laːn], *m* -s/*no pl* vigour.

elast|isch [e'lastiʃ], *adj.* (a) elastic (material, bandage etc.); flexible (wood, metal, *Fig:* person, attitude etc.); (b) springy (steps, walk etc.); supple (movements, limbs etc.). ◆**E~izität** [elastisi'tɛːt], *f* -/*no pl* elasticity; (*also Fig:*) flexibility; springiness.

Elch [ɛlç], *m* -(e)s/-e (European) elk.

Elefant [ele'fant], *m* -en/-en elephant.

elegan|t [ele'gant], *adj.* (a) elegant; (b) *Fig:* neat (solution etc.). ◆**E~z** [-'gants], *f* -/*no pl* (a) elegance; (b) neatness.

elek|trifizieren [elektrifi'tsiːrən], *v.tr.* to electrify (a railway etc.). ◆**E~triker** [e'lektrikər], *m* -s/- electrician. ◆**e~trisch** [e'lektriʃ], *adj.* electric (shock, razor, current etc.); electrical (appliance etc.). ◆**e~trisieren** [-'ziːrən], *v.tr.* to charge (sth.) with electricity; **sich e.,** to get an electric shock. ◆**E~trizität** [-itsi'tɛːt], *f* -/*no pl* electricity. ◆**E~trizi'tätswerk,** *n* power station.

Elektro- [e'lektro-], *comb.fm.* (a) *Ph: Ch: etc:* electro-(magnet etc.); (b) electrical (industry, engineer etc.); (c) electric (boat, drive, vehicle, razor etc.). ◆**E~de** [-'troːdə], *f* -/-n electrode. ◆**E~lyse** [-tro'lyːzə], *f* -/*no pl* electrolysis. ◆**E~n** [e'lektron], *n* -s/-en [-'troːnən], electron. ◆**E~nen-** [-'troːnən], *comb.fm.* electronic (organ etc.); (b) electron (microscope, beam). ◆**E~nik** [-'troːnik], *f* -/*no pl* electronics. ◆**e~nisch,** *adj.* electronic. electronically.

Element [ele'mɛnt], *n* -(e)s/-e element; *El:* cell (of a battery). ◆**e~ar** [-'taːr], *adj.* I. (a) (*wesentlich*) fundamental (needs, requirements); (b) (*primitiv*) rudimentary (knowledge etc.). 2. elemental (force, feeling etc.).

Elend ['e:lɛnt]. I. *n* -s/*no pl* (a) (*Armut*) poverty; (b) misery; distress. II. **e.,** *adj.* miserable; (a) (*jämmerlich*) wretched, (*ärmlich*) poverty-stricken (existence, person etc.); (b) (*erbärmlich*) miserable. ◆**'E~sviertel,** *n* slum.

elf [ɛlf]. I. *num.adj.* eleven. II. **E.,** *f* -/-en *Fb:* eleven; team. ◆**E~'meter,** *m* penalty kick.

Elfe ['ɛlfə], *f* -/-n elf.

Elfenbein ['ɛlfənbain], *n* ivory.

eliminieren [elimi'niːrən], *v.tr.* to eliminate.

elit|är [eli'tɛːr], *adj.* elitist. ◆**E~e** [e'liːtə], *f* -/-n elite.

Ellbogen ['ɛlboːgən], *m* -s/- elbow.

Elle ['ɛlə], *f* -/-n *Anat:* ulna. ◆**'e~nlang,** *adj.* *F:* interminable.

Elsaß ['ɛlzas]. *Pr.n.n* -& -sses Alsace. ◆**Elsässer(in)** ['ɛlzɛsər(in)], *m* -s/- (*f* -/-nen) Alsatian.

Elster ['ɛlstər], *f* -/-n magpie.

elter|lich ['ɛltərliç] *adj.* parental (home etc.). ◆**E~n** ['ɛltərn], *pl* parents. ◆**'E~nhaus,** *n* (parental) home. ◆**'e~nlos,** *adj.* orphaned. ◆**'E~nteil,** *m* parent.

Email [e'mai], *n* -s/-s/**E~le** [e'maljə], *f* -/-n enamel. ◆**e~lieren** [ema(l)'ji:rən], *v.tr.* to enamel (a vase etc.).

Emanzi|pation [emantsipatsi'o:n], *f* -/-en emancipation. ◆**e~i'pieren,** *v.tr.* to emancipate (women etc.).

Embryo ['ɛmbryo], *m* -s/-s & -nen embryo.

Emigr|ant [emi'grant], *m* -en/-en emigrant. ◆**E~ati'on,** *f* -/-en emigration. ◆**e~ieren** [-'gri:rən] *v.i.* (sein) to emigrate.

Emotion [emotsi'o:n], *f* -/-en emotion. ◆**e~al** [-o'na:l], *adj.* emotional.

Empfang [ɛm'pfaŋ], *m* -(e)s/-e receipt (of goods, a letter etc.); reception (of s.o., guests, *TV:* a programme); in **E. nehmen,** to receive (goods, a present etc.), welcome (s.o.). ◆**e~en,** *v.tr.irr.28* (a) to receive (money, a gift, letter, an award, orders, *TV:* a programme, the sacrament etc.); (b) to welcome (a guest etc.); (c) (*Frau*) to conceive (a child). ◆**E~sdame,** *f* receptionist. ◆**E~shalle,** *f* reception area, *N.Am:* lobby (of a hotel).

Empfäng|er [ɛm'pfɛŋər], *m* -s/- 1. (*Pers.*) recipient; addressee. 2. *Rad: TV:* receiver. ◆**e~lich,** *adj.* **für etwas** *acc* **e.,** susceptible/prone to sth. ◆**E~nis,** *f* -/-se conception. ◆**E~nisverhütung,** *f* contraception.

empfehl|en [ɛm'pfe:lən], *v.tr.irr.2* (a) to recommend (s.o., sth.); (b) (*Pers.*) **sich e.,** to take one's leave; **bitte u. Sie mich Ihrer Gattin,** please remember me to your wife. ◆**e~enswert,** *adj.* to be recommended; (*ratsam*) advisable. ◆**E~ung,** *f* -/-en recommendation.

empfind|en [ɛm'pfindən], I. *v.tr.irr.9* to feel (pain, joy etc.). II. **E~,** *n* -s/*no pl* feeling; **meinem E. nach,** in my opinion; the way I feel. ◆**e~lich,** *adj.* (a) sensitive (skin etc.); (*gegen* + *acc,* to); (b) susceptible; (b) (*reizbar*) touchy (person); (c) delicate (child, plant, material etc.); (d) (*spürbar, hart*) severe (pain, penalty, cold etc.); serious (losses). ◆**E~lichkeit,** *f* -/-en (a) sensitivity (*gegen* + *acc,* to); tenderness (of a wound etc.); *Med:* susceptibility; (b) touchiness; (c) delicacy (of a material etc.). ◆**e~sam** [ɛm'pfintzə:m], *adj.* (a) sentimental; (b) (*sensibel*) sensitive. ◆**E~ung,** *f* -/-en feeling; sensation (of cold, pain etc.); (*Gemütsbewegung*) sentiment.

empor [ɛm'po:r], *adv. Lit:* up(wards). ◆**E~kömmling** [ɛm'po:r], *m* -s/-e upstart. ◆**e~steigen,** *v.tr.* & *i.sep.irr.89* (sein) to rise.

Empore [ɛm'po:rə], *f* -/-n gallery.

empör|en [ɛm'pø:rən], *v.tr.* to infuriate (s.o.); **sich (über etwas** *acc*) **e.,** to get into a fury (about sth.). ◆**e~end,** *adj.* outrageous (statement etc.); (*schändlich*) shocking. ◆**E~ung,** *f* -/-en indignation.

emsig ['ɛmziç], *adj.* busy; (*fleißig*) industrious.

End- ['ɛnt-], *comb.fm.* final (phase, state, *Sp:* round, spurt etc.); ultimate (purpose etc.). ◆**E~betrag,** *m* sum total; total amount. ◆**'e~gültig,** *adj.* final (decision, solution etc.); definitive (answer, result etc.); conclusive (proof). ◆**'e~lich.** 1. *adv.* (a) at last; (b) (*schließlich*) finally. 2. *adj. Mth: etc:* finite. ◆**'e~los,** *adj.* (a) endless; interminable (speech etc.); (b) (*unbegrenzt*) boundless (patience etc.). ◆**'E~punkt,** *m* last point (on a scale); end (of a line etc.); destination. ◆**E~spiel,** *n* final. ◆**'E~station,** *f* last stop; (*Endbahnhof*) terminus; *N.Am:* terminal. ◆**'E~summe,** *f* sum total; total amount.

End|e ['ɛndə], *n* -s/-n end; **am E.,** at the end; **E. April,** at the end of April; **sie ist E. Vierzig,** she is in her late forties; **zu E.,** at an end; (*verbraucht*) finished; **zu E. gehen,** to come to an end; (*Vorräte usw.*) to run out; *Fig:* **am E. war er's vielleicht doch nicht,** perhaps it wasn't him after all. ◆**'e~en,** *v.i.* (*haben*) to end; **der Vertrag endet im Mai,** the contract runs out in May. ◆**E~ung,** *f* -/-en ending.

Energie [enɛr'gi:]. I. *f* -/-n energy. II. **E~ie-,** *comb.fm.* energy (requirement etc.); (*source* etc.) of energy. ◆**e~iegeladen,** *adj.* full of energy; dynamic. ◆**e~ielos,** *adj.* listless. ◆**e~isch** ['e'nɛrgiʃ], *adj.* (a) forceful (person, character etc.); (b) (*entschlossen*) resolute (person, tone, step).

eng [ɛŋ], *adj.* (a) narrow (street, valley etc.); *Fig:* **hier ist es mir zu e.,** I feel shut in here; (b) (*nahe*) close (friend etc.); (c) **die Hose ist e.,** the trousers are a tight fit. ◆**E~e** ['ɛŋə], *f* -/-n (a) narrowness; (b) (*Bedrängnis*) tight corner; **j-n in die E. treiben,** to corner s.o. ◆**'e~herzig,** *adj.* petty, small-minded. ◆**'E~paß,** *m* (a) (narrow) pass, defile (between mountains); (b) *Fig:* bottleneck. ◆**e~stirnig** ['ɛŋʃtirniç], *adj.* narrow-minded.

Engag|ement [ãgaːʒə'mãː], *n* -s/-s commitment; *esp. Th:* engagement. ◆**e~ieren** [-'ʒi:rən], *v.tr.* (a) to take (s.o.) on, *Th: etc:* engage (s.o.); (b) **sich (politisch usw.) e.,** to involve oneself heavily (in politics etc.). ◆**e~iert,** *adj.* committed (person).

Engel ['ɛŋəl], *m* -s/- angel. ◆**e~haft,** *adj.* angelic.

England ['ɛŋlant]. *Pr.n.n* -s. England.

Engländer ['ɛŋlɛndər], *m* -s/- 1. Englishman. 2. *Tchn:* adjustable spanner.

♦'E~in, f -/-nen Englishwoman.
englisch ['ɛŋlɪʃ]. I. adj. English. II. E., n
-(s)/no pl (Sprache) English.
Enkel ['ɛŋkəl], m -s/- grandson.
♦'E~in, f -/-nen granddaughter.
♦'E~kind, n grandchild.
enorm [e'nɔrm], adj. (a) enormous; (b)
F: tremendous; fantastic.
Ensemble [ã'sã:bl], n -s/-s Mus: ensemble; Th: company.
entarten [ɛnt'ʔɑːrtən], v.i. (sein) to
degenerate.
entbehr|en [ɛnt'beːrən], v. 1. v.tr. to do
without (s.o., sth.). 2. v.i. (haben) + gen
Lit: dieses Gerücht entbehrt jeder
Grundlage, this rumour is without any
foundation. ♦e~lich, adj. superfluous.
♦E~ung, f -/-en privation.
ent'bind|en, v.tr.irr.9 Med: to deliver (a
woman) of a child. ♦E~ung, f delivery.
entblößen [ɛnt'bløːsən], v.tr. to bare.
ent'dock|en, v.tr. to discover (s.o., sth.);
to detect (a crime, mistakes etc.).
♦E~er, m -s/- discoverer; (Forscher) explorer. ♦E~ung, f -/-en discovery (of);
(Enthüllung) detection.
Ente ['ɛntə], f -/-n 1. duck. 2. (Zeitungs-)
false report.
ent'ehr|en, v.tr. to dishonour. ♦e~end,
adj. degrading.
ent'eign|en, v.tr. to dispossess (s.o.); Jur:
to expropriate (property).
ent'eisen, v.tr. to defrost (a refrigerator).
ent'erben, v.tr. to disinherit (s.o.).
ent'fachen, v.tr. Lit: to inflame (desire,
passions) to provoke (a quarrel etc.).
ent'fall|en, v.i.irr.27 (sein) (a) Lit:
(Sachen) j-m/j-s Händen e., to slip from
s.o.'s hands; Fig: ihr Name ist mir e.,
her name has slipped my mind; (b) Adm:
(auf Formular) entfällt, not applicable; (c)
auf j-n e., to fall to s.o.
ent'falt|en, v.tr. (a) to unfold (a table-
cloth, Fig: a plan etc.); sich e., (Blume
usw.) to open; (c) (entwickeln) (Pers.) to
develop (one's powers, faculties etc.); (c)
(zeigen) to display, show (courage, taste
etc.). ♦E~ung, f -/no pl (a) unfolding;
(b) display (of pomp, courage etc.); (c)
development; zur E. kommen, (Plan
usw.) to come to fruition; (Schönheit) to
blossom.
entfern|en [ɛnt'fɛrnən], v.tr. (a) to re-
move; (herausnehmen) to take (sth.) out;
j-n aus dem Amt/Dienst e., to remove/
dismiss s.o. from office; (b) to move, carry (s.o., sth.) away; sich e., to go away,
leave. ♦e~t, adj. (a) 20 km e., 20 km
away; (b) distant, remote (place, relation); (c) (schwach) faint (resemblance);
ich denke nicht im e~testen daran, I
haven't the slightest intention of doing it.
♦E~ung, f -/-en (Weite) distance.
♦E~ungsmesser, m rangefinder.
ent'fesseln, v.tr. to unleash (feelings
etc.); to provoke (a war, argument etc.).

entflamm|bar [ɛnt'flambɑːr], adj. leicht
e., inflammable; (Pers.) enthusiastic.
♦e~en, v.tr. (a) to inflame (passions,
feelings); to kindle (enthusiasm); to
arouse (anger etc.).
ent'fremden, v.tr. to alienate (s.o.).
ent'frosten, v.tr. to defrost.
ent'führ|en, v.tr. (a) to kidnap, abduct
(s.o.); (b) to hijack (an aeroplane, ship
etc.). ♦E~er, m (a) kidnapper; (b) hijacker. ♦E~ung, f -/-en (a) kidnap-
ping, abduction; (b) hijacking.
entgegen [ɛnt'geːgən], adv. & prep.
+ dat 1. towards. 2. against (the wind
etc.); contrary to (s.o.'s wishes, regulations). ♦e~bringen, v.tr.sep.irr.16 j-
m, etwas dat Verständnis usw. e., to
show understanding etc. for s.o., sth.
♦e~gehen, v.i.sep.irr.36 j-m e., to
go/walk to meet s.o. ♦e~gesetzt,
adj. opposite (direction, effect etc.); contrary, opposing (interests etc.).
♦e~halten, v.tr.sep.irr.45 j-m etwas
e., to hold sth. out to s.o.; dem ist
nichts entgegenzuhalten, there is no objection to that. ♦e~kommen. I.
v.i.sep.irr.53 (sein) (a) j-m, etwas dat e.,
to come towards/approach s.o., sth.; (b)
j-m/j-s Wünschen e., to oblige s.o./
comply with s.o.'s wishes. II. E., n -s/no
pl obligingness, co-operation; (Zugeständnis) concession. ♦e~kommend, adj. 1.
oncoming (vehicle, traffic). 2. obliging
(person); helpful (suggestion etc.).
♦e~nehmen, v.tr.sep.irr.69 to accept
(gifts, orders etc.), take (a telephone call,
message etc.); to receive (congratulations,
a prize etc.). ♦e~sehen, v.i.sep.irr.92
(haben) j-m e., to look towards s.o./in
s.o.'s direction; etwas dat e., to await
sth., (mit Freude) look forward to sth.
♦e~setzen, v.tr.sep. (a) j-m etwas
Widerstand e., to resist s.o., sth.; (b) diesem Vorwurf habe ich nichts entgegen-
zusetzen, I have no reply to this reproach; (b) (gegenüberstellen) to contrast
(sth.). ♦e~treten, v.i.sep.irr.105 (sein)
(a) j-m e., to approach s.o.; dem Feind
usw. e., to face the enemy etc.; (b) Vor-
urteilen usw. e., to oppose prejudices
etc. ♦e~wirken, v.i.sep. (haben) etwas
dat e., to counteract sth.
entgegn|en [ɛnt'geːgnən], v.tr. to reply.
♦E~ung, f -/-en answer, reply; (schlagfertig) retort, rejoinder.
ent'gehen, v.i & i.tr.36 (sein) (a) etwas
dat e., to avoid sth.; (b) (unbemerkt bleiben) j-m e., to escape s.o.'s notice;
sie läßt sich dat nichts e. she doesn't
miss anything.
entgeistert [ɛnt'gaistərt], adj. dumbfounded; (entsetzt) aghast.
Entgelt [ɛnt'gɛlt], n -(e)s/-e payment;
gegen E., for a fee.
entgleis|en [ɛnt'glaizən], v.i. (sein) (Zug)
to be derailed, Fig: (Pers.) to commit a
faux pas. ♦E~ung, f -/-en 1. derail-

ment. 2. *Fig:* faux pas; embarrassing slip.

ent'gräten, *v.tr.* to bone, fillet (a fish).

enthaar|en, *v.tr.* to remove hair from (legs etc.). ◆E~**ungsmittel**, *n* depilatory.

ent'halt|en, *v.tr.irr.45* (*a*) to contain (sth.); **im Preis e.**, included in the price; (*b*) **sich der Stimme e.**, to abstain (from voting). ◆**e~sam**, *adj.* abstemious; (*sexuell*) chaste. ◆E~**samkeit**, *f -/no pl* abstinence. ◆E~**ung**, *f Pol: etc:* abstention (from voting).

enthärten, *v.tr.* to soften (water etc.).

ent'hüllen, *v.tr.* to reveal (sth., *Fig:* a plot etc.); to unveil (a face, monument etc.).

Enthusiasmus [ɛntuzi'asmus], *m -/no pl* enthusiasm.

ent'kernen, *v.tr.* to core (apples); to seed (grapes, raisins etc.); to stone (cherries etc.).

ent'kommen, *v.i.irr.53* (*sein*) to escape, get away (j-m, from s.o.).

ent'korken, *v.tr.* to uncork (a bottle).

entkräften [ɛnt'krɛftən], *v.tr.* to weaken (s.o.); *Fig:* to invalidate (an argument).

ent'laden, *v.tr.irr.56* to unload (luggage, a rifle, lorry etc.); to discharge (a battery etc.); **sich e.**, (*Gewitter*) to break, burst.

ent'lang, *prep. + acc/dat & adv.* along. ◆**e~gehen**, *v.i.sep.irr.36* (*sein*) to walk along.

entlarven [ɛnt'la:rfən], *v.tr.* to unmask (s.o.).

ent'lass|en, *v.tr.irr.57* to dismiss (s.o.); to discharge (a patient etc.); (*befreien*) to release (a prisoner). ◆E~**ung**, *f -/-en* 1. (*a*) discharge; release; (*b*) leaving school. 2. dismissal, *F:* firing.

ent'last|en, *v.tr.* (*a*) to relieve the strain etc.) on (s.o., sth.); to ease (traffic, *Fig:* s.o.'s conscience etc.); (*b*) *Jur:* to exonerate. ◆E~**ung**, *f -/-en* relief; easing; *Jur:* **zu j-s E.**, in s.o.'s defence. ◆E~**ungs-**, *comb.fm.* relief (road, train etc.); *Jur:* exonerating (evidence etc.); defence (witness etc.).

ent'leeren, *v.tr.* to empty.

ent'legen, *adj.* remote; (*einsam*) isolated.

ent'locken, *v.tr.* j-m, etwas dat etwas e., to coax sth. from s.o., sth.

ent'lüften, *v.tr.* to ventilate (a room etc.); *Aut:* to bleed (brakes etc.).

entmutigen [ɛnt'mu:tigən], *v.tr.* to discourage.

Entnahme [ɛnt'na:mə], *f -/-n* taking (**aus** + *dat*, from).

ent'nehmen, *v.tr.irr.69* (*a*) **etwas** (aus) etwas dat e., to take sth. from/out of sth.; (*b*) (*schließen*) to deduce (sth.).

ent'puppen, *v.refl.* **sich als etwas e.**, to turn out to be sth.

ent'rahmen, *v.tr.* to (take the) cream off, skim (milk).

ent'rätseln, *v.tr.* to puzzle out (a mystery etc.).

ent'reißen, *v.tr.irr.4* to snatch (s.o., sth.) away (j-m, from s.o.).

ent'richten, *v.tr.* to pay (taxes etc.).

ent'rinnen, *v.i.irr.73* (*sein*) to escape, get away (etwas dat, from sth.).

ent'rosten, *v.tr.* to derust (sth.).

ent'rüst|en, *v.tr.* to fill (s.o.) with indignation; **sich** (**über etwas** acc) e., to get indignant at sth.; **entrüstet**, indignant (person, face). ◆E~**ung**, *f -/no pl* indignation.

ent'schädig|en, *v.tr.* to compensate (s.o.), *Jur:* pay (s.o.) compensation/(*Schadenersatz*) damages. ◆E~**ung**, *f* compensation; *Jur:* (*Schadenersatz*) damages.

ent'schärfen, *v.tr.* to defuse (a bomb, mine etc.); *Fig:* to take the sting out of (a crisis etc.).

Entscheid [ɛnt'ʃait], *m -(e)s/-e* decision; *Jur:* ruling. ◆**e~en** [-'ʃaidən], *v.tr. & i.tr.65* (*haben*) to decide (**über** + acc, on); **du mußt hier e.**, it's your decision; **sich e.**, (i) (*Pers.*) to decide, make up one's mind; (ii) (*Spiel, Sache usw.*) to be decided. ◆**e~end**, *adj.* decisive (influence, victory, evidence etc.); crucial (point, moment, question); *Sp:* deciding (goal etc.). ◆E~**ung**, *f -/-en* decision; settlement (of a question, problem etc.); *Jur: Adm:* ruling.

entschieden [ɛnt'ʃi:dən], *adj.* decisive (manner, tone etc.); firm (refusal, denial, supporter, opponent).

ent'schließen, *v.refl.irr.31* **sich** (**zu etwas** dat) e., to decide, make up one's mind (to do sth.).

entschlossen [ɛnt'ʃlɔsən], *adj.* determined, resolute (person, action, attitude etc.); **er war zu allem e.**, he was ready to do anything. ◆E~**heit**, *f -/no pl* determination; resolution.

Ent'schluß, *m* decision. ◆E~**kraft**, *f -/no pl* determination; initiative.

entschlüsseln [ɛnt'ʃlysəln], *v.tr.* to decipher (a code, writing), decode (a message etc.).

entschuld|bar [ɛnt'ʃultba:r], *adj.* excusable, pardonable. ◆**e~igen** [-'ʃuldigən], *v.tr.* (*a*) to excuse (s.o.'s behaviour etc.); (*b*) **entschuldige/entschuldigen Sie!** excuse me! to excuse (s.o.); **Sie bitte die Störung**, (I'm) sorry to disturb you; (*b*) (*wegen Abwesenheit*) j-n e., to make s.o.'s excuses; **nicht zu e.**, inexcusable; (*c*) *v.refl.* **sich** (**bei j-m**) e., to apologize (to s.o.). ◆E~**igung**, *f -/-en* 1. apology; (**j-n/für j-n**) um E. bitten, to apologize (to s.o./ for s.o.); (**ich bitte um**) E.! I beg your pardon! (I'm) sorry! 2. (*Ausrede*) excuse.

ent'setz|en. I. *v.tr.* (*a*) to horrify, appal (s.o.); **sich über j-n, etwas e.**, to be horrified/appalled at s.o., sth.; (*b*) *Mil:* to relieve (a fortress etc.). II. **E.**, *n -s/no pl* horror. ◆**e~lich**, *adj. (a*) horrible; appalling (crime); (*b*) *F:* dreadful (weather, person, cold etc.); (*c*) *F: (sehr stark)* terrible. ◆e~t, adj. horrified; appalled; horror-stricken.

ent'sichern, v.tr. to release the safety catch of (a gun).

ent'sinnen, v.refl.irr.3 sich (j-s, etwas) e., to remember, recollect (s.o., sth.).

ent'spann|en, v.tr. & i. (sein) & refl. (sich) e., to relax; Fig: die Lage hat sich entspannt, the situation has eased. ◆E~ung, f -/no pl relaxation; Fig: easing (of a situation etc.); Pol: détente (between East and West). ◆E~ungspolitik, f policy of détente.

ent'sprech|en, v.i.irr.14 (haben) (a) den Tatsachen, einer Beschreibung usw. e., to correspond to/agree with the facts, a description etc.; (b) (gleichkommen) etwas dat e., to be the equivalent of sth.; (c) (nachkommen) einem Wunsch, einer Bitte usw. e., to comply with a wish, request etc.; j-s Erwartungen usw. e., to meet s.o.'s expectations etc. ◆e~end. 1. adj. (a) corresponding; (b) (angemessen) appropriate (authority, payment etc.); suitable (clothes). 2. prep. + dat (je nach) according to (age, height, size etc.); (gemäß) in accordance with (orders, wishes etc.).

ent'springen, v.i.irr.19 (sein) (a) (Fluß) to rise, have its source; (b) Fig: to stem; (c) (entkommen) to escape.

ent'stehen, v.i.irr.100 (sein) to come into being; (geschaffen werden) to be created; (Wärme usw.) to be generated; (Brand) to start; (Ideen, Bewegung usw.) to emerge; (Freundschaft usw.) to arise; (Schaden, Unkosten usw.) aus etwas/durch etwas e., to result from sth. ◆E~ung, f -/no pl coming into being (of sth.); emergence (of an idea, a nation etc.).

ent'stellen, v.tr. (a) (verzerren) to distort (an object, Fig: facts, etc.); (b) (verunstalten) to disfigure (s.o.'s face, body).

ent'stören, v.tr. to suppress (interference (on a radio etc.)).

ent'täusch|en, v.tr. to disappoint (s.o.), dash (s.o.'s hopes), betray (s.o.'s trust). ◆e~t, adj. disappointed. ◆E~ung, f -/en disappointment.

ent'waffnen, v.tr. to disarm (s.o.).

Ent'warnung, f all-clear (signal).

ent'wässer|n, v.tr. to drain (soil, fields etc.). ◆E~ung, f -/en drainage.

entweder [ɛnt'veːdər], conj. & adv. e. ... oder, either ... or.

ent'weichen, v.i.irr.40 (sein) to escape.

ent'wenden, v.tr. to steal.

ent'werf|en, v.tr.irr.110 (a) to design (a building, dress, machine, poster etc.); to make a sketch for (a painting, sculpture etc.); (b) to draft (a novel, lecture etc.), plan (a programme); to devise (a plan).

ent'wert|en, v.tr. (a) to devalue (currency); (b) to cancel (tickets, postage stamps). ◆E~er, m -s/- cancelling machine (for tickets).

ent'wick|eln, v.tr. to develop (sth., Phot:

a film), evolve (a plan etc.); to generate (heat etc.). ◆E~lung, f -/en development; esp. Biol: evolution. ◆E~lungshilfe, f aid to developing countries. ◆E~lungsland, m developing country. ◆E~lungsstufe, f stage (of development).

entwirren [ɛnt'vɪrən], v.tr. to unravel (thread, a knot etc.); Fig: to clarify (a situation), solve (a riddle).

ent'wischen, v.i. (sein) F: to make off (mit + dat, with); j-m e., to give s.o. the slip.

ent'wöhn|en [ɛnt'vøːnən], v.tr. to wean (a child, young animal); to cure (an addict, oneself). ◆E~ung, f -/en (a) weaning; (b) curing of an addiction.

ent'würdigen, v.tr. to degrade.

Ent'wurf, m (a) (Konzept) draft; (Abriß) outline (of a plan etc.); Art: sketch, study; (b) design (of clothes, furniture, machinery); plan (of a building etc.).

ent'wurzeln, v.tr. to uproot (trees, people).

ent'zieh|en, v.tr.irr.113 (a) to take (sth.) away, withdraw (one's hand, support, favour etc.) (j-m, from s.o.); (Pflanzen) dem Boden Wasser e., to draw water from the soil; (b) sich j-m, etwas dat e., to evade s.o., sth. ◆E~ung, f withdrawal. ◆E~ungskur, f (course of) treatment for an addiction.

ent'ziffern, v.tr. to decipher (handwriting, a code etc.), decode (a message).

ent'zück|en. I. v.tr. to delight (s.o.). II. E., n -s/no pl delight, (Freude) joy. ◆e~end, adj. delightful, charming; (Aussehen) ravishing.

Ent'zug, m -(e)s/no pl withdrawal; withholding (of drugs, permission etc.).

entzünd|en [ɛnt'tsyndən], v.tr. (a) to light (a fire, cigarette etc.), ignite (a substance); sich e., (Brennstoff usw.) to ignite; (Feuer) to light; (Heu, Gebäude usw.) to catch fire; (b) Fig: to inflame, excite (passions etc.); (c) Med: (Wunden usw.) sich e., to become inflamed. ◆e~et, adj. Med: inflamed. ◆E~ung, f Med: inflammation.

ent'zwei, adj. broken, in pieces. ◆e~gehen, v.i.sep.irr.36 (sein) to fall apart.

Enzian [ɛntsiaːn], m -s/-e gentian.

Epidemie [epide'miː], f -/-n epidemic.

Epilepsie [epilɛp'siː], f -/-n epilepsy.

episch ['eːpɪʃ], adj. epic.

Episode [epi'zoːdə], f -/-n episode. ◆e~nhaft, adj. episodic.

Epoche [e'pɔxə], f -/-n period; Lit: epoch. ◆e~machend, adj. epoch-making.

Epos ['eːpɔs], n -/Epen epic.

er [eːr], pers.pron. (Pers.) he; (Ding) it.

er'achten. I. v.tr. etwas für/als nötig usw. e., to consider sth. necessary etc. II. E., n meines E~s, in my opinion.

er'arbeiten, v.tr. to earn enough money

to buy (a house etc.).

Erb- ['ɛrp-], *comb.fm.* (a) hereditary (disease, title, monarchy etc.); inherited (property, characteristic etc.); (b) *Biol:* genetic (research etc.). ◆**E~e¹** ['ɛrbə], *m -n/-n* heir; beneficiary (under a will). ◆**'E~e²**, *n -s/no pl* inheritance; geistiges E., spiritual heritage. ◆**'e~en**, *v.tr.* to inherit (sth., *Fig:* a characteristic, *F:* old clothes etc.). ◆**'E~faktor**, *m* heredity factor, gene. ◆**'E~folge**, *f Jur:* succession. ◆**e~in** ['ɛrbin], *f -/-nen* heiress. ◆**e~lich**, *adj.* hereditary. ◆**'E~schaft**, *f -/-en* inheritance. ◆**'E~stück**, *n* heirloom. ◆**'E~sünde**, *f* original sin. ◆**'E~teil**, *n* share in an inheritance.

erbarm|en [ɛr'barmən], I. *v.refl.* sich j-s e., to take pity on s.o. II. E., *n -s/no pl* mercy, compassion. ◆**e~ungslos**, *adj.* merciless; remorseless (persecution). ◆**e~ungsvoll**, *adj.* merciful, compassionate.

erbärmlich [ɛr'bɛrmliç], *adj.* wretched, miserable; (a) (*mitleiderregend*) pitiful (appearance etc.); (b) (*sehr schlecht*) dreadful (quality etc.); (c) *F:* (*sehr groß, stark*) terrible (thirst, hunger etc.). ◆**E~keit**, *f -/no pl* pitifulness; wretchedness.

erbau|en, *v.tr.* (a) to build (sth.), erect (a building); (b) *Lit:* sich (an etwas dat) e., to be edified (by sth.). ◆**E~er**, *m -s/-* builder. ◆**e~lich**, *adj.* edifying (reading etc.). ◆**E~ung**, *f -/no pl* edification; (moral) uplift.

erbeuten [ɛr'bɔʏtən], *v.tr.* (a) *Mil:* to seize (sth.) (as booty); (b) (*Dieb usw.*) to make off with (money, jewels etc.).

erbittern [ɛr'bitərn], *v.tr.* to embitter (s.o.); (*erzürnen*) to anger (s.o.). ◆**e~t**, *adj.* (a) (*verbittert*) embittered (b); (b) stubborn (enemy, opponent); fierce (fight, battle).

erblinden [ɛr'blindən], *v.i. (sein)* to go blind.

erbos|en [ɛr'bo:zən], *v.tr.* sich über j-n, etwas *acc* e., to get angry with s.o., sth. ◆**e~t**, *adj.* angry.

er'brechen, *v.tr. & refl. & i.irr.14 (haben)* (sich) e., to vomit.

Erbse ['ɛrpsə], *f -/-n* pea.

Erd-, ['ɛɪrt-], *comb.fm.* (a) earth's (surface, curvature etc.); (axis, interior etc.) of the earth; (b) *El:* earth, *N.Am:* ground (lead/wire etc.). ◆**'E~beben**, *n* earthquake. ◆**'E~beere**, *f* strawberry. ◆**'E~boden**, *m* ground, earth. ◆**e~** ['ɛːrdə], *f -/-n* (a) earth; auf der E., on earth; auf der ganzen E., all over the world; (b) *El:* earth(-wire), *N.Am:* ground(-wire). ◆**'e~en**, *v.tr. El:* to earth, *N.Am:* ground (an appliance etc.). ◆**'E~gas**, *n* natural gas. ◆**'E~geschoß**, *n* ground/*N.Am:* first floor. ◆**'E~kunde**, *f* geography. ◆**'E~nuß**, *f* peanut. ◆**'E~öl**, *n* (mineral) oil; petroleum. ◆**'E~reich**, *n*

earth, soil. ◆**'E~rutsch**, *m* (*also Fig:*) landslide. ◆**'E~teil**, *m* continent.

er'denklich, *adj.* imaginable, conceivable; alles E~e, everything possible.

er'drosseln, *v.tr.* to choke (s.o.) to death.

er'drücken, *v.tr.* to crush, squeeze (s.o.) to death.

er'dulden, *v.tr.* to endure (pain, injustice).

er'eifern, *v.refl.* sich über etwas *acc* e., to get excited/(*zornig*) heated about sth.

er'eig|nen, *v.refl.* sich e., to occur; (*Veranstaltung*) to take place. ◆**E~nis**, *n -sses/-sse* event. ◆**e~nisreich**, *adj.* eventful.

er'fahr|en, **I.** *v.tr.&i.irr.26 (haben)* (a) to learn, discover (sth.); von etwas dat e., to hear about sth.; (b) (*erleben*) (*Pers.*) to experience (joy, sorrow), meet with (ingratitude, humiliation etc.); to suffer (a defeat, pain etc.). **II.** *adj.* experienced. ◆**E~ung**, *f -/-en* **1.** (*experience*); schlechte E~en (mit j-m, etwas dat) machen, to be let down by s.o., sth. **2.** etwas in E. bringen, to find sth. out. ◆**e~ungsgemäß**, *adv.* judging by (previous) experience.

er'fass|en, *v.tr.* (a) (*Auto usw.*) to drag (s.o.) along; *Fig:* (*Gefühle usw.*) to overcome (s.o.); (b) (*verstehen*) to grasp (sth.); (c) (*registrieren*) to list (sth.); etwas statistisch e., to make a statistical survey of sth. ◆**E~ung**, *f* **1.** inclusion. **2.** (*Ermittlung*) recording.

er'find|en, *v.tr.irr.9* to invent (a machine, *Fig:* stories etc.). ◆**E~er**, *m -s/-* inventor. ◆**e~erisch**, *adj.* inventive; (*findig*) ingenious. ◆**E~ung**, *f -/-en* invention. ◆**e~ungsgabe**, *f* inventiveness.

Erfolg [ɛr'fɔlk], *m -(e)s/-e* **1.** (*Resultat*) result, outcome; (*Wirkung*) effect. **2.** (*positives Ergebnis*) success; E. haben, to be successful; viel E.! good luck! ◆**e~los**, *adj.* unsuccessful; vain; fruitless (attempt etc.). ◆**E~losigkeit**, *f -/no pl* lack of success. ◆**e~reich**, *adj.* successful. ◆**e~versprechend**, *adj.* promising.

erforder|lich [ɛr'fɔrdərliç], *adj.* required, (*nötig*) necessary. ◆**e~n**, *v.tr.* (*Sache*) to require (money, time etc.), call for (patience, courage, quick action etc.).

er'forsch|en, *v.tr.* (a) to explore (a country etc.); (b) (*ermitteln*) to investigate (a mystery, s.o.'s motives etc.). ◆**E~ung**, *f* exploration; investigation.

er'freu|en, *v.tr.* (a) to please, delight (s.o., the eye, ear etc.); (b) sich großer Beliebtheit usw. e., to enjoy great popularity etc. ◆**e~lich**, *adj.* pleasing (sight, result etc.); gratifying (achievement); welcome (news). ◆**e~licherweise**, *adv.* fortunately, luckily. ◆**e~t**, *adj.* pleased, glad; sehr e.! pleased to meet you!

er'frieren, *v.i.irr.32 (sein)* (*Pers., Tier*) to freeze to death; (*Pflanzen*) to be killed by (the) frost; (*Finger, Zehen usw.*) to be frostbitten.

er'frisch|en, v. 1. v.tr. to refresh. ◆**e~end**, adj. refreshing. ◆**E~ung**, f /-en refreshment.

er'füll|en, v.tr. (a) to fill (a room etc.); (b) (nachkommen) to perform (a task, duty etc.), fulfil (a promise, condition etc.); **einen Zweck e.**, to serve a purpose; **sich e./erfüllt werden**, (Prophezeiung) to be fulfilled, (Traum) come true, (Hoffnung) be realized. ◆**E~ung**, f -/no pl (a) fulfilment; (Befriedigung) satisfaction; (b) performance; realization (of a wish, dream etc.).

ergänz|en [er'gentsən], v.tr. (a) to complement (s.o., sth.); **darf ich noch etwas e.?** may I add something to that? (b) (vervollständigen) to complete (a list, sentence etc.), to fill in (missing words etc.), supply (missing parts). ◆**E~ung**, f -/-en (a) no pl complementing; (Vervollständigung) completion; supplying (of missing parts, words etc.); (b) complement; (Hinzufügung) addition

er'geb|en. I. v.tr.irr.35 (a) to result in (sth.), to produce (results, proof); (Rechnung) to come to (a sum, figure); (b) **sich aus etwas dat e.**, to be the result of (sth.); (c) (Schwierigkeit usw.) **sich e.**, to arise, F: crop up; **es hat sich so e.**, it just turned out like that; (d) (Pers., Truppen) **sich e.**, to surrender. **II.** adj. 1. (a) **j-m e. sein**, to be devoted to s.o. 2. (resignierend) resigned (expression etc.). ◆**E~enheit**, f -/no pl devotion. ◆**E~nis** [er'ge:pnis], n -ses/-se result; Mth: (Lösung) solution. ◆**e~nislos**, adj. without result; inconclusive (negotiations etc.); Sp: drawn (game).

er'gehen, v.i.irr.36 (sein) (a) (Verordnung, Befehl usw.) to be issued/(Gesetz) passed; (Einladung) to be sent; **etwas über sich acc e. lassen**, to put up with sth.; (b) impers., **es ist ihm/ihr gut, schlecht usw. ergangen**, he/she got on well, badly etc.; (c) refl. **sich in Vermutungen usw. acc e.**, to indulge in (speculation) etc.

ergiebig [er'gi:biç], adj. rich (source, harvest etc.) (**an+dat**, in); productive (discussion, research etc.).

ergötzen [er'gœtsən], v.tr. to amuse, (entzücken) delight (s.o.).

er'greifen, v.tr.irr.43 (a) to seize (s.o., sth., Fig: power etc.); (festnehmen) to capture (a criminal etc.); Fig: (Furcht usw.) to overcome (s.o.); (innerlich bewegen) (Musik usw.) to move (s.o.); **Maßnahmen e.**, to adopt measures/take steps; **einen Beruf e.**, to take up a profession.

ergriffen [er'grifən], adj. moved.

er'gründen, v.tr. to get to the bottom of (sth., a mystery etc.), to seek out (the cause of sth.).

Er'guß, m 1. Med: effusion (of blood). 2. Fig: outpouring; flood (of tears, abuse).

er'haben, adj. 1. sublime, lofty (thoughts); exalted (state of mind); magnificent (sight). 2. **über jeden Verdacht usw. e.**, above suspicion etc.

Er'halt, m -(e)s/no pl receipt. ◆**e~en. I.** v.tr.irr.45 (a) (bekommen) to receive, get (sth.); to obtain (permission, access, a substance etc.); (b) to maintain (a building, roads); to keep (the peace, one's freedom etc.); to preserve (a work of art etc.); (ernähren) to support (s.o., a family etc.). **II.** adj. **gut e.**, well preserved; **e. bleiben**, to survive. ◆**E~ung**, f -/no pl maintenance, upkeep; preservation (of works of art, one's health etc.).

erhältlich [er'heltliç], adj. obtainable; **schwer e.**, difficult to obtain.

er'hängen, v.refl. **sich e.**, to hang oneself.

er'härten, v.tr. to harden; Fig: to support (a statement etc.).

er'heb|en, v.tr.irr.48 (a) to raise (one's head, voice, glass etc.); (b) to levy (a tax, toll); (c) **sich e.**, (Pers.) to rise (to one's feet), get up; Fig: (Frage, Problem usw.) to arise, F: crop up. ◆**e~lich**, adj. considerable.

erheitern [er'haitərn], v.tr. to amuse (s.o.).

erhellen [er'helən], v.tr. (a) to illuminate (a room, street etc.); **sich e.**, to grow lighter, brighten; (b) to throw light upon (a mystery etc.).

erhitzen [er'hitsən], v.tr. (a) to heat (a liquid, metal etc.); **sich e.**, to get hot; (b) (erregen) to excite (s.o., s.o.'s imagination etc.).

erhöh|en [er'hø:ən], v.tr. (a) to raise (sth.); (b) (steigern) to increase (prices, speed, Med: the dose etc.); to put up (wages etc.). ◆**E~ung**, f -/-en 1. raising. 2. increase.

er'hol|en, v.refl. **sich e.**, (a) (Patient usw.) to recover; (b) (sich ausruhen) to have a rest; (nach einer Krankheit) to convalesce. ◆**e~sam**, adj. restful, relaxing. ◆**E~ung**, f -/no pl recovery; (Periode) convalescence; (Entspannung) relaxation; (Spiel usw.) recreation. ◆**e~ungsbedürftig**, adj. in need of a rest/holiday; run down.

er'hören, v.tr. Lit: to answer (a prayer, request etc.).

Erika [e'ri:ka], f -/-ken heather.

erinner|n [er'?inərn], v.tr. (a) to remind (s.o.) (**an j-n, etwas acc**, of s.o., sth.); (b) **sich an j-n, etwas acc e.**, to remember/recall s.o., sth.; **wenn ich mich recht erinnere**, if I remember rightly. ◆**E~ung**, f -/-en (a) memory; (b) (Andenken) memento (of s.o.); souvenir (of a visit etc.).

erkält|en [er'keltən], v.tr. **sich e.**, to catch (a) cold. ◆**E~ung**, f -/-en cold.

erkenn|bar [er'kenbar], adj. (a) recognizable; (b) (mit dem Auge) e., visible. ◆**e~en**, v.tr.irr.51 (a) to recognize (s.o., s.o.'s voice, a danger etc.); to identify (s.o., sth.); (b) (wahrnehmen) to make out (s.o., sth.). ◆e~tlich, adj. sich (j-m) e. zeigen, to show one's gratitude (to s.o.). ◆E~tnis, f -/se 1. (Wissen) knowledge. 2. (Einsicht) realization, recognition; wissenschaftliche E~tnisse, scientific discoveries. ◆E~ungsdienst, m (police) records department.

Erker ['ɛrkər], m -s/- bay(-window).

erklär|en [ɛr'kleːrən], v.tr. (a) (klarmachen) to explain (sth.); (deuten) to interpret a text, dream; law etc.); (b) (äußern, bekennen) to declare (sth.); er erklärte sich bereit, es zu tun, he said he was willing to do it. ◆e~end, adj. explanatory. ◆e~lich, adj. explicable; (verständlich) understandable. ◆e~t, adj. declared (enemy etc.). ◆E~ung, f -/-en 1. explanation. 2. declaration.

er'klingen, v.i.irr.19 (sein) to sound; (Glocke, Stimme usw.) to ring out.

erkrank|en [ɛr'kraŋkən], v.i. (sein) to be taken ill/N.Am: sick. ◆E~ung, f -/-en illness.

erkunden [ɛr'kundən], v.tr. to investigate (sth.); Mil: to reconnoitre (the terrain, positions).

erkundig|en [ɛr'kundiɡən], v.refl. sich e., to enquire (nach j-m, after s.o.; nach etwas dat, about sth.). ◆E~ung, f -/-en enquiry.

er'lahmen, v.i. (sein) (Gespräch usw.) to flag.

er'langen, v.tr. to obtain (sth.), gain (access, popularity etc.).

Erlaß [ɛr'las], m -sses/-sse 1. decree. 2. exemption (+ gen, from); Jur: remission.

er'lass|en, v.tr.irr.57 (a) to issue (a decree, warrant etc.); to enact (a law); (b) to remit (debts, a punishment etc.).

erlaub|en [ɛr'laubən], v.tr. (a) (j-m) etwas e., to allow (s.o.) sth.; wenn Sie e. ..., if you don't mind ...; (b) sich dat etwas e., to take the liberty of doing sth.; wir können uns kein neues Auto e., we cannot afford a new car. ◆E~nis, f -/no pl permission.

er'läuter|n, v.tr. to elucidate (a problem etc.). ◆E~ung, f -/-en explanation.

Erle ['ɛrlə], f -/-n alder.

er'leb|en, v.tr. (a) to experience (sth.); to undergo (a change, crisis, hardship etc.); (b) (mite.) to witness (sth.); to live to see (sth., a birthday, year etc.). ◆E~nis, n -ses/-se experience.

erledigen [ɛr'leːdigən], v.tr. (a) to deal with (sth.); to get through (one's work, business etc.); to get (a job etc.) done; to settle (a matter, question, problem etc.); sich von selbst e., to take care of itself; (b) F: (vernichten) to do for (s.o.); (finanziell usw.) to ruin (s.o.); (töten) to do (s.o.) in.

erleichter|n [ɛr'laiçtərn], v. 1. v.tr. (a) to lighten (a burden etc.); (b) to relieve (s.o., pain etc.); to ease (s.o.'s conscience, pain, suffering); (c) to facilitate (a task), make (a task, life) easier.

◆e~t, adj. relieved. ◆E~ung, f -/-en relief.

er'leiden, v.tr.irr.59 to suffer (sth.).

er'lernen, v.tr. to learn (a trade, language etc.); to train for (a job).

er'lesen, adj. selected (food, wine etc.); select (company etc.); discerning (taste).

er'leuchten, v.tr. to illuminate (a room etc.). ◆E~ung, f -/-en (sudden) inspiration.

erlogen [ɛr'loːɡən], adj. false, trumpedup (story etc.).

Erlös [ɛr'løːs], m -es/-e proceeds.

er'löschen, v.i.irr.22 (sein) (a) (Feuer, Licht usw.) to go out; (b) Lit: (Liebe, Haß, Stimme usw.) to die; (c) (Vertrag usw.) to expire.

er'lös|en, v.tr. (a) to redeem (man, the human soul etc.); to release (s.o.). ◆E~ung, f -/-en (a) release, deliverance; (b) (Erleichterung) relief; (c) Ecc: redemption.

ermächtig|en [ɛr'mɛçtigən], v.tr. j-n zu etwas e., to authorize s.o. to do sth. ◆E~ung, f -/no pl authorization.

er'mahn|en, v.tr. to exhort (s.o.) (zur Vorsicht usw., to be careful etc.); (rügen) to reprimand (s.o.). ◆E~ung, f -/-en admonition; (Rüge) reprimand.

er'mäßig|en, v.tr. to reduce (prices etc.). ◆E~ung, f reduction.

er'messen, v.tr.irr.25 to assess, (berechnen) calculate (damage etc.). II. E., n -s/ no pl discretion; judgement.

ermitt|eln [ɛr'mitəln], v. 1. v.tr. to establish (facts, the truth, details etc.). 2. v.i. (haben) to investigate, make inquiries. ◆E~lung, f -/-en ascertaining; (Entdeckung) discovery; pl investigations. ◆E~lungsverfahren, n preliminary proceedings.

ermöglichen [ɛr'møːkliçən], v.tr. to make (sth.) possible (j-m, for s.o.).

er'mord|en, v.tr. to murder (s.o.), assassinate (a king, statesman). ◆E~ung, f -/-en murder; assassination.

ermüd|en [ɛr'myːdən], v. 1. v.tr. to tire (s.o.). 2. v.i. (sein) to tire, get tired (s.o.). ◆E~ung, f -/no pl tiredness, (also Tchn:) fatigue. ◆E~ungserscheinung, f sign of fatigue.

ermunter|n [ɛr'muntərn], v.tr. (a) (ermutigen) to encourage (s.o.); (b) (aufmuntern) to cheer (s.o.) up.

ermutigen [ɛr'muːtigən], v.tr. to encourage (s.o.).

er'nähr|en, v.tr. (a) to feed (s.o., sth.); (gesund halten) to nourish (s.o., sth.); sich von etwas e., (Pers.) to live on sth.; (Tier, Pflanze) to feed on sth.; (b) (unterhalten) to support (a family etc.). ◆E~er, m -s/- breadwinner. ◆E~ung, f -/no pl (a) (Ernähren) feeding, nourishment (of s.o.); esp. Med: nutrition; (b) (Kost) diet; (c) (Unterhalt) support of a family etc.).

er'nenn|en, v.tr.irr.51 to appoint (s.o.

◆E~ung, f appointment (zu + dat, as).

erneuer|n [ɛr'nɔʏərn], v.tr. (a) to renovate (a building, furniture); (b) (ersetzen) to replace (a battery, part etc.); to change (Med. a dressing, Aut: the oil etc.); to renew (a friendship, relationship etc.). ◆E~ung, f -/-en (a) renovation; (b) renewal.

erneut [ɛr'nɔʏt], adj. (a) renewed; new; (b) adv. (noch einmal) again.

erniedrig|en [ɛr'ni:drɪgən], v. 1. v.tr. (herabwürdigen) to degrade (s.o., oneself); (demütigen) to humiliate (s.o.). ◆E~ung, f -/-en degradation; humiliation.

ernst [ɛrnst]. I. adj. serious; **meinst du das e.?** do you really mean that? II. E., m -es/no pl seriousness; **es ist mein** (bitterer) **E.**, I am (quite) serious about it; **im E.?** really? honestly? ◆E~**fall**, m (case of) emergency. ◆'e~**gemeint**, adj. sincerely meant; genuine (offer, advice). ◆'e~**haft**, adj. serious. ◆'E~**haftigkeit**, f -/no pl seriousness; genuineness. ◆'e~**lich**, adj. serious; grave (fault, warning, doubts etc.).

Ernte ['ɛrntə], f -/-n (Ertrag) crop, harvest. ◆'e~n, v.tr. to harvest (a crop, corn etc.); to pick (fruit); Fig: to earn (applause, gratitude, praise).

er'nüchter|n, v.tr. to sober (s.o.) up; Fig: to bring (s.o.) down to earth; (enttäuschen) to disillusion (s.o.). ◆E~ung, f -/-en (a) sobering up; (b) Fig: disillusionment.

Erobe|er [ɛr'ʔo:bərər], m -s/- conqueror. ◆e~n, v.tr. to conquer (a country, city, Fig: s.o.'s heart etc.); to capture (a fortress, city). ◆E~ung, f -/-en Mil: & Fig: conquest; capture.

er'öffn|en, v.tr. to open; **j-m etwas e.**, to disclose sth. to s.o. ◆E~ung, f -/-en 1. opening; (feierlich) inauguration; 2. disclosure. ◆E~**ungs-**, comb.fm. opening (ceremony, speech, session etc.).

erörter|n [ɛr'ʔœrtərn], v.tr. to discuss (a case, problem etc.). ◆E~ung, f -/-en discussion.

Eroti|k [e'ro:tɪk], f -/no pl eroticism. ◆e~**sch**, adj. erotic.

erpicht [ɛr'pɪçt], adj. **ich bin nicht sehr e. darauf**, I am not very keen on it.

er'press|en, v.tr. (a) to blackmail (s.o.); (b) to extort (money, a confession etc.). ◆E~er, m -s/- blackmailer. ◆E~ung, f blackmail, extortion.

er'proben, v.tr. to test, try out (a new machine, remedy etc.); Fig: to put (s.o.'s loyalty, honesty etc.) to the test.

er'raten, v.tr.irr.13 to guess (sth.).

erreg|bar [ɛr're:kbarr], adj. excitable; (reizbar) irritable. ◆E~**barkeit**, f -/no pl excitability; irritability. ◆e~**en**, v.tr. to excite (s.o., s.o.'s senses); to arouse (envy, suspicion, sympathy, sexual desire etc.); to cause (anxiety, displeasure,

amusement etc.); **sich e.**, to get excited/worked up. ◆E~er, m -s/- cause (of a disease). ◆e~t, adj. excited; (unruhig) agitated; (zornig) heated (argument, words etc.); emotional (voice). ◆E~**theit**, f -/no pl excitement; (Unruhe) agitation. ◆E~ung, f -/no pl (state of excitement/(Unruhe) agitation.

erreich|bar [ɛr'raiçbarr], adj. (a) within reach; accessible; (b) (Ziel usw.) attainable; (c) (Pers.) available ◆e~en, v.tr. to reach (s.o., sth., a speed, place etc.); to achieve (a purpose, aim); **schwer zu e.**, difficult to get to; **j-n (telefonisch) e.**, to get through to s.o. (on the telephone).

er'richten, v.tr. to erect (a building, barricade etc.), put up (scaffolding etc.).

er'ringen, v.tr.irr.19 to gain, win (sth.) (with a struggle).

erröten [ɛr'rø:tən], v.i. (sein) to blush.

Errungenschaft [ɛr'rʊŋənʃaft], f -/-en achievement; F: (Anschaffung) acquisition.

Er'satz. I. m -es/no pl (a) replacement; substitute; (Pers.) stand-in; (b) (Entschädigung) compensation. II. E~-, comb.fm. replacement (driver, material etc.); spare (tyre, battery etc.). ◆E~**mann**, m stand-in; Sp: substitute.

ersäufen [ɛr'zɔʏfən], v.tr. F. to drown.

er'schaffen, v.tr.irr.77 Lit: to create (sth.).

er'schein|en, v.i.irr.79 (sein) to appear; (Buch, Zeitschrift) to come out. ◆E~ung, f -/-en (a) (Aussehen) appearance; (b) (Sache, Vorgang) phenomenon; (Symptom) symptom; (Gespenst) apparition; (Pers.) **eine elegante E.**, an elegant figure.

er'schießen, v.tr.irr.31 to shoot (s.o., oneself, an animal) (dead).

er'schlaffen, v.i. (sein) (Muskeln usw.) to go limp; (Haut) become flabby; (Pers., Arme usw.) to become weakened.

er'schlagen, v.tr.irr.85 to kill (s.o.).

er'schleichen, v.tr.irr.86 **sich dat etwas e.**, to obtain sth. by underhand methods.

er'schließen, v.tr.irr.31 to open up (an area, country, market etc.).

er'schöpf|en, v.tr. to exhaust (s.o., sth.). ◆e~t, adj. exhausted; (Vorräte) finished; (Geduld) at an end. ◆E~ung, f -/no pl exhaustion.

er'schrecken, v. 1. v.i.irr. (sein) (Angst bekommen) to get a scare. 2. v.tr. to alarm (s.o.), give (s.o.) a fright; (plötzlich) to startle (s.o.); F: **sich e.**, to get a fright/shock.

erschrocken [ɛr'ʃrɔkən], adj. startled, shocked.

erschütter|n [ɛr'ʃʏtərn], v.tr. to shake (a building, Fig: s.o.'s faith etc.); Fig: (Nachricht usw.) to shock/shatter (s.o.). ◆E~ung, f -/-en 1. no pl shaking. 2. (a) shock; tremor (of an earthquake); (b) (Ergriffenheit) (state of) shock.

er'schwer|en, *v.tr.* to make (sth.) more difficult, complicate (a task etc.).

er'schwindeln, *v.tr.* to get (sth.) by trickery.

erschwinglich [ɛrˈʃvɪŋlɪç], *adj.* within one's means.

ersetz|bar [ɛrˈzɛtsbaːr], *adj.* replaceable. ◆e~en, *v.tr.* (a) to replace (s.o., sth.) (durch j-n, etwas, with s.o., sth.); (b) (erstatten) to make good (damage), reimburse (expenses).

ersichtlich [ɛrˈzɪçtlɪç], *adj.* obvious.

er'spar|en, *v.tr.* j-m/sich *dat* Geld, Zeit, Mühe usw. e., to save s.o./oneself money, time, trouble etc.; j-m etwas Unangenehmes e., to spare s.o. sth. unpleasant. ◆E~nis, *f -/-se* saving (an/von etwas *dat*, of sth.); *pl* E~nisse, savings; economies.

erst [ɛrst], *adv.* (a) (*zuerst*) first; (b) (*nicht eher als*) not ... until; (c) (*nicht mehr als*) only; er ist eben e. angekommen, he has only just come; (d) (*steigernd*) wenn du e. einmal so alt bist wie ich, just wait until you're as old as I am; dann wird er e. recht böse sein, then he really will be angry. ◆E~aufführung, *f* first performance; deutsche E., German premiere. ◆E~ausgabe, *f* first edition. ◆e~'beste, *adj.* der/die/das e~e = der/die/das e~e beste. ◆e~ens, *adv.* first(ly), in the first place. ◆e~e(r, s), *num.adj.* first; (a) im e~en Stock, on the first/Am: second floor; fürs e., for the time being; in e~er Linie, first and foremost; (b) (*beste*) best; Waren e~er Wahl, top quality goods; (c) er nahm das e. beste, he took the first thing he could lay his hands on. ◆'e~malig, *adj.* first. ◆e~mals, *adv.* for the first time.

er'starren, *v.i.* (sein) (a) (*Flüssigkeit*) to solidify; (*frieren*) to freeze; (b) (*Glieder usw.*) to stiffen, (*vor Kälte*) go numb; (*Pers.*) vor Schreck erstarrt, petrified with fear.

erstatten [ɛrˈʃtatən], *v.tr.* (a) to refund, reimburse (expenses etc.); (b) Bericht e., to report.

er'staun|en I. *v.tr.* to astonish (s.o.); das erstaunt mich nicht, it doesn't surprise me. II. E., *n -s/no pl* astonishment. ◆e~lich, *adj.* astonishing.

er'stechen, *v.tr.irr.14* to stab (s.o.) to death.

er'stehen, *v.tr.irr.100* etwas billig e., to pick sth. up cheap.

er'stick|en, *v.* 1. *v.tr.* (a) to suffocate (s.o.); *Fig:* to stifle (a sound, laugh etc.); to smother (flames). 2. *v.i.* (sein) to suffocate; *F:* ich ersticke in Arbeit, I'm up to my neck in work. ◆E~ung, *f -/no pl* suffocation.

er'streben, *v.tr. Lit:* to strive for (sth.). ◆e~swert, *adj.* desirable; worthwhile (goal).

er'strecken, *v.refl.* sich e., (*Gebiet*) to stretch; sich auf j-n, etwas *acc* e., to in-

clude, (*Gespräch usw.*) cover (s.o., sth.); (*Vorschrift*) to apply to s.o., sth.

er'suchen. I. *v.tr.* j-n um etwas *acc* e., to request sth. from s.o. II. E., *n -s/-* (*formal*) request.

er'tappen [ɛrˈtapən], *v.tr.* to catch (s.o.).

er'teilen, *v.tr.* to grant (permission etc.); to place (an order).

er'tönen [ɛrˈtøːnən], *v.i.* (sein) to be heard; (*Sirene usw.*) to sound, (*Schuß, Schrei*) ring out.

Ertrag [ɛrˈtraːk], *m -(e)s/-e* Agr: yield; Min: output; (b) (*Gewinn*) return(s), profit. ◆E~s-, *comb.fm.* profit (situation, tax etc.).

er'tragen, *v.tr.irr.85* to stand (s.o., sth.), bear (pain, suffering etc.).

erträglich [ɛrˈtrɛːklɪç], *adj.* bearable.

er'tränken, *v.tr.* to drown.

er'träumen, *v.tr.* sich *dat* etwas e., to dream of/imagine sth.

er'trinken, *v.i.irr.96* (sein) to drown.

er'übrigen, *v.tr.* (a) to spare (money, time); (b) sich e., to be superfluous.

er'wachen, *v.i.* (sein) to awake; *Fig:* (*Gefühle usw.*) to be aroused.

er'wachsen. I. *v.i.irr.107* (sein) to arise. II. *adj.* grown-up (behaviour etc.). ◆e~e(r), *m & f decl. as adj.* adult.

erwäg|en [ɛrˈvɛːɡən], *v.tr.irr.* to consider (sth., whether ...), think (sth.) over. ◆E~ung, *f -/-en* consideration; etwas in E. ziehen, to take sth. into consideration.

erwähn|en [ɛrˈvɛːnən], *v.tr.* to mention. ◆e~enswert, *adj.* worth mentioning. ◆E~ung, *f -/-en* mention(ing).

er'wärmen, *v.tr.* to warm up (a room, liquid etc.); *Fig:* sich für j-n, etwas *acc* e., to warm to s.o., sth.

er'wart|en, *v.tr.* (a) (*rechnen mit*) to expect (s.o., sth., a baby); wider E., contrary to expectation; (b) (*warten auf*) to wait for (s.o., sth.). ◆E~ung, *f -/-en* expectation. ◆e~ungsvoll, *adj.* expectant.

er'wecken, *v.tr. Lit:* to awaken, arouse (s.o., *Fig:* interest, emotions etc.).

er'weichen, *v.tr. & i.* (sein) to soften.

er'weisen, *v.tr.irr.70* (a) to prove (s.o.'s innocence etc.); (b) j-m einen Dienst, ein Gefallen usw. e., to do s.o. a service, favour etc.

Erwerb [ɛrˈvɛrp], *m -s/no pl* (a) (*Gewerbe*) livelihood; (b) (*Aneignung*) acquisition; (*Kauf*) purchase. ◆e~en [-'bən], *v.tr.irr.101* to acquire, (*durch Kauf*) purchase (sth.); *Fig:* (*gewinnen*) to win (fame, respect etc.). ◆e~sfähig, *adj.* (*Pers.*) capable of gainful employment. ◆e~slos, *adj.* unemployed. ◆e~stätig, *adj.* (gainfully) employed.

erwider|n [ɛrˈviːdərn], *v.tr. & i.* (haben) (a) to answer; to reply; (b) to return (a greeting, feeling, visit, *Mil:* fire etc.). ◆E~ung, *f -/-en* 1. answer; reply; (*scharf*) retort. 2. return (of a feeling

etc.).

er'wischen, v.tr. F: to catch (s.o., a thief, a bus etc.); **es hat sie erwischt**, (i) (krank) she's got it; (ii) (tot) she's died; (iii) (verliebt) she's got it bad.

erwünscht [ɛr'vynʃt], adj. desired (effect).

erwürgen, v.tr. to strangle (s.o.).

Erz¹ [ɛrts], n -es/-e ore.

'Erz-, e~-❤️, comb.fm. (a) (Rang) arch(diocese etc.); (b) (steigernd) arch-(conservative etc.); complete, utter (fool etc.).

er'zähl|en, 1. v.tr. to tell (a story etc.), give an account of (an event). 2. v.i. (haben) **er kann gut e.**, he is good at telling stories. ◆**e~end**, adj. narrative (poem, style etc.). ◆**E~er**, m -s/- narrator. ◆**E~ung**, f -/-en story, tale.

er'zeug|en, v.tr. to generate (warmth, electricity, Fig: ideas, feelings); to produce (goods, Fig: an effect etc.); Fig: to engender (interest, hatred etc.); to create (tension etc.). ◆**E~er**, m -s/- (Hersteller) producer. ◆**E~nis**, n product. ◆**E~ung**, f generation; esp. Agr: production; Ind: manufacture.

er'zieh|en, v.tr.irr.113 (in der Familie) to bring up, Sch: educate (a child); **streng erzogen werden**, to have a strict upbringing. ◆**e~erisch**, adj. educational. ◆**E~ung**, f -/no pl upbringing; (Bildung) education; (Schulung) training. ◆**E~ungs-**, comb.fm. educational (system, problem etc.); (method etc.) of upbringing. ◆**E~ungsberechtigte(r)**, m & f decl. as adj. parent or guardian.

er'ziel|en, v.tr. to achieve (success, unanimity, a result etc.); Com: to realize (a profit, price); Sp: to score (a goal).

er'zwingen, v.tr.irr.19 **Geld/ein Versprechen von j-m e.**, to extort money/exact a promise from s.o. (by force); **sich dat Zutritt in ein Gebäude e.**, to force one's way into a building.

es [ɛs], pron. it. 1. subject pron. (Sache, Tier) it; (Kind) he; she. 2. object pron. (a) it; (Kind) him; her.

Esche ['ɛʃə], f -/-n ash (tree).

Esel ['eːzəl], m -s/- 1. donkey; ass. 2. F: fool, ass. ◆**E~sbrücke**, f (Gedächtnis-stütze) mnemonic; Sch: crib. ◆**E~sohr**, n Fig: **Buch mit E~sohren**, dog-eared book.

Eskalation [ɛskalatsi'oːn], f -/-en escalation. ◆**e~'lieren**, v.tr.&i. (haben) to escalate (a war etc.).

Eskimo ['ɛskimo], m -(s)/-(s) Eskimo.

Eß- ['ɛs-], comb.fm. (a) eating (habits etc.); (b) dining (room etc.). ◆**'eßbar**, adj. edible; **noch e.**, still fit to eat/ eatable. ◆**'Eßkastanie**, f sweet chestnut. ◆**'Eßlöffel**, m tablespoon.

ess|en ['ɛsən], 1. v.tr. & i.irr. (haben) to eat; **zu Mittag/Abend e.**, to have lunch/ supper; **wollen wir e. gehen?** shall we go out for a meal? II. E., n -s/- 1. no pl eat-

ing. 2. (Nahrung) food. 3. (Mahlzeit) meal; (offizielles E.) dinner. ◆**'E~en(s)marke**, f meal ticket/ coupon. ◆**E~enszeit**, f mealtime.

Essenz [ɛ'sɛnts], f -/-en essence.

Essig ['ɛsiç], m -s/-e vinegar. ◆**'E~gurke**, f (pickled) gherkin.

Estragon ['ɛstragɔn], m -s/no pl tarragon.

etabl|ieren [eta'bliːrən], v.tr. to establish, set up (a business etc.); **sich e.**, (Pers.) to establish oneself, Com: set up in business. ◆**e~iert**, adj. (well-)established (firm etc.).

Etage [e'taːʒə], f -/-n storey, floor; **auf der dritten E.**, on the third/N.Am: fourth floor. ◆**E~nbett**, n bunk bed. ◆**E~nwohnung**, f (self-contained) flat/N.Am: apartment (in a block).

Etappe [e'tapə], f -/-n stage (of a journey etc.); Sp: stage, leg (of a race). ◆**e~nweise**, adv. by stages.

Etat [e'taː], m -s/-s budget. ◆**E~jahr**, n financial year.

etepetete [eːtəpe'teːtə], adj. F: (penibel) pernickety; (geziert) ladida.

Eth|ik ['eːtik], f -/-en (a) no pl ethics; (b) (Lehre) ethic. ◆**'e~isch**, adj. ethical.

Etikett [eti'kɛt], n -(e)s-e label; (Preis-schild) price tag/ticket. ◆**e~ieren** [-'tiːrən], v.tr. to label (sth., Fig: s.o.).

etliche(r,s) ['ɛtliçə(r,s)], indef.pron. some; pl several. ◆**e~s**, a number of things.

Etui [ɛt'viː], n -s/-s (spectacles/cigarette) case.

etwa ['ɛtva], adv. 1. (ungefähr) approximately; **in e. drei Tagen**, in about three days. 2. (a) (zum Beispiel) **Länder wie e. Indien**, countries such as India (for example); (b) (verstärkend) **er ist doch nicht e. krank?** he isn't ill by any chance? **nicht e., daß ich Angst hatte,** not that I was afraid. ◆**e~ig** ['ɛtvaːç)iç], adj. possible.

etwas ['ɛtvas]. I. indef.pron. something; (in Fragen und Verneinungen) anything; **nimm dir e. davon,** have some (of it). II. indef.adj. (a) some; **sie kann e. Englisch,** she knows some English; (b) adv. a little; **e. schwierig,** rather difficult; F: **ich will noch e. arbeiten,** I want to do a bit more work.

euch [ɔyç]. 1. pers.pron. (acc & dat of ihr) you; **wie geht es e.?**(in letter) E.? how are you? 2. refl.pron. **wascht e.,** wash yourselves.

euer ['ɔyər], poss.adj. your. ◆**eu(e)re(r,s)** ['ɔyrə(r,s)], poss.pron. yours; **ist das eu(e)res?** is that yours/ your kind.

Eule ['ɔylə], f -/-n owl.

eur|e(r,s) ['ɔyrə(r,s)], see eu(e)r, eure(r,s). ◆**e~erseits**, adv. on your part. ◆**e~esgleichen**, pron. (people of) your kind. ◆**e~etwegen/um e~etwillen**, adv. for your sake; because of you.

Europ|a [ɔy'roːpa]. I. n -s/no pl Europe.

II. **E~a~,** comb.fm. European (Pol: Parliament, Sp: champion etc.). ◆**E~äer** ['ro:pɛːər], m ‑s/‑ European. ◆**e~äisch,** adj. European; **die E~äische Gemeinschaft,** the European Community.

Euter ['ɔytər], n ‑s/‑ udder.

evakuier|en [evaku'iːrən], v.tr. to evacuate (s.o., an area etc.). ◆**E~ung,** f ‑/ ‑en evacuation.

evangel|isch [evaŋ'geːliʃ], adj. Protestant (church etc.). ◆**E~ium** [‑'geːlium], n ‑s/‑ien gospel.

eventuell [evɛntu'ɛl], adj. (a) possible; (b) adv. (vielleicht) perhaps.

ewig ['eːviç], adj. **1.** (a) eternal (life, truth, love etc.); everlasting (peace, joy etc.). **2.** F: (ständig) continual; (endlos) endless; **das dauert ja e. (lange)!** this is taking ages! ◆**E~keit,** f ‑/‑en eternity.

exakt [ɛ'ksakt], adj. exact.

Examen [ɛ'ksaːmən], n ‑s/‑ & ‑mina examination; F: exam.

Exemplar [ɛksɛm'plaːr], n ‑s/‑e (a) specimen; (b) copy of a paper, book etc.). ◆**e~isch,** adj. (beispielhaft) exemplary; representative.

exerzieren [ɛksɛr'tsiːrən], v.i. (haben) to drill.

Exil [ɛ'ksiːl], n ‑s/‑e exile; **im E.,** in exile.

Existenz [ɛksis'tɛnts], f ‑/‑en **1.** (Leben, Dasein usw.) existence; **es geht um die nackte E.,** it's a matter of life and death. **2.** (Lebensgrundlage) livelihood. **3.** Pej: **dunkle E~en,** shady characters; **verkrachte/gescheiterte E.,** failure. ◆**E~kampf,** m fight for survival. ◆**E~minimum,** n subsistence level; (Gehalt) living wage.

existieren [ɛksis'tiːrən], v.i. (haben) to exist; (leben) to subsist (von + dat, on).

exklusiv [ɛksklu'ziːf], adj./**E~,** comb.fm. (a) sole (rights etc.); (b) (vornehm) select (hotel, party etc.). ◆**e~e** ['‑ziːvə], prep. + gen esp. Com: excluding.

Exot(e) [ɛ'ksoːt(ə)], m ‑en/‑en exotic person/plant/animal. ◆**e~isch,** adj.

exotic.

Expansion [ɛkspanzi'oːn], f ‑/‑en expansion. ◆**E~spolitik,** f expansionist policy.

Expedition [ɛkspediti'oːn], f ‑/‑en expedition.

Experiment [ɛksperi'mɛnt], n ‑(e)s/‑e experiment (an + dat, on). ◆**e~ell** [‑'tɛl], adj. experimental. ◆**e~ieren** [‑'tiːrən], v.i. (haben) to experiment.

Experte [ɛks'pɛrtə], n ‑n/‑n expert.

explo|dieren [ɛksplo'diːrən], v.i. (sein) to explode; (Kessel usw.) to burst. ◆**E~sion** [‑zi'oːn], f ‑/‑en explosion; **zur E. bringen,** to detonate (a bomb etc.). ◆**e~siv** [‑'ziːf], adj. (also Fig:) explosive.

Export [ɛks'pɔrt], m ‑(e)s/‑e **1.** no pl export(ing). **2.** exports. ◆**E~eur** [‑'tøːr], m ‑s/‑e exporter. ◆**e~ieren** [‑'tiːrən], v.tr. to export (goods etc.). ◆**E~kaufmann,** m export salesman. ◆**E~land,** n exporting country.

Expreßgut [ɛks'prɛsguːt], n Rail: express parcel(s); N.Am: fast freight.

Expression|ismus [ɛksprɛsio'nismus], m ‑/no pl expressionism.

extern [ɛks'tɛrn], adj. external.

extra ['ɛkstra]. **I.** adv. **1.** (a) (gesondert) separately; (b) (eigens) especially; (absichtlich) **das hast du e. gemacht,** you did that on purpose. **2.** (zusätzlich) extra; **e. stark,** extra strong. **II.** inv.adj. additional; extra. ◆**E~blatt,** n extra (edition).

Extrakt [ɛks'trakt], m ‑e(s)‑e extract.

extravagant [ɛkstrava'gant], adj. flamboyant; (ausgefallen) outlandish (person, clothes, taste etc.); far-fetched (idea).

extrem [ɛks'treːm]. **I.** adj. extreme. **II. E~,** n ‑(e)s/‑e extreme.

extrovertiert [ɛkstrover'tiːrt], adj. extrovert.

Exzellenz [ɛkstsɛ'lɛnts], f ‑/‑en Seine/Eure E., His/Your Excellency.

exzentrisch [ɛks'tsɛntriʃ], adj. eccentric.

Exzeß [ɛks'tsɛs], m ‑zesses/‑zesse excess.

F

F, f [ɛf], n ‑/‑ (the letter) F, f.

Fabel ['faːbəl], f ‑/‑n fable; (unglaubliche Geschichte) yarn. ◆**f~haft,** adj. F: fabulous. ◆**F~tier,** n mythical beast.

Fabrik [fa'briːk], f ‑/‑en factory. **II. F~,** comb.fm. factory (worker, owner etc.). ◆**F~ant** [fabri'kant], m ‑en/‑en (a) factory owner; (b) (Hersteller) manufacturer. ◆**F~at** [‑'kaːt], n ‑(e)s/‑e make. ◆**F~ation** [‑katsi'oːn], f ‑/no pl manufacture. ◆**F~gelände,** n factory site. ◆**f~neu,** adj. brand new.

fabrizieren [fabri'tsiːrən], v.tr. F: to concoct.

Fach [fax]. **I.** n ‑(e)s/⸚er **1.** compartment (of a drawer etc.). **2.** (a) Sch: etc: subject; (b) Com: field; line (of business etc.); **ein Meister seines F~es,** a master of his trade; **ein Mann vom F.,** an expert (on the subject). **II. F~,** comb.fm. specialist (bookshop, literature etc.); (beruflich) professional (training etc.); (technisch) technical (jargon etc.). ◆**F~arbeiter,** m skilled worker. ◆**F~arzt,** m/ ◆**F~ärztin,** f specialist (doctor). ◆**F~ausdruck,** m technical term. ◆**F~bereich,** m subject area. ◆**F~hochschule,** f technical/training college. ◆**f~kundig,** adj. expert, with expert knowledge. ◆**f~lich,** adj. technical; (*beruflich*) professional; **f. qualifiziert**, qualified in one's subject. ◆'**F~mann**, *m* expert (**für** + *acc*, on; **auf diesem Gebiet**, in this field). **f~männisch**, *adj.* expert (advice etc.). ◆'**F~schule**, *f* vocational school. ◆'**f~simpeln**, *v.i.* (*haben*) *F:* to talk shop. ◆'**F~welt**, *f* **die F.**, the profession; *Com:* the trade. ◆'**F~werkhaus**, *n* half-timbered house.

fäch|eln ['fɛçəln], *v.tr.* to fan (s.o., sth.). ◆'**F~er**, *m* -s/- fan.

Fackel ['fakəl], *f* /-n torch.

fad(e) [fɑːt(də)], *adj.* (*a*) tasteless, insipid (food, drink); (*b*) *F:* boring.

Faden ['fɑːdən], *m* -s/- thread; *Fig:* **den F. verlieren**, to lose the thread. ◆'**F~nudeln**, *fpl* vermicelli. ◆'**f~scheinig**, *adj.* threadbare (garment); flimsy (excuse).

Fagott [fa'gɔt], *n* -(e)s/-e bassoon.

fähig ['fɛːiç], *adj.* (*a*) capable (**zu etwas** *dat*, of sth.); (*b*) able, competent (teacher etc.). ◆'**F~keit**, *f* /-en ability.

fahl [fɑːl], *adj.* pale (light etc.); pallid (complexion etc.).

fahnd|en ['fɑːndən], *v.i.* (*haben*) (*Polizei usw.*) **nach j-m, etwas** *dat* **f.**, to search/ hunt for s.o., sth. ◆'**F~ung**, *f* /-en search, hunt (**nach** + *dat*, for). ◆'**F~ungsaktion**, *f* manhunt. ◆'**F~ungsliste**, *f* wanted list.

Fahne ['fɑːnə], *f* /-n (*a*) flag; (*b*) (*Rauchf.*) trail; *F:* **er hat eine F.**, his breath reeks of drink. ◆'**F~nflucht**, *f* desertion. ◆'**F~nmast**, *m*/ '**F~nstange**, *f* flagpole.

Fahr|ausweis ['fɑːrausvais], *m* ticket. ◆'**F~bahn**, *f* /-en carriageway; (*Straße*) roadway. ◆'**f~bereit**, *adj.* in running order. ◆'**f~en**, *v.irr.* 1. *v.i.* (*sein*) (*a*) to travel, go; *Aut:* to drive; **mit der Bahn/dem Auto f.**, to go by train/car; **er fährt mit meinem Rad**, he's riding my bicycle; **das Auto fährt gut schlecht**, the car is running well/badly; (*b*) (*abfahren*) **wir f. morgen**, we're going/leaving tomorrow; (*c*) **sich** *dat* **mit der Hand durch das Haar f.**, to run one's fingers through one's hair; *F:* **was ist denn in dich gefahren?** what's got/ *N.Am:* gotten into you? 2. *v.tr.* to drive (s.o., a car etc.); to ride (a bicycle etc.); **das Auto fährt sich gut**, this car is a pleasure to drive. ◆'**F~er(in)**, *m* -s/- (*f* /-nen) driver. ◆'**F~erflucht**, *f* /-no *pl* failure to stop (after an accident); **im Fall von F.**, a case of hit-and-run driving. ◆'**F~gast**, *m* passenger. ◆'**F~geld**, *n* fare. ◆'**F~gelegenheit**, *f* means of transport. ◆'**F~gestell**, *n* 1. *Aut:* chassis. 2. *Av:* undercarriage. ◆'**f~ig**, *adj.* (*geistig*) dithering; (*physisch*) fidgety. ◆'**F~karte**, *f* ticket. ◆'**F~kartenausgabe**, *f*/'**F~kartenschalter**, *m* ticket office. ◆'**f~lässig**, *adj.* careless; *Jur:* negligent; **f~lässige**

Tötung, manslaughter. ◆'**F~lässigkeit**, *f* /-en carelessness; *Jur:* negligence. ◆'**F~lehrer**, *m* driving instructor. ◆'**F~plan**, *m* timetable. ◆'**f~planmäßig**, *adj.* scheduled (service); (*departure*) as scheduled. ◆'**F~preis**, *m* fare. ◆'**F~prüfung**, *f* driving test. ◆'**F~rad**, *n* bicycle. ◆'**F~radweg**, *m* cycle track. ◆'**F~schein**, *m* ticket. ◆'**F~schule**, *f* driving school. ◆'**F~schüler(in)**, *m* (*f*) learner driver. ◆'**F~spur**, *f* traffic lane. ◆'**F~stuhl**, *m* lift, *N.Am:* elevator. ◆'**F~stunde**, *f* driving lesson. ◆'**F~t**, *f* /-en journey, trip; (*im Auto*) drive; **eine F. ins Blaue**, a mystery tour; **in voller F.**, (going) at full speed, flat out. ◆'**F~trichtung**, *f* direction of travel. ◆'**f~tüchtig**, *adj.* (*a*) (person) fit to drive; (*b*) roadworthy (vehicle). ◆'**F~verbot**, *n* driving ban; loss of one's licence. ◆'**F~wasser**, *n* *Nau:* channel, fairway; *Fig:* **in seinem/im richtigen F. sein**, to be in one's element. ◆'**F~zeug**, *n* vehicle. ◆'**F~zeugpapiere**, *npl* (vehicle) registration papers.

Fähr|mann ['fɛːrman], *m* ferryman. ◆'**F~schiff**, *n* ferry (boat). ◆'**F~e**, *f* /-n ferry.

Fährte ['fɛːrtə], *f* /-n (*a*) trail; (*b*) *Fig:* **auf der falschen F.**, on the wrong track.

Faible ['fɛːbəl], *n* -s/-s *F:* soft spot; weakness.

fair [fɛːr], *adj.* fair. ◆'**F~neß**, *f* /-no *pl* fairness.

Fakten ['faktən], *pl* facts, data.

Faktor ['faktɔr], *m* -s/-en [-'toːrən] factor.

Fakultät [fakul'tɛːt], *f* /-en faculty.

Falke ['falkə], *m* -n/-n hawk, *esp.* falcon. ◆'**F~njagd**, *f* hawking.

Fall [fal], *m* -(e)s/-e 1. fall; *Fig:* **j-n zu F. bringen**, to bring about s.o.'s downfall. 2. *esp. Med: Jur:* case; **auf jeden F./alle F~e**, in any case; whatever happens; **auf keinen F.**, under no circumstances; **im F~(e) eines Brandes**, in the event of a fire; **das ist nicht mein F.**, it's not my cup of tea; **klarer F.!** sure thing! ◆'**F~beil**, *n* guillotine. ◆'**F~e**, *f* /-n trap; **in die F. gehen**, to fall into the trap. ◆'**f~en**, *v.i.irr.* (*sein*) (*a*) to fall; **sich aufs Bett f. lassen**, to fall/drop onto the bed; **etwas f. lassen**, to drop sth.; **das fällt unter diese Kategorie**, that comes in this category; (*b*) **er ist im 2. Weltkrieg gefallen**, he was killed in the Second World War; (*c*) **die Entscheidung ist gefallen**, the decision has been made. ◆'**f~enlassen**, *v.tr.sep.irr.51* to drop (a subject, plan, friend, remark etc.). ◆'**F~grube**, *f* pit; *Fig:* pitfall. ◆'**F~obst**, *n* windfalls. ◆'**F~schirm**, *m* parachute. ◆'**F~schirmjäger**, *m* paratrooper. ◆'**F~schirmspringer**, *m* parachutist. ◆'**F~strick**, *m* snare; *Fig:* trap, pitfall. ◆'**F~tür**, *f* trapdoor.

fällen ['fɛlən], v.tr. (a) to fell, cut down (a tree); (b) **ein Urteil f.,** to pass judgement.

fällig ['fɛliç], adj. due; **der f~e Betrag,** the amount due; **schon längst f.,** long overdue; ◆'**F~keit,** f -/no pl Fin: maturity.

falsch [falʃ], adj. (unecht) false (teeth, friend, modesty, smile etc.); imitation, F: fake (jewellery etc.); forged (banknotes etc.); assumed (name); (b) (nicht korrekt) wrong; mis-; **wir sind hier f. (ge-gangen),** we've gone the wrong way; **etwas f. verstehen,** to misunderstand sth. ◆'**F~geld,** n counterfeit money. ◆'**F~heit,** f -/no pl (an insincerity; (b) falsity (of statement etc.). ◆'**F~meldung,** f false report. ◆'**F~spieler,** m cheat.

fälschen ['fɛlʃən], v.tr. to forge. ◆'**f~lich,** adj. wrong. ◆'**f~licher-'weise,** adv. by mistake. ◆'**F~ung,** f -/-en forgery.

Faltblatt ['faltblat], n folder, leaflet. ◆'**F~e,** f -/-n (a) fold (in material, paper etc.); pleat (in a skirt); crease (in trousers etc.); (b) line, wrinkle (in a face). ◆'**f~en,** v.tr. (a) to fold; (b) sich f., to form wrinkles. ◆'**f~enlos,** adj. (a) (Rock) straight; (b) (Gesicht usw.) smooth. ◆'**F~enrock,** m pleated skirt. ◆'**f~ig,** adj. (a) Cl: pleated; (b) (zerknittert) creased; (c) wrinkled (skin).

Falter ['faltər], m -s/- moth.

Falz [falts], m -es/-e fold (in paper), (metal) joint.

familiär [famili'ɛːr], adj. family (worries etc.); **aus f~en Gründen,** for family reasons.

Familie [fa'miːliə], f -/-n family; **er hat F.,** he has children; **zur F. gehören,** to be one of the family. ◆**F~n-,** comb.fm. family (event, planning, life, grave, etc.). ◆**F~nangehörige(r),** m & f decl. as adj. member of a/the family. ◆**F~nbetrieb,** m family business. ◆**F~nkreis,** m family circle; **f~nname,** m surname. ◆**F~noberhaupt,** n head of the family. ◆**F~npackung,** f family size/pack. ◆**F~nstand,** m marital status. ◆**F~nvater,** m family man.

famos [fa'moːs], adj. F: marvellous.

Fan [fɛn], m -s/-s fan.

Fanatiker [fa'naːtikər], m fanatic. ◆**f~isch** [-'naːtiʃ], adj. fanatical.

Fanfare [fan'faːrə], f -/-n fanfare.

Fang [faŋ], m -(e)s/-e 1. no pl (a) capture (of an animal); catching (of fish); (b) (Beute) catch; **ein guter F.,** a good catch. 2. (a) Z: fang; (b) Orn: talon. ◆**f~en,** v.tr.irr. to catch (s.o., sth., an animal etc.); to capture (an animal, a prisoner, soldier etc.); **sich f.,** (i) to get caught; (ii) (beim Fallen) to regain one's balance; Fig: to regain one's composure; ◆'**F~frage,** f trick question.

fantastisch [fan'tastiʃ], adj. fantastic.

Farb- ['farp-], comb.fm. (a) colour (photograph, film, print, etc.); (b) paint (pot etc.). ◆**F~band,** n typewriter ribbon. ◆'**f~e** ['-bə], f -/-n 1. colour; 2. (Kartenspiel) suit; **F. bekennen,** to follow suit; Fig: to put one's cards on the table. 3. (Malerf.) paint; (Farbstoff) dye. ◆'**f~echt,** adj. colour-fast. ◆'**f~enblind,** adj. colour-blind. ◆'**f~enfroh,** adj. colourful. ◆'**f~enprächtig,** adj dazzlingly colourful. ◆'**F~fernsehen,** n colour television. ◆'**f~ig** ['-biç], adj (a) coloured (glass etc.); (b) colourful (shirt, scene etc.); (c) coloured (people); **ein F~iger/ eine F~ige,** a coloured man/woman. ◆'**F~kasten,** m box of paints. ◆'**f~los,** adj. colourless. ◆'**F~losigkeit,** f -/no pl colourlessness. ◆'**F~stift,** m crayon. ◆'**F~stoff,** m dye; (in Lebensmitteln) colouring. ◆'**F~ton,** m tone, shade (of a colour).

färben ['fɛrbən], v.tr. to dye (material, hair etc.); to colour (a picture etc.). ◆'**F~ung,** f -/-en colouring; (Nuance) tinge; (Tendenz) slant.

Farce ['farsə], f -/-n Th: & Fig: farce.

Farm [farm], f -/-en farm. ◆**F~er,** m -s/- farmer.

Farn [farn], m -(e)s/-e/**F~kraut,** n fern; bracken.

Fasan [fa'zaːn], m -(e)s/-e(n) pheasant.

Fasching ['faʃiŋ], m -s/-e carnival.

Faschismus [fa'ʃismus], m -/no pl fascism. ◆**F~t,** m -en/-en fascist. ◆**f~tisch,** adj. fascist.

faseln ['faːzəln], v.tr. & i. (haben) (Pers.) F: to blather, spout nonsense.

Faser ['faːzər], f -/-n fibre. ◆'**f~ig,** adj. fibrous; stringy (meat). ◆'**f~n,** v.i. (haben) to fray; (Holz) to splinter.

Faß [fas], n -sses/-sser barrel; drum (for tar, oil); (butter) churn; (fermentation vat; **Bier vom F.,** draught beer. ◆'**F~bier,** n draught beer.

Fassade [fa'saːdə], f -/-n facade.

faßbar [fas'baːr], adj. (a) (begreiflich) comprehensible; (b) tangible (reason, result).

fassen ['fasən], v.tr. (a) to take hold of, grasp (s.o., sth.); (mit Gewalt) to seize (s.o., sth.); (Polizei) to catch, capture (s.o.); (b) **sich f.,** to get a hold of oneself; **einen Entschluß f.,** to make a decision; **sich kurz f.,** to express oneself concisely; (c) (begreifen) to grasp, comprehend (sth.); **sie kann es noch immer nicht f.,** she still can't take it in; (d) to set, mount (a jewel); (e) to hold (a quantity of sth., people). ◆'**F~ung,** f -/-en 1. (a) mount (of a lens etc.); setting (of a jewel); (b) frame (for spectacles); (c) El: socket. 2. (Form) version (of a work, book etc.); draft (of a document); (Formulierung) wording, phrasing. 3. (Ruhe) composure; **die F. bewahren/verlieren,**

to keep/lose one's head. ◆'f~ungslos, adj. speechless; (außer sich) beside oneself (vor + dat, with). ◆'F~ungsvermögen, n -s/- 1. capacity. 2. Fig: (powers of) comprehension.

Fasson [fa'sõ:], f /-s 1. Cl: etc: style, cut; etwas nach seiner F. tun, to do sth. in one's own way. ◆F~schnitt, m fully-styled (hair)cut.

fast [fast], adv. nearly, almost; f. keins, hardly any.

fasten ['fastən], v.i. (haben) to fast. ◆'F~enzeit, f Lent. ◆'F~nacht, f -/no pl (a) Shrove Tuesday; (b) (Karnevalszeit) carnival.

Faszin|ation [fastsinatsi'o:n], f -/no pl fascination. ◆f~ieren [-'ni:rən], v.tr. to fascinate.

fatal [fa'ta:l], adj. awkward (question, situation); embarrassing (consequences etc.); fatal, disastrous (tendency etc.).

fauchen ['fauxən], v.i. (haben) to spit, hiss.

faul [faul], adj. 1. (a) (schlecht) bad; rotten (fruit, egg etc.); stale (air); f. riechen, to smell rotten/foul; (b) Fig: f~e Ausrede, poor/lame excuse; hier ist etwas f~, there's something fishy about this. 2. (untätig) lazy. ◆'f~en, v.i. (haben) (Gemüse, Fleisch usw.) to rot; (Zähne usw.) to decay; (Leiche) to decompose. ◆f~enzen ['faulɛntsən], v.i. (haben) to laze about. ◆'F~enzer, m -s/- lazybones. ◆'F~heit, f no pl laziness, idleness. ◆'F~pelz, m F: lazybones. ◆'F~tier, n 1. Z: sloth. 2. F: lazybones.

Fäul|e ['fɔʏlə], f -/no pl decay. ◆'F~nis, f -/no pl rot, decay.

Faust [faust], f -/-e fist; Fig: auf eigene F. handeln, to do sth. off one's own bat. ◆'F~handschuh, m mitten. ◆'F~regel, f rule of thumb. ◆'F~schlag, m punch.

Favorit(in) [favo'ri:t(in)], m -en/-en (f /-nen) favourite.

Faxen ['faksən] fpl antics.

Fazit ['fa:tsit], n -s/-e & -s net result.

Februar ['fe:bruar], m -(s)/-e February.

fecht|en ['fɛçtən]. I. v.i.irr. (haben) to fence. II. F., n -s/no pl fencing. ◆'F~er(in), m -s/- (f /-nen) fencer.

Feder ['fe:dər]. I. f -/-n 1. (a) feather; f~n lassen müssen, to suffer in the process; (b) (Schreibgerät) pen. 2. Tchn: spring. II. 'F~, comb.fm. (a) feather (pillow etc.); plumed (hat etc.); (b) pen(-holder etc.); Tchn: spring (tension etc.). ◆'F~ball, m badminton. ◆'F~bett, n feather bed. ◆'f~führend, adj. in charge. ◆'f~leicht, adj light as a feather. ◆'f~n, v.i. (haben) to spring, (Ball usw.) bounce. ◆'F~strich, m stroke of the pen. ◆'F~ung, f /-en springs; Aut: suspension. ◆'F~vieh, n F: poultry. ◆'F~waage, f spring balanced.

Fee [fe:], f -/-n fairy.

Fege|feuer ['fe:gə-], n -s/no pl purgatory. ◆'f~n, v.tr. to sweep (the floor, chimney etc.); to sweep (up/away) (snow, leaves etc.).

Fehde ['fe:də], f -/-n feud.

fehl [fe:l]. I. adj. f. am Platz(e), out of place. II. 'F~, f~, comb.fm. wrong (diagnosis, decision etc.); false (Sp: start etc.); invalid (Sp: jump, throw etc.); mis(calculation etc.). ◆'F~anzeige, f /-n E: (Antwort) negative. ◆'F~betrag, m deficit; (gegenüber dem Geplanten) shortfall. ◆'f~en, v.i. (haben) (a) to be missing; Sch: er fehlt seit einer Woche, he has been away/absent for a week; (b) es fehlt an Geld, Lehrern, usw., there's a shortage/lack of money, teachers etc.; ihm fehlt jedes Feingefühl, he has no tact at all; (c) F: was fehlt Ihnen? what is the matter with you? (d) sein Auto fehlt ihm, he badly misses his car; das hat mir gerade noch gefehlt! that's all I needed! ◆'f~end, adj. missing; (Pers.) absent. ◆'F~er, m -s/- 1. mistake Sp: fault. 2. defect (in goods, a material etc.); körperliche F~, physical defects. ◆'f~erfrei, adj. faultless. ◆'f~erhaft, adj. faulty; flawed (diamond etc.). ◆'f~erlos, adj. faultless. ◆'F~geburt, f miscarriage. ◆'f~gehen, v.i.sep.irr.36 (sein) to go wrong. ◆'F~griff, m wrong decision. ◆'F~konstruktion, f (i) faulty design; (ii) F: botch-up. ◆'F~schlag, m miss; Fig: failure. ◆'f~schlagen, v.i.sep.irr.85 (sein) to fail. ◆'F~schuß, m miss. ◆'F~tritt, m false step; Fig: lapse. ◆'F~zündung, f misfire.

Feier ['faiər], f -/-n celebration; (private) party; (öffentliche) ceremony. ◆'F~abend, m -s/-e F. machen, to stop work for the day, F: knock off (work); nach F., after hours; F: nun ist aber F.! now that's quite enough of that! ◆'f~lich, adj. solemn; (würdevoll) dignified ◆'F~lichkeit, f -/-en (a) no pl solemnity; (b) pl F~en, celebrations. ◆'f~n, v. 1. v.tr. & i. (haben) to celebrate. ◆'F~stunde, f ceremony. ◆'F~tag, m holiday.

feig(e) [faik ('faigə)], adj. cowardly; f. sein, to be a coward. ◆'F~heit, f -/no pl cowardice. ◆'F~ling, m -s/-e coward.

Feige ['faigə], f -/-n fig.

Feil|e ['failə], f -/-n file. ◆'f~en, v.tr. to file.

feilschen ['failʃən], v.i. (haben) to bargain, haggle.

fein [fain], adj. (a) fine; delicate (material); Fig: sharp (hearing, sight); (b) (vornehm) refined; sich f. machen, to make oneself smart; (c) (auserlesen) choice, first class (goods). ◆'f~fühlig, adj. sensitive. ◆'F~gefühl, n sensitivity; tact. ◆'F~heit, f -/-en (a) fineness; (Zartheit delicacy; (*im Geschmack usw.*) refinement; (b) *pl* subtleties, finer points. ◆'F~kost, *f -/no pl* delicatessen (food). ◆'F~kostgeschäft, *n* delicatessen. ◆'F~mechanik, *f* precision engineering. ◆'F~schmecker, *m* gourmet.

Feind(in) ['faint (-din)], *m -(e)s/-e (f -/-nen)* enemy. ◆'f~lich, *adj.* (a) hostile (attitude etc.); (b) enemy (troops, positions etc.). ◆'F~schaft, *f -/-en* hostility, enmity. ◆'f~selig, *adj.* hostile. ◆'F~seligkeit, *f -/-en* (a) hostility; (b) *pl* hostilities.

feist [faist], *adj.* podgy.

Feld [fɛlt], *n -(e)s/-er* (a) field; (b) *Sp:* pitch; (c) (*bei Brettspielen*) square. ◆'F~bett, *n* camp bed. ◆'F~blume, *f* wild flower. ◆'F~flasche, *f* water bottle. ◆'F~herr, *m* commander. ◆'F~lager, *n* camp. ◆'F~stecher, *m -s/-* fieldglasses. ◆'F~verweis, *m Sp:* sending-off. ◆'F~webel, *m -s/-* sergeant. ◆'F~weg, *m* track, path. ◆'F~zug, *m* campaign.

Felge ['fɛlgə], *f -/-n* (wheel) rim.

Fell [fɛl], *n -(e)s/-e* fur (of a cat etc.); coat (of a dog, horse etc.); fleece (of sheep); **ein dickes F. haben,** to be thickskinned.

Fels [fɛls], *m -en/-en* rock. ◆'F~block, *m* large boulder. ◆'F~en ['fɛlzən], *m -s/-* rock; (*Felswand*) cliff. ◆'f~en'fest, *adj.* unshakable; *adv.* steadfastly. ◆'f~ig, *adj.* rocky. ◆'F~vorsprung, *m* rocky ledge. ◆'F~wand, *f* rock face.

feminin [femi'ni:n], *adj.* feminine (clothes etc.); *Pej:* effeminate (man). ◆F~ist(in), *m -en/-en (f -/-nen)* feminist. ◆f~istisch, *adj.* feminist.

Fenchel ['fɛnçəl], *m -s/no pl* fennel.

Fenster ['fɛnstər], *n -s/-* window. ◆'F~brett, *n* window ledge. ◆'F~putzer, *m* window cleaner. ◆'F~rahmen, *m* window frame. ◆'F~scheibe, *f* window pane. ◆'F~sims, *m* window sill.

Ferien ['fe:riən], *pl* holiday(s); *N.Am:* vacation; **F. machen,** to take one's holiday/vacation. ◆'F~, *comb.fm.* holiday, *N.Am:* vacation (house, job, camp etc.). ◆'F~ort, *m* (holiday) resort. ◆'F~wohnung, *f* holiday home/ flat, *N.Am:* vacation apartment. ◆'F~zeit, *f* holiday season, *N.Am:* vacation period.

Ferkel ['fɛrkəl], *n -s/-* piglet.

fern [fɛrn]. **I.** *adj.* far; (*attrib.*) distant (friends etc.); **von f~(e),** from a long way off. **II.** *F~*, *comb.fm.* long-distance (driver, transport etc.); long-range (bomber etc.). ◆'F~bedienung, *f* remote control. ◆'f~bleiben. **I.** *v.i.sep.irr.12 (sein)* j-m, etwas *dat* f., to stay away from s.o., sth. **II.** *F~*, *n -s/no pl Sch: etc:* absence. ◆'F~e, *f -/no pl* distance; **in weiter F~,** a long way off. ◆'f~er. **1.** *adj.* (*zusätz-*

lich) further. **2.** *adv.* f. möchten wir bestätigen, daß ..., we should also like to confirm that ... ◆'f~gelenkt/ 'f~gesteuert, *adj.* remote-controlled; guided (missile). ◆'F~gespräch, *n* long-distance call. ◆'F~glas, *n* binoculars. ◆'f~halten, *v.tr.sep.irr.45* to keep (s.o., sth.) away, (*schützen*) shield (s.o., sth.). ◆'F~lenkung, *f -/no pl* remote control. ◆'F~licht, *n Aut:* full/*N.Am:* high beam. ◆'f~liegen, *v.i. sep.irr.93 (haben)* es lag ihm fern, sie zu beleidigen, he had no intention of offending her ◆'F~melde-, *comb.fm.* telecommunications (satellite, service etc.). ◆'f~mündlich, *adv.* by telephone. ◆'F~ost, *m inv.* in/aus/nach F., in/to/ from the Far East. ◆'f~östlich, *adj.* Far Eastern. ◆'F~rohr, *n* telescope. ◆'F~schreiben, *n* telex ◆'F~schreiber, *m -s/-* telex machine. ◆'F~seh-, *comb.fm.* television (aerial, announcer, film, etc.). ◆'F~sehapparat *m* television set. ◆'F~seher, *m -s/-* **1.** (*Gerät*) *F:* telly, TV. **2.** (*Pers.*) viewer. ◆'F~sehschirm, *m* television screen. ◆'F~sehsender, *m* television station. ◆'F~sehzuschauer, *m* viewer. ◆'f~sehen. **I.** *v.i.sep.irr.92 (haben)* to watch television. **II.** F., *n -s/-* television; **im F.,** on (the) television. ◆'F~sprecher, *m* telephone. ◆'F~sprechzelle, *f* telephone box. ◆'F~steuerung, *f* remote control. ◆'F~studium, *n* study by correspondence. ◆'F~unterricht, *m* **1.** tuition by correspondence. **2.** correspondence course. ◆'F~ziel, *n* long-term aim.

Ferse ['fɛrzə], *f -/-n* heel.

fertig ['fɛrtiç]. **I.** *adj.* (a) (*bereit*) ready; (b) (*vollendet*) finished; **er ist mit seiner Arbeit f.,** he's finished his work; **mit j-m, etwas *dat* f. werden,** to cope/deal with s.o., sth.; (*C: F:* **ich bin ganz f.,** I'm completely worn out. **II.** *F~*, *comb.fm.* ready-made (clothes etc.); prefabricated (building, house etc.); *Ind:* finished (product, goods). ◆'f~bringen, *v.tr.sep.irr.16 (a)* to get (sth.) done, complete (a task); (b) **es f., etwas zu tun,** to manage to do sth. ◆'f~en, *v.tr.* to produce. ◆'F~keit, *f -/-en* skill, proficiency (**in +** *dat,* at). ◆'f~machen, *v.tr.sep. F:* (a) to finish (sth.); (b) to get (s.o., sth.) ready; (c) (*erschöpfen*) to wear (s.o.) out; (d) *P:* to beat (s.o.) up, (*töten*) do (s.o.) in. ◆'f~stellen, *v.tr.sep.* to complete. ◆'F~stellung, *f -/no pl* completion. ◆'F~ung, *f -/no pl* production.

Fessel ['fɛsəl], *f -/-n* bond. ◆'f~n, *v.tr.* (a) to bind; *Fig:* to tie (s.o.); **ans Bett gefesselt,** confined to bed; (b) (*faszinieren*) to enthrall (s.o.). ◆'f~nd, *adj.* fascinating; (*spannend*) riveting.

fest1 [fɛst]. *adj.* (a) solid (rock, *Ph:* body etc.); (*unbiegsam*) rigid; (*nicht flüssig*) solid; set (jelly); hard (wood); (b) (*stark*) strong (material); secure, solid (structure); (*unbeweglich*) tight (cork, screw etc.); sound (sleep); firm (belief, hope etc.); **eine Tür f. verschließen,** to lock a door securely; **f. davon überzeugt,** firmly convinced of sth.; (*c*) fixed (price, income etc.); firm (offer); set (habits); permanent (home, address); stable (relationship); **f~e Freunde,** firm friends; **eine f~e Vorstellung von etwas dat,** a clear idea of sth.; *F:* **in f~en Händen sein,** to be spoken for. ◆**'f~angestellt,** *adj.* permanent. ◆**'f~binden,** *v.tr.sep.irr.9* to tie (s.o., sth.) up; to lash (s.o., sth.) (**an etwas** *acc,* to sth.). ◆**'f~fahren,** *v.refl.&i.sep.irr.26* (*sich*) **f.,** *Aut:* to get stuck; *Fig:* (*Verhandlungen*) to reach deadlock. ◆**'f~halten,** *v.sep.irr.45* **1.** *v.i.* (*haben*) **an Traditionen usw. f.,** to cling to traditions etc. **2.** *v.tr.* (*a*) to keep hold of (s.o., sth.); (*b*) **sich an etwas** *dat* **f.,** to hold/hang on to sth.; (*c*) to record (events); to capture (a scene). ◆**'f~igen,** *v.tr.* to strengthen (an alliance etc.), consolidate (one's position). ◆**'F~igen,** *m* -s/- *Haarf.*) setting lotion. ◆**F~igkeit,** *f* -/no *pl* firmness, solidity; (*Stärke*) strength; (*Härte*) hardness. ◆**'f~klammern,** *v.tr.sep.* to clamp (sth.) (**an etwas** *dat,* to sth.); **sich an j-m, etwas** *dat* **f.,** to cling tightly to s.o., sth. ◆**'f~klemmen,** *v.sep.* **1.** *v.i.* (*sein*) to jam. **2.** *v.tr.* to jam, wedge (sth.). ◆**F~land,** *n* mainland. ◆**'f~legen,** *v.tr.sep.* (*a*) (*bestimmen*) to lay down (principles), stipulate (conditions, a limit etc.); to fix (a date etc.), decide on (a route, plan); **etwas schriftlich f.,** to put sth. down in writing; (*b*) to commit (oneself, s.o.) (**auf etwas** *acc,* to sth.). ◆**'f~liegen,** *v.i.* *sep.irr.62* (*sein*) (*a*) (*Schiff*) to be aground; (*b*) (*Termin, Preis usw.*) to be fixed. ◆**'f~machen,** *v.tr.sep.* (*a*) to fasten (sth.), tie up (a boat, dog etc.); (**an etwas** *dat,* to sth.); (*b*) to settle (a date, price etc.). ◆**'F~nahme,** *f* -/-n arrest. ◆**'f~nehmen,** *v.tr.sep.irr.69* to capture, (*verhaften*) arrest (s.o.). ◆**'f~setzen,** *v.tr.sep.* to settle (a time, date etc.); to fix (a price etc.). ◆**'f~stehen,** *v.i.* *sep.irr.4* (*haben*) (*Termin, Route usw.*) to be decided; **eines steht fest,** one thing is certain. ◆**'f~stellen,** *v.tr.sep.* to establish (a fact etc.), (*bemerken*) to notice (a change etc.). ◆**'F~stellung,** *f* discovery (of a fact etc.), (*Bemerkung*) observation. ◆**F~ung,** *f* -/-en fortress. ◆**'f~ziehen,** *v.tr.sep.* to pull (a knot) tight; to tighten (a belt, screw etc.).

Fest². I. *n* -es/-e **1.** celebration, festivity; (*private Gesellschaft*) party; **frohes F.!** have a good Christmas! **II.** *F~*, *comb.fm.* festive (evening, dress, mood, decorations etc.); gala (concert, performance). ◆**'F~essen,** *n* banquet, din-

ner; *F:* feast. ◆**f~lich,** *adj.* festive (occasion etc.); dressy (clothes). ◆**'F~saal,** *m* assembly hall; (*für Bälle*) ballroom; (*für Festessen*) banqueting hall. ◆**'F~spiel,** *n* festival.

fett [fɛt]. **I.** *adj.* *a* (*dick*) fat; (*b*) fatty (soup, meal etc.); greasy (hair, skin); *F:* **f~e Beute,** rich haul; (*c*) **f. gedruckt,** in bold type. **II.** *F:* **f.** *m* -(e)s/-e fat. **III.** *F~*, *f~*, *comb.fm.* fat (content etc.); grease (mark etc.). ◆**'f~arm,** *adj.* low-fat. ◆**'F~auge,** *n* speck of fat. ◆**'F~creme,** *f* skin cream. ◆**'f~en,** *v.tr.* to grease. ◆**'f~ig,** *adj.* fatty (substance); greasy (hair, dish etc.). ◆**'F~näpfchen,** *n F:* **ins F. treten,** to put one's foot in it.

Fetzen ['fɛtsən], *m* -s/- scrap.

feucht [fɔʏçt], *adj.* damp; moist (lips, earth etc.). ◆**'f~fröhlich,** *adj.* merry. ◆**'F~igkeit,** *f* -/no *pl* damp; moisture (in a substance); (*von Klima*) humidity. ◆**'F~igkeitscreme,** *f* moisturizing cream.

feudal [fɔʏ'dɑːl], *adj.* feudal.

Feuer ['fɔʏər], *n* -s/- fire; (*im Freien*) bonfire; *Fig:* fervour; **F. fangen,** to catch fire; **j-m F. geben,** to give s.o. a light; **das F. eröffnen/einstellen,** to open fire/cease firing; **sie war gleich F. und Flamme (dafür),** she was immediately wild with enthusiasm (about it); **mit dem F. spielen,** to play with fire. **II.** **'F~,** **f~,** *comb.fm.* fire (alarm, -fighting, etc.); (danger etc.) of fire. ◆**'F~eifer,** *m* ardour, zeal. ◆**'f~fest,** *adj.* fireproof; *Cu:* ovenproof. ◆**'F~gefährlich,** *adj.* inflammable. ◆**'F~leiter,** *f* fire escape. ◆**'F~löscher,** *m* fire extinguisher. ◆**'F~melder,** *m* fire alarm. ◆**'f~n,** *v.* **1.** *v.i.* (*haben*) to fire (**auf j-n, an** s.o.). **2.** *v.tr.* (*a*) to stoke (a boiler etc.); (*b*) *F:* to fling (sth.); (*c*) *F:* to fire (s.o.). ◆**'F~probe,** *f* *Fig:* acid test; ordeal. ◆**'f~rot,** *adj.* fiery (red). ◆**'F~schutz,** *m* cover. ◆**'F~stein,** *m* flint. ◆**'F~stelle,** *f* fireplace. ◆**'F~treppe,** *f* fire escape. ◆**'F~wehr,** *f* fire brigade. ◆**'F~wehrauto,** *n* fire engine. ◆**'F~wehrmann,** *m* fire-man. ◆**'F~werk,** *n* fireworks. ◆**'F~werkskörper,** *m* firework. ◆**'F~zange,** *f* fire tongs. ◆**'F~zeug,** *n* (cigarette) lighter.

feurig ['fɔʏrɪç], *adj.* fiery (temperament etc.); ardent (lover etc.).

Fiasko [fi'asko], *n* -s/-s fiasco.

Fichte ['fɪçtə], *f* -/-n spruce (tree); *F:* pine (tree).

fidel [fi'deːl], *adj.* *F:* jolly, cheerful.

Fieber ['fiːbər], *n* -s/- fever. ◆**'f~haft,** *adj.* feverish. ◆**'f~n,** *v.i.* (*haben*) to be feverish. ◆**'fiebrig,** *adj.* feverish.

fies [fiːs], *adj. F:* horrid.

Figur [fi'guːr], *f* -/-en figure; (*in Buch*) character; (*Schachf.*) piece.

Filet [fi'le:], n -s/-s fillet.

Filial|e [fi'lia:lə], f -/-n branch. ◆**F~leiter**, m branch manager.

Film [film]. I. m -(e)s/-e film; N.Am: Cin: movie. II. **F~-**, comb.fm. film, N.Am: movie (studio, critic, actor). ◆**F~aufnahme**, f filming. ◆**f~en**, v.tr.&i. (haben) to film. ◆**F~kamera**, f cine camera. ◆**F~star**, m film/movie star. ◆**F~verleih**, m film/movie distributors. ◆**F~vorführer**, m projectionist.

Filter ['filtər]. I. m -s/- filter. II. **F~-**, comb.fm. filter (paper, bag etc.). ◆**F~kaffee**, m filter coffee. ◆**f~n**, v.tr. to filter. ◆**F~zigarette**, f filter-tipped cigarette.

Filz [filts], m -es/-e felt. ◆**f~en**, v.tr. F: to frisk (s.o.) ◆**F~stift**, m felt-(tip) pen.

Fimmel ['fiməl], m -s/no pl F: mania, craze.

Finale [fi'na:lə], n -s/- 1. Mus: finale. 2. Sp: final.

Finanz [fi'nants], f -/-en finance. ◆**F~amt**, n tax office. ◆**f~iell** [-tsi'el], adj. financial. ◆**f~ieren** [-'tsi:rən], v.tr. to finance. ◆**F~ierung**, f -/-en financing.

find|en ['findən], v.tr.irr.9 (a) to find; **er war nirgends zu f.**, he was nowhere to be found; (b) (der Meinung sein) f. **Sie nicht?** don't you think (so)? (c) **sich f.**, (auftauchen) to turn up; **es wird sich (schon) alles f.**, everything will be all right. ◆**F~er(in)**, m -s/- (f -/-nen) finder. ◆**F~erlohn**, m reward. ◆**f~ig**, adj. resourceful.

Finesse [fi'nesə], f -/-n F: trick.

Finger ['fiŋər], m -s/- finger; **man muß ihnen dauernd auf die F. sehen**, you have to keep an eye on them all the time; **ich kann es mir doch nicht aus den F~n saugen**, I can't produce it out of thin air. ◆**F~abdruck**, m fingerprint. ◆**f~fertig**, adj. deft. ◆**F~hut**, m 1. thimble. 2. Bot: foxglove. ◆**f~n**, v.i. (haben) **an etwas dat f.**, to finger sth. ◆**F~nagel**, m finger-nail. ◆**F~spitze**, f fingertip. ◆**F~spitzengefühl**, n intuition. ◆**F~zeig**, m -(e)s/-e (Hinweis) tip; (Wink) sign.

fingieren [fiŋ'gi:rən], v.tr. to simulate, (erdichten) invent (sth.). ◆**f~t**, adj. fictitious.

Fink [fiŋk], m -en/-en finch.

Finn|e ['finə], m -n/-n/**F~in**, f -/-nen Finn. ◆**f~isch**, adj. Finnish. ◆**F~land**. Pr.n.n -s. Finland.

finster ['finstər], adj. (a) dark; (düster) gloomy; (unheimlich) sinister; **im F~n**, in the dark; (b) Fig: (zwielichtig) shady (business etc.); (c) **f~e Miene/f~er Blick**, black look. ◆**F~nis**, f -/-se 1. darkness. 2. Astr: eclipse.

Finte ['fintə], f -/-n feint; Fig: trick.

Firm|a ['firma], f -/-men firm; company. ◆**F~eninhaber**, m owner of a/the firm. ◆**F~enwagen**, m company car. ◆**F~enzeichen**, n trade mark.

firm|en ['firmən], v.tr. to confirm. ◆**F~ung**, f -/-en confirmation.

Firnis ['firnis], m -ses/-se varnish.

First [first], m -(e)s/-e ridge.

Fisch [fiʃ], m -(e)s/-e (a) fish; **F~e fangen**, to (catch) fish; (b) Astr: Pisces; (c) F: (Pers.) **ein großer F.**, a VIP; **kleine F~e**, small fry; (Sachen) minor matters. ◆**f~en**, v. 1. v.tr. to fish for, (fangen) catch; 2. v.i. (haben) to fish; **f. gehen**, to go fishing; **nach etwas dat f.**, to fish for sth. ◆**F~er**, m -s/- fisherman. ◆**F~erboot**, n fishing boat. ◆**F~erei**, f -/-en fishing. ◆**F~fang**, m fishing. ◆**F~geschäft**, n fishmonger's (shop), N.Am: fish store. ◆**F~gräte**, f fishbone. ◆**F~grätenmuster**, n herringbone pattern. ◆**F~kutter**, m fishing boat. ◆**F~mehl**, n fishmeal. ◆**F~stäbchen**, n fish finger, N.Am: fishstick. ◆**F~teich**, m fishpond. ◆**F~zug**, m catch.

fit [fit], adj. fit. ◆**F~neß**, f -/no pl fitness.

fix [fiks], adj. 1. fixed (prices, salary etc.); 2. (flink) quick; sharp-witted (person). 3. F: **f. und fertig**, (a) (bereit) completely finished; (b) (erschöpft) completely worn out; ◆**F~er**, m -s/- F: junkie. ◆**f~ieren**, v.tr. (a) etwas schriftlich f., to put sth. down in black and white; (b) Phot: to fix.

Fjord [fjort], m -(e)s/-e fjord.

flach [flax], adj. (a) flat; (eben) level; (b) (niedrig) low (building, heel etc.); (c) (nicht tief) shallow (water, dish etc.); Fig: superficial (book, conversation etc.); Fig: shallowness. ◆**F~heit**, f -/no pl (a) flatness; (b) (also Fig:) shallowness. ◆**F~land**, n low-land(s).

Fläch|e ['flɛçə], f -/-n (a) (Oberfläche) surface; Mth: plane (of a figure); (b) (Ausdehnung) area; expanse (of water etc.). ◆**F~eninhalt**, m area. ◆**F~enmaß**, n square measure.

Flachs [flaks], m -es/no pl flax.

flackern ['flakərn], v.i. (haben) to flicker.

Fladen ['fla:dən], m -s/- fritter.

Flagg|e ['flagə], f -/-n flag; ◆**F~schiff**, n flagship.

Flak [flak], f -/-s anti-aircraft gun.

Flakon [fla'kõ:], n -s/-s phial.

flämisch ['flɛ:miʃ], adj. Flemish.

Flamingo [fla'miŋgo], m -s/-s flamingo.

Flamme ['flamə], f -/-n flame; ◆**F~nmeer**, n mass of flames. ◆**F~nwerfer**, m -s/- flamethrower.

Flanell [fla'nɛl], m -s/-e flannel.

Flank|e ['flaŋkə], f -/-n 1. flank. 2. (a) (Turnen) side vault; (b) Fb: centre, cross. ◆**f~ieren** [-'ki:rən], v.tr. to flank.

Flasche ['flaʃə], f -/-n 1. bottle; cylinder

(of gas); **eine F. Bier,** a bottle of beer. **2. F:** (*Pers.*) useless character. ◆**'F~n-, f~n-, comb.fm.** (a) bottle (brush, opener etc.); (b) bottled (beer, wine etc.). ◆**'F~zug, m** block and tackle.

flatter|haft ['flatərhaft], *adj.* capricious. ◆**'f~n,** *v.i.* (*haben*) (a) to flutter, flap; (b) (*Vogel*) to flap its wings; (*Hände*) to shake.

flau [flau], *adj.* (a) (*schwach*) faint (breeze); (b) (*leblos*) slack (holiday season, business); dull, lifeless (conversation, atmosphere); (c) **F: mir ist f.** (**im Magen**), I feel queasy.

Flaum [flaum], *m* **-(e)s/no** *pl* down, fluff.

flauschig ['flauʃiç], *adj.* fleecy, cuddly (toy etc.).

Flausen ['flauzən], *pl* **F:** nonsense; **er hat nur F. im Kopf,** his head is stuffed with silly ideas.

Flaute ['flautə], *f* **-/-n 1.** *Nau:* dead calm. **2.** *Com: etc:* slack period.

Flecht|e ['flɛçtə], *f* **-/-n 1.** *Bot:* lichen. **2.** *Med:* psoriasis. ◆**'f~en,** *v.tr.irr.* to plait, *N.Am:* braid (hair, straw etc.); to weave (a basket etc.). ◆**'F~werk,** *n* wickerwork.

Fleck [flɛk], *m* **-(e)s/-e** (*Schmutz*) mark, spot; (*vom Wein usw*) stain; (*Klecks*) blot; **blauer F.,** bruise; (b) (*Stück Boden*) patch (of ground); (*Ort*) spot; **er rührte sich nicht vom F.,** he didn't stir/budge; *F:* **vom F. weg,** on the spot, there and then. ◆**F~en, m -s/- 1. = Fleck** (a). **2.** (small) market town. ◆**'f~enlos,** *adj.* spotless. ◆**'F~enwasser,** *n* stain remover. ◆**'f~ig,** *adj.* stained (clothes etc.); blotchy (face).

Fledermaus ['fle:dərmaus], *f* bat.

Flegel ['fle:gəl], *m* **-s/-** lout. ◆**F~ei** [-'lai], *f* **-/-en** rudeness. ◆**'f~haft,** *adj.* loutish. ◆**'F~jahre,** *npl* awkward age.

flehen ['fle:ən], *v.i.* (*haben*) to implore; **bei j-m um etwas** *acc* **f.,** to beg s.o. for sth.

Fleisch [flaiʃ], *n* **-es/no** *pl* (a) flesh; (b) (*Nahrungsmittel*) meat. **II. F~-, f~-, comb.fm.** (a) flesh (wound etc.); (b) meat (dish, salad etc.). ◆**'F~brühe,** *f* (beef) stock; (b) (*Suppe*) consommé. ◆**'F~er,** *m* **-s/-** butcher. ◆**F~e'rei,** *f* **-/-en** butcher's (shop). ◆**'F~erhaken,** *m* meat hook. ◆**'f~fressend,** *adj.* carnivorous. ◆**'f~ig,** *adj.* meaty (animal); fleshy (face, soft fruit). ◆**'F~käse,** *m* meat loaf. ◆**'F~klößchen,** *n* meat ball. ◆**'f~lich,** *adj.* carnal. ◆**'F~pastete,** *f* meat pie. ◆**'F~wolf,** *m* mincer, *N.Am:* meat grinder.

Fleiß [flais], *m* **-es/no** *pl* diligence. ◆**'f~ig,** *adj.* hardworking; **f. arbeiten,** to work hard.

fletschen ['flɛtʃən], *v.tr.* **die Zähne f.,** to bare one's teeth.

flex|ibel ['flɛ'ksi:bəl], *adj.* flexible. ◆**F~ibilität** [-ibili'tɛːt], *f* **-/no** *pl* flexi-

bility.

flick|en ['flikən], **f~en. I.** *v.tr.* to mend **II. F.,** *m* **-s/-** patch. ◆**'F~werk,** *n* **-(e)s/no** *pl Pej:* patched up job. ◆**'F~zeug,** *n* (a) (*beim Nähen*) mending things; (b) (*für Fahrrad*) (puncture) repair kit.

Flieder ['fli:dər], *m* **-s/-** lilac.

Flieg|e ['fli:gə], *f* **-/-n 1.** fly. **2.** *Cl:* bow-tie. ◆**'f~en,** *v.tr.&i.irr.30* (*sein*) to fly; **F: alle Mädchen f. auf ihn,** all the girls find him irresistible; *F:* **aus seiner Stellung f.,** to get the sack; **F: in die Luft f.,** to explode, blow up. ◆**'f~end,** *adj.* flying; **f~er Händler,** itinerant trader. ◆**'F~enfänger,** *m* flytrap. ◆**'F~engewicht,** *n* flyweight. ◆**'F~er,** *m* **-s/-** pilot. ◆**'F~eralarm,** *m* air raid warning. ◆**'F~erangriff,** *m* air attack/raid.

flieh|en ['fli:ən], *v.i.irr.* (*sein*) to run away (**vor j-m, etwas** *dat*, from s.o., sth.); (*entkommen*) to escape. ◆**'f~end,** *adj.* **1.** fleeing (troops etc.). **2.** receding (chin, forehead). ◆**'F~kraft,** *f* centrifugal force.

Fliese ['fli:zə], *f* **-/-n** tile.

Fließ|arbeit ['fli:sarbait], *f* **-/no** *pl* production line work. ◆**'F~band,** *n* conveyor belt. ◆**'f~en,** *v.i.irr.* (*sein*) to flow; (*Hahn, Nase usw.*) to run. ◆**'f~end,** *adj.* (a) flowing; **Zimmer mit f~em Wasser,** room with running water; (b) **f. deutsch sprechen,** to speak fluent German.

flimmern ['flimərn], *v.i.* (*haben*) (*Sterne*) to twinkle; (*Luft, Hitze*) to shimmer; (*Fernsehen*) to flicker.

flink [fliŋk], *adj.* agile (movements, person); nimble (fingers).

Flinte ['flintə], *f* **-/-n** shotgun.

Flirt [flœrt], *m* **-s/-s** flirtation. ◆**'f~en,** *v.i.* (*haben*) to flirt.

Flitter ['flitər], *m* **-s/-** (a) *pl* (*auf einem Kleid*) sequins; (b) (*Glitzerschmuck*) tinsel. ◆**'F~wochen,** *fpl* honeymoon.

flitzen ['flitsən], *v.i.* (*sein*) to whizz (along), (*Pers.*) dash.

Flock|e ['flɔkə], *f* **-/-n** flake. ◆**'f~ig,** *adj.* flaky.

Floh [flo:]. **I. m -(e)s/-e** flea. ◆**'F~markt,** *m* flea market; (*Wohltätigkeitsbasar*) jumble sale.

Flor, *m* **-s/-e 1.** gauze; (*Trauerf.*) crêpe. **2.** (*Teppich f.*) pile.

florieren [flo'ri:rən], *v.i.* (*haben*) (*Geschäft*) to flourish.

Flora ['flo:ra], *f* **-/-ren** flora.

Florett [flo'rɛt], *m* **-(e)s/-e** foil.

Floskel ['flɔskəl], *f* **-/-n** set phrase.

Floß [flo:s], *n* **-/-e** raft.

Flosse ['flɔsə], *f* **-/-n** (a) fin; (b) (*Schwimmf.*) flipper.

Flöt|e ['fløːtə], *f* **-/-n 1.** flute. **2.** champagne flute. ◆**'f~ist(in)** [flø'tist(in)], *m* **-en/-en** (*f* **-/-nen**) flautist.

flott [flɔt], *adj.* **F:** (a) (*schnell*) quick, **F:**

speedy (service etc.); (b) (schick) smart (dress, coat etc.); (rasant) sporty (car); (lebendig) lively (music etc.); flamboyant (style); ◆'f~machen, v.tr.sep. to make (a ship, boat) seaworthy/F: (a car) roadworthy.

Flotte ['flɔtə], f -(a -n) fleet. ◆'F~nstützpunkt, m naval base.

Flöz [fløːts], n -es/-e seam.

Fluch [fluːx], m -(e)s/-e curse. ◆'f~en, v.i. (haben) to curse (auf/über + acc, about).

Flucht1 [fluxt]. I. f -/-en escape; die F. ergreifen, to take flight; den Feind in die F. schlagen, to put the enemy to flight; II. F~-, comb.fm. escape (car etc.). ◆'f~artig, adj. hurried, hasty. ◆'F~versuch, m escape attempt. ◆'F~weg, m escape route.

Flucht2, f -/-en (a) alignment (of buildings etc.); (b) suite (of rooms).

flüchten ['flYçtən], v. 1. v.i. (sein) run away; (sich retten) to escape (vor + dat, from). 2. v.refl. sich irgendwohin f., to take refuge somewhere (vor + dat, from). ◆'f~ig, adj. 1. (flüchtend) fleeing; escaped (prisoner etc.); f. sein, to be on the run. 2. (a) (kurz) cursory (acquaintance); fleeting (glance etc.); (b) (oberflächlich) superficial; shoddy (work); j-n f. kennen, to know s.o. slightly. ◆'F~igkeitsfehler, m careless mistake. ◆'F~ling, m -s/-e refugee.

Flug [fluːk]. I. m -(e)s/-e flight (Fliegen) flying; im F., in flight; die Zeit verging (wie) im F~e, the time flew past. II. F~-, comb.fm. (a) flight (deck, captain etc.); flying (boat, weather etc.); (b) air-(speed, traffic etc.). ◆'F~abwehr, f anti-aircraft defence. ◆'F~abwehrkanone, f anti-aircraft gun. ◆'F~begleiter(in), m (f) steward(ess). ◆'F~blatt, n leaflet, pamphlet. ◆'F~gast, m air passenger. ◆'F~gesellschaft, f airline. ◆'F~hafen, m airport. ◆'F~höhe, f altitude. ◆'F~lotse, m air traffic controller. ◆'F~objekt, n unbekanntes F., unidentified flying object. ◆'F~platz, m airfield. ◆'F~reise, f flight. ◆'f~s [fluks], adv. quickly; at once. ◆'F~steig, m gate (at an airport). ◆'F~zeug, n aeroplane, N.Am: airplane. ◆'F~zeugentführung, f hijacking. ◆'F~zeughalle, f hangar. ◆'F~zeugträger, m aircraft carrier.

Flügel ['flyːgəl], m -s/- 1. wing. 2. half (of a window); side (of the lung). 3. sail (of a windmill); Mus: grand piano. ◆'F~schlag, m wing beat. ◆'F~tür, f double door.

flügge ['flygə], adj. fully-fledged.

Flunder ['flundər], f -/-n flounder.

flunkern ['fluŋkərn], v.i. (haben) F: to tell tall stories.

Fluor ['fluːor], n -s/no pl fluorine.

Flur1 [fluːr], m -(e)s/-e hall.

Flur2, f -/-en (a) Fig: allein auf weiter F. sein, to be all alone; (b) Agr: farmland.

Fluß [flus]. I. m -sses/-sse 1. river. 2. (Fließen) flow (of water, traffic etc.); im F. sein, (Sache) to be in a state of flux. II. 'F~-, comb.fm. river (bed, valley, bank etc.). ◆'F~lauf, m course of a river. ◆'F~abwärts, adv. downstream. ◆f~aufwärts, adv. upstream. ◆'F~pferd, n hippopotamus.

flüssig ['flYsɪç], adj. 1. liquid; molten (metal, lava etc.). 2. (fließend) flowing; fluent (speaker, style etc.). 3. Fin: liquid (capital, assets); ready (money). ◆'F~keit, f -/-en 1. liquid; esp. Anat: etc: fluid. 2. (Eigenschaft) fluency. ◆'f~machen, v.tr.sep. to make available.

flüstern ['flYstərn]. I. v.tr. & i. (haben) to whisper. II. F., n -s/no pl whispering, whisper. ◆'F~propaganda, f whispering campaign. ◆'F~ton, m im F., in a whisper.

Flut [fluːt], f -/-en 1. no pl high tide; bei F., at high tide; die F. steigt/fällt, the tide is coming in/going out. 2. Lit: F~en, waters; eine F. von Tränen, Briefen usw., a flood of tears, letters etc. ◆'F~licht, n floodlight. ◆'F~welle, f tidal wave.

Fohlen ['foːlən], n -s/- foal.

Föhn [føːn], m -(e)s/-e warm Alpine wind.

Föhre ['føːrə], f -/-n pine tree.

Folge ['fɔlgə], f -/-n 1. consequence; etwas zur F. haben, to result in sth. 2. (a) (Reihe) series; sequence; in rascher F., in quick succession; (b) Rad: TV: instalment. 3. einem Befehl etc. F. leisten, to obey an order etc.; einer Einladung F. leisten, to accept an invitation. ◆'f~en, v.i. (a) (sein) j-m/etwas dat f., to follow s.o., sth.; (b) (sein) (zeitlich) j-m, etwas dat/auf j-m, etwas acc f., to follow from s.o., sth.; wie folgt, as follows; daraus folgt, daß ..., it follows from this that ...; (c) (haben) (j-m) f., to obey (s.o.). ◆'f~end, adj. following; am f~en Tag, the next day; f~es, the following. ◆'f~ermaßen, adv. as follows. ◆'f~enschwer, adj. (action etc.) with far-reaching consequences. ◆'f~erichtig, adj. logical. ◆'f~ern, v.tr. to conclude (aus + dat, from). ◆'F~erung, f -/-en conclusion, deduction. ◆'f~lich, adv. & conj. consequently. ◆'f~sam, adj. obedient.

Folie ['foːliə], f -/-n (a) (metal) foil; (b) (plastic) film; (Überzug) lamination.

Folklore [fɔlk'loːrə], f -/no pl 1. folklore. 2. folk music. ◆f~istisch [-o'rɪstɪʃ], adj. folk, F: folksy.

Folter ['fɔltər], f -/-n torture; j-n auf die F. spannen, to keep s.o. on tenterhooks. ◆'f~er, m -s/- torturer. ◆'f~n, v.tr. to torture, Fig: torment (s.o.).

Fön [føːn], m -(e)s/-e R.t.m. hairdryer. ◆'f~en, v.tr. sich dat die Haare f., to dry one's hair.

Fonds [fɔ̃ː], m -/- fund.

foppen ['fɔpən], v.tr. j-n f., to pull s.o.'s leg.

forcieren [fɔr'siːrən], v.tr. (a) das Tempo f., to force the pace; (b) to step up (production etc.).

fordern ['fɔrdərn], v.tr. (a) to demand (rights, money etc.); to claim (Jur: damages, Fig: lives, victims etc.); **einen hohen Preis f.**, to charge a high price; (b) (herausf.) to challenge (s.o.). ◆'F~ung, f -/-en demand.

Förder|band ['fœrdərbant], n conveyor belt. ◆'F~er(in), m -s/- (f -/-nen) patron (of the arts etc.); sponsor (of a project etc.). ◆'f~lich, adj. profitable, favourable. ◆'f~n, v.tr. (a) to promote (trade, art, understanding etc.); (finanziell) to sponsor, support (a project etc.); to further (development, science etc.); (b) Min: to extract. ◆'F~turm, m pithead winding tower. ◆'F~ung, f -/-en 1. sponsorship (of art etc.); promotion. 2. Min: production.

Forelle [fo'rɛlə], f -/-n trout.

Form [fɔrm], f -/-en 1. form; (äußere Gestalt) shape; (Plan usw.) **feste F. annehmen**, to take shape; **in aller F.**, with due ceremony; **die F. wahren**, to keep up appearances. 2. Sp: fitness; **gut/groß in F.**, in good/great form. 3. (Gieß- mould; (Backf.) (baking) tin. ◆'f~al [fɔr'maːl], adj. 1. formal (structure etc.). 2. technical (objections, grounds etc.). ◆'F~alität [-i'tɛːt], f -/-en formality. ◆'F~at [-'maːt], n -(e)s/-e 1. size, format (of paper, books etc.). 2. no pl calibre. ◆'F~ation [-atsi'oːn], f formation. ◆'f~bar, adj. malleable. ◆'F~el, f -/-n formula. ◆'f~ell [-'mɛl], adj. formal (agreement etc.). ◆'f~en, v.tr. to form (a concept, sounds etc.); to shape, mould (a material etc.); (Gedanken, Stoff usw.) sich f., to take shape. ◆'F~en [-'maːrən], v.r. to form; Mil: to draw up (troops). ◆'f~los, adj. 1. shapeless. 2. (zwanglos) informal; casual (behaviour). ◆'F~sache, f (reine) F., pure formality; Adm: technicality. ◆'f~schön, adj. beautifully shaped. ◆'F~ular [-u'laːr], n -s/-e Adm: form, N.Am: blank. ◆'f~u'lieren, v.tr. to formulate. ◆'F~u'lierung, f -/-en formulation; (Wortlaut) wording.

förmlich ['fœrmlɪç], adj. 1. formal. 2. (regelrecht) real. ◆'F~keit, f -/-en formality.

forsch [fɔrʃ], adj. dynamic.

forsch|en ['fɔrʃən], v.i. (haben) (a) nach j-m, etwas dat f., to search for/ (fragen nach) inquire after s.o., sth.; f~der Blick, searching glance; (b) to (do) research (**auf einem Gebiet**, in an area/into

a subject). ◆'F~er(in), m -s/- (f -/-nen) 1. research worker, researcher. 2. (F~ungsreisender) explorer. ◆'F~ung, f -/-en research. ◆'F~ungs-, comb.fm. research (work, institute). ◆'F~ungsreise, f voyage of exploration.

Forst [fɔrst], m -(e)s/-e(n) forest. ◆'F~-, comb.fm. forestry (officer, administration etc.); ◆'F~wirtschaft, f forestry.

Förster ['fœrstər], m -s/- forester, N.Am: forest ranger.

Fort¹ [fɔrt], n -s/-s fort.

fort² [fɔrt], adv. 1. away; **das Buch ist f.**, the book has gone; **sie sind schon f.**, they have already gone/left. 2. **und so f.**, and so on; **in einem f.**, on and on. ◆'f~bestehen, v.i.sep.irr.100 (haben) to survive. ◆'f~bewegen, v.tr.sep. to move (sth.) (away); sich f., to move/walk (along). ◆'f~bilden, v.refl.sep. sich f., to continue one's education/training. ◆'F~bildung, f further education/ training. ◆'f~bleiben, v.i.sep.irr.12 (sein) to stay away. ◆'f~bringen, v.tr.sep.irr.16 to take (s.o., sth.) away. ◆'f~dauern, v.i.sep. (haben) to continue. ◆'f~dauernd, adj. continuous; lasting (effect etc.). ◆'f~entwickeln, v.refl. & i. (haben) (sich) f., to continue to develop. ◆'f~fahren, v.i.sep.irr.26 (a) (sein) to drive away/off; (b) (haben/ sein) to continue (**in seiner Rede usw.**, speaking etc.). ◆'f~fallen, v.i.sep.irr.27 (sein) to be omitted. ◆'f~führen, v.tr. sep. to lead/take (s.o., sth.) away; to carry on, continue (sth. begun by s.o. else). ◆'F~gang, m 1. (Verlauf) course. 2. lit: departure. ◆'f~gehen, v.i.sep.irr.36 (sein) to go away, leave. ◆'f~geschritten, adj. advanced. ◆'f~kommen, n -s/no pl progress. ◆'f~können, v.i.sep.irr.54 (haben) er konnte nicht fort, he could not get away. ◆'f~laufen, v.i.sep.irr.58 (sein) to run away. ◆'f~laufend, adj. continuous. ◆'f~müssen, v.i.sep.irr.68 (haben) to have to leave. ◆'f~nehmen, v.tr.sep.irr.69 to take (s.o., sth.) away. ◆'f~pflanzung, f reproduction. ◆'f~schaffen, v.tr.sep. to remove (s.o., sth.). ◆'f~schreiten, v.i.sep.irr.59 (sein) to progress. ◆'f~schritt, m progress; **große F~e machen**, to make considerable progress. ◆'f~schrittlich, adj. advanced (science, student etc.); progressive (person, ideas etc.). ◆'f~setzen, v.tr.sep to continue (sth.). ◆'F~setzung, f -/-en 1. continuation. 2. (a) (Folge) instalment; (b) (anschließender Teil) sequel. ◆'f~während, adj. incessant. ◆'f~werfen, v.tr.sep.irr.110 to throw (sth.) away. ◆'f~ziehen, v.sep.irr.113 1. v.tr. to pull, drag (s.o., sth.) away. 2. v.i. (sein) to move away; (Vögel) to migrate.

Fossil [fɔ'siːl], n -s/-ien fossil.
Foto ['foːto], I. n -s/-s photo. ◆'F~album, n photograph album. ◆'F~apparat, m camera. ◆f~gen [-'geːn], adj. photogenic. ◆'F~graf ['graːf], m -en/-en photographer. ◆'F~grafie [-a'fiː], f -/-n 1. (Bild) photograph. 2. no pl photography. ◆f~gra'fieren, v.tr. & i. (haben) to take a photograph (of s.o., sth.). ◆f~grafisch [-'graːfiʃ], adj. photographic. ◆f~ko'pie, f photocopy. ◆f~ko'pieren, v.tr. to photocopy.
Foyer [foa'jeː], n -s/-s foyer.
Fracht [fraxt], f -/-en 1. freight; (Ladung) load, Av: Nau: cargo. 2. (Transportpreis) freight. ◆'F~er, m -s/- freighter. ◆'F~gut, n freight; Av: Nau: cargo. ◆'F~kosten, pl freight cost. ◆'F~schiff, n freighter.
Frack [frak], m -(e)s/-e tails.
Frage ['fraːɡə], f -/-n question; (j-m) eine F. stellen, to ask (s.o.) a question; außer F. stehen/sein, to be beyond any doubt; etwas in F. stellen, (i) (Pers.) to question sth; (ii) (Sache) to call sth into question; in F. kommen, to come into consideration; (Pers.) to be eligible; das kommt nicht in F., that is out of the question; ohne F., undoubtedly; nur eine F. der Zeit, only a matter of time. ◆'F~ebogen, m questionnaire. ◆'f~en, v.tr. & i. (haben) j-n etwas f., to ask s.o. sth.; um Rat, Erlaubnis usw. f., to ask for advice, permission etc. ◆'f~end, adj. enquiring (look etc.). ◆'F~esteller(in), m -s/- (pl f -/-nen) questioner. ◆'F~ezeichen, n -s/- question mark. ◆'f~lich, adj. 1. questionable. 2. die f~lichen Personen, the people in question. ◆'f~los, adv. unquestionably. ◆'f~würdig, adj. questionable. ◆'F~würdigkeit, f -/no pl dubiousness.
Fragment [frag'mɛnt], n -(e)s/-e fragment. ◆f~arisch [-'taːriʃ], adj. fragmentary.
Fraktion [fraktsi'oːn], f -/-en Pol: parliamentary party; (innerhalb einer Partei usw.) faction.
Franken ['fraŋkən], m -s/- franc.
frankieren [fraŋ'kiːrən], v.tr. to stamp, Adm: frank; es ist nicht genügend frankiert, there are not enough stamps on it.
Frankreich ['fraŋkraiç], Pr.n.n -s. France.
Franse ['franzə], f fringe.
Französe [fran'tsøːzə], m -n/-n Frenchman. ◆'F~ösin [-'tsøːzin], f -/-nen Frenchwoman. ◆f~ösisch I. adj. French. II. F., n -(s)/no pl (Sprache) French.
frappant [fra'pant], adj. striking. ◆f~ieren, v.tr. to strike; f~ierende Ähnlichkeit, striking similarity.
Fräse ['frɛːzə], f -/-n moulding/(für Metall) milling machine. ◆'f~en, v.tr. to

shape (wood); to mill (metal).
Fratze ['fratsə], f -/-n grimace; F~n schneiden/ziehen, to make faces.
Frau [frau], f -/-en woman; (Ehef.) wife; F. Schmidt, (i) (verheiratet) Mrs. Schmidt; (ii) (unverheiratet) Miss Schmidt; F. Präsident, Madam President. ◆'F~enarzt(-ärztin), m (f) gynaecologist. ◆'F~enbewegung, f feminist movement. ◆'F~enheld, m lady-killer. ◆'F~enzeitschrift, f women's magazine. ◆'F~enzimmer, n -s/- Pej: female. ◆'f~lich, adj. womanly.
Fräulein ['frɔylain], n -s/- 1. young lady. 2. F. Schmidt, Miss Schmidt.
frech [frɛç], adj. cheeky; F~e fresh; barefaced (lie etc.); (ungezogen) naughty (children). ◆'F~dachs, m F: cheeky monkey. ◆'F~heit, f -/-en (a) no pl cheek; (b) F~heiten pl, liberties; (Bemerkungen) cheeky remarks.
Fregatte [fre'ɡatə], f -/-n frigate.
frei [frai], adj. (a) free; f~er Mitarbeiter/Journalist, freelance worker/journalist; f. nach Schiller, freely adapted from Schiller; f. erfunden, entirely fictitious; f. sprechen, to speak without notes; (b) (ohne Scheu) frank (person, play etc.); F: ich bin so f.! I'll take the liberty; (sich bedienen) I'll help myself; (c) (offen, unbehindert) open, clear; (bloß) bare (torso etc.); ins F~e gehen, to go outdoors/into the open (air); den Oberkörper f. machen, to strip to the waist; einen Platz f. machen, to clear a space; (d) (unbesetzt) empty (chair etc.); vacant (post); ist hier noch f.? is this seat taken? (e) (kostenlos) free (entrance etc.); Com: f. Haus, free delivery; (f) sich auf einen Tag f. nehmen, to have a day off; (g) f. von + dat, free of/from. ◆'F~bad, n open-air swimming pool. ◆'f~bekommen, v.tr.sep.irr.53 (a) F: to get (a day etc.) off; (b) to secure the release of (s.o., sth.). ◆'f~beruflich, adj. freelance; self-employed. ◆'F~betrag, m tax allowance. ◆'F~brief, m justification. ◆'F~gabe, f -/no pl release. ◆'f~geben, v.tr.sep.irr.35 to release (s.o., a film etc.); to open (a road). ◆'f~gebig, adj. generous. ◆'F~gebigkeit, f -/no pl generosity. ◆'F~gepäck, n (free) baggage allowance. ◆'f~haben, v.tr.&i.sep.irr.44 (haben) F: to have (time, a day) off. ◆'f~halten, v.tr.sep.irr.45 (a) to treat (s.o.); (b) to keep (a road, entrance etc.) clear; (c) to keep, reserve (a seat). ◆'F~handelszone, f free trade area. ◆'f~händig, adj. freehand. f. radfahren, to cycle with no hands. ◆'F~heit, f -/-en freedom; in F. sein, to be free/ (Sträfling) at large; dichterische F., poetic licence. ◆'f~heitlich, adj. free. ◆'F~heitsentzug, m detention. ◆'F~heitsstrafe, prison sentence.

◆'f~he'raus, adv. frankly, bluntly. ◆'f~kommen, v.i.sep.irr.53 (sein) to be released. ◆'f~lassen, v.tr.sep.irr.57 to release, set free. ◆'f~lassung, f -/-en release. ◆'F~lauf, m freewheel; im F. fahren, to freewheel. ◆'f~legen, v.tr.sep. to expose. ◆'f~lich, adj. 1. (allerdings) admittedly. 2. certainty. ◆'f~licht-comb.fm. open-air (theatre, concert etc.). ◆'f~machen, v.tr.sep. (a) to stamp, put a stamp on (a letter); (b) to clear (a road, entrance etc.); to vacate (a seat, building); (c) to bare (one's shoulders etc.); (sich dat) den Oberkörper f., to strip to the waist; Fig: sich von etwas dat f., to rid oneself of sth. ◆'f~mütig, adj. frank. ◆'f~schaffend, adj. freelance, self-employed. ◆'f~setzen, v.tr.sep. to release (workers, Ch: gas, energy etc.). ◆'f~sprechen, v.tr.sep.irr.14 to clear (s.o.); Jur: to acquit (s.o.). ◆'F~spruch, m acquittal. ◆'f~stehen, v.i.sep.irr.100 (haben) (a) es steht dir frei, it is up to you; (b) (Gebäude) to be unoccupied. ◆'f~stellen, v.tr.sep. j-m etwas f., to leave sth. to s.o.'s discretion. ◆'F~stoß, m Fb: free kick. ◆'F~tod, m suicide. ◆'F~umschlag, m stamped envelope. ◆'f~wild, n easy game. ◆'f~willig, adj. voluntary; sich f. melden, to volunteer. ◆'f~zeichen, n ringing tone. ◆'F~zeit, f spare time, ◆'F~zeit-, comb.fm. casual, leisure (clothes etc.). ◆'F~zeitgestaltung, f planning of one's leisure. ◆'F~zeitzentrum, n leisure centre. ◆'f~zügig, adj. 1. (nicht ortsgebunden) (Pers.) free to move; nomadic (life). 2. (a) (großzügig) generous; (b) (liberal) liberal. ◆'F~zügigkeit, f -/no pl generosity; (b) permissiveness.

Freitag ['fraita:k], m Friday. ◆'f~s, adv. on Fridays.

fremd [fremt], adj. 1. (ausländisch) foreign; (nicht vertraut) strange, alien; ein F~er/eine F~e, a stranger/(Ausländer) foreigner; ich bin hier f., I am a stranger here; Lügen ist ihr f., lying is alien to her nature. 2. (andern gehörig) f~es Eigentum/Gut, other people's property. ◆'f~artig, adj. strange. ◆'f~enführer, m (Pers.) guide. ◆'f~enlegion, f foreign legion. ◆'f~enverkehr, m tourism. ◆'f~enzimmer, n 1. (hotel) room. 2. guest/spare room (in a house). ◆'f~gehen, v.i.sep.irr.36 (sein) F: to be unfaithful. ◆'F~körper, m foreign body. ◆'f~ländisch, adj. exotic. ◆'F~sprache, f foreign language. ◆'f~sprachig, adj. (person) speaking a foreign language; (lessons, literature etc.) in a foreign language. ◆'F~wort, n word of foreign origin.

frenetisch [fre'ne:tiʃ], adj. frenzied.

Frequenz [fre'kvɛnts], f -/-en Rad: Ph: frequency.

fressen ['frɛsən], I. v.tr. & i.irr.25 (haben) (a) (Tier) to eat; F: (Pers.) to gobble; Fig: to eat up (money, petrol etc.); (b) (Rost usw.) to corrode. II. F., n -s/no pl food.

Frettchen ['frɛtçən], n -s/- ferret.

Freud|e ['frɔydə], f -/-n joy, delight; (Vergnügen) pleasure; es wird mir eine F. sein, I shall be delighted; j-m (eine) F. machen, to please s.o., make s.o. happy. ◆'F~enhaus, n Lit: brothel. ◆'F~entränen, fpl tears of joy. ◆'f~estrahlend, adj. beaming. ◆'f~ig, adj. joyful, happy; f~iges Ereignis, happy event; f. überrascht sein, to be pleasantly surprised. ◆'f~los, adj. miserable. ◆'f~voll, adj. joyful, happy.

freuen ['frɔyən], v.tr. (a) to please; es freut mich, daß …, I am pleased/glad that …; (b) sich f., to be pleased/glad; er freut sich des Lebens, to enjoy life; sich an Blumen f., to take pleasure in flowers; sich auf etwas acc f., to look forward to sth.

Freund [frɔynt], m -(e)s/-e (a) friend; (b) (Verehrer) boy friend; (c) lover (of art, music etc.); ich bin kein F. davon, I'm not at all keen on it. ◆'f~eskreis, m circle of friends. ◆'f~in, f -/-nen girl friend. ◆'f~lich, adj. 1. (a) kind (person, invitation etc.); (b) friendly (manner etc.); mit f~lichen Grüßen, yours sincerely; 2. pleasant (area, room etc.); fine (weather). ◆'f~licherweise, adv. kindly. ◆'F~lichkeit, f -/no pl kindness. ◆'F~schaft, f -/-en friendship; mit j-m F. schließen, to make friends with s.o. ◆'f~schaftlich, adj. friendly, amicable. ◆'F~schaftsspiel, n friendly match.

Frevel ['fre:fəl], m -s/- Lit: iniquity. ◆'f~haft, adj. Lit: iniquitous.

Fried|en ['fri:dən], m -s/no pl peace; im F., in peacetime; laß mich in F. leave me alone! ◆'F~ens-, comb.fm. peace (movement, plan etc.); ◆'F~ensschluß, m conclusion of a peace treaty. ◆'F~ensverhandlungen, fpl peace talks. ◆'F~ensvertrag, m peace treaty. ◆'f~enszeiten, pl peacetime. ◆'f~fertig, adj. peaceable. ◆'F~fertigkeit, f -/no pl peaceable nature/behaviour. ◆'F~hof, m cemetery. ◆'f~lich, adj. 1. peaceful (times, demonstrations, purposes etc.); peaceable, calm (person, nature). 2. Lit: (ruhig) peaceful. ◆'f~liebend, adj. peace-loving.

frieren ['fri:rən], v.i.irr.32 (a) (haben) to be/feel (very) cold; ich friere/impers. mich friert (es), I am freezing; draußen friert es, it is freezing outside; (b) (sein) (Wasser usw.) to freeze.

Fries [fri:s], m -es/-e frieze.

Friesle ['fri:zə], m -n/-n/ F~in, f -nen Frisian. ◆'f~isch, adj. Frisian.

frigid(e) [fri'gi:t(-də)], adj. frigid.

Frikadelle [frika'dɛlə], f -/-n rissole.

Frikassee [frika'se:], n -s/-s fricassee.

frisch [friʃ], adj. (a) fresh; (sauber) clean (clothes etc.); f. gebackene Eheleute, a newly married couple; f. gestrichen! wet paint! sich f. machen, to freshen up, have a wash; F: f. und munter, fit and well; (b) (kühl) chilly. ◆'F~e, f -/no pl freshness. ◆'F~haltepackung, f vacuum pack. ◆'F~käse, m curd cheese. ◆'F~luft, fresh air.

Frisleur [fri'zø:r], m -s/-s hairdresser. ◆'F~euse, f -/-n hairdresser. ◆'f~ieren, v.tr. (a) to do (s.o.'s) hair; (b) F: to dress up (a report); to fiddle (accounts etc.); to soup up (an engine, a car). ◆F~iertisch, m dressing table.

Frist [frist], f -/-en (Zeitspanne) period; eine Woche F. erhalten, to receive a week's grace; (b) (Termin) time-limit; (äußerste/letzte) F., deadline. ◆'f~en, v.tr. sein Leben/seine Existenz f., to scrape a living. ◆'f~gerecht, adj. punctual. ◆'f~los, adj. immediate; f. entlassen, dismissed without notice.

Frisur [fri'zu:r], f -/-en hairstyle, F: hairdo.

frivol [fri'vo:l], adj. frivolous; risqué (joke, story).

froh [fro:], adj. happy, cheerful; f~e Weihnachten! happy/merry Christmas! ich bin f., daß ..., I am glad/(erleichtert) relieved that ... ◆f~'locken, v.i. (haben) Lit: to rejoice, (hämisch) gloat. ◆'F~sinn, m cheerfulness.

fröhlich ['frø:lic], adj. cheerful (person, mood etc.); jolly (party, games etc.); f~e Weihnachten! happy Christmas! ◆'F~keit, f -/no pl gaiety; jollity.

fromm [frɔm], adj. pious.

Frömm|elei [frœmə'lai], f -/-en no pl bigotry. ◆'F~igkeit, f -/no pl piety.

frönen ['frø:nən], v.i. (haben) Lit: einem Laster usw. f., to indulge a vice etc.

Fronleichnam [fro:n'laiçna:m], m -s/no pl Corpus Christi.

Front [frɔnt]. I. f -/-en front. F. gegen j-n/etwas acc. machen, to resist s.o., sth; Sp: in F. gehen/liegen, to take/be in the lead. II. 'F~-, comb.fm. (a) front (engine etc.); (b) Mil: front line (experience, troops etc.). ◆'f~al [-'ta:l] adj. & F~al-, comb.fm. frontal; f~aler Zusammenstoß, head-on collision. ◆'F~antrieb, m front-wheel drive.

Frosch [frɔʃ], m -es/¨e frog. ◆'F~mann, m frogman. ◆'F~schenkel, m frog's leg.

Frost [frɔst]. I. m -(e)s/¨e frost. II. 'F~-, comb.fm. frost (damage etc.); frosty (night, weather etc.). ◆'F~beule, f chilblain. ◆'f~ig, adj. frosty (weather etc.); icy (remark etc.).

frösteln ['frœstəln], v.i. (haben) mich fröstelt (es), I feel shivery.

Frottlee [frɔ'te:], n -s/-s towelling. ◆'F~eehandtuch, n towel. ◆'f~ieren [-'ti:rən], v.tr. to rub/towel (s.o., oneself) down.

Frucht [fruxt]. I. f -/¨e fruit; F~e tragen, to bear fruit. II. 'F~-, comb.fm. fruit (yoghurt, salad etc.). ◆'f~bar, adj. fertile (soil, plant, imagination etc.); Fig: fruitful (period, talks etc.); prolific (writer). ◆'F~barkeit, f -/no pl fertility. ◆'F~fleisch, n fruit flesh. ◆'f~ig, adj. fruity. ◆'f~los, adj. fruitless. ◆'F~saft, m fruit juice.

früh [fry:], adj. (a) early; er ist f. gestorben, he died young; f~er oder später, sooner or later; (b) f~er, former (time, enemies); previous (owner etc.); er war f~er Journalist, he used to be a journalist; (c) (morgens) morgen/heute f., tomorrow/this morning; von f. bis spät, from dawn till dusk. ◆'F~aufsteher, m early riser. ◆'F~e, f -/no pl in aller F., bright and early. ◆'f~estens, adv. at the earliest. ◆'F~geburt, f premature birth. ◆'f~jahr, n spring. ◆'F~jahrsputz, m -es/no pl spring clean(ing). ◆'F~ling, m -s/-e spring. ◆'f~morgens, adv. early in the morning. ◆'f~reif, adj. precocious. ◆'F~reife, f precociousness. ◆'F~schicht, f early shift. ◆'F~sport, m morning exercises. ◆'F~stück, n breakfast. ◆'f~stücken, v. 1. v.i. (haben) to have breakfast. 2. v.tr. to have for breakfast. ◆'f~zeitig, adj. early; (vorzeitig) premature.

Frust [frust], m -(e)s/no pl F: frustration. ◆'f~rieren [-'tri:rən], v.tr. to frustrate.

Fuchs [fuks], m -es/¨e fox; (Pferd) chestnut. ◆'F~bau, m fox's earth. ◆'f~en, v.tr. F: to make (s.o.) mad; ◆'f~ig, adj. F: furious, mad. ◆'F~jagd, f fox-hunt(ing). ◆'F~schwanz, m handsaw. ◆'f~teufels'wild, adj. F: hopping mad.

Füchsin ['fyksin], f -/-nen vixen.

Fucht|el ['fuxtəl], f -/no pl F: unter der F. sein/stehen, to be kept in check. ◆'f~eln, v.i. (haben) F: mit den Händen f., to wave one's hands.

Fuge ['fu:gə], f -/-n joint; (Spalte) crack; Fig: aus den F~n geraten, to go to pieces. 2. Mus: fugue.

fügen ['fy:gən], v.tr. (a) to join (sth.) (in etwas acc, to sth.), fit (sth.) (in etwas acc, into sth.); (b) sich j-m, etwas dat f., to give in to s.o., sth.; Lit: sich in sein Schicksal f., to resign oneself to one's fate; (c) Lit: es fügte sich, daß ..., it so happened that ... ◆'f~sam, adj. compliant.

fühl|bar ['fy:lba:r], adj. palpable (loss, relief etc.); tangible, noticeable (difference etc.). ◆'F~en, v.tr. (a) to feel; (b) v.refl. sich krank, betrogen usw. f., to feel ill, deceived etc. ◆'F~er, m -s/- feeler; Fig: die F. ausstrecken, to put out feelers. ◆'F~ung, f -/no pl contact; mit j-m F. aufnehmen, to get in touch with s.o.

Fuhre ['fu:rə], f -/-n cartload. ◆'F~mann, m -(e)s/-leute cart driver. ◆'F~park, m fleet (of vehicles). ◆'F~unternehmer, m haulage contractor. ◆'F~werk, n waggon, cart.

führen ['fy:rən], v. 1. v.tr. (a) to lead (s.o.); to take (s.o.) (über die Straße usw., across the road etc.); Hunde müssen an der Leine geführt werden, dogs must be kept on a lead/N.Am: leash; das Glas zum Mund f., to raise the glass to one's lips; (b) (leiten) to command (a regiment etc.); to captain (a team); to run, manage (a business, hotel etc.); Krieg f., to wage war; (c) to carry (water, oil etc.); Com: to stock (goods); er führt kein Geld bei sich, he doesn't have any money on him; (d) (betreiben) to hold (a conversation, talks etc.); to keep (a diary, list etc.); ein elendes Leben f., to lead a miserable life; über etwas acc Buch f., to keep a record of sth.; (e) Adm: to drive (a vehicle); (f) v.refl. sich (gut/schlecht) f., to behave (well/badly). 2. v.i. (haben) to lead; die Straße führt an der Küste entlang, the road runs along the coast; das führt zu weit, that is going too far; unsere Bemühungen führten zu nichts, our efforts got us nowhere. ◆'f~end, adj. leading (newspaper, firm etc.); prominent (personality); in der Entwicklung f. sein, to be in the forefront of development. ◆'F~er(in), m -s/- (f -/-nen) 1. (Pers.) (a) leader; Mil: commander; (b) (im Museum usw.) guide; (c) (Fahrer) driver. 2. (Buch) guidebook. ◆'F~erschein, m driving licence; den F. machen, to take one's driving test; (fahren lernen) to learn to drive. ◆'F~ung, f -/-en 1. no pl Pol: etc: leadership; Com: management; Mil: command. 2. no pl Sp: etc: in F. liegen/gehen, to be in the lead. 3. no pl (Betragen) conduct. 4. (Besichtigung) guided tour (durch ein Museum, of a museum). ◆'F~ungszeugnis, n certificate of good conduct.

Fülle ['fylə], f -/no pl (große Menge) wealth (von Einfällen usw., of ideas etc.). ◆'f~en, v.tr. (a) to fill (sth.); Cu: to stuff; (b) (schütten) to put (sth.) (in Flaschen usw., into bottles etc.); (c) sich f., to fill (up). ◆'F~federhalter/F ◆'F~er, m -s/- fountain pen. ◆'f~ig, adj. plump. ◆'F~ung, f -/-en 1 filling; (in meat etc.). 2. (Türf.) (door) panel.

fummeln ['foməln], v.i. (haben) F: to fumble (an etwas dat, with sth.).

Fund [funt], m -(e)s/-e 1. (Finden)

finding. 2. (Gefundenes) find. ◆'F~büro, n lost property/N.Am: lost and found office. ◆'F~grube, f -/-n (Geschäft usw.) goldmine; (Buch usw.) mine of information. ◆'F~ort, m place where it was/they were found. ◆'F~sache, f object found; pl lost property. ◆'F~stätte, f site of a find.

Fundament [funda'ment], n -(e)s/-e foundation(s); Fig: basis (of a theory etc.). ◆f~amen'tal, adj. fundamental.

fündig ['fyndiç], adj. f. werden, to make a find.

fünf [fynf], num. adj. five. ◆'F~eck, n pentagon. ◆'f~eckig, adj. five-sided. ◆'f~fach, adj. quintuple; fünf mal times. ◆'f~jährig, adj. five-year-old (child, animal); five-year (period). ◆'F~kampf, m pentathlon. ◆'f~mal, adv. five times. ◆'f~stellig, adj. five-figure. ◆'f~t, adv. zu f., in a group of five. ◆'f~te(r, s), num. adj. fifth. ◆'F~tel, n -s/- fifth. ◆'f~tens, adv. fifthly. ◆'f~zehn, num. adj. fifteen. ◆'f~zig, num. adj. fifty.

fungieren [fuŋ'gi:rən], v.i. (haben) to officiate; (Gegenstand) f. als, to function as.

Funk [funk]. I. m -s/no pl radio; über F., by radio. II. 'F~-, comb.fm. radio station, contact etc.). ◆'F~e, m -n/-n spark; glimmer (of hope etc.). ◆'f~eln, v.i. (haben) to sparkle (Licht, Sterne) twinkle; (Edelstein usw.) to glitter. ◆'f~el'nagel'neu, adj. F: brand new. ◆'f~en. I. v.tr. to radio. II. F., m -s/- = Funke. ◆'F~er, m -s/- radio operator. ◆'F~haus, n radio station. ◆'F~spruch, m radio message. ◆'F~streife, f radio patrol.

Funktion [funktsi'o:n], f -/-en (a) (also Mth:) function; (b) no pl working; außer F., out of action. ◆F~är [-o'nε:r], m -s/-e official. ◆f~ieren [-'ni:rən], v.i. (haben) to work. ◆'F~sstörung, f -/-en malfunction.

Funzel ['funtsəl], f -/-n F: dim/dismal light.

für [fy:r]. I. prep. + acc for; das hat viel f. sich, there is much to be said for it; j-n sprechen, to speak on s.o.'s behalf; f~s erste, for now; Tag f. Tag, day by day; Wort f. Wort, word for word; Schritt f. Schritt, step by step; f. sich, alone; ein Volk f. sich, a race apart; an und f. sich, actually; (im Grunde) basically. II. F., n das F. und Wider, the pros and cons. ◆f~ei'nander, adv. for each/one another. ◆'F~sorge, f -/no pl 1. care. 2. (Sozialhilfe) welfare; F: er lebt von der F., he is living on social security. ◆'F~sorger(in), m -s/- (f -/-nen) social worker. ◆'F~sorgeunterstützung, f social security benefit. ◆'f~sorglich, adj. considerate, thoughtful. ◆'F~sprache, f -/no pl plea; (bei j-m) für j-n F. einlegen, to

plead (with s.o.) on s.o.'s behalf.
◆'F~sprecher, m advocate.
◆'F~wort, n pronoun.
Furche ['furçə], f -/-n furrow.
Furcht [furçt], f -/no pl fear; **vor etwas** dat **F. haben,** to be afraid of sth.; **aus F. vor Strafe,** for fear of punishment. ◆'f~bar, adj. terrible; (dreadful); f~baren **Hunger haben,** to be terribly hungry. ◆'f~los, adj. fearless. ◆'F~losigkeit, f -/no pl fearlessness. ◆'f~sam, adj. timid (person, animal); apprehensive (looks etc.). ◆'F~samkeit, f -/no pl timidity.
fürcht|en ['fyrçtən], v. 1. v.tr. (a) to fear, be afraid of; (b) **sich f.,** to be afraid/ frightened (**vor j-m, etwas** dat, of s.o., sth.) 2. v.i. (haben) to be afraid; **um/für j-n, etwas** acc **f.,** to fear for s.o., sth. ◆'f~erlich, adj. terrifying (sight etc.); F: terrible.
Furnier [fur'niːr], n -s/-e veneer.
Furore [fu'roːrə], f & n **F. machen,** to cause a sensation.
Fürst [fyrst], m -en/-en prince. ◆'F~entum, n -s/-er principality. ◆'F~in, f -/-nen princess. ◆'f~lich, adj. royal (family etc.); princely (bearing, Fig: sum etc.); sumptuous (meal etc.); f. **leben/essen,** to live/eat like a prince.
Furt [furt], f -/-en ford.
Fuß [fuːs], m -es/-e 1. (a) foot; **zu F., on** foot; **zu F. gehen,** to walk; (**bei**) **F.!** heel! (also Fig:) **j-n, etwas mit F~en treten,** to trample on s.o., sth. underfoot; (b) Fig: (**festen**) **F. fassen,** (i) (Pers.) to find one's feet; (ii) (Ideen usw.) to become established; **auf großem F. leben,** to live like a lord; **mit j-m auf gutem F. stehen,** to be on good terms with s.o. 2. **foot,** bottom (of a mountain, stairs etc.); base (of a lamp, pillar etc.); stem (of a glass); leg (of a table). ◆'F~abdruck, m footprint. ◆'F~angel, f mantrap. ◆'F~ball, m football. ◆'F~ball-, comb.fm. football (team stadium etc.). ◆'F~ballfeld, n football pitch. ◆'F~ballplatz, m football ground. ◆'F~ballspiel, n football match. ◆'F~ballspieler, m footballer. ◆'F~boden, m floor. ◆'F~bremse, f footbrake. ◆'f~en, v.i. (haben) (Argument, Theorien usw.) to be based (**auf** + dat, on). ◆'F~ende, n foot. ◆'F~gänger, m -s/- pedestrian. ◆'F~gänger-, comb.fm. pedestrian (crossing etc.). ◆'F~gängerzone, f pedestrian precinct. ◆'F~gelenk, n ankle (joint). ◆'f~hoch, adj. ankle-deep. ◆'F~leiste, f skirting board. ◆'F~marsch, m march. ◆'F~matte, f doormat. ◆'F~note, f footnote. ◆'F~pflege, f -/no pl chiropody. ◆'F~pfleger(in), m (f) chiropodist. ◆'F~pilz, m athlete's foot. ◆'F~rücken, m instep. ◆'F~sohle, f sole of the foot. ◆'F~stapfen, m -s/- Fig: **in j-s F. treten,** to follow in s.o.'s footsteps. ◆'F~tritt, m kick. ◆'F~weg, m footpath.
Fussel ['fusəl], f -/-n (bit of) fluff. ◆'f~ig, adj. (Stoff usw.) covered in fluff.
Futter[1] ['futər], n -s/- Cl: etc: lining. ◆'F~stoff, m lining.
Futter[2], n -s/no pl feed. ◆'F~neid, m professional jealousy.
Futteral [futə'raːl], n -s/-e case; (knife) sheath.
füttern[1] ['fytərn], v.tr. to line (clothes).
füttern[2] v.tr. to feed (an animal, patient, computer, F: machine).
Futur [fu'tuːr], n -s/no pl future (tense).

G

G, g [geː], n -/- (the letter) G, g.
Gabe ['gaːbə], f -/-n gift.
Gabel ['gaːbəl], f -/-n (a) fork; (b) Tel: cradle. ◆'g~n, v.refl. **sich g.,** to fork. ◆'G~stapler, m -s/- fork lift truck. ◆'G~ung, f -/-en fork.
gackern ['gakərn], v.i. (haben) to cackle, cluck.
gaffen ['gafən], v.i. (haben) to gape, (starren) stare. ◆'G~er, m -s/- Pej: curious bystander.
Gage ['gaːʒə], f -/-n fee.
gähnen ['geːnən], v.i. (haben) to yawn; **der Abgrund, gaping chasm.
Gala ['gaːla], f -/no pl evening dress. ◆'G~vorstellung, f gala performance.
galant [ga'lant], adj. gallant.
Galerie [galə'riː], f -/-n gallery.
Galgen ['galgən], m -s/- gallows. ◆'G~frist, f (brief) respite. ◆'G~humor, m gallows humour.
Gall|e ['galə], f -/-n (a) bile; Fig: gall; (b) = **Gallenblase.** ◆'G~enblase, f gall bladder. ◆'G~enstein, m gall-stone.
Galopp [ga'lɔp], m -s/-s & -e gallop. ◆'g~ieren [-'piːrən], v.i. (haben/sein) to gallop.
Gamasche [ga'maʃə], f -/-n spat.
gamm|eln ['gaməln], v.i. (haben) F: to loaf about. ◆'G~ler(in), m -s/- (f -/-nen) F: drop-out.
gang [gaŋ], **g. und gäbe sein,** to be the usual thing.
Gang[2], m -(e)s/-e 1. (a) (Art zu gehen) gait; (b) **in G. sein,** to be running; Fig: **etwas in G. bringen/halten,** to keep sth. going; **in G. kommen,** to get under way. 2. (Lauf) course (of duties, business etc.). 3. (Spaziergang) walk; (Boteng.) errand. 4. course (of a meal). 5. Aut: gear.

6. (*Weg*) path; (*im Gebäude*) corridor; (*Flur*) hallway. ◆'G~schaltung, *f Aut:* gearchange, *N.Am:* gearshift.

Gangster ['gɛŋstɐr], *m* -s/- gangster.

gängeln ['gɛŋəln], *v.tr.* to treat (s.o.) like a child.

gängig ['gɛŋiç], *adj.* (*a*) common (opinion, expression); (*b*) *Com:* popular (goods, line).

Ganove [ga'no:və], *m* -n/-n *P:* crook.

Gans [gans], *f* -/¨e ['gɛnzə] goose.

Gänse|blümchen ['gɛnzəbly:mçən], *n* -s/- daisy. ◆'G~braten, *m* roast goose. ◆'G~füßchen, *n* -s/- *F:* quotation marks. ◆'G~haut, *f F:* goose-pimples. ◆'G~marsch, *m* im G., in single file.

ganz [gants]. **I.** *adj.* 1. whole; von g~em Herzen, with all one's heart; g~e Arbeit leisten, to do a thorough job; g~ Deutschland, all/the whole of Germany. meine g~en Sachen, all my things. 2. quite; eine g~e Menge, quite a lot. 3. *F:* (*heil*) intact; etwas wieder g. machen, to mend sth. **II.** *adv.* 1. (*völlig*) completely; quite; er weiß es g. genau, he knows it perfectly well; du hast g. recht, you are quite right; g. wie du denkst, just as you think; sie ist mir g. fremd, she is a complete stranger to me; g. und gar, utterly, completely; g. und gar nicht, not by any means. 2. (*ziemlich*) quite; es war g. schön, it was quite nice. ◆'G~e(s), *n decl. as adj.* (*a*) das G., the whole (thing); (*Summe*) the total; Fig: aufs G. gehen, to force the issue; (*b*) im g~n, in all, altogether. ◆'g~jährig, *adj.* all year (round). ◆'g~tägig, *adj.* whole day's (journey etc.); full-time (employment etc.). ◆'g~tags, *adv.* g. arbeiten, to work full-time.

gänzlich ['gɛntsliç], *adj.* complete; *adv.* completely.

gar [gɑːr]. **I.** *adj. Cu:* g. (gekocht), (well) cooked, done. **II.** *adv.* (*a*) g. nicht, not at all; g. nicht schlecht, not at all bad; g. nichts, nothing at all; g. keiner, nobody at all; (*b*) (*sogar*) oder g. ..., or even ...; ◆'G~aus, *m -/no Pl F:* j-m den G. machen, to finish s.o. off. ◆'g~en, *v.tr.* to cook.

Garage [ga'rɑːʒə], *f* -/-n garage.

Garantie [garan'tiː], *f* -/-n guarantee (auf/für etwas acc. on sth.); bie für etwas acc. übernehmen, to vouch for/guarantee sth. ◆g~ieren [-'tiːrən], *v.tr. & i.* (*haben*) etwas/für etwas acc g., to guarantee sth. ◆G~iezeit, *f* -/-en guarantee.

Garbe ['garbə], *f* -/-n 1. sheaf. 2. *Mil:* cone of fire.

Garde ['gardə], *f* -/-n 1. die G., the Guards. 2. *F:* die alte G., the old faithfuls.

Garderobe [gardə'roːbə], *f* -/-n 1. (*Kleider*) clothes. 2. (*Kleiderablage*) cloakroom, *N.Am:* checkroom. ◆G~nfrau, *f* cloakroom/*N.Am:* checkroom attendant.

◆'G~enmarke, *f* -/-n cloakroom ticket, *N.Am:* hat/coat check.

Gardine [gar'diːnə], *f* -/-n (net)-curtain.

gären ['gɛːrən], *v.i.* (*haben*) to ferment.

Garn [garn], *n* -(e)s/-e yarn, thread.

Garnele [gar'neːlə], *f* -/-n shrimp; (*rote*) G., prawn.

garnier|en [gar'niːrən], *v.tr.* to garnish. ◆G~ung, *f* -/-en garnish.

Garnison [garni'zoːn], *f* -/-en garrison.

Garnitur [garni'tuːr], *f* -/-en (*a*) set; (*b*) *F:* erste/zweite G. sein, to be topnotch/second best.

garstig ['garstiç], *adj.* nasty, horrid.

Garten ['gartən]. **I.** *m* -s/¨ garden. **II.** ◆'G~, *comb.fm.* garden (wall, path etc.). ◆'G~arbeit, *f* gardening. ◆'G~bau, *m* horticulture. ◆'G~fest, *n* garden party. ◆'G~gerät, *n* gardening tool. ◆'G~laube, *f* summerhouse. ◆'G~schau, *f* flower show. ◆'G~schere, *f* secateurs. ◆'G~zwerg, *m* -(e)s/-e (*a*) garden gnome; (*b*) *Pej:* little squirt.

Gärt|ner(in) ['gɛrtnər(in)], *m* -s/- (*f* -/-nen) gardener. ◆G~erei, *f* -/-en 1. *no Pl F:* gardening. 2. nursery; (*für Gemüse*) market garden.

Gärung ['gɛːrʊŋ], *f* -/-en fermentation.

Gas [gɑːs]. **I.** *n* -es/-e (*a*) gas; (*b*) *Aut:* G. geben, to accelerate. **II.** ◆'G~, *comb.fm.* gas (chamber, supply etc.). ◆'G~brenner, *m* gas burner. ◆'G~flasche, *f* gas cylinder. ◆'G~hahn, *m* gas tap. ◆'G~heizung, *f* gas(-fired) central heating. ◆'G~herd, *m* gas cooker/*N.Am:* range. ◆'G~kocher, *m* gas stove. ◆'G~maske, *f* gas mask. ◆'G~meter [gazo'meːtər], *m* -s/- gasometer. ◆'G~pedal, *n* accelerator pedal.

Gasse ['gasə], *f* -/-n *a*) back street, alley; (*b*) *Aus:* street; (*c*) (*durch die Menge*) passage. ◆'G~enjunge, *m* street urchin.

Gast [gast]. **I.** *m* -(e)s/¨e (*a*) guest; bei j-m zu G. sein, to be s.o.'s guest; (*b*) (*im Lokal usw.*) patron. **II.** ◆'G~, *comb.fm.* guest (speaker etc.); visiting (professor, *Sp:* team etc.). ◆'G~arbeiter, *m* foreign worker. ◆'g~freundlich, *adj.* hospitable. ◆'G~freundschaft, *f* hospitality. ◆'G~geber, *m* -s/- host. ◆'G~geberin, *f* -/-nen hostess. ◆'G~haus, *n* small hotel. ◆'G~hof, *m* country hotel. ◆'g~ieren [gas'tiːrən], *v.i.* (*haben*) to make a guest appearance. ◆'G~land, *n* host country. ◆'g~lich, *adj.* hospitable. ◆'G~lichkeit, *f* -/no Pl hospitality. ◆'G~recht, *n* right to hospitality. ◆'G~rolle, *f* guest role. ◆'G~spiel, *n* guest performance. ◆'G~stätte, *f* restaurant. ◆'G~wirt, *m* landlord. ◆'G~wirtschaft, *f* 1. restaurant. 2. (*Schenke*) public house.

Gäste|buch ['gɛstəbuːx], *n* visitors' book.

◆'G~zimmer, n spare/guest room.

Gastritis ['gastri:tɪs], f /-tiden [-'ti:dən] gastritis. ◆G~onomie [-no'mi:], f /-no pl gastronomy. ◆g~onomisch, adj. gastronomic(al).

Gatte ['gatə], m -n/-n husband; Jur: spouse. ◆G~n, f -/-nen wife; Jur: spouse. ◆'G~ung, f -/-en 1. (a) Z: Bot: genus; (b) (Art) kind. 2. Art: Lit: genre.

Gatter ['gatər], n -s/- (a) trellis; (b) (Eisen) grating; (c) (Tor) gate.

Gaukelei [gaukə'lai], f -/-en Lit: trickery. ◆'G~ler, m -s/- Lit: trickster.

Gaul [gaul], m -(e)s/¨e Pej: (old) nag.

Gaumen ['gaumən], m -s/- palate.

Gauner ['gaunər], m -s/- Pej: (a) crook; (b) F: cunning devil. ◆G~ei ['rai], f -/-en (a) no pl coll. crooked dealings; (b) swindle.

Gaze ['ga:zə], f -/-n gauze.

Gazelle [ga'tselə], f -/-n gazelle.

Gebäck [gə'bɛk], n -(e)s/no pl pastries.

Gebälk [gə'bɛlk], n -(e)s/no pl timbers; (im Dach) beams.

geballt [gə'balt], adj. massed (clouds etc.); clenched (fist); Fig: concentrated (power, fury).

gebannt [gə'bant], adj. spellbound.

Gebärde [gə'bɛ:rdə], f -/-n gesture. ◆g~n, v.refl. Lit: sich ... g., to behave ...

Gebaren [gə'bɛ:rən], n -s/no pl conduct.

gebären [gə'bɛ:rən], v.tr.irr.34 (a) to give birth to; (b) geboren werden, to be born. ◆G~mutter, f womb.

Gebäude [gə'bɔydə], n -s/- building; (Gefüge) structure.

Gebeine [gə'bainə], npl (mortal) remains, bones.

Gebell [gə'bɛl], n -(e)s/no pl barking.

geben ['ge:bən], v.tr. & i.irr. (haben) (a) to give; j-m etwas g., to give sth. to s.o.; to give s.o. sth.; F: es j-m g., (i) (die Meinung sagen) to give s.o. a piece of one's mind; (ii) (verprügeln) to let s.o. have it; (b) to hold, give (a party, ball etc.); er gibt Geschichte, he teaches history; (c) (die Karten) g., to deal (the cards); (d) viel/wenig auf etwas acc g., to set great/little store by sth.; einen Schrei von sich dat g., to utter a cry; (e) sich natürlich/freundlich g., to behave naturally/in a friendly way; (f) sich g., (Schmerz usw.) to wear off. 2. v.impers. es gibt ... acc, there is .../are ...; was gibt's? what's the matter?

Gebet [gə'be:t], n -(e)s/-e prayer; F: j-n ins G. nehmen, to take s.o. to task.

Gebiet [gə'bi:t], n -(e)s/-e 1. (a) (Gegend) area; (b) (Staatsg.) territory. 2. Fig: field. ◆g~en, v.tr.irr. & Lit: (a) (befehlen) j-m g., etwas zu tun, to command s.o. to do sth.; (b) (erfordern) to call for, demand. ◆G~er, m -s/- lord; (Herr) master; (Herrscher) ruler. ◆g~isch, adj. imperious.

Gebilde [gə'bildə], n -s/- structure.

gebildet [gə'bildət], adj. (well-)educated; (kultiviert) cultured.

Gebirge [gə'birgə], n -s/- mountains; (Bergkette) mountain range. ◆g~ig, adj. mountainous. ◆G~s, comb.fm. mountain (pass etc.). ◆G~sland-schaft, f mountain scenery. ◆G~szug, m mountain range.

Gebiß [gə'bis], n -sses/-sse (a) (set of) teeth; (b) (künstliches) G., dentures.

Gebläse [gə'blɛ:zə], n -s/- blower.

geblümt [gə'bly:mt], adj. flowery.

geboren [gə'bo:rən]. adj. born; Frau Schmidt, g~e Mayer, Mrs. Schmidt, née Mayer.

geborgen [gə'bɔrgən], adj. safe, sheltered. ◆G~heit, f -/no pl safety, security.

Gebot [gə'bo:t], n -(e)s/-e 1. (a) (Grundsatz) principle; B: die zehn G~e, the Ten Commandments; (b) Adm: regulation; gesetzliches G., legal requirement. 2. bid (at an auction).

Gebrauch [gə'braux], m no pl (a) use; von etwas dat G. machen, to make use of sth.; (b) usage (of a word etc.). ◆g~en, v.tr. to use, make use of; das kann ich gut g., I can make good use of that. ◆G~s-, comb.fm. utility (furniture etc.); ◆G~sanweisung, f directions for use. ◆G~sartikel, m basic commodity. ◆g~sfertig, adj. ready for use.

gebräuchlich [gə'brɔyçlıç], adj. customary (practice, method etc.); common (expression etc.).

gebraucht [gə'brauxt], adj. used, secondhand; (abgenutzt) worn; adv. etwas g. kaufen, to buy sth. secondhand. ◆G~wagen, m secondhand car.

Gebrechen [gə'brɛçən], n -s/- infirmity. ◆g~lich, adj. frail.

Gebrüll [gə'bryl], n -(e)s/no pl roaring (of lion etc.); bawling.

Gebühr [gə'by:r], f -/-en 1. charge, fee; (road etc.) toll; Tel: etc: charges. 2. über G., unduly. ◆g~en, v. Lit: 1. v.i. (haben) ihm gebührt Bewunderung, he deserves admiration. 2. v.refl.impers. wie es sich gebührt, as is fit and proper. ◆g~end, adj. due (respect etc.); seemly (behaviour etc.). ◆g~enfrei, adj. free of charge. ◆g~enpflichtig, adj. subject to a charge.

gebunden [gə'bundən], adj. bound; ◆g~e Ausgabe, hardcover edition.

Geburt [gə'burt], f -/-en birth. ◆G~en-, comb.fm. birth (rate etc.). ◆G~enkontrolle/G~enregelung, f birth control. ◆G~enrate/G~en-ziffer, f birth rate. ◆G~s-, comb.fm. birth ...; (date, place etc.) of birth; ◆G~sanzeige, f birth notice. ◆G~stag, m birthday. ◆G~sur-kunde, f birth certificate. ◆G~swehen, fpl labour pains.

gebürtig [gə'byrtıç], adj. er ist g~er

Engländer, he is English by birth.

Gebüsch [gə'byʃ], *n* -(e)s/-e bushes.

Gedächtnis [gə'dɛçtnis]. **I.** *n* -ses/-se memory; **etwas im G. behalten,** to remember/retain sth. **II.** **G~-,** *comb.fm.* (a) memory (training etc.); (weakness etc.) of memory; (b) (*Gedenk-*) memorial (service, church etc.). **◆G~feier,** *f* commemoration; *Ecc:* memorial service. **◆G~lücke,** *f* gap in one's memory. **◆G~stütze,** *f* mnemonic.

Gedank|e [gə'daŋkə], *m* -ns/-n **1.** thought (**an** + *acc*, of); **j-n auf andere G~n bringen,** to distract s.o.; **das habe ich ganz in G~n getan,** I did it without thinking; **2.** (*Sorgen*) **sich auf G~n über j-n, etwas *acc* machen,** to worry about s.o., sth. **3.** idea; **G~n austauschen,** to exchange ideas; *F:* **auf dumme G~n kommen,** to get silly ideas; **mit einem G~n spielen,** to toy with an idea. **◆G~en-,** *comb.fm.* (a) thought (content, reader etc.); (freedom, chain etc.) of thought; (b) (exchange etc.) of ideas. **◆G~engang,** *m,* train of thought. **◆G~engut,** *n* (stock of) ideas. **◆g~enlos,** *adj.* **1.** unthinking; *adv.* **etwas g. tun,** to do sth. without thinking. **2.** (*zerstreut*) absent-minded. **◆G~enlosigkeit,** *f* -/-en thoughtlessness; absent-mindedness. **◆G~enstrich,** *m* dash. **◆g~enverloren,** *adj.* lost in thought. **◆g~envoll,** *adj.* pensive, thoughtful.

Gedärm [gə'dɛrm], *n* -(e)s/-e intestines; *Z:* entrails.

Gedeck [gə'dɛk], *n* -(e)s/-e **1.** place (setting). **2.** (*im Restaurant*) set menu.

Gedeih [gə'dai], *m* **auf G. und Verderb,** for better or (for) worse. **◆g~en.** I. *v.i.irr.60* (*sein*) to thrive, (*finanziell*) prosper; **II.** *G.,* *n* -s/no pl success.

Gedenk- [gə'dɛŋk-], *comb.fm.* commemorative (exhibition, concert etc.); memorial (stone, tablet etc.). **◆g~en.** **I.** *v.i.irr.17* (*haben*) *Lit:* (a) **j-s, einer Sache gen g.,** to remember s.o., sth.; (b) **etwas *acc* zu tun g.,** to intend. **II.** **G.,** *n* -s/no pl memory, remembrance. **◆G~feier,** *f* commemoration; *Ecc:* memorial service. **◆G~stätte,** *f* memorial. **◆G~tafel,** *f* commemorative plaque. **◆G~tag,** *m* commemoration day.

Gedicht [gə'diçt], *n* -(e)s/-e poem.

gediegen [gə'di:gən], *adj.* pure; solid (gold, silver etc.).

Gedräng|e [gə'drɛŋə], *n* -s/no pl **1.** (*Drängen*) pushing, shoving. **2.** crush; (*Menge*) crowd. **◆g~t,** *adj.* terse, succinct (style).

gedrungen [gə'druŋən], *adj.* stocky. **◆G~heit,** *f* -/no pl stockiness.

Geduld [gə'dult], *f* -/no pl patience (zu **etwas** *dat,* for sth.); **G. haben (mit j-m),** to be patient (with s.o.). **◆g~en** [-dən], *v.refl.* **sich g.,** to be patient. **◆g~ig** [-diç], *adj.* patient.

◆G~sprobe, *f* trial of patience. **◆G~(s)spiel,** *n* puzzle.

gedunsen [gə'dunzən], *adj.* bloated.

geeignet [gə'aignət], *adj.* (**für etwas** *acc*/**zu etwas** *dat*) **g. sein,** to be suited (to sth.)/suitable (for sth.).

Gefahr [gə'fa:r], *f* -/-en danger; **j-n in G. bringen,** to endanger s.o.; **G. laufen, zu ...,** to run the risk of ...; **auf eigene G.,** at one's own risk. **◆G~en-,** *comb.fm.* danger (signal etc.). **◆G~enzulage,** *f* danger money. **◆g~los,** *adj.* safe. **◆G~losigkeit,** *f* -/no pl safeness. **◆g~voll,** *adj.* perilous.

gefähr|den [gə'fɛ:rdən], *v.tr.* to endanger; to jeopardize (the success of sth. etc.). **◆g~dung,** *f* -/-en endangering. **◆g~lich,** *adj.* dangerous. **◆G~lichkeit,** *f* -/no pl dangerous nature. **◆G~te(r),** *m* -n/-n/**G~in,** *f* -/-nen companion.

Gefälle [gə'fɛlə], *n* -s/- slope; gradient, *N.Am:* grade.

gefallen [gə'falən]. **I.** *v.i.irr.27* (*haben*) (a) **j-m g.,** to please s.o.; **das Bild gefällt mir,** I like the picture; *F:* **sich *dat* etwas g. lassen,** to put up with sth. **II.** **G.** **1.** *m* -s/no pl pleasure, delight; (**sein**) **G. an etwas** *dat* **finden/haben,** to take pleasure in sth. **2.** *m* -s/- favour; **j-m einen G. tun/erweisen,** to do s.o. a favour. **◆G~e(r),** *m decl. as adj.* **die G~en,** the dead/fallen.

gefällig [gə'fɛliç], *adj.* **1.** (*angenehm*) pleasant. **2.** (*hilfsbereit*) obliging. **◆g~st,** *adv.* (if you) please; **hör g~st zu!** will you please listen! **◆G~keit,** *f* -/-en **1.** favour. **2.** *no pl* (a) pleasantness; (b) helpfulness.

Gefangen|e(r) [gə'faŋənə(r)], *m & f decl. as adj.* prisoner. **◆G~enlager,** *n* prison camp. **◆g~halten,** *v.tr.sep.irr.45* to hold (s.o.) prisoner; to keep (an animal) in captivity. **◆G~nahme,** *f* -/no pl capture. **◆g~nehmen,** *v.tr.sep.irr.69* (a) to capture (s.o.), take (s.o.) prisoner; (b) *Fig:* to captivate. **◆G~schaft,** *f* -/no pl captivity.

Gefängnis [gə'fɛŋnis], *n* -ses/-se **1.** prison; **im G. sitzen,** to be in prison. **2.** (*G~strafe*) imprisonment. **◆G~strafe,** *f* prison sentence. **◆G~wärter,** *m* prison warder.

Gefasel [gə'fa:zəl], *n* -s/no pl *F:* twaddle, drivel.

Gefäß [gə'fɛ:s], *n* -es/-e **1.** (*Behälter*) receptacle. **2.** *Anat:* vessel.

gefaßt [gə'fast], *adj.* **1.** composed. **2. auf etwas** *acc* **g. sein,** to be prepared for sth.

Gefecht [gə'fɛçt], *n* -(e)s/-e fight; *Mil:* engagement; **den Gegner außer G. setzen,** to put one's opponent out of action. **◆G~s-,** *comb.fm.* combat (training, unit etc.); fighting (strength etc.); battle (line etc.). **◆g~sbereit** *adj.* ready for action.

gefeit [gə'fait], *adj.* **gegen etwas** *acc* **g.**

sein, to be immune to sth.

Gefieder [gə'fiːdər], n -s/- plumage, feathers. ◆**g~t**, adj. feathered.

Geflecht [gə'flɛçt], n -(e)s/-e network.

gefleckt [gə'flɛkt], adj. spotted, speckled.

Geflügel [gə'flyːgəl], n -s/no pl poultry. ◆**G~schere**, f poultry shears.

Geflüster [gə'flystər], n -s/- whispering.

Gefolge [gə'fɔlgə], n -s/- 1. retinue. Fig: im G~e + gen, in the wake of.

gefragt [gə'fraːkt], adj. (sehr) g., (much) in demand.

gefräßig [gə'frɛːsɪç], adj. Pej: greedy.

Gefreite(r) [gə'fraitə(r)], m decl. as adj. lance-corporal; N.Am: private first class.

Gefrier- [gə'friːr-], comb.fm. (a) frozen (meat etc.); (b) refrigeration (chamber etc.). ◆**g~en**, v.i.irr.32 (sein) to freeze. ◆**G~fach**, n freezer compartment. ◆**G~punkt**, m freezing-point. ◆**g~trocknen**, v.tr.sep. to freeze-dry. ◆**G~truhe**, f -/-n (chest) freezer.

Gefüge [gə'fyːgə], n -s/- structure. ◆**g~ig**, adj. pliant; j-n g. machen, to bend s.o. to one's will.

Gefühl [gə'fyːl], n -(e)s/-e feeling; ich habe kein gutes G. dabei, I feel uneasy about it; seinen G~en freien Lauf lassen, to give vent to one's emotions; etwas im G. haben, to know sth. instinctively. ◆**g~los**, adj. 1. numb (fingers etc.). 2. unfeeling (gleichgültig) indifferent. ◆**G~s-**, comb.fm. emotional (content, life, world etc.). ◆**g~sbetont**, adj. emotional. ◆**G~sduselei**, f -/no pl sentimentality. ◆**g~smäßig**, adj. emotional. ◆**g~voll**, adj. sensitive (person); (Musik usw.) emotional.

gefüllt [gə'fylt], adj. filled.

gegeben [gə'geːbən], adj. (vorhanden) present (circumstances etc.); given (quantity etc.); im g~en Fall, in this present case; zur g~en Zeit, at the proper time. ◆**g~enfalls**, adv. if necessary.

gegen [ge:gən]. I. prep. + acc 1. against; (bei Versus; ein Mittel g. Husten, a remedy for coughs. 2. (in Richtung auf) (a) towards; g. Osten, towards the east, eastwards; etwas g. die Wand lehnen, to lean sth. against the wall; (zeitlich) g. Abend/Morgen, towards evening/morning; (b) (ungefähr) about; g. Weihnachten, around Christmas; (c) (gegenüber) to, towards (s.o.); grausam/höflich g. j-n sein, to be cruel/polite to s.o. 3. (verglichen mit) das ist nichts g. seine Party, this is nothing compared with his party. 4. (im Austausch für) in exchange for. II. G~, comb.fm. (a) (entgegengesetzt) opposite (side etc.); (example etc.) of the contrary; opposing (candidate etc.); (b) (entgegenwirkend) counter- (argument, demonstration etc.). ◆**G~angriff**, m counter-attack. ◆**G~darstellung**, f 1. reply (to an article etc.). 2. conflicting version (of an

event etc.). ◆**g~einander**, adv. against one another/each other. ◆**G~fahrbahn**, f opposite traffic lane. ◆**G~frage**, f counter-question. ◆**G~gewicht**, n counterbalance. ◆**G~gift**, n antidote. ◆**G~leistung**, f G., service/favour in return. ◆**G~mittel**, n remedy (gegen + acc, for); (gegen Gift) antidote. ◆**G~probe**, f cross-check. ◆**G~satz**, m 1. contrast (zu etwas dat, with sth.); in scharfem G. zueinander stehen, to be sharply contrasted. 2. (Gegenteil) opposite. ◆**g~sätzlich**, adj. opposing (opinions, forces etc.); opposite (views, terms etc.). ◆**G~schlag**, m retaliation. ◆**g~seitig**, adj. mutual; sich g. helfen, to help each other. ◆**G~seitigkeit**, f -/no pl reciprocity; auf G. beruhen, to be mutual. ◆**G~spieler**, m opponent. ◆**G~stand**, m (a) (Ding, Objekt) object; (b) (Thema) subject. ◆**G~stimme**, f protesting voice; Pol: etc: vote against. ◆**G~stück**, n 1. (Gegenstand) counterpart (zu etwas dat, of sth.). 2. (G~teil) opposite. ◆**G~teil**, n das G., the opposite; im G., on the contrary. ◆**g~teilig**, adj. opposite (opinion etc.); (statement etc.) to the contrary. ◆**g~über**. I. prep. + dat (a) opposite; (b) er ist mir g. sehr freundlich, he is very friendly towards/to me; (c) (verglichen mit) compared with. II. adv. das Haus g., the house opposite. III. G~, n -(s)/- person opposite. ◆**g~überliegen**, v.i.sep.irr.62 (haben) etwas g., to be opposite sth.; g~ übersehen, v.i.sep.irr.100 (haben) (a) j-m, etwas dat g., to be opposite s.o., sth.; Fig: to face sth.; (b) j-m feindlich/freundlich g., to have a friendly/hostile attitude to s.o. ◆**g~überstellen**, v.tr.sep. j-n einem Zeugen usw. g., to confront s.o. with a witness etc.; zwei Sachen (einander) g., to compare two things. ◆**g~übertreten**, v.i.sep.irr.105 (sein) j-m (mutig/entschlossen usw.) g., to face s.o. (with courage/resolution etc.). ◆**G~verkehr**, m oncoming traffic. ◆**G~vorschlag**, m counter-proposal. ◆**G~wart**, f -/no pl 1. die G., the present (time); 2. (Anwesenheit) presence. ◆**g~wärtig**, adj. (jetzig) (a) present, current; (b) adv. at present. ◆**G~wehr**, f -/no pl resistance. ◆**G~wert**, m equivalent (value). ◆**G~wind**, m head wind. ◆**g~zeichnen**, v.tr.sep. to countersign. ◆**G~zug**, m 1. countermove. 2. Rail: oncoming train.

Gegend ['geːgənt], f -/-en area.

geglückt [gə'glykt], adj. successful.

Gegner|(in) ['geːgnər(in)], m -s/- (f -/- nen) opponent. ◆**g~isch**, adj. opposing (team, interests etc.); (*feindlich*) hostile, *Mil:* enemy (forces etc.).

Gehackte(s) [gə'haktə(s)], *n decl. as adj.* mince, minced/*N.Am:* ground meat.

Gehalt¹ [gə'halt], *m -(e)s/-e* content. **◆g~voll**, *adj.* substantial (food etc.); (book etc.) rich in content.

Gehalt², *n -(e)s/-er* salary. **◆G~s-**, *comb.fm.* salary (claim, increase etc.); **◆G~empfänger**, *m* salary earner. **◆G~szulage**, *f* bonus.

geharnischt [gə'harnɪʃt], *adj.* strongly worded (letter etc.).

gehässig [gə'hɛsɪç], *adj.* spiteful, malicious. **◆G~keit**, *f -/-en* 1 *no pl* spitefulness. 2. spiteful remark.

Gehäuse [gə'hɔʏzə], *n -s/-* (*a*) (clock etc.) case; *Rad: TV:* cabinet; *Tchn:* housing; (*b*) (snail etc.) shell; (*c*) (*Kerng.*) core.

Gehege [gə'he:gə], *n -s/-* game preserve; *Fig:* j-m ins G. kommen, to poach on s.o.'s preserves.

geheim [gə'haim]. I. *adj.* secret; im g~en, in secret, secretly. II. **G~-**, *comb.fm.* secret (agreement, agent, organization, police, weapon etc.). **◆G~dienst**, *m* secret service. **◆g~halten**, *v.tr.sep.irr.45* to keep (sth.) secret. (vor j-m, from s.o.). **◆G~haltung**, *f -/no pl* concealment. **◆G~nis**, *n -ses/-se* 1. secret. 2. (*Rätsel*) mystery. **◆G~niskräme'rei**, *f no pl* secretive behaviour. **◆g~nisvoll**, *adj.* mysterious. **◆G~rezept**, *n* secret recipe.

gehemmt [gə'hɛmt], *adj.* inhibited.

gehen [ge:ən]. *v.irr.* I. *v.i.* (*sein*) (*a*) to go; (zu Fuß) to walk; ins Ausland/in die Stadt g., to go abroad/into town; *Fig:* in sich *acc* g., (i) to take stock of oneself, (ii) to decide to mend one's ways; zum Film g., to go into films; (*b*) (*weggehen*) to leave, go; wollen wir g.? shall we go? (*c*) (*funktionieren*) (*Maschine usw.*) to be going; die Uhr geht nicht richtig, the clock is wrong; *Com:* gut g., (*Geschäfte*) to be good; (*Produkt*) to be selling well; (*d*) (*passen*) wieviel geht in den Koffer? how much will go/fit into the suitcase? (*e*) (*sich richten nach*) or geht nach dem Äußeren, he goes by appearances; wenn es nach mir ginge, if I had anything to do with it; (*f*) (*reichen, sich erstrecken*) das Wasser ging ihm bis zum Knie, the water came up to his knees; es geht nichts über ... *acc*, you can't beat ...; es geht auf/gegen Mitternacht, it is nearly midnight; (*g*) das geht zu weit, that's going too far; die Dinge g. lassen, to let things take their course; sich g. lassen, to lose one's self-control; (*h*) (*möglich sein*) das geht nicht, that is impossible; (*nicht akzeptabel*) that won't do; geht es so? is it all right like that? (*i*) es geht ihm gut/schlecht, (i) he is well/ill; (ii) (*finanziell usw.*) he is doing well/badly; wie geht es Ihnen? how are you?; (*j*) es geht um ...

acc, it is a question of ...; worum geht es? what's it about? es geht ihm nur um das Geld, he is only interested in the money. 2. *v.tr.* (*sein*) to walk (a kilometre etc.). **◆g~enlassen**, *v.tr. sep.irr.57* (*haben*) sich g., to lose one's self-control. **◆g~er**, *m -s/-* walker. **◆g~fähig**, *adj.* able to walk. **◆G~steig/ 'G~weg**, *m* pavement, *N.Am:* sidewalk.

geheuer [gə'hɔʏər], *adj.* nicht (ganz) g., eerie; dubious (idea, business).

Geheul [gə'hɔʏl], *n -(e)s/no pl* howling.

Gehilf|e [gə'hɪlfə], *m -n/-n/G~in*, *f -/-nen Com:* trainee.

Gehirn [gə'hɪrn]. I. *n -(e)s/-e* brain. II. **G~-**, *comb.fm.* brain (surgeon, tumour etc.); cerebral (haemorrhage etc.). **◆G~erschütterung**, *f* concussion. **◆G~hautentzündung**, *f -/no pl* meningitis. **◆G~wäsche**, *f F:* brainwashing.

gehoben [gə'ho:bən]. *adj.* superior (position); elevated (language, style etc.).

Gehölz [gə'hœlts], *n -es/-e* copse.

Gehör [gə'hø:r]. I. *n -(e)s/no pl* 1. hearing; ein feines/empfindliches G., a delicate/sensitive ear. 2. sich *dat* G. verschaffen, to gain a hearing/(beim Lärm) make oneself heard. **◆g~los**, *adj.* deaf.

gehorchen [gə'hɔrçən], *v.i.* (*haben*) (+ *dat*) j-m, etwas *dat* g., to obey s.o., sth.

gehören [gə'hø:rən], *v.* 1. *v.i.* (*haben*) (*a*) j-m g., to belong to s.o.; (*b*) (*zählen zu*) er gehört (mit) zur Familie, he is one of the family; (*c*) (*Teil sein von*) es gehört zu meiner Arbeit, it's part of my job; es gehört dazu, it's the done thing; (*d*) (*nötig sein*) dazu gehört viel Mut, that takes a lot of courage. 2. *v.refl.* sich g., to be right; es gehört sich nicht, it isn't done. **◆g~ig**, *adj.* 1. proper (respect, distance etc.). 2. *F:* (*tüchtig*) real.

gehorsam [gə'ho:rza:m]. I. *adj.* obedient. II. **G~**, *m -s/no pl* obedience.

Geier [gaiər], *m -s/-* vulture.

geifern [gaifərn], *v.i.* (*haben*) to slaver; *Fig:* gegen j-n, etwas *acc* g., to bitch about s.o., sth.

Geige [gaigə], *f -/-n* violin. **◆g~n**, *v.tr.&i.* (*haben*) to play on the violin. **◆G~nkasten**, *m* violin case. **◆G~r(in)**, *m -s/- (f -/nen)* violinist.

Geigerzähler [gaigərtsɛ:lər], *m -s/-* Geiger counter.

geil [gail], *adj.* lecherous (person, smile etc.). **◆G~heit**, *f -/no pl* lewdness, lechery.

Geisel [gaizəl], *f -/-n* hostage. **◆G~nahme**, *f -/-n* taking of hostages.

Geißbock [gaisbɔk], *m* billy-goat.

Geißel [gaisəl], *f -/-n* scourge. **◆g~n**, *v.tr.* to denounce.

Geist [gaist], *m -(e)s/-er* 1. (*a*) mind; großer G., a great mind; hier scheiden sich die G~er, opinions differ on this point; *F:* von allen guten G~ern verlassen sein, to have taken leave of one's senses;

(b) (Witz) wit. 2. (a) spirit; **G. der Zeit**, spirit of the age; *esp. Hum:* **den/seinen G. aufgeben**, to give up the ghost; (b) *Ecc:* **der Heilige G.**, the Holy Ghost/ Spirit; **gute/böse G~er**, good/evil spirits; (c) (*Gespenst*) ghost. ◆'**G~er-, comb.fm.** ghost (story, town etc.); ghostly (hand, voice etc.). ◆'**G~erbahn**, *f* ghost train. ◆'**G~erfahrer**, *m F:* driver going the wrong way on a dual carriageway. ◆'**g~erhaft**, adj. ghostly. ◆'**g~ern**, v.i. (*haben/sein*) to wander about like a ghost. ◆'**G~es-, comb. fm.** intellectual (work, life etc.); mental (attitude, illness etc.). ◆'**g~esabwesend**, adj. absent-minded. ◆'**G~esabwesenheit**, *f -/no pl* absent-mindedness. ◆'**G~esblitz**, *m F:* flash of inspiration; brainwave ◆'**g~esgegenwart**, *f* presence of mind. ◆'**g~esgegenwärtig**, adj. quick-witted. ◆'**g~esgestört**, adj. mentally deranged. ◆'**g~eskrank**, adj. mentally ill. ◆'**g~eskrankheit**, *f* mental illness. ◆'**G~eswissenschaften**, *fpl* **die G.**, the humanities, the arts. ◆'**G~eszustand**, *m* mental state; state of mind. ◆'**g~ig**, adj. 1. mental (effort, activity etc.); intellectual (capacity, powers etc.); **g. zurückgeblieben**, mentally retarded. 2. (*nicht körperlich*) spiritual (beings etc.); **g~e Getränke**, spirits. ◆'**g~lich**, adj. religious; (*kirchlich*) (of the) church, ecclesiastical; **g~e Musik**, church music. ◆'**G~liche(r)**, *m decl. as adj.* clergyman. ◆'**G~lichkeit**, *f -/no pl* **die G.**, the clergy. ◆'**g~los**, adj. stupid. ◆'**g~reich**, adj. (a) clever; (b) (*witzig*) witty.

Geiz [gaits], *m -es/no pl* miserliness. ◆'**g~en**, v.i. (*haben*) **mit etwas dat g.**, to be stingy with sth. ◆'**G~hals**, *m F:* miser. ◆'**g~ig**, adj. mean.

Gejammer [gə'jamər], *n -s/no pl* moaning.

Gekicher [gə'kiçər], *n -s/no pl* giggling.

Gekläff [gə'klɛf], *n -(e)s/no pl* yapping.

Geklapper [gə'klapər], *n -s/no pl* clatter(ing).

Geklimper [gə'klimpər], *n -s/no pl* rattling (of chains etc.); clinking (of glasses etc.).

geknickt [gə'knikt], adj. *F:* downhearted.

gekonnt [gə'kɔnt], adj. skilful, accomplished.

gekränkt [gə'krɛŋkt], adj. offended, hurt.

Gekritzel [gə'kritsəl], *n -s/no pl* scribble, scrawl.

gekünstelt [gə'kynstəlt], adj. affected (person, behaviour); artificial (smile, laugh).

Gelächter [gə'lɛçtər], *n -s/no pl* laughter; **in G. ausbrechen**, to burst out laughing.

geladen [gə'la:dən], adj. *F:* (a) (*Atmosphäre*) tense; (b) (*Pers.*) furious.

Gelage [gə'la:gə], *n -s/-* banquet.

Gelände [gə'lɛndə]. **I.** *n -s/-* 1. (a) (*Landschaft*) terrain; (b) *Mil:* **G.**

gewinnen/verlieren, to gain/lose ground. 2. (*Grundstück*) plot; (exhibition, factory) site. **II. G~-, comb.fm.** cross-country (drive, run etc.); ◆**g~gängig**, adj. *Aut:* suitable for cross-country work. ◆**G~wagen**, *m* cross-country vehicle.

Geländer [gə'lɛndər], *n -s/-* railing; (*Treppe.*) banisters.

gelangen [gə'laŋən], v.i. (*sein*) **an etwas acc/zu etwas dat g.**, to reach/*Fig:* attain sth.; **in j-s Besitz g.**, to come into s.o.'s possession.

gelassen [gə'lasən], adj. composed; (*ruhig*) calm (and collected). ◆**G~heit**, *f -/no pl* composure.

Gelatine [gela'ti:nə], *f -/no pl* gelatine; *N.Am:* gelatin.

geläufig [gə'lɔyfiç], adj. common; **das Wort ist mir nicht g.**, I am not familiar with this word.

gelaunt [gə'launt], adj. **gut/schlecht g.**, in a good mood/bad temper.

gelb [gɛlp]. adj. yellow, light; *Aut:* **bei G.**, at amber/*N.Am:* yellow. ◆**g~lich**, adj. ◆**G~sucht**, *f* jaundice.

Geld [gɛlt]. *n -(e)s/-er* 1. *no pl* money, **es geht ins G.**, it gets expensive. 2. *pl* **G~er**, *Fin:* funds; *Jur:* monies. ◆**G~angelegenheiten**, *fpl* money matters. ◆**G~anlage**, *f* investment. ◆**G~beutel**, *m/*◆**G~börse**, *f* purse. ◆**G~buße**, *f* fine. ◆**G~gier**, *f* avarice. ◆**G~mangel**, *m* lack of money. ◆**G~mittel**, *npl* (financial) resources. ◆**G~schein**, *m* (bank) note, *N.Am:* bill. ◆**G~schrank**, *m* safe. ◆**G~strafe**, *f* fine. ◆**G~stück**, *n* coin. ◆**G~wechsel**, *m* exchange (of money). ◆**G~wert**, *m* monetary value.

Gelee [ʒe'le:], *n & m -s/-s* jelly.

Gelege [gə'le:gə], *n -s/-* clutch (of eggs). ◆**g~n**, adj. (a) schön/ungünstig pleasantly/awkwardly situated; (b) (*Zeit usw.*) convenient, suitable; **das kommt mir sehr g.**, that suits me very well; (c) **mir ist viel/nichts daran g.**, it matters a great deal/little to me. ◆**G~nheit**, *f -/-en* 1. opportunity, chance **bei G.**, when there is a chance. 2. (*Anlaß*) occasion. ◆**G~nheitsarbeiter**, *m* casual worker. ◆**G~nheitskauf**, *m* bargain. ◆**g~ntlich**. **I.** adj. occasional. **II.** adv. (*manchmal*) occasionally.

gelehrig [gə'le:riç], adj. quick (to learn). ◆**g~t**, adj. learned. ◆**G~te(r)**, *m & f decl. as adj.* scholar.

Geleit [gə'lait], *n -(e)s/-e* escort; **freies/sicheres G.**, safe conduct. ◆**g~en**, v.tr. *Lit:* to escort (s.o.). ◆**G~schutz**, *m* escort.

Gelenk [gə'lɛŋk], *n -(e)s/-e* joint. ◆**g~ig**, adj. supple.

gelernt [gə'lɛrnt], adj. skilled.

Geliebte(r) [gə'li:ptə(r)], *m & f decl. as adj.* lover.

geliefert [gə'li:fərt], adj. *F:* done for,

ruined.

gelinde [gə'lində], adj. mild; adv. g. gesagt, to put it mildly.

gelingen [gə'liŋən], I. v.i.irr. (sein) to succeed, be successful; **es gelang mir/ihm**, etwas zu tun, I/he succeeded in doing sth.

gellen ['gɛlən], v.i. (haben) to sound shrill; (Schrei usw.) to ring (out).

geloben [gə'lo:bən], v.tr. Lit: to vow (sth.).

Gelöbnis [gə'lø:pnis], n -ses/-se vow.

gelöst [gə'lø:st], adj. relaxed.

gelt|en ['gɛltən], v.i.irr. (a) (Gültigkeit haben) (Fahrkarte, Paß usw.) to be valid/(Gesetz) in force; (Regel usw.) to apply (für + acc, to); **das gleiche gilt für ihn/von ihm**, the same goes for him; **etwas g. lassen**, to accept sth. (as valid); (b) viel/wenig g., to be worth a lot/a little; (c) **als etwas nom g.**, to be considered to be sth.; (d) **j-m, etwas dat g.**, (Beifall usw.) to be meant for s.o., sth.; (Kritik usw.) to be aimed at s.o., sth.; (e) impers. jetzt gilt es, ruhig zu bleiben, the essential thing now is to remain calm. ◆**g~end**, adj. prevailing (opinion, custom etc.) (law) in force; **Rechte, Forderungen usw. g. machen**, to assert rights, demands etc.; **seinen Einfluß g. machen**, to bring one's influence to bear. ◆**G~ung**, f -/no pl (a) (Gültigkeit) validity; **G. haben**, to be valid; (b) etwas zur G. bringen, to show sth. in its best light; **zur G. kommen**, to have its proper effect; **j-m, etwas dat G. verschaffen**, to bring s.o., sth. to prominence. ◆**G~ungsbedürfnis**, n need for recognition.

Gelübde [gə'lypdə], n -s/- vow.

gelungen [gə'luŋən], adj. (a) successful; (b) F: (drollig) funny, quaint.

Gelüst [gə'lyst], n -(e)s/-e Lit: craving (nach + dat/auf + acc, for).

gemächlich [gə'mɛ:çlɪç], adj. leisurely (pace, walk etc.).

Gemahl [gə'ma:l], m -s/-e (formal) spouse; **Ihr Herr G.**, your husband. ◆**G~in**, f -/-nen (formal) spouse.

Gemälde [gə'mɛ:ldə], n -s/- painting; esp. Fig: picture.

gemäß [gə'mɛ:s]. I. prep. + dat in accordance with (regulations, customs etc.); (je nach) according to (size etc.). II. adj. **j-m, etwas dat g. sein**, to be right for s.o., sth.

gemäßigt [gə'mɛ:sikt], adj. moderate; Geog: temperate (zone etc.).

gemein [gə'main], adj. 1. (a) (grob) vulgar, (person, speech etc.); (b) (niederträchtig) mean (person, behaviour); dirty (lie, trick). 2. (a) (häufig) common (housefly, sparrow etc.); (b) (allgemein) common, general; (c) (gemeinsam) **etwas mit j-m, einer Sache g. haben**, to have sth. in common with s.o., sth. ◆**G~besitz**, m public property.

◆**g~gefährlich**, adj. dangerous (to the public). ◆**G~gut**, n public property. ◆**G~heit** f -/-en 1. no pl (a) (Roheit) vulgarity; (b) (Niedertracht) meanness. 2. mean thing (to do/say). ◆**g~hin**, adv. generally. ◆**G~nutz**, m common good. ◆**g~nützig**, adj. for the common good; non-profitmaking (organization etc.). ◆**G~platz**, m platitude. ◆**g~sam**, adj. (a) common (property, interests); shared (garden etc.); joint (account, ownership, efforts etc.); mutual (friend etc.); **etwas (mit j-m, etwas dat) g. haben**, to have sth. in common (with s.o., sth.); (mit j-m) g~same Sache machen, to make common cause (with s.o.); (b) adv. (zusammen) together; es gehört ihnen g., they own it jointly. ◆**G~samkeit**, f -/-en 1. common feature. 2. no pl harmony. ◆**G~schaft**, f -/-en community; (business, political etc.) association. ◆**g~schaftlich**, adj. common (aim, interest etc.); joint (account, effort etc.). ◆**G~schafts-** comb.fm. (a) communal (kitchen, aerial etc.); co-(production, education etc.); joint (task etc.); (b) community (spirit, life etc.); social (education etc.). ◆**G~schaftsarbeit** f, joint effort; ◆**G~schaftsraum**, m recreation room; Sch: etc: common room. ◆**g~sinn**, m public spirit. ◆**g~verständlich**, adj. generally understandable. ◆**G~wesen**, n community (structure). ◆**G~wohl**, n public welfare.

Gemeinde [gə'maində]. I. f -/-n 1. (local) community. 2. Ecc: parish; (in der Kirche) congregation. II. G~-, comb.fm. (a) Adm: local (election etc.); council (property etc.); (b) Ecc: parish (centre etc.). ◆**G~mitglied**, n parishioner. ◆**G~verwaltung**, f local authority.

Gemenge [gə'mɛŋə], n -s/- mixture (aus + dat, of); (Durcheinander) jumble.

gemessen [gə'mɛsən], adj. measured.

Gemetzel [gə'mɛtsəl], n -s/- carnage; ein G., a bloodbath.

Gemisch [gə'mɪʃ], n -(e)s/-e mixture (aus + dat, of). ◆**g~t**, adj. mixed.

Gemse ['gɛmzə], f -/-n chamois.

Gemunkel [gə'muŋkəl], n -s/no pl gossip.

Gemurmel [gə'murməl], n -s/no pl murmuring, muttering.

Gemüse [gə'my:zə], n -s/- vegetable; usu.coll. vegetables. ◆**G~händler**, m greengrocer. ◆**G~laden**, m greengrocer's shop. ◆**G~zwiebel**, f Spanish onion.

Gemüt [gə'my:t], n -(e)s/-er 1. (Natur) disposition; (Gefühle) feeling(s), emotion(s); **erhitzte G~er**, frayed tempers; **sich dat etwas zu G~e führen**, to take sth. to heart. 2. (Mensch) ein einfaches/heiteres G., a simple/cheerful soul. ◆**g~lich**, adj. (a) snug, cosy (room, flat); (zwanglos) relaxed (atmosphere etc.); genial (person); **es sich dat g. ma-**

chen, to make oneself comfortable; (b) (*gemächlich*) leisurely (meal, pace etc.). ◆G~lichkeit, f -/no pl cosiness; in aller G., at one's leisure. ◆G~smensch, m F: unflappable person. ◆G~sruhe, f -/no pl equanimity; in aller G., as calmly as you please; (*gemächlich*) at one's leisure. ◆G~szustand, m frame of mind. ◆g~voll, adj. warm-hearted.

Gen [ge:n], n -s/-e gene.

genau [gə'nau], adj. (a) exact, precise; (clock, scales etc.); ich kenne ihn g., I know exactly what he's like; das weiß ich ganz g., I know that for certain; g.! exactly! (b) detailed (description, information etc.); ich weiß nichts G~es, I don't know any (of the) details; (c) (*Pers.*) meticulous; man darf nicht alles so g. nehmen, you mustn't take everything so seriously; (d) adv. (*gerade*) just; g. das wollte ich sagen, that's just/ exactly what I was going to say; er ist g. der Vater, he is just like his father. ◆g~genommen, adv. strictly speaking. ◆G~igkeit, f -/no pl (a) exactness; accuracy; (b) meticulousness. ◆g~so. I. adv. g. gut, just as good/well; ich hätte es g. gemacht, I would have done exactly the same. II. g~so-, comb.fm. just as (often, far etc.).

genehmig|en [gə'ne:migən], v.tr. to grant (an application, request etc.); (*billigen*) to approve (a plan, budget etc.); j-m etwas g., to allow s.o. sth. ◆G~ung, f -/-en (a) no pl authorization; (b) (*Schriftstück*) permit, licence.

geneigt [gə'naigt], adj. g. sein, etwas zu tun, to be inclined to do sth.

General [genə'ra:l]. I. m -s/-e & -e general. II. G~-, comb.fm. general (strike etc.); (*großangelegt*) full-scale (attack etc.); ◆G~direktor, m managing director. ◆G~probe, f dress rehearsal. ◆G~sekretär, m secretary-general. ◆g~überholen, v.tr.insep. to give (sth.) a thorough overhaul.

Generation [genəratsi'o:n], f -/-en generation. ◆G~sunterschied, m generation gap.

Generator [genə'ra:tɔr], m -s/-en [-'to:rən], generator.

generell [genə'rɛl], adj. general.

genes|en [gə'ne:zən], v.i.irr. (sein) Lit: to convalesce. ◆G~ende(r), m & f decl. as adj. convalescent. ◆G~ung, f -/no pl convalescence.

Genetik [ge'ne:tik], f -/no pl genetics.

Genf [gɛnf]. Pr.n.n -s. Geneva.

genial [geni'a:l], adj. brilliant. ◆G~ität f -/ali'tɛ:t], f -/no pl genius.

Genick [gə'nik], n -(e)s/-e (nape of the) neck.

Genie [ʒe'ni:], n -s/-s genius.

genieren [ʒe'ni:rən], v.tr. to bother (s.o.); sich g., to be/feel embarrassed; sich vor j-m g., to be shy of s.o.

genieß|bar [gə'ni:sba:r], adj. edible;

(*trinkbar*) drinkable. ◆g~en, v.tr.irr.31 (a) to enjoy (rights, s.o.'s respect etc.); (b) to eat, (*trinken*) drink (sth.); F: sie ist heute nicht zu g., she is in a filthy mood today. ◆G~er, m -s/- pleasure lover; (*im Essen und Trinken*) gourmet. ◆g~erisch, adj. appreciative; adv. with great relish.

Genitiv ['ge:niti:f], m -s/-e genitive (case).

Genoss|e [gə'nɔsə], m -n/-n Pol: etc: comrade. ◆G~enschaft, f Co-operative. ◆G~in, f -/-nen Pol: comrade.

genug [gə'nu:k], adj. enough; ich habe g. von seiner Nörgelei, I've had enough of his moaning. ◆G~tuung [-tu:uŋ], f -/no pl satisfaction.

Genüg|e [gə'ny:gə], f zur G., sufficiently; Pej: only too well; j-s Anforderungen G. leisten, to meet s.o.'s requirements. ◆g~en, v.i. (haben) (a) to be enough/sufficient (j-m, for s.o.); (b) Anforderungen usw. g., to meet requirements etc. ◆g~end, adj. enough, sufficient. ◆g~sam, adj. frugal.

Genuß [gə'nus], m -sses/-sse 1. consumption; taking (of drugs). 2. (a) (*Vergnügen*) pleasure; enjoyment. (b) in den G. einer Rente kommen, to receive a pension. ◆G~mittel, n luxury food. ◆g~süchtig, adj. self-indulgent.

genüßlich [gə'nyslic], adj. pleasurable; adv. with great relish.

Geo|graphie [geogra'fi:], f -/no pl geography. ◆G~loge [-'lo:gə], m -n/-n geologist. ◆G~logie [-lo'gi:], f -/no pl geology. ◆G~metrie [-me'tri:], f -/no pl geometry.

Gepäck [gə'pɛk]. I. n -(e)s/no pl luggage, esp. N.Am: baggage. II. G~-, comb.fm. luggage, esp. N.Am: baggage (check, locker etc.). ◆G~annahme, f luggage counter; Av: baggage check-in; ◆G~ausgabe, f baggage checkout ◆G~netz, n luggage rack. ◆G~stück, n piece of luggage. ◆G~träger, m 1. (*Pers.*) porter. 2. (am Fahrrad) carrier; Aut: roof rack. ◆G~wagen, m luggage van, N.Am: baggage car.

Gepard [gə'part], m -s/-e cheetah.

gepflegt [gə'pfle:kt], adj. (a) well-groomed (appearance, person etc.); well cared for (lawn, skin etc.); (b) civilized (atmosphere etc.); (c) high-class (wine, restaurant etc.).

Gepflogenheit [gə'pflo:gənhait], f -/-en custom.

Gepolter [gə'pɔltər], n -s/no pl banging.

gequält [gə'kvɛ:lt], adj. pained (expression); forced (smile etc.).

gerade [gə'ra:də]. I. adj. 1. even (number). 2. straight (line etc.). 3. direct (route etc.). II. adv. 1. straight; g. gegenüber, straight/directly opposite. 2. (*zeitlich*) just; er telefoniert g., he is on the phone just at the moment; **g. erst,** only just. **3.** (*verstärkend*) (a) (*genau*) exactly; **nicht g. groß/schön,** not exactly large/beautiful; (b) (*zufällig*) **er ist g. hier,** he just happens to be here; **g. heute,** today of all days; (c) (*besonders*) **g. auf diesem Gebiet,** particularly in this field. **III.** *G.,* **-/-n** *Mth:* straight line. ◆**g'~aus,** *adv.* straight ahead. ◆**g~heraus,** *adv. F:* frankly, openly. ◆**g~so,** *adv.* (+*adj.*) just as (**lang** *etc.*) ◆**g~stehen,** *v.i.sep.irr.100* (**haben**) (a) to stand straight; (b) **für etwas** *acc* **g.,** to take the responsibility for sth. ◆**g~wegs,** *adv.* directly. ◆**g~zu,** *adv.* virtually.

geradlinig [gə'raːtliːniç], *adj.* straight; direct (descendant).

gerammelt [gə'raməlt], *adv. F:* **g. voll,** crammed (full), chock-a-block.

Geranie [ge'raːniə], *f* -/-n geranium.

Gerät [gə'rɛːt], *n* -(e)s-e (a) piece of equipment; (*Werkzeug*) tool; *Cu:* utensil; (b) (*Vorrichtung*) device; *esp. El:* appliance; *Rad: TV:* set.

geraten [gə'raːtən], *v.i.irr.13* (**sein**) (a) (*irgendwohin*) **in eine Gegend** *acc/***an einen Ort** *acc* **g.,** to end up in a place; (b) **g. in** + *acc,* to get into (difficulties, a situation etc.); **in Vergessenheit, Gefangenschaft usw. g.,** to be forgotten, captured etc.; (c) (*zufällig*) **an j-n g.,** to come across s.o.; (d) (*gelingen*) **gut/ schlecht g.,** to turn out well/badly; (e) **nach j-m g.,** to take after s.o.

Geratewohl [gəratə'voːl], *n* **aufs G.,** on the off chance; (*wahllos*) at random.

geraum [gə'raum], *adj.* considerable.

geräumig [gə'rɔʏmiç], *adj.* spacious.

Geräusch [gə'rɔʏʃ], *n* -(e)s-e noise. ◆**g~los,** *adj.* noiseless. ◆**g~voll,** *adj.* noisy.

gerb|en ['gɛrbən], *v.tr.* to tan. ◆**G~er,** *m* -s/- tanner. ◆**G~e'rei,** *f* -/-en tannery.

gerecht [gə'rɛçt], *adj.* **1.** just (**gegen** + *acc,* to); (*unparteiisch*) fair (teacher, treatment etc.). **j-m, etwas** *dat* **g. werden,** to do s.o., sth. justice. **2.** (*berechtigt*) legitimate. ◆**g~fertigt,** *adj.* justified. ◆**G~igkeit,** *f* -/*no pl* justice.

Gerede [gə'reːdə], *n* -s/*no pl* talk.

ge'regelt [gə'reːgəlt], *adj.* orderly.

ge'reizt [gə'raitst], *adj.* irritated, irritable; **g~e Atmosphäre,** explosive atmosphere. ◆**G~heit,** *f* -/*no pl* irritation.

Gericht¹ [gə'riçt], *n* -(e)s-e *Cu:* dish.

Gericht², *n* -(e)s-e *Jur:* court (of law); **vor G.,** in court; **j-n, etwas vor G. bringen,** to take s.o., sth. to court; **über j-n zu G. sitzen,** to sit in judgement on s.o. ◆**g~lich,** *adj.* court (order, decision etc.); (*authority, verdict etc.*) of the court; **g~e** (legal proceedings etc.); **gegen j-n g. vorgehen,** to take legal proceedings against s.o. ◆**G~s-,** *comb.fm.* court (records, costs etc.); **g~lich** (correspondent, costs etc.); forensic (medicine);

◆**G~sarzt,** *m* forensic expert. ◆**G~shof,** *m* court (of justice). ◆**G~ssaal,** *m* courtroom. ◆**G~sverfahren,** *n* legal proceedings. ◆**G~sverhandlung,** *f* court hearing. ◆**G~svollzieher,** *m* -s/- bailiff.

gerieben [gə'riːbən], *adj. F:* crafty.

gering [gə'riŋ], *adj.* small (number, amount etc.); slight (difference etc.); low (price, temperature, *Fig:* opinion etc.); slim (chance, hope); short (distance, duration etc.); **meine g~ste Sorge,** the least of my worries; **nicht im g~sten,** not in the least; **kein G~erer als X,** no less a person than X. ◆**g~fügig,** *adj.* negligible (difference, damage etc.); marginal (improvement); minor (offence, injury etc.). ◆**g~schätzig,** *adj.* disdainful (look); disparaging (remark etc.). ◆**G~schätzung,** *f* contempt, disdain.

gerinnen [gə'rinən], *v.i.irr.73* (**sein**) (*Blut usw.*) to clot; (*Milch*) to curdle.

Gerippe [gə'ripə], *n* -s/- skeleton; *Fig:* structure.

gerissen [gə'risən], *adj. F:* crafty.

german|isch [gɛr'maːniʃ], *adj.* Germanic. ◆**G~istik,** *f* -/*no pl* German language and literature.

gern(e) ['gɛrn(ə)], *adj.* **1.** (a) **j-n, etwas g. haben,** to like s.o., sth.; **er spielt g. Tennis,** he likes playing tennis; **ich möchte g. ein Pfund Äpfel,** I'd like a pound of apples; **das glaube ich dir g.,** I can well believe that. ◆**G~egroß,** *m* -/-e *F:* show-off.

Geröll [gə'rœl], *n* -(e)s/*no pl* pebbles.

Gerste ['gɛrstə], *f* -/-n barley. ◆**G~nkorn,** *n* sty(e).

Gerte ['gɛrtə], *f* -/-n switch. ◆**g~n'schlank,** *adj.* slender.

Geruch [gə'rux], *m* -(e)s-e **1.** smell (**nach/von** + *dat,* of). **2.** *no pl* (*Sinn*) sense of smell. ◆**g~los,** *adj.* odourless. ◆**G~ssinn,** *m* sense of smell.

Gerücht [gə'ryçt], *n* -(e)s-e rumour; **es geht das G., daß...,** it is rumoured that ...

geruhsam [gə'ruːzaːm], *adj.* peaceful; (*erholsam*) relaxing.

Gerümpel [gə'rympəl], *n* -s/*no pl* junk.

Gerüst [gə'ryst], *n* -(e)s-e scaffold(ing); *Fig:* framework.

ge'salzen, *adj. F:* steep (prices etc.).

ge'sammelt, *adj.* collected.

gesamt [gə'zamt]. **I.** *adj.* whole, entire. **II.** *G~-,* *comb.fm.* (a) total (number, amount etc.); (b) overall (height, length, *Fig:* impression etc.). ◆**G~ausgabe,** *f* complete edition. ◆**g~deutsch,** *adj.* all-German. ◆**G~heit,** *f* -/*no pl* entirety; (*the*) whole. ◆**G~hochschule,** *f* *approx.* polytechnic. ◆**G~schule,** *f* comprehensive school.

Gesandt|e(r) [gə'zantər], *m decl. as adj.* envoy. ◆**G~schaft,** *f* -/-en legation.

Gesang [gə'zaŋ], *m* -(e)s-e **1.** *no pl* singing. **2.** (*Lied*) song; *Ecc:* hymn.

◆**G~buch,** n hymn book. ◆**G~verein,** m choral society.

Gesäß [gə'zɛːs], n -es/-e Anat: buttocks, F: bottom.

Geschäft [gə'ʃɛft], n -(e)s/-e 1. (a) (Laden) shop; esp. N.Am: store; (b) (Firma) business. 2. (Handel) business; **mit j-m ins G. kommen,** to (start to) do business with s.o.; **wie gehen die G~e?** how's business? 3. (Transaktion) deal; **ein gutes/schlechtes G. machen,** to get a good/bad deal. 5. (Aufgabe) job, task; **er versteht sein G.,** he knows his job. ◆**G~emacher,** m -s/- profiteer. ◆**g~ig,** adj. bustling (activity etc.); busy (person). ◆**g~lich,** adj. business (matters etc.); **g. verreist,** away on business. ◆**G~s-,** comb.fm. 1. business (letter, woman, friend, secret, life, methods, trip, world etc.). 2. shopping (street etc.). ◆**g~sführend,** adj. managing (director etc.); executive (committee etc.). ◆**G~sführer(in),** m (f) 1. Com: manager(ess). 2. secretary (of a society etc.). ◆**G~sführung,** f management. ◆**G~sinhaber(in),** m (f) proprietor. ◆**G~sjahr,** n financial year. ◆**G~sleitung,** f management. ◆**G~smann,** m businessman. ◆**g~smäßig,** adj. businesslike. ◆**G~ssinn,** m business sense. ◆**G~sstelle,** f (a) office; (b) (Filiale) branch. ◆**g~stüchtig,** adj. 1. efficient. 2. (getrieft) smart. ◆**G~sviertel,** n shopping area. ◆**G~szeit,** f hours of business. ◆**G~szweig,** m line of business.

geschehen [gə'ʃeːən]. I. v.i.irr. (sein) to happen (j-m, to s.o.). 2. **das geschieht ihm recht,** that serves him right; **es muß etwas G.!** something must be done! II. G., n -s/- (a) happening; (b) coll. events.

gescheit [gə'ʃait], adj. clever; F: **sei doch g.!** do be sensible!

Geschenk [gə'ʃɛŋk], n -(e)s/-e present. ◆**G~artikel,** m usu. pl gifts, fancy goods. ◆**G~papier,** n wrapping paper.

Geschichte [gə'ʃɪçtə], f -/-n 1. no pl history. 2. (Erzählung) story, tale. F: **eine dumme/üble G.,** stupid/nasty business. ◆**G~enerzähler,** m storyteller. ◆**g~lich,** adj. historical. ◆**G~s-,** comb.fm. history (book, teacher etc.); historical (research etc.). ◆**G~sschreiber,** m -s/- historian.

Geschick [gə'ʃɪk], n -(e)s/-e 1. Lit: (Schicksal) fate. 2. no pl skill. ◆**G~lichkeit,** f -/no pl skill (bei + dat, at, in). ◆**g~t,** adj. skilful (in + dat, at).

geschieden [gə'ʃiːdən], adj. divorced.

Geschirr [gə'ʃɪr], n -(e)s/-e 1. no pl (a) crockery; (Porzellan) china. 2. (b) (dirty) dishes. 2. (Pferdeg.) harness; ◆**G~spülen,** n washing up. ◆**G~spülmaschine,** f dishwasher.

◆**G~tuch,** n tea towel, N.Am: dish towel.

Geschlecht [gə'ʃlɛçt], n -(e)s/-er 1. sex; Gram: gender. 2. generation; (Sippe) family. ◆**g~lich,** adj. sexual. ◆**G~s-,** comb.fm. sexual (act etc.); sex (life, organ etc.); genital (gland etc.). ◆**G~skrankheit,** f venereal disease. ◆**G~steile,** pl genitals. ◆**G~sverkehr,** m sexual intercourse.

geschlossen [gə'ʃlɔsən], adj. (a) closed; **g~e Gesellschaft/Vorstellung,** private party/performance; **g~e Ortschaft,** built-up area; (b) adv. unanimously.

Geschmack [gə'ʃmak], m -(e)s/-e taste; **er findet G. an dem Spiel,** the game appeals to him; **langsam kam er auf den G.,** gradually he acquired a taste for it. ◆**g~los,** adj. tasteless; (joke etc.) in bad taste. ◆**G~losigkeit,** f -/-en adj no pl tastelessness; Fig: bad taste; (b) (Bemerkung) tasteless remark. ◆**G~s-,** comb.fm. (question, sense etc.) of taste; ◆**G~ssache,** f matter of taste. ◆**g~voll,** adj. tasteful.

geschmeidig [gə'ʃmaidiç], adj. supple; (biegsam) pliable.

Geschmier(e) [gə'ʃmiːr(ə)], n -s/no pl 1. smear. 2. (Geschriebenes) scribble, scrawl.

Geschöpf [gə'ʃœpf], n -(e)s/-e creature.

Geschoß [gə'ʃɔs], n -sses/-sse 1. missile. 2. (Stock) floor, storey.

geschraubt [gə'ʃraupt], adj. affected (speech etc.); contrived (style, phrase etc.).

Ge'schrei, n -s/no pl (a) shouting; (grell) screaming; (b) **viel G. um etwas acc machen,** to make a lot of fuss about sth.

Geschütz [gə'ʃyts], n -es/-e gun; pl. artillery; Fig: **schweres G. auffahren,** to bring up one's big guns.

Geschwader [gə'ʃvaːdər], n -s/- squadron.

Geschwafel [gə'ʃvaːfəl], n -s/no pl F: twaddle.

Geschwätz [gə'ʃvɛts], n -es/no pl chatter. ◆**g~ig,** adj. garrulous. ◆**G~igkeit,** f -/no pl garrulity.

geschweige [gə'ʃvaigə], conj. **g. (denn)** let alone.

geschwind [gə'ʃvint], adj. quick, fast. ◆**G~igkeit,** f -/-en speed. ◆**G~igkeits-,** comb.fm. speed (check etc.); ◆**G~igkeitsbeschränkung,** f speed limit. ◆**G~igkeitsmesser,** m speedometer. ◆**G~igkeitsüberschreitung,** f exceeding the speed limit.

Geschwister [gə'ʃvistər], n pl brother's and sister's.

geschwollen [gə'ʃvɔlən], adj. pompous.

Geschworene(r) [gə'ʃvoːrənər], m & f decl. as adj. juror; **die G~n,** the jury.

Geschwulst [gə'ʃvulst], f -/-e 1. Med: tumour. 2. (Schwellung) swelling.

geschwungen [gə'ʃvuŋən], adj. curved.

Geschwür [gə'ʃvyːr], n -s/-e ulcer.

Gesell|e [gə'zɛlə], *m* **-n/-n** 1. skilled worker. 2. *F:* fellow, bloke. ◆**g~en,** *v.refl.* **sich zu j-m g.,** to join s.o. ◆**g~ig,** *adj.* 1. sociable (person, nature etc.). 2. social (evening, gathering etc.). ◆**G~igkeit,** *f* **-/en** 1. *no pl* sociability. 2. *(Treffen)* social gathering. ◆**G~schaft,** *f* **-/en** 1. society; 2. *(Begleitung, Umgang)* company; j-m **g. leisten,** to keep s.o. company. 3. *Com: (Firma)* company. 4. *(Veranstaltung)* party. ◆**g~schaftlich,** *adj.* social. ◆**G~schafts-,** *comb.fm.* social (class, order, novel, criticism etc.). ◆**G~schaftsanzug,** *m* dress suit. ◆**G~schaftsspiel,** *n* party game.

Gesetz [gə'zɛts], *n* **-es/-e** law; *Fig:* **sich** *dat* **etwas zum G. machen,** to make sth. a rule. ◆**G~blatt,** *n* legal gazette. ◆**G~buch,** *n* statute book. ◆**G~entwurf,** *m* (draft) bill. ◆**G~geber,** *m* **-s/-** (i) *(Pers.)* legislator; (ii) *(Organ)* legislature. ◆**G~gebung,** *f* **-/no pl** legislation. ◆**g~lich,** *adj.* legal; *(g. festgelegt)* statutory. ◆**g~los,** *adj.* lawless (person, act etc.). ◆**G~losigkeit,** *f* **-/no pl** lawlessness. ◆**g~mäßig,** *adj. (a) Jur: etc:* legal (title, power etc.); legitimate (claim etc.); lawful (right, procedure etc.). ◆**g~widrig,** *adj.* illegal, unlawful.

gesetzt [gə'zɛtst]. 1. *adj.* sedate. 2. *conj.* **g. den Fall, (daß) er käme/kommt,** assuming/supposing (that) he comes.

Gesicht [gə'zɪçt], *n* **-(e)s/-er** 1. (a) face; **der Wahrheit ins G. sehen,** to face (up to) the truth; **das G. wahren/retten,** to save face; **ein dummes G. machen,** to look stupid; (b) *(Aussehen)* look. 2. *no pl* **etwas zu G. bekommen,** to set eyes on sth.; **etwas aus dem G. verlieren,** to lose sight of sth.; **das zweite G. haben,** to have second sight. ◆**G~s-,** *comb.fm.* (a) face (powder, cream); facial (massage etc.); (b) (field, line etc.) of vision. ◆**G~sausdruck,** *m* expression. ◆**G~sfarbe,** *f* complexion. ◆**G~skreis,** *m* outlook. ◆**G~spunkt,** *m* point of view. ◆**G~szüge,** *mpl* (facial) features.

Gesindel [gə'zɪndəl], *n* **-s/no pl** rabble.

gesinnt [gə'zɪnt], *adj.* **demokratisch g.,** democratically minded; **j-m freundlich/übel g. sein,** to be well/ill disposed towards s.o. ◆**G~ung,** *f* **-/en** nature; *(Überzeugungen)* convictions. ◆**g~ungslos,** *adj.* unprincipled. ◆**G~ungslosigkeit,** *f* **-/no pl** lack of principles. ◆**G~ungswandel,** *m* change of heart/*Pol:* direction.

gesittet [gə'zɪtət], *adj.* well-mannered.

Gesöff [gə'zœf], *n* **-(e)s/-e** *P:* evil brew.

gesondert [gə'zɔndərt], *adj.* separate.

Gespann [gə'ʃpan], *n* **-(e)s/-e** team. ◆**g~t,** *adj.* 1. taut (rope etc.). 2. *Fig:* (a) tense (atmosphere, situation etc.); (b)

eager (audience, anticipation); **ich bin g., was er tun wird,** I am curious to know what he will do; **da bin ich aber g.!** I can't wait (for that)! **g. zuhören/zuschauen,** to listen/watch intently.

Gespenst [gə'ʃpɛnst], *n* **-(e)s/-er** 1. ghost. ◆**G~ergeschichte,** *f* ghost story. ◆**g~erhaft/g~isch,** *adj.* ghostly.

Gespött [gə'ʃpœt], *n* **-(e)s/no pl** (a) mockery; (b) *(Pers.)* laughing-stock.

Gespräch [gə'ʃprɛːç], *n* **-(e)s/-e** 1. conversation, talk; **im G. sein,** to be under discussion; **sie war das G. der ganzen Stadt,** she was the talk of the town. 2. *Tel:* (telephone) call. ◆**g~ig,** *adj.* talkative. ◆**G~igkeit,** *f* **-/no pl** talkativeness. ◆**G~sstoff,** *m* topic(s) of conversation.

gesprenkelt [gə'ʃprɛŋkəlt], *adj.* speckled.

Gespür [gə'ʃpyːr], *n* **-s/no pl** feeling.

Gestalt [gə'ʃtalt], *f* **-/en** 1. (a) *(Pers.)* figure; (b) *no pl (Wuchs)* build; **von zierlicher G. sein,** to be slightly built. 2. *(Form)* shape, form; **G. annehmen/gewinnen,** to take shape. ◆**g~en,** *v.tr.* (a) to form, shape (sth., s.o.'s personality etc.); to create (a work of art); to design (a layout etc.); to arrange (a room etc.); to organize (one's time, activities); (b) *v.refl.* **sich anders/günstig/ungünstig g.,** to turn out differently/well/badly. ◆**G~ung,** *f* **-/en** 1. *no pl (Gestalten)* forming; arrangement; creation 2. *(Anordnung)* design; layout.

geständig [gə'ʃtɛndɪç], *adj.* confessed (criminal); **g. sein,** to have confessed. ◆**G~nis** [-tnɪs], *n* **-ses/-se** confession.

Gestank [gə'ʃtaŋk], *m* **-s/no pl** stench.

gestatten [gə'ʃtatən], *v.tr.* to allow, permit (sth.); **g. Sie?** may I?

Geste ['gɛstə], *f* **-/-n** gesture.

ge'stehen, *v.tr. & i.irr.100* (haben) to confess.

Ge'stein, *n* **-(e)s/-e** rock.

Gestell [gə'ʃtɛl], *n* **-(e)s/-e** 1. *(Stütze)* stand, *(für Flaschen usw.)* rack; *(Regal)* shelves. 2. *(Rahmen)* frame (of spectacles etc.); *(Unterbau)* base (of a machine etc.).

gestern ['gɛstərn], *adv.* yesterday; **g. abend,** last night; *F:* **er ist nicht von g.,** he wasn't born yesterday.

Gestik ['gɛstɪk], *f* **-/no pl** gestures. ◆**g~ulieren** [-u'liːrən], *v.i.* (haben) to gesticulate.

Gestirn [gə'ʃtɪrn], *n* **-(e)s/-e** *Lit:* star.

gestochen [gə'ʃtɔxən], *adj.* meticulous; **g. scharf,** needle-sharp.

Gesträuch [gə'ʃtrɔyç], *n* **-(e)s/-e** bushes, shrubs.

gestreift [gə'ʃtraift], *adj.* striped.

gestrichen [gə'ʃtriçən], *adj.* **ein g~er Teelöffel,** a level teaspoonful; **g. voll,** full to the brim.

gestrig ['gɛstrɪç], *adj.* 1. yesterday's (paper etc.); **unser g~es Gespräch,** our conversation yesterday; 2. *(altmodisch)* behind the times.

Gestrüpp [gə'ʃtryp], n -(e)s/-e undergrowth; *Fig:* maze.

Gestüt [gə'ʃty:t], n -(e)s/-e stud.

Gesuch [gə'zu:x], n -(e)s/-e petition, (*Antrag*) application (**um/auf** + *acc*, for). ◆**g~t**, *adj.* sought after (items); **sehr g.**, much in demand.

gesund [gə'zunt], *adj.* healthy; **sie ist wieder ganz g.**, she is quite well/fit again; **g. leben**, to lead a healthy life; *Fig:* **der g~e Menschenverstand**, common sense. ◆**G~heit**, *f -/no pl* health; **auf Ihre G.!** your health! here's to you! **G.!** bless you! ◆**g~heitlich**, *adj.* (relating to) health; (state, reasons etc.) of health; **g. ist er nicht auf der Höhe**, he is not in the best of health. ◆**G~heits-**, *comb.fm.* health (service etc.); (state etc.) of health. ◆**G~heitspflege**, *f -/no pl* hygiene. ◆**g~heitsschädlich**, *adj.* unhealthy. ◆**G~heitszeugnis**, *n* health certificate.

getigert [gə'ti:gərt], *adj.* striped.

Getöse [gə'tø:zə], n -s/ *no pl* din; roar (of waves etc.).

Getränk [gə'trɛŋk], n -(e)s/-e drink.

Getreide [gə'traidə]. **I.** n -s/- grain. **II.** **G~-**, *comb.fm.* grain (harvest, silo etc.); cereal (product). ◆**G~speicher**, m granary.

getrennt [gə'trɛnt], *adj.* separate; **g. leben**, to live apart.

getreu [gə'trɔy], *adj.* (a) faithful (reproduction etc.); (b) *Lit:* loyal (friend etc.).

Getriebe [gə'tri:bə], n -s/- 1. transmission; *Aut:* gearbox. 2. (*Betriebsamkeit*) hustle and bustle.

getrost [gə'tro:st], *adv.* confidently.

Getto ['gɛto], n -s/-s ghetto.

Getue [gə'tu:ə], n -s/ *no pl F:* fuss.

Getümmel [gə'tyməl], n -s/ *no pl* tumult.

getupft [gə'tupft], *adj.* spotted.

geübt [gə'y:pt], *adj.* (*Pers.*) proficient (**in** + *dat*, at); trained (eye, ear).

Gewächs [gə'vɛks], n -es/-e 1. (*Pflanze*) plant. 2. *Med:* growth. ◆**G~haus**, n greenhouse.

gewachsen [gə'vaksən], *adj.* **einer Sache g. sein**, to be up to sth.; **j-m g. sein**, to be a match for s.o.

gewagt [gə'va:kt], *adj.* daring.

gewählt [gə'vɛ:lt], *adj.* elegant, refined; **sich g. ausdrücken**, to use refined language.

Gewähr [gə'vɛ:r], f -/no pl guarantee; (*Verantwortung*) responsibility. ◆**g~en**, *v.tr.* (a) to grant (a request, credit etc.). (b) **j-n g. lassen**, to let s.o. have his way. ◆**g~leisten**, *v.tr.insep.* to guarantee. ◆**G~smann**, m informant. ◆**G~ung**, *f -/no pl* granting.

Gewahrsam [gə'va:rza:m], m -s/no pl (*Obhut*) safekeeping; (*Haft*) custody.

Gewalt [gə'valt]. **I.** f -/-en 1. (a) (*Macht*) power; **die G. an sich** *acc* **reißen**, to seize power; (b) (*Beherrschung*) control;

etwas/sich in der G. haben, to be in control of sth./oneself; (c) (*bezwingende Kraft*) force; **G. anwenden**, to use force; *Fig:* **mit aller G.**, with all one's might; (*was auch geschieht*) at all costs. **II.** **G~-**, *comb.fm.* violent (crime etc.). ◆**G~akt**, m act of violence. ◆**G~anwendung**, f use of force. ◆**G~herrschaft**, f tyranny. ◆**g~ig**, *adj.* colossal (building etc.); tremendous (task, difference etc.); *F:* terrific (quantity, blow, etc.); **da irrst du dich g.!** there you are very much mistaken! ◆**g~los**, *adj.* non-violent. ◆**G~losigkeit**, *f -/no pl* non-violence. ◆**G~marsch**, m forced march. ◆**g~sam**, *adj.* violent (death, deed etc.); forcible (entry etc.). ◆**g~tätig**, *adj.* violent. ◆**G~tätigkeit**, *f 1. no pl* violence. 2. *esp.pl* act of violence.

Gewand [gə'vant], n -(e)s/er robe.

gewandt [gə'vant], *adj.* skilful; confident (manner, style); ◆**G~heit**, *f -/no pl* skill.

Gewässer [gə'vɛsər], n -s/- stretch of water; *pl.* waters.

Gewebe [gə've:bə], n -s/- 1. (*Stoff*) fabric. 2. *Anat:* tissue.

Gewehr [gə've:r], n -(e)s/-e rifle. ◆**G~lauf**, m barrel.

Geweih [gə'vai], n -(e)s/-e antlers.

Gewerb|e [gə'vɛrbə], n -s/- trade; (*Beschäftigung*) occupation; **das graphische G.**, the printing trade. ◆**g~lich**, *adj.* commercial; **g. tätig sein**, to be in business. ◆**g~smäßig**, *adj.* professional; for profit.

Gewerkschaft [gə'vɛrkʃaft], f -/-en trade/*N.Am:* labor union. ◆**G~(l)er(in)**, *m -s/- (f -/-nen)* trade/*N.Am:* labor unionist. ◆**G~s-**, *comb.fm.* union (leader etc.). ◆**G~sbund**, m (German) Trade Union Federation.

Gewicht [gə'viçt], n -(e)s/-e (a) weight; (b) (*Wichtigkeit*) importance; **seine Stimme hat großes G.**, his voice carries a lot of weight. ◆**G~heben**, n -s/no pl weight-lifting. ◆**g~ig**, *adj.* important. ◆**G~s-**, *comb.fm.* (unit etc.) of weight.

gewieft [gə'vi:ft], *adj.* F: crafty.

gewillt [gə'vilt], *adj.* willing.

Gewimmel [gə'viməl], n -s/no pl swarm.

Gewinde [gə'vində], n -s/- (screw) thread.

Gewinn [gə'vin], m -(e)s/-e 1. (*Ertrag*) profit; **er hat es mit G. verkauft**, he sold it at a profit; (b) (*Vorteil*) benefit. 2. (lottery etc.) prize. ◆**G~beteiligung**, f profit-sharing. ◆**g~bringend**, *adj.* profitable, lucrative. ◆**g~en**, *v.irr.73* 1. *v.tr.* (a) to win; (b) to gain (respect, time, control etc.); (c) **j-n für sich/für einen Plan g.**, to win s.o. over to a plan; 2. *v.i.* (*haben*) (a) to win; (b) **an Bedeutung g.**, to gain in importance; **an Klarheit g.**, to become clearer; ◆**g~end**, *adj.* winning. ◆**G~er**, m -s/- winner.

◆G~spanne, f profit margin.
◆G~ung, f -/no pl extraction.

Gewirr [gə'vir], n -(e)s/-e tangle; maze (of streets etc.); jumble (of sounds etc.).

gewiß [gə'vis], adj. certain; seines Sieges g., certain of victory; aber g. (doch)! (but) of course! bis zu einem gewissen Grade, to a certain extent. ◆gewisser'maßen, adv. to some/a certain extent. ◆Ge'wißheit, f -/no pl certainty; G. über etwas acc) erlangen, to find out for certain (about sth.).

Gewissen [gə'visən], n -s/- conscience; j-n, etwas auf dem G. haben, to have s.o., sth. on one's conscience. ◆g~haft, adj. conscientious. ◆G~haftigkeit, f -/no pl conscientiousness. ◆g~los, adj. unscrupulous. ◆G~s-, comb.fm. (conflict etc.) of conscience. ◆G~sbisse, mpl pangs of conscience, remorse.

Gewitter [gə'vitər]. I. n -s/- thunderstorm; Fig: ein häusliches G., a domestic storm. II. G~~, comb.fm. thundery (shower etc.); storm (front, cloud). ◆g~n, v.impers. (haben) es gewittert, it is thundering. ◆g~schwül, adj. thundery, sultry.

gewittrig [gə'vitriç], adj. thundery.

gewitzt [gə'vitst], adj. shrewd.

gewöhnen [gə'vø:nən], v.tr. j-n an etwas acc g., to get s.o. used to sth.; sich an j-n, etwas acc g., to get used to s.o., sth. ◆g~lich, adj. 1. (a) (normal) normal, ordinary; (üblich) usual; adv. usually; wie g., as usual. 2. (ordinär) common. ◆g~t, p.p. an etwas acc g. sein, to be used to sth. ◆G~ung, f -/no pl G. an etwas acc, becoming accustomed to sth.

Gewohnheit [gə'vo:nhait], f -/-en habit; aus G., from (force of) habit; es ist ihm zur G. geworden, it has become a habit with him. ◆G~heits-, comb.fm. (a) (matter etc.) of habit; (b) habitual (drinker, criminal etc.). ◆G~heitsrecht, n common law. ◆g~t, adj. usual; etwas acc g. sein, to be used to sth.

Gewölbe [gə'vœlbə], n -s/- 1. vault. 2. (Keller) vaults.

Gewühl [gə'vy:l], n -(e)s/no pl (Gewimmel) throng.

gewunden [gə'vundən] adj. twisting.

Gewürz [gə'vyrts], n -es/-e spice; (aromatische Zutat) seasoning. ◆G~gurke, f -/-n pickled gherkin. ◆G~nelke, f clove.

Gezeiten [gə'tsaitən]. I. fpl tides. II. G~~, comb.fm. tidal (power station etc.). ◆G~wechsel, m turn of the tide.

gezielt [gə'tsi:lt], adj. (measure etc.) specific.

geziert [gə'tsi:rt], adj. affected. ◆G~heit, f -/no pl affectedness.

Gezwitscher [gə'tsvitʃər], n -s/no pl twittering.

gezwungen [gə'tsvuŋən], adj. forced.

Gicht [giçt], f -/ no pl gout.

Giebel [gi:bəl]. I. m -s/- gable. II. G~-, comb.fm. gable (window etc.); gabled (roof, house).

Gier [gi:r], f -/no pl (Habg.) greed; craving (nach etwas dat, for sth.). ◆g~ig, adj. greedy (nach + dat, for).

gießen [gi:sən], v.irr.31 1. v.tr. (a) to pour, (verschütten) spill; (b) to water (plants etc.); (c) to cast (metal etc.); to make (candles). 2. v.i.impers. (haben) F: es gießt (in Strömen), it's pouring (with rain). ◆G~kanne, f watering can.

Gift [gift]. I. n -(e)s/-e poison; (Schlangeng. & Fig:) venom; darauf kannst du G. nehmen! you can bet your life on that! II. G~~, comb.fm. poisonous (plant, mushroom etc.); poisoned (arrow etc.); poison (gas, cupboard etc.). ◆g~grün, adj. bilious green. ◆g~ig, adj. poisonous; venomous Fig: remark etc.); Ch: toxic (fumes etc.); Fig: spiteful (person, remark etc.). ◆G~zahn, m poison fang.

Gigant [gi'gant], m -en/-en giant. ◆g~isch, adj. gigantic, colossal.

Gilde ['gildə], f -/-n guild.

Gin [dʒin], m -s/-s gin.

Ginster ['ginstər], m -s/- broom.

Gipfel ['gipfəl], m -s/- (Berg.) summit, top (of a mountain); (also Fig:) peak; esp. Pej: height of stupidity etc.); F: das ist (doch) der G.! that's the limit! ◆G~konferenz, f summit conference ◆G~punkt, m peak; Fig: culmination. ◆G~treffen, n summit meeting.

Gips [gips], m -es/-e plaster of Paris; Med: plaster. ◆G~abdruck, m plastercast. ◆G~bein, n F: leg in plaster/ N.Am: a cast. ◆G~verband, m plastercast.

Giraffe [gi'rafə], f -/-n giraffe.

Girlande [gir'landə], f -/-n garland.

Giro ['ʒi:ro]. I. n -s/-s giro (system); (Überweisung) giro transfer. II. 'G~~, comb.fm. giro (account etc.).

Gischt [giʃt], m -(e)s/-e spray

Gitarre [gi'tarə], f -/-n guitar. ◆G~ist [-'ist], m -en/-en guitarist.

Gitter ['gitər], n -s/- (Stäbe) bars; (Zaun, Geländer) railings; (Drahtg.) wire mesh. ◆G~fenster, n barred window. ◆G~stab, m bar. ◆G~zaun, m lattice-work fence.

Glacéhandschuh [gla'se:hantʃu:], m kid glove.

Gladiole [gladi'o:lə], f -/-n gladiolus.

Glanz [glants], m -es/no pl 1. (a) shine; (halbmatt) sheen; (b) (Helligkeit) brightness; 2. Fig: (Pracht) splendour; Hum: mit G. und Gloria fallen, to fail resoundingly. ◆'G~leistung, f brilliant achievement; Sp: etc: outstanding performance. ◆g~los, adj. dull; Fig: lacklustre. ◆G~stück, n pièce de résistance. ◆'g~voll, adj. magnificent (occasion, performance); brilliant (career etc.). ◆'G~zeit, f heyday.

glänzen ['glɛntsən], v.i. (haben) to shine, gleam; (Sterne, Lichter) to twinkle; (Hose, Nase) to be shiny; Fig: (Pers.) to shine. ◆g~d, adj. 1. bright (eyes etc.); shiny (hair, surface etc.). 2. Fig: brilliant (career, idea etc.).

Glas [glɑːs]. I. n -es/ˁer ['glɛːzər]. 1. glass; zwei G. Bier, two glasses of beer; ein G. Marmelade, a jar/pot of jam. 2. (a) (spectacle) lens; (b) (Ferng.) binoculars. II. G~, comb.fm. glass (eye, roof, -paper, wool etc.). ◆'G~bläser, m glass-blower. ◆'G~er, m -s/- glazier. ◆g~'klar, adj. crystal clear. ◆'G~maler, m stained glass artist. ◆G~male'rei, f /-en stained glass painting. ◆'G~scheibe, f pane of glass. ◆'G~scherbe, f piece of (broken) glass.

gläsern ['glɛːzərn], adj. glass.

glasieren [gla'ziːrən], v.tr. (a) to glaze (tiles etc.); (b) Cu: to ice, N.Am: frost (cakes). ◆g~ig ['glɑːziç], adj. glassy, glazed. 2. Cu: icing, N.Am: frosting.

glatt [glat], adj. 1. (a) smooth; (eben) even; level (surface, ground etc.); (b) (glitschig) slippery (road etc.). 2. (eindeutig) clear (victory etc.); downright (lie etc.); flat (refusal); utter (nonsense); sie ging g. darüber hinweg, she completely ignored it; das hatte ich g. vergessen, I had forgotten all about it. ◆'G~eis, n (black) ice; Fig: j-n aufs G. führen, to take s.o. for a ride. ◆g~gehen, v.i.sep.irr.36 (sein) to go off without a hitch. ◆g~weg, adv. g. ablehnen, to refuse pointblank; das ist g. erlogen, that is a downright lie.

Glätte ['glɛtə], f /-n (a) smoothness; (b) slipperiness. ◆g~n, v.tr. to smooth (a blanket, one's hair etc.); to smooth out (creases etc.).

Glatze ['glatsə], f /-n bald head; er hat/ bekommt eine G., he is/is going bald. ◆g~köpfig, adj. bald(-headed).

Glaube ['glaubə], m -ns/no pl belief (an + acc, in); Ecc: faith; j-m G~n schenken, to believe s.o. ◆g~n, v. 1. v.tr. to believe; j-m g., to believe s.o.; das glaube ich dir (gern), I believe you/ what you say; das ist doch kaum zu g.! it is scarcely credible; ich glaubte, sie sei in Paris, I thought she was in Paris; ich glaube nein, I don't think so. 2. v.i. (haben) to believe (an Gott, Wunder usw., in God, miracles etc.); (vertrauen) an j-n, etwas acc g., to have faith in s.o., sth. ◆g~ensbekenntnis, n creed. ◆g~haft ['glauphaft], adj. plausible. ◆'g~würdig, adj. credible; reliable (sources). ◆'G~würdigkeit, f -/no pl credibility.

gläubig ['glɔybiç], adj. 1. (a) believing (Christian etc.); (b) (fromm) religious. 2. (vertrauensselig) trusting. ◆'G~e(r), m

& f decl. as adj. believer; die G~en, the faithful. ◆'G~er, m -s/- creditor.

gleich [glaiç], adj. & adv. 1. (dasselbe) same; zur g~en Zeit, at the same time; das kommt auf das g~e hinaus, it comes/amounts to the same thing; ihr seid alle g., you are all the same/alike; sie sehen ziemlich g. aus, they look fairly alike; (b) (g~wertig) equal; zu g~en Teilen, in equal parts; g. schwer/groß, equally heavy/large; zweimal zwei (ist) g. vier, twice two equals four; (c) (gleichgültig) es ist mir g., was er denkt, I don't care what he thinks; ganz g. wer kommt, no matter who comes. 2. adv. (a) (sofort) immediately, at once; bis g.! see you in a moment! (b) (direkt) g. daneben, right next to it; g. gegenüber, directly opposite; (c) (fast) es ist g. 9 Uhr, it is almost/nearly 9 o'clock. ◆'g~alt|rig [-alt(ə)riç], adj. (of) the same age. ◆'g~artig, adj. similar. ◆'g~berechtigt, adj. having equal rights. ◆'G~berechtigung, f -/no pl equality. ◆'g~bleiben, v.i. sep.irr.12 (sein) (sich dat) g., to remain the same. ◆'g~bleibend, adj. constant; (konsequent) consistent. ◆'g~en, v.i.irr. (haben) j-m/etwas dat g., to be like/resemble s.o., sth. ◆g~ermaßen, adv. equally. ◆'g~falls, adv. also, likewise; danke g.! thank you, the same to you! ◆'g~förmig, adj. uniform. ◆'G~förmigkeit, f -/no pl uniformity. ◆'g~gesinnt, adj. like-minded. ◆'G~gewicht, n balance; Ph: & Fig: equilibrium; im G., balanced. ◆'g~gültig, adj. (a) (Pers.) indifferent; (apathisch) apathetic; (b) (unwichtig) trivial; er ist mir g., he means nothing to me. ◆'G~gültigkeit, f -/no pl indifference. ◆'G~heit, f -/-en 1. identity of interests etc.). 2. no pl (gleiche Stellung) equality. ◆'g~kommen, v.i.sep.irr.53 (sein) etwas dat g., to be tantamount to sth.; ◆'g~lautend, adj. identical. ◆'g~machen, v.tr.sep. (a) to make (people etc.) equal; (b) eine Stadt dem Erdboden g., to raze a city (to the ground). ◆'G~maß, n symmetry, harmony. ◆'g~mäßig, adj. even; regular (breathing, intervals etc.); steady (pressure, speed etc.); etwas g. verteilen, to share sth. out equally. ◆'G~mäßigkeit, f -/no pl evenness. ◆'G~mut, m equanimity. ◆'g~mütig, adj. calm. ◆'g~namig, adj. with the same name. ◆'G~nis, n -ses/ -se parable. ◆g~sam, adv. Lit: as it were. ◆'g~schalten, v.tr.sep. to bring (organizations) into line. ◆'G~schritt, m marching in step. ◆'g~setzen, v.tr.sep. to equate. ◆'g~stellen, v.tr.sep. = ◆setzen. ◆'G~strom, m direct current. ◆'g~tun, v.i.sep.irr.106 (haben) es j-m g., to do the same as s.o. ◆'G~ung, f -/-en equation. ◆g~viel,

adv. no matter (where, whether ... etc.).
◆**g~wertig,** *adj.* of equal value; (*gleich gut*) equally good. ◆**g~wohl,** *adv.* nevertheless. ◆**g~zeitig,** *adj.* simultaneous; *adv.* at the same time; simultaneously. ◆**g~ziehen,** *v.i.sep.irr.113* (*haben*) to draw level.

Gleis [glais], *n* -es/-e line, track; **auf G.** 3, at Platform 3/*N.Am:* on Track 3.

gleit|en ['glaitən], *n v.i.irr.* (*sein*) to glide; (*rutschen*) to slip, slide. ◆**g~flug,** m glide. ◆**g~zeit,** *f F:* flexitime.

Gletscher ['glɛtʃər], *m* -s/- glacier. ◆**G~spalte,** *f* -/-n crevasse.

Glied [gliːt], *n* -(e)s/-er 1. *Anat:* limb; 2. (*Ketteng.*) (*also Fig:*) link. 3. (*Mitglied*) member. 4. *Mil:* rank. ◆**g~ern** [-dərn], *v.tr.* to order (thoughts, ideas etc.); to plan (an essay, a speech etc.); ◆**g~erung,** *f* -/-en organization. ◆**G~maßen,** *fpl* limbs.

glimm|en ['glimən], *v.i.irr.* (*haben*) to glow. ◆**g~stengel,** *m P:* fag.

glimpflich ['glimpfliç], *adj.* lenient; **g. davonkommen,** to get off lightly.

glitschig ['glitʃiç], *adj.* slippery.

glitzern ['glitsərn], *v.i.* (*haben*) to glitter, (*Sterne usw.*) twinkle.

global [glo'baːl], *adj.* 1. global (conflict etc.). 2. (*umfassend*) overall (idea etc.).

Globus ['gloːbus], *m -* & *-busses/-ben* & *-busse* globe.

Glocke ['glɔkə], *f* -/-n bell; *F:* **das brauchst du nicht an die große G. zu hängen,** you needn't tell the whole world about it. ◆**G~n-,** *comb.fm.* bell (founder etc.); (sound) of a bell/bells. ◆**g~ngeläut,** n ringing/pealing of bells. ◆**G~nspiel,** n 1. (*in Türmen usw.*) carillon. 2. *Mus:* glockenspiel. ◆**G~nturm,** m bell tower; belfry.

Glosse ['glɔsə], *f* -/-n (satirical) commentary; *F:* (snide) comment.

glotzen ['glɔtsən], *v.i.* (*haben*) *F:* to gape.

Gluck|e ['glukə], *f* -/-n broody hen. ◆**g~en,** *v.i.* (*haben*) (*a*) (*Henne*) to cluck; (*b*) (*brüten*) (*also P: Pers.*) to brood. ◆**g~ern,** *v.i.* (*haben*) to glug, gurgle.

Glück [glyk], *n* -(e)s/*no pl* 1. (*a*) luck; **G. haben,** to be lucky; **du kannst von G. reden, daß ...,** you can count yourself lucky that ...; **zu meinem G.,** fortunately for me; **auf gut G.,** on the off chance; (*aufs Geratewohl*) at random; (*b*) (*persönlicher*) fortune; **ihm lächelte/lachte das G.,** fortune smiled on him. 2. (*Zustand*) happiness; **sein G. machen,** to make one's fortune. ◆**g~en,** *v.i.* (*sein*) to succeed; **nicht g.,** to fail. ◆**g~lich,** *adj.* happy; **g. ankommen,** to arrive safely; **g. enden,** to end happily; (*c*) *adv. F:* (*endlich*) finally, at last. ◆**g~licher'weise,** *adv.* fortunately, luckily. ◆**G~s-,** *comb.fm.* lucky (penny number etc.).

lucky charm. ◆**G~sfall,** m stroke of luck. ◆**G~spilz,** m lucky devil. ◆**G~ssache,** *f* matter of luck. ◆**G~sspiel,** n gamble. ◆**g~selig,** *adj.* blissfully happy. ◆**g~strahlend,** *adj.* radiant. ◆**G~wunsch,** m best wishes; (*Gratulation*) congratulations. ◆**G~wunsch-,** *comb.fm.* greetings (card, telegram etc.).

Glüh|birne ['glyːbirnə], *f* light bulb. ◆**g~en,** *v.i.* (*haben*) to glow. ◆**g~end,** *adj.* 1. glowing; red-hot (iron, needle etc.); **g. heiß,** scorching hot. 2. *Fig:* fervent; **g~er Verehrer,** ardent admirer. ◆**G~wein,** m mulled wine. ◆**G~würmchen,** n -s/- glowworm.

Glut [gluːt], *f* -/-en 1. (*Hitze*) heat; (*Glühen*) glow. 2. *Fig:* fervour, ardour.

Glyzerin [glytse'riːn], *n* -s/*no pl* glycerine.

Gnade ['gnɑːdə], *f* -/-n 1. favour; **Euer G~n,** Your Grace. 2. (*Barmherzigkeit*) mercy. **G. vor Recht ergehen lassen,** to be lenient. ◆**G~nfrist,** *f* reprieve. ◆**G~ngesuch,** n plea for clemency. ◆**g~nlos,** *adj.* merciless. ◆**G~nstoß,** m coup de grâce. ◆**G~ntod,** m mercy killing.

gnädig ['gnɛːdiç], *adj.* (*a*) gracious; merciful (God); lenient (judge, sentence etc.); (*b*) (*Anrede*) **g~e Frau,** Madam.

Gnom [gnoːm], *m* -en/-en gnome.

Gnu [gnuː], *n* -s/-s gnu.

Gold [gɔlt]. I. *n* -(e)s/*no pl* gold. II. ◆**G~-,** *g~-,* *comb.fm.* gold (braid, medal, reserves etc.). ◆**G~ader,** *f* vein of gold. ◆**G~barren,** m gold ingot/bar. ◆**G~barsch,** m ruff. ◆**g~blond,** *adj.* golden (hair), gold-haired (person). ◆**g~en** [-dən], *adj.* (*a*) gold; *Fig:* ein **g~enes Herz,** a heart of gold; (*b*) (*g~farbig*) golden; **die g~ene Mitte,** the happy medium. ◆**G~gräber,** m gold-digger. ◆**G~grube,** *f* goldmine. ◆**g~ig,** *adj. F:* sweet, lovely, *N.Am:* cute. ◆**G~rausch,** m goldrush. ◆**g~regen,** m *Bot:* laburnum. ◆**g~'richtig,** *adj. F:* absolutely right. ◆**G~schmied,** m goldsmith. ◆**G~waage,** *f F:* jedes Wort auf die **G. legen,** to weigh every word. ◆**G~zahn,** m gold-capped tooth.

Golf [gɔlf], *n* -s/*no pl* golf. ◆**G~platz,** m golf course. ◆**G~schläger,** m golf club. ◆**G~spieler,** m golfer. ◆**G~strom,** m Gulf Stream.

Gondel ['gɔndəl], *f* -/-n 1. (*Boot*) gondola. 2. cabin (of a cable-car); basket (of a balloon).

Gong [gɔŋ], *m* -s/-s gong. ◆**G~schlag,** m stroke of a/the gong.

gönn|en ['gœnən], *v.tr.* (*a*) j-m etwas nicht g., to begrudge s.o. sth.; **ich gönne ihm seinen Erfolg,** I don't begrudge him his success; **die Niederlage gönne ich ihm,** I'm not sorry he was beaten; (*b*) (*gewähren*) **sich** *dat*/j-m eine Ruhepause usw. g., to allow oneself/s.o. a rest etc. ◆G~er(in), m -s/- (f-/-nen) benefactor; Art: etc: patron. ◆g~erhaft, adj. patronizing.

Gorilla [go'rila], m -s/-s gorilla.

Gosse ['gɔsə], f -/-n gutter.

Gott [gɔt], m -es/¨er god; F: das wissen die G~er, heaven knows; um G~es willen! for heaven's sake! G. sei Dank! thank goodness! so G. will, God willing. ◆G~esdienst, m (church) service. ◆G~eshaus, n house of God, church. ◆g~eslästerlich, adj. blasphemous. ◆G~eslästerung, f blasphemy. ◆G~heit, f -/en deity. ◆g~lob, int. thank goodness. ◆g~los, adj. godless. ◆G~losigkeit, f -/no pl godlessness. ◆g~verdammt, adj. damned. ◆g~verlassen, adj. F: godforsaken.

Götterspeise ['gœtər∫paizə], jelly.

Götze ['gœtsə], m -n/-n/◆G~nbild, n idol.

Gouvern|ante [guvεr'nantə], f -/-n governess. ◆G~eur [-'nø:r], m -s/-e governor.

Grab [gra:p], n -(e)s/¨er grave; bis ans G., till/unto death; ◆g~en [-bən]. v.tr.&i.irr. to dig. ◆G~enkrieg, m trench warfare. ◆G~inschrift, f epitaph. ◆G~mal, n 1. monument. 2. (G~stätte) tomb. ◆G~rede, f funeral oration. ◆G~stätte, f burial place. ◆G~stein, m gravestone.

Grad [gra:t], m -(e)s/-e (a) degree; bis zu einem gewissen G., to a certain extent; (b) Mil: rank; ◆G~einteilung, f calibration. ◆G~messer, m -s/- yardstick.

graduell [gradu'εl], adj. 1. (allmählich) gradual (transition etc.). 2. (difference etc.) of degree.

Graf [gra:f], m -en/-en count; Brit: earl. ◆G~schaft, f -/-en county.

Gräfin ['grɛ:fin], f -/-nen countess.

Gram [gra:m], m -(e)s/no pl Lit: grief.

grämen ['grɛ:mən], v.tr. Lit: sich g., to grieve.

Gramm [gram], n -s/-e gram.

Grammat|ik [gra'matik], f -/-en grammar. ◆g~isch/g~ikalisch [-i'ka:li∫], adj. grammatical.

Grammophon [gramo'fo:n], n -s/-e gramophone.

Granat [gra'na:t], m -(e)s/-e (Stein) garnet. ◆G~apfel, m pomegranate.

Granate [gra'na:tə], f -/-n shell.

grandios [grandi'o:s], adj. superb, magnificent.

Granit [gra'ni:t], m -s/-e granite.

Graph|ik ['gra:fik], f -/-en 1. no pl graphic art(s). 2. (Druck) print; (Stich) engraving. ◆G~iker, m -s/- graphic artist. ◆g~isch, adj. graphic.

Gras [gra:s], n -es/¨er grass; F: ins G. beißen, to bite the dust; G. über etwas acc wachsen lassen, to let the dust settle on sth. ◆g~en ['gra:zən], v.i. (haben)

to graze. ◆G~halm, m blade of grass. ◆G~land, n grassland. ◆G~narbe, f turf.

grassieren [gra'si:rən], v.i. (haben) to be rampant.

gräßlich ['grεsliç], adj. ghastly, dreadful.

Grat [gra:t], m -(e)s/-e (Bergg.) ridge.

Gräte ['grɛ:tə], f -/-n (fish)bone.

Gratifikation [gratifikatsi'o:n], f -/-en gratuity; (Christmas) bonus.

gratis ['gra:tis], adv. free (of charge). ◆G~probe, f -/-n free sample.

Gratul|ant [gratu'lant], m -en/-en wellwisher. ◆G~ation, f -/-en congratulation(s). ◆g~ieren [-'li:rən], v.i. (haben) j-m (zu etwas dat) g., to congratulate s.o. (on sth.); j-m zum Geburtstag g., to wish s.o. many happy returns of the day.

grau [grau]. I. adj. (a) grey, N.Am: gray; (b) (trostlos) gloomy (future etc.); (c) in g~er Vorzeit, in the dim and distant past. ◆G~brot, n rye-bread. ◆g~haarig, adj. grey-haired. ◆g~meliert, adj. greying.

grauen ['grauən]. I. v.impers. es graut mir/mir graut vor etwas dat, I dread (the thought of) sth. II. G., n -s/no pl dread (vor dem Tode, of death). ◆g~erregend/g~voll, adj. horrifying, gruesome. ◆g~haft/g~voll, adj. horrifying; F: dreadful.

Graupeln ['graupəln], fpl small (soft) hail.

Graupen ['graupən], fpl pearl barley.

grausam ['grauzam], adj. cruel. ◆G~amkeit, f -/-en 1. no pl cruelty. 2. (act of) cruelty; atrocity. ◆g~ig, adj. 1. gruesome. 2. F: dreadful.

gravier|en [gra'vi:rən], v.tr. to engrave. ◆g~end, adj. serious (mistake, loss etc.); significant (difference etc.). ◆G~ung, f -/-en engraving.

Gravüre [gra'vy:r], f -/-en engraving.

graz|il [gra'tsi:l], adj. slender; (graziös) graceful. ◆g~iös [gratsi'ø:s], adj. graceful.

greif|bar ['graifba:r], adj. 1. ready to hand; in g~barer Nähe, within (easy) reach. 2. (konkret) tangible (results etc.). ◆g~en, v.irr. 1. v.tr. to take hold of (sth.), (fest) grasp (sth., (schnell) grab (sth.); zum G. nah, (Berge usw.) near enough to touch; Fig: (Erfolg usw.) within one's grasp. 2. v.i. (haben) (a) nach etwas dat g., to reach out for sth.; um sich acc g., (i) to feel around; (ii) (Feuer, Epidemie usw.) to spread; (b) zu etwas dat g., to reach out for sth.; zu einer List g., to resort to a trick; (c) Tchn: (Räder, usw.) to grip, (Zahnräder) engage. ◆G~vogel, m bird of prey.

Greis [grais], m -es/-e old man. ◆G~enalter, n old age.

grell [grεl], adj. (a) glaring (light, sun etc.); garish (colour); (b) (Klang) shrill.

Gremium ['gre:mium], n -s/-ien committee; panel (of experts etc.).

Grenz- ['grɛnts-], *comb.fm.* border, frontier (station, official, town, crossing, traffic etc.). ◆'G~e, *f* -/-n 1. border; (*Stadtg. usw.*) boundary; *Fig:* borderline. 2. (*Maximum*) *usw. at* limit; **seiner Macht sind G~en gesetzt,** there is a limit to his power; **seine Begeisterung kannte keine G~en,** his enthusiasm knew no bounds; **sich in G~en halten,** to be limited. ◆'g~en, *v.i.* (*haben*) **an etwas** *acc* **g.,** (*Stadt, Garten usw.*) to border (on), (*Raum usw.*) be adjacent to sth.; *Fig:* **das grenzt an Erpressung** *usw.,* that verges on blackmail etc. ◆'g~enlos, *adj.* boundless. ◆G~fall, *m* borderline case. ◆'G~linie, *f* boundary (line). ◆'G~schutz, *m* (*Polizei*) border police.

Greuel ['grɔyəl], *m* -s/- *Lit:* horror; **es ist mir ein G.,** I loathe/detest it. ◆'G~tat, *f* atrocity.

Grieben ['gri:bən], *fpl* greaves.

Griech|e ['gri:çə], *m* -n/-n Greek. ◆'G~enland, *Pr.n.n* -s. Greece. ◆'G~in, *f* -/-nen Greek (woman/girl). ◆'g~isch, *adj.* Greek.

Gries|gram ['gri:sgrɑːm], *m* -(e)s/-e *F:* grouch. ◆'g~grämig, *adj. F:* grumpy.

Grieß [gri:s], *m* -es/*no pl* semolina. ◆'G~brei, *m* semolina pudding.

Griff [grif], *m* -(e)s/-e 1. (*a*) grasp, hold; *Sp: etc:* grip; *F:* **etwas im G. haben,** to have sth. at one's fingertips/(*unter Kontrolle*) under control; (*b*) (*Handgriff*) movement (of the hand); 2. handle (of a tool, door etc.). ◆'g~bereit, *adj.* handy. ◆'g~ig, *adj.* 1. (*handlich*) handy (tool, etc.). 2. (*Reifen usw.*) with a good grip.

Grill [gril], *m* -s/-s grill; (*im Freien*) barbecue; ◆'g~en, *v.tr.* to grill, barbecue (meat etc.).

Grille ['grilə], *f* -/-n *Z:* cricket.

Grimasse [gri'masə], *f* -/-n grimace.

grimmig ['grimiç], *adj.* (*wütend*) furious; fierce (animal); grim (humour).

grinsen ['grinzən], *V. v.i.* (*haben*) to grin. II. **G.,** *n* -s/*no pl* grin.

Grippe ['gripə], *f* -/-n influenza; *F:* flu.

Grips [grips], *m* -es/-e *F:* gumption.

grob [grɔːp], *adj.* 1. coarse (linen, *Fig:* features, language etc.); rough (treatment); uncouth (person, behaviour etc.); **g~e Arbeit,** rough/dirty work; **j-n g. anfahren,** to snap at s.o. 2. (*ungefähr*) rough (estimate etc.); **g. geschätzt/gerechnet,** roughly, at a rough estimate. 3. (*schlimm*) gross (violation, injustice, error, insult). ◆G~heit, *f* -/-en 1. *no pl* coarseness, roughness; rudeness. 2. rude/coarse remark. ◆G~ian ['grɔːbiɑːn], *m* -(e)s/-e boor, brute. ◆'g~körnig, *adj.* coarse-grained (sand, film etc.).

Grog [grɔk], *m* -s/-s grog. ◆'g~gy ['grɔgi:], *adj. F:* (*erschöpft*) shattered.

grölen ['grø:lən], *v.tr.&i.* (*haben*) *F:* to bawl (out).

Groll [grɔl], *m* -(e)s/*no pl* rancour, resentment; **einen G. gegen j-n hegen,** to bear a grudge against s.o.

Grönland ['grø:nlant]. *Pr.n.n* -s. Greenland.

Gros [gro:], *n* -/- bulk, majority.

Groschen ['grɔʃən], *m* -s/- 1. *Aus:* groschen (coin). 2. *F:* ten pfennig (piece). ◆'G~roman, *m* -s/-e cheap novel.

groß [gro:s]. I. *adj.* 1. (*a*) big, large; (*b*) (*hochgewachsen*) tall; (*c*) (*älter*) elder; (*erwachsen*) grown-up; **meine g~e Schwester,** my big/elder sister; (*d*) (*nicht gering, bedeutend*) great (difficulty etc.; nation etc.); **g~e Angst haben,** to be very frightened. 2. (*grandios*) grand (style, banquet etc.); **in g~em Rahmen,** on a grand scale; *adv.* **g. feiern/ausgehen,** to celebrate/go out in style. 3. **im g~en und ganzen,** on the whole; **g~e Reden schwingen,** to talk big. II. **G~-, g~-,** *comb.fm.* (*a*) large (firm), big (fire, *Z:* cat); *Com:* bulk (order, purchase etc.); (*g~angelegt*) large-scale (attack, industry etc.); (*b*) *Geog:* Great; (*den G~raum bezeichnend*) Greater (Munich etc.); (*c*) (*bei Verwandten*) great-(aunt, uncle etc.). ◆'G~alarm, *m* red alert. ◆'g~angelegt, *adj.* large-scale (project etc.). ◆'g~artig, *adj.* marvellous, splendid; **sich g. amüsieren,** to have a great time. ◆'G~aufnahme, *f* close-up. ◆'G~buchstabe, *m* capital (letter). ◆'G~britannien, *n* Great Britain. ◆'G~einkauf, *m* bulk buying; *F:* **einen G. machen,** to do a big shop. ◆'G~einsatz, *m* large-scale operation. ◆'G~eltern, *pl* grandparents. ◆'G~enkel, *m* great-grandson. ◆'G~enkelin, *f* great-granddaughter. ◆'G~format, *n* large size. ◆'G~handel, *m* wholesale trade. ◆'G~händler, *m* wholesale dealer, wholesaler. ◆'g~jährig, *adj.* of age. ◆'G~kapital, *n* high finance; big business. ◆'G~macht, *f* superpower. ◆'G~maul, *n* *F:* loudmouth. ◆'g~mut, *f* magnanimity. ◆'g~mütig, *adj.* magnanimous. ◆'G~mutter, *f* grandmother. ◆'G~raum, *m* large area; **im G. München,** in the Greater Munich area. ◆'g~räumig [-rɔymiç], *adj.* 1. spacious (flat, car etc.). 2. extensive (area etc.). ◆'g~spurig, *adj.* self-important; high-sounding (words etc.). ◆'G~stadt, *f* (large) city. ◆'G~städter, *m* city-dweller. ◆'g~städtisch, *adj.* city (life etc.). ◆'G~tat, *f* remarkable feat. ◆'G~teil, *m* major part; **zum G.,** mainly. ◆'g~tuerisch, *adj.* boastful, self-important. ◆'g~tun, *v.i.sep.irr.106* (*haben*) to boast (**mit etwas** *dat,* about sth.). ◆'G~unternehmer, *m* big busi-

nessman. ◆'G~**vater**, m grandfather.
◆'G~**wild**, n big game. ◆'g~**ziehen**,
v.tr.sep.irr.113 to bring up (a child), rear
(a child, animal). ◆'g~**zügig**, adj. generous (person etc.); large-scale (planning
etc.). ◆'G~**zügigkeit**, f -/no pl generosity; spaciousness.

Größe ['grø:sə], f -/-n 1. size; (Höhe)
height; **ein Mann mittlerer G.**, a man of
medium height. 2. Mth: etc: quantity. 3.
(a) (Bedeutung) greatness; (b) (Pers.) great
name. ◆'G~**enunterschied**, m difference in size. ◆'G~**enverhältnis**, n
proportion. ◆'G~**enwahn(sinn)**, m
megalomania; Hum: delusions of grandeur. ◆'g~**enwahnsinnig**, adj. megalo-
maniac. ◆'g~**er**, f -/-**te(r,s)**, adj. comp.
& superl. of **groß**. ◆'g~**ten·teils**, adv.
mainly, for the most part.
◆'g~**t·möglich**, adj. greatest/biggest
possible.

Grossist [grɔ'sist], m -en/-en wholesaler.

grotesk [gro'tɛsk], adj. grotesque.

Grotte ['grɔtə], f -/-n grotto.

Grube ['gru:bə], f -/-n pit;
◆'G~**narbeiter**, m miner, mineworker.

grübeln ['gry:bə'ln], v.i. (haben) to
brood. ◆'G~**ler**, m -s/- brooder.
◆'g~**lerisch**, adj. introspective; brood-
ing.

Gruft [gruft], f -/-e burial vault; (Krypta)
crypt.

grün [gry:n], adj. green; g~**er Salat**, lettuce; g~**e Bohnen**, green beans; **ins
G~e fahren**, to go for a drive in the
country; Aut: g~**e Welle**, synchronized
traffic lights; **bei G.**, when the lights are
green; F: **das ist dasselbe in G.**, that
comes to (exactly) the same thing;
◆'G~**donnerstag**, m Maundy Thursday. ◆'g~**en**, v.i. (haben) Lit: to
become/turn green. ◆'G~**fink**, m
greenfinch. ◆'g~**lich**, adj. greenish.
◆'G~**schnabel**, m greenhorn.
◆'G~**span**, m verdigris. ◆'G~**streifen**, m (a) grass verge; (b) (Mittelstreifen)
central reservation.

Grund [grunt]. I. m -(e)s/-e 1. (Erdboden)
ground; **von G. auf geändert**,
completely/radically altered. 2. bottom
(of a river, container etc.); (sea/river)
bed; Nau: **auf G. laufen**, to run
aground; Fig: **im G~e seines Herzens**,
in his heart of hearts; **einer Sache auf
den G. gehen/kommen**, to get to the
bottom of sth.; **im G~e (genommen)**,
actually, strictly speaking. 3. (a) (Ursache) reason; **aus taktischen/persön-
lichen G~en**, for tactical/personal reasons; **aus gutem G.**, with good reason;
auf G. dieser Tatsache, because of this
fact; (b) (Anlaß) cause (**zum Klagen**
usw., for complaint etc.); **das ist ein G.**
zum Feiern, this calls for a celebration.
II. 'G~·, 'g~·, comb.fm. 1. (a) (grundlegend) basic (equipment, training, right,
rule, wage, Sch: course etc.); funda-

mental (truth, characteristic); (b) (durch
und durch) thoroughly (decent, honest,
bad etc.); completely (different etc.);
◆'G~**begriff**, m fundamental concept/
principle. ◆'G~**besitz**, m (a) no pl land
ownership; (b) Jur: real estate.
◆'G~**besitzer**, m landowner.
◆'g~**buch**, n land register.
◆'g~**falsch**, adj. completely/absolutely
wrong. 2. land (purchase, tax etc.).
◆'G~**gebühr**, f basic rate; Tel: rental.
◆'G~**gesetz**, n fundamental law; West
G. Pol: constitution. ◆g~**ieren**
[-'di:rən], v.tr. to prime. ◆'G~·
farbe, f primer. ◆'G~**lage**, f basis,
foundation; (G~wissen) grounding; (Gerücht usw.) **jeder G. entbehren**, to be entirely without foundation.
◆'g~**legend**, adj. fundamental, basic.
◆'g~**los**, adj. groundless (fear etc.);
unfounded (suspicion); adv. without
(any) reason. ◆'G~**mauer**, f
foundation(-wall). ◆'G~**pfeiler**, m cornerstone. ◆'G~**riß**, m (a) ground plan;
(b) (Abriß) outline. ◆'G~**satz**, m principle. ◆'g~**sätzlich**, adj. fundamental;
ich esse g. keine Schokolade, I never
eat chocolate on principle.
◆'G~**schule**, f primary school; N.Am:
grade school. ◆'G~**stein**, m foundation
stone; Fig: cornerstone. ◆'G~**stück**, n
plot of land. ◆'G~**stufe**, f Sch: junior
stage of (primary school). ◆'G~·
wasser, n ground water. ◆'G~**züge**,
mpl basic/essential features.

gründen ['gryndən], v. 1. v.tr. (a) to
found (a university, firm etc.), set up (an
organization etc.), form (a company party etc.); to start (a family etc.); (b) to
base (a verdict etc.) (**auf etwas acc**, on
sth.). 2. v.refl. & i. (haben) (**sich**) **auf etwas acc g.**, to be based on sth.
◆'G~**er**, m -s/- founder. ◆g~**lich**,
adj. thorough. ◆'G~**lichkeit**, f no pl
thoroughness. ◆'G~**ung**, f -/-en foundation; establishment; formation.

grunzen ['gruntsən], v.i. (haben) to
grunt.

Gruppe ['grupə], f -/-n group; (Team)
team (of experts etc.). ◆'G~**en-**,
comb.fm. group (therapy, pictures etc.).
◆'g~**enreise**, f package tour.
◆'g~**enweise**, adv. in groups.
◆g~**ieren** [gru'pi:rən], v.tr. to group
sich g., to form a group/groups.
◆'g~**ierung**, f -/-en grouping.

Grusel- ['gru:zəl-], comb.fm. horror (film,
story etc.). ◆'g~**ig**, adj. spine-chilling,
F: scary. ◆g~**n**, v.i. v.impers. & refl.
ihm gruselte/er gruselte sich, it gave
him the creeps. **II. G.**, n -s/no pl F: the
creeps.

Gruß [gru:s], m -es/-e greeting; Mil: salute; **einen G. an Ihre Frau!** (kind) regards to your wife! **mit freundlichen
G~en Ihr ...**, yours sincerely ...; **liebe**
G~e Dein ..., yours ...; love from ...

grüßen ['gry:sən], *v.tr. & i.* (*haben*) (*a*) to greet (s.o.), say hello to (s.o.); *Mil:* to salute (an officer); **grüß dich!** hello! **grüß Gott!** good morning/afternoon/evening; (*b*) **g~ Sie ihn** (**herzlich**) **von mir,** give him my regards.

Grütze ['grytsə], *f* **-/-n** gruel; **rote G.,** red jelly.

guck|en ['gukən], *v.i.* (*haben*) *F:* to look; **◆'G~loch,** *n* peep-hole.

Gulasch ['gula∫], *n* **-(e)s/-e** & **-s** goulash.

gültig ['gyltiç], *adj.* valid; (*Gesetz*) in force; **der Fahrplan ist am 1. Mai g.,** the timetable comes into effect on 1st May. **◆'G~keit,** *f* **-/no pl** validity.

Gummi ['gumi]. 1. *m & n* **-s/-s** rubber. 2. (*Harz, Klebstoff*) gum. **◆'G~band,** *n* rubber/elastic band. **◆'G~baum,** *m* rubber plant. **◆g~eren** [gu'mi:rən], *v.tr. a*) to gum (paper etc.); (*b*) to rubberize (fabric etc.). **◆'G~erung,** *f* **-/-en** 1. (*a*) gumming; (*b*) rubberizing. 2. (*a*) gum (on envelopes etc.); (*b*) rubber coating. **◆'G~knüppel,** *m* rubber truncheon. **◆'G~stiefel,** *m* gumboot; *Brit:* wellington. **◆'G~zelle,** *f* padded cell.

Gunst [gunst], *f* **-/no pl** favour; **zu j-s G~en,** in s.o.'s favour.

günst|ig ['gynstiç], *adj.* (*vorteilhaft*) favourable; (*passend*) convenient (time, position etc.); **im g~sten Falle,** at best; **etwas g. kaufen,** to buy sth. at a good price.

Gurgel ['gurgəl], *f* **-/-n** throat. **◆'g~n,** *v.i.* (*haben*) to gargle.

Gurke ['gurkə], *f* **-/-n** (*Salatg.*) cucumber; **saure/eingelegte G~n,** pickled gherkins.

gurren ['gurən], *v.i.* (*haben*) to coo.

Gurt [gurt], *m* **-(e)s/-e** (*Gürtel* belt; *Aut: Av:* seat belt. **◆g~en,** *v.i. Aut:* to put on one's seat belt.

Gürtel ['gyrtəl], *m* **-s/-** belt; (*also Fig:*) **den G. enger schnallen,** to tighten one's belt. **◆'G~linie,** *f* waistline; **Schlag unter die G.,** blow below the belt. **◆'G~reifen,** *m* radial(-ply) tyre. **◆'G~rose,** *f* shingles.

Guß [gus], *m* **-sses/-sse** 1. (*a*) (*Gießen*) founding, casting; (*b*) (*Erzeugnis*) casting. 2. gush, stream (of water etc.); *F:* (*Regen.*) downpour. 3. *Cu:* icing, *N.Am:* frosting. **◆'G~eisen,** *n* cast iron. **◆'g~eisern,** *adj* cast-iron.

gut¹ [gu:t]. *I. adj.* good; **zu j-m sein,** to be good (*gütig*) kind to s.o.; **sei so gut und mach die Tür zu,** would you mind shutting the door; **sich im g~en einigen,** to come to an amicable agreement; **ihm ist nicht g.,** he is not feeling well; **wozu ist das g.?** (i) what's the good of that? (ii) what's that for? **Ende g., alles g.,** all's well that ends well; **g~en Morgen,** good morning; **g~e Reise/Fahrt!** have a good journey! **g~en Appetit!** enjoy your meal! **g~es Neues Jahr,** happy New Year; **so g. wie sicher,** as

good as certain; **so g. wie gar nichts,** hardly anything; **wir wollen es g. sein lassen,** let's leave it at that; **eine g~e Stunde/ein g~es Pfund,** a good hour/pound; **das G~e daran ist, daß ...,** the good thing about it is that ... **II.** *adv.* well; **eine g. angezogene Frau,** a well-dressed woman; **sie sieht g. aus,** (i) (*schön*) she is good-looking; (ii) (*gesund*) she looks well; **ich fühle mich nicht g.,** I don't feel well; **das kann ich g. verstehen,** I can well understand that; **er hat es g. bei seiner Mutter,** he is well off living with his mother; **das ist g. möglich/kann gut sein,** that could well be; *F:* **mach's g.!** see you! **das riecht/ schmeckt g.,** that smells/tastes good. **◆'G~achten,** *n* **-s/-** (*expert*) opinion, report. **◆'G~achter,** *m* **-s/-** expert, consultant. **◆g~artig,** *adj.* good-natured; *Med:* benign. **◆'g~aussehend,** *adj.* good-looking. **◆'g~bürgerlich,** *adj.* solidly middle-class (family etc.); plain (food, accommodation). **◆'g~dünken,** *n* **-s/no pl** discretion; **nach (eigenem) G.,** as one thinks fit. **◆g~gehen,** *v.i.sep.irr.36* (*haben*) (*Sache*) to go well; **es geht mir gut,** (i) I am getting along nicely; (ii) (*gesundheitlich*) I am well. **◆'g~gelaunt,** *attrib.adj.* good-humoured; (*Sache*) done in good faith. **◆g~gläubig,** *adj. Jur:* acting/ (*Sache*) done in good faith. **◆G~haben,** *n* **-s/-** *Com:* credit. **◆'g~heißen,** *v.tr. sep.irr.49* to approve. **◆g~herzig,** *adj.* kind (-hearted). **◆'g~machen,** *v.tr.sep.* to make up for (a mistake, wrong etc.) (an j-m, to s.o.); to make good, repair (damage). **◆g~mütig,** *adj.* good-natured. **◆'G~mütigkeit,** *f* **-/no pl** good nature. **◆'G~schein,** *m* voucher; (*für zurückgegebene Ware*) credit note; (*Geschenkg.*) gift token. **◆'g~schreiben,** *v.tr.sep.irr.12* *Fin:* to credit. **◆'G~schrift,** *f* credit; (*Bescheinigung*) credit note. **◆'g~situiert,** *adj.* well off. **◆'g~tun,** *v.i.sep.irr.106* **j-m, etwas dat** g., to do s.o., sth. good. **◆g~willig,** *adj.* willing; (*wohlgesinnt*) well-disposed.

Gut² [gu:t], *n* **-(e)s/-er** 1. (*Besitz*) property; **irdische Güter,** worldly goods. 2. (*Landgut*) estate. **◆'G~sherr,** *m* landowner. **◆'G~shof,** *m* estate.

Güte ['gy:tə], *f* **-/no pl** 1. (*Herzensg.*) kindness, goodness; **ein Vorschlag zur G.,** a conciliatory proposal. 2. (*Qualität*) quality. **◆'G~klasse,** *f Com:* grade of (product).

Güter- ['gy:tər-], *comb.fm.* goods, *esp. N.Am:* freight (train, traffic, transport etc.). **◆'G~abfertigung,** *f* dispatch of goods/freight. **◆'G~bahnhof,** *m* goods/freight depot. **◆'G~wagen,** *m* goods wagon; *N.Am:* freight car.

gütig ['gy:tiç], *adj.* kind, kind-hearted.

◆'g~lich, adj. amicable; adv. sich g. einigen, to come to an amicable agreement.

Gymnasium [gym'nɔːzium], n -s/-ien approx. = grammar/N.Am: high school.

Gymnast|ik [gym'nastik], f -/no pl keepfit exercises, Sch: P.E; (Turnen) gymnastics. ◆g~isch, adj. gymnastic.

Gynäkolog|e [gynɛko'loːgə], m -n/-n gynaecologist. ◆G~ie [-lo'giː], f -/no pl gynaecology.

H

H,h [haː], n -/-. (the letter) H, h.

Haar [haːr]. I. n -(e)s/-e hair; pl H~e, (i) coll. hair; (ii) (einzelne) hairs; sich das H./die H. waschen, to wash one's hair; um ein H. wäre ich gestürzt, I very nearly fell; j-m aufs H. gleichen, to be the spitting image of s.o. II. 'H~-, comb.fm. hair (dryer etc.). ◆'H~bürste, f hairbrush. ◆'h~en, v.i. (haben) sich h., to lose hairs. ◆'H~esbreite, f um H., by a hair's breadth. ◆'h~ge'nau, adj. precise; (detailliert) in minute detail. ◆'h~ig, adj. 1. hairy. 2. F: tricky (business etc.). ◆'H~nadel, f hairpin. ◆'h~scharf, adv. das Auto fuhr h. an ihm vorbei, the car missed him by a hair's breadth. ◆'H~schnitt, m haircut; (Frisur) hairstyle. ◆H~spalte'rei, f -/-en hairsplitting. ◆'H~spange, f hairslide. ◆'h~sträubend, adj. (a) hair-raising; (b) Pej: appalling, (unglaublich) incredible.

Hab|e ['haːbə], f -/no pl belongings. ◆'h~en, v.tr.irr. (a) to have, F: have got (children, patience, blue eyes etc.); Eile/es eilig h., to be in a hurry; was hast du? what is the matter (with you)? ich habe Hunger/Durst, I am hungry/ thirsty; (b) (enthalten) ein Meter hat tausend Millimeter, there are a thousand millimetres in a metre; (c) bei euch hatten wir es gut, we were well off with you; er hat es nicht leicht, it's not easy for him; er hat etwas Unheimliches (an sich), there is something sinister about him; er hat etwas mit ihr, he is carrying on with her; er hat nichts davon, he doesn't get anything out of it; das hat man davon, that's what comes of it. ◆H~gier ['haːpgiːr], f -/no pl greed; (für den Besitz anderer) covetousness. ◆'h~gierig, adj. greedy. ◆H~seligkeiten, fpl belongings. ◆'H~sucht, f Pej: (obsessive) greed. ◆'h~süchtig, adj. Pej: (obsessively) greedy.

Habicht ['haːbiçt], m -s/-e hawk.

Hachse ['haksə], f -/-n Cu: knuckle (of veal/pork).

Hacke1 ['hakə], f -/-n 1. Agr: hoe, mattock. ∴. pickaxe. ◆'h~en, v. 1. v.tr. (a) to chop (meat, vegetables, wood etc.); to hack (sth., a hole) (in + acc, in); (b) to hoe (the ground). 2. v.i. (haben) (Vogel) to peck (nach j-m, at s.o.). ◆'h~fleisch, n mince, minced/N.Am:

ground meat.

'Hacke2, f -/-n/'H~n, m -s/- heel.

Hafen ['haːfən]. I. m -s/⁼ harbour; (H~stadt) port. II. H~-, comb.fm. harbour (basin etc.); port (authority etc.); dock (area etc.). ◆'H~arbeiter, m docker. ◆'H~damm, m harbour mole. ◆'H~stadt, f port.

Hafer ['haːfər], m -s/no pl oats. ◆'H~brei, m porridge. ◆'H~flocken, fpl porridge oats.

Haft [haft], f -/no pl Jur: custody, detention. ◆'h~bar, adj. Jur: liable. ◆'H~befehl, m (arrest) warrant. ◆'h~en, v.i. (haben) (a) an etwas dat h., to stick/(Staub, Geruch) cling to sth. (b) für j-n, etwas h., to be liable for s.o., sth. ◆'h~enbleiben, v.i.sep. irr.12 (sein) an etwas dat h., to stick/cling to sth. ◆'H~pflicht, f liability. ◆'H~pflichtversicherung, third party insurance. ◆'H~ung, f -/-en 1. liability. 2. Tchn: adhesion.

Häftling ['heftliŋ], m -s/-e detainee.

Hagebutte ['haːgəbutə], f -/-n rosehip.

Hagel ['haːgəl], m -s/no pl hail. ◆'h~korn, n hailstone. ◆'h~n, v.i.impers. (haben) to hail.

hager ['haːgər], adj. gaunt; scraggy (neck).

Hahn [haːn], m -(e)s/⁼e 1. cock. 2. (Wasserh. usw.) tap; N.Am: faucet.

Hai(fisch) ['hai(fiʃ)], m -(e)s/-e shark.

Häk|chen ['heːkçən], n -s/- (a) little hook; (b) (Zeichen) tick, N.Am: check. ◆h~eln ['heːkəln], v.tr. to crochet. ◆'H~elnadel, f crochet hook.

Haken ['haːkən] m -s/- (a) hook; peg (for a hat etc.); (b) Fig: (Nachteil) snag. ◆'H~kreuz, n swastika. ◆'H~nase, f hooked nose.

halb [halp]. I. adj. & adv. half; die h~e Nacht, half the night; eine h~e Stunde, half an hour; h. eins, half-past twelve; h. soviel, half as much. II. 'H~-, 'h~-, comb.fm. (a) half-(brother, moon etc.); (b) semi-(darkness etc.). ◆'H~finale, n semi-final. ◆'H~heit, f -/-en (a) halfheartedness; (b) esp. pl. H~en, halfmeasures. ◆'h~ieren, v.tr. to halve (sth.); (schneiden) to cut (sth.) in half. ◆'H~insel, f peninsula. ◆'H~jahr, n half-year. ◆'h~jährlich, adj. halfyearly. ◆'H~kreis, m semicircle. ◆'H~kugel, f hemisphere. ◆'h~lang, adj. half-length (skirt etc.).

◆'h~**laut**, *adj.* low (voice).
◆'H~**schuh**, *m* shoe. ◆'H~**starke(r)**, *m decl. as adj.* teddy boy, *N.Am:* hood.
◆'h~**tags**, *adv.* h. arbeiten, to work part-time. ◆'H~**tagsarbeit**/'H~**tagsbeschäftigung**, *f* part-time work.
◆'h~**trocken**, *adj.* medium dry (wine etc.). ◆'h~**wegs**, *adv.* fairly, *N.Am:* halfway. ◆'h~**wüchsig**, *adj* adolescent; **ein H~wüchsiger/eine H~wüchsige**, an adolescent. ◆'H~**zeit**, *f Sp:* half-time; (*Spielhälfte*) half.

Halde ['haldə], *f -/-n Min:* tip, slag heap.

Hälfte ['hɛlftə], *f -/-n* half; **die H. des Personals**, half the staff.

Halfter[1] ['halftər], *m -s/-* (*Pferde*.) halter.

Halfter[2], *m -s/-* (*für eine Pistole*) holster.

hallen ['halən], *v.i.* (*haben*) to resound (*widerhallen*) to echo.

Halle ['halə], *f -/-n* (*a*) hall, vestibule; (hotel) lobby; (*b*) *Sp:* indoor arena; (*c*) *Av:* hangar. ◆'H~**nbad**, *n* indoor swimming pool.

hallo ['halo]. *int.* (*a*) hey! (*b*) *Tel: etc:* hello.

Halluzination [halutsinatsi'o:n], *f -/-en* hallucination.

Halm [halm], *m -(e)s/-e* blade (of grass); (*Getreide*.) stalk.

Hals [hals], *m -es/-e* (*a*) neck; **H. über Kopf verliebt sein**, to be head over heels in love; **j-n auf dem H. haben**, to be saddled with s.o.; (*b*) (*Kehle*) throat; **aus vollem H. schreien**, to shout at the top of one's voice. ◆'H~**band**, *n* (dog etc.) collar. ◆'H~**brecherisch**, *adj.* breakneck (speed etc.). ◆'H~**kette**, necklace. ◆'H~'**Nasen-'Ohren-Arzt**, *m* ear nose and throat specialist. ◆'H~**schlagader**, *f* carotid artery. ◆'H~**schmerzen**, *mpl* **H. haben**, to have a sore throat. ◆'H~**starrig**, *adj.* obstinate, stubborn, *F:* pigheaded. ◆'H~**tuch**, *n* scarf. ◆'H~**weh**, *n -s/ no pl* sore throat.

Halt[1] [halt], *m -(e)s/-e* **1.** hold; *Fig:* **keinen H. haben**, to be unstable. **2.** stop, halt; **H. machen**, to stop, (*kurz*) pause. ◆'h~**bar**, *adj.* **1.** (*a*) durable (goods), hard-wearing (clothing etc.); (*b*) (*Essen*) non-perishable. **2.** tenable (argument etc.). ◆'H~**barkeit**, *f -/no pl* durability; keeping quality (of food). ◆'h~**en**, *v. irr.* **1.** *v.tr.* (*a*) to hold (s.o., sth.); (*zurückh.*) to retain (sth.); (*aufh.*) to stop (s.o.); (*b*) (*beibehalten*) to keep, maintain (a distance, course etc.); to hold (prices); (*einh.*) to keep (a promise, one's word); (*c*) (*abh.*) to hold (a meeting); to give a lecture, talk, make a speech); (*d*) (*Meinung*) **j-n für ehrlich, usw. h.**, to think s.o. is honest etc.; **ich halte nicht viel davon**, I don't think much of it; (*e*) sich **h.**, (*Essen*) to keep (fresh); (*Blumen*) to last; *Fig:* **sich an j-n h.**, to turn to s.o.;

sich an die Vorschriften h., to stick to the rules. **2.** *v.i.* (*haben*) (*a*) (*Seil, Klebstoff usw.*) to hold, stay (in position); *Fig:* **zu j-m halten**, to remain loyal to s.o.; (*b*) (*Blumen*) to last; (*Wetter*) to stay fine; (*c*) (*haltmachen*) to stop; (**sich**) **links/rechts h.**, to keep left/right. ◆'H~**erung**, *f -/-en Tchn:* mounting; clamp. ◆'H~**estelle**, *f* (bus etc.) stop. ◆'H~**everbot**, *n* parking ban. ◆'h~**los**, *adj.* **1.** (*Pers.*) unstable. **2.** groundless, unfounded (accusation etc.). ◆'h~**machen**, *v.i.* (*haben*) (to make a) halt, stop. ◆'H~**ung**, *f -/-en* **1.** (*des Körpers*) posture. **2.** (*Einstellung*) attitude. **3.** (*Fassung*) composure, poise.

halt[2], *adv. South G:* just, simply.

Halunke [ha'luŋkə], *m -n/-n* rogue, scoundrel.

hämisch ['hɛːmiʃ], *adj.* malicious; malevolent (look).

Hammel ['haməl], *m -s/-* (*a*) (male) sheep, ram; (*b*) *Cu:* (also **H~fleisch**, *n*) mutton. ◆'H~**keule**, *f* leg of mutton.

Hammer ['hamər], *m -s/-* hammer. ◆'H~**werfen**, *v.tr. & i. no pl* throwing the hammer.

hämmern ['hɛmərn], *v.tr. & i.* to hammer.

Hämorrhoiden [hɛmərɔ'itdən], *fpl* piles, haemorrhoids.

Hampelmann ['hampəlman], *m* (*a*) jumping jack; *Fig:* (*Pers.*) puppet.

Hamster ['hamstər], *m -s/-* hamster. ◆'H~**er**, *m -s/-* hoarder. ◆'h~**n**, *v.tr.* to hoard (food etc.).

Hand [hant]. **I.** *f -/-e* hand; **j-m die H. geben/schütteln**, to shake hands with s.o.; **mit der H. nähen, schreiben usw.**, to sew, write etc. by hand; **etwas in die H~e bekommen**, to get hold of sth.; *Com:* **zu H~en**, for the attention of Mr. X; *Fig:* **unter der H.**, in secret; **sich mit H~en und Füßen wehren**, to fight tooth and nail; **j-n in der H. haben**, to have s.o. at one's mercy; **etwas zur H. haben**, to have sth. on hand/*F:* handy; **das liegt auf der H.**, that is perfectly obvious; **Waren aus zweiter H.**, second-hand goods; **an H. von + dat**, by means of (examples etc.); **das ist ohne H. und Fuß**, it doesn't make sense. **II.** 'H~-, *comb.fm.* (*a*) hand (luggage, -cart, -stand etc.); (*b*) manual (worker, control etc.). ◆'H~**arbeit**, *f* **1.** manual work. **2.** handicraft, *esp.* needlework. ◆'H~**bewegung**, *f* movement of the hand; gesture. ◆'H~**ball**, *m* handball. ◆'H~**bremse**, *f* handbrake. ◆'H~**buch**, *n* handbook, *esp. Tchn:* manual. ◆**h~fest**, *adj.* **1.** sturdy, robust (person). **2.** substantial (meal); solid (proof); sound (argument); tangible (result). ◆'h~**gearbeitet**, *adj.* handmade. ◆'H~**gelenk**, *n* wrist. ◆'h~**gemenge**, brawl, scuffle. ◆'h~**geschrieben**, *adj.* handwritten. ◆'h~

greiflich, *adj.* 1. manifest, obvious (lie), palpable (proof, success etc.). 2. (*Pers.*) **h. werden**, to become violent. ◆**'H~griff**, *m* operation. ◆**'h~haben**, *v.tr.insep.irr.44* to handle. ◆**'H~habung**, *f -/-en* handling. ◆**'H~langer**, *m -s/- Pej:* henchman, *F:* stooge. ◆**'h~lich**, *adj.* handy, easy to manage. ◆**'H~pflege**, *f* manicure. ◆**'H~schelle**, *f* handcuff. ◆**'H~schlag**, *m* handshake. ◆**'H~schrift**, *f* handwriting. ◆**'H~schuh**, *m* glove. ◆**'H~schuhfach**, *m* glove compartment. ◆**'H~streich**, *m* surprise attack/raid. ◆**'H~tasche**, *f* handbag. ◆**'H~teller**, *m* palm. ◆**'H~tuch**, *n* towel. ◆**'H~voll**, *f -/no pl* handful. ◆**'h~warm**, *adj.* lukewarm. ◆**'H~wäsche**, *f* 1. washing by hand. 2. hand-laundry. ◆**'H~werk**, *n* craft; (*Gewerbe*) trade. ◆**'H~werker**, *m -s/-* craftsman. ◆**'h~werklich**, *adj.* (skill etc.) of the craftsman. ◆**'H~werkszeug**, *n* toolkit; *esp. Fig:* tools (of the trade). ◆**'H~zettel**, *m* handbill.

Händedruck ['hɛndədruk], *m* handshake.

Handel ['handəl], *m -s/no pl* (*a*) trade, commerce; (*b*) (business) deal. ◆**'h~n**, *v.i.* (*haben*) (*a*) **mit etwas dat h.**, to deal/ trade in sth.; **um etwas** *acc* **h.**, to bargain for/haggle over sth.; (*b*) to act, take action; (*c*) **wovon handelt dieses Buch?** what is this book about? **um was/worum handelt es sich?** what's it all about? ◆**'H~s-**, *comb.fm.* (*a*) trade (agreement, deficit, register, policy etc.); trading (relations, partner); (*b*) commercial (attaché, law, weight, centre etc.); (*c*) merchant (bank, fleet etc.). ◆**'H~sbilanz**, *f* balance of trade. ◆**'h~seinig**, *adj.* **h. werden/sein**, to agree on terms. ◆**'H~skammer**, *f* Chamber of Commerce. ◆**'H~smarine**, *f* merchant navy. ◆**'H~sreisende(r)**, *m* commercial traveller, *N.Am:* travelling salesman. ◆**'H~sschule**, *f* commercial/*esp.N.Am:* business school. ◆**'h~süblich**, *adj.* customary in the trade; commercial (size). ◆**'H~svertreter**, *m* commercial agent. ◆**'H~svertretung**, *f* trade mission.

Händler ['hɛndlər], *m -s/-* dealer.

Handlung ['handluŋ], *f -/-en* 1. (*Tat*) action. 2. plot (of a play, novel etc.); story-line. ◆**'H~sweise**, *f* course of action; (*Benehmen*) conduct.

Hanf [hanf], *m -(e)s/no pl* hemp.

Hang [haŋ], *m -(e)s/-e* 1. slope; (*Bergh.*) hillside. 2. *no pl* (*Neigung*) inclination.

Hänge- ['hɛŋə-], *comb.fm.* hanging (lamp, cupboard etc.); *Constr:* suspension (bridge etc.). ◆**'H~matte**, *f* hammock. ◆**'h~n**, *v.* 1. *v.i.irr.* (*haben*) (*a*) to hang; **an der Wand/der Decke** *dat* **h.**, to hang on the wall/from the ceiling; (*b*)

(*gern haben*) **an j~m** etwas **h.**, to be attached to s.o., sth. 2. *v.tr.* to hang (sth.) (an/in etwas *acc*, on/in sth.). ◆**'h~nbleiben**, *v.i.sep.irr.12* (*sein*) (*Kleid usw.*) to catch; **get caught** (**an etwas** *dat*, on sth.); (*Pers, Bemühungen usw.*) to get stuck; **im Gedächtnis h.**, to stick (in one's mind). ◆**'H~schloß**, *n* padlock.

Hannover [ha'noːfər]. *Pr.n.n* -s. Hanover.

Hänsel [hɛnzə'laɪ], *f -/-en* teasing remark(s). ◆**'h~n**, *v.tr.* to tease (s.o.).

Hantel ['hantəl], *f -/-n* dumb-bell.

hantieren [han'tiːrən], *v.i.* (*haben*) to busy oneself; **mit einem Messer h.**, to handle a knife.

hapern ['haːpərn], *v.i.impers.* (*haben*) es **hapert an etwas** *dat*, there is a shortage/ lack of sth.

Happen ['hapən], *m -s/e* morsel, mouthful.

happig ['hapiç], *adj. F:* steep, stiff (prices etc.).

Harfe ['harfə], *f -/-n* harp.

Harke ['harkə], *f -/-n* rake. ◆**'h~n**, *v.tr.* to rake (the soil etc.).

harmlos ['harmloːs], *adj.* harmless, innocuous (person, remark etc.); innocent (pleasure, question etc.); slight (cold etc.). ◆**'H~igkeit**, *f -/no pl* harmlessness; innocence.

Harmonie [harmo'niː], *f -/-n* harmony. ◆**h~ieren** [-'niːrən], *v.i.* (*haben*) (*Klänge*) to be harmonious; (*Farben*) to match; **mit j-m h.**, to get on with/ agree with s.o. ◆**H~ika** [-'moːnika], *f -/s* (*Mundh.*) mouth-organ, harmonica; (*Ziehh.*) accordion. ◆**h~isch** [-'moːniʃ], *adj.* harmonious (music, colours, *Fig:* atmosphere etc.).

Harn [harn], *m -(e)s/-e* urine. ◆**'H~blase**, *f* bladder.

Harnisch ['harniʃ], *m -(e)s/-e* 1. (suit of) armour. 2. **j-n in H. bringen**, to infuriate s.o.

Harpune [har'puːnə], *f -/-n* harpoon.

harsch [harʃ]. I. *adj.* harsh. II. **H.**, *m -s/ no pl* crusted snow.

hart [hart]. I. *adj.* (*a*) hard; (winter etc.); severe (punishment); harsh (law, conditions etc.); (*b*) (*Pers.*) tough. II. **h.**, *'h~-*, *comb.fm.* hard (rubber, cheese etc.). ◆**'h~gekocht**, *adj.* hard-boiled. ◆**'h~herzig**, *adj.* hard-hearted. ◆**'h~näckig**, *adj.* obstinate, stubborn (person, resistance etc.); persistent (attempts). ◆**'H~näckigkeit**, *f -/no pl* obstinacy, stubbornness; persistence.

Härte ['hɛrtə], *f -/-n* 1. *no pl* (*a*) hardness; toughness; (*b*) harshness; severity. 2. hardship; privation. ◆**'h~n**, *v.tr.* to harden (a metal, etc.), temper (steel).

Harz [harts], *n -es/-e* resin.

Haschisch [haʃiʃ] *n -s/no pl* hashish.

Haschee [ha'ʃeː], *n -s/-s* hash.

haschen [ˈhaʃən], *v.tr.* to snatch, seize (sth.).

Hase [ˈhaːzə], *m -n/-n* hare. ◆'H**~nfuß**, *m F:* coward. ◆'H**~npfeffer**, *m* jugged hare. ◆'H**~nscharte**, *f* harelip.

Hasel|maus [ˈhaːzlmaus], *f* dormouse. ◆'H**~nuß**, *f* hazelnut.

Haspe [ˈhaspə], *f -/-n* hasp, hook.

Haß [has], *m -sses/no pl* hate, hatred (auf/gegen j-n, etwas *acc*, of/towards s.o., sth.).

hassen [ˈhasən], *v.tr.* to hate (s.o., sth.). ◆'h**~swert**, *adj.* odious.

häßlich [ˈhɛslɪç], *adj.* 1. (*unschön*) ugly. 2. (*gemein*) mean, nasty. ◆'H**~keit**, *f -/-en* ugliness, nastiness.

Hast [hast], *f -/no pl* haste, hurry. ◆'h**~ig**, *adj.* hasty; hurried (steps, meal etc.).

Haube [ˈhaubə], *f -/-n* 1. *Cl:* bonnet; (nurse's cap); *F:* unter die H. kommen, to be married off. 2. *Aut:* bonnet; *N.Am:* hood.

Hauch [haux], *m -(e)s/-e* 1. (*Atem*) breath; (*Lufth.*) (gentle) breeze. 2. (*Anflug*) tinge, touch. ◆'h**~dünn**, *adj.* wafer-thin; very fine (thread etc.); sheer (stockings). ◆'h**~en**, *v.i.* (*haben*) to breathe. ◆'h**~fein**, *adj.* extremely delicate/fine.

hauen [ˈhauən], 1. *v.tr.* (*a*) *F:* (*schlagen*) to bash (s.o., sth.); (*prügeln*) to spank (a child etc.); (*b*) (*schneiden*) to cut/hew (rock, steps etc.). 2. *v.i.* (*haben*) (mit etwas *dat*) auf einen Angreifer h., to hit out at an attacker (with sth.); mit der Faust auf den Tisch h., to bang on the table with one's fist.

Haufen [ˈhaufən], *m -s/-* 1. pile, (*unordentlich*) heap; j-n, etwas über den H. rennen/fahren, to knock/run s.o., sth. down; Pläne usw. über den H. werfen, to upset plans etc. 2. *F:* (*a*) ein H. Geld, a lot of money; (*b*) (*Menschen*) crowd; der ganze H., the whole caboodle. ◆'h**~weise**, *adv. F:* in heaps; (*Menschen*) in droves; er hat h. Geld, he's got loads of money.

häuf|en [ˈhɔyfən], *v.tr.* to heap up, pile up (sth.); **sich h.**, (*Briefe usw.*) to pile up; (*Abfälle*) to accumulate. ◆'h**~ig**, *adj.* frequent. ◆'H**~igkeit**, *f -/no pl* frequency. ◆'H**~ung**, *f -/-en* 1. accumulation; piling up. 2. (*Zunahme*) increase; (greater) frequency (of events).

Haupt [haupt], *n -(e)s/-er Lit:* head. II. 'H**~-**, *comb.fm. (a)* main (attraction, entrance, reason, worry, gate, building, meal, difficulty, theme); principal (aim, purpose etc.); (*b*) (*größere*) major (share, part etc.). ◆'H**~bahnhof**, *m* central/main station. ◆'H**~beruf**, *m* chief occupation; main job. ◆'H**~darsteller(in)**, *m(f)*, leading man/lady. ◆'H**~gewinn**, *m* first prize (in a lottery etc.). ◆'H**~mann**, *m -(e)s/-leute Mil:* captain. ◆'H**~person**, *f (a)* central/principal character (in a play

etc.); (*b*) most important person. ◆'H**~post**, *f* main/central post office. ◆'H**~quartier**, *n* headquarters. ◆'H**~rolle**, *f* leading role; main part. ◆'H**~sache**, *f* main thing; (*Frage*) main point. ◆'h**~sächlich**, *adj.* main, chief (question etc.); *adv.* mainly, chiefly. ◆'H**~saison**, *f* high/full season. ◆'H**~satz**, *m* main clause. ◆'H**~stadt**, *f* capital (city). ◆'H**~straße**, *f (a)* main road; (*b*) (*in einer Stadt*) main street. ◆'H**~verkehrszeit**, *f* rush hour. ◆'H**~wort**, *n* noun.

Häuptling [ˈhɔyptlɪŋ], *m -s/-e* chief (of a tribe).

Haus [haus]. I. *n -es/-er* 1. house; (*Gebäude*) building; nach H~e kommen, to go/come home; zu H~e bleiben, to stay at home; außer H. essen, to eat out; *Fig:* auf einem Gebiet zu H~e sein, to be well up in a subject; aus gutem H~e, from a good family; von H~(e) aus, by birth; (*ursprünglich*) originally. 2. *Com:* firm; er ist nicht im H~e, he is not on the premises. 3. *Th:* auditorium. 4. H. einer Schnecke, snail's shell. II. 'H**~-**, *comb.fm. (a)* house (arrest, number etc.); (*b*) (*häuslich*) domestic (cat, pig etc.). ◆'H**~angestellte(r)**, *m & f* domestic servant. ◆'H**~apotheke**, *f* medicine chest. ◆'H**~arbeit**, *f (a)* housework; (*b*) *Sch:* homework. ◆'H**~arzt**, *m* family doctor. ◆'H**~besetzer**, *m* squatter. ◆'H**~besitzer(in)**, *m(f)* house owner; (*Wirt*) landlord; (*Wirtin*) landlady. ◆'H**~bewohner**, *m* occupier. ◆'H**~en**, *v.i.* (*haben*) (*a*) to live, *F:* hang out; (*b*) (*Sturm usw.*) schlimm h., to wreak havoc. ◆'H**~flur**, *m* (entrance) hall; hallway (of flats etc.); (*Gang*) corridor. ◆'H**~frau**, *f* housewife. ◆'h**~gemacht**, *adj.* home-made. ◆'H**~halt**, *m -(e)s/-e* 1. household. 2. *Parl:* budget. ◆'h**~halten**, *v.i.sep.irr.45* (*haben*) to be careful (mit dem Geld usw., with one's money etc.); mit seinen Kräften h., to conserve one's energies. ◆'H**~hälterin**, *f -/-nen* housekeeper. ◆'H**~halts-**, *comb.fm.* 1. household (article, goods, budget etc.); domestic (help etc.). 2. *Parl:* budget (debate, deficit etc.); budgetary (policy etc.). ◆'H**~haltsgerät**, *n* domestic appliance. ◆'H**~haltsgeld**, *n* housekeeping money. ◆'H**~haltsplan**, *m* budget. ◆'H**~haltung**, *f* 1. household. 2. *no pl* (*Führung*) housekeeping. ◆'H**~herr**, *m* householder; master of the house. ◆'h**~hoch**, *adj. (a)* towering, huge (flames etc.); (*b*) *Fig:* haushoher Sieg, overwhelming victory; h. gewinnen, to win hands down. ◆'h**~ieren**, *v.i.* (*haben*) mit etwas *dat* h., to sell sth. from door to door. ◆'H**~ierer** [-ˈziːrər], *m -s/-* door-to-door salesman.

◆'H~meister, *m* caretaker; *N.Am:* janitor. ◆'H~ordnung, *f* house rules. ◆'H~rat, *m* -s/*no pl* household contents. ◆'H~schlüssel, *m* front-door key. ◆'H~schuh, *m* slipper. ◆'H~tier, *n* domestic animal; (*im Haus*) pet. ◆'H~suchungsbefehl, *m* search warrant. ◆'H~tür, *f* front door. ◆'H~verbot, *n Jur:* order restraining a peson from entering (a house etc.). ◆'H~verwalter, *m* house agent; property manager. ◆'H~wirt, *m* landlord. ◆'H~wirtin, *f* landlady. ◆'H~wirtschaft, *f* -/*no pl* (a) housekeeping; (b) (*Fach*) home economics; (*Haushaltsführung*) household management.

Häus|er- ['hɔyzər-], *comb.fm:* (block, row etc.) of houses. ◆'h~lich, *adj.* domestic.

Haut [haut], *f* -/-e (a) skin; **mit H. und Haar**, *Fig:* completely, totally; **sich seiner H. wehren**, to put up a stubborn resistance; **aus der H. fahren**, to be hopping mad; (b) hide of a cow, elephant etc.). ◆'H~arzt, *m* skin specialist; dermatologist. ◆h~eng, *adj.* skin-tight. ◆'H~farbe, *f* colour of the skin; (*Teint*) complexion. ◆'h~nah, *adj.* 1. *Sp:* close (marking etc.). 2. *F:* graphic, sensational (description etc.).

häuten ['hɔytən], *v.tr.* (a) to skin, flay (an animal); (b) **sich h.**, (*Tier*) to shed its skin.

Haxe [haksə], *f* -/-n = Hachse.

Hebamme ['he:p?amə], *f* -/-n midwife.

Heb|el ['he:bəl], *m* -s/- lever. ◆'H~elwirkung, *f* leverage; purchase. ◆h~en ['he:bən], *v.tr.irr.* (*haben*) to lift (s.o., one's hand, a weight etc.), lift up (a child etc.), raise (one's arm, a glass, *Th:* the curtain, *Fig:* one's voice etc.).

Hecht [hɛçt], *m* -(e)s/-e pike.

Heck [hɛk]. I. *n* -(e)s/-e & -s *Nau:* stern; *Av:* tail; *Aut:* rear. II. '**H~-**, *comb.fm: Aut:* rear (drive, engine etc.). ◆'H~scheibe, *f* rear window. ◆'H~tür, *f* tailgate.

Hecke ['hɛkə], *f* -/-n hedge. ◆'H~nrose, *f* -/-n briar/dog rose. ◆'H~nschere, *f* garden shears, *esp:* hedge-clippers.

Heer [he:r], *n* -(e)s/-e (a) *Mil:* army; (b) *Fig:* host, multitude, *Pej:* horde of people, insects etc.).

Hefe ['he:fə], *f* -/-n yeast. ◆'H~teig, *m* leavened dough.

Heft [hɛft], *n* -(e)s/-e (a) *Sch:* exercise book; (b) (*von Zeitschrift*) copy, issue; (c) (*paper-covered*) booklet; (*Prospekt*) brochure. ◆'h~en, *v.tr.* (a) to tack (a hem etc.); to stitch (a book); (b) to fasten, (*mit Klammer*) clip, (*maschinell*) staple, (*mit Nadel*) pin (sheets of paper etc.) together; (c) **etwas an etwas** *acc* **h.**, to fasten/clip/pin sth. to sth. ◆'H~er,

m -s/- folder. ◆'H~klammer, *f* 1. staple. 2. (*Büroklammer*) paper clip. ◆'H~maschine, *f* stapler. ◆'H~pflaster, *n* sticking plaster. ◆'H~zwecke, *f* -/-n drawing pin; *N.Am:* thumbtack.

heftig ['hɛftiç], *adj.* violent; fierce (argument, blow, storm etc.); heavy (rain, snow); furious, vehement (attack). ◆'H~keit, *f* -/-en violence, fierceness; fury, ferocity (of a storm, an attack); vehemence.

hegen ['he:gən], *v.tr.* (a) to conserve, protect (young game etc.); to nurse, tend (plants etc.); (b) *Lit:* to harbour (a grudge etc.); cherish (a desire).

Hehl [he:l], *m & n* **kein(en) H. aus etwas** *dat* **machen**, to make no secret of sth. ◆'H~er(in), *m* -s/- (*f* -/-nen) receiver (of stolen goods), *F:* fence.

Heide¹ ['haidə], *f* -/-n 1. heath; (*große Fläche*) moor. 2. = H~kraut. ◆'H~kraut, *n* heather. ◆'H~lbeere, *f* bilberry.

Heid|e², *m* -n/-n/'Heidin, *f* -/-nen heathen, pagan. ◆'H~en-, *comb.fm. F:* terrific (noise, fright etc.). ◆'H~enangst, *f* -/no pl: to be scared to death. ◆'H~entum, *n* -s/ *no pl* paganism; heathendom. ◆'h~nisch, *adj.* heathen, pagan.

heikel ['haikəl], *adj.* awkward, tricky (problem, situation etc.); delicate, difficult (matter).

heil [hail]. I. *adj.* (a) unhurt; (*sicher*) safe; (b) (*Sache*) intact, undamaged (house etc.); unbroken (cup etc.); *Fig:* **eine h~e Welt**, a perfect world. II. **H.**, *n* -s/ *no pl Lit:* welfare, well-being; *Ecc:* salvation. III. '**H~-**, *comb.fm.* healing, *Med:* therapeutic (power, process etc.); medicinal (herbs, plants etc.); (method etc.) of treatment. ◆'H~and, *m* -(e)s/*no pl* Saviour. ◆'h~bar, *adj.* curable. ◆'h~en, *v.* 1. *v.tr.* to cure (s.o., a disease), heal (a wound, fracture etc.). 2. *v.i.* (*sein*) (*Wunde usw.*) to heal. ◆'h~froh, *adj. F:* to be mightily relieved. ◆'h~ig, *adj.* holy (baptism, land etc.); sacred (songs etc.). ◆'H~ig'abend, *m* Christmas Eve. ◆'H~ige(r), *m & f decl. as adj.* Saint. ◆'h~igen, *v.tr.* to hallow, sanctify (s.o., sth.). ◆'H~igenschein, *m* (saint's) halo. ◆'H~igkeit, *f* -/no pl sanctity; *Ecc:* holiness. ◆'h~igsprechen, *v.tr.sep.irr.14 Ecc:* to canonize (s.o.). ◆'H~igtum, *n* -s/-er (a) holy place; *esp. Fig:* shrine; (b) (*Gegenstand*) (sacred) relic. ◆'h~los, *adj.* unholy (din, muddle, terror); **h. verschuldet**, hopelessly in debt. ◆'H~mittel, *n* remedy, cure (gegen + *acc,* for). ◆'H~praktiker, *m* (non-professional) practitioner of medicine; healer. ◆'h~sam, *adj.* salutary. ◆'H~s-armee, *f* Salvation Army. ◆'H~ung, *f*

f /-en cure; healing.
Heilbutt ['hailbut], m halibut.
Heim [haim]. **I.** n -(e)s/-e (a) home; (b) (Anstalt) institution; (für Geisteskranke) asylum; (für Studenten) hostel. ◆'**H~at**, f -/no pl home; (Land) homeland; native country; in meiner H., where I come from. ◆'**H~at~**, comb.fm. home (country, town etc.); local, regional (poet etc.); (place, country) of origin/birth. ◆'**h~atlich**, adj. native (customs etc.) ◆'**h~atlos**, adj. homeless (person etc.); stateless (alien). ◆'**H~atvertrie-bene(r)**, m & f decl. as adj. displaced person. ◆'**h~fahren**, v.i. (sein) to go/ travel/drive home. ◆'**H~fahrt**, f journey home. ◆'**H~isch**, adj. native (population), indigenous (plants etc.); local, regional (customs, industry etc.); (b) home (surroundings etc.); sich h. fühlen, to feel at home. ◆'**H~kehr**, f return home, homecoming. ◆'**h~kehren**, v.i.sep. (sein) to return home. ◆'**h~lich**, adj. secret. ◆'**H~lichkeit**, f -/no pl secrecy. ◆'**H~reise**, f journey home. ◆'**H~spiel**, n home game. ◆'**h~suchen**, v.tr. (a) F: j-n h., to descend on s.o.; (b) (Krankheit usw.) to afflict (s.o., a country etc.). ◆'**h~tückisch**, adj. malicious; Fig: insidious (illness). ◆'**H~weg**, m way home. ◆'**H~weh**, n -s/no pl homesickness; sie hat H., she is homesick. ◆'**H~werker**, m -s/- F: do-it-yourselfer, handyman. ◆'**h~zahlen**, v.tr.sep. j-m (etwas) h., to pay s.o. back (for sth.).
Heirat ['hairɑːt], f -/-en marriage. ◆'**h~en**, v.tr. & i. (haben) to marry (s.o.), get married (to s.o.). ◆'**H~santrag**, m proposal of marriage); j-m einen H. machen, to propose to s.o.
heiser ['haizər], adj. hoarse. ◆'**H~keit**, f -/no pl hoarseness.
heiß [hais], adj. **1.** hot (weather, drink etc.); Geog: torrid (zone). **2.** (a) (heftig) fierce (battle, competition, debate etc.); heated (argument); h. umstritten/ umkämpft, hotly contested; (b) Sp: hot (favourite, tip). ◆'**h~blütig**, adj. hot-tempered. ◆'**h~ersehnt**, adj. longed-for; eagerly awaited (moment etc.). ◆'**H~hunger**, m voracious appetite. ◆'**h~laufen**, v.i.sep.irr.58 (sein) (Motor usw.) to run hot; (übermäßig) to overheat. ◆'**H~luft**, f hot air. ◆'**H~-'wasserbereiter**, m water-heater.
heißen ['haisən], v.irr. **1.** v.i. (haben) (a) wie heißt du? what's your name? er heißt Peter, he is called Peter. es heißt, er sei krank, I am told he is ill; (c) (bedeuten) to mean; wie heißt es auf Englisch? what is it (called) in English? was soll das h.! what is the meaning of this! F: what's this in aid of? **2.** v.tr. (nennen) to call (s.o. one's friend, a liar etc.); j-n

willkommen h., to welcome s.o.
heiter ['haitər], adj. gay, bright; (froh) cheerful (mood, face etc.); fine, bright (day, weather), clear (sky). ◆'**H~keit**, f -/no pl cheerfulness; (Lachen) merriment.
Heiz- ['haits-], comb.fm. heating (costs, element, oil, etc.). ◆'**h~bar**, adj. heatable. ◆'**H~decke**, f electric blanket. ◆'**h~en**, v. **1.** v.tr. to heat (a room etc.). **2.** v.i. (haben) to turn on the heating; (Feuer machen) to light a fire; der Ofen heizt gut, the stove gives plenty of heat. ◆'**H~er**, m -s/- stoker; Rail: fireman. ◆'**H~gerät**, n heater. ◆'**H~körper**, m (a) (central heating) radiator; (b) heating element. ◆'**H~lüfter**, m fan heater. ◆'**H~ung**, f /-en heating.
hektisch ['hɛktiʃ], adj. hectic.
Held [hɛlt], m -en/-en hero. ◆'**H~en-**[-dən-], comb.fm. heroic (saga, epic, Mus: tenor etc.). ◆'**h~enhaft**, adj. heroic. ◆'**H~entat**, f heroic deed. ◆'**H~in**, f /-nen heroine.
helf|en ['hɛlfən], v.i.irr. (haben) (a) j-m h., to help/assist s.o.; ich kann mir nicht h., aber ..., I can't help it but ...; sich zu h. wissen, to know how to cope; (b) (nützen) to be good/useful; es hilft nichts, it's no use. ◆'**H~er(in)**, m -s/- (f -/-nen) helper, assistant. ◆'**H~ers-helfer**, m accomplice; henchman.
Helium ['heːliʊm], n -s/no pl helium.
hell [hɛl]. **I.** adj. **1.** (a) light; (blaß) pale (colour, hair, skin etc.); fair (complexion, hair); (b) (strahlend) bright (colour, light etc.); h. erleuchtet, brightly lit; (c) es wird schon h., it is getting light; dawn is breaking. **2.** clear (sound, voice etc.). **II.** 'h~-, comb.fm. light (blue, yellow etc.). ◆'**h~blond**, adj. very fair (hair). ◆'**H~e**, f -/no pl light, brightness. ◆'**h~hörig**, adj. **1.** h. sein, to have sharp ears; F: h. werden, to prick up one's ears. **2.** Arch: poorly soundproofed (walls etc.). ◆'**H~igkeit**, f /no pl brightness; intensity (of light). ◆'**h~seher(in)**, m -s/- (f /-nen) clairvoyant. ◆'**h~wach**, adj. wide awake.
Helm [hɛlm], m -(e)s/-e helmet.
Hemd [hɛmt], n -(e)s/-en shirt; (Unter-) vest; N.Am: undershirt. ◆'**H~bluse**, f shirt blouse.
Hemisphäre [hɛmi'sfɛːrə], f hemisphere.
hemm|en ['hɛmən], v.tr. (a) (Fluß gebieten) to halt, stop, (vorübergehend) check (a course of events etc.); to stem (the flow); (b) (einschränken) to inhibit (s.o., development etc.). ◆'**H~ung**, f /-en Psy: etc: inhibition; (Bedenken) scruple. ◆'**h~ungslos**, adj. uninhibited (person).
Hengst [hɛnst], m -(e)s/-e stallion.
Henkel ['hɛŋkəl]. **I.** m -s/- handle (of a cup/jug). **II.** 'H~-, comb.fm. (basket, jug, pot etc.) with a handle.
Henker ['hɛŋkər], m -s/- executioner;

hangman.

Henne ['hɛnə], f -/-n hen.

her [heːr], adv. (a) (Richtung) here; **h. damit!** give it to me! **von weit h.,** from a long way off; (b) (Zeitspanne) ago, since; **es ist lange h.,** it was long ago.

herab [hɛ'rap]. adv. down, downwards; **die Treppe h.,** down the stairs. ◆**h~hängen,** v.i.sep.irr.46 (haben) (a) to hang down; (b) (Beine) to dangle; (Kopf)) to droop. ◆**h~lassen,** v.tr.sep.irr.57 (a) to lower, let down (blinds, a boat etc.); (b) **sich zu etwas dat h.,** to condescend to do sth. ◆**h~lassend,** adj. condescending ◆**H~lassung,** f -/no pl condescension. ◆**h~sehen,** v.i.sep.irr.92 (haben) to look down. ◆**h~setzen,** v.tr.sep. (a) to reduce (price etc.); (b) (schmälern) to belittle. ◆**H~setzung,** f -/-en (a) reduction (des Preises usw., in price etc.); (b) disparagement. ◆**h~würdigen,** v.tr.sep. (a) to speak disparagingly of (s.o.); (b) to treat (s.o.) degradingly.

heran [hɛ'ran]. adv. close; **bis an den Rand h.,** right up to the edge/rim. ◆**h~bilden,** v.tr.sep. to train, educate (s.o.). ◆**h~bringen,** v.tr.sep.irr.16 to bring (s.o., sth.) close **(an + acc,** to). ◆**h~führen,** v.tr.sep. (a) to lead/take (s.o., sth.) up **(an + acc,** to); (b) (einführen) to introduce (s.o.) **an ein Thema,** to a subject). ◆**h~gehen,** v.i.sep.irr.36 (sein) (a) (sich nähern) **h. an + acc,** to go to/approach (s.o., sth.); (b) (beginnen) **an die Arbeit usw. h.,** to get down to work etc. ◆**h~kommen,** v.i.sep.irr.53 (sein) (a) (Pers., Ereignis) to come up **(an + acc,** to); (b) (ergreifen) **an etwas acc h.,** to get hold of, **(mit Mühe)** get at sth. ◆**h~lassen,** v.tr.sep.irr.57 **j-n (nahe) h.,** to let s.o. come close **(an + acc** to). ◆**h~machen,** v.refl.sep. (a) **sich an eine Arbeit h.,** to get down to a job; (b) F: **sich an j-n h.,** to make up to s.o. ◆**h~reichen,** v.i.sep. (haben) **h. an + acc,** to reach (s.o., sth.). Fig: (gleichkommen) be tantamount to (sth.). ◆**h~treten,** v.i.sep.irr.105 (sein) **h. an + acc,** to come up to, approach (s.o., sth.); (Probleme, Zweifel) to beset (s.o.). ◆**h~wachsen,** v.i.sep.irr.107 (sein) to grow up **(zu etwas dat,** into sth.). ◆**h~wachsend,** adj. adolescent; rising (generation); **ein H~wachsender/eine H~wachsende,** an adolescent. ◆**h~ziehen,** v.tr.sep.irr.113 (a) to draw/pull (s.o., sth.) up (close); **(an + acc,** to); (b) to call in (a specialist etc.); to bring in (foreign workers etc.); to consult (a dictionary etc.).

herauf [hɛ'rauf]. adv. up, upwards. ◆**h~beschwören,** v.tr.sep. (a) to conjure up, evoke (memories etc.); (b) to cause (a disaster, quarrel etc.). ◆**h~bringen,** v.tr.sep.irr.16 to bring (s.o., sth.) up(stairs). ◆**h~kommen,**

v.i.sep.irr.53 (sein) to come up/upstairs. ◆**h~setzen,** v.tr. sep. to increase (prices etc.). ◆**h~ziehen,** v.tr.sep.irr.113 1. v.tr. to pull up (sth.). 2. v.i. (sein) (Tag, Nacht) to approach; (Gefahr usw.) to threaten; **ein Gewitter zieht herauf,** a storm is brewing.

heraus [hɛ'raus], adv. out; (a) **aus einer Notlage h. handeln,** to act from necessity; **aus sich h.,** of one's own accord. ◆**h~bekommen,** v.tr.sep.irr.53 (a) to get (sth.) out **(aus etwas dat,** of sth.); (b) (entdecken) to find (sth.) out. ◆**h~bringen,** v.tr.sep.irr.16 (a) to bring/take (s.o., sth.) out(side); (b) to get (an answer, information) **(aus j-m,** out of s.o.). ◆**h~finden,** v.tr.sep.irr.19 to find out. ◆**H~forderer,** m -s/- challenger. ◆**h~fordern,** v.tr.sep. to challenge; ◆**H~forderung,** challenge. ◆**h~geben,** v.tr.sep.irr.35 (a) to hand (sth.) over, give (sth.) up; (b) (Geld) **j-m h.,** to give s.o. change; (c) (veröffentlichen) to publish, (redigieren) edit (a book, periodical etc.); to issue (banknotes, stamps etc.). ◆**H~geber,** m -s/- editor. ◆**h~gehen,** v.i.sep.irr.36 (sein) to go out **(aus dem Haus,** of the house); Fig: **aus sich dat h.,** to come out of one's shell. ◆**h~halten,** v.tr.sep.irr.45 to keep (s.o.) out **(aus etwas dat,** of sth.). ◆**h~holen,** v.tr.sep. to bring/fetch/(mit Mühe) pull (s.o., sth.) out. ◆**h~kommen,** v.i.sep.irr.53 (sein) (a) to come out **(aus + dat,** of); (b) (Buch usw.) to come out, appear; (Briefmarken, Münzen) to be issued; (c) (Geheimnis, Tatsache) to come out/to light; (Plan usw.) to become known; (sich ergeben) **es wird nichts Gutes dabei h.,** no good will come of it. ◆**h~lassen,** v.tr.sep.irr.57 to let (s.o., sth.) out, leave (sth.) out. ◆**h~nehmen,** v.tr.sep.irr.69 (a) to take (sth.) out **(aus etwas dat,** of sth.); (b) **sich dat zuviel/ Freiheiten h.,** to take liberties. ◆**h~ragen,** v.i.sep. (haben) (a) to project, jut out; (b) Fig: to stand out. ◆**h~reißen,** v.tr.sep.irr.4 (a) to tear (sth.) out **(aus etwas dat,** of sth.); Fig: to jolt, startle (s.o.). (aus seiner Lethargie usw., out of his lethargy etc.); Fig: (retten) **j-n h.,** to come to s.o.'s rescue. ◆**h~rücken,** v.tr. **&** i.sep. (sein) F: to part with (sth., money) (reluctantly); **mit der Sprache h.,** (i) to speak up; (ii) (etwas gestehen) to own up. ◆**h~sehen,** v.i.sep. (haben) to look out; **zum Fenster h.,** to look out of the window. ◆**h~schlagen,** v.tr.sep.irr.85 (a) to knock out (a tooth, partition etc.); (b) F: **Geld/Vorteile aus j-m, etwas dat h.,** to make money out of/gain an advantage from s.o., sth. ◆**h~sein,** v.i.sep.irr.93 to be out; **es ist noch nicht heraus, wer gewonnen hat,** it is not yet known who won. ◆**h~springen,** v.i.sep.irr.96 (sein)

(a) to jump out (**aus** etwas *dat*, of sth.);
(b) F: **bei der Sache springt nichts für
mich heraus,** I'll get nothing out of this
affair. ◆**h~stellen,** *v.tr.sep.* (a) to put
(sth.) out; (b) (*betonen*) to stress (the importance of sth.); (c) **sich h.,** to turn out
(**als** falsch, ungenügend usw., to be
wrong, inadequate etc.). ◆**h~suchen,**
v.tr.sep. to   pick   out,
select   (sth.).   ◆**h~wachsen,**
v.i.sep.irr.107 (*sein*) to grow out (**aus** etwas *dat*, of sth.); (*Pers.*) **aus den Kleidern h.,** to outgrow one's clothes.

herb [hɛrp], *adj.* bitter (taste, *Fig:* loss
etc.); tangy, *Pej:* acrid (smell); dry
(wine); (*streng*) harsh (words etc.).

herbei [hɛr'bai], *adv.* here. ◆**h~eilen,**
v.i.sep. (*sein*) hurry up to the spot.
◆**h~führen,** *v.tr.sep.* to bring about a
decision, result etc.); to cause (an accident,   death   etc.).   ◆**h~rufen,**
v.tr.sep.irr.74 to summon (s.o., help
etc.). ◆**h~schaffen,** *v.tr.sep.* to get
(s.o., sth.) to the spot, F: produce (s.o.,
sth.).

herbemühen, *v.tr.sep.* to ask s.o. to
come; **sich h.,** to (be so good as to)
come.

Herberg|e ['hɛrbɛrgə], *f* -/-n (a) lodging;
(b)   (*Jugendh.*)   (youth)   hostel.
◆'**H~svater,** *m* warden of a youth
hostel).

'**herbitten,** *v.tr.sep.irr.10* to ask (s.o.) to
come.

'**herbringen,** *v.tr.sep.irr.16* to bring (s.o.,
sth.) (here).

Herbst [hɛrpst]. **I.** *m* -(e)s/-e autumn;
N.Am: fall. **II.** '**H~-,** *comb.fm.* autumn
(holidays, colours etc.); autumnal (air,
weather etc.). ◆'**h~lich,** *adj.* autumnal.

Herd [hɛːrt], *m* -(e)s/-e **1.** (cooking) stove,
Brit: cooker. **2.** centre (of an earthquake,
of unrest etc.); *Med:* seat (of an infection), focus (of a disease). ◆'**H~platte,**
f El: hotplate.

Herde ['hɛːrdə], *f* -/-n herd (of cattle
etc.); flock (of sheep etc.).

herein [hɛ'rain], *adv.* (in) here; **h.!** come
in! ◆**h~brechen,** *v.i.sep.irr.14* (*sein*)
(a) (**in** etwas *acc* **h.,** to break/
(*Wassermasse*) burst in(to sth.); (b)
(*Abend, Winter usw.*) to close in; (*Nacht*)
to fall. ◆**h~bringen,** *v.tr.sep.irr.16* to
bring (s.o., sth.) in. ◆**h~fallen,**
v.i.sep.irr.27 (*sein*) (a) (**in** etwas *acc* **h.,**
to fall in(to sth.); (*Licht*) to come in; (b)
F: to be cheated/taken in (**auf** j-n, by
s.o.). ◆**h~holen,** *v.tr.sep.* to bring
(sth.) in. ◆**h~kommen,** *v.i.sep.irr.53*
(*sein*) to come in. ◆**h~lassen,**
v.tr.sep.irr.57 **j-n** (**in das Haus**) **h.,** to let
s.o. in(to the house). ◆**h~legen,**
v.tr.sep. F: to take (s.o.) in, take (s.o.)
for a ride. ◆**h~platzen,** *v.i.sep.* (*sein*)
F: (**in** etwas *acc*) **h.,** to barge in(to) sth.
◆**h~schauen,** *v.i.sep.* (*haben*) to look
in. ◆**h~stürzen,** *v.i.sep.* (*sein*) (**in** et-

was *acc*) **h.,** to rush in (to sth.).

'**Herfahrt** *f* journey/*Aut:* drive here.

'**herfallen,** *v.i.sep.irr.27* (*sein*) **über j-n h.,**
to pitch into s.o.

'**Hergang,** *m* course of events.

'**hergeben,** *v.tr.sep.irr.35* to surrender
(sth.); part with (money etc.); (*überreichen*) to hand (sth.) over; (*zurückgeben*)
to give (sth.) back.

'**hergehen,** *v.i.sep.irr.32* (*sein*) (a) **neben/
hinter j-m h.,** to walk next to/behind
s.o.; (b) *impers.* **es ging laut/lustig her,**
there were noisy/gay goings-on.

'**herhalten,** *v.sep.irr.45* **1.** *v.tr.* to hold out
(one's hand etc.). **2.** *v.i.* (*haben*) **für j-n
h.** (**müssen**), to have to take the blame
for s.o.

Hering ['heːriŋ], *m* -s/-e **1.** herring. **2.**
(*Zeltpflock*) tent-peg.

'**herkommen,** *v.i.sep.irr.53* (*sein*) (a) to
come here; to arrive (here); (b) **wo
kommst du her?** where do you come
from? ◆'**h~kömmlich,** *adj.* conventional; (*üblich*) customary; traditional (belief etc.).

Herkunft ['heːrkunft], *f* -/-e origin.
◆'**H~sland,** *n* country of origin.

'**herleiten,** *v.tr.sep.* to derive (a word,
theory etc.).

'**hermachen,** *v.tr.sep.* **sich h. über** + *acc,*
to fall (up)on, attack (s.o., sth.); F: to
pitch into (s.o., one's food etc.); to set
about, tackle (a job, task etc.).

Hermelin [hɛrmə'liːn], *n* -s/-e **1.** stoat. **2.**
(*Pelz*) ermine.

hermetisch [hɛr'meːtɪʃ], *adj.* hermetic;
h. verschlossen, hermetically sealed.

hernach, *adv.* after(wards); subsequently.

'**hernehmen,** *v.tr.sep.irr.69* to take (sth.).

Heroin [hero'iːn], *n* -s/no *pl* heroin.

heroisch [he'roːɪʃ], *adj.* heroic.

Herr [hɛr], *m* -(e)n/-en **1.** man; (*formell*)
gentleman; **200 Meter der H~en,** men's
200 metres; **meine** (**Damen und**) **H~en!**
(ladies and) gentlemen! **H.** Müller, Mr
Müller; **H.** Präsident, Mr Chairman;
Sehr geehrter H., Dear Sir. **2.** master
(of a servant, dog etc.); **sein eigener H.
sein,** to be one's own master; **H. der
Lage sein,** to have the situation under
control. ◆**H~en-,** *comb.fm.* men's
(clothing, fashion etc.); man's (suit,
shirt). ◆'**H~enabend,** *m* stag party.
◆'**H~enbesuch,**   male   visitor.
◆'**h~enlos,** *adj.* (dog etc.) without a
master; ownerless (object). ◆'**H~gott,**
m **der** (**liebe**) **H.,** the (good) Lord.
◆'**H~in,** *f* -/-nen lady; mistress (of a
dog, servant). ◆'**h~isch,** *adj.* domineering;   (*gebieterisch*)   imperious.
◆'**h~lich,** *adj.* magnificent (spectacle,
view etc.); splendid (food, idea etc.);
marvellous (holiday, weather etc.).
◆'**H~lichkeit,** *f* -/no *pl* magnificence,
splendour. ◆'**H~schaft,** *f* -/-en **1.** (a)
(*Regierung*) rule; (*Macht*) power; sovereignty (of the State); (b) (*Beherrschung*)

control (**über etwas** *acc*, of sth.). **2.** *pl*
meine H~en! ladies and gentlemen!
◆'**h~schen**, *v.i.* (*haben*) (*a*) to rule,
(*Fürst*) reign, *Pol:* (*Partei*) be in power;
(*b*) (*Zustände, Meinung usw.*) to prevail;
überall herrschte Trauer, there was sadness everywhere. ◆'**h~schend**, *adj.* **1.**
reigning (monarch); ruling (class etc.). **2.**
(*gegenwärtig*) current, prevailing.
◆'**H~scher**, *m* -s/- ruler; (*Fürst*) monarch, sovereign. ◆'**H~schsucht**, *f* desire to give orders; domineering/*F:* bossy
nature. ◆'**h~schsüchtig**, *adj.* domineering, *F:* bossy.

'**herrichten**, *v.tr.sep.* to prepare (a meal,
room).

'**herrühren**, *v.i.sep.* (*haben*) to derive,
originate.

'**hersein**, *v.i.sep.irr.93* (*sein*) (*a*) **das dürfte
schon Jahre h.**, it must have been years
ago; (*b*) **hinter j-m, etwas** *dat* **h.**, to be
after s.o., sth.

'**herstammen**, *v.i.sep.* (*haben*) **von j-m**
h., to be descended from s.o.; **wo stammen Sie her?** where do you come from?

'**herstell|en**, *v.tr.sep.* (*a*) *Ind:* to produce,
manufacture (goods etc.); (*b*) to establish
(contact, law and order etc.); to create
(good relations etc.). ◆'**H~er**, *m* -s/-
Ind: manufacturer; ◆'**H~ung**, *f* -/no *pl*
Ind: manufacture, production.
◆'**H~ungs—**, *comb.fm.* production
(fault, costs etc.); manufacturing (process
etc.).

herüber [hɛˈryːbər], *adv.* across; over
here (to me). ◆**h~fahren**, *v.tr. &
i.sep.irr.26* (*sein*) to drive (s.o.) over.

herum [hɛˈrʊm], *adv.* (*a*) **um ... acc h.**,
(i) round ...; (ii) *Fig:* (*etwa*) round about;
(*b*) **verkehrt h.**, the wrong way round.
◆**h~ärgern**, *v.refl.sep. F:* sich mit j-m,
etwas *dat* h., to be constantly irritated by
s.o., sth. ◆**h~drehen**, *v.tr.sep.* to turn
(s.o., sth.) round. ◆**h~fahren**,
v.i.sep.irr.26 (*sein*) to travel/*Aut:* drive
around. ◆**h~führen**, *v.tr.sep.* (*a*) **j-n**
(**im Haus usw.**) **h.**, to take/show s.o.
round (the house etc.); (*b*) **etwas mit
sich** *dat* **h.**, to take/carry sth. about with
one. ◆**h~gehen**, *v.i.sep.irr.36* (*sein*) (*a*)
(*Pers.*) to go/walk round; **um etwas** *acc*
h., to walk round sth.; (*b*) (*Sache*) to be
passed round; *F:* (*Nachricht, Krankheit
usw.*) to go the rounds; (*c*) (*Zeit, Urlaub
usw.*) (**schnell**) **h.**, to pass (quickly).
◆**h~kommen**, *v.i.sep.irr.53* (*sein*) (*a*)
h. um + *acc*, to come round (sth.); to get
round (an obstacle, *Fig:* a difficulty etc.),
get out of (a duty etc.); (*b*) **er kommt
viel herum**, he gets around (a lot).
◆**h~kriegen**, *v.tr.sep. F:* to bring/win
(s.o.) round. ◆**h~reden**, *v.i.sep.* (*haben*) *F:* **um die Sache h.**, to evade the
issue. ◆**h~schlagen**, *v.refl.sep.irr.85
F:* sich (*dauernd*) mit j-m h.,
to be forever squabbling with s.o.; **sich
mit einem Problem h.**, to struggle

with a problem. ◆**h~streiten**,
v.refl.sep.irr.59 sich mit j-m h., to squabble with s.o. ◆**h~treiben**,
v.refl.sep.irr.12 F: (*a*) **sich (auf den Straßen usw.**) **h.**, to roam the streets; (*b*) (**an
einem Ort**) to hang out. ◆**h~treiber**, *m*
-s/- *F:* (*a*) loafer; (*b*) tramp, vagabond.
◆**h~ziehen**, *v.i.sep.irr.113* (*sein*) to
wander about.

herunter [hɛˈrʊntər], *adv.* down; down
here; this way; **die Treppe/Straße h.**,
down the stairs/the street. ◆**h~fallen**,
v.i.sep.irr.27 (*sein*) to fall down/
downstairs. ◆**h~gehen**, *v.i.sep.irr.36*
(*sein*) to go down/downstairs; (*Temperatur, Preise*) to drop (**auf** + *acc*, to).
◆**h~gekommen**, *adj.* (*Pers.*) (*materiell*) in reduced circumstances; (*im Aussehen*) down at heel; (*Gebäude*) dilapidated;
(*Gesundheit, Firma*) run down.
◆**h~hauen**, *v.tr.sep. F:* j-m eine h., to
slap s.o. in the face. ◆**h~holen**,
v.tr.sep. to get/fetch (sth.) down.
◆**h~kommen**, *v.i.sep.irr.53* (*sein*) (*a*)
to come down/downstairs; (*b*) *Fig:* (*Pers.*)
(*materiell*) to come down in the world;
(*gesundheitlich, auch Firma*) to get run
down. ◆**h~lassen**, *v.tr.sep.irr.57* to let
(s.o., sth.) down. ◆**h~reißen**,
v.tr.sep.irr.4 to tear down, (*umstoßen*)
knock down (sth.). ◆**h~setzen**,
v.tr.sep. to reduce (prices etc.).
◆**h~stürzen**, *v.i.sep.* (*sein*) to come
hurtling down.

hervor [hɛrˈfoːr], *adv.* out; forward;
hinter/unter/zwischen etwas *dat* **h.**,
from behind/under/between sth.
◆**h~brechen**, *v.i.sep.irr.14* (*sein*) to
break/burst out (**aus** + *dat*, from).
◆**h~bringen**, *v.tr.sep.irr.16* to bring
(sth.) out; to produce (sth.); to get out (a
sound, word etc.). ◆**h~gehen**,
v.i.sep.irr.36 (*sein*) (*a*) **aus etwas** *dat* **h.**,
to result from sth.; (*b*) **als Sieger h.**, to
emerge victorious. ◆**h~heben**, *v.tr.
sep.irr.48* to emphasize (sth.).
◆**h~ragen**, *v.i.sep.* (*sein*) to jut out
(**aus etwas** *dat*, from sth.).
◆**h~ragend**, *adj.* outstanding (achievement etc.); first-rate (quality etc.); excellent (meal, wine etc.); distinguished (actor, artist, scientist etc.). ◆**h~rufen**,
v.tr.sep.irr.74 to cause (sth.); to give rise
to (a feeling, misunderstanding etc.).
◆**h~treten**, *v.i.sep.irr.105* (*sein*) (*a*)
(*Pers.*) to come forward; (*b*) (*Merkmal*) to
show up; (*sich abheben*) to stand out.
◆**h~tun**, *v.refl.sep.irr.106* sich h., (*a*)
to distinguish oneself; (*b*) *Pej:* to show
off.

'**Herweg**, *m* auf dem H., on the way
here.

Herz [hɛrts]. **I.** *n* -ens/-en (*a*) heart;
leichten/schweren H~ens, with a light/
heavy heart; **sie sind ein H. und eine
Seele**, they are inseparable; **ich bringe
es nicht übers H., zu tun**, I haven't

the heart to do it; **sich** *dat* **ein H. fas-sen**, to pluck up courage; **etwas auf dem H~en haben**, to have sth. on one's mind; **j-n in sein H. schließen**, to become fond of s.o.; **von ganzem H~en**, (i) sincerely; with all one's heart; (ii) wholeheartedly; **im H~en der Stadt**, in the heart of the town; (b) (*Karte*) hearts; (*Farbe*) hearts. II. *H~*, *comb./m.* heart (attack, trouble, surgery, specialist etc.); *Med:* cardiac (infarction, muscle etc.). ◆'**H~ensbrecher**, *m Hum:* ladykiller. ◆'**H~enslust**, *f* **nach H.**, to one's heart's content. ◆'**H~enswunsch**, *m* dearest wish. ◆'**H~ergreifend**/'**h~erschütternd**, *adj.* heartrending. ◆'**H~fehler**, *m* heart/cardiac defect. ◆**h~haft**, *adj.* hearty. ◆'**H~klopfen**, *n* pounding heart; *Med:* palpitations. ◆'**h~krank**, *adj.* suffering from heart trouble. ◆**h~lich**, *adj.* cordial, warm (smile, welcome etc.); heartfelt (thanks etc.); hearty (laugh etc.); **h~liches Beileid**, sincere condolences; **h. gern**, with the greatest pleasure; **h. wenig**, precious little. ◆'**H~lichkeit**, *f* -/no *pl* (a) cordiality, geniality; (b) (*Echtheit*) sincerity. ◆'**h~los**, *adj.* heartless (action etc.); unfeeling (remark *etc*) ◆'**H~losigkeit**, *f* -/-en 1. no *pl* heartlessness. 2. heartless act. ◆'**H~schlag**, *m* (a) heartbeat; (b) *Med:* heart failure. ◆'**H~versagen**, *n* heart failure. ◆'**h~zerreißend**, *adj.* heartrending.

'**herziehen**, *v.sep.irr.113* 1. *v.tr.* **hinter sich** *dat* **h.**, to pull/(*schleppen*) drag (s.o., sth.) along. 2. *v.i.* (*sein*) F: **über j-n, etwas** *acc* **h.**, to pull s.o., sth. to pieces.

Herzog ['hɛrtsoːk], *m -s/-e* duke. ◆'**H~in**, *f* -/-nen duchess. ◆'**H~tum**, *n -s/-er* duchy.

Hesse|**n** ['hɛsən]. *Pr.n.m -s. Geog:* Hesse. ◆'**h~isch**, *adj.* Hessian, from Hesse.

Hetze ['hɛtsə], *f* -/-n 1. (*Eile*) rush, scramble. 2. no *pl Pej:* hounding. ◆'**h~en**, *v.* 1. *v.tr.* (a) to pursue (s.o., sth.) (relentlessly); to hunt (s.o., an animal); *Fig:* to hound (s.o.); (b) *zur Eile anreiben*) to rush (s.o.); (c) **die Hunde auf j-n h.**, to set the dogs on s.o. 2 *v.i.* (*haben*) (a) to rush, race; (b) to stir up trouble/hatred (**gegen j-n**, against s.o.). ◆'**H~er**, *m -s/-* agitator. *Pej:* rabble-rouser. ◆**H~e'rei**, *f* -/-en 1. (mad) rush. 2. *F:* Pol: agitation; (*Rede*) (inflammatory) diatribe. ◆'**H~jagd**, *f* a chase; (b) *Pol:* witch-hunt.

Heu [hɔy], *n -(e)s/no pl* hay; *F:* **Geld wie H. haben**, to be stinking rich. ◆'**H~boden**, *m* hay loft. ◆'**H~gabel**, *f* pitchfork. ◆'**H~haufen**, *m* haystack. ◆'**H~schnupfen**, *m* hayfever. ◆'**H~schrecke**, *f* -/-n grasshopper; (*Wanderh.*) locust.

Heuch|**elei** [hɔyçə'lai], *f* -/-en no *pl* hypocrisy. ◆'**h~eln**, *v.* 1. *v.i.* (*haben*) to sham. 2. *v.tr.* to feign.

m -s/- (*f* -/-nen*) hypocrite. ◆'**h~lerisch**, *adj.* hypocritical.

Heuer ['hɔyər], *f* -/-n *Nau:* (seaman's) pay. ◆'**h~n**, *v.tr.* to sign on (seamen); to hire (a boat).

heulen ['hɔylən], *v.i.* (*haben*) to howl; (*Sirene*) to wail; (*Kind*) bawl (**vor Wut**, with rage); **das ist ja zum H.**, it's enough to make one weep.

heut|**e** ['hɔytə], *adv.* (a) today; **h. morgen**, this morning; **die Zeitung von h**, today's paper; (b) (*heutzutage*) nowadays; **das Deutschland von h.**, present-day Germany. ◆'**h~ig**, *adj.* today's (paper, post etc.). ◆'**h~zutage**, *adv.* nowadays.

Hexe ['hɛksə], *f* -/-n witch. ◆'**h~en**, *v.i.* (*haben*) to do magic. ◆'**h~enjagd**, *f Fig:* witch-hunt. ◆'**H~enkessel**, *m Fig:* pandemonium. ◆'**H~enmeister**, *m* sorcerer, wizard; (*Zauberer*) magician. ◆'**H~enschuß** lumbago. ◆**H~e'rei**, *f* -/-en witchcraft; sorcery.

Hieb [hiːp], *m -(e)s/-e* 1. (a) (*Schlag*) blow; (sword) thrust; (b) **H~e bekommen**, to get a hiding/thrashing. 2. (also **H~wunde** *f*) cut, gash. ◆'**h~- und stichfest**, *adj.* watertight (argument, proof etc.).

hier [hiːr], *adv.* here. ◆'**h~an**, *adv.* on/onto this; **h. kann man es erkennen**, it can be recognized by this. ◆'**h~auf**, *adv.* (a) onto this; (b) *h.* **verließ er das Zimmer**, hereupon he left the room. ◆'**h~bei**, *adv.* (*währenddessen*) (while) doing this. ◆'**h~durch**, *adv.* (a) through here; (b) *Fig:* as a result of this; by this means. ◆'**h~für**, *adv.* for this. ◆'**h~gegen**, *adv.* (a) against this; (b) (*im Vergleich*) in comparison with this. ◆'**h~her**, *adv.* here; **bis h.**, as far as this; (up) to here. ◆'**h~hin**, *adv.* here. ◆'**h~hin**, *adv.* here. **setzen wir uns h.**, let's sit down here; **bis h.**, up to this point; this far. ◆'**h~in**, *adv.* in this; *Fig:* in this connection. ◆'**h~mit**, *adv.* (a) with this; (b) (*hierdurch*) by this means; **h. erkläre ich, daß ...**, I hereby declare that ... ◆'**h~über**, *adv.* above/over here; **h. ist nichts bekannt**, nothing is known about this. ◆'**h~unter**, *adv.* under(neath) this; **h. versteht man ...**, by this is meant ... ◆'**h~von**, *adv.* (a) from here; (b) of/from this; **abgesehen h.**, apart from this. ◆'**h~zu**, *adv.* (a) to this; (b) (*hierüber*) about/concerning this (matter); on this point. ◆'**h~zulande**, *adv.* in this country.

hiesig ['hiːziç], *adj.* local (customs, paper etc.); **er ist kein H~er**, he isn't from here.

Hilfe ['hilfə], *f* -/-n (a) help; assistance; **j-m H. leisten**, to help/assist s.o.; **j-m zu H. kommen**, to come to s.o.'s aid; **etwas zu H. nehmen**, to make use of; **Erste H.**, first aid; (b) (*Sache*) aid; (*Pers.*) help. ◆'**H~eruf**, *m* call for help. ◆'**h~los**, *adj.* helpless; (*ratlos*) at a loss. ◆'H~losigkeit, *f no pl* helplessness. ◆'h~reich, *adj.* helpful. ◆'H~s-aktion, *f* relief campaign/scheme. ◆'H~sarbeiter(in), *m* (*f*) temporary/ (*ungelernt*) unskilled worker. ◆'h~s-bedürftig, *adj.* (*a*) in need of help; (*b*) (*notleidend*) destitute, needy. ◆'h~sbereit, *adj.* ready to help; helpful. ◆'H~sbereitschaft, *f* readiness to help; helpfulness. ◆'H~skraft, *f* assistant. ◆'h~smittel, *n* aid. ◆'H~sschule, *f* special school for educationally subnormal children. ◆'H~swerk, *n* welfare institution; social aid (scheme).

Himbeer- ['himbeːr-], *comb.fm.* raspberry (ice, jam etc.). ◆'H~e, *f* raspberry.

Himmel ['himəl], *m* -s/- (*a*) sky; **unter freiem H.**, in the open; **es kam (wie ein Blitz) aus heiterem H.**, it came out of the blue; **das schreit/stinkt zum H.**, that is an absolute scandal; (*b*) *Ecc:* heaven; **in den H. kommen**, to go to heaven; *Fig:* **im sieb(en)ten H. sein**, to be in (one's) seventh heaven; **um H~s willen!** for goodness' sake! ◆'H~bett, *n* four-poster bed. ◆'h~blau, *adj.* sky-blue. ◆'H~fahrt, *f Ecc:* Christi H., the Ascension. ◆'h~hoch, *adj.* skyhigh; towering (peaks etc.). ◆'H~reich, *n* Kingdom of Heaven. ◆'H~schreiend, *adj.* outrageous. ◆'H~srichtung, *f* point of the compass. ◆'h~weit, *adj. F:* ein h~weiter Unterschied, a world of difference.

himmlisch ['himliʃ], *adj. Ecc: & F:* heavenly. **du siehst einfach h. aus**, you look simply divine.

hin [hin], *adv.* **1.** (*Richtung*) to; towards; there; **ich will nicht h.**, I don't want to go there; **h. und zurück**, there and back; **h. und her**, to and fro; back and forth. **2.** *F:* (*verloren, kaputt*) done for.

hinab [hi'nap], *adv.* down, downward(s). ◆h~gehen, *v.i.sep.irr.36* to go down. ◆h~sehen, *v.i.* *irr.92* to look down.

hinauf [hi'nauf], *adv.* upward(s); **den Berg/Fluß h.**, up the mountain/the river. ◆h~gehen, *v.i.sep.irr.36* (*sein*) to go up (*die Treppe h.*) upstairs. ◆h~klettern, *v.tr.sep.* to climb (a ladder etc.); to clamber/scramble up (a rock etc.). ◆h~ziehen, *v.tr.sep.irr.113* to draw/pull (s.th.) up.

hinaus [hi'naus], *adv.* out; **zum Fenster h.**, out of the window; **nach der Straße h.**, looking onto/facing the street; **über etwas** *acc* **h.**, beyond/in addition to sth. ◆h~fahren, *v.sep.irr.26* **1.** *v.i.* (*sein*) to go/*Aut:* drive out. **2.** *v.tr.* to drive/take (the car) out (*aus der Garage*, of the garage). ◆h~finden, *v.i.sep.irr.9* (*haben*) to find one's way out (*aus etwas dat*, of sth.). ◆h~gehen, *v.i.sep.irr.36* (*sein*) (*a*) to go/walk out (*aus dem Haus usw.*,

of the house etc.); **hier geht es hinaus**, this is the way out; (*b*) **über etwas** *acc* **h.**, to go beyond/exceed sth. ◆h~laufen, *v.i.sep.irr.58* (*sein*) (*a*) to run out (-side); (*b*) **auf etwas** *acc* **h.**, to amount to sth. ◆h~schieben, *v.tr.sep.82* (*a*) to push sth. (out)side; (*b*) to put off, postpone (an appointment, decision etc.). ◆h~schmeißen, *v.tr.sep.irr.4 F:* to chuck (s.o.) out. ◆h~sehen, *v.i.sep.irr.92* (*haben*) to look out. ◆h~tragen, *v.tr.sep.irr.85* to carry (s.o., sth.) out. ◆h~wachsen, *v.i.sep.irr.107* (*sein*) **über etwas** *acc* **h.**, to grow higher than sth.; *Fig:* to outgrow sth. ◆h~werfen, *v.tr.sep.irr.110* (*a*) to throw (s.o., sth.) out; (*b*) *F:* to turn/kick (s.o.) out (*aus dem Haus*, of a house); to sack, fire (an employee). ◆h~wollen, *v.i.sep.irr.112* (*haben*) (*a*) to want to go out; (*b*) **auf etwas** *acc* **h.**, to have sth. in mind, *F:* be up to sth. ◆h~ziehen, *v.sep.irr.113* **1.** *v.tr.* (*a*) to pull (s.o., sth.) out(side); (*b*) **sich h.**, to drag on; (*Abfahrt usw.*) to be delayed. **2.** *v.i.* (*sein*) to move out (*aufs Land usw.*, into the country etc.). ◆h~zögern, *v.tr.sep.* to delay, put off (sth.).

Hinblick ['hinblik], *m* -s/*no pl* **im H. auf** + *acc*, in view of ...; considering ...

hinder|**lich** ['hindərliç], *adj.* j-m, etwas *dat* **h. sein**, to be in s.o.'s way/in the way of sth. ◆h~n, *v.tr.* (*stören*) to hinder (s.o., sth.); (*b*) (*abhalten*) to prevent s.o. from doing sth. ◆H~nis, *n* -ses/-se (*a*) obstacle; (*Schwierigkeit*) difficulty; (*b*) *Sp:* obstacle, (*Hürde*) hurdle. ◆H~nislauf, *m* steeplechase; *Fig:* obstacle race.

'hindeuten, *v.i.sep.* (*haben*) **auf j-n, etwas** *acc* **h.**, to point to s.o., sth.; (*Symptome usw.*) to suggest, indicate sth.

hin'durch, *adv.* (*a*) **durch den Wald h.**, through the wood; (*b*) **das ganze Jahr h.**, all through the year.

hinein [hi'nain]. *adv.* in, into; **zur Tür h.**, in through the door; (*bis*) **tief in die Nacht h.**, late into the night. ◆h~bringen, *v.tr.sep.irr.16* **etwas (ins Zimmer) h.**, to bring sth. in/(to the room). ◆h~fahren, *v.sep.irr.26* **1.** *v.i.* (*sein*) (*in die Stadt usw.*) **h.**, to go/ travel/*Aut:* drive (to the town etc.); **2.** *v.tr.* **ein Auto (in die Garage) h.**, to drive a car in(to the garage). ◆h~fallen, *v.i.sep.irr.27* (*sein*) to fall in. ◆h~gehen, *v.i.sep.irr.36* (*sein*) to go in; **ins Zimmer usw. h.**, to go into/ enter the room etc. ◆h~geraten, *v.i.sep.irr.57* (*sein*) **in etwas** *acc* **h.**, to find oneself/*Fig:* get involved in sth. ◆h~laufen, *v.i.sep.irr.58* (*sein*) (**in etwas** *acc*) **h.**, to run in(to sth.). ◆h~legen, *v.tr.sep.* **etwas (in etwas** *acc*) **h.**, to put/place sth. inside (sth.). ◆h~passen, *v.i.sep.* (*haben*) (**in etwas** *acc*) **h.**, to fit in(to sth.). ◆h~platzen, *v.i.sep.* (*sein*) (**ins Zimmer usw.**) h., to burst in(to the room etc.). ◆h~**reden**, *v.i.sep.* (*haben*) (*a*) (**in ein Gespräch**) h., to interrupt (a conversation). ◆h~**stecken**, *v.tr.sep.* to stick/put sth. (**in etwas** *acc*, in sth.). ◆h~**steigern**, *v.refl.sep.* **sich in Wut usw. h.**, to work oneself up into a rage etc. ◆h~**stürzen**, *v.sep.* **1.** *v.i.* (**ins Wasser** *acc*) h., to fall in(to sth.). **2.** *v.refl.* **sich im Wasser**/*Fig:* **in seine Arbeit h.**, to plunge into the water/*Fig:* one's work. ◆h~**treten**, *v.i.sep.irr.105* (*sein*) (**ins Zimmer usw.**) h., to step/walk in(to the room etc.). ◆h~**ziehen**, *v.tr.sep.irr.113* **in etwas** *acc* h., to pull/drag (s.o., sth.) into sth.; *Fig:* (*verwickeln*) to involve, implicate (s.o.) in sth.

'**hinfahr|en**, *v.i.sep.irr.26* (*sein*) to go/travel/*Aut:* drive there. ◆'**H~t**, *f* outward journey/*Nau:* voyage; **auf/bei der H.**, on the way there.

'**hinfallen**, *v.i.sep.irr.27* (*sein*) to fall (down).

'**hinfällig**, *adj.* (*a*) (*Pers.*) infirm; (*gebrechlich*) frail; (*b*) (*ungültig*) invalid.

'**Hin|gabe**, *f -no pl* devotion (**an Gott usw.**, to God etc.); dedication (**an eine Aufgabe**, to a task). ◆'**h~geben**, *v.tr.sep.irr.35* (*a*) to sacrifice (one's life etc.); to give away (one's possessions); (*b*) **sich einer Aufgabe h.**, to devote oneself to a task. ◆'**h~gebungsvoll**, *adj.* devoted.

hin'gegen, *adv.* on the other hand.

'**hingehen**, *v.i.sep.irr.36* (*sein*) to go (there).

'**hingerissen**, *adv.* with rapt attention.

'**hinhalt|en**, *v.tr.sep.irr.45* (*a*) to hold (sth.) out; (*bieten*) to offer (sth.); (*b*) (*warten lassen*) to put (s.o.) off.

'**hinhören**, *v.i.sep.* (*haben*) to listen (intently).

hinken, *v.i.* (*haben*) to limp; *Fig:* **der Vergleich hinkt**, that's a poor comparison.

'**hinknien**, *v.i.* (*haben*) to kneel down.

'**hinkommen**, *v.i.sep.irr.53* (*sein*) (*a*) to arrive; **wo ist es hingekommen?** where has it got to? (*b*) (*hingehören*) to belong, go; (*c*) (*auskommen*) to make do, manage (**mit dem Geld usw.**, with the money etc.).

'**hinlänglich**, *adj.* adequate, sufficient.

'**hinlegen**, *v.tr.sep.* to lay, put (sth.) down; **sich h.**, to lie down; (*sich ausruhen*) to have a rest.

'**hinpassen**, *v.i.sep.* (*haben*) to fit in (there); to be in the right place.

'**hinreichen**, *v.sep.* **1.** *v.tr.* **j-m etwas h.**, to hand/pass sth. to s.o. **2.** *v.i.* (*haben*) (*a*) **bis zu etwas** *dat* **h.**, to extend as far as sth.; (*b*) (*genügen*) to be enough/adequate. ◆'**h~d**, *adj.* adequate.

'**Hinreise**, outward journey; **bei/auf der H.**, on the way there.

'**hinreißen**, *v.tr.sep.irr.43* (*begeistern*) to enthral (s.o.), send (s.o.) into raptures; **sich von seiner Wut usw. h. lassen**, to allow one's anger etc. to get the better of one. ◆'**h~d**, *adj.* enchanting (person, smile), gorgeous (view etc.); enthralling (performance etc.).

'**hinricht|en**, *v.tr.sep.* to execute (s.o.). ◆'**H~ung**, *f* execution.

'**hinschmeißen**, *v.tr.sep.irr.43* *F:* (*a*) to chuck/fling (sth.) down; (*b*) (*aufgeben*) to chuck up, *N.Am:* quit (one's job etc.).

'**hinsehen**, *v.i.sep.irr.92* (*haben*) to look (that way, in that direction); **zu j-m h.**, to look towards s.o.; **bei genauerem H.**, on closer examination.

'**hinsein**, *v.i.sep.irr.93* *F:* (*a*) (*weg sein*) to be gone; (*b*) (*kaputt sein*) **die Vase/Firma ist hin**, the vase/firm has had it; (*c*) (*Pers.*) **ganz h.**, to be all in/(*hingerissen*) in raptures.

'**hinsetzen**, *v.tr.sep.* (*a*) to put (sth.) down; (*b*) **sich h.**, to sit down.

'**Hinsicht**, *f -/-en* respect; **in gewisser H.**, in certain respects; **in finanzieller H.**, from a financial point of view. ◆'**h~lich**, *prep. + gen* with regard to; concerning.

'**hinstellen**, *v.tr.sep.* (*a*) to put (sth.) down; (*b*) **sich h.**, to stand (there), take up one's position (somewhere); (*c*) (*bezeichnen*) to describe (s.o., sth.).

'**hinstrecken**, *v.tr.sep.* (*a*) **j-m die Hand h.**, to hold out one's hand to s.o.; (*b*) **sich h.**, to stretch oneself out, lie down full length.

hintan|setzen [hin'tantsetsən] / **h~stellen**, *v.tr. sep.* to disregard; to neglect (one's duty).

hinten ['hintən], *adv.* behind; at the rear/the back; **h. im Buch**, at the back of the book; **sie sind noch weit h.**, they are still a long way behind; **nach h.**, backwards; **von h.**, the rear/behind; **das dritte Haus von h.**, the third house from the end; *F:* **h. und vorn(e)**, in every respect; **nicht wissen, wo h. und vorn(e) ist**, not to know whether one is coming or going. ◆'**h~herum**, *adv. F:* (*a*) round the back, the back way; (*b*) *Fig:* by devious means.

hinter ['hintər]. **I.** *prep. + dat/acc* behind; **h. j-m herlaufen**, to run after s.o.; **fünf Kilometer h. der Grenze**, five kilometers beyond/the other side of the border; *Fig:* **etwas h. sich** *dat* **haben**, to have got sth. behind one; **eine große Strecke h. sich** *acc* **bringen**, to cover a great distance. **II.** '**H~-**, *comb.fm.* (*a*) back, rear (axle, wheel, seat, exit, entrance, view etc.); (*b*) *Z:* hind (leg, foot, etc.). ◆'**H~bein**, *n* hind leg; *Fig:* **sich auf die H~e setzen**, to resist. ◆'**h~bliebene(r)**, *m & f decl. as adj.* bereaved (person); (surviving) dependent. ◆'**h~e(r,s)**, *adj.* back, rear; **die h. Seite**, the back; **am h~en Ende**, at the far end. ◆'**h~einander**, *adv.* one after the other; (*in der Zeit*) consecutively; **an drei Tagen h.**, on three consecutive days. ◆'**H~gedanke,** *m* ulterior motive. ◆h~'**gehen,** *v.tr.insep.irr.36* to deceive; *F:* doublecross (s.o.). ◆'**H~grund,** *m* background; *Fig:* make or keep a low profile. ◆'**h~grundig,** *adj.* cryptic (question etc.); enigmatic (smile etc.). ◆'**H~halt,** *m* ambush; **j-n aus dem H. überfallen,** to ambush s.o. ◆'**h~hältig,** *adj.* deceitful, underhand. ◆'**H~haus,** *n* back premises; back of the building. ◆h~'**her,** *adv.* (*nachher*) afterwards, subsequently. ◆h~'**hergehen,** *v.i.sep.irr.36* (*sein*) to walk (behind), follow. ◆h~'**herlaufen,** *v.i.sep.irr.58* (*sein*) (j-m) h., to run behind, follow (s.o.); **einem Mädchen usw. h.**, to run after a girl etc. ◆'**H~hof,** *m* backyard. ◆'**H~kopf,** *m* back of the head. ◆h~'**lassen,** *v.tr.sep.irr.57* (*a*) to leave (a widow, a fortune, etc.); (*b*) to leave (behind) (a message, mess etc.). ◆'**H~lassenschaft,** *f -/-en* estate; *Fig:* legacy. ◆h~'**legen,** *v.tr.insep.* to deposit (documents, money etc.). ◆'**H~list,** *f* cunning; (*betrügerische Art*) deceitfulness. ◆'**h~listig,** *adj.* cunning, crafty; deceitful. ◆'**H~mann,** *m* (*a*) der H., the man behind; (*b*) *Fig:* die H~männer eines Verbrechens usw., the brains behind a crime etc. ◆'**H~n,** *m -s/- F:* backside, bottom. ◆'**h~rücks,** *adv.* from behind; *Fig:* treacherously. ◆'**H~seite,** *f* back, rear (of a building). ◆'**h~ste(r,s),** *adj.* rearmost; last (row etc.); hindmost (person). ◆'**H~treffen,** *n F:* **ins H. geraten/kommen,** to fall/get behind. ◆h~'**treiben,** *v.tr.insep.irr.12* to foil, frustrate (s.o.'s plans etc.). ◆'**H~tür,** *f* back door; *Fig:* **durch die H.**, by devious means. ◆h~'**ziehen,** *v.tr.insep.irr.113* to evade (taxes etc.). ◆'**H~ziehung,** *f* (*tax etc.*) evasion; (*Unterschlagung*) embezzlement. ◆'**H~zimmer,** *n* back room.

'**hintreten,** *v.i.sep.irr.105* (*sein*) **vor j-n h.**, to step up to s.o.; to approach s.o.

'**hintun,** *v.tr.sep.irr.106* (*haben*) *F:* to put (sth.) (somewhere).

hinüber [hi'ny:bər], *adv.* across. ◆h~'**blicken,** *v.i.sep.* (*haben*) to look across. ◆h~'**fahren,** *v.i.sep.irr.26* 1. *v.i.* (*sein*) to go/travel/*Aut:* drive across (**über die Brücke usw.**, the bridge etc.). 2. *v.tr.* to drive/run (s.o., sth.) across. ◆h~'**führen,** *v.sep.* 1. *v.tr.* to take (s.o.) across (**über die Straße usw.**, the road etc.). 2. *v.i.* (*haben*) (*Straße usw.*) to go across/over, cross (**über etwas** *acc,* sth.). ◆h~'**gehen,** *v.i.sep.irr.36* (*sein*) to go over/across (**über den Platz usw.**, the square etc.). ◆h~'**sehen,** *v.i.sep.irr.92* (*haben*) to look across. ◆h~'**wechseln,** *v.i.sep.* (*haben*) to move over, to change over.

hinunter [hi'nuntər], *adv.* down; **den Berg/Fluß h.**, down the mountain/river. ◆h~'**fallen,** *v.i.sep.irr.27* (*sein*) to fall down. ◆h~'**gehen,** *v.i.sep.irr.36* (*sein*) to go/walk down; (**die Treppe**) **h.**, to go downstairs. ◆h~'**klettern,** *v.i.sep.* (*sein*) to climb down. ◆h~'**reichen,** *v.sep.* 1. *v.tr.* to pass (sth.) down. 2. *v.i.* (*haben*) **bis zu etwas** *dat* **h.**, to stretch down to sth. ◆h~'**schlucken,** *v.tr.sep.* to swallow (food, *Fig:* anger, an insult etc.). ◆h~'**sehen,** *v.i.sep.irr.92* (*haben*) to look down. ◆h~'**spülen,** *v.tr.sep.* to wash/swill (sth.) down. ◆h~'**stürzen,** *v.sep.* 1. *v.i.* (*sein*) to tumble/crash down; **die Treppe h.**, to tumble/(*eilen*) hurtle downstairs. 2. *v.tr.* (*a*) to gulp down (food, drink); (*b*) **sich (von etwas** *dat*) **h.**, to hurl oneself off (sth.). ◆h~'**ziehen,** *v.tr.sep.irr.113* to pull (s.o., sth.) down.

'**Hinweg**[1], *m* **auf dem H.**, on the way there.

hin'weg[2], *adv.* **über etwas** *acc* **h.**, over (the top of) sth.; **über lange Zeit h.**, over a long period. ◆h~'**gehen,** *v.i.sep.irr.36* (*sein*) **über etwas** *acc* **h.**, to pass over/(*ignorieren*) overlook sth. ◆h~'**helfen,** *v.i.sep.irr.50* (*haben*) **j-m über etwas** *acc* **h.**, to help s.o. to get over sth. ◆h~'**kommen,** *v.i.sep.irr.53* (*sein*) **über eine Krankheit usw. h.**, to get over an illness etc. ◆h~'**sehen,** *v.i.sep.irr.92* (*haben*) **über j-n, etwas** *acc* **h.**, *Fig:* to overlook s.o., shut one's eyes to sth. ◆h~'**sein,** *v.i.sep.irr.93* (*sein*) **über etwas** *acc* **h.**, to have got over sth. ◆h~'**setzen,** *v.refl.sep.* **sich über j-n, etwas** *acc* **h.**, to disregard, turn a blind eye to (s.o., sth.).

Hinweis ['hinvais], *m -es/-e* (*a*) (*Wink*) hint; **H~e für die Benutzung,** instructions/directions for use; (*b*) (*Bemerkung*) comment; (*Andeutung*) indication. ◆'**h~en,** *v.i.sep.irr.88* 1. *v.tr.* **j-n auf etwas** *acc* **h.**, to draw s.o.'s attention to sth. 2. *v.i.* (*haben*) **auf j-n, etwas** *acc* **h.**, to point out, indicate s.o., sth.; (*erwähnen*) to refer to sth.

'**hinwerfen,** *v.tr.sep.irr.110* (*a*) to throw (s.o., sth.) down; (*fallenlassen*) to drop (sth.); (*b*) *F:* (*aufgeben*) to chuck in, *N.Am:* quit (one's job etc.).

'**hinziehen,** *v.sep.irr.113* 1. *v.tr.* (*a*) to pull (s.o., sth.); **sich zu j-m, etwas** *dat* **hingezogen fühlen,** to feel drawn/attracted to s.o., sth.; (*b*) **sich h.**, to drag on; (*sich verzögern*) to be delayed; (*sich erstrecken*) **sich h.**, to stretch, run. 2. *v.i.* (*sein*) to move.

'**hinzielen,** *v.i.sep.* (*haben*) **auf etwas** *acc* **h.**, to aim at sth.

hinzu [hin'tsu:], *adv.* in addition. ◆h~'**fügen,** *v.tr.sep.* to add (sth.) (**etwas** *dat,* to sth.). ◆'**H~fügung,** *f -/-en* in addition. ◆h~'**gesellen,** *v.refl.sep.* **sich**

zu j-m h., to join s.o. ◆**h~kommen,** *v.i.sep.irr.53 (sein) (a) (Pers.)* **(zur Gruppe) h.,** to join the group; **es kamen noch andere Umstände hinzu,** there were additional factors. ◆**h~ziehen,** *v.tr.sep.irr.113* to call in (a specialist etc.).

Hirn [hɪrn]. I. *n -(e)s/-e* brain; *Cu:* brains. II. **H~,** *comb.fm.* brain, cerebral (tumour etc.). ◆**'H~gespinst,** *n* fanciful idea; *(eingebildet)* figment of the imagination. ◆**'H~hautentzündung,** *f* meningitis. ◆**'h~verbrannt,** *adj.* crackbrained; crazy (idea etc.).

Hirsch [hɪrʃ], *m -(e)s/-e (a)* stag; (red) deer; *(b) Cu:* venison. ◆**'H~kuh,** *f* hind.

Hirse ['hɪrzə], *f -/no pl* millet.

Hirte ['hɪrtə], *m -n/-n* shepherd. ◆**H~n-,** *comb.fm.* shepherd's (song etc.).

hissen ['hɪsən], *v.tr.* to hoist (a flag, sail etc.).

Histor|iker [his'toːrikər], *m -s/-* historian. ◆**h~isch,** *adj.* historical (event, novel etc.).

Hit [hɪt], *m -s/-s F:* hit (song etc.).

Hitze ['hɪtsə]. I. *f -/no pl (a)* heat; *(b)* hot weather; *(c) Fig:* **in der H. des Gefechts,** in the heat of the moment. II. **'H~-,** **'h~-,** *comb.fm.* heat (rash etc.); hot (spell). ◆**h~beständig,** *adj.* heat-resistant. ◆**'h~empfindlich,** *adj.* heat-sensitive. ◆**H~welle,** *f* heat wave.

hitz|ig ['hɪtsɪç], *adj. (jähzornig)* hot-tempered (person); heated (argument etc.); *(leidenschaftlich)* fiery (person, temperament). ◆**H~kopf,** *m* hothead. ◆**'h~köpfig,** *adj.* hot-headed; *(jähzornig)* hot-tempered. ◆**'H~schlag,** *m* heat stroke.

Hobby ['hɔbi], *n -s/-s* hobby.

Hobel ['hoːbəl], *m -s/-* plane; *Cu:* slicer. ◆**'H~bank,** *f* carpenter's bench. ◆**'h~n,** *v.tr. (a)* to plane (wood etc.); to polish, smooth (a surface etc.); *(b)* to slice (vegetables etc.). ◆**'H~späne** *mpl* wood/metal shavings.

hoch [hoːx]. I. *adj. (a)* high; *(b)* tall (tree etc.); **zwei Meter h.,** two metres high/ *(Schnee)* deep/(Pers.) tall; *(c)* high-ranking (officer); **hoher Besuch/Gast,** important guest; **hoher Beamter,** senior official/civil servant; **hohe Ehre,** great honour; *Fig:* **das ist zu h. für mich,** that is above my head/beyond me; *(d)* heavy (penalty, fine); **hohe Summe/Schulden,** large sum/debts; *(e)* **hohes Alter,** great age. II. *adv. (a)* **h. oben,** high up; **j-m etwas h. anrechnen,** to appreciate greatly sth. that s.o. has done; **etwas h. und heilig versprechen,** to promise sth. solemnly; *(c)* **zu h. geschätzt,** overestimated; *F:* **wenn es h. kommt,** at a pinch. III. **H.,** *n -s/-s* 1. cheer. 2. *Meteor:* high(-pressure area). ◆**h~achten,**

v.tr.sep. to have a high regard for (s.o., sth.). ◆**'H~achtung,** *f* (high) esteem. ◆**'h~achtungsvoll,** *adv. Com:* yours faithfully. ◆**'H~adel,** *m* higher nobility. ◆**'H~amt,** *n* High Mass. ◆**'h~arbeiten,** *v.refl.sep.* to work one's way up. ◆**'H~bau,** *m* structural engineering. ◆**h~begabt,** *adj.* highly/extremely gifted. ◆**h~be'tagt,** *adj.* advanced in years; aged. ◆**'H~betrieb,** *m F:* frantic activity; **um 5 Uhr ist bei uns H.,** our peak period is around 5 o'clock. ◆**'h~bringen,** *v.tr.sep.irr.16* to bring (s.o., sth.) up/upstairs. ◆**'H~burg,** *f Fig:* stronghold. ◆**'H~deutsch,** High German; *F:* proper German. ◆**'H~druck,** *m* high pressure. ◆**'H~ebene,** *f* (high) plateau. ◆**'h~empfindlich,** *adj.* highly sensitive. ◆**'h~erfreut,** *adj.* highly delighted; extremely pleased. ◆**'h~fahren,** *v.i.sep.irr.26 (sein) (a)* to go up (in a lift etc.); *(b)* to jump up, *(ängstlich)* start up. ◆**'h~fliegend,** *adj.* ambitious (plan etc.). ◆**'H~form,** *f esp. Sp:* in top form. ◆**'H~gebirge,** *n* high mountains. ◆**'h~gehen,** *v.i.sep.irr.36 (sein) (a)* (Vorhang, Preis usw.) to go up, rise; *F:* (Pers.) **die Treppe h.,** to go up(stairs); *(b)* (also *Fig:*) *(explodieren)* to blow up, explode. ◆**'h~gelegen,** *adj.* high-lying. ◆**'h~geschätzt,** *adj.* held in high esteem. ◆**'h~geschlossen,** *adj.* (shirt etc.) buttoned to the neck; high-necked (dress etc.). ◆**'H~gestochen,** *adj. F:* high falutin; pretentious (style etc.). ◆**'h~gewachsen,** *adj.* tall. ◆**'H~glanz,** *m* high gloss; polish; **etwas auf H. bringen,** to polish sth. until it gleams. ◆**'h~gradig,** *adj.* intense, extreme (anxiety etc.). ◆**'h~halten,** *v.tr.sep.irr.45* to hold up (sth., one's arms, head etc.). ◆**'H~haus,** *n* high-rise building; *Brit:* tower block. ◆**'h~heben,** *v.tr. sep.irr.48* to lift (s.o., sth.) up (high); to raise (one's arms, hand etc.). ◆**'h~interessant,** *adj.* extremely interesting. ◆**'h~kant,** *adv.* **1. etwas h. stellen,** to put sth. on end. **2.** *P:* **j-n h. hinausschmeißen,** to kick s.o. out on his ear. ◆**'h~kommen,** *v.i.sep.irr.53 (sein) F:* to come up/(im *Wasser*) to the surface. ◆**'H~konjunktur,** *f* boom. ◆**'H~kultur,** *f* advanced civilization. ◆**'H~land,** *n* uplands *pl*; Highlands. ◆**'h~leben,** *v.i.sep. (haben)* **j-n etwas h. lassen,** to give s.o., sth. three cheers. ◆**'H~leistungs-,** *comb.fm.* high output (engine/motor etc.). ◆**'h~mo'dern,** *adj.* ultra-modern. ◆**'H~mut,** *m* pride; arrogance. ◆**'h~mütig,** *adj.* proud; *(herablassend)* arrogant, haughty. ◆**'h~näsig,** *adj. F:* stuck-up, snooty. ◆**'h~nehmen,** *v.tr.sep.irr.69 (a)* to lift/pick (s.o., sth.) up; *(b) F:* **j-n h.,** to pull s.o.'s leg. ◆'H~ofen, m blast furnace. ◆'H~parterre, n raised ground floor. ◆'h~prozentig, adj. containing a high percentage (of alcohol etc.). ◆'h~'rot, adj. crimson, scarlet. ◆'H~ruf, m cheer. ◆'H~saison, f high season. ◆'H~schul-, comb.fm. university (education etc.). ◆'H~schullehrer(in), m(f) university teacher/lecturer. ◆'H~schule, f university; (college (conferring degrees); academy (of drama/music). ◆'H~seefischerei, f deep sea fishing. ◆'H~seil, n high wire, tightrope. ◆'h~sitz, m (elevated) hide. ◆'h~sommer, m midsummer; high summer. ◆'h~sommerlich, adj. very summery. ◆'H~spannung, f (a) El: high tension; (b) Fig: (state of) considerable tension. ◆'H~spannungsleitung, f high tension cable; power line. ◆'H~spannungsmast, m electricity pylon. ◆'h~spielen, v.tr. sep. to make great play of (sth.). ◆'H~sprache, f standard language. ◆'H~sprung, m high jump. ◆'H~stape'lei, f -/-en imposture. ◆'H~stapler, m -s/- impostor; F: con man. ◆'h~stimmung, f elated (festlich) festive mood. ◆'H~tour, f auf H~touren arbeiten/laufen, (Fabrik) to work at high pressure, (Motor) to run at full speed. ◆'h~tourig, adj. high-speed (engine etc.). ◆'h~trabend, adj. high-sounding, pompous. ◆'H~verrat, m high treason. ◆'H~wasser, n 1. (Flut) high tide/(Fluß) water. 2. (Überschwemmung) flood. ◆'h~wertig, adj. high-grade (goods, materials). ◆'H~würden, m -s/- Ecc: (Anrede) approx. Father; (seine) H. X, the Reverend X. ◆'h~ziehen, v.tr.sep.irr.113 to raise (sth); pull up (one's trousers etc.).

höchst [hø:çst]. I. adv. most, extremely (exaggerated, unfair). II. 'H~-, comb.fm. maximum (amount, weight, price, number etc.); peak (level, consumption, etc.); highest (offer, bid etc.). ◆'H~e(r, s), adj. (a) highest; tallest (building, spire, tree etc.); (b) (h~möglich) maximum, top (price, speed etc.); greatest (danger etc.); utmost (degree, importance); es ist h. Zeit, it is high time. ◆'h~ens, adv. at most. ◆'H~fall, m im H., at the most. ◆'H~geschwindigkeit, f maximum/top speed. ◆'H~grenze, f upper limit. ◆'H~maß, n maximum amount. ◆'H~leistung, f Ind: maximum output; El: peak output; Sp: best performance. ◆'h~'möglich, adj. highest/greatest possible. ◆'h~per'sönlich, adj. in person. ◆'h~wahr'scheinlich, adv. most probably.

Hochzeit ['hɔxtsait], f -/-en wedding. ◆'H~s-, comb.fm. wedding (guest, present, etc.). ◆'H~skleid, n wedding dress. ◆'H~sreise, f honeymoon (trip). ◆'h~stag, m (a) wedding day; (b) (Ju-

biläum) wedding anniversary.

Hocke ['hɔkə], f -/-n squatting position; in die H. gehen, to squat down. ◆'h~n, v.i. (haben) (a) to crouch, (auf dem Boden) squat; (b) F: to sit (around). ◆'H~r, m -s/- stool.

Höcker ['hœkər], m -s/- hump.

Hockey ['hɔki, 'hɔke], n -s/no pl hockey.

Hoden ['ho:dən], pl testicles. ◆'H~sack, m scrotum.

Hof [ho:f]. I. m -(e)s/-e 1. yard; courtyard (of a castle etc.); (Hinterh.) backyard. 2. (Fürstenh.) (royal etc.) court.

hoff|en ['hɔfən], v.tr.&i. (haben) to hope (auf etwas acc, for sth.); das will ich h.! I should hope so! ◆'h~entlich, adv. it is to be hoped; esp. N.Am: hopefully. ◆'H~nung, f -/-en hope; er macht sich H~en, he fancies his chances. ◆'h~nungslos, adj. hopeless. ◆'H~nungslosigkeit, f -/no pl hopelessness. ◆'H~nungsschimmer, m glimmer/ray of hope. ◆'h~nungsvoll, adj. (a) hopeful; confident; (b) (vielversprechend) promising.

höf|lich ['hø:fliç], adj. polite. ◆'H~lichkeit, f -/-en (a) no pl politeness; courtesy; (b) polite remark; compliment. ◆'H~lichkeitsfloskel, f polite formula/phrase.

Höhe ['hø:ə], f -/-n 1. (a) height (of sth.); esp. Av: altitude; F: das ist ja die H.! that's the limit! (b) in die H., up; upwards; auf der H. sein, to be in good form. 2. (a) (Hügel) hill; (b) esp. Fig: (Gipfel) peak (of one's career, fame etc.); (c) Rec: die H~n, the treble. 3. (a) (Größe) level (of income, prices etc.); (Betrag) amount (of damages etc.); ein Schaden in H. von DM 2000 damage to the amount of 2000 marks; (b) Geog: latitude. ◆'H~n-, comb.fm. (a) altitude (sickness, Sp: training etc.); (b) mountain (air, climate etc.). ◆'H~nmesser, m Av: altimeter. ◆'H~nsonne, f Med: sun-lamp. ◆'H~nunterschied, m difference in altitude/height. ◆'H~nzug, m mountain range. ◆'H~npunkt, m highlight; (einmalig) climax; (Gipfel) peak (of one's career etc.).

Hoheit ['ho:hait], f -/-en (a) (Anrede) Your Highness; (b) Fig: majesty, dignity. 2. no pl sovereignty (of a state). ◆'H~s-, comb.fm. sovereign (territory, rights etc.). ◆'H~sgewässer, npl territorial waters. ◆'h~svoll, adj. dignified, majestic.

höher ['hø:ər], adj. higher; upper (branches, window etc.); superior (intelligence, rank etc.); h~e Schule, secondary school; h~e Gewalt, Act of God.

hohl [ho:l]. I. adj. (a) hollow; Fig: dull (sound); Pej: empty (phrase etc.). II. 'H~-, comb.fm. (a) hollow (body etc.); (b) (konkav) concave (surface, mirror etc.). ◆'H~kopf, m numbskull. ◆'H~maß, n measure of capacity; dry measure. ◆'H~raum, m hollow space, cavity.

Höhl|e ['hø:lə], f -/-n (a) cave; (Schacht) pot-hole; (für Tiere) burrow, lair; (b) Anat: cavity. ◆'H~en-, comb.fm. cave (painting etc.). ◆'H~enbewohner, m cavedweller.

Hohn [ho:n], m -(e)s/no pl scorn, disdain; (Spott) mockery, derision. ◆'h~gelächter, n derisive/scornful laughter. ◆'H~ruf, m jeer.

höhnisch ['hø:niʃ], adj. scornful; (spöttisch) derisive.

hold [hɔlt], adj. Poet: charming, demure.

holen ['ho:lən], v.tr. to fetch (s.o., sth.); to go for (bread etc.); (abholen) to collect; (rufen) to call (the doctor); j-n h. lassen, to send for s.o.; sich dat die Grippe usw. h., to catch a cold, the flu etc.

Holl|and ['hɔlant]. Pr.n.n -s. Holland; the Netherlands. ◆'H~änder [-lɛndər], m -s/- 1. Dutchman. 2. (H~käse) Dutch cheese. ◆'H~änderin, f -/-nen Dutchwoman. ◆'h~ändisch, adj. Dutch.

Höll|e ['hœlə], f -/-n hell. ◆'H~en-, comb.fm. F: infernal (noise etc.); hellish (thirst etc.). ◆'H~enangst, f eine H. haben, to be scared to death. ◆'h~isch, adj. hellish; infernal (region, F: noise etc.); F: hellish (row etc.); fiendish (task etc.).

holper|n ['hɔlpərn], v.i. (haben/sein) (Fahrzeug) to jolt, bump. ◆'h~ig, adj. bumpy.

Holunder [ho'lundər], m -s/- elder. ◆'H~beere, f -/-n elderberry.

Holz [hɔlts]. I. n -es/-er wood; (Rauh.) timber; aus H., wooden. II. 'H~-, comb.fm. (a) (aus H. bestehend) of wood; (vom H.) wood (fibre, wool etc.); (b) (aus H. gemacht) wooden (bridge, house, spoon etc.); (c) Com: timber (trade etc.). ◆'H~fäller, m wood-cutter, N.Am: lumberjack. ◆'H~feuer, n log fire. ◆'H~hammer, m mallet. ◆'h~ig, adj. woody. ◆'H~kohle, f charcoal. ◆'H~kohlengrill, m charcoal grill. ◆'H~kopf, m F: blockhead; clot. ◆'H~schnitzer, m woodcarver. ◆'H~schuh, m clog. ◆'H~weg, m F: auf dem H. sein, to be on the wrong track. ◆'H~wurm, m woodworm.

hölzern ['hœltsərn], adj. wooden.

homo|gen [homo'ge:n], adj. homogeneous. ◆'H~sexuali'tät, f homosexuality. ◆'h~sexu'ell, adj. homosexual; ein H~sexueller, a homosexual.

Honig ['ho:niç], m -s/-e honey. ◆'H~kuchen, m honeycake; (mit Ingwer) gingerbread. ◆'H~wabe, f honeycomb.

Honor|ar [hono'ra:r], n -s/-e fee (for professional services). ◆'h~ieren [-'ri:rən], v.tr. (a) Fig: (belohnen) to re-

ward (an achievement etc.); (b) Fin: to honour (a bill, debt etc.).

Hopfen ['hɔpfən], m -s/- hop, Agr: coll. hops.

hopsen ['hɔpsən], v.i. (sein) F: to hop, skip.

hör|bar ['hø:rba:r], adj. audible; (in Hörweite) within earshot. ◆'h~en, v.tr.&i. (haben) to hear; schlecht h., to be hard of hearing; (b) (anhören) to listen to; auf j-n h., to listen to s.o.; sie hört auf den Namen Anna, she answers to the name of Anna; (c) wie ich höre, ist er verreist, I gather/understand that he is away; er läßt nichts von sich h., he hasn't written. ◆'H~er, m -s/- 1. (a) listener; die H., the audience; (b) Sch: student (at a lecture). 2. Tel: receiver. ◆'H~gerät, n hearing aid. ◆'h~ig, adj. j-m, etwas dat h. sein, to be enslaved by s.o., sth. ◆'H~saal, m lecture hall. ◆'H~spiel, n radio play.

horchen ['hɔrçən], v.i. (haben) to listen.

Horde ['hɔrdə], f -/-n horde; Pej: mob.

Horizont [hori'tsɔnt], m -(e)s/-e (a) horizon; skyline; (b) Fig: das geht über meinen H., that's beyond me. ◆h~al [-'ta:l], adj. horizontal.

Hormon [hɔr'mo:n], n -s/-e hormone.

Horn [hɔrn], n -(e)s/-er horn. ◆'H~haut, f cornea. ◆'H~ist [hɔr'nist], m -en/-en horn-player.

Hörnchen ['hœrnçən], n -s/- small horn; Cu: croissant.

Hornisse [hɔr'nisə], f -/-n hornet.

Horoskop [horo'sko:p], n -s/-e horoscope.

Horror ['hɔrɔr], m -s/no pl dread (vor + dat, of).

Hort ['hɔrt], m -(e)s/-e Lit: (a) hoard; (Schatz) treasure; (b) (Zuflucht) refuge; (c) (Kinderh.) children's home. ◆'h~en, v.tr. to hoard (sth.); to stockpile (arms etc.).

Hose ['ho:zə], f -/-n (pair of) trousers, N.Am: pants; eine neue H., a new pair of trousers. ◆'H~n-, comb.fm. trouser (leg, button, pocket, etc.). ◆'H~nanzug, m trouser suit. ◆'H~nträger, mpl braces; N.Am: suspenders.

Hostess/Hosteß [hɔs'tɛs], f -/-ssen hostess; Av: air hostess; esp. N.Am: stewardess.

Hostie ['hɔstiə], f -/-n host; (consecrated) wafer.

Hotel [ho'tɛl], n -s/-s hotel.

Hub|raum ['hu:praum], m (cylinder) capacity. ◆'H~schrauber, m helicopter.

hübsch [hypʃ], adj. pretty, (anziehend) attractive (girl, tune etc.); F: nice (evening, house etc.).

huckepack ['hukəpak], adv. F: j-n h. tragen/nehmen, to give s.o. a piggyback.

Huf [hu:f], m -(e)s/-e hoof. ◆'H~eisen, n horseshoe.

Hüft- ['hyft-], comb.fm. hip (joint etc.). ◆'H~e, f -/-n hip. ◆'H~gürtel/

'H~halter, m girdle. **◆'H~knochen,** m hip-bone. **◆'H~weite,** f hip measurement.

Hügel ['hy:gəl], m -s/- hill. **◆'h~ig,** adj. hilly. **◆'H~kette,** f line/range of hills.

Huhn [hu:n], n -(e)s/=er chicken; (weiblich) hen.

Hühner- ['hy:nər-], comb.fm. chicken (broth, liver etc.); hen (house etc.). **◆'H~auge,** n corn. **◆'H~ei,** n hen's egg. **◆'H~stall,** m hencoop.

huldigen ['huldigən], v.i. (haben) Lit: j-m, etwas dat h., to pay homage/tribute to s.o., sth. **◆'H~ung,** f -/-en Lit: tribute, homage.

Hülle ['hylə], f -/-n (a) cover; (Verpackung) wrapping(s); (record) sleeve; (b) F: in H. und Fülle, in abundance. **◆'h~n,** v.tr. to wrap (s.o., sth.) in Nebel gehüllt, shrouded in mist.

Hülse ['hylzə], f -/-n (pea, seed etc.) pod; (rice etc.) husk. **◆'H~nfrucht,** f pulse.

human [hu'ma:n], adj. humane. **◆h~itär** [-ni'tɛ:r], adj. humanitarian. **◆H~ität** [-ni'tɛ:t], f -/no f humanity; humaneness.

Hummel ['huməl], f -/-n bumble-bee.

Hummer ['humər], m -s/- lobster.

Humor [hu'mo:r], m -s/no f humour; (Sinn für) H. haben, to have a sense of humour. **◆H~ist** [-'rist], m -en/-en humorist. **◆h~istisch** [-'ristiʃ], adj. humorous (writings etc.). **◆h~los,** adj. humourless. **◆h~voll,** adj. humorous.

humpeln ['humpəln], v.i. (a) (haben) to limp; (b) (sein) to hobble (somewhere).

Humpen ['humpən], m -s/- tankard (with a lid).

Hund [hunt], m -(e)s/-e 1. (a) dog; (Jagdh.) hound; F: auf den H. kommen, to go to the dogs. **◆'H~e-** [-də-], comb.fm. dog's (tail, F: life etc.); dog (bite, breeding, food, racing etc.). **◆'h~e'elend,** adj. mir ist h., I feel rotten. **◆'H~ehütte,** f kennel, N.Am: doghouse. **◆'H~ekuchen,** m dog biscuit. **◆'H~eleine,** f (dog) lead, F: leash. **◆'H~emarke,** f dog's identity tag. **◆'h~e'müde,** adj. F: dog-tired. **◆'H~esteuer,** f dog licence (fee). **◆'h~sge'mein,** adj. P: filthy, lowdown. **◆'H~stage,** mpl dog-days, high summer.

hundert ['hundərt]. num.adj. a/one hundred; H~e von Menschen, hundreds of people. **◆'H~er,** m -s/- F: (a) (Zahl) hundred; (b) (Schein) hundred mark note. **◆'h~'jahrfeier,** f centenary (celebration). **◆'h~'jährig,** adj. a hundred years old. **◆'h~'mal,** adv. a hundred times. **◆'H~'meterlauf,** m hundred metres. **◆'h~'prozentig,** adj. a hundred per cent (alcohol, F: success etc.); complete, total (support). **◆'H~stel,** n -s/- hundredth (part). **◆'h~'tausend,** adj. a/one hundred thousand.

Hündin ['hyndin], f -/-nen bitch.

Hüne ['hy:nə], m -n/-n giant. **◆'h~nhaft,** adj. gigantic.

Hunger ['hunər], m -s/no f hunger (auf etwas aee, for sth.); H. haben, to be hungry. **◆'H~lohn,** m miserable pittance. **◆'h~n,** v.tr. & i. (haben) to suffer from hunger, starve; (fasten) to fast. **◆'H~snot,** f famine. **◆'H~tuch,** n Hum: am H. nagen, to be on the breadline.

hungrig ['hunriç], adj. hungry (nach + dat, for).

Hupe ['hu:pə], f -/-n Aut: horn. **◆'h~en,** v.i. (haben) to hoot, N.Am: honk.

hüpfen ['hypfən], v.i. (sein) to hop; (Ball) to bounce; das ist gehüpft wie gesprungen, it comes to exactly the same thing.

Hürde ['hyrdə], f -/-n hurdle. **◆'H~nlauf,** m hurdlerace. **◆'H~nläufer,** m hurdler.

Hure ['hu:rə], f -/-n Pej: whore, F: tart.

hurra [hu'ra:], int. hurra(h), hurray.

huschen ['huʃən], v.i. (sein) to dart; (Schatten, Lächeln) to flit (über + acc, across).

hüsteln ['hy:stəln], v.i. (haben) to give a slight cough, clear one's throat.

husten ['hu:stən]. I. v. 1. v.i. (haben) to cough. 2. v.tr. to cough (up) (blood etc.). II. H., m -s/no f cough. **◆'H~anfall,** m fit of coughing. **◆'H~bonbon,** n cough sweet/N.Am: drop. **◆'H~reiz,** m irritation in the throat. **◆'H~saft,** m cough syrup.

Hut1 [hu:t]. I. m -(e)s/=e (a) hat; F: H. ab! well done! (b) Fig: verschiedene Interessen usw. unter einen H. bringen, to reconcile different interests etc. **◆'H~macher,** m -s/- hatter.

Hut2, f -/no f auf der H. sein, to be on one's guard.

hüten ['hy:tən], v.tr. (a) to guard, watch over (s.o., sth.); to keep (a secret); (aufpassen auf) to look after, mind (a child, animals etc.); to tend (the fire); (b) das Bett/Haus h. müssen, to have to stay in bed/indoors; (c) sich vor j-m, etwas dat h., to be on one's guard against s.o., sth.; sich h., etwas zu tun, to take care not to do sth.

Hütte ['hytə], f -/-n 1. hut; N.Am: (Blockh.) log cabin. 2. Ind: foundry; (ganze Anlage) iron and steel works. **◆'H~n-,** comb.fm. foundry (worker etc.); iron and steel (plant, industry, works). **◆'H~nkäse,** m cottage cheese.

Hyäne [hy'ɛ:nə], f -/-n hyena.

Hyazinthe [hya'tsintə], f -/-n hyacinth.

Hydrant [hy'drant], m -en/-en hydrant.

Hydraulik [hy'draulik], f -/no f hydraulics. **◆h~isch,** adj. hydraulic (brake etc.).

Hygiene [hygi'e:nə], f -/no f hygiene. **◆h~isch,** adj. hygienic.

Hymne ['hymnə], f -/-n hymn; (Natio-

nalh.) national anthem.

Hypno|se [hyp'no:zə], *f* -/-n hypnosis. ◆**h~tisch**, *adj.* hypnotic. ◆**H~tiseur** [-noti'zøːr], *m* -s/-e hypnotist. ◆**h~tis'ieren**, *v.tr.* to hypnotize.

Hypothek [hypo'te:k], *f* -/-en mortgage. **Hypothese** [hypo'te:zə], *f* -/-n hypothesis. **Hyster|ie** [hyste'riː], *f* -/-n hysteria. ◆**h~isch** [hys'teːriʃ], *adj.* hysterical.

I

I, i [iː], *n* -/- (the letter) I, i.

ich [iç]. I. *pers. pron.* 1; **i. selbst**, I myself; **i. bin's**, it's me; **Menschen wie du und i.**, people like you and me; **i. Idiot!** fool that I am! II. **Ich**, *n* -s/*no pl* self; *esp. Psy:* ego. ◆**i~bezogen**, *adj.* self-centred.

ideal [ide'aːl]. I. *adj.* ideal. II. I., *n* -s/-e ideal. ◆**I~fall**, *m* ideal case; **im I.**, ideally. ◆**I~ismus** [-'lismus], *m* -/*no pl* idealism. ◆**I~ist(in)** [-'list(in)], *m* -en/-en (*f* -/-nen) idealist. ◆**i~istisch** [-'listiʃ], *adj.* idealistic.

Idee [i'deː], *f* -/-n (*a*) idea; (*b*) *F:* **eine I. zuviel/zu kurz**, slightly too much/too short. ◆**i~ll** [ide'el], *adj.* theoretical (viewpoint etc.); notional (value, need etc.).

ident|ifizieren [identifi'tsiːrən], *v.tr.* to identify (s.o., sth.); **sich i. mit** + *dat*, to identify with (a cause etc.). ◆**i~isch** [i'dentiʃ], *adj.* identical. ◆**I~i'tät**, *f* -/-en identity.

Ideolog|ie [ideolo'giː], *f* -/-n ideology. ◆**i~isch** [-'loːgiʃ], *adj.* ideological.

idiomatisch [idio'maːtiʃ], *adj.* idiomatic.

Idiot(in) [idi'oːt(in)], *m* -en/-en (*f* -/-nen) idiot. ◆**i~isch** [-'oːtiʃ], *adj.* idiotic.

Idol [i'doːl], *n* -s/-e idol.

Idyll [i'dyl], *n* -s/-e/I~e, *f* -/-n idyll. ◆**i~isch**, *adj.* idyllic.

Igel ['iːgəl], *m* -s/- hedgehog.

Iglu ['iːglu:], *m* & *n* -s/-s igloo.

Ignorant [igno'rant], *m* -en/-en ignoramus. ◆**i~ieren**, *v.tr.* to ignore, take no notice of (s.o., sth.).

ihm [iːm], *pers. pron. dat. of* er/es (*a*) (+ *verb*) to him; (*Sache*) to it; **gib's i.**, give it to him; **wie geht es i.?** how is he? (*b*) (+ *prep.*) him, it; **von i.**, from him/it; **ein Freund von i.**, a friend of his.

ihn [iːn], *pers. pron. acc. of* er, him; (*Sache*) it. ◆**ihnen** ['iːnən], *pers. pron. dat.pl. of* er, sie & es 1. (to) them; **ich sagte es i.**, I told them. 2. I., (*polite address*) (to) you; **wie geht es I.?** how are you?

ihr [iːr]. I. *pers. pron.* 1. *dat. of* sie (*a*) (+ *verb*) (to) her; (*Sache*) (to) it; **ich sagte es i.**, I told her; (*b*) (*with prep.*) her; (*Tier*) it; **von i.**, from her/it; **ein Freund von i.**, a friend of hers. 2. *nom.pl of* du you. II. *poss. pron.* 1. her; (*Tier/Sache*) its; (*von mehreren*) their; **i~e(r,s)/I.** its one; (*von mehreren*) their one, theirs. 2. I., your. ◆**i~erseits**, *adv.* on her/

their/(I.) your part. ◆**i~esgleichen**, *pron.* 1. her/(*Sache*) its/*pl* their kind; (*solche Leute*) people like that; **eine Sache, die i. sucht**, something unparalleled/unequalled. 2. I., people like you, your sort. ◆**i~etwegen/i~etwillen**, *adv.* 1. because of her/(*Sache*) it/*pl* them; for her/its/their sake. 2. I., for your sake, because of you. ◆**i~ige**, *poss. pron. Lit:* **der/die/das i.**, hers, its; *pl* theirs.

Ikone [i'koːnə], *f* -/-n icon.

illeg|al ['ilegaːl], *adj.* illegal. ◆**i~itim** [-i'tiːm], *adj.* illegitimate.

Illus|ion [iluzi'oːn], *f* -/-en illusion. ◆**i~orisch** [-'zoːriʃ], *adj.* (*a*) illusory; (*b*) (*sinnlos*) pointless.

illustr|ieren [ilu'striːrən], *v.tr.* to illustrate (a book etc.). ◆**i~ierte** [-'striːrtə], *f* -/-n illustrated magazine.

Iltis ['iltis], *m* -ses/-se polecat.

im [im], *prep.* = **in dem**. 1. in the. 2. (*zeitlich*) in; **im Oktober**, in October. 3. **im Stehen**, while standing.

imaginär [imagi'nɛːr], *adj.* imaginary.

Imbiß ['imbis], *m* -sses/-sse snack, light meal. ◆**I~stube**, *f* snack bar.

Imi|tation [imitatsi'oːn], *f* -/-en imitation; (*Fälschung*) fake. ◆**i~'tieren**, *v.tr.* to imitate (s.o., sth.).

Imker ['imkər], *m* -s/- beekeeper.

Immatrikulation [imatrikulatsi'oːn], *f* -/-en matriculation, enrolment.

immens [i'mɛns], *adj.* immense; tremendous (achievement etc.).

immer ['imər], *adv.* 1. (*a*) always; **für i.**, for ever, for good; (*b*) (*jedesmal*) every time; **i. wenn**, whenever; **i. wieder**, again and again; (*c*) (*zunehmend*) **i. mehr**, more and more; **i. besser**, better and better; (*d*) **noch i.**, still. 2. **was/wer/wie/wo i.**, whatever/whoever/however/wherever. ◆**i~grün**, *adj.* evergreen (plant). ◆**i~hin**, *adv.* (*wenigstens*) at any rate; (*trotzdem*) all the same; **er ist i. dein Vater**, after all he is your father. ◆**i~'zu**, *adv. F:* constantly.

Immigr|ant(in) [imi'grant(in)], *m* -en/-en (*f* -/-nen) immigrant. ◆**i~ieren** [-'griːrən], *v.i.* (*sein*) to immigrate.

Immobilien [imo'biːliən], *pl* property; *Jur:* real estate.

immun [i'muːn], *adj.* immune (**gegen** + *acc*, from); *Fig:* impervious (**gegen Kritik usw.**, to criticism etc.). ◆**I~i'tät**, *f* -/-en immunity.

Imperativ [impera'tiːf], *m* -s/-e imperative (mood).

Imperfekt ['ɪmpɛrfɛkt], *n* -s/-e imperfect (tense).

Imperialismus [imperia'lɪsmus], *m* -/no *pl* imperialism. ◆I~**ist** ['-list], *m* -en/-en *Pej*: imperialist.

impf|en ['ɪmpfən], *v.tr.* to inoculate, vaccinate (s.o.). ◆I~**schein**, *m* vaccination certificate. ◆I~**stoff**, *m* serum; vaccine. ◆I~**ung**, *f* -/-en inoculation; vaccination.

imponieren [impo'niːrən], *v.i.* (*haben*) j-m i., to impress s.o. ◆i~**d**, *adj.* impressive.

Import [im'pɔrt]. I. *m* -(e)s/-e 1. no *pl* import (**von** + *dat*, of). 2. import, imported article. II. I~>, *comb.fm.* import (licence, duty, trade etc.). ◆I~**teur** [-'tøːr], *m* -s/-e importer. ◆I~**firma**, *f* importing firm, importers. ◆i~**tieren**, *v.tr.* to import (goods etc.).

imposant [impo'zant], *adj.* imposing.

impotent ['ɪmpotɛnt], *adj.* impotent. ◆I~**z**, *f* -/-en impotence.

imprägnieren [imprɛ'gniːrən], *v.tr.* to impregnate, proof, (*gegen Wasser*) waterproof (a material etc.).

Improvi|sation [improviza'tsi̯oːn], *f* -/-en improvisation. ◆i~**sieren**, *v.tr. & i.* (*haben*) to improvise (a meal, music etc.); to extemporize (a speech).

Impuls [im'puls], *m* -es/-e impulse; (*treibende Kraft*) impetus; (*Anregung*) stimulus. ◆i~**siv** ['-'ziːf], *adj.* impulsive; impetuous.

imstande [im'ʃtandə], *adv.* i. sein, etwas zu tun, to be capable of doing sth.

in [in], *prep.* (*a*) (+ *dat*) in; **in der Stadt,** in town; **in der Schule,** at school; **ich war noch nie in Paris,** I've never been to Paris; **in der Nacht,** in/during the night; **gut in Mathematik,** good at mathematics; (*b*) (+*acc*) into, to; **in die Stadt,** (in)to town; **ins Kino/Theater,** to the cinema/theatre.

Inbegriff [im], *m* perfect example (of sth.); embodiment (of evil, kindness etc.). ◆i~**en,** *adj.* included.

indem [in'deːm], *conj.* 1. (*während*) while. 2. (*Zweck*) er spart Geld, i. er zu Fuß geht, he saves money by walking.

Inder(in) ['ɪndər(in)], *m* -s/- (*f* -/-nen) Indian.

indessen [in'dɛsən], *adv.* meanwhile.

Indian|er(in) [indi'aːnər(in)], *m* -s/- (*f* -/-nen) American/*F*: Red Indian. ◆i~**isch,** *adj.* (Red) Indian.

Indien ['ɪndiən]. *Pr.n.n* -s. India.

indigniert [indi'gniːrt], *adj.* indignant.

Indikativ ['ɪndikatiːf], *m* -s/-e *Gram*: indicative (mood). ◆I~**or** ['-'kaːtor], *m* -s/-en indicator.

indirekt ['ɪndirɛkt], *adj.* indirect.

indisch ['ɪndiʃ], *adj.* Indian.

indiskret [indiskre:t], *adj.* indiscreet. ◆I~**ion** [-'tsi̯oːn], *f* -/-en indiscretion.

indiskutabel [indisku'taːbəl], *adj.* out of the question.

Individu|alist [individua'list], *m* -en/-en individualist. ◆I~**alität** [-'tɛːt], *f* -/no *pl* individuality. ◆i~**ell,** *adj.* individual; personal (style, taste etc.); **das ist i. verschieden,** it varies from case to case. ◆I~**um** [-'viːduum], *n* -s/-duen individual.

Indiz [in'diːts], *n* -es/-ien (*a*) *Jur*: relevant circumstances; (*b*) (*Anzeichen*) indication, sign (**für** + *acc*, of). ◆I~**ienbeweis,** *m* circumstantial evidence.

Indonesi|en [indo'neːziən]. *Pr.n.n* -s. Indonesia. ◆i~**isch,** *adj.* Indonesian.

industrial|isieren [industriali'ziːrən], *v.tr.* to industrialize (an area). ◆I~**i'sierung,** *f* -/no *pl* industrialization.

Industrie [indus'triː]. I. *f* -/-n industry; **in der I.,** in industry. II. I~>, *comb.fm.* industrial (worker, building, product, town, centre etc.). ◆I~**betrieb,** *m* industrial plant. ◆i~**ell,** *adj.* industrial. ◆I~**gebiet,** *n* industrial area. ◆I~**gewerkschaft,** *f* industrial (trade) union. ◆I~**staat,** *m* industrial nation. ◆I~**zweig,** *m* branch of industry.

inei'nander, *adv.* in/into one another. ◆i~**fließen,** *v.i.sep.irr.31* (*sein*) to merge, (*Flüsse*) join; (*Farben*) to run (into one other).

infam [in'faːm], *adj.* infamous.

Infanterie [infantə'riː], *f* -/-n infantry.

Infektion [infɛktsi̯oːn], *f* -/-en infection. ◆I~**s-,** *comb.fm.* (*a*) (danger, source etc.) of infection; (*b*) infectious (disease etc.).

Infinitiv ['ɪnfinitiːf], *m* -s/-e infinitive.

infizieren [infi'tsiːrən], *v.tr.* to infect (s.o., a wound etc.); **sich i.,** to become infected.

Inflation [infla'tsi̯oːn], *f* -/-en inflation. ◆i~**är** [-'tsi̯oːnɛːr], *adj.* inflationary. ◆I~**s-,** *comb.fm.* (danger, rate etc.) of inflation; (*b*) inflationary (policy etc.).

infolge, *prep.* + *gen* as a result of. ◆i~**dessen,** *adv.* consequently.

Inform|ation [informatsi̯oːn], *f* -/-en (*a*) (piece/item of) information; I~**en,** (items of) information; (*b*) **erkundigen Sie sich bei der I.,** ask at the information desk. ◆I~**ati'ons-,** *comb.fm.* (*a*) information (bureau, service etc.); (source, flow etc.) of information; (*b*) informative; esp. *Pol*: fact-finding (visit etc.). ◆i~**a'tiv,** *adj.* informative. ◆i~**ieren** [-'miːrən], *v.tr.* to inform (s.o.); **sich über etwas** *acc* **i.,** to gather information/find out about sth.

infrarot ['ɪnfrarot], *adj.* infra-red.

Infusion [infuzi'oːn], *f* -/-en infusion, drip.

Ingenieur [ɪnʒeni'øːr], *m* -s/-e engineer. ◆I~**schule,** *f* college of engineering.

Ingwer ['ɪŋvər], *m* -s/no *pl* ginger.

Inhaber(in) ['ɪnhaːbər(in)], *m* -s/- (*f* -/-nen) holder (of a document, office, *Sp*: record etc.); occupant (of a house, post etc.); (*Besitzer*) owner (of a business

etc.).
inhaftieren [inhaf'ti:rən], v.tr. Jur: to take (s.o.) into custody.
inhalieren [inha'li:rən], v.tr. to inhale.
Inhalt ['inhalt], m -(e)s/-e 1. contents (of a bottle etc.); (Fassungsvermögen) capacity; Mth: volume. 2. (Stoff) content, subject matter (of a book etc.); (I~s-verzeichnis) contents (list). ◆**i~lich**, adv. as far as the content is concerned. ◆**I~sangabe**, f synopsis. ◆**i~slos**, adj. empty (life, speech etc.). ◆**I~sverzeichnis**, n contents list.
Initiat|ive [initsia'ti:və], f -/-n initiative. ◆**I~or** [-'a:tor], m -s/-en initiator.
Injektion [injektsi'o:n], f -/-en injection.
inklusive [inklu'zi:və], adv. i. Porto, including postage; **bis zum 20. März i.**, until March 20th inclusive.
inkognito [in'kɔɡnito], adv. incognito.
inkonsequent, adj. inconsistent.
Inland, n 1. home country; **im In- und Ausland**, at home and abroad. 2. interior (of a country). ◆**I~s-**, comb.fm. inland (letter etc.); domestic (flight, Com: trade etc.); home (market etc.). ◆**I~sporto**, n inland postage rates.
inländisch [in'lendiʃ], adj. indigenous (goods); home (product etc.); domestic, internal (affairs etc.); inland (mail etc.).
inmitten, prep. & adv. Lit: i. + gen/i. von + dat, amidst.
inne|haben ['inəha:bən], v.tr.sep.irr.44 to hold (an office, a title etc.), occupy (a position etc.). ◆**i~halten**, v.i.sep.irr.45 v.i. (haben) to pause. ◆**i~wohnen**, v.i.sep. (haben) etwas dat i., to be inherent in sth.
innen ['inən]. I. adv. inside; **nach i.**, inwards; **von i.**, from inside/within. II. **I~-**, comb.fm. (a) inner (harbour, courtyard, Fig: life etc.); (b) inside (pocket etc.); (c) interior (lighting, wall, Aut: mirror etc.); (im Hause) indoor (aerial, temperature etc.). ◆**I~architekt**, m interior designer/decorator. ◆**I~minister**, m Minister for the Interior/Home Affairs. ◆**I~politik**, f domestic policy. ◆**i~politisch**, adj. concerning domestic policy. ◆**I~raum**, m (a) interior; (b) (Platz) space inside. ◆**I~stadt**, f town/city centre.
inner [in(r)s] ['inər(r)s], adj. 1. inner (edge, circle, room etc.); internal (organization, Pol: affairs, Med: injury, organs etc.); Fig: inner, inward (calm, voice etc.). 2. **das I.**, the interior; the inner being (of s.o.); **im tiefsten I~n**, deep down (inside). ◆**I~eien** [-'raiən], fpl Cu: offal. ◆**i~halb. I.** prep. + gen inside (the house etc.); within (an area, a time, the family etc.). **II.** adv. within. ◆**i~lich**, adj. internal (bleeding etc.); i. unbeteiligt, emotionally detached; **i. lachen**, to laugh inwardly. ◆**i~örtlich**, adj. within a built-up area. ◆**i~parteilich**, adj. within the party

◆**i~städtisch**, adj. inner city (area etc.). ◆**i~ste(r,s)**, adj. (a) innermost (circle etc.); (b) Fig: inmost (being etc.); deepest (conviction etc.); **im I~sten getroffen**, cut to the quick.
innig ['iniç], adj. deep, warm; (echt) sincere (feelings etc.); intimate (friendship etc.); **j-n i. lieben**, to love s.o. with all one's heart.
Innung ['inuŋ], f -/-en guild, corporation.
inoffiziell, adj. unofficial; informal (discussions etc.).
ins [ins], prep. = in das; **i. Theater gehen**, to go to the theatre.
Insasse ['inzasə], m -n/-n/'I~in, f -/-nen inmate; Aut: occupant, passenger.
insbe'sond(e)re, adv. especially, particularly.
Inschrift, f inscription.
Insekt [in'zɛkt], n -s/-en insect. ◆**I~en-**, comb.fm. insect (powder etc.). ◆**i~enstich**, m insect bite/sting. ◆**I~envertilgungsmittel**, n insecticide.
Insel ['inzəl], f -/-n island. ◆**I~bewohner(in)**, m(f) islander. ◆**I~gruppe**, f group of islands.
Inser|at [inze'ra:t], n -(e)s/-e (small) advertisement, F: (small) ad. ◆**I~ent**, m -en/-en advertiser. ◆**i~ieren**, v.tr. & i. (haben) to advertise.
insge'heim, adv. in secret, secretly; F: on the quiet/N.Am: sly.
insge'samt, adv. in all; all told.
inso|fern [in'zo:fern], adv. to this extent; **i. als ...,** in so far as .... ◆**i~weit. I.** [in'zo:vait], adv. = insofern. **II.** [inzo'vait], conj. as far as; (solange) as long as.
Inspekt|ion [inspɛktsi'o:n], f -/-en inspection; Aut: (Wartung) service. ◆**I~or** [in'spɛktor (-'to:rin)], m -s/-en (f -/-nen) inspector.
Inspir|ation [inspiratsi'o:n], f -/-en inspiration. ◆**i~ieren** [-'ri:rən], v.tr. to inspire (s.o.).
inspizieren [inspi'tsi:rən], v.tr. to inspect (troops, a school etc.); to survey (a building).
Install|ateur [instala'tø:r], m -s/-e (gas etc.) fitter; (Elektriker) electrician; (Klempner) plumber. ◆**i~ieren** [-'ti:rən], v.tr. to install, put in (central heating etc.).
instand [in'ʃtant], adv. i. halten, to keep up (a house etc.), maintain (a car etc.); **i. setzen**, to put (a machine etc.) into working order; to restore (furniture etc.). ◆**I~haltung**, f maintenance, upkeep. ◆**I~setzung**, f -/-en repair; restoration.
in'ständig, adj. urgent (request etc.); fervent (prayer).
Instanz [in'stants], f -/-en authority; Jur: court; **erste/zweite I.**, first/second instance.
Instinkt [in'stiŋkt], m -(e)s/-e instinct. ◆**i~iv** [-'ti:f], adj. instinctive.

Institut [insti'tu:t], n -(e)s/-e institute.
◆I~**ion** [-tutsi'o:n], f -/-en institution.

instruieren [instru'i:rən], v.tr. to instruct, brief (s.o.).

Instrument [instru'mɛnt], n -(e)s/-e instrument; (*Werkzeug*) tool, implement. ◆I~**al-** [-tɑ:l], comb.fm. instrumental (music etc.).

Insulin [inzu'li:n], n -s/no pl insulin.

inszenieren [instse'ni:rən], v.tr. to stage, put on (a play etc.); to produce (a play, film etc.); *Fig:* to engineer (a scandal etc.). ◆I~**ung**, f -/-en Th: production.

intakt [in'takt], adj. intact.

Integration [integratsi'o:n], f -/-en integration. ◆i~**rieren** [-'gri:rən], v.tr. to integrate (s.o., sth.). ◆I~**rität** [-gri'tɛ:t], f -/no pl integrity.

Intellekt [intɛ'lɛkt], n -(e)s/no pl intellect. ◆i~**ektuell**, adj. intellectual; ein I~er/eine I~e, an intellectual. ◆I~**igenz** [-i'gɛnts], f -/-en intelligence.

Intendant [intɛn'dant], m -en/-en artistic (and administrative) director; Th: theatre manager.

Intensität [intɛnzi'tɛ:t], f -/no pl intensity; strength. ◆i~**iv** [-'zi:f], adj. intensive (talks etc.); intense (feelings etc.). ◆i~**ivieren** [-zivi:rən], v.tr. to intensify (sth.). ◆I~**ivstation** [-'zi:f-], f intensive care unit.

inter- [intər-], adj.prefix inter-(continental etc.). ◆i~**national**, adj. international.

interessant [intərɛ'sant], adj. interesting; das ist für mich nicht i., that is of no interest to me. ◆i~**anterweise**, adv. interestingly enough. ◆I~**e** [-'rɛsə], n -s/-n interest; I. für j-n, etwas acc haben, to be interested in s.o., sth. ◆I~**ent** [-'sɛnt], m -en/-en interested party; prospective buyer/*Kunde* (customer. ◆i~**ieren** [-'si:rən], v.tr. to interest (s.o.) (für etwas acc, in sth.); das interessiert mich nicht, I am not interested in that. ◆i~**iert** [-'si:rt], adj. interested (an + dat, in); politisch i., interested in politics.

intern [in'tɛrn], adj. internal. ◆I~**at** [-'nɑ:t], n -(e)s/-e boarding school. ◆i~**ieren** [-'ni:rən], v.tr. to intern (prisoners of war). ◆I~**ierung**, f -/-en internment. ◆I~**ist** [-'nist], m -en/-en Med: specialist in internal diseases, internist.

Interpret(in) ['intərprɛt(in)], m -en/-en (f -/-en) interpreter. ◆I~**ation** [-pretatsi'o:n], f -/-en interpretation. ◆i~**ieren**, [-'ti:rən], v.tr. to interpret.

Interpunktion [intərpuŋktsi'o:n], f -/-en punctuation.

Intervall [intər'val], n -s/-e interval.

intervenieren [intərve'ni:rən], v.i. (haben) to intervene (in + dat, in). ◆I~**tion** [-vɛntsi'o:n], f -/-en intervention.

Interview [intər'vju:], n -s/-s interview.

◆i~**en**, v.tr. to interview (s.o.).

intim [in'ti:m], adj. intimate; private (thoughts etc.). ◆I~**ität** [intimi'tɛ:t], f -/-en intimacy. ◆I~**sphäre**, f privacy.

intolerant [intole'rant], adj. intolerant. ◆I~**anz**, f -/-en intolerance.

intransitiv [in'tranziti:f], adj. intransitive.

Intrigant(in) [intri'gant(in)], m -en/-en (f -/-nen) intriguer; schemer. ◆I~**ge** [-'tri:gə], f -/-n intrigue. ◆i~**gieren**, v.i. (haben) to plot.

introvertiert [introver'ti:rt], adj. introverted.

Intuition [intuitsi'o:n], f -/-en intuition. ◆i~**tiv** [-'ti:f], adj. intuitive.

invalid e [inva'li:də], m -n/-n invalid, disabled worker/*Mil:* serviceman. ◆I~**ität** [-lidi'tɛ:t], f -/no pl disability; (*Zustand*) disablement.

Invasion [invazi'o:n], f -/-en invasion.

Inventar [invɛn'ta:r], n -s/-e (a) goods and chattels; assets; (*Lagerbestand*) stock; (b) (*Verzeichnis*) inventory. ◆I~**ur** [-'tu:r], f -/-en stocktaking; I. machen, to take stock.

investieren [invɛs'ti:rən], v.tr. to invest (money, *Fig:* time etc.). ◆I~**ition** [-titsi'o:n], f -/-en capital investment.

inwendig [in'vɛndiç], adj. inside; j-n, etwas in- und auswendig kennen, to know s.o., sth. inside out.

inwiefern [invi:'fɛrn], adv. in what way.

inwieweit [invi:'vait], adv. to what extent.

inzwischen, adv. meanwhile.

Ion [i'o:n], n -s/-en ion.

Irak [i'ra:k], Pr.n.m -s. Iraq. ◆I~**er(in)**, m -s/- (f -/-nen) Iraqi. ◆i~**isch**, adj. Iraqi.

Iran [i'ra:n], Pr.n.m -s. Iran. ◆I~**er(in)**, m -s/- (f -/-nen) Iranian. ◆i~**isch**, adj. Iranian.

irden ['irdən], adj. earthenware. ◆i~**isch**, adj. earthly (goods etc.); worldly (pleasures etc.).

Ire ['i:rə], m -n/-n Irishman. ◆I~**rin**, f -/-nen Irishwoman. ◆**irisch**, adj. Irish. ◆**Irland**. Pr.n.n -s. Ireland; (*Republik*) Eire.

irgend ['irgənt], adv. 1. i. jemand, someone; i. etwas, something; hat er i. etwas gesagt? did he say anything? nicht i. jemand, not (just) anybody. 2. wenn es i. möglich ist, if it is at all possible. ◆i~'**ein**, indef. pron. 1. some; (+ neg./interrog.) any. 2. i~'**er**, someone; besser als i. anderer, better than anyone else. ◆i~'**wann**, adv. sometime (or other). ◆i~'**was**, indef. pron. F: something; kannst du i. tun? can you do anything? ◆i~'**wer**, indef. pron. F: someone, somebody. ◆i~'**wie**, adv. somehow. ◆i~'**wo**, adv. somewhere. ◆i~'**wohin**, adv. i. fahren, to drive somewhere/anywhere.

Ironie [iro'ni:], f -/-n irony. ◆i~**isch** [i'ro:niʃ], adj. ironic.

irr(e) ['ir(ə)], *adj.* crazy. ◆**I~e¹**, *m & f decl. as adj.* lunatic; *F:* **wie ein I~r**, like mad. ◆**I~e²**, *f* **j~n in die I. führen** = **i~eführen**. ◆**i~eführen**, *v.tr.* to mislead (s.o.); (*täuschen*) to deceive (the public etc.). ◆**I~eführung**, *f* deception. ◆**i~en**, *v.i.* (*haben*) & *refl.* (a) **sich in j-m, etwas** *dat* **i.**, to be mistaken about s.o., sth.; **wenn ich** (**mich**) **nicht irre, if I am not mistaken; ich habe mich in der Zeit geirrt**, I got the time wrong; (b) to wander, stray; **durch die Straßen i.**, to roam the streets. ◆**I~enhaus**, *n* lunatic asylum; *F:* madhouse. ◆**I~fahrt**, *f* roundabout journey; *pl* wanderings. ◆**i~ig**, *adj.* mistaken; false (supposition etc.). ◆**I~licht**, *n* will-o'-the-wisp. ◆**I~sinn**, *m* insanity; madness. ◆**i~sinnig**, *adj.* 1. insane; crazy. 2. *F:* terrific, tremendous; (*komisch*) **i. komisch**, screamingly funny. ◆**I~tum**, *m* -s/-er error; mistake; **im I. sein**, to be mistaken. ◆**i~tümlich**, *adj.* erroneous (assertion etc.), mistaken (opinion etc.); *adv.* by mistake. ◆**I~weg**, *m* wrong track.

irritieren [iri'ti:rən], *v.tr.* to distract; (*ärgern*) to irritate.

Ischias ['iʃias], *m* -/no *pl* sciatica.

Islam [is'laːm], *m* -s/no *pl* Islam. ◆**i~isch**, *adj.* Islamic.

Island ['iːslant]. *Pr.n.n* -s. Iceland. ◆**isländisch**, *adj.* Icelandic.

Isol|ation [izolatsi'oːn], *f* -/-en isolation; *El:* insulation. ◆**I~ator** [-'laːtɔr], *m* -s/-en *El: etc:* (a) insulator; (b) insulating material. ◆**I~ier-** [-'liːr-], *comb.fm.* insulating (material etc.). ◆**i~ieren**, *v.tr.* (a) to isolate (a person); *Med:* to quarantine (a patient); (b) to insulate (wires etc., a pipe, wall etc.). ◆**I~ierstation**, *f* isolation ward. ◆**I~ierung**, *f* -/-en *Med: & Fig:* isolation; *El:etc:* insulation.

Israel ['israeːl]. *Pr.n.n* -s. Israel. ◆**I~i** [-'eːli], *m* -s/-s Israeli. ◆**i~isch**, *adj.* Israeli.

Italien [i'taːliən]. *Pr.n.n* -s. Italy. ◆**I~er(in)** [itali'eːnər(in)], *m* -s/- (*f -/-nen*) Italian. ◆**i~isch. I.** *adj.* Italian. **II. I.**, *n* -s/no *pl* (*Sprache*) Italian.

J

J, j [jɔt], *n* -/- (the letter) J, j.

ja [jaː], *adv.* 1. (*Antwort*) yes; **mit Ja antworten**, to answer 'yes'; **wenn ja**, if so. 2. *F:* **sag ja nichts**, don't you dare say anything; **du kennst ihn ja**, you know what he's like; **ich geh ja schon**, don't worry, I'm going; **du bleibst doch, ja?** you will stay, won't you? **ja, dann ...!** of course, in that case ...! ◆**ja'wohl**, *adv.* (*bejahend*) yes, indeed; (*natürlich*) certainly. ◆**'Jawort**, *n* consent; **sein J. geben**, to say yes.

Jacht [jaxt], *f* -/-en yacht.

Jacke ['jakə], *f* -/-n jacket; (*aus Wolle*) cardigan. ◆**J~tt** [ʒa'kɛt], *n* -s/-s jacket.

Jagd [jaːkt]. I. *f* -/-en 1. (*nach Wild*) hunting, (*Schießen*) shooting (auf + *acc,* of); **auf die J. gehen**, to go hunting. 2. (*Verfolgung*) chase. II. **'J~d-**, *comb.fm.* 1. hunting. 2. *Av:* fighter (aircraft, squadron etc.). ◆**'J~beute**, *f* quarry. ◆**'J~gewehr**, *n* hunting/sporting gun. ◆**'J~revier**, *n* shoot; *esp. Fig:* hunting ground.

jagen ['jaːgən], *v.* 1. *v.tr.* (a) to hunt; (b) (*verfolgen*) to chase; to drive (s.o.) (**aus dem Hause usw.**, out of the house etc.); (*hetzen*) to hound (s.o.); *F:* **damit kannst du mich j.!** you can keep it! (c) to drive (a knife, ball etc.). 2. *v.i.* (*haben*) (a) to hunt; to go hunting; (b) (*rasen*) (*Pers.*) to dash, rush; (*Pferd*) to gallop; (*Motor*) to race; (c) *Fig:* **nach Ruhm, Geld usw. j.**, to pursue fame, fortune etc.

Jäger ['jɛːgər], *m* -s/- 1. (a) hunter; (b) (*Verfolger*) pursuer. 2. (*Aufseher*) gamekeeper. 3. *Av: F:* fighter (plane).

jäh [jɛː], *adj.* (a) (*plötzlich*) sudden; abrupt (ending etc.); (b) sheer (drop etc.). ◆**j~lings** ['jɛːliŋs], *adv.* suddenly, abruptly.

Jahr [jaːr], *n* -(e)s/-e year; **in den fünfziger J~en**, in the fifties; **1000 Mark im J.**, 1000 marks a year; **in die J~e kommen**, to be getting on in years; **in den besten J~en**, in the prime of life. ◆**j~'aus, adv.** j., **jahrein**, year in, year out. ◆**j~elang**, *adj.* (lasting) for years; **in j~en Studium**, in years of study. ◆**J~es-**, *comb.fm.* (a) year's (turnover salary etc.); (beginning, end etc.) of the year; (b) (*wiederholt*) annual (report, meeting etc.). ◆**'J~eswechsel**, *m/* **J~eswende**, *f* turn of the year. ◆**'J~eszeit**, *f* season; time of year. ◆**'J~gang**, *m* 1. age group; **der J. 1970**, those born in 1970; **ist mein J.**, he was born the same year as I was. 2. (*Wein usw.*) **ein guter J.**, a good vintage. 3. (*Zeitschrift*) year's issues. ◆**J~'hundert**, *n* -s/-e century. ◆**J~'hundertfeier**, *f* centenary. ◆**'J~markt**, *m* fair. ◆**J~'zehnt**, *n* -(e)s/-e decade.

jährlich ['jɛːrlix], *adj.* yearly, annual; **einmal j.**, once a year.

Jähzorn ['jɛːtsɔrn], *m* violent temper.

Jalousie [ʒalu'ziː], *f* -/-n blind.

Jammer ['jamər], *m* -s/no *pl* (*Elend*) misery; *F:* **es ist ein J.**, it's a crying shame. ◆**j~n**, *v.i.* (*haben*) to complain, *F:* moan (**über j-n, etwas** *acc,* about); **die Kinder j~n nach der Mutter**, the children are crying for their mother. ◆**j~'schade**, *pred.*

adj. es ist j., it's a crying shame.

jämmerlich ['jɛmərlɪç], *adj.* 1. miserable (state etc.); pitiful (cry etc.); wretched (conditions); **er sieht j. aus,** he is a pitiful sight. 2. *F:* (*a*) miserable (work, effort); (*b*) terrible (fear, pain).

Januar ['januːaːr], *m* -(s)/-e January.

Japan ['jaːpan]. *Pr.n.n* -s. Japan. ◆**J~er(in)** [ja'paːnər(ɪn)], *m* -s/- (*f* -/-nen) Japanese. ◆**j~isch** [ja'paːnɪʃ], *adj.* Japanese.

japsen ['japsən], *v.i.* (*haben*) *F:* to gasp (**nach Luft,** for air).

Jargon [ʒar'gõː], *m* -s/-s jargon.

Jasmin [jas'miːn], *m* -s/-e jasmine.

jäten ['jɛːtən], *v.tr.* to weed.

Jauche ['jauxə], *f* -/-n liquid manure. ◆**J~grube,** *f* cesspit.

jauchzen ['jauxtsən], *v.i.* (*haben*) to rejoice (**über etwas** *acc*, over sth.); (**vor Wonne**) **j.,** to shout for joy.

jaulen ['jaulən], *v.i.* (*haben*) to howl.

je [jeː]. **I.** *adv.* (*a*) (*jemals*) ever; (*je-weils*) at a time; each; (*c*) **je nach** according to; **je nach Belieben,** just as/however you like (it); **je nachdem,** as the case may be; (*Antwort*) it all depends; (*d*) **das hat er seit (eh und) je gehabt,** he's always had that. **II.** *prep.* + *acc;* **je zwei Meter Stoff,** (for) every two metres of material; **die Kosten je Teilnehmer,** the cost for each/per participant. **III.** *conj.* **je ..., desto ...,** the ..., the ... .

Jeans [dʒiːnz], *pl.* jeans. ◆**J~stoff,** *m* denim.

jede(r,s) ['jeːdə(r,z)], *indef. pron.* 1. *adj.* every; (*j~s einzelne*) each; **j-n zweiten Tag,** every other day; (*b*) (*j~s beliebige*) any. 2. *s. adj* **j~(r),** everybody, everyone; (*Sache*) each (one); **j~r** (*einzelne*) **von uns,** each (and every one of us; **j~r von den beiden,** each/both of them; (*b*) **j~s** (*beliebige*) anybody, anyone; (*Sache*) anything. ◆**j~nfalls** ['jeːdnfals], *adv.* (*was auch geschieht*) in any case; (*wenigstens*) at least. ◆**j~rmann,** *indef. pron.* everybody, everyone. ◆**j~rzeit,** *adv.* (at) any time. ◆**j~smal,** *adv.* each/every time.

jedoch [je'dɔx], *conj. & adv.* however.

jeher ['jeːheːr], *adv.* **von/seit j.,** always, all along.

jemals ['jeːmaːls], *adv.* ever.

jemand ['jeːmant], *indef. pron.* (*a*) someone, somebody; (*b*) **anders,** somebody else; (*b*) (*fragend/unbestimmt*) anybody; anyone; **ist hier j.?** is (there) anybody here?

jen|e(r,s) ['jeːnə(r,s)], *dem. pron.* that; *pl.* those. ◆**j~seitig,** *adj.* far, opposite (bank etc.). ◆**j~seits. I.** *prep.* + *gen* beyond; **j. des Flusses,** on the other side of the river. **II.** *J.,* *n* -/no *pl Ecc:* **das J.,** the life hereafter.

Jesus ['jeːzus]. *Pr.n.m* -. Jesus. ◆**J~kind,** *n* **das J.,** the Infant Jesus.

jetzig ['jɛtsɪç], *adj.* present.

jetzt [jɛtst], *adv.* now; **er kommt j. gleich,** he'll be coming in a moment.

jeweil|ig ['jeːvaɪlɪç], *adj.* (*a*) particular; **der j~e Präsident usw.,** the president etc. in office/power at the time; (*b*) (*in Frage kommend*) relevant (authority etc.); **sie wurden an die j~en Besitzer zurückerstattet,** they were returned to their respective owners. ◆**j~s,** *adv.* in each case; **Sie erhalten j. 50 Mark,** you each receive 50 marks.

Job [dʒɔp], *m* -s/-s *F:* job. ◆**j~ben** [-bən], *v.i.* (*haben*) *F:* to take a job.

Joch [jɔx], *n* -(e)s/-e yoke.

Jockei ['dʒɔki, -ke], *m* -s/-s jockey.

Jod [joːt], *n* -(e)s/no *pl* iodine.

jodeln ['joːdəln], *v.i.* (*haben*) to yodel.

Joga ['joːga], *n* -s/no *pl* yoga.

Joghurt ['joːgurt], *m & f* -s/-s yoghurt.

Johannisbeere [jo'hanisbeːrə], *f* -/-n schwarze/rote J., blackcurrant/red-currant.

johlen ['joːlən], *v.i.* (*haben*) to bawl, yell.

Jolle ['jɔlə], *f* -/-n dinghy.

Jonglleur [dʒɔŋ'gløːr], *m* -s/-e juggler. ◆**j~lieren,** *v.i.* (*haben*) to juggle.

Joppe ['jɔpə], *f* -/-n loden jacket.

Jordan [jɔr'daːnin]. *Pr.n.m* -s. Jordan. ◆**J~ier** ['daːnjər], *m* -s/- Jordanian.

Jota ['joːta], *n* -(s)/-s *F:* **er wich (um) kein J.,** he wouldn't budge an inch.

Journal [ʒur'naːl], *n* -s/-e journal. ◆**J~ismus** [-a'lismus], *m* -/no *pl* journalism. ◆**J~ist(in),** *m* -en/-en (*f* -/-nen) journalist.

Jubel ['juːbəl], *m* -s/no *pl* jubilation, rejoicing; (*F~rufe*) cheering. ◆**J~jahr,** *n F:* **alle J~e (ein)mal,** once in a blue moon. ◆**j~n,** *v.i.* (*haben*) to rejoice (**über etwas** *acc,* at sth.); (*rufen*) to cheer.

Jubil|ar(in) [jubi'laːr(ɪn)], *m* -s/-e (*f* -/-nen) man/woman celebrating an anniversary. ◆**J~läum** [-'lɛːum], *n* -s/-läen (*pl*) jubilee; **150-jähriges J.,** 150th anniversary.

jucken ['jukən], *v.tr. & i.* (*haben*) to irritate; **es juckt (mich) am ganzen Körper,** my whole body is itching; *Fig:* **das juckt mich nicht,** I couldn't care less; (*b*) *F:* **sich j.,** to scratch oneself.

Jude ['juːdə], *m* -n/-n Jew. ◆**J~ntum,** *n* -s/no *pl* Judaism.

Jüd|in ['jyːdin], *f* -/-en Jewish woman. ◆**j~isch,** *adj.* Jewish.

Jugend ['juːgənt]. **I.** *f* -/no *pl* 1. (*Alter*) youth; (*13–18*) adolescence; **von J. an,** from an early age. 2. (*junge Leute*) young people. **II.** **'J~-,** *comb.fm.* (*a*) youth (club, orchestra etc.); juvenile (court etc.); *Sp:* junior (champion etc.); (*b*) (*von seiner J.*) youthful (writings etc.); (*memory, friend* etc.). ◆**'J~buch,** *n* book for young people. ◆**'J~frei,** *adj.* (book etc.) suitable for young people; *Cin:* = U-certificate/ *N.Am:* G/PG-rated (film). ◆**'J~gefährdend,** *adj.* (literature) tending to corrupt youth; *Cin:* X-certificate/*N.Am:* R-rated (film). ◆'J~**heim**, *n* (residential) youth club. ◆'J~**herberge**, *f* youth hostel. ◆'J~**kriminalität**, *f* juvenile delinquency. ◆'j~**lich**, *adj.* youthful. ◆'J~**liche(r)**, *f(m) decl. as adj.* young person; *Jur:* juvenile. ◆'J~**stil**, *m* art nouveau. ◆'J~**weihe**, *f East G:* dedication of youth. ◆'J~**zeit**, *f* youth.

Jugoslawe [jugo'sla:və], *m* -n/-n Yugoslav. ◆J~**in**, *f* -/-nen Yugoslav (woman). ◆j~**isch**, *adj.* Yugoslavian.

Juli ['ju:li], *m* -s/-s July.

jung [juŋ]. I. *adj.* young. II. 'J~-, *comb.fm.* young (farmer, animal etc.). ◆'J~**e**, *m* -n/-n 1. boy. 2. *F:* (*junger Mann*) lad; **schwerer J.**, tough guy; (*Verbrecher*) hard case. 3. *int. F:* **J.**, **J.!** I'll be blowed! wow! ◆'J~**e(s)**, *n decl. as adj.* (*Tier*) young one; (wolf, bear etc.) cub. ◆'J~**en-**, *comb.fm.* boy's (voice etc.); *pl* boys' (school etc.). ◆'j~**enhaft**, *adj.* boyish. ◆'J~**fer**, *f* -/-n *Pej:* (alte) **J.**, spinster; old maid. ◆'J~**fern-**, *comb.fm.* maiden (flight, speech etc.). ◆'J~**fernfahrt**, *f* maiden voyage. ◆'J~**frau**, *f* 1. virgin; **die (Heilige) J. Maria**, the (Holy) Virgin Mary. 2. *Astr:* Virgo. ◆'J~**geselle**, *m* bachelor. ◆'J~**lehrer(in)**, *m(f)* student teacher.

jünger ['jyŋər]. I. *adj.* (*a*) younger; (*b*) (*ziemlich jung*) fairly young, youngish; (*c*) recent (occurence, history etc.). II. **J.**, *m*

-s/- disciple.

Jüngling ['jyŋliŋ], *m* -s/-e *Lit: & Pej:* youth.

jüngste(r,s) ['jyŋstə(r,s)], *adj.* (*a*) youngest (child etc.); *F:* **sie ist nicht mehr die J.**, she's no spring chicken; (*b*) latest (events etc.); *Ecc:* **der J. Tag**, Doomsday; **das J. Gericht**, the Last Judgement.

Juni ['ju:ni], *m* -s/-s June.

junior ['ju:niɔr]. I. *adj* **Robert Schmidt j.**, Robert Schmidt junior. II. **J.**, *m* -s/-en (a) (*Sohn*) offspring; (*b*) *no pl Com:* junior director/partner; (*c*) *Sp:* junior.

Jura ['ju:ra], *s.inv.* **J. studieren**, to study law.

Jurist(in) [ju'rist(in)], *m* -en/-en (*f* -/-nen) lawyer.

Jury ['ʒy:ri], *f* -/-s panel of judges.

justieren [jus'ti:rən], *v.tr.* (*a*) to adjust, regulate; (*b*) to justify (a line).

Justiz [jus'ti:ts], *f* -/no pl 1. (administration of) justice. 2. (*Behörden*) judiciary. ◆J~**beamte(r)**, *m* officer of the law. ◆J~**irrtum**, *m* miscarriage of justice. ◆J~**minister**, *m* Minister of Justice; *approx.* Attorney General.

Juto ['ju:tə], *f* /no pl jute.

Juwel [ju've:l], *n & m* -s/-en 1. *n & m* jewel, precious stone. 2. *m* (*pl* J~e) *Fig:* gem. ◆J~**ier** [juve'li:r], *m* -s/-e jeweller.

Jux [juks], *m* -es/-e (practical) joke; **aus J.**, for fun/*F:* kicks.

K

K, k [ka:], *n* -/- (the letter) K, k.

Kabarett [kaba'rɛt], *n* -s/-s cabaret, satirical revue. ◆K~**ist(in)** [-'tist(in)], *m* -en/-en (*f* -/-nen) cabaret/revue artist.

Kabel [ka:bəl]. I. *n* -s/- *El:* (*größeres*) cable; (*Leitung*) lead. II. 'K~-, *comb.fm.* cable (television etc.).

Kabeljau [ka:bəljau], *m* -s/-e *& -s* cod.

Kabine [ka'bi:nə], *f* -/-n (*Schiffsk.*) cabin; (*im Schwimmbad, beim Friseur usw.*) cubicle; (telephone) booth.

Kabinett [kabi'nɛt], *n* -s/-e *Pol:* cabinet. ◆K~**s-**, *comb.fm. Pol:* cabinet (minister etc.). ◆K~**ssitzung**, *f* cabinet meeting.

Kabriolett [kabrio'lɛt], *n* -s/-s convertible.

Kachel [ka:xəl], *f* -/-n tile. ◆K~**n**, *v.tr.* to tile. ◆K~**ofen**, *m* tiled stove.

Kadaver [ka'da:vər], *m* -s/- carcass.

Kader ['ka:dər], *m* -s/- cadre (of an army etc.); *Pol:* hard core, nucleus (of a party).

Kadett [ka'dɛt], *m* -en/-en cadet.

Käfer ['kɛ:fər], *m* -s/- beetle.

Kaff [kaf], *n* -s/-s *F:* (deadly) hole, dump.

Kaffee ['kafe, ka'fe:], *m* -s/-s coffee; **zwei K.**, two coffees. II. 'K~-, *comb.fm.*

coffee (bean, cup etc.). ◆'K~**kanne**, *f* coffee pot. ◆'K~**klatsch**, *m* (women's) afternoon coffee party. ◆'K~**löffel**, *m* (*a*) (large) coffee spoon; (*b*) *Meas:* teaspoonful. ◆'K~**maschine**, *f* coffee-maker. ◆'K~**mühle**, *f* coffee-grinder. ◆'K~**pause**, *f* coffee break. ◆'K~**satz**, *m* coffee grounds.

Käfig ['kɛ:fiç], *m* -s/-e cage.

kahl [ka:l], *adj.* (*a*) (*haarlos*) bald; (*b*) (*schmucklos*) bare (room, tree, rock etc.); bleak (landscape etc.). ◆'k~**fressen**, *v.tr.sep.irr.25* (*Tiere*) to strip (a tree etc.). ◆'k~**geschoren**, *adj.* shorn, shaven. ◆'k~**köpfig**, *adj.* bald-headed. ◆'K~**schlag**, *m* clearing (in a forest).

Kahn [ka:n], *m* -(e)s/-e (*a*) (*Ruderboot*) rowing boat, *N.Am:* rowboat; (*b*) (*Lastk.*) barge.

Kai [kai], *m* -s/-s quay. ◆'K~**anlage**, *f* wharf.

Kaiser ['kaizər]. I. *m* -s/- emperor. II. K~-, *comb.fm.* imperial (crown, palace etc.). ◆'K~**in**, *f* -/-nen empress. ◆'k~**lich**, *adj.* imperial. ◆'K~**reich**, *n* empire. ◆'K~**schnitt**, *m Med:* Caesarean (section).

Kajak ['kɑːjak], m -s/-s kayak.

Kajüte [ka'jyːtə], f -/-n cabin.

Kakadu ['kakaduː], m -s/-s cockatoo.

Kakao [ka'kau], m -s/-s cocoa.

Kakerlak ['kɑːkərlak], m -s & -en/-en cockroach.

Kaktee [kak'teːə], f -/-n/Kaktus ['kaktus], m -/-teen & -tusse cactus.

Kalb [kalp], n -(e)s/-er (a) calf; (b) Cu: veal. ◆'k~en [-bən], v.i. (haben) (Kuh usw.) to calve. ◆'K~fleisch, n veal. ◆'K~s-, comb.fm. Cu: (a) calf's, (liver etc.); (b) veal (steak etc.); (breast etc.) of veal. ◆'K~sbraten, m roast veal. ◆'K~sleder, n calf (leather); calfskin.

Kalender [ka'lɛndər], m -s/- 1. calendar. 2. (Taschenk.) diary.

Kali ['kɑːli], n -s/-s potash; Ch: potassium.

Kaliber [ka'liːbər], n -s/- calibre.

Kalium ['kɑːliʊm], n -s/no pl potassium.

Kalk [kalk], m -(e)s/-e (a) lime; ungelöschter K., quicklime; (b) K~(stein) limestone; (c) (Knochensubstanz) calcium. ◆'K~stein, m limestone.

Kalkul|ation [kalkulatsi'oːn], f -/-en calculation; Com: estimate. ◆k~ieren [-'liːrən], v.tr. to calculate (sth.).

Kalorie [kalo'riː], f -/-n [-ən] calorie. ◆k~narm, adj. low-calorie (food).

kalt [kalt], adj. cold; mir ist (es) k., I am cold; etwas k. stellen, to put sth. to cool; Cu: k~e Platte, plate of cold meats; das läßt mich k., it leaves me cold. ◆'k~blütig, adj. cold-blooded; adv. in cold blood. ◆'K~blütigkeit, f -/no pl coolness; Pej: cold-bloodedness. ◆'K~miete, f basic rent (without heating). ◆'K~schale, f fruit purée/whip; (Vorspeise) sweet soup. ◆'k~schnäuzig, adj. F: cold; (grausam) callous. ◆'k~stellen, v.tr.sep. F: to reduce (s.o.) to impotence.

Kälte ['kɛltə], f -/no pl 1. cold; (unter Null) frost; 10 Grad K., 10 degrees below freezing. 2. Fig: coldness, coolness. ◆'K~grad, m (degree of) coldness. ◆'K~welle, f cold spell.

Kalzium ['kaltsiʊm], n -s/no pl calcium.

Kamel [ka'meːl], n -s/-e 1. Z: camel. 2. (Pers.) idiot.

Kamera ['kaməra], f -/-s camera. ◆'K~mann, m cameraman.

Kamerad(in) [kamə'rɑːt (-'rɑːdin)], m -en/-en (f -/-nen) comrade, companion; F: mate; N.Am: buddy. ◆K~schaft, f -/no pl comradeship; companionship. ◆k~schaftlich, adj. comradely; friendly (relationship).

Kamille [ka'milə], f -/-n camomile. ◆K~ntee, m camomile tea.

Kamin [ka'miːn], m -(e)s/-e fireplace; (Schornstein) chimney. ◆K~kehrer, m -s/- chimney-sweep. ◆K~sims, m mantelpiece.

Kamm [kam], m -(e)s/-e 1. comb. 2. crest (of a wave); ridge (of a mountain). 3. Z:

crest (of a bird); comb (of a cock).

kämmen ['kɛmən], v.tr. to comb (hair, wool etc.); sich k., to comb one's hair.

Kammer ['kamər], f -/-n 1. (Abstellraum) boxroom; (für Haushaltsgeräte) broom cupboard. 2. Pol: Com: chamber (of parliament, trade). II. K~-, comb.fm. Mus: chamber (music etc.). ◆'K~konzert, n concert of chamber music. ◆'K~spiele, npl intimate theatre.

Kampagne [kam'panjə], f -/-n campaign.

Kampf [kampf], m I. -(e)s/-e (a) fight; schwere K~e, heavy fighting; (b) Sp: (Wettkampf) contest; (c) Fig: struggle, (Aktion) campaign; etwas dat den K. ansagen, to declare war on sth. II. 'K~-, comb.fm. fighting (troops etc.); battle (song etc.); Mil: combat (zone, troops etc.). ◆'k~bereit, adj. ready for action; esp. Fig: ready for the fray. ◆'K~handlungen, fpl fighting, (military) action. ◆'K~kraft, f fighting strength. ◆'k~los, adj. without a fight. ◆'k~lustig, adj. belligerent. ◆'K~richter, m -s/- Sp: judge. ◆'k~unfähig, adj. (Soldat) unfit for active service; (Panzer usw.) out of action. ◆'K~verband, m fighting/combat force.

kämpf|en ['kɛmpfən], v. 1. v.i. (haben) to fight; um etwas acc k., to fight/esp. Fig: struggle for sth.; Fig: mit sich k., to struggle with oneself. 2. v.refl. sich durch etwas acc k., to fight one's way through sth. ◆'K~er, m -s/- fighter; Fig: crusader. ◆'k~erisch, adj. fighting (spirit, mood etc.).

Kampfer ['kampfər], m -s/no pl camphor.

Kanad|a ['kanada]. Pr.n.n -s. Canada. ◆K~ier(in) [ka'nɑːdiər(in)], m -s/- (f -/-nen) Canadian. ◆k~isch [ka'nɑːdiʃ], adj. Canadian.

Kanal [ka'nɑːl], m -s/-e 1. (für Schiffe) canal; Geog: der K., the (English) Channel. 2. (für Abwässer) drain, sewer. 3. Rad: TV: channel. ◆K~isation [kanalizatsi'oːn], f -/-en (für Abwässer) sewerage (system); main drainage. ◆k~isieren, v.tr. (a) to canalize (a river); (b) to provide (a town etc.) with sewers/drains.

Kanarienvogel [ka'nɑːriənfoːgəl], canary.

Kandi|dat [kandi'dɑːt], m -en/-en candidate; (Bewerber) applicant. ◆K~datur [-da'tuːr], f -/-en candidature. ◆k~'dieren, v.i. (haben) to be a candidate; Pol: etc: to stand, N.Am: run.

kand|ieren [kan'diːrən], v.tr. Cu: to candy (fruit). ◆K~iszucker, m -s/no pl candy sugar.

Känguruh ['kɛnguru], n -s/-s kangaroo.

Kaninchen [ka'niːnçən], n -s/- rabbit.

Kanister [ka'nistər], m -s/- canister; (aus Blech) tin; (für Wasser) water carrier.

Kanne ['kanə], f -/-n (a) (Krug) jug; (b)

(mit *Deckel*) (milk) churn, (*klein*) can; (coffee, tea) pot; (c) (*Gießk.*) (watering-)-can.

Kannibal|e [kani'bo:lə], *m* -*n*/-*n* cannibal. **◆K~ismus** [-a'lismus], *m* -/*no pl* cannibalism.

Kanon ['ka:nɔn], *m* -*s*/-*s* Mus: canon; (*Lied*) round.

Kanone [ka'no:nə], *f* -/-*n* **1.** Mil: (field etc.) gun; *Hist:* cannon. 2. F: (*Pers.*) ace. *Sp:* champ. **◆K~nkugel**, *f* cannon ball.

Kantate [kan'to:tə], *f* -/*n* cantata.

Kant|e ['kantə], *f* -/-*n* edge. **◆k~ig**, *adj.* angular (stone etc.); squared (timber etc.); square (chin etc.).

Kantine [kan'ti:nə], *f* -/-*n* canteen.

Kanu ['ka:nu, ka'nu:], *n* -*s*/-*s* canoe; **K. fahren**, to canoe.

Kanz|el ['kantsəl], *f* -/-*n* **1.** Ecc: pulpit. 2. Av: cockpit. **◆K~ler**, *m* -*s*/- Pol: chancellor.

Kap [kap], *n* -*s*/-*s* cape, headland.

Kapazität [kapatsi'tɛːt], *f* -/-*en* **1.** capacity. 2. (*Pers.*) **eine K. auf diesem Gebiet**, an authority in this field.

Kapelle [ka'pɛlə], *f* -/-*n* **1.** Ecc: chapel. 2. Mus: band.

Kaper ['ka:pər], *f* -/-*n* caper.

kapern ['ka:pərn], *v.tr.* to seize (a ship etc.) (as a prize).

kapieren [ka'pi:rən], *v.tr.* F: to understand, get (sth.).

Kapital [kapi'to:l], *n* -*s*/-*e &* -*len* capital; *Fig:* asset. **II. K~-**, *comb.fm.* capital (*Fin:* investment, market etc.; *Jur:* crime etc.). **◆K~gesellschaft**, *f* -/-*en* joint stock company. **◆K~ismus** [-a'lismus], *m* -/*no pl* capitalism. **◆K~ist** [-a'list], *m* -*en*/-*en* capitalist. **◆k~istisch**, *adj.* capitalist.

Kapitän [kapi'tɛːn], *m* -*s*/-*e* (a) Nau: Av: captain; master (of a merchant vessel); (b) Sp: etc: team leader.

Kapitel [ka'pitəl], *n* -*s*/- chapter.

Kapitul|ation [kapitulatsi'o:n], *f* -/-*en* capitulation, surrender. **◆k~ieren** [-'li:rən], *v.i. (haben)* to capitulate.

Kaplan [ka'plo:n], *m* -*s*/-*e* chaplain; (*Hilfsgeistlicher*) curate.

Kappe ['kapə], *f* -/-*n* cap. **◆k~n**, *v.tr.* to chop (sth.); to top (a tree).

Kapsel ['kapsəl], *f* -/-*n* (*Behälter*) capsule.

kaputt [ka'put], *adj.* (*Sache*) bust; broken (cup, *Hum:* leg etc.); F: (*Auto*) smashed up; (*nicht funktionierend*) on the blink; *Fig:* ruined (firm, marriage etc.). **◆k~gehen**, *v.i.sep.irr.36* (*sein*) F: to bust, (*Teller usw.*) break; (*Uhr usw.*) to go on the blink; (*Birne usw.*) to go; (*Kleider, Schuhe usw.*) to fall to pieces. **◆k~lachen**, *v.refl.sep.* F: **sich k.**, to laugh one's head off. **◆k~machen**, *v.tr.sep.* F: to bust (sth.); *Fig:* to ruin (s.o., a firm etc.); (*erschöpfen*) to wear (s.o.) out.

Kapuze [ka'pu:tsə], *f* -/-*n* hood.

Karaffe [ka'rafə], *f* -/-*n* decanter; (*im Restaurant*) carafe.

Karambolage [karambo'lo:ʒə], *f* -/-*n* F: Aut: smash; (*Massenk.*) pile-up.

Karamel [kara'mɛl], *m* -*s*/- caramel.

Karat [ka'ro:t], *n* -(*e*)*s*/-*e* carat.

Karawane [kara'vo:nə], *f* -/-*n* caravan (of camels etc.).

Kardinal [kardi'no:l], *m* -(*e*)*s*/-*e* cardinal. **◆K~zahl**, *f* cardinal number.

Karfreitag [kar'fraito:k], *m* Good Friday.

karg [kark], *adj.* (a) scanty (vegetation etc.); frugal (meal); (b) poor (soil etc.). **◆kärglich** ['kɛrkliç], *adj.* scanty (vegetation etc.); frugal (meal); niggardly (sum).

Kargo ['kargo], *m* -*s*/-*s* cargo.

Karib|ik [ka'ri:bik], *Pr.n.f.* -. **die K.**, the Caribbean. **◆k~isch**, *adj.* Caribbean.

kariert [ka'ri:rt], *adj.* check (pattern etc.); *Sp:* chequered (flag).

Karies ['ka:ries], *f* -/*no pl* caries.

Karik|atur [karika'tu:r], *f* -/-*en* caricature; (political etc.) cartoon. **◆K~aturist** [-tu'rist], *m* -*en*/-*en* caricaturist, cartoonist.

karitativ [karita'ti:f], *adj.* charitable.

Karneval ['karnəval], *m* -*s*/-*s* carnival.

Karo ['ka:ro]. **I.** *n* -*s*/-*s* (a) (*Viereck*) square; (b) (*Muster*) check; (c) (*Karte*) diamond; (*Farbe*) diamonds. **II. K~-**, *comb.fm.* (a) check (pattern etc.); (b) (ace, king, queen etc.) of diamonds.

Karosse [ka'rɔsə], *f* -/-*n* (state) coach. **◆K~rie** [-'ri:], *f* body(work).

Karotte [ka'rɔtə], *f* -/-*n* carrot.

Karpfen ['karpfən], *m* -*s*/- carp.

Karre ['karə], *f* -/-*n* = **Karren**.

Karree [ka're:], *n* -*s*/-*s* square.

Karren ['karən], *m* -*s*/- **1.** cart; (*Handk.*) barrow. 2. *Pej:* F: (*Auto*) jalopy.

Karriere [kari'ɛːrə], *f* -/-*n* career; **K. machen**, to get to the top of one's profession. **◆K~macher**, *m Pej:* careerist.

Karte ['kartə], *f* -/-*n* **1.** (a) card; esp. postcard; (b) (visiting) card; (c) (*Speisek.*) menu. 2. (*Fahrk., Eintrittsk.*) ticket. 3. (*Spielk.*) (playing) card; **K~n geben**, to deal; **K~n legen**, to tell fortunes from the cards; **alles auf eine K. setzen**, to put all one's eggs in one basket. **4.** (*Landk.*) map. **◆K~n-**, *comb. fm.* (a) card (player, table etc.); (b) map(-reading etc.). **◆K~spiel**, *n* (a) pack of cards; (b) game of cards.

Kartei [kar'tai], *f* -/-*en* card index. **◆K~karte**, *f* index/file card.

Kartell [kar'tɛl], *n* -*s*/-*e* cartel.

Kartoffel [kar'tɔfəl]. **I.** *f* -/-*n* potato. **II. K~-**, *comb.fm.* potato (salad etc.). **◆K~käfer**, *m* Colorado beetle, *N.Am:* potato bug. **◆K~knödel**, *m* potato dumpling. **◆K~puffer**, *m* potato pancake/fritter. **◆K~püree**, *n* mashed potatoes.

Karton [kar'tɔŋ], *m* -*s*/-*s* **1.** (*Material*) card, cardboard. 2. (*Schachtel*) cardboard box, carton.

Karussell [karu'sɛl], *n* -s/-s roundabout, merry-go-round

Karwoche ['kɑːrvɔxə], *f* -/no *pl* Holy Week.

kaschieren [ka'ʃiːrən], *v.tr.* to conceal.

Käse ['kɛːzə], *m* -s/- cheese. ◆**'K~blatt**, *n F: Pej:* rag. ◆**'K~kuchen** *m*, cheese-cake.

Kasern|e [ka'zɛrnə], *f* -/-n barracks. ◆**K~enhof**, *m* barrack square.

Kasino [ka'ziːno], *n* -s/-s 1. casino. 2. *Mil:* officer's mess.

Kasse ['kasə], *f* -/-n 1. (*a*) (*Behälter*) cash register, till; (*Zahlstelle*) cash desk; (*im Supermarkt*) check-out; (*b*) *Th: Cin: etc:* box office. 2. (*a*) *F:* **gut/knapp bei K. sein**, to be flush (with money)/short of cash; (*b*) (*Spielk.*) pool, *F:* kitty. 3. *F:* (*a*) (*Spark.*) savings bank; (*b*) (*Krankenk.*) health insurance (scheme). ◆**K~nbestand**, *m* cash balance. ◆**'K~nsturz**, *m F:* **K. machen**, to count one's worldly wealth. ◆**'K~nzettel**, *m* receipt, sales slip.

Kasserolle [kasə'rɔlə], *f* -/-n cast-iron frying pan.

Kassette [ka'sɛtə], *f* -/-n 1. (*a*) (*Kästchen* small box; (*Schmuck.*) case, casket; (*b*) (*Buchk.*) slipcase. 2. *Phot: Rec:* cassette. ◆**K~nrecorder**, *m* -s/- cassette recorder.

kassier|en [ka'siːrən], *v.tr.* to take (in) (money from customers etc.); to collect (rent etc.); (*Kellner usw.*) **darf ich bitte k.?** can I give you the bill? ◆**K~er(in)**, *m* -s/- (*f* -/-nen) cashier; *Th: etc:* box-office clerk.

Kastagnetten [kastan'jɛtən], *fpl* casta-nets.

Kastanie [kas'tɑːniə], *f* chestnut. ◆**K~nbaum**, *m* chestnut tree.

Kästchen ['kɛstçən], *n* -s/- small box; casket.

Kaste ['kastə], *f* -/-n caste.

Kasten ['kastən], *m* -s/- box; (*Briefk.*) letter/*N.Am:* mail box; (*Schauk.*) show-case; (*für Brot*) bin; **ein K. Bier**, a crate of beer. ◆**'K~wagen**, *m* box cart/*Rail:* car/*Aut:* van.

kastrieren [kas'triːrən], *v.tr.* to castrate (a man); to neuter, *F:* doctor (a pet).

Katalog [kata'loːk], *m* -(e)s/-e catalogue.

Katapult [kata'pʊlt], *n* -(e)s/-e catapult.

Katarrh [ka'tar], *m* -s/-e catarrh.

katastroph|al [katastro'faːl], *adj.* cata-strophic, disastrous. ◆**K~e** [katas'troːfə], *f* -/-n catastrophe, disaster. ◆**K~engebiet**, *n* disaster area.

Kategor|ie [katego'riː], *f* -/-n category. ◆**k~isch** [-'goːrɪʃ], *adj.* categorical (denial etc.); flat (refusal).

Kater ['kɑːtər], *m* -s/- 1. *Z:* tom cat. 2. *F:* **einen K. haben**, to have a hangover.

Katheder [ka'teːdər], *n* -s/- (lecturer's) reading desk; *Sch:* teacher's desk.

Kathedrale [kate'drɑːlə], *f* -/-n cathedral.

Kathode [ka'toːdə], *f* -/-n cathode.

Kathol|ik(in) [kato'liːk(in)], *m* -en/-en (*f* -/-nen) (*Roman*) Catholic. ◆**k~isch** [-'toːlɪʃ], *adj.* (*Roman*) Catholic.

Kätzchen ['kɛtsçən], *n* -s/- 1. kitten. 2. *Bot:* catkin.

Katze ['katsə], *f* -/-n *Z:* cat, *esp.* she-cat; **die K. aus dem Sack lassen**, to let the cat out of the bag; *F:* **das ist alles für die Katz**, that's a waste of effort. ◆**'K~nauge**, *n* 1. cat's eye. 2. *Aut: etc:* reflector. ◆**'k~nhaft**, *adj.* catlike, fe-line (movements etc.). ◆**'K~njammer**, *m* hangover. ◆**'K~nsprung**, *m F:* **es ist nur ein K.** (von hier), it's only a stone's throw (from here). ◆**'K~nwäsche**, *f F:* lick and a promise.

Kauderwelsch ['kaudərvɛlʃ], *n* -(e)s/*no pl F:* gibberish, double Dutch.

kau|en ['kauən], *v.tr. & i.* (*haben*) (*a*) to chew (food); (*b*) **an den Nägeln k.**, to bite one's fingernails. ◆**'K~gummi**, *n* chewing gum.

kauern ['kauərn], *v.i.* (*haben*) & *v.refl.* (**sich**) **k.**, (*Pers.*) to squat, (*Pers., Tier*) crouch (down).

Kauf [kauf]. I. *m* -(e)s/-e (*a*) purchase; *Fig:* **etwas (mit) in K. nehmen**, to put up with sth.; (*b*) (*Sache*) **ein guter/günstiger K.**, a good buy/bargain. II. **'K~-**, *comb.fm.* purchase (price etc.); (conditions etc.) of purchase. ◆**'k~en**, *v.tr.* to buy (sth.); **regelmäßig bei X k.**, to shop regularly at X's. ◆**'K~haus**, *n* department store. ◆**'k~lustig**, *adj.* eager to buy. ◆**'K~mann**, *m* (*a*) business man; (*Händler*) dealer; (*b*) *A:* shop-keeper; **zum K. gehen**, to go to the gro-cer's. ◆**'k~männisch**, *adj.* commercial (training, firm etc.); **k~männische Angestellter**, (clerical) employee in a busi-ness firm. ◆**'K~vertrag**, *m* contract of purchase; *Jur:* deed of sale.

Käuf|er(in) ['kɔyfər(in)], *m* -s/- (*f* -/-nen) buyer; (*Eink.*) shopper. ◆**'k~lich**, *adj.* for sale.

Kaulquappe ['kaulkvapə], *f* -/-n tadpole.

kaum [kaum], *adv.* hardly; ˈ**sie ist k. acht**, she is barely eight.

Kaution [kautsi'oːn], *f* -/-en *Jur:* security, guarantee; (*für einen Gefangenen*) bail.

Kautschuk ['kautʃuk], *n* -s/-e (india) rub-ber.

Kauz [kauts], *m* -es/-e 1. (small) owl. 2. *F:* **komischer K.**, odd bird, *N.Am:* screwball.

Kavalier [kava'liːr], *m* -s/-e gentleman. ◆**k~sdelikt**, *n* trivial offence.

Kavaller|ie [kavalə'riː], *f* -/-n cavalry. ◆**K~ist**, *m* -en/-en cavalryman, troop-er.

Kaviar ['kɑːviar], *m* -s/-e caviar.

keck [kɛk], *adj.* saucy, (*frech*) cheeky; (*vorlaut*) forward; (*forsch*) bold.

Kegel ['keːgəl], *m* -s/- 1. *Mth:* cone. 2. (*Spielk.*) skittle; (*Bowling*) pin. ◆**'K~bahn**, *f* skittle/*N.Am:* bowling al-ley. ◆**'k~förmig**, *adj.* conical.

◆'k~n, v.i. (haben) to play skittles, N.Am: to bowl.

Kehl|e ['ke:lə], f /-n throat. ◆'K~kopf, m larynx. ◆'K~kopfentzündung, f laryngitis.

Kehr|e ['ke:rə], f /-n (Kurve) sharp bend, esp. hairpin. ◆'k~en¹, v.tr. etwas nach außen, oben usw. k., to turn sth. outwards, upwards etc.; (Pers.) in sich gekehrt, withdrawn, lost in thought. ◆'k~en², v.i. & i. (haben) to sweep. ◆'K~icht, m & n -s/no pl sweepings. ◆'K~maschine, f (carpet, street) sweeper. ◆'K~reim, m refrain. ◆'K~seite, f /-n (Rückseite) reverse (of a coin etc.). ◆'k~tmachen, v.i.sep. (haben) to turn on one's heel.

keifen ['kaifən], v.i. (haben) to scold, bicker.

Keil [kail], m -(e)s/-e wedge. ◆'k~en, v.tr. to split (sth.) with a wedge. ◆'K~riemen, m V-belt.

Keiler ['kailər], m -s/- wild boar.

Keim [kaim], m -(e)s/-e Bot: & Fig: germ; Biol: embryo; Fig: etwas im K. ersticken, to nip sth. in the bud. ◆'k~en, v.i. (haben) to germinate. ◆'k~frei, adj. sterile. ◆'k~tötend, adj. germicidal, antiseptic.

kein [kain]. I. indef.art. no, not any; ich habe k. Geld/k~e Zeit, I've no money/time, I haven't any money/time; k. Wort mehr, not another word. II. indef.pron. 1. k~e(r), nobody, no one; k~er von beiden, neither (of them); ich kenne k~en, I don't know anyone/anybody. 2. (Sache) k~er/k~e/k~es, none, not one; ich habe k~e(s) (mehr), I haven't got any (more). ◆'k~es'falls, adv. on no account. ◆'k~es'wegs, adv. by no means; (überhaupt nicht) not in the least.

Keks [ke:ks], m -es/-e biscuit, N.Am: cookie.

Kelch [kɛlç], m -(e)s/-e 1. goblet. 2. Bot: calyx.

Kelle ['kɛlə], f /-n 1. H: ladle (for soup etc.). 2. (Maurerk.) trowel. 3. Rail: signalling disc.

Keller ['kɛlər], m -s/- cellar, (bewohnbar) basement. ◆'K~assel, f woodlouse.

Kellner ['kɛlnər], m -s/- waiter, Nau: Rail: steward. ◆'K~in, f /-nen waitress.

keltern ['kɛltərn], v.tr. to press (grapes, fruit etc.).

kenn|en ['kɛnən], v.tr.irr. to know (s.o., sth.); er kennt keine Rücksicht, he has no idea of consideration (for others); wir k. uns schon, we have already met. ◆'k~enlernen, v.tr.sep. to get to know (s.o., sth.); (treffen) to meet (s.o.); wir haben uns in Rom kennengelernt, we met in Rome. ◆'K~er, m -s/- expert, authority (+ gen/von + dat, on). ◆'k~tlich, adj. recognizable; etwas k. machen, to mark/identify sth. ◆'K~tnis, f /-se knowledge; etwas zur

K. nehmen, to take note of sth. ◆'K~wort, n Mil: etc: password. ◆'K~zeichen, n (a) (Merkmal) (distinguishing) feature; (b) (Zeichen) mark; (Abzeichen) badge; Aut: (polizeiliches) K~, registration number; N.Am: licence number. ◆'k~zeichnen, v.tr.sep. (a) (markieren) to mark (goods, parts etc.); (b) (charakterisieren) to characterize, distinguish (sth.). ◆'K~ziffer, f code number; Com: reference number.

kentern ['kɛntərn], v.tr. & i. (sein) to capsize.

Keramik [ke'rɑ:mik], f /-en 1. no pl ceramics, pottery. 2. eine K., a piece of pottery.

Kerb|e ['kɛrbə], f /-n notch; slot (for a peg etc.). ◆'K~holz, n F: etwas auf dem K. haben, to have blotted one's copybook.

Kerker ['kɛrkər], m -s/- Hist: dungeon; A: & Aus: prison.

Kerl [kɛrl], m -s/-e F: chap, fellow; P: bloke; esp. N.Am: guy.

Kern [kɛrn]. I. m -(e)s/-e 1. (nut) kernel; pip (of an orange, apple, grape); stone, N.Am: pit (of a cherry etc.). 2. Ph: Biol: nucleus. 3. Fig: core; heart (of a city etc.). II. 'K~, comb.fm. (a) Ph: nuclear (fuel, energy etc.); (b) Fig: central (problem, idea etc.); crucial (question, point). ◆'K~forschung, f nuclear research. ◆'K~gehäuse, n core (of an apple etc.). ◆'k~gesund, adj. healthy, as sound as a bell. ◆'k~ig, adj. earthy (words etc.); robust (person, style etc.). ◆'K~kraftwerk, n nuclear power station. ◆'K~obst, n apple-like fruit(s); pomes. ◆'K~physik, f nuclear physics. ◆'K~spaltung, f nuclear fission. ◆'K~waffe, f nuclear weapon.

Kerze ['kɛrtsə], f /-n 1. candle. 2. Aut: (sparking) plug. ◆'k~nge'rade, adj. bolt upright. ◆'K~nhalter, m candleholder. ◆'K~nständer, m candlestick.

keß [kɛs], adj. jaunty (hat); pert (girl, answer).

Kessel ['kɛsəl], m -s/- 1. (a) (Teek.) kettle; (b) (großer Topf) cauldron; (c) (Heizk., Dampfk.) boiler. 2. (Talk.) basin-shaped valley, hollow. ◆'k~treiben, n Fig: round-up (of a gang); Pol: witchhunt.

Kett|e ['kɛtə], f /-n (a) chain; (b) (Halsk.) necklace; string (of pearls), (gold, silver etc.) chain; (c) Fig: series, succession (of events etc.). ◆'k~en¹, v.tr. an j-n, etwas acc gekettet sein, to be bound/tied to s.o., sth. ◆'K~en², comb.fm. (a) chain (drive, Fig: reaction, smoker etc.); (b) tracked (vehicle).

Ketzer ['kɛtsər], m -s/- heretic. ◆'k~isch, adj. heretical.

keuch|en ['kɔyçən], v.i. (haben) to pant. ◆'k~husten, m whooping cough.

Keule ['kɔylə], f /-n 1. club. 2. Cu: leg.

keusch [kɔyʃ], adj. chaste. ◆'K~heit, f

-no pl chastity.
kichern ['kiçərn], *v.i.* (*haben*) to giggle, titter.
kidnappen ['kitnɛpən], *v.tr.* to kidnap.
Kiebitz ['ki:bits], *m -es/-e Orn:* lapwing.
Kiefer[1] ['ki:fər], *f -/-n* pine (tree).
◆**'K~nholz,** *n* pinewood.
Kiefer[2], *m -s/- Anat:* jaw.
Kiel [ki:l], *m -(e)s/-e* **1.** shaft (of a feather). **2.** *Nau:* keel. ◆**'K~wasser,** *n* wake.
Kieme ['ki:mə], *f -/-n* gill.
Kies [ki:s], *m -es/-e* gravel. ◆**'K~grube,** *f* gravel pit. ◆**'K~weg,** *m* gravel path.
Kiesel ['ki:zəl], *m -s/-* pebble. ◆**'K~stein,** *m* pebble.
Kilo ['ki:lo], *n -s/-(s)* kilo. ◆**'K~gramm,** *n* kilogram. ◆**K~meter** [kilo'me:tər], *m* kilometre. ◆**K~'metergeld,** *n* mileage allowance. ◆**K~'meterzähler,** *m* mileometer. ◆**'K~watt,** *n* kilowatt.
Kimme ['kimə], *f -/-n* notch (in a rifle sight).
Kind [kint], *n -(e)s/-er* child; **von K. auf,** from childhood; (*b*) (*Kleink.*) baby; **sie bekommt ein K.,** she's having a baby. ◆**'K~er-** ['kindər-], *comb.fm.* children's (book, shoes, choir, home etc.); (love etc.) of children; child's (voice, toy etc.). ◆**'K~erarzt,** *m*/**'K~erärztin,** *f* paediatrician. ◆**'K~erbett,** *n* junior bed. ◆**'K~e'rei,** *f -/-en* (*a*) childish behaviour; (*b*) triviality. ◆**'K~ergarten,** *m* kindergarten, nursery school. ◆**'K~ergeld,** *n* child allowance. ◆**'K~erkrippe,** *f* crèche, *N.Am:* day care (nursery). ◆**'K~erlähmung,** *f* infantile paralysis, *F:* polio. ◆**'k~er'leicht,** *adj. F:* dead easy. ◆**'k~erlos,** *adj.* childless. ◆**'K~erlosigkeit,** *f -/no pl* childlessness. ◆**'K~ermädchen,** *n* nursemaid. ◆**'k~erreich,** *adj.* large (family). ◆**'K~erspiel,** *n* (*a*) children's game; (*b*) *F:* pushover, cinch. ◆**'K~erstube,** *f* Fig: **er hat keine K.,** he has no manners. ◆**'K~erteller,** *m* dish for children. ◆**'K~erwagen,** *m* pram, *N.Am:* baby carriage. ◆**'K~esalter,** *n* infancy, childhood; **im K.,** in childhood. ◆**'K~heit,** *f -/no pl* childhood. ◆**'k~isch** ['kindiʃ], *adj.* childish (person, behaviour). ◆**'k~lich** ['kintliç], *adj.* childlike (behaviour). ◆**'K~skopf** ['kints-], *m F:* childish person.
Kinn [kin], *n -(e)s/-e* chin. ◆**'K~haken,** *m* hook (to the chin).
Kino ['ki:no], *n -s/-s* cinema, *N.Am:* movie theatre. ◆**'K~besucher,** *m* cinemagoer, *N.Am:* moviegoer.
Kiosk [ki'ɔsk], *m -(e)s/-e* kiosk.
Kippe ['kipə], *f -/-n* **1.** (*Müllk.*) dump, tip. **2.** *F:* **es steht auf der K.,** (*Gegenstand*) it's balanced precariously; *Fig:* (*Erfolg usw.*) it's touch and go. **3.** *F:* (*Stummel*) fag-end, *N.Am:* cigarette- butt.

◆**'k~en,** *v.* **1.** *v.i.* (*sein*) (*Schrank, Stoß Bücher usw.*) to tilt, (*umfallen*) topple (over). **2.** *v.tr.* (*a*) to tilt (sth.); (*b*) to tip (rubbish, gravel etc.). ◆**'K~schalter,** *m* tumbler switch.
Kirche ['kirçə], *f -/-n* church; **in die K. gehen,** to go to church. ◆**'K~en-,** *comb.fm.* church (choir, music etc.). ◆**'K~enlied,** *n* hymn. ◆**'K~gänger(in),** *m -s/-* (*f -/-nen*) churchgoer. ◆**'K~hof,** *m* churchyard. ◆**'k~lich,** *adj.* church (holiday, wedding etc.); ecclesiastical (office, dignitary etc.). ◆**'K~turm,** *m* church tower, steeple.
Kirsch- ['kirʃ-], *comb.fm.* cherry (tree, cake etc.). ◆**'K~kern,** *m* cherry-stone/*N.Am:* pit. ◆**'K~e,** *f -/-n* cherry. ◆**'K~wasser,** *n* kirsch.
Kissen ['kisən], *n -s/-* cushion; (*Kopfk.*) pillow. ◆**'K~bezug,** *m* cushion cover; (*Kopfk.*) pillow case.
Kiste ['kistə], *f -/-n* crate; box (of cigars etc.).
Kitsch [kitʃ], *m -(e)s/no pl* kitsch. ◆**'k~ig,** *adj.* kitschy.
Kitt [kit], *m -(e)s/-e* (adhesive) cement; (*für Fenster, Risse*) putty. ◆**'k~en,** *v.tr.* (*a*) to glue (broken china etc.); (*b*) to fix (a pane etc.) with putty.
Kittchen ['kitçən], *n -s/- F:* clink, jug.
Kittel ['kitəl], *m -s/-* (*a*) (workman's) overall; (*b*) housecoat; (doctor's etc.) (white) coat.
Kitz [kits], *n -es/-e Z:* kid (of a deer, goat).
Kitzel ['kitsəl], *m -s/no pl* tickle. ◆**'k~(e)lig,** *adj.* ticklish; *Fig:* tricky (situation). ◆**'k~eln,** *v.tr.* to tickle.
Kladde ['kladə], *f -/-n* (*Heft*) (rough) notebook; scribbling pad.
klaffen ['klafən], *v.i.* (*haben*) (*Loch, Wunde usw.*) to gape; (*Abgrund usw.*) to yawn.
kläffen ['klɛfən], *v.i.* (*haben*) (*Hund*) to yap, yelp.
Klage ['kla:gə], *f -/-n* (*a*) (*Beschwerde*) complaint; (*b*) *Jur:* action, suit. ◆**'k~n,** *v.i.* (*haben*) (*a*) to complain; (*b*) *Jur:* to take legal action; **auf Schadenersatz usw. k.,** to sue for damages etc.; (*c*) *Lit:* **über j-s Tod k.,** to mourn s.o.'s death.
Kläg|er(in) ['klɛːgər(in)], *m -s/-* (*f -/-nen*) *Jur:* (*Privatrecht*) plaintiff. ◆**'k~lich,** *adj.* (*a*) (*mitleiderregend*) pitiful, piteous (sight, crying etc.); (*b*) (*erbärmlich*) wretched (performance, result etc.); **k. versagen,** to fail miserably.
klamm [klam], *adj.* (*a*) numb, stiff (hands etc.); (*b*) cold and damp, clammy (clothes etc.).
Klammer ['klamər], *f -/-n* **1.** (paper etc.) clip; (*Heftk.*) (wire) staple; *Tchn:* clamp; *H:* (*Wäschek.*) (clothes) peg, *N.Am:* clothespin. **2.** (*Schriftzeichen*) bracket. ◆**'k~n,** *v.tr.* (*a*) to clip (things) together; (*b*) **sich an j-n, etwas** *acc* **k.,** to cling to s.o., sth.
Klang [klaŋ], *m -(e)s/-e* sound; (*Klang-*

farbe/ tone. ◆'k~**farbe**, *f* tone; timbre. ◆'k~**voll**, *adj.* sonorous (voice, language etc.); *Fig:* k~**voller Name**, illustrious name.

Klapp- ['klap-], *comb.fm.* folding (bed, seat etc.); hinged (lid). ◆**K~e** ['klapə], *f* *-/-n* (*a*) flap; drop-leaf (of a table); drop-front (of a desk etc.); *Anat:* valve; (*b*) *P:* (*Mund*) trap. ◆'k~**en**, *v.* 1. *v.tr.* (*haben*) (*a*) (*Tür usw.*) to bang; (*b*) *F:* (*Plan, Versuch usw.*) to work; (*Unternehmen usw.*) to go well; **nicht k.**, to go wrong. 2. *v.tr.* **nach oben k.**, to turn up (a collar etc.); to lift up (a flap etc.), tip up (a cinema seat etc.). ◆'k~**messer**, *n* jack-knife. ◆'K~**stuhl**, *m* folding chair/stool.

Klapper ['klapər], *f* *-/-n* (child's) rattle. ◆'K~**erkasten**, *m* *F:* rattletrap. ◆'k~**ern**, *v.i.* (*haben*) to clatter, (*lose Gegenstände usw.*) rattle. ◆'K~**erschlange**, *f* rattlesnake. ◆'k~(**e**)**rig**, *adj.* *F:* (*Pers.*) shaky; ramshackle (vehicle etc.).

Klaps [klaps], *m* *-es/-e* smack, slap.

klar [klaːr], *adj.* clear; **ich bin mir darüber** (**völlig**) **im k~en, daß ...**, I am (perfectly) aware/(fully) realize that ... ja k.! yes, of course! *N.Am:* sure thing! *Mil: etc:* **k. zum Gefecht**, ready for action. ◆'K~**heit**, *f* *-/no pl* clarity; lucidity. ◆'k~**machen**, *v.tr.sep.* **j-m etwas k.**, to make sth. clear to s.o. ◆'k~**sehen**, *v.i.sep.irr.92* (*haben*) *F:* to see daylight. ◆'k~**sichtfolie**, *f* transparent foil. ◆'k~**stellen**, *v.tr.sep.* to clarify; **k., daß ...**, to make it clear that ...

Klär|anlage ['klɛːrʔanlaːgə], *f* sewage works. ◆'k~**en**, *v.tr.* to clarify (a liquid, *Fig:* problem); to treat (sewage); **sich k.**, to become clear. ◆'K~**ung**, *f* *-/no pl* clarification.

Klarinette [klari'nɛtə], *f* *-/-n* clarinet.

Klasse ['klasə]. I. *f* *-/-n* class; **ein Hotel/Rail: eine Fahrkarte erster K.**, a first-class hotel/*Rail:* ticket; *F:* (*Spieler*) er **ist große K.**! he's great stuff! II. **k.**, *adj.* *F:* smashing, *N.Am:* swell. ◆'K~**n-**, 'k~**n-**, *comb.fm.* class (hatred, distinctions, *Sch:* teacher etc.). ◆'K~**narbeit**, *f* (written) class test. ◆'k~**nbewußt**, *adj.* class-conscious. ◆'K~**nbuch**, *n* class register. ◆'K~**nkamerad(in)**, *m(f)* classmate. ◆'K~**nkampf**, *m* class struggle. ◆'k~**nlos**, *adj.* classless. ◆'K~**nsprecher(in)**, *m(f)* class captain. ◆'K~**nzimmer**, *n* classroom.

Klassifi|kation [klasifikatsi'oːn], *f* *-/-en* classification. ◆k~**i'zieren**, *v.tr.* to classify.

Klass|ik ['klasik], *f* *-/no pl* classicism; (*Zeit*) classical period. ◆'K~**iker**, *m* *-s/-* classical author/*Mus:* composer. ◆'k~**isch**, *adj.* (*a*) classical; (*b*) (*vorbildlich*) classic (example).

Klatsch [klatʃ], *m* *-es/-e* **1.** (*Geräusch*) smack; (*aufs Wasser*) splash; (*Schlag*) slap. **2.** *no pl F:* gossip. ◆'K~**base**, *f* *F:* (*Pers.*) gossip. ◆'K~**e**, *f* *-/-n* (*fly*) swatter. ◆'k~**en**, *v.tr. & i.* (*haben*) (*a*) to slap (sth.); (*b*) to clap; **j-m Beifall k.**, to applaud s.o.; (*c*) *F:* to gossip. ◆'K~**mohn**, *m* field/corn poppy. ◆'k~**naß**, *adj.* *F:* soaking wet (clothes etc.); (*Pers.*) soaked to the skin. ◆'K~**spalte**, *f* gossip column.

Klaue ['klauə], *f* *-/-n* **1.** *Orn: Z:* claw; talon (of bird of prey); *Z:* (*Hand*) paw. **3.** *F:* (*Schrift*) scrawl, scribble. ◆'k~**n**, *v.tr.* *F:* to pinch, swipe (sth.) (*j-m/von j-m*, from s.o.); to crib (an idea etc.).

Klausel ['klauzəl], *f* *-/-n* *Jur: etc:* clause.

Klausur [klau'zuːr], *f* written examination/test.

Klaviatur [klavia'tuːr], *f* *-en* keyboard.

Klavier [kla'viːr], *n* *-s/-e* piano.

kleb|en ['kleːbən], *v.* **1.** *v.tr.* to stick, (*mit Klebstoff*) glue (sth.). **2.** *v.i.* (*haben*) to stick, (*Kleider usw.*) cling (**an/auf etwas dat**, to sth.). ◆'K~**estreifen**, *m* adhesive/*F:* sticky tape. ◆'K~**rig**, *adj.* sticky. ◆'K~**stoff**, *m* adhesive; glue.

kleck|ern ['klɛkərn], *v.tr. & i.* (*haben*) to spill (soup etc.). ◆'K~**s**, *m* *-es/-e* (ink) blot; blob, dab (of paint); splodge (of dirt etc.). ◆'k~**sen**, *v.i.* (*haben*) to make blots.

Klee [kleː], *m* *-s/no pl* clover. ◆'K~**blatt**, *n* clover-leaf.

Kleid [klait], *n* *-(e)s/-er* (*a*) dress; (*b*) *pl* K~**er**, clothes. ◆'k~**en** [-dən], *v.tr.* (*a*) to dress, clothe (s.o.); **sich sportlich usw. k.**, to wear sporting etc. clothes; **der Mantel kleidet dich gut**, the coat suits you. ◆'K~**erbügel**, *m* coat hanger. ◆'K~**erbürste**, *f* clothes brush. ◆'K~**erschrank**, *m* wardrobe, *N.Am:* clothes closet. ◆'k~**sam**, *adj.* becoming. ◆'K~**ung**, *f* *-/no pl* clothes, clothing.

Kleie ['klaiə], *f* *-/-n* bran.

klein [klain]. I. *adj.* (*a*) small, *esp. F:* little; **mein k~er Finger**, my little finger; **ein k. wenig**, a little bit; **unser K~er/unsere K~e**, our youngest son/daughter; **von k. an/auf**, from childhood; (*b*) low (number, figure, cost etc.); **ein Wort k. schreiben**, to write a word with a small (initial) letter; (*c*) (*unbedeutend*) minor (problem etc.); slight (misfortune, illness etc.); **das k~ere Übel**, the lesser evil; **meine k~ste Sorge**, the least of my worries. II. 'K~-, *comb.fm.* small (shareholder, car etc.). ◆'K~**anzeige**, *f* small ad. ◆'K~**arbeit**, *f* detail/painstaking work. ◆'k~**bildkamera**, *f* miniature camera. ◆'k~**bürgerlich**, *adj.* *Pej:* petty bourgeois. ◆'K~**format**, *n* small size. ◆'k~**gedruckt**, *attrib.adj.* in small print. ◆'K~**geld**, *n* (small/loose) change. ◆'K~**holz**, *n* (chopped) firewood; *F:* **aus j-m K. machen**, to make

mincemeat of s.o. ◆'K~igkeit, f -/-en
trifle; minor matter; F: (zum
Verschenken/Essen) a little something.
◆'k~kariert, adj. (material etc.) in
a small check; (b) F: Pej: narrow-minded
(views etc.). ◆'K~kind, n small child.
◆'K~kram, m F: (a) bits and pieces;
(b) Pej: trivia. ◆'k~kriegen, v.tr.sep.
F: to smash (sth.) up; j-n k., to squash
s.o. ◆'k~laut, adj. subdued, meek.
◆'k~lich, adj. petty; (engstirnig) small-
minded. ◆'K~lichkeit, f -/no pl pettiness. ◆'k~mütig, adj. faint-hearted,
pusillanimous. ◆'K~od ['klaino:t], n
-(e)s/-e & -ien Lit: jewel, gem.
◆'k~schneiden, v.tr.sep.irr.59 to chop
(onions, parsley etc.). ◆'K~st-,
comb.fm. smallest possible (amount etc.).
◆'K~stadt, f small town.
◆'k~städtisch, adj. small-town, provincial.

Kleister ['klaistər], f -/ (wallpaper etc.)
paste. ◆'k~n, v.tr. to paste, F: plaster
(sth.).

Klemm|e ['klɛmə], f -/-n 1. clamp, clip.
2. F: tight spot; in der K. sitzen, to be
in a fix. ◆'k~en, v. 1. v.tr. (a) (swän-
gen) to wedge, jam (sth.); (b) to clip
(sth.); (c) F: sich hinter etwas acc k., (i)
to get down to sth.; (ii) (weitermachen) to
get on with sth. 2. v.i. (haben) (Schublade
usw.) to jam, stick.

Klempner ['klɛmpnər], m -s/- plumber.

Klerus ['kle:rus], m -/no pl clergy.

Klette ['klɛtə], f -/-n Bot: burr.

Kletter-, comb.fm. climbing
(plant, pole, shoes etc.). ◆'K~er, m -s/-
climber. ◆'k~n, v.i. (sein) to climb;
(Pers.) (mit Mühe) to clamber, scramble.
◆'K~tour, f climbing trip.

klicken ['klikən], v.i. (haben) to click.

Klient(in) [kli'ɛnt(in)], m -en/-en (f -/
-nen) Jur: client.

Klima ['kli:ma], n -s/-s & -te climate.
◆'K~anlage, f air-conditioning (system). ◆'k~tisch ['kli:ma:tiʃ], adj. climatic. ◆'K~wechsel, m change of
climate/air.

klimpern ['klimpərn], v.i. (haben) (a) Pej:
(Pers.) to strum; (b) (Münzen usw.) to
chink.

Klinge ['kliŋə], f -/-n blade.

Klingel|el ['kliŋəl], f -/-n (bicycle, door
etc.) bell. ◆'K~elknopf, m bellpush.
◆'k~eln, v.i. (haben) (Klingel, Telefon
usw.) to ring; (Pers.) to ring the bell
(nach j-m, for s.o.); es klingelt, s.o./the
doorbell is ringing. ◆'k~en, v.i.irr.
(haben) (a) (Glocke, Gläser usw.) to ring;
(Stimme, Musikinstrument) to sound; (b)
(+ adj.) to sound (good, sad etc.).

Klin|ik ['kli:nik], f -/-en clinic.
◆'k~isch, adj. clinical.

Klinke ['kliŋkə], f -/-n (Griff)
(door)handle; latch.

klipp [klip], adj. k. und klar, clear as daylight; ich habe es ihm k. und klar ge-

sagt, I told him straight.

Klippe ['klipə], f -/-n rock (in the sea).

klirren ['klirən], v.i. (haben) (Gläser, Tas-
sen usw.) to clink, chink; k~de Kälte,
tingling cold.

Klischee [kli'ʃe:], n -s/-s (Wendung)
cliché. ◆'K~vorstellung, f hackneyed
idea.

Klo [klo:], n -s/-s F: loo, N.Am: john.

Kloake [klo'a:kə], f -/-n sewer; (Senkgrube) cesspool.

klobig ['klo:biç], adj. clumsy.

klopf|en ['klɔpfən], v. 1. v.i. (haben) (a)
to knock; es hat geklopft, there was a
knock; (b) j-m auf die Schulter k., to tap
s.o. on the shoulder; (c) (Herz)
(heftig) k., to pound (vor + dat, with);
(d) (Motor) to knock, F: pink, N.Am:
ping. 2. v.tr. (schlagen) to knock, drive (a
nail etc.) (in + acc, into); to beat (a carpet etc.). ◆'K~er, m -s/- (a) (door)
knocker; (b) H: carpet-beater.
◆'K~zeichen, n tap, knock.

Klöppel ['klœpəl], m -s/- clapper (of a
bell).

Klops [klɔps], m -es/- meatball.

Klosett [klo'zɛt], n -s/-s & -e lavatory,
toilet.

Kloß [klo:s], m -es/-e 1. Cu: dumpling. 2.
F: einen K. im Hals haben, to have a
lump in one's throat.

Kloster ['klo:stər], n -s/- (a) (für Mönche)
monastery; (b) (für Nonnen) convent.

Klotz [klɔts], m -es/-e block (of wood);
(zum Brennen) log; F: einen K. am Bein
haben, to have a millstone round one's
neck.

Klub [klup], m -s/-s club. ◆'K~sessel,
m big armchair.

Kluft¹ [kluft], f -/-e 1. (Felsspalte) cleft (in
rock). 2. Fig: gulf (between parties etc.).

Kluft², f -/-en F: Cl: outfit, gear.

klug [klu:k], adj. (a) (gescheit) clever,
bright; N.Am: smart (child, idea etc.);
intelligent (person, animal etc.); daraus/
aus ihm werd ich nicht k., I can't make
it/him out; (b) (einsichtig) wise; k~er
Rat, good advice. ◆'K~heit, f -/no pl
(a) cleverness; astuteness; (b) prudence.

Klump|en ['klumpən], m -s/- lump;
Min: nugget (of gold etc.). ◆'k~ig,
adj. lumpy (sauce etc.).

knabbern ['knabərn], v.tr. & i. (haben) to
nibble (an + dat, at).

Knabe ['kna:bə], m -n/-n A: & Lit: boy.
◆'K~nchor, m boys' choir.
◆'k~nhaft, adj. boyish.

Knack [knak], m -(e)s/-e crack.
◆'k~en, v. 1. v.i. (haben) (Zweige
usw.) to crack. 2. v.tr. (a) to crack (a nut
etc.); (b) F: to pick (a lock), crack (a
safe). ◆'k~ig, adj. F: crisp (salad),
crunchy (roll etc.). ◆'K~s, m -es/-e F:
(a) (Geräusch, Sprung) crack; (b) defect.
◆'K~wurst, f pork sausage.

Knäckebrot ['knɛkəbro:t], n crispbread.

Knall [knal], m -(e)s/-e (a) bang; crack (of

a shot, whip etc.); pop (of a cork); (b) F:
K. und Fall, at once; (auf der Stelle) on
the spot; (c) F: (Pers.) **einen K. haben**,
to be crackers. ◆'**K~bonbon**, n (party)
cracker, N.Am: favor. ◆'**K~effekt**, m
sensation; sensational part. ◆**k~en**, v.
1. v.i. (haben) to (go) bang; (Peitsche) to
crack; (Sektkorken) to pop; (sein) F: to
crash (in/gegen etwas acc, into/against
sth.). 2. v.tr. to slam (sth.); F: **j-m eine
k.**, to clout s.o. ◆**k~hart**, adj. F:
tough (business etc.); (Pers.) hard as
nails; Sp: (shot etc.) like a bullet.
◆'**k~ig**, adj. F: glaring (colour); flashy
(dress etc.). ◆'**k~rot**, adj. F: bright
scarlet.

knapp [knap], adj. **1.** Cl: tight, closefit-
ting. 2. (a) (Waren) scarce, Com: in short
supply; meagre (portion, pay etc.); (b)
(etwas weniger) just under; **eine k~e
Stunde**, barely an hour; (c) Sp: etc: **k~er
Sieg**, narrow win. **3.** (kurz) brief (summary etc.); terse (style etc.). ◆'**K~heit**,
f -/no pl (a) scantiness; shortage (**an Nahrungsmitteln usw.**, of provisions etc.);
(b) terseness.

knarren ['knarən], v.i. (haben) to creak.

Knast [knast], m -(e)s/-e P: clink.

knattern ['knatərn], v.i. (haben) (Gewehr,
Motorrad) to bang away, (MG) crackle.

Knäuel ['knɔʏəl], n -s/- ball (of wool
etc.).

Knauf [knauf], m -(e)s/-e knob (of a door
etc.).

knauserig ['knauzəriç], adj. stingy,
tight-fisted. ◆'**k~n**, v.i. (haben) to
skimp.

knautsch|en ['knautʃən], v.tr. & i. (ha-
ben) to crumple (material, paper etc.).
◆'**K~zone**, f Aut: crumple zone.

Knebel ['kne:bəl], m -s/- gag. ◆'**k~n**,
v.tr. to gag (s.o.).

Knecht [knɛçt], m -(e)s/-e **1.** A: farmhand. 2. Pej: Fig: slave.

kneif|en ['knaifən], v.irr. **1.** v.tr. to pinch
(s.o.). 2. v.i. (haben) F: **vor etwas dat k.**,
to back out of sth. ◆'**K~zange**, f (pair
of) pincers.

Kneipe ['knaipə], f -/-n F: pub; N.Am:
bar.

kneten ['kne:tən], v.tr. to knead (dough
etc.).

Knick [knik], m -(e)s/-e kink, sharp bend;
(Falte) fold, crease. ◆'**k~en**, v. **1.** v.tr.
(a) to bend (wire etc.); to crease (paper
etc.); (brechen) to snap (a twig etc.);
einen geknickten Eindruck machen, to
look dejected. 2. v.i. (sein) to bend (at an
angle); (brechen) to snap.

Knicks [kniks], m -es/-e curtsey; **einen K.
machen**, to curtsey.

Knie [kni:], n -s/- ['kni:ə] knee.
◆'**K~beuge**, f knees-bend, N.Am:
knee-bend. ◆'**K~fall**, m **einen K. tun**,
to go down on one's knees (**vor j-m**, to
s.o.). ◆'**K~gelenk**, n knee joint.
◆'**K~kehle**, f hollow of the knee.

◆**k~n** [kni:ən], v.refl. & i. (haben) to
kneel. ◆'**K~scheibe**, f knee-cap.
◆'**K~strumpf**, m knee-length sock.

Kniff [knif], m -(e)s/-e **1.** crease (in paper,
material etc.). 2. F: knack (of doing
sth.). ◆'**k~lig**, adj. fiddly (task etc.);
(heikel) tricky (question etc.).

knipsen ['knipsən], v.tr. (a) to punch (a
ticket etc.); (b) to flick (a switch etc.); (c)
Phot: F: to snap.

Knirps [knirps], m -es/-e **1.** F: little chap,
Brit: titch. 2. R.t.m. folding umbrella.

knirschen ['knirʃən], v.i. (haben) to
grate, grind; (Sand, Schnee usw.) to
crunch; **mit den Zähnen k.**, to grind/
gnash one's teeth.

knistern ['knistərn], v.i. (haben) (Feuer
usw.) to crackle.

knitter|frei ['knitərfrai], adj. crease-
resistant. ◆'**k~n**, v.i. (haben) to crease.

Knoblauch ['kno:plaux], m -(e)s/no pl
garlic.

Knöchel ['knœçəl], m -s/- (a) (Fuß.)
ankle; (b) (Finger.) knuckle.

Knoch|en ['knɔxən], m -s/- bone.
◆'**K~enbruch**, m (bone) fracture.
◆'**K~enmark**, n (bone) marrow.
◆'**k~ig**, adj. bony.

Knödel ['knø:dəl], m -s/- dumpling.

Knolle ['knɔlə], f -/-n Bot: corm, tuber.

Knopf [knɔpf], m -(e)s/-e (a) button; (b)
knob (on radio etc.). ◆'**K~loch**, n buttonhole.

knöpfen ['knœpfən], v.tr. to button (up)
(a jacket etc.).

Knorpel ['knɔrpəl], m -s/- **1.** Anat: carti-
lage. 2. Cu: gristle. ◆'**k~(e)lig**, adj. (a)
cartilaginous (tissue etc.); (b) gristly
(meat etc.).

knorrig ['knɔriç], adj. gnarled (tree etc.).

Knospe ['knɔspə], f -/-n bud. ◆'**k~n**,
v.i. (haben) (Baum usw.) to bud.

Knot|en ['kno:tən]. **I.** m -s/- (also Nau:)
knot; Bot: node (on a stem); Med: lump
(in the breast etc.). **II. k.**, v.tr. to knot
(string etc.). ◆'**K~enpunkt**, m junction, intersection of roads, railway lines
etc.)

knüll|en ['knylən], v.tr. to crease, crum-
ple (material etc.). ◆'**K~er**, m -s/- F:
(a) (smash) hit; (Zeitungsartikel) sensation; (b) fantastic idea.

knüpfen ['knypfən], v.tr. (a) to knot (a
tie, carpet etc.); to tie (shoelaces); (b)
Fig: to attach (hopes, condition etc.)
(**an + dat**, to).

Knüppel ['knypəl], m -s/- **1.** club, cudgel;
(policeman's) truncheon. 2. Av: joystick;
Aut: gear lever. ◆'**k~n**, v.tr. to beat
(s.o.) with a club/truncheon.

knurren ['knurən], v.i. (haben) (a) (Hund
usw.) to growl, snarl; (Magen) to rumble;
(b) to grumble.

knusprig ['knuspriç], adj. crisp, crunchy
(biscuit etc.); crusty (bread etc.).

k.o. [ka:'o:], pred.adj. (a) knocked out;
(b) F: **ich bin völlig k.o.**, I'm completely

whacked.

Koalition [koalitsi'o:n], *f* -/-en *Pol: etc:* coalition.

Kobalt ['ko:balt], *n* -(e)s/no *pl* cobalt.

Kobold ['ko:bɔlt], *m* -(e)s/-e goblin, imp.

Kobra ['ko:bra], *f* -/-s cobra.

Koch [kɔx], *m* -(e)s/ːe cook.◆**'K~buch**, *n* cookery book, N.Am: cookbook. ◆**'k~en**, *v.* 1. *v.tr.* (a) to cook (meat, vegetables, a meal etc.); (b) *(sieden lassen)* to boil (water etc.); to make (tea, coffee etc.). 2. *v.i. (haben)* (a) to cook, do the cooking; **gut/schlecht k.**, to be a good/bad cook; (b) *(Wasser usw.)* to boil. ◆**'k~end**, *adj.* boiling. ◆**'K~gelegenheit**, *f* cooking facilities. ◆**'K~herd**, *m* cooker, N.Am: stove. ◆**'K~kunst**, *f* art of cooking, cookery. ◆**'K~löffel**, *m* wooden (mixing) spoon. ◆**'K~nische**, *f* kitchenette. ◆**'K~platte**, *f* ring, *esp.* N.Am: hot plate. ◆**'K~salz**, *n* (common) salt. ◆**'K~topf**, *m* saucepan.

Köchin ['kœçin], *f* -/-nen (woman) cook.

Köder ['kø:dər], *m* -s/- bait. ◆**'k~n**, *v.tr.* to lure, entice (fish, *Fig:* s.o.).

Koexistenz ['ko:ɛksis'tɛnts], *f* -/-en co-existence.

Koffein [kɔfe'i:n], *n* -s/no *pl* caffeine. ◆**k~frei**, *adj.* decaffeinated.

Koffer ['kɔfər], *m* -s/- suitcase, case. ◆**'K~radio**, *n* portable radio. ◆**'K~raum**, *m* boot, N.Am: trunk.

Kognak ['kɔnjak], *m* -s/-s brandy, cognac.

Kohl [ko:l], *m* -(e)s/-e cabbage. ◆**'K~dampf**, *m* P: ravenous hunger. ◆**'K~rabi**, *m* -(s)/-(s) kohlrabi. ◆**'K~rübe**, *f* swede, N.Am: rutabaga.

Kohle ['ko:lə], *f* -/-n 1. (a) coal; (b) *(Zeichenk.)* charcoal. 2. P: *(Geld)* K~n, cash, dough. ◆**'K~hydrat**, *n* carbohydrate. ◆**'K~en-**, *comb.fm.* (a) coal (bunker, heating, industry etc.); (b) *Ch:* carbon (dioxide, monoxide etc.). ◆**'K~enbergwerk**, *n*/'**K~engrube**, *f* coalmine. ◆**'K~ensäure**, *f* (a) *Ch:* carbonic acid; (b) *(in Getränken)* fizz, gas. ◆**'K~enstoff**, *m* carbon. ◆**'K~epapier**, *n* carbon paper. ◆**'K~ezeichnung**, *f* charcoal drawing.

Köhler ['kø:lər], *m* -s/- charcoal-burner.

Koje ['ko:jə], *f* -/-n *Nau:* bunk, berth.

Kokain [koka'i:n], *n* -s/no *pl* cocaine.

kokett [ko'ket], *adj.* coquettish, flirtatious. ◆**k~ieren** [-'ti:rən], *v.i. (haben)* to flirt.

Kokos- ['ko:kɔs-], *comb.fm.* coconut (fibre, mat, palm etc.). ◆**'K~nuß**, *f* coconut.

Koks [ko:ks], *m* -es/-e coke.

Kolben ['kɔlbən], *m* -s/- 1. *Tchn:* piston. 2. *(Gewehrk.)* rifle butt. 3. *Ch:* (laboratory) flask. 4. *Bot:* (corn) cob.

Kolchose [kɔl'ço:zə], *f* -/-n collective farm.

Kolibri ['ko:libri], *m* -s/-s humming bird.

Kolik ['ko:lik], *f* -/-en colic.

Kollaps ['kɔlaps], *m* -es/-e collapse.

Kolleg [kɔ'le:k], *n* -s/-s course of lectures. ◆**K~mappe**, *f* slim briefcase.

Kollege [kɔ'le:gə], *m* -n/-n colleague. ◆**k~ial** [-legi'a:l], *adj.* helpful, friendly (attitude etc.). ◆**K~in** [-'le:gin], *f* -/-nen (female) colleague.

Kollekte [kɔ'lɛktə], *f* -/-n collection. ◆**K~i'on** [-tsi'o:n], *f* -/-en collection *(esp.* of dresses, shoes etc.); *Com:* range; selection. ◆**k~iv** [-'ti:f], *adj.* collective.

kolli|dieren [kɔli'di:rən], *v.i. (sein)* to collide. ◆**K~sion** [-zi'o:n], *f* -/-en collision; *Fig:* clash.

Köln [køln]. *Pr.n.n* -s. Cologne. ◆**'k~isch**, *adj.* (of) Cologne; **K. Wasser**, eau de Cologne.

kolonial [koloni'a:l], *adj.* colonial. ◆**K~i'alwaren**, *fpl* (esp. imported) groceries. ◆**K~ie** [-'ni:], *f* -/-n colony. ◆**k~i'sieren**, *v.tr.* to colonize (a country etc.).

Kolonne [ko'lɔnə], *f* -/-n column (of vehicles, troops, *Mth:* figures); *Aut:* string (of vehicles); line (of traffic); *Mil:* convoy; *Ind:* gang (of workers).

Koloß [ko'lɔs], *m* -sses/-sse giant. ◆**k~ossal** [-'sa:l], *adj.* colossal, gigantic (building etc.); *F:* terrific (luck etc.).

Koma ['ko:ma], *n* -s/-s & -ta coma.

Kombi|nation [kɔmbinatsi'o:n], *f* -/-en combination; *Fb: etc:* (concerted) move; *Cl:* overalls. ◆**k~'nieren**, *v.tr.* to combine (qualities etc.). ◆**K~wagen**, *m* estate car; N.Am: station wagon. ◆**K~zange**, *f* combination pliers.

Komet [ko'me:t], *m* -en/-en comet.

Komfort [kɔm'fo:r], *m* -s/no *pl* comfort; *(Luxus)* luxury; **Haus mit allem K.**, house with all mod. cons. ◆**k~abel** [-fɔr'ta:bəl], *adj.* comfortable.

Kom|ik ['ko:mik], *f* -/no *pl* comedy, comic effect. ◆**'K~iker**, *m* -s/- comedian. ◆**'k~isch**, *adj.* funny.

Komitee [komi'te:], *n* -s/-s committee.

Komma ['kɔma], *n* -s/-s comma; **vier K. fünf**, four point five.

Kommand|ant [kɔman'dant], *m* -en/-en commanding officer; commandant (of a fort etc.). ◆**K~eur** [-'dø:r], *m* -s/-e commander (of a large unit). ◆**k~ieren** [-'di:rən], *v.tr. Mil: etc:* to command (an army etc.); *Nau:* to captain (a ship); *F:* to order (s.o.) about. ◆**K~o** [-'mando], *n* -s/-s 1. (word of) command, order. 2. *Mil:* command; **das K. haben/führen**, to be in command **(über** + *acc*, of). 3. *(Verband)* squad, detachment.

kommen ['kɔmən]. I. *v.i.irr.53 (sein)* (a) to come; *(ankommen)* to arrive; **wann k. wir nach Graz?** when do we get to Graz? **sie kommt immer zu spät**, she is always late; **angekrochen k.**, to come crawling along; **ins Gefängnis/in den Himmel k.**, to go to prison/heaven; **jetzt k. Sie an die Reihe**, now it's your turn; **der Regen**

kommt durch diesen Riß, the rain comes (in) through this crack; **die Kisten k. in den Keller,** the crates go in the cellar; **woher kommt es, daß ...?** how is it that ...? *F:* **das kommt davon!** that happens! it serves you/him/her/them right! **einen Installateur usw. k. lassen,** to have sth. sent; **etwas k. lassen,** to have sth. sent; *(bestellen)* to order sth.; *(b)* (impers.) *(geschehen)* to happen; *(sich ergeben)* to result; **es kam zu einer Vereinbarung,** agreement was reached; **es kam ganz anders (als erwartet),** it turned out quite differently (from what we had expected); *(c)* (es schaffen) **ich komme nicht mehr in dieses Kleid,** I can't get into this dress any more; **er kommt einfach nicht dazu,** he just doesn't get round to it; *(d)* (kosten) **wie teuer kommt diese Vase?** how much is this vase? **wenn es hoch kommt,** at the most; *(e)* **j-m grob/frech k.,** to be rude/cheeky to s.o.; **j-m gelegen/ungelegen k.,** to come at the right/wrong moment for s.o.; **zu etwas** dat **k.,** to get hold of sth.; **zu sich** dat **k.,** to regain consciousness, *F:* come round; **in Schwierigkeiten usw. k.,** to get into difficulties etc.; **wie bist du darauf gekommen?** what made you think of that? **um etwas** acc **k.,** to lose/be deprived of sth. **II. K.,** n *-s/no pl* coming, arrival; **im K. sein,** (Pers., Firma) to be on the way up; *(modisch werden)* to become fashionable. ◆**'k~d,** adj. coming; **k~de Generationen,** future generations.

Kommentar [kɔmɛn'taːr], m *-s/-e* commentary *(zu + dat, on)*; *(Bemerkung)* comment. ◆**K~ator** [-'taːtɔr], m *-s/-en* commentator. ◆**k~ieren** [-'tiːrən], v.tr. to comment on (sth.).

kommerziell [kɔmɛrtsi'ɛl], adj. commercial.

Kommilitone [kɔmili'toːnə], m *-n/-n* fellow student.

Kommiß [kɔ'mis], m *-sses/no pl F:* army (life).

Kommissar [kɔmi'saːr], m *-s/-e* (a) (government) commissioner; *(b)* (police) superintendent.

Kommission [kɔmisi'oːn], f *-/-en* commission; board (of examiners etc.); *Com:* **(Waren) in K.,** (goods) on sale or return.

Kommode [kɔ'moːdə], f *-/-n* chest of drawers, *N.Am:* dresser.

Kommun|**al** [kɔmu'naːl], comb.fm. local (politics, election etc.). ◆**K~ikation** [-ikatsi'oːn], f *-/-en* communication. ◆**K~ion** [-ni'oːn], f *-/-en* Communion. ◆**K~iqué** [-yni'ke:], m *-s/-s* communiqué. ◆**K~ismus** [-u'nismus], m */no pl* communism. ◆**K~ist(in),** m *-en/-en* (f *-/-nen*) Communist. ◆**k~istisch,** adj. Communist.

Komödie [kɔ'møːdiə], f *-/-n* comedy.

kompakt [kɔm'pakt], adj. compact.

Kompanie [kɔmpa'niː], f *-/-en* company.

Komparativ ['kɔmparatiːf], m *-s/-e* comparative.

Kompaß ['kɔmpas], m *-sses/-sse* compass.

kompet|**ent** [kɔmpe'tɛnt], adj. competent (authority etc.). ◆**K~enz,** f *-/-en* authority; competence.

komplett [kɔm'plɛt], adj. complete.

komplex [kɔm'plɛks]. **I.** adj. complex. **II. K.,** m *-es/-e also Psy:* complex.

Kompli|**kation** [kɔmplikatsi'oːn], f *-/-en* complication. ◆**k~ziert,** adj. complicated (problem etc.); *(knifflig)* tricky (job etc.).

Kompliment [kɔmpli'mɛnt], n *-(e)s/-e* compliment.

Komplize [kɔm'pliːtsə], m *-n/-n* accomplice.

Komplott [kɔm'plɔt], n *-(e)s/-e* plot, *(Verschwörung)* conspiracy.

kompo|**nieren** [kɔmpo'niːrən], v.tr. to compose (a piece); to write (a song). ◆**k~'nist,** m *-en/-en* composer.

Kompost [kɔm'pɔst], m *-(e)s/-e* compost. ◆**K~haufen,** m compost heap.

Kompott [kɔm'pɔt], n *-(e)s/-e* stewed fruit.

Kompress|**e** [kɔm'prɛsə], f *-/-n* compress. ◆**K~or** [-'prɛsɔr], m *-s/-en* compressor.

Kompromiß [kɔmpro'mis], m *-sses/-sse* compromise. ◆**k~loß,** adj. uncompromising.

Konden|**sation** [kɔndɛnzatsi'oːn], f *-/-en* condensation. ◆**K~sator** [-'zaːtɔr], m *-s/-en* condenser. ◆**k~'sieren,** v.tr. to condense (vapour etc.). ◆**K~smilch** ['-dɛns-], f evaporated milk.

Kondition [kɔnditsi'oːn], f *-/-en* **1.** *Com: usu.pl* **K~en,** terms, conditions. **2.** *no pl Sp:* (physical) fitness. ◆**K~schwäche,** f *Sp:* lack of fitness. ◆**K~straining,** n fitness training.

Konditor [kɔn'diːtɔr], m *-s/-en* confectioner; *(Tortenbäcker)* pastrycook. ◆**K~ei** [-dito'rai], f *-/-en* (confectionery and) cake/*N.Am:* pastry shop.

Kondom [kɔn'doːm], m/n *-s/-s* condom.

Konfekt [kɔn'fɛkt], n *-(e)s/-e* confectionery, *N.Am:* candy.

Konfektion [kɔnfɛktsi'oːn], f *-/-en* ready-to-wear clothes.

Konfer|**enz** [kɔnfe'rɛnts], f *-/-en* **1.** *(Sitzung)* (business) meeting. **2.** *(Tagung)* conference. ◆**k~ieren** [-e'riːrən], v.i. *(haben)* to confer.

Konfession [kɔnfɛsi'oːn], f *-/-en* (religious) denomination. ◆**k~ell** [-io'nɛl], adj. denominational. ◆**k~slos,** adj. belonging to no religious denomination. ◆**K~sschule,** f denominational school.

Konfetti [kɔn'fɛti], n *-s/no pl* confetti.

Konfirm|**and(in)** [kɔnfir'mant(-din)], m *-en/-en* (f *-/-nen*) confirmation candidate. ◆**K~ation** [-atsi'oːn], f *-/-en* confirmation. ◆**k~ieren** [-'miːrən], v.tr. to confirm (s.o.).

konfiszieren [kɔnfis'tsiːrən], v.tr. to confiscate (property).

Konfitüre [kɔnfiˈtyːrə], f -/-n jam.

Konflikt [kɔnˈflikt], m -(e)s/-e conflict; *Ind:* dispute.

konform [kɔnˈfɔrm], adj. concurring (views etc.); **mit j-m k. gehen**, to concur with s.o.

Konfront|ation [kɔnfrɔntatsiˈoːn], f -/-en confrontation. ◆**k~ieren** [-ˈtiːrən], v.tr. to confront (s.o.).

konfus [kɔnˈfuːs], adj. confused, muddled.

Kongreß [kɔnˈgrɛs], m -sses/-sse congress.

König [ˈkøːniç], m -s/-e king. ◆**K~in** [-gin], f -/-nen queen. ◆**k~lich** [-kliç], adj. royal; *F:* **sich k. amüsieren**, to have a whale of a time. ◆**K~reich**, n kingdom. ◆**K~s-**, comb.fm. royal (crown, palace etc.); king's (son, daughter etc.).

konisch [ˈkoːniʃ], adj. conical.

Konjug|ation [kɔnjugatsiˈoːn], f -/-en conjugation. ◆**k~ieren** [-ˈgiːrən], v.tr. to conjugate (a verb).

Konjunktion [kɔnjunktsiˈoːn], f -/-en conjunction.

Konjunktiv [ˈkɔnjunktiːf], m -s/-e subjunctive (mood).

Konjunktur [kɔnjunkˈtuːr]. I. f -/-en 1. economic situation. 2. (Hochk.) boom. II. 'K~-, comb.fm. business (report etc.); economic (policy etc.).

konkav [kɔnˈkaːf], adj. concave.

konkret [kɔnˈkreːt, kɔŋ-], adj. concrete (proposal, example etc.); actual (situation etc.).

Konkurr|ent(in) [kɔnkuˈrɛnt(in)], m -en/-en (f -/-nen) competitor. ◆**K~enz** [-ˈrɛnts], f -/no pl competition; **j-m/sich dat K. machen**, to compete with s.o./one another; **unsere K.**, our competitors. ◆**k~enzfähig**, adj. Com: competitive. ◆**K~enzkampf**, m rivalry. ◆**k~ieren** [-ˈriːrən], v.i. (haben) to compete.

Konkurs [kɔnˈkurs, kɔŋ-], m -es/-e bankruptcy; **K. machen/in K. geraten**, to go bankrupt/(Firma) into liquidation.

könn|en [ˈkœnən]. I. v.irr. 1. v.tr. to know (how to do) (sth.), to be able to do (sth.); **k. Sie Deutsch?** can/do you speak German? **lesen k.**, to know how to/be able to read; **ich kann nichts dafür, I can't help it;** *F:* **er kann nichts für den Unfall,** the accident was not his fault. 2. *modal aux.* (a) to be able to; **ich kann (nicht) kommen,** I can(not) come; (b) (möglich sein) **es könnte verloren gegangen sein,** it could/might have got lost; **man kann nie wissen,** you never know; **kann sein!** maybe! possibly! (c) **er kann nicht anders,** he cannot do anything else; *P:* **du kannst mich (mal)!** get stuffed! (d) (dürfen) **kann ich jetzt gehen?** can/may I go now? II. **K.**, n -s/no pl ability. ◆**K~er,** m -s/- person of ability; ex-

pert.

konsequ|ent [kɔnzeˈkvɛnt], adj. (a) (folgerichtig) consistent (behaviour etc.); (b) (unbeirrbar) persistent, single-minded (person, efforts etc.). ◆**K~enz,** f -/-en (a) consistency; logic; (b) persistence; (c) (Folge) consequence.

konserv|ativ [kɔnzɛrvaˈtiːf], adj. conservative. ◆**K~atorium** [-vaˈtoːrium], m -s/-ien *Mus:* conservatoire, *N.Am:* conservatory. ◆**K~e** [-ˈzɛrvə], f -/-n 1. (Büchse) tin, *esp. N.Am:* can. 2. pl **K~n,** tinned/canned food. ◆**K~endose,** f tin, *esp. N.Am:* can. ◆**k~ieren** [-ˈviːrən], v.tr. to can, (im Glas) preserve (meat, fruit etc.), n preservative.

Konsonant [kɔnzoˈnant], m -en/-en consonant.

konstant [kɔnˈstant], adj. constant (velocity, number etc.); consistent (treatment, *Sp:* form etc.).

Konstitution [kɔnstitutsiˈoːn], f -/-en constitution. ◆**k~ell** [-oˈnɛl], adj. constitutional.

konstru|ieren [kɔnstruˈiːrən], v.tr. to construct, *Tchn:* (entwerfen) design (sth.); *Pej:* to fabricate (a story etc.). ◆**K~ktion** [-ruktsiˈoːn], f -/-en construction; (Bauweise) design (of an engine, car etc.). ◆**k~ktiv** [-ˈtiːf], adj. constructive.

Konsul [ˈkɔnzul], m -s/-n consul. ◆**K~at** [-ˈlaːt], n -(e)s/-e consulate.

konsultieren [kɔnzulˈtiːrən], v.tr. to consult (a doctor, dictionary etc.).

Konsum [kɔnˈzuːm], m -s/no pl consumption. ◆**K~gesellschaft,** f consumer society.

Kontakt [kɔnˈtakt], m -(e)s/-e contact; **mit j-m K. aufnehmen/haben,** to get/be in touch with s.o. ◆**k~arm,** adj. unable to make friends easily. ◆**k~freudig,** adj. sociable. ◆**K~linse,** f contact lens.

Konter- [ˈkɔntər-], comb.fm. counter- (attack, revolution etc.). ◆**k~n,** v.tr. & i. to counter.

Kontinent [ˈkɔntinɛnt], m -(e)s/-e continent.

Kontingent [kɔntinˈgɛnt], n -(e)s/-e quota (of goods); *Mil:* contingent.

kontinuierlich [kɔntinuˈiːrliç], adj. continuous.

Konto [ˈkɔnto]. I. n -s/-s & -ten account. II. **'K~-,** comb.fm. account (number etc.). ◆**K~auszug,** m statement of account. ◆**K~inhaber(in),** m(f), account-holder. ◆**K~stand,** m balance of an account.

Kontra [ˈkɔntra], n -s/-s (im Spiel) double. ◆**K~baß,** n double-bass. ◆**K~hent,** m -en/-en 1. opponent. 2. *Jur: etc:* party to a contract.

Kontrast [kɔnˈtrast], m -(e)s/-e contrast.

Kontroll- [kɔnˈtrɔl-], comb.fm. control (room, *Av:* tower etc.); check (list etc.).

◆K~e, *f* -/-n **1.** check; (*Überprüfung*) inspection (of goods, machinery etc.); checking (of tickets etc.); (*Zollk.*) customs check/control. **2.** *no pl* (*Beherrschung*) control (über j-n, etwas *acc*, of s.o., sth.). ◆K~eur [-'lø:r], *m* -s/-e supervisor, inspector; *Rail: etc:* ticket inspector. ◆k~ieren [-'li:rən], *v.tr.* (*a*) to check (baggage, weight, quality etc.); to supervise, (s.o., s.o.'s work); to inspect (tickets, papers); (*b*) to control (a company, the market etc.).

Kontroverse [kontro'verzə], *f* -/-n dispute.

Kontur [kon'tu:r], *f* -/-en contour, outline.

Konvention [konventsi'o:n], *f* -/-en (social) convention. ◆k~ell [-o'nel], *adj.* conventional.

Konversation [konverzatsi'o:n], *f* -/-en conversation. ◆K~slexikon, *n* popular encyclopedia.

konvex [kon'veks], *adj.* convex.

Konvoi ['konvoy], *m* -s/-s convoy.

Konzentr|**ation** [kontsentratsi'o:n], *f* -/-en concentration. ◆K~ati'onslager, *n* concentration camp. ◆k~ieren [-'tri:rən], *v.tr. & refl.* to concentrate.

Konzept [kon'tsept], *n* -(e)s/-e (*a*) (*Entwurf*) rough copy, draft (of an essay etc.); (*b*) (*Begriff*) concept, idea; das paßt ihm nicht ins K., it doesn't fit in with his plans/ideas.

Konzern [kon'tsern], *m* -s/-e *Ind:* combine, *N.Am:* conglomerate; group (of companies etc.).

Konzert [kon'tsert], *n* -(e)s/-e **1.** concert. **2.** (*Stück*) concerto.

Konzession [kontsesi'o:n], *f* -/-en **1.** *Com:* (trading, publican's etc.) licence. **2.** (*Zugeständnis*) concession.

Konzil [kon'tsi:l], *n* -s/-e council.

konzipieren [kontsi'pi:rən], *v.tr.* to draw up, draft (a document etc.).

Kooperat|**ion** [ko:operatsi'o:n], *f* -/-en co operation. ◆k~iv [-'ti:f], *adj.* co-operative.

Koordin|**ation** [ko:ordinatsi'o:n], *f* -/-en co-ordination. ◆k~ieren [-'ni:rən], *v.tr.* to co-ordinate (measures etc.).

Kopf [kopf], *m* -(e)s/-e head; **K. an K. liegen,** to be neck and neck; **K. hoch!** chin up! **den K. riskieren,** to risk one's neck; **aus dem K.,** from memory; **sich** *dat* **über etwas** *acc* **den K. zerbrechen,** to rack one's brains over sth.; **ich muß es mir durch den K. gehen lassen,** I'll have to think it over; **den K. verlieren,** to lose one's head; **den K. voll haben,** to have a lot on one's mind; **seinen eigenen K. haben,** to have a will of one's own; **sich** *dat* **etwas** *acc* **in den K. setzen,** to take sth. into one's head; **das mußt du dir aus dem K. schlagen,** you must put it right out of your head; **pro K.,** per head. ◆'K~ball, *m Fb:* header. ◆'K~bedeckung, *f* headgear.

◆'K~geld, *n* reward (for s.o.'s capture). ◆'K~haut, *f* scalp. ◆'K~hörer, *m* (pair of) headphones. ◆'K~jäger, *m* headhunter. ◆'K~kissen, *n* pillow. ◆'k~los, *adj.* headless; (*Pers.*) k. (vor Angst), panicstricken; *adv.* in a state of panic. ◆'K~rechnen, *n* mental arithmetic. ◆'K~salat, *m* cabbage lettuce. ◆'K~schmerzen, *mpl* headache. ◆'K schütteln, *n* shake of the head ◆'K~sprung, *m* header, (straight) dive. ◆'K~stand, *m* head stand. ◆'k~stehen, *v.i.sep.irr.100* (*haben*) *F:* to be at sixes and sevens. ◆'K~steinpflaster, *n* cobbled surface, cobbles. ◆'K~stoß, *m Fb:* header. ◆'K~tuch, *n* headscarf. ◆'K~über, *adj.* head first, headlong. ◆'K~weh, *n* -*s/no pl* headache. ◆'K~zerbrechen, *n* -*s/no pl* sich *dat* **K. machen,** to rack one's brains.

köpfen ['kœpfən], *v.tr.* (*a*) to behead (s.o.); to cut off the head of (an animal); (*b*) *Fb:* to head (the ball).

Kopie [ko'pi:], *f* -/-n **1** (an) copy; (*Doppel*) duplicate; (*Nachbildung*) replica; *Phot:* (*Abzug*) print. ◆k~ren [-'pi:rən], *v.tr.* to copy (s.o., sth.), to duplicate (a document). ◆K~rgerät, *n* (photo)copier.

Kopilot [ko:pilo:t], *m* -en/-en co-pilot.

Koppel[1] ['kɔpəl], *f* -/-n (enclosed) pasture; (*für Pferde*) paddock. ◆K~[2], *n* -s/- *Mil:* leather belt. ◆'k~eln, *v.tr.* to couple.

Koralle [ko'ralə], *f* -/-n coral. ◆K~nriff, *n* coral reef.

Korb [korp], *m* -(e)s/-e basket. ◆'K~ball, *m* basketball. ◆'K~sessel, *m* wicker chair.

Kord [kort], *m* -(e)s/-e corduroy.

Kordel ['kordəl], *f* -/-n cord (of a dressing gown etc.); (*Schnur*) string.

Kordon [kor'dõ:], *m* -s/-s (police etc.) cordon.

Korea [ko're:a]. *Pr.n.n* -s. Korea. ◆K~ner(in) [-re'a:nər(in)], *m* -s/- (*f* /-nen) Korean. ◆k~nisch [-re'a:niʃ], *adj.* Korean.

Korinthe [ko'rintə], *f* -/-n currant.

Kork [kork], *m* -(e)s/-no *pl* cork. ◆'K~en, *m* -s/- cork (stopper). ◆'K~enzieher, *m* -s/- corkscrew.

Korn[1] [korn], *n* -(e)s/-er & -e **1.** (*a*) (*Samenk.*) grain (of sand, salt etc.); (*b*) *no pl* (*Getreidek.*) grain, corn. **2.** (*pl* -e) (*front*) sight (of a rifle etc.); *Fig:* j-n, etwas aufs K. nehmen, to hit out at s.o., sth. ◆Korn[2], *n* -(e)s/-e grain spirit. ◆'K~blume, *f* cornflower.

Körn|**chen** ['kœrnçən], *n* -s/- small grain; granule. ◆'k~ig, *adj.* granular.

Körper ['kœrpər], *m* -s/- body. ◆'K~bau, *m* build, physique. ◆'K~behinderte(r), *m & f* (physically) disabled/handicapped person.

◆'K~geruch, m body odour. ◆'K~haltung, f posture. ◆k~lich, adj. physical. ◆'K~pflege, f personal hygiene. ◆'K~schaft, f -/-en Jur: etc: corporation. ◆'K~teil, m part of the body. ◆'K~verletzung, f physical injury; Jur: bodily harm.

Korps [kɔːr], n -/- Mil: corps.

korpulent [kɔrpu'lɛnt], adj. corpulent.

korrekt [kɔ'rɛkt], adj. correct; (Pers.) sehr k., very proper. ◆K~heit, f -/en correctness. ◆K~ur [-'tuːr], f /-en correction.

Korrespond|ent(in) [kɔrɛspɔn'dɛnt(in)], m -en/-en (f -/-nen) correspondent. ◆K~enz [-'dɛnts], f -/-en correspondence. ◆k~ieren [-'diːrən], v.i. (haben) to correspond.

Korridor [kɔri'doːr], m -s/-e corridor, passage.

korrigieren [kɔri'giːrən], v.tr. to correct.

korrupt [kɔ'rupt], adj. corrupt. ◆K~ion [-tsi'oːn], f -/-en corruption.

Korsett [kɔr'zɛt], n -s/-e corset.

Kose|name ['koːzənaːmə], m pet name. ◆'K~wort, n term of endearment.

Kosmet|ik [kɔs'meːtik], f -/no pl beauty culture, cosmetics. ◆K~ikerin, f -/-nen beautician. ◆k~isch, adj. cosmetic.

kosm|isch ['kɔsmiʃ], adj. cosmic. ◆K~onaut [-o'naut], m -en/-en cosmonaut. ◆K~opolit [-opo'liːt], m -en/-en cosmopolitan (person). ◆K~os, m -/no pl cosmos.

Kost [kɔst], f -/no pl food; (Verpflegung) board. ◆k~en¹ ['-], v.tr. to taste, sample (food, wine etc.). ◆K~probe, f sample, taste.

kost|bar ['kɔstbaːr], adj. precious, valuable. ◆'K~barkeit, f -/-en 1. no pl preciousness; high value. 2. treasure, valuable item. ◆'k~en² [-]. I. v.tr. to cost; was/wieviel kostet das Buch? how much is the book? II. K., pl. cost, expenses; (Auslagen) expenses; Jur: etc. costs; es geht auf meine K., it is at my expense/ F: on me; F: auf seine K. kommen, to get one's money's worth. ◆'k~enlos, adj. free (sample etc.); K~, free of charge. ◆'K~envoranschlag, m preliminary estimate/Brit: costing. ◆'k~spielig, adj. expensive, costly.

köstlich ['kœstliç], adj. (a) delicious, luscious (food, wine etc.); (b) delightful (humour etc.); sich k. amüsieren, to enjoy oneself immensely.

Kostüm [kɔs'tyːm], n -s/-e (a) (woman's) suit; (b) Th: costume; (c) (Maske) fancy dress costume. ◆k~ieren [-y'miːrən], v.tr. & refl. to dress (s.o., oneself) up (in a costume).

Kot [koːt], m -(e)s/no pl excrement; droppings (of animals, birds etc.). ◆'K~flügel, m wing, N.Am: fender.

Kotelett [kɔt'lɛt], n -s/-s chop; (vom Hals) cutlet.

Köter ['kœtər], m -s/- F: Pej: wretched hound; (Mischung) mongrel, N.Am: mutt.

Krabbe ['krabə], f -/-n (a) crab; (b) (Garnele) shrimp.

krabbeln ['krabəln], v.i. (sein) (Insekten) to scuttle; (Baby) to crawl.

krach [krax]. I. int. crash! bang! II. K., m -(e)s/-e & -e 1. (Lärm) row, racket. 2. F: (Streit) row; K. miteinander haben, to quarrel/have a row (with one another). ◆'k~en, v.i. (a) (haben) (Donner usw.) to crash; (b) (sein) to crash, smash.

krächzen ['krɛçtsən], v.i. (haben) (Rabe) to caw; F: (Pers.) to croak.

Krad [kraːt], n -(e)s/-er motorcycle.

Kraft [kraft]. I. f -/-e 1. (Stärke) (a) esp.pl strength; mit aller K., with all one's might; bei K~en sein, to be well/in good health; (b) force (of a blow, wind, Fig: an argument etc.); power (of an engine etc.); (c) (Vorschrift usw.) in K. treten, to come into effect/force. 2. (Arbeiter) Ind: worker; Com: employee. II. k., prep + gen by virtue of (one's authority etc.). ◆'K~ausdruck, m swearword. ◆'K~fahrer, m driver. ◆'K~fahrzeug, n motor vehicle. ◆'k~los, adj. weak, feeble; powerless (hand, arm etc.). ◆'K~probe, f trial of strength; showdown. ◆'K~stoff, m fuel (for an engine). ◆'k~voll, adj. powerful. ◆'K~wagen, m motor car, N.Am: automobile. ◆'K~werk, n power station.

kräftig ['krɛftiç], adj. strong (person, arms, voice etc.); sturdy (child, plant etc.); vigorous (growth etc.); heavy (rain); nutritious (food, soup). ◆'k~igen, v.tr. to strengthen (s.o., the body etc.). ◆'K~igung, f -/no pl strengthening; improvement (in one's health).

Kragen ['kraːgən], m -s/- collar. ◆'K~weite, f collar size.

Krähe ['krɛːə], f -/-n crow. ◆'k~n, v.i. (haben) (Hahn) to crow; (Baby) to coo.

Krake ['kraːkə], m -n/-n octopus.

krakeelen [kra'keːlən], v.i. (haben) F: to brawl.

krakeln ['kraːkəln], v.tr. F: to scrawl (words).

Kralle ['kralə], f -/-n claw; (Raubvogel) talon. ◆'k~n, v.tr. sich an etwas dat k., to cling to sth. (Z: with its claws).

Kram [kraːm], m -(e)s/no pl F: junk; Fig: der ganze K., the whole business. ◆'k~en, v.i. (haben) F: nach etwas dat k., to rummage about for sth.

Krampf [krampf], m -(e)s/-e (a) cramp; (b) convulsion; spasm. ◆'K~ader, f varicose vein. ◆'k~haft, adj. convulsive (twitch etc.); forced, desperate (laugh); Fig: frantic (effort etc.).

Kran [kraːn], m -(e)s/-e 1. crane. 2. (Wasserk.) tap.

Kranich ['kraːniç], m -s/-e crane.

krank [kraŋk], *adj.* (a) ill, *esp. N.Am:* sick; **ein K~er,** an invalid; (*unter Behandlung*) a patient; (b) diseased (organ, plant); weak (heart). ◆'**K~enbesuch,** *m* visit to a sick person; (doctor's) call on a patient. ◆'**K~enbett,** *n* sickbed. ◆'**K~engeld,** *n* sickness benefit. ◆'**K~enhaus,** *n* hospital. ◆'**K~enkasse,** *f* (national/private) health insurance scheme. ◆'**K~enpfleger(in),** *m(f)* male (female) nurse. ◆'**K~enschein,** *m* treatment form; certificate entitling a patient to treatment. ◆'**K~enschwester,** *f* nurse. ◆'**K~enversicherung,** *f* health insurance. ◆'**K~enwagen,** *m* ambulance. ◆'**k~haft,** *adj.* pathological (growth, state etc.); *Fig:* obsessive (jealousy, ambition etc.). ◆'**K~heit,** *f* *-/-en* illness, disease. ◆'**K~heitserreger,** *m* germ.

kränk|en ['krɛŋkən], *v.tr.* to hurt, offend (s.o.). ◆'**k~lich,** *adj.* sickly. ◆'**K~ung,** *f* *-/-en* slight.

Kranz [krants], *m* *-es/-e* wreath.

Kränzchen ['krɛntsçən], *n* *-s/-* 1. small wreath. 2. ladies' (coffee etc.) circle.

Krapfen ['krapfən], *m* *-s/-* (a) (meat etc.) fritter; (b) doughnut.

kraß [kras], *adj.* glaring (example, mistake); blatant (lie, injustice); **krasser Außenseiter,** rank outsider.

Krater ['kra:tər], *m* *-s/-* crater.

Kratz|bürste ['krats byrstə], *f* *-/-n* *F:* little shrew/vixen. ◆'**k~en,** *v.tr. & i.* (haben) to scratch; (*Pullover usw.*) to prickle; **das Eis vom Fenster k.,** to scrape the ice off/from the window. ◆'**K~er,** *m* *-s/-* 1. *Tchn:* scraper. 2. *F:* scratch. ◆'**k~ig,** *adj.* prickly, scratchy (wool etc.).

kraulen[1] ['kraulən], *v.i.* (haben) *Sp:* to (do the) crawl.

'kraulen[2], *v.tr.* to fondle (a cat, dog etc.) (with one's fingertips), ruffle (a cat's fur etc.).

kraus [kraus], *adj.* (a) fuzzy, crinkly (hair); creased, wrinkled (dress, brow); (b) *Fig:* muddled (thoughts etc.). ◆**K~e** ['krauzə], *f* *-/-n* *F:* tight perm.

kräuseln ['krɔyzəln], *v.tr.* (a) to curl, crimp (hair); (*Stoff*) to gather (a skirt etc.); *Fig:* (*Wind*) to ruffle, ripple (water etc.); (b) **sich k.,** (*Haare usw.*) to curl; (*Wasser*) to ripple.

Kraut [kraut], *n* *-(e)s/-er* 1. herb. 2. *no pl* (*Blätter*) leaves; tops (of turnips etc.). 3. *no pl* (*Kohl*) cabbage.

Kräuter- ['krɔytər-], *comb.fm.* herb (vinegar, tea etc.); herbal (liqueur etc.); (butter, cheese etc.) containing herbs.

Krawall [kra'val], *m* *-(e)s/-e* (a) (*Tumult*) riot; (b) *F:* (*Lärm*) racket, row.

Krawatte [kra'vatə], *f* *-/-n* tie. ◆'**K~nnadel,** *f* tie pin.

Krea|tion [kreatsi'o:n], *f* *-/-en* creation. ◆**k~tiv** [-ti'f], *adj.* creative. ◆**K~tur** [a'tu:r], *f* *-/-en* creature.

Krebs [kre:ps], *m* *-es/-e* 1. *Z:* crab;

(*Fluß.*) crayfish. 2. *Astr:* Cancer. 3. *Med:* cancer. ◆'**K~kranke(r),** *m & f* *decl. as adj.* cancer patient.

Kredit [kre'di:t], *m* *-(e)s/-e* credit; **auf K.,** on credit. ◆'**K~karte,** *f* credit card.

Kreide ['kraidə], *f* *-/-n* chalk. ◆'**k~bleich,** *adj.* as white as a sheet.

kreieren [kre'i:rən], *v.tr.* to create (a fashion, *Th:* a part etc.).

Kreis [krais]. **I.** *m* *-es/-e* (a) circle; **sich im K.** bewegen, to revolve; (*also Fig: Gespräch usw.*) to go round and round (in circles); *Fig:* (*Affäre*) **K~e ziehen,** to have repercussions; **weite K~e der Bevölkerung,** large sections of the population; (b) *Adm:* administrative district. **II.** '**K~-,** *comb.fm.* 1. (a) circular (motion, line etc.); (b) *Mth:* (area, arc etc.) of a circle. 2. *Adm:* district (authority, administration etc.). ◆**k~en** [-'kraizən], *v.i.* (haben) (*Vogel, Flugzeug usw.*) to circle; (*Planeten, Fig: Gedanken usw.*) **um etwas acc k.,** to revolve around sth. ◆'**k~förmig,** *adj.* circular (movement etc.). ◆'**K~lauf,** *m* circulation (of blood, money etc.); *Fig:* cycle (of life, seasons etc.). ◆'**K~laufstörung,** *f* circulatory disorder. ◆'**K~säge,** *f* circular saw. ◆'**K~stadt,** *f* chief town of a district. ◆'**K~verkehr,** *m* (traffic) roundabout, *N.Am:* traffic circle.

kreischen ['kraiʃən], *v.i.* (haben) to screech; to shriek.

Kreisel ['kraizəl], *m* *-s/-* (*Spielzeug*) top.

Krem [kre:m], *f* *-/-s* cream. ◆'**k~ig,** *adj.* creamy.

Krematorium [krema'to:rium], *n* *-s/-ien* crematorium, *N.Am:* crematory.

Krempe ['krɛmpə], *f* *-/-n* brim (of a hat).

Krempel ['krɛmpəl], *m* *-s/no pl* *F:* stuff, junk.

krepieren [kre'pi:rən], *v.i.* (sein) (a) (*Bombe usw.*) to burst; (b) *F:* (*Tier, P: Pers.*) to die a miserable death.

Krepp [krɛp], *m* *-s/-s* crêpe. ◆'**K~papier,** *n* crêpe paper. ◆'**K~sohle,** *f* crêpe(-rubber) sole.

Kresse ['krɛsə], *f* *-/-n* cress.

Kreta ['kre:ta]. *Pr.n.* *-s* Crete.

Kreuz [krɔyts]. **I.** *n* *-es/-e* 1. cross. 2. *Anat:* small of the back. 3. (*Karte*) club; (*Farbe*) clubs. **II. k.,** *adv.* **k. und quer,** higgledy-piggledy; (*hin und her*) this way and that. **III.** '**K~-,** *comb.fm.* (a) cross-stitch etc.); (b) ace, king etc.) of clubs. ◆'**k~en,** *v.tr.* (a) (*Linie, Straße usw.*) to cross, intersect (another line, road etc.); **sich k.,** (*Straßen, Linien*) to cross; (b) to cross (animals, plants etc.). 2. *v.i.* (haben) *Nau:* to cruise. ◆'**K~er,** *m* *-s/-* cruiser. ◆'**K~fahrt,** *f* *Nau:* cruise. ◆'**K~feuer,** *n* crossfire. ◆'**k~igen,** *v.tr.* to crucify (s.o.). ◆'**K~igung,** *f* *-/-en* crucifixion. ◆'**K~otter,** *f* adder, common viper. ◆'**K~ung,** *f* *-/-en* 1. intersection (of roads, railways); (*Straßenk.*) (road) junc-

tion, crossroads; (*Übergang*) crossing. 2.
Bot: Z: (*a*) crossing (of animals, plants);
(*b*) (*Tier, Pflanze*) cross. ◆'**K~verhör**,
n cross-examination. ◆'**K~worträtsel**,
n crossword puzzle. ◆'**K~zug**, *m* crusade.
kribbel|ig ['kribəliç], *adj. F:* edgy; (*unru-
hig*) fidgety (child etc.). ◆'**K~n**, *n -s/no
pl* tingling; pins and needles.
kriech|en ['kri:çən], *v.i.irr.55* (*sein*) to
crawl, (*sehr langsam*) creep; **vor j-m k.**, to
grovel/toady to s.o. ◆'**K~er**, *m -s/- Pej:*
crawler, creep. ◆'**k~erisch**, *adj. Pej:*
obsequious, grovelling. ◆'**K~spur**, *f*
crawler lane. ◆'**K~tier**, *n* reptile.
Krieg [kri:k], *m -(e)s/-e* war. ◆'**K~er**
['kri:gər], *m -s/-* warrior. ◆'**k~erisch**,
adj. warlike (attitude, people etc.); martial (bearing etc.). ◆'**k~führend**, *adj.*
belligerent. ◆'**K~führung**, *f* warfare.
◆'**K~s-**, *comb.fm.* war (service, damage, crime etc.); (outbreak, costs, state
etc.) of war. ◆'**K~sbemalung**, *f*
warpaint. ◆'**k~sbeschädigt**, *adj.*
(war) disabled. ◆'**K~sdienst-
verweigerer**, *m* conscientious objector.
◆'**K~serklärung**, *f* declaration of war.
◆'**K~sfall**, *m* **im K.**, in the event of
war. ◆'**K~sfuß**, *m F:* **mit j-m auf K.
stehen/leben**, to be at loggerheads with
s.o. ◆'**K~sgebiet**, *n* war zone.
◆'**K~sgefangene(r)**, *m & f decl. as
adj.* prisoner of war.
◆'**K~sgefangenschaft**, *f* captivity.
◆'**K~sgericht**, *n* court martial.
◆'**K~srecht**, *n* martial law.
◆'**K~sschauplatz**, *m* theatre of war.
◆'**K~sschiff**, *n* warship.
◆'**K~steilnehmer**, *m* combatant.
◆'**k~sversehrt**, *adj.* (war) disabled.
kriegen ['kri:gən], *v.tr. F:* to get (sth.);
to catch (a train, criminal, cold etc.).
Krimi ['krimi], *m -s/-s F:* detective story,
whodunnit.
Kriminal|beamte(r) [krimi'no:l-
beamtə(r)], *m* criminal investigator.
◆**K~film**, *m* crime/detective film.
◆**K~ität** [-nali'tɛːt], *f -/no pl* crime
(rate). ◆**K~polizei**, *f* criminal investigation department. ◆**K~roman**, *m*
crime/detective novel.
kriminell [krimi'nɛl], *adj.* criminal.
◆**K~e(r)**, *m & f decl. as adj.* criminal.
Kringel ['kriŋəl], *m -s/-* curl (of smoke
etc.). ◆'**k~n**, *v.tr.* to coil, curl (sth.);
(*Rauch usw.*) **sich k.**, to curl.
Kripo ['kri:po], *f -/no pl F:* = **Kriminalpolizei**.
Krippe ['kripə], *f -/-n* **1.** crib, manger. **2.**
(*Kinderk.*) day nursery.
Krise ['kri:zə], *f -/-n* crisis. ◆'**K~nherd**,
m storm centre, trouble spot.
Kristall [kris'tal]. **I.** *m -s/-e* crystal. **II.** *n
-s/no pl* crystal (glass). ◆**k~i'sieren**,
v.tr. & i. (*haben*) to crystallize.
Kriterium [kri'te:rium], *n -s/-ien* cri-
terion.

Krit|ik [kri'ti:k], *f -/-en* (*a*) (*Rezension*) no-
tice, review; (*b*) *no pl* (*allgemein*) criticism; *F:* **unter aller/jeder K.**, beneath
contempt. ◆**K~iker** ['kri:tikər], *m -s/-*
critic. ◆**k~iklos** [kri:tiklo:s], *adj.* uncritical. ◆**k~isch** ['kri:tiʃ], *adj.* critical. ◆**k~isieren** [kriti'zi:rən], *v.tr.* to
criticize.
kritteln ['kritəln], *v.i.* (*haben*) to find fault
(**an** + *dat*, with).
Kritzel|ei [kritsə'lai], *f -/-en* scrawl, scrib-
ble. ◆'**k~n**, *v.tr.&i.* (*haben*) to scribble, scrawl (sth.).
Krokodil [kroko'di:l], *n -s/-e* crocodile.
Krokus ['kro:kus], *m -/- & -se* crocus.
Kron|e ['kro:nə], *f -/-n* crown.
◆'**K~enkorken**, *m* crown cap.
◆'**K~leuchter**, *m* chandelier.
◆'**K~prinz**, *m* crown prince.
krön|en ['krø:nən], *v.tr.* to crown (s.o.,
Fig: sth.). ◆'**K~ung**, *f -/-en* (*a*) coronation; (*b*) *Fig:* consummation, crowning
achievement.
Kropf [krɔpf], *m -(e)s/-e* **1.** crop. **2.** *Med:*
goitre.
Kröte ['krø:tə], *f -/-n* toad.
Krücke ['krykə], *f -/-n* crutch.
Krug [kru:k], *m -(e)s/-e* jug.
Krümel ['kry:məl], *m -s/-* crumb.
◆'**k~n**, *v.tr.* to crumble (bread, cake
etc.).
krumm [krum], *adj.* **1.** twisted, out of
shape; warped (wood); bent (nail etc.);
curved (line, spine etc.); crooked (stick,
nose, etc.). **2.** *F:* (*unehrlich*) eine **k~e
Sache drehen**, to do sth. crooked.
◆'**k~beinig**, *adj.* bow-legged, bandy-
legged; (*Dackel usw.*) with bent/bandy
legs. ◆'**k~nehmen**, *v.tr.sep.irr.69* to
take (sth.) amiss.
krümm|en ['krymən], *v.tr.* to bend (a
wire, one's back etc.), crook (one's
finger); **sich k.**, to bend, twist; (*Fluß,
Pfad*) to wind. ◆'**K~ung**, *f -/-en* bend;
curve (of an arch, road etc.); curvature
(of the spine etc.).
Krüppel ['krypəl], *m -s/-* cripple.
Kruste ['krustə], *f -/-n* crust.
Kruzifix [krutsi'fiks], *n -es/-e* crucifix.
Kuba ['ku:ba]. *Pr.n* **-s.** Cuba.
◆**K~ner(in)** [ku'ba:nər(in)], *m -s/- (f
-/-nen)* Cuban.
Kübel ['ky:bəl], *m -s/-* bucket, tub (for
plants etc.); bin (for rubbish).
Kubik- [ku'bi:k-], *comb.fm. Meas:* cubic
(metre, centimetre etc.).
Küche ['kyçə], *f -/-n* **1.** kitchen. **2.**
(*Kochen*) cooking; **kalte K.**, hot/cold
food. ◆'**K~n-**, *comb.fm.* kitchen (towel,
furniture, chair, knife etc.).
◆'**K~nchef**, *m* chef. ◆'**K~ngerät**, *n*
kitchen utensil/*coll.* utensils.
◆'**K~nherd**, *m* kitchen range.
◆'**K~nmaschine**, *f* (electric) mixer.
◆'**K~nschabe**, *f -/-n* cockroach.
Kuchen ['ku:xən], *m -s/-* cake.
◆'**K~blech**, *n* baking sheet.

◆'**K~form**, f cake tin/N.Am: pan.
◆'**K~gabel**, f cake/pastry fork.
◆'**K~teig**, m cake mixture.

Kuckuck ['kukuk], m -s/-e (a) cuckoo; (b) P: zum K.! damn it! das weiß der K.! goodness knows! ◆'**K~suhr**, f cuckoo clock.

Kufe ['ku:fə], f -/-n runner (of a sledge etc.); Av: skid.

Kugel ['ku:gəl], f -/-n 1. ball; Mth: sphere; Sp: shot. 2. (Geschoß) bullet. ◆'**k~förmig**, adj. spherical. ◆'**K~kopf**, m golfball. ◆'**K~lager**, n ball bearing. ◆'**k~n**, v.refl. F: sich k., to roll about. ◆'**k~rund**, adj. F: round as a ball, tubby. ◆'**K~schreiber**, m ballpoint pen. ◆'**k~sicher**, adj. bullet-proof.

Kuh [ku:], f -/⁻e cow. ◆'**K~haut**, f cowhide; F: das geht auf keine K.! it's absolutely staggering! ◆'**K~stall**, m cowshed.

kühl [ky:l], adj. 1. (frisch) cool; (unangenehm) chilly. 2. Fig: cool (reception, head etc.). ◆'**K~e**, f -/no pl coolness; cool (of the evening etc.); chilliness (of night etc.). ◆'**k~en**, v.tr. to cool (sth.). ◆'**K~er**, m -s/- Aut: radiator. ◆'**K~erhaube**, f bonnet, N.Am: hood. ◆'**K~raum**, m cold store. ◆'**K~schrank**, m refrigerator. ◆'**K~tasche**, f cooler bag. ◆'**K~truhe**, f (chest) freezer. ◆'**K~turm**, m cooling tower. ◆'**K~ung**, f -/-en (refreshing) coolness; (b) Tchn: cooling.

kühn [ky:n], adj. bold; (gewagt) daring (escape etc.). ◆'**K~heit**, f -/no pl boldness, daring.

Küken ['ky:kən], n -s/- chick.

kulant [ku'lant], adj. obliging, reasonable.

Kuli[1] ['ku:li], m -s/-s coolie.

Kuli[2], m -s/-s F: ballpoint pen.

Kulisse [ku'lisə], f -/-n (a) Th: piece of scenery; pl K~n, (Seite der Bühne) wings; (b) Fig: background; hinter den K~n, behind the scenes.

Kult [kult], m -(e)s/-e (a) (form of) worship, rite; (b) Fig: idolization. ◆'**k~ivieren** [-'vi:rən], v.tr. to cultivate (land, plants, Fig: taste etc.). ◆'**k~i'viert**, adj. refined, cultivated (taste etc.); cultured (person, mind etc.).

Kultur [kul'tu:r], f -/-en 1 (a) culture, civilization; (b) no pl culture; ohne K., uncultured (person). 2. (a) Agr: etc: cultivation; (b) plantation (of trees etc.). II. K~-, comb.fm. 1. cultural (agreement, policy, centre etc.). 2. Agr: cultivated (plants, land, area etc.). ◆'**k~ell** [-tu'rɛl], adj. cultural. ◆'**K~geschichte**, f cultural history; history of civilization.

Kümmel ['kyməl], m -s/- caraway.

Kummer ['kumər], m -s/no pl grief, sorrow; (Sorge) worry, distress.

kümmer|lich ['kymərlıç], adj. miserable,

wretched (conditions, quarters etc.); puny (plant, efforts etc.); paltry, meagre (salary, result etc.). ◆'**k~n**, v.tr. (a) to bother, concern (s.o.); **was kümmert dich das?** what concern is that of yours? (b) **sich um j.n, etwas acc k.**, to take care of s.o., sth.; **ich kümmere mich nicht um diesen Klatsch**, I don't take any notice of this gossip.

Kumpan [kum'pa:n], m -s/-e F: mate, chum, N.Am: buddy; Pej: crony.

Kumpel ['kumpəl], m -s/- mate, N.Am: buddy.

Kunde[1] ['kundə], m -n/-n customer; (zu Beratender) client. ◆'**K~endienst**, m customer service; (für Käufer) after-sales service. ◆'**K~enkreis**, m clientele. ◆'**K~in**, f -/-nen woman customer/ client. ◆'**K~schaft**, f -/no pl 1. (Kundenkreis) clientele. 2. custom.

Kunde[2], f -/-n A: & Lit: tidings. ◆'**k~geben** ['kunt-], v.tr.sep.irr.35 Lit: to announce, make known (one's views etc.). ◆'**K~gebung**, f -/-en demonstration, rally. ◆'**k~ig** [-dıç], adj. knowledgeable; expert (advice, mechanic etc.).

künd|bar ['kyntba:r], adj. Jur: etc: terminable. ◆'**k~igen** ['kyndıgən], v.tr. (a) to terminate, cancel (an agreement, contract etc.); (b) v.tr. & i. (haben) (Firma usw.) j-m k., to give s.o. notice; (Angestellte) (die Stellung) k., to hand in one's notice. ◆'**K~igung**, f -/-en (a) termination, cancellation; (b) (employer's/employee's) notice; (landlord's) notice to quit. ◆'**K~igungsfrist** f period of notice.

künftig ['kynftıç], adj. (a) future; prospective (candidate); coming (event etc.); (b) adv. in future.

Kunst [kunst], I. f -/⁻e 1. art. 2. (Fähigkeit) skill; F: das ist keine K., there is nothing to it. II. K~-, comb.fm. 1. artificial (manure, limb etc.); synthetic (resin etc.). 2. art (gallery, lover, collector etc.). ◆'**K~akademie**, f art college/school. ◆'**K~faser**, f synthetic fibre. ◆'**k~fertig**, adj. skilful. ◆'**K~fertigkeit**, f skilfulness. ◆'**K~geschichte**, f art history. ◆'**K~gewerbe**, n arts and crafts. ◆'**k~gewerblich**, adj. craftsman-made. ◆'**K~griff**, m trick, dodge. ◆'**K~händler**, m art dealer. ◆'**K~seide**, f artificial silk, rayon. ◆'**K~stoff**, m plastic. ◆'**K~stück**, n trick, stunt; (Glanzleistung) feat; F: K.! no wonder! ◆'**k~turnen**, n (competitive) gymnastics. ◆'**K~verstand**, m artistic judgment. ◆'**k~voll**, adj. highly artistic; elaborate (carving etc.); ingenious (machine etc.). ◆'**K~werk**, n work of art.

Künst|ler(in) ['kynstlər(ın)], m -s/- (f -/-nen) artist. ◆'**k~lerisch**, adj. artistic. ◆'**K~lername**, m stage name. ◆'**k~lich**, adj. artificial.

kunterbunt ['kuntərbunt], *adj.* very varied, mixed.

Kupfer ['kupfər], *n -s/no pl* copper. ◆**k~n,** *adj.* (made of) copper. ◆**K~stich,** *m* copper(-plate) engraving.

Kuppe ['kupə], *f -/-n* 1. brow (of a hill). 2. *(a) (Fingerk.)* fingertip; *(b)* rounded head (of a nail etc.).

Kuppel ['kupəl], *f -/-n* dome.

Kupp|elei [kupə'lai], *f -/-en Jur:* procuring. ◆**k~eln,** *v.* 1. *v.tr.* to couple (sth.). 2. *v.i.* (*haben*) *(a) Jur:* to procure; *(b) Aut:* to declutch. ◆**K~ler(in),** *m -s/- (f -/-nen) Jur:* procurer. ◆**K~lung,** *f -/-en Tchn:* coupling; *Aut:* clutch.

Kur [ku:r], *f -/-en* cure, treatment *(esp. at a spa).* ◆**K~gast,** *m* patient at/visitor to a spa. ◆**k~ieren** [ku'ri:rən], *v.tr.* to cure, heal (s.o., a disease etc.). ◆**K~ort,** *m* health resort, spa. ◆**K~pfuscher,** *m -s/- Pej:* quack.

Kür [ky:r], *f -/-en Sp:* free skating; *(Turnen)* voluntary exercise. ◆**K~lauf,** *m Sp:* free skating.

Kurbel ['kurbəl], *f -/-n* crank. ◆**k~n,** *v.tr.* **in die Höhe k.,** to winch up (a load), wind up (a car window etc.). ◆**K~welle,** *f* crankshaft.

Kürbis ['kyrbis], *m -ses/-se* pumpkin; *(Flaschenk.)* (vegetable) marrow; *esp. N.Am:* squash.

Kurier [ku'ri:r], *m -s/-e* courier.

kurios [kuri'o:s], *adj.* queer (story, idea etc.); quaint (person, object etc.).

Kurs [kurs], *m -es/-e* 1. *(a)* course; *(b) Fig:* policy, line. 2. *(a) Börsen:* price; *Fin:* rate of exchange. 3. *Sch:* course, syllabus; *N.Am:* program. ◆**K~buch,** *n* railway timetable. ◆**K~wagen,** *m Rail:* through coach.

kurs|ieren [kur'zi:rən], *v.i.* (*haben*) to circulate. ◆**k~iv** [-'zi:f], *adj.* italic. ◆**K~us** ['kurzus], *m -/Kurse* course.

Kurve ['kurvə], *f -/-n* curve; bend (of a road, river etc.). ◆**k~nreich,** *adj.* (*Straße*) winding, twisting.

kurz [kurts], *adj.* short *(a)* **bis dahinter,** just behind it; *Fig:* **alles k. und klein schlagen,** to smash everything to pieces; **den k~eren ziehen,** to come off worst; *adv.* **zu k. kommen,** to lose out; **vor k~em,**

recently; **k. anhalten,** to stop briefly. ◆**k~arbeit,** *f* short-time work. ◆**k~ärmelig,** *adj.* short-sleeved. ◆**k~atmig,** *adj. (Pers.)* short-winded. ◆**k~er'hand,** *adv.* without hesitation/delay. ◆**K~fassung,** *f* abridged version (of a book etc.). ◆**k~fristig,** *adj.* short-term (credit etc.). ◆**K~geschichte,** *f* short story. ◆**k~haarig,** *adj.* short-haired. ◆**K~halten,** *v.tr.sep.irr.45* to keep (s.o.) short (of money, food etc.). ◆**k~lebig,** *adj.* short-lived; ephemeral (insect, plant etc.). ◆**K~nachrichten,** *fpl* news summary. ◆**K~schluß,** *m El:* short-circuit, *F:* short. ◆**K~schrift,** *f* shorthand. ◆**k~sichtig,** *adj.* (also *Fig:*) short-sighted, *N.Am:* near-sighted. ◆**k~um,** *adv.* in short. ◆**K~waren,** *fpl* haberdashery, *N.Am:* notions. ◆**K~welle,** *f Rad:* short wave.

Kürz|e ['kyrtsə], *f -/no pl (a)* shortness; brevity (of a description etc.); briefness (of a visit etc.); *(b) (Knappheit)* conciseness. ◆**k~en,** *v.tr. (a) (kürzer machen)* to shorten (sth.); *(b) (verringern)* to cut, reduce (taxes, expenses etc.). ◆**k~lich,** *adj.* recently, a short time ago. ◆**K~ung,** *f -/-en* reduction, cut (des Einkommens usw., in income etc.).

kuschelig ['kuʃəliç], *adj.* cuddly. ◆**k~eln,** *v.refl.* **sich an j-n k.,** to cuddle/snuggle up to s.o.

Kusine [ku'zi:nə], *f -/-n* (female) cousin.

Kuß [kus], *m -sses/-sse* kiss.

küssen ['kysən], *v.tr.* to kiss.

Küste ['kystə], *f -/-n* coast. ◆**K~n-,** *comb.fm.* coastal (area etc.). ◆**K~ngewässer,** *n* coastal/inshore waters. ◆**K~nlinie,** *f* coastline. ◆**K~nwache,** *f* coastguard service.

Kutsch|e ['kutʃə], *f -/-n* (horsedrawn) coach, carriage. ◆**K~er,** *m -s/-* coachdriver, coachman.

Kutte ['kutə], *f -/-n* monk's habit.

Kutter ['kutər], *m -s/-* cutter; *(Fischk.)* fishing boat.

Kuvert [ku'vε:r], *n -s/-s* 1. envelope. 2. *(Gedeck)* cover (at table).

L

L, l [εl], *n -/-* (the letter) L, l.

laben ['la:bən], *v.tr.* to refresh (s.o.).

labil [la'bi:l], *adj.* unstable (situation, character etc.); delicate (health etc.).

Labor [la'bo:r], *n -s/-s & -e* laboratory, *F:* lab. ◆**L~ant(in)** [-o'rant(in)], *m -en/-en (f -/-nen)* laboratory assistant. ◆**L~atorium** [-a'to:rium] *n -s/-rien* laboratory.

Labyrinth [laby'rint], *n -(e)s/-e* maze.

Lache ['la:xə], *f -/-n* puddle.

lach|en ['laxən]. **I.** *v.tr. & i.* (*haben*) to laugh (über + *acc,* at); *F:* **er hat nichts zu l.,** he has a hard time (of it); **das wäre ja gelacht, wenn ...,** it'd be ridiculous if ... **II.** *n -s/no pl* laugh; *coll* laughter; **es ist zum L.,** it's ridiculous; **es ist nicht zum L.,** it's no laughing matter. ◆**L~gas,** *n* laughing gas. ◆**l~haft,** *adj.* ludicrous. ◆**L~krampf,** *m* fit of laughter.

lächeln ['lεçəln]. **I.** *v.i.* (*haben*) to smile

(über etwas acc, at sth.; über j-n, about s.o.). II. **L**, n -s/- smile. ◆'**l~erlich**, adj. ridiculous; **j-n l. machen**, to make s.o. look a fool. ◆'**L~erlichkeit**, f -/-en absurdity.

Lachs [laks], m -es/-e salmon. ◆'**l~farben**, adj. salmon pink. ◆'**L~forelle**, f -/-n salmon trout.

Lack [lak], m -(e)s/-e 1. (farblos) varnish. 2. Aut: paintwork, finish. ◆'**l~affe**, m F: conceited ass. ◆'**l~ieren** [-'ki:rən], v.tr. to varnish (wood, fingernails etc.). ◆'**L~schuh**, m patent leather shoe.

Lackmuspapier ['lakmuspapi:r], n -s/no pl litmus paper.

Lad|e-, comb.fm. (a) loading (crane etc.); (b) El: charging (voltage, current etc.). ◆'**L~egerät**, n (battery) charger. ◆'**l~en**1, v.tr.irr. (a) to load (goods, cargo etc.) (auf + acc, onto); (b) to load (a gun etc.); (c) El: to charge (a battery etc.); (c) **Verantwortung usw. auf sich l.**, to burden oneself with responsibility; (d) Jur: **einen Zeugen (vor Gericht) l.**, to summon a witness. ◆'**L~eraum**, m load/cargo space; Nau: hold. ◆'**L~ung**, f -/-en 1. load; Nau: cargo. 2. E.: charge. 3. Jur: L. (vor Gericht), summons.

Laden2 ['la:dən], m -s/- 1. shop, N.Am: store. 2. F: business. 3. (Fensterl.) shutter. ◆'**L~besitzer(in)**, m & f shopkeeper. ◆'**L~dieb(in)**, m & f shoplifter. ◆'**L~diebstahl**, m (case of) shoplifting. ◆'**L~hüter**, m -s/- slow-moving article. ◆'**L~preis**, m retail price. ◆'**L~schluß** m (shop-)closing time. ◆'**L~tisch**, m (shop) counter.

Lafette [la'fɛtə], f -/-n gun carriage.

Lage ['la:gə], f -/-n 1. position, situation; **versetze dich mal in meine L.**, just put yourself in my position/F: in my shoes; **L. der Dinge**, (present) state of affairs; F: **die L. peilen**, to find out how the land lies; **in der L. sein, etwas zu tun**, to be in a position to do sth. 2. (Schicht) layer (of sand etc.). ◆'**L~bericht**, m Mil: etc: report on the situation. ◆'**L~plan**, m plan (of a town etc.).

Lager ['la:gər]. I. n -s/- 1. Mil: etc: camp. 2. (a) Com: store; (L~haus) warehouse; (b) (Vorrat) stock; **einen Artikel auf L. haben**, to have sth. in stock. 3. Tchn: bearing. II. L~-, comb.fm. 1. (a) camp (fire, leader etc.); (b) (für Lagerung) storage (charge, costs etc.); (c) Tchn: bearing (metal etc.). ◆'**L~arbeiter**, m warehouseman. ◆'**L~bestand**, m stock. ◆'**L~haus**, n warehouse. ◆'**l~n**1 v.tr. (a) to place, lay (s.o., sth.) (somewhere); (b) to store (goods, provisions etc.). 2. v.i. (haben) (a) Mil: etc: to camp; (b) (Waren usw.) to be stored; (Wein) to age. ◆'**L~ung**, f -/-en 1. storing (of goods). 2. Tchn: mounting in a bearing/bearings.

Lagune [la'gu:nə], f -/-n lagoon.

lahm [la:m], adj. (a) (Pers.) lame; (b) F: feeble, limp (handshake); Fig: lame, feeble (joke, excuse etc.). ◆'**l~en**, v.i. (haben) (Tier) to be lame. ◆'**l~legen**, v.tr. to bring (production, traffic etc.) to a standstill.

lähm|en ['lɛ:mən], v.tr. (a) (Gift) to paralyse (a muscle), numb (a nerve); (b) to cripple (industry etc.); (b) (Angst usw.) to petrify, paralyse (s.o.); (Schock usw.) to numb (s.o.). ◆'**L~ung**, f -/-en Med: & Fig: paralysis; Fig: immobilization (of industry etc.).

Laib [laip], m -(e)s/-e **ein L. Brot**, a loaf of bread.

Laich [laiç], m -(e)s/-e spawn. ◆'**l~en**, v.i. (haben) to spawn.

Laie ['laiə], m -n/-n also Ecc: layman; Th: Mus: etc: amateur; ◆'**l~nhaft**, adj. Pej: amateurish (performance etc.). ◆'**L~n-**, comb.fm. Th: Mus: etc: amateur (actor, choir, painter etc.); (b) esp. Ecc: lay (brother, preacher etc.).

Lakai [la'kai], m -en/-en (a) lackey, footman; (b) Fig: Pej: bootlicker.

Lake ['la:kə], f -/-n Cu: brine (for pickling).

Laken ['la:kən], n -s/- sheet.

lakonisch [la'ko:niʃ], adj. laconic.

Lakritze [la'kritsə], f -/-n liquorice.

lallen ['lalən], v.tr. & i. (haben) (Betrunkene usw.) to babble (incoherently).

Lama ['la:ma], n -s/-s Z: llama.

Lamelle [la'mɛlə], f -/-n 1. thin plate/ (Scheibe) disc; (Jalousienl.) slat; (Kühlerl.) gill; 2. (Pilzl.) gill, lamella.

lamentieren [lamen'ti:rən], v.i. (haben) F: to moan.

Lametta [la'mɛta], n -s/no pl tinsel.

Lamm [lam], n -(e)s/-er lamb. ◆'**L~fell**, n lambskin. ◆'**l~fromm**, adj. F: as meek as a lamb. ◆'**L~wolle** f lambswool.

Lampe ['lampə], f -/-n (a) lamp; (Deckenl.) light; (b) (Birne) lightbulb. ◆'**L~nfieber**, n stage fright. ◆'**L~nschirm**, m lampshade.

Lampion [lampi'ɔŋ], m & n -s/-s Chinese lantern.

Land [lant]. I. n -(e)s/-er 1. land; Nau: **an L. gehen**, to go ashore. 2. (nicht Stadt) country; **auf dem L./L~e**, in the country. 3. (a) Pol: country; (b) Adm: West G: Land, state; Aus: province. II. '**L~-**, comb.fm. (a) (vom Lande) country (doctor, house, life, people, air etc.); (ländlich) rural (population etc.); (b) land (warfare, forces etc.); ◆'**L~arbeiter**, m farmhand. ◆'**l~aus**, adv. 1., **landein, l~aus**, far and wide. ◆'**L~besitz**, m landed property, real estate. ◆'**L~besitzer**, m landowner. ◆**L~e-** ['landə], comb.fm. landing (Av: light, flap, Nau: place etc.). ◆'**L~ebahn** f, (landing) runway. ◆'**L~eerlaubnis**, f permission to land. ◆'**l~einwärts**, adv. (further) inland. ◆'**l~en**, v. 1. v.tr. & i. (sein) to land.

◆'L~**enge**, f -/-n isthmus. ◆**L~es-**['landəs-], comb.fm. 1. national (custom, frontier, colours, flag etc.); state (police etc.); (language etc.) of a/the country; 2. West G: Land/state, Aus: provincial (boundary, government etc.); ◆'l~**esüblich**, adj. customary in a/the country. ◆'**L~esverrat**, m high treason. ◆'**L~esverräter** m traitor (to one's country). ◆'**L~eswährung**, f currency of the country. ◆'**L~flucht**, f drift from the country to the town. ◆'**L~friedensbruch**, m Jur: breach of the peace. ◆'**L~gut** n country estate. ◆'**L~karte**, f map. ◆'**L~kreis**, m country/rural district. ◆'l~**läufig**, adj. popular, widespread (opinion, view etc.). ◆'**L~plage**, f plague (of insects); ◆'**L~regen**, n steady rain. ◆'**L~schaft**, f -/-en landscape; coll scenery; **die L. um Bonn**, the country-side round Bonn. ◆'l~**schaftlich**, adj. (a) regional (custom, culture etc.); (b) **das Dorf liegt l. sehr schön**, the village is beautifully situated. ◆'**L~sitz**, m country seat. ◆'**L~smann**, m -(e)s/-leute fellow-countryman. ◆'**L~smännin**, f /-nen fellow-countrywoman. ◆'**L~straße**, f country road; (kleiner) minor road. ◆'**L~streicher(in)**, m -s/- (f /-nen) tramp, N.Am: hobo. ◆'**L~strich** m tract of country. ◆'**L~tag**, m West G. Pol: Land/State parliament. ◆'**L~ung**, f /-en Av: Nau: landing; Av: touchdown. ◆'**L~ungsbrücke**, f jetty, pier. ◆'**l~vermesser**, m, land surveyor. ◆'**L~weg**, m auf dem L., overland. ◆'**L~wein**, m local wine. ◆'**L~wirt(in)**, m & f farmer. ◆'**L~wirtschaft**, f /-en farming, agriculture. ◆'**l~wirtschaftlich** adj. ◆'**L~wirtschafts-**, comb.fm. agricultural. ◆'**L~zunge**, f tongue of land.

Länd|ereien [lɛndə'raiən], fpl estates, landed properties. ◆'**L~erspiel** n Sp: international match. ◆'**l~lich**, adj. rural.

lang [laŋ], adj. long; F: **ein l~er Kerl**, a tall fellow; **vor l~er Zeit**, a long time ago; **er wartete drei Jahre l.**, he waited for three years; **sein Leben l.**, all his life. ◆'**l~atmig**, adj. long-winded (speech etc.); lengthy (explanation etc.). ◆'**l~e**, adv. a long time; **das ist schon l. her**, that was a long time ago; **wie l. (dauert es) noch?** how much longer (does it take)? **(noch) l. nicht fertig**, not nearly ready. ◆**L~e'weile**, f -/no pl boredom. ◆'**l~finger**, m F: pilferer (Taschendieb) pickpocket. ◆'**l~fristig**, adj. long-term (loan etc.). ◆'**l~haarig**, adj. long-haired. ◆'**l~jährig**, adj. long (experience etc.); long-standing (friendship etc.). ◆'**L~lauf**, m cross-country skiing. ◆'**l~lebig**, adj. long-lived (person etc.); durable (material). ◆'**l~sam**,

adj. slow; (allmählich) gradual (development, change etc.); **es wird l. Zeit zu gehen**, it is about time to go. ◆'**L~samkeit**, f -/no pl slowness. ◆'**L~schläfer(in)**, m(f) late riser. ◆'**L~spielplatte**, f -/-n long-playing record. ◆'**L~strecken-** comb.fm. long-distance (flight, runner etc.); long-range (rocket, aircraft etc.). ◆'**l~weilen**, v.tr. to bore (s.o.); sich l., to be bored. ◆'**l~weilig**, adj. boring; dull (landscape, person). ◆'**L~welle**, f Rad: etc: long wave. ◆'**l~wierig**, adj. lengthy, protracted.

Läng|e ['lɛŋə], f -/-n a) length; F: height (of a person); b) Geog: longitude. ◆'**L~engrad**, m degree of longitude. ◆'**L~enmaß**, n longitudinal measure. ◆'**l~lich**, adj. oblong. ◆'**L~s-**, comb.fm. longitudinal (stripe, axis etc.). ◆'**l~st**, adv. (schon) l., a long time ago; F: ages ago; (noch) l. nicht so viel, nothing like as much; F: **das reicht l.**, that is more than enough. ◆'**l~ste(r, s)**, adj. longest.

langen ['laŋən], v.i. (haben) (a) to reach; **nach der Zuckerdose l.**, to reach for the sugar; (b) F: (Geld, Nahrung usw.) to be enough; **jetzt langt's mir aber!** now I've had enough!

Languste [laŋ'gustə], f -/-n spiny lobster.

Lanz|e ['lantsə], f -/-n lance. ◆'**L~ette** ['tsetə], f /-n lancet.

lapidar [lapi'daːr], adj.pithy, terse.

Lappalie [la'paːliə], f -/-n trifle.

Lapp|en ['lapən], m -s/- rag, cloth. ◆'**l~isch** ['lɛpiʃ], adj. silly; (kindisch) childish.

Lapsus ['lapsus], m -/- slip.

Lärche ['lɛrçə], f -/-n (common) larch.

Lärm [lɛrm], m -s/no pl (loud) noise. ◆'**L~belästigung**, f noise pollution. ◆'**l~empfindlich**, adj. sensitive to noise. ◆'**l~en**, v.i. (haben) to make a noise; (Radio usw.) to blare. ◆'**l~end**, adj. noisy.

Larve ['larfə], f -/-n larva.

lasch [laʃ], adj. F: (a) listless (person); limp (handshake etc.); (b) (fade) tasteless (food).

Lasche ['laʃə], f -/-n 1. tongue (of a shoe); Cl: flap. 2. Tchn: joint.

Laser ['leːzər], m -s/- laser. ◆'**L~strahl**, m laser beam.

lassen ['lasən], v.tr.irr. (a) **j-n etwas tun l.**, (i) (erlauben) to let s.o. do sth.; (ii) (heißen) to get s.o. to do sth.; **ich ließ es mir schicken**, I had it sent; **laß dich nicht stören**, don't let me disturb you; **das läßt sich machen**, that can be done; **j-m freie Hand l.**, to allow s.o. a free hand; (b) (zurücklassen) to leave (s.o., sth.); **laß mich in Ruhe/Frieden!** leave me alone/in peace! (c) (unterlassen) to stop (doing sth.); **laß das (sein/bleiben)!** stop it! **wir sind dabei/gut sein**, let's leave it at that.

lässig ['lɛsiç], *adj.* casual; *(unbekümmert)* nonchalant. ◆'**L~keit**, *f -/no pl* casualness; nonchalance.

Lasso ['laso], *m & n -s/-s* lasso.

Last [last], *f -/-en* load; *esp. Fig:* burden; **unter der L. des Schnees**, under the weight of the snow; *Fig:* **j-m zur L. fallen**, to be a burden to s.o.; **j-m etwas zur L. legen**, to accuse s.o. of sth. ◆'**L~auto**, *n* lorry, *N.Am:* truck. ◆'**l~en**, *v.i. (haben) (Sorge, Verantwortung usw.)* **auf j-m l.**, to weigh on s.o. ◆'**L~enaufzug** *m* goods lift, *N.Am:* freight elevator. ◆'**L~er¹**, *m -s/-* lorry, *N.Am:* truck. ◆'**L~(kraft)wagen** *m* lorry, *N.Am:* truck.

Laster², *n -s/-* vice. ◆'**l~haft**, *adj.* wicked.

läster|lich ['lɛstərliç], *adj.* blasphemous (words etc.). ◆'**l~n**, *v.i. (haben) (a) F:* **über j-n l.**, to run s.o. down (behind his back); *(b)* **Gott l.**, to blaspheme.

lästig ['lɛstiç], *adj.* troublesome (cough etc.); irksome (task); tiresome (child, visitor etc.); **l. werden**, to become a nuisance.

Latein [la'tain], *n -(s)/no pl* Latin. ◆**L~amerika**. *Pr.n.n -s.* Latin America. ◆**l~amerikanisch**, *adj.* Latin American. ◆**l~isch**, *adj.* Latin.

latent [la'tɛnt], *adj.* latent (talent, ability); potential (danger).

Laterne [la'tɛrnə], *f -/-n (a)* lantern; *(b) (Straßenl.)* streetlamp. ◆'**L~npfahl**, *m* lamppost.

Latrine [la'triːnə], *f -/-n* latrine.

Latsche ['latʃə], *f -/-n* dwarf pine.

latschen ['laːtʃən]. I. *v.i. (sein) F: (a)* ('**latʃən**) to shuffle (along); *(b)* **wir latschten durch die ganze Stadt**, we traipsed through the whole town. II. L., *m -s/- F:* (worn-out) old shoe.

Latte ['latə], *f -/-n (a)* (wooden) slat; *Tchn etc:* batten; rail (of a fence); *(b) Sp:* bar; *Fb:* crossbar. ◆'**L~nzaun**, *m* paling (fence).

Latz [lats], *m -es/-e* bib. ◆'**L~hose**, *f Cl:* dungarees, *N.Am:* overalls.

Lätzchen ['lɛtsçən], *n -s/-* (child's) bib, feeder.

lau [lau], *adj. (a)* mild (breeze, weather); balmy (air, evening etc.); *(b)* lukewarm (water).

Laub [laup], *n -(e)s/no pl* leaves, foliage. ◆'**L~baum**, *m* deciduous tree. ◆'**L~frosch**, *m* treefrog. ◆'**L~säge**, *f* fretsaw. ◆'**L~wald**, *m* deciduous forest.

Laube ['laubə], *f -/-n* summer-house.

Lauch [laux], *m -(e)s/-e* leek.

Lauer ['lauər], *f -/no pl* **auf der L. liegen/sein**, *(Tier)* to lie in wait; *F: (Pers.)* to be on the lookout. ◆'**l~n**, *v.i. (haben) (Pers., Fig: Gefahren usw.)* to lurk (somewhere); **auf j-n, etwas etc l.**, to lie in wait for s.o., sth.; *F:* to look out for s.o., sth.

Lauf [lauf], *m -(e)s/-e* **1.** *(a) no pl (das Laufen)* running; *Sp:* race; **der 200-Meter-L.**, the 200 metres. **2.** *no pl (Verlauf)* course of a river; *Fig:* of events etc.); **der L. der Dinge** the way things go; **im L~e des Tages**, during the day; **im L~e von wenigen Stunden**, within a few hours. **3.** *no pl* running (of a machine, an engine etc.). **4.** *(Gewehrl.)* barrel (of a rifle etc.). ◆'**L~bahn**, *f* career. ◆'**l~en**, *v.irr.* **1.** *v.i. (sein) (a)* to run; **j-m über den Weg l.**, to run/*F:* bump into s.o.; **den Motor l. lassen**, to run the engine; *(b) (gehen)* to walk; *(c)* **der Film läuft im Fernsehen**, the film is being shown on television; *(d) (fließen)* **das Wasser/den Hahn l. lassen**, to run the water/the tap. **2.** *v.tr.* to run (a distance, race etc.). ◆'**l~end**, *adj. (a)* running (commentary); current (account, expenses, tax year etc.); present (month); *(regelmäßig)* regular (payments); **l. steigen**, to increase continually; *(b)* **auf dem l~en sein/bleiben**, to be well-informed/up-to-date. ◆'**l~enlassen**, *v.tr.sep.irr.57* to let (s.o., an animal) go; to set (a prisoner, an animal) free. ◆'**L~feuer**, *n F:* **sich wie ein L. verbreiten**, to spread like wildfire. ◆'**L~kundschaft**, *f* casual customers. ◆'**L~masche**, *f* ladder, *esp. N.Am:* run (in a stocking/tights). ◆'**L~paß**, *m F:* **j-m den L. geben**, to give s.o. the push. ◆'**L~schritt**, *m* **im L.**, at the double. ◆'**L~steg**, *m* catwalk; walkway. ◆'**L~stall**, *m* playpen. ◆'**L~werk**, *n -(e)s/-e (a)* running gear (of a vehicle etc.); *(b)* clockwork (mechanism); *(c) Rec:* turntable unit. ◆'**L~zettel**, *m* circular; distribution sheet.

Läufer ['lɔyfər], *m -s/-* **1.** *(a) Sp:* runner; *(b) Fb:* half-back. **2.** *H:* (strip of) carpet, runner; *(Treppenl.)* stair-carpet. **3.** *(Schach)* bishop.

läufig ['lɔyfiç], *adj. (Hündin, Katze)* on heat.

Lauge ['laugə], *f -/-n* **1.** *(Waschl.)* soapy water. **2.** *Ch:* lye, alkaline solution.

Laun|e ['launə], *f -/-n (a)* mood; **bei guter/schlechter L.**, in a good mood/a bad temper; *(b) (Einfall)* **das war nur so eine L. von ihm**, that was just one of his whims. ◆'**l~isch**, *adj.* moody, petulant.

Laus [laus], *f -/-e* louse. ◆'**L~bub**, *m -en/-en Hum:* little rascal.

lausch|en ['lauʃən], *v.i. (haben)* to listen; *(heimlich)* to eavesdrop. ◆'**l~ig**, *adj. (gemütlich)* snug, cosy; *(ruhig)* quiet (spot etc.).

laut¹ [laut], *prep. + gen/dat* in accordance with; **l. Bericht**, according to reports.

laut². I. *adj. (a)* loud (voice, shout etc.); noisy (area, children etc.); *(b)* **Klagen, Zweifel usw. wurden l.**, complaints, doubts etc. were voiced. II. **L.**, *m -(e)s/*

-e sound. ◆'l~en, v.i. (haben) **genau lautet der Befehl ...**, the exact wording of the order is ...; **das Schreiben lautet wie folgt: ...**, the letter reads as follows: ... ◆'l~hals, adv. at the top of one's voice. ◆'l~los, adj. silent (mechanism, footsteps); deep (silence). ◆'l~malend, adj. onomatopoeic. ◆'L~schrift, f phonetic transcription. ◆'L~sprecher, m loudspeaker. ◆'l~stark, adj. vociferous, noisy. ◆'L~stärke, f loudness; volume.

Laute ['lautə], f -/-n lute.

läuten ['lɔytən], v. 1. v.i. (haben) (Klingel, Telefon) to ring; (Wecker) to go off. 2. v.tr. to ring (the bell).

lauter ['lautər], adj. inv. sheer, utter (despair, greed); pure (joy, pleasure); l. Steine, nothing but stones.

läuter|n ['lɔytərn], v.tr. to purify (liquids); to refine (metals, glass). ◆'L~ung, f -/no pl purification: refinement.

lauwarm ['lauvarm], adj. lukewarm.

Lava ['laːva], f -/Laven lava.

Lavendel [la'vɛndəl], m -s/- lavender.

lavieren [la'viːrən], v.i. (haben) Fig: (Pers.) to manoeuvre.

Lawine [la'viːnə], f -/-n avalanche. ◆l~nartig, adj. like an avalanche. ◆L~ngefahr, f -/no pl danger of avalanches.

lax [laks], adj. lax (morals, principles etc.); slack (leadership, attitude).

Lazarett [latsa'rɛt], n -(e)s/-e military hospital.

leb|en ['leːbən]. I. v.i. (haben) to live; **seine Mutter lebt noch**, his mother is still alive; **er lebt nur für die Wissenschaft**, his life is dedicated to science; **von Wasser und Brot l.**, to live on bread and water. II. L., n -s/- life; **am L.**, alive; **ums L. kommen**, to lose one's life; Fig: **etwas ins L. rufen**, to bring sth. into being; **mein L. lang, all my life**; Fr: **nie im L.!** not on your life! ◆'l~end, adj. living (person, organism); live (fish, animals). ◆'l~endig [le'bɛndiç], adj. (a) (am Leben) living; pred. alive; (b) (lebhaft) lively (child, story). ◆l~endigkeit, f liveliness. ◆'L~ens-, 'l~ens-, comb.fm. (necessities, experience, form etc.) of life; life (story etc.); living (conditions etc.). ◆'L~ensabend, m old age. ◆'L~ensalter, n lifespan. ◆'L~ensdauer, f lifespan; Tchn: working life. ◆'L~enserwartung, f expectation of life. ◆l~ensfähig, adj. (baby etc.) capable of survival; Biol: & Fig: viable (life-form etc.). ◆'L~ensfreude, f zest; **voller L.**, full of the joys of life. ◆'L~ensgefahr, f danger to life; **er schwebt in L.**, his life is in danger. ◆l~ensgefährlich, adj. extremely dangerous (undertaking); critical (illness, injury). ◆'L~ensgefährte, m/l

◆'L~ensgefährtin, f partner for life. ◆'L~ensgröße, f -/no pl actual size; **in L.**, lifesize. ◆'L~enshaltungskosten, pl cost of living. ◆'L~enslage, f situation. ◆'l~enslänglich, adj. life (imprisonment, membership). ◆'L~enslauf, m curriculum vitae. ◆'l~ensmittel, npl food; (Vorräte) provisions. ◆'L~ensmittelgeschäft, n food shop/esp. N.Am: store. ◆'l~ensnah, adj. realistic, true to life. ◆'l~ensnotwendig, adj. essential, vital. ◆'L~ensstandard m standard of living. ◆'L~ensunterhalt, m livelihood; **seinen L. verdienen**, to earn one's living. ◆'L~ensversicherung f life insurance/assurance. ◆'L~enswandel, m/'L~ensweise, f way of life. ◆'L~enswerk, n sein L., his life's work. ◆'l~enswichtig, adj. vitally important, essential. ◆'L~enszeichen, n sign of life. ◆'L~enszeit, f lifetime; **auf L.**, for life. ◆'L~ewesen, n (living) being, creature. ◆'L~e'wohl, n -(e)s/-e goodbye, A: & Hum: farewell. ◆l~haft ['leːphaft], adj. lively; animated (discussion etc.); vivid (colours, description); keen (interest); brisk (business etc.); busy (traffic). ◆'L~haftigkeit, f -/no pl liveliness; vivacity; vividness; keenness (of interest); briskness (of business). ◆'l~los, adj. lifeless; inanimate (object). ◆'L~zeiten, fpl lifetime; **zu seinen L.**, in/ during his lifetime.

Leber ['leːbər], f -/- liver. ◆'L~fleck, m F: mole. ◆'L~käse, m -s/no pl (spiced) meat loaf. ◆'L~knödel, m liver dumpling. ◆'L~pastete, f Cu: liver pâté. ◆'L~tran, m cod-liver oil. ◆'L~wurst, f (continental) liver sausage.

Lebkuchen ['leːpkuːxən], m (kind of) gingerbread.

leck [lɛk]. I. adj. leaky, leaking. II. L., n -(e)s/-e leak. ◆l~en¹, v.i. (haben) to leak.

lecken² ['lɛkən], v.tr. & i. to lick.

lecker ['lɛkər], adj. delicious, tasty. ◆'L~bissen, m -s/- tasty morsel, titbit; (Delikatesse) delicacy. ◆l~en [-'raien], fpl good things to eat, esp. sweets/N.Am: candy. ◆'L~maul, n F: **ein L. sein**, to have a sweet tooth.

Leder ['leːdər], n -s/- leather. ◆'L~hose, f esp.pl leather shorts, lederhosen. ◆'L~jacke, f -/-n leather jacket. ◆'l~n, adj. leather (gloves etc.). ◆'L~waren, fpl leather goods.

ledig ['leːdiç], adj. unmarried, single. ◆l~lich ['leːdiklıç], adv. merely, solely.

leer [leːr], adj. (a) (ohne Inhalt) empty; flat (battery); (menschenleer) deserted, empty (streets); **l~es Blatt**, blank sheet; (b) Fig: empty, idle (talk, threats etc.);

l~er Blick, blank look; (Miene) vacant expression. ◆'L~e, f -/no pl emptiness. ◆'l~en, v.tr. to empty (a glass etc.), clear (a letter box, dustbin); (Saal usw.) sich l., to empty. ◆'l~gewicht, n weight unladen. ◆'L~lauf, m idling; Brit: tickover. ◆'l~stehend, adj. empty, vacant (room, flat etc.). ◆'L~taste, f space-bar.

legal [le'ga:l], adj. legal; legitimate (government, means etc.). ◆l~i'sieren, v.tr. (haben) to legalize (a practice etc.), authenticate (a document, signature). ◆L~i'tät, f -/no pl legality.

legen ['le:gən], v.tr. (a) (hinlegen) to put/lay (s.o., sth.) down; (Henne) Eier l., to lay (eggs); (b) etwas auf/in/unter etwas acc l., to put sth. on/in/under sth.; (c) sich l., (Wind, Fig: Aufregung usw.) to die down; (Lärm, Schmerz) to subside.

legendär [legɛn'dɛ:r], adj. legendary. ◆L~e [le'gɛndə], f -/-n legend.

leger [le'ʒe:r], adj. casual, relaxed.

legieren [le'gi:rən], v.tr. to alloy (metals); ◆L~ung, f -/-en alloy.

legitim [legi'ti:m], adj. legitimate. ◆L~ation [-timatsi'o:n], f -/-en (Ausweis) proof of identity. ◆l~ieren [-ti'mi:rən], v.tr. (a) to authorize (s.o. to do sth.); (b) sich l., to show proof of one's identity.

Lehm [le:m], m -(e)s/-e clay (soil); Agr: loam.

Lehne ['le:nə], f -/-n (Rückenl.) back, (Arml.) arm (of a chair). ◆l~en, v.tr. & i. (haben) to lean (sth.) (gegen/an + acc, against); ◆L~stuhl, m armchair.

Lehr- ['le:r-], comb.fm. teaching (staff, method etc.). ◆L~buch, n Sch: textbook. ◆L~e i, f -/-n 1. Ind: etc: apprenticeship; kaufmännische L., commercial training. 2. (a) (Gelehrtes) die L. Christi/Hegels, the teachings of Christ/Hegel; (b) Fig: (Lektion) lesson; moral (of a story); das soll dir eine L. sein! let that be a lesson to you! ◆l~en, v.tr. to teach (a subject); ◆l~er, m -s/- Sch: teacher; N.Am: & Sp: etc: instructor. ◆'L~erin, f -/-nen Sch: (woman) teacher; (school)mistress; Sp: etc: instructress. ◆'L~erzimmer, n Sch: staff room. ◆'L~gang, m course of instruction); N.Am: program. ◆'L~jahr, n year of apprenticeship. ◆'L~junge, m (boy) apprentice. ◆'L~kraft, f teacher. ◆'L~ling, m -s/-e apprentice; (Auszubildender) trainee. ◆'L~plan, m syllabus. ◆'l~reich, adj. instructive, informative. ◆'L~satz, m Mth: theorem; Ecc: dogma. ◆'L~stelle, f place for an apprentice. ◆'L~stuhl, m chair, professorship. ◆'L~zeit, f -/no pl (term of) apprenticeship.

Lehre² ['le:rə], f -/-n Tchn: gauge.

Leib [laip], m -(e)s/-er (a) esp. Lit: body; mit L. und Seele dabei sein, to put one's (whole) heart into it; ich hielt ihn

mir vom L~e, I kept him at arm's length. ◆'L~eserziehung, f physical education. ◆'L~eskräfte, f aus L~n, with all one's might. ◆'L~esübungen, fpl physical exercises/training. ◆l~gericht, n favourite dish. ◆l~'haftig, adj. personified; (devil etc.) incarnate; adv. as large as life. ◆'l~lich, adj. (a) physical (pleasure, needs etc.); (b) l~licher Bruder, real/full brother. ◆'L~wächter, m bodyguard.

Leiche ['laiçə], f -/-n (dead) body, corpse; Fig: über L~en gehen, to stop at nothing. ◆'L~enbestatter, m undertaker, N.Am: also: mortician. ◆'L~enhalle, f mortuary. ◆'L~enschau, f post mortem (examination). ◆'L~enstarre, f -/no pl rigor mortis. ◆'L~enwagen, m hearse. ◆'L~nam, m -s/-e Lit: (dead) body, corpse.

leicht [laiçt], I. adj. 1. light (load, touch, Mil: artillery etc.); lightweight (material etc.); l. gebaut, lightly built. 2. (einfach) easy (job, decision, life etc.); light (reading, music etc.); er hat es nicht l., things aren't easy for him; das ist l. möglich, that's perfectly possible; l. zerbrechlich, very fragile. 3. (gering) slight (accent, error, exaggeration etc.); light (food, rain etc.); (im Geschmack) mild (cigar etc.); l~e Grippe, mild attack of flu; l. irritiert, slightly irritated II. comb.fm. 1. 'l~-, adj. (a) lightly (dressed, Mil: armed etc.); (b) easily (movable etc.); (c) slightly (damaged etc.). 2. 'L~-, light (metal, industry etc.); lightweight (concrete etc.). ◆'L~athlet(in), m(f) (track/field) athlete. ◆'L~athletik, f -/no pl (track and field) athletics. ◆'l~fallen, v.i.sep.irr.27 (sein) es ist ihm nicht leichtgefallen, he didn't find it easy. ◆'l~fertig, adj. rash (decision etc.); thoughtless, (action, talk); sein Leben l. aufs Spiel setzen, to risk one's life recklessly; ◆'L~fertigkeit, f -/no pl rashness; thoughtlessness. ◆'l~gläubig, adj. gullible (person). ◆'l~hin, adv. casually. ◆'L~igkeit, f -/no pl 1. lightness. 2. easiness (of a task etc.); mit L., casily, with ease. ◆'l~lebig, adj. happy-go-lucky. ◆'l~machen, v.tr.sep. to make (sth.) easy; er macht es sich dat leicht, he's making things easy for himself. ◆'L~metall, n light metal, esp. alloy. ◆'l~nehmen, v.tr.sep.irr.69 to take (sth.) lightly; not to take (work, life etc.) seriously. ◆'L~sinn, m rashness; (Gefahr gegenüber) recklessness. ◆'l~sinnig, adj. careless (mistake etc.); (zu gewagt) reckless (behaviour etc.); foolhardy (action, person etc.); rash (remark etc.).

leid [lait]. I. adj. (a) (es) tut mir l., I'm sorry; er tut mir l., I feel sorry for him; (b) j-n, etwas acc l. sein, to be tired of s.o., sth. **II.** L., *n* -(e)s/*no pl esp. Lit:* grief, sorrow; (*Leiden*) suffering; **dir wird kein L. geschehen,** no harm will come to you. ◆'l~**en. I.** *v.irr.*59 **1.** *v.i.* (*haben*) to suffer (**an einer Krankheit,** from an illness; **die Rosen haben durch den Frost (stark) gelitten,** the roses were (badly) damaged by the frost. **2.** *v.tr.* (*a*) to suffer (thirst, pain etc.); (*b*) **j-n, etwas (nicht) l. können/mögen,** to (dis)like s.o., sth. **II.** L., *n* -s/- (*a*) suffering; **nach langem L.,** after a long illness; (*b*) *Med:* (*Gebrechen*) complaint. ◆'L~**enschaft,** *f* -/-en passion, (*Begeisterung*) fervour, enthusiasm. ◆'l~**enschaftlich,** *adj.* passionate (person, nature, interest etc.); ardent (admirer etc.); fervent (speech etc.); *F:* **er geht l. gern in die Oper,** he adores going to the opera. ◆l~**er** ['laidər], *adv.* unfortunately; **er ist l. krank,** I'm afraid he's ill. ◆'l~**ig** ['laidiç], *adj.* nasty (problem, etc.); tiresome (business). ◆'l~**lich,** *adj.* reasonable (number, weather, knowledge etc.); passable (food etc.). ◆'l~**tragend,** *adj.* suffering; **die L~en** (i) those who suffer; (ii) (*nach einem Todesfall*) the bereaved/(*Trauernde*) mourners. ◆'L~**wesen,** *n* zu **meinem, seinem usw. L.,** to my, his etc. regret.

Leier ['laiər], *f* -/-n **1.** *Mus:* lyre. **2.** *F:* **immer die alte L.,** always the same old story. ◆'L~**kasten,** *m* barrel-organ. ◆'l~**n,** *v.tr. & i.* (*haben*) *F:* (*a*) to wind (a handle etc.); (*b*) to drone through (a poem, song etc.)

Leih- ['lai-], *comb.fm.* lending (fee etc.). ◆'L~**bibliothek,** *f* lending library. ◆'l~**en,** *v.tr.irr.* (*a*) to lend (money, books etc.); to loan (an exhibit etc.); (*b*) **ich habe (mir) bei/von ihm Geld geliehen,** I borrowed money from him. ◆'L~**gabe,** *f* *esp. Art:* loan. ◆'L~**haus,** *n* pawnshop. ◆'L~**wagen,** *m* hire/*N.Am:* rental car. ◆'l~**weise,** *adv.* on loan.

Leim [laim], *m* -(e)s/-e (*a*) glue; *F:* **aus dem L. gehen,** (*Gegenstand*) to come to pieces; (*b*) *F:* **j-m auf den L. gehen,** to fall for s.o.'s tricks. ◆'l~**en,** *v.tr.* (*a*) to glue (sth.); (*b*) *F:* to take (s.o.) in.

Lein|e ['lainə], *f* -/-n (*a*) line; (*b*) (*Hundel.*) leash, lead. ◆'l~**en. I.** *adj.* linen (sheets etc.). **II.** L., *n* -s/- linen. ◆'L~**en-,** *comb.fm.* linen (dress, paper etc.). ◆'L~**öl,** *n* linseed oil. ◆'L~**samen,** *m* linseed. ◆'L~**tuch,** *n* (*esp.* linen) sheet. ◆'L~**wand,** *f* -/-e *Art:* canvas; *Cin:* screen.

leise ['laizə], *adj.* = faint (steps, noise etc.); quiet (voice etc.); soft (music); **1. sprechen,** to talk quietly/in a low voice; **das Radio l~r stellen,** to turn the radio down; (*b*) light, gentle (rain, breeze, touch etc.); slight (mist, *Fig:* hope, doubt etc.); vague, faint (suspicion etc.).

Leiste ['laistə], *f* -/-n (edging) strip; (*Zierl.*) moulding; *Aut: etc:* trim; (*Fußl.*) skirting board.

'leist|en, *v.tr.* (*a*) (*vollbringen*) to achieve, accomplish (sth.); to perform (a task etc.); **gute Arbeit l.,** to do good work; (*b*) to render (a service, help etc.); (*c*) *F:* **sich dat etwas l.,** to treat oneself to sth.; **er kann sich keine Fehler mehr l.,** he can't afford to make any more mistakes. ◆'L~**ung,** *f* -/-en (*a*) (*Errungenschaft*) achievement; (*b*) (*Niveau*) **nach L. bezahlen,** to pay by results/*Ind:* productivity; (*c*) (*Ausstoß*) output of a machine, factory); power of an engine etc.); performance (of a part, car etc.); (*d*) (*Zahlung*) payment (of a sum, damages etc.). ◆'L~**ungs-,** *comb.fm.* (*a*) *Sp:* (*performance* (test etc.); (*b*) *Tchn:* power (output, reactor etc.); (*c*) *Ind:* productivity (check etc.). ◆'L~**ungsdruck,** *m* *Sch:* pressure (on a pupil/student) to reach a high standard. ◆'l~**ungsfähig,** *adj.* (*a*) efficient (worker, machine); powerful, high performance (car, engine); (*b*) (*Pers.*) fit. ◆'L~**ungsfähigkeit,** *f* -/*no pl* efficiency; productivity; *Ind:* output; *Aut:* performance; *Tchn:* power. ◆'L~**ungsprämie, L~ungszulage,** *f* productivity bonus.

Leit- ['lait-], *comb.fm.* (*a*) leading (currency etc.); guiding (star etc.); (*b*) main, central (idea, concept etc.). ◆'L~**artikel,** *m* leading article, leader. ◆'L~**bild,** *n* ideal. ◆'l~**en,** *v.tr.* (*a*) (*führen*) to lead (an expedition, discussion etc.); to manage (a firm etc.); to run (a hotel, shop etc.); to chair (a meeting); *Mus:* to conduct (an orchestra, choir etc.); *Sp:* to referee (a game); (*b*) to lead, guide (s.o.); (*lenken*) to divert (traffic etc.); (*c*) *Ph: etc:* to conduct (electricity, heat etc.). ◆'l~**end,** *adj.* guiding (principle etc.); managerial (position, function); leading (personality, part); topranking (official etc.). ◆'L~**er1,** *m* -s/- **1.** (*Pers.*) (*also* **L~in** *f*) leader (of a group etc.); director (of a firm); manager, *f* manageress (of a shop etc.); head (of a department etc.); *Mus:* conductor. **2.** *Ph:* conductor. ◆'L~**faden,** *m* (*Buch*) manual, guide; **L~fähigkeit,** *f* *Ph:* conductivity. ◆'L~**motiv,** *n* main theme; *Mus:* leitmotif. ◆'L~**planke,** *f* crash barrier, *N.Am:* guardrail. ◆'L~**spruch,** *m* motto. ◆'L~**stelle,** *f* control point. ◆'L~**ung,** *f* -/-en **1.** (*Leiten*) *no pl* leadership; *Com:* management; direction (of a project etc.); administration, control of finances etc.; chairmanship (of a committee, discussion); *Mus:* **unter (der) L. von X** conducted by X; *N.Am:* X conducting. **2.** *Com:* (*Leitende*) management. **3.** (*a*) *El:* cable; (*für Geräte*) wire, lead; (*b*) *Tel:* line; *F:* **er hat eine lange L.,** he's slow on the uptake; (*c*) (*Rohr*) (water, gas etc.) pipe; (*Hauptl.*) main, *N.Am:* line.

◆'L~ungsmast, m (a) Tel: telegraph pole; (b) mast/pylon (for electric cables). ◆'L~ungsrohr, n (water, gas etc.) pipe. ◆'L~ungswasser, n tap water.

Leiter² ['laitər], f -/-n ladder.

Lektion [lɛktsi'oːn], f -/-en Sch: lesson, unit (in a book). ◆L~türe ['-'tyːrə], -/-n 1. (Lesen) no pl reading. 2. reading matter.

Lende ['lɛndə], f -/-n Anat: & Cu: loin. ◆'L~nbraten, m loin; (Rind) sirloin.

lenk|bar ['lɛŋkbaːr], adj. steerable; (steuerbar) controllable; manageable (child). ◆'l~en, v.tr. (a) to steer (a vehicle), turn (a horse etc.); to guide (s.o., a missile etc.); to direct (traffic, a conversation etc.); (b) (regeln) to control (the press, economy etc.); to rule (a state). ◆'L~rad, n Aut: steering wheel. ◆'L~stange, f (von Fahrrad) handlebars. ◆'L~ung, f -/-en 1. Aut: steering. 2. control (of the economy etc.).

Leopard [leo'part], m -en/-en leopard.

Lepra ['leːpra], f -/no pl leprosy.

Lerche ['lɛrçə], f -/-n lark.

Lern- ['lɛrn-], comb.fm. (a) learning (method, process etc.); educational (aim etc.); (b) teaching (programme etc.). ◆'l~bar, adj. learnable; leicht/schwer l., easy/difficult to learn. ◆'l~begierig, adj. eager to learn. ◆'l~en, v.tr. to learn (sth., to do sth.); Klavier spielen l., to learn to play the piano; einen Beruf l., to train for a career; er lernt es nie, he'll never learn.

les|bar ['leːsbaːr], adj. legible (writing etc.); readable (book, style). ◆L~e-¹ ['leːzə-], comb.fm. reading (lamp, circle, desk etc.). ◆'l~en¹, v.irr. v.tr. & i. to read. hier ist zu l., daß ..., it says here ...; in ihren Augen war zu l., daß ..., you could tell from her eyes that ... ◆'l~enswert, adj. worth reading. ◆'l~er(in), m -s/- (f -/-nen) reader. ◆'L~erbrief, m reader's letter. ◆'l~erlich, adj. legible. ◆'L~esaal, m reading room (of a library). ◆'L~ezeichen, n bookmark. ◆'L~ung, f -/-en reading.

Lesb|ierin ['lɛsbiərin], f -/-nen Lesbian. ◆'l~isch, adj. Lesbian.

Lese² ['leːzə], f -/-n harvest, esp. (Weinl.) grape harvest. ◆'l~n², v.tr. to pick, gather (grapes, berries etc.).

letzt- ['lɛtst-], comb.fm. last-born, possible etc.). ◆'l~e(r,s), adj. last; (neueste) latest (news etc.). in letzter Zeit, of late, recently; er wurde als l~er bedient, he was served last; er wurde l~er he came last; F: der Film ist das L., the film is hopeless; sein L~es hergeben, to do one's utmost; bis ins l., to the last detail; ◆'l~emal, adv. das l., the last time; zum l~enmal, for the last time. ◆'l~ens, adv. (a) lastly; (b) (neulich)

recently. ◆'l~jährig, adj. last year's. ◆'l~lich, adv. (a) after all, when it comes to the point; (b) (zum Schluß) finally.

Leucht- ['lɔyçt-], comb.fm. luminous (dial etc.); fluorescent (screen- etc.); (mit L~stoffröhren) neon (writing etc.). ◆'l~e, f -/-n light. ◆'l~en, v.i. (haben) (Mond, Licht usw.) to shine; (Farben, Himmel usw.) to glow; (Meer usw.) in der Sonne l., to gleam in the sun; ◆'l~end, adj. luminous, glowing (colours etc.); vivid (green etc.); shining (eyes etc.). ◆'L~er, m -s/- chandelier; (Kerzenständer) candlestick. ◆'L~farbe, f luminous paint. ◆'L~feuer, n light beacon. ◆'L~kugel, f flare. ◆'L~rakete, f signal rocket. ◆'L~reklame, f neon (advertising) sign. ◆'L~turm, m lighthouse.

leugnen ['lɔygnən], v.tr. to deny (sth.).

Leukämie [lɔykɛ'miː], f -/no pl leukaemia.

Leukoplast [lɔyko'plast], n -(e)s/-e R.t.m. (plain) sticking plaster.

Leumund ['lɔymunt], m -(e)s/no pl (personal) reputation.

Leute ['lɔytə], pl people.

Leutnant ['lɔytnant], m -s/-e second lieutenant.

leutselig ['lɔytzeːliç], adj. affable. ◆'L~keit, f -/no pl affability.

Lexikon ['lɛksikɔn], n -s/-ka (a) encyclopedia. (b) (Wörterbuch) dictionary.

Liban|ese [liba'neːzə], m -n/-n Lebanese. ◆L~esin, f -/-nen Lebanese (woman). ◆l~esisch, adj. Lebanese. ◆L~on ['liːbanɔn]. Pr.n.m -s. Lebanon.

Libelle [li'bɛlə], f -/-n dragonfly.

liberal [libe'raːl], adj. liberal. ◆L~ismus [-ra'lismus], m -/no pl liberalism.

Libyen ['liːbjən]. Pr.n.n -s. Libya. ◆'L~yer(in), m -s/- (f -/-nen) Libyan. ◆'l~ysch ['liːbyʃ], adj. Libyan.

Licht¹ [liçt]. I. n -(e)s/-er light; L. machen, to turn the light(s) on; Fig: ans L. kommen, to come to light. II. 'L~-, 'l~-, comb.fm. light (year, source, conditions etc.); (patch, speed, strip etc.) of light. ◆'L~bild, n (passport-size) photograph. ◆'L~blick, m Fig: bright spot. ◆'l~durchlässig, adj. translucent. ◆'l~empfindlich, adj. light-sensitive. ◆'l~er'loh, adj. blazing; adv. l. brennen, to be blazing fiercely. ◆'L~hupe, f flasher. ◆'L~maschine, f Aut: etc: dynamo. ◆'L~schalter, m light switch. ◆'l~scheu, adj. Fig: shady (character etc.).

licht², adj. 1. (hell) light (room, sky, colour etc.); am l~en Tag, in broad daylight; 2. thin, sparse (hair, vegetation). ◆'l~en¹, v.tr. to thin (out) (trees, undergrowth etc.); sich l., (Wald usw.) to thin out; (Haare) to get(h) thin; (Nebel) to clear. ◆'L~ung, f -/-en

clearing.
lichten[2], *v.tr.* den Anker l., to weigh anchor.
Lid [liːt], *n* -(e)s/-er (eye)lid.
◆**L'~schatten,** *m* eye shadow.
lieb [liːp], *adj.* 1. (*a*) dear; **l'~e Grüße, Dein X,** kind regards, X; *F:* with love from X; **z.** (*a*) (*nett*) kind; *F:* nice (**zu** j-m, to s.o.); (*b*) (*brav*) good; **sei l.!** be a good boy/girl! 3. welcome (guest etc.); **mehr als mir l. war,** more than I wanted. ◆**l'~äugeln,** *v.i.insep. (haben)* **l. mit** + *dat,* to fancy (sth.), have one's eye on (sth.); to toy/flirt with (an idea). ◆**L'~e** [liːbə], *f* -/-n (*a*) (*zu etwas dat,* of sth.; **zu** j-m, of/for s.o.) love; (*b*) (*nett*) kind. ◆**l'~ebedürftig,** *adj.* in need of love. ◆**L'~e'lei,** *f* -/-en flirtation. ◆**l'~en,** *v.tr.* to love (s.o., sth.); **sie l. sich,** they are in love. ◆**l'~enswert,** *adj.* lovable (person); endearing, engaging (manner, smile etc.). ◆**l'~enswürdig,** *adj.* kind (**zu** j-m, to s.o.). ◆**L'~enswürdigkeit,** *f* -/-en 1. kindness. 2. kind remark. ◆**l'~er,** *adv.* 1. **er möchte l. gehen,** he would prefer to/would rather go; **er fährt l. als ich,** he likes driving more than I do; **es wäre mir l., wenn ...,** I would prefer it if ... 2. (*besser*) **wir wollen l. gehen,** we had better go. ◆**L'~es-,** *comb.fm.* love (letter, story, life, scene etc.); (*need,* declaration etc.) of love. ◆**L'~esdienst,** *m* (act of kindness, good turn. ◆**L'~eskummer,** *m* heartache; **sie hat L.,** she is unhappily in love. ◆**L'~espaar,** *n* courting couple; (pair of) lovers. ◆**l'~evoll,** *adj.* loving, affectionate (embrace, look etc.); (*für-sorglich*) devoted (care etc.). ◆**l'~gewinnen** [liːp-], *v.tr.sep.irr.3* to grow fond of (s.o., sth.). ◆**l'~haben,** *v.tr.sep. irr.44* to love (s.o., sth.), be fond of (s.o., sth.). ◆**L'~haber,** *m* -s/- 1. (*Geliebter*) lover. 2. (*also* **L'~haberin** *f*) lover (of art etc.); (*Sammler*) collector; *Sp:* enthusiast. ◆**l'~kosen** [liːp'koːzən], *v.tr.insep. Lit:* to caress (s.o.). ◆**l'~lich** [liːplɪç], *adj.* (*a*) sweet; (*b*) (*sanft*) gentle (landscape etc.); mellow (wine). ◆**l'~ling,** *m* -s/-e (*a*) darling; (*Kind*) pet; (*b*) (*Bevorzugte*) favourite. ◆**L'~lings-,** *comb.fm.* favourite (occupation, food, colour etc.). ◆**l'~los,** *adj.* loveless (childhood etc.); unloving (person, nature etc.); unkind (words etc.). ◆**L'~losigkeit,** *f* -/no pl unkindness; lack of care. ◆**l'~ste(r,s),** *adj.* dearest (friend etc.); favourite (toy etc.).
Lied [liːt], *n* -(e)s/-er song; *Ecc:* hymn. ◆**l'~ermacher(in),** *m* -s/- (*f* -/-nen) writer and composer of topical songs.
liederlich [liːdərlɪç], *adj.* slovenly; slipshod (piece of work etc.); (*ausschweifend*) dissolute, debauched.
Liefer- ['liːfər-], *comb.fm. Com:* delivery (contract, service etc.); (terms etc.) of

delivery. ◆**L'~ant** [-ə'rant], *m* -en/-en supplier. ◆**l'~bar,** *adj. Com:* available. ◆**l'~n,** *v.tr.* (*a*) (*Firma*) (*verkaufen*) to supply (goods, spare parts etc.) (j-m, to s.o.); (*zustellen*) to deliver (goods); (*b*) to provide (food, *Fig:* evidence etc.); (*Tier*) to yield (milk etc.). ◆**L'~schein,** *m* delivery/advice note. ◆**L'~ung,** *f* -/-en *Com:* (*a*) supply; (*Zustellung*) delivery; (*b*) (*Warensendung*) consignment, shipment. ◆**L'~wagen,** *m* van; (*offen*) pick-up truck. ◆**L'~zeit,** *f* period for delivery.
Liege ['liːgə], *f* -/-n day-bed, divan. ◆**l'~en,** *v.i.irr. (haben)* (*a*) to lie; (*b*) (*Stadt, Haus usw.*) to be situated; **das Zimmer liegt nach Süden,** the room faces south. *Fig:* **so wie die Dinge l.,** as things are; (*c*) (*sich befinden*) to lie; **auf dem Tisch lag Staub,** there was dust on the table; (*d*) **er/es liegt mir,** he/it appeals to me; **es liegt mir viel/nichts daran,** it is very important/of no importance to me; **es liegt an ihm,** (i) (*Entscheidung*) it is up to him; (ii) (*ist seine Schuld*) it is his fault. ◆**l'~enbleiben,** *v.i.sep.irr.12* (*sein*) (*a*) to stay in bed; (*b*) (*Schnee*) to settle; (*c*) (*übrigbleiben*) to be left/ (*liegenlassen*) left behind; (*Arbeit*) to be left undone. ◆**l'~enlassen,** *v.tr.sep.irr.57* (*a*) to leave (s.o., sth.) (*lying somewhere*); (*b*) (*vergessen*) to leave (sth.) behind. ◆**L'~esitz,** *m* reclining seat. ◆**L'~estuhl,** *m* deckchair. ◆**L'~estütz,** *m* -es/-e press-up, *N.Am:* push-up. ◆**L'~ewagen,** *m* couchette car.
Lift [lɪft], *m* -(e)s/-e & -s lift.
Liga ['liːga], *f* -/Ligen league.
Likör [li'køːr], *m* -s/-e liqueur.
lila ['liːla], *inv.adj.* lilac; (*tief*) mauve.
Lilie ['liːliə], *f* -/-n lily.
Liliputaner [lilipu'taːnər], *m* -s/- dwarf.
Limonade [limo'naːdə], *f* -/-n fizzy drink, mineral; (*Zitronenl.*) lemonade. ◆**L'~ne** [li'moːnə], *f* -/-n lime.
Limousine [limu'ziːnə], *f* -/-n *Aut:* (*large*) saloon, *N.Am:* sedan; (*mit Trennwand*) limousine.
Linde ['lɪndə], *f* -/-n lime tree.
lindern ['lɪndərn], *v.tr.* to ease, relieve (pain, suffering etc.); to soothe (pain etc.). ◆**L'~ung,** *f* -/no pl relief.
Lineal [line'aːl], *n* -s/-e ruler.
Linie ['liːniə], *f* -/-n line; **in erster L.,** first of all, primarily; **in zweiter L.,** secondarily; *F:* **auf die (schlanke) L. achten,** to watch one's figure. ◆**L'~nrichter,** *m* linesman. ◆**L'~nschiff,** *n* liner.
linieren [li'niːrən], *v.tr.* to rule lines on (paper etc.); **liniertes Papier,** lined paper.
linke(r,s) ['lɪŋkə(r,s)], *adj.* 1. (*a*) left (arm, side etc.); **auf der l'~en Seite/zur L'~en,** on the lefthand side/the left; (*b*) *Pol:* left-wing (politician, views etc.); (*wing*) **die L.,** the left; (*c*) (*von Klei-*

dung l. **Seite**, wrong side; l. **Masche**, purl stitch. 2. *P*: shady, doubtful (dealings, character etc.). ◆l~**isch**, *adj.* clumsy; (*gehemmt*) awkward. ◆l~**s**, *adv.* (*a*) on the left; **die zweite Straße l.**, the second on the left; l. **von mir to my** left; **von/nach l.**, from/to the left; **j-n l. liegenlassen**, to cold-shoulder s.o.; (*b*) *Pol*: l. **stehen**/F: **sein**, to be leftwing. ◆l~**saußen**, m *Fb*: outside left. ◆l~**sherum**, *adv.* to the left, anticlockwise. ◆l~**sradikal**, *adj.* with radical/extreme leftwing views. ◆l~**sverkehr**, m lefthand side of the road.

Linoleum [li'no:leum], n *-s/no pl* linoleum.

Linse ['linzə], f *-/-n* 1. *Bot*: lentil. 2. *Opt*: lens.

Lippe ['lipə], f *-/-n* lip. ◆l~**bekenntnis** n lip-service. ◆l~**nstift**, m lipstick.

liquidieren [likvi'di:rən], *v.tr.* to liquidate (a firm, opponent etc.); to wind up (a firm).

lispeln ['lispəln], *v.tr.&i.* (haben) to lisp (sth.).

List ['list], f *-/-en* 1. *no pl* cunning, craft(iness); guile. 2. trick; subterfuge. ◆l~**ig**, *adj.* cunning, crafty; (*schlau*) sly.

Liste ['listə], f *-/-n* list.

Litanei [lita'nai], f *-/-en* 1. *Ecc*: litany. 2. *F*: rigmarole.

Liter ['li:(t)ər], m & n *-s/-* litre.

liter|arisch [litə'ra:rif], *adj.* literary. ◆L~**atur** [-a'tu:r], f *-/-en* literature. II. L~~, *comb.fm.* literary (criticism, language, prize etc.); (history etc.) of literature.

Litfaßsäule ['litfaszɔylə], f advertisement pillar.

Liturg|ie [litur'gi:], f *-/-n* liturgy. ◆l~**isch** [-'turgif], *adj.* liturgical.

Litze ['litsə], f *-/-n* (gedreht) cord; (geflochten) braid.

live [laif]. I. *inv.adj. & adv.* live. II. 'L~~, *comb.fm.* live (broadcast etc.).

Livree [li'vre:], f *-/-n* livery.

Lizenz [li'tsents], f *-/-en* licence.

Lob [lo:p], n *-(e)s/-e* praise. ◆l~**en** ['lo:bən], *v.tr.* to praise (s.o.); **das lobe ich mir**, that's what I like to see. ◆l~**enswert**, *adj.* praiseworthy, laudable. ◆L~**lied**, n song of praise; Fig: **ein L. auf j-n anstimmen**, to sing s.o.'s praises. ◆L~**rede**, f eulogy.

löblich ['lø:plic], *adj.* praiseworthy, laudable.

Loch [lɔx], n *-(e)s/-er* (*a*) hole; gap (in a hedge etc.); (*b*) *Billiards*: pocket. ◆l~**en**, *v.tr.* to punch (a ticket, *Datapr*: card etc.). ◆L~**er**, m *-s/-* punch (for paper etc.). ◆L~**karte**, f punched card. ◆L~**streifen**, m punched tape.

löcherig ['lœçəriç], *adj.* full of holes.

Lock|e ['lɔkə], f *-/-n* curl. ◆l~**en**[1], *v.tr.*

to curl (s.o.'s hair); (*Haare*) **sich l.**, to curl. ◆'L~**enwickler**, m *-s/-* curler; (*dicker*) roller. ◆l~**ig**, *adj.* curly.

lock|en[2], *v.tr.* (*a*) to attract (a bird etc.); to lure (s.o., an animal); (*b*) (*reizen*) to tempt; **ein L~des Angebot**, a tempting offer. ◆'L~**mittel**, n bait, lure. ◆'L~**ruf**, m mating call. ◆L~**ung**, f *-/-en* lure, attraction; (*Versuchung*) temptation. ◆'L~**vogel**, m (*Vogel, Pers.*) decoy.

locker ['lɔkər], *adj.* loose; light (soil, mixture); relaxed (posture); Fig: casual (relationship etc.); Pej: lax (morals, discipline). ◆l~**lassen**, *v.i.sep.irr.57* (haben) *F*: nicht l., to keep at it. ◆l~**n**, *v.tr.* to loosen (a screw etc.); ◆l~**n**, to slacken (a rope etc.); to relax (one's grip, discipline etc.); **in gelockerter Stimmung**, in a relaxed mood; **sich l.**, (*Zahn, Schraube usw.*) to work loose; (*Nebel*) to lift; (*Disziplin usw.*) to relax; (*Spannung usw.*) to ease. ◆L~**ung**, f *-/no pl* loosening; slackening; relaxation; easing (of tension).

lodern ['lo:dərn], *v.i.* (haben) (*Flamme*) to flare (up); (*Feuer*) to blaze.

Löffel ['lœfəl], m *-s/-* spoon; ◆l~**n**, *v.tr.* to spoon (sth.) (up) ◆l~**weise**, *adv.* by the spoonful.

Logbuch ['lɔkbu:x], n log(book).

Loge ['lo:ʒə], f *-/-n* 1. *Th*: box. 2. (porter's/masonic) lodge.

logieren [lo'ʒi:rən], *v.i.* (haben) to stay, (*als Untermieter*) lodge, *N.Am*: room (bei j-m, with s.o.).

Log|ik ['lo:gik], f *-/no pl* logic. ◆l~**isch**, *adj.* logical.

Lohn [lo:n]. I. m *-(e)s/-e* (*a*) wage; *coll*: pay; (*b*) (*Belohnung*) reward. II. 'L~~, *comb.fm.* wage (increase etc.); wages (office, book); pay (increase, pause, round etc.). ◆'L~**empfänger**, m wage earner. ◆'L~**steuer**, f income tax (on earned income). ◆'L~**stopp**, m wage freeze. ◆'L~**tüte**, f wage/pay packet.

lohnen ['lo:nən], *v.* 1. *v.* refl. & *v.i.* (haben) **(sich) l.**, to be worthwhile/worth it. 2. *v.tr. Lit*: **j-m etwas l.**, to reward s.o. for sth. ◆l~**d**, *adj.* worthwhile; rewarding (job, experience etc.).

Lok [lɔk], f *-s* F: engine. ◆'L~**führer**, m engine driver, *N.Am*: engineer.

lokal [lo'ka:l]. I. *adj.* local. II. L~, n *-(e)s/-e* (*Kneipe*) Brit: pub, *N.Am*: bar; (*Speisel.*) restaurant. ◆l~~, *comb.fm.* local (newspaper etc.). ◆L~**termin**, m *Jur*: visit to the scene of the crime.

Lokomotiv|e [lokomo'ti:və], f *-/-n* locomotive, engine. ◆L~**führer** [-'ti:ffy:rər], m engine driver, *N.Am*: engineer.

Lorbeer ['lorbe:r], m *-s/-en* laurel, bay; (*L~kranz*) laurel wreath; laurels. ◆'L~**baum**, m bay (tree). ◆'L~**blatt**, n *esp. Cu*: bay leaf.

Lore ['lo:rə], f *-/-n* Min: etc: truck.

Los¹ [loːs], n -es/-e 1. (Schein) lottery/raffle ticket; also Fig: das Große L. ziehen, to hit the jackpot. 2. (Schicksal) lot, fate.

los². I. pred.adj. (a) (Hund usw.) free, loose; der Knopf ist l., the button has come off; F: ich bin ihn/es l., I have got rid of him/it; (b) was ist hier l.? what is going on here? was ist (mit dir) l.? what's the matter (with you)? in dieser Stadt ist nichts l., nothing ever happens in this town. II. adv. 1. int. come on! hurry up! 2. ich muß (schon) l., I must go. ◆'l~binden, v.tr. to untie.
◆'l~brechen, v.tr. & i. sep.irr.14 (sein) to break (sth.) off; (Sturm usw.) to break; (Tumult usw.) to break out.
◆'l~fahren, v.i.sep.irr.26 (sein) (a) (abfahren) to start; (Fahrzeug) to move/Aut: drive off. ◆'l~gehen, v.i.sep.irr.36 (sein) (a) (aufbrechen) to set off (on foot); (b) (abgehen) auf j-n l., to go for s.o.; (c) F: (anfangen) to start; jetzt geht's los! here goes! this is it! (d) F: (sich lösen) to come off; (e) (Mine usw.) to go off.
◆'l~kaufen, v.tr.sep. to buy the release of (a prisoner), ransom (s.o.).
◆'l~kommen, v.tr.sep.irr.53 (sein) to get away. ◆'l~lassen, v.tr.sep.irr.57 (a) to let go of (sth.), release (s.o.); b) to release (a prisoner, one's hand, Aut: the brake etc.); die Hunde auf j-n l., to set the dogs on s.o.; (c) F: to deliver oneself of (a speech, joke etc.). ◆'l~legen, v.i.sep. (haben) F: (mit der Arbeit) l., to get cracking/Brit: stuck in. ◆'l~lösen, v.tr.sep. to remove, detach (sth.).
◆'l~reißen, v.tr.sep.irr.4 to tear/pull (sth.) off; sich l., (Tier) to break free/loose. ◆'l~sagen, v.refl.sep. sich von j-m, einer Partei usw. l., to break with s.o., a party etc. ◆'l~schießen, v.i.sep.irr.31 F: (a) (sein) (wegrasen) to shoot off; (b) Fig: (reden) to fire away. ◆'l~sprechen, v.tr.sep.irr.14 to absolve (s.o.) (von einer Schuld usw., from blame etc.). ◆'l~werden, v.tr.sep.irr.109 (sein) to get rid of (s.o., sth.). ◆'l~ziehen, v.i.sep.irr.113 (sein) F: (a) to set out; (b) (kritisieren) gegen j-n l., to pull s.o. to pieces.

lösbar ['løːsbaːr], adj. soluble (problem). ◆**Lösch/blatt** ['lœʃblat], n (sheet of) blotting paper. ◆'l~en1, v.tr. (a) to extinguish, put out (a fire, candle etc.); (b) to quench (one's thirst); (c) (beseitigen) to delete (an entry etc.); to erase (a tape recording); (d) to blot (ink). ◆'L~papier, n blotting paper.

löschen², v.tr. Nau: to unload, discharge (a ship, cargo etc.).

lose ['loːzə], adj. loose; slack (rope etc.); casual (acquaintance etc.).

Lösegeld ['løːzəgɛlt], n ransom.
◆'l~en, v.tr. (a) (entfernen) to remove, get off (dirt etc.); sich l., (Tapete,

Schmutz usw.) to come off; (Pers.) to detach/free oneself; (b) (lockern) to loosen (a screw, one's belt, grip etc.); to undo (a knot etc.); to relieve (tension etc.); sich l., (Schraube usw.) to work loose, (loskommen) come undone; (Spannung usw.) to be relieved; (c) to cancel, terminate (a contract etc.); to break (ties, connections etc.); seine Verlobung l., to break off one's engagement; (d) to solve (a problem, puzzle etc.); (e) to buy (a ticket).
◆'l~lich, adj. soluble. ◆'L~ung, f -/-en (also Ch:) solution;
◆'L~ungsmittel, n solvent.

losen ['loːzən], v.i. (haben) to draw lots (um etwas acc, for sth.).

Losung ['loːzuŋ], f -/-en 1. Mil: etc: password. 2. Pol: etc: (Parole) slogan, watchword.

Lot [loːt], n -(e)s/-e plumb line; Nau: (sounding) lead. ◆'l~en, v.tr. to plumb (a wall etc.); Nau: to sound (depth of water). ◆'l~recht, adj. vertical, perpendicular.

löt|en ['løːtən], v.tr. to solder (sth.). ◆'L~kolben, m soldering iron.

Lothringen ['loːtriŋən]. Pr.n.n -s. Lorraine.

Lotse ['loːtsə], m -n/-n Nau: etc: pilot. ◆'l~n, v.tr. to pilot (a ship etc.); to guide (an aircraft, s.o.).

Lotterie [lotə'riː], f -/-n lottery.

Lotto ['loto], n -s/-s (esp. state) lottery.

Löwe ['løːvə], m -n/-n lion.
◆'L~enanteil, m der L., the lion's share. ◆'L~enmäulchen, n -s/- snapdragon. ◆'L~enzahn, m dandelion.
◆'L~in, f -/-nen lioness.

loyal [loa'jaːl], adj. loyal. ◆**L~ität**
[-jali'tɛːt], f -/-en loyalty.

Luchs [luks], m -es/-e lynx.

Lücke ['lykə], f -/-n gap; (im Formular usw.) blank (space). ◆'L~nbüßer, m -s/- (Pers., Sache) stopgap. ◆'l~nhaft, adj. (a) with gaps; (b) incomplete; fragmentary (knowledge etc.). ◆'l~nlos, adj. complete (set etc.); comprehensive (knowledge).

Luder ['luːdər], n -s/- P: (a) (Mädchen) ein kleines/faules L., a little/lazy soand-so; (b) Pej: (gemeines) L., (Mann) bastard; (Frau) bitch.

Luft [luft]. I. f -/-e (a) air; in die L. gehen, to blow up, explode; in der L. liegen, to be in the air; F: (Pers.) to blow one's top; Fig: etwas liegt in der L., there is sth. in the air; die Geschichte ist völlig aus der L. gegriffen, the story is pure invention; er behandelte mich wie L., he behaved as if I wasn't there; (b) (Atem) breath; tief L. holen, to take a deep breath; er bekam keine L., he could not breathe; F: mir blieb die L. weg, it took my breath away; (c) F: (freier Raum) space (between objects etc.). II. 'L~-, comb.fm. air (freight, hole, cooling, offensive, rifle, battle, traffic etc.); (change etc.) of air,

◆'L~**angriff**, m air raid. ◆'L~**ballon**, m balloon. ◆'L~**blase**, f air bubble/ Min: pocket. ◆'l~**dicht**, adj. airtight. ◆'L~**druck**, m (a) atmospheric pressure; (b) (Druckwelle) blast. ◆'L~**fahrt**, f aviation. ◆'L~**feuchtigkeit**, f humidity. ◆'l~**gekühlt** adj. air-cooled. ◆'L~**hauch**, m breath of air. ◆'l~**ig**, adj. (a) airy (room etc.); (b) cool, light (dress etc.). ◆'L~**kissenfahrzeug**, n hovercraft. ◆'L~**kurort**, m climatic health resort. ◆'l~**leer**, adj. containing no air; l~**leerer Raum**, vacuum. ◆'L~**linie**, f 100 km l., 100 km as the crow flies. ◆'L~**matratze**, f airbed. ◆'L~**pirat**, m hijacker (of aircraft). ◆'L~**post**, f airmail; per/mit L., by airmail. ◆'L~**raum**, m air space (of a country). ◆'L~**röhre**, f windpipe, trachea. ◆'L~**schiff**, f airship. ◆'L~**schlange**, f streamer. ◆'L~**schutz**, comb.fm. air-raid (shelter, siren etc.). ◆'L~**sprung**, m leap, jump (in the air). ◆'L~**verschmutzung**, f air pollution. ◆'L~**waffe**, f air force. ◆'L~**weg**, m air route; **auf dem L.**, by air. ◆'L~**zufuhr**, f air supply. ◆'L~**zug**, m draught, N.Am: draft (of air).

lüft|en ['lyftən], v. 1. v.tr. (a) to air (a room, bed); (b) Fig: to reveal (a secret etc.). 2. v.i. (haben) to let in some air. ◆'L~**ung**, f -/-no pl airing; ventilation.

Lüg|e ['ly:gə], f -/-n lie; **j-n L~n strafen**, (i) to prove s.o. a liar; (ii) Fig: to prove s.o. wrong. ◆'l~**en**, v.i.irr. (haben) to lie. ◆'L~**ner(in)**, m -s/- (f -/-nen) liar.

Luke ['lu:kə], f -/-n (a) (im Dach) skylight; (b) Nau: etc: hatch.

Lümmel ['lyməl], m -s/- Pej: lout, P: slob. ◆'l~**haft**, adj. loutish. ◆'l~**n**, v.refl. **sich l.**, to loll, sprawl.

Lump [lump], m -en/-en F: Pej: scoundrel, P: swine. ◆'l~**en**. I. v.i. (haben) F: **sich nicht l. lassen**, to be openhanded. II. L., m -s/- rag. ◆'l~**ig**, adj. F: measly, paltry (salary, sum etc.).

Lunge ['luŋə], f -/-n lung. ◆'L~**n-**, comb.fm. lung (disease, cancer etc.). ◆'L~**nentzündung**, f pneumonia. ◆'l~**nkrank**, adj. suffering from tuberculosis.

Lunte ['luntə], f F: **L. riechen**, to sense trouble.

Lupe ['lu:pə], f -/-n magnifying glass; F: **j-n, etwas unter die L. nehmen**, to investigate s.o., sth. closely. ◆'l~**nrein**, adj. flawless (diamond etc.).

Lupine [lu'pi:nə], f -/-n lupin.

Lurch [lurç], m -(e)s/-e amphibian.

Lust [lust], f -/"-e (a) no pl desire (etwas zu tun, to do sth.); **ich hatte keine L.** (dazu), (I) don't feel like/fancy it; (b) no pl (Freude) pleasure; **etwas mit L. und Liebe tun**, to love doing sth.; (c) Lit: (Begierde) lust, (carnal) desire; (Wollust) (sensual) pleasure. ◆'l~**ig**, adj. (a) (munter) jolly; gay (person, colour etc.); (b) (komisch) funny, amusing (person, story etc.); **sich über j-n, etwas** acc **l. machen**, to make fun of s.o., sth. ◆'l~**los**, adj. (Pers. usw.) apathetic, listless; adv. half-heartedly. ◆'L~**mord**, m sex murder. ◆'L~**spiel**, n comedy.

Lüster ['lystər], m -s/- chandelier.

lüstern ['lystərn], adj. (a) lascivious, lecherous; **l~er Blick**, leer; (b) (gierig) greedy (**nach** + dat/**auf** + acc, for).

lutsch|en ['lutʃən], v.tr. & i. (haben) **etwas/an etwas** dat **l.**, to suck sth. ◆'L~**er**, m -s/- lollipop.

lux|uriös [luksuri'ø:s], adj. luxurious. ◆'L~**us** ['luksus], m -/no pl luxury; L. **treiben/im L. leben**, to live a life of luxury. ◆'l~**us-**, comb.fm. luxury (article, flat, hotel etc.); de luxe (model, edition etc.).

lynch|en ['lynçən], v.tr. to lynch (s.o.). ◆'L~**justiz**, f lynch law.

Lyr|ik ['ly:rik], f -/no pl lyric poetry. ◆'L~**iker**, m -s/- lyric poet. ◆'l~**isch**, adj. l. lyric (verse, Mus: tenor). 2. (gefühlvoll) lyrical (mood etc.).

M

M, m [εm], n -/- (the letter) M, m.

Maat [ma:t], m -(e)s/-e(n) (ship's) mate.

Mach|art ['max?a:rt], f Cl: etc: style. ◆'**m~bar**, adj. feasible. ◆'**M~e**, f -/ no pl das ist alles nur M., that's all just show/put on. ◆'**m~en**, v. 1. v.tr. (a) (schaffen, herstellen) to make (sth.); aus Holz gemacht, made of wood; **ein Examen/Foto m.**, to take an exam/a photo; **das Essen m.**, to get the meal; **j-n zum General/zu seiner Frau m.**, to make s.o. a general/one's wife; (b) (tun, ausführen) to do (sth., nothing, one's homework etc.); **was macht er?** (i) what

is he doing? (ii) (beruflich) what does he do (for a living)? **so etwas macht man nicht**, that isn't done; **was macht deine Mutter/deine Arbeit?** how is your mother/your work getting on? F: (Abschiedsgruß) **mach's gut!** cheerio! good luck! (c) **das macht zusammen drei Mark**, that comes to three marks (altogether); (d) (verursachen) to cause (sth.); **salzige Speisen m. Durst**, salty food makes you thirsty; **er macht mir viele Sorgen**, he causes me a lot of worry; **das macht mir Freude**, it gives me pleasure; (e) F: **das macht nichts!** that doesn't matter! **mach dir nichts daraus,** don't take it to heart; (*f*) F: to act as (referee etc.); (*g*) F: **sich m.,** (*Pers.*) to do well, (*Kranker*) get well; (*Sache*) to turn out well; (*Wetter*) to improve; **sich an die Arbeit m.,** to get down to work; **sich auf den Weg m.,** to set off, F: get going; **sich bemerkbar m.,** (*Sache*) to become noticeable; (*Pers.*) to make one's presence felt: 2. *v.i.* (*haben*) (*a*) **laß ihn nur m.!** let him do as he pleases; (*b*) F: **macht schon/schnell!** hurry up! **macht, daß ihr bald zurück seid!** see that you are back soon.

Macht [maxt]. I. *f -/-e* power; (*Stärke*) strength; force (of a blow etc.); **mit aller M.,** with all one's might; **die M. der Gewohnheit,** force of habit; **an die M. kommen/an der M. sein,** to come to/be in power; **die verbündeten M~e,** the allied powers. II. **'M~,** *comb.fm.* power (politics etc.); (*position* etc.) of strength. ◆**'M~bereich,** *m* sphere of influence. ◆**'M~haber,** *m -s/-* ruler. ◆**'m~los,** *adj.* powerless. ◆**'M~losigkeit,** *f -/no pl* powerlessness; helplessness. ◆**'M~probe,** *f* trial of strength. ◆**'m~voll,** *adj.* powerful (ruler etc.). ◆**'M~wort,** *n* ein **M.** sprechen, to put one's foot down.

mächtig ['mɛçtɪç], *adj.* **1.** powerful (ruler, enemy etc.); mighty (nation, fleet, river etc.); strong, powerful (blow, build, voice); massive (building etc.); **sich m. freuen,** to be terribly pleased. **2. einer Sprache m. sein,** to be able to speak a language.

Machwerk ['maxvɛrk], *n* concoction.

Macke ['makə], *f -/-n* F: (*Tick*) quirk; **eine M. haben,** to be nutty.

Mädchen ['mɛːtçən]. I. *n -s/-* girl; F: **M. für alles,** maid of all work; *Hum:* girl Friday. II. **'M~,** *comb.fm.* girl's (voice etc.); girls' (voices, school etc.). ◆**'m~haft,** *adj.* girlish. ◆**'M~name,** *m* (i) girl's name; (ii) (*vor der Ehe*) maiden name

Made ['maːdə], *f -/-n* maggot. ◆**'m~ig,** *adj.* maggoty.

Magazin [maga'tsiːn], *n -s/-e* **1.** (*a*) (*Lager*) warehouse; storeroom; *Mil:* (storage) depot; (*b*) (*Behälter*) magazine (of a gun etc.). **2.** (*Zeitschrift*) magazine.

Magen ['maːgən]. I. *m -s/-* & *-* stomach; **mir dreht sich der M. um,** I feel quite sick. II. **'M~,** *comb.fm.* stomach (complaint, acid etc.); (*cancer* etc.) of the stomach; gastric (region, juice, acid etc.). ◆**'M~beschwerden,** *fpl* stomach trouble. ◆**'M~geschwür,** *n* gastric ulcer. ◆**'M~grube,** *f* pit of the stomach. ◆**'M~schmerzen,** *mpl* stomach ache.

mager ['maːgər], *adj.* **1.** (*dünn*) thin, lean (person, face etc.). **2.** (*ohne Fett*) lean (meat); *Agr:* poor (soil, harvest); *Fig:* meagre. ◆**'M~keit,** *f -/no pl* **1.** thin-

ness. **2.** (*a*) leanness; low-fat content; (*b*) *Agr:* poorness (of soil etc.).

Mag|ie [ma'giː], *f -/no pl* magic. ◆**M~ier** ['maːgiər], *m -s/no pl* magician. ◆**'m~isch,** *adj.* magic (spell etc.).

Magistrat [magis'traːt], *m -(e)s/-e* *Adm:* city council.

Magnet [ma'gneːt]. I. *m -en* & *-s/-en* & *-e* magnet. II. **M~,** *comb.fm.* magnetic (field, compass, needle, *Rec:* head etc.). ◆**m~isch,** *adj.* magnetic.

Mahagoni [maha'goːni], *n -s/no pl* mahogany.

Mäh|drescher ['mɛːdrɛʃər], *m -s/-* combine harvester. ◆**'m~en,** *v.tr.* to mow (a lawn); to cut (grass etc.), (*ernten*) reap (corn etc.). ◆**'M~er,** *m -s/-* (*pers.*) **'M~maschine,** *f* (*für Gras*) mower; (*für Getreide*) reaper.

Mahl [maːl], *n -(e)s/-e* meal. ◆**'M~zeit,** *f* meal; *int.* **M.!** (i) I hope you enjoy your meal; (ii) (*Gruß am Mittag*) hello! F: **Prost M.!** that's a fine mess!

mahl|en ['maːlən], *v.tr.&i. irr.* (*haben*) to grind (coffee, corn etc.).

mahn|en ['maːnən], *v.tr.* (*erinnern*) to remind (s.o.) (**wegen etwas gen,** about sth.; **an etwas** *acc,* of sth.), (*warnen*) to warn (s.o.), (*auffordern*) to urge (s.o.) (**zur Vorsicht usw.,** to be careful etc.). ◆**'M~mal,** *n* memorial. ◆**'M~ung,** *f -/-en* (*Aufforderung*) reminder; (*warning*).

Mähne ['mɛːnə], *f -/-n* mane.

Mai [mai], *m -(e)s/-e* May. ◆**'M~baum,** *m* maypole. ◆**'M~feier,** *f* May Day celebration. ◆**'M~glöckchen,** *n -s/-* lily of the valley. ◆**'M~käfer,** *m* cockchafer, maybug.

Mailand ['mailant]. *Pr.n.n -s.* Milan.

Mais [mais], *m -es/no pl* (*a*) maize; *N.Am:* corn; (*b*) *Cu:* (*als Gemüse*) sweet corn. ◆**'M~kolben,** *m -s/-* corncob; *Cu:* corn on the cob.

Majestät [majɛs'tɛːt], *f -/-en* **1.** majesty. **2. Seine/Ihre M.,** His/Her Majesty. ◆**m~isch,** *adj.* majestic.

Major [ma'joːr], *m -s/-e* **1.** *Mil:* major. **2.** *Av:* squadron leader.

Majoran [majo'raːn], *m -s/-e* marjoram.

makaber [ma'kaːbər], *adj.* macabre.

Makel ['maːkəl], *m -s/-* (*Fehler*) blemish (on fruit/*Fig:* s.o.), *Lit:* (*Schmach*) stain, taint. ◆**'m~los,** *adj.* flawless (skin, articles etc.); spotless (appearance, condition); *Fig:* untarnished (reputation); **m. sauber,** spotlessly clean.

mäkeln ['mɛːkəln], *v.i.* (*haben*) F: **an etwas** *dat* **m.,** to find fault with sth.

Makkaroni [maka'roːni], *pl* macaroni.

Makler ['maːklər], *m -s/-* **1.** (*Börsenm.*) broker. **2.** (*Grundstücksm.*) estate agent. ◆**'M~gebühr,** *f* brokerage; broker's commission.

Makrele [ma'kreːlə], *f -/-n* mackerel.

Makrone [ma'kroːnə], *f -/-n* macaroon.

Mal[1] [ma:l]. **I.** *n* -(e)s/-e time; **zum ersten/letzten M**., for the first/last time; **mit einem M~(e)**, all at once; **kein einziges M**., not once. **II. m.**, *adv.* **1.** *Mth:* **acht m. zwei ist sechzehn**, eight times two equals sixteen; **das Zimmer ist acht m. fünf Meter (groß)**, the room is eight metres by five. **2.** *F:* (= *einmal*) once; **warst du schon m. dort?** have you ever been there? **m. hier, m. dort**, sometimes here, sometimes there; **stell dir das m. vor**, just imagine that; **hör m.!** (just) listen!

Mal[2], *n* -(e)s/-e **1.** mark; (*Mutterm.*) birthmark; (*braun*) mole. **2.** *Sp:* marker; base; (*also* **M~feld** *n*) touch.

Malaria [ma'la:ria], *f* -/no pl malaria.

mal|en ['ma:lən]. **I.** *v.tr.* (a) to paint (sth.); (*Kind*) to draw (sth.); (b) *Fig:* (*schildern*) to portray (sth.). **II. m.**, -s/ *no pl* painting. ◆'**M~er(in)**, *m* -s/- (*f -/-nen*) painter; (*Kunstm.*) artist. ◆**M~er**, *comb.fm.* (a) *Art:* artist's (studio, canvas etc.); (b) painting and decorating (business, work etc.). ◆'**M~e'rei**, *f* -/-en painting. ◆'**m~erisch**, *adj.* **1.** picturesque (area, place); quaint (house etc.). **2.** artistic (talent). ◆'**M~kasten**, *m* paintbox. ◆'**M~stift**, *m* crayon.

Malheur [ma'lø:r], *n* -s/-e & -s *F:* mishap.

Mallorca [ma'jɔrka]. *Pr.n.n* -s. Majorca.

Malt|a ['malta]. *Pr.n.n* -s. Malta. ◆**M~eser(in)** ['-'tɛːzər(in)], *m* -s/- (*f -/-nen*) Maltese.

Malz [malts], *n* -es/no pl malt. ◆'**M~bier**, *n* (non-alcoholic) malt beer.

Mammut ['mamut]. **I.** *n* -s/-e & -s *Z:* mammoth. **II.** '**M~-**, *comb.fm.* mammoth (programme, enterprise etc.); gigantic (building etc.).

man [man], *indef.pron.* (a) one; you; **das sagt m. nicht**, one doesn't/you don't say that; **das tut m. nicht**, that isn't done; **das trägt m. wieder**, that is being worn again; (b) people; somebody; **m. sagt**, **daß ...**, they say that ...; it is said that ...

Manager ['mɛnidʒər], *m* -s/- *Com: Th: etc:* manager; *Com:* executive.

manch [manç], *indef.pron. & adj.* (a) *sing.* many (a), several; **in m~em hat er recht**, he is right about quite a few things; (b) *pl* (*mehrere*) **m~e** (*der*) **Kandidaten**, some/several of the candidates; (c) *m.m. Lit:* **m. einer**, many a person. ◆'**m~erlei**, *adj.* various (kinds of); **m. Dinge**, various things. ◆'**m~mal**, *adv.* sometimes.

Mandant(in) [man'dant(in)], *m* -en/-en (*f -/-nen*) *Jur:* client.

Mandarine [manda'ri:nə], *f* -/-n mandarin (orange); (*flach*) tangerine.

Mandat [man'da:t], *n* -(e)s/-e **1.** power of attorney. **2.** (*Parlamentsm.*) (member's) mandate, seat.

Mandel ['mandəl], *f* -/-n **1.** almond. **2.** tonsil. ◆'**M~entzündung**, *f* tonsillitis.

Mandoline [mando'li:nə], *f* -/-n mandoline(e).

Manege [ma'ne:ʒə], *f* -/-n circus ring.

Mangel[1] ['maŋəl]. **I.** *m* -s/- **1.** *no pl* (*Fehlen*) lack (**an** + *dat*, of); (*nicht genug*) shortage (**an Lebensmitteln usw.**, of food etc.); **aus M. an Erfahrung/Beweisen**, due to lack of experience/evidence. **2.** *usu.pl* (*Fehler*) shortcoming. **II.** '**M~-**, *comb.fm. Med:* deficiency (disease, symptom etc.). ◆'**M~beruf**, *m* understaffed profession. ◆'**m~haft**, *adj.* (a) (*fehlerhaft*) defective, faulty (goods etc.); (b) (*schlecht*) poor (light, memory etc.); *Sch: unsatisfactory.* ◆'**m~n**[1], *v.i.* (*haben*) *esp. Lit:* **es mangelt an etwas** *dat*, there is a lack/shortage of sth. ◆'**M~ware**, *f* scarce commodity; **M. sein**, to be in short supply.

Mangel[2], *f* -/-n mangle. ◆'**m~n**[2], *v.tr.* to mangle (washing etc.).

Manie [ma'ni:], *f* -/-n mania; obsession.

Manier [ma'ni:r], *f* -/-en **1.** *no pl* (*Art*) manner; *Art:* style. **2.** *usu.pl* (*gute/schlechte*) **M~en**, (good/bad) manners. ◆'**m~lich**, *adj.* (a) well-behaved (child); proper (appearance etc.); *adv.* **sich m. benehmen**, to behave properly; (b) *F:* reasonable, decent (quality etc.).

Manifest [mani'fɛst], *n* -es/-e manifesto.

Maniküre [mani'ky:rə], *f* -/-n **1.** *no pl* manicure. **2.** (*Pers.*) manicurist.

Manipul|ation [manipulatsi'o:n], *f* -/-en manipulation. ◆'**m~ieren** ['-'li:rən], *v.tr.* to manipulate (s.o., a situation etc.); *F:* to rig (an election etc.).

Manko ['maŋko], *n* -s/-s **1.** disadvantage; drawback. **2.** *Fin:* deficit.

Mann [man], *m* -(e)s/-er (a) man; **M. für M.**, one by one; **Gespräch von M. zu M.**, man-to-man/frank talk; **fünf Mark pro M.**, five marks per person; **seinen M. stehen**, to hold one's own; *F:* **an den M. bringen**, to find a taker for (sth.); (b) *Mil: Ind:* **hundert M.**, a hundred men; *Nau:* **alle M. an Deck!** all hands on deck! (c) (*Ehemann*) husband. ◆'**m~haft**, *adj.* manly (deed etc.); courageous (deed, decision etc.); stout (resistance). ◆'**M~sbild**, *n* *F: Pej:* male. ◆'**M~schaft**, *f* -/-en *Sp: & Fig:* team; (*Besatzung*) crew. ◆'**M~schafts-**, *comb.fm.* team (game, sport, race, captain etc.). ◆'**m~shoch**, *adj.* as tall/high as a man. ◆'**m~stoll**, *adj. F:* nymphomaniac.

Männ|chen ['mɛnçən], *n* -s/- **1.** little man, dwarf. **2.** *Z:* male; *Orn:* cock. **3.** (*Hund*) **M. machen**, to sit up (and beg). ◆'**M~er-**, *comb.fm.* man's (trousers, voice etc.); men's (clothing, ward, club etc.); male (voice, *Ecc:* order etc.). ◆'**M~ersache**, *f* a man's work/business. ◆'**M~erchor**, *m* male voice choir. ◆'**m~lich**, *adj.* (a) male (sex, line, animal etc.); *Gram:* masculine (noun etc.); (b) masculine (behaviour, features etc.). ◆**'M~lichkeit,** f -/no pl manliness, masculinity (*Potenz*) virility.

Mannequin [manəkɛ̃], n -s/-s (fashion) model.

mannig|fach ['maniçfax], adj. esp. Lit: numerous, manifold. ◆**m~faltig,** adj. Lit: diverse.

Manöv|er [ma'nø:vər], n -s/- 1. manoeuvre. 2. Pej: F: gambit; trick. ◆**m~rieren** [-ø'vri:rən], v.tr. & i. (haben) to manoeuvre (a car, ship etc.); Fig: to steer (s.o.). ◆**m~rierfähig,** adj. manoeuvrable.

Mansarde [man'zardə], f -/-n attic room. ◆**M~nwohnung,** f attic flat/N.Am: apartment.

Manschette [man'ʃɛtə], f -/-n (a) Cl: cuff; (b) paper wrapper (around flowers etc.). ◆**M~nknopf,** m cuff-link.

Mantel ['mantəl], m -s/¨- 1. coat (Winterm.) overcoat; Fig: cloak of secrecy etc.). 2. Tchn: outer covering.

manuell [manu'ɛl], adj. manual.

Manuskript [manu'skript], n -(e)s/-e script; manuscript (of a book).

Mappe ['mapə], f -/-n 1. (Aktenm.) briefcase; (Schulm.) satchel; (Schreibm.) writing case. 2. (Sammelm.) folder; (Ordner) file, (loose-leaf) binder.

Marathon- ['ma:ratɔn], comb.fm. marathon (Sp: runner, course, F: sitting, film etc.). ◆**M~lauf,** m marathon.

Märchen ['mɛ:rçən]. I. n -s/- 1. fairy tale. 2. F: tall story; (Lüge) fib. II. 'M~-, comb.fm. fairy-tale (opera, castle, world etc.). ◆**m~haft,** adj. (a) fairy-tale (world, play etc.); (b) F: fabulous (job, journey etc.); adv. er spielt m., he plays like a dream. ◆**M~land,** n fairyland; wonderland. ◆**M~prinz,** m esp. Hum: Prince Charming.

Marder ['mardər], m -s/- marten.

Margarine [marga'ri:nə], f -/-n margarine.

Marienkäfer [ma'ri:ənkɛ:fər], m ladybird, N.Am: ladybug.

Marihuana [marihu'a:na], n -s/no pl marijuana, P: grass.

Marinade [mari'na:də], f -/-n Cu: (a) marinade; (b) (Salatsoße) salad dressing.

Marine [ma'ri:nə]. I. f -/no pl navy. II. M~-, comb.fm. naval (officer, forces etc.). ◆**m~blau,** adj. navy blue. ◆**M~soldat,** m marine.

Marionette [mario'nɛtə], f -/-n marionette; puppet. ◆**M~n-,** comb.fm. puppet (theatre, Pol: government).

Mark¹ [mark], n -(e)s/no pl 1. (Knochenm.) marrow. 2. (a) (Fruchtm.) pulp; (b) Cu: (Tomatenm. usw.) purée. ◆**M~knochen,** m marrowbone.

Mark², f -/- (Geld) mark; sechs M., six marks. ◆**M~stück,** n one-mark piece.

markant [mar'kant], adj. striking, distinctive.

Marke ['markə], f -/-n 1. (Briefm.) stamp. 2. Com: (a) brand (of cigarettes, coffee etc.); make (of car, radio etc.); (b) (Warenzeichen) trade mark. 3. (a) (Bon) voucher; (Lebensmittelm.) coupon; (b) (Spielm.) counter, chip; (c) (Hundem. usw.) identity disc; (cloakroom etc.) tag. 4. (Zeichen) mark (showing level etc.). ◆**M~n-,** comb.fm. branded (article, goods etc.). ◆**M~nfabrikat,** n proprietary brand. ◆**M~nname,** m brand/trade name.

markier|en [mar'ki:rən], v.tr. (a) (also Fig:) to mark (sth.); (b) F: (vortäuschen) to sham, fake (sth.). ◆**M~ung,** f -/-en (a) no pl marking; (Kennzeichen) marking; (identification) mark.

Markise [mar'ki:zə], f -/-n sun (blind); awning (of a shop).

Markt [markt]. I. m -(e)s/¨-e (also Com:) market; (M~platz) market place; ein Produkt auf den M. bringen, to market/ launch a product. II. 'M~-, comb.fm. market (price, value, town, day etc.). ◆**M~bude,** f market stall. ◆**M~platz,** m market place/square. ◆**M~forschung,** f market research. ◆**M~lage,** f state of the market. ◆**M~lücke,** f gap in the market. ◆**M~wirtschaft,** f (freie) M., free market economy.

Marmelade [marmə'la:də], f -/-n jam.

Marmor ['marmor]. I. m -s/-e marble. II. 'M~-, comb.fm. marble (bust, pillar, Cu: cake etc.); (block etc.) of marble.

marokk|anisch [maro'ka:niʃ], adj. Moroccan. ◆**M~o** [ma'rɔko]. Pr.n.n. -s. Morocco.

Marone [ma'ro:nə], f -/-n sweet chestnut.

Marotte [ma'rɔtə], f -/-n whim; fad.

Marsch [marʃ]. I. m -(e)s/¨-e march; (Wanderung) hike, walk; j-m den M. blasen, to give s.o. a piece of one's mind. II. F: m. ins Bett! off to bed with you! III. 'M~-, comb.fm. Mil: marching (song, step etc.). ◆**M~befehl,** m marching orders. ◆**'m~bereit,** adj. ready to march. ◆**m~ieren** [-'ʃi:rən], v.i. (sein) to march; (wandern) to walk, hike.

Marter ['martər], f -/-n torment, agony. ◆**'m~n,** v.tr. to torment (s.o.).

Märtyrer(in) ['mɛrtyrər(in)], m -s/- (f -/-nen) martyr.

Marx|ismus [mar'ksismus], m -/no pl Pol: Marxism. ◆**M~ist(in),** m -en/-en (f -/-nen) Marxist. ◆**m~istisch,** adj. Marxist.

März [mɛrts], m -(es)/-e March.

Marzipan [martsi'pa:n], n -s/no pl marzipan.

Masche ['maʃə], f -/-n 1. stitch. 2. mesh (of a net); Fig: durch die M~n schlüpfen, to slip through the net. 3. F: (Trick) ploy; gimmick. ◆**M~ndraht,** m wire netting.

Maschin|e [ma'ʃi:nə], f -/-n 1. (a)

machine; (b) F: Aut: (Motor) engine 2. (a) (Flugzeug) plane; (b) F: (Motorrad) machine; (c) (Schreibm.) typewriter; **mit/ auf der M.** geschrieben, typewritten. ◆m~ell [maʃi'nɛl], adj. 1. (production etc.) by machine; adv. m. hergestellt, machine-made. 2. mechanical (process etc.). ◆M~en-, comb.fm. machine (part etc.). ◆M~enschlosser, m machine fitter. ◆M~enfabrik, f engineering works. ◆M~enbau, m -(e)s/no pl (Fach) mechanical engineering. ◆M~engewehr, n machine gun. ◆M~enpistole, f sub-machine gun; tommy gun. ◆M~enraum, m Nau: engine room; Mec: etc: machine room. ◆M~enschaden, m mechanical breakdown; Aut: etc: engine trouble. ◆M~enschrift, f typescript; in M., typewritten. ◆M~e'rie, f -/-n (a) no pl machinery; (b) (Apparat) mechanism. ◆M~ist [-'ist], m -en/-en 1. Ind: machinist, machine operative. 2. Nau: (ship's) engineer.

Maser ['maːzər], f -/-n vein (in wood). ◆M~ung, f -/-en texture, grain.

Masern ['maːzərn], pl Med: measles.

Mask|e ['maskə], f -/-n mask; (Verkleidung) disguise. ◆M~enball, m masked/fancy dress ball. ◆M~enbildner(in), m -s/- (f -/-nen) Th: etc: make-up artist. ◆M~erade [-a'raːdə], f -/-n dressing up; Fig: masquerade, pretence. ◆m~ieren [-'kiːrən], v.tr. (verkleiden) to disguise (s.o., oneself).

Maß¹ [maːs]. I. n -es/-e 1. (Einheit) measure; Fig: mit zweierlei M. messen, to apply double standards. 2. (Größe) measurement, dimension; ein Anzug usw. nach M., a tailor-made/made-to-measure suit. 3. (Grad) extent; degree; ein hohes M. an Vertrauen, a high degree of trust; beschränktem/gewissem/hohem M~e, to a limited/certain/large extent; alles mit M.! everything in moderation! über alle M~en glücklich sein, to be happy beyond measure; ohne M. und Ziel, to excess. II. 'M~-, -, comb.fm. Cl: made-to-measure (suit etc.). ◆'M~arbeit, f das ist M., F: that's cutting it fine. ◆'M~einheit, f unit of measure. ◆m~gebend/'m~geblich, adj. (a) authoritative (book, statement etc.); (b) leading (authority etc.); (ausschlaggebend) decisive (factor, influence etc.). ◆'m~geschneidert, adj. made-to-measure, tailor-made. ◆'m~halten, v.i.sep. irr.45 (haben) to be moderate (in etwas dat, in sth.). ◆'m~los, adj. uncontrolled, unrestrained (anger, emotions etc.); excessive (demands etc.); boundless (zeal, curiosity etc.); m. übertrieben, grossly exaggerated; ich habe mich m. geärgert, I was absolutely furious. ◆'M~nahme, f -/-n measure. ◆'m~regeln, v.tr. to reprimand (s.o.).

◆'M~stab, m 1. scale (of map, plan etc.). 2. (Norm) standard; criterion. ◆'m~stab(s)getreu, adj. (map etc.) (drawn) to scale. ◆'m~voll, adj. restrained (behaviour etc.); reasonable (demand etc.).

Maß, f -/-e South G: litre (of beer). ◆M~krug, m one litre beer mug.

Massage [ma'saːʒə], f -/-n massage.

Massak|er [ma'saːkər], n -s/- massacre. ◆m~rieren [-a'kriːrən], v.tr. to massacre (people).

Masse ['masə], f -/-n 1. mass. 2. (Menge) crowd; (Mehrheit) majority; die breite M., the masses; F: eine M. Leute/Geld, masses of people/money. ◆'M~n-, comb.fm. mass (unemployment, demonstration, grave, murder etc.). ◆'M~nartikel, m mass-produced article. ◆'m~nhaft, adj. a vast number/F: masses of; F: wir haben m. Zeit, we've got heaps of time. ◆'M~nmedien, pl mass media.

Masseur [ma'søːr], m -s/-e masseur. ◆M~euse [-'søːzə], f -/-n masseuse. ◆m~ieren [-'siːrən], v.tr. to massage (s.o., s.o.'s back etc.).

massig ['masɪç], adj. massive, huge/F: m. Arbeit, loads of work.

mäßig ['mɛːsɪç], adj. (a) moderate (speed, income, demands etc.); (b) mediocre (work, pupil etc.); limited (intelligence, ability etc.). ◆m~en [-gən], v.tr. esp. Lit: to moderate (one's language, views etc.); to curb (one's impatience etc.); sich m., to restrain/(beherrschen) control oneself. ◆'M~ung, f -/no pl moderation; reduction (of speed).

massiv [ma'siːf]. I. adj. 1. (a) solid (gold etc.); (b) massive, solidly built (statue etc.). 2. heavy, massive (attack, demands etc.); severe, grave (threat, accusation etc.). II. M., n -s/-e massif.

Mast¹ [mast], m -(e)s/-e & -en mast; Tel: etc: (telegraph etc.) pole; El: pylon.

Mast² f -/-en Agr: fattening (of animals). II. 'M~-, comb.fm. fattened (duck, ox etc.). ◆'M~darm, m rectum.

mästen ['mɛstən], v.tr. to fatten (an animal).

Material [materi'aːl], n -s/-ien material; Mil: (Ausrüstung) equipment. ◆M~ismus [-a'lismus], m -/no pl materialism. ◆M~ist [-a'list], m -en/-en materialist. ◆m~istisch [-a'listɪʃ], adj. materialistic.

Materie [ma'teːriə], f -/-n 1. no pl matter. 2. (Thema) subject matter. ◆m~ll [materi'ɛl], adj. (a) material, (finanziell) financial; (b) Pej: materialistic (person etc.).

Mathematik [matəma'tiːk], f -/no pl mathematics. ◆M~matiker [-'maː tikər], m -s/- mathematician. ◆m~'matisch, adj. mathematical.

Matratze [ma'tratsə], f -/-n mattress.

Matrize [ma'tri:tsə], f -/-n (a) (für Ab-
züge) stencil; (b) Rec: etc: matrix.
Matrose [ma'tro:zə], m -n/-n sailor.
Matsch [matʃ], m -(e)s/no pl 1. (a)
(Schnee~) slush; (b) (Schlamm) mud,
sludge. 2. (Brei) mush. ◆**'m~ig,** adj.
F: (a) slushy (snow); soggy (ground etc.);
(b) mushy, squashy (fruit).
matt [mat], adj. 1. (a) (Pers.) exhausted,
worn out; drained of energy; weaky
(limbs); (b) weak, feeble (smile, voice
etc.); lifeless (performance). 2. (glanzlos)
dull (colour, shine, eyes); matt (paint
etc.); pearl (bulb). 3. (Schach, Fig:) i-n
m. setzen, to checkmate s.o.
◆**'M~scheibe,** f F: TV: screen.
Matte ['matə], f -/-n mat.
Mauer ['mauər], f -/-n wall.
◆**'M~blümchen,** n -s/- Fig: (Pers.)
wallflower. ◆**'M~werk,** n -(e)s/no pl
masonry, brickwork.
Maul [maul], n -(e)s/er 1. Z: mouth. 2.
P: (Mund) trap, gob; halt's M.! shut up!
shut your trap! j-m das M. stopfen, to
shut s.o. up; sich dat das M. über j-n
zerreißen, to take s.o. to pieces.
◆**'m~en,** v.i. (haben) F: to grumble,
moan. ◆**'M~esel,** m mule.
◆**'M~korb,** m muzzle. ◆**m~tier,** n
mule. ◆**'M~- und 'Klauenseuche,** f
foot-and-mouth disease. ◆**'M~wurf,** m
mole. ◆**'M~wurfshaufen,** m molehill.
Maurer ['maurər], m -s/- bricklayer; mason.
Maus [maus], f -/e ['mɔyzə], 1. mouse.
2. Pl M~e, (Geld) cash, Brit:
lolly. ◆**M~efalle** ['mauzə-], f mousetrap. ◆**M~eloch,** n mousehole.
◆**'m~e'tot,** adj. F: dead as a doornail.
◆**'m~grau,** adj. mousy (grey).
Mäuschen ['mɔysçən], n -s/- little mouse.
◆**'m~'still,** adj. (Pers.) as quiet as a
mouse; es war m., one could have heard
a pin drop.
mausern ['mauzərn], v.refl. F: (Pers.)
sich (zu etwas dat) m., to blossom (into
sth.).
maxi|mal [maksi'ma:l], adj. maximum.
◆**M~mum** ['maksimum], n -s/-ima
maximum.
Maxime [ma'ksi:mə], f -/-n maxim.
Mayonnaise [majɔ'nɛ:zə], f -/-n mayonnaise.
Mechan|ik [me'çarnik], f -/-en 1. no pl
(science of) mechanics. 2. (Mechanismus)
mechanism. ◆**M~iker,** m -s/- mechanic. ◆**m~isch,** adj. mechanical;
Fig: automatic (action, movement).
◆**M~ismus** [-'nismus], m -/-men
mechanism; F: works (of a watch etc.).
meckern ['mɛkərn], v.i. (haben) (a)
(Ziege) to bleat; (b) F: (nörgeln) to grumble, grouse; (Frau) to nag.
Medaill|e [me'daljə], f -/-n medal.
◆**M~on** [-dal'jö:], n -s/-s (also Cu:) medallion; (Schmuck) locket.
Medikament [medika'mɛnt], n -(e)s/-e

medicine; (Droge) drug.
Medit|ation [meditatsi'o:n], f -/-en medi-
tation. ◆**m~ieren** [-'ti:rən], v.i. (haben) to meditate (über + acc, on).
Medium ['me:dium], n -s/-ien medium;
die Medien, the media.
Medizin [medi'tsi:n], I. f -/-en medicine.
II. M~, comb.fm. medicine (ball etc.);
medical (student etc.). ◆**M~studium**
n, study of medicine. ◆**m~isch,** adj. 1.
medical (research, knowledge etc.). 2.
(mit Heilwirkung) medicinal (preparation
etc.).
Meer [me:r], n -(e)s/-e (a) sea; auf dem
M., at sea; am M., at the seaside; 1000
Meter über dem M., 1,000 metres above
sea level; (b) Fig: sea, mass (of houses
etc.); flood (of light). ◆**'M~busen,** m
gulf. ◆**'M~enge,** f strait, sound.
◆**'M~es-,** comb.fm. sea (coast, air etc.);
marine (climate, plants, animals etc.).
◆**'M~esfrüchte,** fpl seafood.
◆**'M~esgrund,** m sea bed; ocean floor.
◆**'M~esspiegel,** m über dem M.,
above sea level. ◆**'M~esstrand,** m
seashore. ◆**'M~esströmung,** f ocean
current. ◆**'M~jungfrau,** f mermaid.
◆**'M~rettich,** m horseradish.
◆**'M~schweinchen,** n guinea pig.
◆**'M~wasser,** n sea water.
Mega- [mega-], comb.fm. mega-
◆**M~phon** [-'fo:n], n -s/-e megaphone;
(mit Verstärker) loudhailer.
Mehl [me:l], n -(e)s/-e 1. flour; (grobes)
meal. 2. (Pulver) powder. ◆**'m~ig,** adj.
mealy. ◆**'M~speise,** f dessert.
mehr [me:r], I. pron. & adv. more; m.
als, more than; m. denn je, more than
ever; was willst du m.? what more do
you want? um so m., all the more; das
ist ein Grund m., that is yet another reason; nicht m., no more/longer; es dauert
nicht m. lange, it won't be much longer;
es ist nichts m. da, there is nothing left;
nie m., never again. II. M., m -(s)/no pl
ein M. an Kosten, additional costs. III.
'M~-, m~-, comb.fm. (a) (zusätzlich)
additional, extra (expenditure, costs,
amount etc.); (überschüssig) excess
(weight, profit etc.); (b) adj. multi-
layered, coloured etc.); in several
(volumes, parts). ◆**M~arbeit,** f
extra work; (Überstunden) overtime.
◆**'m~deutig,** adj. ambiguous.
◆**'M~deutigkeit,** f -/no pl ambiguity;
polysemy. ◆**'m~ere,** adj. several; aus
m~eren Gründen, for various reasons;
m~eres, adv. several things.
◆**'m~fach,** adj. multiple; (wiederholt)
repeated (attempts etc.); m~facher Mil-
lionär, multimillionaire; in m~facher
Hinsicht, in more than one respect; m.
vergrößert, magnified several times.
◆**'M~familienhaus,** n detached house
divided into flats. ◆**'m~geschossig,**
adj. multi-storey. ◆**'M~heit,** f -/-en
majority. ◆**m~jährig,** adj. 1. several

years' (experience etc.); (stay etc.) of lasting several years. 2. *Bot:* perennial. ◆**'m~malig,** *adj.* repeated. ◆**'m~mals,** *adv.* on several occasions. ◆**'m~sprachig,** *adj.* multilingual; (*Pers.*) polyglot. ◆**'m~stimmig,** *adj. Mus:* in several parts. ◆**'m~stündig,** *adj.* lasting several hours. ◆**'m~tägig,** *adj.* lasting several days. ◆**'M~wertsteuer,** *f* value-added tax. ◆**'M~zahl,** *f* 1. majority. 2. *Gram:* plural. ◆**'m~zweck-,** *comb.fm.* multipurpose (vehicle, furniture etc.).

meiden ['maidən], *v.tr.irr.65* to avoid.

Meile ['mailə], *f -/-n* mile. ◆**'M~nstein,** *m Fig:* milestone. ◆**'m~nweit,** *adv.* miles; **m. von hier entfernt,** miles away.

mein [main], *poss.adj.* my. ◆**'m~e(r,s),** *poss.pron.* mine; **ich habe das M. getan,** I have done my share; **die M~en,** my people. ◆**'m~er,** *pers.pron.* (*gen of* ich) of me; **er erinnerte sich m.,** he remembered me. ◆**'m~erseits,** *adv.* as far as I am concerned; for my part; (*Antwort*) **ganz m.,** the pleasure is all mine. ◆**'m~esgleichen,** *pron.* people like me. ◆**'m~et'wegen,** *adv.* 1. (*mir zuliebe*) because of me; for my sake. *F:* for all I care, **m. kannst du gehen,** it's all right with me/I don't mind if you go. ◆**'m~ige,** *poss.pron. decl. as adj. Lit:* **der/die/das m.,** mine.

Meineid ['mainait], *m* perjury.

mein|en ['mainən], *v.tr.* (*a*) to think (sth., that ...); **das will ich (aber) m.!** I should think so too! **wenn du meinst,** if you think so; (*b*) to mean (s.o., sth.); **du warst nicht gemeint,** the remark was not aimed at you; **wie meinst du das?** what do you mean by that? **es ehrlich/böse m.,** to have honest/evil intentions; **er meint es gut mit uns,** he has our interests at heart; (*c*) (*sagen*) to say (sth.); **was m. Sie?** what did you say? ◆**'M~ung,** *f -/-en* opinion (**über** + *accusativ* + *dat,* of/about); **meiner M. nach,** in my opinion; **ich bin ganz Ihrer M.,** I quite agree with you; *F:* **ich habe ihm gehörig meine M. gesagt,** I really gave him a piece of my mind. ◆**'M~ungs-,** *comb.fm.* opinion (research etc.); (exchange etc.) of views. ◆**'M~ungsumfrage,** *f* opinion poll. ◆**'M~ungsverschiedenheit,** *f* difference of opinion.

Meise ['maizə], *f -/-n* tit.

Meißel ['maisəl], *m -s/-* chisel. ◆**'m~n,** *v.tr.* to chisel (stone etc.).

meist [maist]. **I.** *adj.* most (of); **die m~en** (**Leute**), most people; **er hat das m~e Geld,** he has (the) most money; **die m~e Zeit,** most of the time; **das m~e davon,** most of it. **II.** *adv.* (*a*) = **m~ens;** (*b*) **am m~en,** the most. **III.** '**m~-,** *comb.fm.* most (loved etc.); most often (read, bought etc.). ◆**'m~ens,** *adv.* mostly; **er ist m. pünktlich,** he is

usually on time.

Meister ['maistər], *m -s/-* 1. master. 2. *Sp: etc:* champion. ◆**'m~haft,** *adj.* masterly; **etw. m. spielen,** to play brilliantly. ◆**'M~hand,** *f von M.,* from/by the hand of a master. ◆**'M~leistung,** *f* masterly feat/achievement. ◆**'m~n,** *v.tr.* to master (a subject, situation etc.); to control (feelings, oneself etc.). ◆**'M~schaft,** *f -/-en* 1. *no pl* mastery. 2. *Sp: etc:* championship. ◆**'M~werk,** *n* masterpiece.

Melancho|lie [melaŋko'li:], *f -/no pl* melancholy. ◆**m~isch** ['-ko:liʃ], *adj.* melancholy.

Melasse [me'lasə], *f -/-n* molasses.

Meld|e- ['meldə-], *comb.fm. Adm:* registration (office, fee etc.). ◆**'m~en,** *v.tr.* (*a*) to report (sth.); **sich m.,** to report (**zum Dienst:** for duty; **krank,** sick); to register (**bei der Polizei,** with the police); **sich (freiwillig) zu einer Arbeit m.,** to volunteer for a job; **sich (zu Wort) m.,** to indicate that one wants to speak; (*b*) (*ankündigen*) to announce (s.o., a train etc.); *Meteor:* to forecast (rain, snow etc.); *Lit:* **der Herbst meldet sich,** there are signs of autumn; (*c*) **er hat sich (bei mir) lange nicht gemeldet,** he hasn't been in touch (with me) for a long time; *Tel:* **eine fremde Stimme meldete sich,** a strange voice answered. ◆**'M~epflicht,** *f* obligation to register/report (a disease etc.). ◆**'m~epflichtig,** *adj.* (*a*) (*Pers.*) obliged to register; (*b*) notifiable (disease etc.). ◆**'M~ung,** *f -/-en* 1. *TV: Rad:* report; (*Nachricht*) news (item). 2. *Adm:* notification; registration (of a birth, death etc.).

meliert [me'li:rt], *adj.* mottled, speckled (material etc.); (**grau**) **m~es Haar,** hair streaked with grey.

melken ['melkən], *v.tr.irr.* to milk (a cow, goat etc.).

Melod|ie [melo'di:], *f -/-n* melody; tune (of a song etc.). ◆**m~isch** [me'lo:diʃ], *adj.* tuneful (music etc.); melodious (voice etc.).

Melone [me'lo:nə], *f -/-n* 1. *Bot:* melon. 2. *F:* bowler (hat).

Membran [mɛm'brɑ:n], *f -/-en Tchn:* diaphragm.

Memoiren [memo'ɑ:rən], *pl* memoirs.

Menge ['mɛŋə], *f -/-n* 1. (*a*) quantity; amount; (*b*) **eine (ganze) M.,** a great deal, *F:* a lot; *F:* **eine M. Leute,** a lot/lots of people; **jede M. Äpfel,** any amount/heaps of apples. 2. (*Menschenm.*) crowd. ◆**'M~nlehre,** *f Mth:* theory of sets. ◆**'m~nmäßig,** *adj.* quantitative; (turnover etc.) in numbers/units. ◆**'M~nrabatt,** *m* bulk discount.

mengen ['mɛŋən], *v.tr.* to mix (liquids, foods etc.) (**mit** + *dat,* with).

Mensa ['mɛnza], *f -/-s* & *-sen* student's refectory/*N.Am:* cafeteria.

Mensch [mɛnʃ], *m -en/-en* 1. man; human being; **der M.**, man. 2. person; **junge M~en**, young people; **unter die M~en kommen**, to mix with other people; **jeder M.**, everybody, everyone; **es erschien kein M.**, not a soul turned up. 3. *int. F* 'M., war das eine Hitze! gosh, it was hot! ◆'M~en-, *comb.fm.* human (life, sacrifice, dignity etc.). ◆'M~enaffe *m* ape. ◆'M~enalter, *n* lifetime. ◆'M~enfeind, *m* misanthropist; anti-social. ◆'m~enfeindlich, *adj.* misanthropic; anti-social. ◆'M~enfresser, *m* -s/- cannibal. ◆'M~enfreund, *m* philanthropist; humanitarian. ◆'m~enfreundlich, *adj.* humanitarian. ◆'M~engedenken, *n* seit M., as long as anyone can remember. ◆'M~enkenner, *m* (good) judge of character. ◆'M~enkenntnis, *f* knowledge of human nature. ◆'m~enleer, *adj.* deserted, empty. ◆'M~enliebe, *f* philanthropy; love of one's fellow men. ◆'M~enmenge *f* crowd. ◆'m~enmöglich, *adj.* humanly possible. ◆'M~enrechte, *pl* human rights. ◆'m~enscheu, *adj.* shy, unsociable. ◆'M~enschlag, *m* -(e)s/pl breed (of people). ◆'m~enunwürdig, *adj.* (a) degrading (behaviour etc.); (b) inhumane (treatment etc.). ◆'M~enverstand, *m* human understanding; **gesunder M.**, common sense. ◆'m~enwürdig, *adj.* (a) (behaviour etc.) worthy of a human being; (b) humane (treatment etc.). ◆'M~heit, *f* -/no pl (alle Menschen) humanity; mankind. ◆'m~lich, *adj.* 1. human (nature, society, body etc.). 2. (human) humane; **sich m. zeigen**, to show sympathy. ◆'M~lichkeit, *f* -/no pl humanity; human qualities; **aus reiner M.**, for purely humanitarian reasons.

Menstruation [mɛnstruatsi'oːn], *f* -/-en menstruation.

Mentalität [mɛntali'tɛːt], *f* -/-en mentality.

Menthol [mɛn'toːl], *n* -s/no pl menthol.

Menü [me'nyː], *n* -s/-s menu.

Menuett [menu'ɛt], *n* -(e)s/-e minuet.

merk|bar ['mɛrkbaːr], *adj.* noticeable. ◆'M~blatt, *n Adm:* (explanatory) leaflet. ◆'m~en, *v.tr.* (a) to notice (sth.); **kaum zu m.**, hardly noticeable; (b) to tell, see (sth.) (an + dat, from); **man merkt an seiner Aussprache**(**daß ...)**, one can tell from his accent (that ...); (c) **sich dat etwas m.**, to make a (mental) note of sth.; **das kann ich mir nie m.**, I can never remember that. ◆'m~lich, *adj.* noticeable, marked; **m. kühler**, noticeably cooler. ◆'M~mal, *n* feature; (Zug) characteristic, trait. ◆'m~würdig, *adj.* remarkable; (seltsam) strange. ◆'M~würdigkeit, *f no pl* oddness, strangeness.

Meß- ['mɛs-], *comb.fm.* measuring (instrument etc.). ◆'m~bar, *adj.* measurable. ◆'M~diener, *m* server. ◆'M~ge-

wand, *n* (Mass) vestment, *esp.* chasuble.

Messe[1] ['mɛsə], *f* -/-n *Ecc:* mass; **M. halten**, to say mass.

Messe[2], *f* -/-n (trade) fair. ◆'M~gelände, *n* exhibition site.

Messe[3], *f* -/-n *Mil:* mess.

mess|en ['mɛsən], *v.irr.* 1. *v.tr.* (a) to measure (sth.); (b) to compare (s.o., sth.) (an + dat, with); **sich mit j-m m.**, to match oneself against s.o., take s.o. on. 2. *v.i.* (haben) to measure; **er mißt 1,80 m**, he is 6 feet tall. ◆'M~ung, *f* -/-en measurement.

Messer ['mɛsər]. I. *n* -s/- (a) knife; (b) blade (of a mower etc.); cutter (of a mincer etc.); (c) (Rasierm.) (cut-throat) razor. II. **M~-**, *comb.fm.* knife (blade etc.). ◆'m~scharf, *adj.* razor-sharp (edge etc.); *Fig:* **m~scharfer Verstand**, keen/acute mind. ◆'M~spitze, *f* point of a knife; *Cu:* **eine M. Salz**, a pinch of salt. ◆'M~stich, *m* stab (with a knife); (Wunde) knife wound.

Messing ['mɛsɪŋ], *n* -s/no pl brass.

Metall [me'tal], *n* -s/-e metal. ◆**M~arbeiter**, *m* metalworker. ◆**m~isch**, *adj.* metallic. ◆**m~verarbeitend**, *adj.* metalworking.

Metapher [me'tafər], *f* -/-n metaphor.

Metaphysik [metafy'ziːk], *f* metaphysics.

Meteor [mete'oːr], *n* -s/-e meteor. ◆**M~it** [-o'riːt], *m* -en/-e meteorite. ◆**M~ologe** [-o'loːgə], *m* -n/-n meteorologist. ◆**m~ologisch** [-o'loːgɪʃ], *adj.* meteorological.

Meter ['meːtər], *m & n* -s/- metre. ◆'M~maß, *n* metric tape measure/(Stab) measuring rod.

Methode [me'toːdə], *f* -/-n method. ◆**m~isch**, *adj.* 1. methodical, systematic. 2. (difficulties etc.) of method. ◆**M~ist** [-o'dist], *m* -en/-en Methodist.

Metier [meti'eː], *n* -s/-s profession; *F:* speciality.

Metri|k ['meːtrik], *f* -/-en metre. ◆'m~sch, *adj.* 1. *Mus:* metrical. 2. *Meas:* metric (system etc.).

Metro|nom [metro'noːm], *n* -s/-e metronome. ◆**M~'pole**, *f* -/-n metropolis.

Mett [mɛt], *n* -(e)s/no pl raw minced/N.Am:* ground pork. ◆'M~wurst, *f* smoked (pork/beef) sausage.

Metzger ['mɛtsgər], *m* -s/- butcher. ◆**M~ei** [-'rai], *f* -/-en butcher's (shop).

Meuchel|mord ['mɔyçəlmɔrt], *m* foul murder. ◆'M~mörder(in), *m* foul murderer.

Meute ['mɔytə], *f* -/-n pack (of hounds); *Fig:* mob (of people). ◆'M~rei, *f* -/-en mutiny; (im Gefängnis usw.) revolt, riot. ◆'m~rer, *m* -s/- mutineer. ◆'m~rn, *v.i.* (haben) to mutiny, (Gefangene usw.) riot.

Mexik|aner(in) [mɛksi'kaːnər(ɪn)], *m* -s/- (f -/-nen) Mexican. ◆**m~anisch**, *adj.* Mexican. ◆'M~o. *Pr.n.n* -s. Mexico.

miauen [mi'auən], *v.i.* (haben) to miaow.

mich [miç]. **I.** *pers.pron.* (*acc. of* **ich**) me.
II. *refl.pron.* myself.

mickerig ['mikəriç], *adj.* F: (*Pers.*) puny;
measly, helpless etc.).

Mieder ['mi:dər], *n* -s/- bodice.

Mief [mi:f], *m* -(e)s/*no pl* F: fug.

Miene ['mi:nə], *f* -/-n (facial) expression;
eine finstere M. machen, to look grim.
◆'M~**nspiel**, *n* (range of) facial expres-
sions.

mies [mi:s], *adj.* P: rotten, lousy; **mir ist
m.**, I feel rotten. ◆'m~**machen**,
v.tr.sep. F: to run s.o., sth. down; **j-m
etwas m.**, to spoil sth. for s.o.
◆'M~**macher**, *m* -s/- F: killjoy.

Miet- ['mi:t-], *comb.fm.* (*a*) (*zu mieten*)
(house etc.) to rent; (boat etc.) for hire;
(*gemietet*) rented (house etc.); hired (boat
etc.); (*b*) rent (increase, allowance etc.);
(loss, payment etc.) of rent. ◆'M~**e**, *f*
-/-n 1. renting (of a house etc.); hire (of a
boat etc.); **zur M. wohnen**, to live in
rented accommodation. 2. (*Betrag*) rent.
◆'m~**en**, *v.tr.* to rent (a flat, room
etc.); to hire (a car, boat etc.).
◆'M~**er(in)**, *m* -s/- (*f* -/-nen) (*a*)
tenant; (*Untermieter*) lodger; (*b*) hirer (of
a car etc.). ◆'M~**shaus**, *n* block of
(rented) flats/*N.Am:* apartments.
◆'M~**vertrag**, *m* lease; rental agreement. ◆'M~**wagen**, *m* hire(d) car.
◆'M~**wohnung**, *f* rented flat/*N.Am:*
apartment.

Migräne [mi'grɛ:nə], *f* -/-n migraine.

Mikro- ['mi:kro-], *comb.fm.* micro-.
◆'M~**film**, *m* microfilm. ◆**M~'phon**,
n -s/-e microphone. ◆**M~'skop**
[-'sko:p], *n* -s/-e microscope.
◆**m~'skopisch**, *adj.* microscopic; **etwas m. untersuchen**, to examine sth. under the microscope. ◆'M~**wellenherd**,
m microwave oven.

Milbe ['milbə], *f* -/-n mite.

Milch [milç]. **I.** *f* -/*no pl* milk. **II.** 'M~-,
comb.fm. (*a*) milk (bar, tooth etc.); (*b*)
dairy (products, cow etc.).
◆'M~**brötchen**, *n* *approx.* bun.
◆'M~**glas**, *n* opaque glass. ◆'m~**ig**,
adj. milky (fluid etc.). ◆'M~**kaffee**, *m*
white coffee, *N.Am:* coffee with milk.
◆'M~**kanne**, *f* milk churn; (*kleiner*)
milk can. ◆'M~**pulver**, *n* dried milk.
◆'M~**reis**, *m* rice pudding.
◆'M~**straße**, *f* galaxy; **die M.**, the
Milky Way. ◆'M~**tüte**, *f* milk carton.

mild [milt], *adj.* mild (weather, taste, cigar, criticism etc.); temperate (climate
etc.); balmy (air etc.); lenient (sentence,
judge etc.); **m. gewürztes Essen**, lightly
seasoned food; **m~e Gabe**, charitable
gift; (*Almosen*) alms. ◆'M~**e**, *f* -/*no pl*
leniency; clemency (**gegen** j-n,
towards s.o.). **II. m.**, *adj.* = mild; **j-n
gesagt**, to put it mildly. ◆'m~**ern**,
v.tr. to relieve (pain, tension etc.); to
calm (anger etc.); to tone down (contrasts
etc.); to reduce (intensity etc.); *Jur:*

m~de Umstände, mitigating/extenuating
circumstances. ◆'m~**tätig**, *adj.* charitable.

Milieu [mil'jø:], *n* -s/-s environment.

militant [mili'tant], *adj.* militant.

Militär [mili'tɛ:r]. **I.** *n* -s/*no pl* (*Heer*)
army; (*Streitkräfte*) armed forces; (*Truppen*) troops. **II. M~-,** *comb.fm.* military
(airport, parade, police etc.).
◆'M~**dienst**, *m* military service.
◆**M~gericht**, *n* court martial.
◆**m~isch**, *adj.* military.

Militar|ismus [milita'rismus], *m* -/*no pl*
militarism. ◆**M~ist**, *m* -en/-en milita-
rist.

Miliz [mi'li:ts], *f* -/-en militia.

Milli|arde [mili'ardə], *f* -/-n thousand mil-
lion; *N.Am:* billion. ◆'M~**gramm**, *n*
milligram. ◆**m~'meter**, *m & n* millimetre.

Million [mili'o:n], *f* -/-en million; **zwei
M~en Einwohner**, two million inhab-
itants. ◆**M~är(in)** [-o'nɛ:r(in)], *m* -s/-e
(*f* -/-nen) millionaire, *f* millionairess.
◆**M~enstadt**, *f* city of (over) a million
people.

Milz [milts], *f* -/-en spleen.

Mim|e ['mi:mə], *m* -n/-n *esp. Hum:* actor.
◆'m~**en**, *v.tr.* F: to act (the hero etc.).
◆'M~**ik**, *f* -/*no pl* mimicry.

Mimose [mi'mo:zə], *f* -/-n *Bot:* mimosa.
◆**m~nhaft**, *adj.* hypersensitive.

minder ['mindər], *adv. & comb.fm.* less.
◆'m~**bemittelt**, *adj.* (*a*) of limited
means; (*b*) F: **geistig m.**, not very
bright. ◆'M~**heit**, *f* -/-en minority.
◆'m~**jährig**, *adj.* under age.
◆'M~**jährigkeit**, *f* -/*no pl* minority.
◆'m~**n**, *v.tr. Lit:* to diminish (pain,
strength etc.). ◆**M~ung**, *f* -/-en decrease; easing (of pain). ◆'m~**wertig**,
adj. inferior; third-rate (literature etc.).
◆'M~**wertigkeit**, *f* inferiority; *Com:*
inferior quality. ◆'M~**wertigkeits-
komplex**, *m* inferiority complex.

Mindest- ['mindəst-], *comb.fm.* minimum
(distance, age, weight, wage etc.).
◆'m~**e**, *adj.* least, slightest; **nicht im
m~n**, not in the least. ◆'m~**ens**, *adv.*
at least. ◆'M~**maß**, *n* minimum
(amount/extent).

Mine ['mi:nə], *f* -/-n 1. *Mil:* mine. 2.
refill (for a ballpoint etc.); (pencil) lead.
◆'M~**nfeld**, *n* minefield. ◆'M~**n-
suchboot**, *n* minesweeper.

Mineral [minə'ra:l], *n* -s/-e & -ien min-
eral. ◆'m~**isch**, *adj.* mineral.
◆**M~quelle**, *f* mineral spring.
◆**M~wasser**, *n* mineral water.

Mini- ['mini-], *comb.fm.* mini-.
◆'M~**rock**, *m* miniskirt.

mini|mal [mini'ma:l]. **I.** *adj.* minimal. **II.**
M~-, *comb.fm.* minimum (price, weight
etc.). ◆**M~mum** ['mi:nimum], *n* -s/-
ma minimum (**an** +*dat*, of).

Minister [mi'nistər]. **I.** *m* -s/- *Pol:* minister (**für Handel usw.**, of trade etc.). **II.**

M~-, *comb.fm.* ministerial (office, conference). **◆m~i'ell,** *adj.* ministerial. **◆M~ium** [-'te:riʊm], *n* **-s/-rien** ministry; *N.Am:* department. **◆M~präsident,** *m* prime minister.

minus ['mi:nʊs]. **I.** *adv.* minus; *(Temperatur)* **m. 4 Grad, 4** degrees below zero. **II. M.,** *n* **-/- 1.** *Mth:* minus (sign). **2.** *Com:* (also **M~betrag** *m*) deficit. **3.** *F: (Nachteil)* drawback; shortcoming; **das ist ein M. für mich,** that's a point against as far as I am concerned. **◆M~pol,** *m* negative pole/terminal. **◆M~punkt,** *m Sp: &c:* minus point; *F:* disadvantage. **◆M~zeichen,** *n Mth:* minus sign.

Minute [mi'nu:tə], *f* **-/-n** minute; **in letzter M.,** at the last minute. **◆m~nlang,** *adj.* lasting for several minutes. **◆M~nzeiger** *m* minute hand.

mir [mi:r], *pers.pron. dat of* **ich. 1.** (to) me; **gib's m.,** give it to me; **er half m.,** he helped me; **m. nichts, dir nichts,** just like that; **mit m.,** with me; **bei m.,** at my home/*F:* place; **ein Freund von m.,** a friend of mine. **2.** *refl.* myself; **m. läuft die Nase,** my nose is running.

Mirabelle [mira'belə], *f* **-/-n** small yellow plum; mirabelle.

Misch- ['miʃ-], *comb.fm.* (a) mixing (drum, vessel etc.); (b) mixed (vegetables, fruit etc.). **◆m~en,** *v.tr.* (a) to mix (drinks, colours etc.); to blend (coffee, tobacco etc.); to shuffle (cards); (b) *(Pers.)* **sich in etwas** *acc* **m.,** to interfere in sth. **◆M~ling,** *m* **-s/-e 1.** *(Pers.)* half-caste. **2.** *Biol:* hybrid. **◆M~masch,** *m* **-(e)s/-e** *F:* hotchpotch. **◆M~ung,** *f* **-/-en** mixture; blend (of coffee, tea etc.).

miser|abel [mizə'ra:bəl], *adj. F:* awful; **sie fühlt sich m.,** she feels rotten. **◆M~e** [mi'ze:rə], *f* **-/-n** *(Lage)* miserable position.

mißacht|en [mis'axtən], *v.tr.* to disregard. **◆M~ung,** *f* **-/no pl** disregard; *(Geringschätzung)* disrespect (of s.o.).

'Mißbehagen, *n* **-s/no pl** uneasiness. **'Mißbildung,** *f* **-/-en** deformity, abnormality.

miß'billigen, *v.tr.* to disapprove of (sth.). **'Mißbrauch,** *m* abuse; *(falscher Gebrauch)* misuse. **◆m~en** [mis'braʊxən], *v.tr.* to abuse (power, s.o. etc.); to misuse (drugs etc.); to indulge in (alcohol etc.) to excess.

'Mißerfolg, *m* failure.

miß'fallen. I. *v.i.irr.27 (haben)* **es mißfällt mir,** it displeases me. **II. M.** ['mis-], *n* **-s/no pl** displeasure; **M. erregen,** to meet with disapproval.

'Mißgeschick, *n* **-(e)s/-e** *(Pers.)* misfortune; *(Malheur)* mishap.

'mißgestaltet, *adj.* deformed, misshapen.

miß'glücken, *v.i.* *(sein)* *(Versuch, Plan usw.)* to fail, be unsuccessful.

miß'gönnen, *v.tr.* j-m etwas m., to begrudge s.o. sth.

'Mißgriff, *m* false move, mistake.

'Mißgunst, *f* **-/no pl** envy; resentment (at s.o.'s success).

miß'hand|eln, *v.tr.* to ill-treat (s.o., sth.). **◆M~lung,** *f* **-/-en** ill-treatment.

Mission [misi'o:n], *f* **-/-en** mission; **in geheimer M.,** on a secret mission. **◆M~ar** [-o'na:r] *m* **-s/-e** missionary.

'Mißklang, *m Mus:* discord; *Fig:* discordant/jarring note.

'Mißkredit, *m* j-n, etwas *acc* **in M. bringen,** to discredit s.o., sth.

mißliebig ['misli:biç], *adj.* unpopular.

miß'lingen [mis'liŋən], *v.i.irr.19 (sein)* to fail, *(Plan)* miscarry; *(Überraschung)* to fall flat.

'Mißmut, *m* bad mood/temper. **◆m~ig,** *adj.* sullen.

miß'raten, *v.i.irr.13 (sein)* (a) *(Ernte)* to fail; (b) *(Kind)* to turn out badly; **m~er Sohn,** black sheep of the family.

'Mißstand, *m* anomaly; *(Schande)* disgrace; *(Zustand)* deplorable state of affairs.

'Mißstimmung, *f* ill-feeling; discord. **'Mißton,** *m Mus:* dissonance; *Fig:* discordant note.

miß'trau|en. I. *v.i.* *(haben)* etwas *dat* m., to mistrust (s.o., sth. **II. M.** ['mis-], *n* **-s/no pl** (a) mistrust (**gegen** + *acc,* of); (b) *(Verdacht)* suspicion. **◆M~ensvotum,** *n Pol:* vote of no confidence. **◆m~isch,** *adj.* suspicious (**gegen** + *acc,* of); mistrustful.

'Mißverhältnis, *n* disproportion.

'Miß|verständnis, *n* misunderstanding. **◆m~verstehen,** *v.tr.ir.100* to misunderstand.

Mist [mist], *m* **-(e)s/no pl 1.** (a) dung; (b) *Agr:* (farmyard) manure. **2.** *F:* rubbish; (a) *(Unsinn)* rot; (b) *(Sachen)* junk, trash; (c) **mach keinen M.!** don't do anything stupid; (d) **so ein M.! verdammter M.!** damn it all! **◆M~haufen,** *m* manure heap, dungheap. **◆M~stück,** *n P:* *(Mann)* bastard; *(Frau)* bitch. **◆M~wetter,** *n F:* lousy/rotten weather.

Mistel ['mistəl], *f* **-/-n** mistletoe.

mit [mit]. **I.** *prep.* + *dat* **1.** with. **2.** *(mittels)* by; **m. dem Zug fahren,** to go by train; **m. der Post,** by post; **m. Scheck bezahlen,** to pay by cheque; **m. lauter Stimme,** in a loud voice; **m. anderen Worten,** in other words. **3.** **m. 20** *(Jahren),* (at the age of) 20; **m. 100 Stundenkilometern,** at 100 kilometres per hour. **II.** *adv.* also, as well; **das gehört m. dazu,** that belongs to it.

'Mitarbeit, *f* **-/no pl** collaboration, cooperation; *(Hilfe)* assistance; *(Beteiligung)* participation; **unter M. von X,** with the collaboration/assistance of X. **◆m~en,** *v.i.sep. (haben)* **an/bei etwas** *dat* m., to collaborate on sth. **◆M~er(in),** *m(f)* -/- collaborator (**an einem Projekt usw.,** on a project etc.);

freier M., freelance worker/ journalist; (b) (Arbeitskollege) colleague; fellow worker; (Betriebsangehöriger) member of staff, employee.

'**mitbekommen**, v.tr.sep.irr.53 (a) to be given (sth.) (für die Reise, for the journey; (b) to catch, (aufnehmen) take in (a remark etc.); (c) von etwas dat nichts m., to miss out on sth.

'**mitbestimm|en**, v.i.sep. (haben) to have a say (in etwas dat, in sth.). ◆'M~ung, f -/no pl participation in decision-making.

'**mitbring|en**, v.tr.sep.irr.16 to bring (s.o., sth.) (with one). ◆'M~sel ['mitbrɪŋzl], n -s/- little present (brought back from holiday etc.).

'**Mitbürger(in)**, m(f) fellow citizen.

miteinander [mitaɪ'nandər], adv. with each other/one another; (zusammen) together; **m. bekannt werden**, to get to know one another; **alle m.**, all together.

'**miterleben**, v.tr.sep. to witness (sth.); F: werde ich das noch m.? will I live to see that?

'**Mitesser**, m -s/- blackhead.

'**mitfahr|en**, v i sep irr 26 (sein) to go/come too (by car etc.). ◆'M~er, m passenger.

'**mitführen**, v.tr.sep. to carry (documents etc.) with one.

'**mitgeb|en**, v.tr.sep.irr.35 j-m etwas m., to give s.o. sth. (to take with him).

'**Mitgefühl**, n sympathy.

'**mitgehen**, v.i.sep.irr.36 (sein) to go/come (along) too.

mitgenommen ['mitgənɔmən], adj. battered; (Pers.) run down, worn out.

'**Mitgift**, f -/-en dowry.

'**Mitglied**, n member. ◆'M~sbeitrag, m membership fee; subscription. ◆'M~schaft, f -/no pl membership.

'**mithalten**, v.i.sep.irr.45 (haben) to hold one's own; (schritthalten) to keep up.

'**mit|helfen**, v.i.sep.irr.50 (haben) to help, lend a hand. ◆'M~hilfe, f assistance, co-operation.

'**mithören**, v.tr.sep. to listen (in) to (sth.).

'**mitkommen**, v.i.sep.irr.53 (sein) (a) to come (along) too; (b) (schritthalten) to keep up; F: (verstehen) **da komme ich nicht ganz mit**, I'm not quite with you.

'**Mitläufer**, m Pol: etc: sympathizer, hanger-on; (Kommunist usw.) fellow traveller.

'**Mitleid**, n pity; (Mitgefühl) sympathy, compassion; **M. mit j-m haben**, to feel sorry for s.o., take pity on s.o. ◆'M~enschaft, f -/no pl j-n, etwas in M. ziehen, to affect s.o., sth. (as well). ◆'m~erregend, adj. pitiful, pathetic. ◆'m~ig [diç], adj. sympathetic; pitying. ◆'m~(s)los, adj. unpitying (look), unfeeling, pitiless (person); ruthless (action).

'**mitmachen**, v.sep. 1. v.tr. (a) to join in (a dance etc.); to take part in (a course,

war etc.); **die Mode m.**, to follow the fashion; (b) to go through (difficult times, experiences etc.); **viel m. müssen**, to suffer a lot. 2. v.i. (haben) to join in (bei + dat, in).

'**Mitmensch**, m fellow man.

'**mitnehm|en**, v.tr.sep.irr.69 (a) to take (s.o, sth.) with one; **im Auto m.**, to give s.o. a lift; (b) j-n schwer/sehr m., (Erlebnis usw.) to hit s.o. hard; (Reise, Krankheit usw.) to take it out of one.

'**mitreden**, v.i.sep. (haben) to join in (the conversation); **sie will überall m.**, she wants a say in everything.

'**mitreisen**, v.i.sep. (sein) mit j-m m., to travel with s.o. ◆'M~de(r), m & f decl. as adj. fellow traveller/passenger.

'**mitreiß|en**, v.tr.sep.irr.4 to carry (s.o., sth.) away. ◆'m~end, adj. thrilling (game etc.); stirring, rousing (speech etc.).

mit'samt, prep. + dat together with.

'**Mitschuld**, f -/no pl complicity. ◆'m~ig, adj. an etwas m. sein, to be partly responsible for sth.

'**Mitschüler(in)**, m & f schoolmate.

'**mitsing|en**, v.i.sep.irr.19 1. v.tr. to join in (a song). 2. v.i. (haben) to join in the singing; **in einem Chor m.**, to sing in a choir.

'**mitspiel|en**, v.i.sep. (haben) (a) to join in a game; (b) to play (in a team, orchestra etc.); to act (in a play, film etc.); (c) (Gefühle, Gründe usw.) to play a part. ◆'M~er(in), m & f participant (in a game); Sp: (team) member.

'**Mitspracherecht**, n right to have a say.

Mittag ['mɪtaːk]. I. m -s/-e noon; midday; **zu M.**, at noon/lunchtime; **zu M. essen**, to have lunch. II. m., adv. **heute/morgen m.**, at midday today/tomorrow. ◆'M~essen, n lunch, midday meal. ◆'M~s, adv. at midday/noon. ◆'M~spause, f lunch hour. ◆'M~sruhe, f (time of) quiet after lunch; ◆'M~sschlaf, m siesta, afternoon nap. ◆'M~szeit, f lunchtime; midday.

'**Mittäter(in)**, m & f accomplice.

Mitte ['mitə], f -/no pl middle (of a room, road, week etc.); centre (of a town, circle etc.); **M. Mai**, in the middle of May; **er ist M. fünfzig**, he is in his mid-fifties; **in unserer M.**, in our midst; amongst us.

'**mitteil|en**, v.tr.sep. j-m etwas m., to inform s.o. of sth., tell s.o. sth.; **es wurde amtlich mitgeteilt, daß ...**, it was officially announced that ... ◆'m~sam, adj. communicative; forthcoming. ◆'M~ung, f -/-en communication (an j-n, to s.o.); (Bericht) report; **amtliche M.**, official announcement.

Mittel ['mitəl]. I. n -s/- 1. means, way; **M. und Wege**, ways and means; **mit drastischen M~n vorgehen**, to use drastic methods; **als letztes M.**, as a last resort. 2. Med: preparation; (Heilm.) cure; (zum

Einnehmen) medicine. **3.** *pl* (*Geldm.*) means, funds; **öffentliche M.**, public money. **4.** (*Durchschnitt*) average (**aus** + *dat.*, of). **II.** 'M~-, 'm~-, *comb.fm.* central (part, piece etc.); Central (America, Europe, European etc.); middle (ear, finger etc.); centre (parting, *Fb:* circle etc.). ◆'M~**alter, das M.**, the Middle Ages. ◆'m~**alterlich**, *adj.* (*also Fig:*) medieval. ◆'M~**ding**, *n* cross. ◆'M~**feld**, *n Fb: etc:* midfield. ◆'m~**fristig**, *adj.* medium-term. ◆'m~**groß**, *adj.* medium-sized (*Pers.*) of medium height. ◆'m~**los**, *adj.* penniless, destitute. ◆'m~**maß**, *n* average (standard). ◆'m~**mäßig**, *adj.* (*a*) (*durchschnittlich*) middling, average; (*b*) *Pej:* mediocre, indifferent. ◆'M~**meer**. *Pr.n.n* **das M.**, the Mediterranean (Sea). ◆'M~**punkt**, *m* centre, central point; *Fig:* hub. ◆'m~**s**, *prep.* + *gen* by means of. ◆'M~**stand**, *m* middle class. ◆'M~**strecken-**, *comb.fm.* (*a*) *Sp:* middle-distance (race, runner); (*b*) *Av: etc:* medium-range (aircraft, rocket etc.). ◆'M~**streifen**, *m* central reservation. ◆'M~**stürmer**, *m* centre forward. ◆'M~**welle**, *f* medium wave.

mitten ['mitən], *adv.* **m. auf der Straße/in der Nacht**, in the middle of the road/night; **m. in der Luft**, in mid-air; **m. durch die Stadt**, right through the centre of the town. ◆'m~**durch**, *adv. F:* (right) through the middle (of it/them).

Mitternacht ['mitərnaxt], *f* midnight.

mittler[e(r,s)] ['mitlərə(r,s)], *adj.* (*a*) middle (house, window etc.); central (part, area etc.); (*b*) medium (size, quality etc.); moderate (speed, temperature etc.); medium-sized (town etc.). ◆'m~**'weile**, *adv.* meanwhile.

Mittwoch ['mitvɔx], *m* -(e)s/-e Wednesday. ◆'m~**s**, *adv.* on Wednesdays.

mit'unter, *adv.* occasionally; from time to time.

'**mitverantwortlich**, *adj.* jointly responsible.

'**Mitverfasser**, *m* co-author.

'**Mitwelt**, *f* -/*no pl* **die M.**, one's fellow men/(*Zeitgenossen*) contemporaries.

'**mitwirk**[en, *v.i.sep.* (*haben*) (*a*) **an/bei etwas** *dat* **m.**, (*Pers.*) to help with sth.; (*Faktoren usw.*) to play a part in sth.; (*b*) *Th: etc:* to take part; **die M~enden**, the performers/*Th:* cast/*Mus:* players. ◆'M~**ung**, *f* co-operation.

Mix[becher ['miksbeçər], *m* (cocktail) shaker. ◆'m~**en**, *v.tr.* to mix (drinks). ◆'M~**er**, *m* -s/- *Cu:* liquidizer. ◆'M~**getränk**, *n* mixed drink; cocktail. ◆'M~**tur**, *f* /-en mixture.

Möbel ['mø:bəl]. **I.** *n* -s/- piece of furniture; *usu.pl* **die M.**, the furniture. **II.** 'M~-, *comb.fm.* furniture (shop, industry, polish etc.). ◆'M~**stück**, *n* piece of furniture. ◆'M~**wagen**, *m* furniture/removal/*N.Am:* moving van.

mobil [mo'bi:l], *adj.* **1.** (*a*) mobile (shop etc.); (*b*) *Mil:* mobilized (troops etc.). **2.** *F:* lively (child). ◆**M~iar** [mobili'a:r], *n* -s/*no pl* furniture and fittings.

möblier[en [mø'bli:rən], *v.tr.* to furnish (a room, flat etc.). ◆**m~t**, *adj.* furnished; *adv.* **m. wohnen**, to live in furnished accommodation.

Mode ['mo:də]. **I.** *f* -/-n fashion; (**in**) **M. sein/aus der M.** (**gekommen**) **sein**, to be fashionable/out of fashion. **II.** 'M~-, *comb.fm.* (*a*) fashion (photographer, drawing etc.); (*b*) (*modisch*) fashionable (profession, colour, illness etc.). ◆'M~(**n**)**schau**, *f* fashion show/parade. ◆**M~schmuck**, *m* costume jewellery. ◆'M~**schöpfer**(**in**), *m(f)* fashion/dress designer.

Modell [mo'dɛl]. **I.** *n* -s/-e model; *Art:* **j-m M. sitzen/stehen**, to sit/pose for s.o. **II.** 'M~-, *comb.fm.* model (aeroplane, railway, dress etc.). ◆**M~baukasten**, *m* modelling kit. ◆**m~ieren** [-'li:rən], *v.tr.* to model (a statue, vase etc.); to mould (clay, wax etc.).

Moder ['mo:dər], *m* -s/*no pl* mould.

modern [mo'dɛrn], *adj.* modern; (*modisch*) fashionable; (*fortschrittlich*) progressive (ideas etc.); up-to-date (methods etc.). ◆**m~i'sieren**, *v.tr.* to modernize (sth.).

Modif[ikation [modifikatsi'o:n], *f* /-en modification. ◆**m~i'zieren**, *v.tr.* to modify (sth.).

modisch ['mo:diʃ], *adj.* fashionable, *F:* trendy.

Mofa ['mo:fa], *n* -s/-s (low-powered) moped.

mogeln ['mo:gəln], *F: v.i.* (*haben*) to cheat.

mögen ['mø:gən], *v.tr.irr.* & *modal aux.* to like (s.o., sth.); **was möchten Sie?** what would you like? **ich möchte kommen**, I would like to come; **es mag sein, daß...**, it may well be that ...; **und wie sie alle heißen m.**, and whatever their names might be; **mag kommen, was will**, come what may.

möglich ['mø:kliç], *adj.* possible; **sobald es Ihnen m. ist**, as soon as you can; **das ist doch nicht m.!** it can't be! *F: er* sprach über alles m~e, he talked about all sorts of things. ◆'m~**er'weise**, *adv.* possibly, perhaps. ◆**M~keit**, *f* /-en (*a*) possibility; **nach M.**, if possible; (*möglichst*) as much/far as possible; (*b*) (*Chance*) chance, opportunity. ◆'m~**st**, *adv.* **1.** (*a*) ... as possible; **m. viel/schnell**, as much/quickly as possible; (*b*) (*wenn möglich*) if possible. **2.** **sein m~stes tun**, to do one's utmost.

Mohn [mo:n], *m* -(e)s/-e (*a*) *Bot:* poppy; (*b*) *Cu:* (*Samen*) poppy-seed. ◆'M~**blume**, *f* poppy.

Möhre ['mø:rə], *f* /-n, **Mohrrübe** ['mo:rry:bə], *f* carrot.

Mokka ['mɔka], *m* -s/-s strong black coffee.

Molch [mɔlç], *m* -(e)s/-e newt.

Mole ['mo:lə], *f* -/-n mole, breakwater.

Molek|ül [mole'ky:l], *n* -s/-e molecule.

Molk|e ['mɔlkə], *f* -/no *pl* whey. ◆**M~e'rei**, *f* -/-en dairy.

Moll [mɔl], *n* -s/no *pl* minor (key).

mollig ['mɔliç], *adj.* **1.** (*dick*) plump, chubby. **2.** (*bequem*) cosy, snug.

Moment[1] [mo'mɛnt], *m* -(e)s/-e moment; **im M.,** at the moment; **M. mal!** hang on a minute! (*halt!*) hold it! ◆**m~an** [-'taɪn], *adj.* (*a*) present (situation etc.); (*b*) (*flüchtig*) momentary, fleeting.

Moment[2], *n* -(e)s/-e factor, element.

Monarch [mo'narç(in)], (*f* -/-nen) monarch. ◆**M~ie** [-'çi:], *f* -/-n monarchy.

Monat ['mo:nat], *m* -(e)s/-e month; **im M. Juli,** in the month of July; *F:* sie ist **im vierten M.,** she's four months pregnant. ◆**m~elang,** *adj.* lasting several months; **m. warten,** to wait for (several) months. ◆**m~lich,** *adj.* monthly; **m. einmal,** once a month. ◆**M~s-,** *comb.fm* (*a*) monthly (rent, salary etc.); (*b*) (beginning, end etc.) of the month. ◆**M~skarte,** *f* monthly season (ticket). ◆**M~srate,** *f* monthly instalment.

Mönch [mœnç], *m* -(e)s/-e monk.

Mond [mo:nt]. **I.** *m* -(e)s/-e moon. **II.** '**M~-,** *comb.fm.* lunar (landscape etc.); moon (rock, landing etc.). ◆**M~bahn,** *f* lunar orbit. ◆**M~fähre,** *f* lunar module. ◆**M~finsternis,** *f* lunar eclipse; eclipse of the moon. ◆**m~hell,** *adj.* moonlit. ◆**M~schein,** *m* moonlight. ◆**m~süchtig,** *adj.* somnambulant.

Monitor ['mo:nitɔr], *m* -s/-e monitor.

mono ['mo:no, 'mɔno]. **I.** *adj.* mono. **II.** '**M~-,** *comb.fm.* mono (recording etc.).

Monogramm [mono'gram], *n* -s/-e monogram.

Monolog [mono'lo:k], *m* -s/-e monologue.

Monopol [mono'po:l], *n* -s/-e monopoly.

monoton [mono'to:n], *adj.* monotonous. ◆**M~ie** [-o'ni:], *f* -/-n monotony.

Monstrum ['mɔnstrum], *n* -s/-ren monster.

Monsun [mɔn'zu:n], *m* -s/-e monsoon.

Montag ['mo:nta:k], *m* -(e)s/-e Monday. ◆**m~s,** *adv.* on Mondays.

Mont|age [mɔn'ta:ʒə], *f* -/-n (*a*) assembly; fitting (of a part); (*b*) *Art:* montage. ◆**M~eur** [-'tø:r], *m* -s/-e fitter, mechanic. ◆**m~ieren** [-'ti:rən], *v.tr.* (*a*) to assemble, set up (a machine etc.); to put together (a collage etc.); (*b*) (*anbringen*) to fit (tyres, a handle etc.), mount (a gun, light etc.); to install (sth.)

Monument [monu'mɛnt], *n* -(e)s/-e monument. ◆**m~al** [-'ta:l], *adj.* monumental.

Moor [mo:r], *n* -(e)s/-e fen; (*Sumpf*) bog. ◆**M~bad,** *n* mud-bath.

Moos [mo:s], *n* -es/-e **1.** *Bot:* moss. **2.** *no*

pl F: (*Geld*) cash, lolly; *N.Am:* dough. ◆**m~grün,** *adj.* moss green.

Mop [mɔp], *m* -s/-s mop.

Moped ['mo:pɛt], *n* -s/-s moped.

Mops [mɔps], *m* -es/-e *Z:* pug (dog). ◆**m~en,** *v.tr. F:* to pinch, swipe (sth.).

Moral [mo'ra:l], *f* -/no *pl* **1.** morals; morality. **2.** moral (of a story etc.). **3.** morale (of troops etc.). ◆**m~isch,** *adj.* moral. ◆**M~predigt,** *f* *Pej:* lecture, homily.

Moräne [mo'rɛ:nə], *f* -/-n moraine.

Morast [mo'rast], *m* -(e)s/-e (*a*) bog; quagmire; (*b*) (*Schlamm*) mire, mud.

Mord [mɔrt], *m* -(e)s/-e murder, *esp. N.Am:* homicide (**an j-m,** of s.o.); *F:* es **gibt M. und Totschlag,** all hell will be let loose. **II.** '**M~-,** *comb.fm.* murder (case etc.). ◆**M~kommission,** *f* murder/*N.Am:* homicide squad. ◆**M~verdacht,** *m* suspicion of murder. ◆**M~s-,** '**m~s-,** *comb.fm.* *F:* (*schrecklich*) terrible, awful (noise, heat etc.). ◆**m~smäßig,** *adj. F:* terrible (noise etc.); terrific (fun etc.).

Mörder(in) ['mœrdər(in)], *m* -s/- (*f* -/-nen) murderer, murderess. ◆**m~isch,** *adj. F:* murderous (weapon, plan etc.), *F:* task, pace, heat etc.); *F:* breakneck (speed).

morgen ['mɔrgən]. **I.** *adv.* **1.** tomorrow; **m. früh,** tomorrow morning. **2. heute/ gestern m.,** this/yesterday morning. **II. M.,** *m* -s/- **1.** morning; **am M.,** in the morning. **2.** *Meas:* acre. **III.** '**M~-,** *comb.fm.* morning (star, newspaper etc.). ◆**M~dämmerung,** *f* dawn. ◆**m~dlich,** *adj.* morning (stillness, walk etc.). ◆**M~grauen,** *n* dawn. ◆**M~mantel,** *m*/**M~rock,** *m* housecoat; (*Schlafrock*) dressing gown. ◆**m~rot,** *n* red (morning) sky. ◆**m~s,** *adv.* in the morning; every morning; **von m. bis abends,** from morning to night.

morgig ['mɔrgiç], *adj.* tomorrow's (weather etc.).

Morphium ['mɔrfium], *n* -s/no *pl* morphine.

morsch [mɔrʃ], *adj.* rotten (wood etc.).

Morse|alphabet ['mɔrzə'alfabet], *n* Morse (code). ◆**m~n,** *v.tr.* to send (a message etc.) in Morse.

Mörser ['mœrzər], *m* -s/- *Cu: & Mil:* mortar.

Mörtel ['mœrtəl], *m* -s/- mortar; (*Putz*) plaster.

Mosaik [moza'i:k], *n* -s/-en & -e mosaic.

Moschee [mɔ'ʃe:], *f* -/-n mosque.

Mosel ['mo:zəl]. *Pr.n.f.* -. Moselle.

Moskau ['mɔskau]. *Pr.n.n* -s. Moscow.

Moskito [mɔs'ki:to], *m* -s/-s mosquito.

Most [mɔst], *m* -(e)s/-e **1.** must. **2.** (*Apfelm.*) (rough) cider.

Motiv [mo'ti:f], *n* -s/-e **1.** (*Grund*) motive.

2. (a) *Mus: Lit:* motif, theme; (b) *Art: Phot:* subject. ◆**M~ation** [-ivatsi'oːn], f -/-en motivation. ◆**m~ieren** [-'viːtrən], v.tr. to motivate (a pupil etc.).

Motor ['moːtɔr]. **I.** m -s/-en engine; *El:* motor. **II.** '**M~**, *comb.fm.* (a) (*eines M~s*) engine (oil, noise etc.); (b) (*mit einem M.*) motor (mower, scooter, vessel etc.); power (pump, saw etc.). ◆'**M~boot**, n motorboat. ◆'**M~haube**, f -/-n *Aut: etc:* bonnet, *N.Am:* hood. ◆**m~i'siert**, adj. motorized (troops etc.); motor (traffic); (visitors etc.) in cars. ◆**M~rad** [mo'toːraːt], n motorcycle. ◆'**M~radfahrer**, m motorcyclist. ◆'**M~schaden**, m engine trouble.

Motte ['mɔtə], f -/-n moth. ◆'**M~nkugel**, f mothball.

Motto ['mɔto], n -s/-s motto.

Möwe ['møːvə], f -/-n gull.

Mücke ['mykə], f -/-n mosquito; (*kleine M.*) midge. ◆'**M~nstich**, m mosquito bite.

Mucks [muks], m -es/-e *F:* (a) slight(est) sound; (b) (*Bewegung*) keinen M. tun/machen, not to stir/budge. ◆'**m~en**, v.i. (*haben*) & refl. usu.neg. *F:* (sich) m., to make a sound; (*sich rühren*) to budge. ◆'**m~mäuschen'still**, adj. *F:* as quiet as a mouse.

müd|**e** ['myːdə], adj. tired; weary (smile, movement etc.); **ich bin es m.**, I am tired of it. ◆'**M~igkeit**, f -/no pl tiredness; weariness.

Muff [muf], m -(e)s/-e muff.

Muff|**el** ['mufəl], m -s/- *F:* (*Pers.*) sourpuss, crosspatch. ◆'**m~(el)ig**, adj. *F:* sulky, grumpy.

muffig ['mufiç], adj. *F:* (*moderig*) musty, stale.

muhen ['muːən], v.i. (*haben*) to moo.

Müh|**e** ['myːə], f -/-n trouble; (*Anstrengung*) effort; **er scheut keine M.**, he spares no effort; **sich dat M. geben/machen**, to take trouble/try hard; **mit M. und Not**, with great difficulty; (*gerade noch*) only just. ◆'**m~elos**, adj. effortless (action etc.); easy (victory etc.). ◆'**m~evoll**, adj. laborious; (*schwierig*) difficult (task, work etc.). ◆'**m~sam**, adj. arduous (life etc.); laborious; (*schwierig*) uphill (task etc.). ◆'**m~selig**, adj. *Lit:* arduous.

Mühle ['myːlə], f -/-n mill; (*für Kaffee usw.*) grinder.

Mulde ['muldə], f -/-n hollow; dip (in the road).

Mull [mul], m -(e)s/-e muslin; *Med:* gauze.

Müll [myl]. **I.** m -s/no pl rubbish, refuse; *N.Am:* garbage. **II.** '**M~**, *comb.fm.* refuse, rubbish, *N.Am:* garbage (heap etc.). ◆'**M~abfuhr**, f refuse collection (service). ◆'**M~beutel**, m dustbin liner. ◆'**M~eimer**, m -s/- dustbin,

N.Am: garbage can; (*im Haus*) waste bin. ◆'**M~halde** f/'**M~kippe**, f rubbish/refuse tip. ◆'**M~mann**, m *F:* dustman, *N.Am:* garbage man. ◆'**M~schlucker**, m rubbish chute. ◆'**M~tonne**, f dustbin, *N.Am:* garbage can.

mulmig ['mulmiç], adj. *F:* (a) tricky, precarious (situation etc.); (b) **mir ist m. zumute**, I feel uneasy/(*schlecht*) queasy.

multi-['multi-], *comb.fm.* multi- (millionaire etc.). ◆**m~pli'zieren**, to multiply (figures etc.).

Mumie ['muːmiə], f -/-n mummy.

Mumm [mum], m -s/no pl *F:* spunk.

Mumps [mumps], m -/no pl mumps.

Mund [munt], m -(e)s/-er mouth; **halt den M.!** shut up! pipe down! **j-m über den M. fahren**, to cut s.o. short. ◆'**M~art**, f dialect. ◆'**M~harmonika**, f harmonica; *F:* mouth organ. ◆'**M~stück**, n mouthpiece; tip (of a cigarette). ◆'**M~wasser**, n -s/- mouthwash. ◆'**M~werk**, n -(e)s/no pl *F:* mouth. ◆'**M~winkel**, m corner of the mouth. ◆'**M~-zu-'M~-Beatmung**, f mouth-to-mouth resuscitation; *F:* kiss of life.

Mündel ['myndəl], n -s/- *Jur:* ward.

münd|**en** ['myndən], v.i. (*sein*) (*Fluß*) to flow; (*Straße*) to lead. ◆'**M~ung**, f -/-en 1. (*Flußm.*) mouth, estuary. **2.** (*Gewehrm.*) muzzle.

mündig ['myndiç], adj. of age; **m. werden**, to come of age. ◆'**M~keit**, f -/no pl majority.

mündlich ['myntliç], adj. oral.

Munition [munitsi'oːn], f -/no pl ammunition. ◆**M~slager**, n -s/- ammunition depot.

munkeln ['muŋkəln], v.tr. & i. (*haben*) to whisper furtively; **man munkelt, (daß ...)**, it is rumoured that ...

munter ['muntər], adj. (a) (*lebhaft*) lively (person, eyes, game etc.); (b) (*heiter*) gay, cheerful; (c) (*wach*) awake. ◆'**M~keit**, f -/no pl liveliness; cheerfulness.

Münz|**e** ['myntsə], f -/-n coin. ◆**m~en**, v.tr. (a) to mint, coin (silver, gold etc.); (b) **auf j-n/etwas** acc **gemünzt sein**, to be aimed/directed at s.o., sth.

mürb|**e** ['myrbə], adj. (a) crumbly (cake, pastry etc.); crunchy (apple); mellow (fruit etc.); (b) (*morsch*) rotten (wood, rope etc.); (c) *Fig:* **j-n m. machen**, to wear s.o. down. ◆'**M~teig**, m short (crust) pastry.

Murks [murks], m -es/no pl *F:* botchup.

Murmel ['murməl], f -/-n marble.

murmeln ['murməln]. **I.** v.tr. & i. (*haben*) to murmur (sth.). **II. M.**, n -s/no pl murmur.

Murmeltier ['murməltiːr], n marmot; **wie ein M. schlafen**, to sleep like a log.

murren ['murən], v.i. (*haben*) to grumble, moan.

mürrisch ['myriʃ], adj. grumpy; sulky.

Mus [muːs], n -es/-e purée.

Muschel ['muʃəl], *f* -/-n 1. (a) (*Schale*) (sea) shell; (b) (*Miesm.*) mussel. 2. *Tel:* (*Sprechm.*) mouthpiece; (*Hörm.*) earpiece.
Museum [mu'ze:um], *n* -s/-seen museum.
Musical ['mju:zikəl], *n* -s/-s musical.
Musik [mu'zi:k]. I. *f* -/no pl 1. music. 2. *F:* (*M~kapelle*) band. II. **M~**, *comb.fm.* (a) music (instrument, scene etc.); (b) music (lesson, teacher, critic etc.); (school, history etc.) of music. ◆**m~alisch** [-'ka:liʃ], *adj.* musical. ◆**M~ant** [-'kant], *m* -en/-en (street etc.) musician. ◆**M~er(in)** ['mu:zikər(in)], *m* -s/- (*f* -/-nen) musician. ◆**M~kapelle**, *f* band.
musisch ['mu:ziʃ], *adj.* artistic; **er ist m. veranlagt**, he has an artistic disposition.
musizieren [muzi'tsi:rən], *v.i.* (haben) to make music.
Muskat [mus'ka:t], *m* -(e)s/-e (also **M~nuß** *f*) nutmeg.
Muskel ['muskəl]. I. *m* -s/-n muscle. II. **M~**, *comb.fm.* muscular (pain etc.); muscle (fibre etc.). ◆**M~kater**, *m* (einen) M. haben, to be stiff (as a result of physical effort). ◆**M~zerrung**, *f* pulled muscle.
muskulös [musku'lø:s], *adj.* muscular.
Muße ['mu:sə], *f* -/no pl Lit: leisure. ◆**M~stunde**, *f* leisure/spare time.
müssen ['mysən], *v.irr. modal aux. & v.i.* (haben) to have to; **ich muß jetzt gehen**, I must/have to/*F:* I've got to go now, **wenn es sein muß**, if it's really necessary; **du mußt es ja wissen**, you should know; **Geld müßte man haben!** it would be nice to be rich; **ich mußte in die Stadt**, I must go into town; **er mußte zum Arzt**, he had to go to the doctor.
müßig ['my:sɪç], *adj.* Lit: 1. idle. 2. (sinnlos) futile.
Muster ['mustər]. I. *n* -s/- 1. (a) (*Vorlage*) pattern; (b) (*Vorbild*) model. 2. (*Dessin*) pattern, design. 3. (*Warenprobe*) sample, specimen. II. **M~**, *comb.fm.* 1. model (letter, pupil etc.); perfect (marriage etc.). 2. *Com:* pattern, sample (book etc.). ◆**m~gültig/m~haft**, *adj.* exemplary, model (behaviour, pupil etc.); perfect (example etc.); *adv.* in an exem-

plary fashion. ◆**m~n**, *v.tr.* (a) to eye, study (s.o.); (b) *Mil:* to inspect (troops etc.); (auf Tauglichkeit) **gemustert werden**, to have a medical. ◆**M~ung**, *f* -/-en 1. inspection, scrutiny (of s.o.). 2. *Mil:* medical examination. 3. (*Stoff usw.*) pattern, design.
Mut [mu:t], *m* -(e)s/no pl courage; (*Tapferkeit*) bravery; (*Kühnheit*) boldness; **den M. verlieren**, to lose heart; **j-m M. machen/den M. nehmen**, to encourage/ discourage s.o. ◆**m~ig**, *adj.* courageous, brave. ◆**m~los**, *adj.* fainthearted; (*entmutigt*) despondent.
mutmaßlich ['mu:tma:slɪç], *adj.* probable (result, verdict etc.); suspected (murderer etc.). ◆**M~ung**, *f* -/-en speculation.
Mutter[1] ['mutər]. I. *f* -/¨ mother. II. *comb.fm.* maternal, motherly (love, instinct etc.); mother's (milk, Day etc.); (b) mother (country, ship etc.). ◆**M~boden**, *m*/**M~erde**, *f* topsoil. ◆**M~gesellschaft**, *f* parent company. ◆**M~leib**, *m* womb. ◆**m~los**, motherless. ◆**M~mal**, *n* birthmark; (braun) mole. ◆**M~schaft**, *f* -/no pl motherhood. ◆**M~seelenallein**, *adj.* all alone. ◆**M~sprache**, *f* mother tongue, native language. ◆**M~tier**, *n* dam.
Mutter[2], *f* -/-n Tchn: nut.
mütterlich ['mytərlɪç], *adj.* motherly (love, woman, type etc.); maternal (instincts, care etc.). ◆**m~erseits**, *adv.* on one's mother's side.
Mutti ['muti], *f* -/-s *F:* mummy, mum.
Mutwille [n] ['mu:tvilə], *m* wilfulness; (*Bosheit*) wilful malice. ◆**m~ig**, *adj.* wilful (behaviour etc.); wanton (damage).
Mütze ['mytsə], *f* -/-n cap; (*Wollm.*) woolly hat.
mysteriös [mysteri'ø:s], *adj.* mysterious.
Mystik ['mystik], *f* -/no pl mysticism. ◆**m~isch**, *adj.* (a) mystic (symbol, ceremony); (b) *F:* (geheimnisvoll) mysterious.
Myth|ologie [mytolo'gi:], *f* -/-n mythology. ◆**m~ologisch** [-o'lo:gɪʃ], *adj.* mythological. ◆**M~os** ['my:tɔs], *m* -/ Mythen myth.

N

N, n [ɛn], *n* -/- (the letter) N, n.
na [na], *int. F:* well; (also) so; **na so was!** well I never! I say! **na und? so what? na, also!** there you are! what did I tell you? **na gut!** all right then!
Nabe ['na:bə], *f* -/-n hub.
Nabel ['na:bəl], *m* -s/- navel. ◆**N~schnur**, *f* umbilical cord.
nach [na:x]. I. *prep.* + *dat* 1. (*räumlich*) (a) to; **n. links/rechts**, to the left/right; **n. allen Richtungen**, in all directions; (b)

n. etwas greifen, streben usw., to reach out, strive etc. for sth. 2. (*zeitlich, Folge*) after; **n. der Schule**, after school; **fünf (Minuten) n. drei**, five (minutes) past three; **bitte n. Ihnen!** after you! 3. (*gemäß*) according to; **n. dem, was Sie sagen**, going by/from what you say; **wenn es n. mir ginge**, if I had my way; **n. Litern gemessen**, measured in litres; **etwas n. Gewicht verkaufen**, to sell sth. by weight. II. *adv.* (a) **n. wie vor**, as was always the case; **n. und n.**, gradually; by degrees; (**b**) **mir n.!** follow me!

'**nachäffen**, v.tr.sep. usu. Pej: to ape, mimic (s.o., sth.).

'**nachahm|en**, v.tr.sep. to imitate, copy, (nachäffen) mimic (s.o., sth.). ◆'**N~er**, m -s/- imitator; mimic. ◆'**N~ung**, f -/-en imitation.

'**nacharbeiten**, v.tr. & i.sep. (haben) to make up for (lost time); **zwei Stunden n.**, to do two extra hours' work.

Nachbar|(in) ['naxbɑːr(in)]. I. m -s/-n (f -/-nen) neighbour. II. **N~**-, comb.fm. neighbouring (country etc.); adjoining (building, room etc.); nextdoor (house, garden); next (table, town etc.). ◆'**n~lich**, adj. neighbourly (relations etc.). ◆'**N~schaft**, f -/no pl neighbourhood; **unsere N.**, our neighbourhood/(Nachbarn) neighbours.

'**nachbestell|en**, v.tr.sep. to order some more of (sth.). ◆'**N~ung**, f Com: repeat order.

'**nachbild|en**, v.tr.sep. to reproduce, copy (sth.). ◆'**N~ung**, f reproduction, copy.

'**nachblicken**, v.i.sep. (haben) **jdm n.** to gaze after s.o.

'**nachdatieren**, v.tr.sep. to backdate (a form, cheque etc.).

nach'dem, conj. (a) (zeitlich) after, when; (**b**) (kausal) **n. die Preise gestiegen sind**, since prices have risen.

'**nachdenk|en**. I. v.i.sep.irr.17 (haben) to think (carefully) (**über** + acc, about); **denk mal nach**, try and think; **er dachte (darüber) nach, ob ....**, he wondered whether .... II. **N.**, n -s/no pl thought, meditation. ◆'**n~lich**, adj. pensive.

'**Nachdruck**, m 1. no pl emphasis; **mit N.**, emphatically. 2. (Neudruck) reprint. ◆'**n~en**, v.tr.sep. to reprint.

'**nachdrücklich** ['nɑːxdrʏkliç], adj. emphatic.

'**nacheifern**, v.i.sep. (haben) **jdm n.** to emulate s.o.

nachei'nander, adv. one after the other; **drei Tage n.**, three days running.

'**nachempfinden**, v.tr.sep.irr.9 **j-s Leid, Freude usw. n.**, to share s.o.'s sorrow, joy etc.; **das kann ich dir n.**, I understand how you feel.

'**Nacherzählung**, f Sch: reproduction.

'**Nachfahre**, m -n/-n Lit: descendant.

'**Nachfolge**, f succession (**in einem Amt**, to an office). ◆'**n~n**, v.i.sep. (sein) **j-m n.**, to follow s.o., (im Amt) succeed s.o. ◆'**N~r(in)**, m -s/- (f -/-nen) successor.

'**nachforsch|en**, v.i.sep. (haben) to make enquiries. ◆'**N~ungen**, fpl enquiries, investigations.

'**Nachfrage**, f 1. Com: demand (**nach** + dat, for). 2. F: **danke der N.!** how kind of you to ask! ◆'**n~n**, v.i.sep. (haben) to inquire, make inquiries; **bei j-m n.**, to ask s.o.

'**nachfühlen**, v.tr.sep. to understand (s.o.'s disappointment etc.).

'**nachfüllen**, v.tr.sep. (a) to refill (a glass etc.); to top up (a radiator etc.); (**b**) to top up with (petrol etc.).

'**nachgeben**, v.i.sep.irr.35 (haben) (a) (Pers.) to give in, yield (**etwas** dat, to sth.); **j-s Wünschen n.**, to bow to s.o.'s wishes; (**b**) (Material, Seil) to give, yield; (Boden usw.) to give way; Fin: (Preise, Kurse) to weaken.

'**Nachgebühr**, f postage due (payment); surcharge.

'**Nachgeburt**, f afterbirth.

'**nachgehen**, v.i.sep.irr.36 (sein) **j-m, etwas** dat **n.**, to follow s.o., sth.; **einem Problem n.**, to look into a problem; **seiner Arbeit n.**, to go about one's work; (Uhr) (**fünf Minuten usw.**) **n.**, to be (five minutes etc.) slow.

'**nachgemacht**, p.p. as adj. imitation (jewellery etc.); counterfeit (money, signature).

'**Nachgeschmack**, m aftertaste.

nachgiebig ['nɑːxɡiːbiç], adj. (a) flexible, pliant (material etc.); (**b**) yielding, compliant (person). ◆'**N~keit**, f -/no pl (a) flexibility; (**b**) compliance, yielding nature; indulgence (of parents etc.).

'**Nachhall**, m echo; reverberation. ◆'**n~en**, v.i.sep. (haben) to echo, reverberate.

'**nachhaltig**, adj. lasting; **n. wirken**, to have a lasting effect/influence.

Nachhauseweg [nɑːx'hauzəveːk], m way home.

'**nachhelfen**, v.i.sep.irr.50 (haben) (**j-m**) **n.**, to lend (s.o.) a hand, help (s.o.); **etwas** dat **n.**, to help sth. along.

nachher [nax'heːr], adv. afterwards; (später) later; **bis n.!** see you later.

'**Nachhilfe**, f (also **N~unterricht** m) Sch: coaching; **N. bekommen**, to be coached. ◆'**N~stunde**, f extra (private) lesson.

'**nachhinein**, adv. **im n.**, afterwards; (nachträglich) after the event.

'**nachholen**, v.tr.sep. (a) to make up for (lost time etc.); to catch up on (sleep, work etc.); (**b**) to do (an examination etc.) later.

'**Nachkomme**, m -n/-n descendant. ◆'**n~en**, v.i.sep.irr.53 (sein) (a) to come, follow (on) later; **j-m, etwas** dat **n.**, to follow s.o., sth.; (**b**) (Schritt halten) to keep up; (**c**) (erfüllen) **einem Versprechen usw. n.**, to keep a promise etc.

'**Nachkriegs**-, comb.fm. post-war (generation etc.). ◆'**N~zeit**, f post-war period.

Nachlaß ['nɑːxlas], n -lasses/-lässe 1. (Erbschaft) estate of a dead person). 2. Com: (Preisn.) discount; reduction.

'**nachlassen**, v.sep.irr.57 1. v.i. (haben) (a) to lessen; (Wind) to drop; (Sturm, Schmerz, Druck usw.) to ease, let up; (Fieber) to go down; (Gehör, Augen usw.) to begin to fail; (Interesse usw.) to wane, fall off; (Wirkung) to wear off; (**b**) (aufgeben) to give up; **nicht n.!** keep it up! 2.

v.tr. Com: etwas vom Preis n., to deduct sth. from the price.

'nachlässig, *adj.* careless; slipshod (person, work etc.); lax, casual (behaviour etc.). ◆**'N~keit,** *f* -/-en carelessness, negligence; *F:* sloppiness.

nachlaufen, *v.i.sep.irr.58 (sein)* j-m, etwas *dat* n., to run after s.o., sth.; *F:* einem Mädchen n., to chase a girl.

nachlegen, *v.tr.sep.* to put more (wood etc.) on (the fire).

nachlesen, *v.tr.sep.irr.61 (nachschlagen)* to look/read (sth.) up.

nachmachen, *v.tr.sep. F:* (a) to copy, (*nachäffen*) mimic (s.o., sth.); to reproduce, copy (period furniture etc.); (*unerlaubt*) to forge (a signature etc.), counterfeit (money etc.); (b) (*nachholen*) to catch up on (sth.) later.

Nachmittag. I. *m* afternoon; am N., in the afternoon. **II. n.,** *adv.* heute/gestern n., this/yesterday afternoon. ◆**'n~s,** *adv.* in the afternoon/(jeden N.) afternoons.

Nachnahme, *f* -/-n etwas per/mit N. schicken, to send sth. cash on delivery/ *abbr.* C.O.D.

Nachname, *m* surname.

Nachporto, *n* postage due.

nachprüfen, *v.tr.sep.* to check, verify (a fact, statement etc.).

nachrechnen, *v.tr.sep.* to check (a sum etc.).

Nachrede, *f Jur:* üble N., defamation, slander.

Nachricht ['naːxrɪçt], *f* -/-en news; eine N., a piece of news/information; eine N. hinterlassen, to leave a message; j-m N. geben, to inform s.o.; *Rad: TV:* die N~en, the news. ◆**'N~en-,** *comb.fm.* news (magazine etc.). ◆**'N~enagentur,** *f* news agency. ◆**'N~endienst,** *m esp. Mil:* intelligence (service). ◆**'N~ensprecher(in),** *m(f),* *N.Am:* newscaster. ◆**'N~entechnik,** *f* (tele)communications.

nachrücken, *v.i.sep. (sein) (Pers., Mil: Truppen)* to move up.

Nachruf, *m* obituary.

nachsagen, *v.tr.sep.* j-m etwas n., to say sth. of s.o.; j-m Gutes/Böses n., to speak well/badly of s.o.

Nachsaison, *f* off/low season.

nachschicken, *v.tr.sep.* to forward, send on (a letter etc.) (j-m, to s.o.).

nachschlagen, *v.sep.irr.85* **1.** *v.tr.* to look (sth.) up. **2.** *v.i. (haben)* in einem Wörterbuch usw. n., to consult a dictionary etc. ◆**'N~ewerk,** *n* reference work.

Nachschlüssel, *m* duplicate key.

Nachschub, *m* -(e)s/*no pl Mil:* supply (**an Proviant usw.,** of food etc.); *coll.* **der N.,** supplies. ◆**'N~linie,** *f/***'N~weg,** *m* supply line.

nachsehen. I. *v.sep.irr.92* **1.** *v.i. (haben)* (a) j-m, etwas *dat* n., to look/gaze after s.o., sth.; (b) (*kontrollieren*) to have a look, check up. **2.** *v.tr.* (a) to look (sth.) up (in a book etc.); (b) (*kontrollieren*) to check (homework etc.); (c) j-m seine Fehler usw. n., to overlook s.o.'s mistakes etc. **II. N.,** *n* -*s/no pl* das N. haben, to come off badly.

nachsenden, *v.tr.sep.irr.94* to forward, send on (a letter etc.).

Nachsicht, *f* -/*no pl* leniency, N. üben, to be lenient, show forbearance. ◆**'n~ig,** *adj.* lenient (**gegen** j-n, towards s.o.); forbearing, charitable (attitude etc.).

nachsitzen. I. *v.i.sep.irr.97 (haben)* n. müssen, to be kept in. **II. N.,** *n* -*s/no pl* detention.

Nachspeise, *f* dessert, *Brit:* sweet.

Nachspiel, *n* 1. *Th:* epilogue. 2. (*Folgen*) consequences; **es wird noch ein N. geben,** there will be repercussions. ◆**'n~en,** *v.tr.sep. Fb: etc:* **fünf Minuten n. lassen,** to allow five minutes injury time.

nachsprechen, *v.tr.sep.irr.14* to repeat (s.o.'s words etc.).

nächst [nɛːçst]. **I.** *prep.* + *dat Lit:* next to. **II. n~,** *comb.fm.* next (largest, highest, smallest, possible etc.). ◆**'n~e(r, s),** *adj.* next; (*nächstgelegen*) nearest; **das n. Geschäft,** the nearest shop; **die n~en Verwandten,** the closest relatives, **in den n~en Tagen,** in the next few days; **wer kommt als n~er?** whose turn is it next? ◆**'n~-beste,** *adj.* (a) next best; (b) the first (hotel etc.) one comes across; *F:* any old (restaurant etc.). ◆**'n~emal,** *adv.* **das n./beim nächstenmal,** (the) next time. ◆**'n~enliebe,** *f* charity. ◆**'n~ens,** *adv.* shortly, soon. ◆**'n~gelegene,** *attrib. adj.* nearest (town, house etc.). ◆**'n~liegende(r, s),** *adj.* most obvious, first (question, etc.).

nachstehen, *v.i.sep.irr.100 (haben)* j-m an etwas *dat* n., to be inferior to s.o. in sth. ◆**'n~d,** *adj.* following; *adv.* below.

nachstellen, *v.sep.* **1.** *v.tr.* (a) to adjust (brakes etc.); (b) *Gram:* to postpone (a verb etc.). **2.** *v.i. (haben) F:* einem Mädchen n., to pursue a girl.

nachsuchen, *v.i.sep. (haben)* (a) to search; (b) um etwas n., to ask for sth.

Nacht [naxt]. **I.** *f* -/-e night; **bei N.,** at night; **bei N. und Nebel,** under cover of darkness; (*heimlich*) secretly; **über N.,** overnight. **II. n.,** *adv.* **heute** n., (i) last night; (ii) tonight; **Dienstag** n., on Tuesday night. **III. 'N~-,** *comb.fm.* night (work, blindness, club, flight, life, train etc.); *Cin: TV:* late-night (programme, performance etc.). ◆**'N~hemd,** *n* nightshirt; (*Frauen.*) nightdress, *F:* nightie. ◆**'N~lokal,** *n* nightspot. ◆**'N~portier,** *m* night porter. ◆**'N~quartier,** *n* shelter/

accommodation for the night. ◆'N~ruhe, f night's sleep. ◆'N~s, adv. at night; n. um 3 (Uhr), at 3 (o'clock); n. in the morning. ◆'N~schicht, f night shift. ◆'N~schwester, f night nurse. ◆'N~tisch, m bedside table. ◆'N~topf, m chamber pot. ◆'N~wache, f night watch. ◆'N~wächter, m night watchman. ◆'N~zeit, f night-time; zur N., at night.

'Nachteil, m disadvantage, drawback. ◆'n~ig, adj. disadvantageous; (schädlich) detrimental, damaging.

nächt|elang ['nɛçtəlaŋ], adj. lasting several nights; adv. night after night. ◆'n~lich, adj. nocturnal (habits, visit etc.); (darkness, stillness) of the night; night-time (theft etc.).

Nachtigall ['naxtigal], f /-en nightingale.

'Nachtisch, m dessert, Brit: sweet; zum N., as dessert, Brit: F: for afters.

'Nachtrag, m -(e)s/-e supplement; postscript (to a report etc.). ◆'n~en, v.tr.sep.irr.85 (a) j-m etwas n., (i) to walk behind s.o. carrying sth.; (ii) refuse to forgive s.o. for sth.; (b) (hinzufügen) to add (sth.).

nachträglich ['naːxtrɛːkliç], adj. subsequent (remark, apology etc.); belated (greetings etc.); adv. later; subsequently.

'nachtrauern, v.i.sep. (haben) j-m, etwas dat n., to bemoan the loss of s.o., sth.

'Nachuntersuchung, f Med: (postoperative etc.) checkup.

'Nachwehen, pl Med: afterpains.

'Nachweis, m -es/-e proof, evidence. ◆'n~bar, adj. demonstrable; Med: detectable (disease etc.); es ist nicht n., it cannot be proved. ◆'n~en, v.tr.sep.irr.70 to prove (a fact, one's identity etc.); man konnte ihm nichts n., it was impossible to pin anything on him.

'Nachwelt, f die N., posterity.

'Nachwirkung, f after-effect.

'Nachwort, n postscript (to a book).

'Nachwuchs. I. m I. F: (Kinder) offspring. 2. (a) musikalischer/wissenschaftlicher N., rising generation of musicians/scientists; (b) Com: trainees (in a firm etc.). II. N~-, comb.fm. (a) young, up and coming (player, actor, author etc.); (b) Com: trainee (salesman etc.).

'nachzahl|en, v.tr.sep. to pay (sth.) later/(zusätzlich) extra. ◆'N~ung, f 1. subsequent payment. 2. back-payment.

'nachzählen, v.tr.sep. to re-count (money, votes etc.); to check (change etc.).

Nachzügler ['naːxtsyːklər], m -s/- latecomer; straggler (on a hike etc.).

Nacken ['nakən], m -s/- (nape of the) neck; Fig: j-m im N. sitzen, to breathe down s.o.'s neck; er hatte die Polizei im N., the police were hard on his heels.

nackt [nakt]. I. adj. (a) naked (person,

body etc.); bare (arms, wall etc.); Art: etc: nude (model etc.); mit n~em Oberkörper, stripped to the waist; sich n. ausziehen, to strip (naked); (b) bare (facts, existence etc.); stark (poverty etc.); undisguised (hatred); die n~e Wahrheit, the plain truth. II. 'N~-, comb.fm. nude (bathing, photograph, dancer etc.). ◆'N~heit, f -/no pl nakedness, nudity. ◆'N~kultur, f nudism.

Nadel ['naːdəl]. I. f /-n needle; (Steckn., Hutn., Haarn.) pin; Rec: stylus. II. 'N~-, comb.fm. (a) needle (size etc.); pin-(head etc.); (b) Bot: coniferous (forest etc.) ◆'N~baum, m coniferous tree, conifer. ◆'N~kissen, n pincushion. ◆'N~stich, m (i) pinprick; (ii) (Nähstich) stitch. ◆'N~streifen, mpl pinstripe.

Nagel ['naːgəl]. I. m -s/- nail; seine Stellung usw. an den N. hängen, to chuck in one's job etc.; sich dat etwas unter den N. reißen, to make off with sth. II. 'N~-, comb.fm. nail-(brush, -file etc.). ◆'N~haut, f cuticle. ◆'N~lack, m nail varnish. ◆'n~n, v.tr. to nail (sth.) (an etwas acc, to sth.). ◆'n~neu, adj. F: brand-new. ◆'N~schere, f nail scissors.

nag|en ['naːgən], v. 1. v.i. (haben) (Tier) to gnaw, (Pers.) nibble (an etwas dat, at sth.); Fig: (Kummer, Zweifel usw.) an j-m n., to prey on s.o.; n~de Zweifel, nagging doubt. 2. v.tr. to gnaw (sth.). ◆'N~er, m -s/-/'N~etier, n rodent.

nah(e) ['naː(ə)], adj. 1. (örtlich) near; j-m, etwas dat n~(e), close to s.o., sth.; n~e (gelegen), nearby (town, house etc.); n~(e) bei der Kirche, near the church. 2. (a) (zeitlich) close, impending (event etc.); near (future); imminent (danger, departure etc.); n~e bevorstehen, to be imminent; (b) den Tränen n~e, on the verge of tears. 3. (eng, vertraut) close (relative, contact etc.); adv. n~ verwandt, closely related. ◆'N~aufnahme, f close-up. ◆'n~e'bei, adv. close by. ◆'n~egehen, v.i.sep.irr.36 (sein) to affect s.o. deeply. ◆'n~ekommen, v.i.sep.irr.53 (sein) (a) etwas dat n., to come close to sth.; (b) j-m n., to get to know s.o. well. ◆'n~elegen, v.tr.sep. j-m etwas n., to recommend sth. (strongly) to s.o. ◆'n~eliegen, v.i.sep.irr.62 (haben) to seem likely; (Idee usw.) to suggest itself. ◆'n~eliegend, adj. likely; fair (assumption etc.); aus n~eliegenden Gründen, for obvious reasons. ◆'n~en, v.i. (sein) Lit: to draw near, approach. ◆'n~estehen, v.i.sep.irr.100 (haben) j-m n., to be close to s.o.(sympathisieren) in sympathy with s.o. ◆'n~e'zu, adv. almost, nearly. ◆'N~kampf, m Mil: close combat. ◆'N~ost, inv. the Near East.

◆'N~verkehr, m Rail: Aut: local traffic. ◆'N~ziel, n short-term aim.

Näh- ['nɛ:-], comb.fm. sewing (needle, silk, lesson, table etc.). ◆'n~en, v.tr. & i. (a) to sew; to make (a dress, curtains etc.); (b) to stitch up (a wound etc.). ◆'N~erin, f -/-nen needlewoman. ◆'N~garn, n sewing cotton. ◆'N~korb, m sewing basket, workbasket. ◆'N~maschine, f sewing machine.

Nähe ['nɛ:ə], f -/no pl nearness, proximity; etwas aus der N. betrachten, to have a close look at sth.; in der N., nearby; in der N. der Stadt, near/close to the town; in meiner N., near me/where I live. ◆'n~r, adj. (a) nearer, closer; shorter (route etc.); n~re Verwandtschaft, close relatives; adv. j-n n. kennenlernen, to get to know s.o. better; (b) (genauer) more detailed (examination etc.); N~es/n~e Auskünfte, further details/information. ◆'n~rkommen, v.i.sep.irr.53 (sein) j-m n., to get to know s.o. better. ◆'n~rn, v.tr. (a) to move/bring sth. closer (etwas dat, to sth.); (b) sich n., to come up (j-m, etwas dat, to s.o., sth.).

nähren ['nɛːrən], v.tr. (a) to feed (s.o., a baby etc.); gut/schlecht genährt, well-fed/undernourished; (b) Lit: to nurture (suspicion etc.). ◆'N~mittel, npl cereal products. ◆'N~stoff, m nutrient. ◆'N~wert, m food value.

nahr|haft ['nɑ:rhaft], adj. nourishing, nutritious. ◆'N~ung, f -/no pl food. ◆'N~ungsmittel. I. n food item; pl foodstuffs. II. N~-, comb.fm. food (industry etc.).

Naht [nɑːt], f -/̈e seam; Med: suture; aus allen N~en platzen, to burst at the seams. ◆'N~los, adj. seamless; Fig: smooth (transition etc.).

naiv [na'iːf], adj. naive. ◆N~ität [naivi'tɛːt], f -/no pl naiveté, ingenuousness.

Nam|e ['nɑːmə], m -ns/-n name; nur dem N~en nach, only by name; (nicht wirklich) nominally, in name only; sich dat einen N~en machen, to make a name for oneself. ◆'N~en-, comb.fm. (list, register etc.) of names. ◆'n~enlos, adj. unnamed, nameless (person, thing); unknown (hero etc.). ◆'n~ens, adv. by the name of, called. ◆'N~ensschild, n nameplate. ◆'N~enstag, m name-day. ◆'N~ensvetter, m namesake. ◆'N~enszug, m signature. ◆'n~entlich, adv. 1. j-n n. nennen, to mention s.o. by name. 2. (besonders) especially, particularly. ◆'n~haft, adj. (a) renowned, celebrated (artist etc.); (b) (beträchtlich) considerable (sum, part etc.); (c) Jur: den Täter n. machen, to name the offender.

nämlich ['nɛːmliç], adv. namely; er

konnte nicht kommen, er ist n. krank, he couldn't come as he is ill.

nanu [na'nuː], int. well! well I never!

Napf [napf], m -(e)s/̈e dish, bowl (for a dog etc.).

Narb|e ['narbə], f -/-n Med: scar. ◆'n~ig, adj. scarred.

Narkose [nar'koːzə], f -/-n narcosis; (N~mittel) anaesthetic. ◆N~arzt, m anaesthetist.

Narr [nar], m -en/-en fool, j-n zum N~en halten, to make a fool of s.o. ◆'n~ensicher, adj. F: foolproof.

närrisch ['nɛriʃ], adj. (verrückt) mad, crazy (person, idea etc.).

Narzisse [nar'tsisə], f -/-n narcissus; gelbe N., daffodil.

nasch|en ['naʃən], v.tr. & i. (haben) to nibble (a cake etc.); an etwas dat n., to nibble at sth.; gerne n., to have a sweet tooth. ◆'n~haft, adj. fond of nibbling; sweet-toothed.

Nase ['nɑːzə], f -/-n nose; immer der N. nach, just follow your nose; (direkt) vor der N., (right) under one's nose; F: auf die N. fallen, to fall flat on one's face; also Fig: to come a cropper; von j-m, etwas dat die N. voll haben, to be fed up with s.o., sth.; j-n an der N. herumführen, to pull the wool over s.o.'s eyes; es ging nicht nach meiner N., things didn't go the way I wanted. ◆'N~en-, comb.fm. nose (drops etc.); (tip etc.) of the nose; nasal (spray etc.). ◆'N~enbein, n nasal bone. ◆'N~enbluten, n nose-bleed. ◆'N~enhöhle, f nasal cavity. ◆'N~enloch, n nostril. ◆'N~enrücken, m bridge of the nose. ◆'n~eweis. I. adj. precocious. II. N~, m -es/-e know-all. ◆'N~horn, n rhinoceros.

näseln ['nɛːzəln], v.i. (haben) to speak through one's nose.

naß [nas], adj. wet. ◆'n~kalt, adj. cold and damp.

Nässe ['nɛsə], f -/no pl wetness; bei N., in the wet; when wet. ◆'n~n, v.tr. to wet (one's bed etc.).

Nation [natsi'oːn], f -/-en nation. ◆n~al [-o'nɑːl]. I. adj. national. II. N~al-, comb.fm. national (flag, park, sport, pride etc.). ◆'N~alhymne f, national anthem. ◆'n~alisieren [-ali'ziːrən], v.tr. to nationalize (an industry etc.). ◆N~alisierung, f -/-en nationalization. ◆N~alismus, m -/no pl nationalism. ◆n~alistisch, adj. nationalistic. ◆N~alität, f -/-en nationality. ◆'N~almannschaft, f national team. ◆'N~alsozialismus, m National Socialism, Nazism. ◆'N~alsozialist, m National Socialist, Nazi.

Natter ['natər], f -/-n (esp. non-poisonous) snake, Z: colubrid; (Ringeln.) grass snake.

Natur [na'tuːr]. I. f -/-en 1. no pl nature; (Landschaft) countryside. 2. (a) (Wesen) nature; disposition; **die menschliche N.**, human nature; **sie ist von N. aus schüchtern**, she is shy by nature; (b) (*Mensch*) character. II. **N∼**, **n∼**, *comb.fm.* (a) natural (colour, law, talent, landscape, product etc.); (b) nature (description etc.). ◆**N∼alien** [-'ra:liən], *pl* (a) natural produce; (b) **in N. bezahlen,** to pay in kind. ◆**N∼a'lismus,** *m* -/*no pl* naturalism. ◆**n∼a'listisch,** *adj.* naturalistic. ◆**N∼ell** [-u'rɛl], *m* -s/- temperament, disposition. ◆**N∼erscheinung,** *f* natural phenomenon. ◆**N∼forscher,** *m* naturalist. ◆**n∼gemäß,** *adj.* 1. natural (way of life etc.). 2. *adv.* (*von sich aus*) by its very nature. ◆**N∼katastrophe,** *f* natural disaster. ◆**n∼rein,** *adj.* pure, unadulterated (honey, fruit-juice etc.). ◆**N∼schutz,** *m* nature conservation; **unter N. stehen,** to be a protected species. ◆**N∼schutzgebiet,** *n* nature reserve. ◆**N∼wissenschaft,** *f* (natural) science. ◆**N∼wissenschaftler(in),** *m(f)* scientist. ◆**n∼wissenschaftlich,** *adj.* scientific.

natürlich [na'ty:rliç], *adj.* (a) natural; (*ungekünstelt*) unaffected; **sich n. benehmen,** to behave naturally; (b) *adv.* of course, naturally. ◆**n∼er'weise,** *adv.* naturally. ◆**N∼keit,** *f* -/*no pl* naturalness.

Nautik ['nautik], *f* -/*no pl* navigation, nautical science. ◆**n∼isch,** *adj.* nautical.

Navig|ation [navigatsi'o:n], *f* -/*no pl* navigation. ◆**N∼ator** [-'ga:tor], *m* -s/-en [-ga'to:rən] navigator.

Nazi|i ['na:tsi], *m* -s/-s Nazi. ◆**N∼ismus** [-'tsismus], *m* -/*no pl* Nazism.

Nebel ['ne:bəl]. I. *m* -s/- fog; (*leichter*) N., mist; **bei N.,** in fog. II. '**N∼,** '**n∼,** *comb.fm.* (a) fog (bell, lamp etc.); (b) foggy (day, weather). ◆**N∼horn,** *n* foghorn. ◆**'n∼ig** = **neblig.**

neben ['ne:bən]. I. *prep.* 1. next to, beside; (a) (+) **er saß n. mir,** he sat next to/beside me; (b) (+) **er setzte sich n. mich,** he sat down next to/beside me. 2. (+) (*zusätzlich zu*) apart from, in addition to. 3. (+ *dat*) (*verglichen mit*) compared to/with. II. **N∼,** *comb.fm.* (a) (*zusätzlich*) extra, additional (work etc.); (b) (*untergeordnet*) subsidiary, secondary (meaning, form etc.); minor (figure etc.); (*beiläufig*) incidental, passing (remark etc.); (c) (*benachbart*) next (table, room etc.), nextdoor (house). ◆**'n∼amtlich,** *adj.* second, additional (employment etc.); **er macht das n.,** he does that as a spare-time job/*F:* sideline. ◆**'n∼an,** *adv.* next door; **im Zimmer n.,** in the next room. ◆**'n∼bei,** *adv.* 1. (*zusätzlich*) in addition; as well. 2. **n. bemerkt,** incidentally; **etwas n. erwähnen,** to mention sth. in passing. ◆**'n∼beruflich,** *adj.* spare-time (work); second (job).

◆'**N∼beschäftigung,** *f* second job; (*in der Freizeit*) spare-time job. ◆'**N∼buhler(in),** *m* -s/- (*f* -/-nen) rival. ◆'**n∼einander,** *adv.* next to each other; side by side; **friedlich n. wohnen,** to live together in harmony. ◆'**N∼eingang,** *m* side entrance. ◆'**N∼fach,** *n* subsidiary/*N.Am:* minor subject. ◆'**N∼fluß,** *m* tributary. ◆'**N∼geräusch,** *n* background noise. ◆'**n∼her,** *adv.* in addition; as well. ◆'**N∼kosten,** *pl* additional expenditure/costs. ◆'**N∼mann,** *m* neighbour (at table etc.). ◆'**N∼produkt,** *n* by-product. ◆'**N∼rolle,** *f* minor/supporting part. ◆'**N∼sache,** *f* minor matter. ◆'**n∼sächlich,** *adj.* unimportant. ◆'**N∼satz,** *m* subordinate clause. ◆'**N∼straße,** *f* secondary/minor road; (*in der Stadt*) side street. ◆'**N∼verdienst,** *m* additional income. ◆'**N∼wirkung,** *f esp. Med:* side effect; *Fig:* spin-off.

neblig ['ne:blıç], *adj.* foggy, misty.

Necessaire [nesɛ'sɛ:r], *n* -s/-s 1. (*Reisen.*) toilet bag. 2. (*Näh..*) sewing kit.

neck|en ['nɛkən], *v.tr.* to tease (s.o.). ◆**N∼e'rei,** *f* -/-en 1. teasing. 2. teasing remark. ◆**'n∼isch,** *adj.* teasing (remark, manner etc.).

Neffe ['nɛfə], *m* -n/-n nephew.

negativ ['ne:gati:f]. I. *adj.* negative. II. **N.,** *n* -s/-e *Phot:* negative.

Neger ['ne:gər], *m* -s/- negro. ◆'**N∼in,** *f* -/-nen negress.

negieren [ne'gi:rən], *v.tr.* to negate (a fact etc.).

nehmen ['ne:mən], *v.tr.irr.* to take (s.o., sth.); (a) **ich nehme ein Omelett,** I'll have an omelette; **Verantwortung auf sich n.,** to take on responsibility; **etwas an sich n.,** to take care of sth.; **etwas zu sich n.,** to eat sth.; *j-n* bei sich n., to take s.o. in; **sich *dat* die Zeit für etwas n.,** to make time for sth.; *F:* **wie man's nimmt,** it depends how you look at it; **j-m etwas n.,** to take sth. away from s.o.; **er nahm ihr die Sorgen,** he freed her of her worries; **sich *dat* etwas n.,** to help oneself to sth.; **was n. Sie pro Stunde?** how much do you charge per hour?

Neid [nait], *m* -(e)s/*no pl* envy, jealousy. ◆**N∼er** ['naidər], *m* -s/- **er hat viele N.,** there are many who envy him. ◆'**n∼isch** [-dɪʃ], *adj.* envious, jealous (**auf** *j-n,* **etwas** *acc,* of s.o., sth.). ◆'**n∼los,** *adj.* without envy.

neig|en ['naigən], *v.* 1. *v.tr.* to slant, incline (a surface etc.); to tilt (a glass, bottle etc.); (*beugen*) to bow, bend (one's head, body etc.); **sich n.,** to slant; (*Boden usw.*) to slope. 2. *v.i.* (*haben*) **zu etwas *dat* n.,** to have a tendency/(*anfällig sein*) to be prone to (sth.). ◆'**N∼ung,** *f* -/-en 1. *no pl* inclination, slant; (*zur Seite*

lean, tilt; (*Hang*) (downward) slope. 2.
(*a*) tendency, inclination (**zu** + *dat*, to);
(*Anfälligsein*) susceptibility, (pre)dis-
position (**zur Trunksucht usw.**, to
alcoholism etc.); (*b*) liking, (*Vorliebe*)
predilection (**zu** + *dat*, for); **N. zu i-m
spüren/fühlen**, to feel attracted to s.o.
◆'**N~ungswinkel**, *m* angle of inclination; rake.
nein [nain], *adv.* no; **mit (einem) N.
antworten**, to answer in the negative.
◆'**N~stimme**, *f Pol:* no (vote).
Nelke ['nɛlkə], *f -/-n* **1.** *Bot:* carnation. 2.
Cu: (*Gewürzn.*) clove.
nennen ['nɛnən], *v.tr.irr.* (*a*) to name (a
child, town etc.); to call (s.o. sth.); **sich
... n.**, (*Pers.*) to call oneself ...; (*Sache*)
be called ...; (*b*) to give, state (one's
name, a reason, price etc.); **ein Beispiel
n.**, to give/quote an example.
◆'**n~enswert**, *adj.* significant, appre-
ciable. ◆'**N~er**, *m -s/-* (*a*) *Mth:* denominator; (*b*) **etwas auf einen (gemein-
samen) N. bringen**, to reduce sth.
to a common denominator. ◆'**N~ung**,
f -/-en naming; mention. ◆'**N~wert**,
m Fin: nominal/face value.
Neon- ['ne:ɔn-], *comb.fm.* neon- (light,
tube etc.). ◆'**N~reklame**, *f* neon sign.
Nepp [nɛp], *m -s/no Pej:* daylight robbery. ◆'**n~en**, *v.tr. F:* to fleece (s.o.),
rook (s.o.).
Nerv [nɛrf], *m -s/-en* nerve; **die N~en
verlieren**, to lose one's nerve; **j-m den
N. töten**, to drive s.o. mad; **es geht ihm
auf die N~en**, it gets on his nerves.
◆'**N~en-, 'n~en-**, *comb.fm.* (*a*) (*nervlich*) nervous (illness, system etc.); (*b*)
Anat: nerve (centre, cell etc.).
◆'**N~enarzt**, *m* neurologist.
◆'**N~enbündel**, *n* bundle of nerves.
◆'**N~enkitzel**, *m F:* thrill.
◆'**N~ensäge**, *f F:* pain in the neck;
trial. ◆'**N~enzusammenbruch**, *m*
nervous breakdown. ◆'**n~lich**, *adj.*
nervous (strain etc.); **n. völlig am Ende
sein**, to be a nervous wreck. ◆**n~ös**
[nɛr'vø:s], *adj.* restless, fidgety (person);
highly-strung (person, horse etc.); **dieser
Lärm macht mich n.**, this noise gets on
my nerves.
Nervosität [nɛrvozi'tɛ:t], *f -/no pl* state of
nerves; restlessness; irritability.
Nerz [nɛrts], *m -es/-e* (*a*) *Z:* mink; (*b*)
(*N~mantel*) mink coat.
Nessel ['nɛsəl], *f -/-n* nettle.
Nest [nɛst], *n -(e)s/-er* **1.** nest. 2. *F: Pej:*
(*kleiner Ort*) armseliges N., miserable
hole. ◆'**N~häkchen**, *n F:* baby of the
family; pet. ◆'**N~wärme**, *f Fig:* love
and security (of a home).
nesteln ['nɛstəln], *v.i.* (*haben*) to fumble
(**an etwas** *dat*, with sth.).
nett [nɛt], *adj.* nice; **n. daß du anrufst**,
it's nice of you to call; **seien Sie bitte so
n.**, would you please be so kind.
netto ['nɛto]. **I.** *adv. Com:* net. **II.** '**N~-**,

comb.fm. net (weight, income, profit
etc.).
Netz [nɛts]. **I.** *n -es/-e* **1.** net; (*Spinnen.*)
(spider's) web; *Fig:* web (of lies etc.);
j-m ins N. gehen, to fall into s.o.'s trap.
2. system, network (of roads, railways
etc.); *El: etc:* mains. **II.** '**N~-**, *comb.fm.
El:* mains (connection, voltage etc.).
◆'**N~haut**, *f Anat:* retina. ◆'**N~-
karte**, *f -/-n Rail: etc:* area season ticket.
neu [nɔy]. **I.** *adj.* (*a*) new; **wie n.**, as good
as/like new; **das ist mir n.**, that's news to
me; **er ist ein n~er Mensch geworden**,
he is a different person/a changed man;
(*b*) (*erneut*) fresh (start, hope etc.); (*noch
ein*) another; **aufs n~e/von n~em**,
afresh; (*von vorn*) from scratch; **n. anfangen**, to start (all over) again; **es muß n.
gestrichen werden**, it will have to be re-
painted; (*c*) **die n~esten Nachrichten/
Moden**, the latest news/fashions; **weißt
du das N~este?** do you know the latest?
n. verheiratet, newly married. **II.** '**N~-**,
'**n~-**, *comb.fm.* new (start, snow, creation etc.); (*b*) (*erneut*) re-orientation
etc.). ◆'**N~anschaffung**, *f* (*Sache*)
new acquisition. ◆'**n~artig**, *adj.* novel,
of a new kind. ◆'**N~auflage**, *f reprint;
(N~bearbeitung)* new edition.
◆'**N~bau**, *m* **1.** *no pl* rebuilding, reconstruction. 2. new building/house.
◆'**n~erdings**, *adv.* lately; recently; **n.
geht er allein zur Schule**, he recently
started going to school by himself.
◆'**N~eröffnung**, *f* reopening.
◆'**N~erscheinung**, *f* new publication/
(*Platte*) release. ◆'**N~erung**, *f -/-en*
innovation. ◆'**n~geboren**, *adj.*
n~geborenes Kind, new-born baby;
sich wie n. fühlen, to feel a different
person. ◆'**N~heit**, *f -/-en* **1.** *no pl* newness; novelty (of an idea, design etc.). 2.
innovation, novelty. ◆'**N~igkeit**, *f -/
-en* (*piece of*) news. ◆'**N~jahr**, *n* New
Year's Day; **pros(i)t N.!**, happy New
Year! ◆'**n~lich**, *adv.* recently; the
other day. ◆'**N~ling**, *m -s/-e* (*a*)
novice, tyro; (*b*) newcomer.
◆'**n~modisch**, *adj.* highly fashionable
(clothes etc.); ultra-modern (design etc.);
Pej: newfangled (idea, machine etc.).
◆'**N~mond**, *m* new moon.
◆'**N~ordnung**, *f* reorganization.
◆'**N~regelung**, *f* revision; *Jur:etc:* reform. ◆'**n~reich**, *adj. Pej:* nouveau
riche. ◆**N~seeland**. *Pr.n.n -s.* New
Zealand. ◆'**n~seeländisch**, *adj.* New
Zealand. ◆'**N~wert**, *m* value when
new; *Com:* replacement value.
◆'**n~wertig**, *adj.* (as good) as new.
◆'**N~zeit**, *f* modern times.
◆'**n~zeitlich**, *adj.* up-to-date, modern
(building, thinking etc.).
Neugier ['nɔygiːr], *f* curiosity. ◆'**n~ig**,
adj. curious, *F:* nosey (person) (**auf j-n,
etwas** *acc*, about s.o., sth.); inquisitive
(glance etc.).

neun [nɔyn], *num.adj.* nine. ◆'**n**~**mal**, *adv.* nine times. ◆'**n**~**malklug**, *adj.* F: too clever by half. ◆'**n**~**te(r, s)**, *num.adj.* ninth. ◆'**N**~**tel**, *n -s/-* ninth. ◆'**n**~**zehn**, *num.adj.* nineteen. ◆'**n**~**zig**, *num.adj.* ninety.

Neur|ologe [nɔyro'lo:gə], *m -n/-n* neurologist. ◆**N**~**ologie** [-olo'gi:], *f -/no pl* neurology. ◆**N**~**ose** [-'ro:zə], *f -/-n* neurosis. ◆**n**~**otisch** [-'ro:tiʃ], *adj.* neurotic.

neutral [nɔy'tra:l], *adj.* 1. neutral. 2. *Gram:* neuter. ◆**n**~**isieren** [-ali'zi:rən], *v.tr.* to neutralize (a country, acid etc.). ◆**N**~**i'tät**, *f -/no pl* neutrality.

Neutrum [ˈnɔytrʊm], *n -s/-tra & -tren Gram:* neuter noun.

nicht [nɪçt]. **I.** *adv.* not; **sie raucht n.**, she does not/F: doesn't smoke; (*momentan*) she is not/F: isn't smoking; (*bitte*) **n. füttern!** (please) do not feed! **ich auch n.**, nor I; **n. besser als**, no better than; **n. mehr und n. weniger**, neither more nor less; **n. doch!** don't! **bitte n.!** please don't! **es ist schön hier, n. (wahr)?** it's nice here, isn't it? **II.** '**N**~, '**n**~, *comb.fm.* non-(swimmer, member, recognition etc.). ◆'**N**~**achtung**, *f* disregard (of sth.); ignoring (of s.o.). ◆'**n**~**amtlich**, *adj.* unofficial. ◆**N**~'**angriffspakt**, *m* non-aggression treaty. ◆'**n**~**beachtung**, *f* disregard, ignoring. ◆'**n**~**ig**, *adj.* 1. *Jur:* void, invalid. 2. *Lit:* trivial, insignificant. ◆'**n**~**leitend**, *adj. El:* non-conducting. ◆'**n**~**raucher**, *m* non-smoker.

Nichte [nɪçtə], *f -/-n* niece.

nichts [nɪçts]. **I.** *indef.pron. & adj.* nothing; **ich weiß n. darüber**, I don't know anything about it; **das macht n.**, that doesn't matter; **ich habe n. dagegen**, I don't mind; **n. als Ärger**, nothing but trouble; **das ist n. für dich**, it is not your cup of tea/all wrong for you; **das führt zu n.**, it doesn't get you anywhere; F: **n. zu machen!** it can't be helped! **mir n., dir n.**, without so much as a by your leave; **n. da!** nothing doing! **n. Besonderes**, nothing special. **II.** **N.**, *n -/no pl* 1. nothingness; (*Leere*) void; **wie aus dem N. auftauchen**, to appear from nowhere. 2. (*Pers.*) a nonentity. ◆'**n**~**ahnend**, *adj.* unsuspecting. ◆**n**~**desto'weniger**, *adv.* nevertheless. ◆'**n**~**nutzig**, *adj.* useless. ◆'**n**~**sagend**, *adj.* meaningless (remark etc.); blank (expression). ◆'**N**~**tun**, *n -s/no pl* idleness.

Nickel [ˈnɪkəl], *n -s/no pl* nickel.

nick|en [ˈnɪkən], *v.i.* (*haben*) to nod; **mit dem Kopf n.**, to nod one's head. ◆'**N**~**erchen**, *n -s/- F:* snooze, nap; **ein N. machen**, to have forty winks.

nie [ni:], *adv.* never; **noch n.**, never before; **fast n.**, hardly ever; **n. mehr**, never again; **n. und nimmer**, never in a thousand years; *int.* (*ablehnend*) not on your life!

nieder [ˈni:dər]. **I.** *adj.* low (wall, price, rank etc.); **n**~**e Beamte**, minor officials; low-grade civil servants. **II.** **N**~, *n*~, *comb.fm.* low (pressure, frequency etc.); (to kneel, rain, sink etc.) down. ◆'**n**~**beugen**, *v.tr. sep. sich n**~**beugen**, to bend/bow down. ◆'**N**~**gang**, *m no pl Lit:* decline. ◆'**n**~**gehen**, *v.i.sep.irr.36* (*sein*) (*a*) (*Flugzeug usw.*) to land, touch down; (*b*) (*Boxer*) to go down, be floored; (*c*) (*Regen usw.*) to come down; (*Gewitter*) to burst. ◆'**n**~**geschlagen**, *adj.* dispirited, depressed. ◆'**N**~**geschlagenheit**, *f -/no pl* depression, dejection. ◆'**N**~**lage**, *f* defeat. ◆'**N**~**lande. Pr.n.pl die N.**, the Netherlands. ◆'**n**~**ländisch**, *adj.* (*a*) (*holländisch*) Dutch; Netherlands (government etc.); (*b*) *Hist:* (art etc.) of the Netherlands. ◆'**n**~**lassen**, *v.refl.sep.irr.57* (*a*) **sich (in einem Ort) n.**, to settle (in a place); (*b*) *Lit:* **sich (in einem Stuhl) n.**, to sit down (in a chair). ◆'**N**~**lassung**, *f -/-en* 1. *no pl* settlement (of s.o., a tribe etc.); *Com:* establishment (of a firm etc.). 2. *Com:* (*Zweign.*) branch. ◆'**n**~**legen**, *v.tr.sep.* (*a*) to lay down (one's arms etc.); **die Arbeit n.**, to down tools; **das Amt n.**, to resign; (*b*) **sich n.**, to lie down; (*c*) **etwas (schriftlich) n.**, to put sth. down (in writing). ◆'**n**~**machen**, *v.tr.sep. F:* to slaughter (people etc.). ◆'**N**~**sachsen. Pr.n.n.** s. Lower Saxony. ◆'**N**~**schlag**, *m Meteor:* precipitation; (*Regen*) rainfall; **radioaktiver N.**, (radioactive) fallout. ◆'**n**~**schlagen**, *v.tr. sep.irr.85* (*a*) to knock (s.o.) down; (*senken*) to lower (one's eyes); (*b*) **sich n.**, *Ch:* to precipitate; *Fig:* (*Erlebnisse, Gefühle usw.*) to find expression; (*c*) to suppress (a revolt, strike etc.). ◆'**n**~**schreiben**, *v.tr.sep.irr.12* to write (sth.) down. ◆'**N**~**schrift**, *f* (*a*) writing down, recording; (*b*) written record; (*Protokoll*) minutes. ◆'**n**~**setzen**, *v.tr.sep.* to put (sth.) down; **sich n.**, to sit down. ◆'**n**~**trächtig**, *adj.* base, vile; (*gemein*) mean, low (trick, lie etc.). ◆'**N**~**trächtigkeit**, *f -/-en* (*a*) *no pl* vileness, baseness; (*b*) mean trick. ◆'**N**~**ung**, *f -/-en* (piece of) low ground; (*Mulde*) hollow; **in den N**~**ungen**, on lower ground.

niedlich [ˈni:tlɪç], *adj.* sweet, dear (little); *N.Am:* cute.

niedrig [ˈni:drɪç], *adj.* low; **von n**~**er Geburt/Herkunft**, of low birth/humble origins; **n**~**e Arbeit**, menial work. ◆'**N**~**wasser**, *n* low water.

niemals [ˈni:ma:ls], *adv.* never.

niemand [ˈni:mant]. **I.** *indef.pron.* nobody, no one; **von uns spricht n. Französisch**, none of us speaks French; **n. anders als**, none other than; **sonst n.**, nobody else. **II.** **N.**, *m -s/no pl* ein N., a nobody/nonentity. ◆'N~sland, *n* no man's land.

Niere ['niːrə], *f* -/-n kidney. ◆'N~n-, *comb.fm.* kidney (stone, transplant etc.); renal (disease etc.). ◆'n~nförmig, *adj.* kidney-shaped.

nieseln ['niːzəln], *v.impers.* es nieselt, it is drizzling. ◆'N~regen, *m* drizzle.

niesen ['niːzən], *v.i.* (haben) to sneeze.

Niet [niːt], *m & n* -(e)s/-e/'N~e¹, *f* -/-n *Tchn:* rivet; *Cl:* stud (on jeans etc.) ◆'n~en, *v.tr.* to rivet (metal sheets etc.).

Niete² ['niːtə], *f* -/-n 1. (*Los*) blank. 2. *F:* (*Mißerfolg*) flop, washout; (*Pers.*) dead loss.

Nikotin [niko'tiːn], *n* -s/*no pl* nicotine. ◆'n~arm, *adj.* with a low nicotine content.

Nil [niːl]. *Pr.n.m* -s. the (river) Nile. ◆'N~pferd, *n* hippopotamus.

nimmersatt ['nimɐzat]. I. *adj.* *F:* insatiable. II. N., *m* -(e)s/-e *F:* greedy-guts.

nippen ['nipən], *v.i.* (haben) to take a sip (an einem Glas, from a glass).

Nippes ['nip(ə)s], *pl* knick-knacks.

nirgend|s ['nirgənts]/'n~wo, *adv.* nowhere, not anywhere.

Nische ['niːʃəl, *f* -/-n recess, alcove.

nist|en ['nistən], *v.i.* (haben) to nest. ◆'N~kasten, *m* nesting box.

Nitrat [ni'traːt], *n* -(e)s/-e *Ch:* nitrate.

Niveau [ni'voː], *n* -s/-s level; die Schüler haben ein hohes/niedriges N., the students' standard is high/low; N. haben, to have class/high standards.

Nixe ['niksə], *f* -/-n water nymph.

nobel ['noːbəl], *adj.* (edel) noble, high-minded; *F:* (großzügig) generous (tip etc.).

noch [nɔx]. I. *adv.* (a) still; n. nicht, not yet; es regnet kaum n., it is hardly raining any more; hast du n. Geld? do you have any money left? n. gestern habe ich ihn gesehen, I saw him only yesterday; (b) even; n. wärmer als gestern, even warmer than yesterday; (c) (zusätzlich) as well; (mit Zahlen) another; wer war n. da? who else was there? n. ein Bier bitte, another beer please; n. einmal, once more; again; sonst n. Fragen? (are there) any more questions? n. etwas, something else, another thing; (d) sei es n. so klein, however small it may be. II. *conj.* weder heute n. gestern, neither today nor yesterday. ◆'n~malig, *adj.* repeat, fresh (attempt etc.); (zusätzlich) further, additional. ◆'n~mals, *adv.* (once) again.

Nockenwelle ['nɔkənvɛlə], *f* camshaft.

Nomade [no'maːdə], *m* -n/-n nomad.

Nomin|ativ ['noːminatiːf], *m* -s/-e *Gram:* nominative (case). ◆'n~ieren [-'niːrən], *v.tr.* to nominate (a candidate etc.); *Sp:* to name (a team etc.).

Nonne ['nɔnə], *f* -/-n nun. ◆'N~kloster, *n* nunnery; convent.

Nord [nɔrt]. I. *m* north; aus/von N., from the north. II. 'N~*, 'n~*, *comb.fm.* (a) north (coast, side, bank, wind etc.); *Geog:* North (America, Germany, Pole etc.); (b) (nördlich) northern (frontier, edge, shore etc.); *Geog:* Northern (Ireland, England etc.). ◆N~en ['nɔrdən], *m* -s/*no pl* north; nach N., northwards. ◆'n~isch, *adj.* Nordic (type, landscape etc.). ◆'N~ost(en), *m* north-east. ◆'n~östlich. I. *adj.* north east(ern) (district etc.); north-easterly (wind, direction etc.). II. *prep.* + *gen* n. der Stadt, (to the) north-east of the town. ◆'N~see, *f* North Sea. ◆'N~stern, *m* pole star. ◆'N~west(en), *m* north-west. ◆'n~westlich. I. *adj.* north-west(ern) (district etc.); north westerly (wind, direction etc.). II. *prep.* + *gen* n. der Stadt, (to the) north-west of the town.

nördlich ['nœrtlɪç]. I. *adj.* northern (border, hemisphere etc.); northerly (wind, direction etc.); n. von Berlin, (to the) north of Berlin. II. *prep.* + *gen* n. der Stadt, (to the) north of the town.

Nörg|elei [nœrgə'lai], *f* -/-en grumbling, grousing. ◆'n~eln, *v.i.* (haben) to grumble, grouse, (kleinlich) niggle (an j-m, etwas *dat,* about s.o., sth.). ◆'N~ler, *m* -s/- grumbler.

Norm [nɔrm], *f* -/-en norm; standard (of behaviour, *Ind:* for a product etc.); moralische N~en, moral standards. ◆'n~al [-'maːl]. I. *adj.* normal; (genormt) standard (size, measurement etc.). II. N~al, *m* -s/*no pl* (a) (genormt) standard (weight, size, format etc.); (b) normal (state, temperature etc.). ◆N~al(benzin) *m* regular/two-star petrol; *N.Am:* low-octane gas. ◆'n~alisieren [-ali'ziːrən], *v.tr.* to normalize (a situation etc.); (Lage usw.) sich n., to return to normal. ◆N~alität, *f* -/*no pl* normality. ◆'n~en/'n~ieren [-'miːrən], *v.tr.* to standardize (a product etc.). ◆'N~ung, *f* -/-en standardization.

Norweg|en ['nɔrveːgən]. *Pr.n.n* -s. Norway. ◆N~er(in), *m* -s/- (f -/-nen) Norwegian. ◆'n~isch, *adj./N., n -/no pl* (Sprache) Norwegian.

Nostalg|ie [nɔstal'giː], *f* -/*no pl* nostalgia. ◆n~isch ['talgiʃ], *adj.* nostalgic.

Not [noːt]. I. *f* -/-e 1. *no pl* (a) need; (N~lage) predicament, plight; (Notwendigkeit) necessity; zur N., in a case of necessity/an emergency; (b) (Elend) hardship; (Armut) poverty; N. leiden, to suffer hardship; (c) (Bedrängnis) distress; seelische N., mental anguish. 2. (Schwierigkeit) difficulty; in N~en, in difficulties/trouble; mit knapper N., by the skin of one's teeth. II. 'N~-, *comb.fm.* emergency (lighting, service, operation, switch etc.); (behelfsmäßig) makeshift, temporary (solution, quarters etc.). ◆'N~**ausgang**, m emergency exit. ◆'N~**behelf**, m temporary measure; makeshift. ◆'N~**bremse**, f emergency brake; Rail: communication cord. ◆'N~**durft**, f -/no pl **seine N. verrichten**, to relieve oneself. ◆**n~dürftig**, adj. scanty (clothing etc.); makeshift (repair, shelter etc.); **etwas n. reparieren**, to do a makeshift repair on sth. ◆'N~**fall**, m emergency; **für den N.**, in case of need; **im N.**, in an emergency. ◆**n~falls**, adv. if need be. ◆**n~gedrungen**, adv. out of necessity. ◆'N~**lage**, f plight; predicament. ◆**n~landen**, v.i.insep. (sein) to make a forced landing. ◆'N~**landung**, f emergency/forced landing. ◆'n~**leidend**, adj. needy, destitute. ◆'N~**lüge**, f white lie. ◆'N~**ruf**, m emergency/Nau: Av: mayday call; (Nummer) emergency services number. ◆'N~**signal**, n distress signal. ◆'N~**stand**, m emergency; desperate situation; Pol: state of emergency. ◆'N~**verband**, m temporary bandage. ◆'N~**wehr**, f -/no pl self-defence. ◆'n~**wendig**, adj. necessary (operation, qualities, evil etc.); essential (equipment etc.); **das N~ste**, the bare essentials. ◆'N~**wendigkeit**, f -/-en necessity.

Notar [no'taːr], m -s/-e Jur: notary (public). ◆**n~iell**, adj. notarial; adv. by a notary.

Note ['noːtə], f -/-n 1. note; pl **N~n**, Mus: (printed/sheet) music; **N~n lesen**, to read music. 2. Sch: mark; N.Am: grade. 3. (Merkmal) character, aura; (Stimmung) atmosphere; **persönliche N.**, personal touch. ◆'N~**nblatt**, n sheet of music. ◆'N~**nschlüssel**, m Mus: clef. ◆'N~**nständer**, m music stand.

notier|en [no'tiːrən], v.t.r to make a note of (sth.); Fb: etc: **den Namen eines Spielers n.**, to book a player. 2. v.i. (haben) Com: to be quoted (**mit/zu** + dat, at). ◆**N~ung**, f -/-en Com: quotation.

nötig ['nøːtiç], adj. necessary (zu + dat, for); **j-n, etwas n. haben**, to need s.o., sth.; **hast du das n.?** do you have to? ◆**n~en**, v.tr. to force, compel (s.o.); **ich sah mich genötigt, einzugreifen**, I felt compelled to intervene; **laß dich nicht n.!** don't wait to be asked! ◆'N~**ung**, f -/-en Jur: intimidation (**zu etwas dat**, to commit sth.).

Notiz [no'tiːts], f -/-en 1. (a) note, memo; **sich dat N~en machen**, to take notes; (b) (Zeitungsn.) (short) article, item. 2. **von j-m, etwas dat (keine) N. nehmen**, to take (no) notice of s.o., sth. ◆'N~**block**, m memo pad, jotter. ◆'N~**buch**, n notebook.

notorisch [no'toːriʃ], adj. notorious.

Nougat ['nuːgat], m & n -s/-s nougat.

Novelle [no'vɛlə], f -/-n 1. novella, long

short story. 2. Jur:etc: amendment (to a law).

November [no'vɛmbər], m -(s)/- November.

Nu [nuː], n F: **im N.**, in a jiffy/flash.

Nuance [ny'ãːsə], f -/-n nuance.

nüchtern ['nyçtərn], adj. (nicht betrunken) sober; (sachlich) matter-of-fact; (vernünftig) level-headed (person, appraisal etc.); **n. betrachtet**, viewed dispassionately; **etwas auf n~en Magen trinken**, to drink sth. on an empty stomach. ◆'N~**heit**, f -/no pl sobriety, level-headedness.

Nudel ['nuːdəl], f -/-n 1. Cu: noodle; pl **N~n**, pasta. 2. F: (Pers.) **eine (komische) N.**, a funny creature. ◆'N~**holz**, n rolling pin. ◆'N~**suppe**, f noodle soup. ◆'N~**teig**, m pasta dough.

nuklear [nukle'aːr], adj. nuclear.

null [nul]. I. num.adj. nought, esp. N.Am: zero; **n. Fehler**, no/zero mistakes; **n. Uhr**, midnight; **n. Komma fünf (0,5)**, nought point five (0·5); **n. Grad**, zero (degrees); Sp: **zwei zu n.**, two-nil; (Tennis) **dreißig-n.**, thirty-love; Jur: **n. und nichtig**, null and void. II. N., f -/-en 1. (Ziffer) nought, N.Am: zero; (b) no pl (Zahl) zero; **fünf Grad unter N.**, five degrees below zero; **seine Chancen sind gleich N.**, his chances are nil; (c) Pej: (Pers.) **eine N.**, a nonentity. ◆'N~**diät**, f starvation diet. ◆'N~**punkt**, m zero (point).

numer|ieren [numə'riːrən], v.tr. to number (pages, tickets etc.). ◆**n~isch** [nu'meːriʃ], adj. numerical.

Nummer ['numər], f -/-n (a) number; Aut: **eine Bonner N.**, a Bonn registration/N.Am: plate; (b) issue, copy (of a magazine etc.); (c) size (of shoes etc.); (d) (Darbietung) number, item; (im Zirkus usw.) act. ◆'N~**nschild**, n Aut: number/N.Am: license plate.

nun [nuːn], adv. (a) now; **was n.?** what now/next? **n. gerade!** now more than ever! **das ist n. mal so**, that's just the way it is; (b) well; **n., wie geht's?** well now, how are you? **n. gut/schön**, all right then.

nur [nuːr], adv. only; **warum hat er das n. getan?** why ever did he do that? **n. keine Angst!** just don't you worry! **wenn sie n. käme!** if only she would come! **ich bin nicht krank, n. müde**, I'm not ill, just tired.

Nürnberg ['nyrnbɛrk]. Pr.n.n -s- Nuremberg.

nuscheln ['nuʃəln], v.i. (haben) F: to mumble.

Nuß [nus], f -/Nüsse nut. ◆'N~**baum**, m walnut tree. ◆'N~**knacker**, m -s/- nut-cracker. ◆'N~**schale**, f (a) nutshell; (b) Fig: (Boot) tiny little tub.

Nüster ['nystər], f -/-n usu.pl **N~n**, nostrils.

Nut [nuːt], f -/-en/'N~**e**, f -/-n Tchn: groove, slot.

Nutte ['nutə], f -/-n P: tart; N.Am: broad.

nutz|bar ['nutsbɑːr], adj. usable, exploitable (resources etc.). ◆**~n~en. I.** v.tr. & i. (haben) = **nützen. II.** N., m -s/no pl use; **wenig N. haben**, to be of little use/ benefit; (j-m) **von N. sein**, to be useful/ of use (to s.o.). ◆**'~n~los**, adj. useless; futile, pointless (conversation etc.); vain, futile (attempts, efforts etc.). ◆**'N~losigkeit**, f -/no pl uselessness; pointlessness; futility. ◆**N~nießer**, m -s/- exploiter. ◆**'N~ung**, f -/-en exploitation (of land, resources).

nütz|e ['nytsə], adj. **(zu) etwas/nichts n. sein**, to be some/no use. ◆**'n~en**, v. **1.** v.i. (haben) to be of use/useful (j-m, to s.o.); **das nützt nichts**, that's no use. **2.** v.tr. to make use of (sth.); to take advantage of (an opportunity etc.); to exploit (land, water power etc.). ◆**'n~lich**, adj. useful (j-m, to s.o.); helpful (person, advice etc.). ◆**'N~lichkeit**, f -/no pl usefulness.

Nymph|e ['nymfə], f -/-n nymph. ◆**N~omanin** [-o'mɑːnin], f -/-nen nymphomaniac.

O

O, o [oː], n -/- (the letter) O, o.

Oase [o'ɑːzə], f -/-n oasis.

ob [ɔp], conj. whether; (a) **ob er wohl kommt?** I wonder if he will come? (b) **als ob**, as if/though; (c) F: **(na) und ob!** and how! sure thing! **und ob ich's gelesen habe!** you bet I've read it!

Obacht ['oːbaxt], f -/no pl attention; **auf etwas acc O. geben**, to pay attention to sth.

Obdach ['ɔpdax], n -(e)s/no pl shelter. ◆**'o~los**, adj. homeless. ◆**'O~losigkeit**, f -/no pl homelessness.

Obduktion [ɔpduktsi'oːn], f -/-en post mortem.

O-Beine ['oːbainə], npl bow-legs.

oben ['oːbən], adv. (a) at the top; (o~drauf) on top; (an der Oberfläche) on the surface; **das dritte von o.**, the third from the top; **von o. bis unten**, from top to bottom; (Pers.) from head to foot; (b) (über dem Sprecher) above, overhead; **hier/dort o.**, up here/there; **hoch o.**, high up/above; (c) (Richtung) **nach o.**, upwards; **mit dem Gesicht nach o.**, face up; (d) (im Buch) **siehe o.**, see above. ◆**'o~an**, adv. at the top. ◆**'o~auf**, adv. (a) on (the) top; (b) Fig: (Pers.) **o. sein**, to be in good form. ◆**'o~'drein**, adv. besides; what is more. ◆**'o~genannt**, adj. above-mentioned.

Ober¹ ['oːbər], m -s/- waiter.

Ober-², comb.fm. (a) upper (arm, deck, jaw, lip etc.); (b) (Rang) senior (Sch: classes etc.); (leitend) chief (inspector etc.). ◆**'O~arzt**, m senior registrar. ◆**'O~befehlshaber**, m supreme commander. ◆**'O~begriff**, m generic term. ◆**'O~bekleidung**, f outer garments. ◆**'O~bürgermeister**, m first mayor (of a city). ◆**'o~e(r,s)**, adj. upper; (höchste) top. ◆**'O~fläche**, f surface. ◆**'o~flächlich**, adj. superficial. ◆**'O~flächlichkeit**, f -/no pl superficiality. ◆**'O~geschoß**, n upper storey. ◆**'o~halb**, prep. + gen. above. ◆**'O~haupt**, n head (of state, the family etc.). ◆**'O~haus**, n Pol: Upper House. ◆**'O~hemd**, n (man's) shirt. ◆**'O~in**, f -/-nen (a) Ecc: mother superior; (b) Med: matron. ◆**'O~kellner**, m head waiter. ◆**'O~körper**, m (upper) torso. ◆**'O~leitung**, f El: overhead wires. ◆**'O~licht**, n (Fenster) skylight. ◆**'O~schenkel**, m thigh. ◆**'O~schwester**, f ward sister. ◆**'O~seite**, f upper side; right side (of cloth, wallpaper etc.). ◆**'O~st**, m -en & -en colonel. ◆**'o~ste(r,s)**, adj. (a) top, uppermost; (b) supreme, highest (rank). ◆**'O~teil**, n Cl: etc: top (part). ◆**'O~wasser**, n Fig: **O. haben** to be in a strong position.

obgleich [ɔp'glaiç], conj. although.

Obhut ['ɔphuːt], f -/no pl Lit: care; Jur: custody (of a child etc.); **er ist in guter O.**, he is well looked after.

Objekt [ɔp'jɛkt], n -(e)s/-e object; Com: (Verkaufso.) item.

Objektiv¹ [ɔpjɛk'tiːf], n -s/-e Phot: lens.

objektiv² [ɔpjɛk'tiːf], adj. objective; actual (conditions, facts etc.). ◆**O~ität** [-tivi'tɛːt], f -/no pl objectivity.

Oblate [o'blɑːtə], f -/-n Ecc: wafer.

obligatorisch [ɔbliga'toːriʃ], adj. compulsory.

Oboe [o'boːə], f -/-n oboe.

Obrigkeit ['oːbriçkait], f -/-en A: & Hum: **die O.**, the powers that be.

ob'schon, conj. although.

obskur [ɔps'kuːr], adj. obscure; (zwielichtig) dubious, shady (figure etc.).

Obst [oːpst]. **I.** n -(e)s/no pl coll. fruit. **II.** **'O~-, comb.fm.** fruit (juice, knife, salad, tree etc.). ◆**'O~garten**, m orchard. ◆**'O~händler**, m fruiterer. ◆**'O~kuchen**, m fruit flan/N.Am: pie.

obszön [ɔps'tsøːn], adj. obscene. ◆**O~ität** [-tsøni'tɛːt], f -/-en obscenity.

ob'wohl, conj. although.

Ochs|e ['ɔksə], m -n/-n **1.** ox. **2.** F: (Pers.) fool, oaf. ◆**'O~enschwanz**, m oxtail. ◆**'O~enzunge**, f ox tongue.

Ocker ['ɔkər], m -s/no pl ochre.

Öde ['ø:də]. **I.** f -/no pl (a) desert, wasteland; (b) Fig: desolation, solitude. **II.** ö., adj. barren (landscape); desolate (place, Fig: existence etc.).

oder ['o:dər], conj. or; F: **das magst du doch**, o.? you like that, don't you?

Ofen ['o:fən], m -s/- (a) (zum Heizen) stove; (**elektrischer**) **O.**, electric fire; (b) Ind: furnace, kiln; (c) Cu: (Backo.) oven. ◆'**O~rohr**, n stovepipe.

offen ['ɔfən], adj. open; (nicht abgeschlossen) unlocked; (Haare) loose, untied; o~e **Weine**, wines by the glass; **auf o~er Strecke**, on an open stretch (of road/rail); o~e **See**, open sea; **vacant posts**; (b) (Pers.) frank, candid; o. **gesagt/gestanden**, frankly, to be frank. ◆'**o~bar**, adj. obvious. ◆**o~'baren**, v.tr. insep. to reveal (a secret, oneself etc.) (j-m, to s.o.). ◆**O~'barung**, f -/-en Ecc. revelation. ◆**o~'halten**, v.tr.sep.irr.45 to hold (a door etc.) open (j-m, for s.o.); to keep (one's eyes, a shop etc.) open. ◆'**O~heit**, f -/no pl openness, frankness. ◆'**o~herzig**, adj. 1. open-hearted, unreserved. 2. Hum: (dress) with a plunging neckline. ◆'**o~kundig**, adj. obvious. ◆'**o~lassen**, v.tr.sep.irr.57 (a) to leave (sth.) open; (b) to leave (a space etc.) blank; (c) to leave (a question) undecided. ◆'**o~sichtlich**, adj. obvious, evident. ◆'**o~stehen**, v.i.sep.irr.100 (haben) (a) (Tür usw.) to be open; (b) (Rechnung usw.) to be outstanding/unpaid.

offensiv [ɔfɛn'zi:f], adj. Mil: offensive (weapons etc.); Sp: attacking (game). ◆**O~e** ['-zi:və], f -/-n Mil: offensive; Sp: attack.

öffentlich ['œfəntliç], adj. public; Pol: etc: open (session); **etwas ö. erklären**, to state sth. publicly. ◆'**O~keit**, f -/no pl **die (breite) Ö.**, the (general) public; **unter Ausschluß der Ö.**, behind closed doors; **etwas an die Ö. bringen**, to publicize sth.

Offerte [ɔ'fɛrtə], f -/-n offer.

offiziell [ɔfi'tsiɛl], adj. official.

Offizier [ɔfi'tsi:r], m -s/-e officer.

öffnen ['œfnən], v.tr. (a) to open (sth.); to undo (a zip), unbutton (a coat etc.); (b) j-m o., to open the door to s.o.; (Tür usw.) **sich ö.**, to open. ◆'**O~er**, m s/- opener. ◆'**O~ung**, f -/-en (a) opening; (b) hole, gap (in a wall etc.). ◆'**O~ungszeiten**, fpl hours of opening/Com: business.

oft [ɔft], adv. often, frequently; **des öfteren**, repeatedly.

ohne ['o:nə]. **I.** prep. + acc. (a) without; **o. mich!** count me out! (b) excluding; to. **den Fahrer waren wir sechs Personen**, there were six of us, not counting the driver; (c) F: **nicht o.**, not bad; (schwierig) pretty tough. **II.** conj. **sie tat es**, o. **daß er es merkte**, she did it without his noticing. ◆**o~'gleichen**, pred.adj.

matchless, incomparable. ◆**o~'hin**, adv. anyway, in any case.

Ohnmacht ['o:nmaxt], f -/-en (a) powerlessness, impotence; (b) Med: faint; (Zustand) unconsciousness; **in O. fallen**, to faint. ◆**ohnmächtig** ['o:nmɛçtiç], adj. (a) powerless; (b) Med: unconscious; **o. werden**, to faint/pass out.

Ohr [ø:r], n -(e)s/-e eye (of a needle etc.).

Ohr [o:r], n -(e)s/-en (a) ear; **ganz O. sein**, to be all ears; **es ist mir zu O~en gekommen, daß ...**, it has come to my attention that ...; j-m eins hinter die **O~en hauen**, to box s.o.'s ears; **sich aufs O. legen**, to take a nap; (b) j-n **übers O. hauen**, to rip s.o. off. ◆'**O~enarzt**, m. ear (nose and throat) specialist. ◆'**o~enbetäubend**, adj. ear-splitting. ◆'**o~ensausen**, n noises/singing in the ears. ◆'**O~feige**, f slap in the face. ◆'**o~feigen**, v.tr. to slap (s.o.) (in the face). ◆'**O~läppchen**, n -s/- earlobe. ◆'**O~ring**, m earring. ◆'**O~wurm**, m 1. earwig. 2. F: (catchy) hit tune.

Ökologie [økolo'gi:], f -/no pl ecology. ◆**ö~isch** ['-lo:gif], adj. ecological.

Ökonomie [økono'mi:], f -/-n 1. economics. 2. (Sparsamkeit) economy. ◆**ö~isch** ['-'no:mif], adj. 1. economic. 2. (sparsam) economical.

Oktave [ɔk'ta:və], f -/-n octave.

ökumenisch [øku'me:nif], adj. ecumenical.

Öl [ø:l]. **I.** n -(e)s/-e oil. **II.** 'Öl-, comb.fm. oil-(field, -firing, -can, Aut: change etc.). ◆'**Ölheizung**, f oil-fired (central) heating. ◆'**ölig**, adj. oily. ◆'**Ölmeßstab**, m Aut: dipstick. ◆'**Ölquelle**, f oilwell. ◆'**Ölsardine**, f tinned sardine (in oil). ◆'**Ölschicht**, f film of oil. ◆'**Ölstand**, m oil level. ◆'**Ölteppich**, m oil slick. ◆'**Ölung**, f -/-en anointment; **die letzte Ö.**, extreme unction. ◆'**Ölzeug**, n oilskins.

Olive [o'li:və], f -/-n olive. ◆**O~en-**, comb.fm. olive (tree, oil etc.). ◆**o~grün**, adj. olive-green.

Olympiade [olympi'a:də], f -/-n Sp: Olympic Games. ◆**o~isch**, adj. Olympic.

Oma ['o:ma], f -/-s F: granny.

Omelett [ɔm(ə)'lɛt], n -(e)s/-e & -s omelette.

ominös [omi'nø:s], adj. ominous; (verdächtig) suspicious, odd (taste etc.).

Omnibus ['ɔmnibus], m -ses/-se bus; Brit: (für lange Strecken) coach.

Onkel ['ɔnkəl], m -s/- uncle.

Opa ['o:pa], m -s/-e F: grandpa.

Opal [o'pa:l], m -s/-e opal.

Oper ['o:pər], f -/-n 1. opera. 2. (Gebäude) opera house. ◆'**O~n-**, comb.fm. operatic (aria, composer etc.); opera (guide, singer, house etc.). ◆**O~n-**

glas, *n* opera glasses.
Operation [opəratsi'o:n], *f -/-en Med: Mil: etc:* operation. ◆**O~s-**, *comb.fm.* (a) Mil: (area, plan etc.) of operations; (b) Med: operating (team, table etc.). ◆**O~ssaal**, *m* operating theatre/N.Am: room.

Operette [opə'retə], *f -/-n* operetta.

operieren [opə'ri:rən], *v.* **1.** *v.i.* (haben) *Med: Mil: etc:* to operate. **2.** *v.tr. Med:* to operate on (s.o.); **er wurde gestern operiert,** he had an operation yesterday.

Opfer ['ɔpfər], *n -s/-* (a) sacrifice; (b) victim (of an accident etc.); **einer Täuschung usw. zum O. fallen,** to be the victim of a deception etc. ◆**o~n,** *v.tr.* to sacrifice (Fig: one's health etc.), give up (one's free time etc.); **sein Leben o.,** to lay down one's life. ◆**O~stock,** *m Ecc:* offertory box.

Opium ['o:pium], *n -s/no pl* opium.

opportun [ɔpɔr'tu:n], *adj.* opportune. ◆**O~ist** [-'nist], *m -en/-en* opportunist. ◆**O~ismus** [-'nismus], *m -/no pl* opportunism.

Opposition [ɔpozitsi'o:n], *f -/-en* opposition (**gegen** + *acc*, to); **in O. zu j-m, etwas dat stehen,** to be opposed to s.o., sth.

Optik ['ɔptik], *f -/no pl* optics. ◆**O~er,** *m -s/-* optician.

optimal [ɔpti'ma:l], *adj.* optimum. ◆**O~ismus** [-'mismus], *m -/no pl* optimism. ◆**O~ist(in),** *m -en/-en (f -/-nen)* optimist. ◆**o~istisch,** *adj.* optimistic.

optisch ['ɔptiʃ], *adj.* **1.** optical (system, illusion etc.). **2.** visual (impression, signal etc.).

Orakel [o'ra:kəl], *n -s/-* oracle.

Orange [o'ranʒə], *f -/-n* orange. ◆**o~(farben),** *adj* orange(-coloured). ◆**O~at** [-'ʒa:t], *n -s/-e* candied orange peel. ◆**O~nschale,** *f* orange peel.

Orchester [ɔr'kɛstər]. **I.** *n -s/-* orchestra. **II. O~-,** *comb.fm.* orchestral (concert, music etc.).

Orchidee [ɔrçi'de:(ə)], *f -/-n* orchid.

Orden ['ɔrdən], *m -s/-* **1.** *Ecc:* order. **2.** *Mil: etc:* decoration, medal.

ordentlich ['ɔrdəntliç], *adj.* **1.** (a) neat, tidy (person, room etc.); (b) (anständig) respectable (family etc.); (c) **o~es Mitglied,** ordinary/full member (of an association etc.); **o~er Professor,** (full) professor. **2.** F: (richtig) proper (meal etc.); **eine o~e Tracht Prügel,** a sound thrashing.

ordinär [ɔrdi'nɛ:r], *adj.* common, vulgar (person etc.).

ordnen ['ɔrdnən], *v.tr.* to put (sth.) into order; to order, arrange (sth.).

Ordner ['ɔrdnər], *m -s/-* **1.** file, *esp.* ring binder. **2.** (Pers.) steward.

Ordnung ['ɔrdnuŋ], *f -/-en* (a) order; (b) orderliness, tidiness; **O. schaffen,** to tidy up; (c) **in O.,** all right; (Papiere usw.) in order. ◆**O~samt,** *n* Public Order Office (issuing passports, permits etc.).

◆**'o~sgemäß,** *adj.* correct, according to the regulations. ◆**'o~swidrig,** *adj.* contrary to the regulations. ◆**'O~szahl,** *f* ordinal number.

Organ [ɔr'ga:n], *n -s/-e* **1.** *Anat:* organ. **2.** (a) publication; (b) Pol: **das ausführende O.,** the executive body. ◆**o~isch,** *adj.* organic (disease etc.). ◆**O~ismus** [-ga'nismus], *m. -/-men* organism; *Anat:* system.

Organisation [ɔrganizatsi'o:n], *f -/-en* organization. ◆**O~ator** [-'za:tor], *m -s/-en* organizer ◆**o~ieren** ['zi:rən], *v.tr.* to organize (a conference etc.); **sich o.,** to form an organization/Ind: a union.

Organist(in) [ɔrga'nist(in)], *m -en/-en (f -/-nen)* organist.

Orgel ['ɔrgəl], *f -/-n* organ. ◆**'O~konzert,** *n* organ recital.

Orgie ['ɔrgiə], *f -/-n* orgy.

Orient ['o:riɛnt], *m -s/no pl* **der O.,** the Orient. ◆**O~ale** [oriɛn'ta:lə], *m -n/-n* (Pers.) Oriental. ◆**o~alisch,** *adj.* oriental.

orientier|en [oriɛn'ti:rən], *v.tr.* (a) j-n/ sich über etwas acc o., to inform s.o./ oneself about sth.; **gut orientiert,** well-informed; (b) sich o., to get one's bearings. ◆**o~ung,** *f -/en (a)* orientation; (O~ssinn) sense of direction; (b) Pol: etc: alignment. ◆**O~ungspunkt,** *m* landmark.

Original [origi'na:l]. **I.** *n -s/-e* (a) original; (b) Fig: **er ist ein O.,** he is quite a character. **II. o.,** *adj.* (a) original; (b) (echt) **o. indischer Tee,** genuine Indian tea. ◆**O~ausgabe,** *f* first edition. ◆**O~fassung,** *f* original version; ◆**O~ität** [-nali'tɛ:t], *f -/no pl* originality; (Echtheit) authenticity. ◆**O~übertragung,** *f Rad: TV:* live transmission. ◆**originell** [origi'nɛl], *adj.* original.

Orkan [ɔr'ka:n], *m -(e)s/-e* hurricane.

Ornament [ɔrna'mɛnt], *n -(e)s/-e* ornament.

Ort [ɔrt], *m -(e)s/-e (a) (Stelle)* place; **an O. und Stelle,** (i) in the proper place; (ii) (sogleich) on the spot; **am O. des Verbrechens,** at the scene of the crime; (b) (Ortschaft) village; (Dorf) village; (Stadt) town; **sie wohnen am O.,** they live locally. ◆**'o~en,** *v.tr.* to locate, pinpoint the position of (a ship, aircraft etc.). ◆**'O~s-,** *comb.fm.* local (knowledge, traffic, time etc.). ◆**'O~schaft,** *f -/-en* village; (Stadt) town. ◆**'o~sfremd,** *adj.* **ich bin hier o.,** I am a stranger here. ◆**'O~sgespräch,** *n* local call. ◆**'O~sname,** *m* place name. ◆**'O~snetz,** *n* local telephone system. ◆**'O~sschild,** *n* place-name sign. ◆**'O~ung,** *f -/no pl* position-finding, location.

örtlich ['œrtliç], *adj.* local. ◆**'Ö~keit,** *f -/-en* locality.

orthodox [ɔrto'dɔks], *adj.* orthodox.

Orthographie [ɔrtograi'fi:], *f -/no pl*

orthography, spelling. ◆o~isch
['graːfiʃ], adj. orthographical; o~ischer
Fehler, spelling mistake.
Orthopäd|e [ɔrto'pɛːdə], m -n/-n ortho-
paedic surgeon; o~isch, adj. orthopaedic.
Öse ['øːzə], f -/-n **Haken und Ö.**, hook
and eye.
Ost- [ɔst-], comb.fm. (a) east (coast, side,
bank, wind etc.); East (Germany, Indies
etc.); (b) (östlich) eastern (frontier etc.).
◆'O~block, m Pol: Eastern Bloc.
◆'o~deutsch, adj. East German.
◆'O~en, m -s/no pl east; aus dem/von
O., from the east; nach O., eastwards;
(Lage) to the east. ◆'O~politik, f policy towards Eastern Europe.
◆'O~see, Pr.n.f -. die O., the Baltic.
◆'o~wärts, adv. eastwards.
Oster- ['oːstər-], comb.fm. Easter (Sunday, Monday, rabbit etc.). ◆'O~ei, n

Easter egg. ◆'O~glocke, f daffo-
dil. ◆'O~n, n -/- Easter; zu O., at
Easter.
Österreich ['øːstərraiç], Pr.n.n -s. Aus-
tria. ◆'ö~isch, adj. Austrian.
östlich ['œstliç]. I. adj. eastern (border,
France etc.); easterly (wind, direction
etc.); ö. von Bonn, (to the) east of Bonn.
II. prep. + gen ö. der Stadt, to the east
of the town.
Otter[1] [ɔtər], m -s/-n Z: otter.
Otter[2], f -/-n Z: & Fig: viper.
Ouvertüre [uver'tyːrə], f -/-n overture.
Oval [o'vaːl]. I. n -s/-e oval. II. o., adj.
oval.
Ovation [ovatsi'oːn], f -/-en ovation.
Oxyd [ɔk'syːt], n -(e)s/-e oxide.
◆o~ieren [-y'diːrən], v.tr. & i. (haben)
to oxidize.
Ozean ['oːtseaːn], m -s/-e ocean.
Ozon [o'tsoːn], n -s/no pl ozone.

P

P, p [peː], n -/- (the letter) P, p.
Paar [paːr]. I. n -(e)s/-e pair; (Mann und
Frau) couple. II. p., inv. adj. ein p., a
few; alle p. Tage, every few days; vor
ein p. Tagen, a few/couple of days ago.
◆'p~en v.tr. (a) to mate (animals,
birds); die Vögel p. sich, the birds are
mating; (b) to combine (qualities etc.).
◆'P~lauf, m pairs skating. ◆'p~mal,
adv. ein p., a few times. ◆'P~ung, f
-/-en (a) Z: Orn: mating; (Kreuzung)
crossing; (b) coupling. ◆'p~weise,
adv. in pairs; two by two.
Pacht [paxt], f -/-en lease. ◆'p~en,
v.tr. to lease, rent (a farm etc.).
◆'P~vertrag, m lease, tenancy agreement.
Pächter ['pɛçtər], m -s/- leaseholder,
tenant.
Pack[1] [pak], m -(e)s/-e package, bundle
(of papers). ◆Pack[2], n -(e)s/no pl P:
rabble, riffraff. ◆'P~eis, n pack-ice.
◆'p~en. I. v.tr. (a) to pack (one's
clothes, goods, a suitcase etc.); to wrap
up (a parcel etc.); (b) to grab, seize (s.o.)
(am Kragen usw., by the collar etc.),
grasp (s.o.'s hand etc.); Fig: to thrill (an
audience etc.); Fig: von Angst gepackt,
gripped/seized with fear; (c) F: p. wir's
noch? will we make it? II. 'P~en, m -s/-
(large) pack, bundle (of washing etc.).
◆'p~end, adj. gripping, riveting;
thrilling (spectacle). ◆'P~er(in), m -s/-
(f -/-nen) packer. ◆'P~esel, m F:
(Pers.) beast of burden; drudge.
◆'P~papier, n (brown) wrapping paper. ◆'P~ung, f -/-en 1. packet, esp.
N.Am: pack of cigarettes etc.); 2er-P.,
double pack. 2. Med: pack.
Päckchen ['pɛkçən], n -s/- packet, esp.

N.Am: pack; (Paket) small parcel.
Pädagog|e [pɛda'goːgə], m -n/-n (Lehrer)
educator, N.Am: instructor. ◆P~ik, f
-/no pl educational theory; pedagogy.
◆p~isch, adj. educational, teaching
(methods etc.); p~ische Hochschule,
teacher training college.
Paddel ['padəl], n -s/- paddle.
◆'P~boot, n canoe. ◆p~n, v.i.
(haben/sein) to paddle, canoe.
Page ['paːʒə], m -n/-n page boy.
◆'P~nkopf, m page-boy hairstyle.
Paket [pa'keːt]. I. n -(e)s/-e parcel;
N.Am: package. II. 'P~-, comb.fm. par-
cel (post etc.); parcels (counter etc.).
◆P~annahme, f parcels counter.
Pakistaner(in) [paːki'stɔːnər(in)], m -s/-
(f -/-nen) & p~isch adj. Pakistani.
Pakt [pakt], m -(e)s/-e Pol: etc: pact, (Ver-
trag) treaty.
Palast [pa'last], m -(e)s/-e palace.
Palästin|a [palɛs'tiːna], Pr.n.n -s. Geog:
Palestine. ◆P~enser [-'nɛnzər], m -s/-
& p~ensisch, adj. Palestinian.
Palaver [pa'laːvər], n -s/- endless discussion, palaver. ◆p~n, v.i. (haben) to
discuss endlessly.
Palette [pa'lɛtə], f -/-n 1. Art: palette. 2.
Ind: Rail: pallet.
Palme ['palmə], f -/-n palm (tree); F: j-n
auf die P. bringen, to drive s.o. up the
wall.
Pampelmuse [pampəl'muːzə], f -/-n
grapefruit.
pampig [pampiç], adj. F: (frech) rude,
stroppy.
panieren [pa'niːrən], v.tr. to bread.
Panik ['paːnik], f -/no pl panic.
◆p~sch, adj. panic-stricken, frantic;

p~**sche Angst haben** to be terrified.
Panne ['panə], f -/-n (a) Tchn: & Fig: breakdown; (b) F: (Fehler) cock-up.
Panorama [pano'raːma], n -s/-men panorama.
pan(t)schen ['pan(t)ʃən], v. 1. v.tr. to adulterate; F: doctor (wine, milk etc.). 2. v.i. F: (Kind) to splash about.
Panther ['pantər], m -s/- Z: panther.
Pantoffel [pan'tɔfəl], m -s/-n (bedroom) slipper. ◆**P~held,** m F: henpecked husband.
Pantomime [panto'miːmə]. 1. f -/-n mime (show). 2. m -n/-n (Pers.) mime.
Panzer ['pantsər]. I. m -s/- 1. Hist: armour; ein P., a suit of armour. 2. Mil: tank. 3. Z: shell of a crab etc.). II. P~-, comb.fm. (gepanzert) armoured (Nau: cruiser, Mil: brigade, division, corps, regiment etc.). ◆**P~faust,** f Mil: bazooka. ◆**P~glas,** n bullet-proof glass. ◆**P~n,** v.tr. to armour-plate (a ship, vehicle). ◆**P~ung,** f -/-en armour(-plating). ◆**P~wagen,** m armoured car.
Papa [pa'paː], m -s/-s F: papa, daddy.
Papagei [papa'gai], m -s/-en parrot.
Papier [pa'piːr]. I. n -s/-e 1. no pl paper. 2. pl papers, documents. II. P~-, comb.fm. paper (money etc.). ◆**P~fabrik,** f papermill. ◆**P~korb,** m waste paper basket. ◆**P~krieg,** m F: (yards of) red tape. ◆**P~schlangen,** fpl paper streamers. ◆**P~taschentuch,** n paper handkerchief; tissue.
Papp(en)deckel f ['pap(ən)dekəl], m cardboard. ◆**P~e,** f -/-n cardboard; F: nicht von P. sein, to be quite something. ◆**p~en,** v.tr. & i. (haben) F: to stick, (mit Klebstoff) glue (sth.). ◆**P~enstiel,** m F: das ist keinen P. wert! I wouldn't give twopence for it! **für einen P.,** for a song. ◆**p~ig,** adj. (klebrig) sticky; (breiig) mushy.
Pappel ['papəl], f -/-n poplar.
Paprika ['paprika], m -s/-(s) (a) (sweet) pepper; (b) (Gewürz) paprika. ◆**P~schote,** f (single) pepper.
Papst [paːpst], m -(e)s/-e pope.
päpstlich ['pɛːpstliç], adj. papal.
Parade [pa'raːdə], f -/-n Mil: parade, march-past. ◆**P~stück,** n showpiece.
Paradies [para'diːs], n -es/-e paradise. ◆**p~isch** [-'diːziʃ], adj. heavenly; delightful.
paradox [para'dɔks], adj. paradoxical.
Paragraph [para'graːf], m -en/-en Jur: section, article (of a law); clause (of a contract).
parallel [para'leːl]. I. adj. & adv. parallel (mit/zu etwas dat, with/to sth.). II. P~-, comb.fm. parallel (case, Sch: class etc.). ◆**P~e,** f -/-n parallel. ◆**P~ogramm** [-elo'gram], n -s/-e parallelogram. ◆**P~straße,** f street running parallel.
Paranuß ['paːranus], f brazil nut.

Parasit [para'ziːt], m -en/-en parasite.
parat [pa'raːt], adj. & adv. ready.
Pärchen ['pɛːrçən], n -s/- (esp. young) couple.
Pardon [par'dõː], m -s/-s P.! sorry! excuse me!
Parfüm [par'fyːm], m -s/-e perfume; scent. ◆**p~ieren** [-fy'miːrən], v.tr. to perfume (sth.).
parieren [pa'riːrən], v. 1. v.tr. to ward off (an attack etc.), parry (a blow). 2. v.i. (haben) F: to toe the line.
Parität [pari'tɛːt], f -/-en parity. ◆**p~isch,** adj. with equal rights.
Park [park]. I. m -s/-s park. II. P~-, comb.fm. Aut: parking (light, fee, disc etc.). ◆**p~en,** v.tr. & i. (haben) Aut: (Pers.) to park (a car); (Auto) to be parked. ◆**P~haus,** n multi-storey car park. ◆**P~lücke,** f parking space. ◆**P~platz,** m (a) car park, N.Am: parking lot; (b) (P~lücke) parking space. ◆**P~uhr,** f parking meter. ◆**P~verbot,** n parking ban; hier ist P., there's no parking here.
Parkett [par'kɛt], n -(e)s/-e 1. (P~boden) parquet floor; (Tanzp.) dance floor. 2. Th: Cin: stalls.
Parlament [parla'mɛnt], n -(e)s/-e parliament. ◆**p~arisch** [-'taːriʃ], adj. parliamentary. ◆**P~s-,** comb.fm. parliamentary (committee, elections etc.); parliament (building etc.) ◆**P~smitglied,** n member of parliament.
Paro|die [paro'diː], f -/-n parody (auf etwas acc, of sth.). ◆**p~ieren,** v.tr. to parody (s.o., sth.).
Parole [pa'roːlə], f -/-n (a) Mil: etc: password; (b) Pol: etc: slogan.
Partei [par'tai], f -/-en 1. side; Pol: Jur: Com: party; für/gegen j-n P. ergreifen, to side with/against s.o. 2. (Mieter) tenant. II. P~-, comb.fm. party (leadership etc.). ◆**p~isch,** adj. biased, prejudiced. ◆**p~los,** adj. independent. ◆**p~politisch,** adj. party political. ◆**P~programm,** n party manifesto. ◆**P~tag,** m party conference/N.Am: convention.
Parterre [par'tɛr]. I. n -s/-s 1. ground/ N.Am: first floor. 2. Th: stalls. II. p., adv. on the ground/N.Am: first floor.
Partie [par'tiː], f -/-n 1. part. 2. (a) (Spiel) game (of chess, tennis etc.); round (of golf etc.); (b) Com: batch (of goods); (c) eine gute/schlechte P., a good/bad match; (d) F: mit von der P. sein, to be in on it.
Partikel [par'tiːkəl], n -s/- particle.
Partisan [parti'zaːn], m -s -en/-en partisan, guer(r)illa.
Partitur [parti'tuːr], f -/-en Mus: score.
Partizip [parti'tsiːp], n -s/-ien Gram: participle.
Partner(in) ['partnər(in)], m -s/- (f -/ -nen) partner. ◆**P~schaft,** f -/-en partnership. ◆**p~schaftlich,** adj.

p~schaftliches Verhältnis, partnership.
◆'P~stadt, f twin town.

Party [pa:rti], f /-s party.

Parzelle [par'tsɛlə], f /-n plot (of land),
N.Am: lot.

Paß [pas]. I. m -sses/-sse 1. passport. 2.
(mountain etc.) pass. 3. Fb: etc: pass. II.
'P~-, comb.fm. passport (office, control
etc.). ◆P~bild, n passport photograph.
◆P~straße, f (road leading over a)
pass.

passabel [pa'sa:bəl], adj. reasonable,
tolerable; adv. reasonably well.

Passag|e [pa'sa:ʒə], f /-n passage.
◆P~ier [-a'ʒi:r], m -s/-e passenger.
◆P~ierschiff, n -(e)s/-e passenger
liner.

Passant [pa'sant], m -en/-en passer-by.

passen ['pasən], v. 1. v.i. (haben) (a) (die
richtige Größe haben) to fit; das Kleid
paßt (dir) gut, the dress fits (you)/is a
good fit (on you); (b) (geeignet sein) to be
suitable (zu j-m, etwas dat, for s.o.,
sth.); der Hut paßt zum Kleid, the hat
matches/goes with the dress; sie p./p.
nicht zueinander, (Pers.) they are well/
ill-matched; (c) (gelegen sein) to be convenient (j-m, for s.o.); heute paßt (es) mir
besser, today is better for me; dein Benehmen paßt ihm nicht, he doesn't like
your behaviour; das könnte dir so p.!
you'd like that, wouldn't you! (d) (Kartenspiel) (ich) passe, (I) pass; no bid; F:
da muß ich p., there you have me. 2.
v.tr. (einfügen) to insert (sth.). ◆p~d,
adj. (a) (geeignet) suitable; appropriate
(behaviour, gift etc.); opportune (moment etc.); apt, fitting (remark etc.);
right, proper (place, time, words etc.);
(b) matching (colour, hat, tie etc.).

passier|bar [pa'si:rba:r], adj. passable.
◆p~en, v. 1. v.tr. (a) to pass (a house,
s.o.); to pass through (a town etc.); to
pass over, cross (a bridge, frontier etc.);
(b) Cu: to strain (soup etc.). 2. v.i.
(sein) to happen; ihm ist nichts passiert, he's
all right/unhurt. ◆P~schein, m pass;
permit.

Passion [pasi'o:n], f /-en (a) passion; (b)
Ecc: Passion. ◆p~iert [-o'ni:rt], adj.
enthusiastic, keen.

passiv ['pasi:f]. I. adj. passive; non-active
(member etc.); Com: adverse (balance of
trade). II. P., Gram: passive (voice).

Paste ['pastə], f /-n paste.

Pastell [pas'tɛl]. I. n -(e)s/-e Art: pastel
(drawing). II. P~-, comb.fm. pastel
(colour, painting etc.).

Pastete [pas'te:tə], f /-n Cu: 1. (meat
etc.) pie; (Königin.) vol-au-vent. 2. (Le-
berp.) paté.

pasteurisieren [pastøri'zi:rən], v.tr. to
pasteurize (milk etc.).

Pastille [pas'tilə], f /-n pastille, lozenge.

Pastor ['pastor], m -s/-en pastor, minister.

Pat|e ['pa:tə], m -n/-n godfather; pl
godparents. ◆'P~enkind, n godchild.

◆'P~enonkel, m godfather. ◆'P~en-
sohn, m godson. ◆'P~entochter, f
goddaughter. ◆'P~in, f /-nen godmother.

Patent [pa'tɛnt]. I. n -(e)s/-e Jur: patent.
II. p., adj. F: neat, ingenious; p~er
Kerl, great guy; (Mädchen) good sort.
III. P~-, comb.fm. patent (law etc.);
P~amt, n, Patent Office. ◆p~ieren
[-'ti:rən], v.tr. to patent (an invention).

Pater [pa:tər], m -s/- & Patres Ecc:
father.

path|etisch [pa'te:tiʃ], adj. emotional,
passionate (speech etc.). ◆P~os
['pa:tɔs], n -/no pl emotionalism.

Patholog|e [pato'lo:gə], m -n/-n patholo-
gist. ◆P~ie [-lo'gi:], f /-n pathology.
◆p~isch [-'lo:giʃ], adj. pathological.

Patience [pasi'ɔs], f /-n (Spiel) patience;
P~n legen, to play patience.

Patient(in) [patsi'ɛnt(in)], m -en/-en (f /
-nen) patient.

Patriot(in) [patri'o:t(in)], m -en/-en (f /
-nen) patriot. ◆p~isch, adj. patriotic.
◆P~ismus [-o'tismus], m -/no pl patriotism.

Patron(in) [pa'tro:n(in)], m -s/-e (f /-nen)
Ecc: patron saint.

Patrone [pa'tro:nə], f /-n cartridge.

Patrouill|e [pa'truljə], f /-n Mil: etc:
patrol. ◆p~ieren [-ul'ji:rən], v.i. (haben)
to go (on) patrol.

patsch [patʃ], int. splash! (Schlag) slap!
◆'P~e, f /-n F: mess; in der P.
sitzen/stecken, to be in a jam.
◆'p~en, v.i. (haben/occ. sein) F: (a) (im
Wasser) to splash; (b) (klatschen) to
smack. ◆'p~naß, adj. F: soaking wet.

patz|en ['patsən], v.i. (haben) F: to make
a slip, boob. ◆'P~er, m -s/- F: slip.
◆'p~ig, adj. F: impudent.

Pauk|e ['paukə], f /-n Mus: kettledrum;
pl P~n, timpani; Fig: mit P~n und
Trompeten, Hum: resoundingly; F: auf
die P. hauen, (i) to paint the town red;
(ii) (prahlen) to blow one's own trumpet.
◆'p~en, v. 1. v.i. (haben) Sch: F: to
cram, swot. 2. v.tr. Sch: F: to swot (sth.)
up. ◆'P~er, m -s/- Sch: F: (Lehrer)
teacher; Pej: crammer.

pausbäckig ['paus'bɛkiç], adj. chubby-
faced.

pauschal [pau'ʃa:l], adj. I. P~-,
comb.fm. (einheitlich) flat-rate (fee etc.);
(inklusiv) lump (sum etc.); all-in (price);
Fig: general, Pej: sweeping (judgment
etc.). ◆P~e, f /-n lump sum.
◆P~reise, f package tour.

Pause1 ['pauzə], f /-n (a) pause; Sch: break;
Th: interval; Cin: N.Am: intermission;
Mus: rest. ◆p~enlos, adj. ceaseless,
incessant; p. arbeiten, to work non-stop.
◆p~ieren [-'zi:rən], v.i. (haben) to
take a break/rest.

Pause2, f /-n tracing. ◆'P~papier, n
tracing paper.

Pavian ['pa:vja:n], m -s/-e Z: baboon.

Pavillon [pavil'jɔ̃], m -s/-s pavilion, annexe (of a school, hospital).

Pazifik [pa'tsifik]. Pr.n.m -s. der P., the Pacific. ◆**p~sch**, adj. der P~sche Ozean, the Pacific (Ocean). ◆**P~smus** [-i'fismus], m -/no pl pacifism. ◆**P~st(in)**, m -en/-en (f -/-nen) & **p~stisch**, adj. pacifist.

Pech [pɛç], n -s/no pl 1. pitch. 2. bad luck; **P. haben**, to be unlucky. ◆**p~schwarz**, adj. pitch-black (darkness etc.); jet-black (hair etc.). ◆**P~strähne**, f run of bad luck. ◆**P~vogel**, m unlucky person.

Pedal [pe'da:l], n -s/-e pedal.

Pedant [pe'dant], m -en/-en pedant. ◆**P~erie**, f -/-n pedantry. ◆**p~isch**, adj. pedantic.

Pediküre [pedi'ky:rə], f -/-n no pl chiropody; pedicure.

Pegel [pe:gəl], m -s/- water level indicator. ◆**P~stand**, m water level.

peilen ['pailən], v.tr. & i. (haben) Nau: Av: to take a bearing on a point etc.; Rad: to detect (the direction of) (sth.).

Pein [pain], f -/no pl Lit: anguish; (mental) agony. ◆**p~igen**, v.tr. to torment (s.o.). ◆**p~lich**, adj. embarrassing, awkward (moment, silence etc.); painful (scene etc.); **es ist mir sehr p.**, I feel very embarrassed about it; **p. genau**, scrupulously exact; painstaking. ◆**P~lichkeit**, f -/-en awkwardness, embarrassment.

Peitsche ['paitʃə], f -/-n whip. ◆**p~en**, v.tr. & i. (haben) to whip (s.o., an animal); Fig: (Regen usw.) to lash (gegen + acc., against).

Pekinese [peki'ne:zə], m -n/-n pekinese.

Pelikan ['pe:likan], m -s/-e pelican.

Pelle ['pɛlə], f -/-n peel (of potatoes, fruit); (sausage) skin; F: **j-m auf die P. rücken**, to (bedrängen) to pester s.o. ◆**p~en**, v.tr. to peel (potatoes etc.); to shell (an egg); (Haut) **sich p.**, to peel. ◆**P~kartoffeln**, fpl potatoes boiled in their skins.

Pelz [pɛlts]. I. m -es/-e fur. II. **P~**, comb.fm. fur (jacket, coat etc.). ◆**P~jäger**, m trapper. ◆**P~tier**, n animal with a valuable fur.

Pendel ['pɛndəl], n -s/- pendulum. ◆**p~n**, v.i. (a) (haben) to swing (to and fro); Fig: to vacillate; (b) (sein) (Pers.) to commute. ◆**P~uhr**, f pendulum clock. ◆**P~verkehr**, m Rail: etc: shuttle service; (für Pendler) commuter service.

Pendler ['pɛndlər], m -s/- commuter.

penetrant [pene'trant], adj. penetrating; (also Fig: Pers:) overpowering.

penibel [pe'ni:bəl], adj. (übergenau) pedantic.

Penis ['pe:nis], m -/-se & Penes penis.

pennen ['pɛnən], v.i. (haben) P: to kip, have a kip.

Pension [pãzi'o:n], f -/-en 1. (a) (Rente) pension; (b) (Ruhestand) **in P.**, retired. 2. (a) (Hotel) boarding-house, guesthouse; (b) (Kost) **volle/halbe P.**, full/half board. ◆**P~är(in)** [-io'nɛ:r(in)], m -s/-e (f -/-nen) pensioner. ◆**p~ieren** [-o'ni:rən], v.tr. to retire (s.o.). ◆**P~s-**, comb.fm. retirement (age etc.).

Pensum ['pɛnzum], n -s/-sen & -sa (allotted) material, (Aufgabe) task.

per [pɛr], prep. + acc (a) by. **P. Post, Zug usw.**, by post, train etc ; (b) Com: (ub) as from.

perfekt [pɛr'fɛkt]. I. adj. (a) perfect; faultless (French etc.); (b) (abgemacht) settled. II. P., n -s/-e Gram: perfect (tense). ◆**P~ion** [-tsi'o:n], f -/no pl perfection.

Perfor|ation [pɛrfora:tsi'o:n], f -/-en perforation. ◆**p~ieren** [-'ri:rən], v.tr. to perforate (sth.).

Pergament [pɛrga'mɛnt], n -(e)s/-e parchment. ◆**P~papier**, n greaseproof paper.

Period|e [peri'o:də], f -/-n period. ◆**p~isch**, adj. periodical.

Peripherie [perife'ri:], f -/-n periphery; (Stadtrand) outskirts.

Perl|e ['pɛrlə], f -/-n pearl; (Glasp., Holzp. usw.) head; Fig: gem. ◆**p~en**, v.i. (haben) (Sekt usw.) to bubble; (Tropfen) to run down. ◆**P~en-**, comb.fm. pearl (fisher, diver etc.). ◆**P~enkette**, f, pearl necklace. ◆**P~mutt** [pɛrl'mut], n -s/no pl mother of pearl. ◆**P~wein**, m sparkling wine.

perplex [pɛr'plɛks], adj. perplexed, puzzled.

Pers|er ['pɛrzər], m -s/- (a) (Pers.) Persian; (b) (Teppich) Persian carpet. ◆**P~erin**, f -/-nen Persian woman. ◆**P~erteppich**, m Persian carpet. ◆**P~ianer** [-zi'a:nər], m -s/- Persian lamb (skin/coat). ◆**p~isch**, adj. Persian.

Person [pɛr'zo:n], f -/-en (a) person; **die Geduld in P.**, patience personified; **ich für meine P.**, as for me; I for my part; (b) **zehn P~en**, ten people; (c) Th: Lit: character. ◆**P~al** [-zo'na:l], n -s/ no pl staff; personnel. ◆**P~al-**, comb.fm. 1. personnel (department etc.); staff (costs etc.). 2. personal (description, Gram: pronoun etc.). ◆**P~alausweis**, m identity card. ◆**P~alchef(in)**, m (f) personnel manager. ◆**P~alien** [-o'na:liən], fpl personal data. ◆**P~en-**, comb.fm. passenger (vehicle etc.). ◆**P~enaufzug**, m passenger lift/ N.Am: elevator. ◆**P~enkraftwagen**, m passenger/private car. ◆**P~enkult**, m personality cult. ◆**P~enzug**, m stopping train; N.Am: local train. ◆**p~ifizieren**, v.tr. to personify (beauty etc.).

persönlich [pɛr'zø:nliç], adj. personal; **p. erscheinen**, to appear in person. ◆**P~keit**, f -/-en personality.

Perspektive [pεrspεk'ti:və], f -/-n perspective; (*Blickpunkt*) viewpoint.

Peru [pe'ru:]. Pr.n.n -s. Peru. ❖P~aner(in) [-u'a:nər(in)], m -s/- (f -/-nen) & p~anisch, adj. Peruvian.

Perücke [pe'rykə], f -/-n wig.

pervers [pεr'vεrs], adj. perverse. ❖P~sion [-zi'o:n], f -/-en perversion. ❖P~sität [-zi'tε:t], f -/-en perversity.

Pessimis|mus [pεsi'mismus], m -/no pl pessimism. ❖P~t(in), m -en/-en (f -/-nen) pessimist. ❖p~tisch, adj. pessimistic.

Pest [pεst], f -/no pl Med: plague; **er haßt sie wie die P.**, he hates her guts.

Petersilie [petər'zi:liə], f -/-n parsley.

Petroleum [pe'tro:leum], n -s/no pl paraffin, N.Am: kerosene. ❖P~lampe, f oil lamp.

Petunie [pe'tu:niə], f -/-n petunia.

petzen ['pεtsən], v.tr. & i. (haben) Sch: F: to tell tales.

Pfad [pfa:t], m -(e)s/-e path. ❖P~finder, m -s/- boy scout.

Pfahl [pfa:l], m -(e)s/-e post. ❖P~bau, m pile dwelling.

Pfalz [pfalts], f -/-en die P., the Palatinate.

Pfand [pfant], n -(e)s/-er (*Bürgschaft*) security; (*Flaschenp. usw.*) deposit; (*Spielp.*) forfeit. ❖P~haus, n 'P~leihe, f -/-n pawnshop. ❖P~leiher, m -s/- pawnbroker.

pfänd|en ['pfεndən], v.tr. to seize (property etc.) as security. ❖P~erspiel, n (game of) forfeits. ❖P~ung, f -/-en Jur: seizure.

Pfann|e ['pfanə], f -/-n Cu: (frying) pan. ❖P~kuchen, m -s/- pancake; **Berliner P.**, doughnut.

Pfarr- ['pfar-], comb.fm. Ecc: parish (district, church etc.). ❖P~er, m -s/- vicar; parson; (*katholischer P.*) (parish) priest. ❖P~haus, n vicarage.

Pfau [pfau], m -(e)s/-e peacock. ❖P~enauge, n peacock butterfly.

Pfeffer ['pfεfər], m -s/- 1. pepper. 2. F: (*Schwung*) pep. ❖P~korn, n peppercorn. ❖P~kuchen, m approx. = gingerbread. ❖P~minz(bonbon), n -es/-e peppermint (sweet). ❖P~minze, f peppermint. ❖P~mühle, f peppermill. ❖p~n, v.tr. Cu: to pepper (food); Fig: to spice (a speech etc.) with jokes etc.).

Pfeif|e ['pfaifə], f -/-n 1. whistle; pipe (of an organ). 2. (*Tabaksp.*) pipe. ❖p~en, v.irr. 1. v.tr. to whistle (a tune etc.); to play (a tune) on a (penny) whistle. 2. v.i. (haben) (a) to whistle; (b) F: **ich pfeife auf dein Geld!** you can keep your money! ❖P~en-, comb.fm. pipe (smoker, cleaner, tobacco etc.). ❖P~er, m -s/- whistler; Mus: piper. ❖P~konzert, n chorus of whistles/catcalls.

Pfeil [pfail], m -(e)s/-e arrow.

❖'p~'schnell, adj. as quick as lightning.

Pfeiler ['pfailər], m -s/- pillar; (*Brückenp.*) pier.

Pfennig ['pfεniç], m -s/-e pfennig; Fig: penny. ❖P~absatz, m stiletto heel.

pferchen ['pfεrçən], v.tr. to cram, stuff (people, animals) (in + acc, into).

Pferd [pfe:rt], n -(e)s/-e horse; (b) Sp: (vaulting) horse; (c) (*Schach*) knight. ❖P~efleisch, n horsemeat. ❖P~erennen, n (i) horse racing; (ii) (*einzelnes*) horse race. ❖P~eschwanz, m (*Frisur*) ponytail. ❖P~esport, m equestrian sport. ❖'P~estall, m stable. ❖P~estärke, f horsepower. ❖P~ewagen, m horse-drawn carriage.

Pfiff [pfif], m -(e)s/-e (a) whistle; (b) F: trick; **der letzte P.**, the final touch.

Pfifferling ['pfifərliŋ], m -s/-e 1. chanterelle. 2. F: **das ist keinen P. wert**, it isn't worth a bean.

pfiffig ['pfifiç], adj. smart (child etc.); knowing (face).

Pfingst- ['pfiŋst-], comb.fm. Whit (Sunday, Monday); Whitsun (holiday, week). ❖P~en, n -s/- Whitsun. ❖P~rose, f peony.

Pfirsich ['pfirziç], m -s/-e peach.

Pflanz|e ['pflantsə], f -/-n plant. ❖'p~en, v.tr. to plant. ❖P~en-, comb.fm. plant (milk, protection etc.); vegetable (fibre, fat etc.). ❖P~enreich, n vegetable kingdom. ❖P~enwelt, f plant life. ❖P~enfresser, m -s/- herbivore. ❖P~enkunde, f botany. ❖'p~lich, adj. vegetable (fat etc.). ❖P~ung, f -/-en 1. no pl planting. 2. plantation.

Pflaster ['pflastər], n -s/- 1. Med: (sticking) plaster. 2. (*Fahrbahnbelag*) road surface; (*aus Steinen*) pavement, paving; **ein gefährliches P.**, a dangerous spot. ❖'p~n, v.tr. to surface (the road etc.). ❖P~stein, m paving stone; (*runder P.*) cobble(stone).

Pflaume ['pflaumə], f -/-n plum. ❖P~nkuchen, m plumtart.

Pflege ['pfle:gə]. I. f -/-n care (of s.o., sth.); maintenance (of parks, buildings etc.); cultivation (of the arts etc.); (*ärztliche*) P., medical care, nursing; **ein Kind in P. geben/nehmen**, to put/take a child into care. II. 'P~-, comb.fm. foster (child, mother etc.). ❖'p~bedürftig, adj. in need of care/Med: nursing. ❖P~eltern, pl foster parents. ❖'P~fall, m person in need of nursing. ❖'p~n, v. 1. v.tr. (a) to care for, look after (s.o., sth.); to nurse (a sick person); (b) to cultivate (the arts, friendship etc.). 2. v.i. (haben) **montags pflegt er ins Kino zu gehen**, he usually goes to the cinema on Mondays. ❖'P~r(in), m -s/- (f -/-nen) nurse.

Pflicht [pfliçt]. I. f -/-en duty; **es ist P.**, it is compulsory/obligatory. II. 'P~-, *comb.fm.* compulsory (contribution, *Sp:* exercise, *Sch:* reading etc.). ◆'p~**bewußt**, *adj.* conscientious. ◆'P~**fach**, *n Sch:* compulsory subject. ◆'P~**gefühl**, *n* sense of duty. ◆'p~**gemäß**, *adj.* dutiful; due (care, respect etc.). ◆'p~**vergessen**, *adj.* neglectful of one's duty.

Pflock [pflɔk], *m* -(e)s/⸚e (tent etc.) peg; (*für Tiere*) post, stake.

pflücken ['pflʏkən], *v.tr.* to pick (flowers, fruit). ◆'P~**er(in)**, *m* -s/- (*f* -/-nen) picker.

Pflug [pfluːk], *m* -(e)s/⸚e plough, *N.Am:* plow.

pflügen ['pflyːgən], *v.tr. & i.* (*haben*) to plough (a field).

Pforte ['pfɔrtə], *f* -/-n (*Tor*) gate; (*Tür*) door.

Pförtner ['pfœrtnər], *m* -s/- gatekeeper; *Sch: etc:* porter; doorman.

Pfosten ['pfɔstən], *m* -s/- post; (*wall*) stud; *Fb:* goalpost, upright.

Pfote ['pfoːtə], *f* -/-n paw.

Pfropfen ['pfrɔpfən]. **I.** *m* -s/- stopper, (*Korken*) cork; bung (of a barrel etc.). **II.** *p~*, *v.tr.* (*a*) to cork, stopper (a bottle), bung (a barrel etc.); (*b*) to cram, stuff (sth.) (in etwas *acc*, into sth.).

pfui [pfui], *int. p.* (**Teufel**!) ugh, how disgusting!

Pfund [pfʊnt], *n* -(e)s/-e pound; **zwei P.** Zucker, two pounds of sugar. ◆'p~**weise**, *adv.* by the pound.

pfuschen ['pfuʃən], *v.i.* (*haben*) to bungle (it). ◆'P~**er**, *m* -s/- bungler. ◆P~**e'rei**, *f* -/-en bungling.

Pfütze ['pfʏtsə], *f* -/-n puddle.

Phänomen [fɛnoˈmeːn], *n* -s/-e phenomenon. ◆p~**al** [-meˈnaːl], *adj.* phenomenal; stupendous.

Phantasie [fantaˈziː], *f* -/-n imagination; **eine schmutzige P.**, a dirty mind. ◆p~**sielos**, *adj.* unimaginative. ◆p~**sieren**, *v.i.* (*haben*) (*a*) to fantasize; to dream (**von Erfolg usw.**, of success etc.); (*b*) *Med:* (**im Fieber**) p., to be delirious. ◆p~**sievoll**, *adj.* imaginative. ◆p~**stisch**, *adj.* fantastic. ◆P~**om** [-toːm], *n* -s/-e phantom.

pharma|zeutisch [farmaˈtsɔʏtiʃ], *adj.* pharmaceutical. ◆P~**zie**, *f* -/no *pl* pharmacy.

Phase ['faːzə], *f* -/-n phase.

Philanthrop [filanˈtroːp], *m* -en/-en philanthropist. ◆p~**isch** [-ˈtroːpiʃ], *adj.* philanthropic.

Philatelie [filateˈliː], *f* -/no *pl* philately.

Philologe [filoˈloːgə], *m* -n/-n student of language and literature. ◆P~**ie** [-oˈgiː], *f* -/no *pl* study of language and literature.

Philosoph [filoˈzoːf], *m* -en/-en philosopher. ◆P~**ie** [-oˈfiː], *f* -/-n philosophy. ◆p~**isch** [-ˈzoːfiʃ], *adj.* philosophical.

Phlegma|tiker [fleˈgmaːtikər], *m* -s/- lethargic person. ◆p~**tisch**, *adj.* lethargic etc.

gic, stolid.

Phosphor ['fɔsfɔr], *m* -s/-e phosphorus.

Photo ['foːto]. **I.** *n & m* -s/-s = **Foto. II.** P~-, *comb.fm.* = **Foto-**.

Phrase ['fraːzə], *f* -/-n (*a*) phrase; (*b*) *Pej:* (*Gemeinplatz*) platitude; trite remark. ◆'P~**ndrescher**, *m* -s/- *Pej:* windbag, speechifier.

Physik [fyˈziːk], *f* -/no *pl* physics. ◆p~**alisch** [-iˈkaːliʃ], *adj.* physical (laws etc.); physics (institute, experiment etc.). ◆'P~**er**, *m* -s/- physicist.

Physio|loge [fyzioˈloːgə], *m* -n/-n physiologist. ◆P~**logie** [-loˈgiː], *f* -/no *pl* physiology. ◆p~**logisch** [-ˈloːgiʃ], *adj.* physiological.

physisch ['fyːziʃ], *adj.* physical.

Pianist(in) [piaˈnist(in)], *m* -en/-en (*f* -/-nen) pianist.

Pickel ['pikəl], *m* -s/- **1.** (*Spitzhacke*) pick-axe; (*Eisp.*) ice-pick. **2.** pimple, spot. ◆'p~**ig**, *adj.* spotty (face etc.).

picken ['pikən], *v.tr. & i.* (*haben*) to peck; **nach etwas p.**, to peck at sth.

Picknick ['piknik], *n* -s/-s picnic. ◆'p~**en**, *v.i.* (*haben*) to picnic.

piep|en ['piːpən], *v.i.* (*haben*) (*a*) (*Vögel*) to peep, chirp; *Rad:* to bleep; (*b*) **bei dir piept's wohl?** you must be off your rocker! ◆'p~**sen**, *v.i.* (*haben*) to peep, squeak, *Rad:* bleep.

Pietät [pieˈtɛːt], *f* -/no *pl* reverence (reverential) respect. ◆p~**los**, *adj.* irreverent.

Pik [piːk]. **I.** *n* -s/-s (*Kartenspiel*) (*Farbe*) spades; (*Karte*) spade. **II.** P~-, *comb.fm.* (ace, king etc.) of spades.

pikant [piˈkant], *adj.* spicy (food, *Fig:* story etc.); (*schlüpfrig*) suggestive (joke etc.).

pikiert [piˈkiːrt], *adj.* (*Pers*) put out, needled; *N.Am:* miffed; (*gekränkt*) injured.

Pilger ['pilgər], *m* -s/- pilgrim. ◆'P~**fahrt**, *f* pilgrimage.

Pille ['pilə], *f* -/-n pill.

Pilot(in) [piˈloːt(in)], *m* -en/-en (*f* -/-nen) pilot.

Pils [pils], *n* -/- Pilsener (beer).

Pilz [pilts], *m* -es/-e fungus; (*eßbarer P.*), (edible) mushroom; **giftiger P.**, toadstool. ◆'P~**krankheit**, *f* mycosis.

pingelig ['piŋəliç], *adj.* F: pernickety, fussy.

Pinguin ['piŋguin], *m* -s/-e penguin.

Pinie ['piːniə], *f* -/-n pine.

Pinkel ['piŋkəl], *m* -s/- P: (**feiner P.**), toff, swell; *N.Am:* dude. ◆p~**n**, *v.i.* (*haben*) P: to (have a) pee.

Pinscher ['pinʃər], *m* -s/- pinscher.

Pinsel ['pinzəl], *m* -s/- brush, *esp.* paintbrush. ◆'p~**n**, *v.tr. & i.* (*haben*) F: to paint (sth.).

Pinzette [pinˈtsetə], *f* -/-n tweezers.

Pionier [pioˈniːr], *m* -s/-e **1.** (*Bahnbrecher*) pioneer. **2.** *Mil:* engineer, sapper.

Pirat [piˈraːt], *m* -en/-en pirate.

◆P~**en-**, *comb.fm.* pirate (ship etc.);
P~**ensender**, *m Rad:* pirate station.
Pirsch [pirʃ], *f -/no pl* (deer-)stalking.
◆'**p~en**, *v.i.* (*haben*) to stalk.
Piste ['pistə], *f -/-n Sp:* track; (*Skip.*) run,
piste; *Av:* runway.
Pistole [pis'to:lə], *f -/-n* pistol.
plädieren [plɛ'di:rən], *v.i.* (*haben*) to
plead, put the case. ◆P~**oyer**
[-doa'je:], *n -s/-s Jur:* (counsel's) sum-
ming up; *Fig:* plea.
Plage ['pla:gə], *f -/-n* nuisance; (*Schwierigkeiten*) trouble; **es macht ihm das
Leben zur P.**, it makes his life a
misery. ◆'**p~n**, *v.tr.* (*a*) to plague,
torment (s.o.); (*b*) **sich p.**, to slave away
(**mit etwas** *dat.* at sth.); to struggle
(**mit einem Problem**, with a problem).
Plakat [pla'ka:t], *n -(e)s/-e* poster; (*auf
Pappe*) placard.
Plakette [pla'kɛtə], *f -/-n* (*a*) (*Gedenktafel*)
plaque; (*b*) (*Abzeichen*) badge.
Plan [pla:n]. I. *m -(e)s/-e* (*a*) plan; (*b*)
(*Karte*) (town etc.) map, plan. II. **'P~-**,
comb.fm. planned (economy etc.).
◆'**p~en**, *v.tr.* to plan (sth.). ◆P~**er**,
m -s/- planner. ◆'**p~los**, *adj.* haphazard, unsystematic (procedure etc.); aimless (search etc.). ◆'**p~mäßig**, *adj.* (*a*)
planned (development etc.); scheduled
(arrival etc.); *adv.* according to plan/
schedule; (*b*) systematic (search etc.).
◆'**P~soll**, *n* planned (output) target.
◆'**P~stelle**, *f Adm:* established post.
◆'**P~ung**, *f -/no pl* planning; **in der P.**,
in the planning stage.
Plane ['pla:nə], *f -/-n* tarpaulin.
Planet [pla'ne:t], *m -en/-en* planet.
◆P~**en-**, *comb.fm.* planetary (orbit,
system).
planieren [pla'ni:rən], *v.tr.* to level.
◆P~**raupe**, *f* bulldozer.
Planke ['plaŋkə], *f -/-n* plank.
Plansch|becken ['planʃbɛkən], *n -s/-*
paddling pool. ◆'**p~en**, *v.i.* (*haben*) to
splash about.
Plantage [plan'ta:ʒə], *f -/-n* plantation.
plappern ['plapərn], *v.i.* (*haben*) *F:* to
chatter.
Plastik ['plastik]. I. *f -/-en Art:* sculpture. II. *n -s/no pl* plastic. III. '**P~ik-**,
comb.fm. plastic (cup, bomb etc.).
◆P~**ikbeutel**, *m* plastic/polythene bag.
◆P~**ikfolie**, *f* plastic film; polythene
sheet. ◆'**p~isch**, *adj.* (*a*) three-
dimensional; *Fig:* graphic (description
etc.). 2. (*formbar*) malleable.
Platane [pla'ta:nə], *f -/-n* plane tree.
Platin [pla'ti:n], *n -s/no pl* platinum.
platschen ['platʃən], *v.i.* (*haben/sein*) *F:*
to splash.
plätschern ['plɛtʃərn], *v.i.* (*haben*) to
splash; (*Bach*) to babble; (*Wellen*) to lap
(**an** + *acc.* against).
platt [plat]. I. *adj.* (*a*) flat (roof, nose
etc.); **etwas p. drücken**, to flatten sth.;
(*b*) *Fig:* trite (conversation etc.); (*c*) *F:*

ich war einfach p.! you could have
knocked me down with a feather! II. **P.**,
n -(s)/no pl./'**P~deutsch**, *n -(s)/no pl*
Low German. ◆'**P~e**, *f -/-n* (*a*) plate,
sheet (of metal, glass etc.); (*Holz.*) panel, board; (*Steinp.*) slab; (*Fliese*) tile; (*b*)
(*Kochp.*) ring (of a cooker); (*c*) *Rec:* (gramophone) record; (*d*) (*großer Teller*)
(large) plate, dish; *Cu:* **eine kalte P.**, a
plate of cold meats. ◆'**P~en-**, *comb.fm.*
record (album, collection etc.).
◆'**P~enhülle** *f*, record sleeve.
◆'**P~enspieler** *m*, record player.
◆'**P~enteller** *m*, (record) turntable.
◆'**P~form**, *f* (*a*) platform; (*b*) *Fig:* basis (for discussion). ◆'**P~fuß**, *m* flat
foot. ◆'**P~heit**, *f -/-en* (*a*) no *pl* triteness; (*b*) (*Bemerkung*) platitude.
plätten ['plɛtən], *v.tr.* to iron (clothes
etc.).
Platz [plats], *m -es/-e* 1. (*a*) (*Stelle*) place;
sonniger P., sunny spot; **fehl am P~e**,
in the wrong place/(*Pers.*) job; *F:* out of
place; (*b*) (*Rang*) position; *Sp:* place; **auf
P. drei**, in third place; (*c*) (*Sitzp.*) seat;
(*am Tisch*) place; **P. nehmen**, to sit
down. 2. (*a*) (*Marktp. usw.*) square; (*b*)
Sp: (sports/football) ground; (*golf*)
course; (*tennis*) court. 3. *no pl* (*Raum*)
space; **j-m P. machen**, to make way for
s.o. ◆P~**angst**, *f F:* claustrophobia.
◆'**P~anweiser(in)**, *m (f)* usher, *f* ush-
erette. ◆P~**karte**, *f Rail:* seat ticket/
reservation. ◆P~**mangel**, *m* lack of
space. ◆'**P~verweis**, *m Sp:* sending
off. ◆'**P~wechsel**, *m* change of position.
Plätzchen ['plɛtsçən], *n -s/-* 1. (little)
place, spot. 2. (round) biscuit; *N.Am:*
cookie.
platz|en ['platsən], *v.i.* (*haben*) (*a*) to
burst (**vor** + *dat.* with); (*Bombe*) to explode; (*Naht*) to split; **vor Lachen p.**, to
split one's sides with laughter; **vor Wut
p.**, to be seething with rage; (*b*) *F:* (*Vorhaben*) to fall through. ◆'**P~patrone**, *f*
blank cartridge. ◆'**P~regen**, *m* cloud-
burst; downpour.
Plauder|ei [plaudə'rai], *f -/-en* chat.
◆'**p~n**, *v.i.* (*haben*) to (have a) chat.
plausibel [plau'zi:bəl], *adj.* comprehensible; plausible (explanation).
plazieren [pla'tsi:rən], *v.tr.* to place (s.o.,
an advertisement, *Sp:* the ball etc.); to
position (guards, players etc.); **sich p.**, to
place oneself; *Sp:* to be placed.
Pleite ['plaitə]. I. *adj. F:* broke, *Brit:*
skint; (*Firma*) **p. gehen**, to go bust. II.
P., *f -/no pl F:* (*a*) bankruptcy; **P. machen**, to go bust; (*b*) (*Mißerfolg*) flop,
washout.
Plenar- [ple'na:r-], *comb.fm.* plenary (session, assembly).
Pleuelstange ['pləyəlʃtaŋə], *f* connecting
rod.
Plexiglas ['plɛksiglas], *n R.t.m.* = per-
spex, *N.Am:* plexiglass.

Plomb|e ['plɔmbə], f -/-n **1.** (Zahn.) filling. **2.** lead seal. **◆p~ieren** ['bi:rən], v.tr. (a) to fill (a tooth); (b) to seal (a crate etc.).

plötzlich ['plœtslɪç], adj. sudden; abrupt (change, stop etc.).

plump [plʊmp], adj. (a) (dick) tubby; podgy (fingers etc.); (massig) bulky (shape etc.); (b) (ungeschickt) awkward; (c) Pej: blatant (lie etc.); crude (joke etc.). **◆P~s,** m -es/-e bump. **◆p~sen,** v.i. (haben/sein) to (tall/land with a) thump.

Plunder ['plʊndər], m -s/no pl junk.

Plünder|er ['plyndərər], m -s/- plunderer, looter. **◆p~n,** v.tr. & i. (haben) to loot (a shop, house etc.); Hum: to raid, rifle (the larder etc.). **◆P~ung,** f -/no pl looting; plundering; Hist: pillaging.

Plural ['plu:ra:l], m -s/-e plural.

Plus [plʊs]. **I.** n -/- **1.** (Vorteil) plus, asset. **2.** (Gewinn) profit. **II.** p., adv. & prep. + dat plus. **◆P~pol,** m El: positive pole/terminal. **◆P~punkt,** m plus; Sp: point; Fig: advantage. **◆P~quamperfekt** [-kvam-], n Gram: pluperfect (tense).

Plüsch [ply:ʃ], m -(e)s/-e plush. **◆P~tier,** n soft/F: cuddly toy, N.Am: stuffed animal.

pneumatisch [pnɔy'ma:tiʃ], adj. pneumatic.

Po [po:], m -s/-s P: bottom, behind.

Pöbel ['pø:bəl], m -s/no pl Pej: mob; rabble.

pochen ['pɔxən], v.i. (haben) to knock; (Herz) to pound, thump.

Pocken ['pɔkən], pl Med: smallpox.

Podest [po'dɛst], n & m -(e)s/-e (low) rostrum, platform.

Podium ['po:diʊm], n -s/-dien (speaker's) rostrum, platform.

Poesie [poe'zi:], f -/-ien poetry.

Poet [po'e:t], m -en/-en poet. **◆p~isch,** adj. poetic.

Pointe ['pɛ̃:tə], f -/-n point (of a joke etc.).

Pokal [po'ka:l], m -s/-e goblet; Sp: cup. **◆P~sieger,** m cup winner. **◆P~spiel,** n Sp: cup tie.

Pökel|fleisch ['pø:kəlflaiʃ], n salt meat. **◆p~n,** v.tr. to cure, pickle, (mit Salz) salt (fish, meat).

Pol [po:l], m -s/-e pole; Fig: der ruhende P., the constant factor. **◆p~ar** [po'la:r]. **I.** adj. polar (region etc.); (cold air etc.) from the Arctic. **II.** P~ar-, comb.fm. polar (expeditions, ice, region etc.); arctic (cold, fox etc.). **◆P~arkreis,** m Arctic Circle.

Pol|e ['po:lə], m -n/-n Pole. **◆P~en.** Pr.n.n -s. Poland. **◆P~in,** f -/-nen Polish woman.

Polemi|k [po'le:mik], f -/-en polemics. **◆p~sch,** adj. polemical (attack etc.); provocative, controversial (statement etc.).

Police [po'li:sə], f -/-n (Versicherungsp.) policy.

Polier [po'li:r], m -s/-e foreman.

Polier-², comb.fm. polishing (brush, cloth). **◆p~en,** v.tr. to polish (sth.).

Poliklinik ['po:likli:nik], f outpatients' department.

Politesse [poli'tɛsə], f -/-n (female) traffic warden.

Polit|ik [poli'ti:k], f -/no pl (a) no pl (Bereich) politics; (h) (bestimmte P.) policy; auswärtige P., foreign policy. **◆P~iker(in)** [-'li:tikər(in)], m -s/- (f -/-nen) politician. **◆p~isch** [-'li:tiʃ], adj. political; p. tätig, active in politics. **◆p~isieren,** v.i. (haben) to talk politics.

Politur [poli'tu:r], f -/-en polish.

Polizei [poli'tsai]. **I.** f -/-en (a) no pl police; (b) police force. **II.** P~-, comb.fm. police (operation, dog, state etc.); (chief etc.) of police. **◆P~beamte(r)** m, police officer. **◆p~lich,** adj. police (procedure etc.); sich p. anmelden, to register with the police. **◆P~präsident,** m chief of police; Brit: Chief Constable. **◆P~präsidium,** n police headquarters. **◆P~revier,** n (i) (Bezirk) police district/N.Am: precinct; (ii) (Wache) police station. **◆P~spitzel,** m (police) informer. **◆P~streife,** f police patrol. **◆P~stunde,** f closing time (for bars etc.).

Polizist [poli'tsist], m -en/-en policeman. **◆P~in,** f -/-nen policewoman.

polnisch ['pɔlnɪʃ], adj. & P., m -(s)/no pl Polish.

Polo ['po:lo], n -s/no pl Sp: polo. **◆P~hemd,** n T-shirt with collar.

Polster ['pɔlstər]. **I.** n -s/- (a) (auf Stühlen usw.) upholstery; Cl: pad, padding; (b) Fig: (Geldreserve) cushion. **II.** P~-, comb.fm. upholstered (furniture, chair etc.). **◆P~er,** m -s/- upholsterer. **◆p~n,** v.tr. to upholster (furniture); Cl: to pad (shoulders etc.); F: (Pers.) gut gepolstert, well-padded. **◆P~ung,** f -/no pl upholstery; (Watte usw.) stuffing.

Polter|abend ['pɔltər?a:bənt], m wedding-eve party (with breaking of crockery). **◆p~n,** v.i. (haben/sein) (a) (Pers.) to make a racket; to bang/thump about; (b) (sein (im Fallen) to crash, clatter (down); (Karren) to clatter (along); (c) (schelten) to rant, bluster.

polygam [poly'ga:m], adj. polygamous. **◆P~gamie** [-ga'mi:], f -/no pl polygamy.

Polyp [po'ly:p], m -en/-en **1.** Z: (a) polyp; (b) F: (Krake) octopus. **2.** P: cop, rozzer.

Pomade [po'ma:də], f -/-n hair cream.

Pommes frites [pɔm'frit], pl (potato) chips; esp. N.Am: French fries.

Pomp [pɔmp], m -(e)s/no pl pomp; splendour; Pej: ostentation. **◆p~ös** [-'pø:s], adj. lavish, ostentatious.

Pony ['pɔni]. **I.** n -s/-s pony. **II.** m -s/-s

(Haar) fringe, *N.Am:* bangs.

Pop- ['pɔp-], *comb.fm.* pop (group, music etc.).

Popelin [popə'liːn], *m* -s/-e poplin.

Popo [po'poː], *m* -s/-s *P:* bottom.

poppig ['pɔpiç], *adj. F:* jazzy.

populär [popu'lɛːr], *adj.* popular.

Por|e ['poːrə], *f* -/-n pore. ◆**p~ös** [po'røːs], *adj.* porous.

Porno ['pɔrno]. I. *m* -s/-s *F:* porn. II. **'P~-**, *comb.fm.* pornographic (film etc.). ◆**p~graphisch**, *adj.* pornographic.

Porree ['pɔre], *m* -s/-s leek.

Portal [pɔr'taːl], *n* -s/-e porch.

Portemonnaie [pɔrt(ə)mɔ'neː], *n* -s/-s purse.

Portier [pɔr'jeː], *m* -s/-s (hall) porter; doorman.

Portion [pɔrtsi'oːn], *f* -/-en helping, portion; *F:* (*Pers.*) **eine halbe P.**, a midget/ *Brit:* titch.

Porto ['pɔrto], *n* -s/-s postage. ◆**p~frei**, *adj.* post free, *N.Am:* post paid.

Porträt [pɔr'trɛː], *n* -s/-s portrait. ◆**p~ieren** [-ɛ'tiːrən], *v.tr.* **j-n p.**, to paint s.o.'s portrait; *Fig:* to portray s.o.

Portu|gal ['pɔrtugal]. *Pr.n.n* -s. Portugal. ◆**P~giese**, *m* -n/-n/**P~giesin**, *f* -/- **nen** Portuguese (man/woman). ◆**p~giesisch**, *adj.* & **P~**, *n* -(s)/no pl Portuguese.

Portwein ['pɔrtvain], *m* port.

Porzellan [pɔrtsə'laːn]. I. *n* -s/-e (a) *(Werkstoff)* porcelain; (b) *(Geschirr)* china. II. **P~-**, *comb.fm.* china (figure, cup etc.).

Posaune [po'zaunə], *f* -/-n trombone.

Pos|e ['poːzə], *f* -/-n pose. ◆**p~ieren** [po'ziːrən], *v.i.* (*haben*) to pose.

Position [pozitsi'oːn], *f* -/-en position; (a) *(Stellung)* post; (b) *Com: etc: (Posten)* item. ◆**P~slicht**, *n Nau: Av:* navigation light.

positiv ['poːzitiːf]. I. *adj.* positive; *(günstig)* favourable; **eine p~e Antwort geben**, to answer in the affirmative; *F:* **ich weiß es p.**, I know it for certain. II. **P.**, *n* -s/-e *Phot:* positive.

Positur [pozi'tuːr], *f* -/-en posture.

Poss|e ['pɔsə], *f* -/-n *Th:* burlesque, farce. ◆**p~ierlich** [-'ʃiːrliç], *adj.* (delightfully) comical.

possessiv ['pɔsɛsiːf], *adj. Gram:* possessive. ◆**P~pronomen**, *n* -s/- *Gram:* possessive pronoun.

Post [pɔst]. I. *f* -/no pl (a) *(Briefe usw.)* post, *N.Am:* mail; **mit der P.**, by post/ mail; (b) *(Amt)* post office. II. **'P~-**, *comb.fm.* (a) postal (address, district etc.); (b) post office (employee, administration etc.); (c) mail (steamer, coach, train etc.). ◆**'P~amt**, *n* post office. ◆**P~anweisung**, *f* postal/money order. ◆**P~bote**, *m* postman, *N.Am:* mailman. ◆**'P~fach**, *n* post office box, *usu. abbr.* P.O. Box. ◆**'P~karte**, *f* -/-n

postcard. ◆**'p~lagernd**, *adj.* poste restante. ◆**'P~leitzahl**, *f* postal/*N.Am:* zip code. ◆**'P~scheckkonto**, *n* postal cheque/giro account. ◆**'P~sparkasse**, *f* post office savings bank. ◆**'P~stempel**, *m* postmark. ◆**'p~wendend**, *adj.* by return (of post), *N.Am:* by return mail. ◆**'P~wertzeichen**, *n* postage stamp.

Posten ['pɔstən], *m* -s/- I. *Mil:* (a) *(Stelle)* post; *F:* **auf dem P. sein**, (i) to feel fit; (ii) *(wachsam)* to be on the alert; (b) *(Wachtp.)* sentry. 2. *(Stellung)* post, job. 3. *Com:* item, entry; *(Waren)* lot, batch.

poten|t [po'tɛnt], *adj.* potent. ◆**P~tial** [-tsi'aːl], *n* -s/-e potential. ◆**p~tiell** [-tsi'ɛl], *adj.* potential. ◆**P~z** [po'tɛnts], *f* -/-en I. *no pl* (sexual) potency; *Fig:* strength. 2. *Mth:* power.

Potpourri ['pɔtpuri], *n* -s/-s *Mus:* medley.

Poularde [pu'laːrdə], *f* -/-n pullet.

Pracht [praxt]. I. *f* -/no pl magnificence, splendour. II. **'P~-**, *comb.fm.* magnificent (building etc.). ◆**'P~exemplar** *n*/ **'P~stück**, *n* magnificent specimen, *F:* beauty. ◆**P~voll**, *adj.* magnificent, gorgeous (colours etc.).

prächtig ['prɛçtiç], *adj.* magnificent; gorgeous (colours etc.); *(großartig)* marvellous (weather etc.).

Prädikat [prɛdi'kaːt], *n* -(e)s/-e 1. rating, assessment; **Wein mit P.**, high-quality wine. 2. *Gram:* predicate.

präg|en ['prɛːgən], *v.tr.* (a) to mint (money, coins); to stamp (metal); (b) *(schöpfen)* to coin (a new phrase, word etc.); (c) to form (s.o.'s character etc.); to characterize (a period, style etc.). ◆**'P~ung**, *f* -/no pl coining, minting; stamping.

pragmatisch [prag'maːtiʃ], *adj.* pragmatic.

prägnan|t [prɛg'nant], *adj.* concise, succinct; *(kernig)* pithy. ◆**P~z**, *f* -/no pl conciseness; incisiveness.

prahl|en ['praːlən], *v.i.* (*haben*) to boast, brag (mit + *dat*, about). ◆**P~e'rei**, *f* -/- **-en** (constant) boasting.

Prakt|ik ['praktik], *f* -/-en practice. ◆**P~i'kant(in)**, *m* -en/-en (*f* -/-nen) student trainee. ◆**P~ikum**, *n* -s/-ka practical training. ◆**'p~isch**, *adj.* practical; *(zweckmäßig)* convenient; *(handlich)* handy (tool etc.); **p~ischer Arzt**, general practitioner; **p. unmöglich**, virtually/ practically impossible. ◆**p~i'zieren**, *v.i.* (*haben*) to practise (**als Arzt**, as a doctor).

Praline [pra'liːnə], *f* -/-n chocolate; **Schachtel P~n**, box of chocolates.

prall [pral]. I. *adj.* 1. bulging (muscles, briefcase etc.); well-rounded (breasts etc.); **p. gefüllt**, filled to bursting. 2. blazing (sun). II. **P.**, *m* -(e)s/-e impact. ◆**'p~en**, *v.i.* (*haben*) **auf/gegen j-n, etwas** *acc* **p.**, to bump/(*mit Wucht*) crash into s.o., sth.; (Ball) to bounce against s.o., sth.

Präm|ie ['prɛ:miə], f -/-n (bei Lotterien) prize; (Versicherungsp.) premium; Ind: bonus. ◆**p~ieren** [prɛ'mi:rən], v.tr. to give (s.o.) an award/a prize; to award (a film etc.) a prize.

Pranke ['praŋkə], f -/-n (lion's etc.) paw.

Präpar|at [prɛpa'ra:t], n -(e)s/-e Med: Ch: preparation. ◆**p~ieren**, v.tr. to prepare (a material, work, oneself etc.).

Präposition [prɛpozitsi'o:n], f -/-en preposition.

Prärie [prɛ'ri:], f -/-n prairie.

Präsens ['prɛ:zəns], n -/-'sentia present (tense). ◆**p~t** [prɛ'zɛnt], adj. present; etwas p. haben, to have sth. at one's fingertips. ◆**p~tieren**, v.tr. to present.

Präservativ [prɛzɛrva'ti:f], n -s/-e condom.

Präsid|ent [prɛzi'dɛnt], m -en/-en president. ◆**P~entschaft**, f -/no pl presidency. ◆**P~entschaftskandidat**, m presidential candidate. ◆**P~ium** [-'zi:diʊm], n -s/-ien 1. (a) (Amt) chairmanship; (b) (Gremium) management committee. 2. (Polizeip.) (police) headquarters.

prasseln ['prasəln], v.i. (haben) (a) (Feuer) to crackle; (b) (Regen usw.) to drum, patter.

prassen ['prasən], v.i. (haben) to indulge oneself, F: live it up.

Präteritum [prɛ'te:ritʊm], n -s/-ta preterite, past tense.

Präventiv- [prɛvɛn'ti:f-], comb.fm. preventive (measure etc.).

Praxis ['praksis], f -/-xen 1. no pl practice; (Erfahrung) experience; in der P., in (actual) practice. 2. (a) (doctor's/lawyer's) practice; (b) (Raum) (doctor's) surgery, consulting room, N.Am: doctor's office; (lawyer's) office.

Präzedenzfall [prɛtse'dɛntsfal], m precedent.

präzis(e) [prɛ'tsi:s (-izə)], adj. precise. ◆**P~ion** [-izi'o:n], f -/no pl precision. ◆**P~ions-**, comb.fm. precision (work, instrument etc.).

predig|en ['pre:digən], v.tr. & i. (haben) to preach. ◆**P~er**, m -s/- preacher. ◆**P~t**, f -/-en (a) Ecc: sermon; (b) F: lecture.

Preis [prais]. I. m -es/-e 1. price; zum halben P., at half-price; um jeden/keinen P., at any/not at any price. 2. (bei Wettbewerb usw.) prize. II. **P~-**, 'p~-, comb.fm. 1. price (rise, limit, list etc.). 2. prize (question etc.). ◆**P~ausschreiben**, n (prize) competition. ◆**P~gabe**, f -/no pl abandonment, betrayal. ◆**p~geben**, v.tr.sep.irr.35 to abandon, give up (s.o., sth.), Mil: surrender (ground); (verraten) to betray (a secret). ◆**p~gekrönt**, adj. prizewinning. ◆**p~günstig**, adj. attractively priced; reasonable; adv. at a

low price. ◆**'P~lage**, f price range. ◆**'p~lich**, adj. in price; adv. with regard to price. ◆**'P~nachlaß**, m discount. ◆**P~richter**, m competition judge; adjudicator. ◆**P~schild**, n price tag. ◆**'P~senkung**, f price concession/reduction. ◆**'P~sturz**, m slump in prices. ◆**'P~träger**, m prizewinner. ◆**P~verleihung**, f prize ceremony. ◆**'p~wert**, adj. reasonably priced.

Preiselbeere ['praizəlbe:rə], f -/-n F: cranberry.

preisen ['praizən], v.tr. Lit: to praise, extol (s.o., sth.).

prekär [pre'kɛ:r], adj. awkward; precarious.

Prell|bock ['prɛlbɔk], m Rail: buffer. ◆**'p~en**, v.tr. to hit (sth.) hard; F: die Zeche p., to leave without paying (the bill). ◆**P~ung**, f -/-en contusion; bruise.

Premier|e [prəmi'e:rə], f -/-n first performance; Th: first night. ◆**P~minister** [prəmi'e:-], m Prime Minister.

Press|e ['prɛsə]. I. f -/-n press. II. **P~e-**, comb.fm. press (report, ticket, conference etc.); (freedom, etc.) of the press. ◆**'P~eagentur**, f press/news agency. ◆**'p~en**, v.tr. to press (s.o., sth., flowers, oneself etc.); to squeeze (s.o.'s hand, a lemon etc.); (stopfen) to cram (sth.) (in etwas acc, into sth.). ◆**p~ieren** [-'si:rən], v.i. (haben) South G: etc: to be urgent.

Preßluft ['prɛslʊft], f compressed air. ◆**P~bohrer**, m pneumatic drill.

Prestige [prɛs'ti:ʒə], n -s/no pl prestige.

Preuße ['prɔysə], m -n/-n Prussian. ◆**P~en**. Pr.n.n -s. Prussia. ◆**'p~isch**, adj. Prussian.

prickeln ['prikəln], v.i. (haben) (a) to tingle; Fig: **p~de Spannung**, electric tension; (b) (Sekt) to bubble.

Priester ['pri:stər], m -s/- priest.

prima ['pri:ma], adj. (a) prime (quality); first-class (goods etc.); (b) F: firstrate; tip-top (condition); **das ist p.!** that's great! **mir geht's p.**, I'm fine. II. **P.**, f -/ **Primen** Sch: top form (in a Gymnasium).

primär [pri'mɛ:r], adj. primary (stage etc.); prime (importance).

Primel ['pri:məl], f -/-n primrose; (Gartenp.) primula.

primitiv [primi'ti:f], adj. (a) primitive (conditions, culture, art etc.); (b) (sehr einfach) simple, basic; rough and ready (method etc.).

Prinz [prints], m -en/-en prince. ◆**P~essin** [-'tsɛsin], f -/-nen princess.

Prinzip [prin'tsi:p], n -s/-ien principle; aus P., on principle; im P., in principle; **ein Mann mit P~ien**, a man of principles. ◆**p~iell** [-ipi'ɛl], adj. fundamental (difference, importance etc.); (question etc.) of principle; adv. to agree etc.) in principle (grundsätzlich) on principle.

Priorität [priori'tɛːt], f /-en priority.

Prise ['priːzə], f /-n pinch (of salt, tobacco etc.).

privat [pri'vaːt]. I. *adj.* private (entrance, life etc.); personal (opinion, reasons etc.); **das sage ich dir ganz p.,** I am telling you this in confidence; **j-n p. sprechen,** to speak to s.o. privately/in private. II. P~, *comb.fm.* private (matter, detective, property, life, patient, lessons etc.); personal (matter, use etc.). ◆P~**adresse,** f private/home address. ◆P~**gespräch,** n Tel: personal/private call. ◆p~**isieren** [-ati'ziːrən], *v.tr.* to transfer (a business etc.) to private ownership. ◆P~**recht,** n civil law.

Privileg [privi'leːk], n -s/-ien privilege. ◆p~**iert** [-le'giːrt], *adj.* privileged.

pro [proː]. I. *prep.* + *acc* per; **p. Jahr,** per annum; **einmal p. Tag,** once a day; **5 Mark p. Stück,** 5 marks each. II. *n* **das P. und Kontra,** the pros and cons.

Probe ['proːbə]. I. f /-n 1. (a) (*Versuch*) test; **auf/zur P.,** on trial; (*Angestellter*) on probation; (*Waren*) on approval; **j-n, etwas auf die P. stellen,** to put s.o., sth. to the test; **die P. bei einer Rechnung machen,** to check a calculation; (b) Th: Mus: rehearsal. 2. (*Muster*) sample; Med: specimen (of blood etc.). II. 'P~, *comb.fm.* test (recording, drilling, flight etc.); trial (order, shot, lesson etc.); probationary (year etc.); *esp.* Sp: practice (jump, throw etc.). ◆'p~**exemplar,** n specimen copy. ◆'p~**fahren,** *v.irr.26 v.tr.* to test drive (a car). ◆'P~**fahrt,** f test/trial run. ◆'p~**n,** *v.tr. & i.* (*haben*) to rehearse (a concert, play etc.). ◆'p~**weise,** *adv.* as a test; **j-n p. anstellen,** to employ s.o. on a trial basis. ◆'P~**zeit,** f trial/probationary period.

probier|en [pro'biːrən], *v.tr.* (a) to try, sample (a dish, drink etc.); (b) (*ausprobieren*) to try (out) (sth.).

Problem [pro'bleːm], n -s/-e problem. ◆P~**atik** [-e'maːtik], f /-no *pl* (range of) problems. ◆p~**atisch,** *adj.* problematic; (*zweifelhaft*) doubtful. ◆p~**los,** *adj.* problem-free; *adv.* without any problems.

Produkt [pro'dukt], n -(e)s/-e (*also Fig:*) product; **landwirtschaftliche P~e,** farm produce. ◆P~**ion** [-duktsi'oːn], f /-en production; (*Menge*) output. ◆P~**i'ons-,** *comb.fm.* production (costs, manager, process etc.); (volume etc.) of production. ◆p~**iv** [-'tiːf], *adj.* productive; prolific (writer). ◆P~**ivität** [-tivi'tɛːt], f /-no *pl* productivity.

Produ|zent [produ'tsɛnt], m -en/-en producer; *Ind:* manufacturer. ◆p~**zieren,** *v.tr.* to produce (goods, food etc.).

profan [pro'faːn], *adj.* (*alltäglich*) mundane.

professionell [profesio'nɛl], *adj.* professional.

Professor [pro'fɛsɔr], m -s/-en 1. profes-

sor (**für Biologie,** of biology). 2. *Aus:* Gymnasium teacher.

Profi ['proːfi]. I. m -s/-s Sp: F: pro. II. 'P~, *comb.fm.* professional (boxer etc.).

Profil [pro'fiːl], n -s/-e (a) profile; (*Umriß*) outline; (b) Aut: tread (of a tyre). ◆p~**ieren** [-i'liːrən], *v.tr.* (Pers.) **sich p.,** to make one's mark.

Profit [pro'fiːt], m -(e)s/-e profit. ◆p~**ieren** [-i'tiːrən], *v.i.* (*haben*) to (make a) profit, benefit (**bei/von** + *dat,* from).

Prognose [pro'gnoːzə], f /-n forecast.

Programm [pro'gram]. I. n -s/-e programme; N.Am: program; (a) plan, schedule; agenda (of a conference); **auf dem P. stehen,** to be on the agenda/planned; (b) (*Sender*) Rad: station; TV: channel; (c) (*gedrucktes P.*) programme; N.Am: playbill; (d) Com: (*Angebot*) range (of furniture etc.). II. P~, *comb.fm.* programme (control etc.); (change etc.) of programme. ◆p~**gemäß,** *adj.* according to plan/schedule. ◆p~**ieren** [-a'miːrən], *v.tr.* to set up a schedule for (a visitor etc.), programme (a computer etc.). ◆P~**ierer,** m -s/- Data-pr: programmer.

progressiv [progrɛ'siːf], *adj.* progressive.

Projekt [pro'jɛkt], n -(e)s/-e project. ◆P~**or** [-'jɛktɔr], m -s/-en projector.

projizieren [proji'tsiːrən], *v.tr.* to project (slides).

Proklа|mation [proklamatsi'oːn], f /-en proclamation. ◆p~**mieren,** *v.tr.* to proclaim (sth.).

Prokurist [proku'rist], m -en/-en *Jur:* attorney; Com: *approx.* company secretary.

Prolet [pro'leːt], m -en/-en Pej: F: prole, peasant. ◆P~**ariat** [-letari'aːt], n -(e)s/no *pl* proletariat. ◆P~**arier** [-'taːriər], m -s/- proletarian. ◆p~**arisch** [-'taːriʃ], *adj.* proletarian.

Prolog [pro'loːk], m -(e)s/-e prologue.

Promen|ade [promə'naːdə], f /-n promenade. ◆P~**adenmischung,** f Hum: mongrel.

Promille [pro'milə], n -(s)/- thousandth part (*esp.* of alcohol in the blood).

prominent [promi'nɛnt], *adj.* prominent. ◆P~**z,** f /-en die P., the top people.

promovieren [promo'viːrən], *v.i.* (*haben*) to receive one's doctor's degree.

prompt [prɔmpt], *adj.* prompt; F: *adv.* (*sogleich*) promptly, immediately.

Pronomen [pro'noːmən], n -s/- & -**mina** pronoun.

Propa|ganda [propa'ganda], f /-no *pl* Pol: *etc:* propaganda; Com: publicity. ◆p~**ieren** [-'giːrən], *v.tr.* to propagate (an idea).

Propeller [pro'pɛlər], m -s/- propeller.

Prophet [pro'feːt], m -en/-en prophet. ◆p~**ezeien** [-fe'tsaiən], *v.tr.* to prophesy, predict (sth.).

Proportion [proportsi'oːn], f /-en proportion. ◆p~**al** [-io'naːl], *adj.* propor-

tional; proportionate (**zu** + dat, to).
Prosa ['proːza], f -/no pl prose.
prosit ['proːzit], int. cheers! your health!
p. Neujahr! happy New Year!
Prospekt [pro'spɛkt], m -(e)s/-e
(Broschüre) leaflet; brochure.
prost [proːst], int. = **prosit**.
Prostata ['prɔstata], f -/-ae prostate
(gland).
Prostitu|ierte [prɔstitu'iːrtə], f decl. as
adj. prostitute. ◆**P~tion** [-'tsioːn], f
-/no pl prostitution.
Protest [pro'tɛst], m -(e)s/-e protest.
◆**P~ant(in)** [-ɛs'tant(in)], m -en/-en (f
-/-nen) Ecc: Protestant. ◆**p~antisch**,
adj. Protestant. ◆**p~ieren** [-'tiːrən],
v.i. (haben) to protest.
Prothese [pro'teːzə], f -/-n artificial limb;
(Zahnp.) dentures.
Protokoll [proto'kɔl], n -s/-e 1. Adm: etc:
written record; minutes (of a meeting
etc.); **etwas zu P. geben/nehmen**, to
make/take down a statement. 2. (Zeremoniell) (diplomatic) protocol. ◆**p~ieren**
[-'kiːrən], v. 1. v.i. (haben) to keep the
minutes. 2. v.tr. to enter (sth.) in the
minutes/records; to record (a statement
etc.).
protzen ['prɔtsən], v.i. (haben) F: to
show off; Brit: to swank (**mit** + dat,
about). ◆**p~ig**, adj. F: ostentatious;
flashy (car etc.).
Proviant [provi'ant], m -s/no pl provisions; (food) supplies.
Provinz [pro'vints], f -/-en province; Pej:
die hinterste P., the back of beyond.
◆**p~iell**, adj. usu. Pej: provincial.
Provision [provizi'oːn], f -/-en Com: commission.
provisorisch [provi'zoːriʃ], adj provisional.
provozieren [provo'tsiːrən], v.tr. to provoke (s.o., an attack). ◆**p~d**, adj. provocative.
Prozedur [protse'duːr], f -/-en (lengthy/
complicated) procedure.
Prozent [pro'tsɛnt], n -(e)s/-e per cent.
◆**P~satz**, m percentage (**an** + dat, of).
◆**p~u'al**, adj. percentage (share etc.);
adv. in percentage terms.
Prozeß [pro'tsɛs], m -sses/-sse 1. (Vorgang) process; (b) Jur: (Verfahren) trial;
den P. gewinnen/verlieren, to win/lose a
case; F: **mit etwas** dat **kurzen P. machen**, to make short work of sth.
◆**P~kosten**, pl Jur: legal costs.
prozessieren [protse'siːrən], v.i. (haben)
to be engaged in litigation (**mit**
j-m, with s.o.).
Prozession [protsɛsi'oːn], f -/-en esp. Ecc:
procession.
prüde ['pryːdə], adj. (in der Moral usw.)
straitlaced. ◆**P~rie** [-'riː], f -/no pl prudish-
ness; prudery.
Prüf- ['pryːf-], comb.fm. Tchn: test (report, load, procedure etc.); testing (apparatus, process etc.). ◆**'p~en**, v.tr. (a)

to test (s.o., s.o.'s knowledge, skill etc.)
(**auf etwas** acc, for sth.); Sch: Univ: to
examine (a candidate); (b) (**auf Richtigkeit
hin**) to check (a bill etc.); (c) (untersuchen)
to examine (a document etc.); to investigate (a case etc.); **p~ender Blick**,
searching glance. ◆**'P~er**, m -s/- Sch:
etc: examiner. ◆**'P~ling**, m -s/-e examin-
nee; examination candidate. ◆**'P~-
stein**, m Fig: touchstone. ◆**'P~ung**, f
-/-en (a) test; Sch: etc: (formell) examination, F: exam; **eine P. ablegen/machen**,
to take an examination/exam; (b) checking; (c) examination; investigation.
◆**P~ungsausschuß**, m/**P~ungskom-
mission**, f board of examiners.
Prügel ['pryːɡəl], m -s/- 1. (Knüppel)
club, cudgel. 2. pl beating; **eine gehörige
Tracht P.**, a sound thrashing. ◆**P~ei**
[-'lai], f -/-en brawl(ing); fight(ing).
◆**p~n**, v.tr. to beat, thrash (s.o.); **sich
p.**, to (have a) fight. ◆**'P~strafe**, f corporal punishment.
Prunk [pruŋk], m -(e)s/no pl (great) splendour; sumptuousness; (beim Zeremoniell)
pomp, spectacle. ◆**'P~stück**, n showpiece. ◆**'p~voll**, adj. sumptuous; flamboyant (style etc.).
Psalm [psalm], m -s/-en psalm.
Pseudonym [psɔydo'nyːm], n -s/-e pseudonym.
Psych|iater [psyçi'aːtər], m -s/- psychia-
trist. ◆**'p~isch**, adj. psychological
(illness, reasons etc.); **unter p~ischem
Druck**, under emotional stress; **p.
bedingt**, of a psychological nature.
Psycho- ['psyço-], comb.fm. psy-
cho(therapy etc.). ◆**P~ana'lyse**, f psychoanalysis. ◆**P~loge** [-'loːɡə], m -n/-
n psychologist. ◆**P~logie** [-lo'ɡiː], f -/
no pl psychology. ◆**p~logisch**
[-'loːɡiʃ], adj. psychological.
Pubertät [puber'tɛːt], f -/no pl puberty.
publik [pu'bliːk], adj. public; **etwas p.
machen**, to announce (sth.) (publicly).
◆**P~ikum** [pu'bliːkum], n -s/no pl (a)
(Zuhörer) audience; (Zuschauer) spectators. ◆**p~izieren** [-bli'tsiːrən], v.tr. to
publish (an article etc.).
Pudding ['pudiŋ], m -s/-e & -s Cu: approx. blancmange.
Pudel ['puːdəl], m -s/- poodle.
◆**'p~wohl**, adv. F: **sich p. fühlen**, to
feel on top of the world.
Puder ['puːdər], m & n -s/- powder.
◆**'P~dose**, f powder compact.
◆**'p~n**, v.tr. to powder (a baby, oneself
etc.). ◆**'P~zucker**, m icing/N.Am:
powdered sugar.
Puff [puf]. 1. m -s/-e & -e F: (Schlag)
punch; jab, poke. 2. m -s/-s pouffe,
N.Am: hassock; (Wäschep.) padded
linen-basket. 3. m & n -s/-s P: brothel.
◆**'P~er**, m -s/- Rail: buffer.
◆**'P~erzone**, f Pol: buffer-zone.
◆**'P~reis**, m puffed rice.
Pull|over [pu'loːvər], m -s/-/F: **Pulli**

['pulj], *m* -s/-s pullover, sweater.
◆**P~under** [-'lundər], *m* -s/- sleeveless
sweater, *Brit:* slipover.

Puls [puls], *m* -es/-e pulse; **j-m den P.
fühlen**, to take s.o.'s pulse. ◆**p~ieren**
[-'zi:rən], *v.i.* (*haben*) to pulsate, throb.
◆**P~schlag**, *m* pulse (beat).

Pult [pult], *n* -(e)s/-e desk.

Pulver ['pulfər, -vər], *n* -s/- powder;
(*Schießp.*) gunpowder. ◆**p~isieren**
[-i'zi:rən], *v.tr.* to grind (sth.) to powder.
◆**P~kaffee**, *m* instant coffee.
◆**P~schnee**, *m* powdery snow.

pummelig ['puməliç], *adj.* F: chubby,
tubby (person).

Pump [pump], *m* -(e)s/-e F: credit; **auf
P.**, on credit/*Brit:* F: tick. ◆**P~e**, *f* -/
-n 1. pump. 2. F: (*Herz*) ticker.
◆**p~en**, *v.tr.&i.* (*haben*) (a) to pump
(air, water etc.); (b) F: **sich dat Geld
usw. bei j-m p.**, to borrow money etc.
from s.o.

Punkt [puŋkt], *m* -(e)s/-e 1. spot; *Gram:*
full stop, *N.Am:* period; **P. auf dem i**,
dot on the i; **P. drei Uhr**, on the stroke
of three: 2. (*Thema*) subject, topic; point
(in a debate etc.); **P. auf die Tagesord-
nung**, item on the agenda. 3. *Sp: etc:*
point. ◆**P~sieger**, *m* winner on
points. ◆**P~zahl**, *f* number of points.

pünktlich ['pyŋktliç], *adj.* punctual;
prompt (payment etc.); **p. ankommen**, to
arrive on time. ◆**P~keit**, *f* -/no pl
punctuality.

Punsch [punʃ], *m* -(e)s/-e (hot) punch.

Pupille [pu'pilə], *f* -/-n pupil (of the eye).

Puppe ['pupə], *f* -/-n 1. doll; (*Marionette*)

puppet, marionette. 2. (*von Insekt*) chrysalis; cocoon (of a silkworm). ◆**P~n-,
comb.fm.** doll's (house, face, furniture
etc.). ◆**P~spieler**, *m* puppeteer.

pur [pu:r], *adj.* pure (gold etc.); sheer
(nonsense etc.); **Whisky p.**, neat whisky.

Püree [py're:], *n* -s/-s *Cu:* purée, mash;
(*Kartoffelp.*) mashed potatoes.

Purpur ['purpur], *m* -s/*no pl* (royal) purple; (*sattes P~rot*) crimson. ◆**'p~rot**,
adj. purple; (*sattrot*) crimson.

Purzel|baum ['purtsəlbaum], *m* somer-
sault. ◆**p~n**, *v.i.* (*sein*) to (take a)
tumble.

Puste ['pu:stə], *f* -/no pl F: puff; **außer
P.**, puffed, out of breath. ◆**P~blume**,
f F: dandelion-clock. ◆**p~n**, *v.i.* (*haben*) F: to blow (**in +** *acc*, into).

Put|e ['pu:tə], *f* -/-n turkey (hen).
◆**P~er**, *m* -s/- turkey (cock).
◆**p~er'rot**, *adj.* crimson, scarlet.

Putz [puts], *m* -es/no pl 1. (*an Wand*) plas-
ter(work). 2. **in vollem P.**, all dressed/F:
dolled up. ◆**p~en**, *v.tr.* (*saubermachen*)
to clean, (*polieren*) polish (sth.); **sich dat
die Zähne p.**, to brush one's teeth.
◆**P~frau**, *f* cleaner, *Brit:* charwoman.
◆**p~ig**, *adj.* cute. ◆**P~lappen**, *m*
cleaning rag; floorcloth.

Puzzlespiel ['pazəlʃpi:l], *n* jigsaw puzzle.

Pyjama [py'dʒa:ma], *m* -s/-s (pair of) pyjamas.

Pyramide [pyra'mi:də], *f* -/-n pyramid.

Pyrenäen [pyre'nɛ:ən], *Pr.n.pl* **die P.**,
the Pyrenees.

Pythonschlange ['py:tɔnʃlaŋə], *f*
python.

Q

Q, q [ku:], *n* -/- (the letter) Q, q.

quabb(e)lig ['kvab(ə)liç], *adj.* jelly-like;
flabby (flesh).

Quacksalber ['kvaksalbər], *m* -s/- quack
(doctor).

Quader ['kva:dər], *m* -s/- 1. *Arch:* stone
block, ashlar. 2. *Math:* rectangular solid.

Quadrat [kva'dra:t], I. *n* -(e)s/-e *Mth:
etc:* square; **4 im Q.**, 4 squared. II. **Q~-,
comb.fm.** square (metre, kilometre, number etc.).

quaken ['kva:kən], *v.i.* (*haben*) (*Frosch*)
to croak; (*Ente*) to quack.

quäken ['kvɛ:kən], *v.i.* (*haben*) to
screech, (*Baby usw.*) squawk.

Qual [kva:l], *f* -en agony; (*seelisch*) torment; **Q~en**, sufferings; (*seelisch*) anguish; **sie machte ihm das Leben zur
Q.**, she made his life a misery.
◆**'q~voll**, *adj.* agonizing; excruciating
(pain).

quäl|en ['kvɛ:lən], *v.tr.* to torment, (*fol-
tern*) torture (s.o., an animal); (*plagen*) to
plague, pester (s.o.); **Tiere q.**, to be
cruel to animals; **sich q.**, (*sich abmühen*)

to struggle. ◆**'q~end**, *adj.* agonizing;
excruciating (pain, thirst etc.); nagging
(though, doubt). ◆**Q~e'rei**, *f* -en
(*Schmerz*) agony; torment; (*Folter*) torture; (*Grausamkeit*) cruelty. ◆**'Q~-
geist**, *m* F: (*Kind usw.*) pest; perfect
nuisance.

Qualifi|kation [kvalifikatsi'o:n], *f* -/-en
qualification; (*Fähigkeit*) ability.
◆**Q~kati'ons-, comb.fm.** *Sp:* qualifying
(round, game etc.). ◆**q~'zieren**, *v.tr.
& i.* to qualify; **sich q.**, to become qualified.

Quali|tät [kvali'tɛ:t], *f* -/-en quality; (*von*)
schlechter Q., of poor quality.
◆**Q~'täts-, comb.fm.** (a) quality (control etc.); (b) high-quality (wine etc.).
◆**'Q~tätsware**, *f* (high-) quality product.

Qualle ['kvalə], *f* -/-n jellyfish.

Qualm ['kvalm], *m* -(e)s/no pl (clouds of)
dense smoke. ◆**'q~en**, *v.* 1. *v.i.* (*haben*) (a) (*Feuer usw.*) to give off clouds of
smoke. 2. *v.tr.* to puff away at (a cigarette etc.). ◆**q~ig**, *adj.* smoky; (room

etc.) full of smoke.

Quanten ['kvantən], *npl Hum: (Füße)* (great big) hooves. ◆'**Q~theorie,** *f Ph:* quantum theory.

Quant|ität [kvanti'tɛːt], *f -/-en* quantity. ◆**q~itativ** [-ta'tiːf] *adj.* quantitative; *adv.* in quantity/numbers. ◆'**Q~um,** *n -s/Quanten* amount; *(Anteil)* share (an + *dat,* of).

Quarantäne [karan'tɛːnə], *f -/-n* quarantine.

Quark [kvark], *m -s/no pl* **1.** *Cu:* curd cheese. **2.** *F:* **red keinen Q.!** don't talk rot!

Quart a ['kvarta], *f -/-ten Sch: approx.* third form/year; *Aus:* fourth form/year. ◆'**Q~al** [kvar'taːl], *n -s/-e* quarter (of a year). ◆**Q~ssäufer,** *m F:* habitual drinker, dipso.

Quarte ['kvartə], *f -/-n Mus:* fourth.

Quartett [kvar'tɛt], *n -(e)s/-e* **1.** *Mus:* quartet. **2.** *(Spiel)* Happy Families.

Quartier [kvar'tiːr], *n -s/-e (also Mil:)* quarters; accommodation.

Quarz [kvaːrts], *m -es/-e* quartz.

quasi ['kvaːzi], *adv.* more or less, as good as.

Quassel|ei [kvasə'lai], *f -/-en F:* (endless) jabbering, chatter ◆'**q~n,** *v.i. (haben) F:* to jabber (away), chatter.

Quaste ['kvastə], *f -/-n Cl: etc:* tassel.

Quatsch [kvatʃ], *m -(e)s/no pl F:* (a) *(dummes Gerede)* rubbish, nonsense; (b) *(dumme Späße)* tomfoolery; **Q. machen,** to fool around; (c) *(Torheit)* **mach keinen Q.!** don't do anything stupid! ◆'**q~en,** *v.tr. & i. (haben) F:* (a) *(Unsinn)* q., to talk rubbish/nonsense; (b) *(schwatzen)* to chat, *(abfällig)* gossip, *(dauernd)* chatter (away). ◆'**Q~kopf,** *m F:* windbag.

Quecksilber ['kvɛksilbər], *n -s/no pl* mercury; quicksilver.

Quell|e ['kvɛlə], *f -/-n* source; **heiße Q~n,** hot springs; **aus sicherer/zuverlässiger Q.,** from a reliable source/on good authority; *F:* **an der Q. sitzen,** to be on the spot; to have direct access (to information, goods etc.). ◆'**q~en,** *v.i.irr. (sein)* (a) *(Wasser usw.)* to well up; *(Rauch)* to billow (out); *(Tränen, Fig: Menschen usw.)* to stream, pour; (b) *(Holz, Cu: Reis usw.)* to swell. ◆'**Q~wasser,** *n* spring water.

quengelig ['kvɛŋəliç], *adj. F:* whining. ◆'**q~eln,** *v.i. (haben)* to whine.

quer [kveːr], **I.** *adv.* crosswise; *(rechtwinklig)* at right angles; **das Kleid ist q. gestreift,** the dress has horizontal stripes; **q. auf dem Bett liegen,** to lie across the bed; **der Anhänger stand q. auf der Straße,** the trailer was at an angle across the road. **II.** *comb.fm.* ◆'**Q~,** 'q~,** *comb.fm.* transverse (axis, motion, flute, *Cl:* pleat

etc.); horizontal (stripe etc.). ◆'**Q~balken,** *m* crossbeam; (door, window) transom; *Fb: etc:* crossbar. ◆'**Q~e,** *f -/no pl F:* **j-m in die Q. kommen,** to get in s.o.'s way, *(Auto usw.)* block s.o.'s path; *(hindern)* to thwart s.o. ◆**Q~feld·ein,** *comb.fm.* cross-country (race, course etc.). ◆**q~gestreift,** *adj.* with transverse/horizontal stripes. ◆'**Q~kopf,** *m F:* awkward customer. ◆'**q~köpfig,** *adj. F:* perverse. ◆'**Q~latte,** *f Fb:* crossbar. ◆'**Q~schiff,** *m Ecc.Arch:* transept. ◆'**Q~schnitt,** *m* **1.** *Mth: etc:* (cross-)section; *Tchn:* transverse/cross section. **2.** *(Auswahl)* cross-section (of the population etc.). ◆'**q~schnittsgelähmt,** *adj.* paraplegic. ◆'**Q~straße,** *f* road/street crossing another; *(Abzweigung)* turning. ◆'**Q~verbindung,** *f* direct link/connection (between two places/*Fig:* two facts).

Querulant [kveru'lant], *m -en/-en* (eternal) moaner.

quetsch|en ['kvɛtʃən], *v.tr. F:* (a) to squeeze (s.o., sth., *Cu:* lemons etc.); (b) *(verletzen)* to bruise (sth.), *(zerquetschen)* crush (a foot etc.). ◆'**Q~ung** *-/-en/* '**Q~wunde,** *f* bruise.

quicklebendig [kvikle'bɛndiç], *adj.* sprightly; *F:* full of beans.

quieken ['kviːkən], *v.i. (haben)* to squeal, *(Maus)* squeak.

quietsch|en ['kviːtʃən], *v.i. (haben) (Tür usw.)* to squeak; *(Reifen usw.)* to screech; *(Kind)* **vor Vergnügen q.,** to squeal with delight. ◆'**q~ver'gnügt,** *adj. F:* cheery, chirpy.

Quinta ['kvinta], *f -/-ten Sch: approx.* second form/year; *Aus:* third form/year.

Quint|e ['kvintə], *f -/-en (-/-n) Mus:* fifth. ◆'**q~essenz,** *f -/-en* quintessence. ◆**Q~ett** [kvin'tɛt], *n -(e)s/-e Mus:* quintet.

Quirl [kvirl], *m -(e)s/-e* **1.** *Cu:* (star-shaped) beater. **2.** *Fig:* (Kind) live wire.

quitt [kvit], *pred.adj. F:* **mit j-m q. sein,** to be quits/even with s.o.

Quitte ['kvitə], *f -/-n* quince.

quitt|ieren [kvi'tiːrən], *v.tr. Com:* to give a receipt (for a bill etc.); to acknowledge (receipt of a delivery etc.); **eine Bemerkung mit einem Lächeln q.,** to greet/answer a remark with a smile. ◆'**Q~ung,** *f -/-en* **1.** *Com: etc:* receipt *(über eine Summe, for a sum).* **2.** *Fig:* **das ist die Q. für dein schlechtes Benehmen,** that's what you get for your bad behaviour.

Quiz [kvis], *n -/-* quiz.

Quote ['kvoːtə], *f -/-n* quota.

Quotient [kvotsi'ɛnt], *m -en/-en* quotient.

R

R, r [er], *n -/-* (the letter) R, r.
Rabatt [ra'bat], *m. -(e)s/-e Com:* discount.
◆**R~marke,** *f Com:* trading stamp.
Rabatte [ra'batə], *f -/-n* (flower) border.
Rabe ['rɑːbə], *m -n/-n Orn:* raven.
◆**R~nmutter,** *f* cruel mother.
◆**r~n'schwarz,** *adj.* jet-black.
rabiat [rabi'aːt], *adj. (aggressiv)* violent;
(roh) brutal; *(rücksichtslos)* ruthless.
Rach|e ['raxə], *f -/no pl* revenge, *Lit:* ven-
geance (an j-m für etwas *acc,* on s.o. for
sth.); *(Vergeltung)* retaliation.
◆**R~eakt,** *m* act of revenge.
◆**r~süchtig,** *adj. Lit:* vengeful.
Rachen ['raxən], *m -s/- Anat: (Kehle)*
throat; *Med:* pharynx.
rächen ['rɛçən], *v.tr. (a) (Pers.)* to avenge
(s.o., sth.); **sich r.,** to take one's revenge, *F:* get one's own back (**an j-m,** on
s.o.); *(b) (Sache)* **sich r.,** to take its toll;
dein Leichtsinn wird sich noch r., you
will have to pay the (penalty) for your
recklessness.
Rachitis [ra'xiːtis], *f -/no pl* rickets.
Rad [raːt]. **I.** *n -(e)s/-er* **1.** wheel; *(Zahnrad)* gear. **2.** *F: (Fahrrad)* bike. **II.** '**R~-,
comb.fm. 1.** wheel (rim etc.). **2.** cycle
(race etc.); cycling (tour etc.). ◆**r~eln,**
v.i. (sein) F: to ride a bike, *(irgendwohin)*
go by bike. ◆**r~fahren,** *v.i.sep.irr.
(sein)* to cycle; **er kann r.,** he can ride a
bicycle. ◆**R~fahrer,** *m* cyclist.
◆**R~kappe,** *f Aut:* hub cap. ◆**R~l-
ler,** *m -s/-* cyclist. ◆**R~rennbahn,** *f*
cycle racing track. ◆**R~sport,** *m* cycling. ◆**R~weg,** *m* cycle track.
Radar ['raːdar, ra'daːr], *m & n -s/no pl*
radar. ◆**R~anlage,** *f* radar installation.
Radau [ra'dau], *m -s/no pl F:* row, racket.
Rädchen ['rɛːtçən], *n -s/-* small wheel.
radebrechen ['raːdəbrɛçən], *v.tr.irr.* to
mangle (a language); **Englisch/Deutsch
r.,** to speak broken English/German.
Rädelsführer ['rɛːdəlsfyːrər], *m* ringleader.
Räderwerk ['rɛːdərverk], *n* mechanism,
F: works (of a clock etc.); *Fig:* machinery (of justice etc.).
radier|en [ra'diːrən], *v.tr.&i. (haben) (a)*
to erase, rub (sth.) out; *(b) Art:* to etch (a
landscape etc.). ◆**R~gummi,** *m & n*
(india-) rubber, eraser. ◆**R~ung,** *f
-/-en* etching.
Radieschen [ra'diːsçən], *n -s/-* (red) radish.
radikal [radi'kaːl], *adj.* radical (change,
Pol: idea, etc.); drastic (action, measures
etc.); ruthless (pursuit of aims etc.); *Pol:*
ein R~er, a radical; **etwas r. ausrotten,**
to eradicate sth. completely.
Radio ['raːdio], *n -s/-s* radio; **im R.,** on
the radio. ◆**r~aktiv** [-ak'tiːf], *adj.*
radioactive. ◆**R~aktivität** [-tivi'tɛːt], *f*

radioactivity. ◆'**R~apparat,** *m* radio
(set).
Radium ['raːdium], *n -s/no pl* radium.
Radius ['raːdius], *m -/-ien* radius.
raffen ['rafən], *v.tr. (a)* to snatch, grab
(sth.) up; *(zusammen)* to amass (money); *(b) Cl:* to
gather (material etc.).
Raffin|ade [rafi'naːdə], *f -/-n* refined su-
gar. ◆**R~erie** [-ə'riː], *f -/-n* refinery.
◆**R~esse** [-fi'nɛsə], *f -/-n* **1.** *(Schlauheit)* cunning; ingenuity (of a plan etc.).
2. refinement. ◆**r~iert,** *adj.* **1.** refined
(sugar etc.). **2.** *(a) (schlau)* crafty, cunning; *(b) (fein)* subtle (flavour etc.); sophisticated (system etc.); refined (taste).
ragen ['raːgən], *v.i. (haben)* to rise, tower
(up).
Rahm [raːm], *m -(e)s/no pl South G:*
cream. ◆'**R~käse,** *m -s/no pl* cream
cheese.
rahmen ['raːmən]. **I.** *v.tr.* to frame (a
picture etc.). **II. R.,** *m -s/- (a)* frame;
Aut: chassis (frame); *(b) Fig:* framework
(of a story etc.); *(Kulisse)* setting; *(Text-
zusammenhang)* context; **im R. bleiben,**
to keep within bounds; **aus dem R. fallen,** to be out of place/*(nicht normal)* out
of the ordinary.
Rakete [ra'keːtə], *f -/-n* rocket; *Mil:
(Geschoß)* missile. ◆**R~nwerfer,** *m
Mil:* rocket launcher.
rammen ['ramən], *v.tr.* to ram (a car,
ship etc.).
Rampe ['rampə], *f -/-n* **1.** ramp. **2.**
(Startr.) launching pad. ◆**R~nlicht,** *n
Th:* footlights; *Fig:* **im R. stehen,** to be
in the limelight.
ramponier|en [rampo'niːrən], *v.tr. F:* to
knock about (furniture etc.). ◆**r~t,** *adj.
F:* battered; *(ruiniert)* ruined.
Ramsch [ramʃ], *m -(e)s/-e F: Pej:* junk.
◆**R~laden,** *m Pej:* junk shop.
ran [ran], *adv. F:* = **heran.**
Rand [rant]. **I.** *m -(e)s/-er* edge; *(a)* rim
(of a plate etc.); lip (of a cup etc.); brim
(of a hat, glass etc.); *(b)* **am R~(e) der
Stadt,** on the outskirts of the town; *(c)*
brink (of a precipice, *Fig:* of ruin etc.);
(d) margin (of a page); *Fig:* **etwas am
R~e erwähnen,** to mention sth. in passing; *(e) F:* **außer R. und Band,** *(Kinder)*
out of hand. **II. R~-,** *comb.fm.* peripheral (zone, *Fig:* problem, figure etc.).
◆**R~bemerkung,** *f* marginal note;
(nebenbei) incidental remark. ◆**R~er-
scheinung,** *f* item/aspect of peripheral
importance. ◆'**r~los,** *adj.* rimless.
◆**r~voll,** *adj.* full (to the brim).
randalieren [randa'liːrən], *v.i. (haben)* to
rampage; *(lärmen)* make a racket.
Rang [raŋ], *m -(e)s/-e* **1.** rank; **alles, was
R. und Namen hat,** everybody who is
anybody. **2.** *(Qualität)* quality. **3.** *Sp:*

place. 4. *Th:* **erster/zweiter R.**, dress/upper circle, *N.Am:* first/second balcony. ◆'**R~ältest(r)**, *m & f decl. as adj.* senior officer. ◆'**R~ordnung**, *f* order of precedence.

Rangier|bahnhof [raŋ'ʒiːrbɑːnhoːf], *m Rail:* marshalling yard, *N.Am:* switchyard. ◆**r~en** [-'ʒiːrən], *v. 1. v.i.* (*haben*) to rank, be classed. 2. *v.tr. Rail:* to shunt, *N.Am:* switch (a train etc.). ◆**R~gleis**, *n* siding.

Rank|e ['raŋkə], *f -/-n Bot:* tendril. ◆'**r~en**, *v.refl. & v.i.* (*haben*) (*Pflanze*) to shoot, send out tendrils; (**sich**) **r.**, to climb.

Ränke ['rɛŋkə], *pl.* **R. schmieden**, to scheme, hatch plots.

Ranzen ['rantsən], *m -s/- 1. Sch:* satchel. 2. *P:* (*Bauch*) paunch, belly.

ranzig ['rantsiç], *adj.* rancid.

rapid(e) [ra'piːt(-idə)], *adj.* rapid.

Raps [raps], *m -es/-e* rape.

rar [raːr], *adj.* scarce (commodity etc.); rare (stamp); *F:* **er macht sich r.**, he rarely puts in an appearance. ◆**R~ität** [rari'tɛːt], *f -/-en* rarity.

rasant [ra'zant], *adj. F:* (*schnell*) meteoric (development etc.); *Aut:* very fast, hairy (car, driving); (*im Aussehen*) racy (car, styling); **r~es Tempo**, breakneck speed.

rasch [raʃ], *adj.* quick (movement etc.); swift (decisions, action etc.).

rascheln ['raʃəln], *v.i.* (*haben*) to rustle.

rase|n[1] ['raːzən], *v.i.* (*a*) (*haben*) (*Pers., Fig: Sturm usw.*) to rage; (*Verrückter*) to rave; (*b*) (*sein*) (*Auto, Fahrer*) to tear/ (*Pers.*) dash along. ◆'**r~nd**, *adj.* (*a*) (*schnell*) very fast; (*heftig*) raging (fury etc.); (*b*) raving (madman etc.); (*c*) (*heftig*) violent (jealousy, pain etc.); **r~nde Kopfschmerzen**, a splitting headache; **r~nder Beifall**, tumultuous applause. ◆'**r~rei**, *f -/no pl* (*a*) raving (*Wut*) rage, fury; (*b*) mad rush/*Aut:* speed.

Rasen[2] ['raːzən]. **I.** *m -s/- coll.* grass; (*also* **R~fläche** *f*) lawn. **II.** '**R~**, *comb.fm.* lawn (fertilizer etc.); (*piece* etc.) of grass. ◆'**R~mäher**, *m* lawn mower.

Rasier|er [ra'ziːr-, *comb.fm.* shaving (mirror, cream, soap etc.). ◆**R~apparat**, *m* razor; **elektrischer R.**, electric shaver. ◆**r~en** [ra'ziːrən], *v.tr.* to shave (s.o., one's chin etc.); **sich r.**, to shave. ◆**R~klinge**, *f* razor blade. ◆**R~messer**, *n* cut-throat razor. ◆**R~pinsel**, *m* shaving brush; ◆**R~wasser**, *n* after-shave (lotion).

Rass|e ['rasə], *f -/-n* (*a*) (*Menschenr.*) (human) race; (*b*) *Z:* breed. ◆**R~ehund**, *m* pedigree dog. ◆'**R~en-**, *comb.fm.* racial (discrimination, characteristic etc.). ◆**R~enhaß**, *m*, racial/race hatred. ◆'**R~entrennung** *f* racial segregation. ◆'**R~epferd**, *n* thoroughbred (horse). ◆'**r~ig**, *adj.* vivacious (woman etc.); fiery (wine, temperament etc.).

◆'**r~isch**, *adj.* racial. ◆**R~ismus** [-'sismus], *m -/no pl* racism, racialism. ◆**R~ist** [-'sist], *m -en/-en* racist. ◆**r~istisch**, *adj.* racist.

Rassel ['rasəl], *f -/-n* rattle. ◆'**r~n**, *v.i.* (*haben*) to rattle (**mit etwas** *dat*, sth.); (*Ketten*) to clank.

Rast [rast], *f -/-en* rest. ◆'**R~e**, *f -/-n Tchn:* catch. ◆'**r~en**, *v.i.* (*haben*) to (take a) rest, have a break (on a journey). ◆'**R~haus**, *n* roadhouse, esp. motorway restaurant. ◆'**r~los**, *adj.* ceaseless; (*unermüdlich*) tireless; (*unruhig*) restless. ◆'**R~stätte**, *f* service area.

Rasur [ra'zuːr], *f -/-en* shave.

Rat [raːt], *m -(e)s/-e* 1. (*pl* **R~schläge**) (piece of) advice, **mit j-m zu R. gehen**, to consult s.o.; **j-n/ein Buch zu R~e ziehen**, to consult s.o./a book. 2. *Adm:* (*Gremium*) council; (*R~smitglied*) councillor. ◆**R~geber**, *m -s/-* adviser. ◆**R~haus**, *n* town hall. ◆'**r~los**, *adj.* helpless (look etc.). ◆'**R~losigkeit**, *f -/no pl* helplessness, perplexity. ◆'**r~sam**, *pred. adj.* advisable; (*weise*) prudent. ◆'**R~schlag**, *m* piece of advice. ◆'**R~sherr**, *m* councillor.

Rate ['raːtə], *f -/-n Com:* instalment. ◆'**r~nweise**, *adv.* in/by instalments.

ratifizier|en [ratifi'tsiːrən], *v.tr.* to ratify (a treaty etc.). ◆**R~ung**, *f -/-en* ratification.

Ration [ratsi'oːn], *f -/-en* ration. ◆**r~ieren** [ratsio'niːrən], *v.tr.* to ration (sth.).

rational [ratsio'naːl], *adj.* rational. ◆**r~isieren** [-nali'ziːrən], *v.tr.* to rationalize.

rationell [ratsio'nɛl], *adj.* efficient; (*wirtschaftlich*) economical.

Rätsel ['rɛːtsəl], *n -s/-* (*a*) (*Wortr.*) riddle; (*b*) (*Geheimnis*) mystery; **es ist mir ein R., wie ...**, it is a mystery to me how ... ◆'**r~haft**, *adj.* baffling (problem); enigmatic (person), mysterious (circumstances etc.).

Ratte ['ratə], *f -/-n* rat. ◆**R~ngift**, *n* rat poison.

rattern ['ratərn], *v.i.* (*a*) (*haben*) (*Maschinengewehr usw.*) to chatter; (*b*) (*sein*) (*Auto usw.*) to rattle, clatter (along).

Raub [raup], *m -(e)s/no pl* 1. robbery. 2. (*Beute*) loot, booty. ◆'**R~bau**, *m* overexploitation (of natural resources); **mit seiner Gesundheit R. treiben**, to abuse one's health. ◆**r~en** ['raubən], *v.tr.* (*a*) **j-m etwas r.**, to rob/deprive s.o. of sth.; (*b*) (*entführen*) to kidnap (a child etc.). ◆'**r~gierig**, *adj.* rapacious. ◆'**R~mord**, *m* robbery with murder. ◆'**R~mörder**, *m* robber and murderer.

◆**R~tier**, *n* beast of prey. ◆**R~überfall**, *m* (bank etc.) raid; holdup. ◆**R~vogel**, *m* bird of prey.

Räuber ['rɔybər], *m* -s/- robber. ◆**R~bande**, *f* gang of thieves/robbers.

Rauch [raux]. I. *m* -(e)s/*no pl* smoke; (*Dämpfe*) fumes. II. '**R~**, *comb.fm.* (*a*) smoke (bomb, cartridge, ring, signal etc.); (cloud etc.) of smoke; (*b*) (*geräuchert*) smoked (meat, glass etc.); (*c*) (*für Raucher*) smoking (room, tobacco etc.); smoker's (table etc.). ◆'**r~en.** I. *v.tr. & i.* (*haben*) to smoke. II. **R.**, *n -s/ no pl* smoking; **R. verboten!** no smoking. ◆**R~er**, *m -s/-* 1. (*Pers.*) smoker. 2. *F: Rail:* (*also* **R~erabteil** *n*) smoking compartment. ◆'**R~**: smoker. ◆'**r~ig**, *adj.* smoky. ◆'**R~verbot** *n* smoking ban.

Räucher- ['rɔyçər], *comb.fm.* smoked (eel, ham etc.). ◆'**R~hering**, *m* smoked herring; kipper. ◆'**R~kerze**, *f* aromatic candle. ◆'**r~n**, *v.tr.* to smoke (fish, meat etc.).

räudig ['rɔydiç], *adj.* mangy.

rauf [rauf], *adv. F:* = **herauf/hinauf**.

Raufbold ['raufbɔlt], *m -(e)s/-e Pej:* ruffian. ◆'**r~en,** *v.* 1. *v.tr. Fig:* **sich** *dat* **die Haare r.,** to tear one's hair. 2. *v.refl. & i.* (*haben*) (**sich**) **r.,** to fight, scrap. ◆**R~e'rei,** *f -/-en* fight, scrap; (*Handgemenge*) brawl. ◆'**r~lustig**, *adj.* pugnacious.

rauh [rau]. I. *adj.* 1. (*a*) rough (surface, hands etc.); coarse (cloth etc.); harsh (texture, sound); (*b*) (*heiser*) hoarse (voice). 2. (*unwirtlich*) (*a*) rough (sea); rugged (landscape etc.); (*b*) raw (climate); biting (wind); severe (winter, weather etc.). 3. (*grob*) uncouth (manners, person etc.). 4. **in** *n*~en **Mengen,** in vast quantities. ◆'**R~fasertapete,** *f* rough-textured wallpaper. ◆'**R~haardackel,** *m* wire-haired dachshund. ◆'**r~haarig**, *adj.* wire-haired (dog). ◆'**R~reif**, *m* hoar frost.

Raum [raum]. I. *m -(e)s/-e* (*a*) space; (*b*) (*Gebiet*) *Geog:* area; (*c*) (*Zimmer*) room. II. '**R~**, *comb.fm.* 1. space (flight, station etc.). 2. room, interior (acoustics etc.). ◆**R~fahrt,** *f* space travel. ◆**R~inhalt,** *m* volume, cubic capacity. ◆'**R~maß,** *n* cubic measure. ◆'**R~pflegerin,** *f* (woman) cleaner. ◆'**R~schiff,** *n* spaceship. ◆'**R~sonde,** *f* space probe.

räumen ['rɔymən], *v.tr.* (*a*) to vacate (a house, one's seat etc.); to evacuate (a building, *Mil:* position etc.); (*b*) (*wegr.*) to clear away (snow, rubble, dishes etc.); (*c*) (*leeren*) to clear (a space, road, table etc.). ◆'**r~lich**, *adj.* spatial; three-dimensional (effect etc.). ◆'**R~ung,** *f -/-en* (*a*) *also Com:* clearance; (*b*) vacating; evacuation. ◆'**R~ungsbefehl** *m* eviction order. ◆'**R~ungsverkauf,** *m Com:* clearance sale.

raunen ['raunən], *v.tr. & i.* (*haben*) to murmur (sth.).

Raupe ['raupə], *f -/-n* 1. caterpillar. 2. tracked vehicle, *esp.* bulldozer. ◆'**R~nkette,** *f* (caterpillar) track. ◆'**R~nschlepper,** *m* caterpillar tractor.

raus [raus], *adv. F:* = **heraus/hinaus.** ◆'**r~schmeißen,** *v.tr.sep.irr.4* (*a*) to chuck (s.o., sth.) out; (*b*) (*entlassen*) to fire (s.o.).

Rausch [rauʃ], *m -(e)s/-e* intoxication; **einen R. haben,** to be drunk. ◆'**r~en.** I. *v.i.* (*haben*) to make a rushing sound; (*leise*) to rustle, (*Bach*) murmur; *Rad: etc:* to hiss; **r~der Beifall,** enthusiastic applause; *Fig:* **r~de Feste,** exhilarating parties; (*sein*) to rush (along). II. **R.,** *n -s/no pl* rushing (sound); (*leise*) rustle; *Rad: etc:* hiss. ◆'**R~gift,** *n* (narcotic) drug; *F:* dope. ◆'**R~gifthändler** *m* drug pedlar/pusher. ◆'**r~giftsüchtig**, *adj.* drug-addicted; **ein R~giftsüchtiger,** a drug addict.

räuspern ['rɔyspərn], *v.refl.* **sich r.,** to clear one's throat.

Raute ['rautə], *f -/-n* diamond (shape); *Mth:* rhombus.

Razzia ['ratsia], *f -/-ien* (police) raid, swoop.

Reagenzglas [rea'gɛntsglɑːs], *n* test tube. ◆**r~ieren** [-'giːrən], *v.i.* (*haben*) to react, (*Pers.*) respond (**auf etwas** *acc,* to sth.).

Reaktion [reaktsi'oːn], *f -/-en* reaction, response (**auf etwas** *acc,* to sth.). ◆**r~är** [-o'nɛːr], *adj.* reactionary. ◆**R~sfähigkeit,** *f -/-en* ability to react (quickly); reactions.

Reaktor [re'?aktɔr], *m -s/-en* reactor.

real [re'aːl]. I. *adj.* real, actual (value etc.). II. **R~**, *comb.fm.* real (income, wages, value etc.). ◆**r~i'sieren,** *v.tr.* (*a*) to realize (hopes), put (a plan, ideas etc.) into practice; (*b*) (*einsehen*) to realize (one's mistakes etc.). ◆**R~ismus** [-a'lismus], *m -/no pl* realism. ◆**R~ist,** *m -en/-en* realist. ◆**r~istisch,** *adj.* realistic. ◆**R~i'tät,** *f -/-en* reality. ◆**R~schule,** *f* modern secondary school.

Rebe ['reːbə], *f -/-n* 1. vine-shoot. 2. (*Weinstock*) vine.

Rebhuhn ['rɛphuːn], *n* partridge.

Rebell(in) [re'bɛl(in)], *m -en/-en* (*f -/-nen*) rebel. ◆**r~ieren** [-li'rən], *v.i.* (*haben*) to rebel. ◆**R~ion** [-li'oːn], *f -/-en* rebellion. ◆**r~isch** [-'bɛliʃ], *adj.* rebellious.

Rechen ['rɛçən], *m -s/-* rake.

Rechen|aufgabe [rɛçən'aufgɑːbə], *f* arithmetical problem. ◆'**R~maschine,** *f* calculator. ◆'**R~schaft,** *f -/no pl* account; **von j-m R. fordern,** to demand an explanation from s.o.; **j-n zur R. ziehen,** to call s.o. to account. ◆'**R~zentrum,** *n* computer centre.

rechn|en ['rɛçnən], *v.* 1. *v.i.* (*haben*) (*a*) to calculate; **gut r. können,** to be good at figures; **vom 1. April an gerechnet,** taking April 1st as a starting point; (b) (haushalten) **mit jedem Pfennig** r., to count every penny; (c) (erwarten) **r. mit** + dat, to be prepared for (sth.); (d) (sich verlassen) **auf ihn kann man nicht** r., one cannot rely on him. 2. v.tr. (a) (schätzen) to estimate, allow (sth.); **grob gerechnet,** at a rough estimate; (b) (zählen) to count, include (s.o., sth.) (**zu** + dat, among); **das Trinkgeld nicht gerechnet,** not counting the tip. ◆**R~ar,** m -s/- (Gerät) calculator; Data-pr: computer. ◆**R~ung,** f -/-en 1. calculation. 2. bill; Com: invoice; **das geht auf meine R.,** this is on me; Fig: j-m, **einer Sache R. tragen,** to take s.o., sth. into account. ◆**R~ungsjahr,** n financial year. ◆**R~ungsprüfer,** m auditor.

recht[1] [reçt], adj. right; (a) (richtig) nach dem R~en sehen, to see that all is well; (völlig) **r. haben,** to be (perfectly) right; **ich muß dir r. geben,** I am forced to admit you are right; **r. so!** that's the idea! that's right! **das ist mir r.,** that's all right with me; (b) (gerecht) fair; just; **es ist nicht r. von dir,** it's wrong/unfair of you; **es geschieht dir r.,** it serves you right; (c) (echt) real (pity etc.); **ich habe keine** r~e **Lust,** I don't really feel like it; **r. traurig,** really sad; **r. gut,** pretty good.

Recht[2], n -(e)s/-e 1. no pl law; **R. und Ordnung,** law and order; **R. sprechen,** to administer justice; Fig: **im R. sein,** to be in the right; **mit R.,** rightly, justifiably. 2. (Anspruch usw.) right (**auf** + acc, to). ◆**r~fertigen,** v.tr. to justify (s.o., oneself, sth.). ◆**R~fertigung,** f -/-en justification. ◆**r~haberisch,** adj. opinionated (person). ◆**r~lich,** adj. legal (question, success etc.); legitimate (claim etc.). ◆**r~mäßig,** adj. legal, lawful (practice etc.); legitimate (claim etc.); rightful (owner). ◆**R~s-,** comb.fm. (a) legal (matter, question, claim, protection etc.); (principle etc.) of law; (b) (sense etc.) of justice. ◆**R~sanwalt,** m lawyer; Brit: solicitor; N.Am: attorney. ◆**R~sbrecher,** m law-breaker. ◆**r~schaffen,** adj. upright, decent; (ehrlich) honest. ◆**R~schreib-,** comb.fm. spelling (reform, mistake etc.). ◆**R~schreibung,** f orthography, (correct) spelling. ◆**r~skräftig,** adj. (decision etc.) with the force of law. ◆**R~sprechung,** f -/-en jurisdiction, administration of justice. ◆**R~streit,** m legal action, lawsuit. ◆**r~swidrig,** adj. illegal, against the law. ◆**r~zeitig,** adj. in time; timely (intervention etc.); r. **ankommen/abfahren,** to arrive/leave on time.

recht|e(r, s) ['reçtə(r,s)], adj. (a) right (arm, shoe, angle etc.); **zu meiner R~en,** on my right; (b) Pol: rightwing (politician, views etc.); right (wing). ◆**R~eck,** n rectangle. ◆**r~eckig,** adj. rectangular. ◆**r~s,** adv. (a) on the

right; **von/nach** r., from/to the right; **die erste Straße** r., the first on the right; r. **abbiegen,** to turn right; (b) Pol: **r. stehen**/F: **sein,** to be right-wing. ◆**R~saußen,** m Fb: outside right. ◆**r~sherum,** adv. (round) to the right, clockwise. ◆**r~sradikal,** adj. with radical/extreme rightwing views. ◆**R~sverkehr,** m righthand rule of the road. ◆**r~wink(e)lig,** adj. right-angled

Reck [rɛk], n -(e)s/-e horizontal bar. ◆**r~en,** v.tr. to crane (one's neck); **sich r.,** to stretch oneself.

Redakt|eur(in) [redakt'ø:r(in)], m -s/-e (f -/-nen) editor. ◆**R~ion** [-'tsi̯oːn], f -/-en 1. no pl editing. 2. (a) editorial staff; (b) (Abteilung) editorial department.

Rede ['reːdə], f -/-n a) speech; b) **wovon ist die R.?** what are you talking about? what is it all about? **davon kann keine R. sein,** that is out of the question; (c) Gram: **direkte/indirekte** R., direct/indirect speech; (d) **j-n zur R. stellen,** to demand an explanation from s.o. ◆**r~gewandt,** adj. eloquent. ◆**r~n** ['reːdən], v. 1. v.i. (haben) to talk, speak; (eine Rede halten) to make a speech; **du hast gut** r., it's easy for you to talk; **er läßt mit sich** r., he is open to persuasion. 2. v.tr. to talk (nonsense etc.), speak (the truth etc.); **er redete kein Wort,** he didn't say a word. ◆**R~nsart,** f saying. ◆**R~wendung,** f phrase.

redlich ['reːtliç], adj. honest, sincere; (rechtschaffen) upright.

Redner ['reːdnər], m -s/- speaker.

redselig ['reːtzeːliç], adj. talkative. ◆**R~keit,** f -/no pl talkativeness.

reduzier|en [redu'tsiːrən], v.tr. to reduce (prices, staff etc.). ◆**R~ung,** f -/-en reduction.

Reede ['reːdə], f -/-n Nau: roads. ◆**R~r,** m -s/- shipowner. ◆**R~rei,** f -/-en shipping company.

reell [re'ɛl], adj. 1. honest, straight (deal etc.); r~e **Preise,** reasonable/realistic prices. 2. (wirklich) real, genuine (chance etc.).

Refer|at [refe'raːt], n -(e)s/-e 1. (Aufsatz) paper; (Bericht) report. 2. Adm: (Abteilung) department. ◆**R~ent(in)** [-'rɛnt(in)], m -en/-en (f -/-nen) 1. author of a paper; (Redner) speaker. 2. (Berater) consultant. ◆**r~ieren** [-'riːrən], v.i. (haben) to report, read a paper (**über** + acc, on).

reflektieren [reflɛk'tiːrən], v. 1. v.tr. to reflect (sth.). 2. v.i. (haben) to meditate (**über** + acc, on).

Reflex [re'flɛks], m -es/-e reflex. ◆**r~iv** [-ɛ'ksiːf], adj. Gram: reflexive.

Reform [re'fɔrm], f -/-en reform. ◆**R~ati'on,** f -/-en Reformation. ◆**R~haus,** n health-food shop. ◆**r~ieren** [-'miːrən], v.tr. to reform (sth.).

Refrain [rə'frɛ:], m -s/-s refrain.

Regal [re'ga:l], n -s/-e (set of) shelves; (Bücher-) bookcase.

Regatta [re'gata], f -/-ten regatta.

rege ['re:gə], adj. (a) active (person etc.); busy (traffic, trade etc.); brisk (business, demand etc.); (b) (lebhaft) lively (person, imagination, discussion etc.).

Regel ['re:gəl], f -/-n 1. rule; (scientific) law; (Vorschrift) regulation; **in der R.**, as a rule. 2. Med: period (of a woman). ◆'r~los, adj. disorderly. ◆'r~mäßig, adj. regular; symmetrical (features). ◆'R~mäßigkeit, f -/no pl regularity; symmetry, orderliness. ◆r~n ['re:gəln], v.tr. (a) to regulate (speed, temperature etc.), control (volume, prices, traffic etc.); (b) to put (affairs etc.) in order; (erledigen) to deal with, sort out (a matter). ◆'r~recht, adj. downright, F: out-and-out. ◆'R~ung, f -/-en 1. regulation, control. 2. settlement; (Lösung) solution. 3. (Beschluß) ruling. ◆'r~widrig, adj. against the rules/regulations; irregular (conduct, procedure etc.).

regen[1] ['re:gən], v.tr. (a) to move (one's arm etc.); (b) **sich r.**, to move, (Gefühle) stir.

Regen[2], m -s/no pl rain. ◆'R~bogen, m rainbow. ◆'R~bogenhaut, f iris of the eye). ◆'R~fälle, mpl rainfall. ◆'R~guß, m downpour. ◆'R~mantel, m raincoat. ◆'r~reich, adj. wet, rainy. ◆'R~schauer, m shower of rain. ◆'R~schirm m umbrella. ◆'R~tag, m rainy day. ◆'R~tropfen, m raindrop. ◆'R~wetter, n rain/wet weather. ◆'R~wurm, m earthworm. ◆'R~zeit, f rainy season.

Regent [re'gɛnt], m -en/-en ruler, sovereign. ◆'R~schaft, f -/-en regency.

Regie [re'ʒi:], f -/-n Cin: TV: direction; Th: Rad: production; **R. führen**, to direct/produce; **unter staatlicher R.**, under state control.

regier|en [re'gi:rən], v. 1. v.tr. to rule, govern (a country). 2. v.i. (haben) to rule (über + acc, over). ◆R~ung, f -/-en government; (Tätigkeit) rule; reign (of a king etc.). ◆R~ungs-, r~ungs-, comb.fm. government (official, circles, spokesman etc.); (change etc.) of government. ◆R~ungschef, m head of government.

Regime [re'ʒi:m], n -s/- [-mə] regime.

Regiment [regi'mɛnt], n 1. -(e)s/-er Mil: regiment. 2. -(e)s/-e (Herrschaft) rule.

Region [regi'o:n], f -/-en region; Lit: sphere.

Regisseur [reʒi'sø:r], m -s/-e Cin: TV: director; Th: Rad: producer.

Regist|er [re'gistər], n -s/- 1. (alphabetisch) index. 2. Adm: register (of births etc.). ◆r~rieren [-'tri:rən], v.tr. (a) to register (a birth etc.); (eintragen) to enter

(sth.) (in + dat, in); (b) Tchn: (Meßgerät) to record (temperature etc.); (c) (zur Kenntnis nehmen) to note (sth.). ◆R~rierkasse, f cash register.

Reglement [reglə'mã:], n -s/-s regulations, rules.

Regler ['re:glər], m -s/- regulator; (Hebel) lever.

reglos ['re:klo:s], adj. motionless.

regnen ['re:gnən], v.impers. to rain. ◆'r~nerisch, adj. rainy.

regsam ['re:kza:m], adj. active, lively.

regul|är [regu'lɛ:r], adj. (vorschriftsmäßig) according to the regulations, regular (troops etc.); proper (time, price etc.). ◆r~ieren [-'i:rən], v.tr. to regulate (temperature, a watch etc.), control (speed, prices etc.); (einstellen) to adjust (volume, mixture etc.).

Regung ['re:guŋ], f -/-en Lit: 1. (Bewegung) movement; stirring (of leaves, air etc.). 2. (Gefühl) feeling; (Anwandlung) impulse. ◆r~slos, adj. motionless.

Reh [re:], n -(e)s/-e roe (deer). 2. Cu: (roe) venison. ◆'R~bock, m roebuck. ◆'R~kitz, n fawn. ◆'R~rücken, m Cu: saddle of venison.

rehabilitieren [rehabili'ti:rən], v.tr. to rehabilitate (s.o.).

Reib|e ['raibə], f -/-n Cu: grater. ◆'r~en, v. irr. 1. v.tr. (a) to rub (sth.); (b) Cu: to grate (nuts, cheese etc.). 2. v.i. (haben) (Riemen usw.) to rub, chafe. ◆'r~e'rei, f -/-en usu. pl. friction. ◆'R~fläche, f striking surface (of a matchbox). ◆'R~ung, f -/-en rubbing, Tchn: Fig: friction. ◆'R~ungs-, comb.fm. frictional (electricity, heat etc.). ◆'r~ungslos, adj. smooth (flow etc.); Tchn: frictionless; adv. r~ verlaufen, to go off without a hitch.

reich[1] [raiç], adj. (a) rich; **die R~en**, the rich/wealthy; (b) **r~e Ausstattung**, lavish/opulent furnishings (of a house); **r. geschmückt**, richly decorated; (c) (r~haltig) copious (selection, knowledge etc.); lavish (meal); plentiful (harvest etc.). ◆'r~haltig, adj. extensive, (umfassend) comprehensive; substantial (meal etc.); rich (fauna etc.). ◆'r~lich, adj. ample (means, meal etc.); abundant (supply etc.); liberal (helping, tip etc.); **das ist etwas r.**, that's a bit too much; **r. spät**, jolly late. ◆'R~tum, m -s/-er wealth, esp. Fig: richness (an + dat, in); affluence (of s.o., society etc.).

Reich[2], n -(e)s/-e (a) Hist: empire; **das Dritte R.**, the Third Reich; (b) Fig: realm (of the arts etc.); the world (of dreams etc.); **das R. der Tiere**, the animal kingdom.

reich|en ['raiçən], v. 1. v.tr. to hand (s.o.) sth. **j-m etwas r.**, to hand/pass s.o. sth. 2. v.i. (haben) (a) to reach, extend; (b) (genügen) to be enough/sufficient; (Vorrat usw.) to last; F: **jetzt reicht es mir aber!** I've had enough! that's the end! ◆'R~weite, f reach (of s.o.); range (of vision, *Mil:* a gun, *Av:* an aircraft etc.).

reif [raif], *adj.* ripe (fruit, cheese etc.); mature (wine, *Fig:* personage, views etc.). ◆**'R~e**, *f /no pl* ripeness; *esp. Fig:* maturity. ◆**'r~en1**, *v.i.* (*sein*) to ripen; (*Wein, Fig: Pers. usw.*) to mature. ◆**'R~eprüfung**, *f* school-leaving examination. ◆**'R~ezeugnis**, *n* school-leaving certificate.

Reif2, *m* -(e)s/*no pl* hoarfrost.

Reifen2 [raifən]. **I.** *m* -s/- 1. (barrel etc.) hoop. 2. *Aut: etc* tyre, *N.Am:* tire 3. (*Schmuck*) bangle. **II.** **'R~**, *comb.fm.* tyre, *N.Am:* tire (pressure, change etc.). ◆**'R~panne**, *f* flat tyre, puncture.

Reihe ['raiə], *f* -/-n 1. row; *Fig:* in der Verräter in den eigenen R~n, a traitor in one's own ranks. 2. (*a*) **ich bin an der R./komme an die R.**, it is my turn; (*der R. nach*, one after another, in turn; (*b*) (*Folge*) (*also Mth:*) series; **seit einer R. von Jahren**, for a number of years. ◆**'r~n**, *v.tr.* (*a*) to string (beads etc.); (*b*) **ein Fest reihte sich ans andere**, one celebration followed another. ◆**'R~nfolge**, *f* order; sequence. ◆**'R~nhaus**, *n* terraced house, *N.Am:* row house. ◆**'r~nweise**, *adv.* in rows; *F:* in great numbers.

Reiher ['raiər], *m* -s/- *Orn:* heron.

Reim [raim], *m* -(e)s/-e rhyme. ◆**'r~en**, *v.* 1. *v.tr. & i.* (*haben*) to rhyme (words etc.). 2. *v.refl.* 'klein' reimt sich auf 'fein', 'klein' rhymes with 'fein'.

rein1 [rain], *adv. F:* = **herein/hinein.** ◆**'R~fall**, *m F:* (*Pleite*) washout, flop; (*Enttäuschung*) let-down. ◆**'r~legen**, *v.tr.sep. F:* to take (s.o.) for a ride.

rein2. **I.** *adj.* 1. (*a*) pure (gold, silk, race etc.); unadulterated (wine etc.); *Com:* r~er Gewinn, net/clear profit; (*b*) (*nichts als*) sheer (imagination, coincidence etc.); (*bloß*) mere (thought etc.); *F:* (*völlig*) utter (madness etc.); r. private Angelegenheit, purely/strictly personal matter. 2. (*a*) (*sauber*) clean (clothes, air etc.); *Fig:* clear (conscience etc.); pure (voice etc.); (*b*) **etwas ins r~e schreiben**, to make a fair copy of sth.; **ein Mißverständnis usw. ins r~e bringen**, to clear up a misunderstanding etc. **II.** **'R~**, **'r~**, *comb.fm. Com: etc:* net (amount, weight, profit etc.). ◆**'R~haltung**, *f /no pl* keeping (a room etc.) clean. ◆**'R~heit**, *f /no pl* 1. purity. 2. (*Sauberkeit*) cleanness. ◆**'r~igen**, *v.tr.* to clean (sth.); to cleanse (skin, blood etc.). ◆**'R~igung**, *f /-en* 1. cleaning; purification. 2. (*chemische*) **R.**, (dry) cleaner's. ◆**'R~igungscreme**, *f* cleansing cream. ◆**'r~lich**, *adj.* (immaculately) clean; spotless (clothes, house etc.). ◆**'R~lichkeit**, *f /no pl* cleanness. ◆**'R~(e)machefrau**, *f* cleaner, *Brit:* charwoman. ◆**'R~rassig**, *adj.* 1. pedigree, purebred (dog etc.); thor-

oughbred (horse etc.). 2. pure-blooded (person). ◆**'R~schrift**, *f* fair copy. ◆**'r~waschen**, *v.tr.sep.irr.108 F:* to whitewash (s.o.).

Reis [rais], *m* -es/-e rice. ◆**'R~korn**, *n* grain of rice.

Reise ['raizə]. **I.** *f* -/-n journey; (*auch hin und zurück*) trip; **R. zur See**, sea voyage; **auf R~n sein**, to be away (on a trip). **II.** **'R~**, *comb.fm.* (*a*) travelling (companion, expenses etc.); (*b*) (*Urlaubs-*) holiday (traffic, weather etc.). ◆**'R~andenken**, *n* souvenir. ◆**'R~bericht**, *m* travelogue. ◆**'R~büro**, *n* travel agency/agent's. ◆**'r~fähig**, *adj.* fit to travel. ◆**'R~führer**, *m* (*a*) (*Buch*) guide book; (*b*) (*Pers.*) (travel) guide. ◆**'R~gepäck**, *n* (hand) luggage, *esp. N.Am:* baggage. ◆**'R~gesellschaft**, *f* party of tourists. ◆**'R~leiter(in)**, *m(f)* tour leader. ◆**'r~n**, *v.i.* (*sein*) to travel; **nach Italien, in den Urlaub usw. r.**, to go to Italy, on holiday etc. ◆**'R~nde(r)**, *m & f decl. as adj.* traveller. ◆**'R~paß**, *n* passport. ◆**'R~route**, *f* itinerary. ◆**'R~scheck**, *m* traveller's cheque. ◆**'R~tasche**, *f* travelling bag. ◆**'R~ziel**, *n* destination.

Reisig [raiziç], *n* -s/*no pl* brushwood.

Reiß|aus [rais'ʔaus], *m F:* **R. nehmen**, to scram, hop it. ◆**'R~brett**, *n* drawing board. ◆**'r~en** ['raisən], *v.irr.* 1. *v.tr.* (*a*) to tear (sth.); *Fig:* **die Macht usw. an sich r.**, to seize power etc.; **j-n zu Boden r.**, to pull/drag s.o. to the ground; (*b*) *F:* **sich um etwas acc r.**, to be dead keen on (doing) sth; (*c*) *Witze r.*, to crack jokes. 2. *v.i.* (*a*) (*sein*) (*Papier, Stoff*) to tear, rip; (*Seil usw.*) to break, snap; (*b*) (*haben*) **an etwas dat r.**, to pull on/at sth. ◆**'r~end**, *adj.* torrential (stream, river etc.); searing (pain); *Com:* r~en Absatz finden, to sell like hot cakes. ◆**'R~er**, *m* -s/- *Pej:* (*Roman, Film usw.*) cheap thriller. ◆**'r~erisch**, *adj.* sensational (advertising etc.). ◆**'R~leine**, *f* (parachute) ripcord. ◆**'R~verschluß**, *m* zip(-fastener), *N.Am:* zipper. ◆**'R~zwecke**, *f* drawing pin, *N.Am:* thumb tack.

Reit- ['rait-], *comb.fm.* riding (instructor, whip, school, boot etc.); **R~hose** *f* riding breeches. ◆**'r~en**, *v.irr. v.tr. & i.* (*sein, occ. haben*) to ride. ◆**'R~er**, *m* -s/- (*Pers.*) rider, horseman; *Mil:* cavalryman. ◆**R~e'rei**, *f /-en Mil:* cavalry. ◆**'R~erin**, *f /-nen* horsewoman. ◆**'R~pferd**, *n* saddle-horse. ◆**'R~turnier**, *n* horse show.

Reiz [raits], *m* -es/-e 1. *Psy:* etc stimulus. 2. (*a*) attraction; lure (*des Unbekannten*, of the unknown); (*b*) *usu.pl* **R~e**, charms. ◆**'r~bar**, *adj.* irritable, touchy. ◆**'R~barkeit**, *f /no pl* irritability; sensitiveness. ◆**'r~en**, *v.tr.* to excite, rouse (s.o.); to arouse (curiosity, desire etc.); to stimulate (feelings); **einen Hund r.**, to tease a dog; **der Rauch reizt die Augen**, smoke irritates the eyes; (b) *(anziehen)* to attract (s.o.); **das reizt mich nicht**, that doesn't appeal to me; (c) *also v.i. (haben) (im Skat)* to bid (sth.). ◆'r~end, *adj.* charming; enchanting (girl etc.). ◆**R~husten**, *m* dry (tickling) cough. ◆'r~los, *adj.* unattractive. ◆'R~ung, *f -/-en Med:* irritation. ◆'r~voll, *adj.* delightful; charming; r~volle Aufgabe, attractive/fascinating task. ◆'R~wäsche, *f* sexy underwear.

rekeln ['re:kəln], *v.refl.* **sich r.**, to stretch; *(im Stuhl usw.)* to sprawl.

Reklam|ation [reklamatsi'o:n], *f -/-en* complaint. ◆**R~e** [re'kla:mə]. **I.** *f -/-n* **1.** *(Werbung)* advertising, publicity; **R. für etwas** *acc* **machen**, to advertise/ promote/*F:* push sth. **2.** *F: (Anzeige)* advertisement, *(Plakat)* poster; *Rad: TV:* commercial. **II.** **R~e~**, *comb.fm.* publicity (film, purpose etc.); advertising (sign etc.). ◆**R~esendung**, *f Rad: TV:* commercial. ◆**r~ieren** [-a'mi:rən], *v. 1. v.tr.* (a) *Com: etc:* to complain about (a lost parcel, damaged goods etc.); (b) to reclaim, claim back (money etc.). **2.** *v.i. (haben)* to complain; to protest.

rekonstruieren [rekɔnstru'i:rən], *v.tr.* to reconstruct (sth.).

Rekord [re'kɔrt]. **I.** *m -(e)s/-e Sp: etc:* record. **II.** **R~-**, *comb.fm.* record (attendance, attempt, time etc.). ◆**R~halter**, *m* record holder.

Rekrut [re'kru:t], *m -en/-en Mil:* recruit. ◆**r~ieren** [-u'ti:rən], *v.tr.* to recruit (staff, *A:* soldiers).

Rektor ['rektɔr], *m -s/-en* [-'to:rən] (a) *(Universität)* rector; *Brit:* vice-chancellor, *N.Am:* president; (b) *Sch:* headmaster, *N.Am:* principal.

Relais [rə'le:], *n -/-* [-'le:(s)] relay.

relativ [rela'ti:f], *adj.* relative; **es geht mir r. gut**, I am fairly/reasonably well. ◆**R~ität** [-ivi'tɛːt], *f -/no pl* relativity.

Relief [reli'ɛf], *n -s/-e & -s* relief.

Religi|on [religi'o:n], *f -/-en* religion; *(Konfession)* denomination, *(Schulfach)* religious education, R.E. ◆**R~ons-**, *comb.fm.* religious (freedom, war etc.); (history etc.) of religion. ◆**R~onsstunde**, *f* R.E./scripture lesson. ◆**r~ös** [-gi'ø:s], *adj.* religious.

Reling ['re:liŋ], *f -/-s & -e* (deck) rail.

Remis [rə'mi:], *n -/- & -en* drawn game, draw.

Rempel|ei [rɛmpə'lai], *f -/-en Fb:* jostling; *Fb:* pushing. ◆**r~n**, *v.tr.* to jostle, *Fb:* push (s.o.).

Ren [rɛn], *n -s/-s* reindeer.

Rendezvous [rãde'vu:], *n -/-* [-'vu:(s)] rendezvous.

Renn- ['rɛn-], *comb.fm.* racing (boat, season, *Aut:* tyres etc.); race(-day etc.). ◆**'R~bahn**, *f* race course/track. ◆**'r~en. I.** *v.i.irr. (sein)* to run, *(eilen)*

rush. **II. R.**, *n -s/-* **1.** *no pl* running, racing. **2.** *Sp: (Wettbewerb)* race; *F:* **das R. machen**, to win the race; *Fig:* to come out on top. ◆**'R~rad**, *n* racing cycle. ◆**'R~sport**, *m* racing. ◆**'R~strecke**, *f* racing circuit; race course.

renovier|en [reno'vi:rən], *v.tr.* (a) to renovate (a building etc.); (b) to redecorate (a room etc.). ◆**R~ung**, *f -/-en* (a) renovation; (b) redecoration.

rent|abel [rɛn'ta:bəl], *adj.* profitable. ◆**R~abilität** [-tabili'tɛːt], *f -/no pl* profitability. ◆'**R~e**, *f -/-n* pension. ◆'**R~enversicherung** (insurance) scheme. ◆**r~ieren** [-'ti:rən], *v.refl.* **sich r.**, to be profitable/*(sich lohnen)* worth while. ◆'**R~ner(in)**, *m -s/- (f -/-nen)* (old-age) pensioner.

Rentier ['rɛnti:r], *n* reindeer.

reparabel [repa'ra:bəl], *adj.* repairable.

Repar|atur [repara'tu:r], *f -/-en* repair. ◆**r~a'turbedürftig**, *adj.* in need of repair. ◆**R~a'turwerkstatt**, *f* (repair) workshop. ◆**r~ieren** [-'ri:rən], *v.tr.* to repair (sth.), mend (shoes etc.).

Repertoire [repɛr'toa:r], *n -s/-s Mus: etc:* repertoire; *Th:* repertory.

Report [re'pɔrt], *m -(e)s/-e* report. ◆**R~age** [-'ta:ʒə], *f -/-n* (a) *(esp. eyewitness)* report; *TV:* documentary; (b) *Rad: etc:* (running) commentary. ◆**R~er** [re'pɔrtər], *m -s/-* (a) reporter; (b) *Rad: etc:* commentator.

Repräsent|ant [reprɛzɛn'tant], *m -en/-en Pol: etc:* representative. ◆**r~ativ** [-ta'ti:f], *adj.* **1.** prestige (car, address, building etc.). **2.** *(typisch)* representative. ◆**r~ieren** [-'ti:rən], *v.tr.* to represent (sth.).

Repress|alie [reprɛ'sa:liə], *f -/-n* reprisal. ◆**R~ion** [-si'o:n], *f -/-en* repression. ◆**r~iv** [-'si:f], *adj.* repressive.

Reproduktion [reprodʊktsi'o:n], *f* reproduction. ◆**r~zieren**, *v.tr.* to reproduce (a painting etc.).

Reptil [rɛp'ti:l], *n -s/-ien* reptile.

Republik [repu'bli:k], *f -/-en Pol:* republic. ◆**R~aner** [-i'ka:nər], *m -s/-* republican. ◆**r~anisch** [-i'ka:niʃ], *adj.* republican.

Requiem ['re:kviɛm], *n -s/-s* requiem.

Requisiten [rekvi'zi:tən], *npl Th:* (stage) properties, *F:* props.

Reserv|at [rezɛr'va:t], *n -(e)s/-e* reservation (for an ethnic group etc.). ◆**R~e** [re'zɛrvə]. **I.** *f -/-n* reserve; *Mil:* **die R.**, the reserves; **j-n aus seiner R. locken**, to make s.o. come out of his shell. **II. R~-**, *comb.fm.* spare (battery etc.); reserve *(Mil:* officer, *Aut:* tank etc.). ◆**R~erad**, *n* spare wheel. ◆**r~ieren** [-'vi:rən], *v.tr.* to reserve (a table etc.). ◆**r~iert**, *adj.* reserved. ◆**R~ierung**, *f -/-en* reservation. ◆**R~ist**, *m -en/-en Mil:* reservist. ◆**R~oir** [-'voa:r], *n -s/-e* reservoir.

Residenz [rezi'dɛnts], *f -/-en* (prince's)

residence.

Resign|ation [rezignatsi'o:n], f -/-en resignation. ◆**r~ieren** ['gni:trən], v.i. (haben) to resign oneself, give up.

resolut [rezo'lu:t], adj. resolute, determined. ◆**R~ion** [-'tsi:o:n], f -/-en resolution.

Resonanz [rezo'nants], f -/-en 1. Ph: resonance. 2. Fig: response.

Respekt [re'spɛkt], m -(e)s/no pl respect. ◆**r~abel** ['ta:bəl], adj. 1. respectable (size etc.). 2. reasonable (decision, grounds etc.). ◆**r~ieren** [-'ti:rən], v.tr. to respect. ◆**r~los**, adj. disrespectful. ◆**R~sperson**, f person commanding respect. ◆**r~voll**, adj. respectful.

Ressort [re'so:r], n -s/-s Adm: (government etc.) department.

Rest [rɛst], m -(e)s/-e rest; Fin: balance (of a sum); pl R~e, leftovers, scraps (of food etc.); remains (of a castle etc.); Fig: j-m den R. geben, to finish s.o. off. ◆'**R~bestand**, m Com: etc: remaining stock. ◆'**R~betrag**, m balance. ◆'**r~lich**, attrib. adj. remaining. ◆'**r~los**, adj. complete (confidence, satisfaction etc.); total, utter (exhaustion etc.).

Restaurant [rɛsto'rã:], n restaurant.

Restaur|ation [rɛstauratsi'o:n], f -/-en restoration. ◆**r~ieren** ['ri:rən], v.tr. to restore (a building etc.).

Resultat [rezul'ta:t], n -(e)s/-e result.

Resümee [rezy'me:], n -s/-s summary.

Retorte [re'tɔrtə], f -/-n retort. ◆**R~n-baby**, n test-tube baby.

rett|en ['rɛtən], v.tr. to save, rescue (s.o., an animal etc.); to salvage (a ship etc.); to retrieve (one's honour); r~der Gedanke, solution, way out; F: bist du noch zu r.? are you out of your mind? sich vor Anfragen nicht r. können, to be swamped with enquiries. ◆'**R~er(in)**, m -s/- (f -/-nen) rescuer. ◆'**R~ung**, f -/-en rescue; F: du bist meine letzte R., you are my only hope; das war seine R., that was his salvation. ◆'**R~ungs-comb.fm** rescue (operation, service etc.). ◆'**R~ungsboot**, n lifeboat. ◆'**r~ungslos**, adj.usu.adv. beyond all hope; er ist r. verloren, there is no hope for him. ◆'**R~ungsring**, m lifebelt.

retuschieren [retu'ʃi:rən], v.tr. Phot: etc: to retouch, touch up (a picture etc.).

Reu|e ['rɔyə], f -/no pl remorse; (also Ecc:) repentance. ◆**r~en**, v.tr. Lit: (Tat usw.) to fill (s.o.) with remorse; es reut mich, daß ..., I regret that ... ◆'**r~ig**, adj. Lit: penitent, repentant. ◆'**r~mütig**, adj. esp. Hum: remorseful, rueful.

Revanche [re'vã:ʃ(ə)], f -/-n (a) revenge; (b) Sp: etc: return match/game. ◆**r~ieren** [-'ʃi:rən], v.refl. sich r., to take one's revenge, F: get one's own back (an j-m, on s.o.); sich bei j-m (für seine Güte usw.) r., to reciprocate (s.o.'s

kindness etc.).

Revers [re've:r], n -/- Cl: lapel.

revidieren [revi'di:rən], v.tr. (ändern) to revise (one's opinion etc.).

Revier [re'vi:r], n -s/- 1. (Bereich) territory (of an animal, gang etc.); (policeman's etc.) beat, F: patch; (Kohlen-.) mining district; (Jagdr.) shoot; hunt. 2. (Polizeiwache) police station.

Revision [revizi'o:n], f -/-en 1. (Prüfung) checking, Com: audit. 2. Jur: appeal.

Revolte [re'vɔltə], f -/-n revolt. ◆**R~ution** [-olutsi'o:n], f -/-en revolution. ◆**r~utionär** [-o'ne:r], m -s/-e revolutionary. ◆**r~utio'nieren**, v.tr. to revolutionize (a country, ideas etc.).

Revolver [re'vɔlvər], m -s/- revolver.

Rezens|ent [retsɛn'zɛnt], m -en/-en (book etc.) reviewer; Th: Mus: critic. ◆**r~ieren** [-'zi:rən], v.tr. to review (a book, play etc.). ◆**R~ion** [-zi'o:n], f -/-en review.

Rezept [re'tsɛpt], n -(e)s/-e 1. Med: prescription; Fig: cure, remedy. 2. Cu: & Fig: recipe. ◆**R~ion** [-tsi'o:n], f -/-en reception (desk). ◆**r~pflichtig**, adj. obtainable only on prescription.

rezitieren [retsi'ti:rən], v.tr. to recite (a poem etc.).

Rhabarber [ra'barbər], m -s/no pl rhubarb.

Rhapsodie [rapzo'di:, raps-], f -/-n rhapsody.

Rhein [rain]. Pr.n.m -s. der R., the Rhine. ◆'**r~isch**, adj. Rhenish. ◆'**R~land**. Pr.n.n -s. das R., the Rhineland.

Rhetorik [re'to:rik], f -/no pl rhetoric. ◆**r~sch**, adj. rhetorical.

Rheuma ['rɔyma], n -s/no pl/R~'tismus, m -/-men rheumatism.

Rhinozeros [ri'no:tseros], n -ses/-se rhinoceros.

rhythm|isch ['rytmiʃ], adj. rhythmical. ◆'**R~us**, m -/-men rhythm.

Richt- ['riçt-], comb.fm. guide, guiding (value, figure etc.); (empfohlen) recommended (price etc.). ◆'**R~antenne**, f directional antenna. ◆'**r~en**, v.tr. (a) to aim, point (a gun, telescope etc.) (auf + acc, at); to direct (an aerial, Fig: efforts etc.), turn (one's eyes etc.) (auf + acc, towards); eine Frage an j-n r., to put/address a question to s.o.; (b) (zurechtmachen) to straighten (teeth, wire etc.); to prepare (a meal etc.); (c) (Urteil fällen) to judge, pass sentence on (s.o.); (d) sich nach etwas dat r., to comply/adhere to sth.; (auf etwas ankommen) to depend on sth.; danach kann man sich nicht r., you cannot go by that. ◆'**R~er(in)**, m -s/- (f -/-nen) judge. ◆'**R~geschwindigkeit**, f recommended (maximum) speed. ◆'**R~linie**, f guideline, guiding principle. ◆'**R~ung**, f -/-en (a) direction; (b) Fig: direction, line of thought, research etc.; Art: Pol: movement, trend. ◆'R~ungsanzeiger, m Aut: direction indicator.

richtig ['riçtiç], adj. 1. (nicht falsch) right, correct (answer, assumption etc.); das ist genau das R~e! that's just the job! ich halte es für das r~e, I think it would be the best thing; etwas r. machen, to do sth. correctly; er kam gerade r., he came at just the right moment; (sehr) r.! quite right! 2. (echt) proper (meal, job etc.); real (name, mother, F: coward etc.). ◆'R~keit, f -/no pl correctness; accuracy (of a statement etc.); rightness (of a decision etc.). ◆'r~stellen, v.tr.sep. to correct (a statement etc.), rectify (a mistake etc.). ◆'R~stellung, f -/-en correction.

riechen ['riːçən], v.tr. & i.irr. (haben) to smell; das konnte ich wirklich nicht r., how was I to know? F: ich kann ihn nicht r., I can't stand him.

Ried [riːt], n -(e)s/-e reeds.

Riege ['riːgə], f -/-n squad.

Riegel ['riːgəl], m -s/- 1. bolt (of a door etc.). 2. bar (of soap, chocolate).

Riemen ['riːmən], m -s/- 1. strap; (Gürtel) belt. 2. Nau: (Ruder) oar.

Ries|e ['riːzə], m -n/-n giant. ◆'R~en-, comb.fm. (a) giant (wheel, firm, Ski: slalom, Z: tortoise etc.), gigantic (building, portion etc.); (b) F: tremendous (success, fun etc.); (c) F: Pej: terrible (mistake, stupidity etc.). ◆'r~en-'groß, adj. F: gigantic, enormous; colossal (stupidity). ◆'R~enschlange, f (giant) boa constrictor. ◆'r~ig, adj. enormous, gigantic; tremendous (strength etc.).

rieseln ['riːzəln], v.i. (a) (sein) (Wasser, Sand usw.) to trickle; (b) (haben) (Regen) to drizzle, (Schnee) fall lightly.

Riff [rif], n -(e)s/-e reef.

Rille ['rilə], f -/-n groove.

Rind [rint], n -(e)s/-er 1. (Stier) bull; (Kuh) cow. 2. Cu: beef. ◆'R~er-['rindər-], comb.fm. 1. Cu: beef (goulash etc.). 2. Agr: (herd etc.) of cattle. ◆'R~erbraten, m roast beef. ◆'R~erfilet, n fillet of beef. ◆'R~fleisch, n beef. ◆'R~sleder, n cowhide. ◆'R~vieh, n 1. coll. cattle. F: (pl R~viecher) ass, twit.

Rinde ['rində], f -/-n 1. (Baumr.) bark. 2. (Brotr.) crust; (Käser. usw.) rind.

Ring [riŋ], m -(e)s/-e ring; circle (of people etc.). ◆'r~förmig, adj. ring-shaped, annular. ◆'R~richter, m Sp: referee.

ringeln ['riŋəln], v.tr. to curl (hair), coil (a tail etc.); sich r., to curl, form curls. ◆'R~natter, f grass snake.

ring|en ['riŋən]. I. v.i.irr. (haben) to wrestle; esp. Fig: to struggle; nach Atem/Luft r., to gasp/struggle for breath. II. R~en, n -s/no pl Sp: wrestling; Fig: struggle. ◆'R~kampf, m wrestling bout.

rings [riŋs], adv. round about, all around. ◆r~he'rum/r~um'her, adv. all around, all the way round.

Rinne ['rinə], f -/-n (also Nau:) channel; (Rinnstein, Dachr.) gutter. ◆'r~en, v.i.irr. (sein) (Regen, Tränen usw.) to flow, run; (Sand) to trickle. ◆'r~n-(e)s/-e trickle; (Bächlein) rivulet. ◆'R~stein, m gutter.

Ripp|chen ['ripçən], n -s/- Cu: (esp. spare) rib (of pork). ◆'R~e, f -/-n rib. ◆'R~enbruch, m broken rib. ◆'R~enfellentzündung, f pleurisy.

Risiko ['riːziko], n -s/-s & -ken risk. ◆'r~los, adj. safe, without any risk.

risk|ant [ris'kant], adj. risky, hazardous. ◆r~ieren [-'kiːrən], v.tr. to risk (sth.).

Riß [ris], m -sses/-sse (im Stoff, Papier usw.) tear; (im Felsen) fissure, cleft; Fig: (zwischen Freunden) rift; Pol: split.

rissig ['risiç], adj. cracked; chapped (skin).

Rist [rist], m -(e)s/-e (am Fuß) instep; (an der Hand) back of the hand.

Ritt [rit], m -(e)s/-e ride (on a horse etc.). ◆'R~er, m -s/- knight. ◆'r~erlich, adj. chivalrous; Hist: knightly. ◆'R~ersporn, m -(e)s/-e larkspur, delphinium.

Ritual [ritu'aːl], n -s/-e & -ien ritual. ◆r~u'ell, adj. ritual.

Ritz [rits], m -es/-e scratch. ◆'R~e, f -/-n crack; (im Vorhang usw.) gap, chink. ◆'r~en, v.tr. to scratch (sth.), (schneiden) cut (glass etc.); to carve (one's name etc.).

Rival|e [ri'vaːlə], m -n/-n/R~in, f -/-nen rival; esp. Sp: competitor. ◆r~ität, f -/-en rivalry.

Rizinusöl ['riːtsinus?øːl], n castor oil.

Robbe ['rɔbə], f -/-n seal.

Roboter ['rɔbɔtər], m -s/- robot.

robust [ro'bʊst], adj. robust (material, health etc.); strong, sturdy (person, table etc.).

röcheln ['rœçəln], v.i. (haben) to breathe stertorously; (Sterbende) to give the death rattle.

Rochen ['rɔxən], m -s/- ray.

Rock [rɔk], m -(e)s/-e skirt.

rodeln ['roːdəln], v.i. (sein/haben) to toboggan. ◆'R~schlitten, m toboggan.

roden ['roːdən], v.tr. to clear (woodland).

Rogen ['roːgən], m -s/- (hard) roe.

Roggen ['rɔgən], m -s/- rye. ◆'R~brot, n rye bread.

roh [roː]. I. adj. 1. (a) raw (hide, silk etc.); raw, uncooked (food); (b) crude (oil); unrefined (sugar); (c) rough, uncut (diamond). 2. (ungenau) rough (sketch, shaping estimate). 3. (grob) coarse, uncouth (person, manners etc.); mit r~er Gewalt, with brute force. II. 'R~-, comb.fm. raw (vegetables, silk etc.); uncut (diamond); crude (ore, oil). ◆'R~bau, m shell. ◆'R~eisen, n pig-iron. ◆'R~kost, f raw (vegetarian

food. ◆'R~ling, m -s/-e (Pers.) brute.
◆'R~material, n/'R~stoff, m raw material. ◆'R~zustand, m natural/Ind: crude state.

Rohr [ro:r], n -(e)s/-e 1. (Schilf:) reed; coll. reeds; (Zucker-, Bambus-) cane. 2. (a) tube; (R~leitung) (water etc.) pipe; (b) (Geschütz-) (gun) barrel. ◆'R~bruch, m burst pipe. ◆'r~förmig, adj. tubular. ◆'R~geflecht, n wickerwork. ◆'R~leitung, f (water/gas) pipe, main. ◆'R~post, f pneumatic tube post. ◆'R~stock, m cane (stick). ◆'R~zucker, m cane sugar.

Röhre ['rø:rə], f -/-n 1. (a) Tchn: tube; (für Wasser usw.) pipe; (b) Rad: valve, N.Am: tube. 2. Cu: oven. ◆'r~nförmig, adj. tubular.

Rokoko ['rɔkoko], n -s/no pl rococo.

Roll|bahn ['rɔlbaːn], f -/-en Av: runway. ◆'R~e, f -/-n 1. roll of (paper, film, money etc.); (Garnr.) reel, N.Am: spool (of thread). 2. Tchn: (Walze) roller. 3. Th: Cin: etc: part; esp. Fig: role; Fig: (bei etwas dat) eine große R. spielen, to play an important part/figure prominently (in sth.). ◆'r~en, v. 1. v.i. (sein) to roll; (Fahrzeug) to move, Av: taxi; ins R. kommen, to start to move, (also F: Sache) get under way. 2. v.tr. to roll (a ball, barrel etc.). ◆'R~er, m -s/- 1. (child's) scooter. 2. (Welle) (heavy) roller. ◆'R~feld, n Av: airfield. ◆'R~film, m roll film. ◆'R~kragen, m polo neck/N.Am: collar. ◆'R~mops, m pickled herring, rollmops. ◆'R~schuh, m roller skate. ◆'R~schuhläufer, m roller-skater. ◆'R~splitt, m (rolled) loose chippings. ◆'R~stuhl, m wheelchair. ◆'R~treppe, f escalator.

Rom [roːm]. Pr.n.n -s. Rome.

Roman [ro'maːn], m -s/-e novel. ◆'R~cier [romãsi'e:], m -s/-s/ Pr:schriftsteller, m novelist.

Roman|tik [ro'mantik], f -/no pl romanticism. ◆'r~tisch, adj. romantic. ◆'R~ze, f -/-n romance.

Römer ['rø:mər], m -s/- 1. (Pers.) Roman. 2. (Weinglas) large goblet (with green/brown stem). ◆'R~in, f -/-nen Roman (woman/girl). ◆'r~isch, adj. Roman, of Rome. ◆'r~isch-katholisch, adj. Roman Catholic.

Rommé ['rɔme], n -s/-s rummy.

röntgen ['rœntgən]. I. v.tr. to X-ray (s.o., sth.); sich r. lassen, to have an X-ray. II. R~-, comb.fm. X-ray (treatment, examination etc.). ◆'R~aufnahme, f X-ray (picture). ◆'R~strahlen, mpl X-rays.

rosa ['ro:za], inv.adj. pink. ◆'r~farben/'r~farbig, adj. pink. ◆'r~rot, adj. (esp. deep) pink.

Rose ['ro:zə], f -/-n rose. ◆'R~n-, comb.fm. rose (garden, hedge, oil, water etc.); (scent, bunch etc.) of roses. ◆'R~nkohl, m (Brussels) sprouts.

◆'R~nkranz, m rosary; den R. beten, to say the rosary. ◆'R~n'montag, m Shrove Monday.

rosig ['ro:ziç], adj. rosy (cheeks, Fig: prospects etc.).

Rosine [ro'zi:nə], f -/-n raisin.

Roß [rɔs], n -sses/-sse & -sser Lit: steed. ◆'R~kastanie, f horse-chestnut. ◆'R~kur, f F: drastic/kill-or-cure treatment.

Rost[1] [rɔst], m -(e)s/-e grid (iron), grating; (Feuerstelle) grate; Cu: grill. ◆'R~braten, m grilled steak.

Rost[2], m -(e)s/no pl rust. ◆'r~en, v.i. (haben/sein) to rust. ◆'r~frei, adj. rustproof; stainless (steel). ◆'r~ig, adj. rusty. ◆'r~rot, adj. rust-red. ◆'R~schutzmittel, n anti-rust preparation.

rösten ['rœstən], v.tr. Cu: to grill (meat), roast (coffee), fry (potatoes), toast (bread etc.). ◆'R~er, m -s/- (für Brot) toaster.

rot [roːt]. I. adj. red; sie wurde r., she went red (in the face)/blushed; das R~e Meer, the Red Sea; das R~e Kreuz, the Red Cross; r~e Beete/Rübe, beetroot. II. R~, n -s/- (a) red; (b) Aut: (Ampel) bei R., when the lights are red. III. R~-, 'r~-, comb.fm. red (light, wine etc.). ◆'r~barsch, m rosefish; N.Am: ocean perch. ◆'r~blond, adj. ginger (hair); ginger-haired (person). ◆'r~haarig, adj. red-haired. ◆'R~käppchen. Pr.n.n -s. Little Red Riding Hood. ◆'R~kehlchen, n -s/- robin (redbreast). ◆'R~kohl, m red cabbage. ◆'r~sehen, v.i.sep.irr. 92 (haben) F: to see red, go into a rage. ◆'R~wild, n red deer.

Rotation [rotatsi'o:n], f -/-en rotation.

rotieren [ro'ti:rən], v.i. (haben) to rotate.

Röte ['rø:tə], f -/no pl redness; (im Gesicht) blush; flush (of anger). ◆'R~eln, pl German measles. ◆'r~en, v.tr. to redden (sth.). ◆'r~lich, adj. reddish; ruddy (cheeks etc.).

Rotz [rɔts], m -es/-e P: snot; ◆'r~näsig [-nɛziç], adj. F: (a) snotty-nosed; (b) (frech) cheeky.

Roulade [ru'la:də], f -/-n beef olive.

Route ['ru:tə], f -/-n route.

Routin|e [ru'ti:nə], f -/no pl (a) routine; (b) (Erfahrung) experience. ◆'r~emäßig, adj. routine (examination etc.). ◆'r~iert [-ti'ni:rt], adj. experienced (driver, lecturer etc.); expert (card player etc.).

Rowdy ['raudi], m -s/-s rowdy, hooligan.

Rübe ['ry:bə], f -/-n beet; weiße R., turnip; gelbe R., carrot; rote R., beetroot. ◆'R~nzucker, m beet sugar.

Rubel ['ru:bəl], m -s/- rouble.

rüber ['ry:bər], adv. F: = herüber/ hinüber; komm r.! come over (to us)!

Rubin [ru'bi:n], m -s/-e ruby. ◆'r~rot, adj. ruby(-red).

Rubrik [ru'bri:k], f -/-en heading; (Spalte) column.

Ruck [ruk], *m* -(e)s/-e jerk; (*Stoß*) jolt; (*Zug*) tug, yank; **einen R. geben**, to jerk, (*Fahrzeug*) lurch; *F:* **in einem R.**, in one go. ◆'**r~artig**, *adj.* jerky (movement etc.); sudden (braking etc.); *adv.* suddenly, with a jerk. ◆'**R~sack**, *m* rucksack. ◆'**r~weise**, *adv.* in fits and starts.

Rück-, rück- ['ryk-], *comb.fm.* 1. (*hintere, nach hinten*) rear, back (wall etc.); rear (light etc.). 2. return (flight, flow, march, *Tel:* call etc.). ◆'**R~antwort** *f* reply. ◆'**R~blick**, *m* review of (past events); **im R.**, in retrospect. ◆'**r~blickend**, *adj.* retrospective; *adv.* looking back, in retrospect. ◆'**r~erstatten**, *v.tr.insep.* to refund (expenses, taxes etc.) (j-m, s.o.), to return (property). ◆'**R~erstattung**, *f* refund; return of (property). ◆'**R~fahrkarte**, *f* return ticket. ◆'**R~fahrt**, *f* return journey. ◆'**R~fall**, *m Med: etc:* relapse; *F:* (**in alte Gewohnheiten**) backsliding. ◆'**r~fällig**, *adj.* **r. werden**, to have a relapse; *Fig:* to go back to one's old ways/*Jur:* a life of crime. ◆'**R~frage**, *f* (further) question, query. ◆'**r~fragen**, *v.i. sep.* (*haben*) **bei j-m r.**, to check with s.o. ◆'**R~gabe**, *f* return of (money etc.). ◆'**R~gang**, *m* decrease, decline (in population etc.); drop, fall (in prices etc.); **R. an Geburten**, drop in the number of births. ◆'**r~gängig**, *adj.* **etwas r. machen**, to cancel sth. ◆'**R~grat**, *n Anat:* spine; *Fig:* backbone (of a country etc.); *F:* **j-m das R. brechen**, to break s.o.'s will/resistance. ◆'**R~griff**, *m* recourse (**auf** + *acc*, to). ◆'**R~halt**, *m* (*Unterstützung*) support, backing. ◆'**r~haltlos**, *adj.* unreserved (admiration etc.); complete (support etc.). ◆'**R~kehr**, *f* -/no *pl* return. ◆'**R~lage**, *f Fin: esp.pl* **R~lagen**, reserves. ◆'**r~läufig**, *adj.* declining (number, production etc.); *Com:* downward (tendency etc.). ◆'**r~lings**, *adv.* (*von hinten*) from behind/the rear; **er fiel r. hin**, he fell (over) backwards. ◆'**R~nahme**, *f -/no pl Com: etc:* taking back; withdrawal (of a statement etc.). ◆'**R~porto**, *n* return postage. ◆'**R~reise**, *f* return journey. ◆'**R~schau**, *f* -/-n review (**auf** + *acc*, of). ◆'**R~schlag**, *m* setback. ◆'**R~schluß**, *m* conclusion. ◆'**R~schritt**, *m* retrograde step. ◆'**r~schrittlich**, *adj.* reactionary. ◆'**R~seite**, *f* back; reverse (of a coin). ◆'**R~sendung**, *f* return (of a letter etc.). ◆'**R~sicht**, *f* consideration; **auf j-n R. nehmen**, to show consideration for s.o. ◆'**r~sichtslos**, *adj.* (a) inconsiderate; (*gefährlich*) reckless; (*skrupellos*) ruthless. ◆'**r~sichtsvoll**, *adj.* considerate. ◆'**R~sitz**, *m* back seat. ◆'**R~spiegel**, *m* rear view mirror. ◆'**R~spiel**, *n* return match.

◆'**R~sprache**, *f* consultation. ◆'**R~stand**, *m* 1. (*Rest*) remains; *Ch:* residue. 2. backlog (of work etc.); *Fin:* arrears; **im R. sein**, to be behind. ◆'**r~ständig**, *adj.* 1. backward (country etc.); old-fashioned, outdated (equipment etc.). 2. (*Zahlung*) overdue, outstanding; (*Pers.*) in arrears. ◆'**R~stau**, *m Aut:* tailback. ◆'**R~strahler** *m Aut: etc:* (rear) reflector. ◆'**R~taste**, *f* back spacer. ◆'**R~tritt**, *m* (a) resignation; (*Abdankung*) abdication; (b) withdrawal (**von einem Vertrag**, from a contract). ◆'**R~vergütung**, *f* (partial) refund. ◆'**r~wärtig**, *adj.* back (door, room etc.); rear (part, section etc.). ◆'**r~wärts**, *adv.* backwards; **von r.**, from behind. ◆'**R~wärtsgang**, *m Aut:* reverse gear. ◆'**R~weg**, *m* way back; (*nach Hause*) way home. ◆'**r~wirkend**, *adj. Jur: etc:* retrospective. ◆'**R~wirkung**, *f* -/-en repercussion (**auf** + *acc*, on). ◆'**R~zahlung**, *f* repayment. ◆'**R~zug**, *m* retreat.

rücken[1] ['rykən], *v.* 1. *v.tr.* to move, shift (a table etc.). 2. *v.i.* (*sein*) to move, (*stückweise*) edge; **mit dem Stuhl näher r.**, to pull up one's chair; **an j-s Stelle r.**, to take over from s.o.

Rücken[2]. I. *m* -s/- (*a*) back (of s.o., sth.); (*b*) (*Bergr.*) (mountain) ridge. II. '**R~-**, *comb.fm.* back, *Anat:* dorsal (muscle etc.). ◆'**R~deckung**, *f* 1. *Mil: etc:* rear cover. 2. *Fig:* backing, support. ◆'**R~lehne**, *f* back (of a chair). ◆'**R~schwimmen**, *n* backstroke. ◆'**R~wind**, *m* tail/following wind. ◆'**R~wirbel**, *m* dorsal vertebra.

rüde[1] ['ry:də], *adj.* uncouth.

Rüde[2], *m* -n/-n dog; male (fox/wolf).

Rudel ['ru:dəl], *n* -s/- herd (of deer etc.); pack (of wolves); pride (of lions).

Ruder ['ru:dər]. I. *n* -s/- 1. oar. 2. *Nau:* (*Steuer*.) rudder; *esp. Fig:* helm; *Pol: etc:* **ans R. kommen**, to come to power. II. '**R~-**, *comb.fm.* rowing (club, regatta etc.). ◆'**R~boot**, *n* rowing boat; *N.Am:* rowboat. ◆'**R~er**, *m* -s/- oarsman, rower. ◆'**r~n**. I. *v.i.* 1. *v.i.* (*sein/haben*) to row. 2. *v.tr.* to row (s.o., a boat etc.). II. *R.*, *n* -s/no *pl* rowing.

Ruf [ru:f], *m* -(e)s/-e 1. call (of s.o., a bird); (*Schrei*) cry, shout; *Fig:* **R. nach Freiheit**, call/demand for freedom. 2. reputation; **von R.**, of renown/repute. ◆'**r~en**, *v.irr.* 1. *v.i.* (*haben*) (*Pers., Vogel*) to call (**nach etwas dat**, for sth.); (*schreien*) to cry, shout. 2. *v.tr.* to call (s.o., an animal etc.). ◆'**R~mord**, *m* character assassination. ◆'**R~name**, *m* Christian name (by which one is generally known). ◆'**R~nummer**, *f* telephone number.

Rüge ['ry:gə], *f* -/-n reprimand, rebuke; (*Kritik*) criticism. ◆'**r~n**, *v.tr.* to reprimand, rebuke (s.o.); to criticize, censure (an attitude etc.).

Ruhe ['ruːə], f -/no pl (a) (Stille) quiet, silence; (b) (Gelassenheit) calmness, composure; F: immer mit der R.! take it easy! (c) (Ungestörtheit) peace. **R. und Ordnung,** law and order; F: **laß mich in R.!** leave me alone/in peace! (d) rest; (Schlaf) sleep; angenehme R.! sleep well! ◆'R~gehalt, n pension. ◆'r~los, adj. restless; unsettled (times etc.). ◆'r~n, v.i. (haben) (a) to rest; (b) (zum Stillstand kommen) (Produktion, Verkehr usw.) to have stopped, be at a standstill; (Geschütze) to be silent. ◆'R~pause, f break (from work). ◆'R~stand, m retirement; in den R. treten/versetzt werden, to retire/be retired. ◆'R~stätte, f Lit: (letzte) R., last resting place. ◆'R~störung, f disturbance of the peace.

ruhig ['ruːɪç], adj. (a) (ohne Bewegung) calm, still (water, air etc.); calm (weather, sea); smooth (crossing, flight); r. sitzen/liegen, to sit/lie still; (b) (ohne Lärm) quiet; (c) (friedlich) peaceful (life etc.); (d) (gelassen) calm (voice etc.); steady (hand, voice); man kann das Kind r. allein lassen, it's quite all right to leave the child alone.

Ruhm [ruːm], m -(e)s/no pl fame. ◆'r~reich/'r~voll, adj. esp. Mil: glorious (campaign, history etc.); famous (regiment etc.).

rühmen ['ryːmən], v.tr. Lit: to praise, extol (s.o., sth.); sich einer Sache r., to pride oneself on sth.

Ruhr [ruːr], f -/no pl Med: dysentery.

Rühr|ei ['ryːrʔai], n scrambled eggs. ◆'r~en. 1. v.tr. (a) to stir (soup, paint etc.); (b) (bewegen) to move (an arm, leg etc.); sich r., to move; (Luft usw.) to stir; Fig: (Pers.) (aktiv sein) to be up and doing; rührt euch! (i) Mil: (stand) at ease! (ii) F: (beeil euch) get a move on! (c) (innerlich bewegen) to move, touch (s.o.); es rührte ihn gar nicht, it left him quite unmoved. 2. v.i. (haben) (a) im Kaffee r., to stir one's coffee; (b) Lit: r. an + acc, to touch (sth.), Fig: touch on (a subject). ◆'r~end, adj. touching. ◆'r~ig, adj. active; enterprising, go-ahead (businessman etc.). ◆'r~selig, adj. (sickeningly) sentimental; maudlin, F: tear-jerking (play etc.). ◆'R~ung, f -/no pl emotion.

Ruin [ru'iːn], m -s/no pl ruin. ◆R~e [ru'iːnə], f -/-n ruin(s). ◆r~ieren [-i'niːrən], v.tr. to ruin (s.o., sth.); to wreck (s.o.'s nerve, hopes etc.).

rülpsen ['rylpsən], v.i. (haben) F: to belch.

Rum [rum], m -s/-s rum.

Rumän|e [ru'mɛːnə], m -n/-n Romanian, R(o)umanian. ◆R~ien [ru'mɛːniən], n -s Romania, R(o)umania. ◆r~isch, adj. Romanian, R(o)umanian.

Rummel ['ruməl], m -s/no pl F: (a) (Trubel) hustle and bustle; (mit Lärm) com-

motion; (viel Aufsehen) fuss, to-do; (b) (Jahrmarkt) fair. ◆'R~platz, m fairground.

rumoren [ru'moːrən], v.i. (haben) F: to bang about, make a noise.

Rumpel|kammer ['rumpəlkamər], f F: lumber room, boxroom. ◆'r~n, v.i. (haben/sein) to rumble; (Pers.) to bang about.

Rumpf [rumpf], m -(e)s/-e 1. Anat: trunk; torso. 2. Av: fuselage; Nau: hull.

rümpfen ['rympfən], v.tr. die Nase r., to turn up one's nose (über etwas acc, at sth.).

rund [runt]. I. adj. (a) round; ein r~es Dutzend, a good dozen. II. adv. 1. r. um + acc, (a)round; r. um die Welt, all (a)round the world. 2. r. 50 Mark, about/approximately 50 marks. III. 'R~-, comb.fm. circular (building, tent etc.); round (arch, file, pillar etc.). ◆'R~brief, m circular letter. ◆R~e ['rundə], f -/-n (a) round; circle (of friends etc.); r. Bier usw., a round of beer etc.; R. durch die Stadt, tour of the town; eine R. machen, (a) Sp: (Durchgang) round (of a competition etc.); (bei Rennen) lap. ◆'r~en, v.tr. to round (sth.), one's lips, back etc.); sich r., to become round, fill out. ◆'R~fahrt, f circular tour. ◆'R~frage, f survey, questionnaire. ◆'R~funk, m radio; im R. ◆ on the radio. ◆'R~funk-, comb.fm. radio (programme, announcer, technology etc.); ◆'R~funkgebühr, f radio licence fee. ◆'R~funksender, m radio station. ◆'R~funksendung, f radio broadcast. ◆'R~gang, m 1. round (of a postman, night-watchman etc.); tour of inspection. 2. (in einer Burg usw.) circular gallery/walk. ◆'r~he'raus, adv. straight out, bluntly; (offen) frankly. ◆'r~he'rum, adv. all round. ◆'r~(völlig) completely, thoroughly. ◆'r~lich, adj. plump, chubby. ◆'r~weg, adv. totally.

runter ['runtər], adv. F: = herunter/hinunter.

Runz|el ['runtsəl], f -/-n wrinkle. ◆'r~(e)lig, adj. wrinkled. ◆'r~eln, v.tr. die Stirn r., to knit one's brows, frown; sich r., to wrinkle.

Rüpel ['ryːpəl], m -s/- lout. ◆'r~haft, adj. loutish, uncouth.

rupfen ['rupfən], v.tr. to pluck (a chicken etc.); to pull up (grass, weeds etc.).

ruppig ['rupɪç], adj. (grob) uncouth; gruff (answer).

Rüsche ['ryːʃə], f -/-n frill.

Ruß [ruːs], m -es/no pl soot. ◆'r~en, v.i. (haben) to form soot. ◆'r~ig, adj. sooty.

Russe ['rusə], m -n/-n Russian. ◆'R~in, f -/-nen Russian woman. ◆'r~isch, adj. & R., n -(s)/no pl Russian.

Rüssel ['rysəl], m -s/- (elephant's) trunk;

(pig's) snout.

Rußland ['ruslant]. *Pr.n.n* -s. Russia.

rüst|en ['rystən], *v.* 1. *v.i.* (*haben*) to arm (**zum Krieg**, for war). 2. *v.refl.* **sich zu etwas** *dat* r., to prepare for sth. ◆**r~ig**, *adj.* active, sprightly (elderly person). ◆**R~ung**, *f* -/-en 1. *no pl* armament; (*Waffen*) arms, armaments. 2. *Hist.* (suit of) armour. ◆**R~ungs-, comb.fm.** arms (control, factory etc.); armaments (industry etc.). ◆**R~ungsbeschränkung**, *f* arms limitation. ◆**R~zeug**, *n* (a) (right) tools/equipment for the job; (b) (*Wissen*) know-how.

rustikal [rusti'kɑːl], *adj.* rustic.

Rute ['ruːtə], *f* -/-n (*esp.* birch) rod; (*Gerte*) switch; (*Angelr.*) fishing rod.

Rutsch [rutʃ], *m* -(e)s/-e slip, slide; (*Erdr.*) landslide; *F:* **auf einen R.**, in one go; **guten R. (ins neue Jahr)!** Happy New Year! (**haben**), *f* slide. ◆**R~e**, *f* -/-n *Ind:* chute. ◆**r~en**, *v.i.* (*sein*) to slide; (*Pers., Tchn: Kupplung usw.*) to slip; (*Auto*) to skid. ◆**r~fest**, *adj.* non-slip (mat etc.). ◆**r~ig**, *adj.* slippery.

rütteln ['rytəln], *v.* 1. *v.tr.* to shake (s.o., sth.). 2. *v.i.* (*haben/sein*) (a) to shake, (*Fahrzeug*) jolt: **an der Tür r.**, to rattle at the door; (b) *Fig:* **daran ist nicht zu r.**, that is irrefutable/(*Entschluß*) irrevocable.

S

S, s [ɛs], *n* -/- (the letter) S, s.

Saal [zɑːl], *m* -(e)s/**Säle** hall.

Saat [zɑːt], *f* -/-en 1. *no pl* (*Säen*) sowing. 2. *coll.* (*Samen*) seed. 3. *coll.* (*Pflanzen*) seedlings, *Agr:* young crops. ◆**'S~gut**, *n coll.* seed(s).

sabbern ['zabərn], *v.i.* (*haben*) *F:* to slobber, (*Baby*) dribble.

Säbel ['zɛːbəl], *m* -s/- sabre.

Sabot|age [zabo'tɑːʒə], *f* -/-n sabotage. ◆**S~eur** [-'tøːər], *m* -s/-e saboteur. ◆**s~ieren** [-'tiːrən], *v.tr.* to sabotage.

Sach|bearbeiter ['zaxbəʔarbaitər], *m* person/*Adm:* official responsible. ◆**'S~beschädigung**, *f* damage to property. ◆**'S~buch**, *n* (*esp.* popularly written) non-fiction book. ◆**s~dienlich**, *adj.* relevant, helpful (information etc.). ◆**'S~e**, *f* -/-n 1. *usu. pl* S~n, things. 2. (*Angelegenheit*) (a) matter, affair; **eine schlimme S.**, a bad business; **er hat die ganze S. erfunden**, he made up the whole thing; (b) **das ist ihre S.**, that's her business/affair; **seine S. verstehen**, to know one's job/*F:* stuff; **das gehört nicht/tut nichts zur S.**, that is beside the point; **zur S. kommen**, to come to the point; (c) (*wofür man sich einsetzt*) cause. ◆**'S~gebiet**, *n* (subject) area, field. ◆**s~gemäß**, *adj.* proper, appropriate. ◆**'S~kenntnis**, *f* expertise; *F:* know-how. ◆**'s~kundig**, *adj.* expert (advice etc.); knowledgeable (person). ◆**'S~lage**, *f* -*no pl* state of affairs; (*current*) situation. ◆**'S~lich**, *adj.* (a) (*faktisch*) factual (details etc.); practical (reasons etc.); (b) (*nüchtern*) matter-of-fact (person, attitude, tone etc.); businesslike (person, manner etc.). ◆**'S~schaden**, *m* material damage. ◆**'S~verhalt**, *m* -(e)s/-e facts (of the matter). ◆**'s~verständige(r)**, *m & f decl. as adj.* expert.

sächlich ['zɛçliç], *adj.* neuter (noun etc.).

Sachse ['zaksə], *m* -n/-n Saxon. ◆**'S~n**. *Pr.n.n* -s. Saxony.

Sächs|in ['zɛksin], *f* -/-nen Saxon girl/woman. ◆**'s~isch**, *adj.* Saxon.

sacht [zaxt], *adj.* gentle; (*leise*) soft; (*vorsichtig*) cautious (movement etc.); *F:* **s~e, s~e!** easy does it!

Sack [zak], *m* -(e)s/-e sack; *F:* **mit S. und Pack**, with bag and baggage. ◆**'S~bahnhof**, *m* terminus. ◆**'s~en**, *v.i.* (*sein*) (*Boden, Gebäude* etc.) to subside, sink; (*Pers.*) to slump (**in einen Stuhl** usw., into a chair etc.). ◆**'S~gasse**, *f* cul-de-sac; *Fig:* dead end. ◆**'S~leinen**, *n* sackcloth.

Sadis|mus [za'dɪsmus], *m* -/*no pl* sadism. ◆**S~t**, *m* -en/-en sadist. ◆**s~tisch**, *adj.* sadistic.

säen ['zɛːən], *v.tr.* to sow (seeds, corn, *Fig:* discord); *Fig:* **dünn gesät**, few and far between.

Safari [za'fɑːri], *f* -/-s safari.

Safe [seːf], *m* -s/-s safe (in a bank etc.).

Saft [zaft], *m* -(e)s/-e juice (of fruit, *Cu:* meat); *Bot:* sap (of a tree etc.). ◆**'s~ig**, *adj.* (a) juicy (fruit, meat etc.); (b) lush (plant, grass etc.). ◆**'s~los**, *adj.* juiceless.

Sage ['zɑːgə], *f* -/-n saga; (*klassische*) legend. ◆**'s~n**, *v.tr.* to say (sth.); **die Wahrheit s.**, to speak the truth; **wie sagt man das auf Englisch?** what is the English for that? *F:* **das kann man wohl s.!** that's very true! **was Sie nicht s.!** you don't say! **das ist nicht gesagt**, you can't bank on it; **j-m etwas s.**, (*mitteilen*) to tell s.o. sth.; **er läßt sich** *dat* **nichts s.**, he won't listen; **j-m seine Meinung s.**, to give s.o. a piece of one's mind; *F:* **wem sagst du das!** you're telling me! **was wollen Sie damit s.?** what do you mean by that? **sagt dir das etwas?** does it mean anything to you? **das hat nichts zu s.**, it's of no consequence; **s. Sie ihm, er soll kommen**, tell him to come; *F:* **er hat nichts zu s.**, he has no say (in the matter). ◆**'s~nhaft**, *adj.* (a) legendary; (b) *F:* fabulous; **s. teuer**, terribly expensive.

Säge ['zɛːgə]. I. *f -/-n* saw. II. **'S~**, *comb.fm.* saw (tooth etc.). ◆**'s~n**, *v.tr.* to saw (wood, metal etc.). ◆**'S~werk**, *n* sawmill.

Sahne ['zaːnə], *f -/no pl* cream; (*Schlags.*) whipped cream. ◆**'S~e-bonbon**, *m & n* toffee. ◆**'S~etorte**, *f* cream cake. ◆**'s~ig**, *adj.* creamy.

Saison [zɛˈzɔ̃], I. *f -/-s* season; *Fig:* S. haben, to be popular/in vogue. II. **'S~**, *comb.fm.* seasonal (work, worker, business etc.). ◆**s~bedingt**, *adj.* seasonal.

Saite ['zaitə], *f -/-n* string. ◆**'S~ninstrument**, *n* string instrument.

Sakko ['zako], *m & n -s/-s* sports jacket.

sakral [zaˈkrɑːl], *adj.* religious (art, music etc.).

Sakrament [zakraˈmɛnt], *n -(e)s/-e* sacrament.

Salami [zaˈlɑːmi], *f -/-s* salami.

Salat [zaˈlɑːt], *m -(e)s/-e* 1. (*Kopfs.*) lettuce. 2. *Cu:* salad. 3. *F:* (*Unordnung*) mess; **der ganze S.**, the whole caboodle/ (*Sache*) business. ◆**S~blatt**, *n* lettuce leaf. ◆**S~soße**, *f* salad dressing.

Salbe ['zalbə], *f -/-n* ointment. ◆**S~ung**, *f -/-en* anointing. ◆**s~ungsvoll**, *adj.* unctuous.

Salbei ['zalbai], *m -s/no pl* sage.

Saldo ['zaldo], *m -s/-s & -den* balance.

Salmiak ['zalmiak], *m & n -s/no pl* ammonium chloride.

Salon [za'lɔŋ], *m -s/-s* 1. drawing-room. 2. (*Geschäft*) hairdresser's/beauty salon. ◆**s~fähig**, *adj.* socially acceptable (behaviour); respectable (clothes etc.).

salopp [za'lɔp], *adj.* casual; (*schlampig*) slipshod (dress, manner); easy-going (behaviour etc.).

Salpeter [zal'peːtər], *m -s/no pl* saltpetre. ◆**S~säure**, *f* nitric acid.

Salto ['zalto], *m -s/-s & -ti* somersault.

Salut [za'luːt], *m -(e)s/-e Mil: etc:* (gun) salute. ◆**s~ieren** [-u'tiːrən], *v.i.* (*haben*) (**vor j-m**) **s.**, to salute (s.o.).

Salve ['zalvə], *f -/-n* salvo.

Salz [zalts]. I. *n -es/-e* salt. II. **'S~**, *comb.fm.* salt (mine, content, lake etc.); *Cu:* salted (meat, herring). ◆**'s~en**, *v.tr.* to salt (food). ◆**'s~ig**, *adj.* salty. ◆**'S~kartoffeln**, *fpl* boiled potatoes. ◆**'S~los**, *adj.* salt-free. ◆**'S~säure**, *f* hydrochloric acid. ◆**'S~streuer**, *m* salt shaker. ◆**'S~wasser**, *n* salt water/Cu: salted water.

Samen ['zɑːmən], I. *m -s/-* seed; *Anat:* sperm. II. **'S~**, *comb.fm.* (*a*) seed (shop, capsule etc.); (*b*) *Anat:* sperm (bank, cell etc.); seminal (fluid etc.).

Sammelband ['zaməlbant], *m* omnibus edition. ◆**S~elbecken**, *n* reservoir. ◆**S~elbestellung**, *f* joint order. ◆**S~eln**, *v.tr.* to collect (money, stamps, wood, facts, *Fig:* one's thoughts etc.); to gather (berries etc.); **neue Kräf-**

te s., to build up one's strength; **sich s.**, (*Menschen, Truppen usw.*) to gather, assemble; *Fig:* (*Pers.*) to collect oneself/ one's thoughts. ◆**S~el'surium**, *n -s/no pl F:* conglomeration. ◆**'S~ler**, *m -s/-* (*Pers.*) collector. ◆**'S~lung**, *f -/-en* collection; *Fig:* (*Konzentration*) composure.

Samstag ['zamstaːk], *m* Saturday.

Samt¹ [zamt]. I. *m -(e)s/-e* velvet. II. **'S~**, *comb.fm.* (*aus S.*) velvet (ribbon, suit, glove etc.); (*samtig*) velvety (green, skin, paw etc.). ◆**'s~ig**, *adj.* velvety (skin etc.).

samt². I. *prep. + dat* together/F: complete with. II. *adv.* **s. und sonders**, all (without exception).

sämtlich ['zɛmtlíç], *adj.* all; **s~es vorhandene Material**, all the material available.

Sanatorium [zana'toːrium], *n -s/-ien* sanatorium.

Sand [zant]. I. *m -(e)s/no pl* sand; (*für Straßen usw.*) grit. II. **'S~**, *comb.fm.* sand (dune, -storm etc.); (*sandig*) sandy (beach, soil etc.). ◆**'S~bank**, *f* sandbank. ◆**'s~ig**, *adj.* sandy. ◆**'S~kasten**, *m* (*für Kinder*) sandpit. *N.Am:* sandbox. ◆**'S~kuchen**, *m* Madeira cake. ◆**'S~papier**, *n* sandpaper. ◆**'S~uhr**, *f* hour-glass; (*für Eier*) egg-timer.

Sandale [zan'daːlə], *f -/-n* sandal.

Sandelholz ['zandəlhɔlts], *n* sandalwood.

sanft [zanft], *adj.* gentle; (*leise*) soft (sound, voice etc.); (*friedlich*) peaceful (sleep etc.). ◆**'S~heit**, *f -/no pl* gentleness; softness. ◆**'S~mut**, *f* gentleness, meekness. ◆**'s~mütig**, *adj.* gentle, meek.

Sänger|(in) ['zɛŋər(in)], *m -s/-s (f -/-nen)* singer.

sanier|en [za'niːrən], *v.tr.* (*a*) to renovate (bad housing etc.); to develop (a district etc.), clear (slums); to clean up (a river etc.); (*b*) *Com:* to put (a firm) back on its feet. ◆**S~ung**, *f -/-en* redevelopment; slum clearance.

sani|tär [zani'tɛːr], *adj.* sanitary; **s~täre Anlagen**, sanitation; (*Toiletten*) lavatories. ◆**S~'täter**, *m -s/-* first-aid man; (*im Krankenwagen*) ambulance man; *Mil:* medical orderly. ◆**S~'tätsauto**, *n* ambulance.

Sanktion [zaŋktsi'oːn], *f -/-en* sanction. ◆**s~ieren** [-o'niːrən], *v.tr.* to sanction (a law, plan etc.).

Saphir ['zaːfiːr], *m -s/-e Rec:* sapphire stylus.

Sardelle [zar'dɛlə], *f -/-n* anchovy.

Sardine [zar'diːnə], *f -/-n* sardine.

Sarg [zark], *m -(e)s/-e* coffin.

Sarkas|mus [zar'kasmus], *m -/-men* sarcasm. ◆**s~tisch**, *adj.* sarcastic.

Satan ['zɑːtan], *m -s/-e* Satan. ◆**s~isch** [za'tɑːniʃ], *adj.* satanic.

Satellit [zatɛ'liːt], *m -en/-en* satellite. ◆**S~en-**, *comb.fm.* satellite (state, town

etc.).

Satin [za'tɛn], *m -s/-s* satin.

Satir|e [za'ti:rə], *f -/-n* satire. ◆**S~iker**, *m -s/-* satirist. ◆**s~isch**, *adj.* satirical.

satt [zat], *adj.* 1. (*a*) (*Pers.*) well-fed, satiated; *F:* full; **sich s. essen**, to eat one's fill; **bist du s.?** have you had enough (to eat)? **das macht s.**, that's filling; (*b*) *F:* **j-n, etwas s. sein/haben**, to be fed up with/sick of s.o., sth. 2. rich, deep (colour, blue etc.).

Satt|el ['zatəl], *m -s/-* saddle; *Fig:* **fest im S. sitzen**, to be secure in one's position. ◆**S~eldach**, *n* saddleback roof. ◆**s~elfest**, *adj.* **s. sein**, to know one's job. ◆**s~eln**, *v.tr.* to saddle (a horse etc.). ◆**S~elschlepper**, *m* tractor (of an articulated lorry/*N.Am:* truck). ◆**S~eltasche**, *f* saddlebag.

sättig|en ['zɛtigən], *v.tr.* (*a*) to satisfy (s.o., *Fig:* s.o.'s curiosity etc.); (*Essen*) **sehr s~end**, very filling; (*b*) to saturate (*Ch:* an acid, *Com:* the market etc.). ◆**S~ung**, *f -/-en* (*a*) satisfaction (of hunger); (*b*) *Ch: etc:* saturation.

Satz [zats], *m -es/-e* 1. (*a*) *Gram:* sentence; **abhängiger S.**, subordinate clause; (*b*) (*These*) thesis; *Mth:* theorem. 2. *Mus:* movement (of a symphony etc.). 3. (*Gruppe*) set (of chairs, glasses etc.); kit (of tools etc.); (*Porzellan*) service. 4. (*Tennis*) set. 5. (*Tarif*) rate. 6. (*Rückstand*) sediment; (*Kaffees*) (coffee) grounds. 7. (*Sprung*) leap; **mit einem S.**, with one bound. ◆**S~teil**, *m* clause. ◆**S~ung**, *f -/-en usu. pl S~en, Jur:* articles (of association); regulations. ◆**S~zeichen**, *n* punctuation mark.

Sau [zau]. I. *f /- -/-e* or *Säue* Z: sow; *P:* **unter aller S.**, bloody awful, lousy; (*b*) *P:* (*Pers.*) (dirty) swine, (*Frau*) bitch. 2. *-/-en* female (wild) boar. II. 'S~-, 's~-, comb.fm. *P:* filthy (weather etc.); bloody awful (job etc.); damn, bloody (stupid, rude, cold etc.). ◆**S~bohne**, *f* broad bean. ◆**S~erei**, *f -/-en F:* (*a*) (*Ärgernis*) absolute scandal; (*b*) (*Unordnung, Schmutz*) awful mess; (*c*) (*Anstößiges*) smut. ◆**S~haufen**, *m* scruffy bunch. ◆**s~mäßig**, *adj. P:* filthy (weather etc.); lousy (pay etc.); frightful (bad luck); **s. kalt**, frightfully cold. ◆**S~stall**, *m* pigsty. ◆**s~wohl**, *adj. F:* **sich s. fühlen**, to be on top of the world.

sauber ['zaubər], *adj.* (*a*) (*schmutzfrei*) clean; (*b*) (*ordentlich*) neat (handwriting, appearance etc.); (*c*) (*anständig*) decent. ◆**s~halten**, *v.tr.sep.irr.45* to keep (sth.) clean. ◆**S~keit**, *f -/no pl* (*a*) cleanliness; neatness; (*b*) decency. ◆**s~machen**, *v.tr.sep.* to clean (a room etc.).

säuber|lich ['zɔybərliç], *adj.* accurate (copying etc.); (**fein**) **s. verpackt**, neatly/carefully packed. ◆**s~n**, *v.tr.* (*a*) to clean (a room, shoes, wound etc.); (*b*)

Pol: to purge (a party). ◆**S~ung**, *f -/-en* cleaning; *Pol:* purge.

Saudi-Arabien [zaudi?a'ra:biən]. *Pr.n.n. -s.* Saudi Arabia.

sauer ['zauər], *adj.* sour (fruit, taste etc.; *Fig:* face etc.); *Ch: etc:* acid (solution, soil etc.); *Cu:* (*in Essig usw.*) pickled (cucumber, herrings etc.); **s. verdientes Geld**, hard earned money; *F:* **er ist s. auf mich**, he's cross with/mad at me. ◆**S~braten**, *m* roast marinated beef. ◆**S~kirsche**, *f* sour cherry. ◆**S~kraut**, *n* sauerkraut. ◆**S~stoff**, *m* oxygen. ◆**S~teig**, *m* leaven.

säuerlich ['zɔyərliç], *adj.* (slightly) sour.

sauf|en ['zaufən], *v.tr. & i. irr.* (*haben*) (*Tier*) to drink (water etc.); *F:* **wir haben die ganze Nacht gesoffen**, we were boozing all night. ◆**S~erei**, *f -/-en F:* (*a*) *no pl* boozing; (*b*) booze-up.

Säufer ['zɔyfər], *m -s/-* *F:* boozer.

saug|en ['zaugən], *v.tr. & i. irr.* (*haben*) (*a*) to suck (sth.); (*b*) (*staubsaugen*) to hoover, vacuum (a room etc.). ◆**S~er**, *m -s/-* teat, *N.Am:* nipple (on baby's bottle). ◆**s~fähig**, *adj.* absorbent (paper etc.). ◆**S~wirkung**, *f* suction.

säug|en ['zɔygən], *v.tr.* to suckle (a baby, *Z:* young). ◆**S~etier**, *n* mammal. ◆**S~ling**, *m -s/-e* baby.

Säule ['zɔylə], *f -/-n* column, (round) pillar. ◆**S~ngang**, *m* colonnade.

Saum [zaum], *m -(e)s/-e* hem; *Fig:* edge. ◆**s~selig**, *adj. Lit:* dilatory.

säumen ['zɔymən], *v.tr.* (*a*) to hem (a garment); (*b*) *Fig:* to line (a road etc.).

Sauna ['zauna], *f -/-s* sauna (bath).

Säure ['zɔyrə], *f -/-n* 1. *Ch:* acid. 2. *no pl* acidity (of wine etc.); sourness (of unripe fruit etc.).

säuseln ['zɔyzəln], *v.i.* (*haben*) (*Wind usw.*) to whisper; (*Blätter*) to rustle.

sausen ['zauzən], *v.i.* (*a*) (*haben*) (*Wind usw.*) to rush, roar; (*Ohren, Kopf usw.*) to buzz; (*b*) *F:* (*sein*) (*Pers., Wagen usw.*) to dash, rush (somewhere); (*c*) (*sein*) *P:* **durchs Examen s.**, to plough/flunk the exam; (*d*) *F:* **etwas s. lassen**, to give sth. a miss.

Saxophon [zakso'fo:n], *n -s/-e* saxophone.

S-Bahn ['ɛsba:n], *f* urban railway.

Schabe ['ʃ:bə], *f -/-n* Z: cockroach.

Schab|en ['ʃa:bən], *v.tr.* to scrape (sth.). ◆**S~er**, *m -s/-* scraper.

Schabernack ['ʃa:bərnak], *m -(e)s/-e* practical joke, prank.

schäbig ['ʃɛ:biç], *adj.* (*a*) shabby (clothes, room etc.); tatty (clothes, car etc.); seedy (hotel etc.); (*b*) measly (present etc.).

Schablon|e [ʃa'blo:nə], *f -/-n* (*a*) *Tchn:* template; (*für eine Zeichnung*) stencil; (*b*) *Fig:* fixed pattern. ◆**s~enhaft**, *adj.* stereotyped.

Schach [ʃax], *n -s/no pl* chess; *Fig:* **j-n in S. halten**, to keep s.o. under control.

◆'S~brett, n chessboard. ◆'S~figur, f chessman. ◆'s~matt. I. int. checkmate. II. adj. 1. j-n s. setzen, to checkmate s.o. 2. F: (erschöpft) dead beat. ◆'S~zug, m (also Fig:) move.

schachern ['ʃaxərn], v.i. (haben) to haggle (um den Preis usw.), over the price etc.).

Schacht [ʃaxt], m -(e)s/-e (mine, lift etc.) shaft; (Brunnens:) well; (für Kohlen usw.) chute.

Schachtel ['ʃaxtəl], f -/-n 1. box; S: Zigaretten, packet/N.Am: pack of cigarettes. 2. F: (Frau) alte S., old bag.

schade ['ʃaːdə], adj. (a) (bedauerlich) es ist (sehr) s., it's a (great) pity/shame (um + acc, about); (b) (wertvoll) es ist zu s. zum Wegwerfen, it is too good to throw away; für diese Arbeit ist er sich zu s., he considers this kind of work beneath him.

Schädel ['ʃɛːdəl], m -s/- skull. ◆'S~bruch, m fracture of the skull.

schaden ['ʃaːdən] I. v.i. (haben) to do harm/damage; das schadet der Gesundheit sehr, that is very bad for one's health; F: das schadet ihm nichts, that won't do him any harm/(verdientermaßen) serves him right. II. S., m -s/-damage, (Verletzung) injury; (Mangel) defect; (Verlust) loss; (Nachteil) harm, detriment; j-m S. zufügen, to do s.o. harm; es soll dein S. nicht sein, you won't lose by it. ◆'S~enersatz, m compensation (for damage/injury). ◆'S~enfreude, f malicious pleasure (over s.o.'s misfortune). ◆'s~enfroh, adj. gloating, (maliciously) gleeful. ◆'s~haft, adj. defective, faulty (part etc.); (beschädigt) damaged (goods etc.). ◆'s~los, adj. sich an j-m s. halten, to take advantage of s.o. (für etwas acc, to make up for sth.). ◆schädigen ['ʃɛːdɪɡən], v.tr. to do harm to, harm (one's health, eyes, reputation etc.); to damage (s.o.'s interests etc.). ◆'s~igung, f -/-en harm, damage. ◆'s~lich, adj. harmful, damaging (effect, influence etc.); unhealthy (climate etc.); noxious (chemicals). ◆'S~ling, m -s/-e pest. ◆'S~lingsbekämpfungsmittel, n pesticide.

Schaf [ʃaːf], n -(e)s/-e sheep. ◆'S~bock, m ram. ◆'S~fell, n sheepskin. ◆'S~herde, f flock of sheep. ◆'S~hirt, m shepherd. ◆'S~skäse, m sheep's milk cheese.

Schäfchen ['ʃɛːfçən], n -s/- little sheep, lamb. ◆'S~chenwolken, fpl fleecy clouds. ◆'S~er, m -s/- shepherd. ◆'S~erhund, m -(e)s/-e sheepdog; (Deutscher) S., Alsatian.

schaffen[1] ['ʃafən]. I. v.tr.irr. to create (sth.); to establish (connections, relationships, order etc.); sie sind für einander geschaffen, they were made for each other. II. S., n -s/no pl (Vorgang) creation; (Tätigkeit) activity. ◆'S~skraft, f

creativity.

schaffen[2] v. 1. v.tr. (a) to manage (sth.), get (sth.) done; to manage to catch (a train etc.); (b) to pass (an exam); das schaffe ich nie, I can never (manage) to do that; (zeitlich) I'll never make it; (b) (bringen) to take, get (s.o., sth.) (somewhere); (c) F: (erschöpfen) j-n s., to wear s.o. out, finish s.o. off, (nervlich) get on s.o.'s nerves. 2. v.i. (haben) s.a. (arbeiten) to work; (Sorge machen) j-m zu s. machen, to cause s.o. difficulty/trouble; (c) sich dat zu s. machen, to busy oneself.

Schaffner ['ʃafnər], m -s/- (bus/tram) conductor; Rail: ticket inspector. ◆'S~in, f -/-nen (bus/tram) conductress.

Schaft [ʃaft], m -(e)s/-e shaft (of a column, axe etc.); shank (of a bolt, tool); leg (of a boot). ◆'S~stiefel, m jackboot.

Schakal [ʃa'kaːl], m -s/-e jackal.

schäkern ['ʃɛːkərn], v.i. (haben) A: & Hum: to tease, flirt; (scherzen) to joke.

Schal[1] [ʃaːl], m -s/-s & -e scarf; (für die Schulter) shawl.

schal[2], adj. flat (beer etc.); Fig: stale (joke etc.).

Schale ['ʃaːlə], f -/-n 1. (Hülle) (a) (hart) shell (of an egg etc.); (b) (des Obstes) skin; (abgeschält) peel (of an apple, potato etc.); (Rinde) rind (of a lemon etc.). 2. (Schüssel) bowl; (shallow) dish; pan (of scales). ◆'S~ntiere, npl molluscs.

schälen ['ʃɛːlən], v.tr. (a) to peel (potatoes, apples etc.); skin (tomatoes, almonds); (b) sich s., to peel.

Schall [ʃal], m -(e)s/-e sound. ◆'s~dicht, adj. soundproof. ◆'S~dämpfer, m Aut: silencer; N.Am: muffler. ◆'s~en, v.i. (haben) to resound. ◆'s~end, adj. resounding (applause, blow), ringing (laughter). ◆'S~geschwindigkeit, f speed of sound. ◆'S~mauer, f sound barrier. ◆'S~platte, f (gramophone) record. ◆'S~platten-, comb.fm. record (album, archive, shop etc.).

Schaltbild ['ʃaltbɪlt], n wiring/circuit diagram. ◆'S~brett, n switchboard. ◆'s~en, v.tr. & i. (haben) (a) Aut: to change gear; (b) El: etc: to switch; (c) F: (begreifen) to catch on, click; (reagieren) to react; (d) s. und walten, to do as one pleases. 2. v.tr. El: to switch (an oven etc.), turn (a switch). ◆'S~er, m -s/- 1. El: switch. 2. Rail: Th: ticket-window; (in Postamt usw.) (counter) position. ◆'S~erhalle, f Rail: booking hall. ◆'S~erstunden, fpl counter hours. ◆'S~hebel, m Aut: gear lever. ◆'S~jahr, n leap year. ◆'S~plan, m El: circuit/wiring diagram. ◆'S~tafel, f switchboard, control panel; Ind: console. ◆'S~ung, f -/-en 1. El: (a) connection; (b) (alle Bauteile) circuit. 2. Aut: gearchange, N.Am: gearshift.

Scham [ʃɑːm]. I. f -/no pl shame; ohne S., unashamed. II. 'S~, comb.fm. Anat: pubic (hair, region etc.). ◆'S~bein, n pubic bone. ◆'S~gefühl, n sense of shame. ◆'s~los, adj. shameless; (unanständig) indecent; unscrupulous (trick etc.). ◆S~losigkeit, f -/-en shamelessness; indecency.

schämen [ˈʃɛːmən], v.tr. sich (wegen) etwas gen s., to be ashamed of sth.; s. Sie sich! shame on you!

Schand|e [ˈʃandə], f -/no pl disgrace; j-m S. machen, to bring shame on s.o. ◆'S~fleck, m blot (in der Landschaft usw., on the landscape etc.). ◆'S~tat, f villainous deed.

schänd|en [ˈʃɛndən], v.tr. (a) to disgrace (a family's name etc.); (entweihen) to desecrate (a church, grave etc.). ◆'s~lich, adj. disgraceful (behaviour etc.); shameful (deed etc.).

Schank|erlaubnis [ˈʃaŋkʔɛrlaupnis], f (publican's) licence, N.Am: excise licence. ◆'S~tisch, m bar (counter).

Schanze [ˈʃantsə], f -/-n Sp: ski jump, hill.

Schar [ʃɑːr], f -/-en crowd (of people); troop (of children etc.); flock (of birds); in (hellen) S~en, in droves/hordes. ◆'s~en, v.refl. sich um j-n, etwas acc s., to flock/cluster round s.o., sth. ◆'s~enweise, adv. in droves/hordes.

scharf [ʃarf], adj. 1. (a) sharp (knife, frost, Fig: eyes etc.); keen (edge, wind, Fig: observation etc.); s. nachdenken/hinsehen, to think/look hard; (b) (deutlich) clear-cut (outlines etc.); sharp (photograph etc.); nicht s., unclear, (verschwommen) blurred; (c) (hart, streng) harsh (criticism, measures etc.); s. durchgreifen/vorgehen, to take strong/severe measures. 2. (stark) Cu: spicy (food); hot (curry etc.); strong (mustard); pungent (smell); s. gewürzt, highly seasoned; (b) strong (drink). 3. (a) (heftig) fierce (resistance, protest); (b) live (ammunition). 4. F: wild auf j-n, etwas acc s. sein, to be keen on s.o., sth. ◆'S~blick, m perspicacity. ◆'s~machen, v.tr. F: to incite, rouse (s.o.). ◆'S~richter, m executioner. ◆'S~schütze, m sharpshooter, marksman. ◆'S~sinn, m shrewdness, astuteness. ◆'s~sinnig, adj. shrewd, astute.

Schärfe [ˈʃɛrfə], f -/-n 1. (a) sharpness; keenness (of the wind etc.); Fig: acuteness (of mind etc.); quickness (of hearing); (b) clarity, Phot: etc: definition; (c) harshness, severity. 2. (Stärke) strength; pungency; Cu: spiciness, hotness. 3. (Heftigkeit) fierceness. ◆'s~n, v.tr. to sharpen (a knife etc.).

Scharlach [ˈʃarlax], m -s/no pl 1. (Farbe) scarlet. 2. Med: scarlet fever. ◆'s~rot, adj. scarlet.

Scharlatan [ˈʃarlatan], m -s/-e charlatan, quack.

Scharnier [ʃarˈniːr], n -s/-e hinge.

Schärpe [ˈʃɛrpə], f -/-n sash.

scharren [ˈʃarən], v.i. (haben) to scrape, scratch.

Scharte [ˈʃartə], f -/-n notch (on a blade etc.).

Schaschlik [ˈʃaʃlik], n -s/-s kebab.

Schatt|en [ˈʃatən], m -s/- (a) shadow (of s.o., sth.); (b) no pl shade (of a tree etc.); 30° im S., 30° C in the shade; Fig: j-n, etwas in den S. stellen, to overshadow s.o., sth. ◆'s~enhaft, adj. shadowy (figures etc.). ◆'S~enriß, m silhouette. ◆'S~enseite, f -/-n 1. shady side (of a house etc.). 2. (Nachteil) drawback, negative aspect; dark side (of life). ◆'s~ieren [ʃaˈtiːrən], v.tr. to shade (background etc.). ◆'S~ierung, f -/-en (a) no pl shading; (b) also Fig: nuance. ◆'s~ig, adj. shady.

Schatulle [ʃaˈtulə], f -/-n casket.

Schatz [ʃats], m -es/¨e 1. treasure. 2. F: (Kind, netter Mensch) darling. ◆'S~kammer, f treasure house/ chamber. ◆'S~meister, m treasurer. ◆'S~sucher, m treasure hunter.

schätz|en [ˈʃɛtsən], v.tr. (a) to estimate (sth.); to judge (a distance etc.); (taxieren) to assess, value (a house etc.); grob geschätzt, at a rough estimate; wie alt s. Sie ihn? how old would you say he is? ich schätze, daß er bald kommt, I reckon/N.Am: guess he'll come soon; (b) (achten) to think highly of (s.o.), (würdigen) appreciate (s.o., wine etc.), value (s.o.'s advice etc.). ◆'S~ung, f -/-en estimate, (Vorgang) estimation; valuation (of a house etc.). ◆'s~ungsweise, adv. at a rough estimate. ◆'S~wert, m assessment, valuation.

Schau [ʃau]. I. f -/-en (fashion, theatre etc.) show; etwas zur S. stellen/tragen, to display sth. II. 'S~, comb.fm. Th: show (business, Pol: trial etc.); Com: display (pack etc.). ◆'S~bild, n diagram. ◆'s~en, v.i. (haben) to look; nach j-m, etwas dat s., to look after s.o., sth. ◆'S~fenster, n shop/N.Am: store window. ◆'S~fensterbummel, m einen S. machen, to go window-shopping. ◆'S~fensterdekoration, f window dressing. ◆'S~fensterpuppe, f window dummy. ◆'s~lustig, adj. curious, inquisitive. ◆'S~platz, m setting (of a novel etc.); scene (of an accident, crime etc.); Sp: venue. ◆'S~spiel, n Th: play, drama; Fig: Lit: spectacle. ◆'S~spieler, m actor. ◆'S~spielerin, f actress. ◆'s~spielerisch, adj. acting (ability etc.). ◆'S~spielhaus, n theatre. ◆'S~steller, m (travelling) showman. ◆'S~tafel, f wall chart.

Schauder [ˈʃaudər], m -s/- shiver; (vor Angst usw.) shudder. ◆'s~haft, adj. F: dreadful, appalling. ◆'s~n. I. v.tr. & i. (haben) (frösteln) to shiver; (vor Angst *usw.*) to shudder, tremble. **II. S.,** *-s/ no pl* shiver; (*Grauen*) (feeling of) horror.

Schau|er ['ʃaʊər]. **I.** *m -s/-* shower (of rain etc.). **II.** '**S~**, *comb.fm.* horror (play etc.). ◆'**s~erlich**, *adj.* ghastly, gruesome (crime, sight etc.); spine-chilling (story). ◆'**S~ermärchen**, *n* horror story, spine-chiller. ◆'**s~rig**, *adj.=s~erlich*; **s. schön**, eerily beautiful.

Schaufel ['ʃaʊfəl], *f -/-n* **1.** shovel. **2.** *Tchn:* (*wheel*) paddle, blade (*of a turbine* etc.). ◆'**S~n**, *v.tr.* to shovel (coal, snow etc.).

Schaukel ['ʃaʊkəl], *f -/-n* (child's) swing. ◆'**s~n**, *v.* **1.** *v.i.* (*haben*) (*auf einer Schaukel usw.*) to (have a) swing; (*im Schaukelstuhl usw.*) to rock. **2.** *v.tr.* to rock (a baby, cradle etc.). ◆'**S~pferd**, *n* rocking horse. ◆'**S~stuhl**, *m* rocking chair.

Schaum [ʃaʊm], *m -(e)s/-e* foam; froth (on beer etc.); (*Seifens.*) lather. ◆'**S~gebäck**, *n* meringues. ◆'**S~gummi**, *n* foam rubber. ◆'**s~ig**, *adj.* frothy (liquid); foamy (sea etc.); **s~ schlagen**, to beat eggs (until frothy). ◆'**S~krone**, *f* white horse (on a wave). ◆'**S~schläger**, *m F:* (*Pers.*) show-off. ◆'**S~stoff**, *m* plastic foam. ◆'**S~wein**, *m* sparkling wine.

schäumen ['ʃɔymən], *v.i.* (*haben*) to foam; (*Bier usw.*) to froth; (*Seife*) to lather; (*Sekt usw.*) to sparkle.

Scheck [ʃɛk]. **I.** *m -s/-s* cheque, *N.Am:* check. **II.** '**S~**, *comb.fm.* cheque, *N.Am:* check (card etc.). ◆'**S~buch/**'**S~heft**, *n* cheque/*N.Am:* check book.

scheckig ['ʃɛkɪç], *adj.* dappled (horse, cow); piebald (horse); blotchy (skin etc.).

scheel [ʃeːl], *adj. F:* **s~ ansehen**, to give s.o. an old-fashioned look.

scheffeln ['ʃɛfəln], *v.tr. F:* **Geld s.**, to rake in money.

Scheibe ['ʃaɪbə], *f -/-n* **1.** (*round*) disc; *Sp: (Schieß.)* target. **2.** (*Schnitte*) slice. **3.** (*Glas*) (window etc.) pane. ◆'**S~n-bremse**, *f* disc brake. ◆'**S~n-waschanlage**, *f* windscreen/*N.Am:* windshield washer. ◆'**S~nwischer**, *m* windscreen/*N.Am:* windshield wiper.

Scheich [ʃaɪç], *m -s/-s* sheikh, sheik.

Scheid|e ['ʃaɪdə], *f -/-n* **1.** sheath (for a sword etc.). **2.** *Anat:* vagina. ◆'**s~en**, *v.tr.65* **1.** *v.tr.* (*a*) *Lit:* (*trennen*) to separate, divide (two things/people); **sich s.**, to diverge; (*b*) *Jur:* to dissolve (a marriage), divorce (a married couple); **sich s. lassen**, to get a divorce. **2.** *v.i.* (*sein*) *Lit:* to part. ◆'**S~ung**, *f -/-en* (*a*) separation; (*b*) *Jur:* divorce. ◆'**S~ungs-grund**, *m* grounds for divorce. ◆'**S~ungsprozeß**, *m* divorce proceedings.

Schein [ʃaɪn]. **I.** *m -(e)s/-e* **1.** *no pl* (*Licht*) light. **2.** *no pl* (*Anschein*) appearance, pretence; **er tut es nur zum S.**, he only pre-

tends to do it. **3.** (*a*) (*Bescheinigung*) certificate; (*Zettel*) chit; (*Führers. usw.*) licence; (*b*) (*Gelds.*) (bank)note, *N.Am:* bill. **II.** '**S~**, *comb.fm.* sham, mock (attack etc.); specious (argument, reason). ◆'**s~bar**, *adj.* apparent (contradiction etc.); ostensible (reasons etc.); *adv.* seemingly. ◆'**s~en**, *v.i.irr.* (*haben*) (*a*) (*leuchten*) to shine; (*b*) (*Eindruck erwecken*) to seem, appear; **mir scheint, daß ...**, it seems to me that ... ◆'**s~heilig**, *adj. F:* hypocritical. ◆'**S~tod**, *m* suspended animation. ◆'**S~werfer**, *m -s/- Aut:* headlight; *Th: etc:* spotlight; *Mil: etc:* (*Suchs.*) search-light.

Scheiß- [ʃaɪs-], *comb.fm. P:* bloody, blasted (work etc.). ◆'**S~e**, *f -/no pl & int. V:* shit. ◆'**s~e'gal**, *adj. P:* **das ist mir s.!** I don't give a damn! ◆'**S~kerl**, *m V:* bastard.

Scheitel ['ʃaɪtəl], *m -s/-* (*a*) crown, top (of the head); (*b*) (*Haars.*) parting. ◆'**s~n**, *v.tr.* **das Haar s.**, to part one's hair. ◆'**S~punkt**, *m* apex.

Scheiter|haufen ['ʃaɪtərhaʊfən], *m -s/- Hist:* (*funeral*) pyre. ◆'**s~n**. **I.** *v.i.* (*sein*) to fail (utterly); (*Verhandlungen usw.*) to break down (**an etwas** *dat, due* to sth.); (*Ehe*) to break up. **II. S.,** *n -s/no pl* failure; breakdown.

Schelle ['ʃɛlə], *f -/-n* (small) bell. ◆'**s~n**, *v.i.* (*haben*) to ring.

Schellfisch ['ʃɛlfɪʃ], *m* haddock.

Schelm [ʃɛlm], *m -(e)s/-e* scallywag, rogue. ◆'**s~isch**, *adj.* roguish, mischievous.

Schelte ['ʃɛltə], *f -/-n* scolding. ◆'**s~n**, *v.tr. & i. irr.* (*haben*) to scold, chide (s.o.).

Schema ['ʃeːma], *n -s/-s & -ta* (*a*) (*Entwurf*) draft; (*Zeichnung*) diagram; (*b*) (*Muster, Norm*) pattern. ◆'**s~tisch** [ʃe'maːtɪʃ], *adj.* (*a*) diagrammatic; (*a. abgebildet*, illustrated in a diagram; (*b*) *Pej:* routine, mechanical (work etc.).

Schemel ['ʃeːməl], *m -s/-* stool.

Schenke ['ʃɛŋkə], *f -/-n* tavern.

Schenkel ['ʃɛŋkəl], *m -s/-* **1.** *Anat:* thigh. **2.** *Mth:* side (of an angle).

schenk|en ['ʃɛŋkən], *v.tr.* **j-m etwas s.**, to give s.o. sth. (as a present); **j-m Aufmerksamkeit s.**, to pay attention to s.o.; **j-m Vertrauen s.**, to trust s.o.; *F:* **das können wir uns s.**, we can do without that. ◆'**S~ung**, *f -/-en* donation.

Scherbe ['ʃɛrbə], *f -/-n* broken piece/fragment (of china, glass etc.).

Scher|e ['ʃeːrə], *f -/-n* (*a*) pair of scissors/(*größer*) shears; (*b*) *usu. pl* **S~n**, claws, pincers (of a crab etc.). ◆'**s~en1**, *v.tr.irr.* to shear (sheep etc.). ◆'**s~en2**, *v.refl.* **er schert sich nicht/darum**, he doesn't care/*F:* give a damn about it; **s. dich zum Teufel!** get lost!

Scherflein ['ʃɛrflaɪn], *n* **sein S. beitragen**, to make one's little contribution.

Scherz [ʃerts], *m* -es/-e joke; *etwas im S. sagen,* to say sth. jokingly/in fun. ◆'**S~artikel,** *m* novelty (article). ◆'**s~en,** *v.i.* (haben) to joke; **damit ist nicht zu s.,** that's no laughing matter. ◆'**S~frage,** *f* (comic) catch question. ◆'**s~haft,** *adj.* jocular; *(leichtfertig)* flippant (remark etc.).

scheu [ʃɔy]. **I.** *adj.* shy. **II. S.,** *f* -/no pl shyness; *(Hemmung)* inhibition; *(Angst)* awe (**vor j-m,** of s.o.). ◆'**s~en,** *v.tr.* (a) to shun (publicity etc.), avoid (risks etc.); *keine Mühe/Kosten s.,* to spare no pains/expense; (b) *sich vor etwas dat s.,* to be afraid of sth./to do sth. ◆'**S~klappen,** *fpl* (horse's) blinkers.

Scheuer|**bürste** [ˈʃɔyərbyrstə], *f* scrubbing brush. ◆'**S~lappen,** *m* floorcloth. ◆'**s~n,** *v.tr.* (a) to scour (pots etc.), scrub (a floor etc.); (b) *(Schuh, Riemen usw.)* to chafe. ◆'**S~tuch,** *n* floorcloth.

Scheune [ˈʃɔynə], *f* -/-n barn.

Scheusal [ˈʃɔyzaːl], *n* -s/-e *Pej:* (Pers.) **du S.!** you beast!

scheußlich [ˈʃɔyslɪç], *adj.* *(häßlich)* hideous (sight, building etc.); *(gräßlich)* monstrous (crime etc.); *F:* **s. kalt,** frightfully/terribly cold. ◆'**S~keit,** *f* -/-en hideous appearance; monstrousness.

Schi [ʃiː], *m* -s/-er = **Ski.**

Schicht [ʃɪçt]. **I.** *f* -/-en **1.** layer; coat (of paint). **2.** *Ind:* shift. **3.** (social) class. **II.** '**S~,** *comb.fm. Ind:* shift (work, worker etc.). ◆'**s~en,** *v.tr.* to stack (wood, bricks etc.). ◆'**s~weise,** *adv.* **1.** in layers. **2.** *Ind:* in shifts.

schick [ʃɪk], *adj.* smart, stylish.

schicken [ˈʃɪkən], *v.tr.* (a) to send (sth.); (b) *sich dat in etwas acc s.,* to resign oneself to sth.; (c) *impers.* **es schickt sich nicht,** it is not done/proper. ◆'**s~lich,** *adj. Lit:* proper; seemly.

Schicksal [ˈʃɪkzaːl], *n* -s/-e fate. ◆'**s~haft,** *adj.* fateful. ◆'**S~sschlag,** *m* blow of fate.

Schieb|**edach** [ˈʃiːbədax], *n*, sliding roof, sunroof. ◆'**s~en,** *v.irr.* **1.** *v.tr.* (a) to push (s.o., sth.); to wheel (a bicycle etc.); (b) **die Schuld auf j-n s.,** to lay the blame on s.o. **2.** *v.i.* (haben) (a) to push; (b) *mit Rauschgift usw.* **s.,** to push drugs etc. ◆'**S~er,** *m* -s/- **1.** (baby's) pusher. **2.** *(zum Absperren usw.)* slide. **3.** *F:* (Pers.) racketeer. ◆'**S~ung,** *f* -/-en *F:* *(Geschäft)* racket, fiddle; **das ist alles S.!** the whole thing's a fiddle!

Schieds|**gericht** [ˈʃiːtsɡərɪçt], *n* court of arbitration. ◆'**S~richter,** *m* **1.** arbitrator. **2.** *Sp:* umpire; *Fb: etc:* referee. ◆'**S~spruch,** *m* arbitration award.

schief [ʃiːf], *adj.* (a) *(nicht gerade)* not straight; crooked; *(geneigt)* slanting (wall etc.); *(zur Seite geneigt)* leaning, *F:* lopsided (post etc.); *Mth:* oblique (angle); inclined (plane); *j-n s. ansehen,* to look askance at s.o.; (b) *(falsch)* false, distorted (picture, view). ◆'**s~gehen,**

*v.i.sep.irr.*36 (sein) *F:* (Unternehmen usw.) to go wrong. ◆'**s~lachen,** *v.i.sep.refl. F:* **sich s.,** to laugh oneself silly. ◆'**s~liegen,** *v.i.sep.irr.*62 (haben) *F:* to be mistaken.

Schiefer [ˈʃiːfər], *m* -s/- slate. ◆'**S~tafel,** *f* slate.

schielen [ˈʃiːlən], *v.i.* (haben) (a) *Med:* to squint; (b) *F:* **auf etwas acc s.,** to cast a beady eye on sth.

Schienbein [ˈʃiːnbain], *n* shin(bone).

Schiene [ˈʃiːnə], *f* -/-n (a) *Rail: etc:* rail; (b) track (for curtains etc.); (c) *Med:* splint. ◆'**s~n,** *v.tr. Med:* to splint (a limb). ◆'**S~nstrang,** *m* (stretch of) railway/*N.Am:* railroad track.

schier [ʃiːr], *adj.* **1.** sheer, pure (stupidity etc.). **2.** *adv.* almost; **s. unmöglich,** all but impossible.

Schieß|**bude** [ˈʃiːsbuːdə], *f* shooting gallery. ◆'**s~en,** *v.irr.*31 **1.** *v.i.* to shoot/fire at s.o., sth.; *F:* **schieß los!** fire away! **in die Höhe/aus der Erde s.,** to shoot up. **2.** *v.tr.* (a) to shoot (sth.); (b) *Fb:* **ein Tor s.,** to score a goal. ◆'**S~e'rei,** *f* -/-en shoot-out. ◆'**S~pulver,** *n* gunpowder. ◆'**S~scharte,** *f* embrasure; arrow slit. ◆'**S~stand,** *m* rifle/shooting range.

Schiff [ʃɪf], *n* -(e)s/-e **1.** ship. **2.** *Ecc:* *(Mittels.)* nave; *(Seitens.)* aisle. ◆'**Schiffahrt,** *f* -/no pl (a) *(Schiffe)* shipping; (b) *(Fahren)* navigation. ◆'**Schiffahrts-,** *comb.fm.* shipping (company etc.). ◆'**Schiffahrtslinie,** *f* shipping route/*(Gesellschaft)* line. ◆'**s~bar,** *adj.* navigable (river etc.). ◆'**S~bau,** *m* shipbuilding. ◆'**S~bruch,** *m* shipwreck; **S. erleiden,** to be shipwrecked; *Fig:* *(Pläne usw.)* to fail. ◆'**s~brüchig,** *adj.* shipwrecked. ◆'**S~er,** *m* -s/- boatman; *(Kapitän)* skipper. ◆'**S~s-,** *comb.fm.* ship's (boy, captain, papers etc.); shipping (agent etc.). ◆'**S~sfracht,** *f* ship's cargo. ◆'**S~schaukel,** *f* swing-boat.

Schikan|**e** [ʃiˈkaːnə], *f* -/-n **1.** (usu. *petty)* victimization; *(bloody-minded)* harassment. **2.** *F: Aut: etc:* **mit allen S~n,** with all the extras/trimmings. ◆**s~ieren** [-aˈniːrən], *v.tr.* to victimize (s.o.).

Schild[1] [ʃɪlt], *m* -(e)s/-e *Mil: Tchn: etc:* shield; *F:* **was führt er im S~e?** what's he after? ◆'**S~drüse,** *f* thyroid gland. ◆'**S~kröte,** *f* *(Wassers.)* turtle; *(Lands.)* tortoise.

Schild[2], *n* -(e)s/-er sign; *(Wegweiser)* signpost; *(große Tafel)* signboard (of a firm etc.); *(Etikett)* label. ◆'**s~ern,** *v.tr.* to describe (an occurrence, one's impressions etc.); *(bildhaft)* to depict (s.o., a scene). ◆'**S~erung,** *f* -/-en description, portrayal.

Schiff(rohr) [ˈʃɪf(roːr)], *n* -(e)s/-e reed.

schillern [ˈʃɪlərn], *v.i.* (haben) to shimmer, *(Diamant usw.)* sparkle.

Schimmel ['∫ɪməl], *m* -s/- 1. white horse. 2. *no pl* (*Fäulnis*) mould (on food etc.). ◆'s~ig, *adj.* mouldy. ◆'s~n, *v.i.* (*sein*) to go mouldy.

Schimmer ['∫ɪmər], *m* -s/*no pl* 1. gleam, glint. 2. (*Anflug*) hint, suspicion. ◆'s~n, *v.i.* (*haben*) to gleam, glint; (*Perlen, Seide usw.*) to shimmer.

Schimpanse [∫ɪm'panzə], *m* -n/-n chimpanzee.

schimpf|en ['∫ɪmpfən], *v.* 1. *v.i.* (*haben*) (*a*) to curse, *F:* carry on, *Brit:* create (*auf/über* j-n, etwas *acc*, about s.o., sth.); **mit** j-m s., to tell s.o. off. 2. *v.tr. Lit:* **j-n einen Lügner usw. s.**, to call s.o. a liar etc. ◆'S~wort, *n* swearword.

Schindel ['∫ɪndəl], *f* -/-n shingle.

schind|en ['∫ɪndən], *v.ir.* 1. *v.tr.* (*a*) to drive (s.o.) hard, *F:* slave-drive (s.o.); (*grausam*) to ill-treat (animals, prisoners etc.); (*b*) **Zeit s.**, to play for time; **Eindruck s.**, to try to impress. ◆'S~er, *m* -s/- slave-driver. ◆'S~e'rei, *f* -/-en *F:* hard slog, grind. ◆'S~luder, *n* mit j-m, etwas das S. treiben, to abuse s.o., sth.

Schinken ['∫ɪŋkən]. I. *m* -s/- *Cu:* ham. II. 'S~-, *comb.fm.* ham (roll, sausage etc.).

Schippe ['∫ɪpə], *f* -/-n shovel; *F:* **j-n auf die S. nehmen**, to pull s.o.'s leg.

Schirm [∫ɪrm], *m* -(e)s/-e 1. (*Regens.*) umbrella; (*Sonnens.*) sunshade. 2. (*gegen Hitze usw.*) screen; (*gegen Licht*) shade; *Cl:* peak (of a cap). ◆'S~herr, *m* patron. ◆'S~herrschaft, *f* patronage.

schizophren [∫itso'fre:n], *adj.* schizophrenic.

Schlacht [∫laxt], *f* -/-en battle (**um** + *acc*, for). ◆'s~en, *v.tr.* to slaughter (animals). ◆'S~er, *m* -s/- butcher. ◆'S~feld, *n* battlefield. ◆'S~hof, *m* slaughterhouse. ◆'S~plan, *m* plan of battle/*Fig:* campaign. ◆'S~schiff, *n* battleship. ◆'S~ung, *f* -/*no pl* slaughter(ing).

Schlacke ['∫lakə], *f* -/-n clinker; (*Erzs.*) slag.

Schlaf [∫la:f]. I. *m* -(e)s/*no pl* sleep. II. 'S~-, *comb.fm.* sleeping (tablet, pill, sickness etc.). ◆'S~anzug, *m* pyjamas, *N.Am:* pajamas. ◆'s~en, *v.i.irr.* (*haben*) to sleep; (*Zustand*) to be asleep; **s. gehen**, to go to bed. ◆'S~engehen, *n* -s/*no pl* going to bed. ◆'S~enszeit, *f* bedtime. ◆'s~los, *adj.* sleepless. ◆'S~gelegenheit, *f* sleeping accommodation. ◆'S~losigkeit, *f* *no pl* sleeplessness, insomnia. ◆'S~mittel, *n* sleeping tablet/drug. ◆'S~saal, *m* dormitory. ◆'S~sack, *m* sleeping bag. ◆'S~wagen, *m* sleeping car, sleeper. ◆'S~wandler(in), *m* -s/- (*f* -/-nen) sleepwalker, *Med:* somnambulist. ◆'S~zimmer, *n* bedroom.

Schläf|er(in) ['∫lɛ:fər(in)], *m* -s/- (*f* -/-nen) sleeper. ◆'s~rig, *adj.* sleepy, drowsy.

Schläfe ['∫lɛ:fə], *f* -/-n temple.

schlaff [∫laf], *adj.* (*locker*) slack (rope etc.); flabby (skin, muscles); (*Pers.*) listless; *Fig:* lax (discipline, morals).

Schlag [∫la:k], *m* -(e)s/-e 1. blow; (*a*) (*Treffer*) hit; (*Fausts.*) punch; (*mit einem Stock usw.*) stroke; **S~e bekommen**, to get a hiding/thrashing; **mit einem S.**, with one blow; *Fig:* at one fell swoop; **S. auf S.**, in quick succession; (*b*) (*Geräusch*) chime of a clock, bell etc.); (*c*) beat (of a drum, heart, waves etc.); (*c*) (*Stroms.*) (electric) shock; *Med: F:* (*Anfall*) stroke. 2. *F:* (*Portion*) **ein S. Suppe**, a helping of soup. 3. (*Menschens.*) another breed. **S~e** (*von Menschen*), another breed. ◆'S~ader, *f* artery. ◆'S~anfall, *m* apoplexy; *F:* stroke. ◆'s~artig, *adj.* sudden; *adv.* all of a sudden. ◆'S~baum, *m* barrier (across the road). ◆'S~bohrer, *m* percussion drill. ◆'s~en, *v.irr.* 1. *v.tr.* (*a*) to hit, strike (s.o., sth.); (*dreschen*) to beat, thrash (s.o., an animal); (*b*) **sich** (**mit** j-m) **s.**, to fight (s.o.); (*c*) (*klopfen*) to knock, (*hämmern*) hammer (a nail etc.); (*d*) *Cu:* to whip (cream, whisk (eggwhites); (*e*) (*Uhr*) to strike (the hour); (*f*) (*besiegen*) **den Gegner s.**, to beat/defeat one's opponent/(*Feind*) enemy; (*g*) (*wickeln*) to wrap (sth.). 2. *v.i.* (*a*) (*haben*) (*Pers.*) to strike (a blow); **nach** j-m **s.**, to lash/hit out at s.o.; (*Vogel*) **mit den Flügeln s.**, to beat/flap its wings; (*b*) (*haben*) (*Regen usw.*) to beat, (*Wellen usw.*) pound, (*Tür*) bang; (*c*) (*sein*) (*Flammen*) to shoot, leap; (*Blitz*) **in etwas** *acc* **s.**, to strike sth.; (*d*) (*haben*) (*Uhr*) to strike, chime; (*Glocke*) to toll; (*Herz usw.*) to beat; (*e*) (*sein*) **nach** j-m **s.**, to take after s.o. ◆'s~end, *adj.* 1. (*überzeugend*) convincing (proof, argument etc.). 2. *Min:* **s~e Wetter**, firedamp. ◆'S~er, *m* -s/- *F:* (*Lied*) pop song; (*Erfolg*) hit; (*Ware*) best-selling line. ◆'S~ersänger, *m* pop singer. ◆'s~fertig, *adj.* quick-witted. ◆'S~fertigkeit, *f* -/*no pl* quick-wittedness. ◆'S~instrument, *n* percussion instrument. ◆'S~loch, *n* pot-hole. ◆'S~sahne, *f* whipped cream. ◆'S~seite, *f* *Nau:* list; **S. haben**, (*Schiff*) to list; *F:* (*Pers.*) to be sloshed. ◆'S~wort, *n* slogan, catchword. ◆'S~zeile, *f* headline. ◆'S~zeug, *n* percussion.

Schläger ['∫lɛ:gər], *m* -s/- 1. *Sp:* (*Gerät*) (golf) club; (hockey) stick; (tennis) racket; (cricket, baseball) bat. 2. *Pej:* ruffian, rowdy. ◆'S~ei ['rai], *f* -/-en brawl, *F:* punch-up, *N.Am:* fist-fight.

Schlamassel [∫la'masəl], *m* -s/- *F:* mess.

Schlamm [∫lam], *m* -(e)s/-e mud. ◆'s~ig, *adj.* muddy.

Schlampe ['∫lampə], *f* -/-n *F:* slut. ◆S~e'rei, *f* -/-en *F:* (*a*) slovenly work/behaviour; (*b*) *no pl* slovenliness.

◆'s~ig, adj. slovenly; slipshod (work etc.); sluttish (woman etc.).

Schlange ['ʃlaŋə], f -/-n 1. Z: snake. 2. (lange Reihe) queue, N.Am: line (of people, cars); **S. stehen**, to queue up, N.Am: stand in line. ◆'S~nbiß, m snakebite. ◆'S~ngift, n (snake's) venom. ◆'S~nlinie, f wavy line. ◆'S~nmensch, m contortionist.

schlängeln ['ʃlɛŋəln], v.refl **s. s.**, (Fluß, Weg usw.) to wind, meander; (Pers.) to worm one's way.

schlank [ʃlaŋk], adj. slim, slender. ◆'S~heit, f -/no pl slimness, slenderness. ◆'S~heitskur, f slimming diet.

schlapp [ʃlap], adj. limp, weak. ◆'S~e, f -/-n setback. ◆'S~hut, m squash hat. ◆'s~machen, v.i. sep. (haben) F: (Sportler usw.) to fall by the wayside. ◆'S~schwanz, m F: drip, wet.

Schlaraffenland [ʃlaˈrafənlant], n land of milk and honey.

schlau [ʃlau], adj. (a) (listig) cunning, crafty; (b) usu. F: (klug) clever (person, plan etc.). ◆'S~heit, f -/no pl = Schläue.

Schlauch [ʃlaux], m -(e)s/-e 1. hose(pipe). 2. Aut: etc: (inner) tube. ◆'S~boot, n rubber dinghy. ◆'s~los, adj. tubeless.

Schläue ['ʃlɔyə], f -/no pl cunning, cleverness.

Schlaufe ['ʃlaufə], f -/-n loop; Cl: (Aufhänger) hanger.

schlecht [ʃlɛçt], adj. (a) bad; **s~es Gehalt**, low salary; **sie ist s. in Englisch**, she is bad at English; **s. über j-n reden**, to speak ill of s.o.; **s~er werden**, to get worse, worsen; (b) adv. badly, not well; (mit Mühe) with difficulty; **s. informiert**, badly/ill-informed; **er hat es immer s. gehabt**, he has always had a hard time of it; **sich s. und recht durchschlagen**, to manage as best one can; **es paßt mir heute s.**, it isn't very convenient for me today; (c) F: **mir ist s.**, I feel ill/(Brechreiz) sick; **es steht s. um ihn**, he is in a bad way; (Milch, Fleisch usw.) **s. werden**, to go off, N.Am: spoil. ◆'s~gehen, v.i.sep.irr.36 (sein) **es geht ihm schlecht**, (i) he is up against it/having a hard time; (ii) (gesundheitlich) he is ill/unwell. ◆'S~igkeit, f -/-en 1. no pl badness. 2. bad/evil deed. ◆'s~machen, v.tr.sep. to run (s.o., sth.) down.

schlecken ['ʃlɛkən], v.tr. & i. (haben) **an etwas dat s.**, to lick sth.

Schlehe ['ʃleːə], f -/-n sloe.

schleich|en ['ʃlaiçən], v.i.irr. (sein) to creep, steal; (langsam) to crawl. ◆'s~end, adj. creeping (inflation etc.); Med: insidious (disease). ◆'S~weg, m secret path; Fig: **auf S~wegen**, by surreptitious means. ◆'S~werk, m -(e)s/no pl.

Schleier ['ʃlaiər], m -s/- 1. (also Fig:) veil.

2. (Dunst) haze. ◆'S~eule, f barn owl. ◆'s~haft, adj. F: **es ist mir s.**, it's a mystery to me.

Schleif|e ['ʃlaifə], f -/-n 1. (Knoten) bow (in hair etc.). 2. (Biegung) U-turn. ◆'s~en1, v.tr.irr.43 to grind, sharpen (a knife etc.); to grind (metal, glass etc.). ◆'s~en2, v.tr. (a) to drag (s.o., sth.) (in/über etwas acc. into/across sth.); (b) Aut: **die Kupplung s. lassen**, to slip the clutch. ◆'S~stein, m grindstone.

Schleim [ʃlaim], m -(e)s/-e slime; Med: mucus. ◆'S~haut, f -/-e mucous membrane. ◆'s~ig, adj. slimy; mucous (membrane etc.).

schlemmen ['ʃlɛmən], v.tr. & i. (haben) to feast (on sth.), F: stuff (sth.).

schlendern ['ʃlɛndərn], v.i. (sein) to saunter, stroll (along).

schlenkern ['ʃlɛnkərn], v.tr. & i. (haben) to swing, dangle (one's legs etc.).

Schlepp|e ['ʃlɛpə], f -/-n Cl: train. ◆'s~en, v.tr. (a) (hinter sich herziehen) to tow (a car, ship etc.); (schleifend) to drag (sth., F: s.o.) along; Fig: (Prozeß usw.) **sich über viele Jahre s.**, to drag on for many years; (b) (tragen) to lug, cart (sth. heavy). ◆'s~end, adj. slow (service, sales etc.); long drawn out (process); sluggish (tempo etc.). ◆'S~er, m -s/- 1. Aut: tractor. 2. Nau: towboat, tug (boat). ◆'S~tau, n **ein Schiff/F: j-n ins S. nehmen**, to take a ship/F: s.o. in tow.

Schleuder ['ʃlɔydər], f -/-n 1. catapult, N.Am: slingshot. 2. H: (Wäsche-) spindrier. ◆'s~n, v. 1. v.tr. (a) to fling, hurl (sth.); (b) to spin-dry (clothes etc.). 2. v.i. (sein) (Auto usw.) to skid. ◆'S~preis, m F: giveaway price. ◆'S~sitz, m ejector seat.

schleunigst ['ʃlɔynikst], adv. with all possible haste; (sofort) instantly.

Schleuse ['ʃlɔyzə], f -/-n a) (zum Regulieren) sluice; (b) (für Schiffe) lock. ◆'s~n, v.tr. (a) to lock (a boat etc.); (b) to guide, steer (s.o.). ◆'S~ntor, n lock-gate.

Schliche ['ʃliçə], mpl **j-m auf die S. kommen**, to get wise to s.o.'s tricks.

schlicht [ʃliçt], adj. simple (dress, style etc.); plain (food, Fig: truth); (bescheiden) modest, unpretentious (house etc.). ◆'s~en, v. 1. v.tr. to settle (a dispute etc.). 2. v.i. (haben) to arbitrate. ◆'S~er, m -s/- arbitrator. ◆'S~ung, f -/no pl arbitration, conciliation.

Schlick [ʃlik], m -(e)s/-e silt.

Schließ|e ['ʃliːsə], f -/-n clasp. ◆'s~en, v.irr.31 1. v.tr. to close, shut (a door, one's eyes etc.); to do up (a dress etc.); **sich s.**, to close; (b) to conclude (an agreement etc.); **ein Bündnis s.**, to form an alliance; (c) (beenden) to end, conclude (a letter, article etc.); (d) (folgern) to conclude (that...) (aus etwas dat, from sth.). 2. v.i. (haben) (a) to close, shut; (Geschäft usw.) (endgültig) to close down; (b) (enden) to end; (c) sein Benehmen läßt auf ein hitziges Temperament s., his behaviour suggests a fiery temperament. ◆'S~fach, n Rail: (luggage) locker; (in Bank) safe-deposit box. ◆'s~lich, adv. (a) finally; (endlich) at last; (b) er ist s. mein Bruder, after all, he is my brother. ◆'S~ung, f -/-en (a) closing down (of a shop etc.); closure (of a pit, factory, school etc.); (b) conclusion (of an agreement).

Schliff |ʃlif|, m -(e)s/-e cut of a gem, glass etc.); (Vorgang) cutting; Fig: etwas dat den letzten S. geben, to put the finishing touch to sth.

schlimm |ʃlim|, adj. (a) bad (mistake, news, cold etc.); serious (accident etc.); nasty (illness, wound); im s~sten Fall, at the worst; es könnte s~er kommen, things could get worse; (b) (böse) wicked, (unartig) naughty (person, child); (c) F: (krank) mein s~es Bein, my bad leg. ◆'s~sten'falls, adv. if the worst comes to the worst; (höchstens) at the worst.

Schlinge |ˈʃliŋə|, f -/-n loop; (zum Zuziehen) noose; Med: (Binde) sling; (Falle) snare. ◆'s~n, v.tr.19 1. v.tr. to wind, wrap (sth.). 2. v.tr. & i. (haben) F: to gobble, bolt (one's food).

Schlingel |ˈʃliŋəl|, m -s/- rascal.

schlingern |ˈʃliŋərn|, v.i. (haben) to roll.

Schlips |ʃlips|, m -es/-e F: tie.

Schlitten |ˈʃlitən|, m -s/- sledge, N.Am: sled; S. fahren, to toboggan. ◆'s~ern, v.i. (haben) to slide (on the ice). ◆'S~schuh, m skate; S. laufen, to skate. ◆'S~schuhläufer(in), m (f) skater.

Schlitz |ʃlits|, m -es/-e slit; (Einwurf) slot (for coins etc.); Cl: vent (of a jacket etc.); (Hosens.) fly. ◆'s~äugig, adj. slit-eyed. ◆'S~ohr, n F: sly devil.

Schloß |ʃlos|, n -sses/¨sser 1. (a) (Türs.) lock; (Vorhänges.) padlock; (b) (Schließe) clasp. 2. (Herrenhaus) mansion, stately home; (Palast) palace; (Burg) castle.

Schlosser |ˈʃlosər|, m -s/- (a) locksmith; (b) (Metallarbeiter) metalworker.

Schlot |ʃlot|, m -(e)s/-e (Fabriks.) (factory) chimney.

schlottern |ˈʃlotərn|, v.i. (haben) (Pers.) to shake, shiver (vor + dat, with).

Schlucht |ʃluxt|, f -/-en gully, ravine.

schluchzen |ˈʃluxtsən|, v.i. (haben) to sob.

Schluck |ʃluk|, m -(e)s/-e gulp; in kleinen S~en, in small mouthfuls/sips. ◆'S~auf, m -s/no pl hiccups. ◆'s~en, v.tr. to swallow (water, a pill etc.; Fig: an insult etc.; F: to swallow up (savings etc.). ◆'S~impfung, f oral vaccination. ◆'s~weise, adv. in sips.

schludern |ˈʃludərn|, v.i. (haben) F: to do slipshod work.

Schlummer |ˈʃlumər|, m -s/no pl Lit: slumber. ◆'s~n, v.i. (haben) Lit: to slumber.

Schlund |ʃlunt|, m -(e)s/¨e 1. back of the throat. 2. Fig: (Abgrund) abyss.

schlüpf|en |ˈʃlypfən|, v.i. (sein) to slip; (Vogel) (aus dem Ei) s., to hatch. ◆'s~er, m -s/- knickers. ◆'s~rig, adj. (a) slippery (road, floor etc.); (b) (anstößig) lewd (joke etc.). ◆'S~rigkeit, f -/-en (a) slipperiness; (b) lewdness.

Schlupfloch |ˈʃlupflox|, n hideout, hiding-place.

schlurfen |ˈʃlurfən|, v.i. (sein) to shuffle, shamble (along).

schlürfen |ˈʃlyrfən|, v.tr. to slurp, (vorsichtig) sip (soup etc.).

Schluß |ʃlus|, m -sses/¨sse 1. (Ende) end; ending (of a play, piece of music etc.); zum/am S., at the end; zum S. sagte er..., finally/in conclusion he said...; F: S. machen, (mit der Arbeit) to knock off, call it a day; mit dem Rauchen usw. S. machen, to give up/stop smoking etc.; S. damit! stop it! 2. (Folgerung) conclusion; S~e ziehen, to draw conclusions (aus etwas dat, from sth.). II. 'S~, comb.fm. final (result, round, scene etc.); last (minute, Th: act; Sp: runner etc.); closing (remark, speech etc.). ◆'S~folgerung, f logical conclusion. ◆'S~licht, n (a) Aut: etc: tail light; (b) F: Sp: tailender. ◆'S~strich, m unter etwas dat einen S. ziehen, to put an end to sth. ◆'S~verkauf, m Com: (end of season) sale. ◆'S~wort, n closing remarks.

Schlüssel |ˈʃlysəl| I. m -s/- (also Fig:) key; (Tonart) signature; Mus: clef. II. 'S~, comb.fm. key (ring, Fig: figure, industry, position etc.) ◆'s~bein, n collarbone. ◆'S~blume, f primrose, cowslip. ◆'S~bund, m & n bunch of keys. ◆'S~loch, n keyhole.

schlüssig |ˈʃlysiç|, adj. conclusive (evidence, proof).

schmachten |ˈʃmaxtən|, v.i. (haben) to languish (nach + dat, for sth.).

schmächtig |ˈʃmɛçtiç|, adj. slight; Pej: weedy.

schmackhaft |ˈʃmakhaft|, adj. tasty (food); Fig: j-m etwas s. machen, to make sth. palatable to s.o.

schmäh|en |ˈʃmɛːən|, v.tr. to abuse, revile (s.o.). ◆'s~lich, adj. disgraceful (treatment etc.); ignominious (defeat etc.).

schmal |ʃmaːl|, adj. (a) narrow (street, bridge, hips etc.); slender (figure, hands etc.); thin (lips, face); (b) (geringe) meagre (income, diet etc.). ◆'S~film, m 8 mm or 16 mm cine film. ◆'S~spur-, comb.fm. 1. narrow-gauge (railway, track). 2. F: small-time (academic etc.).

schmälern |ˈʃmɛːlərn|, v.tr. to diminish (values etc.); Pers: to belittle (s.o.'s achievements etc.).

Schmalz¹ |ʃmalts|, n -es/-e lard.

Schmalz², m -es/no pl F: schmaltz.
◆'s~ig, adj. F: schmaltzy, sentimental.
schmarotz|en ['ʃmarɔtsən], v.i. (haben)
F: bei j-m s., to sponge on s.o.
◆S~er, m -s/- also Fig: parasite; F:
(Pers.) sponger.

Schmarren ['ʃmarən], m -s/- 1. Aus: Cu:
fried strips of pancake. 2. F: Pej: (Unsinn) trash.

schmatzen ['ʃmatsən], v.i. (haben) **beim
Essen s.**, to eat noisily.

schmecken ['ʃmɛkən], v.tr. & i. (haben)
to taste; **es schmeckt nach nichts**, it's
tasteless; **schmeckt's Ihnen?** are you enjoying it? is it to your liking? **es hat
geschmeckt!** it was delicious!

Schmeich|elei [ʃmaiçə'lai], f -/-en flat-
tery. ◆'s~elhaft, adj. flattering.
◆'s~eln, v.i. (haben) to flatter.
◆'S~ler, m -s/- flatterer.

schmeiß|en ['ʃmaisən], v.tr. & i.irr.4
(haben) F: (a) to chuck (sth.); **mit Steinen s.**, to throw stones; **aus der Schule
geschmissen werden**, to be kicked out of
school. ◆'S~fliege, f bluebottle.

Schmelz [ʃmɛlts], m -es/no pl (esp. dental) enamel. ◆'s~en, v.irr.1 1. v.i. (sein)
(Schnee, Eis usw.) to melt; Fig: (Vermögen) to shrink. 2. v.tr. Tchn: to smelt
(ore). ◆'S~käse, m (soft) processed
cheese. ◆'S~punkt, m melting point.
◆'S~tiegel, m Fig: melting pot.
◆'S~wasser, n melted snow/ice.

Schmerz [ʃmɛrts], m -es/-en 1. pain;
(dumpf, anhaltend) ache; **wo haben Sie
S~en?** where does it hurt? 2. (Kummer)
sorrow. ◆'s~empfindlich, adj. sensitive (to pain). ◆'s~en, v.tr. & i. (haben) to hurt (s.o.); **mir schmerzt der
Kopf**, my head aches. ◆'S~ensgeld, n
Jur: compensation for personal suffering.
◆'s~haft, adj. painful. ◆'s~lich,
adj. painful. ◆'s~los, adj. painless.
◆'S~losigkeit, f -/no pl freedom from
pain. ◆'s~stillend, adj. ◆s~es Mittel, painkiller.

Schmetter|ling ['ʃmɛtərlɪŋ], m -s/-e but-
terfly. ◆'s~n, v.tr. (a) to hurl (sth.);
(b) (Trompete usw.) to blare out (a signal
etc.); Hum: (Pers.) to bawl out (a song).

Schmied [ʃmiːt], m -(e)s/-e smith, esp.
blacksmith. ◆S~e ['ʃmiːdə], f -/-n
(smith's) forge, smithy. ◆'s~eeisern,
adj. wrought-iron (gate etc.). ◆s~en,
v.tr. to forge (steel etc., Fig: plans).

schmieg|en ['ʃmiːgən], v.refl. (Pers., Tier
usw.) **sich an j-n, etwas acc s.**, to snuggle close up to s.o., sth. ◆'s~sam, adj.
supple (leather, Fig: body etc.).

Schmier|e ['ʃmiːrə], f -/-n 1. lubricant. 2.
F: (Pers.) **S. stehen**, to act as a lookout.
◆'s~en, v. 1. v.tr. (a) to lubricate, (mit
Fett) grease (moving parts); (b) (streichen)
to apply (ointment, grease etc.), spread
(butter, jam etc.); (c) F: to scrawl (a
note, word etc.). 2. v.i. (haben) (Pers.) to
scrawl. ◆'S~e'rei, f -/-en scribble;

(Parolen) graffiti; (Gemälde) daub.
◆'s~fett, n lubricating grease.
◆'S~fink, m F: (a) scrawler; (b)
(schmutziges Kind) filthy brat.
◆'S~geld, n F: bribe. ◆'s~ig, adj.
1. greasy, (schmutzig) grubby (hand,
book). 2. F: Pej: smarmy (person, manner etc.). ◆'S~seife, f soft soap.

Schminke ['ʃmɪŋkə], f -/-n make-up; Th:
greasepaint. ◆'s~en, v.tr. to make up
(one's face, eyes etc.), make (s.o.) up;
sich s., to put on make-up.
◆'S~tisch, m make-up table.

schmirgel|n ['ʃmɪrgəln], v.tr. to rub
down, sand (a surface). ◆'S~papier, n
emery paper; (Sandpapier) sandpaper.

Schmiß [ʃmɪs], m -sses/no pl F: pep,
verve. ◆**schmissig** [ʃmɪsɪç], adj. F:
rousing (music etc.).

Schmöker ['ʃmøːkər], m -s/- F: tome.
◆'s~n, v.tr. & i. (haben) F: to browse.

schmollen ['ʃmɔlən], v.i. (haben) to sulk.

Schmor|braten ['ʃmoːrbraːtən], m
braised beef, pot roast. ◆'s~en, v.tr.
& i. (haben) Cu: to braise (meat, vegetables etc.); Fig: **j-n s. lassen**, to leave
s.o. to stew in his own juice.

Schmuck [ʃmʊk], m -(e)s/no pl 1.
(S~stücke) jewellery. 2. (Verzierung) decoration; Arch: etc: ornamentation.
◆'s~los, adj. unadorned, (kahl) bare.
◆'S~losigkeit, f -/no pl plainness;
bareness. ◆'S~sachen, fpl jewellery.
◆'S~stück, n piece of jewellery; Fig:
gem (of a collection etc.).

schmücken ['ʃmʏkən], v.tr. to decorate
(sth.), Fig: to embellish (a speech etc.).

schmuddelig ['ʃmʊdəlɪç], adj. F: mucky.

Schmuggel ['ʃmʊgəl], m -s/no pl smuggling. ◆'s~n, v.tr. to smuggle (s.o.,
sth.). ◆'S~ler, m -s/- smuggler.

schmunzeln ['ʃmʊntsəln], v.i. (haben) to
smile to oneself.

schmusen ['ʃmuːzən], v.i. (haben) F:
(Liebespaar) to kiss and cuddle.

Schmutz [ʃmʊts], m -es/no pl dirt.
◆'S~fink, m F: filthy brat.
◆'S~fleck, m dirty mark. ◆'s~ig,
adj. dirty; **sich s. machen**, to get dirty;
ein s~iges Geschäft, a shady/crooked
deal.

Schnabel ['ʃnaːbəl], m -s/- 1. beak. 2. F:
(Mund) trap; **den S. halten**, to keep
quiet.

Schnake ['ʃnaːkə], f -/-n 1. crane-fly, F:
daddy-long-legs. 2. F: (Mücke) gnat.

Schnalle ['ʃnalə], f -/-n buckle.

schnalzen ['ʃnaltsən], v.i. (haben) (Pers.)
mit der Zunge s., to click one's tongue;
mit den Fingern s., to snap one's
fingers.

schnapp|en ['ʃnapən], v. 1. v.tr. (a) (sich
dat) **etwas s.**, to snatch/grab sth.; (b) (gefangennehmen) to catch, nab (a thief etc.).
2. v.i. (haben) (a) **nach etwas dat s.**,
(Pers.) to grab at/(Hund usw.) snap at
sth. ◆'S~schuß, m snapshot.

Schnaps [ʃnaps], m -es/=e schnaps; F: (Spirituosen) hard stuff/N.Am: liquor.◆**'S~kochtopf**, m pressure cooker.◆**'s~stens**, adv. as quickly as possible.◆**'S~straße**, f expressway.◆**'S~zug**, m fast(Fernschnellzug) express train.

schnarchen ['ʃnarçən], v.i. (haben) to snore.

schnarren ['ʃnarən], v.i. (haben) to rattle, clatter; (Klingel usw.) to buzz; (Stimme) to rasp.

schnattern ['ʃnatərn], v.i. (haben) to gabble; F: (Frau, Kind) to chatter away.

schnauben ['ʃnaubən], v.i. (haben) to snort.

schnaufen ['ʃnaufən], v.i. (haben) (Pers., Lok usw.) to puff.

Schnauz|bart ['ʃnautsbaːrt], m large/esp. walrus moustache.◆**'S~e**, f -/-n 1. snout (of a bear, fox, fish etc.); muzzle (of a dog); (Maul) mouth. 2. P: (Mund) gob; (halt die) S.! shut your trap! 3. F: nose (of a car etc.).

Schnecke ['ʃnɛkə], f -/-n snail; (ohne Gehäuse) slug.◆**'S~nhaus**, n snail-shell.◆**'S~ntempo**, n F: im S., at a snail's pace.

Schnee [ʃneː], m -s/no pl snow.◆**'S~ball**, m snowball.◆**'S~fall**, m snowfall; fall of snow.◆**'S~flocke**, f snowflake.◆**'S~gestöber**, n snow flurry.◆**'S~glöckchen**, n snowdrop.◆**'S~kette**, f snow chain.◆**'S~mann**, m snowman.◆**'S~pflug**, m snowplough.◆**'S~regen**, m sleet.◆**'S~sturm**, m snowstorm.◆**'s~weiß**, snow-white.

Schneid [ʃnait], m -(e)s/no pl F: guts.

Schneid|brenner ['ʃnaitbrenər], m cutting torch.◆**S~e** ['ʃnaidə], f -/-n (cutting) edge, blade.◆**'s~en**, v.irr.59 1. v.tr. (a) to cut (sth.); (in Scheiben) to slice (bread, sausage etc.); (b) (Pers.) sich s., to cut oneself; sich dir in den Finger s., to cut one's finger; (c) j-n s., (i) (ignorieren) to cut s.o. dead; (ii) Aut: to cut in on s.o.; (d) (Straßen, Linien usw.) to cut across; sich s., to intersect. 2. v.i. (haben) to cut.◆**'s~end**, adj. cutting edge, Fig: tone etc.); biting (wind, cold etc.).◆**'S~er**, m -s/- tailor.◆**'S~erin**, f -/-nen dressmaker.◆**'s~ern**, v.tr. to make (a dress, coat etc.); to tailor (a suit etc.).◆**'S~ezahn**, m incisor.◆**'s~ig**, adj. (Pers.) dashing; snappy (music).

schneien ['ʃnaiən], v.i. (haben) to snow.

Schneise ['ʃnaizə], f -/-n firebreak; Av: flight path/lane.

schnell [ʃnɛl]. I. adj. quick (movement, worker, service etc.); fast (car, train, road, journey, runner etc.); so. laufen, to run fast/quickly; F: mach s.! hurry up! II. 'S~-, 'S~-, comb.fm. express (service, etc.); high-speed (railway, bus etc.); fast(-growing etc.).◆**'s~en**, v.i. (sein) in die Höhe s., to leap up; (Preise) to shoot up.◆**'S~hefter**, m loose-leaf binder.◆**'S~igkeit**, f -/no pl (a) quickness; rapidity (of progress etc.); (b) (Geschwindigkeit) speed.◆**'S~imbiß**, m

snack bar.◆**'S~kochtopf**, m pressure cooker.◆**'s~stens**, adv. as quickly as possible.◆**'S~straße**, f expressway.◆**'S~zug**, m fast(Fernschnellzug) express train.

schneuzen ['ʃnɔytsən], v.refl. sich s., to blow one's nose.

schnipp|en ['ʃnipən], v. 1. v.tr. to flick (sth.) with one's finger etc. 2. v.i. (haben) mit dem Finger s., to snap one's finger.◆**'s~isch**, adj. pert, cheeky.

Schnipsel ['ʃnipsəl], m -s/- snippet.

Schnitt [ʃnit], m -(e)s/-e 1. cut (in one's hand, in cloth etc.). 2. no pl cutting. 3. (S~muster) pattern. 4. Mth: section. 5. F: (Durchs.) average.◆**'S~blumen**, fpl cut flowers.◆**'S~e**, f -/-n (a) open sandwich; (b) (Scheibe) slice.◆**'S~fläche**, f (a) cut surface; (b) Mth: etc: section.◆**'s~ig**, adj. (car, boat) with racy/sleek lines.◆**'S~lauch**, m chives.◆**'S~muster**, n pattern.◆**'S~wunde**, f cut.

Schnitz|el ['ʃnitsəl], n -s/- 1. Cu: escalope. 2. scrap, shred (of paper etc.).◆**'s~en**, v.tr. to carve (wood, a figure etc.).◆**'S~er**, m -s/- 1. carver. 2. F: einen (groben) S. machen, to make a (bad) blunder.

schnodderig ['ʃnɔdəriç], adj. brash.

schnöde ['ʃnøːdə], adj. base, despicable; j-n s. behandeln, to treat s.o. with contempt.

Schnorchel ['ʃnɔrçəl], m -s/- snorkel.

Schnörkel ['ʃnœrkəl], m -s/- curlicue; (schriftlich) flourish; F: squiggle.◆**'s~ig**, adj. ornate; flowery (style); squiggly (handwriting etc.).

schnorren ['ʃnɔrən], v.tr. & i. (haben) F: to scrounge, cadge (sth.).◆**'S~er(in)**, m -s/- (f -/-nen) scrounger, cadger.

schnüff|eln ['ʃnyfəln], v.i. (haben) (a) (Hund) to sniff (an + dat, at); (b) F: (Pers.) to snoop.◆**'S~ler**, m -s/- F: snooper; Pej: nosy parker.

Schnuller ['ʃnulər], m -s/- (baby's) dummy, N.Am: pacifier.

Schnulze ['ʃnultsə], f -/-n F: tearjerker.

Schnupfen ['ʃnupfən], m -s/no pl Med: head cold.

schnuppern ['ʃnupərn], v.i. (haben) an etwas dat s., to sniff at sth.

Schnur [ʃnuːr], f -/-e 1. string. 2. El: flex.◆**'s~gerade**, adj. dead straight.

schnür|en ['ʃnyːrən], v.tr. to lace (sth.); to tie, lace (up) (shoes etc.).◆**'S~schuh**, m lace-up shoe.◆**'S~senkel**, m -s/- shoelace.

Schnurr|bart ['ʃnurbart], m moustache.◆**'s~en**, v.i. (haben) (Katze) to purr.

Schock [ʃɔk], m -(e)s/-e shock; unter S. stehen, to be in a state of shock.◆**s~ieren** [-'kiːrən], v.tr. to shock, scandalize (s.o.).◆**s~ierend**, adj. shocking, scandalous.

Schöff|e ['ʃœfə], m -n/-n lay judge (in a

S~ngericht. ◆**'S~ engericht,** *n* district court composed of two lay judges and a professional judge.

Schokolade [ʃoko'laːdə], *f -/-n* chocolate. ◆**S~ntorte,** *f* chocolate gateau.

Scholle ['ʃɔlə], *f -/-n* **1.** (*a*) *Agr:* clod (of earth); (*b*) (*Eiss.*) ice floe. **2.** (*Fisch*) plaice.

schon [ʃoːn], *adv.* (*a*) (*bereits*) already; **s. im Jahre 1900,** as early as 1900; **s. damals,** even at that time; (*b*) (*endlich*) **komm s.!** come on! (*c*) (*allein*) just; (*sogar*) even; **s. der Gedanke daran ist schrecklich,** the mere thought of it is terrible; **s. deshalb/aus diesem Grund,** for this reason alone; (*d*) (*gewiß*) certainly; really; (*wohl*) probably; **das ist s. möglich,** that is quite possible; **ja s., aber...,** yes of course, but...; **es wird s. besser werden,** it will get better, don't worry; **s. recht!** OK! **ich glaube s., I** think so.

schon|en ['ʃoːnən], *v.tr.* to spare, save (one's strength, s.o.'s feelings etc.); (*Pers.*) to go/(*Sache*) be easy on (the brakes, eyes etc.); (*schützen*) to protect (one's hands, clothes); **sich s.,** to take things gently. ◆**'s~end,** *adj.* gentle (*für + acc,* to); mild (detergent etc.). ◆**'S~kost,** *f* light food. ◆**'S~ung,** *f -/-en* *no pl* sparing, saving; (*Schutz*) protection, care. **2.** (*im Wald*) young plantation. ◆**'s~ungslos,** *adj.* ruthless, (*unbeirrt*) relentless. ◆**'S~zeit,** *f* close season.

schön [ʃøːn], *adj.* **1.** beautiful; **s~es Wetter,** fine weather. **2.** (*a*) (*angenehm*) pleasant, *F:* nice (surprise, holiday etc.); (*b*) **s~e Feiertage/ein s~es Wochenende!** have a good holiday/a nice weekend! **er läßt s. grüßen,** he sends his best wishes; (*c*) (*gut*) **wie s., daß Sie gekommen sind,** how nice of you to come; **zu s., um wahr zu sein,** too good to be true; *F:* **das war nicht sehr s. von ihr,** that wasn't very nice of her. **3.** *F:* (*beträchtlich*) handsome (sum, profit); **ganz s~** (success etc.); **wir mußten ganz s. arbeiten,** we had to work jolly hard; **s. langsam,** nice and slowly. ◆**'S~heit,** *f -/-en* beauty. ◆**'S~heits-,** *comb.fm.* beauty (queen, contest etc.); cosmetic (surgery etc.). ◆**'S~heitsfehler,** *m* blemish, *Fig:* minor/*F:* cosmetic defect. ◆**'s~machen,** *v.tr.sep.* **sich s.,** to smarten oneself up. ◆**'s~tun,** *v.i.sep.irr. 106* (*haben*) *F:* **j-m s.,** to suck up to s.o.

Schoner ['ʃoːnər], *m -s/-* *Nau:* schooner.

schöpf|en ['ʃœpfən], *v.tr.* (*a*) Wasser aus einem Brunnen usw. **s.,** to draw water from a well etc.; **Suppe s.,** to ladle out soup; (*b*) *Lit:* **frische Luft s.,** to get some fresh air; *Fig:* **neue Hoffnung s.,** to gain fresh hope. ◆**'S~er,** *m -s/-* creator. ◆**'s~erisch,** *adj.* creative. ◆**'S~kelle,** *f*/**'S~löffel,** *m* ladle.

◆**'S~ung,** *f -/-en* creation.

Schorf [ʃɔrf], *m -(e)s/-e* scab (on a wound).

Schornstein ['ʃɔrnʃtaɪn], *m -s/-e* chimney; *Nau:* funnel. ◆**S~feger,** *m -s/-* chimney sweep.

Schoß [ʃoːs], *m -es/̈-e* **1.** (*a*) lap; (*b*) (*Mutterleib*) womb. **2.** *Cl:* (*Rocks.*) (coat) tail. ◆**'S~hund,** *m* lap-dog.

Schote [ʃoːtə], *f -/-n* pod.

Schott|e ['ʃɔtə], *m -n/-n* Scot, Scotsman. ◆**'S~in,** *f -/-nen* Scotswoman. ◆**'s~isch,** *adj.* Scots, Scottish. ◆**'S~land.** *Pr.n.n -s.* Scotland.

Schotter ['ʃɔtər], *m -s/-* gravel; *Rail:* ballast. ◆**'S~straße,** *f* (loose) gravel road.

schraff|ieren [ʃra'fiːrən], *v.tr.* to hatch (a drawing etc.).

schräg [ʃrɛːk], *adj.* sloping (ground, surface etc.); slanting (eyes, writing etc.); **s. gegenüber,** diagonally opposite. ◆**'S~e** [-gə], *f -/-n* slant; (*Fläche*) slope; pitch (of a roof). ◆**'S~schrift,** *f* italics.

Schramme ['ʃramə], *f -/-n* scratch. ◆**'s~n,** *v.tr.* to scratch (sth., oneself).

Schrank [ʃraŋk], *m -(e)s/̈-e* cupboard; (*Kleiders.*) wardrobe, *N.Am:* closet; (*Büros.*) filing cabinet. ◆**'S~koffer,** *m* clothes trunk. ◆**'S~wand,** *f* cupboard (wall) unit.

Schrank|e ['ʃraŋkə], *f -/-n* (*a*) (*Sperre*) barrier; (*Bahns.*) level-crossing gates; (*b*) *Fig: usu.pl* **S~en,** limits; **sich in S~en halten,** to restrain oneself. ◆**'s~enlos,** *adj.* unlimited (freedom etc.). ◆**'S~enwärter,** *m* crossing keeper.

Schraube ['ʃraʊbə], *f -/-n* screw; (*mit eckigem Kopf*) bolt. ◆**'s~en,** *v.tr.* to screw. ◆**'S~nmutter,** *f* nut. ◆**'S~nschlüssel,** *m* spanner, *N.Am:* wrench. ◆**'S~nzieher,** *m* screwdriver. ◆**'S~stock,** *m* vice, *N.Am:* vise. ◆**'S~verschluß,** *m* screw top.

Schrebergarten ['ʃreːbərgartən], *m* allotment (*usu.* with summerhouse).

Schreck [ʃrɛk], *m -(e)s/-e* fright, shock. ◆**'S~en.** **I.** *m -s/-* *no pl* (*Schreck*) fright, shock; (*b*) **die S. des Krieges,** the horrors of war. **II.** *v.tr.* to give (s.o.) a fright. ◆**'s~enerregend,** *adj.* terrifying. ◆**'S~ens-,** *comb.fm.* terrifying (sight, news etc.); (night, cry etc.) of terror. ◆**'S~gespenst,** *n* (*a*) (*Pers.*) bogeyman; (*b*) (*Sache*) nightmare. ◆**'s~haft,** *adj.* easily frightened/scared. ◆**'s~lich,** *adj.* terrible. ◆**'S~lichkeit,** *f -/no pl* terribleness. ◆**'S~schuß,** *m* warning shot.

Schrei [ʃraɪ], *m -(e)s/-e* cry (of a person, bird); (*gellender*) scream; **die S~e der Zuschauer,** the shouts of the spectators. ◆**'s~en,** *v.tr.&i.irr.* (*haben*) (*a*) (*Pers.*) to shout, (*laut*) yell (abuse, curses, one's name etc.); *F:* **das ist zum S~en,** it's a scream; (*b*) (*Eule, Affe usw.*) to screech; (*Möwe, Baby*) to cry. ◆**'s~end,** *adj.* glaring, garish (colour); *Fig:* flagrant, glaring (injustice etc.). ◆'S~hals, m F: noisy lout; (Kind) yelling child.

schreib|en ['ʃraibən]. I. v.tr.&ri.irr.12 (haben) (a) to write (sth.); (b) (buchstabieren) wie schreibt man dieses Wort? how does one spell this word? II. S., n -s/- (Brief) letter. ◆'S~er(in), m -s/- (f -/-nen) writer. ◆'s~faul, adj. lazy about writing letters. ◆'S~fehler, m slip of the pen. ◆'S~heft, n exercise book. ◆S~kraft, f clerical assistant, usu. shorthand typist. ◆'S~maschine, f typewriter. ◆'S~stube, f Mil: orderly room. ◆'S~tisch, m (writing) desk. ◆'S~waren, fpl stationery. ◆'S~warenhändler, m stationer. ◆'S~weise, f 1. spelling. 2. (Stil) written style.

Schreiner ['ʃrainər], m -s/- joiner.

schreiten ['ʃraitən], v.i.irr.41 (sein) (a) to stride (along); (b) Lit: zu etwas dat s., to proceed with sth.

Schrift [ʃrift], f -/-en 1. (a) (Alphabet) script; (b) (Geschriebenes) writing; (Handschrift) (hand)writing. 2. (Abhandlung) report, paper. ◆'S~art, f fount, type. ◆'S~führer(in), m (f) secretary. ◆'s~lich, adj. written; j-m etwas s. mitteilen, to inform s.o. of sth. in writing. ◆'S~setzer, m typesetter. ◆'S~sprache, f written language. ◆'S~steller(in), m -s/- (f -/-nen) writer. ◆'S~stück, n a document, Jur: deed. ◆'S~tum, n -s/no pl literature. ◆'S~wechsel, m Adm: correspondence.

schrill [ʃril], adj. shrill, strident.

Schritt [ʃrit], m -(e)s/-e 1. (a) step; S~e hören, to hear footsteps; einen S. machen/tun, to take a step; auf S. und Tritt, at every turn; wherever one goes; Fig: mit j-m, etwas dat S. halten, to keep up with s.o., sth.; (b) (Gangart) gait; (im) S. fahren, to drive at walking pace. 2. Cl: (Hosens.) crotch. ◆'S~macher, m pacemaker. ◆'Schrittempo, n im S., at a walking pace. ◆'s~weise, adv. step by step, gradually.

schroff [ʃrɔf], adj. (a) sheer, precipitous (rock face etc.); (b) abrupt (manner, change etc.); in s~em Gegensatz, in sharp/stark contrast.

schröpfen ['ʃrœpfən], v.tr. F: to fleece (s.o.), bleed (s.o.) white.

Schrot [ʃro:t], m -(e)s/-e 1. (Munition) (small) shot. 2. no pl wholecorn meal, wholemeal. ◆'S~kugel, f pellet.

Schrott [ʃrɔt], m -(e)s/-e scrap (metal). ◆'S~händler, m scrap dealer. ◆'s~haufen, m scrapheap. ◆'s~reif, adj. fit for the scrapheap.

schrubb|en ['ʃrubən], v.tr. to scrub (a floor etc.). ◆'S~r, m -s/- scrubbing brush (with a long handle).

Schrulle ['ʃrulə], f -/-n 1. (Einfall) cranky/crackpot idea; (Laune) odd whim.

2. (Frau) old crone. ◆'s~ig, adj. dotty, cranky.

schrumpfen ['ʃrumpfən], v.i. (sein) to shrink; (Äpfel usw.) to shrivel.

Schub [ʃu:p], m -(e)s/-e ['ʃy:bə]. 1. (Stoß) push, shove. 2. (Gruppe) batch (of bread, people etc.). ◆'S~fach, n = S~lade. ◆'S~karre, f/S~karren, m wheelbarrow. ◆'S~lade, f drawer. ◆s~s [ʃups], m -es/-e F: push, shove (s.o., sth.). ◆'s~sen, v.tr. F: to shove (s.o., sth.). ◆'s~weise, adv. in batches, a few at a time.

schüchtern ['ʃyçtərn], adj. shy (person, smile, manner etc.); (zaghaft) diffident (request, attempt). ◆s~heit, f -/no pl shyness.

Schuft [ʃuft], m -(e)s/-e F: scoundrel. ◆'s~en, v.i. (haben) F: to slave away.

Schuh [ʃu:], m -(e)s/-e shoe. II. ◆'S~-, comb.fm. shoe (brush, nail etc.); (heel, sole) of a shoe. ◆'S~creme, f shoe polish. ◆'S~größe, f shoe size. ◆'S~löffel, m shoehorn. ◆'S~macher, m shoemaker; (für Reparaturen) shoe repairer.

Schul- ['ʃu:l], comb.fm. school (age, bus, friend, class, year, teacher, sport etc.). ◆'S~arbeit, f (a) schoolwork; (b) (Hausaufgabe) homework. ◆'S~besuch, m school attendance. ◆'S~bildung, f schooling. ◆'S~buch, n schoolbook. ◆'S~e, f -/-n 1. school; in die/zur S. gehen, to go to school. S. machen, to set a precedent. ◆'s~en, v.tr. to train (s.o., a horse, troops etc.). ◆'S~fach, n school subject. ◆'S~ferien, pl school holidays/N.Am: vacation. ◆'S~frei, adj. morgen ist s., there is no school tomorrow. ◆'S~funk, m school broadcasting. ◆'S~hof, m school yard/(Spielplatz) playground. ◆'S~junge, m schoolboy. ◆'S~leiter, m head teacher, N.Am: principal. ◆'S~mädchen, n schoolgirl. ◆'S~pflicht, f obligation to attend school. ◆'s~pflichtig, adj. im s~pflichtigen Alter, of school age. ◆'S~schiff, n training ship. ◆'S~stunde, f (school) lesson. ◆'S~ung, f -/-en training; (Lehrgang) training course. ◆'S~weg, m way to/from school. ◆'S~zeit, f schooldays. ◆'S~zeugnis, n school report.

Schuld [ʃult]. I. f -/-en ['ʃuldən]. 1. no pl (a) (Verantwortlichkeit) blame; es ist meine S./die S. liegt bei mir, it is my fault; I am to blame; (b) (Unrecht) guilt. 2. Fin: debt. II. s., adj. er ist/hat s. (daran), he's to blame (for it); it's his fault. ◆'s~bewußt, adj. guilty (look, expression etc.). ◆s~en ['ʃuldən], v.tr. j-m Geld, Fig: eine Erklärung usw. s., to owe s.o. money, Fig: an explanation etc. ◆'s~enfrei, adj. Fin: clear of debt. ◆'S~gefühl, n guilty feeling, sense of guilt. ◆s~ig ['ʃuldiç], adj. 1. Jur: etc:

guilty; **der/die S~ige**, the guilty person; the culprit. **2. j-m Geld/Fig: eine Erklärung/Dank s.** sein, to owe s.o. money/Fig: an explanation/a debt of gratitude; **sie blieb mir die Antwort s.**, she could not give me an answer. ◆**'S~igkeit**, f -/no pl guilt. ◆**'s~los**, adj. innocent (**an**+dat, of). ◆**'S~ner** ['ʃuldnər], m -s/- debtor. ◆**'S~schein**, m I.O.U. ◆**'S~spruch**, m verdict of guilty.

Schüler ['ʃyːlər], m -s/- (a) Sch: schoolboy; (in der Oberstufe) student; pupil (of a school, a teacher etc.); pl schoolchildren; pupils (of a school); (b) Art: etc: pupil. ◆**'S~in**, f -/nen schoolgirl, (girl) pupil.

Schulter ['ʃultər], f -/-n shoulder. ◆**'S~blatt**, n shoulder blade. ◆**'s~n**, v.tr. to shoulder (a rifle etc.). ◆**'S~tasche**, f shoulder bag.

schummeln ['ʃumǝln], v.i. (haben) F: to cheat.

Schund [ʃunt]. I. m -(e)s/no pl junk, rubbish; (Buch usw.) trash. II. **'S~**, comb.fm. F: rubbishy (goods etc.); trashy (literature).

Schuppe ['ʃupǝ], f -/-n (a) Z: etc: scale; (b) flake (of skin); pl (Haars~n) dandruff. ◆**'s~en1**, v.tr. to scale (fish); (Haut) **sich s.**, to flake. ◆**'s~ig**, adj. scaly.

Schuppen2 ['ʃupǝn], m -s/- shed; (Scheune) barn.

Schur [ʃuːr], f -/-en shearing (of sheep etc.). ◆**'S~wolle**, f clipped wool; **reine S.**, pure new wool.

schür|en ['ʃyːrǝn], v.tr. to poke (the fire); Fig: to stir up (hatred). ◆**'S~haken**, m poker.

schürfen ['ʃyrfǝn], v. **1.** v.tr. **sich dat den Ellbogen usw. s.**, to graze one's elbow etc. **2.** v.i. (haben) **nach Gold usw. s.**, to prospect for gold etc.

Schurke ['ʃurkǝ], m -n/-n rogue. ◆**'s~n**, v.tr. (a) to gather/tuck up (one's skirt etc.). ◆**'S~njäger**, m F: womanizer.

Schuß [ʃus], m -sses/-sse **1.** shot; **S. aufs Tor**, shot at goal. **2.** (a) dash (of rum etc.). **3.** Fig: **in S.** sein, to be in fine fettle/(Haus usw.) shipshape. ◆**'S~linie**, f line of fire. ◆**'S~waffe**, f firearm. ◆**'S~wunde**, f gunshot wound.

Schüssel ['ʃysǝl], f -/-n bowl; (serving etc.) dish.

Schuster ['ʃuːstər], m -s/- shoemaker.

Schutt [ʃut], m -(e)s/no pl rubble. ◆**'S~abladeplatz**, m (refuse) tip, dump. ◆**'S~haufen**, m heap of rubble.

Schüttelfrost ['ʃytǝlfrɔst], m (violent) shivering. ◆**'s~n**, v.tr. to shake (s.o., sth., one's head, fist etc.); (Pers.) **sich vor Ekel s.**, to shudder with disgust.

schütt|en ['ʃytǝn], v.tr. to tip (ash etc.), pour (a liquid etc.).

schütter ['ʃytǝr], adj. sparse, thin (hair etc.).

Schutz [ʃuts]. I. m -es/no pl protection (**vor**+dat, from; **gegen**+acc, against); (Zuflucht) shelter; (Abschirmung) shield (**gegen Strahlung**, against radiation); **zum S. gegen Ansteckung**, as a safeguard against infection; **j-n in S. nehmen**, to stand up for s.o.; Fig: **unter dem/im S. der Dunkelheit**, under cover of darkness. II. **'S~**, comb.fm. protective (helmet, layer, film, Z: colouring etc.). ◆**'S~anzug**, m protective clothes. ◆**'S~befohlene(r)**, m & f decl. as adj. Jur: charge, ward. ◆**'S~blech**, n guard; (am Fahrrad) mudguard. ◆**'S~engel**, m guardian angel. ◆**'S~gebiet**, n conservation area; (also Hist:) protectorate. ◆**'S~haft**, f protective custody. ◆**'S~impfung**, f vaccination. ◆**'s~los**, adj. unprotected, insecure. ◆**'S~maßnahme**, f precaution.

Schütz|e ['ʃytsǝ], m -n/-n **1.** (a) marksman; **ein guter S.**, a good shot; (b) Fb: scorer. **2.** Astr: Sagittarius. ◆**'s~en**, v. **1.** v.tr. to protect (s.o., sth.) (**vor etwas** dat, from sth.); to shelter (s.o.) (**vor dem Regen**, from the rain). **2.** v.i. (haben) to provide protection/shelter (**vor**+dat, from). ◆**'s~end**, adj. protective. ◆**'S~ling**, m protégé.

Schwabe ['ʃvaːbǝ], m -n/-n Swabian. ◆**'S~n**. Pr.n.n -s. Swabia.

schwäbisch ['ʃvɛːbiʃ], adj. Swabian.

schwach [ʃvax], adj. (a) weak; poor (hearing, sight, memory etc.); delicate (child, health etc.); frail (old person); (b) (gering) faint (light, resemblance, hope etc.); **ein s~er Trost**, a slight/Pej: poor consolation; **s~e Leistungen/Arbeit**, poor/inferior work; **s. in Englisch**, bad at English. ◆**'S~heit**, f -/no pl weakness. ◆**'S~kopf**, m Pej: dimwit. ◆**'S~sinn**, m mental deficiency. ◆**'s~sinnig**, adj. mentally deficient; F: Pej: moronic. ◆**'S~strom**, m El: low-voltage current.

Schwäch|e ['ʃvɛçǝ], f -/-n (a) weakness; (b) (Mangel) fault, shortcoming (of a book etc.); deficiency (of a plan etc.); (c) no pl (Vorliebe) **eine S. für j-n, etwas** acc **haben**, to have a soft spot for s.o., sth. ◆**'s~en**, v.tr. to weaken (s.o., sth.). ◆**'s~lich**, adj. sickly. ◆**'S~ling**, m -s/-e weakling. ◆**'S~ung**, f -/no pl weakening.

Schwaden ['ʃvaːdǝn], m -s/- cloud (of smoke etc.).

schwafeln ['ʃvaːfǝln], v.i. (haben) F: to blather, (Unsinn reden) drivel.

Schwager ['ʃvaːɡər], m -s/- brother-in-law.

Schwägerin ['ʃvɛːɡǝrin], f -/-nen sister-in-law.

Schwalbe ['ʃvalbǝ], f -/-n swallow.

Schwall [ʃval], m -(e)s/-e (Bewegung) surge; (große Menge) torrent (of water,

Fig: words).

Schwamm [ʃvam], *m* -(e)s/=e **1.** sponge; *F:* **S. drüber!** (let's) forget it! **2.** (*Hauss.*) dry rot. ◆**'s~ig,** *adj.* (*a*) spongy; (*b*) *Pej:* puffy (face etc.).

Schwan [ʃvaːn], *m* -(e)s/=e swan; ◆**'s~en,** *v.i. impers.* (*haben*) **mir schwant nichts Gutes!** I fear the worst!

schwanger [ʃvaŋər], *adj.* pregnant. ◆**'S~schaft,** *f* -/-en pregnancy. ◆**'S~schaftsabbruch,** *m* termination of pregnancy.

schwängern [ʃvɛŋərn], *v.tr.* to make (s.o.) pregnant.

Schwank [ʃvaŋk], *m* -(e)s/=e comical tale; *Th:* farce. ◆**'s~en,** *v.i.* (*haben*) **die Schule s.** to play truant/*N.Am: F:* hooky. ◆**'S~r,** *m* -s/- truant.

Schwank [ʃvaŋk], *m* -(e)s/=e **1.** (*Grashalme usw.*) to sway; wave; (*Gebäude, Boot usw.*) to rock; (*Betrunkener usw.*) to sway, (*taumeln*) stagger, reel; (*b*) (*Preise, Kurse usw.*) to fluctuate; (*Pers.*) to waver. ◆**'S~ung,** *f* -/-en (*a*) swaying; (*b*) fluctuation, variation.

Schwanz [ʃvants], *m* -es/=e tail.

schwänzen [ʃvɛntsən], *v.tr.* (*haben*) **die Schule s.** to play truant/*N.Am: F:* hooky. ◆**'S~r,** *m* -s/- truant.

Schwarm [ʃvarm], *m* -(e)s/=e **1.** swarm (of bees, insects, *Fig:* people); flock (of birds); shoal (of fish). **2.** *no pl Fig:* (*Pers.*) heart-throb.

schwärm|en [ʃvɛrmən], *v.i.* (*a*) (*haben/sein*) (*Bienen usw.*) to swarm; (*b*) (*haben*) (*Pers.*) **für j-n, etwas** *acc* **s.,** to be smitten with s.o., sth.; **von j-m, etwas** *dat* **s.,** to rave about s.o., sth.; ◆**S~e'rei,** *f* -/-en enthusiasm; (*Verzückung*) rapture. ◆**'s~erisch,** *adj.* effusive; gushing (girl).

Schwarte [ʃvartə], *f* -/-n **1.** rind (of bacon); *Cu:* crackling (of pork).

schwarz [ʃvarts], *adj.* black; **ein S~er/ eine S~e,** a black man/woman; a negro/ negress; **ins S~e treffen,** to score a bull's-eye, *Fig:* hit the mark; *F:* sich s. **ärgern,** to be fuming/hopping mad; **s~er Markt,** black market; **s. über die Grenze gehen,** to cross the border illegally. ◆**'S~arbeit,** *f* work on the side (not declared for tax). ◆**'S~brot,** *n* black bread. ◆**'s~fahren,** *v.i.sep. irr.26* (*sein*) (*a*) to travel without a ticket; (*b*) *Aut:* to drive without a licence. ◆**'S~handel,** *m* illicit trade, black market. ◆**'S~händler,** *m* black marketeer. ◆**'s~hören,** *v.i.sep.* (*haben*) to listen to the radio without a licence. ◆**'s~sehen,** *v.i.sep. irr.92* (*haben*) (*a*) to take a pessimistic view; (*b*) to watch television without a licence. ◆**'S~seher,** *m* -s/- **1.** confirmed pessimist. **2.** *TV:* viewer who has no licence. ◆**'s~weiß,** *adj.* black and white (film etc.). ◆**'S~wald.** *m* Black Forest.

Schwärze [ʃvɛrtsə], *f* -/no pl blackness. ◆**'s~n,** *v.tr.* to blacken (shoes etc.).

schwatzen [ʃvatsən], *v.* **1.** *v.i.* (*haben*) to chatter, natter. **2.** *v.tr.* **dummes Zeug**

s., to talk rubbish. ◆**'s~haft,** *adj.* garrulous, talkative.

schwätz|en [ʃvɛtsən], *v.* = schwatzen. ◆**'S~er(in),** *m* -s/- (*f* -/-nen) *Pej:* talker, windbag.

Schwebe [ʃveːbə], *f Fig:* **in der S. sein/ hängen,** to hang in the balance/be undecided. ◆**'S~bahn,** *f* suspension railway. ◆**'S~balken,** *m* (balance) beam. ◆**'s~n,** *v.i.* (*haben*) (*an einem Seil usw.*) to hang. (*Ballon, Wolken*) to float; **zwischen Leben und Tod s.,** to hover between life and death; **in Gefahr s.,** to be in danger.

Schwed|e [ʃveːdə], *m* -n/-n Swede. ◆**'S~en.** *Pr.n.n* -s. Sweden. ◆**'S~in,** *f* -/-nen Swedish woman. ◆**'s~isch,** *adj.* Swedish.

Schwef|el [ʃveːfəl], *m* -s/no pl sulphur. ◆**'s~(e)lig,** *adj.* sulphurous. ◆**'S~el-säure,** *f* sulphuric acid.

Schweif [ʃvaif], *m* -(e)s/-e tail (of a lion, comet etc.). ◆**'s~en,** *v.i.* (*sein*) (*Blick usw.*) to roam, wander.

Schweig|egeld [ʃvaiɡəɡɛlt], *n* hushmoney. ◆**'s~emarsch,** *m* silent protest march. ◆**'s~en. I.** *v.i.irr.* (*haben*) to be silent; (*Pers.*) to say nothing. **kannst du s.?** can you keep a secret? **II. S.,** *n* -s/no pl silence; **j-n zum S. bringen,** to silence s.o., *F:* shut s.o. up. ◆**'s~end,** *adj.* silent. ◆**'s~sam,** *adj.* taciturn. ◆**'S~samkeit,** *f* -/no pl taciturnity.

Schwein [ʃvain], *n* -(e)s/-e **1.** pig. **2.** *F:* (*Pers.*) **armes S.,** poor devil; **kein S.,** not a soul; **3.** *F:* (*Glück*) **S. haben,** to be dead lucky. ◆**'S~e,** *comb.fm.* (*a*) pig (breeding etc.); (*b*) *Cu:* pork (chop, fillet etc.); (belly etc.) of pork. ◆**'S~ebraten,** *m* joint of pork; roast pork. ◆**'S~ehund,** *m* -(e)s/-e *P:* bastard, swine. ◆**S~e'rei,** *f* -/-en (*a*) (*Schmutz*) filthy mess; (*b*) (*Gemeinheit*) mean trick; scandal; (*c*) (*Unanständigkeit*) obscenity; (*Witz*) dirty joke. ◆**'S~efleisch,** *n* pork. ◆**'S~estall,** *m* pigsty. ◆**'s~isch,** *adj. F: Pej:* lewd (joke, behaviour etc.). ◆**'S~sleder,** *n* pigskin.

Schweiß [ʃvais], *m* -es/no pl sweat; (nur vom Menschen) perspiration. ◆**'S~brenner,** *m* welding torch. ◆**'S~drüse,** *f* sweat gland. ◆**'s~en,** *v.tr.* to weld (metals, plastics etc.). ◆**'S~er,** *m* -s/- welder. ◆**'S~füße,** *fpl* sweaty feet. ◆**'s~gebadet,** *adj.* bathed in sweat. ◆**'S~naht,** *f* welded seam.

Schweiz [ʃvaits]. *Pr.n.f* **die S.,** Switzerland. ◆**'S~er. I.** *m* -s/- Swiss. **II.** *adj.* Swiss. ◆**'S~erin,** *f* -/-nen Swiss woman. ◆**'S~erdeutsch,** *n* Swiss German. ◆**'s~erisch,** *adj.* Swiss (town etc.).

schwelen [ʃveːlən], *v.i.* (*haben*) to smoulder.

schwelgen [ʃvɛlɡən], *v.i.* (*haben*) to indulge (in food, Fig: memories etc.).

Schwelle ['ʃvɛlə], f -/-n (also Fig:) threshold.

schwellen ['ʃvɛlən], v.tr. & i.irr. (sein) to swell. ◆'**S~ung**, f -/-en swelling.

Schwengel ['ʃvɛŋəl], m -s/- (a) (bell) clapper; (b) handle of a pump etc.).

Schwenk [ʃvɛŋk], m -(e)s/-s (a) swing; (b) Phot: pan. ◆'**S~bar**, adj. swivelling. ◆'s~en, v. tr. (a) to wave (one's hat, arms, a flag etc.); (b) to swivel (sth.); Phot: to pan (a camera). 2. v.i. (haben) to swing, Mil: wheel. ◆'**S~er**, m -s/- brandy glass. ◆'**S~ung**, f -/-en swing; change of direction; Mil: wheel; Phot: panning.

schwer [ʃveːr], adj. 1. (nicht leicht) heavy; **s. beladen**, heavily loaded. 2. (a) (hart) hard (work, job, life, fate etc.); severe (punishment etc.); **s. arbeiten**, to work hard; (b) (schwierig) difficult (problem, task, decision, language etc.); **es ist s. zu begreifen**, it is hard/difficult to understand; **s. hören**, to be hard of hearing; **s. atmen**, to breathe with difficulty; **es s. haben**, to have a hard/difficult time. 3. (schlimm) serious, bad (accident, injuries, mistake etc.); serious (harm, offence etc.); **s. krank sein**, to be seriously ill. ◆'**S~arbeit**, f hard (physical) work. ◆'**S~athlet**, m weight lifter, wrestler or boxer. ◆'s~bewaffnet, adj. heavily armed. ◆'**S~e**, f -/no pl 1. heaviness; (Gewicht) weight. 2. (Schwierigkeit) difficulty. 3. (Ausmaß) severity; seriousness. ◆'s~elos, adj. weightless. ◆'**S~e-losigkeit**, f -/no pl weightlessness. ◆'s~erziehbar, adj. ◆'erziehbares Kind, problem child. ◆'s~fallen, v.i. sep.irr.27 (sein) die Arbeit fällt ihm schwer, he finds the work difficult. ◆'s~fällig, adj. ponderous. ◆'**S~gewicht**, n 1. Sp: heavyweight. 2. Fig: (Betonung) (main) stress. ◆'s~hörig, adj. hard of hearing. ◆'**S~hörigkeit**, f -/no pl hardness of hearing. ◆'**S~industrie**, f heavy industry. ◆'**S~kraft**, f (force of) gravity. ◆'s~krank, adj. gravely/critically ill. ◆'s~lich, adv. hardly. ◆'s~machen, v.tr.sep. to make (life, work etc.) difficult (j-m, for s.o.). ◆'s~mütig, adj. melancholy. ◆'s~nehmen, v.tr.sep.irr.69 to take (life etc.) (too) seriously. ◆'**S~punkt**, m 1. Ph: centre of gravity. 2. Fig: (main) emphasis. ◆'s~tun, v.refl.sep.irr.106 F: sich dar mit etwas dat s., to have difficulties with sth. ◆'**S~verbrechen**, n major crime. ◆'**S~verbrecher**, m dangerous criminal. ◆'s~verdaulich, adj. indigestible. ◆'s~verletzt, adj. seriously wounded. ◆'s~wiegend, adj. weighty (decisions, reason etc.).

Schwert [ʃveːrt], n -(e)s/-er sword. ◆'**S~lilie**, f iris.

Schwester ['ʃvɛstər], f -/-n 1. sister. 2.

(Krankens.) (female) nurse. ◆'s~lich, adj. sisterly.

Schwieger|eltern ['ʃviːgərʔɛltərn], pl parents-in-law. ◆'**S~mutter**, f mother-in-law. ◆'**S~sohn**, m son-in-law. ◆'**S~tochter**, f daughter-in-law. ◆'**S~vater**, m father-in-law.

Schwiele ['ʃviːlə], f -/-n callus.

schwierig ['ʃviːriç], adj. difficult. ◆'**S~keit**, f -/-en difficulty.

Schwimm|bad ['ʃvimbaːt], n swimming pool/(Hallenbad) baths. ◆'**S~becken**, n swimming pool. ◆'s~en, v.i.irr.90 (sein/haben) (a) (sein) (Pers., Tier) to swim; (Sache) to float; (Pers.) **S. ist gesund**, swimming is good for you; F: **im Geld s.**, to be rolling in money; (b) (haben) F: (überschwemmt sein) **der ganze Boden schwimmt**, the whole floor is awash; (c) (verschwimmen) to blur; (d) F: (Redner usw.) **er ist ins S. geraten**, he floundered/came unstuck. ◆'**S~er**, m -s/- (Pers.) swimmer. ◆'**S~lehrer(in)**, m (f) swimming instructor. ◆'**S~weste**, f lifejacket.

Schwindel ['ʃvindəl], m -s/no pl 1. giddiness; Med: vertigo. 2. (Betrug) swindle, cheat. ◆'s~elerregend, adj. vertiginous (heights etc.). ◆'s~elfrei, adj. (Pers.) free from giddiness/dizziness. ◆'s~eln, v.i. (haben) a Pej: (lügen) to tell stories, F: fib; (b) mir/mich schwindelt es, I feel dizzy; s~elnde Höhen, dizzy heights. ◆'s~ler(in), m -s/- (f -/-nen) swindler; (Lügner) liar. ◆'s~lig, adj. dizzy, giddy; mir ist s., I feel dizzy/giddy.

schwinden ['ʃvindən], v.i.irr.9 (haben) (a) Lit: (Kräfte, Vorräte usw.) to dwindle; (Schönheit, Einfluß usw.) to wane; (Hoffnung usw.) to fade; (b) (verschwinden) to disappear.

schwingen ['ʃviŋən], v.tr.irr.19 1. v.tr. to swing (one's arm, a hammer etc.); (schwenken) to wave (a flag etc.). 2. v.i. (haben) (a) to swing; (b) (Saite usw.) to vibrate. ◆'**S~ung**, f -/-en Ph: oscillation, vibration.

Schwips [ʃvips], m -es/-e F: **einen S. haben**, to be tipsy.

schwirren ['ʃvirən], v.i. (a) (sein) (Insekten usw.) to buzz (along); (Pfeil usw.) to whirr; (b) (haben) **die Stadt schwirrt von Gerüchten**, the town is buzzing with rumours.

schwitzen ['ʃvitsən], v.i. (haben) (Pers. usw.) to sweat, perspire.

schwören ['ʃvøːrən], v.tr. & i.irr. (haben) to swear (an oath, loyalty etc.); F: **auf ein Medikament usw. s.**, to swear by a remedy etc.

schwul [ʃvuːl], adj. F: gay (man, magazine etc.).

schwül [ʃvyːl], adj. sultry. ◆'**S~e**, f -/ no pl sultriness.

Schwulst [ʃvulst], m -(e)s/no pl Pej: bombast.

Schwund [ʃvunt], *m* -(e)s/*no pl* decrease; *Com:* wastage, loss in weight.

Schwung [ʃvuŋ], *m* -(e)s/-e **1.** (*Bewegung*) swing (of the arms, a pendulum etc.); **S. holen,** to get a good swing. **2.** (a) (*Antrieb*) momentum; **in S. kommen,** to get under way, (*Party*) warm up; (*Pers.*) to get into one's stride; (b) (*Elan*) verve, *F:* zip. ◆'**s~rad,** *n* flywheel. ◆'**s~voll,** *adj.* vivid (performance etc.); lively, spirited (music, speech etc.).

Schwur [ʃvuːr], *m* -(e)s/-e oath. ◆'**S~gericht,** *n G.Jur:* court composed of professional and lay judges (*mit Geschworenen*) jury court.

sechs [zɛks], *num.adj.* six. ◆'**S~eck,** *n* hexagon. ◆'**s~eckig,** *adj.* hexagonal. ◆'**s~mal,** *adv.* six times. ◆'**s~ste(r),** *adj.,* *num.adj.* sixth. ◆'**S~tel,** *n* -s/- sixth. ◆'**s~tens,** *adv.* sixthly.

sech|zehn [ˈzɛçtseːn], *num.adj.* sixteen. ◆'**s~zig,** *num.adj.* sixty. ◆'**s~ziger,** *inv.adj.* die s. Jahre, the sixties.

See [zeː]. **I.** *m* -s/-n lake. **II.** *f* -/-n sea; auf S., at sea; **an der S.,** at the seaside. ◆'**S~bad,** *n* seaside resort. ◆'**S~fahrt,** *f* **1.** *no pl* seafaring, navigation. **2.** voyage. ◆'**S~gang,** *m* swell. ◆'**S~hund,** *m* seal. ◆'**s~krank,** *adj.* seasick. ◆'**S~krankheit,** *f* seasickness. ◆'**S~macht,** *f* naval/maritime power. ◆'**S~mann,** *m* -(e)s/-leute seaman, sailor. ◆'**S~ngebiet,** *n* lake district. ◆'**S~not,** *f* distress at sea. ◆'**S~pferdchen,** *n* sea-horse. ◆'**S~räuber,** *m* pirate. ◆'**S~rose,** *f* water-lily. ◆'**S~stern,** *m* starfish. ◆'**S~tang,** *m* seaweed. ◆'**s~tüchtig,** *adj.* seaworthy. ◆'**S~weg,** *m* sea route; **auf dem S.,** by sea. ◆'**S~zunge,** *f* sole.

Seele [ˈzeːlə], *f* -/-n soul; **das ist mir aus der S. gesprochen,** that's just what I feel. ◆'**S~nruhe,** *f* -/*no pl* complete calm. ◆'**S~nfriede,** *m* peace of mind.

seel|isch [ˈzeːliʃ], *adj.* psychological (illness etc.); emotional (balance, state etc.); **s. bedingt,** with psychological causes. ◆'**S~sorge,** *f* pastoral work. ◆'**S~sorger,** *m* -s/- pastor, clergyman.

Segel [ˈzeːgəl]. **I.** *n* -s/- sail. **II.** '**S~,** *comb.fm.* sailing (boat, ship, club etc.). ◆'**S~fahrt,** *f* -/-en sail (trip). ◆'**S~flieger,** *m* glider pilot. ◆'**S~flugzeug,** *n* glider. ◆**s~n. I.** *v.tr.&i.* (*haben/sein*) to sail (a boat, distance etc.); *Av:* to glide. **II.** *S.,* *n* -s/*no pl* sailing. ◆'**S~sport,** *m* sailing. ◆'**S~tuch,** *n* canvas.

Segen [ˈzeːgən], *m* -s/*no pl* blessing. ◆'**s~sreich,** *adj.* beneficial.

Segment [zɛgˈmɛnt], *n* -(e)s/-e segment.

segn|en [ˈzeːgnən], *v.tr.* to bless (s.o., sth.). ◆'**S~ung,** *f* -/-en blessing.

seh|en [ˈzeːən], *v.irr.* **1.** *v.tr.* (a) to see; **niemand war zu s.,** there was nobody to be seen; (b) (*schätzen*) to regard, judge (sth.); **etwas anders s.,** to look at sth. differently; **sich gezwungen/veranlaßt s.,** etwas zu tun, to feel bound to do sth.; **das werden wir ja gleich s.,** we'll soon find out; (c) **er hat sich lange nicht s. lassen,** there hasn't been any sign of him for a long time; (*Pers.*) to like/dislike sth.; **sie ist stets gern gesehen,** she is always welcome; **sich s. lassen können,** (i) to look attractive/(*repräsentativ*) respectable; (ii) *Fig:* (*Leistung usw.*) to be pretty good. **2.** *v.i.* (*haben*) (a) to see; **gut/schlecht s.,** to have good/bad eyesight; (b) (*blicken*) to look (aus dem Fenster, in den Spiegel usw.), out of the window, in the mirror etc.); **lassen Sie mich/laß (mich) mal s.,** let me have a look; (c) *auf* **Pünktlichkeit s.,** to be particular about punctuality. ◆'**s~enswert,** *adj.* worth seeing. ◆'**S~enswürdigkeit,** *f* -/-en sight (worth seeing). ◆'**S~er(in),** *m* -s/- (*f* -/-nen) seer, prophet. ◆'**S~fehler,** *m* eye defect. ◆'**S~schwäche,** *f* poor eyesight. ◆'**S~test,** *m* eye test. ◆'**S~vermögen,** *n* eyesight.

Sehn|e [ˈzeːnə], *f* -/-n tendon. ◆'**s~ig,** *adj.* sinewy; stringy (meat etc.).

sehn|en [ˈzeːnən], *v.refl.* **sich nach etwas** *dat* **s.,** to yearn/long for sth. ◆'**s~lich,** *adj.* ardent (wish etc.). ◆'**S~sucht,** *f* -/no pl longing (nach + *dat,* for). ◆'**s~süchtig,** *adj.* longing; wistful (expression etc.).

sehr [zeːr], *adv.* very; **s. viel,** very much; **s. viel Geld,** a great deal of money; **das tue ich s. gern,** I like doing that very much; **sich s. bemühen,** to try very hard; **danke s.,** thank you very much; **es gefiel ihr so s., daß ...,** she liked it so much that ...

seicht [zaiçt], *adj.* shallow (water); *Fig:* superficial (book etc.).

Seid|e [ˈzaidə], *f* -/-n silk. ◆'**s~en,** *adj.* silk. ◆'**S~enpapier,** *n* tissue paper. ◆'**s~enweich,** *adj.* soft and silky. ◆'**s~ig,** *adj.* silky.

Seidel [ˈzaidəl], *n* -s/- beer mug.

Seif|e [ˈzaifə], *f* -/-n soap. ◆'**S~en-,** *comb.fm.* soap (powder, dish etc.); soapy (water). ◆'**S~nlauge,** *f* soap suds. ◆'**S~nschaum,** *m* (soapy) lather. ◆'**s~ig,** *adj.* soapy.

seihen [ˈzaiən], *v.tr.* to strain (a liquid etc.).

Seil [zail], *n* -(e)s/-e rope; (*Hochs.*) tightrope. ◆'**S~bahn,** *f* cable railway. ◆'**s~springen,** *v.i.* to skip. ◆'**S~tänzer(in),** *m* (*f*) tightrope walker.

sein[1] [zain], *poss.pron.* his; (*Tier, Sache*) its; **das ist s~er/s~e/s~es,** that's his (one)/(*Tier*) its one; **er hat das S~e dazu beigetragen,** he has done his bit; **jedem das S~e,** to each his own. ◆'**s~er,** *pers.pron.* gen of er/es of him/it. ◆'**s~erseits,** *adv.* on his part.

◆'s~erzeit, *adv.* (*damals*) at that time.
◆'s~es'gleichen, *pron.* (*a*) people like him; (*b*) ein Buch, das s. sucht, a unique book. ◆'s~etwegen/um 's~etwillen, *adv.* because of him; (*für ihn*) for his sake. ◆'s~ige, *poss.pron. Lit:* der/die/das s., his/its one.

sein2. I. *v.i.irr.* (*sein*) to be; (*a*) sei brav! be good! du warst es! it was you! keiner will es gewesen sein, nobody will admit to it; (*b*) es ist an dir zu ..., it is up to you to ...; wie dem auch sei, be that as it may; es sei denn, morgen regnet es, unless it rains tomorrow; wie wäre es mit einem Spaziergang? how about a walk? (*c*) mir ist kalt, schlecht usw., I feel cold, ill etc.; (*d*) *F:* (*passieren*) wenn etwas ist, if anything happens; ist was? is anything wrong? (*e*) wenn er nicht gewesen wäre, if it had not been for him. II. S., *n* -s/no *pl Lit:* existence. ◆'s~lassen, *v.tr.sep.irr.57 F:* to stop (doing) sth., (*aufgeben*) drop (sth.).

seit [zait], *prep.* + *dat & conj.* (*a*) since; ich bin s. vier Tagen krank, I have been ill for four days now; s. wann weißt du das? how long have you known this? ich weiß es erst s. kurzem, I only learnt about it recently; s. wir hier sind, since we have been here. ◆'s~'dem. I. *adv.* since then; II. *conj.* since. ◆'s~her, *adv.* = seitdem I.

Seite ['zaitə], *f* -/-n (*a*) side; face of a coin, dice etc.); *Mil:* flank; zur S. treten, to step aside; S. an S., side by side; *F:* seine schwache/starke S., his weak spot/strong point; auf der einen S...., auf der anderen S. ..., on the one hand ..., on the other hand ...; er stand auf ihrer S., he took her side; *Sp:* die S~n wechseln, to change ends; (*b*) (*Buchs.*) page. ◆'S~nansicht, *f* side view; profile. ◆'S~nblick, *m* side/sidelong glance. ◆'S~nhieb, *m* side-swipe (auf + *acc*, at). ◆'s~nlang, *adj.* going on for (several) pages. ◆'s~ns, *prep.* + *gen* on the part of. ◆'S~nschiff, *n* side aisle. ◆'S~nsprung, *m* (extramarital) escapade. ◆'S~nstechen, *n* stitch (in one's side). ◆'S~nstraße, *f* side street. ◆'S~nstreifen, *m* verge (of a road). ◆'s~nverkehrt, *adj.* the wrong way round; (picture etc.) in mirror image. ◆'S~nzahl, *f* number of pages.

seit|lich ['zaitliç]. I. *adj.* side (entrance etc.); s. von mir, to one side of me. II. *prep.* + *gen* to one side of, beside. ◆'s~wärts, *adv.* sideways.

Sekret|är [zekre'tɛːr], *m* -s/-e 1. (*Pers.*) secretary. 2. (*a*) (tall-front) secretaire. ◆S~tariat [-tari'aːt], *n* -(e)s/-e (*a*) administrative office; (*b*) *Pol:* secretariat. ◆S~tärin [-'tɛːrin], *f* -/-nen (female) secretary.

Sekt [zekt], *m* -(e)s/-e (German) champagne.

Sekte ['zektə], *f* -/-n sect.

Sektion [zektsi'oːn], *f* -/-en *Adm:* section, department.

Sektor ['zektɔr], *m* -s/-en (*Bereich*) sector.

Sekund|a [ze'kunda], *f* -/-den *Sch:* sixth and seventh years/second (highest) form (in a *Gymnasium*). ◆s~är [-'dɛːr] *adj.* secondary. ◆S~e [-'kundə], *f* -/-n second. ◆S~enzeiger, *m* second hand.

selber ['zelbər], *dem.pron. F:* = selbst.

selbst [zelpst]. I. *dem.pron.* ich s., I myself; du/Sie s., you yourself; er s., he himself; sie s., she herself; *pl* they themselves; wir s., we ourselves; Ihr/Sie s., you yourselves; die Tür geht von s. zu, the door closes itself/automatically; das versteht sich von s., that goes without saying. II. *adv.* even; s. wenn, even if. ◆'S~achtung, *f* self-esteem. ◆'S~auslöser, *m Phot:* automatic release. ◆'S~bedienung, *f* self-service. ◆'S~befriedigung, *f* masturbation. ◆'S~beherrschung, *f* self-control. ◆'s~bewußt, *adj.* self-confident, self-possessed. ◆'S~bewußtsein, *n* self-confidence. ◆'S~erhaltung, *f* self-preservation. ◆'s~gefällig, *adj.* smug, complacent. ◆'S~gespräch, *n* soliloquy. ◆'s~herrlich, *adj.* high-handed, autocratic. ◆'S~kostenpreis, *m* cost price. ◆'s~los, *adj.* unselfish. ◆'S~losigkeit, *f* -/no *pl* unselfishness. ◆'S~mord, *m* (act of) suicide. ◆'S~mörder(in), *m* (*f*) (*Pers.*) suicide. ◆'s~sicher, *adj.* self-assured. ◆'s~süchtig, *adj.* selfish. ◆'s~tätig, *adj.* automatic. ◆'s~verständlich, *adj.* (*offensichtlich*) self-evident, obvious (truth, fact etc.); *adv.* of course. ◆'S~verteidigung, *f* self-defence. ◆'S~vertrauen, *n* self-confidence. ◆'S~verwaltung, *f* self-administration/government. ◆'s~zufrieden, *adj.* self-satisfied. ◆'S~zweck, *m* end in itself.

selbständig ['zelpʃtendiç], *adj.* independent; (mit eigenem Betrieb) self-employed (person). ◆'S~keit, *f* -/no *pl* independence.

selektiv [zelek'tiːf], *adj.* selective.

selig ['zeːliç], *adj.* (*a*) blissful; (*Pers.*) overjoyed, *F:* on cloud nine; (*b*) *Ecc:* blessed.

Sellerie ['zeləri], *m* -s/-(s) & *f* -/- celeriac; (*Stangens.*) celery.

selten ['zeltən], *adj.* (*a*) rare (books, plants etc.); ich sehe ihn nur s., I seldom/hardly ever see him. (*b*) *adv.* rarely; *F:* ein s. schönes Bild etc.; an exceptionally lovely picture etc. ◆'S~heit, *f* -/no *pl* rarity.

seltsam ['zeltzaːm], *adj.* strange. ◆'s~er'weise, *adv.* strangely/oddly enough. ◆'S~keit, *f* no *pl* strangeness.

Semester [ze'mestər], *n* -s/- semester, (six-monthly) term. ◆S~ferien, *pl* vacation.

Semikolon [zemi'koːlon], *n* -s/-s & -la semicolon.

Seminar [zemi'naːr], *n* -s/-e 1. seminar;

(*Abteilung*) department. **2.** *Ecc:* seminary.

Semmel ['zɛməl], *f* -/-n *South G:* (crusty) roll.

Senat [ze'naːt], *m* -(e)s/-e senate. ◆**S~or** [-'naːtɔr], *m* -s/-en [-'toːrən] senator.

send|en ['zɛndən], *v.tr.* & *i.* **1.** *v.irr.* (*haben*) to send; to dispatch (goods etc.). **2.** (*haben*) *Rad: TV:* to transmit, broadcast (signals, a programme etc.). ◆**'S~epause,** *f Rad: TV:* interlude. ◆**'S~er,** *m* -s/- (*broadcasting*) station; (*Gerät*) transmitter. ◆**'S~ereihe,** *f* radio/ television series. ◆**'S~esaal,** *m* broadcasting studio. ◆**'S~eschluß,** *m* end of broadcasting, close-down. ◆**'S~ung,** *f* -/-en **1.** (*a*) *no pl* dispatch (of goods); (*b*) (*das Gesandte*) consignment; (*Paket usw.*) package. **2.** *Rad: TV:* (*a*) *no pl* broadcasting (of a programme); (*b*) broadcast; programme. **3.** *Fig:* (*Aufgabe*) mission.

Senf [zɛnf], *m* -(e)s/*no pl* mustard.

sengen ['zɛŋən], *v.tr.*&*i.* (*haben*) to scorch, singe (sth.). ◆**'s~d,** *adj.* scorching, sweltering (sun, heat etc.).

senil [ze'niːl], *adj.* senile.

Senior ['zeːnjɔr]. **I.** *m* -s/-en *Sp:* senior; (*ältestes Mitglied*) veteran. ◆**'S~chef,** *m* boss of a family firm. ◆**S~en-** [zeni'oːrən], *comb.fm.* (*a*) *Sp: etc:* senior (team etc.); (*b*) old people's (home, club etc.).

Senk|blei ['zɛŋkblai], *n* lead, plummet. ◆**'S~e,** *f* -/-n hollow, dip (in a landscape). ◆**'S~el,** *m* -s/- shoelace. ◆**'s~en,** *v.tr.* to lower (one's eyes, voice, arms etc.); to bow (one's head); to reduce (taxes, prices etc.); **sich s.,** to sink; (*Boden*) to fall (away), drop; (*Schranke, Vorhang*) to descend. ◆**'S~fuß,** *m* fallen arches. ◆**'s~-recht,** *adj.* vertical. ◆**'S~rechte,** *f* -n/-n *Mth:* perpendicular. ◆**'S~ung,** *f* -/-en (*a*) (*Abfall*) drop, dip (in the terrain, road etc.); (*b*) (*Verminderung*) lowering (of prices etc.) (**um** + *acc*, by).

Sensation [zɛnzatsi'oːn], *f* -/-en sensation. ◆**s~ell** [-'onɛl], *adj.* sensational.

Sense ['zɛnzə], *f* -/-n scythe.

sensi|bel [zɛn'ziːbəl], *adj.* sensitive. ◆**S~bilität** [-ibili'tɛːt], *f* -/*no pl* sensitivity, sensitiveness.

sentimental [zɛntimɛn'taːl], *adj.* sentimental. ◆**S~ität** [-tali'tɛːt], *f* -/*no pl* sentimentality.

separat [zepa'raːt], *adj.* separate; **s~e Wohnung,** self-contained flat.

September [zɛp'tɛmbər], *m* -s/- September.

Serenade [zere'naːdə], *f* -/-n serenade.

Serie ['zeːriə], *f* -/-n series; *Com:* line of goods etc.); *Aut: etc:* range (of models); *Ind:* **in S. hergestellt,** mass-produced. ◆**'S~nproduktion,** *f* series/mass production. ◆**'s~nweise,** *adv.* in series.

seriös [zeri'øːs], *adj.* respectable (person etc.); sound (firm); **ein s~es Angebot,** a

---

genuine offer.

Serpentine [zɛrpɛn'tiːnə], *f* -/-n zigzag (line, road).

Serum ['zeːrum], *n* -s/-ren serum.

Serv|ice [zɛr'viːs], *n* -s/- (tea etc.) service. ◆**s~ieren** [-'viːrən], *v.tr.* & *i.* (*haben*) to serve (sth.). ◆**S~iererin,** *f* -/-nen waitress. ◆**S~iette** [-vi'ɛtə], *f* -/-n (table) napkin.

Servus ['zɛrvus], *int. F: South G: & Aus:* (*a*) hello! *N.Am:* hi! (*b*) (*Abschiedsgruß*) so long! see you!

Sesam ['zeːzam], *m* -s/-s (*a*) sesame; (*b*) (*Samen*) sesame seeds.

Sessel ['zɛsəl], *m* -s/- (upholstered) armchair. ◆**'S~lift,** *m* chair lift.

seßhaft ['zɛshaft], *adj.* (*Pers., Leben*) settled; **s. werden,** to settle down.

Set [sɛt], *m* & *n* -s/-s **1.** (*Satz*) set. **2.** table mat.

setz|en ['zɛtsən], *v.* **1.** *v.tr.* (*a*) to put (sth. somewhere); **etwas auf eine Liste s.,** to enter/put sth. on a list; **sein Geld auf etwas** *acc* **s.,** to put/stake one's money on sth.; (*b*) (*festlegen*) to set (limits, a target etc.); (*c*) **sich s.,** to sit down; (*d*) to plant (a tree etc.); (*e*) **j-m ein Denkmal s.,** to put up a monument to s.o.; **die Segel s.,** to set/hoist the sails; (*f*) to lay (a book etc.). **2.** *v.i.* (*a*) (*sein*) **über eine Hecke s.,** to jump/leap over a hedge; **die Fähre setzte über den Fluß,** the ferry crossed the river; (*b*) (*haben*) to bet; **auf ein Pferd s.,** to back a horse. ◆**'S~er,** *m* -s/- typesetter, compositor. ◆**'S~ling,** *m* -s/-e seedling.

Seuche ['zɔyçə], *f* -/-n epidemic.

seufze|n ['zɔyftsən], *v.i.* (*haben*) to sigh. ◆**'S~r,** *m* -s/- sigh.

Sex [sɛks], *m* -es/*no pl* sex. ◆**s~istisch** [sɛk'sistiʃ], *adj.* sexist.

Sexta ['zɛksta], *f* -/-ten *Sch:* first form/ year (in a *Gymnasium*).

Sextett [zɛks'tɛt], *n* -(e)s/-e *Mus:* sextet.

Sexu|al- [zɛksu'aːl-], *comb.fm.* sex (life, crime etc.). ◆**S~alität** [-ali'tɛːt], *f* -/*no pl* sexuality. ◆**s~ell** [-u'ɛl], *adj.* sexual.

sezier|en [ze'tsiːrən], *v.tr.* to dissect (a corpse etc.).

Shampoo [ʃam'puː], *n* -s/-s shampoo.

Show [ʃoː], *f* -/-s show. ◆**'S~geschäft,** *n* show business.

siam|esisch [zia'meːziʃ], *adj.* Siamese. ◆**S~katze,** *f* -/-n Siamese cat.

Sibirien [zi'biːrjən]. *Pr.n.n* -s. Siberia. ◆**s~isch,** *adj.* Siberian (climate etc.).

sich [ziç], *refl.pron.* (*a*) *3rd pers. sing.* m himself, *f* herself, *n* itself; *pl* themselves; *2nd pers.* polite form yourself, *pl* yourselves; *indef.* oneself; **das Problem löste s. von selbst,** the problem solved itself; **er gab s.** (**selbst**) **die Schuld,** he blamed himself; (*b*) (*einander*) each other, one another; **sie helfen s.** *dat,* they help one another; (*c*) **sie denkt nur an s.,** she only thinks of herself; **er hat es hinter s.,** he has this behind him; **haben Sie Geld bei**

s.? have you any money on you?

Sichel ['ziçəl], f -/-n sickle.

sicher ['ziçər], adj. (a) safe (place etc.); secure (job, investment etc.); **vor Gefahr s. sein,** to be safe/protected from danger; **s. ist s.,** better safe than sorry; (b) sure (sign, judgement etc.); (*getop*) certain; (*zuverlässig*) reliable (method, evidence etc.); **sind Sie s.?** are you sure/certain? **das ist s. richtig,** that is certainly true; **aber s.!** of course! (c) steady (hand etc.), confident (belief, manner etc.). ◆'**s~gehen,** *v.i.sep.irr.36* (sein) to play safe; **um sicherzugehen,** to be on the safe side, make sure. ◆'**S~heit,** f -/-en 1. *no pl* (a) safety; security (of the state etc.); (b) (*Gewißheit*) certainty; **er kommt mit S.,** he is sure to come; (c) (*Selbsts.*) confidence, assurance. 2. *Fin:* security. ◆'**S~heits-,** *comb.fm.* safety (factor, glass, device etc.); safe (car, distance etc.); (b) security (officer, service, forces, police, risk etc.). ◆'**S~heitsgurt,** *m* safety belt; *Av: Aut:* seat belt. ◆'**s~heitshalber,** *adv.* for safety's sake. ◆'**S~heitsnadel,** f safety pin. ◆'**S~heitsschloß,** *n* safety lock. ◆'**s~lich,** *adv.* certainly. ◆'**s~n,** *v.tr.* (a) to safeguard, (*schützen*) protect (sth.) (**vor etwas dat,** from sth.); (b) (*verschaffen*) to secure (sth.); **sich dat einen guten Platz s.,** to make sure of a good seat; (c) to put the safety catch on (a gun). ◆'**s~stellen,** *v.tr.sep.* (a) (*beschlagnahmen*) to seize, confiscate (goods etc.); (b) to safeguard (a position, service etc.). ◆'**S~ung,** f -/-en 1. *no pl* (*Schutz*) protection, safeguard(ing). 2. (a) *El:* fuse; (b) (*von Pistole*) safety catch.

Sicht [ziçt], f -/*no pl* visibility; **die S. sperren,** to obstruct/block one's view; **außer S.,** out of sight; *Com:* **auf/nach S.,** on/after sight; *Fig:* **auf kurze/lange S.,** in the short/long run; **aus meiner S.,** from my point of view. ◆'**s~bar,** *adj.* visible. ◆'**S~barkeit,** f -/*no pl* visibility. ◆'**s~en,** *v.tr.* to sight (a ship etc.). ◆'**S~gerät,** *n Data-pr:* visual display unit. ◆'**s~lich,** *adj.* visible, evident (pleasure, relief etc.). ◆'**S~verhältnisse,** *npl* visibility. ◆'**S~vermerk,** *m* visa (in a passport etc.). ◆'**S~weite,** f -/*no pl* range of visibility.

sickern ['zikərn], *v.i.* (sein) to seep, ooze.

sie [zi:], *pers.pron.* 1. (*Frau usw.*) (nom.) she, (acc) her, (*Ding*) it; pl they, (acc) them. 2. **S~** you.

Sieb [zi:p], *n* -(e)s/-e strainer, sieve. ◆'**s~en¹** ['zi:bən], *v.tr.* to sieve (flour etc.).

sieben² [zi:bən], *num.adj.* seven. ◆'**s~fach,** *adj.* sevenfold. ◆'**s~mal,** *adv.* seven times. ◆'**S~'sachen,** *fpl F:* (personal) belongings.

sieb|te(r,s) ['zi:ptə(r,s)], *num.adj.* seventh. ◆'**s~tel,** *n* -/- seventh. ◆'**s~tens,** *adv.* seventhly. ◆'**s~-**

zehn, *num.adj.* seventeen. ◆'**s~zig,** *num.adj.* seventy. ◆'**s~ziger.** I. *inv.adj.* **die s. Jahre,** the seventies. II. **S~(in),** *m* -s/- (f -/-nen) seventy-year old.

sied|eln ['zi:dəln], *v.i.* (haben) to settle (somewhere). ◆'**S~ler,** *m* -s/- settler. ◆'**S~lung,** f -/-en 1. housing estate/ *N.Am:* development. 2. *esp. Hist:* settlement.

siede|n ['zi:dən], *v.tr.&i.* (haben) to boil (sth.); **s~nd heiß,** boiling hot. ◆'**S~punkt,** *m* boiling point.

Sieg [zi:k], *m* -(e)s/-e victory; *Sp:* win. ◆'**s~en,** *v.i.* (haben) to win a victory; *Sp: Pol: etc:* to win; *Fig:* to triumph. ◆'**S~er(in)** [-gər(in)], *m* -s/- (f -/-nen) victor; *Sp: etc:* winner. ◆'**S~erehrung,** f *Sp:* prize-giving ceremony. ◆'**s~esgewiß/'s~essicher,** *adj.* confident of victory. ◆'**S~eszug,** *m* triumphant/victorious progress. ◆'**s~reich,** *adj.* victorious.

Siegel ['zi:gəl], *n* -s/- seal; (*Stempel*) stamp. ◆'**S~lack,** *m & n* sealing wax. ◆'**S~ring,** *m* signet ring.

siezen ['zi:tsən], *v.tr.* to address (s.o.) formally/as **Sie.**

Signal [zi'gna:l], *n* -s/-e signal. ◆'**s~isieren,** *v.tr.* to signal (a message etc.); *Fig:* to indicate (sth.).

Signatur [zigna'tu:r], f -/-en signature. ◆'**s~nieren,** *v.tr.* to sign (sth.).

Silbe ['zilbə], f -/-n syllable.

Silber ['zilbər]. I. **s~** *no pl* silver; **das S. putzen,** to polish the silver. II. '**S~-,** *comb.fm.* silver (foil, fox, medal, coin, paper etc.). ◆'**s~n,** *adj.* silver (bracelet, wedding etc.); (*silbrig*) silvery (sheen etc.).

silbrig ['zilbriç], *adj.* silvery.

Silhouette [zilu'etə], f -/-n silhouette.

Silizium [zi'li:tsium], *n* -s/*no pl* silicon.

Silo ['zi:lo], *m* -s/-s silo.

Silvester [zil'vɛstər], *n* -s/- New Year's Eve; *Scot:* Hogmanay.

simpel ['zimpəl], *adj.* simple (fact, solution); *Pej:* (*einfältig*) simple-minded (person etc.).

Sims [zims], *m & n* -es/-e (*Fensters. usw.*) ledge, sill; *Arch:* cornice.

simulieren [zimu'li:rən], *v.* 1. *v.tr.* to sham (an illness etc.); *Tchn:* to simulate (processes etc.). 2. *v.i.* (haben) to sham, pretend.

simultan [zimul'ta:n], *adj.* simultaneous.

Sinfonie [zinfo'ni:], f -/-n symphony. ◆'**s~sch** [-'fo:niʃ], *adj.* symphonic.

sing|en ['ziŋən], *v.tr. & i.irr.19* (haben) to sing (a song, alto etc.). ◆'**S~vogel,** *m* song bird.

Singular ['ziŋgula:r], *m* -s/-e singular.

sinken ['ziŋkən], *v.i.irr.* (sein) (a) (Schiff, Wasserspiegel usw.) to sink; (Sonne) to set; (b) (Temperatur, Preise usw.) to drop, fall; (Wert, Einfluß usw.) to decline, diminish; **in j-s Achtung s.,** to go down in s.o.'s estimation.

Sinn [zin], m -(e)s/-e **1.** no pl (*Bedeutung*) sense (of a term, phrase etc.); meaning (of s.o.'s words etc.); (*Zweck*) point; im S~e des Gesetzes, within the meaning of the law. **2.** no pl (a) (*Geist*) mind; es kam mir plötzlich in den S., I suddenly thought of it; es ist nicht nach meinem S., it is not to my liking; (b) (*Gefühl, Verständnis*) feeling; er hat S. für Humor, he has a sense of humour. **3.** sense (of hearing etc.); bist du nicht bei S.en? are you out of your mind? ◆'S~bild, n symbol. ◆S~bildlich, adj. symbolic. ◆S~en, v.i.irr.73 (haben) Lit: über etwas acc s., to meditate on/brood over sth. ◆'S~esorgan, n sense organ. ◆'S~estäuschung, f sense hallucination. ◆'s~gemäß, adj. s~gemäße Wiedergabe einer Geschichte, rendering giving the gist of a story. ◆'s~ig, adj. apt, F: clever (present, action etc.). ◆'s~lich, adj. sensual (pleasures, love, person, etc.); (*sexuell*) sexual (attraction, desire etc.); s~liche Wahrnehmung, sensory perception. ◆'S~lichkeit, f no pl sensuality; sensuousness. ◆'s~los, adj. pointless (enterprise etc.); s~lose Wut, blind rage; s. betrunken, dead drunk. ◆'S~losigkeit, f no pl pointlessness, futility. ◆'s~voll, adj. **1.** meaningful (sentence, Fig: activity etc.); satisfying, fulfilling (work etc.). **2.** (*vernünftig*) sensible; wise (undertaking, use etc.).

Sintflut ['zintflu:t], f die S., the Flood.

Sinus ['zi:nus], m -/-se sine.

Siphon ['zi:fɔn], m -s/-s (soda etc.) siphon.

Sippe ['zipə], f -/-n (whole) family; clan; (bei Naturvölkern) tribe. ◆'S~schaft, f -/-en usu.Pej: clan, tribe.

Sirene [zi're:nə], f -/-n siren.

Sirup ['zi:rup], m -s/-e syrup.

Sisal [zizal], m -s/no pl sisal.

Sitte ['zitə], f -/-n (a) custom; nach alter S., in the old way; (b) die gute S./gute S~en, good manners; etiquette. ◆'s~enstreng, adj. puritanical, strait-laced; ◆'s~enwidrig, adj. immoral (action etc.); morally offensive (advertising etc.). ◆'S~lich, adj. moral. ◆'S~lichkeit, f no pl morality. ◆'S~lichkeitsverbrechen, n sexual assault. ◆'s~sam, adj. demure (girl, behaviour), well-behaved (children).

Situation [zituatsi'o:n], f -/-en situation.

Sitz [zits], m -es/-e **1.** seat. **2.** Cl: & Tchn: fit. ◆'s~en, v.i.irr. (haben) (a) to sit; bitte bleiben Sie s.! please don't get up! er saß vier Jahre (im Gefängnis), he spent four years in jail; F: die Bemerkung/der Hieb saß! that remark/blow went home; die Vokabeln s., the words have been well memorized/F: have stuck; (c) (*Kleidung*) to fit. ◆'s~enbleiben, v.i.sep.irr.12 (sein) (a)

Sch: F: to stay down, repeat a class/ N.Am: grade; (b) Com: F: der Kaufmann blieb auf seinen Waren s~en, the shopkeeper was stuck with his goods. ◆'s~enlassen, v.tr.sep.irr.57 F: to leave (s.o.) in the lurch; to desert (a fiancé(e), wife, husband); to jilt (a girl). ◆'S~gelegenheit, f seat, place to sit down. ◆'S~platz, m seat. ◆'S~ung, f -/-en session (of a court), conference etc.

Sizilianer(in) [zitsili'a:nər(in)], m -s/- (f -/-nen) Sicilian. ◆S~en [zi'tsi:liən]. Pr.n.n -s. Sicily.

Skala ['ska:la], f -/-len (a) scale of sounds, Mus: notes etc.; range (of colours, ability etc.); (b) Meas: scale, dial (of an instrument).

Skalpell [skal'pɛl], n -s/-e scalpel.

Skandal [skan'do:l], m -s/-e scandal. ◆S~ös [-da'løs], adj. scandalous (behaviour etc.). ◆S~presse, f gutter press.

Skandina|vien [skandi'na:viən]. Pr.n.n -s. Scandinavia. ◆S~vier(in), m -s/- (f -/-nen) Scandinavian. ◆s~visch, adj. Scandinavian.

Skelett [ske'lɛt], n -(e)s/-e skeleton.

Skep|sis ['skɛpsis], f -/no pl scepticism. ◆S~tiker, m -s/- sceptic. ◆s~tisch, adj. sceptical.

Ski [ʃi:]. I. m -s/-er ski; S. laufen/fahren, to ski. II. 'S~-, comb.fm. ski (lift, boots, stick etc.); skiing (area, club, competition etc.) ◆S~fahren/'S~laufen, n skiing. ◆S~fahrer/'S~läufer, m skier. ◆'S~lehrer, m skiing instructor. ◆'S~piste, f ski run. ◆'S~springen, n ski jumping.

Skizz|e ['skitsə], f -/-n sketch. ◆s~ieren [-'tsi:rən], v.tr. (a) to sketch, make a sketch of (sth.); to outline (a subject); (b) (*entwerfen*) to draft (a plan etc.).

Sklav|e ['skla:və], m -n/-n slave. ◆'S~enarbeit, f slave-labour. ◆'S~e'rei, f no pl slavery. ◆'S~in, f -/-nen (female) slave. ◆s~isch, adj. slavish.

Skonto ['skɔnto], n & m -s/-s Com: discount.

Skorpion [skɔrpi'o:n], m -s/-e scorpion. Astr: Scorpio.

Skrupel ['skru:pəl], m -s/- usu.pl scruple. ◆'s~los, adj. unscrupulous. ◆'S~losigkeit, f no pl unscrupulousness.

Skulptur [skulp'tu:r], f -/-en sculpture.

skurril [sku'ri:l], adj. bizarre.

Slalom ['slo:lɔm], m -s/-s slalom.

Slaw|e ['slaːvə], m -n/-n Slav. ◆'S~in, f -/-nen Slav (woman). ◆'s~isch, adj. Slav.

Smaragd [sma'rakt], m -(e)s/-e emerald.

Smoking ['smo:kiŋ], m -s/-s dinner jacket; N.Am: tuxedo.

Snob [snɔp], m -s/-s snob. ◆S~ismus

[sno'bismus], m -no pl snobbery.

so [zo:]. **I.** int. F: so! right! that's that! so? really? ach so! oh I see! so that's what/how it is! **II.** adv. 1. (a) (auf diese Weise) in this/that way; like this/that; laß es so, wie es ist, leave it as it is; so oder so, one way or the other; (b) (in solchem Maße) sei so gut, be so kind; (nur eine Geste) es ist so lang, it's this long; das ist so gut wie sicher, that's as good as/virtually certain; es ärgerte ihn so (sehr), daß ..., it annoyed him so much that ...; das ist gar nicht so einfach, it's not that easy; (c) F: such; so ein langes Buch, such a long book; so ein Pech/Unsinn! what bad luck/nonsense! na so was! well really! what next! **2.** F: (ungefähr) about; so um drei Uhr, (somewhere) around three o'clock.

sobald [zo'balt], conj. as soon as.

Socke ['zɔkə], f -/-n sock.

Sockel ['zɔkəl], m -s/- base; Arch: Art: pedestal; plinth (of a statue).

Soda ['zo:da], n -s/no pl **1.** Ch: soda. **2.** (also S~wasser) soda water.

Sodbrennen ['zo:tbrɛnən], n heartburn.

soeben [zo'e:bən], adv. just (now).

Sofa ['zo:fa], n -s/-s sofa, couch.

sofern [zo'fɛrn], conj. s. es euch paßt, as long as it suits you.

sofort [zo'fɔrt], adv. immediately, at once. ◆**s~ig**, adj. immediate.

Sog [zo:k], m -(e)s/-e undertow (of waves etc.); Tchn: suction.

sogar [zo'ga:r], adv. even.

sogenannt ['zo:gənant], adj. so-called.

sogleich [zo'glaiç], adv. immediately.

Sohle ['zo:lə], f -/-n (a) sole (of a foot or shoe); (b) bottom of a ditch etc.); (c) Min: pit level.

Sohn [zo:n], m -(e)s/-e son.

Sojabohne ['zo:jabo:nə], f -/-n soya bean.

solang(e) [zo'laŋ(ə)], conj. as long as.

solch [zɔlç], dem.pron. such; ein s~er Mensch, such a man; a man like that; s. herrliches Wetter, such wonderful weather; ein paar s~e, a few of those; die Musik als s~e, the music as such.

Sold [zɔlt], m -(e)s/-e (soldiers') pay.

Soldat [zɔl'da:t], m -en/-en soldier. ◆**s~isch**, adj. soldierly.

Söldner ['zœldnər], m -s/- mercenary.

solidarisch [zoli'da:riʃ], adj. **s. handeln**, to act with complete solidarity; to show a united front; **sich mit j-m s. erklären**, to identify fully with s.o.'s aims; to give s.o. full support. ◆**S~ität** [-dari'tɛːt], f -/no pl solidarity.

solide [zo'li:də], adj. solid (shoes, material, building); sound (craftsmanship, firm etc.); (anständig) respectable (person etc.).

Solist(in) [zo'list(in)], m -en/-en (f -/-nen) soloist.

Soll [zɔl], n -s/no pl **1.** Com: debit. **2.** Ind: (production etc.) target. ◆**s~en. 1.** modal aux. (p.p. sollen) (a) (Pflicht) ich

soll Hamlet spielen, I am to play Hamlet; **das hättest du nicht sagen s.**, you should not have said that; (b) (Zukunft) was soll man da machen? what is to be done? niemand soll sagen, daß ..., let it not be said that ...; (c) (laut Bericht usw.) to be supposed to; der Film soll sehr gut sein, the film is supposed to be very good; was soll das heißen? (i) what is that supposed to mean? (ii) F: what's all this in aid of? (d) (konditional) sollten Sie ihn sehen, should you/if you see him. **2.** v.i. (haben) (p.p. gesollt) (a) ich weiß nicht, ob ich sollte/sollte, I don't know if I should; (b) was soll (denn) das? what's all this for/F: in aid of?

Solo ['zo:lo], n -s/-li solo.

somit [zo'mit], adv. hence, consequently.

Sommer ['zɔmər]. **I.** m -s/- summer. **II.** S~, comb.fm. summer (clothes, coat, month, term, weather etc.); (beginning etc.) of summer. ◆**s~lich**, adj. summer (temperatures, heat etc.); summery, F: summery (weather, clothes etc.); **sich s. kleiden**, to wear summer clothes. ◆**S~'schlußverkauf**, m summer sale. ◆**S~sprosse**, f freckle. ◆**S~zeit**, f (Jahreszeit) summertime; (Uhrzeit) summer time.

Sonate [zo'na:tə], f -/-n sonata.

Sonde ['zɔndə], f -/-n probe.

Sonder- ['zɔndər-], comb.fm. special (agreement, report, subject, training, mission, stamp, train etc.). ◆**S~angebot**, n special offer. ◆**s~bar**, adj. odd, strange. ◆**S~fahrt**, f special journey; (Ausfahrt) excursion. ◆**S~fall**, m special case. ◆**s~gleichen**, adv. unparalleled, unprecedented. ◆**s~lich**, adj. **1.** (bei Verneinungen) particular; **ohne s~liche Mühe**, without any great effort. **2.** (seltsam) strange. ◆**S~ling**, m -s/-e eccentric, crank. ◆**S~schule**, f school for retarded children.

sondern ['zɔndərn], conj. but; **nicht nur kalt, s. auch naß**, not only cold but wet.

sondieren [zɔn'di:rən], v.tr. to sound out (s.o., public opinion etc.), explore (a situation etc.).

Sonett [zo'nɛt], n -(e)s/-e sonnet.

Sonnabend ['zɔn'a:bənt], m Saturday.

Sonne ['zɔnə], f -/-n sun. ◆**s~n, v.refl. sich s.**, to sun oneself/bask in the sun. ◆**S~n-**, comb.fm. (a) sun-(worshipper, god, hat, oil etc.); (orbit, surface etc.) of the sun; (b) solar (energy, radiation etc.). ◆**S~naufgang**, m sunrise. ◆**S~nbaden**, n sunbathing. ◆**S~blume**, f sunflower. ◆**S~nbrille**, f sunglasses. ◆**S~nfinsternis**, f eclipse of the sun. ◆**S~nschein**, m sunshine. ◆**S~nschirm**, m parasol. ◆**S~nschutzmittel**, n suntan lotion. ◆**S~nstich**, m sunstroke. ◆**S~nstrahl**, m sunbeam. ◆**S~nsystem**, n solar system. ◆**S~nuhr**, f sundial.

◆'S~**nuntergang**, m sunset. ◆'S~n-**wende**, f solstice.

sonnig ['zɔnɪç], adj. (also Fig:) sunny.

Sonn|tag ['zɔntaːk], m -(e)s/-e Sunday. ◆'s~**tags¹**, adv. on Sundays. ◆'S~**tags-²**, comb.fm. Sunday (driver, school, clothes etc.).

sonst [zɔnst], adv. (a) otherwise; (b) (zusätzlich) s. **noch Fragen?** any more questions? s. **noch etwas/jemand?** anything/anybody else (c) (gewöhnlich) usually; **wie s.,** as usual. ◆'s~**iges/a**), adj.; other; (gewöhnlich) normal. ◆s~**jemand,** indef.pron. someone/(ein Beliebiger) anyone else. ◆'s~**wer,** indef.pron. F: = s~**jemand.** ◆'s~**wie,** adv. F: in some/any (other) way. ◆'s~**wo,** adv. F: somewhere/anywhere else. ◆'s~**wohin,** adv. F: anywhere.

sooft [zo'ɔft], conj. whenever.

Sopran [zo'praːn], m -s/-e soprano. ◆S~**istin,** f -/-nen soprano.

Sorge ['zɔrgə], f -/-n (a) worry; **sie machte sich dat S~n um ihn,** she was worried about him; **keine S.!** don't worry! (b) no pl (Fürsorge) care (um/für + acc, for). ◆'s~**n,** v.i. (haben) (a) für j-n, etwas acc s., to take care of/be responsible for s.o., sth.; **dafür s., daß ...,** to ensure that ..., s. **Sie für Ruhe,** make sure everything is quiet; (b) sich um j-n, etwas acc s., to worry about s.o., sth. ◆'s~**nfrei,** adj. carefree ◆'S~**nkind,** n problem child ◆'s~**nvoll,** adj. worried, anxious.

Sorg|falt ['zɔrkfalt], f -/no pl care; (Gründlichkeit) thoroughness. ◆'s~**fältig,** adj. careful; (gewissenhaft) conscientious. ◆'s~**los,** adj. (a) lighthearted, nonchalant (person); carefree (life); (b) (ohne Sorgfalt) careless (treatment etc.). ◆'s~**sam,** adj. careful (handling etc.).

Sorte ['zɔrtə], f -/-n 1. sort, type; (Marke) brand. 2. Fin: pl S~ten, foreign currency. ◆s~**tieren,** v.tr. to sort (letters etc.).

Sortiment [zɔrti'mɛnt], n -(e)s/-e Com: assortment, range.

sosehr [zo'zeːr], conj. however much; s. **ich mich auch bemühte,** however hard I tried.

Soße ['zoːsə], f -/-n sauce; (Bratens:) gravy.

Souffl|eur [zu'fløːr], m -s/-e/-**leuse,** f -/-n 7: prompter. ◆s~**lieren** [-fliːrən], v.i. (haben) Th: to prompt, act as prompter.

Souterrain [zute'rɛ̃], n -s/-s basement.

Souvenir [zuvə'niːr], n -s/-s souvenir.

souverän [zuvə'rɛːn], adj. sovereign (state etc.); **die Lage s. beherrschen,** to be in complete control. ◆S~**ität** [-reni'tɛːt], f -/no pl sovereignty.

soviel [zo'fiːl]. I. adv. so/as much (wie, as); **doppelt s.,** twice as much. II. conj. s. **ich weiß,** as far as I know.

soweit [zo'vait]. I. adv. 1. generally. 2. (a) s. **wie möglich,** as far as possible; (b) F: **ich bin s.,** I am finished/(bereit) ready. II. conj. as far as.

sowenig [zo'veːnɪç], adv. s. **wie,** no more than; s. **wie möglich,** as little as possible.

sowie [zo'viː], conj. 1. as well as. 2. (sobald) as soon as. ◆s~**so** [-'viːzoː], adv. F: anyway, in any case.

Sowjet|union [zo'vjɛt'uniə̃n], f the Soviet Union. ◆s~**isch,** adj. Soviet.

sowohl [zo'voːl], conj. s. **A als auch B,** both A and B.

sozial [zotsi'aːl]. I. adj. social; (Pers:) public-spirited; s~**e Unterschiede,** social/class differences. II. S~-, comb.fm. social (work, worker, policy, studies etc.); welfare (work, state etc.). ◆S~**abgaben,** fpl social security contributions. ◆S~**demokrat(in),** m(f) Social Democrat. ◆s~**demokratisch,** adj. Social Democratic (party etc.). ◆S~**ismus** [-a'lismus], m -/no pl socialism. ◆S~**ist** [-a'list], m -en/-en socialist. ◆s~**istisch** [-a'listif], adj. socialist. ◆S~**versicherung,** f social security.

Soziolog|e [zotsio'loːgə], m -n/-n/S~**gin,** f -/-nen sociologist. ◆S~**gie** [-logiː], f -/no pl sociology. ◆s~**gisch** [-'loːgif], adj. sociological.

Sozius ['zoːtsius], m -/-se Com: partner. ◆S~**sitz,** m pillion.

sozusagen [zotsu'zaːgən], adv. so to speak; as it were.

Spachtel ['ʃpaxtəl], m -s/- (a) Med: spatula; (b) (für Mörtel usw.) putty knife. ◆'s~**n,** v. 1. v.tr. to smooth (a surface). 2. v.i. (haben) F: to dig/tuck in.

Spagat [ʃpa'gaːt], m -(e)s/-e S. **machen,** to do the splits/N.Am: a split.

späh|en ['ʃpeːən], v.i. (haben) to peer (aus dem Fenster usw., out of the window). ◆S~**er,** m -s/- lookout; scout.

Spalier [ʃpa'liːr], n -s/-e (a) (Gitter) trellis; (b) Fig: S. **stehen,** to form a guard of honour/a lane.

Spalt [ʃpalt], m -(e)s/-e crack; (in Vorhang) chink. ◆s~**bar,** adj. Atom.Ph: fissile, fissionable. ◆S~**e,** f -/-n 1. crack; (Gletschers:) crevasse. 2 (Zeitungs:) column. ◆'s~**en,** v.tr. to split (wood, Ph: atoms, Fig: hairs etc.); Fig: to divide (a country, party). ◆'S~**ung,** f -/-en (a) splitting, division; Atom.Ph: fission; (b) Fig: split.

Span [ʃpaːn], m -(e)s/-e chip, shaving (of wood); filing (of metal). ◆S~**ferkel,** n sucking pig. ◆S~**platte,** f chipboard.

Spange ['ʃpaŋə], f -/-n clasp; (am Schuh) buckle; (Haars:) grip; (Zahns:) brace.

Spani|en ['ʃpaːniən], Pr.n.n -s. Spain. ◆'S~**ier(in),** m -s/- (f -/-nen) Spaniard. ◆'s~**isch,** adj. Spanish.

Spann [ʃpan], m -(e)s/-e Anat: instep. ◆'S~**beton,** m pressed concrete.

◆'S~e, f -/-n (a) (Zeits.) length of time; (Zwischenzeit) interval; (b) Com: margin; (Preisunterschied) price difference. ◆'s~en, v. 1. v.tr. to stretch, tauten (a rope etc.), tighten (the violin strings etc.), tense (muscles etc.), draw (a bow). 2. v.i. (haben) Cl: etc: to be (too) tight. ◆'s~end, adj. exciting, thrilling (story etc.). ◆'S~kraft, f -/no pl vigour, resilience. ◆'S~ung, f -/-en 1. no pl (a) tightness; (b) El: voltage; (c) Fig: tension; (Erwartung) suspense. 2. (psychische) S~ungen, (psychological) strains/tensions.

Spar- ['ʃpɑːr-], comb.fm. (a) savings (book, account etc.); (b) economy (measure etc.). ◆'S~büchse, f money box. ◆'s~en, v. 1. v.tr. to save (money, time, one's strength etc.); sich dat die Mühe s., to save/spare oneself the trouble. 2. v.i. (haben) to save (up); an Material, Zutaten usw. s., to economize on materials, ingredients etc. ◆'S~er, m -s/- saver. ◆'S~kasse, f savings bank. ◆'s~sam, adj. economical (use of sth. etc.); mit etwas dat s. umgehen, to be sparing with sth. ◆'S~samkeit, f -/no pl economy; thrift. ◆'S~schwein, n piggy bank.

Spargel ['ʃpargəl], m -s/no pl asparagus.

spärlich ['ʃpɛːrlɪç], adj. meagre (rations, applause); scanty, sparse (vegetation etc.), thin (hair etc.); s. bekleidet, scantily dressed.

Sparte ['ʃpartə], f -/-n branch (of sport, industry etc.); in meiner S., in my field/area.

Spaß [ʃpɑːs], m -es/⁻e (a) (Scherz) joke; (Streich) lark; er versteht keinen S., he has no sense of humour; (b) no pl fun; aus/zum S., for fun; es macht S., it's fun; die Arbeit macht ihm keinen S., he doesn't enjoy the work; viel S.! have fun/a good time! S. beiseite, joking apart; viel S.! have fun/a good time! ◆'s~en, v.i. (haben) to joke; mit ihm ist nicht zu s., he stands no nonsense. ◆'s~eshalber, adv. F: for fun/kicks. ◆'s~ig, adj. funny, comical. ◆'S~macher, m -s/- joker; clown. ◆'S~vogel, m joker, legpuller.

spät [ʃpɛːt]. I. adj. late; wie s. ist es? what's the time/what time is it? II. 'S~-, comb.fm. late (summer, shift etc.). ◆'s~er, adj. later + adv. ◆'s~estens, adv. at the latest.

Spaten ['ʃpɑːtən], m -s/- spade.

Spatz [ʃpats], m -en/-en Orn: sparrow.

Spätzle ['ʃpɛtslə], npl (esp. home-made) noodles.

spazier|en [ʃpaˈtsiːrən], v.i. (sein) to stroll, (go for a) walk. ◆s~enfahren, v.i.sep.irr.26 (sein) to go for a drive. ◆s~engehen, v.i.sep.irr.36 (sein) to go for a walk. ◆'S~fahrt, f outing, drive. ◆'S~gang, m walk, stroll; einen S. machen, to go for a walk. ◆'S~gänger(in), m -s/- (f -/-nen) walker.

◆'S~stock, m walking stick.

Specht [ʃpɛçt], m -(e)s/-e woodpecker.

Speck [ʃpɛk], m -(e)s/-e (a) Cu: (fatty) bacon; (b) F: fat. ◆'s~ig, adj. greasy.

Spedi|teur [ʃpediˈtøːr], m -s/-e shipper; (im Straßenverkehr) carrier, haulage contractor; (Möbel-) (furniture) remover/N.Am: mover. ◆S~tion [-itsiˈoːn], f (also S~sbetrieb m) shippers, carriers; haulage(Möbel-). removal/N.Am: moving firm.

Speer [ʃpeːr], m -(e)s/-e spear; Sp: javelin. ◆'S~werfen, n -s/no pl Sp: javelin (throwing).

Speiche ['ʃpaiçə], f -/-n spoke.

Speichel ['ʃpaiçəl], m -s/no pl saliva.

Speicher ['ʃpaiçər], m -s/- (a) store(house); (für Getreide) silo, granary; (für Wasser) reservoir; (b) (Dachs.) attic, loft; (c) Data-pr: memory. ◆'s~n, v.tr. to store (goods, data etc.).

speien ['ʃpaiən], v.irr.88 1. v.tr. to spit, bring up (blood etc.); (Vulkan usw.) to belch (fire). 2. v.i. (haben) to spit; (sich übergeben) to vomit.

Speis|e ['ʃpaizə], f -/-n food; (Gericht) warme S~en, hot food. ◆'S~eis, f ice cream. ◆'S~ekammer, f larder. ◆'S~ekarte, f menu. ◆'s~en, v. 1. v.i. (haben) Lit: to have a meal, dine. 2. v.tr. to feed (a reservoir etc.). ◆'S~eröhre, f oesophagus, gullet. ◆'S~esaal, m dining hall/(im Hotel) room. ◆'S~ewagen, m dining car.

Spektak|el [ʃpɛkˈtaːkəl], n -s/no pl F: noise, racket. ◆s~ulär [-akuˈlɛːr], adj. spectacular.

Spektrum ['ʃpɛktrum], n -s/-tren Ph: & Fig: spectrum.

Spekul|ant [ʃpekuˈlant], m -en/-en speculator. ◆S~ation [-tsiˈoːn], f -/-en speculation. ◆s~ieren [-'liːrən], v.i. (haben) to speculate; Fig: auf etwas acc s., to hope for sth.

Spelunke [ʃpeˈluŋkə], f -/-n Pej: low dive.

spendabel [ʃpɛnˈdaːbəl], adj. F: generous, open-handed.

Spend|e ['ʃpɛndə], f -/-n donation; (Beitrag) contribution. ◆'s~n, v.tr. to contribute, donate (money etc.), give (blood, warmth, shade etc.). ◆'S~er, m -s/- 1. (Pers.) donor. 2. (Maschine) dispenser.

spendieren [ʃpɛnˈdiːrən], v.tr. F: j-m ein Eis usw. s., to treat s.o. to an ice etc.

Sperling ['ʃpɛrlɪŋ], m -s/-e sparrow.

Sperr|e ['ʃpɛrə], f -/-n (a) Rail: etc: barrier; Tchn: locking device; (b) (Verbot) ban; Sp: suspension. ◆'s~en, v. 1. v.tr. (a) to block (a road etc.); to close (a road, border etc.); Sp: to obstruct (a player); (b) sich gegen etwas acc s., to resist/object to sth. (strongly); (c) to cut off (the electricity, telephone etc.); to place a ban/an embargo on (imports etc.), block (an account); Sp: to suspend (a player); (d) j-n ins Gefängnis, ein

Tier in einen Käfig usw. **s.**, to lock s.o. in prison, an animal in a cage etc. **2.** v.i. (haben) (Tür usw.) to jam, stick; (Räder usw.) to lock. ◆'S~**holz**, n plywood. ◆'s~**ig**, adj. unwieldy, bulky (object, package etc.). ◆'S~**müll**, m bulky refuse. ◆'S~**sitz**, m (im Zirkus) front seat; Cin: rear stall. ◆'S~**stunde**, f closing time; Mil: curfew.

Spesen ['ʃpe:zən], pl expenses.

Spezial- [ʃpetsi'a:l-], comb.fm. special (training, subject, mission etc.); specialist (dictionary etc.). ◆S~**gebiet**, n special field. ◆s~**isieren** [-a'li:zrən], v.refl. sich auf etwas acc s., to specialize in sth. ◆s~**ist(in)** [-a'list(in)], m -en/-en (f -/-nen) specialist. ◆S~**ität** [-ali'tɛ:t], f -/-en speciality esp. N.Am: specialty.

speziell [ʃpetsi'el], adj. special.

spezifisch [ʃpe'tsi:fiʃ], adj. specific.

Sphäre ['sfɛ:rə], f -/-n sphere.

spicken ['ʃpikən], v.tr. Cu: to lard (meat etc.); Fig: **mit Fehlern gespickter Aufsatz**, essay riddled with mistakes. ◆'S~**zettel**, m F: crib.

Spiegel ['ʃpi:gəl], m -s/- **1.** mirror. **2.** (a) surface (of the sea etc.); (b) (Wasserstand) level. ◆'S~**bild**, n reflection; mirror image. ◆'s~**bildlich**, adj. in mirror image. ◆'S~**ei**, n Cu: fried egg. ◆'s~**n**, v. **1.** v.i. (haben) (a) to reflect; (b) (glänzen) to shine. **2.** v.refl. **sich im Wasser s.**, to be reflected in the water. ◆'S~**schrift**, f mirror writing. ◆'S~**ung**, f -/-en reflection.

Spiel [ʃpi:l]. **I.** n -(e)s/-e **1.** no pl (a) playing of children etc.); (b) movement, play of colours, lights, waves etc.). **2.** Sp: etc: game (of tennis, cards, chess etc.); (als Wettkampf) match. **3.** Th: (Stück) play. **4.** (Satz) set; **im S. Karten**, a pack of cards. **5.** Tchn: slack, clearance. **6.** Fig: **auf dem S. stehen**, to be at stake; **etwas aufs S. setzen**, to risk sth. **II.** 's~-, v. **1.** v.i. (haben) (a) to play (street etc.); (b) gambling (casino, debt etc.). **2.** v.tr. to play (a game, Mus: an instrument, Th: a part etc.); to perform (a play, opera etc.). ◆'s~**end**, adv. F: easily. ◆'S~**er(in)**, m -s/- (f -/-nen) (a) player; (b) (um Geld) gambler. ◆S~**e'rei**, f -/-en (a) no pl playing/Pej: fooling around; (Zeitvertreib) amusement, diversion; (b) (etwas Leichtes) trifle, child's play. ◆'s~**erisch**, adj. **1.** playful (movements etc.). **2.** Sp: playing, Th: acting (ability etc.). ◆'S~**feld**, n Sp: pitch. ◆'S~**film**, m feature film. ◆'S~**halle**, f amusement arcade. ◆'S~**marke**, f (gaming) chip.

◆'S~**plan**, m Th: repertory, programme. ◆'S~**platz**, m playground. ◆'S~**raum**, m room to move, elbow-room; Tchn: (free) play, clearance. ◆'S~**regeln**, fpl rules (of the game). ◆'S~**sachen**, fpl toys. ◆'S~**verderber(in)**, m -s/- (f -/-nen) spoilsport. ◆'S~**waren**, fpl toys. ◆'S~**zeit**, f Th: Sp: (a) (Saison) season; (b) (S~dauer) duration of a performance/game. ◆'S~**zeug**, n (a) toy; (b) coll. toys.

Spieß [ʃpi:s], m -es/-e (a) (Waffe) spear; F: **den S. umdrehen**, to turn the tables; (b) Cu: skewer; (Brats.) spit. ◆'S~**bürger**, m Pej: (ultra-conservative) bourgeois (prig.). ◆'s~**en**, v.tr. to skewer (meat etc.). ◆'S~**er**, m -s/- = S~**bürger**. ◆'S~**rute**, f; **s~ruten laufen**, to run the gauntlet.

Spikes [ʃpaiks, sp-], pl (a) Sp: spikes; (b) Aut: studded (snow) tyres.

Spinat [ʃpi'na:t], m -(e)s/-e spinach.

Spind [ʃpint], n -(e)s/-e locker.

Spindel ['ʃpindəl], f -/-n spindle. ◆'s~**dürr**, adj. thin as a rake.

Spinn|**e** ['ʃpinə], f -/-n spider. ◆'s~**en**, v.irr.73 **1.** v.tr. to spin (wool etc.). **2.** v.i. (haben) F: to be crackers/nuts. ◆'S~**(en)gewebe**, n cobweb. ◆'S~**ennetz**, n spider's web. ◆'S~**er(in)**, m -s/- (f -/-nen) F: er ist ein S., he is a crackpot/Brit: nutter. ◆'S~**rad**, n spinning wheel.

Spion(in) [ʃpi'o:n(in)], m -s/-e (f -/-nen) (a) spy; (b) (Guckloch) peephole (in door). ◆S~**age** [-o'na:ʒə]. **I.** f -/no pl espionage, spying. **II.** S~-, comb.fm. spy (film, trial, ring etc.). ◆s~**ieren** [-o'ni:rən], v.i. (haben) to spy.

Spirale [ʃpi'ra:lə], f -/-n spiral; Med: coil.

Spirituosen [ʃpiritu'o:zən], pl spirits, hard drinks. ◆S~**us** ['ʃpiritus], m -/no pl (surgical) spirit.

Spital [ʃpi'ta:l], n -s/-er A: & Aus: hospital.

Spitz¹ [ʃpits], m -es/-e Z: Pomeranian (dog).

spitz², adj. pointed (shoes, arch, Fig: remark etc.); sharp (pencil, Fig: tongue etc.); **s~er Winkel**, acute angle. ◆'S~**bart**, m pointed beard. ◆'S~**bube**, m Pej: & Hum: rogue. ◆'S~**e**, f -/-n **1.** (a) point (of a needle, pencil), tip (of a pen, the nose etc.); (cigar/cigarette holder); (b) (oberes Ende) top (of a tree etc.); (Gipfel) peak; Fig: (Höchstwert) maximum; F: **er/sie/es ist (absolute/einsame) S.**, he/she/it is (absolutely) super/fantastic; (c) (Führung) head (of a procession, train, organization etc.); leadership (of a party), management (of a firm); Sp: **an der S. liegen**, to be in the lead; (d) (Anzüglichkeit) dig, tilt (**gegen j-n**, at s.o.). **2.** (Stoff) lace. ◆'S~**el**, m -s/- informer; (Spion) spy, undercover agent. ◆'s~**en**, v.tr. to sharpen (a pencil etc.). ◆'S~en-, comb.fm. 1. (a) top (speed, team, quality etc.); top-quality, first-class (product, wine etc.); (b) (Höchst-) maximum (amount, output etc.); peak (load, value etc.). 2. CI: lace (blouse, collar, trimming etc.). ◆'S~enreiter, m leader; number one. ◆'s~findig, adj. tortuous (argument etc.); niggling, pedantic (person). ◆'S~hacke, f pick-axe. ◆'S~name, m nickname.

Splitter ['ʃplitər], m -s/- splinter. ◆'S~gruppe, f -/-n splinter group. ◆'s~n, v.i. (sein) to splinter. ◆'s~'nackt, adj. F: stark naked.

spontan [ʃpon'ta:n], adj. spontaneous (response etc.); impulsive (action).

sporadisch [ʃpo'ra:diʃ], adj. sporadic.

Sporen ['ʃpo:rən], mpl spurs.

Sport [ʃport]. I. m -(e)s/no pl (a) sport; Sch: physical education, games; (b) hobby. II. 'S~-, comb.fm. (a) sports (badge, report, fan, club, news etc.); (b) sporting (event, accident etc.). ◆'S~art, f (type of) sport. ◆'S~lehrer(in), m (f) P.E. teacher, Brit: games master/mistress. ◆'S~ler(in), m -s/- (f -/-nen) sportsman, f sportswoman. ◆'s~lich, adj. (a) sporting (occasion, career etc.); casual (clothes); (b) (fair) sportsmanlike (behaviour etc.); good at games; sporty. ◆'S~platz, m sports ground, playing field. ◆'S~wagen, m (i) sports car; (ii) (für Kinder) pushchair, N.Am: stroller.

Spott [ʃpot], m -(e)s/no pl mockery, ridicule. ◆'s~'billig, adj. F: dirt-cheap. ◆'s~en, v.i. (haben) to mock; über j-n, etwas acc s., to poke fun at/(höhnisch) sneer at s.o., sth.

Spött|er ['ʃpœtər], m -s/- mocker; er ist ein S., he pokes fun at everything. ◆'s~isch, adj. mocking, quizzical (smile etc.); s~ische Bemerkung, snide remark.

Sprach- [ʃpra:x-], comb.fm. linguistic (research, exercise etc.); language (course, teacher, school etc.). ◆'S~begabung, f gift for languages. ◆'S~e, f -/-n 1. language; in englischer S., in English. 2. no pl speech; das kam auch zur S., that was also mentioned. ◆'S~fehler, m speech defect. ◆'s~lich, adj. linguistic; grammatical (errors etc.). ◆'s~los, adj. speechless (vor + dat, with); (erstaunt) dumbfounded. ◆'S~raum, m language area. ◆'S~rohr, n (a) megaphone; (b) Fig: (Pers.) mouthpiece.

Spray [ʃpre:], m & n -s/-s spray.

Sprech|anlage f ['ʃprɛçʔanla:gə], f F: intercom. ◆'s~en, v.irr.14 1. v.tr. (a) to speak (a language, the truth etc.); to say (a word, prayer etc.); Jur: to pronounce (judgement); er sprach kein Wort, he didn't say a word; (b) to speak to (s.o.); er ist nicht/für niemanden zu s., he cannot see anybody. 2. v.i. (haben) to speak (über + acc/von + dat, about); mit j-m s.,

to talk to s.o.; es spricht ..., the speaker is ...; Fig: das spricht für ihn, that's a point in his favour. ◆'S~er(in), m -s/- (f -/-nen) speaker; (Wortführer) spokesman; Rad: TV: announcer. ◆'S~stunde, f Med: consulting/Brit: surgery hours. ◆'S~stundenhilfe, f (doctor's) receptionist. ◆'S~zimmer, n consulting room.

spreizen ['ʃpraitsən], v.tr. to splay (one's legs etc.); spread (wings etc.).

spreng|en ['ʃprɛŋən], v.tr. (a) to blast (rock etc.), blow up (a bridge etc.); (b) to burst (chains, a lock etc.); (c) to sprinkle (washing, water etc.). ◆'S~kopf, m warhead. ◆'S~körper, m explosive device. ◆'S~ladung, f explosive charge. ◆'S~stoff, m explosive. ◆'S~ung, f -/-en explosion, blasting.

Spreu [ʃprɔy], f -/no pl chaff.

Sprich|wort ['ʃpriçvort], n proverb. ◆'s~wörtlich, adj. proverbial.

Spring|brunnen ['ʃpriŋbrunən], m -s/- fountain. ◆'s~en, v.i.irr.19 (sein) (a) to jump, (mit einem großen Satz) leap; (b) (Glas usw.) to crack. ◆'S~er, m -s/- (a) jumper; (b) (Schach) knight; (c) Ind: stand-in. ◆'S~reiten, n -s/no pl show jumping.

Sprit [ʃprit], m (e)s F: juice, N.Am: gas.

Spritz|e ['ʃpritsə], f -/-n 1. (Gerät) spray; (Düse) nozzle; Med: etc: syringe. 2. Med: injection, jab. ◆'s~en, v. 1. v.tr. (a) to spray (crops, water, paint, a car etc.); Med: (injizieren) to inject (a drug etc.). 2. v.i. (haben) (Flüssigkeiten) to splash, (in einem Strahl) squirt; (Fett usw.) to spatter. ◆'S~er, m -s/- 1. splash (of water etc.); blob (of paint etc.). ◆'s~ig, adj. tangy (perfume, wine); lively, sparkling (wit, performance etc.); racy (car, style). ◆'S~pistole, f spraygun. ◆'S~tour, f F: eine S. machen, to go for a joyride/Aut: spin.

spröde ['ʃprø:də], adj. (a) brittle (metal, wood, hair etc.); dry, chapped (skin); (b) (Pers.) standoffish.

Sproß [ʃprɔs], m -sses/-sse (a) Bot: sprout, shoot; (b) offspring.

Sprosse ['ʃprɔsə], f -/-n ladder rung; slat (of a chair).

Sprößling ['ʃprœsliŋ], m -s/-e F: offspring.

Sprotte ['ʃprɔtə], f -/-n sprat.

Spruch [ʃprux], m -(e)s/-e (a) saying; maxim; (Parole) slogan; (b) Jur: (Urteil) sentence, ruling; (c) Pej: F: S~e, empty words, hot air.

Sprudel ['ʃpru:dəl], m -s/- (effervescent) mineral water. ◆'s~n, v.i. (haben) (Flüssigkeiten) to effervesce, F: fizz; (Blasen bilden) to bubble. ◆'S~wasser, n = Sprudel.

Sprüh|dose ['ʃpry:do:zə], f spray, aerosol. ◆'s~en, v. 1. v.tr. to spray (water etc.); to give off (sparks etc.). 2. v.i.

(sein) (a) to spray, (Gischt) shower; (b) Fig: (Pers.) to sparkle, scintillate (vor Witz usw., with wit etc.). ◆'S~regen, m drizzle.

Sprung [ʃpruŋ], m -(e)s/⁼e 1. jump, (großer) leap. 2. (Riß) crack. ◆'S~brett, n springboard. ◆'S~feder, f spring. ◆'s~haft, adj. (a) spasmodic, erratic (movement etc.); (b) sudden (change); rapid (increase). ◆'S~schanze, f jumping hill, ski jump. ◆'S~tuch, n jumping sheet.

Spucke ['ʃpukə], f -/no pl F: saliva, spit. ◆'s~en, v.tr.&i. (haben) to spit.

Spuk [ʃpuːk], m -(e)s/no pl 1. haunting; ghostly apparition. 2. Fig: ghastly business, nightmare. ◆'s~en, v.i. (haben) to haunt; hier spukt es, this place is haunted. ◆'s~haft, adj. ghostly.

Spülbecken ['ʃpyːlbekən], n/'S~e, f -/-n sink. ◆'s~en, v.tr.&i. (haben) to rinse (out) (one's mouth, washing etc.); (auf der Toilette) to flush; (Geschirr) s., to wash up, F: & N.Am: do the dishes; etwas an Land s., to wash sth. ashore. ◆'S~maschine, f dishwasher. ◆'S~mittel, n washing-up/N.Am: dishwashing liquid/powder. ◆'S~tuch, n dishcloth. ◆'S~wasser, n dishwater.

Spule ['ʃpuːlə], f -/-n 1. (a) spool, bobbin; (b) El: coil. ◆'s~n, v.tr. to wind (sth.) onto a spool.

Spur [ʃpuːr], f -/-en 1. (a) (im Boden) track(s) (of a person, animal, tyre etc.); (Fährte) trail; (Fig: Rest) trace; (b) F: eine S. Pfeffer, a trace of pepper; von Takt keine S., not a sign/scrap of tact; eine S. zu hart, slightly/a shade too hard. 2. (Fahrs.) lane. 3. Rec: track. ◆'s~en, v.i. (haben) F: to toe the line. ◆'s~los, adj. esp. adv. without a trace. ◆'S~weite, f Aut: track.

spürbar ['ʃpyːrbaːr], adj. noticeable; (deutlich) distinct. ◆'s~en, v.tr. to feel (pain, the heat etc.), sense (s.o.'s fear etc.). ◆'S~hund, m (a) tracker dog, pointer; (b) F: (Detektiv) sleuth. ◆'S~sinn, m (Instinkt) sixth sense.

Spurt [ʃpurt], m -(e)s/-s spurt, sprint. ◆'s~en, v.i. (sein) to spurt, sprint.

Staat [ʃtɑːt], m -(e)s/-en 1. state; (Land) country. 2. F: (festliche Kleidung) finery. ◆'s~enlos, adj. stateless. ◆'s~lich, adj. state, government (grant, control etc.); (sovereignty, interests etc.) of the state; s. anerkannt, officially/state-approved. ◆'S~s~, comb.fm. (a) state (visit, secret, reception, theatre etc.); (affair etc.) of state; (s~eigen) state-owned (business etc.); national (debt, government etc.); (b) government (expenditure, employee etc.); public (property, enemy etc.). ◆'S~sangehörige(r), m & f decl. as adj. national. ◆'S~sangehörigkeit, f -/no pl nationality, citizenship. ◆'S~sanwalt, m public prosecutor; N.Am: district attorney.

◆'S~sbürger(in), m (f) citizen. ◆'S~sdienst, m civil service. ◆'S~smann, m statesman. ◆'S~soberhaupt, n head of state. ◆'S~ssekretär, m permanent secretary; N.Am: secretary of state. ◆'S~sstreich, m coup (d'état).

Stab [ʃtɑːp], m -(e)s/⁼e 1. (a) rod, pole; (Stock) stick; (b) (aus Eisen) bar (of a cage etc.). 2. (Personal) staff. ◆'S~hochsprung, m pole vault. ◆'S~soffizier, m staff officer.

Stäbchen ['ʃtɛːpçən], n -s/- (Eßs.) chopstick.

stabil [ʃta'biːl], adj. (a) stable (currency etc.); (b) sturdy, robust (structure etc.). ◆s~i'sieren, v.tr. to stabilize (prices etc.). ◆S~ität [-ili'tɛːt], f -/no pl stability; sturdiness, solidity.

Stachel ['ʃtaxəl], m -s/-n (a) (Insektens.) sting; (b) spine, quill (of a porcupine etc.; Bot: thorn; (c) barb (of barbed wire etc.). ◆'S~beere, f gooseberry. ◆'S~draht, m barbed wire. ◆'s~ig, adj. prickly. ◆'S~schwein, n porcupine.

Stadion ['ʃtɑːdiɔn], n -s/-ien stadium.

Stadium ['ʃtɑːdium], n -s/-ien stage, phase.

Stadt [ʃtat]. I. f -/⁼e town, (Groß-) city. II. 'S~-, comb.fm. town (wall, gate etc.); city (fathers, wall, gate, state etc.); urban (motorway/N.Am: freeway, population, district, guerilla etc.); municipal (administration, park, library, theatre etc.). ◆'s~bekannt, adj. well-known, Pej: notorious. ◆'S~plan, m town plan/(street) map. ◆'S~rand, m outskirts of the town. ◆'S~teil, m part/district of the town. ◆'S~zentrum, n town/city centre, N.Am: downtown (area).

Städtchen ['ʃtɛːtçən], f -s/- small town. ◆'S~ebau, m town planning. ◆'S~er(in), m -s/- (f -/-nen) town/city dweller. ◆'s~isch, adj. urban (life, transport etc.); city (clothes etc.); Adm: municipal (authorities etc.).

Staffel ['ʃtafəl], f -/-n (a) Sp: relay team; (b) Av: squadron. ◆'S~ei [-ə'lai], f -/-en Art: easel. ◆'S~n, v.tr. to stagger (Ind: hours etc.), grade (wages).

stagnieren [ʃtag'niːrən], v.i. (haben) to stagnate.

Stahl [ʃtɑːl]. I. m -(e)s/⁼e steel. II. 'S~-, 's~-, comb.fm. steel (blue, industry, works, helmet etc.). ◆'s~hart, adj. hard as steel/Fig: (Pers.) as nails.

Stall [ʃtal], m -(e)s/⁼e stable, (Kuhs.) cowshed; (Kaninchens.) hutch.

Stamm [ʃtam]. I. m -(e)s/⁼e 1. (Baums.) trunk (of a tree). 2. (Volkss.) tribe. 3. Gram: stem, root. II. 'S~-, comb.fm. (a) favourite (café etc.); (b) regular (guest etc.). ◆'S~baum, m family tree; Z: & Hum: pedigree. ◆'s~en, v.i. (haben) (a) s. aus + dat, to come from (a place, an old family etc.); die Worte s. nicht

von mir, those are not my words. ◆'S~**halter,** m Hum: son and heir.

stammeln ['ʃtaməln], v.tr. & i. (haben) to stammer (sth.).

stämmig ['ʃtɛmɪç], adj. burly, stocky.

stampfen ['ʃtampfən], v.i. (a) (haben) to stamp; (Maschine, Motor usw.) to pound; (b) (sein) er **stampfte durch den Schnee,** he tramped/stomped through the snow.

Stand [ʃtant], m -(e)s/ᵉe **1.** (a) no pl standing position; stance; (b) (für Taxis) stand, rank; (am Markt usw.) stall; (Messes.) stand. **2.** no pl (Lage) position; (Stadium) stage; (Zustand) state (of finances, a game etc.); **S. der Dinge,** state of affairs; position. ◆'S~**bild,** n statue. ◆'S~**esamt** ['ʃtandəs-], n registry office. ◆'S~**esbeamte,** m registrar (of births etc.). ◆'s~**esgemäß,** adj. in keeping with social status. ◆'s~**fest,** adj. steady, stable (table etc.); Fig: steadfast. ◆'S~**gericht,** n summary court martial. ◆'s~**haft,** adj. steadfast, unwavering (person etc.); stout (denial etc.). ◆'S~**haftigkeit,** f -/no pl steadfastness, staunchness. ◆'s~**halten,** v.i.sep. (haben) (Pers.) to stand firm; **einem Angriff/Druck usw. s.,** to withstand/stand up to pressure etc. ◆'S~**licht,** n Aut: parking light(s). ◆'S~**ort,** m location; position (of a plant, ship etc.); site of a firm etc.); Mil: garrison. ◆'S~**punkt,** m point of view, standpoint. ◆'S~**recht,** n martial law.

Standard ['ʃtandart], m -s/-s norm, standard.

Ständer ['ʃtɛndər], m -s/- stand (for music, hats etc.). ◆'s~**ig,** ['ʃtɛndɪç], adj. permanent (residence etc.); constant (companion etc.); steady, continuous (noise etc.).

Stange ['ʃtaŋə], f -/-n (Holz:) pole; (Metalls.) rod, bar; (Kleiders.) clothes rail; F: **Kleider von der S.,** clothes off the peg; F: **eine S. Geld,** a pretty penny. ◆'S~**nbrot,** n (loaf of) French bread.

Stanniol [ʃtani'o:l], n -s/-e tin foil. ◆S~**papier,** n silver paper.

Stanze ['ʃtantsə], f -/-n Tchn: punch, punching machine. ◆'s~**n,** v.tr. to punch (holes); (prägen) to stamp (metal etc.).

Stapel ['ʃta:pəl], m -s/- **1.** stack, pile (of books, wood etc.). **2.** (beim Schiffbau) stocks; **vom S. laufen,** to be launched. ◆'S~**lauf,** m launching (of a ship). ◆'s~**n,** v.tr. to stack, pile up (goods etc.).

stapfen ['ʃtapfən], v.i. (sein) to trudge.

Star¹ [ʃtaɾ], m -(e)s/-e **1.** Orn: starling. **2.** Med: cataract.

Star², m -s/-s Cin: etc: star.

stark [ʃtaɾk], adj. (a) strong (man, coffee, drink, current etc.); powerful (engine, voice etc.); (b) (zahlenmäßig) big (army, Sp: field etc.); (heftig) violent (storm); in-

tense (pain etc.); heavy (traffic, demand, rain etc.); **s~e Beteiligung,** large attendance/number of people participating; (c) adv. (viel) a lot; (+ adj.) very; s. **übertrieben/vergrößert,** greatly exaggerated/enlarged. ◆'S~**strom,** m high voltage/power current.

Stärk|e ['ʃtɛɾkə], f -/-n **1.** (a) no pl (Kraft) strength (of a person, party, Fig: s.o.'s faith etc.); (Leistung) power (of an engine etc.); violence, intensity (of pain, a storm, reaction etc.); **mit voller S.,** with full force; (b) Fig: strong point; (c) (Dicke) thickness; (d) (Größe) size (of an army etc.); amount (of traffic etc.). **2.** Cu: starch. ◆'s~**en,** v.tr. (a) to strengthen (s.o., s.o.'s position etc.); (b) to starch (shirt collars etc.). ◆'S~**ung,** f -/-en a strengthening, boosting; (b) (Erfrischung) refreshment. ◆'S~**ungsmittel,** n restorative, tonic.

starr [ʃtaɾ], adj. rigid; (steif) stiff (attitude etc.); **s~er Blick,** fixed stare; s. vor Kälte, frozen stiff. ◆'s~**en,** v.i. (haben) (a) to stare; (b) vor Schmutz s., to be absolutely filthy. ◆'s~**köpfig,** adj. obdurate, obstinate; (eigensinnig) self-willed. ◆'S~**sinn,** m obduracy, obstinacy. ◆'s~**sinnig,** adj. = s~köpfig.

Start [ʃtaɾt], m -(e)s/-s **1.** Sp: & Fig: start; (b) Av: take-off; launch (of a rocket). **II.** 'S~-, comb.fm. starting (block, line, signal etc.). ◆'S~**bahn,** f Av: (take-off) runway. ◆'s~**bereit,** adj. ready to go/Av: for take-off. ◆'s~**en,** v. **1.** v.tr. to start (a race, an engine etc.); to launch (a rocket, a campaign etc.). **2.** v.i. (sein) to start in a race etc.); Av: to take off.

Station [ʃtatsi'o:n], f -/-en **1.** (bus/train/tram) stop; **S. machen,** to break one's journey, esp. N.Am: stop over. **2.** Rad: station. **3.** Med: ward. ◆S~**är** [-o'nɛːɾ], adj. Med: (treatment) as an in-patient. ◆s~**ieren** [-o'ni:ɾən], v.tr. to station (troops etc.).

Statist [ʃta'tist], m -en/-en Th: Cin: extra. ◆S~**ik,** f -/-en coll. statistics. ◆S~**iker,** m -s/- statistician. ◆s~**isch,** adj. statistical.

Stativ [ʃta'ti:f], n -s/-e tripod.

statt [ʃtat], conj. & prep. + gen instead of; **s. dessen,** instead (of this). ◆'s~**finden,** v.i.sep.irr.9 (haben) to happen, take place. ◆'s~**haft,** adj. permissible. ◆'s~**lich,** adj. stately, imposing (house, person etc.); magnificent (figure, building etc.); impressive (collection); considerable (number, sum etc.).

Stätte ['ʃtɛtə], f -/-n Lit: place; site (of an event).

Statue ['ʃta:tuə], f -/-n statue. ◆S~**r** [ʃta'u:ɾ], f -/no pl stature, build. ◆S~**s** ['ʃta:tus], m -/no pl status. ◆S~**t** [ʃta'tu:t], n -(e)s/-en statute.

Stau [ʃtau], m -(e)s/-s **1.** no pl = S~ung **1. 2.** tailback (of traffic). ◆'S~**damm,**

m barrage, dam. ◆'s~en, *v.tr.* to dam (a river etc.), staunch (blood); sich s., to accumulate; (*Leute*) form a crowd, (*Autos*) form a tailback. ◆'S~see, *m* artificial lake, reservoir. ◆'S~ung, *f* -en 1. *no pl* damming-up, staunching (of blood). 2. congestion; snarl-up (of traffic etc.).

Staub [ʃtaup], *m* -(e)s/*no pl* dust. ◆~en ['ʃtaubən], *v.i.* (haben) to make dust. ◆s~ig ['ʃtaubiç], *adj.* dusty. ◆'S~korn, *n* speck of dust. ◆'s~saugen, *v.tr.sep.* to hoover, vacuum (a carpet etc.). ◆'S~sauger, *m* vacuum cleaner. ◆'S~tuch, *n* duster.

Staude ['ʃtaudə], *f* -/-n (perennial) herbaceous plant; (*Strauch*) shrub.

staunen ['ʃtaunən], *v.i.* (haben) to be astonished/amazed (über etwas *acc*, at sth.).

stechen ['ʃtɛçən]. I. *v.irr.14* 1. *v.tr. & i.* (haben) (a) (*Insekt*) to sting, (*Mücke usw.*) bite (s.o.), (*Dorn, Nadel usw.*) to prick (s.o.); (*Messerspitze, Dolch usw.*) to stab (s.o.), pierce (holes in sth.); (b) to cut (peat, asparagus etc.); (c) *Art:* ein Bild (in Kupfer) s., to engrave a picture; (d) (*Kartenspiel*) to trump (a card). 2. *v.i.* (haben) (*Sonne*) to blaze/beat down. II. S., *n* -s/*no pl* (a) stinging, pricking; (b) *Sp:* deciding contest/round. ◆'s~end, *adj.* stinging, stabbing (pain etc.); pungent (smell); penetrating (gaze, smell etc.). ◆'S~mücke, *f* gnat, mosquito. ◆'S~palme, *f* holly. ◆'S~uhr, *f* time clock.

Steckbrief ['ʃtɛkbriːf], *m* personal description (*fur:* of s.o. wanted). ◆'s~dose, *f* socket. ◆'s~en, *v.* 1. *v.i.* (haben) to be, (*fests.*) be stuck. 2. *v.tr.* (a) to put (sth.) (in etwas *acc*, into sth.); to stick (a pin etc.), (in etwas *acc*, into sth.); to fix/fasten/(mit Nadeln) pin (a brooch etc.) (an + *acc*, to); (b) to plant (onions etc.). ◆'s~enbleiben, *v.i. sep.irr.12* (sein) (a) to get stuck (im Schlamm usw., in the mud etc.); (*Redner usw.*) to dry up; (*Gräte usw.*) im Halse s., to stick in one's throat. ◆'S~enpferd, *n* 1. hobby horse. 2. hobby; (*Thema*) pet subject. ◆'S~er, *m* -s/- plug. ◆'S~nadel, *f* pin. ◆'S~rübe, *f* turnip. ◆'S~schloß, *n* mortice lock.

Steg [ʃteːk], *m* -(e)s/-e (narrow) footbridge; *Nau:* (*Brett*) gangplank; (*Bootss.*) jetty. ◆'S~reif, *m* aus dem S., impromptu.

stehen ['ʃteːən], *v.i.irr.* (haben) (a) (aufrechts.) (*Pers., Gebäude usw.*) to stand; im S./s~end arbeiten, to work standing up; zu j-m/seinem Versprechen s., to stand by s.o./one's promise; (b) (*stills.*) (*Uhr usw.*) to have stopped; (*Verkehr usw.*) to be stationary/at a standstill; zum S. kommen, to come to a standstill; (c) (sich befinden) to be (somewhere); das Auto steht vor der Tür, the car is (standing)

at the door; (d) (geschrieben s.) es steht in der Zeitung, it's in the paper; auf dem Schild steht, daß ..., the notice says that ...; (e) (*Stellung*) die Uhr steht auf 6, the clock says 6; gut/schlecht s., (*Währung usw.*) to be strong/weak; (*Sache*) to be going well/ badly; es steht schlecht um ihn, things look bad for him; (gesundheitlich) he is in a bad way; *Sp:* das Spiel steht 2:1, the score is 2–1; (f) (passen) die Jacke steht dir, the jacket suits you/ looks good on you. ◆'s~enbleiben, *v.i.sep.irr.12* (sein) to stop; (*Pers., Fig: Zeit*) to stand still; (*Motor*) to stall; (b) to remain, be left. ◆'s~enlassen, *v.tr.sep.irr.57* (a) to leave (sth.) behind; (vergessen) to forget (sth.); (nicht essen) to leave (food) (untouched); (b) sich *dat* einen Bart s., to grow a beard. ◆'S~lampe, *f* standard lamp. ◆'S~platz, *m Th: etc:* (space in the) standing room; (im Bus) space to stand; *pl* S~plätze, standing room.

stehlen ['ʃteːlən], *v.tr.irr.2* to steal (sth.) (j-m, from s.o.).

steif [ʃtaif], *adj.* stiff; *Fig:* stiff, formal (reception, style etc.); etwas s. und fest behaupten, to insist stubbornly on sth.

Steigbügel ['ʃtaikbyːɡəl], *m* stirrup. ◆'S~eisen, *n* crampon. ◆'s~en, *v.i.irr.89* (sein) to climb; auf einen Berg s., to climb a mountain; in ein Flugzeug, einen Bus usw. s., to board/ get on a plane, bus etc.; (b) (*Flut, Sonne, Temperatur usw.*) to rise; (*Nebel*) to lift; (*Preise usw.*) to go up, increase; (*Spannung, Schulden usw.*) to mount; (*Chancen, Stimmung*) to improve. ◆'s~ern, *v.tr.* to increase; to step up (production, demands etc.); (verbessern) improve (a performance, an offer etc.); sich s., to increase; *Gram:* Adjektive s., to form the comparative and superlative of adjectives. ◆'s~erung, *f* -/-en increase; intensification, enhancement; *Gram:* comparison (of adjectives). ◆'S~ung, *f* -/-en (upward) gradient; *N.Am:* grade; (*Hang*) slope.

steil [ʃtail], *adj.* steep; *Fig:* rapid (increase etc.); mercurial (career).

Stein [ʃtain], *m* -(e)s/-e stone. ◆'s~alt, *adj. F:* (*Pers.*) ancient. ◆'s~bock, *m Z:* ibex; *Astr:* Capricorn. ◆'S~bruch, *m* quarry. ◆'S~butt, *m* turbot. ◆'s~ern, *adj.* stone; *Fig:* (heart) of stone; stony (expression). ◆'S~gut, *n* -(e)s/*no pl* earthenware. ◆'s~hart, *adj.* rock-hard. ◆'s~ig, *adj.* stony (ground etc.). ◆'s~igen, *v.tr.* to stone (s.o.). ◆'S~kohle, *f* (hard) coal. ◆'S~metz, *m* -es/-e stone mason. ◆'S~obst, *n* stone fruit. ◆'S~pilz, *m* edible boletus. ◆'s~reich, *adj. F:* rolling (in money). ◆'S~zeit, *f* Stone Age.

Steißbein ['ʃtaisbain], *n* coccyx.

Stelldichein ['ʃtɛldiçʔain], *n* -s/- rendezvous. ◆'S~e, *f* -/-n 1. (a) place; kahle

S., bare patch; **wunde S.,** sore spot; *Fig:*
auf der S., (*sofort*) immediately; (*hier*)
here and now; **zur S. sein,** (*b*) to be on
hand; (*b*) position; **an der richtigen S.,**
in the right position/place; **an S.
von +** *dat,* instead/in lieu of; **an dieser S.
der Geschichte,** at this point in the
story. 2. (*Arbeitss.*) job, post. 3. (*Diensts.*)
office; (*Behörde*) authority. 4. *Mth:* digit;
(*Dezimals.*) (decimal) place. ◆**'s~en,**
v.tr. (*a*) to put (s.o., sth.); (*b*) (*Pers.*)
sich s., to place oneself, take up position
(somewhere); **stell dich neben mich,**
come (and stand) next to me; **wie s. Sie
sich dazu?** what is your view on this? (*c*)
to set (a trap, switch etc.); to put (the
clock) right; **den Wecker auf 7 Uhr s.,**
to set the alarm for 7 o'clock; **das Gas
höher/niedriger s.,** to turn the gas up/
down; (*d*) (*beschaffen, geben*) to provide
(wine, workers etc.); to put forward (a
demand), put (a question); **j-m eine Aufgabe s.,** to set s.o. a task; (*e*) to corner
(an animal, a criminal); **sich (der Polizei)
s.,** to give oneself up to the police; **sich
einem Gegner s.,** to meet an opponent;
(*f*) **sich krank, taub usw. s.,** to pretend
to be ill, deaf etc. ◆**S~enangebot,** *n*
offer of a post; (*in Zeitung*)
S~enangebote, situations vacant.
◆**'S~enangesuch** *n* application for a
post; (*in Zeitung*) **S~engesuche,** situations wanted. ◆**'S~envermittlung,** *f*
employment agency. ◆**'S~enweise,**
adv. here and there. ◆**'S~ung,** *f* **-/-en**
(*a*) position; (*b*) (*Körperhaltung*) posture;
(*c*) *Mil:* **feindliche S~ungen,** enemy
positions/lines; (*d*) (*Posten*) post, job; (*e*)
(*Haltung*) attitude (**zu +** *dat,* to); **zu etwas** *dat* **S. nehmen,** to express an
opinion on sth. ◆**'S~ungnahme,**
f **-/n** view, comment. ◆**'S~ungslos,**
f job-hunting. ◆**'s~vertretend,** *adj.*
deputy; (*vorübergehend*) acting. ◆**'S~-
vertreter(in),** *m* **-f** deputy; (*Ersatzmann*)
substitute; (*an einem anderen Ort*) representative. ◆**'S~werk,** *n* signal box.

Stelze ['ʃtɛltsə], *f* **-/n** *usu.pl* **S~n,** stilts.

Stemm|bogen ['ʃtɛmboːgən], *m Sp:*
stem turn. ◆**'S~eisen,** *n* crowbar.
◆**'s~en,** *v.tr.* (*a*) to lift (a weight etc.)
above one's head; (*b*) to press (one's knee
etc.); **sich gegen etwas** *acc* **s.,** to brace
oneself against sth.; *Fig:* to resist sth.

Stempel ['ʃtɛmpəl], *m* **-s/-** 1. stamp; (*auf
Silber usw.*) hallmark; (*Posts.*) postmark.
2. *Bot:* pistil. ◆**'S~kissen,** *n* inkpad.
◆**'s~n,** *v.* 1. *v.tr.* to stamp (a document etc.), postmark (a letter); cancel (a
stamp), hallmark (precious metals). 2.
v.i. (**haben**) *F:* **s. gehen,** to be on the
dole.

Stengel ['ʃtɛŋəl], *m* **-s/-** *Bot:* stem.

Steno|gramm [ʃteno'gram], *n* **-(e)s/-e**
shorthand version/text. ◆**'s~gra-
'phieren,** *v.tr.* to take (sth.) down in
shorthand. ◆**'s~ty'pist(in),** *m* **-en/-en**

(*f* **-/-nen**) shorthand-typist.

Stepp|decke ['ʃtɛpdɛkə], *f* **-/n** quilt.
◆**'S~e,** *f* **-/-n** (*in Asien*) steppes; *N.Am:*
prairie; *S.Am:* pampas. ◆**'s~en,** *v.tr.*
to machine-stitch (clothes), quilt (material).

Sterb|e- ['ʃtɛrbə-], *comb.fm.* death (cer-
tificate etc); (hour, date, place etc.) of
death. ◆**'S~ebett,** *n* deathbed.
◆**'S~efall,** *m* death. ◆**'s~en,** *v.i.ir.*
(**sein**) to die (**an etwas** *dat,* of sth.); **im S.
liegen,** to be dying. ◆**'s~ens'krank,**
adj. mortally ill. ◆**'s~lich,** *adj.* mortal
(remains etc.); **ein gewöhnlicher
S~licher,** an ordinary mortal.
◆**'S~lichkeit,** *f* **-/no** *pl* mortality.
◆**'S~lichkeitsrate,** *f* death rate.

Stereo- ['ʃteːreo-, 'st-], *comb.fm.* stereo
(record, tape recorder etc.). ◆**'S~-
anlage,** *f* stereo system, *F:* stereo.

steril [ʃteˈriːl], *adj.* sterile. ◆**S~isation**
[-rilizatsiˈoːn], *f* **-/-en** sterilization.
◆**s~iˈsieren** [-ziˈroːn], *v.tr.* to sterilize
(s.o., sth.), neuter (a cat).

Stern [ʃtɛrn], *m* **-(e)s/-e** star. ◆**'S~bild,**
n constellation. ◆**'S~enbanner,** *n* **das
S.,** the stars and stripes. ◆**'s~förmig,**
adj. star-shaped. ◆**'S~kunde,** *f* **-/no** *pl*
astronomy. ◆**'S~schnuppe,** *f* **-/n**
shooting star. ◆**'S~stunde,** *f* great
moment. ◆**'S~warte,** *f* observatory.

stetig ['ʃteːtɪç], *adj.* steady, constant (increase, decrease etc.). ◆**'s~s,** *adv.* always.

Steuer1 ['ʃtɔyər], *n* **-s/-** *Aut:* steering
wheel; *Nau:* rudder; *Av:* etc: controls;
am S., at the wheel/*Av:* controls/*Nau:*
helm. ◆**'S~bord,** *n* starboard.
◆**'S~gerät,** *n Rad:* control unit.
◆**'S~knüppel,** *m Av:* (control)
stick. ◆**'S~mann,** *m Av:* helmsman.
◆**'s~n,** *v.* 1. *v.tr.* (*a*) to steer (a car,
ship, course etc.), navigate (a ship), pilot
(an aircraft); (*b*) *Tchn:* (*regulieren*) to control (a machine, speed, *Fig:* a firm etc.).
2. *v.i.* to steer, be at the controls/*Nau:*
helm. ◆**'S~rad,** *n* steering wheel.
◆**'S~ung,** *f* **-/-en** (*a*) no *pl* steering;
Av: piloting; *Tchn: & Fig:* control; (*b*)
steering (mechanism); *Av:* controls.

Steuer2. I. *f* **-/-n** tax. II. **'S~-,** *comb.fm.*
tax (increase, collector, group, offence
etc.); fiscal (law, policy, secrecy, year
etc.). ◆**'S~behörde,** *f* tax authorities.
◆**'S~berater,** *m* tax consultant.
◆**'S~erklärung,** *f* tax return.
◆**'S~flucht,** *f* tax evasion (by going
abroad). ◆**'s~frei,** *adj.* tax-free, un-
taxed (goods etc.). ◆**'S~hinterzie-
hung,** *f* tax evasion. ◆**'s~pflichtig,**
adj. taxable (income etc.). ◆**'S~satz,**
m tax rate; rate of assessment.
◆**'S~zahler,** *m* taxpayer.

Stewardeß [stjuːˈardɛs], *f* **-/-ssen**
stewardess; *Av:* air hostess.

stibitzen [ʃtiˈbɪtsən], *v.tr. F:* to pinch,
nick (sth.).

Stich [ʃtiç], m -(e)s/-e 1. (a) prick (of a needle); stab (of a knife, dagger etc.); (S~wunde) stab wound; (b) sting, bite (of an insect). 2. (Nähs.) stitch. 3. Art: engraving. 4. (Kartenspiel) einen S. machen, to take a trick. 5. das Kleid hat einen S. ins Rötliche, the dress has a reddish tinge. 6. j-n im S. lassen, to let s.o. down; (verlassen) leave s.o. in the lurch. ◆**S~'elei**, f -/-en F: (a) snide remark; gibe; (b) no pl sneering, gibing. ◆'**s~eln**, v.i. (haben) gegen j-n s., to gibe at s.o., make snide remarks about s.o. ◆**S~flamme**, f leaping flame; jet of flame. ◆'**s~haltig**, adj. sound, valid (reason, argument etc.). ◆**S~probe**, f spot check. ◆**S~waffe**, f stabbing weapon. ◆**S~wahl**, f final ballot. ◆**S~wort**, n -(e)s 1. (pl -er) headword (in a dictionary etc.). 2. (pl -e) (a) Th: cue; (b) pl notes. ◆**S~wunde**, f stab (wound). ◆**S~wortverzeichnis**, n index.

stick|en [ʃtikən], v.tr. to embroider (a cushion etc.). ◆**S~e'rei**, f -/-en embroidery. ◆'**s~ig**, adj. stuffy (air, room), close (atmosphere). ◆**S~stoff**, m nitrogen.

Stief- [ʃtiːf-], comb.fm. step (-mother, -father, -brother etc.). ◆'**S~kind**, n stepchild; Fig: poor cousin. ◆'**S~mütterchen**, n -s/- pansy.

Stiefel [ʃtiːfəl], m -s/- boot.

Stiege [ʃtiːgə], f -/-n (narrow/steep) stairs.

Stiel [ʃtiːl], m -(e)s/-e stalk (of a plant etc.); stem (of a glass etc.); handle (of a broom etc.).

Stier [ʃtiːr], m -(e)s/-e bull; Astr: Taurus. ◆**S~kampf**, m bullfight. ◆'**S~kämpfer**, m bullfighter.

stieren [ʃtiːrən], v.i. (haben) to stare fixedly.

Stift[1] [ʃtift], m -(e)s/-e 1. pin; (Nagel) tack; (Holz-) peg. 2. (Bleis.) pencil; (Farbs.) crayon. 3. F: (Lehrling) apprentice.

Stift[2], n -(e)s/-e (endowed) religious foundation, esp. seminary. ◆**s~en**, v.tr. (a) to endow, found (a convent etc.); (spenden) to donate (a prize etc.); (b) (bewirken) to cause (confusion, disaster etc.); to bring about (peace etc.). ◆**S~er(in)**, m -s/- (f -/-nen) founder; (Spender) donor (of a prize etc.). ◆**S~ung**, f -/-en (a) foundation; (Schenkung) donation, bequest (to a museum etc.); (b) (charitable/religious) foundation, institution.

Stil [ʃtiːl], m -(e)s/-e style; im großen S., in the grand manner; on a grand scale. II. '**S~-**, comb.fm. stylistic (analysis, level, exercise etc.); (conception, dictionary etc.) of style. ◆**S~blüte**, f stylistic blunder. ◆**S~bruch**, m (incongruous) change of style. ◆**S~gefühl**, n sense of style. ◆**s~istisch**, adj. stylis-

tic. ◆**s~los** [ʃtiːllɔːs], adj. lacking in style/taste. ◆**S~möbel**, npl period furniture. ◆'**s~voll**, adj. stylish, tasteful.

still [ʃtil], adj. (lautlos) quiet, silent; (ohne Bewegung) still; (ruhig) quiet (area, life, person etc.), calm (sea); peaceful (day, village etc.); private (hope, wish); sie blieb s., she said nothing; im s~en, secretly, privately; im s~en Teilhaber, sleeping partner. ◆**S~e**, f -/no pl silence, quiet(ness); stillness; in aller S. heiraten, to have a quiet wedding. ◆**s~en**, v.tr. (a) to nurse, breastfeed (a baby); (b) to quench (one's thirst), satisfy (one's hunger, curiosity, desires etc.); (c) to staunch (blood); to stop (pain etc.). ◆'**s~halten**, v.i. v.sep.irr.45 (haben) to keep still/F: quiet. ◆**S~leben**, n Art: still life. ◆'**s~legen**, v.tr.sep. to shut down (a factory, railway line etc.). ◆**S~schweigen**, n silence. ◆'**s~schweigend**, adj. silent, unspoken; s~schweigendes Einverständnis, tacit agreement; etwas s. übergehen, to pass over sth. in silence. ◆**S~stand**, m standstill. ◆'**s~stehen**, v.i.sep.irr.100 (haben) to stand still, (Verkehr, Produktion usw.) to be at a standstill; (Maschinen usw.) to be idle.

Stimm|abgabe [ʃtim'ʔapgaːbə], f voting. ◆**S~bänder**, npl vocal cords. ◆'**s~berechtigt**, adj. entitled to vote. ◆**S~bruch**, m er ist im S., his voice is breaking. ◆**S~e**, f -/-n 1. (a) voice; die S. des Volkes, public opinion. 2. Mus: (Partie) part. 3. Pol: etc: seine S. abgeben, to (cast one's) vote. ◆'**s~en**, v. 1. v.tr. (a) die Nachricht stimmte ihn glücklich, the news made him happy; (b) Mus: to tune (an instrument). 2. v.i. (haben) (a) to be right/correct; da stimmt etwas nicht, there is something wrong/ (suspekt) fishy there; (b) Pol: etc: für/gegen j-n s., to vote for/against s.o. ◆'**S~enthaltung**, f abstention from voting. ◆'**s~gabel**, f tuning fork. ◆'**s~haft**, adj. voiced (consonant etc.). ◆'**S~lage**, f (vocal) register. ◆'**s~los**, adj. unvoiced. ◆**S~ung**, f -/-en (a) (Laune) mood; (b) die S~des Volkes, public feeling; F: sie waren in S., they were in high spirits; (b) atmosphere. ◆'**s~ungsvoll**, adj. full of atmosphere, evocative. ◆**S~zettel**, m voting/ballot paper.

stimu|lieren [ʃtimu'liːrən], v.tr. to stimulate (s.o.).

Stink|bombe [ʃtiŋkbombə], f -/-n stink-bomb. ◆'**s~en**, v.i.irr. (haben) to stink. ◆'**s~faul**, adj. F: bone-idle. ◆'**S~tier**, n skunk.

Stipendium [ʃti'pɛndium], n -s/-ien scholarship, grant.

Stirn [ʃtirn], f -/-en forehead, brow; Fig: j-m die S. bieten, to stand up to/defy s.o.; er hatte die S., mir zu sagen ..., he had the effrontery/nerve to tell me ...

◆'S~höhle, f (frontal) sinus.
◆'S~runzeln, n frown.

stöbern ['ʃtøːbərn], v.i. (haben) to rummage (about).

stochern ['ʃtɔxərn], v.i. (haben) to poke (about).

Stock¹ [ʃtɔk], m -(e)s/¨e 1. stick; (zum Prügeln) cane; Mus: baton. 2. no pl storey; im ersten S., on the first/N.Am: second floor. ◆'S~werk, n floor, storey.

stock-², adj.comb.fm. F: completely and utterly (stupid, normal etc.); arch- (-conservative etc.). ◆'s~'dunkel, adj. pitch dark. ◆'s~'taub, adj. stone-deaf.

stock|en ['ʃtɔkən], v.i. (haben) (Pers.) to falter, hesitate; (Gespräch) to flag; (Verkehr usw.) to be held up, proceed in fits and starts. ◆'s~end, adj. faltering, hesitant. ◆'S~ung, f -/-en hesitation; hold-up (of traffic etc.).

Stoff [ʃtɔf], m -(e)s/-e 1. material. 2. (a) Ch: substance; (pflanzliche S~e, vegetable matter; (b) Lit: material; (Thema) subject; subject-matter (of a book etc.). ◆'S~wechsel, m metabolism.

stöhnen ['ʃtøːnən], v.i. (haben) to groan, moan.

stoisch ['ʃtoːɪʃ], adj. stoic.

Stollen ['ʃtɔlən], m -s/- 1. Min: tunnel; gallery. 2. Cu: (Christmas) fruit loaf, stollen.

stolpern ['ʃtɔlpərn], v.i. (sein) to stumble.

stolz [ʃtɔlts]. I. adj. proud (auf etwas acc, of sth.); eine s~e Leistung, a splendid achievement. II. S., m -es/no pl pride. ◆s~ieren [-'tsiːrən], v.i. (sein) to swagger, strut.

Stopf- ['ʃtɔpf-], comb.fm. darning (thread, wool, needle etc.). ◆'s~en, v. 1. v.tr. (a) to darn (socks etc.); (b) to fill a pipe, sausage etc.), stuff (a pillow, one's pockets etc.); ein Loch/Leck s., to plug a hole/leak. 2. v.i. (haben) to cause constipation.

Stopp [ʃtɔp], m -s/-s 1. (Halt) stop. 2. (Sperre) ban (für + acc, on); (wage etc.) freeze. II. 'S~, comb.fm. stop (sign etc.). ◆'s~en, v.tr. (a) to stop (s.o., sth.); Fb: etc: to tackle (a player); (b) to time (s.o.) (with a stopwatch). ◆'S~straße, f minor road. ◆'S~uhr, f stopwatch.

Stoppel ['ʃtɔpəl], f -/-n stubble.

Stöpsel ['ʃtœpsəl], m -s/- plug; stopper (in a bottle).

Stör¹ [ʃtøːr], m -(e)s/-e sturgeon.

Stör-², comb.fm. disruptive (action, factor, manoeuvre etc.); Mil: harrassing action, fire etc.). ◆'s~en, v. 1. v.tr. (a) to disturb (s.o.), interfere with (a plan, Rad: reception etc.); (unterbrechen) to interrupt (a conversation etc.); (b) (beunruhigen) to bother, worry (s.o.); stört es Sie, wenn ...? do you mind if ...? 2. v.i. (haben) to be in the way, disturb s.o.; störe ich? am I interrupting/in the way? ◆'s~end, adj. disturbing; disruptive

(effect, influence); (lästig) troublesome. ◆'S~enfried, m -(e)s/-e disruptive element. ◆'S~sender, m jamming transmitter. ◆'S~ung, f -/-en (a) disturbance; interruption, disruption (of proceedings etc.); hold-up (of traffic); (b) Tchn: (Fehler) fault; Rad: interference; Med: disorder.

störrisch ['ʃtœrɪʃ], adj. stubborn, pigheaded.

Stoß [ʃtoːs], m -es/¨e 1. (a) push; j-m einen S. mit dem Fuß/der Faust versetzen, to kick/punch s.o.; ein S. mit dem Dolch, a thrust/stab with the dagger; (b) (Anprall) impact, (kräftig) shock; (Erds.) tremor. 2. (Stapel) pile (of washing, books etc.). ◆'S~dämpfer, m shock absorber. ◆'s~en, v.irr. 1. v.tr. to push (s.o., sth.); (schlagen) to hit, (mit dem Fuß) kick; (zufällig) to knock, (plötzlich) jolt (s.o., sth.); to thrust (a knife etc.); sich (an etwas dat) s., to knock oneself (on sth.); Fig: sich an j-s Benehmen usw. s., to take exception to s.o.'s behaviour etc. 2. v.i. (sein) (a) er ist an/gegen das Bett gestoßen, he bumped into/knocked against the bed; nach j-m s., to lunge at/(Stier usw.) butt s.o.; (b) (grenzen) to border (an etwas acc, on sth.); (c) auf etwas acc s., to come across sth.; auf j-n s., to run into s.o. ◆'s~fest, adj. shockproof. ◆'S~stange, f bumper. ◆'S~verkehr, m rush-hour traffic. ◆'S~zeit, f rush hour.

Stotter|er ['ʃtɔtərər], m -s/- stammerer. ◆'s~n, v.tr. & i. (haben) to stammer.

stracks [ʃtraks], adv. straight, directly.

Straf- ['ʃtraːf-], comb.fm. (a) penal (colony etc.); criminal (court, proceedings etc.); (b) Sp: penalty (bench, points etc.). ◆'S~anstalt, f penal institution, prison. ◆'S~anzeige, f charge. ◆'S~arbeit, f Sch: imposition. ◆'s~bar, adj. Jur: punishable, criminal (action etc.); sich s. machen, to commit an offence. ◆'S~e, f -/-n punishment, penalty; (Gelds.) fine; (Freiheitss.) sentence; zur S., as a punishment. ◆'s~en, v.tr. to punish(/prügeln) beat (s.o.). ◆'s~fällig, adj. s. werden, to commit a criminal offence. ◆'s~frei, adj. unpunished; s. ausgehen, to be let off. ◆'S~gefangene(r), m & f decl. as adj. convict, prisoner. ◆'S~gericht, n criminal court. ◆'S~gesetzbuch, n penal/criminal code. ◆'S~mandat, n (esp. parking) ticket. ◆'S~porto, n surcharge. ◆'S~predigt, f F: j-m eine S. halten, to give s.o. a good talking to (s.o.). ◆'S~prozeß, m criminal proceedings/case. ◆'S~recht, n criminal law. ◆'S~raum, m penalty area. ◆'S~stoß, m penalty kick. ◆'S~tat, f criminal act. ◆'S~täter, m offender. ◆'S~vollzug, m execution of a sentence. ◆'S~zettel, m F: = S~mandat.

straff [ʃtraf], adj. taut (rope etc.); tight (reins, trousers; Fig: organization); Fig: strict (discipline). ◆'s~en, v.tr. to tighten (a rope etc.); Fig: tighten up (organization etc.).

sträf|lich ['ʃtrɛːfliç], adj. criminal (negligence etc.). ◆'S~ling, m -s/-e convict.

Strahl [ʃtraːl], m -(e)s/-en (a) ray of light, the sun, Fig: hope etc.; beam (of a torch etc.); (b) jet of water etc.). ◆'s~en, v.i. (a) to shine, (glänzen) gleam; (b) Fig: (Pers.) to beam (vor Freude usw., with joy etc.). ◆'S~en-, comb.fm. ray (treatment etc.); radiation (damage etc.). ◆'s~end, adj. radiant (beauty, appearance, face, smile etc.); brilliant (sun, weather etc.); shining, sparkling (eyes etc.). ◆'S~entherapie, f radiotherapy. ◆'S~ung, f -/-en radiation.

Strähn|e ['ʃtrɛːnə], f -/-n strand (of hair etc.). ◆'s~ig, adj. straggly (hair etc.).

stramm [ʃtram], adj. (a) (aufrecht) upright; (b) (straff) tight (elastic etc.). ◆'s~stehen, v.i.sep.irr.100 (haben) Mil: to stand to attention.

strampeln ['ʃtrampəln], v.i. (haben) (Baby) to kick.

Strand [ʃtrant], m -(e)s/-e beach; shore (of a lake). ◆'S~bad, n (am Fluß/See) bathing place; (am Meer) bathing beach. ◆'s~en, v.i. (sein) (Schiffe) to run aground. ◆'S~gut, n flotsam and jetsam. ◆'S~korb, m roofed wickerwork beach chair. ◆'S~promenade, f promenade, sea front.

Strang [ʃtraŋ], m -(e)s/-e (a) (Seil) rope; (b) über die S~e schlagen, to kick over the traces; (c) Rail: section (of track).

Strapaz|e [ʃtraˈpaːtsə], f -/-n (physical) strain. ◆s~ieren [-aˈtsiːrən], v.tr. to be hard on (shoes, clothes, skin etc.); to tax/put a strain on (s.o., sth.); to take it out of (s.o.). ◆s~ier'fähig, adj. hardwearing, durable. ◆s~i'ös, adj. exhausting, gruelling.

Straße ['ʃtraːsə], f -/-n 1. (a) street; (b) (Lands.) road. 2. (Meeres.) straits. ◆'S~n-, comb.fm. road (dirt, vehicle, map, network, race, conditions etc.); street (corner, fighting, musician, name, cleaning, theatre etc.). ◆'S~nbahn, f tram; N.Am: streetcar. ◆'S~nbau, m road building/construction. ◆'S~nbeleuchtung, f street lighting. ◆'S~ncafe, n pavement cafe. ◆'S~nkehrer, m road/street sweeper. ◆'S~nkreuzer, m -s/- F: large swanky car. ◆'S~nkreuzung, f road junction, crossroads. ◆'S~nrand, m roadside. ◆'S~nschild, n road/street sign. ◆'S~nseite, f side of the street. ◆'S~nsperre, f road block. ◆'S~nverkehr, m (road) traffic; im S~, on the road. ◆'S~nverkehrsordnung,

f traffic regulations.

Strate|ge [ʃtraˈteːgə], m -n/-n strategist. ◆S~gie [-teˈgiː], f -/-n strategy. ◆s~gisch [-ˈteːgiʃ], adj. strategic.

sträuben ['ʃtrɔybən], v.tr. (a) (Vogel) to ruffle (its feathers); (Haare) sich s., to stand on end; (b) (Pers.) sich gegen etwas acc s., to rebel/fight against sth.

Strauch [ʃtraux], m -(e)s/er bush, shrub.

Strauß¹ [ʃtraus], m -es/-e ostrich.

Strauß², m -es/er bunch (of flowers).

Streb|e ['ʃtreːbə], f -/-n brace. ◆'s~en, v.i. (a) (haben) to strive (nach + dat. for). ◆'S~er, m -s/- F: (pupil) Sch: swot, N.Am: grind. ◆'s~sam ['ʃtreːpzaːm], adj. ambitious; keen to get on; (fleißig) industrious.

Streck|e ['ʃtrɛkə], f -/-n (a) (Abschnitt) stretch (of road etc.); Rail: section (of track); Mth: der S., the straight line AB; (b) (Entfernung) distance; Fig: auf der S. bleiben, to retire (from a race). Fig: j-n zur S. bringen, to hunt down (and capture) s.o. ◆'s~en, v.tr. (a) to stretch (sth., one's arms, legs etc.); to crane (one's neck); sich s., to stretch (out); (b) to eke out (supplies etc.); (c) j-n zu Boden s., to knock down/floor s.o.; (d) Fig: die Waffen s., to give up. ◆'s~enweise, adv. in parts.

Streich¹ [ʃtraiç], m -(e)s/-e prank; j-m einen S. spielen, to play a practical joke/Fig: (Gedächtnis usw.) play tricks on s.o.

Streich-², comb.fm. (a) Mus: string (instrument, orchestra etc.); (b) Cu: (sausage etc.) for spreading. ◆'s~eln, v.tr. to stroke (s.o., a cat etc.). ◆'s~en, v.irr.40 1. v.tr. (a) to spread (butter, a roll, face cream etc.); (b) to stroke (s.o.'s face etc.); (c) to paint (a room etc.); (d) (auss.) to delete (a word etc.), strike off (a name etc.). 2. v.i. (a) (haben) to stroke; (b) (sein) (umhergehen) to wander, roam. ◆'S~er, mpl Mus: strings. ◆'s~fähig, adj. easy to spread; (cheese etc.) for spreading. ◆'S~holz, n match. ◆'S~holzschachtel, f matchbox. ◆'S~ung, f -/-en deletion.

Streif|e ['ʃtraifə], f -/-n (army/police) patrol. ◆'s~en¹, v. 1. v.tr. (a) to touch (s.o., sth.) (lightly), brush against (s.o., sth.); Fig: j-n mit dem Blick/den Augen s., to glance at s.o. 2. v.i. (sein) (umherziehen) to wander, roam (about). ◆'S~en², m -s/- (a) stripe (of colour etc.); (b) Stoff, Land usw., strip of cloth, land etc.; (c) F: (Film) movie. ◆'S~enwagen, m (police) patrol car. ◆'S~schuß, m grazing shot. ◆'S~zug, m reconnaissance; pl (ohne Ziel) wanderings.

Streik [ʃtraik], m -(e)s/-e strike. ◆'S~brecher, m strike-breaker; F: blackleg; N.Am: scab. ◆'s~en, v.i. (haben) (a) to strike; (b) F: (Pers.) (nicht mitmachen) to go on strike; (Gerät) to pack up. ◆'S~**ende(r)**, m & f decl. as adj. striker. ◆'S~**posten**, m picket.

Streit [ʃtrait], m -(e)s/no pl quarrel, (heftig) row; (zwischen Parteien usw.) dispute. ◆'s~**bar**, adj. quarrelsome. ◆'s~**en**, v.irr.41.refl. & i. (haben) (sich) über etwas acc s., to quarrel/argue about sth.; to have an argument/(Eheleute) a row about sth. ◆'S~**fall**, m (a) dispute, controversy; (b) Jur: case. ◆'S~**frage**, f matter in dispute, issue (in an argument). ◆'s~**ig**, adj. j-m etwas s. machen, to question s.o.'s right to sth. ◆'S~**igkeiten**, fpl quarrels, disputes. ◆'S~**kräfte**, fpl armed forces. ◆'s~**lustig**, adj. pugnacious, argumentative. ◆'S~**punkt**, m point at issue. ◆'S~**sucht**, f quarrelsomeness. ◆'s~**süchtig**, adj. quarrelsome.

streng [ʃtreŋ], adj. strict (parent, rule etc.); severe (measure, penalty, expression etc.); hard (winter, frost); strong (taste, smell). ◆'S~**e**, f /no pl strictness, severity; harshness (of treatment etc.); Fig: austerity. ◆'s~**genommen**, adv. strictly speaking. ◆'s~**gläubig**, adj. orthodox. ◆'s~**stens**, adv. s. verboten, strictly forbidden.

Streß [ʃtrɛs], m -sses/no pl stress.

Streu [ʃtrɔy], f -/no pl bed of straw/occ. leaves. ◆'s~**en**, v. 1. v.tr. to scatter (seeds etc.), (unordentlich) strew (paper, flowers etc.), spread (dung, Fig: rumours etc.), sprinkle (sugar etc.). 2. v.i. (haben) (mit Sand) to grit. ◆'S~**er**, m -s/- sprinkler; (für Salz) salt cellar.

streunen ['ʃtrɔynən], v.i. (sein) (Tier, Hum: Pers.) to roam; s~**de Katze**, stray cat.

Streusel ['ʃtrɔyzəl], m -s/- crumble. ◆'S~**kuchen**, m yeast cake with crumble.

Strich [ʃtriç], m -(e)s/-e 1. (Linie) line; (Gedankens.) dash; stroke (of the pen etc.); F: S. **drunter!** let's forget it! F: es **geht** (mir) **gegen den S.**, it goes against the grain. 3. F: **auf den S. gehen**, to walk the streets. ◆'s~**weise**, adv. S. **Regen**, rain in places.

Strick [ʃtrik]. I. m -(e)s/-e cord, (Seil) rope. II. 'S~, comb.fm. (a) knitting (needle, machine etc.); (b) (gestrickt) knitted (dress etc.). ◆'s~**en**, v.tr. & i. (haben) to knit (a pullover etc.). ◆'S~**jacke**, f cardigan. ◆'S~**leiter**, f rope ladder.

Striemen ['ʃtriːmən], m -s/- weal.

strikt [ʃtrikt], adj. strict (orders etc.), severe (measures etc.).

strittig ['ʃtritiç], adj. contentious; s~**er Punkt**, point at issue.

Stroh [ʃtroː], n -(e)s/no pl straw. ◆'S~**blume**, f everlasting flower. ◆'S~**dach**, n thatched roof. ◆'S~**halm**, m (a) blade of straw; (b) (drinking) straw. ◆'S~**hut**, m straw hat. ◆'S~**mann**, m -(e)s/-er dummy;

Fig: front man. ◆'S~**witwe(r)**, f (m) F: grass widow(er).

Strolch [ʃtrɔlç], m -(e)s/-e (a) Pej: tramp, N.Am: bum; (b) F: (Kind) rascal.

Strom [ʃtroːm]. I. m -(e)s/-e (a) (large) river; (b) stream (of blood, Fig: people etc.); **es goß in S~en**, it poured with rain. 2. (Strömung) current. 3. no pl El: current; (Elektrizität) electricity; **unter S. stehen**, to be live. II. 'S~, comb.fm. electricity (bill, consumption etc.); power (cable, source etc.); electric (cable etc.). ◆'s~**abwärts**, adv. downstream. ◆'s~**aufwärts**, adv. upstream. ◆'s~**linienförmig**, adj. streamlined.

ström|en ['ʃtrøːmən], v.i. (sein) (Wasser, Fig: Menschen usw.) to stream, pour. ◆'S~**ung**, f -/-en (a) current (in water/air); (b) Art: Pol: etc: movement; (Tendenz) trend.

Strophe ['ʃtroːfə], f -/-n verse (of a poem etc.).

strotzen ['ʃtrɔtsən], v.i. (haben) **vor Energie usw. s.**, to be full of/bursting with energy etc.

Strudel ['ʃtruːdəl], m -s/- 1. whirlpool; Fig: whirl (of events etc.). 2. Cu: strudel.

Struk|tur [ʃtrukˈtuːr], f -/-en structure. ◆s~**turell** [-uˈrɛl], adj. structural.

Strumpf [ʃtrumpf], m -(e)s/-e stocking. ◆'S~**band**, n garter. ◆'S~**hose**, f tights.

Strunk [ʃtruŋk], m -(e)s/-e stalk; (Baums.) stump.

struppig ['ʃtrupiç], adj. shaggy.

Stube ['ʃtuːbə], f -/-n room. ◆'S~**narrest**, m F: (Kind usw.) S. **haben**, to be confined to one's room. ◆'S~**nhocker**, m F: stay-at-home. ◆'s~**nrein**, adj. house-trained.

Stuck [ʃtuk], m -s/no pl stucco.

Stück [ʃtyk], n -(e)s/-e 1. piece; S. **Papier/Kuchen**, piece of paper/cake; (Wurst, Käse usw.) **am/im S.**, in a piece, unsliced; **fünf Mark pro/das S.**, five marks apiece/each; **im S.**, **aus dem Buch**, a passage from the book; S. **für S.**, bit by bit; (eins nach dem anderen) one by one; Fig: **aus freien S~en**, voluntarily; F: **das ist ein starkes S.!** that's going too far! what a cheek! 2. (a) Th: play; (b) Mus: piece. 3. (Gegenstand) item; **mein bestes S.**, my most precious possession; ◆'S~**arbeit**, f piecework. ◆'S~**chen**, n -s/- little bit; scrap (of paper etc.). ◆'S~**lohn**, m piece rate. ◆'S~**preis**, m unit price. ◆'s~**weise**, adv. one by one; individually; (nach und nach) bit by bit. ◆'S~**werk**, n S. **sein/bleiben**, to remain fragmentary.

Student|(in) [ʃtuˈdɛnt(in)], m -en/-en (f /-nen) student. ◆S~**(en)heim**, n student hostel. ◆s~**isch**, adj. student (customs etc.).

Stud|ie ['ʃtuːdiə], f -/-n (a) study; (b) Art:

sketch, study. ◆s~ieren [-'di:rən], v. 1. v.tr. to study (sth.). 2. v.i. (haben) to study; to be a student/at university. ◆S~ierzimmer, n study.

Studio ['ftudio], n -s/-s studio.

Studium ['ftudium], n -s/-ien course of study, studies.

Stuf|e ['ftu:fə], f -/-n 1. step; (im Hause) stair. 2. stage of a rocket, Fig: development etc.); (Niveau) level. ◆'s~en, v.tr. (a) to terrace (a slope etc.); (b) to grade (wages etc.). ◆'s~enleiter, f Stepladder; Fig: hierarchy. ◆'s~enlos, adj. Tchn: infinitely variable. ◆'s~enweise, adv. step by step, in stages.

Stuhl [ftu:l], m -(e)s/-e chair. ◆'S~gang, m movement of the bowels.

stülpen ['ftylpən], v.tr. etwas nach oben/innen/außen/unten s~, to turn sth. up/in/out/down.

stumm [ftum], adj. dumb (person); (schweigend) silent (person, prayer etc.). ◆'S~film, m silent film.

Stummel ['ftuməl], m -s/- stump, stub; (Zigarettens.) (cigarette) butt.

Stümper ['ftympər], m -s/- bungler, botcher. ◆S~ei [-'rai], f -/-en bungled job/coll. work. ◆'s~haft, adj. botched, bungled (job etc.).

Stumpf¹ [ftumpf], m -(e)s/-e stump.

stumpf², adj. (a) blunt (knife, pencil etc.); Mth: truncated (cone, pyramid); s~er Winkel, obtuse angle; (b) (glanzlos) matt, dull (surface, colour etc.); Fig: apathetic, impassive (look etc.). ◆'S~heit, f -/no pl bluntness; dullness; Fig: apathy. ◆'S~sinn, m (a) (Zustand) apathy; (b) dullness (of a job etc.). ◆'s~sinnig, adj. a) apathetic (person, behaviour etc.); b) soul-destroying (job etc.).

Stund|e ['ftundə], f -/-n 1. hour; zu später S., at a late hour; bis zur S., until now. 2. Sch: lesson, period. ◆'s~en, v.tr. j-m einen Betrag, die Miete usw. s., to give s.o. time to pay a sum, the rent etc. ◆'S~engeschwindigkeit, f average speed (in k.p.h.). ◆'S~enkilometer, mpl 40 S., 40 kilometres per hour/abbr. k.p.h. ◆'S~enlang, adj. lasting for hours; s. warten, to wait for hours. ◆'S~enlohn, m hourly wage rate. ◆'s~enplan, m timetable.

stündlich ['ftyntliç], adj. hourly; sich s. verändern, to change from hour to hour.

stupid(e) [ftu'pi:t(-də)], adj. Pej: pointless, soul-destroying (work etc.).

Stups [ftups], m -es/-e F: nudge, jog. ◆'s~en, v.tr. to nudge, jog (s.o.). ◆'S~nase, f F: snub nose.

stur [ftu:r], adj. F:Pej: dour; (unnachgiebig) pig-headed, stubborn (person). ◆'S~heit, f -/no pl F:Pej: pig-headedness.

Sturm [fturm], I. m -(e)s/-e 1. storm; (Wind) gale. 2. Mil: no pl assault, storming (auf + acc., of). II. 'S~, comb.fm. storm (damage etc.); stormy (night, weather etc.); Nau: gale (warning etc.). ◆'S~angriff, m assault; storming. ◆'S~flut, f storm tide. ◆'S~schritt, m im S., at the double.

stürm|en ['ftyrmən], v. 1. v.tr. Mil: to storm (a fortress etc.); Fig: to besiege (a shop etc.). 2. v.i. a) (haben) (Wind) to blow hard; es stürmt, there is a gale blowing; (b) (sein) er stürmte ins Zimmer, he stormed/rushed into the room. ◆'S~er, m -s/- Fb: etc: forward, striker. ◆'s~isch, adj. a) stormy (sea, weather etc.); rough (sea, crossing etc.); Fig: turbulent (time); (b) (lautstark) tumultuous (applause etc.); vociferous, vehement (protest etc.).

Sturz [fturts], m -es/-e fall; (in die Tiefe) plunge; Fig: collapse, fall (of a government etc.). ◆'S~flug, m nose-dive. ◆'S~flut, f torrent. ◆'S~helm, m crash helmet.

stürzen ['ftyrtsən], v. 1. v.i. (sein) (a) to fall; Lit: (in die Tiefe) to plunge, plummet; Fig: (Regierung usw.) to collapse, fall; (Preise usw.) to drop sharply, slump; (b) (Pers.) (eilen) to rush, dash. 2. v.tr. (a) (werfen) to hurl (s.o., sth.); to plunge (s.o., sth.); sich auf j-n s., to pounce on s.o.; (b) to bring down, (durch Gewalt) overthrow (a government etc.).

Stute ['ftu:tə], f -/-n mare.

stutz|en ['ftutsən], v. 1. v.tr. to trim, clip (a beard, hedge etc.), prune, lop (a tree, bush), dock (a dog's tail). 2. v.i. (haben) to stop (short). ◆'s~ig, adj. da wurde ich s., I became suspicious.

Stütz- ['ftyts-], comb.fm. Tchn: supporting (beam, wall, bar etc.). ◆'S~e, f -/-n support, prop; Fig: (Pers.) mainstay (of the family etc.); (Hilfe) helper. ◆'s~en, v.tr. to support, (stärker) brace (sth.); sich auf etwas acc s., (Pers.) to lean on sth. ◆'S~punkt, m Mil: etc: base.

Subjekt [zup'jɛkt], n -(e)s/-e subject. ◆s~iv [-'ti:f], adj. subjective.

Substantiv ['zupstanti:f], n -s/-e noun.

Substanz [zup'stants], f -/-en substance.

subtil [zup'ti:l], adj. subtle (distinction etc.), refined (methods). ◆S~ität [-tili'tɛ:t], f -/no pl subtlety.

subtrahieren [zuptra'hi:rən], v.tr. to subtract (a number).

Subvention [zupvɛntsi'o:n], f -/-en subsidy, grant. ◆s~ieren [-o'ni:rən], v.tr. to subsidize (theatres etc.). ◆S~ierung, f no pl subsidization.

subversiv [zupvɛr'zi:f], adj. subversive (elements etc.).

Such|aktion ['zu:x²aktsio:n], f -/-n (large-scale) search. ◆'S~e, f -/no pl search (nach + dat, for). ◆'s~en, v. 1. v.tr. a) to look/(angestrengt) search for (sth.); (Polizei) to hunt for (a criminal);

to seek (shelter, protection, advice etc.); **Verkäuferin gesucht**, sales lady wanted. **2.** v.i. (haben) to search, look (**nach j-m, etwas** dat, for s.o., sth.). ◆'**S~er**, m -s/- Phot: viewfinder. ◆'**S~trupp**, n search party.

Sucht [zuxt], f -/-e addiction (**nach** + dat, to); Fig: **S. nach Erfolg**, craving for success.

süchtig ['zyçtiç], adj. addicted (**nach** + dat, to); **ein S~er/eine S~e**, an addict.

Süd [zy:t]. **I.** m south; **aus/von S.**, from the south. **II.** '**S~-**, s~-, comb.fm. (a) south (coast, side, bank, wind etc.); Geog: South (Africa, America, Germany, Pole etc.); (b) (südlich) southern (frontier, edge, shore etc.); Geog: Southern (Italy etc.). ◆**S~afri'kaner(in)** m(f)/ **s~afri'kanisch**, adj. South African. ◆**S~en** ['zy:dən], m -s/no pl south; **nach S.**, southwards. ◆'**S~früchte**, fpl tropical fruit. ◆'s~ländisch, adj. mediterranean (climate etc.); Latin (temperament etc.). ◆'s~lich. **I.** adj. (a) southern (border, hemisphere, region etc.); southerly (wind, direction etc); (b) adv. **s. von München**, south of Munich. **II.** prep. + gen **s. der Alpen**, (to the) south of the Alps. ◆'**S~'ost(en)**, m south-east. ◆'s~'östlich. **I.** adj. south-eastern (district etc.); southeasterly (wind, direction). **II.** prep. + gen **s. der Stadt**, (to the) south-east of the town. ◆'**S~'west(en)**, m south-west. ◆'s~'westlich. **I.** adj. south-western (district etc.); south-westerly (wind, direction). **II.** prep. + gen **s. der Stadt**, (to the) south-west of the town.

Sudan [zu'dɑ:n]. Pr.n.m **-s. der S.**, the Sudan. ◆s~esisch, adj. Sudanese.

süffig ['zyfiç], adj. F: very drinkable, (wine) which goes down well.

süffisant [zyfi'zant], adj. smug, complacent.

suggerieren [zuge'ri:rən], v.tr. **j-m etwas s.**, to put sth. into s.o.'s head. ◆**S~stion** [-gɛsti'o:n], f -/-en insinuation, suggestion; (Überredung) hidden persuasion. ◆s~stiv [-'ti:f], adj. suggestive (power); insinuating (remark etc.).

Sühne ['zy:nə], f -/no pl Lit: atonement; (Strafe) penalty. ◆s~en, v.tr. & i. (haben) Lit: to atone, pay the penalty for a crime etc.).

Sultan ['zulta:n], m -s/-e sultan. ◆S~ine [-a'ni:nə], f -/-n sultana (raisin).

Sülze ['zyltsə], f -/-n brawn.

Summe ['zumə], f -/-n sum.

summen ['zumən], v. **1.** v.tr. to hum (a melody etc.). **2.** v.i. (haben) to hum; (Biene usw.) to buzz.

summieren [zu'mi:rən], v.tr. to add up (numbers etc.); **sich s.**, to accumulate, add up (to quite a lot).

Sumpf [zumpf], m -(e)s/-e swamp, bog. ◆'s~ig, adj. boggy, marshy.

Sund [zunt], m -(e)s/-e sound, straits.

Sünde ['zyndə], f -/-n sin. ◆'**S~enbock**, m scapegoat. ◆'**S~er(in)**, m -s/(f -/-nen) sinner. ◆'s~haft, adj. sinful (thoughts, life etc.); F: **s. teuer**, frightfully expensive. ◆'s~ig, adj. sinful. ◆'s~igen, v.i. (haben) to sin.

Super ['zu:pər], n -s/no pl F: super (petrol). ◆**S~lativ** ['zu:pərlati:f], m -s/-e superlative. ◆'**S~markt**, m supermarket.

Suppe ['zupə], f -/-n soup. ◆'**S~ngrün**, n (bunch of) soup-flavouring vegetables and herbs. ◆'**S~nhuhn**, n boiling fowl. ◆'**S~nwürfel**, m stock cube.

Surfbrett ['sə:fbret], n -(e)s/-er surfboard.

Surrealismus [zurea'lismus], m -/no pl Art: Surrealism. ◆s~istisch, adj. surrealist (picture etc.).

surren ['zurən], v.i. (sein) **durch die Luft s.**, (Insekt usw.) to buzz/(Kugel) whizz through the air.

suspekt [zus'pekt], adj. suspect.

süß [zy:s], adj. sweet. ◆'**S~e**, f -/no pl sweetness. ◆'s~en, v.tr. to sweeten (dishes, drinks etc.). ◆'**S~igkeiten**, fpl sweets, N.Am: candy. ◆'s~lich, adj. sickly, cloying (taste, Fig: smile etc.). ◆'**S~speise**, f sweet (dish), pudding. ◆'**S~stoff**, m sweetener. ◆'**S~waren**, fpl confectionery. ◆'**S~wasser**, n freshwater.

Sylvester [zyl'vestər], n -s/no pl = Silvester.

Symbol [zym'bo:l], n -s/-e symbol. ◆s~isch, adj. symbolic. ◆s~isieren [-oli'zi:rən], v.tr. to symbolize (sth.).

symmetrisch [zy'me:triʃ], adj. symmetrical.

Sympathie [zympa'ti:], f -/-n sympathy. ◆**S~isant** [-ti'zant], m -en/-en Pol: etc: sympathizer. ◆s~isch [-'pa:tiʃ], adj. congenial, likeable (person etc.); **er ist mir s.**, I like him. ◆s~isieren [-pati'zi:rən], v.i. (haben) **mit j-m s.**, to sympathize with s.o.

Symphonie [zymfo'ni:], f -/-n Mus: symphony. ◆s~isch [-'fo:niʃ], adj. symphonic (poem etc.).

Symptom [zymp'to:m], n -s/-e Med: etc: symptom; Fig: (Anzeichen) sign, indication. ◆s~atisch [-o'ma:tiʃ], adj. symptomatic, indicative (**für etwas** acc, of sth.).

Synagoge [zyna'go:gə], f synagogue.

synchron [zyn'kro:n], adj. /**S~-**, comb.fm. synchronous (movements, motor etc.). ◆s~isieren [-oni'zi:rən], v.tr. to synchronize (movements etc.); to dub (a film).

Syndikat [zyndi'ka:t], n -(e)s/-e syndicate.

Syndrom [zyn'dro:m], n -s/-e syndrome.

Synode [zyn'o:də], f -/-n synod.

Synonym [zyno'ny:m]. I. *n* -s/-e synonym. II. *s.*, *adj.* synonymous (word etc.).

Syntax ['zyntaks], *f -/no pl* syntax.

synthetisch [zyn'te:tiʃ], *adj.* synthetic; artificial (flavour etc.); man-made (fibres etc.).

Syphilis ['zyfilis], *f -/no pl* syphilis.

Syrien ['zy:riən]. *Pr.n.n* -s. *Geog:* Syria.

S~(i)er(in), *m -s/- (f /-nen)* Syrian. ◆**s~isch**, *adj.* Syrian.

System [zys'te:m], *n* -s/-e system. ◆**S~atisch** [-e'ma:tiʃ], *adj.* systematic, methodical.

Szene ['stse:nə], *f* -/-n scene. ◆**S~e'rie**, *f* -/-n scenery (*Schauplatz*) setting. ◆**s~isch**, *adj. Th:* with regard to the scenery/setting.

T

T, t [te:], *n* -/- (the letter) T, t.

Tabak ['ta(:)bak], *m* -s/-e tobacco. ◆**T~laden**, *m* tobacconist's (shop). ◆**T~sbeutel**, *m* tobacco pouch. ◆**T~sdose**, *f* tobacco tin. ◆**T~waren**, *pl* tobacco products.

tabellarisch [tabe'la:riʃ], *adj.* tabulated; *adv.* in tabular form. ◆**T~e** [ta'belə], *f* -/-n table (of contents, statistics etc.). ◆**T~enführer**, *m* league leaders.

Tablett [ta'blɛt], *n* -(e)s/-s & *-e* tray. ◆**T~e** [ta'blɛtə], *f* -/-n tablet, pill.

tabu [ta'bu:]. I. *adj.* taboo. II. T., *n* -s/-s taboo.

Tacho ['taxo], *m* -s/-s *Aut: F:* speedo. ◆**T~meter**, *m* speedometer.

Tadel ['ta:dəl], *m* -s/- reproach, (*Verweis*) rebuke; (*Kritik*) censure, criticism. ◆**t~los**, *adj.* perfect (accent, *Cl:* fit etc.); impeccable, irreproachable (behaviour etc.). ◆**t~n**, *v.tr.* to reproach, (*scharf*) rebuke, reprimand (s.o.). ◆**t~nswert** *adj.* reprehensible.

Tafel ['ta:fəl]. I. *f* -/-n 1. (wooden) board, panel; (stone) slab; (*Gedenkt.*) (memorial) tablet, plaque; (*Anzeiget.*) notice board; (*Schild*) sign; *Sch:* blackboard; *El:* (*Schalt.*) control panel; eine T. Schokolade, a bar of chocolate. 2. (*Bild*) plate. 3. A: & *Lit:* (*Tisch*) table. II. T~-, *comb.fm.* table (salt, silver, wine etc.). ◆**t~n**, *v.i.* (*haben*) to dine/(*üppig*) feast. ◆**T~wasser**, *n* mineral/table water.

täfeln ['tɛ:fəln], *v.tr.* to panel (a wall, ceiling). ◆**T~(e)lung**, *f* -/-en panelling.

Taft [taft], *m* -(e)s/-e taffeta.

Tag [ta:k], *m* -(e)s/-e day; **am/bei T~e**, in the daytime; **am (hellichten) T~e**, in (broad) daylight; **es wird schon T.**, it is getting light; **etwas an den T. bringen**, to bring sth. to light; **Interesse, Eifer usw. an den T. legen**, to display interest, eagerness etc.; *Min:* **über/unter T~e**, above/below ground; **eines T~es**, one day; **T. für T.**, daily, every day; **(guten) T.!** good morning/afternoon! *F:* hello! *N.Am:* hi! (*bei Vorstellung*) how do you do? ◆**t~aus**, *adv.* t., **tagein**, day in, day out. ◆**T~ebuch**, *n* diary; *Lit:* journal. ◆**T~edieb**, *m* lazybones, loafer. ◆**T~egeld**, *n* daily allowance.

◆**t~elang**, *adj.* lasting for days; *adv.* for days (on end). ◆**t~en**, *v.i.* (*haben*) (*a*) (*Konferenz*) to meet; (*Gericht usw.*) to sit; (*b*) *Lit:* **es tagt, the day is dawning/ breaking. ◆**T~es-**, *comb.fm.* (events, politics, news, *Mil:* order etc.) of the day; day's (work, march, journey etc.). ◆**T~esanbruch, m bei T., at day-break. ◆**T~eskarte**, *f* (*a*) day ticket; (*b*) menu for the day. ◆**T~eslicht**, *n* daylight; **ans T. kommen**, to come to light. ◆**T~esmutter**, *f* child minder. ◆**T~esordnung**, *f* agenda. ◆**T~eszeit**, *f* time of (the) day. ◆**T~eszeitung**, *f* daily newspaper. ◆**t~'hell**, *adj.* as bright as day. ◆**t~s**, *adv.* t. **darauf/zuvor**, the day after/before; the next/previous day. ◆**T~schicht**, *f* day shift. ◆**t~süber**, *adv.* during the day. ◆**T~ung**, *f* -/-en conference.

täglich ['tɛ:klɪç], *adj.* daily; **dreimal t.**, three times a day.

Taifun [tai'fu:n], *m* -s/-e typhoon.

Taille ['taljə], *f* -/-n waist. ◆**t~iert** [ta'ji:rt], *adj. Cl:* close-fitting at the waist; fully fashioned (shirt etc.).

Takel ['ta:kəl], *n* -s/- *Nau:* tackle. ◆**T~age** [taka'la:ʒə], *f* -/-n *Nau:* rigging. ◆**t~n**, *v.tr.* to rig (a ship).

Takt [takt], *m* -(e)s/-e 1. *Mus:* time; rhythm (of a waltz etc.). 2. *no pl* tact, tactfulness. ◆**T~gefühl**, *n* (sense of) tact. ◆**t~los**, *adj.* tactless. ◆**T~losigkeit**, *f* -/-en *no pl* tactlessness. 2. tactless act, indiscretion. ◆**T~stock**, *m* (conductor's) baton. ◆**t~voll**, *adj.* tactful.

Taktik ['taktɪk], *f* -/-en *Mil: etc:* tactics. ◆**t~isch**, *adj.* tactical.

Tal [ta:l], *n* -(e)s/-er valley. ◆**T~fahrt**, *f* downhill trip/(*Ski*) run; descent. ◆**T~kessel**, *m* valley basin. ◆**T~sohle**, *f* valley floor/bottom. ◆**T~sperre**, *f* dam.

Talar [ta'la:r], *m* -s/-e gown; *Jur:* robe.

Talent [ta'lɛnt], *n* -(e)s/-e talent; **er ist ein großes T.**, he is extremely talented. ◆**t~iert** [-'ti:rt], *adj.* talented, gifted.

Talg [talk], *m* -(e)s/-e tallow; *Cu:* suet.

Talisman ['ta:lisman], *m* -s/-e talisman.

Tamburin [tambu'ri:n], *n* -s/-e tambourine.

Tampon ['tampɔn], *m* -s/-s tampon.

Tandem ['tandɛm], *n* -s/-s tandem.

Tang [taŋ], *m* -(e)s/-e seaweed.

Tang|ente [taŋ'gɛntə], *f* -/-n 1. tangent. 2. (*Straße*) by-pass, ring road. ◆t~ieren [-'gi:rən], *v.tr.* (*a*) *Mth:* to form a tangent to (a curve etc.); (*b*) to affect (s.o.).

Tango ['tango], *m* -s/-s tango.

Tank [taŋk], *m* -s/-s tank. ◆t~en ['taŋkən], *v.* 1. *v.i.* (*haben*) to refuel, fill up. 2. *v.tr. Benzin usw.* t., to fill up with petrol etc. ◆T~er, *m* -s/- tanker. ◆T~stelle, *f* filling station; *N.Am:* gas station. ◆T~wart, *m* pump attendant.

Tann|e ['tanə], *f* -/-n fir (tree). ◆T~enbaum, *m* fir tree. ◆T~enzapfen, *m* fir cone.

Tante ['tantə], *f* -/-n aunt.

Tanz [tants]. I. *m* -es/-e dance. II. 'T~-, *comb.fm.* dance (music, orchestra, step etc.); dancing (song, partner, school etc.). ◆'T~boden, *m* dance floor. ◆t~en, *v.tr. & i.* (*haben*) to dance. ◆'T~lokal, *n* dance hall. ◆'T~saal, *m* ballroom. ◆'T~stunde, *f* dancing lesson.

Tänzer(in) ['tɛntsər(in)], *m* -s/- (*f* -/-nen) dancer.

Tapete [ta'pe:tə], *f* -/-n wallpaper. ◆T~nwechsel, *m* F: change of scenery.

tapezier|en [tape'tsi:rən], *v.tr.* to (wall)paper (a room etc.). ◆T~er, *m* -s/- paperhanger. ◆T~tisch, *m* (paperhanger's) trestle table.

tapfer ['tapfər], *adj.* brave; (*kühn*) bold. ◆'T~keit, *f* -/*no pl* bravery, boldness.

tappen ['tapən], *v.i.* (*sein*) to blunder, stumble; (*im Dunkeln*) to grope one's way.

täppisch ['tɛpiʃ], *adj.* awkward, clumsy.

Tarif [ta'ri:f], *m* -s/-e (*a*) (*Gebühr*) rate; charge; (*b*) (*Verzeichnis*) tariff; table of (fixed) charges; (*c*) *Ind:* (wage/salary) scale. ◆T~lohn, *m* standard wage(s). ◆T~verhandlungen, *fpl* collective bargaining. ◆T~vertrag, *m* (collective) wage agreement.

Tarn- ['tarn-], *comb.fm. esp. Mil:* camouflage (paint, net etc.). ◆'t~en, *v.tr.* to camouflage (sth.); *Fig:* to disguise (s.o., oneself). ◆'T~ung, *f* -/-en camouflage; disguise.

Tasche ['taʃə], *f* -/-n 1. pocket. 2. (*zum Tragen*) bag. ◆'T~n-, *comb.fm.* pocket (lighter, dictionary etc.). ◆'T~nbuch, *n* paperback (book). ◆'T~ndieb(in), *m* (*f*) pickpocket. ◆'T~ngeld, *n* pocket money. ◆'T~nlampe, *f* (electric) torch, *N.Am:* flashlight. ◆'T~nmesser, *n* penknife. ◆'T~nrechner, *m* pocket calculator. ◆'T~nspieler, *m* conjurer, juggler. ◆'T~ntuch, *n* handkerchief.

Tasse ['tasə], *f* -/-n cup.

Tast|atur [tasta'tu:r], *f* -/-en keyboard.

◆'T~e, *f* -/-n (piano, typewriter etc.) key; (*Druckt.*) push-button. ◆'t~en, *v.* 1. *v.i.* (*haben*) to feel; **nach dem Lichtschalter usw.** t., to feel/grope for the light switch etc. 2. *v.tr.* to feel (sth.), examine (sth.) by touch. ◆'T~entelefon, *n* push-button telephone. ◆'T~sinn, *m* sense of touch.

Tat [ta:t], *f* -/-en action; *esp. Lit:* deed. ◆'T~bestand, *m* facts of the case; (*Sachlage*) state of affairs. ◆t~enlos, *adj.* inactive, idle; *adv.* without doing anything. ◆'T~kraft, *f* energy, vigour. ◆t~kräftig, *adj.* energetic, active. ◆'T~ort, *m* scene (*esp. Jur:* of the crime). ◆'T~sache, *f* fact. ◆t~sächlich ['-zɛçliç], *adj.* (*a*) real (reason, circumstances etc.); actual (time, costs etc.); (*b*) *adv.* actually, really. ◆'T~verdacht, *m* suspicion (of having committed a crime).

Tät|er ['tɛ:tər], *m* -s/- culprit; **die T.**, those responsible. ◆'t~ig, *adj.* (*a*) active (person, volcano, co-operation etc.); (*b*) **als Lehrer t. sein**, to work as a teacher etc. ◆'T~igkeit, *f* -/-en (*a*) activity; (*Beschäftigung*) occupation; (*Beruf*) profession, job; (*Arbeit*) work; (*b*) *no pl* in/außer T., in/out of operation. ◆'T~igkeitsbereich, *m* field/sphere of activity. ◆'t~lich, *adj.* violent, physical (assault etc.); *Jur:* t~licher Angriff, assault (and battery). ◆'T~lichkeiten, *fpl* violence.

tätowier|en [tɛto'vi:rən], *v.tr.* to tattoo (s.o.). ◆'T~ung, *f* -/-en tattooing; (*Bild*) tattoo.

tatt(e)rig ['tat(ə)riç], *adj. F:* shaky, trembling (hand etc.); doddery (old man etc.).

Tatze ['tatsə], *f* -/-n paw.

Tau¹ [tau], *n* -(e)s/-e *esp. Nau:* (heavy) rope, hawser. ◆T~ziehen, *n* -s/*no pl* tug-of-war.

Tau², *m* -(e)s/*no pl* dew. ◆'t~en, *v.tr. & i.* (*haben/sein*) to thaw, melt (snow etc.). ◆'t~frisch, *adj.* dewy, fresh (as the dew). ◆'T~tropfen, *m* dewdrop. ◆'T~wetter, *n* thaw.

taub [taup], *adj.* 1. deaf (**auf einem Ohr**, in one ear); **die T~en**, the deaf. 2. (*ohne Empfinden*) numb (**vor Kälte**, with cold); **mein Fuß ist t.**, my foot has gone to sleep. 3. empty (nut, ear of grain). ◆'T~heit, *f* -/*no pl* 1. deafness. 2. numbness. ◆t~stumm, *adj.* deaf and dumb; **ein T~stummer/eine T~stumme**, a deaf-mute.

Taube ['taubə], *f* -/-n 1. pigeon, dove. 2. *Fig:* (*Pers.*) dove. ◆T~nschlag, *m* dovecote.

Tauch|boot ['tauxbo:t], *n* submarine (for short dives). ◆t~en ['tauxən]. I. *v.* 1. *v.i.* (*haben/sein*) (*a*) to dive; (*im Flug*) to dip. 2. *v.tr.* (*kurz*) to dip (s.o., sth.); (*auf länger*) to immerse, steep (sth.). II. T., *n* -s/*no pl* diving. ◆'T~er, *m* -s/-

diver. ◆'T~er-, comb.fm. diver's (suit, helmet etc.); diving (bell etc.). ◆'T~sieder, m -s/- (small) coil immersion heater.

Tauf|becken ['taufbɛkən], n font. ◆'T~e, f /-n baptism, Ecc: christening. ◆'t~en, v.tr. (a) to baptize, Ecc: christen (s.o.); (b) (nennen) to name (a dog, ship etc.). ◆'T~name, m Christian/N.Am: given name. ◆'T~pate, m godfather. ◆'T~patin, f godmother. ◆'T~schein, m certificate of baptism. ◆'T~zeuge, m godparent.

taug|en ['taugən], v.i. (haben) zu etwas t., to be good/of use, useful; wenig/nichts t., to be little/no use; zu etwas dat t., to be suitable for sth. ◆'T~enichts, m -(e)s/-e good-for-nothing. ◆'t~lich ['tauklɪç], adj. useful, suitable (zu + dat, for); Mil: fit (for service). ◆'T~lichkeit, f -/no pl usefulness, suitability; Mil: fitness.

Taum|el ['taumǝl], m -s/no pl (feeling of) giddiness; (Benommenheit) grogginess; (Rausch) ecstasy, rapture. ◆'t~eln, v.i. (haben/sein) (a) to reel, totter; (b) (Falter) to flutter.

Tausch [tauʃ], m -(e)s/-e exchange. ◆'t~en, v. 1. v.tr. to exchange (sth.) (für/gegen etwas acc, for sth.). 2. v.i. (haben) to swap. ◆'T~geschäft, n exchange (transaction). ◆'T~handel, m barter.

täusch|en ['tɔyʃən], v. 1. v.tr. (a) to deceive (s.o., oneself); sich t., to delude oneself/(sich irren) be mistaken/wrong; ich habe mich in ihm getäuscht, I am disappointed in him. 2. v.i. (haben) der Schein täuscht, appearances are deceptive. ◆'t~end, adj. deceptive (appearance); sie sehen sich t. ähnlich, one can hardly tell them apart. ◆'T~ung, f /-en f deception. 2. (Sinnest.) illusion; optische t., optical illusion. ◆'T~ungsmanöver, n diversion.

tausend ['tauzənt], num. adj. a/one thousand; T~e von Menschen, thousands of people. ◆'t~er, m -s/- F: (Schein) thousand mark note. ◆'t~fach, adj. a thousandfold; adv. in a thousand different ways; (tausendmal) a thousand times. ◆'T~füßler, m -s/- centipede. ◆'t~'mal, adv. a thousand times. ◆'t~ste(r,s), num.adj. thousandth. ◆'T~stel, n -s/- thousandth (part).

Tax|e ['taksə], f -/-n 1. (Gebühr) charge, fee; (Ortst.) tax. 2. = Taxi. ◆t~ieren [ta'ksiːrən], v.tr. to estimate (the value etc. of sth.).

Taxi ['taksi], n -s/-s taxi, N.Am: cab. ◆'T~fahrer, m taxi/N.Am: cab driver. ◆'T~stand, m taxi/N.Am: cab stand.

Teak [tiːm], n -s/no pl/'T~holz, n teak.

Team [tiːm], n -s/-s team.

Techn|ik ['tɛçnik], f -/-en 1. no pl (a) technology; (b) (Fach) engineering. 2. (a) (Methode) technique; (b) Tchn: (Aufbau)

mechanics, F: works (of a machine). ◆'T~iker(in), m -s/- (f /-nen) technician; (Ingenieur) engineer. ◆'t~isch, adj. technical; t. begabt, technically minded; with a technical flair. ◆'T~ologe [-o'loːgǝ], m -n/-n technologist. ◆'T~ologie [-olo'giː], f /-n technology. ◆t~o'logisch, adj. technological.

Tee [teː], m -s/-s tea. ◆'T~beutel, m teabag. ◆'T~kanne, f teapot. ◆'T~löffel, m teaspoon. ◆'T~sieb, n tea strainer. ◆'T~stunde, f teatime. ◆'T~tasse, f teacup. ◆'T~wagen, m tea trolley.

Teer [teːr], m -(e)s/-e tar. ◆'t~en, v.tr. to tar (a road etc.).

Teich [taiç], m -(e)s/-e pond.

Teig [taik], m -(e)s/-e dough; (Mürbt.) pastry. ◆'t~ig [-giç], adj. doughy; soggy (cake etc.). ◆'T~rolle, f rolling pin. ◆'T~waren, pl food.

Teil [tail]. I. m & n -(e)s/-e 1. (a) m part; der vierte/fünfte T. davon, a quarter/fifth of it; zum T., partly, to some extent; zum größten T., for the most part, mostly; in esp. Tchn: component, part. 2. (Anteil) share, portion; sein T. beitragen, to do one's bit. II. 'T~, ~-, comb.fm. partial (success, result, solution etc.); part (consignment etc.). ◆'T~bar, adj. divisible. ◆'T~bereich, m section. ◆'T~betrag, m part of an amount; (Rate) instalment. ◆'T~chen, n Ph: particle. ◆'t~en, v. 1. v.tr. (a) (trennen) to divide (sth.); sich t., to divide, separate; (Weg) to fork; (Gruppe) to split up; (Meinungen) to differ; 20 geteilt durch 5 ist 4, 20 divided by 5 is 4; (b) (teilhaben an) to share (a room, profits, Fig: opinion, feelings etc.); to divide, split (up) (the profit, booty etc.). 2. v.i. (haben) to share. ◆'t~haben, v.i.sep.irr.44 (haben) an etwas dat t., to participate/have a share in sth. ◆'t~haber(in), m -s/- (f /-nen) Com: partner. ◆'T~nahme, f -/no pl 1. participation (an + dat, in). 2. (Interesse) interest (an + dat, in); Lit: (Mitgefühl) sympathy. ◆'t~nahmslos, adj. indifferent, apathetic (person); expressionless (face). ◆'T~nahmslosigkeit, f -/no pl indifference; apathy. ◆'t~nehmen, v.i.sep.irr.69 (haben) (a) an etwas dat t., to take part in sth.; (b) an j-s Freude/Schmerz t., to share in s.o.'s joy/pain. ◆'T~nehmer, m -s/- participant; Sp: competitor; Tel: subscriber. ◆'t~s, adv. in part, partly; F: wie geht's? t., t., how are you? so-so. ◆'T~stück, n fragment. ◆'T~ung, f /-en division. ◆'t~weise, adj. partial; adv. partly; (da und dort) in places; (ab und zu) now and then. ◆'T~zahlung, f part payment; (Rate) instalment; etwas auf T. kaufen, to buy sth. on hire purchase. ◆'T~zeitbeschäftigung, f part-time job.

Teint [tɛ̃ː], *m* -s/-s complexion.

Telefon [tele'foːn], *n* -s/-e telephone; ◆**T~anruf**, *m* telephone call. ◆**T~at** [-'oːnaːt], *n* -(e)s/-e telephone call. ◆**T~buch**, *n* telephone directory. ◆**t~ieren** [-o'niːrən], *v.i.* (haben) to telephone, F: phone, make a phone call. ◆**t~isch**, *adj.* (enquiry etc.) on the telephone; **j-n t. benachrichtigen**, to inform s.o. by telephone. ◆**T~ist(in)** [-o'nist(in)], *m* -en/-en (*f* -/-nen) telephone operator; telephonist. ◆**T~nummer**, *f* telephone number. ◆**T~zelle**, *f* (tele)phone box. ◆**T~zentrale**, *f* telephone exchange.

Telegraf [tele'graːf], *m* -en/-en telegraph. ◆**T~enmast**, *m* telegraph pole. ◆**T~ie** [-a'fiː], *f* -/no pl telegraphy. ◆**t~ieren** [-'fiːrən], *v.i.* (haben) (j-m) t., to send (s.o.) a telegram/*nach Übersee* cable. ◆**t~isch** [-'graːfiʃ], *adj.* telegraphic (message, remittance etc.); (reply) by telegram.

Telegramm [tele'gram]. I. *n* -s/-e telegram, (*nach Übersee*) cable. II. **T~**, *comb.fm.* telegram (form etc.); telegraphic (address, style).

Teleobjektiv [ˈteːleʔɔpjɛktiːf], *n* telephoto lens.

Telepathie [telepa'tiː], *f* -/no pl telepathy. ◆**t~isch** [-'paːtiʃ], *adj.* telepathic.

Telephon [tele'foːn], *n* -s/-e = **Telefon**.

Teleskop [tele'skoːp], *n* -s/-e telescope.

Telex [ˈteːlɛks], *n* -/no pl telex.

Teller [ˈtɛlər], *m* -s/- plate. ◆**t~förmig**, *adj.* plate-shaped (disc etc.). ◆**T~wäscher**, *m* dishwasher.

Tempel [ˈtɛmpəl], *m* -s/- temple.

Temperament [tempera'mɛnt], *n* -(e)s/-e 1. (*Gemütsart*) temperament, disposition. 2. (a) (*Schwung*) vivacity, high spirits; (b) (*Leidenschaft*) fire. ◆**t~los**, *adj.* spiritless, phlegmatic. ◆**t~voll**, *adj.* spirited (feurig) fiery, hot-blooded; ardent (lover etc.).

Temperatur [tempera'tuːr], *f* -/-en temperature. ◆**T~abfall**, *m* drop in temperature. ◆**T~anstieg**, *m* rise in temperature. ◆**T~regler**, *m* thermostat.

Tempo [ˈtɛmpo], *n* -s/-s 1. speed; **ein gemächliches T.**, a leisurely pace. 2. pl **Tempi** *Mus:* tempo; **das T. angeben**, to beat/mark time; *Sp: etc:* to set the pace.

Tendenz [tɛn'dɛnts], *f* -/-en tendency; (*Neigung*) inclination; **allgemeine T.**, general trend. ◆**t~iell**, *adv.* in keeping with the trend. ◆**t~iös**, *adj.* tendentious; (politically etc.) biased.

Tender [ˈtɛndər], *m* -s/- tender.

tendieren [tɛn'diːrən], *v.i.* (haben) to tend, have a tendency; **nach rechts/links t.**, to have right-/leftwing leanings.

Tennis [ˈtɛnis]. I. *n* -/no pl (lawn) tennis. II. **T~**, *comb.fm.* tennis (ball, club, shoes, player etc.). ◆**T~platz**, *m* ten-

nis court. ◆**T~schläger**, *m* tennis racket.

Tenor [te'noːr], *m* -s/-e tenor.

Teppich [ˈtɛpɪç], *m* -s/-e carpet. ◆**T~boden**, *m* fitted carpet. ◆**T~klopfer**, *m* -s/- carpet beater.

Termin [tɛr'miːn]. I. *m* -s/-e date; (*Zeit*) time; (*beim Arzt usw.*) appointment. ◆**t~gemäß/t~gerecht**, *adj.* on time/schedule. ◆**t~ieren** [-i'niːrən], *v.tr.* to fix the date for (sth.). ◆**T~kalender**, *m* -s/- engagements book.

Terminologie [tɛrminolo'giː], *f* -/-n [-ən] terminology. ◆**T~us** [ˈtɛrminus], *m* -/-ni term, expression.

Termite [tɛr'miːtə], *f* -/-n termite, white ant.

Terpentin [tɛrpɛn'tiːn], *n* -s/no pl turpentine.

Terrain [tɛ'rɛ̃ː], *n* -s/-s *esp. Mil:* terrain; **T. gewinnen**, to gain ground.

Terrasse [tɛ'rasə], *f* -/-n terrace.

Terrier [ˈtɛrier], *m* -s/- terrier.

Terrine [tɛ'riːnə], *f* -/-n tureen.

Territorium [tɛri'toːrium], *n* -s/-rien territory.

Terror [ˈtɛrɔr]. I. *m* -s/no pl terrorism; (*also* **T~herrschaft** *f*) reign of terror; (*Druck*) intimidation. II. **T~**, *comb.fm.* terrorist (act, attack, methods etc.). ◆**t~isieren** [-i'ziːrən], *v.tr.* to terrorize (a community etc.). ◆**T~ismus** [-'rismus], *m* -/no pl terrorism. ◆**T~ist** [-'rist], *m* -en/-en terrorist. ◆**t~istisch**, *adj.* terrorist.

Tertia [ˈtɛrtsia], *f* -/-ien fourth and fifth years (in a *Gymnasium*).

Terz [tɛrts], *f* -/-en third.

Test [tɛst]. I. *m* -(e)s/-s & -e test. II. **T~**, *comb.fm.* test (picture, drive, flight, pilot etc.); trial (game etc.). ◆**t~en**, *v.tr.* to test (s.o., sth.). ◆**T~stopp**, *m* (atomic) test ban.

Testament [tɛsta'mɛnt], *n* -(e)s/-e 1. *Jur:* will. 2. **das Alte/Neue T.**, the Old/New Testament. ◆**t~arisch** [-'taːriʃ], *adj.* testamentary (legacy etc.). ◆**T~svollstrecker**, *m* executor.

Tetanus [ˈteːtanus], *m* -/no pl tetanus, lockjaw.

teuer [ˈtɔyər], *adj.* 1. expensive; (*wertvoll*) valuable; **wie t. ist dieser Stoff?** how much does this material cost? 2. *Lit:* (*lieb*) dear (friend etc.). ◆**T~ung**, *f* -/-en rise in prices.

Teufel [ˈtɔyfəl], *m* -s/- devil; *F: int.* **pfui T.!** ugh! how disgusting! **zum T.** (**nochmal**)! damn it all! **wer zum T. hat das gesagt?** who on earth said that? ◆**T~saustreibung** *f* exorcism. ◆**T~skerl**, *m* F: daredevil. ◆**T~skreis**, *m* vicious circle.

teuflisch [ˈtɔyfliʃ], *adj.* diabolical, devilish (plan etc.); fiendish (smile etc.).

Text [tɛkst], *m* -(e)s/-e (a) text; (*Stück.*) passage; (b) (*Bildt.*) caption; (c) *Mus:* words (of a song); (*Opernt.*) libretto.

◆**t~en** ['tɛkstən], v.tr. (a) Mus: to write lyrics; (b) (Werbung etc.) to write copy. ◆**T~er**, m -s/- (a) Mus: lyrics writer; (b) (Werbet. etc.) copywriter. ◆**T~stelle**, f passage.

Textil- [tɛks'tiːl-], comb.fm. textile (industry, worker). ◆**T~ien** [-'tiːliən], pl textiles.

Thailland ['tailant]. Pr.n. -s. Thailand. ◆**T~länder(in)**, m -s/- (f -/-nen) Thai (man/woman). ◆**t~ländisch**, adj. Thai.

Theater [te'aːtər]. I. n -s/- 1. theatre, N.Am: theater; T. spielen, to act. 2. (Getue) fuss. II. T~-, comb.fm. theatrical (agency, performance etc.); theatre (ticket, critic, programme etc.); drama (group, critic etc.). ◆**T~besucher**, m playgoer. ◆**T~kasse**, f theatre box office. ◆**T~stück**, n (stage) play.

theatralisch [tea'traːlɪʃ], adj. theatrical.

Theke ['teːkə], f -/-n bar; (Ladentisch) counter.

Thema ['teːma], n -s/-men & -mata (a) subject; (Gesprächst.) topic; (b) Mus: theme. ◆**t~atisch**, adj. with regard to the subject.

Themse ['tɛmzə]. Pr.n.f = die T., the (River) Thames.

Theologie [teo'loːgə], m -n/-n theologian. ◆**T~ie** [-o'giː], f -/-n [-ən] theology. ◆**t~isch**, adj. theological.

Theorletiker [teo'reːtikər], m -s/- theorist. ◆**t~etisch** [-'reːtiʃ], adj. theoretical. ◆**T~ie** [teo'riː], f -/-n [-ən] theory.

Therapleut(in) [tera'pɔyt(in)], m -en/-en (f -/-nen) therapist. ◆**t~eutisch**, adj. therapeutic. ◆**T~ie** [-'piː], f -/-n [-ən] therapy.

Therm|albad [tɛr'maːlbaːt], n thermal bath. 2. (Ort) thermal spa. ◆**T~ometer** [-o'meːtər], n thermometer. ◆**T~osflasche**, f R.t.m: thermos (flask). ◆**T~ostat** [-o'staːt], m -(e)s & -en/-e(n) thermostat.

These ['teːzə], f -/-n thesis.

Thrombose [trɔm'boːzə], f -/-n thrombosis.

Thron [troːn], m -(e)s/-e throne. ◆**t~en**, v.i. (haben) to sit in state. ◆**T~erbe**, m heir to the throne. ◆**T~folge**, f (line of) succession. ◆**T~folger(in)**, m -s/- (f -/-nen) successor to the throne.

Thunfisch ['tuːnfɪʃ], m tuna.

Thüringen ['tyːriŋən]. Pr.n.n -s. Thuringia. ◆**T~er(in)**, m -s/- (f -/-nen) Thuringian.

Thymian ['tyːmiaːn], m -s/-e thyme.

Tibet ['tiːbɛt]. Pr.n.n -s. Tibet. ◆**T~aner(in)** [tibe'taːnər(in)], m -s/- (f -/-nen) Tibetan.

Tick [tik], m -(e)s/-s F: quirk; einen T. haben, (i) to be a bit crazy; (ii) to have an obsession (mit + dat, about). ◆**t~en**, v.i. (haben) to tick.

tief [tiːf]. I. adj. 1. (a) deep (gorge, water,

roots, Fig: silence, sleep, voice etc.); zwei Meter t., two metres deep; t. atmen, to breathe deeply, take a deep breath; (b) (sehr stark) intense (hate, pain etc.); im t~sten Winter, in the depth of winter; bis t. in die Nacht, far into the night. 2. (niedrig) low (cloud, blow, Mus: note etc.); t. ausgeschnittenes Kleid, low-cut dress; Av: t. fliegen, to fly low. II. T., n -s/-s Meteor: depression. III. comb.fm. 1. T~-, (a) deep (drilling, ploughing etc.); (b) low (pressure, flying etc.). 2. t~-, adj. (a) deeply (offended, moved, felt etc.); (b) (Farben) deep (blue, red etc.). ◆**T~bau**, n civil engineering; underground and surface level construction. ◆**T~druckgebiet**, n Meteor: depression. ◆**T~e** ['tiːfə], f -/-n (a) depth; aus der T., from far below; (b) (Tiefgründigkeit) profundity, depth (of insight, thoughts etc.); (c) (Stärke) intensity (of love, pain etc.). ◆**T~ebene**, f lowland, low plain. ◆**T~enpsychologie**, f depth psychology. ◆**T~enschärfe**, f Phot: depth of focus. ◆**T~flug**, m low-level flight. ◆**T~gang**, m Nau: draught, N.Am: draft. ◆**T~garage**, f underground car park. ◆**t~greifend**, adj. far-reaching, radical (changes etc.); thorough (investigation etc.). ◆**t~gründig**, adj. profound (observation etc.). ◆**t~kühlen**, v.tr.sep. to (deep) freeze (fruit, vegetables etc.). ◆**T~kühlfach**, n freezer compartment. ◆**T~kühlkost**, f frozen food. ◆**T~kühltruhe**, f deepfreeze, chest freezer. ◆**T~land**, n lowland plain; pl lowlands. ◆**T~punkt**, m low (point); Fig: low ebb. ◆**T~schlag**, m blow below the belt. ◆**T~schürfend**, adj. penetrating, thorough-going. ◆**T~see**, f deep sea. ◆**T~sinn**, m profundity (of thought etc.). ◆**t~sinnig**, adj. (a) profound; (b) (grüblerisch) pensive. ◆**t~sitzend**, adj. deep-seated. ◆**T~st-**, comb.fm. lowest, minimum (price, temperature etc.). ◆**T~stand**, m (also Fig:) low watermark; Com:etc: low (point). ◆**t~stapeln**, v.i.sep. (haben) F: to understate a case.

Tiegel ['tiːgəl], m -s/- 1. Cu: shallow saucepan. 2. Tchn: crucible.

Tier [tiːr]. I. n -(e)s/-e animal. II. T~-, comb.fm. animal (book, story, world etc.); animals' (home etc.). ◆**T~arzt**, m veterinary surgeon, F: vet. ◆**T~freund**, m animal lover. ◆**T~garten**, m zoo. ◆**t~isch**, adj. (a) animal (fat, protein etc.); (b) Pej: bestial, brutal (behaviour etc.); (c) F: adv. t. ernst, deadly serious. ◆**T~kreiszeichen**, n sign of the zodiac. ◆**T~kunde**, f zoology. ◆**t~lieb**, adj. fond of animal. ◆**T~liebe**, f love of animals. ◆**T~park**, m (large) zoo. ◆**T~quälerei**, f cruelty to animals. ◆**T~-

reich, n animal kingdom. ◆'T~schutz-verein, m society for the prevention of cruelty to animals.

Tiger ['ti:gər], m -s/- tiger.

tilg|en ['tɪlgən], v.tr. (a) Fin: to pay off, repay (a debt etc.); (b) Lit: to eradicate, erase (a mistake etc.), obliterate, efface (memories); Fig: traces etc.); ◆'T~ung, f -/-en (a) Fin: repayment; (b) Lit: eradication, obliteration.

Tint|e ['tɪntə], f -/-n ink. ◆'T~enfisch, m squid; (Krake) octopus. ◆'T~enklecks, m ink blot. ◆'T~enstift, m indelible pencil.

Tip [tɪp], m -s/-s tip.

tipp|en¹ ['tɪpən], v.tr. & i. (haben) (a) j-m, j-n auf die Schulter t., to tap s.o. on the shoulder; (b) F: to type (sth.). ◆'T~fehler, m typing mistake.

tippen², v.i. (haben) (a) ich tippe darauf, daß ..., it's my guess that ...; (b) (wetten) to have a flutter; (im Toto) to fill in the pools. ◆'T~zettel, m lottery/ (Toto) pools coupon.

tipptopp ['tɪp'tɔp], adj. F: tip-top, spotless.

Tirol [ti'ro:l]. Pr.n.n -s. T., the Tyrol.

Tisch [tɪʃ]. I. m -(e)s/-e table; **am T. sitzen,** to sit at the table; F: es fiel unter den T., it went by the board; diese Sache muß vom T., this matter must be dealt with. II. 'T~, comb.fm. table (leg, lamp, manners etc.); (ledge etc.) of the table; (neighbour etc.) at table; dinner (guest etc.). ◆'T~decke, f tablecloth. ◆'T~ler, m -s/- joiner; (Kunstt.) cabinet-maker; (Baut.) carpenter. ◆'T~le'rei, f -/-en 1. no pl joinery; carpentry. 2. joiner's/carpenter's workshop. ◆'T~rede, f after-dinner speech. ◆'T~tennis, n table tennis.

Titel ['ti:təl]. I. m -s/- title. II. 'T~, comb.fm. title (figure, Th: role, Sp: holder etc.). ◆'T~bild, n frontispiece; cover picture (of a magazine). ◆'T~blatt, n title page. ◆'T~verteidiger, m defender of the title), defending champion.

Toast [to:st], m -(e)s/-e & -s 1. Cu: (piece of) toast. 2. (Trinkspruch) toast. ◆'t~en, v.tr. to toast (bread).

tob|en ['to:bən], v.i. (a) (haben) (Pers., Fig: Meer usw.) to rage; (Pers.) to rave, rant (gegen j-n, at s.o.); (b) (haben/sein) (Kinder) to romp (about). ◆'T~sucht, f -/no pl frenzy, raving madness. ◆'t~süchtig, adj. raving mad.

Tochter ['tɔxtər], f -¨- daughter. ◆'T~gesellschaft, f subsidiary (company).

Tod [to:t], m -(e)s/-e death. ◆'t~bringend, adj. deadly (poison), fatal (illness); lethal (weapons etc.). ◆'t~ernst, adj. F: deadly serious. ◆'T~es-, ['to:dəs-] comb.fm. death (blow, cell etc.); (year, time, cause etc.) of (s.o.'s) death; fatal (blow etc.).

◆'T~esangst, f (a) fear of death; (b) (große Angst) mortal fear. ◆'T~esanzeige, f notice of death, obituary. ◆'T~esfall, m death, fatality. ◆'T~eskampf, m death throes/agony. ◆'T~esopfer, n casualty. ◆'T~esstrafe, f death penalty. ◆'T~estag, m day/(Jubiläum) anniversary of (s.o.'s) death. ◆'T~esurteil, n death sentence. ◆'T~esverachtung, f (a) contempt for death; (b) utter contempt. ◆'T~feind, m mortal/deadly enemy. ◆'t~krank, adj. fatally ill. ◆'t~langweilig, adj. F: deadly boring. ◆'t~müde, adj. F: dead tired. ◆'t~sicher, adj. F: (a) dead certain; sure-fire (method etc.); (b) (untrüglich) unerring (instinct etc.). ◆'T~sünde, f deadly/Ecc: mortal sin. ◆'t~unglücklich, adj. F: dreadfully unhappy.

tödlich ['tø:tlɪç], adj. fatal (illness, accident, wound etc.); deadly (blow, weapon, poison etc.); lethal (dose etc.); t. verunglücken, to die in an accident; t. beleidigt, mortally offended.

Toilette [toa'lɛtə], f -/-n 1. (Abort) lavatory, toilet; N.Am: john. 2. (a) (Ankleiden usw.) toilet; (b) (Kleidung) dress. ◆T~n-, comb.fm. toilet (article, paper, soap, water etc.). ◆'T~ntisch, m dressing table, N.Am: dresser.

toler|ant [tole'rant], adj. tolerant. ◆T~anz [-'rants], f -/no pl tolerance. ◆t~ieren [-'ri:rən], v.tr. to tolerate (s.o., sth.).

toll [tɔl], adj. 1. (ausgelassen) wild, (verrückt) crazy (pranks, ideas). 2. F: (großartig) super, terrific (idea etc.); smashing (girl), stunning (woman). ◆'T~heit, f/no pl craziness, madness. ◆'T~kirsche, f deadly nightshade, belladonna. ◆'t~kühn, adj. foolhardy, reckless. ◆'T~wut, f rabies.

Tolpatsch ['tɔlpatʃ], m -(e)s/-e F: clumsy fellow.

Tölpel ['tœlpəl], m -s/- F: blockhead. ◆'t~haft, adj. silly.

Tomate [to'ma:tə], f -/-n tomato. ◆T~n-, comb.fm. tomato (juice, sauce etc.). ◆'T~nmark, n tomato puree.

Tombola ['tɔmbola], f -/-s & -en raffle, tombola.

Ton¹ [to:n]. I. m -(e)s/-e clay. II. 'T~, comb.fm. clay (pit, pipe, pigeon etc.); earthenware (pot etc.). ◆'T~waren, fpl earthenware.

Ton². I. m -(e)s/¨e 1. (a) sound; F: große T~e reden/spucken, to talk big; (b) Mus: note; Fig: den T. angeben, to call the tune; (c) (Betonung) stress. 2. (a) (Redeweise, Tonfall) tone (of voice); (b) der gute T., good form/manners. 3. (Farbt.) tone, shade. II. 'T~, comb.fm. sound (film, camera, quality etc.). ◆'T~abnehmer, m cartridge. ◆'t~angebend, adj. trend-setting.

◆'T~arm, m pickup (arm). ◆'T~art,
f Mus: key. ◆'T~band, n (recording)
tape. ◆'T~bandgerät, n tape recorder.
◆'T~fall, m (a) intonation; (Akzent) accent; (b) (Redeweise) tone of voice.
◆'T~höhe, f pitch (of a note).
◆'T~kopf, m recording head.
◆'T~lage, f pitch. ◆'T~leiter, f
scale. ◆'T~los, adj. soundless; toneless
(voice etc.). ◆'T~stärke, f volume.
◆'T~techniker, m sound engineer.

tön|en ['tø:nən], v. 1. v.i. (haben) (a) to
sound, (Glocke) ring; (b) F: (prahlen) to
boast. 2. v.tr. to tint (hair etc.).
◆'T~ung, f /-n tint, shade.

tönern ['tø:nərn], adj. clay.

Tonne ['tɔnə], f /-n 1. (Faß) barrel; (Regent.) butt; (Müllt.) dustbin. 2. Meas:
ton.

Topf [tɔpf]. I. m -(e)s/=e pot; Cu: (sauce)pan. II. 'T~-, comb.fm. pot (plant
etc.); potted (flower, plant); pan (lid,
cleaner etc.). ◆'T~lappen, m oven
cloth.

Töpfer ['tœpfər], m -s/- potter. ◆T~ei
[-'rai], f /-en (Werkstatt) pottery.
◆'t~n, v.i. (haben) to make pottery.
◆'T~scheibe, f potter's wheel.
◆'T~waren, fpl pottery.

Topographie [topogra'fi:], f /-n topo-
graphy.

Tor¹ [to:r]. I. n -(e)s/-e 1. gate; door (of a
garage etc.). 2. Fb: etc: goal. II. 'T~-,
comb.fm. Fb: etc: goal (difference, line
etc.); scoring (chance etc.). ◆'T~-
bogen, m archway. ◆'T~hüter, m
Fb:etc: goalkeeper. ◆'T~pfosten, m
Sp: goalpost. ◆'T~schlußpanik, f
last-minute panic. ◆'T~schütze, m
goal scorer. ◆'T~wart, m goalkeeper.

Tor², m -en/-en fool. ◆'T~heit, f /-en
folly.

Torf [tɔrf], m -(e)s/no pl peat.

töricht ['tø:riçt], adj. foolish, (dumm) stupid.

torkeln ['tɔrkəln], v.i. (sein) F: to reel,
stagger.

torped|ieren [tɔrpe'di:rən], v.tr. to torpe-
do (a ship, Fig: plan). ◆T~o
[-'pe:do], m -s/-s torpedo.

Torte ['tɔrtə], f /-n (a) cream cake, gateau; (b) (Obstt.) (fruit) flan.
◆'T~nboden, m flan case.

Tortur [tɔr'tu:r], f /-en agony, torture.

tosen ['to:zən], v.i. (haben) to roar,
(Sturm) rage.

Toskana [tɔs'ka:na]. Pr.n.f -. die T~,
Tuscany.

tot [to:t], adj. (a) dead; mein t~er Onkel, my late uncle; (b) Fig: lifeless, dull
(eyes etc.); deserted (city etc.); t~er
Winkel, blind spot; (c) t~er Punkt, im-
passe, deadlock; (Stillstand) standstill;
(Pers.) einen t~en Punkt haben, to be
at a low ebb; Sp: t~es Rennen, dead
heat. ◆'t~arbeiten, v.refl. sich t.,
to work oneself to death. ◆'T~e(r), m

& f decl. as adj. dead person; (Todesopfer)
casualty; die 'T~n, the dead. ◆'T~en-,
comb.fm. death(-bed, mask etc.).
◆'t~enblaß, adj. deathly pale.
◆'T~engräber, m gravedigger.
◆'t~enhemd, n shroud.
◆'T~enkopf m death's head, skull.
◆'T~enmesse, f requiem (mass).
◆'T~enschein, m death certificate.
◆'T~enstarre, f rigor mortis.
◆'t~enstill, adj. dead still/silent.
◆'T~enstille, f dead silence.
◆'T~entanz, m dance of death.
◆'t~geboren, adj. ein t~geborenes
Kind, (i) a stillborn child; (ii) F: a
doomed/abortive enterprise. ◆'T~ge-
burt, f stillbirth; (Kind) stillborn child.
◆'t~kriegen, v.tr.sep. F: er/es ist
nicht totzukriegen, he/it just goes on and
on. ◆'t~lachen, v.refl.sep. sich t., to
split one's sides laughing. ◆'T~schlag,
m manslaughter, homicide. ◆'t~-
schlagen, v.tr.sep.irr.85 to kill (s.o., F:
(Pers.) killer. 2. (Stock) life-preserver.
◆'t~schweigen, v.tr.sep.irr.89 to hush
up (sth.), ignore (s.o.) completely.
◆'t~stellen, v.refl.sep. sich t., to pretend to be dead.

total [to'ta:l], adj. total. ◆T~isator
[-ali'za:tor], m -s/-en totalizator, F: tote.
◆t~itär, adj. totalitarian. ◆T~-
schaden, m (Fahrzeug) T. haben, to be
a write-off.

töt|en ['tø:tən], v.tr. to kill (s.o., oneself,
an animal, a nerve). ◆'T~ung, f /no pl
killing; Jur: homicide.

Toto ['to:to], n & m -s/-s (football) pool(s).
◆'T~schein, m pools coupon.

Toup|et [tu'pe:], n -s/-s toupet.
◆t~ieren [-'pi:rən], v.tr. to back-comb
(one's hair).

Tour [tu:r], f /-en 1. (Ausflug) excursion,
tour; (Fahrt) trip. 2. F: (a) (Art und
Weise) way; auf die dumme/langsame
T., stupidly/slowly; (b) (Trick) ploy;
krumme T~en, shady dealings. 3. Tchn:
(Umdrehung) revolution; auf vollen
T~en laufen, to be running flat out;
(Aktion) to be in full swing; j-n auf
T~en bringen, to spur s.o. into action;
in einer T., incessantly; without stopping. ◆'T~ismus ['rismus], m -/no pl
tourism. ◆'T~ist [-'rist], m -en/-en
tourist. ◆T~isten-, comb.fm. tourist
(hotel, class, traffic etc.).◆'T~nee
[tur'ne:], f /-n on tour.

Trab [tra:p], m -(e)s/no pl trot; F: j-n auf
T. bringen, to make s.o. get a move on.
◆'t~en ['tra:bən], v.i. (sein) to trot.
◆'T~er, m -s/- trotter, trotting horse.
◆'T~rennen, n trotting race.

Trabant [tra'bant], m -en/-en satellite.
◆'T~enstadt f satellite town.

Tracht [traxt], f /-en 1. traditional costume; (Amtskleidung) official dress,
(nurse's) uniform. 2. F: eine T. Prügel,

a sound thrashing. ◆**t~en**, v.i. (haben)
Lit: **nach etwas** dat t., to strive for sth.;
j-m nach dem Leben t., to make an attempt on s.o.'s life.

trächtig ['trɛçtiç], adj. pregnant (animal).

Tradi|tion [traditsi'o:n], f -/-en tradition.
◆**t~tio'nell**, adj. traditional.

Trafo ['tra:fo], m -s/-s transformer.

Trag|bahre ['tra:kba:rə], f -/-n stretcher.
◆**t~bar**, adj. (a) portable; Cl: fit to
wear, wearable; (b) (erträglich) bearable;
(annehmbar) acceptable (**für**+acc, to).
◆**t~en** ['tra:gən], v.irr.85 1. v.tr. (a)
to carry (s.o., sth.); (irgendwohin) to take
(sth.) (somewhere); (Baum usw.) to bear
(fruit); Fig: to bear (responsibility, a
name, Fin: losses, costs etc.; **die Schuld
an etwas** dat t., to be guilty of sth.; (b)
(ertragen) to bear (suffering, one's fate
etc.); (c) to wear (clothes, spectacles, a
ring etc.); to have (a beard); (d) refl. **sich
mit einem Gedanken t.**, to toy with an
idea. 2. v.i. (haben) (a) **das Eis trägt
nicht**, the ice won't take your weight; (b)
(Baum) **gut/schlecht t.**, to produce a
good/bad crop. ◆**T~etasche**, f carrier
bag. ◆**t~fähig**, adj. capable of supporting a load. ◆**T~fähigkeit**, f buoyancy (of water). ◆**T~fläche**, f Av:
wing. ◆**T~flächenboot**, n hydrofoil.
◆**T~weite**, f 1. range. 2. Fig: (Bedeutung) significance; (Folgen) consequences
(of an action/decision).

träge ['trɛ:gə], adj. sluggish; (Pers.)
lethargic; Ph: t. **Masse**, inert mass.

Träger(in) ['trɛ:gər(in)], m -s/- (f -/-nen)
1. (Pers.) (a) carrier of a load, illness
etc.); bearer (of a load, news, a title
etc.); (b) wearer (of clothing); (c) holder
(of a prize, office etc.). 2. Tchn: beam;
(aus Stahl) girder; (Stütze) support. 3. Cl:
(shoulder) strap; (Hosent.) braces, N.Am:
suspenders. ◆**T~rakete**, f launch vehicle.

Trägheit ['trɛ:khait], f -/no pl sluggishness; lethargy; Ph: etc: inertia.

Trag|ik ['tra:gik], f -/no pl tragedy.
◆**t~komisch**, adj. tragicomic.
◆**T~ikomödie**, f tragicomedy.
◆**t~isch**, adj. tragic. ◆**T~ödie**
[tra'gø:diə], f -/-n tragedy.

Trainer ['trɛ:nər], m -s/- Sp: trainer; Fb:
(trainer-)manager. ◆**t~ieren**
[-ɛ:'ni:rən], v.tr.&i. (haben) to train
(s.o., a team, horse etc.); to exercise
(muscles). ◆**T~ing** ['trɛ:niŋ], n -s/-s
training. ◆**T~ings-**, comb.fm. training
(camp, method, facilities etc.).
◆**T~ingsanzug**, m track suit.

Trakt [trakt], m -(e)s/-e tract. ◆**T~at**
[-'ta:t], m & n -(e)s/-e (scientific etc.)
treatise. ◆**t~ieren** [-'ti:rən], v.tr. (a) to
give (s.o.) a rough time; (b) (plagen) to
plague, torment (s.o.).

Traktor ['traktɔr], m -s/-en tractor.

trällern ['trɛlərn], v.tr. & i. (haben) to
warble (a tune etc.).

tramp|eln ['trampəln], v. 1. v.i. (a) (ha-
ben) (stampfen) to stamp (one's feet); (b)
(sein) to stomp, stomp (along). 2. v.tr. to
trample (s.o., sth.). ◆**t~en** ['trɛmpən],
v.i. (sein) F: to hitchhike. ◆**T~olin**
['trampoli:n], n -s/-e trampoline.

Tran [tra:n], m -(e)s/-e 1. train oil. 2. F:
im T., dopey.

Trance ['trɑ̃:s(ə)], f -/-n trance.

Tranchier- [trɑ̃'ʃi:r-], comb.fm. carving
(knife etc.). ◆**T~besteck**, n carving
set. ◆**t~en**, v.tr. to carve (meat).

Träne ['trɛ:nə], f -/-n tear. ◆**t~n**, v.i.
(haben) to water. ◆**T~ngas**, n tear
gas. ◆**t~nüberströmt**, adj. tear-
stained.

Tränke ['trɛnkə], f -/-n watering place;
(Trog) drinking trough. ◆**t~n**, v.tr. (a)
to water (animals); (b) to soak (sth.)
(**mit**+dat, with).

Transform|ator [transfɔr'ma:tɔr], m -s/
-en transformer. ◆**t~ieren** [-'mi:rən],
v.tr. to transform (current etc.).

Transistor [tran'zistɔr], m -s/-en (a) El:
transistor; (b) (also **T~gerät** n) transistor
radio.

Transit- [tran'zi:t-, tranzit-], comb.fm.
transit (goods, traffic etc.). ◆**t~iv**
['tranzitiːf], adj. transitive (verb).

transparent [transpa'rɛnt]. I. adj. transparent. II. **T.**, n -(e)s/-e banner.

Transpiration [transpiratsi'o:n], f -/-en
perspiration.

Transplant|ation [transplantatsi'o:n], f -/
-en transplant; (skin) graft. ◆**t~ieren**
[-'ti:rən], v.tr. to transplant (an organ);
to graft (tissue, skin).

Transport [trans'pɔrt]. I. m -(e)s/-e 1.
(Transportieren) transport; Aut: Rail:
haulage (of goods, people). 2. consignment, shipment (of goods). II. **T~-**,
comb.fm. transport (worker, vehicle, aircraft etc.); carriage, freight (costs,
charges, insurance etc.). ◆**t~abel**
[-'ta:bəl], adj. transportable. ◆**T~er**, m
-s/- transport vehicle. ◆**t~fähig**, adj.
movable. ◆**t~ieren** [-'ti:rən], v.tr. to
transport, (per Schiff) ship (goods,
people); to move (a patient).
◆**T~mittel**, n means of transport/
transportation. ◆**T~unternehmen**, n
transport/haulage company.

Transvestit [transvɛs'ti:t], m -en/-en
transvestite.

Trapez [tra'pe:ts], n -es/-e 1. trapeze. 2.
Mth: trapezium.

Trasse ['trasə], f -/-n (marked-out) line,
route (for a road etc.).

Tratsch [tra:tʃ], m -(e)s/no pl F: Pej: gossip. ◆**t~en**, v.i. (haben) to gossip.

Tratte ['tratə], f -/-n Com: draft.

trau|en ['trauən], v. 1. v.tr. to marry (a
couple). 2. v.i. (haben) **j-m, etwas** dat t.,
to trust s.o., sth. 3. v.refl. **sich** t., to
dare (**etwas zu tun**, to do sth.).
◆**T~ring**, m wedding ring.
◆**T~schein**, m marriage certificate.

◆'T~ung, f -/-en wedding/marriage ceremony. ◆'T~zeuge, m/'T~zeugin, f witness.

Traube ['traubə], f -/-n 1. grape. 2. Fig: cluster (of people etc.). ◆'T~nernte f/'T~nlese, f grape harvest. ◆'T~nsaft, m grape juice. ◆'T~nzucker, m glucose.

Trauer ['trauər]. I. f -/no pl sorrow, grief; T. um den Verstorbenen, sorrow/ mourning for the deceased. 2. (a) (T~zeit) (period of) mourning; (b) (T~kleidung) T. tragen, to wear mourning. II. 'T~, comb.fm. mourning (veil, period etc.); (house, year etc.) of mourning; funeral (service, march etc.). ◆'T~fall, m bereavement. ◆'T~feier, f funeral/burial service. ◆'t~n, v.i. (haben) (a) to grieve, mourn (um + acc, for). ◆'T~spiel, n tragedy. ◆'T~weide, f weeping willow. ◆'T~zug, m funeral procession.

träufeln ['trɔyfəln], v. 1. v.tr. to let (sth.) drip/trickle. 2. v.i. (haben/sein) to drip, trickle.

traulich ['traulɪç], adj. intimate, cosy.

Traum [traum], m -(e)s/=e dream. ◆'T~bild, n vision. ◆'t~haft, adj. 1. dreamlike. 2. F: (wunderbar) fabulous, fantastic.

Trauma ['trauma], n -s/-men trauma. ◆t~tisch ['-'maːtɪʃ], adj. traumatic.

träumen ['trɔymən], v.tr.&i. (haben) to dream (sth.); das hätte ich mir nie t. lassen, I would never have imagined that possible. ◆'T~er, m -s/- dreamer. ◆T~e'rei, f -/-en daydream.

traurig ['traurɪç], adj. sad. ◆'T~keit, f -/no pl sadness.

Treck [trɛk], m -s/-s trek; (Zug) trail of refugees etc.

Treff [trɛf], m -s/-s F: (a) get-together; (b) = T~punkt m. ◆'t~en. I. v.irr. 1. v.tr. (a) (schlagen) to hit (s.o., a target etc.); vom Blitz getroffen, struck by lightning; Fig: dieser Vorwurf traf ihn schwer, this reproach hurt him deeply; (b) (richtig erfassen) to get (sth.) right; to hit on (the right thing/tone etc.); (c) refl. es trifft sich gut/schlecht, daß ..., it is convenient/inconvenient that ...; es traf sich so, daß..., it so happened that ...; wie es sich so trifft, as chance would have it; (d) (begegnen) to meet (s.o.); wo wollen wir uns t.? where shall we meet? ihre Blicke trafen sich, their eyes met; (e) (zustande bringen) to make (arrangements, preparations, a choice, decision etc.). 2. v.i. (a) (haben) to hit the mark/ target; (b) (sein) auf j-n, etwas acc t. to meet s.o./come across sth.; auf Widerstand usw. t., to meet with/encounter resistance etc. II. T~, n -s/- meeting. ◆'t~end, adj. fitting, apt. ◆'T~er, m -s/- 1. Sp: hit; Fb: etc. goal. 2. (Lotteriegewinn) winner; F: (Glücksfall) lucky strike. ◆'T~punkt, m meeting place,

rendezvous. ◆'t~sicher, adj. unerring, accurate; (Bemerkung) to the point. ◆'T~sicherheit, f accuracy; (good) marksmanship.

Treib- ['traip-], comb.fm. (a) floating (mine etc.); drift (-ice, -wood etc.); (b) (antreibo) driving (wheel, belt etc.); fuel (gas, oil etc.). ◆'t~en [traibən]. I. v.irr.12 1. v.tr. (a) to drive (s.o., cattle, snow, a machine etc.); (b) (sich beschäftigen mit) to pursue, carry on (a business etc.); to go in for (sport etc.); sein Spiel mit j-m t., to play a game with s.o. 2. v.i. (a) (sein) (Schiff, Wolke usw.) to drift; die Dinge t. lassen, to let things take their course; (b) (haben) (Pflanzen) to sprout, (Knospen) burst; Cu: (Teig) to rise. II. T~, n -s/no pl goings-on, doings; (geschäftig) bustle. ◆'T~haus, n hothouse. ◆'T~jagd, f battue; Pol: witchhunt. ◆'T~sand, m quicksand. ◆'T~stoff, m fuel.

Trend [trɛnt], m -s/-s trend.

trennbar ['trɛnbaːr], adj. separable (prefix etc.); detachable (part etc.). ◆'t~en, v.tr. (a) to separate (s.o., sth., objects) (von + dat, from); (lösen) to detach, take off (a collar etc.); (b) (aufteilen) to divide (sth.); to break/split (sth.) up (in seine Bestandteile, into its component parts); sie leben getrennt, they are separated; (c) sich t., to separate/ part; (Abschied nehmen) to say goodbye; sie trennte sich von ihm, she parted company with/left him; sich von etwas dat t., to part with sth.; (aufgeben) to give sth. up. ◆'T~ung, f separation; (in Teile) division of a room, word etc.); segregation (of races etc.); distinction (zwischen Begriffen, between concepts). ◆'T~wand, f partition (wall).

treppauf [trɛp'?auf], adv. t., treppab laufen, to run up and down the stairs. ◆'T~e, f -/-n staircase, (flight of stairs); (außen) (flight) of steps. ◆'T~engeländer, n banisters. ◆'T~enhaus, n stairwell. ◆'T~enstufe, f stair, step.

Tresor [tre'zoːr], m -s/-e safe, strongroom; (T~raum) strong room.

Tret- ['trɛt-], comb.fm. pedal (car, boat etc.). ◆'T~eimer, m pedal bin. ◆'t~en, v.irr.1 v.i. (a) (sein) (Pers.) to step (nach vorn, auf die Seite usw., forward, aside etc.); ins Zimmer t., to enter/come into the room; (b) (sein) (kommen) to come (aus + dat, out of), (go (hinaus + dat, behind; in + acc, into); Fig: in Aktion/Kraft t., to come into effect; (c) (haben) to kick; gegen die Tür t., to kick the door. 2. v.tr. (a) to kick (s.o., the ball etc.); (b) (trampeln) to tread (sth., water etc.), to trample (sth., a path).

Treu [trɔy], adj. faithful (husband, wife etc.); loyal (subject, friend, servant etc.); sich selber t., true to oneself; seinen Grundsätzen t. bleiben, to stick to one's principles. ◆'T~e, f -/no pl loyalty;

faithfulness. ◆'T~händer, m -s/- trustee. ◆'T~handgesellschaft, f trust company. ◆'t~herzig, adj. ingenuous; innocently trusting. ◆'T~los, adj. faithless. ◆'T~losigkeit, f -/no pl faithlessness.

Triangel ['triːaŋəl], m -s/- Mus: triangle.

Tri|bunal [tribuˈnaːl], n -s/-e tribunal. ◆T~büne [-ˈbyːnə], f -/-n (Podium) platform, rostrum; (Zuschauert.) grandstand. ◆T~but [-ˈbuːt], m -(e)s/-e tribute.

Trichter ['triçtər], m -s/- 1. funnel. 2. (Granat.) crater. ◆'t~förmig, adj. funnel-shaped.

Trick [trik], m -(e)s/-e trick; (List) ploy, dodge. ◆'T~film, m trick film; (gezeichneter) T., animated cartoon film. ◆'t~reich, adj. artful.

Trieb [triːp], m -(e)s/-e 1. (Drang) urge; (innerer Antrieb) impulse; (Verlangen) desire. 2. Bot: sprout, shoot. ◆'T~feder, f mainspring (of a watch etc.); Fig: driving force. ◆'t~haft, adj. impulsive, instinctive (actions etc.). ◆'T~kraft, f motive force. ◆'T~täter/'T~verbrecher, m sexual offender, sex maniac. ◆'T~wagen, m railcar; Rail: railcar. ◆'T~werk, n power plant, engine.

trief|en ['triːfən], v.i. a) (sein) (Regen, Schweiß usw.) to drip; b) (haben) (triefend naß sein) (von/vor Nässe) t., to be dripping wet; (Nase, Auge) to run. ◆'t~naß, adj. dripping/sopping wet.

triftig ['triftiç], adj. valid; (zwingend) cogent (reason, argument etc.).

Trigonometrie [trigonomeˈtriː], f -/no pl trigonometry.

Trikot [triˈkoː], n -s/-s Sp: singlet; Fb: shirt.

Triller ['trilər], m -s/- Mus: trill. ◆'t~n, v.i. (haben) Mus: to trill; (Lerche usw.) to warble. ◆'T~pfeife, f bird whistle.

trimmen ['trimən], v.tr. a) to trim, clip (a dog); b) to train (s.o.); c) Sp: F: sich t., to get oneself into shape.

Trink- [triŋk-], comb.fm. drinking (vessel, glass, song, chocolate, water etc.). ◆'t~en, v.tr. & i. irr.96 (haben) to drink (sth.). ◆'T~er, m -s/- heavy drinker, alcoholic. ◆'t~fest, adj. F: t. sein, to hold one's drink well. ◆'T~geld, n tip. ◆'T~halle, f refreshment stall. ◆'T~spruch, m toast.

Trio ['triːo], n -s/-s trio.

trippeln ['tripəln], v.i. (sein) to trip, mince along; (Baby) to toddle.

trist [trist], adj. dismal (weather, life etc.); dreary (houses etc.); bleak (prospects).

Tritt [trit], m -(e)s/-e a) (Schritt) step; b) (Fußt.) kick. ◆'T~brett, n running board. ◆'T~leiter, f (short) stepladder.

Triumph [triˈʊmf], m -(e)s/-e triumph. ◆t~al [-ˈfaːl], adj. triumphant. ◆t~bogen, m triumphal arch. ◆t~ieren [-ˈfiːrən], v.i. (haben) to

triumph/(schadenfroh) gloat (über etwas acc, over sth.).

trivial [triviˈaːl], adj. commonplace, trite; (unbedeutend) trivial, insignificant. ◆T~literatur, f light fiction; Pej: trashy literature.

trocken ['trɔkən]. I. adj. a) dry; im T~en, in the dry; under cover; F: auf dem trocknen sitzen, to be stuck/(pleite) broke; b) (langweilig) dull, tedious (work etc.); dry-as-dust (book, lecture etc.). II. 'T~-, comb.fm. a) dry (battery, dock, ice, weight, cleaning etc.); b) (getrocknet) dried (vegetables, milk, fruit etc.). ◆'T~boden, m drying loft. ◆'T~element, n dry cell. ◆'T~haube, f drying hood; drier. ◆'T~heit, f -/no pl 1. dryness; Fig: dullness. 2. (Dürre) drought. ◆'t~kurs, m preparatory (indoor) course. ◆'t~legen, v.tr.sep. a) ein Baby t., to change a baby's nappies; b) to drain (a swamp etc.). ◆'T~rasierer, m dry/electric shaver.

trockn|en ['trɔknən], v.tr. & i. (sein/haben) to dry. ◆'T~er, m -s/- drier.

Troddel ['trɔdəl], f -/-n tassel.

Trödel ['trøːdəl], m -s/no pl F: lumber, junk. ◆T~e'lei, f -/no pl F: dawdling. ◆'T~elmarkt, m flea market; (für Wohltätigkeitszwecke) jumble sale. ◆'t~eln, v.i. (haben/sein) F: to dawdle. ◆'T~ler, m -s/- 1. junk dealer. 2. F: dawdler, slowcoach; N.Am: slowpoke.

Trog [troːk], m -(e)s/-e trough.

Trommel ['trɔməl], f -/-n drum. ◆'T~bremse, f drum brake. ◆'T~fell, n Anat: eardrum. ◆'T~feuer, n barrage. ◆'t~n, v.i. (haben) to drum.

Trommler ['trɔmlər], m -s/- drummer.

Trompete [trɔmˈpeːtə], f -/-n trumpet. ◆'T~r, m -s/- trumpeter.

Tropen ['troːpən]. I. pl die T., the tropics. II. 'T~-, comb.fm. tropical (suit, fever, disease etc.). ◆'t~fest, adj. tropicalized. ◆'T~helm, m sun helmet, topee.

Tropf [trɔpf], m -(e)s/-e 1. F: armer T., poor beggar. 2. (pl -e) Med: drip. ◆'T~en. I. m -s/- drop; (herunterfallend) drip. II. t., v.tr. & i. (haben) to drip (sth.). ◆'T~enfänger m drip catcher. ◆'t~enweise, adv. drop by drop. ◆'t~naß, adj. dripping wet. ◆'T~steinhöhle, f cave with stalactites/stalagmites.

tröpfeln ['trœpfəln], v.i. (haben) to trickle; (Regen) to spit; it's spitting.

Trophäe [troˈfɛːə], f -/-n trophy.

tropisch ['troːpiʃ], adj. tropical.

Trost [troːst], m -(e)s/no pl consolation, comfort; F: nicht ganz/recht bei T. sein, to be off one's rocker. ◆'t~bedürftig, adj. in need of consolation. ◆'t~los, adj. bleak, cheerless (countryside, weather etc.); miserable

(conditions); hopeless (situation etc.).
◆'T~losigkeit, f -/no pl bleakness, cheerlessness; hopelessness, desperation. ◆'T~preis, m consolation prize. ◆'T~reich, adj. comforting.

tröst|en ['trø:stən], v.tr. to console, comfort (s.o., oneself); sich damit t., daß ..., to console oneself with the thought that ... ◆'t~lich, adj. comforting, consoling. ◆'T~ung, f -/-en consolation, comfort.

Trott [trɔt], m -(e)s/-e 1. trot. 2. Fig: routine. ◆'T~el, m -s/- F: idiot. ◆'t~elig, adj. F: dithering. ◆'t~en, v.i. (sein) to trot; F: (Pers.) to trudge (along). ◆'T~oir [trɔtoˈaːr], n -s/-e & -s pavement, N.Am: sidewalk.

trotz [trɔts]. I. prep. + gen in spite of). t~ Regen/des Regens, in spite of the rain. II. T., m -es/no pl defiance; (Eigensinn) obstinacy; j-m zum T., in defiance of s.o.; aller Vernunft zum T., contrary to all reason. ◆'t~dem, adv. nevertheless. ◆'t~en, v.i. (haben) (a) j-m/etwas dat t., to defy s.o., sth.; einer Gefahr t., to brave a danger; (b) (trotzig sein) to be obstinate/(Kind) rebellious. ◆'t~ig/ 't~köpfig, adj. defiant; (Kind usw.) pigheaded; (widerspenstig) rebellious. ◆'T~kopf, m pigheaded person/esp. child.

trüb|e ['try:bə], adj. (a) cloudy (liquid, sky etc.); dull (weather, day, eyes etc.); dim (light); (b) (traurig) gloomy (person, times, thoughts, mood etc.); grim (prospect, experience). ◆'t~en, v.tr. (a) to cloud (a liquid); to dull (a window etc.); sich t., to become cloudy/dull; (b) to cast a cloud over (s.o.'s mood etc.). ◆'T~heit ['try:phait], f -/no pl (a) cloudiness; dullness; dimness, sombreness; (b) gloominess. ◆'T~sal, f -/-e Lit: affliction; (Trauer) grief; F: T. blasen, to be down in the dumps. ◆'t~selig, adj. gloomy (person, mood etc.). ◆'T~sinn, m melancholy. ◆'t~sinnig, adj. gloomy, dejected. ◆'T~ung, f -/-en (a) (also Fig:) clouding; dimming; tarnishing; (b) (Beeinträchtigung) marring.

Trubel ['tru:bəl], m -s/no pl bustle, hurly-burly.

trudeln ['tru:dəln], v.i. (sein) to spiral, Av: spin.

Trüffel ['tryfəl], f -/-n truffle.

Trug [tru:k], m -(e)s/no pl Lit: deception. ◆'T~bild, n hallucination. ◆'T~schluß, m wrong conclusion; fallacy.

trüg|en ['try:gən], v.irr.63 1. v.tr. to deceive (s.o.); wenn mich nicht alles trügt, if I am not much mistaken. 2. v.i. (haben) der Schein trügt, appearances are deceptive. ◆'t~erisch, adj. deceptive.

Truhe ['tru:ə], f -/-n chest.

Trümmer ['trymər], pl debris; (von Gebäuden) rubble; Nau: Av: wreckage.

◆'T~haufen, m heap of rubble.

Trumpf [trʊmpf], m -(e)s/-e trump (card); Fig: alle T~e in der Hand haben, to hold all the trumps. ◆'t~en, v.tr.&i. (haben) to trump (a card).

Trunk [trʊŋk], m -(e)s/-e Lit: (a) drink; (b) (T~sucht) drinking. ◆'T~enheit, f -/no pl drunkenness; T. am Steuer, drunken driving. ◆'T~sucht, f alcoholism.

Trupp [trʊp], m -s/-s gang (of workers etc.); detachment, squad (of police etc.); group (of people). ◆'T~e, f -/-n 1. (a) no pl army; (b) (Verband) unit; (c) pl T~en, troops. 2. Th: etc: company, troupe (of acrobats etc.); Sp: squad. ◆'T~en-, comb.fm. troop (movement, transport etc.); military (parade etc.). ◆'T~enführer, m unit commander. ◆'T~enteil, m unit. ◆'T~enübung, f troop manoeuvre, field exercise. ◆'T~enübungsplatz, m military training area.

Truthahn ['tru:tha:n], m turkey(-cock).

Tschech|e ['tʃɛçə], m -n/-n Czech. ◆'T~in, f -/-nen Czech woman. ◆'t~isch, adj. Czech. ◆'T~oslowakei [-oslova'kai]. Pr.n.f -. Czechoslovakia.

tschüs [tʃyːs], int. F: bye now! so long!

Tub|a ['tu:ba], f -/-ben tuba. ◆'T~e, f -/-n tube.

Tuberkulose [tuberku'lo:zə], f -/-n tuberculosis.

Tuch [tu:x], n -(e)s/-er cloth; (Halst.) scarf; (Kopft.) head scarf; (Staubt.) duster.

tüchtig ['tyçtiç], adj. 1. (fähig) able, competent; (leistungsfähig) efficient; (fleißig) hardworking (person). 2. (beträchtlich) sizeable (piece, portion); big (gulp etc.); hard (blow); healthy (appetite). ◆'T~keit, f -/no pl ability, competence; efficiency; excellence (of work); (Fleiß) industry.

Tück|e ['tykə], f -/-n 1. no pl treachery; Fig: fickleness (of fate). 2. (Handlung) trick, ruse; Fig: danger; seine T~n haben, (Maschine) to be temperamental (Berg, Fluß usw.) treacherous. ◆'t~isch, adj. treacherous, pernicious (illness); malicious (glance etc.).

tuckern ['tukərn], v.i. (haben/sein) (Boot) to chug.

Tugend ['tu:gənt], f -/-en virtue. ◆'t~haft, adj. virtuous.

Tüll [tyl], m -(e)s/-e tulle.

Tülle ['tylə], f -/-n spout.

Tulpe ['tulpə], f -/-n tulip. ◆'T~nzwiebel, f tulip bulb.

tummeln ['tuməln], v.refl. sich t., (Kinder) to romp (about).

Tumor ['tu:mor], m -s/-en ['tumo:rən] tumour.

Tümpel ['tympəl], m -s/- pond.

Tumult [tu'mult], m -(e)s/-e tumult, commotion; pl T~e, disturbances.

tun [tu:n]. **I.** v.ir. **1.** v.tr. (a) to do (sth., a job, favour, one's duty etc.); to make (a vow, remark etc.), take (a step); **so etwas tut man nicht**, that sort of thing isn't done; (b) (antun) **was hat er dir getan?** what did he do to you? **der Hund tut dir nichts**, the dog won't hurt you; (c) F: (stellen) to put (sth.) (somewhere); (d) **das tut's auch**, that would do; **das hat damit nichts zu t./tut nichts zur Sache**, that has nothing to do with it/is quite irrelevant; **es mit j-m zu t. haben**, to have dealings with s.o.; **was tut das schon?** what does it matter? **es tut sich etwas** there is something going on. **2.** v.i. (haben) (a) **ich habe zu t.**, I have work to do/do/(Geschäfte) business to attend to; (b) **freundlich t.**, to act/behave in a friendly way; **tu doch nicht so!** stop pretending/putting it on! **so t., als ob...**, to act/behave as if ...; (c) **mit j-m zu t. haben**, to have dealings with s.o.; **mit etwas dat zu t. haben**, to be concerned/connected with sth. **II. T.**, n -s/no pl doings. ◆**t~lichst**, adv. if at all possible.

Tünche ['tynçə], f -/-n whitewash; Fig: (äußerer Schein) veneer. ◆**t~n**, v.tr. to whitewash (sth.).

Tundra ['tundra], f -/-dren tundra.

Tunes|ien [tu'ne:ziən]. Pr.n.n -s. Tunisia. ◆**t~isch**, adj. Tunisian.

Tunke ['tunkə], f -/-n esp. sauce; (Braten.) gravy. ◆**t~n**, v.tr. to dip (sth.).

Tunnel ['tunəl], m -s/- & -s tunnel.

Tüpfel|chen ['typfəlçən], n -s/- tiny spot; (gedruckt usw.) dot. ◆**t~n**, v.tr. to spot (sth.).

tupf|en ['tupfən]. **I.** v.tr. (a) to dab (sth.) (auf etwas acc, onto sth.); (b) (blau) getupftes Kleid, dress with (blue) polka dots. **II. T.**, m -s/- spot; dot. ◆**T~er**, m -s/- 1. dot. 2. Med: swab.

Tür [ty:r], f -/-en door; **j-n vor die T. setzen**, to throw s.o. out; **Weihnachten steht vor der T.**, Christmas is just round the corner. **II. 'T~-**, comb.fm. door (chain, lock, key etc.). ◆**T~angel**, f door hinge. ◆**T~flügel**, m (lefthand/righthand) door (of a pair). ◆**T~klingel**, f doorbell. ◆**T~öffner**, m (electric) door opener. ◆**T~rahmen**, m doorframe. ◆**T~schwelle**, f doorsill, threshold.

Turban ['turba:n], m -s/-e turban.

Turb|ine [tur'bi:nə], f -/-n turbine. ◆**T~omotor**, m turbocharged engine.

turbulen|t [turbu'lent], adj. turbulent. ◆**T~z**, f -/-en turbulence.

Türk|e ['tyrkə], m -n/-n Turk. ◆**T~ei** [-'kai]. Pr.n.f -. **die T.**, Turkey.

◆**'T~in**, f -/-nen Turkish woman. ◆**t~isch**, adj. Turkish.

Türkis [tyr'ki:s], m -es/-e turquoise. ◆**t~(farben)**, adj. turquoise.

Turm [turm], m -(e)s/-e (a) tower; (spitzer Kirch.) steeple; (b) (Schach) castle; (c) (Sprungt.) diving platform. ◆**T~hoch**, adj. towering (waves etc.). ◆**T~spitze**, f spire. ◆**T~uhr**, f tower/esp. (am Kirch.) church clock.

Türm|chen ['tyrmçən], n -s/- small tower, turret. ◆**t~en**, v. **1.** v.tr. to pile, stack (books etc.); **sich t.**, to pile up. **2.** v.i. (sein) F: to clear out, Brit: do a bunk.

Turn- ['turn-], comb.fm. gymnastic (apparatus, 'exercise etc.); Sch: gym/P.E. (teacher, lesson etc.). ◆**t~en. I.** v.i. (haben) to do gymnastics/E: gym/Sch: P.E. **II. T.**, n -s/no pl Sp: gymnastics; Sch: F: gym; P.E. ◆**T~er(in)**, m -s/(f -/-nen) gymnast. ◆**T~halle**, f gymnasium, F: gym. ◆**T~hemd**, n singlet. ◆**T~hose**, f gym shorts. ◆**T~schuhe**, mpl gym shoes, N.Am: sneakers. ◆**T~verein**, m gymnastics club. ◆**T~zeug**, n gym kit.

Turnier [tur'ni:r]. **I.** n -s/-e tournament; (Reit.) (horse) show; (Tanzt.) (dancing) competition. **II. T~-**, comb.fm. tournament (winner etc.); show (horse, rider etc.); competition (dancing, winner etc.).

Turnus ['turnus], m -/-se rota; im **T.**, in rotation.

Turteltaube ['turtəltaubə], f -/-n turtledove.

Tusch [tuʃ], m -(e)s/-e Mus: flourish.

Tusche ['tuʃə], f -/-n Indian ink. ◆**T~zeichnung**, f pen-and-ink drawing.

tuscheln ['tuʃəln], v.tr. & i. (haben) to whisper (sth.).

Tüte ['ty:tə], f -/-n (a) (paper/plastic) bag; (b) (Eist.) ice-cream cone/cornet.

tuten ['tu:tən], v.i. (haben) to toot, hoot.

Tutor ['tu:tɔr], m -s/-en [tu'to:rən] tutor.

Typ [ty:p], m -s/-en type; (a) **sie ist nicht mein T.**, she is not my type/sort; (b) F: (Pers.) character, N.Am: guy; (c) (Modell) type, model. ◆**T~e**, f -/-n **1.** character; pl Typ-n, type. **2.** F: (Pers.) queer bird, odd character. ◆**t~isch**, adj. typical (für j-n, etwas acc, of s.o., sth.); F: **t. Frau/Mann!** how typical of a woman/man!

Typhus ['ty:fus], m -/no pl typhoid (fever).

Typus ['ty:pus], m -/-pen type.

Tyrann [ty'ran], m -en/-en tyrant; Fig: (Chef usw.) bully. ◆**T~ei** [-'nai], f -/-en tyranny. ◆**t~isch**, adj. tyrannical, bullying. ◆**t~i'sieren**, v.tr. to bully (s.o.), tyrannize (a country etc.).

U

U, u [u:], *n -/-* (the letter) U, u.
U-Bahn ['u:ba:n], *f* underground (railway), *N.Am:* subway. ◆**U~-Station,** *f* underground/*N.Am:* subway station.
übel ['y:bəl]. **I.** *adj.* (*a*) (*schlecht*) bad; (*moralisch schlecht*) wicked, evil; (*b*) (*unangenehm*) nasty, (*stärker*) foul (weather, smell etc.); **j-m ü. mitspielen,** to play a nasty trick on s.o.; (*c*) **mir ist/wird ü.,** I feel sick. **II. Ü.,** *n -s/-* evil; (*Mißstand*) anomaly; **zu allem Ü. ...,** to crown it all/make matters worse ... ◆**ü~ge-launt,** *adj.* grumpy. ◆**ü~nehmen,** *v.tr.sep.irr.69* to take (sth.) amiss, take offence at (sth.). ◆**ü~riechend,** *adj.* evil-smelling. ◆**Ü~täter,** *m* wrong-doer. ◆**ü~wollen,** *v.i.sep.irr.112* (*haben*) **j-m ü.,** to be ill-disposed towards s.o.
üben ['y:bən], *v.tr.* & *i.* (*haben*) to practise; **sich (in etwas** *dat*) **ü.,** to practise (sth.).
über ['y:bər]. **I.** *prep.* **1.** (*Lage*) + *dat* above, over; **er wohnt ü. uns,** he lives above us/on the next floor; **ü. dem Durchschnitt,** above average. **2.** + *acc* over; **ü. einen Graben springen,** to jump over/across a ditch; **ü. München fahren,** to go via Munich; **ü. Fernschreiber,** by telex; **ein Scheck ü. DM 100,** a cheque for 100 marks; **das geht ü. meinen Verstand,** it's beyond my comprehension; **ü. j-n herrschen/Macht haben,** to rule/have power over s.o.; **Fehler ü. Fehler machen,** to make one mistake after the other; **übers Wochenende,** over/for the weekend. **3.** + *acc* (*betreffend*) about; **ein Buch ü. Kunst,** a book about/on art. **II.** *adv.* **1.** (*mehr als*) over, more than; **seit ü. einem Jahr,** for more than a year. **2.** **das ganze Jahr ü.,** all (the) year round; **ü. und ü.,** all over. **III.** *adj.* F: **j-m ü. sein,** to be superior to/more than a match for s.o.
überall, *adv.* everywhere, *esp. N.Am:* all over.
über'anstrengen, *v.tr.insep.* to over-exert (s.o., oneself); to overstrain (one's heart etc.).
über'arbeiten, *v.tr.insep.* (*a*) to rework, revise (a text etc.); (*b*) **sich ü.,** to over-work; **überarbeitet,** overworked.
überaus, *adv.* extremely, exceedingly.
über'backen, *v.tr.insep.irr.1* *Cu:* to brown (cauliflower etc.); **mit Käse ü.,** au gratin.
über'bieten, *v.tr.insep.irr.8* (*a*) (*bei einer Auktion*) to outbid (s.o.); (*b*) to excel/surpass (s.o., oneself etc.); **einen Rekord ü.,** to break a record.
'Überbleibsel [-blaipsəl], *n -s/-* remnant.
'Überblick, *m* (*a*) panoramic/*Fig:* overall view (**über etwas** *acc,* of sth.); (*b*) (*Vor-*

trag usw.) survey. ◆**ü~en** [-'blikən], *v.tr.insep.* to overlook, have a view of (sth.); *Fig:* to grasp, take in (a situation etc.).
über'bringen, *v.tr.insep.irr.16* to deliver.
über'brücken, *v.tr.insep.* to get/(*mit Geld*) tide over (a period); **Gegensätze ü.,** to reconcile differences.
über'dauern, *v.tr.insep.* to outlast (sth.), (*überstehen*) survive (wars etc.).
über'denken, *v.tr.insep.irr.17* to think (sth.) over.
überdimensional [y:bərdimɛnzio'na:l], *adj.* huge, outsize.
'Überdosis, *f* overdose.
'Überdruck, *m Ph:* excess pressure.
Überdruß ['y:bərdrus], *m -sses/no pl* surfeit, (*Müdigkeit*) weariness (**an etwas** *dat,* of sth.). ◆**ü~drüssig** [-drysiç], *adj.* **j-s, einer Sache** *gen* **ü.,** tired of/fed up with s.o., sth.
'überdurchschnittlich, *adj.* above average.
übereifrig, *adj.* overeager.
über'eilen, *v.tr.insep.* to rush (matters etc.); to do (sth.) too hastily. ◆**ü~t,** *adj.* (over)hasty, (*leichtsinnig*) rash.
übereinander, *adv. & comb.fm.* (*a*) on top of one another; one above the other; (*b*) **ü. reden,** to talk about one another.
über'einkommen, *v.i.sep.irr.53* (*sein*) *Lit:* to agree, reach agreement. ◆**Ü~kunft,** *f -/-e* agreement, understanding. ◆**ü~stimmen,** *v.i.sep.* (*haben*) to agree, (*Aussagen usw.*) tally, (*Farben*) match (**mit etwas** *dat,* sth.). ◆**ü~stimmend,** *adj.* concurring (reports etc.); **ü. mit** + *dat,* in conformity with. ◆**Ü~stimmung,** *f* agreement.
'überempfindlich, *adj.* over-sensitive.
über'fahr|en, *v.tr.insep.irr.26* (*a*) to run over (s.o., an animal); (*b*) to drive across (a lige etc.), drive through (traffic lights) etc. ◆**'Ü~t,** *f Nau:* crossing.
'Überfall, *m* (surprise) attack (**auf** + *acc,* on); (*auch von Räubern*) raid (**auf eine Bank,** on a bank). ◆**ü~en** [-'falən], *v.tr.insep.irr.27* to attack (s.o., a place); (*suddenly*) to raid, hold up (a bank etc.).
'überfällig, *adj.* overdue.
über'fliegen, *v.tr.insep.irr.7* to fly over.
'Überfluß, *m* abundance; (*zu groß*) surplus, excess (**an etwas** *dat,* of sth.); **im Ü. leben,** to live in luxury.
'überflüssig, *adj.* superfluous; (*unnötig*) unnecessary.
über'fluten, *v.tr.insep.* to flood over.
über'fordern, *v.tr.insep.* to ask too much of (s.o.); to strain, overtax (the heart, *Fig:* s.o.'s patience etc.).
über'führ|en, *v.tr.insep.* (*a*) to transport, convey (s.o., sth.); (*b*) *Jur:* **j-n (eines Verbrechens) ü.,** to find s.o. guilty (of a

crime). ◆**Ü~ung**, f -/-en 1. transport(ation). 2. Jur: conviction. 3. (Brücke) flyover, esp. N.Am: overpass.

überfüllt [-'fylt], adj. crammed full; overcrowded (schools, buses etc.); congested (roads).

'**Ubergabe**, f -/no pl handing over; esp. Mil: surrender (**an** + acc, to).

'**Ubergang**, m 1. (a) no pl crossing; (b) (Brücke) footbridge. 2. (Wechsel) transition (**auf/in** + acc, to). ◆**Ü~s-**, comb.fm: interim (regulation, solution etc.); transitional (stage etc.). ◆**Ü~szeit**, f transitional period/season.

über'geben, v.tr.insep.irr.35 (a) to hand (s.o., sth.) over, (hefern) deliver (sth.), (anvertrauen) entrust (sth.); to pass on (a message etc.); Mil: to surrender (a town etc.); (b) **sich ü.**, to vomit, be sick.

übergehen, v.irr.36 1. ['y:bərge:ən] v.i.sep. (sein) (a) **ins feindliche Lager/zu einer anderen Partei ü.**, to go over to the enemy/another party; (b) (Besitz) **auf j-n ü.**, to pass to s.o.; (c) **zu etwas (anderem) ü.**, to proceed/pass on to sth. (else); (d) **in etwas ü.**, to change (gradually) into sth. 2. [y:bər'ge:ən] v.tr.insep. to ignore (s.o., sth.); (bei der Beförderung usw.) to pass (s.o.) over; (auslassen) to skip (a chapter etc.).

'**übergeschnappt**, adj. F: round the bend.

'**Ubergewicht**, n excess weight/(Gepäck) baggage; **Ü. haben**, to be overweight.

übergießen [-'gi:sən], v.tr.insep.irr.31 **et-was mit Wasser ü.**, to pour water over sth.

'**überglücklich**, adj. overjoyed.

'**übergreifen**, v.i.sep.irr.43 (haben) (Brand usw.) to spread (**auf** + acc, to).

'**Ubergriff**, m infringement; encroachment (**auf** + acc, on); Mil: incursion (**auf** + acc, into).

'**übergroß**, adj. oversize, outsize.

'**Ubergröße**, f Cl: outsize.

über'handnehmen, v.i.sep.irr.69 (haben) to increase/multiply out of all proportion; (Unkraut usw.) to get out of hand.

über'häufen, v.tr.insep. to inundate (s.o.).

über'haupt, adv. 1. (im allgemeinen) altogether. 2. **nicht/nichts**, not/nothing at all; **ü. nicht möglich**, completely impossible; **wie war es ü. möglich?** how was it at all possible?

über'heblich, adj. arrogant; (eingebildet) conceited, self-important. ◆**Ü~keit**, f -/no pl arrogance; conceit.

über'holen, v.tr.insep. (a) to overtake, pass (s.o., a car); (b) Tchn: (instandsetzen) to overhaul (an engine etc.). ◆**ü~t**, adj. obsolete; (veraltet) old-fashioned, out of date. ◆**Ü~verbot**, n overtaking ban; (auf Verkehrsschild) no overtaking.

über'hören, v.tr.insep. not to hear (sth.); (absichtlich) to ignore (sth.).

'**überirdisch**, adj. supernatural; heavenly

(beauty).

überkochen, v.i.sep. (sein) (Milch usw.) to boil over.

über'lagern, v.tr.insep. to cover, overlie, (teilweise) overlap (sth.); **sich ü.**, to overlap.

über'lassen, v.tr.insep.irr.57 **j-m etwas ü.**, to leave sth. to s.o.; (abtreten) to relinquish/yield sth. to s.o.

über'lasten, v.tr.insep. to overload (a lorry etc.), overstrain (the heart).

überlaufen, v.irr.58 1. ['y:bərlaufən] v.i.sep. (sein) (a) (Bad, Topf usw.) to overflow; (b) (Soldaten usw.) **zum Gegner ü.**, to go over to the enemy/other side. 2. [y:bər'laufən] v.tr.insep. **es überläuft mich kalt, wenn ...**, shivers run down my spine when... **von Touristen ü.**, overrun/(stark) inundated with tourists.

'**Uberläufer**, m turncoat, renegade.

über'leben, v.tr.insep. (a) to survive (an accident etc.); (b) to outlive (s.o.) (**um 2 Jahre**, by 2 years). ◆**Ü~de(r)**, m & f decl. as adj. survivor.

über'legen. I. v.tr. & i.insep. (haben) (etwas) **ü.**, to think (about sth.), consider (sth.); **er hat es sich anders überlegt**, he has changed his mind. II. adj. superior (**j-m**, to s.o.), **an Kraft usw.**, in strength etc.); **ein ü~ener Sieg**, a clear victory. ◆**Ü~enheit**, f -/no pl superiority. ◆**Ü~ung**, f -/-en (a) consideration; (b) pl deliberations.

über'leiten, v.i.sep. (haben) **zu etwas dat ü.**, to lead/go on to sth. (else). ◆**Ü~ung**, f transition.

über'liefern, v.tr.insep. to hand (sth.) down. ◆**Ü~ung**, f tradition; (Brauch) old custom.

über'listen [-'listən], v.tr.insep. to outwit (s.o.).

überm ['y:bərm] = **über dem**.

'**Ubermacht**, f -/no pl superiority, superior strength/(zahlenmäßig) numbers.

über'mächtig, adj. (a) superior (in strength); (b) Fig: overwhelming (desire etc.).

über'mannen [-'manən], v.tr.insep. (Gefühle usw.) to overcome (s.o.).

'**Ubermaß**, n excess (**an Arbeit usw.**, of work etc.).

'**übermäßig**, adj. excessive.

'**Ubermensch**, m superman. ◆**ü~lich**, adj. superhuman.

Übermüdung [-'my:duŋ], f overtiredness.

übermitteln [-'mitəln], v.tr.insep. to transmit, pass on (a message etc.). ◆**Ü~lung**, f transmission.

'**übermorgen**, adv. the day after tomorrow.

'**Ubermut**, m exuberance, high spirits.

'**übermütig**, adj. high-spirited, boisterous; frisky, (frech) cocky (child etc.).

'**übernächste(r,s)**, adj. (the) next (house etc.) but one; (the week, year etc.) after next.

über'nacht|en, *v.i.insep.* (haben) to stay/ spend the night (**bei j-m,** with s.o.). ◆**U~ung,** *f* -/-en overnight stay.

über'nächtigt, *adj.* bleary-eyed.

'Übernahme, *f* -/-n taking over; under- taking (of a task etc.); acceptance (of re- sponsibility etc.).

übernatürlich, *adj.* supernatural.

über'nehmen, *v.tr.insep.irr.69* (a) to take over (a business, job etc.); (*selbst anwen- den*) to adopt, F: borrow (ideas, a pas- sage), (*auf sich nehmen*) to undertake, take on (a task, *Jur:* case etc.); to accept (responsibility etc.); (b) **sich ü.,** to over- do it/things; (*beruflich/finanziell*) to take on too much.

über'prüf|en, *v.tr.insep.* (a) to check (s.o., sth.); (b) to screen, vet (suspects); (b) (*von neuem prüfen*) to review (a decision etc.). ◆**U~ung,** *f* (a) check(ing); screening; (b) review.

über'queren, *v.tr.insep.* to cross (a street etc.).

über'ragen, *v.tr.insep.* (a) to tower above (s.o., sth.); (b) *Fig:* to outclass (s.o.).

überrasch|en [y:bər'raʃən], *v.tr.insep.* to surprise (s.o.); **j-n beim Stehlen ü.,** to catch s.o. stealing. ◆**ü~end,** *adj.* sur- prising; (*unerwartet*) unexpected (visit etc.); **es kam ü.,** it came as a surprise. ◆**U~ung,** *f* -/-en surprise. ◆**U~ungs-,** *comb.fm.* surprise (attack, victory, winner etc.).

über'reden, *v.tr.insep.* to persuade (s.o.).

über'reichen, *v.tr.insep.* to hand over, (*feierlich*) present (sth.).

überreizt ['-raitst], *adj.* overexcited, over- wrought.

'Überrest, *m* remnant; (*Spur*) relic (of a civilization etc.); *esp. pl* remains, ruins.

über'rumpeln, *v.tr.insep.* to take (s.o.) by surprise.

übers ['y:bərs] = **über das.**

'Überschall-, *comb.fm.* supersonic (speed, aircraft etc.).

über'schätzen, *v.tr.insep.* to overesti- mate.

über'schau|bar, *adj.* (*Szene*) visible at a glance; (*Sache*) easy to grasp. ◆**ü~en,** *v.tr.insep.* = **übersehen** (a).

über'schlafen, *v.tr.insep.irr.84* F: to sleep (a decision).

überschlagen, *v.irr.85* 1. ['y:bər'ʃla:gən], *v.tr.insep.* (*auslassen*) to skip, miss out (a passage, lunch etc.); (b) (*berechnen*) to estimate (roughly), tot up (costs etc.); (c) **sich ü.,** (*Pers.*) to somersault; (*Auto*) to overturn; *Fig:* **seine Stimme überschlug sich,** his voice cracked/broke. 2. ['y:bərʃla:gən] *v.tr.sep.* to cross (one's legs etc.). 3. ['y:bər'ʃla:gən] *v.i.sep.* (sein) (*Funken usw.*) to jump across; (*Wellen*) to break.

über'schneiden, *v.refl.insep.irr.59* **sich ü.,** (*Linien usw.*) to intersect; *Fig:* (*The- men usw.*) to overlap; (*zeitlich*) (*Ereignisse usw.*) to coincide, clash.

über'schreiben, *v.tr.insep.irr.12* (a) to head (a chapter etc.); (b) (*übertragen*) to make over (property).

über'schreiten, *v.tr.insep.irr.41* to cross (a frontier etc.); *Fig:* to exceed (a limit, one's authority etc.); to pass (its peak); to infringe (a regulation).

'Überschrift, *f* heading, title.

'Überschuß, *m* (a) surplus (**an Frauen usw.,** of women etc.); (b) (*Gewinn*) profit.

überschüssig [y:bər-ʃysiç], *adj.* surplus (heat, energy, goods etc.); excess (profits etc.).

über'schütten, *v.tr.insep.* to cover (s.o., sth.); **j-n mit Geschenken usw. ü.,** to shower s.o. with presents etc.

überschwemm|en [y:bər'ʃvɛmən], *v.tr.insep.* to flood. ◆**U~ung,** *f* -/-en 1. *no pl* overflowing (of a river etc.); (*also Fig:*) flooding. 2. (*Hochwasser*) flood.

überschwenglich ['y:bərʃvɛŋliç], *adj.* ef- fusive; extravagant (style, praise etc.).

'Übersee. I. *inv.* overseas; **aus/von Ü.,** from overseas; **nach Ü. gehen,** to go overseas. **II. 'Ü~-,** *comb.fm.* overseas (trade, traffic etc.).

über'seh|bar, *adj.* easily surveyed; *Fig:* clear (situation); foreseeable (conse- quences). ◆**ü~en,** *v.tr.insep.irr.92* (a) to overlook (a valley etc.); *Fig:* to have an overall view of (a situation etc.); (b) (*nicht sehen*) to overlook; **es ist nicht zu ü.,** you can't miss it.

über'senden, *v.tr.insep.irr.94* **j-m etwas ü.,** to send sth. to s.o.

übersetz|en, *v.* 1. [y:bər'zɛtsən] *v.tr.&i.insep.* (haben) (a) to translate (sth.) (**ins Deutsche usw.,** into German etc.). 2. ['y:bərzɛtsən] *v.i.sep.* (haben/ sein) to cross (over). ◆**U~er** ['-zɛtsər], *m* translator. ◆**U~ung** ['-zɛtsuŋ], *f* -/-en 1. translation. 2. *Tchn:* gearing; (*Ü~ungsverhältnis*) gear ratio.

'Übersicht. 1. overall view. 2. (*Abriß*) outline, survey (**über** + *acc*, of); (*Tabelle*) table. ◆**ü~lich,** *adj.* easily surveyed, *Fig:* clear, lucid (description etc.). ◆**Ü~lichkeit,** *f* -/*no pl* openness; *Fig:* clarity.

übersiedeln, *v.i.sep.* ['y:bərzi:dəln] & *in- sep.* [y:bər'zi:dəln] (sein) (*Pers., Firma*) to (re)move.

'übersinnlich, *adj.* supernatural (powers etc.).

über'spannen, *v.tr.insep.* (a) (*Brücke, Dach*) to span (a river, space etc.); (*be- spannen*) to cover (sth.); (b) (*zu stark*) to overtighten (a bow etc.).

über'spitzt, *adj.* exaggerated; (*allzu fein*) oversubtle.

über'springen, *v.tr.sep.irr.19* (a) to jump over (sth.), clear (a fence, *Sp:* height etc.); (b) (*auslassen*) to skip (a class, chapter etc.).

überstehen, *v.irr.100* 1. ['y:bərʃte:ən] *v.i.sep.* (haben) to project, jut out. 2.

[y:bər'∫te:ən] v.tr.insep. to get over, recover from (an illness etc.); to overcome, surmount (a danger, difficulties); to weather (a storm, crisis etc.); (*überleben*) to survive (a catastrophe, the winter etc.); to come through (an operation etc.).

über'steigen, v.tr.insep.irr.89 (a) to climb over (sth.); (b) to exceed (a sum, expectations).

über'stimmen, v.tr.insep. to outvote (s.o.).

'Überstunden, fpl overtime.

über'stürz|en, v.tr.insep. to rush (into) (sth.); (*Ereignisse usw.*) **sich ü.**, to follow in rapid succession. ◆**ü~t**, adj. overhasty.

über'tönen, v.tr.insep. to drown (a voice etc.).

Übertrag ['y:bərtra:k], m -(e)s/=e sum carried forward. ◆**ü~bar** [-'tra:kba:r], adj. transferable (auf + acc, to); Med: infectious, (*durch Berührung*) contagious. ◆**ü~en** [-'tra:gən], v.tr.insep.irr.85 (a) to transfer (sth.) (**auf etwas** acc, to sth.); to transmit (Med: a disease, Tchn: power etc.) (**auf** + acc, to); to assign (a task etc.); (b) (*übersetzen*) to translate (a text); **in ü~ener Bedeutung**, in a figurative sense, figuratively; (c) Rad: TV: to broadcast, transmit (a programme). ◆**U~ung**, f -/-en (a) transfer; Med: Tchn: transmission; (b) translation; transcription; (c) Rad: TV: transmission, broadcast.

über'treffen, v.tr.insep.irr.104 (a) to surpass, outdo; **er hat sich selbst übertroffen**, he excelled himself; (b) (*übersteigen*) to exceed (expectations etc.).

über'treib|en, v.tr. & i.insep.irr.12 (*haben*) to exaggerate (sth.), carry (demands etc.) too far. ◆**U~ung**, f -/-en exaggeration.

übertret|en v.irr.105 **1.** ['y:bərtre:tən] v.i.sep. (sein) **zur Opposition usw. ü.**, to go over to the opposition etc.; **zum katholischen Glauben ü.**, to be converted to the Catholic faith. **2.** [y:bər'tre:tən] v.tr.insep. to break (a law, rule etc.), infringe (a regulation). ◆**U~ung**, f -/-en infringement; offence; Jur: misdemeanour.

über'trieben, adj. exaggerated.

'Übertritt, m changeover; Ecc: conversion.

übervölker|t [y:bər'fœlkərt], adj. overpopulated. ◆**U~ung**, f -/no pl overpopulation.

'übervoll, adj. overfull.

über'vorteilen, v.tr.insep. to cheat (s.o.).

über'wach|en, v.tr.insep. to supervise; (*Polizei*) to shadow (s.o.), control (traffic etc.). ◆**U~ung**, f -/no pl supervision; control.

überwältigen [y:bər'vɛltigən], v.tr.insep. (*also Fig:*) to overwhelm (s.o.). ◆**ü~d**, adj. overwhelming (victory etc.).

über'weis|en, v.tr.insep.irr.70 to pay, transfer (money). ◆**U~ung**, f -/-en remittance, payment; transfer (of money).

über'wiegen, v.insep.irr.7 **1.** v.i. (*haben*) to predominate, (*Meinung usw.*) prevail. **2.** v.tr. to outweigh (sth.). ◆**ü~d**, adj. (a) predominant (feature, tone etc.); substantial (majority); (b) adv. mainly.

überwind|en [y:bər'vindən], v.tr.insep.irr.9 to overcome (difficulties, one's fear), surmount (an obstacle etc.), get over (shyness, a crisis etc.); **sich ü.**, **etwas zu tun**, to bring oneself to do sth. ◆**U~ung**, f -/no pl willpower, strength of mind.

'Überzahl, f majority.

überzählig ['y:bərtsɛ:liç], adj. superfluous; Com: etc: surplus (to requirements).

über'zeug|en, v.tr.insep. to convince (s.o., oneself) (**von etwas** dat, of sth.); **ü. Sie sich selbst!** see for yourself! ◆**ü~end**, adj. convincing (argument, proof etc.); compelling (reason). ◆**U~ung**, f -/no pl conviction.

überziehen, v.tr.irr.113 **1.** ['y:bərtsi:ən] v.sep. to put on (a coat etc.) (on top). **2.** [y:bər'tsi:ən] v.insep. (a) to cover (sth.); Ind: to coat (sth.); (b) Fin: to overdraw (one's account).

'Überzug, m **1.** coating (of sugar etc.); coat (of varnish etc.). **2.** (*Bezug*) (chair etc.) cover.

üblich ['y:pliç], adj. usual.

'U-Boot, n submarine.

übrig ['y:briç], adj. (a) attrib. (*andere*) remaining, other (parts, things etc.); **das ü~e**, the rest; **die ü~en**, the others; **the rest of them**; **alles ü~s**, everything else; **im ü~en**, for the rest; otherwise; (b) pred. left (over); (c) **er hat viel für sie ü.**, he likes her a lot. ◆**'ü~bleiben**, v.i. sep.irr.12 (*sein*) to remain, be left; **mir bleibt nichts anderes ü. als zu...**, I have no alternative but to... ◆**'ü~ens** [-gəns], adv. by the way, incidentally. ◆**'ü~lassen**, v.tr.sep.irr.57 to leave (sth.).

Übung ['y:buŋ], f -/-en **1.** practice; Mil: Sp: training. **2.** (*Aufgabe*) exercise. ◆**'U~s-**, comb.fm. practice (flight etc.); training (area etc.).

Ufer ['u:fər], n -s/- (*Seeu.*) shore; (*Flußu.*) (river) bank. ◆**'u~los**, adj. endless; (*grenzenlos*) boundless. ◆**'U~straße**, f riverside/lakeside road.

Uhr [u:r], f -/-en clock; (*Armbandu./Taschenu.*) watch; **acht U.**, eight o'clock; **wieviel U. ist es/haben Sie?** what time is it/do you make it? ◆**'U~(arm)band**, n watch strap. ◆**'U~macher**, m watchmaker; clockmaker. ◆**'U~werk**, n clockwork. ◆**'U~zeiger**, m watch/clock hand. ◆**'U~zeigersinn**, m **im U.**, clockwise; **entgegen dem U.**, anticlockwise.

Uhu ['u:hu:], m -s/-s eagle owl.

Ulk [ulk], *m* -(e)s/-e joke; (*Streich*) lark.
◆**u~ig,** *adj.* F: comical, funny; (*seltsam*) odd.

Ulme ['ulmə], *f* -/-n elm.

Ultimatum [ulti'ma:tum], *n* -s/-ten & -s ultimatum.

Ultra- ['ultra-], *comb.fm.* ultra-(conservative, -modern etc.). ◆**U~kurzwelle,** *f Rad:* very high frequency. ◆**U~schall-,** *comb.fm.* ultrasonic (frequency, wave etc.).

um [um]. **I.** *prep.* + *acc* **1.** (*räumlich*) (a)round; **um sich schlagen,** to lash out in all directions. **2.** (*Zeitpunkt*) (a) (*genau*) **um 20 Uhr,** at 8 p.m.; (b) (*ungefähr*) around; (c) (*Folge*) **Tag um Tag/Stunde um Stunde,** day after day/hour after hour. **3.** (a) (*Zweck*) for; **um Geld spielen,** to play for money; (b) (*wegen*) about; **sich um etwas streiten,** to quarrel over/about sth. **4.** (*Maß*) by; **um einen Kopf größer,** taller by a head; **um vieles besser,** far better. **II.** *conj.* **1. um zu** + *infin.,* (in order) to. **2. um so besser/weniger,** all the better/less. **III.** *adv.* (*vorbei*) over. **IV.** *prep.* + *gen* **um ... willen,** for the sake of...

'umänder|n, *v.tr.sep.* to alter (sth.). ◆**U~ung,** *f* -/-en alteration.

'umarbeit|en, *v.tr.sep.* to remake, remodel (a dress etc.); to revise, rewrite (a book etc.). ◆**U~ung,** *f* -/-en revision; adaptation; *Cl:* remodelling.

um'arm|en, *v.tr.insep.* to embrace, (*fest*) hug (s.o.). ◆**U~ung,** *f* -/-en embrace, hug.

'Umbau, *m* (structural) alteration(s); conversion. ◆**u~en,** *v.tr.sep.* to alter, make structural alterations in (a building).

'umbiegen, *v.tr.sep.irr.7* to bend (sth.) over/back.

'umbild|en, *v.tr.sep.* to transform (sth.); *Pol:* to reshuffle (a cabinet). ◆**U~ung,** *f* transformation; reshuffle.

'umblättern, *v.tr. & i.sep.* (*haben*) to turn over (the page).

'umblicken, *v.refl.sep.* **sich u.,** to look round.

'umbringen, *v.tr.sep.irr.16* to kill, (*ermorden*) murder (s.o.); **sich u.,** to kill oneself, commit suicide.

'Umbruch, *m esp. Pol:* radical change; upheaval.

'umbuchen, *v.tr.sep.* to change the reservation for (one's flight etc.).

'umdrehen, *v.sep.* **1.** *v.tr.* (a) (*auf die andere Seite*) to turn over (a stone, page, record etc.); to turn (a mattress etc.); (b) (*um seine Achse*) to turn (sth.) round; to turn (a key); **sich u.,** (*Pers.*) to turn round; (c) **j-m den Hals u.,** to wring s.o.'s neck. **2.** *v.i.* (*sein*) to turn back. ◆**U~ung** ['-dre:uŋ], *f* turn; *Ph: Astr:* rotation; *Tchn:* revolution.

umei'nander, *adv.* (a) around each other; (b) **sie kümmern sich nicht um u.,** they don't bother about each other.

umfahren, *v.tr.irr.26* **1.** ['umfa:rən] *v.sep. Aut: etc:* to knock (s.o., sth.) down. **2.** [um'fa:rən] *v.sep.* to go/*Aut:* drive/*Nau:* sail round (an obstacle etc.), bypass (a town etc.).

'umfallen, *v.i.sep.irr.27* (*sein*) to fall over/ (*zum Boden*) down; (*zusammenbrechen*) to collapse.

'Umfang, *m* -(e)s/no *pl* **1.** circumference (of a tree, circle etc.). **2.** (*Größe*) size; (*Fläche*) area (of an estate etc.); (*Ausmaß*) extent (of a book etc.); volume (of business etc.); * range (of a voice etc.). ◆**u~reich,** *adj.* extensive; long (book).

um'fassen, *v.tr.insep.* (a) to put one's arm round (s.o., s.o.'s waist); (*mit Händen*) to clasp (sth.); (b) (*umgeben*) to surround; (c) (*enthalten*) to contain (200 pages etc.), comprise (four volumes etc.). ◆**u~d,** *adj.* comprehensive (knowledge, powers etc.); full (confession, description etc.).

'umform|en, *v.tr.sep.* to revise, recast (a sentence etc.). ◆**U~er,** *m* -s/- *El:* converter.

'Umfrage, *f* (public) opinion poll; survey.

'umfüllen, *v.tr.sep.* to pour (sth.) (into another container); to decant (wine).

umfunktionieren, *v.tr.sep.* to change the function/purpose of (sth.); to convert (sth.).

'Umgang, *m* association, contact (**mit j-m,** with s.o.); **mit j-m U. haben/pflegen,** to associate with s.o.; **schlechten U. haben,** to keep bad company; der **U. mit Büchern/Tieren,** working with books/dealing with animals. ◆**'umgänglich** [-gɛŋliç], *adj.* sociable, affable. ◆**U~sformen,** *fpl* manners, social graces. ◆**U~ssprache,** *f* colloquial speech. ◆**u~ssprachlich,** *adj.* colloquial.

um'geb|en, *v.tr.insep.irr.35* to surround (s.o., oneself, sth.); (*einschließen*) to enclose (sth.). ◆**U~ung,** *f* -/-en (a) surroundings; (*Gegend*) neighbourhood; **in der (näheren) U.,** in the vicinity; (b) (*Umkreis*) circle.

umgeh|en, *v.irr.36* **1.** ['umge:ən] *v.i.sep.* (*sein*) (a) to circulate; (*Gerücht usw.*) *F:* to go the rounds; **die Grippe geht wieder um,** there's (a lot of) flu about again; (b) **mit j-m, etwas** *dat* **u.,** to handle s.o., sth.; (*behandeln*) to treat (s.o., sth.); (*verkehren*) to associate with s.o.; **er versteht mit Kindern umzugehen,** he knows how to handle children. **2.** [um'ge:ən] *v.tr.insep.* (a) to go round (sth.); *Aut:* to bypass (a town); (b) (*vermeiden*) to avoid (a difficulty etc.); (*nicht beachten*) to evade/get round (a law, regulation). ◆**u~end,** *adj.* immediate; **umgehende Antwort,** reply by return. ◆**U~ung** [um'ge:uŋ], *f* -/no *pl* (a) bypassing; (b) avoidance, evasion. ◆**U~ungsstraße,** *f* bypass.

'umgekehrt, *adj.* opposite; reverse (order

etc.); **es ist gerade u.!** it's exactly the opposite.

um'grenzen, v.tr.insep. to border, (Zaun) enclose (a field etc.).

'Umhang, m wrap, cape.

'umhängen, v.tr.sep. (a) to hang (sth.) somewhere else; (b) **j-m, sich** dat **etwas u.,** to put sth. round s.o.'s/one's shoulders.

um'her, adv. & comb.fm. (to wander, drive etc.) around; (to look etc.) about. ◆**u~gehen,** v.i.sep.irr.36 (sein) to go/walk around.

um'hinkönnen, v.i.sep.irr.54 (haben) **ich kann nicht umhin, es zu tun,** I cannot help/get out of (doing) it.

'umhören, v.refl.sep. **sich u.,** to ask around.

um'hüllen, v.tr.insep. to wrap (s.o., sth.) up. ◆**U~ung,** f **/-en** wrapper, wrapping.

'Umkehr, f **-/no pl** (a) turning back; (b) Pol: etc: about-face. ◆**u~bar,** adj. reversible. ◆**U~en,** v.sep. **1.** v.i. (sein) to turn back. **2.** v.tr. (a) to turn (pockets etc.) inside out; (b) to reverse (the order, a development etc.). ◆**U~ung,** f **-/no pl** reversal.

'umkippen, v. **1.** v.i.sep. (sein) (a) to fall over; (Auto usw.) to overturn; (Boot) to capsize; (b) F: (ohnmächtig werden) to faint; (c) F: (seine Meinung ändern) to give way (under pressure), change one's tune. **2.** v.tr. to tip (sth.) over, upset (a vase etc.).

um'klammern, v.tr.insep. to clasp, cling to (s.o., sth.).

'Umkleide|kabine, f changing cubicle. ◆**u~n,** v.refl.sep. **sich u.,** to change (one's clothes). ◆**U~raum,** m changing room.

'umkommen, v.i.sep.irr.53 to die, be killed.

'Umkreis, m **-es/no pl** (Nähe) vicinity, neighbourhood; **im U. von drei Kilometer(n),** within a radius of three kilometres. ◆**u~en** [um'kraizəs], v.tr.insep. to circle (around) (sth.); (Planet) to revolve around, (Satellit) orbit (a star).

'Umlauf, m circulation (of blood, money etc.); **im U. sein,** (Geld) to be in circulation; Fig: (Gerüchte usw.) to circulate. ◆**U~bahn,** f Astr: orbit.

'Umlaut, m umlaut.

'umlegen, v.tr.sep. (a) **j-m/sich** dat **einen Mantel usw. u.,** to put a coat etc. round s.o./oneself; (b) to transfer, move (a cable, patient etc.); (c) F: (erschießen) to bump (s.o.) off.

'umleit|en, v.tr.sep. to divert (traffic etc.). ◆**U~ung,** f diversion.

um'nachtet, adj. Lit: **geistig u.,** mentally deranged.

um'rahmen, v.tr.insep. to frame (a picture, Fig: face etc.); Fig: **von Wäldern umrahmt,** ringed by woods.

'umrechn|en, v.tr.sep. Mth: to convert **(Mark in Pfund usw.,** marks into pounds etc.). ◆**U~ung,** f conversion. ◆**U~ungskurs,** m rate of exchange.

um'reißen, v.tr.insep.irr.4 to outline (a situation etc.).

um'ringen, v.tr.insep. to surround (s.o., sth.).

'Umriß, m contour, outline.

'umrühren, v.tr.sep. to stir (soup, paint etc.).

ums [ums] **= um das.**

'umsatteln, v.i.sep. (haben) F: to change jobs.

'Umsatz, m turnover. ◆**U~steuer,** f turnover/N.Am: sales tax.

'umschalten, v.sep. **1.** to switch (the TV, radio etc.) (over) (auf + acc, to); to move (a switch, lever etc.) (auf + acc, to). **2.** v.i. (haben) to change, switch over, TV: Rad: retune (auf + acc to).

'Umschau, f **-/no pl** look round; **nach j-m, etwas** dat **U. halten,** to be on the lookout for s.o., sth. ◆**u~en,** v.refl.sep. **sich u. = sich umsehen.**

'Umschlag, m **1.** (dust) jacket (of a book). **2.** (Briefu.) envelope. **3.** Med: compress. **4.** Cl: cuff; (Hosenu.) turn-up, N.Am: cuff (of trousers); (Saum) hem. **5.** (Wetteru. usw.) sudden change. ◆**u~en** [-gən], v.sep.irr.85 **1.** v.tr. (a) (umwenden) to turn over (pages etc.), fold back (the carpet), turn up (one's sleeves); (b) (umhauen) to knock (sth.) down, fell (a tree etc.). **2.** v.i. (sein) (a) (Auto usw.) to overturn, (Boot) capsize; (b) (Wetter, Fig: Stimmung) to change abruptly; (Wind) to veer (round).

umschreiben, v.tr.irr.12 **1.** ['umʃraibən] v.sep. (a) to rewrite, redraft (a text); (b) **etwas auf j-n/ein Konto u.,** to transfer sth. to s.o.'s an account. **2.** [um'ʃraibən] v.insep. (genau) to define (duties etc.); (mit anderen Worten) to paraphrase (a term etc.).

'umschulen, v.tr.sep. (a) to move (a child) to another school; (b) (umerziehen) to re-educate (s.o.); Ind: to retrain (s.o.).

'Umschweife, m pl **etwas ohne U. sagen,** to say sth. bluntly/straight out.

'Umschwung, m reversal (of fortunes, public opinions etc.), about-turn.

'umsehen, v.refl.sep.irr.92 **sich u.,** to look round/back; **sich nach einem passenden Geschenk u.,** to be looking/on the lookout for a suitable present.

umseitig, adj. overleaf.

'umsetzen, v.tr.sep. Com: to sell/turn over (goods).'

'Umsicht, f circumspection, discretion, prudence. ◆**u~ig,** adj. circumspect; (klug) prudent.

'umsiedeln, v.tr.&i.sep. (sein) to resettle (refugees etc.).

um'sonst, adv. for nothing; (vergeblich) in vain.

um'spannen, v.tr.insep. to clasp, (mit den

Armen) reach round (sth.); *Fig:* to encompass (an area), span (a period).

Umstand ['umʃtant], *m* **1.** (*a*) circumstance; **ein entscheidender U.,** a decisive factor; (*b*) *pl* **unter diesen/keinen U~en,** in these/no circumstances; (*c*) **in anderen U~en,** in the family way. **2.** *pl* (*Mühe*) bother; trouble; **ohne U~e,** without ceremony; (*sogleich*) without further ado. ◆'**U~skleid,** *n* maternity dress.

umständ|ehalber ['umʃtɛndshalbər], *adv.* due to circumstances. ◆'**u~lich,** *adj.* awkward; (*übergenau*) fussy (person, manner etc.); complicated, involved (description etc.).

'**umsteigen** *v.i.sep.irr.89* (*sein*) to change (trains/buses).

'**umstellen** *v.tr.* **1.** ['umʃtɛlən] *v.sep.* (*a*) to shift round, rearrange (furniture etc.); (*b*) (*neu einstellen*) to readjust (sth.), reset (a switch, clock etc.); (*c*) (*ändern*) to change (one's diet etc.). **2.** [um'ʃtɛlən] *v.insep.* to surround (a house etc.). ◆'**U~ung,** *f* (*a*) rearrangement; redeployment; (*b*) readjustment, resetting; (*c*) changeover, conversion.

'**umstimmen,** *v.tr.sep.* (*überreden*) to make (s.o.) change his/her mind; to win (s.o.) round.

'**umstoßen,** *v.tr.sep.irr.103* to knock (s.o., a vase etc.) over; *Fig:* to upset, wreck (a plan, calculations etc.).

um'**stritten,** *adj.* disputed (thesis etc.); controversial (subject, issue etc.).

'**Umsturz,** *m Pol:* overthrow (of a regime); coup.

'**umstürzen** *v.sep.* **1.** *v.tr.* to knock over (chairs, tables etc.). **2.** *v.i.* (*sein*) to fall over, (*Mauer usw.*) fall down.

'**Umtausch,** *m* exchange. ◆'**u~en,** *v.tr.sep.* to exchange (sth.) (**gegen etwas** *acc,* for sth.); to change (money).

'**Umtriebe,** *mpl* machinations, intrigues.

'**umwandeln,** *v.tr.sep.* (*a*) to transform (s.o.'s character etc.); (*b*) *Ph: Ch:* to convert (sth.) (**in** + *acc,* into). ◆'**U~lung,** *f* transformation; conversion.

'**Umweg,** *m* detour.

'**Umwelt. I.** *f -/no pl* environment. **II.** '**U~–,** *comb.fm.* environmental (factor, question etc.); *Biol: etc:* ecological (policy etc.). ◆'**u~freundlich,** *adj.* harmless to the environment. ◆'**U~schutz,** *m* conservation. ◆'**U~schützer,** *m* conservationist. ◆'**U~verschmutzung,** *f* (environmental) pollution.

'**umwenden,** *v.tr.sep.irr.94* to turn over (a page etc.); (*Pers.*) **sich u.,** to turn round.

'**umwerfen,** *v.tr.sep.irr.110* to knock over (s.o., a vase etc.), overturn (a table); *Fig:* to upset, wreck (plans). ◆'**u~d,** *adj.* stupendous (success etc.); stunning (beauty).

um'**zäunen.** *v.tr.insep.* to fence in/round (a plot etc.).

'**umziehen,** *v.sep.irr.113* **1.** *v.i.* (*sein*) to

move (**nach X,** to X). **2.** *v.tr.* **ein Kind/ sich u.,** to change a child's/one's clothes.

um**zingeln** [um'tsiŋəln], *v.tr.insep.* to surround, encircle (the enemy, a town etc.).

'**Umzug** ['umtsuːk], *m* **1.** move, removal (**nach** + *dat* to). **2.** procession.

un**abänderlich** [un²ap²ɛndɛrlɪç], *adj.* unalterable (fact etc.); irrevocable (decision etc.).

'**unabhängig,** *adj.* independent. ◆'**U~keit,** *f -/no pl* independence.

unab'kömmlich, *adj.* indispensable.

un**ablässig** ['un²aplɛsɪç], *adj.* incessant, constant (complaints etc.); unremitting (efforts).

un**ab'sehbar,** *adj.* (*a*) unforeseeable (consequences etc.); (*b*) (*unermeßlich*) immeasurable (loss etc.).

'**unabsichtlich,** *adj.* unintentional.

un**abwendbar** [un²ap'vɛntbaːr], *adj.* unavoidable, inevitable.

'**unachtsam,** *adj.* (*nachlässig*) careless, negligent (action etc.).

'**unähnlich,** *adj.* dissimilar; **j-m u.,** unlike s.o.

'**unangebracht,** *adj.* inappropriate, out-of-place (remark etc.).

'**unangemessen,** *adj.* inappropriate.

'**unangenehm,** *adj.* unpleasant; (*peinlich*) embarrassing, awkward (question etc.).

un**an'nehm|bar,** *adj.* unacceptable. ◆'**U~lichkeit,** *f –/-en usu.pl* **j-m U~lichkeiten bereiten,** to cause s.o. difficulties/trouble.

'**unansehnlich,** *adj.* plain (girl etc.); shabby (clothes etc.).

'**unanständig,** *adj.* indecent (behaviour, language, dress etc.); dirty (joke etc.), rude (word).

un**an'tastbar,** *adj.* sacrosanct; *Jur:* inviolable (rights etc.).

'**unappetitlich,** *adj.* unappetizing (food etc.); *Fig:* unsavoury.

'**Unart** ['un²aːrt], *m* bad habit. ◆'**u~ig,** *adj.* naughty.

'**unauffällig,** *adj.* inconspicuous; unobtrusive (colour, behaviour etc.).

'**unauf'findbar,** *adj.* nowhere to be found.

'**unaufgefordert,** *adj.* of one's own accord.

un**aufhaltsam** [un²auf'haltzaːm], *adj.* irresistible, inexorable.

un**aufhörlich** [un²auf'høːrlɪç], *adj.* incessant, ceaseless.

'**unaufmerksam,** *adj.* inattentive.

'**unaufrichtig,** *adj.* insincere.

un**aufschiebbar** [-'ʃiːpbaːr], *adj.* urgent, pressing.

un**ausbleiblich** [un²aus'blaiplɪç], *adj.* inevitable.

'**unausgeglichen,** *adj.* unbalanced, *Fig:* (*Pers.*) unstable.

un**aus'löschlich,** *adj.* indelible (impression etc.).

un**aus'sprechlich,** *adj.* inexpressible; unutterable (misery etc.).

un**ausstehlich** [-'ʃteːlɪç], *adj.* insufferable.

unbändig ['unbɛndiç], *adj.* uncontrollable; unruly (child); **sich u. freuen**, to be jumping for joy.

unbarmherzig, *adj.* merciless.

unbeabsichtigt, *adj.* unintentional.

'unbeachtet, *adj.* unnoticed; unheeded (warning etc.).

unbedenklich, *adj.* harmless (proposal etc.).

'unbedeutend, *adj.* insignificant; minor (damage, poet etc.); trivial (matter).

unbe'dingt [*stressed* 'un-], *adj.* absolute (loyalty, obedience etc.); **kommst du? ja, u.!** are you coming? yes, definitely; **nicht u.**, not necessarily; **das müssen Sie sich u. ansehen**, you really must see that.

'unbefangen, *adj.* 1. (*unparteiisch*) unbiased; impartial. 2. (*natürlich*) unaffected, natural.

'unbefriedigend, *adj.* unsatisfactory.

'unbefugt, *adj.* unauthorized.

unbegabt, *adj.* untalented, ungifted.

unbegreiflich [unbə'graifliç], *adj.* incomprehensible.

unbegrenzt, *adj.* unlimited.

'unbegründet, *adj.* unfounded (optimism etc.); groundless (accusation, fear etc.).

'Unbehag|en, *n* -*s*/*no pl* uneasiness; (*körperlich*) discomfort. ◆**'u~lich**, *adj.* uncomfortable (atmosphere etc.); uneasy (feeling etc.).

'unbeherrscht, *adj.* (*Pers.*) lacking/without self-control.

'unbeholfen, *adj.* awkward, clumsy.

unbeirr|bar [unbə'?irba:r], *adj.* unwavering, unswerving. ◆**u~t** [-'?irt], *adv.* unswervingly; without wavering.

'unbekannt, *adj.* unknown; **ein U~er/eine U~e**, a stranger.

'unbekleidet, *adj.* undressed.

unbekümmert, *adj.* unconcerned; easygoing (person, manner).

unbelehrbar [unbe'le:rba:r], *adj.* not open to reason.

'unbeliebt, *adj.* unpopular. ◆**'U~heit**, *f* unpopularity.

'unbemannt, *adj.* unmanned (satellite etc.).

unbe'merkt, *adj.* unnoticed, unobserved.

'unbequem, *adj.* (*a*) uncomfortable (shoe, chair etc.); (*b*) (*peinlich*) awkward (person, questions etc.).

unbe'rechenbar, *adj.* unpredictable.

'unberechtigt, *adj.* unjustified (criticism, claim etc.).

'unberührt, *adj.* untouched; unspoilt (countryside); **u~es Mädchen**, virgin.

unbescheiden, *adj.* immodest, presumptuous.

unbeschränkt, *adj.* unlimited.

unbeschreiblich [unbə'fraipliç], *adj.* indescribable.

'unbeschwert, *adj.* carefree; lighthearted (mood).

unbe'sehen, *adj.* unseen, unexamined; **etwas u. kaufen**, to buy sth. sight un-

seen.

unbesieg|bar [unbə'zi:kba:r], *adj.* invincible; *Sp:* unbeatable. ◆**u~t**, *adj. Sp:* -unbeaten.

'unbesonnen, *adj.* thoughtless, imprudent; (*übereilt*) rash.

'unbesorgt, *adj.* unconcerned; **seien Sie u.**, don't worry.

'unbeständig, *adj.* changeable (weather etc.); unsettled (weather, *Fin:* market etc.); fluctuating (prices etc.); *Fig:* (*Pers.*) inconsistent.

'unbestechlich, *adj.* incorruptible.

unbe'stimm|bar, *adj.* indeterminate (age etc.); indefinable (feeling etc.). ◆**'u~t**, *adj.* indefinite (period, future, *Gram:* article); indeterminate (age); (*unsicher*) uncertain; (*unklar*) vague (feeling etc.). ◆**'U~theit**, *f* indefiniteness; uncertainty; vagueness.

unbe'streitbar, *adj.* incontestable, indisputable.

'unbestritten, *adj.* uncontested, undisputed.

'unbeteiligt, *adj.* not involved; (*gleichgültig*) detached (observer etc.).

unbeugsam [un'bɔykza:m], *adj.* uncompromising; unshakable (will etc.).

unbeweg|lich, *adj.* (*a*) (*nicht zu bewegen*) immovable, fixed (joint, part etc.); (*b*) (*ganz still*) motionless, immobile (figures etc.). ◆**'u~t**, *adj.* motionless; calm, still (sea etc.); *Fig:* (*unberührt*) unmoved.

'unbewiesen, *adj.* unproved, (*Schuld*) unproven.

unbe'wohn|bar, *adj.* uninhabitable. ◆**'u~t**, *adj.* uninhabited (region etc.); unoccupied (house).

'unbewußt, *adj.* unconscious.

unbe'zahl|bar, *adj.* 1. prohibitively expensive. 2. priceless (painting etc.). ◆**'u~t**, *adj.* unpaid.

'unblutig, *adj.* bloodless (revolution etc.).

'unbrauchbar, *adj.* useless (work, person etc.); unusable, (*defekt*) unserviceable (apparatus etc.).

und [unt], *conj.* and; *F:* **u. ob!** you bet! and how! **na u.?** well? what then? (*wenn schon*) so what!

Undank, *m Lit:* ingratitude. ◆**'u~bar**, *adj.* ungrateful (**gegen** j-n, to s.o.); **u~bare Aufgabe**, thankless task. ◆**'U~barkeit**, *f* -/*no pl* ingratitude.

un'denkbar, *adj.* unthinkable, inconceivable.

'undeutlich, *adj.* unclear; indistinct.

'undicht, *adj.* leaky, leaking.

'Unding, *n* **es ist ein U., zu ...**, it is absurd/preposterous to ...

'unduldsam, *adj.* intolerant.

undurch'führbar, *adj.* impracticable.

'undurchlässig, *adj.* impermeable, impervious.

undurch'schaubar, *adj.* unfathomable; (*Pers.*) inscrutable, baffling.

'undurchsichtig, *adj.* opaque; *Fig:* baffling; (*suspekt*) shady.

'**uneben**, *adj.* uneven (surface etc.); (*holperig*) bumpy, rough (road etc.).

'**unecht**, *adj.* imitation (leather, pearls etc.); artificial (flowers); false (hair etc.).

'**unehelich**, *adj.* illegitimate (child).

'**unehrlich**, *adj.* dishonest, (*betrügerisch*) deceitful.

'**uneigennützig**, *adj.* unselfish, selfless.
◆'**U~keit**, *f* unselfishness.

'**uneinig**, *adj.* (*Gruppe*) divided; **u. sein**, to disagree/be at loggerheads (**mit j-m,** with s.o.). ◆'**U~keit**, *f* disagreement, dissension.

uneins ['ʊn'ains], *adj.* = uneinig.

'**unempfindlich**, *adj.* insensitive (**gegen** + *acc*, to); (*abgehärtet*) hardened, inured. ◆'**U~keit**, *f* insensitivity.

un'endlich, *adj.* infinite; (*Zeit, Weg*) endless; **u. groß/hoch,** enormously large/high. ◆'**U~keit**, *f -/no pl* endlessness; infinity; (*Ewigkeit*) eternity.

unent'behrlich, *adj.* indispensable.

unentgeltlich [ʊn'ɛnt'gɛltlɪç], *adj.* gratis, free.

'**unentschieden**. **I.** *adj.* undecided; (*Frage*) unsettled; *Sp:* drawn (game); **u~es Rennen,** dead heat. **II. U.,** *n -s/- Sp:* draw.

'**unentschlossen**, *adj.* undecided; (*allgemein*) irresolute, indecisive.

unentwegt [ʊn'ɛnt've:kt], *adj.* (*unaufhörlich*) incessant, uninterrupted; (*unermüdlich*) tireless (fighter etc.); (*wiederholt*) constant.

unerbittlich [ʊn'ɛr'bitlɪç], *adj.* unrelenting (critic, struggle etc.); inexorable (fate, law); **u. bleiben,** to remain adamant.

'**unerfahren**, *adj.* inexperienced.
◆'**U~heit**, *f* inexperience.

'**unerfreulich**, *adj.* unpleasant, disagreeable.

uner'gründlich, *adj.* unfathomable.

'**unerheblich**, *adj.* insignificant (quantity etc.).

uner'hört ['ʊnɛr'hø:rt], *adj.* (*a*) (*noch nie dagewesen*) unheard of, unprecedented (achievement etc.); (*b*) (*skandalös*) outrageous, scandalous (behaviour etc.); exorbitant (prices).

uner'klärlich, *adj.* inexplicable.

unerläßlich [ʊn'ɛr'lɛslɪç], *adj.* indispensable.

'**unerlaubt**, *adj.* not allowed, prohibited; (*unbefugt*) unauthorized.

uner'meßlich, *adj.* immeasurable, immense.

unermüdlich [ʊn'ɛr'my:tlɪç, 'un-], *adj.* untiring, tireless.

uner'reichbar, *adj.* unattainable (goal etc.); inaccessible (place etc.). ◆**u~t**, *adj.* unequalled (performance etc.).

unersättlich [ʊnɛr'zɛtlɪç], *adj.* insatiable.

unerschöpflich [-'ʃœpflɪç], *adj.* inexhaustible.

'**unerschrocken**, *adj.* intrepid, fearless.

unerschütterlich [-'ʃytərlɪç], *adj.* unshakable (will etc.).

uner'schwinglich, *adj.* exorbitant, prohibitive (price etc.).

unersetzlich [ʊn²ɛr'zɛtslɪç], *adj.* irreplaceable.

uner'träglich, *adj.* intolerable, unbearable.

'**unerwartet**, *adj.* unexpected.

'**unerwünscht**, *adj.* unwanted, unwelcome (visit, visitor etc.).

'**unerzogen**, *adj.* badly behaved/brought up.

'**unfähig**, *adj.* (*a*) *pred.* incapable (**zu etwas** *dat*, of sth.); (*b*) (*untauglich*) incompetent. ◆'**U~keit**, *f* (*a*) inability; (*b*) incompetence.

Unfall ['unfal]. **I.** *m* accident. **II.** '**U~-,** *comb.fm.* accident (insurance etc.).
◆'**u~frei**, *adj.* accident-free. ◆'**U~ort**, *m* scene of the accident.

unfaßbar [ʊn'fasbaːr], *adj.* incomprehensible.

unfehlbar [ʊn'fe:lbaːr], *adj.* infallible.
◆'**U~keit**, *f -/no pl* infallibility.

'**unfolgsam**, *adj.* disobedient.

'**unfreiwillig**, *adj.* involuntary; (*unbeabsichtigt*) unintentional (joke etc.).

'**unfreundlich**, *adj.* (*a*) unfriendly; unkind (words etc.); unwelcoming (face); *Pol:* hostile (act); (*b*) (*trüb*) cheerless (room etc.); unpleasant, inclement (weather etc.). ◆'**U~keit**, *f* (*a*) unfriendliness; unkindness; (*b*) cheerlessness; inclemency.

'**unfruchtbar**, *adj.* (*a*) infertile (animal, soil); sterile (person); (*b*) *Fig:* fruitless (discussion etc.).

Unfug ['unfu:k], *m -(e)s/no pl* mischief; *F:* monkey business; (*Unsinn*) nonsense, rubbish; *Jur:* **grober U.,** public nuisance.

Ungar(in) ['ʊngar(in)], *m -n/-n (f -/-nen)** Hungarian (man/woman). ◆'**u~isch**, *adj.* Hungarian. ◆'**U~n,** *Pr.n. n. -s.* Hungary.

ungeachtet ['ʊngə²axtət], *prep. + gen Lit:* notwithstanding; (*trotz*) despite.

unge'ahnt, *adj.* unsuspected.

'**ungebeten**, *adj.* unasked, uninvited.

'**ungeboren**, *adj.* unborn.

'**ungebräuchlich**, *adj.* not usual; (*selten*) uncommon.

'**ungedeckt**, *adj.* uncovered, *F:* dud (cheque etc.).

'**Ungeduld**, *f* impatience. ◆'**u~ig**, *adj.* impatient.

'**ungeeignet**, *adj.* unsuitable; wrong, inappropriate (tool, method); inopportune (moment).

unge'fähr ['ʊngəfɛ:r]. **1.** *adj.* approximate, rough. **2.** *adv.* approximately; about.

'**ungefährlich**, *adj.* safe, not dangerous; harmless (animal, drug etc.).

'**ungehalten**, *adj.* annoyed; (*entrüstet*) indignant.

ungeheuer ['ʊngəhɔʏər]. **I.** *adj.* immense, enormous (size, height, wealth etc.); tremendous (strength, luck etc.); (*schrecklich*) terrible (pain etc.); **u. groß**, tremendously large; **u. heiß**, terribly hot. **II. U.**, *n -s/-* monster. ◆'u~lich, *adj.* monstrous (accusation, crime etc.); outrageous (remark).

'**ungehindert**, *adj.* unhindered; (*ungestört*) undisturbed.

'**ungehörig**, *adj.* unseemly, improper. ◆'U~keit, *f -/-en* impropriety.

'**ungehorsam**. **I.** *adj.* disobedient. **II. U.**, *m* disobedience.

'**ungeklärt**, *adj.* not cleared up; unsolved (problem, mystery); unsettled (question).

'**ungekürzt**, *adj.* unabridged.

'**ungeladen**, *adj.* uninvited (guest etc.).

'**ungelegen**, *adj.* inopportune (remark, proposal etc.); inconvenient (time etc.).

'**ungelernt**, *adj.* unskilled (worker).

'**ungemein**, *adj.* extraordinary, prodigious (effort, progress etc.); *adv.* exceedingly.

'**ungemütlich**, *adj.* (a) uninviting, cheerless (room etc.); uncomfortable (atmosphere etc.); (b) unpleasant (situation, meeting etc.); unfriendly (person).

'**ungenau**, *adj.* inaccurate (measurement, calculation etc.).

ungeniert ['unʒeni:rt], *adj.* unconcerned, nonchalant; (*ungehemmt*) uninhibited, free and easy (behaviour etc.); **etwas u. aussprechen**, to say sth. quite openly.

unge'nießbar, *adj.* inedible, uneatable (food); undrinkable (wine etc.); *F:* (*Pers.*) unbearable.

'**ungenügend**, *adj.* inadequate; (*nicht genug*) insufficient; (*mangelhaft*) unsatisfactory.

'**ungenutzt**, *adj.* unused.

'**unge'ordnet**, *adj.* out of order, in disorder.

'**ungepflegt**, *adj.* unkempt; *F:* scruffy (person, appearance etc.).

'**ungerade**, *adj.* odd, uneven (number).

'**ungerecht**, *adj.* unjust (**gegen** j-n, to s.o.); unfair. ◆'u~fertigt, *adj.* unjustified. ◆'U~igkeit, *f* injustice.

'**ungern**, *adv.* unwillingly; (*widerwillig*) reluctantly.

'**ungerührt**, *adj.* unmoved; impassive (face etc.).

'**Ungeschick**, *n*/'U~lichkeit, *f* clumsiness; ineptitude. ◆'u~t, *adj.* (a) clumsy, inept; *F:* ham-fisted; (b) (*taktlos*) tactless.

'**ungeschminkt**, *adj.* without make-up; *Fig:* **die u~e Wahrheit**, the plain/unvarnished truth.

'**ungeschützt**, *adj.* unprotected; unsheltered.

'**ungesetzlich**, *adj.* illegal. ◆'U~keit, *f* illegality.

'**ungesittet**, *adj.* improper, uncivilized.

'**ungestört**, *adj.* undisturbed; uninterrupted (development).

'**ungestraft**, *adj.* unpunished; **u. davonkommen**, to get off scot-free.

'**ungesund**, *adj.* unhealthy.

'**ungeteilt**, *adj.* undivided; united (country etc.); (*einmütig*) unanimous (approval etc.).

'**ungetrübt**, *adj.* perfect (happiness), blissful, unspoilt (days).

Ungetüm ['ungaty:m], *n -(e)s/-e* monster.

'**ungewiß**, *adj.* uncertain. ◆'U~heit, *f* uncertainty.

'**ungewöhnlich**, *adj.* unusual; exceptional (performance, talent etc.).

'**ungewohnt**, *adj.* unaccustomed; **diese Arbeit ist mir u.**, I am not used to this work.

'**ungewollt**, *adj.* unwanted (pregnancy etc.); (*unbeabsichtigt*) unintentional, inadvertent.

Ungeziefer ['ungætsi:fər], *n -s/no pl* vermin.

'**ungezogen**, *adj.* badly behaved, naughty (child); (*frech*) cheeky.

'**ungezwungen**, *adj.* (*Pers.*) natural, unaffected; informal, free and easy (conversation, atmosphere etc.).

unglaub|haft, *adj.* incredible, unconvincing. ◆u~lich [un'glauplɪç], *adj.* incredible; (*unerhört*) appalling (conditions etc.). ◆'u~würdig, *adj.* unbelievable; implausible (story); untrustworthy.

'**ungleich**, *adj.* **1.** unequal (size, struggle etc.); (*unähnlich*) dissimilar; **u~es Paar**, ill-assorted couple. **2.** *adv.* **u. schwerer**, far more difficult. ◆'U~heit, *f* inequality; dissimilarity. ◆'u~mäßig, *adj.* irregular (pulse etc.); uneven, unequal (distribution etc.).

'**Unglück**, *n* (a) misfortune; (*Pech*) bad luck; (*Elend*) distress, misery; **zum U.**, unfortunately; (b) (*Unfall*) accident; (*Mißgeschick*) mishap. ◆u~lich, *adj.* (a) (*unglücvig*) unfortunate, unlucky (person, coincidence, choice etc.); (b) (*traurig*) unhappy (person, ending etc.). ◆'u~licher'weise, *adv.* unfortunately. ◆'u~selig, *adj.* hapless (person); ill-starred, ill-fated (affair etc.); unfortunate (affair, liking etc.). ◆'U~sfall, *m* (great) misfortune; (*Unfall*) (serious) accident.

'**Ungnade**, *f* **bei j-m in U. fallen**, to fall out of favour with s.o.

'**ungültig**, *adj.* invalid.

'**ungünstig**, *adj.* unfavourable; adverse (conditions etc.); (*ungelegen*) inconvenient (time).

'**ungut**, *adj.* bad (impression, memory etc.); **ein u~es Gefühl haben**, to have misgivings/feel uneasy; **nichts für u.!** no hard feelings!

'**unhaltbar**, *adj.* **1.** untenable (assertion etc.). **2.** (*unerträglich*) intolerable (conditions etc.). **3.** *Sp:* unstoppable (ball, shot).

'**unhandlich**, *adj.* unwieldy, cumbersome.

'**Unheil**, *n* *Lit:* **1.** disaster, misfortune; (*Schaden*) damage; **großes U. anrichten**,

to cause havoc. 2. (*Böses*) evil.
◆'u~bar, *adj.* incurable (disease, person). ◆'u~voll, *adj.* disastrous (consequences etc.); malign (influence).

'unheimlich, *adj.* 1. eery, uncanny (experience, atmosphere, feeling etc.); weird (person, story etc.); sinister (appearance). 2. *F:* (*riesig*) terrific, tremendous (appetite, amount etc.); **u. schnell**, incredibly fast.

'unhöflich, *adj.* impolite; (*absichtlich*) rude. ◆'U~keit, *f* impoliteness; rudeness.

'unhygienisch, *adj.* unhygienic.

Uniform [uni'fɔrm], *f* -/-en uniform. ◆u~iert ['-'mi:rt], *adj.* uniformed, in uniform.

'uninteress|ant, *adj.* uninteresting; (*gleichgültig*) immaterial. ◆'u~iert, *adj.* uninterested (**an etwas** *dat*, in sth.); bored (face).

Union [uni'o:n], *f* -/-en union.

univers|al [univer'za:l], *adj.* universal. ◆U~alerbe, *m* sole heir. ◆u~ell [-'zɛl], *adj.* universal. ◆U~ität [-zi'tɛ:t], *f* -/-en university. ◆U~um ['-verzum], *n* -s/*no pl* universe.

'unkenntlich, *adj.* unrecognizable; (*Text*) undecipherable. ◆'U~nis, *f* ignorance

'unklar, *adj.* unclear; cloudy (liquid etc.); indistinct (outline etc.); **j-n über etwas** *acc* **im u.~en lassen**, to leave s.o. in the dark about sth. ◆'U~heit, *f* lack of clarity; vagueness, indistinctness; **darüber herrscht U.**, it is uncertain.

'unklug, *adj.* imprudent, unwise.

'unkompliziert, *adj.* uncomplicated.

'Unkosten, *fpl* expenses.

'Unkraut, *n* (*a*) *no pl coll* weeds; (*b*) (type of) weed.

'unkritisch, *adj.* uncritical.

'unlängst, *adv.* recently, not long ago.

'unleserlich, *adj.* illegible, unreadable (handwriting).

'unliebsam ['unli:pzo:m], *adj.* unpleasant (surprise etc.).

'unlogisch, *adj.* illogical.

un'lösbar, *adj.* 1. inseparable (union, bond etc.). 2. insoluble (problem etc.); impossible (task).

'Unlust, *f* disinclination, reluctance; **mit U.**, reluctantly.

'Unmasse, *f F:* mass; **U~n/eine U.** (**von**) **Geld**, masses/loads of money.

'unmäßig, *adj.* immoderate, excessive; inordinate (desire).

'Unmenge, *f* mass (**an/von** + *dat*, of); **eine U. Geld**, masses of money.

'Unmensch, *m* brute; *F:* **ich bin ja kein U.**, I'm not inhuman. ◆u~lich, *adj.* 1. brutal; inhuman (cruelty); (*menschenunwürdig*) subhuman (conditions etc.). 2. *F:* (*schrecklich*) terrible (heat etc.).

un'merklich, *adj.* imperceptible.

'unmißverständlich, *adj.* unmistakable.

un'mittelbar, *adj.* direct (connection, consequence etc.); immediate (surround-

ings, superior etc.).

'unmöbliert, *adj.* unfurnished (room etc.).

'unmodern, *adj.* old-fashioned, unfashionable.

unmöglich ['un-, *stressed* un'mø:kliç], *adj.* (*a*) impossible; **ich kann u. kommen**, I cannot possibly come; (*b*) *F:* ridiculous, absurd (hat, dress etc.); **sich u. benehmen**, to behave outrageously.

'unmoralisch, *adj.* immoral.

'Unmut, *m Lit:* displeasure.

unnachahmlich ['unna:xʔa:mliç], *adj.* inimitable.

'unnachgiebig, *adj.* unyielding, inflexible.

unnahbar [un'na:ba:r], *adj.* unapproachable, *F:* standoffish (person).

'unnatürlich, *adj.* unnatural.

'unnötig, *adj.* unnecessary; needless (anger, worry). ◆'u~er'weise, *adv.* unnecessarily.

'unnütz, *adj.* useless; (*sinnlos*) pointless; wasted (effort, expenditure).

'unordentlich, *adj.* untidy (person, room, desk etc.); (*nachlässig*) slipshod (work, style etc.).

'Unordnung, *f* disorder, mess.

'unparteiisch, *adj.* impartial, unbiased; *Sp:* **der U~e**, the referee.

'unpassend, *adj.* unsuitable, inept (remark); (*ungelegen*) inconvenient, inopportune.

unpäßlich ['unpɛsliç], *pred.adj.* poorly, under the weather.

'unpersönlich, *adj.* impersonal; (*Pers.*) distant, aloof.

'unpolitisch, *adj.* non-political; (*Pers.*) unpolitical.

'unpraktisch, *adj.* impractical; impracticable (plan etc.).

'unproblematisch, *adj.* problem-free; (*einfach*) straightforward, uncomplicated.

'unpünktlich, *adj.* unpunctual. ◆'U~keit, *f* lack of punctuality; lateness.

'unrasiert, *adj.* unshaven.

'Unrat, *m* (*e*)*s/no pl* refuse, *N.Am:* trash.

'unrealistisch, *adj.* unrealistic.

'unrecht. I. *adj.* wrong. II. *U.*, *n* (*a*) injustice, wrong; **im U. sein**, to be (in the) wrong/mistaken; **mit/zu U.**, unjustly, wrongly; (*b*) **u. haben**, to be wrong; **damit tust du ihm u.**, there you are doing him an injustice. ◆'u~mäßig, *adj.* illegal, unlawful.

'unredlich, *adj.* dishonest.

'unregelmäßig, *adj.* irregular (pulse, *Gram:* verb etc.); uneven (surface etc.). ◆'U~keit, *f* 1. *no pl* irregularity; unevenness. 2. *esp.pl* U~en, irregularities.

'unreif, *adj.* unripe; *Fig:* immature (person etc.). ◆'U~e, *f* -/*no pl* unripeness; *Fig:* immaturity.

'unrein, *adj.* unclean (shirt etc.); dirty (water etc.); impure (alcohol etc.); blemished (skin).

'unrentabel, *adj.* unprofitable.

'**unrichtig**, *adj.* incorrect, wrong.

Unruh ['unru:], *f* -/-en balance wheel.

'**Unruh|e**, *f* 1. *no pl* (*Ruhelosigkeit*) restlessness; (*Unbehagen*) uneasiness; (*Besorgnis*) anxiety, disquiet; **U. stiften**, to stir up trouble. 2. *Pol: etc: usu.pl* **U~n**, disturbances, *esp.* riots. ◆**u~ehrend**, *m* trouble spot. ◆**U~estifter**, *m* troublemaker, agitator. ◆**u~ig**, *adj.* restless (person, people, life etc.); troubled, fitful (sleep); (*besorgt*) anxious, worried; (*nervös*) jittery.

uns [uns], *pers.pron.* 1. (*a*) *acc* us; (*b*) *dat* (to) us; **das gehört u.**, that belongs to us; **ein Freund von u.**, a friend of ours; **bei u.**, (i) at our home/*F:* place; (ii) (*in der Heimat*) where we come from. 2. *refl.* ourselves; (*einander*) each other, one another.

'**unsachgemäß**, *adj.* improper, inexpert. ◆**u~lich**, *adj.* subjective (standpoint etc.); (*nicht zur Sache*) irrelevant (remarks etc.).

un'sagbar/*Lit:* **unsäglich** [un'ze:kliç], *adj.* inexpressible, unutterable; beyond expression.

'**unsanft**, *adj.* rough; abrupt (push etc.).

'**unsauber**, *adj.* 1. (*schmutzig*) dirty; *Fig:* blurred (sound). 2. (*unordentlich*) untidy (handwriting etc.). 3. (*fragwürdig*) shady (practices etc.).

'**unschädlich**, *adj.* harmless; **u. machen**, to render (sth.) harmless; defuse (a bomb); (*ausschalten*) to eliminate (s.o.).

'**unscharf**, *adj.* blurred, fuzzy; *Phot:* out of focus; *Fig:* woolly (definition etc.).

un'schätzbar [un'fɛtsbaːr], *adj.* inestimable (value etc.); invaluable (services etc.).

'**unscheinbar**, *adj.* inconspicuous; nondescript.

un'schlagbar, *adj.* unbeatable (team etc.).

'**unschlüssig**, *adj.* undecided; irresolute.

Unschuld ['unʃult], *f* -/no pl innocence; (*Jungfräulichkeit*) virginity. ◆**u~ig**, *adj.* (*a*) innocent (**an etwas** *dat*, of sth.); *fur:* **sich u. bekennen**, to plead not guilty; (*b*) **sie ist noch u.**, she is still a virgin.

'**unschwer**, *adv.* easily, without difficulty.

'**unselbständig**, *adj.* dependent (on others); lacking in independence.

unser ['unzər], *poss.adj.* our. ◆**u~e(r,s)**, *poss.pron.* ours. ◆**u~eins**, *indef.pron.* F: people like you and me; the likes of us. ◆**u~erseits**, *adv.* for our part. ◆**u~esgleichen**, *inv.indef.pron.* our equals, people like ourselves. ◆**u~(e)twegen**, *adv.* for our sake, on our account.

'**unsicher**, *adj.* 1. (*gefährlich*) unsafe, dangerous; (*bedroht*) insecure (jobs etc.). 2. (*zweifelhaft*) uncertain; (*nicht selbstsicher*) unsure (of oneself); unsteady, shaky (hand etc.); *Pol: etc:* unstable, unsettled (conditions etc.). ◆**U~heit**, *f* 1. un-

safeness, insecurity. 2. uncertainty; unsteadiness.

'**unsichtbar**, *adj.* invisible.

Unsinn ['unzin], *m* nonsense, rubbish; (*Unfug*) tomfoolery. ◆**u~ig**, *adj.* (*sinnlos*) senseless, foolish, stupid (talk, ideas etc.).

'**Unsitt|e**, *f* bad habit/(*Brauch*) practice. ◆**u~lich**, *adj.* immoral.

'**unsozial**, *adj.* anti-social (laws etc.).

'**unsportlich**, *adj.* 1. unsporting (behaviour etc.); unfair (play). 2. **er ist sehr u.**, he is not at all the sporting type.

unsre ['unzrə] = **unsere**.

un'sterblich, *adj.* immortal. ◆**U~keit**, *f* immortality.

'**unstet**, *adj.* restless (person, nature etc.); wandering (glance); unsettled (life).

unstillbar [un'ʃtilba:r, 'un-], *adj.* insatiable (desire); unquenchable (thirst).

'**Unstimmigkeit**, *f* -/-en (*a*) difference of opinion; (*b*) (*Fehler*) inconsistency, discrepancy.

'**Unsumme**, *f* enormous sum, fortune.

'**unsympathisch**, *adj.* uncongenial, disagreeable; **er ist mir u.**, I don't like him.

'**Untat**, *f* atrocity, monstrous crime.

'**untätig**, *adj.* inactive; idle.

'**untauglich**, *adj.* unsuitable, wrong; (*nutzlos*) useless; *Mil:* (*Pers.*) unfit for military service.

un'teilbar, *adj.* indivisible.

unten ['untən], *adv.* (*a*) (*an der Unterseite*) underneath; **u. im Faß/auf der Seite**, at the bottom of the barrel/page; **nach u. hin/zu**, towards the bottom; *F:* **er ist bei mir u. durch**, I'm through with him; (*b*) (*unterhalb*) (down) below; **hier/dort u.**, down here/there; (*c*) (*Richtung*) **nach u.**, downwards; (*d*) (*im Haus*) downstairs.

unter ['untər], *prep.* + *dat/acc* under; (*tiefer als*) below; **u. seiner Würde**, beneath his dignity; **eine Abteilung u. sich haben**, to be in charge of a department; (*mitten*) **u.**, among(st), amidst; **u. anderem**, among other things; **u. uns gesagt**, between you and me; **u. sich sein**, to be in private/undisturbed; **u. der Woche**, during the week; **was versteht man u. diesem Ausdruck?** what is meant by this expression?

'**unterbelichtet**, *adj.* underexposed.

'**unterbewußt**, *adj.* subconscious (motive etc.). ◆**U~sein**, *n Psy:* subconscious (mind).

unter'bieten, *v.tr.insep.irr.8* (*a*) *Com:* to undercut (prices); to undersell (the competition); (*b*) *Sp:* to beat (a record, time).

unter'binden, *v.tr.insep.irr.9* to put a stop to, prevent (sth.).

unter'bleiben, *v.i.insep.irr.12* (*sein*) **das muß u.**, that must not happen again.

'**Unterbodenschutz**, *m* underseal.

unter'brech|en, *v.tr.insep.irr.14* (*a*) to interrupt (s.o., sth.); *El:* to disconnect, switch off (current); to break (a circuit); (*c*) *Sp:* to stop (play); *Med:* to terminate (a pregnancy). ◆**U~ung,** f -/-en interruption; (*Pause*) break.

unter'breiten, *v.tr.insep.* **j-m etwas u.,** to submit sth. to s.o.

'**unterbringen,** *v.tr.sep.irr.16* to accommodate (s.o., sth.); (*lagern*) to store, *N.Am:* stash (sth.) (away); to fit in (sth. extra etc.).

unter'dessen, *adv.* meanwhile, in the meantime.

'**Unterdruck,** *m Ph:* subatmospheric pressure; vacuum.

unter'drück|en, *v.tr.insep.* (*a*) to suppress (a sigh, feelings, news etc.); to stifle (a yawn etc.); to choke back (one's anger); (*b*) to oppress (people etc.). ◆**U~ung,** f -/no pl suppression; oppression.

unterdurchschnittlich, *adj.* below average.

untere(r,s), *adj.* lower.

unterei'nander, *adv.* **1.** (*Lage*) one below/beneath the other. **2.** (*miteinander*) with one another; **das müssen Sie u. ausmachen,** you must decide that amongst yourselves.

'**unterentwickelt,** *adj.* underdeveloped.

'**unterernährt,** *adj.* undernourished.

'**Unterernährung,** f malnutrition.

Unter'fangen, *n -s/no pl* undertaking.

Unter'führung, f underpass; (*für Fußgänger*) subway.

'**Untergang,** *m* **1.** (*a*) sinking (of a ship); (*b*) setting of the sun/moon). **2.** downfall (of a person etc.); end (of the world).

unter'geben, *adj.* **j-m u.,** subordinate to/ under s.o.

'**untergehen,** *v.i.sep.irr.36* (*sein*) (*a*) (*Schiff usw.*) to sink; (*Pers.*) to go under; *Fig:* **im Lärm u.,** to be drowned by the noise; (*b*) (*Sonne usw.*) to set; (*c*) *Lit:* (*Volk usw.*) to perish; (*Welt*) to come to an end.

'**Untergeschoß,** *n* basement.

'**Untergewicht,** *n* **U. haben,** to be underweight.

unter'graben, *v.tr.insep.irr.42* to undermine (public order, one's health etc.).

'**Untergrund,** *m* **1.** *Agr:* subsoil. **2.** (*Farbe*) undercoat. **3.** *Pol:* underground. **II.** '**U~-,** *comb.fm.* underground (railway, movement etc.).

'**unterhalb.** **I.** *prep.* + *gen* underneath; (*tiefer als*) below. **II.** *adv.* **u. von** + *dat,* below.

'**Unterhalt,** *m* -(e)s/no pl **1.** support (of a wife, a family); (*U~sbeitrag*) maintenance, alimony. **2.** (*Instandhaltung*) upkeep. ◆**u~en** [-'haltən], *v.tr.insep.irr.45* (*a*) to support, keep (a family, one's parents etc.); to operate, run (a business etc.); (*instandhalten*) to maintain (roads, *Pol: etc:* relations etc.); (*b*) (*erfreuen*) to entertain, amuse (s.o. oneself); **wir haben uns prächtig u.,** we enjoyed ourselves immensely; we had a splendid time; (*c*) **sich mit j-m über etwas** *acc* **u.,** to (have a) talk to s.o. about

sth. ◆**u~sam,** *adj.* entertaining, amusing. ◆'**U~s-,** *comb.fm.* maintenance (costs, payment etc.). ◆**U~ung,** f **1.** *no pl* (*Pflege*) maintenance, upkeep. **2.** (*Gespräch*) conversation, talk. **3.** entertainment, amusement; **gute U.!** enjoy yourselves!

'**Unterhändler,** *m* -s/- negotiator; (*Vermittler*) mediator.

'**Unterhemd,** *n* vest; *N.Am:* undershirt.

'**Unterholz,** *n* undergrowth.

'**Unterhose,** f (*für Männer*) (pair of) underpants, *Brit:* pants.

'**unterirdisch,** *adj.* underground, subterranean.

'**Unterkiefer,** *m* lower jaw.

'**unterkommen,** *v.i.sep.irr.53* (*sein*) (*a*) to find accommodation; (*b*) *F:* (*eine Stelle finden*) to get a job.

unter'kühlt, *adj. Med:* suffering from hypothermia; *Fig:* cold, detached.

'**Unterkunft,** f -/-e accommodation; *Mil:* quarters.

'**Unterlage,** f **1.** underlay; (*Grundlage*) base. **2.** *pl* **U~n,** (supporting) documents, records.

Unter'laß [-las], *m* **ohne U.,** incessantly.

unter'lass|en, *v.tr.insep.irr.57* (*a*) to refrain from (doing) (sth.); (*b*) (*versäumen*) to omit (sth.). ◆**U~ung,** f -/-en omission, failure (to do sth.); *Jur:* default.

unter'laufen. **I.** *v.i.sep.irr.58* (*sein*) **ihm sind einige Fehler u.,** he has made several mistakes. **II.** *adj.* **mit Blut u.,** bloodshot (eye).

unterlegen. **I.** *v.tr.* ['untərle:gən] *v.sep.* to put (sth.) under(neath). **II.** [untər'le:gən], *adj.* **1.** inferior (j-m, to s.o.; **an Stärke usw.,** in strength etc.). **2.** (*besiegt*) defeated; *Sp:* losing (team etc.).

'**Unterleib,** *m* (*a*) lower abdomen; (*b*) (*der Frau*) womb, uterus.

unter'liegen, *v.i.insep.irr.62* (*sein*) (*a*) (*geschlagen werden*) to be defeated/beaten (j-m, by s.o.); (*b*) (*unterworfen sein*) to be subject to (rules, censorship etc.).

unterm ['untərm], *F:* = **unter dem.**

Unter'miete, f -/no pl **in/zur U. wohnen,** to be a subtenant. ◆**U~r(in),** *m(f)* subtenant, lodger.

unter'nehm|en. **I.** *v.tr.insep.irr.69* to undertake (a journey etc.); to take (a walk, measures etc.); to make (an attempt etc.); **viel zusammen u.,** to do a lot together. **II.** **U.,** *n* -s/- **1.** (*Vorhaben*) enterprise; *esp. Mil:* operation; **gewagtes U.,** risky undertaking, bold venture. **2.** *Com:* (*Betrieb*) enterprise, business concern. ◆**U~er,** *m* -s/- *Com:* entrepreneur; *Ind:* industrialist; (*Arbeitgeber*) employer. ◆**u~ungslustig,** *adj.* enterprising, go-ahead; (*kühn*) adventurous.

'**Unteroffizier,** *m* **1.** non-commissioned officer, NCO. **2.** (*Feldwebel*) sergeant.

'**unterordnen,** *v.tr.sep.* to subordinate (interests etc.); **sich u.,** to accept a subordinate role.

Unter|redung, f -/-en (formal) conversation, discussion.

Unterricht ['untərɪçt], m -(e)s/-e teaching; (privat) tuition; (Stunden) lessons; im U. erteilen, to teach s.o.; im U., in class. ◆**u~en** [-'rɪçtən], v.tr.insep. (a) to teach (s.o., a subject); (b) (informieren) to inform, notify (s.o.); sich u., to inform oneself, (laufend) keep oneself informed. ◆**U~sstunde,** f lesson.

'Unterrock, m petticoat, slip.

unters ['untərs], F: = unter das.

unter'sagen, v.tr.insep. j-m etwas u., to forbid s.o. to do sth.

Untersatz, m stand; (für Gläser) mat, coaster; (Untertasse) saucer.

unter'schätzen, v.tr.insep. to underestimate.

unter'scheid|en, v.insep.irr.65 1. v.tr. (a) to distinguish (two things), tell (two people/things) apart; (b) sich (von j-m, etwas dat) u., to differ (from s.o., sth.). 2. v.i. (haben) to distinguish, make a distinction. ◆**U~ung,** f -/-en distinction, discrimination.

Unterschied ['untərʃiːt], m -(e)s/-e 1. difference. 2. (Unterscheidung) distinction; im U. zu ihm, in contrast with/unlike him. ◆**u~lich,** adj. different; (schwankend) varying, variable. ◆**'u~slos,** adj. indiscriminate.

unter'schlag|en, v.tr.insep.irr.85 to embezzle (money); to suppress (news, evidence etc.). ◆**U~ung,** f -/-en embezzlement.

'Unterschlupf, m -(e)s/¨-e 1. (Versteck) hiding-place, hide-out. 2. (Obdach) shelter.

unter'schreiben, v.tr. & i.insep.irr.12 (haben) to sign (sth.).

'Unterschrift, f signature.

'Unterseeboot, n submarine.

'Unterseite, f bottom, underside.

'Untersetz|er, m mat, coaster. ◆**u~t** [-'zɛtst], adj. stocky, thickset.

'unterste(r, s), adj. lowest; bottom (floor, class etc.).

unterstehen, v.irr.100. 1. ['untərʃteːən] v.i.sep. (haben) to take shelter. 2. [untər'ʃteːən] v.i.insep. (haben) j-m u., to be/come under s.o., be subordinate to s.o. 3. [untər'ʃteːən], v.refl.insep. sich u., etwas zu tun, to have the audacity to do sth.; unterstehe dich! don't you dare!

unterstell|en, v.tr. 1. ['untərʃtɛlən] v.sep. (a) to put, (lagern) store (sth. somewhere); (in einer Garage) to garage (a car); (b) sich unter einem Balkon u., to take shelter under a balcony. 2. [untər'ʃtɛlən] v.insep. (a) j-m eine Abteilung usw. u., to put s.o. in charge of a department etc.; (b) (annehmen) to assume (sth.). ◆**U~ung** [-'ʃtɛl-], f -/-en 1. subordination; placing under supervision. 2. imputation; insinuation.

unter'streichen, v.tr.insep.irr.40 to underline (a word etc.); Fig: (betonen) to

emphasize, stress (s.o.'s merits etc.).

unter'stütz|en, v.tr.insep. to support; (finanziell) to back. ◆**U~ung,** f -/-en (a) no pl support; (Hilfe) assistance, aid; backing (of a project etc.); (b) Adm: benefit (payment).

unter'such|en, v.tr.insep. to investigate, look into (sth.); (durchsuchen) to search (s.o.'s luggage etc.); to examine (an object, a document, Med: patient etc.); (nachprüfen) to check; sich ärztlich u. lassen, to have a medical (examination)/checkup. ◆**U~ung,** f -/-en investigation; examination; (Durchsuchung) search; (Kontrolle) check, inspection. ◆**U~ungsausschuß,** m fact-finding committee; committee of enquiry. ◆**U~ungshaft,** f imprisonment awaiting trial. ◆**U~ungsrichter,** m approx. examining magistrate.

untertan ['untərtaːn]. I. adj. j-m u. sein, to be s.o.'s creature/servant. II. U., m -s & -en/-en A: subject.

'Untertasse, f saucer.

'untertauchen, v.i.sep. (sein) to dive (under water); Fig: (verschwinden) to disappear.

'Unterteil, n & m lower/bottom part. ◆**u~en** [-'tailən], v.tr.insep. to subdivide (an area, text etc.). ◆**U~ung,** f subdivision.

'Untertitel, m subtitle.

'Unterton, m undertone.

Unter'treibung, f -/-en understatement.

'unter'wandern, v.tr.insep. Pol: to infiltrate (a party etc.).

'Unterwäsche, f underwear.

Unter'wasser-, comb.fm. underwater (photography, camera, massage etc.).

unter'wegs, adv. on the way; er ist immer/viel u., he is always on the move/travels a lot.

unter'weis|en, v.tr.insep.irr.70 j-n (in etwas dat) u., to instruct s.o. (in sth.), teach s.o. (sth.). ◆**U~ung,** f -/-en instruction, teaching.

'Unterwelt, f underworld.

unter'werf|en, v.tr.insep.irr.110 to subjugate (a people etc.); sich u., (i) to surrender; (ii) (sich fügen) to submit (der Disziplin usw.) to discipline etc.). ◆**U~ung,** f -/no pl subjugation; subjection, submission.

unterwürfig [untər'vyrfɪç], adj. servile, obsequious.

unter'zeichnen, v.tr.insep. to sign (a treaty, contract etc.).

unter'ziehen, v.tr.insep.irr.113 j-n, etwas einer Prüfung dat u., to subject s.o. to an examination; sich einer Prüfung, Operation usw. u., to undergo an examination, operation etc.

'Untiefe, f shallow, shoal.

un'tragbar, adj. intolerable (conditions etc.).

un'trennbar, adj. inseparable.

'untreu, adj. unfaithful. ◆**'U~e,** f -/no

pl unfaithfulness; (conjugal) infidelity.

un'tröstlich, *adj.* inconsolable.

'Untugend, *f* bad habit; (*Laster*) vice.

un'überlegt, *adj.* ill-considered (action), rash (action, person).

un·über'sehbar, *adj.* vast (forest, crowd etc.); inestimable (difficulties etc.).

un·über'troffen, *adj.* unsurpassed, unmatched.

unum'gänglich, *adj.* unavoidable, inevitable; (*unentbehrlich*) indispensable.

unum'schränkt [unum'frɛŋkt] *adj.* unlimited, absolute (power etc.).

unum'stritten, *adj.* undisputed, unchallenged.

un·unter'brochen, *adj.* unbroken, continuous (succession, flow etc.); incessant (rain, chatter etc.); **sie redet u.,** she talks non-stop/incessantly.

unver'änderlich, *adj.* unchanging. ◆**u~t,** *adj.* unchanged, unaltered.

unver'antwortlich, *adj.* irresponsible.

unver'besserlich, *adj.* incorrigible (optimist etc.).

'unverbindlich, *adj.* 1. *Com:* not binding; (*Angebot usw.*) without obligation. 2. non-committal (words); (*reserviert*) detached (attitude, person etc.).

unver'blümt, *adj.* blunt, downright (manner etc.).

'unverdaulich, *adj.* indigestible.

'unverdient, *adj.* undeserved.

'unverdünnt, *adj.* undiluted; neat (whisky etc.).

unver'einbar, *adj.* incompatible, irreconcilable.

'unverfänglich, *adj.* harmless, innocent.

unverfroren ['unfɛrfroːrən], *adj.* impudent, insolent.

unver'geßlich, *adj.* unforgettable.

unver'gleichlich, *adj.* incomparable; (*einmalig*) unique, matchless.

'unverheiratet, *adj.* unmarried, single.

unver'hofft ['unfɛrhɔft], *adj.* unexpected.

'unverkäuflich, *adj.* not for sale.

unver'kennbar, *adj.* unmistakable.

unver'meidbar, *adj.* unavoidable (encounter, collision etc.); inevitable (happening etc.).

'unvermindert, *adj.* undiminished; unabated (fury etc.).

'Unvermögen, *n* inability.

unver'mutet, *adj.* unexpected (visit etc.); unsuspected (talents etc.).

'Unvernunft, *f* unreasonableness; (*Torheit*) stupidity. ◆**u~nünftig,** *adj.* unreasonable; (*töricht*) stupid, foolish.

unver'schämt, *adj.* outrageous; (*frech*) impertinent, insolent (remark, behaviour etc.). ◆**U~heit,** *f* **-/-en** (*a*) *no pl* outrageousness; (*Frechheit*) insolence; (*b*) impertinence.

unversehens ['unfɛrzeːəns], *adv.* unexpectedly; (*plötzlich*) all of a sudden.

'unversehrt, *adj.* (*Pers.*) unhurt; (*heil*) unscathed, safe and sound.

unver'söhnlich, *adj.* irreconcilable (en-emies, opinions etc.).

'unverständlich, *adj.* (*a*) (*Pers.*) incomprehensible; (*undeutlich*) unintelligible. ◆**'U~nis,** *n* **auf U. stoßen,** to meet with incomprehension.

'unversucht, *adj.* **nichts u. lassen,** to try everything.

unver'träglich, *adj.* (*a*) (*Pers.*) cantankerous; (*b*) incompatible (ideas, drugs etc.), indigestible (food).

unver'wechselbar, *adj.* unmistakable.

unverwüstlich [unfɛr'vyːstlɪç], *adj.* durable; *Fig:* indefatigable (person), irrepressible (humour).

unver'zeihlich, *adj.* inexcusable; unforgivable.

unver'züglich [unfɛr'tsyːklɪç], *adj.* immediate; instant (reaction etc.).

'unvollendet, *adj.* unfinished.

'unvollkommen, *adj.* (*a*) imperfect (performance etc.); (*b*) (*unvollständig*) incomplete.

'unvollständig, *adj.* incomplete.

'unvorbereitet, *adj.* unprepared (**auf** + *acc,* for); impromptu (speech, lecture).

'unvoreingenommen, *adj.* unprejudiced, unbiased.

'unvorhergesehen, *adj.* unforeseen; unexpected (visit etc.).

'unvorsichtig, *adj.* unwary (step); unguarded (remark); (*leichtsinnig*) careless (driving etc.).

unvor'stellbar, *adj.* unimaginable, inconceivable.

'unvorteilhaft, *adj.* unfavourable (conditions etc.); unbecoming (dress etc.).

'unwahr, *adj.* untrue, false. ◆**'U~heit,** *f* **1.** untruth, falsehood. 2. *no pl* untruthfulness, falseness. ◆**u~scheinlich,** *adj.* (*a*) unlikely, improbable (story etc.); (*b*) *F:* (*unglaublich*) incredible, fantastic (luck etc.).

unweigerlich [un'vaigərlɪç], *adj.* inevitable; **das wird u. eintreten,** it is bound to happen.

'unweit, *adv.* **u.** + *gen/*u. **von** + *dat,* not far from.

'Unwesen, *n* curse; public nuisance; **sein U. treiben,** to be up to (one's) mischief.

'unwesentlich, *adj.* insignificant.

'Unwetter, *n* (bad) storm, (*Gewitter*) thunderstorm.

'unwichtig, *adj.* unimportant, insignificant.

unwider'legbar, *adj.* irrefutable.

unwider'ruflich, *adj.* irrevocable (decision etc.).

unwider'stehlich, *adj.* irresistible.

'Unwille, *m* indignation, anger. ◆**u~ig,** *adj.* (*a*) indignant, angry; (*b*) (*widerwillig*) reluctant. ◆**u~'kürlich,** *adj.* involuntary.

'unwirklich, *adj.* unreal.

unwirsch ['unvɪrʃ], *adj.* gruff, surly.

'unwirtlich, *adj. esp. Fig:* inhospitable.
◆**u~schaftlich,** *adj.* wasteful (person etc.); *esp. Com:* uneconomic (method).

'unwissen|d, *adj.* ignorant (person).
◆'U~heit, *f -/no pl* ignorance.
'unwohl, *pred.adj.* unwell; mir ist/ich
fühle mich u., I feel unwell/*Fig:* (*unbehaglich*) uneasy. ◆'U~sein, *n* indisposi-
tion.
'unwürdig, *adj.* unworthy (+ *gen,* of).
'Unzahl, *f* eine U. von + *dat,* an enormous number/a whole host of.
unzählig [un'tsε:liç], *adj.* innumerable.
Unze ['untsə], *f -/-n* ounce.
unzer'brechlich, *adj.* unbreakable.
unzer'störbar, *adj.* indestructible.
unzer'trennlich, *adj.* inseparable (friends
etc.).
'Unzucht, *f* sexual offence.
'unzüchtig, *adj.* lewd (remark), obscene
(literature etc.).
'unzufrieden, *adj.* dissatisfied. ◆'U~-
heit, *f* dissatisfaction; discontent.
'unzulänglich, *adj.* insufficient, inadequate.
'unzulässig, *adj.* inadmissible.
'unzumutbar, *adj.* unreasonable (demand
etc.).
'unzurechnungsfähig, *adj.* not responsible for his/her actions.
'unzureichend, *adj.* insufficient, inadequate.
'unzutreffend, *adj.* incorrect, untrue;
U~es bitte streichen, delete if not applicable.
'unzuverlässig, *adj.* unreliable.
'unzweideutig, *adj.* unequivocal, unambiguous.
üppig ['ypiç], *adj.* (*a*) luxuriant (vegetation etc.); lush (grass etc.); thick (beard,
hair); (*b*) (*reichlich*) lavish (meal etc.); (*c*)
opulent (figure, blonde etc.).
Ur-, ur- ['u:r-], *prefix* **1.** (*ursprünglich*) original (form, text etc.). **2.** (*bei Ver-
wandtschaften*) great-(grandmother,
grandfather etc.).
ur'alt, *adj.* extremely old, ancient.
Uran [u'ra:n], *n -s/no pl* uranium.
'Uraufführung, *f* premiere; first performance.
urbar ['u:rba:r], *adj.* u. machen, to reclaim, cultivate (land, a swamp etc.).
'Ureinwohner, *m* original inhabitant;

Austral: aborigine.
'Urenkel(in), *m(f)* great-grandson/
granddaughter.
'Urgroßeltern, *pl* great-grandparents.
'Urheber(in), *m -s/- (f -/-nen)* originator
(of an idea etc.); (*Schöpfer*) creator;
(*Autor*) author.
Urin [u'ri:n], *m -s/-e* urine.
ur'komisch, *adj.* extremely funny, hilarious.
Urkund|e ['u:rkundə], *f -/-n* document;
Jur: legal instrument; deed (of ownership
etc.). ◆u~lich [-'kuntliç], *adj.* documentary (evidence etc.); u. erwähnt, recorded, documented.
Urlaub ['u:rlaup], *m -(e)s/-e (Ferien)* holi-
day(s), *N.Am:* vacation; *Mil: Adm: etc:*
leave (of absence); auf/im/in U., on
holiday/*N.Am:* vacation/*Mil:* leave.
◆'U~er, *m -s/-* holidaymaker, *N.Am:*
vacationist. ◆'U~szeit, *f* holiday/
N.Am: vacation season.
Urne ['urnə], *f -/-n* **1.** urn. **2.** *Pol:* ballot
box.
'Ursache, *f -/-n* cause; (*Grund*) reason.
'Ursprung, *m* origin; (*Quelle*) source (of a
river, *Fig:* tradition etc.).
ursprünglich ['u:rʃpryŋliç], *adj.* (*a*) original (form etc.); initial (reaction); (*b*) (*unverdorben*) natural, pristine (state).
Urteil ['urtail], *n -s/-e Jur: etc:* judgement; (*Meinung*) opinion; (*Befund*)
findings; (*Strafe*) sentence; *Jur:* ein U.
über j-n fällen, to pronounce/pass sentence on s.o. ◆u~en, *v.i.* (*haben*) to
judge; wie u. Sie darüber? what is your
opinion on/of this? ◆'U~skraft, *f* ability
to judge; judgement; discrimination.
◆'U~sspruch, *m* verdict; (*Strafe*) sentence.
'Urwald, *m* primeval forest; (*tropischer U.*)
jungle.
urwüchsig ['u:rvy:ksiç], *adj.* unpolished, unsophisticated (manners
etc.); untouched, (*rauh*) rugged (landscape).
Utensil [uten'zi:l], *n -s/-ien* utensil, implement.
Utop|ie [uto'pi:], *f -/-n* Utopia.
◆u~isch [u'to:piʃ], *adj.* utopian.

V

V, v [fau], *n -/-* (the letter) V, v.
Vagabund [vaga'bunt], *m -en/-en Lit:* va-
gabond; (*Landstreicher*) vagrant.
vag(e) ['va:g(ə)], *adj.* vague.
Vakuum ['va:kuum], *n -s/-kuen* vacuum.
◆'v~verpackt, *adj.* vacuum-packed.
Vampir [vam'pi:r], *m -s/-e* vampire.
Vandalismus [vanda'lismus], *m -/no pl*
vandalism.
Vanille [va'nil(j)ə], *f -/no pl* vanilla.
◆'V~egeschmack, *m* vanilla flavour.
vari|abel [vari'a:bəl], *adj.* variable.

◆V~ation [-atsi'o:n], *f -/-en* variation.
◆V~eté [-ie'te:], *n -s/-s* (*a*) (*Vorstellung*) variety show; (*b*) (*also* V~theater
n) variety theatre, music hall.
◆v~ieren, *v.tr. & i.* (*haben*) to vary.
Vase ['va:zə], *f -/-n* vase.
Vater ['fa:tər], *m -s/-* father. ◆'V~land,
n home/native country; (*Deutschland*)
fatherland. ◆'V~landsliebe, *f* patriotism. ◆'v~los, *adj.* fatherless.
◆'V~schaft, *f -/no pl* fatherhood; *Jur:*
paternity. ◆'V~stadt, *f* home town.

◆V~'unser, n -s/- Lord's Prayer.

väterlich ['fɛːtərliç], adj. 1. (wie ein Vater) fatherly, paternal (advice, interest etc.). 2. (des Vaters) the/one's father's (house, business etc.). ◆v~erseits, adv. on the/one's father's side.

Vatikan [vati'kaːn]. Pr.n.m -s. der V., the Vatican.

Veget|arier [vege'taːriər], m -s/- vegetarian. ◆v~arisch, adj. vegetarian. ◆V~ation [atsi'oːn], f -/-en vegetation.

Veilchen ['failçən], n -s/- violet.

Vene ['veːnə], f -/-n vein.

Venedig [ve'neːdiç], Pr.n.n -s. Venice.

Venezolaner|in (venezo'laːnər(in)), m -s/- (f -/-nen)v~'o'lanisch, adj. Venezuelan. ◆V~uela [-tsu'eːla], Pr.n.n -s. Venezuela.

Ventil [vɛn'tiːl], n -s/-e valve. ◆V~ation [-ilatsi'oːn], f -/-en ventilation (system). ◆V~ator [-i'laːtor], m -s/-en [-'toːrən] ventilator, (electric) fan.

ver'abreden, v.tr. to arrange, fix (a meeting, time etc.); sich mit j-m v., to make an appointment with s.o. ◆V~ung, f -/-en arrangement; appointment; (mit Freund/Freundin) date.

ver'abscheuen, v.tr. to detest, loathe (s.o., sth.).

ver'abschieden, v.tr. (a) sich (von j-m) v., to take one's leave (of s.o.), say goodbye (to s.o.); (b) to discharge (an officer etc.); (c) Pol: to pass (a bill).

ver'achten, v.tr. to despise (s.o., sth.). ◆V~ung, f -/no pl contempt, disdain.

verächtlich [fɛr'ɛçtliç], adj. disdainful (gesture etc.); disparaging (remark).

verallgemeiner|n [fɛr'algə'mainərn], v.tr. & i. (haben) to generalize (about sth.). ◆V~ung, f -/-en generalization.

veraltet [fɛr'ʔaltət], adj. out of date, obsolete.

Veranda [ve'randa], f -/-den veranda; N.Am: porch.

veränder|lich [fɛr'ʔɛndərliç], adj. changeable (weather etc.); inconstant (nature, behaviour). ◆v~n, v.tr. to change, alter (s.o., sth.); sich v., to change. ◆V~ung, f alteration, change.

verängstigt [fɛr'ʔɛŋstiçt], adj. frightened; scared.

veranlag|t [fɛr'ʔanlaːkt], adj. künstlerisch v. sein, to have an artistic disposition; praktisch v., practically minded. ◆V~ung, f -/-en disposition; (Hang) tendency; künstlerische V., artistic bent.

ver'anlass|en, v.tr. (a) to arrange for (sth.); das Nötige v., to take the necessary steps; (b) j-n v., etwas zu tun, to make s.o. do sth.; sich veranlaßt sehen/fühlen, etwas zu tun, to feel obliged to do it. ◆V~ung, f -/-en cause (zu + dat, of); (Grund) reason (zu + dat, for); auf seine V. hin, at his instigation.

veranschaulichen [fɛr'ʔanʃauliçən], v.tr. to illustrate (sth.).

veranstalt|en [fɛr'ʔanʃtaltən], v.tr. to organize (sth.); to mount, F: put on (a concert, exhibition etc.). ◆V~er, m -s/- organizer. ◆V~ung, f -/-en (a) organization; (b) (Vorstellung) performance, presentation; öffentliche V., public function.

verantwort|en [fɛr'ʔantvɔrtən], v.tr. to answer for, take the responsibility for (an action etc.); sich v., to defend/justify oneself. ◆v~lich, adj. responsible. ◆V~ung, f -/-en responsibility. ◆v~ungsbewußt, adj. conscientious. ◆v~ungslos, adj. irresponsible. ◆V~ungsvoll, adj. responsible; trustworthy.

ver'arbeit|en, v.tr. (a) Ind: to process (raw material etc.); (b) to digest (Fig: facts etc.). ◆V~ung, f -/no pl (a) processing; (b) digestion.

ver'ärgern, v.tr. to annoy, irritate (s.o.).

Verb [vɛrp], n -s/-en verb.

Verband [fɛr'bant], m -(e)s/⁼e 1. (a) (Vereinigung) association; (b) Mil: formation; force. 2. Med: bandage, dressing. ◆V~(s)kasten, m first-aid box/kit.

ver'bann|en, v.tr. to exile (s.o.); to banish (Hist: s.o., Fig: a thought etc.). ◆V~ung, f -/-en exile; banishment.

verbarrikadieren [fɛrbarika'diːrən], v.tr. to barricade (sth., oneself) (in).

ver'bergen, v.tr.irr.5 to conceal, hide (s.o., sth.) (vor j-m, from s.o.); sich v., to hide.

ver'besser|n, v.tr. to improve (s.o., sth.); (korrigieren) to correct (a mistake, text etc.); sich v., (i) (Pers., Sache) to improve; (seine Lage v.) to better oneself; (ii) (Pers.) (beim Sprechen) to correct oneself. ◆V~ung, f -/-en (a) improvement; (b) correction.

ver'beug|en, v.refl. sich v., to bow. ◆V~ung, f -/-en bow.

ver'biegen, v.tr.irr.7 to bend (sth.) (out of shape).

ver'bieten, v.tr.irr.8 to forbid, Adm: prohibit (sth.), Adm: to ban (a demonstration, play etc.), suppress (a publication); Rauchen verboten, no smoking.

ver'billigen, v.tr. to reduce (sth.) (in price).

ver'bind|en, v.tr.irr.9 (a) to connect (two parts/places etc.); to join (two things); (gleichzeitig) to combine (two articles/Ch: substances); (vereinen) to unite (people, nations); damit sind Gefahren usw. verbunden, that involves danger etc.; (b) Tel: to connect (s.o.), put (s.o.) through; (Sie sind) falsch verbunden, (you've got the) wrong number; (c) Med: to bandage (a wound etc.). ◆v~lich, adj. (a) (entgegenkommend) obliging; friendly (smile, words etc.); (b) (bindend) binding (agreement etc.). ◆V~ung, f (a) connection; (b) Tel: communication; Tel: schlechte V., bad line; (c) (Kombination) combination; Ch: compound; Fig: association (of ideas); *Fig:* **j-n mit etwas** *dat* **in V. bringen,** to link/associate s.o. with sth.; (*d*) (*Verein*) association; (*e*) (*Beziehung*) contact; **sich mit j-m in V. setzen,** to get in touch with s.o.

verbissen [fɛr'bɪsən], *adj.* dogged, grim.

ver'bitten, *v.tr.irr.10* **das verbitte ich mir!** I won't stand for that!

ver'bittern, *v.tr.* to embitter (s.o.).

verblassen [fɛr'blasən], *v.i.* (*sein*) (*also Fig:*) to fade.

Verbleib [fɛr'blaip], *m* **-(e)s/***no pl* whereabouts. ◆**v∼en** [-bən], *v.i.irr.12* (*sein*) to remain.

verblüff|en [fɛr'blyfən], *v.tr.* (*erstaunen*) to amaze; (*ratlos machen*) baffle (s.o.). ◆**V∼ung,** *f* **-/***no pl* amazement, stupefaction.

ver'blühen, *v.i.* (*sein*) to fade, wither.

ver'bluten, *v.i.* (*sein*) to bleed to death.

ver'borgen *adj.* hidden (danger, feeling etc.); secluded (place); **im v∼en,** secretly, in secret.

Verbot [fɛr'boːt], *n* **-(e)s/-e** prohibition; ban (**des Rauchens usw.,** on smoking etc.). ◆**V∼sschild,** *n* prohibition sign.

Ver'brauch, *m* **-(e)s/***no pl* consumption (**an/von** *dat,* of). ◆**v∼en,** *v.tr.* to consume, use (fuel etc.); to spend (time, money etc.); (*erschöpfen*) to use up (reserves, provisions etc.). ◆**v∼t,** *adj.* worn (out) (article etc.); stale (air); exhausted (battery etc.). ◆**V∼er,** *m* **-s/-** consumer.

Ver'brech|en, *n* **-s/-** crime. ◆**V∼er(in)**, *m* **-s/- (***f* **-/-nen)** criminal. ◆**V∼erisch,** *adj.* criminal.

verbreit|en [fɛr'braitən], *v.tr.* to spread (news, a disease etc.); to give out (light, heat etc.); **sich v.,** to spread. ◆**v∼en,** *v.tr.* to widen (a road etc.). ◆**v∼et,** *adj.* common, widespread. ◆**V∼ung,** *f* **-/***no pl* spreading; giving out (heat/light).

verbrenn|en [fɛr'brɛnən], *v.tr.irr.15* **1.** *v.tr.* to burn (sth., oneself); to cremate (a corpse); **ich habe mir die Finger/Zunge verbrannt,** I burnt my fingers/tongue. **2.** *v.i.* (*sein*) to burn; (*Pers.*) to burn to death. ◆**V∼ung,** *f* **-/-en** (*a*) *no pl* burning; cremation; *Tchn:* combustion; (*b*) (*Brandwunde*) burn. ◆**V∼ungsmotor,** *m* combustion engine.

ver'bringen, *v.tr.irr.16* to spend (time, one's holidays etc.).

ver'brüh|en, *v.tr.* to scald (s.o.). ◆**V∼ung,** *f* **-/-en** (*a*) *no pl* scalding; (*b*) scald.

ver'buchen, *v.tr.* to enter (an amount etc.); *Fig:* **einen Erfolg v.,** to score a success.

verbunden [fɛr'bundən], *adj.* connected; **ich bin Ihnen sehr v.,** I am much obliged to you.

verbünde|n [fɛr'byndən], *v.refl.* **sich v.,** to enter into an alliance. ◆**V∼te(r),** *m & f decl. as adj.* ally.

ver'bürgen, *v.tr.* to guarantee (sth.); **sich**

für etwas *acc* **v.,** to vouch for sth.

Verdacht [fɛr'daxt], *m* **-(e)s/***no pl* suspicion; **j-n in/im V. haben,** to suspect s.o.

verdächtig [fɛr'dɛçtɪç], *adj.* suspicious; **sich v. machen,** to arouse suspicion. ◆**v∼en** [-gən], *v.tr.* to suspect (s.o.) (**des Mordes usw.,** of murder etc.). ◆**V∼ung,** *f* **-/-en** suspicion; (*Beschuldigung*) accusation.

ver'damm|en, *v.tr.* to condemn (s.o., sth.). ◆**v∼t,** *adj. P:* damned, blasted, *N.Am:* doggone.

ver'dampfen, *v.i.* (*sein*) to vaporize.

ver'danken, *v.tr.* **j-m etwas v.,** to be indebted to s.o. for sth.; **das habe ich dir zu v.,** I have you to thank for that.

verdau|en [fɛr'dauən], *v.tr.* to digest (sth.). ◆**v∼lich,** *adj.* digestible; **leicht v.,** easy to digest. ◆**V∼ung,** *f* **-/***no pl* digestion. ◆**V∼ungsstörung,** *f* indigestion.

Verdeck [fɛr'dɛk], *n* **-(e)s/-e 1.** *Nau:* top deck. **2.** *Aut:* hood; (*fest*) hardtop. ◆**v∼en,** *v.tr.* to cover (sth.) (up); (*verbergen*) to conceal (sth.).

ver'denken, *v.tr.irr.17* **man kann es ihm nicht v.,** one cannot hold it against him.

verderb|en [fɛr'dɛrbən]. **I.** *v.irr.101* **1.** *v.i.* (*sein*) to deteriorate; (*Essen*) to go bad/off. **2.** *v.tr.* to spoil (a child, food, s.o.'s pleasure, one's health etc.); (*völlig*) ruin (an evening, s.o.'s enjoyment etc.); (*moralisch*) to corrupt (s.o., s.o.'s character); **es mit j-m v.,** to fall out with s.o., get on the wrong side of s.o. **II.** *v.,* *n* **-s/***no pl Lit:* ruin; **j-n ins V. stürzen,** to ruin s.o. ◆**v∼lich,** *adj.* (*a*) perishable (food); (*b*) pernicious (influence etc.).

verdeutlichen [fɛr'dɔytlɪçən], *v.tr.* to clarify (sth.).

ver'dichten, *v.tr.* to compress (a gas, *Fig:* events etc.); **sich v.,** (*Nebel usw.*) to become dense.

ver'dien|en, *v.tr. & i.* (*haben*) (*a*) to earn (money etc.); **gut v.,** to have a good income; (*b*) (*zu Recht bekommen*) to deserve (sth.). ◆**V∼st. 1.** *m* **-(e)s/-e** (*Einkommen*) earnings; income; (*Gehalt*) salary. **2.** *n* **-(e)s/-e** merit; **es ist dein V.,** it is (entirely) due/owing to you. ◆**v∼t,** *adj.* deserving (person); (well-)deserved, just (praise etc.); **sich um sein Land v. machen,** to render great services to one's country. ◆**v∼'ter'maßen,** *adv.* deservedly.

ver'doppe|ln, *v.tr.* to double (sth.); to redouble (one's efforts); **sich v.,** to double (in number/size). ◆**V∼ung,** *f* **-/-en** doubling, duplication.

verdorben [fɛr'dɔrbən], *adj.* spoiled; gone off/bad (food); foul, polluted (air); upset (stomach); corrupt (morals etc.).

verdorren [fɛr'dɔrən], *v.i.* (*sein*) to dry up, (*Pflanze*) wither.

ver'dräng|en, *v.tr.* to push/thrust (s.o., sth.) aside; (*vertreiben*) to oust (s.o.); *Fig:* to repress (an emotion etc.). ◆**V∼ung,**

f -*lno pl* ousting; *Psy:* repression.

ver'drehen, *v.tr. (also Fig:)* to twist (sth.); *Fig:* to distort (the meaning etc.); **j-m den Kopf v.**, to turn s.o.'s head.

verdreifachen [fɛr'draifaxən], *v.tr.* to treble (sth.); **sich v.**, to treble.

verdrieß|en [fɛr'driːsən], *v.tr.irr.31* to annoy (s.o.). ◆**v~lich**, *adj.* grumpy; bad-tempered (person, expression).

verdrossen [fɛr'drɔsən], *adj.* morose, sullen.

ver'drücken, *v.tr. F: (a)* to tuck away (food); *(b)* **sich v.**, to slink away.

Verdruß [fɛr'drus], *m* -sses/-sse *Lit:* annoyance.

ver'duften, *v.i. (sein) F: (Pers.)* to make off; **verdufte!** hop it!

ver'dunkeln, *v.tr.* to darken (a colour, room etc.); to dim (a lamp etc.); **sich v.**, to darken.

ver'dünnen [fɛr'dynən], *v.tr.* to dilute (a liquid), water down (wine etc.), thin (paint etc.).

ver'dunsten, *v.i. (haben)* to evaporate.

ver'dursten, *v.i. (sein)* to die/be dying of thirst.

verdutzt [fɛr'dutst], *adj.* taken aback; (perplex) nonplussed, puzzled.

ver'ehr|en, *v.tr.* to admire, look up to (s.o.), *(mit Liebe)* venerate (s.o. older); *(anbeten)* to worship (s.o., a saint). ◆**v~er(in)**, *m* -s/- *(f* -/-nen) admirer; *F:* fan. ◆**V~ung**, *f* -*lno pl* admiration, veneration, *Ecc:* worship.

vereidig|en [fɛr'?aidigən], *v.tr.* to swear (s.o.) in. ◆**V~ung**, *f* -*lno pl* swearing in.

Verein [fɛr'?ain], *m* -(e)s/-e society; *Sp: etc:* club. ◆**v~bar**, *adj.* compatible, *(Aussage)* consistent. ◆**v~baren**, *v.tr. (a)* to agree (on) (sth.), fix (a date etc.); *(b)* to reconcile (facts, opinions etc.). ◆**V~barung**, *f* -/-en agreement, arrangement; **nach V.**, by arrangement/ *(Termin)* appointment. ◆**v~igen**, *v.tr.* to unite (nations etc.); to bring together (a family etc.); to combine (functions, tasks etc.); **sich v.**, to unite, combine (zu etwas *dat*, to form s.th.); *(Firmen usw.)* to merge; **die Vereinigten Staaten**, the United States. ◆**V~igung**, *f* -/-en 1. union; combination; *Com:* merger. 2. *(Organisation)* organization.

ver'einfach|en, *v.tr.* to simplify (sth.). ◆**V~ung**, *f* -/-en simplification.

ver'einheitlichen, *v.tr.* to standardize (a product etc.), unify (a system etc.).

ver'einsam|en, *v.i. (sein)* to grow lonely. ◆**V~ung**, *f* -*lno pl* isolation.

vereinzelt [fɛr'?aintsəlt], *adj.* occasional, scattered (showers etc.).

vereis|en [fɛr'?aizən], *v.i. (sein) (Straße)* to become icy; *(Fenster usw.)* to ice up. ◆**v~t**, *adj.* icy (road etc.); *Av:* iced up.

vereiteln [fɛr'?aitəln], *v.tr.* to foil, thwart (a plan etc.), frustrate (efforts etc.).

ver'enden, *v.i. (sein) (Tiere)* to die (miserably).

verengen [fɛr'?ɛŋən], *v.tr.* to narrow (sth.); **sich v.**, to narrow; *(Pupille)* to contract.

ver'erb|en, *v.tr.* to leave, bequeath (sth.); to pass on (qualities etc.); **sich v.**, to be hereditary. ◆**v~lich**, *adj.* hereditary. ◆**V~ung**, *f* -*lno pl* heredity.

ver'fahren. I. *v.tr.irr.26* 1. *v.i. (sein)* to proceed, act; **mit j-m streng v.**, to deal severely with s.o. 2. *v.refl.* **sich v.**, to lose one's way. **II.** *adj.* hopelessly bungled. **III. V.**, *n* -s/- *(a)* procedure; *Tchn:* process; *(b) Jur:* proceedings.

Verfall [fɛr'fal], *m* -(e)s/*no pl* 1. decay, dilapidation; decline of (civilization etc.). 2. *Jur:* expiry of a period etc.). ◆**v~en**, *v.i.irr.27 (sein) (a) (Gebäude)* to (fall into) decay, become dilapidated; *(Zivilisation, Moral usw.)* to (go into) decline; *(b) (ungültig werden)* to expire; *(Fin: Wechsel usw.)* to lapse; *(c)* **v. in** + *acc*, to lapse into (silence etc.); *(d)* **j-m v.**, *(Pers.)* to fall under s.o.'s spell; **dem Alkohol v.**, to become addicted to drink; *(e)* **auf einen Plan usw. v.**, to hit on a plan etc.

ver'fälschen, *v.tr.* to falsify (documents etc.), distort (facts, truth etc.).

verfänglich [fɛr'fɛŋlɪç], *adj.* awkward, compromising.

ver'färben, *v.refl.* **sich v.**, to change colour, *(Stoff usw.)* discolour.

ver'fass|en, *v.tr.* to write (sth.). ◆**v~er**, *m* -s/- author, writer. ◆**V~ung**, *f* -/-en *(a) (Zustand)* condition, state; *(b) Pol:* constitution. ◆**v~ungswidrig**, *adj.* unconstitutional.

ver'faulen, *v.i. (sein)* to decay, *(Obst, Holz)* rot.

ver'fecht|en, *v.tr.irr.29* to champion (a theory etc.). ◆**V~er**, *m* -s/- advocate, champion.

ver'fehl|en, *v.tr.* to miss (s.o., sth., one's way). ◆**v~t**, *adj.* mistaken, misguided.

verfeiner|n [fɛr'fainərn], *v.tr.* to refine, improve (methods etc.). ◆**v~t**, *adj.* refined, sophisticated.

ver'film|en, *v.tr.* to film, make a film of (a novel etc.). ◆**V~ung**, *f* -/-en film version.

ver'fliegen, *v.i.irr.30 (haben)* to evaporate, *(verschwinden)* vanish; *(Zeit)* to fly past.

ver'fluch|en, *v.tr.* to curse (s.o., sth.). ◆**v~t**, *adj. F:* confounded, damned; *int.* damn! blast!

ver'folg|en, *v.tr.* to pursue (s.o., an aim, etc.); to shadow (a suspect etc.); to follow (events, progress etc.) closely; *esp. Pol:* to persecute (s.o., a minority etc.). ◆**v~er**, *m* -s/- pursuer; *Pol:* persecutor. ◆**V~ung**, *f* -/-en pursuit; *Pol:* persecution.

ver'formen, *v.tr.* to distort (sth.); **sich v.**, to get out of shape, *(Holz)* warp.

verfrachten [fɛr'fraxtən], v.tr. to ship (goods).

verfroren [fɛr'froːrən], adj. frozen (hands etc.).

verfrüht [fɛr'fryːt], adj. premature; untimely (death).

verfüg|bar [fɛr'fyːkbaːr], adj. available. ◆**V~barkeit**, f -/no pl availability. ◆**v~en** [-gən], v. 1. v.tr. to decree (daß..., that...); to order (sth.). 2. v.i. (haben) **über etwas** acc v., to have sth. at one's disposal; **über sein Geld frei v. können**, to do as one likes with one's money. ◆**V~ung**, f -/-en (a) Jur: Adm: (Befehl) decree, order; (Anordnung) instruction; (b) **ich stehe Ihnen zur V.**, I am at your service/disposal; **mein Auto steht Ihnen jederzeit zur V.**, you can use my car whenever you like.

ver'führ|en, v.tr. to lead (s.o.) astray; to seduce (a girl); esp. Hum: (verlocken) to tempt (s.o.). ◆**V~er**, m -s/- seducer. ◆**v~erisch**, adj. seductive (smile, look etc.); tempting (offer etc.). ◆**V~ung**, f -/-en seduction; enticement.

ver'gammeln, v.i. (sein) F: (Speisen) to go bad; (Pers.) to go to seed.

vergangen [fɛr'gaŋən], adj. past (generations etc.); **im v~en Jahr**, last year. ◆**V~heit**, f -/no pl past; Gram: past tense.

vergänglich [fɛr'gɛŋliç], adj. transitory, fleeting. ◆**V~keit**, f -/no pl transitoriness.

vergas|en [fɛr'gaːzən], v.tr. to vaporize (a liquid); to gas (s.o., an animal). ◆**V~er**, m -s/- carburettor.

ver'geb|en, v.tr.irr.35 (a) (verzeihen) **j-m etwas v.**, to forgive s.o. sth.; (b) (überreichen) to give, award (a prize, scholarship etc.); **ein Amt an j-n v.**, to appoint s.o. to an office; **seine Tochter ist schon v.**, his daughter is already spoken for; (c) Sp: to miss (a chance, goal etc.). ◆**v~ens**, adv. in vain. ◆**v~lich**, adj. futile, vain. ◆**V~ung**, f -/no pl forgiveness.

ver'gehen. I. v.irr.36 **1.** v.i. (sein) (a) (Zeit, Schmerz usw.) to pass; (Gefühl usw.) to disappear, go; (b) **vor Angst, Scham usw. v.**, to die of fright, shame etc. 2. v.refl. **sich v.**, to commit an offence; **sich an j-m v.**, to assault s.o. (sexually). **II.** v., n -s/- offence.

ver'gelt|en, v.tr.irr.37 to repay, (belohnen) reward (a kindness etc.); (sich rächen) to retaliate for (a wrong). ◆**V~ung**, f -/no pl retaliation, Mil: reprisals pl.

vergessen [fɛr'gɛsən], v.tr.irr.25 to forget; (liegenlassen) to leave (sth.) behind. ◆**V~heit**, f -/no pl oblivion; **in V. geraten**, to fall into oblivion.

vergeßlich [fɛr'gɛsliç], adj. forgetful. ◆**V~keit**, f -/no pl forgetfulness.

vergeuden [fɛr'gɔydən], v.tr. to squander, waste (money, time etc.).

vergewaltig|en [fɛrgə'valtigən], v.tr. to rape (a woman); Fig: to do violence to (language etc.). ◆**V~ung**, f -/-en rape; Fig: violation.

vergewissern [fɛrgə'visərn], v.refl. **sich v.**, to make sure.

ver'gießen, v.tr.irr.31 to spill (sth.); Lit: to shed (blood, tears).

vergiften [fɛr'giftən], v.tr. to poison (s.o., sth., oneself).

vergilben [fɛr'gilbən], v.i. (sein) to turn yellow.

Vergißmeinnicht [fɛr'gismainniçt], n -(e)s forget-me-not.

verglasen [fɛr'glaːzən], v.tr. to glaze (a window).

Vergleich [fɛr'glaiç], m -(e)s/-e **1.** comparison; **im V. zu + dat**, compared with/to. **2.** Jur: (Einigung) settlement. ◆**v~bar**, adj. comparable. ◆**v~en**, v.tr.irr.40 (a) to compare (s.o., sth.); **es ist nicht zu v. mit...**, you cannot compare it with...; (b) Jur: **sich mit j-m v.**, to settle with s.o. ◆**v~sweise**, adv. comparatively.

vergnüg|en [fɛr'gnyːgən], v.refl. **sich v.**, to enjoy oneself, have a good time. **II. V.**, n -s/no pl pleasure; (Freude) delight; **viel V.!** enjoy yourself! **es war mir ein V.**, I was pleased to do it/meet you. ◆**v~lich**, adj. enjoyable, pleasant. ◆**v~t**, adj. cheerful; (Pers.) in good spirits. ◆**V~ung**, f -/-en entertainment, F: jollification. ◆**V~ungs-**, comb.fm. entertainment (industry, tax etc.); amusement (park etc.); pleasure (steamer etc.). ◆**V~sreise**, f pleasure trip. ◆**v~süchtig**, adj. pleasure-seeking.

ver'golden, v.tr. to gold-plate, (mit Blattgold) gild (sth.).

ver'gönnen, v.tr. **j-m etwas v.**, to grant s.o. sth.

vergöttern [fɛr'gœtərn], v.tr. to idolize, worship (s.o.).

ver'graben, v.tr.irr.42 to bury.

ver'greifen, v.refl.irr.43 (a) **sich v.**, to make a mistake; **sich im Ausdruck usw. v.**, to choose the wrong term etc.; (b) **sich an etwas** dat **v.**, to misappropriate (sth.); **sich an j-m v.**, to lay hands on s.o., (sexuell) violate s.o.

vergriffen [fɛr'grifən], adj. unavailable; (Buch) out of print.

vergrößer|n [fɛr'grøːsərn], v.tr. to enlarge (a photograph etc.); to expand (a business etc.); to increase (a number, danger etc.); **sich v.**, to expand, increase (in size); (Menge) to swell. ◆**V~ung**, f -/-en increase (in size); esp. Phot: enlargement; expansion, extension. ◆**V~ungsglas**, n magnifying glass.

Vergünstigung [fɛr'gynstigʊŋ], f -/-en privilege; concession.

vergüt|en [fɛr'gyːtən], v.tr. to refund, reimburse (expenses). ◆**V~ung**, f -/-en refund.

ver'haft|en, v.tr. to arrest (s.o.).

◆**V~ung,** f -/-en arrest.
ver'hallen, v.i. (sein) to die away.
ver'halten. I. v.tr.irr.45 **sich v.,** to
behave(*handeln*) act; **sich richtig v.,** to
do (the right thing); **es verhält sich so,**
this is how matters stand; **wie verhält es
sich mit...?** what is the position regarding...? **II. V.,** n -s/no pl behaviour, conduct. ◆**V~s-,** comb.fm. behaviour (pattern etc.); behavioural (research, psychology etc.). ◆**V~sweise,** f (kind of) behaviour.
Verhältnis [fɛr'hɛltnis], n -ses/-se 1. (a)
Mth: etc: ratio; Fig: im V. zu früher,
compared with earlier times; **in keinem
V. zu etwas (dat) stehen,** to bear no relation to sth.; (b) relationship (**zu j-m,** with
s.o.); (c) F: (Liebesv.) affair. 2. pl **V~se,**
conditions, (*Umstände*) circumstances;
über seine V~se leben, to live beyond
one's means; **aus ärmlichen V~sen,**
from a poor background/family.
◆**v~mäßig,** adv. comparatively, rela-
tively.
ver'handeln, v.tr. & i. (haben) to negotiate; *Jur:* to hear, try (a case).
◆**V~lung,** f -/-en negotiation, discussion; pl **V~lungen,** negotiations, talks;
Jur: (legal) proceedings.
ver'hängen, v.tr. to impose (a fine etc.).
◆**V~nis,** n -ses/-se disaster, (*Schicksal*)
fate; **j-m zum V. werden,** to be s.o.'s
downfall. ◆**v~nisvoll,** adj. disastrous,
fatal (mistake etc.); fateful (day etc.).
ver'harren, v.i. (haben) **bei/in etwas dat
v.,** to persist in sth.
ver'härten, v.tr. & refl. to harden.
verhaßt [fɛr'hast], adj. hateful, odious;
(*Pers.*) hated.
ver'hauen, v.tr.irr.47 F: to beat (s.o.) up,
(*verdreschen*) thrash (s.o.).
verheerend [fɛr'heːrənt], adj. devastating
(storm etc.); disastrous (fire, consequences etc.); appalling (conditions etc.).
ver'heilen, v.i. (sein) to heal.
verheimlichen [fɛr'haimliçən], v.tr. to
keep (sth.) secret, conceal (sth.) (j-m,
from s.o.).
ver'heiraten [fɛr'haira:tət], adj. married
(man, woman).
ver'heißen, v.tr.irr.49 Lit: to promise
(sth.). ◆**v~ungsvoll,** adj. promising,
auspicious.
ver'helfen, v.i.irr.50 (haben) **j-m zu etwas
dat v.,** to help s.o. to get to sth.
verherrlichen [fɛr'hɛrliçən], v.tr. to glorify (s.o., deeds etc.).
ver'hindern, v.tr. to prevent (sth.); **ver-
hindert sein,** to be prevented from
coming/going.
verhöhnen [fɛr'høːnən], v.tr. to deride,
jeer at (s.o., sth.).
Verhör [fɛr'høːr], n -(e)s/-e (police etc.)
interrogation; *Jur:* hearing. ◆**v~en,**
v.tr. (a) to interrogate, question (a witness etc.); (b) **sich v.,** to hear wrongly.
ver'hüllen, v.tr. to cover (one's head, face

etc.).
ver'hungern, v.i. (sein) to starve (to
death).
ver'hüt|**en,** v.tr. to prevent, avert (sth.).
◆**V~ungsmittel,** n contraceptive.
verirren [fɛr'ʔirən], v.refl. **sich v.,** to get
lost. ◆**v~t,** adj. lost; stray (bullet etc.).
ver'jagen, v.tr. to chase (s.o., sth.) away.
verjüngen [fɛr'jyŋən], v.tr. (a) to rejuvenate (s.o.), make (s.o., oneself) look
younger; (b) **sich v.,** (schmaler werden) to
taper.
verkalken [fɛr'kalkən], v.i. (sein) (a) to
calcify, (Arterien) harden; (b) F: (Pers.)
to become senile; (c) (Kessel usw.) to fur
up.
verkalku'lieren, v.refl. **sich v.,** to miscalculate.
Verkauf [fɛr'kauf], m sale. ◆**v~en,** v.tr.
to sell (sth.); **zu v.,** for sale.
◆**V~spreis,** m selling/retail price.
Verkäuf|**er(in)** [fɛr'kɔyfar(in)], m -s/- (f
-/-nen) (a) seller; (b) (Angestellter) shop
assistant, N.Am: sales clerk. ◆**v~lich,**
adj. saleable; **gut/schlecht v.,** easy/hard
to sell.
Verkehr [fɛr'keːr], m -s/no pl 1. traffic. 2.
(Umgang) association; (social) contact;
(geschäftlich) dealings; (Geschlechtsv.)
(sexual) intercourse; **er ist kein V. für
dich,** he's not suitable company for you.
◆**v~en,** v. 1. v.i. (haben) (a) (Zug, Bus
usw.) to run; (Schiff) ply; (b) (Pers.) to
have contact, associate, (geschlechtlich)
have (sexual) intercourse. 2. v.tr. to turn
(sth.) (ins Gegenteil usw., into the opposite etc.). ◆**V~s-,** comb.fm. (a) traffic
(chaos, density, check, police, policeman, conditions etc.); (b) road (safety,
accident etc.); (c) transport (minister,
network, system etc.). ◆**V~sampel,** f
traffic light(s). ◆**V~sdelikt,** n traffic
offence. ◆**V~sfluß,** m traffic flow.
◆**V~smittel,** n means of transport.
◆**V~sregel,** f traffic regulation.
◆**V~sstau,** m traffic jam.
◆**V~steilnehmer,** m road user.
◆**V~szeichen,** n traffic/road sign.
verkehrt [fɛr'keːrt], adj. wrong (end
etc.); **v. herum,** the wrong way round.
ver'kennen, v.tr. to mistake (motives
etc.); to misjudge (s.o., sth.); Hum: **ver-
kanntes Genie,** unrecognized/
misunderstood genius.
ver'klagen, v.tr. Jur: to sue (s.o.) (**wegen
etwas dat,** for sth.).
ver'kleid|**en,** v.tr. (a) to disguise (s.o.,
oneself); (b) Tchn: to face (an outer wall);
(täfeln) panel (an inner wall etc.).
◆**V~ung,** f (a) disguise; (b) facing, panelling.
verkleinern [fɛr'klainərn], v.tr. to make
(sth.) smaller, reduce (size, volume etc.).
ver'klingen, v.i.irr.96 (sein) to die away.
verkneifen [fɛr'knaifən], v.tr.irr.43 F:
sich dat das Lachen usw. v., to suppress
one's laughter etc.

ver'knüpfen, *v.tr.* (*a*) to knot, tie (string etc.); (*b*) (*verbinden*) to combine (two actions, sth. with sth.); (*in Gedanken usw.*) to associate, connect (s.o., sth.).

ver'kommen. I. *v.i.irr.53* (*sein*) (*Pers.*) to go downhill, (*stärker*) go to the dogs; (*Obst usw.*) to go bad; (*Gebäude usw.*) to decay, (*Garten*) to go wild. **II.** *adj.* dilapidated (building etc.); (*moralisch*) depraved (person); sleazy (hotel etc.). ◆**V~heit**, *f -/no pl* dilapidated state; depravity.

verkörpern [fɛr'kœrpərn], *v.tr.* to embody, personify (an idea, quality).

verkraften [fɛr'kraftən], *v.tr.* to manage (a task etc.); to cope with (the amount of work/traffic); (*bewältigen*) to get over (an experience).

verkrampft [fɛr'krampft], *adj.* clenched (fingers etc.); tense (person); forced (laughter).

ver'kriechen, *v.refl.irr.55* **sich v.,** to crawl, creep; (*sich verstecken*) to hide.

ver'krümmen, *v.tr.* to bend (sth.).

verkrüppelt [fɛr'krypəlt], *adj.* crippled.

verkrusten [fɛr'krustən], *v.i.* (*sein*) to form a crust(*Blut*) scab.

ver'kühlen, *v.refl.* **sich v.,** to catch cold.

ver'kümmern, *v.i.* (*sein*) (*Pflanze, Glied*) to become stunted; (*Tier*) to waste away.

verkünd/en [fɛr'kyndən], *v.tr. Lit:* to proclaim (sth.); *Jur:* to pronounce (judgement). ◆**V~(ig)ung,** *f -/-en* announcement; proclamation; *Jur:* pronouncement.

ver'kürz/en, *v.tr.* to shorten (sth.); to cut (travelling/working time, a script etc.). ◆**v~t,** *adj.* shortened; abridged (book etc.); abbreviated (word, name).

verladen, *v.tr.* to load (goods etc.).

Verlag [fɛr'laːk], *m -(e)s/-e* publisher(s); publishing house/firm.

ver'lagern, *v.tr. & refl.* to shift.

verlangen [fɛr'laŋən]. **I.** *v.tr.* (*fordern*) to demand (sth.); (*bitten um*) to ask for (the bill etc.); (*wollen*) to want (sth.); (*Aufgabe usw.*) to call for (patience, time etc.); **du wirst am Telefon verlangt,** you are wanted on the telephone. **2.** *v.i.* (*haben*) **v. nach +** *dat,* to ask for (the doctor, a drink etc.). **II.** *V., n -s/no pl Lit:* desire (**nach +** *dat,* for); (*b*) **auf V.,** on demand; **auf js V.** (**hin**), at s.o.'s request.

verläng/ern [fɛr'lɛŋərn], *v.tr.* to lengthen (sth.); to extend (a fence, journey, passport etc.). ◆**V~ung,** *f -/-en* extension; *Sp:* extra time. ◆**V~ungsschnur,** *f* extension lead.

verlangsamen [fɛr'laŋzaːmən], *v.tr.* to slow down (traffic etc.); **das Tempo v.,** to slow down.

Verlaß [fɛr'las], *m auf ihn/sie ist kein V.,** there is no relying on him/her.

ver'lassen. I. *v.tr.irr.57* (*a*) to leave (s.o., sth.); (*im Stich lassen*) to abandon, desert (one's family etc.); (*b*) **sich auf j-n,** et-

was *acc* **v.,** to rely on s.o., sth. **II.** *adj.* deserted (house, person etc.); abandoned (vehicle); (*öde*) desolate (place etc.). ◆**V~heit,** *f -/no pl* desolation.

verläßlich [fɛr'lɛslɪç], *adj.* reliable, dependable. ◆**V~keit,** *f -/no pl* reliability.

Ver'lauf, *m -(e)s/no pl* course; **den weiteren V. abwarten,** to await further developments. ◆**v~en,** *v.i.irr.58* (*sein*) (*a*) (*Ereignis usw.*) to go (off); (*vergehen*) (*Tage usw.*) to pass (slowly etc.); (*b*) (*Linie, Straße usw.*) to run (parallel, straight etc.); (*c*) (*Butter, Farbe usw.*) to run; (*d*) **sich v.,** to lose one's way; (*Menge*) to disperse.

verlautbaren [fɛr'lautbaːrən], *v.tr. Adm:* to make (sth.) known.

ver'leben, *v.tr.* to spend (holidays, one's youth etc.).

ver'leg/en. I. *v.tr.* (*a*) to move, transfer (people, one's quarters etc.); (*b*) (*verschieben*) to put off (an appointment etc.) (**auf +** *acc*, until); (*c*) (*verlieren*) to mislay (a key etc.); (*d*) to lay (a cable etc.); (*e*) (*herausgeben*) to publish (a book etc.); (*f*) **sich auf etwas** *acc* **v.,** to specialize in sth.; *Pej:* to resort to sth. **II.** *adj.* (*Pers.*) embarrassed; **er ist nie um eine Antwort v.,** he is never at a loss for an answer. ◆**V~enheit,** *f -/no pl* embarrassment. ◆**V~er,** *m -s/-* publisher.

Verleih [fɛr'lai], *m -(e)s/-e* (*a*) hire, esp. *N.Am:* rental; (*b*) (*Firma*) hire/rental service; *Cin:* (film) distributors. ◆**v~en,** *v.tr.irr.60* (*a*) to lend (sth.); (*b*) (*überreichen*) to award (a prize); to confer (an honour, title etc.) (**j-m,** on s.o.); (*c*) (*geben*) **j-m Mut, Kraft usw. v.,** to give s.o. courage, strength etc. ◆**V~ung,** *f -/-en* (*a*) lending; (*b*) award.

ver'leiten, *v.tr.* to lead (s.o.) astray/on; **j-n zu etwas** *dat* **v.,** to induce/(*verlocken*) tempt s.o. to do sth.

ver'lernen, *v.tr.* to unlearn, forget (sth.).

ver'lesen, *v.tr.irr.61* (*a*) to read out (sth.); (*b*) **sich v.,** to make a mistake (while reading).

verletz/bar [fɛr'lɛtsbaːr], *adj.* vulnerable. ◆**v~en,** *v.tr.* (*a*) to hurt, injure, esp. *Mil:* wound (s.o., oneself, *Fig:* s.o.'s pride etc.); to injure (one's arm, foot etc.); (*b*) to offend against (decency, good taste etc.); to violate (an agreement etc.), infringe (a law, patent). ◆**v~end,** *adj.* hurtful, wounding (manner, remark etc.). ◆**v~t,** *adj.* (*also Fig:*) hurt, injured; wounded (pride, vanity); **ein V~ter,** a casualty. ◆**V~ung,** *f -/-en* (*a*) injury; (*Wunde*) wound; (*b*) infringement; violation.

ver'leugnen, *v.tr.* to deny (a fact etc.); to disown (a friend etc.).

verleumd/en [fɛr'lɔymdən], *v.tr.* to slander, (*schriftlich*) libel (s.o.). ◆**v~erisch,** *adj.* slanderous; libellous. ◆**V~ung,** *f -/-en* slander; (*schriftlich*) libel. ◆**V~ungskampagne,** *f* smear campaign.

ver'lieb|en, v.refl. sich v., to fall in love (in j-n, with s.o.). ◆**v~t**, adj. in love (in + acc, with); amorous (couple, glances etc.). ◆**V~theit**, f -/no pl (state of) being in love.

verlier|en [fɛr'li:rən], v.irr.32 v.tr. & i. (haben) to lose (s.o., sth.); **sich v.**, (Pers.) to get lost; (Angst, Spur usw.) to disappear, vanish; F: **ihr habt hier nichts verloren**, you've got no business (to be) here. ◆**v~er**, m -s/- loser.

Verlies [fɛr'li:s], n -es/-e dungeon.

ver'lob|en, v.refl. sich v., to get engaged. ◆**V~te(r)**, m & f decl. as adj. (Mann) fiancé; (Frau) fiancée. ◆**V~ung**, f -/-en engagement. ◆**V~ungs-**, comb.fm. engagement (ring etc.).

ver'lock|en, v.tr. to entice, lure (s.o.). ◆**v~end**, adj. tempting. ◆**V~ung**, f -/-en temptation, enticement.

verlogen [fɛr'lo:gən], adj. untruthful; hypocritical (morals etc.).

verloren [fɛr'lo:rən], adj. lost (person, object etc.); vain (effort, hope etc.); j-n, etwas v. **geben**, to give s.o., sth. up for lost. ◆**v~gehen**, v.i.sep.irr.36 (sein) to get lost; (Zeit) to be wasted.

verlos|en [fɛr'lo:zən], v.tr. to draw lots for, (durch Tombola) raffle (sth.). ◆**V~ung**, f -/-en draw, raffle.

verlottern [fɛr'lɔtərn], v.i. (sein) to go to the dogs. ◆**v~t**, adj. dissipated, dissolute.

Verlust [fɛr'lust], m -(e)s/-e loss. ◆**V~geschäft**, n loss-making deal.

ver'machen, v.tr. F: j-m etwas v., to leave sth. to s.o. (in one's will). ◆**V~'mächtnis**, n -ses/-se bequest, legacy.

vermählen [fɛr'mɛːlən], v.refl. Lit: sich v., to get married.

ver'mehren, v.tr. to increase (an amount, wages etc.); **sich v.**, to increase, (Tiere) breed, (Pflanzen) propagate.

vermeiden, v.tr. to avoid (sth.).

vermeintlich [fɛr'maintlɪç], adj. supposed (gangster etc.); alleged (father etc.).

Vermerk [fɛr'mɛrk], m -(e)s/-e note; (Eintrag) entry. ◆**v~en**, v.tr. to make a note of (sth.).

ver'mess|en. I. v.tr. to survey (land etc.). **II.** adj. presumptuous; impudent (request etc.). ◆**V~enheit**, f -/no pl presumption, temerity. ◆**V~er**, m -s/- surveyor.

ver'miet|en, v.tr. to let (a flat, house etc.), lease (buildings, land etc.); to hire (out) (a boat, car etc.). ◆**V~er(in)**, m -s/- (f -/-nen) (a) landlord, (Frau) landlady; (b) hirer. ◆**V~ung**, f -/-en (a) letting; (b) hire, hiring.

ver'minder|n, v.tr. to reduce (sth.); **sich v.**, to lessen (Einfluß usw.) to decrease. ◆**V~ung**, f -/no pl reduction, decrease.

ver'mischen, v.tr. to mix (colours, Cu: ingredients etc.); **sich v.**, to mix (Farben) blend, (Personen) mingle.

vermissen [fɛr'misən], v.tr. to miss (s.o., sth.); **ein Vermißter**, a missing person.

vermitt|eln [fɛr'mitəln], v. 1. v.i. (haben) to mediate. 2. v.tr. (a) to obtain, procure (sth.) (j-m, for s.o.); to negotiate (a deal etc.); (b) (übertragen) to convey (an idea, a picture etc.); to pass on (one's acknowledge); Tel: to put through (a call). ◆**V~ler**, m -s/- (a) (Schlichter) mediator; (b) agent. ◆**V~lung**, f -/-en 1. no pl (Schlichtung) mediation. 2. (Stelle) agency; Tel: exchange.

ver'mögen. I. v.tr.irr.67 Lit: **etwas zu tun v.**, to be able to do sth. **II. V.**, n -s/- 1. (Können) ability. 2. (Besitz) property, (Reichtum) fortune, wealth; F: **das kostet ein V.**, it costs a fortune. ◆**v~d**, adj. wealthy, well-off.

vermuten [fɛr'mu:tən], v.tr. to suspect (sth.); (annehmen) to assume (sth.). ◆**v~lich**, adj. presumable, probable (result etc.). ◆**V~ung**, f -/-en supposition.

vernachlässig|en [fɛr'na:xlɛsigən], v.tr. to neglect (s.o., sth.). ◆**V~ung**, f -/no pl neglect.

vernehm|en. I. v.tr.irr.69 (a) to hear (a sound etc., that ...); (b) (Polizei usw.) to question (a witness etc.). **II. V.**, n dem **V. nach**, from what one hears. ◆**V~ung**, f -/-en questioning.

vernein|en [fɛr'nainən], v.tr.&i. (haben) to say no to a question etc.); to deny (the truth of sth.). ◆**v~ung**, f -/-en (a) negative answer; (b) Gram: negation.

vernicht|en [fɛr'niçtən], v.tr. to destroy (sth., Fig: hopes etc.); to exterminate (a pest, weeds etc.), wipe out (an army, a species etc.). ◆**v~end**, adj. crushing (blow, defeat etc.); devastating (criticism etc.); **j-n v. schlagen**, to crush s.o., Sp: beat s.o. hollow. ◆**V~ung**, f -/no pl destruction; extermination.

Vernunft [fɛr'nunft], f -/no pl reason; **V. annehmen/zur V. kommen**, to see reason/come to one's senses.

vernünftig [fɛr'nynftiç], adj. (a) sensible; sound (argument etc.); **sei doch v.!** do be reasonable/sensible! (b) F: (ordentlich) decent; (richtig) proper (meal etc.).

veröffentlich|en [fɛr'?œfəntlɪçən], v.tr. to publish (a book, report). ◆**V~ung**, f -/-en publication.

ver'ordn|en, v.tr. Med: to prescribe (a treatment, rest etc.). ◆**V~ung**, f order, ruling.

ver'pachten, v.tr. to let (sth.) (out), lease (a farm, land etc.).

ver'pack|en, v.tr. to pack, Com: package (sth.); (einwickeln) to wrap (up) (a present, parcel). ◆**V~ung**, f packing, packaging.

ver'passen, v.tr. (a) to miss (a train, chance etc.); (b) F: (geben) **j-m einen Tritt usw. v.**, to give s.o. a kick etc.

verpesten [fɛr'pɛstən], v.tr. to poison, pollute (the air etc.).

ver'pfleg|en, *v.tr.* to feed (s.o., oneself). ◆**V~ung**, *f -/no pl* catering; (*Mahlzeiten*) meals; (*im Hotel usw.*) board; *Mil:* rations.

verpflicht|en [fɛr'pflɪçtən], *v.tr.* (a) to oblige, (*durch Eid usw.*) bind (s.o.); to commit (s.o.) (**zu einer Zahlung**, to make a payment); **j-m** (**zu Dank**) **verpflichtet**, obliged/indebted to s.o.; **sich zu etwas** *dat* **v.**, to commit oneself to sth.; to undertake to do sth.; (b) (*engagieren*) to engage, sign on (an actor etc.). ◆**V~ung**, *f -/-en* (a) obligation (j-m **gegenüber**, to s.o.); **eine V. eingehen**, to take on a commitment; (b) *Th:* engagement.

ver'pfuschen, *v.tr. F:* to bungle, ruin (one's life etc.).

verpönt [fɛr'pøːnt], *adj.* disapproved of, taboo.

ver'prügeln, *v.tr.* to beat (s.o.) up; (*zur Strafe*) to beat/thrash (s.o.).

Verputz [fɛr'pʊts], *m* plaster; (*Rauhputz*) roughcast. ◆**v~en**, *v.tr.* (a) to plaster, (*außen*) render, (*mit Rauhputz*) roughcast (a wall); (b) *F:* to polish off (food).

Verrat [fɛr'raːt], *m -(e)s/no pl* betrayal (*eines Geheimnisses*, of a secret); (*Landesv.*) treason. ◆**v~en**, *v.tr.irr.13* (a) to betray (s.o., one's country etc.), give away (a secret etc.); **sich v.**, to give oneself away; (b) (*mitteilen*) j-m etwas **v.**, to tell s.o. sth. (in confidence).

Verräter [fɛr'rɛːtər], *m -s/-* traitor, betrayer. ◆**V~in**, *f -/-nen* traitress. ◆**v~isch**, *adj.* treacherous; *Fig:* telltale, giveaway (look etc.).

ver'rechn|en, *v.tr.* (a) to charge/ (*gutschreiben*) credit (a sum) to account; to clear (a cheque); **etwas mit etwas** *dat* **v.**, to offset/balance one thing with another; (b) (*also Fig:*) **sich v.**, to miscalculate. ◆**V~ungsscheck**, *m* non-negotiable/crossed cheque.

verregnet [fɛr'reːɡnət], *adj.* spoilt by rain.

ver'reisen, *v.i.* (*sein*) to go away (on a journey/trip).

ver'reißen, *v.tr.irr.4* to tear (a book, play) to pieces, *F:* slate (a book, play).

verrenk|en [fɛr'rɛŋkən], *v.tr.* to dislocate (one's shoulder etc.); to crick (one's neck); **sich** *dat* **den Fuß v.**, to twist one's ankle. ◆**V~ung**, *f -/-en* dislocation; contortion.

ver'richten, *v.tr.* to carry out, perform (a duty, task etc.).

verringer|n [fɛr'rɪŋərn], *v.tr.* to reduce (sth.); **sich v.**, to decrease, diminish. ◆**V~ung**, *f -/-en* reduction; cut (in output, wages etc.).

ver'rost|en, *v.i.* (*sein*) to *rust*. ◆**v~et**, *adj.* rusty.

verrotten [fɛr'rɔtən], *v.i.* (*sein*) to rot, (*Gebäude*) decay.

ver'rückt [fɛr'rykt], *adj.* crazy, mad (**auf** +*acc*, about); (*geistesgestört*) insane; **ein V~er/eine V~e**, a lunatic. ◆**v~heit**,

f -/-en **1.** *no pl* insanity; *esp. Fig:* madness. **2.** folly; crazy idea.

Ver'ruf, *m* **in V. kommen**, to fall into disrepute. ◆**v~en**, *adj.* disreputable.

Vers [fɛrs], *m -es/-e* verse (in the bible/of a hymn); (*Zeile*) line.

ver'sag|en. **I.** *v.* **I.** *v.i.* j-m/sich *dat* etwas **v.**, to deny s.o./oneself sth. **2.** *v.i.* (*haben*) (*Pers., Ding*) to fail; (*Motor usw.*) to break down. **II.** *v.*, *n -s/no pl* failure; **menschliches V.**, human error/fallibility. ◆**V~er**, *m -s/-* failure; *F:* flop.

ver'salzen. **I.** *v.tr.irr.* to put too much salt in (sth.); *Fig:* **j-m etwas v.**, to spoil sth. for s.o. **II.** *adj.* too salty.

ver'samm|eln, *v.tr.* to assemble (people), gather (people) together; **sich um j-n**, **den Kamin usw. v.**, to gather round s.o., the fire etc. ◆**V~lung**, *f -/-en* assembly; (*weniger formell*) gathering.

Versand [fɛr'zant], *m -s/no pl* dispatch. ◆**V~haus**, *n* mail order firm.

versäum|en [fɛr'zɔymən], *v.tr.* to miss (a chance, train etc.); to lose (time etc.); to neglect (one's duty). ◆**V~nis**, *n -ses /-se* neglect; (*Pflichtv.*) omission.

ver'schaffen, *v.tr.* **sich** *dat/*j-m etwas **v.**, to get (hold of) sth. for oneself/s.o.; **j-m eine Arbeit v.**, to provide s.o. with a job; **sich** *dat* **einen Vorteil usw. v.**, to gain an advantage etc.

verschämt [fɛr'ʃɛːmt], *adj.* bashful; shamefaced.

verschandeln [fɛr'ʃandəln], *v.tr. F:* to disfigure (sth.), spoil (a dress etc.).

verschanzen [fɛr'ʃantsən], *v.refl.* **sich v.**, to dig oneself in; (*in Deckung*) to take cover.

ver'schärfen, *v.tr.* to heighten, increase (contrast, tension etc.); to tighten up (censorship, checks etc.); to stiffen (a penalty); to step up (speed, tempo); **sich v.**, to be heightened/increased.

ver'schätzen, *v.refl.* **sich v.**, to miscalculate.

ver'schenken, *v.tr.* to give (sth.) away, throw away (a chance).

ver'scheuchen, *v.tr.* to chase away (s.o., an animal, *Fig:* worries etc.).

ver'schicken, *v.tr.* to send out (invitations etc.); to send (s.o.) away.

verschieb|en, *v.tr.irr.82* (a) to move, shift (cargo, furniture etc.); *Rail:* to shunt (wagons); (b) (*auf später*) to postpone, put off (sth.) (**auf** + *acc*, until).

verschieden [fɛr'ʃiːdən], *adj.* (a) (*unterschiedlich*) different, distinct; **v. groß/schwer**, of different sizes/weights; (b) *pl* **aus v~en Gründen**, for various reasons; **V~es**, miscellaneous (items), sundries. ◆**v~artig**, *adj.* diverse, of various kinds. ◆**V~heit**, *f -/-en* difference, dissimilarity. ◆**v~tlich**, *adv.* on various occasions.

ver'schimmeln, *v.i.* (*sein*) to go mouldy.

ver'schlafen. **I.** *v.irr.84* **1.** *v.refl.* **&** *i.* (*haben*) (**sich**) **v.**, to oversleep. **2.** *v.tr.* to sleep away (the day, time etc.); *F:* **seinen Zug usw. v.,** to miss one's train etc. by oversleeping. **II.** *adj.* sleepy (person, village etc.).

Ver'schlag, *m* shack, shed; (*Kiste*) crate. ◆**v~en. I.** *v.tr.irr.85* (*a*) to board up (an opening etc.); (*b*) **es verschlug ihm die Sprache,** he was struck dumb. **II.** *adj.* sly, underhand (person). ◆**V~enheit,** *f -/no pl* craftiness; slyness.

verschlechter|n [fɛr'ʃlɛçtərn], *v.tr.* to make (sth.) worse; **sich v.,** to worsen; (*Gesundheit*) to deteriorate. ◆**V~ung,** *f -/no pl* worsening, deterioration.

verschleiern [fɛr'ʃlaiərn], *v.tr.* to veil (one's face); *Fig:* (*verbergen*) to conceal (one's intentions).

Verschleiß [fɛr'ʃlais], *m -es/-e* wear and tear; (*Verbrauch*) consumption (an + *dat,* of). ◆**v~en,** *v.tr. & i.irr.4* (*sein*) to wear (sth., *Fig:* s.o.) out.

ver'schleppen, *v.tr.* (*a*) to take (s.o.) away by force; (*entführen*) to abduct (s.o.); (*b*) to drag out (a discussion etc.).

ver'schleudern, *v.tr.* (*a*) to squander (one's fortune etc.); (*b*) *Com:* to sell (goods) at giveaway prices.

ver'schließ|bar, *adj.* lockable. ◆**v~en,** *v.tr.irr.31* to lock (a door etc.), lock up (a house etc.); **sich Argumenten v.,** to close one's mind to arguments.

verschlimm|ern [fɛr'ʃlimərn], *v.tr.* to make (sth.) worse, aggravate (a situation etc.); **sich v.,** to get worse, deteriorate. ◆**V~erung,** *f -/no pl* worsening, deterioration.

ver'schlingen, *v.tr.irr.95* (*a*) to devour (food, *Fig:* a book etc.); *esp. Fig:* to swallow (s.o., sth.), *Lit:* (*Wellen usw.*) engulf (s.o., sth.); (*b*) (*ineinander*) to entwine (threads etc.).

ver'schlissen, *adj.* worn; (*völlig*) worn out.

verschlossen [fɛr'ʃlɔsən], *adj.* (*a*) locked; (*b*) (*zurückhaltend*) reserved, reticent. ◆**V~heit,** *f -/no pl* reserve

ver'schlucken, *v.tr.* to swallow (food, words); **sich v.,** to choke.

Ver'schluß, *m -sses/-sse* (*a*) (door etc.) catch; *Cl:* fastener; (*Flasche usw.*) stopper, bottle top; **hinter/unter V.,** under lock and key; (*b*) *Phot:* shutter.

ver'schmähen, *v.tr.* to disdain, spurn (help, an offer etc.).

ver'schmerzen, *v.tr.* to get over (a loss etc.).

ver'schmieren, *v.tr.* to besmear, (*bekritzeln*) scrawl over (sth.).

verschmutz|en [fɛr'ʃmutsən], *v.tr.* to soil (clothes, a carpet etc.); to pollute (air, water etc.). ◆**V~ung,** *f -/no pl* pollution.

ver'schnaufen, *v.refl.* **sich v.,** to pause for breath.

verschneit [fɛr'ʃnait], *adj.* covered with snow.

Ver'schnitt, *m* blend.

verschnupft [fɛr'ʃnupft], *adj.* suffering from a cold.

ver'schnüren, *v.tr.* to tie up (a parcel etc.).

verschollen [fɛr'ʃɔlən], *adj.* missing (person etc.).

ver'schonen, *v.tr.* to spare (s.o., sth.) (**von/mit** + *dat,* from).

verschönern [fɛr'ʃøːnərn], *v.tr.* to beautify (s.o., sth.), embellish (a dress, story etc.).

verschränken [fɛr'ʃrɛŋkən], *v.tr.* to fold (one's arms), cross (one's legs).

ver'schreiben, *v.tr.irr.88* (*a*) *Med:* to prescribe (a medicine); (*b*) to make a slip of the pen; (*c*) **sich etwas** *dat* **v.,** to devote oneself to sth.

verschroben [fɛr'ʃroːbən], *adj.* eccentric (person); cranky, crackpot (ideas).

verschrotten [fɛr'ʃrɔtən], *v.tr.* to scrap (a car etc.).

ver'schuld|en. I. *v.tr.* to be responsible for (an accident etc.). **II. V.,** *n -s/no pl* fault, blame; **ohne mein V.,** through no fault of mine. ◆**v~et,** *adj.* in debt; insolvent (firm).

ver'schütten, *v.tr.* to spill (sth.); (*b*) (*Lawine usw.*) to bury (people, a village etc.).

ver'schweigen, *v.tr.irr.89* to keep (sth.) secret; to conceal (news, the truth etc.) (**j-m,** from s.o.).

verschwend|en [fɛr'ʃvɛndən], *v.tr.* to waste (money, food etc.). ◆**V~er,** *m -s/-* spendthrift. ◆**v~erisch,** *adj.* extravagant, wasteful; lavish (costumes, feast etc.). ◆**V~ung,** *f -/no pl* (*a*) waste of sth.; (*b*) wastefulness, extravagance.

verschwiegen [fɛr'ʃviːgən], *adj.* discreet (person); secluded (place etc.). ◆**V~heit,** *f -/no pl* discretion, seclusion.

ver'schwimmen, *v.i.irr.90* (*sein*) to become blurred/(*dunstig*) hazy.

ver'schwinden, *v.i.irr.9* (*sein*) to disappear, vanish; *F:* **verschwinde!** get lost! **II. V.,** *n -s/no pl* disappearance.

verschwitzt [fɛr'ʃvitst], *adj.* soaked in perspiration; sweaty.

verschwommen [fɛr'ʃvɔmən], *adj.* blurred (photograph etc.); hazy (outline etc.); vague, woolly (idea etc.).

ver'schwör|en, *v.refl.irr.91* **sich v.,** to conspire. ◆**V~er(in),** *m (f -/-nen)* conspirator. ◆**V~ung,** *f -/-en* conspiracy, plot.

ver'sehen. I. *v.tr.irr.92* (*a*) to provide (s.o.) (**mit** + *dat,* with); (*b*) to perform (a duty etc.); (*c*) **sich v.,** to make a mistake; (*d*) **ehe man sich versieht,** before you know where you are. **II. V.,** *n -s/-* slip, oversight; (*Fehler*) (careless) mistake; **aus V.,** inadvertently. ◆**v~tlich,** *adv.* inadvertently.

Versehrte(r) [fɛr'zeːrtə(r)], *m & f decl. as adj.* disabled (person).

ver'senden, *v.tr.irr.94* to send out (circulars etc.), dispatch (goods etc.).

versenk|en, *v.tr.* to sink (a ship etc.), submerge (sth.); *Fig:* sich **in ein Buch v.**, to bury/immerse oneself in a book. ◆**V~ung**, *f* sinking; submersion; *Fig:* (self-)absorption; *F:* **in der V. verschwinden**, to disappear from the scene.

versessen [fɛrˈzɛsən], *adj.* **auf j-n, etwas** *acc* v., crazy/mad about s.o., sth.

ver'setz|en, *v.tr.* (*a*) to move (sth.) (somewhere); to transfer (sth., an employee etc.) (**nach** + *dat*, to); *Sch:* to move up, **N.Am:** promote (a pupil); (*b*) **v. in** + *acc*, to set (sth.) in (motion etc.); to put (s.o.) into (a good mood); **v. Sie sich in meine Lage**, put yourself in my shoes; (*c*) **j-m einen Schlag/Stoß v.**, to hit/push s.o.; (*d*) (*verpfänden*) to pawn (a watch etc.). ◆**V~ung**, *f -/-en* (*a*) move, transfer; *Sch:* moving up, promotion; (*b*) pawning.

verseuch|en [fɛrˈzɔyçən], *v.tr.* to contaminate (water etc.). ◆**V~ung**, *f -/no pl* contamination.

ver'sicher|n, *v.tr.* (*a*) to insure (s.o., oneself etc.); (*b*) **j-m v., daß ...**, to assure s.o. that...; **sich j-s, einer Sache v.**, to make sure of s.o., sth. ◆**V~ung**, *f* **1.** insurance. **2.** (*Erklärung*) assurance. ◆**V~ungs-**, *comb.fm.* insurance (agent, claim, company, card, cover etc.). ◆**V~spolice**, *f* insurance policy. ◆**V~sprämie**, *f* insurance premium.

ver'siegeln, *v.tr.* to seal (sth.).

ver'siegen, *v.i.* (*sein*) to run dry, (*Brunnen usw.*) dry up.

versiert [vɛrˈziːrt], *adj.* experienced, (well) versed.

ver'sinken, *v.i.irr.96* (*sein*) to sink, (*Sonne usw.*) go down.

versklav|en [fɛrˈsklaːvən], *v.tr.* to enslave (s.o.). ◆**V~ung**, *f -/no pl* enslavement.

versöhn|en [fɛrˈzøːnən], *v.tr.* to reconcile (s.o.); **sich v.**, to become reconciled; **sie haben sich versöhnt**, they have made it up. ◆**v~lich**, *adj.* conciliatory (mood etc.); forgiving (person). ◆**V~ung**, *f -/ -en* reconciliation.

ver'sorg|en, *v.tr.* (*a*) to provide, supply (s.o., an area etc.); (*b*) (*sorgen für*) to look after (children etc.); to provide for (a family etc.). ◆**V~ung**, *f -/no pl* (*a*) supply; (*b*) (*Pflege*) care of (the old, sick etc.); **die V. einer Familie**, looking after/providing for a family.

verspät|en [fɛrˈʃpɛːtən], *v.refl.* **sich v.**, to be late. ◆**v~et**, *adj.* late (arrival etc.); belated (thanks etc.). ◆**V~ung**, *f -/-en* lateness; *Rail:Av:etc:* delay; **mit (10 Minuten) V.**, (10 minutes) late.

ver'sperren, *v.tr.* to block (an entrance, road etc.), obstruct (a view etc.).

ver'spiel|en, *v.tr.* to gamble away (money, chances etc.). ◆**v~t**, *adj.* playful (kitten etc.); cheerful (tune, pattern).

ver'spotten, *v.tr.* to mock at, deride

(s.o., sth.).

ver'sprech|en. I. *v.tr.irr.104* (*a*) **j-m etwas v.**, to promise s.o. sth.; **sich** *dat* **viel von einer Sache v.**, to have high hopes of sth.; (*b*) **sich v.**, to make a slip of the tongue. **II. V.**, *n -s/no pl* promise. ◆**V~er**, *m* slip of the tongue. ◆**V~ungen**, *fpl* leere V., empty promises.

ver'spüren, *v.tr.* to feel (cold, fear, hunger etc.).

verstaatlich|en [fɛrˈʃtaːtlɪçən], *v.tr.* to nationalize (an industry etc.). ◆**V~ung**, *f -/no pl* nationalization.

Verstand [fɛrˈʃtant], *m -(e)s/no pl* (*Geist*) mind, intellect; (*Vernunft*) sense; sanity; **bei V.**, sane, of sound mind; **den V. verlieren**, to go insane; **wieder zu V. kommen**, to come to one's senses; **nimm doch V. an!** be reasonable! ◆**v~esmäßig** [-dəs-], *adj.* rational (process); intellectual (superiority etc.). ◆**V~esmensch**, *m* rational person.

verständig [fɛrˈʃtɛndɪç], *adj.* intelligent, (*vernünftig*) sensible. ◆**v~en**, *v.tr.* (*a*) to inform, notify (s.o.); (*b*) **sich v.**, to make oneself understood; **sich (mit j-m) v.**, (i) to communicate (with s.o.); (ii) (*sich einigen*) to come to an understanding (with s.o.). ◆**V~ung**, *f -/-en* (*a*) informing, notification; (*b*) (*sich verständigen*) communication; (*c*) (*Übereinkunft*) agreement, understanding.

verständlich [fɛrˈʃtɛntlɪç], *adj.* comprehensible; (*begreiflich*) understandable; **leicht/schwer v.**, easy/difficult to grasp; **sich v. machen**, to make oneself understood/(*bei Lärm*) heard. ◆**V~lichkeit**, *f -/no pl* comprehensibility, intelligibility; (*Klarheit*) clarity. ◆**V~nis** [-ˈʃtɛntnɪs], *n -ses/no pl* understanding; **für Unzuverlässigkeit habe ich kein V.**, I have no time for unreliable people. ◆**v~nislos**, *adj.* uncomprehending. ◆**v~nisvoll**, *adj.* understanding, sympathetic.

ver'stärk|en, *v.tr.* to strengthen (sth.); to reinforce (a material, *Mil:* garrison etc.); (*steigern*) to intensify (pressure, effect etc.); to amplify (*Rad:* a signal etc.); **sich v.**, to increase; (*Sturm usw.*) to grow stronger. ◆**V~er**, *m -s/-* amplifier. ◆**V~ung**, *f a:Tchn:* etc: strengthening, reinforcement; (*b*) increase (**des Verkehrs usw.**, in traffic etc.); (*c*) *esp. Mil:* (*Truppen*) reinforcements.

ver'stauben, *v.i.* (*sein*) to get dusty. ◆**v~t**, *adj.* dusty.

ver'stauchen, *v.tr.* **sich** *dat* **den Fuß/die Hand v.**, to sprain one's ankle/wrist.

ver'stauen, *v.tr.* to stow (sth., *Hum:* s.o.), pack (books etc.).

Versteck [fɛrˈʃtɛk], *n -(e)s/-e* hiding-place. ◆**v~en**, *v.tr.* to hide (s.o., sth.); to conceal (one's embarrassment etc.); **sich v.**, to hide, (*Verfolgte usw.*) go into hiding. ◆**V~spiel**, *n* (game of) hide-

and-seek. ◆v~t, *adj.* hidden; (*heimlich*) secret.

ver'stehen, *v.tr. & i.irr.100* (*haben*) to understand (s.o., sth.); **versteh mich nicht falsch,** don't get me wrong; **was v. Sie darunter?** what do you mean by that? **er versteht nichts davon,** he doesn't know anything about it; **er versteht sich von Autos,** he knows all about cars; **es versteht sich (von selbst),** it goes without saying.

ver'steifen, *v.tr.* to stiffen (sth.), brace a structure etc.); **sich v.,** to stiffen, (*Haltung*) harden.

ver'steiger|**n,** *v.tr.* to auction (sth.). ◆V~**ung,** *f* /-**en** auction (sale).

ver'stell|**bar,** *adj.* adjustable. ◆v~**en,** *v.tr.* (*a*) (*versperren*) to block (a road etc.); (*b*) to shift (sth.); (*falsch*) to put (sth.) in the wrong place; (*einstellen*) to adjust; (*Pers.*) **sich v.,** to pretend, playact. ◆V~**ung,** *f* pretence, play-acting; disguise.

ver'stimm|**t** [fɛr'ʃtimt], *adj.* (*a*) *Mus:* out of tune; (*b*) (*Pers.*) in a bad mood; disgruntled. ◆V~**ung,** *f* /-**en** strained atmosphere; (*Unwillen*) ill-feeling.

ver'stockt [fɛr'ʃtɔkt], *adj.* obdurate, stubborn. ◆V~**heit,** *f /no pl* obduracy.

ver'stohlen [fɛr'ʃtoːlən], *adj.* furtive (glance); stealthy (footstep etc.).

ver'stopf|**en,** *v.tr.* to close (up), plug (a crack, hole etc.); to block, choke (a drain, pipe etc.). ◆v~**t,** *adj.* blocked, congested (street); *F:* bunged up (drain, nose etc.). ◆V~**ung,** *f* /-**en** (*im Rohr usw.*) obstruction; (*in den Straßen*) congestion; *Med:* constipation.

ver'storben [fɛr'ʃtɔrbən], *adj.* **der/die V~e,** the deceased.

ver'stört [fɛr'ʃtøːrt], *adj.* distraught, bewildered.

Ver'stoß, *m* infringement, violation (**gegen** + *acc.* of). ◆v~**en,** *v.irr.103* 1. *v.tr.* to drive (s.o.) away; to disown (a child). 2. *v.i.* (*haben*) **v. gegen** + *acc,* to infringe (regulations etc.), break (the law).

ver'streichen, *v.irr.59* 1. *v.tr.* to spread (butter etc.). 2. *v.i.* (*sein*) *Lit:* (*Zeit*) to pass (by).

ver'streut [fɛr'ʃtrɔyt], *adj.* scattered.

ver'stricken, *v.tr. Fig:* to involve (s.o.) (**in** + *acc,* in); **sich in etwas acc v.,** to get involved in sth.

ver'stümmeln [fɛr'ʃtyməln], *v.tr.* to mutilate (s.o.), *Fig:* a text).

ver'stummen [fɛr'ʃtumən], *v.i.* (*sein*) to fall silent; (*Lärm*) to stop.

Versuch [fɛr'zuːx], *m* -**(e)s/-e** 1. attempt. 2. *Ph: etc:* experiment; (*Probe*) test. ◆v~**en,** *v.tr.* (*a*) to try (sth.), to do sth.); to attempt (flight, a climb, the impossible etc.); **es mit j-m v.,** to give s.o. a try; **sich an/in etwas dat v.,** to try one's hand at sth.; (*b*) to tempt (s.o.); **versucht, etwas zu tun,** tempted to do

sth. ◆V~**s-,** *comb.fm.* experimental (stage, purposes etc.); test (drilling, drive etc.). ◆V~**skaninchen,** *n F:* experimental subject, *F:* guinea-pig. ◆v~**sweise,** *adv.* on a trial basis. ◆V~**ung,** *f* /-**en** temptation; **in V. kommen,** to be tempted.

ver'süßen, *v.tr.* to sweeten (sth.).

ver'tagen, *v.tr.* to adjourn (a debate etc.), (*verschieben*) defer (a decision etc.).

ver'tauschen, *v.tr.* (*a*) to exchange (one thing) (**mit** + *dat,* for); (*b*) (*verwechseln*) to mix up (hats etc.).

verteidig|**en** [fɛr'taidigən], *v.tr. & i.* (*haben*) to defend (s.o., oneself, sth.). ◆V~**er,** *m* -**s/-** defender; *Jur:* advocate, counsel for the defence. ◆V~**ung,** *f /no pl* defence. ◆V~**ungs-,** *comb.fm.* defence (alliance, budget, system, weapon etc.); (line, minister etc.) of defence.

ver'teil|**en,** *v.tr.* to distribute (food, the load etc.); (*verstreuen*) to scatter, spread (sand, sugar etc.); to allocate (duties, subsidies etc.); **die Rollen v.,** *Th:* to cast the parts; *Fig:* to allocate tasks. ◆V~**er,** *m* -**s/-** distributor. ◆V~**ung,** *f* distribution.

verteufelt [fɛr'tɔyfəlt], *adj. F:* (*verzwickt*) extremely awkward; *adv.* devilishly (awkward, difficult etc.); fiendishly (clever, cold etc.).

vertief|**en** [fɛr'tiːfən], *v.tr.* to deepen (a channel, *Fig:* rift etc.); *Fig:* to extend (one's knowledge, etc.); **sich in etwas acc v.,** to become engrossed in sth. ◆V~**ung,** *f* /-**en** 1. depression; (*Mulde*) hollow. 2. *no pl* deepening; extension.

vertikal [vɛrti'kaːl], *adj.* vertical (plane etc.).

ver'tilgen [fɛr'tilgən], *v.tr.* to exterminate (vermin etc.); *F:* to demolish (a cake etc.).

ver'tippen, sich v., *v.refl.* to make a typing mistake.

ver'tonen, *v.tr.* to set (a poem etc.) to music.

Vertrag [fɛr'traːk], *m* -**(e)s/-e** contract; *Pol: etc:* treaty. ◆v~**en** [-gən], *v.tr.irr.85* (*a*) (*aushalten*) to bear, stand (s.o., noise, pain etc.); *F:* to take (criticism etc.); **Alkohol v.,** to hold one's drink/*N.Am:* liquor; **sie verträgt keinen Kaffee,** coffee doesn't agree with her; (*b*) **sich mit j-m v.,** to get on (well) with s.o. ◆v~**lich,** *adj.* contractual. ◆V~**sbruch,** *m* breach of contract. ◆V~**spartner,** *m* partner to a contract.

ver'träglich [fɛr'trɛːkliç], *adj.* (*a*) (*Pers.*) easy to get on with; (*friedlich*) peaceable, good-natured; (*b*) (*Essen*) easy to digest. ◆V~**keit,** *f* -**/no pl** 1. easy-going nature. 2. digestibility.

ver'trauen. I. *v.i.* (*haben*) **j-m, etwas** *dat* **v.,** to trust s.o., sth.; **v. auf** + *acc,* to place one's trust in (God, justice etc.). **II. V.,** *n* -**s/no pl** confidence, trust (**zu** + *dat,* in). **◆v~erweckend**, *adj.* dependable, inspiring confidence. **◆V~bruch**, *m* breach of trust. **◆v~sselig**, *adj.* too trusting, gullible. **◆v~svoll**, *adj.* trustful, trusting. **◆v~swürdig**, *adj.* trustworthy.

ver'traulich, *adj.* (*a*) confidential (report etc.); (*b*) (*familiär*) familiar, *F:* pally. **◆V~keit**, *f -/en* **1.** *no pl* confidential nature. **2.** familiarity.

ver'traut, *adj.* (*a*) intimate (circle etc.); (*b*) (*bekannt*) familiar (face, tune etc.); **sich mit etwas** *dat* **v. machen**, to familiarize oneself with sth. **◆V~heit**, *f -/ -en* (*a*) intimacy; (*b*) familiarity, intimate knowledge.

ver'treiben, *v.tr.irr.12* (*a*) to drive/chase away.(s.o., an animal, clouds etc.); (*aus dem Land*) to exile (s.o.); (*b*) *Fig:* to get rid of (a cold, cough etc.); **sich** *dat* **die Zeit v.**, to while away/pass the time; (*c*) *Com:* to sell (goods) (wholesale).

vertret|bar [fɛr'treːtbaːr], *adj.* tenable (standpoint); defensible (costs, risk etc.). **◆v~en**, *v.tr.irr.105* (*a*) (*zeitweise ersetzen*) to stand in/deputize for (s.o.); (*Interessen wahrnehmen*) to represent (s.o., a country etc.); (*verteidigen*) to advocate (an idea etc.); **die Ansicht v., daß** ..., to take the view that ...; (*b*) *F:* **sich** *dat* **die Beine v.**, to stretch one's legs. **◆V~er(in)**, *m -s/- (f -/-nen)* (*also Com:*) (*a*) representative; (chairman's, minister's etc.) deputy; (*b*) (*Verfechter*) advocate. **◆V~ung**, *f -/en* (*a*) *Jur: Pol: etc:* representation; *Com:* agency; **j-s V. übernehmen**, to stand in for s.o.

Vertrieb [fɛr'triːp], *m -(e)s/-e* sales, marketing. **◆V~s-**, *comb.fm.* sales (department etc.); marketing (costs, organization etc.). **◆V~sleiter**, *m* sales manager.

ver'trocknen, *v.i.* (*sein*) to dry up, (*Brot usw.*) go dry.

ver'trödeln, *v.tr.* to dawdle away, waste (time).

ver'trösten, *v.tr.* to string (s.o.) along (with promises etc.).

ver'tun, *v.tr.* (*a*) to waste (money, time); (*b*) *F:* **sich v.**, to make a slip.

ver'tuschen, *v.tr.* to cover up (an error etc.).

verüben [fɛr'ʔyːbəln], *v.tr.* **j-m etwas v.**, to hold sth. against s.o.

ver'üben, *v.tr.* to commit (a crime etc.).

verunglücken [fɛr'ʔunglʏkən], *v.i.* (*sein*) (*Pers.*) to have an accident; (*Auto, Zug usw.*) to crash; **tödlich v.**, to be killed in an accident.

ver'unreinigen, *v.tr.* to pollute (air, water etc.); to soil (clothes etc.).

verunstalten [fɛr'ʔunʃtaltən], *v.tr.* to disfigure (s.o., sth.).

veruntreuen [fɛr'ʔuntrɔyən], *v.tr.* to embezzle (money).

ver'ursachen [fɛr'ʔuːrzaxən], *v.tr.* to cause (sth.).

ver'urteil|en, *v.tr.* to condemn (s.o., sth.); *Jur:* to sentence (s.o.) (**zu** + *dat*, to). **◆V~ung**, *f -/-en Jur:* conviction; *Fig:* condemnation.

vervielfachen [fɛr'fiːlfaxən], *v.tr.* to increase (production etc.) considerably.

vervielfältig|en [fɛr'fiːlfɛltigən], *v.tr.* to duplicate, make copies of (a text etc.). **◆V~ung**, *f -/-en* duplication, copying.

vervollkommnen [fɛr'fɔlkɔmnən], *v.tr.* to perfect (sth.).

vervollständigen [fɛr'fɔlʃtɛndigən], *v.tr.* to complete (sth.).

ver'wackelt, *adj.* shaky, blurred (photograph).

ver'wahr|en, *v.tr.* (*a*) to keep (sth.) safely; (*b*) **sich gegen etwas** *acc* **v.**, to protest against sth. **◆v~losen**, *v.tr./vi(raise,* *v.i.* (*sein*) to be neglected; (*Garten, Fig: Pers.*) to go to seed. **◆V~ung**, *f -/no pl* (*safe*) keeping; custody (of s.o.); **etwas in V. geben/nehmen**, to hand over/accept sth. for safe keeping.

ver'waist [fɛr'vaist], *adj.* orphaned.

ver'walt|en, *v.tr.* to administer (sth.); to manage, run (a business, hotel etc.). **◆V~er**, *m -s/-* administrator; (*Leiter*) manager; (*Treuhänder*) trustee. **◆V~ung**, *f -/-en* **1.** *no pl* administration; (*Leitung*) management, running. **2.** (*Behörde*) (local etc.) authority. **◆V~ungs-**, *comb.fm.* administrative (district, costs etc.). **◆V~sbeamte(r)**, *m* administrative official; civil servant.

ver'wand|eln, *v.tr.* to change, transform (s.o., sth.) (**in** + *acc*, into); **sich in etwas** *acc* **v.**, to change/turn into sth. **◆V~lung**, *f* change, transformation.

verwandt [fɛr'vant], *adj.* related (**mit** + *dat*, to). **◆V~e(r)**, *m & f decl. as adj.* relative, relation. **◆V~schaft**, *f -/-en* **1.** relationship. **2.** *no pl* relatives, relations.

ver'warn|en, *v.tr.* to caution (s.o.), warn (*Sp:* a player etc.). **◆V~ung**, *f* warning, caution.

ver'waschen, *adj.* washed out, faded.

ver'wässern, *v.tr.* to water down (wine, *Fig:* an idea etc.).

ver'wechs|eln, *v.tr.* to confuse, mix up (people, things); to mistake (s.o., sth.) (**mit j-m, etwas** *dat*, for s.o., sth.). **◆V~lung**, *f -/-en* confusion, *F:* mix-up; mistake.

verwegen [fɛr'veːgən], *adj.* bold, daring. **◆V~heit**, *f -/no pl* audacity, daring.

ver'wehren, *v.tr.* **j-m etwas v.**, to refuse s.o. sth.

verweichlichen [fɛr'vaiçliçən], *v.tr.* to make (s.o.) soft, *F:* mollycoddle (a child).

ver'weiger|n, *v.tr.* (**j-m**) **etwas v.**, to refuse (s.o.) sth.; **den Befehl v.**, to refuse to obey orders.

ver'weilen, *v.i.* (*sein*) *Lit:* to stay, (*länger als nötig*) linger.

Verweis [fɛr'vais], *m -es/-e* **1.** (*Tadel*) reprimand, rebuke. **2.** (*Hinweis*) reference.

◆v~**en** [-zən], *v.tr.irr.70 (a)* to expel (s.o.) (**aus/von** + *dat,* from); **j-n des Landes v.,** to deport s.o.; *Sp:* **einen Spieler des Platzes v.,** to send a player off (the field); *(b) (hinweisen)* **j-n auf etwas** *acc* **v.,** to refer s.o. to sth.

ver'welken, *v.i.* (sein) to wilt, wither.

ver'wend|en, *v.tr.irr.94* to use (s.o., sth.); to spend (care, effort, time etc.). ◆**V~ung,** *f -/-en* use. ◆**v~ungsfähig,** *adj.* fit for use, (geeignet) suitable. ◆**V~ungszweck,** *m* purpose, application.

ver'werf|en, *v.tr.irr.110* to reject, turn down (a plan etc.); to dismiss (a complaint etc.). ◆**v~lich,** *adj.* reprehensible.

ver'wert|en, *v.tr.* to make (good) use of (sth.), put (sth.) to good use; to utilize (resources etc.). ◆**V~ung,** *f -/-en* utilization, exploitation.

verwes|en [fer've:zən], *v.i.* (sein) (Leiche) to decompose. ◆**V~ung,** *f -/no pl* decomposition.

ver'wick|eln [fer'vik|əln], *v.tr. (a)* to involve (s.o.); **sich v.,** (Fäden, Wolle) to get into a tangle (also Pers.) **sich in etwas** *acc/dat* **v.,** to get entangled/mixed up in sth. ◆**v~elt,** *adj.* complex, involved. ◆**V~lung,** *f -/-en* **1.** *no pl* entanglement; involvement. **2.** (*Komplikation*) complication.

verwildern [fer'vildərn], *v.i.* (sein) to go wild; (Pflanze) to grow wild.

verwirklichen [fer'virklicən], *v.tr.* to realize (an ambition, idea etc.); to put (a plan) into effect.

verwirr|en [fer'virən], *v.tr. (a)* to entangle (threads etc.); to tousle (hair); *(b)* to bewilder, (durcheinanderbringen) confuse. ◆**V~ung,** *f -/-en* confusion; (Fassungslosigkeit) bewilderment; **j-n in V. bringen,** to confuse/fluster s.o.; **geistige V.,** distraught state.

ver'wischen, *v.tr.* to smudge.

ver'wittern, *v.i.* (sein) to weather.

verwitwet [fer'vitvət], *adj.* widowed.

verwöhn|en [fer'vø:nən], *v.tr.* to spoil, (verhätscheln) pamper (s.o.). ◆**v~t,** *adj.* spoilt (child etc.); fastidious (taste etc.).

verworfen [fer'vorfən], *adj.* depraved. ◆**V~heit,** *f -/no pl* depravity.

verworren [fer'vorən], *adj.* confused; (verwickelt) involved.

verwund|bar [fer'vuntba:r], *adj.* vulnerable. ◆**V~en,** *v.tr.* to wound (s.o.). ◆**V~ete(r),** *m & f decl. as adj.* wounded (man/woman), casualty. ◆**V~ung,** *f -/-en* **1.** *no pl* wounding. **2.** wound.

ver'wunder|lich, *adj.* surprising; (seltsam) strange, odd. ◆**v~n,** *v.tr.* to surprise (s.o.). ◆**V~ung,** *f -/no pl* surprise; amazement.

ver'wünschen, *v.tr.* to curse (s.o., sth.).

verwüst|en [fer'vy:stən], *v.tr.* to devastate, ravage (a country etc.).

◆**V~ung,** *f -/-en* devastation, ravages.

verzagen [fer'tsa:gən], *v.i.* (haben) to lose heart, give up (hope).

ver'zählen, *v.refl.* **sich v.,** to miscount.

ver'zaubern, *v.tr.* to bewitch, enchant (s.o., sth.).

Verzehr [fer'tse:r], *m -(e)s/no pl* consumption. ◆**v~en,** *v.tr.* to consume (food, drink).

ver'zeichn|en, *v.tr.irr.60* to record (sth.), take (sth.) down; (aufführen) to list (items, names etc.). ◆**V~nis,** *n -sses/ -sse* list; (Register) index.

verzeih|en [fer'tsaiən], *v.tr.irr 60* to forgive (sth.); (entschuldigen) to excuse (a fault etc.); **ich verzeihe es dir,** I'll forgive you (for that). ◆**v~lich,** *adj.* excusable, pardonable. ◆**V~ung,** *f -/no pl* forgiveness; **V.!** sorry!

ver'zerren, *v.tr.* to distort (a picture, sound, facts etc.).

Verzicht [fer'tsiçt], *m -(e)s/-e* renunciation, (Opfer) sacrifice (**auf** + *acc,* of). ◆**v~en,** *v.i.* (haben) to do without, abstain; **v. auf** + *acc,* (aufgeben) to give (sth.) up; to waive, relinquish (a claim, right etc.); to abstain from (alcohol, comment etc.).

ver'ziehen, *v.irr.113* **1.** *v.tr. (a)* to screw up (one's face, mouth); **er verzog das Gesicht,** he pulled a face; *(b)* (verwöhnen) to spoil (a child); *(c)* **sich v.,** (die Form verlieren) to get out of shape; (verschwinden) to disappear. **2.** *v.i.* (sein) to move (house).

ver'zier|en, *v.tr.* to decorate (sth.). ◆**V~ung,** *f -/-en* decoration.

verzinsen [fer'tsinzən], *v.tr.* to pay interest on (a loan etc.). ◆**v~lich,** *adj.* bearing interest.

ver'zöger|n, *v.tr.* to delay (sth.); (verlangsamen) to retard, slow down (development etc.); **sich v.,** to be delayed/held up. ◆**V~ung,** *f -/-en* **1.** *no pl* delaying; slowing down. **2.** delay.

ver'zollen, *v.tr.* to pay duty on (sth.); **haben Sie etwas zu v.?** have you anything to declare?

verzück|t [fer'tsykt], *adj.* ecstatic; *adv.* **v. zuhören,** to listen entranced. ◆**V~ung,** *f -/no pl* (state) of ecstasy.

Ver'zug, *m -(e)s/no pl* delay; *Fin:* **in V. sein,** to be in arrears.

ver'zweif|eln, *v.i.* (sein) to despair. ◆**v~elt,** *adj.* desperate; despairing (look etc.). ◆**V~lung,** *f -/no pl* despair.

verzweigen [fer'tsvaigən], *v.refl.* **sich v.,** (Baum, Straße) to branch, divide; *Fig:* (System usw.) to ramify.

verzwickt [fer'tsvikt], *adj.* F: tricky; ticklish (problem etc.).

Veto ['ve:to], *n -s/-s* veto. ◆**V~recht,** *n* (power of) veto.

Vetter ['fɛtər], *m -s/-* cousin. ◆**V~nwirtschaft,** *f* nepotism.

Viadukt [via'dukt], *m -(e)s/-e* viaduct.

Vibr|ation [vibratsi'o:n], *f -/-en* vibration.

◆v~**ieren** [vi'briːrən], *v.i.* (*haben*) to vibrate.

Video ['video]. **I.** *n* -s/*no pl* video. **II.** '**V**~-, *comb.fm.* video (tape, cassette etc.). ◆**V**~**recorder**, *m*, video (tape) recorder.

Vieh [fiː]. **I.** *n* -(e)s/*no pl* **1.** *Agr*: livestock, *esp.* cattle. **2.** *Pej: F:* (*a*) (*Tier*) creature; (*b*) (*Pers.*) beast. **II.** '**V**~-, *comb.fm. Agr*: livestock, *esp.* cattle (trader, dealer, market etc.). ◆'**v**~**isch**, *adj.* brutal, bestial. ◆'**V**~**zucht**, *f* cattle/stock breeding.

viel [fiːl]. **1.** *adj.* much; *pl* many; v~e Freunde, many/a lot of friends; das v~e Geld, all that money; v. Zeit, a lot of time; nicht v. Geld, not much money. **2.** *adv.* v. arbeiten/lachen, to work/laugh a lot; v. größer, much bigger. **3.** *pron.* (*a*) *inv.* er sagt v./nicht v., he says a lot/not much; einer zu v., one too many; gleich v., the same (amount); (*b*) v~es, a lot of things; in v~em, in many respects; um v~es jünger/besser, much younger/better; (*c*) v~e many, a lot; (*Menschen*) a lot of people. ◆'**v**~**deutig**, *adj.* ambiguous. ◆'**V**~**deutigkeit**, *f* -/en ambiguity. ◆**v**~**er'lei**. **1.** *inv.* many (different) kinds of, a great variety of. **2.** *pron.* all kinds of things; a great many things. ◆'**v**~**fach**, *adj.* (*a*) multiple; many different (ways); **auf v~fachen Wunsch**, by popular demand; um ein v~faches, many times; (*b*) many times (over); (*häufig*) frequently. ◆'**V**~**falt**, *f* -/*no pl* diversity; (great) variety. ◆'**v**~**fältig**, *adj.* diverse (problems etc.); multifarious (activities, duties etc.). ◆'**V**~**fraß**, *m* -es/-e glutton. ◆**v**~**leicht** [fi'laiçt], *adv.* perhaps; *F:* das war v. ein Schreck! that (really) was some shock! ◆'**v**~**mals**, *adv.* many times; danke v., thank you very much. ◆'**v**~**mehr**, *conj. & adv.* (or) rather; (*genauer gesagt*) to be more precise; (*im Gegenteil*) on the contrary. ◆'**v**~**sagend**, *adj.* meaning(ful) (look etc.). ◆'**v**~**schichtig**, *adj.* manylayered; *Fig:* many-faceted. ◆'**v**~**seitig**, *adj.* versatile (person, tool etc.); varied (abilities); wide (experience, interests etc.). ◆'**v**~**versprechend**, *adj.* very promising. ◆'**V**~**zahl**, *f* -/*no pl* multiplicity, enormous number. ◆'**V**~**zweck**-, *comb.fm.* multi-purpose.

vier [fiːr], *num.adj.* four; **auf allen v~en**, on all fours; **unter v. Augen**, confidentially, in private. ◆'**V**~**beiner**, *m* -s/- *Hum:* four-footed friend. ◆'**v**~**beinig**, *adj.* four-legged. ◆'**V**~**eck**, *n* quadrilateral; (*Rechteck*) rectangle; (*mit gleichen Seiten*) square. ◆'**v**~**eckig**, *adj.* rectangular; square; *Mth:* quadrilateral. ◆'**v**~**erlei**, *adj.* of four kinds. ◆'**v**~**fach**, *adj.* (*a*) fourfold; quadruple; **das V**~**fache**, four times as much; (*b*)

adv. four times. ◆'**v**~**jährig**, *adj.* four-year-old (child etc.); four-year (period etc.). ◆'**v**~**mal**, *adv.* four times. ◆'**v**~**malig**, *adj.* (repeated) four times. ◆'**v**~**stellig**, *adj.* four-figure (number). ◆'**V**~**taktmotor**, *m* four-stroke engine. ◆'**v**~**te(r,s)**, *num.adj.* fourth. ◆'**v**~**teilig**, *adj.* in four parts. ◆'**V**~**tel** ['firtəl], *n* -s/- quarter; **V. nach vier**, quarter past four. ◆'**V**~**telfinale**, *n* quarter final. ◆'**V**~**tel'jahr**, *n* quarter (of a year). ◆'**v**~**teljährlich**, *adj. & adv.* quarterly; *adv.* every quarter. ◆'**v**~**teln**, *v.tr.* to quarter (sth.). ◆'**V**~**telnote**, *f* crotchet. ◆'**V**~**telstunde**, *f* quarter of an hour. ◆'**v**~**tens**, *adv.* fourthly. ◆'**v**~**türig**, *adj. Aut:* four-door. ◆'**v**~**zehn**, *num.adj.* fourteen. ◆'**v**~**zehntäglich**, *adj.* fortnight's (holiday etc.). ◆'**v**~**zehntägig**, *adj.* fortnightly. ◆'**v**~**zehnte(r,s)**, *num.adj.* fourteenth. ◆'**v**~**zig**, *num.adj.* forty.

Vikar [vi'kaːr], *m* -s/-e curate.

Vill|**a** ['vila], *f* -/**Villen** detached house. ◆**V**~**enviertel**, *n* smart residential district.

violett [vio'lɛt], *adj.* violet.

Violine [vio'liːnə], *f* -/-n violin. ◆**V**~**inkonzert**, *n* violin concerto. ◆**V**~**oncello** [violɔn'tʃɛlo], *n* cello.

Virus ['viːrus], *m* -/**Viren** virus.

Visier [vi'ziːr], *n* -s/-e *Mil:* gun sight.

Vision [vizi'oːn], *f* -/-en vision.

Visit|**e** [vi'ziːtə], *f* -/-n *Med:* (doctor's) round (in a hospital). ◆**V**~**enkarte**, *f* visiting card.

visuell [vizu'ɛl], *adj.* visual.

Visum ['viːzum], *n* -s/**Visa & Visen** visa.

vital [vi'taːl], *adj.* (*Pers. usw.*) dynamic; full of life.

Vitamin [vita'miːn], *n* -s/-e vitamin. ◆**V**~**mangel**, *m* vitamin deficiency.

Vitrine [vi'triːnə], *f* -/-n glass case; (*Schaukasten*) show/display case.

Vize- ['fiːtsə-], *comb.fm.* vice-(admiral, chancellor etc.). ◆'**V**~**präsident**, *m* vice-president.

Vlies [fliːs], *n* -es/-e fleece.

Vogel ['foːgəl], *m* -s/- bird; *F:* (*Pers.*) komischer/seltsamer V., queer bird/customer; einen V. haben, to be cuckoo; j-m den/einen V. zeigen, to tap one's forehead. ◆'**V**~**bauer**, *n* birdcage. ◆'**V**~**futter**, *n* bird feed. ◆'**V**~**kunde**, *f* -/*no pl* ornithology. ◆'**V**~**perspektive**, *f* bird's eye view.

Vokab|**el** [vo'kaːbəl], *f* -/-n word; *pl* **V**~**n**, vocabulary. ◆**V**~**ular** [-abu'laːr], *n* -s/-e (personal) vocabulary.

Vokal [vo'kaːl], *m* -s/-e vowel.

Volk [fɔlk], *n* -(e)s/**-er** (*a*) people; nation; (*b*) *F:* V., crowds of people.

Völker- ['fœlkər-], *comb.fm.* international (friendship, understanding etc.). ◆'**V**~**kunde**, *f* -/*no pl* ethnology. ◆'**V**~**mord**, *m* genocide. ◆'**V**~**recht**, *n* international law. ◆'v~**rechtlich**, *adj.* in/according to international law.

Volks- ['fɔlks-], *comb.fm.* (*a*) popular (edition, custom, front, hero, art etc.); national (income, day of mourning etc.); (enemy, voice etc.) of the people; *esp. Pol:* people's (army, party, republic, representative etc.); (*b*) (öffentlich) public (library, health, welfare etc.); (*c*) *Mus: Lit: etc:* folk (ballad, epic, music, dance etc.). ◆'V~**abstimmung**, *f* national referendum. ◆'V~**fest** *n*, (local) public festival; (*Jahrmarkt*) funfair. ◆'V~**gruppe**, *f* ethnic minority. ◆'V~**hochschule**, *f* adult/*Brit:* further education college. ◆'V~**lied**, *n* folksong. ◆'V~**schule**, *f* basic primary (and secondary) school. ◆'v~**tümlich**, *adj.* popular; (*traditionell*) traditional; *Pej:* folksy. ◆'V~**wirtschaft**, *f* economics; political economy. ◆'v~**wirtschaftlich**, *adj.* economic.

voll [fɔl], *adj.* (*a*) full; v. **von/mit etwas dat,** full of sth.; (*b*) (*ganz*) whole (truth etc.); complete (success, certainty); **in** v~**em Ernst,** in all seriousness; *Fig:* j-n **nicht für v. nehmen,** not to take s.o. seriously; **v. und ganz,** completely. ◆v~**'auf,** *adv.* fully. ◆'v~**automatisch,** *adj.* fully automatic. ◆'V~**bart,** *m* full beard. ◆'v~**blut,** *n* thoroughbred. ◆v~**'bringen,** *v.tr.insep.irr.16 Lit:* to accomplish (sth.), perform (a task etc.). ◆v~**'enden,** *v.tr.insep.* to complete (a task etc.). ◆v~**ends** ['fɔlɛnts], *adv.* completely; (*erst recht*) especially. ◆V~**'endung,** *f* -/no *pl* 1. (*Abschluß*) accomplishment. 2. (*Vollkommenheit*) perfection. ◆v~**er,** *inv.adj.* ein Korb v. Früchte, a basket (full) of fruit. ◆v~**'führen,** *v.tr.insep.* to perform (a deed, trick etc.). ◆'V~**gas,** *n* full throttle; **V. geben,** to open right up. ◆'v~**jährig,** *adj.* of age. ◆'V~**jährigkeit,** *f* -/no *pl* majority. ◆'V~**kaskoversicherung,** *f* comprehensive insurance. ◆v~**'kommen,** *adj.* perfect; flawless (beauty); *adv.* completely. ◆'V~**kornbrot,** *n* coarse wholemeal bread; (*Schwarzbrot*) black bread. ◆'V~**macht,** *f* authority; *Jur:* power of attorney. ◆'V~**mond,** *m* full moon. ◆'V~**pension,** *f* full board. ◆'v~**schlank,** *adj.* buxom, plump. ◆'v~**ständig,** *adj.* complete. ◆'v~**strecken,** *v.tr.insep. Jur:* to execute (a judgment, will etc.), carry out (a sentence). ◆V~**'streckung,** *f* -/no *pl Jur:* execution; enforcement. ◆'v~**tanken,** *v.tr. & i.sep.* (haben) Aut: to fill up (a car). ◆'V~**versammlung,** *f* full/general assembly. ◆'v~**zählig,** *adj.* complete (set etc.); full (turnout). ◆v~**'ziehen,** *v.tr insep.irr.113* to carry out (an order etc.);

sich v., to take place. ◆V~**'zug,** *m* -(e)s/no *pl* execution.

völlig ['fœlic], *adj.* complete; sheer (madness, nonsense); **du hast v. recht,** you are absolutely right/perfectly correct.

Volleyball ['vɔliball], *m* volleyball.

Volt [vɔlt], *n* -s/- volt.

Volumen [vo'lu:mən], *n* -s/- volume.

vom [fɔm], *prep.* = **von dem.**

von [fɔn], *prep.* + *dat.* 1. from; **v. mir aus,** I don't mind; please yourself; **v. jetzt an,** from now on. 2. **ein Gedicht v.** Heine, a poem by Heine; **müde v. der Reise,** tired from the journey; **v. selbst,** by oneself/itself; automatically. 3. **eine Frau v. 40 Jahren,** a woman of 40; **der König v. Spanien,** the King of Spain; **ein Freund v. mir,** a friend of mine; **v. etwas erzählen/sprechen,** to talk about sth. ◆v~**ei'nander,** *adv.* from one another/each other. ◆v~**statten** [-'ftatən], *adv.* **v. gehen,** to take place, (*verlaufen*) proceed.

vor [fo:r], *prep.* 1. (*räumlich*) (+ *dat/acc*) in front of; **v. allem/allen Dingen,** above all. 2. (*zeitlich*) (+ *dat*) before; **fünf Minuten v. sieben,** five minutes to seven; (**heute**) **v. einem Jahr,** a year ago (today). 3. (+) **v. Kälte, Angst, Zorn usw. zittern,** to tremble with cold, fear, rage etc.; **v. Hunger sterben,** to die of hunger.

'**Vorabend,** *m* evening before.

'**Vorahnung,** *f* premonition.

voran [fo'ran], *adv.* (*a*) first, in front; (*b*) (*vorwärts*) forwards. ◆v~**gehen,** *v.i.sep.irr.36* (*sein*) (*a*) (*Pers.*) to lead (the way); to go on ahead (j-m, of s.o.); (*Sache*) **etwas dat v.,** to precede sth.; (*b*) (*Arbeu usw.*) to make progress. ◆v~**kommen,** *v.i.sep.irr.53* (*sein*) to make headway/progress.

'**Voranmeldung,** *f* advance booking.

'**Voranschlag,** *m* estimate.

'**Vorarbeit,** *f* preparatory work, ground work. ◆'V~**er,** *m* foreman.

voraus [fo'raus], *adv.* (*a*) ahead, in front (+ *dat* etc.); (*b*) ['fo:raus] **im v.,** in advance. ◆v~**berechnen,** *v.tr.sep.* to estimate (costs etc.); to forecast (a result etc.). ◆V~**sage,** *f* -/-n prediction, forecast. ◆v~**sagen,** *v.tr.sep.* to forecast, predict (sth.). ◆v~**sehen,** *v.tr.sep.irr.92* to foresee, anticipate (sth.). ◆v~**setzen,** *v.tr.sep.* to presuppose (sth.), take (sth.) for granted; (*Stellung*) to require (sth.); **vorausgesetzt, daß ...,** provided that ... ◆V~**setzung,** *f* -/-en requirement; qualification (for a job); **falsche V.,** wrong assumption/premise; **unter der V., daß ...,** on the condition/understanding that ... ◆V~**sicht,** *f* foresight; **aller V. nach,** in all probability. ◆v~**sichtlich,** *adj.* expected (date, time etc.); **er kommt v. am Montag,** is expected on Monday.

'**Vorbedingung,** *f* precondition, prerequisite.

'**Vorbehalt,** *m* -(e)s/-e reservation; (*Be-denken*) misgiving. ◆'**v~en,** *v.tr.sep.irr.45* **sich dat etwas v.,** to reserve the right to sth.; **alle Rechte v.,** all rights reserved. ◆'**v~los,** *adj.* unconditional; *adv.* unreservedly.

vorbei [for'bai], *adv.* (a) (*räumlich*) past; (b) (*zeitlich*) over, past; **3 Uhr v.,** past/F: gone 3 o'clock. ◆**v~fahren,** *v.i.sep.irr.26* (*sein*) to go/*Aut:* drive past. ◆**v~gehen,** *v.i.sep.irr.36* (*sein*) (a) (*Pers., Fig: Zeit usw.*) to pass; **v. an +** *dat,* to go/(*zu Fuß*) walk past (s.o., sth.); (*Schuß*) to miss (the target); **im V.,** in passing; (*besuchen*) *F:* to drop in (**bei j-m,** on s.o.).

'**vorbereit|en,** *v.tr.sep.* to prepare (s.o., sth.). ◆'**V~ung,** *f* -/-en preparation. ◆**v~ungs-,** *comb.fm.* preparatory (work, measures etc.).

'**vorbestell|en,** *v.tr.sep.* to order (goods etc.) in advance; to book, reserve (a room, seats etc.). ◆'**V~ung,** *f* advance order; *Th:etc:* booking, reservation.

'**vorbestraft,** *adj.* **jur:** (*zweimal/mehrfach*) **v.,** with (two/several) previous convictions.

'**vorbeug|en,** *v.* **1.** *v.i.* (*haben*) **etwas dat v.,** to prevent sth.; **v~de Maßnahmen,** preventive measures. **2.** *v.refl.* **sich v.,** to bend forward. ◆'**V~ung,** *f* -/-en prevention.

'**Vorbild,** *n* model, example. ◆'**v~lich,** *adj.* exemplary (behaviour etc.); model (pupil etc.).

'**Vorbote,** *m esp. Fig:* herald.

'**vorbring|en,** *v.tr.sep.irr.16* to put forward (an argument, a claim etc.); to offer (an excuse, proof).

Vorder- ['fordər-], *comb.fm.* front (axle, wheel, seat, paw, room etc.); fore(-deck etc.). ◆**v~e(r,s)** ['fordərə(r,s)], *adj.* front. ◆'**V~grund,** *m* foreground; *Fig:* **etwas in den V. stellen,** to give sth. prominence/emphasis. ◆'**v~gründig,** *adj.* obvious, transparent (motive etc.); (*oberflächlich*) superficial (treatment etc.). ◆'**V~mann,** *m* -es/¨er man in front. ◆'**V~seite,** *f* front; obverse (of a coin). ◆'**v~ste(r,s),** *adj.* foremost; very first (row etc.).

'**vordring|en,** *v.i.sep.irr.19* (*sein*) to advance. ◆'**v~lich,** *adj.* urgent.

'**Vordruck,** *m* printed form, *N.Am:* blank.

'**vorehelich,** *adj.* pre-marital.

'**voreilig,** *adj.* (over)hasty, rash.

'**voreingenommen,** *adj.* biased, prejudiced. ◆'**V~heit,** *f* -/no pl bias, prejudice.

'**vorenthalten,** *v.tr.sep.irr.45* to withhold (information etc.) (**j-m,** from s.o.).

'**vorerst,** *adv.* for the time being.

'**Vorfahr,** *m* -en/-en ancestor. ◆'**v~en,** *v.tr. & i.sep.irr.26* (*sein*/*vorfahren*) to drive on ahead. ◆'**V~t,** *f* right of way, priority. ◆'**V~t(s)straße,** *f* major

road.

'**Vorfall,** *m* incident, occurrence. ◆'**v~en,** *v.i.sep.irr.27* (*sein*) (*geschehen*) to happen, occur.

'**Vorfilm,** *m* supporting film.

'**vorfinden,** *v.tr.sep.irr.96* to find (s.o., sth.) (waiting for one).

'**Vorfreude,** *f* pleasurable anticipation.

'**vorführ|en,** *v.tr.sep.* (a) (*aufführen*) to put on (an act, show etc.); to show (a film, play etc.); (b) (*ausstellen*) to display (goods etc.), model (clothes); **dem Richter vorgeführt werden,** to be brought before the judge. ◆'**V~raum,** *m Cin:* projection room. ◆'**V~ung,** *f* presentation; *Cin:* showing; *Th:* performance.

'**Vorgabe,** *f* -/no pl Sp: handicap.

'**Vorgang,** *m* course of events; (*Verfahren*) *Tchn: Biol: etc:* process; *Tchn:* operation.

'**Vorgänger(in),** *m* -s/- (*f* -/-nen) predecessor.

'**Vorgarten,** *m* front garden.

'**vorgeb|en,** *v.tr.sep.irr.35* (a) (*zum Vorwand*) to pretend (**krank zu sein usw.,** to be ill etc.); (b) (*festlegen*) to prescribe, lay down (sth.). ◆'**v~lich,** *adj.* alleged; ostensible (reason).

'**Vorgebirge,** *n* -s/- foothills.

'**vorgefaßt,** *adj.* **v~e Meinung,** preconceived idea.

'**Vorgefühl,** *n* presentiment.

'**vorgehen. I.** *v.i.sep.irr.36* (*sein*) (a) to go forward; (*vorausgehen*) to go on ahead; (*Uhr*) to be fast; (*Vorrang haben*) to take precedence (**allem anderen,** over everything else); (c) (*geschehen*) to happen, (*stattfinden*) take place; (d) (*handeln*) to act, take action. **II. V.,** *n* -s/no pl action.

'**vorgerückt,** *adj.* late (hour), advanced (age, stage etc.).

'**Vorgeschmack,** *m* foretaste.

'**Vorgesetzte(r),** *m & f decl. as adj.* superior; *Mil:* superior officer.

'**vorgestern,** *adv.* the day before yesterday.

'**vorgreifen,** *v.i.sep.irr.43* (*haben*) to anticipate (**j-m, einer Entscheidung usw.,** s.o., a decision etc.).

'**vorhaben. I.** *v.tr.sep.irr.44* to have (sth.) in mind; to plan (sth.); **hast du heute abend etwas vor?** have you got anything on tonight? **II. V.,** *n* -s/- plan, project; *Com:* project; (*Absicht*) intention.

'**vorhalt|en,** *v.sep.irr.45* **1.** *v.tr.* (a) to hold up (a dress, *Fig:* s.o. as an example etc.); (b) **j-m einen Fehler usw. v.,** to reproach s.o. with a mistake etc. **2.** *v.i.* (*haben*) *F:* (*Vorrat usw.*) to last (out). ◆'**V~ung,** *f* remonstration.

'**vorhanden** [foːr'handən], *adj.* existing; (*verfügbar*) available; *Com:* (*Ware*) in stock. ◆'**V~sein,** *n* -s/no pl existence.

'**Vorhang,** *m* -(e)s/¨e curtain.

'**Vorhängeschloß,** *n* padlock.

vorher ['foːrheːr], *adv.* before; (*im voraus*) beforehand, in advance. ◆**v~gehen,**

v.i.sep.irr.36 (*sein*) etwas *dat* v., to precede sth. ◆**v~gehend,** *adj.* preceding; previous (chapter etc.). ◆**v~ig** [fɔːrˈhɛriç], *adj.* previous (evening etc.); prior (warning, agreement etc.). ◆**V~sage,** *f* -/-n prediction; (weather etc.) forecast. ◆**v~sagen,** *v.tr.sep.* to predict, forecast (sth.). ◆**v~sehen,** *v.tr.sep.irr.92* to foresee (sth.).

'**Vorherr|schaft,** *f* -/no *pl* predominance; *Pol:etc:* supremacy. ◆**v~schen,** *v.i.sep.* (*haben*) to predominate; (*Meinung usw.*) to prevail.

'**vorhin,** *adv.* a moment ago, just now. ◆**v~ein,** *adv.* im v., beforehand, in advance.

vorig [ˈfoːriç], *adj.* last (month, year etc.); previous (chapter, paragraph etc.); former, previous (boss, job etc.).

'**Vorjahr,** *n* previous year. ◆'**vorjährig,** *adj.* previous year's (fashion etc.).

'**Vorkämpfer(in),** *m(f)* pioneer.

'**Vorkehrungen,** *fpl* precautions.

'**vorkomm|en. I.** *v.i.sep.irr.53* (*sein*) (*a*) (*geschehen*) to happen; (*sich finden*) (*Pflanzen, Tiere usw.*) to occur, be found (somewhere); (*b*) (*scheinen*) **j-m komisch, verdächtig** v., to strike s.o. as odd, suspicious etc.; **ich kam mir überflüssig vor,** I felt unwanted; (*c*) to come to the front; (*hervorkommen*) to come out. **II. V.,** *n* -s/no *pl* occurrence. ◆'**V~nis,** *n* -sses/-sse incident, occurrence.

'**Vorkriegs-,** *comb.fm.* prewar.

'**vorlad|en,** *v.tr.sep.irr.56* *Jur:* to summon(s) (s.o.), *esp N.Am:* subpoena (s.o.). ◆'**V~ung,** *f Jur:* summons, *esp N.Am:* subpoena.

'**Vorlage,** *f* -/-n (*Muster*) pattern; *Lit:* model; (*Gesetzesv.*) bill; *Fb:* forward pass.

'**vorlassen,** *v.tr.sep.irr.57* to let (s.o.) go first; *Aut: Sp:* to let (s.o.) overtake.

'**Vorläuf|er(in),** *m* -s/- (*f* -/-nen) forerunner. ◆'**v~ig,** *adj.* provisional; interim (measure, report etc.); temporary (appointment etc.).

'**vorlaut,** *adj.* cheeky; too full of himself/herself.

'**vorleg|en,** *v.tr.sep.* to present (sth.); to produce, show (one's passport etc.); to submit (evidence, a question etc.). ◆**v~er,** *m* -s/- mat, rug.

'**vorles|en,** *v.tr.&i.sep.irr.61* (*haben*) to read (sth.) aloud; **soll ich (es) dir v.?** shall I read (it) to you? ◆'**V~ung,** *f* -/-en lecture.

'**vorletzte(r,s),** *adj.* last but one; penultimate (syllable etc.); **im v~n Jahr,** the year before last.

'**Vorlieb|e,** *f* -/no *pl* predilection, preference. ◆**v~nehmen** [-'liːpneːmən], *v.i.sep.irr.69* (*haben*) to make do.

'**vorlieg|en,** *v.i.sep.irr.62* (*haben*) to be on hand/(*zur Verfügung*) available; **j-m, dem Gericht usw.** v., to be in s.o.'s hands, the hands of the court etc.; **es liegt/**

liegen ... vor, there is/are ... ◆**v~end,** *adj.* available; **im v~enden Fall,** in this/the present case.

'**vormachen,** *v.tr.sep. F:* (*a*) **j-m etwas** v., to show s.o. how to do sth.; (*b*) **j-m/sich dat etwas** v., to kid s.o./oneself.

'**Vormachtstellung,** *f* supremacy.

'**vormals,** *adv.* formerly.

'**Vormarsch,** *m* advance.

'**vormerken,** *v.tr.sep.* to make a note of (sth.); to book (a room etc.).

'**Vormittag. I.** *m* -s/-e (late) morning. **II. v.,** *adv.* **heute/gestern/morgen v.,** this/yesterday/tomorrow morning. ◆'**v~s,** *adv.* in the morning.

'**Vormund,** *m* -(e)s/-e guardian. ◆'**V~schaft,** *f* -/no *pl* guardianship.

vorn(e) [fɔrn('fɔrnə)], *adv.* in/at the front; (*vor mir/uns*) ahead; **nach v.,** (*i*) (seen) from the front; (*ii*) (*am Anfang*) at the beginning; (*von neuem*) all over again. ◆**v~he'rein,** *adv.* **von v.,** from the start.

'**Vorname,** *m* Christian name, *N.Am:* given name.

vornehm [ˈfoːrneːm], *adj.* (*a*) distinguished (circles, family, appearance etc.); gentlemanly, ladylike (manner); (*b*) (*elegant, modisch*) smart (resort, area, school etc.); (*c*) (*kultiviert*) refined (taste etc.); elegant (dress, interior).

'**vornehmen,** *v.tr.sep.irr.69* (*a*) (*ausführen*) to carry out (an alteration etc.); (*b*) *F:* (*vorknöpfen*) **den werde ich mir v.!** I'll give him a piece of my mind! (*c*) **sich dat etwas** v., to decide to do sth.; (*d*) *F:* **sich dat ein Buch usw.** v., to take up/start a book etc.

'**Vorort. I.** *m* suburb. **II. V~(s)-,** *comb.fm.* suburban (traffic, train etc.).

'**Vorrang,** *m* -(e)s/no *pl* precedence, priority (*vor* + *dat,* over). ◆'**v~ig,** *adj.* of prime importance.

'**Vorrat,** *m* -(e)s/⸚e stock, supply (**an** + *dat,* of). ◆'**V~s-,** *comb.fm.* store, *Com:* stock (room etc.).

'**vorrätig** [ˈfoːrrɛːtiç], *adj.* in stock, available.

'**Vorrecht,** *n* privilege, prerogative.

'**Vorrichtung,** *f* -/-en apparatus, appliance; (*Gerät*) device.

'**vorrücken,** *v.sep.* **1.** *v.tr.* to move (sth.) forward. **2.** *v.i.* (*sein*) to move up; *Mil:* to advance.

'**vorsagen,** *v.tr.* to recite (a poem etc.); to dictate (sth.); *Sch:* to whisper (the answer).

'**Vorsatz,** *m* -es/-e resolution; **gute V~e,** good intentions.

vorsätzlich [ˈfoːrzɛtsliç], *adj.* deliberate (insult etc.); premeditated (action); malicious (damage etc.); wilful (murder).

'**Vorschau,** *f* -/-en preview, esp. *Cin:* trailer.

'**Vorschein,** *m* **zum V. kommen,** to emerge.

'**vorschieben,** *v.tr.sep.irr.82* (*a*) to push

(sth.) forward; to push (a bolt) across; (b) to give (sth.) as an excuse.

Vorschlag, m suggestion, proposal; (*Angebot*) offer; **auf j-s V. (hin),** at s.o.'s suggestion. ◆'**v~en,** v.tr.sep.irr.85 to suggest (s.o., sth.); to propose (s.o.). ◆'**V~hammer,** m sledgehammer.

vorschnell, adj. hasty, rash.

vorschreiben, v.tr.sep.irr.88 (*fordern*) to dictate, lay down (conditions, conduct etc.), (*Gesetz usw.*) decree (that...); **j-m etwas v.,** to order/tell s.o. to do sth.

Vorschrift, f -/-en regulation, rule; (*Befehl*) order, decree; **j-m V~en machen,** to give s.o. orders. ◆'**v~smäßig,** adj. prescribed; adv. as directed; according to regulations.

Vorschuß, m advance (payment).

vorschweben, v.i.sep. (haben) **mir schwebt ... vor,** I have ... in mind.

vorseh|en, v.tr.sep.irr.92 1. v.tr. (a) to plan (improvement etc.); (*berücksichtigen*) to provide/allow for (an eventuality etc.); **das Gesetz sieht vor, daß ...,** the law provides that ...; (b) sich v., to take care; to look out/watch (vor + dat. for). 2. v.i. (haben) to look out; (*Unterrock usw.*) to show. ◆'**V~ung,** f -/no pl providence.

vorsetzen, v.tr. (a) to move (s.o., sth.) forward; (b) to put (sth.) in front (j-m, of s.o.).

Vorsicht, f -/no pl care; (*Behutsamkeit*) caution; discretion; **V.!** look out! **V. Stufe!** mind the step; **V. Hochspannung!** danger high voltage. ◆'**v~ig,** adj. careful; (*behutsam*) cautious; conservative (estimate). ◆'**v~shalber,** adv. as a precaution. ◆'**V~smaßnahme,** f precaution, safeguard.

Vorsilbe, f prefix.

Vorsitz, m chairmanship. ◆'**V~ende(r),** m & f decl. as adj. chairman; f chairwoman; (*bei Sitzungen*) chairperson.

Vorsorg|e, f -/no pl provision, precaution. ◆'**v~en,** v.i. (haben) to make provision. ◆'**v~lich,** adv. as a precaution.

Vorspeise, f hors d'oeuvre, F: starter.

Vorspiel, n Mus: & Fig: prelude; Th: prologue. ◆'**v~en,** v.sep. 1. v.tr. (a) Mus: to play, Th: act (a piece); (b) (*vortäuschen*) to pretend (sth.). 2. v.i. (haben) j-m v., to play/Th: act for s.o.

vorsprechen, v.tr.sep.irr.37 1. v.tr. **j-m etwas v.,** (i) to say sth. for s.o. to repeat; (ii) (*vortragen*) to recite sth. to s.o. 2. v.i. (haben) (a) Th: to audition; (b) **bei j-m v.,** to call to see s.o.

Vorsprung, m -(e)s/-e 1. projection. 2. Sp: & Fig: lead (vor j-m, over s.o.).

Vorstadt. I. f suburb. **II.** 'V~-, comb.fm. suburban (theatre, cinema etc.).

Vorstand, m -(e)s/-e (a) board (of directors/management); governing body (of an institution); (b) (*Pers.*) chairman. ◆'**V~s-,** comb.fm. Com: board (member etc.).

vorstehen, v.i.sep.irr.100 (haben) (a) to project, jut out; (*Ohren, Zähne usw.*) to stick out; (b) etwas dat v., to be in charge of/Com: manager of sth.

vorstell|bar, adj. conceivable, imaginable. ◆'**v~en,** v.tr.sep. (a) to move (sth.) forward; to put (a clock) forward/on; (b) (*bekanntmachen*) to introduce (s.o., oneself, sth.); (c) sich dat j-n, etwas v., to imagine s.o., sth.; (d) (*darstellen*) to portray, represent (s.o., sth.). ◆'**V~ung,** f 1. introduction (of s.o., sth.). 2. Th:Cin: performance; Cin: showing. 3. (*Begriff*) idea; (*Phantasie*) imagination. ◆'**V~ungsgespräch,** n (job) interview. ◆'**V~ungsvermögen,** n (powers of) imagination.

Vorstoß, m Mil: & Fig: advance. ◆'**v~en,** v.sep.irr.103 1. v.tr. to push/thrust (s.o., sth.) forward. 2. v.i. (sein) Mil: & Fig: to advance.

Vorstrafe, f previous conviction.

vorstrecken, v.tr.sep. (a) to stretch out (one's arms etc.), crane (one's head); (b) to advance (money).

Vorstufe, f preliminary stage.

Vortag, m previous day; day before.

vortäusch|en, v.tr.sep. to sham, simulate (sth.); **j-m v., daß...,** to pretend to s.o. that ... ◆'**V~ung,** f pretence.

Vorteil, m advantage; **von V.,** advantageous; **gegenüber j-m, etwas dat im V. sein,** to have the advantage over s.o., sth.; **die Vor- und Nachteile,** the pros and cons. ◆'**v~haft,** adj. advantageous, favourable (offer, terms, position etc.).

Vortrag, m -(e)s/-e 1. (*Rede*) talk; (*wissenschaftlich*) lecture. 2. (*Darbietung*) performance; recital (of music); recitation (of poetry); (*Art und Weise*) delivery. ◆'**v~en,** v.tr.sep.irr.56 (a) to recite (a poem etc.); to perform (music etc.); (b) (*mitteilen*) to submit (a request etc.), convey (one's reasons etc.), express (a wish etc.). ◆'**V~sreise,** f lecture tour.

vor'trefflich, adj. excellent, first-rate.

vortreten, v.i.sep.irr.105 (sein) (a) to step forward; (b) (*hervorragen*) to project, stick out.

vorüber [fo'ry:bər], adv. = vorbei. ◆'**v~gehen,** v.i.sep.irr.36 (sein) = vorbeigehen; (*Krankheit usw.*) nicht spurlos an j-m v., to leave its mark on s.o. ◆'**v~gehend,** adj. passing (phase, symptom etc.); momentary (lapse etc.); temporary (spell etc.).

Vorurteil, n prejudice. ◆'**v~sfrei/'v~slos,** adj. unprejudiced; unbiased (opinion etc.).

Vorverkauf, m Th: etc: advance booking; **im V.,** in advance.

vorverlegen, v.tr.sep. to move(*zeitlich*) bring (sth.) forward.

Vorwahl, f (a) Pol: preliminary election; N.Am: primary; (b) Tel: dialling code.

Vorwand, m -(e)s/-e pretext, excuse.

vorwärts ['fo:rvɛrts]. **I.** adv. forwards.

II. V~-, *comb.fm.* forward (movement, *Aut:* gear etc.). ◆**'v~gehen,** *v.i.sep.irr.36* (*sein*) F: to progress, make progress. ◆**'v~kommen,** *v.i.sep.irr.53* (*sein*) to (make) progress; (*beruflich usw.*) to get on.

vorweg [for'vɛk], *adv.* (*a*) beforehand; (*im voraus*) in advance; (*b*) (*räumlich*) first, in front. ◆**V~nahme,** *f -/no pl* anticipation. ◆**v~nehmen,** *v.tr.sep.irr.69* to anticipate (sth., a result etc.).

'vorweisen, *v.tr.sep.irr.60* to show (one's passport, knowledge of sth. etc.).

'vorwerfen, *v.tr.sep.irr.110* (*a*) to throw (food) (**einem Tier,** to an animal); (*b*) **j-m etwas v.,** to reproach s.o. with sth., (*beschuldigen*) accuse s.o. of (doing sth.); **ich habe mir nichts vorzuwerfen,** I have nothing on my conscience.

'vorwiegend, *adv.* predominantly.

'Vorwort, *n* foreword, preface.

'Vorwurf, *m* reproach; (*Beschuldigung*) accusation; **j-m V~e machen,** to reproach/blame s.o. ◆**'v~svoll,** *adj.* reproachful.

'Vorzeichen, *n* (*a*) omen, sign; (*b*) *Med: etc:* (advance) symptom.

'vorzeigen, *v.tr.sep.* to produce, show (a passport, ticket etc.).

'Vorzeit, *f* prehistoric times, remote past. ◆**'v~ig,** *adj.* premature.

'vorziehen, *v.tr.sep.irr.113* (*a*) to pull (sth.) forward/(*hervor*) out; to pull (a curtain) across; (*b*) (*lieber mögen*) to prefer (s.o., sth.).

'Vorzug, *m* (*Vorrang*) preference; (*Vorteil*) advantage; (*gute Eigenschaft*) merit, virtue; **etwas dat den V. geben,** to give sth. preference. ◆**'V~s-,** *comb.fm.* preferential (treatment, position etc.). ◆**V~spreis,** *m* preferential rate; special price. ◆**'v~sweise,** *adv.* preferably, for preference.

vorzüglich [fo:r'tsy:klıç], *adj.* excellent, first-rate.

vulgär [vul'gɛ:r], *adj.* vulgar.

Vulkan [vul'ka:n], *m -s/-e* volcano. ◆**V~ausbruch,** *m* volcanic eruption. ◆**v~isch,** *adj.* volcanic. ◆**v~isieren** [-ani'zi:rən], *v.tr.* to vulcanize (rubber etc.).

W

W, w [ve:], *n -/-* (the letter) W, w.

Waag|e ['va:gə], *f -/-n* **1.** (pair of) scales. **2.** *Astr:* Libra. ◆**w~(e)recht,** *adj.* horizontal (line, plane etc.); level (surface etc.).

wabb(e)lig ['vab(ə)lıç], *adj.* F: wobbly.

Wabe ['va:bə], *f -/-n* honeycomb.

wach [vax], *adj.* (*a*) awake; **w. werden,** to wake up; **j-n w. machen,** to wake s.o. up; (*b*) *Fig:* alert (mind, senses etc.). ◆**W~e,** *f -/-n* **1.** (*a*) *Mil:* (*Posten*) sentry; (*also coll.*) guard; (*b*) (*Dienst*) *Mil:* guard (duty); *esp. Nau:* watch; **auf W.,** on guard; (*bei j-m*) **W. halten,** to keep watch/guard (over s.o.). **2.** (*Gebäude*) (police) station. ◆**'w~en,** *v.i.* (*haben*) **w.** (**über j-n, etwas acc w.,** to watch/keep an eye on s.o., sth. ◆**'W~hund,** *m* watchdog, guard-dog. ◆**'w~rufen,** *v.tr.sep.irr.74* *Fig:* to awaken (memories, feelings etc.). ◆**'w~sam,** *adj.* watchful, vigilant. ◆**'W~samkeit,** *f -/no pl* watchfulness, vigilance.

Wacholder [va'xɔldər], *m -s/-* juniper (bush).

Wachs [vaks], *n -es/-e* wax. ◆**'W~bohne,** *f -/-n* wax bean. ◆**'w~en1,** *v.tr.* to wax (a floor etc.).

wachs|en2, ['vaksən], *v.i.irr.* (*sein*) to grow; (*zunehmen*) to increase; **sich dat einen Bart/die Haare w. lassen,** to grow a beard/one's hair. ◆**'W~tum,** *n -s/no pl* growth; (*Zunahme*) increase.

Wächter ['vɛçtər], *m -s/-* guard; (night)

watchman; (*museum*) attendant; (*park*) keeper; *Fig:* guardian.

Wacht|meister ['vaxt-maıstər], *m* *Brit:* (police-)constable. ◆**'W~posten,** *m* guard; *Mil:* sentry.

wackel|ig ['vakəlıç], *adj.* (*a*) wobbly; (*im Bau*) rickety; unsteady (ladder etc.); (*b*) F: (*Pers.*) **w.** (**auf den Beinen**), shaky. ◆**W~kontakt,** *m El:* loose connection. ◆**'w~n,** *v.i.* (*haben*) to wobble; (*beben*) to shake.

wacker ['vakər], *adj.* (*tapfer*) bold; (*ordentlich*) hearty (eater etc.).

Wade ['va:də], *f -/-n* calf.

Waffe ['vafə], *f -/-n* weapon; *pl* **W~n,** arms. ◆**'W~n-,** *comb.fm.* arms (trade etc.); weapons (system). ◆**'W~nschein,** *m* firearms licence. ◆**'W~nstillstand,** *m* armistice.

Waffel ['vafəl], *f -/-n* waffle; (*Keks*) wafer.

Wag|emut ['va:gəmu:t], *m* daring, audacity. ◆**'w~emutig,** *adj.* daring, audacious. ◆**'w~en1,** *v.tr.* to risk (one's life etc.); **es w., etwas zu tun,** to dare to do sth. ◆**'w~halsig,** *adj.* daring. ◆**'W~nis,** *n -ses/-se* hazardous enterprise; (*Gefahr*) risk.

Wagen2 ['va:gən]. **I.** *m -s/-* (*a*) *Aut:* car; (*b*) (*Pferdew.*) cart, waggon; (*c*) *Rail:* (*für Pers.*) coach; (*für Güter*) truck; waggon; *N.Am:* car. **II.** **'W~-,** *comb.fm.* *Aut:* car (roof, care etc.); (column etc.) of cars. ◆**'W~heber,** *m* (car) jack. ◆**'W~ladung,** *f* lorryload, *N.Am:* truckload; *Rail:* waggonload.

Wahl [va:l]. **I.** *f -/-en* **1.** choice; **sie hat-**

ten nur zwei zur W., they only had two to choose from; **ich hatte keine andere W.,** I had no alternative. **2.** *Pol: etc:* election; **zur W. gehen,** to go to the polls. **3.** *Com:* Güter erster/zweiter W., top quality goods/second grade goods. II. **'W~,** *comb.fm. Pol:* election (defeat, slogan, speech, victory etc.); electoral (reform, system etc.); polling (day etc.). ◆**W~berechtigt,** *adj.* entitled to vote. ◆**W~beteiligung,** *f* turn-out, poll. ◆**W~ergebnis,** *n* election result. ◆**W~fach,** *n Sch:* optional subject. ◆**W~kampf,** *m* election campaign. ◆**W~kreis,** *m* constituency. ◆**W~lokal,** *n* polling station. ◆**'w~los,** *adj.* indiscriminate; *adv.* at random. ◆**'W~recht,** *n (aktives)* franchise; **allgemeines W.,** universal suffrage. ◆**W~spruch,** *m* motto.

wähl|en ['vɛːlən], *v.tr.&i. (haben) (a)* to choose; *(b) Tel:* to dial (a number); *(c) Pol: etc:* to elect (s.o., a party); *(stimmen)* to vote; **wen haben Sie gewählt?** for whom did you vote? ◆**'W~er,** *m* -s/- voter, elector. ◆**'w~erisch,** *adj.* choosy, particular. ◆**'W~erschaft,** *f no pl* electorate.

Wahn [vaːn], *m* -(e)s/*no pl* delusion; *(Manie)* mania. ◆**'W~sinn,** *m* insanity; *F: (Verrücktheit)* madness. ◆**'w~sinnig,** *adj. (a)* mad, insane; *(b) F:* terrible (pain etc.); *(c)* terrific (shock etc.); **w. schnell,** incredibly fast. ◆**'W~vorstellung,** *f* delusion; *F:* crazy idea.

wahr [vaːr], *adj. (a)* true (story etc.); **w. werden,** to come true; **es ist etwas W~es daran,** there is some truth in it; *(b) (wirklich)* real (reason, feeling etc.); *(richtig)* genuine (art etc.); *Lit:* true (love, friend etc.); *F:* **das ist nicht das W~e,** it's not quite the thing. ◆**'w~haben,** *v.tr.* **etwas nicht w. wollen,** to refuse to admit/believe sth. ◆**'w~haft,** *adj. Lit:* true; *(wirklich)* real. ◆**'w~haftig,** *adj. Lit:* truthful; *adv.* really, truly; *(ehrlich)* honestly. ◆**'W~heit,** *f* -/-en truth; **in W.,** in reality. ◆**'w~heitsgemäß,** *adj.* truthful (statement etc.). ◆**'w~nehmbar,** *adj.* perceptible. ◆**'w~nehmen,** *v.tr.sep.irr.69 (a) (merken)* to notice; *(b) (nutzen)* to avail oneself of an opportunity etc.; *(c) (vertreten)* to look after (s.o.'s interests). ◆**'W~nehmung,** *f* -/-en **1.** perception, awareness. **2.** seizing (of a chance). ◆**'w~sagen,** *v.tr. & i.sep. & insep. (haben)* to predict (the future, that ...). ◆**'W~sager(in),** *m* -s/- *(f* -/-nen) fortune-teller. ◆**w~'scheinlich,** *adj.* probable; *adv.* probably. ◆**w~'scheinlichkeit,** *f* -/-en probability; **aller W. nach,** in all probability. ◆**'W~zeichen,** *n* symbol, emblem (of a town etc.).

wahr|en ['vaːrən], *v.tr. (a)* to protect (interests, rights); *(b)* to keep (a secret,

one's distance etc.), maintain (one's dignity etc.). ◆**'W~ung,** *f -/no pl (a)* protection; *(b)* keeping, maintaining.

währ|en ['vɛːrən], *v.i. (haben) Lit:* to last. ◆**'w~end** [-ənt]. **I.** *prep. + gen* during. **II.** *conj.* **1.** while. **2.** *(wohingegen)* whereas, while. ◆**w~end'dessen,** *adv.* meanwhile, in the meantime.

Währung ['vɛːruŋ], *f* -/-en currency.

Waise ['vaizə], *f* -/-n orphan. ◆**'W~nhaus,** *n* orphanage.

Wal [vaːl], *m* -(e)s/-e whale. ◆**'W~fang,** *m* whaling.

Wald [valt], *m* -(e)s/-er wood; *(große Fläche)* forest. ◆**'W~brand,** *m* forest fire. ◆**'W~meister,** *m* woodruff.

Walis|er [va'liːzər], *m* -s/- Welshman; **die W.,** the Welsh. ◆**W~in,** *f* -/-nen Welshwoman. ◆**w~isch,** *adj.* Welsh.

Wall [val], *m* -(e)s/-e rampart.

Wall|fahrer(in) ['valfaːrər(in)], *m (f)* pilgrim. ◆**'W~fahrt,** *f* pilgrimage.

Wallone [va'loːnə], *m* -n/-n/**W~in,** *f* -/-nen Walloon. ◆**w~isch,** *adj.* Walloon.

Walnuß ['valnus], *f* walnut.

Walroß ['valrɔs], *n* walrus.

walten ['valtən], *v.i. (haben) Lit:* **Vorsicht w. lassen,** to exercise caution.

Walz|e ['valtsə], *f* -/-n roller; cylinder (of a musical box). ◆**'w~en,** *v.tr.* to roll (metal etc.).

wälz|en ['vɛltsən], *v.tr. (a)* to roll, heave (sth. heavy); *(b)* **sich w.,** to roll; *(im Schlamm)* to wallow; *(schlaflos)* to toss and turn; *(c) F:* **Gedanken, Probleme usw. w.,** to turn over thoughts, problems etc. in one's mind; **Bücher w.,** to pore over books. ◆**'W~er,** *m* -s/- *F:* weighty tome.

Walzer ['valtsər], *m* -s/- waltz.

Wand [vant], *f* -/-e wall *(Trennw.)* partition; *(Seitenw.)* side (of a crate etc.); *(rock* etc.) face. ◆**'W~schrank,** *m* built-in cupboard. ◆**'W~tafel,** *f* blackboard. ◆**'W~teppich,** *m* tapestry. ◆**'W~verkleidung,** *f* wall-covering/ *(Täfelung)* panelling.

Wandel ['vandəl], *m* -s/*no pl* change. ◆**'w~bar,** *adj.* changeable. ◆**'w~n,** *v.i. (sein)* **1.** *Lit:* to wander, stroll. **2.** *v.tr.* to change (s.o., sth.); **sich w.,** to change.

Wander- ['vandər-], *comb.fm.* **1.** travelling (exhibition, circus etc.); itinerant (preacher etc.); *Med:* floating (kidney, liver). **2.** walking (shoes, stick etc.); hiking, rambling (club etc.). ◆**W~bühne,** *f* touring company. ◆**'W~er,** *m* -s/- hiker, rambler. ◆**'w~n,** *v.i. (sein) (a)* to hike, ramble; *(b) (Tiere)* to migrate; *(ziellos) (Pers., Fig: Blicke usw.)* to wander, roam. ◆**'W~pokal,** *m* challenge cup/trophy. ◆**'W~schaft,** *f -/no pl* travels; **auf W.,** on one's travels. ◆**'W~ung,** *f* -/-en hike, ramble. ◆**'W~weg,** *m* footpath.

Wandlung ['vandluŋ], *f* -/-en change,

transformation.

Wange ['vaŋə], f -/-n Lit: cheek.

wankelmütig ['vaŋkəlmyːtiç], adj. Lit: irresolute, vacillating. ◆'**w~en**, v.i. (a) (sein) to stagger, totter; (Betrunkener) to reel; (b) (haben) Fig: to waver.

wann [van], adv. when.

Wanne ['vanə], f -/-n (bath-)tub, bath.

Wanze ['vantsə], f -/-n bug.

Wappen ['vapən], n -s/- coat of arms.

wappnen ['vapnən], v.refl. sich gegen etwas acc w., to prepare to face sth.

Ware ['vaːrə], f -/-n commodity, article; (Erzeugnis) product; W~n, goods. ◆'**W~nangebot**, n range of goods. ◆'**W~nhaus**, n (department) store. ◆'**W~nprobe**, f sample. ◆'**W~nzeichen**, n trade mark.

warm [varm], adj. warm; hot (meal, drink, bath etc.); **Essen w. machen**, to heat/warm up food; **w. essen/duschen**, to have a hot meal/shower. ◆'**w~herzig**, adj. warm-hearted. ◆'**w~laufen**, v.i.sep.irr.58 (sein) Aut: (Motor) to warm up. ◆'**W~miete**, f rent including heating. ◆'**W~wasser-**, comb.fm. hot-water (heating, supply etc.).

Wärme ['vɛrmə], f -/no pl (also Fig:) warmth; Ph: etc: heat. ◆'**w~en**, v. 1. v.tr. to warm (one's hands, oneself etc.), to warm up (food). 2. v.i. (haben) to warm one up; to keep/make one warm. ◆'**W~flasche**, f hot-water bottle. ◆'**w~stens**, adv. very/most warmly.

Warn- ['varn-], comb.fm. warning (cry, light, shot, signal etc.). ◆'**W~blinkanlage**, f Aut: hazard warning lights. ◆'**W~dreieck**, n hazard warning/accident triangle. ◆'**w~en**, v.tr. to warn (s.o.) (vor + dat, of/against). ◆'**W~streik**, m token strike. ◆'**W~ung**, f -/-en warning (vor + dat, of/against).

Warschau ['varʃau]. Pr.n.n -s. Warsaw.

Warte[1] ['vartə], f -/no pl 1. Fig: standpoint. 2. (a) Meteor: weather-station; (b) Astr: observatory.

'Warte-[2], comb.fm. waiting (list etc.). ◆'**W~saal**, m/'**W~zimmer**, n waiting room.

warten ['vartən], v. 1. v.i. (haben) to wait (auf + acc, for); j-n w. lassen, to keep s.o. waiting; auf sich w. lassen, to take a long time; (Pers.) take one's time. 2. v.tr. to service (a machine, car). ◆'**W~ung**, f -/-en 1. no pl servicing. 2. service.

Wärter(in) ['vɛrtər(in)], m -s/- (f -/-nen) attendant; (zoo/lighthouse) keeper; (Gefängnisw.) (prison) warder/f wardress.

warum [va'rum], adv. why.

Warze ['vartsə], f -/-n wart.

was [vas]. I. interrog. & rel.pron. what; **w. für ein Lärm!** what a noise! F: **w. stehst du so blöd da?** why do you just stand there and look stupid? **gut, w.?** not bad, eh? **das, w. er sagt**, what he says; **alles/**

vieles, w. ..., everything/much that ...
II. indef.pron. F: (etwas) something; (in Fragen/Verneinungen) anything; **w. Neues**, something new; **ist w.?** is anything wrong?

Waschbär ['vaʃbɛːr], m racoon. ◆'**W~becken**, n washbasin. ◆'**w~echt**, adj. 1. colour-fast (material), fast (colours). 2. Fig: genuine, F: pukka (Berliner etc.). ◆'**w~en**, v.tr.&i.irr. (haben) to wash (s.o., sth.); **sich dat die Hände/Haare w.**, to wash one's hands/hair; (Wäsche) w., to do the washing, sich w., to wash (oneself); W. und Legen, shampoo and set. ◆'**W~küche**, f laundry room. ◆'**W~lappen**, m 1. face flannel, N.Am: washcloth. 2. F: (Pers.) cissy, wet; (Schwächling) weed. ◆'**W~maschine**, f washing machine. ◆'**W~mittel**, n detergent. ◆'**W~pulver**, n washing powder. ◆'**W~salon**, m laundrette. ◆'**W~straße**, f automatic car wash.

Wäsche ['vɛʃə], f -/no pl 1. washing; (Schmutzw.) laundry. 2. (a) (Unterw.) underwear; (b) (Bettw./Tischw.) (bed-/table-)linen. ◆'**W~klammer**, f clothes peg/N.Am: pin. ◆'**W~leine**, f clothes-/washing-line. ◆'**W~rei**, f -/-en laundry. ◆'**W~trockner**, m clothes drier, esp. tumble drier.

Wasser ['vasər], n -s/- water; Fig: **sich über W. halten**, to keep one's head above water; **er kann ihr nicht das W. reichen**, he can't hold a candle to her; **das Fest fiel ins W.**, the party fell through; **F: er ist mit allen W~n gewaschen**, he wasn't born yesterday; **W. lassen**, to pass water. ◆'**W~ball**, m water polo. ◆'**w~dicht**, adj. waterproof (coat etc.); watertight (container etc.). ◆'**W~fall**, m waterfall. ◆'**W~farbe**, f water colour. ◆'**w~gekühlt**, adj. water-cooled. ◆'**W~hahn**, m water tap, N.Am: faucet. ◆'**W~leitung**, f water pipe. ◆'**W~mann**, m Astr: Aquarius. ◆'**w~n**, v.i. (haben) Av: to land on the water, ditch; (Raumschiff) to splash down. ◆'**w~scheu**, adj. afraid of water. ◆'**W~spülung**, f flush (of a WC). ◆'**W~ski**, m water ski; (Sport) water skiing. ◆'**W~stand**, m water level. ◆'**W~stoff**, m hydrogen. ◆'**W~versorgung**, f water supply. ◆'**W~vogel**, m waterfowl. ◆'**W~waage**, f spirit level. ◆'**W~werfer**, m water cannon. ◆'**W~werk**, n waterworks. ◆'**W~zeichen**, n watermark.

wässerig ['vɛsəriç], adj. watery. ◆'**w~n**, v.tr. to water down (wine etc.); (b) to water (a plant etc.) thoroughly. 2. v.i. (haben) (Augen usw.) to water.

wäßrig ['vɛsriç], adj. = wässerig.

waten ['vaːtən], v.i. (sein) to wade.

Watt[1] [vat], n -s/- El: watt.

Watt², n -s/-en North G: mudflats.
Wattle ['vatl], f -/no pl cotton wool.
◆'**W~ebausch**, m wad of cotton wool. ◆**w~ieren** ['tiːrən], v.tr. to pad, line (a garment etc.).
web|en ['veːbən], v.tr. & i. (haben) to weave. ◆'**W~er(in)**, m -s/- (f -/-nen) weaver. ◆'**W~e'rei**, f -/-en 1. no pl weaving. 2. weaving mill. ◆'**W~stuhl**, m loom.
Wechsel ['vɛksəl], m -s/- 1. change; (sich wiederholend) rotation (of the seasons, crop etc.); (Abwechslung) alternation (of day and night etc.); (Spielerw.) substitution. 2. Fin: bill of exchange. ◆'**W~beziehung**, f correlation. ◆'**W~geld**, n change. ◆'**W~haft**, adj. changeable. ◆'**W~jahre**, npl change of life, menopause. ◆'**W~kurs**, m rate of exchange. ◆'**W~n**, 1. v.tr. & i. (haben) to change; die Wohnung w., to move (house); den Platz, Briefe usw. mit j-m w., to exchange places, letters etc. with s.o. 2. v.i. (haben) to change; (Tag und Nacht usw.) to alternate. ◆'**w~nd**, adj. changeable (weather etc.); variable (wind etc.); varying (success etc.). ◆'**w~seitig**, adj. mutual, reciprocal. ◆'**W~spiel**, n interplay. ◆'**W~strom**, m alternating current. ◆'**W~stube**, f exchange office. ◆'**w~weise**, adv. alternately, in turn. ◆'**W~wirkung**, f interaction.
weck|en ['vɛkən], v.tr. to wake (s.o.) (up); Fig: to awaken, arouse (s.o.'s feelings, memories etc.). ◆'**W~er**, m -s/-alarm (clock).
Wedel ['veːdəl], m -s/- (Staubw.) (feather) duster. ◆'**w~n**, v.i. (haben) to wag (its tail); (Hund usw.) to wag (its tail); (Pers.) to wave (a hand, paper etc.).
weder ['veːdər], conj. w. ... noch ..., neither ... nor ...
Weg¹ [veːk], m -(e)s/-e (a) (Gehw.) path; (Fahrw.) track; ich würde ihm nicht über den W. trauen, I wouldn't trust him an inch; (b) (Route) way, route; (Strecke) distance; auf dem kürzesten W., by the shortest route; auf halbem W~e, halfway; sich auf den W. machen, to set off; etwas in die W~e leiten, to get sth. under way; (c) du bist/stehst mir im W., you're in my way; j-n, etwas aus dem W. räumen, to get rid of/eliminate s.o., sth.; der Gefahr aus dem W. gehen, to keep clear of danger; (d) (Weise) auf diesem W~e, in this way; auf diplomatischem W~e, through diplomatic channels. ◆'**W~bereiter**, m -s/- forerunner. ◆'**W~strecke**, f stretch; (Entfernung) distance. ◆'**W~weiser**, m -s/- signpost.
weg² [vɛk], adv. away, off; weit w., far away; Hände w.! hands off! das muß w., that must go. ◆'**w~bleiben**, v.i.sep.irr.12 (sein) to stay away. ◆'**w~bringen**, v.tr.sep.irr.16 to take/

get (s.o., sth.) away, remove (furniture etc.). ◆'**w~fallen**, v.i.sep.irr.27 (sein) to be discontinued/(ausgelassen) omitted; (aufhören) to cease, stop. ◆'**w~gehen**, v.i.sep.irr.36 (sein) (a) (Pers.) to leave, go away/(ausgehen) out; (Fleck) to come out; (b) wie warme Semmeln w., to sell like hot cakes. ◆'**w~kommen**, v.i.sep.irr.53 (sein) (Pers.) to get away; (verlorengehen) to be lost, disappear. ◆'**w~lassen**, v.tr.sep.irr.57 to leave out, omit (s.o., sth.); to let (s.o.) go. ◆'**w~laufen**, v.i.sep.irr.58 to run away. ◆'**w~legen**, v.tr.sep. to put (sth.) away/(beiseite) aside. ◆'**w~machen**, v.tr.sep. F: to remove (dirt, a spot etc.). ◆'**w~müssen**, v.i.sep.irr.68 (haben) to have to go; ich muß weg, I must leave/be off. ◆'**W~nahme**, f -/no pl taking away, removal. ◆'**w~nehmen**, v.tr.sep.irr.69 to take (sth.) away, remove (sth.) (j-m, from s.o.); to take up (light, space, s.o.'s time etc.). ◆'**w~räumen**, v.tr.sep. to clear (sth.) away. ◆'**w~schaffen**, v.tr.sep. to do away with/(entfernen) remove (sth.). ◆'**w~schnappen**, v.tr.sep. to snatch (sth.) away. ◆'**w~tun**, v.tr.sep.irr.106 to clear/(wegwerfen) throw (sth.) away. ◆'**W~werf-**, comb.fm. disposable (bottle, nappy etc.). ◆'**w~werfen**, v.tr.sep.irr.110 to throw (rubbish, one's life etc.) away, throw out (old clothes etc.). ◆'**w~werfend**, adj. disparaging. ◆'**w~wischen**, v.tr.sep. to wipe (sth.) away/(a word etc.) out; to dismiss (objections etc.). ◆'**w~wollen**, v.i.sep. (haben) to want to get away/(ausgehen) go out. ◆'**w~ziehen**, v.tr.sep.irr.113 1. v.tr. to pull (s.o., sth.) away. 2. v.i. (sein) to move (away) (aus/von + dat, from).
wegen ['veːgən], prep. + gen/F: + dat because of; owing to; w. mir, on my account; von Rechts w., by right; F: von w.! it's nothing of the sort! (kommt nicht in Frage) nothing doing!
weh [veː], adj. F: painful, sore (finger etc.); hurting (feet etc.); j-m/sich dat w. tun, to hurt s.o./oneself; mir tut der Fuß w., my foot is hurting. ◆'**w~(e)**, int. alas! w. dir, wenn ...! it'll be the worse for you, if ... ◆'**W~en1**, fpl labour pains; in den W. liegen, to be in labour. ◆'**W~klage**, f Lit: lament(ation). ◆'**w~leidig**, adj. plaintive (voice etc.); sei doch nicht so w., don't make such a fuss. ◆'**W~mut**, f -/no pl melancholy, (Sehnsucht) longing. ◆'**w~mütig**, adj. melancholy; wistful (smile etc.).
Wehe ['veːə], f -/-n (snow etc.) drift. ◆'**w~n2**, v. 1. v.i. (haben) (Wind) to blow; (Fahne usw.) to wave, flutter; (Haare) to blow about. 2. v.tr. to blow (sth.).
Wehr [veːr]. 1. f sich zur W. setzen, to resist, put up a fight. 2. n -(e)s/-e weir.

◆'W~dienst, m military service.
◆'W~dienstverweigerer, m conscientious objector. ◆'w~en, v.refl. sich w., to fight back; to defend oneself (gegen etwas, against sth.). ◆'w~los, adj. defenceless. ◆'W~macht, f armed forces. ◆'W~pflicht, f conscription; compulsory military service. ◆'w~pflichtig, adj. liable to military service.

Weib [vaip], n -(e)s/-er † adj. Pej: female; N.Am: broad. ◆'W~chen, n -s/- Orn: Z: female. ◆'w~isch, adj. Pej: effeminate, womanish. ◆'w~lich, adj. (a) female (sex etc.); Gram: feminine (gender); (b) (frauenhaft) feminine (characteristic etc.). ◆'W~lichkeit, f -/no pl femininity.

weich [vaiç], adj. soft; tender (meat etc.); (w~gekocht) soft-boiled (egg); w. liegen, to lie on something soft. ◆'W~heit, f -/no pl softness; tenderness. ◆'w~lich, adj. soft (thing, person); weak (character); (weiblich) effeminate ◆'W~ling, m -s/-e weakling; F: softy, sissy. ◆'W~spüler, m -s/- (fabric) conditioner.

Weiche ['vaiçə], f -/-n Rail: points, N.Am: switch; die W~n stellen, to set the points/Fig: the course. ◆'w~n, v.i.irr. (sein) to give way, yield (j-m, etwas dat, to s.o., sth.); (Feind) to fall back, retreat (vor + dat, from).

Weide¹ ['vaidə], f -/-n pasture, meadow. ◆'W~land, n pastureland, pasturage. ◆'w~n, v.tr. & i. (haben) to graze, pasture (sheep etc.); Fig: sich an etwas dat w., to take delight in/(Augen usw.) feast on sth.

Weide² f -/-n/'W~nbaum, m willow tree.

weiger|n ['vaigərn], v.refl. sich w., to refuse (to do sth.). ◆'W~ung, f -/-en refusal.

Weihe ['vaiə], f -/-n Ecc: etc: consecration; W. zum Priester, ordination. ◆'w~en, v.tr. to consecrate (ground, a church etc.); to ordain (s.o.); Fig: dem Tode geweiht, doomed to die. ◆'W~nachten [-naxtən] n Christmas. ◆'w~nachtlich, adj. like Christmas; F: Christmassy. ◆'W~nachts-comb.fm. Christmas (tree, card, present etc.). ◆'W~nachtsabend, m Christmas Eve. ◆'W~nachtsfest, n Christmas (holiday). ◆'W~nachtslied, n Christmas carol. ◆'W~nachtsmann, m Father Christmas. ◆'W~nachtstag, m erster W., Christmas Day; zweiter W., Boxing Day. ◆'W~nachtszeit, f Christmas period. ◆'W~rauch, m incense. ◆'W~wasser, n holy water.

Weiher ['vaiər], m -s/- pond.

weil [vail], conj. because; (da) since.

Weile ['vailə], f -/no pl while, (space of) time.

Wein [vain]. I. m -(e)s/-e (a) wine; (b) (W~reben) vines; W. ernten/lesen, to

pick grapes. II. 'W~-, comb.fm. (a) wine (vinegar, bottle, glass, cellar, cooler etc.); (b) (vom W~stock) vine -(leaf etc.). ◆'W~bau, m wine-growing. ◆'W~(bau)gebiet, n wine-growing area. ◆'W~beere, f grape. ◆'W~berg, m (terraced) vineyard. ◆'W~bergschnecke, f (edible) snail. ◆'W~brand, m brandy. ◆'W~geist, m pure alcohol; spirit. ◆'W~karte, f wine list. ◆'W~lese, f grape harvest, vintage. ◆'W~probe, f wine-tasting. ◆'w~rot, adj. burgundy. ◆'W~stein, m tartar. ◆'W~stock, m grapevine. ◆'W~stube, f wine bar/parlour. ◆'W~traube, f grape.

wein|en ['vainən], v.i. (haben) to cry, weep (vor + dat, from; um + acc, over). ◆'w~erlich, adj. tearful; Pej: whining (child etc.).

weise¹ ['vaizə], adj. wise; (umsichtig) prudent.

'Weise², f -/-n 1. manner, way; auf diese W., in this way/manner; auf keine/in keiner W., by no means. 2. Mus: melody, tune.

'weis|en, v.tr.irr.70 j-m den Weg, die Tür usw. w., to show s.o. the way, door etc.; etwas von sich dat w., to reject sth. completely. ◆'W~ung, f -/-en direction, instruction.

Weis|heit ['vaishait], f -/no pl wisdom. ◆'W~heitszahn, m wisdom tooth. ◆'w~machen, v.tr.sep. j-m etwas w., to make s.o. believe sth. ◆'w~sagen, v.tr.insep. to prophesy (disaster etc.).

weiß [vais], adj. white. ◆'W~brot, n white bread/(Laib) loaf. ◆'w~en, v.tr. to whiten (shoes); to whitewash (a room, wall etc.). ◆'w~haarig, adj. white-haired. ◆'W~kohl, m white cabbage. ◆'W~wäsche, f household linen. ◆'W~wein, m white wine. ◆'W~wurst, f veal sausage.

weit [vait], adj. (a) wide (expanse, sleeve etc.); extensive (area, view etc.); im w~esten Sinne, in the broadest sense; w. geöffnet, wide open; (b) (lang) long (way, journey etc.); in weiter Ferne, in the distance; w. und breit, far and wide; haben Sie es noch w.? have you much further to go? das geht zu w.! that's going too far/the limit! (c) adv. (erheblich) w. größer/besser, far larger/better; bei w~em, by far; bei w~em nicht genug, not nearly enough. ◆'w~aus, adv. far (better etc.); by far, much (the best etc.). ◆'W~blick, m far-sightedness, vision. ◆'W~e, f -/-n (a) (Fläche) extent; (b) (Breite) width; (c) esp. Sp: (Entfernung) distance. ◆'w~en, v.tr. to widen sth.; stretch (shoes etc.). ◆'w~er, adj. further (news, orders etc.); (zusätzlich) additional (expense, worry etc.); bis auf w~eres, until further notice; im w~eren, in the following; w. niemand/nichts, nobody/

nothing else; **und so w.**, and so on; **ohne w~eres**, easily; without any trouble. ◆'w~**erbildung**, f further education. ◆'w~**erempfehlen**, v.tr.sep.irr.2 to recommend (s.o., sth.) to others. ◆'w~**erzählen**, v.tr.sep. to pass on (news etc.) to others. ◆'w~**ergeben**, v.tr.sep.irr.35 to pass on (a message, book etc.). ◆'w~**ergehen**, v.i.sep.irr.36 (sein) to go/walk on; (Pers., Sache) to continue. ◆'w~**erhin**, adv. (künftig) further, in future; (außerdem) moreover, furthermore; **etwas w. tun**, to continue doing/to do sth. ◆'w~**erkommen**, v.i.sep. irr.53 (sein) to get on, progress. ◆'w~**erlaufen**, v.i.sep.irr.58 (sein) to go on running (Zahlungen usw.) to continue. ◆'w~**erleiten**, v.tr.sep. to pass on (a request etc.), send on (mail). ◆'w~**ermachen**, v.tr.&i.sep. (haben) **mit etwas dat w.**, to carry on/continue sth. ◆'w~**este(r,s)**, adj. furthest, most distant (point etc.); **am w~esten**, farthest (away). ◆'w~**gehend**, adj. extensive, far-reaching (changes etc.); **wide** (powers etc.); adv. largely. ◆'w~**läufig**, adj. (a) extensive; spacious (grounds etc.); (b) distant (relative). ◆'w~**reichend**, adj. far-reaching. ◆'w~**schweifig**, adj. long-winded, rambling. ◆'w~**sicht**, f Fig: farsightedness, vision. ◆'w~**sichtig**, adj. Med: long-sighted; Fig: far-sighted. ◆'w~**springer**, m long-jumper. ◆'w~**sprung**, m long jump. ◆'w~**verbreitet**, adj. widespread, common. ◆'w~**winkelobjektiv**, n wide-angle lens.

Weizen ['vaitsən], n -s/no pl wheat.

welch [vɛlç], pron. Lit: **w. ein Segen!** what a blessing! ◆'w~**e(r,s)**, pron. 1. interrog. ◆'w~**er von ihnen?** which (one) of them? 2. rel. (Pers.) who, (Sache/Sachen) which. 3. indef. some; **hast du w~es?** have you got some/any? F: **was für w~es?** what sort?

welk [vɛlk], adj. wilting, (verblaßt) faded (flowers etc.). ◆'w~**en**, v.i. (sein) to wilt, fade.

Well|**blech** ['vɛlblɛç], n corrugated iron. ◆'w~**e**, f -/-n 1. wave. 2. Tchn: shaft. ◆'w~**en**, v.tr. to wave (hair), corrugate (tin, paper); **sich w.**, (Haar) to form waves, be wavy; (Teppich usw.) to get ridges. ◆'w~**enbrecher**, m breakwater. ◆'w~**enlänge**, f (also Fig:) wavelength. ◆'w~**enlinie**, f wavy line. ◆'w~**enreiten**, n surfriding, surfing. ◆'w~**enreiter**, m surfrider, surfer. ◆'w~**ensittich**, m budgerigar. ◆'w~**ig**, adj. wavy (hair etc.); bumpy (road, ground etc.). ◆'w~**pappe**, f corrugated cardboard.

Welpe ['vɛlpə], m -n/-n whelp.

Welt [vɛlt]. I. f -/-en world; **etwas aus der W. schaffen**, to do away with/

(bereinigen) clear up sth.; **ein Mann von W.**, a man of the world; F: **es kostet nicht die W.**, it doesn't cost the earth; **alle W.**, everybody. II. 'W~, 'w~, comb.fm. (a) world (atlas, peace, literature, market, order etc.); international (politics etc.); (map etc.) of the world; (b) (weltweit) worldwide (reputation etc.). ◆'W~**all**, n universe; cosmos. ◆'W~**anschauung**, f ideology; philosophy (of life). ◆'w~**fremd**, adj. unworldly. ◆'W~**fremdheit**, f unworldliness. ◆'W~**klasse**, f world's best/elite; **W. sein**, to be world class. ◆'W~**krieg**, m world war. ◆'w~**lich**, adj. worldly (pleasures etc.); mundane (outlook etc.); (nicht religiös) secular (education, art etc.). ◆'W~**macht**, f world power. ◆'w~**männisch**, adj. sophisticated, urban. ◆'W~**meer**, n ocean. ◆'W~**meister(in)**, m(f) world champion. ◆'W~**meisterschaft**, f world championship. ◆'W~**raum**, m (outer) space. ◆'W~**raumfahrt**, f space travel. ◆'w~**reich**, n empire. ◆'W~**reise**, f world tour. ◆'W~**rekord**, m world record. ◆'W~**ruf**, m world-wide renown; international reputation. ◆'W~**stadt**, f metropolis. ◆'W~**untergang**, m end of the world. ◆'w~**weit**, adj. world-wide. ◆'W~**wunder**, n wonder of the world.

wem [veːm], pron. 1. (to) whom. 2. F: (jemandem) (to) someone.

wen [veːn], pron. 1. whom. 2. F: (jemanden) someone.

Wende ['vɛndə], f -/-n turning point; **W. zum Guten/Schlechten**, change for the better/worse. ◆'W~**ekreis**, m 1. Geog: tropic. 2. Aut: lock; turning circle. ◆'W~**eltreppe**, f spiral staircase. ◆'w~**en**, v. 1. v.tr.irr.94 to turn; **sich w.**, (Pers.) to turn (round); **sich an j-n/ eine Behörde w.**, to turn to s.o. (for help)/apply to an authority (**um** + acc, for); **sich zum Guten/Schlechten w.**, to take a turn for the better/worse. 2. v.i. (haben) to turn (round). ◆'W~**epunkt**, m turning point. ◆'W~**ung**, f -/-en 1. turn. 2. = Redewendung.

wenig ['veːnɪç], pron. & adj. 1. sing. little; **das w~e Geld**, the small amount of money; **w. bekannt**, little known; **w. erfreulich**, not very pleasant; **ein w. Schnee**, a bit of/a little snow. 2. pl (a) few; **mit w~en Worten**, in few/(ein paar) a few words; **nicht w~e**, not a few; quite a number. ◆'w~**er**, comp. adj. & pron.inv. 1. less; pl fewer; **w. Geld**, less money. 2. Mth: 4 **w.** 2, 4 minus 2. ◆'W~**keit**, f /no pl trifle; Hum: **meine W.**, yours truly. ◆'w~**ste(r,s)**, superl. adj. least; pl fewest. ◆'w~**stens**, adv. at least.

wenn [vɛn], conj. 1. if; **w. schon!** what of it! F: so what! **w. er nur käme!** if only he would come! 2. (zeitlich) when; **w. er**

kommt, frage ich ihn, I'll ask him when he arrives; immer w., whenever. ◆'w~gleich, *conj.* although. ◆'w~schon, *conj.* s., dennschon, in for a penny, in for a pound.

wer [ve:r]. I. *inter.pron.* who; w. von euch, which of you? 2. *rel.pron.* anyone who; w. mitkommen will, anyone who/ whoever wants to come. 3. *indef.pron.* F: (jemand) falls w. auftaucht, if anyone turns up.

Werbe- ['vɛrbə-], *comb.fm.* advertising (agent, agency, costs, filter etc.); commercial (broadcast etc.). ◆'W~kampagne, *f* advertising campaign. ◆'W~fernsehen, *n* TV commercials. ◆'W~geschenk, *n* free sample. ◆'w~n, *v.tr.101* 1. *v.tr.* to enlist, recruit (members etc.); to canvass, *Hum:* woo (customers etc.). 2. *v.i. (haben)* to campaign (für eine Partei usw., for a party etc.; *Com:* to advertise (für etwas *acc*, sth.); um j-s Vertrauen w., to try to gain s.o.'s trust. ◆'W~spot, *m* -s/-s commercial. ◆'w~wirksam, *adj.* w. sein, to be good publicity/have plenty of pull.

Werbung ['vɛrbʊŋ], *f* -/-en 1. recruitment (of members etc.). 2. *no pl Com:* advertising; publicity; promotion (für + *acc*, of).

Werdegang ['ve:rdəgaŋ], *m* development; *(Laufbahn)* career.

werden ['ve:rdən], *v.i.irr. (sein)* 1. to become (sth., angry, old etc.); to go (blind, mad, red etc.); to turn (pale, sour etc.); to grow (longer, shorter etc.); to get (wet, warm etc.); gesund/krank w., to get well/fall ill; mir wurde schlecht, I began to feel ill; zu etwas *dat* w., to turn into sth.; daraus wird nichts, nothing will come of that; was wird, wenn er nicht kommt? what will happen if he doesn't come? 2. *v.aux.* (a) *(Futur)* er wird kommen, he will come; (b) *(Konditional)* er würde kommen, wenn ..., he would come if ... (c) *(Passiv)* geliebt w., to be loved; er wurde gewählt, he was chosen. ◆'w~d, *adj.* growing, budding (doctor etc.); w~de Mutter, expectant mother.

werfen ['vɛrfən], *v.tr.irr.* (a) to throw (sth.); to cast *(Fig:* a glance, shadow etc.); (b) Blasen/Falten w., to form bubbles/creases.

Werft [vɛrft], *f* -/-en shipyard.

Werk [vɛrk], *n* -(e)s/-e 1. work; *coll.* (artistic etc.) works, output; am W., at work. 2. *Tchn:* mechanism, *F:* works. 3. *Ind:* works; plant; ab W., ex works. ◆'W~bank, *f* workbench. ◆'w~seigen, *adj.* company(-owned). ◆'W~statt *f* -/-stätten workshop; *Art:* studio. ◆'W~stoff, *m* material. ◆'W~stück, *n* workpiece. ◆'W~student, *m* working student. ◆'W~tag, *m* working day. ◆'w~tags, *adv.* on working days. ◆'w~tätig, *adj.* working (population

etc.). ◆'W~tisch, *m* workbench. ◆'W~zeug, *n (also Fig: Pers.)* tool; *coll.* toolkit, tools. ◆'W~zeugkasten, *m* tool box/chest.

Wermut ['ve:rmu:t], *m* -(e)s/*no pl* 1. *Bot:* wormwood. 2. *(Wein)* vermouth.

wert [ve:rt]. I. *adj.* 1. *(a)* (+ *nom*) viel/ wenig/1000 Mark w., worth a lot/a little/ 1000 marks; nichts w., worthless; der Film ist es w., daß man ihn sieht, the film is worth seeing; *(b)* (+ *gen*) worthy of ...; der Mühe w., worth the trouble. 2. *Lit:* esteemed, valued; *Com:* Ihr w~es Schreiben, your kind letter. II. W., *m* -(e)s/-e *(a)* value; im W~e von, to the value of; *(b)* esp. *Fig:* worth (of s.o., sth.); ohne jeden W., valueless, worthless; das hat keinen W., it's pointless/ useless; auf etwas *acc* (großen/viel) W. legen, to lay (great) stress on/attach (great) importance to sth.; *(c) pl* W~e, values; *(W~sachen)* valuables. III. 'W~, *comb.fm.* value (judgement etc.) (standard etc.) of value. ◆'W~angabe, *f* declaration of value. ◆'W~arbeit, *f* quality workmanship. ◆'w~beständig, *adj.* retaining its value; stable (currency, prices). ◆'w~en, *v.tr.* to assess, calculate (a development etc.); to rate (a performance etc.); *Sp:* es wird nicht gewertet, it does not count. ◆'w~los, *adj.* valueless, worthless. ◆'W~losigkeit, *f* -/*no pl* worthlessness. ◆'W~marke, *f* stamp; coupon. ◆'W~papier, *n* security; *pl* W~papiere, stocks and shares. ◆'W~sache, *f* article of value; *pl* valuables. ◆W~ung, *f* -/-en *(a)* assessment, evaluation; *(b) Sp:* score, points. ◆'w~voll, *adj.* valuable.

Wesen ['ve:zən], *n* -s/- 1. *no pl* nature; *(das Wesentliche)* essence. 2. *(Lebewesen)* being; *(Geschöpf)* creature. ◆'w~tlich, *adj. (a)* essential; im w~tlichen, essentially; in the main; *(b) (grundlegend)* basic, fundamental (quality etc.); *(c) (erheblich)* substantial (difference etc.).

weshalb [vɛs'halp]. I. *interrog.adv.* why. II. *conj.* (which is) why.

Wespe ['vɛspə], *f* -/-n wasp. ◆'W~n-, *comb.fm.* wasp's (nest etc.). ◆'W~nstich, *m* wasp sting.

wessen ['vɛsən], *interrog.pron.* whose; w. Buch? whose book?

West- [vɛst-], *comb.fm.* (a) west (coast, side, bank, wind etc.); West (Germany, Africa, Berlin etc.); (b) *(westlich)* western (frontier etc.). ◆'w~deutsch, *adj.* West German. ◆'W~en, *m* -s/*no pl* west; aus dem/von N., from the west; nach W., westwards; *(Lage)* to the west. ◆W~ern ['vɛstən], *m* -s/- *Cin: F:* western. ◆W~falen [-'fa:lən] *Pr.n.n* -s. Westphalia. ◆w~fälisch [-'fe:lɪʃ], *adj.* Westphalian. ◆'w~lich. I. *adj.* western (hemisphere, border, sky etc.); westerly (wind, direction etc.); **v. von Bonn**, (to the) west of Bonn. **II.** prep. + gen **w. der Stadt**, to the west of the town. ◆**W~mächte**, fpl Western Powers. ◆**'w~wärts**, adj. westwards.

Weste ['vɛstə], f /-n waistcoat, N.Am: vest; Fig: **eine weiße W. haben**, to have a clean record.

weswegen [vɛsve:'ge:gən], interrog.pron. = **weshalb**.

wett [vɛt], adj. even, F: quits. ◆**'W~bewerb**, m -(e)s/-e competition; Sp: contest, event. ◆**'W~büro**, n betting office/shop. ◆**'W~e**, f /-n bet; **sie liefen/fuhren um die W.**, they raced each other (on foot/in cars). ◆**'W~eifer**, m competitive spirit. ◆**'w~eifern**, v.i. (haben) to vie, contend (**um etwas** acc, for sth.). ◆**'w~en. I.** v.i. (haben) to bet (**mit j-m um etwas** acc, s.o. sth.); **auf ein Pferd usw. w.**, to bet on/back a horse etc. **II. W.**, n -s/no pl betting. ◆**'W~er(in)**, m -s/- (f /-nen) better. ◆**'W~kampf**, m Sp: contest, match. ◆**'W~kämpfer**, m competitor; contestant. ◆**'W~lauf**, m race. ◆**'w~machen**, v.tr.sep. to make good (an error, a loss etc.); to offset (a deficiency etc.). ◆**'W~rennen**, n race. ◆**'W~rüsten**, n -s/no pl arms race. ◆**'W~streit**, m contest.

Wetter² ['vɛtər]. **I.** n -s/- weather; **bei jedem W.**, in all weathers; F: **was ist für W.?** what's the weather like? **II. 'W~-**, **'w~-**, comb.fm. weather (service, situation, satellite, conditions etc.); meteorological (office etc.). ◆**'W~bericht**, m weather report. ◆**'w~fest**, adj. weatherproof. ◆**'W~karte**, f weather map/chart. ◆**'W~leuchten**, n sheet lightning. ◆**'w~n**, v.i. (haben) Fig: **gegen j-n, etwas** acc **w.**, to fulminate against s.o., sth. ◆**'W~vorhersage**, f weather forecast. ◆**'W~warte**, f weather/meteorological station.

wetzen ['vɛtsən], v. **1.** v.tr. to sharpen, grind (a knife etc.). **2.** v.i. (sein) F: to shoot, rush (along).

Whisky ['viski], m -s/-s whisk(e)y.

wichtig ['vɪçtɪç], adj. important; **sich/etwas w. nehmen**, to take oneself/sth. seriously; **sich w. machen**, to be full of one's own importance. ◆**'W~keit**, f / no pl importance.

Wick|el ['vɪkəl], m -s/- (a) (Haarw.) roller, curler; (b) Med: compress. ◆**'w~eln**, v.tr. to wind (thread, wire, a bandage etc.); to coil (wire); to put (hair) in curlers; (einw.) to wrap (sth., someone); **ein Baby w.**, to put a nappy/N.Am: diaper on a baby. ◆**'W~eltisch**, m (baby's) changing table. ◆**'W~ler**, m -s/- (hair) curler.

Widder ['vɪdər], m -s/- Z: ram; Astr: Aries.

wider ['vi:dər], prep. + acc against; **w. Erwarten**, contrary to expectation.

◆**'w~'fahren**, v.i.insep.irr.26 (sein) to happen (j-m, to s.o.). ◆**'W~haken**, m barb, barbed hook. ◆**'W~legen**, v.tr.insep. to refute, disprove (sth.). ◆**'W~legung**, f -/no pl refutation. ◆**'w~lich**, adj. loathsome (person, behaviour etc.); obnoxious (spectacle, smell etc.); odious (task etc.). ◆**'w~natürlich**, adj. unnatural, perverted. ◆**'w~rechtlich**, adj. unlawful; wrongful (arrest, dismissal). ◆**'W~rede**, f contradiction; **ohne W.**, unquestioningly; **keine W.!** don't argue! ◆**'W~ruf**, m cancellation, revocation; withdrawal; **bis auf W.**, until further notice. ◆**w~'rufen**, v.tr.insep.irr.74 to cancel, revoke (an order etc.); to withdraw (a statement). ◆**'W~sacher**, m adversary. ◆**w~'setzen**, v.refl.insep. **sich j-m, etwas dat w.**, to oppose/resist s.o., sth. ◆**'w~sinnig**, adj. senseless, absurd. ◆**'w~spenstig**, adj. rebellious; unruly, unmanageable (child, hair); (störrisch) obstinate, stubborn. ◆**'W~spenstigkeit**, f -/-en rebelliousness, unruliness; obstinacy. ◆**'w~spiegeln**, v.tr.sep. also Fig: to reflect, mirror (sth.). ◆**w~'sprechen**, v.i.insep.irr.14 (haben) to contradict (j-m, etwas dat, s.o., sth.); (Aussagen usw.) **sich w.**, to be contradictory; to conflict. ◆**w~'sprechend**, adj. conflicting. ◆**'W~spruch**, m contradiction; **ohne W.**, without protest. ◆**'w~spruchslos**, adv. unprotestingly. ◆**'w~sprüchlich** [-ʃprýçlɪç], adj. contradictory, inconsistent. ◆**'W~stand**, m -(e)s/no pl (also El:) resistance; (j-m, etwas dat) **W. leisten**, to resist (s.o., sth.). ◆**'W~stands-**, comb.fm. resistance (movement etc.). ◆**'W~standskämpfer**, m resistance fighter. ◆**'w~standsfähig**, adj. resistant (**gegen** + acc, to); (stark) tough (person, clothing); hardy (plant). ◆**'w~standslos**, adj. unresisting. ◆**w~'stehen**, v.i.insep.irr.100 (haben) **einem Angriff**, Fig: **der Versuchung usw. w.**, to resist an attack, Fig: temptation etc.; (Material) (**dem**) **Druck usw. w.**, to withstand pressure etc. ◆**'W~streit**, m Lit: conflict. ◆**'w~wärtig**, adj. = **widerlich**. ◆**'W~wille**, m aversion (**gegen** + acc, to); (Ekel) disgust, repugnance. ◆**'w~willig**, adj. reluctant, grudging.

widmen ['vɪtmən], v.tr. to dedicate (a book etc.) (j-m, to s.o.); **sich/seine Zeit usw. etwas dat w.**, to devote oneself/one's time etc. to sth. ◆**'W~ung**, f -/-en dedication.

widrig ['vi:drɪç], adj. adverse.

wie [vi:], adv. interrog. how? F: **und w.! und how!** not half! **w.! du hast es vergessen!** what! you've forgotten it! **II.** conj. (a) comp. as; (ähnlich w.) like; **so groß w. du**, as big as you; **w. sein Va-**

ter, like his father; **w. wenn ...,** as if ...; **w. gesagt,** as has been said; as I have said before; (b) how; **du weißt, w. es ist,** you know how it is; **w. reich er auch sein mag,** however rich he may be.

wieder ['vi:dər], adv. again, once more; **er ging w. ins Haus,** he went back into the house. ◆**W~'aufbau,** m rebuilding, reconstruction. ◆**W~'aufnahme,** f resumption; renewal; readmission (**in einen Verein usw.,** to a club etc.). ◆**w~'aufnehmen,** v.tr.sep.irr.69 to resume (work, discussions etc.); Jur: to re-open (a case). ◆**W~beginn,** m recommencement; resumption. ◆**w~bekommen,** v.tr.sep.irr.53 to get (sth.) back. ◆**w~bringen,** v.tr.sep.irr.16 to bring back. ◆**W~entdeckung,** f rediscovery. ◆**w~erinnern, v.refl. sich an etwas** acc **w.,** to recall sth. ◆**w~erkennen,** v.tr.sep.irr.51 to recognize (s.o., sth.). ◆**w~erlangen,** v.tr.sep. to recover, regain (sth.). ◆**w~finden,** v.tr.sep.irr.9 to find (s.o., sth.) again. ◆**W~gabe,** f 1. reproduction; (Übersetzung, Aufführung) rendering; (Schilderung) account, description. 2. (Rückgabe) return. ◆**w~geben,** v.tr.sep.irr.35 (a) to give back, return (sth); (b) (vortragen, übersetzen) to render (a song, text etc.); (schildern) to give an account of (a conversation, event etc.). ◆**w~gewinnen,** v.tr.sep.irr.90 to recover (one's equilibrium etc.). ◆**w~gutmachen,** v.tr.sep. to make good, (entschädigen) compensate for (damage); to make up for (a mistake etc.), (wrong). ◆**W~'gutmachung,** f -/no pl compensation; Pol: reparations. ◆**w~herstellen,** v.tr.sep. to restore (sth.); to re-establish (contact etc.). ◆**w~holen,** v.tr.insep. to repeat (sth.); Sp: to replay (a match), re-run (a race); **sich w.,** (Pers.) to repeat oneself; (Ereignis) to recur. ◆**w~'holt,** adj. repeated. ◆**w~'holung,** f -/-en repetition; reiteration; (Sendung usw.) repeat; Sp: replay. ◆**W~'holungsspiel,** n Sp: replay. ◆**w~hören,** n -s/no pl **auf W.,** goodbye. ◆**W~kehr,** f -/no pl return; recurrence; (Jubiläum) anniversary. ◆**w~kehren,** v.i.sep. (sein) to return, come back. ◆**w~kommen,** v.i.sep.irr.53 (sein) to come back(noch einmal) again. ◆**w~sehen,** n. **W.,** n -s/ reunion; **auf W., goodbye. ◆w~um,** adv. (a) Lit: again; (b) (andererseits) on the other hand. ◆**w~vereinigen,** v.tr.sep. to reunite. ◆**W~vereinigung,** f reunification. ◆**W~verkauf,** m resale. ◆**W~wahl,** f re-election. ◆**w~wählen,** v.tr.sep. to re-elect.

Wiege ['vi:gə], f -/-n (also Fig:) cradle. ◆**'w~n[1],** v.tr. to rock (a baby, boat etc.); Fig: **sich in Sicherheit w.,** to be lulled into a false sense of security. ◆**'W~nlied,** n lullaby, cradle-song.

wiegen[2], v.tr.&i.irr.7 (haben) to weigh (s.o., sth.), oneself etc.); Fig: (Argument usw.) **schwer w.,** to carry a lot of weight.

wiehern ['vi:ərn], v.i. (haben) to neigh.

Wien ['vi:n]. Pr.n.n -s. Vienna. ◆**'W~er,** adj. Viennese.

Wiese ['vi:zə], f -/-n meadow; (Weide) pasture.

Wiesel ['vi:zəl], n -s/- weasel.

wie'so, interrog. adv. why?

wie'viel, interrog.adv. how much? how many? **w. Geld das kostet!** what a lot of money it costs! ◆**w~te(r,s),** interrog.adj. (number, date etc.); **den w~ten haben wir heute?** what is the date today?

wild [vilt]. **I. adj.** (a) wild; savage (tribe etc.); rugged (landscape etc.); fierce, ferocious (battle, dog etc.); F: **das ist halb so w.,** it's not as bad as all that; **wie w. arbeiten,** to work like mad; (b) (unerlaubt) unauthorized (bathing, parking etc.); **w~er Streik,** wildcat strike; **in w~er Ehe leben,** to cohabit, F: live in sin. **II. W.,** n -(e)s/no pl game. ◆**'W~bret,** n -s/no pl game. ◆**'W~erer,** m -s/- poacher. ◆**'w~ern,** v.tr. & i. (haben) to poach (game). ◆**'W~fang,** m (little) scamp; (Mädchen) tomboy. ◆**'w~'fremd,** adj. F: completely strange; **w~fremder Mensch,** total stranger. ◆**'W~hüter,** m gamekeeper. ◆**'w~lebend,** adj. living in the wild. ◆**'W~leder,** n suede. ◆**'W~nis,** f -/-se wilderness; (Wüste) desert. ◆**'W~schwein,** n wild boar. ◆**'W~wechsel,** m game path/crossing.

Wille ['vilə], m -ns/-n will; **mein fester W.,** my firm intention; **bei/mit gutem W~n,** given enough goodwill; **beim besten W~n,** with the best will in the world; **seinen W~n durchsetzen,** to get one's own way; **ich mußte wider W~n lachen,** I couldn't help laughing. ◆**'w~n,** prep. + gen **um js/des Friedens usw. w.,** for s.o.'s sake/the sake of peace etc. ◆**'w~nlos,** adj. weak-willed. ◆**'W~nskraft,** f willpower. ◆**'w~nsstark,** adj. strong-willed, strong-minded. ◆**'w~ntlich,** adv. deliberately, intentionally.

willig ['viliç], adj. willing, docile (animal etc.). ◆**'w~kommen. I. adj.** welcome; **j-n w. heißen,** to welcome s.o. **II. W.,** n -s/- welcome. ◆**'W~kür,** f -/no pl arbitrariness; (Launen) capriciousness. ◆**'w~kürlich,** adj. arbitrary.

wimmeln ['viməln], v.i. (haben) to be teeming/crawling (**von** + dat, with).

wimmern ['vimərn], v.i. (haben) to whimper.

Wimper ['vimpər], f -/-n (eye)lash; Fig: **ohne mit der W. zu zucken,** without batting an eyelid. ◆**'W~ntusche,** f mascara.

Wind [vint], m -(e)s/-e wind; Fig: W. bekommen/haben von + dat, to get wind of sth.; etwas in den W. schlagen, to turn a deaf ear to sth.; viel W. machen, to make a lot of noise, (prahlen) deny speed; sich mit W. verbreiten, to spread like wildfire. ◆'W~hund, m greyhound. ◆'w~ig, adj. 1. windy. 2. F: dubious (business). ◆'W~licht, n storm lantern. ◆'W~mühle, f windmill. ◆'W~pocken, fpl chickenpox. ◆'W~röschen, n -s/- anemone. ◆'W~rose, f Nau: compass rose. ◆'W~schatten, m lee (side). ◆'W~schutzscheibe, f windscreen, N.Am: windshield. ◆'W~stärke, f wind force. ◆'w~still, adj. windless, calm. ◆'W~stille, f calm. ◆'W~stoß, m gust of wind.

Wind|e ['vində], f -/-n 1. winch, Nau: capstan. 2. Bot: bindweed, convolvulus. ◆'w~en, v.tr.irr.9 (a) (hochw.) to winch (up), hoist (a load etc.); (b) (flechten) to bind, weave (a wreath etc.); (c) sich w., (Pers.) to wind (one's way) (durch + acc, through); to writhe (vor Schmerzen, with pain); (Wurm usw.) to wriggle; (Pfad, Fluß usw.) to twist, wind.

Windel ['vindəl], f -/-n (baby's) nappy, N.Am: diaper. ◆'w~weich, adj. F: j-n w. schlagen, to beat s.o. to a pulp.

Wink [viŋk], m -(e)s/-e (a) (mit der Hand) wave, sign; (mit den Augen) wink; (Kopfnicken) nod; (b) (Hinweis) hint; pointer. ◆'w~en, v. 1. v.i. (haben) to wave (j-m, to s.o.); einem Taxi w., to hail a taxi; Fig: ihm winkt eine Belohnung, he has a reward coming to him. 2. v.tr. j-n zu sich dat w., to beckon/signal to s.o. to come over.

Winkel ['viŋkəl], m -s/- (a) Mth: angle; (b) Tchn: (set) square; (c) (Ecke) corner. ◆'w~eisen, n angle iron. ◆'w~ig, adj. full of corners. ◆'W~messer, m protractor.

winseln ['vinzəln], v.i. (haben) (Hund) to whine.

Winter ['vintər]. I. m -s/- winter. II. 'W~-, comb.fm. (a) winter (suit, clothes, months etc.); winter's (night, day); (beginning etc.) of winter; (b) (winterlich) wintry (weather etc.). ◆'W~fest, adj. winterproof, N.Am: winterized; Bot: hardy. ◆'w~lich, adj. wintry. ◆'W~reifen, m snow tyre. ◆'W~schlaf, m hibernation; W. halten, to hibernate. ◆'W~schlußverkauf, m winter sale. ◆'W~sport, m winter sports.

Winzer ['vintsər], m -s/- wine grower.

winzig ['vintsiç], adj. tiny; w. klein, minute.

Wipfel ['vipfəl], m -s/- treetop.

Wippe ['vipə], f -/-n seesaw.

wir [viːr], pers. pron. we; w. beide, both of us; w. waren es, it was us.

Wirbel ['virbəl], m -s/- 1. (in Wasser, Luft) eddy; Fig: whirl (of activity etc.); (Aufruhr) commotion. 2. Anat: vertebra. ◆'w~n, v.i. (haben/sein) (Wasser, Rauch usw.) to eddy, swirl; (Pers.) to whirl. ◆'W~säule, f spinal column, spine. ◆'W~sturm, m cyclone, tornado. ◆'W~tier, n vertebrate. ◆'W~wind, m whirlwind.

wirk|en ['virkən], v. 1. v.i. (haben) (a) (tätig sein) to work, be active (als Arzt usw., as a doctor etc.); (b) (Wirkung haben) to have an effect (auf j-n, on s.o.); (Arznei) to be effective; (Mitteilung usw.) to seem tired/over edge. 2. v.tr. Lit: to work (wonders). ◆'w~lich, adj. real; actual (fact, state of affairs etc.); (echt) genuine (artist, friend etc.); adv. really. ◆'W~lichkeit, f -/-en reality; in W., in actual fact. ◆'w~sam, adj. effective (Vorschrift usw.) w. werden, to come into effect/force. ◆'W~samkeit, f -/no pl effectiveness. ◆'W~ung, f -/-en effect, impression. ◆'W~ungskreis, m sphere of activity; Pol: etc: influence. ◆'w~ungslos, adj. ineffective; w. bleiben, to have no effect. ◆'W~ungsweise, f (mode of) operation. ◆'w~ungsvoll, adj. effective.

wirr [vir], adj. confused (person); (verfilzt) dishevelled (hair); w~es Zeug reden, to talk incoherently. ◆'W~warr, m -s/no pl chaos; (Lärm) hubbub.

Wirsing ['virziŋ], m -s/no pl savoy (cabbage).

Wirt [virt], m -(e)s/-e (Gastwirt, Vermieter) landlord. ◆'W~in, f -/-nen landlady. ◆'W~schaft, f -/-en 1. economy; freie W., free enterprise. 2. (a) (Haushalt) household, housekeeping; (b) F: eine saubere/schöne W., a fine mess. 3. (Gastw.) Brit: = public house, F: pub; N.Am: = saloon. ◆'w~schaften, v.i. (haben) to manage (well, badly etc.); (Haushalt führen) to keep house. ◆'W~schafterin, f -/-nen housekeeper. ◆'w~schaftlich, adj. 1. economic (development, growth etc.). 2. (sparsam) economical (car etc.); thrifty (housewife etc.). ◆'W~schafts-, comb.fm. economic (relations, history, aid, policy, system etc.); business (life, school etc.); trade (agreement, delegation etc.); industrial (sabotage, espionage etc.). ◆'W~schaftsgeld, n housekeeping money. ◆'W~schaftsgemeinschaft, f economic community. ◆'W~schaftslage, f economic situation. ◆'W~schaftsminister, m minister for economic affairs. ◆'W~schaftsprüfer, m accountant; (Buchprüfer) auditor. ◆'W~schaftswunder, n economic miracle. ◆'**W~shaus**, n Brit: public house, F: pub, N.Am: saloon.

Wisch [viʃ], m -(e)s/-e F: scrap of paper. ◆'**w~en**, v.tr. to wipe (sth.). ◆'**W~er**, m -s/- Aut: etc: wiper. ◆'**W~tuch**, n (floor etc.) cloth.

wispern ['vispərn], v.tr.&i. (haben) to whisper (sth.) (hurriedly).

Wißbegier|de ['visbəgi:r(də)], f -/no pl thirst for knowledge; curiosity. ◆**w~ig**, adj. eager to learn.

wissen ['visən]. I. v.tr. & i.irr. (haben) to know (sth.); **das mußt du w.**, that's up to you; **weißt du noch?** do you remember? **nicht, daß ich wüßte**, not that I am aware of; **ich will nichts von ihm/davon w.**, I will have nothing to do with him/it; **oder was weiß ich**, or something of the sort. II. **W**, n -s/no pl knowledge; **meines W~s**, to my knowledge. ◆'**W~schaft**, f -/-en science. ◆'**W~schaftler**, m -s/- scientist. ◆'**w~schaftlich**, adj. scientific (discovery, method etc.); (akademisch) academic (work, education etc.). ◆'**w~swert**, adj. worth knowing; valuable (information). ◆'**w~tlich**, adj. deliberate; adv. deliberately, knowingly.

wittern ['vitərn], v.tr. to scent, get wind of (prey, Fig: danger etc.). ◆'**W~ung**, f -/no pl (Wetter) weather (conditions).

Witwe ['vitvə], f -/-n widow. ◆'**W~nrente**, f widow's pension. ◆'**W~r**, m -s/- widower.

Witz [vits], m -es/-e (a) joke; (b) no pl (Geist) wit. ◆'**W~blatt**, n comic magazine. ◆'**W~bold**, m -(e)s/-e joker (Geist) wit. ◆'**w~eln**, v.i. (haben) to make jokes. ◆'**W~figur**, f figure of fun. ◆'**w~ig**, adj. witty; (spaßig) funny. ◆'**w~los**, adj. unfunny; (sinnlos) pointless.

wo [vo:]. I. interrog. & rel.adv. where; F: (irgendwo) somewhere; **wo immer (auch)**, wherever; **der Tag, wo ...**, the day when ... II. conj. **wo nicht**, if not; **wo du gerade da bist**, seeing you're here. ◆'**w~anders**, adv. elsewhere, somewhere else. ◆**w~bei** [vo:'bai], adv. 1. interrog. at what? doing what? 2. rel. in/in doing which; in the course of which.

Woche ['vɔxə], f -/-n week. ◆'**w~nende**, n weekend. ◆'**w~nlang**, adj. for weeks. ◆'**W~nschau**, f Cin: newsreel. ◆'**W~ntag**, m weekday. ◆'**w~ntags**, adv. on weekdays.

wöchentlich ['vœçəntliç], adj. weekly (report etc.); **einmal w.**, once a week.

Wodka ['vɔtka], m -s/-s vodka.

wo|durch, adv. 1. interr. by what means? how? 2. rel. through/as a result of which. ◆**w~für**, adv. 1. interrog. for what? what ... for? 2. rel. (in return) for which.

Woge ['vo:gə], f -/-n wave.

wo|gegen, adv. 1. interrog. against what? 2. rel. against which.

wo|her, interrog. & rel.adv. from where(?); where from?(?); **w. weißt du**

das? how do you know that?

wo|hin, interrog. & rel.adv. where (to); **w. damit?** where shall I put it? ◆**w~'gegen**, conj. whereas.

wohl [vo:l]. I. adv. 1. well; **sich w. fühlen**, to feel well/(wie zu Hause) at home/ comfortable; **ist dir nicht w.?** aren't you well? **w. oder übel**, willy nilly; whether I/you like it or not; **das kann man w. sagen!** you can say that again! **w. kaum w. sein**, it may well be (true). 2. (vermutlich) presumably, I suppose; **es wird w. besser sein ...**, it will probably be better ...; **w. kaum**, hardly likely. 3. (zwar) perhaps; **er hat es w. gut gemeint, aber ...**, he may have meant well, but ... II. **W**, n -(e)s/no pl well-being; welfare; **auf j-s W. trinken**, to drink s.o.'s health; **zum W.!** cheers! ◆'**w~auf**, pred.adj. well, in good health. ◆'**W~befinden**, n well-being. ◆'**W~behagen**, n (feeling of) well-being, pleasure. ◆'**w~behalten**, adj. (Pers.) safe and sound; (Objekt) in good condition. ◆'**W~fahrt**, f welfare. ◆'**W~fahrts-**, comb.fm. welfare (state etc.); charity (organization etc.). ◆'**W~geruch**, m pleasant smell, fragrance. ◆'**w~habend**, adj. well-to-do, affluent. ◆'**w~ig**, adj. cosy; contented (sigh etc.). ◆'**w~meinend**, adj. well-meaning. ◆'**w~schmeckend**, adj. pleasant-tasting, tasty. ◆'**W~stand**, m prosperity, affluence. ◆'**W~stands-gesellschaft**, f affluent society. ◆'**W~tat**, f (a) good deed; (Erleichterung) relief; (Segen) boon. ◆'**W~täter(in)**, m(f) benefactor, benefactress. ◆'**w~tätig**, adj. charitable. ◆'**W~tätigkeit**, f charity. ◆'**w~tuend**, adj. beneficial (effect etc.); refreshing (breeze etc.); (lindernd) soothing. ◆'**w~tun**, v.i.sep.irr.106 (j-m) w., to do (s.o.) good. ◆'**w~überlegt**, adj. well-considered. ◆'**w~verdient**, adj. well-deserved, well-earned. ◆'**w~weislich**, adv. very wisely. ◆'**w~wollen**, n -s/no pl goodwill. ◆'**w~wollend**, adj. benevolent; kindly (smile etc.).

Wohn|block ['vo:nblɔk], m block of flats, N.Am: apartment house. ◆'**w~en**, v.i. (haben) to live. ◆'**W~gemeinschaft**, f group sharing a house/flat; commune. ◆'**w~haft**, adj. Adm: resident. ◆'**W~haus**, n residential building, dwelling. ◆'**W~heim**, n residential home/hostel; (Studentenw.) hall of residence. ◆'**w~lich**, adj. cosy, home-like. ◆'**W~ort**, m (place of) residence. ◆'**W~raum**, m living space. ◆'**W~sitz**, m (place of) residence; **ohne festen W.**, of no fixed abode. ◆'**W~ung**, f (a) home; Adm: residence; (Unterkunft) accommodation; (b) (Etagenw.) flat, N.Am: apartment. ◆'**W~ungsnot**, f housing shortage.

◆'w~ungssuche, f house-/flat-hunting. ◆'W~wagen, m caravan; N.Am: trailer. ◆'W~zimmer, n living room.

wölb|en ['vœlbən], v.tr. to curve (sth.); to arch (one's back, brows etc.); sich w., to curve, (Bauch usw.) bulge; (Brücke usw.) to arch (über + acc, across). ◆'W~ung, f -/-en curve; curvature (of the spine).

Wolf [vɔlf], m -(e)s/=e 1. Z: wolf. 2. Cu: mincer.

Wölf|in ['vœlfin], f -/-nen she-wolf. ◆'w~isch, adj. wolfish.

Wolke ['vɔlkə], f -/-n cloud; aus allen W~n fallen, to come down to earth with a bump. ◆'W~en-, comb.fm. cloud (bank, formation etc.); (layer, wall etc.) of cloud. ◆'W~enbruch, m cloud-burst. ◆'W~enkratzer, m -s/- skyscraper. ◆'w~enlos, adj. cloudless. ◆'w~ig, adj. cloudy.

Woll|decke ['vɔldɛkə], f woollen blanket/(Reisedecke) rug. ◆'W~jacke, f woollen cardigan. ◆'W~knäuel, m ball of wool. ◆'W~e, f -/-n wool. ◆'w~en1, adj. wool, woollen.

wollen2 ['vɔlən], v.tr.&i.irr. (haben) to want (sth.), to do (sth.); to wish (daß ..., that ...); er will nicht, he doesn't want to; ich will, daß du hier bleibst, I want you to stay here; w. wir aufstehen? shall we get up?

wo'mit, adv. 1. interrog. with what? what ...with? 2. rel. with what.

wo'möglich, adv. possibly.

wo'nach, adv. 1. interrog. after what? 2. rel. after/according to which.

Wonne ['vɔnə], f -/-n delight; vor W., with joy.

wo'ran, adv. 1. interrog. at what? w. arbeiten Sie? what are you working on? 2. rel. about/at/on which.

wo'rauf, adv. 1. interrog. on what? 2. rel. (up)on which; (wonach) whereupon, after which.

wo'raus, adv. 1. interrog. out of what? from what? 2. rel. out of/of/from which.

wo'rin, adv. 1. interrog. in what? 2. rel. in which, wherein.

Wort [vɔrt], n -(e)s/-e & (Vokabeln) =er word; j-m aufs W. glauben/gehorchen, to believe/obey s.o.'s every word; mit anderen W~en, in other words; mir fehlen die W~e, words fail me; j-m ins W. fallen, to interrupt s.o.; das W. haben/führen, to speak; zu W. kommen, to get a chance to speak; j-m das W. geben/erteilen, to let s.o. speak; j-n beim W. nehmen, to take s.o. at his word. ◆'W~art, f part of speech. ◆'W~bruch, m breaking one's word; breach of promise. ◆'w~brüchig, adj. w. werden, to break one's word. ◆'W~führer, m spokesman. ◆'w~karg, adj. taciturn. ◆'W~laut,

m wording. ◆'w~los, adj. silent; adv. without a word. ◆'w~reich, adj. wordy, verbose. ◆'W~schatz, m vocabulary. ◆'W~spiel, n play on words, pun. ◆'W~wahl, f choice of words. ◆'W~wechsel, m heated exchange, altercation. ◆'w~wörtlich, adv. verbatim, word for word; quite literally.

Wört|erbuch ['vœrtərbu:x], n dictionary. ◆'w~lich, adj. literal (translation etc.); verbatim (account etc.); adv. word for word; etwas w. nehmen, to take sth. literally.

wo'rüber, adv. 1. interrog. (a) about what? (b) (Lage) over what? 2. rel. (a) about which; (b) over which.

wo'rum, adv. 1. interrog. (a) about what? (b) (Lage) round what? 2. rel. (a) about which; (b) round which.

wo'runter, adv. 1. interrog. under/among what? 2. rel. under/among which.

wo'von, adv. 1. interrog. from/of what. 2. rel. from/of/about which.

wo'vor, adv. 1. interrog. before what? w. hat er Angst? what is he afraid of? 2. rel. before/(räumlich) in front of which.

wo'zu, adv. 1. interrog. to what? (warum) why? for what (purpose)? 2. rel. to which.

Wrack [vrak], n -(e)s/-s wreck.

wringen ['vriŋən], v.tr. to wring (out) (washing).

Wucher ['vu:xər], m -s/no pl profiteering, extortion. II. 'W~-, comb.fm. exorbitant, extortionate (rent, price etc.). ◆'W~er, m -s/-/'W~in, f -/-nen profiteer. ◆'w~isch, adj. profiteering (practices); exorbitant (prices etc.). ◆'w~n, v.i. (haben) (a) (Pflanzen usw.) to grow profusely; (b) (mit etwas dat) w., to profiteer (with sth.). ◆'W~ung, f -/-en Bot: rank/rampant growth; Med: growth, esp. proud flesh.

Wuchs [vu:ks], m -es/-e growth; (Körperbau) build.

Wucht [vuxt], f -/no pl 1. force, impact (of a blow etc.). 2. F: das ist eine W.! that's terrific!

wühl|en ['vy:lən], v.i. (haben) to dig, (Tier) burrow; (suchend) to rummage (nach etwas dat, for sth.). ◆'W~maus, f Z: vole.

Wulst [vulst], m -es/=e bulge, roll of fat etc.); (im Stoff) (thick) fold.

wund [vunt], adj. sore. ◆'W~e, f -/-n wound. ◆'W~starrkrampf, m tetanus.

Wunder ['vundər], n -s/- miracle; W. tun/wirken, to work miracles/Fig: (Arznei usw.) wonders; kein/was W., daß ..., no wonder (that) ...; ein W an Genauigkeit, a miracle of precision. ◆'w~bar, adj. (a) (wie ein Wunder) miraculous; (b) (herrlich) marvellous, wonderful. ◆'W~kerze, f sparkler. ◆'W~kind, n child prodigy. ◆'w~lich, adj. odd, strange; weird (ideas etc.). ◆'W~mittel, n miracle cure, Hum:

magic potion. ◆'w~n, v.tr. to surprise (s.o.); **sich über j-n, etwas** acc w., to be surprised about/at s.o., sth. ◆'w~schön, adj. (very) beautiful, lovely. ◆'w~voll, adj. wonderful, marvellous. ◆'W~welt, f magic world, wonderland. ◆'W~werk, n marvel.

Wunsch [vunʃ], m -(e)s/=e wish; (Verlangen) desire; (Bitte) request; **auf j-s W.,** at s.o.'s request; **nach W.,** as desired/required. ◆'w~gemäß, adv. as requested/desired. ◆'W~konzert, n (musical) request programme. ◆'w~los, adj. w. glücklich, perfectly happy. ◆'W~traum, m pipe-dream. ◆'W~zettel, m list of wants.

Wünschelrute ['vynʃəlruːtə], f divining rod.

wünschen ['vynʃən], v.tr. to wish; **ich wünsche Sie zu sprechen,** I wish to speak to you; **es wäre sehr zu w.,** it would be highly desirable; **etwas/viel zu w. übrig lassen,** to leave something/much to be desired; **sich** dat **etwas w.,** to want/(bitten um) ask for/(im stillen) wish for sth. ◆'w~swert, adj. desirable.

Würd|e ['vyrdə], f -/-n 1. no pl dignity. 2. title, (Rang) rank ◆'w~elos, adj. undignified. ◆'W~elosigkeit, f -/no pl lack of dignity. ◆'W~enträger, m dignitary. ◆'w~evoll, adj. dignified; adv. with dignity. ◆'w~ig, adj. worthy; **j-s/des Vertrauens w. sein,** to be worthy of s.o./of trust. ◆'w~igen, v.tr. to appreciate (s.o., sth.), (erkennen) recognize (s.o.'s merits etc.); **ohne mich eines Blickes zu w.,** without deigning to look at me. ◆'W~igung, f -/-en appreciation; (Huldigung) tribute.

Wurf [vurf], m -(e)s/=e 1. (a) throw, toss (of the coin); (b) no pl (Werfen) throwing. 2. Z: litter (of puppies etc.). ◆'W~pfeil, m dart. ◆'W~sendung, f direct mailing.

Würfel ['vyrfəl], m -s/- (a) Mth:etc: cube; (b) (Spielw.) dice. ◆'W~becher, m dice shaker. ◆'w~n, v. 1. v.i. (haben) to play/throw dice (um etwas acc, for sth.). 2. v.tr. Cu: to dice (carrots, meat etc.). ◆'W~spiel, n game of dice.

◆'W~zucker, m cube/lump sugar.

Würg|egriff ['vyrgəgrif], m stranglehold. ◆'w~en, v. 1. v.tr. to strangle, throttle (s.o.); (Kragen usw.) to choke (s.o.). 2. v.i. (haben) to choke (**an etwas** dat, on sth.).

Wurm [vurm], m -(e)s/=er worm. ◆'w~en, v.tr. F: **es wurmt mich,** it rankles with me. ◆'W~fortsatz, m appendix. ◆'w~ig/'w~stichig, adj. worm-eaten.

Wurst [vurst]. I. f -/=e sausage; F: **jetzt geht's um die W.!** it's now or never! II. adv. F: **das ist mir (völlig) w.,** it's all the same to me; I couldn't care less (about that). ◆'w~waren, fpl (cold meats and) sausage products. ◆'W~zipfel, m sausage end.

Würstchen ['vyrstçən], n -s/- small sausage, esp. Frankfurter.

Würze ['vyrtsə], f -/-n seasoning; (also Fig:) spice.

Wurzel ['vurtsəl], f -/-n root; **W~n schlagen,** to take root; (esp. Fig: Pers.) to put down roots.

würz|en ['vyrtsən], v.tr. to season, spice (food); Fig: to add spice to (a story etc.). ◆'w~ig, adj. spicy, well-seasoned. ◆'W~stoff, m flavouring, seasoning.

wuschelig ['vuʃəliç], adj. fuzzy; (zerzaust) tousled. ◆'W~kopf, m mop of (fuzzy) hair.

Wust [vuːst], m -(e)s/no pl F: jumble.

wüst [vyːst], adj. (a) (öde) barren, desert (area etc.); (b) (ausschweifend) wild, dissolute (person, life etc.); **w~es Durcheinander,** utter confusion/chaos. ◆'W~e, f -/-n desert. ◆'W~ling, m -s/-e libertine; rake.

Wut [vuːt], f -/no pl fury, rage; **aus/vor W.,** with rage; **eine W. auf j-n haben,** to be furious with s.o.; **in W. geraten,** to fly into a rage. ◆'W~anfall, m fit of rage. ◆'W~ausbruch, m outburst of rage. ◆'w~entbrannt, adj. burning/filled with rage.

wüt|en ['vyːtən], v.i. (haben) (Pers., Fig: Sturm usw.) to rage; Fig: (Feuer usw.) to wreak havoc. ◆'w~end, adj. furious (**auf j-n,** with s.o.); fuming, irate; **j-n w. machen,** to enrage/infuriate s.o.

X

X, x [iks], n -/- (the letter) X, x. ◆'**X-Beine,** npl knock-knees. ◆'x-beinig, adj. knock-kneed. ◆'x-be'liebig, adj. F: any old. ◆'x-mal, adv. F: umpteen times. ◆'x-te(r, s), adj. F: umpteenth.

Xanthippe [ksan'tipə], f -/-n F: shrew.

Xeroko|pie [kseroko'piː], f -/-n Xerox copy. ◆x~'pieren, v.tr. to xerox (a document etc.).

Xylophon [ksylo'foːn], n -s/-e xylophone.

Y

Y, y ['ypsilɔn], *n -/-* (the letter) Y, y. | **Ypsilon** ['ypsilɔn], *n -(s)/-s* (the letter) Y.

Z

Z, z [tsɛt], *n -/-* (the letter) Z, z.

Zack|e ['tsakə], *f -/-n* point; tooth (of a saw, comb etc.); prong (of a fork; (*Bergs.*) jagged peak. ◆**'z~ig,** *adj.* (*a*) jagged (rocks etc.); (*b*) *F:* smart, dashing (soldier etc.); brisk (movements; music).

zaghaft ['tsa:khaft], *adj.* timid; (*zögernd*) hesitant. ◆**'Z~igkeit,** *f -/no pl* timidity.

zäh [tsɛ:], *adj.* (*a*) tough (meat, *Fig:* person etc.); *Fig:* tenacious (resistance etc.); (*b*) = **zähflüssig;** (*schleppend*) slow, laboured (conversation etc.). ◆**'z~flüssig,** *adj.* glutinous (liquid), viscous (oil); slow-moving (traffic). ◆**'Zähigkeit,** *f -/no pl* toughness (of a person); tenacity.

Zahl [tsa:l], *f -/-en* number; **in Z~en geschrieben,** written in figures; **in großer Z.,** in large numbers. ◆**'z~bar,** *adj.* payable. ◆**'z~en,** *v.tr.&vi.* (*haben*) to pay (a bill, debt, sum etc.); **z. bitte! ich möchte z.,** may I have the bill/ *N.Am:* check please? ◆**'Z~karte,** *f* paying-in form for postal giro. ◆**'z~los,** *adj.* innumerable. ◆**'z~reich,** *adj.* numerous; large (family, audience etc.). ◆**'Z~tag,** *m* payday. ◆**'Z~ung,** *f -/-en* payment; **etwas in Z. nehmen,** to take sth. in part exchange. ◆**'Z~ungsempfänger,** *m* payee. ◆**'z~ungsfähig,** *adj. Com:* (Firma) solvent. ◆**'Z~ungsmittel,** *n* means of payment. ◆**'z~ungsunfähig,** *adj.* unable to pay, insolvent. ◆**'Z~wort,** *n* numeral.

zähl|en ['tsɛ:lən], *v.* 1. *v.i.* (*haben*) (*a*) to count; (*b*) **z. zu+dat,** to belong to (a group etc.), rank among/with (the best etc.); (*c*) **auf j-n, etwas acc z.,** to count on s.o., sth. 2. *v.tr.* to count (people, money etc.); **seine Tage sind gezählt,** his days are numbered. ◆**'Z~er,** *m -s/- 1.* counter; *El: etc:* meter. 2. *Mth:* numerator. ◆**'Z~ung,** *f -/-en* count.

zahm [tsa:m], *adj.* tame.

zähmen ['tsɛ:mən], *v.tr.* (*a*) to tame (an animal); (*b*) *Fig:* to restrain (one's impatience etc.).

Zahn [tsa:n], *m -(e)s/¨e* tooth; *F:* **j-m auf den Z. fühlen,** to sound s.o. out; (*streng*) put s.o. through it. ◆**'Z~arzt,** *m* dentist. ◆**'z~ärztlich,** *adj.* dental (treatment etc.). ◆**'Z~belag,** *m* plaque. ◆**'Z~bürste,** *f* toothbrush. ◆**'z~en,** *v.i.* (*haben*) to cut teeth, be teething. ◆**'Z~ersatz,** *m* denture. ◆**'Z~fäule,** *f* dental decay/ caries. ◆**'z~fleisch,** *n* gum; *coll.* gums.

◆**'z~los,** *adj.* toothless. ◆**'Z~pasta,** *f* toothpaste. ◆**'Z~rad,** *n* gearwheel; (*für Ketten*) sprocket (wheel). ◆**'Z~radbahn,** *f* rack-railway. ◆**'Z~schmelz,** *m* enamel. ◆**'Z~schmerzen,** *mpl* toothache. ◆**'Z~spange,** *f* brace. ◆**'Z~stein,** *m* tartar. ◆**'Z~stocher,** *m* toothpick.

zähneknirschend ['tsɛ:nəknirʃənt], *adv.* under protest, with a bad grace.

Zander ['tsandər], *m -s/-* zander.

Zange ['tsaŋə], *f -/-n* (sugar etc.) tongs; *Tchn:* pliers; *Med:* forceps; *Z:* (lobster's etc.) pincers. ◆**'Z~ngeburt,** *f* forceps delivery.

Zank [tsaŋk], *m -(e)s/no pl* squabble, row (**um/über+acc,** over). ◆**'Z~apfel,** *m Fig:* bone of contention. ◆**'z~en,** *v.refl.* **sich z.,** to squabble, have a row (**um+acc,** over). ◆**'Z~e'rei,** *f -/-en* squabbling.

zänkisch ['tsɛŋkiʃ], *adj.* quarrelsome.

Zäpfchen ['tsɛpfçən], *n -s/- 1. Anat:* uvula. 2. *Med:* suppository.

Zapf|en ['tsapfən]. I. *m -s/- 1. Bot:* (pine etc.) cone. 2. bung, spigot (of a barrel). II. *v.,* *v.tr.* to tap, draw off (beer etc.). ◆**'Z~enstreich,** *m Mil:* last post. ◆**'Z~säule,** *f* petrol/*N.Am:* gas pump.

zappel|ig ['tsapəliç], *adj.* fidgety, wriggly. ◆**'z~n,** *v.i.* (*haben*) (Kind usw.) to fidget, wriggle.

Zar [tsa:r], *m -en/-en* tsar.

zart [tsa:rt], *adj.* tender (meat etc.); soft (skin, *Fig:* sound, colour etc.); gentle (touch etc.); (*empfindlich*) delicate (child, material etc.). ◆**'z~heit,** *adj.* hypersensitive. ◆**'Z~heit,** *f -/no pl* tenderness; softness; delicacy.

zärtlich ['tsɛ:rtliç], *adj.* affectionate. ◆**'Z~keit,** *f -/-en 1.* tenderness, affection. 2. *esp. pl* endearments; (*Liebkosungen*) caresses.

Zauber ['tsaubər], *m -s/no pl* magic; (*Bann*) spell; *Fig:* (Reiz, Faszination) charm (of a person). ◆**'Z~er,** *m -s/-* magician. ◆**'z~haft,** *adj.* enchanting, delightful. ◆**'Z~künstler,** *m* conjurer, magician. ◆**'z~n,** *v.* 1. *v.i.* (*haben*) to do magic/(*Zauberkünstler*) conjuring tricks. 2. *v.tr.* to conjure up (sth.). ◆**'Z~spruch,** *m* magic spell. ◆**'Z~stab,** *m* magic wand. ◆**'Z~trick,** *m* conjuring trick.

zaudern ['tsaudərn], *v.i.* (*haben*) to procrastinate.

Zaum [tsaum], *m -(e)s/¨e* bridle; *Fig:*

sich/seinen Zorn im Z. halten, to restrain oneself/one's anger.

Zaun ['tsaun], *m* -(e)s/-e fence; *Fig:* einen Streit vom Z. brechen, to start a quarrel. ◆**Z~gast**, *m* onlooker. ◆**Z~könig**, *m* wren. ◆**Z~pfahl**, *m* fence-post; *Fig:* Wink mit dem Z., broad hint.

Zebra ['tse:bra], *n* -s/-s Z: zebra. ◆**Z~streifen**, *n* zebra crossing.

Zech|e ['tseçə], *f* -/-n 1. (*Rechnung*) bill; *also Fig:* die Z. bezahlen müssen, to have to foot the bill. 2. *Min:* (esp. coal) pit, mine. ◆**z~en**, *v.i.* (haben) A: & Hum: to tipple, knock it back. ◆**Z~er**, *m* -s/- & Hum: tippler.

Zecke ['tsɛkə], *f* -/-n tick.

Zeh [tse:], *m* -s/-en toe. ◆**Z~e**, *f* -/-n 1. toe. 2. *Bot:* clove (of garlic). ◆**Z~ennagel**, *m* toenail. ◆**Z~enspitzen**, *fpl* auf Z., on tiptoe.

zehn [tse:n], *num.adj.* ten. ◆**Z~er**, *m* -s/- F: ten mark note. ◆**z~fach**, *adj.* tenfold; adv. ten times. ◆**z~jährig**, *adj.* ten-year-old (child etc.); ten-year (period etc.). ◆**Z~kampf**, *m Sp:* decathlon. ◆**z~mal**, *adv.* ten times. ◆**z~te(r, s)**, *num.adj.* tenth. ◆**Z~tel**, *n* -s/- tenth (part).

zehren ['tse:rən], *v.i.* (haben) (a) an j-s Kräften z., to sap s.o.'s strength; (h) (*Pers.*) von Ersparnissen usw. z., to live on savings etc.

Zeichen ['tsaiçən]. I. *n* -s/- sign; (*Wink usw.*) signal (zum Anfang usw., to start etc.); (b) (*Markierung*) mark; (c) (*Symbol*) sign (of the Zodiac, cross etc.). II. ◆**Z~**, *comb.fm.* drawing (board, pen, materials, paper, table etc.); *Sch:* art (teacher etc.). ◆**Z~erklärung**, *f* legend (on a map); key. ◆**Z~setzung**, *f* -/-en punctuation. ◆**Z~sprache**, *f* sign language. ◆**Z~trickfilm**, *m* cartoon film.

zeichn|en ['tsaiçnən]. I. *v. 1. v.tr.* (a) to draw (s.o., sth., a picture etc.); (b) (*kennz.*) to mark (laundry, trees etc.). 2. *v.i.* (haben) (a) to draw; (b) A: & Com: to sign. II. **Z~**, *n* -s/no pl drawing. ◆**Z~er**, *m* -s/- Art: & Ind: draughtsman. ◆**Z~ung**, *f* -/-en (a) drawing; (b) (*Kennz.*) markings.

Zeig|efinger ['tsaigəfiŋər], *m* -s/- forefinger, index finger. ◆**z~en**, *v. 1. v.tr.* (a) to show; (b) sich z., to appear; das wird sich z., we shall see. 2. *v.i.* (haben) to point. ◆**Z~er**, *m* -s/- pointer; (*Uhr:*) (watch/clock) hand. ◆**Z~estock**, *m* pointer.

Zeile ['tsailə], *f* -/-n (a) line; (b) (*Häuser:*) (long) row of houses. ◆**Z~nabstand**, *m* line spacing.

Zeisig ['tsaiziç], *m* -s/-e siskin.

Zeit [tsait]. I. *f* -/-en time; (a) *no pl* sich dat Z. für etwas acc nehmen, to make time for sth.; nimm/laß dir Z., take your time; das hat Z., that can wait; (b) mit der Z. gehen, to move with the times; in

der nächsten Z., in the near future; (c) (*Zeitpunkt*) zur Z., at present; in letzter Z., lately; von Z. zu Z., from time to time. II. **z.**, *prep.* + gen z. meines/seines/ihres Lebens, in my/his/her lifetime. III. ◆**Z~**, *comb.fm.* 1. (a) time (bomb, difference etc.); (b) (question, problem, lack etc.) of time. 2. *Com:* (*zeitweilig*) temporary (work etc.). ◆**Z~alter**, *n* age, era. ◆**Z~druck**, *m* in Z. sein/unter Z. stehen, to be pressed for time. ◆**z~gemäß**, *adj.* in keeping with the period; (*modern*) up-to-date; contemporary (views), topical (theme). ◆**Z~genosse**, *m* contemporary. ◆**z~genössisch**, *adj.* contemporary. ◆**Z~geschehen**, *n* das Z. current events. ◆**z~ig**, *adj.* in good time; z. aufstehen, to get up early. ◆**Z~lang**, f eine Z., for a while. ◆**z~lebens**, *adv.* all one's life. ◆**z~lich**, *adj.* in z~licher Reihenfolge, in chronological order; z. begrenzt sein, to have a time limit. ◆**z~los**, *adj.* timeless (beauty etc.). ◆**Z~lupe**, f in Z., in slow motion. ◆**Z~lupentempo**, *n* snail's pace, crawl. ◆**Z~not**, f in Z. sein, to be pressed for time. ◆**Z~punkt**, *m* time; (*Augenblick*) moment. ◆**Z~raffer**, *m* -s/- im Z., speeded up. ◆**z~raubend**, *adj.* time-consuming. ◆**Z~rechnung**, f calendar. ◆**Z~schrift**, f periodical; (*Illustrierte*) magazine. ◆**Z~verschwendung**, f waste of time. ◆**Z~vertreib**, *m* pastime. ◆**z~weilig**, *adj.* temporary. ◆**z~weise**, *adv.* at times. ◆**Z~wort**, *n* verb. ◆**Z~zeichen**, *n Rad:* time signal. ◆**Z~zünder**, *m* time fuse.

Zeitung ['tsaituŋ], *f* -/-en newspaper, F: paper. ◆**Z~shändler**, *m* newsagent. ◆**Z~spapier**, *n* newspaper.

Zell|e ['tsɛlə], *f* -/-n cell. ◆**Z~kern**, *m* nucleus. ◆**Z~stoff**, *m* cellulose.

Zellophan [tsɛlo'fa:n], *n* -s/no pl cellophane.

Zelt [tsɛlt], *n* -(e)s/-e tent. ◆**Z~bahn**, f canvas; (*Plane*) tarpaulin. ◆**Z~en**, *v.i.* (haben) to camp. ◆**Z~lager**, *n* camp. ◆**Z~platz**, *m* camp site.

Zement [tse'mɛnt], *m* -(e)s/-e cement. ◆**z~ieren** [-'ti:rən], *v.tr.* to cement.

zens|ieren [tsɛn'zi:rən], *v.tr.* (a) *Sch:* to mark (work); (b) to censor (a book, film). ◆**Z~ur** [-'zu:r], *f* -/-en 1. *Sch:* mark. 2. censorship.

Zenti|meter ['tsɛnti:me:tər], *m* centimetre. ◆**Z~ner**, *m* -s/- hundredweight.

zentral [tsɛn'tro:l]. I. *adj.* central; adv. gelegen, centrally situated. II. ◆**Z~**, *comb.fm.* central (committee, government etc.); *Geog:* Central (Asia etc.). ◆**Z~e**, f -/-n central/head office; (*Hauptquartier*) headquarters (of police etc.); *Tel:* telephone exchange. ◆**Z~heizung**, f central heating. ◆**z~i'sieren**, *v.tr.* to centralize (power etc.).

zentri|fugal [tsɛntrifu'gɑːl], *adj.* centrifugal. ◆**Z~fuge** ['~fuːgə], *f* -**/-n** Centr: centrifuge.

Zentrum ['tsɛntrum], *n* -**s/-tren** centre; (*Stadtz.*) town/city centre, *N.Am:* downtown.

Zepter ['tsɛptər], *n* -**s/-** sceptre.

zer|brechen, *v.tr. & i.* (*sein*) *irr.14* to break; F:r (*Freundschaft usw.*) to break up. ◆**z~lich**, *adj.* fragile.

zer|bröckeln, *v.tr. & i.* (*sein*) to crumble.

zer|drücken, *v.tr.* to crush (sth.); (*zu Brei*) to mash (potatoes etc.); F: to crumple (clothes).

Zeremonie [tseremo'niː], *f* -**/-n** ceremony. ◆**z~ell** [-moni'ɛl]. **I.** *adj.* ceremonial, formal. **II. Z.**, *n* -**s/-e** ceremonial.

zer|fahren, *adj.* (*Pers.*) distracted.

Zer|fall, *m* -**s/no pl** disintegration; decay (of buildings, F:r culture etc.). ◆**z~en. I.** *v.i.sep.irr.27* (*sein*) (*a*) to disintegrate; (*Gebäude usw.*) to fall into ruins; (*Ph: Atomkern, Fig: Reich usw.*) to decay; (*b*) (*sich teilen*) in drei Kapitel z., to be divided into three chapters. **II.** *adj.* tumbledown, in ruins.

zer|fetzen, *v.tr.* to tear (sth.) up/to pieces. ◆**z~t**, *adj.* torn (to pieces); Cl: tattered.

zer|fließen, *v.i.irr.31* (*sein*) (Eis, Fig: Geld) to melt (away); (Farben) to run, (Konturen) blur.

zer|gehen, *v.i.irr.36* (*sein*) to dissolve, (*schmelzen*) melt.

zer|kleinern, *v.tr.* to cut/chop up (meat etc.); to crush (rock etc.).

zer|klüftet, *adj.* deeply fissured (rock etc.).

zer|knirscht, *adj.* (*Pers.*) rueful, remorseful.

zer|knittern, *v.tr.* to crease (a dress).

zer|kochen, *v.tr. & i.* (*sein*) to overcook.

zer|kratzen, *v.tr.* to scratch (sth.), (*ganz*) cover (sth.) in scratches.

zer|leg|bar, *adj.* collapsible; leicht z., easy to dismantle. ◆**z~en**, *v.tr.* to take (sth.) apart; Cu: to carve up (an animal etc.).

zer|lumpt, *adj.* ragged, tattered (clothes); (beggar etc.) in rags.

zer|malmen, *v.tr.* to crush (s.o., sth.).

zer|mürben, *v.tr.* to wear down (s.o., s.o.'s resistance etc.). ◆**z~end**, *adj.* wearing, trying.

zer|platzen, *v.i.* (*sein*) to burst.

zer|quetschen, *v.tr.* to squash (a fly etc.), crush (s.o.'s leg etc.).

Zerrbild ['tsɛrbɪlt], *n* distorted picture.

zer|reiben, *v.tr.irr.12* to crush, (*zu Pulver*) pulverize (sth.).

zer|reißen, *v.irr.4* **I.** *v.tr.* (*a*) to tear up (a letter etc.); (*b*) to tear (stockings etc.). **2.** *v.i.* (*sein*) to tear; (Seil, Kette usw.) to break.

zerr|en ['tsɛrən], *v.* **1.** *v.i.* (*haben*) an etwas *dat* z., to tug at sth. **2.** *v.tr.* (*a*) to tug, drag (s.o., sth.); (*b*) sich *dat* eine

Sehne/einen Muskel z., to pull a tendon/muscle. ◆**Z~ung**, *f* Med: pull.

zer|rinnen, *v.i.irr.73* (*sein*) = zerfließen.

zer|rütten [tsɛr'rytən], *v.tr.* to ruin (s.o.'s nerves etc.), wreck (a marriage etc.).

zer|schellen, *v.i.* (*sein*) to be dashed to pieces.

zer|schlagen, *v.tr.irr.85* (*a*) to break, smash (china etc.); (*b*) sich z., (Plan usw.) to fall through; (Hoffnungen) to be shattered.

zer|schmettern, *v.tr.sep.* to smash, shatter (sth.).

zer|schneiden, *v.tr.sep.irr.59* to cut up (a cake etc.).

zer|setz|en, *v.tr.sep.* (*a*) to corrode (metal); (Leiche) sich z., to decompose; (*b*) Fig: to undermine (morale etc.). ◆**Z~ung**, *f* -**/no pl** (*a*) corrosion; decomposition; (*b*) Fig: undermining.

zer|splittern, *v.tr. & i.* (*sein*) to splinter; (Glas usw.) to shatter.

zer|springen, *v.i.irr.19* (*sein*) to shatter.

zer|stäuben, *v.tr.* to atomize, spray (a liquid, perfume etc.). ◆**Z~er**, *m* -**s/-** atomizer; spray.

zer|stör|en, *v.tr.* to destroy (sth.); to wreck (a marriage etc.). ◆**Z~er**, *m* -**s/-** destroyer. ◆**Z~ung**, *f* destruction.

zer|streu|en, *v.tr.* (*a*) to scatter, disperse (leaves, a crowd etc.); Fig: to dispel (fears, doubts etc.); (Menge) sich z., to disperse; (*b*) (*ablenken*) j-n/sich z., to take s.o.'s/one's mind off things; (*unterhalten*) to entertain s.o./oneself. ◆**z~t**, *adj.* (*a*) (*Pers.*) distracted; absent-minded, F: scatterbrained; (*b*) scattered (villages etc.). ◆**Z~theit**, *f* -**/no pl** absentmindedness. ◆**Z~ung**, *f* -**/-en** (*a*) *no pl* dispersal, scattering; Fig: dispelling; (*b*) (Unterhaltung) diversion; entertainment.

zer|stückeln, *v.tr.* to divide (sth.) up, dismember (a body).

zer|teilen, *v.tr.* to divide (sth.) up.

Zertifikat [tsɛrtifi'kɑːt], *n* -(e)s/-e certificate.

zer|treten, *v.tr.irr.105* to trample on (flowers, grass etc.).

zer|trümmern, *v.tr.sep.* to smash up (crockery etc.), wreck (a building etc.); to shatter (glass).

zer|zaus|en, *v.tr.sep.* to ruffle (hair etc.). ◆**z~t**, *adj.* dishevelled, tousled.

Zettel ['tsɛtəl], *m* -**s/-** piece/slip of paper; (Notizz.) note; (Handz.) leaflet.

Zeug [tsɔyk], *n* -(e)s/*no pl* F: (*a*) *usw.* Pej: stuff; (Kleider usw.) things; (*b*) F: (*Unsinn*) wirres Z. reden, to ramble, talk incoherently; (*c*) Fig: sich ins Z. legen, to go hard at it; to do one's utmost (für j-n, for s.o.); (*d*) (Anlage) er hat das Z. zum Arzt, he has the makings of a doctor.

Zeuge ['tsɔygə], *m* -**n/-n** witness. ◆**z~en**, *v.* **1.** *v.tr.* to reproduce (offspring); to father (a child). **2.** *v.i.* (*haben*) für: für/gegen j-n z., to give evidence for/against s.o.; (Sache) von etwas *dat* z., to testify to/show sth. ◆'Z~enaussage, f testimony. ◆'Z~enbank, f = witness box/N.Am: stand. ◆'Z~in, f -/-nen (female) witness. ◆'Z~nis, n -ses/-se (a) (Beweise) evidence; Jur: etc: testimony; Z. ablegen, to give evidence; (b) Com: testimonial; (c) Sch: report. ◆'Z~ung, f -/-en procreation, reproduction; fathering. ◆'z~ungsfähig, adj. sterile, impotent.

Zickzack ['tsiktsak], m -s/-e zigzag; im Z. laufen/verlaufen, to zigzag.

Ziege ['tsi:gə], f -/-n Z: goat. ◆'Z~nbock, m he-/F: billy goat. ◆'Z~nkäse, m goat's milk cheese. ◆'Z~npeter, m -s/- Med: mumps.

Ziegel ['tsi:gəl], m -s/- brick; (Dachz.) tile. ◆'Z~ei [-'lai], f -/-en brickworks. ◆'Z~stein, m brick.

ziehen ['tsi:ən], v.irr. 1. v.tr. (a) to pull (sth.); Med: to extract (a tooth); to draw (a card, lottery ticket, Fig: conclusions etc.); die Blicke auf sich acc z., to attract attention; Folgen nach sich dat z., to have consequences; etwas acc ins Lächerliche z., to turn sth. into a joke; (b) (züchten) to breed (cattle, pigs etc.); (c) sich z., to run, stretch (in die Ferne, into the distance); sich (in die Länge) z., to go on and on; (d) to draw (a line etc.). 2. v.i. (a) (+haben) to pull, (zerren) tug (an etwas dat, on/at sth.); an einer Pfeife/Zigarre z., to puff on a pipe/cigar; (b) (+sein) to move, go, (marschieren) march; (umherstreifen) to wander, roam; (auswandern) er zog zu seinen Kindern, he moved to live with his children; (c) (+haben) impers. es zieht, there is a draught/N.Am: draft; (d) (+haben) Cu: (Tee) to draw. ◆'Z~harmonika, f accordion. ◆'Z~ung, f -/-en draw (of a lottery).

Ziel [tsi:l], n -(e)s/-e 1. (a) (Reisez.) destination; Sp: finish; (c) Mil: etc: target. 2. (Zweck) aim, goal; sich etwas zum Z. setzen, to set oneself sth. as one's target. II. 'Z~, comb.fm. (a) target (group etc.); Sp: finishing (line etc.). ◆'z~bewußt, adj. purposeful. ◆'z~en, v.i. (haben) to aim (auf + acc, at). ◆'Z~fernrohr, n telescopic sight. ◆'Z~foto, n Sp: photofinish photograph. ◆'z~los, adj. aimless. ◆'Z~scheibe, f -/-n (practice) target; Fig: (Pers.) butt. ◆'z~strebig, adj. single-minded.

ziemlich ['tsi:mliç], adj. considerable (number, effort etc.); eine z~e Strecke, quite a distance; z. kalt, quite/rather/F: pretty cold; so z. alles, more or less everything; so z. das gleiche, much the same.

Zier- ['tsi:r-], comb.fm. ornamental (fish, garden, plant etc.). ◆'Z~de, f -/-n ornament. ◆'z~en, v.tr. to decorate, Lit: & Fig: adorn (sth.); Fig: (Namen

usw.) to grace (stir.); (b) sich z., to make a fuss. ◆'z~lich, adj. dainty; slight (build etc.). ◆'Z~lichkeit, f -/no pl daintiness.

Ziffer ['tsifər], f -/-n 1. numeral, digit. 2. Jur: clause, sub-section. ◆'Z~blatt, n dial (of a clock etc.).

zig [tsiç], inv.adj. F: umpteen. ◆'z~mal, adv.F: umpteen times.

Zigarette [tsiga'retə], f -/-n cigarette. ◆'Z~n-, comb.fm. cigarette (machine, paper, smoke etc.). ◆'Z~nstummel, m cigarette end.

Zigarillo [tsiga'rilo], m & n -s/-s small cigar, cigarillo.

Zigarre [tsi'garə], f -/-n cigar.

Zigeuner(in) [tsi'gɔynər(in)], m -s/- (f -/-nen) gipsy.

Zimmer ['tsimər]. I. n -s/- room. II. 'Z~-, comb.fm. room (number, service, temperature etc.); (b) indoor (aerial etc.). ◆'Z~mädchen, n chambermaid. ◆'Z~mann, m carpenter. ◆'z~n, v. 1. v.tr. to make (sth.) from wood. 2. v.i. (haben) to do carpentry, work in wood. ◆'Z~pflanze, f indoor/house plant. ◆'Z~vermittlung, f room/accommodation agency.

zimperlich ['tsimpərliç], adj. Pej: (a) (prüde) prudish, N.Am: prissy; (b) (feige) cowardly; sei nicht so z.! don't make such a fuss/be so soft!

Zimt [tsimt], m -(e)s/-e cinnamon.

Zink [tsiŋk], n -(e)s/no pl zinc.

Zinke ['tsiŋkə], f -/-n prong; tooth (of a comb etc.).

Zinn [tsin], n -(e)s/no pl 1. tin. 2. (Z~geschirr) pewter (ware). II. 'Z~-, comb.fm. (a) tin (mine, soldier etc.); (b) pewter (dish, plate etc.).

Zinnober [tsi'no:bər], m -s/- (Farbe) vermilion. ◆'z~rot, adj. vermilion.

Zins [tsins], m -es/-e(n) esp. pl Fin: Z~en, interest. ◆'Z~eszins, m compound interest. ◆'z~los, adj. interest-free. ◆'Z~fuß/'Z~satz, m interest rate.

Zipfel ['tsipfəl], m -s/- corner (of a cloth etc.); end of sausage etc.; (Spitze) tip. ◆'Z~mütze, f (long) pointed cap.

zirka ['tsirka], adv. about, approximate.

Zirkel ['tsirkəl], m -s/- pair of compasses.

Zirkul ation [tsirkulatsi'o:n], f -/-en circulation. ◆'z~ieren [-'li:rən], v.i. (haben) to circulate.

Zirkus ['tsirkus], m -/-se circus. ◆'Z~zelt, n circus tent, big top.

zisch eln ['tsifəln], v.tr. & i. (haben) to whisper (sth.). ◆'z~en, v.i. (haben) to hiss; (Fett usw.) to sizzle.

Zitadelle [tsita'delə], f -/-n citadel.

Zit at [tsi'ta:t], n -(e)s/-e quotation. ◆'z~ieren [-'ti:rən], v.tr. (a) to quote (s.o., sth.); (b) (vorladen) to summon (s.o.).

Zither ['tsitər], f -/-n zither.

Zitron at [tsitro'na:t], n -(e)s/no pl candied lemon peel. ◆Z~e [tsi'tro:nə], f /-en lemon. ◆Z~en-, comb.fm. lemon (tree, juice etc.). ◆'Z~enlimonade, f lemonade. ◆Z~enpresse, f lemon squeezer. ◆Z~ensäure, f citric acid.

Zitrusfrucht ['tsitrusfruxt], f citrus fruit.

zitt(e)rig ['tsit(ə)riç], adj. shaky; tremulous, quavering. ◆Z~ern, v.i. (haben) to tremble (vor + dat, with); (vor Kälte) to shiver; (Gebäude) to shake; (Stimme) to quaver; um j-n, etwas z., to be very worried about s.o. etc.

Zitze ['tsitsə], f /-n teat.

zivil [tsi'vi:l]. I. adj. a civil; (nicht militärisch) civilian (life, population etc.); (b) (anständig) reasonable (terms, prices etc.). II. Z~, n. s/no pl in Z., (Soldat usw.) in civilian/(Polizist) in plain clothes. III. Z~-, comb.fm. (a) civilian (authority, population, life etc.); (b) Jur: civil (court, law etc.). ◆Z~courage, f courage of one's convictions. ◆Z~dienst, m community service (for conscientious objectors). ◆'z~-en civilization [-ilizatsi'o:n], f /-en civilization. ◆Z~isati'onskrankheiten, fpl diseases of modern society. ◆Z~i'sieren, v.tr. to civilize (a people etc.). ◆Z~ist(in) [-i'list(in)], m -en/en (f /-nen) civilian.

zögern ['tsø:gərn], v.i. (haben) to hesitate; mit etwas dat z., to delay sth. ◆'z~d, adj. hesitant.

Zölibat [tsøli'ba:t], n -(e)s/no pl celibacy.

Zoll¹ [tsɔl], m -(e)s/- Meas: inch. ◆'Z~stock, m folding rule.

Zoll². I. m -(e)s/⸚e (Abgabe) (customs) duty. 2. no pl customs. II. 'Z~-, comb.fm. customs (declaration, frontier, union etc.). ◆Z~abfertigung, f customs clearance. ◆Z~amt, n customs house. ◆Z~beamte(r), m customs officer. ◆'z~frei, adj. duty-free. ◆Z~kontrolle, f customs examination. ◆'z~pflichtig, adj. dutiable (goods).

Zone ['tso:nə], f /-n zone.

Zoo [tso:], m -s/-s zoo. ◆z~'logisch, adj. zoological.

Zopf [tsɔpf], m -(e)s/⸚e pigtail; F: alter Z., antiquated view/custom.

Zorn [tsɔrn], m -(e)s/no pl anger. ◆'z~ig, adj. angry (auf j-n, with s.o.).

zott(el)ig ['tsɔt(əl)iç], adj. shaggy.

zu [tsu:]. I. prep. + dat to; zur Stadt hin, towards the town; zu beiden Seiten, on both sides; zu Weihnachten, at Christmas; zum ersten Mal, for the first time; zu Fuß/Pferd, on foot/horseback; zu etwas werden, to turn into/become sth.; j-n zum Vorbild nehmen, to take s.o. as a model; nehmen Sie Milch zum Kaffee? do you take milk with your coffee? er kommt zum Essen, he is coming for lunch; ein Lappen zum Putzen, a rag for cleaning; was sagst du zu dem Vorschlag? what do you say about/to the proposal? zum halben Preis, for half the price; drei zu eins, (Chancen) three to

one; Sp: (Ergebnis) three-one (3–1). II. adv. 1. zu alt, too old; zu sehr, too much. 2. F: (geschlossen) closed, shut.

zu'aller'erst, adv. first of all. ◆z~'letzt, adv. last of all.

Zubehör ['tsu:bəhø:r], n -(e)s/-e fittings; (zusätzlich) accessories.

zubereit|en, v.tr.sep. to prepare (a meal etc.). ◆Z~ung, f /no pl preparation.

'zubringen, v.tr.sep.irr.16 to spend (time, the night etc.). ◆'Z~er, m -s/-(Z~straße) feeder road.

Zucchini ['tsu:ki:ni], pl /- courgette.

Zucht [tsuxt]. I. f /-en 1. (a) no pl (Züchten) Z: breeding; Bot: cultivation; (b) (Rasse) breed. 2. no pl (Disziplin) discipline; j-n in Z. halten, to keep s.o. under control. II. 'Z~-, comb.fm. breeding (bull, animal etc.). ◆'Z~haus, n (long-stay) prison, N.Am: penitentiary.

züchten ['tsyçtən], v.tr. to breed (animals); to grow (roses etc.); to cultivate (pearls, bacteria etc.). ◆'Z~er, m -s/-breeder; grower (of roses etc.).

◆'z~igen, v.tr. to beat, Lit: chastise (s.o.). ◆'Z~igung, f /-en corporal punishment.

zuck|en ['tsukən], v.tr. & i. (haben) to twitch; (Blitz, Fig: Gedanke) to flash; mit den Achseln z., to shrug one's shoulders. ◆'Z~ung, f /-en twitch.

zücken ['tsykən], v.tr. to draw (a sword etc.); Hum: to whip out (one's cheque book etc.).

Zucker ['tsukər], m -s/no pl sugar; Med: F: Z. haben, to be diabetic. ◆'Z~dose, f sugar basin/bowl. ◆'Z~guß, m icing, N.Am: frosting. ◆'Z~krank, adj. diabetic. ◆'z~n, v.tr. to sugar (coffee etc.). ◆'Z~rohr, n sugar cane. ◆'Z~rübe, f sugar beet. ◆'Z~stange, f stick of rock. ◆'z~süß, adj. (a) as sweet as sugar; (b) Pej: sugary (smile etc.). ◆'Z~watte, f candyfloss. ◆'Z~würfel, m sugar lump, lump of sugar. ◆'Z~zange, f sugar tongs.

'zudecken, v.tr.sep. to cover up (s.o., sth.).

'zudrehen, v.tr.sep. to turn off (a tap etc.).

'zudringlich, adj. pushing, pushy; z. werden, to make advances.

zuei'nander, adv. to one another; z. gehören, to belong together.

'zuerkennen, v.tr.sep.irr.51 to award (a right, damages etc.) (j-m, to s.o.).

zu'erst, adv. (a) first; (b) (anfangs) at first, to start with.

Zufahrt, f access; (Einfahrt) drive. ◆'Z~sstraße, f access road.

Zufall, m coincidence. ◆'z~en, v.i.sep.irr.27 (sein) (a) (Tür usw.) to slam shut; (b) j-m z., (Aufgabe usw.) to fall to s.o. ◆'Z~streffer, m lucky hit, F: fluke.

'zufällig, adj. accidental; weißt du z., wo

er ist? do you know by any chance where he is?

'Zuflucht, f refuge (**vor** + dat, from). ◆'**Z~sort,** m (place of) refuge.

'Zufluß, m flow, supply (of water); influx (of capital etc.); (*Nebenfluß*) tributary.

zu'folge, prep. + dat (*laut*) according to.

zu'frieden, adj. content; attrib. contented (face, person etc.). ◆**Z~heit,** f -/no pl contentment. ◆**z~stellen,** v.tr. to satisfy (s.o., s.o.'s wishes etc.); **z~stellende Antwort,** satisfactory answer.

'zufrieren, v.i.sep.irr.32 (sein) to freeze over.

'zufügen, v.tr.sep. to inflict (sth.) (j-m, on s.o.); **j-m Leid z.,** to do s.o. harm.

'Zufuhr f -/-en supply (*Nachschub*) supplies; *Meteor:* influx (of cold air etc.).

'zuführen, v.sep. **1.** v.tr. j-m, einem Gebäude, einer Stadt usw. etwas z., to supply s.o., a building, town etc. with sth. **2.** v.i. (haben) (*Straße*) **z.** auf + acc, to lead to (a town etc.).

Zug [tsu:k], m -(e)s/-e **1.** (*Bahn*) train. **2.** (*Kolonne*) column; (*Umzug*) procession; *Mil:* platoon. **3.** (*Ziehen*) (a) pull (**nach unten usw.,** downwards etc.); (b) *Orn: etc:* migration. **4.** (*Vorrichtung*) (bell, light etc.) pull. **5.** (*Luftzug*) draught, *N.Am:* draft (of air/a chimney). **6.** (a) (*Schluck*) gulp; **in einem Z.,** in one gulp; *Fig:* in one go; (b) (*Atemzug*) breath; *F:* **in den letzten Z~en liegen,** to be at one's last gasp; *Fig:* **etwas in vollen Z~en genießen,** to enjoy sth. to the full; (c) **Z.** an einer Pfeife/Zigarette usw., puff at a pipe, cigarette etc. **7.** (a) usu.pl (*Gesichtsz~e*) features; (b) (*Charakterzug*) characteristic, trait. **8.** (a) (beim Schreiben/Schwimmen) stroke; (b) (Spiel:) move; *Fig:* **zum Z. kommen,** to get a chance. ◆**Z~brücke,** f drawbridge. ◆**z~ig,** adj. draughty. ◆**Z~kräftig,** adj. with popular/a strong appeal. ◆**Z~luft,** f draught, *N.Am:* draft. ◆**Z~maschine,** f tractor. ◆**Z~verkehr,** m train/rail services. ◆**Z~vogel,** m migratory bird.

'Zugabe, f **1.** *Com:* free gift. **2.** *Mus:* encore.

'Zugang, m (a) access (**zu** + dat, to); (b) (*Eingang*) entrance.

zugänglich ['tsu:gɛnliç], adj. accessible, (*offen*) open (+ dat to); (*Pers.*) approachable.

'zugeben, v.tr.sep.irr.35 (a) to give (sth.) as a bonus/*Com:* free gift; *Cu:* to add (salt etc.); (b) (*gestehen*) to admit.

'zugehen, v.i.sep.irr.36 (sein) (a) **auf** j-n, **etwas** acc z., to walk up to/also *Fig:* approach s.o., sth.; **dem Ende z.,** to draw to a close; (b) *F:* (*Tür usw.*) to shut; (c) v.impers. **es ging lebhaft zu,** things went with a swing.

'zugehörig, adj. belonging to (it); matching (colour etc.). ◆**Z~keit,** f -/no pl

membership (**zu** + dat, of).

'zugeknöpft, adj. *F:* tight-lipped, reserved.

Zügel ['tsy:gəl], m -s/- rein. ◆**z~los,** adj. unrestrained; (*unzüchtig*) licentious. ◆**Z~losigkeit,** f -/no pl lack of restraint; licentiousness. ◆**z~n,** v.tr. to rein in (a horse); *Fig:* to check, restrain (oneself, one's temper etc.).

'Zugeständnis, n concession (**an** + acc, to).

'zugestehen, v.tr.sep.irr.100 (u) **j-m ein Recht,** *Com:* **Rabatt usw. z.,** to grant s.o. a right, *Com:* discount etc.; (b) z., **daß ...,** to admit that ...

zügig ['tsy:giç], adj. swift, rapid.

zu'gleich, adv. at the same time.

'zugreifen, v.i.sep.irr.43 (haben) (a) (*sich festhalten*) to grab hold; (b) (*bei einem Angebot*) to jump at it; (*beim Essen*) **bitte greifen Sie zu,** please help yourself.

zu'grunde, adv. (a) z. **gehen,** (*Pers.*) to be ruined; (*sterben*) to die; **eine Firma usw. z. richten,** to ruin a firm etc.; (b) **etwas** dat z. **liegen,** to be the basis of sth.

zu'gunsten, prep. + gen in favour of.

zu'gute, adv. **j-m etwas z. halten,** to make s.o. due allowance for sth.; **j-m, etwas** dat z. **kommen,** to prove beneficial to/benefit s.o., sth.

'zuhalten, v.tr.sep.irr.45 **1.** v.tr. to keep (sth.) shut; **sich** dat **die Nase z.,** to hold one's nose. **2.** v.i. (haben) **auf etwas** acc z., to make for sth.

'Zuhälter, m -s/- pimp.

Zuhause [tsu'hauzə], n -s/no pl home.

Zu'hilfenahme, f -/no pl use (as an aid); **unter Z. von** + dat, with the aid of.

'zuhör|en, v.i.sep. (haben) to listen (**j-m, etwas** dat, to s.o., sth.). ◆**Z~er,** m listener. ◆**Z~erschaft,** f -/no pl audience.

'zujubeln, v.i.sep. (haben) **j-m z.,** to cheer s.o.

'zukleben, v.tr.sep. to seal (a letter etc.).

'zuknöpfen, v.tr.sep. to button up (a coat etc.).

'zukommen, v.i.sep.irr.53 (sein) (a) **auf j-n z.,** to come towards/approach s.o.; **die Dinge auf sich** acc z. **lassen,** to take things as they come; (b) **j-m etwas z. lassen,** to send s.o. sth.; (c) (*gebühren*) **j-m z.,** to be befitting for s.o.

Zukunft ['tsu:kunft], f -/no pl future. ◆**Z~saussichten,** fpl fears/prospects for the future. ◆**Z~smusik,** f *F:* pie in the sky. ◆**z~sweisend,** adj. forward-looking.

'zukünftig, adj. future; adv. in future.

'Zulage, f (additional) allowance, bonus.

'zulass|en, v.tr.sep.irr.57 (a) to allow, permit (sth.); (*dulden*) to tolerate (injustice etc.); (b) to admit, accept (s.o.) (**als Mitglied usw.,** as a member etc.); to license, register (a motor vehicle, s.o. as a doctor etc.); (c) *F:* to leave (a window etc.)

shut. ◆'Z~ung, f admission (zum Studium usw., to follow a course etc.); authorization, licensing; Aut: registration.

'zulässig, adj. permissible.

'Zulauf, m großen Z. haben, to be very popular. ◆'z~en, v.i.irr.58 (sein) (a) z. auf + acc, (Pers.) to run towards (s.o., sth.); (Straße, Weg) to lead to (sth.); (b) die Katze ist uns zugelaufen, the cat just came to us/adopted us; (c) spitz z., to end in a point.

'zulegen, v.sep. F: 1. v.tr. sich dat ein Auto usw. z., to get oneself a car etc. 2. v.i. (haben) to get moving.

zu'leide, adv. j-m etwas z. tun, to harm/hurt s.o.

'zuleiten, v.tr.sep. (a) to supply (water, electricity etc.) (einer Fabrik usw., to a factory etc.); (b) to pass on (a message etc.) (j-m, to s.o.).

zu'letzt, adv. (a) last; (b) (schließlich) finally; (c) nicht z. wegen, weil ..., not least because ...

zu'liebe, adv. ich tat es ihm z., I did it for his sake.

zum [tsum], prep. = zu dem.

'zumachen, v.sep. 1. v.tr. to shut, close (a door etc.); to do up (a coat etc.). 2. v.i. (haben) to shut.

zu'mal, conj. especially as.

zu'meist, adv. mostly, mainly.

zu'mindest, adv. at least.

zumut|bar ['tsu:mu:tba:r], adj. reasonable (load etc.). ◆z~e [tsu'mu:tə], adv. ihm ist traurig z., he feels sad. ◆z~en ['tsu:mu:tən], v.tr.sep. j-m etwas z., to expect/ask sth. of s.o.; sich dat zuviel z., to take on too much. ◆'Z~ung, f -/no pl (unreasonable) demand.

zu'nächst, adv. at first.

'Zunahme, f -/-n increase (gen/an + dat, in).

'Zuname, m surname.

zünd|en ['tsyndən], v.tr. & i. (haben) to ignite; Fig: eine z~ende Rede, a rousing speech. ◆'Z~er, m -s/- fuse, detonator. ◆'Z~holz, n match. ◆'Z~kerze, f sparking plug. ◆'Z~schlüssel, m ignition key. ◆'Z~schnur, f fuse. ◆'Z~ung, f -/-en ignition.

zunehmen, v.i.sep.irr.69 (haben) (a) to increase (an + dat, in); (b) (Pers.) (an Gewicht) z., to put on weight. ◆'z~d, adj. (a) increasing (influence etc.); z~der Mond, waxing moon; (b) adv. increasingly.

'zuneig|en, v.i.sep. (haben) einer Ansicht usw. z., to incline to an opinion etc. ◆'Z~ung, f fondness, affection.

zünftig ['tsynftiç], adj. professional; F: (richtig) proper, pukkah; sound (thrashing etc.).

Zunge ['tsuŋə], f -/-n tongue. ◆'Z~nbrecher, m tongue-twister. ◆'z~nfertig, adj. glib.

zu'nichte, adv. Pläne usw. z. machen, to ruin plans etc.

zu'nutze, adv. sich dat etwas z. machen, to take advantage/(verwenden) make use of sth.

zu'oberst, adv. at the top; on top.

'zupacken, v.i.sep. (haben) (a) to grab hold; (b) (arbeiten) to get/knuckle down to it.

zupfen ['tsupfən], v.tr. to pluck (eyebrows, Mus: a string etc.); to pull up (weeds etc.). ◆'Z~instrument, n plucked instrument.

zur [tsu:r], prep. = zu der.

'zurechnungsfähig, adj. of sound mind, sane.

zurecht|finden [tsu'rεçtfindən], v.refl.sep. irr.9 sich z., to find one's way about/around. ◆z~kommen, v.i.sep.irr.53 (sein) (a) to cope (mit j-m, etwas dat, with s.o., sth.); (b) (rechtzeitig) (gerade noch) z., to arrive just in time. ◆z~legen, v.tr.sep. to put/place (sth.) ready. ◆z~machen, v.tr.sep. F: to get (a meal, bed etc.) ready, prepare (a salad etc.); sich z., to get oneself ready. ◆z~weisen, v.tr.sep.irr.70 to reprimand (s.o.). ◆'Z~weisung, f -/-en reprimand.

'zureden, v.i.sep. (haben) j-m z., to try to persuade s.o.

'zurichten, v.tr.sep. (a) to prepare (a meal etc.); (b) j-n übel z., to beat s.o. up.

zurück [tsu'ryk]. I. adv. (a) back; (b) F: (im Rückstand) behind. II. Z., n es gibt kein Z., there is no going back. ◆z~behalten, v.tr.sep.irr.45 to keep back (money etc.). ◆z~bekommen, v.tr.sep.irr.53 to get (sth.) back. ◆z~bleiben, v.i.sep.irr.12 (sein) to stay behind/hinter j-m z., to fall/drop behind s.o.; hinter den Erwartungen z., not to come up to expectations. ◆z~bringen, v.tr.sep.irr.16 to take/bring (sth.) back. ◆z~drängen, v.tr.sep. to push/force back (s.o., sth.). ◆z~erobern, v.tr.sep. to recapture (a town etc.). ◆z~erstatten, v.tr.sep. to refund (s.o.'s expenses). ◆z~fahren, v.sep.irr.26 1. v.i. (sein) to return. 2. v.tr. to drive (s.o., a car etc.) back. ◆z~fallen, v.i.sep.irr.27 (sein) to fall back/(Sp: Läufer usw.) behind; Fig: in alte Gewohnheiten usw. z., to relapse into old habits etc. ◆z~finden, v.i.sep.irr.9 (haben) to find one's way back. ◆z~fordern, v.tr.sep. to ask for (sth.) back, reclaim (one's property). ◆z~führen, v.tr.sep. (a) to lead/take (s.o.) back; (b) etwas auf seinen Ursprung z., to trace sth. back to its origins. ◆z~geben, v.tr.sep.irr.35 to return (sth.), give (sth.) back. ◆z~geblieben, adj. backward; geistig z., mentally retarded. ◆z~gehen, v.i.sep.irr.36 (sein) (a) to go back; Fig: (herstammen) es geht auf seine Kindheit

zurück, it goes back to his childhood; (b) (abnehmen) to go down; (Einnahmen usw.) to fall off. ◆**z~gezogen,** adj. secluded, retired; adv. **z. leben,** to live a secluded existence. ◆**z~halten,** v.sep.irr.45 **1.** v.tr. to hold (s.o., sth.) back; to keep (anger etc.) in check, restrain (feelings); **sich z.,** to restrain oneself. **2.** v.i. (haben) **mit etwas dat z.,** to withhold sth. ◆**z~haltend,** adj. restrained; (reserviert) reserved. ◆**Z~haltung,** f /no pl restraint; reserve. ◆**z~kehren,** v.i.sep. (sein) to return. ◆**z~kommen,** v.i. sep.irr.53 (sein) to come/get back; to return (**nach Hause,** home). ◆**z~lassen,** v.tr.sep.irr.57 to leave (s.o., sth.) behind. ◆**z~legen,** v.tr.sep. (a) to put (sth.) back; (b) (beiseitelegen) to put aside, put by (money); (c) (hinter sich bringen) to cover (a distance etc.). ◆**z~liegen,** v.i.sep.irr.62 (haben) (a) Sp: **zehn Sekunden usw. z.,** to be ten seconds etc. behind; (b) **das liegt schon lange zurück,** that was a long time ago. ◆**z~nehmen,** v.tr.sep.irr.69 to take back (goods, a remark etc.); to withdraw (an offer etc.). ◆**z~rufen,** v.sep.irr.74 **1.** v.tr. to call (s.o.) back; **j-m etwas ins Gedächtnis z.,** to remind s.o. of sth. **2.** v.i. (haben) Tel: to call back. ◆**z~schrecken,** v.i.sep. (sein) to start back, recoil (in fright); to flinch (**vor** + dat, from); **er schreckt vor nichts zurück,** he stops at nothing. ◆**z~setzen,** v.tr.sep. (a) to put (sth.) back (in its place); to move (a table etc.) back; Aut: to reverse (a car etc.); (b) (benachteiligen) to place (s.o.) at a disadvantage. ◆**z~stehen,** v.i. sep.irr.100 (haben) (a) (Gebäude usw.) to be set back; (b) **hinter j-m z.,** to be inferior/take second place to s.o. ◆**z~stellen,** v.tr.sep. (a) to put (sth.) back (in its place); (b) (reservieren) to reserve an article etc.; (c) (verschieben) to postpone (plans etc.); (beiseite legen) to set (personal wishes etc.) on one side. ◆**z~treten,** v.i.sep.irr.105 (sein) (a) (Pers.) to step back (**von** + dat, from); (b) (von seinem Amt) **z.,** to resign (one's post); (c) Fig: **hinter etwas** dat **z.,** to take second place to sth. ◆**z~weichen,** v.i.sep.irr.86 (sein) to step(/ängstlich) shrink back; (Hochwasser usw.) to recede. ◆**z~weisen,** v.tr.sep.irr.70 (a) to turn (s.o.) away/(an der Grenze usw.) back; (b) (ablehnen) to refuse, reject (an offer, a request etc.). ◆**z~zahlen,** v.tr.sep. to pay back (an amount); to repay (a loan etc.). ◆**z~zahlung,** f repayment. ◆**z~ziehen,** v.tr.sep.irr.113 (a) to pull (sth.) back; to withdraw (one's hand etc., Mil: troops); **sich z.,** to withdraw; to retire (**vom Geschäft,** from business); Mil: to retreat; (b) (rückgängig machen) to withdraw (a statement, an offer, application etc.); Jur: to drop (an action etc.).

'Zuruf, m shout. ◆**'z~en,** v.tr.sep.irr.74 **j-m etwas z.,** to shout sth. to s.o.

Zusage ['tsuːzaːgə], f -/-n (a) acceptance (of an invitation); (b) (Versprechen) promise. ◆**'z~n,** v.sep. **1.** v.tr. (a) **j-m Hilfe usw. z.,** to promise s.o. help etc. **2.** v.i. (haben) (a) to accept (an/the invitation); (b) (gefallen) **j-m z.,** (of food etc.) to agree (**mit etwas** dat, with); (c) (of weather, climate etc.) to agree/suit s.o.

zusammen [tsu'zamən], adv. (a) together; (b) (insgesamt) in all, altogether; **das macht 10 Mark,** altogether that makes 10 marks. ◆**Z~arbeit,** f co-operation. ◆**z~arbeiten,** v.i.sep. (haben) to co-operate (**an etwas** dat, on sth.). ◆**z~bauen,** v.tr.sep. to assemble (a radio etc.). ◆**z~beißen,** v.tr.sep.irr.4 to clench (one's teeth). ◆**z~bleiben,** v.i.sep.irr.12 to stay together. ◆**z~brechen,** v.i.sep.irr.14 (sein) (Gerüst, Brücke, Pers. usw.) to collapse; (Pers., Verhandlungen usw.) to break down; (Verkehr) to come to a standstill. ◆**z~bringen,** v.tr.sep.irr.16 (a) to bring together, unite (people); (b) to find (money). ◆**Z~bruch,** m collapse, breakdown (of negotiations, a system etc.); (Nervenz.) (nervous) breakdown. ◆**z~fallen,** v.i.sep.irr.27 (sein) (a) to collapse; (b) (Pers.) (schwächer werden) to become enfeebled; (c) (gleichzeitig geschehen) to coincide; (zum Teil) overlap; (Termine) to clash. ◆**z~fassen,** v.tr.sep. (a) (vereinigen) to combine, unite (clubs etc.) (**zu** + dat, in); (b) to summarize (a speech etc.); **z~fassend läßt sich feststellen, daß ...,** to sum up it can be said that ... ◆**Z~fassung,** f **1.** combination. **2.** summing-up, summary. ◆**z~finden,** v.refl.sep.irr.9 **sich z.,** to come together, meet. ◆**z~fließen,** v.i.sep.irr.31 to flow together/into one another. ◆**Z~fluß,** m confluence. ◆**z~fügen,** v.tr.sep. to join (parts) together. ◆**z~führen,** v.tr.sep. to bring (people) together. ◆**z~gehören,** v.i.sep. (haben) to belong together; (zueinander passen) to match, go together. ◆**z~gesetzt,** adj. Gram: compound (word); complex (sentence). ◆**z~halt,** m cohesion; Fig: solidarity. ◆**z~halten,** v.sep.irr.45 **1.** v.tr. to hold (sth.) together, keep (people) together. **2.** v.i. (haben) (Freunde usw.) to stick together. ◆**Z~hang,** m connection; (im Text) context; **der Satz ist aus dem Z. gerissen,** the sentence is out of context. ◆**z~hängen,** v.i.sep.irr.46 (haben) to be connected. ◆**z~hanglos,** adj. disjointed; incoherent. ◆**z~klappbar,** adj. collapsible. ◆**z~klappen,** v.sep. **1.** v.tr. to fold up (a chair etc.), close (a knife etc.). **2.** v.i. (sein) F: (Pers.) to crack up. ◆**z~kommen,** v.i.sep.irr.53 (sein) (Freunde usw.) to meet, get together. ◆**z~kunft,** f -/-e meeting, get-together. ◆**z~laufen,** v.i.sep.irr.58 (sein)

(*Menschen*) to come together, gather; (*Ströme, Linien usw.*) to meet, (*Straßen*) converge. ◆z~**legen**, *v.sep.* 1. *v.tr.* (*vereinigen*) to combine (classes etc.), amalgamate (businesses etc.); to pool (money, ideas etc.). 2. *v.i.* (*haben*) to club together. ◆z~**nehmen**, *v.tr.sep.irr.69* (*a*) to collect (one's thoughts); to summon up (strength, courage); (*b*) sich z., to pull oneself together; (*c*) alles zusammengenommen, all things considered. ◆z~**passen**, *v.i.sep.* (*haben*) to match, go together; (*Menschen*) to suit one another. ◆z~**prallen**, *v.i.sep.* (*sein*) to collide, crash. ◆z~**reißen**, *v.refl.sep.irr.4* F: sich z., to pull oneself together. ◆z~**schlagen**, *v.tr.sep.85* F: to smash up (furniture etc.), beat (s.o.) up. ◆z~**schließen**, *v.refl.sep.irr.31* sich z., to join forces; (*Firmen*) to merge. ◆Z~**schluß**, *m* amalgamation; Com: merger; Pol: union. ◆z~**schreiben**, *v.tr.sep.irr.12* to write (sth.) in one word. ◆z~**schrumpfen**, *v.i.sep.* (*sein*) to shrivel up. ◆Z~**sein**, *n* get-together. ◆z~**setzen**, *v.tr.sep.* (*a*) to put together, assemble (parts, a model etc.); sich z. aus + *dat*, to be composed/made up of (sth.); (*b*) (*Pers.*) sich z., (*sich treffen*) to get together, meet. ◆Z~**setzung**, *f -/-en* 1. assembly. 2. composition. ◆Z~**spiel**, *n* (*a*) Sp: etc: teamwork; (*b*) interaction (of forces etc.). ◆z~**stellen**, *v.tr.sep.* to put together (sth.); to assemble (a collection etc.); to compile (a list, book etc.). ◆Z~**stellung**, *f* putting together; assembly; compilation. ◆z~**stoß**, *m* 1. Aut: etc: crash, collision. 2. F: (*Auseinandersetzung*) clash. ◆z~**stoßen**, *v.i.sep.irr.103* (*sein*) (*Autos usw.*) to collide. ◆z~**stürzen**, *v.i.sep.* (*sein*) to collapse. ◆z~**tragen**, *v.tr.sep.irr.85* to collect (material etc.). ◆z~**treffen**, *v.i.sep.irr.104* (*a*) mit alten Bekannten usw. z., to meet up with old friends etc.; (*b*) (*Ereignisse usw.*) to coincide. ◆z~**treten**, *v.i.sep.irr.105* (*sein*) to assemble, meet. ◆z~**wachsen**, *v.i.sep.irr.107* (*sein*) to grow together; (*Wunde*) to heal. ◆z~**zählen**, *v.tr.sep.* to add up (figures etc.). ◆z~**ziehen**, *v.sep.irr.113* 1. *v.tr.* (*a*) to pull/draw (a loop etc.) together; sich z., to contract, (*schrumpfen*) shrink; (*b*) to add up (figures etc.), to concentrate, mass (troops etc.). 2. *v.i.* (*sein*) F: mit j-m z., to move in with s.o. ◆z~**zucken**, *v.i.sep.* (*sein*) to give a start; (*vor Schmerz*) to wince.

Zusatz. I. *m* (*a*) addition; (*b*) (*also* **Z~stoff**) additive. II. '**Z~**-, *comb.fm.* additional (clause etc.); supplementary (agreement, insurance etc.). **zusätzlich** ['tsuːtsɛtslɪç], *adj.* additional, extra; *adv.* in addition.

'**zuschaue|n**, *v.i.sep.* (*haben*) = zusehen. ◆'**Z~r(in)**, *m -s/- (f -/-nen)* onlooker, (*Beistehender*) bystander; Sp: etc: spectator; Th: etc: member of the audience. ◆'**Z~raum**, *m* auditorium.

'**zuschicken**, *v.tr.sep.* to send (a letter, goods etc.) (j-m, to s.o.).

zuschießen, *v.sep.irr.31* 1. *v.i.* (*sein*) auf j-n z., to shoot/rush towards s.o. 2. *v.tr.* (*a*) F: to contribute (money); (*b*) Fb: to shoot, pass (the ball) (j-m, to s.o.).

Zuschlag, *m* 1. (*Gebühr*) surcharge; Rail: etc: supplementary fare, supplement. 2. (*zum Gehalt usw.*) bonus. 3. (*bei Versteigerungen*) knocking down. ◆'**z~en**, *v.sep.irr.85* 1. *v.tr.* (*a*) to shut, (*mit Wucht*) slam shut (a door, book etc.); (*mit Nägeln*) to nail down (a crate etc.). (*b*) Sp: to hit (the ball) (j-m, to s.o.). 2. *v.i.* (*haben*) (*a*) to hit out; (*Feind, Schicksal usw.*) to strike; (*b*) (*Tür usw.*) to slam shut. ◆'**Z~karte**, *f* supplementary fare ticket. ◆'**z~pflichtig**, *adj.* subject to a supplement.

zuschließen, *v.tr.sep.irr.31* to lock.

zuschnappen, *v.i.sep.* (*a*) (*sein*) to snap/click shut; (*b*) (*haben*) (*Hund*) to snap viciously.

zuschneiden, *v.tr.sep.irr.59* to cut (timber etc.) to size; to cut out (a suit, dress etc.); Fig: auf etwas *acc* zugeschnitten, tailormade for sth.

zuschnüren, *v.tr.sep.* to tie up (a parcel, shoes etc.).

zuschrauben, *v.tr.sep.* to screw (a lid etc.) tight, screw on the lid of (a bottle etc.).

zuschreiben, *v.tr.sep.irr.12* j-m etwas *acc* z., to attribute sth. to s.o.; das hast du dir selbst zuzuschreiben, you only have yourself to blame for that.

Zuschrift, *f* reply (auf eine Annonce usw., to an advertisement etc.).

zu'schulden, *adv.* sich *dat* etwas z. kommen lassen, to do wrong, F: blot one's copybook.

Zuschuß, *m* allowance; (*staatlicher*) Z~, subsidy.

zuschütten, *v.tr.sep.* (*a*) to fill in (a ditch etc.); (*b*) F: to add (water etc.).

zusehen, *v.i.sep.irr.92* (*haben*) (*a*) to look on, watch; bei genauerem/näherem Z., on closer examination; (*b*) (*aufpassen*) z., daß ..., to see/take care that ... ◆'**z~ds**, *adv.* noticeably, visibly.

zusein, *v.i.sep.irr.93* (*sein*) to be shut/closed.

zusetzen, *v.sep.* 1. *v.tr.* (*a*) to add (sth.) (einem Getränk usw., to a drink etc.); (*b*) einbüßen) to lose (one's money). 2. *v.i.* (*haben*) j-m z., (i) (*Pers.*) to go on at s.o.; (*plagen*) to pester/plague s.o.; (ii) (*Krankheit*) to take it out of s.o.; (j-s Tod usw.) to affect (s.o.) deeply.

zusichern, *v.tr.sep.* j-m etwas z., to promise s.o. sth. ◆'**Z~ung**, *f* promise, guarantee.

'**zuspielen**, v.tr.sep. Sp: to pass (the ball) (j-m, to s.o.).

'**zuspitzen**, v.tr.sep. to sharpen (sth.); **sich z.**, to come to a point; Fig: (Lage usw.) to worsen, get critical.

'**zusprechen**, v.tr. & i.sep.irr.14 (haben) (a) j-m Mut/Trost z., to give s.o. (words of) encouragement/comfort; (b) (genießen) **dem Wein/Essen z.**, to do justice to the wine/food.

'**Zuspruch**, m 1. words (esp of encouragement). 2. **großen Z. haben**, to be very popular.

'**Zustand**, m (a) no pl condition, state; (b) usu.pl **unhaltbare Z~e**, intolerable conditions/state of affairs. ◆**z~e** [tsu'ʃtandə], adv. etwas z. bringen, to bring about/manage sth.; **z. kommen**, to come about, (stattfinden) take place.

'**zuständig**, adj. relevant, competent (authority etc.); (verantwortlich) responsible. ◆**Z~keit**, f -/no pl competence; responsibility.

zu'statten, adv. j-m z. kommen, to be useful/an advantage for s.o.

zu'stehen, v.i.sep.irr.100 (haben) **das Geld steht ihm zu**, he is entitled to the money.

'**zustellen**, v.tr.sep. (a) (versperren) to block (a doorway etc.); (b) to deliver (mail etc.). ◆**Z~ung**, f delivery.

'**zustimm**en, v.i.sep. (haben) (etwas dat) z., to agree, (einwilligen) consent to sth.). ◆**Z~ung**, f agreement; consent.

'**zustoßen**, v.tr.sep.irr.103 (sein) to happen; **hoffentlich ist ihr nichts zugestoßen**, I hope nothing has happened to her.

'**Zustrom**, m stream (of visitors, Meteor: warm air etc.).

zu'tage, adv. z. treten, to come to light, be revealed.

'**Zutat**, f usu.pl **Z~en**, Cu: etc: ingredients.

'**zuteilen**, v.tr.sep. to allot, allocate (sth.) (j-m, to s.o.).

zu'tiefst, adv. extremely, deeply.

'**zutragen**, v.tr.sep.irr.42 (a) j-m etwas acc z., to take/(erzählen) report sth. to s.o.; (b) Lit: **sich z.**, to occur.

'**zuträglich**, adj. wholesome (food); beneficial (j-m, etwas dat, to s.o., sth.).

'**zutrau**en. I. v.tr.sep. j-m etwas z., to believe s.o. capable of sth.; **dem ist alles zuzutrauen**! I wouldn't put anything past him! II. z., n -s/no pl confidence (zu j-m, in s.o.). ◆**z~lich**, adj. trusting (child etc.); friendly (animal).

'**zutreffen**, v.i.sep.irr.104 (haben) to be correct; z. **auf + acc**, to apply to (s.o., sth.). ◆**z~d**, adj. correct; applicable (auf + acc, to).

zu'treten, v.i.sep.irr.105 (sein) **auf j-n z.**, to approach, come up to s.o.

zu'trinken, v.tr.sep.irr.96 j-m z., to raise one's glass to s.o.

'**Zutritt**, m admittance, admission.

'**Zutun**, n **es geschah ohne mein Z.**, I had no hand in it.

zu'unterst, adv. (right) at the bottom.

'**zuverlässig**, adj. reliable, dependable. ◆**Z~keit**, f -/no pl reliability.

Zu'versicht, f -/no pl confidence, optimism. ◆**z~lich**, adj. confident, optimistic.

zu'viel, indef.pron. too much.

zu'vor, adv. before; (erst einmal) first. ◆**z~kommen**, v.i.sep.irr.53 (sein) j-m z., to forestall s.o.; to get in first (before s.o.). ◆**z~kommend**, adj. obliging; (hilfsbereit) helpful, thoughtful.

'**Zuwachs**, m -es/ʔe increase (an Macht usw., in power etc.); growth (an Bevölkerung usw., of population etc.); Hum: **Meyers haben Z. bekommen**, the Meyers have had an addition to the family. ◆**z~en**, v.i.sep.irr.108 (sein) (a) (Wunde) to heal; (b) **mit Efeu usw. zugewachsen**, overgrown with ivy etc.

'**Zuwander**er, m -s/- immigrant. ◆**z~n**, v.i. (sein) to immigrate.

zu'wege, adv. etwas z. bringen, to bring sth. about, achieve sth.

zu'weilen, adv. occasionally, sometimes.

'**zuweis**en, v.tr.sep.irr.70 to assign (a task etc.), allocate (a room, money etc.) (j-m, to s.o.). ◆**Z~ung**, f -/-en assignment, allocation.

'**zuwend**en, v.tr.sep.irr.94 (a) j-m sein **Gesicht z.**, to turn one's face towards s.o.; **sich j-m z.**, to turn to s.o.; (b) (widmen) **seine Aufmerksamkeit j-m, etwas dat z.**, to turn one's attention to s.o., sth. ◆**Z~ung**, f -/-en (a) payment, (Beitrag) contribution; (b) (Fürsorge) attention, care.

zu'wenig, indef.pron. too little.

'**zuwerfen**, v.tr.sep.irr.110 j-m etwas z., to throw/toss sth. to s.o.

zu'wider. I. adj. j-m z. sein, to be repugnant to s.o. II. prep. + dat contrary to.

'**zuwinken**, v.i.sep. (haben) j-m z., to wave to s.o.

'**zuziehen**, v.tr.sep.irr.113 (a) to pull (a door) shut/(a knot) tight; to draw (curtains); (b) Fig: to consult, bring in (a specialist etc.); (c) **sich dat eine Krankheit z.**, to catch an illness.

zuzüglich ['tsu:tsy:kliç], prep. + gen Com: plus.

Zwang [tsvaŋ], m -(e)s/ʔe compulsion; **körperlicher Z.**, physical force; **wirtschaftliche Z~e**, economic pressures; **Z. auf j-n ausüben**, to put pressure on s.o.; **tu dir keinen Z. an!** (tu es) go ahead! feel free! ◆**z~los**, adj. informal; free and easy; z. **über etwas acc sprechen**, to speak openly/freely about sth. ◆**Z~losigkeit**, f -/no pl informality. ◆**Z~s-**, comb.fm. (a) compulsory (loan, auction etc.); (en)forced (stay, sale etc.); (b) coercive (measure etc.). ◆**Z~sarbeit**, f forced labour.

◆'Z~sjacke, f straitjacket. ◆'Z~slage, f predicament. ◆'z~släufig, adj. inevitable. ◆'z~sweise, adv. compulsory; (zwangsläufig) inevitably.

zwängen ['tsvɛŋən], v.tr. to force, squeeze (sth.).

zwanzig ['tsvantsiç], num.adj. twenty. ◆'z~jährig, adj. twenty year-old (person etc.); twenty-year (period etc.). ◆'z~ste(r,s), num.adj. twentieth.

zwar [tsvɑːr], adv. (a) (freilich) it's true, admittedly; **es ist z. schön, aber auch teuer**, it is very beautiful of course, but also very expensive; (b) **und z., in fact**; ... **und z. sofort!** ... and I mean immediately!

Zweck [tsvɛk], m -(e)s/-e (a) purpose; (Ziel) aim; **zu diesem Z.**, for this purpose, with this aim (in view); **ein wohltätiger Z.**, a charitable cause; (b) (Sinn) point; **es hat keinen Z. (, das zu tun)**, there is no point (in doing that). ◆'z~dienlich, adj. esp. Adm: appropriate; relevant, helpful (information etc.). ◆'z~los, adj. pointless. ◆'z~mäßig, adj. appropriate, functional, suitable (for the purpose). ◆'Z~mäßigkeit, f -/no pl appropriateness, fitness of purpose. ◆'z~s [tsvɛks], prep. + gen for the purpose of. ◆'z~widrig, adj. inappropriate.

zwei [tsvai], num.adj. two. ◆'z~beinig, adj. two-legged. ◆'Z~bettzimmer, n twin-bedded room. ◆'z~deutig, adj. ambiguous; **z~deutige Bemerkung**, suggestive remark. ◆'z~dimensional, adj. two-dimensional. ◆'z~erlei, adj. two sorts/kinds of (material, cheese etc.); two different (possibilities etc.); **das ist z.**, those are two different things. ◆'z~fach, adj. double (crime etc.); in **z~facher Ausfertigung**, in duplicate. ◆'Z~fa'milienhaus, n two-family house. ◆'z~jährig, adj. two-year old (child, wine etc.); biennial (plant); two-year (period). ◆'Z~kampf, m duel. ◆'z~mal, adv. twice; two times. ◆'z~motorig, adj. twin-engined. ◆'Z~rad, n two-wheeler; (Fahrrad) bicycle. ◆'Z~reiher, m -s/- double-breasted suit. ◆'z~schichtig, adj. double-layered. ◆'z~schneidig, adj. double-edged. ◆'z~seitig, adj. (a) two-sided; reversible (coat etc.); adv. on both sides; (b) bilateral (agreement etc.). ◆'Z~sitzer, m -s/- two-seater. ◆'z~sprachig, adj. bilingual. ◆'z~spurig, adj. two-lane (motorway etc.). ◆'z~stellig, adj. two-figure (number). ◆'z~stimmig, adj. Mus: for two voices; in two parts. ◆'z~stöckig, adj. two-storey. ◆z~t [tsvait], adv. **zu z.**, (i) (als Paar) as a couple; (in Gesellschaft) with someone else; (ii) (in Paaren) in twos; **wir waren zu z.**, there were two of us. ◆'Z~t-, 'z~t-, comb.fm. second (car etc.); second-(best,

largest, highest, fastest etc.). ◆'Z~taktmotor, m two-stroke engine. ◆'z~te(r, s), adj. second; **aus z~ter Hand**, secondhand; **jeden z~ten Tag**, every other day; on alternate days. ◆'z~teilen, v.tr.sep. to divide (sth.) in two. ◆'z~teilig, adj. Cl: two-piece (dress etc.). ◆'z~tens, adv. secondly. ◆'z~tklassig/'z~trangig, adj. second-rate. ◆'z~türig, adj. two-door (car). ◆'Z~twohnung, f second home. ◆'z~wöchig, adj. two-week (period); a fortnight's (holiday etc.).

Zweifel ['tsvaifəl], m -s/- doubt; **z. an etwas dat haben**, to be doubtful about sth.; **über etwas acc im Z. sein**, to be uncertain about sth.; **das steht außer Z.**, that is beyond doubt/question. ◆'z~elhaft, adj. doubtful, questionable; (anrüchig) dubious (business etc.). ◆'z~ellos, adv. undoubtedly; without any doubt. ◆'z~eln, v.i. (haben) an etwas (dat) z., to doubt (sth.). ◆'Z~elsfall, m doubtful case; **im Z.**, in case of doubt. ◆'z~els'ohne, adv. undoubtedly.

Zweig [tsvaik], m -(e)s/-e twig; (Trieb) shoot; (Ast) branch. ◆'Z~geschäft, n branch (shop). ◆'Z~stelle, f branch office.

Zwerchfell ['tsvɛrçfɛl], n diaphragm.

Zwerg [tsvɛrk]. I. m -(e)s/-e dwarf. II. 'Z~-, comb.fm. miniature (tree, form, dog etc.); tiny (state, school etc.).

Zwetsch(g)e ['tsvɛtʃ(g)ə], f -/-n damson plum.

zwick|en ['tsvikən], v.tr. to pinch (s.o., sth.). ◆'Z~mühle, f in einer Z. sein/sitzen, to be in a dilemma.

Zwieback ['tsviːbak], m -(e)s/-e rusk.

Zwiebel ['tsviːbəl], f -/-n onion; (Blumenz.) bulb. ◆'Z~kuchen, f (kind of) onion tart. ◆'Z~schale, f onion skin. ◆'Z~turm, m onion tower.

Zwiegespräch ['tsviːgəʃprɛːç], n Lit: dialogue. ◆'Z~licht, n twilight. ◆'z~lichtig, adj. shady (character etc.). ◆'Z~spalt, m (a) (inner) conflict; (b) (Uneinigkeit) discord. ◆'z~spältig, adj. conflicting (feelings etc.); unbalanced (character etc.). ◆'Z~tracht, f -/no pl Lit: discord.

Zwilling ['tsvilɪŋ], m -s/-e twin; Astr: Z~e, Gemini.

zwing|en ['tsviŋən], v.tr.irr.19 to force (s.o., oneself) (**zu etwas dat**, into sth./to do sth.). ◆'z~end, adj. compelling; cogent (reasons etc.); conclusive (proof etc.). ◆'Z~er, m -s/- kennel(s).

zwinkern ['tsviŋkərn], v.i. (haben) to blink, (als Zeichen) wink.

Zwirn [tsvirn], m -(e)s/-e (twisted) yarn; twine.

zwischen ['tsviʃən], prep. + dat/(mit Bewegung) acc between; (mitten) z., amongst, in the middle of. ◆'Z~bemerkung, f interjection.

◆'Z~**bilanz**, f interim balance.
◆'Z~**ding**, n F: cross. ◆'z~'**durch**,
adv. 1. (a) at intervals; (b) (*inzwischen*) in
the meantime; in between (times). 2.
(*räumlich*) here and there.
◆'Z~**ergebnis**, n interim/provisional
result; Sp: latest score. ◆'Z~**fall**, m incident. ◆'Z~**frage**, f interposed question. ◆'Z~**gericht**, n Cu: entrée.
◆'Z~**geschoß**, n mezzanine.
◆'Z~**händler**, m middleman.
◆'Z~**landung**, f intermediate landing,
stopover. ◆'z~**mahlzeit**, f snack (between meals). ◆'z~**menschlich**, adj.
between people; personal (relations etc.).
◆'Z~**raum**, m gap; space; (*Abstand*)
distance. ◆'Z~**ruf**, m interjection;
Z~**rufe**, interruptions; Pol: heckling.
◆'Z~**spiel**, n 1. Mus: & Th: intermez-
zo. 2. Fig: interlude. ◆'z~**staatlich**,
adj. international. ◆'Z~**station**, f intermediate stop, stopover. ◆'Z~-
stecker, m adapter. ◆'Z~**summe**, f

subtotal. ◆'Z~**wand**, f partition.
◆'Z~**zeit**, f interim (period); **in der Z.,**
in the meantime.
Zwist [tsvist], m **-es/-e** Lit: strife; (*Fehde*)
feud.
zwitschern ['tsvitʃərn], v.i. (*haben*) to
twitter, chirp.
Zwitter ['tsvitər], m **-s/-** hermaphrodite.
zwölf [tsvœlf], num.adj. twelve.
◆'z~**te(r, s)**, num.adj. twelfth.
Zyklus ['tsy:klus], m **-/-klen** cycle.
Zylind|er [tsi'lindər], m **-s/-** 1. Tchn: etc:
cylinder. 2. Cl: (also Z~**erhut** m) top
hat. ◆z~**risch**, adj. cylindrical.
Zyn|iker ['tsy:nikər], m **-s/-** cynic.
◆**z~isch**, adj. cynical. ◆**Z~ismus**
[tsy'nismus] m **-/no pl** cynicism.
Zyp|ern ['tsy:pərn]. Pr.n.n **-s.**
Cyprus. ◆**Z~riote** [tsypri'o:tə], m
-n/-n Cypriot. ◆**z~riotisch**, adj.
Cypriot.
Zypresse [tsy'prɛsə], f **-/-n** cypress.
Zyste ['tsystə], f **-/-n** cyst.

part 2

GRAMMATISCHE HINWEISE

1. Plural der Substantive

(1) **Allgemeine Regel.** In der Regel wird der Plural eines Substantivs durch Anhängen von **-s** geformt, z.B. cat, cats; table, tables.

(2) Substantive mit den Endungen **-s, -sh, -ch** und **-x** bilden den Plural durch Anhängen von **-es**, z.B. glass, glasses; brush, brushes; church, churches; box, boxes.

(3) Die meisten Substantive, die in **-o** enden, formen den Plural durch Anhängen von **-s**, einige jedoch durch Anhängen von **-es**, z.B. potato, potatoes. In diesen Fällen ist die Pluralform im Wörterbuch angegeben.

(4) Substantive mit Endung **-y** ersetzen das 'y' bei der Bildung des Plurals durch **-ies**, außer wenn das 'y' auf einen Vokal folgt. In diesem Fall wird der Plural einfach durch Anhängen von **-s** gebildet, also: army, armies; fly, flies; story, stories; aber: boy, boys; storey, storeys; valley, valleys.

(5) Substantive mit Endung auf **-f** bilden den Plural normalerweise durch Anhängen von **-s**, einige jedoch verwenden die Pluralform **-ves**, z.B. calf, calves; knife, knives. Diese abweichenden Formen sind im Wörterbuch angegeben.

(6) Ebenfalls bei den jeweiligen Einträgen angegeben sind unregelmäßige Pluralformen wie: foot, feet; mouse, mice; child, children usw. Zur Beachtung: policeman, policemen; aber: German, Germans.

(7) Folgende Maß- und Mengenbezeichnungen erhalten keine Pluralform, wenn sie auf eine Zahlenangabe folgen: **dozen, hundred, hundredweight, million, stone, thousand**; also: he weighs ten stone; two dozen eggs; aber: dozens of eggs.

(8) **Zusammensetzungen.** Der Plural eines zusammengesetzten Substantivs wird normalerweise durch Anhängen von **-s** an das letzte Element der Zusammensetzung gebildet, also: ticket collector, ticket collectors; forget-me-not, forget-me-nots. Bei einigen Zusammensetzungen jedoch, insbesondere solchen, die mit **man** und **woman** beginnen, bilden beide Wortelemente den Plural: manservant, menservants; woman doctor, women doctors.

Bei einigen zusammengesetzten Substantiven erscheint nur das erste Element im Plural: father-in-law, fathers-in-law; governor-general, governors-general; commander-in-chief, commanders-in-chief.

2. Konjugation der Verben

(1) **Regelmäßige Verben.** Regelmäßige Verben bilden Imperfekt und Perfekt durch Anhängen von **-ed** an den Infinitiv, z.B.: walk, walked. Endet der Infinitiv in **-e**, wird lediglich **-d** angehängt, z.B. dance, danced. Endet der Infinitiv in **-y**, verändert sich die Endung für die Vergangenheitsformen in **-ied**, also: marry, married; try, tried. Das Partizip Präsens wird durch Anhängen von **-ing** gebildet: walk, walking. Endet der Infinitiv in **-e**, entfällt das **-e**: dance, dancing; Ausnahme: singe, singeing (im Gegensatz zu: sing, singing). Bei den Verben auf **-ie** verändert sich die Endung in **-ying**, also: die, dying; lie, lying.

(2) **Einsilbige Verben,** die auf einen Einzelkonsonanten enden, ebenso Verben, die auf einen Vokal + 1 enden, bilden die Vergangenheit und das Partizip Perfekt unter Verdopplung des Endkonsonanten, z.B.: hop, hopped; step, stepped; travel, travelled.

(3) **Unregelmäßige Verben.** Die Stammformen der hauptsächlichen unregelmäßigen Verben sind im folgenden in alphabetischer Reihenfolge zusammengefaßt. Unregelmäßige Verben sind im Text durch *irr.* gekennzeichnet.

Zur Beachtung: (a) to **be**: *pres.* I am; he is; we, you, they are; *p.* I, he was; we, you, they were; *Partizip Perfekt:* been; *Partizip Präsens:* being.

(b) Modale Hilfsverben: Diese Verben bilden weder Infinitiv noch Partizip Perfekt und werden (mit Ausnahme von **ought**) von einer Infinitivform ohne **to** gefolgt.

can, *p.* could (für Infinitiv wird 'to be able to' und für das Partizip Perfekt 'been able' verwendet).
may, *p.* might.
must, *(gefolgt von Infinitiv, keine Vergangenheitsform).*
ought, *(gefolgt von Infinitiv, keine Vergangenheitsform).*
shall, *p.* should.
will, *p.* would.

Liste der englischen unregelmäßigen Verben
List of English irregular verbs

Infinitive	Past Tense	Past Participle
abide	abode, abided	abode, abided
arise	arose	arisen
be	was, were	been
bear	bore	borne
beat	beat	beaten
become	became	become
begin	began	begun
bend	bent	bent
beseech	besought	besought
bet	bet, betted	bet, betted
bid	bade, bid	bidden, bid
bind	bound	bound
bite	bit	bitten
bleed	bled	bled
blow	blew	blown
break	broke	broken
breed	bred	bred
bring	brought	brought
broadcast	broadcast	broadcast
build	built	built
burn	burnt, burned	burnt, burned
burst	burst	burst
buy	bought	bought
cast	cast	cast
catch	caught	caught
choose	chose	chosen
cling	clung	clung
come	came	come
cost	cost	cost
creep	crept	crept
cut	cut	cut
deal	dealt	dealt
dig	dug	dug
dive	dived, *N.Am.:* dove	dived
do	did	done
draw	drew	drawn
dream	dreamed, dreamt	dreamed, dreamt
drink	drank	drunk
drive	drove	driven
dwell	dwelt	dwelt
eat	ate	eaten
fall	fell	fallen
feed	fed	fed
feel	felt	felt
fight	fought	fought
find	found	found
fling	flung	flung
fly	flew	flown
forbid	forbad(e)	forbidden
forecast	forecast	forecast
foresee	foresaw	foreseen
foretell	foretold	foretold
forget	forgot	forgotten
forgive	forgave	forgiven

forsake	forsook	forsaken
freeze	froze	frozen
get	got	got, *N.Am:* gotten
give	gave	given
go	went	gone
grind	ground	ground
grow	grew	grown
hang	hung, hanged	hung, hanged
have	had	had
hear	heard	heard
hide	hid	hidden
hit	hit	hit
hold	held	held
hurt	hurt	hurt
keep	kept	kept
kneel	knelt, kneeled	knelt, kneeled
know	knew	known
lay	laid	laid
lead	led	led
lean	leant, leaned	leant, leaned
leap	leapt, leaped	leapt, leaped
learn	learnt, learned	learnt, learned
leave	left	left
lend	lent	lent
let	let	let
lie	lay	lain
light	lit, lighted	lit, lighted
lose	lost	lost
make	made	made
mean	meant	meant
meet	met	met
mow	mowed	mown, mowed
overcome	overcame	overcome
overhear	overheard	overheard
overtake	overtook	overtaken
pay	paid	paid
prove	proved	proved, proven
put	put	put
quit	quit, quitted	quit, quitted
read	read [red]	read [red]
rid	rid	rid
ride	rode	ridden
ring	rang	rung
rise	rose	risen
run	ran	run
saw	sawed	sawn, sawed
say	said	said
see	saw	seen
seek	sought	sought
sell	sold	sold
send	sent	sent
set	set	set
sew	sewed	sewn, sewed
shake	shook	shaken
shed	shed	shed
shine	shone	shone
shoe	shod	shod
shoot	shot	shot
show	showed	shown, showed
shrink	shrank	shrunk

shut	shut	shut
sing	sang	sung
sink	sank	sunk
sit	sat	sat
slay	slew	slain
sleep	slept	slept
slide	slid	slid
sling	slung	slung
slit	slit	slit
smell	smelt, smelled	smelt, smelled
sow	sowed	sown, sowed
speak	spoke	spoken
speed	sped, speeded	sped, speeded
spell	spelt, spelled	spelt, spelled
spend	spent	spent
spill	spilt, spilled	spilt, spilled
spin	spun	spun
spit	spat	spat
split	split	split
spoil	spoilt, spoiled	spoilt, spoiled
spread	spread	spread
spring	sprang	sprung
stand	stood	stood
steal	stole	stolen
stick	stuck	stuck
sting	stung	stung
stink	stank	stunk
stride	strode	stridden
strike	struck	struck
string	strung	strung
strive	strove	striven
swear	swore	sworn
sweep	swept	swept
swell	swelled	swollen, swelled
swim	swam	swum
swing	swung	swung
take	took	taken
teach	taught	taught
tear	tore	torn
tell	told	told
think	thought	thought
throw	threw	thrown
thrust	thrust	thrust
tread	trod	trodden
undergo	underwent	undergone
understand	understood	understood
undertake	undertook	undertaken
undo	undid	undone
upset	upset	upset
wake	woke	woken
wear	wore	worn
weave	wove	woven
weep	wept	wept
win	won	won
wind	wound	wound
withdraw	withdrew	withdrawn
withhold	withheld	withheld
withstand	withstood	withstood
wring	wrung	wrung
write	wrote	written

Englische Aussprache

Die Betonung wird durch ein Betonungszeichen ['] vor der zu betonenden Silbe angegeben, z.B. **sugar** ['suɡər], **impossible** [im'pɔsibl]. Eingeklammerte Zeichen deuten auf Laute, die manchmal ausgesprochen werden und manchmal nicht.

Vokale

Zeichen	Beispiele	Zeichen	Beispiele
[æ]	*ba*t, *a*dd	[iː]	*he*, *sea*, *bee*,
[ɑː]	*ba*th, *ca*rt		*fe*ver, *po*lice
[ɑ̃, ɑ̃ː]	*ensemble*	[iə]	*bee*r, *rea*l
[ai]	*li*fe, *fl*y, *ai*sle,	[ɔ]	*lo*t, *wa*sp, *wha*t
	*hei*ght	[ɔː]	*a*ll, *hau*l, *sho*rt,
[au]	*fo*wl, *hou*se		*saw*
[e]	*be*t, *sai*d, *bu*ry	[ɔi]	*boi*l, *to*y, *lo*yal
[eə]	*ba*re, *ai*r, *the*re	[əu]	*boa*t, *lo*w, *ro*pe,
[ei]	*ha*te, *da*y, *nai*l		*no*
[ə]	*a*nnoy, *bu*tter,		
	*pho*tograph	[ʌ]	*cu*t, *so*n, *co*ver,
[(ə)]	*na*tion, *o*cean,		*rou*gh
	*rea*son, *su*dden	[u]	*pu*t, *woo*l, *woul*d
[əː]	*lea*rn, *whi*rl, *bu*rn	[uː]	*sho*e, *pro*ve, *too*,
[i]	*wi*nd, *a*dded,		*tru*e
	*phy*sics	[uə]	*su*rely, *tou*rist

Konsonanten

Zeichen	Beispiele	Zeichen	Beispiele
[b]	*b*etter	[r]	*r*ed, b*r*eak, hu*rr*y
[d]	*d*u*d*	[ɾ]	fathe*r*, sailo*r*
[dʒ]	*r*a*g*e, e*dg*e, *j*et,	[s]	*s*at, mou*s*e, le*ss*
	*di*git	[z]	hou*s*es, fu*s*e,
[f]	*f*at, lau*gh*, *ph*oto		bu*zz*, *z*inc
[g]	*g*old, e*gg*, ro*gu*e	[ʃ]	*sh*am, di*sh*, pres-
[gz]	e*x*act		*s*ure, o*c*ean,
[h]	*h*ouse		ma*ch*ine,
[j]	*y*et		na*ti*on
[ʒ]	plea*s*ure, vi*s*ion	[t]	*t*op, ba*t*
[k]	*c*old, *k*ick, a*ch*e	[ts]	*ts*ar, hin*ts*
[ks]	ex*c*ept, a*x*e, a*c*-	[tʃ]	ma*tch*, *ch*at, ri*ch*
	*c*ident	[θ]	*th*atch, brea*th*,
[l]	*l*og, ab*le*		e*th*er
[m]	*m*ast, pri*sm*	[ð]	*th*at, brea*the*,
[n]	*n*ine		o*th*er
[ŋ]	so*ng*, thi*nk*	[v]	*v*ase, ha*ve*
[p]	*p*art, bum*p*	[w]	*w*ig*w*am

A

A, a¹ [ei], s. (der Buchstabe) A, a n.

a² before a vowel **an** [ə/ən], indef. art. ein(e); **five pence a pound,** fünf Pence das Pfund; **five pounds a head,** fünf Pfund pro Kopf; **three times a week,** dreimal in der Woche; **not a,** kein, keine; **what a,** was für ein(e); **he is a doctor,** er ist Arzt.

aback [ə'bæk], adv. **to be taken a.,** überrascht/(puzzled) verblüfft sein.

abandon [ə'bændən], v.tr. (j-n, etwas) verlassen; (einen Plan) aufgeben.

abashed [ə'bæʃt], adj. verlegen.

abate [ə'beit], v.i. nachlassen.

abattoir [æbətwɑːr], s. Schlachthaus n.

abbey ['æbi], s. Abtei f.

abbot ['æbət], s. Abt m.

abbreviate [ə'briːvieit], v.tr. abkürzen. ◆**abbrevi'ation,** s. Abkürzung f.

abdicate ['æbdikeit], v.i. (of king etc.) abdanken. ◆**abdi'cation,** s. Abdankung f.

abdomen ['æbdəmen], s. Bauch m; (esp. of woman) Unterleib m. ◆**abdominal** [-'dɔminəl], adj. abdominal.

abduct [æb'dʌkt], v.tr. entführen. ◆**ab'duction,** s. Entführung f.

aberration [æbə'reiʃ(ə)n], s. **mental a.,** geistige Verwirrung f; (slip) Versehen n.

abet [ə'bet], v.tr. **to (aid and) a. s.o.,** j-m Beihilfe leisten.

abeyance [ə'beiəns], s. **in a.,** unentschieden.

abhor [əb'hɔːr], v.tr. verabscheuen.

abide [ə'baid], v.irr. **1.** v.i. **to a. by a promise,** bei seinem Versprechen bleiben. **2.** v.tr. **I can't a. him,** ich kann ihn nicht ausstehen.

ability [ə'biliti], s. Fähigkeit f.

abject ['æbdʒekt], adj. elend; **a. despair,** tiefste Verzweiflung.

ablaze [ə'bleiz], adv. & adj. in Flammen.

able ['eibl], adj. fähig; (efficient) tüchtig; **to be a. to do sth.,** etwas tun können. ◆**'able-'bodied,** adj. gesund; Mil: tauglich; (well) tüchtig. ◆**ably,** adv. (adroitly) geschickt; (well) tüchtig.

abnormal [æb'nɔːməl], adj. abnorm; (pathological) krankhaft; (more than usual) überdurchschnittlich.

aboard [ə'bɔːd], I. adv. an Bord. II. prep. **a. (a) ship,** an Bord eines Schiffes; **all a.!** alles einsteigen!

abolish [ə'bɔliʃ], v.tr. abschaffen. ◆**abo'lition,** s. Abschaffung f.

abominable [ə'bɔminəbl], adj. abscheulich.

aborigine [æbə'ridʒini], s. Ureinwohner m.

abortion [ə'bɔːʃ(ə)n], s. Abtreibung f. ◆**a'bortive,** adj. mißlungen.

abound [ə'baund], v.i. reichlich vorhanden sein; **to a. in/with sth.,** sehr reich an etwas dat sein.

about [ə'baut], adv. & prep. **1.** (around) (a) um + acc, um ... acc herum; (b) **there's something unusual a. him,** es ist etwas Ungewöhnliches an ihm. **2.** (of boat) **to go a.,** wenden; Mil: **a. turn!** kehrt machen! **3.** (approximately) ungefähr, etwa; **a. three o'clock,** er kann gegen drei Uhr. **4.** (concerning) über + acc. **5. to be a. to do sth.,** im Begriff sein, etwas zu tun.

above [ə'bʌv], I. prep. über + dat. II. adv. oben; **from a.,** von oben; **a. all,** vor allem. ◆**a'bove'board,** adj. ehrlich.

abreast [ə'brest], adv. Seite an Seite; **to keep a. of developments etc.,** mit Entwicklungen usw. Schritt halten.

abridge [ə'bridʒ], v.tr. kürzen.

abroad [ə'brɔːd], adv. **to go a.,** ins Ausland fahren; **to live a.,** im Ausland wohnen.

abrupt [ə'brʌpt], adj. abrupt; (sudden) plötzlich; (of manner) schroff; (of drop, ending) jäh.

abscess ['æbses], pl. -es ['æbses,-iz], s. Abszeß m.

abscond [əb'skɔnd], v.i. entfliehen; (furtively) (von zu Hause, vom Internat) durchbrennen.

absence ['æbs(ə)ns], s. Abwesenheit f. ◆**absent** ['æbs(ə)nt], adj. abwesend; **to be a.,** fehlen. ◆**absen'tee** [æbs(ə)n'tiː], s. Abwesende(r) f(m). ◆**absen'teeism,** s. Fernbleiben n vom Arbeitsplatz. ◆**'absent-'minded,** adj. geistesabwesend.

absolute ['æbsəl(j)uːt], adj. absolut; **a. power,** unbeschränkte Macht; **-ly,** adv. völlig; **a. essential,** unbedingt notwendig; **a. fantastic!** einfach fantastisch! (affirmative) **a.!** genau! ◆**absolve** [əb'zɔlv], v.tr. freisprechen.

absorb [əb'sɔːb], v.tr. (a) (eine Flüssigkeit, usw.) absorbieren; (b) (einen Stoß usw., Fig: Einwanderer usw.) aufnehmen; (Wissen, Eindrücke) in sich aufnehmen; (c) to be **absorbed in a book,** in ein Buch vertieft sein. ◆**ab'sorbent,** adj. absorbierend.

abstain [əb'stein], v.i. sich enthalten (from, gen); (from voting) sich der Stimme enthalten. ◆**abstemious** [əb'stiːmiəs], adj. enthaltsam. ◆**abstention** [əb'sten'ʃ(ə)n], s. (in voting) Stimmenthaltung f. ◆**abstinence** ['æbstinəns], s. Enthaltsamkeit f; (from alcohol) Abstinenz f.

abstract ['æbstrækt]. I. adj. abstrakt. II. s. Abriß m.

abstruse [æb'struːs], adj. abstrus.

absurd [əb'sɜːd], adj. absurd; (ridiculous) unsinnig. ◆**ab'surdity,** s. Absurdität f; (nonsense) Unsinn m.

abundant [ə'bʌndənt], adj. reichlich (vorhanden). ◆**a'bundance,** s. Reichtum *m* (of, an + *dat*).

abuse I. *s.* [ə'bju:s]. 1. (*practice*) Mißbrauch *m*. 2. (*cursing*) Beschimpfung *f*. II. *v.tr.* [ə'bju:z]. (seine Macht, j-s Vertrauen) mißbrauchen; (j-n) mißhandeln.
◆**a'busive**, *adj.* beleidigend.

abysmal [ə'bizm(ə)l], *adj.* miserabel; **a. ignorance**, bodenlose Unwissenheit.

abyss [ə'bis], *s.* Abgrund *m*.

academic [ækə'demik], *adj.* akademisch; *Fig:* **a purely a. question**, eine rein theoretische Frage. ◆**academy** [ə'kædəmi], *s.* Akademie *f*.

accelerate [æk'seləreit], *v.tr. & i.* (einen Vorgang usw.) beschleunigen. ◆**acceleration**, *s.* Beschleunigung *f*. ◆**ac'celerator**, *s.* Gaspedal *n*.

accent ['æksənt], *s.* Akzent *m*. ◆**accentuate** [æk'sentjueit], *v.tr.* betonen; (*emphasize*) hervorheben. ◆**accentu'ation**, *s.* Akzentuierung *f*.

accept [ək'sept], *v.* 1. *v.tr.* (eine Einladung, ein Amt usw.) annehmen; (j-n, sein Schicksal, ein Geschenk usw.) akzeptieren; (j-n als Mitglied usw.) aufnehmen. 2. *v.i.* zusagen. ◆**ac'ceptable**, *adj.* annehmbar. ◆**ac'ceptance**, *s.* Annahme *f*.

access ['ækses], *s.* Zutritt *m*; (road, drive) Zufahrt *f*. ◆**ac'cessible**, *adj.* (also Fig:) zugänglich.

accessory [æk'sesəri], *s.* 1. Zusatz *m*; **accessories**, Zubehör *n*. 2. *Jur:* Mitschuldige(r) *f(m)*.

accident ['æksidənt], *s.* (*a*) Unfall *m*; (*serious*) a, Unglück *n*; (*b*) (*chance*) Zufall *m*; **by a.**, zufällig. ◆**acci'dental**, *adj.* zufällig; (*by mistake*) versehentlich.

acclaim [ə'kleim]. I. *v.tr.* (j-m) zujubeln. II. *s.* Beifall *m*.

acclimatize [ə'klaimətaiz], *v.tr.* to **become acclimatized**, sich akklimatisieren. ◆**acclimati'zation**, *s.* Akklimatisation *f*.

accommodate [ə'kɔmədeit], *v.tr.* a (*assist*) (j-m) entgegenkommen; (*b*) (*put up*) (j-n) unterbringen. ◆**a'commodating**, *adj.* (*of pers.*) entgegenkommend. ◆**accommo'dation**, *s.* Unterkunft *f*.

accompany [ə'kʌmp(ə)ni], *v.tr.* begleiten. ◆**a'companiment**, *s.* Begleitung *f*.

accomplice [ə'kʌmplis], *s.* Komplize *m*, Komplizin *f*.

accomplish [ə'kʌmpliʃ], *v.tr.* erzielen. ◆**a'complished**, *adj.* vollendet; (*of pers.*) gewandt. ◆**a'complishment**, *s.* Leistung *f*.

accord [ə'kɔːd], *s.* Zustimmung *f*, **of one's own a.**, aus eigenem Antrieb. ◆**a'cordance**, *s.* in a. with, gemäß + *dat*. ◆**a'cording**, *adv.* a. to, laut + *dat*; **-ly**, *adv.* to act a., entsprechend handeln.

accordion [ə'kɔːdiən], *s.* Akkordeon *n*.

accost [ə'kɔst], *v.tr.* (j-n) ansprechen.

account [ə'kaunt]. I. *s.* 1. (*a*) (*with bank,*

firm) Konto *n*; **the accounts** (of a firm), die Bücher *npl* (einer Firma); (*b*) (*invoice*) Rechnung *f*. 2. **of no a.**, ohne Bedeutung; **to take sth. into a.**, etwas berücksichtigen; **on a. of**, wegen + *gen*; **on his a.**, seinetwegen; **on no/not on any a.**, keinesfalls. 3. (*description*) Beschreibung *f*; (*report*) Bericht *m*; **by all accounts**, nach allem, was man hört. II. *v.i.* to a. **for sth**, für etwas **acc** Rechenschaft ablegen; (*explain*) etwas erklären. ◆**a'ccountable**, *adj.* verantwortlich (**for**, für + *acc*; **to**, gegenüber + *dat*). ◆**a'ccountant**, *s.* Buchhalter *m*; (*chartered*) **a.**, Wirtschaftsprüfer *m*.

accumulate [ə'kjuːmjuleit], *v.* 1. *v.tr.* (*collect*) ansammeln; (*amass*) (Geld, Vorräte) anhäufen. 2. *v.i.* (*pile up*) sich anhäufen; (*collect*) sich ansammeln.

accurate ['ækjurit], *adj.* genau, exakt; (*with no mistakes*) fehlerfrei. ◆**'accuracy** [-əsi], *s.* Genauigkeit *f*; Präzision *f* (eines Instruments).

accuse [ə'kjuːz], *v.tr.* (j-n) anklagen; (j-n) beschuldigen (**of a crime**, eines Verbrechens; **of doing sth.**, etwas getan zu haben). ◆**accu'sation**, *s.* Anklage *f*. ◆**a'ccused**, *s. Jur:* **the a.**, der/die Angeklagte.

accustom [ə'kʌstəm], *v.tr.* to a. s.o. to sth., j-n an etwas **acc** gewöhnen. ◆**a'ccustomed**, *adj.* 1. to be a. to sth./to doing sth., an etwas gewohnt sein/gewöhnt sein, etwas zu tun; to get a. to sth., sich an etwas **acc** gewöhnen. 2. (*usual*) gewohnt.

ace [eis], *s.* As *n*.

ache [eik]. I. *s.* Schmerz *m*; **I have a stomach a.**, ich habe Magenschmerzen *pl*. II. *v.i.* schmerzen; **my back aches**, mir tut der Rücken weh.

achieve [ə'tʃiːv], *v.tr.* (a) (eine Großtat usw.) vollbringen; (*b*) (etwas, ein Ziel) erreichen; (Erfolg) erzielen. ◆**a'chievement**, *s.* 1. (*action*) Erreichen *n*; Vollendung *f* (eines Plans). 2. Leistung *f*; achievements, Errungenschaften *fpl*.

acid ['æsid], *s.* Säure *f*; **the a. test**, die Feuerprobe. ◆**acidity** [ə'siditi], *s.* Säuregehalt *m*.

acknowledge [ək'nɔlidʒ], *v.tr.* (a) (*recognize*) anerkennen; (*b*) (*admit*) (Schuld usw.) eingestehen; (*c*) (einen Gruß usw.) erwidern; to a. (*receipt of*) a letter, den Eingang eines Briefes bestätigen. ◆**ack'nowledgement**, *s.* Anerkennung *f*; Bestätigung *f* (eines Briefes).

acne ['ækni], *s.* Akne *f*.

acorn ['eikɔːn], *s.* Eichel *f*.

acoustic [ə'kuːstik], *adj.* akustisch. ◆**a'coustics**, *s.pl.* Akustik *f*.

acquaint [ə'kweint], *v.tr.* a (*inform*) to a. s.o./oneself with sth., j-n/sich über etwas **acc** informieren; (*b*) to be acquainted with s.o., j-n kennen. ◆**a'quaintance**, *s.* 1. to make the a. of s.o., j-n kennenlernen. 2. (*pers.*) Bekannte(r) f(m).

acquiesce [ækwiˈes], v.i. einwilligen (**in sth.**, in etwas acc).

acquire [əˈkwaiər], v.tr. erwerben. ◆**acquisition** [ækwiˈzif(ə)n], s. 1. (action) Erwerb m. 2. (object) Anschaffung f. ◆**acquisitive** [əˈkwizitiv], adj. habgierig.

acquit [əˈkwit], v.tr. (a) freisprechen (**of a crime**, von einem Verbrechen); (b) **to a. oneself well/badly**, gut/schlecht abschneiden ◆**a'quittal**, s. Freispruch m.

acre [ˈeikər], s. Morgen m.

acrid [ˈækrid], adj. beißend.

acrimonious [ækriˈməuniəs], adj. bissig.

acrobat [ˈækrəbæt], s. Akrobat(in) m(f). ◆**acrobatic**, adj. akrobatisch.

across [əˈkrɔs]. I. prep. 1. (motion) über + acc. 2. (position) **a. the river is a small town**, auf der anderen Seite des Flusses ist eine kleine Stadt. II. adv. hinüber; **the river is 100 metres a.**, der Fluß ist 100 Meter breit.

act [ækt]. I. s. 1. (a) Handlung f; (deed) Tat f; **to catch s.o. in the a.**, j-n auf frischer Tat ertappen; (b) **A. of Parliament**, (verabschiedetes) Gesetz n. 2. Th: (a) Akt m (eines Stückes); (b) Nummer f (eines Artisten). II. v. 1. v.tr. (ein Stück, eine Rolle) spielen. 2. v.i. a) handeln; (b) (behave) sich benehmen; (c) (function) **to a. as**, fungieren/dienen als; (d) Th: Cin: spielen. ◆**'acting**. I. adj. (deputy) stellvertretend. II. s. Th: Spielen n. ◆**action** [ˈækʃ(ə)n], s. 1. Handlung f; **to take a.**, handeln; **to bring/put sth. into a.**, etwas in Gang setzen; **out of a.**, außer Betrieb. 2. (movement) Bewegung f. 3. (effect) Wirkung f (on, auf + acc). 4. Jur: Verfahren n; (trial) Prozeß m. 5. Mil: Gefecht n. ◆**'actionable**, adj: klagbar.

active [ˈæktiv], adj. aktiv; (of mind, imagination, interest) rege; (of old pers.) rüstig. ◆**ac'tivity**, s. 1. (bustle) Tun n. 2. Tätigkeit f.

actor [ˈæktər], s. Schauspieler m. ◆**'actress**, s. Schauspielerin f.

actual [ˈæktju(ə)l], adj. eigentlich; (real) tatsächlich; **in a. fact**, in Wirklichkeit. -**ly**, adv. eigentlich; **he a. said ...**, (i) er ging so weit zu sagen, ...; (ii) was er eigentlich sagte, war ...

acute [əˈkjuːt], adj. 1. (of observer, mind) scharf. 2. (of problem, shortage etc.) akut; (of pain) heftig.

ad [æd], s. F: Anzeige f; **small a.**, Kleinanzeige f, Inserat n.

Adam [ˈædəm]. Pr.n. **A's apple**, Adamsapfel m.

adamant [ˈædəmənt], adj. unnachgiebig.

adapt [əˈdæpt], v.tr. (etwas, sich) anpassen (**to sth.**, etwas dat/an etwas acc). ◆**adapta'bility**, s. Anpassungsfähigkeit f. ◆**a'daptable**, adj. anpassungsfähig. ◆**adap'tation**, s. Th: etc: Bearbeitung

f. ◆**a'daptor**, s. El: Zwischenstecker m.

add [æd], v. 1. v.tr. (a) (etwas) hinzufügen; (b) **to a. up**, (Zahlen, eine Rechnung) addieren. 2. v.i. **to a. to sth.**, etwas vermehren. ◆**addition** [əˈdif(ə)n], s. (sth. added) Zusatz m; **in a.**, zusätzlich. ◆**a'ditional**, adj. zusätzlich. ◆**'additive**, s. Zusatz m.

adder [ˈædər], s. Kreuzotter f.

addict [ˈædikt], s. Süchtige(r) f(m); **drug a.**, Rauschgiftsüchtige(r) f(m). ◆**ad'dicted** [əˈdiktid], adj. süchtig; **a. to heroin**, heroinsüchtig. ◆**a'ddiction**, s. Sucht f.

address [əˈdres]. I. s. 1. Adresse f; **a. book**, Adreßbuch n. 2. (speech) Ansprache f; **public a. (system)**, Lautsprecheranlage f. II. v.tr (a) **to a. a letter (to s.o.)**, einen Brief (an j-n) adressieren; (b) (j-n) ansprechen. ◆**addressee** [ædreˈsiː], s. Empfänger m.

adenoids [ˈædənɔidz], s.pl. adenoide Wucherungen fpl.

adept [əˈdept], adj. geschickt (**at/in**, in + dat).

adequate [ˈædikwət], adj. hinreichend; **to be a.**, genügen.

adhere [ədˈhiər], v.i. (a) (of thing) kleben (**to sth.**, an etwas dat); (b) (of pers.) festhalten (**to sth.**, an etwas dat). ◆**ad'hesive** [-ˈhiːz-]. I. adj. klebend; **a. tape**, Klebestreifen m; **a. plaster**, Heftpflaster n. II. s. Klebstoff m.

adjacent [əˈdʒeis(ə)nt], adj. angrenzend; **a. to**, direkt neben + dat.

adjective [ˈædʒiktiv], s. Adjektiv n.

adjoining [əˈdʒɔiniŋ], adj. angrenzend.

adjourn [əˈdʒəːn], v.tr. vertagen (**to/until**, auf + acc).

adjudicate [əˈdʒuːdikeit], v.i. entscheiden. ◆**a'djudicator**, s. Preisrichter m.

adjust [əˈdʒʌst], v.tr. (a) (sich, etwas) einstellen (**to**, auf + acc); (adapt) (sich, etwas) anpassen (**to**, dat/an + acc); (b) (einen Mechanismus) einstellen; (Schrauben usw.) justieren; (eine Uhr usw.) regulieren; (Bremsen) nachstellen; (c) (den Hut, den Kragen usw.) zurechtrücken. ◆**a'djustable**, adj. regulierbar. ◆**a'djustment**, s. Regulierung f.

administer [ədˈministər], v.tr. (ein Geschäft usw.) verwalten; (b) **to a. a drug**, eine Droge verabreichen. ◆**adminis'tration**, s. Verwaltung f; **the Kennedy a.**, die Regierung Kennedy. ◆**ad'ministrative**, adj. verwaltend. ◆**administrator**, s. Verwalter m.

admiral [ˈædm(ə)rəl], s. Admiral m.

admire [ədˈmaiər], v.tr. bewundern. ◆**admirable** [ˈædm(ə)rəbl], adj. bewundernswert; (excellent) großartig. ◆**admiration** [ædməˈreiʃən], s. Bewunderung f. ◆**ad'mirer**, s. Bewunderer m; Bewunderin f; Verehrer m (einer Dame).

admission [ædˈmiʃ(ə)n], s. 1. (a) Eintritt

m (to, in + *acc*); (*access*) Zutritt *m* (to, zu + *dat*); (*b*) (*fee*) Eintrittspreis *m*; (*c*) Einlieferung *f* (ins Krankenhaus). 2. Eingeständnis *n* (**of** a crime etc., eines Verbrechens usw.). ◆**ad'mit**, *v.tr.* (*a*) (*let in*) (j-n, Luft usw.) einlassen; (j-m) Eintritt gewähren; **to be admitted to hospital**, ins Krankenhaus eingeliefert werden; (*b*) (*allow*) (Beweise usw.) zulassen; (*c*) (*concede*) (Schuld usw.) zugeben. ◆**ad'mittance**, *s.* Eintritt *m* (to, in + *dat*); Zutritt *m* (to, zu + *dat*); **no a.**, Eintritt verboten. ◆**ad'mittedly**, *adv.* allerdings.

ado [ə'du:], *s.* **without (any) more a.**, ohne weitere Umstände.

adolescence [ædə'les(ə)ns], *s.* Reifezeit *f*. ◆**ado'lescent. I.** *adj.* jugendlich. **II.** *s.* Jugendliche(r) *f(m)*.

adopt [ə'dɔpt], *v.tr.* (*a*) (ein Kind) adoptieren; (*b*) (einen Plan, Kandidaten) annehmen; (Maßnahmen) ergreifen; (eine Handlungsweise) wählen. ◆**a'dopted**, *adj.* adoptiert; **a. son**, Adoptivsohn *m*. ◆**a'doption**, *s.* 1. Adoption *f*. 2. Annahme *f*.

adore [ə'dɔ:r], *v.tr.* (j-n) anbeten; (für etwas *acc*) schwärmen. ◆**a'dorable**, *adj.* entzückend. ◆**ado'ration**, *s.* Anbetung *f*.

adorn [ə'dɔ:n], *v.tr.* (etwas) schmücken. ◆**a'dornment**, *s.* Schmuck *m*.

adrift [ə'drift], *adv.* treibend.

adulation [ædju'leiʃ(ə)n], *s.* Schmeichelei *f*.

adult ['ædʌlt]. **I.** *adj.* erwachsen. **II.** *s.* Erwachsene(r) *m(f)*.

adulterate [ə'dʌltəreit], *v.tr.* verfälschen.

adulterer, **-eress** [ə'dʌltərər, -ərəs], *s.* Ehebrecher(in) *m(f)*. ◆**a'dultery**, *s.* Ehebruch *m*.

advance [əd'vɑ:ns]. **I.** *s.* 1. (*a*) *Mil: etc:* Vormarsch *m*; (*b*) **in a.**, im voraus; **a. booking**, Vorverkauf *m*. 2. Fortschritt *m* (der Wissenschaft usw.); (*improvement*) Verbesserung *f*. 3. **a.** (*payment*), Vorauszahlung *f*. **II.** *v.* 1. *v.tr.* (*further*) (eine Sache) fördern; **to a. s.o. money**, j-m Geld vorschießen. 2. *v.i.* (*a*) *Mil: etc:* vorrücken; (*b*) (*progress*) Fortschritte machen. ◆**ad'vanced**, *adj.* (*a*) (*of age, stage*) vorgerückt; (*b*) (*of animal*) fortgeschritten; (*c*) (*of ideas etc.*) fortschrittlich. ◆**ad'vancement**, *s.* Beförderung *f* (im Rang); Förderung *f* (der Wissenschaft).

advantage [əd'vɑ:ntidʒ], *s.* Vorteil *m* (**over** s.o., j-m gegenüber); (*use*) Nutzen *m*; **to take a. of s.o., sth.**, j-n, etwas ausnutzen. ◆**advan'tageous** [ædvən'teidʒəs], *adj.* vorteilhaft.

advent ['ædvənt], *s.* 1. *Ecc:* **A.**, Advent *m*, Adventszeit *f*. 2. *Fig:* Kommen *n*.

adventure [əd'ventʃər], *s.* Abenteuer *n*. ◆**ad'venturous**, *adj.* abenteuerlich; (*of pers.*) abenteuerlustig.

adverb ['ædvə:b], *s.* Adverb *n*.

adverse ['ædvə:s], *adj.* ungünstig.

◆**adversary** ['ædvəs(ə)ri], *s.* Gegner(in) *m(f)*. ◆**ad'versity**, *s.* Unglück *n*.

advertise ['ædvətaiz], *v.tr.* & *i.* (*a*) (für ein Produkt) werben; **to a. a post**, eine Stelle ausschreiben; (*b*) (in einer Zeitung) inserieren (**for**, um + *acc*). ◆**advertisement** [əd'və:tismənt], *s.* Anzeige *f*. ◆**'advertising**, *s.* Werbung *f*; **a. agency**, Werbeagentur *f*.

advice [əd'vais], *s.* (*no pl.*) Rat *m*; **piece of a.**, Ratschlag *m*. ◆**ad'visable**, *adj.* ratsam. ◆**advise** [əd'vaiz], *v.tr.* (*a*) (j-n) beraten; **to a. s.o. to do sth.**, j-m raten, etwas zu tun; **to a. s.o. against sth.**, j-n von etwas *dat* abraten; (*b*) (*recommend*) (etwas) empfehlen. ◆**ad'viser**, *s.* (*professional*) Berater *m*; (*personal*) Ratgeber *m*. ◆**ad'visory**, *adj.* beratend.

advocate I. ['ædvəkeit] *v.tr.* befürworten. **II.** ['ædvəkət] *s.* (*champion*) Verfechter *m*; Befürworter *m*.

aerial ['eəriəl]. **I.** *adj.* Luft-. **II.** *s.* *Rad: TV:* Antenne *f*.

aero- ['eərəu-], *prefix* Luft-; Flug-. ◆**aero'batics**, *s.pl.* Kunstflug *m*. ◆**'aerodrome**, *s.* Flugplatz *m*. ◆**aerody'namics**, *s.pl.* Aerodynamik *f*. ◆**'aerofoil**, *s.* *Aut:* Heckflügel *m*. ◆**aero'nautics**, *s.pl.* Luftfahrt *f*. ◆**'aeroplane**, *s.* Flugzeug *n*. ◆**'aerosol**, *s.* (*a*) Sprühdose *f*; (*b*) *Ch:* Aerosol *n*.

affable ['æfəbl], *adj.* leutselig.

affair [ə'feər], *s.* 1. Angelegenheit *f*; Sache *f*. 2. (*love*) **a.**, Liebesverhältnis *n*.

affect¹ [ə'fekt], *v.tr.* (*pretend*) vortäuschen. ◆**a'ffected**, *adj.* affektiert. ◆**affec'tation**, *s.* 1. *no pl* Affektiertheit *f*. 2. (*habit*) affektierte Angewohnheit *f*.

affect² [ə'fekt], *v.tr.* (*a*) (*influence*) (auf etwas *acc*) wirken; (ein Ergebnis, eine Lage usw.) beeinflussen; (*b*) (*move*) (j-n) bewegen. ◆**a'ffection**, *s.* Liebe *f* (**for**, zu + *dat*). ◆**a'ffectionate**, *adj.* liebevoll.

affidavit [æfi'deivit], *s.* beeidigte Erklärung *f*.

affinity [ə'finiti], *s.* Verwandtschaft *f*; (*similarity*) Ähnlichkeit *f*.

affirm [ə'fə:m], *v.tr.* (*confirm*) bestätigen; (*state*) erklären. ◆**affirmation** [æfə(:)'meiʃ(ə)n], *s.* Bestätigung *f*. ◆**a'ffirmative**, *adj.* positiv; **to answer sth. in the a.**, etwas bejahen.

afflict [ə'flikt], *v.tr.* heimsuchen. ◆**a'ffliction**, *s.* (*physical*) Leiden *n*; (*psychological*) Kummer *m*.

affluence ['æfluəns], *s.* Reichtum *m*. ◆**'affluent**, *adj.* wohlhabend; **a. society**, Wohlstandsgesellschaft *f*.

afford [ə'fɔ:d], *v.tr.* sich *dat* (etwas) leisten.

affront [ə'frʌnt], *s.* Beleidigung *f*.

afloat [ə'fləut], *adv.* & *adj.* schwimmend; (*of ship*) flott.

afoot [ə'fut], *adv.* im Gange.

afraid [ə'freid], *adj.* **to be a.**, sich fürchten, Angst haben (of s.o., sth., vor j-m, etwas dat); **I am a.** he's not here, er ist leider nicht hier.

afresh [ə'freʃ], adv. von neuem.

Africa ['æfrikə]. Pr. n. Afrika n. ◆**African. I.** adj. afrikanisch. **II.** s. Afrikaner(in) m(f).

aft [ɑ:ft], adv. Nau: achtern.

after ['ɑ:ftər]. **I.** prep. nach + dat; **to run a s.o., j-m** nachlaufen; **the police are a.** him, die Polizei ist hinter ihm her; **day a. day**, Tag für Tag; **the day a. tomorrow**, übermorgen; **the week a. next**, übernächste Woche; a. all, schließlich; **called Brian a. his father**, nach seinem Vater Brian genannt. **II.** adv. danach; **the week a.**, die folgende Woche. **III.** conj. nachdem. ◆**aftereffect**, s. Nachwirkung f. ◆**aftermath**, s. Nachspiel n; (effects) Nachwirkungen fpl. ◆**after'noon**, s. Nachmittag m; **good a.!** guten Tag! ◆**afters**, s.pl. Nachtisch m. ◆**afterthought**, s. nachträglicher Einfall m. ◆**afterwards**, adv. später.

again [ə'gen], adv. **1.** wieder, (once more) noch einmal; **a. and a.**, immer wieder; **now and a.**, ab und zu. **2.** (what is more) außerdem.

against [ə'genst], prep. gegen + acc.

age [eidʒ] **I.** s. **1.** Alter n; **to be under a.**, minderjährig sein; **to come of a.**, großjährig werden; **a. group**, Altersgruppe f; **a. limit**, Altersgrenze f; **old a.**, hohes Alter. **2.** Zeitalter n; **the Middle Ages**, das Mittelalter; **I haven't seen him for ages**, ich habe ihn schon ewig nicht mehr gesehen. **II.** v. **1.** v.i. altern. **2.** v.tr. (j-n) alt werden lassen. ◆**aged**, adj. **a.** a twenty, 20 Jahre alt. ◆**ag(e)ing**, adj. alternd.

agency ['eidʒənsi], s. Com: Vertretung f; travel a., Reisebüro n. ◆**agent** ['eidʒənt], s. Com: Vertreter m; (secret) a., Geheimagent m.

aggravate ['ægrəveit], v.tr. (a) (ein Problem, die Lage) verschlimmern; (b) (j-n) reizen. ◆**aggravating**, adj. ärgerlich. ◆**aggra'vation**, s. **1.** Verschlimmerung f. **2.** (general) Ärger m; (instance) Ärgernis n.

aggregate ['ægrigit], s. Summe f; Mth: Aggregat n.

aggression [ə'greʃ(ə)n], s. Aggression f. ◆**a'gressive**, adj. aggressiv.

aggrieved [ə'gri:vd], adj. gekränkt.

aghast [ə'gɑːst], adj. entsetzt (at, über + acc).

agile ['ædʒail], adj. flink; (of mind etc.) rege.

agitate ['ædʒiteit], v. **1.** v.tr. (j-n) aufregen. **2.** v.i. **to a. for/against sth.**, für/gegen etwas acc Propaganda machen. ◆**agitated**, adj. aufgeregt. ◆**agi'tation**, s. **1.** Pol: etc: Aufwiegelung f. **2.** (of pers.) Aufregung f. ◆**agitator**, s. Aufwiegler m.

ago [ə'gəu], adv. vor; **ten years a.**, vor zehn Jahren; **a little while a.**, vor kur-

zem; **it is long a.**, es ist lange her.

agonizing ['ægənaiziŋ], adj. (of pain) quälend; (of spectacle) qualvoll. ◆**agony**, s. Qual f.

agree [ə'gri:], v. **1.** v.i. (a) einwilligen (to sth., in etwas acc); (b) sich einigen (on sth., über etwas acc); **to a. on a time**, einen Termin ausmachen; (c) (approve) einverstanden sein; (d) (of things) übereinstimmen; (of pers.) gleicher Meinung sein; (e) **oysters do not a. with me**, Austern vertrage ich nicht. **2.** v.tr. (einen Preis, Termin usw.) vereinbaren; **he agreed to come**, er erklärte sich bereit zu kommen. ◆**a'greeable**, adj. (a) (of pers.) einverstanden; (b) (pleasant) angenehm. ◆**a'greement**, s. **1.** (document) Vereinbarung f; (contract) Vertrag m; Pol: Abkommen n. **2.** (a) (consent) Zustimmung f; (b) (accord) Übereinstimmung f; **to be in a. with s.o., sth.**, mit j-m, etwas dat übereinstimmen.

agriculture ['ægrikʌltʃər], s. Landwirtschaft f. ◆**agri'cultural**, adj. landwirtschaftlich.

aground [ə'graund], adv. **to run a.**, stranden.

ahead [ə'hed] adv. **the town was straight a. of us**, die Stadt lag direkt vor uns; **he went on a.**, er ging vor; **to be two hours a.** (of s.o.), zwei Stunden Vorsprung (vor j-m) haben; **a. of time**, vorzeitig.

aid [eid]. **I.** v.tr. (j-m) helfen; (j-n, ein Land usw.) unterstützen. **II.** s. (a) Hilfe f; **in a. of**, zugunsten + gen; (b) (device) Hilfsmittel n.

ailment ['eilmənt], s. Leiden n; pl Beschwerden fpl.

aim [eim]. **I.** v. **1.** v.tr. (etwas) richten (at s.o., sth., auf j-n, etwas acc). **2.** v.i. **to a. at sth.**, (i) (with weapon) auf etwas acc zielen; (ii) (intend) etwas im Auge haben. **II.** s. **1.** Ziel n; **to take a.** zielen. **2.** (purpose) Zweck m. ◆**aimless**, adj. ziellos.

air [ɛər]. **I.** v.tr. (a) (ein Zimmer, Betten usw.) lüften; (b) (eine Meinung) äußern; **to a. grievances**, Beschwerden vorbringen. **II.** s. **1.** Luft f; **in the open a.**, im Freien; **by a.**, auf dem Luftweg; **a. hostess**, Stewardeß f. **2.** (look) Aussehen n; (of pers.) Miene f. ◆**airbase**, s. Luftstützpunkt m. ◆**airborne**, adj. in der Luft. ◆**air-con'ditioning**, s. Klimaanlage f. ◆**air-cooled**, adj. luftgekühlt. ◆**aircraft**, s. Flugzeug n; **a. carrier**, Flugzeugträger m. ◆**aircrew**, s. Flugzeugbesatzung f. ◆**airfield**, s. Flugplatz m. ◆**airforce**, s. Luftwaffe f. ◆**airlift**, s. Luftbrücke f. ◆**airline**, s. Fluggesellschaft f. ◆**airliner**, s. Verkehrsflugzeug n. ◆**airlock**, s. Luftabschluß m. ◆**airmail**, s. Luftpost f; **by a.**, mit Luftpost. ◆**airman**, -men, s. Flieger m. ◆**airplane**, s. N.Am: Flugzeug n. ◆**airpocket**, s. Luftloch n. ◆**airport**, s. Flughafen m. ◆**air-raid**, s. Fliegerangriff m. ◆**air-sickness**, s.

Luftkrankheit f. **airstrip**, s. Av: Landestreifen m. **airtight**, adj. luftdicht. **air-traffic**, s. Flugverkehr m; a.-t. control, Flugsicherung f; a.-t. controller, Fluglotse m.

aisle [ail], s. Th: Av: etc: Gang m.

ajar [ə'dʒɑːr], adv. angelehnt.

alarm [ə'lɑːm]. I. v.tr. erschrecken; to be alarmed at sth., über etwas acc beunruhigt sein. II. s. Alarm m; to give/sound the a., Alarm schlagen; (device) Alarmanlage f; a. (clock), Wecker m. **a'larming**, adj. alarmierend; (frightening) erschreckend; (worrying) beängstigend. **a'larmist**, s. Schwarzseher m.

alas [ə'læs], int. ach!

Albania [æl'beinjə]. Pr. n. Albanien n.

albatross ['ælbətros], s. Albatros m.

album ['ælbəm], s. Album n.

alcohol ['ælkəhol], s. Alkohol m. **alco'holic**. I. adj. alkoholisch. II. s. (pers.) Alkoholiker(in) m(f).

alcove ['ælkəuv], s. Nische f.

ale [eil], s. Ale n; pale a., helles Bier.

alert [ə'lɔːt]. I. adj. wachsam; (of mind) rege, aufgeweckt. II. s. Alarm(zustand) m; to be on the a., (i) alarmbereit sein; (ii) Fig: auf der Hut sein. **a'lertness**, s. Wachsamkeit f.

alfresco [æl'freskəu], adj. & adv. im Freien.

algebra ['ældʒibrə], s. Algebra f.

Algeria [æl'dʒiəriə]. Pr. n. Algerien n.

alias ['eiliəs], adv. sonst ... genannt.

alibi ['ælibai], s. Alibi n.

alien ['eiliən]. I. adj. a (foreign) ausländisch; (b) (strange) fremd. II. s. Ausländer m. **alienate** ['eiliəneit], v.tr. entfremden.

alight1 [ə'lait], v.i. (of pers.) aussteigen; (of bird) sich niederlassen.

alight2, adj. to be a., brennen; to set sth. a., etwas anzünden.

alignment [ə'lainmənt], s. Aufstellung f in einer geraden Linie; political a., politische Orientierung f.

alike [ə'laik], adj. & adv. gleich; (similar) ähnlich; teachers and children a., Lehrer sowie Kinder.

alimentary [æli'mentəri], adj. a. canal, Verdauungskanal m.

alimony ['æliməni], s. Alimente npl.

alive [ə'laiv], adj. lebendig; he is still a., er lebt noch.

alkali ['ælkəlai], s. Alkali n.

all [ɔːl], adj. pron. & adv. 1. (a) adj. (sing.) ganz; (pl) alle; a. his life, sein ganzes Leben lang; (b) (pers.) alle; a. of us, wir alle; we a. love him, wir haben ihn alle gern; Sp: five a., fünf zu fünf; (c) (things) alles; a. that, das alles. 2. once and for a., ein für allemal; for a. I know, soviel ich weiß; not at a., überhaupt nicht; a. but, fast, beinahe; a. in a/a. things considered, alles in allem. 3. adv. ganz; a. in black, ganz in schwarz; a. the better, umso besser; a.

right, in Ordnung; he enjoyed it a. the same, er hat es trotzdem genossen; a. the same, you might have told me, das hättest du mir immerhin sagen können; a. at once, (i) (suddenly) plötzlich; (ii) (at one time) zugleich. **all(-)clear**, s. Entwarnung f. **all-in**, adj. (of pers.) erschöpft; a.-in price, Inklusivpreis m. **all-out**, adj. maximal; to go a.-o. for sth., alles auf etwas acc setzen. **all-purpose**, adj. Allzweck-. **all-round**, adj. umfassend. **all-rounder**, s. Sp: Allroundsportler m. **all-time**, adj. absolut; a.-t. low, absoluter Tiefstand.

allege [ə'ledʒ], v.tr. (a) behaupten; (b) (pretend) vorgeben. **allegation** [æli'geiʃ(ə)n], s. Anschuldigung f. **al'leged**, adj. angeblich.

allegiance [ə'liːdʒ(ə)ns], s. Treue f (to, gegenüber + dat).

allergy ['ælədʒi], s. Allergie f. **al'lergic**, adj. allergisch (to, gegen + acc).

alleviate [ə'liːvieit], v.tr. (Schmerzen) lindern; (ein Problem) erleichtern.

alley ['æli], s. (enge) Gasse f.

alliance [ə'laiəns], s. Pol: Bündnis n. **allied** ['ælaid], adj. 1. Pol: alliiert, verbündet (to/with, mit + dat). 2. (related) verwandt.

alligator ['æligeitər], s. Alligator m.

allocate ['æləkeit], v.tr. to a. s.o. a task, j-m eine Aufgabe zuteilen/Adm: zuweisen; to a. a sum to sth., eine Summe für etwas acc zur Verfügung stellen. **allo'cation**, s. 1. (act) Zuteilung f. 2. Quote f; (money) zugeteilter Betrag m.

allot [ə'lot], v.tr. to a. sth. to s.o., j-m etwas zuteilen; in its allotted place, an seinem vorgeschriebenen Platz. **a'llotment**, s. (ground) Schrebergarten m.

allow [ə'lau], v.tr. (permit) to a. s.o. sth., j-m etwas erlauben; to be allowed to do sth., etwas tun dürfen; (b) to a. (oneself) enough time for sth., (sich dat) genug Zeit zu etwas dat lassen; (c) to a. for sth., etwas berücksichtigen. **allowance**, s. 1. a Quote f; (b) (money) Zuwendung f; (addition to salary) Zuschuß m; child a., Kinderbeihilfe f. 2. to make a. for sth., etwas berücksichtigen/esp. Tchn: einkalkulieren; you have to make allowances for small children, für kleine Kinder muß man schon Verständnis haben.

alloy ['æloi], s. Legierung f.

allude [ə'l(j)uːd], v.i. to a. to s.o., sth., auf j-n, etwas acc anspielen.

alluring [ə'l(j)uəriŋ], adj. verlockend.

allusion [ə'l(j)uːʒ(ə)n], s. Anspielung f.

ally. I. ['ælai], v.tr. & i. (etwas, sich) vereinigen (to/with, mit + dat). II. ['ælai], s. (pl. 'allies). Verbündete(r) f(m), Alliierte(r) f(m).

almanac ['ɔːlmənæk], s. Almanach m.

almighty [ɔːl'maːtɪ]. **I.** *adj.* allmächtig. **II.** *s.* the A., der Allmächtige.

almond ['ɑːmənd], *s.* Mandel *f.*

almost ['ɔːlməʊst], *adv.* beinahe, fast.

alms [ɑːmz], *s. sing.* or *pl.* Almosen *n.*

alone [ə'ləʊn], *adj.* allein; to leave s.o., sth. a., (i) j-n, etwas in Ruhe lassen; (ii) etwas sein lassen.

along [ə'lɒŋ]. **I.** *prep.* (etwas *acc*) entlang. **II.** *adv.* to move a., sich fortbewegen; **come a.!** komm doch! **a. with**, zusammen mit + *dat.* ◆**a'longside.** **I.** *prep.* (a) neben + *dat;* (b) (*compared with*) verglichen mit + *dat.* **II.** *adv.* daneben; *Nau:* längsseits.

aloof [ə'luːf], *adv. & adj.* zurückhaltend; to remain a., sich fernhalten. ◆**a'loofness,** *s.* Zurückhaltung *f.*

aloud [ə'laʊd], *adv.* laut.

alp [ælp], *s.* the Alps, die Alpen.

alphabet ['ælfəbet], *s.* Alphabet *n.* ◆**alpha'betical,** *adj.* alphabetisch.

alpine ['ælpaɪn], *adj.* alpin; a. plants, Alpenpflanzen *fpl.*

already [ɔːl'redɪ], *adv.* schon.

Alsace [æl'sæs]. *Pr.n.* Elsaß *n.* ◆**Alsatian** [æl'seɪʃ(ə)n], *s.* (*dog*) Schäferhund *m.*

also ['ɔːlsəʊ], *adv.* auch, ebenfalls.

altar ['ɔːltər], *s.* Altar *m.*

alter ['ɔːltər], *v.* **1.** *v.tr.* ändern, (Kleider) umändern. **2.** *v.i.* sich ändern; (*in appearance*) sich verändern. ◆**alte'ration,** *s.* (a) Änderung *f;* (b) *Tchn: etc:* Umbau *m.*

alternate. **I.** [ɔːl'tɜːnɪt] *adj.* **1.** abwechselnd; **on a. days,** jeden zweiten Tag. **2.** *N.Am:* an a. date, ein anderer Termin. **II.** ['ɔːltəneɪt] *v.* **1** *v.tr.* (zwei Sachen) abwechseln lassen. **2.** *v.i.* abwechseln. ◆**'alternating,** *adj.* abwechselnd; *El:* a. current, Wechselstrom *m.* ◆**alternative** [ɔːl'tɜːnətɪv]. **I.** *adj.* alternativ. **II.** *s.* Alternative *f;* to have no a., keine Wahl haben; **-ly,** *adv.* andernfalls.

although [ɔːl'ðəʊ], *conj.* obwohl.

altitude ['æltɪtjuːd], *s.* Höhe *f.*

altogether [ɔːltə'geðər], *adv.* (a) (*wholly*) völlig; (b) (*on the whole*) alles in allem; **how much does that come to a.?** was macht das alles zusammen?

aluminium [ælju'mɪnɪəm], *N.Am:* **aluminum** [ə'luːmɪnəm], *s.* Aluminium *n.*

always ['ɔːlwɪz, -weɪz], *adv.* immer.

amalgam [ə'mælgəm], *s. Fig:* Mischung *f.* ◆**amalgamate** [ə'mælgəmeɪt], *v.* **1.** *v.tr.* zusammenschließen, (*combine*) vereinigen. **2.** *v.i.* sich zusammenschließen. ◆**amalga'mation,** *s.* Zusammenschluß *m.*

amass [ə'mæs], *v.tr.* anhäufen.

amateur ['æmətər], *s.* Amateur *m; Pej:* Dilettant *m.* ◆**'amateurish,** *adj.* dilettantisch.

amaze [ə'meɪz], *v.tr.* erstaunen. ◆**a'mazed,** *adj.* erstaunt. ◆**a'mazement,** *s.* Erstaunen *n.* ◆**a'mazing,** *adj.* erstaunlich.

ambassador [æm'bæsədər], *s.* Botschafter(in) *m(f).*

amber ['æmbər], *s.* **1.** Bernstein *m.* **2.** (*colour*) Bernsteinfarbe *f; Aut:* gelbes Licht.

ambiguous [æm'bɪgjuəs], *adj.* zweideutig. ◆**ambi'guity,** *s.* Zweideutigkeit *f.*

ambition [æm'bɪʃ(ə)n], *s.* (*general*) Ehrgeiz *m;* (*particular*) Ambition *f.* ◆**am'bitious,** *adj.* ehrgeizig.

amble ['æmbl], *v.i.* to a. (along), dahinschlendern.

ambulance ['æmbjuləns], *s.* Krankenwagen *m.*

ambush ['æmbuʃ]. **I.** *v.tr.* (j-n) aus dem Hinterhalt überfallen. **II.** *s.* Hinterhalt *m.*

amen ['ɑː'men], *int.* amen.

amenable [ə'miːnəbl], *adj.* zugänglich (to, *dat*).

amend [ə'mend], *v.tr.* (a) ändern; (b) (*correct*) (einen Text usw.) verbessern. ◆**a'mendment,** *s.* (a) Änderung *f;* (b) Verbesserung *f.* ◆**a'mends,** *s.pl.* to make a. for sth., etwas wiedergutmachen.

amenity [ə'miːnɪtɪ], *s.* Annehmlichkeit *f.*

America [ə'merɪkə]. *Pr.n.* Amerika *n.* ◆**A'merican.** **I.** *s.* Amerikaner(in) *m(f).* **II.** *adj.* amerikanisch.

amethyst ['æmɪθɪst], *s.* Amethyst *m.*

amiable ['eɪmjəbl], *adj.* liebenswürdig.

amicable ['æmɪkəbl], *adj.* freundlich; (*of relations, feelings*) freundschaftlich; **-ably,** *adv.* auf gütlichem Wege.

amid(st) [ə'mɪd(st)], *prep.* mitten in + *dat;* (*with pl.*) mitten unter + *dat.*

amiss [ə'mɪs], *adv. & adj.* to take sth. a., etwas übelnehmen.

ammonia [ə'məʊnjə], *s.* Ammoniak *m.*

ammunition [æmju'nɪʃ(ə)n], *s.* Munition *f.*

amnesia [æm'niːzɪə], *s.* Gedächtnisschwund *m.*

amnesty ['æmnɪstɪ], *s.* Amnestie *f.*

among(st) [ə'mʌŋ(st)], *prep.* (mitten) unter; a. other things, unter anderem.

amorous ['æmərəs], *adj.* zärtlich; (*in love*) verliebt.

amount [ə'maʊnt]. **I.** *s.* **1.** (*money*) Betrag *m.* **2.** (*quantity*) Menge *f.* **II.** *v.i.* to a. to £200, 200 Pfund betragen; that amounts to the same thing, das kommt auf das gleiche hinaus; he'll never a. to much, er wird es nie sehr weit bringen.

amphibian [æm'fɪbɪən], *s.* Amphibie *f.* ◆**am'phibious,** *adj.* amphibisch.

amphitheatre ['æmfɪθɪətər], *s.* Amphitheater *n.*

ample ['æmpl], *adj.* (a) reichlich; (b) an a. figure, eine volle Figur.

amplify ['æmplɪfaɪ], *v.tr.* (ein Signal usw.) verstärken. ◆**'amplifier,** *s.* Verstärker *m.*

amputate ['æmpjuteɪt], *v.tr.* amputieren. ◆**ampu'tation,** *s.* Amputation *f.*

amuse [ə'mjuːz], *v.tr.* (j-n, sich) unterhalten. ◆**a'musement,** *s.* Unterhaltung *f; (pleasure)* Vergnügen *n; (pastime)* Zeitvertreib *m;* a. park, Vergnügungspark *m;* a. arcade, Spielhalle *f.* ◆**a'musing,** *adj.* amüsant.

an see a².

anaemia [ə'ni:miə], *s.* Anämie *f,* Blutarmut *f.* ◆**a'naemic,** *adj.* blutarm.

anaesthetic [ænis'θetik], *s.* Betäubungsmittel *n;* **under a.,** in Narkose; **local a.,** örtliche Betäubung. ◆**anaesthetist** [ə'ni:sθətist], *s.* Narkosearzt *m,* Narkoseärztin *f.*

analogy [ə'nælədʒi], *s.* Analogie *f.* ◆**analogous** [ə'næləgəs], *adj.* analog **(to/with,** + *dat).*

analyse ['ænəlaiz], *v.tr.* analysieren. ◆**analysis,** *pl.* **-ses** [ə'nælisis, -si:z], *s.* Analyse *f.* ◆**'analyst,** *s.* Analytiker *m; esp. N.Am:* Psychoanalytiker *m.* ◆**ana'lytic,** *adj.* analytisch.

anarchy ['ænəki], *s.* Anarchie *f.* ◆**'anarchist,** *s.* Anarchist(in) *m(f).*

anathema [ə'næθəmə], *s.* **it's a. to me,** es ist mir ein Greuel.

anatomy [ə'nætəmi], *s.* Anatomie *f.* ◆**anatomical** [ænə'tomik(ə)l], *adj.* anatomisch.

ancestor ['ænsestər], *s.* Vorfahr *m.* ◆**an'cestral,** *adj.* angestammt; **his a. home,** sein Stammsitz *m.* ◆**ancestry** ['ænsistri], *s.* **1.** *(origin)* Abstammung *f.* **2.** *coll.* Vorfahren *mpl.*

anchor ['æŋkər]. **I.** *s.* Anker *m.* **II.** *v.* **1.** *v.tr.* verankern; **to be anchored,** vor Anker liegen. **2.** *v.i.* ankern. ◆**'anchorage,** *s.* Ankerplatz *m.*

anchovy ['æntʃəvi], *s.* Sardelle *f.*

ancient ['einʃ(ə)nt], *adj.* sehr alt; *esp. F:* uralt.

and [ænd, ənd], *conj.* und; **better a. better,** immer besser.

anecdote ['ænikdəut], *s.* Anekdote *f.*

anemone [ə'neməni], *s.* Anemone *f.*

angel ['eindʒəl], *s.* Engel *m.* ◆**angelic** [æn'dʒelik], *adj.* engelhaft.

anger ['æŋgər], *s.* Zorn *m.*

angle¹ ['æŋgl], *s. (a)* Winkel *m;* **at an a.,** schräg (to, zu + *dat)* *(b) (aspect)* Gesichtspunkt *m.*

angle², *v.i.* angeln.

Anglican ['æŋglikən]. **I.** *s.* Anglikaner(in) *m(f).* **II.** *adj.* anglikanisch.

angry ['æŋgri], *adj.* zornig; **a. with s.o. about sth.,** böse auf j-n wegen etwas *gen;* **to make s.o. a.,** j-n ärgern.

anguish ['æŋgwiʃ], *s.* Qual *f.*

angular ['æŋgjulər], *adj.* eckig; *(of features)* knochig.

animal ['æniml]. **I.** *s.* Tier *n.* **II.** *adj.* Tier-; *Pej:* tierisch.

animate ['ænimeit], *v.tr.* beleben. ◆**'animated,** *adj.* lebhaft; **a. cartoon,** Zeichentrickfilm *m.* ◆**ani'mation,** *s.* Lebhaftigkeit *f.*

animosity [æni'mositi], *s.* Feindseligkeit *f; (hatred)* Haß *m.*

aniseed ['ænisi:d], *s.* Anis *m.*

ankle ['æŋkl], *s.* Knöchel *m.*

annex ['æneks], *v.tr.* (ein Land usw.) annektieren. ◆**annex(e)** ['æneks], *s.* Anbau *m.*

annihilate [ə'naiəleit], *v.tr.* vernichten. ◆**annihi'lation,** *s.* Vernichtung *f.*

anniversary [æni'vɔ:s(ə)ri], *s.* Jahrestag *m;* **wedding a.,** Hochzeitstag *m.*

annotate ['ænəteit], *v.tr.* mit Anmerkungen versehen.

announce [ə'nauns], *v.tr. (a)* (eine Nachricht) bekanntgeben; *Rad: TV:* (ein Programm) ansagen; *(b)* (etwas Zukünftiges) ankündigen. ◆**a'nnouncement,** *s.* Meldung *f; Rad: TV:* Ansage *f; (also over loudspeaker)* Durchsage *f; (small ad)* Anzeige *f.* ◆**a'nnouncer,** *s. Rad: TV:* Ansager(in) *m(f).*

annoy [ə'nɔi], *v.tr. (a) (irritate)* ärgern; **to be annoyed,** sich ärgern **(at, about sth.),** über etwas *acc;* **with s.o.,** über j-n); *(b) (inconvenience)* belästigen. ◆**a'nnoyance,** *s.* Ärger *m.* ◆**a'nnoyed,** *adj.* verärgert. ◆**a'nnoying,** *adj.* ärgerlich.

annual ['ænju(ə)l]. **I.** *adj.* jährlich; Jahres-. **II.** *s. (a) Bot:* einjährige Pflanze *f; (b) (book)* Jahrbuch *n.*

annuity [ə'nju:iti], *s.* Jahresrente *f.*

annul [ə'nʌl], *v.tr.* annullieren.

anomaly [ə'nɔməli], *s.* Anomalie *f; (situation)* Mißstand *m.* ◆**a'nomalous,** *adj.* anomal.

anonymous [ə'nɔniməs], *adj.* anonym. ◆**ano'nymity,** *s.* Anonymität *f.*

anorak ['ænəræk], *s.* Anorak *m.*

another [ə'nʌðər], *adj. & pron.* **1.** *(an additional)* noch ein(e); a. **(one),** noch einer/eine/eines; **a. ten years,** noch zehn Jahre. **2.** *(a different)* ein anderer, eine andere; **one way or a.,** auf irgendeine Weise. **3. one a.,** einander; **they greeted one a.,** sie grüßten sich.

answer ['ɑ:nsər]. **I.** *s.* **1.** Antwort *f* **(to a question,** auf eine Frage). **2.** Lösung *f* **(to a problem,** eines Problems). **II.** *v.* **1.** *v.tr.* (einen Brief usw.) beantworten; (j-m) antworten; **to a. the telephone,** (den Hörer) abnehmen; **to a. an advertisement,** auf eine Anzeige antworten; **to a. the door,** aufmachen. **2.** *v.i.* antworten; **to a. to the name of X,** auf den Namen X hören; **to a. for sth.,** für etwas *acc* verantwortlich sein; **to a. (s.o.) back,** (j-m) frech antworten. ◆**'answerable,** *adj.* **to be a. to s.o. for sth.,** j-m für etwas *acc* verantwortlich sein.

ant [ænt], *s.* Ameise *f.*

antagonize [æn'tægənaiz], *v.tr.* sich *dat* (j-n) zum Gegner machen. ◆**an'tagonism,** *s.* Antagonismus *m* (to, gegen + *acc).* ◆**an'tagonist,** *s.* Gegner *m.* ◆**antago'nistic,** *adj.* feindselig (to, gegen + *acc).*

antarctic [ænt'ɑ:ktik]. **I.** *adj.* antarktisch; **the A. Ocean,** das Südliche Polarmeer. **II.** *s.* **the A.,** die Antarktis.

antedate ['ænti'deit], v.tr. (a) (einem Ereignis) vorausgehen; (b) (ein Dokument usw.) nachdatieren.

antelope ['æntiləup], s. Antilope f.

antenatal ['ænti'neitl], adj. vor der Geburt.

antenna, pl. -ae [æn'tenə,-i:], s. 1. Z: Fühler m. 2. Rad: TV: Antenne f.

anthem ['ænθəm], s. national a., Nationalhymne f.

anthology [æn'θɔlədʒi], s. Anthologie f.

anthropology [ænθrə'pɔlədʒi], s. Anthropologie f. ◆anthro'pologist, s. Anthropologe m, Anthropologin f.

anti- ['ænti-], prefix anti-, gegen-.
◆'anti-'aircraft, adj. Fliegerabwehr-.
◆'anti'bi'otic, s. Antibiotikum n.
◆'antibody, s. Antikörper m.
◆'anti'climax, s. Enttäuschung f.
◆'anti'clockwise, adv. gegen den Uhrzeigersinn. ◆'anti'cyclone, s. Hoch(druckgebiet) n. ◆'anti-'dazzle, adj. Blendschutz-. ◆'antidote, s. Gegenmittel n; Gegengift n.
◆'antifreeze, s. Frostschutzmittel n.
◆'anti-se'mitic, adj. antisemitisch.
◆'anti'septic, I. adj. antiseptisch. II. s. Antiseptikum n. ◆'anti'social, adj. unsozial.

anticipate [æn'tisipeit], v.tr. (a) vorwegnehmen; (den Ereignissen) vorauseilen; (b) (expect) erwarten. ◆antici'pation, s. Erwartung f; Vorwegnahme f.

antics ['æntiks], s.pl. Possen fpl.

antipathy [æn'tipəθi], s. Antipathie f (to, gegen + acc); Abneigung f.

antiquarian [ænti'kwɛəriən], adj. a. bookseller, Antiquar m. ◆antique [æn'ti:k]. I. adj. antik; a. furniture, antike Möbel. II. s. Antiquität f; a. dealer, Antiquitätenhändler m. ◆'antiquated, adj. veraltet. ◆an'tiquity, s. (of period) Altertum n, Antike f.

antithesis [æn'tiθisis], pl. -es [-i:z], s. Gegensatz m (to/of, zu + dat).

antler ['æntlər], s. the antlers, das Geweih.

anus ['einəs], s. After m.

anvil ['ænvil], s. Amboß m.

anxiety [æŋ'zaiiti], s. (a) (fear) Angst f; (b) (worry) Sorge f (for, um + acc); (state) Besorgtheit f.

anxious ['æŋ(k)ʃəs], adj. 1. (a) (of pers.) (afraid) ängstlich; (disturbed) unruhig (about, wegen + gen); (worried) besorgt (about, um + acc); (b) (of time) sorgenvoll. 2. to be a. to do sth, darauf aus sein, etwas zu tun; -ly, adv. 1. besorgt. 2. (impatiently) gespannt.

any ['eni]. I. adj. 1. (a) interrog. sing. irgendein(e), pl. irgendwelche; have you a. milk? haben Sie (etwas) Milch? have you a. eggs? haben Sie Eier? (b) neg. not a., kein(e). 2. (no matter which) jeder, jede, jedes; at a. time, jederzeit; in a. case, jedenfalls. II. pron. (a) have you a. left? (i) (sing.) haben Sie noch davon? (ii) (pl.)

haben Sie noch welche? (b) neg. I can't find a., ich kann keinen/keine/keines finden. III. adv. is he a. better? geht es ihm etwas besser? if it gets a. hotter, wenn es noch wärmer wird; she doesn't dance a. more, sie tanzt nicht mehr. ◆'anybody/'anyone, pron. 1. (irgend) jemand. 2. not a., niemand. 3. (no matter who) jeder. ◆'anyhow. I. adv. to do sth. (just) a., etwas recht und schlecht machen. II. conj. (concessive) immerhin; (whatever happens) sowieso. ◆'anything, pron. (irgend) etwas; not a..., nichts; he eats a., er ißt alles. ◆'anyway, adv. & conj.=anyhow. ◆'anywhere, adv. 1. irgendwo; you can buy it a., du kannst es überall kaufen. 2. not ... a., nirgends; nirgendwo.

apart [ə'pɑːt], adv. 1. (of two people) to live a., getrennt leben; you can't tell them a., man kann die beiden nicht auseinanderhalten; (b) (to pieces) auseinander. 2. a. from, abgesehen von + dat; joking a., Spaß beiseite.

apartment [ə'pɑːtmənt], s. Wohnung f.

apathy ['æpəθi], s. Teilnahmslosigkeit f. ◆apathetic [-'θetik], adj. teilnahmslos.

ape [eip]. I. s. Menschenaffe m. II. v.tr. nachäffen.

aperitif [ə'peritif], s. Aperitif m.

aperture ['æpətjuər, -tʃər], s. 1. Öffnung f. 2. Phot: Blende f.

apex ['eipeks], pl. -exes, -ices ['eipeks, -eksiz, -isitz], s. Spitze f.

aphrodisiac [æfrəu'diziæk], s. Aphrodisiakum n.

apiece [ə'pi:s], adv. pro Stück; (pers.) pro Kopf/Person.

aplomb [ə'plɔm], s. Selbstbewußtsein n; with a., selbstsicher.

apocryphal [ə'pɔkrifəl], adj. (of story) erfunden.

apologetic [əpɔlə'dʒetik], adj. to be a. (for/about sth.), sich (für etwas acc) entschuldigen. ◆apologize [ə'pɔlədʒaiz], v.i. to a. to s.o. for sth., sich bei j-m für etwas acc entschuldigen. ◆a'pology, s. Entschuldigung f.

apoplexy ['æpəpleksi], s. Schlaganfall m.

apostle [ə'pɔsl], s. Apostel m.

apostrophe [ə'pɔstrəfi], s. Apostroph m.

appal(l) [ə'pɔːl], v.tr. entsetzen. ◆a'palling, adj. entsetzlich.

apparatus [æpə'reitəs], s. Apparat m.

apparent [ə'pærənt], adj. 1. (clear) offenbar. 2. (seeming) scheinbar; -ly, adv. anscheinend.

apparition [æpə'riʃ(ə)n], s. Erscheinung f.

appeal [ə'pi:l]. I. s. 1. Appell m (to reason, an die Vernunft); Jur: Berufung f. 2. (a) Aufforderung f (for calm, zur Ruhe); (b) Bitte f (for funds, um Spenden). 3. (attraction) Reiz m. II. v.i. (a) appellieren (to s.o., sth., an j-n, etwas acc); to a. for help, (dringend) um Hilfe bitten; Jur: to a. against a sentence, Berufung gegen ein Urteil einlegen; (b) (of *thing*) gefallen (to, *dat*). ◆a'ppealing, *adj.* reizvoll.

appear [ə'piər], *v.i.* (a) (*become visible, be published etc.*) erscheinen; (*on stage etc.*) auftreten; (b) (*seem*) scheinen. ◆a'ppearance, *s.* 1. Erscheinen *n*; Auftritt *m*; to put in an a., sich (kurz) zeigen. 2. (*look*) Aussehen *n*; (*semblance*) Schein *m*.

appease [ə'piːz], *v.tr.* beschwichtigen.

appendix [ə'pendiks], *pl. -ixes, -ices* [-isiz], *s.* 1. Anhang *m* (eines Buches). 2. *Anat:* Blinddarm *m*. ◆appendi'citis, *s.* Blinddarmentzündung *f*.

appetite ['æpitait], *s.* Appetit *m* (for sth., auf etwas *acc*). ◆'appetizing, *adj.* appetitlich; (*delicious*) lecker.

applaud [ə'plɔːd], *v.tr. & i.* (a) (j-m) applaudieren; (*clap*) klatschen; (b) *Fig:* (einen Entschluß usw.) begrüßen. ◆a'pplause, *s.* Beifall *m*.

apple ['æpl], *s.* Apfel *m*.

appliance [ə'plaiəns], *s.* Gerät *n*.

apply [ə'plai], *v.* 1. *v.tr.* (a) (etwas) auflegen (to sth., auf etwas *acc*); (einen Verband) anlegen; (Farbe usw.) auftragen; (b) (*use*) (Kraft, eine Vorschrift usw.) anwenden; (c) to a. one's mind to sth., sich etwas *dat* widmen. 2. *v.i.* (a) *impers:* gelten (to, für + *acc*); (b) to a. to s.o. (for sth.), sich an j-n (um etwas *acc*) wenden; (*request*) to a. for sth., etwas beantragen; to a. for a job, sich um eine Stellung bewerben. ◆applicable [ə'plikəbl, 'æplik-], *adj.* (*usable*) anwendbar; (*relevant*) zutreffend. ◆applicant ['æplikənt], *s.* Bewerber(in) *m(f)*. ◆application [æpli'keiʃ(ə)n], *s.* 1. (*use*) Anwendung *f* (von etwas *dat*). 2. (*concentration*) Fleiß *m*. 3. (*written*) Antrag *m* (for sth., auf etwas *acc*); Bewerbung *f* (for a job, um eine Stellung). ◆a'pplied, *adj.* a. linguistics, angewandte Linguistik.

appoint [ə'point], *v.tr.* (a) (j-n zu etwas *dat*) ernennen; to a. a new headmaster, einen neuen Schuldirektor anstellen. ◆a'ppointed, *adj.* 1. (*agreed*) vereinbart. 2. (*of house*) well a., gut ausgestattet. ◆a'ppointment, *s.* 1. (*meeting*) Verabredung *f*; *Com: etc.* Termin *m*; to make an a., sich anmelden; by a., nach Vereinbarung. 2. Ernennung *f* (to a post, zu einem Posten usw.).

appreciate [ə'priːʃieit], *v.* 1. *v.tr.* (a) (etwas) zu schätzen wissen; I would a. your help, mir wäre für Ihre Hilfe sehr dankbar; (b) (*recognize*) erkennen. 2. *v.i.* im Wert steigen. ◆a'ppreciable, *adj.* merklich; (*considerable*) bedeutend; (*esp.* with *neg.*) nennenswert. ◆appreci'ation, *s.* 1. (a) Würdigung *f*; (b) (*gratitude*) Dankbarkeit *f*; (*recognition*) Anerkennung *f*; (c) (*understanding*) Verständnis *n* (of, für + *acc*). 2. *Fin:* Wertsteigerung *f*. ◆a'ppreciative [-ʃiətiv], *adj.* (*of review, opinion*) positiv; (*of pers.*)

dankbar.

apprehend [æpri'hend], *v.tr.* festnehmen. ◆appre'hension, *s.* 1. Festnahme *f*. 2. (*fear*) Befürchtung *f*. ◆appre'hensive, *adj.* ängstlich; (*concerned*) besorgt.

apprentice [ə'prentis], *s.* 1. Lehrling *m*. ◆a'pprenticeship, *s.* Lehre *f*.

approach [ə'prəutʃ]. I. *s.* 1. (a) Nahen *n* (einer Person, des Frühlings usw.); (b) (*attitude*) Einstellung *f* (to, zu + *dat*); (*introduction*) Einführung *f*. 2. Zugang *m* (zu einem Haus); Zufahrt *f* (zu einer Stadt usw.); *Av:* Anflug *m*. II. *v.* 1. *v.i.* nahen; (*of pers.*) sich nähern. 2. *v.tr.* (a) sich (einem Ort) nähern; (b) sich (an j-n) wenden (with a proposal etc., mit einem Vorschlag usw.); (c) to a. a question, an eine Frage herangehen. ◆a'pproachable, *adj.* leicht zugänglich.

appropriate. I. [ə'prəuprieit] *v.tr.* sich *dat* aneignen. II. [ə'prəupriət] *adj.* angemessen.

approve [ə'pruːv], *v.* 1. *v.tr.* (eine Handlung) billigen; *Adm:* (ein Ansuchen usw.) genehmigen. 2. *v.i.* to a. of sth., etwas gutheißen; I don't a. of your friends, ich bin mit deinen Freunden nicht einverstanden. ◆a'pproval, *s.* Zustimmung *f*; *Com:* on a., zur Ansicht.

approximate [ə'prɔks(i)mit], *adj.* ungefähr; -ly, *adv.* etwa. ◆approxi'mation, *s.* Annäherung *f* (to, an + *acc*); (*figure*) ungefähre Angabe *f*.

apricot ['eiprikɔt], *s.* Aprikose *f*.

April ['eipril], *s.* April *m*.

apron ['eiprən], *s.* Schürze *f*.

apt [æpt], *adj.* 1. (*suitable*) passend, geeignet; (*of remark*) treffend. 2. (*tending*) (*of pers.*) to be a. to do sth., geneigt sein, etwas zu tun. ◆'aptitude, *s.* Eignung *f* (for sth., zu etwas *dat*).

aqualung ['ækwʌlʌŋ], *s.* Preßluft-tauchgerät *n*.

aquarium [ə'kwɛəriəm], *s.* Aquarium *n*. ◆Aquarius [ə'kwɛəriəs]. *Pr.n.* Wassermann *m*.

aquatic [ə'kwætik], *adj.* Wasser-.

aqueduct ['ækwidʌkt], *s.* Aquädukt *m*.

Arab ['ærəb], *s.* Araber(in) *m(f)*. ◆A'rabian, *adj.* arabisch. ◆Arabic ['ærəbik], I. *adj.* arabisch. II. *s.* Arabisch *n*.

arable ['ærəbl], *adj.* urbar; a. land, Ackerland *n*.

arbitrate ['aːbitreit], *v.* 1. *v.tr.* (einen Streit) schlichten. 2. *v.i.* einen Schiedsspruch fällen. ◆'arbitrary, *adj.* willkürlich. ◆arbi'tration, *s.* Schlichtung *f*; (*by tribunal*) Schiedsgerichtsverfahren *n*. ◆'arbitrator, *s.* Schlichter *m*.

arc [aːk], *s. Mth:etc:* Bogen *m*; *El:* Lichtbogen *m*.

arcade [aː'keid], *s.* (a) Arkade *f*; (b) shopping a., Einkaufspassage *f*.

arch¹ [aːtʃ]. I. *v.tr.* (den Rücken) krümmen. II. *s.* Bogen *m*; (*vault*) Gewölbe *n*.

arch², adj. Erz-; a. **enemy**, Erzfeind m. ◆**archangel** ['ɑːkeindʒ(ə)l], s. Erzengel m. ◆**archbishop** ['ɑːt∫'bi∫əp], s. Erzbischof m.

arch(a)eology [ɑːki'ɔlədʒi], s. Archäologie f. ◆**arch(a)e'ologist**, s. Archäologe m, Archäologin f.

archaic [ɑː'keiik], adj. altertümlich; (out of date) altmodisch.

archery ['ɑːt∫əri], s. Bogenschießen n.

archipelago, pl. **-gos**, **-goes** [ɑːki'peləgəu, -əuz], s. Archipel n.

architect ['ɑːkitekt], s. Architekt(in) m(f). ◆**archi'tectural** [-t∫ərəl], adj. architektonisch. ◆**'architecture** [-t∫ər], s. Architektur f.

archives ['ɑːkaivz], s.pl. Archiv n.

arctic ['ɑːktik]. I. adj. arktisch; **A. Ocean**, Nordpolarmeer n. II. s. the **A.**, die Arktis.

ardent ['ɑːdənt], adj. feurig; (of supporter etc.) leidenschaftlich. ◆**ardour** ['ɑːdər], s. 1. (enthusiasm) Begeisterung f. 2. (passion) Leidenschaft f.

arduous ['ɑːdjuəs], adj. (of task etc.) mühsam; (strenuous) anstrengend.

area ['eəriə], s. 1. (measurement) Fläche f. 2. (region, also Fig:) Gebiet n.

arena [ə'riːnə], s. Arena f.

Argentina [ɑːdʒ(ə)n'tiːnə]. Pr.n. Argentinien n. ◆**Argentinian** [ɑːdʒən'tiniən]. I. adj. argentinisch. II. s. Argentinier(in) m(f).

argue ['ɑːgjuː], v. 1. v.tr. (eine Frage usw.) lebhaft diskutieren. 2. v.i. argumentieren; to a. that ..., behaupten, daß ...; to a. with s.o., about sth., mit j-m über etwas acc streiten; to a. for/against sth., für/gegen etwas acc eintreten. ◆**'arguable**, adj. it is a., das könnte man schon behaupten. ◆**'argument**, s. 1. (reasons) Argument n. 2. (quarrel) Streit m; they had an a., sie stritten sich. ◆**argu'mentative**, adj. streitlustig.

arid ['ærid], adj. dürr.

Aries ['eəriːz]. Pr.n. Astr: Widder m.

arise [ə'raiz], v.i.irr. (a) (get up) aufstehen; (b) (occur) auftreten; **should the occasion a.**, sollte sich die Gelegenheit ergeben; (c) (originate) herrühren.

aristocrat ['æristəkræt], s. Aristokrat(in) m(f). ◆**aristocracy** [-'tɔkrəsi], s. Aristokratie f; coll. Adel m. ◆**aristo'cratic**, adj. aristokratisch.

arithmetic [ə'riθmətik], s. Rechnen n.

ark [ɑːk], s. Noah's A., die Arche Noah.

arm¹ [ɑːm], s. 1. Arm m. 2. Armlehne f (eines Sessels). ◆**'arm'chair**, s. Sessel m. ◆**'armful**, adj. Armvoll m. ◆**'armhole**, s. Ärmelloch n. ◆**'armpit**, s. Achselhöhle f.

arm² [ɑːm]. I. v.tr. bewaffnen. II. s. 1. usu. pl. Waffen f.pl.; the arms race, das Wettrüsten. 2. (coat of) arms, Wappen n. ◆**'armed**, adj. bewaffnet; the a. forces, die Streitkräfte f.pl. ◆**'armour**, s. (a) Mil: a. (plate), Panzerung f; (b)

(suit of) a., Rüstung f. ◆**'armoured**, adj. gepanzert; a. car, Panzerwagen m. ◆**'armoury**, s. Arsenal n. ◆**'army**, s. (particular) Armee f; (general) Militär n.

armistice ['ɑːmistis], s. Waffenstillstand m.

aroma [ə'rəumə], s. Aroma n. ◆**aromatic** [ærəu'mætik], adj. aromatisch.

around [ə'raund]. I. adv. ringsumher. II. prep. (a) (round)um + acc; um ... acc herum; (b) (approx.) he paid a. £400, er hat ungefähr £400 bezahlt.

arouse [ə'rauz], v.tr. (Gefühle usw.) erregen.

arrange [ə'reindʒ], v.tr. (a) (set in order) (Bücher) ordnen; (Möbel) stellen; (b) (plan beforehand) (eine Zeit, einen Treffpunkt usw.) festlegen; to a. with s.o. to do sth., mit j-m vereinbaren, etwas zu tun. ◆**a'rrangement**, s. 1. Anordnung f; Einteilung f (eines Hauses); (putting in order) Ordnung f; to make arrangements, Anordnungen/(preparations) Vorbereitungen treffen. 2. (agreement) Vereinbarung f; by a., nach Vereinbarung.

array [ə'rei], s. Aufgebot n (of sth., an etwas dat).

arrears [ə'riəz], s.pl. Rückstände m.pl; to be in a., im Rückstand sein.

arrest [ə'rest]. I. s. Verhaftung f. II. v.tr. (a) (einen Verbrecher) verhaften; (b) (Fortschritt usw.) hemmen.

arrival [ə'raiv(ə)l], s. Ankunft f; (of pers., thing) Eintreffen n. ◆**arrive** [ə'raiv], v.i. (a) ankommen; eintreffen; (b) to a. at an agreement, zu einer Vereinbarung kommen.

arrogant ['ærəgənt], adj. (haughty) hochmütig; (conceited) eingebildet. ◆**'arrogance**, s. Arroganz f.

arrow ['ærəu], s. Pfeil m.

arsenal ['ɑːsən(ə)l], s. Arsenal n.

arsenic ['ɑːsənik], s. Arsen n.

art [ɑːt], s. Kunst f; arts subjects, geisteswissenschaftliche Fächer. ◆**'artful**, adj. Pej: listig. ◆**'artist**, s. Künstler(in) m(f). ◆**ar'tistic**, adj. künstlerisch; (of pers.) kunstverständig. ◆**'artless**, adj. 1. natürlich. 2. naiv. ◆**'arty**, adj. F: usu. Pej: (gewollt) künstlerisch; a. type, Bohemien m.

artery ['ɑːtəri], s. Arterie f.

arthritis [ɑː'θraitis], s. Arthritis f.

artichoke ['ɑːtit∫əuk], s. (globe) a., Artischocke f; **Jerusalem a.**, Erdartischocke f.

article ['ɑːtikl], s. 1. (paragraph) Abschnitt m; (in treaty) Artikel m. 2. (newspaper) a., Zeitungsartikel m; Beitrag m. 3. (object) Gegenstand m; Com: Ware f; a. of clothing, Kleidungsstück n. 4. Gram: Artikel m.

articulate. I. v.tr. (Worte) artikulieren. II. [ɑː'tikjulit] adj. (of language, pers.) leicht verständlich, deutlich

(im Ausdruck). ◆**ar'ticulated**, *adj.* a. **lorry**, Sattelschlepper *m*.
artificial [ɑːti'fiʃ(ə)l], *adj.* 1. künstlich. 2. unnatürlich.
artillery [ɑː'tiləri], *s.* Artillerie *f*.
artisan [ɑːti'zæn, 'ɑːti-], *s.* Handwerker *m*.
as [æz,əz]. I. *adv.* so; **you're not as tall**, du bist nicht so groß; **as from the 15th**, ab dem Fünfzehnten; **as for that**, was das anbetrifft. II. *conj. & rel. adv.* 1. (*comparison*) wie; **as tall as as him**, du bist so groß wie er; **as well as**, sowie, sowohl … wie; **much as I would like** to, so gern ich es auch möchte; **as if/though**, als ob, als wenn. 2. (*manner*) (*a*) wie; **as (is) usual**, wie gewöhnlich; (*b*) als; **to consider s.o. as a friend**, j-n als Freund betrachten. 3. (*time*) während. 4. (*reason*) da. III. *rel. pron.* wie; **beasts of prey (such) as the lion**, Raubtiere wie etwa der Löwe.
asbestos [æs'bestəs], *s.* Asbest *m*.
ascend [ə'send], *v.* 1. *v.i.* (empor)steigen. 2. *v.tr.* besteigen. ◆**A'scension**, *s. Ecc:* (Christi) Himmelfahrt *f*. ◆**a'scent**, *s.* (*a*) Aufstieg *m*; (*b*) Besteigung *f* (eines Berges).
ascertain [æsə'tein], *v.tr.* (etwas) feststellen, (die Wahrheit) ermitteln.
ascetic [ə'setik], *adj.* asketisch.
ascribe [ə'skraib], *v.tr.* zuschreiben (to s.o., sth., j-m, etwas *dat*); zurückführen (**to sth.**, auf etwas *acc*).
ash[1] [æʃ], *s. Bot:* Esche *f*.
ash[2] *s.* Asche *f*. ◆**'ashtray**, *s.* Aschenbecher *m*. ◆**'Ash 'Wednesday**, *s.* Aschermittwoch *m*.
ashamed [ə'feimd], *adj.* **to be/feel a.** (**of sth.**), sich (etwas *gen*) schämen.
ashore [ə'ʃɔːr], *adv.* an Land.
Asia ['eiʃə]. *Pr.n.* Asien *n*. ◆**'Asian, Asiatic** [eiʃi'ætik]. I. *adj.* asiatisch. II. *s.* Asiate *m*, Asiatin *f*.
aside [ə'said], *adv.* (*a*) beiseite; **to put sth. a.**, etwas beiseite legen; **to stand a.**, zur Seite treten; (*b*) **a. from**, abgesehen von + *dat*.
ask [ɑːsk], *v.tr. & i.* (*a*) (j-n etwas) fragen; **to a. s.o. the way**, j-n nach dem Weg fragen; **to a. s.o. a question**, j-m eine Frage stellen; (*b*) **to a. £6 for sth.**, für etwas *acc* 6 Pfund verlangen; (*c*) (*request*) **to a. s.o. for sth.**, j-n bitten, etwas zu tun; **to a. to do sth.**, um Erlaubnis bitten, etwas zu tun; (*d*) (*enquire*) **to a. about sth.**, sich nach etwas *dat* erkundigen; **to a. s.o. about sth.**, j-n wegen etwas *gen* fragen; **to a. after s.o.**, sich nach j-m erkundigen; (*e*) **to a. for sth.**, um etwas *acc* bitten; (*f*) (*invite*) **to a. s.o. to lunch**, j-n zum Mittagessen einladen. ◆**'asking**, *s.* **it's yours for the a.**, Sie brauchen nur ein Wort zu sagen.
askance [ə'skæns], *adv.* **to look a. at s.o.**, j-n schief ansehen.
askew [ə'skjuː], *adv.* schief.

asleep [ə'sliːp], *adj. & adv.* eingeschlafen; **to be a.**, schlafen; **to fall a.**, einschlafen.
asparagus [əs'pærəgəs], *s.* Spargel *m*.
aspect ['æspekt], *s.* 1. (*appearance*) Aussehen *n*. 2. Aspekt *m* (eines Problems).
aspersion [ə'spəːʃ(ə)n], *s.* **to cast aspersions upon s.o.**, j-n verleumden.
asphalt ['æsfælt, -fɔlt], *s.* Asphalt *m*.
asphyxiate [æs'fiksieit], *v.tr.* ersticken.
aspire [ə'spaiər], *v.i.* streben (**to, nach** + *dat*). ◆**aspiration** [-pə'reiʃ(ə)n], *s.* Bestreben *n*. ◆**a'spiring**, *adj.* ehrgeizig.
aspirin ['æsp(ə)rin], *s.* Aspirin *n*.
ass [æs], *s. Z: & F:* Esel *m*.
assailant [ə'seilənt], *s.* Angreifer(in) *m(f)*.
assassin [ə'sæsin], *s.* Mörder(in) *m(f)*. ◆**a'ssassinate**, *v.tr.* ermorden. ◆**assassi'nation**, *s.* Mord *m*.
assault [ə'sɔːlt]. I. *v.tr.* (j-n) (tätlich) angreifen; (*indecently*) (j-n) unsittlich belästigen, (*rape*) vergewaltigen. II. *s.* (*a*) *Mil:* Sturm *m*; (*b*) Angriff *m*; *Jur:* **indecent a.**, unsittliche Belästigung.
assemble [ə'sembl], *v.* 1. *v.tr.* (*a*) (Menschen) versammeln; (eine Sammlung) zusammenstellen; (*b*) (eine Maschine usw.) zusammenbauen. 2. *v.i.* sich versammeln; (*of parliament*) zusammentreten. ◆**a'ssembly**, *s.* 1. Versammlung *f*. 2. Montage *f* (einer Maschine usw.); **a. line**, Fließband *n*.
assent [ə'sent]. I. *v.i.* zustimmen. II. *s.* Zustimmung *f*.
assert [ə'səːt], *v.tr.* (*a*) (*state*) behaupten; (*b*) (ein Recht) geltend machen; **to a. oneself**, sich durchsetzen. ◆**a'ssertion**, *s.* Behauptung *f*. ◆**a'ssertive**, *adj.* selbstbewußt.
assess [ə'ses], *v.tr.* bewerten; (den Wert von etwas) schätzen; *Jur:* (Schadensatz usw.) festlegen. ◆**a'ssessment**, *s.* Einschätzung *f*. ◆**a'ssessor**, *s.* Schätzer *m*.
asset ['æset], *s.* 1. Vorteil *m*. 2. *Fin:* **assets**, Aktiva *pl*; *Jur:* Güter *pl*.
assiduous [ə'sidjuəs], *adj.* fleißig.
assign [ə'sain], *v.tr.* zuweisen (**to s.o.**, j-m). ◆**a'ssignment**, *s.* (*task*) Aufgabe *f*.
assimilate [ə'simileit], *v.tr.* (in sich) aufnehmen. ◆**assimi'lation**, *s.* Aufnahme *f*.
assist [ə'sist], *v.tr. & i.* helfen. ◆**a'ssistance**, *s.* Unterstützung *f*. ◆**a'ssistant**, *s.* Hilfskraft *f*; Assistent *m*; **shop a.**, Verkäufer(in) *m(f)*.
associate. I. [ə'səuʃieit], *v.* 1. *v.tr.* (etwas) assoziieren. 2. *v.i.* **to a. with s.o.**, mit j-m verkehren. II. [ə'səuʃiət]. 1. *s.* Kollege *m*; Mitarbeiter *m*; **business a.**, Geschäftspartner *m*. 2. *adj.* Mit-. ◆**associ'ation**, *s.* (*a*) Verbindung *f*; (*b*) Umgang *m* (**with s.o., mit** j-m); (*c*) (*organization*) Verband *m*; (*club*) Verein *m*.
assorted [ə'sɔːtid], *adj.* gemischt.

◆**a'ssortment**, *s.* Mischung *f*; *(selection)* Auswahl *f*; *Com:* *(samples)* Sortiment *n*.

assume [ə'sjuːm], *v.tr.* (*a*) (ein Amt, die Verantwortung) übernehmen; (*b*) (etwas) annehmen, *(suppose)* vermuten. ◆**a'ssumed**, *adj.* a. name, falscher Name. ◆**a'ssumption**, *s.* Annahme *f*; on the a. that ..., in der Annahme, daß ...

assure [ə'ʃuər], *v.tr.* to a. s.o, that ..., j-m versichern, daß ...; **you can rest assured that ...,** Sie können sicher sein, daß ... ◆**a'ssurance**, *s.* 1. Versicherung *f*. 2. Selbstbewußtsein *n*. ◆**a'ssured**, *adj.* (*a*) *(certain)* sicher; (*b*) *(pers.)* selbstbewußt. ◆**a'ssuredly** [-idli], *adv.* ganz gewiß.

asterisk ['æst(ə)risk], *s.* Sternchen *n*.

astern [ə'stəːn], *adv.* achtern.

asthma ['æsmə], *s.* Asthma *n*. ◆**asth'matic.** I. *adj.* asthmatisch. II. *s.* Asthmatiker(in) *m(f)*.

astonish [ə'stɔniʃ], *v.tr.* erstaunen; to be astonished at sth., über etwas *acc* erstaunt sein. ◆**a'stonishing**, *adj.* erstaunlich. ◆**a'stonishment**, *s.* Erstaunen *n*.

astound [ə'staund], *v.tr.* in Erstaunen setzen. ◆**a'stounding**, *adj.* erstaunlich.

astray [ə'strei], *adj. & adv.* to go a., sich verlaufen; *(of letter)* verlorengehen; to lead s.o. a., j-n irreführen.

astride [ə'straid], *adv. & prep.* rittlings (auf + *dat*).

astrology [ə'strɔlədʒi], *s.* Astrologie *f*. ◆**a'strologer**, *s.* Astrologe *m*, Astrologin *f*.

astronaut ['æstrənɔːt], *s.* Astronaut(in) *m(f)*.

astronomy [ə'strɔnəmi], *s.* Astronomie *f*. ◆**a'stronomer**, *s.* Astronom *m*. ◆**astro'nomic(al)**, *adj.* astronomisch.

astute [ə'stjuːt], *adj.* scharfsinnig; *(of mind)* klug.

asylum [ə'sailəm], *s.* 1. Asyl *n*; to grant s.o. a., j-m Asyl gewähren. 2. *(institution)* Anstalt *f*.

at [æt], *prep.* 1. *(place)* an + *dat*, bei + *dat*; *(with town)* in; at school, in der Schule; at work, bei der Arbeit; at home, zu Hause; at the Schmidts', bei Schmidts; at the tailor's, beim Schneider. 2. *(time)* at 5 o'clock, um 5 Uhr. 3. *(price)* at twenty pence a pound, (zu) zwanzig Pence das Pfund. 4. *(age)* at the age of eighty, im Alter von 80. 5. *(speed)* bei, mit + *dat*; to drive at (a speed of) 100 kph, mit 100 Kilometern fahren. 6. at my request, auf meine Bitte hin; she's at it again, sie tut es schon wieder; while we are at it, wenn wir einmal dabei sind.

atheism ['eiθiizm], *s.* Atheismus *m*. ◆**'atheist**, *s.* Atheist *m*.

Athens ['æθinz]. *Pr. n.* Athen *n*.

athlete ['æθliːt], *s.* Athlet(in) *m(f)*. ◆**athletic** [-'letik], *adj.* athletisch. ◆**ath'letics**, *s.pl.* Leichtathletik *f*.

Atlantic [ət'læntik], *adj. & s.* the Atlantic (Ocean), der Atlantik.

atlas ['ætləs], *s.* Atlas *m*.

atmosphere ['ætməsfiər], *s.* Atmosphäre *f*.

atom ['ætəm], *s.* Atom *n*; a. bomb, Atombombe *f*. ◆**atomic** [ə'tɔmik], *adj.* atomar; a. energy, Atomenergie *f*. ◆**'atomizer**, *s.* Zerstäuber *m*.

atone [ə'təun], *v.i.* to a. for sth., etwas sühnen.

atrocious [ə'trəuʃəs], *adj.* entsetzlich; *F:* scheußlich, *(of crime)* gräßlich. ◆**atrocity** [ə'trɔsiti], *s.* Greueltat *f*.

attach [ə'tætʃ], *v.tr.* to a. sth. to sth., etwas an etwas *acc* befestigen/*(permanently)* anbringen; to a. importance to sth., auf etwas *acc* Wert legen. ◆**attaché** [ə'tæʃei], *s.* Attaché *m*; a. case, Aktentasche *f*. ◆**a'ttached**, *adj.* to be very a. to s.o., sth., j-m, etwas *dat* sehr zugetan sein. ◆**a'ttachment**, *s.* 1. *(affection)* Zuneigung *f* (für j-n). 2. Zusatzgerät *n* (zu einer Maschine usw.).

attack [ə'tæk]. I. *v.tr.* angreifen, *(mug etc.)* überfallen; (ein Problem) in Angriff nehmen. II. *s.* 1. Angriff *m*. 2. *Med:* Anfall *m*. ◆**a'ttacker**, *s.* Angreifer *m*.

attain [ə'tein], *v.tr.* erzielen. ◆**a'ttainable**, *adj.* erreichbar.

attempt [ə'tem(p)t]. I. *v.tr.* versuchen. II. *s.* Versuch *m*.

attend [ə'tend], *n.* 1. *v.i.* (*a*) dabei sein; (*b*) to a. to s.o., sth., sich um j-n, etwas *acc* kümmern; (*c*) *(pay attention)* aufpassen. 2. *v.tr.* (einer Versammlung usw.) beiwohnen; (an einem Kurs usw.) teilnehmen; to a. school, die Schule besuchen. ◆**a'ttendance**, *s.* Besuch *m*; Beteiligung *f* (an einem Kurs usw.); in a., anwesend. ◆**a'ttendant**, *s.* Diener(in) *m(f)*; *(in museum, zoo etc.)* Wärter *m*. II. *adj.* damit verbunden.

attention [ə'ten(ʃ)n], *s.* 1. Aufmerksamkeit *f*; to pay a. to sth., auf etwas *acc* achten; *Com:* for the a. of Mr. X, zu Händen von Herrn X; a. to detail, Berücksichtigung *f* von Einzelheiten; (*b*) *(repair)* needing a., reparaturbedürftig. 2. *Mil:* a.! stillgestanden! ◆**attentive** [ə'tentiv], *adj.* aufmerksam.

attic ['ætik], *s.* Dachgeschoß *n*.

attire [ə'taiər], *s.* Kleidung *f*, *Lit:* Gewand *n*.

attitude ['ætitjuːd], *s.* Haltung *f*.

attorney [ə'təːni], *s. N.Am:* Rechtsanwalt *m*; District A., = Staatsanwalt *m*; A. General, *Brit:* erster Kronanwalt *m*; *U.S:* approx. = Justizminister *m*; power of a., Vollmacht *f*.

attract [ə'trækt], *v.tr.* anziehen; to be attracted to s.o., sich zu j-m hingezogen fühlen. ◆**a'ttraction**, *s.* Reiz *m*. ◆**a'ttractive**, *adj.* attraktiv, reizvoll. ◆**a'ttractiveness**, *s.* Reiz *m*.

attribute. I. *v.tr.* [ə'tribjuːt], to a. a work

etc. **to s.o.**, j-m ein Werk usw. zuschreiben. II. s. ['ætribju:t], Eigenschaft f.

attrition [ə'triʃ(ə)n], s. **war of a.**, Zermürbungskrieg m.

aubergine ['əubəʒi:n], s. Aubergine f.

auburn ['ɔ:bən], adj. (of hair) kupferrot.

auction ['ɔ:kʃ(ə)n], s. I. (etwas) versteigern. II. s. Auktion f, Versteigerung f. ◆**auctio'neer**, s. Auktionator m.

audacious [ɔ:'deiʃəs], adj. kühn, verwegen. ◆**audacity** [ɔ:'dæsiti], s. 1. Wagemut n. 2. Pej: Frechheit f.

audible ['ɔ:dibl], adj. hörbar.

audience ['ɔ:djəns], s. 1. Th: Rad: etc: Publikum n; TV: Zuschauer mpl; (in a concert) Zuhörer mpl. 2. (interview) Audienz f (with, bei + dat).

audio-visual ['ɔ:diəu'vizjuəl], adj. audiovisuell.

audit ['ɔ:dit]. I. v.tr. prüfen. II. s. Buchprüfung f. ◆'**auditor**, s. Buchprüfer m.

auditorium [ɔ:di'tɔ:riəm], s. Auditorium n.

audition [ɔ:'diʃ(ə)n]. I. s. Th: Vorsprechen n. II. v. 1. v.i. Th: vorsprechen. 2. v.tr. Th: (j-n) vorsprechen lassen.

augment [ɔ:g'ment], v.tr. (etwas) vergrößern; (eine Zahl) vermehren.

augur ['ɔ:gər], v.i. **it augurs well for him**, es sieht gut für ihn aus.

August ['ɔ:gəst], s. August m.

aunt [ɑ:nt], F: **auntie** ['ɑ:nti], s. Tante f.

au pair [əu'peər], adj. & s. **a. p. (girl)**, Au-pair-Mädchen n.

auspices ['ɔ:spisiz], s.pl. **under the a. of ...**, unter der Schirmherrschaft von ... dat. ◆**au'spicious** [–ʃəs], adj. günstig; (promising) verheißungsvoll.

austere [ɔs'tiər], adj. (severe) streng; (plain) nüchtern. ◆**austerity** [–'teriti], s. Strenge f; Nüchternheit f; **time of a.**, Zeit f der (wirtschaftlichen) Einschränkungen.

Australia [ɔs'treiliə]. Pr.n. Australien n. ◆**Aus'tralian**, I. adj. australisch. II. s. Australier(in) m(f).

Austria ['ɔstriə]. Pr.n. Österreich n. ◆**Austrian**, I. adj. österreichisch. II. s. Österreicher(in) m(f).

authentic [ɔ:'θentik], adj. authentisch, echt. ◆**au'thenticate**, v.tr. beglaubigen. ◆**authenticity** [–'tisiti], s. Echtheit f.

author ['ɔ:θər], s. Autor(in) m(f).

authoritative [ɔ:'θɔritətiv], adj. 1. (of tone, manner) gebieterisch. 2. (of statement) maßgebend. ◆**au'thority**, s. 1. Autorität f; **to have a. over s.o.**, über j-n gebieten. 2. Ermächtigung f (, etwas zu tun); (document) Vollmacht f. 3. Experte m (on, über + acc); Kenner m (on, von + dat); **on good a.**, aus glaubwürdiger Quelle. 4. **the authorities, die** Behörden fpl. ◆**authorize** ['ɔ:θəraiz], v.tr. bewilligen; **to a. s.o. to do sth.**, j-n ermächtigen, etwas zu tun. ◆**authori'zation**, s. Ermächtigung f.

◆**'authorized**, adj. autorisiert.

auto- ['ɔ:təu–], prefix auto-, selbst–. ◆**autobi'ography**, s. Autobiographie f. ◆**'autocrat**, s. Autokrat m. ◆**auto'cratic**, adj. selbstherrlich. ◆**'autograph**. I. s. Autogramm n. II. v.tr. (ein Buch usw.) signieren. ◆**'automate**, v.tr. automatisieren. ◆**auto'matic**, adj. automatisch; Aut: **a. transmission**, Automatik f. ◆**auto'mation**, s. Automation f. ◆**'automobile**, s. esp. N.Am: Auto n. ◆**autonomous** [ɔ:'tɔnəməs], adj. autonom. ◆**au'tonomy**, s. Autonomie f. ◆**autopsy** ['ɔ:tɔpsi], s. Obduktion f.

autumn ['ɔ:təm], s. Herbst m. ◆**autumnal** [ɔ:'tʌmnəl], adj. herbstlich.

auxiliary [ɔ:g'ziljəri]. I. adj. Hilfs-. II. s. Helfer m.

avail [ə'veil]. I. v.tr. **to a. oneself of sth.**, sich einer Sache bedienen. II. s. **it's of no a.**, es ist nutzlos. ◆**availa'bility**, s. Verfügbarkeit f. ◆**a'vailable**, adj. verfügbar; Com: vorrätig.

avalanche ['ævəlɑ:nʃ], s. Lawine f.

avantgarde [ævã(ŋ)'gɑ:d], s. Avantgarde f.

avarice ['ævəris], s. Habgier f. ◆**ava'ricious**, adj. habgierig.

avenge [ə'ven(d)ʒ], v.tr. (etwas, sich) rächen (**on s.o.**, an j-n).

avenue ['ævinju:], s. Allee f.

average ['ævəridʒ]. I. s. Durchschnitt m; **on (an) a.**, im Durchschnitt. II. adj. durchschnittlich; **above a.**, überdurchschnittlich; **below a.**, unterdurchschnittlich; **the a. Englishman**, der Durchschnittsengländer. II. v.tr. & i. durchschnittlich betragen; **we averaged 120 kph**, wir hatten ein Durchschnittstempo von 120 Stundenkilometern.

averse [ə'və:s], adj. **to be a. to sth.**, etwas dat abgeneigt sein. ◆**a'version**, s. Abneigung f (**to**, gegen + acc).

avert [ə'və:t], v.tr. (a) (den Blick) abwenden; (b) (prevent) verhindern.

aviary ['eiviəri], s. Vogelhaus n.

aviation [eivi'eiʃ(ə)n], s. Luftfahrt f. ◆**'aviator**, s. Flieger m.

avid ['ævid], adj. begierig (**for**, auf + acc).

avocado [ævə'kɑ:dəu], s. **a. (pear)**, Avocado f.

avoid [ə'vɔid], v.tr. (a) (j-n, etwas) meiden; (etwas) vermeiden; **to a. doing sth.**, es vermeiden, etwas zu tun; (b) (einer Gefahr usw.) entgehen. ◆**a'voidable**, adj. vermeidbar. ◆**a'voidance**, s. Vermeidung f; **tax a.**, Steuerhinterziehung f.

await [ə'weit], v.tr. erwarten; (wait for) (auf j-n, etwas acc) warten.

awake [ə'weik]. I. v.ir. 1. v.i. erwachen. 2. v.tr. (j-n) wecken. II. adj. wach; **wide a.**, hellwach. ◆**a'waken**, v. 1. v.tr. (a) (Gefühle usw.) erwecken; (b) (j-n) wecken. 2. v.i. Lit: aufwachen.

◆a'wakening, s. Erwachen n; rude a., unsanftes Erwachen.

award [ə'wɔːd]. I. v.tr. (j-m einen Preis usw.) verleihen. II. s. Auszeichnung f; (prize) Preis m.

aware [ə'wɛər], adj. bewußt; to be a. of sth., sich dat etwas gen bewußt sein. ◆a'wareness s. Bewußtsein n.

away [ə'wei], adv. (a) weg, fort, davon; to go a., weggehen; five paces a., fünf Schritte entfernt; (b) (absent) abwesend; when he is a., wenn er nicht da ist; a. match, Auswärtsspiel n.

awe [ɔː], s. Ehrfurcht f. ◆'awe-inspiring, adj. ehrfurchtgebietend. ◆'awful, adj. furchtbar.

awkward ['ɔːkwəd], adj. 1. (a) (clumsy)

ungeschickt; (b) (ill at ease) verlegen. 2. (a) (unpleasant) peinlich. (b) (difficult) schwierig; (of shape) unhandlich. ◆'awkwardness, s. 1. (a) Ungeschicklichkeit f; (b) Verlegenheit f. 2. Peinlichkeit f.

awning ['ɔːniŋ], s. Plane f; (of shop) Markise f.

awry [ə'rai], adv. & adj. schief; to go (all) a., schiefgehen.

axe [æks]. I. s. Axt f, Beil n. II. v.tr. (ein Projekt) fallenlassen.

axis pl. -es ['æksis, 'æksiːz], s. Achse f.

axle ['æksl], s. Achse f, (shaft) Welle f.

aye [ai]. I. int. ja. II. s. Parl: Jastimme f.

azalea [ə'zeiljə], s. Azalee f.

B

B, b [biː], s. (der Buchstabe) B, b n.

babble ['bæbl]. I. s. Geplapper n. II. v.i. (a) plappern; (b) (of stream) murmeln.

baboon [bə'buːn], s. Pavian m.

baby ['beibi], s. Baby n; to have a b., ein Kind bekommen; F: to be holding the b., die Verantwortung (für etwas acc) tragen; F: that's your b.! das ist deine Sache!; b. sister, kleine Schwester f. ◆'babyish, adj. kindisch, kindisch. ◆'babysit, v.i. babysitten. ◆'babysitter, s. Babysitter m.

bachelor ['bætʃələr], s. Junggeselle m.

back [bæk]. I. s. 1. Rücken m; b. to front, verkehrt; to do sth. behind s.o.'s b., etwas hinter j-s Rücken tun; to break one's b., sich dat das Rückgrat brechen; Fig: to break the b. of the work, den größten Teil der Arbeit erledigen. 2. (a) (of paper, house etc.) Rückseite f; (of chair) Rückenlehne f; (b) he knows London like the b. of his hand, er kennt London wie seine Westentasche; (c) Aut: in the b., hinten; auf dem Rücksitz; (d) at the b., hinten; at the b. of sth./N.Am: b. of sth., hinter etwas dat. 3. Fb: Verteidiger m. II. adj. (a) hinte-re(-r,s), Hinter-; b. door, Hintertür f; b. seat, Rücksitz m; b. wheel, Hinterrad n; to take a b. seat, eine untergeordnete Rolle spielen. III. adv. zurück; to hit b., zurückschlagen; to call s.o. b., j-n zurückrufen; when will you be b.? wann kommst du zurück? some years b., vor einigen Jahren. IV. v. 1. v.i. (a) rückwärts gehen/Aut: fahren; (of house) to b. onto sth., hinten an etwas acc grenzen. 2. v.tr. (a) (support) (j-n) unterstützen; (b) to b. a horse, (Geld) auf ein Pferd setzen; (c) (einen Wagen) rückwärts fahren. ◆'backache, s. Rückenschmerzen mpl. ◆'back-'bencher, s. Brit: Pol: Parlamentsabgeordnete(r) f (m), die (der) nicht zur Führung seiner Partei gehört. ◆'backbiter, s. Verleum-

der(in) m(f). ◆'backbone, s. (a) Rückgrat n; (b) Fig: Stütze f. ◆'back'dated, adj. a rise b. to April 1st, eine Gehaltserhöhung rückwirkend vom 1. April an. ◆'back 'down, v.i. einen Rückzieher machen. ◆'backer, s. Unterstützer m; Com: Fin: Geldgeber m. ◆'back'fire, v.i. (of plan etc.) fehlschlagen; Aut: fehlzünden. ◆'background, s. Hintergrund m; what's his family b.? aus welchen Familienverhältnissen stammt er? ◆'backhand, s. Rückhand f. ◆'back'handed, adj. b. compliment, zweifelhaftes Kompliment. ◆'backing, s. (finanzielle) Unterstützung f. ◆'backlash, s. Fig: starke Gegenreaktion f. ◆'backlog, s. Rückstände mpl. ◆'back 'out, v.i. to b. out of a deal etc., aus einem Geschäft usw. aussteigen. ◆'backside, s. Hintern m. ◆'back 'up, v. 1. v.tr. (a) (support) (j-n) unterstützen; (one Aussage) bestätigen; (b) N.Am: (einen Wagen) rückwärts fahren. 2. v.i. rückwärts fahren. ◆'backward. I. adj. (a.) b. motion, Rückwärtsbewegung f; (b) (of child) zurückgeblieben; (of country etc.) unterentwickelt. II. adv. backward(s), rückwärts. ◆'backwardness, s. (of child) Zurückgebliebenheit f; (of country) Rückständigkeit f. ◆'backwater, s. (stiller) abgelegener Ort m.

bacon ['beikən], s. Speck m.

bacterium [bæk'tiəriəm], s. (pl bacteria) Bakterie f.

bad [bæd], adj. schlecht; (serious) (of accident etc.) schwer, schlimm; (of food) to go b., schlecht werden; he's in a b. way, es geht ihm gar nicht gut; things are going from b. to worse, es wird immer schlimmer; a b. boy, ein schlimmer Junge; b. smell, übler Geruch; b. tempered, schlecht gelaunt; to have a b. cold, einen starken Schnupfen haben; that's too b.! Pech gehabt! my b. leg, mein

schlimmes Bein; **-ly,** *adv.* schlecht; **b. wounded,** schwer verwundet; **to want sth. b.,** (i) etwas sehr gerne wollen; (ii) (*need*) etwas dringend brauchen.
badge [bædʒ], *s.* Abzeichen *n.*
badger[1] ['bædʒər], *s.* Dachs *m.*
badger[2] ['bædʒər], *v.tr.* (j-n) belästigen.
baffle ['bæfl], *v.tr.* verblüffen.
bag [bæg], *s.* **1.** (*handbag*) Tasche *f;* (*paper*) **b.,** Tüte *f;* **plastic b.,** (*small*) Plastiktüte *f,* (*large*) Plastiksack *m.* **2.** *F:* (*woman*) **old b.,** alte Zicke. ◆**baggy,** *adj.* (*of clothes*) bauschig; (*of trousers*) ausgebeult.
baggage ['bægidʒ], *s.* Reisegepäck *n.*
bagpipes ['bægpaips], *s.pl.* Dudelsack *m.*
bail[1] [beil], *s.* Kaution *f;* (*released*) **on b.,** gegen Kaution freigelassen. ◆**bailiff,** *s.* Gerichtsvollzieher *m.*
bail[2] [beil], *v.tr. Nau:* **to b. out,** (Wasser) ausschöpfen; (ein Boot) leerschöpfen.
bait [beit], *s.* Köder *m.*
bake ['beik], *v.tr. & i.* backen. ◆**baker,** *s.* Bäcker *m.;* **b.'s** (**shop**), Bäckerei *f.* ◆**bakery,** *s.* Bäckerei *f.* ◆**baking-powder,** *s.* Backpulver *n.*
balance ['bæləns]. **I.** *s.* **1.** (*scales*) Waage *f;* **on b.,** alles in allem. **2.** Gleichgewicht *n;* **to lose one's b.,** das Gleichgewicht verlieren; **b. of power,** politisches Gleichgewicht. **3.** *Com:* (*in hand*) Saldo *m;* (*amount due*) Restbetrag *m; Fin:* **b. of payments,** Zahlungsbilanz *f;* **b. sheet,** Bilanz *f.* **II.** *v.* **1.** *v.tr.* (*a*) (etwas) ausbalancieren; (*b*) (eine Rechnung, ein Konto) ausgleichen; **to b. the books,** die Bilanz machen. **2.** *v.i.* (*a*) (*of accounts*) sich ausgleichen; (*b*) (*of pers.*) balancieren. ◆**balanced,** *adj.* ausgeglichen.
balcony, *pl* **-ies** ['bælkəni, -iz], *s.* Balkon *m.*
bald [bɔːld], *adj.* **1.** glatzköpfig. **2.** (*of statement*) unverblümt. ◆**baldness,** *s.* Kahlheit *f.*
bale[1] [beil], *s.* Ballen *m.*
bale[2] [beil], *v.i.* **to b. out,** (mit dem Fallschirm) abspringen.
balk [bɔːk], *v.i.* **to b. at sth.,** vor etwas *dat* stutzen.
ball[1] [bɔːl], *s.* Ball *m;* **billiard b.,** Billardkugel *f.* ◆**ball-bearing,** *s.* Kugellager *n.* ◆**ballcock,** *s.* Schwimmerhahn *m.* ◆**ballpoint,** *s.* **b.** (**pen**), Kugelschreiber *m.*
ballad ['bæləd], *s.* Ballade *f.*
ballast ['bæləst], *s.* Ballast *m.*
ballet ['bælei], *s.* Ballett *n;* **b. dancer,** Balletttänzer(in) *m(f).*
balloon [bə'luːn], *s.* (*child's*) Luftballon *m; Av:* Ballon *m.*
ballot ['bælət], *s.* (**secret**) **b.,** geheime Abstimmung/Wahl; **b. box,** Wahlurne *f.*
ballroom ['bɔːlruːm], *s.* Ballsaal *m.*
Baltic ['bɔːltik], *adj. & s.* **the B.** (**Sea**), die Ostsee.
balustrade [bæləs'treid], *s.* Balustrade *f.*
bamboo [bæm'buː], *s.* Bambus *m.*

ban [bæn]. **I.** *s.* Verbot *n.* **II.** *v.tr.* verbieten.
banal [bə'nɑːl], *adj.* banal.
banana [bə'nɑːnə], *s.* Banane *f.*
band[1] [bænd], *s.* Band *n;* **elastic/rubber b.,** Gummiband *n.*
band[2]. **I.** *s.* **1.** (*gang*) Bande *f.* **2.** *Mus:* Band *f.* **II.** *v.i.* **to b. together,** sich zusammenrotten. ◆**bandstand,** *s.* Musikpavillon *m.* ◆**bandwagon,** *s.* **to jump on the b.,** sich einer erfolgreichen Sache anschließen; (*habitually*) seine Fahne nach dem Wind hängen.
bandage ['bændidʒ]. **I.** *s.* Verband *m,* Bandage *f.* **II.** *v.tr.* verbinden.
bandit ['bændit], *s.* Bandit *m.*
bandy[1] ['bændi], *v.tr.* (Worte mit j-m) wechseln.
bandy,[2] *adj.* **b. legs,** O-Beine *npl.* ◆**bandy-legged,** *adj.* O-beinig.
bang [bæŋ]. **I.** *s.* Knall *m;* **to go b.,** knallen. **II.** *int.* bums! peng! *F:* **b. goes my money!** futsch ist mein Geld! **III.** *v.* **1.** *v.i.* knallen. **2.** *v.tr.* (eine Tür usw.) zuknallen. ◆**banger,** *s.* **1.** (*sausage*) Würstchen *n.* **2.** (*firework*) Knallfrosch *m.* **3.** (*car*) **old b.,** alte Kiste *f.*
banish ['bæniʃ], *v.tr.* (j-n) verbannen.
banisters ['bænistəz], *s.pl.* Treppengeländer *n.*
banjo, *pl.* **-oes/N.Am:** **-os** ['bændʒəu, -əuz], *s.* Banjo *n.*
bank[1] [bæŋk]. **I.** *s.* (*embankment*) Wall *m;* (*of river*) Ufer *n;* (*slope*) Hang *m.* **II.** *v.i. Av:* sich in die Kurve legen.
bank[2] [bæŋk]. **I.** *s.* Bank *f;* **b. account,** Bankkonto *n; Brit:* **b. holiday,** gesetzlicher Feiertag. **II.** *v.i. a*) **to b. with the X Bank,** ein Konto bei der X Bank haben; (*b*) *F:* **to b. on sth.,** auf etwas *acc* bauen. ◆**banker,** *s.* Bankier *m.* ◆**banking,** *s.* Bankgeschäft *n,* Bankwesen *n.* ◆**banknote,** *s.* Banknote *f.* ◆**bankrupt. I.** *adj.* bankrott; **to go b.,** Bankrott machen. **II.** *s.* (*pers.*) Bankrotteur *m.* ◆**bankruptcy,** *s.* Bankrott *m.*
banner ['bænər], *s.* Banner *n;* (*in demonstration*) Transparent *n.*
banns [bænz], *s.pl.* Aufgebot *n.*
banquet ['bæŋkwit], *s.* Festessen *n; Lit:* Bankett *n.*
baptize [bæp'taiz], *v.tr.* (j-n) taufen. ◆**baptism,** *s.* Taufe *f.*
bar [bɑːr]. **I.** *s.* **1.** (*a*) (*metal*) Stange *f;* (*on door*) Riegel *m;* (*b*) (*of chocolate*) Tafel *f;* (*of soap*) Stück *n;* (*of gold, silver*) Barren *m;* (*c*) **bars** *pl,* Gitter *n;* **to be behind bars,** hinter Gittern sitzen. **2.** (*obstacle*) Hindernis *n.* **3.** *Jur:* **to be called to the b.,** als plädierender Anwalt zugelassen werden. **4.** (*premises*) Bar *f;* (*b*) (*counter*) Theke *f.* **II.** *v.tr. a*) (den Weg) versperren; (eine Tür) verriegeln; (*b*) (j-n) ausschließen. **III.** *prep.* (*also* **barring**) ausgenommen; **b. none,** ohne Ausnahme.
barbarian [bɑː'bɛəriən], *s.* Barbar(in) *m(f).* ◆**barbaric** [-'bærik], *adj.* barba-

risch. ◆**bar'barity**, s. Barbarei f.
◆**barbarous** ['-ərəs], adj. barbarisch;
(cruel) grausam.

barbecue ['bɑ:bikju:], s. (a) Grill m; (b)
(party) Grillparty f.

barbed [bɑ:bd], adj. b. wire, Stacheldraht m; b. remark, spitze Bemerkung.

barber ['bɑ:bər], s. Herrenfriseur m.

bare ['beər]. I. adj. 1. (a) (uncovered)
nackt; (b) (barren) kahl. 2. b. majority,
knappe Mehrheit; -ly, adv. kaum. II.
v.tr. entblößen; (die Zähne) reiten.
◆**'hareback**, adv. to ride b., ohne Sattel reiten. ◆**'barefaced**, adj. schamlos.
◆**'barefoot**, adv. barfuß.

bargain ['bɑ:gin]. I. s. (a) (transaction)
Geschäft n; into the b., obendrein; (b)
(cheap purchase) Gelegenheitskauf m; at
b. price, zu einem sehr günstigen Preis.
II. v.i. to b. with s.o., mit j-m
(ver)handeln; I didn't b. for that! damit
hatte ich nicht gerechnet!

barge [bɑ:dʒ]. I. s. Lastkahn m; (if
towed) Schleppkahn m. II. v.i. F: to b.
in, hereinplatzen.

baritone ['bæritəun], s. Bariton m.

bark¹ [bɑ:k], s. Baumrinde f.

bark² [bɑ:k]. I. s. Bellen n. II. v.i. bellen. ◆**'barking**, s. Bellen n.

barley ['bɑ:li], s. Gerste f; b. sugar, (esp.
Bonbons aus) Gerstenzucker m.

barmaid ['bɑ:meid], s. Bardame f.

barman, pl -men ['bɑ:mən, -men], s.
Barkeeper m.

barn [bɑ:n], s. Scheune f.

barnacle ['bɑ:nəkl], s. Entenmuschel f.

barometer [bə'rɔmitər], s. Barometer n.

baron ['bærən], s. Baron m. ◆**'baroness**, s. Baronin f.

barrack ['hærək], s, (usu.pl.) Kaserne f.

barrage ['bærɑ:ʒ], s. 1. Staudamm m;
(across valley) Talsperre f. 2. Mil: Sperr-
feuer n.

barrel ['bærəl]. s. 1. Faß n; (large) Tonne
f. 2. (of small gun) Lauf m; (of large gun)
Rohr n.

barren ['bærən], adj. unfruchtbar.

barricade ['bærikeid]. I. s. Barrikade f.
II. v.tr. (etwas) verbarrikadieren.

barrier ['bæriər], s. 1. Schranke f; (ticket
b. etc.) Sperre f. 2. (obstacle) Hindernis
n.

barrister ['bæristər], s. Brit: plädierender
Rechtsanwalt m.

barrow ['bærəu], s. (wheel-)b., Schubkar-
ren m.

barter ['bɑ:tər], s. Tauschhandel m.

base [beis]. I. s. 1. (a) Basis f; (b) (of
statue etc.) Sockel m; (small) Fuß m. 2.
(place) Standort m; Mil: Stützpunkt m.
II. v.tr. (etwas) gründen (on auf + acc);
to be based on sth., sich auf etwas acc
stützen. ◆**'baseless**, adj. grundlos.
◆**'basement**, s. Kellergeschoß n.

bash [bæʃ]. I. s. F: to have a b. at sth.,
etwas mal probieren. II. v.tr. F: to b.

sth. in, etwas einbeulen; to b. s.o.
about, j-n verprügeln.

bashful ['bæʃf(u)l], adj. schüchtern.

basic ['beisik], adj. grundsätzlich; b.
wage, Grundlohn m.

basin ['beisn], s. (a) (pudding) b., Schüssel f; (b) (wash-)b., Waschbecken n.

basis ['beisis], s. Basis f.

bask [bɑ:sk], v.i. sich sonnen.

basket ['bɑ:skit], s. Korb m.
◆**'basketball**, s. Basketball m.

Basle [bɑ:l]. Pr.n. Basel n.

bass [beis]. I. adj. Baß-. II. s. Baß m.

bassoon [bə'su:n], s. Fagott n.

bastard ['bɑ:stəd, 'bæstəd], s. Scheißkerl
m.

baste [beist], v.tr. begießen.

bat¹ [bæt], s. Fledermaus f.

bat² [bæt]. I. s. Sp: Schläger m; Fig: to
do sth. off one's own b., etwas auf eigene Faust tun. II. v.tr. F: he didn't b. an
eyelid, er hat nicht mit der Wimper ge-
zuckt. ◆**'batsman**, pl -men, s. Schläger m.

batch [bætʃ], s. Ladung f; (of letters) Stoß
m.

bated ['beitid], adj. with b. breath, mit
angehaltenem Atem.

bath, pl baths [bɑ:θ, bɑ:ðz]. I. s. 1. Bad
n; to take/have a b., baden. 2 Badewanne f. II. v.tr. baden. ◆**'bathmat**, s. Ba-
dematte f. ◆**'bathroom**, s. Badezimmer
n. ◆**'bath(-)towel**, s. Badetuch n.

bathe [beið], v.tr. & i. baden.
◆**'bather**, s. Badende(r) f(m).
◆**'bathing**, s. Baden n; b. costume/
suit, Badeanzug m.

baton ['bæt(ə)n,-tɔ̃], s. Stab m; Mus:
Taktstock m.

battalion [bə'tæljən], s. Bataillon n.

batter¹ ['bætər], s. Cu: (flüssiger) Teig m.

batter² ['bætər], v.tr. schlagen.
◆**'battered**, adj. stark beschädigt; b.
wife, vom Ehemann mißhandelte Frau; b.
baby, mißhandeltes Kind.

battery ['bæt(ə)ri], s. Batterie f; b.
charger, Batterieladegerät n.

battle ['bætl]. I. s. Schlacht f. II. v.i. to
b. with s.o. for sth., mit j-m um etwas
acc kämpfen. ◆**'battlefield**, s. Schlacht-
feld n. ◆**'battlements**, s.pl. Zinnen fpl.
◆**'battleship**, s. Schlachtschiff n.

Bavaria [bə'veəriə]. Pr.n. Bayern n.
◆**Ba'varian**. I. adj. bay(e)risch. II. s.
Bayer(in) m(f).

bawl [bɔ:l], v.tr. & i. brüllen.

bay¹ [bei], s. b. leaf, Lorbeerblatt n.

bay² [bei], s. Geog: Bucht f. ◆**'bay-
'window**, s. Erkerfenster n.

bay³ [bei], s. at b., gestellt; to keep s.o.
at b., j-n in Schach halten.

bayonet ['beiənit], s. Bajonett n.

bazaar [bə'zɑ:r], s. Basar f.

be [bi:], v.irr. I. v.i. sein; how are you?
wie geht es dir? the town is in the valley, die Stadt liegt im Tal; how much is
that together? was macht das zusammen?

there is/there are, es gibt; **there were twelve of us,** wir waren zwölf; **be that as it may,** wie dem auch sei; **is it you?** – yes, it's me, sind Sie es? – ja, ich bin's. II. *v.aux.* 1. *(continuous tense)* **I am living in London,** ich wohne in London. 2. *(a) (passive)* werden; **he was killed,** er wurde getötet; *(b) (with infin.)* sollen; **I am to tell you …,** ich soll Ihnen sagen, …
◆**be'ing.** I. *adj.* **for the time b.,** vorläufig. II. *s.* 1. **to come into b.,** entstehen. 2. *(creature)* Wesen *n*; **human b.,** Mensch *m*.

beach [biːtʃ]. I. *s.* Strand *m*. II. *v.tr.* *(ein Boot)* auf den Strand setzen.
◆**beachwear,** *s.* Strandkleidung *f*.

beacon ['biːk(ə)n], *s.* **Av:** Funkfeuer *n*; **Nau:** **b.** (light), Leuchtbake *f*.

bead [biːd], *s.* Perle *f*.

beak [biːk], *s.* Schnabel *m*.

beaker ['biːkər], *s.* Trinkbecher *m*.

beam [biːm]. I. *s.* 1. *(of wood, steel)* Balken *m*. 2. *(ray)* Strahl *m*. II. *v.i.* strahlen.
◆**beaming,** *adj.* (freude)strahlend.

bean [biːn], *s.* Bohne *f*.

bear¹ [beər], *s.* Bär *m*.

bear² [beər], *v.tr. & i. (a)* (eine Last, einen Namen, ein Datum) tragen; *(b)* (Schmerz usw.) ertragen; **to b. with s.o.,** mit j-m Geduld haben; *(c)* **Aut:** *etc:* **to b.** (to the) **right,** sich rechts halten; *(d)* **to b. a child,** ein Kind gebären; **to b. fruit,** Früchte tragen. ◆**bearable,** *adj.* erträglich. ◆**bearer,** *s.* Träger *m*. ◆**bearing,** *s. (a)* **E:** Lager *n*; *(b) (usu.pl.)* Orientierung *f*. ◆**bear 'out,** *v.tr.* bestätigen.

beard [biəd], *s.* Bart *m*. ◆**bearded,** *adj.* bärtig.

beast [biːst], *s.* 1. (wildes) Tier *n*. 2. *(of pers.)* **F:** **what a b.!** was für ein Biest! ◆**beastly,** *adj. (of pers., action)* gemein; **F:** eklig; **what b. weather!** was für ein scheußliches Wetter!

beat [biːt]. I. *v.tr. & i.irr.* schlagen; **to b. time,** *(im)* Takt schlagen; **that beats everything!** das schlägt dem Faß den Boden aus! **it beats me,** ich begreife es nicht. II. *s.* 1. *(a)* Schlag *m; (heart)* Herzschlag *m; (b)* **Mus:** Taktschlag *m.* 2. Runde *f* (eines Polizisten). ◆**beat 'down,** *v.tr.* **to b. s.o. down,** j-n (im Preis) drücken. ◆**beaten,** *adj.* **to be off the b. track,** abseits liegen. ◆**beating,** *s.* 1. Schlagen *n;* Klopfen *n* (des Herzens). 2. *(thrashing)* Prügel *f; (defeat)* Niederlage *f*. ◆**beat 'off,** *v.tr.* (einen Angriff) abwehren. ◆**beat 'up,** *v.tr. Cu:* (Eier usw.) schlagen; *(b) F:* (j-n) zusammenschlagen.

beautiful ['bjuːtif(u)l], *adj.* schön; *(emphatic)* wunderschön. ◆**beautify,** *v.tr.* verschönern. ◆**beauty,** *s.* Schönheit *f*.

beaver ['biːvər], *s.* Biber *m*.

because [bi'kɒz]. I. *conj.* weil. II. *prep. phr.* **b. of,** wegen + *gen*.

beckon ['bek(ə)n], *v.i.* winken; **to b.**

s.o., j-m Zeichen geben.

become [bi'kʌm], *v.i.irr.* werden; **what's b. of him?** was ist aus ihm geworden? ◆**be'coming,** *adj.* kleidsam; **her hat is very b.,** der Hut steht ihr sehr gut.

bed [bed], *s.* 1. Bett *n;* **to go to b.,** ins Bett gehen; **to get out of b.,** aufstehen; **b. and breakfast,** Übernachtung *f* mit Frühstück. 2. **river b.,** Flußbett *n;* flower b., Blumenbeet *n*. ◆**bedclothes,** *s.pl.* Bettzeug *n*. ◆**bedding,** *s.* Bettzeug *n*. ◆**bedridden,** *adj.* bettlägerig. ◆**bedroom,** *s.* Schlafzimmer *n*. ◆**bedside,** *s.* **at the b.,** neben dem Bett; **b. table,** Nachttisch *m;* **b. lamp,** Nachttischlampe *f*. ◆**'bed-sitting room,** *F:* **'bed'sitter/'bed'sit,** *s.* Wohn-Schlafzimmer *n*. ◆**bedspread,** *s.* Bettüberwurf *m*. ◆**bedtime,** *s.* Schlafenszeit *f;* **b. story,** Geschichte *f* vor dem Einschlafen.

bedlam ['bedləm], *s.* Chaos *n*.

bee [biː], *s.* Biene *f*. ◆**beehive,** *s.* Bienenstock *m*. ◆**beeline,** *s.* **to make a b. for sth.,** geradewegs auf etwas *acc* zusteuern.

beech [biːtʃ], *s.* Buche *f*.

beef [biːf], *s.* Rindfleisch *n;* **roast b.,** Rinderbraten *m*. ◆**beefy,** *adj. F:* kräftig.

beer [biər], *s.* Bier *n*.

beet [biːt], *s.* **sugar b.,** Zuckerrübe *f*. ◆**beetroot,** *s.* rote Rübe/*North G:* Bete *f*.

beetle [biːtl], *s.* Käfer *m*.

before [bi'fɔːr]. I. *adv.* vorher; **the day b.,** am Tag vorher; **never b.,** noch nie; **I have seen him b.,** ich habe ihn schon mal gesehen. II. *prep.* vor + *dat;* **the day b. yesterday,** vorgestern; **the week b. last,** vorletzte Woche; **b. long,** bald; **b. leaving he gave me this,** ehe er wegging, gab er mir das. III. *conj.* bevor. ◆**be'forehand,** *adv.* im voraus.

befriend [bi'frend], *v.tr.* **to b. s.o.,** sich mit j-m anfreunden.

beg [beg], *v.* 1. *v.i.* betteln **(for sth., um etwas acc).** 2. *v.tr.* (j-n) (dringend) bitten **(for sth., um etwas acc).**

beggar ['begər], *s.* Bettler *m*.

begin [bi'gin], *v.tr. & i.* beginnen, anfangen; **to b. with,** zunächst. ◆**be'ginner,** *s.* Anfänger(in) *m(f)*. ◆**be'ginning,** *s.* Anfang *m;* **at the b.,** am Anfang; **from the b.,** von Anfang an.

behalf [bi'hɑːf], *s.* **on b. of s.o.,** im Namen von j-m.

behave [bi'heiv], *v.i.* sich benehmen. ◆**be'haved,** *adj.* **well-)b.,** *(of child)* artig; **badly-)b.,** ungezogen. ◆**be'haviour,** *s. (a)* Benehmen *n; (b) (of things)* Verhalten *n*.

behead [bi'hed], *v.tr.* enthaupten.

behind [bi'haind]. I. *adv.* hinten; **to stay/remain b.,** zurückbleiben; **to be b. with one's work,** mit der Arbeit im Rückstand sein. II. *prep.* hinter + *dat* & *acc; Fig:* **to be b. s.o.,** j-n unterstützen.

III. s. F: Hintern m.

beige [bei3], adj. beige.

belated [bi'leitid], adj. verspätet.

belch [belt∫]. I. v. 1. v.i. rülpsen. 2. v.tr. to b. (forth) smoke/flames, Rauch/Flammen ausspeien. II. s. Rülpser m.

belfry ['belfri], s. Glockenturm m.

Belgian ['beld3ən]. I. adj. belgisch. II. s. Belgier(in) m(f). ◆**Belgium** ['beld3əm]. Pr.n. Belgien n.

belief [bi'li:f], s. (a) Glauben m (in, an + acc); (b) (personal b.) Überzeugung f.

believe [bi'li:v], v.tr. glauben; to b. s.o., j-m glauben. 2. v.i. to b. in sth., an etwas acc glauben. ◆**be'lievable**, adj. glaubhaft. ◆**be'liever**, s. (a) to be a great b. in, etwas acc schwören; (b) Ecc: Gläubige(r) f(m).

belittle [bi'litl], v.tr. (j-s Leistungen) schmälern; (j-n) herabsetzen.

bell [bel], s. Glocke f; (doorbell) Klingel f; (small handbell etc.) Schelle f; to ring the b., klingeln; F: that rings a b., das kommt mir bekannt vor.

belligerent [bi'lid3ər(ə)nt], adj. (of country etc.) kriegführend; (of pers.) angriffslustig.

bellow ['beləu], v.i. brüllen.

bellows ['beləuz], s.pl. (pair of) b., Blasebalg m.

belly, pl. **-ies** ['beli, -iz], s. Bauch m.

belong [bi'lɔŋ], v.i. (a) gehören (to s.o., j m); (b) (be appropriate) put it back where it belongs, stellen Sie es wieder dorthin, wo es hingehört; (c) (be part of) to b. to sth., zu etwas dat gehören; to b. to a society, einer Gesellschaft angehören. ◆**be'longings**, s.pl. Habe f.

beloved [bi'lʌvid], s. Geliebte(r) f(m).

below [bi'ləu]. I. adv. unten. II. prep. unter + dat; (level) unterhalb + gen; 10° b. (zero), 10 Grad unter Null.

belt [belt]. I. s. 1. Gürtel m; (for safety) Sicherheitsgurt m. 2. E: Riemen m; conveyor b., Förderband n. II. v.tr. F: to b. s.o., j-n verprügeln. ◆**belt 'up**, v.i. P: b. up! halt die Klappe!

bench [ben(t)∫], s. 1. (a) (seat) Bank f; (b) Jur: the B., (i) der Richterstuhl m; (ii) (the judges) das Richterkollegium. 2. (work b.), Werkbank f.

bend [bend]. I. v.tr. 1. v.tr. (das Knie usw.) beugen; (den Rücken) krümmen; (etwas) biegen. 2. v.i. (a) (of pers.) sich bücken; (b) (of thing) sich biegen; (of road, river etc.) eine Biegung machen. II. s. 1. Biegung f; Krümmung f (in einem Rohr); Kurve f (einer Straße); F: round the b., bekloppt. 2. Med: the bends, Druckluftkrankheit f. ◆**bend 'down**, v.i. (sich) bücken. ◆**bent**. I. adj. 1. (a) gebogen; b. (out of shape), verbogen; (b) F: korrupt. 2. to be on doing sth., darauf erpicht sein, etwas zu tun. II. s. Neigung f (for sth., zu etwas dat).

beneath [bi'ni:θ]. I. adv. darunter. II.

---

prep. unter + dat; unterhalb + gen.

benefactor ['benifæktər], s. Wohltäter(in) m(f). ◆**beneficial** [beni'fi∫(ə)l], adj. wohltuend; (to advantage) vorteilhaft. ◆**beneficiary**, pl. **-ies** [beni'fi∫əri, -iz], s. Nutznießer(in) m(f); Begünstigte(r) f(m).

benefit ['benifit]. I. s. 1. Nutzen m. 2. Adm: Unterstützung f; **unemployment** b., Arbeitslosenunterstützung f; **sickness** b., Krankengeld n. II. v. 1. v.i. to b. by/from sth., von etwas dat profitieren/Nutzen ziehen. 2. v.tr. to b. s.o., j-m nützen.

benevolence [bi'nevələns], s. Wohlwollen n. ◆**be'nevolent**, adj. wohlwollend.

benign [bi'nain], adj. gutmütig.

bequeath [bi'kwi:ð], v.tr. to b. sth. to s.o., j-m etwas hinterlassen. ◆**be'quest**, s. Vermächtnis n.

bereaved [bi'ri:vd], s.pl. the b., die Leidtragenden. ◆**be'reavement**, s. Trauerfall m; (state) Verlassenheit f (der Witwe usw.).

beret ['berei], s. Baskenmütze f.

berry ['beri], s. Beere f.

berth [bə:θ], s. 1. to give s.o., sth. a wide b., um j-n, etwas acc einen großen Bogen machen. 2. Liegeplatz m.

beseech [bi'si:t∫], v.tr.irr. anflehen.

beside [bi'said], prep. neben + dat & acc; to be b. oneself (with joy), außer sich (vor Freude) sein.

besides [bi'saidz]. I. adv. außerdem. II. prep. außer + dat; **nobody b. him had seen it**, niemand außer ihm hatte es gesehen.

besiege [bi'si:d3], v.tr. belagern.

bespoke [bi'spəuk], adj. b. tailor, Maßschneider m.

best [best]. I. adj. & s. beste(r,s); b. man approx.=Brautführer m; to do one's b., sein Bestes tun; F: all the b.! alles Gute! at (the) b., bestenfalls. II. adv. am besten. ◆**best'seller**, s. Bestseller m.

bestial ['bestjəl], adj. bestialisch.

bet [bet]. I. s. Wette f. II. v. 1. v.tr. (eine Summe) setzen (on sth., auf etwas acc). 2. v.tr. wetten. ◆**'betting**, s. Wetten n; to b. shop, Wettbüro n.

betray [bi'trei], v.tr. verraten. ◆**be'trayal**, s. Verrat m.

better ['betər]. I. adj. & adv. besser; so much the b., um so besser; to get the b. of s.o., j-n übervorteilen; to think b. of it, sich eines besseren besinnen; I'd b. go now, es ist besser, ich gehe jetzt. II. v.tr. (a) to b. oneself, sich verbessern; (b) (improve on) (etwas) übertreffen.

between [bi'twi:n]. I. prep. 1. (b. two) zwischen + dat & acc. 2. (b. several) unter + dat; b. friends, unter Freunden. II. adv. (in) b., dazwischen.

beverage ['bevəridʒ], s. Getränk n.

beware [bi'weər], v.i. sich hüten (of sth., vor etwas dat). b. of the dog! Vorsicht, bissiger Hund!

bewilder [bi'wildər], *v.tr.* verwirren. ◆**be'wildered,** *adj.* verwirrt. ◆**be'wildering,** *adj.* verwirrend.

bewitching [bi'witʃiŋ], *adj.* bezaubernd.

beyond [bi'jɔnd]. **I.** *adv.* darüber hinaus. **II.** *prep.* jenseits + *gen*; über ... *acc* hinaus; **it's b. me,** das geht über meinen Horizont. **III.** *s. F:* **at the back of b.,** am Ende der Welt.

bias ['baiəs], *s.* Voreingenommenheit *f.* (*prejudice*) Vorurteil *n*; *Jur:* Befangenheit *f.* ◆**'biased,** *adj.* voreingenommen; (*esp. against sth.*) parteiisch; *Jur:* befangen.

bib [bib], *s.* Latz *m*; (*baby's*) Lätzchen *n*.

Bible ['baibl], *s.* Bibel *f.* ◆**'biblical** ['biblikl], *adj.* biblisch.

bibliography [bibli'ɔgrəfi], *s.* Bibliographie *f.*

bicarbonate [bai'kɑːbənit], *s.* **b. of soda,** doppelkohlensaures Natrium *n.*

biceps ['baiseps], *s.* Bizeps *m.*

bicker ['bikər], *v.i.* (sich) zanken.

bicycle ['baisikl], *s.* Fahrrad *n.*

bid [bid]. **I.** *v.tr. & i.tr.* (*at auction*) bieten. **II.** *s.* (*at auction*) Gebot *n*; **to make a b. for freedom,** zu entkommen versuchen. ◆**'bidder,** *s.* Bieter *m.* ◆**'bidding,** *s.* **1.** to do s.o.'s b., j-s Befehle ausführen. **2.** Bieten *n.*

bide [baid], *v.tr.* **to b. one's time,** (eine Gelegenheit) abwarten.

bifocal [bai'fəuk(ə)l], *adj.* **b. spectacles/** *F:* bifocals, Bifokalbrille *f.*

big [big], *adj.* groß. ◆**'bighead,** *s. F:* eingebildeter Kerl *m.*

bigamy ['bigəmi], *s.* Bigamie *f.*

bigot ['bigət], *s.* (*a*) *Ecc:* Frömmler *m*; (*b*) engstirniger Fanatiker *m.* ◆**'bigoted,** *adj.* intolerant; (*narrow*) engstirnig. ◆**'bigotry,** *s.* **1.** *Ecc:* Frömmelei *f.* **2.** Fanatismus *m.*

bigwig ['bigwig], *s. F:* hohes Tier *n.*

bike [baik], *s. F:* Rad *n.*

bikini [bi'kiːni], *s.* Bikini *m.*

bilberry ['bilbəri], *s.* Heidelbeere *f.*

bile [bail], *s.* Galle *f.*

bilge [bildʒ], *s. Nau:* Bilge *f.*

bilingual [bai'liŋgw(ə)l], *adj.* zweisprachig.

bill¹ [bil], *s.* Schnabel *m* (eines Vogels).

bill² [bil], *s.* **1.** *Com:* Rechnung *f.* **2.** (*a*) *N.Am:* Banknote *f*; (*b*) *Fin:* b. of exchange, Wechsel *m.* **3.** *Th:* double b., Doppelprogramm *n.* **4.** b. of fare, Speisekarte *f.* **5.** *Pol:* Gesetzentwurf *n.* ◆**'billfold,** *s. N.Am:* Brieftasche *f.*

billet ['bilit]. **I.** *v.tr.* einquartieren. **II.** *s.* Quartier *n.*

billiard ['biljəd], *s.* **1.** *pl.* **billiards,** Billard *n.* **2.** b. cue, Queue *m.*

billion ['biljən], *s.* (*a*) Billion *f*; (*b*) *N.Am:* (*thousand million*) Milliarde *f.*

bin [bin], *s.* Kasten *m*; (*waste*) b., Abfalleimer *m*; **bread** b., Brotkasten *m.*

bind [baind], *v.tr.irr.* (*a*) binden; **to b. (up) a wound,** eine Wunde verbinden;

(*b*) (*oblige*) verpflichten. ◆**'binding. I.** *adj.* verbindlich. **II.** *s.* **1.** (*of ski*) Bindung *f.* **2.** (*of book*) Einband *m.*

binoculars [bi'nɔkjuləz], *s.pl.* Fernglas *n.*

biodegradable ['baiəudi'greidəbl], *adj.* biologisch abbaubar.

biography [bai'ɔgrəfi], *s.* Biographie *f.* ◆**bi'ographer,** *s.* Biograph *m.*

biology [bai'ɔlədʒi], *s.* Biologie *f.* ◆**biological** [baiə'lɔdʒikl], *adj.* biologisch. ◆**bi'ologist,** *s.* Biologe *m*, Biologin *f.*

birch [bəːtʃ], *s.* **1.** Birke *f.* **2.** b.(-rod), Rute *f.*

bird [bəːd], *s.* **1.** Vogel *m*; **to kill two birds with one stone,** zwei Fliegen mit einer Klappe schlagen. **2.** *P:* (*girl*) Biene *f.* ◆**'bird's-eye,** *adj.* b.-e. view, Vogelperspektive *f.*

birth [bəːθ], *s.* Geburt *f*; b. certificate, Geburtsurkunde *f*; b. control, Geburtenregelung *f*; **to give b. to a child,** ein Kind zur Welt bringen. ◆**'birthday,** *s.* Geburtstag *m.* ◆**'birthmark,** *s.* Muttermal *n.* ◆**'birthplace,** *s.* Geburtsort *m*; (*house*) Geburtshaus *n.* ◆**'birthrate,** *s.* Geburtenziffer *f.*

biscuit ['biskit], *s.* Keks *m.*

bishop ['biʃəp], *s.* **1.** *Ecc:* Bischof *m.* **2.** (*in chess*) Läufer *m.*

bit¹ [bit], *s.* (*horse's*) Gebiß *n.*

bit² [bit], *s.* Stückchen *n*; **a b.** (of), ein wenig/bißchen.

bitch [bitʃ], *s.* **1.** Hündin *f.* **2.** *P:* (*woman*) Luder *n.*

bite [bait]. **I.** *v.tr.irr.* beißen; (*of insect*) stechen; *Fig:* **to b. off more than one can chew,** sich *dat* zuviel zumuten; *F:* **to b. s.o.'s head off,** j-m den Kopf abreißen. **II.** *s.* **1.** Biß *m*; (*of insect*) Stich *m.* **2.** (*of food*) Bissen *m.* ◆**'biting,** *adj.* schneidend.

bitter ['bitər]. **I.** *adj.* bitter; (*of taste*) herb; (*of wind*) scharf; (*pers.*) verbittert. **II.** *s.* Bitterbier *n.* ◆**'bitterness,** *s.* (*a*) Bitterkeit *f*; (*b*) (*of pers.*) Verbitterung *f.*

bizarre [bi'zɑːr], *adj.* bizarr.

black [blæk]. **I.** *adj.* schwarz; b. ice, Glatteis *n*; b. and white photograph, Schwarzweißfoto *n*; **to beat s.o. b. and blue,** j-n grün und blau schlagen; b. pudding, Blutwurst *f.* b. eye, blaues Auge. **II.** *v.tr. Ind:* boykottieren. ◆**'blackberry,** *s.* Brombeere *f.* ◆**'blackbird,** *s.* Amsel *f.* ◆**'blackboard,** *s.* Wandtafel *f.* ◆**'black'currant,** *s.* schwarze Johannisbeere *f.* ◆**'blacken,** *v.tr.* schwärzen; *Fig:* anschwärzen. ◆**'blackhead,** *s.* Mitesser *m.* ◆**'blackleg,** *s.* Streikbrecher *m.* ◆**'blacklist,** *v.tr.* to b. s.o., j-n auf die schwarze Liste setzen. ◆**'blackmail. I.** *s.* Erpressung *f.* **II.** *v.tr.* erpressen. ◆**'blackmailer,** *s.* Erpresser(in) *m(f).* ◆**'blackout,** *s.* **1.** Verdunkelung *f.* **2.** (*faint*) Ohnmachtsanfall *m.* **3.** news b., Nachrichtensperre *f.*

◆**blacksmith**, s. Schmied m.

bladder ['blædər], s. Blase f.

blade [bleid], s. 1. (grass) Halm m. 2. (knife) Klinge f.

blame [bleim]. I. s. Schuld f; to take the b., die Schuld auf sich acc nehmen. II. v.tr. (j-m) die Schuld geben (for sth., an etwas acc); he's to b., er ist schuld daran. ◆'**blameless**, adj. schuldlos.

blanch [blɑːn(t)ʃ], v. 1. v.tr. Cu: blanchieren. 2. v.i. (of pers.) erbleichen.

blancmange [blə'mɒnʒ], s. Pudding m.

bland [blænd], adj. mild; (of taste) neutral; (of style) charakterlos.

blank [blæŋk]. I. adj. 1. (of paper) leer; (of tape) unbespielt; to leave sth. b., etwas freilassen; b. cheque, Blankoscheck m. 2. b. look, ausdrucksloser Blick; to look b., verdutzt dreinblicken. II. s. 1. (a) N.Am: Formular n; (b) (in document) leere Stelle; (c) my mind's a b., ich habe alles vergessen; F: ich habe Mattscheibe. 2. b. (cartridge), Platzpatrone f.

blanket ['blæŋkit], s. Decke f.

blare ['bleər], v.i. (of trumpet) schmettern; the radio is blaring away, das Radio plärrt.

blasé ['blɑːzei], adj. blasiert.

blaspheme [blæs'fiːm], v.tr. & i. (Gott) lästern. ◆**blasphemous** [-fəməs], adj. gotteslästerlich. ◆**blasphemy** [-fəmi], s. Gotteslästerung f.

blast [blɑːst]. I. s. 1. b. of air, heftiger Windstoß; to be going full b., auf Hochtouren laufen. 2. (explosion) Explosion f. II. v.tr. P: b. (it)! verdammt! ◆'**blast-furnace**, s. Hochofen m. ◆'**blast-off**, s. Start m.

blatant ['bleit(ə)nt], adj. eklatant.

blaze [bleiz]. I. s. 1. Feuer n; (house etc.) Brand m. 2. b. of colour, Farbenpracht f. II. v.i. (of fire) lodern; (of sun) strahlen.

blazer ['bleizər], s. Blazer m.

bleach [bliːtʃ]. I. v.tr. & i. bleichen. II. s. Bleichmittel n.

bleak [bliːk], adj. 1. (of place) öde; (bare) kahl. 2. (of weather) rauh. 3. Fig: trübe; b. prospects, trostlose Aussichten.

bleary ['bliəri], adj. b. eyes, trübe/(on waking) verschlafene Augen.

bleat [bliːt], v.i. (of sheep) blöken; (of goat) meckern.

bleed [bliːd], v.irr. 1. v.i. bluten; to b. to death, verbluten. 2. v.tr. Aut: to b. the brakes, die Bremsen entlüften. ◆'**bleeding**, adj. 1. blutend. 2. P: verdammt.

blemish ['blemiʃ], s. 1. Makel m. 2. Fig: Schandfleck m.

blend [blend]. I. v. 1. v.tr. (Kaffee, Tee usw.) mischen; (etwas) vermengen. 2. v.i. sich (ver)mischen (with, mit + dat); (match) zusammenpassen. II. s. Mischung f (von Kaffee, Tee); Verschnitt m (von Whisky usw.).

bless [bles], v.tr. segnen; b. you! Gesund-

heit! ◆**blessed** ['blesid], adj. (a) Ecc: the B. Virgin Mary, die Heilige Jungfrau Maria; (b) F: that b. boy, dieser verflixte Junge. ◆'**blessing**, s. Segen m; to count one's blessings, mit dem zufrieden sein, was man hat.

blight [blait]. I. s. 1. Bot: Brand m; (on potatoes) Kartoffelfäule f. 2. Fig: schädlicher Einfluß m. II. v.tr. (Hoffnungen usw.) zunichte machen.

blind [blaind]. I. adj. blind; b. spot, Aut: etc: toter Winkel; to turn a b. eye, ein Auge zudrücken; b. alley, Sackgasse f; -ly, adv. blindlings. II. v.tr. blenden. ◆'**blindfold**. I. v.tr. (j-m) die Augen verbinden. II. adj. & adv. mit verbundenen Augen. ◆'**blindness**, s. Blindheit f.

blind² [blaind], s. (roller) b., Rollo n; Venetian b., Jalousie f.

blink [bliŋk]. I. v.i. blinzeln. II. s. F: to be on the b., kaputt sein. ◆'**blinkers**, s.pl. Scheuklappen fpl.

bliss [blis], s. Seligkeit f. ◆'**blissful**, adj. selig; -ly, adv. b. ignorant/unaware, völlig ahnungslos/unbewußt.

blister ['blistər]. I. s. Blase f; (small) Bläschen n. II. v.i. Blasen bekommen; (of paint) Blasen werfen.

blithe [blaið], adj. fröhlich.

blitz [blits], s. F: to have a b. on a room, ein Zimmer radikal aufräumen.

blizzard ['blizəd], s. Schneesturm m.

bloated ['bləutid], adj. (of face) aufgedunsen; (of belly) aufgebläht.

blob [blɒb], s. (of colour) Fleck m; (of ink) Klecks m.

bloc [blɒk], s. Block m.

block [blɒk]. I. s. 1. (of marble etc.) Block m; (of wood) Klotz m. 2. b. of flats, Wohnblock m; to walk round the b., um den Block gehen. 3. (a) road b., Straßensperre f; (b) to have a mental b., eine Sperre haben. 4. b. capitals, Blockbuchstaben mpl. II. v.tr. blockieren. ◆'**blo'ckade**. I. s. Blockade f. II. v.tr. blockieren. ◆'**blockage**, s. Verstopfung f. ◆'**block 'up**, v.tr. zustopfen.

blonde [blɒnd]. I. adj. blond. II. s. Blondine f.

blood [blʌd], s. Blut n; in cold b., kaltblütig; industry needs new b., die Industrie braucht Nachwuchs; b. pressure, Blutdruck m; b. vessel, Blutgefäß n; b. transfusion, Blutübertragung f; b. test, Blutprobe f; b. donor, Blutspender m; b. group, Blutgruppe f. ◆'**bloodcurdling**, adj. markerschütternd. ◆'**bloodhound**, s. Bluthund m. ◆'**bloodless**, adj. unblutig. ◆'**bloodshed**, s. Blutvergießen n. ◆'**bloodshot**, adj. b. eyes, blutunterlaufene Augen. ◆'**bloodstained**, adj. blutbefleckt. ◆'**bloodthirsty**, adj. blutrünstig. ◆'**bloody**, adj. 1. blutig; (of tyrant) blutrünstig. 2. P: (a) adj. verdammt, verflucht; (b) adv. **it's b. hot,** es ist verdammt heiß. ◆**'bloody-'minded,** adj. P: boshaft.

bloom [blu:m]. I. s. Blüte f. II. v.i. blühen.

blossom ['blɔsəm]. I. s. Blüte f. II. v.i. blühen.

blot [blɔt]. I. s. (a) Fleck m; (of ink) Klecks m; (b) Pej: **b. on the landscape,** Schandfleck m (in der Landschaft). II. v.tr. (a) (etwas) beflecken; Fig: **to b. one's copybook,** sich blamieren; (b) (Tinte) aufsaugen; (Geschriebenes) löschen. ◆**'blotter,** s. Schreibunterlage f. ◆**'blotting 'paper,** s. Löschpapier n; (sheet) Löschblatt n.

blotchy ['blɔtʃi], adj. fleckig.

blouse [blauz], s. Bluse f.

blow¹ [blou], v.irr. I. v.i. blasen; **it's blowing a gale,** es stürmt. II. v.tr. (a) blasen; **to b. one's nose,** sich dat die Nase putzen; (b) El: **to b. a fuse,** eine Sicherung durchhauen; (c) F: **b. the expense!** zum Teufel mit den Kosten! ◆**'blow a'way,** v.tr. wegblasen. ◆**'blow 'down,** v.tr. umwehen. ◆**'blow 'in,** v.tr. (ein Fenster usw.) eindrücken. ◆**'blowlamp,** s. Lötlampe f. ◆**'blow 'off,** v. 1. v.tr. (einen Hut usw.) wegwehen. 2. v.i. weggeblasen werden. ◆**'blow 'out,** v. 1. v.tr. ausblasen. 2. v.i. ausgehen. ◆**'blow-out,** s. geplatzter Reifen m. ◆**'blow 'over,** v.i. (of storm) vorübergehen; (of scandal etc.) in Vergessenheit geraten. ◆**'blow 'up,** v. 1. v.i. in die Luft gehen. 2. v.tr. (a) (einen Luftballon usw.) aufblasen, (with a pump) aufpumpen; (b) (explode) sprengen; (c) (enlarge) vergrößern.

blow² [blou], s. 1. (with fist) Schlag m; (with stick) Hieb m. 2. Fig: Enttäuschung f.

blue [blu:]. I. adj. blau; **to feel b.,** niedergeschlagen sein; F: (of language, jokes) schlüpfrig. II. s. film, Pej: Pornofilm m. II. s. **out of the b.,** unerwartet. ◆**'bluebell,** s. Glockenblume f. ◆**'bluebottle,** s. Schmeißfliege f. ◆**'blue-print,** s. 1. Blaupause f. 2. Fig: (model) Vorbild f. ◆**'blue-stocking,** s. Blaustrumpf m.

bluff¹ [blʌf], adj. (of manner) rauh aber herzlich.

bluff² [blʌf]. I. s. Bluff m. II. v.tr. & i. bluffen.

blunder ['blʌndər]. I. s. Schnitzer m. II. v.i. einen Schnitzer machen.

blunt [blʌnt], adj. 1. (of knife etc.) stumpf. 2. (of manner) schroff; **-ly,** adv. **to put it b.,** um es offen zu sagen. ◆**'bluntness,** s. 1. Stumpfheit f. 2. Unverblümtheit f.

blur [blə:r], v.tr. verschwommen machen. ◆**'blurred,** adj. verschwommen.

blurb [blə:b], s. Klappentext m.

blurt [blə:t], v.tr. **to b. out a secret etc.,** mit einem Geheimnis usw. herausplatzen.

blush [blʌʃ], v.i. erröten. ◆**'blushing,**

adj. errötend; (demure) züchtig.

boar [bɔ:r], s. Eber m; **wild b.,** Wildschwein n.

board [bɔ:d]. I. s. 1. (a) Brett n; (floor) b., Diele f; (b) Sch: etc: Tafel f; (notice) Schild n. 2. Verpflegung f; (full) b., Vollpension f; **b. and lodging,** Unterkunft und Verpflegung. 3. b. of enquiry, Untersuchungsausschuß m; **b. of directors,** Adm: Aufsichtsrat m; Com: Vorstand m. 4. on b., an Bord; **on b. a ship,** an Bord eines Schiffes. II. v.tr. **to b. a ship/aircraft,** an Bord eines Schiffes/eines Flugzeugs gehen; **to b. a train/bus,** in einen Zug/Bus einsteigen; (b) **to b. up** (a window etc.), (ein Fenster usw.) mit Brettern verschlagen. ◆**'boarder,** s. Mieter/in m(f); (in boarding house) Pensionsgast m; Sch: Internatsschüler/in m(f). ◆**'boarding,** s. b. house, Pension f; **b. school,** Internat n.

boast [boust]. I. s. 1. v.i. prahlen. 2. to b. (etwas gen) rühmen. ◆**'boastful,** adj. angeberisch. ◆**'boastfulness,** s. Angeberei f. ◆**'boasting,** s. Prahlerei f.

boat [bout], s. 1. Boot m; (ship) Schiff n; **we are all in the same b.,** wir sitzen alle in einem Boot; **to miss the b.,** den Anschluß verpassen; **b. race,** Bootsrennen n; **b. train,** Zug m mit Schiffsanschluß. ◆**'boathouse,** s. Bootshaus n.

bob [bɔb], v.i. to b. (up and down) sich auf und ab bewegen; tänzeln.

bobbin ['bɔbin], s. Spule f.

bodice ['bɔdis], s. (a) Mieder n; (b) Oberteil n (eines Kleides).

body ['bɔdi], s. 1. (a) Körper m; (b) (dead) b., Leiche f. 2. Adm: Körperschaft f; **public b.,** Behörde f. 3. (a) (main part) Substanz f (eines Dokumentes); (b) Aut: Karosserie f. ◆**'bodily.** I. adj. körperlich. II. adv. **to remove s.o. b.,** j-n wegschleppen. ◆**'bodyguard,** s. Leibwächter m. ◆**'bodywork,** s. Karosserie f.

bog [bɔg]. I. s. 1. Sumpf m. 2. P: (lavatory) Klo n. II. v.tr. **to get bogged down,** ins Stocken geraten; steckenbleiben. ◆**'boggy,** adj. sumpfig.

boggle ['bɔgl], v.i. F: **to b. at sth.,** vor etwas dat stutzen; **the mind boggles!** da staunt man!

bogus ['bougəs], adj. falsch.

boil¹ [bɔil], s. Med: Furunkel m & n.

boil² [bɔil], v. 1. v.i. kochen. 2. v.tr. kochen lassen; **boiled potatoes,** Salzkartoffeln fpl; **boiled sweet,** Lutschbonbon m & n. ◆**'boil a'way,** v.i. verkochen. ◆**'boil 'down,** v.tr. F: **what it boils down to is that...,** im Endeffekt heißt es, daß... ◆**'boiler,** s. Heizkessel m; **b. suit,** Schlosseranzug m. ◆**'boiling.** I. s. Kochen n; **b. point,** Siedepunkt m. II. adj. kochend; adv. **b. hot,** kochend/siedend heiß. ◆**'boil 'over,** v.i. überkochen.

boisterous ['bɔist(ə)rəs], adj. ungestüm.

(of child) ausgelassen.
bold [bəuld], adj. 1. (of pers.) kühn; (of action) gewagt; (of colours) kräftig. 2. (type) fett gedruckt. ◆**boldness**, s. Kühnheit f.

bolshy ['bɔlʃi], adj. F: störrisch.

bolster ['bəulstər], s. Kissen n; (round) Schlummerrolle f.

bolt [bəult]. I. s. 1. (of door) Riegel m. 2. E: Bolzen m. II. v. 1. v.i. (of horse) durchgehen. 2. v.tr. (a) (sein Essen) herunterschlingen; (b) (eine Tür) verriegeln. III. adv. b. upright, kerzengerade.

bomb [bɔm]. I. s. Bombe f; b. disposal, (i) (removal) Bombenräumung f; (ii) (exploding) Bombensprengung f. II. v.tr. (a) bombardieren; (b) (auf ein Gebäude usw.) ein Bombenattentat machen. ◆**bom'bard**, v.tr. bombardieren. ◆**bom'bardment**, s. Bombardierung f. ◆**bomber**, s. (aircraft) Bomber m; (pers.) Bombenleger m. ◆**bombing**, s. (a) Bombardierung f (aus der Luft); (b) Bombenattentat n (auf ein Gebäude usw.). ◆**bombshell**, s. F: this was a b. to us all, wir waren alle wie vom Schlag getroffen.

bombastic [bɔm'bæstik], adj. (of style) geschwollen.

bona fide ['bəunə'faidi], adj. echt.

bond [bɔnd], s. 1. Fessel f; Band n. 2. Fin: Obligation f.

bone [bəun]. I. s. 1. Knochen m; (of fish) Gräte f; Fig: b. of contention, Zankapfel m; to have a b. to pick with s.o., mit j-m ein Hühnchen zu rupfen haben; b. dry, knochentrocken; b. idle, stinkfaul. 2. pl. (of the dead) Gebeine npl. II. v.tr. (Fleisch) vom Knochen lösen; (einen Fisch) entgräten. ◆**boneless**, adj. ohne Knochen; (of fish) ohne Gräten. ◆**bony**, adj. (of face etc.) knochig; (of pers., animal) mager.

bonfire ['bɔnfaiər], s. Feuer n (im Freien).

bonnet ['bɔnit], s. 1. Cl: Haube f. 2. Aut: Motorhaube f.

bonus, pl. -uses ['bəunəs, -əsiz], s. Bonus m; (on savings) Prämie f; no claims b., Schadenfreiheitsrabatt m.

boo [bu:]. I. int. huh! buh! II. v. 1. v.tr. auspfeifen. 2. v.i. buhen.

book [buk]. I. s. 1. Buch n. 2. (a) exercise b., Schulheft n; (b) pl. Com: to keep the books, die Bücher führen; F: to be in s.o.'s bad books, bei j-m schlecht angeschrieben sein. II. v.tr. (ein Zimmer, Taxi usw.) bestellen. ◆**bookable**, adj. vorbestellbar; (of tickets) im Vorverkauf erhältlich. ◆**bookcase**, s. Bücherregal n. ◆**bookie**, s. F: Buchmacher m. ◆**booking**, s. (a) Buchung f; (b) Th: etc: Vorbestellung f; **b. office**, Fahrkartenschalter m; Th: Theaterkasse f. ◆**book-keeper**, s. Buchhalter m. ◆**book-keeping**, s. Buchhaltung f. ◆**booklet**, s. Broschüre f.

◆**bookmaker**, s. Buchmacher m. ◆**bookmark**, s. Lesezeichen n. ◆**bookseller**, s. Buchhändler m; (secondhand) b., Antiquar m. ◆**bookshelf**, s. Bücherregal n; (single shelf) Bücherbord n. ◆**bookshop**, s. Buchhandlung f. ◆**bookstall**, s. Bücherstand m; (on station) Zeitungskiosk m. ◆**bookworm**, s. Bücherwurm m.

boom [bu:m]. I. s. 1. (of guns etc.) Dröhnen n. 2. Aufschwung m; Fin: Hochkonjunktur f; to be enjoying a b., sich großer Beliebtheit erfreuen. II. v.i. (a) dröhnen; (b) (of business) blühen.

boomerang ['bu:məræŋ], s. Bumerang m.

boon [bu:n], s. Segen m.

boorish ['buəriʃ], adj. lümmelhaft.

boost [bu:st]. I. v.tr. (a) (etwas) fördern, Com: ankurbeln; (b) E: El: (den Druck, die Spannung) erhöhen; (ein Signal) verstärken. II. s. Auftrieb m; to give s.o., sth. a b., j-m, etwas dar Auftrieb geben. ◆**booster**, s. 1. Med: Nachimpfung f. 2. b. (rocket), Startrakete f.

boot [bu:t]. I. s. 1. Stiefel m. 2. Aut: Kofferraum m. II. v.tr. F: to b. s.o. out, j-n rausschmeißen.

booty ['bu:ti], s. Beute f.

booze [bu:z]. I. s. P: Alkohol m. II. v.i. P: saufen. ◆**boozer**, s. P: 1. (pers.) Säufer m. 2. (pub) Kneipe f.

border ['bɔ:dər]. I. s. 1. Grenze f. 2. (a) Cl: Kante f; (b) flower b., Blumenrabatte f. II. v.i. grenzen (on sth., an etwas acc). ◆**borderline**, s. Grenzlinie f; b. case, Grenzfall m.

bore[1] [bɔ:r]. I. v.tr. & i. (ein Loch usw.) bohren. II. s. Kaliber n (eine Feuerwaffe).

bore[2] [bɔ:r]. I. v.tr. (j-n) langweilen; to be bored (stiff to death), sich (zu Tode) langweilen. II. s. langweiliger Mensch m. ◆**boredom**, s. Langeweile f. ◆**boring**, adj. langweilig.

born [bɔ:n], p.p. geboren; **he was b. in 1970**, er wurde 1970 geboren.

borough ['bʌrə], s. Stadtgemeinde f; (in city) Bezirk m.

borrow ['bɔrəu], v.tr. **to b. sth. from s.o.**, etwas von j-m borgen. ◆**borrower**, s. Entleiher m. ◆**borrowing**, s. Borgen n.

bosom ['buzəm], s. Busen m.

boss [bɔs]. I. s. F: the b., der Chef. II. v.tr. F: to b. s.o. around, j-n herumkommandieren. ◆**bossy**, adj. F: herrisch.

botany ['bɔtəni], s. Botanik f. ◆**bo'tanical** [-'tænikl], adj. botanisch. ◆**botanist**, s. Botaniker(in) m(f).

botch [bɔtʃ], v.tr. F: verpfuschen.

both [bəuθ]. I. adj. & pron. beide; beides; b. (of) their children, ihre beiden Kinder; **they b. came**, sie sind (alle) beide gekommen. II. adv. b. you and I, wir beide; **b. ... and ...**, sowohl ... als auch ...

bother ['bɔðər]. I. v. 1. v.tr. belästigen; **that doesn't b. him**, das stört ihn nicht; **I can't be bothered (to do it)**, das ist mir zu viel Mühe. 2. v.i. to b. about s.o., sth., sich um j-n, etwas acc kümmern; **don't b.!** mach dir keine Mühe! II. s. Mühe f. ◆**'bothered**, adj. hot and b., in Aufregung versetzt; **she isn't b.**, das ist ihr egal.

bottle ['bɔtl]. I. s. 1. Flasche f; b. opener, Flaschenöffner m. II. v.tr. (etwas) in Flaschen abfüllen; (Obst) einmachen. ◆**'bottling** s. Abfüllen n. ◆**'bottle-feed**, v.tr. (ein Baby) mit der Flasche aufziehen. ◆**'bottleneck**, s. Flaschenhals m; Fig: Engpaß m. ◆**'bottle 'up**, v.tr. unterdrücken.

bottom ['bɔtəm]. I. s. 1. (a) Fuß m (eines Hügels, der Treppe, einer Seite usw.); (b) Grund m (eines Flusses); Boden m (einer Tasse usw.); **at/on the b.**, unten; **at the b. of the garden**, am hinteren Ende des Gartens; **to be at the b. of sth.**, hinter etwas dat stecken; **to get to the b. of a mystery**, hinter ein Geheimnis kommen. 2. Anat: F: Hintern m. II. adj. unterste; Aut: b. gear, erster Gang; Sch: he is b. in French, er ist der Schlechteste in Französisch. ◆**'bottomless**, adj. bodenlos.

boulder ['bouldər], s. Felsblock m.

bounce [bauns]. I. v. 1. v.i. springen; (a) (of ball etc.) (up) aufprallen; (back) zurückprallen; (b) F: his cheque bounced, sein Scheck platzte. 2. v.tr. (einen Ball) aufprallen lassen. II. s. Sprung m; (of ball) Aufprall m. ◆**'bouncer**, s. F: Rausschmeißer m.

bound¹ [baund], s. (usu.pl.) out of bounds, Betreten verboten. ◆**'boundless**, adj. unbegrenzt; grenzenlos.

bound² [baund], adj. unterwegs (for, nach + dat); homeward b., auf der Heimreise.

bound³ [baund], s. Sprung m; by leaps and bounds, sprunghaft.

bound⁴ [baund], adj. he's b. to be late, er kommt sicher/garantiert zu spät; it was b. to happen, es mußte so kommen.

boundary ['baund(ə)ri], s. Grenze f.

bouquet [bu'kei], s. 1. Blumenstrauß m. 2. Bukett f (des Weins).

bout [baut], s. 1. Sp: Kampf m. 2. (illness) Anfall m.

bow¹ [bau], s. 1. Bogen m. 2. (knot) Schleife f. ◆**'bow-legged**, adj. O-beinig. ◆**'bow-'tie**, s. Fliege f.

bow² [bau]. I. s. Verbeugung f. II. v. v.i. sich verbeugen; to b. to s.o.'s wishes, sich j-s Wünschen fügen. 2. v.tr. (den Kopf) neigen.

bow³ [bau], s. Nau: (often pl.) Bug m.

bowel ['bauəl], s. usu. pl. bowels, Darm m.

bowl¹ [bəul], s. Schüssel f; (small, shallow) Schale f; (for animal) Napf m.

bowl² [bəul]. I. v.tr. & i. (in cricket) wer-

fen. II. s. Kugel f. ◆**'bowler¹**, s. Werfer m. ◆**'bowling**, s. (a) Bowlspiel n; (b) (indoors) Bowling n; b. alley, Kegelbahn f. ◆**'bowl 'over**, v.tr. umwerfen. ◆**bowls**, s. Bowlsspiel n.

bowler² ['bəulər], s. b. (hat), Melone f.

box¹ [bɔks], s. 1. Schachtel f; (small, wooden or metal) Kasten m; (large wooden) Kiste f; (cardboard) Karton m; b. number, Chiffre f; **P.O. Box**, Postfach n. 2. (a) Th: Loge f; (b) (in stable) Box f; (c) Jur: witness b., Zeugenstand m. ◆**Boxing Day**, s. zweiter Weihnachtstag m. ◆**'box-office**, s. Kasse f.

box² [bɔks], v.i. boxen. ◆**'boxer**, s. Boxer m. ◆**'boxing**, s. Boxen n; b. gloves, Boxhandschuhe mpl; b. match, Boxkampf m.

boy [bɔi], s. Junge m; b. scout, Pfadfinder m. ◆**'boyfriend**, s. Freund m. ◆**'boyish**, adj. jungenhaft.

boycott ['bɔikɔt]. I. v.tr. boykottieren. II. s. Boykott m.

bra [brɑː], s. Büstenhalter m, F: BH m.

brace [breis]. I. s. 1. (a) (support) Stütze f; (b) (for teeth) Zahnspange f. 2. pl. Cl: Hosenträger mpl. II. v.tr. to b. oneself for sth., sich auf etwas acc gefaßt machen. ◆**'bracing**, adj. b. climate, Reizklima n.

bracelet ['breislit], s. Armband n.

bracken ['bræk(ə)n], s. Farnkraut n.

bracket ['brækit]. I. s. 1. E: Träger m; Arch: Konsole f; (wall) b., Wandarm m. 2. (a) Klammer f; round/square brackets, runde/eckige Klammern; (b) the middle income b., die mittlere Einkommensklasse. II. v.tr. (einen Ausdruck, Zahlen) einklammern.

brag [bræg], v.i. prahlen (about sth., mit etwas dat).

braid [breid], s. Borte f; gold b., goldene Tresse f.

braille [breil], s. Blindenschrift f.

brain [brein], s. Gehirn n; b. damage, Gehirnschaden m; to rack one's brain(s), sich auf den Kopf zerbrechen. ◆**'brainchild**, s. Geistesprodukt n. ◆**'brainless**, adj. geistlos. ◆**'brainwash**, v.tr. (j-n) einer Gehirnwäsche unterziehen. ◆**'brainwashing**, s. Gehirnwäsche f. ◆**'brainwave**, s. Geistesblitz m. ◆**'brainy**, adj. F: gescheit.

braise [breiz], v.tr. schmoren.

brake [breik]. I. s. Bremse f; b. fluid, Bremsflüssigkeit f; b. lining, Bremsbelag m; b. shoe, Bremsbacke f; to put on/apply the brakes, bremsen. II. v.tr & i. bremsen.

bramble ['bræmbl], s. Brombeerstrauch m.

bran [bræn], s. Kleie f.

branch [brɑːn(t)ʃ]. I. s. 1. Ast m (eines Baumes). 2. (a) Arm m (eines Flusses); (b) Zweig m (einer Familie); (c) Com: Filiale f (einer Firma). II. v.i. to b. out, neue Wege gehen; *Com:* in eine neue Branche einsteigen; *(of road etc.)* **to b. (off),** abzweigen.

brand [brænd]. I. s. *(a) Com:* Marke f; *(b)* Sorte f. II. *v.tr. (a)* (einem Tier) ein Zeichen einbrennen; *(b)* **to b. s.o. as a liar,** j-n zum Lügner stempeln. ◆**'branded,** adj. **s. goods,** Markenartikel mpl. ◆**'brand(-)'new,** adj. nagelneu.

brandish ['brændiʃ], v.tr. (hin und her) schwingen.

brandy ['brændi], s. Weinbrand m; *(French)* Kognak m.

brass [brɑːs], s. Messing n; **b. band** Blaskapelle f.

brassiere [bræsiɛr], s. Büstenhalter m.

brat [bræt], s. *F:* Balg m & n.

bravado [brəˈvɑːdəu], s. *(gespielte)* Kühnheit f.

brave [breiv]. I. adj. tapfer. II. v.tr. (etwas dat) mutig entgegentreten. ◆**'bravery,** s. Tapferkeit f.

bravo [brɑːˈvəu], int. bravo!

brawl [brɔːl]. I. s. Handgemenge n. II. v.i. zanken; raufen.

brawn [brɔːn], s. Muskelkraft f. ◆**'brawny,** adj. kräftig.

bray [brei], v.i. *(of donkey)* iahen.

brazen ['breizən], adj. unverschämt.

Brazil [brəˈzil]. *Pr.n.* Brasilien n, B. nut, Paranuß f. ◆**Brazilian** [brəˈziljən]. I. adj. brasilianisch. II. s. Brasilianer(in) m(f).

breach [briːtʃ], s. 1. Bruch m *(eines Vertrages, des Versprechens usw.);* Verstoß m *(gegen Vorschriften usw.); Jur:* **b. of the peace,** Friedensbruch m. 2. Bresche f *(in einer Mauer).*

bread [bred], s. Brot n; **b. and butter,** Butterbrot n. ◆**'breadcrumbs,** s.pl. Brotkrümel mpl; *Cu:* Paniermehl n. ◆**'breadwinner,** s. Brotverdiener m.

breadth [bredθ], s. Breite f.

break [breik]. I. s. 1. Bruch m; *(gap)* Lücke f; *lucky* **b.,** Glücksfall m; **give him a b.,** (i) gib ihm eine Chance; (ii) laß ihn in Ruhe. 2. *(a) Sch: etc:* Pause f; *(b)* **the coffee b.,** die Kaffeepause; *(c)* **you need a b.,** du brauchst Urlaub; **weekend b.,** Wochenendurlaub m. 3. b. **of day,** Tagesanbruch m. II. v.irr. 1. v.tr. *(a)* brechen; (eine Tasse usw.) zerbrechen; (ein Spielzeug usw.) kaputtmachen; **to b. one's arm,** sich das Arm brechen; *(b)* **b. (out of) gaol,** aus dem Gefängnis ausbrechen; *(c) (interrupt)* (eine Reise, einen Stromkreis) unterbrechen; **the tree broke his fall,** sein Fall wurde vom Baum gebremst; *(d)* **to b. s.o.,** j-n ruinieren; *(e)* **b. it to her gently,** bring es ihr schonend bei. 2. v.i. *(a) (of glass etc.)* zerbrechen; *(of rope etc.)* zerreißen; *(of waves)* sich brechen; *(of storm)* losbrechen; *(of day)* anbrechen; **to b. into a house,** in ein Haus einbrechen. ◆**'breakable,** adj. zerbrechlich. ◆**'breakage,** s. Bruch m. ◆**break**

a'way, v. 1. v.tr. abbrechen. 2. v.i. *(of rock etc.)* losbrechen; *(of pers.)* sich losreißen; *Pol:* *(of group)* sich lossagen; *Pol:* **b.-a. group,** Splitterpartei f. ◆**'break 'down,** v. 1. v.tr. *(a)* (eine Tür) einbrechen; *(Widerstand)* brechen; *(b)* (etwas) (in Kategorien) aufteilen. 2. v.i. *(a) (of pers., system)* zusammenbrechen; *(of plan, negotiations)* scheitern; *(b) (of machine)* versagen; *(of car)* eine Panne haben. ◆**'breakdown,** s. 1. *(a)* Zusammenbruch m; *(nervous)* b., Nervenzusammenbruch m; *(b)* Scheitern n *(der Verhandlungen usw.);* *(c)* Versagen n *(einer Maschine);* *Aut:* Panne f; **b. lorry,** Abschleppwagen m. 2. Aufgliederung f. ◆**'breaker,** s. *(wave)* Brecher m. ◆**'break 'even,** v.i. seine Kosten decken. ◆**'break 'in,** v. 1. v.tr. (eine Tür usw.) aufbrechen. 2. v.i. **to b. in(to a house),** (in ein Haus) einbrechen. ◆**'break-in,** s. Einbruch m. ◆**'break 'loose,** v.i. sich losreißen. ◆**'breakneck,** adj. **at b. speed,** in halsbrecherischem Tempo. ◆**'break 'off,** v. 1. v.tr. (Verbindungen usw.) abbrechen; (eine Verlobung) lösen. 2. v.i. abbrechen. ◆**'break 'open,** v.tr. aufbrechen. ◆**'break 'out,** v.i. ausbrechen. ◆**'break 'through,** v.tr. & i. *(durch etwas acc)* durchbrechen. ◆**'breakthrough,** s. Durchbruch m. ◆**'break 'up,** v. 1. v.tr. *(a)* zerbrechen, zerstören; *(b) (scrap)* (ein Auto, ein Schiff) verschrotten; *(c)* (eine Menge) auseinandertreiben; (einen Kampf) abbrechen. 2. v.i. *(a) (of marriage)* scheitern; *(of crowd)* sich auflösen; *(b) (of couple)* sich trennen; *(c) (of school)* in die Ferien gehen. ◆**'breakwater,** s. Buhne f.

breakfast ['brekfəst], s. Frühstück n; **to have b.,** frühstücken.

breast [brest], s. Brust f; **b. stroke,** Brustschwimmen n. ◆**'breast-'feed,** v.tr. stillen.

breath [breθ], s. Atem m; **a b.,** ein Atemzug m; **to hold one's b.,** den Atem anhalten; **to waste one's b.,** in den Wind reden; **out of b.,** außer Atem; **to go out for a b. of air,** frische Luft schöpfen gehen. ◆**'breathalyse,** v.tr. *F:* (j-n) (ins Röhrchen) pusten lassen. ◆**'breathless,** adj. atemlos.

breathe [briːð], v. 1. v.i. atmen; **to b. in/out,** einatmen/ausatmen. 2. v.tr. **to b. a sigh of relief,** erleichtert aufatmen. ◆**'breather,** s. *F:* Verschnaufpause f. ◆**'breathing,** s. Atmen n; **b. space,** Atempause f.

breed [briːd]. I. v.irr. 1. v.tr. *(a)* (Tiere) züchten; *(b)* (Gewalt, Haß usw.) hervorrufen. 2. v.i. sich vermehren. II. s. Rasse f. ◆**bred** [bred], adj. **well b.,** gut erzogen. ◆**'breeder,** s. 1. Agr: Züchter m. 2. **b. reactor,** Brutreaktor m. ◆**'breeding,** s. 1. Züchtung f; Zucht f; **b. ground,** Nährboden m. 2. Bildung f.

breeze [briːz], s. Brise f. ◆**'breezy**, adj. 1. (of day) windig. 2. (of pers., manner) lebhaft.

brevity ['breviti], s. Kürze f.

brew [bruː]. I. v. 1. v.tr. (Bier) brauen; (Tee) kochen. 2. v.i. (a) (of tea) ziehen; (b) there's a storm brewing, ein Gewitter ist im Anzug. ◆**'brewer**, s. Brauer m. ◆**'brewery**, s. Brauerei f.

bribe [braib]. I. s. Bestechung f; (money) Schmiergeld n; to take a b., sich bestechen lassen. II. v.tr. (j-n) bestechen. ◆**'bribery**, s. Bestechung f.

brick [brik], s. Ziegel m; (esp. red) Backstein m. ◆**'bricklayer**, s. Maurer m.

bride [braid], s. Braut f; the b. and groom, das Brautpaar. ◆**'bridal**, adj. Braut-. ◆**'bridegroom**, s. Bräutigam m. ◆**'bridesmaid**, s. Brautjungfer f.

bridge¹ [bridʒ]. I. s. 1. Brücke f. 2. Nau: Kommandobrücke f. II. v.tr. (eine Schwierigkeit usw.) überbrücken; to b. a gap, eine Lücke füllen.

bridge² [bridʒ], s. (game) Bridge n.

bridle [braidl]. I. s. Zaum m; b. path, Reitweg m. II. v.tr. (ein Pferd) zäumen; (eine Leidenschaft usw.) zügeln.

brief [briːf]. I. adj. kurz; in b., kurz (gesagt). II. s. 1. Jur: Com: Instruktionen fpl; (b) Jur: (case) Mandat n. 2. Cl: briefs, Slip m. III. v.tr. to b. s.o., j-m seine Instruktionen geben. ◆**'briefcase**, s. Aktentasche f. ◆**'briefing**, s. 1. Anweisung f. 2. Jur: Instruktion f. ◆**'briefness**, s. Kürze f.

brigade [bri'geid], s. Brigade f. ◆**brigadier** [brigə'diər], s. Brigadegeneral m.

bright [brait], adj. 1. (a) hell; b. eyes, klare Augen; (b) (of weather) heiter; (of colour) leuchtend; to look on the b. side, die Sache(n) optimistisch betrachten. 2. (of pers.) gescheit; a b. idea, ein guter/kluger Einfall. ◆**'brighten**, v.tr. 1. aufhellen. 2. v.i. to b. (up), (of weather, pers.) sich aufheitern. ◆**'brightness**, s. Helle f; Klarheit f.

brilliant ['briljənt], adj. glänzend; (gifted) hochbegabt; (intellectually) b., geistreich. ◆**'brilliance**, s. (a) (shine) Glanz m; (b) (of pers.) hohe Begabung f; (intellectual) b., hohe Intelligenz f.

brim [brim]. I. s. Rand m; (of hat) Krempe f. II. v.i. to b. over, überfließen.

brine [brain], s. Salzwasser n, Sole f.

bring [briŋ], v.tr.irr. (a) bringen (to s.o., j-m); I cannot b. myself to do it, ich kann es nicht über mich bringen; (b) (b. along) mitbringen. ◆**'bring a'bout**, v.tr. (etwas) verursachen; (einen Vorgang) bewirken. ◆**'bring a'long**, v.tr. mitbringen. ◆**'bring 'back**, v.tr. zurückbringen; to b. back memories, Erinnerungen wachrufen. ◆**'bring 'down**, v.tr. (a) herunterbringen; (of storm) (einen Baum usw.) umwerfen; (eine Regierung usw.) stürzen; (b) (den Preis) herab-

setzen. ◆**'bring 'forward**, v.tr. (einen Termin) vorverlegen. ◆**'bring 'in**, v.tr. (a) hereinbringen; die Polizei usw. einschalten; (b) Com: to b. in interest, Zinsen tragen; (c) (introduce) (eine Maßnahme) einführen. ◆**'bring 'off**, v.tr. zustande bringen. ◆**'bring 'out**, v.tr. (etwas, ein Buch) herausbringen; (eine Eigenschaft) zutage bringen; (eine Farbe) zur Geltung bringen. ◆**'bring 'round**, v.tr. hinüberbringen. ◆**'bring 'round**, v.tr. (a) (j-n) wieder zu sich bringen; (b) (persuade) (j-n) überreden; (c) (die Konversation) lenken (to a subject, auf ein Thema). ◆**'bring to'gether**, v.tr. (Menschen) zusammenbringen; (eine Sammlung) zusammenstellen. ◆**'bring 'up**, v.tr. (a) heraufbringen; (vomit) erbrechen; (b) (Kinder) erziehen; (c) to b. up a subject, ein Thema zur Sprache bringen.

brink [briŋk], s. Rand m.

brisk [brisk], adj. (a) (lively) lebhaft; (b) (quick) schnell. ◆**'briskness**, s. Lebhaftigkeit f.

bristle [brisl]. I. s. Borste f. II. v.i. (a) (of hair etc.) sich sträuben; (b) to b. with sth., von etwas dat strotzen. ◆**'bristly**, adj. borstig; (to touch) stachelig.

Britain ['brit(ə)n]. Pr.n. (Great) B., Großbritannien n.

British ['britiʃ], adj. britisch; s.pl. the British, die Briten. ◆**'Briton**, s. Brite m; Britin f.

brittle [britl], adj. spröde.

broach [brəutʃ], v.tr. (ein Thema) anschneiden.

broad [brɔːd], adj. breit; Fig: it's as b. as it's long, es ist gehüpft wie gesprungen; in b. outline, in groben Umrissen; -ly, adv. b. speaking, allgemein gesprochen. ◆**'broadcast**. I. v.tr. (ein Programm) senden. II. s. Sendung f. III. adj. übertragen. ◆**'broadcaster**, s. Rundfunksprecher(in) m(f). ◆**'broadcasting**, s. Rundfunkwesen n. ◆**'broaden**, v.tr. & i. (sich) verbreitern. ◆**'broad-'minded**, adj. tolerant. ◆**'broad-'shouldered**, adj. breitschultrig.

brocade [brə(u)'keid], s. Brokat m.

broccoli ['brɔkəli], s. Brokkoli m.

brochure [brə'ʃuər, 'brəuʃər], s. Prospekt m.

broiler ['brɔilər], s. Brathuhn n.

broke [brəuk], adj. F: pleite.

broken ['brəuk(ə)n], adj. (of stick, leg etc.) gebrochen; (of cup etc.) zerbrochen; F: kaputt; b. English, gebrochenes Englisch; b. down, außer Betrieb; F: kaputt. ◆**'broken-'hearted**, adj. untröstlich.

broker ['brəukər], s. Makler m.

bromide ['brəumaid], s. Bromid n.

bronchitis [brɔŋ'kaitis], s. Bronchitis f.

bronze [brɔnz], s. Bronze f.

brooch [brəutʃ], s. Brosche f.

brood [bruːd]. I. s. Brut f. II. v.i. brüten; to b. over sth., über etwas acc grübeln. ◆**broody**, adj. brütend.

brook [bruk], s. Bach m.

broom [bruːm], s. Besen m.

broth [brɔθ], s. Brühe f.

brothel [brɔθl], s. Bordell n.

brother ['brʌðər], s. Bruder m; brothers and sisters, Geschwister npl. ◆**brotherhood**, s. Brüderschaft f. ◆**brother-in-law**, s. Schwager m.

hrow [braʊ], s (a) Anat: Stirn f; (b) (of hill) Kuppe f. ◆**browbeat**, v.tr. einschüchtern.

brown [braʊn]. I. adj. (a) braun; b. bread = approx. Grahambrot n; (b) (of pers.) gebräunt. II. v. 1. v.tr. bräunen; F: to be browned off, es satt haben. 2. v.i. braun werden.

brownie ['braʊni], s. 1. junge Pfadfinderin f. 2. N.Am: Schokoladenschnitte f.

browse [braʊz], v.i. in Büchern blättern.

bruise [bruːz]. I. s. Quetschung f; F: blauer Fleck m. II. v.tr. quetschen.

brunette [bruːˈnet], s. Brünette f.

brunt [brʌnt], s. to bear the b. (of the work), die Hauptlast tragen; to bear the b. of his anger, seinen vollen Zorn zu spüren bekommen.

brush [brʌʃ]. I. s. (a) Bürste f; (b) (paint) b., Pinsel m. II. v. 1. v.tr. (a) (Kleider) abbürsten; sich dat (die Haare) bürsten, (die Zähne) putzen; (b) (touch) (etwas) streifen. 2. v.i. to b. against sth., (gegen) etwas acc streifen. ◆**brush a'side**, v.tr. (j-n) beiseite schieben. ◆**brush 'up**, v.tr. to b. up one's German, seine Sprachkenntnisse auffrischen. ◆**brushwood**, s. Gestrüpp n.

brusque [bru(ː)sk], adj. schroff.

Brussels ['brʌslz]. Pr.n. Brüssel n; B. sprouts, Rosenkohl m.

brute [bruːt], s. Rohling m; Unmensch m; b. force, rohe Gewalt. ◆**brutal**, adj. brutal. ◆**bru'tality**, s. Brutalität f.

bubble [bʌbl]. I. s. Blase f. II. v.i. sprudeln. ◆**bubbly**, adj. schäumend. I. s. F: Champagner m.

buck [bʌk]. I. s. 1. (male deer) Bock m. 2. N.Am: F: Dollar m. 3. to pass the b., die Verantwortung abschieben. II. v.i. (of horse) bocken. ◆**buck 'up**, v.i. sich zusammenraffen.

bucket ['bʌkit], s. Eimer m; F: to kick the b., abkratzen. ◆**bucketful**, s. Eimervoll m.

buckle [bʌkl]. I. s. Schnalle f. II. v. 1. v.tr. (a) (einen Gürtel) zuschnallen; (b) (Metall) krümmen. 2. v.i. to b. (up), (of metal etc.) sich verbiegen.

bud [bʌd]. I. s. Knospe f. II. v.i. knospen. ◆**budding**, adj. a b. artist, ein angehender Künstler.

Buddhism ['budiz(ə)m], s. Buddhismus m. ◆**Buddhist**. I. s. Buddhist m. II. adj. buddhistisch.

buddy ['bʌdi], s. esp. N.Am: F: Kumpel m.

budge [bʌdʒ], v. 1. v.tr. (etwas) (vom Fleck) bewegen. 2. v.i. he refused to b., er rührte sich nicht von der Stelle.

budget ['bʌdʒit]. I. s. Budget n; Pol: Haushaltsplan m; to b. for sth., etwas einkalkulieren.

buff [bʌf]. I. s. opera b., Opernfreund m. II. adj. sandfarben.

buffalo, pl. -oes ['bʌfələu, -əuz], s. Büffel m

buffer ['bʌfər], s. esp.pl. (on carriage) Puffer m; (at end of line) Prellbock m.

buffet1 ['bufei], s. Büffett n.

buffet2 ['bʌfit], v.tr. stoßen.

buffoon [bʌˈfuːn], s. Clown m.

bug [bʌg]. I. s. 1. Wanze f; N.Am: F: Insekt n, esp. Käfer m. 2. F: the flu b., der Grippebazillus m. 3. (versteckes) Abhörgerät n. II. v.tr. to b. a room, in einem Zimmer ein Abhörgerät verstecken.

bugle ['bjuːgl], s. Signalhorn n.

build [bild]. I. v.tr.irr. bauen. II. s. Körperbau m; Figur f. ◆**builder**, s. Baumeister m. ◆**build 'in**, v.tr. einbauen. ◆**building**, s. 1. Gebäude n. 2. b. (trade), Bauwesen n; b. site, Baustelle f; b. society, Bausparkasse f. ◆**build 'up**, v.tr. (a) aufbauen; built up area, bebautes Gebiet; Aut: Adm: geschlossene Ortschaft; (b) (eine Sammlung) zusammenstellen. ◆**build-up**, s (preparation) Vorbereitung f; (publicity) einleitende Propaganda f.

bulb [bʌlb], s. 1. Bot: Zwiebel f. 2. El: Birne f.

Bulgaria [bʌlˈgɛəriə]. Pr.n. Bulgarien n. ◆**Bul'garian**. I. adj. bulgarisch. II. s. Bulgare m; Bulgarin f.

bulge [bʌldʒ]. I. s. Ausbuchtung f; (long) Wulst m; (in body) Fettpolster n. II. v.i. to b. (out), bauschen. ◆**bulging**, adj. bauschig; (full) vollgestopft; (projecting) hervorstehend.

bulk [bʌlk], s. Masse f; in b., en gros; to b. buying, Großeinkauf m. 2. (majority) Mehrheit f. ◆**bulky**, adj. (large) umfangreich; (awkward shape) unförmig; (of goods etc.) sperrig.

bull [bul], s. Stier m. ◆**bulldog**, s. Bulldogge f. ◆**bulldozer**, s. Planierraupe f. ◆**bullfight**, s. Stierkampf m. ◆**bullfighter**, s. Stierkämpfer m. ◆**bullock**, s. Ochse m. ◆**bullring**, s. Stierkampfarena f. ◆**bull's-eye**, s. Zentrum n (der Zielscheibe); to score a b.-e., ins Schwarze treffen.

bullet ['bulit], s. Kugel f. ◆**bulletproof**, adj. kugelsicher.

bulletin ['bulitin], s. (a) news b., Nachrichtensendung f; (b) (on sick person) Meldung f über j-s Befinden].

bullion ['buljən], s. (gold) (Gold-/Silber)barren m.

bully ['buli]. I. s. Tyrann m. II. v.tr. tyrannisieren.

bumble-bee ['bʌmblbi:], s. Hummel f.

bump [bʌmp]. I. s. 1. (blow) Stoß m; (sound) Bums m. 2. Beule f; (in road etc.) holprige Stelle f. II. v. 1. v.tr. (sn, et-was) anstoßen. 2. v.i. to b. into sth., gegen etwas acc stoßen; (of vehicle) etwas anfahren; F: to b. into s.o., j-n zufällig treffen. ◆'**bumpy**, adj. holprig; (of ride) holpernd.

bumper ['bʌmpər]. I. s. Stoßstange f. II. adj. Rekord-; b. crop, Rekordernte f.

bun [bʌn], s. 1. (currant) b., Korinthenbrötchen n. 2. (hair) Knoten m.

bunch [bʌntʃ], s. (a) Strauß m (Blumen); b. of grapes, Traube f; b. of keys, Schlüsselbund m; (b) (people) Gruppe f.

bundle ['bʌndl]. I. s. Bündel n (Wäsche, Holz usw.); Stoß m (Papier usw.). II. v.tr. to b. sth. up, etwas (zusammen)bündeln.

bung [bʌŋ], v.tr. F: schmeißen; to b. sth. up, etwas verstopfen.

bungalow ['bʌŋgələu], s. Bungalow m.

bungle ['bʌŋgl], v.tr. verpfuschen.

bunk1 [bʌŋk], s. Schlafkoje f; b. beds, Etagenbetten npl.

bunk2, s. F: to do a b., abhauen.

bunker ['bʌŋkər], s. Bunker m.

bunting ['bʌntiŋ], s. Flaggenschmuck m.

buoy [bɔi]. I. s. Boje f. II. v.tr. to b. s.o. up, j-n stärken. ◆'**buoyancy**, s. 1. Schwimmfähigkeit f; (of water) Auftrieb m. 2. Fig: (of pers.) Schwung m. ◆'**buoyant**, adj. 1. schwimmfähig; (of water) tragend. 2. (of pers.) munter; Com: (of market etc.) lebhaft.

burden ['bə:dn]. I. s. Last f; esp. Fig: Bürde f. II. v.tr. to b. s.o. with sth., j-m etwas aufbürden.

bureau, pl. **-eaux** ['bjuərəu, -əuz], s. 1. (desk) Sekretär m. 2. (office) Büro n. ◆**bureaucracy** [bjuə'rɔkrəsi], s. Bürokratie f. ◆'**bureaucrat** ['bjuərəukræt], s. Bürokrat m. ◆**bureau'cratic**, adj. bürokratisch.

burglar ['bə:glər], s. Einbrecher m; b. alarm, Alarmanlage f. ◆'**burglarize**, v.tr. N.Am: = burgle. ◆'**burglary**, s. Einbruch m. ◆'**burgle**, v.tr. they have been burgled, bei ihnen ist eingebrochen worden.

burial ['beriəl], s. Begräbnis n.

burly ['bə:li], adj. stämmig.

Burma ['bə:mə]. Pr.n. Birma n.

burn [bə:n]. I. v. irr. 1. v.tr. verbrennen. 2. v.i. (of light, fire etc.) brennen; (of food) anbrennen. II. s. (a) (in carpet etc.) Brandstelle f; (b) Med: Verbrennung f. ◆'**burner**, s. Brenner m. ◆'**burn 'down**, v.tr. & i. niederbrennen. ◆'**burnt**, adj. verbrannt; (of food) angebrannt. ◆'**burn 'up**, v.tr. (Kohlen usw.) verbrennen; (Energie) aufzehren.

burp [bə:p], v.i. F: rülpsen.

burrow ['bʌrəu]. I. s. Bau m. II. v.i. (of rabbits etc.) einen Bau/(of pers.) einen Tunnel graben.

bursar ['bə:sər], s. Quästor m.

burst [bə:st]. I. v.irr. 1. v.i. to b. into tears, in Tränen ausbrechen; F: I'm bursting, ich muß dringend aufs Klo. 2. v.tr. (einen Ballon usw.) platzen lassen; the river b. its banks, der Fluß trat über die Ufer. II. s. b. of fire, Feuersalve f; b. of activity, Ausbruch m von Geschäftigkeit; b. of speed, Spurt m. ◆'**burst 'in**, v.i. hereinstürmen. ◆'**burst 'open**, v.i. (of door) auffliegen; (of parcel etc.) aufgehen. ◆'**burst 'out**, v.i. to b. out laughing, in Gelächter ausbrechen.

bury ['beri], v.tr. (j-n) begraben, beerdigen; (etwas) vergraben.

bus, pl. **buses** [bʌs, 'bʌsiz], s. (Auto)bus m; b. conductor, Autobusschaffner m; b. station, Autobusbahnhof m; b. stop, Bushaltestelle f.

bush [buʃ], s. (a) Strauch m; to beat about the b., um den heißen Brei herumreden; (b) pl. Gebüsch n. ◆'**bushy**, adj. buschig.

business ['biznis], s. 1. (matter) Angelegenheit f, Sache f; it's none of your b., das geht dich nichts an; to get down to b., zur Sache kommen. 2. (a) (firm) Betrieb m; Firma f; (b) coll. Geschäfte npl; he's here on b., er ist geschäftlich hier; to do b. with s.o., mit j-m geschäftlich zu tun haben; to mean b., es ernst meinen; b. hours, Geschäftszeiten fpl. ◆'**businesslike**, adj. 1. (of pers.) geschäftstüchtig; praktisch veranlagt. 2. (of manner) sachlich. ◆'**businessman**, s. Geschäftsmann m.

bust1 [bʌst], s. 1. Art: Büste f. 2. Anat: Busen m; b. measurement, Brustumfang m.

bust2. I. v. 1. v.tr. kaputtmachen. 2. v.i. kaputtgehen. II. adj. kaputt; F: to go b., Bankrott machen.

bustle ['bʌsl]. I. v.i. to b. (about), (herum)hantieren. II. s. (geschäftiges) Treiben n. ◆'**bustling**, adj. geschäftig.

busy ['bizi]. I. adj. (a) (of pers.) (sehr) beschäftigt; (b) (of activity etc.) geschäftig; a b. day, ein anstrengender Tag; a b. street, eine belebte Straße. II. v.tr. to b. oneself, sich beschäftigen (with sth., mit etwas dat); -ily, adv. emsig. ◆'**busybody**, s. Wichtigtuer(in) m(f).

but [bʌt]. I. conj. (a) aber; (b) (after negative) sondern; he is not English b. German, er ist kein Engländer, sondern ein Deutscher. II. adv. nur; one can b. try, man kann es wenigstens versuchen. III. conj. & prep. (a) (except) all b. him, alle außer ihm; the last b. one, der vorletzte; (b) b. for, ohne + acc.

butcher ['butʃər], s. 1. Fleischer m, Metzger m; b.'s shop, Fleischerei f, Metzgerei f. II. v.tr. abschlachten.

butler ['bʌtlər], s. Butler m.

butt1 [bʌt], s. 1. (of cigarette) (Zigaretten)stummel m. 2. (of rifle) (Ge-

wehr)kolben m.
butt², s. Fig: (target) Zielscheibe f.
butt³. I. s. Stoß m. II. v.tr. & i. (j-n) mit dem Kopf stoßen; **to b. in,** unterbrechen.
butter ['bʌtər]. I. s. Butter f; b. **dish,** Butterdose f. II. v.tr. (Brot usw.) mit Butter bestreichen. ◆'**buttercup,** s. Butterblume f. ◆'**butter-fingers,** s. F: Dussel m.
butterfly ['bʌtəflai], s. Schmetterling m; b. **(stroke),** Schmetterlingschwimmen n.
buttock ['bʌtək], s. Hinterbacke f; pl. **buttocks,** Gesäß n.
button ['bʌtn]. I. s. Knopf m. II. v.tr. **to b. sth. (up),** etwas zuknöpfen. ◆'**buttonhole,** s. Knopfloch n; **to wear a b.,** eine Blume im Knopfloch tragen.
buttress ['bʌtris], s. Strebepfeiler m; flying b., Strebebogen m.
buy [bai], v.tr.irr. kaufen. ◆'**buyer,** s. Käufer m; Com: Einkäufer m. ◆'**buy out,** v.tr. (einen Teilhaber) auszahlen. ◆'**buy up,** v.tr. aufkaufen.
buzz [bʌz]. I. s. Summen n. II. v.i. summen. ◆'**buzz off,** v.i. P: abhauen. ◆'**buzzer,** s. Summer m. ◆'**buzzing,** s. Summen n; b. **in the ears,** Ohrensausen n.

buzzard ['bʌzəd], s. Bussard m.
by [bai]. I. prep. 1. (near) bei + dat; **by oneself,** alleine. 2. (a) by **car,** mit dem Auto; (b) **to go by s.o.,** (pass) an j-m vorbeigehen. 3. (a) **by night,** nachts; **by day,** am Tage; (b) **this afternoon,** bis heute nachmittag; **by then,** bis dahin. 4. (agency) von + dat; durch + acc; **he is a baker by trade,** er ist Bäcker von Beruf. 5. (a) **he won by five seconds/ten metres,** er gewann mit einem Vorsprung von fünf Sekunden/zehn Metern; (b) **I am paid by the hour,** ich werde pro Stunde bezahlt. 6. a **room six metres by four,** ein Zimmer sechs Meter mal vier. II. adv. dabei; **close by,** in der Nähe; **by and large,** im großen und ganzen. ◆**by-election,** s. Nachwahl f. ◆**bygone,** adj. vergangen; **to let bygones be bygones,** den Streit beilegen. ◆**by-law,** s. Statut n. ◆**bypass.** I. s. Umgehungsstraße f. II. v.tr. umfahren. ◆**by-product,** s. Nebenprodukt n. ◆**bystander,** s. Zuschauer(in) m(f). ◆**byword,** s. Inbegriff m (for, von + dat).
bye [bai], int. F: (b.) b.! tschüs!

C

C, c [si:], s. (der Buchstabe) C, c n.
cab [kæb], s. 1. Taxi n. 2. (of lorry etc.) Führerhaus n ◆'**cabdriver,** F: '**cabby,** s. Taxifahrer m.
cabaret ['kæbərei], s. Kabarett n.
cabbage ['kæbidʒ], s. Kohl m.
cabin ['kæbin], s. 1. Hütte f. 2. Nau: Av: Kabine f.
cabinet ['kæbinit], s. 1. Schrank m; glass c., Vitrine f; c. **maker,** Möbeltischler m. 2. Pol: the C., das Kabinett.
cable ['keibl]. I. s. 1. (a) Tau n; (b) (metal) Drahtseil m; (c) El: Kabel n. 2. Tel: c.(gram), Überseetelegramm n. II. v.tr. (j-m, etwas acc) telegrafieren.
caboodle [kə'bu:dl], s. F: the **whole c.,** (things) der ganze Klimbim.
cache [kæʃ], s. geheimes Lager n.
cackle ['kækl]. I. s. 1. (of hen) Gegacker n. 2. (laughter) Gekicher n. II. v.i. (a) gackern; (b) (laut) kichern.
cactus, pl. -ti ['kæktəs, -tai], s. Kaktus m.
caddie ['kædi], s. Golfjunge m.
caddy, pl. -ies ['kædi, -iz], s. (tea-)c., Teedose f.
cadet [kə'det], s. Kadett m.
cadge [kædʒ], v.tr.&i. F: (etwas) schnorren.
caesarean [si:'zɛəriən], s. Kaiserschnitt m.
café ['kæfei], s. Café n. ◆**cafeteria** [kæfi'tiəriə], s. Selbstbedienungsrestaurant n; (snack bar) Schnellimbiß m.

caffeine ['kæfi:n], s. Koffein n.
cage [keidʒ], s. Käfig m.
cagey ['keidʒi], adj. F: **he was very c.,** er wollte nichts verraten.
cajole [kə'dʒoul], v.tr. (j-m) gut zureden; **to c. s.o. into doing sth.,** j-n dazu überreden, etwas zu tun.
cake [keik]. I. s. 1. Kuchen m; c. **shop,** Konditorei f; F: **it's a piece of c.,** es ist kinderleicht; **to be selling like hot cakes,** wie warme Semmeln weggehen; c. **of soap,** Riegel m Seife. II. v.i. sich verkrusten; **caked with mud,** mit Schmutz verkrustet.
calamity [kə'læmiti], s. Katastrophe f.
calcium ['kælsiəm], s. Kalzium n.
calculate ['kælkjuleit], v. 1. v.i. Mth: rechnen. 2. v.tr. & i. Com: (etwas) kalkulieren. 3. v.tr. (etwas) berechnen. ◆**calculated,** adj. (of effect etc.) berechnet; (of insult) beabsichtigt; (of lie etc.) bewußt; **to take a c. risk,** sich auf ein Risiko einlassen. ◆**calculating.** I. adj. (of pers.) berechnend. II. (also calculation) s. Berechnung f. ◆**calculator,** s. Rechenmaschine f; (pocket) c., Taschenrechner m.
calendar ['kælindər], s. Kalender m; c. **year,** Kalenderjahr n.
calf, pl. calves¹ [kɑ:f, kɑ:vz], s. Kalb n.
calf, pl. calves² s. (of leg) Wade f.
calibre ['kælibər], s. Kaliber n.
call [kɔ:l]. I. s. 1. (shout) Ruf m; c. **for help,** Hilferuf m. 2. **telephone c.,** Anruf

m. 3. **to be on c.**, Bereitschaftsdienst haben. 4. (*visit*) Besuch *m*; **to pay a c. on s.o.**, j-m einen Besuch abstatten. II. *v.* 1. *v.tr.* (*a*) (j-n, ein Tier) rufen; (*b*) (*telephone*) (j-n) anrufen; (*c*) (*wake*) (j-n) wecken; (*d*) **to c. s.o. a liar etc.**, j-n einen Lügner usw. nennen; **to be called X**, X heißen; (*e*) **to c. a meeting**, eine Versammlung einberufen; **to c. a strike**, einen Streik ausrufen. 2. *v.i.* vorbeikommen; *Tel:* anrufen. ◆**'call 'back**, *v.tr.* (j-n) zurückrufen. ◆**'call-box**, *s.* Telefonzelle *f*. ◆**'caller**, *s.* (*a*) Besucher *m*; (*b*) *Tel:* Anrufer *m*. ◆**'call for**, *v.tr.* (*a*) **to c. for s.o.**, nach j-m rufen; **to c. for help**, um Hilfe rufen; (*b*) (j-n, etwas) abholen; (*c*) **this calls for an explanation**, das verlangt eine Erklärung. ◆**'callgirl**, *s.* Callgirl *n*. ◆**'call 'off**, *v.tr.* (*a*) (*not start*) (etwas) absagen; (*b*) (*stop*) (etwas) abbrechen. ◆**'call on**, *v.tr.* (*a*) (*visit*) (j-n) besuchen; (*b*) (*invite*) (j-n) auffordern, etwas zu tun). ◆**'call 'out**, *v.* I. *v.i.* rufen. 2. *v.tr.* (Namen usw.) aufrufen. ◆**'call 'up**, *v.tr.* (*a*) *Tel: esp. N.Am:* (j-n) anrufen; (*b*) *Mil:* (j-n) einberufen.

callous ['kæləs], *adj.* gefühllos.

calm [kɑːm]. I. *adj.* (*a*) (*of pers.*) ruhig; (*b*) (*of wind etc.*) still. II. *s.* (*a*) Stille *f*; (*b*) (*of pers.*) Ruhe *f*. III. *v.* 1. *v.tr.* **to c. s.o. (down)**, j-n beruhigen. 2. *v.i.* **to c. (down)**, sich beruhigen.

calorie ['kæləri], *s.* Kalorie *f*.

camber ['kæmbər], *s.* Wölbung *f*.

Cambodia [kæm'bəudiə]. *Pr.n.* Kambodscha *n*.

camel ['kæməl], *s.* Kamel *n*.

camera ['kæm(ə)rə], *s.* Kamera *f*. ◆**'cameraman**, *pl.* **-men**, *s.* Kameramann *m*.

camomile ['kæməmail], *s.* Kamille *f*.

camouflage ['kæmuflɑːʒ]. I. *s.* Tarnung *f*. II. *v.tr.* tarnen.

camp [kæmp]. I. *s.* Lager *n*; *Mil:* Feldlager *n*; **c. bed**, Feldbett *n*; **c. site**, Campingplatz *m*; (*for tent*) Zeltplatz *m*. II. *v.i.* kampieren; (*in tent*) zelten; *Mil:* lagern. ◆**'camper**, *s.* 1. Camper *m*. 2. *Aut:* Reisemobil *n*. ◆**'camping**, *s.* Camping *n*; **to go c.**, zelten gehen.

campaign [kæm'pein]. I. *s.* *Mil:* Feldzug *m*; *Pol: etc:* Kampagne *f*; **election c.**, Wahlkampf *m*. II. *v.i.* *a*) *Mil:* einen Feldzug unternehmen; (*b*) *Pol:* eine Kampagne führen; *Fig:* sich einsetzen; **to c. against sth.**, gegen etwas *acc* zu Felde ziehen.

campus, *pl.* **-es** ['kæmpəs, -iz], *s.* Universitätsgelände *n*.

can¹ [kæn]. I. *s.* (*tin*) Dose *f*; **c. opener**, Dosenöffner *m*. II. *v.tr.* (in Büchsen) konservieren. ◆**'canned**, *adj.* 1. Büchsen-; **c. fruit**, Obstkonserven *fpl*. 2. *P:* (*drunk*) besoffen.

can² *modal aux. v.irr.* (*a*) (*ability*) können; (*b*) (*permission*) dürfen; **c. I go now?** darf

ich jetzt gehen?

Canada ['kænədə]. *Pr.n.* Kanada *n*. ◆**Canadian** [kə'neidjən]. I. *adj.* kanadisch. II. *s.* Kanadier(in) *m(f)*.

canal [kə'næl], *s.* Kanal *m*.

canary [kə'nɛəri], *s.* Kanarienvogel *m*; **the C. Islands**, die Kanarischen Inseln *fpl*.

cancel ['kæns(ə)l], *v.tr.* (*a*) (eine Abmachung) rückgängig machen; (eine Schuld) tilgen; (*b*) (eine Veranstaltung) absagen; (*of performance*) **to be cancelled**, ausfallen; **to c. an appointment**, absagen; **to c. an order (for sth.)**, (etwas) abbestellen; (*d*) (Briefmarken, Fahrkarten) entwerten; (*d*) (*of two things*) **they c. one another out**, sie gleichen sich aus. ◆**cance'llation**, *s.* Absage *f*; **have you got a c.?** hat jemand abgesagt/abbestellt?

cancer ['kænsər], *s.* *Med: Astr:* Krebs *m*.

candid ['kændid], *adj.* offen.

candidate ['kændideit], *s.* (*a*) Kandidat(in) *m(f)*; (*b*) (*for job*) Bewerber(in) *m(f)*; (*c*) **examination c.**, Prüfling *m*.

candle ['kændl], *s.* Kerze *f*. ◆**'candlestick**, *s.* Kerzenständer *m*.

candour ['kændər], *s.* Offenheit *f*.

candy, *pl.* **-ies** ['kændi, -iz], *s.* 1. (*sugar*) Kandiszucker *m*. 2. *N.Am:* Bonbons *npl*. ◆**'candyfloss**, *s.* Zuckerwatte *f*.

cane [kein]. I. *s.* 1. (*of bamboo, sugar*) Rohr *n*; **c. chair**, Rohrstuhl *m*; **c. sugar**, Rohrzucker *m*. 2. (*of punishment*) Rohrstock *m*; (*b*) (*walking stick*) Spazierstock *m*. II. *v.tr.* (j-n) mit dem Rohrstock züchtigen.

canister ['kænistər], *s.* Kanister *m*.

cannibal ['kænibəl], *s.* Kannibale *m*. ◆**'cannibalism**, *s.* Kannibalismus *m*.

cannon ['kænən], *s.* Kanone *f*.

canoe [kə'nuː], *s.* Paddelboot *n*; *Sp:* Kanu *n*.

canon ['kænən], *s.* 1. Regel *f*. 2. *Ecc:* (*a*) (*of bible*) Kanon *m*; (*b*) (*pers.*) Domherr *m*. ◆**'canonize**, *v.tr.* heiligsprechen.

canopy, *pl.* **-ies** ['kænəpi, -iz], *s.* Baldachin *m*.

cantankerous [kæn'tæŋkərəs], *adj.* streitsüchtig.

canteen [kæn'tiːn], *s.* Kantine *f*.

canter ['kæntər]. I. *s.* Kanter *m*. II. *v.i.* im Handgalopp reiten.

canvas ['kænvəs], *s.* 1. Segeltuch *n*. 2. *Art:* Leinwand *f*.

canvass ['kænvəs], *v.i.* Stimmen werben. ◆**'canvassing**, *s.* Stimmenwerbung *f*.

canyon ['kænjən], *s.* Cañon *m*.

cap [kæp]. I. *s.* 1. Mütze *f*. 2. (*cover*) Deckel *m*; (*of pen*) Kappe *f*; (*of bottle*) Kapsel *f*. II. *v.tr.* (*outdo*) übertreffen.

capable ['keipəbl], *adj.* 1. (*of pers.*) tüchtig (**of**, *gen/zu* + *inf*); **a c. teacher**, ein tüchtiger Lehrer. 2. **to be c. of doing sth.**, (*of pers.*) imstande sein, etwas zu tun; (*of thing*) etwas tun können; *ably, adv.* gekonnt. ◆**capa'bility**, *s.* Fähigkeit *f*.

capacity [kə'pæsiti], *s.* 1. (*a*) *Ph:* Volu-

men *n*; (*b*) (*of a container*) Fassungsvermögen *n*; (*of hall, train etc.*) **filled to**
c., voll besetzt; **c. audience**, ausverkauf-
tes Haus. **2.** (*a*) (*of pers.*) Fähigkeit
f; (*b*) (*of machine*) (**working**) **c.**,
Leistungsvermögen *n*. **3.** (*position*) **in my**
c. as..., in meiner Eigenschaft als ...
cape¹ [keip], *s. Cl*: Cape *n*, Umhang *m*.
cape², *s.* Kap *n*.
caper ['keipər], *s. Cu*: Kaper *f*.
capital ['kæpitl]. **I.** *adj.* **c. city**, Hauptstadt *f*; **c. punishment**, Todesstrafe *f*; **c.**
letter, Großbuchstabe *m*. **II.** *s. 1. Fin*:
Kapital *n*. **2.** (*city*) Hauptstadt *f*.
◆**'capitalism**, *s.* Kapitalismus *m*.
◆**'capitalist**, *s.* Kapitalist *m*.
◆**'capitalize**, *v.i* **to c. on sth.**, aus etwas *dat* Nutzen ziehen.
capitulate [kə'pitjuleit], *v.i.* kapitulieren.
capricious [kə'priʃəs], *adj.* launenhaft.
Capricorn ['kæprikɔːn], *s.* Steinbock *m*.
capsize [kæp'saiz], *v.i.* kentern.
capsule ['kæpsjuːl], *s.* Kapsel *f*.
captain ['kæptin]. **I.** *s. 1.* (*a*) *Mil*: Hauptmann *m*; *Nau*: Kapitän *m*; *Sp*: Mann-
schaftskapitän *m*. **II.** *v.tr.* (*a*) *Mil*: eine
Kompanie, *Nau*: ein Schiff kommandie-
ren; (*b*) *Sp*: (eine Mannschaft) führen.
caption ['kæpʃ(ə)n], *s.* (*a*) (*of picture*)
Bildunterschrift *f*; (*b*) (*heading*) Überschrift *f*.
captivate ['kæptiveit], *v.tr.* bezaubern.
captive ['kæptiv]. **I.** *adj.* gefangen. **II.** *s.*
Gefangene(r) *f(m)* ◆**cap'tivity**, *s.* Gefangenschaft *f*. ◆**capture** ['kæptʃər]. **I.**
s. Gefangennahme *f* (einer Person), Ein-
nahme *f* (einer Stadt). **II.** *v.tr.* (*a*) (ein Tier) fangen; (*b*)
(j-n) gefangennehmen; (*c*) (eine Stadt
usw.) erobern; **to c. the mood**, die
Stimmung einfangen.
car [kɑːr], *s. 1.* Auto *n*; **c. ferry**, Autofäh-
re *f*; **c. park**, Parkplatz *m*; (*multistorey*)
Parkhaus *n*; (*underground*) Tiefgarage *f*.
2. *Rail: esp. N.Am:* Wagen *m*; **dining c.**,
Speisewagen *m*.
carafe [kə'rɑːf, -æf], *s.* Karaffe *f*.
caramel ['kærəmel], *s.* (*a*) Karamel *m*; (*b*)
(*sweet*) Karamelbonbon *n & m*.
carat ['kærət], *s.* Karat *n*; **eighteen c.**
gold, achtzehnkarätiges Gold.
caravan ['kærəvæn], *s.* (*trailer*) Wohnwagen *m*.
caraway ['kærəwei], *s.* Kümmel *m*.
carbohydrate ['kɑːbəu'haidreit], *s.* Kohle-
hydrat *n*.
carbon ['kɑːbən], *s. 1.* Kohlenstoff *m*; **c.**
dioxide, Kohlendioxyd *n*. **2.** *attrib.*
Kohle-; (*paper*) Kohlepapier *n*; **c.**
copy, Durchschlag *m*.
carburettor [kɑːbjuretər], *s.* Vergaser *m*.
carcass ['kɑːkəs], *s. 1.* (*corpse*) Kadaver *m*.
2. Rumpf *m* (eines geschlachteten Tieres).
card [kɑːd], *s. 1.* Karte *f*; **playing c.**,
Spielkarte *f*; **on the cards**, durchaus
möglich; (*visiting*) **c.**, Visitenkarte *f*. **2.**
(*material*) Karton *m*. ◆**'cardboard**, *s.*

pappe *f*.
cardiac ['kɑːdiæk], *adj.* Herz-; **c. arrest**,
Herzstillstand *m*.
cardigan ['kɑːdigən], *s.* Strickjacke *f*.
cardinal ['kɑːdin(ə)l]. **I.** *adj.* grundsätzlich; **c. number**, Kardinalzahl *f*. **II.** *s.*
Kardinal *m*.
care [keər]. **I.** *s. 1.* (*worry*) Sorge *f*. **2.**
(*caution*) Vorsicht *f*; **to take c.**, vorsichtig
sein; **to take c. that ...**, darauf achten,
daß ... **3.** (*trouble*) Sorgfalt *f*. **to take**
c. of s.o., für j-n sorgen; **dental c.**,
Zahnpflege *f*; **the child was taken into**
c., das Kind kam in Fürsorge, (*on letter*)
c. of (*abbr. c/o*), bei. **II.** *v.i.* (*a*) (*feel con-*
cern) sich *dat* etwas daraus machen; **I**
don't c.! das ist mir (völlig) egal! **for all**
I c. ..., meinetwegen ...; (*b*) (*like*) **to c.**
for s.o., j-n mögen; **would you c. for a**
drink? möchten Sie etwas trinken? (*c*)
(*look after*) **to c. for s.o., sth.**, j-n, etwas
pflegen. ◆**'carefree**, *adj.* sorgenfrei.
◆**'careful**, *adj. 1.* (*cautious*) vorsichtig;
(**be**) **c.!** paß auf! **2.** (*thorough*) sorgfältig.
◆**'careless**, *adj.* nachlässig.
◆**'carelessness**, *s.* Nachlässigkeit *f*.
◆**'caretaker**, *s.* (*a*) (*in schools, flats*)
Hausmeister *m*; (*b*) (*in museum etc.*) Aufseher *m*.
career [kə'riər]. **I.** *s.* (*a*) Laufbahn *f*;
(**successful**) **c.**, Karriere *f*. (*b*) (*profes-*
sion) Beruf *m*; **careers adviser** Berufsbe-
rater(in) *m(f)*. **II.** *v.i.* **to c.** (**along**), dahinrasen.
caress [kə'res]. **I.** *s.* Liebkosung *f*. **II.**
v.tr. liebkosen.
cargo, *pl.* **-oes** ['kɑːgəu, -əuz], *s.* Ladung
f; **c. plane**, Transportflugzeug *n*.
Caribbean [kæri'bi(:)ən], *adj.* **C.** (**Sea**),
Karibisches Meer *n*.
caricature ['kærikətjuər]. **I.** *s.* Karikatur
f. **II.** *v.tr.* karikieren.
carnage ['kɑːnidʒ], *s.* Gemetzel *n*.
carnal ['kɑːnəl], *adj.* fleischlich.
carnation [kɑː'neiʃən], *s.* Nelke *f*.
carnival ['kɑːniv(ə)l], *s.* Karneval *m*;
South G: Fasching *m*.
carnivorous [kɑː'nivərəs], *adj.* fleisch-
fressend.
carol ['kærəl], *s.* **Christmas c.**, Weih-
nachtslied *n*.
carp¹ [kɑːp], *s. inv.* Karpfen *m*.
carp², *v.i.* etwas auszusetzen haben (**at**,
an + *dat*).
carpenter ['kɑːpintər], *s.* (*a*) Tischler *m*;
(*b*) (*working on buildings*) Zimmermann
m. ◆**'carpentry**, *s.* Tischlerei *f*.
carpet ['kɑːpit]. **I.** *s.* Teppich *m*. **II.** *v.tr.*
(ein Zimmer) mit (einem) Teppich ausle-
gen.
carriage ['kæridʒ], *s. 1.* Transport *m*;
(*cost*) Transportkosten *pl*. **2.** (*posture*)
Haltung *f*. **3.** (*a*) (*horsedrawn*) Kutsche *f*;
(*b*) (*railway*) *s.* Eisenbahnwagen *m*.
◆**'carriageway**, *s.* Fahrbahn *f*; **dual c.**,
zweibahnige Straße.
carrier ['kæriər], *s. 1.* (*pers.*) (*a*) Träger *m*;

Überbringer m (von Nachrichten usw.); (b) Med: Krankheitsüberträger m; (c) Com: Spediteur m. 2. (on bicycle etc.) Gepäckträger m; c. bag, Tragtasche f.

carrion ['kæriən], s. Aas n.

carrot ['kærət], s. Karotte f.

carry ['kæri], v.tr. (a) tragen; (of pers.) (eine Botschaft) überbringen; (b) Com: (Waren) befördern; (of pipe) (Wasser, Öl) führen; (c) (of newspaper) (einen Artikel, Bericht) bringen; (d) Fig: to c. sth. too far, etwas zu weit treiben; (e) Mth: c. five, merke fünf; (f) Parl: etc: (of motion) to be carried, angenommen werden; (g) abs. his voice carries well, seine Stimme trägt gut. ◆'carry a'way, v.tr. I was quite carried away, ich war ganz hingerissen. ◆'carrycot, s. Babytragetasche f. ◆'carry 'forward, v.tr. (eine Summe) übertragen; (amount) carried f., Übertrag m ◆'carry 'off, v.tr. (a) (einen Preis) gewinnen; (b) he carried it off well, er hat es gut geschafft. ◆'carry 'on, v. 1 v.tr. (ein Geschäft, ein Gespräch) führen. 2. v.i. a (behave) sich aufführen; (fuss) Theater machen; (b) (continue) (eine Tradition usw.) fortführen; c. on! weitermachen! nur weiter! to c. on with sth., etwas weitermachen. ◆'carry 'out, v.tr. (a) hinaustragen; (b) (einen Plan, einen Befehl usw.) ausführen. ◆'carry 'through, v.tr. (einen Plan) durchführen.

cart [kɑːt]. I. s. (a) (horsedrawn) Wagen m; (b) (handcart) Karren m. II. v.tr. schleppen. ◆'carthorse, s. Zugpferd n.

carton ['kɑːtən], s. (a) (material) Pappe f; (b) (box) Pappschachtel f; a c. of cream, ein Becher m Sahne.

cartoon [kɑː'tuːn], s. 1. Karikatur f; (strip) Comic strip m; Cin: c. film, Zeichentrickfilm m. 2. Art: Karton m. ◆car'toonist, s. Karikaturist m.

cartridge ['kɑːtridʒ], s. 1. Patrone f. 2. c. paper, Zeichenpapier n.

carve [kɑːv], v.tr. (a) (in wood) (etwas) schnitzen; (in stone) (ein Bild) (in/aus Stein) hauen; (b) to c. meat, Fleisch aufschneiden; to c. sth. up, etwas in Stücke zerteilen. ◆'carving, s. 1. Schnitzerei f. 2. Aufschneiden n; c. knife, Tranchiermesser n.

cascade [kæs'keid]. I. s. Wasserfall m. II. v.i. herabstürzen.

case¹ [keis], s. (also Med: Gram: Jur:) Fall m; as the c. may be, je nach Sachlage; just in c., für alle Fälle; in c. he comes, falls er kommt; in c. of a breakdown, im Falle einer Panne; in any c. it's too late, es ist sowieso zu spät; c. history, Krankengeschichte f; Jur: he has a good c., er hat schlüssige Beweise; to make out a c. for sth., etwas begründen.

case², s. 1. (a) (box) Kasten m; (small) Kästchen n; (suitcase) Koffer m; cigarette c., Zigarettenetui n; (b) (soft) spectacle

c., Brillenfutteral n; **pillow c.**, Kopfkissenbezug m. 2. (housing) Gehäuse n; **glass c.**, Vitrine f.

cash [kæʃ]. I. s. no pl. 1. Bargeld n; to pay c., (in) bar bezahlen; c. desk, Kasse f; c. box, Geldkassette f; c. register, Registrierkasse f; c. on delivery, per Nachnahme. 2. F: Geld n; to be short of c., knapp bei Kasse sein. II. v.tr. (einen Scheck usw.) einlösen; to c. in on sth., von etwas dat profitieren. ◆ca'shier, s. Kassierer(in) m(f).

casino, pl. -os [kə'siːnəu, -əuz], s. Kasino n.

cask [kɑːsk], s. Faß n.

casserole ['kæsərəul], s. 1. (container) Schmortopf m. 2. (food) Fleischeintopf m.

cassette [kæ'set], s. Kassette f; c. recorder, Kassettenrecorder m.

cast [kɑːst]. I. s. 1. **plaster c.**, Gipsverband m. 2. Th: Besetzung f. II. v.tr. (a) (die Angel, das Netz) auswerfen; to c. anchor, den Anker auswerfen; (b) to c. light/shadow on sth., Licht/einen Schatten auf etwas acc werfen; (c) to c. one's vote, seine Stimme abgeben; (d) (Metall, eine Statue) gießen; c. iron, Gußeisen n; c. iron proof, hieb- und stichfester Beweis m; (e) to c. s.o. as X/for the part of X., j-m die Rolle des X geben. ◆'castaway, s. Schiffbrüchige(r) f(m). ◆'casting, adj. c. vote, entscheidende Stimme f. ◆'cast 'off, v. 1. v.tr. (etwas) wegwerfen; c. off clothes, abgelegte Kleider. 2. v.i. Nau: ablegen.

castanets [kæstə'nets], s. Kastagnetten fpl.

castle ['kɑːsl], s. 1. Burg f; (mansion) Schloß n. 2. (in chess) Turm m.

castor¹ ['kɑːstər], s. Laufrolle f.

castor², c. c. oil, Rizinusöl n.

castrate [kæs'treit], v.tr. kastrieren.

casual ['kæʒju(ə)l], adj. 1. (a) (chance) zufällig; (b) (not permanent) Gelegenheits-. 2. (a) (informal) ungezwungen; c. clothes, zwanglose Kleidung; (b) (uninvolved) gleichgültig; a c. remark, eine beiläufige Bemerkung.

casualty, pl. -ies ['kæʒjualti, -iz], s. (injured) Verletzte(r) f; (dead) Todesopfer n; c. ward, Unfallstation f.

cat [kæt], s. Katze f; to let the c. out of the bag, die Katze aus dem Sack lassen.

catalogue ['kætələg]. I. s. Katalog m. II. v.tr. (Bücher usw.) katalogisieren.

catalyst ['kætəlist], s. Ch: Katalysator m; Fig: auslösendes Moment n.

catapult ['kætəpʌlt]. I. s. Katapult n. II. v.tr. schleudern.

cataract ['kætərækt], s. Med: grauer Star m.

catarrh [kə'tɑːr], s. Katarrh m.

catastrophe [kə'tæstrəfi], s. Katastrophe f. ◆**catastrophic** [kætə'strɔfik], adj. katastrophal.

catch [kætʃ]. I. v.irr. 1. v.tr. (a) fangen;

(capture) (Tiere) einfangen; *(in falling)* (j-n, etwas) auffangen; *c. up with* (j-n) einholen; *(b) (surprise)* (j-n) überraschen; *(c) (be in time for)* (einen Bus, einen Zug) erreichen; *F:* erwischen; *(d) (hear, understand)* I didn't quite c. that, das habe ich nicht ganz mitgekriegt; *(e) Med:* sich *dat* (eine Krankheit) zuziehen; to c. a cold, sich erkälten; *(f)* to c. a dress on a nail, mit dem Kleid an einem Nagel hängenbleiben; to c. one's finger in a door, sich *dat* den Finger in der Tür klemmen. 2. *v.i. (stick)* the door is catching, die Tür klemmt; her dress caught on a nail, ihr Kleid blieb an einem Nagel hängen. II. s. 1. *(action)* Fangen n. 2. *(of fish)* Fang m. 3. *(trap)* Falle f; there's a c. in it, die Sache hat einen Haken. 4. *(closure)* Verschluß m; *(latch)* Klinke f. ◆'catching, *adj.* ansteckend. ◆'catch 'on, *v.i. (a) (be accepted)* Anklang finden; *(b) (understand)* he caught on immediately, er hat es sofort begriffen. ◆'catch 'out, *v.tr. (of pers.)* (j-n) hereinlegen; his question caught me out, seine Frage hat mich überrumpelt. ◆'catch 'up, *v.tr. & v.i. (a)* to c. s.o., sth. up/c. up with s.o., sth., j-n, etwas einholen; to c. up on one's work, seine Arbeit nachholen; *(b)* caught up in sth., (i) *(involved)* in etwas *acc* verwickelt; (ii) *(carried away)* von etwas *dat* mitgerissen.

catechism ['kætikiz(ə)m], s. Katechismus m.

categorical [kætə'gɔrik(ə)l], *adj.* kategorisch. ◆category ['kætigəri, *N.Am:* -gɔri], s. Kategorie f.

cater ['keitər], *v.i. (a)* Lebensmittel liefern; to c. for s.o., j-n mit Lebensmitteln versorgen; *(b) Fig:* to c. for s.o., sth., j-n, etwas berücksichtigen. ◆'caterer, s. Lebensmittellieferant m. ◆'catering, s. c. (industry), Gaststättengewerbe n; who's doing the c.? wer liefert das Essen?

caterpillar ['kætəpilər], s. Raupe f.

cathedral [kə'θi:drəl], s. Kathedrale f.

catholic ['kæθ(ə)lik]. I. *adj.* 1. umfassend; c. tastes, weite Sympathien. 2. *Ecc:* katholisch. II. s. Katholik(in) m(f). ◆catholicism [kə'θɔlisiz(ə)m], s. Katholizismus m.

cattle ['kætl], s. *inv.* Vich n.

catty ['kæti], *adj. F:* gehässig.

cauliflower ['kɔliflauər], s. Blumenkohl m.

cause [kɔːz]. I. s. 1. *(origin)* Ursache f 2. *(reason)* Grund m (for sth., zu etwas dat); no c. for complaint, kein Grund zur Klage; to have good c. for doing sth., seine guten Gründe für etwas *acc* haben. 3. *(a) (purpose)* Zweck m; it's all in a good c., es ist für einen guten Zweck; *(b)* Sache f; in the c. of freedom, um der Freiheit willen; a lost c., eine verlorene Sache. II. *v.tr. (a)* (etwas) verursachen; *(b)* to c. s.o. to do sth., j-n veranlassen,

etwas zu tun.

causeway ['kɔːzwei], s. Damm m.

caustic ['kɔːstik], *adj.* 1. *Ch:* ätzend, Ätz-. 2. *Fig:* beißend.

cauterize ['kɔːtəraiz], *v.tr. Med:* (eine Wunde usw.) ausbrennen.

caution ['kɔːʃ(ə)n]. I. s. 1. *(care)* Vorsicht f; to proceed with c., vorsichtig vorgehen. 2. *(warning)* Warnung f; *Jur: etc:* Verwarnung f. II. *v.tr.* (j-n) warnen; *Jur: etc:* (j-n) verwarnen. ◆'cautious, *adj.* vorsichtig.

cavalier [kævə'liər], *adj.* anmaßend; c. treatment, arrogante Behandlung.

cavalry ['kævəlri], s. Kavallerie f.

cave [keiv]. I. s. Höhle f. II. *v.i.* to c. in, einstürzen.

cavern ['kævən], s. Höhle f. ◆'cavernous, *adj. (a)* höhlenartig. 2. *Fig:* hohl; *(of cheeks)* eingefallen.

caviar(e) ['kæviɑːr], s. Kaviar m.

cavity ['kævəti], s. Hohlraum m; *Anat:* Höhle f; *(in tooth)* Loch n.

cavort [kə'vɔːt], *v.i.* herumtollen.

cease [siːs], *v.* 1. *v.tr.* (mit etwas dat) aufhören; (die Zahlung, das Feuer, die Arbeit usw.) einstellen; it had ceased to exist, es existiert nicht mehr. 2. *v.i. (of rain etc.)* aufhören; *(of production etc.)* eingestellt werden. ◆'ceasefire, s. Waffenruhe f. ◆'ceaseless, *adj.* unaufhörlich.

cedar ['siːdər], s. Zeder f.

cede [siːd], *v.tr.* (etwas) abtreten (to s.o., an j-n).

ceiling ['siːliŋ], s. 1. Decke f (eines Zimmers). 2. *(limit)* (oberste) Grenze f. price c., oberste Preisgrenze f.

celebrate ['selibreit], *v.tr.* feiern. ◆'celebrated, *adj.* berühmt. ◆cele'bration, s. Feier f. ◆celebrity [sə'lebriti], s. Berühmtheit f.

celery ['seləri], s. Stangensellerie m & f.

celestial [si'lestiəl], *adj.* himmlisch.

celibacy ['selibəsi], s. Zölibat n. ◆celibate ['selibət], *adj.* enthaltsam.

cell [sel], s. Zelle f.

cellar ['selər], s. Keller m.

cellist ['tʃelist], s. Cellist(in) m(f). ◆cello, *pl.* -os ['tʃeləu, -əuz], s. Cello n.

cellophane ['seləfein], s. Zellophan n.

cement [si'ment]. I. s. Zement n. II. *v.tr. (a)* (etwas) zementieren; *(b) Fig:* to c. a friendship, eine Freundschaft festigen.

cemetery ['semətri], s. Friedhof m.

censor ['sensər]. I. s. Zensor m. II. *v.tr.* zensieren. ◆'censorship, s. Zensur f.

censure ['senʃər]. I. s. Tadel m; vote of c., Mißtrauensvotum n. II. *v.tr.* (j-n) tadeln.

census ['sensəs], s. Volkszählung f.

cent [sent], s. 1. *(coin)* Cent m; I haven't a c., ich habe keinen Pfennig. 2. per c., Prozent n.

centenary [sen'tiːnəri], s. Hundertjahrfeier f.

centigrade ['sentigreid], *adj.* **20 degrees c.,** 20 Grad Celsius.

centimetre ['senti:mi:tər], *s.* Zentimeter *m.*

central ['sentr(ə)l], *adj.* **1.** *(a)* zentral; *(of house)* zentral gelegen; **c. heating,** Zentralheizung *f; (b) Geog:* Mittel-; **C. America,** Mittelamerika *n; (c)* **c. reservation,** Mittelstreifen *m* (einer Autobahn). **2.** *(main)* Haupt-; **c. (station),** Hauptbahnhof *m; Pol:* **c. government,** Zentralregierung *f;* **-ly,** *adv.* zentral. ◆**'centralize,** *v.tr.* zentralisieren.

centre ['sentər]. **I.** *s.* Zentrum *n;* **town c.,** Innenstadt *f.* **II.** *attrib.* Mittel-; *Sp:* **c. forward,** Mittelstürmer *m;* **c. half,** Mittelläufer *m; Pol:* **c. party,** Partei *f* der Mitte. **III.** *v.* **1.** *v.tr. (a) Tchn:* (etwas) zentrieren; *(b)* **to be centred in London,** London als Zentrum haben. **2.** *v.i.* **to c. on sth.,** sich auf etwas *acc* konzentrieren.

century ['sentʃəri], *s.* Jahrhundert *n.*

ceramic [si'ræmik], *adj.* keramisch.

cereal ['siəriəl], *s.* **1.** *(usu. pl.)* Getreide *n.* **2.** *(breakfast)* **c.,** Cornflakes, Haferflocken *usw.*

ceremony ['serimoni], *s.* **1.** Zeremonie *f.* **2.** *(formality)* Förmlichkeit *f;* **without c.,** ohne Umstände; **to stand on c.,** sehr förmell sein. ◆**cere'monial.** **I.** *adj.* feierlich. **II.** *s.* Zeremoniell *n.* ◆**cere'monious,** *adj.* zeremoniell.

certain ['sə:t(ə)n], *adj.* **1.** sicher; **I know for c.,** ich weiß es genau/ganz bestimmt. **2.** *(not named)* gewiß; **on a c. day,** an einem bestimmten Tag; **-ly,** *adv.* bestimmt; **c.!** aber sicher! **c. not,** das kommt nicht in Frage. ◆**'certainty,** *s.* **1.** *(in one's mind)* Gewißheit *f; (factual)* Sicherheit *f.*

certificate [sə'tifikit], *s.* **1.** Bescheinigung *f; (paper)* Schein *m;* **medical c.,** ärztliches Attest *n.* **2.** *Sch:* Diplom *n.*

certify ['sə:tifai], *v.tr. (a) (confirm* (einen Tod usw.) bestätigen; *(b)* (etwas) bescheinigen; (eine Abschrift) beglaubigen; **this is to c. that ...,** hiermit wird bescheinigt, daß ...; **to c. s.o. (as being insane),** j-n wegen Geisteskrankheit entmündigen.

cervix ['sə:viks], *s.* Gebärmutterhals *m.*

chafe [tʃeif], *v.tr. (a) (of rope, skin etc.)* (an etwas *dat*) scheuern; *(b) (make sore)* (die Haut usw.) wund reiben.

chaffinch ['tʃæfintʃ], *s.* Buchfink *m.*

chain [tʃein]. **I.** *s.* Kette *f; (in WC)* **to pull the c.,** ziehen; **c. reaction,** Kettenreaktion *f;* **c. smoker,** Kettenraucher *m;* **c. store,** Kettengeschäft *n.* **II.** *v.tr.* anketten.

chair [tʃeər]. **I.** *s.* **1.** Stuhl *m; Sch:* **c. lift,** Sessellift *m.* **2.** **to be in the/take the c.,** den Vorsitz führen. **3.** *(professorship)* Lehrstuhl *m.* **II.** *v.tr.* **to c. a meeting,** bei einer Versammlung den Vorsitz führen. ◆**'chairman, 'chairwoman,** *s. (a) (of a meeting etc.) (also* **chairperson**) Vorsitzen-

de(r) *f(m); (b) (of a firm)* Generaldirektor *m.*

chalet ['ʃælei], *s. (Swiss)* Chalet *n; (for holidays)* Ferienhaus *n.*

chalk [tʃɔ:k], *s.* Kreide *f.*

challenge ['tʃælin(d)ʒ]. **I.** *s.* Herausforderung *f.* **II.** *v.tr. (a)* (j-n) herausfordern; **to c. s.o. to a duel,** j-n zum Duell fordern; *(b) (of sentry)* (j-n) anrufen; *(c)* (eine Behauptung usw.) bestreiten. ◆**'challenger,** *s.* Herausforderer *m.* ◆**'challenging,** *adj.* herausfordernd.

chamber ['tʃeimbər], *s.* **1.** Kammer *f;* **c. maid,** Zimmermädchen *n;* **c. pot,** Nachttopf *m;* **c. music,** Kammermusik *f; (in horrors,* Gruselkabinett *n.* **2.** *C: of* **Commerce,** Handelskammer *f.* **3.** *Parl:* **Lower C.,** Unterhaus *n;* **Upper C.,** Oberhaus *n.*

chameleon [kə'mi:ljən], *s.* Chamäleon *n.*

chamois ['ʃæmwa], *s.* Gemse *f;* **c.** *f/F:* **chammy** ['ʃæmi:] leather, Waschleder *n.*

champagne [ʃæm'pein], *s.* Champagner *m; (German)* Sekt *m.*

champion ['tʃæmpjən]. **I.** *s.* **1.** Verfechter *m* (einer Sache). **2.** *Sp:* Meister(in) *m(f);* **boxing c.,** Boxmeister *m.* **II.** *v.tr.* **to c. sth.,** sich für etwas *acc* einsetzen. ◆**'championship,** *s.* Meisterschaft *f.*

chance [tʃɑ:ns]. **I.** *s.* **1.** *(accident)* Zufall *m;* **by c.,** zufällig. **2.** *(luck)* Glück *n;* **to take no chances,** nichts riskieren. **3.** *(prospect)* Chance *f; Aussichten pl; on the* **off c.,** auf gut Glück; **the chances are that ...,** aller Wahrscheinlichkeit nach ...; **to stand a good/fair c. of sth.,** gute Aussichten auf etwas *acc* haben. **4.** *(opportunity)* Gelegenheit *f;* **to give s.o. a c.,** j-m eine Chance geben. **5.** *attrib.* Zufalls-; zufällig. **II.** *v.* **1.** *v.i.* **to c. (up)on s.o., sth.,** auf j-n, etwas *acc* stoßen. **2.** *v.tr.* **we'll have to c. it,** wir müssen es riskieren. ◆**'chancy,** *adj. F:* riskant.

chancellor ['tʃɑ:nsələr], *s.* Kanzler *m; Brit:* **C. of the Exchequer,** Schatzkanzler *m.*

chandelier [ʃændə'liər], *s.* Kronleuchter *m.*

change [tʃein(d)ʒ]. **I.** *s.* **1.** *(a) (alteration)* (Ver)änderung *f;* **c. of heart,** Gesinnungswandel *m; (b) (innovation)* Neuerung *f.* **2.** *(a) (replacement)* Wechsel *m;* **c. of clothes,** Kleider zum Wechseln; *(b) (transition)* Übergang *m.* **3.** *(variety)* Abwechslung *f; for a c.,* zur Abwechslung; **to need a c.,** Abwechslung nötig haben. **4.** *(money)* Wechselgeld *n;* **small c.,** Kleingeld *n;* **to give c. for a pound,** auf ein Pfund herausgeben. **II.** *v.* **1.** *v.tr. (a) (alter)* ändern; (j-n, seine Stimme, die Welt, usw.) verändern; **he has changed his mind,** er hat sich anders entschlossen; *(b) (swop)* wechseln; **to c. hands,** den Besitzer wechseln; **to c. sth. for sth. else,** etwas gegen etwas anderes (um)tauschen; **to c. trains,** umsteigen; **to**

c. **pounds into marks,** Pfund in Mark umwechseln; **to c. gear,** (den Gang) schalten; (c) **to c. one's clothes,** sich umziehen; **to c. the baby,** das Baby trokkenlegen; (d) (transform) **to c. sth. into sth.,** etwas in etwas acc verwandeln. 2. v.i. a (of pers., weather etc.) sich (ver)ändern; (b) **to c. into a frog,** sich in einen Frosch verwandeln; (c) Cl: sich umziehen; (d) Rail: etc: umsteigen; **all c.!** alles aussteigen! (e) **to c. from red to green,** von rot auf grün wechseln; (f) Aut: **to c. into third** (gear), in den dritten Gang schalten. ◆'**changeable,** adj. (of weather) veränderlich; (of pers.) wankelmütig. ◆'**changing,** s. c. room, Umkleideraum m. ◆**change 'down,** v.i. Aut: herunterschalten (into, in + acc). ◆'**change 'up,** v.i. Aut: hinaufschalten (into, in + acc).

channel ['tʃænl]. **I.** s. **1.** (a) (natural) Rinne f; (man-made) Kanal m; (navigation) c., Fahrrinne f (eines Flusses, Hafens usw.); (b) Geog: **the (English) C.,** der Ärmelkanal, F: der Kanal; **the C. Islands,** die Kanalinseln fpl. **2.** Fig: Weg m; **through** (the) **official channels,** auf dem Amtsweg. **3.** Rad: TV: Kanal m. **II.** v.tr. (Energie, Kräfte usw.) lenken.

chant [tʃɑːnt]. **I.** s. (liturgischer) Gesang m. **II.** v.tr. (Schlagworte usw.) rhythmisch rufen.

chaos ['keɪɔs], s. Chaos n. ◆**cha'otic,** adj. chaotisch.

chap[1] [tʃæp], v.i. (of skin, lips etc.) aufspringen.

chap[2], s. F: Kerl m.

chapel ['tʃæpl], s. Kapelle f.

chaperon ['ʃæpərəʊn]. **I.** s. Anstandsdame f. **II.** v.tr. (j-n) als Anstandsdame begleiten.

chaplain ['tʃæplin], s. Ecc: Kaplan m; (in hospital, school) Hausgeistlicher m.

chapter ['tʃæptər], s. Kapitel n.

char[1] [tʃɑːr], v. tr. & i. (Holz usw.) verkohlen.

char[2]. **I.** s. F: Putzfrau f. **II.** v.i. F: als Putzfrau arbeiten.

character ['kærɪktər], s. **1.** Charakter m; **that is quite out of c. for him,** das ist untypisch für ihn. **2.** (person) a (in play etc.) Person f; (b) **he's a** (quite) **a c.,** er ist ein Original. ◆**character'istic. I.** adj. charakteristisch. **II.** s. (a) (trait) Merkmal n; (b) (quality) Eigenschaft f; **-ally,** adv. charakteristischerweise. ◆'**characterize,** v.tr. (j-n) charakterisieren. ◆'**characterless,** adj. charakterlos.

charcoal ['tʃɑːkəʊl], s. (a) Holzkohle f; (b) Art: Zeichenkohle f.

charge [tʃɑːdʒ]. **I.** s. **1.** Ladung f (einer Bombe usw.); **explosive c., explosive c.,** Sprengladung f. **2.** (fee) Gebühr f; **bank charges,** Bankspesen pl; **free of c.,** kostenlos; **there is no c. for that,** das kostet nichts. **3. to take c.,** die Verantwortung

übernehmen (of sth., für etwas acc); **to be in c. of sth.,** für etwas acc verantwortlich sein. **4.** Jur: (accusation) Beschuldigung f; (in criminal law) Anklage f; **on a c. of theft,** des Diebstahls beschuldigt. **5.** Mil: Sturmangriff m. **II.** v.tr. (a) El: (eine Batterie usw.) aufladen; (b) Jur: **to c. s.o. with a crime,** j-n eines Verbrechens anklagen; (c) Com: etc: (eine Gebühr) erheben; **to c. sth. to s.o.,** j-m etwas berechnen; **to c. three pounds an hour,** pro Stunde drei Pfund berechnen. ◆'**charger,** s. (battery) c., Ladegerät n.

chariot ['tʃærɪət], s. Kampfwagen m.

charity ['tʃærɪtɪ], s. **1.** (quality) Nächstenliebe f. **2.** c. (organisation), karitative Einrichtung; Hilfswerk n; **for c.,** zu Wohltätigkeitszwecken; **c. bazaar,** Wohltätigkeitsbasar m. ◆'**charitable,** adj. **1.** (of pers.) gebefreudig; (of institution) karitativ. **2.** (lenient) nachsichtig.

charm [tʃɑːm]. **I.** s. **1.** (magic) a (Zauber)mittel n; (b) Amulett n. **2.** Charme m, Reiz m (einer Person, eines Ortes usw.). **II.** v.tr. (j-n) bezaubern. ◆'**charming,** adj. reizend, charmant.

chart [tʃɑːt], s. **1.** Nau: Seekarte f. **2.** (sheet of information) Tabelle f. **3.** Mus: F: **the charts** pl, die Hitparade.

charter ['tʃɑːtər]. **I.** s. Chartern n (eines Schiffes, Flugzeugs); c. **plane,** Chartermaschine f. **II.** v.tr. (a) (ein Flugzeug) mieten; (b) (ein Schiff usw.) chartern. ◆**chartered accountant,** Wirtschaftsprüfer m; (b) (ein Flugzeug) chartern.

charwoman ['tʃɑːwʊmən], pl. -women ['tʃɑː-wɪmɪn], s. Putzfrau f.

chary ['tʃɛərɪ], adj. **to be c. about doing sth.,** zögern, etwas zu tun.

chase [tʃeɪs]. **I.** v.tr. & i. jagen. **II.** s. Verfolgung f; (hunt) Jagd f.

chasm ['kæz(ə)m], s. Kluft f.

chassis ['ʃæsɪ], s. Fahrgestell n.

chaste [tʃeɪst], adj. keusch. ◆'**chastity** ['tʃæstɪtɪ], s. Keuschheit f.

chastise [tʃæs'taɪz], v.tr. (j-n) züchtigen.

chat [tʃæt]. **I.** v.i. plaudern; F: **to c. s.o. up,** sich an j-n heranmachen. **II.** s. Plauderei f, F: Plausch m.

chatter ['tʃætər]. **I.** v.i. (a) (of pers.) schwatzen; (of child) plappern; (b) (of teeth) klappern. **II.** s. Geschwätz n; Geplapper n (eines Kindes usw.).

chauffeur ['ʃəʊfər], s. Chauffeur m.

cheap [tʃiːp], adj. billig.

cheat [tʃiːt]. **I.** v. **1.** v.tr. (j-n) beschwindeln. **2.** v.i. (at games etc.) mogeln. **II.** s. (pers.) a (of games) Betrüger m; (b) (at games) Mogler m. ◆'**cheating,** s. **1.** Schwindeln n. **2.** (at games) Mogelei f.

check[1] [tʃek]. **I.** v. **1.** v.tr. (a) (den Fluß, eine Entwicklung usw.) hemmen; (den Feind, den Fortschritt usw.) aufhalten; (eine Krankheit usw.) in Schach halten; (b) (examine) (eine Rechnung, Liste usw.) prüfen; (eine Übersetzung, eine Maschine, den Ölstand usw.) überprüfen. **2.** v.i.

nachprüfen; (by looking) nachsehen. II. s.
1. to keep a c. on s.o., sth., j-n, etwas
unter Kontrolle halten; to keep one's
feelings in c., sich beherrschen. 2. (a)
Kontrolle f (von Fahrkarten, Gepäck
usw); (examination) Prüfung f (einer
Rechnung usw.); c. list, Checkliste f; (b)
N.Am: (bill) Rechnung f. 3. N.Am: (cheque) Scheck m. ◆'check 'in, v.i. (in
hotel) sich anmelden; (b) Av: einchecken.
◆'checkmate, s. Matt n; in: Schach-
matt! ◆'check 'out, v. 1. v.i. (at hotel)
sich abmelden; (eine Tatsache) nachprüfen. ◆'check-out, s. (in supermarket)
Kasse f. ◆'checkpoint, s. Kontroll-
punkt m. ◆'checkup, s. Kontrollunter-
suchung f. ◆'check 'up, v.i. nachprüfen; (by looking) nachsehen.

check², s.   (pattern)   Karo   n.
◆'check(ed), adj. (of pattern) kariert.
◆'checkers, s. N.Am: Damespiel n.

cheek [tʃiːk], s. 1. Backe f. 2. F: (impudence) Frechheit f. ◆'cheeky, adj.
frech.

cheer [tʃiər]. I. s. 1. Frohsinn m. 2. (a)
(applause) Hurra n; three cheers for X,
ein dreifaches Hoch auf X acc; (b) int.
cheers! Prost! II. v. 1. v.tr. (a) to c. s.o.
(up), j-n aufmuntern; (b) (of crowd) (j-m)
zujubeln. 2. v.i. (a) to c. up, (of pers.)
fröhlicher werden; (b) (of crowd) Beifall
rufen. ◆'cheerful, adj. (of pers.) heiter;
c. news, erfreuliche Nachrichten; -ly,
adv. (willingly) gern. ◆'cheeri'o! int.
F: tschüs! ◆'cheerless, adj. trostlos.
◆'cheery, adj. heiter.

cheese [tʃiːz]. I. s. Käse m. II. v.tr. P: to
be   cheesed   off,   angeödet   sein.
◆'cheesecake, s. Käsekuchen m.

chef [ʃef], s. (head cook) Küchenchef m;
(cook) Koch m.

chemical [kemik(ə)l]. I. adj. chemisch.
II. s. pl. chemicals, Chemikalien fpl.
◆'chemist ['kemist], s. 1. (expert in chemistry) Chemiker(in) m(f). 2. (non-
dispensing) Drogist(in) m(f); (dispensing)
c., Apotheker(in) m(f); chemist's shop,
(non-dispensing) Drogerie f; (dispensing)
Apotheke f. ◆'chemistry ['kemistri], s.
Chemie f.

cheque [tʃek], s. Scheck m (for £10, über
10 Pfund); c. book, Scheckheft n.

chequered ['tʃekəd], adj. Fig: c. career,
abwechslungsreiche Karriere.

cherish ['tʃeriʃ], v.tr. (einen Wunsch) hegen.

cherry ['tʃeri], s. Kirsche f; c. tree,
Kirschbaum m.

chess [tʃes],   s.   Schach   n.
◆'chessboard, s. Schachbrett n.

chest [tʃest], s. 1. Truhe f; c. of drawers,
Kommode f. 2. Anat: Brust f; F: to get
sth. off one's c., sich dat etwas von der
Seele reden.

chestnut ['tʃesnʌt], s. Kastanie f.

chew [tʃuː], v.tr. kauen. ◆'chewing

gum, s. Kaugummi m.

chic [ʃiːk], adj. schick.

chick [tʃik], s. Küken n. ◆'chick-pea, s.
Kichererbse f.

chicken   ['tʃikin],   s.   Huhn   n.
◆'chickenpox, s. Windpocken fpl.

chicory ['tʃikəri], s. Zichorie f; (as vegetable) Chicorée f.

chief [tʃiːf]. I. s. (a) Mil: c. of staff, Chef
m des Generalstabs; (b) Häuptling m (eines Stammes). II. adj. Haupt-; c. constable, Polizeipräsident m; -ly, adv. 1.
(mostly) meistens. 2. (mainly) hauptsächlich.

chiffon ['ʃifɔn], s. Chiffon m.

chilblain ['tʃilblein], s. Frostbeule f.

child,   pl.   children [tʃaild, 'tʃildrən],
s. Kind n; that's c.'s play, das ist ein Kin-
derspiel; c. benefit, Kindergeld n.
◆'childbirth,   s.   Entbindung   f.
◆'childhood,   s.   Kindheit   f.
◆'childish, adj. kindisch. ◆'childless, adj. kinderlos. ◆'childlike,
adj. kindlich. ◆'childminder, s. Tages-
mutter f.

Chile ['tʃili]. Pr.n. Chile m. ◆'Chilean
['tʃiliən]. I. s. Chilene m; Chilenin f. II.
adj. chilenisch.

chill [tʃil]. I. s. 1. Verkühlung f; to catch
a c., sich verkühlen. 2. Kälte f; to take
the c. off sth., etwas anwärmen. II. v.tr.
abkühlen. ◆'chilly, adj. 1. (a) (of pers.)
to feel c., frösteln; (b) (of wind, air etc.)
frisch. 2. (unfriendly) frostig.

chime [tʃaim]. I. s. Klang m (einer Glok-
ke); Schlag m (einer Uhr). II. v.tr. & i.
(eine Glocke) läuten; a chiming clock,
eine schlagende Uhr; F: to c. in, einfallen.

chimney ['tʃimni], s. Schornstein m.
◆'chimney-pot, s. Schornsteinaufsatz
m. ◆'chimney-sweep, s. Schornsteinfeger m.

chimpanzee [tʃimpæn'ziː], s. Schimpanse
m.

chin [tʃin], s. Kinn n.

china ['tʃainə], s. 1. Porzellan n. 2. Pr.n.
C., China f. ◆Chinese [tʃai'niːz]. I. s.
1. Chinese m; Chinesin f. 2. (language)
Chinesisch n. II. adj. chinesisch.

chink¹ [tʃiŋk], s. Ritze f (in einer Wand,
einer Tür usw.).

chink². I. s. Geklirr n (von Glas); Klimpern n (von Münzen). II. v.i. (of glasses)
klirren; (of coins) klimpern.

chip [tʃip]. I. s. 1. Span m (von Holz,
Metall); Fig: to have a c. on one's
shoulder, einen Komplex haben. 2. (damaged place) angeschlagene Stelle f (eines
Tellers, einer Tasse usw.). 3. Cu: chips,
Pommes frites pl. II. v. 1. v.tr. (Porzellan) anschlagen. 2. v.i. (of paint) absplittern.

chiropodist [ki'rɔpədist], s. Fuß-
pfleger(in) m(f). ◆chi'ropody, s. Fuß-
pflege f.

chirp ['tʃəːp], v.i. (of bird) zwitschern.

chisel ['tʃɪzl], s. Meißel m.

chivalrous ['ʃɪvǝlrǝs], adj. ritterlich. ◆'**chivalry**, s. Ritterlichkeit f.

chives ['tʃaɪvz], s. Schnittlauch m.

chloride ['klɔːraɪd], s. Chlorid n. ◆**chlorine** ['klɔːriːn], s. Chlor n. ◆**chlorinate** ['klɔːrɪneɪt], v.tr. (Wasser) chloren.

chloroform ['klɔrǝfɔːm], s. Chloroform n.

choc-ice ['tʃɔkaɪs], s. Eis n mit Schokoladenüberzug.

chocolate ['tʃɔk(ǝ)lɪt]. I. s. (a) Schokolade f; (b) a c., eine Praline. II. adj. Schokoladen-; **c. cake**, Schokoladenkuchen m.

choice [tʃɔɪs]. I. s. (a) Wahl f; **to make a c.**, eine Wahl treffen; (b) (selection) Auswahl f. II. adj. (of food, fruit etc.) auserlesen.

choir ['kwaɪǝr], s. Chor m. ◆'**choirboy**, s. Chorknabe m.

choke [tʃǝuk]. I. v. 1. v.tr. (strangle) (j-n) erwürgen; (stifle) (j-n) ersticken. 2. v.i. (of pers.) ersticken; **to c. on a bone**, an einem Knochen würgen. II. s. Aut: Choke m.

cholesterol [kǝ'lestǝrɔl], s. Cholesterin n.

choose [tʃuːz], v.tr.irr. wählen. ◆'**choos(e)y**, adj. F: (of pers.) wählerisch.

chop [tʃɔp]. I. s. 1. (a) Schlag m (mit der Axt, mit dem Fleischerbeil); (b) Hieb m (mit der flachen Hand). 2. Cu: Kotelett n. II. v. 1. v.tr. hacken. 2. v.i. **to c. and change**, (of pers.) es sich dat dauernd anders überlegen. ◆'**chop 'down**, v.tr. (einen Baum) fällen. ◆'**choppy**, adj. (of sea) bewegt. ◆'**chop 'off**, v.tr. abhauen. ◆'**chopstick**, s. Stäbchen n. ◆'**chop 'up**, v.tr. (Holz, Fleisch) in Stücke hacken.

choral ['kɔːr(ǝ)l], adj. Chor-; **c. music**, Chormusik f; **c. society**, Gesangverein m.

chord [kɔːd], s. Akkord m.

chore [tʃɔːr], s. lästige Arbeit f; **to do the chores**, die Hausarbeit machen.

choreography [kɔrɪ'ɔgrǝfi], s. Choreographie f.

chorus ['kɔːrǝs], s. pl. **-uses** ['kɔːrǝs, -ǝsɪz], s. 1. Mus: Th: Chor m. 2. Mus: Refrain m (eines Liedes usw.).

Christ [kraɪst]. Pr.n. Christus m.

christen ['krɪsn], v.tr. (j-n) taufen. ◆'**christening**, s. Taufe f.

Christian ['krɪstɪǝn]. I. s. Christ(in) m(f). II. adj. christlich; **C. name**, Vorname m. ◆**Christianity** [-'ænɪti], s. Christentum n.

Christmas ['krɪsmǝs], s. Weihnachten pl; **C. Day**, der erste Weihnachtstag; **C. Eve**, Heiligabend m.

chromium ['krǝumɪǝm], s. Chrom n; **c. plating**, Verchromung f.

chronic ['krɔnɪk], adj. 1. Med: chronisch. 2. F: mies.

chronicle ['krɔnɪkl]. I. s. Chronik f. II. v.tr. **to c. events**, Ereignisse aufzeichnen.

chronological [krɔnǝ'lɔdʒɪk(ǝ)l], adj. chronologisch.

chrysalis, pl. **-es** ['krɪsǝlɪs, -ɪz], s. Puppe f.

chrysanthemum [krɪ'sænθ(ǝ)mǝm], s. Chrysantheme f.

chuck [tʃʌk], v.tr. F: (a) (etwas) schmeißen; (b) **to c. in/up one's job**, seinen Job an den Nagel hängen.

chuckle ['tʃʌkl]. I. v.i. in sich hineinlachen; F: glucksen. II. s. F: Glucksen m.

chuff [tʃʌf], v.i. F: **to be chuffed**, sich sehr freuen.

chug [tʃʌg], v.i. (of engine) tuckern.

chunk [tʃʌŋk], s. Klumpen m; Klotz m (Holz); großes Stück n (Brot).

church [tʃǝːtʃ], s. Kirche f; **to go to c.**, in die Kirche gehen. ◆'**churchyard**, s. Kirchhof m.

churlish ['tʃǝːlɪʃ], adj. **it would be c. to refuse**, es wäre unhöflich abzulehnen.

churn [tʃǝːn]. I. s. Butterfaß n; **milk c.**, Milchkanne f. II. v.tr. **to c. out sth.**, etwas am laufenden Band produzieren.

chute [ʃuːt], s. (for coal etc.) Schacht m; (on playground) Rutsche f.

cider ['saɪdǝr], s. approx. Apfelmost m.

cigar [sɪ'gɑːr], s. Zigarre f.

cigarette [sɪgǝ'ret], s. Zigarette f; **c. end**, Zigarettenstummel m; **c. lighter**, Feuerzeug n.

cinder ['sɪndǝr], s. Asche f.

cine-camera ['sɪnɪkæm(ǝ)rǝ], s. Filmkamera f.

cinema ['sɪnɪmǝ], s. 1. (medium) Film m. 2. (building) Kino n.

cinnamon ['sɪnǝmǝn], s. Zimt m.

cipher ['saɪfǝr], s. (code) Chiffre f; **in c.**, chiffriert.

circle ['sǝːkl]. I. s. 1. Kreis m; N.Am: **traffic c.**, Kreisverkehr m; **to come full c.**, an den Ausgangspunkt zurückkehren; **vicious c.**, Teufelskreis m. 2. Th: Balkon m; **dress c.**, erster Rang; **upper c.**, zweiter Rang. II. v. 1. v.tr. (etwas) umkreisen. 2. v.i. kreisen. ◆'**circuit** ['sǝːkɪt], s. 1. El: Stromkreis m; **c. diagram**, Schaltbild n. 2. (race track) Rennstrecke f. ◆**circuitous** [-'kjuːɪtǝs], adj. **c. route**, Umweg m. ◆'**circular** ['sǝːkjulǝr], adj. (of arrangement, shape etc.) kreisförmig; **c. letter**, Rundschreiben n. ◆'**circulate** ['sǝːkjuleɪt], v. 1. v.tr. (etwas) herumgehen lassen; (ein Gerücht usw.) in Umlauf setzen. 2. v.i. umgehen; (of money, bad news etc.) kursieren; (of blood) kreisen. ◆**circu'lation**, s. (a) Anat: etc: Kreislauf m; (b) Umlauf m (von Zahlungsmitteln); Kursieren n (des Geldes, eines Gerüchts); (c) Auflage f (einer Zeitung).

circumcise ['sǝːkǝmsaɪz], v.tr. (j-n) beschneiden. ◆**circum'cision**, f Beschneidung f.

circumference [sǝ'kʌmf(ǝ)rǝns], s. Umfang m.

circumstances ['sə:kəmstənsiz, -stænsiz], s. pl. Umstände mpl; **in the c.**, unter den Umständen; **in/under no c.**, auf keinen Fall. ◆**circum'stantial**, adj. c. **evidence**, Indizienbeweis m.

circus, pl. **-uses** ['sə:kəs, -əsiz], s. Zirkus m.

cirrhosis [si'rəusis], s. Zirrhose f.

cistern ['sistən], s. (of WC) Wasserkasten m.

citadel ['sitədel], s. Zitadelle f.

cite [sait], v.tr. zitieren.

citizen ['sitizən], s. (a) (in a town) Bürger(in) m(f); (b) (of a state) Staatsbürger(in) m(f). ◆**'citizenship**, s. Staatsangehörigkeit f.

citric ['sitrik], adj. c. **acid**, Zitronensäure f.

citrus ['sitrəs], adj. c. **fruit**, Zitrusfrucht f.

city ['siti], s. Stadt f; (large) Großstadt f.

civic ['sivik]. I. adj. Adm: (a) (citizen's) bürgerlich; c. **rights**, Bürgerrechte npl; (b) (town) **the c. authorities**, die städtischen Behörden; c. **centre**, Stadthalle f. II. s. pl. Sch: **civics**, Staatsbürgerkunde f.

civil ['sivil], adj. 1. (a) bürgerlich; c. **rights**, Bürgerrechte npl; c. **war**, Bürgerkrieg m; (b) c. **engineer**, Tiefbauingenieur m; c. **engineering**, Tiefbau m; (c) c. **service**, Staatsdienst m; c. **servant**, Staatsbeamte(r) m. 2. (polite) höflich. ◆**ci'vilian**. I. adj. Zivil-; **in c. life**, im Zivilleben. II. s. Zivilist(in) m(f). ◆**'civilize** [-aiz], v.tr. zivilisieren. ◆**'civilized**, adj. zivilisiert. ◆**civili'zation**, s. Zivilisation f.

claim [kleim]. I. s. 1. (demand) Forderung f. 2. (right) Anspruch m (**to** sth., auf etwas acc); **to lay c. to** sth., etwas (für sich acc) beanspruchen; Fig: **to stake one's c.**, sein Anrecht geltend machen. II. v.tr. (a) (ein Recht, eine Pension) beanspruchen; (demand) (Schadenersatz) fordern; (b) (recognise) **does anyone c. this umbrella?** gehört dieser Schirm jemandem? (c) **he claims to represent young people**, er gibt vor, die Jugend zu vertreten; **to c. that ...**, behaupten, daß ...; (d) **to c. one's baggage**, sein Gepäck abholen. **clairvoyant** [kleə'vɔiənt], s. Hellseher(in) m(f).

clam [klæm], s. Venusmuschel f.

clamber ['klæmbər], v.i. klettern.

clammy ['klæmi], adj. feuchtkalt.

clamour ['klæmər]. I. s. (protest) Aufschrei m; **to c. for** sth., Schrei m nach etwas dat. II. v.i. **to c. for** sth., nach etwas dat schreien; Fig: auf etwas acc drängen.

clamp [klæmp]. I. s. (with screws) Schraubzwinge f; (small) Klammer f. II. v. 1. v.tr. **to c.** sth. **to** sth., etwas an etwas acc festklammern. 2. v.i. Fig: **to c. down on** s.o., sth., gegen j-n, etwas acc

scharf vorgehen.

clan [klæn], s. Sippe f.

clandestine [klæn'destin, -ain], adj. heimlich.

clang [klæŋ]. I. s. metallischer Ton m; (of bell) tiefes Tönen n. II. v.i. laut schallen; (of bell) tönen. ◆**'clanger**, s. F: **to drop a c.**, ins Fettnäpfchen treten.

clank [klæŋk]. I. s. Klirren n. II. v.tr. & i. klirren.

clap [klæp]. I. s. 1. Klatschen n; **to give s.o. a c.**, j-m Beifall spenden. 2. c. **of thunder**, Donnerschlag m. II. v. 1. v.tr. (a) **to c. one's hands**, klatschen; (b) **to c. eyes on** s.o., j-n zu Gesicht bekommen. 2. v.i. (Beifall) klatschen. ◆**'clapping**, s. Klatschen n.

claret ['klærət], s. Bordeaux-Rotwein m.

clarify ['klærifai], v.tr. klären. ◆**clarinet** [klæri'net], s. Klarinette f. ◆**clarity** ['klæriti], s. Klarheit f.

clash [klæʃ]. I. s. Kollision f (von Ansichten, Interessen usw.). II. v.i. (a) (of opinions etc.) aufeinanderfallen; (of armies) zusammenprallen; (of pers.) **to c. with** s.o., mit j-m aneinandergeraten; (b) (of colours) sich beißen; (c) (of events) zusammenfallen.

clasp [klɑːsp]. I. s. Schließe f (eines Mantels, usw.). II. v.tr. greifen.

class [klɑːs], s. Klasse f; **the middle c.**, der Mittelstand; **first/second c.**, erste/ zweite Klasse; **first c.**, erstklassig. ◆**classifi'cation** [klæ-], s. Klassifikation f. ◆**'classify** ['klæ-], v.tr. klassifizieren; **classified advertisements**, Kleinanzeigen fpl. ◆**'classroom**, s. Klassenzimmer n. ◆**'classy**, adj. F: vornehm; (of clothes etc.) schick.

classic ['klæsik]. I. adj. klassisch; (of garment etc.) zeitlos. II. s. pl. **Classics**, Altphilologie f. ◆**'classical**, adj. klassisch; c. **education**, humanistische Bildung.

clatter ['klætər]. I. s. Geklapper n. II. v.i. klappern.

clause [klɔːz], s. 1. Jur: etc: Klausel f. 2. Gram: Satzteil m.

claustrophobia [klɔːstrə'fəubiə], s. Platzangst f.

claw [klɔː]. I. s. Kralle f. II. v.tr. **to c. at** sth., etwas mit den Krallen bearbeiten.

clay [klei], s. (earth) Lehm m; (for pottery) Ton m.

clean [kliːn]. I. adj. (a) (free of dirt) sauber; (of shirt, linen etc.) frisch; (of pers., animal etc.) reinlich; c. **copy**, Reinschrift f; (b) (of cut, break) glatt; (c) Aut: c. **licence**, Führerschein m ohne Strafeintrag; (d) **to come c.**, F: (of pers.) Farbe bekennen. II. adv. ganz; völlig; **I had c. forgotten (about) it**, das hatte ich glatt vergessen; **they got c. away**, sie sind spurlos verschwunden. III. v.tr. säubern; **to c. one's teeth**, sich dat die Zähne putzen. 2. v.i. saubermachen. ◆**'cleaner**, s. 1. (pers.) Raumpfleger(in) m(f); (char) Putzfrau f; (dry) **cleaner's**, chemische Reinigung *f.* 2. (*fluid*) Putzmittel *n.* ◆'**cleaning**, *s.* **dry c.**, chemische Reinigung *f.* ◆'**clean 'out**, *v.tr.* (ein Zimmer, einen Schreibtisch usw.) ausräumen. ◆'**clean-'shaven**, *adj.* glattrasiert.

cleanse [klenz], *v.tr.* reinigen. ◆'**cleansing**, *adj.* **c. cream**, Reinigungscreme *f.*

clear [kliər]. **I.** *adj.* klar; **a c. sky**, ein heiterer Himmel; **a c. conscience**, ein reines Gewissen; **c. profit**, reiner Gewinn; **c. majority**, absolute Mehrheit; **three c. days**, drei volle Tage; -**ly**, *adv.* (*a*) (*distinctly*) deutlich; (*b*) (*obviously*) offensichtlich. **II.** *adj. & adv.* **to steer/keep c. of s.o., sth.**, j-m, etwas dat aus dem Wege gehen; **stand c. of the doors!** Türe freihalten! **III.** 1. *v.tr.* (*a*) **to c. the air**, (*after row*) die Lage entspannen; (*b*) (j-n) freisprechen; (*c*) (*empty*) (einen Saal) räumen; (eine Straße von Schnee usw.) freimachen; (ein Zimmer, einen Schrank usw.) ausräumen; (einen Wald) roden; **to c. the table**, den Tisch (nach dem Essen) abräumen; **to c. one's throat**, sich räuspern; (*d*) (*remove*) (Teller vom Tisch usw.) wegräumen; (Unkraut usw.) entfernen; **50 pence to c.**, Restposten für 50 Pence; (*e*) (*extend beyond*) (über etwas *acc*) hinausragen; (*not hit*) (an einem Vorsprung usw.) gerade noch vorbeikommen. 2. *v.i.* (*of weather*) **to c. (up)**, sich aufheitern; (*of mist*) **to c. (away)**, sich auflösen. ◆'**clearance**, *s.* 1. (*removal*) Beseitigung *f.*; (*a*) (*customs*) *c.*, Zollabfertigung *f.*; (*b*) Rodung *f* (von Land, Wald); (*c*) **c. sale**, Räumungsverkauf *m.* 2. (*space*) Zwischenraum *m.* ◆'**clear a'way**, *v.* 1. *v.tr.* (etwas) wegräumen; (Teller usw.) abräumen. 2. *v.i.* den Tisch abräumen. ◆'**clear-'cut**, *adj.* scharf umrissen; **c.-c. distinction**, deutlicher Unterschied. ◆'**clearing**, *s.* Lichtung *f.* ◆'**clear 'off**, *v.i. F:* (*of pers.*) abhauen. ◆'**clear 'up**, *v.* 1. *v.tr.* (ein Problem usw.) klarstellen. 2. *v.i.* (*a*) (*of weather*) sich aufklären; (*b*) (*tidy up*) aufräumen.

cleavage ['kliːvidʒ], *s.* Brustansatz *m.*

clench [klenʃ], *v.tr.* (die Zähne) zusammenbeißen; (die Faust) ballen.

clergy ['kləːdʒi], *s. coll.* Geistliche *mpl;* **the c.**, die Geistlichkeit *f.* ◆'**clergyman**, *pl.* -**men**, *s.* Geistlicher *m.*

clerical ['klerik(ə)l], *adj.* 1. *Ecc:* geistlich. 2. **c. work**, Schreibarbeit *f.*; **c. staff**, Schreibkräfte *fpl.*

clerk [klɑːk, *N.Am:* kləːk], *s.* 1. (*in office*) Büroangestellte(r) *f(m);* **bank c.**, Bankangestellte(r) *f(m).* 2. *N.Am:* (*sales person*) Verkäufer(in) *m(f).*

clever ['klevər], *adj.* 1. (*skilful*) geschickt. 2. (*intelligent*) klug.

cliché ['kliːʃei], *s.* Klischee *n.*

click [klik]. **I.** *s.* (*sound*) Klicken *n.* **II.** *v.i.* (*a*) **the door clicked shut**, die Tür fiel ins Schloß; (*b*) *F:* **it suddenly**

---

clicked, auf einmal fiel der Groschen.

client ['klaiənt], *s.* Kunde *m.*, Kundin *f.* ◆**clientele** [klaiɒn'tel, klitdi'tel], *s.* Kundschaft *f.*

cliff [klif], *s.* Klippe *f.*

climate ['klaimæt], *s.* Klima *n.*

climax ['klaimæks], *s.* Höhepunkt *m.*

climb [klaim]. **I.** *s.* Aufstieg *m.* **II.** *v.* 1. *v.tr.* (einen Berg usw.) besteigen; (einen Berg, eine Leiter, Mauer usw.) erklimmen. 2. *v.i.* steigen; (*clamber*) klettern. ◆'**climb 'down**, *v.* 1. *v.tr. & i.* (einen Berg usw.) herabsteigen. 2. *v.i. F:* klein beigeben. ◆'**climber**, *s.* 1. Bergsteiger(in) *m(f).* 2. *Pej:* **social c.**, Karrieremacher *m.* ◆'**climbing**. **I.** *adj.* **c. plant**, Kletterpflanze *f.* **II.** *s.* Klettern *n;* (*mountain*) **c.**, Bergsteigen *n.*

clinch [klinʃ], *v.tr. F:* **to c. a deal**, ein Geschäft festmachen.

cling [kliŋ], *v.i.irr.* (*of dirt etc.*) anhaften (**to**, *dat*); (*of pers.*) **to c. to s.o./**Fig: **to a hope**, sich an j-n/Fig: eine Hoffnung klammern.

clinic ['klinik], *s.* Klinik *f.* ◆'**clinical**, *adj.* klinisch.

clink¹ [kliŋk]. **I.** *s.* Geklirr *n.* **II.** *v.i.* klirren.

clink², *s. P:* (*prison*) Kittchen *n.*

clip¹ [klip]. **I.** *s.* Klammer *f.*, *paper* c., Büroklammer *f.* **II.** *v.tr.* (etwas) anklammern (**to sth.**, an etwas *acc*).

clip². **I.** *s* Ausschnitt *m* (aus einem Film). **II** *v.tr.* (*a*) (ein Schaf) scheren; (eine Hecke usw.) schneiden; (*b*) (*punch*) (eine Fahrkarte usw.) knipsen.

clique [kliːk], *s.* Clique *f.*

cloak [kləuk], *s.* Umhang *m.* ◆'**cloakroom**, *s.* 1. *Th: etc:* Garderobe *f.* 2. (*toilet*) Toilette *f;* (*washroom*) Waschraum *m.*

clobber ['klɒbər]. **I.** *s. F:* (j-n) hauen. **II.** *s. F:* Kram *m.*

clock [klɒk]. **I.** *s.* Uhr *f;* **it's two o'c.**, es ist zwei Uhr; **to work round the c.**, rund um die Uhr arbeiten. **II.** *v.i.* **to c. in/out**, stempeln. ◆'**clockface**, *s.* Zifferblatt *n.* ◆'**clockwise**, *adj. & adv.* im Uhrzeigersinn *m.* ◆'**clockwork**, *s.* Uhrwerk *n.*

clog [klɒg]. **I.** *v.tr.* (ein Rohr usw.) verstopfen. **II.** *s.* Holzschuh *m;* (*modern*) Clog *m.*

cloister ['klɒistər], *s.* Kreuzgang *m.*

close¹ [kləus]. **I.** *adj.* 1. nahe (**to**, + *dat*); **c. together**, nahe/dicht beieinander. 2. (*of atmosphere*) stickig; (*of weather*) schwül. 3. (*a*) (*of connection etc.*) eng; **a c. friend** ein enger Freund; (*b*) **on closer examination**, bei näherer Betrachtung. **II.** *adv.* **c.** (by/at hand), nahe, nahe dabei; **he lives c. to the station**, er wohnt nahe beim Bahnhof; -**ly**, *adv.* eng; genau; **to check sth. c.**, etwas genau nachprüfen; **c. related**, eng verwandt. ◆'**close-up**, *s.* Nahaufnahme *f.*

close² [kləuz]. **I.** *v.tr.* (*a*) (*shut*) (eine Tür, ein Geschäft, die Augen usw.)

schließen; (eine Straße usw.) sperren; (eine Fabrik, eine Eisenbahnlinie) stillegen; (b) (*bring to an end*) (eine Rede, eine Debatte usw.) beenden. **2.** *v.i.* (*of door, shop etc.*) schließen. **II.** *s.* to **draw to a c.**, sich dem Ende nähern; to **bring sth. to a c.**, etwas beenden. ◆'**close 'down**, *v.* **1.** *v.tr.* (einen Betrieb, *Rail:* eine Strecke) stillegen. **2.** *v.i.* stillgelegt werden; *Rad.: TV:* **we c.d. at 11.30 p.m.**, wir haben um 23.30 Uhr Sendeschluß. ◆'**closed**, *adj.* **1.** geschlossen; **road c.**, Straße gesperrt. **2.** *El:* **circuit television**, (*for security*) Fernseh-Überwachungssystem *n.* **3. c. shop**, Gewerkschaftszwang *m.* ◆'**closing**, *adj.* schließend; Schluß-; **c. remark**, Schlußbemerkung *f;* **c. date**, Schlußtermin *m;* (*for competition*) Einsendeschluß *m;* **c. time**, (*of shop*) Ladenschluß *m;* (*of pub*) Polizeistunde *f; Fin:* **c. price**, Schlußkurs *m.* ◆'**closure** [-ʒər], *s.* Stillegung *f* (einer Fabrik usw.).

clot [klɔt]. **I.** *s.* **1.** *Med:* **blood c.**, Blutgerinnsel *n.* **2.** *P:* (*pers.*) Hornochse *m.* **II.** *v.i.* gerinnen.

cloth [klɔθ], *pl.* **cloths** [klɔθs], *s.* **1.** Tuch *n.* **2.** *a)* (*rag*) Lappen *m;* (*b*) (**table**) **c.**, Tischtuch *n.*

clothe [kləuð], *v.tr.* (j-n) kleiden. ◆**clothes** [kləuðz], *s.pl.* Kleider *npl;* to **put on/take off one's c.**, sich anziehen/ausziehen; **c. brush**, Kleiderbürste *f;* **c. line**, Wäscheleine *f;* **c. peg**, Wäscheklammer *f.* ◆'**clothing**, *s.* (*articles of*) **c.**, Kleidungsstücke *npl;* the **c. industry/trade**, die Bekleidungsindustrie *f.*

cloud [klaud]. **I.** *s.* Wolke *f.* **II.** *v.i.* (*of sky*) to **c. over**, sich bewölken. ◆'**cloudburst**, *s.* Wolkenbruch *m.* ◆'**cloudless**, *adj.* wolkenlos. ◆'**cloudy**, *adj.* (*of sky*) bewölkt; (*of liquid*) trübe.

clove[1] [kləuv], *s.* Gewürznelke *f.*

clove[2], *s. c.* **of garlic**, Knoblauchzehe *f.*

clover ['kləuvər], *s.* Klee *m.*

clown [klaun], *s.* Clown *m.*

club [klʌb]. **I.** *s.* **1.** *(a)* (*heavy stick*) Keule *f;* (*b*) (*golfc:*) Schläger *m.* **2.** *pl.* (*in cards*) Kreuz *n.* **3.** Verein *m;* *esp. Sp:* Klub *m.* **II.** *v.* **1.** *v.tr.* (j-n) mit einer Keule schlagen. **2.** *v.i.* to **c. together**, sich zusammentun. ◆'**clubhouse**, *s.* Klubhaus *n.*

cluck [klʌk], *v.i.* glucken.

clue [klu:], *s.* Anhaltspunkt *m;* (*in crossword*) Stichwort *n;* *F:* **I haven't a c.**, ich habe keinen Schimmer. ◆'**clueless**, *adj. F:* doof.

clump [klʌmp], *s. c.* **of trees**, Baumgruppe *f; c.* **of bushes**, Gebüsch *n.*

clumsy ['klʌmzi], *adj.* (*of pers., manner etc.*) ungeschickt; (*awkward*) linkisch.

clutch [klʌtʃ]. **I.** *s.* **1.** to **be in s.o.'s clutches**, in j-s Gewalt sein. **2.** *Aut:* Kupplung *f.* **II.** *v.tr.* (j-n) festhalten. **2.** *v.i.* to **c. at sth.**, nach etwas *dat* greifen.

clutter ['klʌtər]. **I.** *s.* Kram *m.* **II.** *v.tr.* to

c. (up) a **room with sth.**, ein Zimmer mit etwas *dat* vollstopfen.

co- [kəu-], *prefix* Mit-; **co-author**, Mitverfasser *m; Av:* **co-pilot**, Kopilot *m.*

coach [kəutʃ]. **I.** *s.* **1.** *(a)* (*motor*) Omnibus *m;* (*b*) *Rail:* Wagen *m;* (*c*) (*horse-drawn*) Kutsche *f.* **2.** *Sp:* Trainer *m.* **II.** *v.tr.* (*a*) (j-m) Nachhilfestunden geben; (*b*) *Sp:* (j-n) trainieren.

coagulate [kəu'æguleit], *v.tr. & i.* gerinnen.

coal [kəul], *s.* Kohle *f.* ◆'**coalfield**, *s.* Kohlenrevier *m.* ◆'**coalmine**, *s.* Kohlenbergwerk *n.*

coalesce [kəuə'les], *v.i.* (*grow together*) aneinanderwachsen; (*fuse*) verschmelzen.

coalition [kəuə'liʃ(ə)n], *s.* Koalition *f.*

coarse [kɔːs], *adj.* grob; (*of joke*) derb. ◆'**coarseness**, *s.* Grobheit *f.*

coast [kəust], *s.* Küste *f; F:* the **c. is clear**, die Luft ist rein. ◆'**coastal**, *adj.* Küsten-; **c. waters**, Küstengewässer *npl.* ◆'**coaster**, *s.* **1.** *Nau:* Küstenfahrzeug *n.* **2.** (*small mat*) Untersetzer *m.* ◆'**coastguard**, *s.* Küstenwacht *f.* ◆'**coastline**, *s.* Küstenlinie *f.*

coat [kəut]. **I.** *s.* **1.** Mantel *m.* **2. c. of arms**, Wappen *n.* **3.** Fell *n* (einer Katze usw.). **4.** (*layer*) Schicht *f;* (*of paint*) Anstrich *m.* **II.** *v.tr.* (einen Keks, eine Pille mit Schokolade, Zucker usw.) überziehen. ◆'**coat(-)hanger**, *s.* Kleiderbügel *m.* ◆'**coating**, *s.* (*of sugar, chocolate*) Überzug *m.*

coax [kəuks], *v.tr.* (j-m) gut zureden; (*persuade*) (j-n) überreden.

cob [kɔb], *s.* **corn on the c.**, Maiskolben *m.*

cobble [kɔbl], *s. c.* (**stone**), Kopfstein *m;* **cobbles**, Kopfsteinpflaster *n.* ◆'**cobbled**, *adj.* **c. street**, Straße *f* mit Kopfsteinpflaster. ◆'**cobbler**, *s. A:* Flickschuster *m.*

cobra ['kəubrə], *s.* Kobra *f.*

cobweb ['kɔbweb], *s.* Spinngewebe *n.*

cocaine [kəu'kein], *s.* Kokain *n.*

cock [kɔk], *s.* (*fowl*) Hahn *m.* ◆'**cocky**, *adj.* großspurig.

cockerel ['kɔk(ə)rəl], *s.* Hähnchen *n.*

cock-eyed [kɔk'aid], *adj. F:* schief.

cockle [kɔkl], *s.* Herzmuschel *f.*

cockney ['kɔkni], *s.* Cockney *m.*

cockpit ['kɔkpit], *s.* Cockpit *n.*

cockroach ['kɔkrəutʃ], *s.* Küchenschabe *f.*

cocktail ['kɔkteil], *s.* Cocktail *m.*

cocoa ['kəukəu], *s.* Kakao *m.*

coconut ['kəukənʌt], *s.* Kokosnuß *f.*

cocoon [kə'ku:n], *s.* Kokon *m.*

cod [kɔd], *s. c.*(**-fish**), Kabeljau *m; c.*-**liver oil**, Lebertran *m.*

code [kəud], *s.* **1.** (*system of rules*) Code *m;* **highway c.**, Straßenverkehrsordnung *f.* **2. c. word**, Codewort *n;* **a message written in c.**, eine chiffrierte Mitteilung.

co-education ['kəuedju'keiʃ(ə)n], *s.* Koedukation *f.*

coerce [kəu'ə:s], v.tr. (j-n) zwingen (**into doing sth.**, etwas zu tun). ◆**coercion** [-'ə:ʃən], s. Zwang m.

co-existence ['kəuig'zistəns], s. peaceful c., friedliche Koexistenz.

coffee ['kɔfi], s. Kaffee m; **white c.**, Kaffee mit Milch; **instant c.**, löslicher Kaffee m; **c. pot**, Kaffeekanne f; **c. break**, Kaffeepause f; **c. table**, Couchtisch m.

coffin ['kɔfin], s. Sarg m.

cog [kɔg], s. Zahn m. ◆**'cogwheel**, s. Zahnrad n.

cognac ['kɔnjæk], s. Kognak m.

coherent [kəu'hiərənt], adj. (a) zusammenhängend; (of argument) konsequent; (b) (comprehensible) verständlich.

coil [kɔil], s. 1. (of rope etc.) Rolle f. 2. El: Spule f; Aut: (ignition) c., Zündspule f. 3. Med: Spirale f.

coin [kɔin]. I. s. Münze f. II. v.tr. (Geld, Fig: einen Ausdruck) prägen. ◆**'coinbox**, s. c. telephone, Münzfernsprecher m.

coincide [kəuin'said], v.i. (a) (of events etc.) zusammenfallen; (b) (of ideas etc.) übereinstimmen. ◆**coincidence** [kəu'insidəns], s. Zufall m.

coke¹ [kauk], s. Koks m.

coke², s. F: (abbr. for R.t.m coca-cola) Cola f.

colander ['kʌləndər], s. Durchschlag m (für Gemüse).

cold [kəuld]. I. adj. s. 1. kalt; **I feel/I am c.**, mir ist (es) kalt; F: **he got c. feet**, er hat kalte Füße gekriegt. 2. (a) (unfriendly) kühl; F: **to give s.o. the c. shoulder**, j-m die kalte Schulter zeigen; (unfeeling) **that leaves me c.**, das läßt mich kalt; **in c. blood**, kaltblütig. II. s. 1. Kälte f. 2. Med: Erkältung f; **c. in the head**, Schnupfen m; **to catch a cold**, sich erkälten. ◆**'cold-'blooded**, adj. kaltblütig.

collaborate [kə'læbəreit], v.i. zusammenarbeiten. ◆**collabo'ration**, s. Mitarbeit f. ◆**co'llaborator**, s. Mitarbeiter(in) m(f) (an einem Projekt).

collapse [kə'læps]. I. s. (a) Einsturz m (eines Gebäudes usw.); (b) Zusammenbruch m (eines Reiches usw.). II. v.i. (of building, wall) einstürzen; (of plans etc.) auffliegen; (of pers.) zusammenbrechen. ◆**co'llapsible**, adj. zusammenklappbar.

collar ['kɔlər]. I. s. 1. Kragen m. 2. (for dog etc.) Halsband n. II. v.tr. to c. s.o., j-n anhalten; (of police) j-n erwischen. ◆**'collar-bone**, s. Schlüsselbein n.

collate [kə'leit], v.tr. zusammentragen.

colleague ['kɔli:g], s. Kollege m; Kollegin f.

collect [kə'lekt]. v. 1. v.tr. (a) sammeln; (take in) (Schulhefte usw.) einsammeln; (pick up) (Papierabfälle usw.) auflesen; (b) (Beiträge, Schulden usw.) einkassieren; **to c. taxes**, Steuern einziehen; (of pers.) (seine Gedanken) sammeln; **to c. oneself**, sich aufraffen; (d) (fetch) abholen. 2. v.i. (of crowd, dust, water etc.) sich ansammeln. 3. attrib. N.Am: c. call, R-Gespräch n. ◆**co'llected**, adj. (a) c. works, gesammelte Werke; (b) (of pers.) calm and c., ruhig und gefaßt. ◆**co'llection**, s. 1. Sammlung f. 2. Leerung f (eines Briefkastens). 3. (a) Ecc: Kollekte f; (b) (for charity) Sammlung f. ◆**co'llective**, adj. (of property, efforts etc.) gemeinsam. ◆**co'llector**, s. Sammler(in) m(f).

college ['kɔlidʒ], s. 1. Brit: Hochschule f; **c. of technology**, approx. technische Hochschule f; **c. of further education**, approx. Volkshochschule f. 2. N.Am: (kleinere) Universität f.

collide [kə'laid], v.i. zusammenstoßen. ◆**collision** [kə'liʒ(ə)n], s. Zusammenstoß m.

colliery ['kɔljəri], s. Kohlengrube f.

colloquial [kə'ləukwiəl], adj. umgangssprachlich.

collusion [kə'lju:ʒ(ə)n], s. Kollusion f; **to act in c. with s.o.**, in geheimer Absprache mit j-m handeln.

Cologne [kə'ləun]. Pr.n. Köln n.

Colombia [kə'lɔmbiə]. Pr.n. Kolumbien n.

colon ['kəulən], s. 1. Doppelpunkt m. 2. Anat: Dickdarm m.

colonel ['kə:nl], s. Oberst m.

colony ['kɔləni], s. Kolonie f. ◆**colonial** [kə'ləunjəl], adj. kolonial. ◆**'colonist**, s. Kolonist m. ◆**coloni'zation**, s. Kolonisation f. ◆**'colonize**, v.tr. (ein Land usw.) kolonisieren; (ein Gebiet) besiedeln.

color, s. N.Am: = colour.

colossal [kə'lɔs(ə)l], adj. riesig.

colour ['kʌlər]. I. s. 1. (a) Farbe f. (b) scheme, Farbkombination f; c. film, Farbfilm m; c. television, Farbfernsehen n; (b) F: off c., nicht ganz auf der Höhe. II. v.tr. färben. ◆**'colourblind**, adj. farbenblind. ◆**'coloured**. I. adj. (a) farbig; (brightly) c., bunt; (b) Fig: (biased) gefärbt. II. s. pl. coloureds, Buntwäsche f. ◆**'colouring**, s. (dye) Farbstoff m. ◆**'colourless**, adj. farblos.

colt [kault], s. Hengstfohlen m.

column ['kɔləm], s. 1. Arch: Säule f; Anat: spinal c., Wirbelsäule f. 2. Mil: Kolonne f. 3. (a) (in newspaper) Spalte f; (b) c. of figures, Kolonne f von Zahlen. ◆**'columnist**, s. Kolumnist(in) m(f).

coma ['kəumə], s. Koma n.

comb [kəum]. I. s. Kamm m. II. v.tr. kämmen; **to c. one's hair**, sich dat die Haare kämmen; Fig: **to c. the district**, die Gegend absuchen.

combat ['kɔmbæt]. I. s. Kampf m. II. v.tr. bekämpfen.

combine. I. [kəm'bain], v. 1. v.tr. (Eigenschaften usw.) kombinieren; **to c. forces**, die Kräfte vereinigen; **to c. business with pleasure**, das Angenehme mit dem Nützlichen verbinden. 2. *v.i.* sich zusammenschließen. II. ['kɒmbain] *s.* **c.** harvester, Mähdrescher *m.* ◆**combination** [kɒmbi'neiʃ(ə)n], *s.* Kombination *f.* ◆**com'bined,** *adj.* **c.** efforts, gemeinsame Anstrengungen *fpl.*

combustion [kəm'bʌstʃ(ə)n], *s.* Verbrennung *f;* **c.** engine, Verbrennungsmotor *m.*

come [kʌm], *v.i.irr. kommen; F:* **he had it coming to him,** er hat es durchaus verdient; **c. to that,** in dem Fall; **that's what comes of doing nothing,** das kommt davon, wenn man nichts tut; **to c. to nothing,** zu nichts führen; **nothing will c. of this,** da wird nichts draus; **it comes to £5,** das macht £5; **to c. to think of it,** wenn ich's mir überlege; **that comes easily to him,** das fällt ihm leicht; **in years to c.,** in späteren Jahren. ◆'**come a'bout,** *v.i.* geschehen. ◆'**come a'cross,** *v.tr. auf* (j-n, etwas *acc*) stoßen. ◆'**come-back,** *s.* Comeback *n.* ◆'**come 'by,** *v.tr.* zurückkommen **(to** sth., auf etwas *acc*). ◆'**come 'by,** *v.i.* **1.** *v.tr.* (etwas) auftreiben; *(by accident)* zu (etwas *dat*) kommen. **2.** *v.i.* vorbeikommen. ◆'**come 'down,** *v.i. (of ceiling etc.)* herunterfallen; *(of rain, prices etc.)* fallen; **it all comes d. to his pride,** es ist alles auf seinen Stolz zurückzuführen. ◆'**come 'forward,** *v.i. (report)* sich melden. ◆'**come 'in,** *v.i. (a)* hereinkommen; *(of train etc.)* einfahren; *Com: (of mail, order etc.)* eingehen; *(answer to knock)* **c. in!** herein! *(b)* **that will c. in handy,** das wird mir zugute kommen; *(c)* **to c. in for criticism,** Kritik einstecken müssen. ◆'**come 'off,** *v.* **1.** *v.tr. F:* **c. off it!** das glaubst du doch nicht im Ernst! **2.** *v.i. (a) (of thing)* loskommen; *(of button etc.)* abgehen; *(of attempt)* **it came off,** es hat geklappt; *(c) (of pers.)* **to c. off badly,** schlecht abschneiden. ◆'**come 'on,** *v.i. (a) (make progress)* Fortschritte machen; **(b)** *int.* **c. on!** (i) komm schon! (ii) *(in disbelief)* na hör mal! ◆'**come 'out,** *v.i. (a)* herauskommen; *(of stars, book)* erscheinen; **to c. out with the truth,** mit der Wahrheit herausrücken; *(b)* Ind: *(of workers)* **to c. out** (on strike), streiken; *(c) (of stain)* herausgehen; **how did the pictures c. out?** wie sind die Bilder geworden? ◆'**come 'over,** *v.i.* **what has c. o. you?** was ist in dich gefahren? ◆'**come 'round,** *v.i. (a)* **you must c. r. and see us,** Sie müssen uns besuchen kommen; *(b) (regain consciousness)* (wieder) zu sich *dat* kommen. ◆'**come 'to,** *v.i.* zu sich *dat* kommen. ◆'**come 'up,** *v.i. (a)* heraufkommen; *(b)* **to c. up to s.o.,** an j-n herantreten; *(c) (of seeds)* sprießen; *(d)* **to c. up** (for discussion), zur Diskussion kommen; *(e)* **to c. up to s.o.'s expectations,** j-s Erwartungen erfüllen; *(f)* **to c. up against difficulties,**

auf Schwierigkeiten stoßen; *(g) (reach)* **the water comes up to my waist,** das Wasser reicht mir bis zur Taille. ◆'**coming. I.** *adj.* kommend; **the c. year,** das kommende Jahr. **II.** *s.* **a lot of c. and going,** viel Hin und Her.

comedy ['kɒmədi], *s.* Komödie *f.* ◆**comedian** [kə'mi:diən], *s.* Komiker *m.*

comet ['kɒmit], *s.* Komet *m.*

comfort ['kʌmfət]. **I.** *s.* **1.** Trost *m;* **to take c.,** Trost finden. **2.** *(a)* **the comforts of life,** die Annehmlichkeiten des Lebens; *(b) (luxury)* Komfort *m.* **II.** *v.tr.* (j-n) trösten. ◆**comfortable** ['kʌmftəbl], *adj.* bequem; **c.** off, wohlhabend. ◆'**comforting,** *adj.* tröstlich. ◆'**comfy,** *adj. F:* bequem.

comic ['kɒmik]. **I.** *adj.* komisch; **c.** strip, Comic Strip *m.* **II.** *s. (a) (pers.)* Komiker *m; (b)* Comic-Heft *n.*

comma ['kɒmə], *s.* Komma *n.*

command [kə'mɑːnd]. **I.** *s.* **1.** *(order)* Befehl *m.* **2.** *Mil: etc:* Kommando *n;* **to be in c.,** das Kommando haben. **3.** Beherrschung *f* (einer Sprache, einer Situation usw.). **II.** *v.tr. (a)* (j-m) befehlen, (etwas zu tun); *(b)* (ein Regiment usw.) führen; *(c)* (über ein großes Wissen, große Geldsummen usw.) verfügen; **to c. respect,** Achtung gebieten. ◆**comman'deer,** *v.tr.* beschlagnahmen. ◆**co'mmander,** *s.* Befehlshaber *m.* ◆**co'mmanding,** *adj.* **c.** officer, befehlshabender Offizier; *(of battalion)* Kommandeur *m.* ◆**co'mmandment,** *s.* Gebot *n.* ◆**co'mmando,** *s.* Mitglied *n* einer Kommandotruppe.

commemorate [kə'meməreit], *v.tr.* das Andenken (von j-m, etwas *dat*) feiern.

commence [kə'mens], *v.tr. & i.* anfangen. ◆**co'mmencement,** *s.* Anfang *m.*

commend [kə'mend], *v.tr. (a) (praise)* (j-n) loben; *(b) (recommend)* (j-m etwas) empfehlen; ◆**co'mmendable,** *adj.* lobenswert. ◆**commen'dation,** *s.* Lob *n.* **2.** Empfehlung *f.*

commensurate [kə'menʃərət], *adj.* angemessen **(to/with** sth., etwas *dat*).

comment ['kɒment]. **I.** *s.* Bemerkung *f;* **no c.!** Kommentar überflüssig! **II.** *v.i. (casually)* Bemerkungen machen **(on** sth., über etwas *acc*); **to c. on a text,** einen Text kommentieren. ◆'**commentary,** *s.* Kommentar *m.* ◆'**commentator,** *s.* Kommentator *m.*

commerce ['kɒmɜːs], *s.* Handel *m.* ◆**co'mmercial. I.** *adj.* Handels-; **c.** traveller, Handelsreisende(r) *m;* **c.** vehicle, Nutzfahrzeug *n.* **II.** *s. TV:* Werbespot *m; (script)* Werbetext *m.* ◆**co'mmercialize,** *v.tr.* kommerzialisieren.

commiserate [kə'mizəreit], *v.i.* **to c. with** s.o., j-m sein Mitgefühl aussprechen.

commission [kə'miʃ(ə)n]. **I.** s. 1. (*board of enquiry*) Kommission f. 2. Mil: Offizierspatent n. 3. (*order etc.*) Auftrag m. 4. **my car is out of c.**, mein Auto ist außer Betrieb. 5. Com: Provision f; **to work on c.**, auf Provision arbeiten. **II.** v.tr. (einen Künstler usw.) beauftragen; (ein Porträt usw.) in Auftrag geben. ◆**commis'sionaire**, s. Portier m. ◆**co'mmissioner**, s. **c. of police**, approx. Polizeikommissar m.

commit [kə'mit], v.tr. (a) (ein Verbrechen, Selbstmord usw.) begehen. (b) **to c. oneself**, sich festlegen; **a committed person**, ein engagierter Mensch; (c) **to c. sth. to memory**, sich etwas einprägen; **to c. s.o. for trial**, j-n dem Gericht überweisen. ◆**co'mmitment**, s. (a) Engagement f; (*obligation*) Verpflichtung f.

committee [kə'miti], s. Ausschuß m.

commodity [kə'mɔditi], s. Gebrauchsartikel m; pl. Gebrauchsgüter npl.

common ['kɔmən]. **I.** adj. 1. (*of property, interests etc.*) gemeinsam; **c. ground**, Diskussionsgrundlage f; Jur: **c. law**, Gewohnheitsrecht n; **C. Market**, Gemeinsamer Markt; Sch: **c. room**, Lehrerzimmer n. 2. (a) (*ordinary*) gewöhnlich; **the c. man**, der einfache Mann; F: **c. or garden**, ganz gewöhnlich; (b) (*frequent*) häufig; (*of views, practice etc.*) verbreitet; (*of expression, word*) geläufig; (c) **c. sense**, gesunder Menschenverstand. 3. Pej: (*of pers., manners etc.*) ordinär. **II.** s. 1. **to have sth. in c. with s.o.**, etwas mit j-m gemeinsam haben. 2. **c.** (*land*), Gemeindeland n. ◆**commoner**, s. Bürgerliche(r) f(m). ◆**commonplace**, adj. banal; (*frequent*) häufig. ◆**commons**, s. pl. **the** (*House of*) **C.**, das (britische) Unterhaus n. ◆**commonwealth**, s. **the C.**, das (britische) Commonwealth.

commotion [kə'məuʃ(ə)n], s. Aufruhr f.

communal [kə'mju:n(ə)l], adj. 1. (*shared*) gemeinschaftlich. 2. (*community*) Gemeinde-.

communicate [kə'mju:nikeit], v. 1. v.tr. (eine Nachricht, seine Gefühle usw.) mitteilen (to s.o., j-m). 2. v.i. (a) (*contact*) sich in Verbindung setzen; (b) (*make oneself understood*) sich verständlich machen. ◆**communication** [-i'keiʃ(ə)n], s. 1. Verständigung f; **c. cord**, Notbremse f. 2. (*message*) Mitteilung f. 3. pl. **communications**, (a) (*transport*) Verkehrsverbindungen fpl; Mil: **lines of c.**, Nachschublinien fpl; (b) (*telephone etc.*) Nachrichtenwesen n. ◆**co'mmunicative** [-ikətiv], adj. mitteilsam. ◆**co'mmunion** [-jən], s. (*Holy*) **C.**, das (heilige) Abendmahl; (*Catholic*) Kommunion f.

communism ['kɔmjunizm], s. Kommunismus m. ◆**communist. I.** s. Kommunist m. **II.** adj. kommunistisch.

community [kə'mju:niti], s. Gemein-

schaft f; **c. centre**, Freizeitzentrum n.

commute [kə'mju:t], v.i. pendeln. ◆**co'mmuter**, s. Pendler m.

compact¹ [kəm'pækt], adj. kompakt.

compact² ['kɔmpækt], s. (*powder*) c., Puderdose f.

companion [kəm'pænjən], s. Gefährte m; Gefährtin f. ◆**com'panionship**, s. Kameradschaft f; Gesellschaft f.

company ['kʌmpəni], s. 1. (a) Gesellschaft f; **to keep s.o. c.**, j-m Gesellschaft leisten; **to part c.** (**with s.o.**), sich (von j-m) trennen; (b) **we are expecting c.**, wir erwarten Besuch. 2. Com: Gesellschaft f; (*firm*) Firma f; (*large company*) Konzern m. 3. (a) Th: Schauspielertruppe f; (b) **ship's c.**, Besatzung f. 4. Mil: Kompanie f.

compare [kəm'peər], v. 1. v.tr. (j-n, etwas) vergleichen (to/with, mit + dat). 2. v.i. **to c. badly with s.o.**, sth., gegen j-n, etwas acc schlecht abschneiden. ◆**comparable** ['kɔmp(ə)rəbl], adj. vergleichbar (to/with, mit + dat). ◆**com'parative**, adj. 1. (*linguistics etc.*) Vergleichend. 2. (*of wealth etc.*) relativ; -ly, adv. verhältnismäßig. ◆**com'parison**, s. Vergleich m; **in c. to**, im Vergleich zu + dat.

compartment [kəm'pɑ:tmənt], s. 1. Rail: Abteil n. 2. (*of cupboard etc.*) Fach n; (*larger*) Abteilung f.

compass ['kʌmpəs], s. 1. Kompaß m. 2. (pair of) **compasses**, Zirkel m.

compassion [kəm'pæʃ(ə)n], s. Mitleid n. ◆**com'passionate**, adj. mitleidig; (*of pers., deed etc.*) erbarmungsvoll.

compatible [kəm'pætibl], adj. (a) (*of things*) vereinbar; (b) (*of pers.*) **they are very c.**, sie passen gut zusammen; (c) (*computers*) kompatibel. ◆**compatibility**, s. (a) (*of things*) Vereinbarkeit f; (b) Verträglichkeit f; (c) Kompatibilität f.

compatriot [kəm'pætriət], s. Landsmann m; Landsmännin f.

compel [kəm'pel], v.tr. (j-n) zwingen (etwas zu tun). ◆**com'pelling**, adj. (*of story, film etc.*) fesselnd.

compensate ['kɔmpənseit], v. 1. v.tr. (j-n) entschädigen. 2. v.i. **to c. for a disadvantage**, einen Nachteil ausgleichen. ◆**compen'sation**, s. Entschädigung f.

compère ['kɔmpeər], s. Conférencier m.

compete [kəm'pi:t], v.i. (a) konkurrieren; (b) **to c. for a prize**, sich einen Preis bewerben.

competent ['kɔmpitənt], adj. 1. (*of worker etc.*) tüchtig. 2. Jur: Adm: etc: kompetent. ◆**'competence**, s. 1. Tüchtigkeit f. 2. Jur: Adm: Kompetenz f.

competition [kɔmpi'tiʃ(ə)n], s. 1. Com: etc: Konkurrenz f. 2. Wettbewerb m; (in magazine etc.) Preisausschreiben n. ◆**com'petitive**, adj. (a) Wettbewerbs-; (b) (*of prices, products etc.*) konkurrenzfähig. ◆**com'petitor**, s. Konkurrent m; Sp: Teilnehmer m.

compile [kəm'pail], *v.tr.* zusammenstellen. ◆**compi'lation**, *s.* Zusammenstellung *f.*

complacent [kəm'pleis(ə)nt], *adj.* selbstzufrieden. ◆**com'placency**, *s.* Selbstzufriedenheit *f.*

complain [kəm'plein], *v.i.* (a) klagen; (b) (*formally*) sich beschweren. ◆**com'plaint**, *s.* 1. Klage *f.* 2. Beschwerde *f.*; **to lodge a c. against s.o.**, sth., gegen j-n, über etwas *acc* Beschwerde führen. 3. (*illness*) Leiden *n.*

complement ['kɔmplimənt]. I. *s.* 1. full c., volle Anzahl/Menge. 2. Ergänzung *f.* II. *v.tr.* ergänzen. ◆**comple'mentary**, *adj.* ergänzend.

complete [kəm'pli:t]. I. *adj.* 1. (a) vollständig; (b) (*concluded*) abgeschlossen. 2. **he is a c. stranger to me**, er ist mir völlig fremd; **it came as a c. surprise to me**, es kam für mich ganz überraschend. II. *v.tr.* (a) (eine Sammlung usw.) vervollständigen; (eine Arbeit, ein Buch usw.) abschließen; (b) **to c. a form**, ein Formular ausfüllen; **-ly**, *adv.* völlig. ◆**com'pletion**, *s.* 1. Fertigstellung *f.*; **it is nearing c.**, es wird bald fertig. 2. *Jur: Com:* **on c. of contract**, nach Vertragserfüllung.

complex ['kɔmpleks]. I. *adj.* (of situation etc.) verwickelt; (of structure etc.) komplex. II. *s.* Komplex *m.*; **Minderwertigkeitskomplex** *m.* ◆**com'plexity**, *s.* Kompliziertheit *f.*

complexion [kəm'plekʃ(ə)n], *s.* Teint *m.*

complicate ['kɔmplikeit], *v.tr.* (etwas) komplizieren. ◆**complicated**, *adj.* kompliziert. ◆**compli'cation**, *s.* Komplikation *f.*

complicity [kəm'plisiti], *s.* Mitschuld *f.*

compliment ['kɔmplimənt]. I. *s.* Kompliment *n.*; **to pay s.o. a c.**, j-m ein Kompliment machen; **with compliments**, mit besten Empfehlungen. II. *v.tr.* (j-m) ein Kompliment machen; **to c. s.o. on his success**, j-n zu seinem Erfolg beglückwünschen. ◆**complimentary** [-'ment(ə)ri], *adj.* (a) (of remark etc.) schmeichelhaft; (b) **c. ticket**, Freikarte *f.*

comply [kəm'plai], *v.i.* **to c. with a rule**, sich einer Regel fügen; **to c. with a request**, einer Bitte nachkommen.

component [kəm'pəunənt]. I. *s.* Bestandteil *m.* II. *adj.* **c. parts**, Einzelteile *npl.*

compose [kəm'pəuz], *v.tr.* (a) *Mus:* komponieren; (b) **to c. oneself**, sich fassen. ◆**com'posed**, *adj.* 1. (of pers.) gefaßt; (of manner etc.) gelassen. 2. **to be c. of sth.**, aus etwas *dat* bestehen. ◆**com'poser**, *s.* Komponist *m.* ◆**composition** [kɔmpə'ziʃ(ə)n], *s.* 1. Komposition *f.*; (essay) Aufsatz *m.* 2. Zusammensetzung *f* (eines Stoffes, einer Arznei usw.). ◆**composure** [-'pəuʒər], *s.* Gelassenheit *f.*

compost ['kɔmpɔst], *s.* Kompost *m.*

compound ['kɔmpaund]. I. *adj.* zusammengesetzt; **c. fracture**, komplizierter Bruch; **c. interest**, Zinseszins *m.* II. *s. Ch:* Verbindung *f.*

comprehend [kɔmpri'hend], *v.tr.* begreifen. ◆**comprehension** [kɔmpri-'henʃ(ə)n], *s.* Verständnis *n;* (capacity) Fassungsvermögen *n.* ◆**comprehensible**, *adj.* verständlich. ◆**comprehensive**, *adj.* umfassend; **c. school**, Gesamtschule *f;* **c. insurance**, Vollkasko *n.*

compress. I. [kəm'pres], *v.tr.* verdichten; **compressed air**, Druckluft *f.* II. ['kɔmpres], *s.* Kompresse *f.* ◆**compression** [-'preʃ(ə)n], *s.* Kompression *f.*

comprise [kəm'praiz], *v.tr.* **to c. sth.**, aus etwas *dat* bestehen.

compromise ['kɔmprəmaiz]. I. *s.* Kompromiß *m.* II. *v.* 1. *v.tr.* (j-n) kompromittieren. 2. *v.i.* einen Kompromiß schließen. ◆**compromising**, *adj.* kompromittierend.

compulsion [kəm'pʌlʃ(ə)n], *s.* Zwang *m.* ◆**compulsive** [-siv], *adj.* Zwangs-. ◆**compulsory** [-səri], *adj.* obligatorisch; Pflicht-.

computer [kəm'pju:tər], *s.* Computer *m,* Rechner *m.*

comrade ['kɔmreid, -rid], *s.* (a) Kamerad *m,* Kameradin *f;* (b) *Pol:* Genosse *m,* Genossin *f.*

con [kɔn]. *P:* I. *adj.* **c. man**, Hochstapler *m.* II. *v.tr.* (j-n) reinlegen; **to c. s.o. into sth.**, j-m etwas andrehen.

concave ['kɔnkeiv], *adj.* konkav.

conceal [kən'si:l], *v.tr.* verbergen (from s.o., vor j-m). ◆**con'cealed**, *adj.* versteckt; **c. lighting**, indirekte Beleuchtung.

concede [kən'si:d], *v.tr.* **to c. that ...**, einräumen/zugeben, daß ...; **to c. a point**, in einem Punkt nachgeben.

conceit [kən'si:t], *s.* Eingebildetheit *f.* ◆**con'ceited**, *adj.* eingebildet.

conceive [kən'si:v], *v.tr.* (a) (ein Kind) empfangen; (b) sich *dat* (einen Plan usw.) ausdenken; (c) (understand) begreifen. ◆**con'ceivable**, *adj.* denkbar; **the worst c. result**, das denkbar schlechteste Ergebnis; **-ably**, *adv.* **he could (not) c. ...**, es ist (nicht) möglich/denkbar, daß er ...

concentrate ['kɔnsəntreit], *v.* 1. *v.tr.* konzentrieren. 2. *v.i.* **to c. (on sth.)**, sich auf etwas *acc* konzentrieren. ◆**concen'tration**, *s.* Konzentration *f.*

concept ['kɔnsept], *s.* Begriff *m.* **conception** [kən'sepʃ(ə)n], *s.* 1. Empfängnis *f* (eines Kindes). 2. (idea) Vorstellung *f.*

concern [kən'sə:n]. I. *s.* 1. (matter) Angelegenheit *f.* 2. (worry) Besorgnis *f. Com:* Unternehmen *n.* II. *v.tr.* (a) (j-n) angehen; **as far as I'm concerned**, mich betrifft; **the persons concerned**, die Beteiligten; (b) (*worry*) (j-n) beunruhigen; **we are concerned for her safety,** wir sind um ihre Sicherheit besorgt. ◆**con'cerning,** *prep.* bezüglich *gen.*

concert ['kɔnsət], *s.* Konzert *n; c.* **hall,** Konzertsaal *m.* ◆**concerted** [kən'səːtid], *adj.* **c. efforts,** vereinte Anstrengungen.

concertina [kɔnsə'tiːnə], *s.* Konzertina *f.*

concerto [kən'tʃəːtəu], *s.* Konzert *n.*

concession [kən'seʃ(ə)n], *s.* **to make a c.** **to s.o.,** j-m ein Zugeständnis machen.

conciliatory [kən'siliət(ə)ri], *adj.* (*calming*) beschwichtigend; (*reconciling*) versöhnend.

concise [kən'sais], *adj.* knapp (gefaßt); (*of style, expression*) prägnant.

conclude [kən'kluːd], *v.* 1. *v.tr.* (a) (*finish*) beenden; (b) (*deduce*) folgern. ◆**con'clusion** [-ʒən], *s.* 1. Abschluß *m* (einer Rede, eines Vertrags usw.). 2. Folgerung *f;* **to come to the c. that ...,** zu dem Schluß kommen, daß ... ◆**con'clusive** [-siv], *adj.* entscheidend.

concoct [kən'kɔkt], *v.tr.* (a) (in einem Gericht) selber erfinden; (ein Getränk) zusammenbrauen; (b) (einen Plan usw.) aushecken. ◆**con'coction,** *s.* 1. (*dish*) selbsterfundenes Gericht *n;* (*drink*) Gebräu *n.* 2. (*tale*) Lügengeschichte *f.*

concrete ['kɔnkriːt]. I. *adj.* 1. (*of form, proposal*) konkret. 2. (*of surface etc.*) betoniert, e.g. **pillar,** Betonpfeiler *m.* II. *s.* Beton *m;* **reinforced c.,** Stahlbeton *m.*

concur [kən'kəːr], *v.i.* (*agree*) übereinstimmen.

concussion [kən'kʌʃ(ə)n], *s.* Gehirnerschütterung *f.*

condemn [kən'dem], *v.tr.* (a) (j-n) verurteilen; (b) (ein Haus usw.) für untauglich erklären. ◆**condem'nation,** *s.* Verurteilung *f.*

condense [kən'dens], *v.* 1. *v.tr.* (einen Bericht) zusammenfassen. 2. *v.i.* (*of vapour*) sich kondensieren. ◆**conden'sation,** *s.* (*moisture*) Kondensat *n;* (*process*) Kondensation *f.* ◆**con'densed,** *adj.* **c. milk,** Kondensmilch *f.*

condescend [kɔndi'send], *v.i.* sich herablassen (**to do sth.,** etwas zu tun). ◆**condes'cending,** *adj.* herablassend.

condition [kən'diʃ(ə)n]. I. *s.* 1. (*requirement*) Bedingung *f;* **on c. that,** unter der Bedingung, daß ... 2. *pl.* (*circumstances*) Verhältnisse *npl.* 3. (*state*) Zustand *m.* II. *v.tr.* (einen Stoff, j-n) konditionieren. ◆**con'ditional,** *adj.* (a) (*of agreement etc.*) bedingt; (b) **c. on sth.,** von etwas *dat* abhängig. ◆**con'ditioner,** *s.* (a) (*hair*) c., Haarkur *f;* (b) (*fabric*) c., Weichspüler *m.*

condolence [kən'dəuləns], *s.* **to offer s.o. one's condolences,** j-m sein Beileid aussprechen.

condone [kən'dəun], *v.tr.* (etwas) stillschweigend dulden.

conducive [kən'djuːsiv], *adj.* **to be c. to sth.,** etwas *dat* förderlich sein.

conduct I. ['kɔndʌkt], *s.* (*behaviour*) Benehmen *n;* Verhalten *n; Sch:* Betragen *n.* II. [kən'dʌkt], *v.tr.* (a) (j-n) führen; **conducted tour (of a town etc.),** Führung *f* (durch eine Stadt usw.); (b) **to c. s.o.'s affairs,** j-s Geschäfte führen; (c) (ein Orchester) dirigieren; (d) (Wärme, Strom) leiten. ◆**con'ductor,** *s.* 1. (a) *Mus:* Dirigent *m;* (b) (*f* con'ductress) (*on bus*) Schaffner(in) *m(f).* 2. *El:* Leiter *m;* **lightning c.,** Blitzableiter *m.*

cone [kəun], *s.* 1. Kegel *m;* (*ice-cream*) c., Tüte *f.* 2. *Bot:* Zapfen *m.*

confectioner [kən'fekʃ(ə)nər], *s.* Konditor *m.* ◆**confectionery** [kən'fekʃ(ə)n(ə)ri], *s.* Süßwaren *fpl.*

confederation [kənfedə'reiʃ(ə)n], *s.* Bund *m; esp.* Staatenbund *m.*

confer [kən'fəːr], *v.* 1. *v.tr.* **to c. a title etc. on s.o.,** j-m einen Titel usw. verleihen. 2. *v.i.* sich beraten. ◆**conference** ['kɔnfərəns], *s.* Konferenz *f;* **press c.,** Pressekonferenz *f.*

confess [kən'fes], *v.tr. & i.* (a) **to c. to a crime,** ein Verbrechen gestehen; (b) (*admit*) (etwas) zugeben; **I must c. that ...,** ich muß gestehen, daß ...; (c) *Ecc:* (seine Sünden) beichten. ◆**con'fessed,** *adj.* (**self-)c.,** erklärt. ◆**confession** [-'feʃ(ə)n], *s.* 1. Geständnis *n.* 2. *Ecc:* Beichte *f.*

confide [kən'faid], *v.tr.* **to c. in s.o.,** sich j-m anvertrauen. ◆**confidence** ['kɔnfid(ə)ns], *s.* (a) Vertrauen *n* (in, zu + dat) **in c.,** im Vertrauen; (b) (**self-)c.,** Selbstvertrauen *n.* ◆**'confident,** *adj.* (a) (**self-)c.,** selbstbewußt; (b) (*optimistic*) zuversichtlich; **to be c. that ...,** überzeugt sein, daß ... ◆**confidential** [-'denʃ(ə)l], *adj.* vertraulich; **-ly,** *adv.* im Vertrauen.

confine [kən'fain], *v.tr.* (a) **confined to bed,** ans Bett gefesselt; (b) **confined space,** enger Raum; (c) **to confine oneself to doing sth.,** sich darauf beschränken, etwas zu tun. ◆**con'finement,** *s.* 1. *solitary* c., Einzelhaft *f.* 2. (*of pregnant woman*) Niederkunft *f.*

confirm [kən'fəːm], *v.tr.* (a) (ein Gerücht, einen Auftrag usw.) bestätigen; (b) *Ecc:* (j-n) konfirmieren. ◆**confirmation** [kɔnfə'meiʃ(ə)n], *s.* 1. Bestätigung *f.* 2. *Ecc:* Konfirmation *f.* ◆**con'firmed,** *adj.* **c. bachelor,** eingefleischter Junggeselle.

confiscate ['kɔnfiskeit], *v.tr.* beschlagnahmen. ◆**confis'cation,** *s.* Beschlagnahmung *f.*

conflagration [kɔnflə'greiʃ(ə)n], *s.* Feuersbrunst *f.*

conflict I. *s.* ['kɔnflikt]. I. *s.* 1. (*fight*) Kampf *m.* 2. Konflikt *m* (von Interessen usw.). II. [kən'flikt] *v.i.* **to c. with sth.,** zu etwas *dat* in Widerspruch stehen. ◆**con'flicting,** *adj.* sich widersprechend; (*of feelings*) widerstreitend.

conform [kənˈfɔːm], v.i. sich anpassen (to, dat). ◆**conformity**, s. Anpassung f (to, an + dat).

confront [kənˈfrʌnt], v.tr. (einer Gefahr usw.) ins Auge sehen; **to c. s.o. with the truth**, j-n mit der Wahrheit konfrontieren. ◆**confrontation** [kən–], s. Konfrontation f.

confuse [kənˈfjuːz], v.tr. (a) (eine Sache mit einer anderen) verwechseln; (b) (j-n) verwirren. ◆**confused**, adj. (of pers.) verwirrt; (of report etc.) verworren; **to get c.**, in Verwirrung geraten. ◆**confusion** [-ʒ(ə)n], s. Verwirrung f.

congeal [kənˈdʒiːl], v.i. (of blood) gerinnen.

congenital [kənˈdʒenitl], adj. angeboren.

conger [ˈkɒŋgər], s. c. **eel**, grauer Meeraal.

congested [kənˈdʒestid], adj. (of roads, nose) verstopft; (of traffic) gestaut; (overcrowded) überfüllt. ◆**congestion**, [-ˈdʒestʃ(ə)n], s. Verstopfung f; (traffic) c., Verkehrsstauung f.

conglomeration [kənglɒmǝˈreiʃ(ə)n], s. Ansammlung f, Pej: (hotchpotch) Mischmasch m.

congratulate [kənˈgrætjuleit], v.tr. (j-m) gratulieren (**on sth.**, zu etwas dat). ◆**congratulations**, s. pl. c.! herzlichen Glückwunsch!

congregate [ˈkɒŋgrigeit], v.i. sich versammeln. ◆**congregation**, s. (versammelte) Gemeinde f.

congress [ˈkɒŋgres], s. Kongreß m. ◆**congressman**, s. N.Am: Pol: Mitglied in den Repräsentantenhauses.

conical [ˈkɒnikl], adj. kegelförmig.

conifer [ˈkɒnifər], s. Nadelbaum m.

conjecture [kənˈdʒektʃər]. I. s. Mutmaßung f; pure c., reine Vermutung f. II. v.i. Vermutungen anstellen.

conjunction [kənˈdʒʌŋkʃ(ə)n], s. 1. Gram: Konjunktion f. 2. **in c. with**, in Verbindung mit + dat.

conjunctivitis [kəndʒʌŋkti'vaitis], s. Bindehautentzündung f.

conjure [ˈkʌndʒər], v. 1. v.tr. **to c. up memories etc.**, Erinnerungen usw. heraufbeschwören. 2. v.i. zaubern. ◆**conjuring**, s. Zauberei f. ◆**conjurer**, s. Zauberkünstler m.

conk [kɒŋk], v.i. P: **to c. out**, den Geist aufgeben.

conker [ˈkɒŋkər], s. F: Roßkastanie f.

connect [kəˈnekt], v.tr. (a) verbinden; (zwei Teile usw. aneinander) anschließen; **to c. sth. to sth.**, etwas mit etwas dat verbinden; esp. Tchn: etwas an etwas acc anschließen; (b) (associate) (etwas) verknüpfen. ◆**connecting**, adj. verbindend; c. **train**, Anschlußzug m. ◆**connection** [kəˈnekʃ(ə)n], s. (a) Verbindung f; El: Tel: Rail: Anschluß m; (b) (context) Zusammenhang m; **in c. with my application**, bezüglich meiner Bewerbung; (c) **to have connections**, Be-

ziehungen haben (**with**, zu + dat).

connoisseur [kɒnəˈsəːr], s. Kenner m.

conquer [ˈkɒŋkər], v.tr. (a) (j-n, Land) erobern; (b) (seiner Eifersucht usw.) Herr werden. ◆**conqueror**, s. Sieger m. ◆**conquest** [ˈkɒŋkwest], s. Eroberung f.

conscience [ˈkɒnʃəns], s. Gewissen n; **to have sth. on one's c.**, etwas auf dem Gewissen haben. ◆**conscientious** [-ʃiˈenʃəs], adj. gewissenhaft; c. **objector**, Kriegsdienstverweigerer m.

conscious [ˈkɒnʃəs], adj. 1. **to be c. of sth.**, (sich dat) etwas gen bewußt sein; c. **attempt**, bewußter Versuch m. 2. **to be c.**, bei Bewußtsein sein. ◆**consciousness**, s. **to lose c.**, das Bewußtsein verlieren; **to regain c.**, (wieder) zu Bewußtsein kommen.

conscript [ˈkɒnskript], s. Einberufene(r) f(m). ◆**conscription**, s. Einberufung f.

consecrate [ˈkɒnsikreit], v.tr. weihen.

consecutive [kənˈsekjutiv], adj. **on three c. days**, an drei aufeinanderfolgenden Tagen; adv. hintereinander.

consensus [kənˈsensəs], s. Übereinstimmung f.

consent [kənˈsent]. I. v.i. **to c. to sth.**, in etwas acc einwilligen. II. s. **to give (one's) c.**, seine Zustimmung geben; **by common c.**, nach allgemeiner Ansicht; **age of c.**, sexuelle Mündigkeit f.

consequence [ˈkɒnsikwəns], s. 1. Folge f; **to take the consequences**, die Folgen/die Konsequenzen tragen. 2. (importance) **it's of no c.**, es hat keinerlei Bedeutung. ◆**consequent**, adj. daraus folgend; **-ly**, adv. & conj. folglich.

conserve [kənˈsəːv], v.tr. **to c. energy**, Kräfte sparen. ◆**conservation** [kɒnsəˈveiʃ(ə)n], c. **(of the environment)**, Umweltschutz m. ◆**conservative** [-ˈətiv]. I. adj. (a) Pol: etc: konservativ; (b) **at a c. estimate**, niedrig geschätzt. II. s. Konservative(r) f(m). ◆**conservatory** [-ətri], s. Wintergarten m.

consider [kənˈsidər], v.tr. (a) (examine) (eine Frage usw.) erwägen; sich dat (eine Möglichkeit usw.) überlegen; (ein Angebot, eine Bewerbung usw.) berücksichtigen; **when you c. that ...**, wenn man bedenkt, daß ... (b) (take into account) (j-s Alter usw.) berücksichtigen, in Betracht ziehen; **all things considered**, wenn man alles in Betracht zieht; (c) (think) **I c. him crazy**, ich halte ihn für verrückt; **to c. oneself lucky**, sich glücklich schätzen. ◆**considerable**, adj. beträchtlich. ◆**considerate**, adj. rücksichtsvoll. ◆**consideration**, s. 1. **to take sth. into c.**, etwas berücksichtigen; **after careful c.**, nach reiflicher Überlegung; **that is a c.**, das ist schon eine Erwägung. 2. (thoughtfulness) Rücksicht f; **out of c. for s.o.**, aus Rücksicht auf j-n. 3. (payment) **for a small c.**, gegen ein geringes Ent-

gelt. ◆**con'sidered,** *adj.* my c. opinion, meine wohlüberlegte Meinung.
◆**con'sidering. I.** *prep.* c. his age, in
Anbetracht seines Alters. **II.** *adv.* F: it's
not so bad, c., unter den Umständen ist
das gar nicht so schlecht.

consignment [kən'sainmənt], *s.* Lieferung *f*.

consist [kən'sist], *v.i.* to c. of sth., aus
etwas *dat* bestehen. ◆**con'sistent,** *adj.*
1. (*a*) (*argument etc.*) konsequent; (*b*) (*un-
varying*) gleichmäßig. **2.** c. with, im
Einklang/vereinbar mit + *dat*.
◆**con'sistency,** *s.* **1.** (*a*) Konsequenz *f*;
(*b*) Gleichmäßigkeit *f* (der Leistungen).
2. (*thickness etc.*) Konsistenz *f*.

console [kən'səul], *v.tr.* trösten.
◆**consolation** [kɔnsə'leiʃ(ə)n], *s.* Trost
m; c. prize, Trostpreis *m*.

consolidate [kən'sɔlideit], *v.tr.* konsoli-
dieren.

consonant [kɔnsənənt], *s.* Konsonant *m*.

consortium [kən'sɔ:tiəm], *s.* Konsortium
n.

conspicuous [kən'spikjuəs], *adj.* auffallend; it is very c., es fällt sehr auf; to be
c. by one's absence, durch Abwesenheit
glänzen.

conspire [kən'spaiər], *v.i.* sich verschwö-
ren. ◆**conspiracy** [-'spirəsi], *s.* Verschwörung *f*. ◆**con'spirator,** *s.* Ver-
schwörer *m*.

constable [ˈkʌnstəbl], *s.* Polizist *m*.
◆**constabulary** [kən'stæbjuləri], *s.* Polizei *f*.

constant [ˈkɔnst(ə)nt]. **I.** *adj.* ständig. **II.**
s. Konstante *f*; **-ly,** *adv.* ständig.

constellation [kɔnstə'leiʃ(ə)n], *s.* Stern-
bild *n*.

consternation [kɔnstə'neiʃ(ə)n], *s.* Bestürzung *f*.

constipation [kɔnsti'peiʃ(ə)n], *s.* Verstopfung *f*.

constituent [kən'stitjuənt], *s.* Pol: Wähler *m*. ◆**constituency,** *s.* Wahlkreis *m*.

constitute [ˈkɔnstitjut], *v.tr.* (*a*) (*represent*) darstellen; (*b*) (*make up*) (eine Summe usw.) ausmachen. ◆**consti'tution,**
s. **I.** Pol: Verfassung *f*. **2.** (*physical*) Konstitution *f*. ◆**consti'tutional,** *adj.*
verfassungsmäßig.

constraint [kən'streint], *s.* Zwang *m*.

construct [kən'strʌkt], *v.tr.* bauen.
◆**con'struction,** *s.* Bau *m*; unter e. im
Bau. ◆**con'structive,** *adj.* konstruktiv.

consul [ˈkɔns(ə)l], *s.* Konsul *m*.
◆**consulate** [-julət], *s.* Konsulat *n*.

consult [kən'sʌlt], *v.tr.* (j-n) zu Rate ziehen; to c. a book/a timetable, in einem
Buch/einem Fahrplan nachsehen.
◆**con'sultant,** *s.* Berater *m*; Med:
Facharzt *m*. ◆**consultation**
[kɔnsəl'teiʃ(ə)n], *s.* Beratung *f*.

consume [kən'sju:m], *v.tr.* (*a*) (Essen,
Getränke) zu sich *dat* nehmen; (*b*) (Kräfte, Geld) verbrauchen; **he is consumed
with envy,** ihn frißt der Neid.

◆**con'sumer,** *s.* Verbraucher *m*; c.
goods, Verbrauchsgüter *npl*; c. protection, Verbraucherschutz *m*.

consummate [kən'sʌmət], *adj.* with c.
ease, mit größter Leichtigkeit.

consummation [kɔnsə'meiʃ(ə)n], *s.* Voll-
ziehung *f* (einer Ehe).

consumption [kən'sʌm(p)ʃ(ə)n], *s.* Genuß *m* (von alkoholischen Getränken
usw.); Verbrauch *m* (*Aut:* von Benzin
usw.).

contact [ˈkɔntækt]. **I.** *s.* Kontakt *m*; to
come into c. with s.o., sth., mit j-m, etwas *dat* in Berührung kommen, to make
c., Kontakt aufnehmen; c. lens, Kon-
taktlinse *f*; he is a business c. of mine,
ich kenne ihn geschäftlich. **II.** *v.tr.* to c.
s.o., sich mit j-m in Verbindung setzen.

contagious [kən'teidʒəs], *adj.* anstek-
kend.

contain [kən'tein], *v.tr.* (*a*) enthalten; (*b*)
(*restrain*) (Gefühle usw.) unterdrücken; to
c. oneself, sich beherrschen.
◆**con'tainer,** *s.* Behälter *m*; Com: Container *m*; c. port, Containerhafen *m*.

contaminate [kən'tæmineit], *v.tr.* (Wasser usw.) verseuchen.
◆**contami'nation,** *s.* Verseuchung *f*.

contemplate [ˈkɔntempleit], *v.tr.* (*a*) (*regard*) (etwas) betrachten; (der Zukunft)
entgegensehen; (*b*) (*consider*) (an etwas
acc) denken. ◆**contemplation,** *s.*
Nachsinnen *n*.

contemporary [kən'temp(ə)rəri]. **I.** *adj.*
zeitgenössisch. **II.** *s.* Zeitgenosse *m*, Zeit-
genossin *f*.

contempt [kən'tem(p)t], *s.* **1.** Verachtung
f. **2.** Jur: c. of court, Mißachtung *f* des
Gerichts. ◆**con'temptible,** *adj.* verachtenswert. ◆**con'temptuous,** *adj.* geringschätzig.

contend [kən'tend], *v.i.* to c. with s.o.,
sth., mit j-m, etwas *dat* kämpfen.

content[1] [ˈkɔntent], *s. also pl.* contents,
Inhalt *m*.

content[2] [kən'tent]. **I.** *v.tr.* to c. oneself
with sth., sich mit etwas *dat* begnügen.
II. *adj.* zufrieden. **III.** *s.* to one's heart's
c., nach Herzenslust. ◆**con'tented,**
adj. zufrieden. ◆**con'tentment,** *s.* Zu-
friedenheit *f*.

contention [kən'tenʃ(ə)n], *s.* bone of c.,
Zankapfel *m*.

contest. I. [ˈkɔntest], *v.tr.* (ein Testament) anfechten. **II.** [ˈkɔntest], *s.* (*a*) Sp:
Wettkampf *m*; (*b*) (*competition*) Wettbewerb *m*. ◆**con'testant,** *s.* Bewerber(in)
m(f); (*in competition*) Teilnehmer(in) *m(f)*.

context [ˈkɔntekst], *s.* Zusammenhang *m*.

continent [ˈkɔntinənt], *s.* **1.** Kontinent
m. **2.** *Brit:* on the C., auf dem europä-
ischen Festland. ◆**conti'nental,** *adj.*
(*a*) Kontinental-; c. drift, Kontinental-
verschiebung *f*; (*b*) *Brit:* kontinentaleuro-
päisch; c. quilt, Federbett *n*.

contingent [kən'tindʒənt], *s.* Kontingent
n; F: Schub *m* (von Menschen).

◆**con'tingency**, s. c. **plan**, Eventualplan m.

continue [kən'tinju(:)], v. 1. v.tr. (a) (etwas) fortsetzen; (b) to c. to do sth./doing sth., in etwas dat fortfahren; **he continues** to work/to read, er arbeitet/las weiter. 2. v.i. (of speaker etc.) fortfahren; (of weather etc.) anhalten; (on a journey) weiterfahren; (with a job) weitermachen. ◆**con'tinual**, adj. dauernd; **-ly,** adv. dauernd; (repeatedly) immer wieder. ◆**continu'ation,** s. Fortsetzung f. ◆**continuity** [kɔnti'nju:)iti], s. (logische) Folge f; **there's no c.,** es fehlt der Zusammenhang. ◆**con'tinuous,** adj. ununterbrochen.

contour ['kɔntuər], s. Kontur f; c. **line,** Höhenlinie f.

contraband ['kɔntrəbænd], s. Schmuggelware f.

contraception [kɔntrə'sepʃ(ə)n], s. Empfängnisverhütung f. ◆**contra'ceptive** [-tiv]. I. s. Empfängnisverhütungsmittel n. II. adj. empfängnisverhütend.

contract. I. [kən'trækt], v. 1. v.i. sich zusammenziehen. 2. v.tr. to c. **an illness,** sich dat eine Krankheit zuziehen. II. ['kɔntrækt], s. Vertrag m; **breach of c.,** Vertragsbruch m. ◆**con'traction,** s. Zusammenziehung f. ◆**con'tractor,** s. Unternehmer m. ◆**con'tractual,** adj. vertraglich.

contradict [kɔntrə'dikt], v.tr. (j-m, etwas dat) widersprechen. ◆**contra'diction,** s. Widerspruch m. ◆**contra'dictory,** adj. widersprüchlich.

contralto, pl. -os [kən'træltəu, -trɑ:ltəu, -əuz], s. Alt m.

contraption [kən'træpʃ(ə)n], s. F: Pej: primitiver Apparat m; Machwerk n.

contrary ['kɔntrəri]. I. adj. entgegengesetzt (**to,** dat). II. s. Gegenteil n; **on the c.,** im Gegenteil; **proof to the c.,** gegenteilige Beweise. III. adv. c. **to,** gegen + acc; c. **to expectation(s),** wider Erwarten.

contrast. I. [kən'trɑ:st], v. 1. v.i. to c. **with sth.,** einen Gegensatz zu etwas dat bilden; (of colours) sich gegen etwas abstechen. 2. v.tr. to c. **sth. with sth.,** etwas einer Sache dat gegenüberstellen. II. ['kɔntrɑ:st], s. Gegensatz m; **in c. with,** im Gegensatz zu.

contravene [kɔntrə'vi:n], v.tr. (gegen ein Gesetz usw.) verstoßen.

contribute [kən'tribju(:)t], v. 1. v.tr. (etwas) beitragen (**to,** zu + dat). 2. v.i. (dazu) beitragen (etwas zu tun). ◆**contri'bution** [kɔn-], s. Beitrag m; **to make a c.,** einen Beitrag leisten. ◆**con'tributor,** s. Beiträger m. ◆**con'tributory,** adj. c. **factor,** Mitursache f.

contrite ['kɔntrait], adj. Lit: reuig.

contrive [kən'traiv], v. 1. v.tr. (einen Plan usw.) aushecken. 2. v.i. to c. **to do sth.,** es fertigbringen, etwas zu tun.

◆**con'trived,** adj. gewollt.

control [kən'trəul]. I. s. 1. (mastery) Beherrschung f; (power) Gewalt f; **due to circumstances beyond our c.,** wegen nicht vorauszusehender Umstände; **out of/under c.,** außer/unter Kontrolle; **he lost c. of/over his car,** er verlor die Herrschaft über seinen Wagen. 2. (regulation) **under government c.,** unter Staatsaufsicht; **import controls,** Importbeschränkungen fpl. 3. **at the controls,** (of car) am Steuer; c. **panel,** Schalttafel f; c. **tower,** Kontrollturm m; **volume c.,** Lautstärkeregler m. II. v.tr. (etwas) kontrollieren; Kontrolle (über j-n, etwas acc) haben; (den Verkehr, die Wirtschaft, ein Flugzeug usw.) lenken; **to c. oneself,** sich beherrschen.

controversial [kɔntrə'və:ʃ(ə)l], adj. (of issue, figure etc.) umstritten; (of writings, critic etc.) polemisch; c. **question,** Streitfrage f. ◆**controversy** [kɔntrə'və:si, kən'trɔvəsi], s. Meinungsstreit m; **a subject of great c.,** ein heiß umstrittenes Thema.

convalesce [kɔnvə'les], v.i. sich erholen. ◆**conva'lescence,** s. Erholungszeit f.

convene [kən'vi:n], v. 1. v.tr. (eine Versammlung usw.) einberufen. 2. v.i. sich versammeln.

convenience [kən'vi:njəns], s. 1. Bequemlichkeit f; **at your c.,** wann (immer) es Ihnen paßt; **a c. food,** ein Schnellgericht n. 2. (public) c., öffentliche) Toilette f. 3. **with all conveniences,** mit allen Annehmlichkeiten. ◆**con'venient,** adj. (of time) gelegen; (of arrangement etc.) praktisch; **if it is c. for you,** wenn es Ihnen paßt.

convent ['kɔnvənt], s. Kloster n.

convention [kən'venʃ(ə)n], s. 1. Tagung f; N. Am: Pol: Parteitag m. 2. Pol: Konvent m. 3. (custom) Sitte f; **social conventions,** gesellschaftliche Formen fpl. ◆**con'ventional,** adj. konventionell; (customary) herkömmlich.

converge [kən'və:dʒ], v.i. (of lines, roads) zusammenlaufen.

converse [kən'və:s], v.i. sich unterhalten. ◆**conver'sation,** s. Gespräch n.

convert. I. [kən'və:t], v.tr. (a) (j-n) bekehren; (b) (etwas) umwandeln (**into** sth., in etwas acc); to c. **a house into flats,** ein Haus in Wohnungen umbauen. II. ['kɔnvə:t], s. Bekehrte(r) f(m). ◆**con'version,** s. 1. Eccl: Bekehrung f. 2. Umwandlung f (von Wasser in Dampf usw.); Umbau m (eines Gebäudes). ◆**con'vertible,** s. Kabriolett n.

convex ['kɔnveks], adj. konvex.

convey [kən'vei], v.tr. (a) (Güter, Personen usw.) befördern; (Wasser, Strom usw.) leiten; (b) (den Sinn, seine Meinung usw.) ausdrücken. ◆**con'veyor,** s. c. **belt,** Förderband n.

convict. I. [kən'vikt], v.tr. (j-n) verurteilen; **to c. s.o.** (of a crime), j-n (eines

Verbrechens) für schuldig befinden. **II.** ['kɔnvikt], s. Strafgefangene(r) f(m). ◆con'viction, s. 1. Jur: Verurteilung f. 2. (belief) Überzeugung f.

convince [kən'vins], v.tr. (j-n) überzeugen (of sth., von etwas dat). ◆con'vincing, adj. überzeugend.

convoy ['kɔnvɔi], s. (a) (escort) Geleit n; (b) (escorted ships) Geleitzug m.

convulsion [kən'vʌlʃ(ə)n], s. Med: to get convulsions, Krämpfe bekommen.

cook [luk]. **I.** v. 1. v.tr. (a) kochen; (roast, fry) (Fleisch, Würste usw.) braten; is it cooked? ist es gar? F: Com: to c. the books, die Bücher frisieren. 2. v.i. kochen. **II.** s. Koch m; Köchin f. ◆'cookbook, s. N.Am: Kochbuch n. ◆'cooker, s. Herd m. ◆'cookery, s. Kochen n; c. book, Kochbuch n. ◆'cookie, s. N.Am: Plätzchen n. ◆'cooking. **I.** s. Kochen n. **II.** adj. c. apple, Kochapfel m; c. utensil, Küchengerät n.

cool [ku:l]. **I.** adj. kühl; (calm) ruhig; gelassen. **II.** s. 1. Kühle f. 2. F: to keep one's c., die Ruhe bewahren. **III.** v.tr. & i. abkühlen; to c. down, sich abkühlen; Fig: (of pers.) sich beruhigen; to c. off, (of enthusiasm etc.) abkühlen.

coop [ku:p]. **I.** s. Hühnerstall m. **II.** v.tr to c. s.o., sth. up, j-n, etwas einsperren.

co-operate ['kəu'ɔpəreit], v.i. zusammenarbeiten. ◆co-ope'ration, s. Zusammenarbeit f; (help) Mithilfe f. ◆co-'operative. **I.** adj. 1. (of pers.) hilfsbereit. 2. (of organization etc.) genossenschaftlich. **II.** s. Genossenschaft f.

co-ordinate [kəu'ɔ:dineit], v.tr. (etwas) koordinieren. ◆co-ordi'nation, s. Koordination f.

cop [kɔp], s. P: 1. (policeman) Polyp m; the cops, die Polente f. 2. it's not much c., damit ist es nicht weit her.

cope [kəup], v.i. to c. with s.o., sth., mit j-m, etwas dat fertig werden.

copper ['kɔpər], s. 1. Kupfer n. 2. attrib. kupfern. 3. P: (policeman) Polyp m.

copse [kɔps], s. Gehölz n.

copulate ['kɔpjuleit], v.i. sich begatten; (of male) begatten. ◆copu'lation, s. Begattung f.

copy ['kɔpi]. **I.** v. 1. v.tr. (a) kopieren; to c. sth. (down/out), etwas abschreiben; (b) (imitate) nachahmen. 2. v.i. Sch: abschreiben. **II.** s. 1. Kopie f. 2. (written or typed) Abschrift f; rough c., Kladde f; fair c., Reinschrift f; carbon c., Durchschlag m. 3. (of book etc.) Exemplar n; (of newspaper) Nummer f. ◆'copyright, s. Copyright n.

coral ['kɔrəl], s. Koralle f. **II.** adj. c. reef, Korallenriff n.

cord [kɔ:d], s. 1. Strick m. 2. vocal cords, Stimmbänder npl. 3. Cl: F: cords, Cordhose f.

cordial ['kɔ:djəl]. **I.** adj. herzlich. **II.** s. Fruchtsirup m.

cordon ['kɔ:dən]. **I.** s. Kette f; police c., Polizeikette f. **II.** v.tr. to c. off an area etc., eine Gegend usw. absperren.

corduroy ['kɔ:dərɔi], s. Cord m.

core [kɔ:r], s. Kern m; (of apple etc.) Kerngehäuse n.

cork [kɔ:k]. **I.** s. 1. (material) Kork m. 2. (for a bottle etc.) Korken m. **II.** adj. Kork-. ◆'corkscrew, s. Korkenzieher m.

corn¹ [kɔ:n], s. Korn n; N.Am: Mais m; c. on the cob, Maiskolben m. ◆'cornflour, s. Stärkemehl n.

corn², s. Med: Hühnerauge n.

cornea ['kɔ:niə], s. Hornhaut f.

corned [kɔ:nd], adj. c. beef, Corned beef n.

corner ['kɔ:nər]. **I.** s. 1. Ecke f; F: c. shop, Tante-Emma-Laden m; Fb: c. (kick), Eckball m; Fig: to be in a tight c., in der Klemme sitzen. 2. (bend) Kurve f. **II.** v. 1. v.tr. (j-n) in die Enge treiben; Com: to c. the market, den Markt aufkaufen. 2. v.i. Aut: eine/die Kurve nehmen.

cornet ['kɔ:nit], s. 1. Mus: Kornett n. 2. (ice-cream) c., Eistüte f.

corny ['kɔ:ni], adj. F: (a) (of joke) abgedroschen; (b) (of film etc.) kitschig.

coronary ['kɔrənəri], adj. Med: c. (thrombosis), Koronarthrombose f.

coronation [kɔrə'neif(ə)n], s. Krönung f.

coroner ['kɔrənər], s. richterliche(r) Beamte(r) m für die Leichenschau.

corporal ['kɔ:p(ə)r(ə)l], s. Mil: Stabsunteroffizier m.

corporal², adj. c. punishment, körperliche Züchtigung f.

corporation [kɔ:pə'reif(ə)n], s. Aktiengesellschaft f.

corpse [kɔ:ps], s. Leiche f.

corpuscle ['kɔ:pʌsl], s. Körperchen n.

correct [kə'rekt]. **I.** v.tr. (j-n, etwas) korrigieren. **II.** adj. (a) richtig; (b) (of pers., dress etc.) korrekt. ◆co'rrection, s. Korrektur f.

correspond [kɔris'pɔnd], v.i. (a) sich entsprechen; (of two accounts etc.) sich decken; to c. with/to sth., etwas dat entsprechen; (b) to c. with s.o., mit j-m korrespondieren. ◆corres'pondence, s. Briefwechsel m; to deal with one's c., seine Post erledigen; c. course, Fernkurs m. ◆corres'pondent, s. 1. (regular) Briefpartner(in) m(f). 2. (reporter) Korrespondent(in) m(f). ◆corres'ponding, adj. entsprechend.

corridor ['kɔridɔ:r], s. Korridor m.

corroborate [kə'rɔbəreit], v.tr. (eine Aussage usw.) bestätigen.

corrode [kə'rəud], v. 1. v.tr. (of rust etc.) (Metall usw.) zerfressen; (of chemical etc.) (Metall usw.) ätzen. 2. v.i. korrodieren. ◆co'rrosion [-ʒ(ə)n], s. Korrosion f. ◆co'rrosive [-siv]. **I.** s. Ätzmittel n. **II.** adj. zerfressend.

corrugated ['kɔrəgeitid], *adj.* gewellt; c. iron, Wellblech *n.*

corrupt [kə'rʌpt]. **I.** *v.tr.* (Jugendliche) verderben. **II.** *adj.* korrupt. ◆co'**rruption**, *s.* Korruption *f.*

corset ['kɔːsit], *s.* Mieder *n; esp. Med:* Korsett *n.*

cosh [kɔʃ]. **I.** *s.* Knüppel *m.* **II.** *v.tr.* (j-n) mit einem Knüppel schlagen.

cosmetic [kɔz'metik]. **I.** *adj.* kosmetisch. **II.** *s.pl.* **cosmetics**, Kosmetika *npl.*

cosmopolitan [kɔzmə'pɔlit(ə)n], *adj.* kosmopolitisch; (*of city*) international; (*of pers.*) weltbürgerlich.

cost [kɔst]. **I.** *v. 1. v.i.* kosten; **it c. him five pounds,** es hat ihn fünf Pfund gekostet. *2. v.tr.* to c. **a project,** eine Kostenberechnung für ein Projekt anstellen. **II.** *s.* Kosten *pl;* **c. of living,** Lebenshaltungskosten *pl;* **c. price,** Selbstkostenpreis *m; Fig:* **I know that to my c.,** das weiß ich aus bitterer Erfahrung; **at all costs,** um jeden Preis; **whatever the c.,** koste es, was es wolle. ◆'**costly,** *adj.* kostspielig.

costume ['kɔstjuːm], *s. 1.* (**national**) c., Tracht *f. 2.* (*fancy dress*) Kostüm *n.*

cosy ['kəuzi]. **I.** *adj.* gemütlich. **II.** *s.* (**tea-**)c., Teewärmer *m.*

cot [kɔt], *s.* Kinderbett *n; (with bars)* Gitterbett *n.*

cottage ['kɔtidʒ], *s.* Häuschen *n,* Cottage *f;* **c. cheese,** Hüttenkäse *m;* **c. industry,** Heimindustrie *f.*

cotton ['kɔtn], *s. 1.* Baumwolle *f;* (**sewing-**)c., Nähgarn *n;* **c. reel,** Garnrolle *f;* **c. wool,** Watte *f.* **II.** *adj.* baumwollen.

couch [kautʃ], *s.* Couch *f.*

cough [kɔf]. **I.** *s.* Husten *m.* **II.** *v.i. (a)* husten; *(b) F:* (*pay*) **to c. up,** blechen.

could [kud], *see* **can**[2].

council ['kauns(i)l], *s.* (*a*) (*assembly*) Rat *m;* **town** c., Stadtrat *m;* (*b*) (*local authority*) Gemeinde *f;* **c. flat,** Sozialwohnung *f.* ◆'**councillor,** *s.* Rat *m;* (**town**) c., Stadtrat *m.*

counsel ['kauns(ə)l]. **I.** *s. 1.* (*advice*) Rat *m. 2. Jur:* Anwalt *m;* **c. for the defence,** Verteidiger *m;* **c. for the prosecution,** Anklagevertreter *m.* **II.** *v.tr.* (j-n) beraten; **to c. caution,** zur Vorsicht raten. ◆'**counsellor,** *s.* Berater *m.* ◆'**counsellor,** *s. N.Am:* Anwalt *m.*

count[1] [kaunt]. **I.** *v.tr. (a)* zählen; *(b)* to c. **oneself lucky,** sich glücklich schätzen; to c. **on s.o.,** sich auf j-n verlassen; to c. **on sth.** mit etwas rechnen. *2. v.i.* zählen. **II.** *s.* Zählung *f.* ◆'**count-down,** *s.* Countdown *m.* ◆'**countless,** *adj.* unzählig.

count[2], *s.* Graf *m.*

counter[1] ['kauntər], *s. 1. (a)* (*in shop*) Ladentisch *m;* (*b)* (*in bank, post office*) Schalter *m. 2. E:* Zähler *m.*

counter[2], *v. 1. v.tr.* (einen Angriff) erwi-

dern; (j-s Plänen usw.) entgegenarbeiten. *2. v.i.* kontern. ◆'**counter'act,** *v.tr.* (etwas *dat*) entgegenwirken. ◆'**counter-attack.** **I.** *s.* Gegenangriff *m.* **II.** *v.tr. & i.* einen Gegenangriff (gegen j-n) unternehmen. ◆'**counter-'espionage,** *s.* Gegenspionage *f.* ◆**counterfeit** ['kauntəfit]. **I.** *adj.* gefälscht. **II.** *v.tr.* (Geld usw.) fälschen. ◆'**counterfoil,** *s.* Kontrollabschnitt *m.* ◆'**counterpart,** *s.* Gegenstück *n.* ◆'**counter'sign,** *v.tr.* (einen Scheck usw.) gegenzeichnen.

countess ['kauntis], *s.* Gräfin *f.*

country ['kʌntri], *s. (a)* Land *n; Pol:* Staat *m;* (*countryside*) **in the c.,** auf dem Land; **c. house,** Landhaus *n;* (*b)* (*terrain*) Gelände *n.* ◆'**countryside,** *s.* Landschaft *f.*

county ['kaunti], *s. 1. Brit:* Grafschaft *f;* **c. council,** Grafschaftsrat *m. 2. N.Am:* Verwaltungsbezirk *m.*

coup [kuː], *s.* Coup *m.*

couple ['kʌpl], *s. 1.* Paar *n;* **married c.,** Ehepaar *n. 2.* (*a few*) **a c. of days,** ein paar Tage.

coupon ['kuːpɔn], *s. 1.* (*form*) Coupon *m. 2.* (*voucher*) Gutschein *m.*

courage ['kʌridʒ], *s.* Mut *m;* **to pluck up c.,** Mut aufbringen. ◆**courageous** [kə'reidʒəs], *adj.* mutig.

courgette [kuə'ʒet], *s.* Zucchini *f.*

courier ['kuriər], *s. 1.* Reiseleiter *m. 2.* (*messenger*) Kurier *m.*

course [kɔːs], *s. 1. (a)* Lauf *m* (der Ereignisse usw.); **in the c. of time,** im Laufe der Zeit; **in due c.,** zu seiner Zeit; **to let things take their c.,** den Dingen ihren Lauf lassen; *(b)* **of c.,** natürlich, selbstverständlich; **of c. not,** natürlich nicht; **a matter of c.,** eine Selbstverständlichkeit. *2. (a) Sch:* Kurs *m;* Lehrgang *m;* (*b) Med:* **c. of treatment,** Behandlung *f. 3.* (*a*) Richtung *f; Nau:* Kurs *m;* *(b)* to **follow a c. of action,** eine Linie verfolgen. *4. Cu:* Gang *m. 5. (a)* Golf *m;* golf **c.,** Golfplatz *m;* *(b)* **race c.,** Rennstrecke *f.*

court [kɔːt]. **I.** *s. 1.* (*royal*) Hof *m; Jur:* Gericht *m. 3. tennis* c., Tennisplatz *m.* **II.** *v.tr.* (einer Frau) den Hof machen; **to c. disaster,** Unheil herausfordern. ◆**courteous** ['kəːtjəs], *adj.* höflich. ◆'**courtesy** ['kəːtisi], *s.* Höflichkeit *f.* ◆'**court-'martial.** **I.** *s.* Militärgericht *n.* **II.** *v.tr.* (j-n) vor ein Militärgericht stellen. ◆'**courtship,** *s.* Werbung *f* (of, um + *acc*). ◆'**courtyard,** *s.* Hof *m.*

cousin ['kʌzn], *s.* (*male*) Vetter *m;* (*female*) Kusine *f.*

cove [kəuv], *s.* kleine Bucht *f.*

cover ['kʌvər]. **I.** *s. 1.* **cushion c.,** Kissenbezug *m. 2.* (*lid*) Deckel *m* (eines Kochtopfs usw.). *3.* (*a*) Deckel *m* (eines Buches); *(b)* Titelseite *f* (einer Zeitschrift); **c. girl,** Covergirl *n. 4.* **under separate c.,** mit getrennter Post. *5.* (*protection*) Schutz *m;* **to take c.,** Schutz suchen, *Mil:* in Deckung gehen; (*insurance*)

c. note, Deckungszusage f. II. v.tr. (a)
bedecken; (b) (eine Strecke) zurücklegen;
(c) (den Bedarf, die Kosten) decken; (d)
(ein Thema usw.) (umfassend) behandeln; (in media) (über etwas acc) berichten. ◆'coverage, s. (in media) Bericht-
erstattung f. ◆'cover 'up, v.tr. (a) zudecken; (b) (eine Spur, einen Fehler
usw.) verbergen; (eine peinliche Angelegenheit usw.) vertuschen.

cow [kau], s. Kuh f. ◆'cowboy, s.
Cowboy m.

coward ['kauəd], s. Feigling m.
◆'cowardice, s. Feigheit f.
◆'cowardly, adj. feige.

cower ['kauər], v.i. sich ducken.

cowslip ['kauslip], s. Schlüsselblume f.

cox [kɔks], s. Nau: Steuermann m.

coy [kɔi], adj. (a) scheu; (b) (affectedly
modest) zimperlich.

crab [kræb], s. Krabbe f.

crack [kræk]. I. s. 1. (of gun, whip etc.)
Knall m. 2. Riß m; (in glass etc.) Sprung
m. 3. F: I'll have a c. at it, ich werde es
mal versuchen. II. adj. F: erstklassig; c.
shot, Meisterschütze m. III. v. 1. v.tr.
(a) (eine Nuß) knacken; to c. a plate,
einen Sprung in einen Teller machen; (b)
F: (einen Safe, einen Kode) knacken; (c)
to c. jokes, Witze reißen. 2. v.i. (of glass
etc.) einen Sprung bekommen; (of wall
etc.) einen Riß/Risse bekommen; F: get
cracking, mach dich dran; (hurry) mach
fix! ◆'cracked, adj. (a) (of glass etc.)
gesprungen; (of wall, skin etc.) rissig; (b)
F: (of person) übergeschnappt. ◆'crack
'down, v.tr. to c. down on sth., harte
Maßnahmen gegen etwas acc treffen.
◆'crack 'up, v. 1. v.tr. F: he's not all
he's cracked up to be, er ist nicht so gut
wie sein Ruf. 2. v.i. (of pers.) zusammenbrechen.

crackle ['krækl]. I. v.i. (of fire etc.) knistern. II. s. Knistern n. ◆'crackling, s.
knusprige Schwarte f (des Schweinebra-
tens).

cradle ['kreidl], s. Wiege f.

craft¹ [krɑ:ft], s. Handwerk n.
◆'craftsman, pl. -men, s. Handwerker
m. ◆'craftsmanship, s. handwerkliches
Geschick n. ◆'crafty, adj. schlau; Pej:
(hinter)listig.

craft², s. Fahrzeug n; coll. Fahrzeuge npl.

crag [kræg], s. Felszacke f.

cram [kræm], v. 1. v.tr. (etwas in einen
Koffer, in den Mund usw.) hineinstopfen. 2. v.i. (a) sich hineinzwängen; (b) F:
to c. for an examination, für eine Prüfung pauken.

cramp [kræmp]. I. s. Krampf m. II. v.tr.
F: to c. s.o.'s style, hemmend auf j-n
wirken. ◆'cramped, adj. eng.

crane [krein]. I. s. 1. Z: Kranich m. 2.
Tchn: Kran m. II. v.tr. to c. one's neck,
den Hals recken.

crank [kræŋk], s. verschrobener Typ m;
Sonderling m. ◆'crankshaft, s. Kurbel-

welle f.

crash [kræʃ]. I. s. 1. Krach m. 2. Fin:
Sturz m. 3. (a) Aut: Rail: Unglück n;
(collision) Zusammenstoß m; c. helmet,
Sturzhelm m; (b) Av: Absturz m. 4. attrib. c. course, Intensivkurs m. II. v.i.
(a) krachen; (b) Aut: Rail: verunglücken;
(of two cars) zusammenstoßen; to c. into
a tree, gegen einen Baum fahren; (c) Av:
abstürzen. ◆'crash-land, v.i. Av: eine
Bruchlandung machen.

crate [kreit], s. Kiste f.

crater ['kreitər], s. (a) Krater m; (b)
(bomb) c., Trichter m.

craving ['kreivin], s. Begierde f, (of pregnant woman) Gelüste npl (for,
nach + dat).

crawl [krɔ:l]. I. v.i. (a) (of worm, car,
pers.) kriechen; (of baby) krabbeln; (b)
to be crawling with vermin, von Ungeziefer wimmeln. II. s. (swimming) Kraulen n; to do the c., kraulen.

crayon ['kreiən,-ɔn], s. Farbstift m.

craze [kreiz], s. F: Masche f. ◆'crazy,
adj. verrückt; to be c. about s.o., verrückt nach j-m sein.

creak [kri:k], v.i. knarren. II. s. Knarren n.

cream [kri:m], s. 1. Sahne f; c. cheese,
Rahmkäse m. 2. Elite f; the c. of society, die Spitzen der Gesellschaft. 3. (face
c.) Creme f. 4. attrib.
c.(-coloured), cremefarben. ◆'creamy,
adj. sahnig.

crease [kri:s]. I. v. 1. v.tr. (a) (Papier
usw.) falten; (b) (ein Kleid usw.) zerknittern. 2. v.i. (of material etc.) knittern.
II. s. Falte f.

create [kri'eit], v.tr. schaffen; (einen Eindruck) machen; (Schwierigkeiten usw.)
hervorrufen. ◆cre'ation, s. Schöpfung
f. ◆cre'ative, adj. schöpferisch.
◆cre'ator, s. Schöpfer m. ◆'creature
['kri:tʃər], s. 1. Geschöpf n. 2. c. comforts, Bequemlichkeiten fpl.

crèche [kreiʃ], s. Kinderkrippe f.

credentials [kri'denʃ(ə)lz], s.pl. 1. Papiere npl; (references) Zeugnisse npl. 2. Fig:
(qualifications) Voraussetzungen fpl.

credible ['kredibl], adj. glaubwürdig.
◆credi'bility, s. Glaubwürdigkeit f.

credit ['kredit]. I. s. 1. Com: Kredit m; to
buy sth. on c., etwas auf Kredit kaufen;
c. note, Gutschein m; c. card, Kredit-
karte f. 2. Ehre f; it does him c., es
macht ihm Ehre; to take the c. for sth.,
sich dafür etwas als Verdienst anrechnen.
II. v.tr. (a) to c. s.o. with a sum, j-m
einen Betrag gutschreiben; (b) I credited
you with more sense, ich hielt dich für
vernünftiger. ◆'creditor, s. Gläubiger
m.

creed [kri:d], s. Kredo m.

creep [kri:p]. I. v.i.irr. schleichen. II. s.
F: it gives me the creeps, mir gruselt es
davor. ◆'creepy, adj. gruselig.

cremate [kri'meit], v.tr. einäschern.

◆cre'mation, s. Einäscherung f.
◆crematorium, [kremə'tɔːriəm], s. Krematorium n.

crêpe [kreip], s. 1. c. bandage, elastische Binde f. 2. c.(-rubber) sole, Kreppsohle f.

cress [kres], s. Kresse f; water-c., Brunnenkresse f.

crest [krest], s. 1. (of bird) Haube f. 2. (of hill, wave) Kamm m. 3. (coat of arms) Wappen n. ◆'crestfallen, adj. (of pers.) betreten.

Crete [kriːt], Pr.n. Kreta n.

crew [kruː], s. 1. Nau: Besatzung f. 2. Pej: Bande f. 3. c. cut, Bürstenschnitt m.

crib [krib]. 1. s. Krippe f. 2. (baby's) c., Kinderbett n.

crick [krik], s. to have a c. in one's neck/back, sich dat den Hals/den Rücken verrenkt haben.

cricket ['krikit], s. Sp: Kricket n. ◆'cricketer, s. Kricketspieler m.

crime [kraim], s. Verbrechen n. ◆'criminal ['kriminl]. I. adj. kriminell; (punishable) strafbar; to have a c. record, vorbestraft sein. II. s. Verbrecher m.

crimson ['krimz(ə)n], adj. purpurrot.

cringe [krindʒ], v.i. (in fear) sich ducken.

crinkle ['kriŋkl], v.tr. & i. (Papier) knittern.

cripple ['kripl]. I. s. Krüppel m. II. v.tr. (a) (j-n) zum Krüppel machen; crippled with arthritis, durch Arthritis gelähmt; (b) Fig: lähmen.

crisis ['kraisis], pl. crises ['kraisiːz], s. Krise f.

crisp [krisp]. I. adj. 1. knusprig. 2. (of air, weather) frisch. 3. (of literary style) knapp. II. s. (potato) crisps, Chips pl.

criterion ['kraiˈtiəriən], pl. -ia [kraiˈtiəriən, -iə], s. Kriterium n.

critic ['kritik], s. Kritiker m. ◆'critical, adj. kritisch; -ly, adv. c. ill, schwerkrank. ◆'criticism [-isiz(ə)m], s. Kritik f. ◆'criticize [-isaiz], v.tr. kritisieren.

croak [krəuk], v.i. (of frog) quaken; (of raven, pers.) krächzen. II. s. Krächzer m. ◆'croaky, adj. krächzend.

crochet ['krəuʃei], v.tr. & i. häkeln.

crockery ['krɔkəri], s. Geschirr n.

crocodile ['krɔkədail], s. Krokodil n.

crocus ['krəukəs], pl. crocuses ['krəukəs, -əsiz], s. Krokus m.

crony ['krəuni], s. P: Kumpan m.

crook [kruk], s. F: Gauner m. ◆crooked ['krukid], adj. 1. (bent) krumm; (at the wrong angle) schief. 2. Fig: (of pers.) unehrlich.

crop [krɔp], s. 1. Ernte f. 2. (riding) c., Reitstock m. ◆'crop 'up, v.i. F: auftauchen.

cross [krɔs]. I. s. 1. Kreuz n. 2. Bot: Z: Kreuzung f. II. v.tr. 1. (die Straße usw.) überqueren; (die Wüste) durchqueren; it crossed my mind that ... der Ge-

danke ging mir durch den Kopf, daß ...; (b) (die Beine) übereinanderschlagen; to keep one's fingers crossed for s.o., j-m die Daumen drücken; (c) (Tierrassen usw.) kreuzen; (d) crossed cheque Verrechnungsscheck m. 2. v.i. (a) (of lines, roads etc.) sich kreuzen; (b) to c. from Dover to Calais, die Überfahrt von Dover nach Calais machen. III. adj. 1. F: böse. 2. in (compounds) Quer-. ◆'cross-'country. I. adv. querfeldein. II. s. c.-c. (run), Geländelauf m. ◆'cross-exami'nation, s. Kreuzverhör n. ◆'cross-e'xamine, v.tr. (j-n) ins Kreuzverhör nehmen. ◆'cross-eyed, adj. schielend. ◆'crossfire, s. Kreuzfeuer n. ◆'crossing, s. 1. (sea journey) Überfahrt f. 2. (road, railway) Kreuzung f; level c., Bahnübergang m; (pedestrian) c., Fußgängerübergang m. ◆'cross-'legged, adv. mit gekreuzten Beinen. ◆'cross-'purposes, s. to talk at c.-p., aneinander vorbeireden. ◆'crossroads, s. Straßenkreuzung f. ◆'crossword, s. c. (puzzle), Kreuzworträtsel n.

crotchet ['krɔtʃit], s. Viertelnote f. ◆'crotchety, adj. mürrisch.

crouch [krautʃ], v.i. hocken.

crow [krəu], s. Krähe f; as the c. flies, in der Luftlinie.

crowd [kraud]. I. s. Menge f. II. v. 1. v.i. to c. (together), sich drängen. 2. v.tr. to c. (into) a room, sich in ein Zimmer hineindrängen. ◆'crowded, adj. überfüllt.

crown [kraun]. I. s. Krone f. II. v.tr. to c. s.o. king, j-n zum König krönen.

crucial ['kruːʃ(ə)l], adj. entscheidend.

crucifix ['kruːsifiks], s. Kruzifix n. ◆crucifixion [-'fikʃ(ə)n], s. Kreuzigung f. ◆'crucify, v.tr. kreuzigen.

crude [kruːd], adj. 1. (of raw material) roh; c. oil, Rohöl n. 2. (of pers., manners etc.) grob; (of structure etc.) primitiv. ◆'crudeness/'crudity, s. primitive Art f; (of pers., language etc.) Grobheit f.

cruel [kruəl], adj. grausam. ◆'cruelty, s. Grausamkeit f; c. to animals, Tierquälerei f.

cruet ['kruːit], s. H: c.(-stand) Menage f.

cruise [kruːz]. I. s. Nau: Kreuzfahrt f. II. v.i. Nau: kreuzen; cruising speed, Reisegeschwindigkeit f. ◆'cruiser, s. (a) Nau: Kreuzer m; (b) motor c./(cabin) c., Kajütboot n.

crumb [krʌm], s. Krümel m. ◆crumble ['krʌmbl], v.tr. & i. (Brot usw.) zerbröckeln; (of walls, Fig: of empire) zerfallen.

crumpet ['krʌmpit], s. salziges Hefegebäck n.

crumple ['krʌmpl], v.tr. (etwas) zerdrücken; (ein Kleid, Papier usw.) zerknittern.

crunch [krʌn(t)ʃ]. I. v. 1. v.tr. (einen Keks usw.) geräuschvoll essen. 2. v.i. (of snow, gravel etc.) knirschen. II. s. F:

when it comes to the c., wenn es darauf ankommt.

crusade [kru:'seid], s. Kreuzzug m.

crush [krʌʃ]. I. v.tr. zerdrücken. II. s. 1. (crowd) Gedränge n. 2. F: to have a c. on s.o., für j-n schwärmen. ◆'**crushing**, adj. (of defeat, reply etc.) vernichtend.

crust [krʌst], s. Kruste f. ◆'**crusty**, adj. (of bread etc.) krustig.

crutch [krʌtʃ], s. (for disabled) Krücke f.

crux [krʌks], s. the c. (of the matter), der springende Punkt.

cry [krai]. I. v. 1. v.i. (a) (weep) weinen; (b) to c. (out), schreien; (c) (exclaim) rufen. 2. v.tr. weinen. II. s. 1. Ruf m. 2. to have a good c., sich ausweinen.

cryptic ['kriptik], adj. rätselhaft.

crystal ['kristl], s. 1. Kristall m. 2. c. (-glass), Kristall n; c. ball, Kristallkugel f; c.-clear, kristallklar. ◆'**crystallize**, v.i. kristallisieren; (of plan etc.) feste Form annehmen.

cub [kʌb], s. 1. Junge(s) n; bear c., Bärenjunge(s) n. 2. (scout) Wölfling m.

cube [kju:b], s. Würfel m. ◆'**cubic**, adj. Kubik-; c. meter, Kubikmeter m & n; c. capacity, Kubikinhalt m; Aut: Hubraum m.

cubicle ['kju:bikl], s. Kabine f.

cubism ['kju:biz(ə)m], s. Kubismus m.

cuckoo ['kuku:], s. Kuckuck m.

cucumber ['kju:kʌmbər], s. Gurke f.

cuddle ['kʌdl], v. 1. v.tr. (ein Kind usw.) herzen. 2. v.i. to c. up to s.o., sich an j-n kuscheln. ◆'**cuddly**, adj. F: kuschelig; c. toy, Kuscheltier n.

cue¹ [kju:], s. Th: Stichwort n.

cue², s. billiard c., Billardqueue n.

cuff [kʌf], s. 1. (of shirt etc.) Manschette f; F: off the c., aus dem Stegreif. 2. N.Am: trouser c., Hosenaufschlag m. ◆'**cuff-links**, s.pl. Manschettenknöpfe mpl.

cuisine [kwi'zi:n], s. Kochkunst f.

cul-de-sac ['kʌldəsæk], s. Sackgasse f.

culinary ['kʌlinəri], adj. kulinarisch.

culminate ['kʌlmineit], v.i. to c. in sth., in etwas dat gipfeln. ◆culmi'**nation**, s. Gipfelpunkt m.

culprit ['kʌlprit], s. Täter m.

cult [kʌlt], s. Kult m.

cultivate ['kʌltiveit], v.tr. a) (das Land) bebauen; (Getreide, Wein usw.) anbauen; (b) (die Musik usw.) pflegen. ◆'**cultivated**, adj. (of pers.) kultiviert. ◆culti'**vation**, s. Kultivierung f.

culture ['kʌltʃər], s. Kultur f. ◆'**cultural**, adj. kulturell. ◆'**cultured**, adj. kultiviert.

cumbersome ['kʌmbəsəm], adj. unhandlich.

cumulative ['kju:mjulətiv], adj. kumulativ.

cunning ['kʌniŋ]. I. s. Schlauheit f. II. adj. schlau; Pej: listig.

cup [kʌp], s. 1. Tasse f; a c. of tea, eine

Tasse Tee; F: that's not my c. of tea, das ist nicht mein Fall. 2. Sp: Pokal m; c. final, Pokalendspiel n. ◆'**cupful**, s. c. of sugar, Tasse f Zucker.

cupboard ['kʌbəd], s. Schrank m.

curator [kjuə'reitər], s. Kustos m (eines Museums usw.).

curb [kə:b]. I. s. = kerb. II. v.tr. (sich, seinen Zorn usw.) im Zaum halten.

curdle ['kə:dl], v. 1. v.i. (of milk etc.) gerinnen. 2. v.tr. zum Gerinnen bringen.

cure ['kjuər]. I. v.tr. (a) heilen; (b) (smoke) räuchern; (salt) einsalzen. II. s. 1. (process) Heilung f. 2. (a) (treatment) Kur f; (b) (remedy) Heilmittel n (for, gegen + acc).

curfew ['kə:fju], s. Ausgehverbot n.

curiosity [kjuəri'ɔsiti], s. Neugier f. ◆'**curious**, adj. 1. (of pers.) neugierig. 2. (strange) merkwürdig.

curl [kə:l]. I. s. (of hair) Locke f. II. v. 1. v.tr. to c. one's hair, sich dat Locken drehen; (of hair) sich locken. ◆'**curler**, s. Lockenwickler m. ◆'**curl 'up**, v.i. (of cat etc.) sich zusammenrollen; (of pers.) F: es sich gemütlich machen. ◆'**curly**, adj. lockig.

currant ['kʌrənt], s. Korinthe f.

currency ['kʌrənsi], s. Währung f; foreign c., Devisen pl.

current ['kʌrənt]. I. s. 1. (in water, also Fig:) Strömung f. 2. (electric) c., (elektrischer) Strom m. II. adj. 1. (of words etc.) geläufig; (of opinions etc.) herrschend. 2. (present) gegenwärtig; (topical) aktuell; c. affairs, aktuelle Fragen; c. account, Girokonto; -ly, adv. gegenwärtig.

curriculum [kə'rikjuləm], s. (a) Lehrplan m; (b) c. vitae, Lebenslauf m.

curry¹ ['kʌri], s. Curry n.

curry², v.tr. to c. favour with s.o., sich in j-s Gunst einschmeicheln.

curse [kə:s]. I. s. Fluch m. II. v. 1. v.tr. (j-n) verfluchen. 2. v.i. fluchen.

cursory ['kə:səri], adj. flüchtig.

curt [kə:t], adj. barsch.

curtail [kə:'teil], v.tr. abkürzen.

curtain ['kə:t(ə)n], s. (a) Gardine f; (b) Th: Vorhang m.

curve [kə:v]. I. s. Kurve f. II. v.i. sich biegen. ◆'**curved**, adj. gebogen.

cushion ['kuʃ(ə)n]. I. s. Kissen n. II. v.tr. (einen Stoß) dämpfen. ◆'**cushy** ['kuʃi], adj. F: bequem.

custard ['kʌstəd], s. Vanillesoße f.

custody ['kʌstədi], s. 1. Obhut f; Sorgerecht n (of a child, über ein Kind). Jur: Haft f. ◆'**custodian** [-'təudiən], s. Wächter m.

custom ['kʌstəm], s. 1. (tradition) Brauch m; (habit) Gepflogenheit f. 2. Com: Kundschaft f. 3. **customs**, Zoll m. ◆'**customary**, adj. gewohnt; (of walk, drink etc.) gewohnheitsmäßig. ◆'**custom-'built**, adj. in Sonderausführung gebaut. ◆'**customer**, s. Kunde m.

◆'custom-'made, *adj.* in Sonderausführung; (*of clothes*) maßgeschneidert.

cut [kʌt]. **I.** *v.tr.* **1.** *v.i.* (*of knife etc.*) schneiden; *Fig:* that cuts both ways, das ist ein zweischneidiges Schwert. **2.** *v.tr.* (*a*) schneiden; (Gras, Getreide usw.) mähen; (Holz) hacken; (einen Schlüssel) anfertigen; (ein Stück Kuchen) abschneiden; to. c. one's finger, sich *dat* in den Finger schneiden; (*b*) (Preise, Steuern usw.) herabsetzen; (j-s Gehalt usw.) kürzen; (c) to c. (the cards), abheben; (d) to c. s.o. (dead), j-n schneiden; *Fig:* to c. corners, sich leicht machen; (of builder etc.) an allen Ecken und Enden sparen. **II.** *s.* **1.** Schnitt *m;* (wound) Schnittwunde *f.* **2.** (reduction) Kürzung *f* (in salary etc., des Gehalts usw.); power c., Stromsperre *f.* **3.** Schnitt *m* (eines Anzuges usw.). **4.** Cu: c. (of meat), Fleischstück *n.* **5.** short c., Abkürzung *f.* **6.** *F:* (share) Anteil *m.* **III.** *adj.* c. glass, Kristall *n;* c. and dried, (of opinion) vorgefaßt; (of plans etc.) fix und fertig. **◆'cutback,** *s.* Kürzung *f* (in expenditure, der Ausgaben). **◆'cut 'down** *v.tr.* (*a*) (einen Baum) fällen; (*b*) (seine Ausgaben usw.) reduzieren. **◆'cut 'in,** *v.i.* *Aut:* to c. in on s.o., j-n schneiden; (*b*) to c. in on a conversation, ein Gespräch unterbrechen. **◆'cut 'off,** *v.tr.* abschneiden; *Tel:* we've been c. o., wir sind unterbrochen worden. **◆'cut 'out,** *v.* **1.** *v.i.* (of engine) aussetzen. **2.** *v.tr.* (*a*) ausschneiden; (ein Kleid usw.) zuschneiden;

(*b*) *Fig:* (of pers.) to be c. o. for sth., zu etwas *dat* geeignet sein; *F:* c. it o.! laß das sein! **◆'cut 'short,** *v.tr.* abkürzen; to c. a long story s., um es kurz zu machen. **◆'cutting. I.** *s.* **1.** Ausschnitt *m.* **2.** (of plant) Ableger *m.* **II.** *adj.* *Fig:* schneidend; c. edge, Schneide *f;* c. remark, bissige Bemerkung. **◆'cut 'up,** *v.tr.* (*a*) (Fleisch, Wurst) aufschneiden; (Papier, Stoff usw.) zerschneiden; (*b*) *F:* to c. up rough, aggressiv werden.

cute [kjuːt], *adj.* niedlich.

cutlery ['kʌtləri], *s.* Besteck *n.*

cutlet ['kʌtlit], *s.* Kotelett *n.*

cyanide ['saiənaid], *s.* Zyanid *n.*

cycle ['saikl]. **I.** *s.* **1.** Zyklus *m.* **2.** (bicycle) Fahrrad *n;* c. track, Radweg *m.* **II.** *v.i.* (mit dem Rad) fahren. **◆'cyclist,** *s.* Radfahrer *m.*

cyclone ['saikləun], *s.* Zyklon *m.*

cylinder ['silindər], *s.* (*a*) Zylinder *m;* (*b*) oxygen c., Sauerstoffflasche *f.* **◆'cy'lindrical,** *adj.* zylindrisch.

cynic ['sinik], *s.* Zyniker *m.* **◆'cynical,** *adj.* zynisch. **◆'cynicism,** *s.* Zynismus *m.*

cypress ['saiprəs], *s.* Zypresse *f.*

Cyprus ['saiprəs]. *Pr.n.* Zypern *n.*

cyst [sist], *s.* Zyste *f.*

Czech [tʃek]. **I.** *s.* **1.** Tscheche *m;* Tschechin *f.* **2.** (language) Tschechisch *n.* **II.** *adj.* tschechisch. **◆'Czechoslovakia** ['tʃekəusləu'vækiə]. *Pr.n.* die Tschechoslowakei *f.*

D

D, d [diː], *s.* (der Buchstabe) D, d *n.*

dab [dæb]. **I.** *s.* **1.** (tap) Tupfer *m.* **2.** (of paint etc.) Klecks *m.* **3.** *F:* to be a d. hand at sth., in etwas *dat* sehr geschickt sein. **II.** *v.tr.* abtupfen.

dabble ['dæbl], *v.i.* *F:* to d. in law/politics, sich oberflächlich mit Recht/Politik befassen.

dachshund ['dækshund], *s.* Dackel *m.*

dad [dæd], **daddy** ['dædi], *s.* *F:* Vati *m.* **◆'daddy-'long-legs,** *s.* (*a*) Brit: Schnake *f;* (*b*) N.Am: Weberknecht *m.*

daffodil ['dæfədil], *s.* Osterglocke *f;* gelbe Narzisse *f.*

daft [dɑːft], *adj.* *F:* verrückt; *P:* doof.

dagger ['dægər], *s.* Dolch *m.*

dahlia ['deiliə], *s.* Dahlie *f.*

daily ['deili], *adj. & adv.* täglich; Tages-; d. (paper), Tageszeitung *f.*

dainty ['deinti], *adj.* zierlich.

dairy ['dɛəri], *s.* **1.** Molkerei *f;* d. farming, Milchwirtschaft *f.* d. produce, Molkereiprodukte *npl.* **2.** (shop) Milchgeschäft *n.*

daisy ['deizi], *s.* Gänseblümchen *n;* (large) Margerite *f.*

dam [dæm]. **I.** *s.* Staudamm *m;* (across

valley) Talsperre *f.* **II.** *v.tr.* to d. (up) a river etc., einen Fluß usw. stauen.

damage ['dæmidʒ]. **I.** *s.* **1.** Schaden *m.* **2.** *pl. Jur:* Schadenersatz *m.* **II.** *v.tr.* beschädigen; *Fig:* (einer Person, dem Ruf) schaden. **◆'damaged,** *adj.* beschädigt. **◆'damaging,** *adj.* schädlich.

damn [dæm]. **I.** *s.* *P:* I don't give a d., das kümmert mich einen Dreck. **II.** *adj.* *P:* verdammt; this d. job! diese Scheißarbeit! **III.** *int.* d. it! verdammt! **IV.** *v.tr.* verdammen. **◆'damned,** *adj.* **1.** verdammt. **2.** *F:* (*a*) what a d. nuisance, verflucht unangenehm; to do one's damnedest, sein möglichstes tun; (*b*) adv. (intensive) it's d. hard! es ist verflucht schwer! a d. sight better, bei weitem besser. **◆'damning,** *adj.* (of criticism etc.) vernichtend.

damp [dæmp]. **I.** *s.* Feuchtigkeit *f.* **II.** *adj.* feucht. **◆'dampen,** *v.tr.* (Eifer usw.) dämpfen. **◆'damper,** *s.* to put a d. on the celebrations, den Festlichkeiten einen Dämpfer aufsetzen.

dance [dɑːns]. **I.** *s.* **1.** Tanz *m.* **2.** (occasion) Tanzabend *m;* (smart) Ball *m.* **II.** *v.tr. & i.* tanzen. **◆'dancer,** *s.* Tän-

zer(in) m(f). ◆'**dancing**, s. Tanzen n.
dandelion ['dændilaiən], s. Löwenzahn
m.
dandruff ['dændrʌf], s. Schuppen pl.
Dane [dein], s. 1. Däne m; Dänin f. 2.
(dog) (Great) D., Dänische Dogge f.
◆'**Danish. I.** adj. dänisch; D. pastry,
Hefeteilchen n; (coiled) Schnecke f. **II.** s.
(language) Dänisch n.
danger ['deindʒər], s. Gefahr f (to sth.,
für etwas acc). ◆'**dangerous**, adj. gefährlich.
dangle ['dængl], v. 1. v.i. baumeln. 2.
v.tr. (etwas) baumeln lassen; (Beine,
Arme) schlenkern.
Danube ['dænju:b], Pr.n. the D., die Donau.
dare [dɛər], v. 1. modal aux. (es) wagen;
how d. you! was fällt dir ein! **I d. say**
(that) ..., ich glaube schon, daß ... 2.
v.tr. (a) to d. to do sth., (es) wagen, etwas zu tun; (b) to d. s.o. to do sth., j-n
herausfordern, etwas zu tun. ◆'**dare**-
devil, s. Draufgänger m. ◆'**daring. I.**
adj. (a) (of pers.) kühn; (b) (of action) gewagt. **II.** s. Kühnheit f.
dark [dɑ:k]. **I.** adj. dunkel; (sombre) düster; (pitch) d., finster; d. green, dun-
kelgrün; F: to keep sth. d., etwas geheimhalten; d. horse, unbekannte Größe.
II. s. 1. Dunkelheit f. 2. F: to keep s.o.
in the d., j-n im Ungewissen lassen.
◆'**darken**, v. 1. v.tr. verdunkeln. 2. v.i.
sich verdunkeln. ◆'**darkness**, s. Dunkelheit f; (pitch) d., Finsternis f.
darling ['dɑ:liŋ], s. Liebling m.
darn [dɑ:n], v.tr. stopfen.
dart [dɑ:t]. **I.** s. Pfeil m. **II.** v.i. to d. in/
out, herein-/hinausflitzen.
dash [dæʃ]. **I.** s. 1. Schuß m (Rum, Whisky); d. of colour, Farbklecks m. 2. (line)
Strich m; Gedankenstrich m. 3. (a) (rush)
Sturz m; to make a d. for sth., sich auf
etwas acc stürzen; (b) N.Am: Sp: Sprint
m. **II.** v.i. (sich) stürzen; **I have to d.,**
ich muß lossausen. ◆'**dashboard**, s.
Armaturenbrett n. ◆'**dash 'off**, v. 1.
v.i. lossausen. 2. v.tr. (einen Aufsatz
usw.) hinhauen.
data ['dɑ:tə, 'deitə], s.pl. Daten pl; d.
processing, Datenverarbeitung f.
date¹ [deit], s. (fruit) Dattel f.
date². **I.** s. 1. Datum n; what's the d. to-
day? der wievielte ist heute? **to fix a d.,**
einen Termin festsetzen; **to be up to d.,**
auf dem laufenden sein; **to bring sth. up**
to d., etwas auf den neuesten Stand bringen; **out of d.,** (i) überholt; veraltet; (ii)
(expired) ungültig; this is my d. heute. 2. F:
Verabredung f; **to have a d. with s.o.,**
mit j-m verabredet sein. **II.** v. 1. v.tr.
(einen Brief, ein Kunstwerk usw.) datieren; (b) v.i. **to d. back to,** zurückreichen
bis. ◆'**dated**, adj. (a) (of letter etc.) (b)
(old-fashioned) veraltet.
dative ['deitiv], s. Dativ m.
daub [dɔ:b], v.tr. beschmieren; (Farbe)

schmieren.
daughter ['dɔ:tər], s. Tochter f.
◆'**daughter-in-law**, s. Schwiegertoch-
ter f.
daunting ['dɔ:ntiŋ], adj. überwältigend;
d. task, gewaltige Aufgabe.
dawdle ['dɔ:dl], v.i. trödeln.
dawn [dɔ:n]. **I.** s. Morgengrauen n; **at d.,**
bei Tagesanbruch. **II.** v.i. (a) (of day) anbrechen; (b) Fig: **at last it dawned on**
me that ..., endlich kam es mir zum Bewußtsein, daß ...
day [dei], s. 1. (a) Tag m; **to call it a d.,**
für heute Schluß machen; **that made my**
d., da habe ich mich königlich gefreut;
that'll be the d.! das möchte ich mal erleben! (b) attrib. d. shift, Tagschicht f;
d. return (ticket), Tagesrückfahrkarte f.
2. those were the days! das waren noch
Zeiten! **in our d.,** zu unserer Zeit; **I was**
a student in those days, damals war ich
Student; **these days,** heutzutage.
◆'**daybreak**, s. Tagesanbruch m.
◆'**daydream**, s. Wachtraum m. **II.**
v.i. Luftschlösser bauen. ◆'**daylight**, s.
Tageslicht n; **in broad d.,** am hellichten
Tag. ◆'**daytime**, s. Tageszeit f; **in the**
d., bei Tage.
daze [deiz], s. **in a d.,** benommen.
dazzle ['dæzl], n tr (j-n) blenden.
◆'**dazzling**, adj. blendend.
dead [ded]. **I.** adj. 1. (a) tot; (of flower)
verwelkt; **d. body,** Leiche f; (b) (of limb)
to go d., taub werden; Geog: at the d. at
weekends, Köln ist am Wochenende wie
ausgestorben. 2. (complete) völlig, ganz;
d. loss, Totalverlust m; **d. on time,** auf
die Minute pünktlich; **d. heat,** totes Rennen. **II.** s. 1. pl. the d., die Toten mpl.
2. at d. of night, mitten in der Nacht; **in**
the d. of winter, im tiefsten Winter. **III.**
adv. (a) völlig; ganz; (b) F: beat,
todmüde; (b) **to stop d.,** plötzlich stehenbleiben; (c) **I am d. against it,** ich bin
ganz dagegen. ◆'**deaden**, v.tr. (den
Schall usw.) dämpfen; (Schmerz) betäuben. ◆'**dead-'end,** s. (a) Sackgasse f;
(b) attrib. ohne Ausweg; ohne Chancen.
◆'**deadline**, s. (äußerster) Termin m.
◆'**deadlock**, s. **to reach d.,** sich fest-
fahren. ◆'**deadly,** adj. tödlich.
◆'**dead'pan,** adj. ausdruckslos.
deaf [def], adj. taub. ◆'**deafen**, v.tr.
(j-n) taub machen. ◆'**deafening**, adj.
ohrenbetäubend. ◆'**deaf-'mute,** s.
Taubstumme(r) f(m). ◆'**deafness**, s.
Taubheit f.
deal¹ [di:l], s. (a) (part) **a good d. of the**
time, im Großteil der Zeit; (b) (amount)
a great d. of money, eine Menge Geld;
he is a good d. better, ihm geht es viel
besser.
deal². **I.** v.irr. **1.** v.tr. (a) **to d. out** (gifts
etc.), (Geschenke usw.) austeilen; (b) **to**
d. s.o. a blow, j-m einen Schlag versetzen; (c) (Karten) geben. 2. v.i. **a) to d.**
with sth., (i) (of book etc.) von etwas dat

handeln; (ii) (of pers.) etwas erledigen; **to d. with s.o.,** mit j-m fertig werden; **Com: to d. with a firm,** mit einer Firma Geschäfte machen; (b) (at cards) geben. II. s. Geschäft n; (agreement) Abmachung f; F: **it's a d.!** abgemacht! **he got a raw d.,** er hat schlecht dabei abgeschnitten. ◆**'dealer,** s. 1. (at cards) Kartengeber m. 2. Com: Händler m. ◆**'dealing,** s. pl. **to have dealings with s.o.,** mit j-m (geschäftlich) zu tun haben.

dean [di:n], s. Dekan m.

dear [diər]. I. adj. 1. lieb; (in letter) **D. Mr. Smith,** Sehr geehrter Herr Smith; **D. David,** Lieber David. 2. (expensive) teuer; **-ly,** adv. **to love s.o., sth. d.,** j-n, etwas sehr lieben. II. s. Liebe(r,s) f(m,n); **my d.,** mein Lieber m, meine Liebe f. III. int. F: **d. me!** du meine Güte! **oh d.!** ach je!

dearth [də:θ], s. Mangel m (of, an + dat).

death [deθ], s. 1. Tod m; **frozen to d.,** erfroren; **burnt to d.,** verbrannt; **d. penalty,** Todesstrafe f; F: **d. trap,** Todesfalle f. 2. (with number) **five deaths,** fünf Todesfälle mpl; (in accident) fünf Todesopfer npl. ◆**'deathbed,** s. Sterbebett n.

debate [di'beit]. I. s. Debatte f. II. v. 1 v.tr. (ein Thema) debattieren. 2. v.i. **to d. whether to do sth.,** überlegen, ob man etwas tun sollte. ◆**de'batable,** adj. (of question) strittig; **it's d.,** es ist fraglich.

debauched [di'bɔ:tʃt], adj. liederlich.

debility [di'biliti], s. Entkräftung f.

debit ['debit]. I. s. Soll n; (amount) Debetposten m. II. v.tr. **to d. s.o./s.o.'s account with a sum,** j-s Konto mit einer Summe belasten.

debris ['debri:], s. Trümmer npl.

debt [det], s. Schuld f; **to be in d.,** verschuldet sein. ◆**'debtor,** s. Schuldner m.

debut ['deibju:, de-], s. Debüt n.

decade ['dekeid], s. Jahrzehnt n.

decadence ['dekəd(ə)ns], s. Dekadenz f. ◆**'decadent,** adj. dekadent.

decaffeinated [di:'kæfineitid], adj. koffeinfrei.

decanter [di'kæntər], s. Karaffe f.

decay [di'kei]. I. s. 1. (decline) Verfall m. 2. (of matter, teeth) Fäulnis f. II. v.i. a (of building) verfallen; (b) (of vegetable matter, teeth) verfaulen; (of flesh) verwesen.

deceased [di'si:st], s. **the d.,** der/die Verstorbene.

deceit [di'si:t], s. Betrug m. ◆**de'ceitful,** adj. falsch; (cunning) hinterlistig.

deceive [di'si:v], v. 1. v.tr. (a) betrügen; (b) (mislead) täuschen. 2. v.i. täuschen.

December [di'sembər], s. Dezember m.

decent ['di:s(ə)nt], adj. anständig; F: **are you d.?** bist du angezogen? **the food is quite d.,** das Essen ist ganz annehmbar. ◆**'decency** [-si], s. Anstand m; **he**

didn't even have the **d.** to thank me, er hat es nicht einmal für nötig gehalten, mir zu danken.

deception [di'sep/(ə)n], s. (a) Betrug m; (b) (misleading) Täuschung f. ◆**de'ceptive,** adj. trügerisch; (misleading) irreführend.

decibel ['desibel], s. Dezibel n.

decide [di'said], v. 1. v.tr. entscheiden; **to d. to do sth.,** beschließen, etwas zu tun. 2. v.i. sich entschließen; **to d. on sth.,** sich zu etwas dat entscheiden. ◆**de'cidedly,** adv. **d.** fat, entschieden zu fett. ◆**de'ciding,** adj. entscheidend.

deciduous [di'sidjuəs], adj. **d.** tree, Laubbaum m.

decimal ['desim(ə)l]. I. adj. dezimal; **d. point,** Dezimalpunkt m; **to three d. places** auf drei Dezimalstellen. II. s. Dezimalzahl f.

decipher [di'saifər], v.tr. entziffern; (einen Code) entschlüsseln.

decision [di'siʒ(ə)n], s. 1. (a) (of pers.) Entscheidung f; (resolve) Entschluß m; **to reach a d.,** zu einem Entschluß kommen; **to take/make a d.,** (i) einen Entschluß fassen; (ii) eine Entscheidung treffen; (b) (of group, assembly) Beschluß m; Jur: Urteil n. 2. (manner) Entschlossenheit f. ◆**decisive** [-'saisiv], adj. 1. ausschlaggebend; (of action etc.) entscheidend. 2. (of pers., manner) entschlossen; **-ly,** adv. entscheidend.

deck [dek], s. Deck n; **a d.** of cards, ein Spiel Karten. ◆**'deck-chair,** s. Liegestuhl m.

declare [di'kleər], v.tr. **d.** i. erklären; (at customs) **have you anything to d.?** haben Sie etwas zu verzollen? **to d. s.o. the winner,** j-n zum Sieger erklären. ◆**declaration** [deklə'reiʃ(ə)n], s. Erklärung f; (statement) Behauptung f.

decline [di'klain]. I. s. (a) Niedergang m (eines Reiches usw.); Abfall m (der Preise); **to go into a d./be on the d.,** zur Neige gehen; (b) (deterioration) Verschlechterung f (in morals, der Moral); **d.** in standards, Abfall m des Niveaus; Sch: Leistungsabfall m. II. v. 1. v.tr. ablehnen; **he declined to comment,** er enthielt sich eines Kommentars. 2. v.i. sinken; (of prices) abfallen.

decode [di:'kəud], v.tr. entschlüsseln.

decompose [di:kəm'pəuz], v.i. verwesen. ◆**decomposition** [-kəmpə-'zif(ə)n], s. Verwesung f.

décor ['dekɔ:r], s. Dekor m. ◆**decorate** ['dekəreit], v.tr. a (etwas) schmücken; (eine Torte usw.) verzieren; (ein Zimmer) neu streichen (und tapezieren); (c) (j-n) (mit einem Orden) auszeichnen. ◆**deco'ration,** s. 1. a Verzierung f; Dekoration f; interior d., Innenausstattung f. 2. (medal) Auszeichnung f. ◆**'decorative,** adj. dekorativ. ◆**'decorator,** s. (a) interior d., Innenarchitekt m; (b) painter and d., Maler und Tapezierer m.

decoy [di'kɔi], s. (object) Köder m; (pers., bird) Lockvogel m.

decrease I. [di:'kri:s], s. (in size) Abnahme f; (in number, price) Rückgang m. II. [di:'kri:s], v. 1. v.tr. (den Preis) herabsetzen; (etwas) verringern. 2. v.i. (in size) abnehmen; (in number) weniger werden; (of numbers) sinken. ◆de'creasing, adj. abnehmend; **-ly**, adv. in abnehmendem Maße.

decree [di'kri:]. I. s. 1. Adm: Erlaß m. 2. Jur: Entscheid m; (judgement) Urteil n. II. v.tr. (etwas) verordnen.

decrepit [di'krepit], adj. 1. (of pers.) altersschwach. 2. (of thing) heruntergekommen; (of house etc.) verfallen.

dedicate ['dedikeit], v.tr. a) (ein Gebäude) einweihen; (b) to d. sth. to s.o., j-m etwas widmen. ◆**dedi'cation**, s. 1. Einweihung f (einer Kirche usw.). 2. Widmung f (eines Buches usw.). 3. (sense of) d., Hingabe f.

deduce [di'dju:s], v.tr. folgern (from, aus + dat).

deduct [di'dʌkt], v.tr. (einen Betrag) abziehen. ◆**de'duction**, s. 1. Abzug m. 2. (conclusion) Folgerung f.

deed [di:d], s. 1. Tat f. 2. Jur: Urkunde f.

deep [di:p], adj. & adv. tief; **d. sleep**, fester Schlaf; **d. blue**, tiefblau. ◆**'deepen**, v. 1. v.tr. a) vertiefen; (b) (ein Gefühl) verstärken. 2. v.i. sich vertiefen; (strengthen) sich verstärken. ◆**deep-'freeze**, s. Tiefkühltruhe f. ◆**deep-'fry**, v.tr. in tiefem Fett ausbacken. ◆**'deeply**, adv. d. hurt, schwer gekränkt. ◆**deep-'rooted**, adj. tief verwurzelt. ◆**deep-'seated**, adj. tiefsitzend.

deer [diər], s. inv. Hirsch m.

deface [di'feis], v.tr. beschädigen; (etwas Schriftliches) unleserlich machen.

defamation [defə'meiʃ(ə)n], s. Verleumdung f. ◆**defamatory** [di'fæmətri], adj. verleumderisch.

default [di'fɔ:lt]. I. s. Jur: by d., durch Nichterscheinen vor (des Gegners). II. v.i. (a) (seinen Verpflichtungen usw.) nicht nachkommen; (b) Jur: etc: nicht erscheinen.

defeat [di'fi:t]. I. s. Niederlage f. II. v.tr. (a) (j-n, eine Armee) besiegen; Sp: (j-n) schlagen; (b) Parl: (einen Vorschlag) ablehnen; (die Regierung) überstimmen. ◆**de'featist**. I. s. Defätist m. II. adj. defätistisch.

defect¹ [di'fekt], s. Fehler m; physical d., Gebrechen n. ◆**de'fective**, adj. mangelhaft; d. brakes, defekte Bremsen.

defect² [di'fekt], v.i. (zu einer anderen Partei usw.) übertreten; abtrünnig werden.

defence [di'fens], s. (a) Verteidigung f; (justification) Rechtfertigung f; (b) Sp: Abwehr f. ◆**de'fenceless**, adj. wehrlos.

◆**defend** [di'fend], v.tr. (j-n, etwas) verteidigen (**from/against**, gegen + acc); (eine Tat) rechtfertigen. ◆**de'fendant**, s. Jur: Angeklagte(r) f(m). ◆**de'fender**, s. Verteidiger m; Sp: Abwehrspieler m; (of title) Titelverteidiger m. ◆**de'fensive**. I. adj. defensiv; **d. measure**, Abwehrmaßnahme f. II. s. Defensive f; **to go on to the d.**, in die Defensive gehen.

defer [di'fə:r], v.tr. verschieben. ◆**de'ferment**, s. Aufschub m.

deference ['def(ə)rəns], s. Ehrerbietung f. ◆**deferential** [-'renʃ(ə)l], adj. ehrerbietig.

defiance [di'faiəns], s. Trotz m; (act of) d., Herausforderung f. ◆**de'fiant**, adj. trotzig.

deficiency [di'fiʃənsi], s. 1. Mangel m (of/in, an + dat). 2. (quality) Mangelhaftigkeit f. ◆**de'ficient**, adj. ungenügend; (of work) mangelhaft; **to be d. in**, mangeln an + dat.

deficit ['defisit], s. Defizit n.

define [di'fain], v.tr. (a) definieren; **to d. one's position**, seinen Standpunkt klarstellen; (b) (Grenzen) festlegen; (c) (of outlines, ideas) clearly defined, klar umrissen. ◆**definite** ['definit], adj. bestimmt; **is that d.? is that so sicher?** **-ly**, adv. bestimmt. ◆**defi'nition**, s. 1. Definition f (eines Wortes). 2. Schärfe f (des Bildes, des Tones).

deflate [di'fleit], v.tr. (a) (aus einem Reifen usw.) die Luft ablassen; (b) F: that's deflated him! das hat ihm den Wind aus den Segeln genommen! ◆**de'flation**, s. Fin: Deflation f.

deflect [di'flekt], v.tr. ablenken.

deformed [di'fɔ:md], adj. mißgestaltet. ◆**de'formity**, s. Mißbildung f.

defraud [di'frɔ:d], v.tr. **to d. s.o. of sth.**, j-n um etwas acc betrügen.

defray [di'frei], v.tr. **to d. the cost of sth.**, die Kosten von etwas dat tragen.

defrost [di:'frɔst], v.tr. (den Kühlschrank) abtauen; (Tiefgekühltes) auftauen lassen.

deft [deft], adj. geschickt, gewandt.

defunct [di'fʌŋkt], adj. (of firm, railway etc.) stillgelegt; **to be d.**, nicht mehr bestehen.

defy [di'fai], v.tr. (a) (j-m, etwas dat) trotzen; (challenge) (j-n) herausfordern; (b) **to d. description**, jeder Beschreibung spotten.

degenerate. I. [di'dʒenəreit], v.i. degenerieren. II. [di'dʒen(ə)rit], adj. entartet; (of pers.) degenerieren.

degradation [degrə'deiʃ(ə)n], s. Entwürdigung f. ◆**de'grading**, adj. entwürdigend.

degree [di'gri:], s. 1. Grad m; **by degrees**, allmählich, nach und nach; **to get a d.**, sein Studium abschließen.

dehydrate [di:'haidreit], v.tr. (etwas dat) das Wasser entziehen; (Gemüse) dörren.

◆dehy'dration, s. Wasserentzug m.

de-ice ['di:'ais], v.tr. enteisen. ◆'de-'icer, s. Enteisungsmittel n.

deign [dein], v.tr. to d. to do sth., sich herablassen, etwas zu tun.

dejected [di'dʒektid], adj. niedergeschlagen. ◆de'jection, s. Niedergeschlagenheit f.

delay [di'lei]. I. s. 1. Verzögerung f; without (further) d., unverzüglich. 2. (lateness) Verspätung f. II. v. 1. v.tr. (a) verzögern; (eine Zahlung usw.) aufschieben; (b) (j-n) aufhalten. 2. v.i. zögern. ◆de'layed, adj. to be d., sich verzögern; (of pers.) aufgehalten werden.

delegate. I. ['deligit], s. Delegierte(r) f(m). II. ['deligeit], v.tr. (j-n) delegieren; to d. sth. to s.o., j-m etwas anvertrauen. ◆dele'gation, s. Delegation f.

delete [di'li:t], v.tr. streichen. ◆de'letion, s. Streichung f.

deliberate. I. [di'lib(ə)rit], adj. 1. (intentional) absichtlich; (conscious) bewußt. 2. (of pers., manner) bedächtig; (of speech, tread) gemessen. II. [di'libəreit], v.tr. & i. nachdenken (on, über + acc); (of group) sich beraten (on, über + acc). ◆delibe'ration, s. (a) Überlegung f; (b) pl. Beratung f (einer Versammlung usw.).

delicacy [delikəsi], s. Cu: Delikatesse f. ◆delicate ['delikit], adj. (a) (of colours, feelings etc.) zart; (b) (tricky) heikel; (c) (of health, mechanism, pers.) empfindlich; (d) a d. taste, ein feiner Geschmack.

delicatessen [delikə'tes(ə)n], s. (shop) Feinkostgeschäft n.

delicious [di'liʃəs], adj. köstlich; (of food) lecker.

delight [di'lait]. I. s. Freude f. II. v. 1. v.tr. (j-n) erfreuen. 2. v.i. to d. in doing sth., sich damit vergnügen, etwas zu tun. ◆de'lighted, adj. to be d. with/at sth., sich über etwas acc freuen; (I shall be) d., mit dem größten Vergnügen. ◆de'lightful, adj. entzückend.

delinquency [di'liŋkwənsi], s. Kriminalität f. ◆de'linquent. I. adj. straffällig. II. s. Straftäter m.

delirious [di'liriəs], adj. (im Fieber) phantasierend; d. with joy, außer sich vor Freude. ◆de'lirium, s. Delirium n.

deliver [di'livər], v.tr. (a) (Waren usw.) liefern; (ein Paket) abgeben; (Post) zustellen; F: to d. the goods, seinen Verpflichtungen nachkommen; (b) to d. a speech, eine Rede halten. ◆de'liverance, s. Erlösung f. ◆de'livery, s. 1. Lieferung f (von Waren); Zustellung f (von Post). 2. Med: Entbindung f.

delta ['deltə], s. Flußdelta n.

delude [di'lju:d], v.tr. (j-n) täuschen; to d. oneself, sich dat Illusionen machen. ◆de'lusion, s. Täuschung f.

deluge ['delju:dʒ]. I. s. (a) Wolkenbruch m; (b) Fig: Flut f (von Briefen usw.). II. v.tr. (j-n) überschwemmen.

de luxe [di'lʌks]. adj. Luxus-; d. l. version/model, Luxusausführung f.

delve [delv], v.i. to d. into sth., sich in etwas acc vertiefen.

demand [di'mɑ:nd]. I. s. 1. Forderung f; on d., auf Verlangen. 2. Com: Nachfrage f; in d., gefragt. 3. pl. to make (many) demands on s.o.'s time, j-n sehr in Anspruch nehmen. II. v.tr. verlangen.

demented [di'mentid], adj. wahnsinnig.

democracy [di'mɔkrəsi], s. Demokratie f. ◆democrat ['deməkræt], s. Demokrat(in) m(f). ◆demo'cratic, adj. demokratisch.

demolish [di'mɔliʃ], v.tr. zerstören; (Gebäude usw.) niederreißen. ◆demolition [demə'liʃ(ə)n], s. Abbruch m.

demon ['di:mən], s. Dämon m.

demonstrate ['demənstreit], v. 1. v.tr. (a) (etwas Wahres) beweisen; (b) (ein System) darlegen; Com: (ein Gerät, ein Auto) vorführen. 2. v.i. Pol: demonstrieren. ◆demon'stration, s. 1. (a) Beweis m; (b) Darlegung f; Com: Vorführung f. 2. Pol: Demonstration f. ◆demonstrative [di'mɔnstrətiv], adj. demonstrativ; she's not very d., sie zeigt selten ihre Gefühle. ◆'demonstrator, s. Pol: Demonstrant m.

demoralize [di'mɔrəlaiz], v.tr. entmutigen.

demote [di'məut], v.tr. degradieren.

den [den], s. 1. (a) Höhle f; (b) Bau m (eines Fuchses usw.). 2. (room) Bude f.

denial [di'naiəl], s. Leugnung f; (refusal) Verweigerung f; Ablehnung f (einer Bitte); official d., Dementi n.

Denmark ['denmɑ:k]. Pr.n. Dänemark n.

denim ['denim], s. Jeansstoff m; denims, Jeans pl.

denomination [dinɔmi'neiʃ(ə)n], s. 1. Ecc: Bekenntnis n. 2. Nennwert m (von Münzen usw.). ◆de'nominator, s. Nenner m.

denote [di'nəut], v.tr. bedeuten.

denounce [di'nauns], v.tr. (j-n, etwas) öffentlich verurteilen.

dense [dens], adj. 1. dicht. 2. F: (of pers.) schwer von Begriff; dumm. ◆'density, s. Dichte f.

dent [dent]. I. s. (in metal) Beule f; (also in wood etc.) Delle f. II. v.tr. (etwas) einbeulen; dented, verbeult.

dental ['dentl], adj. dental, Zahn-. ◆'dentist, s. Zahnarzt m. ◆'dentistry, s. Zahnheilkunde f. ◆'denture, s. Zahnprothese f, F: Gebiß n.

deny [di'nai], v.tr. (a) (eine Tat) leugnen; (ein Gerücht) dementieren; (esp. with neg.) (ein Gefühl) abstreiten; there's no denying (the fact) that ..., es läßt sich nicht leugnen, daß ...; (b) (refuse) to d. s.o. sth., j-m etwas verweigern; to d.

oneself sth., sich *dat* etwas nicht gönnen.

deodorant [diː'oudərənt], *s.* Deo(dorant) *n.*

depart [di'pɑːt], *v.i.* (*a*) (*of pers.*) abreisen; (*of train*) abfahren; (*b*) to d. (from a rule etc.), (von einer Regel usw.) abweichen. ◆de'**parture**, *s.* 1. Abreise *f*, Abfahrt *f*. 2. Abweichung *f*; a new d., eine Neuerung.

department [di'pɑːtmənt], *s.* 1. (*a*) Abteilung *f*; d. store, Kaufhaus *n*; (*at university*) Institut *n*. 2. *Pol:* Ministerium *n*; *N.Am:* State D., Außenministerium *n*. ◆de'**part'mental**, *adj.* 1. Abteilungs-. 2. *Pol:* Ministerial-.

depend [di'pend], *v.i.* (*a*) abhängen (on sth., von etwas *dat*); depending on ..., je nach + *dat*; (*b*) (*rely*) to d. (up)on s.o., sth., sich auf j-n, etwas *acc* verlassen. ◆de'**pendable**, *adj.* (*of pers.*) verläßlich; (*of source etc.*) zuverlässig. ◆de'**pendant**, *s.* = dependent II. ◆de'**pendence**, *s.* 1. Abhängigkeit *f* (on, von + *dat*). 2. (*trust*) Vertrauen *n* (on, auf + *acc*). ◆de'**pendent**. I. *adj.* angewiesen (on, auf + *acc*). II. *s. Adm:* Unterhaltsberechtigte(r) *f(m)*.

depict [di'pikt], *v.tr.* schildern.

deplete [di'pliːt], *v.tr.* (*Vorräte usw.*) aufbrauchen; (*Reserven*) verzehren. ◆de'**pletion**, *s.* Schwund *m* (von Reserven).

deplore [di'plɔːr], *v.tr.* bedauern. ◆de'**plorable**, *adj.* bedauernswert; (*disgraceful*) schändlich.

deploy [di'plɔi], *v.tr.* (*use*) einsetzen; (*position*) verteilen; (*base*) stationieren.

deport [di'pɔːt], *v.tr.* ausweisen. ◆depor'**tation**, *s.* Ausweisung *f.*

depose [di'pəuz], *v.tr.* vom Thron absetzen.

deposit [di'pozit]. I. *s.* 1. (*safe*) d., Depot *n*; d. account, Sparkonto *n*. 2. (*a*) (*down payment*) Anzahlung *f* (on, auf + *acc*); (*b*) (*guarantee*) Pfand *n*. 3. (*left by liquid*) Bodensatz *m*. 4. Vorkommen *n* (von Erz usw.). II. *v.tr.* to d. valuables (with a bank), Wertgegenstände (bei einer Bank) hinterlegen.

depot ['depəu, *N.Am:* 'diːpəu], *s.* (*a*) Depot *n*; (*b*) *bus:*, Autobusgarage *f*; *Rail:* goods d., Güterbahnhof *m*; (*building*) Güterhalle *f.*

depraved [di'preivd], *adj.* (*moralisch*) verdorben. ◆de'**pravity** [-'præv-], *s.* Verdorbenheit *f.*

depreciate [di'priːʃieit], *v.i. Fin:* an Wert verlieren. ◆depreci'**ation**, *s.* Wertverlust *m.*

depress [di'pres], *v.tr.* (*a*) (einen Knopf, ein Pedal usw.) herunterdrücken; (*b*) (j-n) deprimieren; (*c*) *Com:* (den Markt, Handel) ungünstig beeinflussen. ◆de'**pressed**, *adj.* (*of pers.*) deprimiert; (*of market etc.*) flau; d. area, (wirtschaftliches) Notstandsgebiet *n*. ◆de'**pressing**,

adj. deprimierend. ◆de'**pression**, *s.* 1. *Fin:* Wirtschaftskrise *f.* 2. (*of pers.*) Depression *f.*

deprive [di'praiv], *v.tr.* to d. s.o. of sth., j-n etwas *gen* berauben. ◆de'**prived**, *adj.* benachteiligt. ◆depri'**vation** [depri'veiʃ(ə)n], *s.* Entbehrung *f.*

depth [depθ], *s.* 1. Tiefe *f.* 2. (*a*) Stärke *f* (von Farben, Gefühlen usw.); (*b*) (*of study etc.*) in d., gründlich, eingehend. 3. in the depths of despair, in tiefster Verzweiflung.

deputation [depju(ː)'teiʃ(ə)n], *s.* Deputation *f.* ◆'**deputize**, *v.i.* to d. for s.o., j-n vertreten. ◆'**deputy**, *s.* Stellvertreter(in) *m(f)*, Beauftragte(r) *f(m)*; d. chairman, stellvertretende(r) Vorsitzende(r) *f(m)*.

derail [di'reil], *v.tr.* to be derailed, entgleisen. ◆de'**railment**, *s.* Entgleisung *f.*

derange [di'rein(d)ʒ], *v.tr.* he is deranged, er ist geistesgestört.

derelict ['derilikt], *adj.* verwahrlost.

derision [di'riʒ(ə)n], *s.* Hohn *m*, Spott *m.* ◆de'**risive** *adj.* höhnisch.

derive [di'raiv], *v.tr. & i.* (*a*) to d. sth. from sth., etwas aus etwas *dat* gewinnen; (Nutzen usw.) aus etwas *dat* ziehen; to d. pleasure from sth., Freude an etwas *dat* haben; (*b*) to be derived/d. from sth., von etwas *dat* stammen. ◆deri'**vation** [deri-], *s.* Abstammung *f.* ◆de'**rivative** [di'rivətiv]. I. *adj.* (*a*) (*of substance*) abgeleitet; (*b*) (*of style etc.*) eklektisch. II. *s.* 1. Ableitung *f*; *Ch:* Derivat *n.*

dermatologist [dəːmə'tɔlədʒist], *s.* Hautarzt *m.*

derogatory [di'rɔgət(ə)ri], *adj.* abträglich; (*of remark*) abfällig; (*of word*) abwertend.

descend [di'send], *v.* 1. *v.i.* (*of thing*) herunterkommen; (*drop*) herunterfallen; (*of pers.*) heruntersteigen; to be descended from s.o., von j-m abstammen. 2. *v.tr.* (eine Treppe) hinuntergehen. ◆de'**scendant**, *s.* Nachkomme *m.* ◆de'**scent**, *s.* 1. Abstieg *m.* 2. (*in family etc.*) Abstammung *f.*

describe [dis'kraib], *v.tr.* beschreiben; to d. s.o. as ..., j-n als ... bezeichnen. ◆des'**cription**, *s.* Beschreibung *f*; people of this d., Leute dieser Art. ◆des'**criptive**, *adj.* (*a*) beschreibend; (*b*) (*quality*) anschaulich.

desert[1] ['dezət], *s.* Wüste *f.*

desert[2] [di'zəːt], *v.* 1. *v.i.* to d. (from the army), (vom Heer) desertieren. 2. *v.tr.* (j-n) verlassen. ◆de'**serted**, *adj.* verlassen; (*of home etc.*) leer. ◆de'**serter**, *s.* Deserteur *m.* ◆de'**sertion**, *s.* Fahnenflucht *f.*

deserts [di'zəːts], *s. pl.* to get one's just deserts, seinen wohlverdienten Lohn empfangen.

deserve [di'zəːv], *v.tr.* verdienen. ◆de'**serving**, *adj.* verdienstvoll. ◆de'**servedly** [-idli], *adv.* verdienter-

maßen; (rightly) mit Recht.
design [di'zain]. **I.** s. 1. (intention) Absicht f; **by d.**, absichtlich. 2. (a) (pattern) Muster n; (b) (shape) Form f. 3. Ind: etc: (a) (plan) Entwurf m; (b) Bauart f; E: etc: Konstruktion f; **the latest d.**, die neueste Ausführung. **II.** v.tr. (ein Kleid, eine Maschine usw.) entwerfen; (eine Brücke usw.) konstruieren; **that's not what it is designed for**, es ist nicht zu diesem Zweck bestimmt. ◆**de'signer**, s. Ind: Konstrukteur m; Cl: Modedesigner(in) m(f).

designate ['dezigneit], v.tr. usu. Adm: (a) **to d. s.o. (as) sth.**, j-n zu etwas dat ernennen; (b) (etwas) bezeichnen; (Bedingungen usw.) nennen; (Grenzen usw.) kennzeichnen.

desire [di'zaiər]. **I.** s. 1. (a) (particular wish) Wunsch m; (b) (craving) Verlangen n (for, nach + dat); **I have no d. to travel**, ich habe keine Lust zum Reisen. 2. (sensual) d., Begierde f. **II.** v.tr. (etwas) wünschen, esp. Lit: begehren; **it leaves much to be desired**, es läßt viel zu wünschen übrig. ◆**de'sirable**, adj. (a) (of thing) begehrenswert; (attractive) reizvoll; (b) (of action) wünschenswert.

desk [desk], s. (in office etc.) Schreibtisch m; Sch: Pult n.

desolate ['desələt], adj. (of place) wüst, trostlos.

despair [dis'peər]. **I.** s. Verzweiflung f (at, über + acc). **II.** v.i. verzweifeln.

desperate ['despərət], adj. 1. (a) (of illness etc.) gefährlich; (b) (extreme) äußerst; **d. need**, dringendes Bedürfnis. 2. (of pers.) verwegen; zu allem fähig; (of conflict, attempt etc.) verzweifelt; **-ly**, adv. sehr; (urgently) dringend; **to want sth. d.**, etwas unbedingt (haben) wollen. ◆**despe'ration**, s. in d., aus Verzweiflung.

despicable ['despikəbl, dis'pik-], adj. verachtenswert. ◆**despise** [dis'paiz], v.tr. verachten.

despite [dis'pait], prep. trotz (+ gen).

despondent [dis'pɔndənt], adj. verzagt.

despotic [des'pɔtik], adj. despotisch.

dessert [di'zə:t], s. Nachtisch m; **d. spoon**, Dessertlöffel m.

destination [desti'neiʃ(ə)n], s. (of train etc.) Bestimmungsort m; (of pers.) Reiseziel n.

destine ['destin], v.tr. **to be destined for sth.**, zu etwas dat bestimmt sein. ◆**'destiny**, s. Schicksal n.

destitute ['destitju:t], adj. notleidend; (poor) verarmt.

destroy [dis'trɔi], v.tr. zerstören; (Papiere, Ungeziefer, eine Armee) vernichten; (ein Tier) töten. ◆**de'stroyer**, s. Zerstörer m. ◆**destruction** [dis'trʌkʃ(ə)n], s. Vernichtung f; Zerstörung f (eines Gebäudes usw.). ◆**des'tructive**, adj. destruktiv.

detach [di'tætʃ], v.tr. entfernen; **to d.**

itself/become detached, sich (los)lösen. ◆**de'tachable**, adj. abnehmbar. ◆**de'tached**, adj. 1. abgetrennt; **d. house**, Einfamilienhaus n. 2. (of pers.) distanziert; (uninvolved) unbeteiligt; (unbiased) objektiv. ◆**de'tachment**, s. 1. (of pers.) Distanziertheit f; Objektivität f. 2. Mil: etc: Abteilung f.

detail ['di:teil, N.Am: di'teil], s. Detail n; **in d.**, ausführlich; **to go into d.**, näher auf etwas acc eingehen.

detain [di'tein], v.tr. (a) Jur: (j-n) in Haft behalten; (b) (delay) (j-n) aufhalten. ◆**detai'nee**, s. Häftling m.

detect [di'tekt], v.tr. (a) (find out) entdecken; (b) (notice) wahrnehmen. ◆**de'tection**, s. (a) Entdeckung f; (b) Wahrnehmung f. ◆**de'tective**, s. Detektiv m; **d. story**, Kriminalroman m. ◆**de'tector**, s. Suchgerät n.

detente [dei'tɑ:t], s. Entspannung f.

detention [di'tenʃ(ə)n], s. Jur: Haft f; Sch: Nachsitzen n.

deter [di'tə:r], v.tr. abhalten.

detergent [di'tə:dʒ(ə)nt], s. Waschmittel n.

deteriorate [di'tiəriəreit], v.i. (become worse) sich verschlechtern. ◆**deterio'ration**, s. Verschlechterung f.

determine [di'tə:min], v.tr. (a) (fix) bestimmen; (discover) (das Wesen einer Sache) ermitteln; **to d. the sex of a baby**, das Geschlecht eines Babys feststellen; (b) (decide) **to d. to do sth.**, sich entschließen, etwas zu tun. ◆**de'termined**, adj. (of pers.) resolut; entschlossen. ◆**determi'nation**, s. (of pers.) Entschlossenheit f.

deterrent [di'terənt], s. Abschreckungsmittel n.

detest [di'test], v.tr. verabscheuen.

detonate ['detəneit], v.tr. explodieren lassen. ◆**deto'nation**, s. Detonation f. ◆**'detonator**, s. Sprengkapsel f.

detour ['di:tuər], s. Umweg m.

detract [di'trækt], v.i. **to d. from sth.**, etwas beeinträchtigen.

detriment ['detrimənt], s. Nachteil m; (damage) Schaden m; **to the d. of ...**, zum Schaden + gen. ◆**detri'mental**, adj. schädlich (**to**, für).

deuce [dju:s], s. (Tennis) Einstand m.

devalue [di:'vælju], v.tr. abwerten. ◆**devalu'ation**, s. Abwertung f.

devastate ['devəsteit], v.tr. verwüsten. ◆**'devastating**, adj. verheerend. ◆**devas'tation**, s. Verwüstung f.

develop [di'veləp], v. 1. v.tr. entwickeln; **to d. a district**, ein Gebiet erschließen; **to d. an illness**, eine Krankheit bekommen. 2. v.i. sich entwickeln; **to d. into sth.**, zu etwas dat werden. ◆**de'veloper**, s. (pers.) (a) Erschließer m (eines Gebiets); Pej: Spekulant m; (b) late Phot: Entwickler m. ◆**de'veloping**, adj: **d. country**, Entwicklungsland n. ◆**de'velopment**, s. 1.

Entwicklung *f.* 2. Erschließung *f* (eines Gebiets).

deviate ['diːvieit], *v.i.* abweichen. ◆**devi'ation,** *s.* Abweichung *f.*

device [di'vais], *s.* 1. to leave s.o. to his own devices, j-n sich *dat* selbst überlassen. 2. *(apparatus)* Gerät *n.*

devil ['devl], *s.* Teufel *m;* **what the d. are you doing?** was zum Teufel machst du da? **talk of the d.!** wenn man vom Teufel spricht! **be a d.!** wag's doch mal!

devious ['diːviəs], *adj.* 1. *(complex)* umständlich. 2. *(of pers.)* hinterlistig.

devise [di'vaiz], *v.tr.* (einen Plan) ersinnen; (eine Methode, ein Gerät) erfinden.

devoid [di'vɔid], *adj.* **d. of,** frei von + *dat; (neg. sense)* bar + *gen.*

devote [di'vəut], *v.tr.* (Zeit, ein Buch usw.) widmen (**to** s.o., sth., j-m, etwas *dat*); **to d. oneself to sth.,** sich etwas *dat* widmen. ◆**de'voted,** *adj.* ergeben (**to,** *dat*); *(loving)* liebevoll. ◆**de'votion,** *s.* Hingabe *f* (**to** sth., an etwas *dat*); Liebe *f* (**to** s.o., für j-n).

devour [di'vauər], *v.tr.* verschlingen.

devout [di'vaut], *adj.* fromm.

dew [djuː], *s.* Tau *m.*

dexterity [deks'teriti], *s.* Geschicklichkeit *f.*

diabetes [daiə'biːtiːz], *s.* Zuckerkrankheit *f.* ◆**diabetic** [-'betik]. I. *adj.* zuckerkrank; **d. chocolate,** Diabetikerschokolade *f.* II. *s.* Diabetiker(in) *m(f).*

diabolical [daiə'bɔlik(ə)l], *adj.* teuflisch.

diagnose ['daiəgnəuz], *v.tr.* (eine Krankheit) diagnostizieren. ◆**diagnosis,** *pl.* **-oses** [-'nəusis, -əusiːz], *s.* Diagnose *f.*

diagonal [dai'ægənəl], *adj.* diagonal; **-ly,** *adv.* schräg.

diagram ['daiəgræm], *s.* Diagramm *n.*

dial ['daiəl]. I. *s.* Wählscheibe *f* (eines Telefons). II. *v.tr.* (eine Nummer) wählen; **can I d. America?** kann ich nach Amerika durchwählen? ◆**dialling,** *s.* **d. tone,** Amtszeichen *n.*

dialect ['daiəlekt], *s.* Dialekt *m.*

dialogue ['daiəlɔg], *s.* Dialog *m.*

diameter [dai'æmitər], *s.* Durchmesser *m.* ◆**dia'metrically,** *adv.* **d. opposed,** genau entgegengesetzt.

diamond ['daiəmənd], *s.* 1. Diamant *m.* 2. *(a) (shape)* Raute *f; (b) (in cards)* Karo *n.* ◆**'diamond-shaped,** *adj.* rautenförmig.

diaper ['daiəpər], *s. N.Am:* Windel *f.*

diarrhoea [daiə'riə], *s.* Durchfall *m.*

diary ['daiəri], *s.* 1. *(written record)* Tagebuch *n.* 2. *(for appointments etc.)* Kalender *m.*

dice [dais], *s. pl.* Würfel *m.*

dictate [dik'teit]. I. *v.tr. & i.* diktieren; (Maßnahmen usw.) vorschreiben. II. *s. usu. pl.* Gebot *n.* ◆**dic'tation,** *s.* Diktat *n.* ◆**dic'tator,** *s.* Diktator *m.* ◆**dicta'torial,** *adj. (of power)* diktatorisch; *(of tone)* gebieterisch. ◆**dic'tatorship,** *s.* Diktatur *f.*

dictionary ['dikʃ(ə)nri], *s.* Wörterbuch *n.*

diddle ['didl], *v.tr. F:* (j-n) übers Ohr hauen.

die [dai], *v.i. (a) (of pers.)* sterben (**of** sth., an etwas *dat); (of plants, animals)* eingehen; *(of flowers)* verwelken; *(b) F:* **I am dying of thirst,** ich verdurste; **to be dying to do sth.,** darauf brennen, etwas zu tun; *(c) F: (of car, machine)* **it died on me,** es hat den Geist aufgegeben. ◆**'die a'way,** *v.i.* verhallen. ◆**'die 'down,** *v.i. (of fire)* ausgehen; *(of wind)* nachlassen. ◆**'diehard,** *s.* Hartnäckige(r) *f(m).* ◆**'die 'out,** *v.i.* aussterben.

diesel [diːz(ə)l], *s.* **d. (oil),** Diesel(öl) *n;* **d. engine,** (i) *E:* Dieselmotor *m;* (ii) *Rail:* Diesellok *f.*

diet ['daiət]. I. *s.* 1. *(food)* Kost *f.* 2. *(regime)* Diät *f;* **to be on a d.,** *(to slim)* eine Schlankheitskur machen. II. *v.i.* eine Schlankheitskur machen.

differ ['difər], *v.i. (a)* sich unterscheiden (**from,** von + *dat); (b) (disagree)* **to d. about sth.,** über etwas *acc* anderer Meinung sein. ◆**'difference** ['difr(ə)ns], *s. (a)* Unterschied *m;* **d. in age/colour,** Alters-/Farbunterschied *m;* **it makes no d.** (**to me**), es ist (mir) gleich; *(b) (of opinion),* Meinungsverschiedenheit *f.* ◆**'different,** *adj. (pred.)* anders (**from,** als + *nom); (attrib.)* andere(r,s); *(with pl.) (distinct, various)* verschieden; **they are d.,** (i) *(both)* sie sind anders; (ii) *(from one another)* sie sind verschieden. ◆**differentiate** [-'renʃieit], *v.tr. & i.* unterscheiden.

difficult ['difikəlt], *adj.* schwierig. ◆**'difficulty,** *s.* Schwierigkeit *f.*

diffidence ['difid(ə)ns], *s.* Schüchternheit *f.* ◆**'diffident,** *adj.* schüchtern.

dig [dig]. I. *s.* **to give s.o. a d. in the ribs,** j-m einen Rippenstoß geben. II. *v.tr.* 1. *(a)* (Erde, ein Beet) umgraben; *(b)* (ein Loch) graben. 2. *v.i.* graben (**for** sth., nach etwas *dat); (in garden)* umgraben. ◆**digs,** *s.pl. F:* Bude *f;* **to live in d.,** in Untermiete wohnen. ◆**'dig 'up,** *v.tr.* (a) (eine Pflanze, eine Schatz) ausgraben; (den Garten) umgraben; *(b) F:* (Informationen) ans Licht bringen.

digest [dai'dʒest], *v.tr.* (a) (Essen) verdauen; *(b)* (Tatsachen) verarbeiten. ◆**di'gestible,** *adj.* verdaulich. ◆**di'gestion,** *s.* Verdauung *f.*

dignify ['dignifai], *v.tr.* ehren. ◆**'dignified,** *adj.* würdevoll. ◆**'dignitary,** *s.* Würdenträger *m.* ◆**'dignity,** *s.* Würde *f;* **beneath his d.,** unter seiner Würde.

digress [dai'gres], *v.i.* abschweifen. ◆**di'gression,** *s.* Abschweifung *f.*

dike [daik], *s.* Deich *m.*

dilapidated [di'læpideitid], *adj.* verwahrlost. ◆**dilapi'dation,** *s.* Verwahrlosung *f.*

dilatory ['dilət(ə)ri], *adj.* säumig.

dilemma [di'lemə], s. Dilemma n.

diligence ['dilidʒ(ə)ns], s. Fleiß m. ◆**diligent**, adj. fleißig.

dilute [dai'lju:t], v.tr. verdünnen.

dim [dim]. I. adj. 1. (a) (of light) trübe; (of image) verblaßt; to grow d., (of light, sight) trübe werden; (of recollection) verblassen; (b) F: to take a d. view of sth., von etwas dat nicht erbaut sein. 2. F: (of pers.) dumm; -ly, adv. d. lit, mit düsterer Beleuchtung. II. v. 1. v.tr. (ein Licht) abblenden. 2. v.i. (of light, sight) trübe werden; (of outlines) verblassen.

dimension [di'menʃ(ə)n], s. 1. Dimension f; pl. Maße npl (eines Zimmers usw.); (b) Fig: Seite f (eines Problems usw.). ◆**di'mensional**, adj. two-/three-d., zwei-/dreidimensional.

diminish [di'miniʃ], v. 1. v.tr. vermindern. 2. v.i. sich vermindern. ◆**di'minutive**, adj. winzig.

dimple ['dimpl], s. Grübchen n.

din [din], s. Krawall m.

dine [dain], v.i. speisen; **to d. out**, auswärts essen. ◆**'diner**, s. 1. (pers.) Tischgast m. 2. N.Am: Speiselokal n; Rail: Speisewagen m. ◆**'dining**, s. **d. room**, Speisezimmer n; **d. table**, Eßtisch m; Rail: **d. car**, Speisewagen m.

dinghy [diŋ(g)i], s. Dingi n; **rubber d.**, Schlauchboot n; **sailing d.**, kleines Segelboot n.

dingy ['dindʒi], adj. düster; (dark) dunkel.

dinner ['dinər], s. (evening meal) Abendessen n; (midday meal) Mittagessen n; (banquet) Festessen n; **to give a d. party**, eine Gesellschaft zum Abendessen einladen; ◆**d. jacket**, Smoking m.

dinosaur ['dainəsɔ:r], s. Dinosaurier m.

dip [dip]. I. s. 1. F: to go for/have a d., (kurz) schwimmen gehen. 2. (in road) Mulde f; (in landscape) Senke f. II. v. 1. v.tr. (a) (into liquid) (ein)tauchen; (b) Aut: to d. the headlights, abblenden. 2. v.i. (a) (of sun etc.) sich senken; (b) to d. into one's pocket, in die Tasche greifen. ◆**'dipstick**, s. Ölmeßstab m.

diphtheria [dif'θiəriə], s. Diphtherie f.

diploma [di'pləumə], s. Diplom n.

diplomacy [di'pləuməsi], s. Diplomatie f. ◆**'diplomat** ['dipləmæt], s. Diplomat m. ◆**diplo'matic**, adj. diplomatisch.

dire ['daiər], adj. 1. (urgent) dringend; **to be in d. need of sth.**, etwas dringend brauchen. 2. (terrible) entsetzlich.

direct [dai'rekt, di-]. I. v.tr. (a) (ein Unternehmen) leiten; to d. a play/film, bei einem Stück/Film Regie führen; (b) (Aufmerksamkeit, Anstrengungen) lenken (to sth., auf etwas acc); (c) could you d. me to the station? können Sie mir den Weg zum Bahnhof sagen? (d) to d. s.o. to do sth., j-m Anweisungen geben, etwas zu tun. II. adj. & adv. 1. direkt; (of cause, taxes etc.) unmittelbar; (b) (of train) durchgehend; **d. hit**, Volltreffer m; **d. current**, Gleichstrom m. 2. (exact) genau; **the d. opposite**, das genaue Gegenteil; -ly, adv. (exactly) genau; (time) he's coming d., er kommt sofort/gleich. ◆**di'rection**, s. 1. Richtung f; **sense of d.**, Orientierungssinn m. 2. Leitung f (eines Unternehmens usw.); Th: etc: Regie f. 3. (instructions) Anleitungen fpl; **directions for use**, Gebrauchsanweisung f. ◆**di'rector**, s. Direktor m; Th: Cin: Regisseur m; Com: (board member) Vorstandsmitglied n. ◆**di'rectory** [-t(ə)ri], s. Tel: Telefonbuch n; Com: **trade d.**, Firmenverzeichnis n.

dirt [də:t], s. Schmutz m; **it's d. cheap**, es ist spottbillig. ◆**'dirty**. I. adj. schmutzig; F: dreckig; **d. mind**, dreckige Phantasie; **d. old man**, Lustmolch m; **d. trick**, Gemeinheit f; **to do the d. on s.o.**, j-m übel mitspielen; **d. look**, mißbilligender Blick. II. v.tr. schmutzig machen.

disability [disə'biliti], s. (physical) körperliche Behinderung f.

disable [dis'eibl], v.tr. (j-n) untauglich machen. ◆**dis'abled**, adj. körperbehindert; (of serviceman) kriegsversehrt.

disadvantage [disəd'vɑ:ntidʒ], s. Nachteil m; **to be at a d.**, im Nachteil sein. ◆**disadvan'tageous**, adj. nachteilig (to, für + acc).

disagree [disə'gri:], v.i. (a) nicht übereinstimmen; (of two reports etc.) sich widersprechen; (b) (of pers.) anderer Meinung sein; (c) (argue) sich streiten; (d) cherries d. with me, Kirschen bekommen mir nicht. ◆**disa'greeable**, adj. unangenehm; (of pers.) unfreundlich. ◆**disa'greement**, s. 1. (between statements, etc.) Widerspruch m. 2. (between people) Meinungsverschiedenheit f; (quarrel) Streit m.

disappear [disə'piər], v.i. verschwinden. ◆**disa'ppearance**, s. Verschwinden n.

disappoint [disə'point], v.tr. enttäuschen. ◆**disa'ppointing**, adj. enttäuschend. ◆**disa'ppointment**, s. Enttäuschung f.

disapprove [disə'pru:v], v.i. to d. of sth., etwas mißbilligen. ◆**disa'pproval**, s. Mißbilligung f; look of d., mißbilligender Blick.

disarm [dis'ɑ:m], v.i. abrüsten. ◆**dis'arming**, adj. entwaffnend. ◆**dis'armament**, s. Abrüstung f.

disarray [disə'rei], s. Unordnung f.

disaster [di'zɑ:stər], s. Katastrophe f. ◆**di'sastrous**, adj. katastrophal.

disbelief [disbi'li:f], s. Unglaube m.

disc [disk], s. (a) Scheibe f; slipped d., Bandscheibenschaden m; (b) (record) Schallplatte f; **d. jockey**, Diskjockey m.

discard [dis'kɑ:d], v.tr. (Kleider, Karten usw.) ablegen; (einen Plan) aufgeben.

discern [di'sə:n], v.tr. erkennen. ◆**dis'cernible**, adj. erkennbar. ◆**di'scerning**, adj. (of pers.) scharfsinnig; (of taste) erlesen; **a d. eye**, ein Kennerblick.

discharge. I. ['dist∫ɑ:dʒ], s. 1, (a) Abfluß m (von Wasser); Ausstoß m (von Rauch); (b) El: Entladung f; (c) Med: Ausfluß m; (from wound) Eiterung f. 2. Entlassung f (eines Angestellten, Jur: eines Gefangenen, Med: eines Patienten). II. [dis't∫ɑ:dʒ], v.tr. (a) Med: (Eiter usw.) absondern; (b) einen Angestellten, Med: einen Patienten, Jur: einen Gefangenen entlassen; (c) (eine Aufgabe) erfüllen; (einer Pflicht) nachkommen; (eine Schuld) begleichen.

disciple [di'saipl], s. Jünger m.

discipline ['disiplin]. I. s. Disziplin f. II. v.tr. to d. s.o., j-n strafen.

disclaimer [dis'kleimər], s. Widerruf m.

disclose [dis'kləuz], v.tr. bekanntgeben; (ein Geheimnis) enthüllen. ◆dis'closure [-ʒər], s. Bekanntgabe f (einer Nachricht); Enthüllung f (eines Geheimnisses usw.).

disco ['diskəu], s. F: Diskothek f.

discomfort [dis'kʌmfət], s. (a) (inconvenience) Unbequemlichkeit f; (b) (slight pain etc.) Unbehagen n.

disconcert [diskən'sə:t], v.tr. (j-n) aus der Fassung bringen. ◆discon'certing, adj. beunruhigend.

disconnect [diskə'nekt], v.tr. (a) trennen; (b) El: etc: (den Strom, das Telefon) abschalten. ◆discon'nected, adj. 1. (a) getrennt; (b) El: etc: abgeschaltet. 2. (of thoughts, speech) zusammenhanglos.

disconsolate [dis'kɔnsəlit], adj. untröstlich.

discontent [diskən'tent], s. Unzufriedenheit f. ◆discon'tented, adj. unzufrieden.

discontinue [diskən'tinju], v.tr. (a) beenden; (b) Com: (ein Produkt) nicht mehr führen.

discord ['diskɔ:d], s. Zwietracht f.

discotheque ['diskəutek], s. Diskothek f.

discount. I. s. ['diskaunt], s. Rabatt m; to sell sth. at a d., etwas mit Rabatt verkaufen. II. [dis'kaunt], v.tr. (j-s Meinung) nicht beachten; (eine Möglichkeit) ausschließen.

discourage [dis'kʌridʒ], v.tr. (a) (of future etc.) (j-n) entmutigen; (b) (of pers.) (j-m) abraten (from doing sth., etwas zu tun). ◆dis'couraging, adj. entmutigend; (of difficulty etc.) abschreckend. ◆dis'couragement, s. (a) (state) Entmutigung f; (b) (process, thing) Abschreckung f.

discover [dis'kʌvər], v.tr. entdecken. ◆dis'covery, s. Entdeckung f.

discredit [dis'kredit], v.tr. (a) (eine Theorie usw.) umstoßen; (b) (j-n) in Mißkredit bringen.

discreet [dis'kri:t], adj. diskret. ◆discretion [-'kre∫(ə)n], s. 1. (judgement) Ermessen n. 2. (tact) Diskretion f.

discrepancy [dis'krepənsi], s. Diskrepanz f.

discriminate [dis'krimineit], v.i. (a) to d.

between two things, zwischen zwei Dingen unterscheiden; (b) to d. against s.o., j-n benachteiligen. ◆discrimi'nation, s. (unfair) d., Benachteiligung f; racial d., Rassendiskriminierung f.

discuss [dis'kʌs], v.tr. (etwas) besprechen; (eine Frage) erörtern. ◆dis'cussion [-∫(ə)n], s. Besprechung f; Diskussion f; to be under d., zur Debatte stehen.

disdain [dis'dein], s. Verachtung f. ◆dis'dainful, adj. verächtlich.

disease [di'zi:z], s. Krankheit f.

disembark [disem'bɑ:k], v.i. an Land gehen.

disfigure [dis'figər], v.tr. (j-s Gesicht) entstellen; (eine Landschaft usw.) verunstalten. ◆dis'figurement, s. Entstellung f; Verunstaltung f.

disgrace [dis'greis]. I. s. Schande f; (object) Schandfleck m; in d., in Ungnade. II. v.tr. (etwas dat) Schande machen; to d. oneself, sich blamieren. ◆dis'graceful, adj. schändlich; F: unerhört.

disgruntled [dis'grʌntld], adj. verstimmt (at sth., über etwas acc).

disguise [dis'gaiz]. I. s. Verkleidung f; in d., verkleidet, Fig: getarnt. II. v.tr. (j-n, sich) verkleiden; (etwas) tarnen; (seine Stimme usw.) verstellen; (conceal) (Gefühle) verhehlen.

disgust [dis'gʌst], s. 1. (physical) Abscheu m, Ekel m (at, vor etwas dat). 2. (intense annoyance) Empörung f; in d., empört. ◆dis'gusting, s. (horrible) widerlich; (physically) ekelhaft.

dish [di∫]. I. v.tr. (a) to d. up (a meal), (das Essen) auftragen; (b) F: to d. out money etc., Geld usw. austeilen. II. s. 1. (a) (shallow) Platte f; (usu. glass) Schale f; (deeper) Schüssel f; to do the dishes, coll. das Geschirr. 2. (food) Gericht n. ◆'dishcloth, s. Spültuch n. ◆'dishwasher, s. Geschirrspülmaschine f.

dishearten [dis'hɑ:tn], v.tr. (j-n) entmutigen. ◆dis'heartening, adj. entmutigend; (of task) deprimierend.

dishevelled [di'∫ev(ə)ld], adj. 1. (of hair) zerzaust. 2. (of clothes) schlampig.

dishonest [dis'ɔnist], adj. unehrlich. ◆dis'honesty, s. Unehrlichkeit f.

dishonour [dis'ɔnər], v.tr. entehren.

disillusion [disil'lju:ʒ(ə)n], v.tr. (j-n) desillusionieren; (disappoint) (j-n) enttäuschen.

disinfect [disin'fekt], v.tr. desinfizieren. ◆disin'fectant, s. Desinfektionsmittel n.

disinherit [disin'herit], v.tr. enterben.

disintegrate [dis'intigreit], v.i. zerfallen; (of structure) auseinanderfallen. ◆disinte'gration, s. Zerfall m.

disinterested [dis'intristid], adj. selbstlos; (unbiased) unparteiisch.

disjointed [dis'dʒɔintid], adj. (of style,

speech) unzusammenhängend.

disk [disk], *s.* (*a*) *see* **disc**; (*b*) *Data-pr:* Diskette *f.*

dislike [dis'laik]. **I.** *s.* Abneigung *f* (**of/for** s.o., sth., gegen j-n, etwas *acc*). **II.** *v.tr.* (j-n, etwas) nicht mögen; **to d. doing sth.**, etwas ungern tun.

dislocate ['disləkeit], *v.tr.* sich *dat* (ein Glied) ausrenken.

dislodge [dis'lɔdʒ], *v.tr.* verschieben.

dismal ['dizməl], *adj.* trübe, trist.

dismantle [dis'mæntl], *v.tr.* auseinandernehmen.

dismay [dis'mei]. **I.** *s.* Bestürzung *f.* **II.** *v.tr.* (j-n) bestürzen.

dismiss [dis'mis], *v.tr.* (*a*) (j-n aus einer Stellung) entlassen; (j-n von einem Amt) absetzen; (*b*) (*let go*) (j-n) entlassen; (eine Versammlung) auflösen; *Mil:* **d.!** wegtreten! (*c*) *Fig:* **to d. sth. as worthless**, etwas als wertlos abtun; (*d*) (einen Vorschlag) zurückweisen; *Jur:* **to d. a case**, eine Klage abweisen. ◆**dis'missal**, *s.* Entlassung *f* (aus einer Stellung); Absetzung *f* (von einem Amt).

dismount [dis'maunt], *v.i.* (vom Pferd usw.) absteigen.

disobey [disə'bei], *v.tr.* (j-m) nicht gehorchen. ◆**diso'bedience**, *s.* Ungehorsam *m* (**to** s.o., gegenüber j-m). ◆**diso'bedient**, *adj.* ungehorsam.

disorder [dis'ɔːdər], *s.* **1.** Unordnung *f.* **2.** (*riot*) (**civil**) **d.**, öffentliche Unruhen *fpl.* **3.** *Med:* Störung *f.* ◆**dis'orderly**, *adj.* **1.** unordentlich. **2.** (*a*) *Jur:* (*of pers.*) zuchtlos; (*b*) (*of crowd*) aufrührerisch.

disorganize [dis'ɔːgənaiz], *v.tr.* (etwas) durcheinanderbringen; **she's completely disorganized**, sie ist völlig unorganisiert.

disown [dis'əun], *v.tr.* (ein Kind) verstoßen.

disparaging [dis'pæridʒiŋ], *adj.* verächtlich.

dispatch [dis'pætʃ]. **I.** *v.tr.* (*a*) (Waren) absenden; (j-n, etwas) wegschicken; (*b*) (j-n, ein Tier) töten. **II.** *s.* **1.** Versand *m* (von Waren); Abschicken *n* (von Post); *Com:* **d. note**, Versandanzeige *f.* **2. d. rider**, Meldefahrer *m.*

dispel [dis'pel], *v.tr.* (Zweifel usw.) vertreiben.

dispense [dis'pens], *v.i.* **to d. with sth.**, auf etwas *acc* verzichten. ◆**dis'pensary**, *s.* Apotheke *f.* ◆**dis'pensing**, *s.* **d. chemist**, Apotheker(in) *m(f).*

disperse [dis'pəːs], *v.* **1.** *v.tr.* zerstreuen. **2.** *v.i.* (*of crowd*) sich zerstreuen.

dispirited [di'spiritid], *adj.* niedergeschlagen.

display [dis'plei]. **I.** *s.* **1.** (*a*) Ausstellung *f* (von Waren); (*b*) (*demonstration*) Vorführung *f;* **air d.**, Flugschau *f.* **2.** Zurschaustellung *f* (von Wissen, Zuneigung usw.). **II.** *v.tr.* (*a*) (Waren usw.) ausstellen; **to d. a notice**, eine Bekanntmachung aushängen; (*b*) (Dummheit, Wissen, Zuneigung) zur Schau stellen; (Wissen) zeigen.

displeasure [dis'pleʒər], *s.* Mißfallen *n.*

dispose [dis'pəuz], *v.i.* **to d. of**, (etwas) loswerden; (eine Leiche usw.) wegschaffen; (eine Bombe) unschädlich machen; (Probleme) beseitigen. ◆**dis'posable**, *adj.* Wegwerf-; Einweg-. ◆**dis'posal**, *s.* **1.** (*a*) (*throwing away*) Wegwerfen *n;* (*removal*) Beseitigung *f;* (*b*) Ablagerung *f* (von Müll). **2. to be at s.o's d.**, j-m zur Verfügung stehen. ◆**dis'posed**, *adj.* **to be well/ill d. towards s.o.**, j-m gut/schlecht gesinnt sein. ◆**dispo'sition**, *s.* Veranlagung *f;* **he is of a nervous d.**, er ist nervös veranlagt.

disproportionate [disprə'pɔːʃənit], *adj.* übermäßig.

disprove [dis'pruːv], *v.tr.* widerlegen.

dispute [dis'pjuːt]. **I.** *s.* Streit *m;* **industrial d.**, Arbeitskonflikt *m.* **II.** *v.tr.* (*a*) (eine Frage) erörtern; (*b*) (eine Feststellung) anfechten.

disqualify [dis'kwɔlifai], *v.tr.* (j-n) disqualifizieren; **to d. s.o. from driving**, j-m den Führerschein entziehen.

disregard [disri'gɑːd]. **I.** *s.* Nichtbeachtung *f* (einer Vorschrift usw.); Gleichgültigkeit *f* (**for**, gegenüber + *dat*). **II.** *v.tr.* ignorieren; **to d. a rule**, eine Vorschrift nicht beachten.

disrepair [disri'peər], *s.* **to fall into d.**, verfallen; **in a state of d.**, baufällig.

disrepute [disri'pjuːt], *s.* **to bring sth. into d.**, etwas in Verruf bringen. ◆**disreputable** [dis'repjutəbl], *adj.* (*of pers.*) in schlechtem Ruf stehend; (*of area etc.*) verrufen.

disrespect [disri'spekt], *s.* Respektlosigkeit *f.* ◆**disre'spectful**, *adj.* respektlos.

disrupt [dis'rʌpt], *v.tr.* unterbrechen.

dissatisfaction [dissætis'fækʃ(ə)n], *s.* Unzufriedenheit *f.* ◆**dis'satisfied**, *adj.* unzufrieden.

dissent [di'sent], *v.i.* **to d.** (**about sth.**), (über etwas *acc*) anderer Meinung sein.

disservice [di(s)'səːvis], *s.* **to do s.o. a d.**, j-m einen schlechten Dienst erweisen.

dissident ['disidənt]. **I.** *adj.* andersdenkend. **II.** *s.* Dissident *m.*

dissipate ['disipeit], *v.tr.* (Angst, Zweifel) zerstreuen. ◆**'dissipated**, *adj.* ausschweifend.

dissociate [di'səuʃieit], *v.tr.* **to d. oneself from a statement etc.**, sich von einer Äußerung usw. distanzieren.

dissolute ['disəluːt], *adj.* ausschweifend.

dissolve [di'zɔlv], *v.* **1.** *v.tr.* auflösen. **2.** *v.i.* sich auflösen.

dissuade [di'sweid], *v.tr.* (j-m) abraten.

distance ['distəns], *s.* (*a*) Entfernung *f;* **from a d.**, aus einiger Entfernung; **in the d.**, in der Ferne; (*also Fig:*) **to keep one's d.**, Distanz halten; **to cover a long/short d.**, eine lange/kurze Strecke zurücklegen. ◆**distant** ['distənt], *adj.* **1.** (*of place, country*) entfernt, fern; **a d. relation**, ein entfernter

Verwandter. 2. (of pers.) zurückhaltend; (of manner) kühl.

distaste [dis'teist], s. Abneigung f (for, gegen + acc). ◆**dis'tasteful**, adj. widerwärtig.

distil [dis'til], v.tr. destillieren (Schnaps usw.) brennen. ◆**dis'tillery**, s. Branntweinbrennerei f.

distinct [dis'tiŋ(k)t], adj. 1. (different) verschieden. 2. (clear) deutlich; -ly, adv. deutlich; to remember d., sich genau erinnern. ◆**dis'tinction**, s. 1. (difference) Unterschied m. 2. (excellence) Auszeichnung f. ◆**dis'tinctive**, adj. charakteristisch.

distinguish [dis'tiŋgwiʃ], v. 1. v.tr. (a) (discern) (etwas) erkennen; (b) (etwas) unterscheiden; to d. oneself, sich auszeichnen. 2. v.i. unterscheiden. ◆**dis'tinguished**, adj. a d. writer, ein Schriftsteller von Rang.

distort [dis'tɔ:t], v.tr. (a) (das Gesicht, Rad.: TV: den Ton, das Bild usw.) verzerren; (Metall) verformen; (b) (Wahrheit, Tatsachen) verfälschen/ (unintentionally) entstellen.

distract [dis'trækt], v.tr. (Aufmerksamkeit usw.) ablenken. ◆**dis'traction**, s. Ablenkung f; noise is a d., Lärm lenkt ab.

distraught [dis'trɔ:t], adj. verzweifelt.

distress [dis'tres], s. 1. (grief) Kummer m. 2. (of ship) in d., in Seenot; d. signal, Notsignal n. ◆**dis'tressing**, adj. peinlich; to be d. (to s.o.), (j-m) Kummer machen.

distribute [dis'tribju(:)t], v.tr. verteilen (to/among, an + acc); (Waren) vertreiben. ◆**distri'bution**, s. Verteilung f; Com: Vertrieb m. ◆**dis'tributor**, s. 1. Cin: Verleiher m; Com: Vertreter m. 2. El: Aut: Verteiler m.

district [distrikt], s. 1. Gegend f. 2. Adm: Bezirk m; d. nurse, Bezirkskrankenschwester f.

distrust [dis'trʌst]. I. s. Mißtrauen n. II. v.tr. (j-m, etwas dat) mißtrauen. ◆**dis'trustful**, adj. mißtrauisch.

disturb [dis'tə:b], v.tr. (a) stören; (b) (worry) (j-n) beunruhigen. ◆**dis'turbance**, s. 1. Störung f. 2. Pol: Unruhe f; Aufruhr m. ◆**dis'turbed**, adj. (a) gestört; (b) (of child) verhaltensgestört; (b) (worried) beunruhigt. ◆**dis'turbing**, adj. beunruhigend.

disuse [dis'ju:s], s. to fall into d., außer Gebrauch kommen. ◆**disused** [-'ju:zd], adj. außer Gebrauch; d. mine, stillgelegtes Bergwerk.

ditch [ditʃ]. I. s. Graben m. II. v.tr. F: (a) (ein Flugzeug) notwassern; (b) she ditched him, sie hat ihn abgehängt.

dither [di:ðə], v.i. F: zaudern.

ditto [di:təu], adv. ebenfalls, ebenso.

dive [daiv]. I. s. (under water) Tauchen n; (of pers. into water) Kopfsprung m. II. v.i. (a) to d. into the water, einen

Kopfsprung ins Wasser machen; he dived into the bushes, er stürzte ins Gebüsch; (b) (of submarine, diver) tauchen. ◆**'diver**, s. (a) Taucher m; (b) (from board) Kunstspringer m.

'diving, s. (a) Tauchen n; d. suit, Taucheranzug m; (b) d. board, Sprungbrett n.

diverge [dai'və:dʒ], v.i. (of opinions etc.) auseinandergehen; to d. from sth., von etwas dat abweichen.

diverse [dai'və:s], adj. verschiedenartig. ◆**di'version** [dai'və:ʃ(ə)u], s. Umleitung f (des Verkehrs, eines Flusses); Ablenkung f (der Aufmerksamkeit); to create a d., ein Ablenkungsmanöver durchführen. ◆**di'vert** [dai'və:t], v.tr. (einen Fluß, den Verkehr usw.) umleiten; (die Aufmerksamkeit) ablenken.

divide [di'vaid], v. 1. v.tr. (a) (etwas) teilen; (b) (eine Zahl) dividieren (by, durch + acc); (c) (separate) (etwas) trennen (from, von + dat). 2. v.i. (of thing) sich teilen. ◆**dividend** [dividend], s. Dividende f; Fig: Bonus m; Fig: to pay dividends, sich bezahlt machen.

divine [di'vain], adj. göttlich.

division [di'viʒ(ə)n], s. 1. Spaltung f (into several parts, in mehrere Teile). 2. Aufteilung f (von Besitz, der Arbeit usw.). 3. Mth: Division f. 4. (a) Adm: Abteilung f; (b) Mil: Division f; (c) Sp: Liga f. ◆**di'visible** [-'viznbl], adj. teilbar.

divorce [di'vɔ:s]. I. s. Scheidung f; to get a d., sich scheiden lassen. II. v.tr. to d. one's husband/wife, sich von seinem Mann/seiner Frau scheiden lassen. ◆**divorcee** [-'si:], s. Geschiedene(r) f(m).

divulge [di'vʌldʒ], v.tr. ausplaudern.

dizziness ['dizinis], s. Schwindel m. ◆**'dizzy**, adj. 1. schwindlig; I feel d., mir ist schwindlig. 2. (of heights etc.) schwindelnd.

do [du:]. I. v. 1. v.tr. & i. irr. machen, tun; what do you do (for a living)? was machen Sie (beruflich)? well done! gut gemacht! he was doing over a hundred, er fuhr mit mehr als hundert; to do s.o. out of sth., j-n um etwas acc bringen; (after making a bargain) done! abgemacht! how do you do? (i) wie geht es Ihnen? (ii) (on being introduced) sehr erfreut; (suffice) that will do, das genügt; this room will do for an office, dieses Zimmer kann als Büro dienen. 2. verb substitute he writes better than I do, er schreibt besser als ich; may I open these letters? - please do, darf ich die Briefe öffnen? - bitte; I like coffee - do you? ich mag Kaffee - Sie auch? you like him, don't you? Sie mögen ihn, nicht wahr? don't! nicht! you like London? so do I, Sie mögen London? ich auch. 3. v.aux. (a) (emphasis) he did go, er ist doch hingegangen; (b) do sit down! bitte setzen Sie sich doch! (b) do you see him? sehen Sie ihn? **we do not know,** wir wissen es nicht. **4. to have to do with s.o., sth.,** mit j-m, etwas *dat* zu tun haben**; I could do with a cup of tea,** ich könnte eine Tasse Tee gebrauchen**; to do without sth.,** auf etwas *acc* verzichten. **II.** s. *F:* (*event*) Party *f;* Veranstaltung *f;* **a big do,** eine große Angelegenheit. ◆**do a'way, v.i. to do away with sth.,** etwas abschaffen. ◆**'doing,** s. **that takes some d.,** da gehört schon allerhand dazu**; that was your d.,** das war Ihr Werk. ◆**do-it-yourself** [duːitjɔ'self]. **I.** s. *F:* Eigenbau *m;* Heimwerken *n.* **II.** *adj.* Heimwerker-; **d.-i.-y. shop,** Heimwerkerladen *m.* ◆**'do 'up, v.tr. F:** (*a*) (ein Haus usw.) renovieren, *F:* aufmöbeln**; to do oneself up,** sich herausputzen**;** (*b*) (etwas) einpacken**;** (*button*) (einen Mantel usw.) zuknöpfen**;** (Knöpfe) zumachen.

docile ['dousail], *adj.* fromm.

dock¹ [dɔk], **I.** s. Dock *n;* **the docks,** die Hafenanlagen *fpl.* **II.** *v.i.* ins Dock gehen. ◆**'docker,** s. Hafenarbeiter *m.* ◆**'dockyard,** s. Werft *f.*

dock², s. *Jur:* Anklagebank *f.*

doctor ['dɔktər], s. (*abbr. Dr.*) Doktor *m; Med:* Arzt *m;* **woman d.,** Ärztin *f.*

doctrine ['dɔktrin], s. Lehre *f.*

document ['dɔkjumənt], s. Dokument *n; pl.* Papiere *f.* ◆**docu'mentary. I.** *adj.* dokumentarisch. **II.** s. Dokumentarfilm *m.*

dodge [dɔdʒ], *v.tr.* (*a*) (einem Schlag) ausweichen**;** (*b*) to a **task,** sich vor einer Aufgabe drücken. ◆**'dodgy,** *adj. F:* (*a*) (*tricky*) knifflig; (*b*) (*faulty*) defekt.

dog [dɔg]. **I.** s. Hund *m.* **II.** *v.tr.* (j-n) verfolgen. ◆**'dog-'tired,** *adj.* hundemüde. ◆**'dog-house,** s. *F:* to be in the **d.-h.,** in Ungnade sein.

dogged ['dɔgid], *adj.* verbissen.

dogmatic [dɔg'mætik], *adj.* dogmatisch.

dole [doul]. **I.** s. *F:* Arbeitslosenunterstützung *f;* to go on the **d.,** stempeln gehen. **II.** *v.tr. F:* to **d. sth. out,** etwas austeilen.

doll [dɔl]. **I.** s. Puppe *f.* **II.** *v.tr. F:* to **d. oneself up,** sich herausputzen.

dollar ['dɔlər], s. Dollar *m.*

dolphin ['dɔlfin], s. Delphin *m.*

dome [doum], s. Kuppel *f.*

domestic [də'mestik], *adj.* (*a*) Haus-; **d. animal,** Haustier *n;* (*b*) (*d. in character*) häuslich; **d. bliss,** häusliches Glück; (*c*) *Econ: etc:* (*of produce, news*) inländisch; **d. flight,** Inlandsflug *m.* ◆**do'mesticate,** *v.tr.* (ein Tier) zähmen. ◆**do'mesticated,** *adj.* (*of pers.*) häuslich.

dominant ['dɔminənt], *adj.* (vor)herrschend. ◆**'dominance,** s. Vorherrschaft *f.* ◆**'dominate** ['dɔmineit], *v.* **I.** *v.tr.* (*a*) (j-n) beherrschen; (über etwas *acc*) dominieren; (*b*) (einen Ort usw.) überragen. **2.** *v.i.* dominieren. ◆**domi'nation,** s. Beherrschung *f.*

domineering [dɔmi'niəriŋ], *adj.* herrisch.

donate [də'neit, dəu-], *v.tr.* spenden. ◆**do'nation,** s. Spende *f.* ◆**donor** ['dəunər], s. Spender *m.*

donkey ['dɔŋki], s. Esel *m; Fig:* d. **work,** Schwerarbeit *f; F:* **donkey's years,** eine Ewigkeit.

doodle ['duːdl]. **I.** *v.i.* kritzeln. **II.** s. Gekritzel *n.*

doomed [duːmd], *adj.* (*of plan etc.*) d. to **failure,** zum Scheitern verurteilt.

door [dɔːr], s. **I. 1.** (*a*) Tür *f;* next **d.,** nebenan; **to d. to d. selling,** Hausieren *f;* (*b*) out of doors, im Freien. **2.** (*entrance*) Eingang *m;* **tickets at the d.,** Karten beim Eingang. ◆**'doorbell,** s. Türklingel *f.* ◆**'doorhandle,** s. Türklinke *f.* ◆**'doorknob,** s. **1.** (*turning*) Türgriff *m.* **2.** (*fixed*) Türknopf *m.* ◆**'doorman,** s. Portier *m.* ◆**'doormat,** s. Abtreter *m.* ◆**'doorstep,** s. Schwelle *f.* ◆**'doorway,** s. Türöffnung *f;* in the **d.,** in der Tür.

dope [dəup]. **I.** s. *F:* Rauschgift *n.* **II.** *v.tr.* to **d. oneself,** Drogen nehmen. ◆**'dop(e)y,** *adj.* **1.** (*a*) (*dazed*) benommen; (*b*) (*sleepy*) schläfrig. **2.** *F:* (*stupid*) dämlich.

dormitory ['dɔːmitri], s. Schlafsaal *m.*

dose [dəus]. **I.** s. Dosis *f.* **II.** *v.tr.* to **d. s.o. with sth.,** j-m eine (starke) Dosis von etwas *dat* verabreichen.

dot [dɔt]. **I.** s. Punkt *m; F:* he arrived on **the d.,** er kam auf die Minute; **on the d. of two,** Punkt zwei. **II.** *v.tr.* **dotted line,** punktierte Linie; *Fig:* a **hillside dotted with houses,** ein Berghang mit vereinzelten Häusern.

dote [dəut], *v.i.* to **d. on/upon s.o.,** in j-n vernarrt sein.

double [dʌbl]. **I.** *adj.* **1.** doppelt; **d. bed,** französisches Bett; **d. room,** Doppelzimmer *n.* **2.** (*twice*) d. **the number,** die doppelte Anzahl, zweimal soviel. **II.** *adv.* to **see d.,** doppelt sehen. **III.** s. **1.** at the **d.,** im Laufschritt *m; Fig:* schnellstens. **2.** *Sp:* **doubles,** Doppel *n.* **IV.** *v.* **1.** *v.tr.* verdoppeln. **2.** *v.i.* sich verdoppeln. ◆**'double-'bass,** s. Kontrabaß *m.* ◆**'double-'breasted,** *adj.* (*of suit*) zweireihig. ◆**'double-'cross,** *v.tr. F:* (j-n) hintergehen. ◆**'double-'decker,** s. (*bus*) Doppeldecker *f.* ◆**'double-park,** *v.tr. & i.* doppelreihig parken.

doubt [daut]. **I.** *v.tr.* (j-s Worte) anzweifeln**; I d. whether he will come,** ich zweifle, ob er kommen wird. **2.** *v.i.* zweifeln. **II.** s. Zweifel *m;* **no d.,** zweifellos. ◆**'doubtful,** *adj.* **1.** (*of thing*) zweifelhaft. **2.** (*of pers.*) nicht sicher; to be **d.** (**about sth.**), (an etwas *dat*) zweifeln. ◆**'doubtless,** *adv.* zweifellos.

dough [dəu], s. Teig *m.* ◆**'doughnut,** s. Berliner *m; South G:* Krapfen *m.*

dove [dʌv], s. Taube *f.*

dowdy ['daudi], *adj.* unschick.

down [daun]. **I.** *adv.* **1.** (*a*) (*direction*) hinunter; (b) **£100 d.**, £100 als Anzahlung; (c) (written) **did you get it d.?** hast du alles mitschreiben können? (d) int. **d. with the traitors!** nieder mit den Verrätern! (to a dog) **d.!** sitz! 2. (position) (on the ground) am Boden; **d. below,** unten; F: **d. there,** dort unten; **face d.,** mit dem Gesicht/(of thing) der Vorderseite nach unten; F: **d. under,** in Australien. 3. (as far as) **d. to here,** bis hier herunter; I'm **d. to my last cigarette,** ich habe nur noch eine Zigarette. 4. F: **d. and out,** verkommen. II. prep. (a) hinab; **d. the mountain,** den Berg hinunter; (b) (along) **d. the street,** die Straße entlang; (c) N.Am: **d. town,** im/(direction) ins Stadtzentrum. III. adj. **d. payment,** Anzahlung f. IV. s. **ups and downs,** Höhen und Tiefen. V. v.tr. (a) to **d. tools,** die Arbeit niederlegen; (b) (drink) F: to **d. a gin,** sich auf eine Gin hinter die Binde gießen. ◆'**down-at-'heel,** adj. heruntergekommen. ◆'**downcast,** adj. niedergeschlagen. ◆'**downfall,** s. Untergang m (eines Reiches usw.); **love of drink was his d.,** die Trunksucht war sein Verderben. ◆'**down'hill. I.** adv. to go **d.,** (of road) abwärts führen; (of car etc.) bergab fahren; Fig: **he's going d.,** es geht bergab mit ihm. II. adj. Sp: **d. race,** Abfahrtslauf m. ◆'**downpour,** s. Platzregen m. ◆'**downright. I.** adj. ausgesprochen; **d. lie,** glatte Lüge. II. adv. **d. rude,** ausgesprochen frech. ◆**down'stairs. I.** adv. unten; to go **d.,** (die Treppe) hinuntergehen. II. adj. **the d. rooms,** die Zimmer im Erdgeschoß. ◆'**down-to-'earth,** adj. sachlich. ◆'**downward,** adj. abwärts führend; **d. slope,** Abhang m; **d. trend (of prices),** fallende Tendenz f (der Preise). ◆'**downwards,** adv. abwärts; (downhill) bergab.

doze [dəuz], v.i. dösen; to **d. off,** einnicken.

dozen ['dʌzn], s. Dutzend n; **half a d.,** ein halbes Dutzend; **dozens of people,** ein Haufen Leute.

drab [dræb], adj. (colour) graubraun; Fig: eintönig.

draft [drɑːft]. **I.** s. 1. Mil: N.Am: Einberufung f. 2. Com: Tratte f. 3. Skizze f (eines Planes usw.); Entwurf m (eines Briefes usw.). II. v.tr. (Truppen) einberufen; (einen Brief usw.) aufsetzen; (einen Plan usw.) skizzieren.

drag [dræg]. **I.** v. 1. v.tr. schleppen 2. v.i. (of conversation, lawsuit etc.) sich in die Länge ziehen. II. s. 1. F: **an awful d.,** eine schreckliche Plage. 2. **in d.,** als Frau gekleidet. ◆'**drag 'on,** v.i. sich (in die Länge) ziehen.

dragon ['drægən], s. Drache m. ◆'**dragonfly,** s. Libelle f.

drain [drein]. **I.** s. 1. Abfluß m; (underground) Kanal m; **d. pipe,** Abflußrohr n; Kanalrohr n. 2. Fig: Verlust m; **d. on**

---

one's strength, Kräfteverschleiß m; Fin: **d. on reserves,** Abfluß m von Geldern. II. v. 1. v.tr. (a) to **d. water (off/away),** Wasser ableiten; (b) (ein Glas usw.) austrinken; (Land) entwässern; (einen Teich, Aut: den Kühler usw.) ablassen; Med: (eine Wunde) dränieren. 2. v.i. (of water etc.) to **d. (away),** versickern. ◆'**drainage,** s. main **d.,** Kanalisation f. ◆'**draining,** s. H: **d. board,** Abtropfbrett n.

drama ['drɑːmə], s. 1. Schauspiel n. 2. (event) Drama n. ◆**dramatic** [drə'mætik], adj. dramatisch. ◆'**dramatist,** s. Dramatiker m. ◆'**dramatize,** v.tr. (etwas) dramatisieren; (einen Roman usw.) für die Bühne bearbeiten.

drastic ['dræstik], adj. drastisch.

draught [drɑːft], s. 1. pl. **draughts,** Damespiel n; **d. board,** Damebrett n. 2. (in a room) Zugluft f. 3. **beer on d./d. beer,** Bier n vom Faß. ◆'**draughty,** adj. zugig; **it's d.,** es zieht.

draughtsman, pl. -**men** ['drɑːftsmən], s. technischer Zeichner m.

draw [drɔː]. **I.** s. 1. Ziehung f (einer Lotterie); Verlosung f (für eine Tombola). 2. (of pers., event) Attraktion f (of play) **to be a (box office) d.,** ein Kassenschlager sein. 3. Sp: Unentschieden n; to **end in a d.,** unentschieden ausgehen. II. v. 1. v.tr. (a) (auf) (den Vorhang usw.) zuziehen; (of horse etc.) (einen Wagen usw.) ziehen; to **d. water,** Wasser holen; to **d. breath,** (ein)atmen; (b) (attract) (Zuhörer, Kunden usw.) anziehen; **to draw s.o.'s attention to sth.,** die Aufmerksamkeit auf etwas acc lenken; (c) Com: (Geld) abheben; (einen Scheck) einlösen (an Bild, einen Plan usw.) zeichnen; (c) Sp: **the game was drawn,** das Spiel war unentschieden. 2. v.i. (a) to **d. near (to s.o.),** j-m nahekommen; (of train) to **d. into a station,** in einen Bahnhof einfahren; (b) to **d. to an end,** dem Ende entgegengehen; (of day etc.) sich neigen; (c) to **let the tea d.,** den Tee ziehen lassen. ◆'**draw a'head,** v.i. einen Vorsprung gewinnen. ◆'**draw a'side,** v.tr. (a) (j-n) beiseite nehmen; (b) (einen Vorhang usw.) zur Seite ziehen. ◆'**draw 'back,** v. 1. v.tr. (einen Vorhang, seine Hand usw.) zurückziehen. 2. v.i. sich zurückziehen. ◆'**drawback,** s. Nachteil m. ◆'**drawer,** s. Schublade f; **chest of drawers,** Kommode f. ◆'**draw 'in,** v.i. **the days are drawing in,** die Tage werden kürzer. ◆'**drawing,** s. Zeichnung f; **d. board,** Reißbrett n; **d. pin,** Reißzwecke f. ◆'**drawing-room,** s. Salon m. ◆'**drawn,** adj. 1. (of pers.) tired and drawn, müde und abgespannt. 2. Sp: **d. match,** unentschiedenes Spiel. ◆'**draw 'on,** v.tr. (Reserven) angreifen; **he can d. on fifty years' experience,** er kann auf die Erfahrung von fünfzig Jahren zurückgreifen. ◆'draw 'out, v.tr. (a) (etwas aus etwas dat) herausholen; **I could not d. her o.**, ich konnte nichts aus ihr herauslocken; (b) (eine Diskussion usw.) hinausziehen. ◆'draw 'up, v.tr. 1. v.tr. (ein Dokument) aufsetzen; (eine Liste) aufstellen. 2. v.i. (of vehicle) halten.

dread [dred], v.tr. fürchten. ◆'**dreadful**, adj. furchtbar.

dream [dri:m]. I. s. Traum m; **to have a d.**, träumen; **like a d.**, traumhaft; **my d. house**, mein Traumhaus. II. v.tr. & i. irr. träumen (**about/of**, von + dat); F: **I shouldn't d. of doing it**, das würde mir nicht im Traum einfallen.

dreary ['driəri], adj. (of weather etc.) trostlos; (of work etc.) langweilig.

dregs [dregz], s.pl. Bodensatz m.

drench [dren(t)ʃ], v.tr. (j-n) durchnässen; **drenched**, klatschnaß.

dress [dres]. I. s. 1. (a) Kleidung f; (b) **d. circle**, erster Rang; **d. rehearsal**, Generalprobe f. 2. (women's d.) Kleid n; **d. designer**, Modedesigner(in) m(f); (creating fashions) Modeschöpfer(in) m(f). II. v. 1. v.tr. (a) (j-n) anziehen; (b) (decorate) schmücken; (c) (eine Wunde) verbinden. 2. v. refl. & i. to d. (oneself), sich anziehen. ◆'**dresser**, s. H: Anrichte f; (kitchen) d., (Küchenbüfett n mit) Tellerbord n. ◆'**dressing**, s. 1. Ankleiden n. 2. Cu: (salad) d., Salatsoße f. 3. Med: Verband m. 4. attrib. **d. gown**, Morgenrock m; **d. room**, (i) Ankleideraum m; (ii) Th: Garderobe f; **d. table**, Frisiertisch m. ◆'**dressmaker**, s. Schneiderin f. ◆'**dressmaking**, s. Schneidern n. ◆'**dress 'up**, v.i. (of pers.) (a) sich festlich anziehen; F: sich aufbrezeln; (b) to **d. up as X**, sich als X verkleiden.

dribble ['dribl], v.i. 1. (a) (of baby etc.) sabbern; (b) Sp: to **d. (the ball)**, (mit dem Ball) dribbeln.

dried [draid], adj. getrocknet; **d. fruit**, Dörrobst n; **d. milk**, Trockenmilch f.

drift [drift]. I. s. 1. (of argument) Gedankengang m; Tendenz f. 2. (snow-)d., Schneewehe f. II. v.i. (a) (of pers.) sich treiben lassen; (of thing) getrieben werden; Nau: Av: abgetrieben werden; (of couple) to **d. apart**, sich auseinanderleben; (b) (of snow) Wehen bilden.

drill [dril]. I. s. 1. Tchn: Bohrer m. 2. Mil: Exerzieren n. II. v. 1. v.tr. (a) (ein Loch) bohren; (b) (j-n) drillen. 2. v.i. bohren (**for sth.**, nach etwas dat).

drink [driŋk]. I. s. 1. **food and d.**, Essen und Trinken; (b) **to give s.o. a d.**, j-m etwas zu trinken geben; to **have a d.**, etwas trinken. 2. Getränk n; **soft d.**, alkoholfreies Getränk; (alcoholic) d., Drink m. 3. Alkohol m; **the worse for d.**, betrunken. II. v.tr. irr. trinken; to **d. to s.o.**, auf j-s Wohl trinken. ◆'**drinkable**, adj. trinkbar. ◆'**drinker**, s. Trinker(in) m(f). ◆'**drinking**, s. **d. fountain**, Trinkbrunnen m; **d. water**,

Trinkwasser n. ◆'**drink 'up**, v.tr. & i. austrinken.

drip [drip]. I. s. 1. (a) Tropfen m; (b) Med: Infusion f. 2. F: (pers.) Niete f. II. v.i. tropfen. ◆'**drip-'dry**, adj. bügelfrei.

drive [draiv]. I. s. 1. Fahrt f; **to go for a d.**, spazierenfahren; **an hour's d.**, eine Stunde Fahrt. 2. (entrance) Auffahrt f; (short) Einfahrt f. 3. **left-hand d.**, Linkssteuerung f. 4. E: **d. shaft**, Antriebswelle f. 5. (of pers.) Energie f; **to have plenty of d.**, viel Tatkraft haben. II. v.irr. 1. v.tr. (a) (Vieh) treiben; (b) (ein Fahrzeug) fahren; to **d. s.o. home**, j-n nach Hause fahren; **can you d.?** kannst du Auto fahren? (c) (einen Motor, ein Fahrzeug) betreiben; (d) to **d. s.o. to sth.**, j-n zu etwas dat treiben; to **d. s.o. mad**, j-n zum Wahnsinn treiben. 2. v.i. fahren; to **d. on the right**, rechts fahren. ◆'**drive at**, v.tr. **what are you driving at?** worauf willst du hinaus? ◆'**drive a'way**, v. 1. v.tr. vertreiben. 2. v.i. abfahren. ◆'**drive 'back**, v. 1. v.tr. (a) (j-n, ein Heer) zurücktreiben; (b) (ein Auto) zurückfahren. 2. v.i. zurückfahren. ◆'**drive-in**, s. d.-i. (cinema), Autokino n. ◆'**driver**, s. Fahrer m (eines Autos usw.); Führer m (einer Lokomotive). ◆'**driveway**, s. Auffahrt f. ◆'**drive 'up**, v.i. vorfahren. ◆'**driving**. I. adj. **d. force**, treibende Kraft; **d. rain**, strömender Regen. II. s. Fahren n; **d. school**, Fahrschule f; **d. test**, Fahrprüfung f; **d. licence**, Führerschein m.

drizzle ['drizl]. I. s. Sprühregen m. II. v.i. **it is drizzling**, es nieselt.

droop [dru:p], v.i. (a) (of eyelids) sich senken; (b) (of flowers) verwelken.

drop [drop]. I. s. 1. (liquid) Tropfen m. 2. (fall) Abfall m; **d. in prices**, Preissenkung f; **sudden d. in temperature**, plötzlicher Temperatursturz; Fig: **at the d.** of a hat, auf der Stelle. II. v. 1. v.i. (a) (of leaves, blossom etc.) fallen; (of ground) abfallen; (of pers.) umfallen; (c) (of prices) sinken; (of wind) nachlassen; (of voice) leiser werden. 2. v.tr. (a) (etwas) fallen lassen; (Bomben) abwerfen; to (let) **d. a remark**, eine Bemerkung fallen lassen; (b) F: (set down) **I'll d. you at the station**, ich setze Sie am Bahnhof ab; (c) (omit) (eine Silbe, Sp: einen Spieler usw.) auslassen; (give up) (eine Idee usw.) aufgeben; (d) (die Stimme, die Augen) senken. ◆'**drop 'in**, v.i. vorbeikommen. ◆'**drop 'off**, v.i. (a) (of thing) abfallen; (b) (of pers.) einnicken. ◆'**drop 'out**, v.i. (of pers.) to **d. o. of a contest**, aus einem Wettkampf ausscheiden.

drought [draut], s. Dürre f.

drown [draun], v. 1. v.tr. (a) (ein Tier usw.) ertränken; **to be drowned**, ertrinken; (b) (einen Laut) übertönen. 2. v.i. ertrinken.

drowse [drauz], v.i. dösen. ◆'**drowsy**, adj. schläfrig.

drudgery ['drʌdʒəri], s. Schinderei f.

drug [drʌg]. I. s. 1. Med: Droge f. 2. Rauschgift n; d. addict, Rauschgiftsüchtige(r) f(m). II. v.tr. (j-m) Drogen verabreichen. ◆**druggist**, s. N.Am: Apotheker(in) m(f). ◆**drugstore**, s. N.Am: Drugstore m.

drum [drʌm]. I. s. Trommel f; coll. the drums, das Schlagzeug. II. v. 1. v.i. (of rain, fingers etc.) trommeln. 2. v.tr. to d. sth. into s.o., j-m etwas einpauken. ◆**drummer**, s. Schlagzeuger m. ◆**drumstick**, s. Mus: Trommelschlegel m.

drunk [drʌŋk], adj. to get d., sich betrinken. ◆**drunkard**, s. Säufer(in) m(f). ◆**drunken**, adj. betrunken; in a d. stupor, sinnlos betrunken. ◆**drunkenness**, s. Rausch m.

dry [drai]. I. adj. 1. trocken. 2. Fig: (a) (boring) langweilig; (b) a d. sense of humour, ein trockener Humor. II. v. 1. v.tr. (a) trocknen; to d. the dishes, das Geschirr abtrocknen; to d. one's eyes, die Tränen abwischen; (b) (Obst) dörren. 2. v.i. trocknen. ◆**dry-'clean**, v.tr. chemisch reinigen. ◆**'dry 'cleaner's**, s. chemische Reinigung f. ◆**'dry 'off**, v.i. trocknen. ◆**'dry 'out**, v.i. austrocknen. ◆**'dry-'rot**, s. Hausschwamm m. ◆**'dry 'up**, v.i. (a) (of spring) versiegen; (of ideas etc.) sich erschöpfen; (c) F: (dishes) abtrocknen.

dual ['dju(:)əl], adj. doppelt; d. carriageway, zweispurige Straße.

dubious ['dju:biəs], adj. (a) (of pers.) unsicher; (b) (of undertaking) zweifelhaft.

duchess ['dʌtʃis], s. Herzogin f.

duck [dʌk]. I. s. Ente f. II. v.i. sich ducken. ◆**duckling**, s. Entlein n; Cu: junge Ente f.

dud [dʌd], F: adj. wertlos; d. cheque, ungedeckter Scheck.

due [dju:]. I. adj. 1. (a) (of payment etc.) fällig; the balance d. to us, der uns geschuldete Saldo; (b) the train is due at two o'clock, der Zug soll (laut Fahrplan) um zwei Uhr ankommen. 2. (appropriate) angemessen; in d. course, zu gegebener Zeit; with d. respect, bei aller Achtung. 3. d. to, wegen + gen. 4. adv. d. north, genau nördlich. II. s. 1. to give him his d. he can really sing, er kann schon singen, das muß man ihm lassen. 2. pl. (fees) Abgaben fpl.

duel ['dju(:)əl], s. Duell n.

duet [dju(:)'et], s. Duett n.

duke [dju:k], s. Herzog m.

dull [dʌl]. I. adj. 1. (a) (of day, weather, light) trüb; (of colour) matt; (b) (of sound, pain) dumpf; (of sight, hearing) schwach. 2. (boring) langweilig. II. v.tr. (die Sinne usw.) abstumpfen; (Schmerz) mildern.

duly ['dju:li], adv. 1. (correctly) ordnungsgemäß. 2. (punctually) rechtzeitig.

dumb [dʌm], adj. 1. stumm. 2. F: esp. N.Am: dumm.

dummy ['dʌmi], s. 1. Attrappe f; (tailor's) d., Schneiderpuppe f; (in window) Schaufensterpuppe f. 2. (for baby) Schnuller m. 3. d. run, Probe f.

dump [dʌmp]. I. s. 1. Abladeplatz m; (rubbish) d., (small) Müllhaufen m; (big) Müllhalde f. 2. F: what a d.! was für ein trauriger Laden! II. v.tr. (a) (Müll usw.) deponieren; (b) F: (etwas) hinschmeißen.

dumps [dʌmps], s.pl. F: down in the d., deprimiert, (esp. after failure etc.) niedergeschlagen.

dunce [dʌns], s. Ignorant m; F: Niete f.

dune [dju:n], s. Düne f.

dung [dʌŋ], s. Mist m.

dungarees [dʌŋgə'ri:z], s.pl. Latzhose f.

dungeon ['dʌn(d)ʒ(ə)n], s. Verlies n.

duplicate. I. ['dju:plikət], 1. adj. Duplikat-; d. key, Nachschlüssel m. 2. s. Duplikat n; in d., in doppelter Ausfertigung. II. ['dju:plikeit], v.tr. (a) (one copy) (ein Dokument usw.) kopieren; (several copies) (Schriftstücke) vervielfältigen; (b) (etwas) wiederholen. ◆**duplicator**, s. Vervielfältigungsapparat m.

durable ['djuərəbl], adj. haltbar; (of material) strapazierfähig. ◆**dura'bility**, s. Haltbarkeit f.

duration [dju(ə)'reiʃ(ə)n], s. Dauer f.

during ['djuəriŋ], prep. während + gen.

dusk [dʌsk], s. Dämmerung f; at d., bei Einbruch der Dunkelheit.

dust [dʌst]. I. s. Staub m; F: to bite the d., ins Gras beißen. II. v.tr. (Möbel usw.) abstauben. ◆**'dustbin**, s. Mülltonne f ◆**'dust-cart**, s. Müll(abfuhr)wagen m. ◆**'duster**, s. Staubtuch m. ◆**'dustman**, pl. -men, s. Müllmann m; the dustmen, die Müllabfuhr. ◆**'dustpan**, s. Müllschippe f. ◆**'dusty**, adj. staubig.

Dutch [dʌtʃ]. I. adj. holländisch; Fig: to go D., getrennte Kasse machen. II. s. 1. the Dutch, die Holländer pl. 2. Holländisch n. ◆**'Dutchman**, pl. -men, Holländer m.

duty ['dju:ti], s. 1. Pflicht f. 2. (task) duties, Aufgaben fpl; to take up one's duties, sein Amt antreten; (b) to be on d., Dienst haben; off d., dienstfrei. 3. (customs) d., Zoll m. ◆**'dutiable**, adj. zollpflichtig. ◆**'dutiful**, adj. pflichtbewußt; -ly, adv. pflichtgemäß. ◆**'duty-'free**, adj. zollfrei.

duvet ['du:vei], s. Daunendecke f.

dwarf [dwɔ:f]. I. s. Zwerg m. II. v.tr. (etwas) winzig erscheinen lassen.

dwell [dwel], v.i.irr. to d. on a subject, bei einem Thema verweilen.

dwindle ['dwindl], v.i. dahinschwinden.

dye [dai]. I. s. Farbstoff m. II. v.tr. färben.

dyke [daik], s. see dike.

dynamic [dai'næmik], adj. dynamisch.

dynamite ['dainəmait], s. Dynamit n.

dynamo ['dainəməu, -əuz], s. Dynamo m.

dynasty ['dinəsti], s. Dynastie f.
dysentery ['disəntri], s. Ruhr f.
dyslexia [dis'leksiə], s. Legasthenie f.

◆**dys'lexic**, adj. legasthenisch.
dyspepsia [dis'pepsiə], s. Verdauungsstörung f.

E

E, e [i:], s. (der Buchstabe) E, e n.
each [i:tʃ]. **I.** adj. jeder, jede, jedes; e. year, jedes Jahr; e. one of us, jede(r) (einzelne) von uns. **II.** pron. 1. (ein) jeder, (eine) jede, (ein) jedes; they earn £10 e./e. earn £10, jeder von ihnen verdient zehn Pfund. 2. e. other, einander; to be afraid of e. other, Angst voreinander haben; they hate e. other, sie hassen sich. **III.** adv. je; (of pers.) pro Person; (of thing) pro Stück; 10 pence e., je zehn Pence/zehn Pence pro Stück.
eager ['i:gər], adj. eifrig. ◆**'eagerness,** s. Eifer m.
eagle ['i:gl], s. Adler m.
ear¹ ['iər], s. Ohr n; to play by e., nach dem Gehör spielen; F: to play it by e., je nach Lage der Dinge entscheiden. ◆**'earache,** s. Ohrenschmerzen mpl. ◆**'eardrum,** s. Trommelfell n. ◆**'earlobe,** s. Ohrläppchen n. ◆**'earmark,** v.tr. to e. funds for a purpose, Gelder für einen Zweck vorsehen. ◆**'earphones,** s.pl. Kopfhörer m. ◆**'earplug,** s. Ohrenwatte f. ◆**'earring,** s. Ohrring m. ◆**'earshot,** s. within e., in Hörweite. ◆**'earwig,** s. Ohrwurm m.
ear², s. (of corn) Ähre f.
earl [ə:l], s. Graf m.
early ['ə:li]. **I.** adj. früh; **II.** adv. früh; to come (too) e., zu früh kommen.
earn [ə:n], v.tr. verdienen. ◆**'earnings,** s.pl. 1. (of pers.) Einkommen n. 2. (profit) Ertrag m.
earnest ['ə:nist]. **I.** adj. ernst. **II.** s. in e., im Ernst.
earth [ə:θ], s. Erde f; F: where on e. have you been? wo in aller Welt bist du gewesen? **down** to e., nüchtern. ◆**'earthenware,** s. Töpferwaren pl. ◆**'earthly,** adj. 1. irdisch. 2. there is no e. reason for this, es besteht kein erdenklicher Grund dafür. ◆**'earthquake,** s. Erdbeben n.
ease [i:z]. **I.** s. 1. at e., behaglich; ill at e., unbehaglich. 2. Leichtigkeit f; with e., mühelos. **II.** v. 1. v.tr. a) (das Gemüt) beruhigen; (Schmerzen) lindern; (c) (die Spannung, Belastung) erleichtern; (c) to e. sth. into position, etwas vorsichtig in die richtige Lage bringen. 2. v.i. (a) (of situation) sich entspannen; (b) (of storm etc.) to e. off, nachlassen.
easel ['i:zl], s. Staffelei f.
east [i:st]. **I.** s. Osten m; the Far/Middle E., der Ferne/Nahe Osten. **II.** adv. nach Osten. **III.** adj. Ost-, östlich; e. wind, Ostwind m. ◆**'easterly,** adj. = east III.

◆**'eastern,** adj. östlich; (oriental) orientalisch; E. Bloc, Ostblock m. ◆**'eastwards,** adv. ostwärts, nach Osten.
Easter ['i:stər], s. Ostern n; E. egg, Osterei n.
easy ['i:zi]. **I.** adj. leicht; on e. terms, auf Raten; -ily, adv. 1. leicht. 2. e. the best, bei weitem die Beste. **II.** adv. F: to take it/things e., sich schonen; sich dat Ruhe gönnen. ◆**'easy-'chair,** s. Lehnstuhl m. ◆**'easy-'going,** adj. (a) unbekümmert; (b) (lax) lässig.
eat [i:t], v.irr. 1. v.tr. (of pers.) essen; (of animal) fressen. 2. v.i. a) to e. out, auswärts essen; (b) to e. into sth., etwas allmählich wegfressen. ◆**'eating.** **I.** s. Essen n. **II.** adj. attrib. e. apple, Eßapfel m; e. habits, Eßgewohnheiten fpl. ◆**'eat 'up,** v.tr. (a) (eine Speise) aufessen; (b) F: (Benzin, Geld usw.) fressen.
eaves [i:vz], s.pl. Dachüberhang m. ◆**'eavesdrop,** v.i. lauschen. ◆**'eavesdropper,** s. Lauscher(in) m(f).
ebb [eb]. **I.** s. 1. e. (tide), Ebbe f. 2. Fig: things were at a low e., es herrschte Tiefstand. **II.** v.i. (of tide) zurückgehen; (of life etc.) to e. away, dahinschwinden.
ebony ['ebəni], s. Ebenholz n.
eccentric [ek'sentrik, ik-]. **I.** adj. exzentrisch. **II.** s. (pers.) Sonderling m. ◆**eccen'tricity,** s. Verschrobenheit f; (eccentric act) Exzentrizität f.
echo ['ekəu]. **I.** s. (pl. echoes) Echo n. **II.** v. 1. v.tr. (einen Ton usw.) widerhallen lassen; (j-s Worte) nachbeten. 2. v.i. widerhallen.
eclipse [i'klips]. **I.** s. Finsternis f; e. of the moon, Mondfinsternis f. **II.** v.tr. (einen Stern) verfinstern; Fig: (j-n) in den Schatten stellen.
ecology [i:'kolədʒi], s. Ökologie f.
economic [i:kə'nomik], adj. wirtschaftlich. ◆**eco'nomical,** adj. sparsam. ◆**eco'nomics,** s.pl. Volkswirtschaft f. ◆**e'conomist** [i(:)'kɔnəmist], s. Volkswirt m. ◆**e'conomize,** v.i. sparen (on, an + dat). ◆**e'conomy,** s. 1. (of pers., car etc.) Sparsamkeit f; (a saving) Sparmaßnahme f. 2. (of country) Wirtschaft f; (political) e., Volkswirtschaft f.
ecstasy ['ekstəsi], s. Ekstase f.
edge [edʒ]. **I.** s. 1. (of a blade) Schneide f; Fig: to take the e. off sth., etwas dat die Schärfe nehmen; on e., (of pers.) nervös; to have the e. (on s.o.), (j-m) gerade noch voraus sein. 2. Rand m (des Waldes usw.); Kante f (des Tisches usw.). **II.** v.tr. & i. (a) the street wa

cdgcd with trees, die Straße war mit Bäumen eingesäumt; (b) to e. one's way forwards, Schritt für Schritt vorrücken; to e. away, sich zurückziehen. ◆**edgeways,** adv. seitlich; F: I can't get a word in e., ich kann kein Wort anbringen. ◆**edgy,** adj. F: nervös.

edible ['edibl], adj. genießbar.

edit ['edit], v.tr. (a) (ein Buch, eine Zeitung) herausgeben; (b) (einen Text) redigieren; (c) (einen Film, eine Aufnahme) schneiden. ◆**edition** [i'diʃən], s. 1. Ausgabe f. 2. (printing) Auflage f. ◆**editor** ['editar], s. 1. Herausgeber m (eines Buches, einer Zeitung). 2. Redakteur m (bei einer Zeitung, bei einem Verlag). ◆**edi'torial.** I. adj. redaktionell; e. staff, Redaktion f. II. s. Leitartikel m.

educate ['edjukeit], v.tr. (a) bilden; (of university etc.) ausbilden; (b) (bring up) erziehen. ◆**education** [edju'keiʃən], s. 1. Sch: Bildung f; (at university) Ausbildung f. 2. (upbringing) Erziehung f. ◆**edu'cational,** adj. (a) (of methods etc.) pädagogisch; (b) (valuable) pädagogisch wertvoll. 2. Bildungs-; e. film, Lehrfilm m.

eel [i:l], s. Aal m.

eerie, eery ['iari], adj. 1. (of feeling, story) unheimlich. 2. (of house, atmosphere) gespenstisch.

effect [i'fekt]. I. s. 1. Wirkung f; to have an e. on s.o., auf j-n wirken; to take e., (i) wirksam werden; (ii) (of regulation) in Kraft treten; (iii) (of drugs) wirken; to no e., ohne Resultat; calculated for e., auf Effekt berechnet. 2. (meaning) words to that e., Worte in diesem Sinne. 3. pl. personal effects, persönliche Habe f. 4. in e., in Wirklichkeit. II. v.tr. bewirken. ◆**e'ffective,** adj. 1. wirkungsvoll. 2. (impressive) eindrucksvoll.

effeminate [i'feminit], adj. unmännlich.

effervescent [efa'vesant], adj. sprudelnd.

efficiency [i'fiʃənsi], s. 1. (a) (of pers.) Tüchtigkeit f; (b) (of firm, machinery etc.) Leistungsfähigkeit f. ◆**e'fficient,** adj. (a) (of pers.) tüchtig; (b) (of firm, factory) leistungsfähig; -ly, adv. to work e., (of machine) rationell/(of pers.) tüchtig arbeiten.

effort ['efat], s. (a) Anstrengung f; to make an e., sich anstrengen; (b) Bemühungen fpl. ◆**'effortless,** adj. mühelos.

effusive [i'fju:siv], adj. (of feelings, thanks etc.) überschwenglich.

egg1 [eg], s. Ei n; e. yolk, Eidotter n; e. cup, Eierbecher m. ◆**'eggshell,** s. Eierschale f.

egg2, v.tr. to e. s.o. on, j-n anstacheln.

egoism ['egauizm], s. Egoismus m. ◆**'egoist,** s. Egoist(in) m(f).

Egypt ['i:dʒipt]. Pr.n. Ägypten n. ◆**Egyptian** [i'dʒipʃ(ə)n]. I. adj. ägyptisch. II. s. Ägypter(in) m(f).

eiderdown ['aidədaun], s. Daunendecke

f.

eight [eit], num. adj. acht. ◆**eighteen** ['ei'ti:n], num. adj. achtzehn. ◆**eigh'teenth,** num. adj. achtzehn-te(r,s). ◆**eighth** ['eitθ]. I. num. adj. achte(r,s). II. s. Achtel n. ◆**eighty** ['eiti], num. adj. achtzig.

either ['aiðər]. I. adj. jeder, jede, jedes (von zweien). II. pron. (a) eine(r,s) (von zweien); e. of them, einer von den beiden. III. conj. e. ... or, entweder ... oder. IV. adv. F: not ... e./nor ... e., (und) auch nicht.

ejaculate [i'dʒækjuleit], v.tr. (also Biol:), ausstoßen. ◆**ejacu'lation,** s. 1. Ausruf m. 2. Biol: Ejakulation f.

eject [i'dʒekt], v.tr. hinauswerfen.

eke [i:k], v.tr. e. out, (Vorräte usw.) strecken; to e. out a meagre existence, sich dürftig durchschlagen.

elaborate. I. [i'læbrit], adj. (a) kompliziert; (b) (of decoration) kunstvoll. II. [i'læbəreit], v. 1. v.tr (einen Plan) sorgfältig ausarbeiten. 2. v.i. can you e.? können Sie ausführlicher sein?

elapse [i'læps], v.i. verstreichen.

elastic [i'læstik], adj. 1. elastisch; e. band, Gummiband n. II. s. Gummiband n.

elbow ['elbau], s. Ellbogen m. ◆**elbow-room,** s. Bewegungsfreiheit f.

elder ['eldər]. I. adj. älter. II. s. (der, die) Ältere m, f. ◆**'elderly,** adj. ältlich. ◆**'eldest,** adj. älteste(r,s).

elect [i'lekt]. I. v.tr. (a) to e. to do sth., sich entschließen, etwas zu tun; (b) (j-n zu einem Amt) wählen. II. adj. President e., zukünftiger Präsident. ◆**e'lection,** s. Wahl f; e. campaign, Wahlkampf m. ◆**e'lectorate,** s. Wählerschaft f.

electric [i'lektrik], adj. elektrisch; e. motor, Elektromotor m; e. shock, elektrischer Schlag. ◆**e'lectrical,** adj. elektrisch. ◆**electrician** [-'triʃ(ə)n], s. Elektriker m. ◆**electricity** [-'trisiti], s. Elektrizität f; (current) Strom m. ◆**e'lectrocute,** v.tr. to be electro-cuted, durch einen elektrischen Schlag getötet werden. ◆**e'lectrode,** s. Elektrode f. ◆**e'lectrolysis,** s. Elektrolyse f. ◆**e'lectron,** s. Elektron n. ◆**elec'tronic.** I. adj. elektronisch. II. s.pl. electronics, Elektronik f.

elegance ['eligans], s. Eleganz f. ◆**'elegant,** adj. elegant.

element ['elimənt], s. (a) Element n; (b) an e. of truth, ein Körnchen Wahrheit. ◆**elementary** [-'ment(ə)ri], adj. elementar; (simple) einfach; e. school, Grundschule f.

elephant ['elifant], s. Elefant m.

elevate ['eliveit], v.tr. (a) (etwas) hochheben; (b) (j-n in Rang) erhöhen (to, zu + dat). ◆**'elevated,** adj. (of position) hoch (gelegen). 2. (of thoughts) erhaben. ◆**'elevator,** s. N.Am: Fahrstuhl m.

eleven [i'levn]. I. num. adj. elf. II. s.pl.

elevenses, approx. zweites Frühstück.
◆**e'leventh,** num. adj. elfte(r,s); **at the e. hour,** in letzter Minute.

elicit [i'lisit], v.tr. **to e. the facts,** die Tatsachen ans Licht bringen; (**a reply from s.o.,**) j-m eine Antwort entlocken.

eligible ['elidʒibl], adj. berechtigt; **e. for a pension,** pensionsberechtigt; **e. bachelor,** gute Partie.

eliminate [i'limineit], v.tr. beseitigen; Sp: **to be eliminated in the first round,** in der ersten Runde ausscheiden.
◆**elimi'nation,** s. Beseitigung f; Sp: Ausscheiden n.

elm [elm], s. Ulme f.

elocution [elə'kju:ʃ(ə)n], s. Sprechtechnik f.

elongate ['i:lɔŋgeit], v.tr. verlängern.

elope [i'ləup], v.i. durchgehen.

eloquence ['eləkwəns], s. Beredsamkeit f. ◆**'eloquent,** adj. (of pers.) beredt.

else [els], adv. 1. sonst; **do as I say, or e.!** tu, was ich sage, sonst passiert was! 2. adj. or adv. **did you see anybody e.?** hast du sonst noch jemand gesehen? **something e.,** etwas anderes; (in shop) **anything e.?** sonst noch etwas? **someone e.,** jemand anders; **nothing e.,** sonst nichts; **everything e.,** alles andere; **somewhere e.,** irgendwo anders; **nowhere e.,** sonst nirgends. ◆**'else'where,** adv. anderswo; **to go e.,** woandershin gehen.

elucidate [i'lu:sideit], v.tr. (ein Problem usw.) erläutern.

elude [i'lju:d], v.tr. (a) ausweichen; (b) (escape) (j-m) entkommen.

elusive [i'lu:siv], adj. schwer erfaßbar.

emaciated [i'meiʃieitid], adj. abgezehrt.

emancipate [i'mænsipeit], v.tr. emanzipieren.

embalm [im'bɑ:m], v.tr. (einen Leichnam) einbalsamieren.

embankment [im'bæŋkmənt], s. Böschung f; **railway e.,** Bahndamm m.

embargo [im'bɑ:gəu], pl. **-oes** [im'bɑ:gəu, -əuz], s. Embargo n; **trade e.,** Handelssperre f.

embark [im'bɑ:k], v.i.(a) (of pers.) sich einschiffen; (b) **to e. on sth.,** mit etwas dat beginnen.

embarrass [im'bærəs], v.tr. (j-n) in Verlegenheit bringen. ◆**em'barrassed,** adj. (of pers.) verlegen. ◆**em'barrassing,** adj. peinlich. ◆**em'barrassment,** s. Verlegenheit f.

embassy ['embəsi], s. Botschaft f.

embellish [im'beliʃ], v.tr. (a) verschönern; (b) (eine Geschichte usw.) ausschmücken. ◆**em'bellishment,** s. 1. Verschönerung f. 2. Fig: Ausschmückung f.

embers ['embəz], s.pl. glühende Kohlen fpl.

embezzle [im'bezl], v.tr. unterschlagen.

embittered [im'bitəd], adj. verbittert.

emblem ['embləm], s. (symbol) Sinnbild n; (of town etc.) Wahrzeichen n.

embody [im'bɔdi], v.tr. verkörpern.

◆**em'bodiment,** s. Verkörperung f.

embrace [im'breis]. I. v.tr. (a) (j-n) umarmen; (b) (include) (etwas) umfassen; (c) **to e. a cause,** sich einer Sache annehmen. II. s. Umarmung f.

embroider [im'brɔidər], v.tr. (a) (einen Muster) sticken; (b) (eine Geschichte usw.) ausschmücken. ◆**em'broidery,** s. Stickerei f.

embryo, pl. **-os** ['embriəu, -əuz], s. Embryo m.

emerald ['emərəld]. I. s. Smaragd m. II. adj. smaragdgrün.

emerge [i'mɜːdʒ], v.i. (a) (aus dem Wasser usw.) auftauchen; (aus einem Zimmer usw.) herauskommen; (b) (be discovered) zum Vorschein kommen; (c) (come into being) entstehen. ◆**e'mergence,** s. Entstehung f (einer Theorie usw.).

emergency [i'mɜːdʒənsi], s. Notfall m; **in (case of) an e.,** im Notfall; **e. exit,** Notausgang m; **e. state of e.,** Ausnahmezustand m; **e. landing,** Notlandung f.

emery ['eməri], s. **e. board,** Sandblattfeile f.

emigrant ['emigrənt], s. Auswanderer m. ◆**emigrate** ['emigreit], v.i. auswandern. ◆**emi'gration,** s. Auswanderung f.

eminence ['eminəns], s. hoher Rang m. ◆**'eminent,** adj. berühmt; **-ly,** adv. eminent.

emit [i'mit], v.tr. (a) (Strahlen, Wärme, usw.) ausstrahlen; (Rauchwolken usw.) ausstoßen; (b) (of pers.) (einen Seufzer, einen Ton) von sich geben.

emotion [i'məuʃ(ə)n], s. 1. (feeling) Gefühl n. 2. (state of) e., Erregung f. ◆**e'motional,** adj. (of pers., voice) erregt; (of attitude etc.) gefühlsbetont; **-ly,** adv. (with adj.) gefühlsmäßig; (with verb) erregt. ◆**e'motive,** adj. gefühlsgeladen.

emperor ['empərər], s. Kaiser m.

emphasis ['emfəsis], s. Betonung f. ◆**'emphasize,** v.tr. betonen. ◆**emphatic** [im'fætik], adj. betont; (of warning etc.) nachdrücklich; (of refusal, denial) entschieden.

empire ['empaiər], s. Reich n.

employ [im'plɔi], v.tr. (a) (j-n) beschäftigen; (take on) (j-n) anstellen; (b) (etwas) verwenden. ◆**em'ployee,** s. Arbeitnehmer(in) m(f). ◆**em'ployer,** s. Arbeitgeber(in) m(f). ◆**em'ployment,** s. (a) (work) Beschäftigung f; **e. agency,** Stellenvermittlungsbüro n; **full e.,** Vollbeschäftigung f; (b) (taking on) Anstellung f (von Arbeitskräften).

empress ['empris], s. Kaiserin f.

empty ['empti]. I. v. 1. v.tr. (etwas) (aus)leeren; (einen Tank) ablassen; (ein Zimmer usw.) ausräumen. 2. v.i. sich leeren. II. adj. leer; **on an e. stomach,** auf nüchternen Magen. ◆**'empty-'handed,** adj. mit leeren Händen. ◆**'emptiness,** s. Leere f.

enable [i'neibl], v.tr. to c. s.o. to do sth., es j-m ermöglichen, etwas zu tun.

enamel [i'næməl], s. Email n.

enamoured [i'næməd], adj. angetan (of, von + dat).

enchant [in'tʃɑːnt], v.tr. (j-n) bezaubern. ◆en'chanting, adj. entzückend. ◆en'chantment, s. Zauber m.

encircle [in'səːkl], v.tr. (j-n, etwas) umzingeln; (den Feind usw.) einkreisen.

enclose [in'kləuz], v.tr. (a) (surround) (etwas mit etwas dat) umgeben; (ein Grundstück) einfrieden; (b) to e. sth. with a letter, etwas einem Brief beifügen. ◆en'closure [-ʒər], s. (a) (paddock) Koppel f; (in zoo etc.) Gehege n; (b) Com: Anlage f.

encompass [in'kʌmpəs], v.tr. umfassen.

encore [ɔŋ'kɔːr], int. & s. Zugabe f.

encounter [in'kauntər]. I. v.tr. (j-m, etwas dat) begegnen; (auf Schwierigkeiten usw.) stoßen. II. s. Begegnung f.

encourage [in'kʌridʒ], v.tr. (a) (j-n) ermutigen (to do sth., etwas zu tun); (b) (die Forschung usw.) fördern. ◆en'couragement, s. 1. (act) Ermutigung f; (thing) Ansporn m. 2. Förderung f. ◆en'couraging, adj. ermutigend.

encroach [in'krəutʃ], v.i. übergreifen (on s.o.'s property, auf j-s Besitz; on s.o.'s rights, in j-s Rechte).

encyclopaedia [insaiklə'piːdiə], s. Enzyklopädie f.

end [end]. I. s. 1. Ende n; to put an e. to sth./make an e. of sth., mit etwas dat Schluß machen; to come to an e., enden; in the e., zum Schluß; for two hours on e., zwei Stunden lang ununterbrochen; my hair stood on e., mir standen die Haare zu Berge; cigarette e., Zigarettenstummel m; Aut: big e., Pleuelfuß m. 2. (purpose) Zweck m; to this e., zu diesem Zweck; for his own ends, für seine eigenen Zwecke. II. v. 1. v.tr. beenden. 2. v.i. (a) enden; (b) to e. up with sth., zum Schluß etwas bekommen; you'll e. up in jail, du wirst noch im Gefängnis landen.

endanger [in'deindʒər], v.tr. gefährden.

endear [in'diər], v.tr. beliebt machen. ◆en'dearing, adj. gewinnend.

endeavour [in'devər]. I. s. Bemühen n. II. v.i. to e. to do sth., sich darum bemühen, etwas zu tun.

endorse [in'dɔːs], v.tr. (a) (j-s Meinung usw.) bestätigen; (b) (einen Scheck) indossieren. ◆en'dorsement, s. Strafvermerk m (auf einem Führerschein).

endow [in'dau], v.tr. endowed with great talents, mit großem Talent ausgestattet. ◆en'dowment, s. e. insurance, Erlebensfallversicherung f.

endure [in'djuər], v.tr. aushalten. ◆en'durance, s. (powers of) e., Durchhaltevermögen n.

enemy ['enəmi], s. Feind m.

energetic [enə'dʒetik], adj. energisch.

◆**energy** ['enədʒi], s. Energie f.

enforce [in'fɔːs], v.tr. (ein Gesetz) durchführen; (eine Vorschrift) in Kraft setzen. ◆en'forcement, s. Durchführung f.

engage [in'geidʒ], v. 1. v.tr. (a) (employ) (j-n) anstellen; (b) to e. s.o. in conversation, j-n ins Gespräch ziehen. 2. (of pers.) sich befassen (in, mit + dat); (b) (of gears etc.) ineinandergreifen. ◆en'gaged, adj. 1. (a) (of couple) verlobt; to get e., sich verloben; (b) (occupied) beschäftigt (in sth., mit etwas dat). 2. Tel: besetzt. ◆en'gagement, s. 1. (appointment) Verabredung f. 2. (to be married) Verlobung f; e. ring, Verlobungsring m. ◆en'gaging, adj. (of manner etc.) gewinnend.

engine ['endʒin], s. 1. Rail: Lokomotive f; e. driver, Lokomotivführer m. 2. (of car etc.) Motor m. ◆engineer [endʒi'niər]. I. s. Ingenieur m. II. v.tr. organisieren, arrangieren. ◆engi'neering, s. Ingenieurwesen n; (mechanical) e., Maschinenbau m.

England ['ingland]. Pr.n. England n. ◆English ['inglif]. I. adj. englisch. II. s. 1. Englisch n. 2. the E., die Engländer pl. ◆'Englishman, pl. -men, s. Engländer m. ◆'Englishwoman, pl. -women, s. Engländerin f.

engrave [in'greiv], v.tr. eingravieren.

engross [in'grəus], v.tr. to be engrossed in sth., in etwas acc vertieft sein.

engulf [in'gʌlf], v.tr. überschütten.

enhance [in'hɑːns], v.tr. (den Wert) erhöhen; (Aussehen) verschönern.

enigma [i'nigmə], s. Rätsel n. ◆enigmatic [enig'mætik], adj. rätselhaft.

enjoy [in'dʒɔi], v.tr. (a) (an etwas dat) Vergnügen finden; to e. oneself, sich gut unterhalten; to e. doing sth., etwas gern machen; (b) (Rechte usw.) genießen. ◆en'joyable, adj. erfreulich. ◆en'joyment, s. Vergnügen n; Unterhaltung f.

enlarge [in'lɑːdʒ], v.tr. vergrößern. 2. v.i. to e. upon a subject, sich über ein Thema verbreiten. ◆en'largement, s. Vergrößerung f.

enlighten [in'laitn], v.tr. aufklären.

enlist [in'list], v. 1. v.tr. (Soldaten) anwerben; to e. s.o.'s aid, j-n zu Hilfe ziehen. 2. v.i. sich (zum Militärdienst) melden.

enmity ['enmiti], s. Feindschaft f; e. towards/for s.o., Feindseligkeit f gegen j-n.

enormous [i'nɔːməs], adj. riesig; an e. success, ein Riesenerfolg.

enough [i'nʌf], adj. & adv. genug; e. money, genug Geld; that's e., (no more thanks) das genügt; that's e.! das reicht!; good e., gut genug.

enquire [in'kwaiər], v. 1. v.tr. to e. the way etc., sich nach dem Weg usw. erkundigen. 2. v.i. sich erkundigen (about/after s.o., sth., nach j-m, etwas dat). ◆**en'quiry**, s. 1. Nachfrage f; **to make enquiries (about s.o., sth.)**, (über j-n, etwas acc) Erkundigungen einziehen. 2. (by police etc.) Untersuchung f.

enrich [in'ritʃ], v.tr. bereichern.

enrol(l) [in'rəul], v.i. (of students) sich immatrikulieren.

en route [ɑ:(n)'ru:t], adv. unterwegs.

enslave [in'sleiv], v.tr. versklaven.

ensue [in'sju:], v.i. folgen; **the ensuing discussion**, die darauf folgende Diskussion.

ensure [in'ʃuɔr], v.tr. gewährleisten; **to e. that ...**, dafür sorgen, daß ...

entail [in'teil], v.tr. (Folgen) mit sich bringen; (Ausgaben) verursachen.

enter [in'rit], v. 1. v.tr. (a) (a) eintreten; (b) **to e. for a competition**, sich an einem Wettbewerb beteiligen. 2. v.tr. (a) (ein Haus, ein Zimmer) betreten; (b) **to e. university**, auf die Universität gehen; (c) **to e. a name on a list**, einen Namen in eine Liste eintragen.

enterprise ['entəpraiz], s. 1. (project, firm) Unternehmen n; **private** e., Privatwirtschaft f. 2. (spirit of e., Unternehmungsgeist m. ◆**'enterprising**, adj. unternehmungslustig.

entertain [entə'tein], v. 1. v.tr. (a) (amuse) (j-n) unterhalten; (b) (einen Gast) bewirten; (c) (einen Vorschlag) in Erwägung ziehen. 2. v.i. Gäste empfangen. ◆**enter'taining**, adj. unterhaltend. ◆**enter'tainment**, s. Unterhaltung f.

enthuse [in'θju:z], v.i. to e. about/over s.o., sth., für j-n, etwas acc schwärmen. ◆**en'thusiasm**, s. Begeisterung f. ◆**en'thusiast**, s. Enthusiast m; Anhänger m (einer Sportart); **football e.**, Fußballfreund m. ◆**enthusi'astic**, adj. begeistert.

entice [in'tais], v.tr. (j-n) verlocken; **to e. s.o. into sth.**, j-n zu etwas dat verleiten.

entire [in'taiɔr], adj. ganz; (of amount, population etc.) gesamt; (of confidence, attention) voll; -ly, adv. völlig. ◆**entirety** [in'tai(ɔ)rɔti], s. Gesamtheit f; the population in its e., die gesamte Bevölkerung.

entitle [in'taitl], v.tr. to e. s.o. to sth., j-n zu etwas dat berechtigen. ◆**en'titled**, adj. to be e. to sth., ein Anrecht auf etwas acc haben; to be e. to do sth., dazu berechtigt sein, etwas zu tun.

entrance¹ ['entrɔns], s. 1. (of pers.) Eintritt m. 2. (a) (of building, cave etc.) Eingang m; (b) (for vehicle) Einfahrt f.

entreat [in'tri:t], v.tr. (j-n) anflehen.

entrust [in'trʌst], v.tr. to e. a secret, a child etc. to s.o., j-m ein Geheimnis, ein Kind usw. anvertrauen.

entry ['entri], s. 1. (a) (of pers.) Eintritt m; (b) (into country) Einreise f; e. visa, Einreisevisum n; no e., (i) (for traffic) keine Einfahrt; (ii) (for people) Zutritt verboten. 2. (in list etc.) Eintrag m; Com:

Buchung f.

enunciate [i'nʌnsieit], v. 1. v.tr. (Meinungen, Worte) aussprechen. 2. v.i. to e. clearly, eine deutliche Aussprache haben. ◆**enunci'ation**, s. Aussprache f.

envelop [en'veləp], v.tr. einhüllen (in sth., in etwas acc). ◆**envelope** ['envələup], s. Umschlag m.

enviable ['enviəbl], adj. beneidenswert. ◆**envious** ['enviəs], adj. neidisch (of, auf + acc).

environment [in'vaiərənmənt], s. Umwelt f; (surroundings) Umgebung f. ◆**environ'mental**, adj. Umwelt-.

envisage [in'vizidʒ], v.tr. voraussehen.

envoy ['envɔi], s. Gesandte(r) m.

envy ['envi]. I. s. Neid m (of, auf + acc); **she is the e. of her friends**, sie wird von ihren Bekannten beneidet. II. v.tr. to e. s.o. sth., j-n um etwas acc beneiden.

epic ['epik], s. Epos n.

epidemic [epi'demik]. I. adj. epidemisch. II. s. Epidemie f.

epilepsy ['epilepsi], s. Epilepsie f. ◆**epi'leptic** adj. epileptisch.

episode ['episəud], s. (a) Episode f; (b) TV: in four episodes, in vier Folgen.

epitaph ['epitɑ:f], s. Grabinschrift f.

epitome [i'pitəmi], s. Verkörperung f.

epoch ['i:pɔk], s. Epoche f.

equal ['i:kwəl]. I. adj. 1. (a) gleich; (b) **to be e. to the occasion/to a task**, dem Anlaß/einer Aufgabe gewachsen sein; -ly, adv. gleich; e. good, gleich/genauso gut; e., ..., gleichermaßen ... II. s. Gleichgestellte(r) f(m). III. v.tr. (j-m, etwas dat) gleichen; to e. s.o./be s.o.'s e., j-m gleichkommen. ◆**equality** [i'kwɔliti], s. Gleichheit f. ◆**'equalize**, v.tr. gleichmachen. 2. v.i. Sp: ausgleichen. ◆**'equalizer**, s. Sp: Ausgleichstreffer m.

equanimity [ekwə'nimiti], s. Gleichmut m.

equate [i'kweit], v.tr. to e. sth. with sth., etwas mit etwas dat gleichsetzen. ◆**e'quation**, s. Gleichung f.

equator [i'kweitər], s. Äquator m. ◆**equatorial** [ekwə'tɔ:riəl], adj. äquatorial.

equilibrium [i:kwi'libriəm], s. Gleichgewicht n.

equinox ['ekwinɔks], s. Tagundnachtgleiche f.

equip [i'kwip], v.tr. ausrüsten; (ein Labor, eine Fabrik usw.) ausstatten. ◆**e'quipment**, s. 1. Ausrüstung f. 2. (apparatus) Geräte npl; Apparatur f.

equitable ['ekwitəbl], adj. gerecht.

equity ['ekwiti], s. 1. Gerechtigkeit f. 2. equities, Dividendenpapiere npl.

equivalent [i'kwivələnt]. I. adj. (a) (of equal value) gleichwertig; (b) (corresponding) entsprechend. II. s. Entsprechung f; (in value) Gegenwert m; (counterpart) Gegenstück n.

era ['iərə], s. Zeitalter n.

eradicate [i'rædikeit], v.tr. ausrotten.

erase [i'reiz], v.tr. (Geschriebenes) ausradieren; (eine Aufnahme) löschen. ◆**e'raser**, s. Radiergummi m.

erect [i'rekt]. I. adj. aufrecht. II. v.tr. (a) (einen Mast usw.) aufrichten; (b) (ein Gebäude) errichten. ◆**e'rection**, s. 1. Errichtung f. 2. Anat: Erektion f.

erode [i'roud], v.tr. (by water) auswaschen, (by wind etc.) aushöhlen. ◆**erosion** [i'rouʒ(ə)n], s. Erosion f.

erotic [i'rotik], adj. erotisch.

errand ['erənd], s. Botengang m; to run errands, Besorgungen machen.

erratic [i'rætik], adj. (of things) unregelmäßig; (of pers., conduct) unberechenbar.

error ['erər], s. Irrtum m; (tangible mistake) Fehler m. ◆**erroneous** [i'rəuniəs], adj. (of opinion etc.) irrig; (of accusation) falsch; **-ly**, adv. irrtümlich.

erudite ['erudait], adj. gelehrt.

erupt [i'rʌpt], v.i. ausbrechen. ◆**e'ruption**, s. Ausbruch m.

escalate ['eskəleit], v.tr. & i. (sich) eskalieren. ◆**esca'lation**, s. Eskalation f. ◆**escalator**, s. Rolltreppe f.

escape [is'keip]. I. s. 1. (a) Flucht f; to have a narrow e., gerade noch davonkommen; e. route, Fluchtweg m; e. clause, Ausweichklausel f; (of pers.) Feuerleiter f; (c) (of gas, fluid) Ausströmen n. 2. Fig: Ausweg m (aus einer Situation). II. v. 1. v.i. (a) (of pers.) entkommen; to e. from prison, aus dem Gefängnis entfliehen; (b) (of gas) entweichen; (of liquid) ausströmen. 2. v.tr. (j-m) entkommen; (einer Gefahr usw.) entgehen; to e. notice, unbemerkt bleiben; the name escapes me, der Name fällt mir nicht ein. ◆**escapade**, s. Eskapade f. ◆**es'capism**, s. Flucht f vor der Wirklichkeit.

escarpment [is'kɑ:pmənt], s. Böschung f.

escort. I. ['eskɔ:t], s. (of several pers.) Geleit n; (individual) Begleiter(in) m(f). II. [is'kɔ:t], v.tr. geleiten.

especially [i'speʃəli], adv. besonders.

espionage ['espiənɑ:ʒ], s. Spionage f.

essay ['esei], s. Aufsatz m.

essence ['esəns], s. (a) (of thing) Wesen n; in e., im wesentlichen; (b) Ch: Cu: Essenz f. ◆**essential** [i'senʃəl]. I. adj. (a) (unbedingt) notwendig; (of qualifications) erforderlich; (of pers.) unentbehrlich; (of food, industry) lebenswichtig; (b) (of feature etc.) wesentlich. II. s. the essentials, das Wesentliche; **-ly**, adv. im wesentlichen; (chiefly) hauptsächlich.

establish [is'tæbliʃ], v.tr. (a) (set up) (eine Organisation) bilden; (ein Geschäft) gründen; (Ordnung) schaffen; to e. oneself, (i) (settle) sich niederlassen; (ii) (achieve fame) sich dat einen Namen machen; (b) (prove) beweisen. ◆**es'tablishment**, s. 1. Bildung f, Gründung f. 2. educational e., Bildungs-anstalt f. 3. the E., das Establishment.

estate [is'teit], s. (land) Gut n; (housing) e., Wohnsiedlung f; e. agent, Grundstücksmakler m; e. car, Kombiwagen m.

esteem [is'ti:m], s. Achtung f.

estimate. I. ['estimət], s. Schätzung f; (of cost) Kostenvoranschlag m. II. ['estimeit], v.tr. schätzen. ◆**esti'mation**, s. 1. Schätzung f. 2. in my e., meiner Ansicht nach.

estuary ['estjuəri], s. Flußmündung f.

etching ['etʃin], s. Radierung f.

eternal [i'tə:nl], adj. ewig. ◆**e'ternity**, s. Ewigkeit f.

ether ['i:θər], s. Äther m.

ethics ['eθiks], s.pl. Ethik f. ◆**'ethical**, adj. (of values etc.) ethisch; (of conduct etc.) sittlich.

Ethiopia [i:θi'oupiə]. Pr.n. Äthiopien n.

etiquette ['etiket], s. Etikette f.

etymology [eti'mɔlədʒi], s. Etymologie f.

euphemism ['ju:fimiz(ə)m], s. Euphemismus m.

Europe ['juərəp]. Pr.n. Europa n. ◆**Euro'pean**. I. adj. europäisch. II. s. Europäer(in) m(f).

evacuate [i'vækjueit], v.tr. (a) (Personen, Truppen) evakuieren; (b) (ein Gebäude, ein Stadtteil usw.) räumen.

evade [i'veid], v.tr. ausweichen; sich (um eine Frage) drücken; (j-s Wachsamkeit) entgehen; to e. the issue, der Streitpunkt umgehen.

evaluate [i'væljueit], v.tr. den Wert (von etwas dat) berechnen; (eine Leistung) bewerten.

evangelical [i:væn'dʒelik(ə)l], adj. evangelisch. ◆**e'vangelist**, s. Evangelist m.

evaporate [i'væpəreit], v. 1. v.tr. (eine Flüssigkeit) verdunsten lassen; **evaporated milk**, Kondensmilch f. 2. v.i. verdunsten.

evasion [i'veiʒən], s. Ausweichen n. ◆**e'vasive**, adj. (of answer) ausweichend.

eve [i:v], s. Vorabend m; on the e. of his departure, am Vortag seiner Abreise.

even[1] ['i:vən], adv. 1. (a) sogar, selbst; e. his enemies, sogar seine Feinde; e. so, trotzdem; e. if, selbst/auch wenn; (b) not e., nicht einmal. 2. e. better, noch besser.

even[2]. I. adj. 1. (level) eben. 2. (a) (of breathing) regelmäßig; (b) (of temperament) ausgeglichen. 3. (equal) gleich; (of two people) to be e., quitt sein; Fig: to get e. with s.o., es j-m heimzahlen. 4. e. number, gerade Zahl. II. v.tr. to e. things out, die Gleichgewicht wiederherstellen.

evening ['i:vnin], s. Abend m; in the e., abends; e. dress, Abendtoilette f; (man's) Abendanzug m; (lady's) Abendkleid n; e. class, Abendkurs m.

event [i'vent], s. 1. (case) Fall m; in the e., wie es sich herausstellt? 2. (happening) Ereignis n; the course of events, der Verlauf der Dinge. 3. *esp. Sp:* (type of) e., Disziplin *f.* ◆e'**ventful**, *adj.* ereignisreich. ◆**eventual** [i'ventjuəl], *adj.* it led to his e. ruin, es führte schließlich zu seinem Untergang; -ly, *adv.* schließlich. ◆**eventu'ality**, *s.* Möglichkeit *f;* for all eventualities, für alle Fälle.

ever ['evər], *adv.* 1. *(a)* je; have you e. been to Munich? waren Sie schon einmal in München? he hardly e. smokes, er raucht fast nie; it was raining harder than e., es regnete stärker denn je; *(b)* e. since then, seitdem. 2. *(a)* immer; for e., für immer; *(b)* e. larger, immer größer. 3. *F:* e. so difficult, furchtbar schwer. ◆**evergreen**. **I.** *adj. Bot:* immergrün. **II.** *s. Bot:* immergrüne Pflanze *f.* ◆**ever'lasting**, *adj.* ewig.

every ['evri], *adj.* jeder, jede, jedes. ◆'**everybody/everyone**, *indef. pron.* jeder. ◆'**everyday**, *adj.* alltäglich. ◆'**everything**, *s. indef. pron.* alles. ◆'**everywhere**, *adv.* überall.

evict [i(ː)'vikt], *v.tr.* auf die Straße setzen. ◆**e'viction**, *s.* Vertreibung *f.*

evidence ['evidəns], *s.* 1. much in e., überall zu sehen. 2. *(sign)* Anzeichen *n;* *(trace)* Spur *f.* 3. *Jur:* *(a)* *(proof)* Beweis *m;* *(b)* *(statement)* Zeugenaussage *f;* to give e., *(as witness)* aussagen. ◆'**evident**, *adj.* offensichtlich.

evil ['iːv(ə)l]. **I.** *adj.* böse; *(of pers., character, reputation etc.)* übel. **II.** *s.* 1. Übel *n.* 2. *(forces of e.)* das Böse.

evoke [i'vouk], *v.tr.* ein Bild usw.) heraufbeschwören; *(Gefühle)* wachrufen. ◆**evocative** [i'vokətiv], *adj.* an e. picture, ein Bild, das Erinnerungen wachruft.

evolve [i'volv], *v.* 1. *v.tr.* (etwas) entwickeln. 2. *v.i.* *(a)* sich entwickeln *(into, zu + dat);* *(b)* *(come into being)* entstehen *(from, aus + dat).* ◆**evolution** [iːvə'luː(f)(ə)n], *s.* Entwicklung *f; Biol:* Evolution *f.*

ewe [juː], *s.* Mutterschaf *n.*

ex- [eks-], *prefix* ex-, Ex-.

exact [eg'zækt, ig-]. **I.** *adj.* genau; the e. opposite, das genaue Gegenteil. **II.** *v.tr.* (ein Versprechen usw.) erzwingen; -ly, *adv.* 1. genau; not e. ideal, nicht gerade ideal. 2. *(as answer)* eben! genau! ◆**e'xacting**, *adj.* anspruchsvoll.

exaggerate [ig'zædʒəreit], *v.tr. & i.* übertreiben. ◆**exagge'ration**, *s.* Übertreibung *f.*

exam [eg'zæm, ig-], *s. Sch: F:* = **examination** 2. *(a).* ◆**exami'nation**, *s.* 1. *(investigation)* Untersuchung *f.* 2. *(a) Sch:* Prüfung *f,* Examen *n;* *(b) Jur:* Verhör *n.* ◆**e'xamine**, *v.tr.* *(a)* untersuchen; *(b) Sch:* (einen Kandidaten) prüfen. ◆**e'xaminer**, *s.* Prüfer(in) *m(f).*

example [ig'zaːmpl], *s.* Beispiel *n* (of, für + *acc*); for e., zum Beispiel; to set an e., ein (gutes) Beispiel geben; to make

an e. of s.o., an j-m ein Exempel statuieren.

exasperate [ig'zaːspəreit], *v.tr.* (j-n) zur Verzweiflung bringen. ◆**ex'asperated**, *adj.* außer sich *dat.* ◆**exaspe'ration**, *s.* Verzweiflung *f.*

excavate ['ekskəveit], *v.tr.* ausgraben. ◆**exca'vation**, *s.* Ausgrabung *f.*

exceed [ek'siːd, ik-], *v.tr.* *(a)* (eine Grenze usw.) überschreiten; (eine Summe, eine Zahl) übersteigen; *(b)* (j-s Erwartungen) übertreffen. ◆**ex'ceedingly**, *adv.* äußerst.

excel [ek'sel, ik-], *v.* 1. *v.tr.* he excelled himself, er hat sich selbst übertroffen. 2. *v.i.* sich auszeichnen. ◆**excellence** ['eks(ə)ləns], *s.* Vorzüglichkeit *f;* hervorragende Qualität *f.* ◆**'excellency**, *s.* Your E., (Ihre) Exzellenz *f.* ◆**'excellent**, *adj.* ausgezeichnet.

except [ek'sept, ik-], *prep.* außer + *dat;* e. for a few corrections, bis auf einige Korrekturen; e. that ..., außer daß ... ◆**ex'ception**, *s.* Ausnahme *f;* with the e. of, mit Ausnahme von + *dat,* bis auf + *acc.* 2. to take e. to sth., an etwas *dat* Anstoß nehmen. ◆**ex'ceptional**, *adj.* *(a)* außergewöhnlich; *(b)* *(unusual)* ungewöhnlich.

excerpt ['eksəːpt], *s.* Auszug *m.*

excess [ik'ses], *s.* 1. Übermaß *n* (of, an + *dat*); *(surplus)* Überschuß *m;* to e., übermäßig; in e. of, über + *dat.* 2. *attrib.* e. baggage, Übergewicht *n;* e. fare, Zuschlag *m* (zum Fahrpreis). 3. *pl.* excesses, Ausschreitungen *fpl.* ◆**ex'cessive**, *adj.* übermäßig; *(of caution, cleanliness etc.)* übertrieben.

exchange [eks'tʃeindʒ, iks-]. **I.** *s.* *(of goods, students etc.)* Austausch *m;* *(of purchased article etc.)* Umtausch *m;* in e. (for sth.), im Tausch (gegen etwas *acc*) 2. *Fin:* rate of e., Wechselkurs *m.* 3. *(telephone) e.,* Fernsprechzentrale *f.* **II.** *v.tr.* *(a)* tauschen (for, gegen + *acc*); (Worte) wechseln; *(b)* (Geld) wechseln (for, gegen + *acc*).

exchequer [iks'tʃekər], *s.* the E., der Fiskus; the Chancellor of the E., der Schatzkanzler.

excite [ik'sait], *v.tr.* aufregen. ◆**ex'citable**, *adj.* leicht erregbar. ◆**ex'citement**, *s.* *(a)* Aufregung *f;* *(b)* (state of) e., Erregung *f.* ◆**ex'citing**, *adj.* erregend.

exclaim [eks'kleim, iks-], *v.i.* ausrufen. ◆**exclamation** [eksklə'meiʃ(ə)n], *s.* Ausruf *m;* e. mark, Ausrufezeichen *n.*

exclude [eks'kluːd, iks-], *v.tr.* ausschließen; **excluding**, mit Ausnahme von + *dat.* ◆**ex'clusion**, *s.* Ausschluß *m.* ◆**ex'clusive**, *adj.* 1. *(excluding)* ausschließlich. 2. *(elitist)* exklusiv; -ly, *adv.* ausschließlich.

excommunicate [ekskə'mjuːnikeit], *v.tr.* exkommunizieren.

excruciating [iks'kruːʃieitiŋ, eks-],

grauenhaft.

excursion [eks'kə:ʃ(ə)n, iks-], s. Ausflug m.

excuse. I. [iks'kju:s], s. **1.** Entschuldigung f. **2.** (pretext) Vorwand m. **II.** [iks'kju:z], v.tr. entschuldigen; **e. me!** entschuldigen Sie bitte! ◆**ex'cusable** [-zəbl], adj. zu entschuldigen.

execute ['eksikju:t], v.tr. (a) (etwas) ausführen; (b) (einen Verbrecher) hinrichten. ◆**exe'cution,** s. **1.** Ausführung f. **2.** Hinrichtung f (eines Verbrechers). ◆**exe'cutioner,** s. Scharfrichter m. ◆**executive** [ig'zekjutiv]. **I.** adj. Pol: etc: **e. power,** ausübende Gewalt. **II.** s. **1.** (body) Verwaltung f; Pol: Exekutive f. **2.** (pers.) Adm: Verwaltungsbeamte(r) m; Com: Manager m.

exemplary [ig'zempləri], adj. **1.** (of conduct etc.) musterhaft. **2.** (of punishment) exemplarisch. ◆**exemplify** [ig'zemplifai], v.tr. to e. sth., für etwas acc als Beispiel dienen.

exempt [ig'zem(p)t, eg-]. **I.** v.tr. befreien. **II.** adj. (von etwas dat) befreit; **e. from taxation,** steuerfrei. ◆**e'xemption,** s. Befreiung f.

exercise ['eksəsaiz]. **I.** s. **1.** (movement) Bewegung f; **physical exercises,** Leibesübungen pl. **2.** (a) Sch: Mus: etc: Übung f; **e. book,** Schulheft n; (b) Mil: Manöver n. **II.** v.tr. (a) (einen Beruf, ein Amt usw.) ausüben; (Geduld) üben; **to e. one's right,** von seinem Recht Gebrauch machen; (b) (ein Bein usw.) bewegen.

exert [ig'zə:t, eg-], v.tr. (a) (eine Kraft, einen Einfluß) ausüben; (b) **to e. oneself,** sich anstrengen. ◆**e'xertion,** s. Anstrengung f.

exhaust [ig'zɔ:st, eg-]. **I.** v.tr. erschöpfen. **II.** s. Aut: **e. (system),** Auspuff m; **e. pipe,** Auspuffrohr n. ◆**e'xhausted,** adj. erschöpft. ◆**e'xhausting,** adj. erschöpfend ◆**e'xhaustion,** s. Erschöpfung f. ◆**e'xhaustive,** adj. eingehend.

exhibit [ig'zibit, eg-]. **I.** s. (a) Ausstellungsstück n; (b) Jur: Beweisstück n. **II.** v.tr. ausstellen. ◆**exhibition** [eksi'biʃ(ə)n], s. Ausstellung f.

exhilarating [ig'ziləreitiŋ], adj. aufregend. ◆**exhila'ration,** s. freudige Erregung f.

exile ['eksail]. **I.** s. **1.** Exil n. **2.** (pers.) Verbannte(r) f(m). **II.** v.tr. verbannen.

exist [ig'zist, eg-], v.i. existieren. ◆**e'xistence,** s. (of pers.) Dasein n, Existenz f; (of thing) Vorhandensein n; **in e.,** vorhanden. ◆**e'xisting,** adj. vorhanden. (of law etc.) gegenwärtig.

exit ['eksit], s. **1.** Abgang m; **e. visa,** Ausreisevisum n. **2.** (door) Ausgang m.

exonerate [ig'zɔnəreit, eg-], v.tr. entlasten.

exorbitant [ig'zɔ:bit(ə)nt, eg-], adj. unverschämt; **e. price,** Wucherpreis m.

exotic [eg'zɔtik], adj. exotisch.

expand [iks'pænd, eks-], v. **1.** v.tr. vergrößern, ausdehnen. **2.** v.i. sich ausdehnen. ◆**ex'panding,** adj. an **e. market,** ein wachsender Markt. ◆**expanse** [-'pæns], s. Weite f. ◆**ex'pansion,** s. Ausdehnung f.

expatriate. I. [eks'pætrieit], v.tr. ausbürgern. **II.** [eks'peitriət], s. Ausgebürgerte(r) f(m). **III.** adj. ausgebürgert.

expect [iks'pekt, ek-], v.tr. (a) erwarten; F: **she's expecting,** sie ist in anderen Umständen; (b) (demand) **I e. you to be punctual,** ich erwarte Pünktlichkeit von dir; **to e. a lot of s.o.,** j-m viel zumuten; (c) **I e. so,** ich denke schon. ◆**ex'pectant,** adj. erwartungsvoll; **e. mother,** werdende Mutter. ◆**expec'tation,** s. **1.** Erwartung f. **2.** usu.pl. **expectations,** Aussichten fpl.

expediency [iks'pi:diənsi, eks-], s. Zweckmäßigkeit f. ◆**ex'pedient,** adj. zweckmäßig.

expel [iks'pel, eks-], v.tr. (einen Ausländer) aus einem Land ausweisen; (einen Schüler) von der Schule verweisen.

expendable [iks'pendəbl, eks-], adj. entbehrlich. ◆**ex'penditure,** s. Ausgaben fpl. ◆**ex'pense,** s. **1.** Ausgabe fpl; **at my e.,** auf meine Kosten. **2.** pl. Spesen pl; **e. account,** Spesenkonto n. ◆**ex'pensive,** adj. teuer.

experience [iks'piəriəns, eks-]. **I.** s. **1.** Erfahrung f. **2. an e.,** ein Erlebnis n. **II.** v.tr. erleben. ◆**ex'perienced,** adj. erfahren.

experiment [iks'periment, eks-]. **I.** s. Experiment n. **II.** v.i. experimentieren. ◆**experi'mental,** adj. Versuchs-; **e. car,** Versuchsauto n.

expert ['ekspə:t]. **I.** adj. sachkundig; (of professional) fachkundig. **II.** s. Fachmann m. ◆**expertise** [-'ti:z], s. Sachkenntnis f; (professional) Fachkenntnis f.

expire [iks'paiər, eks-], v.i. (of period, licence) ablaufen. ◆**ex'piry,** s. Ablauf m.

explain [iks'plein, eks-], v.tr. erklären. ◆**explanation** [eksplə'neiʃ(ə)n], s. Erklärung f. ◆**explanatory** [iks'plænətri, eks-], adj. erklärend.

explicable [eks'plikəbl, iks-], adj. erklärlich.

explicit [iks'plisit, eks-], adj. (of answer etc.) deutlich; (of command etc.) ausdrücklich; **-ly,** adv. ausdrücklich.

explode [iks'pləud, eks-], v. **1.** v.tr. (a) (eine Bombe usw.) explodieren; (b) Fig: (eine Theorie usw.) umstoßen. **2.** v.i. explodieren.

exploit¹ ['eksplɔit], s. Großtat f.

exploit² [iks'plɔit, eks-], v.tr. ausnutzen. ◆**exploi'tation,** s. Ausnutzung f.

explore [iks'plɔ:r, eks-], v.tr. (a) (ein Land usw.) erforschen; (b) (Möglichkeiten usw.) untersuchen. ◆**explo'ration,** s. Erforschung f. ◆**exploratory** [eks'plɔrətri, iks-], adj. **e. talks,** Sondierungsgespräche npl. ◆**ex'plorer,** s. Forscher m.

explosion [iks'plɔuʒ(ə)n, eks-], s. Explosion f. ◆**ex'plosive** [-ziv]. I. adj. explosiv. II. s. Sprengstoff m.

export. I. [eks'pɔːt], v.tr. exportieren. II. ['ekspɔːrt], s. Export m. ◆**expor'tation**, s. Export m. ◆**ex'porter**, s. Exporteur m.

expose [iks'pɔuz], v.tr. (a) (etwas) bloßlegen; (b) (j-n) aussetzen (**to** sth., etwas dat); (c) (ein Verbrechen) aufdecken; (einen Betrüger) entlarven. ◆**ex'posed**, adj. an e. position, eine ungeschützte Lage. ◆**exposure** ['-pɔuʒər], s. (a) to die of e., erfrieren; (b) Phot: Belichtung f; e. meter, Belichtungsmesser m; (on film) 36 exposures, 36 Aufnahmen.

express[1] [iks'pres, eks-]. I. adj. 1. ausdrücklich; 2. e. train, Schnellzug m; e. letter, Eilbrief m. II. adv. durch Eilboten. III. s. Schnellzug m; -ly, adv. ausdrücklich.

express[2], v.tr. ausdrücken. ◆**expression** [-'preʃ(ə)n], s. Ausdruck m; (facial) e., Gesichtsausdruck m. ◆**ex'pressive**, adj. ausdrucksvoll.

expulsion [iks'pʌlʃ(ə)n, eks-], s. Ausweisung f (aus einem Lande); Verweisung f (von der Schule).

exquisite [eks'kwizit], adj. auserlesen.

extend [iks'tend, eks-], v.tr.v. (a) verlängern; (Grenzen, j-s Einfluß usw.) ausdehnen; (einen Betrieb) vergrößern; (ein Haus) ausbauen; (b) (die Hand usw.) ausstrecken. II. v.i sich ausdehnen. ◆**ex'tension**, s. 1. Verlängerung f (einer Frist, einer Straße usw.). 2. (on house) Anbau m. 3. Tel: Nebenanschluß m. ◆e. lead, Verlängerungsschnur f. ◆**ex'tensive**, adj. e. knowledge, umfassendes Wissen; e. research, weitreichende Forschungen; -ly, adv. weitgehend.

extent [iks'tent, eks-], s. Ausdehnung f; Weite f (einer Fläche); Umfang m (eines Schadens usw.); to some/a certain e., gewissermaßen.

extenuating [eks'tenjueitiŋ, iks-], adj. e. circumstances, mildernde Umstände.

exterior [eks'tiəriər]. I. adj. äußere(r,s), Außen-. II. s. (a) das Äußere; (outside) Außenseite f; on the e., außen; (b) (appearance) Erscheinung f.

exterminate [eks'təːmineit], v.tr. ausrotten. ◆**extermi'nation**, s. Ausrottung f.

external [eks'təːn(ə)l], adj. äußere(r,s), Außen-; -ly, adv. äußerlich.

extinct [iks'tiŋ(k)t, eks-], adj. (a) (of volcano) erloschen; (b) (of species) ausgestorben. ◆**ex'tinction**, s. Aussterben n.

extinguish [iks'tiŋgwiʃ, eks-], v.tr. lö-

schen. ◆**ex'tinguisher**, s. Feuerlöscher m.

extort [iks'tɔːt, eks-], v.tr. erpressen. ◆**ex'tortion**, s. Erpressung f. ◆**ex'tortionate**, adj. e. price, Wucherpreis m.

extra ['ekstra]. I. adj. zusätzlich; e. charge, Zuschlag m. II. adv. (a) extra; you have to pay e. for the wine, der Wein ist nicht im Preis inbegriffen; (b) besonders; F: e. strong, besonders stark. III. s. (a) (payment) Zuschlag m; Cin: Statist m; (c) pl. extras, Nebenausgaben fpl.

extract. I. ['ekstrækt], s. 1. Extrakt m. 2. (from a book etc). Auszug m. II. v.tr. [iks'trækt, eks-], herausziehen; (einen Zahn) ziehen. ◆**ex'traction**, s. 1. Herausziehen n. 2. (origin) Herkunft f.

extradition [ekstrə'diʃ(ə)n], s. Auslieferung f.

extraordinary [iks'trɔːd(i)nri, eks-], adj. (a) außerordentlich; (b) F: (amazing) erstaunlich.

extravagance [iks'trævəgəns, eks-], s. Verschwendung f. ◆**ex'travagant**, adj. (of pers. etc.) verschwenderisch; (of claims, actions etc.) extravagant.

extreme [iks'triːm, eks-]. I. adj. (a) extrem; (b) Pol: etc: radikal. II. s. Extrem n; in the e., äußerst; to go to extremes, es zu weit treiben; -ly, adv. äußerst. ◆**extremity** [iks'tremiti, eks-], s. 1. äußerstes Ende n (eines Seils usw.). 2. in an e., im äußersten Notfall. 3. one's extremities, seine Gliedmaßen fpl.

extricate ['ekstrikeit], v.tr. befreien.

extrovert ['ekstrəuvəːt]. I. adj. extrovertiert. II. s. extrovertierter Mensch.

exuberance [ig'zuːbərəns, eg-], s. Ausgelassenheit f. ◆**e'xuberant**, adj. ausgelassen.

eye [ai]. I. s. 1. Auge n; keep your eyes open! paß gut auf! to be up to one's eyes in work, bis über die Ohren in Arbeit stecken; to set eyes on sth., etwas zu Gesicht bekommen; to see e. to e. with s.o., mit j-m gleicher Meinung sein; to keep an e. on sth., (i) auf etwas acc aufpassen; (ii) etwas im Auge behalten. 2. (of needle) Öhr n. II. v.tr. to e. s.o., j-n mustern. ◆**'eyeball**, s. Augapfel m. ◆**'eyebrow**, s. Augenbraue f. ◆**'eyelash**, s. Augenwimper f. ◆**'eyelid**, s. Augenlid n. ◆**'eyeopener**, s. Überraschung f. ◆**'eyeshadow**, s. Lidschatten m. ◆**'eyesight**, s. good/bad e., gute/schlechte Augen pl. ◆**'eyesore**, s. that house is an e., das Haus ist ein Schandfleck. ◆**'eyewitness**, s. Augenzeuge m.

F

F, f [ef], (der Buchstabe) F,f *n.*
fable ['feibl], *s.* Fabel *f.* ◆**fabulous** ['fæbjuləs], *adj.* F: fantastisch.
fabric ['fæbrik], *s.* 1. Gefüge *n* (der Gesellschaft). 2. (*material*) Stoff *m.* ◆**fabricate**, *v.tr.* (eine Geschichte usw.) erfinden.
facade [fə'sɑːd], *s.* Fassade *f.*
face [feis], *s.* 1. Gesicht *n*; to be f. to f. with s.o., j-m gegenüberstehen; ◆**cloth/f.** flannel, Waschlappen *m.* 2. (*expression*) Gesichtsausdruck *m*; (*put on*) Miene *f*; to make/pull faces, Gesichter schneiden; to keep a straight f., ernst bleiben. 3. on the f. of it, auf den ersten Blick; *Fin:* f. value, Nennwert *m*; *Fig:* I took it at its f. value, ich habe es für bare Münze genommen; to lose f., das Gesicht verlieren. 4. (*surface*) Fläche *f*; Zifferblatt *n* (einer Uhr). II. *v.tr. & i.* (*a*) (*of pers.*) (j-m, etwas *dat*) gegenüberstehen; (j-m, der Gefahr) ins Gesicht sehen; to be faced with sth., mit etwas *dat* konfrontiert werden; (*b*) (*of house etc.*) to face the street/the sea, auf die Straße/das Meer hinausgehen. ◆**face-lift** *s.* 1. Gesichtsstraffung *f.* 2. to give sth. a f.-l., etwas aufmöbeln.
facet ['fæsit], *s.* 1. Schliff *m* (eines Edelsteins). 2. Aspekt *m* (eines Problems).
facetious [fə'siːʃəs], *adj.* (*of remark etc.*) scherzhaft.
facial ['feiʃəl], *adj.* Gesichts-.
facile ['fæsail], *adj.* oberflächlich.
facilitate [fə'siliteit], *v.tr.* erleichtern.
facility [fə'siliti], *s.* 1. (*a*) (*ease*) Leichtigkeit *f*; (*b*) (*skill*) Gewandtheit *f.* 2. *esp.pl.* Möglichkeiten *fpl*, Einrichtungen *fpl.*
fact [fækt], *s.* Tatsache *f*; in f./in point of f., tatsächlich; (*actually*) eigentlich.
faction ['fækʃ(ə)n], *s.* Splittergruppe *f.*
factor ['fæktər], *s.* Faktor *m.*
factory ['fæktəri], *s.* Fabrik *f.*
factual ['fæktjuəl], *adj.* sachlich; f. report, Tatsachenbericht *m.*
faculty ['fæk(ə)lti], *s.* 1. Fähigkeit *f.* 2. (*department*) Fakultät *f.*
fad [fæd], *s.* F: Marotte *f.*
fade [feid], *v.i.* verblassen; (*of flowers, beauty*) verwelken; (*of hope*) schwinden; (*of memory*) verblassen; to f. (away), (*of sound*) verklingen.
fag [fæg], *s.* F: 1. Schinderei *f.* 2. (*cigarette*) Glimmstengel *m.* ◆**fagged 'out**, *adj.* F: völlig k.o.
fail [feil]. I. *adv.phr.* without f., unbedingt; was auch geschieht. II. *v.* 1. *v.i.* (*a*) (*of attempt, plan*) scheitern; (*of crops*) mißraten; if all else fails, wenn alle Stricke reißen; (*b*) (*of pers., voice, machinery, heart etc.*) versagen; *Sch:* durchfallen; he failed to persuade her, es gelang ihm nicht, sie zu überreden; (*c*)

(*of memory, eyesight etc.*) nachlassen; (*of health*) sich verschlechtern; **the light is failing**, es dämmert; (*d*) (*of business*) Konkurs machen. 2. *v.tr.* to f. s.o., j-n im Stich lassen; (*in exam*) j-n durchfallen lassen; to f. an examination, bei einer Prüfung durchfallen. ◆**failing**. I. *s.* (*of pers.*) Fehler *m.* II. *prep.* mangels *+ gen.*
◆**failure**, *s.* 1. Versagen *n* (der Nieren, einer Maschine usw.); f. to appear, Nichterscheinen *n.* 2. (*pers.*) Versager *m.* 3. (*thing*) Mißerfolg *m.*
faint [feint]. I. *adj.* 1. (*a*) (*of light, Fig: comfort*) schwach; (*b*) (*of colour*) zart; a f. sound, ein leises Geräusch; I haven't the faintest idea, ich habe keine blasse Ahnung. 2. I feel f., ich werde gleich ohnmächtig. II. *s.* Ohnmacht *f.* III. *v.i.* ohnmächtig werden; -ly, *adv.* leise (sprechen, klingen); schwach (leuchten); f. visible, kaum sichtbar. ◆**faintness**, *s.* (*of sound, light etc.*) Schwäche *f.*
fair¹ [feər], *s.* (*a*) Jahrmarkt *m*; (*b*) (*trade*) f., Messe *f.*
fair² [feər]. I. *adj.* 1. (*of skin*) hell; (*of hair*) blond. 2. (*just*) gerecht; *F:* f. enough, na gut. 3. (*quite good*) ziemlich gut. 4. f. copy, Reinschrift *f.* II. *adv.* to play f., fair spielen; -ly, *adv.* 1. (*justly*) gerecht. 2. (*honestly*) ehrlich. 3. (*quite*) ziemlich. ◆**fair 'hairod**, *adj.* blond. ◆**fairness**, *s.* Fairneß *f*; in all f., um gerecht zu sein.
fairy [feəri], *s.* Fee *f*; f. tale, Märchen *n.* ◆**fairyland**, *s.* Märchenland *n.*
faith [feiθ], *s.* 1. (*a*) Vertrauen *n*; to have f. in s.o., zu j-m Vertrauen haben; (*b*) the Christian f., der christliche Glaube. 2. in good f., gutgläubig. ◆**faithful**. I. *adj.* (*a*) (*of friend*) treu; (*b*) (*of reproduction, translation*) genau. II. *s.* *Ecc:* the f., die Gläubigen *mpl*; -ly, *adv.* 1. treu; *Com:* yours f., hochachtungsvoll *m.* 2. genau. ◆**faithfulness**, *s.* Treue *f* (to s.o., zu j-m). ◆**faithless**, *adj.* treulos.
fake [feik]. I. *s.* Fälschung *f.* II. *v.tr.* fälschen.
falcon ['fɔːlkən], *s.* Falke *m.*
fall [fɔːl]. I. *s.* 1. Fall *m*; (*heavy*) Sturz *m*; a heavy f. of snow, starker Schneefall *m*. *N.Am:* the f., der Herbst. 3. Sinken *n* (der Preise, der Temperatur). 4. Untergang *m* (eines Menschen); *Pol:* Sturz *m* (einer Regierung). II. *v.i. irr.* (*a*) (*of thing*) fallen; (*of building*) to f. (in), einstürzen; to f. to pieces, zusammenfallen; (*b*) (*of pers.*) (hin)fallen; (*heavily*) stürzen; night is falling, die Nacht bricht an; his face fell, er machte ein langes Gesicht; (*c*) Christmas falls on a Thursday, Weihnachten fällt auf einen Donnerstag; (*d*) (*of barometer, price*) sinken; (*of wind*) nachlassen; (*e*) to f. ill,

krank werden; ◆**'fall 'back**, v.i. to f. b. **on sth.**, auf etwas *acc* zurückgreifen. ◆**'fall be'hind**, v.i. (hinter j-m) zurückbleiben; (*with work*) in Rückstand geraten. ◆**'fall 'down**, v.i. (a) (of pers.) hinfallen; (of object) hinunterfallen; (of building) einstürzen. ◆**'fall for**, v.i. F: (a) to f. a trick, auf einen Trick hereinfallen; (b) to f. f. s.o., sth., sich in j-n, etwas verlieben. ◆**'fall 'in**, v.i. (a) (of roof etc.) einstürzen; (b) Mil: (in Linie) antreten; (c) to f. in with s.o., mit j-m gemeinsame Sache machen. ◆**'fall 'off**, v. 1. v.tr. to f. o. (a wall), (von einer Mauer) herunterfallen. 2. v.i. nachlassen; (in numbers) weniger werden. ◆**'fall 'out**, v.i. (a) to f. o. (of a window), (zum Fenster) hinausfallen; (b) (of hair) ausfallen; (c) Mil: wegtreten; (d) (disagree) in Streit geraten. ◆**'fallout**, s. (radioactive) f., (radioaktiver) Niederschlag m. ◆**'fall 'over**, v. 1. v.tr. to f. o. **sth.**, über etwas *acc* stolpern. 2. v.i. (of pers.) umfallen; (of jug, glass etc.) umkippen. ◆**'fall 'through**, v.i. ins Wasser fallen.

fallacy ['fæləsi], s. irrige Ansicht f.

false [fɔls], adj. 1. (wrong) falsch; 2. (artificial) (of hair, teeth) künstlich; f. teeth, (künstliches) Gebiß n. ◆**'falsehood**, s. Unwahrheit f. ◆**'falsify**, v.tr. fälschen.

falter ['fɔltər], v.i. (esp. of voice) stocken; (of pers.) zögern.

fame [feim], s. Ruhm m.

familiar [fə'miliər], adj. (a) (intimate) vertraut; (b) (known) bekannt (to, dat). (c) to be f. with sth., mit etwas dat vertraut sein. ◆**famili'arity**, s. 1. Vertraulichkeit f. 2. Vertrautheit f (with sth., mit etwas dat.). ◆**fa'miliarize**, v.tr. to f. oneself/s.o. with sth., sich/j-n mit etwas dat vertraut machen.

family ['fæmili], s. Familie f; f. doctor, Hausarzt m; f. man, Familienvater m; f. tree, Stammbaum m; f. allowance, Kindergeld n; f. planning, Familienplanung f.

famine ['fæmin], s. Hungersnot f. ◆**'famished**, adj. ausgehungert.

famous ['feiməs], adj. berühmt.

fan¹ [fæn]. I. s. 1. Fächer m. 2. (mechanical) Ventilator m; f. belt, Keilriemen m. II. v. 1. v.tr. to f. oneself, sich fächeln. 2. v.i. to f. (out), sich (fächerförmig) ausbreiten.

fan², s. F: Fan m; f. mail, Verehrerpost f.

fanatic [fə'nætik], s. Fanatiker(in) m(f). ◆**fa'natical**, adj. fanatisch. ◆**fa'naticism**, s. Fanatismus m.

fancy ['fænsi]. I. s. to take a f. to s.o., sth., an j-m, etwas dat Gefallen finden. II. adj. (a) f. cake, Törtchen n (mit Zukkerguß usw.); (b) f. dress, Kostüm n; f.-dress ball, Kostümfest n; (c) Pej: (of ideas etc.) ausgefallen; f. prices, Phantasiepreise mpl. III. v.tr. (a) f. that! was Sie nicht sagen! (b) I f. a biscuit, ich

hätte Lust auf einen Keks; (c) F: he fancies himself, er hält sich für weiß Gott wen. ◆**'fanciful**, adj. phantastisch.

fanfare ['fænfɛər], s. Fanfare f.

fang [fæŋ], s. (a) Reißzahn m; (b) (of snake) Giftzahn m.

fantasy ['fæntəsi,-zi], s. Phantasie f; f. world, Phantasiewelt f. ◆**fan'tastic**, adj. F: fantastisch.

far [fɑːr]. I. adv. 1. (a) (of place) weit; f. away/off, weit entfernt; Fig: he will go f., er wird es weit bringen; (b) as f. as I know, soviel ich weiß; in so f. as, insofern; f. from it, keineswegs. 2. (of time) so f., bisher. 3. viel; it's f. better, es ist viel besser; by f., weitaus. II. adj. at the f. end of the street, am anderen Ende der Straße; the Far East, der Ferne Osten. ◆**'faraway**, adj. weit entfernt. ◆**far-'fetched**, adj. an den Haaren herbeigezogen. ◆**far-'reaching**, adj. weitreichend. ◆**far-'sighted**, adj. weitblickend.

farce [fɑːs], s. Farce f. ◆**'farcical**, adj. lächerlich.

fare [fɛər]. I. s. (a) (cost) Fahrpreis m; (money) Fahrgeld n. 2. (food) Kost f.

farewell [fɛə'wel]. int. & s. Lebewohl n; to bid s.o./sth. f., von j-m/etwas dat Abschied nehmen.

farm [fɑːm]. I. s. Bauernhof m; f. labourer, Landarbeiter m; f. produce, landwirtschaftliche Produkte npl. II. v. 1. v.tr. (Land) bewirtschaften. 2. v.i. Landwirtschaft betreiben. ◆**'farmer**, s. Bauer m. ◆**'farmhouse**, s. Bauernhaus n. ◆**'farming**, s. Landwirtschaft f. ◆**'farmyard**, s. Hof m.

fart [fɑːt], P: I. s. Furz m. II. v.i. furzen.

farther ['fɑːðər], adj. 1. adv. f. (than), weiter (als). II. adj. entfernt. ◆**'farthest**, adv. am weitesten.

fascinate ['fæsineit], v.tr. faszinieren. ◆**'fascinating**, adj. faszinierend. ◆**fasci'nation**, s. Faszination f.

fascism ['fæʃiz(ə)m], s. Faschismus m. ◆**'fascist**, s. Faschist m.

fashion ['fæʃ(ə)n]. I. s. 1. (manner) Art f. 2. Cl: etc: Mode f; in f., (in) Mode; out of f., unmodern; f. magazine, Modejournal n. II. v.tr. formen. ◆**'fashionable**, adj. modern; (of clothes, resort) modisch.

fast¹ [fɑːst]. I. v.i. fasten n. II. v.i. fasten.

fast² I. adj. schnell; the clock is f., die Uhr geht vor. II. adv. 1. f. asleep, in tiefem Schlaf. 2. schnell.

fasten ['fɑːsn], v. 1. v.tr. befestigen (to sth., an etwas dat.). 2. v.i. the dress fastens at the back, das Kleid ist hinten zuzumachen. ◆**'fastener, 'fastening**, s. Verschluß m.

fastidious [fæs'tidiəs], adj. wählerisch.

fat [fæt]. I. adj. 1. (of pers., cigar etc.) dick. 2. (of meat) fett. II. s. Fett n.

fatal [feit(ə)l], adj. 1. (of accident etc.) tödlich. 2. f. mistake, verhängnisvoller Irrtum; -ly, adv. f. injured, tödlich verletzt. ◆**fatality** [fə'tæliti], s. Todesopfer n. ◆**fate** [feit], s. Schicksal n. ◆**fated**, adj. (a) f. (to do sth.) vom Schicksal bestimmt, (etwas zu tun); (b) F: (of plan) zum Scheitern verurteilt.

father ['fɑːðər], I. s. Vater m. ◆**fatherland**, s. Vaterland n. ◆**father-in-law**, s. Schwiegervater m. ◆**fatherless**, adj. vaterlos. ◆**fatherly**, adj. väterlich.

fathom ['fæðəm]. I. s. Klafter f. II. v.tr. (a) (Wasser) loten; (b) Fig: (etwas) begreifen.

fatigue [fə'tiːg]. I. s. Ermüdung f. II. v.tr. ermüden. ◆**fatiguing**, adj. ermüdend.

fatten ['fæt(ə)n], v. 1. v.tr. (Tiere) mästen. 2. v.i. fett werden. ◆**fattening**, adj. that's f., das macht dick. ◆**fatty**, adj. fett; f. foods, fetthaltige Nahrungsmittel.

fatuous ['fætjuəs], adj. albern.

faucet ['fɔːsət], s. N.Am: Wasserhahn m.

fault [fɔːlt]. I. s. 1. (a) (defect) Fehler m; (b) Tchn: Defekt m; TV: etc: Störung f. 2. to be at f., im Unrecht sein; it's your f., es ist Ihre Schuld. 3. Geog: Verwerfung f. II. v.tr. (j-m) einen Fehler nachweisen. ◆**faultfinding**, s. Krittelei f. ◆**faultless**, adj. fehlerfrei; f. German, tadelloses Deutsch. ◆**faulty**, adj. fehlerhaft; f. brakes, schlechte Bremsen.

fauna ['fɔːnə], s. Fauna f.

favour ['feivər]. I. s. 1. to find f. (with s.o.) (j-m) gefallen; in f. of sth., für etwas acc. 2. (act) Gefallen m; to do s.o. a f., j-m einen Gefallen tun. II. v.tr. (a) to f. sth., für etwas acc sein; (b) (prefer) bevorzugen. ◆**favourable**, adj. günstig. ◆**favourite**. I. adj. Lieblings-; f. dish, Leibgericht n. II. s. (n) (pers.) Liebling m; (b) Sp: Favorit(in) m(f). ◆**favouritism**, s. (unfaire) Bevorzugung f.

fawn[1] [fɔːn]. I. s. Hirschkalb n; Rehkitz n. II. adj. rehbraun.

fawn[2], v.i. to f. on s.o., sich bei j-m einschmeicheln. ◆**fawning**, adj. kriecherisch.

fear ['fiər]. I. s. Angst f; Furcht f (of s.o., sth., vor j-m, etwas dat); F: no f.! keine Angst! fears, Befürchtungen f. v. 1. v.tr. to f. the worst, das Schlimmste befürchten. 2. v.i. fürchten (for sth., um etwas acc). ◆**fearful**, adj. 1. (terrible) furchtbar. 2. (apprehensive) furchtsam. ◆**fearless**, adj. furchtlos. ◆**fearlessness**, s. Furchtlosigkeit f.

feasible ['fiːzəbl], adj. durchführbar. ◆**feasibility**, s. Durchführbarkeit f [f. study, Durchführbarkeitsanalyse f.

feast [fiːst]. I. s. 1. Ecc: f. (day), Fest n. 2. (meal) Festessen n. II. v.i. to f. on sth., etwas ausgiebig genießen.

feat [fiːt], s. Großtat f; (achievement) Leistung f.

feather ['feðər], s. Feder f.

◆**featherbrained**, adj. she is f., sie hat ein Spatzenhirn.

feature ['fiːtʃər]. I. s. 1. esp. pl. (of face) Gesichtszüge mpl. 2. (characteristic) Merkmal n. 3. (article) Bericht m; f. (film), Hauptfilm m. II. v. 1. v.tr. Cin: TV: etc: (j-n, einen Bericht usw.) bringen. 2. v.i. (of things) vorkommen; (of pers.) eine (führende) Rolle spielen.

February ['februəri], s. Februar m.

fed [fed], adj. F: to be f. up, es satt haben.

federal ['fedərəl], adj. Bundes-; the F. Republic of Germany, die Bundesrepublik Deutschland. ◆**fede'ration**, s. Bund m.

fee [fiː], s. Gebühr f.

feeble ['fiːbl], adj. (a) schwach; (of old pers.) gebrechlich; (b) (of excuse etc.) lahm; (c) F: (bad) mies. ◆**feeble-'minded**, adj. schwachsinnig. ◆**feebleness**, s. Schwäche f.

feed [fiːd]. I. s. (for animal) Futter n; (for baby) Nahrung f. II. v. irr. 1. v.tr. (a) (ein Tier, ein Kind) füttern (on sth., mit etwas dat); (einen Menschen) zu essen geben; (b) to f. sth. into the computer, etwas in den Computer eingeben. 2. v.i. fressen; to f. on sth., (of pers.) sich von etwas dat ernähren; (of animal) etwas fressen. ◆**feedback**, s. 1. El: Rückkopplung f. 2. Reaktionen fpl (auf eine Umfrage usw.). ◆**feedpipe**, s. Tchn: Zuleitungsrohr n. ◆**feed up**, v.tr. (ein Tier) mästen.

feel [fiːl]. I. s. (a) it has a rough f., es fühlt sich rauh an; (b) to get the f. of sth., sich an etwas acc gewöhnen. II. v. irr. 1. v.tr. (a) (physically) fühlen; (Kälte, eine Bewegung, eine Wirkung) spüren; (Schmerz) empfinden. b to f. one's way forward, sich nach vorn tasten; (b) (emotionally) (Liebe, Abscheu usw.) empfinden; (c) (consider) meinen. 2. v.i. (of pers.) (a) sich (wohl, besser, glücklich, fremd usw.) fühlen; I f. cold/ill, mir ist kalt/schlecht; (b) I felt like crying, ich hätte weinen können; I f. like a cup of tea, ich hätte Lust auf eine Tasse Tee; (c) to f. for s.o., mit j-m Mitleid haben; (d) to f. for sth., nach etwas dat tasten; (e) to f. up to sth., sich für etwas acc stark genug fühlen. ◆**feeling**, s. Gefühl n.

feign [fein], v.tr. vortäuschen.

fell [fel], v.tr. (einen Baum) fällen.

fellow ['feləu], s. 1. f. citizen, Mitbürger m; f. countryman, Landsmann m; f. traveller, Mitreisende(r) f (m); Fig: Mitläufer m; F: Kerl m. ◆**fellowship**, s. Forschungsstipendium n.

felony ['feləni], s. schweres Verbrechen n.

felt [felt], s. Filz m; f. pen, Filzstift m.

female ['fiːmeil]. I. adj. weiblich. II. s. Weibchen n. ◆**feminine** ['feminin], adj. weiblich; (of dress etc.) feminin. ◆**feminism**, s. Feminismus m.

◆'feminist. I. s. Feminist(in) m(f). II. adj. feministisch.

fence [fens]. I. s. Zaun m. II. v. 1. v.tr. to f. in sth., etwas einzäunen. 2. v.i. Sp: fechten. ◆'fencing, s. 1. Sp: Fechten n. 2. (material) Zaun m.

fend [fend], v.tr. & v.i. to f. off an attack, einen Angriff abwehren. 2. v.i. to f. for oneself, sich allein durchschlagen.

fender ['fendər], s. (a) Kaminvorsetzer m; (b) N.Am: Aut: Kotflügel m.

ferment. I. s. ['fə:ment]. 1. Aufruhr m. II. [fə'ment]. v.i. gären. ◆fermen'tation, s. Gärung f.

fern [fə:n], s. Farnkraut n.

ferocious [fə'rəuʃəs], adj. (of pers.) grimmig; (of animal) wild; a f. attack, ein heftiger Angriff. ◆ferocity [-'rɔsiti], s. Wildheit f Heftigkeit f.

ferret ['ferit]. I. s. Z: Frettchen n. II. v.i. to f. about, herumsuchen.

ferry ['feri]. I. s. f. (boat), Fähre f. II. v.tr. übersetzen.

fertile ['fə:tail], adj. fruchtbar; f. imagination, reiche Phantasie. ◆fertility. [-'tiliti], s. Fruchtbarkeit f. ◆fertilization [-ilai'zeif(ə)n], s. Befruchtung f. ◆'fertilize, v.tr. a) befruchten; (b) (den Boden) düngen. ◆'fertilizer, s. Dünger m.

fervent ['fə:vənt], adj. leidenschaftlich; (of request etc.) inständig. ◆'fervour, s. Leidenschaft f.

fester ['festər], v.i. eitern.

festival ['festival], s. Fest n; Mus: Th: Festspiele npl; film f., Filmfestival n. ◆'festive, adj. festlich; the f. season = Weihnachten n. ◆fes'tivity, s. the festivities, die Festlichkeiten fpl.

fetch [fetʃ], v.tr. (a) (etwas) holen; (j-n) abholen; (b) to f. a good price, einen guten Preis erzielen. ◆'fetch 'back, v.tr. zurückholen. ◆'fetch 'in, v.tr. hereinbringen. ◆'fetch 'down, v.tr. herunterholen. ◆'fetch 'in, v.tr. hereinbringen. ◆'fetching, adj. attraktiv; (of smile) gewinnend.

fête [feit], s. Fest n.

fetish ['fetiʃ], s. Fetisch m.

fetter ['fetər], s. usu. pl. fetters, Fesseln fpl.

feud [fju:d], s. Fehde f.

feudal ['fju:dl], adj. feudal.

fever ['fi:vər], s. Fieber n. f. ◆'feverish, adj. fieberhaft; Med: fiebrig.

few [fju:], adj. (a) wenige; (b) (several) a f. (books etc.), ein paar (Bücher usw.); a f. more, noch ein paar; quite a f., ziemlich viele. ◆'fewer, adj. weniger. ◆'fewest, adj. he had the f. points, er hatte die wenigsten Punkte; I got (the) f., ich bekam am wenigsten.

fiancé [fi'ã:nsei], s. Verlobte(r) m. ◆fi'ancée, s. Verlobte f.

fiasco, pl. -os [fi'æskəu, -əuz], s. Fiasko n.

fib [fib]. I. s. F: kleine Lüge f. II. v.i. F: flunkern.

fibre ['faibər], s. (a) Faser f; (b) moral f., moralische Stärke f. ◆'fibreglass, s. Glasfaser f.

fickle [fikl], adj. unbeständig; (of pers.) wankelmütig. ◆'fickleness, s. Unbeständigkeit f; Wankelmut m.

fiction ['fikʃ(ə)n], s. 1. (not truth) Erfindung f. 2. (art, category) Belletristik f; (works of) f., Unterhaltungsliteratur f. ◆'fic'titious, adj. (frei) erfunden.

fiddle [fidl]. I. s. 1. Mus: F: Geige f. 2. F: Schwindel m. II. v. 1. v.i. F: to f. with sth., mit etwas dat herumspielen. 2. v.tr. F: (etwas) arrangieren; to f. the accounts, die Bücher frisieren. ◆'fiddler, s. 1. Mus: Geiger m. 2. F: Schwindler m. ◆'fiddling, adj. geringfügig. ◆'fiddly, adj. F: knifflig.

fidelity [fi'deliti], s. Treue f.

fidget ['fidʒit]. I. s. F: Zappelphilipp m. II. v.i. to f. (about), (herum)zappeln. ◆'fidgeting, s. Zappelei f. ◆'fidgety, adj. zappelig.

field [fi:ld], s. 1. Feld n. to have a f. day, einen erfolgreichen Tag haben. 2. (area of study etc.) Gebiet n. ◆'fieldglasses, s.pl. Feldstecher m. ◆'Field-'Marshal, s. Feldmarschall m. ◆'fieldmouse, s. Feldmaus f.

fiend [fi:nd], s. (a) Teufel m; (b) (pers.) Unmensch m; (c) F: (enthusiast) Fanatiker m. ◆'fiendish, adj. teuflisch.

fierce [fiəs], adj. (a) (of battle, competition etc.) heftig; (b) (of animal) bösartig. ◆'fierceness, s. Heftigkeit f; Bösartigkeit f.

fiery ['faiəri], adj. feurig.

fifteen [fif'ti:n], num. adj. fünfzehn. ◆fif'teenth, num. adj. fünfzehnte(r,s).

fifth [fifθ]. I. num. adj. fünfte(r,s). II. s. Fünftel n.

fifty ['fifti], num. adj. fünfzig; let's go f., machen wir's halbe-halbe.

fig [fig], s. Feige f.

fight [fait]. I. s. Kampf m; (brawl) Schlägerei f. II. v. 1. v.i. a) kämpfen (for/over/about sth., um etwas acc); (b) (brawl) sich prügeln; (of children) sich raufen; to f. back, sich wehren. 2. v.tr. bekämpfen; (gegen j-n) kämpfen. ◆'fighter, s. 1. Kämpfer m. 2. Av: Jagdflugzeug n. ◆'fighting, s. 1. Kämpfen n; Mil: fierce f., heftige/ schwere Kämpfe. 2. (brawling) Prügelei f.

figment ['figmənt], s. a f. of your imagination, ein Auswuchs m Ihrer Phantasie.

figure ['figər]. I. s. 1. (shape) Figur f. 2. (a) (pers. of importance) Persönlichkeit f; (b) a ghostly f., eine gespenstische Gestalt. 3. (d) (number) Zahl f; to be good at figures, gut im Rechnen sein; (b) (amount) Betrag m. 4. (in book) Abbildung f. II. v. 1. v.i. a) (auf einer Liste usw.) vorkommen; (b) N.Am: meinen. 2. v.tr. I can't f. him/it out, ich kann ihn/es nicht begreifen. ◆'figurative, *adj.* metaphorisch; **f. meaning**, übertragene Bedeutung; **-ly**, *adv.* **to speak f.**, bildlich sprechen.

filament ['filəmənt], *s.* 1. *Bot:* Staubfaden *m.* 2. *El:* Glühfaden *m.*

file¹ [fail]. I. *s. (tool)* Feile *f.* II. *v.tr.* feilen.

file² [fail]. I. *s.* 1. *(containing documents etc.)* Ordner *m.* 2. *(dossier)* Akten *fpl;* **on f.**, bei den Akten. 3. *Data-pr:* Datei *f.* II. *v.tr. (etwas)* zu den Akten legen, *(sort)* (ein)ordnen. ◆**'filing**, *s.* Einordnen *n;* **f. cabinet**, Aktenschrank *m.*

file³ [fail]. I. *s.* **in single f.**, im Gänsemarsch. II. *v.i.* **to f. in/out**, einer nach dem anderen hinein-/hinaustreten.

filial ['filiəl], *attrib. adj.* Kindes-; **f. devotion**, Liebe *f* zu den Eltern.

filibuster ['filibʌstər], *v.i. N. Am:* Obstruktion treiben.

fill [fil]. I. *s.* **to eat one's f.**, sich satt essen; **to have one's f. of sth.**, genug von etwas *dat* haben. II. *v.* 1. *v.tr. (a)* füllen; **to be filled with admiration**, mit Bewunderung erfüllt sein; *(b)* (einen Posten) besetzen. 2. *v.i.* sich füllen. ◆**'fill 'in**, *v.tr. (a)* (ein Loch) ausfüllen, (einen Graben) zuschütten; *(b)* (in Formular) ausfüllen; (das Datum) einsetzen. ◆**'filling**. I. *adj.* sättigend. II. *s.* 1. *(in tooth, food)* Füllung *f.* 2. *Aut:* **f. station**, Tankstelle *f.* ◆**'fill 'out**, *v.tr. esp. N.Am:* (in Formular) ausfüllen. ◆**'fill 'up**, *v.* 1. *v.tr. (a)* (ein Glas usw.) füllen; *Aut:* **to f. a car up (with petrol)**, ein Auto volltanken; *(b)* (in Loch ein Formular) ausfüllen. 2. *v.i. (a)* sich füllen; *(b) Aut:* volltanken.

fillet ['filit]. I. *s.* Filet *n.* II. *v.tr.* in Filets zerlegen.

filly ['fili], *s.* Jungstute *f.*

film [film]. I. *s.* 1. *(layer)* (dünne) Schicht *f.* 2. Film *m;* **to make a f.**, einen Film drehen; **f. star**, Filmstar *m.* II. *v.* 1. *v.tr.* (eine Szene) drehen. 2. *v.i.* filmen.

filter ['filtər]. I. *s.* Filter *m.* II. *v.* 1. *v.tr.* filtern. 2. *v.i. (of news etc.)* **to f. through**, durchsickern.

filth ['filθ], *s.* Dreck *m.* ◆**'filthy**, *adj.* dreckig.

fin [fin], *s.* Flosse *f.*

final ['fainl]. I. *adj. (a)* letzte(r,s); End-; *(b) (of decision etc.)* endgültig. II. *s.* 1. *Sp:* Endspiel *n.* 2. *Sch:* **finals**, Abschlußprüfung *f;* **-ly**, *adv.* schließlich. ◆**finale** [fi'nɑ:li], *s.* Finale *n.* ◆**'finalist**, *s. Sp:* Finalist(in) *m(f).* ◆**'finalize**, *v.tr. (etwas)* vollenden; (Vorbereitungen usw. *dat)* abschließen.

finance I. ['fainæns]. *s.* 1. Finanz *f.* 2. *pl* Finanzen *pl.* II. [fi'næns, 'fai-], *v.tr.* finanzieren. ◆**fi'nancial**, *adj.* finanziell; **f. year**, (i) *Com:* Geschäftsjahr *n;* (ii) *Pol:* Finanzjahr *n.* ◆**fi'nancier**, *s.* Finanzmann *m.*

find [faind]. I. *s.* Fund *m.* II. *v.tr. irr.* finden; **they will f. it easy/difficult**, es wird

ihnen leicht-/schwerfallen; **to f. s.o. guilty**, j-n für schuldig befinden. ◆**'find 'out**, *v.* 1. *v.tr.* herausfinden. 2. *v.i.* **to f. out (about sth.)**, *(learn)* (etwas) erfahren; *(discover)* (etwas) entdecken.

fine¹ [fain]. I. *s.* Geldstrafe *f.* II. *v.tr.* (j-n) mit einer Geldstrafe belegen; **to be fined (£50)**, eine Geldstrafe (von £50) bekommen.

fine² [fain]. *adj.* 1. *(of weather etc.)* schön; *F:* **that's f.!** (i) *(OK)* das geht in Ordnung; (ii) *(excellent)* das ist prima! **that's f. with me**, das paßt mir gut; *(of health)* **I'm f.**, mir geht's gut. 2. *(a) (of mesh etc.)* fein; *(b) (of fabric, skin)* zart; **f. distinction**, feiner Unterschied. II. *adv.* fein; *F:* **to cut it f.**, sich *dat* recht wenig Zeit lassen; **-ly**, *adv.* **f. chopped**, fein gehackt. III. *int.* **f.!** gut!

finger ['fiŋgər], *s.* 1. Finger *m;* **he wouldn't lift a f. (to help them)**, er würde den keinen Finger rühren (, ihnen zu helfen). II. *v.tr.* betasten. ◆**'fingernail**, *s.* Fingernagel *m.* ◆**'fingerprint**, *s.* Fingerabdruck *m.* ◆**'fingertip**, *s.* Fingerspitze *f;* **to have sth. at one's fingertips**, etwas griffbereit haben.

finicky ['finiki], *adj. F: (of pers.)* heikel; *(pedantic)* übertrieben genau.

finish ['finiʃ]. I. *s.* 1. Ende *n.* 2. *Sp:* Ziel *n.* 3. *(of products etc.)* Ausführung *f.* II. *v.* 1. *v.tr. (of author usw.)* beenden; (ein Buch) zu Ende lesen; (Getränk) austrinken. 2. *v.i. (of period, performance etc.)* zu Ende gehen; *(of pers.)* fertig werden; *(c) Sp:* **to f. third**, als dritter durchs Ziel gehen. ◆**'finished**, *adj.* 1. *Ind:* **f. goods/products**, Fertigprodukte *npl.* 2. **beautifully f.**, schön gearbeitet/lackiert *(of paintwork).* 3. *F: (of pers.)* erledigt. ◆**'finishing**, *adj.* **f. touch**, der letzte Schliff; **f. line**, Ziellinie *f.* ◆**'finish 'off**, *v.tr.* (eine Aufgabe) zu Ende führen; *(eat up)* (etwas) aufessen. ◆**'finish 'up**, *v.i. F:* **we finished up in a pub**, zum Schluß landeten wir in einer Kneipe.

finite ['fainait], *adj.* begrenzt.

Finland ['finlənd]. *Pr. n.* Finnland *n.* ◆**Finn**, *s.* Finne *m,* Finnin *f.* ◆**'Finnish**. I. *adj.* finnisch. II. *s.* Finnisch *n.*

fir [fəːr], *s.* Tanne *f.*

fire ['faiər]. I. *s.* 1. *(a)* Feuer *n;* **electric f.**, elektrischer Ofen *m; (b) (conflagration)* Brand *m;* **to catch f.**, Feuer fangen; **to set f. to a house**, ein Haus in Brand stecken; **to be on f.**, brennen; in Flammen stehen; **f. alarm**, Feueralarm *m;* **f. brigade**, Feuerwehr *f;* **f. engine**, Feuerwehrauto *n;* **f. escape**, Feuertreppe *f;* **f. extinguisher**, Feuerlöscher *m;* **f. station**, Feuerwache *f.* 2. *Mil:* **to cease f.**, das Feuer einstellen. II. *v.* 1. *v.tr. (a) Fig:* **to be fired with enthusiasm (for sth.)**, von Begeisterung (für etwas *acc)* erfüllt sein; *(b)* **to f. a revolver at s.o.**, mit einem

Revolver auf j-n schießen; **to f. a shot,** einen Schuß abfeuern; **to f. questions at s.o.,** j-n mit Fragen bombardieren; (c) F: (einen Angestellten) entlassen, F: feuern. 2. *v.i.* schießen (**at** s.o., **auf** j-n).
◆**'firearm,** *s.* Schußwaffe *f.* ◆**'fire a'way,** *v.i.* F: f. a.! leg los!
◆**'firefighter,** *s.* Feuerwehrmann *m.*
◆**'firefighting,** *s.* Brandbekämpfung *f.*
◆**'fireguard,** *s.* Schutzgitter *n.*
◆**'firelight,** *s.* Feuerschein *m.*
◆**'firelighter,** *s.* Feueranzünder *m.*
◆**'fireman,** *s.* Feuerwehrmann *m.*
◆**'fireplace,** *s.* Kamin *m.* ◆**'fireproof,** *adj. (of dish etc.)* feuerfest; *Cl:* feuerbeständig; **f. door,** feuersichere Tür.
◆**'fireside,** *s.* by/at the f., am Kamin.
◆**'firewood,** *s.* Brennholz *n.*
◆**'firework,** *s.* Feuerwerkskörper *m; pl* fireworks, Feuerwerk *n.*

firm¹ [fə:m], *s.* Firma *f.*

firm² [fə:m]. I. *adj.* (a) fest; (b) *(strict)* streng; **-ly,** *adv.* fest. ◆**'firmness,** *s.* Festigkeit *f; (of pers., treatment)* Strenge *f.*

first [fə:st]. I. *adj.* erste(r,s); **in the f. place,** erstens; *(to start with)* gleich am Anfang; **f. thing (in the morning),** zuallererst (nach dem Aufstehen); **f. aid,** Erste Hilfe *f; Aut:* f. (gear), erster Gang. II. s. 1. (the) first, der, die, das Erste; **to f. to do sth.,** etwas als erster tun; *Sp:* to be f., Erster sein. 2. **at first,** zuerst. III. *adv.* (a) erstens; zuerst; **f. of all,** zuallererst; (b) **when I f. saw him,** als ich ihn zum ersten Mal sah; **he arrived f.,** er kam als erster an; **-ly,** *adv.* erstens. ◆**'first-(')class.** I. *adj.* erstklassig; **a f.-c. compartment,** ein Abteil erster Klasse. II. *adv.* to travel f.-c., erster Klasse reisen. ◆**'first-'rate,** *adj.* erstklassig.

fish [fiʃ]. I. s. Fisch *m;* **f. and chips,** Bratfisch *m* mit Pommes Frites. II. *v.i.* fischen; *(with rod)* angeln. ◆**'fishbone,** *s.* Fischgräte *f.* ◆**'fisherman,** *s.* Fischer *m.* ◆**'fishery,** *s.* Fischerei *f.* ◆**'fishhook,** *s.* Angelhaken *m.* ◆**'fishing,** *s.* Fischen *n; (with rod)* Angeln *n;* **f. boat,** Fischerboot *n;* **f. limit,** Fischereigrenze *f;* **f. net,** Fischnetz *n;* **f. tackle,** Angelgeräte *npl; f.* **line,** Angelschnur *f;* **f. rod,** Angel(rute) *f.* ◆**'fishmonger,** *s.* Fischhändler *m;* **f.'s (shop),** Fischgeschäft *n.* ◆**'fishy,** *adj.* F: verdächtig.

fission ['fiʃ(ə)n], *s.* Spaltung *f.*

fissure ['fiʃər], *s.* Spalte *f.*

fist [fist], *s.* Faust *f;* **to clench one's fists,** die Fäuste ballen.

fit¹ [fit], *s.* (a) *Med: etc:* Anfall *m;* (b) **to be in fits of laughter,** sich vor Lachen krümmen; *Fig:* f. of generosity etc., Anwandlung *f* von Großzügigkeit usw.; (c) **by fits and starts,** schubweise (arbeiten, vorwärtskommen). ◆**'fitful,** *adj.* unbeständig; *(of sleep)* unruhig.

fit² [fit]. I. *adv.* 1. (a) *(suitable)* geeignet (**for sth.,** zu etwas *dat*); (b) **f. to eat/drink,**

eßbar/trinkbar. 2. *(healthy)* (gut) in Form, *esp.Sp:* fit; **to keep f.,** sich in Form halten. II. *s.* Sitz *m;* **to be a tight/loose f.,** knapp/lose sitzen; *(of dress)* **to be a good/bad f.,** gut/schlecht sitzen. III. *v.* 1. *v.tr.* (a) *(suit)* (j-m) passen; (b) *(attach)* (etwas) anbringen (**to sth.,** an etwas *acc*); (Reifen usw.) montieren. 2. *v.i.* passen; **your dress fits well,** Ihr Kleid sitzt gut. ◆**'fit 'in,** *v.i.* to fit in (**with** sth.), (zu etwas *dat*) dazupassen; **he doesn't f. in here,** er paßt nicht hierher; **I will have to f. you/it in somehow,** ich werde Sie/es irgendwie einschieben müssen. ◆**'fitness,** *s.* 1. *(of pers.)* Tauglichkeit *f* (**for** sth., zu etwas *dat*). 2. *(physical)* f., Form *f; Sp:* Fitneß *f.* 2. ◆**'fitted,** *adj. Cl:* tailliert; **f. carpet,** Teppichboden *m;* **f. cupboard,** Einbauschrank *m.* ◆**'fitter,** *s.* Installateur *m.* ◆**'fitting.** I. *adj. (suitable)* passend; *(of remark)* treffend. II. s. 1. (a) Anbringung *f; E:* Montage *f;* (b) *Cl:* Anprobe *f.* 2. *esp. pl.* **fittings,** Einrichtungen *fpl.*

five [faiv], *num.adj.* fünf. ◆**'fiver,** *s. Brit:* F: Fünfpfundschein *m; N.Am:* Fünfdollarschein *m.*

fix [fiks]. I. s. 1. F: Klemme *f;* **to be in a f.,** in der Klemme sitzen. 2. *P: (drugs)* **to have a f.,** fixen. II. *v.tr.* (a) (etwas) befestigen (**to sth.,** an etwas *dat*); (b) *(decide)* (einen Termin, einen Preis usw.) festsetzen; **how are you fixed for money?** wie steht es mit den Finanzen? (c) F: *(arrange)* **he'll f. it,** er wird's schon machen; organisieren; (d) *(repair)* **to f. sth.,** etwas herrichten; (e) *N.Am: (prepare)* (eine Mahlzeit) zubereiten. ◆**'fixed,** *adj.* **f. smile,** starres Lächeln. ◆**'fixture,** *s.* 1. eingebautes Möbelstück *n; pl.* **fixtures,** eingebautes Mobilar *n.* 2. *Sp:* Veranstaltung *f.* ◆**'fix 'up,** *v.tr.* F: organisieren; **to f. s.o. up with** sth., etwas für j-n besorgen.

fizz [fiz], *v.i.* sprudeln. ◆**'fizzle 'out,** *v.i.* sich im Sand verlaufen. ◆**'fizzy,** *adj.* sprudelnd.

flabbergast ['flæbəga:st], *v.tr.* erstaunen; **I was flabbergasted,** ich war erstaunt/F: platt.

flabby ['flæbi], *adj.* schlaff.

flag¹ [flæg], *s.* Fahne *f;* esp. *Nau:* Flagge *f.* ◆**'flagship,** *s.* Flaggschiff *n.* ◆**'flag-signal,** *s.* Flaggensignal *n.* ◆**'flagstaff,** *s.* Fahnenstange *f.*

flag², *v.i.* *(of zeal, energy)* nachlassen; *(of conversation)* erlahmen.

flagrant ['fleigrənt], *adj. (of offence)* schamlos; **f. injustice,** schreiende Ungerechtigkeit.

flair [flɛər], *s.* (a) *(gift)* Talent *n;* (b) *(instinct)* Flair *m.*

flake [fleik]. I. s. (a) *(of snow, oatmeal)* Flocke *f;* (b) *(of rust)* Schuppe *f.* II. *v.i. (of paint etc.)* **to f. (away/off),** abblättern. ◆**'flaky,** *adj.* **f. pastry,** Blätterteig *m.*

flamboyant [flæm'bɔiənt], adj. (of pers., style) extravagant; (of clothing) auffallend.

flame [fleim], s. Flamme f; **to burst into/go up in flames**, in Flammen aufgehen. ◆**'flameproof**, adj. flammensicher. ◆**'flamethrower**, s. Flammenwerfer m. ◆**'flaming**, adj. (a) f. row, heftiger Streit; (b) P: verdammt.

flamingo, pl. -o(e)s [flə'miŋgəu, -əuz], s. Flamingo m.

flan [flæn], s. Torte f.

flange [flændʒ], s. (on pipe etc.) Flansch m.

flank [flæŋk]. I. s. Flanke f. II. v.tr. flankieren.

flannel ['flæn(ə)l], s. (a) Flanell m; f. trousers/flannels, Flanellhosen fpl; (b) face f., Waschlappen m.

flap [flæp]. I. s. 1. F: to get in a f., sich aufregen. 2. (of table, envelope etc.) Klappe f. II. v. 1. v.tr. (of bird) to f. its wings, mit den Flügeln schlagen. 2. v.i. (a) (of sail, flag) flattern; (b) F: (of pers.) sich aufregen.

flare ['flɛər].flare I. s. 1. (signal) Leuchtsignal n. 2. pl. flares, ausgestellte Hosen fpl. II. v.i. to f. up, s. (of flame etc.) (auf)lodern; (of pers.) aufbrausen. ◆**'flared**, adj. Cl: ausgestellt. ◆**'flare-up**, s. (of flame etc.) Wutausbruch m.

flash [flæʃ]. I. s. (a) Blitz m; f. bulb, Blitzlicht n; Fig: f. of inspiration, Erleuchtung f; F: Geistesblitz m; in a f., im Nu m; a f. in the pan, ein Strohfeuer; (b) (news) f., Sondermeldung f. II. v. 1. v.i. blitzen. 2. v.tr. to f. (one's lights) at s.o., j-n anblinken. ◆**'flashback**, s. Rückblende f. ◆**'flashing**, adj. (of eyes) funkelnd. ◆**f. light**, Blinklicht n. ◆**'flashy**, adj. auffällig; F: knallig.

flask [flɑːsk], s. Flasche f.

flat [flæt]. I. adj. 1. flach; to have a f. tyre, Reifenpanne f haben. 2. Fig: a f. refusal, eine glatte Absage. 3. (of conversation etc.) langweilig; (of drink) schal; f. battery, leere Batterie. 4. f. rate, Einheitspreis m. 5. Mus: A f., As; B f., B; D f., Des; E f., Es. II. adv. 1. flach. 2. F: to be f. broke, völlig pleite sein. 3. Fig: to fall f., (of performance etc.) danebengehen; (of idea, joke) verpuffen. 4. to sing f., zu tief singen; ♦y, adv. rundweg; he f. refused, er weigerte sich glattweg. III. s. 1. Aut: F: Reifenpanne f. 2. Wohnung f. ◆**'flatlet**, s. Kleinwohnung f. ◆**'flatness**, s. (a) Flachheit f (einer Fläche); (b) Eintönigkeit f (des Lebens usw.). ◆**'flatten**, v.tr. (etwas) flachmachen; (den Boden) einebnen; F: to f. s.o., (j-n) k.o. schlagen.

flatter ['flætər], v.tr. (j-m) schmeicheln. ◆**'flatterer**, s. Schmeichler(in) m(f). ◆**'flattering**, adj. schmeichelhaft. ◆**'flattery**, s. Schmeichelei f.

flaunt [flɔːnt], v.tr. to f. sth., mit etwas dat protzen.

flavour ['fleivər]. I. s. Geschmack m; pl

Geschmacksrichtungen fpl. II. v.tr würzen; **vanilla-flavoured**, mit Vanillegeschmack. ◆**'flavouring**, s. Würzstoff m. ◆**'flavourless**, adj. geschmacklos.

flaw [flɔː], s. Defekt m; (in material, Fig: character) Fehler m; (in argument) Lücke f. ◆**'flawless**, adj. tadellos.

flea [fliː], s. Floh m. ◆**'fleabite**, s. 1. Flohstich m. 2. Fig: Bagatelle f.

fleck [flek], s. (of colour) Tupfen m; (mark) Fleck m; f. of dust, Staubkorn n.

fledg(e)ling ['fledʒliŋ], s. Orn: eben flügge gewordener Vogel m.

flee [fliː], v.tr. & i. irr. to f. (from) s.o., sth., vor j-m, etwas dat fliehen.

fleece [fliːs], s. Schaffell n. ◆**'fleecy**, adj. (of lining etc.) wollig.

fleet [fliːt], s. 1. Flotte f. 2. (firm's) f., (cars) Wagenpark m.

fleeting ['fliːtiŋ], adj. flüchtig.

Flemish ['flemiʃ]. I. adj. (a) (people) flämisch; (b) (land) flandrisch. II. s. Flämisch n.

flesh [fleʃ], s. 1. Fleisch n. 2. in the f., in Person. ◆**'fleshy**, adj. fleischig.

flex [fleks]. I. v.tr. (Muskeln) spielen lassen. II. s. Schnur f. ◆**flexi'bility**, s. Biegsamkeit f; (of pers.) Anpassungsfähigkeit f. ◆**'flexible**, adj. (of material) biegsam; (of adaptable) anpassungsfähig. ◆**'flexitime**, s. Gleitzeit f.

flick [flik], I. s. Schnippen n. II. v.tr. schnippen.

flicker ['flikər], v.i. (a) flackern; El: flimmern; (b) (of eyelid) zucken.

flight [flait], s. 1. (a) (flying) Flug m; an hour's f., eine Flugstunde; f. path, Flugbahn f; f. recorder, Flug(daten)schreiber m; (b) Fig: f. of fancy, Phantasiegebilde n. 2. f. of stairs, Treppenflucht f. 3. (escape) Flucht f.

flimsy ['flimzi], adj. (a) schwach; (of structure) wackelig; (of material, paper) dünn; (of excuse) fadenscheinig.

flinch [flintʃ], v.i. zurückzucken.

fling [fliŋ], v.tr. irr. (a) (etwas) schleudern; (b) to f. oneself, sich stürzen (at s.o., auf j-n).

flint [flint], s. Feuerstein m.

flip [flip], v.tr. to f. sth. into the air, etwas hochschnellen. 2. v.i. to f. through a book, ein Buch schnell durchblättern.

flippant ['flipənt], adj. leichtfertig. ◆**'flippancy**, s. Leichtfertigkeit f.

flirt [fləːt]. I. s. Flirt m. II. v.i. flirten. ◆**flir'tation**, s. Flirt m.

float [fləut]. I. v. 1. v.i. (a) (of thing) schwimmen; (of swimmer, boat) treiben; (b) (in air) schweben. 2. v.tr. (a) (ein Schiff) flottmachen; (b) to f. a company, eine Gesellschaft gründen. II. s. 1. Schwimmer m. 2. (in procession) Wagen m. ◆**'floating**, adj. treibend; schwimmend; (in air) schwebend; f. voter, Wechselwähler m.

flock [flɔk]. I. s. (of animals) Herde f; (of

birds) Schwarm m; (of people, geese etc.) Schar f. II. v.i. **everyone is flocking to see the exhibition**, alle strömen in die Ausstellung.

flog [flɔg], v.tr. (a) auspeitschen; Fig: **to f. a subject to death**, ein Thema zu Tode reiten; (b) F: (sell) verschachern.

flood [flʌd]. I. s. (a) (disaster) Überschwemmung f; (b) f. of tears, Tränenstrom m. II. v. 1. v.tr. (ein Gebiet, Com: den Markt) überschwemmen. 2. v.i. (of river) über die Ufer treten. ◆'**flooding**, s. Überschwemmung f. ◆'**floodlight**, s. Flutlicht n.

floor [flɔːr], s. 1. Fußboden m. 2. (storey) Stock m; ground f., Erdgeschoß n; first f., (i) erster Stock m; (ii) N.Am: Erdgeschoß n. ◆'**floorboard**, s. Dielenbrett n. ◆'**floorcloth**, s. Scheuertuch n. ◆'**floorshow**, s. Kabarettvorstellung f.

flop [flɔp]. I. s. Th: Durchfall m. II. v.i. (a) (of pers.) **to f. (down)**, (hin)plumpsen; (b) F: (fail) durchfallen. ◆'**floppy 'disk**, s. Diskette f.

florid ['flɔrid], adj. überladen.

florist ['flɔrist], s. Blumenhändler m; **florist's (shop)**, Blumengeschäft n.

flotilla [flə'tilə], s. Flottille f.

flounce [flauns]. I. s. Cl: Volant m. II. v.i. **to f. out of a room**, (gereizt) aus einem Zimmer rauschen.

flounder ['flaundər], s. I. Flunder f. II. Fig: F: schwimmen.

flour ['flauər], s. Mehl n.

flourish ['flʌriʃ], v.i. (of plant, pers. etc.) gedeihen; (of trade, arts etc.) blühen.

flout [flaut], v.tr. mißachten.

flow [fləu]. I. s. Fluß m. II. v.i. fließen.

flower ['flauər]. I. s. Blume f; f. bed, Blumenbeet n; f. pot, Blumentopf m. II. v.i. blühen. ◆'**flowering**, s. Blüte f.

flu [fluː], s. F: Grippe f.

fluctuate ['flʌktjueit], v.i. schwanken. ◆'**fluctuating**, adj. schwankend. ◆**fluctu'ation**, s. Schwankung f.

fluency ['fluːənsi], s. Geläufigkeit f. ◆'**fluent**, adj. fließend.

fluff [flʌf], s. (a) (on clothes etc.) Fussel f; (b) (down, soft fur) Flaum m. ◆'**fluffy**, adj. flaumig; f. toy, Plüschtier n.

fluid ['fluːid]. I. s. Flüssigkeit f. II. adj. flüssig; a f. situation, eine veränderliche Lage.

fluke [fluːk], s. F: Zufall m.

fluoride ['fluːəraid], s. Fluor n.

flurry ['flʌri], s. 1. (of wind) Windstoß m; snow f., Schneegestöber n. 2. (agitation) Aufregung f.

flush¹ [flʌʃ]. I. s. (in face) Erröten n; hot flushes, Wallungen fpl. II. v.i. (a) (of face) erröten; (b) (in WC) spülen. ◆'**flushed**, adj. errötet.

flush², adj. 1. F: **to be f.** (with money), gut bei Kasse sein. 2. **f. with the floor**, in gleicher Ebene mit dem Fußboden.

fluster ['flʌstər]. I. s. Verwirrung f. II. v.tr. (j-n) aus der Fassung bringen.

◆'**flustered**, adj. verwirrt.

flute [fluːt], s. Flöte f.

flutter ['flʌtər], v.i. flattern.

fly¹ [flai], s. Fliege f.

fly², s. (also flies) Hosenschlitz m.

fly³, v. irr. 1. v.i. fliegen. **time flies**, die Zeit verfliegt; **the door flew open**, die Tür flog auf; **to f. into a rage**, in Wut geraten. 2. v.tr. (a) (eine Fahne) hissen; (einen Drachen) steigen lassen; (b) (ein Flugzeug) fliegen. ◆'**flying**, adj. (a) f. boat, Flugboot n; f. saucer, fliegende Untertasse f; f. fish, fliegender Fisch m; (b) (police) f. squad, Überfallkommando n; (c) f. jump, Sprung m (mit Anlauf); Sp: f. start, fliegender Start m; F: f. visit, Stippvisite f. ◆'**flyover**, s. Überführung f. ◆'**flypast**, s. Flugparade f.

foal [fəul], s. Fohlen n.

foam [fəum]. I. s. Schaum m; f. rubber, Schaumgummi m. II. v.i. schäumen.

focal ['fəukəl], adj. f. point, Brennpunkt m. ◆'**focus** ['fəukəs]. I. s. Brennpunkt m; in f., scharf eingestellt; out of f., unscharf. II. v. 1. v.tr. (a) (ein Fernrohr, einen Fotoapparat) scharf einstellen; (b) to f. attention on sth., die Aufmerksamkeit auf etwas acc konzentrieren. 2. v.i. to f. on an object, einen Gegenstand fixieren. ◆'**focusing**, s. Scharfeinstellung f.

fodder ['fɔdər], s. Futter n.

foetus ['fiːtəs], s. Fötus m.

fog [fɔg], s. (dichter) Nebel m. ◆'**foggy**, adj. nebelig. ◆'**foghorn**, s. Nebelhorn n. ◆'**foglamp**, s. Nebelscheinwerfer m.

foil¹ [fɔil], s. Folie f; Cu: baking f., Alufolie f.

foil², s. Sp: Florett n.

foil³, v.tr. vereiteln.

foist [fɔist], v.tr. F: **to f. sth. on s.o.**, j-m etwas andrehen.

fold [fəuld]. I. s. Falte f. II. v.tr. (a) falten; (b) to f. sth. in sth., etwas in etwas dat einwickeln; (c) to f. one's arms, die Arme verschränken. ◆'**folder**, s. Mappe f. ◆'**folding**, adj. Klapp-; f. chair, Klappstuhl m. ◆'**fold 'up**, v. 1. v.tr. (a) (etwas) zusammenklappen; (Papier usw.) zusammenfalten. 2. v.i. F: (of firm) pleite gehen.

foliage ['fəuliidʒ], s. (of trees) Laub n; (of plants) Blätter npl.

folk [fəuk], s. (a) Leute pl; (b) Mus: f. dance, Volkstanz m; f. (music), Volksmusik f. ◆'**folklore**, s. Folklore f. ◆'**folksong**, s. Volkslied n.

follow ['fɔləu], v. 1. v.tr. (a) (j-m, etwas dat) folgen; (b) (of period etc.) auf (etwas acc) folgen; (c) to f. s.o.'s advice, j-s Rat befolgen; to f. instructions, Anweisungen dat Folge leisten; (d) F: I don't quite f. you, da komme ich nicht ganz mit. 2. v.i. (nach)folgen; as follows, wie folgt. ◆'**follower**, s. Anhänger m. ◆'**following**. I. adj. folgend; the f. day, am nächsten Tag. II. s. Anhängerschaft f. ◆**follow 'up. I.** v.tr. to f. up a matter, eine Sache weiterverfolgen. **II. 'f.-up,** s. Nachfassen n.

folly ['fɔli], s. Torheit f.

fond [fɔnd], adj. **1.** (a) (loving) liebevoll; (b) to be f. of s.o., sth., j-n, etwas gern haben. **2.** (of hope, belief etc.) töricht. ◆**'fondness,** s. (a) Liebe f (for s.o., zu j-m); (b) Schwäche f (for sth., für etwas acc.)

fondle ['fɔndl], v.tr. liebkosen.

food [fu:d], s. (a) Nahrung f; (at meal) Essen n; (for animals) Futter n; f. poisoning, Lebensmittelvergiftung f; f. for thought, Grund m zum Nachdenken; (b) (fare, diet) Kost f; (c) (groceries) Lebensmittel pl; f. shop, Lebensmittelgeschäft n. ◆**'foodstuff,** s. Nahrungsmittel n.

fool [fu:l]. **I.** s. Narr m, Dummkopf m; to make a f. of s.o./oneself, j-n/sich lächerlich machen. **II. 1.** v.i. **I was only fooling,** ich habe nicht ernst gemeint. **2.** v.tr. (j-n) betrügen; you could have fooled me, was du nicht sagst! ◆**'foolery,** s. Dummheiten fpl. ◆**'foolhardy,** adj. tollkühn. ◆**'foolish,** adj. dumm. ◆**'foolishness,** s. Dummheit f. ◆**'foolproof,** adj. narrensicher.

foot [fut]. **I.** s. (pl feet [fi:t]). **1.** Fuß m; on f., zu Fuß; to put one's f. down, (i) ein Machtwort sprechen; (ii) Aut: F: aufs Gas treten; F: to put one's f. in it, ins Fettnäpfchen treten. **2.** Fußende n (des Bettes); Fuß m (eines Strumpfes, eines Berges usw.). **II.** v.tr. to f. the bill, für die Rechnung aufkommen. ◆**'football,** s. Fußball m; f. pitch, Fußballfeld n. ◆**'footballer,** s. Fußballspieler m. ◆**'footbridge,** s. Fußgängerbrücke f. ◆**'footing,** s. to be on a good f. with s.o., sich mit j-m gut stehen. ◆**'footlights,** s.pl. Rampenlicht n. ◆**'footmark,** s. Fußabdruck m. ◆**'footnote,** s. Fußnote f. ◆**'footpath,** s. Pfad m. ◆**'footprint,** s. Fußabdruck m. ◆**'footstep,** s. Schritt m; F: to follow in s.o.'s footsteps, in j-s Fußstapfen treten. ◆**'footwear,** s. Schuhwerk n.

for [fɔːr]. **I.** prep. **1.** für + acc. to eat sth. f. supper, etwas zum Abendbrot essen; **2.** (purpose) what f.? wozu? to jump f. joy, vor Freude hüpfen. **3.** (time) I'm going away f. a fortnight, ich verreise für vierzehn Tage; he was missing f. a fortnight, er war vierzehn Tage (lang) verschwunden; I've been here f. three days, ich bin seit drei Tagen hier. **II.** conj. denn.

forage ['fɔridʒ], v.i. to f. for sth., nach etwas dat suchen.

forbearance [fɔː'bɛərəns], s. Nachsicht f. ◆**for'bearing,** adj. nachsichtig.

forbid [fə'bid], v.tr. verbieten; to f. s.o. to do sth., j-m verbieten, etwas zu tun. ◆**for'bidden,** adj. verboten.

◆**for'bidding,** adj. abschreckend.

force [fɔːs]. **I.** s. **1.** by f. of habit, aus alter Gewohnheit. **2.** (a) (of pers.) Kraft f; Wucht f (eines Schlages, Sturms usw.); to use f., Gewalt anwenden; (b) f. of gravity, Schwerkraft f. **3.** Mil: etc: Verband m (von Truppen); to join the Forces, zum Militär gehen; to join forces with s.o., sich mit j-m zusammentun. (of law) to come into f., in Kraft treten. **II.** v.tr. (a) (j-n) zwingen; (b) (eine Tür) aufbrechen; (c) to f. sth. on s.o., j-m etwas aufdrängen. ◆**force 'back,** v.tr. zurückdrängen. ◆**'forced,** adj. (a) erzwungen; f. labour, Zwangsarbeit f; f. landing, Notlandung f; (b) (of laugh, smile) gezwungen. ◆**'forceful,** adj. (of pers.) energisch. **2.** (of language) eindringlich. **3.** (of argument) überzeugend. ◆**'forcible,** adj. gewaltsam.

ford [fɔːd], s. Furt f.

fore [fɔːr]. **I.** s. to come to the f., in den Vordergrund treten. ◆**'forearm,** s. Unterarm m. ◆**fore'boding,** s. (böse) Vorahnung f. ◆**'forecast. I.** s. Voraussage f; weather f., Wetterbericht m. **II.** v.tr. (etwas) voraussagen. ◆**'forecourt,** s. (of building) Vorhof m; (of garage) Vorplatz m. ◆**'forefather,** s. Vorfahr m. ◆**'forefinger,** s. Zeigefinger m. ◆**'forefront,** s. in the f., in der vordersten Reihe; Fig: (most) obig; the f., das Vorangehende. ◆**'foregone,** adj. it was a f. conclusion (that…), es war von vornherein klar (, daß…). ◆**'foreground,** s. Vordergrund m. ◆**'forehand,** s. Vorhand f. ◆**'forehead** ['fɔrid,'fɔːhed], s. Stirn f. ◆**'foreleg,** s. Vorderbein n. ◆**'foreman,** s. Vorarbeiter m. ◆**'foremost. I.** adj. (of place) vorderste(r,s); the f. authority, der führende Experte (on sth., für etwas acc). **II.** adv. first and f., zuallererst. ◆**'forename,** s. esp. N.Am: Vorname m. ◆**'forerunner,** s. Vorläufer m. ◆**fore'see,** v.tr. voraussehen. ◆**fore'shadow,** v.tr. (ein Ereignis) vorausahnen lassen. ◆**'foresight,** s. Voraussicht f. ◆**fore'stall,** v.tr. (j-m, j-s Plänen) zuvorkommen. ◆**'foretaste,** s. Vorgeschmack m. ◆**fore'tell,** v.tr.irr. (etwas) voraussagen. ◆**'foreword,** s. Vorwort n.

foreign ['fɔrin], adj. **1.** (abroad) ausländisch; f. language, Fremdsprache f; f. currency, Devisen fpl; f. trade, Außenhandel m; f. affairs, auswärtige Angelegenheiten; the F. Office, das (britische) Außenministerium. **2.** (strange) fremd; f. body, Fremdkörper m. ◆**'foreigner,** s. Ausländer(in) m(f).

forensic [fə'rensik], adj. gerichtlich; f. medicine, Gerichtsmedizin f.

forest ['fɔrist], s. Wald m; f. fire, Waldbrand m; esp. N.Am: f. ranger, Förster m. ◆**'forestry,** s. Forstwirtschaft f.

forfeit ['fɔːfit]. **I.** s. Pfand n. **II.** v.tr. verwirken.

forge¹ [fɔːdʒ]. **I.** s. Schmiede f. **II.** v.tr. (a) schmieden; (b) (eine Unterschrift, Banknoten usw.) fälschen. ◆**forger,** s. Fälscher m. ◆**forgery,** s. Fälschung f.

forge², v.i. to f. ahead, große Fortschritte machen.

forget [fəˈget], v.tr. irr. vergessen. ◆**forˈgetful,** adj. vergeßlich. ◆**forˈgetfulness,** s. Vergeßlichkeit f. ◆**forˈget-me-not,** s. Vergißmeinnicht n.

forgive [fəˈgiv], v.tr. irr. to f. s.o. for sth., j-m etwas verzeihen/vergeben. ◆**forˈgivable,** adj. verzeihlich. ◆**forˈgiveness,** s. Verzeihung f. ◆**forˈgiving,** adj. versöhnlich.

forgo [fɔːˈgəu], v.tr. irr. to f. sth., auf etwas acc verzichten.

fork [fɔːk]. **I.** s. 1. Gabel f. 2. Gabelung f (einer Straße). **II.** v. 1. v.i. (of road) sich gabeln. 2. v.tr. P: to f. out/N.Am: to f. over/up money, blechen. ◆**ˈfork-ˈlift ˈtruck,** s. Gabelstapler m.

forlorn [fəˈlɔːn], adj. verlassen.

form [fɔːm]. **I.** s. 1. Form f; F: you know the f., du weißt schon, wie das geht; to be in (good) f./off f., in Form/nicht in Form sein. 2. (printed) Formular n. **II.** v. 1. v.tr. (a) (mould) formen (into sth., zu etwas dat); (b) (create) (einen Kreis, Wörter, Sätze, eine Regierung usw.) bilden; (c) (eine Firma) gründen; (d) (einen Plan usw.) ausarbeiten. 2. v.i. (a) (take on a particular shape) sich formen; (of idea, plans) Gestalt annehmen; (b) (come into being) sich bilden. ◆**forˈmation,** s. Formung f; Bildung f; Gründung f; Av: Formation f. ◆**ˈformative,** adj. f. years, Entwicklungsjahre npl.

formal [ˈfɔːm(ə)l], adj. (following conventions, impersonal) formell; (of occasion, dress) feierlich; (of design) symmetrisch. ◆**forˈmality,** s. 1. (social convention) Förmlichkeit f. 2. Adm: etc: Formalität f.

former [ˈfɔːmər], adj. 1. ehemalig; in f. times, in früheren Zeiten. 2. the f., der, die, das erstere; -ly, adv. früher.

formidable [ˈfɔːmidəbl], adj. (of pers., character) ehrfurchtgebietend; (of opponent, task etc.) gewaltig.

formula [ˈfɔːmjulə], s. Formel f. ◆**ˈformulate,** v.tr. formulieren.

forsake [fəˈseik], v.tr. irr. (a) (j-n, etwas) verlassen; (b) (give up) (etwas) aufgeben.

fort [fɔːt], s. Fort n.

forth [fɔːθ], adv. back and f., hin und her; and so f., und so weiter. ◆**ˈforthcoming,** adj. 1. bevorstehend; (of book) in Kürze erscheinend. 2. (of pers.) mitteilsam.

fortify [ˈfɔːtifai], v.tr. (a) (eine Stadt) befestigen; (b) (j-n) stärken. ◆**ˈfortiˈcation,** s. Festungswerk n.

fortitude [ˈfɔːtitjuːd], s. Standhaftigkeit f.

fortnight [ˈfɔːtnait], s. vierzehn Tage mpl. ◆**ˈfortnightly. I.** adj. vierzehntägig. **II.**

adv. alle vierzehn Tage.

fortress [ˈfɔːtrəs], s. Festung f.

fortuitous [fɔːˈtjuːitəs], adj. zufällig.

fortune [ˈfɔːtʃən,-tjuːn], s. 1. (a) (luck) Glück n; by good f., durch glücklichen Zufall; (b) (fate) Schicksal n; to tell fortunes, wahrsagen; f. teller, Wahrsager(in) m(f). 2. (wealth) Vermögen n. ◆**ˈfortunate,** adj. glücklich; to be f., Glück haben. -ly, adv. glücklicherweise.

forty [ˈfɔːti], num.adj. vierzig.

forward [ˈfɔːwəd]. **I.** adj. 1. f. movement, Vorwärtsbewegung f. 2. (of pers.) keck. **II.** adv. (also forwards) 1. vorwärts. 2. (of pers.) to come f., sich melden. **III.** s. Fb: Stürmer m. **IV.** v.tr. (einen Brief) nachschicken.

fossil [ˈfɔs(ə)l], s. Fossil n.

foster [ˈfɔstər], v.tr. (a) (ein Kind) in Pflege nehmen; (b) (einen Wunsch) hegen. ◆**ˈfosterchild,** s. Pflegekind n. ◆**ˈfoster-mother,** s. Pflegemutter f.

foul [faul]. **I.** adj. 1. (a) (putrid) (of smell, taste) faulig; (b) (nasty) (of taste, pers. etc.) widerlich; (of language) unflätig. 2. adv. to fall f. of s.o., es sich dat mit j-m verderben. **II.** s. Sp: Foul n. **III.** v.tr. (a) (die Luft usw.) verschmutzen; (b) Sp: (j-n) foulen; (c) (of dog etc.) (den Gehsteig) beschmutzen.

found [faund], v.tr. (eine Firma, Schule, Gesellschaft usw.) gründen. ◆**founˈdation,** s. 1. Gründung f (einer Stadt usw.). 2. Grundmauer f (eines Gebäudes). 3. Fig: Grundlage f; (of rumour) without f., unbegründet. ◆**founderˈ**, s. Gründer m.

founder² [ˈfaundər], v.i. (of ship) sinken.

foundry [ˈfaundri], Gießerei f.

fountain [ˈfauntin], s. (a) (artificial) Springbrunnen m; (natural) Quelle f; (drinking) f., Trinkbrunnen m; (b) f. pen, Füllfederhalter m.

four [fɔːr], num.adj. vier. to go on all fours, auf allen Vieren gehen. ◆**ˈfourfold,** adj. & adv. vierfach. ◆**ˈfour-footed,** adj. Hum: f.-f. friend, Vierbeiner m. ◆**ˈfour-seater,** s. Aut: Viersitzer m. ◆**ˈfourteen,** num.adj. vierzehn. ◆**ˈfourteenth,** num.adj. vierzehnte(r, s). ◆**ˈfourth. I.** num.adj. vierte(r, s). **II.** s. Viertel n.

fowl [faul], s. coll. Geflügel n.

fox [fɔks]. **I.** s. Fuchs m. **II.** v.tr. (j-n) verblüffen, (deceive) täuschen. ◆**ˈfoxglove,** s. Fingerhut m. ◆**ˈfoxhound,** s. Meutehund m. ◆**ˈfoxhund(ing),** s. Fuchsjagd f. ◆**ˈfox-ˈterrier,** s. Fox(terrier) m. ◆**ˈfoxtrot,** s. Foxtrott m.

foyer [ˈfɔiei], s. Foyer n.

fraction [ˈfrækʃ(ə)n], s. Bruchteil m.

fracture [ˈfræktʃər]. **I.** s. Bruch m; (point of) f., Bruchstelle f. **II.** v.tr. brechen.

fragile [ˈfrædʒail], adj. zerbrechlich.

fragment ['frægmənt], s. Fragment n.

fragrance ['freigrəns], s. Duft m. ◆**'fragrant**, adj. duftend.

frail [freil], adj. gebrechlich.

frame [freim]. I. s. 1. (a) Rahmen m; (b) Fassung f (einer Brille). 2. (a) (of pers.) Körperbau m; (b) f. of mind, Gemütsverfassung f. II. v.tr. (a) (ein Bild) einrahmen; (b) P: to f. s.o., j-m ein Verbrechen anhängen. ◆**'frame-up**, s. P: abgekartetes Spiel n. ◆**'framework**, s. 1. (of building) Gerippe n. 2. Fig: Gefüge n (der Regierung usw.); (structure) Aufbau m; within the f. of the United Nations, im Rahmen der Vereinten Nationen.

France [frɑːns]. Pr.n. Frankreich n.

franchise ['fræn(t)faiz], s. 1. Pol: Wahlrecht n; Com: Lizenz f.

frank¹ [fræŋk], adj. offen; to be f./-ly, adv. offen gestanden. ◆**'frankness**, s. Offenheit f.

frank², v.tr. (einen Brief) frankieren.

frankfurter ['fræŋkfəːtər], s. Frankfurter Würstchen n.

frantic ['fræntik], adj. (a) to be f., außer sich dat sein (with joy/fear etc., vor Freude/Angst usw.); (b) f. efforts, verzweifelte Bemühungen fpl.

fraternal [frə'təːnl], adj. brüderlich. ◆**fraternize** ['frætənaiz], v.i. fraternisieren.

fraud [frɔːd], s. Schwindel m; esp. Jur: Betrug m. ◆**'fraudulent**, adj. betrügerisch.

fraught [frɔːt], adj. f. with danger, gefahrvoll.

fray¹ [frei], s. Schlägerei f.

fray², v.tr. & i. ausfransen. ◆**frayed**, adj. (a) Cl: ausgefranst; (b) f. tempers, erhitzte Gemüter npl.

freak [friːk], s. (a) einmaliges Phänomen n; (b) (pers.) Mißgeburt f. ◆**f. storm**, ungeheurer Sturm.

freckle ['frekl], s. Sommersprosse f.

free [friː]. I. adj. 1. frei; to set s.o. f., (i) (of government) j-n freilassen; (ii) (of rescuer etc.) j-n befreien; he is not f. to do it, es steht ihm nicht frei, das zu tun; f. from pain, ohne Schmerzen; f. from worry, sorgenfrei; duty f., zollfrei; f. enterprise, Privatwirtschaft f. 2. (no cost) kostenlos, f. gift/sample, Gratisprobe f.; -ly, adv. (a) frei; to move f., sich frei bewegen; to speak f., offen reden; (b) (voluntarily) freiwillig. II. v.tr. (a) (j-n, ein Volk usw.) befreien; to f. a prisoner, (of government) einen Gefangenen freilassen; (by force etc.) einen Gefangenen befreien; (b) (etwas Verklemmtes) freibekommen. ◆**'freedom**, s. Freiheit f; f. of speech, Redefreiheit f. ◆**'freehand**, adj. f. drawing, Freihandzeichnen n. ◆**'freehold**, s. freier Grundbesitz. ◆**'freelance**, adj. freiberuflich. ◆**'freemason**, s. Freimaurer m. ◆**'freemasonry**, s. Freimaurerei f. ◆**'freestyle**, s. Freistilschwimmen n.

◆**'freeway**, s. N.Am: Schnellstraße f.

freeze [friːz]. I. v.irr. 1. v.i. (a) (of liquid etc.) frieren; (b) (of pers.) to f. to death, erfrieren. 2. v.tr. (Obst usw.) tiefkühlen; (b) to f. wages, Löhne stoppen. II. s. wage f., Lohnstopp m. ◆**'freezer**, s. (upright) Tiefkühlschrank m; (chest) f., Tiefkühltruhe f. ◆**'freezing**. I. adj. f. temperatures, Temperaturen fpl unter dem Nullpunkt; f. fog, Eisnebel m; F: it's f., es ist eiskalt. II. s. above/below f., über/unter Null; f. point, Gefrierpunkt m.

freight [freit], s. Fracht f; esp. N.Am: f. train, Güterzug m; air f., Luftfracht f.

French [fren(t)f]. I. adj. französisch; F. bread, Stangenbrot n; F. dressing, Salatsoße f nach französischer Art; F. fries, Pommes frites fpl; F. window, Glastür f (zum Garten); F. horn, Horn n. II. s. 1. Französisch n. 2. pl. the F., die Franzosen. ◆**'Frenchman**, s. Franzose m. ◆**'Frenchwoman**, s. Französin f.

frequency ['friːkwənsi], s. 1. Häufigkeit f. 2. Ph: Frequenz f. ◆**frequent**. I. adj. ['friːkwənt], 1. häufig; -ly, adv. oft. II. v.tr. [fri'kwent] (eine Kneipe usw.) (regelmäßig) aufsuchen.

fresh [fref]. I. adj. 1. frisch. 2. (cheeky) F: frech. ◆**'freshen**, v. 1. v.i. (of wind) frischer werden. 2. v.tr. (das Gedächtnis) auffrischen. ◆**'freshman**, F: fresher, s. Sch: Student m im ersten Jahr. ◆**'freshness**, s. Frische f. ◆**'freshwater**, adj. Süßwasser-, f. fish, Süßwasserfisch m.

fret [fret], v.i. sich sorgen. ◆**'fretful**, adj. weinerlich.

friar ['fraiər], s. Mönch m.

friction ['frik∫(ə)n], s. 1. Reibung f. 2. Fig: Reiberei f.

Friday ['fraidi], s. Freitag m; Good F., Karfreitag m.

fridge [fridʒ], s. F: Kühlschrank m.

friend [frend], s. 1. Freund(in) m(f); (acquaintance) Bekannte(r) f(m); to make friends (with s.o.), sich (mit j-m) anfreunden. ◆**'friendless**, adj. ohne Freund. ◆**'friendliness**, s. Freundlichkeit f. ◆**'friendly**, adj. freundlich; to be f. with s.o., mit j-m befreundet sein; Sp: f. match, Freundschaftsspiel n. ◆**'friendship**, s. Freundschaft f.

frieze ['friːz], s. Arch: Fries m; (on wallpaper) Zierstreifen m.

frigate ['frigət], s. Fregatte f.

fright [frait], s. Schreck(en) m; to give s.o. a f., j-n erschrecken. ◆**'frighten**, v.tr. (j-m) Angst machen, (startle) (j-n) erschrecken. ◆**'frightening**, adj. erschreckend. ◆**'frightful**, adj. F: schrecklich; -ly, adv. F: f. nice, furchtbar nett.

frigid ['fridʒid], adj. frigide.

frill [fril], s. 1. Cl: Rüsche f. 2. F: frills, Verzierungen fpl; a meal without frills, ein einfaches Essen.

fringe [frɪndʒ], *s.* 1. Franse *f.* 2. *(edge)* Rand *m;* f. **benefits,** zusätzliche Sozialaufwendungen *fpl.*

frisk [frɪsk], *v.tr.* (j-n) durchsuchen, *F:* filzen. ◆**frisky,** *adj.* lebhaft.

fritter¹ [ˈfrɪtər], *s.* Fettgebäck *n;* **apple** f., Apfelkrapfen *m.*

fritter², *v.tr.* to f. **(away),** (Zeit, Geld usw.) verplempern.

frivolous [ˈfrɪvələs], *adj.* leichtfertig; frivol. ◆**frivolity** [-ˈvɔlɪti], *s.* Leichtfertigkeit *f;* Frivolität *f.*

frizz(l)y [ˈfrɪz(l)i], *adj.* kraus.

frock [frɔk], *s.* Kleid *n.*

frog [frɔg], *s.* Frosch *m;* **f.'s legs,** Froschschenkel *mpl.* ◆**frogman,** *s.* Froschmann *m.*

frolic [ˈfrɔlik], *v.i.* herumtollen.

from [frɔm, frəm], *prep.* 1. von + *dat;* f. **now on,** von nun an. 2. (a) *(out of, with place)* aus + *dat;* to **take a glass f. the cupboard,** ein Glas aus dem Schrank nehmen; **he comes f. London,** er stammt aus London; **made f. wood,** aus Holz (gemacht). 3. f. **what I hear,** nach dem, was ich höre.

front [frʌnt]. I. *s.* 1. Vorderseite *f;* at **the f. of the train,** vorn im Zug; in f. of, vor + *dat;* *(opposite)* gegenüber + *dat;* in f./at the f., vorne. 2. *Mil: Meteor:* Front *f.* 3. *(seafront)* Strandpromenade *f.* 4. *Com: etc: (cover-up)* Tarnorganisation *f.* II. *adj.* vorder, Vorder-; f. **door,** Haustür *f;* f. **page,** Titelseite; f. **seat,** Vordersitz *m;* f. **line,** Front(linie) *f.* ◆**frontage,** *s.* Front *f.*

frontier [ˈfrʌntiər], *s.* Grenze *f.*

frost [frɔst], *s.* Frost *m.* ◆**frostbite,** *s.* Erfrierung *f.* ◆**frostbitten,** *adj.* erfrorenen. ◆**frosted,** *adj.* (a) f. **over,** vereist; (b) f. **glass,** Milchglas *n.*

froth [frɔθ]. I. *s.* Schaum *m.* II. *v.i.* schäumen. ◆**frothy,** *adj.* schaumig.

frown [fraun]. I. *s.* finsterer Blick *m.* II. *v.i.* die Stirn runzeln; to f. at s.o., j-n finster anblicken.

frozen [ˈfrəuzən], *adj.* (a) gefroren; (b) f. to **death,** völlig erfroren; **I'm f.,** mir ist eiskalt; (b) *(of food)* tiefgekühlt; f. **food,** Tiefkühlkost *f.*

frugal [ˈfruːg(ə)l], *adj. (of pers.)* sparsam; *(of meal etc.)* kärglich.

fruit [fruːt], *s. coll.* Obst *n.* f. **juice,** Obstsaft *m;* f. **salad,** Obstsalat *m.* 2. *Bot: & Fig:* Frucht *f.* ◆**fruiterer,** *s.* Obsthändler *m.* ◆**fruitful,** *adj. (also Fig:)* fruchtbar. ◆**fru'ition,** *s.* to **come to f.,** in Erfüllung gehen. ◆**fruitless,** *adj.* fruchtlos; f. **efforts,** vergebliche Mühe/Bemühungen. ◆**fruit-machine,** *s.* Spielautomat *m.*

frumpish [ˈfrʌmpɪʃ], *adj.* unmodisch (gekleidet).

frustrate [frʌsˈtreɪt], *v.tr.* (j-n) frustrieren. ◆**frustrating,** *adj.* frustrierend. ◆**frus'tration,** *s.* Frustration *f.*

fry [fraɪ], *v.* 1. *v.tr.* (in der Pfanne) bra-

ten; **fried egg,** Spiegelei *n.* 2. *v.i.* braten. **frying pan,** Bratpfanne *f.*

fuddled [ˈfʌdld], *adj.* (a) *(tipsy)* beschwipst; (b) *(confused)* konfus.

fuel [ˈfjuəl], *s.* 1. *(for fire)* Brennstoff *m.* 2. *(for engine)* Kraftstoff *m;* *Aut:* f. **gauge,** Benzinuhr *f.*

fug [fʌg], *s. F:* Mief *m.*

fugitive [ˈfjuːdʒɪtɪv], *s.* Flüchtling *m.*

fulfil [fulˈfil], *v.tr.* (a) (etwas) erfüllen; *(of wish)* to **be fulfilled,** in Erfüllung gehen; (b) *(ein Versprechen)* einlösen. ◆**ful'filment,** *s.* Erfüllung *f.*

full [ful]. I. *adj.* voll; (a) f. up, voller + *gen,* voll mit + *dat;* (b) f. **(up),** *(of bus)* voll besetzt; *(of pers.)* satt; *(of report)* ausführlich; *(d) (complete)* ganz; f. **moon,** Vollmond *m;* f. **stop,** Punkt *m.* II. *s.* (a) in f., vollständig; (b) to **enjoy sth. to the f.,** etwas in vollen Zügen genießen. ◆**full'back,** *s.* Verteidiger *m.* ◆**full-blown,** *adj.* vollwertig. ◆**full-length.** I. *adj. (of skirt)* lang; f.-l. **portrait,** ganzes Porträt; f.-l. **film,** abendfüllender Film. II. *adv.* to **lie f.-l. on the floor,** voll ausgestreckt auf dem Fußboden liegen. ◆**fullness,** *s.* 1. Fülle *f;* in **the f. of time,** zur gegebenen Zeit. 2. Weite *f* (eines Rocks). 3. Ausführlichkeit *f* (eines Berichts usw.). ◆**full-scale,** *adj. (of rescue etc.)* großangelegt; *(thorough)* gründlich; f.-s. **attack,** Großangriff *m.* ◆**full-time.** I. *adj.* f.-t. **work,** ganztägige Arbeit *f:* **it's a f.t. job,** es ist keine Zeit übrig. II. *adv.* ganztags. ◆**fully,** *adv.* völlig.

fumble [ˈfʌmbl], *v.i.* (mit den Fingern) fummeln; to f. **with sth.,** an etwas herumfummeln.

fume [fjuːm]. I. *s. usu.pl.* **fumes,** Dämpfe *mpl; Aut:* **exhaust fumes,** Abgase *npl.* II. *v.i. F: (of pers.)* vor Wut kochen. ◆**fuming,** *adj.* wütend.

fun [fʌn], *s.* Spaß *m;* to **make f. of s.o.,** j-n zum besten halten; **for/in f.,** zum Spaß; **it's good/great f.,** es macht viel Spaß; to **have f. doing sth.,** sich bei etwas *dat* gut unterhalten. ◆**funfair,** *s.* Jahrmarkt *m.*

function [ˈfʌŋkʃ(ə)n]. I. *s.* 1. Funktion *f.* 2. *(party etc.)* (a) *(private)* Feier *f;* (b) *(public)* (öffentliche) Veranstaltung *f;* *(reception)* Empfang *m.* II. *v.i.* funktionieren. ◆**functional,** *adj.* zweckmäßig.

fund [fʌnd]. I. *s.* 1. (a) Fonds *m;* **pension f.,** Pensionskasse *f;* (b) *pl* **funds,** Geldmittel *npl;* to **be in funds,** gut bei Kasse sein. 2. *Fig: (store)* Vorrat *m.* II. *v.tr.* (etwas) finanzieren; (für ein Projekt) aufkommen.

fundamental [fʌndəˈmentl]. I. *adj.* grundlegend; *(essential)* wesentlich (to, für + *acc.*). II. *s.* Grundsatz *m;* **-ly,** *adv.* grundsätzlich.

funeral [ˈfjuːn(ə)rəl], *s.* Begräbnis *n;* f. **service,** Trauergottesdienst *m;* f. **procession,** Leichenzug *m.*

fungus, *pl* **fungi** ['fʌŋgəs, -gaɪ]. *s.* Pilz *m.*

funicular [fju'nikjulər], *adj. & s.* **f.** (**railway**), Seilbahn *f.*

funk [fʌŋk], *s. P:* Schiß *m;* **to be in a blue f.**, einen Mordsschiß haben.

funnel ['fʌnl], *s.* **1.** (*for pouring*) Trichter *m.* **2.** (*of ship etc.*) Schornstein *m.*

funny ['fʌni], *adj.* komisch; **-ily**, *adv.* **f. enough**, komischerweise.

fur [fəːr], *s.* (*a*) (*on animal*) Fell *n;* (*b*) *Cl:* Pelz *m;* **f. coat**, Pelzmantel *m.*

furious ['fjuəriəs], *adj.* (*a*) (*angry*) wütend (**with s.o.**, auf j-n); (*b*) (*violent*) heftig; **at a f. pace**, mit rasender Geschwindigkeit.

furnace ['fəːnis], *s.* (*a*) Brennofen *m;* **blast f.**, Hochofen *m;* (*b*) *Fig:* Backofen *m.*

furnish ['fəːniʃ], *v.tr.* (*a*) (eine Wohnung usw.) einrichten; **furnished room**, möbliertes Zimmer; (*b*) **to f. evidence/an example**, Beweise/ein Beispiel liefern. ◆**'furnishings**, *spl* Einrichtungsgegenstände *mpl.* ◆**'furniture** ['fəːnitʃər], *s.* Möbel *npl;* **piece of f.**, Möbelstück *n.*

furrow ['fʌrəu], *s.* Furche *f.* ◆**'furrowed**, *adj.* **f. brow**, gerunzelte Stirn *f.*

further ['fəːðər]. **I.** *adv.* **1.** weiter. **2.** (*besides*) ferner. **II.** *adj.* weiter. **III.** *v.tr.* fördern. ◆**further'more**, *adv.* außerdem ◆**'furthest. I.** *adj.* am weitesten ent-

fernt. **II.** *adv.* am weitesten.

furtive ['fəːtiv], *adj.* verstohlen.

fury ['fjuəri], *s.* (*a*) (*anger*) Wut *f;* (*b*) *Fig:* Heftigkeit *f.*

fuse ['fjuːz]. **I.** *s. El:* Sicherung *f;* **f. box**, Sicherungskasten *m;* **f. wire**, Sicherungsdraht *m;* **the f. has gone/blown**, die Sicherung ist durchgebrannt. **II.** *v.i.* (*a*) **the lights have fused**, die Sicherung für das Licht ist durchgebrannt; (*b*) *Fig:* verschmelzen. ◆**fusion** ['fjuːʒ(ə)n], *s.* **1.** *Ph:* Fusion *f.* **2.** *Fig:* Vereinigung *f.*

fuselage ['fjuːzilɑːʒ], *s.* Rumpf *m.*

fusillade [fjuːzi'leid], *s.* Gewehrsalve *f.*

fuss [fʌs]. **I.** *s.* **1.** Getue *n;* **to make a f.**, Umständ/F: Theater machen. **2. to make a f. of s.o.**, viel Aufhebens um j-n machen; (*spoil*) j-n verhätscheln. **II.** *v.i.* Umständ/F: Theater machen. ◆**'fussiness**, *s.* Umständlichkeit *f.* ◆**'fussy**, *adj.* umständlich; (*particular*) heikel.

fusty ['fʌsti], *adj.* moderig; (*of smell*) muffig.

futile ['fjuːtail], *adj.* sinnlos. ◆**futility** [-'tiliti], *s.* Sinnlosigkeit *f.*

future ['fjuːtʃər]. **I.** *adj.* künftig. **II.** *s.* Zukunft *f.* ◆**futu'ristic**, *adj.* futuristisch.

fuzzy ['fʌzi], *adj.* (*of hair*) kraus. **2.** (*of outlines, photo*) unscharf.

G

G, g [dʒiː], *s.* (der Buchstabe) G, g *n.*

gab [gæb], *s. F:* **to have the gift of the g.**, ein gutes Mundwerk haben.

gabble ['gæbl], *v.i.* plappern.

gable ['geibl], *s.* Giebel *m.*

gadget ['gædʒit], *s.* (kleines) Gerät *n.*

Gaelic ['geilik]. **I.** *adj.* gälisch. **II.** *s.* Gälisch *n.*

gag [gæg]. **I.** *s.* **1.** Knebel *m.* **2.** *F:* (*joke*) Gag *m*, Witz *m.* **II.** *v.tr.* (j-n) knebeln.

gaily ['geili], *adv.* fröhlich; **g. coloured**, farbenfroh.

gain [gein]. **I.** *s.* **1.** (*profit*) Gewinn *m;* (*advantage*) Vorteil *m.* **2.** (*in resources, capital etc.*) Zuwachs *m.* **II.** *v.tr.* (*a*) (etwas, einen Freund usw.) gewinnen; (*b*) **to g. strength, popularity etc.**, an Stärke, Beliebtheit usw. gewinnen; **to g. weight**, zunehmen. **2.** *v.i.* (*a*) (*catch up*) aufholen; (*b*) (*of clock*) vorgehen.

gala ['gɑːlə], *s.* Fest *n;* **swimming g.**, Schauschwimmen *n;* **g. performance**, Galavorstellung *f.*

galaxy ['gæləksi], *s.* Milchstraße *f.*

gale [geil], *s.* (*a*) Sturm *m;* (*b*) *Fig:* **g. of laughter**, Lachsalve *f.*

gall [gɔːl], *s.* Galle *f;* **g. bladder**, Gallenblase *f.* ◆**'galling**, *adj.* ärgerlich; **it's g. to me**, es wurmt mich. ◆**'gallstone**, *s.* Gallenstein *m.*

gallant ['gælənt], *adj.* galant. ◆**'gallant-**

-ry, *s.* Tapferkeit *f.*

gallery ['gæləri], *s.* Galerie *f.*

galley ['gæli], *s.* **1.** *Hist:* Galeere *f.* **2.** *Nau:* Kombüse *f.*

gallon ['gælən], *s.* Gallone *f.*

gallop ['gæləp]. **I.** *s.* Galopp *m.* **II.** *v.i.* galoppieren.

gallows ['gæləuz], *s.* Galgen *m.*

galore [gə'lɔːr], *adv.* in Hülle und Fülle.

gamble ['gæmbl]. **I.** *s.* Risiko *n.* **II.** *v.tr. & i.* (um Geld) spielen; **to g. away a fortune**, ein Vermögen verspielen. ◆**'gambler**, *s.* Spieler(in) *m(f).* ◆**'gambling**, *s.* Spielen *n.*

game [geim]. **I.** *s.* **1.** Spiel *n;* (*a*) *of cards, chess etc.*) Partie *f;* **2.** *Sch:* **games**, Sport *m.* **2.** (*Hunting*) Wild *n.* **II.** *adj.* **g. for anything**, bereit, alles mit zumachen; *F:* **I'm g.**, ich mache mit. ◆**'gamekeeper**, *s.* Wildhüter *m.*

gammon ['gæmən], *s.* (geräucherter) Schinken *m.*

gang [gæŋ]. **I.** *s.* (*a*) Kolonne *f* (von Arbeitern); (*b*) Bande *f* (von Verbrechern, Kindern). **II.** *v.i.* *F:* **to g. up on s.o.**, sich gegen j-n zusammenrotten. ◆**'gangster**, *s.* Gangster *m.*

gangrene ['gæŋgriːn], *s.* Wundbrand *m.*

gangway ['gæŋwei], *s.* (*a*) Gang *m;* **g. please!** Platz machen, bitte! (*b*) *Nau:* Fallreep *n.*

gaol [dʒeil]. I. s. Gefängnis n; F: Kittchen n. II. v.tr. (j-n) ins Gefängnis werfen. ◆'gaoler, s. Gefängniswärter m.

gap [gæp], s. 1. (space with sth. missing) Lücke f. 2. Fin: trade g., Handelsdefizit n; to close the g., den Vorsprung aufholen. 3. (time) Zwischenraum m.

gape [geip], v.i. (a) (of things) gähnen; (of hole) klaffen; (b) (of pers.) den Mund aufreißen; (in surprise etc) gaffen; to g. at s.o., sth., j-n, etwas begaffen. ◆'gaping, adj. (of wound, hole) klaffend.

garage ['gæra:ʒ], s. (a) (for storage) Garage f; (b) (for repairs) Werkstatt f; (c) (for petrol) Tankstelle f.

garbage ['gɑ:bidʒ], s. Müll m; esp. N. Am: Küchenabfälle mpl; g. can, Mülleimer m.

garble ['gɑ:bl], v.tr. (einen Text) entstellen; (eine Nachricht) verstümmeln.

garden ['gɑ:dn]. I. s. Garten m; public gardens, öffentliche Anlagen fpl.; g. produce, Gartenbauerzeugnisse npl. II. v.i. im Garten arbeiten. ◆'gardener, s. Gärtner(in) m(f). ◆'gardening, s. Gartenarbeit f.

gargle ['gɑ:gl], v.i. gurgeln.

garish ['gɛəriʃ], adj. grell.

garland ['gɑ:lənd], s. Girlande f.

garlic ['gɑ:lik], s. Knoblauch m.

garment ['gɑ:mənt], s. Kleidungsstück n.

garnish ['gɑ:niʃ]. I. v.tr. garnieren. II. s. Garnierung f.

garrison ['gærisən], s. Garnison f.

garrulous ['gærələs, -juləs], adj. geschwätzig.

garter ['gɑ:tər], s. (a) Strumpfband n; (b) N. Am: Sockenhalter m.

gas [gæs]. I. s. 1. Gas n; g. cooker, Gasherd m; g. fire, Gasofen m; g. meter, Gasuhr f. 2. N.Am: Benzin n; g. station, Tankstelle f. II. v.tr. (j-n) vergasen; to g. oneself, sich mit Gas umbringen. ◆'gasoline, s. N. Am: Benzin n. ◆'gasworks, s. pl. Gaswerk n.

gash [gæʃ]. I. s. (tiefe) Schnittwunde f. II. v.tr. (j-m) eine tiefe Schnittwunde zufügen; he gashed his arm, er hat sich tief in den Arm geschnitten.

gasket ['gæskit], s. Dichtung f.

gasp [gɑ:sp]. I. s. Keuchen n. II. v.i. keuchen; to g. for breath, nach Luft schnappen.

gastric ['gæstrik], adj. Magen-. ◆gas'tritis, s. Gastritis f.

gate [geit], s. (a) Tor n (eines Gartens, einer Stadt usw.); (of farm, across road etc.) Gatter n; (b) Av: Flugsteig m. ◆'gatecrash, v.tr. (eine Party) uneingeladen mitmachen. ◆'gatecrasher, s. Eindringling m. ◆'gateway, s. (also Fig:) Tor n.

gather ['gæðər], v. 1. v.tr. (a) (etwas) sammeln; (Blumen) pflücken; (Beeren) lesen; (Weizen, Heu usw.) ernten; to g. strength, Kräfte sammeln; to g. speed,

in Fahrt kommen; to g. dust, Staub fangen; (b) (conclude) (etwas) folgern; (understand) (Gesagtes, einen Namen usw.) mitkriegen. 2. v.i. (a) (of crowd etc.) sich versammeln; (b) a storm is gathering, ein Gewitter zieht sich zusammen. ◆'gathering, s. Versammlung f; family g., Familientreffen n.

gaudy ['gɔ:di], adj. bunt; Pej: grell.

gauge [geidʒ]. I. s. (a) Meßinstrument n; Mec. E: Lehre f; (b) (indicator) Anzeiger m; petrol g., Benzinuhr f. II. v.tr. Fig: schätzen.

gaunt [gɔ:nt], adj. hager.

gauze [gɔ:z], s. Gaze f.

gay [gei], adj. 1. (of pers.) (a) lustig; (b) F: (homosexual) schwul. 2. (of things) heiter; g. colours, bunte Farben.

gaze [geiz]. I. s. (starrer) Blick m. II. v.i. to g. at s.o., sth., j-n, etwas anstarren.

gazelle [gə'zel], s. Gazelle f.

gazetteer [gæzə'tiər], s. geographisches Namenverzeichnis n.

gear [giər]. I. s. 1. coll. (a) Gerät n; Zubehör n; camping g., Campingausrüstung f; swimming g., Badesachen fpl; all my g., mein ganzes Zeug; (b) F: (clothes) Kluft f. 2. Aut: Gang m; in g., mit eingelegtem Gang; to change g., (den Gang) schalten; g. lever, Schalthebel m. II. v.tr. (etwas) anpassen (to sth., etwas dat). ◆'gearbox, s. Getriebe n.

Geiger ['gaigər], s. G. counter, Geigerzähler m.

gelatine ['dʒelətin], s. Gelatine f.

gelignite ['dʒelignait], s. Gelatinedynamit n.

gem [dʒem], s. Edelstein m; esp. Fig: Juwel n.

Gemini ['dʒeminai]. Pr. n. pl. Zwillinge mpl.

gen [dʒen], s. P: Informationen fpl. ◆genned up, adj. phr. P: to be g. up, Bescheid wissen.

gender ['dʒendər], s. Geschlecht n.

gene [dʒi:n], s. Gen n. ◆genealogy [dʒi:ni'ælədʒi], s. Genealogie f. ◆genealogical [-ə'lɔdʒikl], adj. genealogisch.

general ['dʒen(ə)rəl]. I. adj. allgemein; the g. public, die breite Öffentlichkeit; g. knowledge, Allgemeinbildung f; g. practitioner, praktischer Arzt; (b) in g., im allgemeinen, im großen und ganzen. II. s. Mil: General m. ◆generali'zation, s. Verallgemeinerung f. ◆'generalize, v.i. verallgemeinern. ◆'generally, adv. allgemein.

generate ['dʒenəreit], v.tr. erzeugen. ◆gene'ration, s. 1. (a) (people) Generation f; g. gap, Generationsunterschied m; (b) (time) Menschenalter n. 2. Erzeugung f. ◆'generator, s. Generator m.

generous ['dʒenərəs], adj. großzügig. ◆generosity [-'rɔsiti], s. Großzügigkeit f.

genetics [dʒə'netiks], s. Genetik f.

Geneva [dʒə'ni:və]. Pr. n. Genf n.

genial ['dʒi:niəl], adj. jovial.

genitals ['dʒenitlz], s. pl. (äußere) Geschlechtsteile npl.

genius ['dʒi:niəs], s. (pers.) Genie n; (quality) Genialität f; **work of g.**, geniale Arbeit.

gent [dʒent], s. abbr. P: = gentleman; F: **the gents**, die Herrentoilette f.

gentle ['dʒentl], adj. sanft; g. **hint**, zarter Wink. ◆**'gently**, adv. sachte; (carefully) vorsichtig.

gentleman, pl. **-men** ['dʒentlmən, -men], s. 1. (smart man) Gentleman m. 2. (any man) Herr m; **Gentlemen**, Herren.

gentry ['dʒentri], s. (nieder) Adel m; **landed g.**, Landadel m.

genuine ['dʒenjuin], adj. (a) echt; (b) (of pers.) aufrichtig; **-ly**, adv. wirklich.

geography [dʒi'ɔgrəfi], s. Geographie f. ◆**geographical** [-ə'græfikl], adj. geographisch.

geology [dʒi'ɔlədʒi], s. Geologie f. ◆**geological** [-ə'lɔdʒikl], adj. geologisch. ◆**ge'ologist**, s. Geologe m, Geologin f.

geometry [dʒi'ɔmətri], s. Geometrie f. ◆**geometrical** [-ə'metrikl], adj. geometrisch.

geranium [dʒə'reinjəm], s. Geranie f.

geriatric [dʒeri'ætrik], adj. geriatrisch.

germ [dʒə:m], s. 1. Biol: Bot: Keim m. 2. Med: Bakterie f. ◆**germi'nation**, s. Keimung f. ◆**'germinate** v.i. keimen.

German ['dʒə:mən]. I. adj. deutsch; G. **measles**, Röteln f. II. s. 1. Deutsche(r) f(m). 2. (language) Deutsch n; **in G.**, auf deutsch. ◆**'Germany**, Pr. n. Deutschland n; **West G.**, die Bundesrepublik Deutschland n; **East G.**, Ostdeutschland n; (official name) die Deutsche Demokratische Republik, usu. abbr. DDR f.

gesticulate [dʒes'tikjuleit], v.i. gestikulieren.

gesture ['dʒestʃər]. I. s. Geste f. II. v.i. gestikulieren.

get [get], v. irr. 1. v.tr. (a) (receive) (etwas, eine Krankheit) bekommen, F: kriegen; (einen Brief) erhalten; (b) (obtain) (etwas) besorgen, F: kriegen; (c) (catch) (einen Dieb) fassen; F: **that really gets me** das macht mich wild; **what's got (into) him?** was ist in ihn gefahren? (d) F: (understand) (j-n, etwas) verstehen; (e) (fetch) **to go and g. s.o., sth.,** j-n, etwas holen (gehen); (f) (j-m etwas) zukommen lassen; **how can I g. it to you?** wie kann ich es dir zukommen lassen? (g) **to g. lunch** (ready), das Mittagessen zubereiten; (g) **to g. s.o. to do sth.,** (i) j-n etwas tun lassen; (ii) (by persuasion) j-n dazu bringen, etwas zu tun; **to g. the house painted,** das Haus streichen lassen; (h) **what have you got there?** was hast du da? (i) (obligation) **you've got to do it,**

du mußt es (unbedingt) tun. 2. v.i. (a) (become) (reich, alt usw.) werden; (b) (arrive) **he'll g. here tomorrow,** er wird morgen hier ankommen. ◆**'get a'cross,** v.tr. & i. **here couldn't g. it across,** er hat es nicht klarmachen können. ◆**'get at,** v.tr. & i. difficult **to g. at,** schwer zugänglich; F: **what are you getting at?** worauf willst du hinaus? **to g. at s.o.,** es auf j-n abgesehen haben. ◆**'get a'long,** v.i. **they g. a. very well together,** sie kommen gut miteinander aus. ◆**'get a'way,** v.i. (escape) entkommen; **to g. a. with it,** ungeschoren davonkommen. ◆**'getaway,** s. Flucht f; **g. car,** Fluchtauto n. ◆**'get 'back,** v. 1. v.i. **to g. b. (home),** (nach Hause) zurückkommen. 2. v.tr. (etwas) zurückbekommen; F: **to g. one's own b.,** sich revanchieren. ◆**'get 'by,** v.i. sich zurechtfinden; F: durchkommen. ◆**'get 'down,** v. 1. v.i. (a) absteigen (**from,** von + dat); (b) **to g. d. to work/business,** sich an die Arbeit machen. 2. v.tr. (a) (from shelf etc.) (etwas) herunterholen; (b) (write) (etwas) aufschreiben; (c) (swallow) (etwas) herunterschlucken; (d) F: **it gets you d.,** es ist deprimierend. ◆**'get 'in,** v. 1. v.i. (a) (i. car etc.) einsteigen; (b) **when does the train g. in?** wann kommt der Zug an? (c) Pol: gewählt werden. 2. v.tr. (die Wäsche usw.) hereinholen; (die Ernte) einbringen. ◆**'get 'into,** v.i. **to g. i. a car** etc., in einen Wagen usw. einsteigen; **to g. i. bad company,** in schlechte Gesellschaft geraten. ◆**'get 'off,** v. 1. v.tr. & i. (a) **to g. o. (the bus/train),** (aus dem Bus/Zug) aussteigen; (b) davonkommen; **to g. o. lightly,** glimpflich davonkommen; (c) (leave) abfahren; (leave work) Feierabend machen. 2. v.tr. (a) (ein Paket) abschicken; (b) **to g. the day o.,** den Tag freibekommen. ◆**'get 'on,** v. 1. v.tr. (Kleider) anziehen. 2. v.i. **time's getting on,** die Zeit vergeht; **to be getting on for forty,** auf die Vierzig zugehen; (b) **she is getting on well,** sie macht gute Fortschritte; **how are you getting on? wie geht's?** (c) **to g. on well with s.o.,** gut mit j-m auskommen. ◆**'get 'out,** v. 1. v.tr. (a) (einen Nagel usw.) herausziehen; F: herauskriegen; (b) **to g. sth. o. of the drawer,** etwas aus der Schublade herausnehmen; **I got nothing o. of it,** ich hatte nichts davon. 2. v.i. **to g. o. of sth.,** aus etwas darauf herauskommen. ◆**'get 'over,** v.tr. & i. (a) **to g. o. a wall,** über eine Mauer klettern; (b) **to g. sth. o. with,** etwas hinter sich acc bringen; (c) über (eine Krankheit, eine Überraschung usw.) hinwegkommen. ◆**'get 'round,** v.i. **I never g. r. to it,** ich komme nie dazu. ◆**'get 'through,** v.tr. & i. (a) Tel: Anschluß bekommen; (b) (eine Arbeit) erledigen. ◆**'get-together,** s. (meeting) Zusammenkunft f; (social) zwangloses Beisammensein n.

◆**'get 'up**, *v.i.* aufstehen. ◆**'getup**, *s.*
F: Aufmachung *f.*

geyser ['gaizǝr, *N. Am:* gaizǝr], *s.* **1.** Gey-
sir *m.* **2.** *H:* Durchlauferhitzer *m.*

ghastly ['gɑːstli], *adj.* gräßlich.

gherkin ['gǝːkin], *s.* Essiggurke *f.*

ghetto *pl.* **-os** ['getǝu, -ǝuz], *s.* Getto *n.*

ghost [gǝust], *s.* **1.** Gespenst *n*; g. story,
Gespenstergeschichte *f*; g. town, Geister-
stadt *f.* **2.** the Holy G., der Heilige
Geist. ◆**'ghostly**, *adj.* geisterhaft.

giant ['dʒaiǝnt]. **I.** *s.* Riese *m.* **II.** *adj.* riesig.

gibe [dʒaib], *s.* Seitenhieb *m*; *pl.* gibes,
Spott *m.*

giblets ['dʒiblits], *s. pl.* Geflügelklein *n.*

giddy ['gidi], *adj.* schwindlig; **I feel g.**,
mir ist schwindlig. ◆**'giddiness**, *s.*
Schwindelgefühl *n.*

gift [gift], *s.* (*a*) Geschenk *n*; *Com:* free
g., Zugabe *f*; (*b*) Begabung *f*; **he has a g.
for languages**, er ist sprachbegabt.
◆**'gifted**, *adj.* begabt.

gigantic [dʒai'gæntik], *adj.* riesig.

giggle ['gigl]. **I.** *s.* Gekicher *n.* **II.** *v.i.* kichern.

gild [gild], *v.tr.* vergolden. ◆**gilt. I.** *adj.*
vergoldet. **II.** *s.* Vergoldung *f.*

gill [gil], *s. Z:* Kieme *f.*

gimmick ['gimik], *s. F:* Trick *m*; *advertising g.*, Reklamegag *m.*

gin [dʒin], *s.* Gin *m.*

ginger ['dʒindʒǝr]. **I.** *s.* Ingwer *m.* **II.**
adj. rotblond. ◆**'gingerly**, *adv.* vorsichtig.

gipsy ['dʒipsi], *s.* Zigeuner(in) *m(f).*

giraffe [dʒi'rɑːf], *s.* Giraffe *f.*

girder ['gǝːdǝr], *s.* Tragbalken *m.*

girdle ['gǝːdl], *s.* Mieder *n.*

girl [gǝːl], *s.* Mädchen *n*; g. guide, Pfadfinderin *f*; his g./g. friend, seine Freundin. ◆**'girlish**, *adj.* mädchenhaft.

giro ['dʒairǝu], *s.* Giro *n.*

girth [gǝːθ], *s.* Umfang *m*; (*of pers.*) Taille
f.

gist [dʒist], *s.* Hauptinhalt *m*; **I got the g.
of it**, ich habe das Wesentliche mitgekriegt.

give [giv]. **I.** *v.* **1.** *v.tr.* (*a*) geben; **to g.
sth. to s.o./ s.o. sth.**, j-m etwas geben;
(einen Vortrag) halten. **2.** *v.i.* (*a*) geben;
(*b*) *(yield)* nachgeben. **II.** *s.* **g. and take**,
Kompromiß *m.* ◆**'give a'way**, *v.tr.* (*a*)
(etwas) verschenken; (*b*) *(betray)* (j-n, etwas) verraten; *F:* **to g. the game** *s.a.* alles
verraten. ◆**give 'back**, *v.tr.* zurückgeben. ◆**give 'in**, *v.* **1.** *v.i.* nachgeben
(**to s.o., sth.**, j-m, etwas *dat*). **2.** *v.tr.*
(Bücher, eine Arbeit) einreichen.
◆**'given**, *adj.* **1.** (*particular*) bestimmt. (*b*) *N. Am:* g. name, Vorname
m. **2.** (*of pers.*) ergeben (to, *dat*). ◆**'give
'off**, *v.tr.* (Gas, Dampf usw.) abgeben.
◆**'give 'out**, *v.* **1.** *v.tr.* (Bücher, Preise
usw.) verteilen; (eine Mitteilung) bekanntgeben. **2.** *v.i.* (*of supplies etc.*) ausgehen. ◆**'give 'up**, *v.tr.* (*a*) (Hoffnung,

einen Plan usw.) aufgeben; (*b*) **to g. oneself up**, sich (freiwillig) ergeben; (*to police*) sich der Polizei stellen. ◆**'give
'way**, *v.i.* (*a*) nachgeben (**to s.o.**, j-m; to
temptation, pressure etc.**, der Versuchung, dem Druck usw.); **the roof gave
w.**, das Dach stürzte ein; **her love gave
w. to hatred**, ihre Liebe verwandelte sich
in Haß; (*b*) *Aut:* Vorfahrt gewähren.

glacier ['glæsiǝr], *s.* Gletscher *m.*

glad [glæd], *adj.* froh (**of/at**, über + *acc*);
-ly, *adv.* gern(e).

glamour ['glæmǝr], *s.* Glanz *m*; (*of person*)
Reiz *m.* ◆**'glamorous**, *adj.* (*of girl*)
traumhaft schön; (*of job etc.*) glanzvoll.

glance [glɑːns]. **I.** *s.* (*flüchtiger*) Blick *m.*
II. *v.i.* **a**) **to g. at s.o.**, einen Blick auf
j-n werfen; **to g. through a text**, einen
Text überfliegen; (*b*) **to g. off**, abprallen.

gland [glænd], *s.* Drüse *f.* ◆**'glandular**,
adj. **g. fever**, Drüsenfieber *n.*

glare [glɛǝr]. **I.** *s.* (*dazzle*) Blenden *f*;
grelles Licht *f* (der Sonne). **2.** (*look*) wü-
tender Blick *m.* **II.** *v.i.* (*a*) grell
leuchten; **to g. at s.o.**, j-n böse anstarren. ◆**'glaring**, *adj.* **1.** (*of sun etc.*)
grell. **2.** (*of injustice*) schreiend; (*of example, mistake*) kraß.

glass [glɑːs], *s.* **1.** Glas *n.* **2.** (**a pair of**)
glasses, eine Brille.

glaze [gleiz]. **I.** *v.tr.* (*a*) (ein Fenster
usw.) verglasen; (*b*) (eine Oberfläche, ein
Gemälde) lasieren; *Fig:* glazed look, gla-
siger Blick. **II.** *s.* Lasur *f.* ◆**'glazier**, *s.*
Glaser *m.*

gleam [gliːm]. **I.** *s.* (*a*) Schimmer *m*;
(*schwacher*) Schein *m*; (*b*) Glänzen *n* (eines Messers, der Augen). **II.** *v.i.* schimmern; (*of water, eyes*) glänzen.

glean [gliːn], *v.tr.* (Informationen) entnehmen.

glib [glib], *adj.* zungenfertig; (*superficial*)
oberflächlich.

glide [glaid], *v.i.* gleiten; (*of glider*) segeln. ◆**'glider**, *s.* Segelflugzeug *n.*
◆**'gliding**, *s. Av:* Segelfliegen *n.*

glimmer ['glimǝr], *s.* Glimmen *n*; **g. of
hope**, Hoffnungsschimmer *m.*

glimpse [glimps]. **I.** *s.* flüchtiger Blick *m*;
to catch a g. of s.o., sth., j-n, etwas
flüchtig zu sehen bekommen. **II.** *v.tr.*
(etwas, -n) flüchtig sehen.

glint [glint]. **I.** *s.* Schimmer *m.* **II.** *v.i.*
schimmern.

glisten ['glisn], *v.i.* glitzern.

glitter ['glitǝr]. **I.** *s.* Glitzern *n.* **II.** *v.i.*
glitzern.

gloat [glǝut], *v.i.* **to g. (over sth.)**, sich
hämisch (über etwas *acc*) freuen.

globe [glǝub], *s.* Globus *m.* **g. artichoke**,
Artischocke *f.* ◆**'global**, *adj.* global.

gloom [gluːm], *s.* **1.** Dunkelheit *f.* **2.**
(*state of mind*) Schwermut *f*; Trübsinn *m.*
◆**'gloomy**, *adj.* **1.** (*dark*) dunkel, düster. **2.** (*a*) (*of pers.*) schwermütig; (*b*)
pessimistisch.

glory ['glɔːri], *s.* **1.** Ruhm *m.* **2.** (*splen-*

dour) Pracht *f.* ◆'**glorify**, *v.tr.* verherrlichen. ◆'**glorified**, *adj.* F: it was only a g. shed, es war nur eine bessere Hütte. ◆'**glorious**, *adj.* 1. prächtig. 2. *(of victory etc.)* glorreich.

gloss [glɔs], *v.tr.* **to g. over**, (Fehler, Wahrheiten) vertuschen. ◆'**glossy**, *adj.* glänzend; **g. magazine**, Illustrierte *f.* ◆'**glossary** ['glɔsəri], *s.* Glossar *n.*

glove [glʌv], *s.* Handschuh *m*; **g. compartment**, Handschuhfach *n.*

glow [gləu]. I. *s.* Glühen *n.* II. *v.i.* (a) *(of metal, coal)* glühen; (b) **to be glowing with health**, vor Gesundheit strotzen. ◆'**glowing**, *adj.* *(of coals etc.)* glühend; *(of face etc.)* strahlend; **g. report**, begeisterter Bericht.

glucose ['glu:kəuz, -əus], *s.* Traubenzucker *m.*

glue [glu:]. I. *s.* Klebstoff *m.* II. *v.tr.* (etwas) kleben (**to sth.**, an etwas *acc*.)

glum [glʌm], *adj.* trübsinnig.

glut [glʌt], *s.* Überfluß *m* (**of sth.**, an etwas *dat*).

glutton ['glʌtn], *s.* Vielfraß *m*; **you're a g. for punishment!** du kannst nie genug kriegen!

gnarled [nɑːld], *adj.* *(of tree)* knorrig; *(of hands etc.)* knotig.

gnash [næʃ], *v.tr.* **to g. one's teeth**, mit den Zähnen knirschen.

gnat [næt], *s.* Mücke *f.*

gnaw [nɔː], *v.tr. & i.* **to g. (at) sth.**, an etwas *dat* nagen.

go [gəu]. I. *v.i. irr.* 1. (a) *(walk)* gehen; (b) *(travel)* fahren; **the train goes at 10**, der Zug fährt um 10 Uhr; (c) *(lead)* **this road goes to Munich**, diese Straße führt nach München. 2. *(of machinery)* gehen, funktionieren. 3. *(leave)* (fort)gehen; *(on a journey)* abreisen; **it's all gone**, es ist nichts mehr übrig; **a fuse went**, eine Sicherung brannte durch. 4. **all has gone well so far**, bisher ist alles glatt verlaufen. 5. **are you going to make a speech?** werden Sie eine Rede halten? **I was going to walk there but it was too far**, zu wollte zu Fuß hingehen, aber es war zu weit. 6. **it won't go into my case**, es geht/paßt nicht in meinen Koffer; **the key won't go into the lock**, der Schlüssel will nicht ins Schloß; **where does this book go?** wohin gehört dieses Buch? 7. *(become)* **to go mad**, verrückt werden. 8. **to let (sth.) go**, (etwas) loslassen. II. *s.* F: 1. **to be always on the go**, immer auf Trab sein. 2. (a) *(try)* Versuch *m*; **to have a go at sth.**, etwas probieren; (b) *(turn)* **it's your go**, du bist dran; **at one go**, auf einmal. 3. **he made a go of it**, er machte einen Erfolg daraus. ◆'**go a'bout**, *v.* 1. *v.i.* herumgehen. 2. *v.tr.* **how do you go a. it?** wie nimmst man das in Angriff? ◆'**go-ahead**. I. *adj.* fortschrittlich. II. *s.* **to give s.o. the g.**, j-m grünes Licht geben. ◆'**go a'way**, *v.i.* fortgehen. ◆'**go back**, *v.i.* zurückgehen. ◆'**go**

between, *s.* Vermittler(in) *m(f)*. ◆'**go by**, *v.tr. & i.* (a) *(pass)* vorbeigehen; *(of time)* vergehen; (b) **to go by appearances**, nach dem äußeren Schein urteilen. ◆'**go down**, *v.i.* (a) hinuntergehen; *(of ship, sun)* untergehen; *(of prices)* sinken; (b) *(in quality)* sich verschlechtern; *(of area)* herunterkommen; (c) **the suggestion went down well**, der Vorschlag hat Anklang gefunden. ◆'**go for**, *v.tr.* F: *(attack)* **to go f. s.o.**, auf j-n losgehen. ◆'**go 'in**, *v.i.* (a) *(into room)* eintreten; *(into house)* hineingehen; (b) **to go in for sth.**, sich mit etwas *dat* befassen. ◆'**going**. I. *adj.* **a g. concern**, ein gutgehendes Unternehmen; **the g. price**, der Marktpreis. II. *s.* (a) **while the g. is good**, solange es noch geht; (b) F: **goings on**, Vorfälle *mpl* Pej: Umtriebe *mpl*. ◆'**go 'off**, *v.i.* (a) *(of pers.)* fortgehen; (b) *(of gun)* losgehen; *(of bomb)* explodieren; (c) **everything went o. well**, alles ist gut verlaufen; (d) F: *(of food)* verderben; (e) F: **I've gone o. Gruyere**, Schweizer Käse schmeckt mir nicht mehr. ◆'**go 'on**, *v.i.* (a) weitergehen; **to go on speaking**, weitersprechen, weiterarbeiten usw.; **go on! weiter!** (b) **what's going on here?** was geht hier vor? (c) F: **to go on at s.o.**, mit j-m dauernd schimpfen. ◆'**go 'out**, *v.i.* (a) *(into garden etc.)* hinausgehen; *(with friend etc.)* ausgehen; (b) *(of fire)* ausgehen; (c) *(of tide)* zurückgehen. ◆'**go 'over**, *v.tr.* (eine Arbeit, ein Dokument) durchsehen. ◆'**go 'round**, *v.i.* *(of wheel etc.)* sich drehen; *(of pers., rumours)* herumgehen; **to go round**, Bummelstreik *m.* ◆'**go 'through**, *v.* 1. *v.tr.* (a) (durch eine Tür usw.) durchgehen; (b) (Dokumente) durchsehen; (c) (Erlebnisse) durchmachen. 2. *v.i.* durchgehen. ◆'**go 'up**, *v.i.* *(of pers.)* hinaufgehen; *(of prices)* steigen. ◆'**go with'out**, *v.* 1. *v.tr.* (auf etwas *acc*) verzichten. 2. *v.i.* ohne (es) auskommen. ◆'**go 'wrong**, *v.i.* *(of plan etc.)* schiefgehen.

goal [gəul], *s.* 1. *(aim)* Ziel *n.* 2. *Sp:* Tor *n*; **to score a g.**, ein Tor schießen. ◆'**goalkeeper**, *s.* Torwart *m.* ◆'**goalpost**, *s.* Torpfosten *m.*

goat [gəut], *s.* Ziege *f.*

gobble [gɔbl], *v.tr.* gierig herunterschlingen.

god [gɔd], *s.* Gott *m*; **thank G.!** Gott sei Dank! **for God's sake**, um Gottes willen; F: **G. knows how**, weiß Gott, wie. ◆'**godchild**, *pl.* -**children**, *s.* Patenkind *n.* ◆'**goddaughter**, *s.* Patentochter *f.* ◆'**goddess**, *s.* Göttin *f.* ◆'**godfather**, *s.* Pate *m.* ◆'**godforsaken**, *adj.* gottverlassen. ◆'**godmother**, *s.* Patin *f.* ◆'**godparents**, *s.pl.* Paten *pl.* ◆'**godsend**, *s.* Geschenk *n* des Himmels; F: Segen *m.* ◆'**godson**, *s.* Patensohn *m.*

goggles, ['gɔglz], s. pl. Schutzbrille f.

gold [gəuld], s. Gold n. ◆**'golden**, adj. golden; Gold-; g. **handshake**, Abfindung f (eines abgehenden Direktors); g. **rule**, goldene Regel. ◆**'goldfish**, s. Goldfisch m. ◆**'gold-mine**, s. Goldmine f. ◆**'gold-plated**, adj. vergoldet.

golf [gɔlf], s. Golf(spiel) n; g. **club**, (i) Golfschläger m; (ii) Golfklub m; g. **course**, Golfplatz m. ◆**'golfball**, s. Golfball m. ◆**'golfer**, s. Golfspieler(in) m(f).

gong [gɔŋ], s. Gong m.

good [gud]. I. adj. gut; g. **morning/evening!** guten Morgen/Abend! g. **at** French, gut in Französisch; a g. **hour**, eine gute Stunde; a g. **10 kilometres**, gute zehn Kilometer; a g. **deal**, ziemlich viel; **to make g.**, (einen Schaden, Verlust usw.) wiedergutmachen. II. s. 1. das Gute n, Gutes n; (a) (of pers.) **to do g.**, Gutes tun; **he's up to no g.**, er führt nichts Gutes im Schilde; (b) (of thing) **to do s.o. g.** j-m guttun; **that isn't much g.**, das taugt/nützt nicht viel; **it's no g.!** da ist nichts zu machen! es hilft nichts! **no g. talking about it**, es hat keinen Sinn, darüber zu reden; (c) adv. phr. **for g. (and all)**, für immer; **he is leaving the country for g.**, er verläßt das Land für immer/auf Dauer. 2. pl. Com: Güter npl; Waren fpl; **to deliver the goods**, F: Wort halten; **goods train**, Güterzug m. ◆**good'bye**, int. auf Wiedersehen! ◆**good-'looking**, adj. gutaussehend. ◆**good-'natured**, adj. gutmütig. ◆**'goodness**. I. s. (a) (kindness) Güte f; (b) (virtue) Tugend f. II. int. (my) g.! du meine Güte! **for g. sake!** um Gottes willen! **thank g.**, Gott sei Dank.

goose, pl **geese** [guːs, giːs], s. Gans f. ◆**'gooseflesh**, s. ◆**'goosepimples/** N.Am: **'goose bumps**, s.pl. Gänsehaut f.

gooseberry ['guzbəri], s. Stachelbeere f.

gory ['gɔːri], adj. blutig; (of story etc.) blutrünstig.

gorgeous ['gɔːdʒəs], adj. herrlich.

gorilla [gə'rilə], s. Gorilla m.

gormless ['gɔːmləs], adj. F: begriffsstutzig.

gosh [gɔʃ], int. G: mein Gott! Mensch!

gospel ['gɔspəl], s. Evangelium n; Fig: **to take sth. as g.** (truth), etwas für bare Münze nehmen.

gossip ['gɔsip], I. s. 1. (pers.) Klatschbase f. 2. Klatsch m; g. **column**, Klatschspalte f. II. v.i. klatschen.

Gothic ['gɔθik], adj. gotisch.

gourmet ['guəmei], s. Feinschmecker m.

gout [gaut] s. Gicht f.

govern ['gʌvən], v.tr. (a) (ein Land) regieren; (b) (determine) (seine Haltung usw.) bestimmen. ◆**'government**, s. Regierung f. ◆**'governor**, s. Gouverneur m; Statthalter m (einer Provinz); Sch: etc: Vorstandsmitglied n.

gown [gaun]. 1. **evening** g., Abendkleid n. 2. Talar m (der Professoren, Richter usw.); **dressing** g., Morgenrock m.

grab [græb], v. 1. v.tr. (a) (etwas) packen; **to g. hold of sth.**, etwas (hastig) ergreifen; (b) P: **how does that g. you?** wie findest du das? 2. v.i. **to g. at sth.**, nach etwas dat greifen.

grace [greis], I. s. 1. (of movement) Anmut f; **social graces**, (gute) Umgangsformen fpl. 2. **to say g.**, das Tischgebet sprechen; F: **to have ten days' g.**, zehn Tage Aufschub haben. ◆**'graceful**, adj. anmutig. ◆**gracious** ['greiʃəs], adj. 1. (with condescension) gnädig; (kind) gütig; (b) g. **living**, luxuriöser Lebensstil.

grade [greid]. I. s. 1. (also Sch:) Klasse f; **good grades**, gute Noten fpl; F: **to make the g.**, es schaffen. 2. (incline) N. Am: Gefälle n. II. v.tr. (Waren usw.) einteilen; (Schularbeiten) bewerten.

gradient ['greidiənt], s. **up(ward)** g., Steigung f; **down(ward)** g., Gefälle n.

gradual ['grædju(ə)l], adj. allmählich.

graduate. I. ['grædjuət] s. Hochschulabsolvent m. II. ['grædjueit] v.i. graduieren.

graft [grɑːft]. I. s. 1. Med: Transplantat n; (process) Transplantation f. 2. (work) Schwerarbeit f, F: Schufterei f. II. v.tr. (Haut) verpflanzen.

grain [grein], s. 1. Korn n; coll. Getreide n. 2. Maserung f (von Holz); F: **it goes against the g.**, es geht (mir) gegen den Strich.

gram(me) [græm], s. Gramm n.

grammar ['græmər], s. Grammatik f; g. **school**, approx. Gymnasium n.

gramophone ['græməfəun], s. Grammophon n.

grand [grænd], adj. 1. (large) (a) groß; (main) Haupt-; g. **piano**, Flügel m; (b) g. **total**, Gesamtsumme f. 2. (magnificent) grandios; (smart) vornehm; (elaborate) prunkvoll. 3. F: wunderbar. ◆**'grandchild**, pl. **-children**, s. Enkelkind n. ◆**'granddaughter**, s. Enkelin f. ◆**grandeur** ['grændʒər], s. Herrlichkeit f. ◆**'grandfather**, s. Großvater m; g. **clock**, Standuhr f. ◆**'grandma**, s. F: Oma f. ◆**grandiose** ['grændiəus], adj. grandios. ◆**'grandpa**, s. F: Opa m. ◆**'grandmother**, s. Großmutter f. ◆**'grandparents**, s. pl. Großeltern pl. ◆**'grandson**, s. Enkel m. ◆**'grandstand**, s. (überdachte) Tribüne f.

granite ['grænit], s. Granit m.

granny ['græni], s. F: Oma f.

grant [grɑːnt]. I. s. (finance) (finanzielle) Unterstützung f; Sch: Studienbeihilfe f. II. v.tr. (a) (j-m etwas) gewähren; (j-m Erlaubnis) erteilen; (b) **to take sth. for granted**, etwas als selbstverständlich nehmen; (c) (eine Bitte) erfüllen; (d) admit (etwas) zugeben.

grape [greip], s. Weintraube f. ◆**'grape-**

fruit, s. Grapefruit f. ◆**'grapevine,** s. F: **I heard it through the g.,** ich habe es munkeln hören.

graph [grɑːf], s. Diagramm n; graphische Darstellung f; **g. paper,** Millimeterpapier n. ◆**graphic** ['græfik], adj. graphisch; **g. description,** anschauliche Beschreibung.

grapple ['græpl], v.i. ringen **(with s.o., sth.,** mit j-m, etwas dat); **to g. with a problem,** sich mit einem Problem auseinandersetzen.

grasp [grɑːsp]. I. s. (a) **within his g.,** in seiner Reichweite; (b) **to have a thorough g. of a subject,** eine Sache beherrschen. II. v.tr. (a) (etwas) ergreifen; (b) (understand) (etwas) begreifen. ◆**'grasping,** adj. habgierig.

grass [grɑːs], s. (a) Gras n; (b) (lawn) Rasen m. ◆**'grasshopper,** s. Heuschrecke f. ◆**'grassy,** adj. grasbedeckt.

grate¹ [greit], s. Kamin m. ◆**'grating,** s. Gitter n.

grate², v. 1. v.tr. (a) (Käse) reiben; (b) **to g. one's teeth,** mit den Zähnen knirschen. 2. v.i. knirschen. ◆**'grater,** s. Reibe f.

grateful ['greitful], adj. dankbar **(to s.o. for sth.,** j-m für etwas acc). ◆**gratitude** ['grætitjuːd], s. Dankbarkeit f.

gratifying ['grætifaiiŋ], adj. erfreulich.

gratuity [grə'tjuːiti], s. Trinkgeld n. ◆**gra'tuitous,** adj. überflüssig.

grave¹ [greiv]. I. s. Grab n. II. adj. ernst, **g. mistake,** schwerwiegender Fehler; **-ly,** adv. **g. ill,** schwer krank. ◆**'gravestone,** s. Grabstein m. ◆**'graveyard,** s. Friedhof m.

gravel ['grævl], s. Kies m.

gravity ['græviti], s. 1. Ernst m. 2. Ph: (force of) g., Schwerkraft f. ◆**'gravitate,** v.i. **to g. towards sth.,** allmählich zu etwas dat tendieren.

gravy ['greivi], s. Soße f (zum Braten usw.); (juice) Bratensaft m.

gray [grei] see **grey.**

graze¹ [greiz], v.i. (of animal) weiden.

graze², I. s. Abschürfung f. II. v.tr. (a) (die Haut, den Finger) abschürfen; (b) (touch lightly) (j-n, etwas) streifen.

grease [griːs]. I. s Fett n. II. v.tr. (mit Fett) schmieren. ◆**'grease-proof,** adj. **g.-p. paper,** Butterbrotpapier n. ◆**'greasy,** adj. fettig; Pej: schmierig.

great [greit], adj. (a) groß; **G. Britain,** Großbritannien n; **a g. many people,** sehr viele Leute; (b) (important) bedeutend; **g. occasion,** wichtiger Anlaß; F: **that's g.!** das ist großartig! **-ly,** adv. sehr. ◆**'great-'aunt,** s. Großtante f. ◆**'great-'grandfather,** s. Urgroßvater m. ◆**'great-'grandmother,** s. Urgroßmutter f. ◆**'greatness,** s. Größe f; (importance) Bedeutung f. ◆**'great-'uncle,** s. Großonkel m.

Greece [griːs]. Pr. n. Griechenland n.

◆**Greek.** I. adj. griechisch. II. s. Grieche m, Griechin f. III. s. Griechisch n.

greed [griːd], s. (a) Gier f; Habsucht f; (b) (for food) Gefräßigkeit f. ◆**'greedy,** adj. (a) gierig; (covetous) habsüchtig; (b) gefräßig.

green [griːn]. I. adj. grün; Fig: **g. with envy,** gelb vor Neid. II. s. (a) (colour) Grün n; (b) **greens,** grünes Gemüse n; (c) (lawn etc.) Grünfläche f; **village g.,** Dorfwiese f. ◆**'greenery,** s. F: Grün n; (foliage) Laub n. ◆**'greengage,** s. Reneklode f. ◆**'greengrocer,** s. Obst- und Gemüsehändler m. ◆**'greenhouse,** s. Gewächshaus n.

greet [griːt], v.tr. (a) (j-n) grüßen; (b) (welcome) (j-n, etwas) begrüßen. ◆**'greeting,** s. Gruß m.

gregarious [gri'gɛəriəs], adj. gesellig.

grenade [grə'neid], s. (hand) g., Handgranate f.

grey [grei], adj. grau. ◆**'grey-'haired** adj. grauhaarig. ◆**'greyhound,** s. Windhund m.

grid [grid], s. 1. (iron) g., Gitter n. 2. El: (national) g., Überlandleitungsnetz n. 3. (for maps) Gitternetz n.

grief [griːf], s. (worry) Kummer m; (pain) Leid n; **to come to g.,** verunglücken; (of plan) scheitern. ◆**'grievance,** s. Beschwerde f. ◆**grieve,** v. 1. v.tr. (j-n) betrüben. 2. v.i. sich dat Kummer machen (over, über + acc); **to g. for s.o.,** um j-n trauern.

grill [gril]. I. s. 1. (appliance) Grill m. 2. (meat etc.) (mixed) g., Gemischtes vom Grill. II. v.tr. (Fleisch usw.) grillen.

grim [grim], adj. grimmig; **g. determination,** eiserne Entschlossenheit.

grimace ['griməs]. I. s. Grimasse f. II. v.i. Grimassen schneiden.

grime [graim], s. (eingefressener) Schmutz m. ◆**'grimy,** adj. schmutzig.

grin [grin]. I. s. Grinsen n. II. v.i. grinsen; F: **to g. and bear it,** gute Miene zum bösen Spiel machen.

grind [graind]. I. s. F: Schinderei f. II. v. irr. 1. v.tr. (a) (Kaffee usw.) mahlen; (b) (Metall, Glas, Klingen) schleifen; **to g. one's teeth,** mit den Zähnen knirschen; (c) N.Am: (Fleisch) durchdrehen. 2. v.i. **to g. to a halt,** zum Stillstand kommen.

grip [grip]. I. s. Griff m; Fig: **to get/keep a g. on oneself,** sich beherrschen; **to come to grips with a problem,** sich mit einem Problem auseinandersetzen. II. v.tr. (etwas) festhalten. ◆**'gripping,** adj. fesselnd.

gristle ['grisl], s. Knorpel m.

grit [grit]. I. s. 1. Sand m; **road g.,** Streugut n. 2. Fig: Mut m, F: Schneid m. II. v.tr. (a) (Straßen) streuen; (b) **to g. one's teeth,** die Zähne zusammenbeißen.

groan [grəun]. I. s. Stöhnen n. II. v.i. stöhnen.

grocer ['grəusər], s. Lebensmittelhändler m; **g.'s (shop),** Lebensmittelgeschäft n.

◆'**groceries**, *s. pl.* Lebensmittel *npl.*

groin [grɔin], *s.* Leiste *f.*

groom [gruːm]. I. *s.* **1.** Pferdeknecht *m.* **2.** (*at wedding*) Bräutigam *m.* II. *v.tr.* (*j-n*) (als Nachfolger usw.) einarbeiten.

groove [gruːv], *s.* Furche *f*; (*in wood, record*) Rille *f.*

grope [grəup], *v.i.* tasten (**for sth.**, nach etwas *dat*); **to g. one's way,** sich vorwärtstasten.

gross [grəus], *adj.* **1.** (*of error, negligence*) grob. **2.** *Com: etc:* Brutto-; **-ly,** *adv.* höchst; **g. exaggerated,** stark übertrieben.

grotty ['grɔti], *adj. P:* schäbig; (*of area*) heruntergekommen.

grotesque [grəu'tesk], *adj.* grotesk.

ground¹ [graund], *adj.* gemahlen; *N.Am:* **g. beef,** gehacktes Rindfleisch.

ground² [graund]. I. *s.* **1.** (*a*) Boden *m*; **g. floor,** Erdgeschoß *n*; **g. control,** Flugleitung *f*; **to hold/stand one's g.,** nicht nachgeben; **to gain/lose g.,** Boden gewinnen/verlieren; **to break new g.,** Neuland betreten; (*b*) *sports* **g.,** Sportplatz *m*; (*large*) Sportgelände *n*; (*c*) *pl.* grounds, Anlagen *fpl* (eines Schlosses usw.). **2.** (*reason*) Grund *m*; **g. for complaint,** Anlaß *m* zur Klage; **on what grounds?** mit welcher Begründung? **4.** *N. Am: El:* Erde *f.* II. *v.tr.* (einem Flugzeug) Startverbot erteilen. ◆'**grounding**, *s.* Grundlage *f* (in einem Fach). ◆'**groundless**, *adj.* grundlos. ◆'**groundsheet**, *s.* Bodenplane *f.* ◆'**groundwork**, *s.* Vorarbeiten *fpl.*

group [gruːp]. I. *s.* Gruppe *f.* II. *v.tr.* (etwas) gruppieren.

grove [grəuv], *s.* Hain *m.*

grovel ['grɔv(ə)l], *v.i.* (*of pers., dog*) kriechen (**to s.o.,** vor j-m).

grow [grəu], *v.irr.* **1.** *v.i.* (*a*) (*of pers., animals, plants etc.*) wachsen; (*b*) (*increase*) zunehmen (**in sth.,** an etwas *dat*); (*c*) **this music grows on you,** mit der Zeit gefällt einem diese Musik doch; (*d*) (*become*) werden; **to g. old,** alt werden. **2.** *v.tr.* (*a*) (Getreide, Gemüse) anbauen; (Rosen usw.) züchten; (*b*) **to g. a beard,** sich *dat* einen Bart wachsen lassen. ◆'**grown-up,** *adj.* Erwachsene(r) *f(m).* ◆'**growth,** *s.* **1.** (*process*) Wachsen *n.* **2.** (*increase*) Wachstum *n*; (*in numbers*) Zunahme *f*; **g. industry,** Wachstumsindustrie *f.* **3.** Wuchs *m* (der Haare usw.). **4.** *Med:* Tumor *m.* ◆'**grow 'up,** *v.i.* (*of pers.*) aufwachsen; (*of town etc.*) entstehen.

growl [graul], *v.i.* (*of dog*) knurren; (*bear*) brummen.

grub [grʌb], *s. P:* Futter *n.* ◆'**grubby,** *adj. F:* schmuddelig; (*filthy*) dreckig.

grudge [grʌdʒ]. I. *s.* **to bear s.o. a g.,** einen Groll gegen j-n hegen. II. *v.tr.* **to g. s.o. his success,** j-m seinen Erfolg mißgönnen. ◆'**grudging,** *adj.* (*of nature etc.*) mißgünstig; (*of praise, gift*

etc.) widerwillig.

gruelling ['gruːəliŋ], *adj.* strapaziös.

gruesome ['gruːsəm], *adj.* schauerlich.

gruff [grʌf], *adj.* (*ill-tempered*) barsch; (*of voice*) rauh.

grumble ['grʌmbl], *v.i.* murren.

grumpy ['grʌmpi], *adj.* mürrisch.

grunt [grʌnt]. *v.i.* knurren; (*of pig etc.*) grunzen.

guarantee [gærən'tiː]. I. *s.* **1.** Garantie *f*; (*document*) Garantieschein *m.* II. *v.tr.* garantieren.

guard [gɑːd]. I. *s.* **1.** (*a*) Wache *f*; (*pers.*) *Mil: etc:* Wachposten *m*; (*in prison*) Wärter *m*; **to be on g./stand g.,** Wache stehen; **g. dog,** Wachhund *m*; (*b*) **to be on one's g.,** auf der Hut sein; **to be caught off one's g.,** überrumpelt werden. **2.** *Rail:* Zugführer *m*; **g.'s van,** Dienstwagen *m.* **3.** (*on machine*) Schutzblech *n*; (*fire*) g., Kamingitter *n.* II. *v.tr.* **1.** (*a*) (Gefangene, ein Lager usw.) bewachen; (*b*) (*protect*) (einen Mechanismus, seinen Ruf usw.) schützen. **2.** *v.i.* **to g. against sth.,** sich vor etwas *dat* hüten. ◆'**guarded,** *adj.* behutsam; **g. answer,** vorsichtige Antwort. ◆'**guardian,** *s.* Vormund *m* (eines Minderjährigen); **g. angel,** Schutzengel *m.*

guer(r)illa [gə'rilə], *s.* Guerillakämpfer *m.*

guess [ges]. I. *s.* Vermutung *f*; **at a g.,** schätzungsweise. II. *v.tr.* **1.** (etwas) erraten. **2.** *v.i.* (*a*) raten; (*b*) *N. Am:* glauben, denken. ◆'**guesswork,** *s.* (reine) Vermutung *f.*

guest [gest], *s.* Gast *m.* ◆'**guesthouse,** *s.* Pension *f.*

guidance ['gaidəns], *s.* **1.** Leitung *f*; Führung *f.* **2.** (*a*) (*information*) Orientierung *f*; (*b*) (*advice*) Rat *m.* ◆'**guide.** I. *s.* **1.** (*pers.*) Führer *m*; **girl g.,** Pfadfinderin *f.* **2.** (*book*) travel g., Reiseführer *m.* **3.** (*guideline*) Richtlinie *f*; (*model*) Vorbild *n.* II. *v.tr.* (j-n) führen, leiten; (etwas) lenken. ◆'**guidebook,** *s.* Führer *m*; *esp.* (*travel*) g., Reiseführer *m.* ◆'**guided,** *adj.* **g. tour,** Führung *f* (durch ein Schloß usw.); (*b*) **g. missile,** Fernlenkgeschoß *n.* ◆'**guide-dog,** *s.* Blindenhund *m.* ◆'**guideline,** *s.* Richtlinie *f.*

guillotine [gilə'tiːn], *s.* Guillotine *f*; (*for paper*) Schneidemaschine *f.*

guilt [gilt], *s.* Schuld *f.* ◆'**guilty,** *adj.* schuldig (**of,** + *gen*); **g. conscience,** schlechtes Gewissen *n.*

guinea-pig ['ginipig], *s.* **1.** Meerschweinchen *n.* **2.** *F:* (*pers.*) Versuchskaninchen *n.*

guitar [gi'tɑːr], *s.* Gitarre *f.* ◆**gui'tarist,** *s.* Gitarrenspieler(in) *m(f).*

gulf [gʌlf], *s.* **1.** *Geog:* Golf *m.* **2.** *Fig:* Kluft *f.*

gull [gʌl], *s.* Möwe *f.*

gullible ['gʌləbl], *adj.* leichtgläubig.

gulp [gʌlp]. I. *s.* Schluck *m.* II. *v.tr.* **to g. sth. (down),** etwas hinunterschlucken.

gum¹ [gʌm]. I. *s.* **1.** (*adhesive*) Klebstoff

m. 2. (chewing) g., Kaugummi *m.* II.
v.tr. (a) (Papier) gummieren; (b) (etwas)
kleben (on/to, an + *acc*).
gum², *s.* Zahnfleisch *n.*

gun [gʌn]. I. *s.* 1. (a) (large) Geschütz *n;*
(b) (rifle) Gewehr *n;* (c) Revolver *m.* II.
v.tr. **to g. s.o. down,** j-n niederschießen.
◆**gunfire,** *s.* Geschützfeuer *n.*
◆**gunman,** *pl.* *-men,* *s.* bewaffneter
Bandit *m.* ◆**gunpoint,** *s.* **at g.,** (threatening) mit vorgehaltener Pistole.
◆**gunpowder,** *s.* Schießpulver *n.*
◆**gunshot,** *s.* Gewehrschuß *m;* g.-
wound, Schußwunde *f.*

gurgle [ˈɡɔːɡl], *v.i.* gluckern.

gush [gʌʃ], *v.i.* **to g. (out),** heraus-
strömen. ◆**gushing,** *adj.* (*of pers.,*
praise) überschwenglich.

gust [gʌst], *s.* Windstoß *m;* (at sea) Bö *f.*

gusto [ˈɡʌstəu], *s.* *F:* **with g.,** mit Genuß *m;*
(singing) aus voller Kehle.

gut [gʌt]. I. *s.* (a) Darm *m;* **guts,** Eingeweide *npl;* (b) *F:* **to have guts,** Schneid
haben. II. *v.tr.* (a) (Fisch, Geflügel) ausnehmen; (b) (of house) **gutted by fire,**
völlig ausgebrannt.

gutter [ˈɡʌtər], *s.* 1. Dachrinne *f.* 2. (in
street) Gosse *f;* Rinnstein *m; F:* g.-press,
Schmutzpresse *f.*

guttural [ˈɡʌtərəl], *adj.* kehlig.

guy [ɡai], *s.* *F:* Kerl *m.*

gym [dʒim], *s.* *F:* 1. Turnhalle *f.* 2. Turnen *n;* g. **shoes,** Turnschuhe *mpl.*
◆**gymnasium** [-ˈneiziəm], *s.* Turnhalle
f. ◆**gymnast** [-næst], *s.* Turner(in
m(f)). ◆**gym'nastics,** *s. pl.* Gymnastik
f, Turnen *n;* (in competition) Kunstturnen
n.

gynaecology [gaini'kɔlədʒi], *s.* Gynä-
kologie *f.* ◆**gynae'cologist,** *s.* Gynä-
kologe *m,* Frauenarzt *m,* Frauenärztin
f.

H

H, h [eitʃ], *s.* (der Buchstabe) H, h *n.*

haberdashery [ˈhæbədæʃəri], *s.* Kurz-
waren *fpl; N. Am:* Herrenartikel *mpl.*

habit [ˈhæbit], *s.* 1. Gewohnheit *f;* **to be
in the h. of doing sth.,** die Gewohnheit
haben/gewöhnt sein, etwas zu tun; **to get
into the h. (of doing sth.),** es sich *dat*
angewöhnen (, etwas zu tun). 2. *Ecc:* Habit *n.* ◆**habitual** [həˈbitjuəl], *adj.* gewohnt; (automatic) gewohnheitsmäßig;
-ly, *adv.* aus Gewohnheit; (constantly)
ständig.

habitable [ˈhæbitəbl], *adj.* bewohnbar.
◆**habitat,** *s.* Habitat *m.*

hack [hæk], *v.tr. & i.* (etwas) hacken; **to
h. sth. to pieces,** etwas zerhacken/in
Stücke hacken. ◆**hacking,** *adj.* h.
cough, trockener Husten.

hackneyed [ˈhæknid], *adj.* abgedroschen.

haddock [ˈhædək], *s.* Schellfisch *m.*

haemorrhage [ˈheməridʒ], *s.* Blutung *f.*

haggard [ˈhægəd], *adj.* abgezehrt; (from
worry) abgehärmt.

haggle [ˈhægl], *v.i.* feilschen (over,
um + *acc*).

Hague (the) [ðəˈheig]. *Pr.n.* Den Haag.

hail¹ [heil]. I. *s.* Hagel *m.* II. *v.i.* hageln.
◆**hailstone,** *s.* Hagelkorn *n.*

hail², *v.tr.* (a) (ein Taxi usw.) rufen;
(b) (greet) (j-n, etwas) begrüßen; *Fig:* he
was hailed as the new star, man feierte
ihn als den neuen Star. 2. *v.i.* **he hails
from X,** er stammt aus X.

hair [hɛər], *s.* (human) Haar *n;* coll. Haare *npl;* **to do one's h.,** sich frisieren; h.
dryer, Fön *m;* **by a h.'s breadth,** um
Haaresbreite. ◆**hairbrush,** *s.* Haarbür-
ste *f.* ◆**haircut,** *s.* Haarschnitt *m;* **to
have a h.,** sich *dat* die Haare schneiden
lassen. ◆**hairdo,** *s.* *F:* Frisur *f.*
◆**hairdresser,** *s.* Friseur *m,* Friseuse *f.*

◆**hairpin,** *s.* Haarnadel *f;* (in road) h.
bend, Haarnadelkurve *f.* ◆**hair-
raising,** *adj.* haarsträubend.
◆**hairspray,** *s.* Haarspray *n.*
◆**hairstyle,** *s.* Frisur *f.* ◆**hairy,** *adj.*
(a) behaart; (b) *F:* (of situation) brenzlig.

half, *pl.* **halves** [hɑːf, hɑːvz]. I. *s.* (a)
Hälfte *f;* **to cut sth. in h.,** etwas halbieren; (b) **one and a h.,** eineinhalb, ander-
halb; (c) *Fb: etc:* **the first h.,** die erste
Halbzeit. II. *adj.* halb; **h. an hour,** eine
halbe Stunde. III. *adv.* (a) halb; zur
Hälfte; **the glass was h. full,** das Glas
war halb voll; **not h.!** und wie! (b) **it's h.
past two,** es ist halb drei; (c) **h. as big,**
halb so groß. ◆**half-and'half,** *adv.*
halb und halb. ◆**half-brother,** *s.* Halb-
bruder *m.* ◆**half-caste,** *s.* *adj.* halbblü-
tig. II. *s.* Mischling *m.* ◆**half-'fare,** *s.*
halber Fahrpreis *m.* ◆**half-'hearted,**
adj. zaghaft; (of pers.) lustlos. ◆**half-
'hourly,** *adj. &. adv.* halbstündlich.
◆**halfpenny** [ˈheipni], *s.* *A:* halber Penny *m.* ◆**half-sister,** *s.* Halbschwester *f.*
◆**half-'term,** *s.* *Brit:* schulfreie Tage in
der Mitte eines Trimesters. ◆**half-
'time,** *s. Fb: etc:* Halbzeit *f.* ◆**half-
'way,** *adj. & adv.* 1. auf halbem Weg;
we have only got h.-w., wir
haben erst den halben Weg
zurückgelegt/(with work) nur die Hälfte
gemacht; *Fig:* **to meet s.o. h.-w.,** j-m
auf halbem Weg entgegenkommen; 2. *N.
Am:* **'halfway,** halbwegs; h. **decent,** eini-
germaßen anständig. ◆**halfwit,** *s.* Ein-
faltspinsel *m.*

halibut [ˈhælibət], *s.* Heilbutt *m.*

hall [hɔːl], *s.* 1. (for concerts etc.) Saal *m;*
(dining) h., Speisesaal *m.* 2. (entrance-)
h., Flur *m;* (large) Diele *f.* 3. **h. of residence,** Studentenheim *n.* ◆**hallmark,**

s. (a) (on gold, silver) Beschauzeichen n; (b) Fig: Kennzeichen n (eines Genies usw.).

hallo see **hello**.

hallowed ['hæləud], adj. geheiligt.

Hallowe'en ['hæləu'i:n], s. Abend m vor Allerheiligen.

hallucination [həlju:si'neiʃən], s. Halluzination f.

halo, pl. -oes ['heiləu, -əuz], s. Heiligenschein m.

halt [hɔːlt]. I. s. Stillstand m; Mil: etc: Halt m. II. v. 1. v.tr. (j-n, etwas) anhalten; (den Verkehr) zum Stehen bringen. 2. v.i. haltmachen; int. Mil: etc: halt! ◆**halting**, adj. zögernd.

halve [hɔːv], v.tr. (a) (cut in two) (etwas) halbieren; (b) (cut down) (etwas) um die Hälfte reduzieren.

ham [hæm], s. Cu: Schinken m. ◆**h. sandwich**, Schinkenbrot n. 2. F: (a) (actor), Kulissenreißer m; (b) (radio) h., Hobbyfunker m.

hamburger ['hæmbəːgər], s. Hamburger m.

hammer ['hæmər]. I. s. Hammer m. II. v. 1. v.tr. hämmern. 2. v.i. to h. at the door, an die Tür hämmern.

hammock ['hæmək], s. Hängematte f.

hamper ['hæmpər], v.tr. behindern.

hamster ['hæmstər], s. Hamster m.

hamstring ['hæmstriŋ], s. Kniesehne f.

hand [hænd]. I. s. 1. Hand f; hands up! Hände hoch! **hands off!** Hände weg! to give s.o. a h., j-m behilflich sein. 2. (a) (near) at h., nahe; the matter in h., die in Bearbeitung befindliche Sache; on the one h., einerseits; on the other h., andererseits; to get out of h., außer Kontrolle geraten; to win hands down, spielend gewinnen; to live from h. to mouth, von der Hand in den Mund leben. 3. (pers.) F: to be an old h. at sth., in etwas dat sehr geübt sein. 4. F: (applause) Beifall m; to give s.o. a big h., j-m begeistert Beifall spenden. 5. (in cards) to have a good/bad h., gute/schlechte Karten haben. 6. (of watch, clock) Zeiger m. II. v.tr. to h. sth. to s.o., j-m etwas reichen; F: you've got to hand it to him, das muß man ihm lassen. ◆**handbag**, s. Handtasche f. ◆**handbrake**, s. Handbremse f. ◆**handbook**, s. 1. (manual) Handbuch n. 2. (guide) Führer m. ◆**handcuff**, v.tr. (j-m) Handschellen anlegen. ◆**handcuffs**, s.pl. Handschellen fpl. ◆**handful**, s. Handvoll f. ◆**hand-grenade**, s. Mil: Handgranate f. ◆**hand 'in**, v.tr. (ein Paket usw.) abgeben; (ein Formular, ein Gesuch usw.) einreichen. ◆**handkerchief** ['hæŋkətʃiːf], s. Taschentuch n. ◆**hand-'made**, adj. handgemacht. ◆**hand 'out**, v.tr. austeilen. ◆**handout**, s. 1. (publicity) Werbezettel m. 2. (charity) Almosen n. ◆**hand 'over**, v.tr. (etwas) übergeben (to s.o.,

an j-n) . ◆**hand 'round**, v.tr. (eine Flasche usw.) herumreichen; (Bonbons usw.) austeilen. ◆**handshake**, s. Händedruck m. ◆**handwriting**, s. Handschrift f. ◆**handwritten**, adj. handgeschrieben. ◆**handy**, adj. 1. (a) (convenient) praktisch; zweckmäßig; (b) (of pers.) geschickt. 2. to keep sth. h., etwas zur Hand haben. ◆**handyman**, pl. -men, s. Mann m, der allerlei (kleine) Arbeiten verrichtet.

handicap ['hændikæp]. I. s. Handikap n; (mental or physical) Behinderung f; (disadvantage) Nachteil m. II. v.tr. to be mentally/physically handicapped, geistig/körperlich behindert sein.

handicraft ['hændikrɑːft], s. (a) (craft) Handwerk n; (b) (work) Handarbeit f; **handicrafts**, Handarbeiten fpl.

handle ['hændl]. I. s. (of tool, weapon etc.) Griff m; (of door) Klinke f; (of cup) Henkel m; (of broom etc.) Stiel m. II. v. 1. v.tr. (a) (etwas) handhaben; (touch) (etwas) anfassen, berühren; (b) (eine Angelegenheit) handhaben. 2. v.i. this car handles well/badly, der Wagen fährt sich gut/schwer. ◆**handlebar**, s. Lenkstange f.

handsome ['hænsəm], adj. (a) gutaussehend; (b) (of reward etc.) großzügig.

hang [hæŋ]. I. v.irr. 1. v.tr. (a) (etwas) hängen (on/from sth., an etwas acc); to h. (down) one's head, den Kopf hängen lassen; (b) (p. & p.p. hanged) (einen Verbrecher) hängen; to h. oneself, sich erhängen. 2. v.i. (a) hängen (on/from sth., an etwas dat); (b) (of criminal) gehängt werden. II. s. F: to get the h. of sth., kapieren, wie etwas funktioniert/wie man etwas macht. ◆**hang a'bout/a'round**, v.i. herumstehen; F: herumlungern; (wait) warten. ◆**hang 'back**, v.i. zurückbleiben; (hesitate) zögern. ◆**hang 'down**, v.i. herunterhängen. ◆**hanger**, s. (a) (on coat etc.) Aufhänger m; (b) (for coat etc.) Kleiderbügel m. ◆**hanger-'on**, s. (pers.) Pol: etc: Mitläufer m. ◆**hang-glider**, s. Drachenflieger m. ◆**hang-gliding**, s. Drachenfliegen n. ◆**hanging**, s. (execution) Hinrichtung f am Galgen. ◆**hang 'on**, v.i. (a) sich festhalten (to sth., an etwas dat); to h. on to one's job, seine Stelle behalten; (b) (persevere, wait) can you h. on until I come? kannst du warten, bis ich komme? F: h. on! Moment mal! ◆**hang 'out**, v.tr. (Wäsche usw.) (draußen) aufhängen. ◆**hangover**, s. F: Kater m. ◆**hang 'up**, v. 1. v.tr. (a) (etwas) aufhängen; (b) P: hung up, gehemmt. 2. v.i. Tel: F: auflegen. ◆**hangup**, s. F. Komplex m.

hangar ['hæŋər], s. Hangar m.

hanker ['hæŋkər], v.i. sich sehnen (after sth., nach etwas dat).

haphazard [hæp'hæzəd], adj. willkürlich; (accidental) zufällig.

happen ['hæpən], v.i. (a) (of accident etc.) passieren; (of event etc.) geschehen; (b) what's happened to him? was ist mit ihm passiert/aus ihm geworden? to know whether ... ? wissen Sie zufällig, ob ..? as it happens, zufälligerweise; (d) to h. upon sth., (zufällig) auf etwas acc stoßen; (e) (take place) stattfinden. ◆'happening, s. Ereignis n.

happy ['hæpi], adj. (a) glücklich; (b) (satisfied) zufrieden; -ily, adv. glücklich; (luckily) glücklicherweise. ◆'happiness, s. Glück n.

harass ['hærəs], v.tr. (j-n) plagen; (mentally) quälen.

harbour ['hɑːbər]. I. s. Hafen m. II. v.tr. (a) (einem Verbrecher usw.) Obdach gewähren; (b) Fig: (Gefühle) hegen.

hard [hɑːd]. I. adj. 1. (of pers.) hart. 2. (difficult) schwer; h. of hearing, schwerhörig. 3. (a) to be h. on s.o., streng mit j-m sein; (b) h. facts, nackte Tatsachen fpl; h. luck, Pech n. II. adv. 1. (a) (with effort) kräftig; to try h./harder, sich dat große/mehr Mühe geben; to think h., scharf nachdenken; to work h./be h. at work, schwer arbeiten; it's raining h., es regnet heftig/stark; (b) F: to be h. up, knapp bei Kasse sein. 2. schwer; h. earned wages, schwer/sauer verdienter Lohn. ◆'hardboard, s. Hartfaserplatte f. ◆'hard-'boiled, adj. hartgekocht. ◆'harden, v.tr. (a) (Metalle, Fette usw.) härten; (b) (of pers.) to h. oneself, sich abhärten; hardened to sth., an etwas acc gewöhnt. 2. v.i. hart werden. ◆'hard-'hearted, adj. hartherzig. ◆'hardly, adv. kaum. ◆'hardness, s. Härte f. ◆'hardship, s. Not f; (privation) Entbehrung f. ◆'hardware, s. 1. Haushaltswaren fpl. 2. Tchn: Hardware f. ◆'hard-'wearing, adj. (of material etc.) dauerhaft; (of clothes etc.) strapazierfähig. ◆'hard-'won, adj. schwer erkämpft. ◆'hard-'working, adj. fleißig. ◆'hardy, adj. (of pers.) abgehärtet; (b) (of plant) ausdauernd; mehrjährig.

hare ['hɛər], s. Z: Hase m. ◆'harelip, s. Hasenscharte f.

harm [hɑːm]. I. s. Schaden m; out of h.'s way, in Sicherheit. II. v.tr. (j-m, etwas dat) schaden. ◆'harmless, adj. harmlos. ◆'harmful, adj. schädlich.

harmony ['hɑːməni], s. Harmonie f. ◆har'monious, adj. harmonisch. ◆'harmonize. 1. v.tr. (eine Melodie) harmonisieren. 2. v.i. (of colour etc.) harmonieren (with sth., mit etwas dat).

harness ['hɑːnis]. I. s. (of horse etc.) Geschirr n. II. v.tr. (a) (ein Pferd usw.) anschirren; (b) (Wasserkraft) nutzbar machen.

harp [hɑːp], s. Harfe f.

harpoon [hɑː'puːn], s. Harpune f.

harrowing ['hærouiŋ], adj. grauenvoll.

harsh [hɑːʃ], adj. 1. (of texture, sound etc.) rauh; (of colour) grell. 2. (of pers., Jur: sentence etc.) hart. ◆'harshness, s. 1. Rauheit f. 2. Härte f.

harvest ['hɑːvist]. I. s. Ernte f. II. v.tr. ernten. ◆'harvester, s. combine h., Mähdrescher m.

hash [hæʃ], s. 1. F: to make a h. of sth., etwas vermasseln/verpfuschen. 2. F: (drug) Hasch n.

hassle ['hæsəl], s. F: Ärger m.

haste [heist], s. Eile f. ◆'hasten, v.i. eilen, sich beeilen. ◆'hasty, adj. (of departure) hastig; (of decision) übereilt.

hat [hæt], s. Hut m; that's old h., das sind olle Kamellen.

hatch¹ [hætʃ], s. 1. Nau: etc: Luke f. 2. service f. ◆'hatchback, s. Wagen m mit Hecktür.

hatch², v. 1. v.tr. (Eier, Fig: einen Plan) ausbrüten. 2. v.i. to h. (out), ausschlüpfen.

hatchet ['hætʃit], s. Beil n; to bury the h., das Kriegsbeil begraben.

hate [heit]. I. s. Haß m. II. v.tr. (a) (j-n, etwas) hassen; (b) to h. to do sth., etwas sehr ungern tun. ◆'hateful, adj. hassenswert. ◆'hatred, s. Haß m (for/of s.o., sth., gegen j-n, etwas acc).

haughty ['hɔːti], adj. hochmütig.

haul [hɔːl]. I. v.tr. ziehen, (with effort) schleppen. II. s. 1. (of robber) Beute f. 2. (distance) Strecke f. ◆'haulage, s. 1. Spedition f; h. contractor, Spediteur m. 2. (cost) Frachtkosten fpl. ◆'haulier, s. Spediteur m.

haunt [hɔːnt]. I. s. Lieblingsaufenthalt m. II. v.tr. this house is haunted, in diesem Haus spukt es; (of pers.) to be haunted by memories (of sth.), von Erinnerungen (an etwas acc) verfolgt werden.

have [hæv], v.tr.irr. haben; F: he had it, mit ihm ist es aus; to h. sth. done, etwas machen lassen; to h. to do sth., etwas tun müssen; I h. come, ich bin gekommen; he has burnt it, er hat es verbrannt; I h. lived in London for three years, ich wohne seit drei Jahren in London; I had better say nothing, ich sage lieber nichts. ◆'have 'in, v.tr. to h. it in for s.o., es auf j-n abgesehen haben. ◆'have 'on, v.tr. (a) to h. a coat on, einen Mantel anhaben; to h. nothing on, unbekleidet sein; (b) I h. nothing on tonight, ich bin heute abend frei; what do you h. on this evening? was haben Sie heute abend auf dem Programm? (c) F: to h. s.o. on, F: j-n anführen. ◆'have 'out, v.tr. to h. it out with s.o., j-n zur Rede stellen. ◆'have 'up, v.tr. F: to be had up for sth., wegen etwas gen vors Gericht kommen.

haven ['heivn], s. (a) Hafen m; (b) (refuge) Zufluchtsort m.

haversack ['hævəsæk], s. Rucksack m.

havoc ['hævək], s. Chaos n; Fig: to cause

h., eine verheerende Wirkung haben.
hawk [hɔːk], s. Falke m.
hawthorn ['hɔːθɔːn], s. Hagedorn m.
hay [hei], s. Heu n. ◆**'hay-fever**, s. Heuschnupfen m. ◆**'haystack**, s. Heuschober m. ◆**'haywire**, adj. F: durcheinander; to go h., durcheinandergeraten.
hazard ['hæzəd]. I. s. Gefahr f (to health etc.) für die Gesundheit usw.); (risk) Risiko n. II. v.tr. (etwas) riskieren. ◆**'hazardous**, adj. riskant.
haze [heiz], s. Dunst m. ◆**'hazy**, adj. (of weather etc.) dunstig; Fig: (of ideas etc.) unklar.
hazel-nut ['heizlnʌt], s. Haselnuß f.
he [hiː], pers. pron. er.

head [hed]. I. s. 1. Kopf m; they put their heads together, sie steckten die Köpfe zusammen; it's above my h., das geht über meinen Verstand; to keep one's h., den Kopf nicht verlieren. 2. Spitze f (eines Zuges usw.); Kopfende n (eines Tisches, eines Betts); (on beer) Blume f; at the h. of the list, (ganz) oben auf der Liste; Fig: to come to a h., sich zuspitzen. 3. (a) (pers.) Oberhaupt n (einer Familie); Sch: Direktor(in) m(f); (b) attrib. Haupt-; h. office, Hauptsitz m; h. waiter, Oberkellner m. 4. thirty h. of cattle, dreißig Stück Vieh; to pay so much per h./a h., soundsoviel pro Person zahlen. 6. (of coin) heads or tails? Kopf oder Wappen? F: I can't make h. or tail of this, daraus werde ich nicht schlau. II. v. 1. v.tr. (a) (lead) (eine Partei, Kolonne usw.) anführen; (b) h. the ball, den Ball köpfen. 2. v.i. to h. for sth., auf etwas acc zugehen/Naut: & Fig: zusteuern. ◆**'headache**, Kopfschmerzen mpl. ◆**'header**, s. Fb: Kopfball m ◆**'head-'first**, adv. kopfüber. ◆**'heading**, s. Überschrift f (of letter) Briefkopf m. ◆**'headlamp, 'headlight**, s. Scheinwerfer m. ◆**'headline**, s. Schlagzeile f; to hit the headlines, Schlagzeilen machen. ◆**'headlong**, adv. kopfüber. ◆**'head'master**, s. Schulleiter m. ◆**'head'mistress**, s. Schulleiterin f. ◆**'head-'on**, adj. frontal. ◆**'headphones**, s.pl. Kopfhörer m. ◆**'head'quarters**, s.pl. 1. Mil: Hauptquartier n. 2. (of bank, police etc.) Zentrale f. ◆**'headrest**, s. Kopfstütze f. ◆**'headscarf**, s. Kopftuch n. ◆**'headstrong**, adj. eigenwillig. ◆**'headway**, s. to make h., Fortschritte machen.
heal [hiːl], v.tr. & i. heilen.
health [helθ], s. 1. Gesundheit f; h. foods, Reformkost f; h. food store, Reformhaus n; h. insurance, Krankenversicherung f; h. resort, Kurort m. 2. to drink (to) the h. of s.o., auf j-s Wohl trinken. ◆**'healthy**, adj. gesund.
heap [hiːp]. I. s. (a) Haufen m; (b) F: pl. (large number) jede Menge f; heaps of time, jede Menge Zeit. II. v.tr. (Sachen)

aufhäufen; **to h. s.o.'s plate with straw-berries**, Erdbeeren auf j-s Teller häufen; **heaped spoonful**, gehäufter Löffel; Fig: **to h. praises/insults on s.o.**, j-n mit Lob/Beleidigungen überschütten.
hear [hiər], v.tr. 1. v.tr. (a) hören; (b) (listen to) (j-m) zuhören. 2. v.i. (a) to h. from s.o., von j-m hören; (b) to h. of/about sth., etwas erfahren; to have heard of s.o., von j-m gehört haben; father won't h. of it, Vater will nichts davon wissen. ◆**'hearing**, s. (a) Jur: etc: Verhandlung f; (b) Gehör n; h. aid, Hörgerät n. ◆**'hearsay**, s. Hörensagen n.
hearse [həːs], s. Leichenwagen m.
heart [hɑːt], s. Herz n. 1. h. attack, Herzanfall m; at h., im Grunde; to have a change of h., seine Meinung ändern; I did not have the h. to disturb him, ich konnte es nicht über mich bringen, ihn zu stören; F: have a h.! sei nicht so! to take h., sich dat ein Herz fassen; to lose h., den Mut verlieren; to know sth. by h., etwas auswendig können. 2. (core) das h. of the matter, der Kern der Sache; in the h. of, im Herzen + gen. 3. (in cards) hearts, Herz n. ◆**'heartbeat**, s. Herzschlag m ◆**'heartbreaking**, adj. herzzerreißend. ◆**'heartbroken**, adj. untröstlich. ◆**'heartburn**, s. Sodbrennen n. ◆**'hearten**, v.tr. (j-n) ermutigen. ◆**'heartfelt**, adj. herzlich. ◆**'heartless**, adj. herzlos. ◆**'heartrending**, adj. herzzerreißend. ◆**'hearty**, adj. 1. (of feeling etc.) herzlich. 2. (of meal, appetite) herzhaft; -ily, adv. 1. herzlich. 2. herzhaft (empfinden). 2. herzhaft (essen).
hearth [hɑːθ], s. Herd m.
heat [hiːt]. I. s. 1. Wärme f; (intense) Hitze f. 2. it happened in the h. of the moment, es geschah in der Hitze des Gefechts. 3. Sp: (i) (in sprinting etc.) Vorlauf m; (ii) (in swimming etc.) Runde f. II. v.tr. (a) (etwas) heiß machen; (Wasser, Metall usw.) erhitzen; (ein Zimmer usw.) heizen. ◆**'heated**, adj. (a) (of water etc.) erhitzt; (b) (of room etc.) geheizt; (c) (of discussion) hitzig. ◆**'heater**, s. Heizgerät n; (in car etc.) Heizanlage f. ◆**'heating**, s. Heizung f. ◆**'heatwave**, s. Hitzewelle f.
heath [hiːθ], s. Heide f.
heathen ['hiːðən]. I. adj. heidnisch. II. s. Heide m; Heidin f.
heather ['heðər], s. Heidekraut n.
heave [hiːv], v. 1. v.tr. (a) (lift) (eine Last) (mit großer Anstrengung) heben; (b) to h. a sigh, einen Seufzer ausstoßen. 2. v.i. (a) (of sea, breast) sich heben (und senken); (b) to h. at a rope, an einem Tau ziehen.
heaven ['hev(ə)n], s. Himmel m; for h.'s sake, um Himmels willen; h. knows where it is, der Himmel weiß wo das ist. ◆**'heavenly**, adj. himmlisch.

heavy ['hevi], adj. (a) schwer; (b) (of traffic, eating etc.) stark; (c) (of style, tread) schwerfällig; -ily, adv. schwer; to **sleep h.**, tief schlafen. ◆**'heavyweight.** Sp: I. adj. Schwergewichts-. II. s. Schwergewichtler m.

Hebrew ['hi:bru:]. I. adj. hebräisch. II. s. (language) Hebräisch n.

heckle ['hekl], v.tr. (den Redner) (durch Zwischenrufe) unterbrechen. ◆**'heckler**, s. Zwischenrufer m.

hectic ['hektik], adj. hektisch.

hedge [hedʒ]. I. s. Hecke f. II. v.i. Ausreden suchen. ◆**'hedgehog**, s. Igel m.

heed [hi:d]. I. v.tr. beachten. II. s. to **take h. of s.o., sth.**, j-m, etwas dat Beachtung schenken.

heel [hi:l]. I. s. (a) Ferse f; (of shoe) Absatz m; **down at h.**, heruntergekommen. II. v.tr. to **h. a shoe**, einen Absatz an einen Schuh machen.

hefty ['hefti], adj. F: (of pers.) stämmig; (of blow) schwer; **a h. sum**, eine saftige Summe.

height [hait], s. 1. (a) Höhe f; (b) (of pers.) Größe f. 2. Fig: Höhepunkt m (einer Karriere usw.). **the h. of fashion**, die neueste Mode.

heir ['ɛər], s. Erbe m. ◆**'heiress**, s. Erbin f. ◆**'heirloom**, s. Erbstück n.

helicopter ['helikɔptər], s. Hubschrauber m.

helium ['hi:ljəm], s. Helium n.

hell [hel], s. Hölle f; **what the h. do you want?** was zum Teufel wollen Sie? **oh h.!** verdammt! ◆**'hellish**, adj. teuflisch; -ly, adv. F: **h. difficult**, verdammt schwierig.

hello ['heləu], int. (a) (guten) Tag/Morgen/Abend; (b) Tel: hallo.

helm [helm], s. Ruder n.

helmet ['helmit], s. Helm m.

help [help]. I. s. Hilfe f. II. v.tr. (a) (j-m) helfen; **h. yourself**, bedienen Sie sich; (b) **if I can h. it**, wenn ich es vermeiden kann; **I can't h. it**, ich kann nichts dafür; **I couldn't h. laughing**, ich mußte lachen. ◆**'helper**, s. Helfer(in) m(f). ◆**'helpful**, adj. (a) (of pers.) hilfsbereit; (b) (of advice etc.) nützlich. ◆**'helping.** I. adj. to **lend** (s.o.) **a h. hand**, j-m dat behilflich sein. II. s. Portion f (einer Speise). ◆**'helpless**, adj. hilflos. ◆**'helplessness**, s. Hilflosigkeit f. ◆**'help out**, v.tr. (j-m) aushelfen.

hem [hem]. I. s. Saum m. II. v.tr. (a) (ein Kleid) säumen; (b) to **h. in**, (j-n, etwas) umzingeln.

hemisphere ['hemisfiər], s. Hemisphäre f.

hen [hen], s. 1. (fowl) Huhn n. 2. (female) Henne f) **h. party**, Damengesellschaft f. ◆**'henpecked**, adj. F: **h. husband**, Pantoffelheld m.

hence [hens], adv. 1. (from now) **five years h.**, in fünf Jahren. 2. (thus) daher.

hepatitis [hepə'taitis], s. Leberentzündung f.

her [hər, hə:r]. I. pers. pron. 1. (object) (a) acc sie; for **h.**, für sie; (b) dat ihr; **give h. this**, gib ihr das. 2. **it's h.**, sie ist es. II. poss. adj. ihr.

heraldry ['herəldri], s. Heraldik f.

herb [hə:b], s. (a) Bot: Kraut n; (b) Cu: Gewürz n. ◆**'herbal**, adj. Kräuter-; **h. remedy**, Kräuterkur f.

herd [hə:d]. I. s. Herde f. II. v.tr. (Vieh usw.) hüten.

here [hiər], adv. hier. **h. goes!** also los! **h. you are**, das ist für Sie; **h. we are**, da sind wir; **that's neither h. nor there**, das ist völlig belanglos.

hereditary [hi'reditri], adj. erblich.

heresy ['herəsi], s. Ketzerei f. ◆**'heretic**, s. Ketzer m.

heritage ['heritidʒ], s. Erbe n.

hermit ['hə:mit], s. Einsiedler m.

hernia ['hə:niə], s. Bruch m.

hero, pl. -oes ['hiərəu, -əuz], s. Held m. ◆**heroic** [hə'rəuik], adj. heldenhaft. ◆**heroine** ['herəuin], s. Heldin f. ◆**'heroism**, s. Heldentum n.

heroin ['herəuin], s. Heroin n.

heron ['herən], s. Reiher m.

herring ['heriŋ], s. Hering m; F: **a red h.**, eine falsche Fährte.

hers [hə:z], poss. pron. ihrer, ihre, ihres; pl. ihre.

herself [hə:'self], pers. pron. (a) selbst; (b) (refl.) sich.

hesitate ['heziteit], v.i. zögern. ◆**'hesitant**, adj. zögernd. ◆**hesi'tation**, s. Zögern n.

hey-day ['heidei], s. Blütezeit f; Glanzzeit f.

hibernate ['haibəneit], v.i. Winterschlaf halten. ◆**hiber'nation**, s. Winterschlaf m.

hiccup, hiccough ['hikʌp]. I. s. 1. Schluckauf m. 2. F: (hitch) Stockung f. II. v.i. Schluckauf haben.

hide[1] [haid], v.tr. 1. v.tr. (j-n, etwas) verstecken (**from s.o.**, vor j-m). 2. v.i. sich verstecken. ◆**'hide-and-'seek**, s. Versteckspiel n. ◆**'hide-out**, s. Versteck m. ◆**'hiding**[1], s. to **go into h.**, sich verstecken; to **be in h.**, sich versteckt halten; **h. place**, Versteck n.

hide[2], s. (skin) Haut f. ◆**'hiding**[2], to **give s.o. a h.**, j-n verdreschen.

hideous ['hidiəs], adj. (ugly) scheußlich; (of crime, noise etc.) gräßlich.

hierarchy ['haiərɑ:ki], s. Hierarchie f.

high [hai]. I. adj. hoch; **a wall two metres h.** eine zwei Meter hohe Mauer; **h. jump**, Hochsprung m; Fig: **it's h. time he started school**, es ist höchste Zeit, daß er in die Schule kommt; -ly, adv. to **think h. of s.o.**, j-n sehr schätzen. 2. **h. amusing**, höchst amüsant; **h. paid**, sehr gut bezahlt. 3. **h. strung**, überempfindlich. II. adv. hoch; **feelings ran h.**, die Gemüter erhitzten sich. ◆**'high-'heeled**, adj. mit hohen Absätzen. ◆**'highlands**, s.pl. **the H. of Scotland**, das Schottische Hochland. ◆'high-'level, *attrib. adj.* (Besprechung usw.) auf höchster Ebene. ◆'highlight. I. *s.* 1. (*in hair*) helle Strähne *f.* 2. Höhepunkt *m* (von etwas). II. *v.tr.* hervorheben. ◆'Highness, *s.* His H., Seine Hoheit *f.* ◆'high-'pitched, *adj.* (*of voice*) hoch; (*of scream*) schrill. ◆'high-'ranking, *adj.* ranghoch. ◆'high-'rise, *adj.* h.-r. flats, Hochhäuser *npl.* ◆'highway, *s.* Landstraße *f;* N.Am: Schnellstraße *f;* the H. Code, die Straßenverkehrsordnung.

hijack ['haidʒæk], *v.tr.* entführen. ◆'hijacker, *s.* Entführer *m;* (*of aircraft*) Luftpirat *m.* ◆'hijacking, *s.* Entführung *f* (eines Flugzeuges usw.).

hike [haik]. I. *s.* Wanderung *f.* II. *v.i.* wandern. ◆'hiker, *s.* Wanderer *m.* ◆'hiking, *s.* Wandern *n.*

hilarious [hi'lɛəriəs], *adj.* urkomisch. ◆hilarity [-'læriti], *s.* Gelächter *n.*

hill [hil], *s.* 1. Hügel *m.* 2. (*incline*) Steigung *f.* ◆'hillside, *s.* Hang *m.* ◆'hilly, *adj.* hügelig.

hilt [hilt], *s.* Griff *m* (eines Schwertes usw.); Fig: to the h., voll und ganz.

him [him], *pers. pron. object.* 1. (*a*) (acc) ihn; for h., für ihn; (*b*) (dat) ihm; give h. this, gib ihm das. 2. it's h., er ist es. ◆him'self, *pers. pron.* (*a*) selbst; (*b*) (*refl.*) sich.

hind [haind], *adj.* h. leg, Hinterbein *n.* ◆'hindsight, *s.* verspätete Einsicht *f;* with h., rückblickend.

hinder ['hindər], *v.tr.* (j-n, etwas) hindern; (eine Entwicklung) hemmen. ◆'hindrance, *s.* Hindernis *n.*

Hindi ['hindi:], *s.* (*language*) Hindi *n.* ◆'Hindu [hin'du]. I. *s.* (*pers.*) Hindu *m.* II. *adj.* Hindu-. ◆'Hinduism, *s.* Hinduismus *m.*

hinge [hindʒ]. I. *s.* Scharnier *n;* (*large*) Angel *f* (einer Tür usw.). II. *v.i.* abhängen (on sth., von etwas *dat*).

hint [hint]. I. *s.* 1. (*a*) Wink *m;* to drop a h., eine Andeutung fallen lassen; (*b*) (*tip*) Hinweis *m.* II. *v.i.* to h. at sth., auf etwas *acc* anspielen.

hip [hip], *s.* Hüfte *f.*

hippopotamus, *pl.* -muses, -mi [hipə'pɔtəməs, -masiz, -mai], *s.* Nilpferd *n.*

hire ['haiər]. I. *s.* (*action*) Verleih *m;* h. car, Mietwagen *m;* for h., zu mieten; (*of taxi*) frei; h. purchase, Ratenkauf *m;* to buy sth. on h. purchase, etwas auf Raten/Abzahlung kaufen. II. *v.tr.* (*a*) (ein Auto, einen Saal usw.) mieten; (Arbeiter usw.) einstellen; (*b*) to h. out, verleihen.

his [hiz]. I. *poss. adj.* sein(e). II. *poss. pron.* seiner, seine, seines; *pl.* seine; this is h., das ist seins.

hiss [his]. I. Zischen *n.* II. *v.tr. & i.* zischen.

history ['hist(ə)ri], *s.* Geschichte *f.* ◆historian [-'tɔːriən], *s.* Historiker(in) *m(f).* ◆historic [-'tɔrik], *adj.* historisch.

◆his'torical, *adj.* geschichtlich.

hit [hit]. I. *v.irr.* 1. *v.tr.* (*a*) (j-n) schlagen; (*b*) (*missile, stone etc.*) (j-n, etwas) treffen; hard h. by financial losses, durch finanzielle Verluste schwer getroffen. II. *s.* 1. (*a*) Schlag *m;* direct h., Volltreffer *m;* (*b*) F: (*song, play*) Hit *m.* ◆'hit 'off, *v.tr.* to h. it off with s.o., mit j-m gut auskommen. ◆'hit 'on, *v.tr.* to h. on an idea, auf eine Idee kommen. ◆'hit 'out, *v.i.* Fig: to h. o. at s.o., sth., über j-n, etwas *acc* herziehen.

hitch [hitʃ]. I. *s.* Störung *f;* to go without a h., reibungslos/ F: wie geschmiert gehen; technical h., Panne *f.* II. *v.tr.* (*a*) to h. sth. (on) to sth., etwas an etwas *acc* festknüpfen; (*b*) to h. (up) one's trousers, sich *dat* die Hose hochziehen. ◆'hitch-hike, *v.i.* trampen, per Anhalter fahren. ◆'hitch-hiker, *s.* Tramper *m.*

hive [haiv], *s.* (bee)h., Bienenkorb *m.*

hoard [hɔːd]. I. *s.* Hort *m.* II. *v.tr.* horten.

hoarding ['hɔːdiŋ], *s.* Bauzaun *m;* advertisement h., Reklamewand *f.*

hoarse [hɔːs], *adj.* heiser.

hoax [həuks], *s.* (*false alarm*) blinder Alarm *m;* (*false report*) Ente *f.*

hobble ['hɔbl], *v.i.* humpeln.

hobby ['hɔbi], *s.* Hobby *n.*

hockey ['hɔki], *s.* Hockey *n.*

hoe [həu]. I. *s.* Hacke *f.* II. *v.tr. & i.* hacken.

hog [hɔg]. I. *s.* (*pig*) Schwein *n;* Fig: to go the whole h., aufs Ganze gehen. II. *v.tr.* F: to h. sth., auf etwas *dat* sitzen.

hoist [hɔist], *v.tr.* (eine Fahne, Flagge) hissen; (*b*) to h. sth. (up), etwas hochziehen.

hold [həuld]. I. *v.irr.* 1. *v.tr.* (*a*) (j-n, etwas) halten; (*b*) (*contain*) fassen; (*c*) (*conduct*) (eine Sitzung, Ausstellung usw.) abhalten; (ein Fest usw.) veranstalten; (*d*) (den Atem) anhalten; h. it! halt! Moment! (*e*) (*consider*) to h. s.o. responsible, j-n verantwortlich machen; to h. (the view) that ..., die Meinung vertreten, daß ...; (*f*) (*possess*) (einen Titel, Land, Aktien) haben; to h. an office, ein Amt bekleiden. 2. *v.i.* (*a*) (*of glue, rope etc.*) halten; (*b*) (*of weather*) anhalten; to h. good (for sth.), (für etwas *acc*) gelten. II. *s.* Halt *m;* to have a h. over s.o., j-n in seiner Hand haben; to take h. of sth., etwas fassen; F: to get h. of sth., etwas aufreißen; to get h. of s.o., (*on phone etc.*) j-n erreichen. ◆'hold-all, *s.* Reisetasche *f.* ◆'hold 'back, *v.tr.* (etwas) zurückhalten. 2. *v.i.* sich zurückhalten. ◆'holder, *s.* 1. (*pers.*) Inhaber *m* (einer Karte, Lizenz); Träger *m* (eines Titels usw.). 2. (*device*) Halter *m.* ◆'hold 'off, *v.tr.* (den Feind) abwehren. 2. *v.i.* (*of rain etc.*) ausbleiben. ◆'hold 'on, *v.i.* to h. on to sth., sich an etwas *dat* festhalten. h. on! (i) festhalten! (ii) F: (warten Sie) einen Augenblick. ◆'hold 'out, v. 1. v.tr. (etwas) hinhalten. 2. v.i. durchhalten. ◆'hold 'up, v. 1. v.tr. (a) (die Hand usw.) hochheben; (b) (delay) (den Verkehr usw.) aufhalten; (c) (of robber) (j-n) überfallen. 2. v.i. (of story, evidence) stichhaltig sein. ◆'hold-up, s. 1. Stockung f (des Verkehrs usw.). 2. Überfall m (auf j-n, eine Bank usw.).

hold², s. Laderaum m (eines Schiffes).

hole [houl], s. Loch n.

holiday ['holidei], s. (a) (public) h., Feiertag m; to take a h., (i) sich dat einen Tag frei nehmen; (ii) Urlaub machen; (b) (period) Urlaub m; (esp. school) holidays, Ferien pl; on h., auf Urlaub. ◆'holidaymaker, s. Urlauber m.

Holland ['holənd]. Pr. n. Holland n.

hollow ['holəu], adj. hohl.

holly ['holi], s. Stechpalme f.

holster ['houlstər], s. Pistolentasche f.

holy ['houli], adj. heilig.

homage ['homidʒ], s. Huldigung f; to pay h. to s.o., j-m huldigen.

home [houm]. I. s. 1. (a) Heim n; (b) at h., zu Hause; make yourself at h., fühlen Sie sich wie zu Hause. 2. (birthplace) Heimat f. 3. (institution or place) Heim n; old people's h., Altersheim n. II. adv. 1. nach Hause. 2. to bring sth. h. to s.o., j-m etwas klarmachen. III. adj. 1. h. address, Privatadresse f; h. help, Haushaltshilfe f; h. game, Heimspiel n; h. truth, ungeschminkte Wahrheit. 2. h. affairs, innere Angelegenheiten fpl; Brit: H. Office, Innenministerium n; H. Secretary, Innenminister m; H. Secretary, Innenminister m. ◆'homeland, s. Heimatland n. ◆'homeless, adj. obdachlos. ◆'homely, adj. 1. (of house, pers.) gemütlich; (of food) bürgerlich. 2. N. Am: (of pers.) unscheinbar. ◆'home-'made, adj. (of food) hausgemacht; (of object) selbstgemacht; (amateurish) (selbst) gebastelt. ◆'homesick, adj. she's h., sie hat Heimweh. ◆'homesickness, s. Heimweh n. ◆'homework, s. Hausaufgaben fpl.

homicide ['homisaid], s. Totschlag m; (murder) Mord m. ◆homi'cidal, adj. mörderisch.

homosexual [homəu'seksjuəl]. I. adj. homosexuell. II. s. Homosexuelle(r) m.

honest ['onist], adj. aufrichtig; (of pers., intentions) ehrlich; an h. opinion, eine offene Meinung; -ly, adv. ehrlich; int. h.! wirklich! ◆'honesty, s. Ehrlichkeit f.

honey ['hani], s. Honig m. ◆'honeycomb, s. Honigwabe f. ◆'honeymoon, s. (period) Flitterwochen fpl; (trip) Hochzeitsreise f. ◆'honeysuckle, s. Geißblatt n.

honorary ['onərəri], adj. (of position) ehrenamtlich.

honour ['onər]. I. s. 1. Ehre f; in s.o.'s h., zu j-s Ehren; word of h., Ehrenwort n. 2. (award, medal etc.) Auszeichnung f.

II. v.tr. ehren. ◆'honourable, adj. ehrenhaft.

hood [hud], s. 1. Kapuze f. 2. Aut: N. Am: Kühlerhaube f.

hoof, pl. -s, hooves [hu:f, -s, hu:vz], s. Huf m.

hook [huk]. I. s. Haken m. II. v.tr. (a) to h. sth. to sth., etwas an etwas acc festhaken; (b) (einen Fisch usw.) angeln. ◆'hooked, adj. F: to be h. on sth., etwas dat verfallen sein.

hooligan ['hu:ligən], s. Rowdy m.

hoop [hu:p], s. Reifen m.

hoot [hu:t], v.i. (a) (of owl etc.) rufen; (b) Aut: hupen. ◆'hooter, s. Sirene f (einer Fabrik); Aut: Hupe f.

hoover ['hu:vər]. I. s. R.t.m. Staubsauger m. II. v.tr. & i. (mit dem Staubsauger) saugen.

hop¹ [hop], s. Bot: Hopfen m.

hop² [hop], s. Hüpfer m. II. v.i. hüpfen. ◆'hopping, adj. F: h. mad, wütend.

hope [houp]. I. v.tr. & i. hoffen; to h. for sth., auf etwas acc hoffen. II. s. Hoffnung f; (prospect) Aussicht f. ◆'hopeful, adj. hoffnungsvoll; -ly, adv. hoffentlich. ◆'hopeless, adj. hoffnungslos; (of situation) aussichtslos. ◆'hopelessness, s. Hoffnungslosigkeit f.

horde [ho:d], s. Horde f.

horizon [hə'raiz(ə)n], s. Horizont m.

horizontal [hori'zont(ə)l], adj. horizontal.

hormone ['ho:məun], s. Hormon n.

horn [ho:n], s. 1. (of animal) Horn n. 2. Mus: (French) h., Horn n. 3. Aut: Hupe f.

hornet ['ho:nit], s. Hornisse f.

horoscope ['horəskəup], s. Horoskop n.

horrible ['horibl], adj. schrecklich.

horrid ['horid], adj. scheußlich.

horrify ['horifai], v.tr. entsetzen. ◆ho'rrific, adj. gruselig. ◆horror ['horər], s. Entsetzen n; h. story, Schauergeschichte f; h. film, Horrorfilm m.

horse [ho:s], s. Pferd n; h. racing, Pferderennen n. ◆'horseback, s. on h., zu Pferde. ◆'horseman, s. Reiter m. ◆'horsewoman, s. Reiterin f. ◆'horseplay, s. Herumalbern n. ◆'horsepower, s. Pferdestärke f (abbr. PS). ◆'horseradish, s. Meerrettich m. ◆'horseshoe, s. Hufeisen n.

horticulture ['ho:tikaltʃər], s. Gartenbau m.

hose [houz]. I. s. Schlauch m. II. v.tr. (den Garten usw.) spritzen. ◆'hosiery, s. Strumpfwaren fpl.

hospitable [hos'pitəbl], adj. gastfreundlich. ◆hospi'tality, s. Gastfreundschaft f.

hospital ['hospitl], s. Krankenhaus n.

host¹ [houst], s. Gastgeber m. ◆'hostess, s. Gastgeberin f; air h., Stewardeß f.

host², s. Ecc: Hostie f.

hostage ['hostidʒ], s. Geisel f.

hostel ['hɔstəl], s. (a) (for students etc) Heim n; (b) **youth h.,** Jugendherberge f.

hostile ['hɔstail], adj. feindselig (to, gegen + acc). ◆**hos'tility,** s. 1. (a) (enmity) Feindschaft f (to, gegen); (b) (animosity) Feindseligkeit f. 2. pl. Mil: Feindseligkeiten fpl.

hot [hɔt]. I. adj. 1. (a) heiß; (of water, meal etc.) warm; **I am h.,** mir ist heiß; (b) Cu: (of curry etc.) scharf. 2. **to be h. on discipline,** auf Disziplin scharf sein; **he's not very h. on geography,** Geographie ist nicht seine Stärke. II. v.tr. **to h. sth. up,** etwas erhitzen. ◆**'hot-'tempered,** adj. (of pers.) hitzig, jähzornig. ◆**'hot-'water 'bottle,** s. Wärmflasche f.

hotel [hou'tel], s. Hotel n.

hound [haund]. I. s. Jagdhund m. II. v.tr. jagen.

hour ['auər], s. Stunde f, F: **to take hours over sth.,** eine Ewigkeit für etwas acc brauchen; **office hours,** Dienststunden fpl; Bürozeit f; **after (working) hours,** nach Dienstschluß m; **in the small hours,** in den frühen Morgenstunden. ◆**'hourly.** I. adj. stündlich. II. adv. stündlich, jede Stunde.

house, pl. **-ses** [haus, 'hauziz]. I. s. 1. (a) Haus n; **at/in my h.,** bei mir; **to my h.,** zu mir; **to move h.,** umziehen; **h. plant,** Zimmerpflanze f; (b) **a drink on the h.,** ein Glas auf Kosten des Hauses. 2. Th: **h. full,** ausverkauft. II. v.tr. (hauz) unterbringen. ◆**'houseboat,** s. Hausboot n. ◆**'housecoat,** s. Morgenrock m. ◆**'household,** s. Haushalt m. ◆**'house-hunting,** s. Haussuche f. ◆**'housekeeper,** s. Haushälterin f. ◆**'housekeeping,** s. (money/F: h., Haushaltsgeld n. ◆**'house-warming,** **h.-w. party,** Einzugsfeier f. ◆**'housewife,** pl. **-wives,** s. Hausfrau f. ◆**'housework,** s. Hausarbeit f. ◆**'housing** ['hauziŋ], s. 1. coll. Wohnungen fpl; Häuserbestand m (einer Stadt); **h. estate,** Wohnsiedlung f; **the h. problem,** das Wohnungsproblem. 2. Tchn: Gehäuse n.

hovel ['hɔvl], s. Schuppen m.

hover ['hɔvər], v.i. (a) (of hawk etc.) rütteln; (b) (of pers.) zögernd herumstehen. ◆**'hovercraft,** s. Luftkissenfahrzeug n.

how [hau], adv. 1. wie; **h. are you?** wie geht es Ihnen? **h. do you do?** sehr erfreut(, Sie kennenzulernen); **h. about a drink?** wie wär's mit einem Drink? 2. (a) **h. much,** wieviel; **h. many,** wie viele; (b) **h. I wish I could!** wenn ich doch nur könnte!

however [hau'evər]. I. adv. wie ... auch; **h. good his work is,** wie gut seine Arbeit auch ist. II. conj. (je)doch.

howl [haul]. I. v.i. heulen. II. s. Heulen n. ◆**'howler,** s. F: Schnitzer m.

hub [hʌb], s. 1. Nabe f. 2. Fig: Mittelpunkt m. ◆**'hub-cap,** s. Radkappe f.

hubbub ['hʌbʌb], s. Tumult m.

huddle ['hʌdl]. I. v.i. **to h. (together),** sich zusammendrängen; **to be huddled together,** dicht zusammengedrängt sein. II. s. Häufchen n.

huff [hʌf], s. F: **to be in a h.,** die gekränkte Leberwurst spielen.

hug [hʌg]. I. v.tr. umarmen. II. s. Umarmung f.

huge [hju:dʒ], adj. riesig; **-ly,** adv. **h. enjoyable,** höchst unterhaltsam.

hull [hʌl], s. Rumpf m.

hum [hʌm], v.tr. & i. summen.

human ['hju:mən], adj. menschlich; **h. (being),** Mensch m; **-ly,** adv. **everything h. possible,** alles menschenmögliche. ◆**humane** [hju(:)'mein], adj. (of methods etc.) human; (b) (of pers.) menschlich. ◆**humanity** [-'mæniti], s. 1. (quality) Menschlichkeit f. 2. (mankind) die Menschheit. 3. pl. Sch: Geisteswissenschaften fpl.

humble ['hʌmbl]. I. adj. (a) demütig; (b) (of circumstances, house etc.) bescheiden. II. v.tr. (j-n) demütigen.

humdrum ['hʌmdrʌm], adj. eintönig.

humid ['hju:mid], adj. feucht. ◆**hu'midity,** s. Feuchtigkeit f; (atmospheric) h., Luftfeuchtigkeit f.

humiliate [hju(:)'milieit], v.tr. (j-n) erniedrigen. ◆**humili'ation,** s. Erniedrigung f. ◆**hu'mility,** s. Demut f.

humour ['hju:mər]. I. s. 1. Humor m; **to have a sense of h.,** Humor haben. 2. (state of mind) Laune f; **to be in a good/bad h.,** guter/schlechter Laune sein. II. v.tr. **to h. s.o.,** j-m seinen Willen lassen. ◆**'humorist,** s. Humorist m. ◆**'humorous,** adj. (of pers.) humorvoll; (of writer) humoristisch.

hump [hʌmp], s. Buckel m; (of camel) Höcker m.

hunch [hʌn(t)ʃ], s. F: **I have a h. that ...,** ich habe so eine Ahnung, daß ... ◆**'hunchback,** s. (pers.) Bucklige(r) f(m).

hundred ['hʌndrəd]. I. num. adj. hundert. II. s. 1. (unit) Hundert n; **hundreds of people,** Hunderte von Menschen. ◆**'hundredth.** I. adj. hundertste(r, s). II. s. (fraction) Hundertstel n. ◆**'hundredweight,** s. Zentner m.

Hungarian [hʌŋ'gɛəriən]. I. s. 1. Ungar(in) m(f). 2. Ungarisch n. II. adj. ungarisch. ◆**Hungary** ['hʌŋgəri]. Pr. n. Ungarn n.

hunger ['hʌŋgər], s. Hunger m; **h. strike,** Hungerstreik m. ◆**'hungry,** adj. hungrig.

hunt [hʌnt]. I. s. Jagd f; (by police) Fahndung f (for, nach + dat). II. v.tr. & i. (a) jagen; (b) **to h. for sth.,** etwas eifrig suchen; (c) **h. a criminal,** nach einem Verbrecher fahnden. ◆**'hunter,** s. Jäger m. ◆**'hunt 'down,** v.tr. (a) (ein Tier) hetzen; (b) (einen Verbrecher) zur Strecke bringen. ◆**'hunting,** s. Jagd f.

hurdle ['hə:dl], s. (a) Sp: Hürde f; **100 metres hurdles**, 100-Meter-Hürdenlauf m; (b) (obstacle) Hindernis n.

hurl [hə:l], v.tr. (etwas) schleudern (at s.o., sth., gegen j-n, etwas acc).

hurrah [hu'rɑ:], **hurray** [hu'rei], int. hurra!

hurricane ['hʌrikən], s. Orkan m.

hurry ['hʌri]. I. v. 1. v.tr. (j-n) antreiben; (etwas) beschleunigen. 2. v.i. (a) sich beeilen; **h. up!** beeile dich! (b) **h. somewhere**, irgendwohin eilen. II. s. Eile f; **to be in a h.**, es eilig haben. ◆**'hurried**, adj. eilig; (superficial) flüchtig.

hurt [hə:t], v.irr. 1. v.tr. 1. v.tr. (j-n, sich) verletzen; **to get h.**, verletzt werden; (feelings) (j-n) kränken; **to h. s.o.'s feelings**, j-s Gefühle verletzen. 2. v.i. schmerzen; **does it h.?** tut es weh? **my foot hurts** mir tut der Fuß weh. ◆**'hurtful**, adj. verletzend.

husband ['hʌzbənd], s. Ehemann m; **my h.**, mein Mann.

hush [hʌʃ]. I. s. Schweigen n. II. int. still! ◆**'hush-'hush**, adj. F: streng geheim. ◆**'hush 'up**, v.tr. vertuschen.

husk [hʌsk], s. Hülse f; Spelze f (von Getreide).

husky[1] ['hʌski], adj. heiser.

husky[2], s. (dog) Eskimohund m.

hut [hʌt], s. Hütte f.

hutch [hʌtʃ], s. **(rabbit-)h.**, Kaninchenstall m.

hyacinth ['haiəsinθ], s. Hyazinthe f.

hybrid ['haibrid], s. 1. Biol: Hybride f. 2.

(thing) Mischling m.

hydrant ['haidrənt], s. Hydrant m.

hydraulic [hai'drɔ:lik], adj. hydraulisch.

hydroelectric ['haidrəui'lektrik], adj. hydroelektrisch.

hydrofoil ['haidrəufɔil], s. Tragflächenboot n.

hydrogen ['haidrədʒ(ə)n], s. Wasserstoff m.

hyena [hai'i:nə], s. Hyäne f.

hygiene ['haidʒi:n], s. Hygiene f. ◆**hy'gienic**, adj. hygienisch.

hymn [him], s. Kirchenlied n; **h.-book**, Gesangbuch n.

hyper- ['haipə], prefix über-; **hypercritical**, adj. überkritisch; **hypersensitive**, adj. überempfindlich.

hyphen ['haif(ə)n], s. Bindestrich m.

hypnosis [hip'nəusis], s. Hypnose f. ◆**'hypnotism** [-nətizm], s. Hypnotismus m. ◆**'hypnotize** [-nətaiz], v.tr. hypnotisieren.

hypochondriac [haipəu'kɔndriæk], s. Hypochonder m.

hypocrisy [hi'pɔkrisi], s. Heuchelei f. ◆**'hypocrite** [-əkrit], s. Heuchler m. ◆**hypo'critical**, adj. heuchlerisch.

hypothesis, pl. **-ses** [hai'pɔθisis, -si:z], s. Hypothese f. ◆**hypothetical** [haipə'θetikl], adj. theoretisch.

hysteria [his'tiəriə], s. Hysterie f. ◆**hysterical** [-'terikl], adj. hysterisch. ◆**hys'terics**, s.pl. hysterischer Anfall m; F: (laughter) **we were in h.**, wir haben uns gerollt vor Lachen.

I

I[1], **i** [ai], s. (der Buchstabe) I, i n.

I[2], pers.pron. ich.

ice [ais]. I. s. Eis n; **i. hockey**, Eishockey n; **i. rink**, Eisbahn f; **i. skating**, Schlittschuhlaufen n. II. v. 1. v.tr. to a cake, einen Kuchen mit Zuckerguß überziehen. 2. v.i. (of window etc.) **to i. up**, vereisen. ◆**'iceberg**, s. Eisberg m. ◆**'icebox**, s. N.Am: Kühlschrank m. ◆**'ice-'cream**, s. Eis n. ◆**'ice-cube**, s. Eiswürfel m. ◆**'icicle**, s. Eiszapfen m. ◆**'icing**, s. Cu: Zuckerguß m. ◆**'icy**, adj. eiskalt; (of wind, welcome etc.) eisig; **i. road**, vereiste Straße.

Iceland ['aislənd], Pr.n. Island n.

icon ['aikɔn], s. Ikone f.

idea [ai'diə], s. 1. Idee f. 2. (concept) Vorstellung f; **he hasn't the faintest i.**, er hat keine blasse Ahnung. 3. (intention) Absicht f.

ideal [ai'di:əl]. I. adj. ideal. II. s. Ideal n; **-ly**, adv. im Idealfall. ◆**i'dealist**, s. Idealist(in) m(f). ◆**i'dealize**, v.tr. idealisieren.

identical [ai'dentik(ə)l], adj. identisch (with/to, mit + dat). ◆**identifi'cation**,

s. Identifizierung f. ◆**i'dentify**, v. 1. v.tr. (a) identifizieren; (b) **to i.** oneself, sich ausweisen. 2. v.i. (of pers.) **to i. with s.o., sth.**, sich mit j-m, etwas dat identifizieren. ◆**i'dentity**, s. Identität f; **i. card**, Personalausweis m; **mistaken i.**, Personenverwechslung f.

ideology [aidi'ɔlədʒi], s. Ideologie f. ◆**ideo'logical**, adj. ideologisch.

idiom ['idiəm], s. Redewendung f. ◆**idio'matic**, adj. idiomatisch.

idiosyncrasy [idiəu'siŋkrəsi], s. persönliche Eigenart f.

idiot ['idiət], s. Idiot m. ◆**idiotic** [-'ɔtik], adj. idiotisch.

idle ['aidl]. I. adj. 1. (a) (of pers.) untätig; (of worker) **to be i.**, nicht arbeiten; (b) (of machines etc.) **standing i.**, außer Betrieb. 2. (lazy) faul. 3. **i. threats**, leere Drohungen. II. v.i. (a) (of pers.) faulenzen; (b) (of engine) leer laufen. ◆**'idly**, adv. **to stand i. by**, untätig dastehen.

idol ['aidl], s. Idol n. ◆**'idolize**, v.tr. (j-n) vergöttern.

idyll ['idil], s. Idylle f. ◆**i'dyllic**, adj. idyllisch.

if [if]. **I.** *conj.* **1.** wenn; **if not,** wenn nicht; **you'll only get five pence for it, if that,** dafür bekommst du höchstens fünf Pence; **if only I had known!** wenn ich das bloß gewußt hätte! **as if,** als ob. **2.** (=*whether*) ob. **II.** *s.* **with no ifs and buts,** ohne Wenn und Aber.

igloo ['iglu:], *s.* Iglu *m & n.*

ignite [ig'nait], *v.* **1.** *v.tr.* (etwas) entzünden. **2.** *v.i.* sich entzünden; (catch fire) Feuer fangen. ◆**ig'nition** [-'niʃən], *s.* Zündung *f*; **i. key,** Zündschlüssel *m.*

ignorance ['ignərəns], *s.* Unkenntnis *f* (of sth., + gen); Unwissenheit *f* (on/about sth., über etwas acc). ◆**ignorant,** *adj.* unwissend. ◆**ignore** [ig'nɔ:r], *v.tr.* ignorieren.

ill [il]. **I.** *adj.* krank; **i. health,** schlechte Gesundheit; **i. effects,** schädliche Auswirkungen; **of i. repute,** von üblem Ruf. **II.** *s.* Übel *n.* **III.** *adv.* schlecht; **he is i. at ease,** er fühlt sich unbehaglich. ◆**ill-ad'vised,** *adj.* (of action) nicht ratsam; (foolish) unklug. ◆**ill-'fated,** *adj.* unglückselig; (of attempt) mißglückt. ◆**ill-'feeling,** *s.* Feindseligkeit *f.* ◆**ill-'gotten,** *adj.* **i.-g. gains,** unredlich erworbenes Geld. ◆**illness,** *s.* Krankheit *f.* ◆**ill-'timed,** *adj.* ungelegen. ◆**ill-'treat,** *v.tr.* schlecht behandeln, (maltreat) mißhandeln. ◆**ill-'treatment,** *s.* schlechte Behandlung; Mißhandlung *f.* ◆**ill-'will,** *s.* böses Blut *n.*

illegal [i'li:g(ə)l], *adj.* illegal.

illegible [i'ledʒibl], *adj.* unleserlich.

illegitimate [ili'dʒitimit], *adj.* (of child) unehelich.

illicit [i'lisit], *adj.* (gesetzlich) unerlaubt.

illiteracy [i'lit(ə)rəsi], *s.* Analphabetentum *n.* ◆**il'literate,** *adj.* des Lesens und Schreibens unkundig.

illogical [i'lɔdʒik(ə)l], *adj.* unlogisch.

illuminate [i'l(j)u:mineit], *v.tr.* beleuchten. ◆**il'luminating,** *adj.* (of talk etc.) aufschlußreich. ◆**illumi'nation,** *s.* Beleuchtung *f; pl.* festliche Beleuchtung *f.*

illusion [i'u:ʒ(ə)n], *s.* Illusion *f.* ◆**i'llusionist,** *s.* Zauberer *m.* ◆**i'llusory,** *adj.* trügerisch.

illustrate ['iləstreit], *v.tr.* (a) (eine Lehre usw.) veranschaulichen; (b) (Bücher usw.) illustrieren. ◆**illus'tration,** *s.* **1.** (erklärendes) Beispiel *n.* **2.** Illustration *f.*

image ['imidʒ], *s.* **1.** Bild *n;* (of saints etc.) Bildnis *n.* **2.** *Fig:* **to improve one's i.,** sein Image aufpolieren.

imagine [i'mædʒin], *v.tr.* (a) (sth. possible) sich dat (j-n, etwas) vorstellen; (b) (sth. untrue) sich dat (etwas) einbilden. ◆**i'maginary,** *adj.* imaginär. ◆**imagi'nation,** *s.* Phantasie *f.* ◆**i'maginative,** *adj.* phantasievoll; (of work etc.) einfallsreich.

imbecile ['imbəsi:l], *s.* Schwachsinnige(r) *f(m).*

imitate ['imiteit], *v.tr* nachahmen.

◆**imi'tation,** *s.* Nachahmung *f*; **i.** jewellery, falscher Schmuck.

immaculate [i'mækjulit], *adj.* makellos, (perfect) tadellos.

immaterial [imə'tiəriəl], *adj.* unwichtig.

immature [imə'tjuər], *adj.* unreif.

immediate [i'mi:djət], *adj.* **1.** unmittelbar. **2.** (at once) unverzüglich; **-ly. I.** *adv.* (a) (place etc.) unmittelbar; (b) (time) sofort. **II.** *conj.* **i. he received the money,** sobald er das Geld bekam.

immense [i'mens], *adj.* enorm; ungeheuer; **-ly,** *adv.* **to enjoy oneself i.,** sich prächtig unterhalten.

immerse [i'mə:s], *v.tr.* (j-n, etwas) untertauchen, (dip) eintauchen. ◆**i'mmersion,** *s.* **i.** heater, Wasserboiler *m.*

immigrate ['imigreit], *v.i.* einwandern. ◆**'immigrant. I.** *adj.* eingewandert. **II.** *s.* Einwanderer *m;* Immigrant(in) *m(f).* ◆**immi'gration,** *s.* Einwanderung *f.*

imminent ['iminənt], *adj.* unmittelbar bevorstehend.

immobile [i'məubail], *adj.* unbeweglich. ◆**i'mmobilize,** *v.tr.* bewegungsunfähig machen; (den Verkehr) lahmlegen.

immodest [i'mɔdist], *adj.* unbescheiden.

immoral [i'mɔrəl], *adj.* unmoralisch. ◆**immo'rality,** *s.* Unmoral *f.*

immortal [i'mɔ:tl], *adj.* unsterblich. ◆**immor'tality,** *s.* Unsterblichkeit *f.* ◆**i'mmortalize,** *v.tr.* unsterblich machen.

immune [i'mju:n], *adj.* immun (to, gegen + acc); *Fig:* gefeit (to, gegen + acc). ◆**i'mmunity,** *s.* Immunität *f.* ◆**immuni'zation,** *s.* Immunisierung *f.* ◆**'immunize,** *v.tr.* (j-n) immunisieren.

impact ['impækt], *s.* **1.** Aufprall *m* (against/on sth., auf etwas acc); (of two moving objects) Zusammenprall *m.* **2.** Wucht *f* (einer Explosion usw.). **3.** *Fig:* Wirkung *f* (on s.o., auf j-n).

impair [im'pɛər], *v.tr.* (etwas dat) schaden; (Beziehungen) verschlechtern.

impartial [im'pɑ:ʃ(ə)l], *adj.* unparteiisch.

impatient [im'peiʃənt], *adj.* ungeduldig. ◆**im'patience,** *s.* Ungeduld *f.*

impeccable [im'pekəbl], *adj.* tadellos.

impede [im'pi:d], *v.tr.* (j-n) hindern; (prevent) (j-n, etwas) behindern. ◆**im'pediment** [im'pedimənt], *s.* (speech) **i.,** Sprachfehler *m.*

impending [im'pendiŋ], *adj.* (nahe) bevorstehend.

impenetrable [im'penitrəbl], *adj.* undurchdringlich.

imperative [im'perətiv], *adj.* **I.** *adj.* unerläßlich. **II.** *s. Gram:* Imperativ *m.*

imperceptible [impə'septəbl], *adj.* nicht wahrnehmbar.

imperfect [im'pə:fikt]. **I.** *adj.* fehlerhaft. **II.** *s. Gram:* Imperfekt *n.* ◆**imper'fection,** *s.* Fehler *m.*

imperial [im'piəriəl], *adj.* kaiserlich. ◆**im'perialism,** *s.* Imperialismus *m.*

imperious [im'piəriəs], *adj.* anmaßend.
impersonal [im'pə:sənəl], *adj.* unpersönlich.
impersonate [im'pə:səneit], *v.tr.* to 1. s.o., sich für j-n ausgeben; *Th:* j-n imitieren. ◆**imperso'nation**, *s.* Nachahmung *f.* ◆**im'personator**, *s.* Imitator *m.*
impertinence [im'pə:tinəns], *s.* Unverschämtheit *f.* ◆**im'pertinent**, *adj.* unverschämt.
impervious [im'pə:viəs], *adj.* 1. *(of materials etc.)* undurchlässig. 2. *Fig: (of pers.)* i. to criticism, keiner Kritik zugänglich.
impetuous [im'petjuəs], *adj. (of pers.)* ungestüm; *(of action)* unbesonnen.
impetus ['impitəs], *s.* Auftrieb *m.*
impinge [im'pindʒ], *v.i.* einwirken (on/ upon, auf + acc).
implant [im'plɑ:nt], *v.tr.* einpflanzen.
implement¹ ['implimənt], *s.* Gerät *n*; *(tool)* Werkzeug *n.*
implement² ['impliment], *v.tr.* (einen Plan usw.) ausführen; (einen Vertrag) erfüllen.
implicate ['implikeit], *v.tr.* (j-n) verwickeln (**in sth.**, in etwas *acc*). ◆**impli'cation**, *s.* Implikation *f.*
implicit [im'plisit], *adj.* 1. inbegriffen (**in sth.**, in etwas *dat*); *(unexpressed)* unausgesprochen. 2. i. **faith**, blinder Glaube. **-ly**, *adv.* **to obey** (s.o.) i., (j-m) bedingungslos gehorchen.
implore [im'plɔ:r], *v.tr.* anflehen.
imply [im'plai], *v.tr.* (a) *(assume)* voraussetzen; (b) *(indicate)* andeuten.
impolite [impə'lait], *adj.* unhöflich.
import I. *s.* ['impɔ:t]. Einfuhr *f*, Import *m*; *(article)* Einfuhrartikel *m.* II. *v.tr.* [im'pɔ:t] einführen, importieren. ◆**im'porter**, *s.* Importeur *m.*
importance [im'pɔ:t(ə)ns], *s.* Wichtigkeit *f*; *(significance)* Bedeutung *f.* ◆**im'portant**, *adj.* wichtig; *(significant)* bedeutend.
impose [im'pəuz], *v.* 1. *v.tr.* (eine Steuer, Bedingungen usw.) auferlegen; (eine Geldstrafe) verhängen. 2. *v.i.* to i. **on** s.o., sich j-m aufdrängen. ◆**im'posing**, *adj.* eindrucksvoll. ◆**impo'sition**, *s.* (a) Auferlegung *f*; Verhängung *f*; (b) it's an i., es ist eine Zumutung.
impossible [im'pɔsəbl], *adj.* unmöglich. ◆**impossi'bility**, *s.* Unmöglichkeit *f.*
impostor [im'pɔstər], *s.* Hochstapler *m.*
impotence [im'pɔt(ə)ns], *s.* (a) Unfähigkeit *f*; (b) *Med:* Impotenz *f.* ◆**impotent**, *adj.* (a) unfähig; (b) *Med:* impotent.
impoverished [im'pɔv(ə)riʃt], *adj.* verarmt.
impracticable [im'præktikəbl], *adj.* (a) *(of plan etc.)* undurchführbar; (b) *(of design)* unpraktisch.
impress [im'pres], *v.tr.* (j-n) beeindrucken; **to i. sth. upon s.o.**, j-m etwas

einschärfen. ◆**im'pression**, *s.* 1. Eindruck *m.* 2. Abdruck *m* (eines Siegels usw.). ◆**im'pressionable**, *adj.* leicht beeinflußbar. ◆**im'pressionist**, *s.* Impressionist(in) *m(f).* ◆**im'pressive**, *adj.* eindrucksvoll.
imprison [im'prizn], *v.tr.* (j-n) ins Gefängnis bringen. ◆**im'prisonment**, *s.* Haft *f.*
improbable [im'prɔbəbl], *adj.* unwahrscheinlich.
impromptu [im'prɔm(p)tju:]. I. *adj.* i. **speech**, Stegreifrede *f.* II. *adv.* aus dem Stegreif.
improper [im'prɔpər], *adj.* 1. *(wrong)* falsch. 2. *(unseemly)* ungehörig; *(unfitting)* unpassend; **-ly**, *adv.* **1. a word i. used**, ein falsch gebrauchtes Wort. 2. to behave i., sich ungehörig benehmen.
improve [im'pru:v], *v.* 1. *v.tr.* verbessern. 2.[*v.i.* *(of pers.)* sich bessern; to i. (**up)on** sth., (etwas) übertreffen. ◆**im'provement**, *s.* Verbesserung *f*; *(in health)* Besserung *f.*
improvise ['imprəvaiz], *v.tr.* improvisieren. ◆**improvi'sation**, *s.* Improvisation *f.*
imprudent [im'pru:dənt], *adj.* unklug. ◆**im'prudence**, *s.* Unklugheit *f.*
impudent ['impjudənt], *adj.* unverschämt. ◆**im'pudence**, *s.* Unverschämtheit *f.*
impulse ['impʌls], *s.* Impuls *m.* ◆**im'pulsive**, *adj.* impulsiv.
impunity [im'pju:niti], *s.* Straffreiheit *f*; **with i.**, ungestraft.
impure [im'pjuər], *adj.* 1. *(of air etc.)* unrein. 2. *(of thoughts etc.)* unsittlich. ◆**im'purity**, *s.* Unreinheit *f*; **impurities**, Verunreinigungen *fpl* *(in* Blut usw.).
in [in]. I. *prep.* 1. *(of place)* (a) *(position)* **in** + *dat*; (b) *(into)* **in** + *acc.* 2. *(of time)* **in the evening**, am Abend; *(every evening)* abends; **in August**, im August; *(since)* **not in 6 years** seit 6 Jahren nicht mehr; **to do sth. in three hours**, etwas in drei Stunden erledigen. 3. *(manner)* **in this way**, auf diese Weise; **in English**, auf Englisch. 4. *(while)* **in** + *dat*; **in coming downstairs he tripped and fell**, beim Herunterkommen stolperte er und fiel. II. *adv.* 1. zu Hause. 2. **to be** (well) **in with** s.o., mit j-m auf gutem Fuße stehen. 3. *F:* **he is in for it!** der kann sich auf etwas gefaßt machen! 4. (a) **day in, day out**, tagein, tagaus; (b) **all in**, alles zusammen. III. s. **he knows the ins and outs (of the matter)**, er ist mit allen Feinheiten (der Sache) vertraut.
inability [inə'biliti], *s.* Unfähigkeit *f.*
inaccessible [inæk'sesəbl], *adj. (of place, pers.)* unzugänglich.
inaccurate [in'ækjurit], *adj.* ungenau.
inactive [in'æktiv], *adj.* untätig. ◆**inac'tivity**, *s.* Untätigkeit *f.*
inadequate [in'ædikwit], *adj.* unzulänglich; *(of number, quantity)* ungenügend; **to**

feel i., sich der Situation nicht gewachsen fühlen.

inadmissible [inəd'misəbl], *adj.* unzulässig.

inadvertent [inəd'vɜːt(ə)nt], *adj.* unbeabsichtigt.

inadvisable [inəd'vaizəbl], *adj.* nicht ratsam.

inane [i'nein], *adj.* albern.

inanimate [in'ænimit], *adj.* leblos.

inappropriate [inə'prəupriit], *adj.* unpassend.

inarticulate [inɑː'tikjulit], *adj.* (*of speech*) undeutlich; (*of pers.*) **to be i.**, sich nicht ausdrücken können.

inattentive [inə'tentiv], *adj.* unaufmerksam.

inaudible [in'ɔːdəbl], *adj.* unhörbar.

inaugurate [i'nɔːgjureit], *v.tr.* (*a*) (eine Veranstaltung) eröffnen; (ein Gebäude usw.) einweihen; (*b*) (einen Präsidenten) ins Amt einsetzen. ◆**i'naugural**, *adj.* Eröffnungs-.

incalculable [in'kælkjuləbl], *adj.* unermeßlich.

incapable [in'keipəbl], *adj.* unfähig, (of, + *gen*). ◆**incapa'bility**, *s.* Unfähigkeit *f.*

incapacitate [inkə'pæsiteit], *v.tr.* (j-n) untauglich machen, (*for work*) arbeitsunfähig machen.

incendiary [in'sendjəri], *s.* **i.** (**bomb**), Brandbombe *f.*

incense¹ [insens], *s.* Weihrauch *m.*

incense² [in'sens], *v.tr.* (j-n) in Wut bringen. ◆**in'censed**, *adj.* wütend.

incentive [in'sentiv], *s.* Anreiz *m.*

incessant [in'sesənt], *adj.* unaufhörlich.

incest [insest], *s.* Blutschande *f.*

inch [in(t)ʃ], *s.* Zoll *m* (2,54 cm); *Fig:* **not to give an i.**, keinen Fußbreit nachgeben.

incidence [insidəns], *s.* Vorkommen *n* (einer Krankheit usw.).

incident [insidənt], *s.* Zwischenfall *m.* ◆**inci'dental**, *adj.* beiläufig, Neben-; **-ly**, *adv.* übrigens.

incinerator [in'sinəreitər], *s.* Müllverbrennungsofen *m.*

incipient [in'sipiənt], *adj.* beginnend.

incision [in'siʒən], *s.* Einschnitt *m.*

incisive [in'saisiv], *adj.* (*of mind*) scharf; (*of remark*) scharfsinnig; (*of style*) prägnant.

incite [in'sait], *v.tr.* (j-n) aufhetzen (**to sth.**, zu etwas *dat*). ◆**in'citement**, *s.* Aufhetzung *f.*

inclement [in'klemənt], *adj.* (*of weather, climate*) unfreundlich.

inclination [inkli'neiʃn], *s.* Neigung *f.* ◆**incline** ['inklain], *s.* Hang *m.* ◆**in'clined**, *adj.* **1.** (*of pers.*) geneigt; **she's i. to be lazy**, sie neigt zur Faulheit. **2.** (*of thing*) schräg.

include [in'kluːd], *v.tr.* (*a*) (j-n, etwas) einschließen (**in**, in + *acc*); (j-n) einbeziehen (**in a conversation**, in ein Gespräch); (*b*) **to i. s.o. in a team/a fact in a book**, j-n in eine Mannschaft/eine Tatsache in ein Buch aufnehmen. ◆**in'cluding**, *adj.* einschließlich; **i. VAT**, inklusive Mehrwertsteuer. ◆**in'clusion** [-ʒən], *s.* **1.** Einbeziehung *f.* **2.** Aufnahme *f* in eine Mannschaft usw.). ◆**in'clusive** [-siv], *adj.* einschließlich (**of**, + *gen*).

incognito [inkɔg'niːtəu], *adv.* inkognito.

incoherent [inkəu'hiərənt], *adj.* (*of statement, talk etc.*) zusammenhanglos; (*of pers.*) **to be i.**, wirres Zeug reden.

income ['inkəm], *s.* Einkommen *n*; **i. tax**, Einkommensteuer *f.*

incoming ['inkʌmiŋ], *adj.* **i. mail**, Posteingang *m*; *Tel:* **i. call**, Gespräch *n* von auswärts.

incomparable [in'kɔmp(ə)rəbl], *adj.* unvergleichlich.

incompatible [inkəm'pætibl], *adj.* (*of views, proposals etc.*) unvereinbar; (*of drugs, blood groups*) unverträglich; (*of people*) **they are i.**, sie passen nicht zueinander.

incompetent [in'kɔmpitənt], *adj.* (*of pers.*) unfähig; (*of worker*) untauglich. ◆**in'competence**, *s.* Unfähigkeit *f*; Untauglichkeit *f.*

incomplete [inkəm'pliːt], *adj.* unvollständig.

incomprehensible [inkɔmpri'hensibl], *adj.* unverständlich.

inconceivable [inkən'siːvəbl], *adj.* undenkbar.

inconclusive [inkən'kluːsiv], *adj.* (*of negotiations*) ergebnislos; (*of result, evidence*) nicht schlüssig.

incongruous [in'kɔŋgruəs], *adj.* unpassend.

inconsiderate [inkən'sid(ə)rit], *adj.* rücksichtslos.

inconsistent [inkən'sistənt], *adj.* *a*) (*contradicting*) widersprüchlich; unvereinbar (**with the evidence**, mit den Beweisen); (*b*) (*of pers.*) unbeständig; (*illogical*) inkonsequent. ◆**incon'sistency**, *s.* (*a*) Unvereinbarkeit *f* (**with sth.**, mit etwas *dat*); (*b*) (*of pers.*) Unbeständigkeit *f.*

inconspicuous [inkən'spikjuəs], *adj.* unauffällig.

inconvenience [inkən'viːnjəns], *s.* **I.** *s.* Unannehmlichkeit *f.* **II.** *v.tr.* (j-m) Umstände machen. ◆**incon'venient**, *adj.* ungünstig.

incorporate [in'kɔːpəreit], *v.tr.* (*a*) (einen Staat, ein Gebiet) einverleiben (**into**, + *dat*); (*b*) (einen Vorschlag usw.) aufnehmen (**in a plan**, in einen Plan).

incorrect [inkə'rekt], *adj.* falsch.

incorrigible [in'kɔridʒəbl], *adj.* unverbesserlich.

increase. I. *s.* ['inkriːs] Erhöhung *f* (von Preisen usw.); Zunahme *f* (der Bevölkerung usw.); Steigerung *f* (von Leistungen usw.); **to be on the i.**, zunehmen. **II.** *v.* [in'kriːs] **1.** *v.i.* (*a*) (*in size*) wachsen; (*of* *price etc.*) steigen; (*of population etc.*) zunehmen; **to i. in value**, im Wert steigen; (*b*) (*in number*) (*of difficulties etc.*) sich vermehren. 2. *v.tr.* (Preise usw.) erhöhen; (die Leistung) steigern. ◆**in'creasingly**, *adv.* immer mehr; **it is becoming i. difficult**, es wird immer schwieriger.

incredible [in'kredibl], *adj.* unglaublich; **-ibly,** *adv.* **i. he was unharmed**, wie durch ein Wunder blieb er unverletzt; *F:* **i. hot**, unglaublich warm.

incredulous [in'kredjuləs], *adj.* ungläubig.

increment ['inkrimənt], *s.* Lohnerhöhung *f.*

incriminate [in'krimineit], *v.tr.* belasten. ◆**in'criminating,** *adj.* belastend.

incubation [inkju'beiʃən], *s.* Ausbrüten *n;* **i. period**, Inkubationszeit *f.* ◆**'incubator,** *s.* Brutkasten *m.*

incur [in'kəːr], *v.tr.* sich dat (j-s Unwillen usw.) zuziehen; **to i. debts**, Schulden machen.

incurable [in'kjuərəbl], *adj.* (*of disease*) unheilbar; **i. optimist**, unverbesserlicher Optimist.

indebted [in'detid], *adj.* (zu Dank) verpflichtet (**to s.o.**, j-m); **to be i. to s.o. for sth.**, j-m für etwas *acc* Dank schulden.

indecent [in'diːsənt], *adj.* anstößig; *Jur:* unzüchtig.

indecision [indi'siʒən], *s.* Unentschlossenheit *f.*

indecisive [indi'saisiv], *adj.* unentschlossen.

indeed [in'diːd], *adv.* (*a*) tatsächlich; (*b*) (*intensifying*) **I'm very glad i.**, ich bin wirklich sehr froh; (*c*) (*as comment*) **i.?** wirklich? **yes i.!** tatsächlich!

indefinite [in'definit], *adj.* unbestimmt.

indent [in'dent], *v.tr.* (eine Zeile usw.) einrücken.

independence [indi'pendəns], *s.* Unabhängigkeit *f.* ◆**inde'pendent,** *adj.* unabhängig (**of**, von + *dat*).

indescribable [indis'kraibəbl], *adj.* unbeschreiblich.

indestructible [indis'trʌktəbl], *adj.* unzerstörbar.

indeterminate [indi'təːminit], *adj.* unbestimmt.

index ['indeks], *s. pl.* **-es** & *Mth: Tchn:* **indices** [-isiːz]. 1. **i.** (**finger**) Zeigefinger *m.* 2. (*in book*) Register *n.* 3. (**card**) **i.**, Kartei *f;* **i. card**, Karteikarte *f.* **4. cost of living i.**, Lebenshaltungsindex *m.* ◆**'index-linked,** *adj.* dem Lebenshaltungsindex angepaßt; **i.-l. pension**, dynamische Rente.

India ['indjə]. *Pr.n.* Indien *n.* ◆**'Indian. I.** *adj.* 1. indisch. 2. *N. & S.Am:* indianisch. **II. s.** 1. Inder(in) *m(f).* 2. *N. & S.Am:* Indianer(in) *m(f).*

indicate ['indikeit], *v.tr.* (*a*) (*show*) (etwas) zeigen; (*of instrument*) (einen Wert)

anzeigen; (*b*) (*point out*) (auf etwas *acc*) hinweisen. ◆**indi'cation,** *s.* 1. (*sign*) Anzeichen *n; Med:* Indikation *f.* 2. (*hint*) Hinweis *m.* ◆**in'dicative. I.** *adj.* **to be i. of sth.**, auf etwas *acc* hindeuten. **II.** *s. Gram:* Indikativ *m.* ◆**'indicator,** *s.* (*device*) Anzeiger *m; Aut:* Blinker *m.*

indictment [in'daitmənt], *s. Jur:* Anklage *f; Fig:* **i. of government policy**, Verurteilung der Regierungspolitik.

Indies ['indiz]. *Pr.n.* **the West I.**, die Antillen *fpl.*

indifferent [in'difrənt], *adj.* 1. (*of pers.*) gleichgültig. 2. (*of thing*) mittelmäßig. ◆**in'difference,** *s.* Gleichgültigkeit *f.*

indigenous [in'didʒinəs], *adj.* einheimisch.

indigestion [indi'dʒestʃ(ə)n], *s.* Verdauungsstörung *f.* ◆**indi'gestible,** *adj.* unverdaulich.

indignant [in'dignənt], *adj.* empört (**at**, über + *acc*). ◆**indig'nation,** *s.* Empörung *f.*

indignity [in'digniti], *s.* Demütigung *f.*

indirect [indi'rekt, indai-], *adj.* indirekt. ◆**indi'rectly,** *adv.* indirekt.

indiscreet [indis'kriːt], *adj.* (*of disclosure*) indiskret; (*of remark*) taktlos. ◆**indis'cretion,** *s.* Indiskretion *f;* Taktlosigkeit *f.*

indiscriminate [indis'kriminit], *adj.* wahllos.

indispensable [indis'pensəbl], *adj.* unentbehrlich.

indisposed [indis'pəuzd], *adj.* **to be i.**, sich nicht wohl fühlen.

indistinct [indis'tiŋkt], *adj.* undeutlich.

indistinguishable [indis'tiŋgwiʃəbl], *adj.* nicht zu unterscheiden.

individual [indi'vidjuəl]. **I.** *adj.* individuell; **i. case**, Einzelfall *m.* **II. s.** Individuum *n.* ◆**indivi'duality,** *s.* Individualität *f.* ◆**indi'vidually,** *adv.* einzeln.

indoctrinate [in'dɔktrineit], *v.tr.* (j-n) indoktrinieren. ◆**indoctri'nation,** *s.* Indoktrination *f.*

indolence ['indələns], *s.* Faulheit *f.* ◆**'indolent,** *adj.* faul.

Indonesia [ində(u)'niːzjə]. *Pr.n.* Indonesien *n.* ◆**Indo'nesian,** *adj.* indonesisch.

indoor ['indɔːr], *adj.* (*a*) Innen-; **i. plant**, Zimmerpflanze *f;* (*b*) *Sp:* Hallen-; **i. (swimming) pool**, Hallenbad *n.* ◆**in'doors,** *adv.* (*a*) im Hause. (*b*) ins Haus; **to go i.**, ins Haus gehen.

induce [in'djuːs], *v.tr.* (*a*) (j-n) dazu bewegen (**to do sth.**, etwas zu tun); (*b*) *Med:* **to i. labour**, die Wehen einleiten. ◆**in'ducement,** *s.* Anreiz *m.*

indulge [in'dʌldʒ], *v.* 1. *v.tr* (einer Neigung usw.) nachgeben; **to i. oneself**, sich verwöhnen. 2. *v.i.* **to i. in sth.**, sich etwas *dat* hingeben. ◆**in'dulgence,** *s.* **i. in drink**, übermäßiges Trinken. ◆**in'dulgent,** *adj.* nachsichtig.

industrial [in'dʌstriəl], *adj.* industriell, Industrie-, Betriebs-; **i. dispute**, Arbeitskonflikt *m;* **i. estate**, Industriegelände *n.*

◆in'dustrialist, s. Industrieller m.
◆in'dustrious, adj. fleißig.
◆industry ['indəstri], s. 1. (of pers.) Fleiß m. 2. Industrie f.
ineffective [ini'fektiv], ineffectual [ini'fektju(ə)l], adj. unwirksam; (of pers.) untauglich.
inefficient [ini'fiʃənt], adj. 1. (of pers.) untüchtig; nicht leistungsfähig. 2. (of firm, factory) unwirtschaftlich.
◆ine'fficiency s. 1. (of pers.) Untüchtigkeit f; mangelnde Leistungsfähigkeit f. 2. Com: Unwirtschaftlichkeit f.
inept [i'nept], adj. ungeschickt.
◆i'neptitude, s. Ungeschicktheit f.
inequality [ini:'kwɔliti], s. Ungleichheit f.
inert [i'nə:t], adj. (of pers.) reglos; Ph: träge. ◆inertia [i'nə:ʃ(i)ə], s. Trägheit f.
inescapable [inis'keipəbl], adj. unentrinnbar; (of conclusion etc.) unvermeidlich.
inevitable [in'evitəbl], adj. unvermeidlich. ◆inevita'bility, s. Unvermeidlichkeit f.
inexcusable [iniks'kju:zəbl], adj. unverzeihlich.
inexorable [in'eksərəbl], adj. unerbittlich.
inexpensive [iniks'pensiv], adj. preisgünstig.
inexperienced [iniks'piəriənst], adj. unerfahren.
inexplicable [ineks'plikəbl], adj. unerklärlich.
infallible [in'fæləbl], adj. unfehlbar.
infamous ['infəməs], adj. berüchtigt.
infant ['infənt], s. (a) Kleinkind n; Baby n; i. mortality, Säuglingssterblichkeit f; (b) i. school, Anfängerstufe f der Grundschule. ◆'infancy [-si], s. (a) frühe Kindheit f; Fig: Anfangsstadium n. ◆'infantile, adj. kindisch.
infantry ['infəntri], s. Infanterie f.
infatuated [in'fætjueitid], adj. vernarrt (with s.o., in j-n). ◆infatu'ation, s. Vernarrtheit f; (blind) Betörung f.
infect [in'fekt], v.tr. (also Fig:) (j-n) anstecken; Med: (j-n, eine Wunde, ein Tier usw.) infizieren. ◆in'fection, s. Infektion f. ◆in'fectious, adj. ansteckend.
infer [in'fə:r], v.tr. (conclude) (daraus) schließen; (gather) entnehmen (from, aus + dat). ◆'inference [-fərəns], s. Folgerung f.
inferior [in'fiəriər], adj. 1. i. to s.o. (in rank etc.), j-m (im Rang usw.) untergeordnet. 2. (a) (of thing) minderwertig; (b) (of pers.) unterlegen. ◆inferi'ority, s. Unterlegenheit f; i. complex, Minderwertigkeitskomplex m.
infernal [in'fə:nəl], adj. höllisch, Höllen-; F: i. row, Höllenlärm m.
inferno [in'fə:nəu], pl. -os [in'fə:nəu, -əuz], s. Inferno n.
infested [in'festid], adj. verseucht.
infidelity [infi'deliti], s. (eheliche) Un-

treue f.
in-fighting ['infaitiŋ], s. (interne) Querelen fpl.
infiltrate ['infiltreit], v.tr. (ein Land, eine Partei) unterwandern. ◆infil'tration, s. Unterwanderung f.
infinite ['infinit], adj. unendlich. ◆infini'tesimal, adj. unendlich klein. ◆in'finitive, s. Infinitiv m. ◆in'finity, s. Unendlichkeit f.
infirmary [in'fə:məri], s. 1. Krankenhaus n. 2. (room) Krankenzimmer n. ◆in'firmity, s. Gebrechlichkeit f.
inflame [in'fleim], v.tr. (eine Wunde usw.) entzünden. ◆in'flammable, adj. brennbar; (esp. as warning) feuergefährlich. ◆infla'mmation, s. Entzündung f. ◆in'flammatory, adj. (of speech etc.) aufrührerisch.
inflate [in'fleit], v.tr. (einen Luftballon usw.) aufblasen; (einen Gummireifen) aufpumpen. ◆in'flatable, adj. aufblasbar. ◆in'flated, adj. aufgeblasen. ◆in'flation, s. Inflation f. ◆in'flationary, adj. inflationär.
inflexible [in'fleksəbl], adj. unnachgiebig.
inflict [in'flikt], v.tr. (eine Wunde, ein Leid usw.) zufügen (on s.o., j-m).
influence ['influəns]. I. s. Einfluß m (upon/over s.o., sth., auf j-n, etwas occ). II. v.tr. beeinflussen. ◆influ'ential, adj. einflußreich.
influenza [influ'enzə], s. Grippe f.
influx ['inflʌks], s. Zustrom m (von Menschen); Zufuhr f (von Waren).
inform [in'fɔ:m], v.tr. informieren; to i. s.o. of sth., j-m etwas mitteilen. ◆in'formant, s. Informant m. ◆information [infə'meiʃ(ə)n], s. Information f; (piece of) i., Auskunft f; several items Informationen fpl. ◆in'formative, adj. aufschlußreich. ◆in'formed, adj. informiert. ◆in'former, s. police i., Polizeispitzel m.
informal [in'fɔ:məl], adj. zwanglos; (of meeting, Sp: match) inoffiziell; -ally, adv. informell. ◆infor'mality, s. Zwanglosigkeit f.
infra-red ['infrə'red], adj. infrarot.
infrastructure ['infrəstrʌktʃər], s. Infrastruktur f.
infrequent [in'fri:kwənt], adj. selten.
infringe [in'frindʒ], v. 1. v.tr. (gegen ein Gesetz usw.) verstoßen; (ein Patent) verletzen. 2. v.i. to i. on/upon s.o.'s rights, in j-s Rechte eingreifen. ◆in'fringement, s. Verstoß m (of, gegen + acc); i. (of the law) Gesetzesübertretung f.
infuriate [in'fjuərieit], v.tr. (j-n) wütend machen. ◆in'furiating, adj. sehr ärgerlich.
ingenious [in'dʒi:njəs], adj. (of pers.) einfallsreich; (of thing) raffiniert. ◆inge'nuity [-dʒi'nju:iti], s. Einfallsreichtum m; Raffiniertheit f.

ingenuous [in'dʒenjuəs], *adj.* naiv.

ingot [iŋgət], *s.* Barren *m.*

ingratiate [in'greiʃieit], *v.tr.* **to i. oneself with s.o.,** sich bei j-m einschmeicheln.

ingratitude [in'grætitjuːd], *s.* Undankbarkeit *f.*

ingredient [in'griːdiənt], *s.* Bestandteil *m.*; **ingredients of a cake,** Backzutaten *fpl*; *Fig:* **the ingredients of success,** die Voraussetzungen für den Erfolg.

inhabit [in'hæbit], *v.tr.* bewohnen. ◆**in'habitant,** *s.* Einwohner(in) *m(f).*

inhale [in'heil], *v.tr.* einatmen.

inherent [in'hiər(ə)nt], *adj.* innewohnend (**in, + *dat*).

inherit [in'herit], *v.tr.* erben. ◆**in'heritance,** *s.* Erbe *n*; Erbschaft *f.*

inhibit [in'hibit], *v.tr.* hemmen; **inhibited,** (*of pers.*) gehemmt. ◆**inhi'bition,** *s.* Hemmung *f.*

inhospitable [inhɔs'pitəbl], *adj.* unwirtlich.

inhuman [in'hjuːmən], *adj.* unmenschlich.

initial [i'niʃəl]. **I.** *adj.* anfänglich, Anfangs-. **II.** *s.* (*s.o.'s*) **initials,** (j-s) Initialen *pl*; **-ally,** *adv.* am Anfang.

initiate [i'niʃieit] *v.tr.* (*a*) (etwas) beginnen; (*b*) **to i. s.o. into a mystery,** j-n in ein Geheimnis einweihen. **II.** [i'niʃiit], *s.* Eingeweihte(r) *f(m).* ◆**initi'ation,** Einführung *f*; Einweihung *f.* ◆**initiative** [i'niʃiotiv], *s.* Initiative *f*; **to act on one's own i.,** aus eigener Initiative handeln; **to take the i.,** die Initiative ergreifen.

inject [in'dʒekt], *v.tr.* **to i. s.o. with a drug,** j-m ein Medikament injizieren. ◆**in'jection,** *s.* Injektion *f*; *Fig:* **i. of capital,** Kapitalspritze *f.*

injunction [in'dʒʌŋkʃən], *s.* einstweilige Verfügung *f.*

injure ['indʒər], *v.tr.* verletzen. ◆**'injured. I.** *adj.* verletzt. **II.** *s.* **the i.,** die Verletzten *pl.* ◆**'injury,** *s.* Verletzung *f*; **to add insult to i.,** das Maß vollmachen.

injustice [in'dʒʌstis], *s.* Ungerechtigkeit *f*; **you do him an i.,** Sie tun ihm unrecht.

ink [iŋk], *s.* (*a*) (*for writing*) Tinte *f*; (*for drawing*) Tusche *f.* ◆**'inkwell,** *s.* Tintenfaß *n.*

inkling ['iŋkliŋ], *s.* (leise) Ahnung *f.*

inland. I. *adj.* (*a*) binnenländisch; Binnen-; **i. waterways,** Binnengewässer *npl*; (*b*) *Brit:* **I. Revenue,** Steuerbehörde *f.* **II.** [in'lænd], *adv.* landeinwärts.

in-laws ['inlɔːz], *s.pl. F:* Schwiegereltern *pl.*

inlet ['inlet], *s.* **1.** Einlaß *m.* **2.** *Geog:* Meeresarm *m.*

inmate ['inmeit], *s.* Insasse *m,* Insassin *f.*

inn [in], *s.* Wirtshaus *n.*

innate [i'neit], *adj.* angeboren.

inner ['inər], *adj.* innere(r,s), Innen-; **i.**

tube, Luftschlauch *m.*

innings ['iniŋz], *s.* Spielzeit *f.*

innocent ['inəsənt], *adj.* (*a*) (*not guilty*) unschuldig; (*b*) (*unsuspecting*) arglos; (*ingenuous*) naiv. ◆**'innocence,** *s.* (*a*) Unschuld *f* (eines Angeklagten); (*b*) Arglosigkeit *f.*

innocuous [i'nɔkjuəs], *adj.* harmlos.

innovation [inəu'veiʃ(ə)n], *s.* Neuerung *f.*

innuendo, *pl.* **-oes** [inju(ː)'endəu, -əuz], *s.* versteckte Anspielung *f.*

innumerable [i'njuːmərəbl], *adj.* zahllos.

inoculate [i'nɔkjuleit], *v.tr.* impfen. ◆**inocu'lation,** *s.* Impfung *f.*

inoffensive [inə'fensiv], *adj.* harmlos.

inopportune [in'ɔpətjuːn], *adj.* ungelegen; (*of remark etc.*) unpassend.

inordinate [i'nɔːdinit], *adj.* unmäßig.

input ['input], *s.* *Data-pr:* Eingabe *f.*

inquest ['inkwest], *s.* *Jur:* amtliche Untersuchung *f* (zur Feststellung der Todesursache).

inquire [in'kwaiər], *v.* **1.** *v.tr.* sich (nach dem Preis, Weg usw.) erkundigen. **2.** *v.i.* sich erkundigen (**about/after s.o., sth.,** nach j-m, etwas *dat*); **to i. into sth.,** etwas untersuchen. ◆**in'quiring,** *adj.* fragend. ◆**in'quiry,** *s.* **1.** Nachfrage *f*; **to make inquiries (about s.o.),** (über j-n) Erkundigungen einziehen. **2.** (*police*) **i.,** (polizeiliche) Untersuchung *f.* **3.** *Tel:* **Inquiries,** Auskunft *f.*

inquisitive [in'kwizitiv], *adj.* neugierig.

insane [in'sein], *adj.* (*a*) geisteskrank, (*b*) *F:* verrückt. ◆**in'sanity** [-'sæniti], *s.* Geisteskrankheit *f.*

insanitary [in'sænit(ə)ri], *adj.* unhygienisch.

insatiable [in'seiʃəbl], *adj.* unersättlich.

inscription [in'skripʃ(ə)n], *s.* Inschrift *f*; Gravur *f* (auf einer Münze).

inscrutable [in'skruːtəbl], *adj.* unergründlich.

insect ['insekt], *s.* Insekt *n.* ◆**in'secticide,** *s.* Insektengift *n.*

insecure [insi'kjuər], *adj.* unsicher. ◆**inse'curity,** *s.* Unsicherheit *f.*

insemination [insemi'neiʃ(ə)n], *s.* **artificial i.,** künstliche Befruchtung *f.*

insensitive [in'sensitiv], *adj.* gefühllos. ◆**insensi'tivity,** *s.* Gefühllosigkeit *f.*

inseparable [in'sep(ə)rəbl], *adj.* untrennbar; (*of friends*) unzertrennlich.

insert [in'səːt], *v.tr.* (etwas) einfügen; **to i. a coin,** eine Münze einwerfen.

inside ['in'said]. **I.** *s.* (*a*) Innenseite *f*; (*inner surface*) Innenfläche *f*; **on the i.,** innen; **i. out,** verkehrt herum; **turned i. out,** (*of pockets*) umgestülpt; *Fig:* **to know sth. i. out,** etwas in- und auswendig kennen; (*b*) (das) Innere *n* (eines Hauses usw.). **II.** *adj.* Innen-, innere(r,s); **i. information,** vertrauliche Informationen; **i. job,** *F:* von Angestellten begangener Diebstahl. **III.** *adv.* im Innern, innen. **IV.** *prep.* innerhalb + *gen.*

◆**in'sider**, *s.* Eingeweihte(r) *f (m)*.

insidious [in'sidiəs], *adj.* heimtückisch.

insight ['insait], *s.* (*a*) Einblick *m*; **to gain an i. into sth.**, Einblick in eine Sache gewinnen; (*b*) (*realization*) Einsicht *f*.

insignificant [insig'nifikənt], *adj.* unbedeutend.

insincere [insin'siər], *adj.* unaufrichtig; (*of smile etc.*) falsch. ◆**insincerity** [-'seriti], *s.* Unaufrichtigkeit *f*.

insinuate [in'sinjueit], *v.tr.* andeuten. ◆**insinu'ation**, *s.* Andeutung *f*.

insipid [in'sipid], *adj.* (*of food*) geschmacklos; (*of book etc.*) langweilig.

insist [in'sist], *v.i.* bestehen (**on/upon**, auf + *acc*); **to i. on doing sth.**, darauf bestehen, etwas zu tun. ◆**in'sistence**, *s.* Beharren *n* (**on**, auf + *acc*). ◆**in'sistent**, *adj.* (*a*) beharrlich; (*b*) (*pushing*) aufdringlich.

insolent ['insələnt], *adj.* frech. ◆'**insolence**, *s.* Frechheit *f*.

insoluble [in'sɔljubl], *adj.* **1.** *Ch: etc:* unlöslich. **2.** (*of problem etc.*) unlösbar.

insomnia [in'sɔmniə], *s.* Schlaflosigkeit *f*.

inspect [in'spekt], *v.tr.* (*a*) (Lebensmittel, Maschinen usw.) prüfen; (*b*) (eine Schule, *Hum:* ein Haus usw.) inspizieren; *Mil:* **to i. troops**, die Parade abnehmen. ◆**in'spection** [-'spekʃ(ə)n], *s.* Inspektion *f*; (*examination*) Überprüfung *f*. ◆**in'spector**, *s.* Inspektor(in) *m(f)*.

inspire [in'spaiər], *v.tr.* (j-n) inspirieren; **to i. s.o. with confidence**, j-m Vertrauen einflößen. ◆**inspi'ration** [-spi'reiʃ(ə)n], *s.* Inspiration *f*. ◆**in'spired**, *adj.* genial.

instability [instə'biliti], *s.* (*a*) (*of boat, car etc.*) Unausgewogenheit *f*; (*b*) *Fig:* Unbeständigkeit *f*; (*esp. of character*) Labilität *f*.

install [in'stɔːl], *v.tr.* installieren. ◆**installation** [instə'leiʃ(ə)n], *s.* (*a*) Installierung *f*; (*b*) (*system*) Anlage *f*.

instalment [in'stɔːlmənt], *s.* **1.** (*of serial etc.*) Fortsetzung *f*. **2.** (*part payment*) Rate *f*.

instance ['instəns], *s.* Beispiel *n* (of sth., für etwas *acc*); (*case*) Fall *m*; **for i.**, zum Beispiel.

instant ['instənt]. **I.** *s.* Moment *m*. **II.** *adj.* sofortig; **i. coffee**, Schnellkaffee *m*. ◆**instan'taneous**, *adj.* unverzüglich.

instead [in'sted]. **I.** *prep.* **i. of s.o.**, anstelle von j-m, etwas *dat*; **of him**, an seiner Stelle. **II.** *adv.* statt dessen.

instigate ['instigeit], *v.tr.* (j-n, etwas) anregen; (etwas Böses) anstiften. ◆**insti'gation**, *s.* (*a*) Anregung *f*; **at his i.**, auf seine Anregung (hin); (*b*) Anstiftung *f* (von etwas Bösem). ◆**instigator**, *s.* Anstifter(in) *m(f)*.

instil [in'stil], *v.tr.* **to i. sth. into s.o.**, j-m etwas einflößen.

instinct ['instiŋ(k)t], *s.* Instinkt *m*. ◆**in'stinctive**, *adj.* instinktiv.

institute ['institjuːt]. **I.** *v.tr.* (einen Brauch, eine Vorschrift usw.) einführen;

Jur: **to i. an inquiry**, eine Untersuchung einleiten. **II.** *s.* Institut *n*. ◆**insti'tution**, *s.* (*a*) (*tradition*) Brauch *m*; (*b*) Anstalt *f*.

instruct [in'strʌkt], *v.tr.* (*a*) (j-n) unterrichten; (*b*) (j-n) anweisen (**to do sth.**, etwas zu tun). ◆**in'struction**, *s.* **1.** (*teaching*) Unterricht *m*; (*training*) Ausbildung *f*. **2.** *usu.pl.* Anweisung *f*. ◆**in'structive**, *adj.* aufschlußreich. ◆**in'structor**, *s.* Lehrer(in) *m(f)*.

instrument ['instrəmənt], *s.* Instrument *n*. ◆**instru'mental**, *adj.* **1.** **to be i. in doing sth.**, eine entscheidende Rolle bei etwas *dat* spielen. **2.** *i. music*, Instrumentalmusik *f*.

insubordinate [insəbɔːdinit], *adj.* ungehorsam. ◆**insubordi'nation**, *s.* Gehorsamsverweigerung *f*.

insufferable [in'sʌf(ə)rəbl], *adj.* unerträglich.

insufficient [insə'fiʃənt], *adj.* ungenügend.

insular ['insjulər], *adj.* (*a*) insular, Insel-; (*b*) (*of pers.*) engstirnig.

insulate ['insjuleit], *v.tr.* isolieren. ◆**insu'lation**, *s.* Isolierung *f*. ◆**insulating**, *adj.* **i. tape**, Isolierband *n*.

insulin ['insjulin], *s.* Insulin *n*.

insult. **I.** ['insʌlt] *s.* Beleidigung *f*. **II.** [in'sʌlt] *v.tr.* (j-n) beleidigen. ◆**in'sulting**, *adj.* beleidigend.

insuperable [in'sjuːp(ə)rəbl], *adj.* unüberwindlich.

insure [in'ʃuər], *v.tr.* (*a*) versichern; (*b*) (*guarantee*) (Erfolg usw.) gewährleisten. ◆**in'surance**, *s.* Versicherung *f*; **i. policy**, Versicherungspolice *f*.

insurmountable [insə(ː)'mauntəbl], *adj.* unüberwindlich.

insurrection [insə'rekʃən], *s.* Aufstand *m*.

intact [in'tækt], *adj.* unversehrt.

intake ['inteik], *s.* **1.** (*opening*) Einlaß *m*, Einlaßöffnung *f*. **2.** (*amount admitted*) **food i.**, Nahrungsaufnahme *f*.

integral ['intigrəl], *adj.* wesentlich. ◆**'integrate** [-greit], *v.* **1.** *v.tr.* (j-n) integrieren (**into society etc.**, in die Gesellschaft usw.). **2.** *v.i.* sich integrieren. ◆**inte'gration**, *s.* Integration *f*.

integrity [in'tegriti], *s.* Integrität *f*.

intellect ['intəlekt], *s.* Verstand *m*. ◆**inte'llectual.** **I.** *adj.* intellektuell; (*of work etc.*) geistig. **II.** *s.* Intellektuelle(r) *f(m)*.

intelligence [in'telidʒəns], *s.* **1.** Intelligenz *f*. **2.** *esp. Mil:* (*service*) Nachrichtendienst *m*. ◆**in'telligent**, *adj.* intelligent.

intelligible [in'telidʒəbl], *adj.* verständlich.

intend [in'tend], *v.tr.* **to i. to do sth.**, beabsichtigen, etwas zu tun. ◆**in'tended**, *adj.* **1.** (*a*) beabsichtigt; (*of journey etc.*) geplant; (*b*) (*intentional*) absichtlich. **2. i. for s.o.**, für j-n gedacht,

(of remark etc.) an j-n gerichtet.
intense [in'tens], adj. (a) (of colour, feelings etc.) intensiv, stark; (b) (of pers., expression) angespannt; **-ly,** adv. äußerst; höchst; ◆**in'tensify,** v. 1. v.tr. (a) (eine Wirkung, einen Kontrast usw.) steigern; (b) to i. one's efforts/a search, seine Bemühungen/eine Suche intensivieren 2. v.i. (of feelings etc.) stärker werden. ◆**in'tensity,** s. Intensität f. ◆**in'tensive,** adj. intensiv; **i. care unit,** Intensivstation f.
intent [in'tent]. I. adj. to be i. on sth., in etwas acc ganz vertieft sein; to be i. on doing sth., fest entschlossen sein, etwas zu tun. II. s. 1. Absicht f. 2. **to all intents and purposes,** so gut wie. ◆**intention** [in'tenʃən], s. Absicht f. ◆**in'tentional,** adj. absichtlich.
interact [intər'ækt], v.i. aufeinander wirken. ◆**inter'action,** s. Wechselwirkung f.
intercede [intə(:)'si:d], v.i. to i. with s.o. for s.o., bei j-m für j-n Fürsprache einlegen.
intercept [intə(:)'sept], v.tr. abfangen. ◆**inter'ception,** s. Abfangen n.
interchange. I. ['intətʃeindʒ], s. (of ideas etc.) Austausch m; traffic i., Kreuzung f. II. [intə'tʃeindʒ], v.tr. austauschen. ◆**inter'changeable,** adj. austauschbar.
intercom ['intəkɔm], s. Sprechanlage f.
intercontinental [intəkɔnti'nentl], adj. interkontinental.
intercourse ['intə(:)kɔ:s], s. (a) social i., gesellschaftlicher Umgang m; (b) (sexual) i., Geschlechtsverkehr m.
interest ['int(ə)rest]. I. s. 1. (a) Interesse n (in music etc., an der Musik dat usw.); to take an i. in sth., sich für etwas acc interessieren; (b) (advantage) Vorteil m; to act in one's own i., zum eigenen Vorteil handeln. 2. Com: Beteiligung f (in a firm, an einer Firma). 3. Fin: Zinsen mpl; i. rate, Zinssatz m. II. v.tr. (j-n) interessieren (in sth., für etwas acc). ◆'**interested,** adj. interessiert (in sth., an etwas dat); to be i. in sth., sich für etwas acc interessieren. ◆'**interesting,** adj. interessant.
interface ['intəfeis], s. Data-pr: Schnittstelle f.
interfere [intə'fiər], v.i. (in einen Streit usw.) eingreifen; to i. in other people's business, sich in fremde Angelegenheiten einmischen. ◆**inter'ference,** s. 1. Eingreifen n; Einmischung f (in sth., in etwas acc). 2. Rad: Störung f. ◆**inter'fering,** adj. he's very i., er mischt sich dauernd ein.
interim ['intərim]. I. s. in the i., in der Zwischenzeit. II. adj. Zwischen-.
interior [in'tiəriər]. I. adj. inner, Innen-; i. decorator, Innenarchitekt m. II. s. (space) Innenraum m; (of country) Binnenland n.
interlude ['intəlju:d], s. Zwischenspiel n.

intermediary [intə'mi:djəri], s. Vermittler(in) m(f).
intermediate [intə'mi:diət], adj. Zwischen-.
interminable [in'tə:minəbl], adj. endlos.
intermission [intə'miʃən], s. Pause f.
intermittent [intə'mitənt], adj. in Abständen (auftretend/erscheinend).
internal [in'tə:nəl], adj. innere(r, s); i. combustion engine, Verbrennungsmotor m. 2. Innen-; inländisch; i. trade, Binnenhandel m; N.Am: i. revenue, inländische Steuereinnahmen; **-ally,** adv. innen; to bleed i., innerlich bluten.
international [intə'næʃ(ə)nəl], adj. international.
interplay ['intəplei], s. Wechselspiel n.
interpret [in'tə:prit], v.tr. (a) (einen Text usw.) auslegen; Mus: (ein Stück) interpretieren; (b) (translate) (ein Gespräch usw.) dolmetschen. ◆**interpre'tation,** s. 1. Interpretation f. 2. (mündliche) Übersetzung f. ◆**in'terpreter,** s. Dolmetscher(in) m(f).
interrogate [in'terəgeit], v.tr. (j-n) ausfragen; Jur: (Zeugen usw.) verhören. ◆**interro'gation,** s. Vernehmung f, Verhör n.
interrupt [intə'rʌpt], v.tr. unterbrechen; (disturb) (j-n) stören. ◆**inte'rruption,** s. Unterbrechung f; Störung f.
interval ['intəvəl], s. (a) Zwischenraum m; at intervals, in Abständen; (b) Meteor: bright i., kurze Aufheiterung f; (c) Th: etc: Pause f.
intervene [intə'vi:n], v.i. (a) (of pers.) eingreifen (in, in + acc); Pol: Mil: etc: intervenieren; (b) (of events) dazwischenkommen; (c) (of time) ten years intervened, zehn Jahre lagen dazwischen. ◆**inter'vention** [-'venʃ(ə)n], s. Eingreifen n; Pol: Mil: etc: Intervention f.
interview ['intəvju:]. I. s. (a) TV: Interview n; (b) (for job) Vorstellungsgespräch n. II. v.tr. (a) (j-n) interviewen; (b) (mit j-m) ein Vorstellungsgespräch führen. ◆'**interviewer,** s. Interviewer m.
intestine [in'testin], s. Darm m.
intimacy ['intiməsi], s. Intimität f. ◆**intimate¹** ['intimit], adj. (a) vertraut; (of room etc.) intim; (of manner, talk) vertraulich; (b) (of knowledge etc.) gründlich; **-ly,** adv. **to know sth. i.,** etwas genau kennen.
intimate² ['intimeit], v.tr. (etwas) zu verstehen geben.
intimidate [in'timideit], v.tr. (j-n) einschüchtern. ◆**in'timidating,** adj. einschüchternd. ◆**intimi'dation,** s. Einschüchterung f.
into ['intu, intə], prep. in + acc, in ... hinein.
intolerable [in'tɔl(ə)rəbl], adj. unerträglich. ◆**in'tolerant,** adj. intolerant.
intoxicate [in'tɔksikeit], v.tr. berauschen. ◆**in'toxicated,** adj. berauscht; (drunk) betrunken. ◆**intoxi'cation,** s. Rausch

m.

intravenous [intrə'viːnəs], *adj.* intravenös.

intrepid [in'trepid], *adj.* unerschrocken.

intricate ['intrikit], *adj.* kompliziert; *F:* (tricky) knifflig. ◆**in'tricacy,** *s.* Kompliziertheit *f;* Kniffligkeit *f.*

intrigue [in'triːg]. I. *v.* [in'triːg]. 1. *v.i.* intrigieren. 2. *v.tr.* to i. s.o., j-n faszinieren. II. *s.* ['intriːg] Intrige *f.* ◆**in'triguing,** *adj.* faszinierend.

intrinsic [in'trinsik], *adj.* innere(r,s); (real) wirklich.

introduce [intrə'djuːs], *v.tr.* (a) (etwas Neues) einführen; (b) **he introduced me to her,** er stellte mich ihr vor; to i. s.o. to sth., j-n in etwas *acc* einführen. ◆**intro'duction,** *s.* Einführung *f.* 2. (of pers.) Vorstellung *f.* ◆**intro'ductory,** *adj.* einführend; Einführungs-.

introspective [intrə'spektiv], *adj.* (of pers.) introspektiv.

introvert ['intrəuvəːt], *s.* introvertierter Mensch *m.*

intrude [in'truːd], *v.i.* to i. on s.o., sich bei j-m eindrängen. ◆**in'truder,** *s.* Eindringling *m.* ◆**in'trusion,** *s.* Eindringen *n;* (disturbance) Störung *f.* ◆**in'trusive,** *adj.* aufdringlich.

intuition [intju(ː)'iʃən], *s.* Intuition *f.* ◆**in'tuitive,** *adj.* intuitiv.

inundate ['inʌndeit], *v.tr.* inundated with tourists, von Touristen überlaufen; inundated with requests, mit Bitten überhäuft.

invade [in'veid], *v.tr.* einfallen. ◆**in'vader,** *s.* Eindringling *m.*

invalid[1] [in'vælid], *adj.* ungültig. ◆**in'validate,** *v.tr.* (eine Behauptung usw.) entkräften; *Jur:* (einen Vertrag) nichtig machen.

invalid[2] ['invəlid, -liːd]. I. *adj.* (of pers.) krank. II. *s.* Invalide *m.*

invaluable [in'vælju(ə)bl], *adj.* unbezahlbar.

invariable [in'vɛəriəbl], *adj.* unveränderlich; **-ly,** *adv.* ständig; (each time) jedes Mal.

invasion [in'veiʒən], *s.* Invasion *f.*

invective [in'vektiv], *s.* Beschimpfungen *fpl.*

invent [in'vent], *v.tr.* erfinden. ◆**in'vention,** *s.* Erfindung *f.* ◆**in'ventive,** *adj.* erfinderisch. ◆**in'ventor,** *s.* Erfinder(in) *m(f).*

inventory ['invəntri], *s.* Bestandsaufnahme *f.*

inverse [in'vəːs], *adj.* umgekehrt. ◆**in'vert** [in'vəːt], *v.tr.* umkehren; inverted commas, Anführungszeichen *npl.*

invertebrate [in'vəːtibreit], *s.* wirbelloses Tier *n.*

invest [in'vest], *v.tr. & i.* investieren (in sth., in etwas *acc*). ◆**in'vestment,** *s.* 1. Investition *f.* 2. (money etc.) Anlage *f.* ◆**in'vestor,** *s.* Kapitalanleger *m;* small

i., Kleinsparer *m.*

investigate [in'vestigeit], *v.tr.* untersuchen. ◆**investi'gation,** *s.* Untersuchung *f.* ◆**in'vestigator,** *s.* Ermittlungsbeamte(r) *m.*

inveterate [in'vet(ə)rit], *adj.* **i. gambler,** Gewohnheitsspieler *m.*

invigorating [in'vigəreitiŋ], *adj.* belebend.

invincible [in'vinsəbl], *adj.* unbesiegbar.

invisible [in'vizəbl], *adj.* unsichtbar.

invite [in'vait], *v.tr.* einladen. ◆**invitation** [-vi'teiʃ(ə)n], *s.* Einladung *f.* ◆**in'viting,** *adj.* einladend; (of food) appetitlich.

invoice ['invɔis]. I. *s.* Rechnung *f.* II. *v.tr.* to i. s.o. for an amount, j-m einen Betrag in Rechnung stellen.

involuntary [in'vɔlənt(ə)ri], *adj.* unwillkürlich.

involve [in'vɔlv], *v.tr.* (a) (often passive) (j-n) hineinziehen (in sth., in etwas *acc*); to be involved in a dispute/in a plot, an einem Streit/an einer Verschwörung beteiligt sein; the car involved (in the accident), das an dem Unfall beteiligte Auto; (b) (entail) (Unkosten usw.) mit sich bringen. ◆**in'volved,** *adj.* kompliziert. ◆**in'volvement,** *s.* Beteiligung *f.*

inwardly ['inwəli], *adv.* innerlich. ◆**inwards,** *adv.* nach innen (gerichtet).

iodine ['aiədiːn], *s.* Jod *n.*

Iran [i'rɑːn]. *Pr.n.* Iran *m.* ◆**Iranian** [i'reinjən]. I. *adj.* iranisch. II. *s.* Iraner(in) *m(f).*

Iraq [i'rɑːk]. *Pr.n.* Irak *m.* ◆**I'raqi.** I. *adj.* irakisch. II. *s.* Iraker(in) *m(f).*

irate [ai'reit], *adj.* wütend.

Ireland ['aiələnd]. *Pr.n.* Irland *n.*

iris ['aiəris], *s. Anat: Bot:* Iris *f.*

Irish ['aiəriʃ]. I. *adj.* irisch. II. *s.* 1. (language) Irisch *n.* 2. *pl.* the I., die Iren *mpl.* ◆**'Irishman,** *pl.* **-men,** *s.* Ire *m.* ◆**'Irishwoman,** *pl.* **-women,** *s.* Irin *f.*

irksome ['əːksəm], *adj.* lästig.

iron ['aiən]. I. *s.* 1. (a) Eisen *n;* i. ore, Eisenerz *n;* (b) I. Curtain, eiserner Vorhang *m.* 2. *H:* Bügeleisen *n.* II. *v.tr.* (Wäsche) bügeln. ◆**'ironing,** *s.* Bügeln *n;* i. board, Bügelbrett *n.* ◆**'ironmonger,** *s.* Eisenwarenhändler *m.*

irony ['aiərəni], *s.* Ironie *f.* ◆**i'ronical,** *adj.* ironisch.

irrational [i'ræʃənəl], *adj.* irrational.

irreconcilable [irekən'sailəbl], *adj.* (a) (of enemy etc.) unversöhnlich; (b) (of ideas) unvereinbar (with, mit).

irrefutable [iri'fjuːtəbl], *adj.* unwiderlegbar.

irregular [i'regjulər], *adj.* 1. (a) (of bus service etc.) unregelmäßig; (b) (of surface) uneben. 2. (of conduct etc.) ungehörig; (against rules) unvorschriftsmäßig. ◆**irregu'larity,** *s.* 1. Unregelmäßigkeit *f.* 2. (a) Ungehörigkeit *f;* (b) (infringement) Verstoß *m* (gegen eine Vorschrift).

irrelevance [i'relivəns], s. Nebensächlichkeit f. ◆**i'rrelevant**, adj. nebensächlich; that's i., das hat nichts damit zu tun.

irreparable [i'rep(ə)rəbl], adj. nicht wiedergutzumachen.

irreplaceable [iri'pleisəbl], adj. unersetzlich.

irrepressible [iri'presəbl], adj. he is i., er ist nicht unterzukriegen.

irresistible [iri'zistəbl], adj. unwiderstehlich.

irresolute [i'rezəl(j)u:t], adj. unentschlossen.

irrespective [iris'pektiv], adj. & adv. i. of, ungeachtet + gen.

irresponsible [iris'pɔnsəbl], adj. (of person) verantwortungslos; (of action) unverantwortlich.

irreverent [i'rev(ə)rənt], adj. ehrfurchtslos.

irrevocable [i'revəkəbl], adj. unwiderruflich.

irrigate ['irigeit], v.tr. bewässern. ◆**irri'gation**, s. Bewässerung f.

irritate ['iriteit], v.tr. (a) (die Haut usw.) reizen; (b) (j-n) irritieren. ◆**irritable**, adj. reizbar; ◆**irritant**, s. Reizmittel n. ◆**irritating**, adj. irritierend. ◆**irri'tation**, s. 1. Ärger m. 2. Med: Reizung f.

Islamic [iz'læmik], adj. islamisch.

island ['ailənd], s. Insel f. ◆**isle**, s. (esp.in Pr.n.) Insel f.

isobar ['aisoubɑ:], s. Isobare f.

isolate ['aisəleit], v.tr. isolieren ◆**iso'lation**, s. Isolierung f.

Israel ['izrei(ə)l]. Pr.n. Israel n. ◆**Is'raeli**. I. adj. israelisch. II. s. Israeli m.

issue ['isju:]. I. s. 1. Frage f; (in argument) Streitfrage f; **to force the i.**, eine Entscheidung erzwingen. 2. (a) Ausgabe f (von Münzen, Briefmarken usw.); Ausstellung f (eines Passes usw.); Emission f (von Aktien); (b) Nummer f (einer Zeitschrift). II. v.tr. a herausgeben; (Pässe, Schecks usw.) ausstellen; (Aktien) ausgeben; (b) Mil: **to i. an order,** einen Befehl erteilen.

it [it], pers.pron. 1. (a) (subject) es n; er m; sie f; (b) (direct object) es n; ihn m; sie f; (c) (indirect object) ihm m, n; ihr f. 2. **it's me,** ich bin's; **it's the children,** es sind die Kinder; **that's just it!** das ist es ja gerade! **it's said that...,** man sagt, daß...

Italian [i'tæljən]. I. adj. italienisch. II. s. (a) Italiener(in) m(f); (b) Italienisch n. ◆**Italy** ['itəli]. Pr.n. Italien n.

italics [i'tæliks], s.pl. Kursivschrift f.

itch [itʃ]. I. v.i. jucken; Fig: **to be itching to do sth.,** darauf brennen, etwas zu tun. II. s. (also **itching**) Jucken n. ◆**itchy,** adj. juckend.

item ['aitəm], s. 1. (a) (object) Gegenstand m; i. of clothing, Kleidungsstück m; (b) (matter) Sache f. 2. (a) (on agenda etc.) Punkt m; (b) Com: etc: (in budget etc.) Posten m. 3. **news i.,** (einzelne) Nachricht f; (article) Artikel m.

itinerary i'tinərəri,ai-], s. Reiseroute f.

its [its], poss.adj. m, n sein; f ihr.

it's [its]. F: = 1. **it is.** 2. **it has.**

itself [it'self], pers.pron. 1. (reflexive) sich. 2. (emphatic) selbst.

I've [aiv]. F: = **I have.**

ivory ['aiv(ə)ri], s. 1. Elfenbein n. 2. attrib. (a) elfenbeinern; (b) (colour) elfenbeinfarbig.

ivy ['aivi], s. Efeu m.

J

J, j [dʒei], s. (der Buchstabe) J, j n.

jab [dʒæb]. I. v.tr. & i. (j-n) stoßen, (with sth. sharp) stechen. II. s. 1. Knuff m. 2. Med: F: Spritze f.

jack [dʒæk], s. 1. (in cards) Bube m. 2. Aut: Wagenheber m. ◆**jackdaw,** s. Dohle f. ◆**jackknife,** v.i. the trailer **jackknifed,** der Anhänger scherte aus und stellte sich quer. ◆**jackpot,** s. Hauptgewinn m; F: **to hit/win the j.,** den Haupttreffer machen; Fig: den Vogel abschießen. ◆**'jack'up,** v.tr. (ein Auto usw.) aufbocken.

jackal ['dʒækɔːl], s. Schakal m.

jacket ['dʒækit], s. 1. (a) Jacke f; (b) j. potatoes, gebackene Kartoffeln fpl. 2. book j., Schutzumschlag m.

jade [dʒeid], s. Jade m.

jaded ['dʒeidid], adj. abgekämpft.

jagged ['dʒægid], adj. zackig; (of rock, coastline) zerklüftet.

jail [dʒeil], s. see gaol.

jam¹ [dʒæm]. I. v. 1. v.tr. (a) F: (etwas) hineinzwängen; **to get one's finger jammed,** sich dat den Finger einquetschen; (b) F: **to j. on the brakes,** (heftig) auf die Bremsen steigen; (c) (block) (eine Maschine) blockieren. 2. v.i. (a) (stick) klemmen; (b) (of key etc.) steckenbleiben. II. s. (a) (traffic) j., Verkehrsstauung f; (b) F: **to be in a j.,** in der Klemme sitzen.

jam², s. Marmelade f.

Jamaica [dʒə'meikə]. Pr.n. Jamaika n. ◆**Ja'maican.** I. adj. jamaikisch. II. s. Jamaikaner(in) m(f).

jangle ['dʒæŋgl], s. 1. v.i. klimpern. 2. v.tr. **to j. the keys,** mit den Schlüsseln klimpern.

janitor ['dʒænitər], s. Hausmeister m.

January ['dʒænjuəri], s. Januar m.

Japan [dʒə'pæn]. Pr.n. Japan n. ◆**Japa'nese.** I. adj. japanisch. II. s. 1. Japaner(in) m(f). 2. Japanisch n.

jar¹ [dʒɑːr], v. 1. v.i. nicht harmonieren. 2. v.tr. (die Nerven, das Rückgrat usw.) erschüttern.

jar², s. Glas n.

jargon ['dʒɑːgən], s. Jargon m.

jasmine ['dʒæzmin], s. Jasmin m.

jaundice ['dʒɔːndis], s. Gelbsucht f.

jaunt [dʒɔːnt], s. Spritztour f.

javelin ['dʒævlin], s. (a) Speer m; (b) (event) Speerwurf m.

jaw [dʒɔː], s. Kiefer m.

jay [dʒei], s. Eichelhäher m. ◆**jaywalker**, s. leichtsinniger Fußgänger.

jazz [dʒæz], s. Jazz m. ◆**jazz 'up**, v.tr. verjazzen. ◆**jazzy**, adj. (of music) verjazzt; F: (of tie etc.) poppig; Pej: schreiend.

jealous ['dʒeləs], adj. eifersüchtig (of, auf + acc). ◆**jealousy**, s. Eifersucht f.

jeans [dʒiːnz], s. pl. Jeans pl.

jeep [dʒiːp], s. Jeep m.

jeer [dʒiər]. I. v.i. (of crowd) johlen; (of pers.) to j. at s.o., sth., j-n, etwas verhöhnen. II. s. Hohnruf m. ◆**jeering**. I. adj. johlend; (scornful) höhnisch. II. s. Johlen n.

jelly ['dʒeli], s. Gelee m. ◆**jelly-fish**, s. Qualle f.

jeopardize ['dʒepədaiz], v.tr. gefährden. ◆**jeopardy**, s. Gefahr f.

jerk [dʒəːk]. I. s. 1. Ruck m. 2. P: (pers.) Lümmel m. II. v. 1. v.tr. (etwas) ruckweise ziehen. 2. v.i. einen Ruck geben. ◆**jerky**, adj. ruckartig.

jerry-built ['dʒeribilt], adj. schlecht gebaut.

jersey ['dʒəːzi], s. Pullover m.

jest [dʒest], s. Scherz m.

jet [dʒet], s. 1. Strahl m; j. of water, Wasserstrahl m. 2. j. (plane), Düsenflugzeug n; j. engine, Strahltriebwerk n; j. fighter, Düsenjäger m.

jettison ['dʒetis(ə)n], v.tr. über Bord werfen.

jetty ['dʒeti], s. Landungssteg m.

Jew [dʒuː], s. Jude m. ◆**Jewish**, adj. jüdisch.

jewel ['dʒuːəl], s. (a) Edelstein m; esp. Fig: Juwel n; (b) pl. Schmuck m. ◆**jeweller**, s. Juwelier m. ◆**jewel(l)ery**, s. Schmuck m.

jiffy ['dʒifi], s. in a j., im Nu; (soon) gleich.

jigsaw ['dʒigsɔː], s. j. (puzzle), Puzzle(spiel) n.

jilt ['dʒilt], v.tr. F: (einem Mann) den Laufpaß geben; (ein Mädchen) sitzenlassen.

jingle ['dʒiŋgl], v. 1. v.i. klingeln; (of keys, money) klimpern. 2. v.tr. (etwas) klingeln lassen; (mit Geld, Schlüsseln) klimpern.

jitter ['dʒitər], s. F: to get the jitters, Schiß kriegen. ◆**jittery**, adj. nervös.

job [dʒɔb], s. 1. (a) Arbeit f; Aufgabe f; F: it's a good j. you came, es ist gut,

daß du gekommen bist; (b) F: I had a (hard) j. to convince him, ich konnte ihn nur mit Mühe überzeugen. 2. (position etc.) Stellung f; F: Job m.

jockey ['dʒɔki], s. Jockei m.

jocular ['dʒɔkjulər], adj. scherzhaft.

jodhpurs ['dʒɔdpəːz], s.pl. Reithosen fpl.

jog [dʒɔg], v.tr. & i. (a) (shake) (j-n) durchrütteln; (b) (knock) j-n stupsen; to j. s.o.'s memory, j-s Gedächtnis auffrischen. ◆**jogging**, s. Jogging n.

join [dʒɔin]. I. s. Verbindungsstelle f. II. v. 1. v.tr. (a) (etwas) verbinden (to sth., mit etwas dat); (zwei Teile) zusammenfügen; (b) (j-m) Gesellschaft leisten; (c) (einem Verein, einer Partei usw.) beitreten; (in eine Firma) eintreten; to j. the army, zur Armee gehen. 2. v.i. (of lines) zusammenlaufen; (of roads) sich treffen. ◆**joiner**, s. Tischler m. ◆**joinery**, s. Tischlerarbeit f. ◆**join 'in**, v. 1. v.i. mitmachen. 2. v.tr. sich (an etwas dat) beteiligen. ◆**joint**. I. s. 1. (a) Tchn: Fuge f; (b) Anat: Gelenk n. 2. Cu: Braten n. 3. F: esp. N. Am: Lokal n; Pej: Bude f. III. adj. 1. gemeinsam; j. account, Gemeinschaftskonto n. 2. Mit-; j. owner, Miteigentümer m. ◆**join 'up**, v. 1. v.i. (a) Mil: zum Militär gehen; (b) (of lines etc.) zusammenlaufen. 2. v.tr. (zwei Sachen) zusammenfügen.

joist [dʒɔist], s. Dielenbalken m; pl. Gebälk n.

joke [dʒəuk]. I. s. Scherz m; Witz m; (practical) j., Streich m; F: it's no j.! das ist keine Kleinigkeit! II. v.i. scherzen; (tell jokes) Witze reißen; you must be joking! das meinst du doch nicht im Ernst! ◆**joker**, s. 1. Spaßvogel m. 2. (in cards) Joker m. ◆**joking**, s. j. apart, Scherz beiseite.

jolly ['dʒɔli]. I. adj. fröhlich; lustig. II. adv. F: j. glad, sehr froh.

jolt [dʒəult]. I. s. Ruck m. II. v. 1. v.tr. (j-m, etwas dat) einen Ruck geben. 2. v.i. holpern.

Jordan ['dʒɔːd(ə)n]. Pr. n. Jordanien n. ◆**Jordanian** [-'deiniən], I. adj. jordanisch. II. s. Jordanier(in) m(f).

jostle ['dʒɔsl], v.tr. & i. drängeln.

jot [dʒɔt], v.tr. to j. sth. down, sich dat etwas notieren.

journal ['dʒəːn(ə)l], s. 1. Journal n (einer Reise usw.); (diary) Tagebuch n. 2. (periodical) Zeitschrift f. ◆**journalism**, s. Journalismus m. ◆**journalist**, s. Journalist(in) m(f).

journey ['dʒəːni], s. Reise f.

jovial ['dʒəuvjəl], adj. jovial.

joy [dʒɔi], s. Freude f. ◆**joyful**, adj. freudig. ◆**joy-ride**, s. F: Spritztour f. ◆**joy-stick**, s. Steuerknüppel m.

jubilant ['dʒuːbilənt], adj. hocherfreut. ◆**jubi'lation**, s. Jubel m.

jubilee ['dʒuːbiliː], s. Jubiläum n.

judge [dʒʌdʒ]. I. s. Jur: Richter m. 2. Sp: Schiedsrichter m. II. v. 1. v.tr. (a) Jur: (einen Fall) entscheiden; (b) (eine Sache) beurteilen; to j. a competition, in

einem Wettbewerb entscheiden; (c) (eine Entfernung usw.) schätzen. 2. v.i. urteilen (by/from), nach + dat).
◆'**judg(e)ment**, s. 1. Urteil n. 2. (ability) Urteilsvermögen n. ◆**judicial** [dʒu:'diʃəl], adj. gerichtlich. ◆**ju'dicious**, adj. klug.

jug [dʒʌg], s. Krug m; (for milk etc.) Kanne f; (small) Kännchen n.

juggle [dʒʌgl], v.i. jonglieren. ◆'**juggler**, s. Jongleur m.

Jugoslavia [ju:gə(u)'slɑːvjə]. Pr. n. Jugoslawien n.

juice [dʒu:s], s. Saft m.

jukebox [dʒu:kbɔks], s. Musikbox f.

July [dʒu'lai], s. Juli m.

jumble [dʒʌmbl]. I. v.tr. to j. sth. up, etwas durcheinanderbringen. II. s. Durcheinander n; j. sale, approx. = Flohmarkt m.

jumbo [dʒʌmbəu], s. j. (jet), Jumbo-Jet m.

jump [dʒʌmp]. I. s. 1. Sprung m. 2. (fence) Hindernis n. II. v. 1. v.i. (a) springen; you made me j.! du hast mich erschreckt! (b) to j. to conclusions, voreilig Schlüsse ziehen. 2. v.tr. (etwas) überspringen; to j. the queue, sich vordrängen. ◆**jump at**, v.tr. (a) to j. at sth., sich auf etwas acc stürzen; (b) F: to j. at an offer, ein Angebot sofort ergreifen. ◆'**jumper**, s. Pullover m. ◆'**jump-lead**, s. Starthilfekabel n. ◆'**jumpy**, adj. F: nervös.

junction [dʒʌŋ(k)ʃ(ə)n], s. 1. Verbindungsstelle f. 2. (a) (road) j., Kreuzung f; T-j., Einmündung f; (b) Rail: Bahnknotenpunkt m.

juncture [dʒʌŋ(k)tʃər], s. at this j., in diesem Augenblick.

June [dʒu:n], s. Juni m.

jungle [dʒʌŋgl], s. Dschungel m.

junior [dʒu:njər]. I. s. (a) Junior m. (b) he is two years my j., er ist zwei Jahre jünger als ich. II. adj. jünger; j. school, Grundschule f; j. events, Juniorenwettkampf m.

junk [dʒʌŋk], s. Pej: Ramsch m; j. shop, Trödlerladen m.

jurisdiction [dʒuəris'dikʃ(ə)n], s. (authority) Gerichtsbarkeit f; (area of authority) Kompetenzbereich m.

jury [dʒuəri], s. Jur: the j., die Geschworenen pl. 2. (of competition) Jury f. ◆'**juror, 'juryman**, s. Geschworener m.

just [dʒʌst]. I. adj. (a) (fair) gerecht; (b) (deserved) verdient; -ly, adv. j. famous, mit Recht berühmt. II. adv. 1. gerade; I saw him j. now/have j. seen him, ich habe ihn gerade gesehen; j. as he was leaving, gerade als er wegging. 2. (exactly) genau; it's j. the same, es ist genau das gleiche; he can do it j. as well, er kann es ebenso gut. 3. I was (only) j. in time/F: I only j. made it, ich habe es gerade noch geschafft; only j. enough, gerade noch genug. 4. (only) nur; j. tell me, sag's mir doch. 5. F: j. marvellous, einfach großartig.

justice [dʒʌstis], s. Gerechtigkeit f; to do s.o. j., j-m gerecht werden.

justify [dʒʌstifai], v.tr. rechtfertigen. ◆**justi'fiable**, adj. berechtigt; (of action) zu rechtfertigen; (of conduct) entschuldbar. ◆**justifi'cation**, s. Rechtfertigung f. ◆'**justified**, adj. (of decision etc.) gerechtfertigt; (of pers.) to be j. in doing sth., berechtigt sein, etwas zu tun.

jut [dʒʌt], v.i. to j. (out), vorspringen.

juvenile [dʒu:vənail], adj. jugendlich; Jugend-; j. court, Jugendgericht n; j. delinquent, jugendlicher Straftäter m.

K

K, k [kei], s. (der Buchstabe) K, k n.

kaleidoscope [kə'laidəskəup], s. Kaleidoskop n.

kangaroo [kæŋgə'ru:], s. Z: Känguruh n.

kayak [kaiæk], s. Kajak m.

keel [ki:l]. I. s. Kiel m. II. v.i. to k. over, kentern.

keen [ki:n], adj. 1. (of interest, feeling) stark; Com: k. competition, scharfe Konkurrenz. 2. (of pers.) eifrig; to be k. on sth., von etwas dat begeistert sein. 3. (of eye, ear) scharf.

keep [ki:p]. I. v.irr. 1. v.tr. (a) (retain) (etwas) behalten; to k. a seat for s.o., einen Platz für j-n freihalten; to k. a secret, ein Geheimnis bewahren; (b) (look after) (Geflügel, Schweine usw.) halten; to k. a hotel, ein Hotel führen; to k. one's parents, für seine Eltern sorgen; (c) (hold up) (j-n) aufhalten; to k. s.o. waiting, j-n warten lassen; the noise kept

me from sleeping, der Lärm ließ mich nicht schlafen; (d) to k. a promise, ein Versprechen halten; (e) to k. sth. secret, etwas geheimhalten; (f) (store) (etwas) aufbewahren. 2. v.i. (a) to k. doing sth., (i) etwas immer wieder machen; (ii) (continue) etwas weitermachen; (b) (on sign) k. left, links halten; (c) (of food etc.) sich halten; (d) to k. warm/well/fit, warm/gesund/fit bleiben; F: how are you keeping? wie geht es Ihnen? II. s. to earn one's k., seinen Unterhalt verdienen. ◆**keep a'way**, v. 1. v.tr. (j-n, etwas) fernhalten. 2. v.i. sich fernhalten. ◆**keep 'back**, v. 1. v.tr. (a) (den Feind, die Menge) zurückhalten; (b) (die Wahrheit) verschweigen; (c) (Geld) (zurück)behalten. 2. v.i. k. back! zurücktreten! ◆'**keeper**, s. (of zoo, lighthouse) Wärter m; (of park etc.) Wächter m. ◆**keep 'in**, v. 1. v.tr. (a) (j-n) nicht hinauslassen; (b) (Zorn usw.) zurückhalten; (c) to k. one's hand in, in Übung bleiben. 2. v.i. (a) (on road) sich am Rand halten; (b) to k. in with s.o., mit j-m auf gutem Fuß bleiben. ◆'keeping, s. 1. Aufbewahrung f; for (your) safe k., zur Verwahrung. 2. in k. with sth., etwas dat entsprechend. ◆'keep 'off, v.tr. (etwas) nicht anrühren; k. o. the grass! Betreten des Rasens verboten! k. your hands o.! Hände weg! ◆'keep 'on, v.1. v.tr. (a) (seinen Hut) aufbehalten; (b) (j-n) (in einer Stellung) behalten. 2. v.i. to k. on doing sth., (i) (repeat) etwas immer wieder machen; (ii) (continue) etwas weitermachen; F: to k. on at s.o., an j-m dauernd herumnörgeln. ◆'keep 'out, v.1. v.tr. (j-n) nicht hereinlassen. 2. v.i. to k. o. of the way, sich fernhalten; K. o.! Betreten verboten! F: k. o. of this! misch dich nicht ein! ◆'keep 'to, v.tr. (a) to k. to a rule/promise, sich an eine Regel/ein Versprechen halten; (b) to k. to the left, links halten; he keeps (himself) to himself, er ist ein Einzelgänger. ◆'keep 'up, v.1. v.tr. (a) (look after) (einen Garten usw.) instandhalten; (b) he won't be able to k. it up, er wird es nicht durchhalten können; k. it up! nur so weiter! nicht nachlassen! (c) (maintain) (Interessen, eine Freundschaft usw.) aufrechterhalten; (d) to k. s.o. up, j-n vom Schlafen abhalten. 2. v.i. schritthalten (with, mit + dat).

kennel ['ken(ə)l], s. (a) Hundehütte f; (b) pl. (for boarding) Tierpension f.

kerb [kə:b], s. Bordkante f.

kernel ['kə:n(ə)l], s. Kern m; (of cereal) Korn n.

ketchup ['ketʃəp], s. Ketchup m & n.

kettle ['ketl], s. Kessel m.

key [ki:], s. 1. Schlüssel m. k. ring, Schlüsselring m; Fig: k. word, Schlüsselwort n. 2. Mus: Tonart f. 3. Taste f (einer Schreibmaschine, des Klaviers usw.). ◆'keyboard, s. (of typewriter, piano) Tastatur f. ◆'keyhole, s. Schlüsselloch n.

khaki ['ka:ki]. I. adj. khakifarben. II. s. (material) Khaki m.

kick [kik]. I. v. 1. v.i. (of pers.) (of baby) strampeln; (of horse etc.) ausschlagen. 2. v.tr. (j-n, etwas dat) einen Fußtritt geben; to k. the ball, den Ball treten. II. s. 1. Tritt m. 2. F: P: (just) for kicks, nur zum Spaß. ◆'kick 'off, v.i. (a) Fb: anstoßen; (b) F: (start) loslegen. ◆'kick-off, s. Anstoß m. ◆'kick 'out, v.tr. F: (j-n) rausschmeißen. ◆'kick 'up, v.tr. F: to k. up a fuss, Theater machen.

kid¹ [kid], s. 1. Z: Kitz n. 2. k. gloves, Glacéhandschuhe mpl. 3. F: Kind n.

kid² [kid], F: (j-n) foppen; don't k. yourself, mach dir nichts vor.

kidnap ['kidnæp], v.tr. (j-n) entführen; F: (j-n) kidnappen. ◆'kidnapper, s. Ent-

führer m; F: Kidnapper m.

kidney ['kidni], s. Niere f.

kill [kil], v.tr. töten; to k. oneself, sich umbringen; to k. time, die Zeit totschlagen. ◆'killer, s. 1. (murderer) Mörder m. 2. F: (of drug) tödlich sein; k. disease, tödliche Krankheit. 2. k. whale, Schwertwal m. ◆'killing, s. 1. Tötung f (eines Menschen); Schlachten n (eines Tieres). 2. Morden n.

kiln [kiln], s. Brennofen m.

kilogram(me) ['kiləu)græm], s. Kilogramm n.

kilometre ['kiləu)mi:tər, ki'ləmitər], s. Kilometer m.

kilt [kilt], s. Kilt m.

kin [kin], s. next of k., nächste(r) Verwandte(r) f(m).

kind¹ [kaind], s. Art f; this k. of music, diese Art Musik; F: I k. of expected it, ich habe das irgendwie schon erwartet.

kind² [kaind], adj. nett; gut. ◆'kind-'hearted, adj. gutherzig. ◆'kindly. I. adj. (of pers.) gütig. II. adv. freundlicherweise; will you k. remove your foot! nimm gefälligst deinen Fuß weg! ◆'kindness, s. Güte f; (helpfulness) Gefälligkeit f.

kindergarten ['kindəgɑːtn], s. Vorschule f.

kindle ['kindl], v.tr. (a) (ein Feuer usw.) anzünden; (b) (Leidenschaft) entflammen.

king [kiŋ], s. König m. ◆'kingdom, s. 1. Königreich n; the United K., das Vereinigte Königreich. 2. Reich n; animal k., Tierreich n. ◆'kingfisher, s. Eisvogel m. ◆'king-size(d), adj. im Großformat.

kink [kiŋk], s. Knick m. ◆'kinky, adj. P: abnorm.

kiosk ['ki:ɔsk], s. Kiosk m.

kipper ['kipər], s. Räucherhering m.

kiss [kis]. I. s. Kuß m. II. v.tr. küssen.

kit [kit], s. 1. (equipment) Ausrüstung f. 2. (set of parts) Bausatz m; (model) k., Baukasten m. ◆'kit-bag, s. Seesack m.

kitchen ['kitʃən], s. Küche f; k. unit, Küchenelement n; k. sink, Spülbecken n.

kite [kait], s. Drachen m.

kitten ['kitn], s. Kätzchen n.

kitty ['kiti], s. Kasse f.

knack [næk], s. Kniff m; F: Dreh m.

knapsack ['næpsæk], s. Rucksack m; Mil: Tornister m.

knead [ni:d], v.tr. kneten.

knee [ni:], s. Knie n. ◆'knee-cap, s. Kniescheibe f.

kneel [ni:l], v.i.irr. knien.

knickers ['nikəz], s.pl. Damenschlüpfer m.

knife, pl. **knives** [naif, naivz], I. s. Messer n. II. v.tr. (j-n, etwas) mit dem Messer angreifen.

knight [nait]. I. s. 1. Hist: Ritter m. 2. (in chess) Springer m. II. v.tr. (j-n) in den Adelsstand erheben. ◆'knighthood, s. to receive a k., in den Adelsstand erhoben werden.

knit [nit], *v.tr & i.* stricken. ◆'**knitting**, *s.* 1. (*action*) Stricken *n.* 2. Strickarbeit *f*; **k. machine**, Strickmaschine *f*. ◆'**knitting-needle**, *s.* Stricknadel *f.* ◆'**knitwear**, *s.* Strickwaren *fpl.*

knob [nɔb], *s.* 1. (*on door etc.*) Griff *m*; (*on drawer, radio etc.*) Knopf *m.* 2. Stückchen *n* (Butter usw.).

knock [nɔk]. I. *s.* Klopfen *n*; (*blow*) Schlag *m*; **there was a k. (at the door)**, es hat geklopft. II. *v.* 1. *v.tr.* (*a*) (*j-n, etwas*) schlagen; (*b*) F: (*criticize*) **to k. sth.**, etwas heruntermachen. 2. *v.i.* (*a*) **to k. against sth.**, gegen etwas *acc* stoßen; (*b*) (*of pers., Aut: of engine*) klopfen. ◆'**knock 'down**, *v.tr.* (*a*) (*j-n*) niederschlagen; (*etwas*) umstoßen; **to be knocked down by a car**, von einem Auto angefahren werden; (*b*) (*ein Haus*) niederreißen. ◆'**knocker**, *s.* Türklopfer *m.* ◆'**knocking**, *s.* Klopfen *n.* ◆'**knock-'kneed**, *adj.* X-beinig. ◆'**knock 'off**, *v.* 1. *v.tr.* F: **to k. off an essay etc.**, einen Aufsatz usw. schnell hinhauen. 2. *v.i.* F: Feierabend machen. ◆'**knock 'out**, *v.tr.* (*a*) (einen Zahn) (her)ausschlagen; (*b*) (j-n) k.o. schlagen.

knock 'over, *v.tr.* (j-n, etwas) umstoßen.

knot [nɔt]. I. *s.* Knoten *m.* II. *v.tr.* (eine Schnur) verknoten.

know [nəu]. I. *v.tr. & i.irr.* (*a*) (j-n, einen Ort, ein Buch usw.) kennen; **to get to k. s.o., sth.**, j-n, etwas kennenlernen; (*b*) (etwas) wissen; **as far as I k.**, soviel ich weiß; (*c*) **to k. about sth.**, über etwas *acc* Bescheid wissen; **I k. nothing about it**, davon weiß ich nichts. II. *s.* F: **to be in the k.**, im Bilde sein. ◆'**know-all**, *s.* F: Besserwisser *m.* ◆'**know-how**, *s.* F: Sachkenntnis *f*; Technik *f.* ◆'**knowing**. I. *adj.* wissend; **-ly**, *adv.* 1. (*intentionally*) wissentlich. 2. **to look k. at s.o.**, j-m einen wissenden Blick zuwerfen. II. *s.* **there's no k. what will happen**, es ist nicht vorauszusehen, was jetzt geschieht. ◆**knowledge** ['nɔlidʒ], *s.* 1. (*in general*) Wissen *n.* 2. (*of sth. particular*) Kenntnisse *fpl.* ◆'**knowledgeable** *adj.* bewandert (**about, in** + *dat*).

knuckle [nʌkl], *s.* Fingerknöchel *m.*

Korea [kə'riə]. *Pr. n.* Korea *n.* ◆**Ko'rean.** I. *adj.* koreanisch; **the K. War**, der Koreakrieg. II. *s.* Koreaner(in) *m(f)*.

L

L, l [el], *s.* (der Buchstabe) L, l *n*; **L plate**, Fahrschülerschild *n.*

lab [læb], *s.* F: Labor *n.*

label ['leibl]. I. *s.* 1. Etikett *n*; (*tag*) Schildchen *n*; (*luggage*) l., (*tie-on*) Gepäckanhänger *m.* II. *v.tr.* (*a*) (Flaschen usw.) etikettieren; (*b*) (j-n als etwas) bezeichnen.

laboratory [lə'bɔrətri], *s.* Labor *n.*

laborious [lə'bɔːriəs], *adj.* mühsam.

labour ['leibər], *s.* 1. (*work, task*) Arbeit *f.* 2. (*a*) (*workers*) *coll.* Arbeiter *mpl*; l. **force**, Arbeiterschaft *f*; (*b*) *Pol:* **the L. party**, die Labour Party. 3. *Med:* l. (**pains**), Geburtswehen *fpl.* ◆'**labourer**, *s.* (ungelernter) Arbeiter *m.* ◆'**laboursaving**, *adj.* arbeitssparend.

labyrinth ['læbirinθ], *s.* Labyrinth *n.*

lace [leis]. I. *s.* 1. (*for tying*) Schnürband *n*; (*shoe*) l., Schnürsenkel *m.* 2. (*material*) Spitze *f.* II. *v.tr.* **to l. (up) one's shoes**, sich *dat* die Schuhe zuschnüren.

lacerate ['læsəreit], *v.tr.* zerfleischen.

lack [læk]. I. *s.* Mangel *m* (**of, an** + *dat*); II. *v.tr. & i.* **he lacks/is lacking in experience**, es fehlt ihm an Erfahrung.

lacquer ['lækər], *s.* Lack *m*; **hair l.**, Haarspray *m.*

lad [læd], *s.* Junge *m*, (junger) Bursche *m.*

ladder ['lædər]. I. *s.* 1. Leiter *f.* 2. (*in stocking*) Laufmasche *f.* II. *v.i.* Laufmasche machen.

ladle ['leidl], *s.* Schöpflöffel *m.*

lady ['leidi], *s.* (*a*) Dame *f*; (*in title*) Lady

f; **l. in waiting**, Hofdame *f*; (*b*) F: **the ladies'**, die Damentoilette. ◆'**ladybird**, *s.* Marienkäfer *m.* ◆'**ladylike**, *adj.* damenhaft.

lag [læg], *v.i.* **to l. behind (s.o.)**, (mit j-m) nicht Schritt halten; (j-m) nachhinken.

lager ['lɑːgər], *s.* Lagerbier *n.*

lagoon [lə'guːn], *s.* Lagune *f.*

lair [lɛər], *s.* Lager *n.*

lake [leik], *s.* See *m.*

lamb [læm], *s.* Lamm *n.*

lame [leim], *adj.* lahm.

lament [lə'ment]. I. *s.* Klage *f.* II. *v.tr.* beklagen. ◆**lamentable** ['læməntəbl], *adj.* beklagenswert. ◆**lamentation** [-'teiʃən], *s.* Wehklage *f.*

lamp [læmp], *s.* Lampe *f.* ◆'**lamp-post**, *s.* Laternenpfahl *m.* ◆'**lampshade**, *s.* Lampenschirm *m.*

lance [lɑːns]. I. *s.* Lanze *f.* II. *v.tr.* *Med:* aufschneiden.

land [lænd]. I. *s.* Land *n.* v. 1. *v.tr.* (*a*) (ein Flugzeug) landen; (*b*) F: (eine Stellung) kriegen. 2. *v.i.* landen. ◆'**landing**, *s.* 1. Landung *f.* 2. (*in house*) Treppenflur *m*; (**half**) l., Treppenabsatz *m.* ◆'**landlady**, *s.* Wirtin *f.* ◆'**landlord**, *s.* (*a*) Hauseigentümer *m*; (*of estate*) Grundbesitzer *m*; (*of pub*) Wirt *m.* ◆'**landmark**, *s.* Orientierungspunkt *m*; (*famous building*) Wahrzeichen *n*; *Fig:* Markstein *m* (**in** history etc., der Geschichte usw.). ◆'**landowner**, *s.*

Grundbesitzer *m.* ◆**landscape,** *s.* Landschaft *f.* **l. gardener,** Gartenarchitekt *m.* ◆**landslide,** *s.* **1.** Erdrutsch *m.* **2.** *Pol:* **l. victory,** überwältigender Wahlsieg.

lane [lein], *s.* **1.** (*a*) (*in town*) Gasse *f;* (*b*) (*in country*) enge Landstraße *f;* Weg *m.* **2.** (*a*) *Aut:* Spur *f;* (*b*) *Sp:* Bahn *f* (einer Rennbahn).

language [ˈlæŋgwidʒ], *s.* Sprache *f.*

languid [ˈlæŋgwid], *adj.* träge.

lanky [ˈlæŋki], *adj.* schlaksig.

lantern [ˈlæntən], *s.* Laterne *f.*

lap¹ [læp], *s.* Schoß *m.*

lap², *s. Sp:* Runde *f.*

lap³, *v.* **1** *v.tr. F:* **he lapped it up,** *Fig:* (*praise etc.*) er hat sich darin gesonnt. **2.** *v.i.* (*of water*) plätschern.

lapel [ləˈpel], *s.* Aufschlag *m.*

lapse [læps], *s.* **1.** (*a*) (*slip*) Versehen *n;* (*b*) (*moral*) Fehltritt *m.* **2.** (*of time*) Verlauf *m;* Zeitspanne *f.*

larceny [ˈlɑːsəni], *s.* Diebstahl *m.*

lard [lɑːd], *s.* Schmalz *n.*

larder [ˈlɑːdər], *s.* Speisekammer *f.*

large [lɑːdʒ]. **I.** *adj.* groß. **II.** *s.* **at l.,** auf freiem Fuß; **the people at l.,** die breite Masse. **III.** *adv.* **by and l.,** im großen und ganzen; **-ly,** *adv.* größtenteils. ◆**large-'scale,** *adj.* großangelegt.

lark¹ [lɑːk], *s. Orn:* Lerche *f.*

lark², *s. F:* Jux *m.* **II.** *v.i. F:* **to l.** (**about**), herumtollen.

larva, *pl.* **-ae** [ˈlɑːvə, -viː], *s.* Larve *f.*

larynx [ˈlæriŋks], *s.* Kehlkopf *m.* ◆**laryngitis** [lærinˈdʒaitis], *s.* Kehlkopfentzündung *f.*

laser [ˈleizər], *s.* Laser *m.*

lash¹ [læʃ]. **I.** *s.* Peitschenhieb *m.* **II.** *v.tr. & i.* peitschen. ◆**lash 'out,** *v.i.* (*a*) um sich *acc* schlagen; (*verbally*) **to l. o.** (**against/at s.o., sth.**), (über) j-n, etwas *acc*) herfallen; (*b*) *F:* es sich *dat* was kosten lassen.

lash², *v.tr.* (*tie*) festbinden.

lass [læs], *esp. Scot:* **lassie** [ˈlæsi], *s.* Mädel *n.*

lasso, *pl.* **-os** [læˈsuː, -uːz]. **I.** *s.* Lasso *n & m.* **II.** *v.tr.* mit einem Lasso einfangen.

last¹ [lɑːst]. **I.** *adj.* letzte(r,s); **she was the l.** to arrive, sie kam als letzte; **the l. but one,** der/die/das vorletzte; **l. night,** gestern abend. **II.** *adv.* (*a*) **when I saw him l./l.** saw him, als ich ihn das letzte Mal sah; (*b*) **he came l.,** er kam als letzter (*Sp:* ans Ziel); **-ly,** *adv.* zuletzt.

last², *v.i.* dauern; (*of food, weather etc.*) sich halten. ◆**lasting,** *adj.* (*of peace, friendship etc.*) dauernd, von Dauer; (*of effect etc.*) anhaltend.

latch [lætʃ], *s.* Klinke *f;* (*on lock*) Schnapper *m;* **on the l.,** nur (zu) spät eingeklinkt; nicht verschlossen.

late [leit], *adj.* **1.** (*too l.*) (zu) spät; **the train is ten minutes l.,** der Zug hat zehn Minuten Verspätung. **2.** (*not early*) spät. **3. my l. father,** mein verstorbener Vater. **4.** **of l.,** in letzter Zeit; **the latest model,**

das neueste Modell. **II.** *adv.* (*a*) **to arrive too l./an hour l.,** zu spät/mit einer Stunde Verspätung ankommen; (*b*) **to stay up l.,** bis spät (in die Nacht) aufbleiben; **l. in life,** im vorgerückten Alter; **at the latest,** spätestens; **-ly,** *adv.* in letzter Zeit. ◆**latecomer,** *s.* Nachzügler *m.*

latent [ˈleit(ə)nt], *adj.* verborgen; *Psy: Ph:* latent.

lateral [ˈlætərəl], *adj.* seitlich.

lathe [leið], *s.* Drehbank *f.*

lather [ˈlæðər]. **I.** *s.* Seifenschaum *m.* **II.** *v.i.* schäumen.

Latin [ˈlætin]. **I.** *s.* Latein *m.* **II.** *adj.* **1.** lateinisch. **2.** (*of temperament*) südländisch; **L. America,** Lateinamerika *n.*

latitude [ˈlætitjuːd], *s.* **1.** Spielraum *m.* **2.** *Geog:* Breite *f.*

latter [ˈlætər], *adj.* **1.** **the l.,** der/die/das letztere. **2.** **the l. half of June,** die zweite Junihälfte.

laudable [ˈlɔːdəbl], *adj.* lobenswert.

laugh [lɑːf]. **I.** *s.* Lachen *n.* **II.** *v.* **1.** *v.i.* (*a*) lachen; **to l. at s.o.,** j-n auslachen. **2.** *v.tr.* **he tried to l. the matter off,** er versuchte, die Sache mit einem Scherz abzutun. ◆**laughable,** *adj.* lächerlich. ◆**laughing. I.** *adj.* lachend. **II.** *s.* Lachen *n;* **it's no l. matter,** da gibt's nichts zu lachen. ◆**laughing-stock,** *s.* **to be a l.-s.,** ausgelacht werden. ◆**laughter,** *s.* Gelächter *n.*

launch [lɔːntʃ]. **I.** *s.* Barkasse *f.* **II.** *v.tr.* (*a*) (eine Rakete usw.) abschießen; (*b*) (ein neues Schiff) vom Stapel lassen; (*c*) *Mil:* **to l. an attack,** einen Angriff starten; (*d*) *esp. Com:* (ein neues Erzeugnis, Modell usw.) herausbringen; (ein Unternehmen) starten. ◆**launching,** *s.* **1.** (*a*) Stapellauf *m* (eines Schiffes); (*b*) Abschuß *m* (einer *Rakete*); **l. pad,** Abschußrampe *f.* **2.** Herausbringen *n* (eines Erzeugnisses usw.).

laundry [ˈlɔːndri], *s.* **1.** (*place*) Wäscherei *f.* **2.** (*clothes etc.*) Wäsche *f.* ◆**launderette** [lɔːnˈdret], *s.* Waschsalon *m.*

laurel [ˈlɒrəl], *s.* Lorbeer *m.*

lava [ˈlɑːvə], *s.* Lava *f.*

lavatory [ˈlævətri], *s.* Toilette *f.*

lavender [ˈlævindər], *s.* Lavendel *m.*

lavish [ˈlæviʃ]. **I.** *adj.* (*of pers.*) verschwenderisch. **2.** (*of entertainment etc.*) aufwendig. **II.** *v.tr.* **to l. attention on s.o.,** j-n mit Aufmerksamkeit überschütten; **-ly,** *adv.* **to entertain l.,** mit viel Aufwand empfangen.

law [lɔː], *s.* **1.** Gesetz *n.* **2.** (*subject*) Jura *npl;* **l. school,** Rechtsakademie *f.* **3.** (*justice*) Recht *n;* **under British l.,** nach britischem Recht. ◆**law-abiding,** *adj.* gesetzestreu. ◆**lawless,** *adj.* gesetzlos. ◆**lawsuit,** *s.* Prozeß *m.* ◆**lawyer,** *s.* Rechtsanwalt *m;* Jurist *m.*

lawn [lɔːn], *s.* Rasen *m.* ◆**lawnmower,** *s.* Rasenmäher *m.*

lax [læks], *adj.* (*of morals, discipline etc.*)

locker; (of pers. etc.) nachlässig. ◆**laxative**, s. Abführmittel n.

lay¹ [lei], attrib. adj. laienhaft; Laien-. ◆**layman**, pl. -men, s. Laie m.

lay², v.irr. I. v.tr. legen; (einen Teppich, Rohre usw.) verlegen; (eine Falle) aufstellen; **to l. the table**, den Tisch decken. 2. v.i. (of hen) Eier legen. ◆**layabout**, s. Faulenzer m. ◆**layby**, s. (large) Rastplatz m; (small) Parkstreifen m. ◆**lay 'down**, v.tr. a) hinlegen; **to l. d. one's arms**, die Waffen niederlegen; (b) (Grundsätze, Regeln) festsetzen; (Bedingungen) stellen. ◆**layer**, s. Schicht f; (of clothing) Lage f. ◆**lay 'into**, v.tr. F: **to l. i. s.o.**, auf j-n losgehen; (criticize) über j-n herziehen. ◆**lay 'off**, v.tr. (Arbeiter) entlassen. ◆**lay 'on**, v.tr. (Gas, Wasser usw.) anlegen; (ein Essen) bereitstellen. ◆**lay 'out**, v.tr. a) (einen Leichnam) aufbahren; (b) (Geld) auslegen; (c) (einen Garten) anlegen; (d) (with blow) (j-n) niederstrecken. ◆**layout**, s. Anordnung f; (of magazine etc.) Layout n (einer Seite usw.).

laziness ['leizinəs], s. Faulheit f. ◆**lazy**, adj. faul. ◆**lazybones**, s. F: Faulpelz m.

lead¹ [led], s. Blei n.

lead² [liːd]. I. v.tr. & i.irr. führen. II. s. 1. Führung f; **to take the l.**, die Führung übernehmen. 2. (clue) Anhaltspunkt m; (of police) Hinweis m. 3. Th: Hauptrolle f. 4. (for dog) Leine f. 5. (flex) Kabel n. ◆**lead a'stray**, v.tr. verführen. ◆**lead a'way**, v.tr. wegführen. ◆**lead 'back**, v.tr. zurückführen. ◆**leader**, s. 1. Führer m; Anführer m (eines Aufruhrs usw.). 2. (in newspaper) Leitartikel m. ◆**leadership**, s. Führung f. ◆**leading**, adj. I. l. question, Suggestivfrage f. 2. führend; l. article, Leitartikel m; l. man (lady), Hauptdarsteller(in) m(f). ◆**lead 'up**, v.i. **to l. up to a subject**, auf ein Thema hinführen; **I know what you are leading up to**, ich weiß, worauf Sie hinauswollen.

leaf, pl. **leaves** [liif, liivz], s. 1. Blatt n. 2. (of table) Klappe f. ◆**leaflet**, s. Com: Prospekt m; Pol: Flugblatt n. ◆**leafy**, adj. belaubt.

league [liːg], s. Liga f; **in l. with s.o.**, mit j-m verbündet.

leak [liːk]. I. s. undichte Stelle f; (hole) Loch n; (in ship etc.) Leck n. II. v. 1. v.i. (of joint) undicht sein; (of tank, ship) ein Leck haben; **to l. away**, auslaufen; **the roof is leaking**, das Dach läßt den Regen durch. 2. v.tr. (Nachrichten) durchsickern lassen. ◆**leak 'out**, v.i. (of news) durchsickern. ◆**leaky**, adj. (of ship, tank) leck; (of roof, shoes etc.) undicht.

lean¹ [liːn], adj. mager.

lean², v.irr. 1. v.i. (a) sich lehnen (against/on sth., an etwas acc); (position) **he is/was leaning on the wall**, er lehnt/

lehnte an der Wand; (b) (bend over) sich beugen, **to l. out of the window**, sich zum Fenster hinauslehnen; **to l. back**, sich zurücklehnen; (c) (of wall etc.) schief stehen. 2. v.tr. **to l. a ladder against a wall**, eine Leiter an eine Mauer anlehnen. ◆**leaning**, adj. schief. ◆**lean-to**, s. (shed) angebauter Schuppen m.

leap [liːp]. I. s. Sprung m. II. v. 1. v.i. irr. springen. 2. v.tr. (einen Graben) überspringen. ◆**leapfrog**, s. Bocksprung m; **to (play at) l.**, bockspringen. ◆**leap-year**, s. Schaltjahr n.

learn [ləːn], v.tr.irr. (a) lernen; (b) (einen Beruf usw.) erlernen; (c) (Nachrichten usw.) erfahren. ◆**learned** [ˈləːnid], adj. gelehrt. ◆**learner**, s. 1. **to be a quick l.**, leicht lernen. 2. Anfänger(in) m(f); **l. driver**, Fahrschüler(in) m(f). ◆**learning**, s. 1. (process) Lernen n. 2. (knowledge) Wissen n; (erudition) Gelehrtheit f.

lease [liːs]. I. s. Pacht f; (rental agreement) Mietvertrag m. II. v.tr. (a) verpachten (**to s.o.**, an j-n); (b) (take on l.) pachten; (ein Auto) mieten. ◆**leasehold**, s. 1. flat, Pachtwohnung f. ◆**leaseholder**, s. Pächter m.

leash [liːʃ], s. Hundeleine f.

least [liːst]. I. adj. geringste(r,s). II. s. das Geringste/Wenigste/Mindeste; **at l. £10**, mindestens zehn Pfund; **I can at l. try**, ich kann's wenigstens versuchen. III. adv. am wenigsten.

leather [ˈleðər], s. Leder n.

leave [liːv]. I. s. 1. (permission) Erlaubnis f. 2. Mil: etc: l. (of absence), Urlaub m; **on l.**, auf Urlaub. 3. **to take one's l.**, Abschied nehmen. II. v.irr. 1. v.tr. (a) (j-n, etwas) lassen; (Essen) stehenlassen; (b) (eine Nachricht, Spur) hinterlassen; (eine Narbe) zurücklassen; **to l. one's money to s.o.**, j-m sein Geld vermachen/hinterlassen; (c) (forget) **I left it in the office**, ich habe es im Büro liegenlassen; (d) **to l. a decision** etc. to s.o., j-m eine Entscheidung usw. überlassen; (e) **is there any left?** ist etwas übrig? (f) (j-n, seine Frau, eine Stellung, ein Zimmer) verlassen. 2. v.i. (of pers.) abreisen; (of train, bus etc.) abfahren; (of plane) starten; (of employee) **he is leaving next week**, er geht nächste Woche ab. ◆**leave be'hind**, v.tr. (a) (j-n) zurücklassen; (b) (forget) (etwas) liegenlassen. ◆**leave 'out**, v.tr. (a) (j-n) übergehen; (b) (etwas) auslassen.

Lebanon [ˈlebənən]. Pr. n. der Libanon.

lecherous [ˈletʃ(ə)rəs], adj. lüstern.

lecture [ˈlektʃər]. I. s. Vortrag m; (at university) Vorlesung f (**on, über** + acc). II. v.i. einen Vortrag/eine Vorlesung halten (**on, über** + acc). ◆**lecturer**, s. Vortragende(r) f(m); (university) l., Dozent(in) m(f).

ledge [ledʒ], s. (window l.) Sims m; (on rock) Felsvorsprung m.

ledger ['ledʒər], s. Hauptbuch n.

lee [li:], s. Nau: Lee(seite) f; **in the l. of a rock**, im Windschatten eines Felsens. ◆**'leeway**, s. (freedom) Spielraum m.

leech [li:tʃ], s. Blutegel m.

leek [li:k], s. Lauch m, Porree m.

leer ['liər]. I. s. lüsterner Blick m. II. v.i. **to l. at s.o.**, lüstern/boshaft nach j-m schielen.

left1 [left]. I. adj. linke(r,s). II. adv. links. III. s. Linke f; (a) **on the l.**, links, auf der linken Seite; **from/to the l.**, von/ nach links; (b) Pol: **the L.**, die Linke. ◆**'left-hand**, adj. **on the l.-h. side**, auf der linken Seite. ◆**'left-'handed**, adj. linkshändig. ◆**'leftist**. I. s. Linksgerichtete(r) m. II. adj. linksgerichtet. ◆**'left-'wing**, adj. linksgerichtet.

left2, adj. & p.p. of **leave** q.v. ◆**'left-overs**, s.pl. Reste mpl. ◆**'left-'luggage (office)**, s. Gepäckaufbewahrung f.

leg [leg], s. 1. Bein n; **to pull s.o.'s leg**, j-n auf den Arm nehmen. 2. Cu: Keule f. 3. Sp: **the first l.**, die erste Etappe. ◆**'leg-room**, s. Knieraum m.

legacy ['legəsi], s. Erbschaft f.

legal ['li:g(ə)l], adj. gesetzlich; **is it l.?** ist es (gesetzlich) erlaubt? 1. **documents, Rechtsurkunden** fpl; **-ly**, adv. **l. binding/ valid**, rechtskräftig. ◆**le'gality**, s. Gesetzlichkeit f; (of claim etc.) Rechtmäßigkeit f. ◆**'legalize**, v.tr. legalisieren.

legend ['ledʒənd], s. Legende f. ◆**'legendary**, adj. legendär.

legible ['ledʒibl], adj. leserlich.

legion ['li:dʒ(ə)n], s. Legion f.

legislate ['ledʒisleit], v.i. Gesetze erlassen. ◆**legis'lation**, s. Gesetzgebung f. ◆**'legislative** [-lətiv], adj. gesetzgebend. ◆**'legislator**, s. Gesetzgeber m.

legitimacy [li'dʒitiməsi], s. Rechtmäßigkeit f; Ehelichkeit f (eines Kindes). ◆**le'gitimate**, adj. 1. Jur: rechtmäßig; (of child) ehelich. 2. (justified) berechtigt.

leisure ['leʒər, N.Am: li:-], s. (restful) Muße f; (spare time) Freizeit f; **at l.**, mit Muße. ◆**'leisurely**, adj. gemächlich.

lemon ['lemən]. I. s. Zitrone f. II. adj. zitronengelb. ◆**lemo'nade**, s. Zitronenlimonade f.

lend [lend], v.tr.irr. (a) (Geld, Bücher usw.) leihen (to s.o., j-m); (b) **this style lends itself to imitation**, dieser Stil läßt sich leicht nachahmen. ◆**'lender**, s. Verleiher m; (of loan) Darlehensgeber m. ◆**'lending**, s. Leihen n; **l. library**, Leihbücherei f.

length [leŋθ], s. 1. (distance) Länge f. 2. l. of time, Zeitspanne f, Zeit f; l. of service, Dienstalter n; **at l.**, (i) (at last) endlich; (ii) (in detail) ausführlich. 3. **to go to great lengths**, sich dat viel Mühe geben. ◆**'lengthen**, v. 1. v.tr. verlängern. 2. v.i. länger werden. ◆**'lengthways, 'lengthwise**, adv. der Länge nach. ◆**'lengthy**, adj. langwierig.

leniency ['li:niənsi], s. Nachsicht f; Milde f (einer Strafe). ◆**lenient**, adj. (of pers.) nachsichtig; (of sentence) mild.

lens [lenz], s. Linse f; Phot: Objektiv n.

Lent [lent], s. Fastenzeit f.

lentil ['lentil], s. Linse f.

Leo ['li:əu], s. Astr: Löwe m.

leopard ['lepəd], s. Leopard m.

leper ['lepər], s. Aussätzige(r) f(m). ◆**'leprosy**, s. Lepra f.

lesbian ['lezbiən]. I. s. Lesbierin f. II. adj. lesbisch.

less [les]. I. adj. weniger; (smaller) geringer. II. prep. **purchase price l. 10%**, Kaufpreis weniger/abzüglich 10%. III. adv. weniger. ◆**'lessen**, v. 1. v.i. abnehmen; (of wind, resistance etc.) nachlassen. 2. v.tr. verringern. ◆**'lesser**, adj. geringer.

lesson ['les(ə)n], s. (a) Sch: Stunde f; (in book) Lektion f; (b) Fig: Lehre f; (c) Ecc: Bibellesung f.

let1 [let], v.tr. 1. v.tr. lassen; **to l. s.o. do sth.**, j-n etwas tun lassen; **to l. s.o. through/past etc.**, j-n durchlassen/ vorbeilassen usw.; **to l. go of sth.**, etwas loslassen; Fig: **to l. oneself go**, sich gehenlassen. II. v. aux. **let's hurry!** beeilen wir uns! ◆**'let a'lone**, prep. phr. geschweige denn. ◆**'let 'down**, v.tr. (a) Th: (den Vorhang) herunterlassen; (b) (ein Kleid) verlängern; (c) F: (j-n) im Stich lassen, (disappoint) enttäuschen. ◆**'letdown**, s. F: Reinfall m. ◆**'let 'in**, v.tr. (j-n, etwas) hereinlassen. ◆**'let 'off**, v.tr. (a) (Feuerwerk, eine Schußwaffe) abfeuern; (b) **to l. s.o. o.**, j-n laufenlassen. ◆**'let 'on**, v.tr. & i. F: (etwas) verraten. ◆**'let 'out**, v.tr. herauslassen. ◆**'let 'up**, v.i. nachlassen. ◆**'letup**, s. Pause f.

let2, v.tr. (ein Haus usw.) vermieten (to s.o., an j-n).

lethal ['li:θ(ə)l], adj. tödlich.

lethargic [le'θɑ:dʒik], adj. träge.

letter ['letər], s. 1. (of alphabet) Buchstabe m. 2. (message) Brief m; **l. box**, Briefkasten m.

lettuce ['letis], s. Kopfsalat m.

leukaemia [lu:'ki:miə], s. Leukämie f.

level ['lev(ə)l]. I. s. 1. (height) Höhe f; (also Fig: Ebene f; (standard) Niveau n; Med: Spiegel m (von Zucker usw.). 2. **on the l.**, (i) auf der Ebene; (ii) F: (of pers.) ehrlich. II. adj. (a) (flat) eben; l. **crossing**, Bahnübergang m; (b) **l. with**, auf gleicher Höhe mit + dat. III. v.tr. (a) (den Erdboden) ebnen; (b) **to l. a gun/ Fig: a criticism at s.o.**, ein Gewehr/ Kritik gegen j-n richten. ◆**'level-'headed**, adj. vernünftig; nüchtern.

lever ['li:vər], s. Hebel m. II. v.tr. **to l. sth. up/open**, etwas mit einem Hebel heben/öffnen.

levy ['levi]. I. s. capital l., Kapitalabgabe f. II. v.tr. (a) (Steuern usw.) erheben; (b) (Truppen) ausheben.

lewd [lju:d], adj. unzüchtig.

liable ['laiəbl], *adj.* **1.** (*responsible*) haftbar; **to be l.,** haften (**for sth.,** für etwas *acc.*). **2.** (*inclined*) **to be l. to do sth.,** dazu neigen, etwas zu tun; **difficulties are l. to occur,** man muß mit Schwierigkeiten rechnen. ◆**lia'bility,** *s.* **1.** (*a*) Haftung *f*; (*b*) *pl.* Schulden *fpl.* **2.** F: **he is a l.,** er ist eine Belastung.

liaison [li'eizɔn], *s.* Verbindung *f.* ◆**li'aise,** *v.i.* eine Verbindung aufnehmen (**with s.o.,** mit j-m).

liar ['laiər], *s.* Lügner(in) *m(f).*

libel ['laibl]. **I.** *s.* (schriftliche) Verleumdung *f.* **II.** *v.tr.* (j-n) (schriftlich) verleumden. ◆**'libellous,** *adj.* verleumderisch.

liberal ['libərəl]. **I.** *adj.* liberal; (*open-minded*) aufgeschlossen; **l. education,** Allgemein -ly, *adv.,* reichlich. **II.** *s.* Liberale(r) *f(m).* ◆**'liberalism,** *s.* Liberalismus *m.*

liberate ['libəreit], *v.tr.* befreien. ◆**libe'ration,** *s.* Befreiung *f.*

liberty ['libəti], *s.* Freiheit *f.*

Libra ['li:brə], *s. Astr:* Waage *f.*

library ['laibrəri], *s.* Bibliothek *f*; (*public*) **lending l.,** Leihbücherei *f.* ◆**librarian** [lai'breəriən], *s.* Bibliothekar(in) *m(f).*

Libya ['libiə]. *Pr. n.* Libyen *n.*

licence ['lais(ə)ns], *s.* **1.** (*a*) Lizenz *f*; (*permit*) Genehmigung *f*; (*b*) (*actual form*) Schein *m*; (*driving*) l., Führerschein *m.* **2.** *poetic* l., dichterische Freiheit *f.* ◆**'license,** *v.tr.* (etwas) amtlich genehmigen, *Cum.* (einen Händler usw.) konzessionieren. **licensed premises,** Schankwirtschaft *f.* ◆**licentious** [-'senfəs], *adj.* unzüchtig.

lick [lik]. **I.** *v.* **1.** *v.tr. & i.* lecken. **II.** *s.* Lecken *n.*

lid [lid], *s.* Deckel *m.*

lie¹ [lai]. **I.** *s.* Lüge *f.* **II.** *v.i.* lügen; **to l. to s.o.,** j-n belügen.

lie² *v.i.irr.* liegen. ◆**'lie 'down,** *v.i.* sich hinlegen. ◆**'lie-in,** *s.* F: **to have a l.-i.,** ausschlafen.

lieutenant [lef'tenənt, *N.Am:* lu:-], *s.* Oberleutnant *m.*

life, *pl.* **lives** [laif, laivz], *s.* Leben *n*; **l. assurance/insurance,** Lebensversicherung *f*; **for l.,** auf Lebenszeit; **l. sentence,** lebenslängliche Freiheitsstrafe. ◆**'lifebelt,** *s.* Rettungsring *m.* ◆**'lifeboat,** *s.* Rettungsboot *n.* ◆**'lifeguard,** *s.* Rettungsschwimmer *m.* ◆**'lifejacket,** *s.* Schwimmweste *f.* ◆**'lifeless,** *adj.* leblos. ◆**'lifelike,** *adj.* naturgetreu. ◆**'lifeline,** *s. Nau:* Rettungsleine *f*; *Fig:* Lebensader *f.* ◆**'life-size(d),** *adj.* lebensgroß. ◆**'lifetime,** *s.* in his l., zu seinen Lebzeiten.

lift [lift]. **I.** *v.* **1.** *v.tr.* (*a*) heben; **to l. s.o., sth. up,** j-n, etwas aufheben/(*above head*) aufheben; (*b*) **to l. a ban etc.,** ein Verbot usw. aufheben. **2.** *v.i.* (*of fog etc.*) sich lichten. **II.** *s.* **1.** *Aut:* **to give s.o. a**

l., j-n (im Auto) mitnehmen; **to get a l.,** mitgenommen werden. **2.** Aufzug *m*; (*ski-lift*) Lift *m.* **3.** *Av:* Auftrieb *m.*

light¹ [lait]. **I.** *s.* **1.** Licht *n*; (*of crime*) **to come to l.,** ans Licht kommen; **to bring sth. to l.,** etwas ans Licht bringen; **to throw l. on sth.,** eine Sache aufklären; **in the l. of your remarks,** angesichts Ihrer Bemerkungen. **2.** (*electric etc.*) (*a*) (*lamp*) Lampe *f*; (*head-, spotlight*) Scheinwerfer *m*; (*b*) (*traffic*) l./ **lights,** Ampel *f*; (*c*) *Fig:* (*person*) **a leading l. in science,** eine Leuchte der Wissenschaft. **3. have you got a l.?** haben Sie Feuer? **II.** *v.irr.* **1.** *v.tr.* (*a*) (eine Lampe, eine Zigarette; ein Feuer usw.) anzünden; (*b*) (*illuminate*) (einen Saal usw.) erleuchten; (eine Treppe usw.) beleuchten. **2.** *v.i.* **to l. up,** (*of eyes, face, etc.*) aufleuchten. **III.** *adj.* (*of sky, colour, hair etc.*) hell; **l. green,** hellgrün. ◆**'lighten¹,** *v.tr.* heller machen. ◆**'lighter,** *s.* Feuerzeug *n.* ◆**'lighthouse,** *s.* Leuchtturm *m.* ◆**'lighting,** *s.* Beleuchtung *f.*

light². **I.** *adj.* (*not heavy*) leicht. **II.** *adv.* **to travel l.,** mit wenig Gepäck reisen; -ly, *adv.* leicht; **to get off l.,** billig davonkommen. ◆**'lighten²,** *v.tr.* leichter machen. ◆**'light-'headed,** *adj.* schwindlig. ◆**'light-'hearted,** *adj.* sorglos, unbeschwert. ◆**'lightweight,** *adj.* leicht.

lightning ['laitnin], *s.* Blitz *m*; **l. conductor,** Blitzableiter *m.*

like¹ [laik]. **I.** *prep.* (*resembling*) wie; **what is he/the weather l.?,** wie ist er/das Wetter?; **l. this,** so. **II.** *s.* the **l.,** dergleichen; *F:* **the likes of us,** unsereins. ◆**'likelihood,** *s.* Wahrscheinlichkeit *f.* ◆**'likely. I.** *adj.* (*a*) wahrscheinlich; (*b*) (*suitable*) geeignet. **II.** *adv.* **most l./very l.** as not, höchstwahrscheinlich; *F:* **not l.!** kommt nicht in Frage! ◆**'like-minded,** *adj.* gleichgesinnt. ◆**'likeness,** *s.* **1.** (*similarity*) Ähnlichkeit *f.* **2.** (*portrait*) Porträt *n.* ◆**'likewise,** *adv.* gleichfalls.

like². **I.** *v.tr.* (*with noun*) (j-n, etwas) mögen, gern haben; **I l. that,** das gefällt mir; **as much as you l.,** soviel du willst. **2. to l. to do/doing sth.,** etwas gern tun; **I would/I'd l. to come too,** ich möchte mitkommen; **as you l.,** wie Sie wollen. **II.** *s.* **likes and dislikes,** Neigungen und Abneigungen *fpl.* ◆**'likable,** *adj.* sympathisch. ◆**'liking,** *s.* Vorliebe *f.*

lilac ['lailək]. **I.** *s.* Flieder *m.* **II.** *adj.* lila.

lily ['lili], *s.* Lilie *f.* **l. of the valley,** Maiglöckchen *n.*

limb [lim], *s.* **1.** Glied *n.* **2.** Ast *m* (eines Baumes); *Fig:* **out on a l.,** für sich allein.

limber ['limbər], *v.i.* **l. up,** Lockerungsübungen machen.

limbo ['limbəu], *s.* *Fig:* **in l.,** in der Schwebe.

lime¹ [laim], *s.* Kalk *m.* *m.* ◆**'limestone,** *s.* Kalkstein *m.*

lime², *s.* Limone *f;* **l. juice,** Limonensaft *m.*

lime³, *s.* **l.** (tree), Linde *f.*

limelight ['laimlait], *s.* Rampenlicht *n.*

limit ['limit]. **I.** *s.* Grenze *f;* **(time) l.,** Frist *f;* **F: that's the l.!** da hört doch alles auf! **II.** *v.tr.* beschränken (to, auf + acc). ◆**limited,** *p.p. & adj.* beschränkt; **l. company,** Gesellschaft *f* mit beschränkter Haftung. ◆**limi'tation,** *s.* Beschränkung *f.* ◆**limitless,** *adj.* grenzenlos.

limousine ['limu:zi:n], *s.* Limousine *f.*

limp¹ [limp]. **I.** *s.* Hinken *n;* **to have a l.,** hinken. **II.** *v.i.* hinken.

limp², *adj.* schlaff.

limpet ['limpit], *s.* Napfschnecke *f; Fig:* Klette *f.*

line¹ [lain]. **I.** *s.* **1.** *(a) Nau:* Leine *f; fishing* l., Angelschnur *f; washing* l., Wäscheleine *f; (b) Tel:* Leitung *f;* **a bad l.,** eine schlechte Verbindung; **hold the l.,** bleiben Sie am Apparat. **2.** *(a) (on paper etc)* Linie *f;* **enemy lines,** feindliche Stellungen *fpl; (b) (row)* Reihe *f; esp. N.Am: (queue)* Schlange *f;* **in/out of l.,** in einer/außerhalb der Reihe; **this is in l. with my ideas,** das steht im Einklang mit meinen Ideen; *(c) (wrinkle)* Falte *f; (writing)* Zeile *f; F:* **to drop s.o. a l.,** j-m ein paar Zeilen schreiben; *Th:* **to learn/forget one's lines,** seine Rolle lernen/vergessen; *(e) railway* l., Eisenbahnlinie *f; (route)* Eisenbahnstrecke *f; (tracks)* Gleise *npl; (f) (family)* Geschlecht *n; (g)* **l. of argument,** Beweisführung *f;* **I take the l. that ...,** ich vertrete den Standpunkt, daß ...; **(h) (principles)** *pl.* **along/on the right lines,** nach den richtigen Grundsätzen. **3.** **l. of business,** Branche *f.* **II.** *v.tr.* **to l. the street,** die Straße säumen. ◆**liner,** *s.* Linienschiff *n.* ◆**linesman,** *s.* Linienrichter *m.* ◆**line 'up,** *v.i.* sich in einer Reihe aufstellen; *(b) (queue)* Schlange stehen.

line², *v.tr. Cl:* füttern. ◆**lining,** *s.* Futter *n.*

linen ['linin], *s.* **1.** *(cloth)* Leinen *n.* **2.** *(washing)* Wäsche *f.*

linger ['liŋgər], *v.i.* verweilen. ◆**lingering,** *adj. (of glance)* sehnsüchtig; **a l. doubt,** ein nicht zu verdrängender Zweifel.

lingerie ['lɛ̃ʒəri(:)], *s.* Damenunterwäsche *f.*

linguist ['liŋgwist], *s.* Linguist *m.* ◆**lin'guistics,** *s.pl.* Linguistik *f.*

link [liŋk]. **I.** *s.* **(a)** Glied *n* (einer Kette); *(b) Fig: (connection)* Verbindung *f.* **II.** *v. 1.* *(etwas)* verbinden (with, mit + dat). **2.** *v.i.* **to l. up with s.o./sth.,** sich j-m, an etwas *acc* anschließen.

linoleum [li'nəuljəm], *F:* **lino** ['lainəu], *s.* Linoleum *n.*

linseed ['linsi:d], *s.* **l. oil,** Leinöl *n.*

lint [lint], *s.* Mull *m.*

lion ['laiən], *s.* Löwe *m.* ◆**lioness,** *s.*

Löwin *f.*

lip [lip], *s.* **1.** Lippe *f.* **2.** Rand *m* (einer Tasse usw.); Schnauze *f* (eines Krugs). ◆**lip-read,** *v.tr. & i.* (Worte) von den Lippen ablesen. ◆**lip-service,** *s.* **to pay l.-s. to sth.,** zu etwas *dat* ein Lippenbekenntnis ablegen. ◆**lipstick,** *s.* Lippenstift *m.*

liqueur [li'kjuər], *s.* Likör *m.*

liquid ['likwid]. **I.** *adj.* flüssig. **II.** *s.* Flüssigkeit *f.* ◆**liquidate,** *v.tr.* liquidieren. ◆**liqui'dation,** *s. Fin:* Liquidation *f.* ◆**liquidizer,** *s.* (elektrischer) Mixer *m.*

liquor ['likər], *s. esp. N.Am:* Alkohol *m;* **l. store,** Wein- und Spirituosenhandlung *f.*

liquorice ['likəris], *s.* Lakritze *f.*

lisp [lisp]. **I.** *s.* Lispeln *n.* **II.** *v.i.* lispeln.

list¹ [list]. **I.** *s.* Liste *f.* **II.** *v.tr. (enter)* (etwas) (in eine Liste) eintragen; *(mention)* (Sachen, Vorteile usw.) aufführen.

list², *v.i. (of ship)* Schlagseite haben.

listen ['lisn], *v.i.* **to l. to s.o., sth.,** j-m, etwas *dat* zuhören. ◆**listen 'in,** *v.i.* **to l. i. (to the radio),** Radio hören; **to l. i. to a telephone conversation** etc., ein Telefongespräch usw. mithören. ◆**listener,** *s.* Zuhörer(in) *m(f); Rad:* Hörer(in) *m(f).*

listless ['listlis], *adj.* teilnahmslos.

literate ['lit(ə)rət], *adj.* des Lesens und Schreibens kundig; *(educated)* gebildet.

literal ['litərəl], *adj.* wörtlich; **-ly,** *adv.* wörtlich; **they l. starved to death,** sie sind buchstäblich verhungert.

literary ['lit(ə)rəri], *adj.* literarisch; **l. language,** Schriftsprache *f.* ◆**literature** ['litrətʃər], *s.* Literatur *f.*

lithe [laið], *adj.* geschmeidig.

litigation [liti'geiʃən], *s.* Prozeß *m,* Rechtsstreit *m.*

litre ['li:tər], *s.* Liter *m.*

litter ['litər], *s.* **1.** *(waste paper etc.)* Abfälle *mpl.* **2.** *Z:* Wurf *m.* **II.** *v.tr.* **to l. the room with papers/l. papers all over the room,** Papiere (überall) im Zimmer verstreuen.

little ['litl]. **I.** *adj.* **1.** *(of size)* klein. **2.** *(of amount)* wenig; **l. money,** wenig Geld; **a l. money,** ein wenig/*F:* ein bißchen Geld. **II.** *s.* **I see very l. of him,** ich sehe ihn (sehr) selten; **l. by l.,** nach und nach.

live. I. *adj.* [laiv] **1.** lebend; **l. broadcast,** Live-Sendung *f; a) El:* unter Strom; *attrib.* stromführend; *b) Mil: (of ammunition)* scharf. **II.** *v.* [liv] **1.** *v.i.* **a)** leben; **to l. on sth.,** von etwas leben; *(b) (reside)* wohnen. **2.** *v.tr.* **to l. a happy life,** ein glückliches Leben führen. ◆**live 'down,** *v.tr.* **he'll never l. this d.,** man wird es ihn nie vergessen lassen. ◆**livelihood** ['laivlihud], *s.* Lebensunterhalt *m.* ◆**lively** ['laivli], *adj.* lebhaft. ◆**liven** ['laivən] **'up,** *v. 1. v.i. (of pers.)* in Stimmung kommen; **the party is livening up,** jetzt kommt die Party in Schwung. **2.** *v.tr.* (etwas) beleben.

◆**livestock** ['laivstɔk], s. Vieh n.
◆**'live 'up**, v.i. to l. up to one's reputation, seinem Ruf gerecht werden; to l. it up, ein tolles Leben führen. ◆**living** ['liviŋ]. I. adj. lebend. II. s. to earn/make one's l., seinen Lebensunterhalt verdienen; l. wage, Existenzminimum n. ◆**'living-room**, s. Wohnzimmer n.

liver ['livər], s. Leber f.

livid ['livid], adj. (angry) wütend.

lizard ['lizəd], s. Eidechse f.

llama ['lɑːmə], s. Lama n.

load [ləud]. I. s. 1. Last f.; (cargo) Ladung f; work l., Arbeitsbelastung f; Fig: that's a l. off my mind, mir ist ein Stein vom Herzen gefallen. 2. F: loads of money, ein Haufen Geld. II. v. 1. v.tr. (a) to l. s.o., sth. with sth., j-n, etwas mit etwas dat beladen; (b) (ein Gewehr usw.) laden; (einen Film, eine Kassette) einlegen; (c) P: he's loaded, er hat Geld wie Heu. 2. v.i. to l. (up), (auf)laden.

loaf[1], pl. **loaves** [ləuf, ləuvz], s. 1. Brot n. 2. P: (head) use your l.! streng mal dein Hirn an!

loaf[2], v.i. to l. (about), herumlungern.

loan [ləun]. I. s. 1. Leihgabe f. 2. Fin: Darlehen n. II. v.tr. to l. s.o. sth., j-m etwas leihen.

loath [ləuθ], adj. to be l. to do sth., etwas nur ungern tun.

loathe [ləuð], v.tr. (j-n, etwas) verabscheuen, nicht ausstehen können. ◆**'loathing**, s. Abscheu m. ◆**'loathsome**, adj. abscheulich.

lobby ['lɔbi]. I. s. (a) Vorraum m; (b) Pol: Interessengruppe f, Lobby f. II. v.tr. to l. M.P.s, Parlamentsabgeordnete zu beeinflussen versuchen.

lobster ['lɔbstər], s. Hummer m.

local ['ləuk(ə)l]. I. adj. örtlich, Orts-; l. government, Kommunalverwaltung f; l. authority, Ortsbehörde f; l. call, Ortsgespräch n; l. anaesthetic, örtliche Betäubung. II. s. (a) 1. (inhabitant) Ortsansässige(r) f(m); the locals, die Hiesigen pl; (b) F: the l., die Kneipe an die Ecke; -ly, adv. well-known l., allgemein bekannt in ir Gegend. ◆**'locality**, s. Gegend f. ◆**lo'cate**, v.tr. (a) (find) ausfindig machen; (b) (place) plazieren; (in building) unterbringen; to be located, sich befinden. ◆**lo'cation**, s. (situation) Lage f; Cin: shot on l., als Außenaufnahme gedreht.

lock[1] [lɔk], s. (of hair) Locke f.

lock[2]. I. s. (of door, rifle etc.) Schloß n. 2. (on canal etc.) Schleuse f. II. v. 1. v.tr. (a) (die Tür usw.) zuschließen; to l. (up) the house, das Haus abschließen; to l. s.o. into a room, j-n in ein Zimmer einschließen; Tchn: (ein Teil) sperren. 2. v.i. (a) (of door etc.) sich verschließen lassen; (b) (of moving parts) sperren; (of wheels, brakes) blockieren. ◆**'locker**, s. kleiner Schrank m; Nau: Mil: Spind m; (on station etc.) Schließfach n. ◆**'lock-**

out, s. Aussperrung f. ◆**'locksmith**, s. Schlosser m. ◆**'lock 'up**, v.tr. (a) (j-n) einsperren; (b) (das Haus) abschließen.

locket ['lɔkit], s. Medaillon n.

locomotive ['ləukə'məutiv], s. Lokomotive f.

locust ['ləukəst], s. Heuschrecke f.

lodge [lɔdʒ]. I. s. Loge f. II. v. 1. v.tr. to l. a complaint, eine Beschwerde einreichen. 2. v.i. (a) (of pers.) (bei j-m) logieren; (b) (of thing) steckenbleiben. ◆**'lodger**, s. Untermieter m. ◆**'lodgings**, s.pl. möblierte Zimmer npl.

loft [lɔft], s. Dachboden m.

log [lɔg], s. 1. Holzscheit n; l. cabin, Blockhütte f; Fig: to sleep like a l., wie ein Sack schlafen. 2. l. (book), Logbuch n; Aut: l. book, approx. Zulassungsschein m.

logarithm ['lɔgəriθ(ə)m], s. Logarithmus m.

loggerheads ['lɔgəhedz], s. they are constantly at l., sie liegen sich ständig in den Haaren.

logic ['lɔdʒik], s. Logik f. ◆**'logical**, adj. logisch.

loin [lɔin], s. (usu. pl.) Lenden fpl.

loiter ['lɔitər], v.i. herumlungern.

loll [lɔl], v.i. (sich) lümmeln.

lollipop ['lɔlipɔp], F: **lolly** ['lɔli], s. Lutscher m; ice l., Eis n am Stiel.

lone [ləun], adj. einsam. ◆**'lonely**, adj. einsam; a l. spot, eine abgelegene Stelle. ◆**'loneliness**, s. Einsamkeit f. ◆**'lonesome**, adj. einsam.

long[1] [lɔŋ]. I. adj. lang; a l. time, lange; for a l. time, seit langem. II. s. 1. the l. and the short of it is ..., mit einem Wort/kurzum ... 2. before l., bald; it's not for l., es dauert nicht lange. III. adv. 1. has he been gone l.? ist er schon lange fort? I won't be long, ich bin bald wieder da; as l. as I live, solange ich lebe. 2. all day l., den ganzen Tag. 3. no longer, nicht mehr; how much longer? wie lange noch? ◆**'long-'distance**, adj. l.-d. runner, Langstreckenläufer m; l.-d. call, Ferngespräch n. ◆**'long-'haired**, adj. langhaarig. ◆**'long 'jump**, s. Weitsprung m. ◆**'long-'playing**, adj. l.-p. record, Langspielplatte f. ◆**'long-'range**, adj. (a) (long-distance) Langstrecken-; l.-r. missile, Ferngeschoß n; (b) (of plan, forecast) auf lange Sicht. ◆**'long-'sighted**, adj. weitsichtig. ◆**'long-'standing**, adj. seit langem bestehend. ◆**'long-'suffering**, adj. geduldig. ◆**'long-'term**, adj. langfristig. ◆**'long-'winded**, adj. langatmig; (lengthy) langwierig.

long[2], v.i. sich sehnen (for s.o., sth., nach j-m, etwas dat). ◆**'longing**. I. s. Sehnsucht f. II. adj. sehnend.

longitude ['lɔŋgitjuːd, 'lɔndʒi-], s. Länge f.

loo [luː], s. F: Klo n.

look [luk]. **I.** s. **1.** (*glance*) Blick m; (*expression*) Miene f; **to have a l. at sth.**, sich dat etwas ansehen. **2.** (*appearance*) (*a*) Aussehen n. **II. 1.** v.tr. **to l. of it**, allem Anschein nach; (*b*) F: pl **good looks**, gutes Aussehen n. **II. 1.** v.tr. & i. sehen; South G: schauen; North G: gucken; F: **l. here!** na hör mal! **2.** v.i. (*appear*) aussehen (like, nach + dat.). ◆**'look 'after**, v.tr. **to l. a. s.o., sth.**, sich um j-n, etwas acc kümmern; (*carefully*) (etwas) pflegen; **please l. a. my bag for a moment**, bitte passen Sie einen Augenblick auf meine Tasche auf. ◆**'look a'round**, v.i. **1.** sich umsehen (for sth., nach etwas dat). **2.** v.tr. **to l. a. a place**, sich in einem Ort umsehen. ◆**'look 'at**, v.tr. (j-n, etwas) ansehen; (j-n) anblicken ◆**'look a'way**, v.i. den Blick abwenden. ◆**'look 'back**, v.i. zurückblicken (at s.o., sth., auf j-n, etwas acc). ◆**'look 'down**, v.i. (*also Fig:*) herabsehen (on s.o., sth., auf j-n, etwas acc). ◆**'look 'for**, v.tr. suchen. ◆**'look 'forward**, v.i. **to l. f. to sth.**, sich auf etwas acc freuen. ◆**'look-in**, s. F: **he won't get a l.-i.**, dabei springt nichts für ihn heraus. ◆**'look 'into**, v.tr. (eine Angelegenheit) untersuchen. ◆**'look 'on**, v.i. zusehen. ◆**'look 'out**, v.i. (*a*) hinaussehen; **to l. o. of the window**, zum Fenster hinaussehen/hinausblicken; **a room that looks out on the garden**, ein Zimmer mit Ausblick auf den Garten; (*b*) Ausschau halten (for s.o., nach j-m); (*c*) (*take care*) aufpassen; **l. o.!** Vorsicht! ◆**'look-out**, s. **1. to be on the l.-o. for s.o., sth.**, nach j-m, etwas auf Ausschau halten. **2.** F: **that's his l.-o.**, das ist seine Angelegenheit. ◆**'look 'round**, v.tr. & i. **to l. r. (a museum etc)**, sich (im einem Museum usw.) umsehen; **don't l. r.**, dreh dich nicht um. ◆**'look 'up**, v. **1.** v.i. (*a*) aufblicken (Fig: to s.o., zu j-m); (*b*) (*improve*) sich bessern. **2.** v.tr. (*a*) (ein Wort usw.) nachschlagen; (*b*) (*visit*) (j-n) aufsuchen.

loom[1] [lu:m], s. Webstuhl m.

loom[2] [lu:m], v.i. (plötzlich) aufragen.

loop [lu:p], s. Schleife f; (*of rope etc.*) Schlinge f. ◆**'loophole**, s. Fig: Lücke f; F: Hintertürchen n.

loose [lu:s]. **I.** adj. **1.** (*a*) (*detached, undone*) lose; **l. change**, Kleingeld n; (*b*) (*free*) frei. **2.** (*slack*) locker; **-ly**, adv. **1. l.** tied, locker gebunden. **2. l.** translated, frei übersetzt. ◆**'loose-'leaf**, adj. **l.-l.** binder, Schnellhefter m. ◆**'loosen**, v. **1.** v.tr. lockern; (einen Knoten usw.) lösen. **2.** v.i. sich lockern.

loot [lu:t]. **I.** s. Beute f. **II.** v. **1.** v.tr. (eine Stadt) ausplündern. **2.** v.i. plündern.

lop [lop], v.tr. **to l. off a branch**, einen Ast absägen. ◆**'lop-'sided**, adj. schief.

lord [lo:d], s. **1.** (*master, also Ecc:*) Herr m; **the L.'s Prayer**, das Vaterunser. **2.**

(*title*) Lord m. ◆**'lordship**, s. **Your L.**, Euer Gnaden.

lorry ['lori], s. Lastwagen m, F: Laster m; **l. driver**, Lastwagenfahrer m.

lose [lu:z], v.tr.irr. (*a*) verlieren; **to l. in value**, an Wert verlieren; Sp: **to l. by 2 goals to 1**, 2 zu 1 verlieren; **to l. weight**, abnehmen; **to l. oneself/one's way**, sich verirren; (*of car driver*) sich verfahren; (*b*) (*of clock etc.*) nachgehen. ◆**'lose 'out**, v.i. verlieren. ◆**'loser**, s. Verlierer m. ◆**'lost**, adj. (*of thing*) verloren; **to get l.**, verlorengehen; **l. property office**, Fundbüro n; (*b*) (*of pers.*) verirrt; **to get l.**, sich verirren; **I am l.**, ich habe mich verirrt; (*of Mil: of pers.*) verschollen; (*of ship*) untergegangen.

loss [los], s. Verlust m; **to be at a l.**, nicht weiter wissen.

lot [lot], s. **1.** (*fate*) Los n; **to draw lots for sth.**, um etwas acc losen. **2.** (*a*) (*at auction*) Posten m; (*b*) F: **the l., alles, das Ganze**. **3.** F: **a l., viel(e), eine Menge**; **a l. of money, viel Geld, eine Menge Geld**; **I see quite a l. of him**, ich sehe ihn ziemlich oft; **aber times have changed a l.**, die Zeiten haben sich sehr geändert. **4.** F: lots, jede Menge.

lotion ['louʃ(ə)n], s. Lotion f.

lottery ['lotəri], s. Lotterie f; **l. ticket**, Los n.

loud [laud], adj. laut; **-ly**, adv. laut; **to protest l.**, lautstark protestieren. ◆**'loudness**, s. Lautstärke f. ◆**'loud'speaker**, s. Lautsprecher m.

lounge [laundʒ]. **I.** s. (*in house*) Wohnzimmer n; (*in hotel*) Gesellschaftsraum m. **II.** v.i. sich lümmeln.

louse, pl. **lice** [laus, lais], s. Laus f. ◆**'lousy** ['lauzi], adj. F: miserabel.

lout [laut], s. Flegel m.

love [lʌv]. **I.** s. **1.** Liebe f; **in l.**, verliebt; **to fall in l. with s.o.**, sich in j-n verlieben; **to make l.**, zusammen schlafen; **l. letter**, Liebesbrief m; **l. song**, Liebeslied n; **l. story**, Liebesgeschichte f. **l. affair**, (Liebes)verhältnis n. **2.** (*pers.*) **my l.**, mein Schatz; mein Liebster, meine Liebste. **3.** Sp: Null f. **II.** v.tr. lieben; F: **to l. doing sth.**, etwas schrecklich gern tun. ◆**'lovable**, adj. liebenswert. ◆**'lovely**, adj. (*a*) (*of girl, picture etc.*) reizend; (*b*) F: (*of party, meal etc.*) großartig. ◆**'lover**, s. **1.** Geliebte(r) f(m); *esp. Th:* Liebhaber m. **2.** Freund m (der Künste usw.); **music l.**, Musikfreund m. ◆**'loving**, adj. liebevoll.

low [lou]. **I.** adj. (*a*) niedrig; **l. speed**, geringe Geschwindigkeit; **supplies are (running) l.**, die Vorräte werden knapp; (*b*) (*of note, sound*) tief; (*soft*) leise; (*c*) Fig: (*mean*) niederträchtig; (*d*) Fig: (*bad*) **l. opinion**, schlechte Meinung. **II.** adv. (*a*) tief (fliegen, liegen, sinken usw.); **to lie l.**, sich versteckt halten; (*b*) **the lowest paid workers**, die am schlechtesten bezahlten Arbeiter. **III.** s. **all-time l.**, ab-

soluter Tiefstand *m.* ◆**'low-down,** *s.*
P: **to give s.o. the l.-d.,**
j-n aufklären (**on sth.,** über etwas *acc*).
◆**'lower,** *v.tr.* (*a*) (j-n, etwas) herunterlassen; (eine Fahne) niederholen; (*b*) (die
Augen, den Preis usw.) senken.
loyal ['lɔiəl], *adj.* treu (**to s.o., sth.,** j-m,
etwas *dat*). ◆**'loyalty,** *s.* Treue *f.*
lozenge ['lɔzindʒ], *s.* Pastille *f.*
lubricate ['lu:brikeit], *v.tr.* schmieren.
◆**'lubricant,** *s.* Schmiermittel *n.*
◆**lubri'cation,** *s.* Schmierung *f.*
lucid ['lu:sid], *adj.* klar; (*of pers., mind*)
scharfsinnig.
luck [lʌk], *s.* 1. (*fortune*) (**good**) **l.,** Glück
n; **bad/hard l.,** Pech *n;* **good**
l.! viel Glück! **piece/stroke of l.,** Glücksfall *m;* **worse l.!** leider! 2. (*chance*) Zufall
m. ◆**'lucky,** *adj.* glücklich; (*of thing*)
glückbringend; **to be l.,** (*of pers.*) Glück
haben; (*of thing*) Glück bringen; **l. day,**
Glückstag *m;* **-ily,** *adv.* zum Glück.
lucrative ['lu:krətiv], *adj.* lukrativ.
ludicrous ['lu:dikrəs], *adj.* lächerlich.
lug [lʌg], *v.tr. F:* schleppen.
luggage ['lʌgidʒ], *s.* Gepäck *n;* **l. rack,**
Gepäcknetz *n;* **l. locker,** Schließfach *n.*
lugubrious [lu:'gu:briəs], *adj.* düster.
lukewarm ['lu:kwɔ:m], *adj.* lauwarm.
lull [lʌl]. **I.** *s.* (*in a storm*) kurze Flaute *f;*
a l. in the conversation, eine Gesprächs-
pause. **II.** *v.tr. Fig:* **to be lulled into a**
(**false**) **sense of security,** sich in einem
Sicherheitsgefühl wiegen. ◆**'lullaby**
['lʌləbai], *s.* Wiegenlied *n.*
lumbago [lʌm'beigəu], *s.* Hexenschuß *m.*
lumber ['lʌmbər], *v.tr. F:* (j-n) belasten
(**with sth.,** mit etwas *dat*).
◆**'lumberjack,** *s.* Holzfäller *m.*
luminous ['lu:minəs], *adj.* leuchtend,
Leucht-.
lump [lʌmp]. **I.** *s.* (*a*) (*of clay, wood etc.*)

Klumpen *m;* **l. of sugar,** Zuckerwürfel
m; **l. sum,** Pauschalbetrag *m;* (*b*) (*swell-*
ing etc.) Schwellung *f.* **II.** *v.tr. F:* **to l.**
everything together, alles in einen Topf
werfen. ◆**'lumpy,** *adj.* (*of sauce*) klum-
pig.
lunacy ['lu:nəsi], *s.* Wahnsinn *m.*
◆**'lunatic. I.** *s.* Verrückte(r) *f(m).* **II.**
adj. wahnsinnig.
lunar ['lu:nər], *adj.* Mond-; **l. module,**
Mondfähre *f.*
lunch [lʌn(t)ʃ], *s.* Mittagessen *n;* **l. hour,**
Mittagspause *f.* ◆**'luncheon,** *s.* Mittagessen *n;* **l. voucher,** Essensbon *m.*
lung [lʌn], *s.* Lunge *f.*
lunge [lʌndʒ], *v.i.* vorwärts stoßen.
lupin ['lu:pin], *s.* Lupine *f.*
lurch1 [lə:tʃ], *s.* **to leave s.o. in the l.,**
j-n im Stich lassen.
lurch2, *v.i.* (*a*) (*of vehicle*) einen Ruck geben; (*b*) (*of ship*) schlingern; (*c*) (*of pers.*)
taumeln.
lure ['ljuər]. **I.** *s. Fig:* Verlockung *f.* **II.**
v.tr. (*a*) (ein Fisch, Tier) ködern; (*b*)
(j-n, ein Tier) anlocken.
lurid ['ljuərid], *adj.* 1. (*of colours*) grell. 2.
(*of film etc.*) reißerisch.
lurk [lə:k], *v.i.* lauern.
luscious ['lʌʃəs], *adj.* köstlich.
lush [lʌʃ], *adj.* üppig.
lust [lʌst], *s.* (*a*) (*geschlechtliche*) Begierde *f;* (*b*) **l. for power,** Machtgier *f.*
◆**'lusty,** *adj.* rüstig.
lute [lu:t], *s.* Laute *f.*
luxuriant [lʌg'zjuəriənt], *adj.* üppig.
◆**lux'urious,** *adj.* luxuriös. ◆**luxury**
['lʌkʃəri], *s.* Luxus *m.*
lynch [lin(t)ʃ], *v.tr.* (j-n) lynchen.
lyric ['lirik]. **I.** *adj.* lyrisch; **l. poetry,** Lyrik *f.* **II.** *s.* (*a*) lyrisches Gedicht *n;* (*b*)
Mus: **lyrics,** Text *m.* ◆**'lyrical,** *adj.*
lyrisch.

M

M, m [em], *s.* (der Buchstabe) M, m *n.*
mac [mæk], *s. abbr. F:* = **mackintosh.**
macabre [mə'kɑ:br], *adj.* makaber.
macaroni [mækə'rəuni], *s.* Makkaroni *pl.*
machinations [mæki'neiʃ(ə)nz], *s.pl.* Ma-
chenschaften *fpl.*
machine [mə'ʃi:n], *s.* (*a*) Maschine *f;* **m.**
tool, Werkzeugmaschine *f;* (*b*) (*small de-*
vice) Apparat *m.* ◆**ma'chinery,** *s.* Ma-
schinerie *f;* (*mechanism*) Mechanismus *m.*
mackerel ['mæk(ə)rəl], *s.* Makrele *f.*
mackintosh ['mækintɔʃ], *s.* Regenmantel
m.
mad [mæd], *adj.* 1. verrückt. 2. *F:* **m.**
about/on sth., auf etwas *acc* versessen;
m. about s.o., in j-n vernarrt. 3. (*angry*)
böse. ◆**'maddening,** *adj.* aufreizend.
◆**'madness,** *s.* Wahnsinn *m.*
madam ['mædəm], *s.* gnädige Frau.
magazine [mægə'zi:n], *s.* Zeitschrift *f;*

(*illustrated*) Illustrierte *f.*
maggot ['mægət], *s.* Made *f.*
magic ['mædʒik]. **I.** *s.* Zauber *m.* **II.** *adj.*
magisch. ◆**'magical,** *adj.* zauberhaft.
◆**magician** [mə'dʒiʃ(ə)n], *s.* Zauberkünstler *m.*
magistrate ['mædʒistreit], *s.* Friedensrichter *m.*
magnanimous [mæg'næniməs], *adj.*
großmütig.
magnate ['mægneit], *s.* Magnat *m.*
magnet ['mægnit], *s.* Magnet *m.*
◆**magnetic** [-'netik], *adj.* magnetisch.
◆**'magnetism** [-nətizm], *s.* Magnetis-
mus *m; Fig:* (*personal*) **m.,** Anziehungs-
kraft *f.*
magnify ['mægnifai], *v.tr.* (ein Bild usw.)
vergrößern; **magnifying glass,** Vergröße-
rungsglas *n.*
magnificent [mæg'nifisənt], *adj.* herrlich.

magnitude ['mægnitju:d], s. 1. Größe f. 2. Fig: Ausmaß n (einer Katastrophe).

magpie ['mægpai], s. Elster f.

mahogany [mə'hɔgəni], s. Mahagoni n.

maid [meid], s. 1. Dienstmädchen n. 2. **old m.**, alte Jungfer f. ◆**'maiden**, attrib. adj. 1. (unmarried) **m. aunt**, unverheiratete Tante f; **m. name**, Mädchenname m. 2. (first) **m. voyage**, Jungfernfahrt f; **m. speech**, Jungfernrede f.

mail [meil]. I. s. Post f; **m. order firm**, Versandhaus n. II. v.tr. esp. N.Am: (etwas) mit der Post schicken; (einen Brief) aufgeben. ◆**'mailbag**, s. Postsack m. ◆**'mailbox**, s. N.Am: Briefkasten m.

maim [meim], v.tr. verstümmeln.

main [mein]. I. s. 1. in the m., im ganzen; im wesentlichen. 2. (a) (water) m., Hauptwasseranschluß m; (b) (gas m.) Hauptleitung f; El: Stromnetz n. II. attrib. adj. Haupt-; **m. road**, Hauptstraße f; **m. thing**, Hauptsache f; **-ly**, adv. hauptsächlich; (mostly) größtenteils. ◆**'mainland**, s. Festland n. ◆**'mainstay**, s. Fig: Hauptstütze f.

maintain [mein'tein], v.tr. (a) (Recht und Ordnung, Kontakt usw.) aufrechterhalten; (eine Geschwindigkeit) beibehalten; (b) (Straßen, Anlagen usw.) instand halten; (eine Maschine) warten; (c) (j-n, eine Familie) unterhalten; (d) **he maintained that ...**, er behauptete, daß ... ◆**'maintenance** [-tinəns], s. Instandhaltung f; Aut: etc: Wartung f.

maisonette [meizə'net], s. Maisonettewohnung f.

maize [meiz], s. Mais m.

majesty ['mædʒisti], s. Majestät f. ◆**ma'jestic** [mə'dʒestik], adj. majestätisch.

major¹ ['meidʒər], s. Major m.

major², adj. 1. (a) (larger) Haupt-; **the m. part**, der größte Teil; (b) (serious) ernst; **m. operation**, schwere Operation; (c) (important) bedeutend; **a m. change**, eine große Veränderung. 2. **m. road**, Hauptverkehrsstraße f; (having priority) Vorfahrtstraße f. 3. Mus: Dur; **in A m.**, in A-Dur. ◆**majority** [mə'dʒɔriti], s. Mehrheit f.

make [meik]. I. s. Marke f. II. v.irr. 1. v.tr. (etwas) machen; (earn) verdienen; (reach) (eine Stadt usw.) erreichen; **to m. sth. into sth.**, etwas zu etwas dat machen; **to m. s.o. do sth.**, j-n veranlassen, etwas zu tun; F: **we've made it!** wir haben's geschafft! 2. v.i. **what do you m. of it?** was halten Sie davon? ◆**'make 'do**, v.i. sich begnügen (with s.o., sth., mit j-m, etwas dat). ◆**'make 'for**, v.i. (a) (aim for) **he was making f. London**, sein Ziel war London; **where are you making f.?** wohin wollen Sie? (b) (contribute to) **it makes for good relations**, es fördert gute Beziehungen. ◆**'make 'off**, v.i. F: sich davonmachen (with s.o., sth., mit j-m, etwas dat). ◆**'make 'out**,

v.tr. (a) (einen Scheck) ausstellen; (b) (eine Handschrift) entziffern; **I cannot m. it o.**, ich werde nicht klug daraus; (c) **I could not m. o. his features in the dark**, ich konnte seine Züge im Dunkeln nicht erkennen. ◆**'makeshift**, adj. behelfsmäßig; **a m. shelter**, eine Notunterkunft f. ◆**'make 'up**, v. 1. v.tr. (a) **to m. up lost ground**, Versäumtes nachholen; (in race) aufholen; (b) **to m. up a prescription**, eine verschriebene Arznei zubereiten; (c) Cl: (einen Anzug) anfertigen; (d) (invent) (eine Geschichte) erfinden; (e) (from) (ein Ganzes usw.) bilden; (f) **to m. (s.o., oneself) up**, (j-n, sich) schminken; (g) **to m. up one's mind**, sich entschließen; (h) **to m. up it up with s.o.**, sich mit j-m versöhnen. 2. v.i. **to m. up for sth.**, etwas wiedergutmachen; **to m. up for lost time**, verlorene Zeit aufholen. ◆**'make-up**, s. Make-up n; Th: (result) Maske f.

malaria [mə'lɛəriə], s. Malaria f.

male [meil]. I. s. 1. Mann m; (animal) Männchen n. II. adj. männlich.

malfunction [mæl'fʌŋkʃ(ə)n], s. Funktionsstörung f.

malice ['mælis], s. Bosheit f. ◆**ma'licious**, adj. (of damage etc.) böswillig; (of remarks) boshaft.

malign [mə'lain], v.tr. (j-n) verleumden. ◆**malignant** [mə'lignənt], adj. **m. tumour**, bösartige Geschwulst f.

mallet ['mælit], s. Holzhammer m.

malnutrition [mælnju'triʃ(ə)n], s. Unterernährung f.

malpractice [mæl'præktis], s. Mißbrauch m.

malt [mɔ:lt], s. Malz n.

mammal ['mæməl], s. Säugetier n.

mammoth ['mæməθ]. I. s. Z: Mammut n. II. adj. Fig: riesig, ungeheuer.

man [mæn]. I. s. pl. **men** [men]. 1. (human) Mensch m; **the m. in the street**, der Durchschnittsmensch. 2. (male) Mann m. II. v.tr. (ein Schiff usw.) bemannen. ◆**'manhole**, s. Einstiegeschacht m. ◆**'mankind**, s. die Menschheit. ◆**'man'kind**, s. die Menschheit. ◆**'manpower**, s. coll. Arbeitskräfte fpl. ◆**'manslaughter**, s. Totschlag m.

manage ['mænidʒ], v. 1. v.tr. (a) (einen Betrieb, ein Hotel) führen, leiten; (b) F: (etwas) schaffen; **she managed to see him**, es gelang ihr, ihn zu sehen. 2. v.i. zurechtkommen. ◆**'manageable**, adj. 1. (of tool etc.) handlich. 2. (of pers.) fügsam. ◆**'management**, s. (a) (managers) Leitung f (eines Geschäfts, usw.); (b) (practice) Geschäftsführung f. 2. (handling) Handhabung f (einer Angelegenheit). ◆**'manager**, s. Leiter m, Manager m. ◆**'manageress**, s. Geschäftsführerin f (eines Restaurants usw.); Leiterin f (einer Abteilung); Direktorin f (einer Firma). ◆**mana'gerial**, adj. führend, leitend; **m. staff**, Führungskräfte *fpl.* ◆'**managing,** *adj.* m. director, Geschäftsführer *m.*

mandarin(e) ['mændərin], *s.* Mandarine *f.*

mandate ['mændeit], *s.* Mandat *n; Jur:* Vollmacht *f.* ◆'**mandatory** [-dətri], *adj.* verbindlich.

mane [mein], *s.* Mähne *f.*

mangle ['mæŋgl]. I. *s.* Mangel *f.* II. *v.tr.* verstümmeln.

mango, *pl.* **-oes** ['mæŋgəu, -əuz], *s.* Mango *f.*

mania ['meiniə], *s.* Manie *f.* ◆'**maniac,** *s. F:* Verrückte(r) *f(m); sex* m., (a) Triebtäter *m; Hum:* Lustmolch *m.*

manicure ['mænikjuər]. I. *s.* Maniküre *f.* II. *v.tr.* maniküren.

manifest ['mænifest]. I. *adj.* offensichtlich. II. *v.tr.* (etwas) aufweisen; to m. itself, sich zeigen. ◆**manifes'tation,** *s.* Erscheinung *f.* ◆**mani'festo,** *pl.* **-os,** *s.* election m., Wahlprogramm *n.*

manipulate [mə'nipjuleit], *v.tr.* manipulieren. ◆**manipu'lation,** *s.* Manipulation *f.*

manner ['mænər], *s.* 1. (a) Weise *f;* in this m., auf diese Weise; (b) (of pers.) Art *f.* 2. *pl.* Manieren *pl;* (good) manners, gute Manieren/gutes Benehmen. ◆'**mannerism,** *s.* Tick *m.*

manoeuvre [mə'nu:vər]. I. *s.* Manöver *n.* II. *v.tr. & i.* manövrieren.

manor ['mænər], *s.* m. (house), Herrenhaus *n;* Schloß *n.*

mansion ['mænʃən], *s.* Schloß *n.*

mantelpiece ['mæntlpi:s], *s.* Kaminsims *m.*

manual ['mænjuəl]. I. *adj.* manuell; Hand-. II. *s.* Handbuch *n.*

manufacture [mænju'fæktʃər]. I. *s.* Herstellung *f;* country of m., Herstellungsland *n.* II. *v.tr.* herstellen; **manufactured goods,** Industriewaren *fpl.* ◆**manu'facturer,** *s.* Hersteller *m.*

manure [mə'njuər], *s.* Dünger *m;* (farmyard) m., Mist *m.*

manuscript ['mænjuskript], *s.* Manuskript *n.*

many ['meni]. I. *adj.* 1. viel(e); **how m.?** wie viele? 2. *Lit:* m. a, mancher, manche, manches. II. *s.* viele *pl.*

map [mæp]. I. *s.* Landkarte; (of town) Stadtplan *m.* II. *v.tr.* kartieren.

maple ['meipl], *s.* Ahorn *m;* m. syrup, Ahornsirup *m.*

mar [ma:r], *v.tr.* verderben.

marathon ['mærəθən], *s.* Marathonlauf *m.*

marble ['ma:bl], *s.* 1. Marmor *m.* 2. Murmel *f.*

March¹ [ma:tʃ], *s.* März *m.*

march². I. *s.* Marsch *m.* II. *v.* 1. *v.i.* marschieren. 2. *v.tr.* **to m. s.o. off,** j-n abführen. ◆'**marching,** *s.* m. orders, Marschbefehl *m.*

mare [meər], *s.* Stute *f.*

margarine [ma:dʒə'ri:n], *s.* Margarine *f.*

margin ['ma:dʒin], *s.* 1. Rand *m* (einer Seite usw.). 2. m. of error, Fehlerbereich *m;* profit m., Gewinnspanne *f.* ◆'**marginal,** *adj.* (a) am Rande; m. note, Randbemerkung *f;* (b) (slight) geringfügig; m. seat, Wahlkreis *m* mit knapper Mehrheit.

marigold ['mærigəuld], *s.* Ringelblume *f.*

marijuana [mæri'(h)wa:nə], *s.* Marihuana *f.*

marinade [mæri'neid], *s.* Marinade *f.* ◆'**marinate,** *v.tr.* marinieren.

marine [mə'ri:n]. I. *adj.* (a) (sea) Meeres-; (b) (shipping) See-. II. *s.* Marinesoldat *m.*

marital ['mæritl], *adj.* ehelich; m. status, Familienstand *m.*

maritime ['mæritaim], *adj.* See-.

marjoram ['ma:dʒ(ə)rəm], *s.* Majoran *m.*

mark¹ [ma:k]. I. *s.* 1. (target) *Fig:* to hit the m., ins Schwarze treffen; to be wide of the m., danebentreffen. 2. (trace) Spur *f;* (dirty) m., Fleck *m;* birth m., Muttermal *n.* 3. (a) (sign) Zeichen *n;* (b) (feature) Kennzeichen *n.* 4. *Sch:* Note *f.* II. *v.tr.* (a) (eine Grenze usw.) markieren; (b) (Schularbeiten) benoten; (c) to m. time, Zeit schinden; (d) (you) m. my words! paß nur auf! du wirst noch an meine Worte denken! (e) *Fb:* (einen Spieler) decken. ◆'**marked,** *adj.* a m. improvement, eine merkliche Besserung. ◆'**markup,** *s.* Kalkulationsaufschlag *m.*

mark², *s.* (money) Mark *f;* **ten marks,** zehn Mark.

market ['ma:kit]. I. *s.* Markt *m.;* m. place, Marktplatz *m;* m. research, Marktforschung *f.* II. *v.tr.* (a) (introduce) (etwas) auf den Markt bringen; (b) (sell) (etwas) vertreiben. ◆'**marketable,** *adj.* marktfähig. ◆'**marketing,** *s.* Marketing *n;* (sale) Vertrieb *m.*

marksman ['ma:ksmən], *pl.* **-men** ['ma:ksmən], *s.* Scharfschütze *m.*

marmalade ['ma:məleid], *s.* Orangenmarmelade *f.*

maroon¹ [mə'ru:n], *adj.* dunkelrot.

maroon², *v.tr.* **to be marooned,** (on an island) ausgesetzt werden; *F:* (be stuck) festsitzen.

marquee [ma:'ki:], *s.* Festzelt *n.*

marriage ['mæridʒ], *s.* (a) (state) Ehe *f,* m. guidance, Eheberatung *f;* (b) (ceremony) Trauung *f;* m. certificate, Heiratsurkunde *f;* (c) (act of marrying) Heirat *f;* m. bureau, Ehevermittlung *f.* ◆'**married,** *adj.* verheiratet; m. couple, Ehepaar *n.* ◆'**marry,** *v.tr & i.* heiraten.

marrow ['mærəu], *s.* 1. bone m., Knochenmark *m.* 2. (vegetable) m., Speisekürbis *m.*

marsh [ma:ʃ], *s.* Sumpf *m.*

marshal ['ma:ʃəl]. I. *s.* field m., Feldmarschall *m.* II. *v.tr.* (Truppen usw.) aufstellen; (Gedanken, Tatsachen) ordnen.

martial ['mɑːʃ(ə)l], *adj.* m. law, Kriegsrecht *n.*

Martian ['mɑːʃən], *s.* Marsmensch *m.*

martyr ['mɑːtər]. I. *s.* Märtyrer(in) *m(f).* II. *v.tr.* (j-n) zum Märtyrer machen. ◆'**martyrdom**, *s.* Martyrium *n.*

marvel ['mɑːv(ə)l]. I. *s.* Wunder *n.* II. *v.i.* sich wundern (**at** sth., über etwas *acc*.) ◆'**marvellous**, *adj.* wunderbar; *F:* fabelhaft.

Marxist ['mɑːksist]. I. *s.* Marxist(in) *m(f).* II. *adj.* marxistisch.

marzipan [mɑːzi'pæn], *s.* Marzipan *n.*

mascara [mæs'kɑːrə], *s.* Wimperntusche *f.*

mascot ['mæskət], *s.* Maskottchen *n.*

masculine ['mæskjulin], *adj.* männlich.

mash [mæʃ], *v.tr.* (etwas) zu Brei zerdrücken; **mashed potatoes**, Kartoffelbrei *m.*

mask [mɑːsk]. I. *s.* Maske *f.* II. *v.tr.* maskieren. ◆'**masking**, *adj.* m. tape, Abdeckband *n.*

masochist ['mæsəkist], *s.* Masochist *m.*

mason ['meisən], *s.* 1. Steinmetz *m.* 2. *(freemason)* Freimaurer *m.* ◆'**masonic** [mə'sɔnik], *adj.* freimaurerisch. ◆'**masonry**, *s.* Mauerwerk *n.*

masquerade [mæskə'reid]. I. *s.* Maskerade *f.* II. *v.i.* to m. as s.o., sich für j-n ausgeben.

mass¹ [mæs], *s. Ecc:* Messe *f.*

mass², *s.* Masse *f;* m. production, Massenproduktion *f.* ◆'**mass-pro'duce**, *v.tr.* (einen Artikel) in Massenproduktion herstellen.

massacre ['mæsəkər]. I. *s.* Massaker *n.* II. *v.tr.* massakrieren.

massage ['mæsɑːʒ]. I. *s.* Massage *f.* II. *v.tr.* massieren.

massive ['mæsiv], *adj.* massiv.

mast [mɑːst], *s.* Mast *m.*

master ['mɑːstər]. I. *s.* 1. Herr *m.* 2. *Sch:* (a) *(teacher)* Lehrer *m;* (b) Rektor *m* (eines Colleges). 3. *(of subject etc.)* Meister *m;* m. copy, Original *n;* m. key, Hauptschlüssel *m.* II. *v.tr.* (eine Aufgabe, Schwierigkeiten) meistern; (ein Fach usw.) beherrschen. ◆'**masterful**, *adj.* gebieterisch. ◆'**masterly**, *adj.* meisterhaft. ◆'**mastermind**, *v.tr.* to m. a project, der führende Kopf eines Projekts sein. ◆'**masterpiece**, *s.* Meisterwerk *n.* ◆'**mastery**, *s.* Beherrschung *f.*

masturbate ['mæstəbeit], *v.i.* onanieren.

mat [mæt], *s.* (a) Matte *f;* (door) m., Abtreter *m;* (b) (rug) Vorleger *m;* (c) (under plates, vases etc.) Untersetzer *m;* beer m., Bierdeckel *m.* ◆'**matted**, *adj.* verfilzt.

match¹ [mætʃ]. I. *s.* 1. *Sp:* Spiel *n.* 2. to be a m. for s.o., sth., j-m, etwas *dat* gewachsen sein; to meet one's m., seinen Meister finden. 3. these colours are a good m., diese Farben passen gut zusammen/vertragen sich gut. II. *v.tr. & i.* (a) he can m. anyone for speed, er kann es mit jedem an Schnelligkeit auf

nehmen; to be evenly matched (for strength etc.), einander (an Stärke usw.) gleich sein; (b) *(adapt)* (Tchn: Teile) aufeinander abstimmen; (c) the curtains m. the carpet, die Vorhänge passen zum Teppich. ◆'**matching**, *adj.* zusammenpassend. ◆'**matchless**, *adj.* unvergleichlich.

match², *s.* Streichholz *n.* ◆'**matchbox**, *s.* Streichholzschachtel *f.*

mate [meit]. I. *s.* (a) *(assistant)* Gehilfe *m* (eines Arbeiters); (b) *P:* Kumpel *m.* II. *v.i.* sich paaren. ◆'**mating**, *s. Z:* Paarung *f;* m. season, Paarungszeit *f.*

material [mə'tiəriəl]. I. *adj.* materiell. II. *s.* (fabric) Stoff *m.* 2. (a) (basis) Material *n;* raw m., Rohstoff *m;* building m., Baumaterial *n;* (b) usu. pl. writing materials, Schreibmaterialien *npl;* teaching materials, Lehrmittel *npl.* ◆**ma'terialist**, *s.* Materialist *m.* ◆**materia'listic**, *adj.* materialistisch. ◆**ma'terialize**, *v.i.* (a) (of idea, project etc.) sich verwirklichen; (b) *F:* (of pers.) to fail to m., nicht auftauchen.

maternal [mə'tɔːnəl], *adj.* mütterlich. ◆**ma'ternity**, *s.* Mutterschaft *f;* m. dress, Umstandskleid *n.*

mathematics [mæθə'mætiks], *s.pl.* Mathematik *f.* ◆**mathe'matical**, *adj.* mathematisch. ◆**mathema'tician**, *s.* Mathematiker *m.* ◆**maths**, *s.pl. F:* Mathe *f.*

matinée ['mætinei], *s.* Matinee *f.*

matrimony ['mætriməni], *s.* Ehestand *m.*

matron ['meitrən], *s.* (in school etc.) Hausmutter *f;* (in hospital) Oberin *f.*

matter ['mætər]. I. *s.* 1. (a) (material) Materie *f;* (b) reading m., Lesestoff *m.* 2. no m. how, egal wie. 3. (affair) Sache *f,* Angelegenheit *f;* as a m. of course, selbstverständlich; as a m. of fact, in der Tat; eigentlich; for that m., was das anbelangt; what is the m.? was ist los? to make matters worse ..., zu allem Unglück ...; und obendrein ... II. *v.i.* von Bedeutung sein (to s.o., für j-n acc); it doesn't m., es spielt keine Rolle; it doesn't m. to me, es macht mir nichts aus. ◆'**matter-of-'fact**, *adj.* sachlich.

mattress ['mætris], *s.* Matratze *f.*

mature [mə'tjuər]. I. *adj.* reif. II. *v.tr. & i.* (a) reifen; (b) (of policy etc.) fällig werden. ◆**ma'turity**, *s.* Reife *f.*

mauve [məuv], *adj.* lila.

maxim ['mæksim], *s.* Maxime *f;* (principle) Grundsatz *m.*

maximize ['mæksimaiz], *v.tr.* steigern. ◆'**maximum**. I. *s.* Maximum *n.* II. *adj.* maximal; m. speed, Höchstgeschwindigkeit *f.*

may¹ [mei], *v. aux.* (a) (possibility) können; be that as it m., wie dem auch sei; (b) (permission) dürfen; m. I? darf ich? (c) (wish) mögen. ◆'**maybe**, *adv.* vielleicht.

May², *s.* Mai *m.*

mayonnaise [meiəˈneiz], s. Mayonnaise f.

mayor ['mɛər], s. Bürgermeister m. ◆'**mayoress**, s. Bürgermeisterin f.

maze [meiz], s. Irrgarten m; esp. Fig: Labyrinth n.

me [miː], pers. pron. 1. (object) (a) acc mich; for me, für mich; (b) dat mir; he gave me money, er gab mir Geld. 2. it's me, ich bin's.

meadow ['medəu], s. Wiese f.

meagre ['miːgər], adj. dürftig.

meal, s. Mahlzeit f.

mean1 [miːn], adj m. temperature, mittlere Temperatur f. ◆'**means**, s. the m., das/die Mittel; by all m., aber natürlich; by m. of sth., durch etwas acc.

mean2, adj. 1. (small) gering. 2. (unkind) gemein. 3. (miserly) geizig. ◆'**meanness,** s. 1. Gemeinheit f. 2. Geiz m.

mean3, v.tr.irr. 1. (a) (intend) (etwas) beabsichtigen; (esp. with remark) (etwas) meinen; he didn't m. (to do) it, er hat es nicht absichtlich getan; to m. well es gut meinen; do you m. me? meinen Sie mich? this book was meant for you, dieses Buch war für dich gedacht/bestimmt; (b) (signify) bedeuten; what does this m.? was bedeutet das? ◆'**meaning. I.** adj. well-m., (of pers.) wohlmeinend; (of action, words) wohlgemeint. **II.** s. (a) Bedeutung f (eines Wortes usw.); Sinn m (eines Satzes, einer Rede usw.). ◆'**meaningful,** adj. sinnvoll. ◆'**meaningless,** adj. bedeutungslos.

meander [miˈændər], v.i. sich schlängeln.

meantime ['miːntaim]/**meanwhile** ['miːn(h)wail], s. & adv. (in the) m., inzwischen.

measles ['miːzlz], s.pl. Masern pl.

measure ['meʒər]. **I.** s. 1. Maß n. made to m., nach Maß gearbeitet. 2. (action) Maßnahme f. **II.** v. 1. v.tr. (a) messen; (ein Zimmer) ausmessen; (b) to m. s.o. (for a suit), j-m (für einen Anzug) Maß nehmen. 2. v.i. (a) the table measures three metres by two, der Tisch mißt drei mal zwei Meter; (b) to m. up to expectations, den Erwartungen entsprechen. ◆'**measurement. s.** 1. (act) Messung f; to take measurements, Messungen vornehmen. 2. (length etc.) Maß n; to take s.o.'s measurements, j-m Maß nehmen.

meat [miːt], s. Fleisch n.

mechanic [miˈkænik], s. 1. Mechaniker m; motor m., Autoschlosser m. 2. pl. mechanics, Mechanik f. ◆me'**chanical,** adj. mechanisch; (by machine) maschinell. ◆'**mechanism** ['mekənizm], s. Mechanismus m. ◆'**mechanize** [-naiz], v.tr. mechanisieren.

medal ['medl], s. Sp: etc: Medaille f; Mil: Orden m. ◆'**medallist,** s. Medaillengewinner(in) m(f). ◆**medallion** [-'dæljən],

s. Medaillon n.

meddle ['medl], v.i. (a) (interfere) sich einmischen (in/with sth., in etwas acc); (b) (mess about) who has been meddling with my papers? wer hat sich an meine Papiere herangemacht?

media ['miːdiə], s. the (mass) m., die (Massen)medien.

medi(a)eval [medi'iːvəl], adj. mittelalterlich.

mediate ['miːdieit], v.i. vermitteln. ◆'**mediator,** s. Vermittler m. ◆**medi'ation,** s. Vermittlung f.

medical ['medik(ə)l], adj. ärztlich; m. certificate, ärztliches Attest; m. student, Medizinstudent(in) m(f); m. practitioner, praktischer Arzt m; the m. profession, die Ärzteschaft. **II.** s. f: ärztliche Untersuchung; -ly, adv. ärztlich. ◆'**medicine** ['meds(i)n], s. Medizin f; medicines, Medikamente npl. ◆**medicinal** [-'disinl], adj. medizinisch.

mediocre [miːdiˈəukər], adj. mittelmäßig. ◆**mediocrity** [-'ɔkriti], s. Mittelmäßigkeit f.

meditate ['mediteit], v.i. meditieren. ◆**medi'tation,** s. Meditation f.

Mediterranean [meditə'reiniən], adj. the M. (Sea), das Mittelmeer.

medium ['miːdiəm]. **I.** s. pl. -s, -ia [-iə]. 1. Mitte f. 2. (means) Mittel n. 3. (spiritualist) Medium n. **II.** adj. mittlere(r,s), Mittel-.

medley ['medli], s. Potpourri m.

meek [miːk], adj. Pej: duckmäuserisch.

meet [miːt], v.tr.irr. 1. v.tr. (a) (j-n) treffen; (by chance) (j-m) begegnen; (b) (for the first time) (j-n) kennenlernen; (c) (Gefahren, Schwierigkeiten usw. dat) begegnen; (d) (fulfil) (einer Anforderung) entsprechen; (eine Bedingung) erfüllen; (einer Verpflichtung) nachkommen. 2. v.i. (a) sich treffen; (b) to m. with sth., etwas erleben. ◆'**meeting,** s. 1. (by chance) Begegnung f; (arranged) Treffen n; esp. place, Treffpunkt m. 2. (gathering) Versammlung f; (of committee etc.) Sitzung f.

melancholy ['melənkəli]. **I.** s. Melancholie f. **II.** adj. melancholisch.

mellow ['meləu]. **I.** adj. (a) (of wine) ausgereift; (b) (of sound, colour) sanft. **II.** v.i. ausreifen; Fig: (of pers.) milder werden.

melodious [mi'ləudiəs], adj. melodiös. ◆'**melody** ['melədi], s. Melodie f.

melodrama ['melədrɑːmə], s. Melodrama n. ◆**melodra'matic,** adj. melodramatisch.

melon ['melən], s. Melone f.

melt [melt], v. 1. v.i. schmelzen. 2. v.tr. (etwas) schmelzen lassen; to m. down metals, Metalle einschmelzen. ◆'**melting,** s. m. point, Schmelzpunkt m.

member ['membər], s. Mitglied n; M. of Parliament, Parlamentsabgeordnete(r) f(m). ◆'**membership,** s. 1. Mitgliedschaft f; m. card, Mitgliedskarte f. 2.

(*number*) Mitgliederzahl *f*.

memento, *pl.* **-o(e)s** [mə'mentəu, -əuz], *s.* Andenken *n*.

memo, *pl.* **-os** ['meməu, -əuz], *s. F:* (*abbr. of* **memorandum**) Mitteilung *f*.

memoirs ['memwɑːz], *s.pl.* Memoiren *fpl*.

memorable ['mem(ə)rəbl], *adj.* denkwürdig.

memorandum, *pl.* **-da, -dums** [memə'rændəm, -də, -dəmz], *s.* 1. Memorandum *n.* 2. (*note*) Mitteilung *f*.

memorial [mə'mɔːriəl]. I. *s.* Denkmal *n*. II. *attrib. adj.* Gedächtnis-. ◆'**memorize**, *v.tr.* auswendig lernen. ◆'**memory** ['meməri], *s.* 1. (*faculty*) Gedächtnis *n.* 2. (*thing remembered*) Erinnerung *f*.

menace ['menəs, -nis], *s.* (*threat*) Drohung *f*; (*danger*) drohende Gefahr *f*. ◆'**menacing**, *adj.* drohend; (*of silence*) bedrohlich.

menagerie [mə'nædʒəri], *s.* Menagerie *f*.

mend [mend], *v.tr.* reparieren; (*Kleider*) ausbessern; (*Löcher, Strümpfe*) stopfen.

menial ['miːniəl], *adj.* niedrig.

meningitis [menin'dʒaitis], *s.* Gehirnhautentzündung *f*.

menopause ['menəupɔːz], *s.* Wechseljahre *npl*.

menstruate ['menstrueit], *v.i.* die Regel haben. ◆**menstru'ation**, *s.* Menstruation *f*, monatliche Regel *f*.

mental ['ment(ə)l], *adj.* geistig. **m. illness**, Geisteskrankheit *f*; **m. hospital/home**, Krankenhaus *n*/Heim *n* für Geisteskranke; **-ly**, *adv.* geistig. ◆**mentality** [-'tæliti], *s.* Mentalität *f*.

mention ['menʃ(ə)n]. I. *s.* Erwähnung *f*. II. *v.tr.* erwähnen; **not to m. ...**, ganz zu schweigen von ... *dat; F:* **don't m. it!** gern geschehen!

menu ['menju], *s.* Speisekarte *f*.

mercantile ['mɜːk(ə)ntail], *adj.* kaufmännisch; Handels-.

mercenary ['mɜːsin(ə)ri]. I. *s.* Söldner *m*. II. *adj.* gewinnsüchtig.

merchant ['mɜːtʃ(ə)nt]. I. *s.* Kaufmann *m*; (*dealer*) Händler *m*. 2. *attrib.* Handels-; **m. bank**, Handelsbank *f*; **m. navy**, Handelsmarine *f*. ◆'**merchandise**, *s.* Handelsgüter *npl*; Waren *fpl*.

Mercury ['mɜːkjuri]. 1. *Pr.n.* Merkur. 2. **m.**, *s. Ch:* Quecksilber *n*.

mercy ['mɜːsi], *s.* Barmherzigkeit *f; Ecc: etc:* Gnade *f*; **to be at s.o.'s m.** j-m ausgeliefert sein. ◆'**merciful**, *adj.* barmherzig; **-ly**, *adv.* zum Glück. ◆'**merciless**, *adj.* erbarmungslos.

mere ['miər], *adj.* (a) bloß; **the m. thought**, der bloße Gedanke; (*b*) (*pure*) rein; **-ly**, *adv.* bloß.

merge [mɜːdʒ], *v.tr.* (*Firmen*) fusionieren. 2. *v.i.* (a) (*of roads etc.*) zusammenlaufen; (*of rivers etc.*) zusammenfließen; (*b*) **to m. into sth.**, in etwas *dat* verschmelzen; ◆'**merger**, *s.* Fusion *f*.

meringue [mə'ræg], *s.* Baiser *n*.

merit ['merit]. I. *s.* 1. (a) *usu. pl.* (*of person*) Verdienst *m*; (*b*) (*advantage*) Vorteil *m.* 2. (*worth*) Wert *m*. II. *v.tr.* verdienen.

mermaid ['mɜːmeid], *s.* Meerjungfrau *f*.

merry ['meri], *adj.* (a) fröhlich; (*b*) (*tipsy*) angeheitert.

mesh [meʃ], *s.* (*of net etc.*) Masche *f*.

mess [mes], *s.* 1. Unordnung *f*; (*muddle*) Durcheinander *n*; **to make a m. of a job**, eine Arbeit verpfuschen. 2. (*dirt*) Dreck *m.* 3. *Mil:* Messe *f*. ◆'**mess a'bout**, *v.* 1. *v.i. F:* herumkursen; *mit* etwas *dat* herumspielen. 2. *v.tr. F:* (j-n) hinhalten. ◆'**mess 'up**, *v.tr. F:* (a) (etwas) dreckig machen; (*b*) (*Pläne usw.*) durcheinanderbringen. ◆'**messy**, *adj.* 1. (*untidy*) unordentlich. 2. (*dirty*) dreckig.

message ['mesidʒ], *s.* Botschaft *f*; **to give s.o. a m.**, j-m etwas ausrichten. ◆'**messenger** ['mesindʒər], *s.* Bote *m*.

metabolism [me'tæbəlizm], *s.* Metabolismus *m*.

metal [metl], *s.* Metall *n*. ◆**metallic** [mi'tælik], *adj.* metallisch. ◆**me'tallurgy**, *s.* Metallurgie *f*.

metaphor ['metəfər], *s.* Metapher *f*. ◆**metaphorical** [-'fɔrikl], *adj.* metaphorisch.

meteor ['miːtiər], *s.* Meteor *m*. ◆**meteoric** [-'ɔrik], *adj.* **m. rise**, kometenhafter Aufstieg.

meteorology [miːtjə'rɔlədʒi], *s.* Meteorologie *f*.

meter ['miːtər], *s.* Meßgerät *n*; **parking m.**, Parkuhr *f*; **electricity/gas m.**, Strommzähler/Gaszähler *m*.

methane ['miːθein], *s.* Methan *n*.

method ['meθəd], *s.* Methode *f*. ◆**methodical** [mi'θɔdikl], *adj.* systematisch.

methylated ['meθileitid], *adj.* **m. spirits**, *F:* **meths**, Brennspiritus *m*.

meticulous [mi'tikjuləs], *adj.* äußerst genau.

metre ['miːtər], *s.* Meter *m* & *n.* ◆**metric** ['metrik], *adj.* metrisch.

Mexico ['meksikəu]. *Pr. n.* Mexiko *n*. ◆'**Mexican**, *s.* Mexikaner(in) *m(f)*.

miaow [mi(ː)'au]. I. *s.* Miau *n*. II. *v.i.* miauen.

micro- ['maikrəu-], *comb./m.* Mikro-; **microfilm**, Mikrofilm *m*; **microprocessor**, Mikroprozessor *n*.

microbe ['maikrəub], *s.* Mikrobe *f*.

microphone ['maikrəfəun], *s.* Mikrofon *n*.

microscope ['maikrəskəup], *s.* Mikroskop *n*. ◆**microscopic** [-'skɔpik], *adj.* mikroskopisch klein.

microwave ['maikrəuweiv], *s.* **m. oven**, Mikrowellenherd *m*.

mid [mid], *attrib. adj.* **in m. air**, in der Luft; **in m. June**, Mitte Juni; **he is in his m.-fifties**, er ist Mitte fünfzig. ◆'**mid'day**, *s.* Mittag *m*. ◆**middle**

['midl]. **I.** *adj.* mittlere(r,s), Mittel-; **the m. class(es)**, der Mittelstand; **m. aged/in m. age**, im mittleren Alter; **the M. Ages**, das Mittelalter; **the M. East**, der Nahe Osten. **II.** *s.* (*a*) Mitte *f;* **in the m.**, in der Mitte von, mitten in + *dat;* (*b*) *F:* (*waist*) Taille *f.* ◆**'the 'Midlands**, *s.pl.* Mittelengland *n.* ◆**'midnight**, *s.* Mitternacht *f.* ◆**midst**, *s.* **in the m.**, mitten in + *dat.* ◆**'mid'stream**, *s.* **in m.**, in der Mitte des Flusses/Stromes. ◆**'mid'summer**, *s.* Hochsommer *m.* ◆**'mid'way**, *adv.* auf halbem Wege; **m. between**, in der Mitte zwischen + *dat.* ◆**'mid'week**, *s.* & *adv.* Mitte *f* der Woche. ◆**'Mid'west**. *Pr.n.* Mittelwesten *m* (von Amerika).

midwife, *pl.* **-wives** ['midwaif, -waivz], *s.* Hebamme *f.* ◆**'midwifery** [-'wif(ə)ri], *s.* Geburtshilfe *f.*

might[1] [mait], *s.* Macht *f.*

might[2], *v. aux.* (*past tense of* **may**) könnte(n); **you m. have asked!** Sie hätten doch fragen können! ◆**'mighty. I.** *adj.* (*powerful*) mächtig; (*enormous*) gewaltig. **II.** *adv.* höchst.

migraine ['mi:grein], *s.* Migräne *f.*

migrate [mai'greit], *v.i.* (*of pers.*) abwandern; (*of birds*) ziehen. ◆**'migrant. I.** *adj.* wandernd; **m. worker**, Wanderarbeiter *m;* (*from abroad*) Gastarbeiter *m;* **s. of birds**) Wanderer *m;* (*pers.*) Umsiedler(in) *m(f).* ◆**mi'gration**, *s.* (*of pers.*) Abwanderung *f;* (*of peoples*) Völkerwanderung *f;* (*of birds, fish*) Zug *m.*

mike [maik], *s. F:* Mikro *n.*

Milan [mi'læn]. *Pr.n.* Mailand *n.*

mild [maild], *adj.* mild; (*of illness, cigar etc.*) leicht; **-ly**, *adv.* leicht; **to put it m.**, gelinde gesagt. ◆**'mildness**, *s.* Milde *f.*

mile [mail], *s.* Meile *f; F:* **he's miles faster**, er ist viel schneller. ◆**'mileage**, *s.* (*zurückgelegte*) Meilenzahl *f;* (*of car*) Meilenstand *m;* **unlimited m.**, unbegrenzte Kilometerleistung. ◆**'milestone**, *s.* Meilenstein *m.*

militant ['militənt]. **I.** *adj.* militant. **II.** *s.* Kämpfer *m; Pol:* Aktivist *m.* ◆**'military. I.** *adj.* militärisch, Militär-. **II.** *s.* **the m.**, das Militär.

milk [milk]. **I.** *s.* Milch *f.* **II.** *v.tr.* melken. ◆**'milkman**, *s.* Milchmann *m.*

mill [mil]. **I.** *s.* Mühle *f.* **II.** *v.tr.* mahlen. 2. *v.i.* **to m.** (*about*), hin- und hertreiben.

milligramme ['miligræm], *s.* Milligramm *n.* ◆**'millimetre**, *s.* Millimeter *m.*

million ['miljən], *s.* Million *f.* ◆**'millio'naire**, *s.* Millionär(in) *m(f).* ◆**'millionth**, *adj.* millionste(r).

mime [maim], *v.tr.* & *i.* mimen.

mimic ['mimik]. **I.** *s.* Imitator *m* (von Stimmen). **II.** *v.tr.* nachäffen. ◆**'mimicry**, *s.* Nachäffung *f.*

mince [mins]. **I.** *s.* 1. *Cu:* Hackfleisch *n.* 2. **m. pie**, mit 'mincemeat' gefüllte Pastete. **II.** *v.tr.* (*a*) (Fleisch usw.)

durchdrehen; **minced meat**, Hackfleisch *n;* (*b*) *Fig:* **not to m. one's words**, kein Blatt vor den Mund nehmen. ◆**'mincemeat**, *s.* Pastetenfüllung *f* aus Rosinen, Korinthen, Äpfeln usw.; *Fig:* **to make m. of s.o.**, aus j-m Hackfleisch machen. ◆**'mincer**, *s.* Fleischwolf *m.*

mind [maind]. **I.** *s.* 1. Sinn *m;* Kopf *m;* (*intellect*) Geist *m;* **you're/you must be out of your m.!** du bist (wohl) nicht bei Trost! 2. **to bear/keep sth. in m.**, sich *dat* etwas merken; (*consider*) etwas berücksichtigen; *F:* **it went clean out of my m.**, ich habe es total vergessen. 3. (*opinion*) Meinung *f;* **to my m.**, meiner Ansicht nach; **to give s.o. a piece of one's m.**, j-m gehörig die Meinung sagen; **to make up one's m.**, sich entschließen; **to change one's m.**, sich *dat* etwas überlegen; **to have an open m.**, unvoreingenommen sein. 4. (*attention*) **to take his m. off it**, um ihn davon abzulenken. **II.** *v.* 1. *v.tr.* (*a*) (*look after*) **to m. s.o., sth.**, sich um j-n, etwas *acc* kümmern; **m. your own business**, kümmere dich um deine eigenen Angelegenheiten; (*b*) (*look out*) **m. the step!** Achtung Stufe! **m.** (**that**) **you don't lose it**, paß auf/gib acht, daß du es nicht verlierst; (*c*) (*object*) **do you m. my smoking?** stört es Sie, wenn ich rauche? **would you m. shutting the door?** würden Sie bitte die Tür schließen? **I don't m.**, mir macht es nichts aus; **never m.**, mach dir nichts draus; (*d*) **the dirt is bad enough, never m. the noise**, der Schmutz ist schlimm genug, von dem Lärm ganz zu schweigen. 2. *v.i. F:* **to m.** (**out**), aufpassen; **m. out!** Achtung! ◆**'minded**, *adj.* gesinnt.

mine[1] [main], *poss. pron.* meiner, meine, mein(e)s; *pl.* meine.

mine[2]. **I.** *s.* 1. Bergwerk *n;* (**coal**) Kohlengrube *f; Fig:* **a m. of information**, eine Fundgrube des Wissens. 2. *Mil:* Mine *f.* **II.** *v.tr.* (*a*) **to m. coal, ores etc.**, Kohle, Erze usw. abbauen; (*b*) *Mil:* verminen. ◆**'minefield**, *n. Mil:* Minenfeld *n.* ◆**'miner**, *s.* Bergarbeiter *m.* ◆**'mining**, *s.* Bergbau *m.*

mineral ['minərəl], *s.* 1. Mineral *n.* 2. **m. water**, Mineralwasser *n.*

mingle ['miŋgl], *v.i.* sich mischen.

mini ['mini]. **I.** *s. m.* (**skirt**), Minirock *m.* **II.** *adj.* & *prefix* klein, Mini-; **minibus**, Kleinbus *m.*

miniature ['minitʃər, 'minjətʃər], *adj.* Klein-.

minimal ['miniməl], *adj.* minimal. ◆**'minimize**, *v.tr.* (etwas) auf ein Minimum beschränken. ◆**'minimum. I.** *s.* Minimum *n* (**of**, an + *dat*). **II.** *attrib. adj.* Mindest-; **m. wage**, Mindestlohn *m.*

minister ['ministər], *s.* 1. *Pol:* Minister *m.* 2. *Ecc:* Pastor *m.* ◆**mini'sterial**, *adj.* ministeriell; **at m. level**, auf Ministerebene. ◆**'ministry**, *s.* Ministerium *n.*

mink [miŋk], s. Nerz m.

minor ['mainər]. **I.** adj. **1.** (a) klein(er); (negligible) geringfügig; **m. injury**, leichte Verletzung; **a m. offence**, ein leichtes Vergehen; (b) (less important) unbedeutend, Neben-; **m. matter/point**, Nebensache f. **2.** Mus: Moll; **A m.**, a-Moll. **II.** s. Minderjährige(r) f(m). ◆**mi'nority**, s. Minderheit f.

mint¹ [mint]. **I.** adj. **in m. condition**, in neuwertigem Zustand. **II.** v.tr. prägen.

mint², s. (a) Bot: Minze f; (b) (peppermint) Pfefferminzbonbon s.

minus ['mainəs], prep. (a) minus, weniger; (b) F: ohne + acc; (c) **it is m. 10 degrees**, es ist 10 Grad unter Null.

minute¹ ['minit], s. **1.** Minute f; F: **wait a/just a m.!** Moment mal! einen Augenblick! **2.** pl. **minutes**, Protokoll n (einer Sitzung).

minute² [mai'nju:t], adj. winzig.

miracle ['mirəkl], s. Wunder n. ◆**mi'raculous** [-'rækjuləs], adj. wunderbar; **to have a m. escape/recovery**, wie durch ein Wunder entkommen/genesen.

mirage ['mira:ʒ], s. Fata Morgana f.

mirror ['mirər]. **I.** s. Spiegel m. **II.** v.tr. wiederspiegeln.

misapprehension [misæpri'henʃ(ə)n], s. Mißverständnis n.

misbehave [misbi'heiv], v.i. & refl. **to m.** (oneself), sich schlecht benehmen.

miscalculate [mis'kælkjuleit], v. **1.** v.tr. (etwas) falsch berechnen. **2.** v.i. sich verrechnen.

miscarriage [mis'kæridʒ], s. **1.** m. of justice, Justizirrtum m. **2.** Med: Fehlgeburt f.

miscellaneous [misə'leiniəs], adj. (of writings etc.) vermischt; (of goods etc.) divers.

mischief ['mistʃif], s. Unfug m; **to get up to m.**, Unfug anstellen. ◆**'mischievous**, adj. **m. child**, Schlingel m; **a m. smile**, ein schelmisches Lächeln.

misconception ['miskən'sepʃən], s. falsche Auffassung f.

misdemeanour ['misdi'mi:nər], s. Vergehen n.

miser ['maizər], s. Geizhals m. ◆**'miserly**, adj. geizig.

miserable ['miz(ə)rəbl], adj. (a) (of existence etc.) elend; (b) (of pers.) trübsinnig; (c) F: Pej: (of pay, weather etc.) miserabel; **-ably**, adv. **to fail m.**, kläglich versagen. ◆**'misery**, s. (a) Elend n; (b) F: (pers.) Miesepeter m.

misfire [mis'faiər], v.i. (a) (of gun) versagen; (of engine) fehlzünden; (b) (of joke, plan) danebengehen.

misfit ['misfit], s. Außenseiter m.

misfortune [mis'fɔ:tʃ(ə)n, -tju:n], s. Unglück n; pl. Unglücksfälle mpl.

misgiving [mis'giviŋ], s. Bedenken n.

mishap [mishæp], s. Mißgeschick n.

misinform ['misin'fɔ:m], v.tr. (j-n) falsch unterrichten.

misjudge ['misdʒʌdʒ], v.tr. falsch beurteilen.

mislay [mis'lei], v.tr.irr. verlegen.

mislead [mis'li:d], v.tr.irr. (j-n) irreführen; (misinform) (j-n) falsch unterrichten. ◆**mis'leading**, adj. irreführend.

misplace [mis'pleis], v.tr. verlegen. ◆**mis'placed**, adj. unangebracht.

misprint ['misprint], s. Druckfehler m.

misrepresent ['misrepri'zent], v.tr. (Tatsachen usw.) falsch darstellen.

miss¹ [mis]. **I.** s. (blow) Fehlschlag m; (shot) Fehlschuß m; (throw) Fehlwurf m; **I'll give that film a m.**, den Film werde ich mir schenken. **II.** v. **1.** v.tr. (a) (einen Schlag, das Ziel usw.) verfehlen; (eine Verabredung, eine Gelegenheit, einen Zug usw.) verpassen; F: **to m. the boat**, den Anschluß verpassen; (b) **to m. the point**, nicht begreifen, worum es eigentlich geht; (c) (j-n, etwas) vermissen; (d) (escape) **he just missed being run over**, er wäre fast überfahren worden; (e) **to m. (out) s.o., sth.**, j-n etwas auslassen. **2.** v.i. (a) das Ziel verfehlen; (of shot) danebengehen; (b) F: **he feels he's missing out on something**, er glaubt, er versäumt etwas. ◆**'missing**, adj. **1.** fehlend; **to be m.**, fehlen. **2.** (of pers., esp. soldier) vermißt.

miss², s. Fräulein n.

missile ['misail], s. (thrown) Wurfgeschoß n; (fired) Geschoß n.

mission ['miʃ(ə)n], s. **1.** (a) (task) Aufgabe f; (b) Mil: Av: Einsatz m. **2.** Ecc: Mission f. ◆**'missionary**, s. Missionar m.

mist [mist]. **I.** s. (haze) Dunst m; (thick) Nebel m. **II.** v.i. (of glass) **to m. up/over**, beschlagen; **misted up**, beschlagen. ◆**'misty**, adj. neblig; (hazy) dunstig.

mistake [mis'teik]. **I.** s. Fehler m; (abstract) Irrtum m; **by m.**, irrtümlich. **II.** v.tr.irr. (j-n, etwas) verwechseln (for s.o., sth., mit j-m, etwas dat). ◆**mis'taken**, adj. **1. to be m.**, sich irren (about sth., in etwas dat). **2. m. opinion**, irrtümliche Meinung; (case of) **m. identity**, Personenverwechslung f; **-ly**, adv. irrtümlicherweise.

mistletoe ['misltou], s. Mistel f.

mistress ['mistris], s. **1.** (a) Herrin f; (b) Sch: Lehrerin f; (c) (lover) Geliebte f.

mistrust [mis'trʌst]. **I.** s. Mißtrauen n. **II.** v.tr. (j-m, etwas dat) mißtrauen.

misunderstand ['misʌndə'stænd], v.tr.irr. mißverstehen. ◆**'misunder'standing**, s. Mißverständnis n.

misuse. I. ['mis'ju:s], s. Mißbrauch m. **II.** ['mis'ju:z], v.tr. (a) mißbrauchen; (b) (Worte, Werkzeuge usw.) falsch anwenden.

mitten ['mit(ə)n], s. Fausthandschuh m.

mix [miks]. **I.** s. Mischung f. **II.** v. **1.** v.tr. mischen. **2.** v.i. (a) (of substance) sich mischen; (b) (of pers.) **to m. (with other people)**, mit anderen Leuten verkehren. ◆**mixed**, adj. gemischt.

◆'mixer, s. 1, H: Küchenmaschine f. 2. (of pers.) a good/bad m., ein geselliger/ungeselliger Mensch. ◆mixture ['mikstʃər], s. Mischung f. ◆'mix'up, v.tr. (a) (Papiere usw.) durcheinanderbringen; (b) (j-n, etwas) verwechseln; (c) to be mixed up in sth., in etwas dat verwickelt sein; (d) F: mixed up, (confused) verwirrt. ◆'mix-up, s. Durcheinander n; Verwechslung f.

moan [məun]. I. s. 1. (a) (groan) Stöhnen n; (b) F: (complaint) Klage f. II. v.i. (a) ächzen; (groan) stöhnen; (b) F: (complain) jammern.

moat [məut], s. Burggraben m.

mob [mɔb]. I. s. (wilde) Horde f. II. v.tr. (a) (of angry crowd) (j-n) anpöbeln; (b) he was mobbed by his fans, er wurde von seinen Fans umdrängt.

mobile ['məubail], adj. (a) (of pers.) beweglich; (b) (of thing) fahrbar; m. home, Wohnmobil n. ◆mobility [məu'biliti], s. Beweglichkeit f. ◆'mobilize, v.tr. & i. mobilisieren.

mock [mɔk]. I. attrib. adj. (a) (false) falsch; (b) (pretend) Schein-. II. v.tr. & i. to m. (at) s.o., sth., j-n, etwas verspotten. ◆'mockery, s. Spott m. 2. (travesty) Farce f.

mode [məud], s. (Art und) Weise f.

model ['mɔdl]. I. s. 1. Modell n; m. aeroplane, Modellflugzeug n. 2. (for imitation) (a) Vorbild n; (b) (ideal) Muster n; m. husband, Mustergatte m. 3. (pers.) Mannequin n; male m., Dressman m. II. v.tr. (a) (in clay etc.) (einen Kopf usw.) modellieren; (b) (Kleider) vorführen.

moderate I. adj. ['mɔd(ə)rət], (a) mäßig; (of views etc.) gemäßigt; (b) (medium) mittlere(r, s). II. v.tr. ['mɔdəreit], mäßigen; -ly, adv. mäßig. ◆mode'ration, s. Mäßigung f; everything in m., alles mit Maß.

modern ['mɔdən], adj. modern; m. languages, neuere Sprachen. ◆'modernize, v.tr. modernisieren.

modest ['mɔdist], adj. bescheiden; (of price) mäßig. ◆'modesty, s. Bescheidenheit f.

modify ['mɔdifai], v.tr. (einen Entwurf) (Pläne) ändern.

module ['mɔdju:l], s. (space m.) Raumkapsel f; lunar m., Mondfähre f.

moist [mɔist], adj. feucht. ◆'moisten ['mɔisən], v.tr. befeuchten. ◆'moisture, s. Feuchtigkeit f. ◆'moisturizer, s. Feuchtigkeitscreme f. ◆'moisturizing, adj. m. cream, Feuchtigkeitscreme f.

mole¹ [məul], s. (on skin) Leberfleck m.

mole² [məul], s. Z: Maulwurf m.

molecule ['mɔlikju:l], s. Molekül n. ◆molecular [-'lekjulər], adj. molekular.

molest [məu'lest], v.tr. belästigen.

mollycoddle ['mɔlikɔdl], v.tr. F: verhätscheln.

moment ['məumənt], s. Moment m, Augenblick m. ◆'momentary, adj. vorübergehend; -ily, adv. einen Augenblick (lang). ◆mo'mentous, adj. bedeutsam. ◆mo'mentum, s. Moment n; to gather m., esp. Fig: allmählich in Fahrt kommen.

monarch ['mɔnək], s. Monarch m. ◆'monarchy, s. Monarchie f.

monastery, ['mɔnəstri], s. Kloster n. ◆mo'nastic, adj. mönchisch.

Monday ['mʌndi], s. Montag m.

monetary ['mʌnit(ə)ri], adj. Geld-; m. policy, Währungspolitik f.

money ['mʌni], s. Geld n. ◆'money-box, s. Sparbüchse f. ◆'moneylender, s. Geldverleiher m. ◆'money-spinner, s. F: Kassenschlager m.

Mongolia [mɔŋ'gəuliə]. Pr. n. Mongolei f.

mongrel ['mʌŋgrəl], s. (dog) Bastard m; F: Promenadenmischung f.

monitor ['mɔnitər]. I. s. 1. Monitor m. II. v.tr. (Ereignisse, Entwicklungen) verfolgen.

monk [mʌŋk], s. Mönch m.

monkey ['mʌŋki], s. Affe m; m. wrench, Engländer m.

monocle ['mɔnəkl], s. Monokel n.

monogram ['mɔnəgræm], s. Monogramm n.

monologue ['mɔnələg], s. Monolog m.

monopolize [mə'nɔpəlaiz], v.tr. monopolisieren. ◆mo'nopoly, s. Monopol n.

monotone ['mɔnətəun], s. in a m., mit monotoner Stimme. ◆monotonous [mə'nɔtənəs], adj. monoton; (of landscape) eintönig; (boring) langweilig. ◆mo'notony, s. Monotonie f; Eintönigkeit f.

monsoon [mɔn'su:n], s. Monsun m.

monster ['mɔnstər], s. (a) Ungeheuer n; (b) Pej: (pers.) Scheusal n. ◆monstrosity [-'strɔsiti], s. Mißgeburt f. ◆'monstrous, adj. unerhört.

month [mʌnθ], s. Monat m; once a m., einmal im Monat; for (several) months, monatelang. ◆'monthly I. adj. & adv. monatlich; m. season (ticket), Monatskarte f. II. s. (periodical) Monatsheft n.

monument ['mɔnjumənt], s. Denkmal n. ◆monu'mental, adj. monumental.

moo [mu:]. I. s. Muh n. II. v.i. muhen.

mood [mu:d], s. (of pers.) Laune f; (esp. of group) Stimmung f; in a good/bad m., gut/schlecht gelaunt; I am not in the m. for it, mir ist nicht danach zumute. ◆'moody, adj. 1. (fickle) launenhaft. 2. (gloomy) mürrisch.

moon [mu:n], s. Mond m; F: over the m., im siebten Himmel. ◆'moonlight. I. s. Mondlicht n; in the/by m., im Mondschein. II. v.i. eine Nebenbeschäftigung haben.

moor¹ [muər], s. Heide f.

moor² [muər], v.tr. (ein Schiff) festmachen. ◆'moorings, s.pl. Anlegestelle f.

moose [muːs], s. Elch m.

moot [muːt], v.i. it's a m. point, darüber läßt sich streiten.

mop [mɔp]. I. s. 1. Mop m. 2. m. of hair, Wuschelkopf m. II. v.tr. (den Fußboden) wischen. ◆'mop 'up, v.tr. aufwischen.

mope [məup], v.i. Trübsal blasen.

moped ['məuped], s. Moped n.

moral ['mɔrəl]. I. adj. 1. sittlich. 2. (of life, tone, support etc.) moralisch. II. s. 1. Moral f (einer Geschichte). 2. pl. morals, Moral f; -ly, adv. moralisch. ◆'mo'rality, s. Sittlichkeit f. ◆'moralize, v.i. Moral predigen.

morale [mɔ'rɑːl], s. Moral f.

morass [mə'ræs], s. Morast m.

morbid ['mɔːbid], adj. morbid; (pathological) krankhaft.

more [mɔːr]. I. adj. (a) mehr; (b) (additional) noch; one m. week, noch eine Woche. II. s. is there any m.? gibt es noch etwas davon? what is m., außerdem/noch dazu. III. adv. (a) m. and m., immer mehr; m. or less, mehr oder weniger; (b) (again) noch; once m., noch einmal; I don't want to go there any m., ich will nicht wieder/nicht mehr dort hingehen; (c) (comparative) m. critically, kritischer; even m. beautiful, noch schöner. ◆more'over, adv. außerdem.

morning ['mɔːniŋ], s. Morgen m; (later part) Vormittag m; tomorrow m., morgen früh; yesterday/this m., gestern/heute morgen; in the m., am Morgen; am Vormittag.

Morocco [mə'rɔkəu]. Pr. n. Marokko n.

moron ['mɔːrɔn], s. F: Idiot m.

morose [mə'rəus], adj. (grumpy) mürrisch; griesgrämig; (sullen) verstockt.

Morse [mɔːs], s. M. (code), Morsealphabet n.

mortal ['mɔːt(ə)l], adj. (a) sterblich; (b) (causing death) a m. blow, ein tödlicher Schlag; (c) a.m. tödlich (verletzt, beleidigt). ◆mor'tality, s. Sterblichkeit f.

mortar ['mɔːtər], s. 1. (bowl, also Mil:) Mörser m. 2. (cement) Mörtel m.

mortgage ['mɔːgidʒ]. I. s. Hypothek f. II. v.tr. (ein Haus usw.) mit einer Hypothek belasten.

mortician [mɔː'tiʃən], s. N.Am: Leichenbestatter m.

mortify ['mɔːtifai], v.tr. (j-n) demütigen.

mortuary ['mɔːtjuəri], s. Leichenhalle f.

mosaic [mə(u)'zeiik], s. Mosaik n.

Moscow ['mɔskəu]. Pr. n. Moskau n.

mosque [mɔsk], s. Moschee f.

mosquito, pl. -oes [məs'kiːtəu, -əuz], s. Moskito m.

moss [mɔs], s. Moos n. ◆'mossy, adj. moosig.

most [məust]. I. adj. meist; m. people, die meisten Leute; for the m. part, zum größten Teil. II. s. & indef. pron. (a) she won m., sie hat am meisten gewonnen; m. of my friends, die meisten meiner

Freunde; m. of the work, der größte Teil der Arbeit; to make the m. of an opportunity, das Beste aus einer Gelegenheit machen; (b) twenty at (the) m., höchstens zwanzig. III. adv. 1. (comparison) (a) (with verb) am meisten; (b) (with adj. & adv.) the m. beautiful woman, die schönste Frau. 2. (intensive) höchst; (extremely) äußerst; -ly, adv. (a) (in most cases) meistens; (b) (for the most part) zum größten Teil.

motel [məu'tel], s. Motel n.

moth [mɔθ], s. 1. Nachtfalter m. 2. (clothes) m., Motte f. ◆'motheaten, adj. mottenzerfressen.

mother ['mʌðər], s. 1. Mutter f; m.-in-law, Schwiegermutter f II. v.tr. (j-n) bemuttern. ◆'motherhood, s. Mutterschaft f. ◆'motherly, adj. mütterlich.

motif [məu'tiːf], s. Motiv n.

motion ['məuʃ(ə)n]. I. s. 1. (a) (movement) Bewegung f; (b) (sign) Zeichen n. 2. Pol: etc: Antrag m. II. v.tr. & i. to m. (to) s.o. to do sth., j-m ein Zeichen geben, etwas zu tun. ◆'motionless, adj. bewegungslos.

motive ['məutiv], s. 1. Motiv n (einer Handlung). 2. (motif) Motiv n. ◆'motivate, v.tr. (eine Handlung) motivieren. ◆moti'vation, s. Motivation f.

motley ['mɔtli], adj. bunt gemischt.

motor ['məutər], s. (a) Motor m; (b) m. car, Automobil n; m. vehicle, Kraftfahrzeug n. ◆'motorboat, s. Motorboot n. ◆'motorcycle, F: 'motorbike, s. Motorrad n. ◆'motorcyclist, s. Motorradfahrer m. ◆'motorist, s. Autofahrer m. ◆'motorize, v.tr. (intensive) motorisieren. ◆'motorway, s. Autobahn f.

motto, pl. -o(e)s ['mɔtəu, -əuz], s. Motto n.

mould¹ [məuld]. I. s. Form f. II. v.tr. formen (into sth., zu etwas dat).

mould², s. (on food, wall) Schimmel m. ◆'mouldy, adj. schimm(e)lig.

moult [məult], v.i. (of birds etc.) sich mausern.

mound [maund], s. (of earth) Erdhügel m; (of stones) Steinhaufen m.

mount [maunt], v. 1. v.i. (rise) steigen; (grow) wachsen. 2. v.tr. (a) (ein Pferd usw.) besteigen; (of car) to m. the pavement, auf den Bürgersteig hinauffahren; (b) Tchn: (einen Apparat usw.) montieren; (on sth., auf etwas acc); (c) (ein Bild, ein Juwel einfassen; (d) to m. guard, Wache halten. ◆'mounted, adj. (on horse etc.) beritten. ◆'mount 'up, v.i. sich häufen.

mountain ['mauntin], s. Berg m; m. range, Gebirgskette f. ◆mountai'neer, s. Bergsteiger m. ◆mountai'neering, s. Bergsteigen n. ◆'mountainous, adj. gebirgig.

mourn [mɔːn], v. 1. v.i. trauern (for/over s.o., sth., um j-n, etwas acc). 2. v.tr. trauern. ◆'mourner, s. Trauernde(r) *f(m)*; **the mourners,** die Leidtragenden *mpl.* ◆**'mournful,** *adj.* trauervoll; *(sad)* traurig. ◆**'mourning,** *s.* Trauer *f*; *(dress)* Trauerkleidung *f.*

mouse, *pl.* **mice** [maus, mais], *s.* Maus *f.* ◆**'mousetrap,** *s.* Mausefalle *f.* ◆**'mousy,** *adj.* graubraun.

moustache [məs'taːʃ], *s.* Schnurrbart *m.*

mouth. I. [mauθ], *s.* **1.** Mund *m.* **2.** Z: Maul *n;* *(of dog etc.)* Schnauze *f.* **3.** Mündung *f* (eines Flusses, Gewehrs); Öffnung *f* (einer Flasche usw.); Eingang *m* (eines Tunnels, einer Höhle); Einfahrt *f* (eines Hafens). **II.** [mauð], *v.tr.* *(Worte)* lautlos formen. ◆**'mouthful,** *s.* (a) Mundvoll *m;* (b) *(word)* Zungenbrecher *m.* ◆**'mouth-organ,** *s.* Mundharmonika *f.* ◆**'mouthpiece,** *s.* **1.** Mundstück *n* (eines Blasinstruments); Tel: Sprechmuschel *f* (eines Telefons). **2.** *(speaker)* Sprachrohr *n.*

move [muːv]. **I.** *s.* **1.** (a) *(in game)* Zug *m;* (b) *Fig:* Schritt *m;* **what is the next m.?** was machen wir jetzt? **2.** *(movement)* **on the m.,** unterwegs; **to make a m.,** aufbrechen; **F: to get a m. on,** sich beeilen. **3.** *(moving house)* Umzug *m.* **II.** *v.* **1.** *v.tr.* (a) *(shift)* (etwas) von der Stelle bewegen; (einen Stuhl usw.) rücken; *(misplace)* (etwas) verrücken; *(remove)* (etwas) entfernen; *(to another place)* (Möbel) umstellen; **to m. house,** umziehen; (set in motion) (den Kopf, die Hand usw.) bewegen; (c) *(emotionally)* (j-n) rühren. **2.** *v.i.* (a) sich bewegen; (b) *(move house)* umziehen. ◆**move a'way,** *v.i.* wegrücken *(from,* von + *dat);* *(move house)* wegziehen. ◆**move 'forward,** *v.tr. & i.* vorrücken. ◆**'move 'in,** *v.i.* (in ein Haus) einziehen. ◆**'movement,** *s.* Bewegung *f.* ◆**'move 'out,** *v.i.* (aus einem Haus) ausziehen. ◆**'movie,** *s.* *esp N.Am:* Film *m.* ◆**'moving,** *adj.* **1.** **m. parts,** bewegliche Teile. **2.** *(of book, play etc.)* ergreifend.

mow [mau], *v.tr.irr.* mähen. ◆**'mower,** *s.* (lawn) m., Rasenmäher *m.*

Mrs ['misiz], *s.* Mrs. Smith, Frau Smith.

Mr ['mistər], *s.* Mr. Smith, Herr Smith.

Ms [məz], *s.* Ms Brown, Frau Brown.

much [mʌtʃ]. **I.** *adj.* viel; **how m. bread?** wieviel Brot? **II.** *adv.* viel; **m. better,** viel besser; **as I like him,** so gern ich ihn auch mag; **m. to my surprise,** sehr zu meiner Überraschung. **III.** *s.* (a) *(a lot)* viel; *(many things)* vieles; (b) **as/so m.,** soviel; **so m. the better,** umso besser; (c) **too m.,** zuviel. ◆**'muchness,** *s. F:* **much of a m.,** ziemlich das gleiche.

muck [mʌk]. **I.** *s.* *(dung)* Mist *m;* F: *(filth)* Dreck *m.* **II.** *v.* **1.** *v.tr. F:* **to m. up a job,** eine Arbeit verpfuschen. **2.** *v.i. F:* **to m. about,** herumspielen. ◆**'mucky,** *adj. F:* dreckig.

mud [mʌd], *s.* *(liquid)* Schlamm *m;* *(sticky)* Morast *m;* *(on street etc.)* Kot *m;* *(on clothes)* Schmutz *m;* F: Dreck *m.* ◆**'muddy,** *adj.* *(of river etc.)* schlammig; *(of liquid)* trüb; *(of floor, shoes, colour etc.)* schmutzig. ◆**'mudguard,** *s.* Schutzblech *n.*

muddle ['mʌdl]. **I.** *s.* Durcheinander *n.* **II.** *v.tr.* (Dinge) durcheinanderbringen. ◆**'muddled,** *adj.* durcheinander; *(of pers.)* verwirrt; *(of thinking, situation)* wirr. ◆**'muddle 'through,** *v.i.* sich durchwursteln.

muffle ['mʌfl], *v.tr.* dämpfen. ◆**'muffler,** *s.* **1.** *(scarf)* (dicker) Schal *m.* **2.** *N.Am:* Aut: Auspufftopf *m.*

mug¹ [mʌg], *s.* Becher *m* (mit Henkel).

mug², *s. (fool)* Trottel *m.*

mug³, *v.tr.* überfallen. ◆**'mugging,** *s.* Straßenraub *m.*

muggy ['mʌgi], *adj. F:* schwül.

mule [mjuːl], *s.* Maultier *n.*

mull [mʌl], *v.tr.* (a) **to m. sth. over,** über etwas *acc* nachdenken; (b) **mulled wine,** Glühwein *m.*

multi ['mʌlti], *prefix* viel-, mehr-; **multilingual,** mehrsprachig; **multimillionaire,** Multimillionär *m.*

multicoloured ['mʌltikʌləd], *adj.* vielfarbig.

multiple ['mʌltipl], *adj.* vielfach; *(with pl)* mehrere; **m. sclerosis,** multiple Sklerose *f.* ◆**multipli'cation,** *s.* Multiplikation *f.* ◆**'multiply,** *v.* **1.** *v.tr. & i. Mth:* multiplizieren. **2.** *v.i.* sich vermehren.

multistorey ['mʌlti'stɔːri], *adj.* **m. car park,** Parkhaus *n.*

multitude ['mʌltitjuːd], *s.* Menge *f.*

mum [mʌm], *s. F:* Mama *f.*

mumble ['mʌmbl], *v.tr. & i.* undeutlich sprechen.

mummy¹ ['mʌmi], *s.* *(in tomb)* Mumie *f.*

mummy², *s. F:* Mutti *f.*

mumps [mʌmps], *s.pl.* Mumps *m.*

mundane [mʌn'dein], *adj.* alltäglich.

municipal [mju(ː)'nisip(ə)l], *adj.* städtisch; **m. council,** Stadtrat *m;* **m. elections,** Gemeindewahlen *fpl.*

mural ['mjuərəl], *s.* Wandmalerei *f.*

murder ['məːdər]. **I.** *s.* Mord *m;* Ermordung *f* (of s.o., j-s). **II.** *v.tr.* (j-n) ermorden. ◆**'murderer,** *s.* Mörder *m.* ◆**'murderous,** *adj.* mörderisch.

murky ['məːki], *adj.* düster; *(dark)* finster.

murmur ['məːmər]. **I.** *s.* Gemurmel *n.* **II.** *v.tr. & i.* murmeln.

muscle ['mʌsl], *s.* Muskel *m.* ◆**muscular** ['mʌskjulər], *adj.* **1.** Muskel-. **2.** *(of pers., body etc.)* muskulös.

museum [mju(ː)'ziːəm], *s.* Museum *n.*

mushroom ['mʌʃrum]. **I.** *s.* (eßbarer) Pilz *m, esp.* Champignon *m.* **II.** *v.i. F:* *(of buildings etc.)* aus dem Boden schießen.

music ['mjuːzik], *s.* (a) Musik *f;* (b) *(printed)* Noten *fpl.* ◆**'musical. I.** *adj.* **1.** musikalisch; *(of sound)* melodisch; **m. instrument,** Musikinstrument *n.* **II.** *s.* Musical *n;* **-ly,** *adv.* musikalisch.

◆'music-hall, *s.* Varieté(theater) *n.*

◆'musician [mjuː'ziʃən], *s.* Musiker(in) *m(f).*

Muslim ['muzləm]. I. *s.* Mohammedaner(in) *m(f).* II. *adj.* mohammedanisch.

mussel ['mʌsl], *s.* Muschel *f.*

must [mʌst]. I. *modal aux. v.* 1. müssen. 2. *neg.* you m. not do that, das darfst du nicht tun. II. *s. F:* it's a m., man muß es einfach tun/sehen usw.

mustard ['mʌstəd], *s.* Senf *m.*

muster ['mʌstər], *v.tr.* m. (Kraft, Mut) aufbringen.

mute [mjuːt], *adj.* stumm.

mutilate ['mjuːtileit], *v.tr.* verstümmeln. ◆muti'lation, *s.* Verstümmelung *f.*

mutiny ['mjuːtini]. I. *s.* Meuterei *f.* II. *v.i.* meutern. ◆muti'neer, *s.* Meuterer *m.*

mutter ['mʌtər], *v.tr. & i.* murmeln.

mutton ['mʌt(ə)n], *s.* Hammelfleisch *n.*

mutual ['mjuːtjuəl], *adj.* (a) (*reciprocal*) gegenseitig; (b) (*shared*) gemeinsam.

muzzle ['mʌzl]. 1. *s.* 1. (*of dog etc.*) (a) Schnauze *f;* (b) (*guard*) Maulkorb *m.* 2. (*of gun*) Mündung *f.* II. *v.tr.* (a) (einem Hund) einen Maulkorb anlegen; (b) *F:* (die Presse usw.) knebeln.

my [mai], *poss. adj.* mein.

myself [mai'self], *pers. pron.* (a) selbst; (b) *refl.* mich (selbst).

mystery ['mistəri], *s.* Geheimnis *n;* (*puzzle*) Rätsel *n.* ◆**mysterious** [-'tiəriəs], *adj.* geheimnisvoll; (*puzzling*) rätselhaft.

mystic ['mistik], *s.* Mystiker *m.* ◆'**mysticism**, *s.* Mystik *f.*

mystify ['mistifai], *v.tr.* it mystified me, es war mir ein Rätsel. ◆'mystified, *adj.* perplex.

myth [miθ], *s.* Mythos *m.* ◆'mythical, *adj.* mythisch. ◆my'thology, *s.* Mythologie *f.*

N

N, n [en], *s.* (der Buchstabe) N, n *n.*

nab [næb], *v.tr. F:* schnappen.

nag [næg], *v.tr. & i.* meckern (about sth., über etwas *acc*); to n. (at) s.o., an j-m (dauernd herumnörgeln. ◆'nagging, *adj.* (*of pers.*) meckernd; (*of doubt, pain*) nagend.

nail [neil]. I. *s.* Anat: Tchn: Nagel *m;* n. file, Nagelfeile *f;* n. scissors, Nagelschere *f;* n. varnish, Nagellack *m.* II. *v.tr.* (etwas) nageln (to sth., an/auf etwas *acc*). ◆'nailbrush, *s.* Nagelbürste *f.*

naïve [naː'iːv, nai-], *adj.* naiv.

naked ['neikid], *adj.* nackt. ◆'nakedness, *s.* Nacktheit *f.*

name [neim]. I. *s.* 1. Name *m;* Christian/first/N.Am: given n., Vorname *m;* my n. is…, ich heiße…; to call s.o. names, j-n beschimpfen. 2. (*reputation*) Ruf *m.* II. *v.tr.* nennen. ◆'nameless, *adj.* namenlos. ◆'namely, *adv.* nämlich. ◆'namesake, *s.* Namensvetter *m.*

nanny ['næni], *s.* 1. Kindermädchen *n.* 2. *F:* n. goat, Ziege *f.*

nap [næp]. I. *s. F:* Nickerchen *n;* to have a n., ein Nickerchen machen. II. *v.i. F:* to catch s.o. napping, j-n überrumpeln.

nape [neip], *s.* n. of the neck, Nacken *m.*

napkin ['næpkin], *s.* (a) (table) n., Serviette *f;* (b) (baby's) n., Windel *f.*

Naples ['neiplz], *Pr.n.* Neapel *n.*

nappy ['næpi], *s. F:* Windel *f.*

narcotic [naː'kɔtik], *s.* Betäubungsmittel *n.*

nark [naːk], *v.tr. F:* to be/feel narked, verschnupft sein.

narrate [nə'reit], *v.tr.* (etwas) erzählen. ◆'narrative ['nærətiv], *s.* Erzählung *f.* ◆na'rrator, *s.* Erzähler *m.*

narrow ['nærəu]. I. *adj.* (a) (*not wide*) eng; (b) (*with a small margin*) knapp; to

have a n. escape, mit knapper Not davonkommen; (c) (*of pers., views*) engstirnig. II. *v.* 1. *v.i.* (*Sp: of lead, gap*) kleiner werden; (*of pipe, road etc.*) sich verengen. 2. *v.tr.* (eine Straße usw.) enger machen; (in Arbeitsgebiet) einengen; -ly, *adv.* (*with a small margin*) he n. escaped death, er entging mit knapper Not dem Tod. ◆'narrow-'minded, *adj.* engstirnig.

nasal ['neiz(ə)l], *adj.* nasal.

nasturtium [nəs'təːʃəm], *s.* Kapuzinerkresse *f.*

nasty ['naːsti], *adj.* 1. ekelhaft; a n. job, eine unangenehme Arbeit; a n. accident, schwerer Unfall; n. cold, üble Erkältung. 2. (*of pers.*) gemein (to s.o., zu j-m); *F:* a n. piece of work, ein Ekel.

nation ['neiʃ(ə)n], *s.* Nation *f;* (*people*) Volk *n.* ◆'national ['næʃ(ə)nəl]. I. *adj.* national, National-; n. anthem, Nationalhymne *f.* II. *s.* Staatsbürger(in) *m(f);* -ly, *adv.* national. ◆'nationalism, *s.* Nationalismus *m.* ◆'nationalist, *s.* Nationalist *m.* ◆natio'nality, *s.* Staatsangehörigkeit *f.* ◆nationali'zation, *s.* Verstaatlichung *f.* ◆'nationalize, *v.tr.* (Industrie usw.) verstaatlichen. ◆'nationwide, *adj. & adv.* überregional; (*in W. Germany*) bundesweit.

native ['neitiv]. I. *adj.* (a) (*of quality, talent etc.*) angeboren; (b) (*of place*) Geburts-; n. tongue, Muttersprache *f;* (c) (*of population etc.*) einheimisch. II. *s.* Einheimische(r) *f(m);* a n. of Munich, ein gebürtiger Münchner.

nativity [nə'tiviti], *s.* Christi Geburt *f.*

Nato ['neitəu], *s.* Nato *f.*

natter ['nætər], *v.i.* schwatzen.

natural ['nætʃər(ə)l], *adj.* natürlich; n. gas, Erdgas *n;* -ly, *adv.* natürlich.

◆**'naturalist,** s. Naturwissenschaftler m. ◆**natura'lization,** s. Einbürgerung f. ◆**'naturalize,** v.tr. einbürgern.

nature ['neitʃər], s. Natur f; **by n.,** von Natur aus; **something of that n.,** etwas in der Art.

naughty ['nɔːti], adj. (of child) ungezogen.

nausea ['nɔːsiə], s. Brechreiz m. ◆**'nauseate,** v.tr. (j-n) anekeln. ◆**'nauseating,** adj. ekelerregend.

nautical ['nɔːtik(ə)l], adj. nautisch, See-; **n. mile,** Seemeile f.

naval ['neiv(ə)l], adj. Marine-; **n. officer,** Marineoffizier m.

nave [neiv], s. Kirchenschiff n.

navel ['neiv(ə)l], s. Nabel m.

navigable ['nævigəbl], adj. schiffbar. ◆**navigate** ['nævigeit], v. 1. v.i. (a) navigieren; (b) (map-read) die Karte lesen. 2. v.tr. (a) (einen Fluß) befahren; (b) (ein Schiff, Flugzeug) navigieren. ◆**navi'gation,** s. Navigation f. ◆**'navigator,** s. Navigator m.

navvy ['nævi], s. Bauarbeiter m.

navy ['neivi], s. Marine f; **n. blue,** Marineblau n.

Nazi ['nɑːtsi]. I. s. Nazi m. II. adj. nazistisch, Nazi-. ◆**'Nazism,** s. Nazismus m.

near ['niər]. I. adv. nah(e); **n. at hand,** (ganz) in der Nähe; **to come/draw n. to s.o., sth.,** sich j-m, etwas dat nähern. II. prep. (etwas dat) nahe; in der Nähe (von etwas dat); **n. the end,** (of period) kurz vor dem Ende; (of line etc.) fast am Ende; **n. (to) the shops,** in der Nähe der Geschäfte. III. adj. nah; **the nearest hospital,** das nächste Krankenhaus; Aut: **the n. side,** die rechte Seite; Brit: die linke Seite. IV. v.tr. sich (dem Ende, Ziel usw.) nähern. ◆**-ly,** adv. fast, beinahe. ◆**'nearby.** I. ['niəbai] adj. nahegelegen. II. [niə'bai] adv. in der Nähe. ◆**near-'sighted,** adj. kurzsichtig.

neat [niːt], adj. 1. (unmixed) pur. 2. (tidy) ordentlich; (of pers.) gepflegt; **n. solution,** elegante Lösung. ◆**-ly,** adv. ordentlich. ◆**'neatness,** s. Ordentlichkeit f.

necessary ['nesis(ə)ri, -seri], adj. (a) nötig, notwendig (for sth., zu etwas dat); **if n.,** notfalls; (b) (inevitable) zwangsläufig. ◆**-arily** [also -'serili], adv. (of necessity) notwendigerweise; (inevitably) zwangsläufig. ◆**necessitate** [nə'sesiteit], v.tr. (er)fordern. ◆**ne'cessity,** s. Notwendigkeit f; **of n.,** notwendigerweise; **for me a car is a n.,** ein Auto ist für mich unentbehrlich.

neck [nek]. I. s. 1. (a) Hals m; **to run n. and n.,** Kopf an Kopf laufen; **low n.,** tiefer Ausschnitt. 2. (a) Hals m (einer Flasche); (b) (of land) Landenge f. II. v.i. P: knutschen. ◆**'necklace,** s. Halskette f. ◆**'neckline,** s. Ausschnitt m. ◆**'necktie,** s. N.Am: Schlips m.

nectarine ['nektəri(ː)n], s. Nektarine f.

née [nei], adj. n. **Meyer,** geborene Meyer.

need [niːd]. I. s. 1. (a) Notwendigkeit f; **there's no n. to go there,** es ist nicht nötig, hinzugehen; (b) Bedarf m (of sth., an etwas dat); **to have n./be in n. of sth.,** etwas benötigen. 2. (suffering, starvation etc.) Not f; **those in n.,** die Notleidenden. 3. (particular n.) Bedürfnis n. II. v. 1. v.tr. (etwas) brauchen, (formal) benötigen. 2. aux. v. n. **he go?** muß er gehen? **you needn't wait,** du brauchst nicht zu warten. ◆**'needless,** adj. unnötig; (superfluous) überflüssig; **n. to say,** selbstverständlich. ◆**'needy,** adj. notleidend.

needle ['niːdl], s. Nadel f. ◆**'needlework,** s. Handarbeit f.

negative ['negətiv]. I. adj. negativ. II. s. 1. **to answer in the n.,** eine negative Antwort geben. 2. Phot: Negativ n.

neglect [ni'glekt]. I. s. Vernachlässigung f (of s.o., sth., j-s, etwas gen); **in a state of n.** in einem Zustand der Verwahrlosung. II. v.tr. (a) (j-n, etwas) vernachlässigen; (pass over) (j-n) übersehen; (b) (eine Pflicht, eine Gelegenheit usw.) versäumen. ◆**ne'glected,** adj. verwahrlost.

negligence ['neglidʒəns], s. Nachlässigkeit f; Jur: Fahrlässigkeit f. ◆**'negligent,** adj. nachlässig; Jur: fahrlässig. ◆**'negligible,** adj. unbedeutend; (of quantity, sum) geringfügig.

negotiate [ni'gəuʃieit], v. 1. v.tr. (einen Vertrag, Bedingungen usw.) aushandeln. 2. v.i. verhandeln (for/about sth., über etwas acc). ◆**ne'gotiable,** adj. **salary n.,** Gehalt nach Vereinbarung. ◆**negoti'ation,** s. Verhandlung f. ◆**ne'gotiator,** s. Unterhändler m.

negress ['niːgres], s. Negerin f. ◆**negro,** pl. **-oes** ['niːgrəu, -əuz]. I. adj. Neger-. II. s. Neger m.

neigh [nei], v.i. wiehern.

neighbour ['neibər], s. Nachbar(in) m(f). ◆**'neighbourhood,** s. Nachbarschaft f. ◆**'neighbouring,** adj. benachbart; Nachbar-. ◆**'neighbourly,** adj. nachbarlich.

neither ['naiðər, N.Am: 'niːðər]. I. adv. & conj. **n. ... nor ...** weder ... noch ...; **she was not there and n. was her sister,** sie war nicht da und ihre Schwester auch nicht. II. adj. & pron. **in n. case,** in keinem der Fälle; **n. of them has come,** keine(r) von beiden ist gekommen.

neon ['niːon], s. Neon n; **n. light,** Neonlicht n; **n. sign,** Leuchtschrift f; (advert) Leuchtreklame f.

nephew ['nevju:, nef-], s. Neffe m.

nerve [nəːv], s. Nerv m; **to get on s.o.'s nerves,** j-m auf die Nerven gehen; **to lose one's n.,** die Nerven verlieren; **what a n.!** so eine Frechheit! ◆**'nerveracking,** adj. nervenaufreibend. ◆**'nervous,** adj. 1. **n. system,** Nervensystem n. 2. (of pers.) (a) (on edge) nervös; (b) (timid) ängstlich; **to be n.,** Angst haben. ◆'**nervousness**, s. (a) Nervosität f; (b) Ängstlichkeit f.

nest [nest]. I. s. Nest n; n. of tables, Dreisatztisch m. II. v.i. nisten.

nestle ['nesl], v.i. es sich dat bequem machen; **to n. up to s.o.**, sich an j-n kuscheln.

net¹ [net]. I. s. Netz n. II. v.tr. (Fische, Vögel usw.) mit dem Netz fangen. ◆'**netting**, s. wire n., Maschendraht m. ◆'**network**, s. Netz n; road n., Straßennetz n.

net², adj. netto, Netto-; £250 n., £250 netto.

Netherlands ['neðələndz]. Pr.n. the N., die Niederlande.

nettle ['netl], s. Nessel f.

neuralgia [njuə'rældʒə], s. Neuralgie f.

neurology [njuə'rɔlədʒi], s. Neurologie f. ◆**neu·rologist**, s. Neurologe m.

neurosis, pl. -ses [njuə'rəusis, -siːz], s. Neurose f. ◆**neurotic** [-'rɔtik], adj. neurotisch.

neuter ['njuːtər]. I. adj. sächlich. II. s. Neutrum n. III. v.tr. (einen Kater usw.) kastrieren; (eine Katze usw.) sterilisieren. ◆'**neutral**. I. adj. neutral. II. s. Aut: in n., im Leerlauf. ◆**neu·trality**, s. Neutralität f. ◆'**neutralize**, v.tr. neutralisieren.

never ['nevər], adv. nie; **n. again**, nie wieder; **he'll n. believe that**, das glaubt er dir doch nie; F: **well I n.!** na, so was! **n. mind**, mach dir nichts draus, macht doch nichts. ◆'**never-'ending**, adj. endlos. ◆'**never-'never**, s. F: **to buy sth. on the n.-n.**, etwas auf Pump kaufen. ◆**nevertheless**, adv. trotzdem.

new [njuː], adj. neu; **n. moon**, Neumond m; Com: **as n.**, neuwertig; Cu: adv. neu; **a n. painted door**, eine frisch gestrichene Tür; **n.-weds**, frischgebackenes Ehepaar n. ◆'**newborn**, adj. neugeboren. ◆'**newcomer**, s. Neuankömmling m. ◆**New England**. Pr.n. Neuengland n. ◆'**new-'laid**, adj. **n.-l. eggs**, frische Eier. ◆'**newness**, s. Neuheit f. ◆'**New 'Year**, s. das Neue Jahr; **N. Y.'s Day**, Neujahr n; **N. Y.'s Eve**, Silvester n. ◆**New 'Zealand**. Pr.n. Neuseeland n.

news [njuːz], s. 1. Neuigkeit f; **we have had no n. from him**, wir haben nichts von ihm gehört; **have you heard the n.?** haben Sie das Neueste gehört? **what (is the) n.?** was gibt's Neues? **a sad piece of n.**, eine traurige Nachricht. 2. Rad: TV: Nachrichten pl; **n. flash**, Kurzmeldung f. ◆'**newsagent**, s. Zeitungshändler m. ◆'**newspaper** ['njuːs-], s. Zeitung f.

next [nekst]. I. adj. nächste(r,s); **the n. room**, das nächste Zimmer; **n. to**, neben + dat; **the n. day she went home**, am nächsten Tag fuhr sie nach Hause; **the week after n.**, übernächste Woche; **this time n. year**, heute in einem Jahr; **the n. time I see him**, das nächste Mal,

wenn ich ihn sehe; **who's n.?** wer ist als nächster dran? II. adv. **what shall we do n.?** was wollen wir als nächstes machen? **when I n. saw him**, als ich ihn das nächste Mal sah. ◆'**next(-)door**, adv. nebenan.

nib [nib], s. Feder f.

nibble ['nibl], v.tr. & i. **to n. (at) sth.**, an etwas dat knabbern.

nice [nais], adj. F: (a) (of pers.) nett; sympathisch; **to be n. to s.o.**, zu j-m nett sein; (b) (of thing) nett; (of weather) schön; **a n. meal**, ein gutes Essen; **it's n. and warm**, es ist schön warm; (of weather) F: **that will do n.**, das paßt ausgezeichnet; **he is doing n.**, (i) (of patient) er macht gute Fortschritte; (ii) (financially) es geht ihm nicht schlecht; (in job) er macht sich. ◆**nicety** ['naisəti], s. pl. niceties feine Unterschiede mpl.

niche [niːʃ], s. Nische f.

nick [nik]. I. s. 1. (notch) Kerbe f. 2. Fig: **in the n. of time**, im letzten Augenblick. II. v.tr. P: (etwas) klauen.

nickel ['nikl], s. 1. Nickel n. 2. N.Am: Fünfcentstück n.

nickname ['nikneim]. I. s. Spitzname m. II. v.tr. **to n. s.o. X**, j-m den Spitznamen X geben.

nicotine ['nikətiːn], s. Nikotin n.

niece [niːs], s. Nichte f.

Nigeria [nai'dʒiəriə]. Pr.n. Nigeria n.

nigger ['nigər], s. Pej: Neger m.

niggle ['nigl], v.tr. (j-n) ärgern, reizen. ◆'**niggling**, adj. n. details, belanglose Einzelheiten.

night [nait], s. Nacht f; **last n.**, heute/ letzte Nacht; (up to bedtime) gestern abend; **the n. before**, am Abend vorher; (late) in der Nacht davor; **ten o'clock at n.**, zehn Uhr abends; **good n.!** gute Nacht! **at/by n.**, nachts; **in the n.**, in der Nacht; **n. watchman**, Nachtwächter m; **n. school**, Abendschule f; **n. shift**, Nachtschicht f; Th: **first n.**, Premiere. ◆'**nightcap**, s. Schlaftrunk m. ◆'**nightclub**, s. Nachtklub m. ◆'**nightdress**, s. Nachthemd n. ◆'**nightfall**, s. **at n.**, bei Einbruch der Dunkelheit. ◆'**nightie**, s. Nachthemd n. ◆'**nightingale**, s. Nachtigall f. ◆'**nightly**. I. adj. nächtlich. II. adv. jede Nacht; (evening) jeden Abend. ◆'**nightmare**, s. Alptraum m. ◆'**nightshade**, s. deadly n., Belladonna f.

nil [nil], s. null.

nine [nain], num. adj. neun. ◆'**nine'teen**, num. adj. neunzehn. ◆'**nine'teenth**, num. adj. neunzehnte(r,s). ◆'**ninety**, num. adj. neunzig. ◆'**ninth**. I. num. adj. neunte(r,s). II. s. (fraction) Neuntel n.

ninny ['nini], s. Trottel m.

nip [nip]. I. s. (pinch) Kniff m; (bite) kleiner Biß m; Fig: **there was a n. in the air**, die Luft war merklich kühl. II. v. 1.

v.tr. (j-n in den Arm usw.) kneifen. 2. *v.i. F:* **n. round to the baker's,** lauf mal schnell zum Bäcker. ◆**'nippy,** *adj. it's a bit n. today,** es ist ziemlich kalt heute.

nipple ['nipl], *s.* Brustwarze *f.*

nitrate ['naitreit], *s.* Nitrat *n.* ◆**'nitric,** *adj.* **n. acid,** Salpetersäure *f.* ◆**'nitrogen** [-rɔdʒən], *s.* Stickstoff *m.*

no [nəu]. **I.** *adj.* kein(e). **no admittance,** kein Eintritt; Betreten verboten; **no smoking,** Rauchen verboten; **it's no good/use,** es nützt nichts; in no time, im Nu; **no one—nobody. II.** *adv.* **I am no richer than he is,** ich bin nicht reicher als er; **he is no longer here,** er ist nicht mehr hier. **III.** *adv.* **to answer no,** mit einem Nein antworten.

noble ['nəubl]. **I.** *adj.* 1. (*aristocratic*) adlig. 2. (*of sentiments, bearing etc.*) edel. **II.** *s.* Adlige(r) *f(m).* ◆**'no'bility,** *s.* Adel *m.*

nobody ['nəubədi], *pron.* niemand; keine(r) *f(m);* **n. else** keiner sonst.

nod [nɔd]. **I.** *s.* Nicken *n;* **he gave me a friendly n.,** er nickte mir freundlich zu. **II.** *v.* 1. *v.i.* nicken; *F:* **to n. off,** einnicken. 2. *v.tr.* **he nodded his head,** er nickte mit dem Kopf.

noise [nɔiz], *s.* 1. (*loud*) Lärm *m;* **to make a n.,** Lärm/*F:* Krach machen. 2. Geräusch *n.* ◆**'noiseless,** *adj.* geräuschlos. ◆**'noisy,** *adj.* laut.

nomad ['nəumæd], *s.* Nomade *m.* ◆**no'madic,** *adj.* nomadisch.

nominal ['nɔmin(ə)l], *adj.* 1. nominell; **n. value,** Nennwert *m.* 2. (*of amount*) unbedeutend.

nominate ['nɔmineit], *v.tr.* (*a*) (j-n) ernennen; **as director etc.,** zum Direktor usw.); (*b*) (j-n als Kandidat) aufstellen. ◆**nomi'nation,** *s.* (*a*) **his n. for the post of/as minister,** seine Ernennung zum Minister; (*b*) Aufstellen *n* (einer Person) als Kandidat. ◆**nomi'nee,** *s.* 1. (**for president etc.,** zum Präsidenten usw.) Ernannte(r) *f(m).* 2. aufgestellter Kandidat *m.*

non [nɔn], *comb. fm.* nicht-; -los.

non-alcoholic ['nɔnælkə'hɔlik], *adj.* alkoholfrei.

nonchalant ['nɔnʃələnt], *adj.* (*a*) (*of pers.*) gleichgültig; *Pej:* sorglos; (*b*) (*of gesture* &c.) lässig.

non-commissioned ['nɔnkə'miʃ(ə)nd], *adj. Mil:* **n.-c. officer,** Unteroffizier *m.*

noncommittal ['nɔnkə'mit(ə)l], *adj.* **he was n.,** er legte sich nicht fest.

nondescript ['nɔndiskript], *adj.* nichtssagend; **a n. person,** ein unscheinbarer Mensch.

none [nʌn]. **I.** *pron.* keiner, keine, kein(e)s; **how much money have you got? — n. at all,** wieviel Geld hast du? — gar keins; **I know n. of them,** ich kenne keinen von ihnen; **have you any apples? — no, n.,** haben Sie Äpfel? — nein, keine; **n. of your impudence!** laß die Frechheiten! **II.** *adv.* (*a*) **I like him n.**

the worse for it, ich mag ihn deshalb nicht weniger; (*b*) **he came n. too soon,** er kam keine Minute zu früh.

nonentity [nɔ'nentiti], *s.* (*pers.*) Null *f.*

nonexistent ['nɔnig'zist(ə)nt], *adj.* nicht vorhanden.

non-fiction ['nɔn'fikʃən], *s.* Sachliteratur *f.*

non-iron ['nɔn'aiən], *adj.* bügelfrei.

nonplus ['nɔn'plʌs], *v.tr.* **to be n. plussed,** verblüfft/perplex sein.

nonsense ['nɔnsəns], *s.* Unsinn *m; F:* Quatsch *m;* **no n.!** nur keinen Blödsinn! ◆**'non'sensical,** *adj.* unsinnig; *F:* blödsinnig.

non-skid ['nɔn'skid], *adj.* rutschfest.

non-smoker ['nɔn'sməukər], *s.* Nichtraucher *m.*

nonstop ['nɔn'stɔp]. **I.** *adj.* Nonstop-; **n. train,** durchgehender Zug. **II.** *adv.* **to talk n.,** ununterbrochen reden.

non-union ['nɔn'juːniən], *adj.* (*of workers*) nicht gewerkschaftlich organisiert.

non-violent ['nɔn'vaiələnt], *adj.* gewaltlos.

noodles ['nuːdlz], *s.* Nudeln *pl.*

nook [nuk], *s.* Ecke *f; Fig:* Schlupfwinkel *m.*

noon [nuːn], *s.* Mittag *m;* **at 12 o'clock n.,** um zwölf Uhr mittags.

noose [nuːs], *s.* Schlinge *f.*

nor [nɔːr], *conj.* **he was not hungry, n. was I,** er hatte keinen Hunger, und ich auch nicht.

norm [nɔːm], *s.* Norm *f;* **above the n.,** über dem Durchschnitt. ◆**'normal. I.** *adj.* normal. **II.** *s.* Normalzustand *m;* **to get back to n.,** sich normalisieren; -ly, *adv.* normalerweise.

north [nɔːθ]. **I.** *s.* Norden *m;* **in the n.,** im Norden; **to the n. (of),** nördlich (+ *gen*). **II.** *adj.* nördlich; **n. of London,** nördlich von London; **to travel n.,** nach Norden fahren; **the window faces n.,** das Fenster geht nach Norden. **III.** *adj.* Nord-; **the N. Sea,** die Nordsee; **the N. Pole,** der Nordpol. ◆**'north-'east. I.** *s.* Nordosten *m.* **II.** *adj.* Nordost-. **III.** *adv.* nordöstlich. ◆**'northerly** ['nɔːðəli], *adj.* nördlich. ◆**'northern** ['nɔːð(ə)n], *adj.* nördlich; **N. Ireland,** Nordirland *n;* **n. lights,** Nordlicht *n.* ◆**'northwards,** *adv.* nach Norden. ◆**'north-'west. I.** *s.* Nordwesten *m.* **II.** *adj.* Nordwest-. **III.** *adv.* nordwestlich. ◆**'north-'western,** *adj.* nordwestlich.

Norway ['nɔːwei], *Pr.n.* Norwegen *n.*

Nor'wegian [nɔː'wiːdʒən]. **I.** *adj.* norwegisch. **II.** *s.* 1. Norweger(in) *m(f).* 2. (*language*) Norwegisch *n.*

nose [nəuz]. **I.** *s.* 1. Nase *f; Fig:* **to have a (keen) n. for sth.,** eine feine Nase/*F:* einen guten Riecher für etwas haben. **II.** *v.* 1. *v.tr. F:* **to n. out** (a secret etc.), (ein Geheimnis usw.) ausschnüffeln. 2. *v.i.* **to n. about/around,** herumschnüffeln. ◆**'nosebleed,** *s.* Nasenbluten *n.*

◆'nosedive, s. Sturzflug m. ◆'nosy, adj. F: neugierig; a n. parker, ein Schnüffler.

nostalgia [nɔs'tældʒiə], s. Nostalgie f; Sehnsucht f (for, nach + dat). ◆nos'talgic, adj. nostalgisch.

nostril ['nɔstril], s. Nasenloch n.

not [nɔt], adv. nicht. 1. she is n./F: isn't here, sie ist nicht da; n. at all, gar nicht; thank you very much — n. at all, vielen Dank — nichts zu danken; n. including the wine, Wein nicht inbegriffen; F: n. to worry! keine Sorge! das macht nichts! n. that I am afraid of him, nicht etwa, daß ich Angst vor ihm habe. 2. n. any/n. a(n), kein(e); n. a hope, keine Chance.

notable ['nəutəbl], adj. (of fact etc.) bemerkenswert; (of pers.) bedeutend; ◆'ably, adv. (a) bemerkenswert; (b) many politicians, n. the Prime Minister, viele Politiker, insbesondere der Premierminister.

notch [nɔtʃ], s. Kerbe f.

note [nəut]. I. s. 1. Mus: Note f; (sound) Ton m. 2. usu. pl. notes, Notizen fpl; to make a n. of sth., sich dat etwas notieren; to leave a n. for s.o., j-m einen Zettel hinlegen. 3. (commentary) Anmerkung f. 4. credit n., Gutschein m; bank n., Banknote f; ten mark n., Zehnmarkschein m. 5. to take n. of sth., von etwas dat Notiz nehmen. II. v.tr. (a) (pay attention to) zur Kenntnis nehmen; (b) (write down) aufschreiben. ◆'notebook, s. Notizbuch n. ◆'notecase, s. Brieftasche f. ◆'noted, adj. bekannt. ◆'notepaper, s. Briefpapier n. ◆'noteworthy, adj. bemerkenswert.

nothing ['nʌθiŋ]. I. s. nichts. 1. to say n. of the others, von den anderen ganz zu schweigen; she is n. if not discreet, diskret ist sie auf jeden Fall; n. new, nichts Neues; n. much, nicht viel; n. but, nichts als; he does n. but complain, er beschwert sich dauernd; for n., umsonst; he is n. to me, er bedeutet mir nichts. II. adv. n. near/n. like as good, längst nicht so gut.

notice ['nəutis]. I. s. 1. (public) Anschlag m; official n., amtliche Bekanntmachung f; (b) (in newspaper) Anzeige f. n. of birth/death, Geburtsanzeige/Todesanzeige f. 2. (warning) Kündigung f; to give an employee a month's n., einen Angestellten mit einmonatiger Frist kündigen; (of employee) to give in one's n., kündigen; without n., ohne Warnung; (of dismissal) fristlos; at short n., kurzfristig; until further n., bis auf weiteres. 3. (attention) to take n. of s.o., sth., auf j-n, etwas acc achten. II. v.tr. (j-n, etwas) bemerken; to n. that ..., merken, daß ... ◆'noticeable, adj. bemerkbar; it's not n., es fällt nicht auf. ◆'notice-board, s. Anschlagtafel f; Sch: etc: schwarzes Brett n.

notify ['nəutifai], v.tr. (j-n) benachrichtigen (of sth., von etwas dat).

◆notifi'cation, s. Benachrichtigung f (der Polizei usw.).

notion ['nəuʃ(ə)n], s. Idee f; he has no n. of time, er hat keinen Zeitbegriff.

notorious [nəu'tɔːriəs], adj. berüchtigt. ◆notoriety [-tə'raiəti], s. schlechter Ruf m.

nought [nɔːt], s. Mth: Null f.

noun [naun], s. Substantiv n.

nourish ['nʌriʃ], v.tr. (a) (j-n) ernähren, (eine Pflanze usw.) nähren; (b) Fig: (Hoffnungen usw.) hegen. ◆'nourishing, adj. nahrhaft. ◆'nourishment, s. Nahrung f.

novel[1] ['nɔv(ə)l], s. Roman m. ◆'novelist, s. Romanschriftsteller m.

novel[2], adj. neuartig; (original) originell. ◆'novelty, s. Neuheit f.

November [nəu'vembər], s. November m.

novice ['nɔvis], s. 1. Neuling m. 2. Ecc: Novize m; Novizin f.

now [nau]. I. adv. jetzt; in three days from n., heute in drei Tagen; it is going to begin n., es wird (jetzt) gleich beginnen; I saw him just n., ich habe ihn eben gesehen; n. here, n. there, einmal hier, einmal dort; n. and then, hin und wieder; come n.! nun hör mal; n. then! what's all this about? nanu, was ist denn hier los? II. conj. n. that I am older, jetzt, wo ich älter bin. ◆'nowadays, adv. heutzutage.

nowhere ['nəuweər], adv. nirgends; n. near as pretty as ..., nicht annähernd so hübsch wie ...

nozzle ['nɔzl], s. Düse f.

nucleus ['njuːkliəs], s. Kern m. ◆'nuclear, adj. nuklear, Kern-; n. power station, Kernkraftwerk n.

nude [njuːd]. I. adj. nackt; n. photograph, Aktaufnahme f. II. s. (a) in the n., nackt; (b) (pers.) Nackte(r) f(m); Art: Akt m. ◆'nudist, s. Nudist m. ◆'nudity, s. Nacktheit f.

nudge [nʌdʒ]. I. v.tr. (j-n) mit dem Ellbogen anstoßen. II. s. Stoß m.

nuisance ['njuːs(ə)ns], s. (a) (pers.) lästiger Mensch; (tormentor) Quälgeist m; to make a n. of oneself, lästig/aufdringlich werden; (b) (thing) Plage f; public n., öffentliches Ärgernis n; what a n.! wie ärgerlich!

null [nʌl], adj. Jur: n. and void, nichtig. ◆'nullify, v.tr. für nichtig erklären.

numb [nʌm]. I. adj. (of limb etc.) gefühllos; esp. pred. taub. II. v.tr. betäuben.

number ['nʌmbər]. I. s. 1. Mth: (a) Zahl f; (b) (numeral) Ziffer f. 2. (quantity) Anzahl f; a n. of people voted for him, mehrere Leute stimmten für ihn; in large/small numbers, in großer/geringer Anzahl. 3. (of room, house etc.) Nummer f; telephone n., Telefonnummer f; Aut: (registration) n., Kennzeichen n; n. plate, Nummernschild n. 4. (of periodical) Ausgabe f. II. v.tr. (a) numerieren

(b) I n. him among my friends, ich zähle ihn zu meinen Freunden; (c) his days are numbered, seine Tage sind gezählt. ◆'numberless, adj. zahllos.

numeral ['nju:mərəl], s. Ziffer f. ◆nu'merical, adj. numerisch; in n. order, zahlenmäßig geordnet. ◆'numerous, adj. zahlreich.

nun [nʌn], s. Nonne f.

nuptial ['nʌpʃ(ə)l], adj. Hochzeits-.

nurse [nəːs]. I. s. (a) Krankenschwester f; male n., Krankenpfleger m; (b) (children's) n., Kindermädchen n. II. v.tr. (a) pflegen; (b) (Zweifel, Verdacht usw.) hegen. ◆'nursemaid, s. Kindermädchen n. ◆'nursery, s. 1. Kinderzimmer n; n. rhyme, Kinderreim m; day n., Kindertagesstätte f; n. school, Vorschule f. 2. (for flowers) Gärtnerei f; (for trees) Baumschu-

le f. ◆'nursing, s. Krankenpflege f; n. home, Privatklinik f.

nurture ['nəːtʃər], v.tr. (j-n, ein Tier) nähren; (Gefühle) hegen.

nut [nʌt], s. 1. Nuß f. 2. F: she's nuts, sie spinnt. 3. Tchn: Mutter f. ◆'nutcase, s. F: he's a n., er spinnt. ◆'nutcracker, s. Nußknacker m. ◆'nutmeg, s. Muskat m. ◆'nutshell, s. Nußschale f; Fig: in a n., kurz gesagt.

nutrient ['nju:triənt], s. Nährstoff m. ◆nu'trition, s. Ernährung f. ◆nu'tritious, adj. nahrhaft. ◆'nutritive, adj. n. value, Nährwert m.

nylon ['nailɔn], s. Nylon n.

nymph [nimf], s. Nymphe f. ◆nymphomaniac [nimfəu'meinjæk], s. Nymphomanin f.

O

O, o [əu], s. 1. (der Buchstabe) O, o n. 2. Tel: Null f.

oaf [əuf], s. Lümmel m.

oak [əuk], s. o (tree), Eiche f.

oar [ɔːr], s. Ruder n. ◆'oarsman, s. Ruderer m.

oasis, pl. oases [əu'eisis, əu'eisiːz], s. Oase f.

oat [əut], s. usu. pl. Hafer m; Fig: to sow one's wild oats, sich dat die Hörner abstoßen. ◆'oatmeal, s. Hafermehl n.

oath [əuθ], pl. oaθz], s. 1. Eid m; to take an o., einen Eid leisten. 2. (curse) Fluch m.

obdurate ['ɔbdjurət], adj. verstockt; (stubborn) starrköpfig.

obedience [ə'biːdjəns], s. Gehorsam m. ◆o'bedient, adj. gehorsam.

obese [əu'biːs], adj. fettleibig.

obey [ə'bei], v.tr. & i. (j-m, einem Befehl) gehorchen.

obituary [ə'bitjuəri], s. Todesanzeige f.

object. I. ['ɔbdʒikt] s. 1. (a) (also Gram:) Objekt n; (b) (purpose) Zweck m, the o. of the exercise, der Sinn der Sache; (c) expense is no o., Geld spielt keine Rolle. II. [əb'dʒekt] v.i. to o. to s.o., sth., gegen j-n, etwas acc sein; do you o. to my smoking? haben Sie etwas dagegen, wenn ich rauche? ◆ob'jection, s. Einwand m; I've no o. to that, ich habe nichts dagegen. ◆ob'jectionable, adj. widerwärtig. ◆ob'jective. I. adj. objektiv. II. s. (aim) Ziel n. ◆objec'tivity, s. Objektivität f. ◆ob'jector, s. Gegner(in) m(f) (to, gen).

oblige [ə'blaidʒ], v.tr. to o. s.o. to do sth., j-n zwingen/nötigen, etwas zu tun; to be obliged to do sth., etwas tun müssen; much obliged! danke bestens! ◆obli'gation [ɔbli'geiʃ(ə)n], s. Verpflichtung f; without o., unverbindlich. ◆obligatory [ə'bligətri], adj. obligato-

risch. ◆o'bliging, adj. entgegenkommend.

oblique [ə'bliːk], adj. schräg.

obliterate [ə'blitəreit], v.tr. (efface) (etwas) auslöschen; (Geschriebenes) ausstreichen. ◆oblite'ration, s. Auslöschung f.

oblivion [ə'bliviən], s. Vergessenheit f.

oblong ['ɔblɔŋ]. I. adj. länglich; Mth: rechteckig. II. s. Rechteck n.

oboe ['əubəu], s. Oboe f.

obnoxious [əb'nɔkʃəs], adj widerwärtig.

obscene [əb'siːn, -'ɔb-], adj. obszön. ◆obscenity [-'seniti], s. Obszönität f.

obscure [əb'skjuər]. I. adj. 1. (of argument etc.) unklar. 2. (of writer etc.) unbekannt; (forgotten) vergessen; Pej: unbedeutend. II. v.tr. (etwas) verdunkeln; (hide) verbergen. ◆ob'scurity, s. 1. (darkness) Dunkelheit f. 2. Unklarheit f. 3. Unbekanntheit f; to sink into o., in Vergessenheit geraten.

obsequious [əb'siːkwiəs], adj. (of pers.) unterwürfig; (of manner) kriecherisch.

observe [əb'zəːv], v.tr. (a) (einen Brauch) pflegen; (b) (watch) (j-n, etwas) beobachten; (notice) (etwas) bemerken. ◆ob'servant, adj. aufmerksam; he's very o., er merkt alles. ◆obser'vation, s. 1. Beobachtung f. 2. (remark) Bemerkung f. ◆ob'servatory, s. Sternwarte f. ◆ob'server, s. Beobachter m.

obsess [əb'ses], v.tr. to be obsessed with an idea/a fear, von einer Idee/Angst besessen sein. ◆ob'session, s. (state) Besessenheit f; (idea) Zwangsvorstellung f.

obsolete ['ɔbsəlit], adj. veraltet. ◆obsolescent [-'lesənt], adj. veraltend.

obstacle ['ɔbstəkl], s. Hindernis n; Sp: o. race, Hindernisrennen n.

obstetrics [əb'stetriks], s. pl. Geburtshilfe f.

obstinate ['ɔbstinət], *adj.* starrköpfig; störrisch. ◆**'obstinacy,** *s.* Starrsinn *m.*

obstreperous [əb'strep(ə)rəs], *adj.* aufsässig.

obstruct [əb'strʌkt], *v.tr.* (a) (eine Straße usw.) versperren; (eine Einfahrt, ein Rohr usw.) blockieren; **to o. s.o.'s view,** j-m die Sicht versperren; (b) hemmen; **to o. the police,** die Polizei behindern. ◆**ob'struction,** *s.* 1. (a) Versperrung *f;* Blockierung *f;* (b) Hemmung *f;* Behinderung *f;* (c) *Pol:* (policy of) o., Obstruktion *f.* 2. (obstacle) Hindernis *n* ◆**ob'structive,** *adj.* hinderlich.

obtain [əb'tein], *v.tr.* erhalten; (get for oneself) sich *dat* (etwas) verschaffen. ◆**ob'tainable,** *adj.* erhältlich.

obtrusive [əb'tru:siv], *adj.* aufdringlich.

obtuse [əb'tju:s], *adj.* 1. *Mth:* stumpf. 2. (of pers.) begriffsstutzig.

obviate ['ɔbvieit], *v.tr.* vermeiden. ◆**'obvious,** *adj.* offensichtlich; o. fact, selbstverständliche Tatsache; **-ly,** *adv.* offensichtlich.

occasion [ə'keiʒ(ə)n], *s.* (a) Gelegenheit *f;* **on this o.,** bei dieser Gelegenheit; (b) Anlaß *m;* **to rise to the o.,** sich der Lage gewachsen zeigen. ◆**o'ccasional,** *adj.* gelegentlich; o. showers, vereinzelte Regenschauer *mpl;* **-ly,** *adv.* hin und wieder.

occupant ['ɔkjupənt], *s.* Bewohner *m.* ◆**occu'pation,** *s.* 1. *Mil:* Besetzung *f* (eines Landes). 2. (task) Beschäftigung *f;* (profession) Beruf *m.* ◆**occu'pational,** *adj.* Berufs-. ◆**'occupied,** *adj.* (a) (busy) beschäftigt; (b) (taken) besetzt. ◆**'occupier,** *s.* Bewohner *m.* ◆**'occupy,** *v.tr.* (a) (live in) (ein Haus usw.) bewohnen; *Mil:* besetzen; (b) (Zeit) in Anspruch nehmen; (Platz) einnehmen; (c) (keep busy) (j-n, sich) beschäftigen.

occur [ə'kə:r], *v.i.* (a) geschehen, sich ereignen; (b) **the word only occurs twice,** das Wort kommt nur zweimal vor; (c) **it occurs to me that ...,** es fällt mir ein, daß ... ◆**o'ccurrence,** *s.* (event) Ereignis *n.*

ocean ['əuʃ(ə)n], *s.* Ozean *m.* ◆**oceanic** [əuʃi'ænik], *adj.* ozeanisch. ◆**ocean'ography,** *s.* Meereskunde *f.*

ochre ['əukər], *s.* Ocker *m.*

o'clock [ə'klɔk], *adv.* one/six o'clock, ein/sechs Uhr.

octagon ['ɔktəgən], *s.* Achteck *n.* ◆**octagonal** [-'tægən(ə)l], *adj.* achteckig.

octave ['ɔktiv], *s. Mus:* Oktave *f.*

October [ɔk'təubər], *s.* Oktober *m.*

octogenarian [ɔktəudʒi'neəriən], *s.* Achtzigjährige(r) *f(m).*

octopus, *pl.* -ses ['ɔktəpəs, -siz], *s.* Krake *m.*

oculist ['ɔkjulist], *s.* Augenarzt *m.*

odd [ɔd], *adj.* 1. (a) (of number) ungerade; (b) **fifty** o., über fünfzig; **to be the o. man/one out,** überzählig/(exception) die

Ausnahme sein. 2. (a) (single) einzeln; (b) **at o. times,** hin und wieder; bei Gelegenheit; o. **job man,** Gelegenheitsarbeiter *m.* 3. (unusual) seltsam; *F:* komisch; **-ly,** *adv.* o. (enough), seltsamerweise. ◆**'oddity,** *s.* 1. (characteristic) Eigenart *f.* 2. (thing) etwas Seltsames/Komisches. ◆**'oddness,** *s.* Seltsamkeit *f.* ◆**odds,** *s.pl.* 1. (a) (chances) Aussichten *fpl;* **the o. are in his favour,** er hat gute Chancen; (b) 2. o. **and ends,** Kram *m.*

ode [əud], *s.* Ode *f.*

odious ['əudiəs], *adj.* (of pers.) verhaßt; (of task etc.) widerlich.

odour ['əudər], *s.* (a) (smell) Geruch *m;* (b) (scent) Duft *m.* ◆**'odourless,** *adj.* geruchlos.

of [accented ɔv, unaccented əv], *prep.* 1. gen or von + dat; (a) (belonging to) **the head of the horse,** der Kopf des Pferdes; **the Queen of England,** die Königin von England; (b) (by) **the works of Shakespeare,** die Werke Shakespeares/von Shakespeare; (c) (quantity) **many of these mistakes,** viele dieser Fehler; (d) (from) **south of the river,** südlich des Flusses; (e) (characteristic) **a matter of principle,** eine Prinzipienfrage; **it's very kind of you,** das ist sehr nett von Ihnen; (f) **a glass of wine,** ein Glas Wein; **the first of June,** der erste Juni. 2. **to die of sth.,** an etwas *dat* sterben; **to think of sth.,** an etwas *acc* denken. 3. (made of) aus + *dat;* **a fence of wood,** ein Zaun aus Holz.

off [ɔf]. I. *adv.* 1. (away) (a) (position) weg; (specific distance) entfernt; **a long way o.,** weit weg; (b) (movement) fort; **I must be o.,** ich muß gehen; (c) (down) **to fall o.,** herunterfallen. 2. (a) (switched) o., *El:* ausgeschaltet; (of gas, water) abgestellt; (b) *Cl:* ausgezogen; (c) (in restaurant) **chicken is o.,** Huhn gibt es nicht mehr; (d) *F:* (of deal etc.) **it's all o.,** die ganze Sache ist abgeblasen; (e) **the meat is o./has gone o.,** das Fleisch ist schlecht (geworden). 3. **well o.,** gut dran; (rich) reich. **II.** *prep.* 1. (a) von + *dat;* **to fall o. a horse,** vom Pferd fallen; **to take sth. o. the table,** etwas vom Tisch nehmen; (b) **a street o. Oxford Street,** eine Seitenstraße von Oxford Street; o. **Dover,** vor der Küste bei Dover. 2. (a) *F:* **to be o. one's food,** keinen Appetit haben; (b) **to have a day o.,** einen Tag frei haben. **III.** *adj.* (a) *Aut:* o. **side,** rechts; (when driving on the right) links; (b) **an o. day,** ein schlechter Tag; on the o. **chance,** aufs Geratewohl. ◆**'off'hand.** I. *adv.* I don't know o., das kann ich nicht so ohne weiteres sagen. **II.** *adj.* (of pers.) brüsk; (of answer) kurz angebunden; (b) (casual) lässig. ◆**'off-licence,** *s.* (shop) Wein- und Spirituosengeschäft *n.* ◆**'off-'peak,** *adj.* außerhalb der Stoßzeit. ◆**'off'set,** *v.tr.irr.* (etwas usw.) wettmachen. ◆**offshore** [ɔf'ʃɔ:r], *adv.* vor der Küste. ◆**'off'side.** *Fb:* abseits.

& adv. abseits. ◆'offspring, s. 1. coll.
Nachkommen mpl. 2. F: (child) Sprößling m.
offal ['ɔf(ə)l], s. Innereien fpl (vom Rind
usw.).
offence [ə'fens], s. 1. to take o. at sth.,
an etwas dat Anstoß m. nehmen; no o.
(meant)! nichts für ungut! 2. (crime) Vergehen n. 3. (attack) Angriff m.
◆o'ffend, v.tr. beleidigen.
◆o'ffender, s. Täter(in) m(f); Jur:
Straffällige(r) f(m). ◆o'ffending, adj.
(a) (of thing) anstößig; (b) (of words etc.)
beleidigend. ◆o'ffensive. I. adj. anstößig (to s.o., für j-n.); (b) (of smell etc.)
ekelhaft. II. s. Mil: Offensive f.
offer ['ɔfər]. I. s. Angebot n; o. of marriage, Heiratsantrag m. II. v.tr. to offer
s.o. sth., j-m etwas anbieten; to o. resistance, Widerstand leisten. ◆'offering,
s. Ecc: Spende f; (to god) Opfer n.
◆'offertory, s. Kollekte f.
office ['ɔfis], s. 1. (a) Büro n; head o.,
Hauptgeschäftsstelle f; o. hours, Büro-
stunden fpl; (b) Brit: Pol: Foreign/Home
O., Außen/Innenministerium n. 2. (post)
Amt n. ◆officer ['ɔfisər], s. 1. (official)
Beamte(r) f(m); (police) o., Polizist m;
medical o., Amtsarzt m. 2. Mil: Offizier
m. ◆official [ə'fiʃ(ə)l]. I. adj. (a) o.
business, dienstlich; (b) (of news etc.) offiziell. II. s. Funktionär m; (state employee) Beamter, Beamtin f.
◆offi'cialese, s. F: Amtssprache f.
◆o'fficiate, v.i. (a) fungieren (as host
etc., als Gastgeber usw.); (b) Ecc: den
Gottesdienst leiten. ◆o'fficious, adj.
diensteifrig. ◆o'fficiousness, s. (über-
triebener) Diensteifer m.
often ['ɔftən, 'ɔfn], adv. oft; every so o.,
von Zeit zu Zeit.
oh [əu], int. oh! oh, I see! ach so!
oil [ɔil], s. 1. (a) Öl n; (mineral) o., Erdöl n;
o. well, Erdölquelle f; o. rig, Bohrinsel
f; o. slick, Ölteppich m; o. level, Ölstand m; o. can, Ölkanne f; o. colours/
paints, oils, Ölfarben fpl; o. painting,
Ölgemälde n; Fig: to pour o. on
troubled waters, Öl auf die Wogen gießen. II. v.tr. (eine Maschine usw.) ölen;
P: (of pers.) well oiled, besoffen.
◆'oilfield, s. Ölfeld n. ◆'oilskins, s.
pl. Ölzeug n. ◆'oily, adj. (a) ölig;
(b) Fig: (of manner) aalglatt.
ointment ['ɔintmənt], s. Salbe f.
OK (also okay) [əu'kei]. F: I. int. in
Ordnung! okay! II. adj. that's OK, das
geht in Ordnung.
old [əuld], adj. alt; to grow o., alt werden; altern; an o. maid, eine alte Jungfer; o. age, das Alter; o. age pensioner,
Rentner m; F: the/my o. man/woman,
mein Alter/meine Alte; F: an o. flame,
eine alte Flamme. ◆'old-'fashioned,
adj. 1. altmodisch; (clothes) unmodern. 2.
(of ideas) überholt; (of pers.) rückständig.
◆'old-'hat, adj. F: unmodern.

olive ['ɔliv]. I. s. 1. Olive f; o. oil,
Olivenöl n; o. (tree), Ölbaum m; o.
branch, Olzweig m; Fig: to hold out
the o. branch, ein Friedensangebot
machen. 2. Cu: beef o., Rindsroulade f.
II. adj. o.(-green), olivgrün.
Olympic [ə'limpik]. I. adj. olympisch;
the O. Games, die Olympischen Spiele.
II. s. the Olympics, die Olympiade f.
omelet(te) ['ɔmlit], s. Cu: Omelett n.
omen ['əumen], s. Omen n. ◆ominous
['ɔminəs], adj. ominös; (evil) unheilvoll.
omit [ə'mit, əu'mit], v.tr. o (etwas) auslassen; (j-n) übergehen; (b) to o. to do
sth., es unterlassen, etwas zu tun.
◆o'mission, s. (of thing) Weglassung f;
(of action) Unterlassung f.
omnipotence [ɔm'nipətəns], s. Allmacht
f. ◆om'nipotent, adj. allmächtig.
omniscient [ɔm'nisiənt], adj. allwissend.
omnivorous [ɔm'nivərəs], adj. allesfres-
send.
on [ɔn]. I. prep. 1. (a) auf + dat/
(motion) + acc; it is on the table, es ist
auf dem Tisch; it fell on the roof, es fiel
auf das Dach; F: have you enough
(money) on you? haben Sie genug Geld
bei sich? on the shore, am Strand; to
hang on the wall, an der Wand hängen;
(b) (direction) on the left/right, links/
rechts, on the way, auf dem Weg, unterwegs; (c) (means) on the train/bus, mit
dem Zug/Bus; on foot, zu Fuß; on the
radio, im Radio; on television, im Fernsehen. 2. (time) on Monday, am Montag;
on Mondays, montags; on time, pünktlich; on (his) arrival in Helsinki, bei seiner Ankunft in Helsinki; on waking up,
beim Aufwachen. 3. F: the drinks are on
me, die Drinks gehen auf meine Rechnung. 4. (concerning) über + acc; a talk
on Luther, ein Vortrag über Luther. 5.
(condition) unter + dat; on this condition,
unter dieser Bedingung; on no account,
auf keinen Fall. II. adv. 1. (a) (of event)
to be on, stattfinden; what's on at the
cinema? was wird im Kino gespielt?
have you anything on tonight? haben Sie
heute abend etwas vor? (b) (of switch, apparatus) eingeschaltet; don't leave the
light on, laß das Licht nicht brennen;
Tchn: 'on-off', 'Ein-Aus'. 2. to have a
coat on, einen Mantel anhaben. 3. (continuation) (a) to work on, weiterarbeiten;
and so on, und so weiter; on and on,
immer weiter; (b) later on, später; from
then on, von dem Zeitpunkt an.
once [wʌns], adv. 1. einmal; not o., kein
einziges Mal; o. more, noch einmal; for
o., ausnahmsweise; o. in a while, hin
und wieder; o. and for all, ein für allemal; o. (upon a time) there was ..., es
war einmal .... 2. at o., (i) (immediately)
sofort; (ii) (at the same time) zugleich;
auf einmal.
oncoming ['ɔnkʌmiŋ], adj. o. traffic,
Gegenverkehr m.
one [wʌn]. I. adj. ein, eine; o. day, eines

Tages. **II.** *s.* **1.** (*number*) eins. **2.** (*a*) **there's only o. left**, es ist nur einer/eine/eins übrig; **all in o.**, alles in einem; (*b*) **at o.** (**o'clock**), um ein Uhr/*F:* um eins. **III.** *dem. pron.* (*a*) **this o.**, dieser/diese/dieses; **which o. do you like best?** welcher/welche/welches gefällt dir am besten? (*b*) **a red dot and a blue o.**, ein roter Punkt und ein blauer. **IV.** *indef. pron.* **1.** (*pl. some, any*) einer/eine/ein(e)s; **I haven't a pencil, have you got o.?** ich habe keinen Bleistift, hast du einen? **o. of them**, einer von ihnen; **not o.** (**of them**), keiner (von ihnen); **o. by o.**, einer nach dem anderen. **2.** (*you*) (*a*) (*subject*) man; (*object*) einen; **o. never knows**, man weiß nie; (*b*) **one's**, sein(e); **to cut one's finger**, sich in den Finger schneiden. ◆**one-'armed**, *adj.* **F:** **o.-a. bandit**, Spielautomat *m.* ◆**one-'eyed**, *adj.* einäugig. ◆**one-'horse**, *adj.* **F:** **o.-h. town**, armseliges Nest. ◆**one-'parent**, *adj.* **o.-p. family**, Halbfamilie *f.* ◆**one'self**, *pron.* (*a*) *refl.* sich; **to talk to o.**, mit sich selbst reden; **by o.**, allein; (*b*) **one must do it o.**, man muß es selbst machen. ◆**one-'sided**, *adj.* einseitig. ◆**one-'track**, *adj.* **to have a o.-t. mind**, immer nur das eine im Kopf haben. ◆**one-'up**, *adj.* (*a*) *Sp:* **to be o.-up**, einen Punkt/*Fb:* ein Tor usw. voraus sein; (*b*) **to be o.-up on s.o.**, j-m voraus sein. ◆**one'upmanship**, *s. Hum:* Kunst *f*, den anderen immer voraus zu sein. ◆**one-'way**, *adj.* Einbahn-; **o.-w. street**, Einbahnstraße *f.*

onerous ['ɔnərəs, 'aʊn-], *adj.* (*of task*) mühsam; (*of duties*) lästig.

onion ['ʌnjən], *s.* Zwiebel *f*; **o. skin**, Zwiebelschale *f.*

onlooker ['ɔnlukər], *s.* Zuschauer(in) *m(f).*

only ['əʊnli]. **I.** *adj.* einzig; **o. son**, einziger Sohn. **II.** *adv.* (*a*) nur; **I've o. three**, ich habe nur drei; (*b*) (*with time*) erst; **o. just**, gerade erst; **o. yesterday**, erst gestern. **III.** *conj.* aber; **o. it's too big**, es ist nur zu groß.

onslaught ['ɔnslɔːt], *s.* (heftiger) Angriff *m.*

onus ['əʊnəs], *s.* Last *f*; (*responsibility*) Verantwortung *f.*

onward(s) ['ɔnwəd(z)], *adv.* (*a*) (*forwards*) vorwärts; (*b*) **from tomorrow o.**, ab morgen.

ooze [uːz]. **I.** *s.* (*mud*) Schlamm *m.* **II.** *v.i.* sickern.

op [ɔp], *s.* **F:** **1.** *Med:* Operation *f.* **2.** *Mil:* **combined op(s)**, vereintes Unternehmen *n.*

opal ['əʊp(ə)l], *s.* Opal *m.*

opaque [əʊ'peik], *adj.* undurchsichtig.

open ['əʊp(ə)n]. **I.** *adj.* **1.** offen; (*of shop etc.*) geöffnet; **o. to the public**, für die Öffentlichkeit zugänglich. **2.** (*a*) **in the o.** (**air**), im Freien; **on the o. road**, auf freier Strecke; **the o. sea**, das offene Meer; (*b*) *Fig:* **o. to question**, fraglich; (*of verdict*) anfechtbar. **3.** (*frank*) offen; **to keep an o. mind**, sich nicht beeinflussen lassen. **4.** **the job is still open**, die Stelle ist noch frei. **II.** *v.* **1.** *v.tr.* (*a*) öffnen; (ein Buch usw.) aufschlagen; (*b*) (ein Land, neue Märkte usw.) erschließen; **to o.** (**up**) **a way/path through sth.**, sich dat einen Weg durch etwas *acc* bahnen; (*c*) (ein Fest, ein Geschäft, ein Gespräch, ein Konto usw.) eröffnen. **2.** *v.i.* (*of flower etc.*) sich öffnen; (*of shop etc.*) öffnen; **aufmachen; the door opens into the garden**, die Tür führt in den Garten; **-ly**, *adv.* offen; **to speak o. about sth.**, offen über etwas *acc* sprechen. ◆**open-'air**, *adj.* Frei-; **o.-a. pool**, Freibad *n*; **o.-a. theatre**, Freilichtbühne *f.* ◆**'opener**, *s.* **can/tin o.**, Büchsenöffner *m.* ◆**open-'heart**, *adj. Med:* **o.-h. surgery**, Eingriff *mpl* am offenen Herzen. ◆**'opening**, *s.* **1.** (*a*) Öffnen *n* (einer Flasche, der Post usw.); (*b*) Eröffnung *f* (von Verhandlungen, von einem Gebäude usw.); **o. speech**, Eröffnungsrede *f.* **2.** (*gap*) Öffnung *f*; (*in a forest*) Lichtung *f.* **3.** (*possibility, esp. job*) Möglichkeit *f.* ◆**'open-'minded**, *adj.* aufgeschlossen. ◆**'openness**, *s.* Offenheit *f.* ◆**'open-'plan**, *adj. Arch:* ohne Trennwände. ◆**open 'out**, *v.* **1.** *v.tr.* (ein Blatt Papier usw.) ausbreiten. **2.** *v.i.* (*of valley etc.*) sich ausbreiten; (*of view*) sich erstrecken. ◆**'open 'up**, *v.* **1.** *v.tr.* (ein Land, einen Markt usw.) erschließen. **2.** *v.i.* **o. up!** aufmachen!

opera ['ɔp(ə)rə], *s.* Oper *f*; **o. glasses**, Opernglas *n.* ◆**o'peratic**, *adj.* (*of opera*) Opern-. ◆**o. music**, Opernmusik *f.*

operate ['ɔpəreit], *v.* **1.** *v.i.* (*a*) (*of machine*) in Betrieb sein; (*of Med:*) **to o.** (**on s.o.**), (j-n) operieren. **2.** *v.tr.* (*of pers.*) (eine Maschine) bedienen; (eine Bremse, einen Hebel) betätigen. ◆**'operating**, *s. Ind: etc:* Betrieb *m*; **o. instructions**, Bedienungsanleitung *f*; **o. theatre**, Operationssaal *m.* ◆**ope'ration**, *s.* **1.** (*running*) Betrieb *m*; (*control*) Bedienung *f* (einer Maschine); Betätigung *f* (einer Bremse usw.). **2.** (*single process*) Arbeitsvorgang *m; Mth:* Prozeß *m.* **3.** *Med:* Operation *f*; **to have an o.**, operiert werden. ◆**ope'rational**, *adj.* (*ready for use*) betriebsfertig/*Mil:* einsatzfähig; (*in use*) im Betrieb/*Mil:* Einsatz. ◆**'operative** ['ɔp(ə)rətiv], *adj.* (*a*) (*effective*) wirksam; (*of law etc.*) **to become o.**, in Kraft treten; (*b*) (*relevant*) zutreffend. ◆**'operator**, *s.* (*a*) *Ind:* Maschinist *m*; (*b*) *Tel:* Telefonist(in) *m(f)*; *Nau: Av: etc:* **radio o.**, Funker *m.*

opinion [ə'pinjən], *s.* Meinung *f*; **in my o.**, meiner Meinung nach; **that's a matter of o.**, das ist Ansichtssache *f*; **o. poll**, Meinungsumfrage *f.* ◆**o'pinionated**, *adj.* rechthaberisch.

opium ['əʊpjəm], *s.* Opium *n.*

opponent [ə'pəunənt], s. Gegner m.

**oppor`tunity** [ɔpɔ`tjuːniti], s. Gelegenheit f.

oppose [ə'pəuz], v.tr. (a) sich (j-m, etwas dat) widersetzen; (eine Ansicht, eine Bewegung usw.) bekämpfen; (b) (compare) gegenüberstellen. ◆**op`posed**, adj. abgeneigt; **to be o. to sth.**, gegen etwas acc sein. ◆**op`posing**, adj. entgegengesetzt. ◆**opposite** ['ɔpəzit, -sit]. I. adj. (a) (facing) gegenüberstehend; **the house o.**, das Haus gegenüber; (b) (of directions, poles, meaning etc.) entgegengesetzt; **the o. sex, das andere Geschlecht. II. s.** Gegenteil n. III. adv. gegenüber; **she lives o., sie wohnt gegenüber. IV. prep.** gegenüber + dat. ◆**oppo`sition** s. Widerstand m; (b) Pol: Opposition f.

oppress [ə'pres], v.tr. (a) (ein Volk) unterdrücken; (b) (of anxiety, heat etc.) (j-n) bedrücken. ◆**o`ppression**, s. 1. Unterdrückung f. 2. (feeling) Bedrücktheit f. ◆**o`ppressive**, adj. 1. (of rule etc.) tyrannisch. 2. (of atmosphere) bedrückend; (of weather, heat) schwül. ◆**o`ppressor**, s. Unterdrücker m.

'**optical** ['ɔptikəl], adj. optisch. ◆**op`tician**, s. Optiker m. ◆**'optics**, s. pl. Optik f.

optimist ['ɔptimist], s. Optimist(in) m(f). ◆**'optimism**, s. Optimismus m. ◆**opti`mistic**, adj. optimistisch.

option ['ɔpʃ(ə)n], s. (choice) Wahl f; Alternative f; **to leave one's options open, sich nicht festlegen. ◆'optional, adj.** wahlweise.

opulence ['ɔpjuləns], s. Üppigkeit f. ◆**'opulent**, adj. üppig.

or [ɔːr], conj. oder; **he can't read or write, er kann weder lesen noch schreiben.**

oracle ['ɔrəkl], s. Orakel n.

oral ['ɔːr(ə)l]. I. adj. mündlich. II. s. Sch: F: mündliche Prüfung.

orange ['ɔrin(d)ʒ]. I. s. Apfelsine f, Orange f. II. adj. orange(farben).

oration [ɔ'reiʃ(ə)n], s. feierliche Rede f. ◆**orator** ['ɔrətər], s. Redner(in) m(f). ◆**'oratory**, s. Redekunst f.

oratorio, pl. -os [ɔrə'tɔːriəu, -əuz], s. Mus: Oratorium n.

orbit ['ɔːbit]. I. s. Umlaufbahn f (eines Satelliten); **to go into o., in die Umlaufbahn gelangen; II. v.tr. (einen Planeten)** umkreisen.

orchard ['ɔːtʃəd], s. Obstgarten m.

orchestra ['ɔːkistrə], s. Orchester n. ◆**or`chestral** [-`kes-], adj. Orchester-. ◆**'orchestrate**, v.tr. (ein Werk) orchestrieren. ◆**orche`stration**, s. Orchesterbearbeitung f.

orchid ['ɔːkid], s. Orchidee f.

ordain [ɔː'dein], v.tr. (a) Ecc: **to o. s.o. priest, j-n zum Priester weihen; (b) (decree) (etwas) verfügen, Fig: (of fate etc.)** bestimmen.

ordeal [ɔː'diːl], s. (schwere) Probe f, Fig:

Feuerprobe f.

order ['ɔːdər]. I. s. 1. Ordnung f; (sequence) Reihenfolge f; **in o., in Ordnung; out of o., (of machine) außer Betrieb; (defective) defekt; in good o., in gutem Zustand. 2. in o. to, um zu + inf; in o. that, damit. 3. (class, also medal) Orden m. 4. (a) (command) Befehl m; until further orders, bis auf weiteren Befehl; (b) Com: Auftrag m; (act of ordering) Bestellung f; to form, Bestellschein m; (c) money/postal o., Postanweisung f. II.** v.tr. (a) **to o. s.o. to do sth., j-m befehlen, etwas zu tun; (b) (Waren, Essen, ein Taxi usw.) bestellen; (in restaurant) have you ordered? haben Sie schon bestellt?** ◆**'orderly. I. adj. (a) (tidy) ordentlich; (of riding) geordnet; (b) (of crowd etc.) friedlich. II. s. medical o., Krankenwärter m; Mil: Sanitäter m.**

ordinal ['ɔːdin(ə)l], adj. o. (number), Ordnungszahl f.

ordinary ['ɔːdin(ə)ri], adj. normal; (also Pej:) gewöhnlich; **-ily, adv. normalerweise.**

ordnance ['ɔːdnəns], s. 1. Mil: Artillerie f. 2. Brit: **O. Survey map, Meßtischblatt n (der Nationalen Landesvermessung).**

ore [ɔːr], s. Erz n.

organ ['ɔːgən], s. 1. Mus: Orgel f. 2. Anat: Organ n. ◆**organic** [ɔː'gænik], adj. organisch. ◆**'organism**, s. Organismus m. ◆**'organist**, s. Mus: Organist m. ◆**organi`zation**, s. Organisation f. ◆**'organize**, v.tr. organisieren. ◆**'organizer**, s. Organisator m; (of event) Veranstalter m.

orgy ['ɔːdʒi], s. Orgie f.

orient ['ɔːriənt], s. **the O., der Orient.** ◆**ori`ental. I. adj. orientalisch. II. s.** Orientale m; Orientalin f. ◆**'orientate**, v.tr. **to o. oneself, sich orientieren.**

origin ['ɔridʒin], s. 1. Ursprung m; (source) Quelle f (eines Gerüchts usw.); (of pers.) Herkunft f; **country of o., Herkunftsland n. ◆original [ə'ri-]. I. adj. (a) (first) ursprünglich; (unaltered) original; (b) (new) originell. II. s. Original n (eines Bildes usw.). ◆**orig`inality**, s. Originalität f. ◆**o'riginate**, v. 1. v.tr. (create) (etwas) schaffen; (found) (eine Bewegung, Stilrichtung) begründen. 2. v.i. (of thing) entstehen (from/in, aus + dat), (of war, quarrel etc.) seinen Ausgang nehmen.**

Orkneys ['ɔːkniz]. Pr.n.pl. **the O., die** Orkneyinseln fpl.

ornament ['ɔːnəmənt]. I. s. Ornament n; Fig: (pers. etc.) Zierde f. II. v.tr. (etwas) verzieren. ◆**ornate** [ɔː'neit], adj. (of style) überladen; (of object) reich verziert, verschnörkelt; (of language) blumig.

ornithology [ɔːni'θɔlədʒi], s. Vogelkunde f.

orphan ['ɔːf(ə)n], s. Waise f. ◆**'orphanage**, s. Waisenhaus n.

orthodox ['ɔːθədɔks], adj. orthodox.

orthography [ɔː'θɔgrəfi], s. Rechtschreibung f.

orthopaedic [ɔːθəˈpiːdik], adj. orthopädisch.

oscillate [ˈɔsileit], v.i. schwingen; (of needle etc.) ausschlagen. ◆**oscil'lation**, s. Schwingung f.

ostensible [ɔsˈtensibl], adj. angeblich; (apparent) scheinbar.

ostentation [ɔstenˈteiʃ(ə)n], s. Protzigkeit f. ◆**osten'tatious**, adj. protzig.

osteopath [ˈɔstiəpæθ], s. Osteopath m.

ostracism [ˈɔstrəsizm], s. Achtung f. ◆**'ostracize**, v.tr. (j-n) ächten.

ostrich [ˈɔstritʃ], s. Strauß m.

other [ˈʌðər], s. indef. I. adj. (a) andere(r,s), die o. one, der/die/das andere; (b) the o. night, neulich abends/nachts; (c) (alternate) every o. day, jeden zweiten Tag; (d) (different) o. than, anders als. II. pron. andere(r,s); one after the o., einer nach dem anderen; the others, die anderen; each o., einander; F: someone or o., irgend jemand. ◆'otherwise, adv. 1. (differently) anders. 2. (in other respects) sonst; o. he's quite sane, sonst ist er ganz normal.

otter [ˈɔtər], s. Otter m.

ought [ɔːt], v. aux. sollte(n); you o. to go now, Sie sollten jetzt gehen; you o. to see the exhibition, Sie sollten sich die Ausstellung ansehen; it would be enough for three, das müßte für drei Personen genügen.

our [ɑːr, ˈauər], poss. adj. unser. ◆**ours**, poss. pron unsere, unsere, unseres; this is o., das gehört uns; a friend of o., ein Freund von uns. ◆**our'selves**, pers. pron. pl. selbst.

oust [aust], v.tr. (j-n) verdrängen.

out [aut], adv. hinaus; (a) to go o., hinausgehen; to come o., herauskommen; o. you go! raus mit dir! (b) (away) weg; to throw sth. o., etwas wegwerfen; (c) my father is o., mein Vater ist nicht zu Hause. 2. (wrong) to be o. in one's calculations, sich verrechnet haben. 3. (of fire) ausgegangen. 4. (finished) zu Ende. 5. o o. (a) aus + dat; o. of the window, aus dem Fenster/zum Fenster hinaus; o. of doors, im Freien; o. of the way, (i) int. aus dem Weg! (ii) (of place) abgelegen; (b) (outside) a mile o. of (the) town, eine Meile außerhalb der Stadt. ◆'outback, s. Austral: the o., das Landesinnere. ◆**out'bid**, v.tr.irr. (at auction) (j-n) überbieten. ◆**out'board**, adj. o. motor, Außenbordmotor m. ◆**outbreak**, s. Ausbruch m (einer Krankheit usw.). ◆**'outbuilding**, s. Nebengebäude n. ◆**'outburst**, s. Ausbruch m (von Zorn usw.). ◆**'outcast**. I. s. Ausgestoßene(r) f(m). II. adj. ausgestoßen. ◆**'outcome**, s. Ergebnis n. ◆**'outcry**, s. (lautstarker) Protest m. ◆**out'distance**, v.tr. Sp: (j-n) weit hinter sich lassen. ◆**out'do**, v.tr.irr.

(j-n) übertreffen. ◆**'outdoor**, adj. im Freien. ◆**'outer**, adj. äußere(r,s), Außen-; o. space, Weltraum m. ◆**'outfit**, s. Ausrüstung f. ◆**'outgoings**, s.pl. Ausgaben fpl. ◆**out'grow**, v.tr.irr. herauswachsen (aus Kleidern usw.); (Gewohnheiten) ablegen. ◆**'outing**, s. Ausflug m. ◆**out'landish**, adj. (of dress) ausgefallen; (of behaviour, ideas) seltsam. ◆**'outlaw**. I. s. Geächtete(r) f(m). II. v.tr. (a) (j-n) ächten; (b) Fig: (etwas) verbieten. ◆**'outlay**, s. Auslagen fpl. ◆**'outline**. I. s. Umriß m. II. v.tr. (etwas) umreißen; to o. sth. roughly, etwas in groben Zügen darstellen. ◆**out'live**, v.tr. (j-n, etwas) überleben. ◆**'outlook**, s. (a) (view) Aussicht f; (b) Fig: (prospect) Aussichten fpl; (opinion) Ansicht f. ◆**'outlying**, adj. (of villages etc.) entlegen. ◆**out'number**, v.tr. (dem Feind usw.) zahlenmäßig überlegen sein. ◆**'output**, s. (a) Ind: Produktion f; Min: Ertrag m; Lit: etc: Werk n; (b) (of engine, machine etc.) Leistung f. ◆**'outrage**. I. s. 1. (atrocity) Greueltat f. 2. (sth. shocking) Unverschämtheit f. ◆**out'rageous**, adj. unerhört; (of prices) unverschämt; (of remark) empörend. ◆**'outright**, adv. glatt; to refuse o., glattweg ablehnen. ◆**'outset**, s. Anfang m. ◆**out'shine**, v.tr.irr. (j-n, etwas) in den Schatten stellen. ◆**out'side**. I. s. Außenseite f. II. adj. äußere(r,s); Außen-; Fb: o. right, Rechtsaußen m. III. adv. (viewed from inside) draußen. IV. prep. außerhalb + gen. ◆**out'sider**, s. Außenseiter m. ◆**'outskirts**, s.pl. Rand m; (of town) Stadtrand m. ◆**out'standing**, adj. 1. (excellent) hervorragend. 2. (a) (not paid) offenstehend; o. debts, Außenstände mpl; (b) (of work etc.) unerledigt. ◆**'outstay**, v.tr. to o. one's welcome, länger als erwünscht bleiben. ◆**out'stretched**, adj. ausgestreckt. ◆**out'vote**, v.tr. (j-n) überstimmen. ◆**'outward**. I. adj. (a) Hin-; o. journey, Hinreise f; (b) (external) äußerlich; (attrib. only) äußere(r, s). II. adv. nach außen; -ly, adv. (apparently) allem Anschein nach. ◆**'outwards**, adv. nach außen. ◆**out'wit**, v.tr. (j-n) überlisten.

oval [ˈəuv(ə)l]. I. adj. oval. II. s. Oval n.

ovary [ˈəuvəri], s. Eierstock m.

ovation [əuˈveiʃ(ə)n], s. Ovation f.

oven [ˈʌv(ə)n], s. 1. (baker's etc.) Backofen m; (of cooker) Backrohr n. 2. (kiln) Ofen m. ◆**'ovenware**, s. feuerfestes Geschirr n.

over [ˈəuvər]. I. prep. (a) über + dat/ (motion) + acc; (beyond) o. the frontier, über die Grenze; the house o. the road, das Haus gegenüber; (b) (more than) über + acc; (during) o. the weekend, übers Wochenende; (c) (about) to worry o. sth., sich wegen etwas gen Sorgen machen. II. adv. 1. all o., (i) (of pers.) am

ganzen Körper; (ii) (of thing) an der ganzen Oberfläche; all o. again, wieder von vorne; o. and o. again, immer wieder. 2. (a) (away) hinüber; to cross o., die Straße überqueren; (b) o. there, (da) drüben; (c) (towards speaker) herüber; F: come o. to our place, komm rüber zu uns. 3. (more) children of 12 and o., Kinder über 12 Jahre. 4. (past) vorbei; (at an end) zu Ende; it's all o. with me, mit mir ist es aus. ◆over'all. I. [əuvər'ɔːl] adv. gesamt; Gesamt-. II. ['əuvərɔːl] s. Kittelschürze f.
◆over'bearing, adj. an o. manner, eine herrische Art. ◆'overboard, adv. über Bord. ◆over'burden, v.tr. überlasten. ◆over'cast, adj. (of sky) bedeckt. ◆'over'charge, v.tr. & i. to o. (s.o.), (j-m) zu viel berechnen. ◆'overcoat, s. Mantel m. ◆over'come, v.tr.irr. überwinden. II. adj. to be o. with/by sth., von etwas dat übermannt werden. ◆over'crowded, adj. überfüllt. ◆over'crowding, s. Überfüllen n. ◆over'do, v.tr.irr. (etwas) zu weit treiben; (exaggerate) übertreiben. ◆'overdose, s. Überdosis f. ◆'overdraft, s. I have an o., ich habe mein Konto überzogen. ◆over'draw, v.tr.irr. (das Konto) überziehen. ◆'overdrive, s. Aut: Schongang m. ◆'over'due, adj. überfällig. ◆over'eat, v.i.irr. (of pers.) sich überessen. ◆over'estimate. I. s. Überschätzung f. II. v.tr. (etwas) überschätzen. ◆'overflow. I. ['əuvəfləu] s. 1. (of liquid etc.) Überlaufen n. 2. (pipe) Überlauf m. II. [əuvə'fləu] v. 1. v.tr. (of river) to o. its banks, über die Ufer treten. 2. v.i. (of water etc.) überfließen; (of cup etc.) überlaufen. ◆over'grown, adj. überwuchert. ◆overhaul. I. ['əuvəhɔːl] s. Überholung f (einer Maschine usw.). II. [əuvə'hɔːl] v.tr. (eine Maschine usw.) überholen. ◆'over'head, adv. oben. ◆over'hear, v.tr. (eine Konversation usw.) zufällig mit anhören. ◆over'heat, v. 1. v.tr. überhitzen. 2. v.i. (of bearing etc.) heißlaufen. ◆'over'land, adv. auf dem Landwege. ◆overlap [əuvə'læp], v.tr. & i. to o. (one another), sich überschneiden. ◆over'load. I. [əuvə'ləud] v.tr. (a) überladen; (b) (einen Motor usw., El: das Netz) überlasten. II. ['əuvələud] s. Überlastung f. ◆over'look, v.tr. (a) (das Meer usw.) überblicken; (b) (j-n, eine Tatsache) übersehen; we'll o. it, wir werden darüber hinwegsehen. ◆'over'night. I. adv. über Nacht; to stay o., übernachten. II. adj. o. stay/ stop, Übernachtung f (at, in + dat). ◆'overpass, s. Überführung f. ◆over'power, v.tr. überwältigen. ◆over'powering, adj. überwältigend. ◆over'rate, v.tr. (etwas) überbewerten; (j-n) überschätzen. ◆'overrider, s. Aut:

Stoßstangenhorn n. ◆over'rule, v.tr. (a) (j-u) überstimmen; (b) (einen Einwand) zurückweisen; Jur: (ein Urteil) verwerfen. ◆over'run, v.tr. v.tr. (a) Mil: (über ein Land) herfallen; (b) the house is o. with mice, in dem Haus wimmelt es von Mäusen; (c) (die Zeit, die Grenzen) überschreiten. ◆over'seas. I. adv. nach Übersee; to go o., ins Ausland fahren. II. adj. Übersee-; o. trade, Überseehandel m. ◆over'shadow, v.tr. überschatten. ◆over'shoot, v.tr.irr. to o. a turning, an einer Abzweigung (versehentlich) vorbeifahren. ◆over'sleep, v.i.irr. verschlafen. ◆over'steer, s. Übersteuerung f. ◆'over'step, v.tr. (die Grenzen, seine Befugnisse) überschreiten. ◆over'take, v.tr. (a) überholen; (b) Lit: (of accident) ereilen. ◆over'taking, s. Überholen n; no o., Überholverbot n. ◆over'tax, v.tr. (a) Fin: (j-n) übersteuern; (b) (j-n) überbeanspruchen. ◆over'throw v.tr.irr. (eine Regierung usw.) stürzen; (einen Plan) zunichte machen. ◆'overtime. I. s. Ind: Überstunden fpl. II. adv. to work o., Überstunden machen. ◆over'whelm, v.tr. (a) (den Feind, j-n) überwältigen; to be overwhelmed with work, mit Arbeit überhäuft sein. ◆over'whelming, adj. (of majority etc.) überwältigend. ◆'over'work. I. s. Überlastung f. II. v. 1. v.tr. (j-n) mit Arbeit überlasten. 2. v.i. (of pers.) sich überarbeiten.

overture ['əuvətjuər], s. 1. Mus: Ouvertüre f. 2. usu. pl. to make overtures to s.o., bei j-m Annäherungsversuche machen.

owe [əu], v.tr. (a) to o. s.o. money/o. money to s.o., j-m Geld schulden/schuldig sein; (b) v.i. I still o. you for the petrol, ich bin Ihnen noch das Benzin schuldig; (c) (j-m sein Leben, seinen Erfolg usw.) verdanken; I o. you an explanation, ich bin Ihnen eine Erklärung schuldig. ◆'owing. prep. o. to, wegen + gen; o. to the rain, wegen des Regens.

owl [aul], s. Eule f.

own [əun]. I. v.tr. (etwas) besitzen. II. adj. eigen; the house is my o., das Haus gehört mir. III. s. (a) he has a copy of his o., er hat ein eigenes Exemplar; F: to get one's o. back, sich revanchieren; (b) to be (all) on one's o., (ganz) allein sein. ◆'owner, s. Besitzer(in) m(f); Eigentümer(in) m(f) (eines Hauses, einer Firma); parking at o.'s risk, Parken auf eigene Gefahr.

ox, pl. oxen [ɔks, 'ɔks(ə)n], s. Ochse m; Cu: o. tongue, Ochsenzunge f. ◆'oxtail, s. Ochsenschwanz m.

oxide ['ɔksaid], s. Oxyd m. ◆oxidize ['ɔksidaiz], v.tr. & i. oxydieren.

oxygen ['ɔksidʒən], s. Sauerstoff m.
oyster ['ɔistər], s. Auster f; Orn: o.

catcher, Austernfischer m.
ozone ['ɔuzəun], s. Ozon n.

P

P, p [pi:], s. (der Buchstabe) P, p n.

pace [peis]. I. s. 1. (step) Schritt m. 2. (speed) Tempo n; at a walking p., im Schrittempo; Sp: etc: to set the p., das Tempo angeben. 3. v.i. to p. up and down, auf und ab schreiten. ◆'pacemaker, s. Med: & Sp: Schrittmacher m.

pacific [pə'sifik], s. the P. (Ocean), der Pazifik, der Stille Ozean. ◆'pacifism, s. Pazifismus m. ◆'pacifist, s. Pazifist(in) m(f). ◆'pacify ['pæsifai], v.tr. (j-n) beruhigen; (Zorn, Ärger) beschwichtigen.

pack [pæk]. I. v.tr. a) (Kleider usw.) einpacken; Ind: (Waren) verpacken; **packed lunch**, Lunchpaket n; to p. one's **suitcase**/abs. to p., (den Koffer) packen; (b) (fill) to p. sth. with sth., etwas mit etwas dat vollstopfen; (c) (squeeze) stopfen; **the hall was packed**, der Saal war gerammelt voll; (d) F: **I'm packing it in**, ich schmeiße den Kram/die Arbeit hin. II. s. 1. Pack m; (on back) Tornister m; Mil: Gepäck n. 2. (of people) Pack n, Bande f; (of hounds, wolves etc.) Meute f; a p. of cards, ein Kartenspiel n; Fig: to **tell s.o. a p. of lies**, j-m die Hucke voll lügen. ◆'package. I. s. (parcel, also Pol: etc.) Paket n; Com: Packung f; p. **tour**, Pauschalreise f. II. v.tr. Com: (Waren) verpacken. ◆'packaging, s. (material) Verpackung f. ◆'packet, s. Päckchen n; a p. of cigarettes, ein Päckchen Zigaretten. ◆'packing, s. 1. (a) (action) Verpacken n; (b) (wrappings) Verpackung f; p. case, Kiste f.

pact [pækt], s. Pol: Mil: etc: Pakt m.

pad [pæd]. I. s. 1. Cl: etc: Polster n. 2. **writing p.**, Schreibblock m. II. v.tr. (a) (einen Stuhl usw.) polstern; (eine Jacke in den Schultern) auspolstern; (b) Fig: (eine Rede usw.) mit Füllwörtern usw. strecken. ◆'padding, s. a) Polsterung f; Cl: Wattierung f; (b) F: (in book etc.) Füllsel n.

paddle1 ['pædl]. I. s. 1. Paddel n. 2. (on wheel) Schaufel f; p. **steamer**, Raddampfer m. II. v.tr. & i. (ein Kanu) paddeln.

paddle2, v.i. planschen; **paddling pool**, Planschbecken n.

paddock ['pædɔk], s. (a) (field) Koppel f; (b) Rac: Führring m.

paddy ['pædi], s. p. **field**, Reisfeld n.

padlock ['pædlɔk], s. Vorhängeschloß n.

paediatrician [pi:diə'triʃ(ə)n], s. Kinderärztin f.

pagan ['peigən]. I. s. Heide m, Heidin f. II. adj heidnisch.

page1 ['peidʒ]. I. s. p.-**boy**, Hotelpage m.

page2, s. Seite f; **on p. 6**, auf Seite 6; p. **by p.**, Seite für Seite.

pageant ['pædʒənt], s. Festzug m.

paid [peid], adj. bezahlt.

pail [peil], s. Eimer m.

pain [pein]. s. 1. (physical, also Fig:) Schmerz m; (mental) Qual f; to **be in great p.**, starke Schmerzen haben; F: **he's a p. in the neck**, er ist nicht auszuhalten. 2. pl. Mühe f; to **take pains**, sich dat Mühe geben (over sth., bei etwas dat). ◆'painful, adj. (of wound, treatment etc.) schmerzhaft; (of memories etc.) schmerzlich. ◆'painkiller, s. schmerzstillendes Mittel n. ◆'painless, adj. schmerzlos. ◆'painstaking, adj. he is very p., er scheut keine Mühe; p. work, mühsame Kleinarbeit.

paint [peint]. I. s. (a) Farbe f; (of car) Anstrich m; (notice) **wet p.** frisch gestrichen! II. v. 1. v.tr. (ein Zimmer usw.) streichen; (ein Bild) malen. 2. v.i. (of artist etc.) malen. ◆'paintbrush, s. Farbpinsel m. ◆'painter, s. 1. (artist) Maler(in) m(f). 2. (house) p., Anstreicher m. ◆'painting, s. 1. (art) Malerei f. 2. (picture) Gemälde n. ◆'paintwork, s. Aut: Lack m.

pair [pɛər], s. Paar n.

Pakistan [pɑːkis'tɑːn, pæk-]. Pr.n. Pakistan n. ◆'Paki'stani. I. adj. pakistanisch. II. s. Pakistaner(in) m(f).

pal [pæl], s. F: (guter) Freund m.

palace ['pælis], s. Schloß n; (royal) Königsschloß n.

palate ['pælit], s. Anat: Gaumen m. ◆'palatable [-ətəbl], adj. wohlschmeckend.

palatial [pə'leiʃ(ə)l], adj. prunkvoll.

pale [peil], adj. (a) (of face etc.) blaß; (of moonlight etc.) fahl; (b) (of colour) hell.

Palestine ['pælistain]. Pr. n. Palästina n. ◆'Pales'tinian. I. adj. palästinensisch. II. s. Palästinenser(in) m(f).

palings ['peiliŋz], s.pl. Lattenzaun m.

pall [pɔːl], s.p. **bearer**, Sargträger m.

pallet ['pælit], s. Ind: & Paint: Palette f.

palliative ['pæliətiv], s. schmerzlinderndes Mittel n.

pallid ['pælid], adj. (of face, light etc.) blaß; (of sky) fahl.

pallor ['pælər], s. Blässe f.

palm1 [pɑːm], s. 1. p. (tree), Palme f. 2. Ecc: P. **Sunday**, Palmsonntag m.

palm2, s. Handfläche f. ◆'palmistry, s. Handlesekunst f.

palpable ['pælpəbl], adj. (of result etc.) greifbar; (of difference, relief etc.) fühlbar; (of error) eindeutig.

palpitate ['pælpiteit], v.i. (a) (of heart) heftig klopfen; wild schlagen. ◆palpi'tation, s. Herzklopfen n.

paltry ['pɔːltri], *adj.* dürftig; *(of excuse)* fadenscheinig.
pamper ['pæmpər], *v.tr.* verhätscheln.
pamphlet ['pæmflit], *s.* Broschüre *f; esp. Pol:* Flugblatt *n.*
pan [pæn], *s. Cu:* Kochtopf *m;* frying *p.,* Bratpfanne *f.* ◆**'pancake,** *s.* Pfannkuchen *m;* P. Day, Faschingsdienstag *m.*
panacea [pænə'siːə], *s.* Allheilmittel *n.*
panache [pə'næʃ], *s.* Schwung *m; (elegance)* Eleganz *f.*
pancreas ['pæŋkriəs], *s.* Bauchspeicheldrüse *f.*
panda ['pændə], *s. Z:* Panda *m; F:* p. car, Streifenwagen *m.*
pander ['pændər], *v.i.* frönen (**to** sth., etwas *dat*).
pane [pein], *s.* Fensterscheibe *f.*
panel ['pæn(ə)l]. **I. s. 1.** *(wood)* Holztafel *f; (glass)* Glasscheibe *f; (in door)* Türfüllung *f; (metal)* Verkleidungsblech *n.* **2.** *(committee)* Ausschuß *m; TV: Rad: etc:* Team *n; (in quiz)* Rateteam *n.* **II.** *v.tr.* (eine Wand usw.) täfeln. ◆**'panelling,** *s.* Täfelung *f.*
pang [pæŋ], *s.* pangs of conscience, Gewissensbisse.
panic ['pænik]. **I. s.** Panik *f.* **II.** *v.i.* von Panik erfaßt werden. ◆**'panicky,** *adj. F: (of pers.)* in Panikstimmung.
panorama [pænə'rɑːmə], *s.* Panorama *n.* ◆**pano'ramic** ['-'ræmik], *adj.* p. view, Rundblick *m.*
pansy ['pænzi], *s. Bot:* Stiefmütterchen *n.*
pant [pænt], *v.i.* keuchen.
panther ['pænθər], *s.* Panther *m.*
panties ['pæntiz], *s. pl.* Damenslip *m.*
pantomime ['pæntəmaim], *s. Th:* Märchenspiel *n* (im Varietéstil).
pantry ['pæntri], *s.* Speisekammer *f.*
pants [pænts], *s. pl. (a)* (pair of) p., Unterhose *f; (b) N.Am:* Hose *f.*
papal ['peipəl], *adj.* päpstlich.
paper ['peipər]. **I. s. 1.** Papier *n;* piece of p., Zettel *m; (large)* Bogen *m;* p. clip, Büroklammer *f;* p. mill, Papierfabrik *f;* p. weight, Briefbeschwerer *m.* **2.** *(a)* (exam paper) Dokumente *npl;* (records) Akten *fpl; (proving identity etc.)* npl. **3.** *(newspaper)* Zeitung *f.* **4.** (wall) p., Tapete *f.* **II.** *v.tr.* (ein Zimmer usw.) tapezieren. ◆**'paperback,** *s.* Taschenbuch *n.* ◆**'paperwork,** *s.* Schreibarbeit *f; F:* Papierkrieg *m.*
par [pɑːr], *s.* **1.** Gleichheit *f; (a)* to be on a p. with s.o., j-m gleichstehen; *(b) F:* to feel below p., nicht ganz auf der Höhe sein. **2.** *(Golf)* Par *n.*
parable ['pærəbl], *s.* Gleichnis *n.*
parachute ['pærəʃuːt], *s.* Fallschirm *m.* **II.** *v.i.* mit dem Fallschirm abspringen.
parade [pə'reid]. **I. s.** *Mil: etc: (static)* Parade *f; (marching)* Aufmarsch *m; (procession)* Festzug *m.* **II.** *v.i. Mil:* vorbeimarschieren.
paradise ['pærədais], *s.* Paradies *n.*
paradox ['pærədɔks], *s.* Paradox *n.*

◆**para'doxical,** *adj.* paradox; -ally, *adv.* paradoxerweise.
paraffin ['pærəfin], *s.* Paraffin *n.*
paragon ['pærəgən], *s.* Muster *n.* p. of virtue, Ausbund *m* der Tugend.
paragraph ['pærəgrɑːf], *s.* Absatz *m.*
parallel ['pærəlel]. **I.** *adj.* parallel (**with/to,** zu + *dat*). **II.** *s. (comparison)* Parallele *f,* Vergleich *m.*
paralyse ['pærəlaiz], *v.tr.* lähmen. ◆**pa'ralysis,** *s.* Lähmung *f.*
paramount ['pærəmaunt], *adj.* höchste(r,s); oberste(r,s)
parapet ['pærəpit], *s.* Brüstung *f; (railing)* Geländer *n.*
paraphernalia [pærəfə'neiliə], *s.pl. F:* Kram *m; (personal)* Siebensachen *fpl.*
paraphrase ['pærəfreiz]. **I. s.** Paraphrase *f,* Umschreibung *f.* **II.** *v.tr.* umschreiben.
parasite ['pærəsait], *s.* Parasit *m.*
paratrooper ['pærətruːpər], *s.* Fallschirmjäger *m.* ◆**'paratroops,** *s.pl. Mil:* Fallschirmtruppen *fpl.*
parcel ['pɑːs(ə)l], *s.* Paket *n.*
parch [pɑːtʃ], *v.tr. (of sun, wind)* (etwas) austrocknen; *F:* **I'm parched!** ich komme um vor Durst!
parchment ['pɑːtʃmənt], *s.* Pergament *n.*
pardon ['pɑːd(ə)n]. **I. s.** *(a)* to beg s.o.'s p., j-n um Verzeihung bitten; **I beg your p.!** Entschuldigung! *(b) Jur:* free p., Begnadigung *f.* **II.** *v.tr. (a)* (j-m) verzeihen; *(b) Jur:* (j-n) begnadigen.
parent ['pɛərənt], *s.* Elternteil *m;* pl. **parents,** Eltern *pl.*
parenthesis [pə'renθəsis], *pl.* **-eses** [pə'renθəsis, -siːz], *s.* Parenthese *f;* **in parentheses,** in Klammern.
Paris ['pæris]. *Pr. n.* Paris *n.* ◆**Parisian** [pə'riziən]. **I.** *adj.* Pariser. **II.** *s.* Pariser(in) *m(f).*
parish ['pæriʃ], *s. Ecc:* Gemeinde *f.*
parity ['pæriti], *s. Com: Fin:* Parität *f.*
park [pɑːk]. **I. s.** Park *m.* **II.** *v.tr.* (ein Auto usw.) parken. ◆**'parking,** *s.* Parken *n;* no p., Parken verboten; p. space, Parklücke *f;* p. meter, Parkuhr *f;* p. ticket, Strafzettel *m.*
parliament ['pɑːləmənt], *s.* Parlament *n.* ◆**parlia'mentary,** *adj.* parlamentarisch.
parlour ['pɑːlər], *s.* **1.** beauty p., Schönheitssalon *m.* **2.** *A: (best room)* gute Stube *f.*
parochial [pə'rəukiəl], *adj.* **1.** *Ecc:* parochial. **2.** *Pej:* provinziell.
parody ['pærədi]. **I. s.** Parodie *f* (**on/of** auf + *acc*). **II.** *v.tr.* parodieren.
parole [pə'rəul], *s.* **on** p., auf Ehrenwort.
parquet [pɑː'kei], *s.* Parkett *n.*
parrot ['pærət], *s.* Papagei *m.*
parsimonious [pɑːsi'məuniəs], *adj.* sparsam; *(miserly)* knauserig.
parsley ['pɑːsli], *s.* Petersilie *f.*
parsnip ['pɑːsnip], *s.* Pastinake *f.*
parson ['pɑːsn], *s.* Gemeindepfarrer *m.* ◆**'parsonage,** *s.* Pfarrhaus *n.*
part [pɑːt]. **I. s. 1.** *(a)* Teil *m & n;* **in** p.,

zum Teil/teilweise; *Ind:* spare parts, Ersatzteile *npl;* (*b*) *Gram:* to p. of, Wortart *f;* (*c*) (*in newspaper etc.*) Fortsetzung *f* (*eines Romans usw.*); (*volume*) Band *m;* (*d*) p.-time work, Teilzeitarbeit *f;* to work p.-time, halbtags arbeiten. 2. (*a*) to take p. in sth., an etwas *dat* teilnehmen; (*b*) *Th:* Rolle *f;* (*c*) *Mus:* Partie *f.* 3. on the p. of, seitens + *gen.* II. *adv.* teilweise. III. *v.* 1. *v.tr.* (*separate*) (etwas) trennen; to p. one's hair, sich *dat* einen Scheitel ziehen. 2. *v.i.* sich trennen. ◆**parting.** I. *s.* (*a*) Trennung *f;* (*b*) (*farewell*) Abschied *m.* 2. (*in the hair*) Scheitel *m.*

partial ['pɑːʃ(ə)l], *adj.* 1. (*a*) (*biased*) voreingenommen; *Jur:* befangen; (*b*) to be p. to sth., eine Schwäche für etwas *acc* haben. 2. Teil-; teilweise; p. acceptance, Teilakzept *n.* ◆**participate** [pɑːˈtisipeit], *v.i.* to p. in sth., an etwas *dat* teilnehmen. ◆**partici'pation,** *s.* Teilnahme *f* (in, an + *dat*). ◆**participle** ['pɑːtisipl], *s. Gram:* Partizip *n.* ◆**particle** ['pɑːtikl], *s.* 1. *Gram:* Partikel *f.* 2. *Ph: etc:* Teilchen *n.* ◆**particular** [pəˈtikjulər]. I. *adj.* 1. (*special*) besondere(r,s); in p., besonders. 2. (*fussy*) eigen; -ly, *adv.* besonders. II. *s. esp.* pl. particulars, Einzelheiten *fpl.* ◆**partisan** [pɑːtiˈzæn], *s.* Partisan *m.* ◆**partition** [pɑːˈtiʃ(ə)n]. I. *s.* 1. Trennwand *f.* II. *v.tr.* (*ein Feld, Land usw.*) teilen; (*b*) (*ein Zimmer*) aufteilen. **partly** ['pɑːtli], *adv.* zum Teil, teilweise. **partner** ['pɑːtnər], *s.* 1. Partner *m* (*mf*). 2. *Com:* Teilhaber(in) *m(f).* ◆**partnership,** *s.* 1. Partnerschaft *f;* (*combination*) Kombination *f.* 2. *Com:* Assoziation *f.* **partridge** ['pɑːtridʒ], *s.* Rebhuhn *n.* **party** ['pɑːti], *s.* 1. *Pol:* Partei *f.* 2. Party *f;* birthday p., Geburtstagsfeier *f.* 3. (*group of people*) Gesellschaft *f;* Gruppe *f;* rescue p., Rettungsmannschaft *f.* 4. a third p., ein Dritter.

pass [pɑːs]. I. *v.* 1. *v.i.* (*a*) (*of pers.*) vorbeigehen; (*in vehicle*) vorbeifahren; to let s.o. p., j-n vorbeilassen; if you're passing this way, falls Sie hier vorbeikommen; to let a remark p., eine Bemerkung durchgehen lassen; (*b*) (*of time*) to p. (by), vergehen; (*in examination, test*) bestehen. 2. *v.tr.* (*a*) to p. s.o., sth., an j-m, etwas *dat* vorbeigehen/(*in vehicle*) vorbeifahren; (*b*) (*exceed*) überschreiten; (*c*) *Sch:* (*eine Prüfung*) bestehen; *Parl:* to p. a bill, ein Gesetz verabschieden; (*d*) (*hand*) (j-m etwas) reichen; *Fb:* to p. the ball to s.o., j-m den Ball zuspielen; *Med:* to p. water, Wasser lassen; (*e*) to p. the time, die Zeit verbringen. II. *s.* 1. (mountain) p., (Gebirgs)paß *m.* 2. (*document*) *Adm: etc:* Passierschein *m.* 3. *Fb: etc:* Vorlage *f.* ◆**passable,** *adj.* (*a*) passabel; (*b*) (*of road*) passierbar.

◆**passage** ['pæsidʒ], *s.* 1. (*in a building*) Flur *m,* Korridor *m;* (*between buildings etc.*) Durchgang *m.* 2. (*in music, book etc.*) Stelle *f.* ◆**passenger** ['pæsindʒər], *s.* Passagier *m.* ◆**passer-by,** (*pl* passers-by), *s.* Passant *m.* ◆**passing.** I. *adj.* (*of remark etc.*) beiläufig; a p. fancy, eine (vorübergehende) Laune. II. *s.* (*death*) Hinscheiden *n.* ◆**pass 'off,** *v.* 1. *v.i.* ablaufen. 2. *v.tr.* to pass o. off as an actor, sich als Schauspieler ausgeben. ◆**pass 'on,** *v.* 1. *v.tr.* (Informationen, ein Buch usw.) weitergeben. 2. *v.i. Fig:* (*die*) hinscheiden. ◆**pass 'out,** *v.i.* ohnmächtig werden. ◆**pass 'over,** *v.i.* (etwas) ich legen. ◆**Passover,** *s. Ecc:* Passah *n.* ◆**passport,** *s.* Paß *m.* ◆**pass 'round,** *v.tr.* to p. r. the wine etc., die Weinflasche usw. herumreichen. ◆**password,** *s. Mil: etc:* Kennwort *n.* ◆**passion** ['pæʃ(ə)n], *s.* Leidenschaft *f.* ◆**passionate,** *adj.* leidenschaftlich. ◆**passive** ['pæsiv]. I. *adj.* passiv. II. *s. Gram:* Passiv *n.*

past¹ [pɑːst]. I. *adj.* (*a*) vergangen; in times p., in früheren Zeiten; (*b*) *Gram:* p. participle, Partizip Perfekt *n.* II. *s.* Vergangenheit *f;* in the p., früher. **past²**. I. *prep.* (*a*) an ... dat vorbei; to walk p. s.o., an j-m vorbeigehen; (*b*) a quarter p. four, Viertel nach vier; *F:* to be p. it, zu alt dafür sein. II. *adv.* to walk/go p., vorbeigehen.

pasta ['pæstə], *s.* Teigwaren *fpl.* **paste** [peist]. I. *s.* 1. (*for sticking paper etc.*) Kleister *m.* II. *v.tr.* to p. sth. in/on sth., etwas in/auf etwas *acc* festkleben.

pastel ['pæst(ə)l], p. shades, Pastelltöne *mpl.* **pasteurize** ['pɑːstjəraiz], *v.tr.* (Milch) pasteurisieren.

pastime ['pɑːstaim], *s.* Zeitvertreib *m.* **pastor** ['pɑːstər], *s. Ecc:* Pastor *m.* ◆**pastoral,** *adj. Art:* p. scene, ländliche Szene.

pastry ['peistri], *s.* 1. (*dough*) Teig *m.* 2. (*cake*) Gebäck *n.* **pasture** ['pɑːstjər], *s.* Weide *f.* **pasty¹** ['pɑːsti], *F:* to look p., käseweiß sein. **pasty²** ['pæsti], *s. Cu:* Pastete *f.*

pat [pæt]. I. *s.* 1. Klaps *m.* 2. p. of butter, Stückchen *n* Butter. II. *v.tr.* (j-n, ein Tier) tätscheln. III. *adv.* to have an answer off p., eine Antwort parat haben. **patch** [pætʃ]. I. *s.* 1. (*for repair*) Flicken *m.* 2. (*small area*) (*a*) Fleck *m;* (*b*) (*land*) (kleines) Stück *m.* 3. (*on eye*) Augenklappe *f.* II. *v.tr.* (ein Kleid, einen Reifen usw.) flicken; *F:* to p. it up with s.o., sich wieder aussöhnen (mit j-m). ◆**patchy,** *adj.* (*a*) fleckig; p. fog, strichweise Nebel; (*b*) *Fig:* (*uneven*) ungleichmäßig; (*of knowledge etc.*) lückenhaft.

pâté ['pætei], *s.* Pastete *f.* **patent** ['pætənt, 'peitənt]. I. *adj.* 1. p.

medicine, Markenpräparat n; **p. leather**, Lackleder n. 2. (obvious) offensichtlich; **-ly**, adv. offensichtlich. II. s. Patent n; **p. pending**, Patent angemeldet. III. v.tr. (eine Erfindung usw.) patentieren.

paternal [pə'tə:nl], adj. väterlich. ◆**pa'ternity**, s. Vaterschaft f.

path, pl. [pɑ:ðz], s. 1. Pfad m; esp. Fig: Weg m. 2. Bahn f (der Sonne, eines Planeten usw.).

pathetic [pə'θetik], adj. 1. mitleiderregend; **a p. sight**, ein rührender Anblick. 2. F: Pej: **p. effort**, ein kläglicher Versuch.

pathology [pə'θɔlədʒi], s. Pathologie m. ◆**pa'thologist**, s. Pathologe m.

pathos ['peiθɔs], s. **the p. of the situation**, das Rührende an der Situation.

patience ['peiʃ(ə)ns], s. 1. Geduld f. 2. (game) Patience f. ◆**'patient**. I. adj. geduldig; **to be p.**, Geduld haben. II. s. Med: Patient(in) m(f).

patriot ['peitriət, 'pæ-], s. Patriot(in) m(f). ◆**patri'otic**, adj. patriotisch. ◆**'patriotism**, s. Patriotismus m.

patrol [pə'trəul]. I. s. (a) Mil: etc: Patrouille f (b) (police) Streife f; **p. car**, Streifenwagen m. II. v. 1. v.i. auf Patrouille/(police) Streife gehen. 2. v.tr. patrouillieren.

patron ['peitrən], s. 1. (a) Förderer m (der Künste usw.); (b) Schirmherr m (einer Wohltätigkeitsveranstaltung usw.); (c) Ecc: **p. saint**, Schutzheilige(r) f(m). 2. Com: Th: Cin. Besucher m (eines Kinos usw.); Kunde m (eines Geschäfts). ◆**patronage** ['pætrənidʒ], s. Förderung f. ◆**patronize** ['pæ-], v.tr. **to p. s.o.**, j-n herablassend behandeln. ◆**patronizing**, adj. **p. tone**, herablassender Ton.

patter ['pætər]. I. v.i. (of feet) trappeln; (of rain, hail etc.) prasseln. II. s. Getrappel n; Prasseln n.

pattern ['pætən], s. Muster n.

paunch [pɔ:n(t)ʃ], s. Wanst m.

pause [pɔ:z]. I. s. Pause f. II. v.i. eine Pause machen; (in conversation) innehalten; (hesitate) zögern.

pave [peiv], v.tr. (eine Straße) pflastern; Fig: **to p. the way for s.o., sth.**, j-m, etwas den Weg bahnen. ◆**'pavement**, s. Bürgersteig m. ◆**'paving**, s. Pflaster n; **p. stone**, Pflastersteine m.

pavilion [pə'viljən], s. Sp: Klubhaus n.

paw [pɔ:]. I. s. Z: (also F:=hand) Pfote f. II. v.tr. (a) (of cat, dog etc.) mit den Pfoten stupsen; (b) F: (of pers.) betasten.

pawn¹ [pɔ:n], v.tr. (Wertsachen) verpfänden. ◆**'pawnbroker**, s. Pfandleiher m.

pawn², s. (in chess) Bauer m.

pay [pei]. I. v.irr. 1. v.tr. (a) bezahlen; (j-m eine Summe) zahlen; (b) **to p. attention to sth.**, etwas dat Aufmerksamkeit schenken; **p. attention!** aufpassen! **to p. s.o. the honour**, j-m die Ehre erweisen.

2. v.i. (a) (of pers.) zahlen, bezahlen; (b) (of thing) sich lohnen; **crime doesn't p.**, Verbrechen zahlt sich nicht aus. II. s. Lohn m; p. **packet**, Lohntüte f. ◆**'payable**, adj. zahlbar; **to become p.**, fällig werden. ◆**'pay 'back**, v.tr. zurückzahlen. ◆**'pay-day**, s. Zahltag m. ◆**'pay-ee**, s. Zahlungsempfänger m. ◆**'pay 'for**, v.tr. (etwas) bezahlen; F: **you'll p. for this!** das wird dir teuer zu stehen kommen! ◆**'pay 'in**, v.tr. (einen Scheck usw.) einzahlen (**into an account**, auf ein Konto). ◆**'payload**, s. Nutzlast f (eines Flugzeugs, eines Schiffs usw.). ◆**'payment**, s. (act, amount) Zahlung f; (of pers.) Bezahlung f. ◆**'pay 'off**, v. 1. v.tr. (Schulden usw.) abzahlen. 2. v.i. **it'll p. off in the end**, am Ende macht sich das bezahlt. ◆**'pay 'out**, v.tr. (Geld) ausgeben. ◆**'payroll**, s. Gehaltsliste f. ◆**'payslip**, s. Lohnzettel m. ◆**'pay 'up**, v.i. zahlen.

pea [pi:], s. Erbse f.

peace [pi:s], s. 1. Frieden m; (of country etc.) **at p.**, im Frieden (**with**, mit + dat). 2. Jur: **to keep the p.**, den öffentlichen Frieden aufrechterhalten. 3. **p. and quiet**, Ruhe f. ◆**'peaceful**, adj. friedlich. ◆**'peacefulness**, s. Friedlichkeit f. ◆**'peacetime**, s. Friedenszeiten fpl.

peach [pi:tʃ], s. Pfirsich m.

peacock ['pi:kɔk], s. Pfau m.

peak [pi:k]. I. s. 1. Schirm m (einer Mütze). 2. (a) Gipfel m (eines Berges usw.); Fig: Höhepunkt m; (b) attrib: Höchst-; **p. hours**, Stoßzeit f.

peal [pi:l]. I. s. 1. **p. of bells**, Glockengeläut n. 2. **p. of laughter**, Lachsalve f. II. v.i. (of bells) läuten.

peanut ['pi:nʌt], s. Erdnuß f.

pear [peər], s. Birne f.

pearl [pə:l], s. Perle f.

peasant ['pez(ə)nt], s. Bauer m.

peat [pi:t], s. Torf m.

pebble ['pebl], s. Kieselstein m. ◆**'pebbly**, adj. kiesig.

peck [pek], v.i. (of bird etc.) hacken (**at**, nach + dat). ◆**'peckish**, adj. F: **to feel (a bit) p.**, (ein bißchen) Appetit haben.

peculiar [pi'kju:liər], adj. 1. besondere(r,s). 2. (odd) eigenartig. ◆**pe'culi'arity**, s. 1. Besonderheit f. 2. (also pe'cularness) Eigenartigkeit f.

pedal ['pedl]. I. s. Pedal n. II. v.i. in die Pedale treten.

pedantic [pe'dæntik], adj. pedantisch.

peddle ['pedl], v. 1. v.i. hausieren. 2. v.tr. Pej: **to p. drugs etc.**, mit Drogen usw. handeln. ◆**'peddler/'pedlar**, s. Hausierer m.

pedestal ['pedist(ə)l], s. Sockel m; Fig: **to put s.o. on a p.**, j-n aufs Podest stellen.

pedestrian [pi'destriən]. I. adj. prosaisch; (unimaginative) einfallslos. II. s. Fußgänger m; **p. precinct**, Fußgängerzone f; **p. crossing**, Fuß-gängerübergang m.

pedigree ['pedigri], s. (a) Stammbaum m; (b) **p. dog**, Rassehund m.

peel [pi:l]. I. s. Schale f. II. v. 1. v.tr. (eine Frucht, Kartoffeln usw.) schälen. 2. v.i. (of paint etc.) abblättern; (of skin, nose etc.) sich schälen. ◆**'peeler**, s. potato p., Kartoffelschäler m. ◆**'peelings**, s.pl. Schalen fpl.

peep [pi:p]. I. s. (glance) verstohlener Blick m; F: to get a p. at sth., etwas kurz zu Gesicht bekommen. II. v.i. to p. at sth., etwas kurz angucken; to p. out, hervorgucken.

peer [piər], v.i. to p. over the wall, über die Mauer spähen.

peerage ['piːridʒ], s. Brit: (a) Peerswürde f; (b) Adelsstand m.

peeved [pi:vd], adj. verärgert.

peewit ['pi:wit], s. Kiebitz m.

peg [peg]. I. s. (a) (for tent etc.) Pflock m; (b) (hat, coat) p., Haken m; clothes p., Wäscheklammer f; Cl: off the p., von der Stange. II. v.tr. (etwas) anpflocken (to, an + acc).

pejorative [pi'dʒɔrətiv], adj. abwertend.

pelican ['pelikən], s. Pelikan m.

pellet ['pelit], s. 1. Kügelchen n. 2. (for gun) Schrotkugel f.

pelt [pelt]. I. s. 1. v.tr. (j-n) bewerfen (with stones, mit Steinen). 2. v.i. (of rain etc.) to p. (down), niederprasseln. II. s. (skin) Balg m.

pelvis ['pelvis], s. Becken n.

pen¹ [pen], s. (for sheep etc.) Pferch m.

pen², s. (for writing) Feder f; p. friend, Brieffreund(in) m(f).

penal ['pi:n(ə)l], adj. Straf-; p. code, Strafgesetzbuch n. ◆**'penalize**, v.tr. (punish) (j-n) bestrafen; Sp: Strafpunkte geben. ◆**penalty** ['pen(ə)lti], s. 1. Strafe f; to pay the p. (for sth.), (für etwas acc) büßen (müssen). 2. Fb: Elfmeter m.

penance ['penəns], s. Buße f; to do p., Buße tun.

pence [pens], s.pl. Pence mpl.

pencil ['pens(i)l], s. Bleistift m.

pending ['pendiŋ], prep. bis auf + acc; p. further instructions, bis auf weiteres.

pendulum ['pendjuləm], s. Pendel n.

penetrate ['penitreit], v.tr. & i. (in etwas acc) eindringen; (permeate) (etwas) durchdringen. ◆**'penetrating**, adj. durchdringend; (of pers.) scharfsinnig.

penguin ['peŋgwin], s. Pinguin m.

penicillin [peni'silin], s. Penizillin n.

peninsula [pi'ninsjulə], s. Halbinsel f.

penis ['pi:nis], s. Penis m.

penitence ['penit(ə)ns], s. Reue f. ◆**peni'tration**, s. Perforation f.

penknife, ['pennaif], s. Taschenmesser n.

penny ['peni], s. Penny m; Fig: he hasn't a p. to his name, er hat keinen Pfennig; the penny's dropped, der Groschen ist gefallen. ◆**'penniless**, adj. mittellos.

pension ['penʃ(ə)n]. I. s. Rente f; (from employer/fund) Pension f. II. v.tr. to p. s.o. off, j-n pensionieren. ◆**'pensionable**, adj. p. age, Pensionsalter n. ◆**'pensioner**, s. Pensionär(in)

m(f); (old-age) p., Rentner(in) m(f).

pensive ['pensiv], adj. nachdenklich.

pentagon ['pentəgən], s. Fünfeck n.

penthouse ['penthaus], s. Dachterrassenwohnung f.

penultimate [pən'Altimət], adj. vorletzte(r,s).

people ['pi:pl]. I. s. coll. (with pl. construction) 1. (a) Leute pl; (esp. with number) Menschen mpl; a thousand p., tausend Menschen; (b) (impers.) p. say, man sagt. 2. Pol: Volk n. II. v.tr. (ein Land usw.) bevölkern.

pep [pep], s. F: Schwung m; p. talk, anspornende Rede f.

pepper ['pepər], s. 1. Cu: Pfeffer m. 2. Bot: (green, red) p., (grüner, roter) Paprika m; (single fruit) Paprikaschote f. ◆**'peppercorn**, s. Pfefferkorn n. ◆**'peppermill**, s. Pfeffermühle f. ◆**'peppermint**, s. Pfefferminz(bonbon) n.

per [pər], prep. 1. (a) pro; ten pence p. pound, zehn Pence das Pfund; sixty kilometres p. hour, sechzig Kilometer in der Stunde. 2. gemäß + gen; as p. invoice, gemäß Rechnung.

perceive [pə'siːv], v.tr. Lit: wahrnehmen. ◆**per'ceptible**, adj. wahrnehmbar. ◆**per'ception**, s. 1. Wahrnehmung f. 2. (faculty) Auffassungsvermögen n. ◆**per'ceptive**, adj. aufmerksam; (astute) scharfsinnig; (understanding) einsichtig.

percentage [pə'sentidʒ], s. Prozentsatz m.

perch¹ [pəːtʃ]. I. s. (for birds) Vogelstange f. II. v.i. (a) (of birds etc.) sitzen; (b) the hut is perched on the mountainside, die Hütte liegt hoch am Berghang.

perch², s. (fish) Barsch m.

percolate ['pəːkəleit], v.i. (of liquid) durchsickern; (of coffee) durchlaufen. ◆**'percolator**, s. Kaffeemaschine f.

percussion [pə'kAʃ(ə)n], s. Mus: Schlagzeug n.

perennial [pə'renjəl]. I. adj. immer wiederkehrend. II. s. Bot: perennierende Pflanze f.

perfect. I. ['pəːfikt], adj. 1. (a) perfekt; (ideal) ideal; (b) F: (complete) völlig. 2. Gram: p. (tense) Perfekt n. II. [pə'fekt] v.tr. (eine Maschine usw.) perfektionieren; (Sprachkenntnisse usw.) vervollkommnen. ◆**per'fection**, s. Perfektion f.

perforate ['pəːfəreit], v.tr. perforieren. ◆**perfo'ration**, s. Perforation f.

perform [pə'fɔːm], v. 1. v.tr. (a) (eine Bewegung) ausführen; (einen Dienst) leisten; (eine Aufgabe, eine Pflicht) erfüllen; (b) Th: Mus: aufführen; Th: (eine Rolle) spielen; Mus: (ein Lied usw.) vortragen. 2. v.i. (a) (of actor) spielen; (b) (of machine) funktionieren. ◆**per'formance**, s. 1. Leistung f (eines Arbeiters, eines Sportlers, einer Maschine usw.). 2. Th: Mus: Aufführung f; Th:

Vorstellung f. ◆**per'former,** s. Th: etc: Darsteller(in) m(f).

perfume, s. ['pə:fju:m] Parfüm n.

perfunctory [pə'fʌŋkt(ə)ri], adj. flüchtig.

perhaps [pə'hæps, præps], adv. vielleicht.

peril ['peril], s. Gefahr f.; **at your p.,** auf eigene Gefahr. ◆**'perilous,** adj. gefährlich.

perimeter [pə'rimitər], s. Umgrenzung f.

period ['piəriəd], s. **1.** (time) (a) Zeitraum m, Zeitspanne f; (fixed) Frist f; (b) Sch: Schulstunde f. **2.** Epoche f; Art: etc: Periode f. **3.** Gram: Punkt m. **4.** Med: (monatliche) Regel f (einer Frau). ◆**peri'odical. I.** adj. (also **peri'odic**) periodisch; **-ly,** adv. von Zeit zu Zeit. **II.** s. (publication) Zeitschrift f.

periscope ['periskəup], s. Periskop n.

perish ['periʃ], v.i. (a) A: (die) umkommen; (b) (of goods etc.) verderben; (of rubber) altern. ◆**'perishable,** adj. (of goods etc.) leicht verderblich. ◆**'perishing,** adj. F: it's p., es ist saukalt.

perjure ['pə:dʒər], v.tr. Jur: **to p.** oneself, einen Meineid leisten. ◆**'perjury,** s. Meineid m.

perk [pə:k]. **I.** s. F: Vorteil m (in einer Stellung). **II.** v.i. F: **to p. (up),** wieder aufleben.

perm [pə:m], s. F: Dauerwelle f.

permanent ['pə:mənənt], adj. (a) (lasting) bleibend; esp. Tchn: Dauer-; **p. address,** ständiger Wohnsitz; (constant) (of fear etc.) ständig; **-ly,** adv. auf immer (und ewig); **p. employed,** fest angestellt. ◆**'permanence,** s. Dauerhaftigkeit f.

permeate ['pə:mieit], v.tr. & i. **to p. (through) sth.,** (of moisture, flavour) in etwas acc einziehen.

permissible [pə'misibl], adj. zulässig. ◆**per'mission,** s. Erlaubnis f. ◆**per'missive** adj. **p. society,** permissive Gesellschaft.

permit. I. ['pə:mit] v.tr. (j-m etwas) erlauben. **II.** ['pə:mit] s. Genehmigung f; **work p.,** Arbeitserlaubnis f.

pernicious [pə'niʃəs], adj. schädlich. ◆**per'nickety** [pə'nikiti], adj. F: pingelig.

perpendicular [pə:pən'dikjulər], adj. Mth: senkrecht (**to,** zu + dat).

perpetrate ['pə:pitreit], v.tr. (ein Verbrechen usw.) begehen. ◆**'perpetrator,** s. Täter m.

perpetual [pə'petjuəl], adj. ewig; (unending) endlos; (not stopping) unaufhörlich. ◆**per'petuate,** v.tr. (eine Lage usw.) fortbestehen lassen.

perplex [pə'pleks], v.tr. (j-n) verblüffen. ◆**per'plexed,** adj. (of pers.) perplex, verblüfft. ◆**per'plexing,** adj. verblüffend.

persecute ['pə:sikju:t], v.tr. (j-n) verfolgen. ◆**perse'cution,** s. Verfolgung f. ◆**'persecutor,** s. Verfolger m.

persevere [pə:si'viər], v.i. durchhalten; **to p. with sth.,** mit etwas dat (beharrlich) weitermachen. ◆**perse'verance,** s. Ausdauer f.

Persia ['pə:ʃə]. Pr. n. Persien n. ◆**'Persian. I.** adj. persisch. **II.** s. Perser(in) m(f).

persist [pə'sist], v.i. (a) (of pers.) **to p. in sth.,** auf etwas dat beharren; (b) (of condition etc.) anhalten. ◆**per'sistence,** s. **1.** (of pers.) Beharrlichkeit f. **2.** Anhalten n (des Fiebers usw.). ◆**per'sistent,** adj. **1.** (of rain, fever) anhaltend. **2.** (of pers.) beharrlich; (obstinate) hartnäckig; (importunate) aufdringlich.

person ['pə:s(ə)n], s. Person f; **in p.,** persönlich. ◆**'personable,** adj. (of pers.) gutaussehend. ◆**'personage,** s. Persönlichkeit f. ◆**'personal,** adj. persönlich; **-ly,** adv. persönlich. ◆**perso'nality,** s. Persönlichkeit f. ◆**personifi'cation,** s. Verkörperung f. ◆**per'sonify,** v.tr. (etwas) verkörpern; **he was innocence personified,** er war die Unschuld in Person. ◆**perso'nnel,** s. Personal n.

perspective [pə'spektiv], s. Perspektive f.

perspire [pə'spaiər], v.i. schwitzen. ◆**perspiration** [pə:spi'reiʃ(ə)n], s. (sweat) Schweiß m.

persuade [pə'sweid], v.tr. (a) **to p. s.o. of sth.,** j-u von etwas dat überzeugen; (b) **to p. s.o. to do sth.,** j-n überreden, etwas zu tun; **he persuaded me not to,** er redete es mir aus. ◆**per'suasion,** s. (a) Überredung f; (powers of) p., Überredungskünste fpl; (b) (conviction) Überzeugung f. ◆**per'suasive,** adj. überzeugend.

pertinent ['pə:tinənt], adj. (of remark) zur Sache; (of literature etc.) einschlägig.

perturb [pə'tə:b], v.tr. (j-n) beunruhigen.

Peru [pə'ru:]. Pr. n. Peru n. ◆**Pe'ruvian. I.** adj. peruanisch. **II.** s. Peruaner(in) m(f).

peruse [pə'ru:z], v.tr. (ein Buch usw.) durchlesen.

pervade [pə'veid], v.tr. (durch etwas acc) durchdringen. ◆**per'vasive,** adj. durchdringend.

perverse [pə'və:s], adj. (of pers., idea etc.) pervers. ◆**per'versity,** s. Perversität f. ◆**per'version,** s. Perversion f. ◆**pervert. I.** [pə'və:t] v.tr. (j-n) pervertieren; (etwas) entstellen. **II.** ['pə:və:t] s. Perverse(r) f(m).

pessimism ['pesimizm], s. Pessimismus m. ◆**'pessimist,** s. Pessimist(in) m(f). ◆**pessi'mistic,** adj. pessimistisch.

pest [pest], s. (nuisance) Plage f; (child, animal etc.) Quälgeist m. ◆**'pester,** v.tr. (j-n) belästigen. ◆**'pesticide,** s. Schädlingsbekämpfungsmittel n.

pet [pet]. **I.** s. **1.** (a) Haustier n; **to have a p. rabbit,** ein Kaninchen als Haustier halten; (b) (child) Engel m. **2.** attrib. (favourite) Lieblings-. **II.** v.tr. streicheln. ◆**'petting,** s. Petting n.

petal ['pet(ə)l], s. Bot: Blütenblatt n.

peter ['pi:tər], v.i. to p. out, sich im Sande verlaufen.

petition [pi'tiʃ(ə)n], s. Jur: etc: Gesuch n; p. for divorce, Scheidungsklage f.

petrify ['petrifai], v.tr. (a) (etwas) versteinern; (b) (terrify) (j-n) entsetzen; I was petrified, ich war starr vor Entsetzen.

petrol ['petr(ə)l], s. Benzin n; p. station, Tankstelle f.

petticoat ['petikəut], s. Unterrock m.

petty ['peti], adj. 1. (a) geringfügig; p. theft, Bagatelldiebstahl m; (b) p. (-minded), kleinlich. 2. Com: p. cash, Kleingeld n. 3. Nau: p. officer, Bootsmann m. ◆**'pettiness**, s. Kleinlichkeit f.

petulant ['petjulənt], adj. launisch; (irritated) gereizt.

pew [pju:], s. Kirchenbank f.

pewter ['pju:tər], s. Zinn n.

phantom ['fæntəm], s. Phantom n.

pharmaceutical [fɑ:mə'sju:tik(ə)l], adj. pharmazeutisch. ◆**pharmacist**, s. Pharmazeut m. ◆**'pharmacy**, s. Pharmazie f; (shop) Apotheke f.

phase [feiz]. I. s. Phase f. II. v.tr. esp. Com: to p. out a model etc., ein Modell usw. auslaufen lassen.

pheasant ['feznt], s. Fasan m.

phenomenon, pl. **-ena** [fi'nɔminən, -inə], s. (everyday) Erscheinung f; (remarkable) Phänomen n. ◆**phe'nomenal**, adj. phänomenal.

philanthropy [fi'lænθrəpi], s. Philanthropie f. ◆**phi'lanthropist**, s. Menschenfreund m.

philately [fi'lætəli], s. Philatelie f. ◆**phi'latelist**, s. Philatelist m.

Philippines ['filipi:nz]. Pr. n. the P., die Philippinen fpl.

philology [fi'lɔlədʒi], s. Philologie f.

philosopher [fi'lɔsəfər], s. Philosoph m. ◆**philo'sophical**, adj. philosophisch. 2. Fig: (of pers.) gelassen. ◆**phi'losophy**, s. Philosophie f.

phobia ['fəubjə], s. Phobie f.

phone [fəun]. I. s. Tel: Telefon n. II. v.tr. & i. anrufen.

phonetic [fə'netik], adj. phonetisch. ◆**pho'netics**, s.pl. (sing. constr.) Phonetik f.

phoney ['fəuni], adj. F: unecht; (forged) gefälscht.

phosphorus ['fɔsf(ə)rəs], s. Phosphor m.

photo ['fəutəu]. I. s. F: Foto n. II. comb. fm. Foto-, foto-. ◆**'photocopier**, s. Fotokopiergerät n. ◆**'photocopy.** I. s. Fotokopie f. II. v.tr. (etwas) fotokopieren. ◆**photogenic** [-'dʒi:nik], adj. fotogen. ◆**photograph.** I. s. Fotografie f; to take a p., eine Aufnahme machen. II. v.tr. fotografieren. ◆**photographer** [fə'tɔgrəfər], s. Fotograf m. ◆**photographic** [-'græfik], adj. fotografisch. ◆**photography** [fə'tɔgrəfi], s. Fotografie f.

phrase [freiz]. I. s. Ausdruck m; set p., Redewendung f; turn of p., Ausdrucksweise f. II. v.tr. (etwas) in Worte fassen, formulieren.

physical ['fizik(ə)l], adj. (a) Ph: physikalisch; (b) physisch; (bodily) körperlich; p. training Leibesübungen fpl. -ly, adv. (a) physikalisch; (b) physisch; p. impossible, praktisch unmöglich; p. handicapped, körperbehindert. ◆**physician** [fi'ziʃ(ə)n], s. Arzt m, Ärztin f. ◆**physics** ['fiziks], s.pl. (sing. constr.) Physik f. ◆**'physicist**, s. Physiker(in) m(f).

physiognomy [fizi'ɔnəmi], s. Physiognomie f.

physiological [fiziəu'lɔdʒikəl], adj. physiologisch.

physiotherapy [fiziəu'θerəpi], s. Krankengymnastik f. ◆**'physio'therapist**, s. Krankengymnast(in) m(f).

physique [fi'zi:k], s. Körperbau m.

piano, pl. **-os** ['piænəu, -əuz], s. Klavier n; grand p., Konzertflügel m. ◆**pianist** ['pi:ənist], s. Pianist(in) m(f).

pick [pik]. I. v.tr. & i. (a) (choose) (j-n, etwas) auswählen; to p. and choose, wählerisch sein; to p. a quarrel, Streit suchen; (b) (Blumen, Obst usw.) pflücken; (lift) aufheben (off, von + dat); (c) to p. at one's food, im Essen herumstochern; to p. one's nose, in der Nase bohren; Fig: I've a bone to p. with you, mit dir habe ich noch ein Hühnchen zu rupfen; (d) to p. a lock, ein Schloß knacken. II. s. 1. Spitzhacke f. 2. (thing) das Beste. ◆**'pickaxe**, s. Spitzhacke f. ◆**'pick on**, v.tr. sich dat (j-n) aufs Korn nehmen. ◆**'pick 'out**, v.tr. (select) (j-n, etwas) aussuchen. ◆**'pickpocket**, s. Taschendieb(in) m(f). ◆**'pick 'up**, v. 1. v.tr. (a) (etwas) (vom Boden) aufheben; (b) (collect) (eine Warensendung usw.) abholen; to p. s.o. up, (i) j-n (im Auto) mitnehmen/(fetch) abholen; (ii) F: j-n aufgabeln; (c) Rad: (Signale usw.) auffangen; (d) (learn) (eine Sprache, Ausdrücke usw.) lernen; (e) (of vehicle) to p. up speed, beschleunigen. 2. v.i. (of pers.) (wieder) zu Kräften kommen; business is picking up, das Geschäft erholt sich. ◆**'pick-up**, s. 1. F: (pers.) Gelegenheitsbekanntschaft f; (prostitute) Flittchen n. 2. (collection) Abholung f. 3. Rec: Tonabnehmer m.

picket ['pikit]. I. s. Ind: (strike) p., Streikposten m. II. v.tr. & i. Ind: to p. (a factory etc.), (vor einer Fabrik usw.) Streikposten stehen.

pickle ['pikl]. I. s. Marinade f. II. v.tr. (Gurken, Zwiebeln, Fisch usw.) einlegen; (Fleisch) pökeln.

picnic ['piknik]. I. s. Picknick n. II. v.i. picknicken.

picture ['piktʃər]. I. s. (a) Bild n; (painting) Gemälde n; he's the p. of health, er strotzt vor Gesundheit; Fig: to be in the p., im Bilde sein; (b) Cin: Film m; to go

to the pictures, ins Kino gehen. II. v.tr. (imagine) sich dat (j-n, etwas) vorstellen. ◆**pictu'resque,** adj. malerisch.
pie [pai], s. Pastete f; p. crust, Kruste f.
piebald ['paibɔ:ld], adj. gescheckt.
piece [pi:s]. I. s. 1. Stück n; a p. of news, eine Neuigkeit; a p. of information, eine Information; a p. of furniture, ein Möbelstück; Fig: I gave him a p. of my mind, ich habe ihm gehörig die Meinung gesagt. 2. (part) Teil m & n; in pieces, zerlegt; (broken) zerbrochen; to take sth. to pieces, etwas auseinandernehmen/zerlegen; to come to pieces, (i) zerlegbar sein; (ii) (fall apart) auseinanderfallen; Fig: she went to pieces, sie brach zusammen. 3. (a) (coin) Münze f; 50p p., 50-Pence-Stück n; (b) (in chess) Figur f. II. v.tr. **to p. together,** zusammenstückeln. ◆**piecemeal,** adv. stückweise.
pier [piər], s. 1. (a) Brit: Pier m; (b) (landing) p., Landungsbrücke f; 2. Civ.E: Pfeiler m (einer Brücke usw.).
pierce [piəs], v.tr. (a) (enter) (in etwas acc) hineinstechen; (b) (go through) (etwas) durchstechen; (of light) to p. the darkness, die Dunkelheit durchdringen. ◆**'piercing,** adj. (of scream etc.) durchdringend.
piety ['paiəti], s. Frömmigkeit f.
pig [pig], s. Schwein n. ◆**'piggy-bank,** s. Sparschwein n. ◆**'pig'headed,** adj. F: störrisch. ◆**'piglet,** s. Ferkel n. ◆**'pigsty,** s. Schweinestall m. ◆**'pigtail,** s. Zopf m.
pigeon ['pidʒin], s. Taube f. ◆**'pigeonhole,** s. Brieffach n.
pigment ['pigmənt], s. Pigment n.
pike [paik], s. Hecht m.
pile¹ [pail], s. (for building) Pfahl m.
pile² [pail]. I. s. Haufen m; (tidy) Stapel m. II. v. 1. v.tr. to p. up, (Holz) aufschichten; (Bücher, Kisten) stapeln; (amass) (Vermögen usw.) anhäufen. 2. v.i. to p. up, sich häufen. ◆**'pile-up,** s. Aut: F: Karambolage f.
pile³, s. (of velvet, carpet etc.) Flor m.
piles [pailz], s.pl. Med: Hämorrhoiden fpl.
pilfer ['pilfər], v.tr. (etwas) stehlen, F: klauen.
pilgrim ['pilgrim], s. Pilger m. ◆**'pilgrimage,** s. Pilgerfahrt f.
pill [pil], s. Pille f; (sugar-coated) Dragée n; F: to be on the p., die Pille nehmen.
pillage ['pilidʒ], v.tr. & i. plündern.
pillar ['pilər], s. Pfeiler m; (round) Säule f; Fig: (pers.) a p. of society, eine Stütze der Gesellschaft. ◆**'pillar-box,** s. Briefkasten m.
pillion ['piliən], s. Soziussitz m; p. passenger, Soziusfahrer(in) m(f).
pillow ['piləu], s. Kopfkissen n; p.-case, Kopfkissenbezug m.
pilot ['pailət]. I. s. 1. (a) Av: Pilot(in) m(f); (b) Nau: Lotse m. 2. p. light, (gas)

Zündflamme f. 3. p. scheme, Modellversuch m; p. study, Pilotstudie f. II. v.tr. (a) Av: (ein Flugzeug) führen; (b) Nau: (ein Schiff, Fig: j-n) lotsen.
pimento [pi'mentəu], s. Piment m & n.
pimp [pimp], s. Zuhälter m.
pimple ['pimpl], s. Pickel m.
pin [pin]. I. s. 1. (Steck)nadel f; p. cushion, Nadelkissen n; I have pins and needles, mir kribbelt es. 2. Sp: (in bowling) Kegel m. II. v.tr. (a) (etwas) mit einer Nadel heften; (b) to p. one's hope on sth., seine Hoffnung auf etwas acc setzen; (b) (j-n) (an Boden, gegen die Wand usw.) festhalten; Fig: to p. s.o. down, (j-n) auf ein Angebot usw.) festnageln. ◆**'pinpoint,** v.tr. (a) (ein Flugzeug usw.) genau orten; (b) (etwas) genau feststellen. ◆**'pinprick,** s. Nadelstich m. ◆**'pinstripe,** s. Nadelstreifen m.
pinafore ['pinəfɔ:r], s. p. (dress), Trägerrock m.
pincer ['pinsər], s. (a) pair of pincers, Kneifzange f; (b) Z: Schere f.
pinch [pin(t)ʃ]. I. v.tr. (a) (j-n) kneifen; (abs. (of shoe) drücken; (b) F: (steal) (etwas) klauen. 2. (a) Kneifen n; Fig: at a p., im Notfall; (b) a p. (of salt etc.), eine Prise (Salz usw.); Fig: to take sth. with a p. of salt, etwas nicht für bare Münze nehmen.
pine¹ [pain], s. p.(-tree), Kiefer f; p. cone, Kienapfel m.
pine², v.i. to p. away, sich (vor Leid usw.) verzehren; to p. for s.o., sth., sich nach j-m, etwas dat sehnen.
pineapple ['painæpl], s. Ananas f.
pink [piŋk], adj. rosa inv.
pinnacle ['pinəkl], s. 1. (summit) Gipfel m; (rock) Felsnadel f. 2. Arch: Spitzturm m.
pint [paint], s. Meas: Pint m (Brit: 0·568 Liter); a p. of beer, approx. eine Halbe (Bier).
pioneer [paiə'niər], s. Pionier m.
pious ['paiəs], adj. fromm.
pip [pip], s. (in fruit) Obstkern m.
pipe [paip]. I. s. 1. (for liquid, gas) Rohr n; (mains) Leitung f; burst p., Rohrbruch m. 2. Mus: Pfeife f; pl. (bag)pipes, Dudelsack m. 3. (for tobacco) Pfeife f; p. dream, Wunschtraum m. II. v.tr. (Wasser, Gas usw.) durch Rohre leiten. ◆**'pipeline,** s. Pipeline f. ◆**'piping,** adj. p. hot, kochend heiß.
piquant ['pi:kənt], adj. pikant.
pique [pi:k], s.; in a fit of p., pikiert.
pirate ['paiərət]. I. s. Pirat m. II. adj. Rad: p. station, Piratensender m; (book etc.) pirate(d) edition, Raubdruck m. ◆**'piracy,** s. Piraterie f.
Pisces ['paisi:z], s.pl. Astr: Fische mpl.
piss [pis], s.; in V: Pisse f. II. v.i. V: pissen; p. off! hau ab! ◆**'pissed,** adj. P: stockbesoffen.
pistachio [pis'ta:ʃiəu], s. Pistazie f.
pistol ['pist(ə)l], s. Pistole f.

piston ['pistən], s. Kolben m.

pit [pit]. **I.** s. (hole in ground, mine) Grube f; Th: etc: **orchestra** p., Orchesterraum m. **II.** v.tr. to p. one's wits, strength etc. against s.o., seinen Geist, seine Kraft usw. mit j-m messen. ◆'**pitted**, adj. (of metal) angefressen; (of skin) narbig.

pitch[1] [pitʃ], s. Pech n; p. **black**, pechschwarz; **it is p. dark**, es ist stockdunkel.

pitch[2]. **I.** v. 1. v.tr. (a) (ein Zelt, Lager) aufschlagen; **pitched battle**, F: regelrechte Schlacht; (b) Sp: (einen Ball usw.) schleudern. 2. v.i. F: **to p. into sth.**, sich über etwas acc hermachen. **II.** s. 1. (a) Mus: (of voice) Tonhöhe f (einer Stimme); Tonlage f (eines Instruments); (b) Fig: (degree) Grad m. 2. (throw) Wurf m. 3. Sp: Spielfeld n; **football** p., Fußballfeld n. 4. (slope) Gefälle n (eines Daches usw.). ◆'**pitchfork**, s. Heugabel f.

piteous ['pitiəs], adj. kläglich.

pitfall ['pitfɔ:l], s. esp. Fig: Falle f.

pith [piθ], s. das Weiße (einer Orangenschale). ◆'**pithy**, adj. (of style) markig.

pittance ['pitəns], s. Hungerlohn m.

pity ['piti]. **I.** s. (a) Mitleid n; **to take/ have p. on s.o., sth.**, mit j-m, etwas dat Erbarmen haben; **to feel p. for s.o.**, Mitleid mit j-m haben; (b) **what a p.!** wie schade! **II.** v.tr. (j-n) bedauern. ◆'**pitiful**, adj. (a) (of pers.) jämmerlich; **it's p. to see him**, es jammert einen, wenn man ihn sieht; (b) Pej: kläglich.

pivot ['pivət]. **I.** s. Drehpunkt m. **II.** v.i. sich drehen (**on an axis**, um eine Achse).

placard ['plækɑ:d], s. Plakat n.

placate [plə'keit], v.tr. (j-n) beschwichtigen.

place [pleis]. **I.** s. 1. (a) (village, town) Ort m; (small town) Ortschaft f; **the most expensive hotel in the p.**, das teuerste Hotel am Ort; (b) F: (restaurant etc.) Lokal n; F: **at our p.**, bei uns zu Hause; (c) **p. of business**, Geschäftssitz m; Adm: **p. of residence**, Wohnsitz m. 2. (a) Pl: Bücher liegen überall herum; **out of p.**, fehl am Platze; (b) (square) Platz m. 3. (seat at table etc.) Platz m; **p. mat**, Set m & n; **to change places with s.o.**, mit j-m den Platz tauschen. 4. (position) (a) Mth: Stelle f; **in your p.**, an deiner Stelle; **in (the) p. of ...**, anstelle von ... dat; (b) **he knows his p.**, er weiß, wo er hingehört; (c) Sp: **in first/second p.**, auf dem ersten/zweiten Platz. **II.** v.tr. (etwas) stellen, legen (**on, in etc.**, auf, in usw. + acc); **to p. an order**, einen Auftrag erteilen; **to be well placed**, (well able) gut imstande sein (**to ..., zu ...**); Sp: **to be placed**, sich plazieren.

placid ['plæsid], adj. (of pers.) gelassen; (of child) friedlich.

plagiarism ['pleidʒiərizm], s. Plagiat n.

plague [pleig]. **I.** s. 1. (nuisance) Plage f.

2. Med: Pest f. **II.** v.tr. (j-n) plagen.

plaice [pleis], s. Scholle f.

plain [plein]. **I.** adj. 1. (clear) klar, deutlich; **it's as p. as day** es liegt auf der Hand/ist sonnenklar; **p. speaking**, unverblümte Worte. 2. (simple) (a) (of style, dress etc.) einfach, schlicht; **p. truth**, ungeschminkte Wahrheit; (b) (of material etc.) einfarbig; (c) **p. chocolate**, Bitterschokolade f. 3. (of pers.) unansehnlich; **-ly**, adv. klar; (obviously) offensichtlich; **I can see it p.**, ich sehe es genau. **II.** s. Geog: etc: Ebene f. ◆'**plain-'clothes**, adj. **p.-c. policeman**, Polizeibeamter m in Zivil. ◆'**plainness**, s. (of pers.) unvorteilhaftes Aussehen n; (b) Einfachheit f, Schlichtheit f.

plaintiff ['pleintif], s. Kläger(in) m(f).

plaintive ['pleintiv], adj. klagend.

plait [plæt]. **I.** s. Zopf m. **II.** v.tr. (Haare usw.) flechten.

plan [plæn]. **I.** s. 1. Plan m; (of building) Grundriß m; **according to p.**, planmäßig/nach Plan. **II.** v.tr. (etwas) planen; **to p. to do sth.**, vorhaben, etwas zu tun. ◆'**planning**, s. Planung f; **p. permission**, Baugenehmigung f.

plane[1] [plein], s. Mth: etc: Ebene f.

plane[2]. **I.** s. Tchn: Hobel m. **II.** v.tr. (Holz) hobeln.

plane[3], s. **p.(-tree)**, Platane f.

plane[4], s. Av: F: Flugzeug n.

planet ['plænit], s. Planet m.

plank [plæŋk], s. Planke f.

plant [plɑ:nt]. **I.** s. 1. Pflanze f. 2. Ind: (factory) Werk n; (b) (machinery) Maschinen fpl. **II.** v.tr. (a) pflanzen; (etwas) (b) **to p. a bomb**, eine Bombe legen. ◆'**plan'tation**, s. Plantage f.

plaque [plɑ:k, plæk], s. 1. (tablet) Gedenktafel f. 2. (on teeth) Zahnbelag m.

plaster ['plɑ:stər]. **I.** s. 1. Med: sticking p., Klebe(e)pflaster n. 2. (a) Arch: Putz m; (b) Med: **p.** (of paris), Gips m; **his leg is in p.**, sein Bein ist in Gips/in einem Gipsverband. **II.** v.tr. (a) Arch: (eine Wand, Decke usw.) verputzen; (b) (cover) bedecken; (c) P: plastered, besoffen. ◆'**plasterer**, s. Arch: etc: Gipser m.

plastic ['plæstik]. **I.** adj. 1. Med: **p. surgery**, plastische Chirurgie f. 2. Plastik-; **p. cup**, Plastiktasse f. 3. Kunststoff m, esp. Plastik n.

plate [pleit]. **I.** s. 1. (for food) Teller m; F: **he has a lot on his p.**, er hat viel um die Ohren. 2. (sheet of metal etc.) (a) Platte f; **p. glass**, Schaufensterglas n; (b) (with name etc.) Schild n; Aut: (number) p., Nummernschild n. 3. (book illustration) Bildtafel f. **II.** v.tr. (chromium) (etwas) verchromen; (silver) (etwas) versilbern. ◆'**plateful**, s. Tellervoll m. ◆'**plating**, s. silver p., Versilberung f.

plateau, pl. **-x, -s** ['plætəu, -z], s. Plateau n.

platform ['plætfɔ:m], s. 1. (a) (for speaker) Podium n; (stage) Bühne f; **drilling**

p., Bohrinsel f; (b) Rail: Bahnsteig m.

platinum ['plætinəm], s. Platin n.

platitude ['plætitjuːd], s. Gemeinplatz m.

platoon [plə'tuːn], s. Mil: Zug m.

plausible ['plɔːzibl], adj. (a) (of theory) plausibel; p. **explanation**, glaubwürdige Erklärung; (b) (of pers.) überzeugend.

play [plei]. I. s. 1. Spiel n; p. on words, Wortspiel n; Sp: p. **began at one o'clock**, das Spiel begann um ein Uhr. 2. Th: Stück n. II. v. tr. & i. spielen; to p. **safe**, sichergehen. ◆'play 'at, v.tr. (a) (Karten usw.) spielen; (b) F: **what are they playing at?** was treiben denn die da? ◆'play 'back, v.tr. (ein Tonband) überspielen. ◆'play 'down, v.tr. bagatellisieren. ◆'player, s. Spieler m. ◆'playful, adj. (of pers.) zum Spielen aufgelegt; (of kitten, child) verspielt; (of remark) neckend. ◆'playground, s. Spielplatz m; Sch: Schulhof m. ◆'plaything, s. Spielzeug n. ◆'play 'up, v.i. (give trouble) Mätzchen machen. ◆'playwright, s. Dramatiker m.

plea [pliː], s. 1. Jur: Bekenntnis f (of guilty, zur Schuld). 2. (request) Bitte f; p. **for mercy**, Gnadengesuch n.

plead [pliːd], v. 1. v.i. (a) Jur: (of barrister) plädieren (for s.o., für j-n); (of prisoner) to p. **guilty/not guilty**, sich schuldig/nicht schuldig bekennen; to p. **with s.o.**, j-n anflehen; to p. **for mercy**, um Gnade bitten. 2. to p. **ignorance**, sich auf Unwissenheit berufen.

pleasant ['plez(ə)nt], adj. angenehm; (of pers.) freundlich, F: nett.

please [pliːz], v.tr. (a) (j-m) gefallen; (satisfy) (j-n) zufriedenstellen; p. **yourself!** (ganz) wie Sie wünschen/wollen! (b) bitte; p. **tell me ...**, bitte sagen Sie mir ...; may I?—do! darf ich?—bitte sehr! ◆'pleased, adj. erfreut; (satisfied) zufrieden (with, mit + dat); he's very p. **about it**, er freut sich darüber; I'm p. **to see you**, es freut mich, Sie zu sehen. ◆'pleasing, adj. angenehm; (of result etc.) erfreulich. ◆'pleasure ['pleʒər], s. Vergnügen n; pl Freuden fpl; with p., gern.

pleat [pliːt]. I. s. Cl: etc: Falte f. II. v.tr. (einen Rock, Stoff usw.) in Falten legen; **pleated skirt**, Faltenrock m.

pledge [pledʒ]. I. s. (promise) Versprechen n. II. v.tr. **pledged to do sth.**, verpflichtet, etwas zu tun.

plenty ['plenti], s. Überfluß m; p. **of time/shirts**, reichlich Zeit/viele Hemden; there's p. **more**, es ist noch viel übrig; five will be p., fünf sind mehr als genug. ◆'plentiful, adj. reichlich vorhanden.

pliable ['plaiəbl], adj. biegsam.

pliers ['plaiəz], s.pl. Zange f.

plight [plait], s. Notlage f.

plinth [plinθ], s. Arch: Plinthe f.

plod [plɔd], v.i. schwerfällig gehen; to p. **on**, mühsam weitermachen.

plonk[1] [plɔŋk], v.tr. F: (etwas) hinpflan-

zen.

plonk[2], s. F: Gesöff n, esp. billiger Wein m.

plot [plɔt]. I. s. 1. (kleines) Grundstück n. 2. Handlung f (eines Romans usw.). 3. (conspiracy) Verschwörung f. II. v. 1. v.tr. (a) Mth: (eine Kurve usw.) konstruieren; graphisch darstellen; to p. a **course**, einen Kurs abstecken; (b) (plan) (einen Mord usw.) planen. 2. v.i. to p. **against s.o., sth.**, gegen j-n, etwas intrigieren.

plough [plau]. I. s. Pflug m. II. v.tr. (a) (einen Acker) pflügen; (b) F: to p. **through a book etc.**, ein Buch usw. durchackern.

ploy [plɔi], s. F: Trick m.

pluck [plʌk], v.tr. (a) (Geflügel) rupfen; (Augenbrauen) (aus)zupfen; Mus: (eine Saite usw.) zupfen; (b) Lit: (Früchte, Blumen) pflücken. ◆'pluck 'up, v.tr. to p. **up (one's) courage**, sich dat ein Herz fassen.

plug [plʌg]. I. s. 1. (in basin etc.) Stöpsel m. 2. (a) El: Stecker m; (b) Aut: (spark) p., Zündkerze f. II. v. 1. v.tr. (a) (ein Loch) zustopfen; (b) Com: F: to p. a **product**, die Werbetrommel für ein Produkt rühren; (c) to p. **in the TV**, den Fernseher einstecken. 2. v.i. to p. **away**, sich abplagen (at sth., mit etwas dat).

plum [plʌm], s. Pflaume f.

plumage ['pluːmidʒ], s. Gefieder n.

plumb [plʌm]. I. s. p. **line**, Lotleine f. II. adv: p. **in the middle**, genau in der Mitte. ◆'plumber, s. Installateur m. ◆'plumbing, s. Rohrleitungen fpl (in einem Haus).

plump [plʌmp]. I. adj. (of child, woman) mollig; (of man, woman) rundlich; (of chicken, arm etc.) fleischig. II. v.i. F: to p. **for s.o., sth.**, sich für j-n, etwas acc entscheiden.

plunder ['plʌndər]. I. s. (booty) Beute f. II. v.tr. (eine Stadt usw.) plündern.

plunge [plʌn(d)ʒ]. I. v. 1. v.tr. (etwas ins Wasser usw.) tauchen; **plunged into darkness**, in Dunkelheit getaucht. 2. v.i. (a) (ins Wasser usw.) tauchen, Fig: sich (in ein Abenteuer usw.) stürzen; (c) (drop) (of cliff) (steil) abfallen; (of prices) stark fallen. II. s. Sturz m; (dive) Tauchen n; Fig: to take the p., den Sprung wagen.

pluperfect [pluː'pəːfikt], adj. & s. p. (tense), Plusquamperfekt n.

plural ['pluər(ə)l], adj. & s. Plural m.

plus [plʌs], prep. plus; p. **VAT**, zuzüglich Mehrwertsteuer.

plush [plʌʃ], adj. F: luxuriös; (smart) vornehm.

ply[1] [plai], v.tr. (a) to p. a **trade**, ein Gewerbe betreiben; (b) to p. **s.o. with drink**, j-m Alkohol aufdrängen.

ply[2], s. three p. wool, dreifache Wolle. ◆'plywood, s. Sperrholz n.

pneumatic [njuː'mætik], adj. pneumatisch; **p. drill,** Preßluftbohrer *m.*

pneumonia [nju(:)'məuniə], *s.* Lungenentzündung *f.*

poach¹ [pəutʃ], *v.tr. Cu:* (Eier) pochieren; **poached eggs,** verlorene Eier.

poach², *v.tr. & i.* to p. (game), wildern. ◆**'poacher,** *s.* Wilderer *m.*

pocket ['pɔkit]. I. *s.* 1. Tasche *f*; **p. edition,** Taschenausgabe *f*; **p. knife,** Taschenmesser *n*; **p. money,** Taschengeld *n.* 2. (*in billiards etc.*) Loch *n.* II. *v.tr.* (Geld usw.) einstecken.

pod [pɔd], *s.* Schote *f*; (*of seeds*) Hülse *f.*

poem ['pəuim], *s.* Gedicht *n.* ◆**poet** ['pəuit], *s.* Dichter *m.* ◆**po'etic,** *adj.* poetisch; **p. licence,** dichterische Freiheit. ◆**'poetry,** *s.* Gedichte *npl*; (*lyric*) p., Lyrik *f.*

poignant ['pɔinjənt], *adj.* rührend.

point [pɔint]. I. *s.* 1. Punkt *m*; (*a*) (*place*) Stelle *f*; **p. of view,** Gesichtspunkt *m*; (*attitude*) Standpunkt *m*; (*b*) Frage *f,* Sache *f*; **p. at issue,** Streitpunkt *m*; **to make one's p.,** seinen Standpunkt klarmachen; **to make a p. of doing sth.,** darauf bedacht sein, etwas zu tun; **that's the p.,** darum geht es ja; (*c*) (*sense*) **what would be the p. of ...,** welchen Sinn hätte es, zu ...; **there's no p.,** es hat keinen Zweck; (*d*) **to be on the p. of doing sth.,** im Begriff sein, etwas zu tun; (*e*) (*degree*) **up to a (certain) p.,** bis zu einem gewissen Grad; (*f*) **to refuse p. blank,** glatt ablehnen. 2. (*end*) Spitze *f* (einer Nadel usw.); *Geog:* Landspitze *f.* 3. *Rail:* **pl points,** Weiche *f.* II. *v.* 1. *v.tr.* (eine Waffe usw.) richten (at s.o., auf j-n). 2. *v.i.* (*a*) **to p. at s.o., sth.,** auf j-n, etwas *acc* zeigen; *Fig:* **all the evidence points to him,** alle Beweise deuten auf ihn; (*b*) **to p. sth. out,** auf etwas *acc* hinweisen. ◆**'pointed,** *adj.* (*sharp, also of remark*) spitz. ◆**'pointer,** *s.* (*a*) Zeiger *m* (eines Meßgerätes); (*b*) *F:* Tip *m.* ◆**'pointing,** *s.* Ausfugung *f* (einer Mauer). ◆**'pointless,** *adj.* sinnlos.

poise [pɔiz]. I. *s.* (*balance*) Gleichgewicht *n*; (*attitude*) Haltung *f* (des Körpers). II. *v.tr.* balancieren.

poison ['pɔiz(ə)n]. I. *s.* Gift *n.* II. *v.tr.* (*a*) (j-n) vergiften; *Fig:* (j-s Charakter, ein Verhältnis usw.) verderben. ◆**'poisoning,** *s.* Vergiftung *f.* ◆**'poisonous,** *adj.* giftig.

poke [pəuk]. 1. *v.tr.* (*a*) (j-n) anstoßen; (*b*) (das Feuer) schüren; (*c*) (einen Schirm usw.) (in etwas *acc*) stecken; (*d*) **to p. fun at s.o.,** sich über j-n lustig machen. 2. *v.i.* **to p. about,** herumstochern. ◆**'poker¹,** *s.* Schürhaken *m.*

poker² [pəukər], *s.* (*game*) Poker *n.*

Poland ['pəulənd]. *Pr. n.* Polen *n.*

polar ['pəulər], *adj.* polar, Polar-; **p. bear,** Eisbär *m.*

Pole¹ [pəul], *s.* Pole *m,* Polin *f.*

pole², *s.* Stange *f*; (*post*) Pfahl *m*; (*for flag etc.*) Mast *m*; *Sp:* **p. vault,** Stabhoch-

sprung *m.*

pole³, *s. Geog:* Pol *m*; *Fig:* **poles apart,** grundverschieden.

police [pə'li:s], *s.* **the p. (force),** die Polizei; **p. officer,** Polizist(in) *m(f)*; **p. station,** Polizeiwache *f.* ◆**po'liceman,** *pl.* **-men,** *s.* Polizist *m.* ◆**po'licewoman,** *pl.* **-women,** *s.* Polizeibeamtin *f,* Polizistin *f.*

policy ['pɔlisi], *s.* 1. (*a*) Politik *f*; **foreign p.,** Außenpolitik *f*; (*b*) *Com: etc:* Grundsatz *m.* 2. *Ins:* (**insurance**) p., Police *f.*

polio ['pəuliəu], *s.* Kinderlähmung *f.*

polish ['pɔliʃ]. I. *s.* Politur *f*; (*shine*) Hochglanz *m*; **shoe p.,** Schuhcreme *f.* II. *v.tr.* polieren. ◆**'polished,** *adj.* poliert; *Fig:* (*of style, manners etc.*) geschliffen. ◆**'polish 'off,** *v.tr. F:* (eine Arbeit) hinhauen; (Essen) wegputzen. ◆**'polish 'up,** *v.tr.* **to p. up one's French,** sein Französisch auffrischen.

Polish ['pəuliʃ]. I. *adj. Geog:* polnisch. II. *s.* (*language*) Polnisch *n.*

polite [pə'lait], *adj.* höflich. ◆**po'liteness,** *s.* Höflichkeit *f.*

politics ['pɔlitiks], *s.pl.* Politik *f.* ◆**political** [pə'litik(ə)l], *adj.* politisch. ◆**poli'tician,** *s.* Politiker(in) *m(f).*

poll [pəul], *s.* 1. Wahl *f*; **to go to the polls,** zur Wahl gehen. 2. (**opinion**) p., Meinungsumfrage *f.* ◆**'polling,** *s.* **p. station,** Wahllokal *n.*

pollen ['pɔlin, -ən], *s.* Blütenstaub *m.*

pollute [pə'l(j)u:t], *v.tr.* verschmutzen. ◆**po'llution,** *s.* (**environmental**) p., Umweltverschmutzung *f.*

polo ['pəuləu], *s.* 1. *Sp:* Polo *n.* 2. *Cl:* **p. neck,** Rollkragen *m.*

polystyrene [pɔli'stairi:n], *s.* Polystyrol *n.*

polytechnic [pɔli'teknik], *s. approx.* Technische Hochschule *f.*

polythene ['pɔliθi:n], *s.* **p. bag,** Plastikbeutel *m.*

pomegranate ['pɔm(i)grænit], *s.* Granatapfel *m.*

pompous ['pɔmpəs], *adj.* (*a*) (*of style etc.*) schwülstig; (*b*) (*of pers.*) aufgeblasen.

pond [pɔnd], *s.* Teich *m.*

ponder ['pɔndər], *v.tr.* (etwas) überlegen. ◆**'ponderous,** *adj.* schwerfällig.

pony ['pəuni], *s.* Pony *n*; **p. tail,** Pferdeschwanz *m.*

poodle ['pu:dl], *s.* Pudel *m.*

pool [pu:l]. I. *s.* (*a*) (*natural*) Weiher *m*; (*small*) Tümpel *m*; (*man-made*) Becken *m*; (*swimming*) p., Schwimmbad *n*; (*c*) **p. of blood/oil,** Blutlache/Ollache *f.* (*d*) (*football*) **pools,** Fußballtoto *m* & *n.* II. *v.tr.* (Gewinne, Gelder usw.) zusammenlegen; **to p. one's resources,** sich zusammentun.

poor [puər, pɔr], *adj.* 1. (*needing money or help*) arm; **the p.,** die Armen. 2. (*bad*) schlecht; **p. excuse,** faule Ausrede; **to have a p. opinion of s.o.,** nicht viel von j-m, etwas *dat* halten. ◆**'poorly.** I.

adv. schlecht. II. *adj.* (*ill*) unpäßlich; **he is p.**, es geht ihm nicht gut.

pop[1] [pɒp]. I. *v.i.* (*a*) (*of cork etc.*) knallen; (*b*) **to p. in to see s.o.**, bei j-m vorbeischauen; **to p. out**, (i) (*jump*) hinausspringen; (ii) *go out*) einen Moment weggehen. II. *s.* Knall *m* (eines Korkens). ◆**'popcorn**, *s.* Popkorn *n*. ◆**'popgun**, *s.* Platzpistole *f*.

pop[2], *adj.* **p.** (*music*), Popmusik *f*; **p. song**, Schlager *m*.

pop[3], *s. F:* (*drink*) Brause *f*.

pope ['pəʊp], *s.* Papst *m*.

poplar ['pɒplər], *s.* Pappel *f*.

poppy ['pɒpi], *s.* Mohnblume *f*.

popular ['pɒpjulər], *adj.* (*a*) (*of the people*) Volks-; (*b*) (*much liked*) beliebt; (*c*) (*prevalent*) **p. view**, herrschende Meinung; **-ly**, *adv.* **it is p. believed that ...,** man nimmt allgemein an, daß ... ◆**popu'larity**, *s.* Beliebtheit *f.* ◆**'popularize**, *v.tr.* popularisieren.

populate ['pɒpjuleit], *v.tr.* (ein Land usw.) bevölkern; **densely populated,** dicht bevölkert. ◆**popu'lation**, *s.* Bevölkerung *f.*

porcelain ['pɔːslin], *s.* Porzellan *n.*

porch [pɔːtʃ], *s.* (*a*) (*on houses*) Windfang *m*; (*b*) *N.Am:* Veranda *f.*

porcupine ['pɔːkjupain], *s.* Stachelschwein *n.*

pore[1] [pɔːr], *s.* Pore *f.*

pore[2], *v.i.* **to p. over a book**, über einem Buch hocken.

pork [pɔːk], *s.* Schweinefleisch *n.*

pornography [pɔː'nɒgrəfi], *s.* Pornographie *f.*

porous ['pɔːrəs], *adj.* porös.

porpoise ['pɔːpəs], *s.* Tümmler *m.*

porridge ['pɒridʒ], *s.* Haferbrei *m*; **p. oats,** Haferflocken *fpl.*

port[1] [pɔːt], *s. Nau:* Hafen *m.*

port[2], *s. Nau:* (*direction*) Backbord *m.*

port[3], *s.* (*wine*) Portwein *m.*

portable ['pɔːtəbl], *adj.* tragbar.

porter[1] ['pɔːtər], *s.* (*doorman*) Pförtner *m.*

porter[2], *s. Rail:* Gepäckträger *m*; (*in hotels*) Hoteldiener *m.*

portfolio, *pl.* **-oes** [pɔːt'fəuljəu, -z], *s.* (*folder*) Mappe *f.*

porthole ['pɔːthəul], *s. Nau:* Bullauge *n.*

portion ['pɔːʃ(ə)n]. I. *s.* (*a*) Teil *m*; (*share*) Anteil *m* (**of sth.**, von etwas dat); (*b*) *Cu:* Portion *f* (von Speisen). II. *v.tr.* **to p. sth. out,** etwas austeilen.

portly ['pɔːtli], *adj.* beleibt.

portrait ['pɔːtrit], *s.* Porträt *n*; (*description*) Schilderung *f.* ◆**por'tray**, *v.tr.* darstellen; (*describe*) schildern.

Portugal ['pɔːtjug(ə)l]. *Pr. n.* Portugal *n.* ◆**Portuguese** [-'giːz]. I. *adj.* portugiesisch. II. *s.* (*a*) Portugiese *m*, Portugiesin *f*; (*b*) (*language*) Portugiesisch *n.*

pose [pəuz]. I. *s.* Pose *f.* II. *v.* 1. *v.tr.* (eine Frage) stellen; **this poses a problem,** das ist problematisch. 2. *v.i. Art:* **to p. for s.o.**, für j-n Modell stehen;

(*b*) **to p. as a Frenchman,** sich als Franzose ausgeben.

posh [pɒʃ], *adj. F:* vornehm.

position [pə'ziʃ(ə)n]. I. *s.* (*a*) Position *f*; Stellung *f* (des Körpers, *Tchn:* eines Hebels, *Mil:* einer Batterie usw.); (*mental attitude*) Standpunkt *m*; (*b*) (*situation*) Lage *f* (eines Hauses usw.); Standort *m* (eines Schiffes usw.); **in p.**, an der richtigen Stelle; (*c*) (*relative to others*) Stellung *f*; *Sp:* Stelle *f*; **in first p.**, an erster Stelle; (*d*) (*job*) Stelle *f.* II. *v.tr.* (etwas) in die richtige Lage/Stellung bringen.

positive ['pɒzitiv], *adj.* 1. (*of result, reply etc.*) positiv. 2. (*a*) (*certain*) **are you p.?** sind Sie ganz sicher? (*b*) *F:* (*definite*) **a p. advantage,** ein eindeutiger/ausgesprochener Vorteil; **-ly,** *adv.* 1. sicher, mit Gewißheit. 2. *F:* ganz, völlig.

possess [pə'zes], *v.tr.* (*a*) (*own*) (etwas) besitzen; (*b*) **what possessed you?** was ist in Sie gefahren? **like a man possessed,** wie ein Besessener. ◆**po'ssession,** *s.* 1. **to take p. of sth.**, etwas in Besitz nehmen. 2. **all my possessions,** mein ganzes Hab und Gut. ◆**po'ssessive**, *adj.* (*jealous*) eifersüchtig; (*b*) *Gram:* Possessiv-.

possible ['pɒsibl], *adj.* möglich; **as many details as p.**, möglichst viele Einzelheiten. ◆**'possibly,** *adv.* 1. (*emphatic*) **I cannot p. do it**, das kann ich unmöglich tun. 2. (*perhaps*) **yes, p.**, ja, vielleicht. ◆**possi'bility**, *s.* Möglichkeit *f.*

post[1] [pəust], *s.* Pfosten *m*; (*stake*) Pfahl *m*; (*tall*) Mast *m*; *Fig:* **as dead as a p.**, stocktaub; **starting p.**, Startpfosten *m*; **winning p.**, Ziel *n.*

post[2]. I. *s. Mil:* Posten *m*; at his p., auf seinem Posten. 2. (*job*) Stelle *f*; (*office*) Amt *n.* II. *v.tr. Mil:* (*a*) **to p. sentries,** Wachen aufstellen; (*b*) **to be posted to Germany**, nach Deutschland versetzt werden.

post[3]. I. *s.* (*mail, service, post office*) Post *f*; (*a*) **by return of p.**, postwendend; **to send sth. by p.**, etwas mit der Post schicken; **p. office**, Postamt *n*; **p. box,** Briefkasten *m*; **P.O. Box,** Postfach *n.* II. *v.tr.* (*a*) **to p. a letter**, einen Brief zur Post bringen/(*in letter box*) einwerfen; (*b*) *Fig:* **to keep s.o. posted,** j-n auf dem laufenden halten. ◆**'postage**, *s.* Porto *n*; **p. stamp**, Briefmarke *f.* ◆**'postal,** *adj.* Post-; **p. code,** Postleitzahl *f.* ◆**'postcard,** *s.* Postkarte *f.* ◆**'postman,** *s.* Briefträger *m.* ◆**'postmark,** *s.* Poststempel *m.*

post- [pəust-], *prefix* Nach-. ◆**'postmortem,** *s.* Obduktion *f.* ◆**'postwar,** *adj.* Nachkriegs-.

poster ['pəustər], *s.* Plakat *n*, Poster *n.*

posterity [pɒs'teriti], *s.* die Nachwelt; (*s.o.'s descendants*) Nachkommenschaft *f.*

posthumous ['pɒstjuməs], *adj.* postum.

postpone [pəus'pəun], *v.tr.* (etwas) aufschieben.

postscript ['pousskript], s. Nachschrift f.

posture ['post∫ər], s. (*pose*) Positur f; (*position*) Stellung f.

pot [pot]. I. s. (a) Topf m; (*for tea, coffee*) Kanne f; **a p. of jam**, ein Glas n Marmelade; (b) P: **to go to p.**, auf den Hund kommen. II. v.tr. (Pflanzen) eintopfen. ◆**'potted**, adj. p. plant, Topfpflanze f. ◆**'pot-hole**, s. (*in road*) Schlagloch n. ◆**'pot-luck**, s. F: **to take p.-l.**, mit dem vorliebnehmen, was es gerade gibt.

potash ['potæ∫], s. Kali n.

potassium [pə'tæsiəm], s. Kalium n.

potato, pl. **-oes** [pə'teitəu, -əuz], s. Kartoffel f; **p. crisps**, Chips mpl.

potency ['pəutənsi], s. Stärke f (eines Drinks, eines Motors usw.); Wirksamkeit f (eines Medikaments). ◆**'potent**, adj. stark; (*of drug*) wirksam; Fig: (*of argument*) stichhaltig. ◆**po'tential**. I. adj. potentiell. II. s. esp. Potential n; (*of pers.*) Fähigkeiten fpl. ◆**po'tentially**, adv. **p. dangerous**, unter Umständen gefährlich.

potter[1] ['potər], v.i. **to p. (about)**, (*aimlessly*) herumtrödeln; (*in house, garden*) herumhantieren.

potter[2], s. Töpfer(in) m(f); **p.'s wheel**, Töpferscheibe f. ◆**'pottery**, s. 1. (*workshop*) Töpferei f. 2. (*vessels etc.*) Töpferwaren fpl.

potty ['poti], s. F: (*for child*) Töpfchen n.

pouch [paut∫], s. Beutel m.

poultry ['pəultri], s. coll. Geflügel n.

pounce [pauns], v.i. sich stürzen (**on** auf + acc).

pound[1] [paund], s. (*weight, money*) Pfund n; (a) **by the p.**, pfundweise; (b) **p. note**, Pfundnote f.

pound[2], v.i. (*of heart*) pochen.

pour [po:r], v. 1. v.tr. (eine Flüssigkeit) gießen (**into/over sth.**, in/über etwas acc). 2. v.i. (a) **it's pouring (with rain)**, es gießt; es regnet in Strömen; (b) (*of water*, Fig: *of people etc.*) strömen (**into**, in + acc; **out of**, aus + dat). ◆**'pour 'in**, v. 1. v.i. (*of applications etc.*) in großen Mengen eintreffen. 2. v.tr. (eine Flüssigkeit) eingießen. ◆**'pour 'out**, v.tr. Fig: **to p. out one's heart**, sein Herz ausschütten.

pout [paut], v.i. (*of pers.*) schmollen.

poverty ['povəti], s. Armut f. ◆**'poverty-stricken**, adj. verarmt.

powder ['paudər]. I. s. Pulver n; (*cosmetic*) Puder m. II. v.tr. (a) **to p. one's face**, sich das Gesicht pudern; (b) **powdered milk**, Trockenmilch f.

power ['pauər]. I. s. 1. Macht f; **it is beyond my p.**, es liegt nicht in meiner Macht; **to fall into s.o.'s p.**, in j-s Gewalt kommen; Pol: (*of party*) **in p.**, an der Macht. 2. (*ability*) Fähigkeit f; **p. of speech**, Sprechvermögen n. 3. (*strength, force*) (a) Tchn: Stärke f (eines Motors); (*of vehicle*) **under its own p.**, mit eigener Kraft; (b) El: Strom m. ◆**'cable/line**, Starkstromleitung f; **p. point**,

Steckdose f; **p. station**, Kraftwerk n. 4. F: **the powers that be**, Vater Staat. 5. Mth: **three to the p. of four**, drei hoch vier. II. v.tr. (eine Maschine usw.) antreiben. ◆**'powerful**, adj. (a) (*of engine, pers., animal etc.*) stark; (*of car*) leistungsfähig; (*of blow*) heftig; (b) (*influential*) mächtig. ◆**'powerless**, adj. (*without influence*) machtlos.

practicable ['præktikəbl], adj. (*of plan, idea*) durchführbar; (*possible*) möglich.

practical ['præktik(ə)l], adj. praktisch; **p. joke**, Streich m; **-ly**, adv. 1. praktisch. 2. F: (*virtually*) fast.

practice ['præktis], s. 1. (*action*) Praxis f; **in p.**, in der Praxis. 2. (a) (*habit*) Gewohnheit f; (*custom*) Brauch m; (b) **illegal p.**, illegale Handlungsweise. 3. (*repeated exercise*) (a) Übung f; **out of p.**, aus der Übung; **choir p.**, Chorprobe f; (b) Sp: etc: Training n. 4. Jur: Med: etc: Praxis f. ◆**'practise** ['præktis], v.tr. (a) (Klavier, Schwimmen) üben; **to p. what one preaches**, seine Lehren in die Tat umsetzen; (b) (einen Beruf) ausüben. ◆**'practitioner**, s. Med: **general p.**, praktischer Arzt m.

pragmatic [præg'mætik], adj. pragmatisch.

prairie ['prɛəri], s. Prärie f.

praise [preiz]. I. s. Lob n; **in p. of s.o.**, sth., j-n, etwas dat zu Ehren. II. v.tr. loben. ◆**'praiseworthy**, adj. lobenswert.

pram [præm], s. Kinderwagen m.

prance [prɑːns], v.i. (*of child etc.*) hüpfen; (*of horse*) tänzeln.

prank [præŋk], s. Streich m.

prawn [prɔːn], s. Garnele f.

pray [prei], v.tr. & i. beten (**for sth., um etwas acc**). ◆**'prayer**, s. Gebet n; **the Lord's P.**, das Vaterunser.

pre- [priː], prefix Vor-.

preach [priːt∫], v. 1. v.tr. **to p. a sermon**, eine Predigt halten. 2. v.i. predigen (**about sth.**, von etwas dat). ◆**'preacher**, s. Prediger m.

precarious [pri'kɛəriəs], adj. unsicher; (*dangerous*) gefährlich.

precaution [pri'kɔː∫(ə)n], s. Vorsichtsmaßnahme f; **to take precautions**, Vorsichtsmaßnahmen treffen; **as a p.**, vorsichtshalber.

precede [pri(ː)'siːd], v.tr. (j-m, etwas dat) vorausgehen. ◆**'precedence** ['presidəns], s. **to take p.**, den Vorrang haben (**over s.o.**, vor j-m). ◆**'precedent** ['presid(ə)nt], s. Präzedenzfall m. ◆**'preceding** [pri'siːdiŋ]. I. adj. vorhergehend; **the p. day**, der vorige Tag. II. prep. **the week p. the match**, die Woche vor dem Spiel.

precept ['priːsept], s. Gebot n.

precinct ['priːsiŋkt], s. Gelände n; **shopping p.**, Einkaufszentrum n; **pedestrian p.**, Fußgängerzone f.

precious ['pre∫əs]. I. adj. (a) (*of great value*) kostbar; **p. stones**, Edelsteine mpl;

II. *adv.* p little, herzlich wenig.
precipice ['presipis], *s.* Steilwand *f.* ◆**pre'cipitous,** *adj. (of cliff)* abschüssig.
precipitate I. [pri'sipiteit] *v.tr. (hasten)* (in order) to p. matters, um die Sache zu beschleunigen. **II.** [-itit] *adj.* übereilt. ◆**pre'cipitation,** *s. Meteor: & Ch:* Niederschlag *m.*
precise [pri'sais], *adj.* genau; you must be p., Sie müssen präzise sein. ◆**precision** [-'siʒ(ə)n], *s.* Genauigkeit *f;* p. engineering, Feinmechanik *f.*
precocious [pri'kəuʃəs], *adj.* frühreif; *Pej: (of small child)* altklug.
preconceived [pri:kən'si:vd], *adj.* p. idea *(also* precon'ception), vorgefaßte Meinung *f.*
precursor [pri(:)'kə:sər], *s.* Vorläufer(in) *m(f).*
predator ['predət(ə)r], *s.* Raubtier *n.*
predecessor ['pri:disesər], *s.* Vorgänger(in) *m(f).*
predetermine [pri:di'tə:min], *v.tr.* vorherbestimmen.
predicament [pri'dikəmənt], *s.* mißliche Lage *f.*
predict [pri'dikt], *v.tr.* voraussagen. ◆**pre'dictable,** *adj.* leicht vorauszusagen. ◆**pre'diction,** *s.* Voraussage *f.*
predilection [pri:di'lekʃ(ə)n], *s.* Vorliebe *f.*
predispose [pri:dis'pəuz], *v.tr.* predisposed to sth., zu etwas disponiert sein. ◆**predispo'sition,** *s.* Neigung *f* (to, zu + dat).
predominate [pri'dɔmineit], *v.i. (numerically)* überwiegen; *(of feature)* vorherrschen. ◆**pre'dominance,** *s. (in numbers)* Überwiegen *n.*
preeminent [pri(:)'eminənt], *adj.* to be p., den Vorrang haben.
prefabricated [pri'fæbrikeitid], *adj.* p. house, Fertighaus *n.*
preface ['prefis], *s. (of book)* Vorwort *n.*
prefect ['pri:fekt], *s. Sch: Brit:* Aufsichtsschüler(in) *m(f).*
prefer [pri'fə:r], *v.tr. (etwas)* vorziehen; I would p. to go without, ich würde lieber darauf verzichten. ◆**preferable** ['pref-], *adj.* p. (to sth.), *(etwas dat)* vorzuziehen; -**ably,** *adv.* vorzugsweise. ◆**preference** ['pref-], *s.* Vorliebe *f* (for sth., für etwas *acc*). ◆**prefe'rential** [pref-], *adj.* p. treatment, Vorzugsbehandlung *f.*
prefix ['pri:fiks], *s.* Präfix *n;* Vorsilbe *f.*
pregnancy ['pregnənsi], *s.* Schwangerschaft *f.* ◆**'pregnant,** *adj.* schwanger.
prehistoric [pri:hi'stɔrik], *adj.* vorgeschichtlich.
prejudice ['predʒudis], *s.* **I.** *s.* Vorurteil *n.* **II.** *v.tr.* to p. s.o. for/against sth., j-n für/gegen etwas beeinflussen. ◆**'prejudiced,** *adj. (of pers.)* voreingenommen (for/against s.o., sth., für/gegen j-n, etwas *acc); (of judge, judgement)* befangen.

preliminary [pri'liminəri], *adj.* Vor-; *(preparatory)* vorbereitend; p. remarks, einleitende Bemerkungen.
prelude ['prelju:d], *s. Mus:* Vorspiel *n; Fig:* Auftakt *m* (to, zu + dat).
premature ['premətjuər], *adj.* frühzeitig; p. birth, Frühgeburt *f.*
premeditated [pri'mediteitid], *adj.* vorsätzlich. ◆**premier** ['premjər]. **I.** *adj.* führend. **II.** *s. Pol:* Premierminister *m.*
première [premieər], *s. Th:* Premiere *f,* Uraufführung *f.*
premises ['premisiz], *s.pl.* Räumlichkeiten *fpl; (restaurant)* Lokal *n;* business p., Geschäftslokal *n;* on the p., im Hause.
premium ['pri:miəm], *s.* **1.** insurance p., Versicherungsprämie *f.* **2.** to be at a p., sehr gesucht sein.
premonition [pri:mə'niʃ(ə)n], *s.* Vorahnung *f.*
preoccupation [pri:ɔkju'peiʃ(ə)n], *s. (distraction)* Zerstreutheit *f;* Vertieftsein *n* (with sth., in etwas *dat).* ◆**pre'occupied,** *adj.* in Gedanken vertieft.
prepaid ['pri:'peid], *adj.* im Voraus bezahlt.
prepare [pri'peər], *v.* **1.** *v.tr.* vorbereiten; *(ein Gericht)* zubereiten; to p. to do sth., sich anschicken, etwas zu tun. **2.** *v.i.* to p. for sth., sich auf etwas *acc* vorbereiten. ◆**prepa'ration,** *s.* Vorbereitung *f.* ◆**pre'paratory,** *adj.* vorbereitend. ◆**pre'pared,** *adj. (ready)* bereit.
preponderance [pri'pond(ə)rəns], *s.* Überwiegen *n.*
preposition [prepə'ziʃ(ə)n], *s.* Präposition *f.*
prepossessing [pri:pə'zesiŋ], *adj.* anziehend.
preposterous [pri'pɔst(ə)rəs], *adj.* absurd.
prerequisite [pri'rekwizit], *s.* Vorbedingung *f.*
prescribe [pri'skraib], *v.tr. Med:* to p. sth. for s.o., j-m etwas verordnen/verschreiben. ◆**prescription** [-'skripʃ(ə)n], *s. Med:* Rezept *n.*
presence ['prez(ə)ns], *s.* Gegenwart *f,* Anwesenheit *f;* in the p. of danger, angesichts der Gefahr; p. of mind, Geistesgegenwart *f.* ◆**present¹. I.** *adj.* **1.** *(place) (of pers.)* anwesend *(at,* bei + dat); the people p., die Anwesenden *mpl;* to be p. at a ceremony, einer Zeremonie beiwohnen. **2.** *(time)* gegenwärtig; at the p. time, zur Zeit; *(b) (existing, current)* jetzig; *(c) Gram:* p. tense, Gegenwart *f;* -**ly,** *adv. (soon)* bald. **II.** *s.* the p., die Gegenwart; up to the p., bis heute; at p., zur Zeit; for the p., vorläufig.
present². **I.** ['prez(ə)nt], *s. (gift)* Geschenk *n.* **II.** [pri'zent] *v.tr. (a) (hand over) (ein* Gesuch usw.) einreichen; to p. sth. to s.o., j-m etwas überreichen; *(b) (offer)* (eine Gelegenheit, Schwierigkeiten usw.) bieten; *Th:* to p. a play, ein Stück dar-

bieten; (c) (introduce) (j-n, sich) vorstellen; (ein Thema, eine Geschichte usw.)
darstellen. ◆pre'sentable [pri-], adj.
präsentabel. ◆presen'tation [prezə-],
s. 1. Th: etc: Darbietung f. 2. (feierliche)
Überreichung f (eines Preises usw.).
presentiment [pri'zentimənt], s. (böse)
Vorahnung f.
preserve [pri'zə:v]. I. v.tr. (a) (ein Gebäude, den Frieden usw.) erhalten; (Dokumente) aufbewahren; well preserved,
gut erhalten; (b) (Obst usw.) einmachen.
II. s usu. pl. Cu: Eingemachtes n; (jam)
Konfitüre f. ◆pre'servative, s. 1. (in
foods) Konservierungsmittel n. 2. (for
wood etc.) Schutzmittel n.
preside [pri'zaid], v.i. den Vorsitz haben
(at/over a meeting, über eine Versammlung). ◆'president, s. (a) N.Am: Com:
Vorsitzende(r) m (eines Konzerns); (b)
Pol: Präsident m.
press [pres]. I. s. (also newspapers) Presse
f; p. cutting, Zeitungsausschnitt m; to
have a good/bad p., eine gute/schlechte
Presse haben; to go to p., in Druck gehen. II. v. 1. v.tr. (a) (etwas) drücken;
(Trauben usw.) keltern; to p. the button, auf den Knopf drücken; to p.
clothes, Kleider bügeln; (b) (j-n) bedrängen; to be pressed for time, unter Zeitdruck stehen; hard pressed, schwer
unter Druck. 2. v.i. to p. on sth., etwas acc drücken; to p. for sth., etwas
fordern. ◆'pressing, adj. (urgent) dringend. ◆'press 'on, v.i. (a) (walking)
weitergehen; (b) (working) weitermachen.
◆pressure ['preʃər], s. Druck m; to
bring p. to bear, Druck ausüben.
◆'pressurize, v.tr. unter Druck setzen.
prestige [pres'ti:ʒ], s. Prestige n.
presume [pri'zju:m], v.tr. (a) (etwas) vermuten; (b) to p. to do sth., sich dat erlauben, etwas zu tun. ◆pre'sumably,
adv. vermutlich. ◆pre'sumption, s.
Vermutung f. ◆pre'sumptuous, adj.
anmaßend.
presuppose [pri:sə'pəuz], v.tr. (etwas)
voraussetzen.
pretence [pri'tens], s. Vortäuschung f; by
false pretences, unter Vorspiegelung falscher Tatsachen. ◆pre'tend. I. v.tr.
(feign) (etwas) vortäuschen; to p. to be
sth., vorgeben, etwas zu sein; he pre-
tended to be in pain, er tat, als ob er
Schmerzen hätte; he does not p. to be
an expert, er gibt sich nicht als Experte
aus. 2. v.i. he's only pretending, er tut
nur so. ◆pre'tentious, adj. überheblich.
pretext ['pri:tekst], s. Vorwand m; on the
p. of consulting me, unter dem Vorwand, mich zu Rate zu ziehen.
pretty ['priti]. I. adj. hübsch. II. adv. F:
ziemlich; p. well finished/the same, so
ziemlich fertig/das gleiche.
prevail [pri'veil], v.i. (a) to p. on s.o. to
do sth., j-n dazu bringen, etwas zu tun;

(b) (of situation etc.) herrschen; calm pre-
vails, es herrscht Ruhe. ◆pre'vailing,
adj. p. winds, vorherrschende Winde.
◆'prevalent, adj. vorherrschend.
prevaricate [pri'værikeit], v.i. Ausflüchte
machen.
prevent [pri'vent], v.tr. (a) (j-n) hindern
(from doing sth., an etwas dat); (b) (etwas) verhindern; (einen Unfall usw.) ver-
hüten. ◆pre'vention, s. Verhinderung
f; p. of accidents, Unfallverhütung f.
◆pre'ventive, adj. vorbeugend.
preview ['pri:vju:], s. Vorbesichtigung f
(einer Ausstellung usw.); Th: Cin: Vorschau f.
previous ['pri:viəs], adj. (a) vorhergehend; on the p. day, am Tag vorher; (b)
(earlier) früher; -ly, adv. vorher; (formerly) früher.
pre-war ['pri:'wɔ:r], adj. Vorkriegs-.
prey [prei]. I. s. Beute f; bird of p.,
Raubvogel m. II. v.i. to p. upon insects
etc., Insekten usw. jagen; Fig: something is preying on his mind, etwas bedrückt ihn/F: liegt ihm im Magen.
price [prais]. I. s. Preis m; p. list, Preisli-
ste f; p. reduction, Preissenkung f. II.
v.tr. den Preis (einer Ware) festsetzen;
(estimate) schätzen. ◆'priceless, adj.
(a) von un schätzbarem Wert; (b) F: (of
pers., story etc.) unbezahlbar.
prick [prik]. I. s. Stich m. II. v.tr. (a) to
p. one's finger, sich dat in den Finger
stechen; (b) to p. up one's ears, die Ohren spitzen. ◆'prickle. l. s. Stachel m.
II. v.i. stechen; (of skin etc.)
prickeln. ◆'prickly, adj. stachlig; Fig:
(of pers., temper) reizbar.
pride [praid]. I. s. Stolz m; to take a p. in
sth., auf etwas acc stolz sein. II. v.tr. to
p. oneself on sth., auf etwas acc stolz
sein.
priest [pri:st], s. Priester m; (parish) p.,
Pfarrer m. ◆'priesthood, s. (a) coll.
the p., der Klerus; (b) (office) Priesteramt
n.
priggish ['prigiʃ], adj. selbstgefällig.
prim [prim], adj. (of pers.) spröde; (of
manner) geziert.
primary ['praiməri]. I. adj. 1. (basic)
Grund-; p. colours, Grundfarben fpl; p.
school, Grundschule f. 2. (main) Haupt-;
p. concern, Hauptsorge f.
prime¹ [praim]. I. adj. 1. (first) Haupt-;
of p. importance, von höchster Wichtigkeit; P. Minister, Premierminister m. 2.
Mth: p. number, Primzahl f. II. s. Blütezeit f; in the p. of life, in den besten
Jahren.
prime² [praim], v.tr. (a) Mil: (eine Bombe, Handgranate) scharfmachen; (b) (in decorating
etc.) (etwas) grundieren.
primitive ['primitiv], adj. primitiv; Pej:
tiv; (original) ursprünglich.
primrose ['primrəuz], s. Bot: Primel f.
prince [prins], s. (royal) Prinz m; (noble-
man & Fig:) Fürst m. ◆prin'cess, s.

Prinzessin f. ◆**princi'pality**, s. Fürstentum n.

principal ['prinsip(ə)l]. I. adj. Haupt-; -ly, adv. hauptsächlich. II. s. 1. (a) Sch: etc: Direktor m; (b) Th: Hauptdarsteller(in) m(f). 2. Fin: Kapital n.

principle ['prinsipl], s. Prinzip n; in p., im Prinzip; grundsätzlich; to do sth. on p., etwas aus Prinzip tun.

print [print]. I. s. 1. Druck m; in p., im Druck; (available) vorrätig; out of p., vergriffen. 2. (mark) Abdruck m. 3. Phot: Abzug m. II. v.tr. (a) (ein Buch, eine Zeitung) drucken; printed matter, Drucksache f; (b) (write in capitals) in Druckbuchstaben schreiben. ◆**'printer**, s. Drucker m. ◆**'printing**, s. (process) Drucken n; p. press, Druckerpresse f; p. works, Druckerei f. ◆**'print-out**, s. Data-pr: Ausdruck m.

prior ['praiər]. I. adj. früher (to, als). II. adv. p. to, vor + dat; p. to my departure, bevor ich abreise. ◆**priority** [prai'ɔriti], s. Priorität f; Aut: Vorfahrt f; to give sth. p., etwas dat den Vorrang geben.

priory ['praiəri], s. Ecc: Priorat n.

prism ['prizm], s. Prisma n.

prison ['priz(ə)n], s. Gefängnis n; to send s.o. to p., j-n ins Gefängnis stecken, j-n einsperren. ◆**'prisoner**, s. Gefangene(r) f(m); to take s.o. p., j-n gefangennehmen.

pristine ['pristi:n], adj. unberührt; in p. condition, makellos.

private ['praivit]. I. adj. privat; Privat-; (confidential) vertraulich; to keep a matter p., etwas für sich acc behalten; p. parts, Geschlechtsteile npl; (on notice) P., kein Zutritt! -ly, adv. privat; (secretly) insgeheim; p. owned, in Privatbesitz. II. s. 1. in p., privat; (of conversation) unter vier Augen; (of meeting) hinter geschlossenen Türen. 2. Mil: einfacher Soldat m; P. Smith, Soldat Smith. ◆**'privacy** ['praivəsi, 'pri-], s. Zurückgezogenheit f; in the p. of one's home, bei sich zu Hause.

privet ['privit], s. Liguster m.

privilege ['priviliʤ], s. Privileg n; (honour) Ehre f. ◆**'privileged**, adj. privilegiert; to be p. to do sth., die Ehre haben, etwas zu tun.

prize [praiz]. I. s. Preis m. II. v.tr. (j-n, etwas) schätzen. ◆**'prizewinner**, s. Preisträger(in) m(f).

pro[1] [prəu]. I. prep. 1. F: für + acc; the pros and cons, das Für und Wider. 2. p. rata, anteilmäßig. II. prefix -freundlich; p. German, deutschfreundlich.

pro[2], s. Sp: F: Profi m.

probable ['prɔbəbl], adj. wahrscheinlich; the p. answer, die vermutliche Antwort. ◆**proba'bility**, s. Wahrscheinlichkeit f; in all p., höchstwahrscheinlich. ◆**'probably**, adv. wahrscheinlich.

probation [prəu'beiʃ(ə)n], s. Probezeit f;

Jur: Bewährung f; on p., auf Probe/Jur: Bewährung; p. officer, Bewährungshelfer m. ◆**pro'bationary**, adj. Probe-; p. period, Probezeit f.

probe [prəub]. I. v. 1. v.tr. (einen Gegenstand) forschend untersuchen; (eine Angelegenheit) erforschen. 2. v.i. to p. into sth., etwas forschend untersuchen. II. s. (investigation) Untersuchung f.

problem ['prɔbləm], s. Problem n. ◆**proble'matic**, adj. problematisch.

procedure [prə'si:dʒər], s. Verfahren n.

proceed [prə'si:d], v.i. (a) (go) sich (irgendwohin) begeben; (continue) (i) weiterfahren; (ii) (on foot) weitergehen; (b) (act) verfahren; how shall we p.? wie sollen wir verfahren/(continue) weitermachen? to p. with a job, (start) eine Arbeit in Angriff nehmen; (c) (of thing) vor sich gehen; things are proceeding as usual, alles geht seinen üblichen Gang. ◆**pro'ceedings**, s.pl. (a) Parl: etc: Vorgänge mpl; (b) Jur: legal p., Gerichtsverfahren n; to take p. against s.o., gegen j-n gerichtlich vorgehen. ◆**proceeds** ['prəusi:dz], s.pl. Erlös m (of a sale, aus einem Verkauf).

process ['prəuses]. I. s. Vorgang m; esp. Ind: Verfahren n; he is in the p. of moving, er ist gerade dabei, umzuziehen. II. v.tr. (a) Ind: (Rohstoffe) verarbeiten; (b) Phot: (einen Film) entwickeln; (c) Adm: (einen Fall, eine Anmeldung) bearbeiten.

procession [prə'seʃ(ə)n], s. Umzug m; Ecc: etc: Prozession f.

proclaim [prə'kleim], v.tr. proklamieren. ◆**proclamation** [prɔklə'meiʃ(ə)n], s. Proklamation f.

procrastinate [prəu'kræstineit], v.i. (of pers.) zaudern.

procure [prə'kjuər], v. 1. v.tr. (a) (Arbeit usw.) beschaffen. 2. v.i. Jur: kuppeln.

prod [prɔd]. I. v.tr. (a) to p. s.o., sth., j-n, etwas stoßen/F: knuffen; (b) Fig: (j-n) anspornen (into doing sth., zu etwas dat). II. s. leichter Stoß m.

prodigal ['prɔdig(ə)l], adj. verschwenderisch; the p. son, der verlorene Sohn.

prodigy ['prɔdidʒi], s. child/infant p., Wunderkind n. ◆**pro'digious**, adj. erstaunlich.

produce. I. [prə'dju:s] v.tr. (a) (bring out) (den Paß usw.) vorzeigen; (ein Taschentuch usw.) herausholen; (b) Th: (ein Stück) inszenieren; Rad: TV: (ein Programm) leiten; Cin: (bei einem Film) Regie führen; (c) (manufacture) (Waren usw.) produzieren, herstellen; (Blüten, Früchte) hervorbringen; (d) Fig: (eine Wirkung) erzielen; (eine Stimmung, ein Gefühl usw.) hervorrufen. II. ['prɔdju:s] s. Produkte npl. ◆**pro'ducer**, s. 1. Com: Erzeuger m. 2. Th: Regisseur m; Cin: Produzent m; Rad: Spielleiter m. ◆**product** ['prɔdʌkt], s. Produkt n. ◆**pro'duction**, s. 1. Ind: Herstellung f; Produktion f; p. line, Fließband n; to be in p., hergestellt werden. 2. *Th:* Inszenierung *f.* ◆**pro'ductive,** *adj. (of activity)* produktiv; *(of mine, period etc.)* ergiebig. ◆**produc'tivity,** *s.* Produktivität *f.*

profane [prə'fein], *adj. (a) (of language)* lästerlich; *(b) (not sacred)* profan.

profess [prə'fes], *v.tr.* (seine Liebe usw.) erklären; (seine Unschuld usw.) beteuern; **I do not p. to be a scholar,** ich gebe mich nicht als Gelehrter aus. ◆**profession** [-'feʃ(ə)n], *s. 1. (declaration)* Erklärung *f* (der Liebe usw.). 2. *(occupation)* Beruf *m;* **by p.,** von Beruf; **the professions,** die freien Berufe. ◆**pro'fessional. I.** *adj. (a)* beruflich; Berufs-; *(of practice etc.)* professionell; *(piece of work etc.)* fachmännisch. **II.** *s.* Fachmann *m; Sp: & F:* Profi *m.* ◆**pro'fessor,** *s.* Professor *m.* ◆**pro'fessorship,** *s.* Professur *f.*

proficient [prə'fiʃənt], *adj.* tüchtig; **to be p. in sth.,** in etwas *dat* bewandert sein. ◆**pro'ficiency,** *s.* Fertigkeit *f.*

profile ['prəufail], *s.* 1. Profil *n.* 2. *(article)* Porträt *n.*

profit ['prɔfit]. **I.** *s. (gain)* Gewinn *m; (advantage)* Vorteil *m;* **to sell at a p.,** etwas mit Gewinn verkaufen. **II.** *v.i.* **to p. by sth.,** aus etwas *dat* Gewinn ziehen. ◆**'profitable,** *adj.* rentabel; *(advantageous)* vorteilhaft.

profound [prə'faund], *adj. (a) (deep)* tief; *(b) (of knowledge)* gründlich; *(of thought etc.)* tiefgründig; **p. respect,** größte Hochachtung; **-ly,** *adv.* sehr, stark.

profuse [prə'fju:s], *adj.* überschwenglich; **-ly,** *adv.* **to perspire p.,** übermäßig schwitzen. ◆**pro'fusion,** *s.* Fülle *f.*

program(me) ['prəugræm]. **I.** *s.* Programm *n.* **II.** *v.tr.* (einen Computer usw.) programmieren. ◆**'programmer,** *s. Data-pr:* Programmierer *m.*

progress. I. ['prəugres] *s.* Fortschritt *m;* **to make p.,** Fortschritte machen; **to make quick/slow p.,** schnell/langsam vorankommen; **in p.,** im Gange. **II.** [prə'gres] *v.i. (a) (proceed) (of work etc.)* weitergehen; *(b) (make progress)* vorwärtskommen; *(develop)* sich entwickeln. ◆**pro'gression,** *s. (a)* Fortschritt *m* (von einer Sache zur anderen); *(sequence)* Folge *f;* *(movement)* Fortbewegung *f.* ◆**pro'gressive,** *adj. (a) (in ideas)* fortschrittlich; *(b) (increasing)* progressiv; **-ly,** *adv.* zunehmend.

prohibit [prə'hibit], *v.tr.* (etwas) verbieten; **to p. s.o. from doing sth.,** j-m verbieten, etwas zu tun; **smoking prohibited,** Rauchen verboten. ◆**prohibition** [prəuhi'biʃ(ə)n], *s.* Verbot *n; N.Am. Hist:* Prohibition *f.* ◆**pro'hibitive,** *adj.* unerschwinglich.

project. I. ['prɔdʒekt] *s.* 1. *v.tr. (a) Phot:* (Dias, ein Bild) projizieren; *Th:* **to p. (one's voice),** seine Stimme weit tragen lassen. 2. *v.i.* vorstehen; **to p. from/out of sth.,** aus etwas *dat* hervorragen. **II.**

['prɔdʒekt] *s.* Projekt *n.* ◆**pro'jection,** *s.* 1. Projektion *f.* 2. *(forecast)* Vorhersage *f.* 3. *(sticking out)* Vorsprung *m; (rock)* Überhang *m.* ◆**pro'jector,** *s.* Projektor *m.*

proletariat [prəuli'teəriət], *s.* Proletariat *n.*

prolific [prə'lifik], *adj. (of writer etc.)* produktiv; *(of period etc.)* fruchtbar.

prologue ['prəuləg], *s.* Prolog *m.*

prolong [prə'lɔŋ], *v.tr.* (ein Treffen usw.) verlängern. ◆**pro'longed,** *adj.* anhaltend; **a p. period,** eine längere Zeit.

promenade [prɔmən'ɑ:d], *s.* Promenade *f.*

prominence ['prɔminəns], *s. (fame)* Berühmtheit *f; (importance)* Bedeutung *f.* ◆**'prominent,** *adj. (noticeable)* auffallend; *(projecting)* vorstehend; *(of pers.)* prominent; **p. position,** *(of pers.)* führende Stellung; **a p. figure,** eine wichtige Persönlichkeit.

promiscuity [prɔmis'kju:iti], *s.* Promiskuität *f.*

promise ['prɔmis]. **I.** *s. (a)* Versprechen *n* (**to help etc.,** zu helfen usw.); *(b) (prospect)* Aussicht *f;* **to show great p.,** viel versprechen. **II.** *v.* 1. *v.tr. (a)* **to p. s.o. sth.,** j-m etwas versprechen; *(b) Fig:* (etwas) in Aussicht stellen. 2. *v.i.* **I p.,** ich verspreche es. ◆**'promising,** *adj.* vielversprechend.

promontory ['prɔmənt(ə)ri], *s.* Küstenvorsprung *m.*

promote [prə'məut], *v.tr. (a)* (j-n) befördern (**to the rank of,** zu + *dat*); *(b)* (eine Sache, gute Beziehungen, die Künste usw.) fördern; *Com:* **to p. a product,** für ein Produkt werben. ◆**pro'motion,** *s.* 1. Beförderung *f* (von j-m); **to gain p.,** befördert werden. 2. Förderung *f* (einer Sache); *Com:* Werbung *f* (für ein Produkt); **sales p.,** Absatzförderung *f.*

prompt [prɔm(p)t]. **I.** *adj. (a) (immediate)* prompt; *(b) (punctual)* pünktlich. **II.** *v.tr. (a)* **to p. s.o. to do sth.,** j-n veranlassen/*(persuade)* dazu animieren, etwas zu tun; *(b) Th:* (einem Schauspieler) soufflieren.

prone [prəun], *adj.* **to be p. to sth.,** zu etwas *dat* neigen.

prong [prɔŋ], *s.* Zinke *f* (einer Gabel); *(sharp point)* Zacke *f.* ◆**'pronged,** *adj.* **two-/three p.,** zwei-/dreizinkig.

pronoun ['prəunaun], *s. Gram:* Pronomen *n,* Fürwort *n.*

pronounce [prə'nauns], *v.tr. (a) (declare)* (etwas) erklären; **to p. s.o. fit,** j-n für gesund erklären; *(b) Jur:* (ein Urteil) verkünden; *(c)* (ein Wort usw.) aussprechen. ◆**pro'nounced,** *adj. (a) (noticeable)* auffallend; *(b) (distinct)* deutlich; **p. improvement,** ausgesprochene Verbesserung. ◆**pro'nouncement,** *s.* 1. *Jur:* Verkündigung *f.* 2. Erklärung *f.* ◆**pronunci'ation** [-nʌn-], *s.* Aussprache *f.*

proof [pruːf]. I. s. 1. Beweis m. 2. (of alcohol) Alkoholgehalt m. 3. (a) p. (stage),
Korrektur f; (galley) p., Korrekturfahne
f; (b) Phot: Probeabzug m. II. adj. -fest;
p. against the weather, wetterfest.

prop¹ [prɔp]. I. s. Stütze f. II. v.tr. **to p.**
(up) sth., etwas stützen.

prop², s. Th: usu. pl. **props,** Requisiten
npl.

propaganda [prɔpə'gændə], s. Propaganda f.

propel [prə'pel], v.tr. (j-n, etwas) (vorwärts)treiben; **propelled by steam,** mit
Dampfantrieb. ◆**pro'peller,** s. Propeller m.

propensity [prə'pensiti], s. Hang m (**for/**
to sth., zu etwas dat).

proper ['prɔpər], adj. richtig; **they're**
very p., sie sind sehr korrekt; **p. name,**
Eigenname m; **in the hotel** p., im Hotel
selbst; **-ly,** adv. richtig; **not p. shut,**
nicht richtig geschlossen; **to behave** p.,
sich anständig benehmen.

property ['prɔpəti], s. 1. (a) (thing owned)
Eigentum n; **lost** p., Fundsachen fpl; (b)
(house etc.) Besitz m; (small) Haus n; (c)
coll. (land, buildings) Immobilien pl. 2.
(attribute) Eigenschaft f (eines Stoffes).

prophecy ['prɔfisi], s. Prophezeiung f.
◆**'prophesy** [-sai], v.tr. & i. prophe-
zeien. ◆**'prophet** [-fit], s. Prophet m.

proportion [prə'pɔːʃ(ə)n]. I. s. 1. (a)
(part) Teil m; 2. (b) Ch: Cu: etc: (amount in
mixture) Anteil m. 2. (relation) Verhältnis
n; Proportion f; **in** p., im richtigen Verhältnis; **to lose all sense of** p., jeglichen
Maßstab/Überblick verlieren. 3. pl. a
debt of enormous proportions, eine
Schuld von gewaltigem Ausmaß. II. v.tr.
well proportioned, gut proportioniert.
◆**pro'portional,** adj. be p. proportional (to,
zu + dat); of (figures) **to be** p., im Verhältnis zueinander stehen; Pol: p. **representation,** Verhältniswahlrecht n.
◆**pro'portionate,** adj. im richtigen
Verhältnis; **to be** p. **to** sth., etwas dat
entsprechen.

propose [prə'pəuz], v. 1. v.tr. (a) (suggest) (j-n, etwas) vorschlagen; **to** p. a
toast, einen Toast ausbringen; (b) (intend) (etwas) vorhaben; **how do you** p. **to**
do it? wie wollen Sie es tun? 2. v.i. **to** p.
to a girl, einem Mädchen einen Heiratsantrag machen. ◆**pro'posal,** s. (suggestion) Vorschlag m. ◆**proposition**
[prɔpə'ziʃ(ə)n], s. (suggestion) Vorschlag
m; (plan) Vorhaben n; (in debate) Antrag
m.

proprietor [prə'praiətər], s. Besitzer m.

propriety [prə'praiəti], s. 1. Anstand m.
2. (rightness) Angemessenheit f (einer Bemerkung usw.).

propulsion [prə'pʌlʃ(ə)n], s. Antrieb m.

prosaic [prəu'zeiik], adj. prosaisch.

prose [prəuz]. I. s. 1. Prosa f. 2. Sch:
Übersetzung f (in eine Fremdsprache).

prosecute ['prɔsikjuːt], v.tr. & i. Jur: to

p. s.o., gegen j-n gerichtlich vorgehen.
◆**prose'cution** [-'kjuːʃ(ə)n], s. Jur: (a) (action)
strafrechtliche Verfolgung f (eines Verbrechens); (h) (prosecuting party) An-
klagevertretung f. ◆**'prosecutor,** s.
Jur: Ankläger m.

prospect ['prɔspekt], s. Aussicht f; **job**
with good prospects, Stellung mit guten
Aufstiegsmöglichkeiten. ◆**pros'pective,**
adj. (future) möglich; (possible) eventuell;
p. client, potentieller Kunde.

prospectus, pl -uses [prə'spektəs, -əsiz],
s. Prospekt m.

prosper ['prɔspər], v.i. (of business etc.)
blühen. ◆**pros'perity** n. Wohlstand m.
◆**'prosperous,** adj. (of pers.) wohlhabend; (of business) erfolgreich.

prostitute ['prɔstitjuːt], s. Prostituierte f.
◆**prosti'tution** n. Prostitution f.

prostrate ['prɔstreit], adj. 1. **p. on the**
floor, auf dem Boden hingestreckt. 2.
Fig: **p. with grief,** vor Gram gebrochen.

protagonist [prəu'tægənist], s. Hauptfigu-
gur f.

protect [prə'tekt], v.tr. (j-n, etwas) schützen (**from sth.,** vor etwas dat); **to** p.
one's interests, seine Interessen wahren.
◆**pro'tection,** s. Schutz m.
◆**pro'tective,** adj. (a) Schutz-; p.
layer, Schutzschicht f; (b) (of pers.)
schützend. ◆**pro'tector,** s. Schützer m.

protein ['prəutiin], s. Eiweiß n.

protest. I. ['prəutest], s. Protest m; **to**
make a p., protestieren; Jur: Einspruch
einlegen; **under** p., unter Protest. II.
[prə'test] v. 1. v.i. protestieren. 2. v.tr.
to p. **one's innocence,** seine Unschuld
beteuern. ◆**Protestant** ['prɔtistənt]. I.
s. Protestant(in) m(f). II. adj. protestantisch.

protocol ['prəutəkɔl], s. Protokoll n.

protract [prə'trækt], v.tr. (Verhandlungen
usw.) in die Länge ziehen.
◆**pro'tracted,** adj. langwierig.

protrude [prə'truːd], v.i. hervorstehen;
(of ears) abstehen; (of teeth) vorstehen.
◆**pro'trusion,** s. Vorsprung m.

proud [praud], adj. 1. stolz (**of** s.o., sth.,
auf j-n, etwas acc). 2. Pej: hochmütig.

prove [pruːv], v. irr. 1. v.tr. (a) (Schuld,
eine Tatsache) beweisen; (seine Identität
usw.) nachweisen; (b) (confirm) (etwas)
bestätigen; (c) **to** p. **itself/oneself,** sich
bewähren; **to** p. **oneself to be a good**
friend, sich als treuer Freund erweisen.
2. v.i. sich herausstellen.

proverb ['prɔvɜːb], s. Sprichwort n.
◆**pro'verbial** [prə'vɜːbjəl], adj. sprichwörtlich; (in negative contexts) notorisch.

provide [prə'vaid], v. 1. v.i. **to** p. **for,**
(foresee) (eine Möglichkeit) voraussehen;
(satisfy) (Bedürfnisse) befriedigen; (Kosten) decken; **to** p. **for a family,** für eine
Familie sorgen. 2. v.tr. (Unterstützung
usw.) zur Verfügung stellen; (eine Gelegenheit) bieten; **to** p. **s.o., sth. with**
sth., j-n, etwas mit etwas dat versehen/

(*supply*) beliefern. ◆**pro'vided**, *conj.* p. (that) ..., vorausgesetzt, (daß) ...

providence ['prɔvidəns], *s.* Vorsehung *f*.

province ['prɔvins], *s.* Provinz *f*. ◆**provincial** [prə'vinʃ(ə)l], *adj.* provinziell; **p. town**, Provinzstadt *f*.

provision [prə'viʒ(ə)n]. I. *s.* 1. (a) (*providing*) Versehen *n* (of sth., mit etwas *dat*); (b) **to make p. for sth.**, Vorkehrungen für etwas *acc* treffen. 2. *pl* Lebensmittel *npl*; (*supplies*) Vorräte *mpl*. 3. *Jur:* Bestimmung *f* (eines Vertrags usw.). ◆**pro'visional**, *adj.* provisorisch.

proviso, *pl.* **-oes** [prə'vaizəu, -əuz], *s.* Vorbehalt *m*.

provocation [prɔvə'keiʃən], *s.* Provokation *f*; Herausforderung *f*. ◆**provocative** [prə'vɔk-], *adj.* herausfordernd. ◆**provoke** [prə'vəuk], *v.tr.* (j-n) provozieren; **to p. s.o. to do sth.**, j-n dazu herausfordern, etwas zu tun.

prowess ['prauis], *s.* (*skill*) Tüchtigkeit *f*.

prowl [praul]. I. *v.i.* **to p. (around)**, herumschleichen. II. *s.* **to be on the p.**, herumstreichen.

proximity [prɔk'simiti], *s.* Nähe *f*.

proxy ['prɔksi], *s.* **by p.**, in Vertretung.

prude [pruːd], *s.* Prüde(r) *f(m)*. ◆**prudish**, *adj.* prüde.

prudence ['pruːd(ə)ns], *s.* Umsicht *f*. ◆**prudent**, *adj.* umsichtig; **-ly**, *adv.* klugerweise.

prune[1] [pruːn], *s.* Backpflaume *f*.

prune[2], *v.tr.* (einen Baum usw.) beschneiden.

Prussia ['prʌʃə]. *Pr. n.* Preußen *n*. ◆**Prussian**. I. *adj.* preußisch. II. *s.* Preuße *m*, Preußin *f*.

pry [prai], *v.i.* **to p. into sth.**, seine Nase in etwas *acc* stecken.

psalm [sɑːm], *s.* Psalm *m*.

pseudo ['sjuːdəu]. I. *prefix* pseudo-. II. *adj. F:* unecht.

pseudonym ['sjuːdənim], *s.* Pseudonym *n*.

psychiatry [sai'kaiətri], *s.* Psychiatrie *f*. ◆**psy'chiatrist**, *s.* Psychiater *m*.

psychic ['saikik], *adj.* (*of phenomena*) übersinnlich.

psychoanalysis [saikəuə'nælisis], *s.* Psychoanalyse *f*.

psychology [sai'kɔlədʒi], *s.* Psychologie *f*. ◆**psycho'logical**, *adj.* psychologisch; (*of illness, pressure, reasons etc.*) psychisch. ◆**psy'chologist**, *s.* Psychologe *m*, Psychologin *f*.

pub [pʌb], *s.* (= **public house**) *F:* Wirtschaft *f*; p. crawl, Kneiperunde *f*.

puberty ['pjuːbəti], *s.* Pubertät *f*.

public ['pʌblik]. I. *adj.* öffentlich; **p. demand**, allgemeine Nachfrage; **p. house**, Wirtshaus *n*; **p. relations**, Öffentlichkeitsarbeit *f*. II. *s.* 1. **the (general) p.**, die (breite) Öffentlichkeit; **in p.**, in der Öffentlichkeit. 2. (*audience*) Publikum *n*. ◆**publican** ['pʌblikən], *s.* Wirt *m*.

publication [pʌbli'keiʃ(ə)n], *s. Lit: etc:* Veröffentlichung *f*.

publicity [pʌb'lisiti], *s.* Publicity *f*; Werbung *f*. ◆**publicize**, *v.tr.* (a) (etwas) öffentlich bekanntmachen; (b) (*advertize*) Reklame machen (für etwas *acc*).

publish ['pʌbliʃ], *v.tr.* (einen Roman usw.) veröffentlichen. ◆**publisher**, *s.* Verleger *m*. ◆**publishing**, *s.* **p. house**, Verlag *m*.

pudding ['pudiŋ], *s.* 1. *Cu:* Pudding *m*; **rice p.**, Milchreis *m*. 2. (*dessert*) Nachtisch *m*.

puddle ['pʌdl], *s.* Pfütze *f*.

puerile ['pjuərail], *adj.* infantil.

puff [pʌf]. I. *s.* 1. (a) **p. of wind**, leichter Windstoß *m*; (b) Zug *m* (an einer Zigarette); **p. of smoke**, Rauchwölkchen *n*. 2. *Cu:* **p. pastry**, Blätterteig *m*. II. *v.* 1. *v.i.* (a) (*of smoke*) paffen; (b) (*of pers., steam train*) keuchen. 2. *v.tr.* **to p. (out) smoke**, Rauch ausstoßen. ◆**puffed**, *adj.* (*of pers.*) außer Atem. ◆**puffy**, *adj.* (*of face*) aufgedunsen.

pugnacious [pʌg'neiʃəs], *adj.* kampflustig.

puke [pjuːk], *v.i. P:* kotzen.

pull [pul]. I. *s.* Zug *m*; **to give sth. a p.**, an etwas *dat* ziehen. II. *v.* 1. *v.tr.* (a) (etwas) ziehen; (b) **to p. a muscle**, sich *dat* einen Muskel zerren. 2. *v.i.* ziehen. ◆**pull down**, *v.tr.* (ein Gebäude) niederreißen. ◆**pull 'in**, *v.i. Aut:* (*of car*) einfahren; *Aut:* **to p. in (to the kerb)**, (am Randstein) anhalten. ◆**pull 'off**, *v.* 1. *v.tr. F:* **to p. o. a victory**, den Sieg erringen. 2. *v.i. Aut:* (*start*) losfahren. ◆**pull 'out**, *v.* 1. *v.tr.* (einen Zahn usw.) herausziehen. 2. *v.i.* (*of train*) abfahren; (*of car etc.*) ausscheren. ◆**pullover**, *s. Cl:* Pullover *m*. ◆**pull 'round/through**, *v.i.* (*of patient*) durchkommen. ◆**pull to'gether**, *v.tr.* **to p. oneself t.**, sich zusammennehmen. ◆**pull 'up**, *v.* 1. *v.tr.* (die Rolläden usw.) hochziehen. 2. *v.i.* (*of rider, vehicle*) anhalten.

pulley ['puli], *s.* Rolle *f*.

pulp [pʌlp], *s.* (a) (*of fruit*) Fruchtfleisch *n*. 2. (**paper**) **p.**, Papierbrei *m*.

pulpit ['pulpit], *s.* Kanzel *f*.

pulse [pʌls], *s.* Puls *m*; **to feel s.o.'s p.**, j-m den Puls fühlen. ◆**pul'sate**, *v.i.* pulsieren.

pulverize ['pʌlvəraiz], *v.tr.* (eine Substanz) pulverisieren; (Gestein) zerkleinern.

pumice ['pʌmis], *s.* **p. (-stone)**, Bimsstein *m*.

pump [pʌmp]. I. *s.* Pumpe *f*; *Aut:* **p. attendant**, Tankwart *m*. II. *v.tr.* (a) (Wasser usw.) pumpen; *Aut:* **to p. (up) a tyre**, einen Reifen aufpumpen; (b) *F:* **to p. s.o.**, j-n ausfragen.

pumpkin ['pʌm(p)kin], *s.* Kürbis *m*.

pun [pʌn], *s.* Wortspiel *n*.

punch[1] [pʌntʃ]. I. *s.* 1. (*tool*) Stempel *m*.

(*for paper etc.*) Locher *m.* 2. (*blow*) Faustschlag *m.* II. *v.tr.* (*a*) (*Papier usw.*) lochen; (*b*) (j-n, etwas) mit der Faust schlagen; to p. s.o.'s face, j-m eine ins Gesicht geben/langen, ◆'**punch-up,** *s. F:* Schlägerei *f.*

punch2, *s.* (*drink*) Punsch *m.*

punctual ['pʌŋktju(ə)l], *adj.* pünktlich.

punctuate ['pʌŋktjueit], *v.tr. & i.* (einen Text) interpunktieren. ◆**punctu'ation,** *s.* Interpunktion *f.*

puncture ['pʌŋktʃər]. I. *s. Aut: etc:* Reifenpanne *f;* to mend a p., einen Reifen flicken. II. *v.tr.* (ein Luftkissen usw.) durchstechen.

pungent ['pʌndʒənt], *adj.* 1. (*of smell*) stechend. 2. (*of remark, satire etc.*) beißend.

punish ['pʌniʃ], *v.tr.* (*a*) bestrafen; (*b*) *Fig:* (einen Motor usw.) strapazieren. ◆'**punishable,** *adj.* strafbar; it is p. by a fine, darauf steht eine Geldstrafe. ◆'**punishing,** *adj.* strapazierend. ◆'**punishment,** *s.* Strafe *f;* (*process*) Bestrafung *f.*

punk [pʌŋk], *s.* (*a*) (*Pers.*) Punker *m;* (*music*) Punk *m. ◆ Sp:* Wetter *m.*

punter ['pʌntər], *s.* Punter(in) *m(f).*

puny ['pju:ni], *adj.* kümmerlich.

pupil1 ['pju:p(i)l], *s. Sch:* Schüler(in) *m(f).*

pupil2, *s.* Pupille *f* (des Auges).

puppet ['pʌpit], *s.* Marionette *f.*

puppy ['pʌpi], *s.* junger Hund *m;* p. fat, Babyspeck *m.*

purchase ['pəːtʃəs]. I. *s.* Kauf *m;* (*article*) Anschaffung *f;* p. price, Kaufpreis *m.* II. *v.tr.* (etwas) kaufen; **purchasing power,** Kaufkraft *f.* ◆'**purchaser,** *s.* Käufer(in) *m(f).*

pure ['pjuər], *adj.* rein.

purgatory ['pəːgət(ə)ri], *s.* Fegefeuer *n.*

purge [pəːdʒ]. I. *s. esp. Pol:* Säuberungsaktion *f.* II. *v.tr.* (ein Land, eine politische Partei usw.) säubern. ◆'**purgative** [-gə-], *s. Med:* Abführmittel *n.*

purify ['pjuərifai], *v.tr.* (etwas) reinigen. ◆**purifi'cation,** *s.* Reinigung *f.* ◆'**purist,** *s.* Purist *m.* ◆'**purity,** *s.* Reinheit *f.*

Puritan ['pjuərit(ə)n]. I. *s.* Puritaner(in) *m(f).* II. *adj.* (*also* **puri'tanical**) puritanisch.

purl [pəːl], *s.* p. stitch, Linksmasche *f.*

purple ['pəːpl]. I. *s.* Purpur *m.* II. *adj.* purpurrot.

purpose ['pəːpəs], *s.* (*aim*) Zweck *m;* (*intention*) Absicht *f;* on p., absichtlich; for this p., zu diesem Zweck. ◆'**purposeful,** *adj.* zielbewußt. ◆'**purposely,** *adv.* absichtlich.

purr [pəːr], *v.i.* (*of cat*) schnurren.

purse [pəːs]. I. *s.* 1. Portemonnaie *n.* II. *v.tr.* to p. one's lips, die Lippen schürzen. ◆'**purser,** *s. Nau:* Zahlmeister *m.*

pursue [pəˈsjuː], *v.tr.* (j-n, etwas) verfolgen; (dem Vergnügen, seinem Studium

usw.) nachgehen. ◆**pur'suit,** *s.* (*a*) Verfolgung *f;* (*b*) Ausübung *f* (eines Gewerbes; Betreiben *n* (von Studien); *Fig:* the p. of happiness, die Jagd nach dem Glück.

purveyor [pəːˈveiər], *s.* Lieferant *m.*

pus [pʌs], *s.* Eiter *m.*

push [puʃ]. I. *s.* 1. Stoß *m; F:* to give s.o. the p., j-n rausschmeißen. 2. *F:* at a p., im Notfall. II. *v.* 1. *v.tr.* (*a*) (etwas) schieben; p. the button, (auf den Knopf drücken; to p. oneself forward, sich nach vorne drängen; (*b*) *F:* I'm pushed (for time), ich stehe unter Zeitdruck; (*c*) *F:* he's pushing forty, er wird (bald) vierzig. 2. *v.i.* drängen. ◆'**pusher,** *s.* (*drug*) p., Rauschgifthändler *m.* ◆'**push-bike,** *s. F:* Fahrrad *n.* ◆'**push 'off,** *v.i. F:* (*leave*) abhauen.

puss/pussy [pus, 'pusi], *s. F:* Miezekatze *f.*

put [put], *v.tr.* (*a*) (*place*) (etwas) setzen, stellen, *F:* tun (**on/in,** auf/in+ *acc*); p. it on the table, setzen/legen/stellen Sie es auf den Tisch; to p. sth. in a cupboard, etwas in einen Schrank stecken/*F:* tun; to p. milk in one's tea, Milch in seinen Tee tun; to p. the matter right, die Angelegenheit ins reine bringen; to p. a law into operation, ein Gesetz in Kraft setzen; to stay p., sich nicht vom Fleck rühren; (*b*) (*express*) (etwas) ausdrücken; to p. it mildly, gelinde gesagt; to p. a question to s.o., j-m eine Frage stellen; I'll p. it to him, ich werde es ihm vorschlagen; (*c*) (*estimate*) I p. the population at 10,000, ich schätze die Bevölkerung auf 10000. ◆'**put a'cross,** *v.tr.* (eine Idee usw.) verständlich machen. ◆'**put a'way,** *v.tr.* (*a*) (seine Sachen) wegräumen; (*b*) *F:* to p. s.o. a., j-n einsperren. ◆'**put 'back,** *v.tr.* (*a*) (etwas) zurückstecken (in sth., in etwas *acc*); (etwas) zurücklegen (on sth., auf etwas *acc*). ◆'**put 'by,** *v.tr.* (etwas) weglegen; (Geld) auf die hohe Kante legen. ◆'**put 'down,** *v.tr.* (*a*) (etwas) niedersetzen; (*b*) (*write*) (etwas) notieren; (*c*) (*attribute*) you can p. it d. to his ignorance, man kann es seiner Unwissenheit zuschreiben; (*d*) to p. d. an animal, ein Tier einschläfern. ◆'**put 'forward,** *v.tr.* (j-n, einen Plan usw.) vorschlagen; (einen Vorschlag) unterbreiten. ◆'**put 'in** *v.* 1. *v.tr.* (etwas) hineinsetzen. 2. *v.i. a*) *Nau:* to p. in to a port, in einen Hafen einlaufen; (*b*) to p. in for a post, sich um eine Stelle bewerben. ◆'**put 'off,** *v.* 1. *v.tr.* (*a*) (*postpone*) (etwas) verschieben (for a week, um eine Woche); (*b*) to p. s.o. o. with an excuse, j-n mit einer Ausrede abspeisen; *F:* (*dissuade*) to p. s.o.o. doing sth., j-n von etwas *dat* abbringen; the noise puts me o., der Lärm stört mich. ◆'**put 'on,** *v.tr.* (*a*) to p. the kettle/the potatoes on, Wasser/die Kartoffeln aufsetzen; to p. on a record/a tape, eine Platte auflegen/ein Band spielen; (b) (organize) (eine Ausstellung usw.) veranstalten; Th: (ein Stück) aufführen; (c) (switch on) (ein Licht usw.) einschalten; Aut: to p. the brakes on, bremsen; (d) (Kleider, Schuhe) anziehen; to p. on one's clothes, sich anziehen; to p. on one's hat, den Hut aufsetzen; (e) to p. on weight, zunehmen. ◆'put 'out, v.tr. (a) (stretch out) (die Hand usw.) ausstrecken; (b) (switch off) (das Licht usw.) ausschalten; he p. himself o. for me, er machte sich meinetwegen viel Mühe. ◆'put 'over, v.tr. = put across. ◆'put 'through, v.tr. Tel: can you p. me t. to X? können Sie mich bitte mit X verbinden? ◆'put to'gether, v.tr. (a) (mehrere Teile) zusammensetzen; (b) (assemble) (eine Maschine usw.) zusammenbauen; Fig: to p. two and two t., seine Schlüsse ziehen. ◆'put 'up, v.tr. (a) (einen Schirm) aufspannen; (einen Vorhang usw.) aufhängen; (b) (ein Plakat usw.) anbringen; (c) (increase) (Preise) erhöhen; (d) (accommodate) (j-n) unterbrin-

gen; (e) to p. up with sth., sich mit etwas dat abfinden; (f) to p. s.o. up to sth., j-n zu etwas dat anstiften; (g) (ein Gebäude) errichten; (ein Zelt usw.) aufschlagen. ◆'put u'pon, p.p. only to be p. u., ausgenutzt werden.

putrefy ['pju:trifai], v.i. (of object) faulen.
putrid ['pju:trid], adj. (of food etc.) faulig.
putt [pʌt]. I. s. (in golf) Putt m. II. v.i. putten.
putty ['pʌti], s. Kitt m.
puzzle ['pʌzl]. I. s. Rätsel n; (jigsaw) p., Puzzlespiel n. II. v.tr. (j-n) verdutzen; it puzzles me, es ist mir ein Rätsel. ◆'puzzled, adj. verdutzt. ◆'puzzling, adj. rätselhaft.
pygmy ['pigmi], s. Pygmäe m, Pygmäin f.
pyjamas [pi'dʒɑːməz], s.pl. Schlafanzug m.
pylon ['pailən], s. Hochspannungsmast m.
pyramid ['pirəmid], s. Pyramide f.
Pyrenees [pirə'niːz]. Pr. n. the P., die Pyrenäen pl.
python ['paiθ(ə)n], s. Pythonschlange f.

Q

Q, q [kjuː], s. (der Buchstabe) Q, q n.
quack[1] [kwæk], v.i. (of duck) quaken.
quack[2], s. (a) q. (doctor), Kurpfuscher m; (b) (charlatan) Scharlatan m.
quad [kwɔd], s. F: abbr. (child) Vierling m.
quadrangle ['kwɔdræŋgl], s. Arch: (viereckiger) Hof m.
quadruped ['kwɔdruped], s. Vierfüßler m.
quadruple ['kwɔdrupl]. I. adj. vierfach; (in four parts) vierteilig. II. v.tr. vervierfachen. ◆'quadruplet, s. Vierling m.
quagmire ['kwægmaiər, 'kwɔg-], s. Morast m.
quail [kweil], s. Wachtel f.
quaint [kweint], adj. (a) (of house, village) malerisch; (b) (curious) kurios; N.Am: drollig.
quake [kweik], v.i. zittern, (with fear, vor Angst).
Quaker ['kweikər], s. Quäker m.
qualify ['kwɔlifai], v.i. & tr. to q. s.o. for sth., (entitle) j-n zu etwas dat berechtigen; (make suitable) j-n für etwas acc geeignet machen; (b) (modify) to q. a statement etc., eine Behauptung einschränken. 2. v.i. (a) (be suitable) sich eignen (for, zu + dat); to q. for assistance, zur Unterstützung berechtigt sein; (b) (train, pass test) sich qualifizieren (as an engineer, zum Ingenieur). ◆qualification [-i'keiʃ(ə)n], s. Qualifikation f. ◆'qualified, adj. (a) (of pers.) qualifiziert; geeignet; (b) (entitled) berechtigt.
quality ['kwɔliti], s. 1. Qualität f (einer

Ware usw.); Com: q. goods, Qualitätswaren fpl; of good/bad q., von guter/schlechter Qualität. 2. (characteristic) Eigenschaft f; (consistency) Beschaffenheit f.
qualm [kwɑːm], s. to have no qualms about doing sth., keine Bedenken haben, etwas zu tun.
quandary ['kwɔndəri], s. to be in a q., sich in einem Dilemma befinden.
quantity ['kwɔntiti], s. (a) Quantität f; (amount) Menge f; (number) Anzahl f; (b) q. surveyor, Baukostensachverständige(r) m.
quarantine ['kwɔrəntiːn]. I. s. Quarantäne f. II. v.tr. (j-n, ein Tier) unter Quarantäne stellen.
quarrel ['kwɔrəl]. I. s. Streit m; to have a q., sich streiten. II. v.i. (sich) streiten (with s.o. over/about sth., mit j-m über etwas acc). ◆'quarrelsome, adj. streitsüchtig.
quarry ['kwɔri]. I. s. Steinbruch m. II. v.tr. (Steine) brechen.
quart [kwɔːt], s. Meas: Quart n (Brit: = 1,14 Liter; N.Am: = 0,95 Liter).
quarter ['kwɔːtər]. I. s. 1. (a) (also district) Viertel n; three quarters of our food, drei Viertel unserer Nahrungsmittel; (b) Z: hind quarters, Hinterteil n. 2. (a) (three months) Quartal n; Vierteljahr n; (b) q. of an hour, Viertelstunde f; three quarters of an hour, eine Dreiviertelstunde; a q. to/past eight, Viertel vor/nach acht. 3. at close quarters, dicht beieinander; seen at/from close quarters, aus der Nähe betrachtet. 4. pl. Mil: Quartiere npl. II. v.tr. (a) (einen Apfel

usw.) vierteln; (b) Mil: (Truppen) einquartieren. ◆'quarter-'final, s. Sp:
Viertelfinale n. ◆'quarterly. I. adj. (of
payment etc.) vierteljährlich. II. s. (publication) Vierteljahresschrift f.

quartet [kwɔː'tet], s. Mus: Quartett n.

quartz [kwɔːts], s. Quarz m.

quash [kwɔʃ], v.tr. (a) Jur: (ein Urteil)
widerrufen; (b) (einen Aufstand) niederschlagen.

quaver ['kweivər] I. s. Mus: Achtelnote f.
II. v.i. zittern.

quay [kiː], s. Kai m.

queasy ['kwiːzi], adj. unwohl; (sick) übel.

queen ['kwiːn], s. 1. Königin f. 2. (in
cards, chess) Dame f.

queer ['kwiər], adj. 1. (strange) seltsam;
F: komisch. 2. (homosexual) P: schwul; a
q., ein Schwuler.

quell [kwel], v.tr. Lit: (einen Aufstand,
Fig: Gefühle) unterdrücken.

quench [kwen(t)ʃ], v.tr. to q. one's
thirst, seinen Durst löschen.

query ['kwiəri]. I. s. Frage f; (on work
done) Rückfrage f; to raise a q., eine
Frage aufwerfen. II. v.tr. (eine Behauptung) in Frage stellen.

quest [kwest], s. Suche f (for,
nach + dat).

question ['kwestʃ(ə)n]. I. s. Frage f; (a)
to ask s.o. a q., j-m eine Frage stellen;
q. mark, Fragezeichen n; without q.,
zweifellos; (b) (matter) that's out of the
q. das kommt nicht in Frage; a q. of
time, eine Frage der Zeit. II. v.tr. (a)
(j-n) befragen; (of police) (j-n) verneh-
men; Jur: (einen Zeugen, Angeklagten)
verhören; (b) (etwas) bezweifeln.
◆'questionable, adj. fragwürdig; it is
q. whether ..., es ist fraglich, ob ...
◆questio'nnaire, s. Fragebogen m.

queue [kjuː]. I. s. Schlange f (von Menschen, Autos). II. v.i. to q. (up), Schlange
stehen, sich anstellen.

quibble ['kwibl], v.i. kritteln.

quick [kwik]. I. adj. schnell; a q. child,
ein aufgewecktes Kind; q. wit, schlagfer-
tiger Humor; she has a q. temper, sie ist
jähzornig. II. s. Fig: cut to the q., im
Innersten getroffen. ◆'quick-'acting,
adj. schnellwirkend. ◆'quicken, v. 1.
v.tr. (a) (im Gang) beschleunigen. 2. v.i.
(of pulse etc.) sich beschleunigen.
◆'quicksand, s. Treibsand m.
◆'quick-'tempered, adj. jähzornig.
◆'quick-'witted, adj. aufgeweckt; (of

answer etc.) schlagfertig.

quid [kwid], s. F: Pfund n.

quiet ['kwaiət]. I. s. 1. (rest, peace) Ruhe
f; (silence) Stille f; (privacy) Ungestörtheit
f. 2. F: on the q., heimlich. II. adj. ruhig; (a) (silent) still; (of talk, voice) leise;
be q.! (shut up) sei still! (b) keep q.,
behalte es für dich. ◆'quieten, v. 1.
v.tr. (j-n, ein Kind) beruhigen, (pacify)
besänftigen. 2. v.i. to q. down, sich beruhigen. ◆'quietness, s. (a) Ruhe f;
Stille f; (b) Besonnenheit f (eines Menschen usw.).

quill [kwil], s. q. (pen), Federkiel m.

quilt [kwilt], s. Steppdecke f.

quintet [kwin'tet], s. Mus: Quintett n.

quintuple ['kwintjupl]. I. adj. fünffach.
II. v.tr. verfünffachen. ◆'quintuplet, s.
Fünfling m.

quirk [kwəːk], s. Laune f (der Natur,
des Schicksals usw.).

quit [kwit]. I. adj. F: to be quit, los
sein. II. v. 1. v.tr. (j-n, einen Ort) verlassen; to q. doing sth., mit etwas dat aufhören. 2. v.i. F: (of employee) seine Stellung aufgeben.

quite [kwait], adv. (a) ganz; (fairly) ziemlich; (entirely) völlig; q. new, ganz/
ziemlich neu; not q. as much, nicht ganz
so viel; q. enough, schon genug; I don't
q. know what he will do, ich weiß nicht
recht, was er tun wird; (b) (with noun) q.
a surprise, eine ziemliche Überraschung.

quiver ['kwivər], v.i. (of voice, movement)
zittern (with, vor + dat).

quiz, pl. quizzes [kwiz, 'kwiziz]. I. s.
Quiz n. II. v.tr. (j-n) ausfragen.

quizzical ['kwizik(ə)l], adj. (teasing) (of remark, manner) neckisch; (of look, smile)
spöttisch.

quorum ['kwɔːrəm], s. Quorum n.

quota ['kwəutə], s. (of money, immigrants)
Quote f; (of goods) Kontingent n.

quote [kwəut]. I. v.tr. (a) (einen Schriftsteller, eine Stelle usw.) zitieren; to q.
(from) the Bible, aus der Bibel zitieren;
to q. an instance of sth., ein Beispiel für
etwas acc anführen; Com: please q. this
number/reference, bitte geben Sie diese
Nummer/dieses Zeichen an; (b) Com:
(einen Preis) nennen. II. v.i. to q. for
sth. einen Preis für etwas acc nennen.
III. s. F: = quotation. ◆quo'tation, s.
1. Zitat n; q. marks, Anführungszeichen
npl. 2. Com: (estimate) Kostenvoranschlag
m; (of price) Preisangabe f.

R

R, r [ɑːr], s. (der Buchstabe) R, r n.

rabbi ['ræbai], s. Rabbiner m.

rabbit ['ræbit], s. Kaninchen n; (N.Am:
also) Hase m; r. hole, Kaninchenbau m;
r. hutch, Kaninchenstall m.

rabble ['ræbl], s. (a) (mob) Pöbel m; (b)

Pej: Gesindel n.

rabies ['reibiːz], s. Tollwut f.

race[1] [reis]. I. s. Sp: Rennen n; to go to
the races, zum Pferderennen gehen; r.
meeting, (horse r.) Renntag m; Fig: r.
against time, Wettlauf m mit der Zeit;

arms r., Wettrüsten *n.* **II.** *v.* **1.** *v.i. (a)* an einem Rennen teilnehmen; *(b) (of car etc.)* to r. **along,** dahinrasen. **2.** *v.tr. (a)* to r. s.o., mit j-m um die Wette laufen; *(b)* (ein Pferd) rennen lassen. ◆'**racecourse,** *s.* Rennplatz *m.* ◆'**racehorse,** *s.* Rennpferd *n.* ◆'**race-track,** *s.* Rennbahn *f; (for motor racing)* Rennstrecke *f.* ◆'**racing,** *s. (a) (activity)* Rennen *n; (sport)* Rennsport *m; (b) attrib.* Renn-; r. **driver,** Rennfahrer *m;* r. **car,** Rennwagen *m.* ◆'**racy,** *adj. (a) (of car etc.)* sportlich; *(b) (of style)* spritzig.

race², *s.* Rasse *f;* the human r., das Menschengeschlecht. ◆'**racial** ['reiʃ(ə)l], *adj.* rassisch; r. **discrimination,** Rassendiskriminierung *f;* r. **minorities,** Rassenminderheiten *fpl.* ◆'**racialism/racism** ['reisizm], *s.* Rassismus *m.* ◆'**racialist/ 'racist. I.** *s.* Rassist *m.* **II.** *adj.* rassistisch.

rack¹ [ræk], *s. (frame)* Gestell *n; (stand)* Ständer *m;* Rail: **luggage** r., Gepäckablage *f.*

rack², *v.tr.* to r. **one's brains,** sich daf den Kopf zerbrechen.

racket¹ ['rækit], *s. Sp:* Schläger *m.*

racket², *s.* **F. 1.** *(noise)* Krach *m.* **2.** *(shady business)* Schiebergeschäft *n;* it's a r.! das ist ein Schwindel! ◆'**racke'teer,** *s.* Schieber *m.*

radar ['reidɑːr], *s.* Radar *m, n.*

radiance ['reidjəns], *s.* strahlender Glanz *m.* ◆'**radiant,** *adj.* strahlend. ◆'**radiate** ['reidieit], *v.* **1.** *v.i. (a)* ausstrahlen *(from,* aus + *dat); (emit rays)* Strahlen aussenden; *(of lines, roads etc.)* strahlenförmig (von einem Punkt) ausgehen. **2.** *v.tr.* ausstrahlen. ◆**radi'ation,** *s.* Strahlung *f;* **nuclear** r., Kernstrahlung *f.* ◆'**radiator,** *s.* **1.** *(for heating)* Heizkörper *m.* **2.** *Aut:* Kühler *m.*

radical ['rædik(ə)l]. **I.** *adj.* radikal. **II.** *s. (pers.)* Radikale(r) *f(m).*

radio ['reidiəu], *s. (a)* Radio *n;* on the r., im Radio; *(b) (institution)* Rundfunk *m;* r. **station,** Rundfunksender *m;* r. **play,** Hörspiel *n.* ◆'**radioactive,** *adj.* radioaktiv. ◆'**radioac'tivity,** *s.* Radioaktivität *f.* ◆**radi'ographer,** *s.* Röntgenassistent(in) *m(f).* ◆**radi'ologist,** *s.* Röntgenologe *m.* ◆**radi'ology,** *s.* Röntgenologie *f.*

radish ['rædiʃ], *s. (red)* Radieschen *n.*

radium ['reidiəm], *s.* Radium *n.*

radius, *pl.* **-ii** ['reidiəs, -iai], *s. Mth:* Radius *m; within a r. of three kilometres,* im Umkreis von drei Kilometern.

raffle ['ræfl], *s.* Tombola *f;* r. **ticket,** Los *n.*

raft [rɑːft], *s.* Floß *n.*

rafter ['rɑːftər], *s.* Dachsparren *m.*

rag¹ [ræg], *s. (a) (torn piece)* Fetzen *m,* Lumpen *m; (for cleaning)* Lappen *m.* ◆'**ragamuffin** ['rægəmʌfin], *s.* zerlumpter Kerl *m; (esp. child)* Strolch *m.*

◆'**ragged** ['rægid], *adj.* zerlumpt.

rag², *s. (students')* Studentenkarneval *m.*

rage [reidʒ]. **I.** *s.* Wut *f;* **(fit of)** r., Wutanfall *m;* to be in a r. **(with** s.o.), (auf j-n) wütend sein; **to fly into a** r., in Wut geraten; **to be all the** r., große Mode sein. **II.** *v.i. Fig: (of storm, wind)* toben; *(of epidemic)* wüten.

raid [reid]. **I.** *s.* Raubzug *m* (von Banditen); Razzia *f* (der Polizei); *Mil: etc:* Überfall *m;* **air** r., Luftangriff *m.* **II.** *v.tr. Mil:* (ein Lager usw.) überfallen; *(of police)* to r. **an area,** eine Razzia auf ein Viertel vornehmen.

rail [reil], *s.* **1.** *(for clothes etc.)* Stange *f;* Geländer *n* (einer Treppe usw.). **2.** *(fence) Nau:* Reling *f; esp. pl.* Gitterzaun *m.* **3.** *Rail: (a) (track)* Schiene *f; pl.* **rails,** Gleise *npl; F: (of pers.)* **to go off the rails,** aus dem Gleis kommen; *(b) (railway)* **to go/travel by** r., mit der Bahn fahren. ◆'**railings,** *s.pl.* Gitter *n;* Sitterzaun *m; (on bridge)* Geländer *n.* ◆'**railway,** *N.Am:* '**railroad,** *s.* Eisenbahn *f;* r. **station,** Bahnhof *m.*

rain [rein]. **I.** *s.* Regen *m.* **II.** *v.tr. & i. (a)* regnen, *F:* to r. **cats and dogs,** gießen, in Strömen regnen; *Sp: etc:* **to be rained off,** wegen Regen abgesagt werden; *(b) Fig: (of blows etc.)* to r. **(down),** niederprasseln. ◆'**rainbow,** *s.* Regenbogen *m.* ◆'**raincoat,** *s.* Regenmantel *m.* ◆'**raindrop,** *s.* Regentropfen *m.* ◆'**rainfall,** *s.* Regenfälle *mpl; (quantity)* Niederschlagsmenge *f.*

rainy, *adj.* regnerisch; **to keep sth. for a** r. **day,** etwas für den Notfall aufheben.

raise [reiz]. *v.tr. (a) (lift)* (die Hand, den Arm usw.) heben; (eine Last) hochheben, *(with crane)* hochwinden; (Rolläden, den Vorhang usw.) hochziehen; (sein Glas, seinen Kopf, den Blick usw.) erheben; *(b) (erect)* to r. **a monument** to s.o., j-m ein Denkmal setzen; *(c) (bring up)* (eine Familie) aufziehen; (Tiere) züchten; *(d)* to r. **false hopes,** falsche Hoffnungen erwecken; *(e)* to r. **one's voice,** seine Stimme erheben; to r. **the alarm,** Alarm schlagen; *(f)* (eine Frage) aufwerfen; to r. **an objection,** Einspruch erheben; *(g) (increase)* j-s Gehalt, einen Preis usw.) erhöhen; *(h)* to r. **money,** Geld aufbringen; *(for charity)* Geld eintreiben. **II.** *s. N.Am:* Gehaltserhöhung *f.*

raisin ['reizn], *s.* Rosine *f.*

rake [reik]. **I.** *s.* Harke *f.* **II.** *v.tr. (a)* (Blätter) zusammenharken; (den Boden, einen Weg) (glatt) harken; *(b)* (das Feuer) schüren. ◆'**rake 'in,** *v.tr. F:* to r. **in money,** Geld scheffeln. ◆'**rake 'up,** *v.tr. Fig:* to r. **up s.o.'s past,** j-s Vergangenheit aufwärmen.

rally ['ræli]. **I.** *s.* **1.** Zusammenkunft *f; (demonstration)* Massenkundgebung *f; Aut:* **(car)** r., Rallye *f.* **2.** *(in tennis)* Ballwechsel *m.* **II.** *v.* **1.** *v.tr.* (Truppen, Anhänger usw.) zusammenrufen. **2.** *v.i. (of* *troops, supporters etc.)* zusammenkommen; **they rallied round their leader,** sic scharten sich um ihren Führer.

ram [ræm]. I. *s. Z:* Widder *m.* II. *v.tr.* to r. (in) a post etc., einen Pfahl usw. einrammen; *Aut:* to r. another car, einen anderen Wagen rammen.

ramble ['ræmbl]. I. *s. (hike)* Wanderung *f.* II. *v.i. (a) (hike)* wandern; *(b) Fig:* vom Thema abschweifen. ◆'**rambling,** *adj.* 1. *(of story, speech)* weitschweifig; *(incoherent)* unzusammenhängend. 2. r. house, weitläufiges Haus.

ramifi'cation [ræmifi'keiʃ(ə)n], *s.* **ramifications of a problem,** Verwicklungen *spl* eines Problems.

ramp [ræmp], *s.* Rampe *f; (for loading)* Laderampe *f.*

rampage [ræm'peidʒ], *s.* to be on the r., randalieren.

rampant ['ræmpənt], *adj. (of evils etc.)* um sich greifend; *(unrestrained)* zügellos.

rampart ['ræmpɑːt], *s.* Wall *m.*

ramshackle ['ræmʃækl], *adj.* baufällig.

ranch [rɑːn(t)ʃ], *s. N.Am:* Ranch *f.*

rancid ['rænsid], *adj.* ranzig.

random ['rændəm]. I. *s.* at r., aufs Geratewohl; to walk out at r., blindlings drauflosschlagen. II. *adj.* ziellos; *(chance)* zufällig; r. **sample,** Stichprobe *f.*

range [reindʒ]. I. *s.* 1. *(a)* r. of **mountains/hills,** Gebirgskette *f*/Hügelkette *f; (b) (selection) Com:* Auswahl *f (of, an + dat);* wide r., große Auswahl. 2. *(distance, area) Mil.etc:* Schußweite *f* (einer Kanone usw.) Reichweite *f* (einer Rakete, eines Autos usw.) Flugbereich *m* (eines Flugzeugs); **at a r. of 800 metres,** in einer Entfernung von 800 Metern; *(b) Fig:* Bereich *m; (c) Com:* price r., Preislage *f; (d) Mus:* Umfang *m* (einer Stimme, eines Instruments). II. *v.i. (extend)* sich erstrecken, *(from … to …,* von … *dat* bis … *dat);* **the temperatures r. from ten to thirty degrees,** die Temperaturen liegen zwischen zehn und dreißig Grad.

rank¹ [ræŋk]. I. *s.* 1. *Mil:* Reihe *f,* Linie *f; Pol:* the party r. and file, das Fußvolk der Partei. 2. *(position) Mil: etc:* Rang *m.* 3. **taxi r.,** Taxistand *m.* II. *v.* 1. *v.tr. (j-n)* zählen *(with/among the great writers etc.,* zu den großen Schriftstellern usw.); *Sp:* he is ranked fifth, er steht an fünfter Stelle. 2. *v.i.* zählen *(among/ with, zu + dat);* to r. as …, als … gelten; to r. above s.o., vor j-m rangieren.

rank², *adj.* übelriechend; *(rancid)* ranzig.

rankle ['ræŋkl], *v.i.* his undeserved success rankles with me, sein unverdienter Erfolg wurmt mich.

ransack ['rænsæk], *v.tr. (a)* (ein Zimmer, eine Schublade usw.) durchwühlen; *(b)* (eine Stadt) plündern.

ransom ['rænsəm]. I. *s. (sum)* Lösegeld *n;* to be held to r., gegen Lösegeld gefangengehalten werden. II. *v.tr.* (j-n) freikaufen.

rant [rænt], *v.i. (in anger)* toben.

rap [ræp]. I. *s.* Klaps *m; (knock)* lautes Klopfen *n; Fig:* to take the r., die Schuld auf sich *acc* nehmen. II. *v.tr. & i.* klopfen *(at, an + acc;* on, auf *+ acc).*

rapacious [rə'peiʃəs], *adj.* habgierig.

rape [reip]. I. *s.* Vergewaltigung *f.* II. *v.tr.* vergewaltigen.

rapid ['ræpid]. I. *adj.* schnell; **-ly,** *adv.* schnell. II. *s. (usu. pl.) (in river)* Stromschnelle *f.* ◆**ra'pidity,** *s.* Schnelligkeit *f.*

rapt [ræpt], *adj.* hingerissen. ◆**rapture** ['ræptʃər], *s.* Entzücken *n.* ◆**'rapturous,** *adj.* r. applause, stürmischer Beifall.

rare ['rɛər], *adj.* 1. *(infrequent)* selten; *(valuable)* rar. 2. *(of air)* dünn. 3. *(of meat)* nicht gar; *(of steak)* englisch. ◆**'rarefied** [-ifaid], *adj. (of air)* verdünnt.

rascal ['rɑːsk(ə)l], *s.* Gauner *m; (esp. child)* Schlingel *m.*

rash¹ [ræʃ], *s. Med:* Hautausschlag *m.*

rash², *adj. (hasty)* übereilt; *(ill-considered)* unüberlegt; *(risky)* leichtsinnig. ◆**'rashness,** *s.* Übersürztheit *f;* Unbesonnenheit *f;* Leichtsinn *m.*

rasher ['ræʃər], *s. Cu:* r. of bacon, Scheibe *f* Speck.

rasp [rɑːsp], *v.i. (of voice etc.)* krächzen; *(of sound)* schnarren.

raspberry ['rɑːsb(ə)ri, 'rɑːz-], *s.* Himbeere *f.*

rat [ræt], *s.* 1. *Z:* Ratte *f.* 2. *Pej: (pers.)* Schuft *m.*

ratchet ['rætʃit], *s. Tchn:* Ratsche *f; (bar)* Sperrstange *f.*

rate [reit]. I. *s.* 1. *(a)* Rate *f;* Satz *m;* r. of **growth,** Wachstumsrate *f;* birth/death r., Geburtenziffer *f*/Sterblichkeitsziffer *f; Fin:* r. of **interest,** Zinssatz *m; (b) (fixed charge)* Tarif *m;* postal rates, Postgebühren *fpl.* 2. *(a) (speed)* Geschwindigkeit *f; F:* Tempo *n;* at this r., wenn es so weitergeht; at any r., jedenfalls. 3. *pl.* rates, *(tax)* Gemeindeabgaben *fpl.* 4. *(class)* first/second r., erstrangig/ zweitrangig. II. *v.tr. (estimate)* einschätzen. ◆**'rating,** *s. (a) (valuation)* Bewertung *f; (b) TV:* programme r., Einschaltquote *f* (eines Programms).

rather ['rɑːðər], *adv.* 1. ziemlich; r. pretty, recht hübsch. 2. lieber *(than,* als); I'd r. not, (ich möchte) lieber nicht. 3. eher; he is r. to be pitied than feared, er ist eher/vielmehr zu bemitleiden als zu fürchten; or r., I did have it, genauer gesagt, ich hatte es.

ratify ['rætifai], *v.tr.* (einen Vertrag) ratifizieren; *(eine Abmachung)* bestätigen. ◆**ratifi'cation,** *s.* Ratifizierung *f,* Bestätigung *f.*

ratio, *pl.* **ratios** ['reiʃiəu, -əuz], *s.* Verhältnis *n.*

ration ['ræʃ(ə)n]. I. *s.* Ration *f; (allowance)* Zuteilung *f.* II. *v.tr.* (Lebensmittel) rationieren.

rational ['ræʃən(ə)l], *adj.* **1.** (*of pers.*) vernünftig; (*sane*) zurechnungsfähig. **2.** (*of thought etc.*) rational, (*of explanation*) vernunftgemäß.

rattle ['rætl]. **I.** *s.* **1.** (*toy*) Klapper *f.* **2.** (*a*) (*noise*) Geklapper *n*; Rasseln *n* (von Ketten usw.); (*b*) **death** *r.*, Röcheln *n.* **II.** *v.* **1.** *v.i.* klappern. **2.** *v.tr.* (*a*) **to** *r.* **chains**, mit Ketten rasseln; (*b*) *F:* (j-n) aus der Fassung bringen. ◆'**rattlesnake**, *s.* Klapperschlange *f.*

raucous ['rɔːkəs], *adj.* (*of voice*) rauh; *r.* **laughter**, rohes Gelächter.

ravage ['rævidʒ]. **I.** *v.tr.* (ein Land, eine Stadt, *Fig:* ein Gesicht) verwüsten. **II.** *s.* *usu. pl.* verheerende Wirkung *f* (der Zeit usw.).

rave [reiv], *v.i.* (*a*) (*of madman*) phantasieren; **a raving lunatic**, ein Rasender; (*b*) *F:* **to** *r.* **about sth.**, von etwas *dat* schwärmen. ◆'**raving**, *s.* *usu. pl* irres Gerede *n.*

raven ['reiv(ə)n], *s.* Rabe *m.*

ravenous ['rævinəs], *adj.* heißhungrig; *F:* **to be** *r.*, einen Bärenhunger haben.

ravine [rə'viːn], *s.* Schlucht *f.*

ravishing ['ræviʃiŋ], *adj.* hinreißend (schön).

raw [rɔː], *adj.* **1.** (*uncooked*) roh; *r.* **state**, Rohzustand *m.* **2.** *Ind:* Roh-; *r.* **material**, Rohstoff *m.* **3.** (*a*) (*sore*) wund; **r.** **wound**, offene Wunde; (*b*) *r.* **weather**, naßkaltes Wetter; (*c*) *F:* **to get a** *r.* **deal**, unfair behandelt werden.

ray [rei], *s.* Strahl *m*; *r.* **of light**, Lichtstrahl *m*; **a** *r.* **of hope**, ein Hoffnungsschimmer *m.*

rayon ['reiɔn], *s.* Kunstseide *f.*

raze [reiz], *v.tr.* **to** *r.* **to the ground**, dem Erdboden gleichmachen.

razor ['reizər], *s.* (*a*) (**cut-throat**) *r.*, Rasiermesser *n*; (*b*) (**safety**) *r.*, Rasierapparat *m*; *r.* **blade**, Rasierklinge *f.*

re¹ [riː], *prep. Com:* betrifft; *abbr.* betr.; **re your letter of June 10th**, mit Bezug auf Ihren Brief vom 10. Juni.

re² ['riː-], *prefix* wieder, noch einmal; **to re-read sth.**, etwas noch einmal lesen.

reach [riːtʃ]. **I.** *s.* **1.** **within s.o.'s** *r.*, in j-s Reichweite; **out of** *r.*, außer Reichweite; **within easy** *r.* **of the station**, vom Bahnhof leicht zu erreichen. **2.** Flußstrecke *f* (zwischen zwei Krümmungen). **II.** *v.* **1.** *v.tr.* (*a*) erreichen; **to** *r.* **agreement/a conclusion**, zu einer Einigung/zu einem Schluß gelangen; (*b*) (*come as far as*) bis zu (etwas *dat*) reichen; (*c*) **to** *r.* **out**, (die Hand usw.) ausstrecken. **2.** *v.i.* sich erstrecken, reichen (**to/as far as**, bis/bis zu + *dat*); **will it** *r.* (**this far**)? reicht es (bis dahin)? (*of pers.*) hinkommen; (*c*) **to** *r.* **out for sth.**, nach etwas *dat* greifen.

react [ri'ækt], *v.i.* reagieren (**to**, auf + *acc*). ◆**re'action**, *s.* Reaktion *f*; (*statement*) Stellungnahme *f.*

◆**re'actionary**. **I.** *adj.* reaktionär. **II.** *s.* Reaktionär *m.* ◆**re'actor**, *s.* Reaktor *m.*

read [riːd]. **I.** *v.tr. & i. irr.* (*a*) (etwas) lesen; **to** *r.* **to s.o.**, j-m vorlesen; *El:* **to** *r.* **the meter**, den Zähler ablesen; (*b*) (*study*) **to** *r.* **up a subject**, über eine Sache nachlesen; (*at university*) **he's reading French**, er studiert Französisch; (*c*) **this sentence does not** *r.* **well**, dieser Satz liest sich nicht gut; (*of instrument*) anzeigen. **II.** *s.* *F:* Lektüre *f*; **this book is a good** *r.*, das Buch liest sich gut. **III.** *adj.* [red] **well-r.**, belesen; bewandert. ◆'**readable**, *adj.* **1.** (*legible*) lesbar; (*of writing*) leserlich. **2.** (*enjoyable*) lesenswert. ◆'**reader**, *s.* **1.** Leser(in) *m(f).* **2.** *Sch:* Lesebuch *n.* ◆'**readership**, *s.* Leserkreis *m.* ◆'**reading**, *s.* **1.** (*action*) Lesen *n*; Lektüre *f.* **2.** (*figure etc.*) Anzeige *f* (eines Meßinstruments). ◆'**readingmatter**, *s.* Lesestoff *m.*

readjust [riːə'dʒʌst], *v.* **1.** *v.tr.* (*a*) **to** *r.* **sth.** (**to sth.**), etwas (etwas *dat*) wieder anpassen; (*b*) *Tchn:* (etwas) neu einstellen. **2.** *v.i.* (*of pers.*) **to** *r.* (**to sth.**), sich (etwas *dat*) wieder anpassen. ◆**rea'djustment**, *s.* (*a*) Wiederanpassung *f*; (*b*) *Tchn:* Neueinstellung *f.*

ready ['redi]. **I.** *adj.* **1.** (*mentally prepared*) (*of pers.*) bereit (**to do sth.**, etwas zu tun); **to get** *r.*, sich vorbereiten (**for sth.**, auf etwas *acc*); (*b*) (*finished*) (*of pers., thing*) fertig; **lunch is** *r.*, das Mittagessen ist fertig; *Sp:* *r.*, **steady, go!** Achtung, fertig, los! **2.** (*quick*) (*of answer*) prompt. **II.** *adv.* *r.* **made**, fertig; *Cu:* Fertig-; *r.* **cooked**, fertig gekocht; **-ily**, *adv.* **1.** (*willingly*) gern. **2.** (*easily*) leicht. ◆'**readiness**, *s.* **1.** **to be in** *r.*, bereit sein. **2.** Bereitwilligkeit *f* (**to do sth.**, etwas zu tun).

real ['riəl]. **I.** *adj.* wirklich; (*genuine*) echt; (*true*) wahr; *r.* **silk**, echte Seide; **in** *r.* **life**, im wirklichen Leben. **2.** *Jur:* *r.* **estate**, Immobilien *pl*; **-ly**, *adv.* (*a*) (*genuinely*) wirklich; (*b*) (*emphatic*) **you** *r.* **must go there**, Sie müssen unbedingt hingehen. ◆'**realism**, *s.* Realismus *m.* ◆'**realist**, *s.* Realist(in) *m(f).* ◆**rea'listic**, *adj.* realistisch; (*of model etc.*) wirklichkeitsgetreu. ◆**reality** [ri'æliti], *s.* Wirklichkeit *f.*

realize ['riəlaiz], *v.tr.* (*a*) (*achieve*) (eine Ambition usw.) verwirklichen; (*b*) (*recognize*) (etwas) einsehen, erkennen; **I** *r.* **that**, das sehe ich schon ein. ◆**reali'zation**, *s.* **1.** Verwirklichung *f* (eines Plans). **2.** Einsicht *f*; Erkenntnis *f.*

realm [relm], *s.* **1.** Königreich *n.* **2.** *Fig:* (*sphere*) Bereich *m.*

ream [riːm], *s.* (*paper*) Ries *n.*

reap [riːp], *v.tr.* (Getreide usw.) ernten; (ein Feld) mähen.

reappear [riːə'piər], *v.i.* wieder erscheinen. ◆'**rea'ppearance**, *s.* Wiedererscheinen *n.*

rear¹ ['riər]. I. s. (a) hinterer Teil m; Rückseite f (eines Hauses usw.), Heck n (eines Autos); (b) **he stood at the r.** (of the crowd), er stand ganz hinten (in der Menge). II. adj. hinter, Hinter-; **r. light,** Hecklicht n; **r.- view mirror,** Rückspiegel m. ◆'**rear-'admiral,** s. Konteradmiral m.

rear², v. 1. v.tr. (a) (ein Kind) aufziehen; (Tiere) züchten; (b) **Fig: to r. its ugly head,** (of question) sich erheben; (of jealousy etc.) erwachen. 2. v.i. (of horse) sich aufbäumen.

rearm [ri:'ɑ:m], v.tr. & i. aufrüsten. ◆**re'armament,** s. Aufrüstung f.

re-arrange ['ri:ə'reindʒ], v.tr. (differently) (etwas) umstellen; (again) (etwas) neu ordnen.

reason ['ri:z(ə)n]. I. s. 1. Grund m (for, gen); (cause) Ursache f (for, gen); (occasion) Anlaß m (for, zu + dat); **with (good) r.,** mit Recht. 2. (mental powers) Verstand m. 3. (good sense) Vernunft f; **it stands to r. that...,** es leuchtet ein, daß... II. v. 1. v.i. **to r. with s.o.,** j-m zureden. 2. v.tr. **to r. that...,** folgern, daß... ◆'**reasonable,** adj. 1. (sensible) vernünftig; (understanding) verständig. 2. (a) (of article) preiswert; (of price) angemessen; (low) niedrig; (b) **in r. condition,** in ganz gutem Zustand. **-bly,** adv. 1. vernünftig. 2. (quite) ziemlich; **I know him r. well,** ich kenne ihn ganz gut. ◆'**reasoning,** s. Argumentation f.

reassemble ['ri:ə'sembl], v. 1. v.tr. (eine Maschine usw.) wieder zusammenbauen. 2. v.i. (of people) wieder zusammenkommen.

reassure ['ri:ə'ʃuər], v.tr. (j-n) beruhigen; **he reassured me that...,** er versicherte mir (nochmals), daß... ◆'**rea'ssuring,** adj. beruhigend.

rebate ['ri:beit], s. (a) (discount) Rabatt m; (b) (on tax, rent) Rückvergütung f.

rebel. I. ['reb(ə)l]. s. Rebell(in) m(f). II. [ri'bel] v.i. rebellieren. ◆**re'bellion,** s. Rebellion f. ◆**re'bellious,** adj. rebellisch.

rebirth ['ri:'bə:θ], s. Wiedergeburt f.

rebound. I. [ri'baund] v.i. zurückprallen. II. ['ri:baund] s. **on the r.,** Fig: als Reaktion.

rebuff [ri'bʌf]. I. s. Abfuhr f. II. v.tr. (j-n) abweisen; (of girl) (j-n) abblitzen lassen.

rebuild ['ri:'bild], v.tr.irr. wiederaufbauen.

rebuke [ri'bju:k]. I. s. Rüge f. II. v.tr. (j-n) rügen.

recall [ri'kɔ:l]. I. s. (memory) Erinnerungsvermögen n. II. v.tr. (a) (j-n) zurückrufen; (einen Botschafter) abberufen; (b) **I don't r. his name,** ich kann mich nicht an seinen Namen erinnern.

recapitulate [ri:kə'pitjuleit], v.tr. & i. (Hauptpunkte einer Rede) rekapitulieren, wiederholen. ◆**'recapitu'lation,** F: 'recap, s. Rekapitulation f.

recapture ['ri:'kæptʃər]. I. v.tr. (einen Verbrecher) wieder gefangennehmen; (eine Stadt usw.) zurückerobern. II. s. Wiedergreifung f; Wiedereinnahme f (einer Stadt usw.).

recede [ri'si:d], v.i. (of flood etc.) zurückgehen. ◆**re'ceding,** adj. 1. zurückgehend. 2. (of forehead) fliehend.

receipt [ri'si:t], s. 1. Empfang m; **on r. of this letter,** nach Erhalt/Com: Eingang dieses Briefes. 2. Com: pl. receipts, Einnahmen fpl. 3. (document) (for goods) Empfangsbestätigung f; (for money) Quittung f; (from till) Kassenzettel m; **to give a r. for a sum/a payment,** eine Geldsumme/Zahlung quittieren.

receive [ri'si:v], v.tr. (a) erhalten; (eine Wunde, Rad: eine Sendung, Ecc: das Sakrament usw.) empfangen; (b) (greet) (Gäste) empfangen. ◆**re'ceiver,** s. 1. (in bankruptcy) Konkursverwalter m. 2. (a) Tel:/Rad: Hörer m; (b) Rad: Empfänger m.

recent ['ri:s(ə)nt], adj. (of event) unlängst/vor kurzem stattgefunden; **in r. years,** in den letzten Jahren; **r. events,** die jüngsten Ereignisse; **-ly,** adv. kürzlich, neulich; **he has r. become lazy,** er ist in letzter Zeit faul geworden.

receptacle [ri'septəkl], s. Behälter m.

reception [ri'sep(ə)n], s. Empfang m; (in hotel etc.) **r. (desk),** Empfang m, Rezeption f. ◆**re'ceptionist,** s. (in hotel etc.) Empfangsdame f; (male) Empfangschef m; Med: Sprechstundenhilfe f. ◆**re'ceptive** [ri'septiv], adj. (of pers.) empfänglich (to, für + acc).

recess, pl. -esses [ri'ses, 'ri:ses, -esiz], s. 1. (in wall) Nische f. 2. Ferien pl (des Parlaments usw.). ◆**re'cession,** s. Com: Konjunkturrückgang m.

recipe ['resipi], s. Rezept n.

recipient [ri'sipiənt], s. Empfänger(in) m(f).

reciprocate [ri'siprəkeit], v.tr. **to r. s.o.'s feelings/good wishes,** j-s Gefühle/ Glückwünsche erwidern. ◆**re'ciprocal,** adj. gegenseitig.

recite [ri'sait], v.tr. & i. (ein Gedicht usw.) aufsagen, (in public) vortragen. ◆**re'cital,** s. Mus: Solistenkonzert n. ◆**recitation** [resi'tei(ə)n], s. Vortrag m.

reckless ['reklis], adj. (of driving etc.) rücksichtslos; (of behaviour) leichtsinnig.

reckon ['rek(ə)n], v.tr. & i. (a) (calculate) (Kosten) berechnen; (b) (estimate) (Kosten, den Wert) schätzen; (c) (think) meinen; (rate) (j-n, etwas) einschätzen; (d) **to r. on sth.,** auf etwas acc rechnen. ◆**'reckoning,** s. **to be out in one's r.,** sich verrechnet haben; **day of r.,** Tag der Abrechnung.

reclaim [ri'kleim], v.tr. (a) (claim back) (Eigentum) zurückfordern; (b) **to r. land from the sea,** Neuland vom Meer gewinnen. **II.** ['ri:klaim] *s. Av:* baggage r., Gepäckausgabe *f.*

recline [ri'klain], *v.i.* liegen (**on/upon**, auf + *dat*); **reclining on a couch**, ausgestreckt auf einer Couch; **reclining seats**, Liegesitze *mpl.*

recluse [ri'klu:s], *s.* Einsiedler(in) *m(f).*

recognize ['rekəgnaiz], *v.tr.* (a) (j-n, etwas) erkennen (**by sth.**, an etwas *dat*); (b) (einen Staat, j-s Rechte, Leistungen) anerkennen. ◆**recog'nition**, *s.* **1.** Erkennen *n.* **2.** Anerkennung *f* (eines Staates usw.). ◆**'recognizable**, *adj.* erkennbar. ◆**'recognized**, *adj.* (*of expert etc.*) anerkannt.

recoil [ri'koil] *s.* Rückstoß *m* (eines Gewehrs); Rücklauf *m* (eines Geschützes). **II.** [ri'koil] *v.i.* (a) (*of firearm*) zurückstoßen; (b) (*of pers.*) zurückspringen; (*in horror*) zurückschrecken (**from**, vor + *dat*).

recollect [rekə'lekt], *v.tr.* to r. sth., sich an etwas *acc* erinnern. ◆**reco'llection**, *s.* Erinnerung *f.*

recommend [rekə'mend], *v.tr.* to r. sth. to s.o., j-m etwas empfehlen; to r. s.o. to do sth., j-m empfehlen/raten, etwas zu tun. ◆**recommen'dation**, *s.* Empfehlung *f.*

recompense ['rekəmpens]. **I.** *s.* Belohnung *f*; Entschädigung *f* (für einen Verlust usw.). **II.** *v.tr.* (j-n) belohnen (**for sth.**, für etwas *acc*).

reconcile ['rekənsail], *v.tr.* (a) (zwei Personen miteinander) versöhnen; **to become reconciled**, sich versöhnen; **to r. oneself to sth.**, sich mit etwas *dat* abfinden; (b) (Gegensätze usw.) in Einklang bringen. ◆**recon'cilable**, *adj.* (*of pers.*) versöhnbar; (*of things*) vereinbar. ◆**reconcili'ation** [-sili-], *s.* Versöhnung *f* (zwischen zwei Personen).

recondition [ri:kən'diʃ(ə)n], *v.tr.* (etwas) überholen.

reconnaissance [ri'kɔnis(ə)ns], *s. Mil: etc:* Erkundung *f* (der feindlichen Stellungen); Aufklärung *f.*

reconnoitre [rekə'nɔitər], *v.* **1.** *v.tr.* (ein Gelände) erkunden. **2.** *v.i.* Erkundungen anstellen.

reconsider [ri:kən'sidər], *v.tr.* sich *dat* (eine Frage usw.) nochmals überlegen.

reconstruct [ri:kən'strʌkt], *v.tr.* (ein Gebäude usw.) wiederaufbauen. ◆**'recon'struction**, *s.* (a) Wiederaufbau *m*; (b) Rekonstruktion *f* (eines Verbrechens usw.).

record. I. ['rekɔ:d] *s.* **1.** (a) Aufzeichnung *f* (von Tatsachen usw.); (*document*) Aktenstück *n*; (*list*) Register *n*; **to make/keep a r. of sth.**, etwas protokollieren/aufzeichnen; (b) *pl.* records, Akten *fpl*; *Hist:* Archiv *n.* **2.** (*reputation*) Leumund *m*; **to have a criminal r.**, vorbestraft sein. **3.** *Sp: etc:* Rekord *m*; **4.** *Rec:* Schallplatte, *f:* Platte *f*; **r. player**, Plattenspieler *m*. **II.** [ri'kɔ:d] *v.tr.* (a) (eine

Tat, ein Geschehen) aufzeichnen; (b) *Tchn:* (*of meter etc.*) (einen Wert) registrieren; (c) **recorded delivery**, *approx.*=Einschreiben *n*; (d) *Rec:* (etwas) aufnehmen. ◆**re'corder**, *s.* **1.** *Rec:* (tape) r., Tonbandgerät *n*; **cassette r.**, Kassettenrecorder *m.* **2.** *Mus:* Blockflöte *f.* ◆**re'cording**, *s. Rec:* Aufnahme *f.*

recount¹ [ri'kaunt], *v.tr.* (etwas) erzählen.

recount² **I.** [ri'kaunt] *v.tr.* (Stimmen usw.) nachzählen. **II.** ['ri:kaunt] *s. Pol:* nochmalige Zählung *f* (der Stimmen).

recoup [ri'ku:p], *v.tr.* to r. one's losses, seine Verluste wiedergutmachen.

recourse [ri'kɔ:s], *s.* **to have r. to sth.**, Zuflucht zu etwas *dat* nehmen.

recover [ri'kʌvər], *v.* **1.** *v.tr.* (einen verlorenen Gegenstand) zurückbekommen; (eine Schuld) eintreiben; (einen Verlust) wiedergutmachen. **2.** *v.i.* sich erholen. ◆**re'covery**, *s.* **1.** (*of sth. lost etc*) Wiedererlangung *f.* **2.** (*of pers.*) Erholung *f*; (*from illness*) Genesung *f.*

recreation [rekri'eiʃ(ə)n], *s.* Erholung *f*; (*entertainment*) Unterhaltung *f*; (*pastime*) Zeitvertreib *m.*

recrimination [rikrimi'neiʃ(ə)n], *s. usu. pl.* gegenseitige Beschuldigungen *fpl.*

recruit [ri'kru:t]. **I.** *s.* Rekrut *m.* **II.** *v.tr.* (a) *Mil:* rekrutieren; (b) (neue Mitglieder) werben. ◆**re'cruitment**, *s. Com:* Anwerbung *f* (von Arbeitskräften usw.).

rectangle ['rektæŋgl], *s.* Rechteck *n.* ◆**rec'tangular**, *adj.* rechteckig.

rectify ['rektifai], *v.tr.* (einen Fehler) korrigieren; (eine Aussage) richtigstellen; (Mißstände) beseitigen.

rector ['rektər], *s.* **1.** *Ecc:* Pfarrer *m.* **2.** (*of university*) Rektor *m.*

recumbent [ri'kʌmbənt], *adj.* liegend.

recuperate [ri'ku:pəreit], *v.i.* (*of pers.*) sich erholen.

recur [ri'kə:r], *v.i.* (*of event, problem etc.*) wiederkehren; (*be repeated*) sich wiederholen. ◆**recurrence** ['kʌrəns] *s.* Wiederkehr *f*, Wiederauftreten *n* (einer Krankheit usw.). ◆**re'current**, *adj.* immer wieder auftretend.

recycle [ri:'saikl], *v.tr.* wiederverwerten.

red [red]. **I.** *adj.* (a) rot; **r. light district**, Bordellviertel *n*; (b) *F:* **r. herring**, (*action*) Ablenkungsmanöver *n*; (*clue*) falsche Spur *f*; (c) *Adm:* r. tape, Bürokratie *f.* **II.** *s.* (a) (*colour*) Rot *n*; (b) *F:* **to be in the r.**, in den roten Zahlen stecken. ◆**'redden**, *v.i.* (*of sky, leaves etc.*) rot werden; (*of pers.*) erröten (at, über + *acc*; with, vor + *dat*). ◆**'reddish**, *adj.* rötlich. ◆**'red-'haired**, *adj.* rothaarig. ◆**'red-'handed**, *adj.* **to catch s.o. r.-h.**, j-n auf frischer Tat ertappen. ◆**'redhead**, *s.* Rothaarige(r) *f(m).* ◆**'red-'hot**, *adj.* (*of metal*) glühend heiß. ◆**'redness**, *s.* Röte *f.*

redecorate [ri:'dekəreit], *v.tr.* neu streichen und tapezieren.

redeem [ri'di:m], *v.tr.* (a) *Ecc:* (j-n) erlösen; (b) (Fehler usw.) ausgleichen; (save) (seinen guten Ruf usw.) wiederherstellen. ◆re'deemer, s. the R., der Erlöser. ◆re'deeming, adj. the only r. feature is that..., das einzig Gute daran ist, daß ... ◆re'demption [ri'dempf(ə)n], s. Ecc: Erlösung f (der Menschheit).

redirect ['ri:dai'rekt, -di-], v.tr. (einen Brief usw.) nachsenden.

redress [ri'dres], v.tr. (a) (ein Unrecht) wiedergutmachen; (einen Mißstand) beseitigen; (b) to r. the balance, das Gleichgewicht wiederherstellen.

reduce [ri'dju:s], v.tr. (a) (etwas) reduzieren, (in length) verkürzen, (scale down) verkleinern (to, auf + acc); (eine Zahl) vermindern; (die Temperatur) senken; (den Preis) herabsetzen; Fig: to r. s.o. to silence/despair, j-n zum Schweigen/zur Verzweiflung bringen. ◆re'duced, adj. reduziert; (of speed, number) vermindert; r. fare, ermäßigter Fahrpreis. ◆reduction [ri'dʌkʃ(ə)n], s. Verminderung f, Reduzierung f; Herabsetzung f (der Preise); Rückgang m (der Temperatur); Com: Rail: etc: Ermäßigung f.

redundant [ri'dʌndənt], adj. überschüssig; (of worker) überzählig; to be made r., entlassen werden. ◆re'dundancy, s. Com: Entlassung f (von überzähligen Arbeitern); r. pay(ment), Abfindung f.

reed [ri:d], s. 1. Bot: Schilfrohr n; esp. pl. reeds, Schilf n. 2. Mus: Rohrblatt n.

reef [ri:f], s. Riff n; coral r., Korallenriff n.

reek [ri:k]. I. s. Gestank m. II. v.i. stinken (of nach).

reel [ri:l]. I. s. (a) r. of cotton, Garnrolle f; (b) (for fishing) Rolle f; (c) Rec: Cin: Spule f; (d) Mus: schottischer Reigentanz m. II. v. 1. v.tr. F: to r. off answers etc., Antworten usw. herunterrasseln. 2. v.i. taumeln.

re-elect [ri:i'lekt], v.tr. (j-n) wiederwählen. ◆re-e'lection, s. Wiederwahl f.

re-enter ['ri:'entər], v.tr. & i. wieder eintreten

refectory [ri'fektəri], s. Speisesaal m; (for students) Mensa f.

refer [ri'fɔ:r], v. 1. v.tr. to r. a matter to s.o./to a tribunal etc., eine Sache an j-n/ein Gericht usw. weiterleiten; his doctor referred him to a specialist, sein Arzt überwies ihn zu einem Facharzt. 2. v.i. (a) to r. to s.o., sth., auf j-n, etwas acc hinweisen; (mention) j-n, etwas erwähnen; (b) to r. to s.o., sth. as (one's authority), sich auf j-n, etwas acc berufen. ◆referee [refə'ri:]. I. s. 1. Sp: Schiedsrichter m. 2. to give s.o. as a r., j-n als Referenz angeben. II. v.tr. (einen Spiel) als Schiedsrichter leiten. ◆reference ['ref(ə)rəns], s. 1. Verweisung f (einer Frage usw.) (to, an + acc). 2. (a) (mention) Erwähnung f (to, gen); Hinweis m (to, auf + acc); with r. to...,

mit Hinsicht auf + acc; Com: bezugnehmend auf + acc; (b) Com: Adm: (on letter, file etc.) Aktenzeichen n. 3. r. work, Nachschlagewerk n. 4. (for job) Referenz f. ◆refe'rendum, s. Volksentscheid m.

refill. I. ['ri:'fil] v.tr. (etwas) nachfüllen. II. ['ri:fil] s. Nachfüllung f; (for ballpoint) (neue) Mine f.

refine [ri'fain], v.tr. (a) (Zucker, Petroleum usw.) raffinieren; (b) (seinen Geschmack, Methoden usw.) verfeinern. ◆re'fined, adj. (of taste etc.) verfeinert; (of pers.) kultiviert. ◆re'finement, s. (quality) Feinheit f (der Sprache, Manieren usw.). ◆re'finery, s. Raffinerie f.

reflect [ri'flekt], v. 1. v.tr. (of surface) (Licht, ein Bild) wiederspiegeln; (Hitze, Strahlen) reflektieren. 2. v.i. (a) (meditate) nachdenken (on/upon sth., über etwas acc); (b) (of action) to r. on s.o., ein schlechtes Licht auf j-n werfen. ◆re'flection, s. 1. (a) (process) Wiederspiegelung ; (image) Spiegelbild n; (b) Reflexion f (von Strahlen usw.). 2. (thought) Überlegung f; on r., wenn ich es mir überlege.

reflex ['ri:fleks], s. Reflex m.

reflexive [ri'fleksiv], adj. Gram: r. pronoun, Reflexivpronomen n.

reform [ri'fɔ:m]. I. v.tr. (Verwaltung usw.) reformieren. v. 1. v.i. sich bessern. II. s. Reform f; pl Reformbestrebungen fpl. ◆refor'mation [refə'meiʃ(ə)n], s. 1. Reformierung f, Besserung f (des Charakters usw.). 2. Hist: the R., die Reformation. ◆re'former, s. Reformer(in) m(f); Ecc: Hist: Reformator m.

refrain [ri'frein], v.i. to r. from sth., von etwas dat absehen; he could not r. from smiling, r. konnte sich des Lächelns nicht enthalten.

refresh [ri'freʃ], v.tr. (a) (j-n) erfrischen; (b) to r. oneself, sich erfrischen; (with drink, food) sich stärken. ◆re'freshing, adj. erfrischend; (of sleep) erquickend. ◆re'freshment, s. Erfrischung f.

refrigerate [ri'fridʒəreit], v.tr. (Nahrungsmittel) kühlen. ◆re'frigerator, s. Kühlschrank m.

refuel ['ri:'fjuəl], v.tr. Nau: Av: (ein Schiff, ein Flugzeug) betanken.

refuge ['refju:dʒ], s. 1. Zuflucht f; (protection) Schutz m (from, vor + dat); to seek/take r. with s.o., Zuflucht bei j-m nehmen. 2. (place) Zufluchtsort m; (home) Zufluchtsstätte f; Asyl n. ◆refu'gee, s. Flüchtling m.

refund. I. [ri:'fʌnd] v.tr. (Geld) zurückzahlen (to s.o., an j-n). II. ['ri:fʌnd] s. Rückzahlung f.

refurbish ['ri:'fɔ:biʃ], v.tr. (ein Haus usw.) renovieren.

refuse¹ ['refju:s], s. Müll m; garden r., Gartenabfälle mpl; r. collection, Müllabfuhr f; r. tip, Müllkippe f.

refuse² [ri'fju:z], v.tr. (a) to r. s.o. sth.,

j-m etwas verweigern; **to r. an application, a gift etc.,** einen Antrag, ein Geschenk usw. ablehnen; (b) **to r. to do sth.,** sich weigern, etwas zu tun. ◆re'fusal, s. Ablehnung f (eines Antrags usw.); Verweigerung f (einer Bitte usw.).

refute [ri'fjuːt], v.tr. widerlegen.

regain [ri(ː)'gein], v.tr. (die Freiheit usw.) wiedergewinnen; **to r. consciousness,** wieder zu Bewußtsein kommen.

regal ['riːg(ə)l], adj. königlich. ·

regard [ri'gɑːd]. I. s. 1. **with/having r. to,** hinsichtlich + gen; **with r. to payment,** was die Zahlung betrifft ... 2. (consideration) Rücksicht f (for, auf + acc); (concern) Beachtung f (for, gen); **without r. for expense,** ohne Rücksicht auf die Kosten. 3. (a) (esteem) Achtung f; (b) (end of letter) **regards,** Peter, herzliche Grüße, Peter. II. v.tr. (a) (etwas) ansehen (as, als); (b) (concern) (j-n) betreffen; **as regards the money,** was das Geld betrifft; (c) (j-s Wünsche) berücksichtigen. ◆re'garding, prep. hinsichtlich + gen; **r. your enquiry,** mit Bezug auf Ihre Anfrage. ◆re'gardless, adj. r. of, ungeachtet + gen.

regenerate [ri'dʒenəreit], v.tr. Fig: (etwas) neu beleben.

regent ['riːdʒənt], s. Regent(in) m(f). ◆'regency, s. Regentschaft f.

regime [rei'ʒiːm], s. Pol: Regime n.

regiment ['redʒimənt], s. Regiment n.

region ['riːdʒ(ə)n], s. 1. (a) Gebiet n, Region f; (b) (district) Gegend f; Adm: Bezirk m. 2. (sphere) Bereich m; **a sum in the r. of £1000,** eine Summe von ungefähr 1000 Pfund. ◆'regional, adj. regional.

register ['redʒistər]. I. s. 1. (list) Register n; Sch: (class) r., Klassenbuch n. 2. (vocabulary etc.) Sprachgebrauch m (eines Fachbereichs usw.). 3. **cash r.,** Registrierkasse f. II. v.tr. (a) (einen Namen) einschreiben; (eine Geburt) anmelden; (b) (of meter) (einen Wert) anzeigen. 2. v.i. (a) sich (in ein Register) eintragen; sich (bei der Polizei usw.) anmelden; (b) F: **it didn't r. (with her),** sie hat es nicht mitgekriegt. ◆'registered, adj. (of letter etc.) eingeschrieben. ◆regis'trar, s. 1. (r. of births etc.) Standesbeamte(r) m 2. (at university) Registerführer m. 3. Med: Oberarzt m. ◆regis'tration, s. Eintragung f; **r. number,** (polizeiliches) Kennzeichen n. ◆'registry, s. r. office, Standesamt n.

regret [ri'gret]. I. s. Bedauern n; **to have no regrets** keine Reue empfinden. II. v.tr. (a) (etwas) bedauern; **I r. to have to tell/inform you that ...,** ich muß Ihnen leider mitteilen, daß ...; (b) (eine Tat, Vergangenes) bereuen. ◆re'grettable, adj. bedauerlich. ◆re'gretful, adj. bedauernd; (sad) traurig; (remorseful) reuevoll; **-ly,** adv. mit Bedauern.

regular ['regjulər]. I. adj. (a) regelmäßig; (b) (systematic) geregelt, geordnet; (c) (usual) üblich; Gram: **r. verb,** regelmäßiges Verb; (d) **r. staff,** ständiges Personal. II. s. F: (in shop) Stammkunde m, Stammkundin f; (in pub) Stammgast m. ◆regu'larity, s. Regelmäßigkeit f. ◆'regulate, v.tr. regulieren; (den Verkehr, die Geschwindigkeit usw.) regeln. ◆regu'lation, s. (rule) Vorschrift f; attrib. vorschriftsmäßig.

rehabilitate [riːhə'biliteit], v.tr. (a) (j-n) rehabilitieren; (b) (Versehrte, Flüchtlinge, Verbrecher) wieder (in die Gesellschaft) eingliedern. ◆rehabili'tation, s. Rehabilitierung f; Wiedereingliederung f (in die Gesellschaft).

rehearse [ri'həːs], v.tr. & i. (ein Stück) proben. ◆re'hearsal, s. Probe f.

reign [rein]. I. s. Herrschaft f; **r. of terror,** Schreckensherrschaft f. II. v.i. regieren (over, über + acc).

reimburse [riːim'bəːs], v.tr. **to r. s.o. (for his costs)/s.o.'s costs,** j-m die Kosten rückerstatten.

rein [rein], s. Zügel m; Fig: **to give free r. to sth.,** etwas dat freien Lauf lassen.

reindeer ['reindiər], s. Rentier n.

reinforce [riːin'fɔːs], v.tr. (einen Bau, einen Stoff, Mil: eine Besatzung usw.) verstärken; **reinforced concrete,** Stahlbeton m. ◆rein'forcement, s. Mil: usu. pl. Verstärkungstruppen fpl.

reinstate [riːin'steit], v.tr. (j-n) wiedereinstellen.

reiterate [riː'itəreit], v.tr. (etwas) wiederholen.

reject [ri'dʒekt] v.tr. (of pers.) (etwas) ablehnen; (eine Methode, ein Urteil) verwerfen; (einen Freier, einen Kandidaten usw.) abweisen. II. ['riːdʒekt] s. Ausschußware f. ◆re'jection, s. Ablehnung f; Verwerfung f; Zurückweisung f.

rejoice [ri'dʒɔis], v.i. sich (über) freuen, (at/over sth., über etwas acc).

rejoin [ri'dʒɔin], v.tr. sich (j-m) wieder anschließen.

rejuvenate [ri'dʒuːvineit], v.tr. (sich, j-n) verjüngen.

relapse [ri'læps], s. Rückfall m.

relate [ri'leit], v.tr. (a) (etwas) erzählen; (Tatsachen) berichten; (b) (zwei Sachen) aufeinander beziehen, in Beziehung bringen. 2. v.i. **to r. to sth.,** (i) sich auf etwas acc beziehen; (ii) (of pers.) eine Beziehung zu etwas dat haben. ◆re'lated, adj. 1. (of things) verbunden (to, mit + dat). 2. (of pers.) verwandt (to, mit + dat). ◆re'lation, s. 1. (relationship) Beziehung f; Verhältnis n; **in r. to,** im Verhältnis zu + dat. 2. (pers.) Verwandte(r) f(m). ◆re'lationship, s. (a) Verhältnis n (to/with, zu + dat); (b) (to relative) Verwandtschaft f.

relative ['relətiv]. I. adj. 1. (a) (of terms, success etc.) verhältnismäßig; (b) **r. to sth.,** im Verhältnis zu etwas dat. 2.

Gram: r. pronoun, Relativpronomen *n.*
II. *s.* Verwandte(r) *f(m);* **-ly,** *adv.* verhältnismäßig; r. **happy,** ganz/ziemlich glücklich.

relax [ri'læks], *v.* 1. *v.tr.* (den Griff, die Disziplin, ein Verbot usw.) lockern; (Muskeln) entspannen. 2. *v.i.* sich entspannen. ◆**relax'ation,** *s.* Lockerung *f;* Entspannung *f.* ◆**re'laxing,** *adj.* entspannend.

relay. **I.** [ri'lei] *v.tr.irr.* (eine Nachricht) weitergeben; *Rad:* übertragen. **II.** ['ri:lei] *s.* (*relief team*) Ablösung *f;* **to work in relays,** sich (bei der Arbeit) ablösen; *Sp:* r. (*race*), Staffellauf *m.*

release [ri'li:s]. **I.** *s.* 1. (*of pers.*) Befreiung *f;* Freilassung *f* (eines Gefangenen). 2. (*a*) Freigabe *f* (*Com:* eines neuen Modells, *Cin:* eines Films); (*b*) (*press*) *Pr.,* Verlautbarung *f.* **II.** *v.tr.* (*a*) (j-n) befreien; (einen Gefangenen) freilassen; (*b*) (*Com:* einen neuen Wagen usw., *Cin:* einen Film) freigeben; (*publish*) (einen Text usw.) veröffentlichen; (*c*) (*let go*) loslassen; (die Bremse) lösen.

relegate ['religeit], *v.tr.* (j-n, etwas) verbannen (**to,** in + *acc*); *Fb:* **to be relegated,** absteigen (**to,** in + *acc*).

relent [ri'lent], *v.i.* sich erweichen lassen. ◆**re'lentless,** *adj.* (*of pers.*) schonungslos; (*pitiless*) erbarmungslos; r. **struggle,** erbitterter Kampf.

relevant ['relivənt], *adj.* einschlägig; **to be r. to sth.,** sich auf etwas *acc* beziehen. ◆**'relevance,** *s.* Relevanz *f.*

reliable [ri'laiəbl], *adj.* zuverlässig; (*trustworthy*) vertrauenswürdig; (*of machine*) betriebssicher. ◆**relia'bility,** *s.* Zuverlässigkeit *f;* Vertrauenswürdigkeit *f;* Betriebssicherheit *f* (einer Maschine usw.) ◆**re'liant,** *adj.* **to be r. on s.o.,** sich auf j-n verlassen müssen.

relic ['relik], *s.* 1. *Ecc:* Reliquie *f.* 2. (*remains*) Überrest *m;* relics of the past, Altertümer *npl.*

relief¹ [ri'li:f], *s.* 1. Erleichterung *f.* 2. (*a*) (*aid*) r. **fund,** Unterstützungsfonds *m;* (*b*) (*substitute*) Entlastung *f;* (*c*) *Mil: etc:* Ablösung *f* (einer Wache usw.). 3. *Fin:* tax r., Steuererleichterung *f.* ◆**re'lieve,** *v.tr.* (*a*) (Leiden) erleichtern; (Schmerzen) lindern; (j-s Gewissen) beruhigen; (*b*) *Mil:* **to r. a town/fortress,** eine Stadt/Festung entsetzen; **to r. s.o. of a duty/responsibility,** j-n von einer Pflicht/Verantwortung entbinden. ◆**re'lieved,** *adj.* erleichtert.

relief², *s.* **to stand out in (sharp) r.,** sich scharf abheben (**against sth.,** von etwas *dat*).

religion [ri'lidʒən], *s.* Religion *f;* *Fig:* Kult *m.* ◆**re'ligious,** *adj.* religiös; (*pious*) fromm.

relinquish [ri'liŋkwiʃ], *v.tr.* einen Plan usw. aufgeben; (auf ein Recht) verzichten.

relish ['reliʃ]. **I.** *s.* 1. (*spice*) Würze *f.*
Fig: **with great r.,** mit großem Vergnü-

gen. **II.** *v.tr.* **to r. doing sth.,** etwas sehr gern/mit Vergnügen tun.

reluctance [ri'lʌktəns], *s.* Widerwille *m;* Abneigung *f* (, etwas zu tun). ◆**re'luctant,** *adj.* 1. (*of pers.*) **to be r. to do sth.,** abgeneigt, etwas zu tun. 2. (*of consent etc.*) widerwillig; (*hesitant*) zögernd; **-ly,** *adv.* widerstrebend.

rely [ri'lai], *v.i.* **to r. (up)on s.o., sth.,** sich auf j-n, etwas *acc* verlassen.

remain [ri'mein], *v.i.* bleiben; **only ten ...,** es sind nur noch zehn übrig; **to r. sitting/seated,** sitzen bleiben; **to r. behind,** zurückbleiben. ◆**re'mainder,** *s.* the r., der Rest; *coll.* die Übrigen *pl;* the r. of his life, der Rest seines Lebens. ◆**re'maining,** *adj.* übrig; (*surviving*) übriggeblieben. ◆**re'mains,** *s.pl.* Reste *mpl;* Überbleibsel *npl* (einer Mahlzeit); Überreste *mpl,* Spuren *fpl* (einer Zivilisation usw.).

remand [ri'mɑ:nd], *s.* *Jur:* on r., in Untersuchungshaft.

remark [ri'mɑ:k]. **I.** *s.* Bemerkung *f.* **II.** *v.* 1. *v.tr.* bemerken. 2. *v.i.* **to r. on sth.,** auf etwas *acc* hinweisen. ◆**re'markable,** *adj.* bemerkenswert; (*strange*) merkwürdig; (*extraordinary*) außerordentlich.

remedial [ri'mi:djəl], *adj.* Hilfs-. ◆**remedy** ['remidi]. **I.** *s.* (*a*) Abhilfe *f;* Mittel *n* (**for/against,** gegen + *acc*); (*b*) *Med:* Heilmittel *n.* **II.** *v.tr.* (etwas *dat*) abhelfen, in Ordnung bringen; (einen Mißstand) beseitigen.

remember [ri'membə], *v.tr.* (*a*) **to r. s.o., sth.,** sich an j-n, etwas *acc* erinnern; **as far as I r.,** soviel/soweit ich mich entsinne; (*b*) (*make a mental note of*) sich *dat* (etwas) merken; (*c*) (*bear in mind*) (etwas) bedenken. ◆**re'membrance,** *s.* Andenken *n;* in r. of s.o., zur Erinnerung/(on grave etc.) zum Andenken an j-n; **R. Day,** Heldengedenktag *m.*

remind [ri'maind], *v.tr.* **to r. s.o. of s.o., sth.,** j-n an j-n, etwas *acc* erinnern; **that reminds me (...)!** dabei fällt mir ein (,...)! ◆**re'minder,** *s.* Mahnung *f.*

reminisce [remi'nis], *v.i.* in Erinnerungen schwelgen. ◆**remi'niscence,** *s.* Erinnerung *f.* ◆**remi'niscent,** *adj.* **to be r. of s.o., sth.,** an j-n, etwas *acc* erinnern.

remit [ri'mit], *v.tr. Com:* (*pay*) (j-m eine Summe) überweisen. ◆**re'mittance,** *s. Com:* Überweisung *f.*

remnant ['remnənt], *s.* (letzter) Rest *m.*

remonstrate ['remənstreit], *v.i.* protestieren (**against sth.,** gegen etwas *acc*).

remorse [ri'mɔ:s], *s.* Reue *f.* ◆**re'morseful,** *adj.* reumütig. ◆**re'morseless,** *adj.* (*a*) reuelos; (*b*) (*pitiless*) erbarmungslos.

remote [ri'məut], *adj.* 1. (*a*) (*distant*) fern; (*weit*) entfernt; *Rad:* r. **control,** Fernlenkung *f;* (*b*) (*of situation*) abgelegen. 2. *Fig:* a r. resemblance, eine entfernte Ähnlichkeit.

remove [ri'muːv], *v.tr.* (*a*) (*take off*) abnehmen; (ein Kleidungsstück) ablegen; (*take away*) (etwas) wegnehmen/ entfernen; (*b*) (*eliminate*) (Flecken) entfernen; (Fehler, ein Hindernis usw.) beseitigen; (Schwierigkeiten, einen Mißstand) beheben. ◆**re'movable**, *adj.* abnehmbar. ◆**re'moval**, *s.* 1. Entfernen *n* (eines Flecks usw.); Beseitigung *f* (eines Mißstandes). 2. (*to another house*) Umzug *m;* furniture r., Möbelspedition *f.* ◆**re'mover**, *s.* (*liquid*) Entferner *m;* paint r., Abbeizmittel *n.*

remunerate [ri'mjuːnəreit], *v.tr.* (*pay*) (j-n) bezahlen; (*reward*) belohnen (for, für + *acc*). ◆**remune'ration**, *s.* Bezahlung *f;* Belohnung *f* (for, für + acc).

renaissance [re'neisɔ̃ns], *s.* the R., die Renaissance.

render ['rendər], *v.tr.* (*a*) to r. a service to s.o., j-m einen Dienst erweisen; (*b*) (*with adj.*) (j-n, etwas) ... machen; to r. sth. unusable, etwas unbrauchbar machen.

rendezvous ['rɔndivuː], *s.* Rendezvous *n;* (*place*) Treffpunkt *m.*

renew [ri'njuː], *v.tr.* (etwas) erneuern; (*at library*) (ein Buch) verlängern; (eine Bekanntschaft) wieder aufnehmen. ◆**re'newal**, *s.* 1. Erneuerung *f;* Wiederaufnahme *f.*

renounce [ri'nauns], *v.tr.* (auf ein Recht, einen Titel usw.) verzichten.

renovate ['renəuveit], *v.tr.* renovieren. ◆**reno'vation**, *s.* Renovierung *f.*

renown [ri'naun], *s.* Berühmtheit *f.* ◆**re'nowned**, *adj.* berühmt (for, für + acc).

rent [rent]. **I.** *s.* (*for house etc.*) Miete *f.* **II.** *v.tr.* (*a*) (*let*) (ein Haus) vermieten; (*b*) (*hire*) (eine Wohnung) mieten; (ein Fernsehgerät usw.) leihen. ◆**'rental**, *s.* (*amount*) Miete *f.*

reopen [riː'əup(ə)n], *v.tr.* (*a*) wieder aufmachen; (*b*) (Verhandlungen usw.) wiedereröffnen.

reorganize [riː'ɔːgənaiz], *v.tr.* (etwas) neu organisieren, (*alter*) umorganisieren.

rep [rep], *s. F: Com:* Vertreter(in) *m* (*f*).

repair [ri'pɛər]. **I.** *s.* Reparatur *f* (einer Maschine usw.); Ausbesserung *f* (von Kleidern usw.). **II.** *v.tr.* (etwas) reparieren; (Kleider) ausbessern; (einen Reifen) flicken; to r. damage/a loss, Schaden/einen Verlust wiedergutmachen. ◆**re'pairable**, *adj.* reparierbar; *pred.* zu reparieren.

repatriate [riː'pætrieit], *v.tr.* (j-n) repatriieren.

repay [riː'pei], *v.tr.irr.* (*a*) (Geld, eine Schuld) zurückzahlen; (j-n) entschädigen; to r. s.o. for sth., j-m etwas vergelten; (*b*) to r. a favour, eine Gefälligkeit erwidern. ◆**re'payment**, *s.* (*a*) Rückzahlung *f;* (*b*) Entschädigung *f.*

repeal [ri'piːl]. **I.** *s.* Aufhebung *f* (eines Gesetzes). **II.** *v.tr.* (ein Gesetz) aufheben.

repeat [ri'piːt]. **I.** *s.* Wiederholung *f.* **II.** *s. Com:* r. order, Nachbestellung *f.* ◆**re'peated**, *adj.* wiederholt.

repel [ri'pel], *v.tr.* (den Feind usw.) zurücktreiben; (einen Angriff, einen Schlag) abwehren; (Insekten) vertreiben. ◆**re'pellent**, *adj.* abstoßend; water r., wasserabstoßend.

repent [ri'pent], *v.* 1. *v.tr.* (etwas) bereuen. 2. *v.i.* Reue empfinden. ◆**re'pentance**, *s.* Reue *f.* ◆**re'pentant**, *adj.* reuig.

repercussion [riːpə'kʌʃ(ə)n], *s.* Rückwirkung *f.*

repertoire ['repətwɑːr], *s.* Repertoire *n.* ◆**repertory** ['repət(ə)ri], *s. Th:* Repertoire *n.*

repetition [repi'tiʃ(ə)n], *s.* Wiederholung *f.*

replace [ri'pleis], *v.tr.* (*a*) (etwas) wieder an seinen Platz stellen/setzen; (*b*) (*substitute*) (j-n, etwas) ersetzen (by/with, durch + acc); (Maschinenteile) auswechseln. ◆**re'placeable**, *adj.* ersetzbar; *Tchn:* auswechselbar. ◆**re'placement**, *s.* Ersatz *m;* (*a*) (*pers.*) (*temporary*) Stellvertreter(in) *m*(*f*); (*b*) *Ind:* r. (part), Ersatzteil *n.*

replay ['riːplei], *s.* 1. *Sp:* Wiederholungsspiel *n.* 2. *Rec:* Abspielen *n.*

replenish [ri'pleniʃ], *v.tr.* (ein Glas, einen Tank usw.) wieder auffüllen (with, mit + dat); to r. one's supplies, neue Vorräte anlegen.

replica ['replikə], *s.* (genaue) Kopie *f; Art:* Replik *f.*

reply [ri'plai]. **I.** *s.* Antwort *f.* **II.** *v.i.* antworten (to sth., auf etwas acc; to s.o., j-m).

report [ri'pɔːt]. **I.** *s.* Bericht *m* (on, über + acc); (*verbal*) Meldung *f;* to make a r., Bericht erstatten (on sth., über etwas acc). **II.** *v.* 1. *v.tr.* (*a*) (eine Tatsache) berichten/(on radio) melden; (*b*) to r. an accident to the police, einen Unfall der Polizei melden; (*c*) *Gram:* reported speech, indirekte Rede. 2. *v.i.* (*a*) to r. on sth., über etwas acc Bericht erstatten/berichten; (*b*) to r. to s.o., sich bei j-m melden. ◆**re'porter**, *s.* Reporter *m.*

repose [ri'pəuz]. **I.** *s.* Ruhe *f.* **II.** *v.i.* ruhen.

reprehensible [repri'hensəbl], *adj.* tadelnswert.

represent [repri'zent], *v.tr.* (*a*) (*portray*) (etwas, *Th:* eine Rolle usw.) darstellen; (*b*) (*act for*) (eine Firma, einen Wahlbezirk usw.) vertreten. ◆**represen'tation**, *s.* 1. (*portrayal*) Darstellung *f.* 2. *Com: etc:* Vertretung *f.* ◆**repre'sentative. I.** *adj.* 1. (*symbolical*) symbolisch (of, für + acc). 2. (*typical*) repräsentativ. **II.** *s. esp. Com:* Vertreter(in) *m*(*f*); *Jur:* Beauftragte(r) *m & f.*

repress [ri'pres], *v.tr.* (einen Aufstand, Emotionen) unterdrücken; (Wünsche, Gedanken) verdrängen. ◆**re'pression**, *s.* Unterdrückung *f;* Verdrängung *f.* ◆**re'pressive**, *adj.* repressiv.

reprieve [ri'priːv]. I. *s. Jur: etc: (temporary)* Aufschub *m; (permanent)* Begnadigung *f.* II. *v.tr.* (a) *(permanently)* (j-n) begnadigen; (b) *Fig:* (j-m) eine Gnadenfrist geben.

reprimand ['reprimɑːnd]. I. *s.* Verweis *m.* II. *v.tr.* (j-m) einen Verweis erteilen.

reprint. I. ['riːprint] *s.* (eines Buch) neu auflegen. II. ['riːprint] *s.* Neuauflage *f.*

reprisal [ri'praiz(ə)l], *s.* Vergeltungsmaßnahme *f.*

reproach [ri'prəutʃ]. I. *s.* Vorwurf *m;* beyond r., ohne Tadel. II. *v.tr.* to r. s.o. about sth., j-m wegen etwas *gen* Vorwürfe machen. ◆**re'proachful**, *adj.* vorwurfsvoll.

reproduce ['riːprə'djuːs], *v.* 1. *v.tr.* (ein Modell usw.) nachbilden; (Musik) wiedergeben; (ein Bild) nachdrucken. 2. *v.i.* *(multiply)* sich vermehren. ◆**'repro'duction**, *s.* 1. Reproduktion *f* (eines Gemäldes, der menschlichen Rasse); *Rec: etc:* Wiedergabe *f* (von Tönen, Farben usw.). 2. Nachbildung *f.*

reptile ['reptail], *s.* Reptil *n.*

republic [ri'pʌblik], *s.* Republik *f.* ◆**re'publican.** I. *adj.* republikanisch. II. *s.* Republikaner(in) *m(f).*

repudiate [ri'pjuːdieit], *v.tr.* (eine Beschuldigung usw.) zurückweisen; (j-s Autorität) nicht anerkennen.

re'pugnant [ri'pʌgnant], *adj.* widerlich; to be r. to s.o., j-m zuwider sein.

repulse [ri'pʌls], *v.tr.* (einen Feind) zurücktreiben; (einen Angriff) abwehren. ◆**re'pulsion**, *s.* Abscheu *f* (to/for s.o., sth., vor j-m, etwas *dat*). ◆**re'pulsive**, *adj.* widerlich.

reputable ['repjutəbl], *adj.* angesehen; *(respectable)* anständig. ◆**repu'tation**, *s.* Ruf *m.* ◆**re'puted**, *adj. (supposed)* vermeintlich.

request [ri'kwest]. I. *s.* Bitte *f* (for, um + *acc*); *(formal)* Ersuchen *n* (for, um + *acc*); **on/by r.,** auf Wunsch; *Rad: etc:* r. **programme,** Wunschsendung *f.* II. *v.tr.* (um etwas *acc*) bitten; **to r. sth. from s.o.,** j-n um etwas *acc* ersuchen.

require [ri'kwaiər], *v.tr.* (a) *(demand)* **to r. sth. of s.o.,** etwas von j-m verlangen; (b) *(need)* (etwas) brauchen, nötig haben. ◆**re'quired**, *adj. (necessary)* nötig; *(desired)* gewünscht; **if r.,** notfalls. ◆**re'quirement,** *s. (demand)* Forderung *f.* 2. *(need)* Bedürfnis *n; pl.* Bedarf *m.* 3. *(condition)* Voraussetzung *f.*

requisite ['rekwizit], *adj. (necessary)* erforderlich. ◆**requi'sition,** *s. v.tr. Mil: etc:* beschlagnahmen.

rescind [ri'sind], *v.tr. Jur: Adm:* (ein Gesetz usw.) aufheben; (einen Vertrag) für

ungültig erklären.

rescue ['reskjuː]. I. *s.* Rettung *f;* Bergung *f* (von Schiffbrüchigen); **to come to s.o.'s r.,** j-m zu Hilfe kommen. II. *v.tr.* retten; *Nau:* bergen (from, aus + *dat*).

research [ri'səːtʃ]. I. *s.* Forschung *f* (**on/into sth.,** über etwas *acc*). II. *v.* 1. *v.i.* **to r. (into a subject),** Forschung (über eine Sache) betreiben. 2. *v.tr.* (ein Gebiet) erforschen.

resemble [ri'zembl], *v.tr.* (j-m, etwas *dat*) ähnlich sein. ◆**re'semblance,** *s.* Ähnlichkeit *f* (to, mit + *dat*).

resent [ri'zent], *v.tr.* (etwas) übelnehmen; (j-n) ablehnen. ◆**re'sentful,** *adj.* **to be r. of sth.,** etwas nicht vertragen können. ◆**re'sentment,** *s.* Ressentiment *n* (against/at, gegen + *acc*).

reserve [ri'zəːv]. I. *v.tr.* (einen Platz) reservieren; **to r. the right to do sth.,** sich *dat* das Recht vorbehalten, etwas zu tun. II. *s.* 1. Reserve *f* (von Geld, Energie usw.); *(store)* Vorrat *m* (von Lebensmitteln). 2. *Sp:* Reservespieler *m.* 3. *(area)* **nature** r., Naturschutzgebiet *n.* 4. *(reticence)* Zurückhaltung *f.* ◆**reser'vation** [rezə-], *s.* 1. Reservierung *f.* 2. *(doubt)* Bedenken *n;* **without r.,** ohne Vorbehalt. 3. *(for animals)* Naturschutzgebiet *n.* ◆**re'served,** *adj.* 1. **r. seats,** reservierte Plätze. 2. *(of pers.)* zurückhaltend. ◆**reservoir** ['rezəvwɑːr], *s.* Reservoir *n; (container)* Speicher *m.*

reshuffle [riː'ʃʌfl], *s. Pol:* Umbildung *f.*

reside [ri'zaid], *v.i.* wohnen. ◆**residence** ['rezidəns], *s.* (a) *(place of)* r., Wohnsitz *m;* (b) *(house etc.)* Wohnung *f;* Residenz *f* (eines Fürsten); **(students') hall of** r., Studentenheim *n.* ◆**'resident.** I. *adj.* **r. in X,** wohnhaft in X. II. *s.* Einwohner(in) *m(f);* (in hotel) Hotelgast *m.* ◆**resi'dential,** *adj.* Wohn-; **r. area,** Wohnviertel *n.*

residue ['rezidjuː], *s.* Rest *m; Ch:* Rückstand *m.*

resign [ri'zain]. I. *s.* 1. *v.tr.* (a) (eine Stelle) aufgeben; (b) **to r. oneself to doing sth.,** sich damit abfinden, etwas tun zu müssen. 2. *v.i.* von einem Posten) zurücktreten; (aus einem Verein) austreten. ◆**resignation** [rezig'neiʃ(ə)n], *s.* 1. Rücktritt *m* (from a post, von einem Posten). 2. *(state of mind)* Resignation *f.* ◆**re'signed,** *adj.* resigniert.

resilient [ri'ziliənt], *adj.* elastisch; *(of pers.)* nicht unterzukriegen.

resin ['rezin], *s.* Harz *n.*

resist [ri'zist], *v.tr. & i.* (a) (etwas *dat*) widerstehen; (b) *(oppose)* (j-m) Widerstand leisten; sich (einem Projekt usw.) widersetzen. ◆**re'sistance,** *s.* Widerstand *m* (to, gegen + *acc*); Widerstandsfähigkeit *f* (von Stahl usw.). ◆**re'sistant,** *adj. (of material)* widerstandsfähig; **heat-**r., hitzebeständig.

resolute ['rezəl(j)uːt], *adj. (of pers., man-*

ner) resolut; *(of resistance etc.)* fest.

reso'lution, s. 1. *(a) (corporate decision)* Beschluß *m* (einer Versammlung); *(b) (personal decision)* Entschluß *m*; **good re-solutions,** gute Vorsätze *mpl.* 2. *(decisiveness)* Entschlossenheit *f.* 3. r. of a problem, Lösung *f* eines Problems.
◆**resolve** [ri'zɔlv]. I. *v.* 1. *(decisiveness)* Entschlossenheit *f.* II. *v.* 1. *v.tr. (solve)* (ein Problem) lösen; (einen Zweifel) beseitigen. 2. *v.i.* sich entschließen (**to do sth.,** etwas zu tun).

resonant ['rezənənt], *adj.* resonant.

resort [ri'zɔrt]. I. s. 1. **as a last r.,** als letzter Ausweg, *F:* wenn alle Stricke reißen. 2. **(holiday) r.,** Ferienort *m*; **seaside r.,** Seebad *n.* II. *v.i.* **to r. to violence, force etc.,** Gewalt, Zwang usw. anwenden.

resound [ri'zaund], *v.i.* erschallen; widerhallen. ◆**re'sounding,** *adj. (of success etc.)* glänzend; r. **blow,** heftiger/*Fig:* schwerer Schlag; r. **victory,** überwältigender Sieg.

resource [ri'sɔrs], s. 1. Hilfsmittel *n*; *Sch:* Lehrmittel *n.* 2. *pl. (money, labour etc.)* Mittel *npl*; *(wealth)* Reichtümer *mpl* (eines Landes); **natural resources,** Naturschätze *mpl*; *(minerals)* Bodenschätze *mpl.*
◆**re'sourceful,** *adj.* findig.

respect [ri'spekt]. I. s. 1. *(aspect)* Hinsicht *f*; **with r. to/in r. of,** hinsichtlich + *gen.* 2. *(esteem)* Achtung *f*; **to have r. for s.o.,** j-n respektieren. II. *v.tr.* (j-n) respektieren; **to r. s.o.'s wishes,** j-s Wünsche berücksichtigen. ◆**respecta'bility,** s. *(status)* Ansehen *n*; *(quality)* Anständigkeit *f.* ◆**re'spectable,** *adj. (of pers., firm etc.)* solide; safely, *adv.* r. dressed, anständig gekleidet. ◆**re'spectful,** *adj.* ehrerbietig; *(of pers.)* respektvoll *(towards, gegen + acc);* **-ly,** *adv.* höflichst. ◆**re'spective,** *adj.* jeweilig; **-ly,** *adv.* **the concerts are in London and Manchester r.,** die Konzerte finden jeweils in London und Manchester statt.

respiration [respi'reiʃ(ə)n], s. Atmung *f.*

respite ['respait, 'respit], s. *(breathing space)* Atempause *f*; *(rest)* Ruhepause *f.*

resplendent [ri'splendənt], *adj.* prächtig.

respond [ri'spɔnd], *v.i. (of pers.)* antworten **(to a question etc.,** auf eine Frage usw.); *(react)* reagieren **(to sth.,** auf etwas *acc;);* *(of machine, instrument)* ansprechen **(to sth.,** auf etwas *acc);* *(of illness, patient)* **to r. to treatment,** auf die Behandlung ansprechen.
◆**re'sponse,** *(answer)* Antwort *f*; *(to advertisement etc.)* Zuschrift *f*; *coll.* Reaktion *f.* ◆**responsi'bility,** s. Verantwortung *f.* ◆**re'sponsible,** *adj.* 1. *(accountable)* verantwortlich **(to s.o. for sth.,** j-m für etwas *acc).* 2. *(of job, attitude etc.)* verantwortungsvoll; *(of pers.)* verantwortungsbewußt; *(reliable)* zuverlässig. ◆**re'sponsive,** *adj.* empfänglich **(to in-**

fluences, für Einflüsse); *(of audience)* mitgehend.

rest¹ [rest]. I. s. 1. *(a) (repose)* Ruhe *f*; *Fig:* **to set s.o.'s mind at r.,** j-n beruhigen; *(b) (halt)* Rast *f*; *(break)* Ruhepause *f* **(from,** von + *dat);* **to have/take a r.,** sich ausruhen; *(take a break)* Pause machen. 2. *Mus:* Pause *f.* 3. *(support)* Stütze *f.* II. *v.* 1. *v.i. (a)* ruhen; *(in bed etc.)* sich ausruhen; *(b)* **to r. on sth.,** sich auf/gegen etwas *acc* stützen/lehnen. 2. *v.tr. (a)* (die Augen, die Stimme) schonen; *Sp:* (einen Spieler) aussetzen lassen; *(b) (support)* (die Ellbogen usw.) stützen. ◆**'restful,** *adj.* erholsam; *(peaceful)* ruhig, friedlich. ◆**'restless,** *adj.* ruhelos; *(uneasy)* unruhig. ◆**'restlessness,** s. Ruhelosigkeit *f*; Unruhe *f.*

rest², s. *(a)* Rest *m*; **the r. of the money,** das übrige Geld; *(b) (pers.) pl.* die Übrigen; **the r. of us,** wir anderen.

restaurant ['rest(ə)rɔŋ], s. Restaurant *n.*

restive ['restiv], *adj.* unruhig; *(on edge)* nervös.

restore [ri'stɔr], *v.tr. (a) (return)* (etwas Gestohlenes usw.) wiedergeben **(to s.o.,** j-m); *(b) (renovate)* (ein Gebäude, Gemälde usw.) restaurieren; (Möbel) erneuern; *(c) (re-establish)* (die öffentliche Ordnung) wiederherstellen. ◆**restoration** [restə'reiʃ(ə)n], s. 1. Rückerstattung *f* (von Eigentum). 2. Restaurierung *f* (eines Kunstwerkes usw.). 3. Wiederherstellung *f* (der Gesundheit, Ordnung usw.).

restrain [ri'strein], *v.tr.* (j-n, sich) zurückhalten; (einen Hund) bändigen; *Fig:* (Gefühle) unterdrücken; *(limit)* (Freigebigkeit usw.) einschränken; **to r. s.o. from doing sth.,** j-n davon abhalten, etwas zu tun. ◆**re'strained,** *adj. (of expression etc.)* verhalten; *(of pers., manner)* zurückhaltend. ◆**re'straint,** s. *(a)* Beschränkung *f* (der Freiheit, des Handels); *(b) (manner)* Zurückhaltung *f.*

restrict [ri'strikt], *v.tr. (a)* beschränken **(to, auf + acc);** *(b) (of things)* (Bewegungen) hemmen. ◆**re'stricted,** *adj.* beschränkt; *(of movements)* gehemmt. ◆**re'striction,** s. *(a)* Beschränkung *f*; **speed r.,** Geschwindigkeitsbegrenzung *f*; *(b)* Hemmung *f* (der Bewegungen usw.). ◆**re'strictive,** *adj.* einschränkend.

result [ri'zʌlt]. I. s. *(a)* Ergebnis *n*; *(consequence)* Folge *f*; *(b)* **to produce results,** Erfolg bringen; **the desired r.,** die gewünschte Wirkung. II. *v.i. (a)* sich ergeben **(from,** aus + *dat);* *(b)* enden **(in, in + dat).** ◆**re'sultant,** *adj.* resultierend.

resume [ri'zjuːm], *v.* 1. *v.tr. (a)* (Verhandlungen, Beziehungen usw.) wiederaufnehmen; *(b)* (den Kampf, das Spiel) fortsetzen. 2. *v.i.* wieder anfangen. ◆**resumption** [ri'zʌmpʃən], s. Wiederaufnahme *f*; Fortsetzung *f* (eines Spiels usw.).

resurface ['riː'səːfis], *v.* 1. *v.tr.* **to r. the**

road, den Straßenbelag erneuern. 2. *v.i.* (*of diver, submarine*) wieder auftauchen.

resurrection [rezə'rek∫(ə)n], *s.* Auferstehung *f.*

resuscitate [ri'sʌsiteit], *v.tr.* (j-n) wiederbeleben.

retail ['ri:teil], *s.* *r.* (**trade**), Einzelhandel *m.*

retain [ri'tein], *v.tr.* (*a*) (etwas) behalten; (eine Sitte, eine Gewohnheit usw.) beibehalten; (*b*) (*remember*) (etwas im Gedächtnis) behalten; (*c*) (Wasser usw.) zurückhalten. ◆**re'tainer**, *s.* (*fee*) Honorar *n.*

retaliate [ri'tælieit], *v.i.* sich revanchieren. ◆**retali'ation**, *s.* Vergeltung *f;* (*act*) Vergeltungsmaßnahme *f.*

retarded [ri'tɑːdid], *adj.* (**mentally**) r., zurückgeblieben.

retention [ri'ten∫(ə)n], *s.* Behalten *n;* Beibehaltung *f* (alter Bräuche usw.); (*memory*) Merkfähigkeit *f.*

reticent ['retis(ə)nt], *adj.* (*of character*) zurückhaltend. ◆**'reticence**, *s.* Verschwiegenheit *f.*

retire [ri'taiər], *v.* 1. *v.i.* (*a*) sich zurückziehen (from, von + *dat*); (*b*) (*stop working*) aufhören zu arbeiten; (*esp. of civil servant*) in den Ruhestand treten. 2. *v.tr.* (j-n) pensionieren. ◆**re'tired**, *adj.* im Ruhestand. ◆**re'tirement**, *s.* Ruhestand *m.* ◆**re'tiring**, *adj.* (*of pers.*) zurückhaltend.

retort [ri'tɔːt]. I. *s.* (schlagfertige) Antwort *f.* II. *v.tr.* schlagfertig antworten (to sth., auf etwas *acc*).

retrace [ri'treis], *v.tr.* (j-s Bewegungen) zurückverfolgen; to r. one's steps, denselben Weg zurückgehen.

retract [ri'trækt], *v.tr.* (*a*) (die Klauen, *Av:* das Fahrgestell) einziehen; (*b*) (eine Anklage) zurückziehen; (eine Aussage) widerrufen; (eine Behauptung) zurücknehmen.

retreat [ri'tri:t]. I. *s.* *Mil:* Rückzug *m; Fig:* to beat a hasty r., eiligst das Feld räumen. II. *v.i.* sich zurückziehen.

retribution [retri'bju:∫(ə)n], *s.* Vergeltung *f.*

retrieve [ri'tri:v], *v.tr.* (*a*) (*recover*) (Verlorenes) wiederbekommen; (*from awkward position*) herausholen (from, aus + *dat*); *Data-pr:* (Informationen) abfragen; (*b*) (*put right*) (einen Verlust) wettmachen. ◆**re'trieval**, *s.* Wiedergewinnung *f;* *Data-pr:* Abfragen *n.* ◆**re'triever**, *s.* (*dog*) Apportierhund *m.*

retrospect ['retrəuspekt], *s.* in r., rückblickend, im Rückblick.

return [ri'tə:n]. I. *s.* 1. Rückkehr *f;* Heimkehr *f* (aus dem Krieg); (*recurrence*) Wiederkehr *f* (*Mus:* eines Themas usw.); **many happy returns (of the day)!** herzlichen Glückwunsch zum Geburtstag! *f.* **journey,** Rückreise *f.* **r. ticket,** Rückfahrkarte *f.* 2. (*profit*) Com: esp. *pl.* Ertrag *m.* 3. (*a*) (*giving back*) Rückgabe *f;* (*sending back*) Rücksendung *f.* 4. tax r.,

Steuererklärung *f.* II. *v.* 1. *v.i.* zurückkehren; (*recur*) wiederkehren; to r. home, heimkehren. 2. *v.tr.* (*a*) (etwas Geborgtes usw.) zurückgeben; (*send back*) zurückschicken; (Geld) zurückzahlen (to s.o., j-m); (*b*) (Dank, einen Gruß, einen Schlag) erwidern. ◆**re'turnable,** *adj.* rückgabepflichtig; (*of deposit etc.*) rückzahlbar; (*of goods*) umtauschbar.

reunion [ri:'ju:njən], *s.* Treffen *n* (von ehemaligen Schülern usw.).

rev [rev]. I. *s.* *F: Aut: abbr. of revolution*) Umdrehung *f* (pro Minute). II. *v. F: Aut:* to r. up the engine, den Motor auf Touren bringen. 2. *v.i.* auf Touren kommen.

reveal [ri'vi:l], *v.tr.* (ein Geheimnis usw.) enthüllen; (*betray*) (seine Absicht, ein Versteck usw.) verraten. ◆**re'vealing,** *adj.* aufschlußreich; *Hum:* (*of dress*) offenherzig. ◆**revelation** [revə'lei∫(ə)n], *s.* Offenbarung *f.*

reveille [ri'væli], *s.* *Mil:* Wecksignal *n.*

revel ['rev(ə)l], *v.i.* (*celebrate*) feiern; (*carouse*) zechen. ◆**'reveller,** *s.* Feiernde(r) *f(m);* Zecher *m.* ◆**'revelry,** *s.* Feiern *n;* (*drinking*) Gelage *n.*

revenge [ri'vendʒ]. I. *s.* Rache *f;* (*in games etc.*) Revanche *f;* to get one's r. on s.o. for sth., sich an j-m für etwas *acc* rächen. II. *v.tr.* (j-n, ein Unrecht usw.) rächen; to r. oneself/be revenged, sich rächen (on s.o., an j-m; for sth., für etwas *acc*).

revenue ['revinju:], *s.* Einnahmen *fpl, esp.* (*of state*) Staatseinnahmen *fpl.*

reverberate [ri'və:b(ə)reit], *v.i.* (*of sound*) hallen; (*echo*) widerhallen. ◆**reverbe'ration,** *s.* Widerhall *m.*

revere [ri'viər], *v.tr.* (j-n) verehren. ◆**'reverend,** *adj.* ehrwürdig; *Ecc:* (*as title*) **the** (**Very**) **R. Father Brown,** Hochwürden Brown. ◆**'reverent,** *adj.* ehrfürchtig.

reverie ['revəri], *s.* Träumerei *f.*

reversal [ri'və:s(ə)l], *s.* (*a*) Umkehrung *f* (der Reihenfolge usw.); (*b*) Umstoßung *f* (einer Entscheidung, *Jur:* eines Urteils). ◆**reverse** [ri'və:s]. I. *adj.* (*of order etc.*) umgekehrt; (*of direction*) entgegengesetzt. II. *s.* 1. (*opposite*) Gegenteil *n.* 2. (*back*) Rückseite *f* (eines Blatts); Kehrseite *f* (einer Münze usw.). 3. *Aut:* r. (**gear**), Rückwärtsgang *m.* III. *v.tr.* (*a*) (*turn over*) (etwas) umdrehen; (*b*) (*change to opposite*) (die Reihenfolge) umkehren; (eine Entscheidung, *Jur:* ein Urteil) umstoßen; (*c*) *Aut:* to r. (**one's car**), rückwärts fahren; (*d*) *Tel:* to r. the charges, ein R-Gespräch führen. ◆**re'versible,** *adj.* umkehrbar.

revert [ri'və:t], *v.i.* (*a*) (*of property*) heimfallen (to s.o., an j-m); (*b*) to r. to a custom etc., in einen Brauch usw. zurückfallen.

review [ri'vju:]. I. *s.* 1. *Mil:* Parade *f.* 2.

(a) (of past events) Rückschau f; (b) (survey) Übersicht f; (report) Bericht m; (c) Rezension f (eines Buches, Films usw.); **good/bad r.**, gute/schlechte Kritik f; (d) (periodical) Rundschau f. **II.** v.tr. (a) (Truppen usw.) inspizieren; (b) Gehälter, die Lage usw.) überprüfen; (c) (ein Buch, einen Film) besprechen.

revile [ri'vail], v.tr. (j-n) schmähen.

revise [ri'vaiz], v.tr. (a) (alter) (seine Meinung) ändern; (b) (correct) (ein Buch usw.) überarbeiten. ◆**revision** [ri'viʒ(ə)n], s. Revision f.

revive [ri'vaiv], v. 1. v.i. (regain consciousness) wieder zu sich dat kommen. 2. v.tr. (a) (j-n) wiederbeleben; (b) (einen alten Brauch) wieder einführen. ◆**re'vival**, s. Neubelebung f (einer Kunst, des Handels); Wiederbelebung f (eines Gefühls usw.); Wiedereinführung f (eines Brauches usw.); Th: Wiederaufnahme f.

revoke [ri'vəuk], v.tr. (eine Anordnung usw.) widerrufen; (einen Befehl usw.) aufheben; (einen Vertrag) annullieren.

revolt [ri'vəult]. **I.** s. Aufstand m. **II.** v. 1. v.i. revoltieren. 2. v.tr. (disgust) (j-n) anwidern; (make indignant) empören. ◆**re'volting**, adj. widerlich.

revolution [revə'l(j)uːʃ(ə)n], s. 1. (rotation) Umdrehung f. 2. Pol: etc: Revolution f. ◆**revo'lutionary I.** adj. revolutionär. **II.** s. Revolutionär(in) m(f).

revolve [ri'vɔlv], v. 1. v.tr. (a) (ein Rad usw.) drehen. 2. v.i. kreisen (round sth., um etwas acc); (of wheel etc.) sich drehen. ◆**re'volving**, adj. tr. door, Drehtür f.

revolver [ri'vɔlvər], s. Revolver m.

revulsion [ri'vʌlʃ(ə)n], s. (feeling of) r., Ekel m.

reward [ri'wɔːd]. **I.** s. Belohnung f; (to finder) Finderlohn m. **II.** v.tr. (j-n) belohnen.

rewrite ['riː'rait], v.tr.irr. überarbeiten.

rhetoric ['retərik], s. 1. Rhetorik f. 2. Pej: Schwulst m. ◆**rhetorical** [ri'tɔrikəl], adj. (of question etc.) rhetorisch; (of style) hochtrabend, Pej: schwülstig.

rheumatism ['ruːmətizm], s. Rheuma m. ◆**rheumatic** [-'mætik], adj. rheumatisch; (of pers.) rheumakrank.

Rhine [rain]. Pr. n. the R., der Rhein.

rhinoceros [rai'nɔsərɔs], F: **rhino** ['rainəu], s. Z: Nashorn n.

rhubarb ['ruːbɑːb], s. Rhabarber m.

rhyme [raim]. **I.** s. Reim m; **in r.**, gereimt. **II.** v.i. sich reimen.

rhythm ['rið(ə)m], s. Rhythmus m.

rib [rib]. **I.** s. Rippe f. **II.** v.tr. F: (j-n) necken.

ribbon ['ribən], s. (a) Band n; (b) (typewriter) Farbband n.

rice [rais], s. Reis m; **r. pudding**, Milchreis m.

rich [ritʃ], adj. 1. reich (**in**, an + dat). 2. (a) (of soil) fruchtbar; (of harvest) ergiebig; (b) (of food) gehaltvoll; (fatty) fett;

(c) (of colours) satt; (of sound) voll.

rick [rik], s. r. of hay, Heuschober m.

rickets ['rikits], s. Med: Rachitis f. ◆**'rickety**, adj. F: (of house) baufällig; (of furniture) wackelig.

ricochet ['rikəʃei], v.i. abprallen.

rid [rid], v.tr.irr. (j-n, etwas) befreien (of s.o., sth., von j-m, etwas dat); to get r. of s.o., sth., j-n, etwas loswerden. ◆**'riddance**, s. good r.! den/die/das sind wir glücklich los!

ridden ['rid(ə)n], comb. fm. von ... dat geplagt; bed-r., bettlägerig.

riddle¹ ['ridl], s. Rätsel n.

riddle², v.tr. riddled with holes, ganz durchlöchert.

ride [raid]. **I.** s. (on horse) Ritt m; (in car, train etc.) Fahrt f. **II.** v. 1. v.i. (on horse); (b) to r. on a bicycle, mit dem Rad fahren; to r. in a bus/car/train, im Autobus/Auto/Zug fahren. 2. v.tr. to r. a horse, ein Pferd reiten; to r. a bicycle/motorcycle, radfahren/Motorrad fahren. ◆**'rider**, s. Reiter(in) m(f) (eines Pferdes); Fahrer(in) m(f) (eines Fahrrads, Motorrads). ◆**'riding**, s. Reiten n.

ridge [ridʒ], s. Rücken m (der Nase, eines Berges usw.); (raised area) Erhöhung f; (line of hills) Hügelkette f.

ridicule ['ridikjuːl]. **I.** s. Spott m. **II.** v.tr. (j-n) lächerlich machen. ◆**ri'diculous**, adj. lächerlich.

rife [raif], adj. (of disease) to be r., grassieren.

rifle¹ ['raifl], v.tr. to r. through sth. etwas durchwühlen.

rifle², s. Gewehr n.

rift [rift], s. (a) (gap) Ritze f; (b) Fig: (between friends) Riß m.

rig¹ [rig]. **I.** s. oil/drilling r., Bohrinsel f. **II.** v.tr. (ein Schiff) auftakeln. ◆**'rigging**, s. Nau: (a) (type) Takelung f; (b) coll. Takelage f. ◆**'rig out**, v.tr. (sich, j-n) ausstaffieren. ◆**'rig 'up**, v.tr. F: (einen Apparat usw.) aufstellen, (amateurishly) zusammenbasteln.

rig², v.tr. F: manipulieren; **the fight was rigged**, der Kampf war ein abgekartetes Spiel.

right [rait]. **I.** adj. 1. **r. angle**, rechter Winkel. 2. (a) (appropriate; just) (right) gerecht; **the r. thing (to do)**, das Richtige; (b) (correct) richtig; (exact) genau; to be r., (of pers.) recht haben; (of amount, remark etc.) stimmen; (of watch etc.) richtig gehen. 3. (in order) **to put things r.**, die Dinge (wieder) in Ordnung bringen. 4. (direction) rechte(r,s); **on the r. (hand) side**, auf der rechten Seite; Pol: r. wing, rechter Flügel. 5. int. r.! also gut! **-ly**, adv. (correctly) richtig; (justly) mit Recht; **I can't r. say**, das kann ich nicht genau sagen. **II.** s. 1. (justice) Recht n. 2. (a) (claim) Anrecht n (to sth., auf etwas acc); **what gives you the r. to do this?** was berechtigt Sie dazu? **in one's own r.**, von sich aus; **r. of way**, Vorfahrt f; (b) pl.

rights, Rechte *npl.* **3.** (*right hand & Pol:*) Rechte *f;* **on the r.,** rechts/zur Rechten; **to the r.,** nach rechts; **to the r. of,** rechts von + *dat.* **III.** *adv.* **1.** (*a*) **go r. on,** gehen Sie immer geradeaus; (*b*) **r. away,** sofort; (*c*) ganz; **to sink r. to the bottom,** bis auf den Grund sinken; **r. at the top,** ganz oben; **r. in the middle,** genau in der Mitte. **2.** (*to* **answer/guess r.,** richtig antworten/raten. **IV.** *v.tr.* (*a*) (*ein* Unrecht) wiedergutmachen; (*b*) (*ein* Boot usw.) aufrichten. ◆**'righteous,** *adj.* (*a*) rechtschaffen; *Pej:* (*self-r.*) selbstgerecht. ◆**'righteousness,** *s.* Rechtschaffenheit *f.* ◆**'rightful,** *adj.* rechtmäßig. ◆**'right-'hand,** *adj.* (*a*) rechte(r,s); **the r.-h. drawer,** die rechte Schublade; (*b*) nach rechts, Rechts-; **r.-h. bend,** Rechtskurve *f.* ◆**'right-'handed,** *adj.* rechtshändig. ◆**'right-'wing,** *adj. Pol:* rechtsgerichtet; **he's very r.-w.,** er steht sehr weit rechts.

rigid ['rid3id], *adj.* starr, *Fig:* (*of pers.*) unbeugsam.

rigour ['rigər], *s.* Strenge *f.* ◆**'rigorous,** *adj.* streng.

rim [rim], *s.* **1.** Felge *f* (eines Rades). **2.** Rand *m* (einer Vase usw.).

rind [raind], *s.* (*of cheese*) Rinde *f;* (*of fruit*) Schale *f;* (*of bacon*) Schwarte *f.*

ring¹ [riŋ], *s.* Ring *m;* **r. road,** Umgehungsstraße *f.* ◆**'ringleader,** *s.* Rädelsführer *m.* ◆**'ringlet,** *s.* Ringellocke *f.*

ring² [riŋ]. **I.** *s.* **1.** (*sound*) (*a*) Klang *m* (der Gläser, der Stimme); (*b*) **there's a r. at the door,** es läutet/klingelt. **2.** *F:* **I'll give you a r.,** ich werde dich anrufen. **II.** *v.* **1.** *v.i.* (*a*) (*of bells*) läuten; (*of small bell*) klingeln; **to r. for service,** nach der Bedienung klingeln; (*b*) (*echo*) ertönen (**with,** von + *dat.*). **2.** *v.tr.* **to r. the bell,** (i) (*large*) die Glocke läuten; (ii) (*doorbell*) läuten. ◆**'ring 'up,** *v.tr. Tel:* (j-n) anrufen.

rink [riŋk], *s.* (*skating*) *r.,* Eisbahn *f.*

rinse [rins]. **I.** *v.tr.* spülen. **II.** *s.* Spülen *n;* (*colour*) *r.,* Tönung *f.*

riot ['raiət]. **I.** *s.* Aufruhr *f;* **r. police,** Bereitschaftspolizei *f;* **to run r.,** (*of children*) sich austoben. **II.** *v.i.* aufständisch werden; (*football fans*) randalieren. ◆**'rioter,** *s.* Aufrührer *m.* ◆**'rioting,** *s.* Unruhen *fpl.* ◆**'riotous,** *adj.* (*a*) (*of crowd*) aufrührerisch; (*b*) (*of laughter*) ausgelassen; (*hilarious*) urkomisch.

rip [rip]. **I.** *s.* Riß *m.* **II.** *v.tr. & i.* (etwas) reißen. ◆**'rip 'off,** *v.tr. Fig: F:* **to r. s.o. off,** j-n übers Ohr hauen.

ripe [raip], *adj.* (*of fruit*) reif. ◆**'ripen,** *v.* **1.** *v.tr.* (Obst usw.) reifen lassen. **2.** *v.i.* reifen; *esp. Fig:* zur Reife kommen.

ripple ['ripl]. **I.** *v.* **1.** *v.i.* sich kräuseln. **2.** *v.tr.* (Wasser) kräuseln. **II.** *s.* Kräuselung *f;* kleine Welle *f.*

rise [raiz]. **I.** *v.i.* sich erheben; (*of sun etc., Th: curtain*) aufgehen; (*of temperature, prices etc.*) steigen. **II.** *s.* (*a*) (*in*

ground*) Erhebung *f;* (*small hill*) Anhöhe *f;* (*h*) (*increase*) Erhöhung *f* (der Preise usw); (*c*) (*cause*) **to give r. to sth., Anlaß zu etwas *dat* geben; etwas veranlassen. ◆**'rising. I.** *adj.* (*of prices, temperature etc.*) steigend. **II.** *s.* (*revolt*) Aufstand *m.*

risk [risk]. **I.** *s.* Risiko *n;* Gefahr *f;* **to take/run a r.,** ein Risiko eingehen; **at one's own r.,** auf eigene Gefahr. **II.** *v.tr.* (etwas) riskieren. ◆**'risky,** *adj.* riskant; (*dangerous*) gefährlich.

rite [rait], *s.* Ritus *m; Ecc:* **the last rites,** die Sterbesakramente *npl.* ◆**'ritual** ['ritjuəl]. **I.** *adj.* rituell. **II.** *s.* Ritual *n.*

rival ['raiv(ə)l]. **I.** *s.* Rivale *m,* Rivalin *f;* (*competitor*) Konkurrent(in) *m(f).* **II.** *adj.* rivalisierend; *Com:* Konkurrenz-. **III.** *v.tr.* (j-m) Konkurrenz machen. ◆**'rivalry,** *s.* Rivalität *f.*

river ['rivər], *s.* Fluß *m;* (*large*) Strom *m;* **down/up (the) r.,** flußabwärts/flußaufwärts; stromabwärts/stromaufwärts.

rivet ['rivit]. **I.** *s. Tchn:* Niete *f.* **II.** *v.tr.* (etwas) nieten. ◆**'riveting,** *adj. Fig:* fesselnd.

road [rəud], *s.* Straße *f; esp. Fig:* Weg *m;* **r. transport,** Straßentransport *m;* **r. surface,** Fahrbahn *f;* **r. sign,** Straßenschild *n.* ◆**'road-block,** *s.* Straßensperre *f.* ◆**'roadside,** *s.* Straßenrand *m.* ◆**'roadway,** *s.* Fahrbahn *f.* ◆**'roadworks,** *s.pl.* Straßenbauarbeiten *fpl.* ◆**'roadworthy,** *adj.* fahrtüchtig.

roam [rəum], *v.i.* wandern; (*stray*) streunen.

roar [rɔːr]. **I.** *s.* **1.** Gebrüll *n* (eines Löwen usw.). **2.** Donnern *n* (einer Kanone); Toben *n* (des Meeres, des Sturms). **II.** *v.i.* brüllen; (*of sea, storm*) toben; (*of thunder*) krachen; (*of fire*) lodern; *Aut: Av:* **to r. past,** vorbeibrausen.

roast [rəust]. **I.** *v.tr.* (*a*) (Fleisch, Kartoffeln) (im Ofen) braten; (*b*) (Kaffee, Kastanien) rösten. **II.** *v.i. Cu: & Fig:* (*of pers.*) braten; *F:* **I'm roasting,** ich komme um vor Hitze. **II.** *s. Cu:* Braten *m; r.* beef, Rinderbraten *m,* Roastbeef *n.*

rob [rɔb], *v.tr.* (j-n) bestehlen; (eine Bank usw.) ausrauben. ◆**'robber,** *s.* Räuber *m.* ◆**'robbery,** *s.* Raub *m; F:* **it's sheer r.,** das ist der reinste Wucher.

robe [rəub], *s.* (*loose garment*) Gewand *n;* (*ceremonial*) Robe *f.*

robin ['rɔbin], *s.* (*redbreast*) Rotkehlchen *n.*

robot ['rəubɔt], *s.* Roboter *m.*

robust [rəu'bʌst], *adj.* robust; (*of structure*) stabil.

rock¹ [rɔk], *s.* **1.** (*a*) Felsen *m;* (*in sea*) Klippe *f;* (*b*) (*material*) Gestein *n.* **2.** (*a*) (*sweet*) Zuckerstange *f.* **3.** *attrib:* **r. plant,** Steinpflanze *f.* ◆**'rock-'bottom,** *s.* **to touch r.-b.,** den Tiefpunkt erreichen. ◆**'rockery,** *s.* Steingarten *m.* ◆**'rocky,** *adj.* felsig.

rock² [rɔk], *v.* **1.** *v.tr.* (die Wiege, ein Kind usw.) schaukeln. **2.** *v.i.* (*of cradle etc.*)

schaukeln; *(of building etc.)* schwanken. ◆'**rocking**, adj. r. chair, Schaukelstuhl m.

rocket ['rɔkit], s. Rakete f.

rod [rɔd], s. Stange f; *(bar, short stick)* Stab m; *(stick)* Rute f; *(fishing)* r., Angelrute f.

rodent ['rəud(ə)nt], s. Nagetier n.

roe[1] [rəu], s. Z: r. (deer), Reh n.

roe[2], s. *(of fish)* Rogen m.

rogue [rəug], s. *(a)* Pej: Schurke m; *(b)* Schelm m.

rôle [rəul], s. Th: etc: Rolle f.

roll [rəul]. I. s. 1. *(a)* *(of paper, film etc.)* Rolle f; *(b)* *(of bread)* Brötchen n. 2. *(list)* Liste f, esp. Namensliste f. II. v. 1. v.tr. rollen; (eine Zigarette) drehen; **rolled gold**, Dubleegold n. 2. v.i. *(a)* *(forwards, down)* rollen; *(b)* *(sideways)* of ship, car) schlingern. ◆'**roller**, s. Tchn: Rolle f; *(cylinder)* Walze f. ◆'**roller-'skate. I.** s. Rollschuh m. **II.** v.i. Rollschuh laufen. ◆'**rolling. I.** adj. *(a)* r. country, hügelige Gegend; *(b)* F: **to be** r. (in money), im Geld schwimmen. **II.** s. Cu: r. pin, Teigrolle f; Rail: r. stock, rollendes Material. ◆'**roll 'over**, v. 1. v.tr. (j-n, etwas) umdrehen. 2. v.i. *(of pers.)* sich (im Liegen) umdrehen; *(of dog)* sich auf den Rücken wälzen.

Roman ['rəumən]. **I.** s. Römer(in) m(f). **II.** adj. römisch; R. numerals, römische Ziffern; **R. Catholic**, (römisch-)katholisch; *(pers.)* Katholik(in) m(f).

romance [rəu'mæns], s. Romanze f; *(love story)* Liebesgeschichte f. ◆**ro'mantic**, adj. romantisch; Art: Lit: R. Movement, Romantik f.

Rome [rəum]. Pr.n. Rom n.

romp [rɔmp], v.i. *(of children)* **to** r. (about), herumtoben.

roof [ru:f], s. Dach n; Aut: r. rack, Dachgepäckträger m.

rook[1] [ruk], s. Orn: Krähe f; esp. Saatkrähe f.

rook[2], s. *(in chess)* Turm m.

room [ru:m, rum]. s. 1. Zimmer n; *(esp. very large)* Raum m; r. mate, Zimmergenosse *(-genossin)* m(f). 2. *(space)* Platz m. ◆'**roomy**, adj. geräumig.

roost [ru:st], s. *(of birds)* Sitzplatz m; *(of hens)* Hühnerstange f; **to rule the r.**, das Regiment führen. **II.** v.i. *(of hens)* auf der Stange sitzen.

root [ru:t]. **I.** s. 1. Wurzel f; **to take** r., Wurzel fassen; r. **cause**, Grundursache f. 2. Mth: **square** r., Quadratwurzel f. ◆'**rooted**, adj. *(of prejudice etc.)* **deeply** r., tief verwurzelt.

rope [rəup], s. Seil n; esp. Nau: Tau n; *(hangman's)* Strick m. ◆'**rope 'in**, v.tr. F: **they roped me in**, sie haben mich rangekriegt. ◆'**ropey**, adj. P: mies.

rosary ['rəuzəri], s. Ecc: Rosenkranz m.

rose[1] [rəuz]. s. 1. Rose f; r. bush, Rosenstrauch m; r. hip, Hagebutte f. 2. Brause f (einer Gießkanne). 3. *(colour)* Rosa n. **II.** adj. r. (coloured), rosa.

◆'**rosemary**, s. Bot: Rosmarin m.

◆'**rosy**, adj. rosig.

rosette [rəu'zet], s. Rosette f.

rosin ['rɔzin], s. Kolophonium n.

roster ['rɔstər], s. Dienstplan m.

rostrum ['rɔstrəm], s. Podium n.

rot [rɔt]. **I.** s. Fäule f. **II.** v.i. faulen; *(of corpse)* verwesen. ◆'**rotten**, adj. *(of fruit, egg etc.)* faul; verfault; *(of wood)* morsch; *(b)* F: miserabel; **I feel** r., mir ist mies.

rota ['rəutə], s. abwechselnder Dienst; duty r., Dienstplan m.

rotate [rəu'teit], v. 1. v.i. sich drehen. 2. v.tr. (ein Rad usw.) drehen. ◆'**rotary**, adj. drehend. ◆**ro'tation**, s. Drehung f; in r., der Reihe nach. ◆'**rotor**, s. Läufer m (einer Turbine); Av: Rotor m (eines Hubschraubers).

rote [rəut], s. **to learn by** r., auswendig lernen.

rotund [rəu'tʌnd], adj. rundlich.

rough [rʌf]. **I.** adj. 1. *(a)* *(of surface, sound)* rauh; *(coarse)* grob; *(b)* *(of road)* holprig; *(of ground)* uneben; F: **to feel pretty** r., sich ziemlich mies fühlen. 2. *(a)* *(stormy)* stürmisch; r. **sea**, bewegte See; *(b)* *(of treatment, manner)* grob. 3. *(a)* *(approximate)* grob, annähernd; **I can give you a** r. **idea**, ich kann es Ihnen ungefähr/*(of scheme)* in groben Umrissen sagen; *(b)* r. **copy**, Konzept n; -ly, adv. 1. grob. 2. *(approximately)* ungefähr; r. **speaking**, so ungefähr. **II.** s. *(in golf)* **to get into the** r., den Ball ins lange Gras schlagen. **III.** adv. **to live/sleep** r., im Freien leben/schlafen. **IV.** v.tr. F: **to** r. **it**, auf Bequemlichkeit verzichten. ◆'**roughage**, s. grobe Nahrung f; Ballaststoffe mpl. ◆'**rough-and-'ready**, adj. primitiv. ◆'**roughen**, v.tr. (eine Fläche) aufrauhen.

roulette [ru:'let], s. Roulett(e) n.

round [raund]. **I.** adj. rund. **II.** s. 1. Runde f; **to stand a** r. **of drinks**, eine Runde ausgeben; *(of doctor, postman etc.)* **to do one's rounds**, seine Runde machen; r. **of applause**, Beifallssturm m. 2. Mil: Salve f; r. **of ammunition**, Schuß m. 3. Mus: Kanon m. **III.** adv. 1. *(a)* **to turn** r., sich umdrehen; r. **and** r., im Kreis; **to go** r., (i) *(not straight there)* herumgehen; (ii) *(rotate)* sich drehen; (iii) *(to see s.o.)* vorbeigehen; *(b)* **to hand** r. **the cake**, den Kuchen herumreichen; **there isn't enough to go** r., es reicht nicht für alle; *(c)* **all the year** r., das ganze Jahr hindurch; r. **about**, rund herum. **IV.** prep. um + acc *(herum)*; *(a)* r. **the table**, rings um den Tisch; um den Tisch herum; r. **the world**, rund um die Welt; **to go** r. **the corner**, um die Ecke gehen; *(b)* *(approximately)* r. **(about)** £100, ungefähr £100. **V.** v.tr. *(a)* (etwas) rund machen; (eine Kante) abrunden; *(b)* **to** r. **a bend**, um eine Kurve fahren.

◆'roundabout. I. s. 1. (at fair) Karussell n. 2. Aut: Kreisverkehr m. II. adj. (of pers. etc.) umständlich. ◆'rounded, adj. (ab)gerundet. ◆'round 'off, v.tr. (eine Rede usw.) abschließen. ◆'round 'up, v.tr. (a) (eine Herde) zusammentreiben; (Verbrecher) einfangen; (b) (Ziffern) aufrunden.

rouse [rauz], v.tr. (a) to r. s.o. (from sleep), j-n (aus dem Schlaf) wecken; (b) Fig: (j-n) aufrütteln; to r. oneself, sich aufraffen; (c) (anger) (j-n) aufbringen. ◆'rousing, adj. r. speech, mitreißende Rede.

rout [raut], v.tr. Mil: (eine Armee) in die Flucht schlagen.

route [ru:t], s. v. Route f; (itinerary) Reiseroute f; Av: Rail: Strecke f.

routine [ru:'ti:n], s. (a) Routine f; (b) attrib. routinemäßig; Pej: (of performance etc.) schablonenhaft.

row¹ [rau], s. Reihe f; in Reihen, reihenweise.

row², v.tr. & i. (in boat) rudern. ◆'rower, s. Ruderer m. ◆'rowing, s. Rudern n; Sp: Rudersport m; r. boat, Ruderboot n.

row³ [rau], s. 1. (noise) Krach m. 2. (quarrel) Streit m; to have a r., sich streiten.

rowdy ['raudi], adj. rauflustig; (noisy) randalierend.

royal ['rɔiəl], adj. königlich. ◆'royalty, s. 1. (a) königliche Person(en) f(pl); (b) (status etc.) Königswürde f. 2. esp. pl. (for publication etc.) Tantiemen fpl.

rub [rʌb], v. 1. v.tr. (j-n, etwas) reiben; Fig: to r. shoulders with s.o., mit j-n zusammenkommen. 2. v.i. (sich) reiben (against, gegen + acc). ◆'rubber, s. Gummi m & n; (India) r., Radiergummi m; r. band, Gummiband n. ◆'rub 'down, v.tr. (a) abreiben; (with sandpaper) abschmirgeln. ◆'rub 'in, v.tr. (eine Salbe usw.) einreiben; F: don't r. it in! du brauchst es mir nicht unter die Nase zu reiben! ◆'rub 'out, v.tr. (etwas) ausradieren.

rubbish ['rʌbiʃ], s. 1. (a) (waste) Abfälle mpl; (refuse) Müll m; (debris) Schutt m; r. bin, Abfalleimer m; r. dump, Müllkippe f; (b) (worthless goods) Ausschußware f; F: Mist m. 2. (nonsense) Unsinn m, F: Quatsch m.

rubble ['rʌbl], s. (debris) Schutt m. (for roadmaking etc.) Bruchstein m.

ruby ['ru:bi], s. 1. Rubin m. 2. (colour) Rubinrot n.

rucksack ['rʌksæk], s. Rucksack m.

rudder ['rʌdər], s. Ruder n.

ruddy ['rʌdi], adj. 1. (a) (of cheeks) rot; r. complexion, frische Gesichtsfarbe; (b) rötlich. 2. P: verdammt.

rude [ru:d], adj. 1. (a) (impolite) unhöflich (to s.o., zu j-m); (b) (indecent) unanständig; Hum: r. drawing, obszöne Zeichnung. 2. (abrupt) unsanft.

rudiments ['ru:dimənts], s.pl. Anfänge

mpl; Grundbegriffe mpl (einer Wissenschaft). ◆'rudi'mentary, adj. (of knowledge) elementar; (simple) einfach.

ruffian ['rʌfiən], s. Rohling m.

ruffle ['rʌfl], v.tr. (a) (Haare, Federn) zerzausen; (b) Fig: (j-n) aus der Fassung bringen; ruffled, gereizt.

rug [rʌg], s. 1. (blanket) Decke f. 2. (on floor) kleiner Teppich m; (by bed) Bettvorleger m.

rugby ['rʌgbi], s. r. (football), F: rugger ['rʌgər], Rugby n.

rugged ['rʌgid], adj. (a) (of terrain) wild; (of cliffs) zerklüftet; (b) r. features, markante Züge.

ruin ['ru:in]. I. s. 1. (building etc.) Ruine f; to be in ruins, eine Ruine sein; Fig: (of plan) völlig zerstört sein. 2. (esp. of pers.) Ruin m. II. v.tr. ruinieren; (Pläne) vereiteln. ◆'rui'nation, s. Vernichtung f. (of pers.) Ruin m. ◆'ruinous, adj. (causing ruin) ruinös.

rule [ru:l]. I. s. 1. (regulation) Regel f; as a (general) r., in der Regel, im allgemeinen; r. of thumb, Faustregel f; rules and regulations, Vorschriften fpl. 2. (government) Regierung f (einer Partei); (domination) Herrschaft f. II. v. 1. v.tr. (ein Land, ein Volk) regieren. 2. v.i. (of king etc.) regieren; to r. over a country, über ein Land herrschen. ◆'ruler, s. 1. (pers.) Herrscher(in) m(f). 2. Mth: Lineal n. ◆'ruling. I. adj. herrschend; the r. class, die herrschende Schicht. II. s. (amtliche/gerichtliche) Verordnung f.

rum [rʌm], s. Rum m.

Rumania [ru(:)'meiniə]. Pr. n. Rumänien n. ◆Ru'manian. I. adj. rumänisch. II. s. 1. (pers.) Rumäne m, Rumänin f. 2. (language) Rumänisch n.

rumble ['rʌmbl]. I. s. Grollen n (des Donners); Rumpeln n (eines Lastwagens); Rec: Rumpelgeräusch n. II. v.i. (of thunder etc.) grollen; (of stomach) knurren.

ruminate ['ru:mineit], v.i. (a) (of cow) wiederkäuen; (b) (of pers.) grübeln (on/over sth., über etwas acc).

rummage ['rʌmidʒ], v.i. to r. through old papers, alte Papiere durchstöbern.

rumour ['ru:mər], s. Gerücht n. ◆'rumoured, adj. it is r. that..., man munkelt, daß...

rump [rʌmp], s. (of cattle) Hinterteil n; r. steak, Rumpsteak n.

rumple ['rʌmpl], v.tr. (Papier) zerknüllen; (ein Kleid) zerknittern; (Haare) zerraufen.

rumpus ['rʌmpəs], s. F: (a) (noise) Krawall m; (b) (fuss) Spektakel m.

run [rʌn]. I. v. 1. v.i. & v.tr. (a) laufen; (fast, in race) rennen; (b) Sp: teilnehmen (in a race, an einem Rennen); Pol: to r. for an office, für ein Amt kandidieren; (c) (travel) fahren; this train is not running **today**, dieser Zug verkehrt heute nicht; (d) (flow) fließen; (of eyes) tränen; (of tap, nose, colour) laufen; Fig: it runs in the family, es liegt in der Familie; (of work) funktionieren, laufen; (f) (stretch) sich erstrecken; (of road) verlaufen. 2. v.tr. (a) to r. a race, um die Wette laufen; (b) (drive) (j-n, ein Auto) fahren; to r. s.o. into town, j-n in die Stadt fahren; (c) (einen Motor, einen Hahn usw.) laufen lassen; (ein Bad) einlaufen lassen; (d) (manage) (ein Geschäft usw.) führen. II. s. (a) Lauf m; (of criminal) to be on the r., auf der Flucht sein; (in cricket, baseball) to score/make a r., einen Lauf machen; (b) Aut: etc: Fahrt f; to go for a r., eine Spazierfahrt machen; trial r., Probefahrt f; (c) (succession) Reihe f; Th: to have a long/short r., lange/kurze Zeit laufen. ◆'run a'cross, v.i. (meet etc) (j-m) zufällig begegnen. ◆'run a'way, v.i. davonlaufen. ◆'runaway, s. Ausreißer m. ◆'run 'down, v. 1. v.i. (of clock) ablaufen. 2. v.tr. (a) (die Straße, den Berg usw.) hinunterlaufen; (b) Aut: (j-n) anfahren; (c) (criticize) herabsetzen; (d) (einen Betrieb) abbauen; Fig: (of pers.) run down, (gesundheitlich) herunter. ◆'run-down, s. (report) Bericht m. ◆'run 'into, v.i. (a) to r. i. sth., in etwas acc hineinrennen/(of car) hineinfahren; (b) to r. i. difficulties, auf Schwierigkeiten stoßen. ◆'runner, s. 1. (athlete) Läufer(in) m(f); (competitor, horse etc.) Teilnehmer(in) m(f). 2. Bot: (shoot) Trieb m; r. bean, Stangenbohne f. 3. Kufe f (eines Schlittens usw.). ◆'runner-'up, s. Sp: Zweite(r) f(m). ◆'running. I. adj. (of commentary, expenses etc.) laufend; (one after another) nacheinander; three days r., drei Tage hintereinander. II. s. 1. Sp: & Fig: to be in/out of the r., Aussicht/keine Aussichten haben. 2. (a) (operation) Betrieb m (einer Maschine, usw.); Laufen n (eines Motors). ◆'runny, adj. flüssig; (of nose) laufend; ◆'run

'off, v.i. (a) davonrennen; (b) (of water) ablaufen. ◆'run 'out, v.i. (of supplies) ausgehen; time is running out, die Zeit wird knapp. ◆'run 'over, v.tr. Aut: (j-n) überfahren. ◆'run 'through, v.tr. (ein Dokument usw.) schnell durchlesen. ◆'run 'up, v. 1. v.i. (approach) herbeilaufen; to come running up, herangelaufen kommen. 2. v.tr. (eine Schuld) auflaufen lassen; to r. up a bill, eine Rechnung anwachsen lassen. ◆'runway, s. Av: (for take-off) Startbahn f; (for landing) Landebahn f.

rung [rʌŋ], s. Sprosse f (einer Leiter).

rupture ['rʌptʃər]. I. s. (all senses) Bruch m. II. v.tr. & i. (etwas) brechen.

rural ['ruərəl], adj. ländlich.

ruse [ru:z], s. List f.

rush¹ [rʌʃ], s. (reed) Binse f.

rush². I. s. 1. Ansturm m (for sth., auf etwas acc); r. hour, Stoßzeit f; r. hour traffic, Stoßverkehr m. 2. (hurry) Eile f. II. v. 1. v.i. stürzen (at s.o., auf j-n). 2. v.tr. (hurry) (j-n) drängen.

rusk [rʌsk], s. Zwieback m.

russet ['rʌsit], adj. rostbraun.

Russia ['rʌʃə]. Pr. n. Rußland n. ◆'Russian. I. s. (a) Russe m, Russin f; (b) (language) Russisch n. II. adj. russisch.

rust [rʌst]. I. s. Rost m. II. v.i. verrosten. ◆'rusty, adj. rostig; Fig: I am r., ich bin aus der Übung.

rustic ['rʌstik], adj. ländlich; (of furniture, pers.) rustikal; esp. Hum: bäuerlich.

rustle ['rʌsl], v. 1. v.i. (of wind etc.) rauschen; (of leaves) rascheln; (of paper, silk) knistern. 2. v.tr. (a) F: to r. up a meal, ein Essen herzaubern; (b) N.Am: (Vieh) stehlen.

rut [rʌt], s. Furche f; Fig: (of pers.) to be in a r., im alten Gleis festgefahren sein.

ruthless ['ru:θlis], adj. mitleidlos; (relentless) rücksichtslos. ◆'ruthlessness, s. Rücksichtslosigkeit f.

rye [rai], s. Roggen m; r. bread, Roggenbrot n.

S

S, s [es], s. (der Buchstabe) S, s n.

Sabbath ['sæbəθ], s. Sabbat m.

sable ['seibl], s. (animal/fur) Zobel m.

sabotage ['sæbətɑːʒ]. I. s. Sabotage f. II. v.tr. (ein Projekt, Maschinen usw.) sabotieren. ◆sabo'teur, s. Saboteur m.

saccharin ['sækərin], s. Saccharin n.

sachet ['sæʃei], s. (plastic) Sachet n.

sack¹ [sæk]. I. s. Sack m. II. v.tr. F: to s. s.o., j-n an die Luft setzen.

sack², v.tr. (eine Stadt usw.) plündern.

sacrament ['sækrəmənt], s. Ecc: Sakrament n.

sacred ['seikrid], adj. heilig; s. music, geistliche Musik.

sacrifice ['sækrifais]. I. s. Opfer n; to make sacrifices, Opfer bringen. II. v.tr. (etwas) opfern.

sacrilege ['sækrilidʒ], s. Sakrileg n. ◆sacri'legious, adj. frevlerisch; (blasphemous) gotteslästerlich.

sacrosanct ['sækrousæŋkt], adj. sakrosankt; (untouchable) unantastbar.

sad [sæd], adj. traurig; (of colours etc.) trist; (dilapidated) verkommen; -ly, adv. (a) traurig; (b) (before statement) traurigerweise. ◆'sadden, v.tr. (j-n) betrüben. ◆'sadness, s. Traurigkeit f.

saddle ['sædl]. I. s. (seat) Sattel m. II. v.tr. (a) (ein Pferd) satteln; F: to s. s.o.

with sth., j-m etwas aufbürden.
sadism ['seɪdɪzm], s. Sadismus m.
◆**sadist**, s. Sadist m. ◆**sadistic**
[sə'-], adj. sadistisch.

safari [sə'fɑːri], s. Safari f.
safe [seɪf]. I. adj. sicher; (unhurt) heil; s. **and sound,** wohlbehalten; **-ly,** adv. sicher; **to arrive s.,** wohlbehalten ankommen. II. s. Safe m. ◆**safeguard.** I. s. Vorsichtsmaßnahme f; (protection) Schutz m (against, gegen + acc). II. v.tr. sichern; (interests, rights) schützen. ◆**safe keeping,** s. (sichere) Aufbewahrung f. ◆**safety,** s. Sicherheit f; **s. measures,** Sicherheitsmaßnahmen fpl. **s. pin,** Sicherheitsnadel f; Aut: **Av: s. belt,** Sicherheitsgurt m.

saffron ['sæfrən]. I. s. Safran m. II. adj. **s. (yellow),** safrangelb.

sag [sæg], v.i. (of roof, bed etc.) durchhängen.

sage [seɪdʒ], s. Bot: Salbei m.

Sagittarius [sædʒɪ'teəriəs], s. Astr: Schütze m.

sago ['seɪgəu], s. Sago m.

sail [seɪl]. I. s. 1. Nau: s. (a) Segel n; **to set s.,** in See stechen; (b) (trip) Segelfahrt f. 2. Flügel m (einer Windmühle). II. v.i. segeln; (of steamer etc.) fahren. ◆**sailing.** I. adj. **s. dinghy,** (kleines) Segelboot; **s. ship,** Segelschiff n. II. s. Segeln n; F: **it was all plain s.,** es ging alles ganz glatt. ◆**sailor,** s. Matrose m.

saint [seɪnt], s. (a) Heilige(r) f(m); Fig: **the patience of a s.,** eine Engelsgeduld; (b) attrib. **St. Peter,** der Heilige Petrus. ◆**saintly,** adj. heilig; (of smile etc.) engelhaft.

sake [seɪk], s. **for the s. of,** wegen + gen; **for s.o's s.,** j-m zuliebe; **for my/your/her s.,** um meinetwillen/deinetwillen/ihretwillen; **for heaven's/God's/goodness' s.,** um Gottes willen.

salad ['sæləd], s. Salat m; **s. dressing,** Salatsoße f.

salary ['sæləri], s. Gehalt n.

sale [seɪl], s. Verkauf m; (a) **for s.,** zu verkaufen; (b) Com: pl. Absatz m; (c) (clearance) s., Ausverkauf m; **summer s.,** Sommerschlußverkauf m; attrib. **sales,** Verkaufs-; F: **sales talk,** Verkaufsjargon m. ◆**salesgirl,** s. Verkäuferin f. ◆**salesman, pl. -men,** s. Verkäufer m; (travelling) s., Handelsreisende(r) m.

salient ['seɪliənt], adj. hervorstehend; **s. point,** springender Punkt.

saline ['seɪlaɪn], adj. salzhaltig.

saliva [sə'laɪvə], s. Speichel m.

sallow ['sæləu], adj. gelblich(-blaß).

salmon ['sæmən]. I. s. Lachs m. II. adj. **s. pink,** lachsfarben.

saloon [sə'luːn], s. (a) N.Am: Schankwirtschaft f; F: Kneipe f; Brit: **s. bar,** (vornehmere) Bar f; (b) Aut: **s. (car),** Limousine f.

salt [sɔːlt]. I. s. (a) Cu: Salz n; Fig: **to take a story with a pinch of s.,** eine Ge-

schichte nicht wörtlich nehmen. II. adj. **salzig;** **s. water,** Salzwasser n. III. v.tr (etwas) salzen. ◆**salty,** adj. salzig; Cu: versalzen.

salubrious [sə'luːbriəs], adj. gesund.

salutary ['sæljutəri], adj. heilsam.

salute [sə'l(j)uːt]. I. s. esp. Mil: Gruß m. II. v.tr. (j-n) grüßen; abs. Mil: salutieren.

salvage ['sælvɪdʒ]. I. s. 1. (a) Bergung f (eines Schiffes usw.); (b) Wiederverwertung f (von Abfällen, Resten usw.). 2. (property saved) Bergungsgut n. II. v.tr (ein Schiff usw.) bergen; (Abfälle usw.) wiederverwerten.

salvation [sæl'veɪʃ(ə)n], s. Rettung f; Ecc: Erlösung f; **S. Army,** Heilsarmee f.

same [seɪm]. I. adj. gleiche(r,s); **the s. ...,** derselbe/dieselbe/dasselbe ...; der/die/das gleiche ...; **the s. thing,** dasselbe; das gleiche; **he's the s. age as I am,** er ist ebenso alt wie ich; **it's all the s. to me,** es ist mir gleich/egal; **the s. to you!** gleichfalls! II. adv. gleich (aussehen usw.); **all the s.,** immerhin. ◆**sameness,** s. 1. Gleichheit f. 2. (dullness) Eintönigkeit f.

sample ['sɑːmpl]. I. s. 1. (specimen) Probe f (eines Minerals, von Blut usw.); Kostprobe f (von Wein usw.). 2. (example) Beispiel n. II. v.tr. (etwas) probieren; (try out) (eine neues Restaurant usw.) ausprobieren.

sanctify ['sæŋ(k)tɪfaɪ], v.tr. (j-n, etwas) heiligen. ◆**sanctimonious** [-'məunɪəs], adj. frömmelnd. ◆**sanctuary,** s. 1. Heiligtum n. 2. (refuge) Zufluchtsort m. 3. **bird s.,** Vogelschutzgebiet n.

sanction ['sæŋ(k)ʃ(ə)n]. I. s. 1. (punishment) Bestrafung f; Pol: Sanktion f. 2. (approval) Billigung f; (permission) Erlaubnis f. II. v.tr. billigen.

sand [sænd]. I. s. 1. Sand m. 2. (also pl. sands) (beach) Sandstrand m. II. v.tr. **to s. (down),** etwas abschmirgeln/abschleifen. ◆**sandbag,** s. Sandsack m. ◆**sandbank,** s. Sandbank f. ◆**sandune,** s. Sanddüne f. ◆**sandpaper,** s. Sandpapier n. ◆**sandpit,** s. Sandkasten m. ◆**sandstone,** s. Sandstein m. ◆**sandy,** adj. (of soil, beach etc.) sandig.

sandal ['sænd(ə)l], s. Sandale f.

sandwich ['sænwɪdʒ, -wɪtʃ]. I. s. (a) Sandwich n; **ham s.,** Schinkenbrot n; (b) Sch: **s. course,** Lehrgang m mit theoretischem und praktischem Teil. II. v.tr. (j-n) einklemmen.

sane [seɪn], adj. vernünftig; (of pers.) bei Verstand. ◆**sanity** ['sænɪti], s. Vernunft f; **to lose one's s.,** den Verstand verlieren.

sanguine ['sæŋgwɪn], adj. (of temperament) heiter; (of views, policy etc.) zuversichtlich.

sanitation [sænɪ'teɪʃ(ə)n], s. sanitäre Einrichtungen fpl. ◆**sanitary,** adj. sanitär; **s. towel,** Damenbinde f.

Santa Claus ['sæntəklɔːz]. *Pr.n. Brit:* der Weihnachtsmann.

sap [sæp]. I. *s.* Saft *m* (eines Baumes usw.). II. *v.tr.* to s. s.o.'s strength, an j-s Kräften zehren.

sapling ['sæplɪŋ], *s.* junger Baum *m*.

sapphire ['sæfaɪər], *s.* Saphir *m*.

sarcasm ['sɑːkæzm], *s.* Sarkasmus *m*. ◆**sar'castic**, *adj.* sarkastisch.

sardine [sɑː'diːn], *s.* Sardine *f*.

Sardinia [sɑː'dɪnɪə]. *Pr.n.* Sardinien *n*.

sardonic [sɑː'dɔnɪk], *adj.* sardonisch.

sash [sæʃ], *s.* (*clothing*) Schärpe *f*.

satanic [sə'tænɪk], *adj.* satanisch.

satchel ['sætʃ(ə)l], *s.* Schulranzen *m*.

satellite ['sætəlaɪt], *s.* Satellit *m*; **s. town**, Trabantenstadt *f*.

satiate ['seɪʃɪeɪt], *v.tr.* (j-n) sättigen; (*to excess*) übersättigen.

satin ['sætɪn], *s.* Satin *m*.

satire ['sætaɪər], *s.* Satire *f*. ◆**satirical**, [sə'tɪrɪk(ə)l] *adj.* satirisch.

satisfaction [sætɪs'fækʃ(ə)n], *s.* 1. (*action*) Befriedigung *f* (eines Gläubigers). 2. (*a*) (*state*) Befriedigung *f*; (*b*) (*feeling*) Genugtuung *f* (**at/with**, über + *acc*). ◆**satis'factory**, *adj.* zufriedenstellend; (*just good enough*) befriedigend; **not s.**, unbefriedigend. ◆**satisfy** ['sætɪsfaɪ], *v.tr.* (*a*) (*fulfil*) (einer Verpflichtung) nachkommen; (eine Bedingung, einen Wunsch) erfüllen; (Ansprüche) befriedigen; (*b*) (*make content*) (j-n) befriedigen; **to s. one's hunger**, sich sättigen; (*c*) (*convince*) (j-n) überzeugen. ◆**'satisfied**, *adj.* 1. zufrieden. 2. (*convinced*) überzeugt. ◆**'satisfying**, *adj.* befriedigend; (*of food*) sättigend; (*of arguments, reasons*) überzeugend.

saturate ['sætjureɪt], *v.tr.* (*a*) (*wet*) (etwas) durchtränken; (*b*) (*Ch:* eine Substanz, *Com:* den Markt) sättigen.

Saturday ['sætədɪ], *s.* Samstag *m*, Sonnabend *m*.

sauce [sɔːs], *s. Cu:* Soße *f*. ◆**'saucepan**, *s.* Kochtopf *m*. ◆**'saucer**, *s.* Untertasse *f*. ◆**'saucy**, *adj. F:* frech.

Saudi Arabia ['saudɪ ə'reɪbɪə]. *Pr.n.* Saudi-Arabien *n*.

sauna ['sɔːnə], *s.* Sauna *f*.

saunter ['sɔːntər]. I. *v.i.* **to s.** (**along**), (dahin)schlendern. II. *s.* Bummel *m*.

sausage ['sɔsɪdʒ], *s.* Wurst *f*; **s. meat**, Bratwurstmasse *f*.

savage ['sævɪdʒ]. I. *adj.* (*a*) (*of people, tribe etc.*) wild; primitiv; (*b*) (*fierce*) (*of animal*) bösartig; (*of pers., attack etc.*) brutal; **-ly**, *adv.* brutal; bösartig. II. *s.* Wilde(r) *f(m)*. III. *v.tr.* (*of animal*) (j-n) anfallen.

save [seɪv]. I. *v.tr.* (*a*) (*rescue*) (j-n) retten (**from sth.**, vor etwas *dat*); **to s. s.o.'s life**, j-m das Leben retten; (*b*) (*keep*) (etwas) aufheben; (*c*) (*economize*) (Geld, Zeit usw.) sparen; **I'm saving up for a new car**, ich spare auf ein neues Auto; (*d*) (*avoid*) **that will s. us a lot of**

trouble, das erspart uns viel Mühe. II. *s. Fb: etc:* Abwehraktion *f*; **to make a s.**, den Ball abwehren. ◆**'saving**. I. *adj.* (*a*) sparend; **labour-s.**, arbeitssparend; (*b*) **it's his s. grace**, das ist ein versöhnender Zug an ihm. II. *s.* (*a*) Ersparnis *f*; **s. of time**, Zeitersparnis *f*; (*b*) *pl.* savings, Ersparnisse *fpl*; **savings bank**, Sparkasse *f*.

saviour ['seɪvjər], *s.* **the S.**, der Heiland.

savour ['seɪvər], *v.tr. Lit:* (Wein, eine Speise) kosten/(*enjoy*) genießen. ◆**'savoury**, *adj. Cu:* (*a*) (*tasty*) schmackhaft; (*b*) (*spicy*) pikant.

saw [sɔː]. I. *s.* Säge *f*. II. *v.tr. & i.* (Holz usw.) sägen. ◆**'sawdust**, *s.* Sägemehl *n*. ◆**'sawmill**, *s.* Sägemühle *f*.

Saxon ['sæksən]. I. *s.* Sachse *m*; Sächsin *f*. II. *adj.* sächsisch. ◆**'Saxony.** *Pr.n.* Sachsen *n*.

saxophone ['sæksəfəun], *s.* Saxophon *n*.

say [seɪ]. I. *v.tr.irr.* (*a*) sagen; **it said on the radio …**, im Radio wurde gemeldet …; (*in book etc.*) **it says here …**, hier heißt es …; **people s./they s.** es heißt/man sagt; **there's a lot to be said for it**, es spricht vieles dafür; **that's to s.**, das heißt; (**let's**) **s. you are alone**, nehmen wir an, Sie sind allein; (*b*) (*speak*) (ein Gebet) sprechen; (ein Gedicht) aufsagen. II. *s.* **to have a s.**, ein Wort mitzureden haben. ◆**'saying**, *s.* 1. **it goes without s. that …**, es versteht sich ganz von selbst, daß … 2. (*common*) **s.**, Sprichwort *n.*

scab [skæb], *s.* 1. (*on wound*) Schorf *m.* 2. *F:* (*pers.*) Streikbrecher *m*.

scaffold ['skæf(ə)ld], *s.* 1. Baugerüst *n.* 2. (*for executions*) Schafott *n*. ◆**'scaffolding**, *s.* Baugerüst *n.*

scald [skɔːld], *v.tr.* **to s. oneself/one's foot**, sich/sich *dat* den Fuß verbrühen. ◆**'scalding**, *adj.* **s. hot**, brühheiß.

scale¹ [skeɪl]. I. *s.* 1. Schuppe *f* (eines Fisches). 2. (*a*) (*in boiler etc.*) Kesselstein *m*; (*b*) (*on teeth*) Zahnstein *m*. II. *v.tr.* (einen Fisch) schuppen.

scale² [skeɪl], *s.* 1. Skala *f*; (*of a map, model etc.*) Maßstab *m*; **to a s.** of 1:10, im Maßstab von 1:10; **s. model**, maßstabgetreues Modell; (*b*) (*relative size*) Umfang *m* (einer Katastrophe usw.); (**on a**) **large/small s.**, im Großen/im Kleinen. 2. *Mus:* Tonleiter *f*. II. *v.tr.* scaled down, in verkleinertem Maßstab.

scale³, *v.tr.* (*climb*) (eine Mauer usw.) erklimmen; (einen Berg) besteigen.

scales [skeɪlz], *s.pl.* (**pair of**) **s.**, Waage *f*.

scallop ['skɔləp], *s. Z:* Kammuschel *f*.

scalp [skælp], *s.* Kopfhaut *f*.

scalpel ['skælp(ə)l], *s.* Skalpell *n.*

scamper ['skæmpər], *v.i.* huschen; **to s. off**, weghuschen.

scan [skæn]. I. *v.* 1. *v.tr. & i.* (einen Vers) skandieren. 2. *v.tr.* (den Horizont) absuchen (**for sth.**, nach etwas *dat*); (die Zeitung usw.) durchsehen. II. *s.* Abta-

stung *f*; *Med:* Scan *m*.
scandal ['skænd(ə)l], *s.* **1.** (*action*) Skandal *m*. **2.** (*gossip*) Klatsch *m*. ◆**'scandalize**, *v.tr.* (j-n) schockieren. ◆**'scandalous**, *adj.* skandalös.

Scandinavia [skændi'neivjə]. *Pr. n.* Skandinavien *n.* ◆**Scandi'navian.** **I.** *adj.* skandinavisch. **II.** *s.* Skandinavier(in) *m(f)*.

scant [skænt], *adj.* recht wenig. ◆**'scanty**, *adj.* dürftig; (*of vegetation etc.*) kärglich; **-ily**, *adv.* **s. dressed,** dürftig/spärlich bekleidet.

scapegoat ['skeipgəut], *s.* Sündenbock *m*.

scar [skɑːr]. **I.** *s.* Narbe *f*. **II.** *v.tr.* (*a*) (ein Gesicht usw.) mit Narben entstellen; (*b*) *Fig:* (*damage*) (etwas) beschädigen. **2.** *v.i.* eine Narbe hinterlassen.

scarce [skɛəs], *adj.* (*rare*) selten; (*not plentiful*) knapp; *F:* **make yourself s.!** verdufte! **-ly**, *adv.* kaum. ◆**'scarcity**/**'scarceness**, *s.* Knappheit *f*; (*lack*) Mangel *m*.

scare ['skɛər]. **I.** *s.* (*a*) (*fright*) Schrecken *m*; (*b*) Alarm *m*; (*hoax*) blinder Alarm; **bomb s.,** Bombenalarm *m*. **II.** *v.tr.* (j-n) erschrecken; **to s. s.o./an animal away,** j-n/ein Tier verscheuchen. ◆**'scarecrow**, *s.* Vogelscheuche *f*. ◆**'scared**, *adj.* ängstlich; **to be s.** (*of sth.*), Angst (vor etwas *dat*) haben; **to be s. to death,** Todesangst haben. ◆**'scaremonger**, *s.* Bangemacher *m*. ◆**'scary**, *adj. F:* gruselig.

scarf [skɑːf], *s.* Schal *m*; (*headscarf*) Kopftuch *n*.

scarlet ['skɑːlət], *adj.* scharlachrot; **s. fever,** Scharlach *m*.

scathing ['skeiðiŋ], *adj.* kritisch; (*of criticism etc.*) vernichtend.

scatter ['skætər], *v.* **1.** *v.tr.* (*a*) (*make run/fly away*) (Vögel, Leute usw.) zerstreuen; (*b*) (Konfetti usw.) streuen; (Samen) ausstreuen. **2.** *v.i.* (*of crowd*) sich zerstreuen. ◆**'scatterbrained**, *adj.* (*of pers.*) zerstreut. ◆**scattered**, *s.* **showers,** vereinzelte Schauer. ◆**'scatty**, *adj. F:* verrückt.

scavenger ['skævindʒər], *s.* Aasfresser *m*.

scenario [si'nɑːriəu], *s.* **-os** [si'nɑːriəu,-əuz], *s. Cin: etc:* Drehbuch *n*; *Th:* Textbuch *n*.

scene [siːn], *s.* **1.** *Th: etc:* Szene *f*; **behind the scenes,** hinter den Kulissen. **2.** (*place*) Schauplatz *m*; **s. of the crime,** Tatort *m*; **s. of the accident/disaster,** Unfallort *m*. **3.** (*view, sight*) **a touching s.,** ein rührender Anblick. **4.** (*emotional outburst*) Szene *f*. ◆**'scenery**, *s.* **1.** *Th:* Kulissen *fpl*; (*design*) Bühnenbild *n*. **2.** (*landscape*) Landschaft *f*. ◆**'scenic**, *adj.* landschaftlich schön.

scent [sent]. **I.** *s.* **1.** (*pleasant smell*) Duft *m*; (*perfume*) Parfüm *n*. **2.** Witterung *f*; (*track*) Fährte *f*; (*of hounds, police etc.*) **to be on the right s.,** auf der richtigen Spur sein. **II.** *v.tr.* (*a*)

(ein Tier) wittern; (*b*) (etwas) parfümieren; (*die Luft*) mit Duft erfüllen.

sceptic ['skeptik], *s.* Skeptiker(in) *m(f)*. ◆**'sceptical**, *adj.* skeptisch. ◆**'scepticism**, *s.* Skepsis *f*.

sceptre ['septər], *s.* Zepter *n*.

schedule ['ʃedjul, *esp. N.Am:* 'ske-]. **I.** *s.* **1.** (*list*) Verzeichnis *n*. **2.** (*a*) Plan *m*; **to work to s.,** nach Plan arbeiten; **on s.,** (*of train etc.*) fahrplanmäßig; **to be behind s. with sth.,** mit etwas *dat* zurück sein; (*b*) (*of pers.*) Programm *n*; **crowded s.,** volles Programm. **II.** *v.tr.* (etwas) planen; *Rail:* **scheduled service,** fahrplanmäßiger Verkehr *m*.

scheme [skiːm]. **I.** *s.* **1.** (*combination*) Schema *n*; (*system*) System *n*. **2.** (*a*) (*plan*) Plan *m*; (*b*) (*dishonest*) Intrige *f*. **II.** *v.* **1.** *v.i.* planen (**to do sth.,** etwas zu tun); **to s. against s.o.,** gegen j-n intrigieren. **2.** *v.tr.* Ränke schmieden; ein Komplott anzetteln. ◆**'scheming.** **I.** *adj.* intrigant. **II.** *s.* Intrigieren *n*.

schizophrenic [skitsəu'frenik]. **I.** *adj.* schizophren. **II.** *s.* Schizophrene(r) *f(m)*.

scholar ['skɔlər], *s.* **1.** (*student*) Studierende(r) *f(m)*; *A:* (*pupil*) Schüler(in) *m(f)*. **2.** (*pers. with much knowledge*) Gelehrte(r) *f(m)*. ◆**'scholarly**, *adj.* gelehrt. ◆**'scholarship**, *s.* **1.** Gelehrsamkeit *f*. **2.** *Sch:* Stipendium *n*.

school [skuːl], *s.* Schule *f*; **s. leaver,** Schulabgänger *m*; **driving s.,** Fahrschule *f*; *Fig:* **s. of thought,** Denkart *f*. ◆**'schoolboy**, *s.* Schüler *m*. ◆**'schoolgirl**, *s.* Schülerin *f*. ◆**'schooling**, *s.* (*education*) Ausbildung *f*; (*instruction*) Schulunterricht *m*. ◆**'schoolteacher**, *s.* Lehrer(in) *m(f)*.

science ['saiəns], *s.* Wissenschaft *f*; *esp.* Naturwissenschaft *f*; **s. fiction,** Science-Fiction *f*. ◆**scien'tific**, *adj.* (*a*) naturwissenschaftlich; (*b*) (*of method*) wissenschaftlich; (*of pers.*) systematisch. ◆**'scientist**, *s.* Naturwissenschaftler(in) *m(f)*.

scintillate ['sintileit], *v.i. Fig:* (*of wit etc.*) sprühen; *Th: etc:* **scintillating performance,** glänzende Aufführung

scissors ['sizəz], *s.pl.* (**pair of**) **s.,** Schere *f*.

scoff¹ [skɔf], *v.i.* spotten (**at s.o., sth.,** über j-n, etwas *acc*).

scoff², *v. P:* (*eat*) **1.** *v.i.* fressen. **2.** *v.tr.* (etwas) verputzen.

scold [skəuld], *v.tr.* ausschimpfen.

scone [skɔn, skəun], *s. approx.* Milchbrötchen *n*.

scoop [skuːp]. **I.** *v.tr.* **to s. (out),** (Wasser usw.) ausschöpfen; **to s. up,** (etwas) aufschaufeln. **II.** *s.* **1.** (*kitchen*) Schaufel *f*. **2.** *F:* (*report*) Exklusivmeldung *f*.

scooter ['skuːtər], *s.* Roller *m*.

scope [skəup], *s.* (*a*) (*range*) Bereich *m*; (*extent*) Umfang *m*; (*b*) (*opportunity*) **to give s.o. plenty of s.,** j-m viel Spielraum geben; **it leaves s. for improvement,** es ließe sich noch verbessern.

scorch [skɔːtʃ], *v.tr.* (etwas) versengen. ◆'**scorching**, *adj. & adv.* sengend; s. **hot**, glutheiß.

score [skɔːr]. **I.** *s.* 1. (*scratch*) Kratzer *m*; (*notch*) Kerbe *f*; (*cut*) Einkerbung *f*. 2. *Sp:* (*no. of points*) Punkt(e)zahl *f*; (*position of game*) Spielstand *m*; (*result*) Ergebnis *n*; **what's the s.?** wie steht das Spiel? 3. (*debt*) *Fig:* **to settle/pay off old scores**, alte Rechnungen begleichen. 4. *Mus:* Partitur *f*. 5. (*a*) *A:* (*inv. in pl.*) **a s.**, zwanzig; (*b*) *pl.* jede Menge; **scores of people**, Scharen *pl* von Menschen. **II.** *v.* 1. *v.tr.* (*a*) (*mark with cuts*) (Metall, Stein usw.) ritzen; (*b*) *Sp:* (of match) erzielen; *Fb:* **to s. a goal**, ein Tor schießen. 2. *v.i.* (*a*) *Sp:* die Punkte anschreiben; (*b*) *Sp:* (*of player*) Punkte erzielen. ◆'**scoreboard**, *s. Sp:* Anzeigetafel *f*. ◆'**scorer**, *s. Fb:* Torschütze *m*.

scorn [skɔːn]. **I.** *s.* 1. Hohn *m*. **II.** *v.tr.* (*a*) (*deride*) verhöhnen; (*reject*) (ein Angebot usw.) verschmähen. ◆'**scornful**, *adj.* höhnisch.

Scorpio ['skɔːpiəu], *s. Astr:* Skorpion *m*.

scorpion ['skɔːpjən], *s.* Skorpion *m*.

Scot [skɔt], *s.* Schotte *m*; Schottin *f*; **to get off s.(-)free**, straffrei ausgehen. ◆'**Scotch** [skɔtʃ]. **I.** *adj.* schottisch. **II.** *s.* (*whisky*) Scotch *m*, schottischer Whisky *m*, Scotch *m*. **III.** *v.tr.* (j-s Pläne usw.) durchkreuzen. ◆'**Scotland** ['skɔtlənd], *Pr. n.* Schottland *n*. ◆'**Scots**, *adj.* schottisch. ◆'**Scotsman**, *pl. -men*, *s.* Schotte *m*. ◆'**Scotswoman**, *pl. -women*, *s.* Schottin *f*. ◆'**Scottish**, *adj.* schottisch.

scoundrel ['skaundrəl], *s.* Schuft *m*.

scour[1] ['skauər], *v.tr.* (Töpfe usw.) scheuern.

scour[2], *v.tr.* **to s. the district for s.o.**, **sth.**, die Gegend nach j-m, etwas *dat* absuchen.

scourge [skəːdʒ], *s.* Geißel *f*; *Fig:* Plage *f*.

scout [skaut]. **I.** *s.* (*a*) *Mil:* Kundschafter *m*; (*b*) (*boy*) s., Pfadfinder *m*. **II.** *v.i.* **to s. about/around for sth.**, nach etwas *dat* herumsuchen.

scowl [skaul]. **I.** *s.* finsterer Blick *m*. **II.** *v.i.* finster blicken; **to s. at s.o.**, j-n finster anblicken.

scraggy ['skrægi], *adj.* mager.

scramble ['skræmbl]. **I.** *v.* 1. *v.i.* (*a*) (*climb*) klettern; (*b*) **to s. for the ball**, sich um den Ball raufen. 2. *v.tr.* (*a*) (*code*) (eine Nachricht) verschlüsseln; (*b*) *Cu:* **scrambled eggs**, Rührei *n*. **II.** *s.* (*rush*) Hetze *f*; Gedränge *n* (**for sth.**, um etwas *acc*).

scrap[1] [skræp]. **I.** *s.* 1. (*a*) (*small piece*) Stückchen *n*; (*of cloth*, *paper*) Fetzen *m*; (*b*) (*fragment*) Bruchstück *n*. 2. (*a*) *pl.* **scraps**, (*remains*) Überbleibsel *npl*; (*uneaten food*) Reste *mpl* (einer Mahlzeit); (*b*) **s.** (**metal**), Schrott *m*; **s. heap**, Schrotthaufen *m*. **II.** *v.tr.* (*a*) (etwas) wegwerfen;

(ein Auto usw.) verschrotten; (*b*) (einen Plan usw.) aufgeben. ◆'**scrappy**, *adj.* bruchstückhaft.

scrap[2]. *s.* (*fight*) *F:* Rauferei *f*; (*quarrel*) Streit *m*.

scrape [skreip]. **I.** *s.* 1. Kratzen *n*; (*result*) Schramme *f*. 2. (*awkward situation*) *F:* **to be in a s.**, in der Klemme sitzen. **II.** *v.* 1. *v.tr.* (*a*) (Schmutz, Farbe usw.) abkratzen; (*b*) (*damage*) (Möbel, Lackierung usw.) schrammen; **to s. one's knee etc.**, sich *dat* das Knie usw. aufschürfen. 2. *v.i.* kratzen; **to s. through an exam**, ein Examen mit knapper Not bestehen. ◆'**scraper**, *s.* Schabmesser *n*.

scratch [skrætʃ]. **I.** *s.* 1. (*a*) (*mark*) Kratzer *m*; (*b*) (*wound*) Schramme *f*. 2. (*a*) **to start from s.**, ganz von vorne anfangen; (*b*) **to come up to s.**, den Erwartungen entsprechen. **II.** *v.tr.* (*a*) (j-n, etwas) kratzen; *Fig:* **to s. the surface (of a subject)**, ein Thema nur oberflächlich berühren; (*b*) (*of animal*) (im Sand usw.) scharren. ◆'**scratchy**, *adj.* (*of wool etc.*) kratzig.

scrawl [skrɔːl]. **I.** *v.tr.* **to s. sth. on sth.**, etwas auf etwas *acc* kritzeln/schmieren. **II.** *s.* Kritzelei *f*.

scream [skriːm]. **I.** *s.* (gellender) Schrei *m*; **s. of pain**, Schmerzensschrei *m*. **II.** *v.i.* schreien (**with fright**, vor Angst).

scree [skriː], *s.* Geröllhalde *f*.

screech [skriːtʃ]. **I.** *s.* gellender Schrei *m*. **II.** *v.i.* kreischen.

screen [skriːn]. **I.** *s.* 1. (*shield*) Schirm *m*; (*against draughts*) Wandschirm *m*. 2. (*a*) *Phot: Cin:* Leinwand *f*; (*medium*) **the s.**, der Film; **s. test**, Probeaufnahmen *fpl*; (*b*) *TV: etc:* Bildschirm *m*. **II.** *v.tr.* (*a*) (*hide*, *protect*) (etwas) abschirmen (**from sth.**, gegen etwas *acc*); (*b*) *Cin:* (einen Roman usw.) verfilmen; *TV:* (ein Programm) (auf dem Bildschirm) zeigen. ◆'**screening**, *s.* 1. (*protection*, *also El:*) Abschirmung *f* (**from/against**, gegen + *acc*). 2. *Pol:* Durchleuchten *n*. ◆'**screenplay**, *s. Cin:* Drehbuch *n*.

screw [skruː]. **I.** *s.* 1. Schraube *f*. 2. *P:* (*warder*) Gefängniswärter *m*. **II.** *v.tr.* (*a*) **to s. sth. (on) to sth.**, etwas an etwas *acc* schrauben; (*b*) **to s. up one's handkerchief**, sein Taschentuch zusammenknüllen; **to s. up one's eyes**, die Augen zusammenkneifen; (*c*) *V:* (*copulate*) (j-n) ficken. ◆'**screwdriver**, *s.* Schraubenzieher *m*.

scribble ['skribl]. **I.** *v.tr.* (etwas) kritzeln. **II.** *s.* Gekritzel *n*.

script [skript], *s.* 1. (*a*) (*manuscript*) Manuskript *n*; (*b*) *Cin:* Drehbuch *n*; **s. writer**, Drehbuchautor *m*. 2. (*alphabet*) Schrift *f*.

scripture ['skriptʃər], *s.* (**Holy**) **S.**, Heilige Schrift *f*.

scroll [skrəul], *s.* Schriftrolle *f*.

scrounge [skraundʒ], *v.tr. & i: F:* (*beg*) (etwas) schnorren. ◆'**scrounger**, *s.*

Schnorrer m.

scrub [skrʌb], v.tr. (den Fußboden usw.)
schrubben. ◆**'scrubbing-brush**, s.
Scheuerbürste f.

scruff [skrʌf], s. **1.** to seize s.o. by the s.
of the neck, j-n beim Kragen packen.
◆**'scruffy**, adj. F: ungepflegt.

scrum [skrʌm], s. Sp: & F: Gedränge n.

scruple ['skruːpl], s. Skrupel m; pl. **scru-
ples**, Bedenken npl. ◆**'scrupulous**, adj.
(a) (conscientious) gewissenhaft (about to,
mit + dat); (b) (precise) genau.

scrutinize ['skruːtinaiz], v.tr. (j-n, etwas)
prüfend ansehen. ◆**'scrutiny**, s. Untersuchung f.

scuffle ['skʌfl]. **I.** s. Rauferei f. **II.** v.i.
raufen.

scullery ['skʌləri], s. Spülküche f.

sculptor ['skʌlptər], s. Bildhauer m.
◆**'sculpture**, s. Art: Plastik f.

scum [skʌm], s. Schaum m; Pej: (people)
Abschaum m (der Menschheit).

scurrilous ['skʌriləs], adj. gemein; (of
language etc.) unflätig.

scurry ['skʌri], v.i. huschen; to s. off/
away, davonhasten.

scuttle[1] ['skʌtl], s. (coal) s., Kohlen-
schütte f.

scuttle[2], v.tr. (ein Schiff) versenken.

scuttle[3], v.i. to s. off = scurry off.

scythe [saið], s. Sense f.

sea [siː], s. **1.** (a) Meer n; See f; at s., auf
See; by the s., am Meer; by s., auf dem
Seeweg; (b) (motion of sea) heavy s.,
schwerer Seegang m. **2.** Fig: (expanse) a
s. of faces, ein Meer von Gesichtern.
◆**'sea'breeze**, s. Seebrise f.
◆**'seafarer**, s. Seefahrer m.
◆**'seafood**, s. Meeresfrüchte fpl.
◆**'seafront**, s. Strandpromenade f.
◆**'seagull**, s. Möwe f. ◆**'seashell**,
Muschel f. ◆**'seashore**, s. Meeres-
strand m. ◆**'sea-sickness**, s. Seekrank-
heit f. ◆**'seaside**, s. Meeresküste f; at
the s., am Meer; s. resort, Seebad n.
◆**'sea-water**, s. Meerwasser n.
◆**'seaweed**, s. Seetang m.
◆**'seaworthy**, adj. seetüchtig.

seal[1] [siːl], s. Seehund m.

seal[2]. **I.** s. (a) (on document, letter etc.) Siegel n; to give th. the s. of approval, et-
was dat persönlich billigen; (b) (closure)
Verschluß m. **II.** v.tr. (with wax) versie-
geln; (gum down) (einen Brief usw.) zukleben; (make airtight) luftdicht verschließen. ◆**'seal 'off**, v.tr. (ein Gebiet)
abriegeln.

seam [siːm], s. **1.** Naht f; Fig: bursting
at the seams, zum Bersten voll. **2.** Min:
(of coal) Flöz n; (of ore) Ader f.

search [səːtʃ]. **I.** s. (a) Suche f; (for
s.o. missing) Suchaktion f; (manhunt)
Fahndung f; s. party, Suchtrupp m; Jur:
s. warrant, Haussuchungsbefehl m. **2.**
(examination) Durchsuchung f (von Gepäck usw.). **II.** v. **1.**
v.tr. (a) (eine Schublade usw.) durchsu-

chen, (j-n, einen Ort) absuchen (for sth.,
nach etwas, usw.); Jur: (Gepäck, ein Haus
usw.) durchsuchen; (b) P: s. me! keine
Ahnung! **2.** v.i. to s. (for sth.), (nach etwas dat) suchen. ◆**'searchlight**, s.
Suchscheinwerfer m.

season ['siːz(ə)n]. **I.** s. **1.** Jahreszeit f;
holiday s., Urlaubszeit f; to be in s., (of
fruit) reif sein. **2.** Th: Sp: etc: Saison f;
Rail: etc: s. ticket, Zeitkarte f. **II.** v.tr.
(a) (eine Speise) würzen; (b) (Holz) ablagern. ◆**'seasonal**, adj. saisonbedingt.
◆**'seasoned**, adj. **1.** gewürzt. **2.** (of
timber) abgelagert; Fig: (of pers.) erfahren. ◆**'seasoning**, s. Cu: Würze f.

seat [siːt]. **I.** s. (a) Sitz m; Rail: etc: Sitzplatz m; Th: Platz m; Aut: s. belt, Sicherheitsgurt m; (b) (part of body) Gesäß
n; s. of trousers, Hosenboden m; (c) s.
of government, Regierungssitz m. **II.**
v.tr. (j-n, sich) setzen; to be seated, sitzen; please be seated, nehmen Sie bitte
Platz; (of building) to s. 500, 500 Sitz-
plätze haben. ◆**'seating**, s. (seats) Sitz-
plätze mpl; s. capacity, Zahl f der Sitz-
plätze.

secluded [si'kluːdid], adj. (of place etc.)
ruhig gelegen; (lonely) einsam.
◆**seclusion** [-'kluːʒ(ə)n], s. Ruhe f; ru-
hige Lage f (eines Hauses).

second[1] ['sekənd], s. Sekunde f.

second[2], adj. zweiter, zweite, zweites;
the s. of January, der zweite Januar; the
s. largest, der/die/das zweitgrößte; Sp: to
come s. (to s.o.), den zweiten Platz
(hinter j-m) belegen; to have s.
thoughts, es sich dat anders überlegen;
-ly, adv. zweitens. **II.** s. **1.** Zweite m & f;
n; Charles the S., Karl der Zweite. **2.**
Com: seconds, Waren fpl zweiter Wahl.
III. v.tr. Pol: to s. a motion, einen Vorschlag befürworten. ◆**'secondary**, adj.
1. sekundär; of s. importance, nebensächlich. **2.** Sch: Brit: s. school/
education, höhere Schule/Schulbildung.
◆**'second(-)hand**, adj. aus zweiter
Hand; s.-h. car, Gebrauchtwagen m.
◆**'second-'rate**, adj. zweitrangig; (mediocre) mittelmäßig.

secret ['siːkrit]. **I.** adj. (a) (officially) geheim; (b) (of whisper, smile, feeling etc.)
heimlich; -ly, adv. heimlich. **II.** s. Geheimnis n; in s., heimlich; to let s.o.
into a s., j-n in ein Geheimnis einweihen. ◆**'secrecy**, s. (a) Heimlichkeit f
(eines Planes usw.); (b) sworn to s., zur
Verschwiegenheit verpflichtet.
◆**secrete** [si'kriːt], v.tr. (a) Biol: (ein
Sekret) absondern; (b) (hide) (j-n, etwas)
verbergen (from, von + dat.)
◆**'secretive**, adj. (of pers.) geheimtue-
risch.

secretary ['sekrətri], s. Sekretär(in) m(f);
Pol: S. of State, (i) Brit: Minister m; (ii)
N.Am: Außenminister m.

sect [sekt], s. Sekte f.

section ['sekʃ(ə)n], s. **1.** (a) (part) Teil m;

(b) Abschnitt m (eines Textes usw.); Rail: Streckenabschnitt m; (c) (department) Abteilung f; Mil: Gruppe f; (d) Jur: Paragraph m (eines Gesetzes). 2. Mth: Med: Schnitt m; (cross) s., Querschnitt m.

sector ['sektər], s. Sektor m.

secular ['sekjulər], adj. weltlich.

secure [si'kjuər]. I. adj. 1. (safe, certain) sicher (against, vor + dat); to feel s., sich geborgen fühlen. 2. (firm) fest. II. v.tr. (a) (make safe) (etwas) sichern; (protect) schützen (against/from, gegen + acc); (b) (fix) (etwas) festmachen (to, an + acc); (c) (obtain) sich dat (einen Platz, j-s Dienste usw.) beschaffen. ◆se'curity, s. 1. Sicherheit f. 2. (guarantee) Bürgschaft f; Com: (deposit) Kaution f; (for loan etc.) Sicherheit f; (c) Fin: usw. pl. securities, Wertpapiere npl.

sedate [si'deit], adj. gesetzt.

sedative ['sedətiv]. I. s. Beruhigungsmittel n. II. adj. beruhigend.

sedentary ['sedəntri], adj. sitzend.

sediment ['sedimənt], s. (a) Sediment n; (b) (in wine etc.) Bodensatz m.

sedition [si'diʃ(ə)n], s. Aufruhr m. ◆se'ditious, adj. aufrührerisch.

seduce [si'djuːs], v.tr. (j-n) verführen. ◆se'duction [-'dʌkʃ(ə)n], s. Verführung f. ◆se'ductive, adj. verführerisch.

see [siː], v.tr. & i.irr. (a) (j-n, etwas) sehen; see you on Thursday! bis Donnerstag! F: I'll go and s., ich werde mal nachsehen; (b) (visit) to go to/F: s. s.o., j-n besuchen; (c) (einen Besucher) empfangen; I can't s. him today, ich kann ihn heute nicht sprechen; (d) (accompany) (j-n) begleiten; I'll s. you home/to the door, ich begleite Sie nach Hause/(bis) zur Tür; (e) (recognize) (etwas) erkennen; (understand) (etwas) verstehen; (f) to s. that everything is in order, danach sehen/dafür sorgen, daß alles in Ordnung ist. ◆'see a'bout, v.tr. to s. a. sth., sich um etwas acc kümmern. ◆'see 'off, v.tr. to s.o. o. on a train/a plane, j-n zur Bahn/zum Flughafen bringen. ◆'see 'through, v.tr. (a) Fig: (j-s Absichten usw.) durchschauen; (b) (support) to s. s.o. t., j-m (bis zum Ende) helfen; to s. sth. t., (die Sache) durchhelfen. ◆'see 'to, v. tr. (nach j-m, etwas dat) sehen. ◆'seeing. I. s. Sehen n; worth s., sehenswert. II. conj. phr. s. that ..., angesichts der Tatsache, daß ...

seed [siːd], s. 1. Samen m; coll. Saat f; s. potato, Saatkartoffel f; to go to s., F: (of pers.) herunterkommen. 2. Sp: gesetzter Spieler m. ◆'seedy, adj. F: (of pers., place etc.) schäbig.

seek [siːk], v.tr. (a) (look for) (etwas) suchen; (b) (ask for) to s. sth. from s.o., etwas von j-m erbitten.

seem [siːm], v.i. scheinen; (a) how does

it s. to you? wie erscheint Ihnen das? wie kommt Ihnen das vor? (b) impers. it seems as though/as if, es scheint, als ob. ◆'seeming, adj. -ly, adv. (not real) scheinbar; (perhaps real) anscheinend.

seep [siːp], v.i. sickern; (s. through) durchsickern.

see-saw ['siːsɔː]. I. s. Wippe f. II. v.i. wippen.

seethe [siːð], v.i. (of place) wimmeln (with, von + dat); to be seething with anger, vor Wut kochen.

segment ['segmənt], s. Abschnitt m; orange s., Orangenspalte f.

segregate ['segrigeit], v.tr. trennen.

seize [siːz], v. 1. v.tr. (a) (etwas gen) bemächtigen; (take possession of) Jur: beschlagnahmen; (b) (capture) (j-n) festnehmen; Mil: (eine Stadt usw.) einnehmen; (c) (take hold of) (etwas) packen; Fig: to s. the opportunity, die Gelegenheit ergreifen; to s. power, die Macht an sich reißen. 2. v.i. (of piston etc.) to s. (up), sich festfressen. ◆'seizure [siːʒər], s. 1. Beschlagnahme f (von Waren). 2. Med: plötzlicher Anfall m.

seldom ['seldəm], adv. selten.

select [si'lekt]. I. v.tr. (etwas) auswählen (from, aus + dat). II. adj. (of school etc.) ausgesucht; Elite-. ◆se'lection, s. Auswahl f; to make a s., eine Auswahl treffen. ◆se'lective, adj. selektiv.

self [self], s. (pl. selves [self, selvz], s. Selbst m; F: he's his old s. again, er ist wieder der alte. ◆'self-a'ssertive, adj. selbstbehauptend. ◆'self-a'ssurance, s. Selbstsicherheit f. ◆'self-a'ssured, adj. selbstsicher. ◆'self-'centred, adj. selbstsüchtig. ◆'self-con'fessed, adj. erklärt. ◆'self-'confidence, s. Selbstbewußtsein n. ◆'self-'conscious, adj. verlegen. ◆'self-'consciousness, s. Befangenheit f. ◆'self-con'tained, adj. 1. (independent) unabhängig. 2. s.-c. flat, abgeschlossene Wohnung f. ◆'self-con'trol, s. Selbstbeherrschung f. ◆'self-de'fence, s. Selbstverteidigung f; Jur: Notwehr f. ◆'self-em'ployed, adj. selbständig. ◆'self-es'teem, s. Selbstachtung f. ◆'self-'evident, adj. selbstverständlich. ◆'self-'government, s. Selbstverwaltung f. ◆'self-im'portant, adj. überheblich. ◆'self-in'dulgent, adj. (of pers.) genußsüchtig. ◆'self-in'flicted, adj. s.-i. wound, Selbstverstümmelung f. ◆'self-'interest, s. Eigennutz m. ◆'self-ish, adj. selbstsüchtig. ◆'selfishness, s. Selbstsucht f. ◆'self-po'ssessed, adj. selbstbewußt. ◆'self-re'liance, s. Selbständigkeit f. ◆'self-re'spect, s. Selbstachtung f. ◆'self-'same, adj. genau der/die/dasselbe. ◆'self-'service, I. s. Selbstbedienung f. II. adj. s.-s. shop, Selbstbedienungsgeschäft n. ◆'self-su'fficient, adj. sich selbst versorgend (in, mit + dat).

sell [sell], *v.irr.* **1.** *v.tr.* verkaufen (**to**, an + *acc*.) **2.** *v.i.* **will it s.?** wird es sich gut verkaufen? **the picture sold for £500,** das Bild wurde für £500 verkauft. ◆**'seller,** *s.* (*a*) (*pers.*) Verkäufer(in) *m(f)*; (*b*) (*article*) **a good s.,** eine gutgehende Ware. ◆**'selling,** *s.* Verkauf *m*; **s. price,** Verkaufspreis *m.* ◆**'sell 'off,** *v.tr. Com:* (Waren usw.) unter Preis abstoßen. ◆**'sell 'out,** *v.tr. Com:* (Waren) ausverkaufen.

sellotape ['seləuteip], *s. R.t.m.* = Tesafilm *m R.t.m.*

semaphore ['seməfɔ:r], *s.* (*signals*) Winkzeichen *npl.*

semblance ['sembləns], *s.* Anschein *m.*

semi ['semi], *prefix* halb-. ◆**'semi-auto'matic,** *adj.* halbautomatisch. ◆**'semicircle,** *s.* Halbkreis *m.* ◆**'semi'circular,** *adj.* halbkreisförmig. ◆**'semi'colon,** *s.* Semikolon *n.* ◆**'semi'conscious,** *adj.* halb bei Bewußtsein. ◆**'semi-de'tached,** *adj.* **s.-d. house,** Doppelhaus *n.* ◆**'semi-'final,** *s.* Halbfinale *n.* ◆**'semi-'skilled,** *adj.* (*of worker*) angelernt.

seminary ['seminəri], *s.* Priesterseminar *n.*

semolina [semə'li:nə], *s.* Grieß *m.*

senate ['senit], *s.* Senat *m.* ◆**'senator,** *s.* Senator *m.*

send [send], *v.tr.irr.* (*a*) schicken; **she sent me for bread,** sie schickte mich Brot holen; **to s. sth. crashing to the ground,** etwas zusammenstürzen lassen. ◆**'send a'way,** *v.tr.* (j-n) fortschicken. ◆**'sender,** *s.* Absender *m* (eines Briefes usw.). ◆**'send 'for,** *v.tr.* (j-n) holen lassen; **I shall s. f. it,** ich werde es mir schicken lassen/(*order it*) es bestellen. ◆**'send 'off.** I. *v.tr.* (j-n) fortschicken; (*b*) (einen Brief usw.) abschicken. II. *s. F:* **they gave him a terrific s.-o.,** sie haben ihn ganz groß verabschiedet. ◆**'send 'on,** *v.tr.* (j-m einen Brief usw.) nachschicken. ◆**'send 'up,** *v.tr. F:* **to s. up s.o., sth.,** j-n, etwas verulken. ◆**'send-up,** *s. F:* Karikatur *f;* (*performance*) Parodie *f.*

senile ['si:nail], *adj.* senil. ◆**se'nility** [si'niliti], *s.* Senilität *f.*

senior ['si:niər]. I. *adj.* (*a*) ältere(r, s); **s. citizen,** Senior *m;* (*pensioner*) Rentner *m;* **William Jones S.,** William Jones senior; (*b*) **s.** (*in rank*), ranghöher. II. *s.* **to be s.o.'s s.,** (*in age*) älter als j-d sein; (*in rank*) j-s Vorgesetzter sein. ◆**seniority** [-i'ɔriti], *s.* **1.** (*in age*) höheres Alter; *Adm: Com: etc:* Dienstalter *n.* **2.** (*in rank*) höherer Rang.

sensation [sen'sei∫(ə)n], *s.* **1.** (*feeling*) Gefühl *n* **2.** Sensation *f;* **to create/cause a s.,** Sensation machen. ◆**sen'sational,** *adj.* sensationell.

sense [sens]. I. *s.* **1.** (*a*) Sinn *m;* **a keen s.** of smell, ein guter Geruchssinn; (*b*) (*feeling*) Gefühl *n* (der Freude, der Sicherheit usw.); **s. of justice,** Gerechtigkeitssinn *m.* **2.** (*a*) *pl.* **to come to one's senses,** (i) Vernunft annehmen; (ii) (*regain consciousness*) wieder zu Bewußtsein kommen; **to bring s.o. to his senses,** j-n zur Besinnung bringen; (*b*) (*reason*) Vernunft *f;* **common s.,** gesunder Menschenverstand; **there is no s. in (doing) that,** das hat keinen Sinn. **3.** (*meaning*) Bedeutung *f* (eines Wortes). II. *v.tr.* (etwas) spüren. ◆**'senseless,** *adj.* (*pointless*) sinnlos. ◆**'sensible,** *adj.* vernünftig. ◆**'sensitive** ['sensitiv], *adj.* (*a*) (*of pers., skin, tooth etc.*) empfindlich; **s. to cold,** kälteempfindlich; (*b*) (*positive sense*) (*of pers.*) sensibel. ◆**'sensual** ['sensjuəl], *adj.* sinnlich. ◆**sensu'ality,** *s.* Sinnlichkeit *f.* ◆**'sensuous,** *adj.* (*of pleasure etc.*) sinnlich; (*voluptuous*) wollüstig.

sentence ['sentəns]. I. *s.* **1.** *Gram:* Satz *m.* **2.** *Jur:* (*a*) (*statement*) Urteil *n;* **to pass s.,** das Urteil sprechen (on s.o., über j-n); (*b*) (*punishment*) Strafe *f;* **s. of death,** Todesstrafe *f.* II. *v.tr. Jur:* (j-n) verurteilen.

sentiment ['sentimənt], *s.* **1.** (*a*) (*feeling*) Gefühl *n;* (*b*) *esp. pl.* Ansicht *f;* **my sentiments entirely!** ganz meine Meinung! **2.** (*sentimentality*) Sentimentalität *f.* ◆**senti'mental,** *adj.* sentimental; *Pej:* (*of book, film*) rührselig; **s. value,** Erinnerungswert *m.*

sentry ['sentri], *s.* Posten *m.* ◆**'sentry-box,** *s. Mil:* Schilderhaus *n.*

separate. I. ['sep(ə)rət] *adj.* (*a*) (*not connected*) getrennt (**from**, von + *dat*); (*b*) (*different*) verschieden; **a s. question,** eine andere Frage; **-ly,** *adv.* getrennt; (*individually*) einzeln. II. ['sepəreit] *v.tr. & i.* (j-n, etwas) trennen; (*of two or more people*) sich trennen. ◆**sepa'ration,** *s.* **1.** Trennung *f.* **2.** (*distance*) Entfernung *f.*

September [sep'tembər], *s.* September *m.*

septic ['septik], *adj. Med:* septisch; **s. tank,** Senkgrube *f.*

sequel ['si:kwəl], *s.* (*a*) Fortsetzung *f* (eines Romanes usw.); (*b*) (*consequence*) Folge *f.*

sequence ['si:kwəns], *s.* **1.** Folge *f;* (*order*) Reihenfolge *f;* **in s.,** der Reihe nach. **2.** (*series*) Reihe *f; Cin: etc:* Stelle *f.*

serenade [serə'neid]. I. *s.* Serenade *f.* II. *v.tr.* to s.o., (j-m) ein Ständchen bringen.

serene [sə'ri:n], *adj.* (*of pers.*) abgeklärt; (*unperturbed*) gelassen; (*of sky, landscape etc.*) heiter. ◆**serenity** [-'reniti], *s.* Abgeklärtheit *f;* heitere Gelassenheit *f.*

sergeant ['sɑ:dʒənt], *s.* Feldwebel *m.* ◆**sergeant-'major,** *s. Mil:* Hauptfeldwebel *m.*

serial ['siəriəl]. I. *adj.* **s. number,** laufende Nummer *f.* II. *s.* **s.** (*story*) Fortsetzungsgeschichte *f.* ◆**'series** ['siəri:z], *s. inv.* Serie *f; Rad: TV:* Sendereihe *f.*

serious ['siəriəs], *adj.* (*a*) ernst; (*earnest*) ernsthaft; (*of offer*) ernstgemeint; **I'm s.,** ich meine es im Ernst; (*b*) **s. injury,**

schwere Verletzung; **s. mistake**, schwerwiegender Fehler; **-ly**, *adv.* (*a*) **to take sth. s.**, etwas ernst nehmen; (*b*) **s. ill, s. schwer krank.** ◆'**seriousness**, *s.* (*a*) Ernst *m* (einer Lage usw.); (*of pers.*) Ernsthaftigkeit *f*; **in all s.**, allen Ernstes; (*b*) Schwere *f* (einer Krankheit usw.).

sermon ['sə:mən], *s.* **1.** *Ecc:* Predigt *f.* **2.** *F:* Moralpredigt *f.*

serpent ['sə:p(ə)nt], *s. Z:* Schlange *f.*

serrated [sə'reitid], *adj.* gezackt.

serum ['siərəm], *s.* Serum *n.*

serve [sə:v], *v.* **1.** *v.tr.* (*a*) (*of pers.*) **to s. a master/a cause**, einem Herrn/einer Sache dienen; (*b*) (*of thing*) (etwas *dat*) dienlich sein; **it will s. the purpose**/*abs.* **it will s.**, es erfüllt den Zweck; (*c*) (*in shop, at table*) (j-n) bedienen; **to s. the soup**, die Suppe servieren; (*d*) *F:* **it serves you right!** es geschieht dir recht! **2.** *v.i.* (*a*) dienen (**as**, als); *Adm:* amtieren; (*b*) (*in tennis*) aufschlagen. ◆'**servant**, *s.* (**domestic**) **s.**, Diener(in) *m(f).* ◆'**service**, *s.* **I.** *s.* **1.** Dienst *m*; (*a*) **I'm at your s.**, ich stehe Ihnen zur Verfügung; (*b*) (*regular transport*) Verkehr *m*; **railway s.**, Eisenbahnverbindung *f*; (*c*) *esp. pl.* (**public**) **services**, öffentliche Einrichtungen *fpl*; **social services**, Sozialeinrichtungen *pl*. **2.** (*a in shop, hotel etc.*) Bedienung *f*; **s. charge**, Bedienungsgeld *n*; (*b*) *Aut:* Wartung *f.* **3.** *Ecc:* Gottesdienst *m.* **4.** (*in tennis*) Aufschlag *m.* **5.** (*china*) **tea/dinner s.**, Tee-service/Speiseservice *n.* **II.** *v.tr.* (ein Auto usw.) warten. ◆'**serviceman**, *s. Mil:* Soldat *m*; *pl.* **servicemen**, Militärpersonal *n.*

serviette [sə:vi'et], *s.* Serviette *f.*

servile ['sə:vail], *adj.* (*of pers.*) unterwürfig.

servitude ['sə:vitju:d], *s.* Knechtschaft *f.*

session ['seʃ(ə)n], *s.* Sitzung *f.*

set [set]. **I.** *s.* **1.** (*a*) Satz *m*; Set *n* (von Unterwäsche); (*china*) Service *n*; **s. of teeth**, Gebiß *n*; (*b*) *TV:* Rad: etc: Apparat *m*; (*c*) *Sp:* Satz *m*; (*d*) (*series*) Reihe *f.* **2. shampoo and s.**, Waschen und Legen *n.* **3.** *Cin:* Filmkulisse *f*; *Th:* Bühnenbild *n.* **II.** *v.* **1.** *v.tr.* (*a*) (*put*) (etwas auf etwas *acc*) stellen/setzen; **to s. the table**, den Tisch decken; (*b*) (*adjust*) einstellen (to, auf + *acc*); (eine Falle, den Wecker, eine Aufgabe usw.) stellen; (*c*) **to s. sth. on fire**, etwas in Brand stecken; **to s. s.o. free**, j-n befreien; **to s. the fashion**, den Ton angeben; *Th:* **the scene is s. in the street**, die Handlung spielt sich auf der Straße ab; (*d*) *Mus:* (ein Gedicht usw.) vertonen. **2.** *v.i.* (*a*) (*of sun*) untergehen; (*of jelly, cement etc.*) fest werden; (*c*) **to s. to work**, sich an die Arbeit machen. **III.** *adj.* fest; **s. phrase**, stehende Redewendung; **he's s. in his ways**, er ist in die Gewohnheitsmensch; *F:* **to be all s.**, ganz bereit sein. ◆'**set a'bout**, *v.i.* (*a*) **to s. a. (doing) sth.**, etwas in Angriff nehmen; (*b*) **to s.**

a. s.o., über j-n herfallen. ◆'**set a'side**, *v.tr.* (*save*) (Geld) beiseite legen. ◆'**setback**, *s.* Rückschlag *m.* ◆'**set 'back**, *v.tr.* (*a*) (*move back*) (etwas) zurückstellen; (*b*) (*delay*) verzögern; (j-n) aufhalten; (*c*) *F:* **it set me b. £20**, es hat mich um £20 ärmer gemacht. ◆'**set 'down**, *v.tr.* (etwas) hinsetzen; (einen Fahrgast) absetzen. **2.** *v.tr.* (Gründe usw.) darlegen. ◆'**set 'in**, *v.i.* (*start*) einsetzen. ◆'**set 'off**, *v.* **1.** *v.tr.* (eine Bombe usw.) zur Explosion bringen. **2.** *v.i.* sich aufmachen (**on a journey**, zu einer Reise). ◆'**set 'out**, *v.tr.* (*a*) (*display*) (Waren usw.) auslegen, (*arrange*) anordnen; (seine Gründe) darlegen; (*b*) **to s. o. to do sth.**, sich *dat* vornehmen, etwas zu tun. ◆'**set-square**, *s.* Zeichendreieck *n.* ◆'**setting**, *s.* **1.** (*a*) Schauplatz *m* (eines Romans usw.); Milieu *n*; (*b*) Fassung *f* (eines Edelsteins usw.). **2.** *Mus:* Vertonung *f* (eines Gedichtes usw.). **3.** (*adjustment*) Einstellung *f* (eines Gerätes usw.). ◆'**set-'to**, *s. F:* Schlägerei *f.* ◆'**set 'up**, *v.tr.* aufstellen; (eine Maschine) montieren; **to s. up house**, einen (eigenen) Hausstand gründen; **to s. up a business/in business**, ein Geschäft etablieren. ◆'**set-up**, *s. F:* (*structure*) Aufbau *m* (einer Firma usw.); **what's the s. up here?** wie ist das hier organisiert?

settee [se'ti:], *s.* Sofa *n.*

setter ['setər], *s.* (*dog*) Setter *m.*

settle ['setl], *v.* **1.** *v.tr.* (*a*) (*colonize*) (ein Land usw.) besiedeln; (*b*) (*decide*) regeln; (einen Streit) beilegen; **that settles it!** das wär's! (*c*) (*calm*) beruhigen; (*d*) (*fix*) festsetzen; (*e*) (*pay*) (eine Rechnung usw.) begleichen; **to s. (up) with s.o.**, mit j-m abrechnen. **2.** *v.i.* (*a*) (*of pers., bird etc.*) **to s. somewhere**, sich irgendwo niederlassen; (*b*) (*of dust*) sich legen; (*c*) (*of liquid*) sich klären; (*of dregs, sediment*) sich absetzen; (*of foundations, soil*) sich senken; (*d*) (*decide*) **to s. on/for sth.**, sich für etwas *acc* entscheiden, (*agree*) sich auf etwas *acc* einigen. ◆'**settled**, *adj.* (*a*) (*of weather etc.*) beständig; (*b*) (*decided*) entschieden; (*of matter*) erledigt; (*c*) (*of pers.*) ruhig. ◆'**settle 'down**, *v.i.* sich niederlassen. ◆'**settlement**, *s.* **1.** (*a*) (*act*) Besiedlung *f* (eines Landes usw.); (*b*) (*place*) Siedlung *f.* **2.** Erledigung *f* (einer Angelegenheit); Begleichung *f* (einer Schuld usw.); **they have reached a s.**, sie haben sich geeinigt.

seven ['sev(ə)n]. **I.** *num. adj.* sieben. **II.** *s.* Sieben *f.* ◆'**seven'teen**. **I.** *num. adj.* siebzehn. **II.** *s.* Siebzehn *f.* ◆'**seven'teenth**. **I.** *num. adj.* siebzehnte(r, s). **II.** *s.* Siebzehntel *n.* ◆'**seventh**. **I.** *num. adj.* siebente(r, s). **II.** *s.* Siebentel *n.* ◆'**seventieth**. **I.** *num. adj.* siebzigste(r, s). **II.** *s.* Siebzigstel *n.* ◆'**seventy**. **I.** *num. adj.* siebzig. **II.** *s.* Siebzig *f*; **in the seventies**, in den siebziger Jahren.

sever ['sevər], *v.tr.* (etwas) abtrennen.

several ['sev(ə)rəl], *adj.* mehrere.

severe [si'viər], *adj.* **1.** (*strict*) streng; (*of criticism, punishment etc.*) hart. **2.** (*of pain, storm*) stark, (*of weather*) rauh; **s. illness**, schwere Krankheit; **-ly,** *adv.* **1.** streng. **2.** stark. ◆**severity** [-'veriti], *s.* **1.** Strenge *f.* **2.** Stärke *f,* Heftigkeit *f* (*Med:* eines Anfalls usw.).

sew [sou], *v.tr.irr.* nähen; **to s. on a button,** einen Knopf annähen. ◆**'sewing,** *s.* **1.** Nähen *n;* **s. machine,** Nähmaschine *f.* **2.** Näharbeit *f.*

sewage ['s(j)u:idʒ], *s.* Abwasser *n;* **s. works,** Kläranlage *f.* ◆**'sewer** ['s(j)u:ər], *s.* Abwasserkanal *m.* ◆**'sewerage,** *s.* Kanalisation *f.*

sex [seks], *s.* Sex *m;* (*gender*) Geschlecht *n;* **s. education,** Sexualaufklärung *f; Sch:* Sexualkunde *f;* **s. sexual,** *adj.* geschlechtlich; **s. intercourse,** Geschlechtsverkehr *m.* ◆**'sexy,** *adj. F:* (*of film, book etc.*) erotisch; (*of girl* sexy.

sextet [seks'tet], *s.* Sextett *n.*

shabby ['ʃæbi], *adj.* schäbig.

shade [ʃeid]. **I.** *s.* **1.** Schatten *m.* **2.** (*a*) **s.** (*of a colour*), Farbton *m;* (*nuance*) Schattierung *f; Fig:* **s. of meaning,** Nuance *f;* (*b*) (*slightly*) **a s. too big,** eine Spur zu groß. **3.** (*lamp*) **s.,** Lampenschirm *m.* **II.** *v.tr.* (*a*) (einen Ort) beschatten; (*make dark*) (etwas) überschatten; (*b*) (*screen*) (ein Licht, die Augen) abschirmen. ◆**'shading,** *s.* Schattierung *f.* ◆**'shady,** *adj.* **1.** schattig. **2.** *F:* zwielichtig; (*suspicious pers.*) verdächtig; **a s. business,** eine anrüchige Sache.

shadow ['ʃædou]. **I.** *s.* Schatten *m.* **II.** *v.tr. Fig:* (*follow* to **s.** s.o.), jn beschatten. ◆**'shadowy,** *adj.* schattenhaft; (*b*) (*shady*) schattig.

shaft [ʃɑ:ft], *s.* **1.** Stiel *m* (eines Werkzeuges usw.); Schaft *m* (eines Pfeiles). **2.** (*ray*) Strahl *m* (der Sonne usw.). **3.** *Tchn:* (*spindle, axle*) Welle *f.* **4.** (*of mine, lift*) Schacht *m.*

shaggy ['ʃægi], *adj.* (*of hair etc.*) struppig; (*of dog*) zottig.

shake [ʃeik]. **I.** *s.* **1.** Schütteln *n.* **2.** (**milk**) **s.,** Milchshake *m.* **II.** *v.tr.* **1.** *v.tr.* (*a*) schütteln; **to s. one's head,** den Kopf schütteln; **to s. hands with s.o.,** j-m die Hand schütteln; (*b*) *F:* (j-n, j-s Glauben usw.) erschüttern. **2.** *v.i.* beben, (*of building etc.*) wackeln; (*tremble*) (*of pers., voice*) zittern. ◆**'shaken,** *adj.* (*of pers.*) erschüttert; (*trembling*) zitternd; **badly s. (up),** stark mitgenommen. ◆**'shake 'off,** *v.tr.* (einen Verfolger, etwas) abschütteln. ◆**'shake 'up,** *v.tr.* (a) (eine Flüssigkeit) (gut) schütteln; (b) *Fig:* (j-n) aufrütteln. ◆**'shake-up,** *s. F:* (*of pers.*) Aufrüttelung *f;* **a big s.-up,** eine große Umwälzung. ◆**'shaky,** *adj.* (*of pers.*) zitterig; (*of hand, voice*) zitternd; (*of chair etc.*) wackelig; (*b*) (*uncertain*) unsicher; *F:* wackelig.

shall [ʃæl,ʃ(ə)l], *modal aux. v.* (*p.* **should**

[ʃud], *q.v.*) (*a*) (*command*) sollen; **s. I open the window?** soll ich das Fenster öffnen? (*b*) *1st pers. future* werde(n).

shallow ['ʃælou]. **I.** *adj.* (*of water, also Fig:*) seicht; (*of dish etc.*) flach. **II.** *s.pl.* **shallows,** Untiefen *fpl.* ◆**'shallowness,** *s.* Seichtheit *f.*

sham [ʃæm]. **I.** *adj.* (*a*) (*pretend*) vorgetäuscht; (*b*) (*false*) falsch. **II.** *s.* (a) (*thing*) Täuschung *f;* (*b*) (*pers.*) Scharlatan *m.*

shamble ['ʃæmbl], *s.pl.* **shambles** (*with sing. constr.*) *F:* (*mess*) Schlamassel *m;* (*fiasco*) Reinfall *m.*

shame [ʃeim]. **I.** *s.* (a) (*disgrace*) Schande *f;* **to my s.,** zu meiner Schande; **have you no sense of s.?** schämen Sie sich nicht? **to put s.o. to s.,** j-n beschämen; (*b*) *F:* **what a s.!** wie schade! **II.** *v.tr.* (j-n) beschämen. ◆**'shamefaced,** *adj.* beschämt. ◆**'shameful,** *adj.* schändlich. *f.* ◆**'shameless,** *adj.* schamlos.

shampoo [ʃæm'pu:]. **I.** *s.* Shampoo *n.* **II.** *v.tr.* (Haar) schamponieren.

shamrock ['ʃæmrɔk], *s.* irischer Dreiblattklee *m.*

shandy ['ʃændi], *s. approx. = North G:* Alsterwasser *n, South G:* Radler *m.*

shan't [ʃɑ:nt], = **shall not.**

shanty ['ʃænti], *s.* **1. s. town,** Barackenvorstadt *f.* **2.** (*song*) (**sea**) **s.,** Seemannslied *n.*

shape [ʃeip]. **I.** *s.* **1.** (a) (*outer form*) Form *f;* (*of plan, structure etc.*) **to take s.,** Gestalt annehmen; (*b*) (*pers. or being*) Gestalt *f.* **2.** *F:* (*state*) Zustand *m; Sp: etc:* Kondition *f;* **in good/poor s.,** (*pers., team etc.*) gut/schlecht in Form. **II.** *v.* **1.** *v.tr.* (Ton usw.) formen. **2.** *v.i.* (*develop*) sich entwickeln. ◆**'shapeless,** *adj.* formlos. ◆**'shapely,** *adj.* (*of thing*) formschön; (*of pers.*) gut proportioniert.

share [ʃeər]. **I.** *s.* **1.** (a) Anteil *m;* **fair s.,** gerechter Anteil; (*b*) (*part played*) Beteiligung *f;* **he doesn't do his s.,** er trägt sein Teil nicht bei. **2.** *Fin:* Aktie *f;* **s. prices,** Börsenkurse *mpl.* **II.** *v.* **1.** *v.tr.* (etwas, *Fig:* Ansichten usw.) teilen; **to s. sth. out,** etwas aufteilen (**among,** *unter* + *dat*). **2.** *v.tr.* & *i.* **to s. (in) sth.,** an etwas *dat* teilnehmen. ◆**'shareholder,** *s. Fin:* Aktionär(in) *m(f).*

shark [ʃɑ:k], *s.* Hai *m; F:* (*pers.*) Gauner *m.*

sharp [ʃɑ:p]. **I.** *adj.* (a) scharf; (*of point*) spitz; (*of drop*) steil; (*b*) *Fig:* (*of pers.*) scharfsinnig; *Pej:* gerissen; **s. practices,** unsaubere Geschäftsmethoden; Gaunerei *f;* (*c*) (*of wind*) schneidend; (*d*) (*of sound*) durchdringend; schrill; (*e*) (*of taste*) herb; (*f*) *Mus:* zu hoch; **C s., F s.** etc., Cis, Fis usw.; **-ly,** *adv.* scharf; **the road dips s.,** die Straße fällt steil ab; **to answer s.o. s.,** j-m schroff antworten. **II.** *adv.* **1.** scharf. **2.** pünktlich; **at four o'clock s.,** pünktlich um vier Uhr. ◆**'sharpen,** *v.tr.* schärfen; (einen Bleistift) spitzen.

◆**'sharpness**, s. Schärfe f; (severity) Heftigkeit f (des Schmerzes); (of pers.) Scharfsinn m; (cunning) Schlauheit f. ◆**sharp'witted**, adj. scharfsinnig.

shatter ['ʃætər], v.tr. (a) (Glas usw.) zerschmettern; Fig: (Hoffnungen usw.) zerstören; (Nerven usw.) zerrütten. 2. v.i. zersplittern. ◆**'shattering**, adj. a s. blow, ein vernichtender Schlag.

shave [ʃeiv]. I. s. 1. to have a s., sich rasieren. 2. to have a close/narrow s., mit knapper Not davonkommen. II. v. 1 v.tr. (a) (j-n, sein Kinn usw.) rasieren; to s. (oneself), sich rasieren; (Holz) ab-schälen; to s. sth. off, etwas abschaben. 2 v.i. sich rasieren. ◆**'shaven**, adj. clean-s., glatt rasiert. ◆**'shaving**, s. 1. s. brush, Rasierpinsel m. 2. usu. pl. shavings, Späne mpl (von Holz usw.).

shawl [ʃɔːl], s. Dreieckstuch n.

she [ʃi, ʃiː]. pers. pron. f. 1. (pers.) sie. 2. (car, ship) es; **she sails tomorrow**, es/das Schiff fährt morgen ab.

sheaf, pl. **sheaves** [ʃiːf, ʃiːvz], s. Garbe f (von Korn usw.).

shear [ʃiər], v.tr. (ein Schaf usw.) sche-ren. ◆**shears**, s.pl. (pair of) s., große Schere f.

sheath [ʃiːθ], s. (a) Scheide f (eines Schwertes usw.); Futteral n (eines Mes-sers usw.); (b) Tchn: Hülle f; (contraceptive) s., Kondom n. ◆**sheathe** ['ʃiːð], v.tr. (ein Schwert usw.) in die Scheide stecken.

shed [ʃed], v.tr. (a) (of tree) (Laub) verlie-ren; (of lorry etc.) to s. its load, seine Ladung verlieren; (b) (Tränen, Blut) ver-gießen; Fig: to s. light on a matter, eine Sache aufklären.

sheen [ʃiːn], s. Glanz m.

sheep [ʃiːp], s. inv. Schaf n; coll. Schafe npl. ◆**'sheepdog**, s. Schäferhund m. ◆**'sheepish**, adj. 1. (feeling foolish) verle-gen. 2. (timid) furchtsam; (shy) schüch-tern. ◆**'sheepskin**, s. Schaffell n.

sheer [ʃiər], adj. (a) (complete) völlig; (b) (of rock) senkrecht; (of drop) jäh.

sheet [ʃiːt], s. 1. (for bed) Bettuch n. 2. (paper) Bogen m, (small) Blatt n. 3. s. metal, Blech n.

sheik(h) [ʃeik], s. Scheich m.

shelf, pl. **shelves** [ʃelf, ʃelvz], s. Brett n, Bord n; (in cupboard) Fach n; (set of) shelves, Regal n (für Bücher usw.).

shell [ʃel]. I. s. 1. Schale f (eines Eies, einer Muschel, einer Nuß usw.; Haus n (einer Schnecke); Panzer m (einer Schild-kröte). 2. (outer structure) Rohbau m (ei-nes Gebäudes). 3. Mil: Granate f. II. v.tr. (a) (Erbsen) enthülsen; (b) Mil: beschie-ßen. ◆**'shellfish**, s. coll. Schalentiere npl.

shelter ['ʃeltər]. I. s. 1. (concept) Obdach n; (protection) Schutz m; (place) Unter-schlupf m. 2. (hut) Schutzhütte f; (roof) Schutzdach n. II. v. 1 v.tr. (j-n, etwas) schützen (from, vor + dat); (take into

one's home) (j-m) Obdach geben. 2. v.i. Schutz suchen (from, vor + dat); sich unterstellen. ◆**sheltered**, adj. ge-schützt (against/from, vor + dat).

shelve [ʃelv], v.tr. (einen Plan usw.) auf-schieben. ◆**'shelving**, s. Regale npl.

shepherd ['ʃepəd], s. Schäfer m.

sheriff ['ʃerif], s. N.Am: Sheriff m.

sherry ['ʃeri], s. Sherry m.

Shetland ['ʃetlənd]. Pr. n. the Shet-lands/S. Islands, die Shetlandinseln fpl.

shield [ʃiːld]. I. s. Schild m; Fig: Schutz m. II. v.tr. (j-n, seine Augen usw.) ab-schirmen (from, gegen + acc); (protect) (j-n) schützen (from, vor + dat).

shift [ʃift]. I. s. 1. (movement) Verschie-bung f; (change) Veränderung f; Wechsel m. 2. Ind: Schicht f; to s. work, Schicht-arbeit f. II. v. 1 v.tr. (move) (etwas) ver-schieben; (eine Last usw.) verlagern; (Möbel usw.) umstellen; Th: to s. the scenery, die Kulissen schieben. 2. v.i. (move) (of cargo etc.) sich verschieben; (of wind) umspringen. ◆**'shifty**, adj. (of pers.) verschlagen; s. look, ausweichender Blick.

shimmer ['ʃimər], v.i. schimmern.

shin [ʃin], s. Anat: s. (bone), Schienbein n.

shine [ʃain], s. v.i.irr. (a) (of sun etc.) scheinen; (of eyes etc.) strahlen; (of po-lished surface, hair etc.) glänzen; (of sun, lamp etc.) to s. on sth., etwas anstrahlen; (illuminate) etwas beleuchten; (b) Fig: (of pers.) glänzen. II. v. s. 1. Schein m (der Sonne usw.). 2. (polish) Glanz m. ◆**'shining**, adj. glänzend; a s. exam-ple, ein leuchtendes Beispiel. ◆**'shiny**, adj. glänzend.

shingle ['ʃiŋl], s. Strandkies m.

shingles ['ʃiŋlz], s.pl. Med: Gürtelrose f.

ship [ʃip]. I. s. Schiff n. II. v.tr. (a) (load) (eine Fracht usw.) verladen; (b) (send) (Güter) verschiffen/(by air) befördern/(by road, rail) verfrachten. ◆**'shipbuilding**, s. Schiffbau m. ◆**'shipment**, s. 1. (a) (loading) Einschiffung f; (b) (sending) Verschiffung f. 2. (a) (shipload) Schiffs-ladung f; (b) (batch of goods) Lieferung f. ◆**'shipping**, s. 1. Verfrachtung f; (in ship) Verschiffung f. 2. s. company/line, Reederei f; s. lane/route, Schiffahrtsstra-ße f. 2. coll. Schiffe pl. ◆**'shipshape**, adj. in tadelloser Ordnung; (spotless) blitzsauber. ◆**'shipwreck**. I. s. (a) Schiffbruch m; (b) (ship) Wrack n. II. v.tr. to be shipwrecked, schiffbrüchig werden; **shipwrecked sailors**, Schiffbrü-chige pl.

shirk [ʃəːk], v.tr. to s. a task, sich vor einer Aufgabe drücken.

shirt [ʃəːt], s. Hemd n; in (one's) sleeves, in Hemdsärmeln.

shit [ʃit]. I. s. V: Scheiße f. II. v.i. V: scheißen.

shiver ['ʃivər]. I. v.i. zittern (with cold/ fear, vor Kälte/Angst). II. s. Schauer m.

◆'shivery, adj. F: to feel s., frösteln.
shoal [ʃəul], s. Schwarm m (von Fischen, Fig: von Menschen).
shock [ʃɔk]. I. s. 1. (jolt) Stoß m; s. wave, Druckwelle f; Aut: s. absorber, Stoßdämpfer m. 2. (a) Med: Fig: Schock m; to be suffering from s., unter Schock stehen; (b) Fig: (fright) Schreck m; (blow) Schlag m. 3. El: (elektrischer) Schlag m. II. v.tr. 1. (a) (j-n) schockieren; (b) (frighten) (j-n) erschrecken. ◆'shocking, adj. schockierend; it's s., es ist entsetzlich.
shoddy ['ʃɔdi], adj. schäbig, (bad) minderwertig.
shoe [ʃuː]. I. s. 1. Schuh m; s. polish, Schuhcreme f. 2. (horse's) Hufeisen n. II. v.tr.irr. (ein Pferd) beschlagen. ◆'shoebrush, s. Schuhbürste f. ◆'shoehorn, s. Schuhlöffel m. ◆'shoelace, s. Schnürsenkel m.
shoot [ʃuːt]. I. v.irr. 1. v.i. (a) (with gun, also Fb:) schießen (at s.o., sth., auf j-n, etwas acc); (b) (move fast) schießen; (of car etc.) to s. (along), (dahin)rasen. 2. v.tr. (ein Tier usw.) schießen; (eine Pistole, Fig: Fragen usw.) abfeuern (at s.o., auf j-n); to s. dead, j-n erschießen; (c) Cin: (einen Film) drehen. II. s. Bot: Schößling m. ◆'shoot down, v.tr. abschießen. ◆'shooting. I. adj. s. star, Sternschnuppe f; s. pain, stechender Schmerz. II. s. (a) Breach-Schießen n; (b) Cin: (of flames etc.) emporschießen; (of prices) (rapide) in die Höhe gehen; (of plant) schnell wachsen.
shop [ʃɔp]. I. s. 1. Laden m; Geschäft n; s. assistant, Verkäufer(in) m(f); s. window, Schaufenster n. 2. Ind: Werkstatt f; s. steward, Vertrauensmann m (der Gewerkschaft); on the s. floor, in der Fabrikhalle; unter den Arbeitern. 3. F: to talk s., fachsimpeln. II. v.i. einkaufen. ◆'shopkeeper, s. Ladenbesitzer(in) m(f), ◆'shoplifter, s. Ladendieb m. ◆'shoplifting, s. Ladendiebstahl m. ◆'shopping, s. (a) (purchases) Einkäufe mpl; (activity) Einkaufen n; to go s., einkaufen gehen; s. centre, Einkaufszentrum n. ◆'shop-soiled, adj. Com: (leicht) angeschmutzt.
shore¹ [ʃɔːr], s. Ufer n (eines Sees); (sea) s., Strand m, Küste f (des Meeres); Nau: on s., an Land; (two miles) off s., (zwei Meilen) vor der Küste.
shore², v.tr. to s. (sth.) up, (etwas) abstützen.
short [ʃɔːt]. I. adj. kurz; a s. man, ein kleiner Mann; at s. range, aus kurzer Entfernung; El: s. circuit, Kurzschluß m; at s. notice, kurzfristig; you have a s. memory, Sie vergessen schnell; a s. time ago, vor kurzem; s. story, Kurzgeschichte f; in s., kurz; to have a s. temper, leicht aufbrausen/in Zorn geraten; s.

weight/measure, Fehlgewicht n; s. (of money), knapp bei Kasse; I'm 20p s., mir fehlen 20 Pence; to be s. of breath, außer Atem sein; -ly, adv. (soon) bald; s. after(wards), kurz danach. II. s. a) Cl: shorts, Shorts pl; (b) Cin: F: Kurzfilm m. III. adv. 1. to stop s., plötzlich stehenbleiben; (in speaking) innehalten; to cut s.o.s., j-m das Wort abschneiden. 2. to fall s. of sth., etwas nicht erreichen; (not fulfil) etwas dat nicht nachkommen. ◆'shortage, s. Knappheit f (of food, an Nahrungsmitteln); Mangel m (of labour, money etc., an Arbeitskräften, Geld usw.). ◆'shortbread/'shortcake, s. (Art) Mürbeteiggebäck n. ◆'short-circuit, v.tr. El: (einen Kreis usw.) kurzschließen. ◆'shortcomings, s.pl. Mängel mpl. ◆'shorten, v. 1. v.tr. (etwas) verkürzen; (Kleider) kürzen. 2. v.i. kürzer werden. ◆'shorthand, s. Kurzschrift f; s.-typist, Stenotypistin f. ◆'short-lived, adj. (of fashion etc.) kurzlebig. ◆'shortness, s. Kürze f. ◆'short-sighted, adj. kurzsichtig. ◆'short-tempered, adj. reizbar. ◆'short-term, adj. kurzfristig.
shot [ʃɔt], s. 1. (discharge) Schuß m; Fig: a long s., reine Vermutung; not by a long s., noch lange nicht. 2. (missile) Geschoß n; (small) s., Schrot m. 3. Sp: (a) Fb: Schuß m; (throw) Wurf m; (b) (heavy ball) Kugel f. 4. Phot: Aufnahme f. 5. F: (try) Versuch m; I'll have a s. at it, ich werde es mal probieren. ◆'shotgun, s. Schrotbüchse f.
should [ʃud]. 1. pret. of shall (ought to) sollte(n), solltest, sollten; you s. do it at once! Sie sollten es sofort tun! you s. have seen him, Sie hätten ihn sehen sollen. 2. s. the occasion arise, sollte sich die Gelegenheit ergeben.
shoulder ['ʃəuldər]. I. s. Schulter f; s. blade, Schulterblatt n; s. strap, Schulterriemen m; (on bra etc.) Träger m; (on motorway) hard s., Randstreifen m. II. v.tr. Fig: to s. a responsibility, eine Verantwortung auf sich acc nehmen.
shout [ʃaut]. I. s. a) (loud call) Ruf m; (b) (loud cry) Schrei m. II. s. 1. v.i. (speak loudly) schreien; (call out) rufen; to s. at s.o., j-n anschreien; to s. for joy, jauchzen. 2. v.tr. (etwas) schreien; to s.o. down, j-n überschreien. ◆'shouting, s. Geschrei n.
shove [ʃʌv]. I. s. Schubs m. II. v.tr. schubsen; to s. sth. into a drawer, etwas in eine Schublade hineinstopfen.
shovel ['ʃʌv(ə)l]. I. s. Schaufel f. II. v.tr. schaufeln.
show [ʃəu]. I. s. 1. (a) Ind: Com: (display) Ausstellung f (von Waren); motor s., Automobilausstellung f; fashion s., Modenschau f; (b) Th: Vorstellung f; esp. Cin: TV: Show f. 2. (appearance) Schau f; it's only for s., es ist nur fürs Auge. II. v.irr. 1. v.tr. (etwas) zeigen (s.o./to

s.o., j-m); (a) (Fahrkarten usw.) vorzeigen; **to s. s.o. how to do sth.** (teach) j-m etwas beibringen; (b) (exhibit) (etwas) ausstellen; (demonstrate) (etwas) vorführen; (c) (indicate) (etwas) anzeigen; **to s. a profit,** einen Gewinn aufweisen; (d) **to s. s.o. to his room,** j-n zu seinem Zimmer bringen; (e) (prove) **he showed himself to be unreliable,** er erwies sich als unzuverlässig. 2. v.i. (a) (of thing) hervorsehen (**under sth.,** unter etwas dat); it shows, man sieht es; (b) (of film) **to be showing,** laufen. ◆'showdown, s. (endgültige) Auseinandersetzung f; (trial of strength) Kraftprobe f. ◆'show'in, v.tr. (j-n) hereinführen. ◆'showing, s. 1. Cin: Vorstellung f. 2. Sp: etc: **on this s.,** nach dieser Leistung zu urteilen. ◆'show-jumping, s. Springreiten n. ◆'show 'off, v. 1. v.tr. (j-s Vorzüge) zur Geltung kommen lassen; Pej: (mit einem Auto usw.) angeben. 2. v.i. (of pers.) angeben. ◆'show-off, s. F: Angeber m. ◆'showroom, s. Ausstellungsraum m. ◆'show 'up, v. 1. v.tr. (j-n, j-s Heuchelei usw.) bloßstellen. 2. v.i. (of feature) hervortreten; F: (of visitor etc.) auftauchen. ◆'showy, adj. auffällig; (splendid) prunkvoll; (of performance etc.) effektvoll.

shower ['ʃauər]. I. s. (a) Schauer m (von Regen usw.); **heavy s.,** Regenguß m; (b) (bath), Dusche f; **to take a s.,** duschen. II. v.tr. (a) (mit Wasser usw.) übergießen; **to s. compliments/presents on s.o.,** j-n mit Komplimenten/ Geschenken überschütten. ◆'showery, adj. (of weather) mit häufigen Schauern.

shred [ʃred]. I. s. Streifen m; Fetzen m (von Stoff, Papier usw.); **to tear sth. to shreds,** etwas in kleine Stücke zerreißen; Fig: **there isn't a s. of evidence,** man hat keinen einzigen Beweis. II. v.tr. (a) (etwas) in Stücke schneiden; (b) (tear) zerreißen; (Gemüse) raspeln.

shrewd [ʃruːd], adj. (of pers.) scharfsinnig; klug. ◆'shrewdness, s. Scharfsinn m; Klugheit f.

shriek [ʃriːk]. I. s. (schriller) Schrei m; **shrieks of laughter,** kreischendes Gelächter n. II. v.i. schrill kreischen; **(with laughter,** vor Lachen) kreischen.

shrill [ʃril], adj. schrill.

shrimp [ʃrimp], s. Garnele f.

shrine [ʃrain], s. Schrein m (eines Heiligen).

shrink [ʃriŋk], v.i.irr. (a) schrumpfen; (of clothes etc.) einlaufen; (of other materials) sich zusammenziehen; (b) **to s. (back) from danger etc.,** vor einer Gefahr usw. zurückschrecken.

shrivel ['ʃriv(ə)l], v.i. schrumpfen; **to s. up,** zusammenschrumpfen; (of skin etc.) runzelig werden.

shroud [ʃraud], s. Leichentuch n. ◆'shrouded, adj. eingehüllt.

Shrove [ʃrəuv], adj. S. Tuesday, Fast-

nachtsdienstag m.

shrub [ʃrʌb], s. Strauch m. ◆'shrubbery, s. Gesträuch n; (planted) Sträucherrabatte f.

shrug [ʃrʌg]. I. v.tr. **to s. (one's shoulders),** mit den Achseln zucken. II. s. Achselzucken n.

shrunken ['ʃrʌŋk(ə)n], adj. geschrumpft.

shudder ['ʃʌdər]. I. s. Zittern n; Beben n; Schauder m (von Entsetzen, Furcht usw.). II. v.i. (tremble) zittern; (shake) beben **(with horror, fear etc.,** vor Entsetzen, Furcht usw.).

shuffle ['ʃʌfl], v. 1. v.i. **to s.** (along), (dahin)schlurfen. 2. v.tr. & i. **to s. one's feet,** mit den Füßen scharren. 3. v.tr. (Karten) mischen.

shun [ʃʌn], v.tr. (j-n, etwas) meiden.

shunt [ʃʌnt], v.tr. Rail: rangieren.

shut [ʃʌt], v.irr. 1. v.tr. schließen, zumachen; **to be s.,** zusein; **the shops are s.,** die Geschäfte sind/haben zu. ◆'shut 'down, v.tr. & i. (eine Fabrik usw.) schließen. ◆'shut-down, s. Schließung f (einer Fabrik usw.). ◆'shut 'in, v.tr. einschließen; (lock in) einsperren. ◆'shut 'off, v.tr. (a) (Strom, Wasser usw.) absperren; (b) (j-n) absondern (**from,** von dat). ◆'shut 'out, v.tr. (a) (exclude) (etwas) ausschließen; (b) (lock out) (j-n) aussperren. ◆'shut 'up, v. 1. v.tr. (a) (j-n, etwas) einschließen; (b) (ein Haus usw.) verschließen; (c) F: **to s. s.o. up,** j-m das Maul stopfen. 2. v.i. F: **s. up!** halt's Maul! ◆'shutter, s. 1. Fensterladen m. 2. Phot: Verschluß m.

shuttle ['ʃʌtl], s. s. service, Pendelverkehr m. ◆'shuttlecock, s. Federball m.

shy1 [ʃai], v.i. (of horse) scheuen.

shy2, adj. (of pers.) scheu; (timid) schüchtern. ◆'shyness, s. Scheu f; Schüchternheit f.

Siberia [sai'biəriə]. Pr. n. Sibirien n. ◆Si'berian, adj. sibirisch.

Sicily ['sisili]. Pr. n. Sizilien n. ◆Si'cilian. I. s. Sizilianer(in) m(f). II. adj. sizilianisch.

sick [sik], adj. 1. krank. 2. **to be s.,** (vomit) sich übergeben; **I feel s.,** mir ist schlecht. 3. F: **to be s. of sth.,** etwas satt haben; **it makes you s.,** es ekelt einen an; P: **es ist zum Kotzen.** ◆'sicken, v. 1. v.i. erkranken (**with,** an + dat); **he's sickening for sth.,** er brütet etwas aus. 2. v.tr. (j-n) anekeln. ◆'sickening, adj. widerlich; **it's s.,** es ekelt einen an. ◆'sickly, adj. (a) (of pers. etc.) kränklich; (weakly) schwächlich; (b) s. smell/ taste, widerlich süßer Geruch/Geschmack m. ◆'sickness, s. 1. Krankheit f. 2. (vomiting) Übelkeit f.

sickle ['sikl], s. Sichel f.

side [said]. I. s. 1. Seite f; **by s.o.'s s.,** an j-s Seite, neben j-m; **s. by s.,** Seite an Seite, nebeneinander; **s. of bacon,** Speckseite f; **to move to one s.,** zur Seite treten; **to put sth. on one s.,** etwas beiseite legen/*(save)* auf die hohe Kante legen; *F:* **to make sth. on the s.**, etwas nebenbei verdienen; **the right/wrong s.**, die Oberseite/Rückseite (eines Stoffs usw.); **to get on the right s.** of s.o., sich mit j-m gut stellen; **you must look on the bright s.**, Sie müssen das Gute an der Sache sehen. 2. *(a)* **he's on our s.**, er ist auf unserer Seite; **to take sides (with s.o.)**, (j-s) Partei ergreifen; *(b) Sp: etc:* Partei; *(team)* Mannschaft *f*; *(c)* **on his mother's/father's s.**, mütterlicherseits/väterlicherseits. 3. *attrib. (a)* seitlich; Seiten-; **s. entrance**, Seiteneingang *m*; *(b) (secondary)* Neben-; **s. issue**, Nebenfrage *f*; *Med:* **s. effect**, Nebenwirkung *f*. II. *v.i.* **to s. with s.o.**, j-s Partei ergreifen. ◆**sideboard**, *s.* Büfett *n*; Anrichte *f* (in einem Eßzimmer). ◆**sideburns**, *s.pl.* Koteletten *fpl.* ◆**sidelight**, *s. Aut:* Standlicht *n.* ◆**sideline**, *s.* **as a s.**, nebenbei. ◆**sidestep**, *v.tr. & i.* (einem Schlag usw.) ausweichen. ◆**sidestreet**, *s.* Seitenstraße *f*, Nebenstraße *f.* ◆**sidewalk**, *s. N.Am:* Bürgersteig *m.* ◆**sideways**, *adv.* seitwärts. ◆**siding**, *s.* Abstellgleis *n.*

sidle ['saidl], *v.i.* **to s. up to** s.o., sich an j-n heranschleichen.

siege [si:dʒ] *s.* Belagerung *f.*

sieve [siv]. I. *s.* Sieb *n.* II. *v.tr.* sieben.

sift [sift], *v.tr. (a)* (etwas) sieben; *(b) (Be-*weismaterial usw.) sichten.

sigh [sai]. I. *s.* Seufzer *m.* II. *v.i.* seufzen.

sight [sait]. I. *s.* 1. *(a)* Sehvermögen *n*; **short s.**, Kurzsichtigkeit *f*; **to lose one's s.**, erblinden; *(b)* **to catch s. of** s.o., sth., j-n, etwas erblicken; **to lose s. of** s.o., sth., j-n, etwas aus den Augen verlieren; **at first s.**, zunächst; **to know s.o. by s.**, j-n (nur) vom Sehen kennen; *(c)* **to come into s.**, sichtbar werden; **out of s.**, außer Sicht; unsichtbar. 2. *(a) (sth. seen)* Anblick *m*; *(b)* **to see the sights**, die Sehenswürdigkeiten besichtigen. 3. *Mil:* Visier *n* (eines Gewehrs usw.). II. *v.tr.* (j-n, etwas) erblicken; **to s. land**, Land sichten. ◆**sighting**, *s.* Sichten *n*; Sichtung *f* (von Vögeln usw.). ◆**sight-read**, *v.tr. & i. Mus:* (ein Stück) vom Blatt singen/spielen. ◆**sightseeing**, *s.* Besichtigung *f*; **to go s.**, Sehenswürdigkeiten besichtigen.

sign [sain]. I. *s.* 1. Zeichen *n.* 2. *(a) (indication)* Anzeichen *n*; *(trace)* Spur *f*; *(b) (proof)* Beweis *m*; **as a s. of confidence**, als Vertrauensbeweis. 2. *(a) (notice)* Schild *n*; Aushängeschild *n* (eines Wirtshauses); *(road)* s., Verkehrszeichen *n*; **s. of the Zodiac**, Tierkreiszeichen *n.* II. *v.tr.* (einen Brief usw.) unterschreiben; (ein Gemälde) signieren. ◆**sign 'on**, *v.* 1. *v.tr.* (jdn.) einstellen. 2. *v.i.* sich (in eine Liste) eintragen; *(take a job)* sich verpflichten (eine Stellung anzunehmen); *(of unemployed pers.)* stempeln gehen. ◆**signpost**. I. *s.* Wegweiser *m.* II.

v.tr. (eine Straße) ausschildern.

signal ['signəl]. I. *s.* Signal *n*; *(indication, gesture)* Zeichen *n*; *Rail:* **s. box**, Stellwerk *n.* II. *v.i.* ein Signal/Zeichen geben; *(wave)* winken (**to** s.o.; -j-m). ◆**signalman**, *pl* -**men**, *s. Rail:* Weichensteller *m.*

signature ['signətʃər], *s.* Unterschrift *f*; *Rad: etc:* **s. tune**, Kennmelodie *f*; Indikativ *n.*

signify ['signifai], *v.tr. (a) (mean)* bedeuten; *(b) (indicate)* (Zustimmung usw.) zu verstehen geben. ◆**significance** [-'nifikəns], *s.* Bedeutung *f*; **of (no) s.**, von (keinerlei) Bedeutung. ◆**sig'nificant**, *adj.* bedeutend; *(typical)* bezeichnend; **-ly**, *adv.* bezeichnenderweise; **to change s.**, sich bedeutend/erheblich ändern.

silence ['sailəns]. I. *s.* Stille *f*; *(esp. of pers.)* Schweigen *n*; *(command)* **s.!** Ruhe! II. *v.tr.* (j-n) zum Schweigen bringen; *(by force etc.)* (j-n) mundtot machen. ◆**silencer**, *s. Aut:* Auspufftopf *m.* ◆**silent**, *adj. (a) (of mechanism, steps etc.)* geräuschlos; *(of night, countryside)* still; *Cin:* **s. film**, Stummfilm *m*; *(b) (of pers.)* schweigsam; **to keep s. about sth.**, über etwas *acc* schweigen; **-ly**, *adv.* geräuschlos; schweigend.

silhouette [silu:'et]. I. *s. (a) (outline)* Umriss *mpl; (b) Art:* Silhouette *f.* II. *v.tr.* **to be silhouetted against the sky**, sich gegen den Himmel abheben.

silicon ['silikən], *s. Ch:* Silizium *n*; **s. chip**, Siliziumchip *m.*

silk [silk], *s. (a)* Seide *f*; *(b) attrib.* Seiden-. ◆**silkworm**, *s.* Seidenraupe *f.* ◆**silky**, *adj.* seidig; *(soft)* seidenweich.

sill [sil], *s. (window)* s., Fenstersims *m*; *(internal)* Fensterbank *f.*

silly ['sili], *adj.* dumm; *F:* blöd; **don't do anything s.**, mach keine Dummheiten. ◆**silliness**, *s.* Dummheit *f.*

silt [silt]. I. *s.* Schlick *m.* II. *v.tr. & i. (of river, harbour)* **to s. up**, verschlammen.

silver ['silvər], *s.* 1. *(metal, also articles)* Silber *n.* 2. *attrib.* silbern, Silber-; **s. spoon**, Silberlöffel *m*; **s.-plated**, versilbert. 3. *(coins)* Silber *n*; *(change)* Kleingeld *n.*

similar ['similər], *adj.* ähnlich (**to**, *dat*). ◆**similarity** [-'læriti], *s.* Ähnlichkeit *f.*

simile ['simili], *s.* Gleichnis *n.*

simmer ['simər], *v.i. (a) Cu:* sanft kochen; *(b) Fig: (of revolt)* schwelen; *(of pers.)* **to s. down**, sich beruhigen.

simple ['simpl], *adj.* 1. *(of thing, problem)* einfach; *(plain)* schlicht; *(not complicated)* unkompliziert. 2. *(of pers.)* einfältig. ◆**simple-'minded**, *adj. (of pers.)* einfältig. ◆**sim'plicity**, *s. (a)* Einfachheit *f* (einer Methode, eines Problems usw.); Unkompliziertheit *f* (eines Charakters); *(b)* Schlichtheit *f* (eines Kleides usw.). 2. *(of pers.)* Einfalt *f.* ◆**simplify**, *v.tr.* (etwas) vereinfachen. ◆**simply**, *adv.* 1.

einfach. 2. (a) F: (absolutely) you s. must go, du mußt unbedingt gehen; (b) (only) nur; I s. said that ..., ich sagte nur, daß ...

simulate ['simjuleit], v.tr. simulieren.

simultaneous [sim(ə)l'teiniəs], adj. gleichzeitig.

sin [sin]. I. s. Sünde f; Hum: to live in s., in wilder Ehe leben. II. v.i. sündigen. ◆**sinful**, adj. (of pers.) sündig; (of act, waste etc.) sündhaft.

since [sins]. I. adv. (a) seitdem; ever s., von der Zeit an; it is many years s., es ist viele Jahre her; (b) (meanwhile) inzwischen. II. prep. seit + dat; he's been up s. dawn, er ist schon seit der Morgendämmerung auf; s. then, seitdem. III. conj. (a) (time) seitdem; seit; s. I've been here, seit(dem) ich hier bin; (b) (consequence) da; weil.

sincere [sin'siər], adj. (of pers., feelings etc.) aufrichtig; (warm) herzlich; -ly, adv. aufrichtig; (in letter) yours s., mit freundlichen Grüßen. ◆**sincerity** [-'seriti], s. Aufrichtigkeit f; Herzlichkeit f.

sinew ['sinju:], s. Sehne f.

sing [siŋ], v.tr. & i.irr. singen. ◆**singer**, s. Sänger(in) m(f). ◆**singing**. I. adj. singend. II. s. Gesang m.

singe [sindʒ], v.tr. (Haare usw.) versengen.

single ['siŋgl]. I. adj. 1. (a) (only one) einzig; (of payment) einmalig; not a s. one, kein einziger; (b) (individual) einzeln; every s. one of us, jeder einzelne von uns. 2. (a) (one pers.) Einzel-; s. bed, Einzelbett n; Rail: s. ticket, einfache Fahrkarte; (b) (of pers.) ledig; alleinstehend. II. Sp: singles, Einzel n. III. v.tr. to s. s.o., sth. out, j-n, etwas auslesen. ◆**single-'breasted**, adj. Cl: einreihig. ◆**single-'handed**, adj. allein; he did it s.-h., er hat es im Alleingang gemacht. ◆**single-'minded**, adj. (of pers.) zielstrebig. ◆**single-'track**, adj. (a) Rail: eingleisig; (b) (of road) einspurig. ◆**singly**, adv. 1. (separately) getrennt; einzeln. 2. (alone) allein.

singlet ['singlit], s. 1. (vest) Unterhemd n. 2. Sp: Trikot n.

singular ['siŋgjulər]. I. adj. (uncommon) einzigartig; (remarkable) merkwürdig. II. s. Gram: Einzahl f, Singular m.

sinister ['sinistər], adj. finster; s. story, unheimliche Geschichte.

sink[1] [siŋk], s. Spülbecken n.

sink[2], v.irr. 1. v.i. (a) sinken; (of ship, sun) untergehen; his heart sank, der Mut verließ ihn; (b) (of ground) sich senken, (slope) abfallen; (c) to s. (in value), im Wert sinken. 2. v.tr. (a) (einen Schiff) versenken; (b) einen Pfahl usw.) einsenken; Min: (einen Schacht) abteufen. ◆**sink 'in**, v.i. (of words) Wirkung haben; it hasn't sunk in yet, er/sie hat es noch nicht ganz begriffen.

sinuous ['sinjuəs], adj. gewunden.

sinus ['sainəs], s. Nebenhöhle f. ◆**sinu'sitis**, s. Nebenhöhlenentzündung f.

sip [sip]. I. s. kleiner Schluck m. II. v.tr. (etwas) in kleinen Schlucken trinken.

siphon ['saif(ə)n]. I. s. Siphon m. II. v.tr. to s. (off) a liquid, eine Flüssigkeit absaugen.

sir [sə:r, sər], s. Herr; (in letter) (Dear) Sir, Sehr geehrter Herr!

siren ['saiərən], s. Sirene f.

sister ['sistər], s. Schwester f; Med: (ward) s., Oberschwester f. ◆**'sister-in-law**, s. Schwägerin f.

sit [sit], v.irr. 1. v.i. (a) sitzen; (b) to s. on a committee, in einem Ausschuß tätig sein; to s. for an exam(ination), eine Prüfung ablegen; (c) (of court, assembly etc.) tagen. 2. v.tr. (ein Kind auf einen Stuhl usw.) setzen usw. ◆**'sit 'back**, v.i. sich zurücklehnen. ◆**'sit 'down**, v.i. sich (auf einen Stuhl usw.) setzen; please s. d., nehmen Sie bitte Platz. ◆**'sit-in**, s. Sit-in n. ◆**'sitting**. I. s. Sitzung f. II. adj. sitzend; s. target, leichte Beute. ◆**'sitting-room**, s. Wohnzimmer n. ◆**'sit 'up**, v.i. (a) aufrecht sitzen; (b) (not go to bed) aufbleiben.

site [sait], s. (of building, town etc.) Lage f; camping s., Campingplatz m; (building) s., Baustelle f.

situated ['sitjueitid], adj. the house is s. by the sea, das Haus liegt am Meer; pleasantly s., schön gelegen. ◆**situ'ation**, s. 1. Lage f. 2. (job) Stelle f; situations vacant, Stellenangebote npl.

six [siks]. I. num. adj. sechs. II. s. Sechs f. ◆**six'teen**. I. num. adj. sechzehn. II. s. Sechzehn f. ◆**six'teenth**. I. num. adj. sechzehnte(r, s). II. s. Sechzehntel n. ◆**sixth**. I. num. adj. sechste(r, s). II. s. (fraction) Sechstel n. ◆**'sixtieth**. I. num. adj. sechzigste(r, s). II. s. Sechzigstel n. ◆**'sixty**. num. adj. sechzig; (of pers.) in his sixties, in den Sechzigern; in the sixties (= 1960s), in den sechziger Jahren.

size [saiz]. I. s. Größe f; Umfang m (eines Problems); (of book, paper) Format n. II. v.tr. to s. s.o., sth. up, sich dat über j-n, etwas acc eine Meinung bilden. ◆**siz(e)able**, adj. a s. sum, eine beträchtliche Summe.

sizzle ['sizl], v.i. (of sausages etc.) brutzeln.

skate[1] [skeit], s. (fish) Glattrochen m.

skate[2]. I. s. Schlittschuh m. II. v.i. Schlittschuh laufen. ◆**'skateboard**, s. Rollbrett n, Skateboard n. ◆**'skater**, s. Schlittschuhläufer m. ◆**'skating**, s. s. rink, Eisbahn f.

skeleton ['skelit(ə)n], s. (a) Skelett n; (b) s. key, Nachschlüssel m; (c) s. staff/crew, Minimalbelegschaft f.

sketch [sketʃ]. I. s. 1. Skizze f; to give a s. of sth. (in words), etwas kurz umreißen. 2. Th: Sketch m. II. v.tr. (eine Szenc usw.) skizzieren. **◆'sketchy,** adj. (of description etc.) skizzenhaft; (of knowledge etc.) oberflächlich

skewer ['skju:(:)ər], s. Spieß m.

ski [ski:]. I. s. Ski m; s. jumping, Skispringen n; s. lift, Skilift m. II. v.i. skilaufen. **◆'skier,** s. Skiläufer m. **◆'skiing,** s. Skilaufen n; s. instructor, Skilehrer m.

skid [skid]. I. s. Rutschen n; Aut: Schleudern n. II. v.i. rutschen; Aut: schleudern.

skill [skil], s. Geschick n. **◆'skilful,** adj. geschickt. **◆'skilfulness,** s. Geschicklichkeit f. **◆'skilled,** adj. (of pers.) geschickt (at sth., in etwas dat); Ind: s. worker, gelernter Arbeiter.

skim [skim], v.tr. (den Rahm usw.) abschöpfen; **skimmed milk,** Magermilch f. 2. v.i. to s. through a letter, einen Brief flüchtig durchlesen.

skimp [skimp], v. 1. v.tr. (an Material, am Essen dat usw.) sparen. 2. v.i. knausern. **◆'skimpy,** adj. (of meal) mager; (of garment) dürftig.

skin [skin]. I. s. 1. Haut f; (with fur) Fell n. 2. (of fruit) Schale f. II. v.tr. (ein Tier) häuten. **◆'skinflint,** s. Geizhals m. **◆'skinny,** adj. mager. **◆'skin-tight,** adj. hauteng.

skint [skint], adj. F: pleite.

skip [skip]. I. v. 1. v.i. (a) hüpfen; (b) (with rope) seilspringen. 2. v.tr. (ein Kapitel im Buch usw.) überspringen. II. s. Ind: etc: Kübel m.

skirmish ['skə:miʃ], s. Geplänkel n.

skirt [skə:t]. I. s. Cl: Rock m. II. v.tr. (eine Stadt, einen Wald usw.) umranden. **◆'skirting,** adj. s. board, Fußleiste f.

skittle ['skitl], s. Kegel m; to play skittles, kegeln. **◆'skittle alley,** s. Kegelbahn f.

skulk [skʌlk], v.i. sich versteckt halten; (with evil purpose) lauern.

skull [skʌl], s. Schädel m; s. and crossbones, Totenkopf m.

skunk [skʌŋk], s. Z: Stinktier n.

sky [skai], s. Himmel m; in the s., am Himmel. **◆'sky-blue,** adj. himmelblau. **◆'skylight,** s. Dachluke f. **◆'skyline,** s. Horizont m; Skyline f. **◆'skyscraper,** s. Wolkenkratzer m.

slab [slæb], s. (a) (of stone etc.) Platte f; (b) (slice) dicke Scheibe f.

slack [slæk]. I. s. (of rope) Lose n; to take up the s., (ein Seil usw.) straffen. II. adj. 1. (of pers.) nachlässig (at, in + dat); (of attitude etc.) lässig; (of discipline, morals) locker. 2. (not tight) lose; (of rope) schlaff. 3. (of business etc.) flau. III. v.i. (of pers.) F: faulenzen. **◆'slacken,** v.i. (of rope etc.) sich lockern. **◆'slacken off,** v.i. nachlassen. **◆'slackness,** s. 1. (of pers.) Nachlässigkeit f (of attitude etc.) Lässigkeit f. 2. (of rope etc.) Schlaffheit f. 3. (of business etc.) Flauheit f.

slag [slæg], s. Schlacke f; s. heap, Halde

f.

slam [slæm]. I. s. (of door etc.) Knall m. II. v. 1. v.i. (of door etc.) knallen. 2. v.tr. (eine Tür usw.) zuknallen.

slander ['slɑ:ndər]. I. s. Verleumdung f. II. v.tr. (j-n) verleumden. **◆'slanderous,** adj. verleumderisch.

slang [slæŋ], s. Slang m.

slant [slɑ:nt]. I. s. Schräge f; at a s., schräg. F: (point of view) Blickwinkel m. II. v. 1. v.i. schräg sein; (of surface etc.) sich neigen. 2. v.tr. (etwas) neigen; (b) Fig: (einen Bericht usw.) färben. **◆'slanting,** adj. schräg.

slap [slæp]. I. s. Klaps m. II. v.tr. (ein Kind usw.) klapsen; to s. s.o.'s face, j-m eine Ohrfeige geben. **◆'slapdash/slap-happy,** adj. liederlich. **◆'slapstick,** s. (comedy) Slapstick m. **◆'slap-up,** adj. s.-up meal, feudales Essen.

slash [slæʃ]. I. s. 1. Hieb m (mit dem Messer usw.). 2. (cut) Hiebwunde f. II. v.tr. (a) to s.o.'s face, j-m das Gesicht zerschneiden; (b) Fig: (Preise usw.) stark herabsetzen.

slat [slæt], s. Latte f.

slate [sleit], s. Schiefer m; s. roof, Schieferdach n.

slaughter ['slɔ:tər]. I. s. (a) (act) Schlachten n (von Vieh); Abschlachten n (von Menschen); (b) (carnage) Gemetzel n. II. v.tr. (Vieh) schlachten; (Menschen) abschlachten. **◆'slaughterhouse,** s. Schlachthaus n

Slav [slɑ:v]. I. s. Slawe m, Slawin f. II. adj. slawisch. **◆Slavonic** [slə'vɔnik], adj. slawisch.

slave [sleiv]. I. s. Sklave m; Sklavin f. II. v.i. to s. (away) at sth., sich mit etwas dat abschinden/abplagen. **◆'slavery,** s. Sklaverei f.

slay [slei], v.tr.irr. A: & Lit: (j-n) umbringen.

sleazy ['sli:zi], adj. F: verkommen.

sledge [sledʒ]. I. s. Schlitten m. II. v.i. to s./go sledging, Schlitten fahren. **sledge-hammer** ['sledʒhæmər], s. Vorschlaghammer m.

sleek [sli:k], adj. (a) (of hair etc.) seidenglänzend; (b) s. lines, schnittige Form (eines Autos usw.).

sleep [sli:p]. I. s. Schlaf m; (of pers., F: of leg etc.) to go to s., einschlafen; to put an animal to s., ein Tier einschläfern. II. v. 1. v.i. (a) schlafen; (b) (spend night) (im Hotel usw.) übernachten. 2. (accommodate) (Leute) unterbringen; **the hotel sleeps 100,** das Hotel bietet Schlafgelegenheiten für 100 Personen. **◆'sleeper,** s. 1. to be a light/heavy s., einen leichten/tiefen Schlaf haben. 2. Rail: (on track) Schwelle f. 3. Rail: Schlafwagen m. **◆'sleep 'in,** v.i. (intentionally) ausschlafen; (unintentionally) verschlafen. **◆'sleepiness,** s. 1. Schläfrigkeit f. 2. (lethargy) Verschlafenheit f. **◆'sleeping,**

I. *adj.* schlafend; *Com:* **s. partner**, stiller Teilhaber *m.* II. **s.** Schlafen *n;* **s. bag,** Schlafsack *m; Rail:* **s. pill,** Schlaftablette *f.* ◆**'sleep-walking, s.** Schlafwandeln *n.* ◆**'sleepy, adj.** verschlafen.

sleet [sliːt], s. Schneeregen *m.*

sleeve [sliːv], *s.* 1. Ärmel *m.* 2. (record) s., Plattenhülle *f.*

sleigh [slei], *s.* Pferdeschlitten *m.*

sleight [slait], **s. s. of hand,** Fingerfertigkeit *f.*

slender ['slendər], *adj.* 1. *(of pers.)* schlank. 2. *(a) (of income etc.)* schmal; *(b) (of hope, excuse etc.)* schwach.

slice [slais], I. *s.* Scheibe *f.* II. *v.tr.* (Brot usw.) in Scheiben) schneiden.

slick [slik], I. *s.* **(oil)** s., Ölteppich *m.* II. *adj. (a) (of businessman etc.)* clever; *(b) (of performance)* routiniert.

slide [slaid]. I. *s.* 1. *(action)* Rutschen *n; (landslide)* Erdrutsch *m.* 2. *(on ice, in playground)* Rutschbahn *f.* 3. *Phot: F:* Dia *n; (for microscope)* Objektträger *m.* 4. *(a) (hair)* s., Haarspange *f; (b) Tchn:* Schieber *m; Mth:* **s. rule,** Rechenschieber *m.* II. *v.irr.* 1. *v.i. (a) (of bolt, drawer etc.)* gleiten; *(b) (of pers.) (on ice etc.)* rutschen; *(by accident)* ausrutschen. 2. *v.tr. (etwas)* schieben. ◆**'sliding, adj.** gleitend; **s. door,** Schiebetür *f.*

slight [slait]. I. *adj. (a) (of pers., build)* zierlich; *(frail-looking)* schmächtig. 2. *(not great)* leicht; *(insignificant)* gering(fügig); **s. smell,** schwacher Geruch; -**ly,** *adv.* 1. *(of pers.)* **s. built,** von zierlichem Körperbau. 2. leicht; **s. better,** ein bißchen/ etwas besser. II. *s.* Kränkung *f.*

slim [slim]. I. *adj. (a) (of pers.)* schlank; *(b) (of chance, hope etc.)* gering. II. *v.i. (lose weight)* abnehmen. ◆**'slimline, adj.** *(of TV etc.)* superflach.

slime [slaim], *s. (mud)* Schlamm *m.* ◆**'slimy, adj.** 1. *(muddy)* schlammig. 2. *(slippery, also Fig:)* schleimig.

sling [sliŋ]. I. *s. (weapon)* Schleuder *f.* 2. *Med:* Armschlinge *f.* II. *v.tr.irr. (a)* (einen Ball usw.) schleudern; *(b)* **to s. a rifle over one's shoulder,** ein Gewehr umhängen.

slink [sliŋk], *v.i.irr.* schleichen; **to s. off,** wegschleichen. ◆**'slinky, adj.** *(of dress)* verführerisch; *(tight)* hauteng.

slip [slip]. I. *s.* 1. *(a) (on ice etc.)* Rutsch *m; (b)* **to give s.o. the s.,** j-m entkommen. 2. *(mistake)* Versehen *n; (conduct)* Fehltritt *m;* **it was a s. of the tongue,** ich habe mich versprochen. 3. *(pillow-)* s., Kopfkissenbezug *m.* 4. *Cl:* Unterrock *m.* 5. **s. of paper,** Zettel *m.* II. *v.* 1. *v.i. (a) (move out of position)* rutschen; *(slide)* gleiten; *(b) F: (go quickly)* **to s. away,** davonschleichen; **to s. into a dress,** in ein Kleid schlüpfen; *(c) F:* **he's slipping,** er hat nachgelassen; *(of time)* **to s. by,** verstreichen. 2. *v.tr. (a)* **to s. off a ring/a dress,** einen Ring/ein Kleid abstreifen; *(b)* **it slipped my mind,** es ist mir entfal-

len; *(c)* **he slipped it into his pocket,** er ließ es in die Tasche gleiten. ◆**'slipper,** *s.* Hausschuh *m;* **(bedroom) s.,** Pantoffel *m.* ◆**'slippery, adj.** 1. glitschig; *(icy)* glatt. 2. *F: (of pers.)* gerissen. ◆**'slip-road,** *s.* Zufahrtstraße *f.* ◆**'slip 'up,** *v.i.* einen Schnitzer machen. ◆**'slip-up,** *s. F:* Panne *f.* ◆**'slipway,** *s.* Helling *f.*

slit [slit]. I. *s.* Schlitz *m.* II. *v.tr.* (j-m die Kehle) aufschneiden; **to s. open a sack etc.,** einen Sack usw. aufschlitzen.

slither ['sliðər], *v.i.* glitschen; *(of snake etc.)* gleiten.

sliver ['slivər], *s. (of wood etc.)* Streifen *m; (of cheese etc.)* hauchdünne Scheibe *f.*

slob [slɔb], *s. P:* Lümmel *m.*

slobber ['slɔbər], *v.i.* geifern.

slog [slɔg]. I. *v.i.* **to s. away at sth.,** sich mit etwas *dat* abplagen. II. **s. hard s.,** Schinderei *f.*

slogan ['slougən], *s.* Slogan *m.*

slop [slɔp]. I. *s.pl.* **slops,** Schmutzwasser *n.* II. *v.* 1. *v.i. (of liquid)* **to s. (over),** überschwappen. 2. *v.tr.* (Bier, Wasser usw.) verschütten. ◆**'sloppy, adj.** *(a) (untidy)* schlampig; *(b) (sentimental)* rührselig.

slope [sloup]. I. *s. (a) (gradient)* on/at a s., geneigt; *(b) (sloping ground)* Hang *m.* II. *v.* 1. *v.i. (a) (of ground)* sich neigen; **to s. down,** abfallen; **to s. upwards,** ansteigen; *(b) (of writing)* **to s. forwards/ backwards,** sich nach rechts/links neigen. 2. *v.tr. (etwas)* neigen. ◆**'sloping, adj.** *(of ground)* geneigt; *(of writing etc.)* schräg; *(of shoulders)* abfallend.

slot [slɔt], *s.* 1. *(for money etc.)* Einwurf *m;* **s. machine,** Münzautomat *m.* 2. *(for peg etc.)* Kerbe *f.*

slouch [slautʃ], *v.i.* mit hängenden Schultern stehen/sitzen/gehen.

slovenly ['slʌvənli], *adj.* liederlich.

slow [slou]. I. *adj.* 1. langsam; *Rail:* **s. train,** Personenzug *m; F:* Bummelzug *m; Cin: TV:* **in s. motion,** in Zeitlupe. 2. *(mentally)* schwerfällig. 3. **business is s.,** das Geschäft geht schleppend. 4. **the clock is (ten minutes) s.,** die Uhr geht (10 Minuten) nach. III. *v.* 1. *v.i.* **to s. up/down,** langsamer fahren/gehen. 2. *v.tr.* **to s. sth. down/up,** etwas verlangsamen; -**ly,** *adv.* langsam. ◆**'slowness,** *s.* Langsamkeit *f.*

slug [slʌg], *s.* Nacktschnecke *f.*

sluggish ['slʌgiʃ], *adj. (of pers., engine)* träge. ◆**'sluggishness, s.** Trägheit *f.*

sluice [sluːs], *s.* Schleuse *f;* **s. gate,** Schleusentor *n.*

slum [slʌm], *s.* Elendsviertel *n.*

slumber ['slʌmbər], *s.* Schlummer *m.*

slump [slʌmp]. I. *s. Com:* Kurssturz *m; economic* s., Konjunkturrückgang *m.* II. *v.i. (a) (of pers.)* sacken; *(b) Com: (of prices etc.)* (plötzlich) stürzen.

slur¹ [sləː], *s.* Makel *m;* **to cast a s. upon s.o.,** j-s Ehre beflecken.

slur², *v.tr.* (Buchstaben, Silben) verschleifen; **to s. one's words,** mit schwerer Zunge reden. ◆**'slurred,** *adj.* undeutlich.

slush [slʌʃ], *s.* **1.** Matsch *m.* **2.** *Fig:* Kitsch *m.* **3.** *F:* s. fund, Schmiergelder *pl.* ◆**'slushy,** *adj.* **1.** matschig. **2.** *Fig:* kitschig.

slut [slʌt], *s.* Schlampe *f.*

sly [slai], *adj. (of pers., look etc.)* listig.

smack¹ [smæk], *v.i.* **to s. of sth.,** leicht nach etwas *dat* schmecken.

smack². **I.** *s.* **1.** *(sound)* Klatsch *m.* **2.** *(slap)* Klaps *m;* **s. in the face,** Ohrfeige *f.* **II.** *v.tr. (a)* **to s. s.o.,** j-m einen Klaps geben; *(b)* **to s. one's lips,** (mit den Lippen) schmatzen.

small [smɔːl]. **I.** *adj.* klein; **s. number,** geringe Anzahl; **the s. print,** das Kleingedruckte; **s. business,** Kleinbetrieb *m;* **s. talk,** Geplauder *n;* **a s. matter,** eine Kleinigkeit; **on a s. scale,** in kleinem Maßstab; **to make s.o. look s.,** j-n blamieren; **to feel s.,** sich schämen. **II.** *s. Anat:* **s. of the back,** Kreuz *n.* ◆**'smallpox,** *s. Med:* Pocken *fpl.* ◆**'small-'scale,** *adj. (of model)* in verkleinertem Maßstab (angefertigt).

smart [smɑːt]. **I.** *v.i. (of wound, eyes etc.)* brennen. **II.** *adj.* **1.** *(of pers., clothes)* elegant; *F:* schick. **2.** *(clever)* klug; **s. answer,** fixe Antwort. **3.** *(brisk)* **s. pace,** flottes Tempo. **4.** *(of blow)* hart; **-ly,** *adv.* **s. dressed,** elegant/flott angezogen. ◆**'smarten,** *v.tr.* **to s. sth. up,** etwas aufmöbeln; **to s. s.o./oneself up,** j-n/sich feinmachen. ◆**'smartness,** *s. (of clothes, pers. etc.)* Schick *m.*

smash [smæʃ]. **I.** *s.* **1.** *(loud noise)* Krach *m; (blow)* heftiger Schlag *m.* **2.** *(crash)* heftiger Zusammenstoß *m;* **car s.,** Autounfall *m.* **II.** *v.tr. (a)* **to s. sth. (to pieces),** etwas zerschlagen/*(shatter)* zerschmettern; *(b)* **(den Feind)** vernichtend schlagen; **(of windaw etc.)** zerbrechen; *(b) (of car)* **to s. into a wall,** gegen eine Wand prallen. ◆**'smashing,** *adj. F:* klasse. ◆**'smash-'up,** *v.tr.* (etwas) zertrümmern; *F:* (ein Auto) zu Schrott fahren.

smattering ['smæt(ə)riŋ], *s.* oberflächliche Kenntnisse *fpl* (of, in + *dat*).

smear [smiər]. **I.** *s.* Klecks *m; Fig:* **s. campaign,** Verleumdungskampagne *f.* **2.** *Med:* Abstrich *m.* **II.** *v.tr. (a)* (j-n, etwas) beschmieren; *(b)* **(Tinte usw.)** verwischen.

smell [smel]. **I.** *s.* Geruch *m; (bad)* **s.,** Gestank *m.* **II.** *v.irr.* **1.** *v.tr. (a) (involuntarily)* (etwas) riechen; *(b) (voluntarily)* **to s. a flower,** an einer Blume riechen. **2.** *v.i.* **to s. nice/bad,** gut/schlecht riechen; **to s. of garlic,** nach Knoblauch *dat* riechen. ◆**'smelly,** *adj.* stinkend.

smelt [smelt], *v.tr.* (Erz) schmelzen.

smile [smail]. **I.** *s.* Lächeln *n.* **II.** *v.i.* lächeln; **to s. at s.o.,** j-m zulächeln.

smirk [smɔːk]. **I.** *s.* (selbstgefälliges)

Grinsen *n.* **II.** *v.i.* feixen.

smith [smiθ], *s.* Schmied *m.*

smithereens [smiðə'riːnz], *s.pl. F:* **to be smashed to s.,** in tausend Stücke zerspringen.

smock [smɔk], *s.* Hänger(kleid) *m(n).*

smog [smɔg], *s.* Smog *m.*

smoke [sməuk]. **I.** *s.* Rauch *m.* **II.** *v.* **1.** *v.tr. (a)* (eine Zigarette usw.) rauchen; *(b)* (Fleisch usw.) räuchern. **2.** *v.i.* rauchen. ◆**'smokeless,** *adj.* **s. fuel,** raucharmer Brennstoff. ◆**'smoking,** *s.* Rauchen *n;* **no s.,** Rauchen verboten; *Rail:* **s. compartment,** Raucherabteil *n.* ◆**'smoky,** *adj.* rauchig.

smooth [smuːð]. **I.** *adj.* glatt; *(of flight, crossing)* ruhig; *(of drink)* mild. **II.** *v.tr.* **to s. sth.** (down/out), etwas glätten; **-ly,** *adv.* glatt; **to run s.,** (i) *(of machine)* ruhig laufen; (ii) *(of event etc.)* reibungslos verlaufen. ◆**'smoothness,** *s.* Glätte *f;* ruhiger Verlauf *m* (eines Fluges usw.); Laufruhe *f* (einer Maschine usw.).

smother ['smʌðər], *v.tr.* (j-n, etwas) ersticken.

smoulder ['sməuldər], *v.i.* schwelen.

smudge [smʌdʒ]. **I.** *s.* Schmutzfleck *m; (in writing etc.)* verwischte Stelle *f.* **II.** *v. v.tr.* (etwas) beschmutzen; (die Unterschrift, Farben usw.) verwischen. **2.** *v.i. (of ink, paint etc.)* schmieren.

smug [smʌg], *adj.* selbstgefällig.

smuggle ['smʌgl], *v.tr. & i.* schmuggeln. ◆**'smuggling,** *s.* Schmuggel *m.*

smut [smʌt], *s.* Schmutz *m.* ◆**'smutty,** *adj.* schmutzig.

snack [snæk], *s.* Imbiß *m;* **to have a s.,** eine Kleinigkeit essen. ◆**'snack-bar,** *s.* Schnellimbiß *m.*

snag [snæg], *s. F:* Haken *m;* **that's the s.,** das ist der Haken (dabei/daran).

snail [sneil], *s.* Schnecke *f;* **at a s.'s pace,** im Schneckentempo.

snake [sneik], *s.* Schlange *f.*

snap [snæp]. **I.** *s.* **1.** *(a) (bite)* Schnappen *n. (b) (sound)* Knacks *m.* **2. cold s.,** Kälteeinbruch *m.* **3.** *Phot:* s.(shot), Schnappschuß *m.* **II.** *adj.* **to make a s. decision/judgement,** Knall und Fall entscheiden/urteilen. **III.** *v.* **1.** *v.tr. (a)* **to s. sth. shut,** etwas zuklappen; *(b)* **to s. one's fingers,** mit den Fingern schnalzen; *(c) (break)* (etwas) durchbrechen; *(d) Phot: F:* (j-n, etwas) knipsen. **2.** *v.i. (a)* **to s. at s.o.,** *(of dog)* nach j-m schnappen; *(of pers.)* j-n anfahren; *(b) (of lock etc.)* **to s. to/shut,** zuschnappen; *(c) (break)* entzweibrechen; *(of rope)* reißen. ◆**'snap 'up,** *v.tr.* (etwas) ergattern.

snare ['sneər]. **I.** *s.* Falle *f.* **II.** *v.tr.* (ein Tier usw.) in einer Falle fangen.

snarl [snɑːl]. **I.** *v.i. (of animal, pers.)* knurren; **to s. at s.o.,** j-n anknurren. **II.** *s.* Knurren *n.* ◆**'snarl 'up,** *v.i. (of traffic etc.)* einen Stau bilden. **2.** *v.tr.* (den Verkehr usw.) zum Stocken bringen.

snatch [snætʃ], v. 1. v.i. greifen (at, nach + dat). 2. v.tr. (a) (j-n, etwas) wegreißen; (b) Fig: (eine Gelegenheit) ergreifen.

sneak [sni:k], v. 1. v.i. to s. about, herumschleichen; to s. off, wegschleichen. 2. v.tr. F: (etwas hinterhältig) klauen. ◆'**sneakers**, s. (shoes) N.Am: F: Leibtreter mpl. ◆'**sneaking**, adj. a s. suspicion, ein leiser Verdacht. ◆'**sneaky**, adj. hinterhältig.

sneer [snɪər]. I. s. spöttisches Lächeln n. II. v.i. spöttisch lächeln; to s. at s.o., sth., über j-n, etwas acc spotten.

sneeze [sni:z]. I. s. Niesen n. II. v.i. niesen.

sniff [snɪf]. I. s. Schnüffeln n. II. v. 1. v.i. schnüffeln; to s. at sth., (of pers.) an etwas dat riechen; (of animal) etwas beschnuppern. 2. v.tr. (of pers.) an etwas dat) riechen; (of animal) (etwas) beschnuppern. ◆'**sniffle**, v.i. schnüffeln.

snigger ['snɪgər]. I. s. Kichern n. II. v.i. kichern.

snip [snɪp]. I. v.tr. to s. (at) sth., (an etwas dat) schnippeln. II. s. (a) (cut) Schnitt m; (b) (piece) Schnipsel m.

sniper ['snaɪpər], s. Heckenschütze m.

snivel ['snɪvl], v.i. (a) (with runny nose) schnüffeln; (b) (cry) wimmern. ◆'**snivelling**, adj. (a) schnüffelnd; (b) wimmernd; (of child) weinerlich.

snob [snɒb], s. Snob m. ◆'**snobbery** s. Snobismus m. ◆'**snobbish**, adj. snobistisch.

snooker ['snu:kər], s. Snooker n.

snoop [snu:p], v.i. to s. (around), (herum)schnüffeln. ◆'**snooper**, s. Schnüffler m.

snooty ['snu:ti], adj. F: hochnäsig.

snooze [snu:z], v.i. ein Nickerchen machen.

snore [snɔ:r], v.i. schnarchen.

snorkel ['snɔ:kl], s. Schnorchel m.

snort [snɔ:t], v.i. schnauben.

snout [snaut], s. Schnauze f.

snow [snəu]. I. s. Schnee m. II. v. impers. schneien; F: **I'm snowed under with work**, ich bin mit Arbeit überhäuft. ◆'**snowball**. I. s. Schneeball m. II. v.i. Fig: (grow quickly) lawinenartig anwachsen. ◆'**snowbound**, adj. eingeschneit. ◆'**snowdrift**, s. Schneewehe f. ◆'**snowdrop**, s. Schneeglöckchen n. ◆'**snowfall**, s. Schneefall m. ◆'**snowflake**, s. Schneeflocke f. ◆'**snowplough**, s. Schneepflug m. ◆'**snowy**, adj. (of landscape etc.) schneebedeckt.

snub[1] [snʌb]. I. s. schroffe Abweisung f. II. v.tr. (j-n) schroff abweisen.

snub[2], adj. F: s.-nose, Stupsnase f.

snuff [snʌf], s. Schnupftabak m.

snug [snʌg], adj. gemütlich; (of bed etc.) mollig warm; -ly, adv. gemütlich; (of garment etc.) to fit s., wie angegossen passen.

snuggle ['snʌgl], v.i. to s. up to s.o., sich an j-n anschmiegen; to s. down in bed, sich ins Bett kuscheln.

so [səu]. I. adv. 1. so; so much, so (sehr); so far, so weit; so far as I know, soviel ich weiß; so much, so viel; (unspecified quantity) so many articles at 10 marks, soundsoviele Artikel zu 10 Mark; so much so that ..., derart/dermaßen, daß ... 2. (a) and so, und so weiter; (b) I think so, ich glaube (schon); I don't think so, ich glaube nicht; so to speak, sozusagen; is that so? tatsächlich? (c) (also) he is clever and so is she, er ist intelligent und sie auch. 3. conj. phr. so that ..., (i) (result) so daß ...; (ii) (intent) damit ...; so as to ..., damit ...; he hurried, so as not to be late/so that he would not be late, er beeilte sich, um nicht zu spät zu kommen. 4. (about) a week or so, ungefähr eine Woche. II. conj. also; he wasn't there, so I came back, er war nicht da, also/daher bin ich zurückgekommen; F: so what? na und? ◆'**so-called**, adj. sogenannt. ◆'**so-'so**, adv. F: he's s., es geht ihm so la-la.

soak [səuk], v. 1. v.tr. (a) (Brot, Wäsche usw.) einweichen (in, in + dat); (b) (etwas) durchtränken (in sth., mit etwas dat); (of rain) (j-n, etwas) durchnässen; soaked to the skin, völlig durchnäßt. 2. v.i. (a) (of washing etc.) eingeweicht werden; (b) (of moisture) to s. through, durchkommen. ◆'**soaking**, s. (of pers.) to get a good s., völlig durchnäßt werden. ◆'**soak 'up**, v.tr. (of sponge etc.) (Wasser usw.) aufsaugen.

soap [səup]. I. s. Seife f. II. v.tr. einseifen; s. powder, Waschpulver n. ◆'**soapy**, adj. seifig.

soar [sɔ:r], v.i. (of bird, plane etc.) in die Höhe steigen; (of spire etc.) hochragen; (of prices) in die Höhe schnellen.

sob [sɒb]. I. s. Schluchzer m. II. v.i. schluchzen.

sober ['səubər]. I. adj. nüchtern; (matter of fact) sachlich. II. v. 1. v.i. to s. up, nüchtern werden. 2. v.tr. to s. s.o. up/down, j-n ernüchtern. ◆**so'briety** [-'braɪətɪ], s. Nüchternheit f.

soccer ['sɒkər], s. Fußball m.

sociable ['səuʃəbl], adj. gesellig.

social ['səuʃ(ə)l]. I. adj. (a) (of society) gesellschaftlich; Gesellschafts-; s. class, Gesellschaftsschicht f; (b) (aiding society) sozial; s. security, Sozialversicherung f; s. worker, Sozialarbeiter(in) m(f); s. services, Sozialeinrichtungen fpl; -ly, adv. to meet s., gesellschaftlich zusammenkommen. II. s. geselliges Beisammensein n.

socialism ['səuʃəlizm], s. Sozialismus m. ◆'**socialist**. I. s. Sozialist m. II. adj. sozialistisch.

society [sə'saiəti], s. Gesellschaft f; (club) Verein m.

sock [sɔk], s. Socken m; long/knee s.,

Kniestrumpf m.

socket ['sɔkit], s. (power) s., Steckdose f.

soda ['saudǝ], s. Soda n; baking-s., (doppeltkohlensaures) Natron n.

sofa ['saufǝ], s. Sofa n.

soft [sɔft], adj. 1. weich. 2. (a) (of voice, light, breeze etc.) sanft; (b) (quiet) leise; s. music, gedämpfte Musik. 3. to have a spot for s.o., für j-n etwas übrig haben. 4. s. drugs, weiche Drogen; s. drinks, alkoholfreie Getränke. 5. (of pers.) F: (a) s. (in the head), schwachsinnig; (b) (physically) verweichlicht; -ly, adv. to speak/tread s., leise sprechen/gehen ◆'**soften** ['sɔfn], v. 1. v.tr. (etwas) weich machen; (das Licht, die Musik usw.) dämpfen. 2. v.i. weich werden; (of pers.) sich erweichen lassen. ◆'**softhearted**, adj. weichherzig. ◆'**softness**, s. Weichheit f; (of voice etc.) Sanftheit f. ◆'**software**, s. Datapr: Software f.

soggy ['sɔgi], adj. matschig; (soaked) durchnäßt.

soil[1] [sɔil], s. Boden m.

soil[2], v.tr. (etwas) beschmutzen. ◆'**soiled**, adj. schmutzig.

solar ['saulǝr], adj. Sonnen-; s. system, Sonnensystem n.

solder ['sǝuldǝr, 'sɔldǝr]. I. s. Lötmittel n. II. v.tr. löten.

soldier ['sǝuldʒǝr], s. Soldat m.

sole[1] [sǝul]. I. s. Sohle f; s. of the foot, Fußsohle f. II. v.tr. (Schuhe usw.) besohlen.

sole[2], s. Seezunge f.

sole[3], adj. einzig; -ly, adv. einzig und allein; (merely) lediglich.

solemn ['sɔlǝm], adj. 1. (of music, ceremony etc.) feierlich. 2. (of pers., mood etc.) ernst. ◆'**solemnity** ['lemniti], s. Feierlichkeit f.

solicit [sǝ'lisit], v.tr. & i. a) to s. (for) sth., um etwas acc werben; (b) (of prostitute) sich anbieten. ◆**so'licitor**, s. Rechtsanwalt m.

solid ['sɔlid]. I. adj. 1. (not liquid) fest. 2. (not hollow) massiv. 3. (firm, reliable) (of pers., thing) solid(e). 4. (of argument, proof etc.) handfest. 5. a s. hour, eine volle Stunde. II. s. 1. Ph: Ch: fester Körper m. 2. pl. (food) solids, feste Nahrung f; -ly, adv. 1. s. built, (i) (of pers.) kräftig gebaut; (ii) (of building etc.) stabil gebaut. 2. they are s. behind us, sie stehen geschlossen hinter uns. ◆**soli'darity**, s. Solidarität f. ◆**so'lidify**, v. 1. v.i. fest werden. 2. v.tr. (etwas) fest werden lassen.

soliloquy [sǝ'lilǝkwi], s. Selbstgespräch n; Th: Monolog m.

solitary ['sɔlit(ǝ)ri], adj. (only one) einzig; (lonely) einsam; s. confinement, Einzelhaft f. ◆'**solitude**, s. Einsamkeit f.

solo, pl. -os ['saulǝu, -ǝuz]. I. s. Solo n. II. adj. Solo-. III. adv. Mus: to play s.,

solo spielen. ◆'**soloist**, s. Solist(in) m(f).

solstice ['sɔlstis], s. Sonnenwende f.

soluble ['sɔljubl], adj. 1. Ph: Ch: löslich. 2. (of problem) lösbar. ◆**solution** [sǝ'lu:ʃ(ǝ)n], s. Lösung f.

solve [sɔlv], v.tr. (ein Problem usw.) lösen. ◆'**solvent**. I. adj. Com: (of firm) zahlungsfähig. II. s. Ch: etc: Lösungsmittel n.

some [sʌm]. I. adj. 1. (usu. not translated) I bought s. coffee, ich habe (etwas) Kaffee gekauft; s. more meat, noch (etwas) Fleisch. 2. (a certain amount) einige(r, s); after s. time, nach einiger Zeit; s. days ago, vor einigen Tagen. 3. (about) etwa; s. twenty people, etwa zwanzig Leute; in s. cases, in manchen Fällen. 4. (unspecified) s. man (or other), irgendein Mann; s. time, irgendwann. 5. F: N.Am: toll; that was s. party! das war vielleicht eine Party! II. pron. 1. (partitive) welche(s); take s. bread – I've already got s., nimm dir Brot – ich habe schon welches; take s.! nimm (dir) davon! 2. (not all) einige, s. of them, einige von ihnen/(things) davon.

somebody ['sʌmbǝdi], pron. jemand; s. or other, irgend jemand.

somehow ['sʌmhau], adv. s. (or other), irgendwie.

someone ['sʌmwʌn], pron. & s. = somebody.

somersault ['sʌmǝsɔːlt]. I. s. Purzelbaum m, Sp: Salto m. II. v.i. (a) einen Purzelbaum schlagen; Gym: einen Salto machen; (b) (accidentally) (of pers., car etc.) sich überschlagen.

something ['sʌmθiŋ]. 1. pron. etwas; F: was; s. nice, etwas Schönes; s. to drink, etwas zu trinken; s. or other, irgend etwas; s. which you ought to know, etwas, was Sie wissen sollten; F: he is an architect or s., er ist Architekt oder so was (Ähnliches). II. adv. it looks s. like a rose, es sieht so ähnlich wie eine Rose aus.

sometime ['sʌmtaim], adv. s. (or other), irgendwann; F: see you s., bis dann.

sometimes ['sʌmtaimz], adv. manchmal.

somewhat ['sʌmwɔt], adv. (a) (with adj.) etwas; (b) s. of a surprise, eine ziemliche Überraschung.

somewhere ['sʌmwεǝr], adv. s. (or other), irgendwo; s. else, (irgend)wo anders.

son [sʌn], s. Sohn m. ◆'**son-in-law**, s. Schwiegersohn m.

sonata [sǝ'nɑːtǝ], s. Sonate f.

song [sɔŋ], s. Lied n. ◆'**songwriter**, s. Liedermacher m; (classical) Liederkomponist m.

sonic ['sɔnik], adj. Sp: Schall-.

sonnet ['sɔnit], s. Sonett n. 1.

sonorous ['sɔnǝrǝs], adj. (of voice etc.) klangvoll.

soon [suːn], adv. 1. bald; s. after, bald

darauf/danach; **as** s. **as possible**, möglichst bald. 2. (*early*) **too** s., zu früh; **how** s. **can you be ready?** wie schnell kannst du fertig sein? 3. (*a*) **I would just as** s. **stay**, ich würde ebensogern bleiben; (*b*) **sooner,** (*rather*) lieber.

soot [sut], s. Ruß *m.* ◆**'sooty,** *adj.* rußig.

soothe [su:ð], *v.tr.* (*a*) (j-n, j-s Zorn usw.) beruhigen; (*b*) (Schmerzen usw.) lindern.

soppy ['sɔpi], *adj.* F: (*silly*) doof; (*sentimental*) kitschig.

sophisticated [sə'fistikeitid], *adj.* 1. (*of pers.*) weltklug; (*of tastes etc.*) verfeinert, anspruchsvoll; *Cl: etc:* hochelegant. 2. (*of machine etc.*) hochentwickelt; (*of system*) raffiniert. ◆**sophisti'cation,** s. 1. (*of pers.*) Weltklugheit *f.* 2. Raffiniertheit *f;* hochentwickelter Stand (der Technik).

soporific [sɔpə'rifik]. I. s. Schlafmittel *n.* II. *adj.* einschläfernd.

soprano, *pl.* **-os** [sə'prɑ:nəu, -əuz], s. *Mus:* (*a*) (*voice*) Sopran *m;* (*b*) (*pers.*) Sopranistin *f.*

sorcerer ['sɔ:sərər], s. Zauberer *m.* ◆**'sorcery,** s. Zauberei *f.*

sordid ['sɔ:did], *adj.* elend; (*dirty*) dreckig; (*of story*) trist; (*unpleasant*) unschön.

sore [sɔ:r]. I. *adj.* 1. wund; **my finger is** s., mein Finger tut weh. 2. F: (*a*) (*of pers.*) ärgerlich; (*hurt*) gekränkt. II. s. wunde Stelle *f;* **a** s., adv. sehr; s. **needed,** dringend gebraucht.

sorrow ['sɔrəu], s. (*a*) (*suffering*) Leid *n;* Kummer *m;* (*b*) (*regret*) Bedauern *n.* ◆**'sorrowful,** *adj.* kummervoll; (*of expression etc.*) traurig. ◆**'sorry,** *adj.* 1. **he is** s. **that** ..., es tut ihm leid, daß ...; er bedauert, daß ...; **he was** s. **for her,** sie tat ihm leid; **I am** s. **to say,** ich muß leider sagen. 2. **(I'm) s.!** Entschuldigung! 3. (*pitiable*) **a** s. **sight/state,** ein erbärmlicher Anblick/Zustand.

sort [sɔːt]. I. s. 1. (*a*) Sorte *f;* **two sorts of apple,** zwei Sorten Äpfel; **all sorts of people,** allerlei Leute; (*b*) Art *f;* **what** s. **of car have you got?** was für ein Auto haben Sie? **something of that** s., etwas in der Art; (*c*) F: s. **of hot,** ziemlich warm. 2. (*of pers.*) **he/she is a good** s., er/sie ist ein guter Kerl. 3. F: **out of sorts,** (i) (*health*) nicht ganz auf der Höhe; (ii) (*temper*) schlecht gelaunt. II. *v.tr.* (Gegenstände, Briefe usw.) sortieren. ◆**'sort 'out,** *v.tr.* (*a*) (etwas) aussortieren; (*b*) (eine Angelegenheit, Frage usw.) erledigen. ◆**'sorting,** s. Sortieren *n;* s. **office,** Sortierstelle *f.*

soul [səul], s. 1. Seele *f;* **to put one's heart and** s. **into it,** mit Leib und Seele dabei sein; **he was the life and** s. **of the party,** er hielt die Party in Schwung. 2. (*person*) **there wasn't a** s. **to be seen,** es war keine Menschenseele zu sehen; **poor** s.! armes Geschöpf! ◆**'soul-**

destroying, *adj.* geisttötend. ◆**'soulful,** *adj.* (*of eyes, look etc.*) traurig; (*of music*) gefühlvoll; *Pej:* gefühlsselig.

sound¹ [saund]. I. s. 1. (*a*) (*noise*) Geräusch *n;* (*b*) Schall *m* (einer Glocke usw.); *esp. Cin:* Ton *m;* s. **track,** Tonspur *f;* (*recording*) Filmmusik *f;* (*c*) (*uttered by pers. or animal*) Laut *m;* (*d*) (*tone*) Klang *m* (einer Stimme, eines Instruments usw.) 2. **I don't like the** s. **of it,** es gefällt mir nicht. II. *v.* 1. *v.i.* (*a*) (*of trumpet etc.*) schallen; (*of music*) erklingen; (*b*) klingen; **that sounds good,** das hört sich gut an; **it sounds like** Mozart, es klingt nach Mozart. 2. *v.tr.* **to** s. **the alarm,** Alarm läuten. ◆**'soundless,** *adj.* lautlos. ◆**'soundproof.** I. *adj.* schalldicht. II. *v.tr.* (einen Raum usw.) schalldicht machen.

sound², *v.tr. Nau:* (die Wassertiefe usw.) loten. ◆**'sounding,** s. **to take soundings,** loten.

sound³, s. *Geog:* Meerenge *f;* (*with name*) Sund *m.*

sound³, *adj.* 1. (*healthy*) gesund. 2. (*a*) (*sensible*) vernünftig; (*of judgement etc.*) folgerichtig; (*of argument etc.*) stichhaltig; s. **advice,** guter Rat; (*b*) *Com: Fin:* (*of investment*) solide; (*c*) (*thorough*) tüchtig. 3. (*of sleep*) fest.

soup [su:p], s. Suppe *f;* **clear** s., Bouillon *f;* s. **plate,** Suppenteller *m.*

sour [sauər]. I. *adj.* sauer; **to turn** s., sauer werden. II. *v.tr.* (*a*) (etwas) säuern; (*b*) (j-n) verbittern. ◆**'sourness,** s. 1. (*of fruit etc.*) Säure *f.* 2. (*of pers.*) mürrisches Wesen *n.*

source [sɔːs], s. Quelle *f* (eines Flusses, *Fig:* der Freude usw.); (*origin*) Ursprung *m.*

south [sauθ]. I. s. Süden *m;* **in the** s., im Süden; **to the** s. (of), südlich (+ *gen*). II. *adv.* südlich; s. **of London,** südlich von London; **to travel** s. nach (dem) Süden fahren. III. *adj.* Süd-; **S. Africa,** Südafrika *n;* **S. African,** (i) *adj.* südafrikanisch; (ii) s. Südafrikaner(in) *m(f)*. ◆**'south-'east.** I. s. Südosten *m.* II. *adj.* Südost-; (*of wind*) südöstlich. III. *adv.* südöstlich (**of,** + *gen*/with Pr. n. von + *dat*); (*direction*) nach Südosten. ◆**'south-'eastern,** *adj.* südöstlich. ◆**'southerly** ['sʌðəli], *adj.* südlich. ◆**'southern** ['sʌðən], *adj.* südlich; ◆**'south-'west.** I. s. Südwesten *m.* II. *adj.* Südwest-. III. *adv.* südwestlich (**of,** + *gen*/with Pr. n. von + *dat*); (*direction*) nach Südwesten. ◆**'south-'western,** *adj.* südwestlich.

souvenir [su:və'ni(:)ər], s. Andenken *n.*

sovereign ['sɔvrin], s. 1. Herrscher(in) *m(f).* 2. (*gold coin*) Sovereign *m.* II. *adj.* s. **state,** unabhängiger Staat. ◆**'sovereignty,** s. Souveränität *f.*

Soviet ['sauviət, 'sɔvjət], s. Sowjet *m;* **S. Union,** Sowjetunion *f;* **Union of S.**

Socialist Republics (USSR), Union *f* der Sozialistischen Sowjetrepubliken (UdSSR).

sow¹ [sau], *v.tr.irr.* säen

sow² [sau], *s. Z:* Sau *f.*

soya ['sɔiə], *s. Cu:* **s. bean,** Sojabohne *f.*

spa [spɑ:], *s.* Kurort *m.*

space [speis]. **I.** *s.* **1.** *(a) (concept)* Raum *m; (between objects, lines)* Abstand *m;* **blank s.,** Lücke *f; (b) (room)* Platz *m; (c) (area)* Fläche *f;* **in a confined s.,** auf engem Raum. **2.** *(outer)* s., Weltraum *m;* **s. travel,** Weltraumfahrt *f.* **3.** *s. (of time),* Zeitraum *m;* **in the s. of a few minutes,** innerhalb weniger Minuten. **II.** *v.tr. (etwas)* in regelmäßigen Abständen verteilen. ◆**'spaceman,** *pl.* **-men,** *s.* Raumfahrer *m.* ◆**'spaceship,** *s.* Raumschiff *m.* ◆**'spacing,** *s.* Abstand *m* (zwischen den Zeilen usw.); **single/double s.,** einfacher/doppelter Zeilenabstand. ◆**'spacious,** *adj.* geräumig.

spade¹ [speid], *s.* Spaten *m.*

spade², *s. Pik m; queen of spades,* Pikdame *f.*

spaghetti [spə'geti], *s.* Spaghetti *pl.*

Spain [spein]. *Pr.n.* Spanien *n.*

span [spæn]. **I.** *s.* **1.** Spannweite *f* (einer Brücke usw.). **2. s. (of time),** Zeitspanne *f;* **life s.,** Lebensdauer *f.* **II.** *v.tr. (a) (of bridge etc.)* to s. sth., sich über etwas *acc* spannen; *(b) (of life, reign etc.) (einen Zeitraum)* umspannen.

Spaniard ['spænjəd], *s.* Spanier(in) *m(f).*

spaniel ['spænjəl], *s.* Spaniel *m.*

Spanish ['spæniʃ]. **I.** *adj.* spanisch. **II.** *s.* Spanisch *n.*

spank [spæŋk], *v.tr.* **to s. a child,** einem Kind den Hintern versohlen.

spanner ['spænər], *s.* Schraubenschlüssel *m.*

spar [spɑ:r], *v.i. (a) Sp:* sparren; *(b) Fig:* **to s. with s.o.,** mit j-m argumentieren.

spare ['speər]. **I.** *adj. (a)* überschüssig; **s. time,** Freizeit *f;* **s. room,** Gästezimmer *n; (b) Aut: etc:* **s. part,** Ersatzteil *m;* **s. wheel,** Reserverad *n.* **II.** *v.tr. (a) (do without) (etwas)* entbehren; **to have nothing to s.,** nichts übrig haben; *(b) (not hurt)* (j-n, j-s Gefühle usw.) schonen; *(c) (save)* **to s. you the trouble,** um Ihnen die Mühe zu (er)sparen. **III.** *s. Aut: etc:* Ersatzteil *n.* ◆**'sparing,** *adj.* sparsam

spark [spɑ:k]. **I.** *s. (a)* Funke *m; (b) Fig:* Funken *m.* **II.** *v.i.* funken; *(b) adj.* Zündkerze *f.* ◆**'spark 'off,** *v.tr. (etwas)* auslösen.

sparkle ['spɑ:kl]. **I.** *s.* Funkeln *n.* **II.** *v.i.* funkeln; *(of wine)* perlen. ◆**'sparkling,** *adj.* funkelnd; **s. wine,** Schaumwein *m.*

sparrow ['spærəu], *s.* Spatz *m.*

sparse [spɑ:s], *adj. (a) (of population etc.)* dünn; **s. hair,** schütteres Haar; **s. vegetation,** spärlicher Pflanzenwuchs; *(b) (rare)* selten; **-ly,** *adv.* dünn.

spasm ['spæz(ə)m], *s. Med:* Krampf *m.* ◆**spas'modic,** *adj. (a) Med:* krampfar-

tig; *(b)* unregelmäßig; **-ally,** *adv.* hin und wieder.

spastic ['spæstik]. *Med.* **I.** *adj.* spastisch; *(of pers.)* spastisch gelähmt. **II.** *s.* Spastiker *m.*

spate [speit], *s.* **1.** *the river is in (full) s.,** der Fluß führt Hochwasser. **2.** *Fig:* Flut *f* (von Worten, Briefen usw.)

spatial ['speiʃ(ə)l], *adj.* räumlich.

spatter ['spætər], *v.tr.* bespritzen.

spatula ['spætjulə], *s.* Spachtel *f.*

spawn [spɔ:n]. **I.** *s.* Laich *m; frog* s., Froschlaich *m.* **II.** *v.* **1.** *v.i. (of fish, frog etc.)* laichen. **2.** *v.tr. (of fish, frog etc.)* (Eier) ablegen.

speak [spi:k], *v.irr.* **1.** *v.i. (a)* sprechen; **to s. to s.o.,** (i) *(address)* j-n ansprechen; (ii) *(converse with)* mit j-m sprechen (about, über + *acc*); *Tel:* **who is (it) speaking?** wer ist am Apparat? *(b)* **generally speaking,** im allgemeinen; **strictly speaking,** genaugenommen; *(c) (make a speech)* sprechen; eine Rede halten. **2.** *v.tr. (a)* **to s. the truth,** die Wahrheit sagen; *(b)* **to s. German,** Deutsch sprechen. ◆**'speaker,** *s.* Redner *m;* **to be a fluent s.,** flüssig reden; *Pol: Brit:* **the S.,** der Präsident (des Unterhauses). ◆**'speak 'for,** *v.i.* **to s. f. s.o.,** *(support)* j-n unterstützen; *(on behalf of)* in j-s Namen sprechen; **s. f. yourself!** das ist (wohl) Ihre Meinung! ◆**'speaking,** *adj.* **English-s.,** englischsprechend. ◆**'speak of,** *v.i. (in, etwas)* erwähnen. ◆**'speak 'out,** *v.i.* seine Meinung offen sagen. ◆**'speak 'up,** *v.i. (a)* lauter sprechen; *(b)* **to s. up for s.o.,** für j-n eintreten.

spear [spiər]. **I.** *s.* Speer *m.* **II.** *v.tr.* mit dem Speer durchbohren.

special ['speʃ(ə)l]. **I.** *adj.* besondere; *s;* Sonder-; **s. case,** Sonderfall *m; Com:* **s. offer,** Sonderangebot *n.* **II.** *s.* **1.** Sondernummer *f* (einer Zeitung usw.). **2.** *(train)* Sonderzug *m.* **3.** *(in restaurant) F:* **today's s.,** Spezialität *f* des Tages; **-ly,** *adv. (a)* besonders; **s. good,** besonders gut; *(b)* **I came s.,** ich bin extra gekommen. ◆**'specialist,** *s.* Spezialist *m.* ◆**speciality** [-i'æliti], *s.* Spezialität *f.* ◆**specialization** [-əlai'zeiʃ(ə)n], *s.* Spezialisierung *f; (subject)* Spezialfach *n.* ◆**'specialize,** *v.i.* sich spezialisieren (in, auf + *acc*).

species ['spi:ʃi:z], *s. Z: etc:* Art *f.*

specific [spə'sifik], *adj. (of statement, orders etc.)* genau; **a s. purpose,** ein bestimmter Zweck; **-ally,** *adv.* genau; **he s. mentioned it,** er hat es ausdrücklich erwähnt. ◆**specifi'cation,** *s. (a)* Spezifizierung *f; (description)* Beschreibung *f; (b) (data)* **technical s.,** technische Daten. ◆**'specify,** *v.tr. (a) (state)* (Zweck usw.) genau angeben; (seine Gründe usw.) nennen; *(b) (prescribe)* (etwas) vorschreiben.

specimen ['spesimin], *s. (a) (example)* Exemplar *n; (b) (sample)* Probe *f.*

speck [spek], s. (kleiner) Fleck m; **s. of dust**, Staubkorn n. ◆**'speckled,** adj. gesprenkelt.

spectacle ['spektəkl], s. 1. (a) (public show) Schau f; Fig: Schauspiel n; **to make a s.** of oneself, sich auffällig benehmen/kleiden; (b) (sight) Anblick m. 2. (pair of) spectacles, Brille f ◆**spec'tacular** [-'tækjulər], adj. spektakulär. ◆**spec'tator** [-'teitər], s. Zuschauer(in) m(f).

spectre ['spektər], s. Gespenst n.

spectrum, pl. -**tra** ['spektrəm, -trə], s. Spektrum n.

speculate ['spekjuleit], v.i. (a) **to s. about sth.,** Mutmaßungen über etwas acc anstellen; (b) Fin: spekulieren (**on, auf** + acc). ◆**specu'lation,** s. 1. Mutmaßung f (**about, über** + acc). 2. Fin: Spekulation f. ◆**'speculative** [-lətiv], adj. (a) (of pers., mood etc.) grüblerisch; (b) Fin: spekulativ.

speech [spi:tʃ], s. 1. (a) Sprache f; freedom of s., Redefreiheit f; (b) (way of talking) Sprechweise f; (c) Gram: indirect s., indirekte Rede; **part of s.,** Wortart f. 2. (address) Rede f; **to make a s.,** eine Rede halten. ◆**'speechless,** adj. sprachlos (**with, vor** + dat).

speed [spi:d]. I. s. 1. Geschwindigkeit f; **at s.,** in voller Fahrt. 2. Aut: etc: (gear) Gang m. n II. v.i.irr schnell fahren; F: **to s. along,** dahinsausen. ◆**'speedboat,** s. Schnellboot n. ◆**'speeding,** s. Überschreitung f der zulässigen Geschwindigkeit. ◆**spee'dometer,** s. Tachometer m. ◆**'speed 'up,** v. 1. v.i. schneller werden; (accelerate) beschleunigen. 2. v.tr. **to s. sth. up,** etwas beschleunigen. ◆**'speedy,** adj. zügig; (fast) schnell; **s. reply/recovery,** baldige Antwort/ Genesung.

spell¹ [spel], s. Zauberspruch m; Fig: Bann m; **to cast a s. over s.o.,** j-n verzaubern. ◆**'spellbound,** adj. (wie) gebannt.

spell², v.irr. 1. v.tr. (a) (ein Wort) schreiben; **how do you s. it?** wie wird es geschrieben? **to s. a word (out),** (aloud) ein Wort buchstabieren; (b) (mean) bedeuten. 2. v.i. rechtschreiben. ◆**'spelling,** s. Rechtschreibung f. ◆**'spell 'out,** v.tr. (a) (Worte) buchstabieren; (b) (etwas) im einzelnen darlegen.

spell³, s. Periode f; **cold s.,** Kältewelle f; **for a s.,** eine Zeitlang.

spend [spend], v.tr. (a) (Geld) ausgeben (**on, für** + acc); (b) **to s. a lot of time on sth.,** etwas dat viel Zeit widmen; (c) (Zeit) verbringen. ◆**'spending,** s. Ausgaben npl (von Geld); **s. power,** Kaufkraft f. ◆**'spendthrift,** s. Verschwender m. ◆**spent,** adj. (of pers., powers etc.) erschöpft; (of bullet etc.) verbraucht.

sperm [spə:m], s. Samen m. ◆**'sperm whale,** s. Pottwal m.

spew [spju:], v.tr. **to s. sth. (out),** etwas ausspeien.

sphere ['sfi(:)ər], s. 1. Mth: Kugel f. 2. Bereich m; **in the political s.,** in der politischen Sphäre; **s. of activity,** Tätigkeitsbereich m. ◆**'spherical** ['sfe-], adj. kugelförmig.

spice [spais]. I. s. Gewürz n. ◆**'spicy,** adj. (a) (of food) würzig; (b) (of story etc.) pikant.

spick and span ['spik ən(d) 'spæn], adj. (of room etc.) blitzblank; (of pers.) geschniegelt.

spider ['spaidər], s. Spinne f.

spike [spaik], s. (on railing, stick etc.) Spitze f; (on barbed wire etc.) Stachel m. ◆**'spiky,** adj. stachelig; (pointed) spitz.

spill [spil], v.irr. 1. v.tr. (Wasser, Milch usw.) verschütten. 2. v.i. (of liquid) verschüttet werden.

spin [spin]. I. v.irr. 1. v.tr. (a) (Garn usw.) spinnen. 2. v.i. (of top, wheel etc.) sich drehen; (of aircraft) trudeln; (of pers.) **to s. round,** sich plötzlich umdrehen. II. s. Sp: Drall m; **to put s. on the ball,** dem Ball einen Drall geben. ◆**'spin-drier,** s. Wäscheschleuder f. ◆**'spinning,** s. Spinnen n; Ind: Spinnerei f; **s. wheel,** Spinnrad n. ◆**'spin-off,** s. Abfallprodukt m; Fig: Nebenwirkung f. ◆**'spin 'out,** v.tr. (eine Geschichte) in die Länge ziehen.

spinach ['spinidʒ], s. Spinat m.

spindle [spindl], s. Spindel f; (shaft) Welle f.

spine [spain], s. 1. Anat: Wirbelsäule f. 2. (of book) Rücken m. 3. (prickle) Stachel m. ◆**'spine-chilling,** adj. gruselig. ◆**'spineless,** adj. **he's s.,** er hat kein Rückgrat.

spinster ['spinstər], s. unverheiratete Frau f; (old) alte Jungfer f.

spiral ['spaiərəl]. I. s. Spirale f. II. adj. gewunden; **s. staircase,** Wendeltreppe f. III. v.i. (in Spiralen) hochwirbeln; (of prices etc.) in die Höhe schießen.

spire ['spaiər], s. Turmspitze f.

spirit ['spirit]. I. s. 1. Geist m; (of pers.) **kindred spirits,** verwandte Seelen. 2. (mood) Stimmung f; **to enter into the s. of sth.,** etwas mit Hingabe mitmachen; (b) pl. **spirits,** Gemütsverfassung f; **in high spirits,** übermütig. 3. (alcohol) usu. pl. Spirituosen pl; **surgical s.,** Wundbenzin n. II. v.tr. **to s. s.o. away,** j-n, etwas wegzaubern. ◆**'spirited,** adj. (of pers.) temperamentvoll; (of discussion) lebhaft; (of horse, defence, speech) feurig. ◆**'spiritual.** I. adj. 1. (of the spirit) geistig. 2. Ecc: geistlich. II. s. (negro) s., Spiritual n. ◆**'spiritualism,** s. Spiritismus m.

spit¹ [spit], s. 1. Cu: Bratspieß m. 2. Geog: Landzunge f.

spit², v.i.irr. spucken; (of cat) fauchen; **it's spitting (with rain),** es tröpfelt. ◆**'spittle,** s. Speichel m.

spite [spait]. **I.** s. 1. Bosheit f. 2. prep. phr. **in s. of**, trotz g gen; **in s. of everything**, trotz allem. **II.** v.tr. **he did it to s. her**, er tat es ihr zum Trotz. ◆**'spiteful**, adj. gehässig.

splash [splæʃ]. **I.** s. 1. (a) (sound) Klatsch m; Platschen n; (b) (mark) Spritzer m. 2. (of colour, light) Fleck m. **II.** v. 1. v.i. (of waves etc.) platschen; (of tap) spritzen; **to s. about**, planschen. 2. v.tr. (j-n, etwas, sich) bespritzen. ◆**'splash 'down**, v.tr. (of spacecraft) wassern. ◆**'splash-down**, s. Wasserung f.

splendid ['splendid], adj. herrlich; (magnificent) prächtig. ◆**'splendour**, s. Pracht f.

splint [splint], s. Schiene f.

splinter ['splintər]. **I.** s. Splitter m. **II.** v.i. splittern.

split [split]. **I.** s. 1. Riß m (im Stoff usw.); Pol: a **s. in the party**, eine Spaltung innerhalb der Partei; Sp: **to do the splits**, Spagat machen. **II.** v.irr. 1. v.tr. (a) spalten; (when bargaining) **to s. the difference**, sich in der Mitte treffen. 2. v.i. (of wood etc.) sich spalten; (of seam etc.) platzen. **III.** adj. gespalten; **s. peas**, geschälte Erbsen. ◆**'split-'level**, adj. auf zwei Ebenen. ◆**'split 'up**, v. 1. v.i. (of couple) auseinandergehen. 2. v.tr. (etwas) aufteilen (**into**, in + acc).

splutter ['splʌtər], v.i. (of pers., engine) stottern.

spoil [spɔil]. **I.** v.irr. 1. v.i. (a) (of food) schlecht werden; (b) (of pers.) **spoiling for a fight**, streitlustig. 2. v.tr. (a) (etwas) verderben; (b) (ein Kind usw.) verwöhnen. **II.** s. usu. pl. Beute f. ◆**'spoilsport**, s. Spielverderber m. ◆**'spoilt**, adj. verdorben; a **s. child**, ein verwöhntes Kind.

spoke [spəuk], s. (of wheel) Speiche f.

spoken ['spəukən], adj. Hum: **s. for**, vergeben.

spokesman, pl. **-men** ['spəuksmən, -men], s. Wortführer m; **government s.**, Regierungssprecher m.

sponge [spʌn(d)ʒ]. **I.** s. 1. Schwamm m. 2. Cu: **s.(-cake)**, Biskuitkuchen m. **II.** v.tr. (etwas) mit einem Schwamm abwischen. ◆**'sponger**, s. F: Schmarotzer m. ◆**'spongy**, adj. schwammig; (of ground) sumpfig.

sponsor ['spɔnsər]. **I.** s. (backer) Förderer m; Com: Bürge m; Sp: Sponsor m. **II.** v.tr. (j-n, etwas) fördern; Com: (für j-n) bürgen; Rad: TV: (eine Sendung) (als Sponsor) finanzieren; Sp: (j-n, eine Mannschaft usw.) sponsern. ◆**'sponsorship**, s. Unterstützung f; Com: Bürgschaft f; Sp: Sponsern n.

spontaneous [spɔn'teinjəs], adj. spontan. ◆**spontaneity** [spɔntə'niːiti]/◆**spon'taneousness**, s. Spontaneität f.

spool [spuːl], s. Spule f.

spoon [spuːn]. **I.** s. Löffel m. **II.** v.tr. **to s. sth. (up)**, etwas löffeln. ◆**'spoonful**, s. a **s. of soup**, ein Löffel Suppe.

sporadic [spə'rædik], adj. sporadisch.

sport [spɔːt]. **I.** s. 1. (a) Sport m; **(type of) s.**, Sportart f; (b) attrib. Sport-; **sports car**, Sportwagen m, **sports jacket**, Sakko m. 2. (fun) Spaß m. 3. (pers.) a **good s.**, ein guter Kerl. **II.** v.tr. (eine Blume im Knopfloch usw.) tragen. ◆**'sporting**, adj. sportlich; **s. chance**, ziemlich gute Chance. ◆**'sportsman**, pl. **-men**, ◆**'-woman**, pl. **-women**, s. 1. Sportler(in) m(f). 2. (fair player) Sportsmann m. ◆**'sporty**, adj. sportlich.

spot [spɔt]. **I.** s. 1. Punkt m; Fleck m. 2. (a) (place) Ort m; (b) (exact position) Stelle f; **on the s.**, (i) zur Stelle; (ii) (there and then) an Ort und Stelle; (iii) (immediately) auf der Stelle; **s. check**, Stichprobe f; F: **to put s.o. on the s.**, j-n in Verlegenheit bringen. 3. (on face etc.) Pickel m; pl. (rash) Ausschlag m. 4. (drop) Tropfen m (Regen). **II.** v. 1. v.i. **it's spotting with rain**, es tröpfelt. 2. v.tr. (catch sight of) (j-n, etwas) erkennen. ◆**'spotless**, adj. fleckenlos; (immaculate) makellos. ◆**'spotlight**. **I.** s. Th: etc: Spotlight m. **II.** v.tr. Fig: (j-n, etwas) herausstellen. ◆**'spot-'on**, adj. genau richtig. ◆**'spotted**, adj. (of material) getupft; (of animal) gefleckt; (speckled) gesprenkelt. ◆**'spotty**, adj. (of face etc.) pickelig.

spouse [spauz], s. Jur: Ehepartner(in) m(f); Hum: Gatte m, Gattin f.

spout [spaut]. **I.** s. 1. Schnauze f (einer Kanne usw.); (for rainwater) Ausguß m; (of pump) Hahn m. **II.** v.i. (her-ausspritzen.

sprain [sprein]. **I.** s. Verstauchung f. **II.** v.tr. **to s. one's ankle/wrist**, sich dat den Fuß/die Hand verstauchen.

sprat [spræt], s. Sprotte f.

sprawl [sprɔːl], v.i. (a) (of pers.) (behaglich) ausgestreckt liegen/sitzen; F: (sich) rekeln; (b) (of town) sich weit ausdehnen.

spray¹ [sprei], s. **s. of flowers**, Blütenzweig m.

spray². **I.** s. 1. (of sea etc.) Gischt f. 2. (a) (for hair, plants etc.) Spray m or n; (b) (atomizer) Sprühdose f. **II.** v. 1. v.i. (of liquid) sprühen. 2. v.tr. (a) (eine Flüssigkeit) sprühen; Agr: (Bäume, Getreide usw.) spritzen; Ind: (in Auto usw.) spritzen.

spread [spred]. **I.** s. 1. Fig: (range) Umfang m. 2. (process) Verbreitung f (des Wissens, der Krankheit usw.). 3. F: (meal) Schmaus m. 4. (on bread) Aufstrich m. **II.** v. 1. v.i. (of news, disease etc.) sich verbreiten; (of fire, area of land) sich ausbreiten. 2. v.tr. (a) **to s. sth. (out)**, etwas ausbreiten; (b) (Krankheit, eine Nachricht usw.) verbreiten; (c) (Brot mit Butter usw.) bestreichen; **to s. butter on bread**, Butter aufs Brot streichen.

spree [spriː], s. **shopping s.**, Einkaufsbummel m.

sprig [sprig], s. Zweig m.

sprightly ['spraitli], adj. lebhaft; (of old pers.) rüstig.

spring [sprin]. I. s. 1. (jump) Sprung m. 2. (of water) Quelle f. 3. (season) Frühling m. 4. s. tide, Springflut f. 5. (a) (elasticity) Elastizität f; (b) (device) Feder f. II. v.irr. 1. v.i. (a) springen; (b) (arise) entstammen (from, dat.). 2. v.tr. (a) to s. sth. on s.o., j-n mit etwas dat überraschen; (b) to s. a leak, ein Leck bekommen. ◆'**springboard**, s. Sprungbrett n. ◆'**spring-cleaning**, s. Frühjahrsputz m. ◆'**spring 'up**, v.i. (of breeze, Fig: doubt etc.) aufkommen; (of plant) aufschießen. ◆'**springy**, adj. (of gait etc.) federnd.

sprinkle ['sprinkl], v.tr. (a) (Wasser usw.) sprengen; (Sand, Zucker) streuen; (b) to s. s.o., sth. with water, j-n, etwas mit Wasser besprengen/berieseln. ◆'**sprinkler**, s. Sprinkler m.

sprint [sprint]. I. s. (a) (race) Sprint m; (b) (spurt) Spurt m. II. v.i. (a) sprinten; (b) (spurt) spurten. ◆'**sprinter**, s. Sprinter m; Kurzstreckenläufer m.

sprout [spraut]. I. v.i. (a) (of seed) treiben; (of plant) sprießen; (b) (of plant etc.) hochschießen. II. s. Sproß m; (Brussels) sprouts, Rosenkohl m.

spruce [spru:s], s. (tree) Fichte f.

sprung [sprʌŋ], adj. well/badly s., gut/schlecht gefedert.

spur [spə:r]. I. s. 1. Sporn m. 2. (incitement) Ansporn m; on the s. of the moment, ganz spontan; (of decision) plötzlich. 3. Geog: Ausläufer m. II. v.tr. Fig: to s. s.o. on, j-n anspornen.

spurious ['spjuariəs], adj. falsch.

spurn [spə:n], v.tr. verschmähen.

spurt [spə:t]. I. v.i. (a) (of liquid, flames etc.) to s. out, hervorschießen; to s. up, emporschießen; (b) Sp: spurten. II. s. 1. s. of water, plötzlich hervorschießender Wasserstrahl; 2. Sp: Spurt m.

spy [spai]. I. s. Spion(in) m(f). II. v. 1. v.i. spionieren; to s. on s.o., j-m nachspionieren. 2. v.tr. (see) erspähen. ◆'**spying**, s. Spionage f.

squabble ['skwɔbl]. I. v.i. zanken. II. s. Zank m. ◆'**squabbling**, s. Gezänk n.

squad [skwɔd], s. Mil: etc: Kommando n; firing s., Exekutionskommando n. Mannschaft f.

squadron ['skwɔdrən], s. (a) Mil: (armoured) Kompanie f; (cavalry) Schwadron n; (b) Nau: Geschwader n; (c) Av: Staffel f.

squalid ['skwɔlid], adj. elend. ◆'**squalor**, s. Elend n.

squall [skwɔ:l], s. Bö f. ◆'**squally**, adj. böig.

squander ['skwɔndər], v.tr. vergeuden.

square [skwɛər]. I. s. (a) (figure) Quadrat n; (on chessboard, map etc.) Feld n. 2. (in town) Platz m. 3. Mth: the s. of a number, die zweite Potenz einer Zahl. 4.

(set) s., Winkel m. II. adj. 1. (a) quadratisch; (b) (of shoulders, chin etc.) eckig. 2. Mth: Quadrat-; s. root, Quadratwurzel f; two metres s., zwei Meter im Quadrat. 3. (a) to get things s., alles in Ordnung bringen; (b) to give s.o. a s. deal, j-n fair behandeln; (c) a s. meal, ein ordentliches Essen. III. adv. Fig: fair and s., (above-board) einwandfrei. IV. v. 1. v.tr. (a) Mth: (eine Zahl) zur zweiten Potenz erheben; (b) (etwas mit etwas dat) in Einklang bringen. 2. v.i. to s. up with s.o., mit j-m abrechnen. ◆'**squared**, adj. s. paper, kariertes Papier.

squash [skwɔʃ]. I. v. 1. v.tr. (etwas) zerdrücken. 2. v.i. (a) (of fruit etc.) zerdrückt werden; (b) (of people) sich quetschen (into a car etc., in einen Wagen usw.). II. s. 1. Gedränge n. 2. orange s., Orangengetränk n. 3. Sp: s. (rackets), Squash n.

squat [skwɔt]. I. v.i. (a) hocken; to s. down, sich hinkauern; (b) to s. in a house, ein Haus besetzt haben. II. adj. untersetzt. ◆'**squatter**, s. Hausbesetzer m.

squawk [skwɔ:k]. I. v.i. kreischen. II. s. Kreischen n.

squeak [skwi:k]. I. v.i. (a) (of mouse etc.) piepsen; (b) (of hinge, shoes, etc.) quietschen. II. s. (a) Piepser m; (b) Quietschen n.

squeal [skwi:l], v.i. (a) (of child etc.) quietschen; to s. with fear, vor Angst schreien; (b) (of pig) quieken; (c) P: (turn informer) singen.

squeamish ['skwi:miʃ], adj. überempfindlich.

squeeze [skwi:z], v.tr. (a) drücken; (Saft, eine Zitrone usw.) auspressen; (b) (force) (etwas in einen Koffer usw.) quetschen.

squelch [skweltʃ], v.i. to s. through the mud, durch den Morast quatschen.

squib [skwib], s. Knallfrosch m.

squint [skwint]. I. v.i. schielen (at, auf + acc). II. s. Schielen n.

squirm [skwə:m], v.i. (of worm, Fig: of pers. etc.) sich winden.

squirrel ['skwirəl], s. Eichhörnchen n.

squirt [skwə:t]. I. v. 1. v.tr. (of liquid) to s. (out), (heraus)spritzen. 2. v.tr. (Wasser, Sahne usw.) spritzen. II. s. (jet) Strahl m; a s. of soda, ein Spritzer m Soda.

stab [stæb]. I. v.tr. to s. s.o., auf j-n einstechen; to s. s.o. to death, j-n erstechen. II. s. Stoß m (mit dem Dolch usw.); (wound) Stichwunde f; Fig: s. in the back, Dolchstoß m.

stable[1] ['steibl]. I. s. Stall m. II. v.tr. (ein Pferd) einstallen.

stable[2], adj. stabil, (lasting) dauerhaft; (of pers.) ausgeglichen. ◆'**stability** [stə'biliti], s. Stabilität f; Ausgeglichenheit f (einer Person). ◆'**stabilize**, v.tr. stabilisieren.

stack [stæk]. I. s. 1. s. of wood/books

etc., Stapel *m* Holz/Bücher usw. 2. Schornstein *m*; (*of factory*) Fabrikschlot *m*. II. *v.tr.* to s. sth. (up), etwas auf/stapeln.

stadium, *pl.* -ia, -iums ['steidiəm, -iə, -iəmz], s. Stadium *n*.

staff [stɑːf], s. 1. (*pole*) Stab *m*. 2. (*a*) Personal *n*; *Sch*: (**teaching**) s., Lehrkörper *m*; **editorial** s., Redaktion *f*; (*b*) *Mil*: Stab *m*. II. *v.tr.* (ein Büro usw.) mit Personal besetzen.

stag [stæg], s. Hirsch *m*.

stage [steidʒ]. I. s. 1. *Th*: Bühne *f*; s. **directions,** Bühnenanweisungen *fpl*; s. **fright,** Lampenfieber *n*. 2. (*a*) Stadium *n*; (*in development*) Entwicklungsstufe *f*; **at an early** s., in einem frühen Stadium; (*b*) Etappe *f* (einer Reise, eines Rennens); **by** (**easy**) **stages,** etappenweise. 3. **landing** s., Landungssteg *m*. II. *v.tr.* (ein Stück, eine Demonstration usw.) inszenieren.

stagger ['stægər], *v.* 1. *v.i.* schwanken; (*nearly fall*) taumeln. 2. *v.tr.* (*a*) (j-n) erschüttern; (*b*) *Tchn*: (etwas) versetzt anordnen. ◆**staggered,** *adj.* (*a*) erstaunt; (*b*) (*of hours, holidays*) gestaffelt; (*c*) *Tchn*: versetzt. ◆**staggering,** *adj.* (*of news*) umwerfend.

stagnant ['stægnənt], *adj.* (*a*) s. **water,** stehendes Wasser; (*b*) (*of trade etc.*) to be s., stocken. ◆**stag'nate,** *v.i.* (*of water, also Fig:*) stagnieren; (*of pers.*) geistig abstumpfen.

staid [steid], *adj.* (*of pers.*) gesetzt.

stain [stein]. I. s. 1. (*a*) Fleck *m*; s. **remover,** Fleckenentferner *m*; (*b*) *Fig:* Makel *m* (**on,** an + *dat*). 2. (*for wood*) Beize *f*. II. *v.tr.* (*a*) (ein Kleid, *Fig:* j-s Ruf) beflecken; (*b*) (Glas usw.) färben; (Holz) beizen; **stained glass,** bemaltes Glas. ◆**'stainless,** *adj.* unbefleckt; s. **steel,** rostfreier Stahl.

stair [stɛər], s. (*a*) Stufe *f*; (*b*) *pl.* **stairs** (*also* **staircase**) Treppe *f*.

stake [steik]. I. s. 1. (*post*) Pfahl *m*. 2. (*money*) Einsatz *m*; **to have a** s. **in sth.,** an etwas *dat* (finanziell) beteiligt sein; *Fig:* **to be at** s., auf dem Spiel stehen. II. *v.tr.* (eine Geldsumme usw.) setzen (**on,** auf + *acc*).

stalactite ['stæləktait], s. Stalaktit *m*.

stalagmite ['stæləgmait], s. Stalagmit *m*.

stale [steil], *adj.* (*a*) (*of bread*) alt/(backen), (*of beer*) abgestanden; (*of air*) verbraucht; (*b*) (*of smell etc.*) muffig. ◆**'stalemate,** s. 1. (*in chess*) Patt *n*. 2. *Fig:* the talks **have reached a** s., die Verhandlungen sind in eine Sackgasse geraten.

stalk[1] [stɔːk], *v.* 1. *v.i.* stolzieren. 2. *v.tr.* sich (an) j-n, etwas *acc*) anschleichen.

stalk[2], s. Stiel *m*.

stall [stɔːl]. I. s. 1. (*for horses & at market etc.*) Stand *m*. 2. *Ecc:* Stuhl *m*. 3. *Th:* **stalls,** Parkett *n*. II. *v.* 1. *v.tr.* (*a* *Aut:* (den Motor) abwürgen; (*b*) *F:* **to** s. **s.o.,** j-n hinhalten. 2. *v.i.* (*a* *Aut:* (*of engine*) absterben; (*b*) *Fig:* (*of pers.*) Ausflüchte machen.

stallion ['stæljən], s. Hengst *m*.

stamina ['stæminə], s. Durchhaltevermögen *n*; *esp. Sp:* Ausdauer *f*.

stammer ['stæmər]. I. *v.i.* stottern. II. s. Stottern *n*.

stamp [stæmp]. I. s. 1. (*mark, instrument*) Stempel *m*; **date** s., Datumsstempel *m*. 2. (*postage*) s., Briefmarke *f*. II. *v.* 1. *v.tr.* (*a*) **to** s. **one's foot,** mit dem Fuß aufstampfen; (*b*) (einen Brief, einen Paß) (ab)stempeln; (*c*) (*affix stamp*) **to** s. **a letter,** einen Brief freimachen. 2. *v.i.* stampfen; **to** s. **about,** herumtrampeln; **to** s. **on sth.,** etwas zertrampeln. ◆**stamped,** *adj.* s. **addressed envelope,** frankierter Rückumschlag. ◆**'stamping,** s. s.-**ground,** Lieblingsaufenthalt *m* (eines Tieres, einer Person). ◆**stamp 'out,** *v.tr.* (ein Feuer) austreten; (einen Aufstand) niederschlagen; (eine Epidemie) ausrotten.

stampede [stæm'piːd]. I. s. (*a*) (*of animals*) panische Flucht *f*; (*b*) (*of people*) Ansturm *m*. II. *v.i.* (*a*) (*of animals*) (in wilder Flucht) davonstürmen; (*b*) (*of people*) losstürmen (**for/towards,** auf + *acc*).

stance [stɑːns], s. Haltung *f*; *Fig:* **to take up a** s., einen Standpunkt beziehen.

stand [stænd]. I. s. 1, *Fig:* **to take a firm** s., eine entschlossene Haltung einnehmen. 2. (*support*) Ständer *m*; **hat** s., Kleiderständer *m*. 3. (*at market, exhibition etc.*) Stand *m*; **news** s., Zeitungsstand *m*. 4. (*for spectators*) Tribüne *f*. II. *v.irr*. 1. *v.i.* (*a*) (*of pers., building etc.*) stehen; **to** s. **still,** (i) (*cease to move*) stehenbleiben; (ii) (*not fidget*) still stehen; **to** s. **firm/fast,** nicht nachgeben; (*b*) (*remain valid*) (*of offer etc.*) bestehenbleiben; *Sp:* **the record stands at 5 metres,** der Rekord liegt bei 5 Metern; **I'd like to know where I** s., ich möchte wissen, woran ich bin; **as things** s./as **it stands at the moment,** wie die Dinge stehen/zur Zeit liegen; **to** s. **as candidate,** sich als Kandidat aufstellen lassen; (*c*) **it stands to reason that …,** es liegt auf der Hand/ist nur natürlich, daß … 2. *v.tr.* (*a*) (*place*) stellen; (*b*) (*bear*) (etwas) ertragen; **I can't** s. **the heat,** ich kann die Hitze nicht vertragen; **I can't** s. **him,** ich kann ihn nicht ausstehen; (*c*) **he stands a good/poor chance,** seine Chancen stehen gut/schlecht. ◆**'stand** a'side, *v.i.* zur Seite treten. ◆**'stand 'back,** *v.i.* (*of pers.*) zurücktreten. ◆**'stand 'by,** *v.* 1. *v.i.* (*of troops etc.*) in Alarmbereitschaft stehen. 2. *v.tr.* (*a*) (j-m) beistehen; (*b*) **to** s. **by a promise,** ein Versprechen einhalten. ◆**'standby,** s. (*a*) *Av:* s. **flight,** Standby-Flug *m*; (*b*) *Reserve f*; s. **troops,** Reservetruppen *fpl*; *Rail:* s. **engine,** Ersatzlokomotive *f*. ◆**'stand 'down,** *v.i.* **to** s. **d. in favour of s.o. else,** zugunsten eines anderen zurücktreten. ◆**'stand**

'for, v.tr. (a) (of abbreviation) (etwas) bedeuten; (b) (tolerate) sich dat (etwas) gefallen lassen. ◆'stand 'in, v.i. to s. i. for s.o., für j-n einspringen. ◆'stand-in, s. Sp: etc: Ersatzmann m; Cin: Double n. ◆'standing. I. adj. 1. to be left s., überhaupt nicht mithalten können. 2. (permanent) to become a s. joke, sprichwörtlich werden; Fin: s. order, Dauerauftrag m. II. s. 1. (in bus etc.) s. room for three passengers, drei Stehplätze. 2. (a) (position) Rang m; social s., gesellschaftlicher Rang; (b) (high s.), Ansehen n. 3. Dauer f; of long s., langjährig. ◆'stand'offish, adj. F: (of pers.) unfreundlich, kühl. ◆'stand 'out, v.i. (a) (of pers., thing) sich abheben (against, gegen + acc; from, von + dat); he stands o. among his contemporaries, er ragt unter seinen Zeitgenossen hervor. ◆'standpoint, s. Standpunkt m. ◆'standstill, s. Stillstand m; to come to a s., zum Stillstand kommen; (of car) stehenbleiben. ◆'stand 'up, v.i. (a) aufstehen; (b) Fig: to s. up for s.o., sth., für j-n, etwas acc eintreten; to s. up to s.o., sich gegen j-n wehren; (of materials etc.) to s. up to hard use, strapazierfähig sein; (c) F: to s. s.o. up, j-n sitzenlassen.

standard ['stændəd], s. 1. Mil: Fahne f. 2. Meas: Eichmaß n; Ind: Norm f; to apply/set high standards, hohe Maßstäbe anlegen/setzen; to be up to s., den Anforderungen/Ind: der Norm entsprechen; below s., ungenügend; (of goods) von minderwertiger Qualität. 3. (level of achievement) Niveau n; s. of living, Lebensstandard m; (c) pl. (values) moral standards, moralische Werte. 4. attrib. (a) Standard-; s. work, Standardwerk n; (b) Ind: (of equipment etc.) serienmäßig. 5. lamp s., Laternenpfahl m; H: s. lamp, Stehlampe f. ◆standardi'zation, s. Standardisierung f; Ind: Normierung f; Meas: Eichung f. ◆'standardize, v.tr. (etwas) standardisieren; Ind: (Produkte usw.) normieren.

stanza ['stænzə], s. Strophe f.
staple¹ ['steipl]. I. s. Klammer f. II. v.tr. (mit einer Klammer) zusammenheften. ◆'stapler, s. Heftmaschine f.
staple², adj. Haupt-; s. diet, Hauptnahrung f.
star [stɑːr]. I. s. 1. Stern m. 2. Cin: Th: etc: Star m; s. part, Starrolle f. II. v. 1. v.tr. Cin: Th: a film starring X, ein Film mit X in der Hauptrolle. 2. v.i. (of actor usw.) die Hauptrolle spielen (in einem Film usw.) ◆'starlight, s. Sternenlicht n. ◆'starlit, adj. sternhell. ◆'starry, adj. (of sky, night etc.) sternklar; (of eyes) leuchtend; s.-eyed, (naive) blauäugig.
starboard ['stɑːbɔd], s. Steuerbord n; to s./the s. side, nach Steuerbord.
starch [stɑːtʃ]. I. s. Stärke f. II. v.tr.

(Wäsche) stärken.
stare [stɛər]. I. s. starrer Blick. II. v.i. starren; to s. at s.o., j-n anstarren.
stark [stɑːk]. I. adj. (bare) kahl; in s. contrast with ..., in scharfem Gegensatz zu ... dat. II. adv. s. naked, splitternackt.
starling ['stɑːliŋ], s. Star m.
start [stɑːt]. I. s. 1. (a) Anfang m; Rac: Start m; for a s., erstens; from s. to finish, von Anfang bis Ende; (b) Antritt m (einer Reise); Abfahrt f; (c) Sp: to give s.o. twenty metres s., j-m zwanzig Meter Vorsprung geben. 2. (a) (fright) to give s.o. a s., j-n erschrecken; (b) by fits and starts, schubweise (arbeiten); ruckweise (vorwärtskommen). II. v. 1. v.i. (a) anfangen (doing sth./to do sth.), etwas zu tun; on sth., mit etwas dat); to s. with, (i) (at the beginning) zuerst; (ii) (in the first place) erstens; (b) Aut: etc: (of engine) anspringen; (c) (in race) starten; (on journey) to s. (out), aufbrechen; (of bus etc.) losfahren. 2. v.tr. (a) (eine Arbeit usw.) anfangen; (b) to s. (up) a business, ein Unternehmen gründen; to s. a fire, (i) (of thing) einen Brand verursachen; (ii) (of pers.) (arson) Feuer legen; (c) Sp: to s. a race, ein Rennen starten; (d) Aut: (das Auto) starten; to s. the engine, den Motor anlassen; Ind: etc: to s. (up) a machine, eine Maschine in Gang setzen. ◆'starter, s. 1. Sp: Starter m (eines Rennens). 2. Aut: Anlasser m. 3. (a) Cu: Vorspeise f. (b) that'll do for starters, das genügt für den Anfang. ◆'starting, s. attrib. s. point, Ausgangspunkt m; Sp: s. post, Startpfosten m.
startle ['stɑːtl], v.tr. (j-n) erschrecken. ◆'startling, adj. alarmierend; (amazing) erstaunlich; (of resemblance) frappant.
starve [stɑːv], v. 1. v.i. hungern; to s. to death, verhungern. 2. v.tr. (j-n) hungern lassen. ◆star'vation, s. Hungern n. ◆'starved, adj. ausgehungert; to be s. of sth., nach etwas dat hungern.
state [steit]. I. s. 1. (condition) Zustand m (einer Person, eines Gegenstands); s. of health, Gesundheitszustand m. 2. (status) married s., Ehestand m. 3. (ceremony) Pomp m; (of body) to lie in s., feierlich aufgebahrt sein. 4. (nation) Staat m; Head of S., Staatsoberhaupt n; affairs of s., Staatsangelegenheiten fpl; the United States (of America)/F: the States, die Vereinigten Staaten (von Amerika); s. school, staatliche Schule. II. v.tr. (seinen Namen, seine Gründe usw.) angeben; (Tatsachen) feststellen; (seine Meinung) äußern; he stated that ..., er sagte, daß ... ◆'stated, adj. on s. days, an festgesetzten Tagen. ◆'stateless, adj. (of pers.) staatenlos. ◆'stately, adj. (of pers., building etc.) stattlich; (of manner, walk etc.) gemessen; s. home, herrschaftliches Haus, esp. Landschloß n.

◆**'statement,** s. Feststellung f; (remark) Behauptung f; esp Jur: Aussage f; **public** s., öffentliche Erklärung f; Fin: s. of **account/bank** s., Kontoauszug m.

◆**'statesman,** pl. **-men,** s. Staatsmann m.

static ['stætik]. I. adj. (a) Ph: El: statisch; (b) (immobile) unbeweglich. II. s. Ph: statische Elektrizität; Rad: atmosphärische Störung.

station ['steiʃ(ə)n]. I. s. 1. (position) Platz m; Fig: s. in life, gesellschaftliche Stellung. 2. (a) Rad: Sender m; (b) (police) s., Polizeiwache f; **lifeboat** s., Rettungsstation f; Pol: **polling** s., Wahllokal n; **weather** s., Wetterwarte f. 3. (railway) s., Bahnhof m; **bus/coach** s., Omnibusbahnhof m; **underground/F: tube** s., U-Bahnhof m. II. v.tr. (a) (j-n, sich) aufstellen; (b) Mil: **to** s. **troops,** Truppen stationieren. ◆**'stationary,** adj. unbeweglich; **to be** s., (still) stehen; **a** s. **car,** ein haltendes Auto. ◆**'station-master,** s. Bahnhofsvorsteher m.

stationer ['steiʃənər], s. Schreibwarenhändler m. ◆**'stationery,** s. Schreibwaren fpl; (paper) Schreibpapier n; **office** s., Bürobedarf m.

statistics [stə'tistiks], s.pl. Statistik f. ◆**sta'tistical,** adj. statistisch. ◆**statisti'cian** [stætis'tiʃ(ə)n], s. Statistiker m.

statue ['stætju:], s. Standbild n. ◆**statu'esque** [-ju'esk], adj. wie eine Statue

stature ['stætʃər], s. Gestalt f.

status ['steitəs], s. (a) Adm: **marital** s., Familienstand m; Jur: **legal** s., Rechtsstellung f; **with no official** s., nicht amtlich anerkannt; (b) **social** s., gesellschaftlicher Rang; s. **symbol,** Statussymbol n; (c) s. **quo,** Status quo m.

statute ['stætju:t], s. (a) Jur: Gesetz n; (b) (of corporation etc.) Satzung f. ◆**'statutory,** adj. gesetzlich; s. **requirement,** Vorschrift f.

staunch [stɔ:n(t)ʃ], adj. treu.

stave [steiv]. I. s. Mus: Notensystem n. II. v.tr. **to** s. **off danger/a disaster,** eine Gefahr/eine Katastrophe abwehren.

stay [stei]. I. s. Aufenthalt m. II. v.i. (a) bleiben; (b) sich aufhalten (in a place, an einem Ort; with s.o., bei j-m); **to** s. **at a hotel,** in einem Hotel wohnen. 2. v.tr. (of pers., horse) **to** s. **the course/distance,** (bis zum Schluß) durchhalten. ◆**'stay** a**'way,** v.i. wegbleiben. ◆**'stay** 'in, v.i. zu Hause bleiben. ◆**'staying,** s. s. **power,** Ausdauer f. ◆**'stay** 'on, v.i. länger bleiben. ◆**'stay** 'out, v.i. ausbleiben; Ind: **the men are staying o.,** die Arbeiter setzen den Streik fort. ◆**'stay** 'up, v.i. **to** s. **up late,** lange aufbleiben.

stead [sted], s. 1. **to stand s.o. in good** s., j-m zustatten kommen. 2. **in his** s., an seiner Stelle.

steadfast ['stedfɑːst], adj. (of pers.) beständig (in, in + dat); (in courage etc.) standfest.

steady ['stedi]. I. adj. 1. fest; (of table, ladder etc.) standfest, (of voice) ruhig; **to have a** s. **hand,** eine sichere Hand haben. 2. (unchanging) gleichmäßig; (of prices etc.) stabil; (continuous) ständig; s. **girlfriend,** feste Freundin; s. **job,** regelmäßige Arbeit. 3. (of pers.) solide; (reliable) zuverlässig. II. v. 1. v.tr. (a) (ein Boot, einen Tisch usw.) festhalten; **to** s. **oneself against sth.,** sich auf etwas acc stützen; (b) (j-n, sich, die Nerven) beruhigen. 2. v.i. (of prices, etc.) sich festigen; **-ily,** adv. 1. fest; **he looked at her** s., er sah sie mit ruhigem Blick an 2. ständig; **to work** s. **at sth.,** beharrlich an etwas dat arbeiten. ◆**'steadiness,** s. 1. Festigkeit f (der Hand, der Stimme usw.). 2. Gleichmäßigkeit f; Com: Stabilität f (der Preise).

steak [steik], s. Steak n.

steal [sti:l], v.irr. 1. v.tr. **to** s. **sth. from s.o.,** j-m etwas stehlen. 2. v.i. **to** s. **away/off,** sich davonschleichen/wegstehlen. ◆**'stealing,** s. Stehlen n.

stealthy ['stelθi], adj. verstohlen.

steam [sti:m]. I. s. Dampf m; **to let off** s., Fig: seinen Gefühlen Luft machen; s. **engine,** (i) Dampfmaschine f; (ii) Rail: Dampflokomotive f. II. v. 1. v.tr. (Fisch, Gemüse usw.) dünsten. 2. v.i. (a) (emit steam) dampfen; (b) (of glass) **to** s. **up,** (sich) beschlagen. ◆**'steamer,** s. Nau: Dampfer m. ◆**'steamroller,** s. Dampfwalze f. ◆**'steamy,** adj. dampfig; (of climate) feuchtheiß.

steel [sti:l]. I. s. Stahl m. II. v.tr. **to** s. **oneself to do sth.,** sich überwinden, etwas zu tun. ◆**'steelworks,** s.pl. Stahlwerk n.

steep¹ [sti:p], adj. steil; s. **drop,** jäher Abfall.

steep² [sti:p], v.tr. (a) (etwas) einweichen (in sth., mit etwas dat); (b) Fig: steeped in **tradition,** traditionsreich.

steeple ['sti:pl], s. (spitzer) Kirchturm m; (spire) Kirchturmspitze f. ◆**'steeplejack,** s. Turmarbeiter m.

steer ['stiər], v.tr. & i. (a) (ein Auto usw.) lenken; (ein Schiff) steuern; (b) Fig: **to** s. **clear of sth.,** etwas vermeiden. ◆**'steering,** s. (a) Nau: Steuerung f; (b) Aut: Lenkung f; s. **wheel,** Lenkrad n.

stem¹ [stem]. I. s. 1. Bot: Stengel m. 2. Stiel m (eines Glases, einer Pfeife). 3. Stamm m (eines Wortes usw.). II. v.i. **to** s. **from sth.,** von etwas dat herstammen.

stem², v.tr. **to** s. **the flow,** den Fluß dämmen; (of blood) das Blut stillen.

stench [sten(t)ʃ], s. Gestank m.

stencil ['stensil]. I. s. (a) (plate) Schablone f; (b) (design) Schablonenzeichnung f. II. v.tr. (a) (etwas) schablonieren.

step¹ [step]. I. s. 1. (walking) Schritt m; **to take a** s., einen Schritt machen; s.

by s., Schritt für Schritt; (b) *Fig:* **a big s. forward**, ein großer Fortschritt. 2. (*measure*) Maßnahme *f*; **to take the necessary steps**, die erforderlichen Maßnahmen ergreifen/treffen. 3. Stufe *f* (einer Treppe); (*door*) s., Schwelle *f*. II. *v.i.* treten; **s. this way**, folgen Sie mir bitte. ◆'**stepladder**, *s.* Stehleiter *f*, (*small*) Trittleiter *f*. ◆'**step 'up**, *v.tr.* (Produktion usw.) steigern.

step-², *prefix* Stief-; **stepbrother**, Stiefbruder *m*; **stepchild**, Stiefkind *n*.

stereo ['steriəu, 'stiəriəu]. I. *s.* (a) **in s.**, in Stereo; (b) *F:* (*system*) Stereoanlage *f*. II. *adj.* Stereo-. ◆**stereo'phonic** *adj.* stereophon. ◆'**stereotype**, *s.* 1. Druckplatte *f.* 2. *Fig:* Klischee *n.* ◆'**stereotyped**, *adj.* stereotyp; *s. phrase*, Klischee *n.*

sterile ['sterail], *adj.* steril; (*germ-free*) keimfrei. ◆**ste'rility** [stə'riliti], *s.* Sterilität *f.* ◆'**sterilize**, *v.tr.* (j-n usw.) sterilisieren. ◆'**sterilizer**, *s.* Sterilisator *m.*

sterling ['stə:liŋ], *adj.* 1. Sterling-; **s. silver**, Standardsilber *n.* 2. **pound s.**, Pfund *n* Sterling.

stern¹ [stə:n], *adj.* streng.

stern², *s. Nau:* Heck *n.*

stethoscope ['steθəskəup], *s.* Stethoskop *n.*

stew [stju:]. I. *s.* Eintopf *m.* II. *v.* 1. *v.tr.* (Fleisch) schmoren; (Obst) kochen. 2. *v.i.* (*of meat*) schmoren. ◆**stewed**, *adj.* **s. meat**, Schmorfleisch *n*; **s. fruit**, Kompott *n.*

steward ['stju:əd], *s.* 1. (*estate manager*) Verwalter *m.* 2. (*attendant*) *Nau: Av:* Steward *m*; *Rail:* Kellner *m.* 3. (*official*) Ordner *m.* ◆'**stewar'dess**, *s.* Stewardeß *f.*

stick¹ [stik], *s.* 1. (a) (*for walking, hitting etc.*) Stock *m*; (*for peas, beans etc.*) Stange *f*; *hockey* s., Hockeyschläger *m*; (b) (*drumstick*) Schlegel *m*; (c) *pl.* **sticks**, Kleinholz *n*; (*firewood*) Reisig *n.* 2. Stange *f* (Sellerie, Rhabarber usw.). 3 *Av:* (*control*) s., Steuerknüppel *m.*

stick², *v.irr.* 1. *v.tr.* (a) (eine Nadel usw.) (hinein)stechen (**into sth.**, in etwas *acc*); **to s. a knife into s.o.**, j-n mit einem Messer stechen; (b) *F:* (*put*) (etwas) stecken (**in/on etc.**, in/auf usw. + *acc*); (c) (*fix with glue etc.*) (etwas) kleben (**to**, an + *acc*); (d) *F:* (*bear*) (j-n, etwas) ertragen; **to s. it out**, es durchhalten. 2. *v.i.* (a) (*of lid, drawer etc.*) festsitzen; (*of door*) klemmen; (b) kleben (**to sth.**, an etwas *acc*); **to s. to a friend/one's word**, einem Freund/seinem Wort treu bleiben; **to s. together**, (*of people*) zusammenhalten; **to s. to the subject/point**, bei der Sache bleiben; (c) **to s. be stuck**, steckenbleiben; (*between two objects*) (fest) eingeklemmt sein. ◆'**sticker**, *s.* Aufkleber *m.* ◆'**stickiness**, *s.* Klebrigkeit *f.* ◆'**sticking**, *adj.* **s. plaster**, Heftpflaster

n. ◆'**stick-in-the-mud**, *s. F:* Rückschrittler *m.* ◆'**stick 'on**, *v.tr.* (a) (*affix*) (eine Briefmarke usw.) aufkleben; (b) *F:* (*add*) (eine weitere Summe) dazurechnen. ◆'**stick 'out**, *v.* 1. *v.tr.* **to s. o. one's tongue**, die Zunge herausstrecken. 2. *v.i.* (a) vorstehen; (*of ears*) abstehen; **to s. o. beyond sth.**, über etwas *acc* hinausragen; (b) *Fig:* (*be noticeable*) auffallen. ◆'**stick 'up**, *v.* 1. *v.tr.* (hang *up* etwas) aufhängen; (*put up*) (etwas) anbringen. 2. *v.i.* (a) **to s. up (above sth.)**, über etwas *acc* hinausragen; (b) *F:* **to s. up for s.o.**, sich für j-n einsetzen. ◆'**sticky**, *adj.* 1. (a) klebrig; (b) (*gummed*) Klebe-; **s. tape**, Klebestreifen *m*; (c) *Fig:* warmes, schwüles Wetter. 2. *F:* (*difficult*) schwierig.

stickler ['stiklər], *s.* Pedant *m.*

stiff [stif]. I. *adj.* (a) steif; (*of fingers*) **s. with cold**, starr vor Kälte; **s. breeze**, steife Brise; (b) *Fig:* (*competition*) scharfe Konkurrenz; (c) (*difficult*) schwierig. II. *s. P:* (*corpse*) Leiche *f.* ◆'**stiffen**, *v.* 1. *v.tr.* (etwas) versteifen. 2. *v.i.* (a) sich versteifen; (*of pers.*) (plötzlich) erstarren; (b) (*of wind*) auffrischen. ◆'**stiffness**, *s.* (a) Steifheit *f*; (b) (*difficulty*) Schwierigkeit *f.*

stifle ['staifl], *v.* 1. *v.tr.* (a) (j-n, ein Feuer usw.) ersticken; (b) (*suppress*) (ein Gefühl) unterdrücken. 2. *v.i.* ersticken. ◆'**stifling**, *adj.* erstickend; **it's s. in here**, hier ist es zum Ersticken (heiß).

stigma ['stigmə], *s.* Stigma *n*; (*disgrace*) Schande *f.*

stile [stail], *s.* Zauntritt *m.*

still¹ [stil]. I. *adj.* still; (*quiet*) ruhig; (*of cider etc.*) nicht schäumend; **to stand s.**, stillstehen; *Art:* **s. life**, Stilleben *n.* II. *s. Cin:* Standfoto *n.* ◆'**stillborn**, *adj.* totgeboren. ◆'**stillness**, *s.* Stille *f.*

still². I. *adv.* a. noch; **he's s. here**, er ist (immer) noch da; (b) (*even so*) **you s. have to pay**, Sie müssen trotzdem zahlen; (c) **s. better**, noch besser. II. *conj.* dennoch; **but s., I did see her**, aber wenigstens habe ich sie gesehen.

still³, *s.* Destillierapparat *m.*

stilt [stilt], *s.* (*pair of*) **stilts**, Stelzen *fpl.* ◆'**stilted**, *adj.* steif; **s. language**, gezierte Sprache.

stimulate ['stimjuleit], *v.tr.* stimulieren; (den Handel) ankurbeln. ◆'**stimulant**, *s.* Anregungsmittel *n.* ◆'**stimulating**, *adj.* stimulierend. ◆**stimu'lation**, *s.* Anregung *f.* ◆'**stimulus**, *s.* Antrieb *m*; *Psy:* Reiz *m.*

sting [stiŋ], *s.* 1. Stachel *m* (einer Biene usw.). 2. (*wound*) Stich *m.* II. *v.* 1. *v.tr.* (a) (*of bee etc.*) (j-n) stechen; (b) *F:* **to s. s.o. for a fiver**, j-n um £5 neppen. 2. *v.i.* **my eyes were stinging**, mir brannten die Augen. ◆'**stinging**, *adj.* stechend; **s. nettle**, Brennessel *f.*

stingy ['stin(d)ʒi], *adj.* knauserig.

stink [stiŋk]. I. *s.* Gestank *m.* II. *v.i.* stinken (of, nach + dat). ◆'stinking, adj. stinkend; Pej: (awful) widerlich; F: s. rich, steinreich.

stint [stint]. I. v.tr. (a) to s. oneself, sich einschränken; (b) to s. (on) sth., mit etwas dat knausern. II. s. to do one's s., seinen Teil beitragen.

stipulate ['stipjuleit], v. 1. v.tr. (eine Bedingung usw.) voraussetzen; (einen Termin usw.) festsetzen. 2. v.i. he stipulated that ..., er machte es zur Bedingung, daß ... ◆stipu'lation, s. Bedingung f.

stir [stə:r]. I. s. 1. (a) (movement) Bewegung f; (b) (excitement) Aufregung f. II. v. 1. v.tr. (a) (Kaffee, Teig usw.) rühren; (b) (move) (etwas) bewegen; (c) Fig: to s. up trouble, böses Blut machen. 2. v.i. sich rühren. ◆'stirring, adj. (of tune, speech etc.) mitreißend; s. times, aufregende Zeiten.

stirrup ['stirəp], s. Steigbügel m.

stitch [stitʃ]. I. s. 1. (a) (in sewing) Stich m; (b) (in knitting) Masche f; (c) Med: to put stitches in a wound, eine Wunde nähen. 2. s. (in the side), Seitenstechen n. II. v.tr. (ein Kleidungsstück, Med: eine Wunde) nähen; to s. up a tear, einen Riß flicken.

stoat [stəut], s. Hermelin m.

stock [stɔk]. I. s. 1. (race) Stamm m. 2. (store) Vorrat m; Com: Lagerbestand m; in/out of s., vorrätig/nicht vorrätig; to take s., Fig: Bilanz ziehen; to take s. of the situation, die Lage abschätzen. 3. Agr: (live)s., Vieh n; Viehbestand m. 4. (for soup) Brühe f. 5. Fin: Aktien fpl; stocks and shares, Wertpapiere npl; the S. Exchange, die Börse. II. v. 1. v.tr. (a) Com: (of shop) (eine Ware) führen; (b) (einen Bach usw.) (mit Fischen) besetzen. 2. v.i. to s. up (with sth.), sich (mit etwas dat) eindecken. ◆'stockbroker, s. Börsenmakler m. ◆'stockist, s. Fachhändler m (of, für + acc). ◆'stockpile. I. s. großer Vorrat m. II. v. 1. v.tr. (Waren) aufstapeln. 2. v.i. einen großen Vorrat anlegen. ◆'stocktaking, s. Com: Inventur f. ◆'stocky, adj. (of pers.) untersetzt; (strong) stämmig.

stocking ['stɔkiŋ], s. Strumpf m.

stodge [stɔdʒ], s. F: Mehlpampe f. ◆'stodgy, adj. (of food) schwer verdaulich.

stoical ['stəuik(ə)l], adj. stoisch. ◆'stoicism [-sizm], s. Stoizismus m.

stoke [stəuk], v.tr. (ein Feuer) schüren; (einen Ofen) bedienen.

stolid ['stɔlid], adj. stur.

stomach ['stʌmək]. I. s. (a) Magen m; (b) (belly) Bauch m. II. v.tr. vertragen.

stone [stəun]. I. s. (a) Stein m; s. quarry, Steinbruch m; a s.'s throw, ein Katzensprung m; (precious), s. Edelstein m; (in fruit) Kern m, Stein m; Opera's, Kirschkern m; (c) Meas: = 6,35 Kilo; (d) s. cold, eiskalt; Fig: a heart of s., ein

steinernes Herz. II. v.tr. (a) to s. s.o. (to death), j-n (zu Tode) steinigen; (b) (Obst) entsteinen (Kirschen, Datteln) entkernen. ◆stoned, adj. 1. P: besoffen. 2. (of fruit) entsteint. ◆'stonemason, s. Steinmetz m. ◆'stonework, s. Mauerwerk n. ◆'stony, adj. 1. (of path etc.) steinig. 2. Fig: steinern; s. silence, eisiges Schweigen.

stool [stu:l], s. 1. Hocker m; folding s., Klappstuhl m; wooden (foot)s., Schemel m. 2. Med: Stuhl m; (bowel movement) Stuhlgang m.

stoop [stu:p]. I. s. krumme Haltung f; to walk with a s., krumm gehen. II. v.i. (a) sich bücken; (habitually) sich krumm halten; (b) Fig: I won't s. to (doing) that, ich werde mich nicht dazu erniedrigen.

stop [stɔp]. I. s. 1. (a) (state) Stillstand m; to put a s. to sth., (mit) etwas dat ein Ende machen; (b) (during journey) Halt m; (longer) Aufenthalt m; to make a s., haltmachen; (c) (for bus etc.) Haltestelle f. 2. (full) s., Punkt m. 3. (organ) s., Register n. 4. Phot: Blende f. II. v. 1. v.tr. (a) (j-n, einen Wagen, den Verkehr) anhalten/(briefly) aufhalten; (eine Tätigkeit) einstellen; (den Ball, eine Uhr) stoppen; (eine Maschine, Aut: den Motor) abstellen; (den Kampf) abbrechen; (einem Vorgang) ein Ende machen; to s. doing sth., aufhören, etwas zu tun; to s. s.o. doing sth., j-n daran hindern, etwas zu tun; Fin: to s. a cheque, einen Scheck sperren; (b) (fill, block) (ein Loch) zustopfen; (eine Lücke) ausfüllen. 2. v.i. (a) (stop moving) (of car etc.) halten; (of pers., watch) stehenbleiben; (b) (stop action) aufhören; (stop talking) innehalten; (c) F: to s. at home, zu Hause bleiben. ◆'stopcock, s. Absperrhahn m. ◆'stopgap, s. Lückenbüßer m. ◆'stoplight, s. Aut: Stopplicht n. ◆'stoppage, s. 1. Stockung f (des Verkehrs usw.). 2. (interruption) Unterbrechung f; Ind: (by workers) Arbeitseinstellung f. ◆'stopper, s. Verschluß m. ◆'stopping, s. s. place, (for tourists etc.) Aufenthaltsort m; (for bus etc.) Haltestelle f. ◆'stopwatch, s. Stoppuhr f.

storage ['stɔ:ridʒ], s. 1. (storing) Lagerung f (von Waren); Speicherung f (von Energie usw.); to take goods out of s., Waren auslagern; El: s. heating, Speicherheizung f. 2. (space) Lagerraum m.

store [stɔ:r]. I. s. 1. (a) Vorrat m (of sth., an etwas dat); (b) (warehouse) Lagerhaus n; (furniture), s. Möbeldepot n; s. room, Lagerraum m. 2. (shop) esp. N.Am: Geschäft n; (department) s., Kaufhaus n. II. v.tr. lagern. ◆'storehouse, s. Lagerhaus n; (b) Fig: Schatzkammer f.

storey ['stɔ:ri], s. Stockwerk n; on the third s./N.Am: on the fourth s., im dritten Stock.

stork [stɔ:k], s. Storch m.

storm [stɔ:m]. I. s. 1. Sturm m; (thunder)s., Gewitter n. 2. *Mil:* to take a **town by s.**, eine Stadt im Sturm nehmen. **II** *v.tr. & i.* stürmen. ◆'**stormy**, *adj.* stürmisch; **s. wind**, Sturmwind *m;* **s. sky**, drohender Himmel.

story¹ ['stɔːri], *s.* Geschichte *f;* (*plot*) Handlung *f* (eines Romans usw.) ◆'**storyline**, *s.* Handlung *f.* ◆'**storyteller**, *s.* Erzähler *m.*

story², *s. N.Am:* = **storey**.

stout¹ [staut], *adj.* **1.** (*strong*) stark; (*of shoes*) fest. 2. (*fat*) beleibt; **-ly**, *adv.* **s. built**, fest gebaut.

stout², *s.* Stout *n* (dunkles Starkbier).

stove [stəuv], *s.* (*a*) (*for heating*) Ofen *m;* (*b*) (*cooker*) Herd *m.*

stow [stəu], *v.* **1.** *v.tr.* **to s. (away) goods, cargo etc.**, Güter, die Ladung usw. verstauen. 2. *v.i.* **to s. away**, as blinder Passagier fahren. ◆'**stowaway**, *s.* blinder Passagier *m.*

straddle ['strædl], *v.tr.* **to s. a horse/a chair**, rittlings auf einem Pferd/einem Stuhl sitzen; (*of bridge*) **to s. a river etc.**, einen Fluß usw. überspannen.

straggle ['strægl], *v.i.* (*of pers.*) umherstreifen; (*of plants*) wuchern; **to s. (behind)**, hinterherzotteln. ◆'**straggling**, *adj.* (*of hair*) strähnig.

straight [streit]. **I.** *adj.* **1.** gerade; **s. hair**, glattes Haar; **with a s. face**, mit ernstem Gesicht; **to put sth. s.**, etwas geradestellen. 2. (*of pers.*) aufrichtig. 3. **s. whisky**, Whisky pur; *Th:* **s. play**, (konventionelles) Theaterstück *n.* **II.** *s. Sp:* Gerade *f.* **III.** *adv.* **1.** gerade; **to keep s. on**, immer geradeaus gehen. 2. (*a*) direkt; **to look s.o. s. in the face/in the eye**, j-m gerade ins Gesicht sehen; **to come s. to the point**, direkt zur Sache kommen; (*b*) (*at once*) gleich; **I'll come s. back**, ich bin gleich wieder da. ◆'**straighten**, *v.* **1.** *v.tr. (a)* (etwas) geradestellen/(by bending) geradebiegen; (*b*) (*tidy*) (ein Zimmer, eine Angelegenheit usw.) in Ordnung bringen; **to s. out a problem**, ein Problem regeln. 2. *v.i.* (*of pers.*) **to s. (up)**, sich aufrichten. ◆**straight'forward**, *adj.* (*frank*) offen; (*b*) (*uncomplicated*) einfach; **a s. answer**, eine direkte Antwort. ◆**straight'forwardness**, *s.* (*a*) Offenheit *f;* (*b*) Einfachheit *f.*

strain¹ [strein]. **I.** *s.* **1.** Spannung *f* (eines Seils); *Tchn: Fig:* (*physical*) Anstrengung *f* (**on s.o.**, für j-n); Belastung *f* (eines Teils); **to reduce the s. on a part**, ein Teil entlasten; **mental/nervous s.**, nervliche Überanstrengung. 2. *Med:* Zerrung *f.* **II.** *v.* **1.** *v.tr. (a)* (ein Seil usw.) spannen; **to s. one's ears**, angestrengt lauschen; (*b*) *Med:* (einen Muskel) zerren; (ein Gelenk) verstauchen; (das Herz, die Augen) überanstrengen; (*c*) (eine Flüssigkeit) filtrieren. 2. *v.i.* zerren (**at**, an+*dat*). ◆'**strained**, *adj.* **1. s. relations**, gespannte Beziehungen; *Med:* **s. muscle**, Muskelzerrung *f.* ◆'**strainer**, *s.* Sieb *n.*

strain², *s.* **1.** Zug *m;* **a s. of weakness/mysticism**, ein Hang zur Schwäche/zur Mystik. 2. (*a*) (*breed*) Rasse *f;* (*b*) (*plant, virus*) Art *f.*

strait [streit], *s.* (*a*) Meeresstraße *f;* **the Straits of Dover**, die Straße von Dover; (*b*) **in dire straits**, in einer Notlage sein. ◆'**straitjacket**, *s.* Zwangsjacke *f.* ◆'**strait'laced**, *adj.* sittenstreng; prüde.

strand [strænd], *s.* Strang *m* (eines Seils usw.); **s. of hair**, Haarsträhne *f.*

stranded ['strændid], *adj.* (*a*) (*of ship*) (auf Grund) aufgelaufen; (*b*) (*of pers.*) **to be s.**, auf dem trockenen sitzen; *Aut:* steckengeblieben sein.

strange [streindʒ], *adj.* **1.** (*alien*) fremd; (*unfamiliar*) unbekannt. 2. (*peculiar*) seltsam; **-ly**, *adv.* **s. dressed**, seltsam angezogen; **s. (enough)**, seltsamerweise. ◆'**stranger**, *s.* Fremde(r) *f(m);* **I'm a s. here**, ich bin hier fremd.

strangle ['stræŋgl], *v.tr.* erwürgen. ◆**strangu'lation**, *s.* Strangulierung *f.*

strap [stræp]. **I.** *s.* Riemen *m;* (*for watch*) Armband *n;* (*over shoulder*) Träger *m.* **II.** *v.tr.* **to s. sth. (down)**, (etwas) (mit einem Riemen) festschnallen. ◆'**strapping**, *adj. F:* stramm.

strategic [strə'tiːdʒik], *adj.* strategisch. ◆'**strategy** ['strætədʒi], *s.* Strategie *f.*

stratum, *pl.* **-a** ['strɑːtəm, -ə], *s.* Schicht *f.*

straw [strɔː], *s.* **1.** *coll.* Stroh *n.* 2. (*single*) Strohhalm *m; Fig:* **to clutch at straws**, sich an einen Strohhalm klammern.

strawberry ['strɔːb(ə)ri], *s.* Erdbeere *f; s. jam*, Erdbeermarmelade *f.*

stray [strei]. **I.** *adj.* (*of dog etc.*) streunend; **s. bullet**, verirrte Kugel. **II.** *s.* streunendes Tier. **III.** *v.i. (a)* (*of pers., animal*) streunen; (*of thoughts*) abschweifen; (*b*) **to s. from the point**, vom Thema abschweifen.

streak [striːk]. **I.** *s.* **1.** (*strip*) Streifen *m.* 2. (*a*) (*element*) **s. of cowardice**, feiger Zug; (*b*) **a s. of luck/bad luck**, eine Glückssträhne/Pechsträhne. **II.** *v.i.* **to s. past**, vorbeisausen. ◆'**streaked**, *adj.* **s. with red**, mit roten Streifen. ◆'**streaky**, *adj.* streifig; **s. bacon**, durchwachsener Speck.

stream [striːm]. **I.** *s.* (*a*) Bach *m;* (*b*) (*current & Fig:*) Strom *m;* **in a continuous s.**, unaufhörlich. **II.** *v.i.* strömen. ◆'**streamer**, *s.* (*paper*) **streamers**, Papierschlangen *fpl.* ◆'**streamline**, *v.tr.* (*a*) (etwas *dat*) eine Stromlinienform geben; (*b*) (eine Firma usw.) rationalisieren. ◆'**streamlined**, *adj.* stromlinienförmig.

street [striːt], *s.* Straße *f;* **in the s.**, auf der Straße; **s. lighting**, Straßenbeleuchtung *f;* **s. sweeper**, (*pers.*) Straßenkehrer *m.* ◆'**streetcar**, *s. N.Am:* Straßenbahn *f.*

strength [streŋθ], *s.* **1.** (*a*) Stärke *f;*

(*physical*) Kraft *f*; **with all one's s.**, mit aller Kraft; (*b*) Intensität *f* (der Farbe, des Gefühls). **2. to be present in great s.**, in großen Mengen anwesend sein. ◆**strengthen,** *v.tr.* stärken; (eine Mauer usw.) verstärken.

strenuous ['strenjuəs], *adj.* anstrengend; **-ly,** *adv.* energisch.

stress [stres]. **I.** *s.* **1.** (*a*) *Tchn:* (starke) Beanspruchung *f*; (*load*) Belastung *f*; (*pressure*) Druck *m*; (*b*) *Psy:* Streß *m.* **2.** (*emphasis*) (*a*) Nachdruck *m*; (*b*) *s.* (accent), Betonung *f.* **II.** *v.tr.* (*a*) *Tchn:* (ein Teil) (stark) beanspruchen; (*b*) (den Wert von etwas, eine Silbe usw.) betonen.

stretch [stretʃ]. **I.** *s.* **1.** (*a*) (*road, rail etc.*) Strecke *f*; **s. of water**, Gewässer *n*; **s. of forest**, Waldgebiet *n*; (*b*) (*time*) Zeitspanne *f*; **at a/one s.**, ununterbrochen. **2.** (*quality*) Elastizität *f*; *attrib.* elastisch; *Cl:* Stretch-. **II.** *v.* **1.** *v.tr.* (*a*) (*expand*) dehnen; (*stretch tight*) (ein Tuch usw.) spannen; (*b*) **that's stretching it a bit!** das ist ein bißchen übertrieben! **2.** *v.i.* (*a*) (*of elastic etc.*) sich dehnen; **material that stretches**, dehnbarer Stoff; (*b*) (*of landscape etc.*) sich erstrecken; (*c*) (*of pers.*) sich strecken; **to s. for sth.**, nach etwas *dat* langen. ◆**stretcher,** *s. Med:* Tragbahre *f.* ◆**stretch 'out,** *v.* **1.** *v.tr.* (sich, die Beine, die Hand) ausstrecken. **2.** *v.i.* (*reach*) langen (for sth., nach etwas *dat*).

strict [strikt], *adj.* streng; (*precise*) genau; **-ly,** *adv.* **s.** (speaking), genaugenommen; **s. forbidden/prohibited**, strengstens verboten. ◆**strictness,** *s.* Strenge *f.*

stride [straid]. **I.** *s.* langer Schritt *m.* **II.** *v.i.* (*of pers.*) mit langen Schritten gehen; **to s. along**, dahinschreiten.

strident ['straidənt], *adj.* (*of voice*) kreischend; (*of sound*) schrill.

strife [straif], *s.* Streit *m.*

strike [straik]. **I.** *s.* **1.** *Ind:* Streik *m*; **to go on/come out on s.**, in Streik treten. **2.** *Mil:* Angriff *m.* **II.** *v.irr.* **1.** *v.tr.* (*a*) (*hit*) schlagen; (das Ziel) treffen; **his head struck the pavement**, sein Kopf ist aufs Pflaster aufgeschlagen; **to s. a match**, ein Streichholz anzünden; **to s. oil**, auf Öl stoßen; *F:* **to s. lucky**, Glück haben; (*fig*) **to s. terror into s.o.**, j-m Schrecken einjagen; (*c*) (*impress*) (j-n) auffallen; (*d*) **to s. a balance**, das Gleichgewicht herstellen; **to s. a bargain**, einen Handel abschließen; (*e*) (*delete*) **to s.** (off/out), (etwas) streichen. **2.** *v.i.* (*a*) (*of clock, hour*) schlagen; (*of enemy*) zuschlagen; **to s. back**, zurückschlagen; **to s. out**, losschlagen; (*in words*) loslegen; (*c*) (*of employees*) streiken. ◆**striker,** *s.* **1.** *Ind:* Streikende(r) *f(m)*. **2.** *Fb:* Stürmer *m.* ◆**striking,** *adj.* (*a*) (*of similarity etc.*) auffallend; (*b*) (*impressive*) eindrucksvoll. ◆**strike 'up,** *v.tr.* (eine Bekanntschaft usw.) anknüpfen. **2.** *v.tr. & i. Mus:* **to s. up (a tune)**, (mit einer Melo-

die) einsetzen.

string [striŋ]. **I.** *s.* **1.** Schnur *f*; *Fig:* **to pull strings**, seine Beziehungen spielen lassen; **s. vest**, Netzhemd *n.* **2.** *Mus:* Saite *f*; *Mus: coll.* **the strings**, (*b*) die Streicher *mpl*; **s. instrument**, Streichinstrument *n.* **3.** (*a*) **s. of beads**, Perlenkette *f*; (*b*) (*queue*) Schlange *f*; Kolonne *f* (von Autos usw.). **II.** *v.* **1.** *v.tr.* (*a*) *Fig:* (*of pers.*) **highly strung**, nervös; (*b*) (Perlen) (auf eine Schnur) aufziehen; (*c*) *F:* **to s. s.o. along**, (deceive) j-n an der Nase herumführen. **2.** *v.i. F:* **to s. along with s.o.**, sich mit j-m auf kurz oder lang zusammentun. ◆**stringy,** *adj.* (*of meat*) sehnig.

stringent ['strin(d)ʒ(ə)nt], *adj.* streng. ◆**stringency,** *s.* Strenge *f.*

strip [strip]. **I.** *s.* **1.** Streifen *m*; **s. cartoon/comic s.**, Comic-strip *m*; **s. lighting**, Neonröhren *fpl.* **2.** *Cl:* Dreß *m.* **II.** *v.* **1.** *v.tr.* (*a*) (*j-n*) ausziehen; (*violently*) (j-m) die Kleider vom Leibe reißen; **stripped to the waist**, mit nacktem Oberkörper; (*b*) **to s. s.o. of sth.**, j-n etwas *gen* berauben; (*c*) (ein Bett) abziehen; (einen Zimmer) ausräumen; (*burgle*) ausplündern; (Farbe, Lack) abziehen, (*with liquid*) abbeizen; (eine Maschine, ein Gewehr) auseinandernehmen. **2.** *v.i.* (*of pers.*) sich ausziehen. ◆**stripper,** *s.* **1.** (*pers.*) Stripperin *f.* **2.** (*paint s.*) Abbeizmittel *n.*

stripe [straip], *s.* Streifen *m.* ◆**striped/'stripy,** *adj.* gestreift.

strive [straiv], *v.i.irr.* **to s.** (to do sth.), sich bemühen, (etwas zu tun); **to s. after/for sth.**, nach etwas *dat* streben.

stroke [strəuk]. **I.** *s.* (*a*) (*blow*) Schlag *m*; (*with whip*) Hieb *m*; (*b*) (*in swimming*) Schwimmart *f*; (*c*) **s. of the brush/pen**, Pinselstrich/Federstrich *m*; (*d*) *Med:* Schlaganfall *m.* **II.** *v.tr.* (j-n, etwas) streicheln.

stroll [strəul]. **I.** *s.* Spaziergang *m*; *F:* (*sightseeing etc.*) Bummel *m.* **II.** *v.i.* schlendern; (*go for a s.*) bummeln.

strong [strɔŋ]. **I.** *adj.* (*a*) stark; (*of colour, health, expression, voice etc.*) kräftig; **s. feelings**, feste Überzeugungen; (*b*) **s. cheese**, scharfer Käse. **II.** *adv. F:* (*machine etc.*) **it's still going s.**, es funktioniert noch tadellos; **-ly,** *adv.* (*a*) **I feel s. that ...**, ich bin fest davon überzeugt, daß ...; (*b*) stark (riechen, schmecken). ◆**stronghold,** *s. Mil:* Festung *f*; *Fig:* Hochburg *f.* ◆**strong-'minded,** *adj.* willensstark. ◆**strongroom,** *s.* Tresor *m.*

stroppy ['strɔpi], *adj. F:* ungehalten.

structure ['strʌktʃər], *s.* **1.** Struktur *f*; (*manner of construction*) Bauart *f* (eines Hauses); Bauweise *f*; (*building*) Bauwerk *n*; (*social*) *s.*, Gesellschaftsstruktur *f*; **s. of a sentence**, Satzbau *m.* ◆**structural,** *adj.* Struktur-; baulich; Bau-; **s. engineering**, Hochbau *m.*

struggle ['strʌgl]. I. s. Kampf m. II. v.i. kämpfen (**for sth.**, um etwas acc); **we struggled through**, wir haben uns durchgekämpft.

strum [strʌm], v.tr. & i. **to s. (on) the piano/the guitar**, auf dem Klavier/auf der Gitarre klimpern.

strut[1] [strʌt]. I. s. stolzer Gang m. II. v.i. stolzieren.

strut[2], s. (for building) Strebe f.

stub [stʌb]. I. s. (short piece) Stummel m; (of tree) Baumstrumpf m; (ticket) s., Kontrollabschnitt m. II. v.tr. (a) **to s. one's toe**, sich dat die Zehe anstoßen; (b) **to s. out a cigarette**, eine Zigarette ausdrücken. ◆**'stubby**, adj. kurz und dick; **s. fingers**, Wurstfinger mpl.

stubble ['stʌbl], s. Stoppel f. ◆**'stubbly**, adj. stoppelig.

stubborn ['stʌbən], adj. hartnäckig; Pej: (of pers.) eigensinnig.

stucco ['stʌkəu], s. Stuck m.

stud[1] [stʌd]. I. s. 1. (nail) Nagel m; Fb: (on boot) Stollen m. 2. **collar s.**, Kragenknopf m. ◆**'studded**, adj. mit Nägeln beschlagen.

stud[2], s. s. (farm) Gestüt n; (stallion) Zuchthengst m.

student ['stju:d(ə)nt], s. Student(in) m(f).

studio, pl. **-os** ['stju:diəu, -əuz], s. Studio n.

studious ['stju:diəs], adj. lernbegierig.

study ['stʌdi]. I. s. 1. (a) Studie f; **to make a s. of sth.**, etwas studieren; **the s. of physics**, das Studium der Physik; (b) pl. **studies**, Studium n. 2. Mus: Etüde f. 3. (room) Arbeitszimmer n. II. v.tr. & i. studieren; **to s. for an examination**, sich auf eine Prüfung vorbereiten. ◆**'studied**, adj. absichtlich.

stuff [stʌf]. I. s. F: Zeug n; **he knows his s.**, er kennt sich aus; (b) **have you got all your s.?** hast du deine ganzen Sachen? (ein Kissen, Cu: Geflügel usw.) füllen; (ein Sofa) polstern; (c) **to s. up a hole**, ein Loch zustopfen; (c) **to s. sth. into sth.**, etwas in etwas acc stopfen. ◆**'stuffing**, s. (all senses) Füllung f.

stuffy ['stʌfi], adj. (a) (of air) stickig; (of room) muffig; (b) (of pers.) spießig.

stumble ['stʌmbl], v.i. (a) stolpern; **to s. (in one's speech)**, sich verhaspeln; Fig: **stumbling block**, (obstacle) Hindernis n; (b) **to s. on s.o., sth.**, zufällig auf j-n, etwas acc stoßen.

stump [stʌmp]. I. s. 1. (of tree, tooth etc.) Stumpf m; (of pencil, cigar etc.) Stummel m. 2. (in cricket) Torstab m. II. v.tr. F: (j-n) verblüffen; **to be stumped**, aufgeschmissen sein. ◆**'stumpy**, adj. stumpfartig; (of pers.) untersetzt.

stun [stʌn], v.tr. betäuben; **the news stunned me**, ich war von der Nachricht wie betäubt. ◆**'stunning**, adj. F: toll.

stunt[1] [stʌnt], v.tr. **to s. the growth of**

s.o., sth., j-n, etwas im Wachstum hemmen. ◆**'stunted**, adj. (of pers. etc.) verkümmert.

stunt[2], s. s. **flying**, Kunstflug m; Cin: s. **man**, Stuntman m; Pej: **publicity s.**, Werbetrick m.

stupefy ['stju:pifai], v.tr. (j-n) erstaunen.

stupendous [stju:'pendəs], adj. umwerfend.

stupid ['stju:pid], adj. dumm, F: blöd. ◆**stu'pidity**, s. Dummheit f.

stupor ['stju:pər], s. Betäubung f; **to be in a s.**, betäubt sein.

sturdy ['stə:di], adj. kräftig; (of pers.) robust; (of structure) stabil.

stutter ['stʌtər]. I. s. Stottern n. II. v.tr. & i. (etwas) stottern.

sty, pl. **sties** [stai, staiz], s. (pig's) S., Schweinestall m.

sty(e) [stai], s. Med: Gerstenkorn n.

style [stail]. I. s. 1. Stil m; (kind) Art f; (manner) Weise f; Cl: **the latest s.**, die neueste Mode; **to live in s.**, auf großem Fuß leben. II. v.tr. (das Haar) modisch frisieren; (for men) (Haare) im Fassonschnitt schneiden. ◆**'stylish**, adj. schick. ◆**'stylist**, s. (hair) s., Friseur m, Friseuse f. ◆**'stylize**, v.tr. (etwas) stilisieren.

sub- [sʌb]. I. prefix Unter-. II. s. Nau: F: U-Boot m.

subconscious [sʌb'kɔnʃəs], adj. unterbewußt; **-ly**, adv. im Unterbewußtsein.

subcontract [sʌb'kɔntrækt], s. Nebenvertrag m. ◆**subcon'tractor**, s. Unterkontrahent m; (supplier) Lieferant m.

subdivide [sʌbdi'vaid], v. 1. v.tr. (etwas) unterteilen. 2. v.i. sich unterteilen. ◆**subdi'vision**, s. (category) Unterabteilung f.

subdue [səb'dju:], v.tr. (a) (j-n, etwas) unterwerfen; (b) (das Licht usw.) dämpfen. ◆**sub'dued**, adj. (quiet) ruhig; (gloomy) bedrückt; (b) (of colour, lighting etc.) gedämpft.

sub-edit ['sʌb'edit], v.tr. redigieren. ◆**'sub-'editor**, s. zweiter (zweite) Redakteur(in) m(f).

subheading ['sʌbhediŋ], s. Untertitel m.

subject I. ['sʌbdʒikt], s. 1. (pers.) Staatsbürger(in) m(f). 2. Gram: Subjekt n. 3. (a) Thema n (eines Aufsatzes usw.); (b) (matter) Gegenstand m (eines Buches usw.); (b) Sch: Fach n. II. ['sʌbdʒikt] adj. 1. **s. to s.o.**, j-m unterworfen. 2. Adm: -pflichtig; **s. to modification**, Änderungen vorbehalten. III. [səb'dʒekt] v.tr. (ein Volk) unterwerfen; **to s. s.o. to sth.**, j-n etwas dat aussetzen. ◆**sub'jective**, adj. subjektiv.

subjunctive [səb'dʒʌŋ(k)tiv], s. Gram: Konjunktiv m.

sublet [sʌb'let], v.tr. (ein Zimmer usw.) untervermieten.

sublime [sə'blaim], adj. (a) (lofty) erhaben; (extremely beautiful) himmlisch; (b) **s. ignorance**, selige Unwissenheit.

◆**sublimate** ['sʌblimeit], v.tr (Gefühle) sublimieren.

submarine ['sʌbməri:n], s. Unterseeboot n, U-Boot n.

submerge [səb'mə:dʒ], v. 1. v.tr. (a) untertauchen; (b) (flood) (ein Feld usw.) überschwemmen. 2. v.i. (of submarine, diver) tauchen. ◆**sub'merged**, adj. unter Wasser; (by flood) überschwemmt. ◆**sub'mersion**, s. Untertauchen n.

submission [səb'miʃ(ə)n], s. 1. (a) Unterwerfung f (von Rebellen usw.); (b) (obedience) Ergebenheit f. 2. Unterbreitung f (einer Frage usw.); Vorlegen n (einer Sache). 3. (claim) Behauptung f. ◆**sub'missive**, adj. fügsam; (servile) unterwürfig. ◆**sub'mit**, v. 1. v.i. sich fügen (to s.o., sth., j-m, etwas dat). 2. v.tr. to s. sth. to s.o., j-m etwas vorlegen; to s. a question, eine Frage unterbreiten.

subnormal [sʌb'nɔ:m(ə)l], adj. (of pers.) geistig zurückgeblieben.

subordinate [sə'bɔ:dinət]. I. adj. untergeordnet (to s.o., j-m); Gram: s. clause, Nebensatz m. II. s. Untergebene(r) f(m).

subpoena [sʌb'pi:nə], Jur: esp. N.Am: v.tr. (j-n) unter Strafandrohung vorladen.

subscribe [səb'skraib], v. 1. v.tr. (eine Summe) spenden; to s. £10, £10 stiften. 2. v.i. (a) to s. to a charity, einem Wohltätigkeitsverein einen Beitrag zahlen; (b) to s. to a newspaper, eine Zeitung abonnieren. ◆**sub'scriber**, s. 1. (to newspaper etc.) Abonnent(in) m(f). 2. (telephone) s., Teilnehmer(in) m(f). ◆**subscription** [-'skripʃ(ə)n], s. 1. (member's) s., Mitgliedsbeitrag m. 2. (for theatre, magazine etc.) Abonnement n.

subsequent ['sʌbsikwənt], adj. folgend; (later) später; -ly, adv. später; (as a result) infolgedessen.

subside [səb'said], v.i. (a) (of ground) sich senken; (b) (of water level) sinken; (c) (of storm, anger, fever, noise) nachlassen. ◆**subsidence** ['sʌbsidəns], s. Bodensenkung f.

subsidiary [səb'sidjəri]. I. adj. untergeordnet. II. s. Com: Filiale f; Tochtergesellschaft f.

subsidy ['sʌbsidi], s. Subvention f; government s., Staatszuschuß m. ◆**subsidize**, v.tr. subventionieren.

subsistence [səb'sistəns], s. Lebensunterhalt m; s. allowance, Unterhaltsbeihilfe f.

substance ['sʌbstəns], s. 1. Substanz f; Fig: the s. (of an argument etc.), das Wesentliche n (an einem Argument usw.). 2. (wealth) a man of s., ein wohlhabender Mann. ◆**substantial** [səb'stænʃ(ə)l], adj. 1. (real) wirklich. 2. (large) beträchtlich. 3. a s. meal, ein reichliches Essen; (b) (of structure) solide; -ally, adv. (a) beträchtlich; (b) (essentially) in the same, im wesentlichen gleich. ◆**sub'stantiate**, v.tr. (einen Anspruch

usw.) begründen.

substandard ['sʌb'stændəd], adj. unter der Norm.

substitute ['sʌbstitju:t]. I. s. 1. (pers.) Stellvertreter m; Fb: Auswechselspieler m. 2. (material, foodstuff) Ersatz m; coffee s., Kaffee-Ersatz m. II. v.tr. to s. concrete for stone, Stein durch Beton ersetzen.

subterfuge ['sʌbtəfju:dʒ], s. List f; (evasion) Ausflucht f.

subterranean [sʌbtə'reiniən], adj. unterirdisch.

subtitle ['sʌbtaitl], s. Untertitel m.

subtle ['sʌtl], adj. 1. fein. 2. (a) (ingenious) raffiniert; (b) (crafty) schlau. ◆**subtlety**, s. (a) Feinheit f; (b) Raffiniertheit f; Schlauheit f.

subtract [səb'trækt], v.tr. (eine Zahl usw.) abziehen, subtrahieren (from, von + dat). ◆**sub'traction**, s. Mth: Subtraktion f.

suburb ['sʌbə:b], s. Vorort m. ◆**su'burban** [sə-], adj. vorstädtisch; Vorstadt-. ◆**su'burbia**, s. usu. Pej: Vorstadt f.

subversion [səb'və:ʃ(ə)n], s. Pol: Staatsgefährdung f; Fig: Untergrabung f (der Moral usw.). ◆**sub'versive**, adj. subversiv.

subway ['sʌbwei], s. 1. Unterführung f (für Fußgänger). 2. N.Am: Rail: U-Bahn f.

succeed [sək'si:d], v. 1. v.i. to s. to s.o. (in office), j-m (im Amt) nachfolgen. 2. v.i. (a) (of project) gelingen; (of pers.) if I s., wenn es mir gelingt. (b) to s. in doing sth., etwas erfolgreich tun. ◆**suc'ceeding**, adj. (nächst)folgend. ◆**suc'cess**, s. Erfolg. ◆**suc'cessful**, adj. (of pers.) erfolgreich; he was s. (in doing sth.), es gelang ihm, etwas zu tun). ◆**suc'cession**, s. 1. (a) (sequence) Folge f; in s., hintereinander; (b) (series) Reihe f. 2. (to title etc.) Erbfolge f; s. to the throne, Thronfolge f. ◆**suc'cessive**, adj. aufeinanderfolgend; -ly, adv. to win two games s., zwei Spiele nacheinander gewinnen. ◆**suc'cessor**, s. Nachfolger(in) m(f); s. to s.o., j-s Nachfolger.

succinct [sʌk'siŋ(k)t], adj. prägnant.

succulent ['sʌkjulənt], adj. saftig.

succumb [sə'kʌm], v.i. to s. to an illness, Fig: temptation etc., einer Krankheit, Fig: einer Versuchung usw. erliegen.

such [sʌtʃ], adj. & adv. 1. solch; s. a man, so ein Mann; he drives at s. a speed that ..., er fährt so schnell, daß ...; s. a thing, so etwas, F: so was; s. big houses, so große/solche große Häuser; s. a long time, so lange; s. was his courage that ..., so groß war sein Mut, daß ...; some s. plan, irgend so ein Plan. 2. s. as, (so) wie; men s. as you/s. men as you, Männer wie Sie; F: s. as? zum Beispiel? ◆**'suchlike**. I. adj. F: derartig. II. pron. usu. pl. and s., und dergleichen.

suck [sʌk], v.tr. & i. (a) (etwas) saugen (out of, aus + dat); (b) **to s. sweets/an ice-cream,** Bonbons/ein Eis lutschen. ◆'**suck 'down,** v.tr. (of current, bog etc.) (j-n, etwas) hinunterziehen. ◆'**sucker,** s. P: (pers.) Dussel m. ◆'**suckle,** v.tr. (ein Jungtier) säugen; (ein Baby) stillen. ◆'**suck 'up,** v. 1. v.tr. (Flüssigkeit usw.) aufsaugen. 2. v.i. F: **to s. up to s.o.,** j-m um den Bart gehen. ◆'**suction,** s. (action) Saugen n; (effect) Saugwirkung f; s. **pump,** Saugpumpe f.

Sudan [suːˈdæn, suːˈdɔːn]. Pr. n. the S., der Sudan m. ◆**Sudanese** [-dəˈniːz]. I. adj. sudanesisch. II. s. Sudanese m; Sudanesin f.

sudden ['sʌdn]. I. adj. plötzlich. II. adv. phr. **all of a s.,** ganz plötzlich; **-ly,** adv. plötzlich.

suds [sʌdz], s.pl. **(soap-)s.,** Seifenlauge f.

sue [suː, sjuː], v.tr. Jur: **to s. s.o.,** gegen j-n gerichtlich vorgehen.

suede [sweɪd], s. Wildleder n.

suet ['suːɪt], s. Rindertalg m.

suffer ['sʌfər], v. 1. v.tr. (a) (Verluste, Schmerzen, den Tod usw.) erleiden; **to s. damage,** beschädigt werden; (b) (bear) (j-s Launen usw.) ertragen. 2. v.i. leiden **(from an illness,** an einer Krankheit; **from neglect** etc., unter Vernachlässigung usw.). ◆'**sufferer,** s. Leidende(r) f(m). ◆'**suffering.** I. adj. leidend. II. s. Leiden n.

suffice [səˈfaɪs], v.i. genügen; **s. it to say,** kurz und gut. ◆**su'fficient,** adj. genügend; **£100 will be s.,** hundert Pfund werden genügen/reichen.

suffix ['sʌfɪks], s. Gram: Nachsilbe f.

suffocate ['sʌfəkeɪt], v.tr. & i. ersticken. ◆'**suffocating,** adj. erstickend. ◆**suffo'cation,** s. Ersticken n.

suffrage ['sʌfrɪdʒ], s. Wahlrecht n.

sugar ['ʃugər]. I. s. Zucker m; s. **cane,** Zuckerrohr n; s. **lump,** Stück n Zucker. II. v.tr. zuckern. ◆'**sugary,** adj. (a) zuckrig; (too) s., zu süß; (b) Pej: (of smile, words etc.) zuckersüß.

suggest [səˈdʒest], v.tr. (a) **to s. sth. to s.o.,** j-m etwas vorschlagen/(recommend) nahelegen; (b) (indicate) (of evidence etc.) (auf etwas acc) hindeuten; **this shape suggests a rabbit,** diese Form erinnert an ein Kaninchen; (c) (assert) (etwas) behaupten. ◆**su'ggestion,** s. (a) Vorschlag m; **to make a s.,** etwas vorschlagen; **at his s.,** auf seinen Vorschlag hin; (b) Behauptung f; (c) (trace) Spur f. ◆**su'ggestive,** adj. (a) vielsagend; (b) (of remark etc.) zweideutig.

suicide ['sjuːɪsaɪd], s. (act) Selbstmord m; **to commit s.,** Selbstmord begehen; **attempted s.,** Selbstmordversuch m. ◆**sui'cidal,** adj. s. **tendencies,** selbstmörderische Neigungen; F: **I feel s.,** ich könnte mich umbringen.

suit [suːt, sjuːt]. I. s. 1. Jur: Klage f. 2. Cl: (man's) Anzug m; (woman's) Kostüm n. 3. (in cards) Farbe f; **to follow s.,** Fig: dasselbe tun. II. v.tr. (a) (of pers.) **to be suited to sth.,** für etwas acc geeignet sein; (b) (of thing) (j-m) passen; **I shall do it when it suits me,** ich werde es tun, wenn es mir paßt; **this colour suits you,** diese Farbe steht Ihnen gut. ◆'**suita'bility,** s. Eignung f; Schicklichkeit f (einer Bemerkung, des Benehmens usw.). ◆'**suitable,** adj. passend; **to be s. to/for sth.,** zu etwas dat/für etwas acc geeignet sein/passen. ◆'**suitcase,** s. Koffer m.

suite [swiːt], s. 1. (a) s. **of rooms,** Zimmerflucht f; (in hotel) Suite f; (b) s. **of furniture,** Möbelgarnitur f; **lounge s.,** Sitzgarnitur f. 2. Mus: Suite f.

sulk [sʌlk], v.i. schmollen. ◆'**sulky,** adj. mürrisch; (esp. of child) trotzig.

sullen ['sʌlən], adj. verdrossen; s. **expression,** verdrießliche Miene.

sulphur ['sʌlfər], s. Schwefel m. ◆'**sulphate,** s. Sulfat m. ◆**sulphuric** [-'fjuːrɪk], adj. Schwefel-.

sultan ['sʌltən], s. Sultan m. ◆**sultana** [-'tɑːnə], s. 1. Sultanin f. 2. (raisin) Sultanine f.

sultry ['sʌltrɪ], adj. schwül; (of temperament) heißblütig.

sum [sʌm], s. 1. (a) (total) Summe f; s. **total,** Gesamtsumme f; (b) s. (of money), Betrag m, Summe f. 2. Mth: F: Rechenaufgabe f; **to do sums,** rechnen. ◆'**summarize,** v.tr. zusammenfassen. ◆'**summary.** I. adj. (immediate) unverzüglich; (of dismissal) fristlos; Jur: summarisch. II. s. Zusammenfassung f. ◆'**sum 'up,** v.tr. (a) (kurz) zusammenfassen; (b) **to s. up I would like to say …,** zusammenfassend möchte ich sagen, …

summer ['sʌmər], s. Sommer m; **in (the) s.,** im Sommer. ◆'**summertime,** s. Sommerzeit f. ◆'**summery,** adj. sommerlich.

summit ['sʌmɪt], s. Gipfel m; Pol: s. **meeting,** Gipfeltreffen n.

summon ['sʌmən], v.tr. (a) j-n (zu sich dat) bestellen; (die Feuerwehr usw.) rufen; Jur: **to s. s.o. (as a witness),** j-n (als Zeugen) vorladen; (b) **to s. a meeting,** eine Versammlung einberufen; (c) **to s. up one's courage/all one's strength,** seinen Mut/seine ganzen Kräfte zusammenraffen. ◆'**summons,** s. 1. Aufforderung f (to s.o., zu j-m zu kommen). 2. Jur: Vorladung f.

sumptuous ['sʌm(p)tjuəs], adj. (of clothes, feast) prächtig; **a s. meal,** ein üppiges Mahl.

sun [sʌn]. I. s. Sonne f. II. v.tr. **to s. oneself,** sich sonnen. ◆'**sunbathe,** v.tr. sich sonnen. ◆'**sunbathing,** s. Sonnenbaden n. ◆'**sunbeam,** s. Sonnenstrahl m. ◆'**sunburn,** s. Sonnenbrand m.

◆'sunburnt, *adj. (tanned)* sonnengebräunt; *(esp. excessively)* sonnenverbrannt. ◆'Sunday, *s.* Sonntag *m.*

◆'sundial, *s.* Sonnenuhr *f.*

◆'sunflower, *s.* Sonnenblume *f.*

◆'sunglasses, *s.pl.* Sonnenbrille *f.*

◆'sunlight, *s.* Sonnenlicht *n.*

◆'sunlit, *adj.* sonnenbeschienen.

◆'sunny, *adj.* sonnig. ◆'sunrise, *s.* Sonnenaufgang *m.* ◆'sunset, *s.* Sonnenuntergang *m.* ◆'sunshine, *s.* Sonnenschein *m;* in the s., in der Sonne. ◆'sunstroke, *s.* Sonnenstich *m.* ◆'suntan, *s.* Sonnenbräune *f.* ◆'suntanned, *adj.* sonnengebräunt.

sundry ['sʌndri]. I. *adj.* verschiedene; s. expenses, diverse Unkosten. II. *s. (a)* all and s., jedermann; *(b) pl.* sundries, Verschiedenes *s; (with meal)* Beilagen *fpl.*

sunken ['sʌŋkən], *adj. (of wreck etc.)* versunken; *(of garden, bath etc.)* versenkt.

super ['su:pər]. I. *adj. F:* toll. II. *prefix* Super-, Über-.

superannuation [su:pərænju'eiʃən], *s.* Pension *f.*

superb [su:'pə:b], *adj. (outstanding)* hervorragend; *(beautiful)* herrlich.

supercilious [su:pə'siliəs], *adj. (of manner)* hochnäsig; *(of remark)* geringschätzig.

superficial [su:pə'fiʃ(ə)l], *adj.* oberflächlich.

superfluous [su:'pə:fluəs], *adj.* überflüssig.

superimpose [su:pərim'pouz], *v.tr.* (etwas) darüberlegen; to s. sth. on sth., etwas über etwas *acc* legen.

superintendent [su:pərin'tendənt], *s.* Direktor *m; Adm:* Aufsichtsbeamte(r) *m;* police s., Polizeikommissar *m.*

superior [su:'piəriər]. I. *adj.* 1. *(a) (better) (of pers.)* überlegen (to s.o., j-m); *(of thing)* besser (to, als). 2. *(higher) Mil: etc:* s. officer, Vorgesetzter *m; Jur:* s. court, höhere Instanz. 3. *(supercilious)* überheblich. II. *s. (a) (at work etc.)* Vorgesetzte(r) *f(m); (b) Ecc:* Mother S., Oberin *f.* ◆superiority [-'ɔriti], *s.* 1. Überlegenheit *f* (over, über + *dat);* s. in strength, Übermacht *f.* 2. Überheblichkeit *f.*

superlative [su:'pə:lətiv]. I. *adj.* unübertrefflich. II. *s. Gram:* Superlativ *m.*

superman, *pl.* -men ['su:pəmæn, -men], *s.* Übermensch *m.*

supermarket ['su:pəma:kit], *s.* Supermarkt *m.*

supernatural [su:pə'nætʃ(ə)rəl], *adj.* übernatürlich.

superpower ['su:pəpauər], *s. Pol:* Supermacht *f.*

supersede [su:pə'si:d], *v.tr.* (etwas) ersetzen (by sth., durch etwas *acc);* a method now superseded, eine jetzt überholte Methode.

supersonic [su:pə'sɔnik], *adj.* Überschall-.

superstition [su:pə'stiʃ(ə)n], *s.* Aberglau-

be *m.* ◆super'stitious, *adj.* abergläubisch.

superstructure ['su:pəstrʌktʃər], *s.* Oberbau *m; Nau:* Aufbauten *mpl.*

supervise ['su:pəvaiz], *v.tr.* beaufsichtigen. ◆supervision [-'viʒ(ə)n], *s.* Beaufsichtigung *f;* under police s., unter Polizeiaufsicht *f.* ◆'supervisor, *s.* Aufseher *m.*

supper ['sʌpər], *s.* Abendessen *n;* to have s., zu Abend essen; *Ecc:* the Last S., das letzte Abendmahl.

supple ['sʌpl], *adj.* geschmeidig; *(flexible)* biegsam.

supplement. I. ['sʌplimənt] *s.* 1. *(addition)* Ergänzung *f* (to, gen). 2. *(a)* Beilage *f; (to book, report)* Nachtrag *m; (b) Rail: etc: (to fare)* Zuschlag *m.* II. ['sʌplimənt] *v.tr.* to s. one's income by sth., sein Einkommen durch etwas *acc* ergänzen. ◆supple'mentary, *adj.* zusätzlich.

supply [sə'plai]. I. *s.* 1. *(act)* Versorgung *f* (of, mit + *dat); (delivery)* Lieferung *f; Tchn:* Zufuhr *f* (von Öl usw.); in short s., knapp. 2. *(store)* Vorrat *m* (of, an + *dat);* supplies, Vorräte *mpl; (food)* Proviant *m;* office supplies, Bürobedarf *m.* II. *v.tr. (a)* to s. s.o. with sth./sth. to s.o., j-n mit etwas *dat* versorgen; *(b) Com:* (j-n) beliefern; (Waren) liefern. ◆su'pplier, *s.* Lieferant *m* (von Waren).

support [sə'pɔ:t]. I. *s.* 1. *(a) (act)* Unterstützung *f;* to be without means of s., mittellos sein. 2. *(object)* Stütze *f; (of arch etc.)* Träger *m.* II. *v.tr. (a)* (j-n, einen Bogen usw.) stützen; *(b) Fig: (with money, help)* unterstützen; *(with comfort)* (j-m) beistehen; *(eine Theorie, einen Anspruch)* bestätigen; *(c)* (j-n, eine Familie) erhalten/*feed* ernähren. ◆su'porter, *s.* Verfechter *m* (einer Sache); *Fb: etc:* Anhänger *m.* ◆su'pporting, *adj. (a)* stützend; Stütz-; s. wall, Stützmauer *f; (b) Th: Cin:* s. cast, Mitspieler *mpl;* s. role, Nebenrolle *f.*

suppose [sə'pouz], *v.tr. (a) (treat as fact)* (etwas) annehmen; I s./supposing (that) ... angenommen, daß ...; *(b) (imagine)* (etwas) vermuten, *(think)* glauben, I s. so, es ist wohl anzunehmen; *(c)* to be supposed to do sth., etwas tun sollen; I'm not really supposed to be here, eigentlich dürfte ich nicht hier sein. ◆su'pposed, *adj.* vermeintlich; -ly, *adv.* vermutlich. ◆suppo'sition [sʌpə'ziʃ(ə)n], *s.* Vermutung *f; (assumption)* Annahme *f.*

suppress [sə'pres], *v.tr.* unterdrücken; *(eine Veröffentlichung)* verbieten; *(einen Skandal, die Wahrheit)* vertuschen. ◆su'ppression, *s.* 1. Unterdrückung *f.* 2. Verbot *m; (hushing up)* Vertuschen *n.* ◆su'ppressor, *s.* 1. Unterdrücker *m.* 2. *El:* Entstörer *m.*

supreme [su:(')pri:m], *adj. (a) (highest)* höchste(r,s); *(in rank)* oberste(r,s); *(b)* (*unbeatable*) unübertrefflich; *Sp:* unschlagbar; (*c*) (*ultimate*) äußerste(r,s). ◆**supremacy** [-'preməsɪ], *s.* Vorherrschaft *f* (*over*, über + *acc*); Oberhoheit *f* (der Kirche, des Staates).

surcharge ['sə:tʃɑ:dʒ], *s.* Zuschlag *m.*

sure [ʃuər]. I. *adj.* sicher; *s.* of oneself, selbstsicher; **he's s. to know**, er wird es bestimmt wissen; **to make s. of sth.**, sich einer Sache vergewissern; (*check*) etwas prüfen; **just to make s.**, (einfach) um sicherzugehen; **s. footing**, fester Halt. II. *adv.* **s. enough he was there**, er war wie erwartet/tatsächlich da; **-ly**, *adv.* 1. sicher; **slowly but s.**, langsam aber sicher. 2. (*intensive*) doch; **s. you don't believe that!** das glauben Sie doch nicht im Ernst! ◆**'sure-'footed**, *adj.* mit sicherem Tritt.

surf [sə:f]. I. *s.* Brandung *f.* II. *v.i.* wellenreiten. ◆**'surfboard**, *s.* Surfbrett *n.* ◆**'surfing**, *s.* Wellenreiten *n*, Surfing *n.*

surface ['sə:fis]. I. *s.* 1. (*top, exterior*) Oberfläche *f;* (*road*) **s.**, Straßendecke *f.* 2. (*area*) Fläche *f.* II. *v.* 1. *v.tr.* (eine Straße) asphaltieren. 2. *v.i.* auftauchen.

surge [sə:dʒ]. I. *s.* (*a*) Schwall *m* (des Wassers usw.); **s. of power**, Kräftestoß *m;* (*b*) *Fig:* Aufwallung *f* (von Freude, Zorn usw.). II. *v.i.* (*of sea*) wogen; (*of crowd*) **to s. forward**, nach vorn drängen.

surgeon ['sə:dʒən], *s.* Chirurg *m.* ◆**'surgery**, *s.* 1. Chirurgie *f; further s. is not necessary*, weitere chirurgische Eingriffe sind nicht nötig. 2. (*place*) Praxis *f; s.* (*hours*), Sprechstunden *fpl.* ◆**'surgical**, *adj.* chirurgisch; **s. appliances**, Sanitätsartikel *mpl.*

surly ['sə:lɪ], *adj.* griesgrämig; (*in speech*) schroff; (*rude*) grob.

surmise [sə(:)'maɪz], *v.tr.* (etwas) vermuten.

surmount [sə(:)'maunt], *v.tr.* überwinden.

surname ['sə:neɪm], *s.* Familienname *m.*

surpass [sə(:)'pɑ:s], *v.tr.* übertreffen.

surplice ['sə:plɪs], *s.* Chorhemd *n.*

surplus ['sə:pləs], *s.* (*a*) Überschuß *m* (of sth., an etwas *dat*); (*b*) *attrib.* überschüssig; Über-.

surprise [sə'praɪz]. I. *s.* 1. Überraschung *f;* **to take s.o. by s.**, j-n überraschen/*Mil:* überrumpeln; **s. visit**, unerwarteter Besuch. II. *v.tr.* (j-n) überraschen; **surprised at sth.**, von etwas *dat* überrascht; **I'm surprised at you!** ich staune über Sie! ◆**sur'prising**, *adj.* überraschend.

surrealism [sə'rɪəlɪzm], *s.* Surrealismus *m.* ◆**su'realist**. I. *s.* Surrealist(in) *m(f).* II. *adj.* surrealistisch.

surrender [sə'rendər]. I. *s.* 1. (*handing over*) Übergabe *f* (einer Sache, *Mil:* einer Festung usw.); Auslieferung *f* (von Gefangenen usw.). 2. *Mil:* Kapitulation *f* (eines Heeres). II. *v.* 1. *v.tr.* (*a*) (etwas) übergeben; (Gefangene usw.) ausliefern; (*b*) (*give up*) (einen Besitz) aufgeben; **to**

s. a right, auf ein Recht verzichten. 2. *v.i.* **to s.** (**to the enemy**), sich (dem Feind) ergeben; **to s.** (**to the police**), sich der Polizei stellen.

surreptitious [sʌrəp'tɪʃəs], *adj.* heimlich.

surround [sə'raund]. I. *s.* Umrandung *f.* II. *v.tr.* (*a*) (j-n, etwas) umgeben; (*b*) *Mil:* umzingeln. ◆**su'rrounding**, *adj.* umliegend. ◆**su'rroundings**, *s.pl.* Umgebung *f.*

surveillance [sə(:)'veɪləns], *s.* Überwachung *f.*

survey. I. ['sə:veɪ] *s.* 1. (*a*) (*esp. written*) Übersicht *f* (of, über + *acc*); (*b*) (*examination*) Untersuchung *f;* (*c*) (*opinion poll*) Umfrage *f.* 2. (*of land etc.*) Vermessung *f;* **air/aerial s.**, Luftbildmessung *f.* II. [sə(:)'veɪ] *v.tr.* (*a*) (from high point) überblicken; (*b*) (*examine*) (etwas) untersuchen; (*c*) (*land usw.*) vermessen. ◆**sur'veying**, *s.* Vermessung *f.* ◆**sur'veyor**, *s.* (**land**) **s.**, Landvermesser *m.*

survival [sə'vaɪv(ə)l], *s.* Überleben *n.* ◆**sur'vive**, *v.tr. & i.* überleben. ◆**sur'vivor**, *s.* Überlebende(r) *f(m).*

susceptible [sə'septɪbl], *adj.* empfindlich; **s. to pain**, schmerzempfindlich; **s. to a disease**, für eine Krankheit anfällig. ◆**suscepti'bility**, *s.* Anfälligkeit *f* (**to an illness etc.**, gegen/für eine Krankheit usw.); **s. to impressions**, Empfänglichkeit *f* für Eindrücke.

suspect. I. ['sʌspekt]. 1. *adj.* (*of pers.*) verdächtig; (*of thing*) suspekt. 2. *s.* Verdächtige(r) *f(m).* II. [sə'spekt] *v.tr.* (*a*) verdächtigen (**of a murder etc.**, eines Mordes usw.); (*b*) (*etwas*) vermuten.

suspend [sə'spend], *v.tr.* (*a*) (*hang*) (etwas) aufhängen; **suspended in midair**, in der Luft hängend; (*b*) (*stop*) (Zahlungen, ein Verfahren usw.) einstellen; (*c*) *Jur:* **suspended sentence**, Urteil *n* mit Bewährung; (*d*) (*ban*) (ein Mitglied) suspendieren; *Sp:* (einen Sportler) sperren. ◆**sus'pender**, *s.* (*a*) Strumpfhalter *m;* **s. belt**, Strumpfbandgürtel *m;* (*b*) *pl. N.Am:* Hosenträger *mpl.* ◆**sus'pense**, *s.* Spannung *f.* ◆**sus'pension**, *s.* 1. (*a*) **s. bridge**, Hängebrücke *f;* (*b*) *Aut:* Radaufhängung *f.* 2. Ausschließen *n* (eines Vereinsmitglieds usw.); *Sp:* Sperrung *f* (eines Spielers).

suspicion [sə'spɪʃ(ə)n], *s.* 1. (*a*) Verdacht *m;* (*b*) (*state*) Mißtrauen *n;* **to regard s.o. with s.**, j-n mit Mißtrauen betrachten. 2. (*trace*) Spur *f.* ◆**sus'picious**, *adj.* (*a*) (*of behaviour etc.*) verdächtig; (*b*) (*of glance, attitude, pers.*) mißtrauisch (**about s.o., sth.**, gegen j-n, etwas *acc*); **to be s. of s.o.**, j-n verdächtigen; **-ly**, *adv.* (*a*) **to behave s.**, sich verdächtig benehmen; (*b*) **to look s. at s.o.**, j-n mißtrauisch ansehen.

sustain [sə'steɪn], *v.tr.* (*a*) (*keep going*) (j-n) erhalten; (*b*) (*suffer*) (eine Niederlage, eine Verletzung usw.) erleiden; (*c*) *(withstand)* (einen Druck usw.) aushalten; (einem Angriff) standhalten. ◆**sus'tained**, *adj.* Dauer-; *(of interest etc.)* anhaltend.

sustenance ['sʌstinəns], *s. (food)* Nahrung *f.*

swab [swɔb]. **I.** *s. Med: (a)* Tupfer *m; (b) (specimen)* Abstrich *m.* **II.** *v.tr.* (das Deck) schrubben.

swagger ['swægər]. **I.** *s.* **1.** stolzierender Gang *m.* **2.** *(boasting)* Prahlerei *f.* **II.** *v.i. (a)* stolzieren; *(b) (boast)* prahlen.

swallow[1] ['swɔləu]. **I.** *s.* **1.** Schluck *m.* **II.** *v.tr. (a)* schlucken; *Fig:* (eine Beleidigung, seinen Stolz usw.) herunterschlucken; *(b)* **to s. sth. (up),** *(also Fig:)* etwas verschlingen.

swallow[2], *s. Orn:* Schwalbe *f.*

swamp [swɔmp]. **I.** *s.* Sumpf *m.* **II.** *v.tr.* überschwemmen; *(of waves)* **to s. a boat,** über einem Boot zusammenschlagen; *Fig: (of pers.)* **to be swamped with work,** mit Arbeit überhäuft sein.

swan [swɔn], *s.* Schwan *m.*

swap [swɔp]. **I.** *s.* Austausch *m.* **II.** *v.tr.* **to s. sth. for sth.,** etwas gegen etwas *acc* austauschen; **shall we s.?** tauschen wir?

swarm [swɔːm]. **I.** *s.* Schwarm *m; s.* **of bees,** Bienenschwarm *m.* **II.** *v.i. (a) (of bees)* schwärmen; *(of people, ants)* strömen; *(b)* **to s. with sth.,** von etwas *dat* wimmeln.

swarthy ['swɔːði], *adj.* dunkelhäutig.

swastika ['swɔstikə], *s.* Hakenkreuz *n.*

swat [swɔt], *v.tr.* (eine Fliege usw.) totschlagen.

swathe [sweið], *v.tr.* (j-n, etwas) einwickeln.

sway [swei]. **I.** *s.* **1.** Schwanken *n.* **2.** *Lit: (rule)* Herrschaft *f; (influence)* Einfluß *m;* **to hold s.,** herrschen **(over,** über + *acc).* **II.** *v.* **1.** *v.i.* schwanken; *(gently)* sich wiegen; *(of boat)* schaukeln. **2.** *v.tr.* (j-n, j-s Meinung) beeinflussen; (das Publikum) mitreißen.

swear [sweər], *v.irr.* **1.** *v.tr.* (einen Eid, Treue usw.) schwören; **to s. to do sth.,** sich (eidlich) verpflichten, etwas zu tun; **to be sworn in,** vereidigt werden. **2.** *v.i. (a)* schwören; **to s. by s.o.,** auf j-n, etwas *acc* schwören; *(b) (curse)* fluchen; **to s. at s.o.,** auf j-n schimpfen. ◆**'swear-word,** *s.* Fluch *m.*

sweat [swet]. **I.** *s.* Schweiß *m;* **to be in a s.,** schwitzen. **II.** *v.tr. & i. (a)* schwitzen; *F:* **to s. it out,** es (mit Hangen und Bangen) durchstehen; *(b) (work)* **to s. blood,** Blut schwitzen. ◆**'sweater,** *s. Cl:* Pullover *m.* ◆**'sweaty,** *adj.* verschwitzt.

Sweden ['swiːd(ə)n], *Pr.n.* Schweden *n.* ◆**Swede,** *s.* **1.** *(pers.)* Schwede *m;* Schwedin *f.* **2.** *Agr:* **s.,** Kohlrübe *f.* ◆**'Swedish.** **I.** *adj.* schwedisch. **II.** *s.* Schwedisch *n.*

sweep [swiːp]. **I.** *s.* **1.** *Fig:* **to make a clean s.,** reinen Tisch machen. **2.** *(movement) (a)* Schwung *m* (des Arms usw.);

(b) (of radar) Abtasten *n.* **3.** *(a)* geschwungene Kurve *f* (einer Bucht, Straße usw.); *(b) (stretch)* weite Strecke *f.* **4.** *(pers.) (chimney)* **s.,** Schornsteinfeger *m.* **II.** *v.irr.* **1.** *v.tr. (a)* (das Zimmer, den Schornstein usw.) kehren, fegen; *(b) (of current)* **to s. s.o., sth. along,** j-n, etwas mitreißen; **to s. away obstacles etc.,** Hindernisse usw. aus dem Weg räumen; **I was swept off my feet,** ich war ganz hingerissen. **2.** *v.i. (with broom)* kehren, fegen; *(of wind, rain)* fegen; *(of water)* strömen; *(of pers., vehicle)* **to s. (along,** dahinfegen; **to s. into/out of a room,** in ein Zimmer hineinrauschen/aus einem Zimmer hinausrauschen; **to s. past,** vorbeirauschen. ◆**'sweeper,** *s. (for street, carpet etc.)* Kehrmaschine *f.* ◆**'sweeping.** **I.** *adj. (grand)* großangelegt; *(far-reaching)* weitgehend; **s. gesture,** weit ausholende Geste; **s. statement,** Verallgemeinerung *f;* **s. changes,** tiefgreifende Änderungen. ◆**'sweepstake,** *s.* Rennwette *f.*

sweet [swiːt]. **I.** *adj.* süß; *(a) F:* **to have a s. tooth,** ein Leckermaul sein; *(b)* **s.-(smelling),** wohlriechend; *(c) (of food, water)* frisch; *(d) (of sound)* wohlklingend; *(e) (of child, girl)* lieb, süß. **II.** *s. (a)* Bonbon *n & m;* **sweets,** Süßigkeiten *fpl; (b) (course)* Nachtisch *m;* **-ly,** *adv.* **1.** süß. **2.** *(of machine)* **to run s.,** glatt laufen. ◆**'sweeten,** *v.tr.* (ein Getränk usw.) süßen. ◆**'sweetener/'sweetening,** *s.* Süßstoff *m.* ◆**'sweetheart,** *s.* Schatz *m.* ◆**'sweetie,** *s.* Bonbon *n & m.* ◆**'sweetness,** *s.* Süße *f.* ◆**'sweet-'tempered,** *adj.* gutmütig.

swell [swel]. **I.** *s. Nau:* Dünung *f.* **II.** *adj. esp. N.Am: F:* klasse. **III.** *v.irr.* **1.** *v.tr. (a)* **the river was swollen with flood-water,** der Fluß war vom Hochwasser angeschwollen; *(b) (increase)* (eine Anzahl) erhöhen; (eine Menschenmenge) vergrößern. **2.** *v.i.* anschwellen; *(of sail etc.)* blähen; *(grow in number)* sich vermehren; *(of numbers)* ansteigen. ◆**'swelling,** *s. Med:* Schwellung *f.*

swelter ['sweltər], *v.i. (of pers.)* vor Hitze verschmachten/*F:* kochen. ◆**'sweltering,** *adj.* drückend heiß.

swerve [swəːv]. **I.** *s.* Abschwenkung *f; (skid)* Schleudern *n.* **II.** *v.i. (of pers., vehicle)* (plötzlich) abschwenken.

swift [swift], *adj.* schnell. **II.** *s. Orn:* Segler *m.*

swig [swig]. *F:* **I.** *s.* tüchtiger Schluck *m.* **II.** *v.tr.* (etwas) (gierig) saufen.

swill [swil]. **I.** *s. (pig)* **s.,** Schweinefutter *n.* **II.** *v.tr. (a)* (den Fußboden) abschwemmen; **to s. (out) a glass,** ein Glas ausspülen; *(b) P:* (ein Glas Bier usw.) saufen.

swim [swim]. **I.** *s.* **to go for a s.,** schwimmen gehen. **II.** *v.i.irr.* schwimmen; **to s. (across) the river,** den Fluß durchschwimmen. ◆**'swimmer,** *s.*

Schwimmer(in) *m(f)*. ◆'**swimming**, *s*.
Schwimmen *n*; **s. pool**, (*complex*)
Schwimmbad *n*; (*actual pool*) Schwimm-
becken *n*; (*outdoor*) Freibad *n*; (*indoor*)
(*also* **s. bath(s)**), Hallenbad *n*; **s. trunks**,
Badehose *f*. ◆'**swimsuit**, *s*. Badeanzug
m.

swindle ['swindl]. I. *s*. Schwindel *m*. II.
v.tr. **to s. s.o.** (**out of sth.**), j-n (um etwas *acc*) betrügen. ◆'**swindler**, *s*.
Schwindler(in) *m(f)*.

swine [swain], *s. inv.* (*also Pej: of pers.*)
Schwein *n*; *Pej:* **dirty s.!** Drecksau!

swing [swiŋ]. I. *s*. 1. (*a*) Schwingen *n*;
(*one movement*) Schwung *m*; (*b*) (*change*)
Umschwung *m* (der öffentlichen Meinung). 2. (*rhythm etc.*) Schwung *m*; **to be
in full s.**, in vollem Gang sein. 3.
(**child's**) **s.**, Schaukel *f*. 4. *Mus:* Swing
m. II. *v.irr*. 1. *v.i.* (*a*) schwingen; (*of
hanging object*) baumeln; (*of pers. on
swing*) schaukeln; (*of door*) **to s. open**,
aufgehen; (*b*) (*turn*) **to s. round**, sich umdrehen; **he swung round the corner**, er
schwenkte um die Ecke; (*c*) **to s. at s.o.**,
zum Schlag gegen j-n ausholen. 2. *v.tr*.
(*a*) (etwas) schwingen; (*above one's head*)
(ein Schwert usw.) schwenken; (seine
Beine) baumeln lassen; **to s. one's arms**,
mit den Armen schlenkern; (*b*) (*turn*) (etwas) drehen; **to s. sth. round**, etwas umdrehen. ◆'**swing-bridge**, *s*. Drehbrü-
cke *f*. ◆'**swing-door**, *s*. Pendeltür *f*.
◆'**swinging**, *adj.* (*a*) schwingend; (*b*)
F: flott, schwungvoll.

swipe [swaip]. I. *s*. (*wuchtiger*) Schlag *m*.
II. *v.tr*. (*a*) *Sp:* (den Ball) (mit Wucht)
schlagen; (*b*) *P:* **to s. sth.** (**from s.o.**),
(j-m) etwas klauen.

swirl [swə:l]. I. *s*. Wirbel *m*; (*water*) (kleiner) Strudel *m*. II. *v.i.* (*of dust etc.*) wir-
beln; (*of water*) strudeln.

swish [swiʃ]. I. *s*. Rascheln *n* (von Seide
usw.); Zischen *n* (einer Peitsche, eines
Stocks). II. *v.i.* (*rustle*) rascheln; (*of
whip, stick*) zischen. III. *adj. F:* nobel.

Swiss [swis]. I. *adj.* schweizerisch,
Schweizer; **S. German**, Schweizer-
deutsch *n*. II. *s. inv.* Schweizer(in) *m(f)*.

switch [switʃ]. I. *s*. 1. (*stick*) Gerte *f*. 2.
El: Schalter *m*. 3. (*change*) Wechsel *m*.
II. *v.* 1. *v.tr.* (*a*) *El:* **to s. sth. on/off**, etwas einschalten/ausschalten; (*b*) (*change*)
(das Thema usw.) wechseln; (die Produk-
tion) umstellen (**to**, auf + *acc*). 2. *v.i.* (*a*)
to s. on/off, einschalten/ausschalten;
(*change*) **to s.** (**over**), umstellen (**to**,
auf + *acc*). ◆'**switchboard**, *s*. (*in
office etc.*) Zentrale *f*; *Tp:* Apparat, Telefo-
nist(in) *m(f)*; (*b*) *El:* Schaltbrett *n*.

Switzerland ['switsələnd]. *Pr. n.* die
Schweiz.

swivel ['swiv(ə)l]. I. *v.* 1. *v.i.* sich drehen. 2. *v.tr.* (etwas) drehen, (*swing*)
schwenken. II. *s. attrib.* Dreh-;
Schwenk-; **s. chair**, Drehstuhl *m*.

swollen ['swəulən], *adj.* geschwollen.

swoop [swu:p]. I. *s*. (*a*) (*of bird of prey*)
Sturzflug *m*; (*b*) (*raid*) Überfall *m*; (*by police*) Razzia *f*; *Fig:* **at one fell s.**, mit einem Schlag. II. *v.i.* (*of bird*) **to s. on its
prey**, auf seine Beute herabstoßen; (*of
pers.*) **to s.** (**on sth.**), (auf etwas *acc*) stürzen; (*of police*) **to s. on an area**, in einem
Bezirk Razzia machen.

sword [sɔ:d], *s*. Schwert *n*.

sworn [swɔ:n], *adj.* geschworen; **s. en-
emies**, Todfeinde *mpl*.

swot [swɔt], *F:* I. *s*. Büffler *m*. II.
v.tr. **to s.** (**up**) maths, Mathematik büffeln.

syllable ['siləbl], *s*. Silbe *f*.

syllabus ['siləbəs], *pl.* -**uses** ['siləbəs, -əsiz], *s*.
Lehrplan *m*.

symbol ['simb(ə)l], *s*. Symbol *n*; *Mth: etc:*
Zeichen *n*. ◆**symbolic** [-'bɔlik], *adj.*
symbolisch. ◆'**symbolism**, *s*. Symbolik
f. ◆'**symbolize**, *v.tr.* symbolisieren.

symmetry ['simitri], *s*. Symmetrie *f*.
◆**symmetrical** [-'metrikl], *adj.* symmetrisch.

sympathetic [simpə'θetik], *adj.* (*a*) mitfühlend; (*b*) (*understanding*) verständnisvoll; **s. to new ideas**, für neue Ideen
empfänglich; (*c*) (*congenial*) sympathisch.
◆'**sympathize**, *v.i.* **to s.** (**with s.o.**),
(*be sorry*) (mit j-m) Mitleid haben; (*understand*) (mit j-m) sympathisieren.
◆'**sympathizer**, *s*. Sympathisant(in)
m(f). ◆'**sympathy**, *s*. 1. (*sorrow*) Mitleid *n*; (*concern*) Mitgefühl *n*; **to have s.
for/with s.o.**, mit j-m Mitleid haben. 2.
Sympathie *f*; **popular s. is on his side**,
er genießt die Sympathie der Öffentlichkeit.

symphony ['simfəni], *s*. Symphonie *f*.

symptom ['simptəm], *s*. Anzeichen *n*;
Med: Symptom *n* (**of**, für + *acc*).

synagogue ['sinəgɔg], *s*. Synagoge *f*.

synchronize ['siŋkrənaiz], *v.tr.* synchro-
nisieren; **s. your watches**, stimmen Sie
Ihre Uhren aufeinander ab.

syndicate ['sindikit], *s*. Syndikat *n*.

synonym ['sinənim], *s*. Synonym *n*.
◆**synonymous** [-'nɔniməs], *adj.* synonym; **s. with sth.**, gleichbedeutend mit
etwas *dat.*

synopsis, *pl.* -**ses** [si'nɔpsis, -si:z], *s*. In-
haltsangabe *f*.

syntax ['sintæks], *s*. Syntax *f*.

synthesis, *pl.* -**ses** ['sinθisis, -si:z], *s*.
Synthese *f*.

synthetic [sin'θetik], *adj.* synthetisch,
Kunst-; **s. fibre**, Kunstfaser *f*.

syphilis ['sifilis], *s*. Syphilis *f*.

Syria ['siriə]. *Pr. n.* Syrien *n*. ◆'**Syrian.
I.** *s*. Syrer(in) *m(f)*. II. *adj.* syrisch.

syringe ['sirindʒ]. I. *s*. Spritze *f*. II. *v.tr.*
(*a*) (eine Flüssigkeit) spritzen; (*b*) *Med:*
(die Ohren) ausspritzen.

syrup ['sirəp], *s*. Sirup *m*.

system ['sistəm], *s*. (*a*) System *n*; (*b*) (*of
railways, roads etc.*) Netz *n*; **motorway s.**,
Autobahnnetz *n*; **one way s.**, Einbahn-

straßensystem n; *Data pr:* **systems analysis,** Systemanalyse f; F: **to get sth. out** of one's s., etwas ganz loswerden.
◆**syste'matic,** adj. systematisch.

T

T, t [tiː], s. (der Buchstabe) T, t n; *Fig:* **it suits me to a T,** es paßt mir ausgezeichnet; **T-junction,** Einmündung f (in eine Vorfahrtsstraße).

ta [taː], *int.* F: danke.

tab [tæb], s. (a) (*material, cardboard*) Strippe f; (*metal*) Zunge f; (b) *Cl:* (*loop*) Schlaufe f; (*for hanging up*) Aufhänger m; (c) (*label*) Anhänger m.

tabby ['tæbi], s. t. (**cat**), getigerte Katze.

tabernacle ['tæbənækl], s. Tabernakel m.

table ['teibl]. I. s. 1. Tisch m; **to lay the t.,** den Tisch decken; **to clear the t.,** (den Tisch) abräumen; **t. mat,** Set n; **t. wine,** Tafelwein m; **t. tennis,** Tischtennis n. 2. (*list*) Tafel f; (*conversion etc.*) Tabelle f. II. v.tr. *Parl:* **to t. a motion,** einen Antrag einbringen. ◆**'tablecloth,** s. Tischtuch n. ◆**'tablespoon,** s. Eßlöffel m.

tablet ['tæblit], s. 1. *Med:* Tablette f. 2. **t. of soap,** Stück n Seife. 3. *N.Am:* Notizblock m.

taboo [tə'buː]. I. s. Tabu n. II. *adj.* tabu.

tabulate ['tæbjuleit], v.tr. (Resultate) in Tabellen aufzeichnen; (Ziffern) tabellarisch anordnen.

tacit ['tæsit], *adj.* stillschweigend. ◆**'taciturn,** *adj.* (*silent*) schweigsam; (*of few words*) wortkarg.

tack [tæk]. I. s. 1. (*nail*) Zwecke f; *carpet* t., Teppichnagel m. 2. *Cl:* Heftstich m. 3. *Nau:* **to be on a starboard t.,** auf Steuerbordhalsen liegen; *Fig:* **on the right/wrong t.,** auf dem richtigen/falschen Wege. II. v. 1. v.tr. (a) **to t. sth. (down),** etwas festnageln; (b) *Cl:* (einen Saum usw.) heften. 2. v.i. *Nau:* kreuzen.

tackle ['tækl]. I. s. 1. Gerät n; (*equipment*) Ausrüstung f; **fishing t.,** Angelgerät n. 2. (*ropes*) *Nau:* Takel n; *Tchn:* **block and t.,** Flaschenzug m. 3. *Fb:* Tackling m. II. v.tr. (a) (j-n) (mit Fragen usw.) angehen; (ein Problem) anpacken; (b) *Fb:* angreifen.

tacky ['tæki], *adj.* klebrig.

tact [tækt], s. Takt m, Feingefühl n. ◆**'tactful,** *adj.* taktvoll. ◆**'tactless,** *adj.* taktlos. ◆**'tactlessness,** s. Taktlosigkeit f.

tactical ['tæktik(ə)l], *adj.* taktisch. ◆**tactician** [tæk'tiʃən], s. Taktiker m. ◆**'tactics,** *s. pl.* Taktik f.

tadpole ['tædpəul], s. Kaulquappe f.

taffeta ['tæfitə], s. Taft m.

tag [tæg]. I. s. 1. Anhängsel n; (*label*) Etikett n; *price* t., Preisschild n. 2. (*quotation*) geflügeltes Wort n. 3. (*children's game*) Haschen n. II. v.i. **to t. along** (be-

hind), hinterherlaufen.

tail [teil]. I. s. (a) Schwanz m; Schweif m (eines Kometen); (b) *Aut:* **t. light,** Schlußlicht n; (c) **t. end,** Schluß m (einer Prozession usw.); Ende n (der Saison). II. v.tr. **to t. s.o.,** j-m auf den Fersen folgen; (*of police*) j-n beschatten. ◆**'tailback,** s. *Aut:* Rückstau m. ◆**'tailgate,** s. *Aut:* Heckklappe f. ◆**'tail 'off,** v.i. abklingen, schwächer werden.

tailor ['teilər]. I. s. Schneider m. II. v.tr. (einen Anzug) nach Maß schneidern; **well tailored,** tadellos gearbeitet. ◆**'tailoring,** s. (*job*) Schneiderei f; (*process*) Schneidern n. ◆**'tailor-'made,** *adj. Cl: & Fig:* maßgeschneidert.

taint [teint], v.tr. (j-n, Fleisch) verderben; *esp. Fig:* (j-n) anstecken (**with sth.,** von etwas *dat*). ◆**'tainted,** *adj.* verdorben.

take [teik], v.tr.irr. nehmen; (a) **to t. sth. from s.o.,** j-m etwas (weg)nehmen; **to t. a passage from a book,** einem Buch einem Buch entnehmen; **to t. an opportunity,** eine Gelegenheit wahrnehmen; (b) (*capture*) (j-n) festnehmen; *Mil:* (eine Stadt) einnehmen; **to t. s.o. prisoner,** j-n gefangennehmen; **to be taken ill,** erkranken; (c) **to t. a paper,** eine Zeitung abonnieren; (*of seat, table*) **taken,** besetzt; **t. a seat/your seats,** nehmen Sie bitte Platz; **to t. the wrong road,** die falsche Straße einschlagen; **to t. an examination,** eine Prüfung ablegen; (d) (einen Preis) gewinnen; (e) (Nahrung) zu sich nehmen; *Com:* **to t. £3000 per week,** £3000 wöchentlich einnehmen; **to t. a photograph,** eine Aufnahme machen; **to t. sth. to pieces,** etwas auseinandernehmen; (f) (*accept*) (ein Geschenk) annehmen; **the car can t. six people,** in dem Auto haben sechs Leute Platz; **t. it from me!** glaube (es) mir! **to t. sth. the wrong way,** etwas falsch auffassen; (g) (*assume*) **I t. it that you are coming,** ich nehme an, daß du kommst; **I took him for an Englishman,** ich hielt ihn für einen Engländer; **to t. a dislike to s.o.,** gegen j-n eine Abneigung entwickeln; (h) (*require*) (Geduld usw.) erfordern; (Zeit) (eine Woche usw.) dauern; **the journey takes five days,** die Reise dauert fünf Tage; *Gram:* **this verb takes the dative,** dieses Verb wird mit dem Dativ konstruiert; (i) **to t. s.o. somewhere,** j-n irgendwohin führen/(*in car etc.*) mitnehmen; **to t. s.o. to the hospital/to the station,** j-n ins Krankenhaus/zum Bahnhof bringen; **to t. sth. to s.o.,** etwas zu j-m hintragen; **t. it with you,** nehmen Sie es mit. ◆**'take**

'**after**, *v.i.* she doesn't t. a. her father, sie gerät nicht nach ihrem Vater. ◆'**take** a'**way**, *v.tr.* wegnehmen; (*in café*) is it to t.a.? ist es zum Mitnehmen? ◆'**takeaway**, *s.* (*shop*) Restaurant *n* mit Straßenverkauf. ◆'**take** '**back**, *v.tr.* (*a*) (etwas) zurücknehmen (**to** s.o., j-m); (*b*) (j-n) zurückführen; (einen Angestellten) wiedereinstellen. ◆'**take** '**down**, *v.tr.* (*a*) (*from shelf etc.*) herunternehmen; (Vorhänge usw.) abnehmen; (*b*) (*write*) to t. d. a few notes, sich *dat* einige Notizen machen. ◆'**take** '**in**, *v.tr.* (*a*) (*admit*) (j-n) einlassen; (ein Mitglied, einen Untermieter) aufnehmen; (*b*) to t. in a dress at the waist, ein Kleid in der Taille enger machen; (*c*) (*include*) (etwas) umfassen; (*d*) (*grasp*) (eine Idee) begreifen; (*e*) F: (j-n) hereinlegen; **to be taken in**, reinfallen (**by** sth., auf etwas *acc*). ◆'**take** '**off**, *v.* **1.** *v.tr.* (*a*) (etwas) wegnehmen; (*b*) (den Hut) abnehmen; (Kleider) ausziehen; **to** t. o. **one's clothes**, sich ausziehen; (*c*) (j-n) wegbringen; (*d*) F: (*mimic*) (j-n) nachäffen. **2.** *v.i. Av:* starten. ◆'**take-off**, *s. Av:* Abflug *m*, Start *m*. ◆'**take** '**on**, *v.tr.* (*a*) (eine Arbeit) annehmen; (einen Kampf) aufnehmen; (*b*) (*engage*) (einen Arbeiter) einstellen; (*c*) (Passagiere usw.) einsteigen lassen; (Fracht) laden. ◆'**take** '**out**, *v.tr.* (*a*) herausnehmen; **to** t. o. a stain, einen Fleck entfernen; **to** t. o. a tooth, einen Zahn ziehen; (*from bank*) to t. o. **money**, Geld abheben; (*from library*) to t. o. a book, ein Buch ausleihen; (*b*) **the heat takes it o. of one**, die Hitze macht einen ganz matt; **don't** t. it o. on me, laß deine Wut nicht an mir aus; (*c*) (j-n, einen Hund) ausführen; (*d*) to t. o. an **insurance policy**, eine Versicherung abschließen. ◆'**take** '**over**, *v.* **1.** *v.tr.* (etwas) übernehmen. **2.** *v.i.* to t. o. **from** s.o., j-m (in einem Amt) nachfolgen; (*relieve* s.o.) j-n ablösen. ◆'**take-over**, *s.* (*a*) *Com:* etc: Übernahme (eines Betriebes usw.); t. **bid**, Übernahmeangebot *n*; (*b*) *Pol:* Machtübernahme *f*. ◆'**take to**, *v.i.* (*a*) to t. to **flight/to one's heels**, die Flucht ergreifen; **to t. to the road**, losfahren; **to t. to one's bed**, das Bett hüten; (*b*) **to t. to drink**, sich dem Alkohol ergeben; (*c*) **to t. to s.o.**, sich zu j-m hingezogen fühlen. ◆'**take** '**up**, *v.tr.* (*a*) (etwas) aufnehmen; (*raise*) (einen Teppich) aufrollen; (eine Straße) aufreißen; (*b*) (einen Rock usw.) kürzer machen; (*c*) (*absorb*) (Wasser) aufsaugen; (*d*) (einen Beruf) ergreifen; (eine Tätigkeit) beginnen; (*e*) (Zeit, j-s Aufmerksamkeit, Platz usw.) in Anspruch nehmen. ◆'**taking**, *adj.* t. **ways**, gewinnende Art. ◆'**takings**, *s.pl. Com:* Einnahmen *fpl*.

talc [tælk], *s.* talcum. ◆'**talcum**, *s.* t. **powder**, Körperpuder *m*.

tale [teil], *s.* (*a*) (*story*) Erzählung *f*; (*b*) (*untruth*) Lügengeschichte *f*.

talent ['tælənt], *s.* Talent *n*; (*ability*) Fähigkeit *f*; *esp. Iron:* Gabe *f*. ◆'**talented**, *adj.* begabt.

talk [tɔːk]. I. *s.* **1.** (*a*) (*action*) Reden *n*; (*b*) (*what is said*) Gerede *n*; (*idle*) t., Geschwätz *n*; (*conversation*) Gespräch *n*; (*casual*) Plauderei *f*; **to have a** t. **with s.o.**, sich mit j-m unterhalten. **2.** (*lecture*) Vortrag *m*. II. *v.* **1.** *v.i.* (*a*) reden, sprechen (**on/about** sth., über etwas *acc*; **of** sth., von etwas *dat*); **it's easy to** t. du hast gut reden! (*b*) **talking of which…**, da wir gerade davon sprechen…; t. **about luck!** was für ein Glück! (*c*) **to** t. **to s.o.**, sich mit j-m unterhalten; (*d*) (*give away a secret*) reden; **somebody must have talked**, es muß einer geschwatzt haben. **2.** *v.tr.* (*a*) (Deutsch, Französisch usw.) sprechen; (Unsinn, wirres Zeug) reden; **to** t. **sense**, vernünftig reden; **to** t. **oneself hoarse**, sich heiser reden; **to** t. **s.o. into doing sth.**, j-m einreden, etwas zu tun; **to** t. **s.o. round/over**, j-n überreden. ◆'**talkative**, *adj.* geschwätzig. ◆'**talker**, *s. Pej:* Schwätzer(in) *m(f)*; **he's a great** t., er redet viel. ◆'**talking**, *s.* Reden *n*; **no** t. **please!** Ruhe bitte! F: **to give s.o. a good** t. **to**, j-m die Leviten lesen.

tall [tɔːl], *adj.* **1.** (*of pers.*) groß; (*of thing*) hoch. **2.** F: a t. **story**, eine unglaubliche Geschichte; **that's a** t. **order!** das ist ein bißchen viel verlangt! ◆'**tallboy**, *s.* Aufsatzkommode *f*. ◆'**tallness**, *s.* Größe *f*, Höhe *f*.

tallow ['tæləu], *s.* Talg *m*.

tally ['tæli]. I. *s.* (*bill etc.*) Rechnung *f*. II. *v.i.* übereinstimmen.

talon ['tælən], *s.* Kralle *f*.

tambourine [tæmbə'riːn], *s.* Tamburin *n*.

tame [teim]. I. *adj.* **1.** (*of animal*) zahm; (*tamed*) gezähmt. **2.** *Fig:* (*of pers.*, *affair etc.*) lahm; (*boring*) fade. II. *v.tr.* (ein Tier) zähmen; (einen Löwen) bändigen. ◆'**tameness**, *s.* **1.** Zahmheit *f* (eines Tieres). **2.** *Fig:* Lahmheit *f*.

tamper ['tæmpər], *v.i.* **to** t. **with sth.**, an etwas *dat* herumhantieren; (*alter*) etwas unbefugt abändern.

tan [tæn]. I. *s.* **1.** (*colour*) Hellbraun *n*. **2.** (*suntan*) Bräune *f*. II. *adj.* hellbraun. III. *v.* **1.** *v.tr.* (*a*) (Leder) gerben; (*b*) (die Haut) bräunen. **2.** *v.i.* (*of pers.*) sich bräunen; **she tans easily**, sie wird schnell braun.

tandem ['tændəm], *s.* Tandem *n*.

tang [tæŋ], *s.* scharfer Beigeschmack *m*; (*smell*) Geruch *m*.

tangent ['tæn(d)ʒənt], *s.* Tangente *f*.

tangerine [tæn(d)ʒə'riːn], *s.* Mandarine *f*.

tangible ['tæn(d)ʒibl], *adj.* konkret.

tangle ['tæŋgl]. I. *s.* Gewirr *n*; (*in ball*) wirrer Knäuel *m* (von Garn, Haaren); **in a** t., ganz durcheinander. II. *v.tr.* durcheinanderbringen.

tango ['tæŋgəu], *s.* Tango *m*.

tank [tæŋk], s. 1. (container) Tank m. 2. Mil: Panzer m. ◆**'tanker**, s. (a) Nau: Tanker m; (b) Aut: Tankwagen m.

tankard ['tæŋkəd], s. Bierkrug m; (pewter) t., Zinnkrug m.

tantalize ['tæntəlaiz], v.tr. (j-n) quälen, (keep in suspense) (j-n) zappeln lassen. ◆**'tantalizing**, adj. quälend; (of smile) provozierend.

tantamount ['tæntəmaunt], adj. t. to, gleichbedeutend mit + dat.

tantrum ['tæntrəm], s. Wutanfall m.

tap1 [tæp]. I. s. Hahn m. II. v.tr. anzapfen.

tap2. I. s. leichter Schlag m, Klaps m; t. **dance/dancing**, Steptanz m. II. v.tr. klopfen.

tape [teip]. I. s. 1. Band n; (adhesive) t., Klebestreifen m; Rec: (recording) t., Tonband n; t. **recorder**, Tonbandgerät n; t. **measure**, Bandmaß n. II. v.tr. Rec: (etwas) auf Tonband aufnehmen. ◆**'tapeworm**, s. Bandwurm m.

taper ['teipər]. I. s. (candle) dünne Wachskerze f. II. v.i. sich verjüngen. ◆**'tapering**, adj. spitz zulaufend; (conical) kegelförmig.

tapestry ['tæpistri], s. Gobelin m.

tapioca [tæpi'əukə], s. Tapioka f.

tappet ['tæpit], s. Aut: Ventilstößel m.

tar [tɑːr]. I. s. Teer m. II. v.tr. teeren.

tarantula [tə'ræntjulə], s. Tarantel f.

target ['tɑːgit], s. Ziel n; (in archery etc.) Schießscheibe f.

tariff ['tærif], s. 1. Zolltarif m. 2. (price list) Preisverzeichnis n.

tarmac ['tɑːmæk], s. Av: Rollfeld; t. (surface), Teerdecke.

tarn [tɑːn], s. (kleiner) Bergsee m.

tarnish ['tɑːniʃ], v.tr. trüben; Fig: (j-s Ruf usw.) beflecken.

tarpaulin [tɑː'pɔːlin], s. Plane f; Nau: Persenning f.

tart1 [tɑːt], s. 1. Cu: Torte f; (small) Törtchen n. 2. F: (prostitute) Dirne f.

tart2, adj. sauer; (of answer) bissig.

tartan ['tɑːt(ə)n], s. Schottenstoff m; (pattern) Schottenmuster n.

tartar ['tɑːtər], s. 1. Ch: Weinstein m. 2. Med: Zahnstein m. 3. Cu: t. **sauce**, Tatarsoße f.

task [tɑːsk], s. Aufgabe f; Mil: t. **force**, Spezialtruppe f.

tassel ['tæs(ə)l], s. Quaste f.

taste [teist]. I. s. Geschmack m; (a) (sense of) t., Geschmackssinn m; (b) (small quantity) kleiner Bissen m (Käse usw.); Schlückchen n (Wein); (c) (liking) **to have a t. for sth.**, eine Vorliebe für etwas acc haben; (d) **to have (good) t.**, (guten) Geschmack haben; **in bad t.**, geschmacklos; (bad manners) unangebracht. II. v. 1. v.tr. (a) (etwas) schmecken; (ein Gewürz usw.) herausschmecken; (b) (sample) (etwas) kosten; (Weine) probieren. 2. v.i. **to t. of sth.**, nach etwas dat schmecken. ◆**'tasteful**,

adj. geschmackvoll. ◆**'tasteless**, adj. 1. (of food) ohne Geschmack. 2. (of furnishings etc.) geschmacklos ◆**'tastelessness**, s. Geschmacklosigkeit f. ◆**'tastiness**, s. Schmackhaftigkeit f (einer Speise). ◆**'tasty**, adj. schmackhaft.

ta-ta [tæ'tɑː], int. F: Wiedersehen!

tatters ['tætəz], s. pl. **in t.**, zerlumpt. ◆**'tattered**, adj. zerfetzt.

tattoo1 [tə'tuː], s. Mil: 1. (drumming) Zapfenstreich m. 2. (entertainment) Tattoo n.

tattoo2. I. s. (on body) Tätowierung f. II. v.tr. tätowieren.

tatty ['tæti], adj. F: schäbig.

taunt [tɔːnt]. I. s. spöttische Bemerkung f. II. v.tr. (j-n) verspotten.

Taurus ['tɔːrəs], s. Astr: Stier m.

taut [tɔːt], adj. (of rope etc.) straff; gespannt; (of nerves) angespannt.

tavern ['tævən], s. esp. A: Schenke f.

tawdry ['tɔːdri], adj. kitschig-bunt; geschmacklos.

tawny ['tɔːni], adj. gelbbraun; t. **owl**, Waldkauz m.

tax [tæks]. I. s. Steuer f; t. **collector**, Steuereinnehmer m; t. **return**, Steuererklärung f. II. v.tr. (a) (j-n, etwas) besteuern; (b) (weary) (j-n, j-s Kräfte, Geduld) strapazieren. ◆**'taxable**, adj. (of income) steuerpflichtig. ◆**tax'ation**, s. Besteuerung f; **subject to t.**, steuerpflichtig. ◆**'tax-'free**, adj. steuerfrei. ◆**'taxing**, adj. strapazierend. ◆**'taxpayer**, s. Steuerzahler m.

taxi ['tæksi]. I. s. Taxi n, Taxe f; t. **driver**, Taxifahrer m; t. **rank**/Scot: **stance**, Taxistand m. II. v.i. Av: rollen.

taxidermy ['tæksidəːmi], s. Taxidermie f. ◆**'taxidermist**, s. Tierpräparator m.

tea [tiː], s. Tee m; t. **break**, Teepause f; t. **service/set**, Teeservice n; (afternoon) t., Nachmittagstee m; (high) t., frühes Abendbrot n; t. **party**, Teegesellschaft f; t. **trolley**, Teewagen m. ◆**'teabag**, s. Teebeutel m. ◆**'teacaddy**, s. Teedose f. ◆**'teacake**, s. flaches, weiches Brötchen n. ◆**'teacloth**, s. 1. (kleine) Tischdecke f. 2. = **tea towel**. ◆**'teacosy**, s. Teewärmer m. ◆**'teacup**, s. Teetasse f. ◆**'tealeaf**, s. Teeblatt n. ◆**'teapot**, s. Teekanne f. ◆**'tearoom**, s. Teestube f. ◆**'teashop**, s. 1. (café) Teestube f. 2. (shop) Teegeschäft n. ◆**'teaspoon**, s. Teelöffel m. ◆**'teaspoonful**, s. Teelöffel(voll) m. ◆**'teatowel**, s. Geschirrtuch n.

teach [tiːtʃ], v.tr.irr. (j-n, ein Fach) unterrichten, lehren; t. **s.o. sth.**, j-n etwas lehren/F: beibringen; (in school) j-n in etwas dat unterrichten; F: that will t. **him!** das wird ihm eine Lehre sein! ◆**'teacher**, s. Lehrer(in) m(f).

◆**'teaching**, s. 1. Unterricht m. 2. esp. pl. **teachings**, Lehre f, Lehren fpl.

teak [tiːk], s. Teakholz n.

team [tiːm], s. 1. Sp: etc: Mannschaft f;

t. spirit, Mannschaftsgeist m. 2. Gespann n (von Pferden usw.). ◆**'teamwork,** s. 1. Zusammenarbeit f, Teamwork n.

tear¹ [tiər], s. Träne f. ◆**'tearful,** adj. (of pers., voice) weinerlich; (of parting etc.) tränenreich. ◆**'tear-gas,** s. Tränengas n.

tear² [tɛər]. I. s. Riß m (in einem Kleid usw.). II. v.irr. 1. v.tr. (a) (etwas) zerreißen; Fig: torn between two possibilities, zwischen zwei Möglichkeiten hin und her gerissen; F: that's torn it! jetzt ist alles im Eimer! (b) to t. sth. (away) from s.o./out of s.o.'s hands, j-m etwas entreißen. 2. v.i. (a) (of paper etc.) reißen; (b) (rush) to t. along/down/up, dahinrasen/hinunterrasen/hinaufrasen. ◆**'tear a'way,** v.tr. (etwas) wegreißen; I could not t. myself a., ich konnte mich nicht losreißen. ◆**'tear 'down,** v.tr. herunterreißen; (ein Haus) niederreißen. ◆**'tearing,** adj. reißend; to be in a t. hurry, es furchtbar eilig haben. ◆**'tear 'up,** v.tr. (einen Brief usw.) zerreißen.

tease [tiːz], v.tr. (j-n) necken, (maliciously) aufziehen. ◆**'teaser,** s. F: (problem) harte Nuß f. ◆**'teasing,** I. adj. neckend. II. s. Neckerei f.

teat [tiːt], s. Anat: Brustwarze f; Z: Zitze f; (on bottle) Sauger m.

technical ['teknik(ə)l], adj. technisch; t. terms, Fachausdrücke mpl; -ly, adv. 1. technisch. 2. (actually) genaugenommen. ◆**techni'cality,** s. 1. Tchn: technische Einzelheit f. 2. Jur: Adm: etc: Formsache f. ◆**tech'nician,** s. Techniker m. ◆**technique** [tek'niːk], s. Technik f. ◆**tech'nology,** s. Technologie f.

teddy (bear) ['tedi (bɛər)], s. Teddy(bär) m.

tedious ['tiːdiəs], adj. langweilig. ◆**'tediousness/'tedium,** s. Langweiligkeit f.

tee [tiː], s. Sp: (area) Abschlag m; (peg) Aufsatz m.

teem [tiːm], v.i. to be teeming with people, ants etc., von Leuten, Ameisen usw. wimmeln; teeming rain, strömender Regen.

teens [tiːnz], s. pl. Jugendjahre npl. ◆**'teenager,** s. Teenager m.

teeter ['tiːtər], v.i. taumeln; (sway) wanken.

teeth [tiːθ], s. pl. of tooth q.v. ◆**teethe** [tiːð], v.i. zahnen.

teetotal [tiː'təutl], adj. abstinent. ◆**tee'totaller,** s. Abstinenzler(in) m(f).

telecommunications [telikəmjuː-niˈkeiʃ(ə)nz], s. pl. Fernmeldewesen n.

telegram ['teligræm], s. Telegramm n. ◆**telegraph** ['teligrɑːf], s. Telegraf m; t. pole, Telegrafenmast m. ◆**telegraphic** [-'græfik], adj. telegrafisch. ◆**telegraphy** [ti'legrəfi], s. Telegrafie f.

telepathy [ti'lepəθi], s. Gedankenübertragung f. ◆**telepathic**

[teliˈpæθik], adj. telepathisch.

telephone ['telifəun]. I. s. Telefon n; t. number, Telefonnummer f; t. box, Telefonzelle f; t. call, Telefonanruf m; t. directory, Telefonbuch n; t. exchange, Telefonzentrale f; t. operator, Telefonist(in) m(f). II. v. 1. v.i. telefonieren. 2. v.tr. (eine Nachricht) telefonieren. ◆**telephonist** [ti'lefənist], s. Telefonist(in) m(f).

telephoto [teli'fəutəu], s. t. (lens), Teleobjektiv n.

teleprinter [teli'printər], s. Fernschreiber m.

telescope ['teliskəup]. I. s. Teleskop n. II. v. (Teile) ineinanderschieben. ◆**telescopic** [-'skɔpik], adj. (a) teleskopisch; (b) (collapsible) ineinanderschiebbar; (of aerial, strut) ausziehbar.

television [teli'viʒ(ə)n], s. Fernsehen n; on (the) t., im Fernsehen; t. set, Fernsehapparat m; t. announcer, Fernsehansager(in) m(f). ◆**televise,** v.tr. (etwas) im Fernsehen übertragen.

telex ['teleks], s. Telex n.

tell [tel], v. 1. v.tr. (a) (etwas, die Wahrheit usw.) sagen; (etwas, eine Geschichte usw.) erzählen; to t. a lie, lügen; to t. tales, aus der Schule plaudern; Sch: F: petzen; to t. s.o. sth., j-m etwas sagen/erzählen; (b) (pass on) (eine Neuigkeit) mitteilen; (ein Geheimnis) verraten; (c) (inform) to t. s.o. about sth., j-m von etwas dat erzählen; j-n über etwas acc informieren; (d) to t. s.o. to do sth., j-m sagen/j-n bitten, etwas zu tun; (e) (distinguish) (etwas) unterscheiden; (recognize) erkennen; (f) (know) (etwas) wissen; who can t.? wer weiß? 2. v.i. (a) seine Wirkung haben; this tells in his favour, das spricht für ihn; (b) to t. on s.o., j-n verpetzen; ◆**'teller,** s. 1. Erzähler(in) m(f). 2. Com: Kassierer(in) m(f). ◆**'telling,** adj. wirksam; t. blow, wuchtiger Schlag. ◆**'tell 'off,** v.tr. ausschimpfen. ◆**'telltale,** adj. t. signs, verräterische Zeichen.

telly ['teli], s. F: Flimmerkiste f.

temerity [ti'meriti], s. Kühnheit f.

temper ['tempər]. I. s. 1. (a) Temperament n; to lose one's t., ärgerlich werden; (lose patience) die Geduld verlieren; (b) (state of mind) Laune f; to be in a good/bad t., guter/schlechter Laune sein; (c) (anger) Zorn m. 2. Tchn: Härte f (des Stahls). II. v.tr. (a) (Stahl) härten; (b) (seinen Eifer usw.) mäßigen. ◆**'temperament,** s. 1. (excitability) Temperament n. 2. (character) Veranlagung f. ◆**tempera'mental,** adj. launenhaft.

temperance ['temp(ə)rəns], s. Mäßigkeit f; (abstinence) Enthaltsamkeit f. ◆**'temperate,** adj. (of pers.) mäßig; enthaltsam; (of language, climate) gemäßigt.

temperature ['tempritʃər], s. Temperatur f; Med: to have a t., Fieber haben.

tempest ['tempist], s. A: & Lit: (wilder) Sturm m. ◆**tempestuous** [-'pestjuəs], adj. stürmisch; (of pers., nature) ungestüm.

template ['templit], s. Tchn: Schablone f.

temple¹ ['templ], s. Tempel m.

temple², s. Anat: Schläfe f.

tempo ['tempəu], s. Tempo n.

temporal ['tempərəl], adj. 1. zeitlich. 2. (secular) weltlich.

temporary ['temp(ə)rəri], adj. (provisional) vorläufig, provisorisch; **-ily**, adv. vorübergehend.

tempt [tem(p)t], v.tr. to t. s.o. to do sth., j-n verlocken, etwas zu tun; to be tempted, in Versuchung kommen. ◆**temp'tation**, s. Versuchung f. ◆**'tempting**, adj. verführerisch; (of offer, food) verlockend.

ten [ten], num. adj. zehn.

tenable ['tenəbl], adj. (of opinion) vertretbar.

tenacious [tə'neiʃəs], adj. zäh. ◆**tenacity** [-'næsiti], s. Zähigkeit f.

tenant ['tenənt], s. (of house etc.) Mieter m; (of estate) Pächter m. ◆**'tenancy**, s. Mieten f (eines Hauses usw.); Pachtung f (eines Gutes usw.).

tend¹ [tend], v.tr. (einen Garten, einen Kranken) pflegen; (eine Maschine) bedienen.

tend², v.i. (a) to t. towards sth., zu etwas dat/in eine gewisse Richtung tendieren; (b) to t. to do sth., dazu neigen, etwas zu tun. ◆**'tendency** s. Tendenz f; (of pers.) Neigung f (to, zu + dat).

tender¹ ['tendər], adj. (a) zart; t. meat, zartes/weiches Fleisch; (b) (of pers.) zärtlich; Fig: t. heart, weiches/empfindsames Herz. ◆**'tenderness**, s. Zartheit f; (of pers.) Zärtlichkeit f, Weichherzigkeit f.

tender² I. s. Com: Angebot n. II. v. tr. (seine Dienste) anbieten; to t. one's resignation, sein Abschiedsgesuch einreichen.

tendon ['tendən], s. Anat: Sehne f.

tenement ['tenimənt], s. Mietskaserne f.

tenfold ['tenfəuld], adj. & adv. zehnfach.

tennis ['tenis], s. Tennis n; t. court, Tennisplatz m; t. racket, Tennisschläger m.

tenor ['tenər], s. 1. Lit: (sense) wesentlicher Sinn; (content) Inhalt m. 2. Mus: Tenor m; (voice) Tenorstimme f.

tense¹ [tens], s. Gram: Zeitform f.

tense² adj. gespannt. ◆**'tenseness**, s. Gespanntheit f (des Muskels, der Verhältnisse); das Spannende (an einem Drama usw.). ◆**tension** ['tenʃ(ə)n], s. 1. (also El:) Spannung f. 2. Gespanntheit f (der Muskeln).

tent [tent], s. Zelt n; t. peg, Zeltpflock m.

tentacle ['tentəkl], s. Z: Fühler m.

tentative ['tentətiv], adj. zögernd; (provisional) provisorisch; **-ly**, adv. versuchsweise.

tenterhooks ['tentəhuks], s. pl. Fig: to be on t., auf die Folter gespannt sein.

tenth [tenθ], num. adj. zehnte(r, s). 2. (fraction) Zehntel n.

tenuous ['tenjuəs], adj. (of thread) dünn; (of distinction) subtil.

tenure ['tenjər], s. Bekleidung f (eines Amtes); (period) Amtszeit f.

tepid ['tepid], adj. lauwarm.

term [tə:m], s. 1. (a) (fixed) Frist f; (b) (period) Zeit f, Dauer f; in the short/long t., auf kurze/lange Sicht (gesehen); (c) Sch: etc: Trimester n/Semester n; (d) Jur: Sitzungsperiode f. 2. pl. (a) (conditions) Bedingungen fpl. Fig: to come to terms with death, sich mit dem Tod abfinden; (b) (relationship) Beziehungen fpl; to be on friendly/good terms with s.o., mit j-m befreundet sein/auf gutem Fuße stehen. 3. (expression) Ausdruck m; (b) in terms of, in Hinsicht auf + acc. ◆**'terminal** I. adj. (a) End-; (b) Med: (of illness) unheilbar. II. s. 1. Rail: Endstation f; Av: Terminal m; coach t., Omnibusbahnhof m. ◆**'terminate**, v. 1. v.tr. beenden. 2. v.i. zum Abschluß kommen. ◆**termi'nation**, s. Ende n; Abschluß m (der Verhandlungen usw.); ◆**termi'nology**, s. Terminologie f, (specialized) Fachsprache f. ◆**'terminus**, pl. **-i, -uses** [-minəs, -mini:, -əsiz], s. Rail: Endstation f.

termite ['tə:mait], s. Termite f.

terrace ['terəs, -ris], s. 1. Terrasse f. 2. Häuserreihe f; t. house, Reihenhaus n.

terrain [tə'rein], s. Gelände n.

terrestrial [ti'restriəl], adj. irdisch.

terrible ['teribl], adj. schrecklich, furchtbar; **-ibly**, adv. F: furchtbar, schrecklich.

terrier ['teriər], s. Terrier m.

terrific [tə'rifik], adj. (a) (enormous) enorm, ungeheuer; **-ally**, adv. enorm.

terrify ['terifai], v.tr. (j-n) in Angst und Schrecken versetzen. ◆**'terrifying**, adj. fürchterlich.

territory ['terit(ə)ri], s. Gebiet n. ◆**terri'torial**, adj. territorial; t. waters, Hoheitsgewässer npl.

terror ['terər], s. Schrecken m (of, vor + dat); ◆**'terrorism**, s. Terrorismus m. ◆**'terrorist**, s. Terrorist m. ◆**'terrorize**, v.tr. terrorisieren.

terse [tə:s], adj. knapp; (of pers.) kurz und bündig; (of sentences etc.) gedrängt.

test [test]. I. s. 1. Probe f; esp. Tchn: Test m; (examination) Untersuchung f; (check) Kontrolle f; to put s.o., sth. to the t., j-n, etwas auf die Probe stellen; Av: t. pilot, Testpilot m; Ch: etc: t. tube, Reagenzglas n; t. (match), Länderspiel n. 2. Sch: etc: Test m; Prüfung f. II. v.tr. (j-n, etwas) prüfen (for sth., auf etwas acc hin); (etwas) einer Prüfung unterziehen; (eine Maschine usw.) testen, (examine) untersuchen; (ein Verfahren) auf die Probe stellen; Ch: (einen Stoff) analysieren; Med: (Blut) untersuchen.

testament ['testəmənt], s. Testament n.

testicle ['testikl], s. Hoden m.

testify ['testifai], v. 1. v.tr. (etwas) aussa-gen. 2. v.i. to t. to sth., etwas bezeugen. ◆**testimonial** [-'məunjəl], s. (evidence) Zeugnis n; (for job etc.) Empfehlungs-schreiben n. ◆**testimony** [-məni], s. Jur: etc: Zeugnis n; (statement) (mündliche) Zeugenaussage f.

testy ['testi], adj. reizbar.

tetanus ['tetənəs], s. Wundstarrkrampf m.

tether ['teðər]. I. s. Halterstrick m (eines Pferdes usw.); Fig: at the end of one's t., am Ende seiner Kräfte; (impatient) am Ende seiner Geduld. II. v.tr. (ein Tier) anbinden.

text [tekst], s. Text m. Sch: Lehrbuch n. ◆**textbook** n.

textile ['tekstail], s. Gewebe n; pl. tex-tiles, Textilien pl. ◆**texture** ['tekstʃər], s. Beschaffenheit f.

Thai [tai]. I. s. Thailänder(in) m(f). II. adj. thailändisch. ◆**Thailand**. Pr. n. Thailand n.

Thames [temz]. Pr. n. Themse f.

than [ðæn, ðən], conj. als.

thank [θæŋk]. I. s. pl. thanks, Dank m; F: thanks! danke! many thanks! vielen Dank! (b) thanks to, dank + gen. II. v.tr. (a) (j-m) danken, sich (bei j-m) bedanken (for sth., für etwas acc); t. goodness! Gott sei Dank! (b) to have s.o. to t. for sth., j-m etwas zu verdanken haben. ◆**thankful**, adj. dankbar. ◆**thankfulness**, s. Dankbarkeit f. ◆**thankless**, adj. undankbar. ◆**thanksgiving**, s. Danksagung f; Ecc: (Harvest) T., Erntedankfest n. ◆**thankyou**, s. Dankeschön n.

that[ðæt]. I. dem. pron. (pl. those [ðəuz]) 1. das, pl. die; give me t., gib mir das; how much are those? wieviel kosten die (da)? t. is (to say) ..., das heißt, ...; after t., danach, darauf; what do you mean by t.? was willst du damit sagen? at t., noch dazu; and t.'s t.! und damit basta! 2. (opposed to this, these) je-ner, jene, jenes; this is new, t. is old, dies(es) ist neu, jenes ist alt. II. dem. adj. (pl. those) jener, jene, jenes; pl. jene; t. one, jenes dort; everyone agrees on t. point, die sind sich in dem Punkt einig. III. dem. adv. t. high, so hoch.

that[ðət], rel. pron. sing. & pl. der, die, das; everything/all t. ..., alles, was ...; the best t. he could do, das Beste, was er machen konnte.

that[ðæt, ðət], conj. daß.

thatch [θætʃ], v.tr. (ein Dach) mit Stroh decken; thatched cottage, strohgedecktes Landhaus.

thaw [θɔː]. I. s. Tauwetter n; (process) Tauen n. II. v. 1. v.tr. (Schnee) tauen; (Fleisch usw.) auftauen. 2. v.i. (of snow etc.) tauen; (of frozen food; Fig: of pers.) auftauen.

the [ðə], before vowel [ðiː]. I. def. art. der, die, das; pl. die. II. adv. so much

the better, umso besser; the sooner the better, je eher, desto besser. ◆**theatre** ['θiətər], s. 1. Theater n; to go to the t., ins Theater gehen. 2. Med: (operating) t., Operationssaal m. ◆**theatregoer**, s. Theaterbesucher(in) m(f). ◆**theatrical** [θi'ætrik(ə)l], adj. 1. Theater-. 2. (as in the theatre) theatralisch.

theft [θeft], s. Diebstahl m.

their [ðeər], poss. adj. ihr, ihre; ◆**theirs** [ðeəz], poss. pron. ihrer, ihre, ihres; pl. ihre.

them [ðəm], pers. pron. pl. (objective case) (acc) sie; (dat) ihnen; I like t., ich habe sie gern; I shall tell t., ich werde es ih-nen sagen; it's t.! sie sind's! ◆**them'selves**, pers. pron. 1. (reflexive) sich. 2. (emphatic) selbst.

theme [θiːm], s. Thema n; t. song, Titel-melodie f.

then [ðen], adv. dann; (a) (at that time) damals; t. and there, auf der Stelle, so-fort; now and t., dann und wann; (b) (after that) danach, darauf; now t.! (i) aufpassen! (ii) hören Sie mal! before t., vorher; by t., bis dahin; bis zu der Zeit; till t., bis dahin.

theology [θi'ɔlədʒi], s. Theologie f. ◆**theologian** [θiə'ləudʒən], s. Theolo-ge m. ◆**theological** [-'lɔdʒikl], adj. theologisch.

theorem ['θiərəm], s. Lehrsatz m. ◆**theoretical** ['θiə'retikl], adj. theore-tisch. ◆**theorize**, v.i. Theorien aufstel-len. ◆**theory** ['θiəri], s. Theorie f; in t., theoretisch.

therapy ['θerəpi], s. Therapie f. ◆**therapist**, s. Therapeut(in) m(f).

there [ðeər]. I. adv. (place) dort, da; (di-rection) dorthin, dahin. 2. (unstressed) [ðər] t. is/are, es ist/sind; es gibt + acc. 3. da; t. you are mistaken, da irrst du dich. II. int. da! (look) sieh mal! t. now! na also! (calming) schon gut! t.! t.! don't worry! schon gut, mach dir keine Sor-gen! ◆**thereabouts**, adv. 1. in der Nähe. 2. (with number) so ungefähr. ◆**there'by**, adv. dadurch. ◆**'therefore**, adv. deswegen. ◆**thereu'pon**, adv. darauf(hin).

thermal ['θəːməl], adj. esp. Ph: Wärme-; t. unit, Wärmeeinheit f. ◆**thermometer** [θə'mɔmitər], s. Ther-mometer n. ◆**thermos** s. R.t.m. t. (flask), Thermosflasche f. ◆**thermostat** ['θəːməstæt], s. Thermostat m.

these [ðiːz], pl. of **this** q.v.

thesis, pl. **theses** ['θiːsis, 'θiːsiːz], s. These f; (for doctorate) Doktorarbeit f.

they [ðei]. 1. pers. pron. nom. pl. sie. 2. indef. pron. (= one) man.

thick [θik]. I. adj. 1. (of forest, fog, hair etc.) dicht; (of crowd) dichtge-drängt. 3. (a) (of liquid) dickflüssig; (b) F: t.(-headed), begriffsstutzig. II. s. in the t. of it, mittendrin. ◆**thicken**, v. 1. v.tr. (etwas) dicker machen; Cu: (eine

Soße) eindicken. 2. v.i. dicker werden; (of fog etc.) dichter werden. ◆'thicket, s. Dickicht n. ◆'thickness, s. 1. (a) Dicke f (eines Gegenstandes); (b) Dichte f (des Nebels, eines Waldes usw.); Dichtheit f (der Haare usw.). 2. (layer) Schicht f. ◆'thickset, adj. (of pers.) untersetzt. ◆'thick-skinned, adj. dickhäutig; F: (of pers.) dickfellig.

thief, pl. thieves [θiːf, θiːvz], s. Dieb(in) m(f); (crook) Gauner m. ◆'thieve, v.tr. & i. stehlen. ◆'thieving. I. adj. diebisch. II. s. Diebstahl m.

thigh [θai], s. Oberschenkel m.

thin [θin]. I. adj. dünn; (of thread) fein; (of pers.) mager; (slim) schlank; (of population) spärlich; t. excuse, fadenscheinige Entschuldigung. -ly, adv. dünn. II. v. 1. v.tr. (a) (einen Gegenstand) dünner machen; (b) (eine Farbe, eine Soße usw.) verdünnen. 2. v.i. (a) dünn(er) werden; (of pers.) abnehmen. ◆'thinness, s. Dünnheit f; Feinheit f; Magerkeit f; Schlankheit f; Spärlichkeit f.

thing [θiŋ], s. (object) Ding n; pl. F: (possessions) Sachen fpl. 2. (matter) Sache f. last t. at night, als letztes (vor dem Schlafengehen); as things are, wie die Dinge liegen.

think [θiŋk]. I. v.tr. & i.irr. (a) denken; (consider) überlegen; (meditate) nachdenken; (b) (believe) glauben; just t.! stell dir nur vor! (c) (express opinion) meinen; what do you t.? was sollte ich Ihrer Ansicht nach machen? I t. she's pretty, ich finde sie hübsch; everyone thought he was mad, jeder hielt ihn für verrückt; I t. so, ich glaube ja. 2. v.tr. to t. of/about sth., an etwas acc denken; (meditate) über etwas acc nachdenken; (imagine) sich dat etwas vorstellen; I can't t. of the right word, ich komme nicht auf das richtige Wort; the best I can t. of, das beste, was mir einfällt; (just) t. of that! stell dir (nur) vor! to t. of s.o.'s feelings, Rücksicht auf j-s Gefühle nehmen; to be thinking of doing sth., vorhaben, etwas zu tun; what do you t. of/about it? was halten Sie davon/meinen Sie dazu? ◆'thinker, s. Denker(in) m(f). ◆'thinking. I. adj. denkend. II. s. Denken n. ◆'think 'over, v.tr. (etwas) überdenken. ◆'think 'up, v.tr. sich (etwas) ausdenken.

third [θəːd]. I. num. adj. dritter, dritte, drittes; t. person, (also t. party) Dritte(r) m; t. party insurance, Haftpflichtversicherung f. II. s. (fraction) Drittel n; -ly, adv. drittens. ◆'third-'rate, adj. drittrangig.

thirst [θəːst], s. Durst m; Fig: t. for knowledge, Wißbegier f. ◆'thirsty, adj. durstig; to be (very) t., (großen) Durst haben; this is t. work, diese Arbeit macht Durst/durstig.

thirteen [θəː'tiːn]. I. num. adj. dreizehn. II. s. Dreizehn f. ◆thir'teenth, num.

adj. dreizehnte(r,s).

thirty ['θəːti], num. adj. dreißig. ◆'thirtieth, num. adj. dreißigste(r,s).

this [ðis]. I. dem. pron. pl. these [ðiːz] 1. dies(es); pl. diese; II. dem. adj (pl. these) dieser, diese, dieses; pl. diese; t. one, dieses; t. evening, heute abend. III. dem. adv. t. high, so hoch; t. far, bis hierher.

thistle ['θisl], s. Distel f.

thong [θɔŋ], s. Lederstreifen m.

thorn [θɔːn], s. Dorn m; (bush) Dornbusch m. ◆'thorny, adj. dornig; Fig: t. problem, heikles Problem.

thorough ['θʌrə], adj. gründlich; (of search) genau; (careful) sorgfältig; -ly, adv. gründlich; (completely) vollkommen (begreifen); völlig (neu gestalten); I t. enjoyed the meal, das Essen schmeckte mir ausgezeichnet. ◆'thoroughbred, s. I. adj. (of horse) vollblütig, Vollblut-; (of dog) reinrassig. II. s. Vollblut(pferd) n. ◆'thoroughfare, s. esp. Adm: Durchgangsstraße f. ◆'thoroughness, s. Gründlichkeit f; (care) Sorgfalt f; (completeness) Vollkommenheit f.

those [ðəuz], pron. & adj. pl. of that¹.

though [ðəu], conj. 1. obwohl. 2. as t., as ob + subj.

thought [θɔːt], s. 1. Gedanke m; the mere t. (of it), der bloße Gedanke (daran). 2. (process) Denken n; (meditation) Nachdenken n; lost in t., in Gedanken vertieft. 3. (idea) Idee f; (consideration) Überlegung f. ◆'thoughtful, adj. 1. (pensive) nachdenklich. 2. (considerate) rücksichtsvoll; -ly, adv. (pensively) nachdenklich. ◆'thoughtfulness, s. 1. Nachdenklichkeit f. 2. Rücksicht(nahme) f; (attention) Aufmerksamkeit f. ◆'thoughtless, adj. (a) unüberlegt; (b) (inconsiderate) rücksichtslos; -ly, adv. rücksichtslos. ◆'thoughtlessness, s. (a) Unüberlegtheit f; (b) Rücksichtslosigkeit f.

thousand ['θauz(ə)nd]. I. num. adj. tausend. II. s. Tausend n. ◆'thousandth. I. num. adj. tausendste(r,s). II. s. (fraction) Tausendstel n.

thrash [θræʃ], v.tr. (a) (j-n) verprügeln; (b) Sp: etc: (j-n, eine Mannschaft) vernichtend schlagen. ◆'thrashing, s. 1. eine tüchtige Prügel. 2. Sp: etc: Niederlage f. ◆'thrash 'out, v.tr. (ein Problem) ausführlich erörtern.

thread [θred]. I. s. 1. (a) Faden m; sewing t., Nähfaden m; (b) Cl: Garn n; Fig: to lose the t., den Faden verlieren. 2. Gewinde n. II. v.tr. Tchn: to t. a needle, (den Faden in) eine Nadel einfädeln. ◆'threadbare, adj. (also Fig:) fadenscheinig.

threat [θret], s. Drohung f. ◆'threaten, v.tr. o t. s.o., sth. (with sth.), j-m, etwas dat (mit etwas dat) drohen; j-n t. to do sth., drohen, etwas zu tun. ◆'threatening, adj. (of tone) drohend.

three [θriː]. I. num. adj. drei; t.-

cornered, dreieckig; *Cl:* t.-piece suit, dreiteiliger Anzug; *Aut:* t.-wheeler, Dreiradauto *n.* **II.** *s.* *(figure)* Drei *f.* ◆**threefold,** *adj. & adv.* dreifach.

thresh [θreʃ], *v.tr.* (Weizen) dreschen. ◆**thresher,** *s.* Dreschmaschine *f.*

threshold ['θreʃ(h)əuld], *s.* Schwelle *f.*

thrift [θrift], **'thriftiness,** *s.* Sparsamkeit *f.* ◆**thrifty,** *adj. (economical)* sparsam.

thrill [θril]. **I.** *s.* **1.** *(trembling)* Zittern *n.* **2.** *(excitement)* Erregung *f.* **II.** *v.* **1.** *v.tr.* *(a) (excite)* (j-n) erregen; *(b) (delight)* (j-n, das Publikum) begeistern. **2.** *v.i.* beben (**with,** vor + *dat*). ◆**thriller,** *s.* Thriller *m.* ◆**thrilling,** *adj.* aufregend; *(tense)* spannend; *(of spectacle)* packend.

thrive [θraiv], *v.i.* *(of child, plant etc.)* gedeihen; *(of business)* blühen. ◆**thriving,** *adj.* gedeihend; *(of pers., business)* blühend.

throat [θrəut], *s.* *(outside)* Hals *m;* *(inside)* Kehle *f; (of animal)* Rachen *m;* **to have a sore t.,** Halsschmerzen haben; **to clear one's t.,** sich räuspern.

throb [θrɔb]. **I.** *s.* Klopfen *n;* Pochen *n* (des Herzens). **II.** *v.i.* klopfen. ◆**throbbing,** *s. (pain)* pochende/(*in the head*) hämmernde Schmerzen *mpl.*

throes [θrəuz], *s. pl.* death t., Todeskampf *m; Fig:* **in the t. of,** mitten in + *dat.*

thrombosis [θrɔm'bəusis], *s.* Thrombose *f.*

throne [θrəun], *s.* Thron *m.*

throng [θrɔŋ]. **I.** *s. (people)* Menschenmenge *f; (crush)* Gedränge *n.* **II.** *v.i.* **to t. together,** sich zusammendrängen.

throttle [θrɔtl]. **I.** *s. Aut: etc: (pedal)* Gaspedal *n.;* **to open the t.,** Gas geben. **II.** *v.tr.* (j-n) erwürgen.

through [θruː]. **I.** **1.** *prep. (a)* durch + *acc;* *(b) (time)* während, hindurch; *(c) (because of)* wegen + *gen; (with emotions etc.)* aus + *dat.* **2.** *adv.* **1.** durch; *Tel:* **to get t.,** eine Verbindung bekommen; **you're t.,** Sie sind verbunden. **2.** *(finished)* fertig; **I'm t. with him,** ich will nichts mehr mit ihm zu tun haben. ◆**through'out.** **I.** *prep. ... acc* hindurch; **t. the year,** das ganze Jahr hindurch/während des ganzen Jahres. **II.** *adv. (all the time)* die ganze Zeit. ◆**throughway,** *s. N.Am.* Autobahn *f.*

throw [θrəu]. **I.** *s.* Wurf *m.* **II.** *v.tr./v.i. (a)* werfen, *(hurl)* schleudern, *(b)* **to t.** *v.tr.* wegwerfen; *(waste)* (Worte, Zeit) verschwenden. ◆**throw a'way,** *v.tr.* wegwerfen; *(waste)* (Worte, Zeit) verschwenden. ◆**throwaway,** *adj.* Wegwerf-. ◆**throw 'in,** *v.tr.* hineinwerfen; *Fb:* (den Ball) einwerfen. ◆**throw 'out,** *v.tr.* hinauswerfen; (Hitze) ausstrahlen. ◆**throw 'up,** *v.* **1.** *v.tr.* (etwas) in die Höhe werfen, hochwerfen; (die Hände) hochwerfen. **2.** *v.i. F: (vomit)* kotzen.

thru [θruː], *N.Am.* = through.

thrush [θrʌʃ], *s.* Drossel *f.*

thrust [θrʌst]. **I.** *s. (a)* Stoß *m; (Tchn)* Schubleistung *f.* **II.** *v.* **1.** *v.tr. (a)* (etwas) (heftig) stoßen; (j-n) schieben; **to t. one's hands into one's pockets,** die Hände in die Taschen stecken; *(b)* **to t. sth. on s.o.,** j-m etwas aufdrängen.

thud [θʌd], *s.* dumpfer Schlag *m.*

thug [θʌg], *s. F:* Schläger *m; (bully)* Tyrann *m.*

thumb [θʌm]. **I.** *s.* Daumen *m.* **II.** *v.tr. (a)* **to t. (through)** a book, ein Buch durchblättern; *(of book)* well-thumbed, abgegriffen; *(b) F:* **to t. a lift,** per Anhalter fahren. ◆**thumbnail,** *s.* Daumennagel *m.* ◆**thumbtack,** *s. N.Am:* Reißzwecke *f.*

thump [θʌmp]. **I.** *s.* dumpfer Schlag *m, F:* Plumps *m; (blow)* Puff *m.* **II.** *v.tr. & i. (a)* (j-n) schlagen; *(b) (of heart)* heftig pochen.

thunder ['θʌndər]. **I.** *s.* Donner *m.* **II.** *v.tr. & i. (also Fig:)* donnern; ◆**thunderbolt,** *s.* Donnerkeil *m; Fig: (news)* Blitzstrahl *m.* ◆**thundering,** *adj.* donnernd. ◆**thunderous,** *adj. (of applause)* donnernd. ◆**thunderstorm,** *s.* Gewitter *m.* ◆**thunderstruck,** *adj.* wie vom Blitz getroffen. ◆**thundery,** *adj. F: (of weather)* gewitterschwül.

Thursday ['θəːzdi], *s.* Donnerstag *m.*

thus [ðʌs], *adv.* **1.** *(in this way)* so. **2.** *(therefore)* also, folglich.

thwart [θwɔːt], *v.tr.* (j-m) in die Quere kommen; **to t. s.o.'s plans,** j-s Pläne durchkreuzen; **to be thwarted,** gehindert sein.

thyme [taim], *s.* Thymian *m.*

thyroid ['θairɔid], *s.* **t.** (gland), Schilddrüse *f.*

tiara [ti'ɑːrə], *s.* Diadem *n.*

Tibet [ti'bet]. *Pr.n.* Tibet *n.* ◆**Ti'betan.** **I.** *adj.* tibetisch. **II.** *s.* Tibeter(in) *m(f).*

tick[1] [tik]. **I.** *s.* **1.** *(a) (sound)* Ticken *n; (b) F:* Moment *m; just a/half a t.!* ich komme gleich! **2.** *(mark)* Häkchen *n.* **II.** *v.* **1.** *v.i. (sound)* ticken. **2.** *v.tr.* abhaken. ◆**'ticking,** *s.* **1.** Ticken *n.* **2.** Bezugsstoff *m* (für Kissen usw.); (bed-) t., Inlett *n.* ◆**tick 'over,** *v.i. (of engine)* leerlaufen.

tick[2], *s. (insect)* Zecke *f.*

tick[3], *s. F:* Kredit *m;* **to buy sth. on t.,** etwas auf Pump kaufen.

ticket ['tikit], *s.* **1.** Karte *f; (entrance)* t., Eintrittskarte *f; (bus, train)* t., Fahrkarte *f;* left luggage t., Gepäckschein *m;* cloakroom t., Garderobenmarke *f;* lottery t., Lotterielos *m;* **t. collector,** Fahrkartenkontrolleur *m;* t. machine, Fahrkartenautomat *m;* t. office, Fahrkartenschalter *m.* **2.** *(label)* Etikett *n; (price)* t., Preisschild *n; Aut: F:* **to get a (parking) t.,** einen Strafzettel bekommen.

tickle ['tikl]. **I.** *s.* Kitzel *m.* **II.** *v.tr. (a)* (j-n) kitzeln; *Fig:* **to t. s.o.'s fancy,** j-m zusagen; *(b) F:* (j-n) erheitern. ◆**ticklish,** *adj.* **1.** *(of pers.)* kitzlig. **2.**

(*tricky*) heikel.

tide [taid], *s*. *esp. coll. or pl.* tides, Gezeiten *pl*; high t., Flut *f*; the t. is out/it is low t., es ist Ebbe *f*. ◆'**tidal**, *adj*. l. t. wave, Flutwelle *f*. 2. Gezeiten-. ◆'**tide 'over**, *v.tr*. that will t. us over, das wird uns solange über Wasser halten.

tidy ['taidi]. l. *adj*. ordentlich; (*orderly*) geordnet. II. *v*. 1. *v.tr*. (etwas) ordnen, in Ordnung bringen; to t. a room, in einem Zimmer aufräumen; to t. sth. away, etwas wegräumen. 2. *v.i.* to t. up, aufräumen. ◆'**tidily**, *adv*. t. dressed, ordentlich angezogen. ◆'**tidiness**, *s*. Ordentlichkeit *f*; (*order*) Ordnung *f*.

tie [tai]. l. *s*. 1. Band *n*; (*connection*) Verbindung *f*; family ties, Familienverpflichtungen *fpl*. 2. *Cl:* Krawatte *f*; binden. ◆'**tie 'up**, *v.tr*. (a) (Schnürsenkel, einen Knoten usw.) binden; (ein Paket) zubinden; (ein Bündel) zusammenbinden; (*bandage*) (einen verletzten Arm, usw.) verbinden; (b) (einen Hund) anbinden (**to a post**, an einen Pfahl); (j-n) fesseln; (c) just now I'm tied up, augenblicklich bin ich beschäftigt.

tier [tiər], *s*. Etage *f*; *Th: etc:* Rang *m*; in tiers, etagenförmig.

tiff [tif], *s*. kleine Unstimmigkeit *f*, *F:* Krach *m*.

tiger ['taigər], *s*. Tiger *m*. ◆'**tigress**, Tigerin *f*.

tight [tait]. l. *adj*. 1. (a) (of *clothes etc.*) eng; t. fit, knapper Sitz *m*; (of *money*, *time, etc.*) knapp; (c) (of *cork, screw etc.*) fest; (*stiff*) steif; (d) (*taut*) gespannt. 2. *F:* blau; ◆'**tights**, *s. pl.* Strumpfhose *f*; *Th: etc:* Trikot *n*.

tile [tail], *s*. (a) (*floor*) t., Fliese *f*; (*on walls etc.*) Kachel *f*; (*on roof*) Dachziegel *m*; tiled roof, Ziegeldach *n*; tiled floor, Fliesenboden *m*.

till¹ [til], *v.tr*. *A: & Lit:* (Land usw.) bestellen.

till², *s*. (cash) t., Ladenkasse *f*.

till³, *prep. & conj*. (a) bis; t. now/then, bis jetzt/dahin; (b) (*with noun*) bis zu | dat; t. the next time, bis zum nächsten Mal; (c) he won't come t. after dinner, er kommt erst nach dem Essen.

tiller ['tilər], *s*. *Nau:* Ruderpinne *f*.

tilt [tilt], *v*. 1. *v.i.* (of *surface*) to t. (up), sich neigen; (of *pile*) to t. over, kippen; (*fall*) umkippen. 2. *v.tr*. (etwas) kippen.

timber ['timbər], *s*. Holz *n*; standing t./t. trees, Nutzholzbäume *mpl*.

time [taim]. l. *s*. (a) Zeit *f*; in a short t., binnen kurzem, in drei Wochen; I haven't seen him for a long t., ich habe ihn (schon) lange/seit langem nicht gesehen; for some t. (past), seit einiger Zeit; all the t., die ganze Zeit; to take one's t. over sth., sich für etwas *acc* Zeit lassen; F: I've no t. for him, (i) ich habe keine Geduld mit ihm; (ii) er ist mir unsympathisch; (b) (*moment*) Zeit *f*; Zeitpunkt *m*; at that t., zu der Zeit, damals; at the present t., gegenwärtig; at times, manchmal; some t. or other, irgendwann einmal; by the t. I got there, bis ich dort ankam; from t. to t., ab und zu; von Zeit zu Zeit; what's the t.? wieviel Uhr ist es? wie spät ist es? to arrive on t., pünktlich ankommen; in good t., rechtzeitig; I was just in t., ich kam gerade (noch) rechtzeitig; it's high t., es ist höchste Zeit; we had a good t., wir haben uns bestens amüsiert; next t., nächstes Mal; several times over, mehrere Male; four times as big, viermal so groß; at the same t., gleichzeitig; t. lag, Verzögerung *f*; t. limit, Frist *f*; Zeitbeschränkung *f*; (c) *Mus:* Takt *m*; to beat/keep t., (den) Takt schlagen; II. *v.tr*. (a) den Zeitpunkt festlegen/wählen für (etwas *acc*); he didn't t. it right, er hat den richtigen Zeitpunkt nicht erwischt; (b) *Sp:* to t. s.o., j-n stoppen. ◆'**timekeeper**, *s*. *Sp:* Zeitnehmer *m*. ◆'**timeswitch**, *s*. Schaltuhr *f*. ◆'**timetable**, *s*. 1. *Rail: etc:* Fahrplan *m*. 2. *Sch:* Stundenplan *m*. ◆'**timing**, *s*. 1. (ignition) t., Zündeinstellung *f*. 2. *Sp:* Zeitnahme *f*. 3. (*fixing of time*) Zeitbestimmung *f*; Zeitwahl *f*

timid ['timid], *adj*. scheu. ◆'**ti'midity**, *s*. Scheu *f*.

timpani ['timpəni], *s. pl.* Kesselpauken *fpl*. ◆'**timpanist**, *s*. Pauker *m*.

tin [tin], *s*. 1. Zinn *n*; (*tinplate*) Blech *n*; 2. Dose *f*; t. opener, Dosenöffner *m*. ◆'**tinfoil**, *s*. Stanniol *n*. ◆'**tinny**, *adj*. (of *sound etc.*) blechern. ◆'**tin'plate**, *s*. Weißblech *n*.

tinge [tin(d)ʒ]. l. *s*. 1. (zarte) Tönung *f*; with a t. of red, mit einem Stich ins Rote; rötlich getönt. 2. *Fig:* (*trace*) Spur *f*; a t. of sadness, ein Anflug *m* von Trauer. II. *v.tr*. (Haare usw.) leicht tönen.

tingle ['tiŋgl], *v.i.* prickeln; (*with cold*

etc.) (leicht) brennen.

tinker ['tiŋkər] I. *s.* Kesselflicker *m.* II. *v.i.* **to t.** (**about**), herumpfuschen (**with**, an + *dat*).

tinkle ['tiŋkl] I. *s.* (*also* **tinkling**) Geklingel *n.* II. *v.* 1. *v.i.* klingeln. 2. *v.tr.* (mit etwas *dat*) klingeln.

tinsel ['tins(ə)l], *s.* Lametta *n;* (*loose*) Flitter *m.*

tint [tint]. I. *s.* Farbton *m;* Tönung *f;* (*of black*) Schattierung *f.* II. *v.tr.* (Haar usw.) tönen.

tiny ['taini], *adj.* winzig.

tip¹ [tip], *s.* Spitze *f; Fig:* **it is on the t. of my tongue,** es liegt mir auf der Zunge. ◆**'tiptoe.** I. *s. & adv.* (**on**) **t.,** auf Zehenspitzen *fpl.* II. *v.i.* auf Zehenspitzen gehen. ◆**'tip'top,** *adj. F:* klasse, prima.

tip² I. *s.* 1. (*money*) Trinkgeld *n.* 2. *Sp: etc:* Tip *m.* II. *v.* 1. *v.tr.* (*a*) (j-n ins Wasser usw.) stoßen; (*tilt*) (etwas) kippen; (*knock over*) (etwas) umstoßen; (*b*) **to t. s.o. off,** j-m einen Wink geben; (*c*) (j-m) ein Trinkgeld geben. 2. *v.i.* kippen; **to t. over,** umkippen; **to t. up,** hochkippen. ◆**'tip-lorry/***F:* **'tipper,** *s.* Kipper *m.* ◆**'tip-off,** *s. F:* Tip *m;* **to give s.o. a/ the t.-o.,** j-m einen Wink geben.

tipple ['tipl]. I. *s. F:* Gesöff *n.* II. *v.i.* zechen.

tipsy ['tipsi], *adj.* beschwipst; **to get t.,** sich *dat* einen Schwips antrinken.

tire¹ ['taiər], *v.* 1. *v.tr.* (j-n, ein Tier) ermüden. 2. *v.i.* müde werden; **he soon tired of it,** ihm wurde es bald langweilig. ◆**'tired,** *adj.* müde; **t. out,** erschöpft; **t. to death,** todmüde; **to be t. of sth.,** etwas *gen* müde sein. ◆**'tiredness,** *s.* Müdigkeit *f.* ◆**'tireless,** *adj.* unermüdlich. ◆**'tiresome,** *adj.* aufreibend; (*of child*) lästig. ◆**'tiring,** *adj.* ermüdend (*of day, pers. etc.*) anstrengend.

tire², *s. N. Am:* = **tyre.**

tissue ['tisju:], *s.* 1. *Anat: etc:* Gewebe *n.* 2. (*paper*) **t.,** Papiertaschentuch *n;* **t. paper,** Seidenpapier *n.*

tit¹ [tit], *s. Orn:* Meise *f;* **blue t.** Blaumeise *f.*

tit², *s. F:* **t. for tat,** wie du mir, so ich dir.

titbit ['titbit], *s.* Leckerbissen *m.*

titillate ['titileit], *v.tr.* (den Gaumen, die Sinne usw.) kitzeln.

titivate ['titiveit], *v.tr.* schön machen.

title ['taitl], *s.* 1. Titel *m; Th:* **t. rôle,** Titelrolle *f.* 2. *Jur:* Rechtstitel *m;* (*to property*) Eigentumsrecht *n;* **t. deed,** Eigentumsurkunde *f.* ◆**'titled,** *adj.* adelig.

titter ['titər]. I. *s.* Kichern *n.* II. *v.i.* kichern. ◆**'tittering,** *s.* Gekicher *n.*

to [tu:]. I. *prep.* 1. zu + *dat;* (*esp. with town, country*) nach + *dat;* **he went to France/to the USA,** er reiste nach Frankreich/in die USA; **to go to school/ university,** in die Schule/auf die Universität gehen; **to clasp s.o. to one's heart,**

j-n ans Herz drücken; **to this end,** zu diesem Zweck; **to everyone's surprise,** zur Überraschung aller. 2. (*a*) (*until*) bis; **to this day,** bis heute, zum heutigen Tag; **ten (minutes) to six,** zehn (Minuten) vor sechs; (*b*) bis auf + *acc;* **soaked to the skin,** naß bis auf die Haut. 3. **to speak to s.o.,** mit j-m sprechen; **he said to me ...,** er sagte mir, ... II. (*with the infinitive*) zu; (*in order*) to, um zu; **he came to help me,** er kam, um mir zu helfen; **too hot to drink,** zu heiß zum Trinken; **he wants/is able to go,** er will/ kann gehen. III. *adv.* (*stressed*) 1. **to come t.,** (wieder) zu sich *dat* kommen. 2. **movement to and fro,** Hin- und Herbewegung *f.*

toad [toud], *s.* Kröte *f.* ◆**'toadstool,** *s.* Giftpilz *m.*

toady ['toudi], *v.i.* **to t. to s.o.,** vor j-m kriechen.

toast [toust]. I. *s.* 1. (**a piece of**) **t.,** (eine Scheibe) Toast *m.* 2. Trinkspruch *m,* Toast *m.* II. *v.* 1. *v.tr. & i.* (Brot) toasten. 2. *v.tr.* **to t. s.o.,** auf j-s Wohl trinken. ◆**'toaster,** *s.* Toaster *m.*

tobacco [tə'bækou], *s.* Tabak *m;* **t. pouch,** Tabak(s)beutel *m.* ◆**to'bacconist,** *s.* Tabakhändler *m;* **t.'s (shop),** Tabakwarenladen *m.*

toboggan [tə'bɔgən]. I. *s.* Rodelschlitten *m.* II. *v.i.* rodeln.

today [tə'dei], *adv. & s.* heute; *of t./* **today's,** heutig; **t.'s paper,** die Zeitung von heute.

toddle ['tɔdl], *v.i.* (*of child*) watscheln. ◆**'toddler,** *s.* Kleinkind *n.*

toddy ['tɔdi], *s.* Grog *m.*

to-do [tə'du:], *s. F:* (*fuss*) Getue *n;* **what a t.!** was für eine Aufregung!

toe [tou]. I. *s.* Zehe *f.* II. *v.tr.* **to t. the line,** sich an die Hausordnung/*Pol:* Parteilinie halten. ◆**'toecap,** *s.* Schuhspitze *f.* ◆**'toehold,** *s.* Halt *m* (für die Zehen). ◆**'toenail,** *s.* Zehennagel *m.*

toffee ['tɔfi], *s.* Toffee *n;* (*weiches*) Karamelbonbon *n.*

together [tə'geðər], *adv.* zusammen; **to go/belong t.,** zusammengehören; **t. with,** zusammen mit + *dat.*

toggle ['tɔgl], *s.* Knebel(verschluß) *m.*

toil [toil]. I. *s.* (mühselige) Arbeit *f.* II. *v.i.* sich abplagen.

toilet ['tɔilit], *s.* Toilette *f;* **t. soap,** Toilettenseife *f;* **t. paper,** Toilettenpapier *n;* **t. roll,** Rolle *f* Toilettenpapier.

token ['touk(ə)n], *s.* 1. Zeichen *n.* 2. (*for books, records*) Gutschein *m;* (*at games*) Spielmarke *f.*

tolerable ['tɔlərəbl], *adj.* (*a*) erträglich; (*b*) (*reasonable*) passabel, **-ably,** *adv.* ziemlich. ◆**'tolerance,** *s.* Toleranz *f.* ◆**'tolerant,** *adj.* tolerant. ◆**'tolerate,** *v.tr.* (*a*) (j-n, etwas) dulden; (Ansichten usw.) tolerieren; (*b*) (*bear*) (etwas) aushalten. ◆**tole'ration,** *s.* Duldung *f.*

toll¹ [toul], *s.* (*a*) Zoll *m;* **t. bridge/road,**

gebührenpflichtige Brücke/Straße; (b) *Fig:* (of epidemic etc.) to take a heavy t., viele Opfer fordern.

toll², v.tr. & i. (eine Glocke) läuten.

tomato, pl. -oes [təˈmɑːtəu, əuz], s. Tomate f.

tomb [tuːm], s. Grab n; (monument) Grabmal n; (vault) Gruft f. ◆'**tombstone,** s. Grabstein m.

tombola [tɔmˈbəulə, ˈtɔmbələ], s. Tombola f.

tomboy [ˈtɔmbɔi], s. jungenhaftes Mädchen n; *F:* wilde Range f.

tome [təum], s. dicker Band m, *F:* Wälzer m.

tomfool [tɔmˈfuːl], adj. *F:* dämlich. ◆tom'foolery, s. *F:* Unfug m.

tommy gun [ˈtɔmi ɡʌn], s. *F:* Maschinenpistole f.

tomorrow [təˈmɔrəu]. I. adv. morgen; t. evening, morgen abend; the day after t., übermorgen. II. s. Morgen n; t.'s/of t., von morgen.

ton [tʌn], s. Tonne f; *F:* there's tons of it, es gibt jede Menge davon. ◆'**tonnage,** s. *Nau:* (a) (of ship) Tonnage f; (b) (duty) Frachtgeld n.

tonal [ˈtəunəl], adj. *Mus:* tonal.

tone [təun]. I. s. (sound) Ton m; *Fig:* to set the t., den Ton angeben. II. v.i. to t. with sth., mit etwas harmonieren. ◆tone 'down, v.tr. (einen Ausdruck, Farben, usw.) abschwächen. ◆'**toneless,** adj. tonlos.

tongs [tɔŋz], s.pl. Zange f; fire-t., Feuerzange f.

tongue [tʌŋ], s. 1. Zunge f; to put one's t. out at s.o., j-m die Zunge herausstrecken; to hold one's t., den Mund halten; t. in cheek, nicht ernst gemeint. 2. *A:* (language) Sprache f. ◆'**tongue-tied,** adj. sprachlos. ◆'**tongue-twister,** s. Zungenbrecher m.

tonic [ˈtɔnik]. I. adj. t. water, Tonic n. II. s. 1. *Med:* Tonikum n; *Fig:* Stimulans n. 2. *Mus:* Grundton m.

tonight [təˈnait], adv. & s. heute abend; (after bedtime) heute nacht.

tonsil [ˈtɔns(i)l], s. *Anat:* Mandel f. ◆'**tonsillitis** [ˈlaitis], s. *Med:* Mandelentzündung f.

too [tuː], adv. 1. zu; t. much money, zuviel Geld. 2. (as well) auch; I'm coming t., ich komme auch mit.

tool [tuːl], s. 1. Werkzeug n; gardening tools, Gartengeräte npl. ◆'**toolbag,** s. Werkzeugtasche f. ◆'**toolbox,** s. Werkzeugkasten m.

tooth, pl. teeth [tuːθ, tiːθ], s. Zahn m; set of teeth, Gebiß n; to have a t. out, sich dat einen Zahn ziehen lassen. ◆'**toothache,** s. Zahnschmerzen mpl. ◆'**toothbrush,** s. Zahnbürste f. ◆'**toothless,** adj. zahnlos. ◆'**toothpaste,** s. Zahnpasta f. ◆'**toothpick,** s. Zahnstocher m.

top¹ [tɔp]. I. s 1. Spitze f (eines Daches usw.); Gipfel m (eines Berges usw.); Wipfel m (eines Baumes); at the t., (ganz) oben; *Fig:* an der Spitze; *Fig:* at the t. of his voice, aus vollem Halse; from t. to toe, von Kopf bis Fuß; on t., obenauf; on t. of it (all), noch dazu/obendrein. 2. *Aut:* (gear) höchster Gang m. II. adj. oberste(r,s), höchste(r,s); t. coat, letzter Anstrich; m; t. speed, Höchstgeschwindigkeit f; t. secret, streng geheim. III. v.tr. (a) (lop) (einen Baum usw.) kappen; (b) (cover) (etwas) bedecken, (crown) krönen; and to t. it all..., und um dem ganzen die Krone aufzusetzen...; (c) (exceed) (eine Zahl, Summe) übersteigen; (d) to t. the list, die Liste anführen; *Fig:* (take priority) den Vorrang haben. ◆'**topless,** adj. oben ohne; attrib. Oben-ohne-. ◆'top 'up, v.tr. nachfüllen.

top², s. Kreisel m.

topaz [ˈtəupæz], s. Topas m.

topic [ˈtɔpik], s. Thema n. ◆'**topical,** adj. aktuell.

topple [ˈtɔpl], v. 1. v.i. to t. (down/over), umkippen; (of tree, building etc.) umstürzen. 2. v.tr. to sth. over, etwas umstoßen.

topsy-turvy [ˈtɔpsiˈtəːvi], adj. & adv. verkehrt; (confused) durcheinander; to turn everything t.-t., alles auf den Kopf stellen.

torch [tɔːtʃ], s. 1. Fackel f. 2. (electric) t., Taschenlampe f.

torment. I. [ˈtɔːment] s. Qual f. II. [tɔːˈment] v.tr. (j-n) quälen.

tornado, pl. -oes [tɔːˈneidəu, -əuz], s. Tornado m.

torpedo, [tɔːˈpiːdəu]. I. s. (pl. -oes) [-əuz] Torpedo m. II. v.tr. (ein Schiff) torpedieren.

torrent [ˈtɔrənt], s. (reißender) Strom m; (mountain stream) Sturzbach m. ◆'**torrential** [-ˈren(ə)l], adj. (of rain) strömend.

torrid [ˈtɔrid], adj. (a) (of heat, passion etc.) glühend; (b) (of land, plain etc.) ausgedörrt.

torso, pl. -os [ˈtɔːsəu, -əuz], s. Rumpf m.

tortoise [ˈtɔːtəs], s. Schildkröte f. ◆'**tortoiseshell** [-ˈtɔːʃel], s. Schildpatt n.

tortuous [ˈtɔːtjuəs], adj. 1. (of path etc.) verschlungen. 2. *Fig:* (of argument) spitzfindig.

torture [ˈtɔːtʃər]. I. s. Folter f; *Fig:* Marter f. II. v.tr. (j-n) foltern.

toss [tɔs], s. 1. Wurf m (einer Münze usw.). II. v. 1. v.tr. (a) (einen Ball usw.) in die Luft werfen; to t. a coin, mit einer Münze knobeln (for sth., um etwas acc). 2. v.i. to t. (about)/t. and turn in bed, sich im Bett hin und her wälzen. ◆'**toss-up,** s. (a) Knobeln n (mit einer Münze); (b) *F:* it's a t.-up, es steht auf der Kippe.

tot¹ [tɔt], s. 1. F: (child) tiny t., kleiner Wicht m. 2. a t. of rum, ein Schluck m Rum.

tot², v.tr. to t. up, (Zahlen, Ausgaben usw.) zusammenrechnen.

total ['təut(ə)l]. I. adj. (a) (whole) gesamt; t. amount, Gesamtsumme f; (b) (complete) völlig; (of eclipse, war etc.) total; t. silence, absolute Stille; -ly, adv. völlig. II. s. (a) (money) Gesamtbetrag m; grand t., Gesamtsumme f; (b) (number) Endresultat n. III. v.tr. (Summen usw.) zusammenrechnen. ◆**totalitarian** [təutæli'tɛəriən], adj. totalitär. ◆**totali'tarianism**, s. Totalitarismus m. ◆**totality** [-'tæliti], s. Gesamtheit f.

totalisator ['təutəlaizeitər], F: **tote** [təut], s. Totalisator m.

totem ['təutəm], s. Totem n.

totter ['tɔtər], v.i. (a) (of pers.) taumeln; (b) (of structure) wanken, wackeln.

touch [tʌtʃ]. I. s. 1. (a) (sense of) t., F: it was t. and go, es hing an einem Faden; (b) to give sth. the finishing t., einer Sache den letzten Schliff geben. 2. (sense of) t., Tastsinn m. 3. (feature) Zug m; the t. of the master, die Hand des Meisters; personal t., persönliche Note. 4. t. of garlic, eine Spur Knoblauch; with a t. of bitterness, mit einem Anflug von Bitterkeit; a t. of flu, eine leichte Grippe. 5. Kontakt m; to be in t. with s.o., mit j-m in Verbindung stehen/Kontakt haben; 6. Sp: (at rugby) Malfeld n; Fb: Aus n; t. line, (at rugby) Mallinie f; Fb: Seitenlinie f. II. v.tr. (a) (j-n, etwas) berühren; (esp. neg.) (etwas) anrühren; t. wood! toi, toi, toi! Fig: to t. (on) a subject, ein Thema (kurz) berühren; (b) (j-n) rühren; his kindness touched me deeply, ich war von seiner Güte sehr gerührt. ◆**'touch 'down**, v.i. Av: landen; (at rugby) den Ball im gegnerischen Malfeld niederlegen. ◆**touched**, adj. (a) (moved) gerührt; (b) F: (slightly mad) nicht ganz richtig im Kopf. ◆**'touchiness**, s. Reizbarkeit f. ◆**'touching**, adj. rührend. ◆**'touch 'up**, v.tr. (Lack) ausbessern; Phot: (eine Aufnahme) retuschieren. ◆**'touchy**, adj. (of pers.) reizbar.

tough [tʌf]. I. adj. 1. (strong) stark, widerstandsfähig; (of pers., meat) zäh. 2. (inflexible) (of pers.) hart, unnachgiebig. 3. (difficult) F: a t. job, ein schwieriger Job; t. luck! Pech! II. s. F: Rowdy m. ◆**toughen**, v. 1. v.tr. (j-n) abhärten; (einen Stoff) fester machen. 2. v.i. sich abhärten. ◆**'toughness**, s. 1. Stärke f; Zähheit f. 2. Härte f. 3. Schwierigkeit f.

tour [tuər]. I. s. 1. (a) Tour f, Reise f (of, durch + acc); walking t., Wandertour f; (b) Th: etc: Tournee f (of, durch + acc). II. v.tr. & i. Th: etc: to t. the provinces, Gastspiele in der Provinz geben. ◆**'tourism**, s. Fremdenverkehr m. ◆**'tourist**, s. Tourist m; t. office, Ver-

kehrsamt n.

tournament ['tuənəmənt], s. Turnier n.

tousle ['tauzl], v.tr. (Haare) zerzausen.

tow [təu]. I. s. to take a ship/a car in t., ein Schiff ins Schlepptau nehmen/ein Auto abschleppen. II. v.tr. (ein Fahrzeug) abschleppen; (ein Schiff) schleppen. ◆**'towing**, s. Schleppen n; Aut: Abschleppen n. ◆**'towpath**, s. Leinpfad m. ◆**'tow-rope**, s. Aut: Abschleppseil n.

towards [tə'wɔ:dz], prep. 1. auf ... acc zu; he came t. me, er kam auf mich zu/ mir entgegen; 2. (for) für + acc; his feelings t. me, seine Gefühle mir gegenüber; 3. (time) gegen + acc; t. noon, gegen Mittag.

towel ['tauəl], s. Handtuch n.

tower ['tauər]. I. s. Turm m; t. block, Hochhaus n; (flats) Wohnturm m; Fig: he's a t. of strength, er ist eine große Stütze. II. v.i. hochragen; to t. over/ above s.o., sth, j-n, etwas weit überragen/Fig: übertreffen. ◆**'towering**, adj. haushoch.

town [taun], s. Stadt f; to go into t., in die Stadt gehen; t. council, Stadtrat m; t. hall, Rathaus n; t. planning, Städteplanung f. ◆**'township**, s. (a) Stadtgemeinde f; (b) N.Am: Verwaltungsbezirk m.

toxic ['tɔksik], adj. giftig.

toy [tɔi]. I. s. Spielzeug n; toys, Spielsachen fpl. II. v.i. to t. with an idea, mit einem Gedanken spielen. ◆**'toyshop**, s. Spielwarengeschäft n.

trace [treis]. I. s. Spur f; we lost all t. of them, wir haben sie völlig aus den Augen verloren; to disappear without (a) t., spurlos verschwinden. II. v.tr. (a) (draw) (Linien usw.) nachziehen; (Muster usw.) durchpausen; (b) (find) (j-n, etwas) aufspüren. ◆**tracery**, s. Flechtwerk n; Arch: (window) t., Maßwerk n. ◆**'tracing**, s. (act) Durchpausen n; t. paper, Pauspapier n.

track [træk], s. 1. t. (trace) Spur f; Fährte f (eines Tieres); to follow in s.o's tracks, in j-s Fußstapfen treten; to keep t. of s.o., j-n nicht aus den Augen verlieren; F: to make tracks, sich auf den Weg machen (for, nach + dat). 2. (a) (path) Weg m; it's off the beaten t., es liegt abseits; (b) Sp: Piste f; (motorracing) t., Rennstrecke f; t. racing, Rundstreckenrennen n. 3. Rail: Gleis n. II. v.tr. (einen Täter, eine Spur usw.) verfolgen; to t. s.o. down, j-n aufspüren. ◆**'tracker dog**, s. Spürhund m.

tract¹ [trækt], s. 1. t. (of country), Landstrich m.

tract², s. Ecc: Traktat n.

tractor ['træktər], s. Agr: Traktor m; (for towing) Zugmaschine f.

trade [treid]. I. s. Handel m; (occupation) Beruf m; (craft) Handwerk n; (business) Geschäft n, Gewerbe n; t. directory, Firmenverzeichnis n; t. union, Gewerkschaft f; t. **unionism,** Gewerkschaftswesen n; t. **unionist,** Gewerkschaftler m; t. **mark,** Warenzeichen n; t. **name,** Handelsbezeichnung f. **II.** v. 1. v.i. handeln (in sth., mit etwas dat). 2. v.tr. Com: to t. in one's old car, sein altes Auto in Zahlung geben. ◆**'trader,** s. Händler m. ◆**'tradesman,** pl. **-men,** s. Händler m; (shopkeeper) Geschäftsinhaber m. ◆**'tradewind,** s. Passat m. ◆**'trading,** s. Handel m; t. **stamp,** Rabattmarke f; t. **estate,** Gewerbegebiet n.

tradition [trə'diʃ(ə)n], s. (a) Tradition f; (custom) Brauch m; (b) oral t., mündliche Überlieferung f. ◆**tra'ditional,** adj. traditionell; t-ly, adv. nach altem Brauch.

traffic ['træfik]. **I.** s. 1. (trade) Handel m; (illegal) Schleichhandel m. 2. Verkehr m; t. **jam,** Verkehrsstauung f; t. **lights,** Ampel f; t. **warden,** (female) Politesse f; (male) Hilfspolizist m (für den ruhenden Verkehr). **II.** v.i. Pej: to t. in sth., mit etwas dat Schwarzhandel treiben.

tragedy ['trædʒidi], s. Tragödie f. ◆**'tragic,** adj. tragisch.

trail [treil]. **I.** s. 1. Spur f; t. of smoke, Rauchfahne f. 2. esp. N.Am: (unbefestigte) Straße f; Weg m. **II.** v. 1. v.tr. (a) to t. **sth.** (along) behind one, (etwas) hinter sich dat herschleppen; (b) (follow) (j-n) verfolgen; (shadow) (einen Verbrecher usw.) beschatten; to t. an animal, der Fährte eines Tieres folgen. 2. v.i. (a) to t. **(behind),** (i) Sp: (drop back) Boden verlieren; (ii) (be far behind) zurückliegen; (b) (of pers.) to t. **along,** sich dahinschleppen; (of skirt) to t. **along the ground,** am Boden schleifen; (c) (of plant) herunterhängen. ◆**'trailer,** s. Aut: (a) Anhänger m; (b) N.Am: Wohnwagen m. 2. Cin: Voranzeige f.

train [trein]. **I.** s. 1. Rail: Zug m; t. **ferry,** Zugfähre f. 2. Fig: Folge f (von Ereignissen usw.); t. of thought, Gedankengang m. 3. Cl: Schleppe f. **II.** v. 1. v.tr. (a) (j-n) ausbilden; (ein Kind) erziehen; (ein Tier) dressieren; (ein Pferd) trainieren; (b) (eine Pflanze) ziehen; (c) (eine Waffe, Kamera usw.) richten (on, auf + acc). 2. v.i. Sp: etc: trainieren (for, für + acc). ◆**trained,** adj. (of soldier etc.) ausgebildet; (of animal) dressiert; (of eye etc.) geschult; (of athlete) trainiert. ◆**trai'nee,** s. Lehrling m. ◆**'trainer,** s. 1. Dompteur m (eine Löwen usw.); Dresseur m (von Hunden). 2. Sp: Trainer m. ◆**'training,** s. (a) Ausbildung f; Schulung f (des Auges usw.); (teacher) t. **college,** Pädagogische Hochschule f; (b) Sp: Training n; in t., in Kondition; (c) Dressur f (eines Tieres).

traipse [treips], v.i. F: latschen.

trait [trei], s. Charakterzug m.

traitor ['treitər], s. Verräter(in) m(f).

trajectory [trə'dʒektəri], s. Flugbahn f.

tram [træm], s. Straßenbahn f. ◆**'tramcar,** s. Straßenbahnwagen m.

◆**'tramline,** s. Straßenbahnschiene f.

tramp [træmp]. **I.** s. 1. (sound) Getrampel n (von Füßen, Hufen usw.). 2. Fußmarsch m; (hike) Wanderung f. 3. (pers.) (a) Landstreicher m; (b) N.Am: (prostitute) Straßenmädchen n. **II.** v.i. (a) trampeln (on sth., auf etwas dat); (b) (hike) wandern; (wander) herumvagabundieren.

trample ['træmpl], v. 1. v.i. to t. **on s.o.,** sth., j-n, etwas mit Füßen treten. 2. v.tr. to t. **sth. underfoot,** etwas zertrampeln.

trampoline ['træmpəlin], s. Trampolin n.

trance [trɑːns], s. Trance f.

tranquil ['træŋkwil], adj. ruhig; (peaceful) friedlich; (of pers., attitude etc.) gelassen. ◆**tran'quillity,** s. Ruhe f. ◆**'tranquillizer,** s. Beruhigungsmittel n.

trans- [træns, trænz], prefix trans-. ◆**transact** [træn'sækt], v.tr. (ein Geschäft) durchführen. ◆**tran'saction,** s. 1. Durchführung f (einer Sache). 2. (a) Com: (business) t., Geschäft n; (process) Geschäftsvorgang m; (b) pl. (negotiations) Verhandlungen fpl. ◆**transatlantic** [trænzət'læntik], adj. (a) (of flight etc.) transatlantisch; (b) amerikanisch. ◆**transcend** [træn'send], v.tr. (a) (den Verstand, j-s Kräfte usw.) übersteigen; (b) (excel) (etwas) übertreffen. ◆**transcontinental** [trænzkɔnti'nentl], adj. transkontinental. ◆**transcribe** [træn'skraib], v.tr. (a) (copy) (etwas Geschriebenes) abschreiben; (b) (Stenogramm, eine Aufnahme usw.) übertragen ◆**'transcript/tran'scription,** s. (a) Abschrift f; Übertragung f (einer Aufnahme usw.); (b) (recording) Aufzeichnung f. ◆**transept** ['trænsept], s. Querschiff n. ◆**transfer.** **I.** [træns'fə(r)] v.1. v.tr. (a) (move) (eine Geschäftsstelle usw.) verlegen (to, nach + dat); (Beamte usw.) versetzen (to, nach + dat); (b) (hand over) (ein Recht, ein Eigentum, Fig: Zuneigung usw.) übertragen (to s.o., auf j-n); (Geld) überweisen (to s.o., j-m). 2. v.i. übergehen (to sth., zu etwas dat). **II.** ['trænsfər] s. 1. (a) Verlegung f; (b) Versetzung f. 2. (a) Übertragung f (von Eigentum); (b) Überweisung f (von Geld). 3. (change) Wechsel m; Av: etc: Umsteigen n. 4. (picture) Abziehbild n. ◆**trans'ferable,** adj. übertragbar (to, auf + acc). ◆**transform** [træns'fɔːm], v.tr. (a) verwandeln (into sth., in etwas acc); (b) Ch: (Energie usw.) umsetzen; El: (Strom) umspannen. ◆**transfor'mation,** s. Verwandlung f. ◆**trans'former,** s. El: Transformator m. ◆**transfuse** [træns'fjuːz], v.tr. Med: (Blut) übertragen. ◆**trans'fusion,** s. (blood) t., Bluttransfusion f. ◆**transient** ['trænziənt]. **I.** adj. vorübergehend; (of happiness) vergänglich. **II.** s.pl. N.Am: (travellers) Durchreisende mpl. ◆**transistor** [træn'sistə], s. El: Transistor m; t. (radio), Transistorradio n. ◆**transit** ['trænsit, -zit], s. Durchreise f; passengers in t., Durchreisende mpl; t. camp, Durchgangslager n. ◆**transition** [træn'siʃ(ə)n], s. Übergang m (to, zu + dat). ◆**tran'sitional**, adj. Übergangs-. ◆**'transitive**, adj. t. verb, transitives Verb. ◆**'transitory**, adj. vorübergehend. ◆**translate** [træns'leit], v.tr. übersetzen. ◆**trans'lation**, s. Übersetzung f. ◆**trans'lator**, s. Übersetzer(in) m(f). ◆**trans'lucent**, adj. lichtdurchlässig. ◆**transmission** [trænz'miʃ(ə)n], s. (a) Übertragung f; Übermittlung f (von Nachrichten usw.); (b) Aut: Getriebe n; (c) Rad: Übertragung f. ◆**trans'mit**, v.tr. (a) (Krankheiten, Rad: eine Sendung usw.) übertragen (to, auf + acc); (b) (Nachrichten usw.) übermitteln. ◆**trans'mitter**, s. Rad: etc: Sender m. ◆**transparency** [træns'pɛər(ə)nsi], s. 1. (quality) Durchsichtigkeit f. 2. Phot: Diapositiv n. ◆**trans'parent**, adj. durchsichtig; **-ly**, adv. t. obvious, ganz offensichtlich. ◆**transplant**. I. [træns'plɑːnt] v.tr. (a) umpflanzen; (b) Med: transplantieren. II. ['trænsplɑːnt] s: Med: Transplantation f. ◆**transport**. I. ['trænspɔːt] s. (a) Transport m, Beförderung f; (b) **(means of)** t., Transportmittel n. II. [træns'pɔːt] v.tr. (a) transportieren, befördern. ◆**transpor'tation**, s. Transport m, Beförderung f. ◆**trans'porter**, s. (vehicle) Transporter m. ◆**transverse** ['trænzvɜːs], adj. querlaufend; Quer-. ◆**transvestite** [trænz'vestait], s. Transvestit m.

trap1 [træp]. I. s. 1. Falle f. 2. P: (mouth) Klappe f. II. v.tr. (a) (ein Tier usw.) (mit einer Falle) fangen; **trapped by the flames**, von den Flammen eingeschlossen; (b) (j-m) eine Falle stellen. ◆**'trapdoor**, s. Falltür f.

trap2, s. (pony) t., Ponywagen m.

trapeze [trə'piːz], s. Trapez n.

trappings ['træpiŋz], s. pl. **all the t.**, das ganze Drum und Dran.

trash [træʃ], s. 1. N.Am: Abfälle mpl. 2. Pej: (literature etc.) Schund m; (worthless stuff) Plunder m. ◆**'trashy**, adj. wertlos.

traumatic [trɔː'mætik], adj. traumatisch; F: erschütternd.

travel ['trævl]. I. s. Reisen n; t. agency, Reisebüro n. II. v. 1. v.i. reisen. 2. v.tr. (eine Strecke) zurücklegen. ◆**'traveller**, s. Reisende(r) f(m); **t.'s cheque**, Reisescheck m. ◆**'travelling**. I. adj. reisend; t. salesman, Handelsreisende(r) m. II. s. Reisen n; **t. bag**, Reisetasche f. ◆**'travelogue**, s. Reisebeschreibung f.

traverse [trə'vɜːs], v.tr. durchqueren.

trawler ['trɔːlər], s. Trawler m, Fischdampfer m.

tray [trei], s. Tablett n.

treacherous ['tretʃ(ə)rəs], adj. (of pers., disease etc.) heimtückisch; (of action) ver-

räterisch; Fig: **a t. surface**, eine glitschige Fahrbahn. ◆**'treachery**, s. Verrat m.

treacle ['triːkl], s. (dunkler) Sirup m.

tread [tred]. I. s. 1. Schritt m, Tritt m. 2. (of stair) Treppenstufe f. 3. Aut: etc: Profil n (eines Reifens). II. v.irr. 1. v.i. treten; **to t. on s.o.'s toes**, j-m auf die Zehen treten. 2. v.tr. **to t. under foot**, (etwas) mit Füßen treten.

treason ['triːz(ə)n], s. Landesverrat m.

treasure ['treʒər]. I. s. Schatz m; **t. hunt**, Schatzsuche f. II. v.tr. (a) (etwas) (wie einen Schatz) hüten; (b) Fig: (j-s Freundschaft usw.) sehr schätzen. ◆**'treasurer**, s. Schatzmeister m. ◆**'treasury**, s. Schatzamt n; Brit: Adm: Finanzministerium n.

treat [triːt]. I. s. (besonderes) Vergnügen n; (meal) Schmaus m; **to stand s.o. a t.**, j-m etwas spendieren; **school t.**, Schulausflug m. II. v.tr. (a) behandeln; (b) **to t. s.o. to sth.**, j-m etwas spendieren; **to t. oneself to sth.**, sich dat etwas gönnen. ◆**'treatise** ['triːtiz], s. Abhandlung f (on, über + acc). ◆**'treatment**, s. Behandlung f. ◆**'treaty**, s. Vertrag m.

treble ['trebl]. I. adj. 1. dreifach. 2. Mus: **t. voice**, Sopranstimme f; **t. clef**, Diskantschlüssel m. II. s. 1. das Dreifache. 2. Mus: (a) (pers., voice) Sopran m; (b) (range) Diskant m. III. v.tr. (etwas) verdreifachen.

tree [triː], s. Baum m. ◆**'treetop**, s. Baumkrone f; (tip) Baumwipfel m.

trek [trek]. I. s. Treck m. II. v.i. F: (irgendwohin) latschen.

trellis ['trelis], s. Gitter n; (for plants) Spalier n.

tremble ['trembl], v.i. zittern (with, vor + dat); (of voice etc.) beben. ◆**'trembling**. I. adj. zitternd. II. s. Zittern n; Beben n.

tremendous [tri'mendəs], adj. (a) enorm; (b) (splendid) prächtig.

tremor ['tremər], s. 1. Zittern n. 2. (earth) t., Erschütterungswelle f.

trench [tren(t)ʃ], s. Graben m; Mil: Schützengraben m.

trend [trend]. I. s. Trend m. II. v.i. tendieren **(to/towards**, zu + dat). ◆**'trendy**, adj. F: modisch.

trepidation [trepi'deiʃ(ə)n], s. Angst f.

trespass ['trespəs], v.i. (in Grundstück) unbefugt betreten. ◆**'trespasser**, s. **trespassers will be prosecuted**, unbefugtes Betreten wird strafrechtlich verfolgt.

tress [tres], s: Lit: Locke f.

trestle ['tresl], s. Bock m; **t. table**, (langer) Klapptisch m.

trial ['traiəl], s. 1. Jur: Prozeß m. 2. (test) Probe f; **on t.**, auf/zur Probe; **by t. and error**, durch wiederholtes Versuchen; Com: **t. order**, Probeauftrag m; Aut: **t. run**, Probefahrt f.

triangle ['traiæŋgl], s. 1. Dreieck m. 2. Mus: Triangel m. ◆**tri'angular**, adj. dreieckig.

tribe [traib], s. Volksstamm m. ◆**tribal,** adj. Stammes-. ◆**tribesman,** pl. -men, s. Stammesangehörige(r) m.

tribulation [tribjuˈleiʃən], s. Lit: Drangsal n.

tribunal [tr(a)iˈbju:n(ə)l], s. Tribunal n; (for appeals) Appellationsgericht n; Ind: Arbeitsgericht n.

tribute [ˈtribju:t], s. (respect) Huldigung f; (praise) Lob n. ◆**tributary,** s. Nebenfluß m.

trice [trais], s. in a t., im Nu.

trick [trik]. I. s. 1. Trick m; to play a t. on s.o., j-m einen Streich spielen. 2. (habit) Angewohnheit f; F: Tick m. 3. (at cards) Stich m. II. v.tr. (j-n) betrügen. ◆**trickery,** s. Betrug m. ◆**tricky,** adj. (of job etc.) kompliziert; (of situation etc.) heikel.

trickle [ˈtrikl]. I. s. Rinnsal n; (drip) Tröpfeln n. II. v.i. rieseln; (seep) sickern; (of tap) tröpfeln.

tricycle [ˈtraisikl], s. Dreirad n.

tried [traid], adj. (well) t., bewährt.

trier [ˈtraiər], s. F: he's a (hard) t., er bemüht sich sehr.

trifle [ˈtraifl], s. 1. (a) Kleinigkeit f; (b) a t. too short, etwas zu kurz. 2. Cu: Trifle n. ◆**trifling,** adj. unbedeutend.

trigger [ˈtrigər]. I. s. (a) (of gun) Abzug m; to pull the t., abdrücken; (b) Phot: etc: Auslöser m. II. v.tr. to t. sth. (off), etwas auslösen.

trigonometry [trigəˈnɔmitri], s. Trigonometrie f.

trill [tril]. I. s. Mus: Triller m. II. v.i. trillern.

trilogy [ˈtrilədʒi], s. Trilogie f.

trim [trim]. I. s. 1. (condition) (guter) Zustand m; **in good t.,** in gutem Zustand; (of pers.) gut beisammen; Sp: in guter Form; Sp: to get into t., in Kondition kommen. 2. (cutting) to give sth. a t., etwas (nach)schneiden. 3. Aut: Zierleisten fpl; (interior) Innenausstattung f. II. adj. (neat) ordentlich; sauber; (smart) schmuck; (of lawn, beard) gepflegt; a t. figure, eine schlanke Figur. III. v.tr. a (cut) (Haare usw.) (nach)schneiden; (eine Hecke, den Bart) stutzen; (einen Hund) trimmen; (b) (decorate) Cl: verzieren; trimmed with lace, mit Spitze besetzt; (c) Fig: to t. one's sails to the wind, sich nach dem Winde drehen. ◆**trimming,** s. 1. Cl: Besatz m. 2. Cu: Garnierung f; F: with all the trimmings, mit allem Drum und Dran.

Trinity [ˈtriniti], s. the T., die Dreifaltigkeit; **T. (Sunday),** Dreifaltigkeitsfest n.

trinket [ˈtriŋkit], s. (wertloses) Schmuckstück n.

trio, pl. -os [ˈtri:ɔu, -ɔuz], s. Trio n.

trip [trip]. I. s. 1. (excursion) Ausflug m; (journey) Reise f; (short) Fahrt f; esp. N.Am: (holiday) Urlaubsreise f; Aut: t. (recorder), Kilometerzähler m (für kurze Entfernungen). 2. (a) (stumble) Stolpern

n; (b) (tripping s.o.) Beinstellen n. II. v. 1. v.i. (a) to t. along, dahertrippeln; (b) to t. (up), stolpern; Fig: to t. up (badly), einen (schweren) Fehler machen. 2. v.tr. to t. s.o. (up), (i) j-m ein Bein/Fig: eine Falle stellen; (ii) (catch out) Fig: j-n bei einem Fehler ertappen. ◆**tripper,** s. Ausflügler(in) m(f).

tripe [traip], s. 1. Cu: Kutteln fpl. 2. F: (rubbish) Mist m.

triple [ˈtripl], adj. dreifach. ◆**triplet,** s. (pers.) Drilling m. ◆**triplicate,** s. in t., in dreifacher Ausfertigung.

tripod [ˈtraipɔd], s. Dreifuß m; Phot: Stativ n.

trite [trait], adj. banal; (of phrase) abgedroschen.

triumph [ˈtraiəmf, -ʌmf]. I. s. Triumph m; (victory) Sieg m. II. v.i. triumphieren. ◆**triumphal** [-ˈʌmf(ə)l], adj. Triumph-. ◆**tri'umphant,** adj. triumphierend; (victorious) siegreich.

trivial [ˈtriviəl], adj. unbedeutend; (a) (of reason, complaint etc.) geringfügig; (b) (of work of art) banal. ◆**trivi'ality,** s. Unwichtigkeit f; (b) Banalität f.

trolley [ˈtrɔli], s. (a) Handwagen m; shopping t., Einkaufswagen m; Rail: Av: luggage t., Kofferkuli m; (b) (tea) t., Teewagen m. ◆**trolleybus,** s. Oberleitungsbus m, F: O-Bus m.

trombone [trɔmˈbɔun], s. Mus: Posaune f.

troop [tru:p]. I. s. 1. (group) Schar f. 2. Mil: pl. **troops,** Truppen fpl; **t. ship,** Truppentransportschiff n. II. v.i. to t. in/out/off, in Scharen hereinströmen/hinausströmen/losziehen. ◆**trooper,** s. Mil: Kavallerist m.

trophy [ˈtrɔufi], s. Trophäe f.

tropic [ˈtrɔpik], s. (a) Wendekreis m (b) pl. **the tropics,** die Tropen pl. ◆**tropical,** adj. tropisch.

trot [trɔt]. I. s. Trab m. II. v.i. traben.

trouble [ˈtrʌbl]. I. s. 1. (a) (worry) Sorge f; (b) (difficulties) Schwierigkeiten fpl; (unpleasantness) Unannehmlichkeiten fpl; to get into t. with the police, mit der Polizei in Konflikt kommen; to be in t., in Nöten sein; to make t., Unruhe stiften. 2. (bother) Mühe f; to take the t./go to the t. of doing sth., sich dat die Mühe machen, etwas zu tun; it's not worth the t., das ist nicht der Mühe wert; to go to a lot of t., sich dat viel Mühe machen; it's no t.! das ist nicht der Rede wert! 3. (a) he has heart t., er hat es mit dem Herzen; (b) engine t., Maschinenschaden m; (c) pl. Pol: Unruhen pl. II. v. 1. v.tr. (a) (worry) (j-n) beunruhigen; to be troubled about s.o., um j-n in Sorge sein; (b) (j-n) belästigen; I'm sorry to t. you, es tut mir leid; Sie stören zu müssen; to t. (oneself) to do sth., sich dat die Mühe machen, etwas zu tun. 2. v.i. (worry) beunruhigt sein (about, wegen + gen); don't t. about it, machen Sie sich keine Sorgen darum. ◆'**troubled**, *adj.* **1.** (*of water*) aufgewühlt. **2.** (*of sleep etc.*) unruhig. **t. period**, turbulente/bewegte Zeit. ◆'**troublemaker**, *s.* Unruhestifter *m.* ◆'**troubleshooter**, *s.* (*a*) *Ind:* Störungssucher *m;* (*b*) *Fig:* (*peacemaker*) Friedensstifter *m.* ◆'**troublesome**, *adj.* **1.** lästig. **2.** (*of task*) mühsam.

trough [trɒf], *s.* **1.** Trog *m.* **2.** *Meteor:* **t. of low pressure**, Tiefdruckgebiet *n.*

trounce [trauns], *v.tr. Sp:* (j-n, eine Mannschaft) haushoch besiegen.

troupe [tru:p], *s. Th: etc:* Truppe *f.*

trousers ['trauzəz], *s.pl.* (**pair of**) **t.**, Hose *f.*

trousseau ['tru:səu], *s.* Aussteuer *f.*

trout [traut], *s. inv.* Forelle *f.*

trowel ['trau(ə)l], *s.* Kelle *f.*

truant ['tru:ənt], *s. Sch:* Schwänzer *m;* **to play t.**, die Schule schwänzen.

truce [tru:s], *s.* Waffenstillstand *m.*

truck[1] [trʌk], *s.* **1. I have no t. with him**, mit ihm will ich nichts zu tun haben. **2.** *N.Am:* (**garden**) **t.**, Gemüse und Obst; **t. farmer**, Gemüsegärtner *m.* **t. farm**, Gemüsegärtnerei *f.*

truck[2], *s.* (*a*) *Aut: esp. N.Am:* Lastwagen *m, F:* Laster *m;* **delivery t.**, Lieferwagen *m;* **t. driver**, Lastwagenfahrer *m;* (*b*) *Rail: esp. Brit:* Wagen *m;* **goods t.**, Güterwagen *m.*

truculence ['trʌkjuləns], *s.* Trotz *m.* ◆'**truculent**, *adj.* trotzig.

trudge [trʌdʒ], *v.i.* (mühselig) stapfen.

true [tru:]. *adj.* **1.** wahr; **that's t.!** das stimmt! **to come t.**, sich verwirklichen; (*of dream*) in Erfüllung gehen. **2.** (*real*) echt, wirklich; **a t. friend**, ein wahrer Freund. **3.** (*faithful*) treu (**to**, *dat*); **to one's word**, seinem Wort getreu; **t. to life**, lebensecht.

truffle ['trʌfl], *s.* Trüffel *f.*

truly ['tru:li], *adv. (a)* treu, aufrichtig; (*b*) **I am t. grateful to you**, ich bin Ihnen wirklich dankbar; (*c*) **yours t.**, Ihr ergebener.

trump [trʌmp], *s.* **1.** Trumpf *m.* **II.** *v.tr.* **to t. up an excuse**, eine Entschuldigung erfinden.

trumpet ['trʌmpit]. **I.** *s.* Trompete *f.* **II.** *v.i.* trompeten.

truncheon ['trʌn(t)ʃ(ə)n], *s.* Knüppel *m;* **rubber t.**, Gummiknüppel *m.*

trundle ['trʌndl], *v.* **1.** *v.tr.* (eine Schubkarre usw.) schieben. **2.** *v.i. Aut:* **to t. along**, dahingondeln.

trunk [trʌŋk], *s.* **1.** (*a*) Stamm *m* (eines Baumes); (*b*) (*of pers., animal*) Rumpf *m;* *Tel:* **t. call**, Ferngespräch *n.* **2.** (*large case*) Schrankkoffer *m.* **3.** Rüssel *m* (eines Elefanten). **4.** *pl. Cl:* Unterhose *f;* (*for swimming*) Badehose *f.*

truss [trʌs]. **I.** *s.* Bruchband *n.* **II.** *v.tr.* **to t. s.o. up**, j-n fesseln.

trust [trʌst]. **I.** *s.* **1.** Vertrauen *n* (**in**, auf + *acc*). **2.** *Jur:* Treuhandverhältnis *n.* **II.** *v.tr.* (j-m) vertrauen; (j-m) trauen; **to**

t. s.o. with sth./sth. to s.o., j-m etwas anvertrauen; **t. him to spend it all on drink!** das sieht ihm ähnlich, alles für Alkohol auszugeben! ◆'**trus'tee**, *s. Jur:* Treuhänder *m;* Verwalter *m* (eines Vermögens). ◆'**trustful**/'**trusting**, *adj.* vertrauensvoll. ◆'**trustworthiness**, *s.* **1.** Zuverlässigkeit *f.* **2.** Glaubwürdigkeit *f.* ◆'**trustworthy**, *adj.* **1.** zuverlässig. **2.** (*credible*) glaubwürdig. ◆'**trusty**, *adj.* zuverlässig; (*faithful*) treu.

truth [tru:θ], *s.* **1.** Wahrheit *f;* **the t. is/to tell the t., I forgot**, ehrlich gesagt, ich habe es vergessen. ◆'**truthful**, *adj.* (*a*) (*of pers.*) wahrheitsliebend; (*b*) (*of story etc.*) wahr; **-ly**, *adv.* wahrheitsgemäß. ◆'**truthfulness**, *s.* (*a*) Wahrheitsliebe *f;* (*b*) Wahrhaftigkeit *f.*

try [trai]. **I.** *s.* Versuch *m;* **to have a t. at doing sth**, es mit etwas *dat* versuchen. **II.** *v.* **1.** *v.tr.* (*a*) versuchen; (*b*) (*test*) ausprobieren; (*c*) *Fig:* (j-n, etwas) prüfen; (*d*) *Jur:* **to t. a case**, über eine Sache gerichtlich verhandeln. **2.** *v.i.* (*a*) (*take trouble*) **you're not trying**, du strengst dich nicht an; (*b*) (*es*) versuchen; **t. again**, versuch es noch einmal; **it's worth trying**, der Versuch lohnt sich; (*c*) **to t. for sth.**, sich um etwas *acc* bemühen. ◆'**trying**, *adj.* aufreibend; (*laborious*) mühsam. ◆'**try 'on**, *v.tr.* (ein Kleidungsstück) anprobieren. ◆'**try 'out**, *v.tr.* ausprobieren. ◆'**try-out**, *s.* Probe *f.*

tsar [zɑr, tsɑr], *s.* Zar *m.*

tub [tʌb], *s.* (*a*) (*for plants etc.*) Kübel *m;* **bath t.**, Badewanne *f;* (*b*) (*small*) Becher *m.* ◆'**tubby**, *adj. F:* (*of pers.*) pummelig.

tuba ['tju:bə], *s.* Tuba *f.*

tube [tju:b], *s.* **1.** Rohr *n,* Röhre *f; T.V:* Bildröhre *f;* (*flexible, also Aut:*) Schlauch *m.* **2.** **t. of toothpaste etc.**, Tube *f* Zahnpasta usw. **3.** *Rail:* **the t.**, die U-Bahn; **t. station**, U-Bahnhof *m.* ◆'**tubeless**, *adj. Aut:* schlauchlos. ◆'**tubular**, *adj.* röhrenförmig.

tuber ['tju:bər], *s. Bot:* Knolle *f.* ◆**tuberculosis** [tjubɜːkju'ləusis], *s. Med:* Tuberkulose *f.*

tuck [tʌk]. **I.** *s.* **1** *Cl:* Abnäher *m.* **2.** *F: Sch:* **t. shop**, Süßwarengeschäft *n.* **II.** *v.tr.* (*a*) *Cl:* Abnäher (in den Stoff) machen; (*b*) (etwas) (irgendwohin) stecken. ◆'**tuck 'a'way**, *v.tr.* (*a*) (etwas) wegstecken, (*hide*) verstecken; (*b*) *F:* (Essen) verdrücken. ◆'**tuck 'in**, *v.* **1.** *v.tr.* (*a*) (etwas) einstecken; **to t. in the sheet**, das Bettuch unterschlagen/feststecken; (*b*) **to t. the children in**, die Kinder im Bett gut zudecken. **2.** *v.i. F:* (tüchtig) zulangen. ◆'**tuck 'up**, *v.tr.* (*a*) (die Ärmel) hochkrempeln; (den Rock) schürzen; (*b*) (j-n) im Bett gut zudecken.

Tuesday ['tju:zdi], *s.* Dienstag *m.*

tuft [tʌft], *s.* (*of hair, grass etc.*) Büschel *m.*

tug [tʌg]. **I.** *s.* **1.** Zerren *n; Sp:* (*also Fig:*

t. of war, Tauziehen *n.* 2. *Nau:* t. (boat), Schlepper *m.* II. *v.tr* & *i.* ziehen; to t. sth. along, etwas hinter sich *dat* herziehen.

tuition [tju(:)'ıʃ(ə)n], *s.* Unterricht *m.*

tulip ['tju:lıp], *s.* Tulpe *f.*

tumble ['tʌmbl]. I. *s.* Fall *m.*, Sturz *m;* to take a t., stürzen. II. *v.i.* (a) *(fall)* stürzen; (b) F: to t. to it, es kapieren. ◆**'tumbledown**, *adj.* baufällig. ◆**'tumble-'drier**, *s.* Wäschetrockner *m.* ◆**'tumbler**, *s.* *(glass)* Trinkglas *n.*

tummy ['tʌmı], *s.* F: Magen *m;* (belly) Bauch *m;* t. ache, Bauchschmerzen *pl.*

tumour ['tju:mər], *s.* Tumor *m.*

tumult ['tju:mʌlt], *s.* Tumult *m.* ◆**tu'multuous**, *adj.* turbulent; *(of applause etc.)* stürmisch.

tumulus, *pl.* **-li** ['tju:mjuləs, -laı], *s.* Hügelgrab *n.*

tuna ['tju:nə], *s.* Thunfisch *m.*

tundra ['tʌndrə], *s.* Tundra *f.*

tune [tju:n]. I. *s.* 1. Melodie *f.* 2. *(a* the piano is in t./out of t., das Klavier ist gestimmt/verstimmt; (to sing/play) out of t./in t., falsch/richtig (singen/spielen); *Fig:* to be in t./out of t. with one's surroundings, mit seiner Umwelt im Einklang/im Widerspruch stehen. 3. *Aut: (of engine)* **(state of)** t., Einstellung *f.* II. *v.tr.* (a) (ein Instrument) stimmen; (b) *Aut:* to t. the ignition/engine etc., die Zündung/den Motor usw. einstellen. ◆**'tuneful**, *adj. (of voice etc.)* melodisch; *(of music)* melodienreich. ◆**'tuneless**, *adj.* ohne Melodie. ◆**'tuner**, *s.* 1. piano t., Klavierstimmer *m.* 2. *Rad:* Tuner *m.* ◆**'tune 'in**, *v.tr.* & *i. Rad:* (a radio) einstellen (to a station, auf einen Sender). ◆**'tune 'up**, *v.* 1. *v.i. Mus:* die Instrumente stimmen. 2. *v.tr. Aut:* (den Motor) frisieren. ◆**'tuning**, *s.* 1. *Mus:* Stimmen *n.* 2. *Aut:* Einstellen *n.* 3. *Rad:* Sendereinstellung *f.*

tungsten ['tʌŋstən], *s.* Wolfram *n.*

tunic ['tju:nık], *s.* 1. *(of soldier, policeman)* Uniformjacke *f.* 2. *(blouse)* Kasack-Bluse *f.*

Tunisia [tju(:)'nızıə], *Pr. n.* Tunesien *n.* ◆**Tu'nisian**, I. *adj.* tunesisch. II. *s.* Tunesier(in) *m(f).*

tunnel ['tʌn(ə)l]. I. *s.* Tunnel *m.* II. *v.i.* einen Tunnel bohren. ◆**'tunnelling**, *s.* Tunnelbau *m.*

tunny(-fish) ['tʌnı(fiʃ)], *s.* Thunfisch *m.*

turban ['tə:bən], *s.* Turban *m.*

turbid ['tə:bıd], *adj.* (a) *(thick)* zähflüssig; (b) *(not clear)* trüb.

turbine ['tə:baın], *s.* Turbine *f.*

turbot ['tə:bət], *s.* Steinbutt *m.*

turbulent ['tə:bjulənt], *adj.* turbulent. ◆**turbulence**, *s.* Turbulenz *f.*

tureen [tə'ri:n, tju-], *s.* Terrine *f.*

turf, *pl.* **turves** [tə:f, tə:vz], *s.* 1. Rasen *m;* (sod) Grassode *f.* 2. *(peat)* Torf *m.*

turgid ['tə:dʒıd], *adj. Med:* & *Fig:* geschwollen.

Turkey[1] ['tə:kı], *Pr. n.* die Türkei. ◆**Turk**, *s.* Türke *m,* Türkin *f.* ◆**'Turkish**. I. *adj.* türkisch; T. bath, Dampfbad *n;* t. delight, Türkischer Honig *m.* II. *s.* (language) Türkisch *n.*

turkey[2], *s.* (bird) Truthahn *m; Cu:* Pute(r) *f (m).*

turmoil ['tə:moıl], *s.* Tumult *m.*

turn [tə:n]. I. *s.* 1. *(revolution)* Umdrehung *f,* Drehung *f* (eines Rades usw.). 2. (a) *(change of direction)* Richtungswechsel *m;* t. of the tide, Gezeitenwechsel *m; Fig:* Wendepunkt *m; (of tide, weather etc.)* **to be on the t.**, umschlagen; (b) *(in road)* Abbiegung *f; (bend)* Kurve *f; (change of condition)* Wendung *f;* at the t. of the century, um die Jahrhundertwende; to take a t. for the better/worse, sich zum Guten/Schlechten wenden; (d) *F:* the sight gave me quite a t., der Anblick versetzte mir einen ziemlichen Schock. 3. (a) in t., der Reihe nach; by turns, abwechselnd; they take (it in) turns, sie wechseln sich ab; it is my t., ich bin an der Reihe/F: dran; (b) *Th: etc:* Nummer *f.* 4. to do s.o. a good t., j-m einen Gefallen tun. II. *v.* 1. *v.tr.* (a) *(rotate)* drehen; to t. a page, umblättern; (b) they turned the whole house upside down, sie haben das ganze Haus auf den Kopf gestellt; (c) *(direct)* (Augen, Gedanken usw.) richten (to, towards, auf + *acc*); (d) to t. the corner, um die Ecke biegen; *(of invalid etc.)* über dem Berg sein; (e) (j-n, etwas) machen (into, zu + *acc*); this weather has turned the milk sour, bei diesem Wetter ist die Milch sauer geworden. 2. *v.i.* (a) *(rotate)* *(of wheel etc.)* sich drehen; to toss and t. in bed, sich im Bett hin und her wälzen; (b) sich wenden (to, zu + *dat*); to t. to the right/left, sich nach rechts/links drehen; *Aut:* nach rechts/links abbiegen; the wind is turning, der Wind dreht sich; to t. to s.o., sich j-m zuwenden; (c) *(change)* sich verwandeln (into, in + *acc*); (become) werden (zu + *dat*); the tide is turning, die Gezeiten schlagen um; the milk has turned (sour), die Milch ist sauer geworden; the leaves are beginning to t., die Blätter verfärben sich. ◆**'turn a'way**, *v.* 1. *v.tr.* (a) (das Gesicht, einen Schlag usw.) abwenden; (b) (j-n, esp Zuschauer) abweisen. 2. *v.i.* sich abwenden. ◆**'turn 'back**, *v.* 1. *v.tr.* (a) (j-n) umkehren lassen; (b) (die Bettdecke usw.) zurückschlagen. 2. *v.i.* umkehren. ◆**'turn 'down**, *v.tr.* (a) (eine Bettdecke usw.) zurückschlagen; (den Kragen usw.) herunterschlagen; (eine Buchseite) umknicken; (b) (die Gasflamme usw.) kleiner stellen; (das Radio usw.) leiser stellen; (c) (j-n abweisen; to t. d. an offer etc., ein Angebot usw. ablehnen. ◆**'turn 'in**, *v.tr.* (die Füße usw.) nach innen drehen; (Stoff usw.) nach innen falten. ◆**'turning**. I. *adj.* (sich) drehend; *Fig:* t. point, Wendepunkt *m.* **II.** *s.* Abbiegen *n;* **take the first t. to the right,** die erste Straße rechts abbiegen. ◆'turn 'off, *v.* 1. *v.tr.* (das Wasser, den Strom usw.) abstellen; (das Licht) ausmachen; (das Radio, den Fernseher usw.) ausschalten; (den Wasserhahn usw.) zudrehen. 2. *v.i.* (von einer Straße) abbiegen. ◆'turn 'on, *v.tr.* (das Gas, den Strom usw.) anstellen; (das Wasser) andrehen; (das Licht) anmachen; (ein Gerät) einschalten; (den Wasserhahn usw.) aufdrehen. ◆'turn 'out, *v.* 1. *v.tr.* (a) (j-n) hinauswerfen (**off/from,** aus + *dat*); (b) (eine Schublade, ein Zimmer usw.) ausräumen; (c) *Ind:* (Waren) herstellen; (d) (das Licht usw.) ausmachen. 2. *v.i.* **everything turned o. well in the end,** es ist alles gut ausgegangen; **it turned out that...,** es stellte sich heraus, daß...; ◆'turn-out, *s.* **there was a good t.-o. at the meeting,** die Versammlung war gut besucht. ◆'turn 'over, *v.tr.* (a) umdrehen; (eine Seite) umblättern; ◆'turnover, *s. Com:* Umsatz *m.* ◆'turn 'round, *v.* 1. *v.tr.* umdrehen. 2. *v.i.* (of pers., etc.) sich umdrehen. ◆'turnstile, *s.* 1. Drehkreuz *n.* ◆'turntable, *s.* 1. *Rail: etc:* Drehscheibe *f.* 2. *Rec:* Plattenteller *m;* (complete unit) Laufwerk *n.* ◆'turn 'to, *v.i.* to t. to s.o. (for help), sich an j-n wenden. ◆'turn 'up, *v.* 1. *v.tr.* (a) nach oben drehen; (den Kragen) hochschlagen; **turned up nose,** Stupsnase *f; Fig:* **to t. up one's nose at sth.,** über etwas *acc* die Nase rümpfen; (c) **to t. up the gas,** das Gashöher stellen; *Rad: etc:* **can you t. it/the volume up?** können Sie es bitte lauter stellen? 2. *v.i. F: (appear)* auftauchen. ◆'turn-up, *s.* Aufschlag *m* (an einer Hose usw.).

turnip ['tə:nip], *s.* (weiße) Rübe *f.*
turpentine ['tə:p(ə)ntain], *s.* Terpentin *n.*
turquoise ['tə:kwɔːz, -kwɔiz]. **I.** *s.* 1. Türkis *m.* 2. (colour) Türkis *n.* **II.** *adj.* türkisfarben.
turret ['tʌrit], *s.* Türmchen *n.*
turtle ['tə:tl], *s.* 1. Schildkröte *f;* **t. soup,** Schildkrötensuppe *f.* 2. **t. dove,** Turteltaube *f.*
tusk [tʌsk], *s.* Stoßzahn *m.*
tussle ['tʌsl], *s.* Handgemenge *n.*
tutor ['tju:tər], *s.* 1. (private) t., Privatlehrer *m.* ◆tu'torial, *s.* Tutorenstunde *f.*
tuxedo, *pl.* **-os** [tʌk'si:dəu, -əuz], *s. N.Am:* Smoking *m.*
twaddle ['twɔdl], *s. F:* Quatsch *m;* **to talk t.,** quatschen.
twang [twæŋ]. **I.** *s.* 1. Vibrierton *m* (eines Saiteninstruments). 2. **to talk with a nasal t.,** näseln. **II.** *v.* 1. *v.tr.* **to t. a guitar,** auf der Gitarre zupfen. 2. *v.i.* (of string) vibrieren.
tweak [twi:k], *v.tr.* (etwas) zwicken.
tweed [twi:d], *s.* Tweed *m.*

tweezers ['twi:zəz], *s.pl.* Pinzette *f.*
twelve [twelv], *num. adj.* zwölf. ◆'twelfth, *num. adj.* zwölfte(r, s).
twenty ['twenti], *num. adj.* zwanzig; ◆'twentieth. **I.** *num. adj.* zwanzigste(r, s). **II.** *s. (fraction)* Zwanzigstel *n.*
twerp [twə:p], *s. P:* Blödian *m.*
twice [twais], *adv.* zweimal; **t. as big,** doppelt so groß; **he's t. my age,** er ist doppelt so alt wie ich.
twig[1] [twig], *s.* Zweig *m.*
twig[2], *v.tr. P:* (etwas) kapieren.
twilight ['twailait], *s. (evening)* Zwielicht *n;* Abenddämmerung *f; occ. (morning)* Morgendämmerung *f.*
twin [twin]. **I.** *s.* 1. Zwilling *m.* 2. **t. beds,** zwei Einzelbetten; **t. town,** Partnerstadt *f.* **II.** *v.tr.* (zwei Städte) zu Partnerstädten machen. ◆'twinning, *s.* Partnerschaft *f* (zweier Städte).
twine [twain]. **I.** *s.* Bindfaden *m.* **II.** *v.* 1. *v.tr.* (Fäden usw.) drehen; (together) zusammendrehen. 2. *v.i.* sich winden.
twinge [twin(d)ʒ], *s.* (a) Stich *m;* (b) **twinges of conscience,** Gewissensbisse *mpl.*
twinkle ['twiŋkl]. **I.** *s.* Funkeln *n.* **II.** *v.i.* funkeln. ◆'twinkling, *s.* Funkeln *n; F:* **in the t. of an eye/in a t.,** im Nu.
twirl [twə:l]. **I.** *s.* 1. (action) Drehen *n.* 2. (decoration) Schnörkel *m.* **II.** *v.* 1. *v.tr.* (Daumen, Locken usw.) drehen. 2. *v.i.* sich drehen.
twist [twist]. **I.** *s.* Windung *f; (rotating)* Drehung *f; also Fig:* Verdrehung *f;* **strange t. of fate,** seltsame Wendung des Schicksals. **II.** *v.* 1. *v.tr.* (a) drehen; (b) (out of shape) (etwas, *Fig:* die Wahrheit) verdrehen, verzerren; **to t. one's ankle,** sich *dat* den Fuß verrenken. 2. *v.i.* (of worm, road etc.) sich winden. ◆'twisted, *adj.* (a) (contorted) verzerrt; (of ankle etc.) verrenkt; (b) (of pers., views etc.) verdreht; (esp. sexually) pervers; **t. mind,** perverse Veranlagung. ◆'twister, *s. F:* Gauner *m.*
twit [twit], *s. P:* Idiot *m.*
twitch [twitʃ], *s.* 1. Zucken *n.* **II.** *v.i.* zucken.
twitter ['twitər]. **I.** *s.* Zwitschern *n.* **II.** *v.i.* (of bird etc.) zwitschern. ◆'twittering, *s.* Gezwitscher *n.*
two [tu:]. **I.** *s.* 1. **the t. of us** wir zwei; wir beide; **by t./in twos,** zu zweit; *Fig:* **to put t. and t. together,** es sich *dat* zusammenreimen. 2. (figure) Zwei *f.* **II.** *adj.* zwei; **the t. boys,** die beiden Jungen; *Fig:* **to be in t. minds about sth.,** über etwas *acc* im Zwiespalt sein. ◆'two-'faced, *adj.* heuchlerisch. ◆'two-'piece, *adj.* zweiteilig. ◆'two-'seater, *s.* Zweisitzer *m.* ◆'two-stroke, *adj.* Zweitakt-. ◆'two-'time, *v.tr. esp. N.Am:* (seinen Mann usw.) betrügen. ◆'two-'way, *adj. El:* **t.-w. adapter/**plug, Doppelstecker *m.*
tycoon [tai'ku:n], *s.* Industriemagnat *m.*

type ['taip]. **I.** s. 1. Typ *m*; (a) (of pers.) **an unpleasant t.,** ein unangenehmer Typ; (b) (of thing) **that t. of thing,** etwas in dieser Art. 2. (in printing) Type *f*. **II.** *v.tr. & i.* (a) (etwas) mit der Maschine schreiben, F: tippen; **typed,** maschinegeschrieben; (b) to **t. s.o.,** j-n typisieren. ◆'**typecast,** *v.tr.* Th: etc: (einem Schauspieler) eine Rolle zuordnen, die seinem Charakter entspricht. ◆'**typescript,** s. (Schreibmaschinen)manuskript *n*. ◆'**type-writer,** s. Schreibmaschine *f*. ◆'**typewritten,** *adj.* maschinegeschrieben, F: getippt. ◆'**typing,** s. Maschineschreiben *n*, F: Tippen *n*; ◆'**typist,** s. Stenotypist(in) *m(f)*.

typhoid ['taifɔid], s. Typhus *m*.
typhoon [tai'fuːn], s. Taifun *m*.
typhus ['taifəs], s. Flecktyphus *m*.
typical ['tipik(ə)l], *adj.* typisch; **that's t. of him,** das ist typisch für ihn. ◆'**typify,** *v.tr.* (etwas) charakterisieren.
tyranny ['tirəni], s. Tyrannei *f*. ◆**tyrannical** [ti'rænik(ə)l] tyrannisch. ◆'**tyrannize,** *v.tr.* tyrannisieren. ◆'**tyrant** ['taiər(ə)nt], s. Tyrann(in) *m(f)*.
tyre ['taiər], s. Reifen *m*; **t. pressure,** Reifendruck *m*.
Tyrol [ti'rɔːl]. *Pr. n.* (in the T., (in) Tirol *n*. ◆**Tyrolean** [tirə'liːən] *adj.* T. **Alps,** Tiroler Alpen. ◆**Tyrolese** [tirə'liːz] s. Tiroler(in) *m(f)*.

U

U, u [juː], s. 1. (der Buchstabe) U, u *n*. 2. F: **U and non-U,** das Feine und das Unfeine.
ubiquitous [juː'bikwitəs], *adj.* allgegenwärtig.
udder ['Adər], s. Euter *n*.
ugh [uh], *int.* pfui!
ugly ['Agli], *adj.* häßlich; **in an u. mood,** übler Laune. ◆'**ugliness,** s. Häßlichkeit *f*.
ulcer ['Alsər], s. Geschwür *n*.
ulterior [Al'tiəriər], *adj.* u. **motive,** Hintergedanken *f*.
ultimate ['Altimət], *adj.* äußerste(r, s); (final) endgültig; **-ly,** *adv.* (a) schließlich; (b) im Endeffekt. ◆**ultimatum** [Alti'meitəm], s. Ultimatum *n*.
ultra- ['Altrə], *prefix* Ultra-. ◆**ultra'sonic,** *adj.* Ultraschall-. ◆**ultra'violet,** *adj.* ultraviolett.
umbilical [Am'bilik(ə)l], *adj.* u. **cord,** Nabelschnur *f*.
umbrage ['Ambridʒ], s. Ärgernis *n*; to **take u. at sth.,** an etwas *dat* Anstoß nehmen.
umbrella [Am'brelə], s. Schirm *m*.
umpire ['Ampaiər]. **I.** s. Sp: Schiedsrichter *m*. **II.** *v.tr.* Sp: (ein Spiel) als Schiedsrichter leiten. ◆'**umpiring,** s. Schiedsrichtern *n*.
umpteen [Am(p)'tiːn], *adj.* F: zig; u. **times,** x-mal.
un-, [An], *prefix* un-, nicht.
unabashed [Anə'bæʃt], *adj.* unerschrocken.
unabated [Anə'beitid], *adj.* unvermindert.
unable [An'eibl], *adj.* to be u. to do sth., etwas nicht tun können.
unacceptable [Anək'septəbl], *adj.* unannehmbar.
unaccompanied [Anə'kAmpənid], *adj.* unbegleitet.
unaccountable [Anə'kauntəbl], *adj.* unerklärlich; **-ably,** *adv.* unerklärlicher-

weise.
unaccustomed [Anə'kAstəmd], *adj.* ungewohnt; **u. to sth.,** an etwas *acc* nicht gewöhnt.
unadulterated [Anə'dAltəreitid], *adj.* unverfälscht, rein.
unaffected [Anə'fektid], *adj.* 1. (genuine) ungekünstelt; (of feelings) aufrichtig; (of pers., style) natürlich. 2. (a) (of pers.) (unmoved) unberührt; (b) (unchanged) unverändert.
unaided [An'eidid], *adj.* ohne Hilfe; **(alone and) u.,** ganz allein.
unaltered [An'ɔːltid], *adj.* unverändert.
unambitious [Anæm'biʃəs], *adj.* 1. (of pers.) nicht ehrgeizig. 2. (of project) anspruchslos.
unanimous [ju(ː)'næniməs], *adj.* (of decision) einstimmig.
unanswerable [An'ɑːnsərəbl], *adj.* (of criticism) unwiderlegbar; (of question, problem) unlösbar.
unappetizing [An'æpitaiziŋ], *adj.* unappetitlich.
unapproachable [Anə'prəutʃəbl], *adj.* unzugänglich; (of pers.) unnahbar.
unarmed [An'ɑːmd], *adj.* unbewaffnet.
unashamed [Anə'feimd], *adj.* schamlos.
unasked [An'ɑːskt], *adj.* ungebeten.
unassuming [Anə'sjuːmiŋ], *adj.* anspruchslos; (modest) bescheiden.
unattached [Anə'tætʃt], *adj.* ungebunden.
unattainable [Anə'teinəbl], *adj.* unerreichbar.
unattended [Anə'tendid], *adj.* unbeaufsichtigt.
unattractive [Anə'træktiv], *adj.* unattraktiv.
unauthorized [An'ɔːθəraizd], *adj.* unbefugt.
unavoidable [Anə'vɔidəbl], *adj.* unvermeidlich.
unaware [Anə'wɛər], *adj.* to be u. of sth., sich *dat* einer Sache nicht bewußt

sein. ◆una'wares, adv. to take s.o. u., j-n überraschen.

unbalanced [ʌn'bælənst], adj. unausgeglichen; (of mind) gestört.

unbearable [ʌn'bɛərəbl], adj. unerträglich.

unbeatable [ʌn'bi:təbl], adj. unschlagbar.

unbecoming [ʌnbi'kʌmiŋ], adj. 1. unschicklich. 2. (of garment) unkleidsam.

unbelievable [ʌnbi'li:vəbl], adj. unglaublich.

unbend [ʌn'bend], v.irr. 1. v.i. sich gerade biegen; Fig: (of pers.) auftauen. 2. v.tr. (etwas) geradebiegen. ◆un'bending, adj. unbiegsam; Fig: (of will etc.) unbeugsam.

unbias(s)ed [ʌn'baiəst], adj. unparteiisch.

unbounded [ʌn'baundid], adj. unbegrenzt.

unbreakable [ʌn'breikəbl], adj. unzerbrechlich.

unbridled [ʌn'braidld], adj. (of passion) zügellos.

unbroken [ʌn'brəuk(ə)n], adj. (a) nicht gebrochen; (b) (uninterrupted) ununterbrochen; (c) Sp: u. record, unübertroffener Rekord.

unbutton [ʌn'bʌt(ə)n], v.tr. aufknöpfen.

uncalled [ʌn'kɔ:ld], adj. u. for, (inappropriate) fehl am Platze; (unjustified) unbegründet.

uncanny [ʌn'kæni], adj. unheimlich.

uncared for [ʌn'kɛəd fɔ:r], adj. vernachlässigt.

unceasing [ʌn'si:siŋ], adj. unaufhörlich.

unceremonious [ʌnseri'məuniəs], adj. (of treatment) unsanft; (of pers., rebuke) brüsk; -ly, adv. ohne viel Federlesens.

uncertain [ʌn'sə:t(ə)n], adj. unsicher; (of future etc.) ungewiß; (of time, amount) unbestimmt; (varying) unbeständig; I am u. whether ..., ich bin nicht sicher, ob ... ◆un'certainty, s. Unsicherheit f; Ungewißheit f; Unbestimmtheit f; (doubt) Zweifel m.

unchangeable [ʌn'tʃein(d)ʒəbl], adj. unveränderlich. ◆un'changed, adj. unverändert. ◆un'changing, adj. gleichbleibend.

uncharted [ʌn'tʃɑ:tid], adj. nicht kartiert.

unchecked [ʌn'tʃekt], adj. 1. (not held up) ungehemmt; (of fire, epidemic) to continue u., unvermindert fortdauern. 2. (not examined) nicht kontrolliert.

uncivil [ʌn'sivl], adj. unhöflich. ◆uncivilized [ʌn'sivilaizd], adj. unzivilisiert; (of conditions) primitiv; (of behaviour) ungehobelt.

unclaimed [ʌn'kleimd], adj. (of letter etc.) nicht abgeholt.

uncle ['ʌŋkl], s. Onkel m.

unclouded [ʌn'klaudid], adj. (of sky) unbewölkt; (of vision) klar; (of liquid) ungetrübt.

uncoil [ʌn'kɔil], v. 1. v.tr. (ein Kabel usw.) abspulen. 2. v.i. (of snake) sich ausringeln.

uncomfortable [ʌn'kʌmf(ə)təbl], adj. (of things) unbequem; (unpleasant) unangenehm.

uncommon [ʌn'kɒmən], adj. ungewöhnlich; (of word, bird, flower etc.) selten; -ly, adv. außerordentlich.

uncommunicative [ʌnkə'mju:nikətiv], adj. verschlossen.

uncomplaining [ʌnkəm'pleiniŋ], adj. nicht klagend; -ly, adv. klaglos.

uncomplimentary [ʌnkɒmpli'ment(ə)ri], adj. wenig schmeichelhaft.

uncompromising [ʌn'kɒmprəmaiziŋ], adj. kompromißlos; (inflexible) unnachgiebig.

unconcerned [ʌnkən'sə:nd], adj. (not worried) unbesorgt; unbekümmert (about, wegen + gen).

unconditional [ʌnkən'diʃənəl], adj. vorbehaltlos.

unconfirmed [ʌnkən'fə:md], adj. unbestätigt.

uncongenial [ʌnkən'dʒi:niəl], adj. (of pers.) unsympathisch.

unconnected [ʌnkə'nektid], adj. nicht miteinander verbunden; (separate) getrennt; (not related) nicht verwandt.

unconscious [ʌn'kɒnʃəs], adj. 1. (unaware) unbewußt (of, + gen); the u., das Unbewußte. 2. (senseless) bewußtlos; to become u., das Bewußtsein verlieren; -ly, adv. unbewußt. ◆un'consciousness, s. 1. Unbewußtheit f. 2. Bewußtlosigkeit f.

uncontrollable [ʌnkən'trəuləbl], adj. (of child, anger) unbändig; (of desire) unwiderstehlich; u. laughter, unbeherrschtes Gelächter.

unconventional [ʌnkən'venʃən(ə)l], adj. unkonventionell.

unconvinced [ʌnkən'vinst], adj. nicht überzeugt (of sth., von etwas dat).

uncooked [ʌn'kukt], adj. ungekocht, roh.

uncork [ʌn'kɔ:k], v.tr. entkorken.

uncouth [ʌn'ku:θ], adj. ungehobelt; (of remark) grob; (awkward) linkisch.

uncover [ʌn'kʌvər], v.tr. (a) (etwas) freilegen; (einen Körperteil) entblößen; (b) Fig: to u. a plot, eine Verschwörung aufdecken.

uncultivated [ʌn'kʌltiveitid], adj. 1. (of field) unbebaut. 2. Fig: (of pers.) unkultiviert.

undamaged [ʌn'dæmidʒd], adj. unbeschädigt.

undaunted [ʌn'dɔ:ntid], adj. unverzagt.

undecided [ʌndi'saidid], adj. (a) (of game, issue etc.) unentschieden; (b) (of pers.) unschlüssig.

undecipherable [ʌndi'saif(ə)rəbl], adj. nicht zu entziffern.

undefinable [ʌndi'fainəbl], adj. undefinierbar. ◆unde'fined, adj. (a) nicht definiert; (b) (vague) unbestimmt.

undemonstrative [ˌʌndiˈmɔnstrətiv], *adj.* zurückhaltend.

undeniable [ˌʌndiˈnaiəbl], *adj.* unbestreitbar.

under ['ʌndər]. **I.** *prep.* unter + *dat(with motion)* + *acc*; from u. the table, unter dem Tisch hervor; he's u. thirty, er ist unter dreißig (Jahren); u. age, minderjährig; u. these circumstances, unter diesen Umständen; u. construction, im Bau; to be u. repair, in Reparatur sein. **II.** *adv.* unten. ◆**under'carriage**, *s. Av:* Fahrgestell *n.* ◆**under'clothes**, *s. pl.* /**underclothing**, *s.* Unterwäsche *f.* ◆**undercoat**, **I.** *s.* Grundierung *f.* **II.** *v.tr.* grundieren. ◆**under'cover**, *adj.* **u. agent**, Geheimagent *m.* ◆**undercurrent**, *s.* Unterströmung *f.* ◆**under'cut**, *v.tr.irr.* (j-n im Preis) unterbieten. ◆**under'veloped**, *adj.* unterentwickelt; **u. countries**, Entwicklungsländer *npl.* ◆**underdog**, *s.* the u., der Unterlegene. ◆**under'done**, *adj.* nicht gar; *(of meat)* nicht durch(gebraten). ◆**under'estimate**. **I.** [-mət] *s.* Unterschätzung *f.* **II.** [-meit] *v.tr.* (j-n, etwas) unterschätzen. ◆**underex'pose**, *v.tr.* (einen Film) unterbelichten. ◆**under'fed**, *adj.* unterernährt. ◆**under'foot**, *adv.* unter den Füßen. ◆**under'go**, *v.tr.irr.* (eine Erfahrung, einen Prozeß usw.) durchmachen; (einen Verlust) erleiden; *Med:* to u. an operation, sich einer Operation unterziehen. ◆**under'graduate/F:undergrad**, *s.* Student(in) *m(f)* (einer Universität). ◆**underground. I.** *adj.* Untergrund-; **u. railway**, Untergrundbahn *f.* **II.** *s. Rail:* Untergrundbahn *f; F:* U-Bahn *f. R:* ◆**undergrowth**, *s.* Unterholz *n;* Gestrüpp *n.* ◆**underhand**, *adj.* hinterhältig. ◆**under'line**, *v.tr.* unterstreichen. ◆**underling**, *s. Pej:* Handlanger *m.* ◆**under'lying**, *adj.* (a) darunterliegend; *(b) Fig:* zugrundeliegend. ◆**under'mine**, *v.tr.* (a) (etwas) unterminieren; (ein Ufer) aushöhlen; *(b) Fig:* (Autorität usw.) untergraben. ◆**under'neath. I.** *prep.* unter + *dat (with motion)* + *acc*; from u. sth., unter etwas *dat* hervor. **II.** *adv.* (a) unten; *(b) (below)* darunter. **III.** *s.* Unterseite *f.* ◆**under'nourished**, *adj.* unterernährt. ◆**under'paid**, *adj.* unterbezahlt. ◆**underpass**, *s.* Unterführung *f.* ◆**under'privileged**, *adj.* unterprivilegiert; (gesellschaftlich) benachteiligt. ◆**under'rate**, *v.tr.* unterschätzen. ◆**underseal**, *s. Aut:* Bodenschutz *m.* ◆**underside**, *s.* Unterseite *f.* ◆**under'signed**, *s.* the u., der/die Unterzeichnete. ◆**underskirt**, *s.* Unterrock *m.* ◆**under'stand**, *v.tr. & i.irr.* verstehen; to u. business, sich in geschäftlichen Angelegenheiten auskennen; **I u. your impatience**, ich habe Ver-

ständnis für Ihre Ungeduld; **what do you u. by that?** was verstehen Sie darunter? **am I to u. that ...?** wollen Sie damit sagen, daß ...? ◆**under'standable**, *adj.* verständlich; **ably**, *adv.* begreiflicherweise. ◆**under'standing**. **I.** *s.* **1.** Verständnis *n (of,* für + *acc); (insight)* Einsicht *f (of,* in + *acc).* **2.** *(agreement)* Vereinbarung *f;* **on the u. that**, unter der Bedingung/Voraussetzung, daß ... **II.** *adj. (of pers.)* verständnisvoll. ◆**under'statement**, *s.* Untertreibung *f.* ◆**under'stood**, *adj.* **1.** verstanden; **easily u.**, leicht verständlich; **to make oneself u.**, sich verständlich machen. **2.** *(agreed)* abgemacht. ◆**understudy. I.** *s.* zweite Besetzung *f.* **II.** *v.tr.* (einen Schauspieler) vertreten. ◆**under'take**, *v.tr.irr.* (a) (eine Reise usw.) unternehmen; (eine Aufgabe) auf sich nehmen; *(b)* to u. to do sth., sich verpflichten, etwas zu tun. ◆**undertaker**, *s.* Leichenbestatter *m.* ◆**under'taking**, *s.* **1.** *(taking on)* Übernehmen *n* (einer Aufgabe); Unternehmen *n* (einer Reise usw.). **2.** *a Com: (business)* Unternehmen *n; (b) (task)* Aufgabe *f.* **3.** *(promise)* Verpflichtung *f.* ◆**under'value**, *v.tr.* unterbewerten. ◆**underwear**, *s.* Unterwäsche *f.* ◆**underworld**, *s.* the (criminal) u., die Unterwelt. ◆**under'write**, *v.tr.irr.* (eine Summe usw.) garantieren. ◆**underwriter**, *s.* Versicherungsgeber *m.*

undeserved [ˌʌndiˈzɜːvd], *adj.* unverdient; **-ly** [-idli], *adv.* unverdient(erweise).

undesirable [ˌʌndiˈzaiərəbl], *adj.* unerwünscht.

undies ['ʌndiz], *s. pl. F:* Unterwäsche *f.*

undignified [ʌnˈdignifaid] *adj.* würdelos.

undiscovered [ˌʌndisˈkʌvəd], *adj.* unentdeckt.

undiscriminating [ˌʌndisˈkrimineitiŋ], *adj. (of pers., taste etc.)* anspruchslos.

undisputed [ˌʌndisˈpjuːtid], *adj.* unbestritten.

undistinguished [ˌʌndisˈtiŋgwiʃt], *adj.* durch nichts ausgezeichnet; *(ordinary)* gewöhnlich.

undisturbed [ˌʌndisˈtɜːbd], *adj.* ungestört.

undo [ʌnˈduː], *v.tr.irr. (a) (destroy)* to u. all the good, alles zunichte machen; *(b) (open)* aufmachen; *(unbutton)* (ein Kleid) aufknöpfen. ◆**un'done**, *adj.* **1.** offen. **2.** *(of work etc.)* unerledigt; **what's done cannot be u.**, Geschehenes kann man nicht ungeschehen machen.

undoubted [ʌnˈdautid], *adj.* unbestritten; **-ly**, *adv.* zweifellos.

undress [ʌnˈdres], *v.* **1.** *v.i.* sich ausziehen. **2.** *v.tr.* ausziehen.

undue ['ʌndjuː], *adj.* ungebührlich; *(excessive)* übertrieben. ◆**un'duly**, *adv.* übermäßig.

undulate ['ʌndjuleit], *v.i.* wogen.

◆**'undulating**, *adj.* wogend.

unearth [ʌn'ɜːθ], *v.tr.* (etwas) ausgraben; (ein Manuskript usw.) aufstöbern.

unearthly [ʌn'ɜːθli], *adj.* (*supernatural*) übernatürlich; *F:* **at an u. hour,** in aller Herrgottsfrühe.

uneasy [ʌn'iːzi], *adj.* (*worried*) besorgt; (*embarrassed*) verlegen; **he was u.** (**in his mind**), ihm war unbehaglich zumute. ◆**un'easiness**, *s.* Unbehagen *n;* (*worry*) Unruhe *f.*

uneatable [ʌn'iːtəbl], *adj.* ungenießbar.

uneconomic [ʌniːkə'nɔmik], *adj.* unwirtschaftlich. ◆**uneco'nomical**, *adj.* nicht sparsam.

uneducated [ʌn'edjukeitid], *adj.* ungebildet; (*of accent etc.*) unkultiviert.

unemployed [ʌnim'plɔid], *adj.* (*a*) unbeschäftigt; (*b*) (*out of a job*) arbeitslos; **the u., die** Arbeitslosen *pl.* ◆**unem'ployment**, *s.* Arbeitslosigkeit *f; Adm:* **u. benefit,** Arbeitslosenunterstützung *f.*

unending [ʌn'endiŋ], *adj.* endlos.

unenviable [ʌn'enviəbl], *adj.* wenig beneidenswert.

unequal [ʌn'iːkwəl], *adj.* ungleich; **to be u. to the task,** der Aufgabe nicht gewachsen sein; **-ly,** *adv.* ungleich. ◆**un'equalled**, *adj.* einmalig; (*of pers.*) ohnegleichen.

unerring [ʌn'ɜːriŋ], *adj.* unfehlbar; (*of sense*) untrüglich.

uneven [ʌn'iːv(ə)n], *adj.* (*a*) (*of surface*) uneben; (*bumpy*) holperig; (*b*) *Fig:* (*variable*) ungleichmäßig; (*of pulse*) nicht regelmäßig; *Mth:* **u. number,** ungerade Zahl.

uneventful [ʌni'ventful], *adj.* ereignislos; **u. life,** ruhiges Leben.

unexpected [ʌnik'spektid], *adj.* unerwartet; (*of result*) unvermutet; (*of meeting*) unverhofft.

unexploded ['ʌniks'spləudid], *adj.* nicht explodiert.

unexpressed [ʌniks'prest], *adj.* unausgesprochen.

unfailing [ʌn'feiliŋ], *adj.* unfehlbar.

unfair [ʌn'fɛər], *adj.* ungerecht, also *Sp:* unfair; (*morally*) unfair; (*wrongly*) zu Unrecht; **to act u.,** ungerecht handeln. ◆**un'fairness,** *s.* Ungerechtigkeit *f.*

unfaithful [ʌn'feiθful], *adj.* untreu. ◆**un'faithfulness,** *s.* Untreue *f.*

unfamiliar [ʌnfə'miljər], *adj.* (*a*) (*of thing*) unbekannt (**to s.o.,** j-m); (*strange*) fremd; (*b*) (*of pers.*) **to be u. with sth.,** etwas nicht kennen.

unfashionable [ʌn'fæʃ(ə)nəbl], *adj.* altmodisch; *esp. Cl:* unmodern.

unfasten [ʌn'fɑːsn], *v.tr.* (*a*) (etwas) losmachen; (*b*) (*open*) aufmachen.

unfavourable [ʌn'feiv(ə)rəbl], *adj.* ungünstig; (*of terms etc.*) unvorteilhaft (**for/to,** für + *acc*).

unfeeling [ʌn'fiːliŋ], *adj.* gefühllos.

unfinished [ʌn'finiʃt], *adj.* nicht fertig; (*of work of art*) unvollendet.

unfit [ʌn'fit], *adj.* (*a*) ungeeignet (**for**

sth., für etwas *acc*); (*unworthy*) nicht würdig (**to do sth.,** etwas zu tun); (*b*) (*in poor health*) bei schlechter Gesundheit, *Sp: & F:* nicht fit.

unflagging [ʌn'flægiŋ], *adj.* unermüdlich.

unflappable [ʌn'flæpəbl], *adj.* *F:* **she is u.,** sie ist nicht aus der Ruhe zu bringen.

unflattering [ʌn'flæt(ə)riŋ], *adj.* wenig schmeichelhaft; (*of dress*) unvorteilhaft.

unflinching [ʌn'flin(t)ʃiŋ], *adj.* unerschütterlich; (*resolute*) entschlossen; **-ly,** *adv.* ohne mit der Wimper zu zucken.

unfold [ʌn'fəuld], *v.* 1. *v.tr.* (*a*) (etwas) entfalten; (eine Zeitung) auseinanderfalten; (*b*) (einen Plan) darlegen. 2. *v.i.* sich entfalten; (*of plot etc.*) sich entwickeln.

unforeseeable [ʌnfɔː'siːəbl], *adj.* nicht voraussehbar. ◆**unfore'seen**, *adj.* unvorhergesehen.

unforgettable [ʌnfə'getəbl], *adj.* unvergeßlich.

unforgivable [ʌnfə'givəbl], *adj.* unverzeihlich.

unfortunate [ʌn'fɔːtʃənət], *adj.* (*a*) (*of pers.*) unglücklich; **to be u.,** Pech haben; (*b*) (*of mistake, coincidence etc.*) bedauerlich; **-ly,** *adv.* leider.

unfounded [ʌn'faundid], *adj.* unbegründet.

unfriendly [ʌn'frendli], *adj.* unfreundlich. ◆**un'friendliness,** *s.* Unfreundlichkeit *f.*

unfurnished [ʌn'fɜːniʃt], *adj.* unmöbliert.

ungainly [ʌn'geinli], *adj.* unbeholfen.

unget-at-able ['ʌnget'ætəbl], *adj.* *F:* schwer erreichbar/zugänglich.

ungodly [ʌn'gɔdli], *adj.* 1. gottlos; (*sinful*) sündhaft. 2. *F:* **at an u. hour,** in aller Hergottsfrühe.

ungracious [ʌn'greiʃəs], *adj.* unliebenswürdig; (*impolite*) unhöflich.

ungrateful [ʌn'greitful], *adj.* undankbar.

ungrudging [ʌn'grʌdʒiŋ], *adj.* bereitwillig.

unguarded [ʌn'gɑːdid], *adj.* 1. unbewacht. 2. (*of pers., remark*) unachtsam.

unhappy [ʌn'hæpi], *adj.* unglücklich. ◆**un'happily,** *adv.* unglücklicherweise.

unharmed [ʌn'hɑːmd], *adj.* unversehrt.

unhealthy [ʌn'helθi], *adj.* (*a*) ungesund; (*b*) (*of pers.*) nicht gesund.

unheard [ʌn'hɜːd], *adj.* 1. **to go u.,** nicht gehört werden; (*be ignored*) nicht beachtet werden. 2. **that's u. of,** das ist noch nie dagewesen/(*outrageous*) unerhört.

unhelpful [ʌn'helpful], *adj.* (*of pers.*) nicht hilfsbereit, unfreundlich; (*of criticism*) nicht konstruktiv.

unhesitating [ʌn'heziteitiŋ], *adj.* prompt, unverzüglich.

unhurt [ʌn'hɜːt], *adj.* unverletzt.

unidentified [ʌnai'dentifaid], *adj.* nicht identifiziert; **u. flying object,** unbekanntes Flugobjekt.

unification [juːnifi'keiʃ(ə)n], *s.* Vereinigung *f.*

uniform ['juːnifɔːm]. **I.** adj. (same) gleich; (same shape) gleichförmig; (of dress etc.) einheitlich. **II.** s. Uniform f. ◆**uni'formity**, s. Gleichförmigkeit f; Einheitlichkeit f (der Kleidung, des Stils usw.); Pej: Eintönigkeit f.

unify ['juːnifai], v.tr. vereinigen.

unilateral [juːni'læt(ə)rəl], adj. einseitig.

unimaginable [ʌni'mædʒinəbl], adj. unvorstellbar. ◆**uni'maginative**, adj. phantasielos.

unimportant [ʌnim'pɔːtənt], adj. unwichtig.

unimpressed [ʌnim'prest], adj. nicht beeindruckt. ◆**unim'pressive**, adj. nicht eindrucksvoll; (small) unscheinbar.

uninhabitable [ʌnin'hæbitəbl], adj. unbewohnbar. ◆**unin'habited**, adj. unbewohnt.

uninjured [ʌn'in(d)ʒəd], adj. unverletzt.

unintelligent [ʌnin'telidʒənt], adj. unintelligent. ◆**unin'telligible**, adj. unverständlich.

unintentional [ʌnin'tenʃ(ə)nəl], adj. unabsichtlich.

uninterested [ʌn'intristid], adj. uninteressiert (in, an + dat); (indifferent) gleichgültig. ◆**un'interesting**, adj. uninteressant.

uninterrupted [ʌnintə'rʌptid], adj. ununterbrochen; (of work) ungestört (by, von + dat).

uninviting [ʌnin'vaitiŋ], adj. wenig verlockend.

union ['juːnjən], s. **1.** (joining) Vereinigung f; Pol: Zusammenschluß m (von Parteien usw.). **2.** (body) (a) Verein m; Com: Verband m; Pol: Union f; (b) Ind: (trade) u., Gewerkschaft f. ◆**Union 'Jack**, s. Union Jack m (die britische Nationalflagge).

unique [juː'niːk], adj. einmalig; (of its kind) einzigartig.

unison ['juːnisən], s. Mus: (a) Einklang m; in u., unisono; (b) attrib. einstimmig.

unit ['juːnit], s. Einheit f; Fin: u. trust, Investmenttrust m; u. furniture, Anbaumöbel pl; kitchen u., Küchenelement n.

unite [juː'nait], v. **1.** v.tr. (a) vereinigen; (Elemente, Bestandteile) verbinden; (Eigenschaften) in sich vereinigen. **2.** v.i. (a) sich vereinigen; (b) (of states) sich verbünden. ◆**u'nited**, adj. vereint; (esp. of states etc.) vereinigt; **the U. Kingdom**, das Vereinigte Königreich; **the U. States (of America)**, die Vereinigten Staaten (von Amerika); **the U. Nations**, die Vereinten Nationen. ◆**unity** ['juːniti], s. (a) Einheit f (einer Partei, eines Landes usw.); Einheitlichkeit f (der Handlung eines Romans usw.); (b) (agreement) Einigkeit f; (harmony) Eintracht f.

universe ['juːnivəːs], s. Universum n. ◆**uni'versal**, adj. universal, Universal-; (of knowledge) allumfassend; (of rule etc.) allgemeingültig; **-ly**, adv. allgemein.

unjust [ʌn'dʒʌst], adj. ungerecht (to, gegen + acc); ◆**un'justifiable**, adj. nicht zu rechtfertigen(d). ◆**un'justified**, adj. ungerechtfertigt.

unkempt [ʌn'kem(p)t], adj. (of hair) zerzaust; (of appearance) ungepflegt; (of garden) verwahrlost.

unkind [ʌn'kaind], adj. lieblos; (unfeeling) gefühllos; (cruel) grausam; **that's u. of him**, das ist nicht nett von ihm. ◆**un'kindly**, adv. unfreundlich. ◆**un'kindness**, s. Lieblosigkeit f; Unfreundlichkeit f.

unknown [ʌn'nəun], adj. **I.** adj. unbekannt (to, dat). **II.** adv. **u. to me**, ohne mein Wissen. **III.** s. (pers.) Unbekannte(r) f(m); Mth: Unbekannte f.

unladen [ʌn'leidn], adj. unbeladen; **weight u./u. weight**, Leergewicht n.

unlawful [ʌn'lɔːful], adj. ungesetzlich; (of transaction etc.) illegal.

unleash [ʌn'liːʃ], v.tr. (j-n, etwas) entfesseln; (Hunde) loskoppeln.

unless [ʌn'les], conj. wenn/falls ... nicht; es sei denn, (daß + subj.); **u. I am mistaken**, wenn ich mich nicht irre.

unlicensed [ʌn'laisənst], adj. unbefugt; (of action) unerlaubt; Com: (of sale etc.) nicht konzessioniert.

unlike [ʌn'laik]. **I.** adj. verschieden. **II.** prep. **not u. s.o.**, j-m nicht unähnlich; **u. his father ...**, er, im Gegensatz zu seinem Vater ... ◆**un'lik(e)able**, adj. unsympathisch. ◆**un'likely**, adj. unwahrscheinlich; **an u. tale**, eine unglaubwürdige Geschichte; **he's u. to come**, wahrscheinlich kommt er nicht.

unlimited [ʌn'limitid], adj. unbegrenzt; Com: (of liability etc.) unbeschränkt.

unlined [ʌn'laind], adj. (a) (of clothes) ungefüttert; (b) (of paper) unliniert; (of face) faltenlos.

unload [ʌn'ləud], v.tr. entladen, (eine Fracht) ausladen. ◆**un'loading**, s. Entladen n.

unlock [ʌn'lɔk], v.tr. aufschließen.

unlucky [ʌn'lʌki], adj. **1.** (of pers.) unglücklich; **to be u.**, kein Glück haben; F: Pech haben; (b) (of thing) unglückbringend. ◆**un'luckily**, adv. unglücklicherweise.

unmanageable [ʌn'mænidʒəbl], adj. nicht zu handhaben; (of child) widerspenstig.

unmarketable [ʌn'mɔːkitəbl], adj. unverkäuflich.

unmarried [ʌn'mærid], adj. unverheiratet; **u. mother**, ledige Mutter.

unmask [ʌn'mɑːsk], v. **1.** v.tr. (j-n) demaskieren; Fig: (j-n) entlarven. **2.** v.i. sich demaskieren.

unmerited [ʌn'meritid], adj. unverdient.

unmistakable [ʌnmis'teikəbl], adj. unmißverständlich; (easily recognized) unverkennbar.

unmitigated [ʌn'mitigeitid], adj. (undiminished) ungemindert; (thorough) hundertprozentig.

unnatural [ʌn'næt∫rəl], *adj.* unnatürlich; (*of crime*) widernatürlich; (*of style etc.*) künstlich.

unnecessary [ʌn'nesis(ə)ri], *adj.* unnötig; (*superfluous*) überflüssig.

unnoticed [ʌn'nəutist], *adj.* unbemerkt.

unobservant [ʌnəb'zə:vənt], *adj.* unaufmerksam. ◆**unob'served**, *adj.* unbemerkt.

unobtainable [ʌnəb'teinəbl], *adj.* nicht erhältlich.

unobtrusive [ʌnəb'tru:siv], *adj.* (*of pers., manner*) unaufdringlich; (*of thing*) unauffällig.

unoccupied [ʌn'ɔkjupaid], *adj.* 1. (*of pers.*) unbeschäftigt. 2. (*empty*) leerstehend; (*of house etc.*) unbewohnt; (*of seat*) frei.

unofficial [ʌnə'fi∫(ə)l], *adj.* inoffiziell; (*of report*) unbestätigt.

unopposed [ʌnə'pəuzd], *adj.* (*of pers.*) ohne Konkurrenz; *Sp:* ohne Gegner; *Parl:* ohne Gegenkandidat(en); (*of proposal etc.*) unbeanstandet.

unorthodox [ʌn'ɔ:θədɔks], *adj.* unorthodox.

unostentatious ['ʌnɔsten'tei∫əs], *adj.* (*a*) (*of building, dress*) schlicht; (*b*) (*of pers., behaviour*) unauffällig.

unpack [ʌn'pæk], *v.tr. & i.* auspacken.

unpaid [ʌn'peid], *adj.* unbezahlt; (*honorary*) ehrenamtlich.

unpalatable [ʌn'pælitəbl], *adj.* nicht schmackhaft; *Fig:* (*of truth etc.*) unangenehm.

unparalleled [ʌn'pærəleld], *adj.* (*of intensity etc.*) unvergleichlich; (*of action*) beispiellos; (*of luck etc.*) ohnegleichen.

unpardonable [ʌn'pɑ:dnəbl], *adj.* unverzeihlich.

unperturbed [ʌnpə'tə:bd], *adj.* ungestört; (*calm*) gelassen.

unpleasant [ʌn'plez(ə)nt], *adj.* unangenehm; (*of sight, meeting etc.*) unerfreulich.

unpolished [ʌn'pɔli∫t], *adj.* unpoliert; (*of gem, marble etc.*, *Fig:* *of pers., style*) ungeschliffen.

unpopular [ʌn'pɔpjulər], *adj.* unbeliebt.

unpractical [ʌn'præktik(ə)l], *adj.* unpraktisch.

unprecedented [ʌn'presidentid], *adj.* beispiellos; noch nie dagewesen.

unprejudiced [ʌn'predʒudist], *adj.* vorurteilslos; (*of pers., judgement*) unparteiisch.

unprepared [ʌnpri'peəd], *adj.* unvorbereitet.

unpretentious [ʌnpri'ten∫əs], *adj.* anspruchslos; (*modest*) bescheiden.

unprincipled [ʌn'prinsipld], *adj.* skrupellos.

unprofitable [ʌn'prɔfitəbl], *adj.* unrentabel; *Fig:* (*of effort etc.*) unnütz.

unprotected [ʌnprə'tektid], *adj.* ungeschützt.

unprovided for [ʌnprə'vaidid fɔːr], *adj.* (*a*) (*of child etc.*) ohne Mittel; (*b*) (*of

**eventuality*) nicht vorgesehen.

unpunctual [ʌn'pʌŋ(k)tju(ə)l], *adj.* unpünktlich.

unpunished [ʌn'pʌni∫t], *adj.* ungestraft; **to go u.**, (*of pers.*) straflos ausgehen; (*of deed*) ungestraft bleiben.

unqualified [ʌn'kwɔlifaid], *adj.* 1. (*of pers.*) unqualifiziert; (*not fully trained*) nicht ausgebildet. 2. (*unlimited*) uneingeschränkt; (*of statement*) ohne Vorbehalt; **not an u. success**, kein durchgreifender Erfolg.

unquestionable [ʌn'kwest∫ənəbl], *adj.* unbestreitbar; **-ably**, *adv.* ohne jeden Zweifel. ◆**un'questioning**, *adj.* ohne Frage; (*absolute*) bedingungslos; **u. obedience**, blinder Gehorsam; **-ly**, *adv.* ohne zu fragen; ohne Zögern.

unravel [ʌn'ræv(ə)l], *v.tr.* (*a*) (Fäden) entwirren; (ein Gewebe, Gestricktes) auftrennen; (*b*) *Fig:* (ein Geheimnis) enträtseln.

unreadable [ʌn'ri:dəbl], *adj.* (*a*) (*of handwriting*) unleserlich; (*b*) (*of book*) unlesbar.

unreal [ʌn'riːəl], *adj.* unwirklich; phantastisch. ◆**'unrea'listic**, *adj.* unrealistisch; (*of pers., attitude*) wirklichkeitsfremd. ◆**unreality** [-'æliti], *s.* Unwirklichkeit *f*.

unreasonable [ʌn'ri:znəbl], *adj.* (*a*) (*of pers.*) **don't be so u.**, sei doch vernünftig; (*b*) (*of request etc.*) unzumutbar; **u. demands**, übertriebene Forderungen; **it's u. to expect that**, das ist zu viel verlangt.

unrecognizable [ʌn'rekəgnaizəbl], *adj.* unerkennbar; **he was u.**, er war nicht wiederzuerkennen.

unrehearsed [ʌnri'hə:st], *adj.* (*a*) *Th:* ungeprobt; (*b*) (*of speech etc.*) aus dem Stegreif.

unrelated [ʌnri'leitid], *adj.* (*of facts, concepts*) nicht miteinander verbunden; (*of pers.*) nicht miteinander verwandt.

unrelenting [ʌnri'lentiŋ], *adj.* (*of pers.*) unnachgiebig; (*of struggle*) unerbittlich; (*of persecution*) schonungslos; (*of pace*) unvermindert.

unreliable [ʌnri'laiəbl], *adj.* unzuverlässig; (*of character*) nicht vertrauenswürdig; (*of information*) nicht glaubwürdig.

unrelieved [ʌnri'liːvd], *adj.* 1. (*of pain*) ungemindert. 2. (*uniform*) einheitlich; (*monotonous*) monoton; (*of colour etc.*) ohne Abwechslung.

unrepentant [ʌnri'pentənt], *adj.* reuelos.

unreserved [ʌnri'zə:vd], *adj.* 1. (*of praise, support etc.*) uneingeschränkt. 2. (*of pers., nature*) offenherzig. 3. **u. seats**, nicht reservierte Plätze; **-ly** [-idli], *adv.* ohne Vorbehalt.

unresponsive [ʌnris'pɔnsiv], *adj.* (*of pers.*) teilnahmslos.

unrest [ʌn'rest], *s.* Unruhe *f*; **industrial u.**, Unzufriedenheit *f* unter der Arbeiterschaft.

unrestricted [ʌnrɪˈstrɪktɪd], *adj.* uneingeschränkt; *(of speed)* unbegrenzt; *(of view)* ungehindert.

unripe [ʌnˈraɪp], *adj. (of fruit etc.)* unreif.

unrivalled [ʌnˈraɪv(ə)ld], *adj.* unvergleichlich; *(of pers.)* ohne Rivalen; *(of ability, performance etc.)* unerreicht.

unroll [ʌnˈrəʊl], *v.* 1. *v.tr.* (einen Teppich usw.) aufrollen. 2. *v.i.* *(of flag etc.)* sich aufrollen.

unruffled [ʌnˈrʌfld], *adj. (of pers.)* gelassen; **u. composure,** unerschütterliche Gelassenheit.

unruly [ʌnˈruːlɪ], *adj. (of child)* widerspenstig; *(wild)* ungestüm.

unsafe [ʌnˈseɪf], *adj.* unsicher; *(of action)* gefährlich; *(of undertaking)* riskant; *(of pers.)* in Gefahr.

unsaid [ʌnˈsed], *adj.* unausgesprochen.

unsal(e)able [ʌnˈseɪləbl], *adj.* unverkäuflich.

unsanitary [ʌnˈsænɪt(ə)rɪ], *adj.* unhygienisch.

unsatisfactory [ʌnsætɪsˈfækt(ə)rɪ], *adj.* unbefriedigend; *(of explanation)* nicht überzeugend. ◆**unsatisfied** [ʌnˈsætɪsfaɪd], *adj.* 1. *(of pers.)* unzufrieden. 2. *(of desire etc.)* unbefriedigt; *(of appetite)* nicht gesättigt.

unsavoury [ʌnˈseɪv(ə)rɪ], *adj.* 1. *(of dish)* unschmackhaft; **u. smell,** übler Geruch. 2. *(of affair etc.)* zwielichtig; **u. reputation,** übler Ruf.

unscrew [ʌnˈskruː], *v.tr.* abschrauben.

unscrupulous [ʌnˈskruːpjʊləs], *adj.* skrupellos.

unseen [ʌnˈsiːn]. I. *adj.* 1. ungesehen. 2. *(invisible)* unsichtbar. II. *s. Sch:* unvorbereitete Übersetzung *f.*

unselfish [ʌnˈselfɪʃ], *adj. (of pers.)* selbstlos. ◆**un'selfishness,** *s.* Selbstlosigkeit *f.*

unsettle [ʌnˈsetl], *v.tr.* (j-n) beunruhigen. ◆**un'settled,** *adj.* 1. *(disturbed)* unruhig; *(of weather)* veränderlich. 2. (a) *(undecided)* unentschlossen; *(of questions)* unentschieden; (b) *(of bill)* unbezahlt; *(of estate)* noch nicht abgewickelt.

unshak(e)able [ʌnˈʃeɪkəbl], *adj.* unerschütterlich.

unshaven [ʌnˈʃeɪvn], *adj.* unrasiert.

unsightly [ʌnˈsaɪtlɪ], *adj.* häßlich.

unskilful [ʌnˈskɪlfʊl], *adj.* ungeschickt. ◆**un'skilled,** *adj.* ungeübt; *Ind:* **u. worker,** ungelernter Arbeiter.

unsociable [ʌnˈsəʊʃəbl], *adj.* ungesellig.

unsolved [ʌnˈsɒlvd], *adj.* ungelöst.

unsophisticated [ʌnsəˈfɪstɪkeɪtɪd], *adj.* ungekünstelt; *(genuine)* unverfälscht; *(naive)* arglos; *(simple)* schlicht.

unsound [ʌnˈsaʊnd], *adj. (defective)* fehlerhaft; *(of wood)* morsch; *(of fruit)* verdorben; *(of structure etc.)* unsicher, *(dangerous)* gefährlich; *esp. fur:* **of u. mind,** unzurechnungsfähig.

unsparing [ʌnˈspeərɪŋ], *adj.* **to be u. in one's efforts,** keine Mühe scheuen.

unspeakable [ʌnˈspiːkəbl], *adj.* unbeschreiblich; *F:* *(terrible)* entsetzlich.

unspoilt [ʌnˈspɔɪlt], *adj.* unverdorben; *(of countryside)* unberührt.

unspoken [ʌnˈspəʊk(ə)n], *adj.* unausgesprochen; *(of agreement)* stillschweigend.

unstable [ʌnˈsteɪbl], *adj.* nicht stabil; *(of pers.)* labil.

unsteady [ʌnˈstedɪ], *adj.* 1. *(of object)* wacklig; *(of footsteps)* wankend; *(of hand)* unsicher; **u. on one's feet,** wacklig auf den Beinen. 2. *(varying)* unbeständig; *(of prices)* schwankend; *(of pulse etc.)* unregelmäßig. ◆**un'steadiness,** *s.* 1. Wackligkeit *f;* Wanken *n* (der Schritte); Unsicherheit *f* (der Hand). 2. Unbeständigkeit *f;* Schwanken *n* (der Preise usw.). 3. Unregelmäßigkeit *f* (des Pulses).

unstinting [ʌnˈstɪntɪŋ], *adj.* großzügig.

unstuck [ʌnˈstʌk], **to come u.,** (i) *(of envelope)* aufgehen; (ii) *F:* *(of plan)* schiefgehen.

unsuccessful [ʌnsəkˈsesfʊl], *adj.* 1. erfolglos. 2. *(of pers.)* nicht erfolgreich; *(in examination)* durchgefallen.

unsuitable [ʌnˈsjuːtəbl], *adj.* 1. *(of pers., thing)* ungeeignet *(for, für + acc);* *(of behaviour)* unangemessen. 2. *(of thing)* unpassend; *(of several things, married couple)* nicht zusammenpassend.

unsuspected [ʌnsəˈspektɪd], *adj. (of pers.)* unverdächtigt. 2. *(of qualities)* ungeahnt. ◆**unsus'pecting,** *adj.* ahnungslos; *(by nature)* nicht argwöhnisch; *(naive)* arglos.

unswerving [ʌnˈswɜːvɪŋ], *adj.* unbeirrbar; **u. devotion,** unerschütterliche Liebe.

unsympathetic [ʌnsɪmpəˈθetɪk], *adj.* 1. mitleidslos. 2. *(uncongenial)* unsympathisch.

untamed [ʌnˈteɪmd], *adj.* ungezähmt.

untapped [ʌnˈtæpt], *adj.* unangezapft; **u. source,** ungenutzte Quelle.

unthinkable [ʌnˈθɪŋkəbl], *adj.* undenkbar; *(unimaginable)* unvorstellbar.

untidy [ʌnˈtaɪdɪ], *adj.* unordentlich. ◆**un'tidiness,** *s.* Unordentlichkeit *f.*

untie [ʌnˈtaɪ], *v.tr.* aufbinden; (einen Knoten) lösen; (ein Tier) losbinden.

until [ʌnˈtɪl]. I. *prep. & conj.* bis; **u. the evening,** bis zum Abend; **not u.,** erst; **he won't come u. two o'clock,** er wird erst um zwei Uhr kommen.

untimely [ʌnˈtaɪmlɪ], *adj. & adv. (early)* *(of death etc.)* vorzeitig; *(of arrival etc.)* verfrüht.

untiring [ʌnˈtaɪərɪŋ], *adj.* unermüdlich.

untold [ʌnˈtəʊld], *adj.* 1. *(of story)* unerzählt. 2. *Fig:* unsäglich.

untoward [ʌnˈtəʊəd], *adj. (of circumstances)* ungünstig; *(of accident)* unglücklich.

untrained [ʌnˈtreɪnd], *adj.* ungeschult.

untranslatable [ˈʌntrænsˈleɪtəbl], *adj.* unübersetzbar.

untried [ʌnˈtraɪd], *adj.* ungeprüft; *(of*

pers., method etc.) unerprobt; **we left nothing u.**, wir haben alles versucht.

untroubled [ʌn'trʌbld], *adj. (of mind etc.)* ruhig; *(of happiness etc.)* ungestört.

untrue [ʌn'tru:], *adj.* unwahr.

untrustworthy [ʌn'trʌstwəːði], *adj.* unzuverlässig; *(of witness etc.)* nicht vertrauenswürdig.

untruth [ʌn'tru:θ], *s.* Unwahrheit *f.* ◆**un'truthful**, *adj. (of pers.)* lügnerisch; *(of statement etc.)* unwahr; *(of report)* falsch.

unusable [ʌn'juːzəbl], *adj.* unbrauchbar. ◆**un'used**, *adj.* ungebraucht; *(of stamp)* ungestempelt.

unusual [ʌn'juːʒu(ə)l, -ʒəl], *adj.* ungewöhnlich; *(rare)* selten; *(of word etc.)* ungebräuchlich; **nothing u.**, nichts Ungewöhnliches; **-ly**, *adv.* ungewöhnlich.

unveil [ʌn'veil], *v.tr.* enthüllen.

unwanted [ʌn'wɔntid], *adj.* unerwünscht.

unwary [ʌn'wɛəri], *adj.* unvorsichtig.

unwavering [ʌn'weivəriŋ], *adj.* unerschütterlich; **-ly**, *adv.* unbeirrt.

unwelcome [ʌn'welkəm], *adj.* unwillkommen; *(of news)* unangenehm.

unwell [ʌn'wel], *adj.* krank.

unwholesome [ʌn'həulsəm], *adj.* unbekömmlich; *(esp. of appearance)* unappetitlich.

unwieldy [ʌn'wiːldi], *adj. (of equipment, tool)* unhandlich; *(of package etc.)* sperrig. **2.** *(of structure)* unförmig; *(topheavy)* kopflastig.

unwilling [ʌn'wiliŋ], *adj. (of pers., agreement etc.)* widerwillig; **u. to do sth.**, unwillig, etwas zu tun. **-ly**, *adv.* ungern.

unwind [ʌn'waind], *v.irr.* **1.** *v.tr.* (ein Kabel usw.) abwickeln. **2.** *v.i. Fig: (of pers.)* sich entspannen.

unwise [ʌn'waiz], *adj.* unklug; *(foolish)* töricht.

unwitting [ʌn'witiŋ], *adj.* unbewußt; *(unintentional)* unabsichtlich; **-ly**, *adv.* unwissentlich.

unworkable [ʌn'wəːkəbl], *adj. (of plan)* undurchführbar.

unworthy [ʌn'wəːði], *adj.* unwürdig (**of**, + *gen.*: **to do sth.**, etwas zu tun).

unwrap [ʌn'ræp], *v.tr.* (ein Geschenk) auspacken; (ein Paket usw.) aufmachen; (einen Verband usw.) abwickeln.

unwritten [ʌn'rit(ə)n], *adj.* ungeschrieben.

unyielding [ʌn'jiːldiŋ], *adj.* nicht nachgebend; *(of pers.)* unnachgiebig.

up [ʌp]. **I.** *adv.* **1.** nach oben; *(upwards)* aufwärts; *(into the air)* in die Höhe; **to go up**, hinaufgehen; *(explode)* in die Luft gehen; **to walk up and down**, auf und ab gehen. **2.** *(position)* oben; **up on the roof**, oben auf dem Dach; **halfway up**, in halber Höhe; **up above (sth.)**, oberhalb (von etwas *dat*); **the moon is up**, der Mond ist aufgegangen; **road up**, (Vorsicht) Bauarbeiten. **3.** *(a)* **to go up**, *(of*

prices, temperature etc.) steigen; *(b)* **his blood was up**, er war ganz aufgeregt/empört; *(c)* **to be up against s.o.**, mit j-m zu tun haben; *F:* **to be up against it**, in der Klemme sein. **4.** *(not in bed)* auf; **is he up yet?** ist er schon aufgestanden? **to be up and about**, auf den Beinen sein; **to be/stay up all night**, die ganze Nacht aufbleiben. **5.** **what's up?** was ist los? **6.** *(your)* **time's up**, Ihre Zeit ist um; **his leave's up**, sein Urlaub ist zu Ende; *F:* **the game's up**, das Spiel ist aus; **it's all up with him**, mit ihm ist es aus. **7.** **up to;** *(a)* *(place, time)* bis; **to go up to s.o.**, auf j-n zugehen; **up to now**, bis jetzt; *(b)* **to be up to a task**, einer Aufgabe gewachsen sein; **he's up to something**, er führt etwas im Schilde; *(c)* **it's up to him to decide**, die Entscheidung liegt bei ihm. **II.** *prep.* **1.** **to go up a hill**, einen Berg hinaufsteigen/*(of car)* hinauffahren; **he went up the stairs**, er ging die Treppe hinauf; **the cat is up the tree**, die Katze ist *(oben)* auf dem Baum. **2.** **up the river**, den Fluß hinauf, flußaufwärts. **III.** *s. F:* **ups and downs**, das Auf und Ab. **IV.** *v.tr. F:* (Preise) erhöhen. ◆**'up-and-'coming**, *adj.* vielversprechend. ◆**'up-and-'up**, *s. F:* **he is on the up-a.-up**, er macht sich. ◆**upbringing** ['ʌpbriŋiŋ], *s.* Erziehung *f.* ◆**up-end** ['ʌp'end], *v.tr.* (etwas) hochkant stellen. ◆**upgrade** [ʌp'greid], *v.tr. (a) (improve)* verbessern; *(b) (promote)* (j-n) befördern; (eine Stellung) höher einstufen. ◆**upheaval** [ʌp'hiːv(ə)l], *s. (a) (fuss)* Getue *n;* *(b) (violent)* Aufruhr *f; Pol: etc:* Umwälzung *f.* ◆**uphill** ['ʌp'hil]. **I.** *adj.* bergauf; *Fig: (of task)* mühsam. **II.** *adv.* bergauf. ◆**uphold** [ʌp'həuld], *v.tr.irr. (a)* (eine Tradition) aufrechterhalten; *(b) (approve)* (j-s Verhalten), einen Einspruch) billigen; (eine Entscheidung) bestätigen. ◆**up'holstery**, *s.* Polsterung *f.* ◆**upkeep** ['ʌpkiːp], *s.* Instandhaltung *f.* ◆**up-market** [ʌp'mɑːkit], *adj. Com: (of product)* für höhere Ansprüche. ◆**upon** [ə'pɔn], *prep. (a) esp. Lit: (on)* auf + *dat/ (motion)* + *acc;* **once u. a time**, es war einmal. ◆**upper** ['ʌpər]. **I.** *adj.* obere(r,s); *Ober-:* **u. jaw**, Oberkiefer *m;* **the u. storeys**, die oberen Stockwerke; **u. part**, Oberteil *m* & *n;* **the u. classes**, *(i)* die Oberschicht (der Gesellschaft); *(ii) Sch:* die Oberklassen; *Fig:* **to get the u. hand**, die Oberhand gewinnen. **II.** *s. usu. pl.* Oberleder *n* (am Schuh). ◆**uppermost** ['ʌpəməust]. **I.** *adj.* oberste(r,s). **II.** *adv.* zuoberst. ◆**upright** ['ʌprait]. **I.** *adj.* **1.** aufrecht; *(vertical)* senkrecht; *(straight)* gerade. **2.** *(of conduct)* aufrichtig; *(of pers.)* rechtschaffen. **II.** *adv.* aufrecht. ◆**uprising** ['ʌpraiziŋ], *s.* Aufstand *m.* ◆**uproar** ['ʌprɔːr], *s.* Tumult *m;* **the town is in an u.**, die Stadt ist in Aufruhr. ◆**uproot** [ʌpˈruːtl], v.tr. (einen Baum, Fig: j-n) entwurzeln; (eine Pflanze) ausreißen. ◆upset. I. [ˈʌpset] s. 1. Umkippen n (eines Wagens usw.); Kentern n (eines Bootes); (of pers.) seelische Erschütterung f. 2. (confusion) Verwirrung f. II. [ˈʌpˈset] v.tr.irr. (a) (knock over) umkippen; (b) (destroy) (die Gesellschaftsordnung) umstürzen; (j-s Pläne) vereiteln; (c) (disturb) (Verhältnisse, j-s Pläne) stören; (d) (confuse) (j-n) verwirren. III. adj. (a) (of pers.) aufgeregt; aus der Fassung; (b) he has an u. stomach, er hat einen verdorbenen Magen. ◆upshot [ˈʌpʃɔt], s. Ausgang m; the u. was that..., der Endeffekt war, daß... ◆upside down [ˈʌpsai(d)ˈdaun], adv. phr. auf den Kopf gestellt; (in a muddle) drunter und drüber. ◆upstairs [ʌpˈstɛəz]. I. adv. (a) (position) oben; (b) to go u., nach oben gehen. II. adj. (of room) im oberen Stockwerk. ◆upstart [ˈʌpstɑːt], s. Emporkömmling m. ◆upstream [ˈʌpstriːm], adv. stromaufwärts. ◆uptake [ˈʌpteik], s. slow on the u., schwer von Begriff; to be quick on the u., schnell begreifen. ◆uptight [ʌpˈtait], adj. F: (tense) nervös; (angry) sauer. ◆up-to-date [ʌptəˈdeit], adj. (of pers., clothes etc.) modern; (of report, subject) aktuell; (of attitude) zeitgemäß; (of machine) auf dem neuesten Stand; to be/ keep up-to-d., auf dem laufenden sein. ◆upturn [ˈʌptəːn], s. Aufwärtsbewegung f (der Preise usw.); Fig: (in fortune) Aufschwung m. ◆upward [ˈʌpwəd], adj. Aufwärts- u. movement, Aufwärtsbewegung f; an u. tendency, eine steigende Tendenz. ◆upwards [ˈʌpwədz], adv. 1. aufwärts. 2. (facing u.) nach oben. 3. (more) mehr; a hundred pounds and u., hundert Pfund und mehr; from ten (years old) u., ab zehn Jahren.

Urals [ˈjuərəlz]. Pr. n. the U., der Ural.

uranium [juˈreiniəm], s. Uran n.

urban [ˈəːbən], adj. städtisch, Stadt-. ◆urbani'zation, s. Verstädterung f.

urbane [əːˈbein], adj. weltmännisch; (smart) elegant.

urchin [ˈəːtʃin], s. 1. (boy) Gassenjunge m. 2. Z: sea u., Seeigel m.

urge [əːdʒ]. I. v. Drang m. II. v.tr. (a) to u. s.o/a horse (on), j-n/ein Pferd vorwärts treiben/anspornen; (b) to u. s.o. to do sth., j-n drängen, etwas zu tun. ◆urgent, adj. dringend. ◆urgency, s. Dringlichkeit f.

urinal [juˈrainəl], s. (a) Pissoir n; (b) (for invalid) Urinflasche f. ◆urine [ˈjuərin], s. Urin m, Harn m. ◆urinate, v.i. urinieren.

urn [əːn], s. (a) Vase f; (b) (burial) u., Urne f; (b) tea u., Teemaschine f.

us [ʌs], pers. pron. uns; he sees us, er sieht uns; give us some, gib uns davon; there are three of us, wir sind drei.

usable [ˈjuːzəbl], adj. brauchbar. ◆usage [ˈjuːsidʒ], s. 1. (treatment) Behandlung f. 2. (custom) Brauch m. 3. (of language) Sprachgebrauch m; (of word) Wortgebrauch m.

use. I. [juːs], s. 1. Gebrauch m; (for a particular purpose) Verwendung f; (application) Anwendung f (von Gewalt usw.); I'll find a u. for it, ich werde es schon irgendwie verwenden können; to make u. of sth., Gebrauch von etwas dat machen; not in u., nicht in Gebrauch; (of lift etc.) außer Betrieb; ready for u., gebrauchsfertig; directions for u., Gebrauchsanweisung f. 2. (ability, right) he has the u. of the garden, er darf den Garten benutzen. 3. (help) Nutzen m; of u., nützlich; it's no u., es hat keinen Sinn; to have no u. for sth., mit etwas dat nichts anfangen können; I have no u. for him, für ihn habe ich nichts übrig; what's the u.? wozu (das)? II. [juːz] v.tr. (etwas) gebrauchen; (ein Gerät, einen Gegenstand) benutzen, (for a purpose) verwenden; (Zeit usw.) nutzen; to u. sth. (up), etwas aufbrauchen/verbrauchen; this car uses a lot of petrol, dieses Auto (ver)braucht viel Benzin. ◆used¹ [juːzd], adj. gebraucht; u. car, Gebrauchtwagen m; hardly u., fast neu; u. up, (of supplies) verbraucht. ◆used² [juːst]. I. adj. to be u. to sth., an etwas acc gewöhnt sein, etwas gewohnt sein; to get u. to sth., sich an etwas acc gewöhnen. II. aux. I used to do it, ich habe es früher immer getan. ◆useful [ˈjuːsful] adj. (a) nützlich; (of clothing) praktisch; (b) (usable) verwendbar. ◆'usefulness, s. Nützlichkeit f, Verwendbarkeit f. ◆useless [ˈjuːslis], adj. (unusable) (of object) unbrauchbar; (of pers., actions) unnütz; (pointless) sinnlos; (of efforts) vergeblich. ◆'uselessness, s. Nutzlosigkeit f. ◆user [ˈjuːzər], s. Benutzer(in) m(f).

usher [ˈʌʃər], s. Platzanweiser m. ◆ushe'rette, s. Platzanweiserin f.

usual [ˈjuːʒu(ə)l], adj. gewöhnlich; (generally accepted) üblich; it's the u. practice, das ist gang und gäbe; as u., wie immer; -ly, adv. gewöhnlich; meistens.

usurp [juːˈzəːp], v.tr. (j-s Besitz) widerrechtlich an sich reißen; (of throne) Thronräuber m.

usury [ˈjuːʒuri], s. Wucher m.

utensil [juˈtens(i)l], s. (a) Gerät n, (b) (tool) Werkzeug n.

uterus [ˈjuːtərəs], s. Gebärmutter f.

utilitarian [juːtiliˈteəriən]. I. adj. utilitär. II. s. Utilitarist m. ◆utility [juˈtiliti], s. (a) (usefulness) Nutzen m; Com: u. goods, Gebrauchsgegenstände mpl; (b) public u./N.Am: u., gemeinnütziges Unternehmen n. ◆utilization [-aiˈzeiʃ(ə)n], s. Verwendung f; Nutzbarmachung f (des Bodens, Fig: von Talenten usw.); Verwertung f (von Rohstoffen usw.) ◆'utilize [-aiz], v.tr. (a) (etwas) verwenden; (b) (exploit) (den Boden, Fig:

Talente usw.) nutzbar machen; (Zeit, eine Gelegenheit) ausnutzen.

utmost ['ʌtmoust]. **I.** *adj.* (*of care etc.*) äußerste(r,s); (*of need etc.*) größte(r,s); it is of the u. importance that..., es ist äußerst wichtig, daß... **II.** *s.* das Äußerste; **to the u. of one's ability**, nach be-

sten Kräften.

utter[1] ['ʌtər], *adj.* vollkommen; **u. bliss**, die höchste Seligkeit; **u. nonsense**, völliger Unsinn; **-ly**, *adv.* völlig.
◆**'uttermost**, *adj.* äußerste(r,s).

utter[2], *v.tr.* (ein Wort, Gefühle, Gedanken) äußern, aussprechen.

V

V, v [viː], *s.* (der Buchstabe) V, v *n*; *Cl:* **V neck**, V-Ausschnitt *m*.

vacant ['veik(ə)nt], *adj.* (*a*) (*empty*) leer; (*not occupied*) frei; (*of expression etc.*) geistlos. ◆**'vacancy**, *s.* **1.** (*emptiness*) Leere *f*. **2.** (*a*) (*on board-ing house*) 'v.', Zimmer frei; (*b*) (*job*) offene Stelle *f*. ◆**vacate** [vəˈkeit], *v.tr.* (*a*) (eine Stelle usw.) aufgeben; (*b*) (ein Zimmer usw.) räumen. ◆**va'cation**, *s.* (*a*) *Sch:* Ferien *fpl*; (*b*) *esp. N.Am:* Urlaub *m*.

vaccinate ['væksineit], *v.tr.* (j-n) impfen. ◆**vacci'nation**, *s.* Schutzimpfung *f*.

vacuum ['vækjuəm], *s. Ph: & Fig:* Vakuum *n*; **v. cleaner**, Staubsauger *m*; **v. flask**, Thermosflasche *f*.

vagina [vəˈdʒainə], *s.* Scheide *f*.

vagrant ['veigrənt], *s.* Landstreicher *m*.

vague [veig], *adj.* vage; (*unclear*) unklar; **v. outlines**, verschwommene Umrisse; **I haven't the vaguest idea**, ich habe nicht die geringste Ahnung; **-ly**, *adv. esp. F:* vage. ◆**'vagueness**, *s.* Vagheit *f*; Un-klarheit *f*; (*of pers.*) vage Art.

vain [vein], *adj.* **1.** (*of pers.*) eitel. **2.** (*of effort etc.*) vergeblich. **3. in v.** (*also* **-ly**, *adv.*), vergeblich.

valentine ['væləntain], *s.* (*card*) Valentins-gruß *m*.

valiant ['væljənt], *adj.* tapfer; (*in attack*) mutig; (*of effort etc.*) heldenhaft.

valid ['vælid], *adj.* gültig; (*of argument, reason*) stichhaltig. ◆**va'lidity**, *s.* Gültig-keit *f* (eines Dokuments); Stichhaltigkeit *f* (eines Arguments, eines Grundes).

valley ['væli], *s.* Tal *n*.

value ['væljuː]. **I.** *s.* (*a*) Wert *m*; **v. added tax**, Mehrwertsteuer *f*; (*b*) **this is good v.**, das ist preiswert; **to get good v. for** (one's) money, preiswert einkaufen. **II.** *v.tr.* schätzen. ◆**'valuable. I.** *adj.* wert-voll. **II.** *s.pl.* **valuables**, Wertgegenstände *mpl*. ◆**valu'ation**, *s.* **1.** (*value*) Schätz-wert *m*. **2.** (*process*) Bewertung *f*. ◆**'valueless**, *adj.* wertlos. ◆**'valuer**, *s.* Schätzer *m*.

valve [vælv], *s.* **1.** *Tchn:* Ventil *n*; (*cock*) Hahn *m*. **2.** *Anat: & Mus:* Klappe *f* (des Herzens, eines Instruments usw.). **3.** *Rad:* Röhre *f*.

vampire ['væmpaiər], *s.* Vampir *m*.

van [væn], *s.* **1.** *Aut:* (**delivery**) v., Liefer-wagen *f*. **2.** *Rail:* Güterwagen *m*; (**luggage**) v., Gepäckwagen *m*.

vandal ['vænd(ə)l], *s.* Vandale *m*. ◆**'vandalism**, *s.* Vandalismus *m*. ◆**'vandalize**, *v.tr.* mutwillig beschädi-gen.

vanilla [vəˈnilə], *s.* Vanille *f*.

vanish ['væniʃ], *v.i.* verschwinden; **F: to v. into thin air**, spurlos verschwinden.

vanity ['væniti], *s.* Eitelkeit *f*; **v. case**, Kosmetikkoffer *m*.

vantage ['vɑːntidʒ], *s.* (*a*) (*in tennis*) Vor-teil *m*; (*b*) **v. point**, Aussichtspunkt *m*.

vaporize ['veipəraiz], *v.* **1.** *v.tr.* verdamp-fen lassen. **2.** *v.i.* (*of liquid*) verdampfen. ◆**'vapour**, *s.* Dampf *m*; *Av:* **v. trail**, Kondensstreifen *m*.

variable ['veəriəbl], *adj.* (*a*) veränderlich; (*of weather, mood*) wechselhaft; (*of cost*) schwankend; (*b*) *Tchn:* (*adjustable*) ver-stellbar. ◆**'variance**, *s.* **to be at v. with s.o.**, mit j-m uneinig sein. ◆**'variant**, *s.* Variante *f*. ◆**vari'ation**, *s.* (*change*) Schwankung *f*; **v. of/in temperature**, Temperaturschwankung *f*.

varicose ['værikous], *adj.* **v. veins**, Krampfadern *fpl*.

variety [vəˈraiəti], *s.* **1.** (*a*) (*richness*) Ab-wechslung *f*; (*b*) (*large number*) Vielzahl *f*; (*selection*) Auswahl *f*. **2.** (*type*) Art *f*; (*variant*) Variante *f*. **3.** *Th:* Varieté *n*; **v. show**, Varietévorstellung *f*.

various ['veəriəs], *adj.* verschieden; **for v. reasons**, aus verschiedenen Gründen.

vary ['veəri], *v.* **1.** *v.tr.* abändern; *Mus:* (ein Thema usw.) variieren. **2.** *v.i.* (*a*) (*of temperature etc.*) schwanken; (*b*) (*differ-ent*) verschieden sein; (*disagree*) nicht übereinstimmen; **opinions v. on this**, da teilen sich die Meinungen. ◆**'varied**, *adj.* verschiedenartig; (*of work, career etc.*) abwechslungsreich. ◆**'varying**, *adj.* (*a*) (*different*) verschieden; (*of weight, de-gree etc.*) unterschiedlich; (*b*) (*inconstant*) veränderlich; **v. prices**, schwankende Preise.

vase [vɑːz], *s.* Vase *f*.

vast [vɑːst], *adj.* riesig; (*of plain etc.*) ausgedehnt.

vat [væt], *s.* Bottich *m*; (*barrel*) Faß *n*.

Vatican ['vætikən]. *Pr. n.* **the V.**, der Va-tikan.

vault[1] [vɔ(ː)lt], *s.* **1.** (*roof*) Gewölbe *n*. **2.** (*underground*) Kellergewölbe *n*; (*of bank*) Tresorraum *m*; **wine** v., Weinkeller *m*. ◆**'vaulted**, *adj.* gewölbt.

vault[2]. **I.** *s. Sp:* Sprung *m*. **II.** *v.tr. & v.i.*

to v. (over) sth., über etwas *acc* springen.

vaunt [vɔːnt], *v.tr. Lit*: (etwas) rühmen.

veal [viːl], *s.* Kalbfleisch *n*.

veer [ˈviər], *v.i.* (*of wind*) sich drehen; (*of ship*) abdrehen.

vegetable [ˈvedʒ(i)təbl], *s.* Gemüse *n*; **v. garden**, Gemüsegarten *m*. ◆**vege'tarian. I.** *adj.* vegetarisch. **II.** *s.* Vegetarier(in) *m(f)*. ◆**vege'tate**, *v.i.* vegetieren. ◆**vege'tation**, *s.* Vegetation *f*.

vehemence [ˈviːəməns], *s.* Heftigkeit *f*. ◆**'vehement**, *adj.* heftig.

vehicle [ˈviːikl], *s.* 1. Fahrzeug *n*. 2. *Fig:* Mittel *n*.

veil [veil]. **I.** *s.* Schleier *m*. **II.** *v.tr.* (das Gesicht) verschleiern; *Fig:* (seine Gefühle usw.) verhüllen.

vein [vein], *s.* 1. *Anat:* Vene *f*. 2. *Bot:* Rippe *f*. 3. (*a*) (*in marble, wood*) Maser *f*; (*b*) *Min:* Ader *f* (von Erz usw.); (*seam*) Flöz *n*. 4. *Fig:* (*a*) Stimmung *f*; (*b*) poetic v., poetische Ader.

velocity [viˈlɔsiti], *s.* Geschwindigkeit *f*.

velvet [ˈvelvit], *s.* Samt *m*.

vendetta [venˈdetə], *s.* Blutrache *f*.

veneer [vəˈni(ː)ər], *s.* 1. Furnier *n*. 2. *Fig:* Anschein *m*.

venerable [ˈven(ə)rəbl], *adj.* ehrwürdig. ◆**'venerate** [-əreit], *v.tr.* (j-n) verehren. ◆**vene'ration**, *s.* Verehrung *f*.

venereal [viˈniəriəl], *adj.* **v. disease** (*abbr. F:* VD), Geschlechtskrankheit *f*.

Venetian [viˈniːʃ(ə)n]. **I.** *adj.* venezianisch; **v. blind**, Jalousie *f*. **II.** *s.* Venezianer(in) *m(f)*.

Venezuela [veneˈzweilə]. *Pr. n.* Venezuela *n*. ◆**Vene'zuelan. I.** *adj.* venezolanisch. **II.** *s.* Venezolaner(in) *m(f)*.

vengeance [ˈven(d)ʒəns], *s.* Rache *f*; **to take v. on s.o.**, sich an j-m rächen.

Venice [ˈvenis]. *Pr. n.* Venedig *n*.

venison [ˈvenizn], *s.* 1. Reh(fleisch) *n*; **roast v.**, Rehbraten *m*.

venom [ˈvenəm], *s.* (*a*) Schlangengift *n*; (*b*) *Fig:* Giftigkeit *f*. ◆**'venomous**, *adj.* giftig.

vent [vent]. **I.** *s.* 1. (*round*) Luftloch *n*; (*long*) Luftschlitz *m*; (*in barrel*) Spundloch *n*. 2. *Cl:* Schlitz *m* (an einem Jackett usw.). **II.** *v.tr.* **to v. one's anger on s.o.**, seinen Ärger an j-m auslassen.

ventilate [ˈventileit], *v.tr.* (*a*) (ein Zimmer usw.) lüften; (*b*) *Fig:* (eine Beschwerde, eine Frage) zur Sprache bringen. ◆**venti'lation**, *s.* 1. Lüftung *f* (eines Zimmers usw.); (*intake*) Belüftung *f*; (*extraction*) Entlüftung *f*. 2. Erörterung *f* (einer Frage). ◆**'ventilator**, *s.* Ventilator *m*.

ventriloquist [venˈtriləkwist], *s.* Bauchredner *m*.

venture [ˈventʃər]. **I.** *s.* Unternehmen *n*. **II.** *v.* 1. *v.tr.* (*a*) (etwas) wagen; (*b*) (sein Leben, Geld) riskieren. 2. *v.i.* **to v. out of doors**, sich hinauswagen.

venue [ˈvenjuː], *s.* (*meeting place*) Treff-

punkt *m*; (*of conference*) Tagungsort *m*; *Sp: etc:* (*scene of event*) Schauplatz *m*.

veranda(h) [vəˈrændə], *s.* Veranda *f*.

verb [vəːb], *s.* Verb *n*. ◆**'verbal**, *adj.* 1. *Gram:* verbal. 2. (*oral*) mündlich. 3. (*literal*) wörtlich. ◆**ver'batim** [vəˈbeitim]. **I.** *adj.* wörtlich. **II.** *adv.* Wort für Wort.

verdict [ˈvəːdikt], *s.* Urteil *n*.

verge [vəːdʒ]. **I.** *s.* (*a*) Rand *m*; Einfassung *f* (eines Blumenbeets); (*beside road*) (grass) v., Grasstreifen *m*; (*b*) **on the v.** of tears, den Tränen nahe. **II.** *v.i.* **to v. on sth.**, an etwas *acc* grenzen.

verger [ˈvəːdʒər], *s. Ecc:* Kirchendiener *m*.

verify [ˈverifai], *v.tr.* überprüfen. ◆**verification** [-fiˈkeiʃ(ə)n], *s.* Nachprüfung *f*.

vermicelli [vəːmiˈtʃeli], *s.* Fadennudeln *fpl*.

vermin [ˈvəːmin], *s.* Ungeziefer *n*; *Fig:* Abschaum *m*.

vermouth [ˈvəːməθ], *s.* Wermut *m*.

versatile [ˈvəːsətail], *adj.* (*of pers. etc.*) vielseitig. ◆**versa'tility**, *s.* Vielseitigkeit *f*.

verse [vəːs], *s.* 1. (*unit*) Strophe *f*; (*in bible*) Vers *m*. 2. (*a*) Verse *mpl*; (*lyric*) v., Lyrik *f*; (*b*) (*metre*) Versmaß *n*.

version [ˈvəːʃ(ə)n], *s.* 1. (*a*) Fassung *f* (eines Werkes usw.); (*b*) *F:* (*of a story*) Version *f*. 2. *Ind:* (*model*) Ausführung *f*.

versus [ˈvəːsəs], *prep.* gegen + *acc*.

vertebra, *pl.* **-brae** [ˈvəːtibrə, -briː], *s.* Wirbel *m*.

vertical [ˈvəːtik(ə)l], *adj.* senkrecht, vertikal; *Av:* **v. take-off aircraft**, Senkrechtstarter *m*.

vertigo [ˈvəːtigəu], *s.* Schwindel *m*.

verve [vəːv], *s.* Schwung *m*.

very [ˈveri]. **I.** *adj.* (*a*) (*exact*) genau; **you're the v. man!** du bist genau der Richtige! **the v. opposite**, genau das Gegenteil; **at that v. moment**, genau in dem Augenblick; (*b*) (*emphatic*) **at the v. beginning/end**, ganz am Anfang/Ende; **caught in the v. act**, auf frischer Tat ertappt; (*c*) **the v. thought** (of it), der bloße Gedanke (daran). **II.** *adv.* sehr; **v. good**, sehr gut; **at the v. latest**, spätestens.

vespers [ˈvespəz], *s.pl.* Vesper *f*.

vessel [ˈvesl], *s.* 1. *Nau:* Schiff *n*. 2. (*container*) Gefäß *n*.

vest [vest], *s.* 1. Unterhemd *n*. 2. *N.Am:* Weste *f*.

vested [ˈvestid], *adj.* **v. rights/interests**, angestammte Rechte.

vestige [ˈvestidʒ], *s.* Spur *f*.

vestments [ˈvestmənts], *s. pl. Ecc:* Meßgewand *n*. ◆**'vestry**, *s.* Sakristei *f*.

vet [vet]. **I.** *s. F:* Tierarzt *m*. **II.** *v.tr. F:* (j-s Arbeit usw.) überprüfen.

veteran [ˈvetərən]. **I.** *s.* Veteran *m*. **II.** *adj.* (*of things*) uralt.

veterinary [ˈvetərinri], *adj.* tierärztlich.

veto ['vi:təu]. **I.** s. Veto n. **II.** v.tr. (etwas) verbieten, (reject) durch ein Veto zurückweisen.

vex [veks], v.tr. (j-n) irritieren, (annoy) ärgern. ◆**vex'ation**, s. Ärger m. ◆**'vexing**, adj. ärgerlich; (troublesome) lästig.

via [vaiə], prep. über + acc.

viable ['vaiəbl], adj. Biol: lebensfähig; Fig: (of project etc.) durchführbar.

viaduct ['vaiədʌkt], s. Viadukt m.

vibrate [vai'breit], v.i. vibrieren; (of tone, string) schwingen; (of voice) beben. ◆**vi'bration**, s. Vibration f; Ph: Schwingung f.

vicar ['vikər], s. Pfarrer m. ◆**'vicarage**, s. Pfarrhaus n.

vice[1] [vais], s. Laster n.

vice[2], s. Tls: Schraubstock m.

vice-[3], prefix Vize-; **v.-chairman**, stellvertretender Vorsitzender; **v.-president**, Vizepräsident m.

vice versa ['vaisi'vəːsə], adv. phr. umgekehrt.

vicinity [vi'siniti], s. Nähe f; nähere Umgebung f (der Stadt usw.).

vicious ['viʃəs], adj. (a) bösartig; (of attack, criticism etc.) gemein; (b) v. kick, boshafter Fußtritt; (c) Fig: v. circle, Teufelskreis m.

victim ['viktim], s. Opfer n. ◆**victimi'zation**, s. Schikane f. ◆**'victimize**, v.tr. (j-n) schikanieren.

victor ['viktər], s. Sieger m. ◆**victorious** [vik'tɔːriəs], adj. siegreich. ◆**'victory**, s. Sieg m.

Victorian [vik'tɔːriən], adj. viktorianisch.

video ['vidiəu], s. v. tape, Videoband n; **v. tape recorder**, Videorecorder m; **v. cassette**, Videokassette f.

vie [vai], v.i. to v. with s.o., mit j-m wetteifern.

Vienna [vi'enə]. Pr. n. Wien n. ◆**Viennese** [viːə'niːz]. **I.** adj. Wiener; (in character) wienerisch. **II.** s. (pers.) Wiener(in) m(f).

view [vjuː]. **I.** s. **1.** (a) Besichtigung f; (b) in v., in Sicht; **to come into v.**, sichtbar werden. **2.** (scene) Aussicht f; (particular aspect) Ansicht f; **views of the town**, Blicke mpl auf die Stadt; (pictures) Bilder npl/Ansichten fpl von der Stadt. **3.** Fig: (a) point of v., Gesichtspunkt m; (b) in v. of the fact that..., angesichts der Tatsache, daß... **4.** (opinion) Ansicht f; **in my v.**, meiner Ansicht/Meinung nach. **II.** v.tr. (a) ansehen; (b) Fig: (j-n, etwas) betrachten (as, als). ◆**'viewer**, s. **1.** (pers.) Betrachter m; TV: Fernsehzuschauer m. **2.** Phot: Diabetrachter m. ◆**'viewfinder**, s. Phot: Sucher m. ◆**'viewpoint**, s. Gesichtspunkt m.

vigilance ['vidʒiləns], s. Wachsamkeit f. ◆**'vigilant**, adj. wachsam.

vigour ['vigər], s. Energie f; Vitalität f; Fig: Nachdruck m. ◆**'vigorous**, adj.

energisch.

vile [vail], adj. **1.** (of pers.) widerwärtig. **2.** F: (of weather, temper etc.) scheußlich.

villa ['vilə], s. Villa f.

village ['vilidʒ], s. Dorf n. ◆**'villager**, s. Dorfbewohner(in) m(f).

villain ['vilən], s. Schurke m.

vindicate ['vindikeit], v.tr. (a) (j-n, Handlungen usw.) rechtfertigen; (b) (einen Anspruch) geltend machen.

vindictive [vin'diktiv], adj. (vengeful) rachsüchtig; (unforgiving) nachtragend.

vine [vain], s. Weinstock m; **v. grower**, Winzer m; **v. growing**, Weinbau m. ◆**'vineyard** ['vinjəd], s. (on hill) Weinberg m; (on flat) Weingarten m.

vinegar ['vinigər], s. Essig m.

vintage ['vintidʒ], s. **1.** Weinlese f; (crop) Weinernte f. **2.** (year) Jahrgang m; **v. wine**, Qualitätswein m. **3.** v. car, Oldtimer m.

viola [vi'əulə], s. Bratsche f.

violate ['vaiəleit], v.tr. (a) (eine Regel) verletzen; (ein Gesetz) übertreten; (b) (rape) vergewaltigen. ◆**vio'lation**, s. (a) Verletzung f; Übertretung f; (b) Vergewaltigung f. ◆**violence** ['vaiələns], s. **1.** (action) Gewalt f. **2.** (quality) Heftigkeit f (einer Reaktion, des Windes usw.). ◆**'violent**, adj. (a) heftig, stark; **v. temper**, tobend vor Wut; (b) (of act, pers.) gewalttätig.

violet ['vaiələt]. **I.** s. **1.** Veilchen n. **2.** (colour) Violett n. **II.** adj. violett.

violin [vaiə'lin], s. Violine f, Geige f. ◆**vio'linist**, s. Geiger(in) m(f).

viper ['vaipər], s. Giftschlange f.

virgin ['vəːdʒin]. **I.** s. Jungfrau f. **II.** adj. jungfräulich; Fig: unberührt. ◆**vir'ginity**, s. Jungfräulichkeit f.

Virgo ['vəːgəu], s. Astr: Jungfrau f.

virile ['virail], adj. (a) (sexually) viril; (b) robust; (manly) männlich. ◆**vi'rility**, s. (a) Virilität f; (b) Männlichkeit f; Robustheit f.

virtual ['vəːtjuəl], adj. eigentlich; praktisch; **this was a v. confession**, das war praktisch ein Geständnis; **-ly**, adv. praktisch; (nearly) beinahe.

virtue ['vəːtjuː], s. **1.** Tugend f. **2.** prep. phr. **by v. of**, auf Grund + gen. ◆**'virtuous**, adj. tugendhaft; (in character) rechtschaffen.

virtuoso, pl. -os [vəːtju'əuzəu, -əuz], s. Virtuose m, Virtuosin f.

virulent ['virjulənt], adj. Med: bösartig.

virus ['vaiərəs], s. Virus m.

visa ['viːzə], s. Visum n.

vis-à-vis ['viːza:'viː]. prep. gegenüber + dat.

viscount ['vaikaunt], s. Vicomte m.

visible ['vizəbl, -ibl], adj. sichtbar. ◆**visi'bility**, s. (a) Sichtbarkeit f; (b) Sichtverhältnisse npl. ◆**vision** ['viʒ(ə)n], s. **1.** (a) Sehkraft f (eines Auges); **field of v.**, Blickfeld n; (b) Fig: **a man of v.**, ein Mann mit Weitblick. **2.**

(a) Traumbild *n*; *(b) Ecc: etc:* Vision *f*; **to see visions,** Visionen haben.

visit ['vizit]. **I.** *s.* Besuch *m* (to, in + *dat*), (stay) Aufenthalt *m*; **on a v.,** zu/auf Besuch; **to pay s.o. a v.,** j-n besuchen. **II.** *v.tr.* besuchen; *(seek out)* (j-n) aufsuchen. ◆**'visiting. I.** *adj.* zu/auf Besuch; Gast-; **v. professor,** Gastprofessor *m.* **II.** *s.* Besuchen *n*; **v. card,** Visitenkarte *f.* ◆**'visitor,** *s.* Besucher *m* (to, gen); (to house, restaurant) Gast *m* (to, in + *dat*); **she's got visitors,** sie hat Besuch; **visitors' book,** Gästebuch *n.*

vista ['vistə], *s.* Aussicht *f.*

visual ['vizjuəl], *adj.* visuell; *Sch:* **v. aids,** Anschauungsmaterial *n.* ◆**'visualize,** *v.tr.* **to v. s.o., sth.,** sich *dat* etwas vorstellen; **I can't v. it,** ich kann mir davon kein Bild machen.

vital ['vait(ə)l], *adj.* **1.** *(essential)* lebenswichtig. **2.** *(full of life)* vital. ◆**vitality** [-'tæliti], *s.* Vitalität *f.*

vitamin ['vitəmin, vait-], *s.* Vitamin *n.*

vitiate ['vifieit], *v.tr.* (etwas) beeinträchtigen; (Argumente) hinfällig machen.

vivacious [vi'veifəs], *adj.* lebhaft. ◆**vi'vaciousness, vivacity** [-'væsiti], *s.* Lebhaftigkeit *f.*

vivid ['vivid], *adj. (a) (bright)* hell, leuchtend; **v. colours,** leuchtende Farben; *(b) (clear)* deutlich; *(c) (lively)* lebhaft *(of description etc.)* lebhaft; *(of picture)* lebendig; **v. imagination,** rege Phantasie. ◆**'vividness,** *s.* Lebhaftigkeit *f*; Lebendigkeit *f.*

vivisection [vivi'sekʃ(ə)n], *s.* Vivisektion *f.*

vizor ['vaizər], *s.* **1.** Visier *n.* **2.** *Aut: & Cl: (on cap)* Blende *f.*

vocabulary [və'kæbjuləri], *s.* Wortschatz *m*; *(list)* Wörterverzeichnis *n.*

vocal ['vouk(ə)l], *adj.* Stimm-, Gesang-; *Anat:* **v. cords,** Stimmbänder *npl.*

vocation [və(u)'keiʃ(ə)n], *s. (a) (calling)* Berufung *f* (for, zu + *dat*); *(b) (aptitude)* Begabung *f* (for, für + *acc*); *(c) (profession)* Beruf *m.* ◆**vo'cational,** *adj.* Berufs-; **v. guidance,** Berufsberatung *f.*

vociferate [və'sifəreit], *v.i. (of pers.)* schreien. ◆**vo'ciferous,** *adj.* lautstark.

vogue [voug], *s.* Mode *f*; **to be in v.,** Mode sein.

voice [vois]. **I.** *s. (a)* Stimme *f*; **in a low v.,** mit leiser Stimme; **with one v.,** einstimmig; *(b) Gram:* **active/passive v.,** Aktiv *n*/Passiv *n*; *Fig:* **to v.** (eine Meinung, Zweifel usw.) äußern. ◆**voiced,** *adj.* stimmhaft.

void [void]. **I.** *adj.* **1.** *(empty)* leer. **2.** *Jur:* **null and v.,** null und nichtig. **3. v. of,**

ohne + *acc.* **II.** *s.* Leere *f.*

volatile ['vɔlətail], *adj.* **1.** *Ch:* flüchtig. **2.** *(of pers.) (excitable)* überschäumend; *(inconstant)* flatterhaft.

volcano, *pl.* **-oes** [vɔl'keinou, -ouz], *s.* Vulkan *m.* ◆**volcanic** [-'kænik], *adj.* vulkanisch.

volition [və'liʃ(ə)n], *s.* Willenskraft *f*; **of one's own v.,** aus freien Stücken.

volley ['vɔli], *s. (a) Mil:* Geschützsalve *f*; *(b) Sp:* Flugball *m*, Volley *n.* ◆**'volleyball,** *s.* Volleyball *m.*

volt [vault], *s.* Volt *n.* ◆**'voltage,** *s.* Spannung *f.*

voluble ['vɔljubl], *adj.* redselig.

volume ['vɔljuːm], *s.* **1.** *(book)* Band *m.* **2.** *(quantity)* **the v. of exports,** das Ausfuhrvolumen. **3.** *(measure) Ph: etc:* Volumen *n*; Rauminhalt *m.* **4.** *(loudness)* Lautstärke *f*; **to turn up the v. of the radio,** das Radio lauter stellen.

voluntary ['vɔlənt(ə)ri], *adj.* freiwillig. ◆**volunteer** [vɔlən'tiːər]. **I.** *s. Mil:* Freiwillige(r) *m.* **II.** *v.i.* sich freiwillig melden (**for sth.,** zu etwas *dat*).

voluptuous [və'lʌptjuəs], *adj. (of thoughts, pleasures etc.)* wollüstig.

vomit ['vɔmit]. **I.** *s.* Erbrochenes *n.* **II.** *v.* **1.** *v.tr.* erbrechen. **2.** *v.i.* sich übergeben. ◆**'vomiting,** *s.* Erbrechen *n.*

voracious [və'reiʃəs], *adj.* gierig; **v. appetite,** unersättlicher Appetit.

vote [vaut]. **I.** *s. (a)* Abstimmung *f*; *(b) (individual)* v., Stimme *f*; **to have the/a v.,** das Stimmrecht haben. **II.** *v.tr. & i.* wählen; **to v. for s.o., sth.,** für j-n, etwas stimmen. ◆**'voter,** *s.* Wähler *m.* ◆**'voting,** *s.* Abstimmung *f*; *(at election)* Wählen *n.*

vouch [vautʃ], *v.i.* **to v. for s.o./for the truth of sth.,** für j-n/für die Wahrheit von etwas *dat* bürgen. ◆**'voucher,** *s.* Gutschein *m.*

vow [vau]. **I.** *s.* Gelübde *n.* **II.** *v.tr.* geloben.

vowel ['vauəl], *s.* Vokal *m*; **v. sound,** Vokallaut *m.*

voyage ['vɔiidʒ]. *s.* Seereise *f.* ◆**'voyager,** *s.* Seereisende(r) *f (m).*

vulgar ['vʌlgər], *adj.* vulgär; *(of language, pers.)* ordinär. ◆**vul'garity,** *s.* Gewöhnlichkeit *f*; **to lapse into v.,** ins Ordinäre verfallen.

vulnerable ['vʌln(ə)rəbl], *adj.* (leicht) verletzbar; *Fig:* anfällig **(to sth.,** für etwas *acc*). ◆**vulnera'bility,** *s.* Verletzbarkeit *f*; *Fig:* Anfälligkeit *f* **(to,** für + *acc*).

vulture ['vʌltʃər], *s.* Geier *m.*

W

W, w ['dʌblju:], *s.* (der Buchstabe) W, w *n.*

wad [wɔd], *s.* (*a*) (*ball*) Ball *m;* Knäuel *n* (Papier); (*pad*) Polster *n;* **w. of cotton wool,** Wattebausch *m;* (*b*) **w. of (bank)notes,** Bündel *n* Banknoten.

waddle ['wɔdl], *v.i.* watscheln.

wade [weid], *v.i.* (*a*) (durch einen Bach usw.) waten.

wafer ['weifər], *s.* **1.** (*biscuit*) Waffel *f.* 2. *Ecc:* Hostie *f.*

waft [wɑ:ft], *v.tr. & i.* **a scent (was) wafted into the room,** ein Duft wehte ins Zimmer.

wag [wæg], *v.tr.* **the dog wagged its tail,** der Hund wedelte mit dem Schwanz.

wage[1] [weidʒ], *s.* (*sing. or pl.*) Lohn *m;* **w. earner,** Lohnempfänger *m;* **w. packet,** Lohntüte *f;* **w. freeze,** Lohnstopp *m.*

wage[2], *v.tr.* **to w. war/a campaign,** Krieg/einen Feldzug führen.

wager ['weidʒər]. **I.** *v.i.* wetten. **II.** *s.* Wette *f.*

waggle ['wægl], *v.tr.* **to w. its tail,** mit dem Schwanz wedeln.

wag(g)on ['wæg(ə)n], *s.* **1.** (*cart*) Pferdewagen *m.* **2.** *Rail:* (*goods*) **w.,** Güterwagen *m.*

wail [weil]. **I.** *v.i.* (*a*) (*of child, siren etc.*) heulen; (*b*) (*lament*) klagen. **II.** *s.* (*a*) Heulen *n;* (*b*) Klage *f.*

waist [weist], *s.* (*of pers., dress*) Taille *f.* ◆**'waistcoat,** *s.* Weste *f.* ◆**'waistline,** *s.* Taille *f;* **to watch one's w.,** auf die Linie achten.

wait [weit]. **I.** *v.i.* (*a*) warten; **to w. for s.o., sth.,** auf j-n, etwas *acc* warten; **w. and see!** nur Geduld! (*threat*) **just you w.!** warte nur! (*b*) **to w.** (**at table**), (bei Tisch) bedienen. **II.** *s.* Wartezeit *f.* ◆**'waiter,** *s.* Kellner *m;* (*calling*) **w.!** Herr Ober! ◆**'waiting,** *s.* **w. list,** Warteliste *f;* **w. room,** (*at doctor's etc.*) Wartezimmer *n;* *Rail:* Wartesaal *m.* ◆**'waitress,** *s.* Kellnerin *f;* (*calling*) **w.!** Fräulein!

waive [weiv], *v.tr.* **to w. a claim/one's rights,** auf einen Anspruch/seine Rechte verzichten.

wake[1] [weik], *v.irr.* **1.** *v.i.* **to w.** (**up**), aufwachen. **2.** *v.tr.* **to w. s.o.** (**up**), j-n wecken. ◆**'waken,** *v.* **1.** *v.i.* aufwachen; *Fig:* erwachen. **2.** *v.tr.* (*a*) (*b*) wecken; (*b*) (Gefühle usw.) wecken; (Erinnerungen) wachrufen.

wake[2], *s.* (*a*) *Nau:* Kielwasser *n;* (*b*) *Fig:* **in the w. of the storm,** unmittelbar nach dem Sturm; (*c*) (*for dead*) Totenwache *f.*

walk [wɔ:k]. **I.** *v.i.* **1.** *v.i.* gehen; (*for pleasure*) spazierengehen; (*longer distances*) wandern. **2.** *v.tr.* **to w. a dog,** einen Hund spazierenführen. **II.** *s.* **1.** Weg *m;* **it's an hour's w. from here,** von hier aus geht man eine Stunde zu Fuß. **2.** Spaziergang *m;* **to go for a w.,** spazierengehen. **3.** (*gait*) Gang *m.* **4.** (*in garden etc.*) Spazierweg *m.* **5. people from all walks of life,** Angehörige *pl* aller Gesellschaftsschichten. ◆**'walker,** *s.* Spaziergänger *m;* (*hiker*) Wanderer *m.* ◆**'walkie-'talkie,** *s.* tragbares Funksprechgerät *n,* Walkie-talkie *n.* ◆**'walking,** *s.* Gehen *n;* Laufen *n;* (*for pleasure*) Spazierengehen *n;* (*hiking*) Wandern *n;* **w. stick,** Spazierstock *m.* ◆**'walkout,** *s.* spontane Arbeitsniederlegung *f.* ◆**'walk 'over,** *v.i.* **to w. o. to s.o.,** zu j-m hinübergehen. ◆**'walkover,** *s. Sp:* leichter Sieg *m.*

wall [wɔ:l]. **I.** *s.* (*a*) Mauer *f;* (*b*) (*of building, room*) Wand *f.* **II.** *v.tr.* **to w. sth.** (**in**), etwas ummauern. ◆**'wallflower,** *s.* (*a*) *Bot:* Goldlack *m;* (*b*) *F:* (*at dance*) **to be a w.,** Mauerblümchen spielen. ◆**'wallpaper,** *s.* Tapete *f.*

wallet ['wɔlit], *s.* Brieftasche *f.*

wallow ['wɔləu], *v.i.* (*a*) (*of animal*) **to w. in the mud,** sich im Schlamm wälzen; (*b*) (*of pers.*) *Fig:* **to w. in sentiment etc.,** in Gefühlen usw. schwelgen.

walnut ['wɔ:lnʌt], *s.* (*a*) Walnuß *f;* (*b*) (*tree*) Nußbaum *m;* (*c*) (*wood*) Nußbaumholz *n.*

walrus ['wɔ:lrəs], *s.* Walroß *n.*

waltz [wɔ:l(t)s]. **I.** *s.* Walzer *m.* **II.** *v.i.* Walzer tanzen.

wan [wɔn], *adj.* (*a*) (*of pers., face*) bleich; (*b*) (*of light, sky*) fahl.

wand [wɔnd], *s.* (*magic*) **w.,** Zauberstab *m.*

wander ['wɔndər], *v.i.* wandern; **to w. about,** herumschweifen; (*stray*) irren; **to w. from the subject,** vom Thema abschweifen. ◆**'wanderer,** *s.* Wanderer *m.* ◆**'wandering. I.** *adj.* wandernd. **II.** *s.* Wandern *n.*

wane [wein]. *v.i.* abnehmen; (*of interest etc.*) nachlassen; (*of beauty*) schwinden.

want [wɔnt]. **I.** *v.tr.* **a** (*desire*) (etwas) wollen, wünschen; **he wants a bike for Christmas,** er wünscht sich ein Fahrrad zu Weihnachten; **you're wanted (on the phone),** Sie werden (am Telefon) verlangt; (*b*) **to w. to do sth.,** etwas tun wollen; **he wants me to go with him,** er will, daß ich mitgehe; (*c*) (*need*) (j-n, etwas) brauchen; **have you got everything you w.?** haben Sie alles, was Sie brauchen? (*d*) (*seek*) (eine Stelle, einen Verbrecher) suchen; **cook wanted,** Koch/Köchin gesucht. **II.** *s.* **1.** (*lack*) Mangel *m* (**of,** an *+ dat*); **for w. of anything better,** mangels eines Besseren. **2.** (*poverty*) Not *f;* **to be in w.,** Not leiden. **3.** (*need*) Bedürfnis *n;* (*desire*) Wunsch *m.* ◆**'wanting,** *adj.* **he is w. in intelli-**

gence, tact etc., es fehlt ihm an Intelligenz, Takt usw.

wanton ['wɔntən], *adj.* 1. (*wilful*) w. destruction, mutwillige Zerstörung. 2. (*unchaste*) unkeusch.

war [wɔːr], *s.* Krieg *m;* **to make w.** on s.o., gegen j-n Krieg führen. ◆**warfare,** *s.* Kriegführung *f.* ◆**warhead,** *s.* Sprengkopf *m;* **nuclear w.,** Atomsprengkopf *m.*

warble ['wɔːbl]. I. *v.i.* (*of bird*) trillern. II. *s.* Triller *m.* ◆**warbler,** *s.* Grasmücke *f.*

ward [wɔːd]. I. *s.* 1. *Jur:* Mündel *n.* 2. (*in hospital*) Station *f;* **w. sister,** Stationsschwester *f.* II. *v.tr.* **to w. off** a blow, a danger etc., einen Schlag, eine Gefahr usw. abwehren. ◆**warden,** *s.* Aufseher *m;* Leiter *m* (eines Studentenheims); (*of youth hostel*) Herbergsvater *m;* (*female*) Herbergsmutter *f;* **traffic w.,** (*male*) Verkehrspolizist *m;* (*female*) Politesse *f.* ◆**warder/wardress,** *s.* Gefängniswärter(in) *m(f).* ◆**wardrobe,** *s.* 1. Kleiderschrank *m.* 2. (*clothes*) Garderobe *f.*

ware [weər], *s.* Waren *fpl;* (*china etc.*) Geschirr *n.* ◆**warehouse,** *s.* Lager.

warm [wɔːm]. I. *adj.* warm; **I am w.,** mir ist warm; **to give s.o.** a w. welcome/reception, j-m einen warmen/herzlichen Empfang bereiten. II. *v.* 1. *v.tr.* (ein Zimmer, eine Flüssigkeit usw.) wärmen, (*gradually*) erwärmen. 2. *v.i.* sich erwärmen; **-ly,** *adv.* 1. w. dressed, warm angezogen. 2. **to thank s.o.** w., j-m herzlich danken. ◆**warm-hearted,** *adj.* warmherzig. ◆**warmth,** *s.* 1. Wärme *f.* 2. (*cordiality*) Herzlichkeit *f* (eines Empfanges usw.). ◆**'warm 'up,** *v.* 1. *v.tr.* (etwas) erwärmen; (Speisen) aufwärmen. 2. *v.i.* warm werden; (*of engine*) warmlaufen.

warn [wɔːn], *v.tr.* (j-n) warnen (**of/ against,** vor + *dat*). ◆**warning.** I. *adj.* warnend; w. light, Warnlicht *n.* II. *s.* Warnung *f;* **to arrive without** w., unangemeldet kommen.

warp [wɔːp], *v.i.* (*of wood*) sich verziehen. ◆**warped,** *adj.* (*of wood*) verzogen. 2. (*of mind, humour etc.*) verdreht.

warrant ['wɔrənt]. *s.* (*order*) Befehl *m;* (*authority*) Vollmacht *f; Jur:* w. of arrest, Haftbefehl *m.* ◆**warranty,** *s. Com:* Garantie *f.*

warren ['wɔrən], *s.* (**rabbit**) w., Kaninchenbau *m.*

warrior ['wɔriər], *s.* Krieger *m.*

Warsaw ['wɔːsɔː]. *Pr. n.* Warschau *n.*

wart [wɔːt], *s.* Warze *f.*

wary ['weəri], *adj.* vorsichtig; **to be w. of** doing sth., sich hüten, etwas zu tun; **-ily,** *adv.* vorsichtig; **to tread w.,** behutsam vorgehen.

wash [wɔʃ]. I. *v.* 1. *v.tr.* (*a*) (etwas) waschen; **to w. oneself,** sich waschen; **to w. one's hands/hair,** sich *dat* die Hände/ Haare waschen; (*b*) (*of sea*) (Felsen) um-

spülen. 2. *v.i.* (*of pers.*) sich waschen. II. *s.* (*a*) (*of pers.*) to have a w., sich waschen; **to give sth.** a w., etwas waschen; (*b*) (*dirty clothes etc.*) Wäsche *f.* ◆**washable,** *adj.* waschbar. ◆**wash a'way,** *v.tr.* (etwas) wegspülen. ◆**wash-basin,** *N.Am:* **washbowl,** *s.* Waschbecken *n.* ◆**washcloth,** *s. N.Am:* Waschlappen *m.* ◆**washer1,** *s.* 1. (*pers.*) w. up, Tellerwäscher *m.* 2. *Aut:* (**windscreen/***N.Am:* **windshield**) **w.,** Scheibenwaschanlage *f.* ◆**washing,** *s.* 1. Waschen *n.* 2. (*a*) Wäsche *f;* **dirty w.,** Schmutzwäsche *f;* w. machine, Waschmaschine *f;* w. powder, Waschpulver *n;* (*b*) *Aut:* w. bay, Waschanlage *f.* 3. w. up, Abwasch *m;* **to do the** w.-up, den Abwasch machen. ◆**wash-leather,** *s.* Waschleder *f.* ◆**wash 'out,** *v.tr.* (*a*) (*remove*) (einen Fleck usw.) auswaschen; (*b*) (*rinse*) (eine Flasche usw.) ausspülen. ◆**washout,** *s. F:* (*of event etc.*) Pleite *f;* (*of pers.*) Niete *f.* ◆**washroom,** *s.* Waschraum *m.* ◆**washstand,** *s.* Waschtisch *m.* ◆**wash 'up,** *v.* 1. *v.tr.* (*a*) (das Geschirr usw.) abwaschen; (*b*) (*of sea*) (etwas) an Land spülen. 2. *v.i.* abwaschen.

washer2, *Tchn:* Dichtungsring *m.*

wasp [wɔsp], *s.* Wespe *f.*

waste [weist]. I. *v.* 1. *v.tr.* (Geld usw.) verschwenden, (seine Kräfte usw.) vergeuden (**on,** an + *acc*). 2. *v.i.* (*of pers.*) to w. away, dahinschwinden, (*die*) dahinsiechen. II. *adj.* 1. w. land/ground, wüstes/unbebautes Gelände. 2. *fig:* w. paper basket, Papierkorb *m.* III. *s.* 1. Verschwendung *f* (von Geld, Licht usw.); w. of time/space, Zeit/Platzvergeudung *f.* 2. (*rubbish*) Abfälle *mpl;* w. disposal unit, (*chute*) Müllschlucker *m;* (*in sink*) Abfallzerkleinerer *m.* 3. *usu. pl.* (*deserted land*) Einöde *f.* ◆**wastage,** *s.* Verschwendung *f.* ◆**wasteful,** *adj.* (*of pers.*) verschwenderisch; (*of methods etc.*) unwirtschaftlich.

watch [wɔtʃ]. I. *s.* 1. (*also Nau:*) Wache *f;* **to be on the w. for** s.o., sth., nach j-m, etwas *dat* Ausschau halten; **to keep w. over** s.o., sth., auf/j-n, etwas *acc* aufpassen. 2. (*for time*) Uhr *f.* II. *v.* 1. *v.tr.* (*a*) (j-n, etwas) beobachten; **to w.** s.o. **do** sth., beobachten, wie j-d etwas macht; **to w. television,** fernsehen; (*b*) **could you** w. **the baby for** a moment? würdest du einen Moment auf das Baby aufpassen? *F:* w. **your step!** w. it! paß auf! Vorsicht! 2. *v.i.* (*a*) **to w. (out) for** s.o., sth., nach j-m, etwas *dat* ausschauen; (*wait*) j-n, etwas abwarten; (*b*) (*take care*) **to w. out,** aufpassen; **w. out!** Vorsicht! paß auf! ◆**watchdog,** *s.* Wachhund *m.* ◆**watchful,** *adj.* wachsam. ◆**watchmaker,** *s.* Uhrmacher *m.* ◆**watchman,** *s.* Wächter *m;* **night w.,** Nachtwächter *m.*

water ['wɔ:tər]. I. *s.* Wasser *n*; *pl* waters, Gewässer *npl* (eines Sees, eines Flusses usw.); **w. level**, Wasserstand *m*; **w. lily**, Seerose *f*; **w. melon**, Wassermelone *f*; **w. polo**, Wasserball *m*; **w. skiing**, Wasserski *n*. II. *v.* 1. *v.tr.* (*a*) (die Blumen, den Garten usw.) gießen; (*of river etc.*) (eine Landschaft) bewässern; (*b*) **to w. sth. down**, etwas verwässern; (*c*) (Tiere) tränken. 2. *v.i.* (*a*) (*of eyes*) tränen; (*b*) **my mouth watered**, das Wasser lief mir im Mund zusammen. ◆**'water-colour**, *s.* 1. (*paint*) Wasserfarbe *f*. 2. (*painting*) Aquarell *n*. ◆**'watercress**, *s.* Brunnenkresse *f*. ◆**'waterfall**, *s.* Wasserfall *m*. ◆**'waterhole**, *s.* Wasserstelle *f* (in den Tropen). ◆**'watering**, *s.* Gießen *n* (der Blumen usw.); **w. can**, Gießkanne *f*. ◆**'waterline**, *s.* Wasserlinie *f* (eines Schiffes). ◆**'waterlogged**, *adj.* (*of boat*) voll Wasser; (*of ground, wood*) (von Wasser) durchtränkt. ◆**'waterproof**. I. *adj.* wasserdicht. II. *v.tr.* (etwas) imprägnieren. ◆**'watershed**, *s.* (*a*) *Geog:* Wasserscheide *f*; (*b*) *Fig:* Wendepunkt *m*. ◆**'watertight**, *adj.* (*a*) wasserdicht; (*b*) *Fig:* (*of argument etc.*) stichhaltig. ◆**'waterworks**, *s.* Wasserwerk *n*. ◆**'watery**, *adj.* wässerig.

watt [wɔt], *s.* Watt *n*.

wave [weiv]. I. *s.* 1. (*also Ph: & Fig:*) Welle *f*; **permanent w.**, Dauerwelle *f*. 2. Winken *n*; **to give s.o. a w.**, j-m mit der Hand (zu)winken. II. *v.* 1. *v.i.* (*a*) (*of flag etc.*) wehen; (*b*) **to w. to s.o.**, j-m zuwinken; (*c*) (*of hair*) sich wellen. 2. *v.tr.* (die Arme, eine Fahne usw.) schwenken; **to w. one's hand**, mit der Hand winken; **to w. goodbye to s.o.**, j-m zum Abschied zuwinken. ◆**'wavelength**, *s.* *Rad: & Fig:* Wellenlänge *f*. ◆**'wavy**, *adj.* wellig; gewellt.

waver ['weivər], *v.i.* (*a*) (*of flame etc.*) flackern; (*b*) (*of pers.*) schwanken; (*of courage*) wanken.

wax¹ [wæks]. I. *s.* Wachs *n*; **ear w.**, Ohrenschmalz *m*. II. *v.tr.* wachsen. ◆**'waxwork**, *s.* Wachsfigur *f*; **waxworks**, Wachsfigurenkabinett *n*. ◆**'waxy**, *adj.* (*a*) (*pale*) wachsbleich; (*b*) (*waxlike*) wachsartig.

wax², *v.i.* (*of moon*) zunehmen.

way [wei], *s.* 1. (*path*) Weg *m*; (*road*) Straße *f*; **over/across the w.**, gegenüber; **which is the best w. to the station?** wie kommt man am besten zum Bahnhof? **to lose one's w.**, sich verirren; **to go the wrong w.**, (i) (*on foot*) sich verlaufen; (ii) (*in car etc.*) sich verfahren; **to find one's w.**, den Weg finden; **to know one's w. about**, sich auskennen; **on the w.**, unterwegs (**to**, nach + *dat*); **on the w. home/to school**, auf dem Heimweg/Schulweg; **to go out of one's w.**, einen Umweg machen; *Fig:* **to go out of one's w. to help s.o.**, sich *dat* besondere Mühe geben, j-m zu helfen; (*of village etc.*) **out of the w.**,

abgelegen; **by the w.**, übrigens; **w. in**, Eingang *m*; **w. out**, Ausgang *m*; **it's a long w. (from here)**, es liegt weit weg/weit entfernt (von hier); **all the w.**, den ganzen Weg; **to be in s.o.'s w.**, j-m im Wege stehen; **to keep out of s.o.'s w.**, j-m aus dem Wege gehen; **to make w. for s.o.**, j-m Platz machen; **give w.!** Vorfahrt beachten! 2. (*direction*) (*a*) Richtung *f*; **which w. are you going?** in welche Richtung gehen Sie? (*b*) **the wrong w. round**, verkehrt herum; (*of photograph etc.*) seitenverkehrt; **the other w. round**, anders herum. 3. (*manner*) Weise *f*; Art *f*; **in this w.**, auf diese Weise; so; **is this the w. to do it?** macht man es so? **no w.!** ganz ausgeschlossen! **to get one's own w.**, seinen Willen durchsetzen; **if I had my w.**, wenn es nach mir ginge; (*respect*) **in many ways**, in vieler Hinsicht. 4. **what have you got in the w. of drinks?** was haben Sie an Getränken? 5. (*motion*) Fahrt *f*; **under w.**, (*of ship*) in Fahrt; (*of work*) im Gange. ◆**way'lay**, *v.tr.irr.* (j-m) auflauern. ◆**'wayward**, *adj.* (*capricious*) launenhaft; (*self-willed*) eigensinnig.

we [wi:], *pers. pron.* wir.

weak [wi:k], *adj.* schwach. ◆**'weaken**, *v.* 1. *v.tr.* (j-n, etwas) schwächen; (j-n, ein Argument) entkräften. 2. *v.i.* schwach/schwächer werden; (*of power, influence etc.*) nachlassen. ◆**'weakling**, *s.* Schwächling *m*. ◆**'weakly**. I. *adj.* schwach. II. *adj.* kränklich. ◆**'weakness**, *s.* Schwäche *f*; Unzulänglichkeit *f* (einer Leistung).

wealth [welθ], *s.* 1. Reichtum *m*. 2. **a w. of material/ideas**, eine Fülle von Material/Anregungen. ◆**'wealthy**, *adj.* reich, wohlhabend.

wean [wi:n], *v.tr.* entwöhnen.

weapon ['wepən], *s.* Waffe *f*.

wear [wεər]. I. *v.irr.* 1. *v.tr.* (einen Hut, ein Kleid, eine Brille) tragen; **what shall I w.?** was soll ich anziehen? 2. *v.i.* (*a*) (*of tyres etc.*) sich abnutzen; (*b*) (*of material etc.*) **to w. well**, strapazierfähig sein; **these shoes have worn well**, diese Schuhe haben gut gehalten. II. *s.* 1. (*clothes*) **men's w.**, Herrenkleidung *f*. 2. (*a*) **there's still a lot of w. in this dress**, dieses Kleid läßt sich noch lange tragen; (*b*) Abnutzung *f*; *Tchn:* Verschleiß *m*; **fair w. and tear**, (normale) Abnutzung. ◆**'wear a'way**, *v.* 1. *v.tr.* (etwas) (Farbe) abtragen; (eine Inschrift usw.) wegwischen. 2. *v.i.* abgenutzt werden; (*of steps*) ausgetreten werden; (*of rocks etc.*) ausgewaschen werden. ◆**'wear 'down**, *v.* 1. *v.tr.* (*a*) (etwas) abnutzen; (Absätze) abtreten; (*b*) **to w. d. s.o.'s resistance**, j-n zermürben. 2. *v.i.* abgenutzt werden; (*of heels*) abgetreten werden. ◆**'wearer**, *s.* Träger(in) *m(f)* (eines Mantels usw.). ◆**'wearing**, *adj.* (*of thing*) ermüdend; (*of pers.*) anstrengend. ◆'wear 'off, v. 1. v.tr. (etwas) abtragen. 2. v.i. (a) abgetragen werden; (of pile etc.) sich abnutzen; (b) (of effect etc.) nachlassen; the novelty will soon w. o., der Reiz der Neuheit wird sich bald verlieren. ◆'wear 'out, v. 1. v.i. (of things) abgenutzt werden. 2. v.tr. (a) (etwas) abnutzen; (Kleider) abtragen; (b) to w. oneself o., sich erschöpfen.

weary ['wiəri]. I. adj. müde (of sth., + gen); w. of life, lebensmüde. II. v.tr. (j-n) ermüden. 2. v.i. to w. of sth., etwas gen müde/überdrüssig werden. ◆'weariness, s. Müdigkeit f. ◆'wearisome, 'wearying, adj. ermüdend; (tedious) langweilig.

weasel ['wiːz(ə)l], s. Wiesel n.

weather ['weðər]. I. s. Wetter n; w. forecast, Wettervorhersage f; F: (of pers.) under the w., unpäßlich; nicht ganz auf der Höhe. II. v. 1. v.tr. (a) (Holz) austrocknen; (b) to w. a storm, (of ship) einen Sturm abwettern; Fig: (of pers.) eine Krise überstehen. 2. v.i. (of stone etc.) verwittern. ◆'weatherbeaten, adj. (of building etc.) vom Wetter angegriffen; (of face) verwittert. ◆'weathercock, s. Wetterhahn m.

weave [wiːv], v.irr. 1. v.tr. (a) (Stoff) weben; (b) (Körbe usw.) flechten; (c) (of pers., river etc.) sich winden. 2. v.i. (a) weben; (b) F: get weaving! mach dich dran! ◆'weaver, s. Weber m. ◆'weaving, s. Weberei f.

web [web], s.1. spider's w., Spinnennetz n; Fig: Gewebe n. 2. Z: (of webbed foot) Schwimmhaut f; (of bat's wing) Flughaut f. ◆webbed, adj. Z: w. foot, Schwimmfuß m. ◆'webbing, s. Cl: Gurt m.

wed [wed], v. 1. v.tr. Lit: (a) (j-n) heiraten; (b) (of priest) (ein Brautpaar) trauen. 2. v.i. (of pers.) heiraten. ◆'wedding, s. (a) Hochzeit f; (ceremony) Trauung f; silver/golden w., silberne/goldene Hochzeit; (b) attrib. Hochzeits-; w. day, Hochzeitstag m; w. ring, Trauring m.

wedge [wedʒ]. I. s. 1. Keil m. 2. w. of cake, ein Stück Kuchen. 3. w. heel, Keilabsatz m. II. v.tr. to w. sth. into sth., etwas in etwas acc hineinzwängen; wedged in position, festgeklemmt.

Wednesday ['wenzdi], s. Mittwoch m.

wee [wiː], adj. esp. Scot: klein

weed [wiːd]. I. s. Unkraut n. II. v.i. Unkraut jäten. ◆'weedkiller, s. Unkrautvertilgungsmittel n. ◆'weedy, adj. 1. (of garden) von Unkraut bewachsen. 2. (of pers.) schmächtig.

week [wiːk], s. Woche f; once a w., einmal in der Woche; a w. from now/today w., heute in acht Tagen. ◆'weekday, s. Wochentag m. ◆'weekend, s. Wochenende n. ◆'weekly. I. adj. & adv. wöchentlich; w. wage, Wochenlohn m. II. s. (newspaper) Wochenzeitung f.

weep [wiːp], v. 1. v.i.irr. weinen (over/about, über + acc). II. s. to have a good w., sich ausweinen.

weigh [wei], v. 1. v.tr. (a) wiegen; (b) Nau: to w. anchor, den Anker lichten. 2. v.i. how much do you w.? wieviel wiegen Sie? ◆'weighbridge, s. Brückenwaage f. ◆'weigh 'down, v.tr. (etwas) niederdrücken. ◆'weight, s. (a) Gewicht n; (of pers.) to lose w., abnehmen; to gain/put on w., zunehmen; (b) (burden) Last f; Fig: that's a great w. off my mind, damit ist mir ein Stein vom Herzen gefallen. ◆'weightlessness, s. Schwerelosigkeit f. ◆'weight-'lifter, s. Gewichtheber m. ◆'weighty, adj. schwer; Fig: (of reason etc.) schwerwiegend. ◆'weigh'watcher, s. Linienbewußte(r) f(m). ◆'weigh 'up, v.tr. to w. up advantages and disadvantages, Vorund Nachteile abwägen; to w. s.o. up, j-n abschätzen.

weir [wiər], s. Wehr n.

weird [wiəd], adj. (a) (uncanny) unheimlich; (b) (strange) seltsam; (of pers.) verschroben; F: komisch.

welcome ['welkəm]. I. adj. (a) willkommen; to make s.o. w., j-n freundlich aufnehmen; (b) int. w.! herzlich willkommen! thank you – you're w.! vielen Dank – nichts zu danken! II. s. to give s.o. a warm/hearty w., j-n freundlich/herzlich aufnehmen. III. v.tr. (j-n) willkommen heißen.

weld [weld]. I. v.tr. schweißen; welded seam, Schweißnaht f. II. s. Schweißstelle f. ◆'welder, s. Schweißer m. ◆'welding, s. Schweißen n.

welfare ['welfɛər], s. (of state etc.) Wohlfahrt f; (of pers.) Wohlergehen n; (social) w., öffentliche Fürsorge; the W. State, der Wohlfahrtsstaat.

well¹ [wel], s. 1. Brunnen m. 2. oil w., Ölquelle f.

well². I. adv. 1. (a) gut; to behave w., sich gut benehmen; you would do w. to forget about it, am besten vergißt du das; to wish s.o. w., j-m alles Gute wünschen; (b) to think w. of s.o., j-n schätzen. 2. (a) you may w. laugh, du hast gut lachen; (b) we might (just) as w. have stayed at home, wir hätten ebensogut zu Hause bleiben können. 3. (intensifying) he's w. over fifty, er ist weit über fünfzig. 4. as w., auch. 5. w. off, gut dran; (rich) wohlhabend. II. adj. 1. (healthy) gesund; I'm not w., es geht mir nicht gut. 2. all is w., es ist alles in Ordnung. III. int. w! w. I never! na, so was! (oh) w., it can't be helped, na ja, das ist nun mal so. ◆'well-ad'vised, adj. (of pers.) you would be w.-a. to forget this, es wäre ratsam, das zu vergessen. ◆'well-be'haved, adj. artig. ◆'well-'being, s. Wohlergehen n (eines Einzelnen); Wohl n (der Familie, des Staates usw.); a feeling of w.-b., ein

Wohlgefühl n. ◆'**well-'bred**, adj. gut erzogen. ◆'**well-'known**, adj. bekannt. ◆'**well-'read**, adj. (of pers.) belesen. ◆'**well-'timed**, adj. it was w.-t., es geschah gerade im richtigen Augenblick. ◆'**well-to-'do**, adj. wohlhabend. ◆'**well-wisher**, s. Wohlgesinnte(r) f(m).

wellington ['weliŋtən], s. boots/**wellingtons**/F: wellies, Gummistiefel mpl.

Welsh [welʃ]. **I.** adj. walisisch; Cu: W. **rabbit/rarebit**, überbackener Käsetoast m. **II.** s. (a) the W., die Waliser; (b) (language) Walisisch. ◆'**Welshman**, s. Waliser m. ◆'**Welshwoman**, s. Waliserin f.

west [west]. **I.** s. Westen m; to the w. (of), westlich + gen/(with names) von + II. adj. West-; the w. coast, die Westküste; **W. Indian**, s. westindisch; (b) s. Westinder(in) m(f). **III.** adv. the room faces w., das Zimmer geht nach Westen. ◆'**westerly**, adj. in a w. direction, in westlicher Richtung. ◆'**western**. **I.** adj. westlich; **W. Europe**, Westeuropa n. **II.** s. F: Cin: Western m. ◆'**westwards**, adv. nach Westen.

wet [wet]. **I.** adj. (a) naß; w. **paint**, frisch gestrichen; (b) w. **weather**, Regenwetter n; F: (pers.) a w. **blanket**, ein Spielverderber. **II.** v.tr. (etwas) naß machen. ◆'**wetness**, s. Nässe f. ◆'**wet-suit**, s. Kälteschutzanzug m (für Taucher).

whack [wæk]. **I.** v.tr. F: (a) to w. s.o., (thrash) j-n verprügeln; (hit) j-m eine langen; (b) Sp: (seine Gegner) in die Pfanne hauen. **II.** s. Schlag m. ◆'**whacking**, s. to give s.o. a w., j-m eine Tracht Prügel verabreichen.

whale [weil], s. **I.** Wal m. **2.** F: we had a w. of a time, wir hatten einen Mordsspaß. ◆'**whaling**, s. Walfang m. ◆'**whaler**, s. (pers., ship) Walfänger m.

wharf pl. **-ves** ['wɔːf -vz], s. Kai m.

what [wɔt]. **I.** adj. welche(r, s); he gave me w. **money he had**, er gab mir alles, was er an Geld hatte; w. **size do you take?** welche Größe haben Sie? w. **good/use is it?** wozu dient es/ist es gut? w. **sort of (an) animal is that?** was ist das für ein Tier? w. **an idea!** was für eine Idee! w. **a lovely picture!** welch ein schönes Bild! **II.** pron. was. w. **I have just said** ..., das, was ich eben gesagt habe ...; w. **are you doing here?** was machst du denn hier? w**hat's his name?** wie heißt er? w. **is the weather like?** wie ist das Wetter? w. **about a cup of tea?** wie wär's mit einer Tasse Tee? w. **about you?** wie steht's mit Ihnen? w**ell**, w. **about it?** ja, und? w. **if it rains?** was geschieht, wenn es regnet? w. **did you say?** wie bitte? w. **with?** womit? w. **on?** worauf? **over w.?** worüber? w. **for?** (purpose) wozu? (reason) wieso? warum? F: **so w.?** na, und? ◆**what'ever. I.** pron. w. **happens**, was auch geschieht; w. **hap-**

pened to Susan? was in aller Welt ist aus Susan geworden? **II.** adj. w. **price they are asking**, welchen Preis sie auch immer verlangen; **no hope w.**, gar/überhaupt keine Hoffnung; **is there any hope w.?** gibt es überhaupt noch Hoffnung?

wheat [wiːt], s. Weizen m.

wheedle ['wiːdl], v.tr. to w. **sth. out of s.o.**, j-m etwas abschmeicheln.

wheel [wiːl]. **I.** s. (a) Rad n; Nau: Steuerrad n; Aut: (steering) s. Lenkrad n; at the w., am Steuer; (b) potter's w., Töpferscheibe f. **II.** v.tr. (ein Fahrrad, eine Karre usw.) schieben. **2.** v.i. (a) (of bird) kreisen; (b) (of pers.) to w. **round**, sich jäh umdrehen. ◆'**wheelbarrow**, s. Schubkarre(n) f(m). ◆'**wheelchair**, s. Rollstuhl m.

wheeze [wiːz]. **I.** v.i. pfeifend atmen. **II.** s. pfeifender Atemzug. ◆'**wheezy**, adj. (of breath) pfeifend; (of pers.) asthmatisch.

when [wen]. **I.** adv. **1.** interrog. wann? **2.** rel. the **days w. the shops are closed**, die Tage, an denen die Geschäfte geschlossen sind; the **time w.** ..., die Zeit, wo ... **II.** conj. **1.** (in the past) als; w. he **saw her**, als er sie sah. **2.** (whenever) wenn; we **always had fun w. he came**, wir hatten immer viel Spaß, wenn er kam. **3.** (future) **I find it I'll let you know**, sobald ich es finde, sage ich dir Bescheid. ◆**when'ever**, adv. (a) (any time that) wann immer; (b) (each time that) immer wenn.

where [wɛər], adv. **1.** interrog. wo? w. **(to)?** wohin? w. **from?** woher? w. **do you live?** wo wohnen Sie? w. **are you going?** wohin gehen Sie? w. **do you come from?** woher kommen Sie? **2.** rel. wo; (direction) wohin; (at the place) w. **it happened**, an der Stelle/dort, wo es passiert ist; he **doesn't know w. to go**, er weiß nicht, wohin er gehen soll. ◆**whereabouts. I.** ['wɛərəbauts] interrog. adv. w. **do you live?** wo wohnen Sie? **II.** ['wɛər-] s. Aufenthaltsort m. ◆**where'as**, conj. während. ◆**wher'ever**, adv. w. he **is**, wo (immer) er auch ist; we **you go you see them**, überall, wo man hinkommt, sieht man sie.

whet [wet], v.tr. Fig: to w. **the appetite**, den Appetit anregen.

whether ['weðər], conj. ob.

which [witʃ], adj. & pron. **1.** interrog. welche(r, s); w. **have you chosen?** welche/welchen/welches hast du gewählt? **2.** rel. (a) der, die, das; the **house w. is for sale**, das Haus, das zu verkaufen ist; (b) (with prep.) **about w.**, worüber; **for w.**, wofür; (c) (referring to a clause) was; **I have lost my money, w. is very annoying**, ich habe mein Geld verloren, was sehr ärgerlich ist. ◆**which'ever**, adj. & pron. welche(r,s) auch; **take w. book you like**, nehmen Sie sich welches Buch Sie wollen.

whiff [wif]. s. (leichter) Hauch m; (scent) Duft m; (smell) Geruch m.

while [wail]. I. s. Weile f; for a w., eine Zeitlang; once in a w., hin und wieder. 2. it's not worth your w., es ist nicht der Mühe wert; es lohnt sich nicht (für Sie). II. conj. (time) während.

whim [wim], s. Laune f. ◆'whimsical, adj. (of pers.) launenhaft; (of ideas) schrullig.

whimper ['wimpər]. I. v.i. wimmern; (esp. of dog) winseln. II. s. Wimmern n; Winseln n.

whine [wain]. I. v.i. (of engine etc.) heulen; (complain) (wehleidig) jammern; (of child) quengeln; (of dog) jaulen. II. s. (also 'whining) Geheul n; Gejammer n; Quengelei f; Jaulen n.

whip [wip]. I. v.tr. (a) (j-n, ein Pferd) peitschen; (b) Cu: (Sahne usw.) schlagen; (c) he whipped the revolver out of his pocket, er riß den Revolver aus der Tasche. s. 1. Peitsche f. 2. Parl: (pers.) Einpeitscher m. ◆'whip 'round. I. v.i. sich blitzartig umdrehen. II. s. F: to have a quick 'w.-r., den Hut herumgehen lassen. ◆'whip 'up, v.tr. (Leidenschaften) aufpeitschen.

whirl [wə:l]. I. v.tr. & i. (herum)wirbeln. II. s. Wirbel m. ◆'whirlpool, s. Wasserstrudel m. ◆'whirlwind, s. Wirbelwind m.

whirr [wə:r]. I. s. Schwirren n (der Flügel); Brummen n (einer Maschine); Surren n (eines Propellers). II. v.i. schwirren; (of machinery etc.) brummen; (of propeller etc.) surren.

whisk [wisk]. I. v.tr. (Eiweiß, Sahne) schlagen. II. s. Cu: Schneebesen m.

whisker ['wiskər], s. Schnurrhaar n (einer Katze usw.); F: (of pers.) whiskers, Backenbart m.

whisk(e)y ['wiski], s. Whisky m.

whisper ['wispər]. I. s. Flüstern n. II. v.tr. & i. flüstern (to s.o., mit j-m).

whist [wist], s. Whist n; w. drive, Whistturnier n.

whistle ['wisl]. I. s. 1. (sound) Pfeifen n; (single) Pfiff m. 2. (instrument) Pfeife f. II. v.tr. & i. pfeifen.

white [wait]. I. adj. (a) weiß; w. coffee, Milchkaffee m; w. horse, Schimmel m; a w. man, ein Weißer; (b) (pale) a w. face, ein bleiches/blasses Gesicht; (c) Fig: w. lie, Notlüge f. II. s. 1. Weiß n; dressed (all) in w., (ganz) in Weiß gekleidet; (ganz) weiß angezogen. 2. (pers.) Weiße(r) f(m). 3. Cu: w. of egg, Eiweiß n. ◆'whitebait, s. Breitling m. ◆'white-'collar, adj. w.-c. worker, Büroangestellte(r) f(m). ◆'whiten, v.tr. (etwas) weiß machen; (whitewash) (eine Mauer usw.) weißen; (bleach) (Kleider usw.) bleichen. ◆'whiteness, s. Weiße f. 2. (pallor) Blässe f. ◆'whitewash. I. s. Tünche f. II. v.tr.

(a) (eine Mauer usw.) weißen; (b) Fig: (j-n) (von einer Anschuldigung) reinwaschen.

whiting ['waitiŋ], s. Merlan m.

Whitsun(tide) ['witsən(taid)], s. Pfingsten n.

whittle ['witl], v.tr. (a) to w. away, (Ersparnisse usw.) allmählich aufzehren; (b) to w. down, (etwas) stark reduzieren.

whizz [wiz], v.i. sausen; to w. past, vorbeisausen; (of bullet etc.) vorbeizischen; to w. along, dahinflitzen. ◆'whizzkid, s. F: Senkrechtstarter m.

who [hu:], nom. pron. 1. interrog. wer? 2. rel. der, die, das; the friend w. came yesterday, der Freund, der gestern gekommen ist. ◆who'dunit, s. F: Krimi m. ◆who'ever, pron. wer (auch) immer; w. finds it may keep it, wer es findet, darf es behalten.

whole [həul]. I. adj. ganz. II. s. the w., das Ganze; to form a w., ein Ganzes/eine Einheit bilden; on the w., im großen und ganzen. ◆'whole-'hearted, adj. aufrichtig; w. support, rückhaltlose Unterstützung; -ly, adv. von ganzem Herzen; I agree w., ich bin ganz Ihrer Meinung. ◆'wholemeal, adj. w. bread, Vollkornbrot n. ◆'wholesale. I. adj. Com: 1. Großhandels-. 2. w. slaughter, Massenmord m. II. adv. im Großhandel, en gros. ◆'wholesaler, s. Großhändler m. ◆'wholly, adv. (entirely) ganz völlig.

wholesome ['həulsəm], adj. gesund; (of food, drink) bekömmlich.

whom [hu:m], pron. 1. interrog. acc wen; dat wem; w. did you see? wen haben Sie gesehen? of w. …? von wem/(whose) wessen …? 2. rel. acc. den, die, das; dat dem, der; pl denen; the man w. you saw, der Mann, den du gesprochen hast; the friend to w. I lent the book, der Freund, dem ich das Buch geliehen habe; of w., von dem/pl. denen; (whose) dessen, pl. deren.

whoop [hu:p], v.i. keuchen. ◆'whooping cough, s. Keuchhusten m.

whopper ['wɔpər], s. P: Mordsding n; (giant) Riese m. ◆'whopping, adj. P: enorm; w. lie, faustdicke Lüge.

whore [hɔ:r], s. Hure f. II. v.i. huren.

whose [hu:z], poss. pron. 1. interrog. wessen? w. daughter are you? wessen Tochter bist du? 2. rel. dessen; pl. & f deren; the pupil about w. work I complained, der Schüler, über dessen Arbeit ich mich beklagt habe.

why [wai]. I. adv. warum; the reason w. (he came), der Grund s, weshalb er gekommen ist. II. int. w., of course! aber natürlich!

wick [wik], s. Docht m.

wicked ['wikid], adj. (a) (of pers., intentions) böse; (of remarks) boshaft; (b) (of child) schlimm. ◆'wickedness, s. Bosheit f.

wicker ['wikər], s. w. (work), Flechtwerk n; (articles) Korbwaren fpl.

wicket ['wikit], s. 1. Pförtchen n. 2. (in cricket) Dreistab m; Tor n; w. keeper, Torhüter m.

wide [waid]. I. adj. 1. (of river, road) breit; how w. is the room? welche Breite hat das Zimmer? 2. (extensive) weit; the w. world, die weite Welt; Fig: w. experience, reiche Erfahrung; w. reading, große Belesenheit. II. adv. weit; w. apart, weit auseinander; far and w., weit und breit; open w.! weit aufmachen! w. awake, hellwach; -ly, adv. weit; w. known, weit und breit bekannt; he has travelled w., er ist von weit gereister Mann. ◆'wide-'angle, attrib.adj. w.-a. lens, Weitwinkelobjektiv n. ◆'widen, v. 1. v.tr. (a) (etwas) breiter machen; (eine Straße) verbreitern; (b) (ein Loch) ausweiten; (c) Fig: to w. one's horizons, seinen Gesichtskreis erweitern. 2. v.i. breiter werden. ◆'widespread, adj. weitverbreitet. ◆'width [widθ], s. Breite f.

widow ['widəu], s. Witwe f. ◆'widowed, adj. verwitwet. ◆'widower, s. Witwer m.

wield [wi:ld], v.tr. (ein Schwert usw.) handhaben.

wife, pl. **wives** [waif, waivz], s. Frau f; (formal) Gattin f.

wig [wig], s. Perücke f.

wiggle ['wigl], v. 1. v.i. (of path etc.) sich schlängeln; (b) (move) wackeln. 2. v.tr. to w. one's toes, hips, etc., mit den Zehen, Hüften usw. wackeln.

wigwam ['wigwæm], s. Wigwam m.

wild [waild]. I. adj. 1. (of animals) wild; (of plants) to grow w., wild wachsen; (b) (of wind) heftig; a w. night, eine stürmische Nacht; (c) (untamed) ungezähmt; w. animals, wilde Tiere; (of pers.) ausgelassen; it makes me w., das macht mich wild/wütend; (of girl) w. about s.o., verrückt nach j-m; (of idea etc.) verrückt. II. s. (a) in the w., in der Natur; (b) pl the wilds, die Wildnis; -ly, adv. wild; (at random) aufs Geratewohl. ◆'wildcat, adj. Ind: w. strike, wilder Streik. ◆'wilderness ['wildənis], s. Wildnis f; (desert) Wüste f. ◆'wildfire, s. to spread like w., sich wie ein Lauffeuer verbreiten. ◆'wildfowl, s. Wildvögel mpl. ◆'wild 'goose, s. Wildgans f; F: w.-g. chase, nutzloses Unterfangen. ◆'wildlife, s. Tiere npl (in der freien Natur); w. sanctuary, Tierschutzgebiet n. ◆'wildness, s. Wildheit f; Toben n (eines Sturmes); Unsinnigkeit f (der Ideen, des Geredes).

wilful ['wilful], adj. 1. (of pers.) eigensinnig. 2. (intentional) absichtlich.

will [wil]. I. s. 1. (a) Wille m; strength of w., Willensstärke f; (b) (desire) Wunsch m; of one's own free w., aus freien

Stücken. 2. Jur: Testament n; to leave s.o. sth. in one's w., j-m etwas testamentarisch vermachen. II. modal aux. v. (a) (want) wollen; the engine won't start, der Motor will nicht anspringen; (b) (future) werden. ◆ w./F: I'll come, ich werde kommen. ◆'willing, adj. to be w., to do sth., bereit sein, etwas zu tun; -ly, adv. bereitwillig; I would w. go, but ..., ich würde gerne hingehen, aber ... ◆'willingness, s. Bereitschaft f (etwas zu tun). ◆'willpower, s. Willenskraft f.

willow ['wiləu], s. w. (tree), Weide f.

wilt [wilt], v.i. (of plant) verwelken; (b) (of pers.) schlapp werden.

wily ['waili], adj. listig; F: gerissen.

win [win]. I. v.tr. & i.irr. gewinnen. II. s. 1. Sieg m. ◆'winner, s. Gewinner(in) m(f); Sp: Sieger(in) m(f). ◆'winning. I. adj. 1. (of pers., team) siegreich; (in lottery etc.) w. number, Gewinnummer f. 2. (of pers.) w. ways, anziehendes Wesen. II. s. 1. Sieg m; Nt: w. post, Ziel n. 2. pl winnings, Gewinn m (beim Spiel, Toto usw.). ◆'win 'over, v.tr. (j-n) für sich acc gewinnen. ◆'win 'through, v.i. to w. t. in the end, sich am Ende durchsetzen.

wince [wins]. I. v.i. (vor Schmerz) zusammenzucken; (make a face) das Gesicht verziehen (at, bei + dat). II. s. Zusammenzucken n.

winch [wintʃ], s. Winde f.

wind[1] [wind]. I. s. 1. Wind m; to get w. of sth., etwas wittern; to put the w. up s.o., j-m angst und bange machen. 2. (a) (breath) Atem m; to get one's second w., wieder zu Atem kommen; (b) (flatulence) Blähungen fpl. 3. Mus: w. instrument, Blasinstrument n. II. v.tr. it winded me, es hat mir den Atem verschlagen. ◆'windbreak, s. Windschutz m. ◆'windcheater, s. Windjacke f. ◆'windfall, s. 1. (fruit) windfalls, Fallobst n. 2. Fig: unverhoffter Gewinn. ◆'windless, adj. windstill. ◆'windmill, s. Windmühle f. ◆'windpipe, s. Luftröhre f. ◆'windscreen/N.Am: 'windshield, s. Aut: Windschutzscheibe f; w. wiper, Scheibenwischer m. ◆'windswept, adj. dem Wind ausgesetzt; (of sea etc.) windgepeitscht. ◆'windward, adj. Wind-; Nau: Luv-. ◆'windy, adj. windig; (of day, weather) stürmisch.

wind[2] [waind]. I. v.irr. 1. v.i. sich winden. 2. v.tr. (a) (etwas) winden (round sth., um etwas acc); to w. wool into a ball, Wolle zu einem Knäuel wickeln; (b) (eine Uhr) aufziehen. II. s. Windung f; (single bend) Biegung f. ◆'winding. I. adj. sich schlängelnd; (of road) kurvenreich; w. staircase, Wendeltreppe f. II. s. Aufziehen n (einer Uhr). ◆'wind 'up, v. 1. v.tr. (a) (ein Seil usw.) aufwinden; (Garn) aufwickeln; (eine Uhr) aufziehen; (b) (finish) (eine Rede usw.)

schließen; *Com:* (eine Firma) liquidieren. 2. *v.i.* enden.

windlass ['windləs], *s.* Winde *f; Nau:* Ankerspill *n.*

window ['windəu], *s.* (a) Fenster *n; w.* **pane,** Fensterscheibe *f;* **w. ledge/sill,** Fenstersims *n;* (*internal*) Fensterbrett *n;* **w. box,** Blumenkasten *m,* (b) (**shop**) **w.,** Schaufenster *n;* **w. shopping,** Schaufensterbummel *m.*

wine [wain], *s.* Wein *m;* **w. production,** Weinbau *m;* **w. cellar,** Weinkeller *m;* **w. list,** Weinkarte *f;* **w. merchant,** Weinhändler *m;* **w. tasting,** Weinprobe *f;* **w. waiter,** Weinkellner *m.* ◆**wineglass,** *s.* Weinglas *n.*

wing [wiŋ], *s.* (a) Flügel *m;* (b) *Th:* **the wings,** die Kulissen *fpl;* (c) *Fb: etc:* (*pers.*) Außenstürmer *m.*

wink [wiŋk], **I.** *s.* Wink *m* (mit den Augen); **with a w.,** mit einem Zwinkern; *F:* **to have forty winks,** ein Nickerchen machen. **II.** *v.i.* (a) (*of pers.*) zwinkern; **to w. at s.o.,** j-m zuzwinkern; (b) (*of light*) blinken. ◆**winking,** *s.* Zwinkern *n.*

winkle ['wiŋkl], *s.* Strandschnecke *f.*

winter ['wintər]. **I.** *s.* Winter *m;* **w. clothes,** Winterkleidung *f;* **w. sports,** Wintersport *m.* **II.** *v.i.* überwintern. ◆**wintry,** *adj.* winterlich.

wipe [waip]. **I.** *v.tr.* (etwas) wischen; (eine Fläche) abwischen; **to w. sth. clean/dry,** etwas sauberwischen/abtrocknen. **II.** *s.* Wischen *n;* **give it a w.!** wisch es ein bißchen ab! ◆**wiper,** *s. Aut:* (**windscreen**/*N.Am:* **windshield**) **w.,** Scheibenwischer *m.* ◆**wipe out,** *v.tr.* (a) (eine Schuld) tilgen; (b) (*erase*) (ein Bild, Wörter) ausradieren; (*destroy*) (eine Armee usw.) vernichten; (eine Rasse, Tierart) ausrotten.

wire ['waiər]. **I.** *s.* Draht *m;* (a) (**barbed**) **w.,** Stacheldraht *m;* (b) (**telephone**) **w.,** Telefonleitung *f;* **w. tapping,** Anzapfen *n* von Telefonleitungen; (c) (*telegram*) Telegramm *n.* **II.** *v.tr.* (eine Nachricht) telegrafieren. ◆**wireless,** *s.* **w.** (**set**), Radio(apparat) *n(m);* **on the w.,** im Rundfunk. ◆**wirepulling,** *s. Fig:* Drahtzieherei *f.* ◆**wiry,** *adj.* drahtig.

wisdom ['wizdəm], *s.* Weisheit *f;* **w. tooth,** Weisheitszahn *m.* ◆**wise** [waiz], *adj.* weise; (*in particular instance*) klug; **-ly,** *adv.* klugerweise, vernünftigerweise. ◆**wisecrack,** *s.* Witz *m.*

wish [wiʃ]. **I.** *v.tr.* (a) **to w. to do sth.,** etwas tun wollen; **I don't w. to do it,** ich möchte nicht, daß du es tust; **I w. I were in your place,** ich wünschte, ich wäre an deiner Stelle; (b) (*greeting*) (j-m etwas) wünschen. **II.** *s.* Wunsch *m;* **my best wishes on your retirement/for a rapid recovery,** die besten Wünsche zu Ihrer Pensionierung/für eine baldige Genesung; (*end of letter*) **with best wishes,** herzliche Grüße. ◆**wishful,** *adj. F:* **that's w. thinking,** das ist reines

Wunschdenken.

wishy-washy ['wiʃiwɔʃi], *adj. F:* (*of soup etc.*) wäßrig; (*of colour*) verwaschen; (*of idea*) vage; (*of book etc.*) seicht.

wisp [wisp], *s.* **w.** of hair, Haarsträhne *f;* **w. of smoke,** Rauchfahne *f.*

wistful ['wistful], *adj.* wehmütig; (*longing*) sehnsüchtig.

wit [wit], *s.* **1.** *pl.* **wits,** Verstand *m;* **to have one's wits about one,** geistesgegenwärtig sein; **to be at one's wits' end,** am Ende seiner Weisheit sein. **2.** (*pers.*) Witzbold *m.*

witch [witʃ], *s.* Hexe *f;* **w. doctor,** Medizinmann *m.* ◆**witchcraft,** *s.* Hexerei *f.*

with [wið], *prep.* with *+ dat:* **he stays with his mother,** er wohnt bei seiner Mutter; **I'll be w. you in a moment,** ich komme gleich; *Fig:* **I'm not quite w. you,** ich komme nicht ganz mit; **it's a habit w. me,** das ist Gewohnheit bei mir; **have you a pencil w. you?** hast du einen Bleistift bei dir? (*in spite of*) **w. all his faults,** trotz aller seiner Fehler; **to tremble w. rage,** vor Wut zittern.

withdraw [wið'drɔː], *v.irr.* **1.** *v.tr.* (*remove*) (etwas) entfernen, wegnehmen; (die Hand, *Fur:* eine Klage, *Com:* ein Angebot usw.) zurückziehen (**from,** von/ aus *+ dat*); **to w. money from the bank,** Geld von der Bank abheben. **2.** *v.i.* (*of pers.*) sich zurückziehen (**from,** von/ aus *+ dat*); *Sp:* (*of competitor*) **to w. from a competition,** aus einem Wettkampf ausscheiden. ◆**with'drawal,** *s.* Zurückziehen *n;* Abhebung *f* (von Geld); Zurücknahme *f* (eines Angebotes usw.); *Mil:* Rückzug *m; Sp:* Ausscheiden *n;* **w. symptoms,** Entzugserscheinungen *fpl.*

wither ['wiðər], *v.i.* (*of plant*) verwelken; (*dry up*) verdorren. ◆**withered,** *adj. Bot:* verwelkt. ◆**withering,** *adj. Fig:* **w. look,** vernichtender Blick.

withhold [wið'həuld], *v.tr.irr.* (a) (*refuse*) (seine Einwilligung usw.) verweigern; (b) (Tatsachen usw.) vorenthalten.

within [wið'in], *prep.* innerhalb *+ gen;* **w. one's four walls,** innerhalb seiner vier Wände; **w. sight,** in Sichtweite; **w. a week,** innerhalb einer Woche.

without [wið'aut], *prep.* ohne *+ acc;* **w. seeing me,** ohne mich zu sehen; **that goes w. saying,** das versteht sich von selbst; **to do w. sth.,** auf etwas *acc* verzichten.

withstand [wið'stænd], *v.tr.irr.* (Schmerzen usw.) aushalten; *Mil:* (einem Angriff) widerstehen.

witness ['witnis], **I.** *s.* Zeuge *m;* Zeugin *f;* **w. box**/*N.Am:* **stand,** Zeugenbank *f.* **II.** *v.tr.* (a) **to w. an occurrence,** bei einem Vorfall zugegen sein; (b) (eine Unterschrift) beglaubigen.

witty ['witi], *adj.* witzig, geistreich. ◆**witticism,** *s.* witzige Bemerkung *f.*

wizard ['wizəd], *s.* Zauberer *m.* ◆**wizardry,** *s.* Zauberei *f.*

wizened ['wizənd], adj. runz(e)lig; (shrunken) zusammengeschrumpft.

wobble ['wɔbl], v.i. wackeln; (sway) schwanken. ◆'**wobbly**, adj. F: wack(e)lig.

woe [wəu], Leid n, Kummer m. ◆'**woebegone**, adj. jammervoll.

wog [wɔg], s. P: Pej: (esp. Arab) Kameltreiber m; (black) Nigger m.

wolf, pl. **wolves** [wulf, wulvz]. I. s. 1. Wolf m; (she) Wölfin f; Fig: **to cry w.**, blinden Alarm schlagen. 2. (pers.) F: Schürzenjäger m. II. v.tr. **to w. one's food**, sein Essen hinunterschlingen.

woman, pl. **women** ['wumən, 'wimin], s. Frau f; **w. libber**, Frauenrechtlerin f; **w. doctor**, Ärztin f; **w. friend**, Freundin f.

womb [wu:m], s. Gebärmutter f.

wonder ['wʌndər]. I. s. 1. (miracle) Wunder n; **no w.!** kein Wunder! 2. (surprise) Erstaunen n. II. v.i. 1. sich wundern; erstaunt sein (**at/about**, über + acc); **I don't w. at it**, das wundert mich nicht. 2. v.tr. **I w. whether he will come**, ich frage mich/bin gespannt, ob er kommen wird. ◆'**wonderful**, adj. wunderbar. ◆'**wonderment**, s. Verwunderung f.

wood [wud], s. 1. Wald m; **we're not out of the w.** yet, wir sind noch nicht über den Berg. 2. (material) Holz n. ◆'**wood-carving**, s. Holzschnitzerei f. ◆'**woodcut**, s. Holzschnitt m. ◆'**wood-cutter**, s. Holzfäller m. ◆'**wooded**, adj. (of area, slope) bewaldet. ◆'**wooden**, adj. hölzern, Holz-; **w.-headed**, begriffsstutzig. ◆'**woodland**, s. Wald m; (area) Waldfläche f. ◆'**woodlouse**, s. Kellerassel f. ◆'**woodman**, pl. **-men**, s. 1. Förster m. 2. (lumberjack) Holzfäller m. ◆'**woodpecker**, s. Specht m; **spotted w.**, Buntspecht m. ◆'**woodshed**, s. Holzschuppen m. ◆'**woodwind**, s. Mus: die Holzbläser mpl (eines Orchesters); **w. instrument**, Holzblasinstrument n. ◆'**woodwork**, s. Holzarbeit f. ◆'**woodworm**, s. Holzwurm m.

wool [wul], s. Wolle f. ◆'**woollen**, adj. wollen; **w. goods**, Wollwaren fpl. ◆'**woollens**, s. pl. (materials) Wollstoffe mpl; (goods) Wollwaren fpl. ◆'**woolly**, adj. wollig; Fig: (of ideas etc.) verschwommen.

word [wə:d]. I. s. 1. Wort n; **in other words**, mit anderen Worten; anders ausgedrückt; **a man of few words**, ein wortkarger Mensch; **to have words with s.o.**, eine Auseinandersetzung mit j-m haben; **by w. of mouth**, mündlich; (news) **to send s.o. w. of sth.**, j-n (brieflich) über etwas acc benachrichtigen; **to keep/break one's w.**, sein Wort halten/brechen. II. v.tr. (etwas) formulieren. ◆'**wording**, s. (a) Wortlaut m (eines Dokuments); (b) (choice of words) Wortwahl f; (manner) Formulierung f.

work [wə:k]. I. s. 1. Arbeit f; **at w.**, bei der Arbeit; (in office) im Büro; **to set to w.**, sich an die Arbeit machen; **out of w.**, arbeitslos; **a piece of w.**, (task) eine Aufgabe; (completed) eine Leistung. 2. Lit: Mus: etc: Werk n; **a w. of art**, ein Kunstwerk. 3. **road works**, Straßenbauarbeiten fpl. 4. (machinery) Räderwerk n; (gears) Getriebe n; **the works of a watch**, ein Uhrwerk. 5. pl. (factory) Werk n, Betrieb m. II. v. 1. v.i. (a) arbeiten (**on sth.**, an etwas dat); **to w. hard**, schwer/fleißig arbeiten; (b) (of machine etc.) funktionieren; (c) **this medicine really works**, diese Medizin wirkt garantiert; **his plan didn't w.**, sein Plan ist nicht gelungen/F: hat nicht geklappt. 2. v.tr. **to w. one's way up**, sich nach oben arbeiten; **he worked his way through college**, er verdiente sich dat sein Studium. ◆'**workable**, adj. (of project) durchführbar. ◆'**workbench**, s. Werkbank f; (small) Arbeitstisch m. ◆'**worker**, s. Arbeiter(in) m(f). ◆'**working**, adj. 1. (of pers.) berufstätig; **the w. class**, die Arbeiterklasse. 2. (a) (of machine) **w./in w. order**, betriebsfähig; **not w.**, außer Betrieb. ◆'**workman**, s. Arbeiter m. ◆'**workmanship**, s. Arbeit f, Ausführung f. ◆'**work off**, v.tr. **to w. off**, (a) (Schulden usw.) abarbeiten; (b) **to w. o. one's energy**, überflüssige Energie loswerden. ◆'**work on**, v. 1. v.i. **to w.** ['wə:k'ɔn] weiterarbeiten. 2. v.tr. ['wə:kɔn] **to w. on a project**, an einem Projekt arbeiten. ◆'**work 'out**, v. 1. v.tr. (a) (eine Idee, einen Plan usw.) ausarbeiten; (b) (ein Problem) lösen. 2. v.i. (a) (gut/schlecht) ausgehen; (b) (of sum) **how much does it w. o. at?** auf wieviel beläuft es sich? ◆'**workshop**, s. Werkstatt f. ◆'**work 'up**, v.tr. (a) (develop) (einen Gedanken, eine Situation usw.) entwickeln; (ein Geschäft) hochbringen; (excite) (das Publikum) aufregen; **to w. oneself up into a rage**, sich in Wut hineinsteigern; F: **don't get worked up**, reg dich nicht auf.

world [wə:ld], s. Welt f; **all over the w./the w. over**, in der ganzen Welt; **what in the w. is the matter with you?** was in aller Welt fehlt dir? **w. war**, Weltkrieg m; Sp: **w. record**, Weltrekord m; **man of the w.**, Mann von Welt; **to feel on top of the w.**, in bester Form sein; **that will do you a w. of good**, das wird dir ungemein gut tun; **to think the w. of s.o.**, j-n sehr hoch einschätzen; **she is/means the w. to him**, sie ist sein ein und alles. ◆'**world-'famous**, adj. weltberühmt. ◆'**worldly**, adj. weltlich. ◆'**world'wide**, adj. weltweit; **w. reputation**, Weltruf m.

worm [wə:m]. I. s. 1. Wurm m; esp. (earth) w., Regenwurm m; Fig: **w.'s eye view**, Froschperspektive f. 2. **w. gear**,

Schneckengetriebe *n.* II. *v.tr.* to w. a secret out of s.o., j-m ein Geheimnis entlocken. ◆'**wormeaten**, *adj.* (a) wurmstichig; (b) *Fig:* uralt.

worn ['wɔːn], *adj.* (a) *(of clothes)* abgetragen; w. out, (i) *(of thing)* (ganz) abgenutzt; (ii) *(of pers.)* erschöpft.

worry ['wʌri]. I. *v.* 1. *v.tr.* (a) (j-n) beunruhigen; *(of pers.)* belästigen; **to w. oneself**, sich *dat* Sorgen/Kummer machen; (b) *(of dog)* (Schafe usw.) hetzen. 2. *v.i.* sich *dat* Sorgen machen; **don't w.!** mach dir keine Sorgen! **it's not worth worrying about**, es lohnt sich nicht, sich *dat* darüber Gedanken zu machen. II. *s.* Sorge *f;* *(stronger)* Kummer *m.* ◆'**worried**, *adj.* besorgt. ◆'**worrying**, *adj. (of thing)* beunruhigend.

worse [wɔːs]. I. *adj.* schlechter, schlimmer. II. *s.* 1. Schlimmeres *n,* Schlechteres *n;* **to change for the w.**, sich zum Schlechteren wenden. III. *adv.* schlechter, schlimmer. ◆'**worsen**, *v.* 1. *v.tr.* (Beziehungen usw.) verschlechtern. 2. *v.i.* sich verschlechtern.

worship ['wɔːʃip]. I. *v.tr.* anbeten II. *s.* Anbetung *f; Ecc:* Kult *m.* ◆'**worshipper**, *s.* Anbeter(in) *m(f); Ecc:* Kirchgänger(in) *m(f).*

worst [wɔːst]. I. *adj.* schlechteste(r, s); schlimmste(r, s); **his w. enemy**, sein ärgster Feind; **the w. part of/about it is that ...**, das Schlimmste daran ist, daß ... II. *s.* **the w.**, der, die, das Schlechteste/Schlimmste; **that's the w. of cheap shoes**, das ist der Nachteil von billigen Schuhen; **at the w.**, schlimmstenfalls; **if the w. comes to the w.**, wenn alle Stricke reißen. III. *adv.* am schlechtesten/schlimmsten.

worsted ['wustid], *s.* Kammgarn *n.*

worth [wɔːθ]. I. *adj.* (a) **to be w. £10,** £10 wert sein; **it's not w. that much**, so viel ist es nicht wert; (b) **it's w. the trouble/w. it**, es lohnt sich; es ist der Mühe wert; **nothing w. mentioning**, nichts Erwähnenswertes. II. *s.* Wert *m;* **five pounds' w. of petrol**, für fünf Pfund Benzin; **to get one's money's w.**, auf seine Kosten kommen. ◆'**worthless**, *adj.* wertlos. ◆**worth'while**, *adj.* der Mühe wert, lohnend.

worthy ['wɔːði], *adj.* würdig; *(esp. of thing)* wert *(of sth., etwas gen).*

would [wud], *aux. v.* **what w. you like?** was möchten Sie? **he w. come if he were invited**, er käme schon, wenn man ihn einladen würde; **she w. often come home tired out**, oft kam sie total erschöpft nach Hause. ◆**would-be** ['wudbi], *adj.* (a) *(unsuccessful)* w. assassin, erfolgloser Attentäter *m;* (b) *(so-called)* sogenannt.

wound [wuːnd]. I. *s.* Wunde *f.* II. *v.tr.* (j-n) verwunden; *Fig:* (j-s Gefühle) verletzen.

woven ['wəuv(ə)n], *adj.* w. goods, Web-

waren *fpl.*

wrangle ['ræŋgl]. I. *v.i.* sich streiten. II. *s.* Zank *m,* 'Streit *m.*

wrap [ræp]. I. *v.tr.* (a) **to w. sth. (up)**, (etwas) einwickeln; (b) **to w.** *(oneself)* **up**, sich warm anziehen; (c) *Fig:* **wrapped up in one's work**, ganz in seine Arbeit vertieft; (d) **he wrapped his arms round her**, er hielt sie umschlungen. II. *s. (scarf)* Schal *m; (rug)* Decke *f.* ◆'**wrapper**, *s.* Hülle *f;* Umschlag *m* (eines Buches). ◆'**wrapping**, *s.* Hülle *f; esp. pl.* Verpackung *f;* **w. paper**, Packpapier *n.*

wreath [riːθ], *s.* Kranz *m; (flowers)* Girlande *f.*

wreck [rek]. I. *s.* 1. (a) *(ship, car)* Wrack *n; (building)* Ruine *f;* **my car's a complete w.**, mein Wagen hat Totalschaden; (b) *Fig: (of pers.)* **to be a nervous w.**, ein Nervenbündel sein. 2. *(occurrence)* Schiffbruch *m.* II. *v.tr.* (ein Schiff) zum Wrack machen; (ein Auto) zu Schrott fahren; (ein Gebäude usw.) (total) zerstören; **to be wrecked**, *(of ship)* auflaufen; *(of pers.)* Schiffbruch erleiden. ◆'**wreckage**, *s.* Wrackteile *npl* (eines Schiffes); Trümmer *pl* (eines Autos, Flugzeugs usw.).

wren [ren], *s. Orn:* Zaunkönig *m.*

wrench [rentʃ]. I. *s.* 1. *(heftiger)* Ruck *m;* **he gave his ankle a w.**, er hat sich *dat* den Knöchel verstaucht; *Fig:* **it will be a w. to leave**, man trennt sich schweren Herzens. 2. *Tchn:* Schraubenschlüssel *m.* II. *v.tr.* (etwas) mit Wucht drehen; *(tear away)* plötzlich wegreißen; **to w. oneself free (from s.o.)**, sich gewaltsam (von j-m) befreien; **to w. one's ankle/shoulder**, sich *dat* den Knöchel/die Schulter verrenken.

wrestle [resl], *v.i.* ringen; *Fig:* **to w. with difficulties etc.**, mit Schwierigkeiten usw. kämpfen. ◆'**wrestler**, *s.* Ringer *m.* ◆'**wrestling**, *s.* Ringen *n.*

wretch [retʃ], *s. (poor)* w., armer Teufel *m.* ◆'**wretched** [-id], *adj.* 1. *(of pers.)* elend. 2. *Pej:* **where's my w. umbrella?** wo ist denn der blöde Schirm?

wriggle [rigl], *v.* 1. *v.i.* sich winden; *(of child etc.)* zappeln; **he tried to w. out of it**, er versuchte, sich davor zu drücken. 2. *v.tr.* **to w. one's way into/through sth.**, sich in etwas *acc* einschleichen/ durch etwas *acc* durchschlängeln. ◆'**wriggly**, *adj.* zappelig.

wring [rɪŋ], *v.tr.irr* **to w. (out)** the washing, die Wäsche (aus)wringen; **to w. the neck of a chicken**, einem Huhn den Hals abdrehen. ◆'**wringing**, *adj.* w. wet, *F:* klatschnaß.

wrinkle ['rɪŋkl]. I. *s.* (a) *(on face)* Runzel *f,* Falte *f;* *(furrow)* Furche *f;* (b) *(in clothes)* Falte *f.* II. *v.* 1. *v.tr.* (in etwas *dat)* Falten machen; *(crumple)* (etwas) zerknittern; **to w. one's forehead**, die Stirn runzeln. 2. *v.i.* Falten werfen; *(of face)* runzlig werden. ◆'**wrinkled**, *adj.*

faltig; (*crumpled*) zerknittert; (*of face*) runzelig.

wrist [rist], *s.* Handgelenk *n*; w. watch, Armbanduhr *f.*

writ [rit], *s.* gerichtlicher Befehl *m*; to serve a w. on s.o., j-n vorladen.

write [rait], *v.tr. & i.irr.* schreiben; he writes for a living, er ist von Beruf Schriftsteller; he wrote to me yesterday, er hat mir gestern geschrieben. ◆'write **down**, *v.tr.* (*etwas*) aufschreiben. ◆'write **'off**, *v.i.* 1. *Fin.:* (eine Summe usw.) abschreiben; (*b*) *F:* to w. off a car, ein Auto zu Schrott fahren. 2. *v.i.* to w. off for sth., sich schriftlich um etwas *acc* bewerben. ◆'write-off, *s.* Totalverlust *m*; the car's a w.-o., der Wagen hat Totalschaden. ◆'writer, *s.* Schriftsteller(in) *m(f)*; (*author*) Verfasser(in) *m(f)*. ◆'write 'up, *v.tr.* (über ein Ereignis usw.) berichten; (ein Thema) behandeln. ◆'write-up, *s.* Bericht *m* (über ein Ereignis). ◆'writing, *s.* 1. (*process*) Schreiben *n.* 2. Schrift *f*; w. paper, Schreibpapier *n*, *esp.* Briefpapier *n.* 3. writings, Schriften *fpl.* ◆'written [ritn], *adj.* geschrieben; (*in writing*) schriftlich.

writhe [raiδ], *v.i.* sich krümmen (**in/with**

pain, vor Schmerzen).

wrong [rɔŋ]. I. *adj.* 1. unrecht; it's w. (of him) to do that, es ist unrecht (von ihm), das zu tun. 2. (*incorrect*) (*a*) (*of fact etc.*) falsch; (*of view*) irrig; (*b*) (*of pers.*) to be w., sich irren; unrecht haben; (*c*) in the w. place, am falschen Ort/Platz; your sweater's w. side out, du hast den Pullover verkehrt herum an; (*d*) what's w. with you last, was hast du? there's something w. with this car, etwas stimmt nicht an diesem Auto. -**ly**, *adv.* (*a*) (*unjustly*) zu Unrecht; (*by mistake*) irrtümlicherweise; (*b*) (*incorrectly*) falsch. II. *s.* (*injustice*) Unrecht *n*; to do s.o. w., j-m unrecht tun/ein Unrecht zufügen; to be in the w., unrecht haben; im Unrecht sein. III. *adv.* 1. falsch. 2. to go w., (i) (*of pers.*) sich verlaufen; (ii) (*of plan*) schiefgehen; (*of machinery*) nicht richtig funktionieren. IV. *v.tr.* (j-m) unrecht tun. ◆'wrong'doer, *s.* Übeltäter(in) *m(f).* ◆'wrongful, *adj.* ungerecht.

wrought [rɔːt], *adj.* w. iron, Schmiedeeisen *n.*

wry [rai], *adj.* a w. smile, ein ironisches Lächeln; w. humour, trockener Humor; to pull a w. face, ein schiefes Gesicht ziehen.

X

X, x [eks], *s.* (der Buchstabe) X, x *n.*
Xmas ['eksməs], *s. F:* Weihnachten *fpl.*
X-ray ['eksrei]. I. *s.* Röntgenstrahl *m*; to

have an X-r., sich röntgen lassen. II. *v.tr.* (j-n, ein Organ) röntgen.
xylophone ['zailəfəun], *s.* Xylophon *n.*

Y

Y, y [wai], *s.* (der Buchstabe) Y, y *n.*
yacht [jɔt], *s.* Jacht *f*; y. club, Jachtklub *m.* ◆'yachting, *s.* Segelsport *m.* ◆'yachtsman, *s.* Sportsegler *m.*
yank[1] [jæŋk]. *F:* I. *v.tr.* (an etwas *dat*) zerren; (j-n) (aus dem Bett usw.) zerren); to y. out a tooth etc., einen Zahn usw. mit einem Ruck herausziehen. II. *s.* Ruck *m.*
Yank[2], **Yankee** ['jæŋki], *s. F:* Ami *m.*
yap [jæp]. I. *v.i.* kläffen. II. *s.* Kläffen *n.* ◆'yapping, *s.* Gekläff *n.*
yard[1] [juːd], *s. Meas:* Yard *n* (=0,914 m).
yard[2], *s.* Hof *m*; *Scotland* Y.: die Londoner Kriminalpolizei, Scotland Yard.
yarn [jɑːn], *s.* 1. Garn *n.* 2. *Fig:* (*story*) Seemannsgarn *n.*
yawn [jɔːn]. I. *v.i.* (*of pers. & Fig: gap*) gähnen. II. *s.* Gähnen *n.*
year [jəːr, jiər], *s.* Jahr *n*; in the y. 1850, im Jahre 1850; y. after y., Jahr für Jahr; (*of wine etc.*) a good y., ein guter Jahrgang. ◆'yearbook, *s.* Jahrbuch *n.* ◆'yearly, *adj.* jährlich.
yearn [jəːn], *v.i.* to y. for sth., sich nach

etwas *dat* sehnen. ◆'yearning, *s.* Sehnen *n* (for, nach + *dat*).
yeast [jiːst], *s.* Hefe *f.*
yell [jel]. I. *v.tr. & i.* (etwas) schreien. II. *s.* (gellender) Schrei *m.*
yellow ['jeləu]. I. *adj.* (*a*) gelb; *Med:* y. fever, Gelbfieber *n*; (*b*) *F:* (*of pers.*) feige. II. *s.* Gelb *n.* ◆'yellowhammer, *s.* Goldammer *f.*
yelp [jelp]. I. *v.i.* (*of dog*) kläffen; (*in pain*) jaulen. II. *s.* Kläffen *n*; Jaulen *n.*
yes [jes]. I. *adv.* ja; y. man, Jasager *m.* II. *s.* Ja *n*; (*esp. to proposal*) Jawort *m.*
yesterday ['jestədi]. I. *adv.* gestern. II. *s.* yesterday's paper, die gestrige Zeitung/ Zeitung von gestern; the day before y., vorgestern.
yet [jet]. I. *adv.* (*a*) noch; has he gone y.? ist er schon gegangen? not y., noch nicht; he'll win y., er wird schon noch gewinnen; (*b*) (*even*) y. further, noch weiter; y. again, schon wieder. II. *conj.* dennoch; (and) y. I like him, (und) trotzdem mag ich ihn.
yew [juː], *s.* y. (tree), Eibe *f*; (*wood*) Ei-

benholz n.

Yiddish ['jidiʃ]. **I.** adj. jiddisch. **II.** s. (language) Jiddisch n.

yield [jiːld]. **I.** s. Ertrag m; (a) (harvest) Ernte f; (b) Fin: (interest) Zinsertrag m. **II.** v. 1. v.tr. Agr: Min: etc: (Getreide, Kohlen, Öl usw.) liefern; Fin: (einen Gewinn) abwerfen; (eine Ernte) einbringen; Fin: to y. interest, Zinsen tragen. 2. v.i. nachgeben (to s.o., j-m). ◆'**yielding. I.** adj. nachgebend; (of pers.) nachgiebig. **II.** s. Nachgeben n; Fig: Nachgiebigkeit f.

yodel ['joudl], v.i. jodeln.

yoga ['jougə], s. Joga n.

yoghurt ['jɔgət, 'jou-], s. Joghurt m.

yoke [jouk], s. Joch n.

yolk [jouk], s. Eidotter n, Eigelb n.

you [juː], pers. pron. 1. (subject) Sie; (to close friend, relative, child, animal etc.) du/pl ihr; **y. poor thing!** Sie/du Ärmste(r)! **y. poor things!** Sie/ihr Ärmsten! **y. Germans,** ihr Deutschen. 2. (object) (a) acc Sie, dich; pl Sie, euch; **I love y.,** ich liebe dich; (b) dat Ihnen, dir; pl Ihnen, euch; **I'll give y. this,** ich gebe Ihnen/dir/euch das; **between y. and me,** unter uns. 3. refl. **have y. any money on y.?** haben Sie Geld bei sich? hast du Geld bei dir? habt ihr Geld bei euch? 4. (indefinite) man; acc einen; dat einem; **it does y. good,** es tut gut. ◆**you'd=you** would. ◆**you'll=you** will.

young [jʌŋ]. **I.** adj. jung; **y. children,** kleine Kinder; **y. people,** Jungendliche/junge Leute. **II.** s. inv. **the y.,** die Jugend. ◆'**youngster,** s. Jugendliche(r) f(m); (boy) Junge m.

your [jɔːr], poss. adj. Ihr(e); (familiar) sing. dein(e); pl. euer, eure. ◆**yours,** poss. pron. Ihrer, Ihre, Ihre; (familiar) deiner, deine, deines; pl deine; (familiar pl.) eurer, eure, eures; pl eure; **this is y.,** das gehört Ihnen/dir/euch; **a friend of y.,** ein Freund von Ihnen/dir/euch. ◆**your'self,** pl. **your'selves,** pers. pron. (a) selbst; **you said so y./yourselves,** Sie haben/du hast/ihr habt es selbst gesagt; (b) refl. sich dat & acc; dich acc; dir dat; euch dat & acc; dich acc; **you have hurt y./yourselves,** Sie haben sich/du hast dich/ihr habt euch verletzt; (c) **you're not quite y.,** Sie sind/du bist nicht ganz auf der Höhe.

youth, pl. -s [juːθ, pl. juːðz], s. 1. (period) Jugend f. 2. (pers.) Jugendliche(r) f(m). 3. coll. junge Leute, die Jugend; **y. hostel,** Jugendherberge f. ◆'**youthful,** adj. (of pers.) jugendlich. ◆'**youthfulness,** s. Jugendlichkeit f.

Yugoslavia [juːgəu'slɑːviə]. Pr. n. Jugoslawien n. ◆'**Yugoslav. I.** adj. jugoslawisch. **II.** s. Jugoslawe m, Jugoslawin f.

Z

Z, z [zed, N.Am: ziː], s. (der Buchstabe) Z, z n.

Zambia ['zæmbiə]. Pr.n. Sambia n. ◆'**Zambian. I.** s. Sambier m. **II.** adj. sambisch.

zany ['zeini], adj. F: burlesk.

zeal [ziːl], s. Eifer m. ◆**zealous** ['zeləs], adj. eifrig.

zebra ['zebrə, 'ziːbrə], s. Zebra n; **z. crossing,** Zebrastreifen m.

zenith ['zeniθ], s. Zenit m; Fig: Höhepunkt m.

zero, pl. -os ['ziərəu, -əuz], s. (number) Null f; (point on scale etc.) Nullpunkt m; **z. hour,** die Stunde Null.

zest [zest], s. (enthusiasm) Begeisterung f; (verve) Schwung m; **to eat with z.,** mit Genuß essen.

zigzag ['zigzæg], s. Zickzack m; **in zigzags,** im Zickzack.

zinc [ziŋk], s. Zink n.

Zionism ['zaiənizm], s. Zionismus m.

zip [zip]. **I.** s. 1. Surren n (einer Kugel usw.). 2. **z. (fastener),** Reißverschluß m. 3. N.Am: **z. code,** Postleitzahl f. **II.** v. 1. v.i. (of bullet etc.) surren. 2. v.tr. F: **can you z. me up?** kannst du mir den Reißverschluß zumachen?

zither ['ziðər], s. Zither f.

zodiac ['zəudiæk], s. Tierkreis m.

zombie ['zəmbi], s. F: apathischer Typ m; (moron) Schwachkopf m.

zone [zəun], s. Zone f.

zoo [zuː], s. Zoo m. ◆**zoology** [zuː'ɔlədʒi], s. Zoologie f. ◆**zoo'logical** [zuː(ə)-], adj. zoologisch. ◆**zoologist** [zuː'ɔ-], s. Zoologe m, Zoologin f.

zoom [zuːm]. **I.** s. Phot: z. (lens), Zoom(objektiv) n. **II.** v.i. F: **to z. along,** dahinbrausen.

Zurich ['zjuərik]. Pr. n. Zürich n.

Deutsche Abkürzungen
German Abbreviations

A *Ampere* ampere
AA *Auswärtiges Amt approx.* Foreign Office
a.a.O. *am angeführten Ort* loc.cit.
Abb. *Abbildung* illustration, figure, *abbr.* fig.
Abf. *Abfahrt* departure
Abg. *Abgeordnete(r)* deputy; *West G:* member of the Bundestag/Landtag
Abk. *Abkürzung* abbreviation, *abbr.* abbr.
Abs. 1. *Absatz* paragraph, *abbr.* par. 2. *Absender* sender
Absch. *Abschnitt* section
Abt. *Abteilung* department, *abbr.* dept.
abzgl. *abzüglich* less
a.D. 1. *außer Dienst* retired. 2. *an der Donau* on the Danube
ADAC *Allgemeiner Deutscher Automobilclub* (W.German motoring association)
Adr. *Adresse* address
AG *Aktiengesellschaft* joint-stock company
akad. *akademisch* academic, university (trained)
allg. *allgemein* general
a.M. *am Main* on the Main
amtl. *amtlich* official
Angest. *Angestellte(r)* employee
Anh. *Anhang* appendix
Ank. *Ankunft* arrival
Anm. *Anmerkung* note
Antw. *Antwort* answer
a.O. *an der Oder* on the Oder
AOK *Allgemeine Ortskrankenkasse* local health insurance
a.o.Prof. *außerordentlicher Professor approx.* associate professor
a.Rh. *am Rhein* on the Rhine
ARD *Arbeitsgemeinschaft der öffentlichen Rundfunkanstalten der BRD* (umbrella organization of West German radio and TV)
ärztl. *ärztlich* medical
ASTA *Allgemeiner Studentenausschuß* (student's union)
A.T. *Altes Testament* Old Testament
AT-Motor *Austauschmotor* exchange reconditioned engine
atü *Atmosphärenüberdruck* pressure above atmospheric pressure
AUA *Austrian Airlines*
Aufl. *Auflage* edition
ausschl. *ausschließlich* exclusive(ly)
AvD *Automobilclub von Deutschland* (W.German motoring association)
a.W. *ab Werk* ex works
Az *Aktenzeichen* file number, reference

B *Bundesstraße* Federal Highway, main road
BASF *Badische Anilin- und Sodafabrik* (leading W.German chemical firm)
Bauj. *Baujahr* year of manufacture
Bd., Bde., *Band, Bände* volume, volumes
BDI *Bundesverband der Deutschen Industrie* Confederation of (West) German Industry (employers' organization)
Bearb. *Bearbeitung;* in B., being dealt with
Bed. *Bedarf* demand
befr. *Sch: befriedigend* satisfactory, *approx.* C
begl. *beglaubigt* certified
beisp. *beispielsweise* for example
bes. *besonders* especially
Betr. *Betreff* reference, *abbr.* re
betr. *betreffend* concerning, *abbr.* re
Bez. *Bezirk* district
BGB *Bürgerliches Gesetzbuch* (W.German Civil Code)
BH *Cl: F: Büstenhalter* bra
Bhf. *Bahnhof* station
BM *Bundesministerium* Federal Ministry
BND *Bundesnachrichtendienst* W.German Intelligence Service
BP *Bundespost* Federal Post Office
BRD *Bundesrepublik Deutschland* Federal Republic of Germany
BRT *Bruttoregistertonnen* gross tonnage
b.w. *bitte wenden* please turn over, *abbr.* P.T.O.
bzgl. *bezüglich* with reference to
bzw. *beziehungsweise* and . . . respectively; or
C *Celsius* centigrade
cal *(Gramm-)Kalorie* calorie
cand. *Kandidat* candidate
cbm *Kubikmeter* cubic metre
ccm *Kubikzentimeter* cubic centimetre, *abbr.* c.c.
CDU *Pol: Christlich-Demokratische Union* Christian Democratic Union
Cie. *Com: Kompanie* company
cm *Zentimeter* centimetre, *abbr.* cm
Co. *Com: Kompanie* company
CSU *Pol: Christlich-Soziale Union* Christian Social Union
c.t. *cum tempore* starting a quarter of an hour later
CVJM *Christlicher Verein Junger Männer* Young Men's Christian Association, *abbr.* Y.M.C.A.
d. 1. *Mth: Durchmesser* diameter. 2. *der/die/das* the
DB *Deutsche Bundesbahn* Federal German Railways
DBP *Deutsche Bundespost* Federal Post Office

DDR *Deutsche Demokratische Republik* German Democratic Republic, *abbr.* GDR

DER *Deutsches Reisebüro* (West) German Travel Agency

DGB *Deutscher Gewerkschaftsbund* Federation of (West) German Trade Unions

d.h. *das heißt* that is, *abbr.* i.e.

Di *Dienstag* Tuesday, *abbr.* Tues.

DIN *Deutsche Industrienorm* German Industrial Standard

Dipl. *(a) Diplom* diploma; *(b) Diplom-* holding a diploma, (academically) qualified; **Dipl.Kfm.** *Diplomkaufmann* person with a commercial diploma; **Dipl.Ing.** *Diplomingenieur* fully trained engineer

Dir. 1. *Direktor* director. 2. *Mus: Dirigent* conductor

Diss. *Dissertation* dissertation

DJH *Deutsches Jugendherbergswerk* German Youth Hostel Association

DM *Deutsche Mark* (West) German mark ·
dm *Dezimeter* decimetre (10 cm)

d.M. *dieses Monats* of this month, *Com:* instant

DNA *Deutscher Normenausschuß* German Standards Committee

do. *ditto* ditto

Do *Donnerstag* Thursday, *abbr.* Thurs.

Doz. *Dozent* university lecturer

dpa *Deutsche Presseagentur* German Press Agency

d.Red. *die Redaktion* the editor(s)

Dr. *Doktor* Doctor; **Dr.h.c.** *Doctor honoris causa* honorary doctorate; **Dr.jur.** *Doctor juris doctor* of law, *abbr.* LLD; **Dr.med.** *Doctor medicinae* Doctor of Medicine, *abbr.* M.D.; **Dr.phil.** *Doktor der Philosophie* Doctor of Philosophy, *abbr.* Ph.D.

DRK *Deutsches Rotes Kreuz* (West) German Red Cross

DSG *Deutsche Schlafwagen- und Speisewagengesellschaft* (West) German Sleeping and Dining Car Company

ds.J. *dieses Jahres* of this year

dz. *derzeit* at present

E *Eilzug* semi-fast train

Ed. *Edition* edition

EG *Europäische Gemeinschaft* European Community

· **e.h.** *ehrenhalber;* **Dr. e.h.** honorary doctor

ehem. *ehemals* formerly

eigtl. *eigentlich* in fact, strictly speaking

einschl. *einschließlich* inclusive of

EKG *Elektrokardiogramm* electrocardiogram

Empf. 1. *Empfänger* addressee. 2. *adj. empfohlen* recommended

entspr. *entsprechend* corresponding(ly)

entw. *entweder* either

erstkl. *erstklassig* first-rate

Eßl. *Eßlöffel* tablespoon

etw. 1. *etwaig* possible. 2. *etwas* something

ev. *evangelisch* protestant

e.V. *eingetragener Verein* registered society

EVP *Einzelhandelsverkaufspreis/ Endverbraucherpreis* retail price

evtl. *eventuell* perhaps, possibly

E-Werk *Elektrizitätswerk* power station

EWG *Europäische Wirtschaftsgemeinschaft* European Economic Community

exkl. *exklusive* exclusive of

f. 1. *für* for. 2. *(und) folgende (Seite)* and following page

Fa. *Firma* firm; *Fa. X* Messrs. X

Fak. *Fakultät* faculty

Fam. *Familie* family

F.A.Z. *Frankfurter Allgemeine Zeitung* (leading West German daily newspaper)

FC *Fußballclub* Football Club

FDGB *Freier Deutscher Gewerkschaftsbund* (East German Trade Union Federation)

FDJ *Freie Deutsche Jugend* Free German Youth (East German youth organization)

FDP *Pol: Freie Demokratische Partei* Free Democratic Party (West German centre party)

Fernschr. *Fernschreiber* telex

F.f. *Fortsetzung folgt* to be continued

ff *sehr fein* extra fine (quality)

FHZ *Freihandelszone* Free Trade Area

Fil. *Com: Filiale* branch

FKK *Freikörperkultur* nudism; **FKK-Kolonie** nudist colony

fl.W. *fließendes Wasser* running water

Forts. *Fortsetzung* continuation

Fr. 1. *Frau* Mrs. 2. *Freitag* Friday, *abbr.* Fri.

fr. *franko* post-paid

Frfr. *Freifrau* Baroness

Frhr. *Freiherr* Baron

Frl. *Fräulein* Miss

frz. *französisch* French

FU *Freie Universität* Free University (of Berlin)

g 1. *Meas: Gramm* gram. 2. *Aus: Groschen* groschen (smallest Austrian coin)

geb. *(a) geboren* born; *(b) geborene* née

Gebr. *Com: Gebrüder* Brothers

gefl. *Com: gefällig* kind

gegr. *gegründet* founded

gem. *gemäß* according to

Gem. *Gemeinde* municipality; *(kleine Ortschaft)* parish

Gen. *Genossenschaft* co-operative society

Geogr. *Geographie* geography

gepr. *geprüft* tested

Ges. *Gesellschaft* company

gesch. *geschieden* divorced

ges.gesch. *gesetzlich geschützt* patented (invention); registered (trade mark)

geschl. *geschlossen* closed; private (performance etc.)

Geschw. 1. *Geschwister* brother(s) and sister(s). 2. *Geschwindigkeit* speed

gest. *gestorben* deceased; *(mit Datum)* died

gez. *gezeichnet* signed

GG *Grundgesetz* Basic (constitutional) Law

GmbH *Gesellschaft mit beschränkter Haftung* limited (liability) company; *abbr. (nach dem Firmennamen)* Co.Ltd.

Gymn. *Gymnasium approx.* grammar/*N.Am:* high school

gzj. *ganzjährig* all year (round)

h *Stunde* hour

H *(Schild) Haltestelle* (bus/tram) stop

ha *Meas:* Hektar hectare

habil. *habilitiert* qualified as a university teacher

Hbf. *Hauptbahnhof* main railway station

h.c. *honoris causa* as an honour, honorary

herg. *hergestellt* manufactured

HF *Hochfrequenz* high frequency

HG *Handelsgesellschaft* trading company

HGB *Jur:* Handelsgesetzbuch commercial code

hj. *halbjährlich* half-yearly

hl *Meas:* Hektoliter 100 litres

Hl., hl. *heilige; der* hl. **Martin** St.Martin

HO *East G: Handelsorganisation (a)* State Trading Organization; *(b) F:* state-owned shop

Hochw. *Ecc: Hochwürden* Reverend

höfl. *höflichst* kindly

Hptst. *Hauptstadt* capital

Hr. *Herr* Mr

Hrsg. *Herausgeber* editor; hrsg. v. *herausgegeben von* edited by

HTL *Höhere Technische Lehranstalt approx.* polytechnic

Hz *Ph:Rad:* Hertz hertz

i. *in/im* in/in the

i.A. . . . *im Auftrag* on behalf of . . ., *abbr.* p.p.

i.allg. *im allgemeinen* in general

i.D. *im Durchschnitt* on average

IG *Industriegewerkschaft* industrial union

i.J. *im Jahre* in (the year)

ill. *illustriert* illustrated

inbegr. *inbegriffen* included

Ing. *Ingenieur* engineer

Inh. *Inhaber* owner

inkl. *inklusive* including, inclusive of

Insp. *Inspektor* inspector

Inst. 1. *Instanz* instance. 2. *Institut* institute

int. *international* international

inzw. *inzwischen* in the meantime

IR- *Infrarot-* infra red

i.R. *im Ruhestand* retired

i.V. 1. *in Vertretung* per pro, *abbr.* p.p. 2. *in Vorbereitung* in preparation

i.W. *in Worten* in words

Jb. *Jahrbuch* yearbook

Jg. *Jahrgang* year/age group

JH *Jugendherberge* youth hostel

Jh *Jahrhundert* century

jun. *junior* junior

jur. *juristisch* legal

kath. *katholisch* catholic

Kfm. *Kaufmann* business man

Kfz *Kraftfahrzeug* motor vehicle

KG *Kommanditgesellschaft* limited partnership

kg *Kilogramm* kilogram

kgl. *königlich* royal

khz *Kilohertz* kilocycles per second, kilohertz

k.J. *künftigen Jahres* of next year

Kl. *Klasse* class

k.M. *künftigen Monats* of next month

km *Kilometer* kilometre(s), *abbr.* km; km/h *Kilometer pro Stunde* kilometres per hour, *abbr.* k.p.h.

kn *Nau:* Knoten knot(s)

kompl. *komplett* complete

Konf. *Konfession* denomination

Kpt *Kapitän* captain

Kr. *Adm: Kreis* administrative district

Kt. *Kanton* Canton

k.u.k. *Aus:Hist: kaiserlich und königlich* Imperial and Royal, i.e. Austro-Hungarian

kv. *kriegsverwendungsfähig* fit for war service

KW *Kurzwelle* short wave

kW *Kilowatt* kilowatt(s), *abbr.* kW

kWh *Kilowattstunde(n)* kilowatt hour(s), *abbr.* kWh

KZ *Hist: Konzentrationslager* concentration camp

Kzf. *Kurzform* abbreviated form

l 1. *Meas:* Liter litre. 2. *links* on the left

landw. *landwirtschaftlich* agricultural

Ldkr. *Landkreis* rural district

led. *ledig* unmarried, single

lfd. *laufend* current

LG *Landgericht* District Court

Lit. *Literatur* literature

Lkw., LKW *Lastkraftwagen* lorry

LPG *East G: landwirtschaftliche Produktionsgenossenschaft* agricultural co-operative

lt. *laut* according to

luth. *Ecc: lutherisch* Lutheran

LW *Rad: Langwelle* long wave

M *East G: Mark* mark(s)

m *Meas: Meter* metre; m² square metre; m³ cubic metre

MA. *Mittelalter* middle ages

ma. *mittelalterlich* medieval

Mag. *Magister* Master (degree)

Math. *Mathematik* mathematics

m.a.W. *mit anderen Worten* in other words

max. *maximal* maximum

mb *Millibar* millibar

mdal. *mundartlich* dialect

MdB *Mitglied des Bundestages* Member of the Bundestag (West German parliament)

mdl. *mündlich* verbal(ly)

m.E. *meines Erachtens* in my opinion

mech. *mechanisch* mechanical

med. *medizinisch* medical

mehrf. *mehrfach* multiple; *adv.* several times

MEZ *Mitteleuropäische Zeit* Central European Time

mfG *mit freundlichen Grüßen* kind regards

mg *Milligramm* milligram(s)

MG *Maschinengewehr* machine gun

MHz *Megahertz* megahertz

Mi *Mittwoch* Wednesday, *abbr.* Wed.

Mill. *Million(en)* million(s)

Min. *Minute(n)* minute(s)

min. *minimal* minimum

ml *Milliliter* millilitre

mm *Millimeter* millimetre

Mo *Montag* Monday, *abbr.* Mon.

möbl. *möbliert* furnished

Mrd. *Milliarde* thousand million, *N.Am:* billion

mtl. *monatlich* monthly

M-und-S, M + S *Aut: Matsch-und-Schnee (Reifen)* snow (tyres)

MWSt. *Mehrwertsteuer* value-added tax, *abbr.* VAT

Mz. *Mehrzahl* plural

N *Nord* north

Nachf. *Com: Nachfolger* successor

nachm. *nachmittags* in the afternoon, *abbr.* p.m.

nat. *national* national

n.Br. *nördlicher Breite* of northern latitude

n.Chr. *nach Christus* after Christ, *abbr.* A.D.

NDR *Norddeutscher Rundfunk* North German Radio

NF 1. *Niederfrequenz* low frequency. 2. *East G:Pol: Nationale Front* National Front

n.J. *nächsten Jahres* of next year

n.M. *nächsten Monats* of next month

N.N. *Name unbekannt* name unknown

NO *Nordost* northeast

NR *Aus: Mitglied des Nationalrats* Member of the National Assembly

Nr. *Nummer* number

NS 1. *Nachschrift* postscript, *abbr.* PS. 2. *Hist: nationalsozialistisch* National Socialist, Nazi

N.T. *Neues Testament* New Testament

NW *Nordwest* northwest

O *Ost* east

o. 1. *oder* or. 2. *ohne* without. 3. *oben* above

ö. *öffentlich* public

o.a. *oben angeführt* above-mentioned

o.ä. *oder ähnlich* or similar

o.A. *ohne Adresse* of no fixed abode

ÖAMTC *Österreichischer Auto-, Motorrad- und Touring-Club* Austrian Automobile, Motorcycle and Touring Club

OB 1. *Oberbürgermeister* first mayor. 2. *Mil: Oberbefehlshaber* commander-in-chief, *abbr.* C.-in-c.

o.B. *Med: ohne Befund* (test) result negative

Obb. *Oberbayern* Upper Bavaria

ÖBB *Österreichische Bundesbahnen* Austrian Federal Railways

od. *oder* or

OEZ *Osteuropäische Zeit* East European time

öff(entl). *öffentlich* public

OHG *Offene Handelsgesellschaft* general partnership

o.J. *ohne Jahr* no date

ö.L. *östlicher Länge* of eastern longitude

OÖ. *Oberösterreich* Upper Austria

OP 1. *Originalpackung* original pack. 2. *Med: Operationssaal* operating theatre

o.Pr. *ordentlicher Professor* full professor

ORF *Österreichischer Rundfunk* Austrian Radio

örtl. *örtlich* local(ly)

o.V. *ohne Verfasser* author unknown, *abbr.* anon.

ÖVP *Österreichische Volkspartei* Austrian Peoples' Party

P. *Ecc:* 1. *Pastor* pastor. 2. *Pater* Father

p.A(dr). *per Adresse* care of, *abbr.* c/o

Part. *Parterre* ground floor

pat. *patentiert* patented

Pf *Pfennig* pfennig(s)

Pfd. *Pfund* pound (weight)

PH *Pädagogische Hochschule* teachers' training college

pharm. *pharmazeutisch* pharmaceutical

phot. *photographisch* photographic

Pkt. *Punkt* point

PKW, Pkw. *Personenkraftwagen* passenger car

Pl. *Platz* square

pl., Pl. *Plural* plural

pol. 1. *politisch* political. 2. *polizeilich* police

pop. *populär* popular

Postf. *Postfach* post-office box

P.P *praemissis praemittendis* to whom it may concern

p.p., p.pa., ppa. *per procura* per pro, *abbr.* p.p.

Präp. *Präposition* preposition

priv. *privat* private

Prof. *Professor* professor

prot. *protestantisch* Protestant

Prov. *Provinz* province

PS 1. *Pferdestärke(n)* horse-power. 2. *postscriptum, Nachschrift* postscript

qkm *Quadratkilometer* square kilometre, *abbr.* sq.km.

qm *Quadratmeter* square metre, *abbr.* sq.m.

Quitt. *Quittung* receipt

r. 1. *rechts* on the right. 2. *Mth: Radius* radius

rd. *rund* roughly

Red. *Redakteur* editor; *Redaktion* editorial staff

Reg. 1. *Regierung* government. 2. *Register* register

Reg.Bez. *Regierungsbezirk* administrative district

Rel. *Religion* religion

Rep. *Republik* republic

resp. *respektive* or . . . as the case may be

Rhld. *Rheinland* Rhineland

RIAS *Rundfunk im amerikanischen Sektor* Radio in the American Sector (of Berlin)

rk., r.-k. *römisch-katholisch* Roman Catholic

rm *Raummeter* cubic metre

röm. *römisch* Roman
Rzpt. *Med: Rezept* prescription
S *Süd* south
S. 1. *Seite* page. **2.** *Aus: Schilling* schilling
s. *siehe* see, *abbr.* v.; **s.a.** *siehe auch* see also
Sa *Samstag* Saturday, *abbr.* Sat.
S-Bahn *Schnellbahn* urban railway
SB *Selbstbedienung* self-service
SBB *Schweizerische Bundesbahn* Swiss Federal Railways
s.Br. *südlicher Breite* of southern latitude
s.d. *siehe dies* see this
SDR *Süddeutscher Rundfunk* South German Radio
SED *East G:Pol: Sozialistische Einheitspartei Deutschlands* Socialist Unity Party (of Germany)
Sek., sek. *Sekunde* second
Sekr. *Sekretär(in)* secretary
Sem. (a) *Semester* term; (b) *Seminar* seminar
Sen. *Senator* senator•
sen. *senior* senior
SFB *Sender Freies Berlin* Free Berlin Radio
sfr., **sFr.** *Schweizer Franken* Swiss francs
sm *Seemeile* nautical mile
SO *Südost* south-east, *abbr.* SE
s.o. *siehe oben* see above
So *Sonntag* Sunday, *abbr.* Sun.
sog. *sogenannt* so-called
SOS *internationales Notsignal* SOS
soz. *sozial(istisch)* social, socialist
SPD *Sozialdemokratische Partei Deutschlands* Social Democratic Party of Germany
spez. (a) *speziell* special(ly); (b) *spezifisch* specific(ally)
SPÖ *Sozialistische Partei Österreichs* Socialist Party of Austria
SR *Saarländischer Rundfunk* Saar Radio
SSD *East G: Staatssicherheitsdienst* State Security Service
St. 1. *Stück* piece. **2.** *Sankt* Saint
staatl.gepr. *staatlich geprüft* who has passed a state examination
städt. *städtisch* urban, municipal
Std. *Stunde* hour
stdl. *stündlich* every hour
stellv. *stellvertretend* assistant
StGB *Strafgesetzbuch* Penal Code
StKl *Steuerklasse* tax class
StPO *Strafprozeßordnung* Code for Criminal Proceedings
Str. *Straße* street, road
stud. *studiosus, Student* student
StVO *Straßenverkehrsordnung* traffic regulations
s.t. *sine tempore* sharp, on time
s.u. *siehe unten* see below
SV *Sportverein* sports club
svw. *soviel wie* as good as; much the same as
SW *Südwest* south-west, *abbr.* SW.
SWF *Südwestfunk* South-West German Radio

s.Z. *seinerzeit* at that time
SZ *Sommerzeit* summer time
t *Tonne* ton
TA 1. *Rec: Tonabnehmer* pick-up. **2.** *Aus: Tierarzt* veterinary surgeon
Tab. *Tabelle* table, chart
tägl. *täglich* daily, per day
Tb, Tbc *Tuberkulose* tuberculosis
TEE *Trans-Europ-Express* Trans-European Express
Teilh. *Teilhaber* partner
Teilz. *Teilzahlung* part-payment
Tel. (a) *Telefon* telephone; (b) *Telegramm* telegram
Temp. *Temperatur* temperature
TF-Boot *Tragflächenboot* hydrofoil
TH *Technische Hochschule* technical university
Tsd. *Tausend* thousand
TSV *Turn- und Sportverein* gymnastics and sports club
TU *Technische Universität* Technical University
TÜV *Technischer Überwachungsverein* Association for Technical Inspection; (*Prüfung*) *approx. Brit:* MOT test
TV 1. *Turnverein* gymnastics club. **2.** *Tarifvertrag* wage agreement. **3.** *Television* television
u. *und* and
u.a. *und andere/anderes* and others/other things; *unter anderem/anderen* among other things
u.ä. *und ähnliche(s)* and the like
u.A.w.g. *um Antwort wird gebeten* an answer is requested, *abbr.* R.S.V.P.
Übers. *Übersetzer* translator
übl. *üblich* usual
u.dsgl.(m.)/u.dgl.(m). *und desgleichen/dergleichen (mehr)* and things like that
u.d.M./ü.d.M. *unter/über dem Meeresspiegel* below/above sea level
UdSSR *Union der Sozialistischen Sowjetrepubliken* Union of Soviet Socialist Republics
u.E. *unseres Erachtens* in our opinion
UHF *Rad: Ultra-Hochfrequenz* ultra high frequency
UKW *Rad: Ultrakurzwelle* very high frequency, *abbr.* VHF
ult. *ultimo* on the last day of (the month)
U/min. *Umdrehungen in der Minute* revolutions per minute, *abbr.* r.p.m.
Univ. *Universität* university
unverk. *unverkäuflich* not for sale
urspr. *ursprünglich* original(ly)
US(A) *Vereinigte Staaten (von Amerika)* United States (of America)
usf. *und so fort* and so forth
usw. *und so weiter* and so on, *abbr.* etc.
u.U. *unter Umständen* circumstances permitting
UV- *ultraviolett* ultra-violet
u.v.a. *und viele(s) andere* and many others
u.W. *unseres Wissens* as far as we know

v. *von, vom* of; from; by

V 1. *Volt* volt. **2.** *Volumen* volume

V. *Vers* line, verse

VAR *Vereinigte Arabische Republik* United Arab Republic

var. *variabel* variable

v.Chr. *vor Christus* before Christ, *abbr.* B.C.

VDS *Verband deutscher Studentenschaften* Association of German Students

VEB *East G: Volkseigener Betrieb* nationalized/people's concern

verb. *verbessert* corrected

Verf., Vf. *Verfasser* author

verh. *verheiratet* married

Verl. *(a) Verlag* publishing firm; *(b) Verleger* publisher

Verm. *Vermerk* note

versch. 1. *verschieden* different. **2.** *verschollen* missing

verst. *verstorben* deceased

vgl. *vergleiche* compare, *abbr.* cf.

v.H., vH *vom Hundert* per cent

VHS *Volkshochschule approx.* College of Further Education

v.J. *vorigen Jahres* of last year

v.l.n.r. *von links nach rechts* from left to right

v.M. *vorigen Monats* of last month

v.o. *von oben* from above

Vollm. *Vollmacht* authority

vollst. *vollständig* complete

vorl. *vorläufig* provisional

vorm. 1. *vormittags* in the morning, *abbr.* a.m. **2.** *vormals* formerly

Vors. *Vorsitzender* chairman

VR *Volksrepublik* People's Republic

v.r.n.l. *von rechts nach links* from right to left

v.T., vT *vom Tausend* per thousand

W 1. *West* west. **2.** *El: Watt* watt(s)

Wb. *Wörterbuch* dictionary

WDR *Westdeutscher Rundfunk* West German Radio

WEU *Westeuropäische Union* Western European Union

WEZ *westeuropäische Zeit* West European time, Greenwich mean time

Whg. *Wohnung* flat

Wkst. *(a) Werkstatt* workshop; *(b) Werkstück* workpiece

w.L. *westlicher Länge* of western longitude

w.o. *wie oben* as above

WSP *Wasserschutzpolizei* river police

Wwe. *Witwe* widow

Wwr. *Witwer* widower

Wz. *Warenzeichen* trademark

Z. 1. *Zahl* number. **2.** *Zeile* line

z. *zu, zum* at; to

z.A. *zur Ansicht* for inspection; (sent) on approval

z.B. *zum Beispiel* for instance, *abbr.* e.g.

z.d.A. *zu den Akten* to be filed

ZDF *Zweites Deutsches Fernsehen* Second Channel of West German Television

zgl. *zugleich* at the same time

z.H(d). *Com: zu Händen* for the attention of

Zi *Zimmer* room

Ziff. *Ziffer* figure

ZK *Pol: Zentralkomitee* Central Committee

z.K. *zur Kenntnisnahme* for information

ZPO *Jur: Zivilprozeßordnung* Code for Civil Actions

z.S. *zur See* naval

z.T. *zum Teil* partly

Ztg. *Zeitung* newspaper

Ztr. *Zentner* approx. hundredweight

Zub. *Zubehör* accessories

zuf. *zufolge* as a result of

zus. *zusammen* together

z.V. *zum Verkauf* for sale

zw. *zwischen* between, among

zzgl. *zuzüglich* plus

z.Z(t). *zur Zeit* at the time; *(jetzt)* at present

English Abbreviations
Englische Abkürzungen

A.A. *Automobile Association* (britischer Automobilclub)

A.A.A. 1. *N.Am: American Automobile Association* (führender Automobilclub) **2.** *Brit: Amateur Athletics Association* Leichtathletikverband *m*

ABC 1. *American Broadcasting Company* (amerikanische Rundfunkgesellschaft). **2.** *Australian Broadcasting Corporation* Australischer

Rundfunk

AC *El: alternating current* Wechselstrom *m*

a/c *account* Konto *n*

A.D. *anno Domini* nach Christi Geburt, *abbr.* n.Chr.

AFN *American Forces Network* Rundfunk der amerikanischen Streitkräfte

A.G.M. *Annual General Meeting* Jahresvollversammlung f

a.m. *ante meridiem* vormittags

anon *anonymous* Autor unbekannt

appro. *Com: on appro.* = *on approval* zur Ansicht/Probe

approx. *approximately* ungefähr

arr. *Rail: etc: arrive(s)* . . . an, Ankunft . . .

ASAP *as soon as possible* sobald wie möglich

ass(oc). *association* Verband m

asst. *assistant* Mitarbeiter m; *attrib.* stellvertretend

Aug. *August* August m

Av., Ave. *Avenue* Chaussee f

b. *born* geboren, *abbr.* geb.

B.A. 1. *Bachelor of Arts* (Grad). 2. *Av: British Airways* Britische Fluggesellschaft

b. & b. *bed & breakfast* Zimmer mit Frühstück

Bart *Baronet* Baron m

B.A.O.R. *British Army of the Rhine* Britische Rheinarmee

BBC *British Broadcasting Corporation* Britische Rundfunkgesellschaft

BC *before Christ* vor Christi Geburt, *abbr.* v.Chr.

B.C.G. *Bilié de Calmette et Guérin* (TBC-Impfstoff)

Beds. *Bedfordshire* (Grafschaft)

Berks. *Berkshire* (Grafschaft)

B.F.N. *Rad: British Forces Network* Rundfunk der Britischen Streitkräfte

b.h.p. *Mec.E: brake horse power* Brems-PS

bldg(s). *building(s)* Gebäude n

B.M.A. *British Medical Association* Britischer Ärzteverband

B.O. *F: body odour* Körpergeruch m

Br. *Ecc: Brother* Frater m

BR *British Rail* Britische Eisenbahngesellschaft

Bros. *Com: Brothers* Gebrüder

BS *British Standard approx.* = DIN

B.Sc. *Bachelor of Science* (Grad)

B.S.I. *British Standards Institution* Britisches Normungsinstitut

B.S.T. *British Summer Time* Britische Sommerzeit

bt. fwd. *Com: brought forward* Übertrag

B.T.U. *British Thermal Unit* Britische Wärmeeinheit

Bucks. *Buckinghamshire* (Grafschaft)

C *Ph: centigrade* Celsius

c. 1. *N.Am: etc: cent* Cent m. 2. *circa* zirka

Cantab. *Cantabrigiensis* = *of Cambridge* von Cambridge

Capt. *captain Mil:* Hauptmann m; *Nau:* Kapitän m

CB *Rad: Citizens' Band* Privatfunk (CB)

CBC *Canadian Broadcasting Company* Kanadischer Rundfunk

C.B.E. *Commander of the (Order of the) British Empire* Komtur des Ordens des British Empire

C.B.I. *Confederation of British Industries* Briti-

scher Industrieverband

C.B.S. *Columbia Broadcasting System* (amerikanische Rundfunkgesellschaft)

C.C. 1. *County Council* Verwaltung der Grafschaft. 2. *Cricket Club*

c.c. *cubic centimetre(s)* Kubikzentimeter m

C.D. 1. *Civil Defence* ziviler Bevölkerungsschutz. 2. *corps diplomatique* diplomatisches Korps

Cdr. *Nau: Commander* Fregattenkapitän m

cent. *hundred* hundert

cert. *certificate* Bescheinigung f; *Sch:* Zeugnis n, Zertifikat n

CET *Central European Time* Mitteleuropäische Zeit, *abbr.* MEZ

cf. *confer* vergleiche, *abbr.* vgl.

C.H. *Companion of Honour* Mitglied des Ehrenordens

chw. *constant hot water* fließendes Warmwasser zu jeder Tages- und Nachtzeit

C.I. *Channel Islands* Kanalinseln fpl

C.I.A. *Central Intelligence Agency* (amerikanischer Geheimdienst)

C.I.D. *Brit: Criminal Investigation Department* Kriminalpolizei f

C-in-C. *Commander-in-Chief* Oberbefehlshaber m

cl. *Meas: centilitre* Zentiliter m

cm *Meas: centimetre* Zentimeter m

CND *Campaign for Nuclear Disarmament* Bewegung für atomare Abrüstung

C.O. *Commanding Officer* Kommandeur m

c/o *(on letter) care of* bei

Co. *Company* Gesellschaft

COD *cash on delivery* per Nachnahme

C. of E. *Church of England* anglikanische Kirche

Col. *Mil: Colonel* Oberst m

Cons. *Pol: Conservative* konservativ

cp. *compare* vergleiche, *abbr.* vgl.

cr. *Fin: credit* Haben

Cres. *Crescent* (bogenförmig geschwungene Straße)

cu. *cubic* kubik

c.v. *curriculum vitae* Lebenslauf m

cwt. *Meas: hundredweight* Zentner m

d. 1. *deceased* gestorben. 2. *A: (coin) penny/pl pence* Penny

D.A. *N.Am: district attorney* Bezirksstaatsanwalt m

D.C. 1. *El: direct current* Gleichstrom m. 2. *N.Am: Geog:* District of Columbia

deb. *Fin: debit* Soll n

Dec. *December* Dezember m

dep. *departure* Abfahrt f

Dept. *Department* Abteilung f

Dip.Ed. *Diploma of Education* Lehrerdiplom n

DIY *do-it-yourself* Heimwerken n; *DIY shop* Heimwerkerladen m

D.J. *dinner jacket* Smoking m

do. *ditto* dito, desgleichen

dol. *dollar* Dollar *m*

doz. *dozen* Dutzend *n*

D.Phil. *doctor of Philosophy* Doktor der Philosophie

Dr. *doctor* Doktor *m*

D.S.C. *Distinguished Service Cross* (militärisches Verdienstkreuz)

D.S.O. *Distinguished Service Order* (militärischer Verdienstorden)

D.T. *delirium tremens* Delirium tremens *n*

E. *East* Ost

E. & O.E. *Com: errors and omissions excepted* Irrtümer und Auslassungen vorbehalten

E.C. *European Community* Europäische Gemeinschaft, *abbr.* EG

E.C.G. *electrocardiogram* Elektrokardiogramm *n*, *abbr.* EKG

Ed. *Editor* Redakteur *m*

ed(it). *edited (by)* herausgegeben (von)

E.E.C. *European Economic Community* Europäische Wirtschaftsgemeinschaft, *abbr.* EWG

EFTA *European Free Trade Association* Europäische Freihandelszone

e.g. *for example* zum Beispiel, *abbr.* z.B.

encl. *Com: enclosure(s)* Anlage *f*

eng(r). *engineer* Ingenieur, *abbr.* Ing.

Esq. *Esquire;* (*in address*) *J. Smith Esq.* Herrn J. Smith

est. *established* gegründet

E.T.A. *Estimated Time of Arrival* geschätzte Ankunftszeit

et. al. *et alia* und andere

etc. *etcetera* und so weiter, *abbr.* usw.

Euratom *European Atomic Energy Community* Europäische Atomgemeinschaft

ex. *example* Beispiel *n*

Exc. *Excellency* Exzellenz *f*

excl. *exclusive* ausschließlich

F *Meas: Fahrenheit* (Temperaturskala)

F.A. *Football Association* Fußballbund *m*

F.B.I. *N.Am: Federal Bureau of Investigation* Bundeskriminalamt *n*

F.C. *football club* Fußballclub *m*

Feb. *February* Februar *m*

fem. *feminine* weiblich

ff. (*and*) *following* (*pages etc.*) (und) folgende (Seiten usw.)

fig. 1. *figure* Abbildung *f.* 2. *figurative* figurativ, übertragen

fl. *florin* Florin *m*

FM *frequency modulation* Frequenzmodulation *f*; *Rad:* (=*VHF*) UKW

F.O. *Foreign Office* (britisches) Außenministerium *n*

f.o.b. *Com: free on board* frei Schiff

f.o.c. *Com: free of charge* frankn

Fr. *Ecc: Father* Pater *m*

F.R.G. *Federal Republic of Germany* Bundesrepublik Deutschland

Fri. *Friday* Freitag *m*, *abbr.* Fr.

F.R.S. *Fellow of the Royal Society* Mitglied der königlichen Gesellschaft (für Naturwissenschaften)

ft. *Meas: foot* Fuß *m*

fwd. *forward;* (*amount*) *brought fwd.* Übertrag *m*

gal. *Meas: gallon* Gallone *f*

G.B. *Great Britain* Großbritannien *n*

G.C. *George Cross* (Tapferkeitsorden für die Zivilbevölkerung)

Gdn(s). *Garden(s)* (in Straßennamen)

G.D.R. *German Democratic Republic* Deutsche Demokratische Republik, *abbr.* DDR

Gen. *Mil: etc: General* General *m*

G.I. *N.Am: general infantryman* einfacher Soldat

G.L.C. *Greater London Council* Verwaltungsrat für Groß-London

G.M.T. *Greenwich Mean Time* westeuropäische Zeit, *abbr.* WEZ

G.N.P. *gross national product* Bruttosozialprodukt *n*

govt. *government* Regierung *f*

G.P. *general practitioner* praktischer Arzt *m*

G.P.O. *A: General Post Office* Britische Postverwaltung

gr. *Meas: gram* Gramm *n*

h. *hour(s)* Stunde(n) *f(pl)*

h. & c. *hot and cold* fließendes Warm- und Kaltwasser

Hants. *Hampshire* (Grafschaft)

hect. *Meas: hectolitre* Hektoliter, *abbr.* hl.

Herts. *Hertfordshire* (Grafschaft)

H.F. *high frequency* Hochfrequenz *f*

H.M. *His/Her Majesty* Seine/Ihre Majestät

H.M.S. *His/Her Majesty's Ship* Schiff der königlichen Marine

H.M.S.O. *His/Her Majesty's Stationery Office* Staatsdruckerei und -verlag

Hon. (*in titles*) *Honourable* ehrenwert (jüngerer Sohn eines Adligen).

H.P. *Hire Purchase* Ratenkauf *m*

h.p. *Mec: horsepower* Pferdestärke, *abbr.* PS

H.Q. *Mil: headquarters* Hauptquartier *n*

H.R.H. *His/Her Royal Highness* Seine/Ihre Königliche Hoheit

ibid. *ibidem* ebenda

i/c *in charge; to be i/c* die Leitung/Verantwortung haben

ID *identity/identification* Identität *f/* Identitätsausweis *m*

i.e. *id est = that is to say* das heißt

I.L.O. *International Labour Organization* Internationale Arbeitsorganisation

I.M.F. *International Monetary Fund* Internationaler Währungsfonds

in./ins. *Meas: inch/inches* Zoll *m(pl)*

Inc. *Incorporated* (*of company etc.*) eingetragen

incl. *inclusive* inklusive, einschließlich

Ind. *Pol: Independent* Unabhängige(r) *f(m)*

inst. *Com: instant* dieses Monats

I.O.M. *Isle of Man* die Insel Man

I.O.U. *I owe you* Schuldschein *m*

I.O.W. *Isle of Wight* die Insel Wight

I.Q. *intelligence quotient* Intelligenzquotient *m*, *abbr.* IQ *m*

IRA *Irish Republican Army* Irisch-Republikanische Armee, *abbr.* IRA *f*

ITV *Independent Television* Unabhängiges Fernsehen

Jan. *January* Januar *m*

J.C. *Jesus Christ* Jesus Christus

J.P. *Justice of the Peace* Friedensrichter *m*

Jul. *July* Juli *m*

Jr. *Junior* Junior

k. *kilogram* Kilogramm *n*, *abbr.* kg

kc. *El: kilocycle* Kilohertz *n*, *abbr.* kHz

K.C.B. *Knight Commander of the Order of the Bath* Großmeister *m* des Bath-Ordens

KHz *kilohertz* Kilohertz *n*, *abbr.* kHz

km *kilometre* Kilometer *m*, *abbr.* km

K.O. *knockout* K.O. *n*

k.p.h. *kilometres per hour* Stundenkilometer *pl*, *abbr.* km/h

kv *El: kilovolt* Kilovolt *n*, *abbr.* kV

kw *El: kilowatt* Kilowatt *n*, *abbr.* kW

l. 1. *Meas: litre* Liter *m abbr.* 1. 2. *left* links

Lab. *Pol: Labour* Labour(partei *f*)

lat. *Geog: latitude* geographische Breite

lb. *Meas: pound* Pfund *n* (Gewicht)

l.b.w. *(Cricket) leg before wicket* (unerlaubtes) Schützen des Tores durch die Beine

Leics. *Leicestershire* (Grafschaft)

L.F. *low-frequency* Niederfrequenz *f*

l.h. *lefthand* linke(r, s)

Lib. *Pol: Liberal* Liberale(r) *f(m)*

Lieut. *Mil: Lieutenant* Oberleutnant *m*

Lieut.-Col. *Mil: Lieutenant-Colonel* Oberstleutnant *m*

Lincs. *Lincolnshire* (Grafschaft)

loc.cit. *loco citato = at the place cited* am angeführten Orte, *abbr.* a.a.O.

long. *Geog: longitude* geographische Länge

L.P. *long-playing record* Langspielplatte *f*

L.P.O. *London Philharmonic Orchestra* Londoner Philharmoniker *pl*

L.S.D. *lysergic acid diethylamide* LSD *n*

L.S.E. *London School of Economics* Londoner Wirtschaftshochschule *f*

L.S.O. *London Symphony Orchestra* Londoner Symphonieorchester *n*

Lt. *Mil: Lieutenant* Oberleutnant *m*

Ltd. *Com: Limited (company)* approx. (Gesellschaft *f*) mit beschränkter Haftung, *abbr.* GmbH *f*

m. 1. *male, Gram: masculine* männlich, *abbr.* m. 2. *Meas:* (a) *metre* Meter *m*, *abbr.* m; **m²** *square metre* Quadratmeter *m*, *abbr.* m²; **m³** *cubic metre* Kubikmeter *m*, *abbr.* m³; (b) *mile(s)* Meile(n) *f(pl)*

M.A. *Master of Arts* (Magistergrad)

Maj. *Mil: Major* Major *m*

masc. *masculine* männlich

math *N.Am:/maths Brit: mathematics* Mathematik *f*

max. *maximum* Maximum *n*

M.C. *Master of Ceremonies* Zeremonienmeister *m*

M.C.C. *Marylebone Cricket Club* (führender Cricketverein)

M.D. *Medicinae Doctor = Doctor of Medicine* Doktor *m* der Medizin, *abbr.* Dr.med.

mg. *Meas: milligram* Milligramm *n*, *abbr.* mgr

Mgr. *Ecc: Monsignor* Monsignore *m*, *abbr.* Mgr.

Middx. *Middlesex* (Grafschaft)

min. *minimum* Minimum *n*

mm *Meas: millimetre(s)* Millimeter *m*, *abbr.* mm

M.O. *Mil: Medical officer* Stabsarzt *m*

mod.cons. *modern conveniences* (moderner) Komfort

Mon. *Monday* Montag *m*, *abbr.* Mo

M.O.T. (a) *A: Ministry of Transport* Transportministerium *n*; (b) *Aut:F: MOT (test)* approx. TÜV *m*

M.P. 1. *Member of Parliament* Parlamentsabgeordnete(r) *f(m)*. 2. *Military Police* Militärpolizei *f*

m.p.g. *Aut: miles per gallon* Meilen pro Gallone

m.p.h. *miles per hour* Meilen pro Stunde

MS. *manuscript* Manuskript *n*; **MSS.** *manuscripts* Manuskripte *npl*

MS *Nau: Motor Ship* Motorschiff *n*

Mt. *Mount* Berg *m* (in Eigennamen)

N. *north* Nord, *abbr.* N

NASA ['næsə] *N.Am: National Aeronautics and Space Administration* Nationale Luft- und Raumfahrtbehörde

NATO ['neitəu] *North Atlantic Treaty Organization* Nato *f*

N.B. *nota bene* wohlgemerkt

NBC *National Broadcasting Corporation* (amerikanische Rundfunkgesellschaft)

N.C.O. *Mil: non-commissioned officer* Unteroffizier *m*

NE, N.E. *north-east* Nordost, *abbr.* NO

N.H.S. *Adm: National Health Service* Staatlicher Gesundheitsdienst

no. *number* Nummer *f*, *abbr.* Nr.

Northants. *Northamptonshire* (Grafschaft)

Notts. *Nottinghamshire* (Grafschaft)

Nov. *November* November *m*

nr. *near* (in address) bei

N.S.P.C.C. *National Society for the Prevention of Cruelty to Children* Kinderschutzbund *m*

N.T. *New Testament* Neues Testament

NUJ *National Union of Journalists* (Journalistengewerkschaft)

NUR *National Union of Railwaymen* (Eisenbahnergewerkschaft)

NUS *National Union of Students* (Studentengewerkschaft)

NUT *National Union of Teachers* (Lehrergewerkschaft)

NW *north-west* Nordwest, *abbr.* NW

N.Y. *New York*

N.Y.C. *New York City*

N.Z. *New Zealand* Neuseeland *n*

OAP *old age pensioner* Rentner *m*

OAS *Organization of American States* Organisation der amerikanischen Staaten

OAU *Organization of African Unity* Organisation der afrikanischen Einheit

ob. *obit* gestorben, *abbr.* gest.

O.B.E. *(Officer of the) Order of the British Empire* (Auszeichnung für Beamte und Zivilisten)

Oct. *October* Oktober *m*

OECD *Organization for Economic Cooperation and Development* Organisation für wirtschaftliche Zusammenarbeit und Entwicklung

OHMS *On His/Her Majesty's Service* im Dienste seiner/ihrer Majestät; *(Post)* Dienstsache

O.M. *Order of Merit* (hohe Auszeichnung)

o.n.o. *or nearest offer* oder höchstes Angebot

op. *Mus: opus* Opus

op.cit. *opere citato = in the work quoted* im zitierten Werk, *abbr.* op.cit.

ord. *ordinary* gewöhnlich, normal

Oxon. 1. *Oxoniensis = of Oxford* von Oxford. 2. *Oxfordshire* (Grafschaft)

oz. *Meas: ounce* Unze *f*

p. 1. *page* Seite. 2. *per pro.* 3. *(money)* pence Pence *pl*

p.a. *per annum* pro Jahr

P.A. *Press Association* Presseverband *m*

P.A.Y.E. *pay as you earn* direkt einbehaltene Einkommensteuer

P.C. 1. *police constable* Polizist *m*, Schutzmann *m.* 2. *postcard* Postkarte *f.* 3. *personal computer* Personal Computer *m*

p.c. 1. *per cent* Prozent. 2. *postcard* Postkarte *f*

P.D.S.A. *People's Dispensary for Sick Animals* tierärztliche Fürsorge für weniger wohlhabende Tierhalter

P.E. *Physical Education* Leibesübungen und Sport

Ph.D. *Doctor of Philosophy* Doktor der Philosophie

PLC/plc *public limited company* Gesellschaft *f* mit beschränkter Haftung, *abbr.* GmbH *f* (mit börsenfähigen Aktien)

P.L.O. *Palestine Liberation Organization* Vereinigung für die Befreiung Palästinas

P.M. *Prime Minister* Premierminister *m*

p.m. *post meridiem* nachmittags, abends

P.O. *Post Office* Postamt *n*

P.O.W. *prisoner of war* Kriegsgefangene(r) *m*

pp. *pages* Seiten *fpl*

p.p. *per pro(curationem)* im Auftrag, *abbr.* i.A.

P.R. *public relations* Öffentlichkeitsarbeit *f*

pr(s). *pair(s)* Paar(e) *n(pl)*

Pres. *president* Präsident *m*

Prof. *professor* Professor *m*

P.S. *postscript* Postskriptum *n*, Nachschrift *f*, *abbr.* PS

P.T. *physical training* Leibesübungen *fpl*

P.T.A. *Parent-Teacher Association* Elternvereinigung *f*, Elternbeirat *m*

Pte. *Mil: Private* einfacher Soldat

P.T.O. *please turn over* bitte wenden, *abbr.* b.w.

pub. *published* veröffentlicht

PVC *polyvinylchloride* PVC *n*

PX *N.Am:Mil: Post Exchange* (Geschäft für das Militär)

Q.C. *Jur: Queen's Council* Justizrat *m*

Q.E.D. *quad erat demonstrandum* was zu beweisen war, *abbr.* q.e.d.

q.v. *which see* siehe unten, *abbr.* s.u.

R. 1. *River* Fluß *m.* 2. *Road* Straße *f*

r. *right* rechts

R.A. *Royal Academy* Königliche Kunstakademie

R.A.C. *Royal Automobile Club* (britischer Automobilclub)

RADA ['rɑːdə] *Royal Academy of Dramatic Art* Königliche Schauspielschule

R.A.F. *Royal Air Force* (Britische Luftwaffe)

R.C. *Roman Catholic* römisch-katholisch

Rd. *road* Straße *f*, *abbr.* Str.

R.E. 1. *Mil: Royal Engineers* (Pioniertruppe). 2. *Sch: religious education* Religion *f* (als Fach)

ref. *reference* Aktenzeichen *n*; *(on letter)* your ref*f.*, Ihr Zeichen

regd. *registered* eingetragen; *(of letter)* eingeschrieben

REME *Royal Electrical and Mechanical Engineers* auf Elektronik und Mechanik spezialisierte Pioniertruppe

rep. *representative* Com: Vertreter *m*

retd. *retired* in Pension

Rev. *Ecc: Reverend* Hochwürden

rev. *revolution* Umdrehung *f*

r.h. *righthand* rechte(r,s)

rly. *railway* Eisenbahn *f*

rm(s). *room(s)* Zimmer *n(pl)*

R.N. *Royal Navy* Königliche Marine

R.N.L.I. *Royal National Lifeboat Institution* Königlich-Nationales Institut für Rettungsboote

r.p.m. *revolutions per minute* Umdrehungen pro Minute

R.P.O. *Royal Philharmonic Orchestra* Königliches Philharmonisches Orchester

RSPCA *Royal Society for the Prevention of Cruelty to Animals* Königlicher Tierschutzverein

R.S.V.P. *répondez s'il vous plaît* um Antwort wird gebeten, *abbr.* u.A.w.g.

Rt.Hon. *Right Honourable* Sehr Ehrenwert

S. *south* Süd

s.a.e. *stamped addressed envelope* frankierter Umschlag mit Adresse

SALT [sɔlt] *Strategic Arms Limitation Treaty* Vertrag über die Beschränkung von strategischen Waffen

SDP *Social Democratic Party* Sozialdemokratische Partei

SE *south-east* Südost, *abbr.* SE

SEATO ['siːtəu] *South East Asia Treaty Organization* Südostasienpakt-Organisation *f*

sec. 1. *second* Sekunde *f.* **2.** *secretary* Schriftführer(in) *m(f)*

Sen. 1. *(with names) Senior* Senior, der Älteste. **2.** *N.Am: Senator* Senator *m*

Sept. *September* September *m*

S.F. *science fiction* Science-fiction *f*

Sgt. *sergeant* Feldwebel *m*

SLR *Phot: single-lens reflex* (einäugige) Spiegelreflexkamera *f*

SNP *Scottish National Party* Schottisch-Nationale Partei

snr. *senior* Senior, der Älteste

Soc. *Society* Gesellschaft *f,* *(club)* Verein *m*

Som. *Somerset* (Grafschaft)

S.O.S. SOS *n* (Seenotzeichen)

Sq. *Square* Platz *m*

sq. *square* Quadrat *n*

SRN *state-registered nurse* staatlich anerkannte Krankenschwester

St. 1. *Saint* Sankt. **2.** *Street* Straße *f*

Sta. *station* Bahnhof *m*

Staffs. *Staffordshire* (Grafschaft)

S.T.D. *Subscriber Trunk Dialling* Selbstwählferndienst *m*

sub. *subscription* Beitrag *m*

Sun. *Sunday* Sonntag *m*

Supt. *superintendent (of police)* approx. Kommissar *m*

SW. *south-west* Südwest, *abbr.* SW

t. *Meas:* *ton* Tonne *f*

T.B. *Med: tuberculosis* Tuberkulose *f*

tel. *telephone (number)* Telefon(nummer) *n (f)*

temp. 1. *temperature* Temperatur *f.* **2.** *f: temporary secretary* Aushilfssekretärin *f*

Ter(r). *Terrace* Häuserreihe *f*

Thurs. *Thursday* Donnerstag, *abbr.* Do

TNT *trinitrotoluene* TNT *n*

Tues. *Tuesday* Dienstag, *abbr.* Di

TUC *Trade Union Congress* (britischer) Gewerkschaftsbund *m*

TV *television* Fernsehen *n,* TV *n*

U.A.R. *United Arab Republic* Vereinigte Arabische Republik

UFO ['juːfəu] *unidentified flying object* unbekanntes Flugobjekt, *abbr.* UFO *n*

UHF *ultra high frequency* Ultra-Hochfrequenz *f*

U.K. *Geog: United Kingdom* Vereinigtes Königreich

ult. *ultimo* des letzten Monats

UN, U.N. *United Nations* Vereinte Nationen *pl,* *abbr.* UNO *f*

UNESCO *United Nations Educational, Scientific*

and Cultural Organization Organisation der Vereinten Nationen für Erziehung, Wissenschaft und Kultur

UNICEF *United Nations International Children's Emergency Fund* Kinderhilfswerk *n* der Vereinten Nationen

Univ. *university* Universität *f*

UNO *United Nations Organization* Organisation der Vereinten Nationen, *abbr.* UNO *f*

US *United States* Vereinigte Staaten *pl, abbr.* US(A) *pl*

USA *United States of America* Vereinigte Staaten von Amerika, *abbr.* USA *pl*

USAF *United States Air Force* US-Luftwaffe *f*

USN *United States Navy* US-Marine *f*

USS *United States Ship* US-Schiff *n*

USSR *Union of Socialist Soviet Republics* Union der Sozialistischen Sowjetrepubliken, *abbr.* UdSSR *f*

v. 1. *El:* volt Volt *n.* **2.** *Sp: & Jur:* *versus* gegen *acc.* **3.** *vide* siehe. **4.** *Poet:* *verse* Vers *m*

V. & A. F: *Victoria and Albert Museum* (Kunstmuseum in London)

VAT *value added tax* Mehrwertsteuer *f, abbr.* MWSt.

V.C. 1. *Vice-Chancellor* Vizekanzler *m.* **2.** *Victoria Cross* (höchste Tapferkeitsmedaille)

VD *venereal disease* Geschlechtskrankheit *f*

VDU *visual display unit* Sichtgerät *n*

VHF *Rad: very high frequency* Ultrakurzwelle *f, abbr.* UKW

VIP *F: very important person* hohes Tier

viz. *videlicet* nämlich

vocab. *F: vocabulary* Wortschatz *m;* *(with translations)* Glossar *n*

vol. *volume* Band *m;* **vols.** *volumes* Bände *pl*

vs. *versus* gegen *acc*

W. *(a)* West; *(b) adj. western* West-, westlich

W., w. *El:* *watt(s)* Watt *n(pl)*

WC *water closet* WC *n*

Wed. *Wednesday* Mittwoch *m, abbr.* Mi

WHO *World Health Organization* Weltgesundheitsorganisation *f*

Worcs. *Worcestershire* (Grafschaft)

wpm *words per minute* Worte pro Minute

WRAF *Women's Royal Air Force* (Frauendienst der Luftwaffe)

WRNS *Women's Royal Naval Service* (Frauendienst der Marine)

yd. *Meas:* *yard* Yard *n* (0.914 m)

YHA *Youth Hostel Association* Jugendherbergsverband *m*

YMCA *Young Men's Christian Association* Christlicher Verein junger Männer, *abbr.* CVJM

YWCA *Young Women's Christian Association* Christlicher Verein junger Frauen, *abbr.* CVJF

yrs. *(in letter) yours* Ihr(e), Dein(e)